RAND McNALLY
NEW
COSMOPOLITAN
WORLD
ATLAS

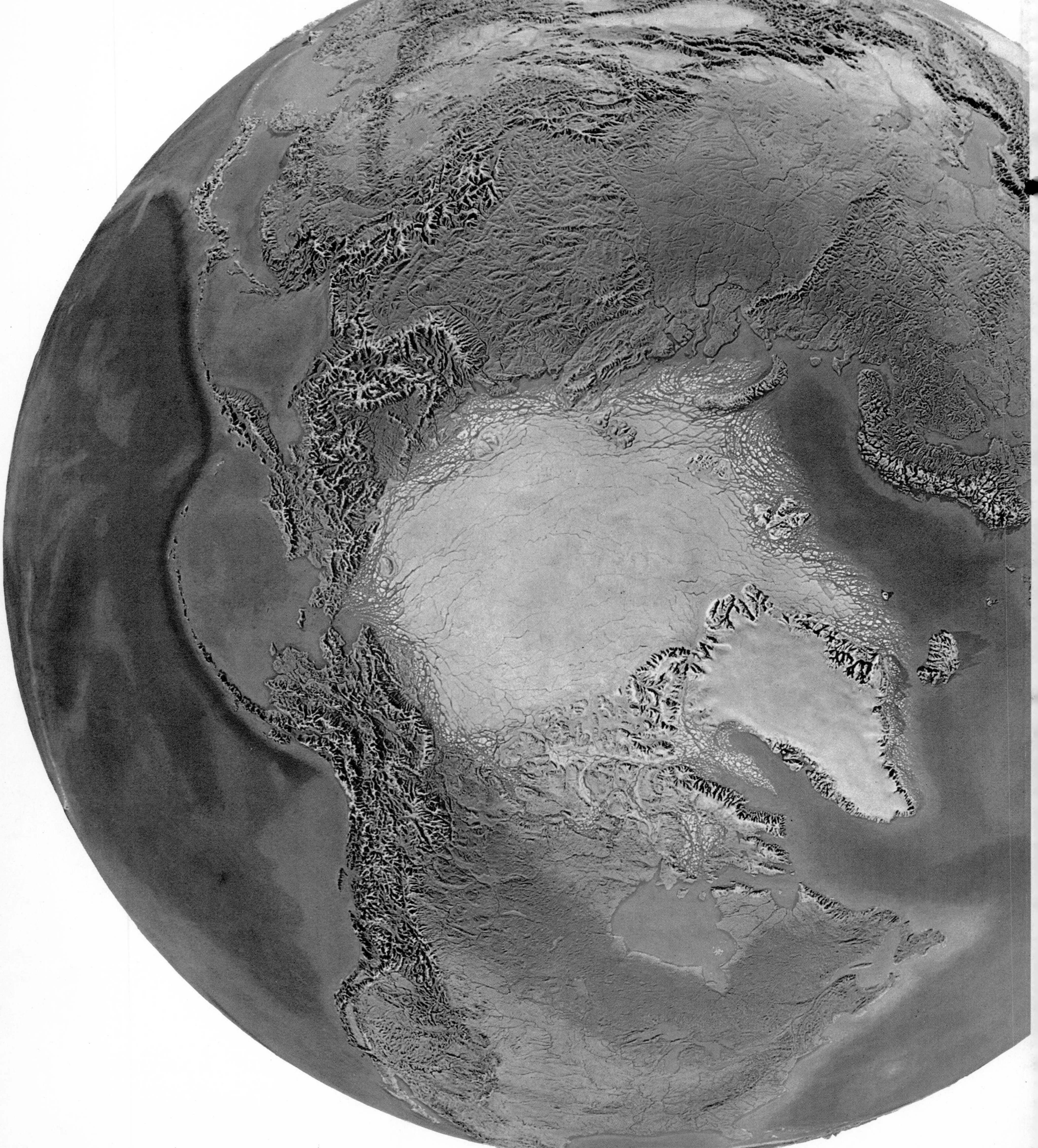

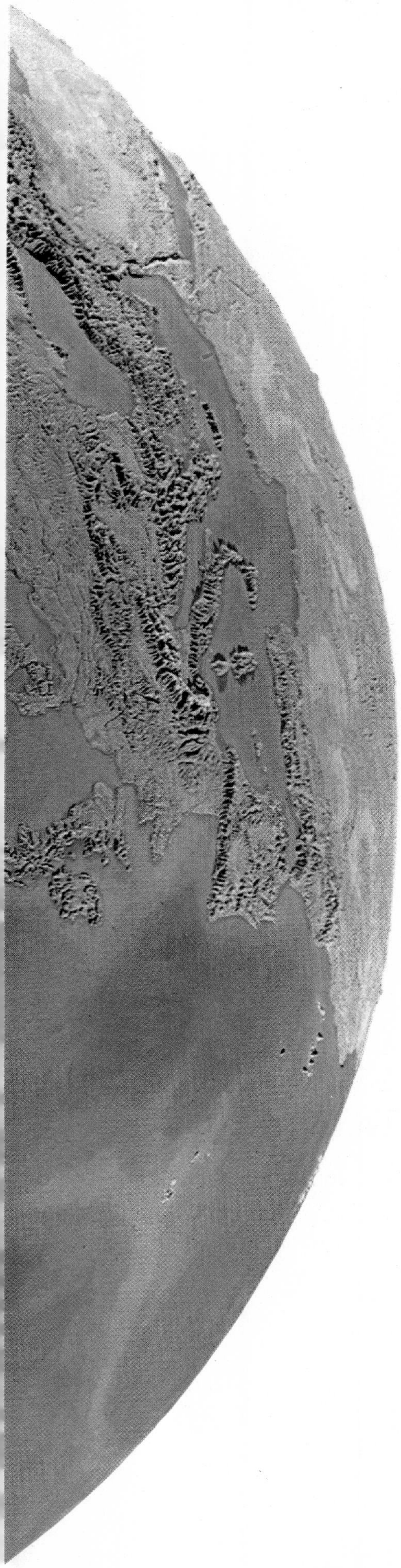

RAND McNALLY
NEW
COSMOPOLITAN
WORLD
ATLAS

RAND McNALLY & COMPANY   Chicago   New York   San Francisco

INTRODUCTION TO THE ATLAS

Since the first Cosmopolitan Atlas was planned, more than a decade ago, man's knowledge of his world has benefited from improved scientific techniques in the recording of geographical data. The public has developed a keener awareness of the expanse of the globe and a widespread curiosity about far-away places. The exploration of space has fired imaginations—everyone is concerned with an astronaut's-eye-view of our sphere.

To keep pace with the times and the changed reader direction, and to provide an atlas as modern as tomorrow, the publishers have enlarged the scope of the map reference material in this NEW COSMO-POLITAN WORLD ATLAS. The heart of the atlas, the Cosmo Series Maps (which are grouped on a broad regional basis, not country by country) are now introduced, region by region, with full-color global views of the regions as they might appear from space. With each global view a short sketch of the region is provided, along with a locator map indicating the political divisions of that region.

Within the regions the basic plan for grouping the Cosmo Series Maps is retained. Each of the great landmasses of the Earth is shown as a whole and then broken down into major continental regions. All the regional maps for a given continent are drawn on the same scale. Thus it is possible to make direct visual comparisons of the sizes of countries and the distances between places by turning from one map to another. Smaller areas are shown in greater detail

on larger scale maps which use even multiples of these regional scales. Small marginal maps show the location of areas covered by the sectional maps. No detail has been neglected that will help the user compare areas or see the world relationships of the area in which he is interested.

The value of any atlas depends almost as much upon the quality of its index as upon the quality of its maps. For this reason the publishers of the NEW COSMOPOLITAN WORLD ATLAS have given to the index the same careful attention they have given to the maps, and in this new edition they have expanded the number of index entries.

The "Index to Political-Physical Maps" includes in one alphabetical listing the names that appear on the Cosmo Series Maps. Often the form of a name commonly used in English-speaking countries differs from the official name. Whenever the anglicized form of the name of a capital city differs from the official spelling, the official name is included on the maps in parentheses. Both forms appear in the index. For other cities, the local, official form is given first on the map, with the customary English form in parentheses. Wherever two forms of a name are in common use because of a recent change in sovereignty, an official change in name, or for any other reason, both forms are given on the map and in the index. This policy has been followed as an aid to English-speaking readers.

In general, place-name spellings follow the recommendations of the United States Board on Geographic Names of the Department of the Interior, which determines the official spelling of foreign geographical names. For some areas and languages, however, more anglicized names are used than the Board recommends for official maps. For the spelling of place-names in the United States, the United States Postal Guide is the authority that is followed.

Three special alphabetical lists increase the usefulness of the maps and index. These are the "Historical Gazetteer," a listing of names that do not appear on modern maps, a "Glossary of Foreign

Geographical Terms" which provides the English equivalents of foreign terms that appear in names of physical features, and a "Glossary of Map Terminology" which explains geographic terms frequently found on maps or needed for their interpretation.

For those who are interested in the relationship of the Earth to the Universe, the introductory pages of the atlas provide discussion and illustrative material on the "Solar System," "The Moon," and "Space." And for the readers' greater enjoyment of the atlas and an appreciation of the painstaking work which has gone into its preparation, there are text, diagrams, and sample maps covering "Map Projections," "Map Scale," "Map Symbols," and the "Index Reference System."

Following the "World Reference Maps" (global views and Cosmo Series Maps) are two sections of specialized, supplementary maps. "The Physical World in Maps" treats the world, each continent, and the United States and Canada with a map emphasizing the elevations of the land and the depth of the surrounding bodies of water. In "The Topical World in Maps" section each of six world maps deals with an important aspect of the Earth's physical or cultural landscape: climate, vegetation, population, race, language, and religion. And so that people can better understand the world today by knowing what came before, the publishers have included two more special map sections. "World History in Maps" presents, by contemporary mapping, the geography of the world through the ages (200 A.D. to 1950). "America's Heritage in Maps" develops a chronicle of the mapping of the New World with maps drawn by outstanding cartographers from 1540 to 1855.

The supplementary material includes for both the world and the United States tables of areas and populations, climatic and economic data, and largest cities. It also includes tables of steamship, railroad, and air distances, as well as a table of "Principal Discoveries and Explorations," a state by state listing with text of "Places of Interest in the United States," and much other useful information.

CONTENTS

AMERICA'S HERITAGE IN MAPS
pages 175 through 188

Geographical Facts, Figures, and Information about the World and the United States
pages 189 through 243

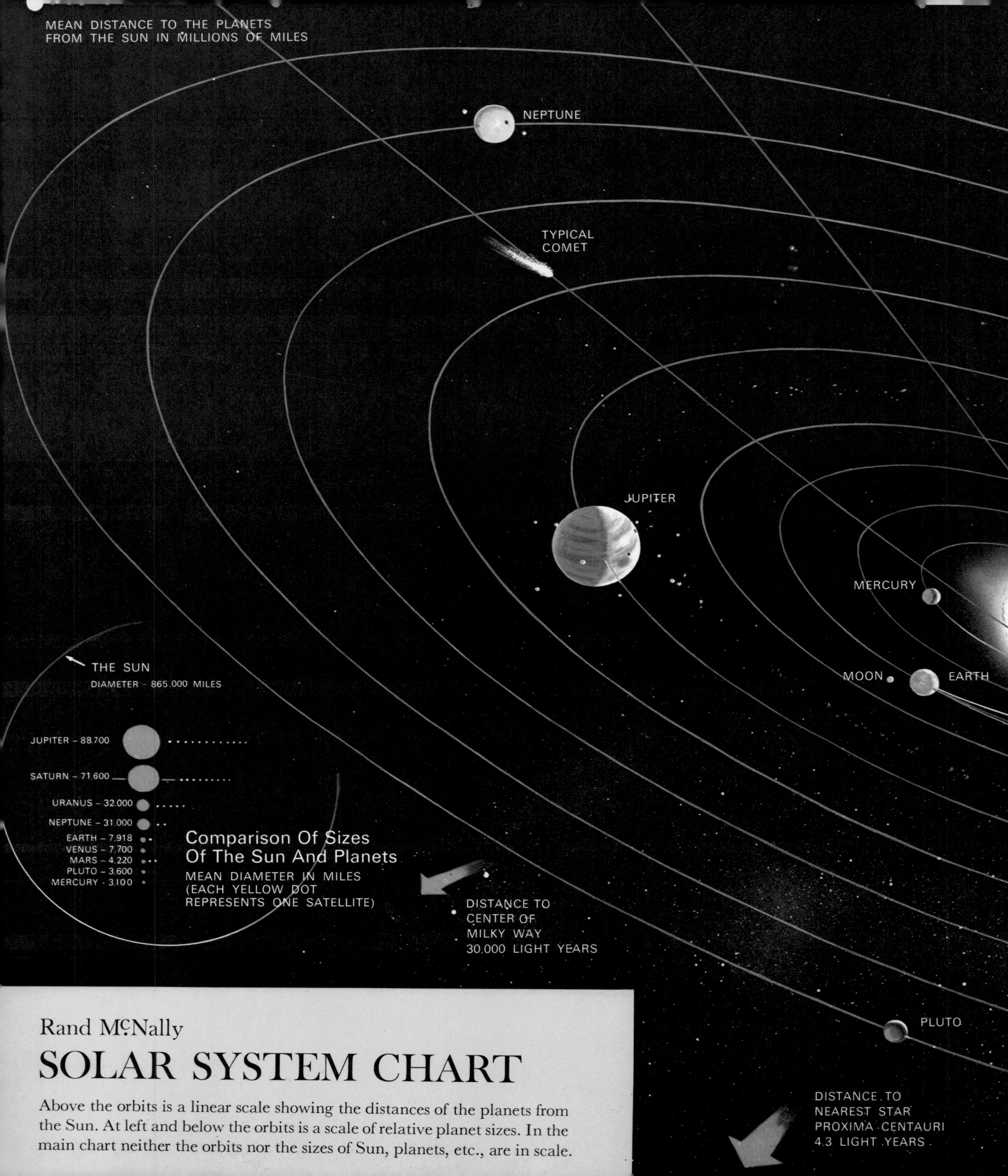

MEAN DISTANCE TO THE PLANETS
FROM THE SUN IN MILLIONS OF MILES

NEPTUNE

TYPICAL
COMET

JUPITER

MERCURY

MOON   EARTH

THE SUN
DIAMETER – 865,000 MILES

JUPITER – 88,700

SATURN – 71,600

URANUS – 32,000

NEPTUNE – 31,000

EARTH – 7,918
VENUS – 7,700
MARS – 4,220
PLUTO – 3,600
MERCURY – 3,100

Comparison Of Sizes
Of The Sun And Planets
MEAN DIAMETER IN MILES
(EACH YELLOW DOT
REPRESENTS ONE SATELLITE)

DISTANCE TO
CENTER OF
MILKY WAY
30,000 LIGHT YEARS

PLUTO

Rand McNally
SOLAR SYSTEM CHART

Above the orbits is a linear scale showing the distances of the planets from
the Sun. At left and below the orbits is a scale of relative planet sizes. In the
main chart neither the orbits nor the sizes of Sun, planets, etc., are in scale.

DISTANCE TO
NEAREST STAR
PROXIMA CENTAURI
4.3 LIGHT YEARS

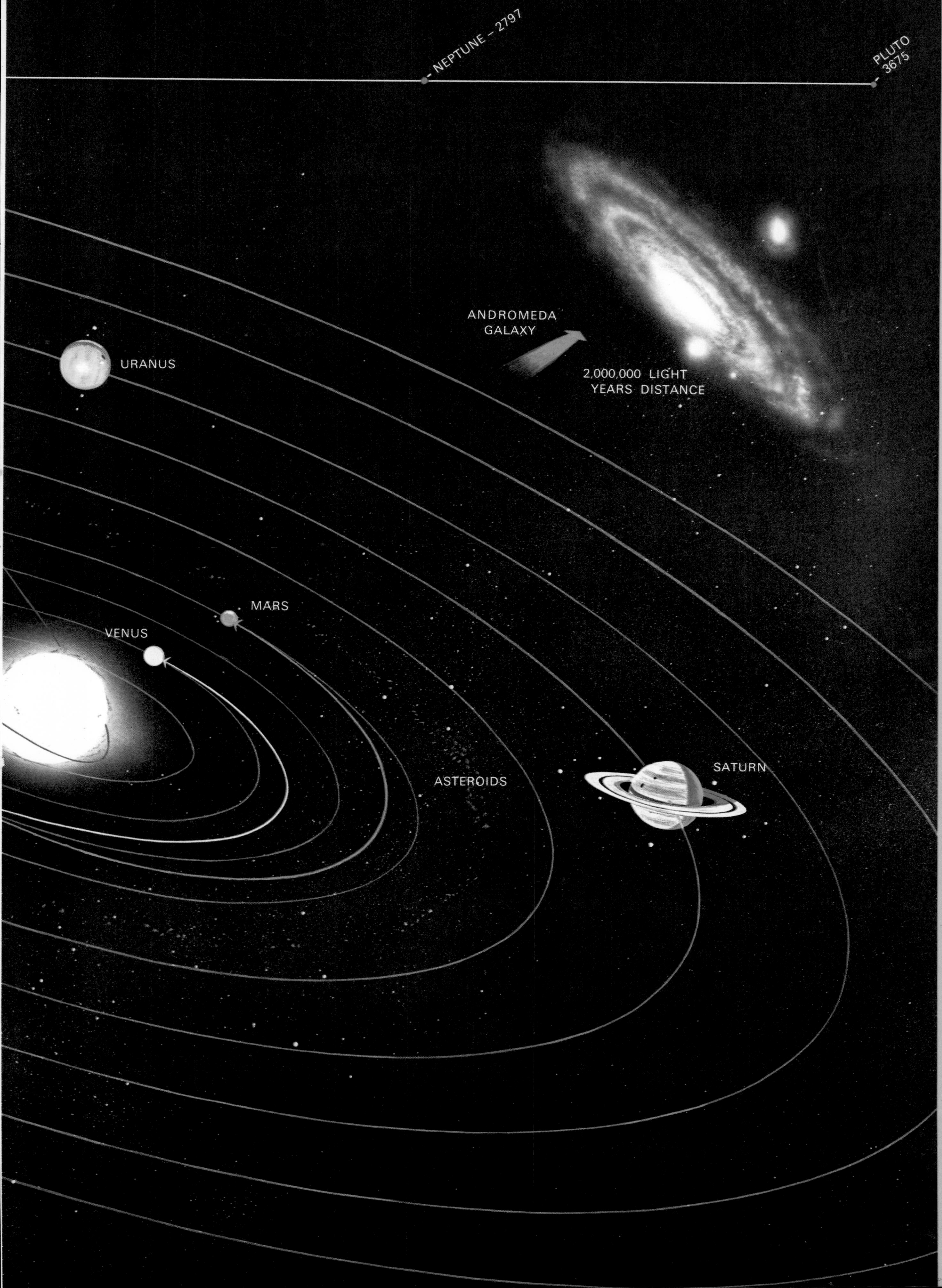

NEPTUNE – 2797

PLUTO 3675

URANUS

ANDROMEDA GALAXY

2,000,000 LIGHT YEARS DISTANCE

MARS

VENUS

ASTEROIDS

SATURN

THE SOLAR SYSTEM

The Solar System, of which the Earth is a part, is depicted graphically on the preceding two pages. This chart simulates the view an observer might expect if situated at a point in space. The system consists of a central star, the Sun, about which moves a family of nine planets, thirty-two moons, thousands of asteroids (or planetoids), and numerous comets and meteor clusters. The planets move around the Sun in nearly circular orbits, lying in approximately the same plane. All revolve in the same direction which is also the direction in which the Sun rotates on its own axis. As the planets' distances from the Sun increase, their respective orbital velocities proportionately decrease. Nearly all of the moons revolve in almost circular orbits along the equatorial planes of their respective planets. One of the exceptions to this rule is the Earth's Moon.

The Planet Information Table below, showing the planets' significant characteristics, will aid in making comparisons between them. The following text sets down further distinguishing characteristics of each. There is one omission, the Earth, which is amply described through the maps of this atlas.

MERCURY: Owing to its small size and consequent low surface gravity, most of its atmosphere escaped into space eons ago. This factor, coupled with a relatively short mean distance from the Sun, has turned Mercury into an arid, Sun-drenched, and most inhospitable world of extremes. On the illuminated side the surface temperature reaches 650° F.

VENUS: It is often called the Earth's "twin sister" because it is so nearly the same size. Venus is shrouded by so dense an atmosphere that its surface has never been seen through telescopes. In 1962, Mariner II spacecraft flew past Venus at a distance of 21,648 miles, and probed the environment of the planet. Thus, it was tentatively determined that the surface temperature might be 800° F., a much higher figure than had been anticipated. It was also ascertained that the dense cloud masses begin at an altitude of 45 miles above the planet's surface, reaching upward to an altitude of 60 miles. Earth-based radar analyses indicate that the surface of Venus might be sandy; alternately some scientists believe that the surface might have oceans and swamps as well as rocky landmasses. Other scientists maintain that the surface might be rocky and wind beaten.

MARS: Mars is the fourth planet in distance from the Sun, and the first located past the Earth. It has several Earth-like features, among them climatic seasons, seasonal water cycles, a surface temperature believed to range from a high of 80° F. to a low of −100° F. Its bright regions suggest the presence of vegetation which changes according to the seasons. Its atmosphere is believed to be thin, yet it is dense enough for clouds to form. Mars has two moons, each less than 10 miles in diameter and located rather near the planet.

JUPITER: Largest of the planets, it is a world of turmoil and change. It rotates so fast that the gases at its surface are forced into bands of turbulent motion. It is believed that it has a small rocky interior surrounded by a huge shell of ice, which in turn is surrounded by layers of solid, then liquid, then gaseous hydrogen topped with clouds of deadly methane and ammonia. The average surface temperature might be about −190° F. Jupiter has twelve moons, three of which are larger than our own.

SATURN: Physically similar to Jupiter, it has a family of nine moons. Due to its greater distance from the Sun, its surface temperature is lower yet, −235° F. Surrounding the planet along its equatorial plane is a ring system with an outside diameter of 175,000 miles. The rings are made up of small solid particles.

URANUS, NEPTUNE, and PLUTO: These are the outer planets of the Solar System. They are also the least-known ones. It is estimated that their surface temperatures drop considerably below −300° F.

PLANET INFORMATION TABLE

PLANET	Mercury	Venus	Earth*	Mars	Jupiter†	Saturn	Uranus	Neptune	Pluto
Number of Natural Satellites per Planet	0	0	1	2	12	9	5	2	0
Mean Diameter (in Miles)	3,100	7,700	7,918	4,220	88,700	71,600	32,000	31,000	3,600
Mean Distance to the Sun (in millions of miles)	36.0	67.25	93.0	141.7	484.0	887.0	1,787.0	2,797.0	3,675.0
Comparative Volume (Earth = 1.00)	0.06	0.92	1.00	0.15	1,318	736	64	60	0.09
Comparative Mass (Earth = 1.00)	0.04	0.81	1.00	0.11	316.94	94.9	14.7	17.2	0.1
Necessary Escape Velocity	2.66	6.38	6.95	3.16	37.0	22.10	13.70	15.40	3.30(?)
Mean Surface Gravity (Earth = 1.00)	0.29	0.86	1.00	0.37	2.64	1.17	0.91	1.12	<0.5
Weight of a Human Being (in pounds)	38	88	100	39	265	117	105	123	55
Rotation on Planet's Own Axis	88.0 days	Unknown	23ʰ56ᵐ	24ʰ37ᵐ	9ʰ50ᵐ	10ʰ14ᵐ	10ʰ45ᵐ	15ʰ48ᵐ	6.39 days
Revolution Around the Sun	88.0 days	224.7 days	365.2 days	687.0 days	11.9 years	29.5 years	84.0 years	164.8 years	248.4 years
Mean Orbital Velocity (in miles per second)	29.76	21.78	18.52	15.00	8.12	6.00	4.23	3.37	2.95
Inclination of Planet's Orbit to the Ecliptic	7°00′	3°24′	0°00′	1°51′	1°18′	2°29′	0°46′	1°47′	17°09′
Inclination of Planet's Equator	0°(?)	32°(?)	23°27′	25°10′	3°07′	26°45′	97°53′	29°	Unknown

*EARTH   †LARGEST PLANET

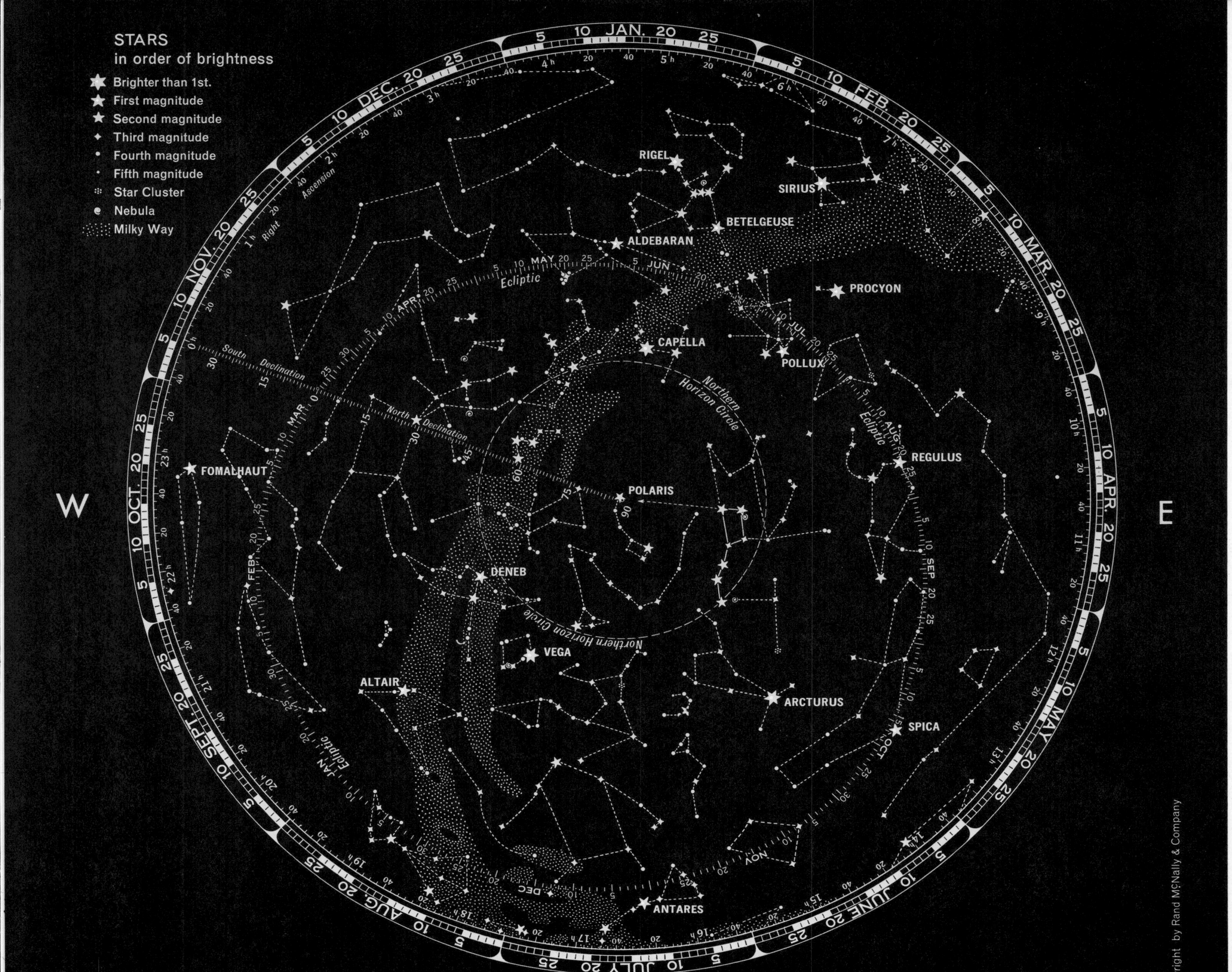

Star Chart for the NORTHERN SKIES

THE PLANETS 1966

Date	MERCURY R.A.	Decl.	VENUS R.A.	Decl.	MARS R.A.	Decl.	JUPITER R.A.	Decl.	SATURN R.A.	Decl.
Jan. 1	17 19	22 S	21 02	16 S	20 38	20 S	5 36	23 N	22 58	9 S
15	18 47	24 S	20 53	13 S	21 23	17 S	5 29	23 N	23 03	8 S
Feb. 1	20 44	20 S	20 12	12 S	22 15	12 S	5 23	23 N	23 09	8 S
15	22 22	12 S	19 55	13 S	22 56	8 S	5 22	23 N	23 15	7 S
Mar. 1	23 48	0	20 09	14 S	23 37	3 S	5 23	23 N	23 21	6 S
15	0 13	5 N	20 46	14 S	0 17	1 N	5 27	23 N	23 28	6 S
Apr. 1	23 34	2 S	21 45	12 S	1 04	6 N	5 35	23 N	23 35	5 S
15	23 54	3 S	22 40	8 S	1 44	10 N	5 44	23 N	23 41	4 S
May 1	1 04	4 N	23 45	3 S	2 30	15 N	5 56	23 N	23 48	3 S
15	2 32	13 N	0 43	3 N	3 10	18 N	6 08	23 N	23 52	3 S
June 1	4 58	24 N	1 56	10 N	4 00	21 N	6 23	23 N	23 57	3 S
15	6 58	25 N	2 59	15 N	4 42	23 N	6 37	23 N	0 00	2 S
July 1	8 27	19 N	4 15	20 N	5 30	24 N	6 52	23 N	0 02	2 S
15	8 52	14 N	5 25	22 N	6 11	24 N	7 06	23 N	0 02	2 S
Aug. 1	8 15	15 N	6 54	24 N	7 01	23 N	7 22	22 N	0 01	2 S
15	8 20	18 N	8 06	21 N	7 40	22 N	7 35	22 N	0 03	2 S
Sept. 1	10 07	13 N	9 31	16 N	8 27	20 N	7 50	21 N	23 55	3 S
15	11 47	3 N	10 38	10 N	9 03	18 N	8 00	21 N	23 52	4 S
Oct. 1	13 23	9 S	11 52	2 N	9 42	15 N	8 11	20 N	23 47	4 S
15	14 39	18 S	12 57	5 S	10 16	12 N	8 18	20 N	23 43	4 S
Nov. 1	15 54	23 S	14 16	13 S	10 54	9 N	8 25	20 N	23 40	5 S
15	15 42	20 S	15 27	19 S	11 24	7 N	8 27	20 N	23 38	5 S
Dec. 1	15 07	15 S	16 49	23 S	11 57	2 N	8 27	20 N	23 38	5 S
15	16 12	16 S	18 06	24 S	12 24	1 S	8 24	20 N	23 39	5 S

THE PLANETS 1967

Date	MERCURY R.A.	Decl.	VENUS R.A.	Decl.	MARS R.A.	Decl.	JUPITER R.A.	Decl.	SATURN R.A.	Decl.
Jan. 1	18 00	24 S	19 39	23 S	12 55	4 S	8 17	20 N	23 42	4 S
15	19 37	24 S	20 53	19 S	13 18	6 S	8 10	21 N	23 45	4 S
Feb. 1	21 37	15 S	22 16	12 S	13 42	8 S	8 00	21 N	23 51	3 S
15	22 58	6 S	23 21	6 S	13 57	9 S	7 54	21 N	23 56	3 S
Mar. 1	23 04	2 S	0 24	2 N	14 06	10 S	7 49	22 N	0 02	2 S
15	22 24	8 S	1 27	9 N	14 07	10 S	7 46	22 N	0 08	1 S
Apr. 1	22 59	8 S	2 45	17 N	13 54	9 S	7 47	22 N	0 16	1 S
15	0 06	2 S	3 53	22 N	13 36	8 S	7 50	22 N	0 22	0
May 1	1 47	9 N	5 13	25 N	13 13	6 S	7 56	21 N	0 29	1 N
15	3 40	20 N	6 24	26 N	13 00	5 S	8 04	21 N	0 35	1 N
June 1	6 02	26 N	7 45	24 N	12 56	3 S	8 15	20 N	0 41	2 N
15	7 15	23 N	8 46	20 N	13 03	3 S	8 26	20 N	0 45	2 N
July 1	7 29	19 N	9 45	15 N	13 20	9 S	8 39	19 N	0 48	3 N
15	6 57	18 N	10 24	9 N	13 41	12 S	8 51	18 N	0 49	3 N
Aug. 1	7 20	21 N	10 51	5 N	14 14	16 S	9 06	17 N	0 50	3 N
15	8 57	19 N	10 48	1 N	14 44	17 S	9 18	16 N	0 49	3 N
Sept. 1	11 06	7 N	10 13	2 N	15 26	20 S	9 33	15 N	0 46	2 N
15	12 31	3 S	9 51	6 N	16 04	22 S	9 44	14 N	0 42	2 N
Oct. 1	13 53	14 S	10 01	7 N	16 50	24 S	9 57	13 N	0 38	1 N
15	14 47	20 S	10 33	7 N	17 34	25 S	10 07	12 N	0 34	1 N
Nov. 1	15 04	19 S	11 22	6 N	18 29	25 S	10 21	11 N	0 30	0
15	14 07	10 S	12 22	4 N	19 14	24 S	10 27	10 N	0 27	0
Dec. 1	15 24	17 S	13 28	7 S	20 07	22 S	10 29	10 N	0 25	0
15	16 53	23 S	14 29	12 S	20 52	20 S	10 32	10 N	0 25	0

THE PLANETS 1968

Date	MERCURY R.A.	Decl.	VENUS R.A.	Decl.	MARS R.A.	Decl.	JUPITER R.A.	Decl.	SATURN R.A.	Decl.
Jan. 1	18 50	25 S	15 49	18 S	21 45	15 S	10 32	10 N	0 26	0
15	20 29	21 S	16 59	21 S	22 26	11 S	10 29	11 N	0 29	1 N
Feb. 1	22 06	11 S	18 28	22 S	23 15	6 S	10 20	11 N	0 33	1 N
15	21 51	9 S	19 42	21 S	23 55	1 S	10 16	12 N	0 38	2 N
Mar. 1	21 17	14 S	20 59	18 S	0 37	4 N	10 09	13 N	0 44	2 N
15	21 59	14 S	22 07	13 S	1 16	8 N	10 02	13 N	0 50	3 N
Apr. 1	23 27	6 S	23 26	5 S	2 03	12 N	9 57	14 N	0 50	3 N
15	0 56	4 N	0 30	2 N	2 43	16 N	9 54	14 N	0 58	4 N
May 1	3 00	18 N	1 43	9 N	3 29	19 N	9 54	14 N	1 05	4 N
15	4 50	25 N	2 49	15 N	4 10	21 N	9 57	14 N	1 12	5 N
June 1	6 04	24 N	4 14	21 N	5 00	23 N	10 03	13 N	1 18	6 N
15	5 58	21 N	5 27	23 N	5 42	24 N	10 10	12 N	1 25	6 N
July 1	5 32	19 N	6 53	24 N	6 29	24 N	10 19	12 N	1 30	7 N
15	6 09	21 N	8 07	21 N	7 09	23 N	10 28	11 N	1 34	7 N
Aug. 1	8 16	21 N	9 33	16 N	7 57	22 N	10 41	9 N	1 38	7 N
15	10 13	18 N	10 39	10 N	8 35	20 N	10 51	8 N	1 38	7 N
Sept. 1	11 56	0	11 56	2 N	9 19	17 N	11 05	7 N	1 37	7 N
15	13 03	9 S	12 59	5 S	9 54	14 N	11 16	6 N	1 34	6 N
Oct. 1	13 50	15 S	14 13	13 S	10 32	11 N	11 29	4 N	1 30	6 N
15	13 23	11 S	15 19	19 S	11 05	7 N	11 40	2 N	1 26	6 N
Nov. 1	13 18	16 S	16 46	24 S	11 44	3 N	12 01	1 N	1 17	5 N
15	14 33	14 S	18 00	25 S	12 11	1 N	12 01	1 N	1 17	5 N
Dec. 1	16 14	22 S	19 24	24 S	12 50	4 S	12 10	0	1 14	5 N
15	17 49	25 S	20 36	22 S	13 21	7 S	12 17	0	1 13	5 N

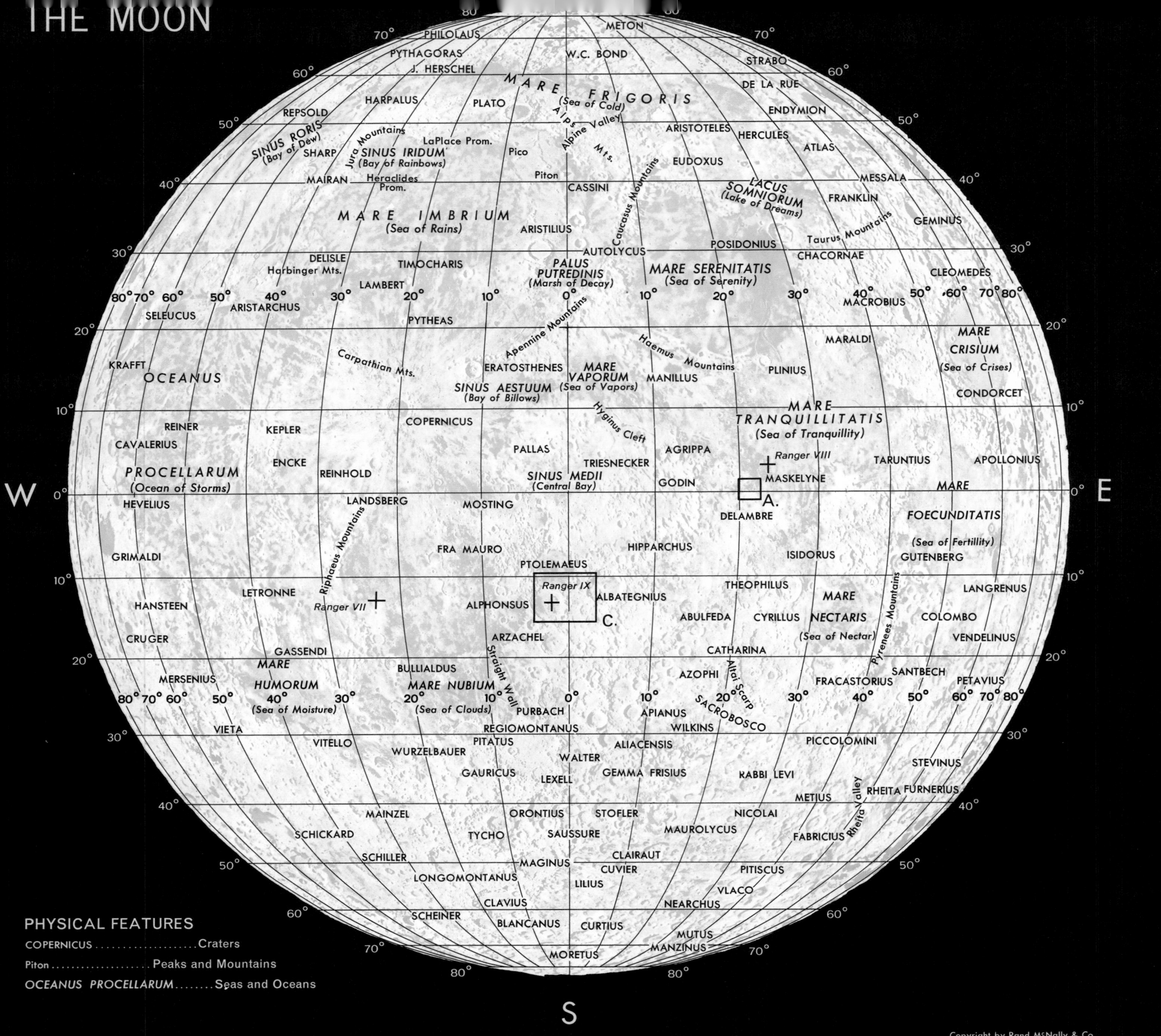

THE MOON

PHYSICAL FEATURES

COPERNICUS ....Craters

Piton ....Peaks and Mountains

OCEANUS PROCELLARUM........Seas and Oceans

+ = Impact sites of Ranger Spacecraft

The Moon is the only natural satellite of the Earth. In comparison to our planet, the Moon is considerably smaller; its diameter is only 2,160 miles. It travels around the Earth once every 27⅓ days, at an average distance of 238,862 miles. Due to the nature of its orbital behavior, only one half of its surface can be seen from Earth. This half is commonly known as the "face side" or "near side." The relatively short distance to it has made it possible to study its surface details through telescopes. The above map was made from numerous photographs taken through various telescopes.

The Moon is a compact world of steep moun-tain peaks, mountain ranges, craters of all sizes, barren plains, valleys, clefts, and rills. Among these, the plains are commonly but erroneously called seas and oceans since Galileo thought these plains to be oceans. As part of its environ-ment, the Moon has a very thin atmosphere consisting of rare gases such as argon and kryp-ton. Therefore, there is no weather, no wind. Sound does not propagate. Due to the absence of wind and weather, its surface features have not eroded and consequently have remained unchanged through the ages except for the dam-age done by meteoroids falling on its surface. Water, which is fundamental to life as we con-ceive it, is thought to be almost nonexistent. Therefore, astronauts on exploratory ventures, will have to carry their own water, air, and other elements necessary for man's existence.

In recent years some inconclusive evidence shows that the Moon is still undergoing some of its distant-past volcanic activity to which are attributed the large majority of the lunar craters.

The "far side" of the Moon, which is not visible from Earth, remains comparatively un-known save for the photographic evidence gath-ered by the Russian Lunik III in 1959, which tends to indicate that the "hidden side" isn't very different from the "face side."

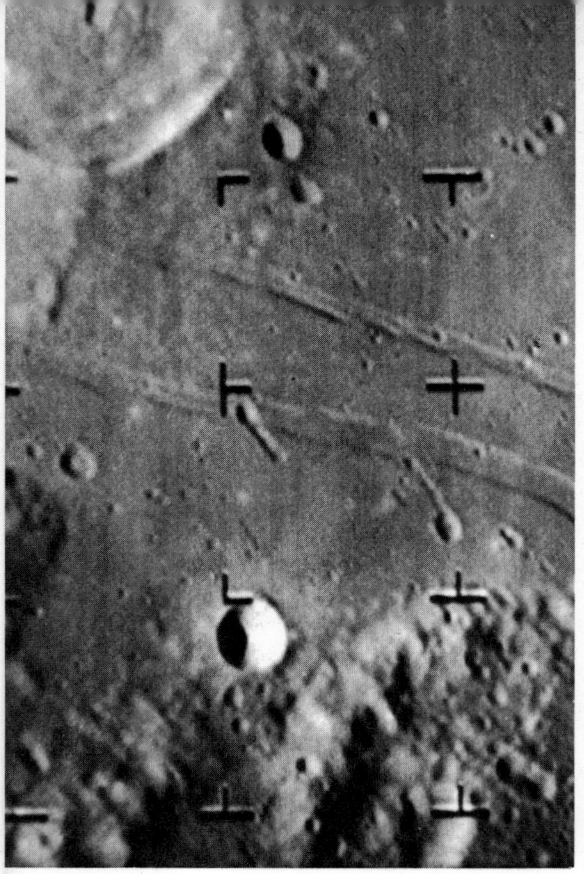

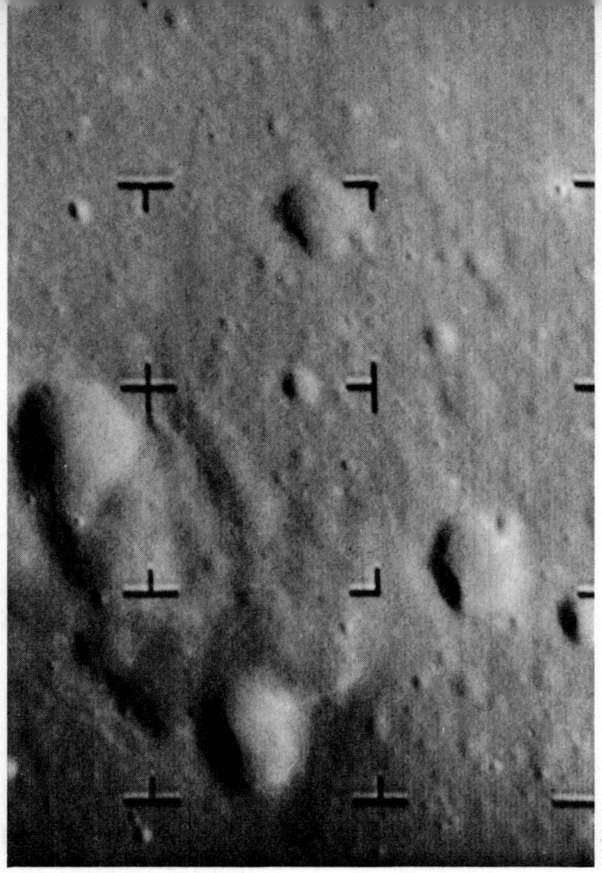

A.

Two photographs by Ranger VIII, February 20, 1965

B.

NASA

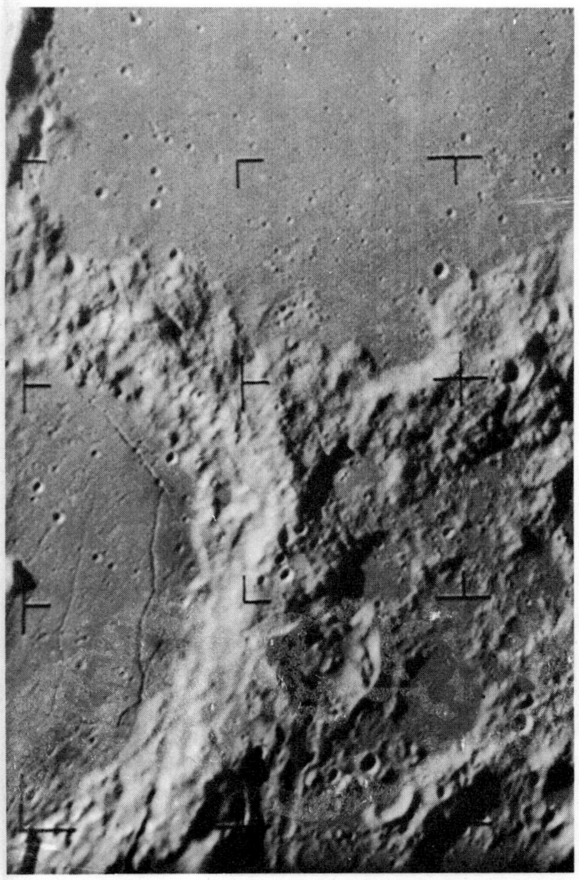

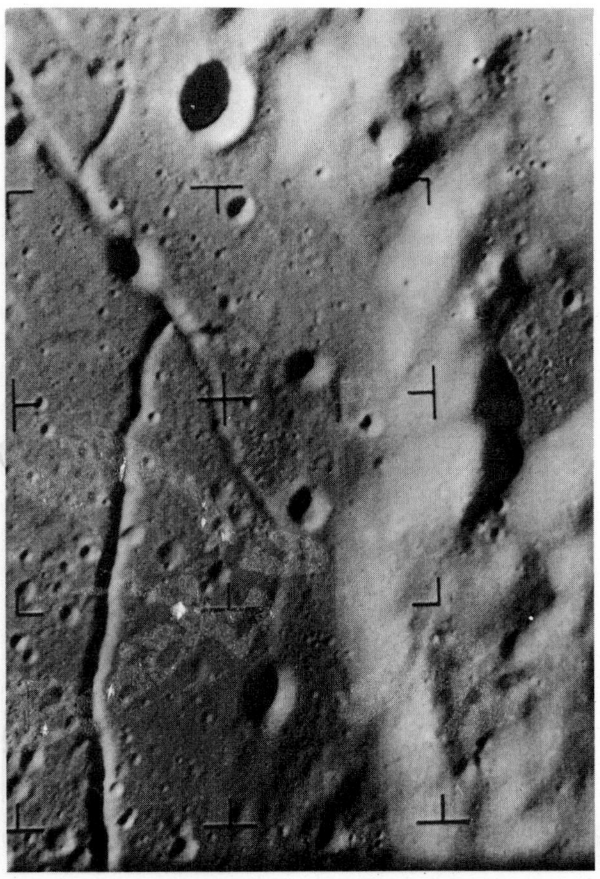

C.

Two photographs by Ranger IX, March 24, 1965

D.

NASA

THE ECLIPSES

ECLIPTIC—ORBIT OF EARTH AROUND SUN

MOON

UMBRA

MOON

SUN

ORBIT OF MOON

UMBRA

PENUMBRA

PENUMBRA

TOTAL ECLIPSE OF THE MOON

Eclipse of the moon occurs only when moon is full. Moon usually appears dull red during the eclipse due to the refraction of the red rays of the sun by the atmosphere of the earth.

TOTAL ECLIPSE OF THE SUN

Eclipse of the sun occurs only during new moon. Sun is invisible in *umbra* and partly invisible in *penumbra*. Total eclipse is visible only in portion of earth touched by shadow of moon (umbra).

THE TIDES

NEAP TIDES

SPRING TIDES

ECLIPTIC—ORBIT OF EARTH AROUND SUN

MOON

SUN

MOON

ORBIT OF MOON

FIRST AND LAST QUARTER

The moon's attraction works against that of the sun. The range of tides decreased.

FULL AND NEW MOON

The moon's attraction works with that of the sun. The range of tides increased.

VERNAL EQUINOX

Noon sun is directly overhead at the Equator on its apparent migration north. Day and night are equal.

APRIL 20

MARCH 21

FEBRUARY 19

MAY 21

JANUARY 20

SUMMER SOLSTICE
Noon sun is directly overhead at 23½°N. Longest day of year.

JUNE 21

July 3—Aphelion 94,560,000 miles

SUN

January 3—Perihelion 91,450,000 miles

DECEMBER 22

WINTER SOLSTICE
Noon sun is directly overhead at 23½°S. Shortest day of year.

JULY 23

NOVEMBER 22

AUGUST 23

SEPTEMBER 23

OCTOBER 23

AUTUMNAL EQUINOX

Noon sun is directly overhead at the Equator on its apparent migration south. Day and night are equal.

THE SEASONS

Northern Hemisphere

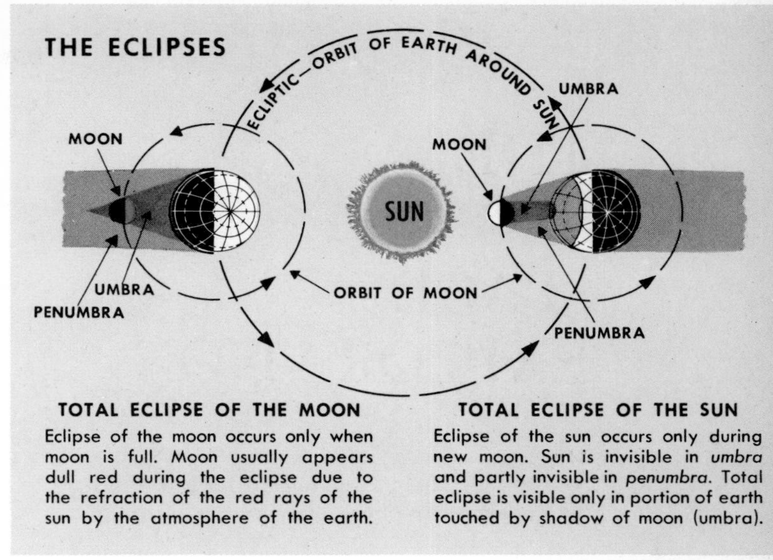

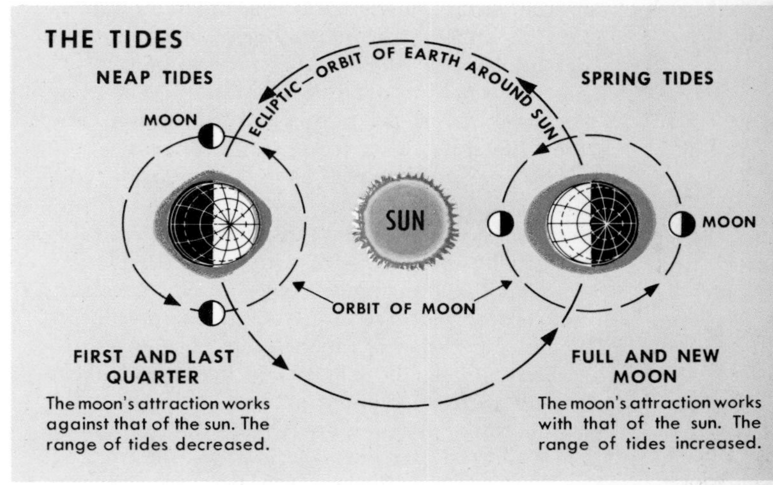

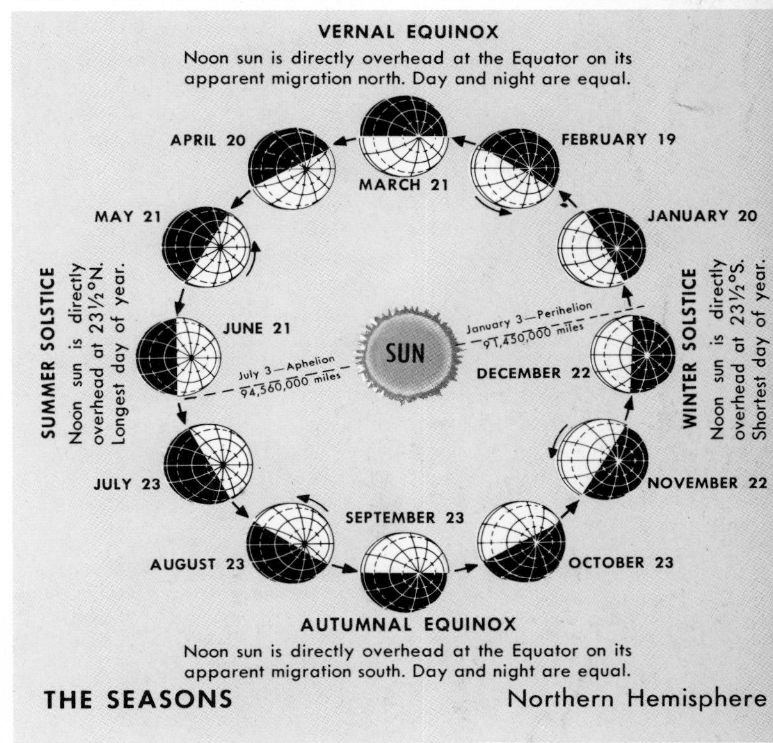

The Ranger program was a National Aeronautics and Space Administration (NASA) project designed to examine the surface of the Moon by means of unmanned spacecraft. Each spacecraft was equipped with a high-resolution, six-camera television system that provided both wide- and narrow-angle coverage. There were three successful Ranger missions. Of these, the last two Rangers, VIII and IX, provided the close-up views shown above. Both missions took place in early 1965.

A. This photograph was taken at an altitude of 151 miles over the lunar surface. The over-all north-south distance is 43 miles. It shows the shoreline of the Sea of Tranquillity, with part of crater Sabine in the northwest corner and the two parallel Hypatia Rills, which extend across the center. Toward the south lies rugged and difficult terrain containing numerous craters.

B. This exposure was taken at an altitude of 27.5 miles. The distance, from north to south, is 4.5 miles. It shows a particularly interesting irregular cluster of depressions which feature gentler slopes than had been anticipated. The surrounding landscape has a frothy appearance of undetermined consistency.

C. This photograph was taken at an altitude of 775 miles. It covers a north-south distance of 123 miles. It shows slightly more than half of two major craters: Ptolomaeus at the top (without significant floor features) and Alphonsus (target of Ranger IX) on the left which shows a rill system and a 3,300-foot central peak.

D. This photograph was taken at an altitude of 115 miles. The over-all north to south distance is 19 miles. It shows the northeastern edge of the floor of the crater Alphonsus and part of the crater's wall. The floor is cut prominently by rills (shown in less detail on figure C.) which are lined with small craterlets that have pocked part of the rills. Surprisingly, the crater walls have gentle slopes and rolling terrain.

THE SAGA OF SPACE EXPLORATION

Man's exploration of the space above the surface of the Earth, first in, and then beyond the life-giving atmosphere, has been a dramatic experience. In the scientific era in which we live, fundamental knowledge of the Earth's relationship to space will increasingly determine the destiny of man. Already the exploration of space has provided important information concerning the true nature of matter, time, motion, and even life itself. Vast scopes of basic data about many terrestrial as well as extraterrestrial realities are being gathered and processed. Unpredictable benefits for men on Earth will inevitably result from this complex effort.

Man is, now, capable of producing the enormous force required to place a human being in space. Nevertheless, to achieve this goal adequately and safely, it has been necessary first to start with instrumented probes and satellites to gather data helpful in developing the technological ability and equipment. These instrumented probes and satellites have come to number in the hundreds. It is appropriate here to note only the major efforts so far, and their practical returns to man.

Satellites equipped with television cameras and infrared sensors, by observing changing atmospheric conditions which man has no other way of knowing, have made possible vastly improved weather forecasts. These meteorological satellites provide advance warnings of tornadoes, floods, blizzards, and hurricanes, thus enabling people to minimize material loss. Below are examples of the Nimbus and Tiros satellites' photography, which is useful to a great number of Earth scientists in furthering man's understanding of his own planet.

Another example of the practical application of space technology are the communications satellites which have greatly augmented the world's radio and telecommunications facilities. Such satellites as Telstar, Relay, Syncom, and Early Bird have made possible global telecasts which measurably improve the degree of understanding between nations and peoples.

Other applications are navigation satellites which will provide accurate information to any of the hundreds of aircraft that crowd the world's skies, or to the 20,000 surface ships that are estimated to be on the Atlantic Ocean alone at certain times.

There are numerous other benefits which are not of direct application to everyday life, but which are just as important to research in other fields. For example, the astronomical satellites help astronomers overcome the distorting effects of the Earth's atmosphere while studying the heavens. And satellites in general assist in determining exact distances, locations, and precise shapes of land and sea areas on Earth, a boon to the mapmakers.

Beside satellites, there are the space probes through which much information has been gathered. These probes differ from satellites in that they are not intended to achieve moon or planetary orbit. Their purpose is to obtain new data via their instruments. In late 1962 Mariner II was launched and guided toward Venus. As it flew by that planet, Mariner II probed the Venusian environment for new data, and transmitted it back to Earth through 48,000,000 miles of interplanetary space. More recently another Mariner probe has been launched, this time in the direction of Mars. Besides data, it scanned photographically a small portion of the Martian surface. The photographs on the preceding page attest to the success of the Ranger missions to the Moon.

In the not-too-distant future man will launch probes in search of extraterrestrial life. The question of life in space and the question of the origin of life are interwoven. The full understanding of this relationship has innumerable implications in the study of human health and disease.

While these probes are being carried on today, man has taken a few steps toward space on his own. For comparatively brief periods of time astronauts and cosmonauts have reached the fringes of space (Projects Mercury and Vostok) and have even maneuvered outside their spacecraft in orbital flights around the Earth (Projects Gemini and Voskhod). For all purposes, man has been orbited in an artificial moon. In revolving about the Earth, a manned satellite has to obey the same physical laws that a natural satellite must. Consequently, man is being exposed to these new conditions and is, through these orbital missions, in the process of learning how to maneuver and behave effectively while in space.

Project Gemini and two-thirds of Project Apollo are devoted to developing the technical ability to navigate in space prior to a landing on the Moon. Project Apollo with a crew of three is designated to accomplish that. The final objective will be that, upon reaching the Moon's vicinity, the Apollo spacecraft will be swerved into a circular orbit about 100 miles above the lunar surface. Two astronauts will then enter the lunar excursion module portion of Apollo, detach it, and land on a previously chosen location on the Moon, while the third crewman remains in the parent craft which continues to orbit the Moon. After exploring the lunar surface near the landing site, taking pictures, etc., the two astronauts will depart from the Moon and rendezvous with the parent craft. After joining the third astronaut in the parent craft, they will detach from the lunar excursion module and return to Earth.

As man's increasing interest, knowledge, and control of inanimate energy has lead him to exploratory ventures here outlined, so it will carry him to a rendezvous with the secrets of the Universe and to a life still unimaginable.

Nimbus I took this clear picture of the Italian Peninsula and Sicily. Clouds on the right obscure the view of Yugoslavia, Albania, and Greece.

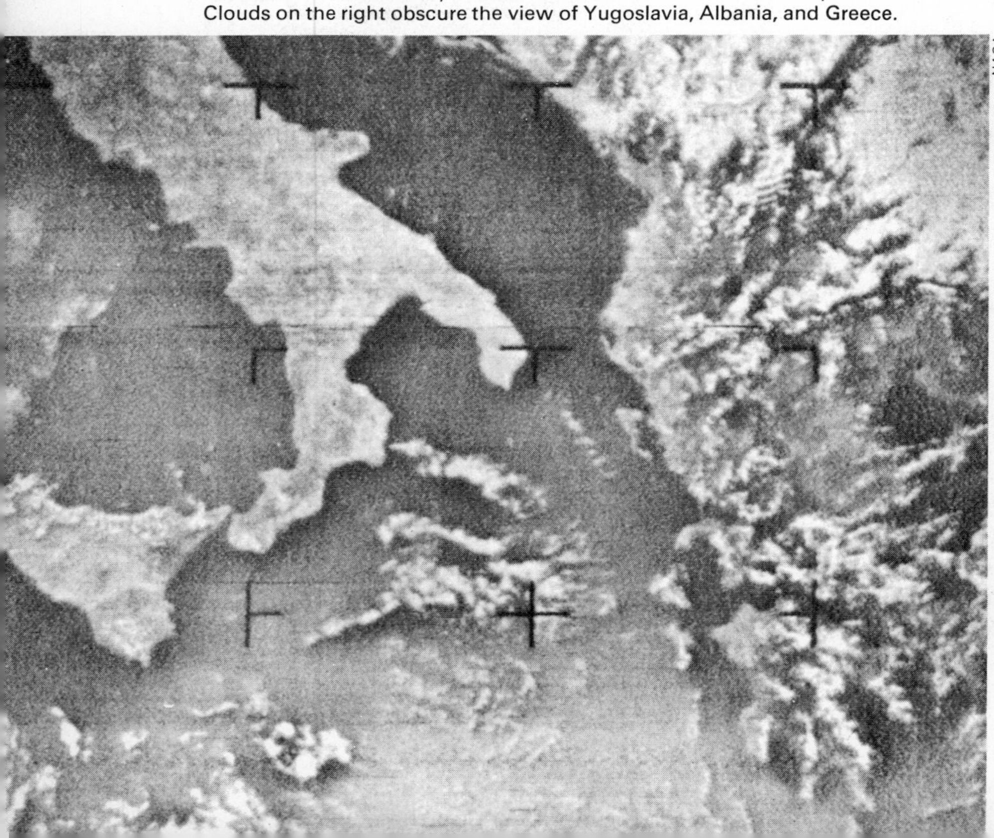

NASA

A photograph of the Red Sea area taken by Tiros I. Major features have been labeled for reference.

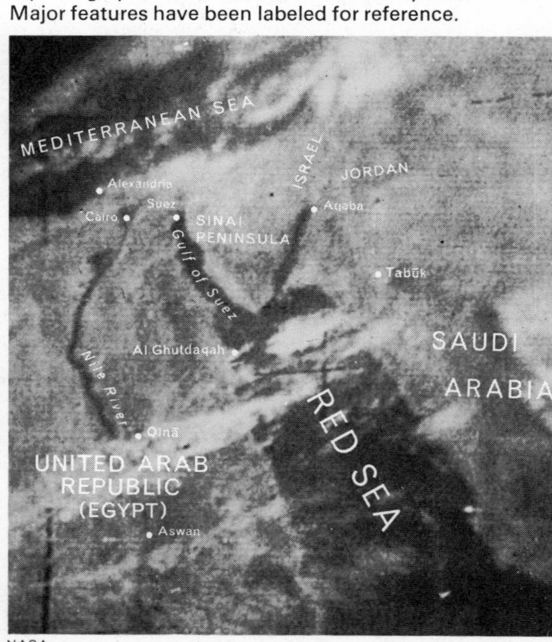

A reference map showing the same area photographed by Tiros I.

NASA

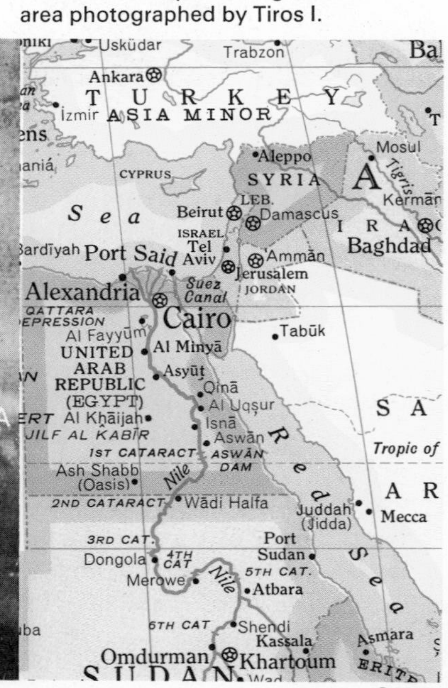

© RMcN

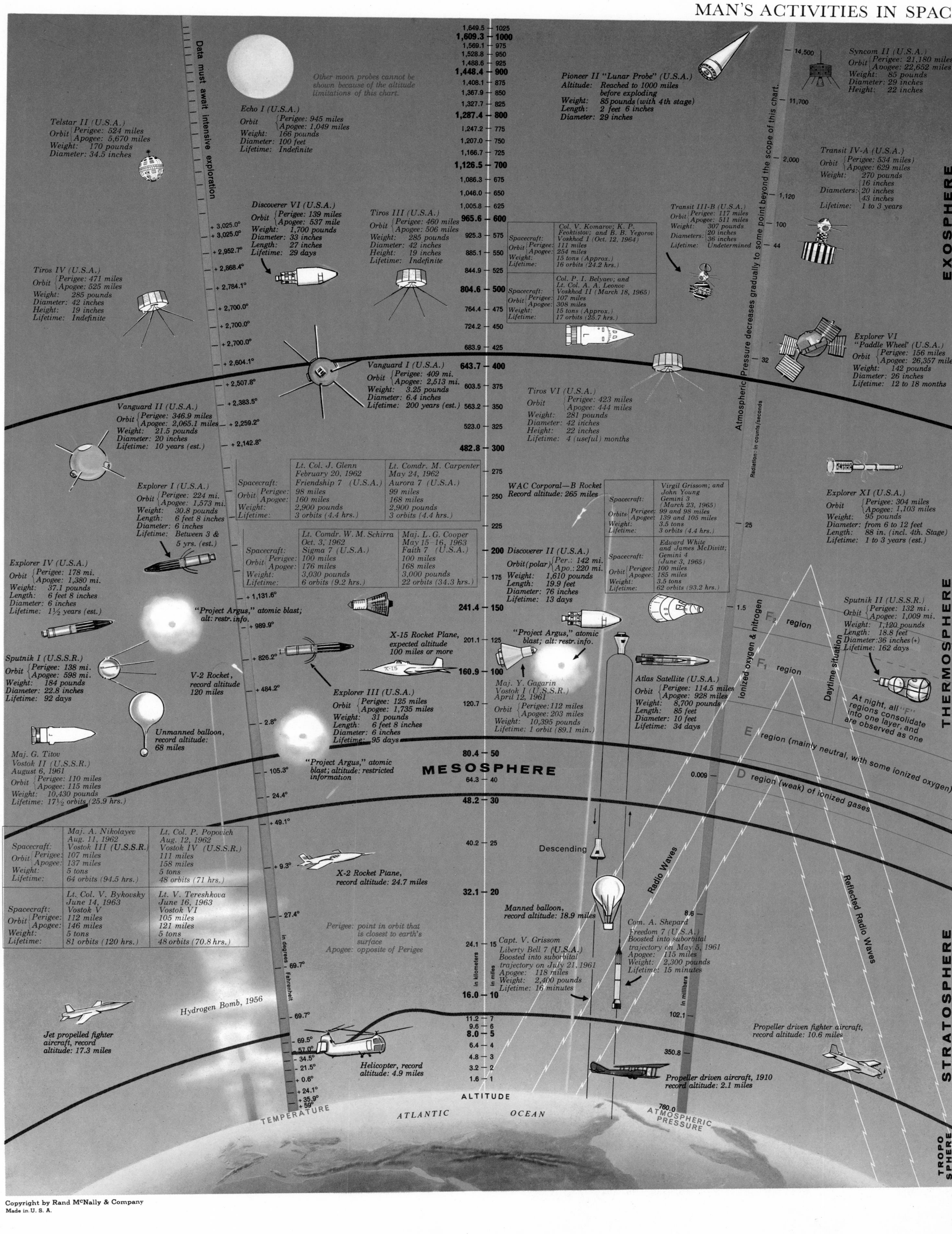

Data must await intensive exploration
Other moon probes cannot be shown because of the altitude limitations of this chart.
Echo I (U.S.A.) Orbit Perigee: 945 miles Apogee: 1,049 miles Weight: 166 pounds Diameter: 100 feet Lifetime: Indefinite
Telstar II (U.S.A.) Orbit Perigee: 524 miles Apogee: 5,670 miles Weight: 170 pounds Diameter: 34.5 inches
Pioneer II "Lunar Probe" (U.S.A.) Altitude: Reached to 1000 miles before exploding Weight: 85 pounds (with 4th stage) Length: 2 feet 6 inches Diameter: 29 inches
Syncom II (U.S.A.) Orbit Perigee: 21,180 miles Apogee: 22,652 miles Weight: 85 pounds Diameter: 29 inches Height: 22 inches
Transit IV-A (U.S.A.) Orbit Perigee: 534 miles Apogee: 629 miles Weight: 270 pounds Diameters: 16 inches 20 inches 43 inches Lifetime: 1 to 3 years
Discoverer VI (U.S.A.) Orbit Perigee: 139 miles Apogee: 537 mile Weight: 1,700 pounds Diameter: 33 inches Length: 27 inches Lifetime: 29 days
Tiros III (U.S.A.) Orbit Perigee: 460 miles Apogee: 506 miles Weight: 285 pounds Diameter: 42 inches Height: 19 inches Lifetime: Indefinite
Spacecraft: Col. V. Komarov; K. P. Feoktistov; and B. B. Yegorov Voskhod I (Oct. 12, 1964) Orbit Perigee: 111 miles Apogee: 254 miles Weight: 15 tons (Approx.) Lifetime: 16 orbits (24.2 hrs.)
Spacecraft: Col. P. I. Belyaev; and Lt. Col. A. A. Leonov Voskhod II (March 18, 1965) Orbit Perigee: 107 miles Apogee: 308 miles Weight: 15 tons (Approx.) Lifetime: 17 orbits (25.7 hrs.)
Transit III-B (U.S.A.) Orbit Perigee: 117 miles Apogee: 511 miles Weight: 307 pounds Diameters: 20 inches 36 inches Lifetime: Undetermined
Tiros IV (U.S.A.) Orbit Perigee: 471 miles Apogee: 525 miles Weight: 285 pounds Diameter: 42 inches Height: 19 inches Lifetime: Indefinite
EXOSPHERE
Explorer VI "Paddle Wheel" (U.S.A.) Orbit Perigee: 156 miles Apogee: 26,357 miles Weight: 142 pounds Diameter: 26 inches Lifetime: 12 to 18 months
Vanguard I (U.S.A.) Orbit Perigee: 409 mi. Apogee: 2,513 mi. Weight: 3.25 pounds Diameter: 6.4 inches Lifetime: 200 years (est.)
Tiros VI (U.S.A.) Orbit Perigee: 423 miles Apogee: 444 miles Weight: 281 pounds Diameter: 42 inches Height: 22 inches Lifetime: 4 (useful) months
Vanguard II (U.S.A.) Orbit Perigee: 346.9 miles Apogee: 2,065.1 miles Weight: 21.5 pounds Diameter: 20 inches Lifetime: 10 years (est.)
Atmospheric Pressure decreases gradually to some point beyond the scope of this chart.
Radiation: in counts/seconds
Spacecraft: Lt. Col. J. Glenn February 20, 1962 Friendship 7 (U.S.A.) Orbit Perigee: 98 miles Apogee: 160 miles Weight: 2,900 pounds Lifetime: 3 orbits (4.4 hrs.)
Lt. Comdr. M. Carpenter May 24, 1962 Aurora 7 (U.S.A.) 99 miles 168 miles 2,900 pounds 3 orbits (4.4 hrs.)
WAC Corporal—B Rocket Record altitude: 265 miles
Spacecraft: Virgil Grissom; and John Young Gemini 3 (March 23, 1965) Orbits Perigee: 99 and 98 miles Apogee: 139 and 105 miles Weight: 3.5 tons Lifetime: 3 orbits (4.4 hrs.)
Spacecraft: Edward White and James McDivitt; Gemini 4 (June 3, 1965) Orbit Perigee: 100 miles Apogee: 185 miles Weight: 3.5 tons Lifetime: 62 orbits (93.2 hrs.)
Explorer XI (U.S.A.) Orbit Perigee: 304 miles Apogee: 1,103 miles Weight: 95 pounds Diameter: from 6 to 12 feet Length: 88 in. (incl. 4th. Stage) Lifetime: 1 to 3 years (est.)
Explorer I (U.S.A.) Orbit Perigee: 224 mi. Apogee: 1,573 mi. Weight: 30.8 pounds Length: 6 feet 8 inches Diameter: 6 inches Lifetime: Between 3 & 5 yrs. (est.)
Spacecraft: Lt. Comdr. W. M. Schirra Oct. 3, 1962 Sigma 7 (U.S.A.) Orbit Perigee: 100 miles Apogee: 176 miles Weight: 3,030 pounds Lifetime: 6 orbits (9.2 hrs.)
Maj. L. G. Cooper May 15–16, 1963 Faith 7 (U.S.A.) 100 miles 168 miles 3,000 pounds 22 orbits (34.3 hrs.)
Discoverer II (U.S.A.) Orbit (polar) Per.: 142 mi. Apo.: 220 mi. Weight: 1,610 pounds Length: 19.9 feet Diameter: 76 inches Lifetime: 13 days
Explorer IV (U.S.A.) Orbit Perigee: 178 mi. Apogee: 1,380 mi. Weight: 37.1 pounds Length: 6 feet 8 inches Diameter: 6 inches Lifetime: 1½ years (est.)
"Project Argus," atomic blast; alt: restr. info.
F2 region
F1 region
ionized oxygen & nitrogen
Daytime situation
Sputnik II (U.S.S.R.) Orbit Perigee: 132 mi. Apogee: 1,009 mi. Weight: 1,120 pounds Length: 18.8 feet Diameter: 36 inches (+) Lifetime: 162 days
At night, all "F" regions consolidate into one layer, and are observed as one
THERMOSPHERE
X-15 Rocket Plane, expected altitude 100 miles or more
"Project Argus," atomic blast; alt: restr. info.
Sputnik I (U.S.S.R.) Orbit Perigee: 138 mi. Apogee: 598 mi. Weight: 184 pounds Diameter: 22.8 inches Lifetime: 92 days
V-2 Rocket, record altitude 120 miles
Explorer III (U.S.A.) Orbit Perigee: 125 miles Apogee: 1,735 miles Weight: 31 pounds Length: 6 feet 8 inches Diameter: 6 inches Lifetime: 95 days
Maj. Y. Gagarin Vostok I (U.S.S.R.) April 12, 1961 Orbit Perigee: 112 miles Apogee: 203 miles Weight: 10,395 pounds Lifetime: 1 orbit (89.1 min.)
Atlas Satellite (U.S.A.) Orbit Perigee: 114.5 miles Apogee: 928 miles Weight: 8,700 pounds Length: 85 feet Diameter: 10 feet Lifetime: 34 days
Unmanned balloon, record altitude: 68 miles
Maj. G. Titov Vostok II (U.S.S.R.) August 6, 1961 Orbit Perigee: 110 miles Apogee: 115 miles Weight: 10,430 pounds Lifetime: 17½ orbits (25.9 hrs.)
"Project Argus," atomic blast; altitude: restricted information
MESOSPHERE
E region (mainly neutral, with some ionized oxygen)
D region (weak) of ionized gases
Spacecraft: Maj. A. Nikolayev Aug. 11, 1962 Vostok III (U.S.S.R.) Orbit Perigee: 107 miles Apogee: 137 miles Weight: 5 tons Lifetime: 64 orbits (94.5 hrs.)
Lt. Col. P. Popovich Aug. 12, 1962 Vostok IV (U.S.S.R.) 111 miles 158 miles 5 tons 48 orbits (71 hrs.)
Spacecraft: Lt. Col. V. Bykovsky June 14, 1963 Vostok V Orbit Perigee: 112 miles Apogee: 146 miles Weight: 5 tons Lifetime: 81 orbits (120 hrs.)
Lt. V. Tereshkova June 16, 1963 Vostok VI 105 miles 121 miles 5 tons 48 orbits (70.8 hrs.)
X-2 Rocket Plane, record altitude: 24.7 miles
Descending
Radio Waves
Reflected Radio Waves
Manned balloon, record altitude: 18.9 miles
Perigee: point in orbit that is closest to earth's surface
Apogee: opposite of Perigee
Capt. V. Grissom Liberty Bell 7 (U.S.A.) Boosted into suborbital trajectory on July 21, 1961 Apogee: 118 miles Weight: 2,400 pounds Lifetime: 16 minutes
Com. A. Shepard Freedom 7 (U.S.A.) Boosted into suborbital trajectory on May 5, 1961 Apogee: 115 miles Weight: 2,300 pounds Lifetime: 15 minutes
Hydrogen Bomb, 1956
Jet propelled fighter aircraft, record altitude: 17.3 miles
Helicopter, record altitude: 4.9 miles
Propeller driven aircraft, 1910 record altitude: 2.1 miles
Propeller driven fighter aircraft, record altitude: 10.6 miles
STRATOSPHERE
TROPOSPHERE
in degrees Fahrenheit
in kilometers
in miles
in millibars
TEMPERATURE
ALTITUDE
ATMOSPHERIC PRESSURE
ATLANTIC OCEAN

MAPS AND MAP PROJECTIONS

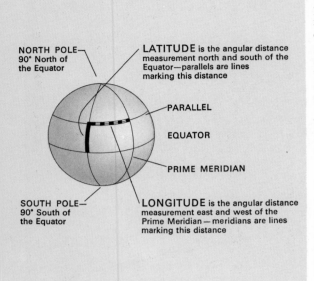

NORTH POLE—
90° North of
the Equator

LATITUDE is the angular distance
measurement north and south of the
Equator—parallels are lines
marking this distance

PARALLEL

EQUATOR

PRIME MERIDIAN

SOUTH POLE—
90° South of
the Equator

LONGITUDE is the angular distance
measurement east and west of the
Prime Meridian—meridians are lines
marking this distance

CONIC PROJECTIONS

Simple Conic

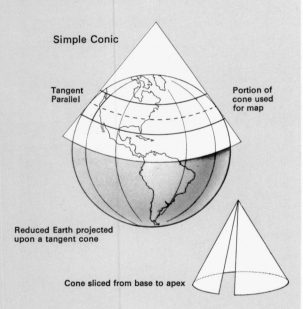

Tangent
Parallel

Portion of
cone used
for map

Reduced Earth projected
upon a tangent cone

Cone sliced from base to apex

Cone developed
onto a flat surface

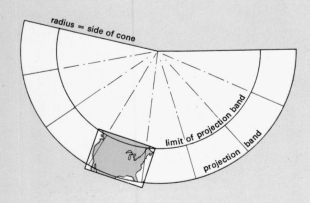

radius = side of cone

limit of projection band

projection band

From the earliest crude drawing to the latest highly accurate, skillful execution, maps have played a very important part in man's understanding of the planet upon which he lives. For only through the map, a reduced representation of the Earth's surface, can man visualize information about the location of places and things. Cities, rivers, mountain ranges, and transportation routes take on new meaning when viewed in relation to one another. Maps expand our conceptions about areas. The following pages are designed to point up some significant elements of maps which are useful in intelligently interpreting them and the variety of information they contain. These sections are *Map Projections, Map Scale, Map Symbols,* and the *Index Reference System.*

MAP PROJECTIONS

The systematic arrangement of parallels and meridians on a plane or flat surface is the framework upon which a map is constructed, and this orderly network is called a map projection. Projections are actually developed through the use of mathematical formulae. The process can best be comprehended by visualizing the following four steps.

1. The earth reduced to a small sphere.
2. Geometric forms—cone, cylinder, plane surface—placed upon or around this sphere.
3. Transferral of the Earth's imaginary grid of parallels and meridians to one of these forms.
4. The form flattened, producing the projection.

When projecting the Earth's curved surface to a flat surface, the *scale* of the map is never consistent throughout, and there may be some distortion of *shapes* of landmasses, and of *area* and *direction* representation. By planning the arrangement of the parallels and meridians some of these important properties can be preserved undistorted. However, to do so, one or more of the other properties must be sacrificed, for only the spherically shaped globe can represent all the characteristics and properties of the Earth's grid absolutely.

The text and diagrams on these pages treat some of the projections found in this atlas, their development, their properties, and characteristics.

Conic Projections

The Simple Conic or Conic as it is often called, the Lambert Conformal Conic, and the Polyconic, as their names imply, are all conically derived. Most of the maps in the atlas utilize these three conic projections. Parallels and meridians are projected onto a cone that is tangent to the reduced earth. Slicing the cone from its base to apex and flattening it onto a flat surface results in the *Simple Conic Projection.* Along the line that is tangent to the surface, the scale of the map is true. This line, usually a parallel, is called a *standard parallel.* As regions away from this line are mapped, the alterations of scale, shape, areal size, and direction increase. (See page 10 for example.)

The *Lambert Conformal Conic Projection* is similar to the Simple Conic, but it is modified so that the cone intersects the sphere in two places and thus provides two lines along which scale is true. Unlike the simple conic, the parallels and meridians are arranged in such a way as to retain correct shapes of regions throughout the map. This is *conformality.* Though the scale does vary as one moves away from the standard parallels, by selecting parallels that are closely spaced and by avoiding a region with a great north-south extent, relatively little distortion occurs. (See page 11 for example.)

The *Polyconic Projection* is formed by combining the surface of many cones to produce a projection with many standard parallels, in the fashion illustrated here. When flattening the surfaces of the cones, there is considerable stretching and consequent distortion toward the periphery. Again, by utilizing only the central portion of the projection (colored part of the diagram) the distorted area can be avoided and a map which minimizes scale alteration, shape, area, and direction distortion results. (See page 39 for example.)

Cylindrical Projections

By projecting the Earth's grid onto a tangent cylinder, we can achieve a series of parallels and meridians at right angles to one another, as they are on the Earth.

Lambert Conformal Conic

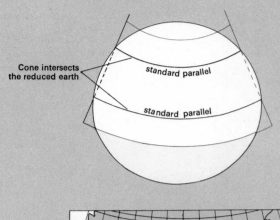

Cone intersects
the reduced earth

standard parallel

standard parallel

standard parallel

standard parallel

After flattening the cone, minor mathematical
adjustments create the Lambert Conformal
Conic with two standard parallels

Polyconic Projection

pole

Map developed
upon the
portion of the projection
with least distortion

CYLINDRICAL PROJECTIONS

Line of tangency

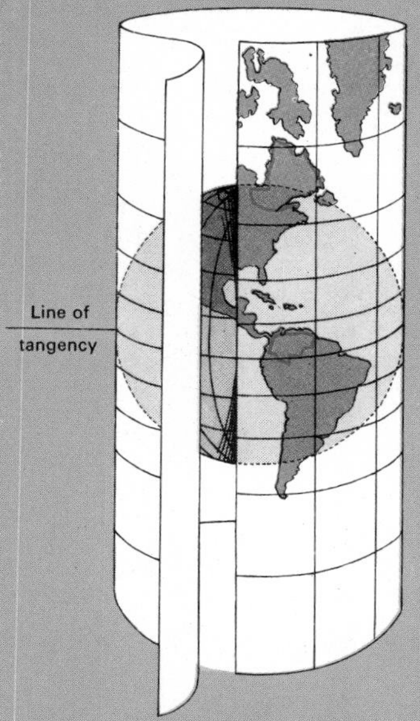

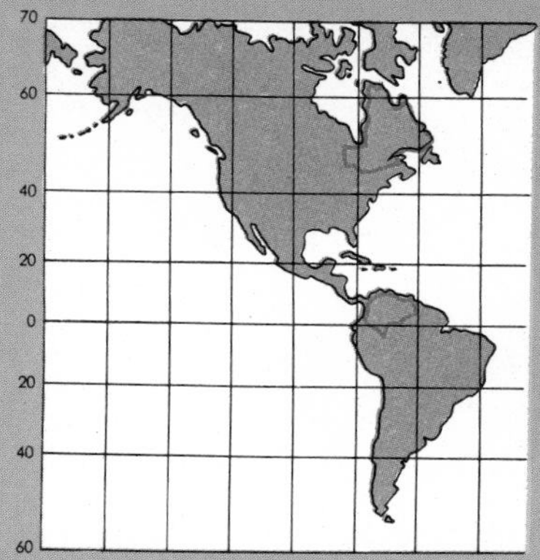

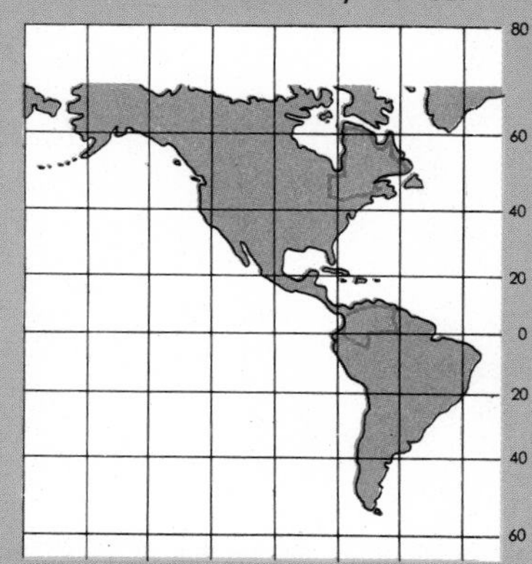

Simple projection of Earth grid to a cylinder tangent at the Equator. The poles are at infinity

Mercator Conformal

Miller Cylindrical

PLANE PROJECTIONS

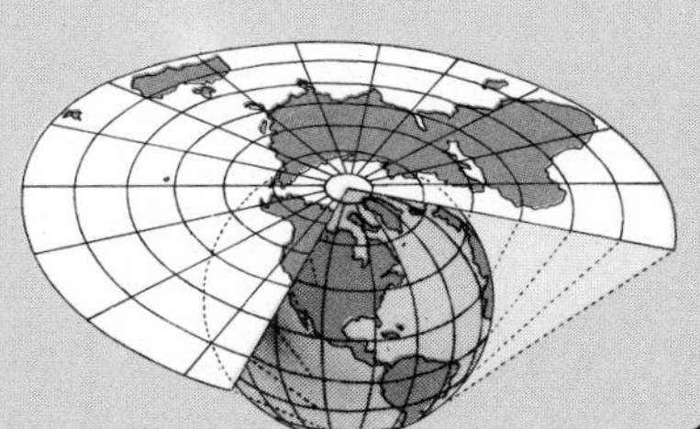

Plane tangent at the North Pole and the resultant projection

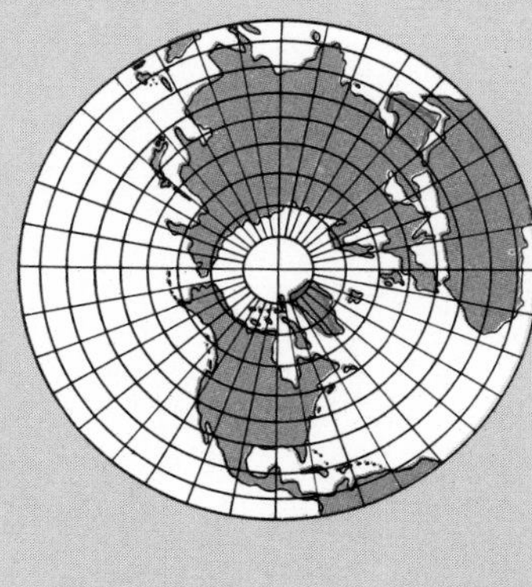

Lambert Equal Area Projection

However, sizes of areas and scales are extremely distorted as regions away from the line of tangency are mapped.

The *Mercator Conformal Projection* is a modification of this method of projecting. On it latitudinal distances are increased in the same proportion as longitudinal distances increase. The chief use of this familiar Mercator Projection has been in navigation because upon it straight lines represent constant compass directions. It shows the correct shapes of limited regions, but exaggerates areas in polar regions.

The *Miller Projection* was developed for general reference maps showing the entire world. Here, too, the parallels and meridians meet at right angles, but the latitudinal distances are not increased in proportion to the longitudinal distances, and for this reason shapes of landmasses are distorted toward polar regions, as is direction representation. However, exaggeration of area and scale has been reduced.

The three cylindrical projections illustrated here show how the same outlined regions look on all three. Notice that on all the maps there is a difference between the regions' areal extent; however, the difference is minimized by the Miller Projection. Comparison of the shapes of the regions with those on a globe shows the Mercator indicating this property most accurately. Other cylindrical projections enable the areas to be correctly shown while distorting the shapes of the landmasses; the cylinder may be tangent to the reduced earth at a position other than the Equator, thereby shifting the zone of least distortion to that region. There is a Miller Projection used on pages 2-3, and a Mercator Projection on page 172.

Plane Projections

Here transformation of the sphere directly to a tangent flat surface is the method of projection. The *Lambert Azimuthal Equal Area Projection* is one upon which the correct relationships between areas have been maintained. For instance, Greenland and the lower portion of the Arabian Peninsula, which are approximately the same in areal extent, appear to be so on the Lambert Azimuthal Equal Area Projection. Notice, however, that although Africa's area is shown correctly, it has been stretched in one direction and compressed in another, thus altering its shape and the scale of the projection. By arranging the spacing of the parallels and meridians differently on the plane surface, true shape (conformality), consistent scale, or correct directions from the center in all directions may also be obtained instead of the equal area property. In any case, retention of the one important property of the sphere creates extreme distortion of all the other properties as regions away from the center of the projection (the point of tangency) are mapped. See page 4 for an example of the Lambert Azimuthal Equal Area projection and page 7 for one that maintains consistent scale from the center of the projection in all directions along the meridians.

Equal Area Projections of the World

To show the world in its entirety on a flat surface so that areas may be compared intelligently, is extremely difficult without altering the shapes of areas beyond recognition. Cylindrical projections do not accomplish this, and plane and conic projections also do not represent the whole world this way. Two projections are frequently used today to accomplish this—the *Homolographic* and the *Sinusoidal*. Each retains the equal area property of the sphere, although each sacrifices uniform scale and invites some extreme shape compression and shearing in the polar areas of the projections.

Using the Homolosine from 40° to the poles and the Sinusoidal from the Equator to 40°, J. Paul Goode took advantage of each of these projections to create the *Goode's Interrupted Homolosine Projection*. This technique of interrupting a projection can be better understood by visualizing the surface of the earth peeled and laid flat. Splitting in the oceanic regions enables the land areas to remain relatively free from shape distortion and allows the land areas to be realistically compared for size.

In summary, where maps cover approximately a hemisphere of the Earth's surface, extreme distortion of some type is evidenced. On most of the maps of the NEW COSMOPOLITAN WORLD ATLAS, however, individual choices of projections have been made to present a realistic picture of the Earth. With these maps the user may compare sizes of areas, shapes of landmasses, and measure distances and directions as accurately as necessary.

EQUAL AREA PROJECTIONS OF THE WORLD

Mollweide Homolographic (Equal Area)

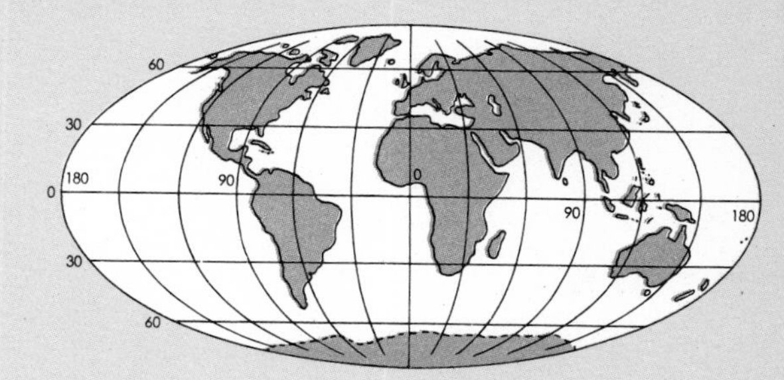

Sinusoidal

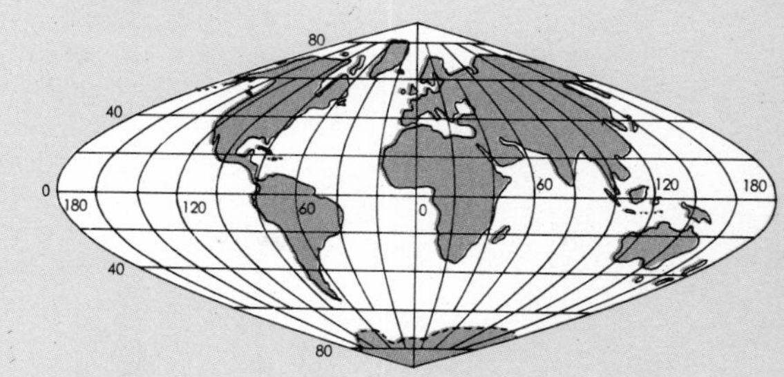

Goode's Interrupted Homolosine

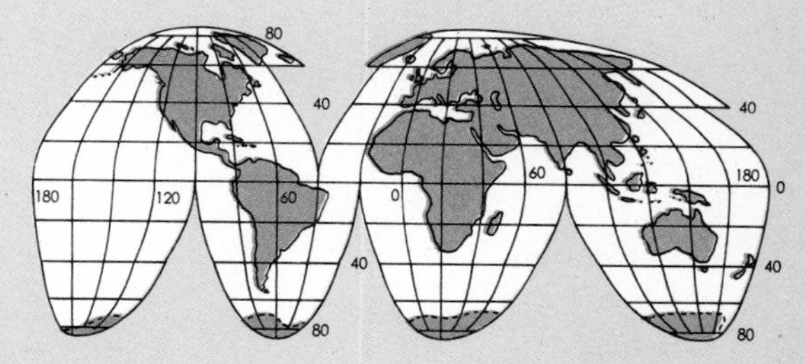

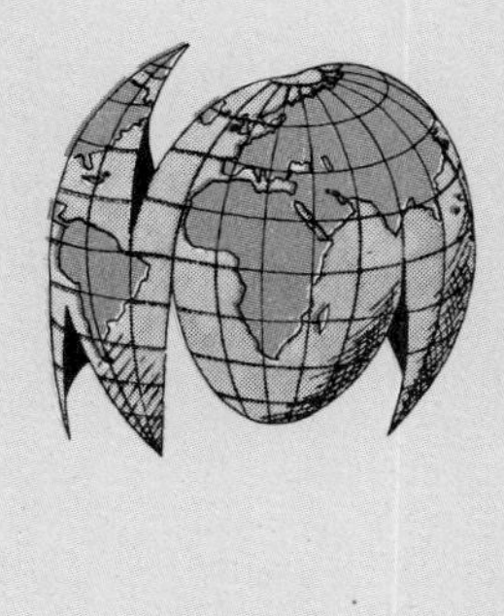

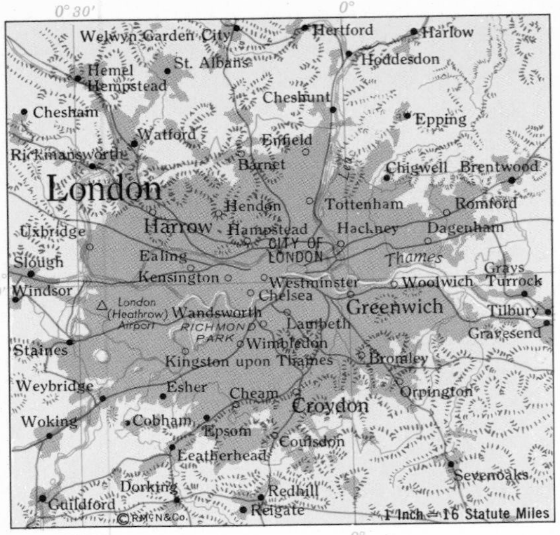

LONDON
1:1,000,000
1 inch = 16 statute miles

Statute Miles 5 0 5 10 15

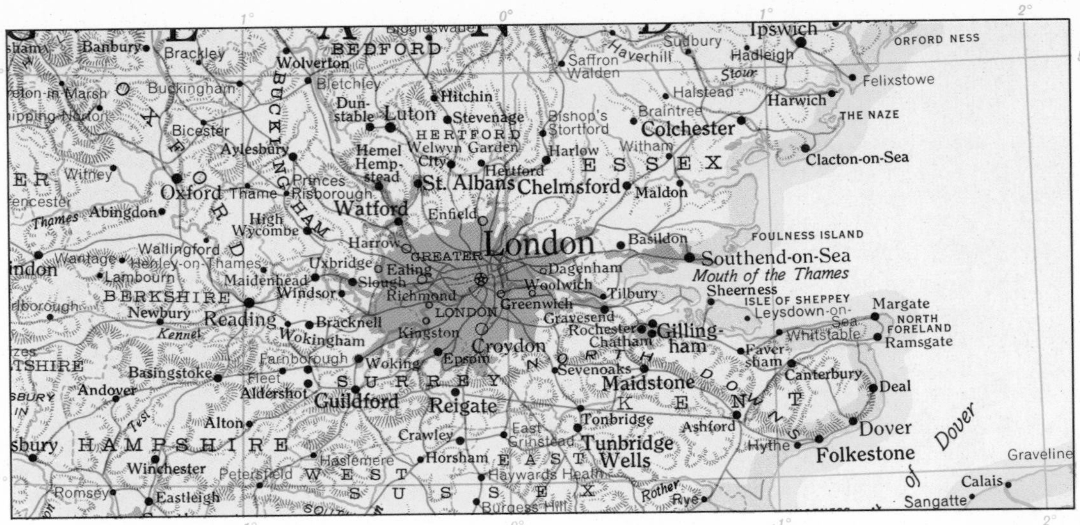

LONDON AND VICINITY
1:2,000,000
1 inch = 32 statute miles

Statute Miles 5 0 5 10 20 30

MAP SCALE

The scale of a map is the relationship it has with the area it represents. It usually is determined by measuring the distance between two places on the map and relating this to the distance between the same two places on the Earth's surface. This relationship may be stated in a number of different ways. Three commonly used methods are the representative fraction, a written statement, and a graphic portrayal. Each of the four maps on this page has its scale stated by these three methods.

The *representative fraction* is written either $\frac{1}{1,000,000}$ or 1:1,000,000. The map unit is always given as one, and the number of similar units this map unit represents on the Earth's surface is written as the denominator of the fraction, or after the colon. Thus, 1 inch or 1 centimeter on the London map in the upper left of the page represents 1,000,000 inches or 1,000,000 centimeters on the Earth's surface. In order to determine how many miles on the Earth 1 inch on the map represents, divide 63,360 (the number of inches in one mile) into 1,000,000. This results in the *written scale* being stated 1 inch represents approximately 16 miles. To further simplify the written scale by a *graphic portrayal*, a distance measured on the map may be converted to the Earth miles it represents by reading directly off the scale. The measured distance from London to Glasgow on the 1:16,000,000 scale map is 1.35 inches, which represents approximately 340 miles, the actual distance on the Earth's surface.

Because the Earth is spherical in shape and the map representing this sphere is flat, a degree of stretching and compressing has taken place in the projection of the sphere to the flat surface. (See the preceding section on projections). Inconsistency of scale from place to place on all maps is one of the results of this flattening process. The size relationship of map measurement to Earth measurement (scale) may not be exactly as stated on all parts of the map. Generally, as one moves away from the standard parallels, or the midsection of the map, toward the periphery, the stated scale changes. Because most of the Cosmo Series Maps encompass relatively small portions of the Earth's surface, the change in scale is of little consequence for general map use.

On world maps, however, where the scale varies greatly from one latitude to another, a varying graphic scale is employed. See the Graphic Linear Scale employed on the world map on pages 2 and 3. This permits accurate measurements at various parallels of latitude. At parallel 45°, 1 inch represents approximately 1,000 miles; at parallel 60° 1 inch represents approximately 700 miles.

As the scale of a map increases, the amount of information and detail shown increases, that is, the representative fraction and scale become larger. Notice in the four examples on this page how the increase in scale makes possible an increase in the number of cities shown, in the detail of the coastline, and in the intricacy and number of rivers.

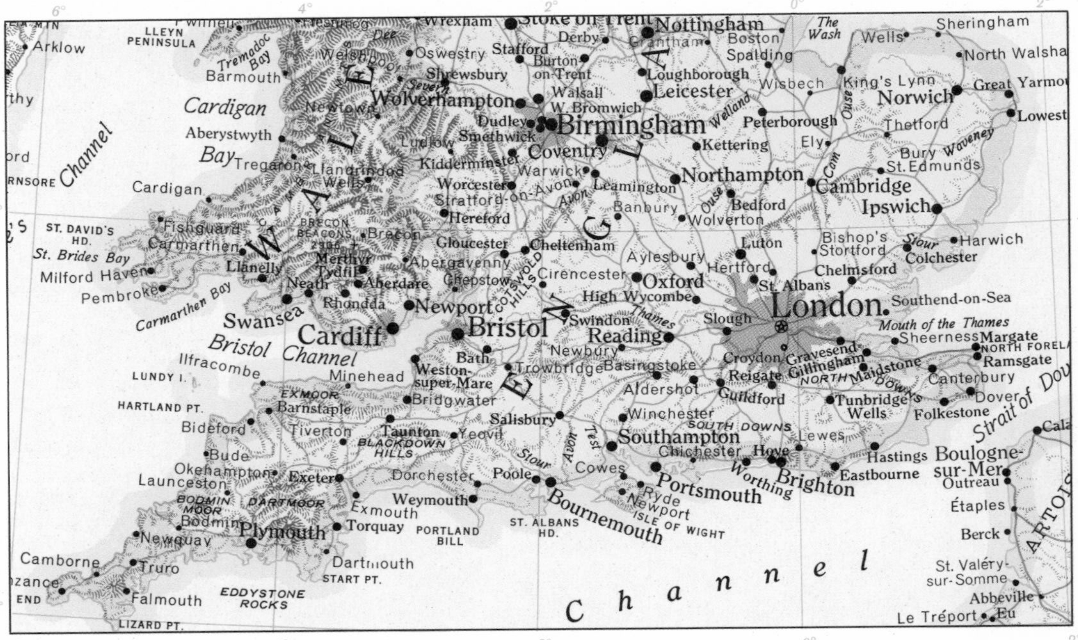

SOUTHERN ENGLAND
1:4,000,000
1 inch = 64 statute miles

Statute Miles 25 0 25 50 75

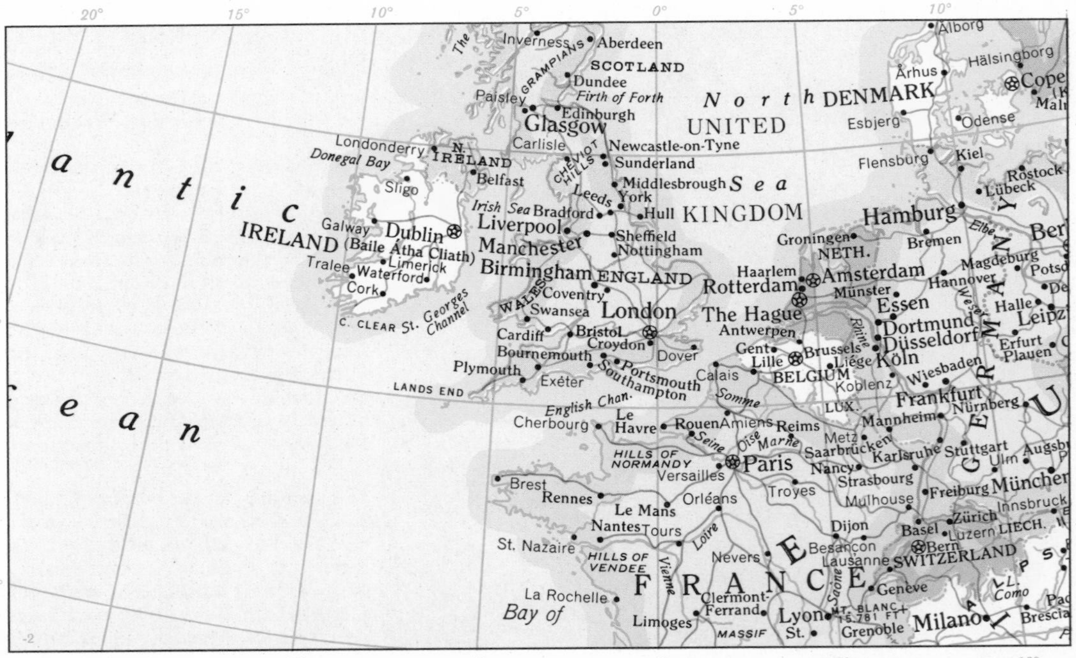

NORTHWEST EUROPE
1:16,000,000
1 inch = 252 statute miles

Statute Miles 100 0 100 200 300

MAP SYMBOLS

CULTURAL FEATURES

Political Boundaries

- International
- Secondary (State, province, etc.)
- County

Populated Places

Cities, towns, and villages
Symbol size represents population of the place

Chicago
Gary
Racine
Glenview
Edgewood

Type size represents relative importance of the place.

Corporate area of large U.S. and Canadian cities and urban area of other foreign cities

Major Urban Area
Area of continuous commercial, industrial, and residential development in and around a major city

- Community within a city
- Capital of major political unit
- Capital of secondary political unit
- Capital of U.S. state or Canadian province
- County Seat
- Military Installation
- Scientific Station

Miscellaneous

- National Park
- National Monument
- Provincial Park
- Indian Reservation
- Point of Interest
- Ruins
- Buildings
- Race Track
- NYC Railroad (Initialed in U.S. and Canada)
- Tunnel
- Underground or Subway
- Dam
- Bridge
- Dike

LAND FEATURES

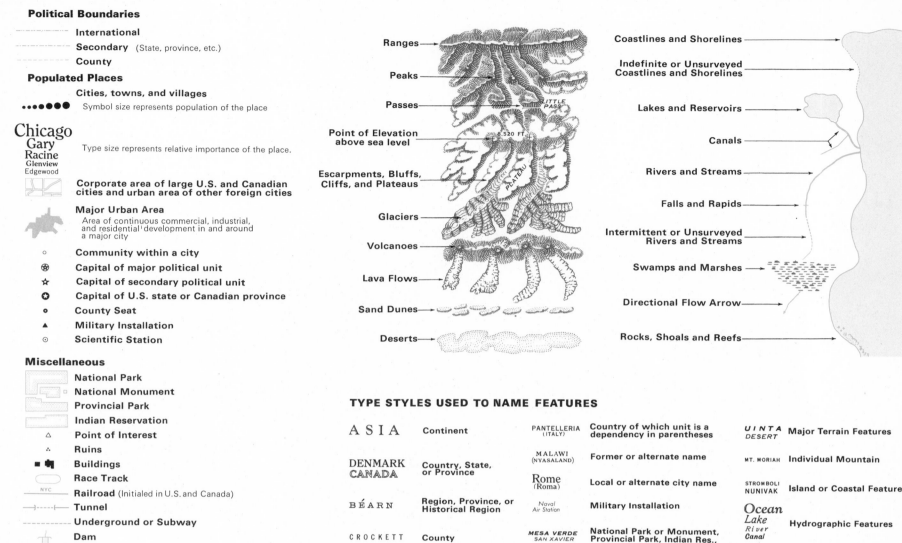

WATER FEATURES

TYPE STYLES USED TO NAME FEATURES

Sample	Meaning
ASIA	Continent
DENMARK / CANADA	Country, State, or Province
BÉARN	Region, Province, or Historical Region
CROCKETT	County
PANTELLERIA (ITALY)	Country of which unit is a dependency in parentheses
MALAWI (NYASALAND)	Former or alternate name
Rome (Roma)	Local or alternate city name
Naval Air Station	Military Installation
MESA VERDE / SAN XAVIER	National Park or Monument, Provincial Park, Indian Res.,
UINTA DESERT	Major Terrain Features
MT. MORIAH	Individual Mountain
STROMBOLI / NUNIVAK	Island or Coastal Feature
Ocean / Lake / River / Canal	Hydrographic Features

Note: Size of type varies according to importance and available space. Letters for names of major features are spread across the extent of the feature.

THE INDEX REFERENCE SYSTEM

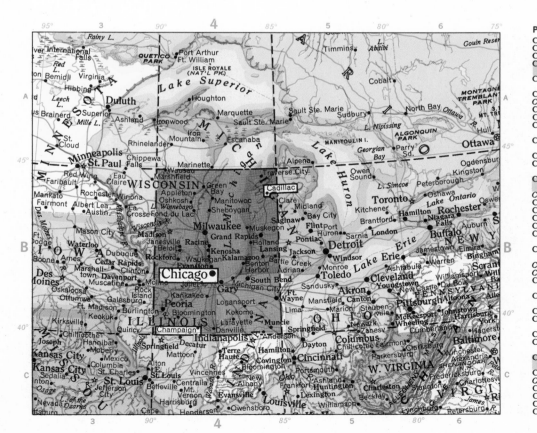

Place Location Pop.	Index Key	Page
Cadillac, Que., Can., 1,077	*E9	72
Cadillac, Sask., Can., 245	H2	70
Cadillac, Fr., 2,324	E3	14
Cadillac, Wexford, Mich., 10,112	B4	98
Cadiz, San Bernardino, Calif., 50	E6	79
Cadiz, Trigg, Ky., 1,980	D2	94
Cadron, creek, Ark	B3	81
Caen, Fr., 91,336 (*120,000)	C3	14
Caetité, Braz., 4,823	D2	57
Chamblee, DeKalb, Ga., 6,635	A5	87
Chambly Canton, Que., Can., 1,885	*D4	73
Chamdo (Changtu), China	E4	34
Champagne, former prov., Fr., 1,504,000	C5	14
Champaign, Champaign, Ill., 49,583	B4	90
Champdore, lake, Que., Can	g8	75
Champerico, Guat., 982	C2	62
Champéry, Switz., 810	D2	19
Champex, Switz	D3	19
Champigneulles, Fr., 5,854	F6	15
Champion, Chase, Nebr., 140	D4	103
Champlain, co., Que., Can., 111,953	B4	73
Champlain, lake, Que., Can	E4	73
Champlain, lake, N.Y., Vt.	B2	120
Chiapa de Corzo, Mex., 6,972	D6	63
Chiapas, state, Mex., 1,215,475	D6	63
Chiba, Jap., 241,615	I10, n19	37
Chiba, pref., Jap., 2,306,010	*I10	37
Chibemba, Ang., 354	E1	48
Chibougamau, Que., Can., 4,765	G18 61, B2	73
Chicago, Cook, Ill., 3,550,404 (*6,517,600)	B4, F3	90
Chichaoua, Mor	C3	44
Chichen-Itzá, ruins, Mex.	C7	63
Chichester, Eng., 20,118	D7	12
Chickasaw, co., Iowa, 15,034	A5	92
Chiclana, Sp., 21,524	D2	20
Chiclayo, Peru, 38,517	C2	58

The indexing system used in this atlas is based upon the conventional pattern of parallels and meridians used to indicate latitude and longitude. The index samples beside the map indicate that the cities of *Chicago*, *Cadillac*, and *Champaign* are all located in *B4*. Each index key letter, *in this case "B,"* is placed between corresponding degree numbers of latitude in the vertical borders of the map. Each index key number, *in this case "4,"* is placed between corresponding degree numbers of longitude in the horizontal borders of the map. Crossing of the parallels above and below the index letter with the meridians on each side of the index number forms a confining "box" in which the given place is certain to be located. It is important to note that location of the place may be anywhere in this confining "box."

Insets on many foreign maps are indexed independently of the main maps by separate index key letters and figures. All places indexed to these insets are identified by the lower case reference letter in the index key. A diamond-shaped symbol in the margin of the map is used to separate the insets from the main map and also to separate key letters and numbers where the spacing of the parallels and meridians is great.

Place-names are indexed to the location of the city symbol. Political divisions and physical features are indexed to the location of their names on the map.

WORLD
REFERENCE
MAPS

In the NEW COSMOPOLITAN ATLAS the world has been mapped on a broad regional basis, not country by country. Introducing each of the regions is a global view of that region, showing how the land might appear in its summer mantle of vegetation if viewed from far out in space. Accompanying text characterizes the region's physical geography, and a simple multicolored outline map identifies the countries of this world region.

Following each of these global views are the Cosmo Series Maps of the region, with each great landmass shown as a whole and subsequently broken down into major continental regions.

THE AMERICAS

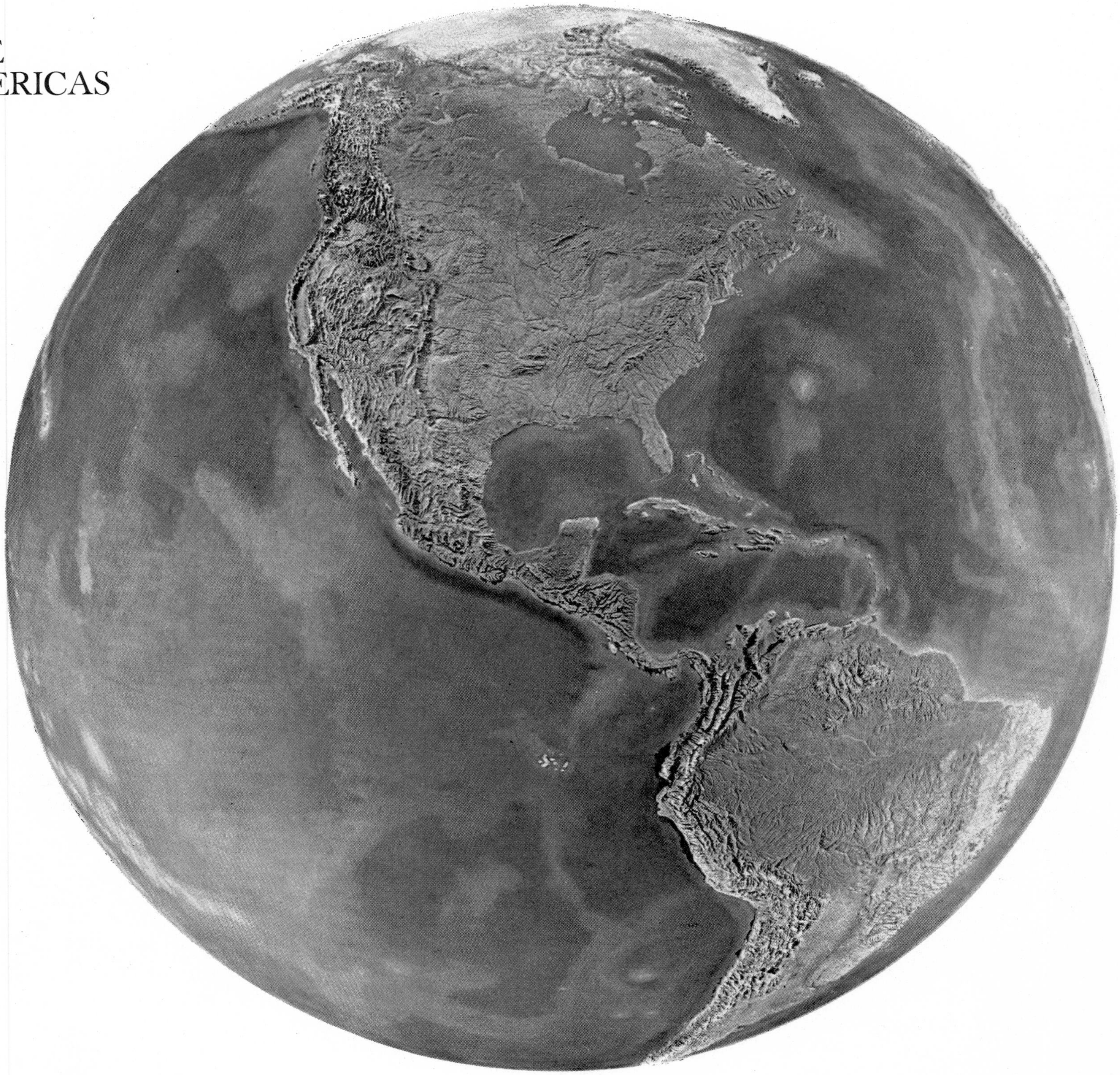

A continuous mountain chain, extending from Cape Horn to the icy peaks of Alaska, links the two Americas. The somber, mysterious Andes jut almost straight up from the blue Pacific to reach the highest elevations in the Western Hemisphere. The mountains continue north at much lower level through Central America, and in Mexico they divide into the west and east Sierra Madre. They join again to become the rugged Rockies that dominate the west of the United States and Canada, where they are flanked by lower parallel ranges to the sea.

The eastern portions of both Americas are marked by lower land—some wasteland, other portions rich for grazing or crops—and each is threaded with mighty river systems. The Amazon has its headwaters in the Andes, and the Missouri-Mississippi river system rises from the drainage flowing east of the Continental Divide.

As an example, pages xx-xxiv are global views which introduce the Cosmo Series Maps on pages 1-7; and pages 7A-7B, the global view of Europe, introduce maps on pages 8-32.

All the regional maps for each continent are drawn on the same scale. Thus it is possible to make direct visual comparisons of the sizes of countries and the distances between places by turning from one map to another. For instance, North America is mapped in three regions—Mexico, United States, Canada—all at the scale of 1:12,000,000. South America's regions are shown at the scale of 1:8,000,000, Europe's, Asia's, and Australia's re-

gions at the scale of 1:16,000,000, and Africa's at the scale of 1:11,400,000. Smaller areas are shown in detail on larger scale sectional maps, which are even multiples of the regional scales.

The maps carry as many political subdivisions as space will permit. Counties are shown on all U.S. state maps and on the maps of appropriate Canadian provinces. Other countries may not be mapped on a large enough scale to show administrative subdivisions. For some of these countries, the names of larger administrative subdivisions appear without the boundaries. In others, regions with historical significance are shown.

AFRICA–EURASIA

Complexes of high ranges run almost continuously from the Atlas in northwestern Africa, through the Alps, across the Balkans, Turkey, Iran, and Afghanistan to the Himalayas, physically linking Africa, Europe, and Asia, the area upon which this global view is focused.

Only by the Mediterranean, Black, Caspian, Baltic, and Red seas is this extensive landmass interrupted. In this expanse a tremendous variety of contrasts in landscapes may be found: the lush, uninhabited growth of vegetation of the lowlands of equatorial Africa is in sharp contrast to the bleak Sa-

haran deserts. The well cultivated, and densely settled lowlands of Eurasia contrast with the barren steppes and tundra of Central Asia. The highest and the lowest points, and the wettest and hottest spots in the world are all found in this great and historic multicontinental area.

EASTERN ASIA

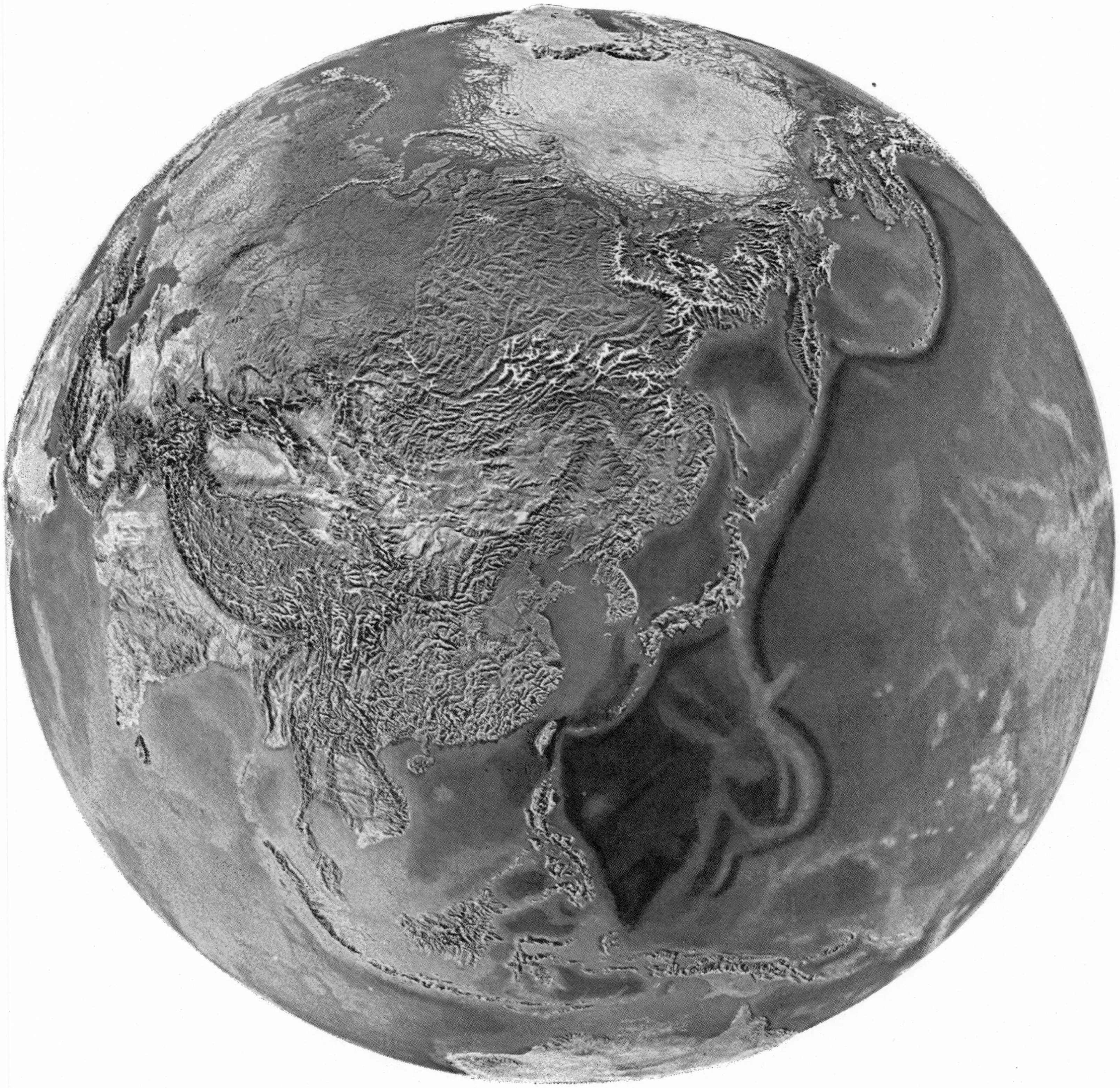

From a vantage point in space above the Fiji, the magnificent sweep of the island-fringed seaboard of Asia appears protected from the Pacific by bastions of lagoons.

Going along the seaboard from the Bering Strait, the first bastion is the Bering Sea, then the Sea of Okhotsk, clearly outlined by the Kamchatka Peninsula of the Soviet Union, the Kurile Islands, and the island of Sakhalin. Next, the Sea of Japan is hemmed in by the islands of Japan and the peninsula of Korea; and the Yellow Sea washes the shores of China, Taiwan, and the western edges of the Ryuku Islands.

As the China coast rounds to the west, the open water beyond the Philippines becomes the South China Sea of typhoon fame. Here the island of Hainan guards the approaches through the Gulf of Tonkin to China and Indochina (the Vietnams, Laos, Cambodia). From the Malay Peninsula the islands of the East Indies form a crescent-shaped, containing line, defining the southern limits of Eastern Asia.

The eastern mainland of Asia spans more than sixty degrees of latitude. South of the mountains of eastern Siberia forested lowlands and great fertile plains extend inland along 2,400 miles of this latitude.

In the southeastern portion of the continent lie the monsoon lands of Asia, where the summer monsoon, borne by the winds from the Indian and Pacific oceans, pours a phenomenal amount of moisture upon the land, more than 95 inches each month during June and July.

The immense landmass of Antarctica, which is almost once again as big as Australia, remains the most isolated of all the continents. It was the last of the world's continents to be sighted by man, and it was a good three centuries after the Age of Discovery, not until 1841, that the Englishman, James Clark Ross, gazed at Mt. Erebus in what he named Victoria Land.

The discovery of Antarctica was impeded by the protective barrier of pack ice clogging the sea approaches to it, and its settle-ment has been thwarted by the severest of natural conditions—an ice cap two miles thick which masks the continent almost completely, ranges of mountains rivaling the Rockies and the Alps, temperatures which very seldom rise above 0° and often plummet to −100°, and winds that blow up to 200 miles an hour.

In the International Geophysical Year, 1958-59, a group of the world's nations cooperated in an intensive study of the continent at the bottom of the world. Modern scientific equipment was employed to measure the ice cap, record the temperature, and survey the mineral wealth. The United States maintained a station at the Pole to observe weather and terrestrial magnetism. The mineral surveys recorded that deposits of coal, tin, lead, and copper were locked in below the ice cap, maybe never to be liberated from their frozen prison.

Modern science has provided adequate shelter and special machines for man and with them study of Antarctica continues.

THE
POLAR NORTH

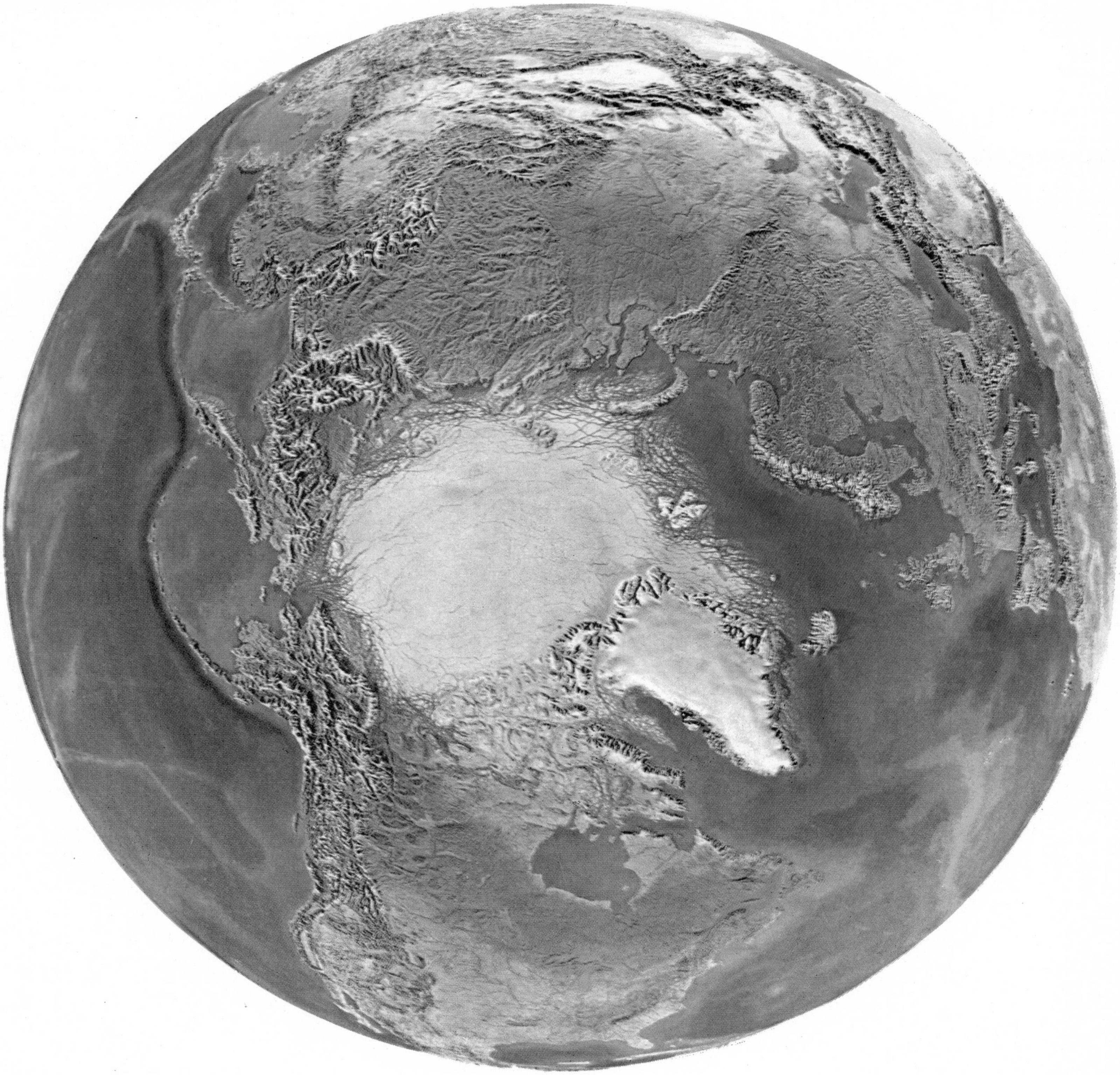

Only a strong inference of the land bridge which once linked North America with Asia remains in the Bering Strait region. But the North Polar ice cap still links the East with the West and dominates the northern portions of the two landmasses by extending its permanent ice and snow around the islands and peninsulas of both continents. As this global view shows, the warmer currents of the North Atlantic hold back this ice and snow from the northern coast of Scandinavia and a part of the Soviet Union.

The North Pole, 90° N. latitude, is located in the midst of perpetually frozen waters of the Arctic Ocean, and there is no North Polar continent. There are Arctic lands, however. Across the northern reaches of Alaska, Canada, and Norway lies tundra where moss and lichen thrive, and a spread of evergreen forests in Siberia and Canada benefit from a brief and chilly summer.

The Arctic lands of North America—Baffin Island and the many glaciered Greenland—are sparsely peopled, mostly by Eski-

mos. The Eurasian islands of Iceland, Svalbard (Spitsbergen), Novaya Zemlya, Severnaya Zemlya, and the New Siberian Islands are mostly ice- and snow-covered. Although there is a small population in a few of the islands, they are peopled mostly by natives and men who have come to tap the mineral wealth. The sea below the Arctic's ice has been crossed, and airlines regularly fly over it, but in most of the area, dominated by the extreme Polar climate, little exploration or development has taken place.

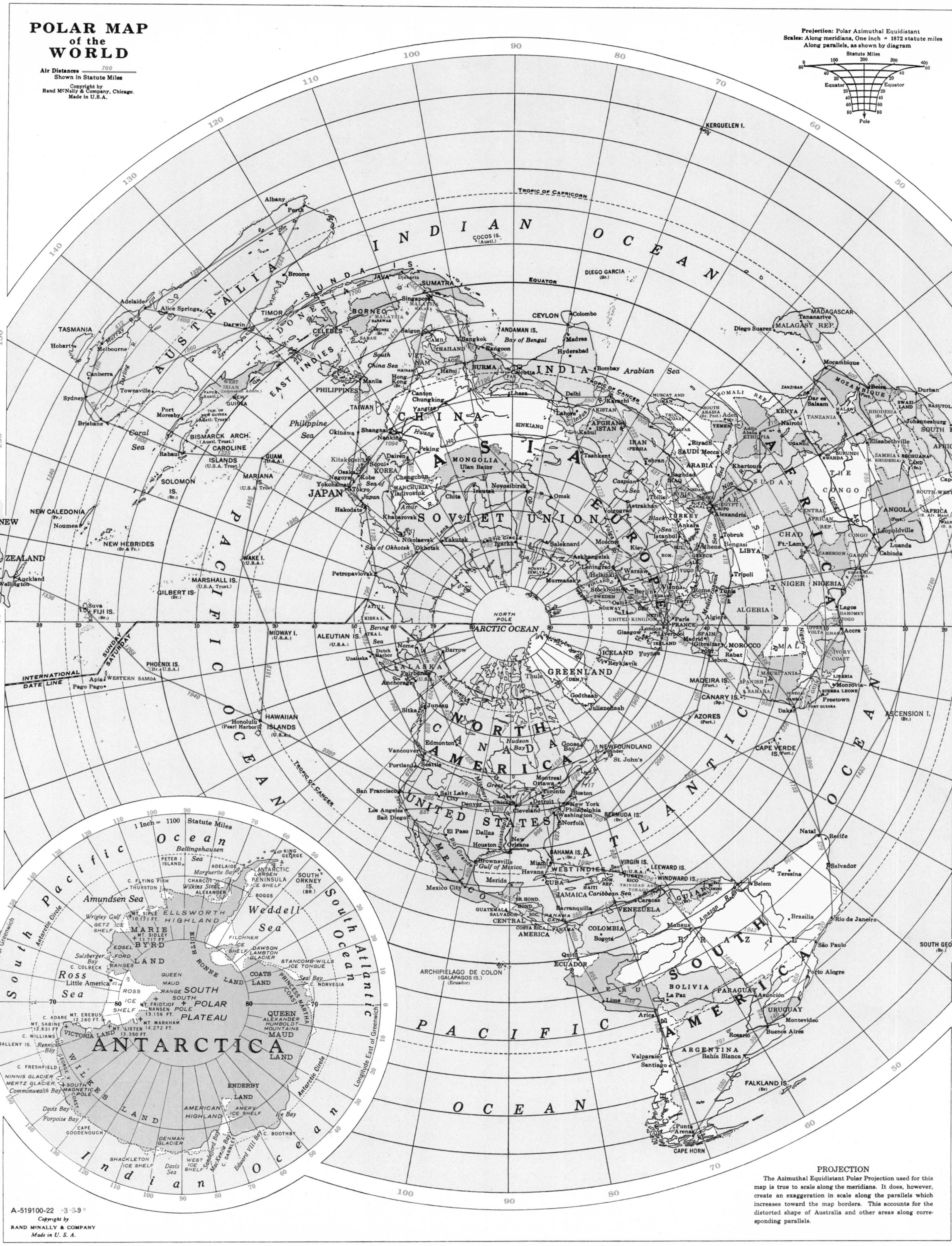

Polar Map of the WORLD

Air Distances ——— 700
Shown in Statute Miles
Copyright by
Rand McNally & Company, Chicago
Made in U.S.A.

Projection: Polar Azimuthal Equidistant
Scales: Along meridians, One inch = 1872 statute miles
Along parallels, as shown by diagram

Statute Miles

PROJECTION

The Azimuthal Equidistant Polar Projection used for this map is true to scale along the meridians. It does, however, create an exaggeration in scale along the parallels which increases toward the map borders. This accounts for the distorted shape of Australia and other areas along corresponding parallels.

A-519100-22 -3-3-9"
Copyright by
RAND McNALLY & COMPANY
Made in U. S. A.

1

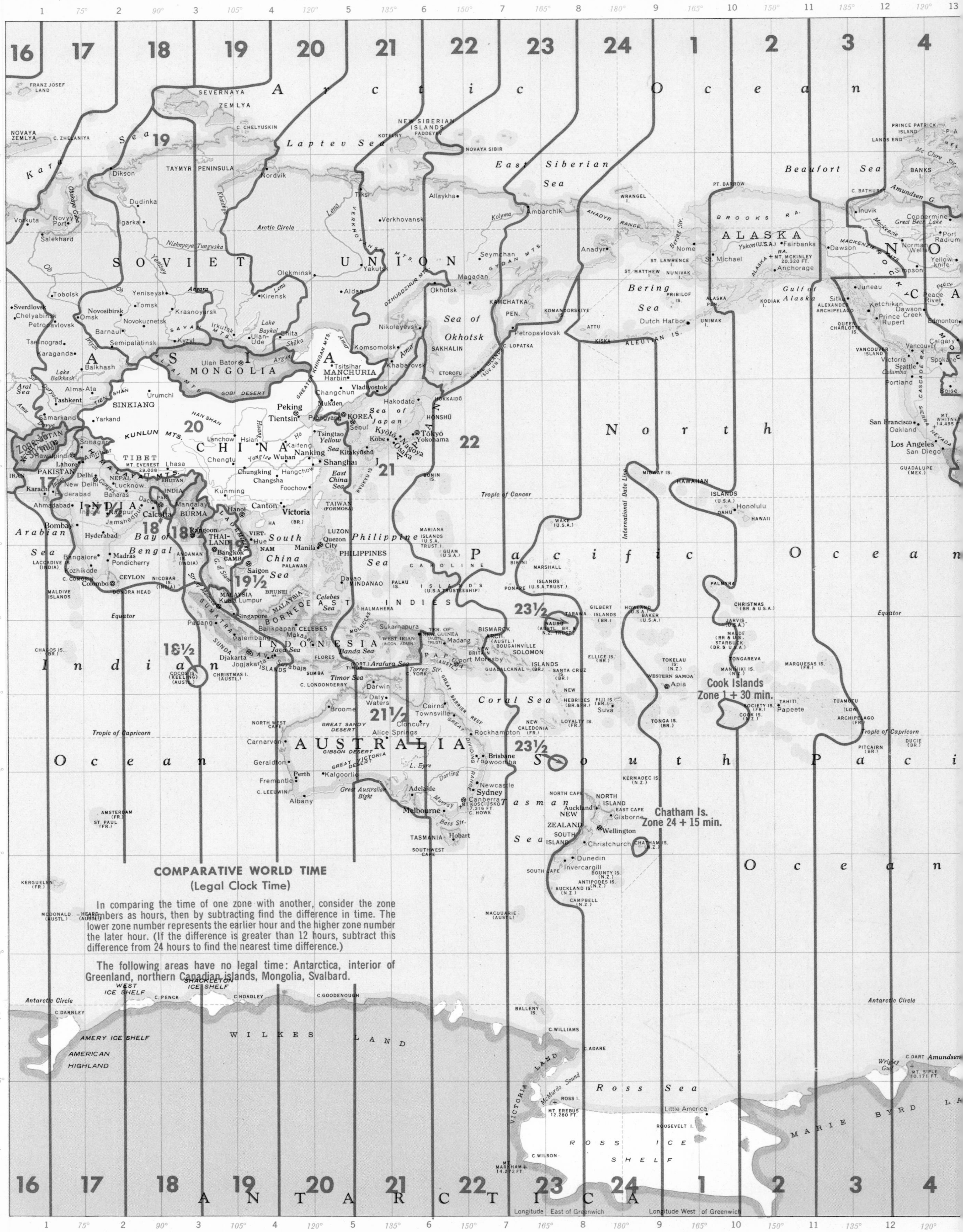

COMPARATIVE WORLD TIME
(Legal Clock Time)

In comparing the time of one zone with another, consider the zone numbers as hours, then by subtracting find the difference in time. The lower zone number represents the earlier hour and the higher zone number the later hour. (If the difference is greater than 12 hours, subtract this difference from 24 hours to find the nearest time difference.)

The following areas have no legal time: Antarctica, interior of Greenland, northern Canadian islands, Mongolia, Svalbard.

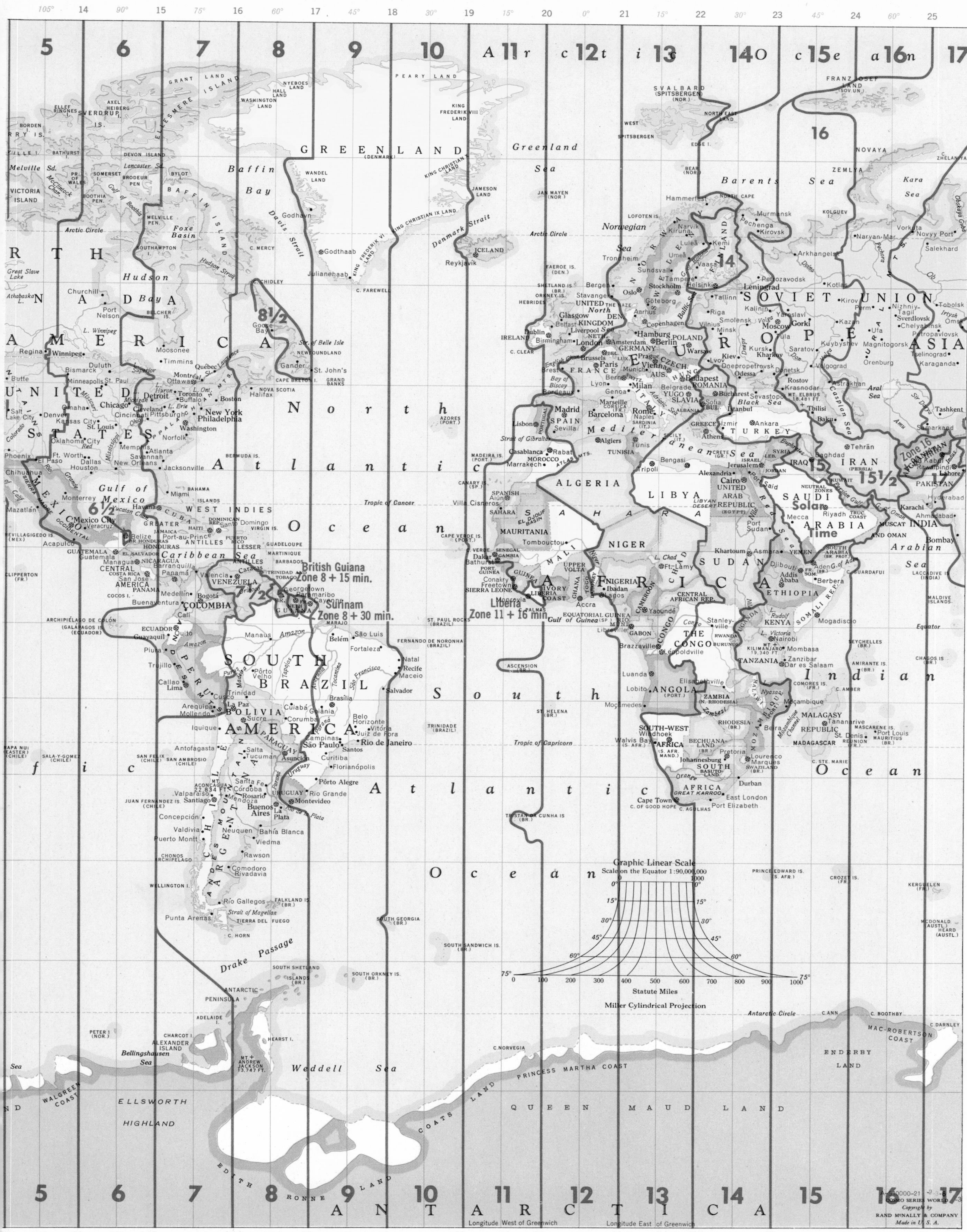

5 6 7 8 9 10 11 12 13 14 15 16 17
Arctic Ocean
GREENLAND (DENMARK)
Greenland Sea
Baffin Bay
Davis Strait
Denmark Strait
Hudson Bay
Norwegian Sea
Barents Sea
Kara Sea
SVALBARD (SPITSBERGEN) (NOR.)
ICELAND
8 1/2
NORTH AMERICA
CANADA
UNITED STATES
MEXICO
6 1/2
Gulf of Mexico
WEST INDIES
Caribbean Sea
British Guiana Zone 8 + 15 min.
Surinam Zone 8 + 30 min.
SOUTH AMERICA
BRAZIL
VENEZUELA
COLOMBIA
PERU
BOLIVIA
ARGENTINA
CHILE
URUGUAY
PARAGUAY
North Atlantic Ocean
South Atlantic Ocean
Tropic of Cancer
Tropic of Capricorn
Equator
Arctic Circle
Antarctic Circle
Drake Passage
Weddell Sea
Bellingshausen Sea
ANTARCTICA
QUEEN MAUD LAND
ELLSWORTH HIGHLAND
ENDERBY LAND
EUROPE
SOVIET UNION
ASIA
UNITED KINGDOM
FRANCE
SPAIN
GERMANY
POLAND
TURKEY
Mediterranean Sea
Black Sea
Caspian Sea
AFRICA
ALGERIA
LIBYA
SAHARA
NIGER
NIGERIA
SUDAN
ETHIOPIA
KENYA
TANZANIA
THE CONGO
ANGOLA
SOUTH-WEST AFRICA
SOUTH AFRICA
MALAGASY REPUBLIC
Liberia Zone 11 + 16 min.
Gulf of Guinea
SAUDI ARABIA
Saudi Solar Time
IRAN
15 1/2
Zone 16
PAKISTAN
INDIA
Arabian Sea
Indian Ocean
Graphic Linear Scale
Scale on the Equator 1:90,000,000
Statute Miles
0 100 200 300 400 500 600 700 800 900 1000
Miller Cylindrical Projection
Longitude West of Greenwich
Longitude East of Greenwich
Copyright by RAND McNALLY & COMPANY
Made in U. S. A.

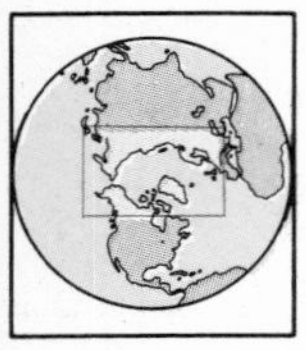

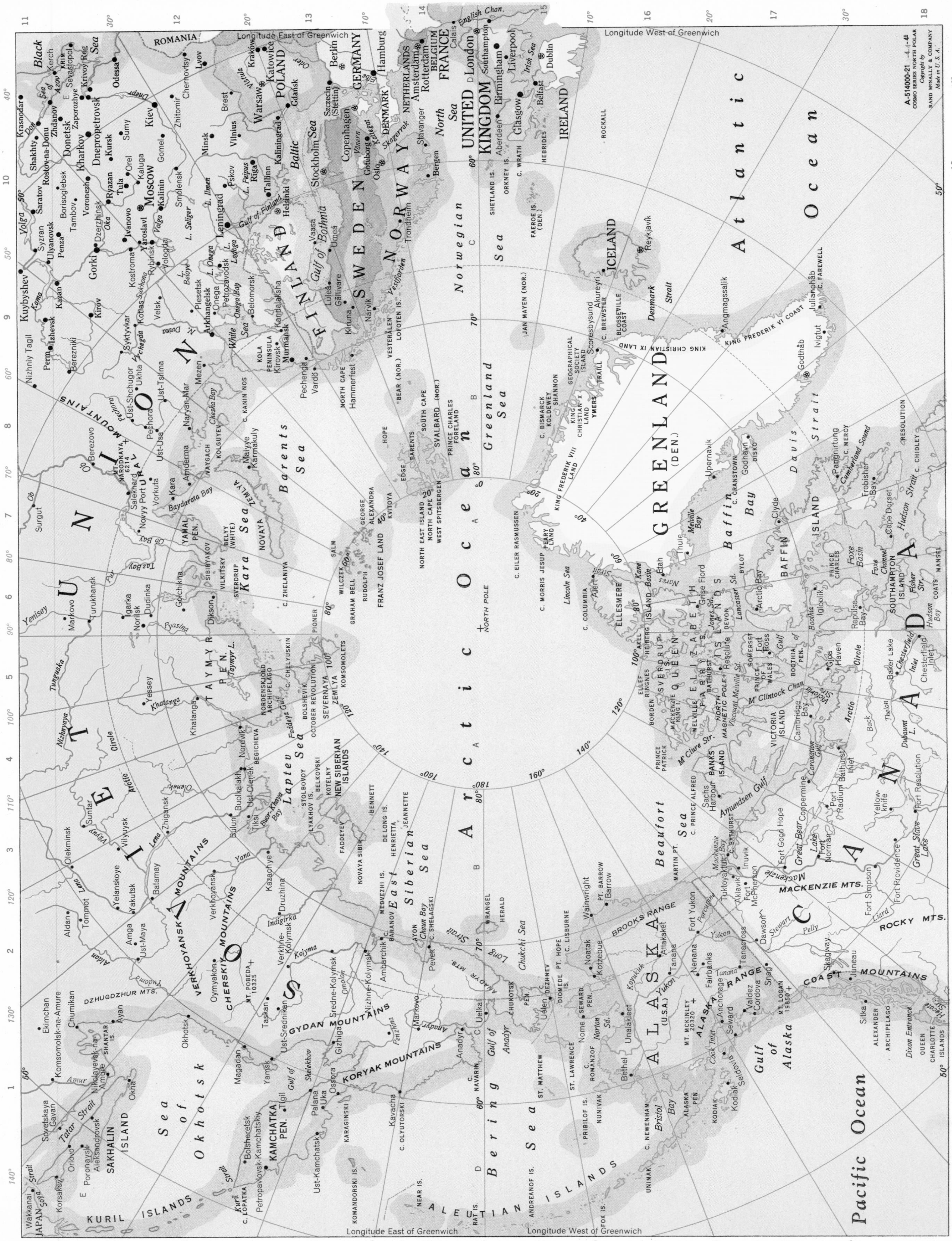

Statute Miles
100 0 100 200 300 400 500

Kilometers
100 0 100 300 500 700

Lambert Azimuthal Equal Area Projection
SCALE 1:28,000,000 1 Inch = 442 Statute Miles

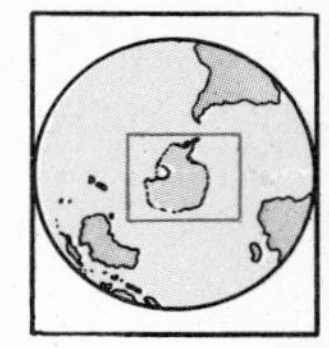

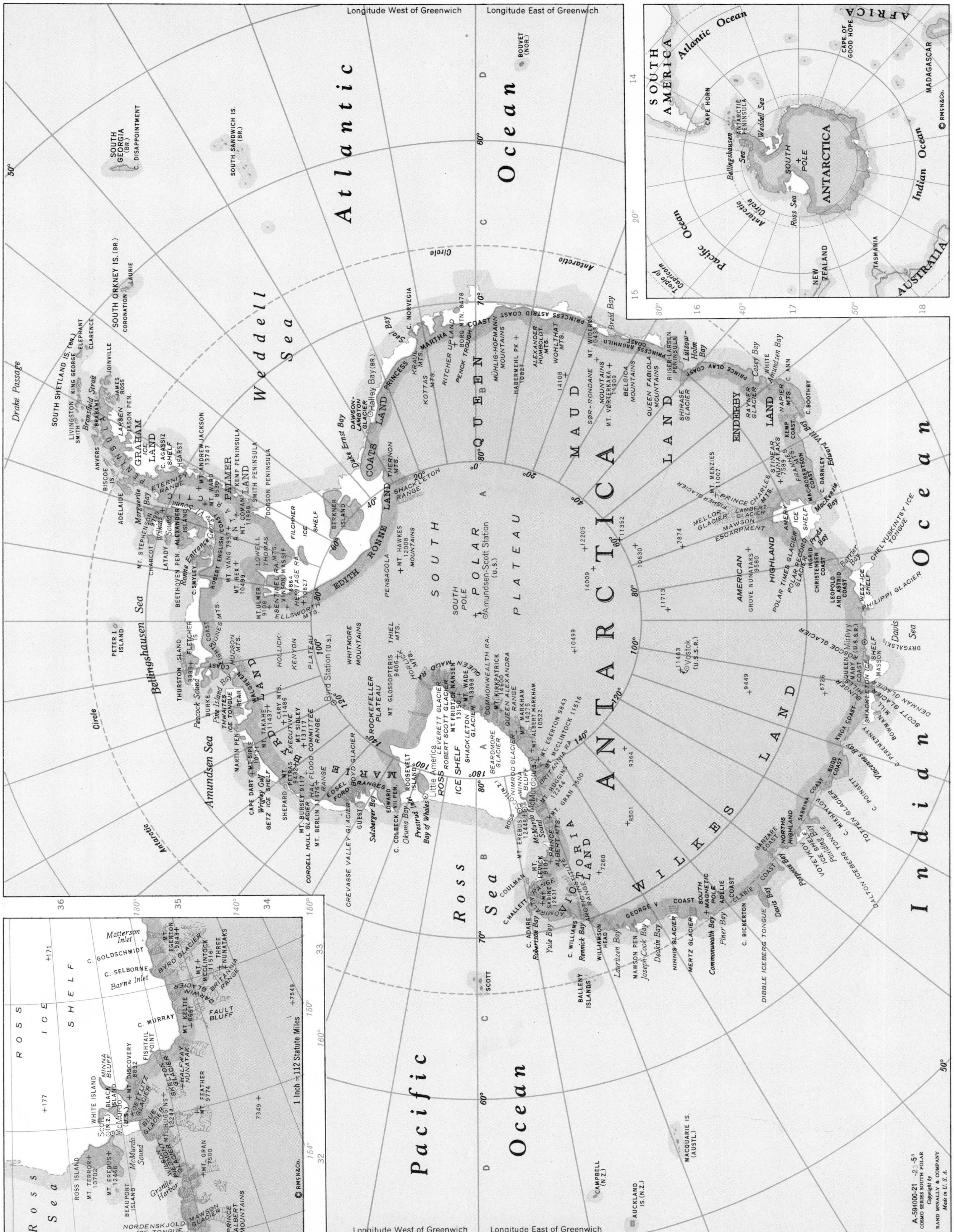

Lambert Azimuthal Equal Area Projection
SCALE 1:28,000,000   1 Inch = 442 Statute Miles

Statute Miles

Kilometers

ATLANTIC OCEAN

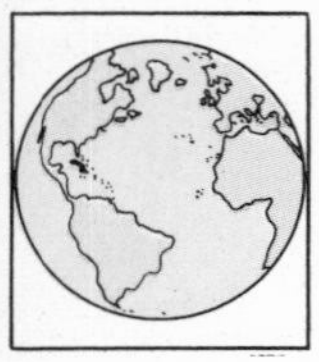

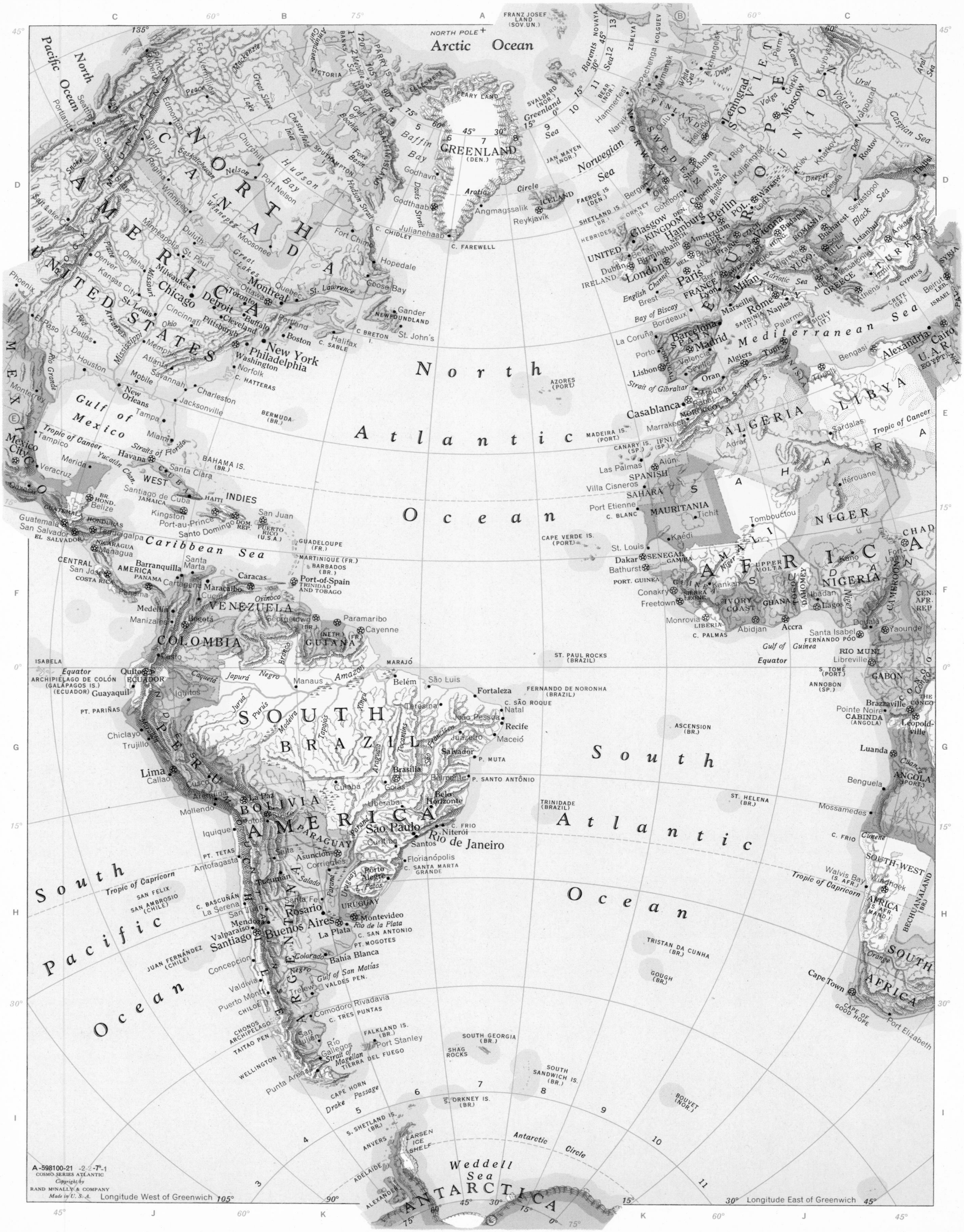

Statute Miles 200 0 200 600 1000 1400
Kilometers 200 0 200 600 1000 1400 1800 2200

Modified Polyconic Projection
SCALE 1:60,728,000 1 Inch = 960 Statute Miles

A-598100-21 -2- -7- -1
COSMO-SERIES ATLANTIC
Copyright by
RAND McNALLY & COMPANY
Made in U. S. A.

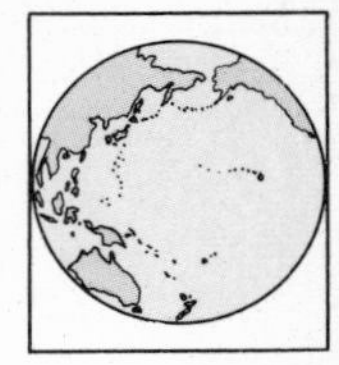

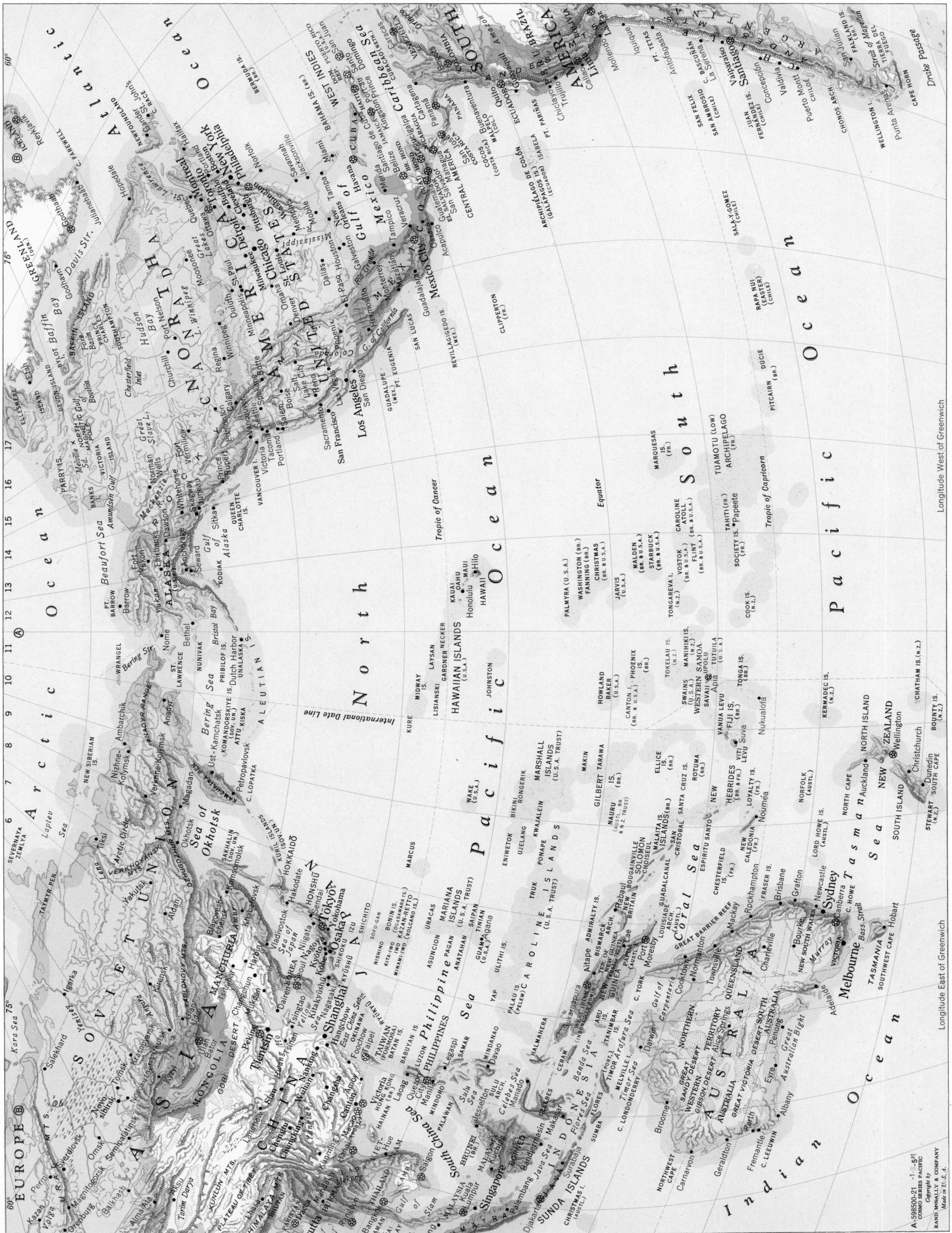

Modified Secant Conic Projection
SCALE 1:66,800,000 1 Inch = 1,040 Statute Miles

Statute Miles
200   0   200   600   1000   1400

Kilometers
200 0 200   600   1000   1400   1800   2200

A-598500-21 -1-.-5⁸¹¹
Copyright by
COSMO SERIES PACIFIC
RAND McNALLY & COMPANY
Made in U.S.A.

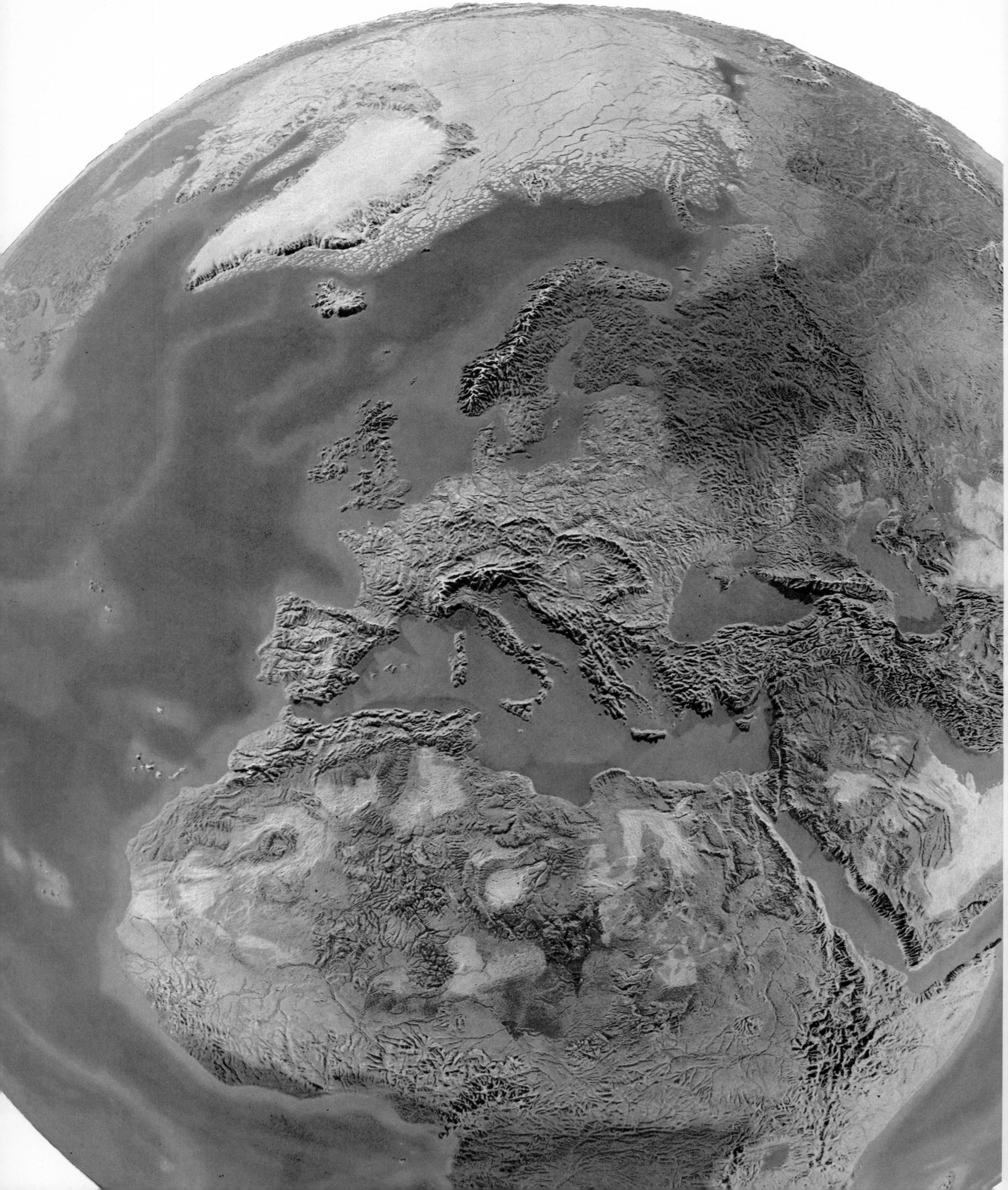

EUROPE

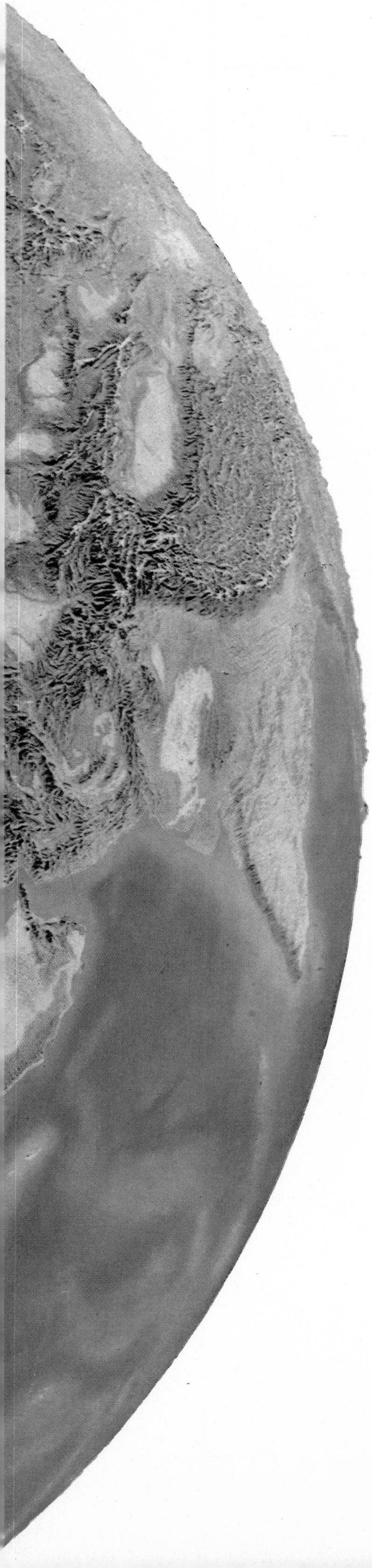

This global view centers on the western extension of Asia, the region the world knows as the continent of Europe. Often the two are linked together under the name Eurasia. This peninsula, or arm, of the great Asian landmass, itself is comprised of numerous peninsulas—those of Scandinavia, Iberia, Italy, and the Balkans—and many offshore islands, the most important group being the British Isles.

The thrust of this arm of Asia into the Atlantic Ocean, the North and Mediterranean seas provides a clear-cut western terminus. But the limits of Europe are not so clearly defined on its eastern flank where no natural barriers exist. For the sake of a "boundary" geographers have come to recognize the low Ural Mountains and the Ural River, the Caspian Sea, the Caucasus Mountains, and the Black Sea as the eastern and southeastern border.

From Europe's eastern limits, where the north to south dimension is approximately 2,500 miles, the irregularly shaped continent tapers toward the southwest and the surrounding bodies of water. Through Europe's history its miles of coastline encouraged contact with the other continents, and the seas became avenues of exchange for culture, politics, and technology with other regions of the world.

Internally Europe embraces a varied landscape comparable to no other region of its size in the world: In a total area of only 3,850,000 square miles are found extremes from zero winters and dry steppes in the east to year-round humid, mild climates in the west; extremes in elevation from the heights of the Alps to the below-sea-level Belgian and Netherlands coasts; and a variation in the distribution of inhabitants from the densely populated, industrialized northwest to the sparsely peopled areas in the agricultural south and east. Thirty-three independent nations, each with its own national, religious, cultural, and political heritage, adds to this variegated landscape.

Because much of Europe is neither too hot or cold, or too high or low, a great extent of its land has been developed, aided by an impressive river-canal system, dominated by the Rhine and Danube. Its natural and cultural wealth has made possible an economic-social-political system which has long influenced the economic, political, and social structure of the rest of the world.

Today, because of its density of population, strategic location, politics, history, economic strength, and cultural tradition, Europe still may rightfully and strongly claim to be one of the hubs of the world.

7B

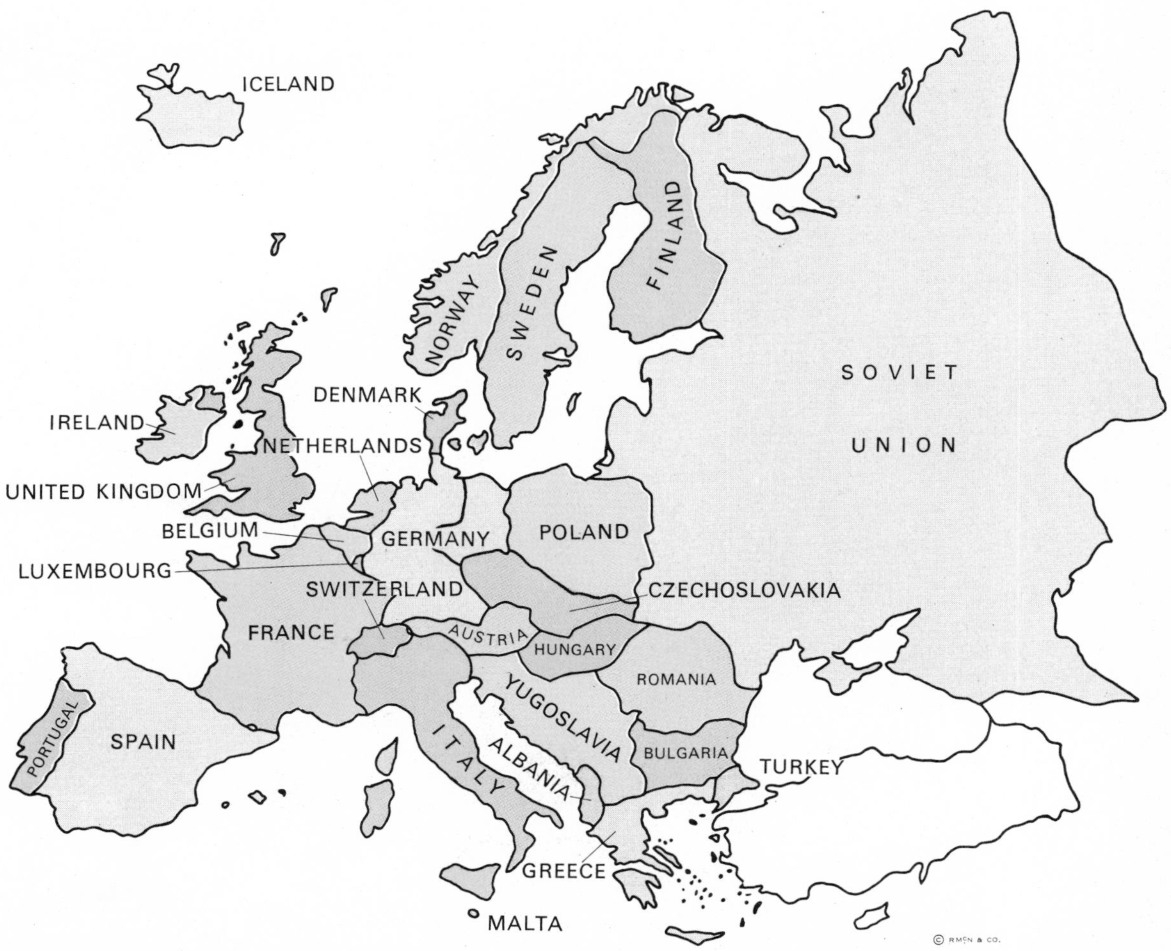

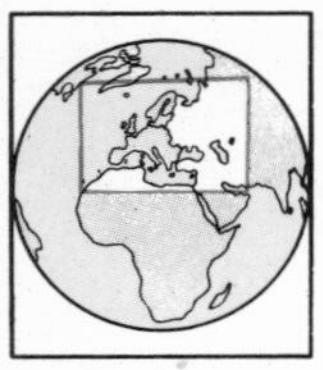

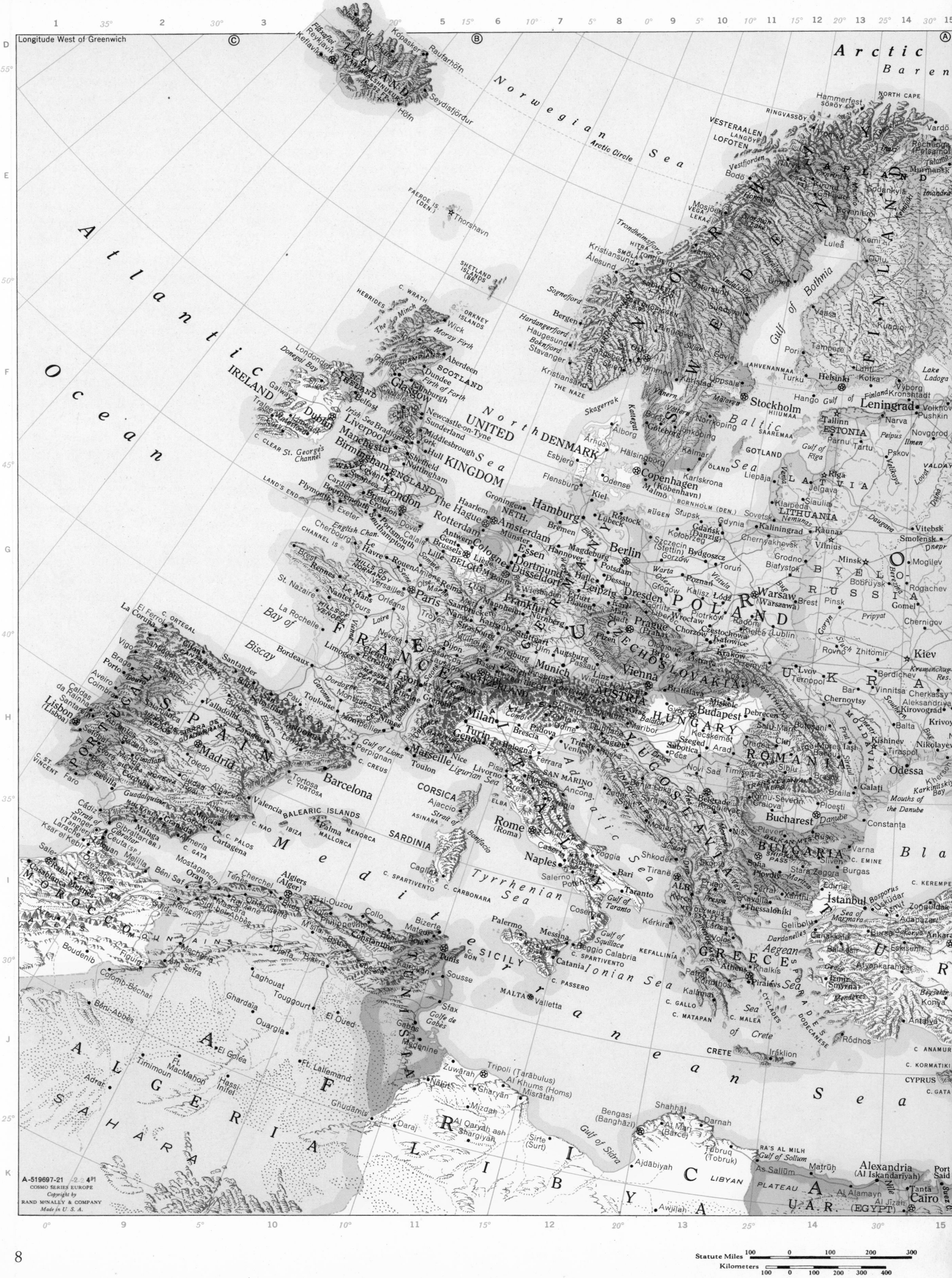

EUROPE AND WESTERN ASIA

8

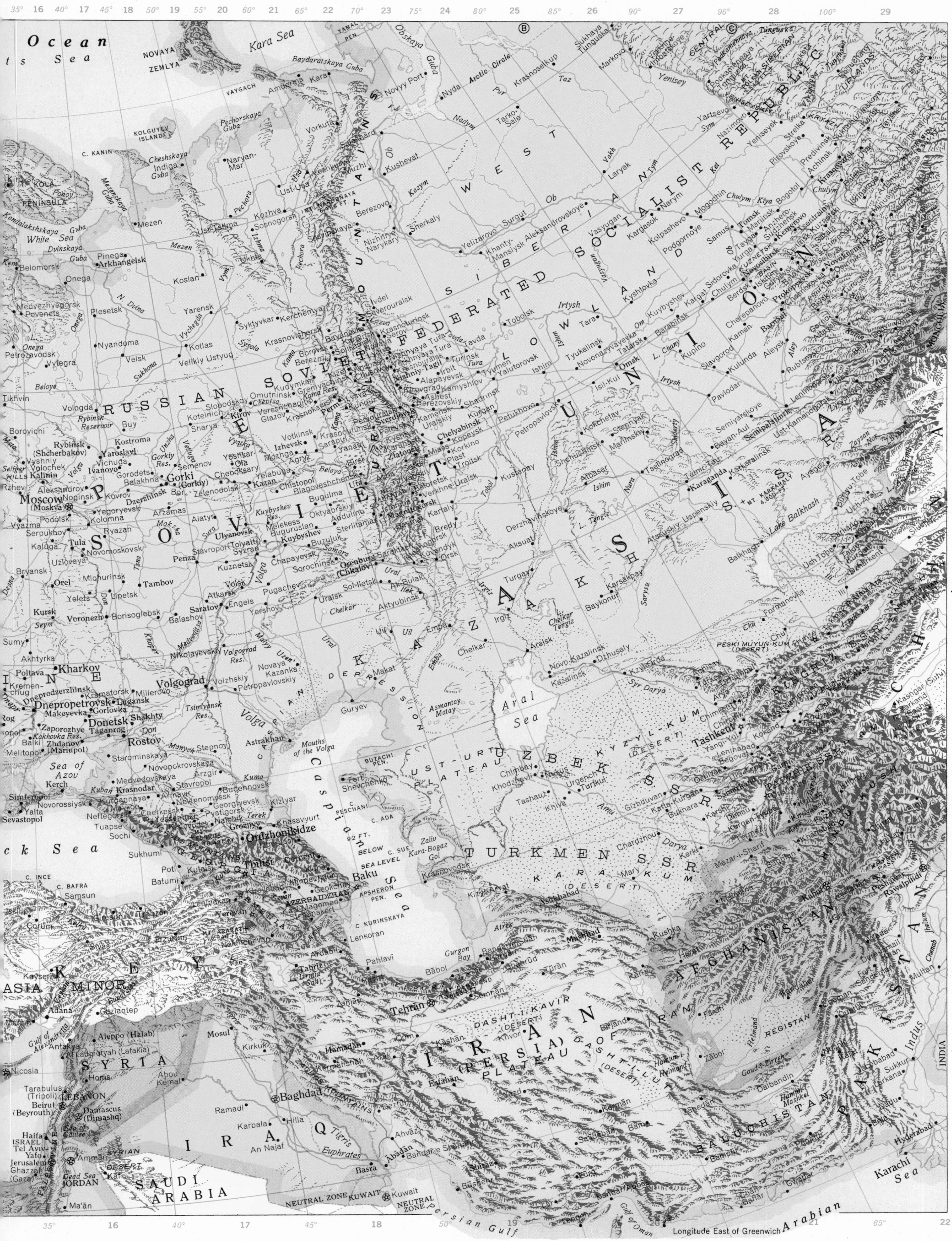

Ocean

ts Sea

Kara Sea

NOVAYA
ZEMLYA

SOVIET FEDERATED SOCIALIST REPUBLIC

RUSSIAN

SOVIET

KAZAKH S.S.R.

UZBEK S.S.R.

TURKMEN S.S.R.

Moscow
(Moskva)

Volgograd

Kharkov

Dnepropetrovsk
Donetsk
Rostov

Sea of
Azov

ck Sea

ASIA MINOR

SYRIA

Aral
Sea

Caspian
Sea

Baku

Tbilisi

ARMENIA
AZERBAIDZHAN

Tehran

IRAN
(PERSIA)
PLATEAU

DASHT-I-KAVIR
(DESERT)

DASHT-I-LUT
(DESERT)

Baghdad

IRAQ

SAUDI
ARABIA

NEUTRAL ZONE   KUWAIT
Kuwait

AFGHANISTAN

PAKISTAN

BALUCHISTAN
REGISTAN

Karachi

INDIA

CHINA

Lake Balkhash

TASHKENT

PESKI MUYUN-KUM
(DESERT)

KYZYL-KUM
(DESERT)

KARA-KUM
(DESERT)

Arabian

Persian Gulf   Longitude East of Greenwich   Gulf of Oman

BRITISH ISLES

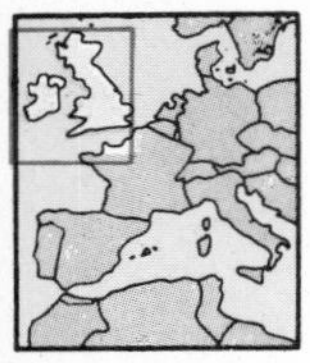

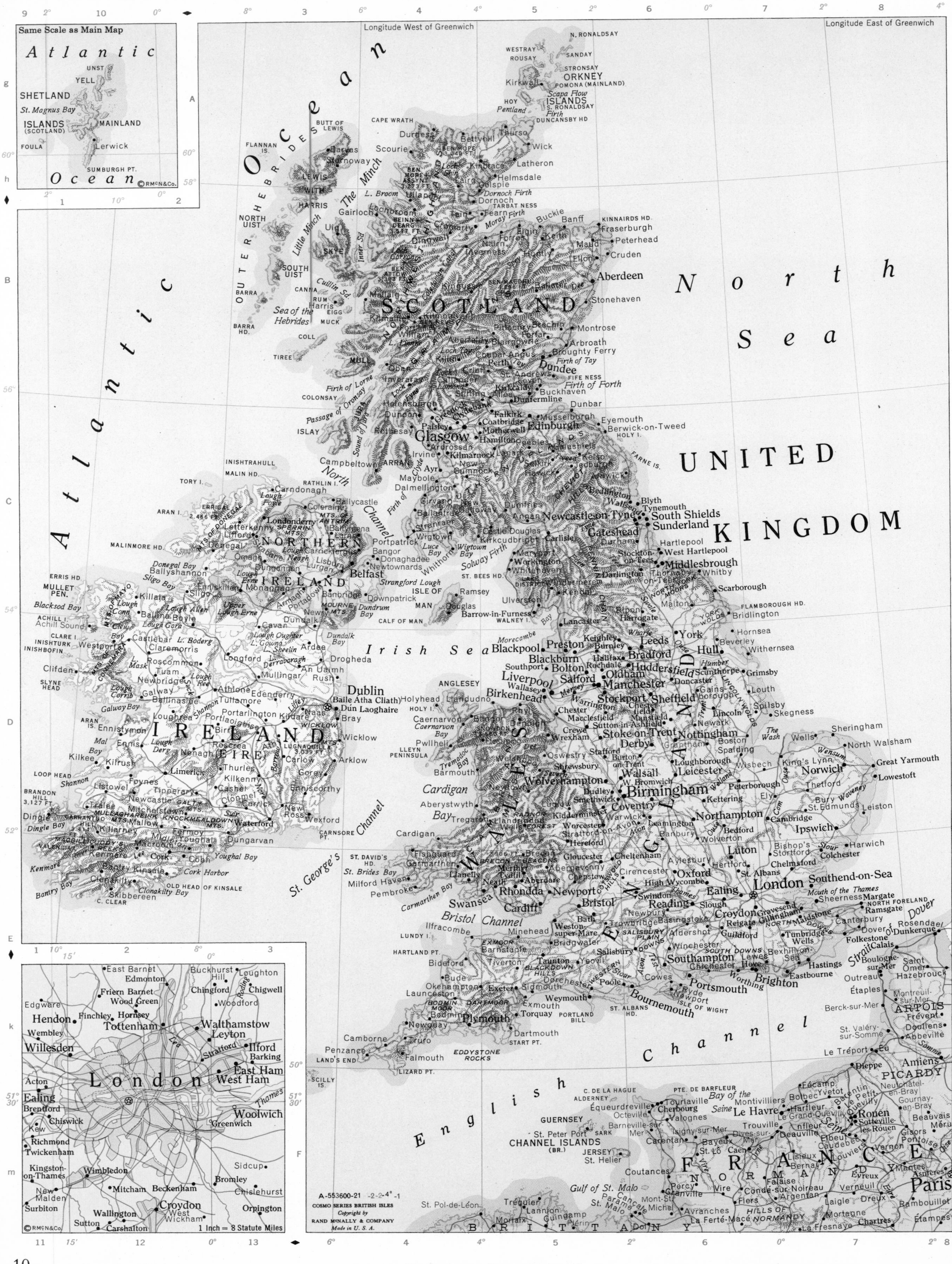

Statute Miles
Kilometers

Conic Projection
SCALE 1:4,000,000 1 Inch = 63 Statute Miles

IRELAND

11

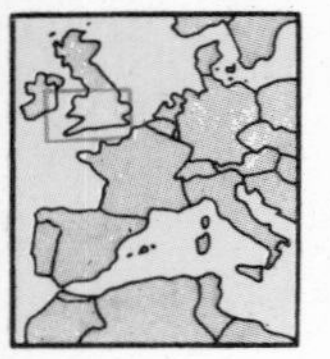

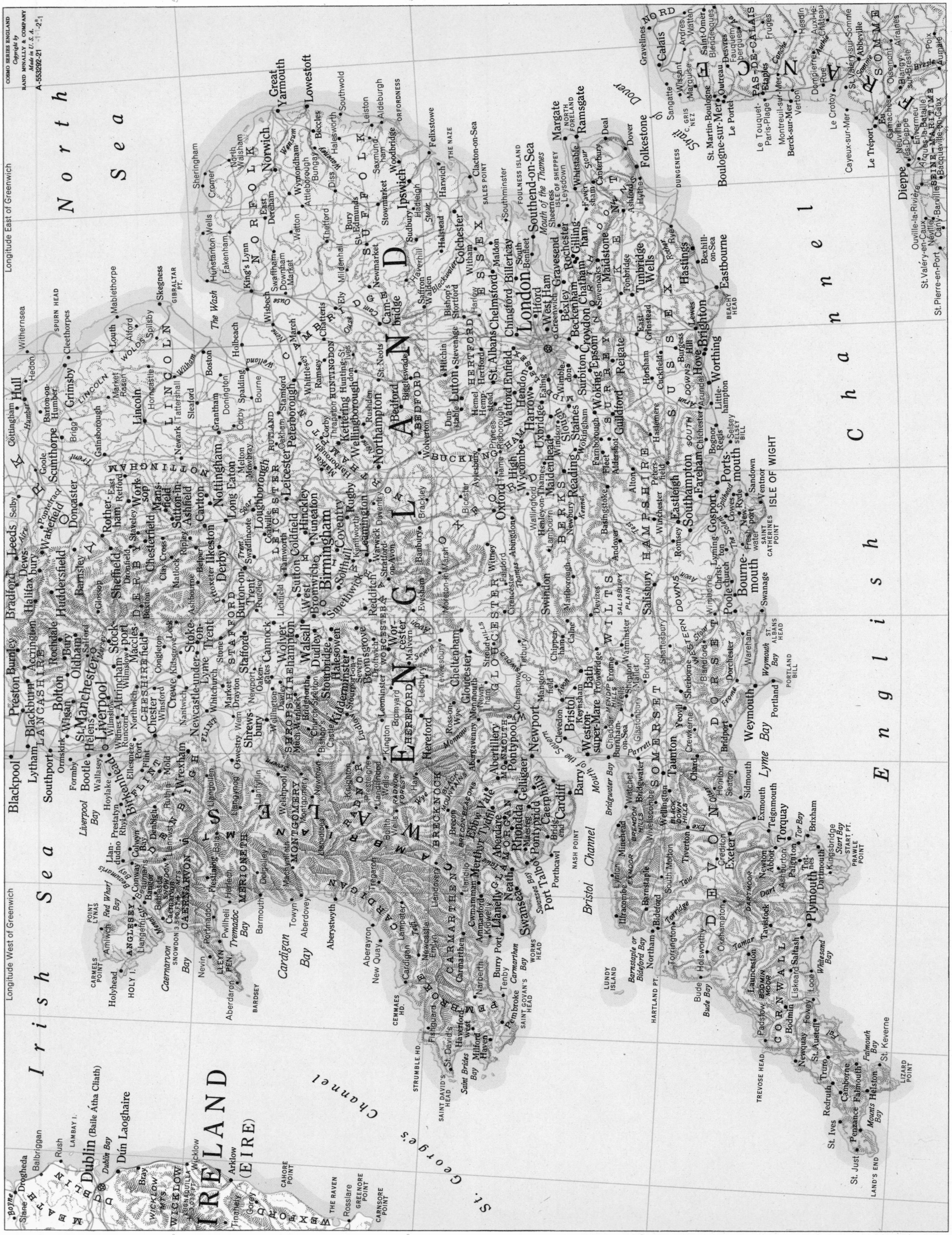

Statute Miles 5 0 5 10 20 30 40 50
Kilometers 5 0 5 10 20 30 40 50 60

Lambert Conformal Conic Projection
SCALE 1:2,000,000 1 Inch = 32 Statute Miles

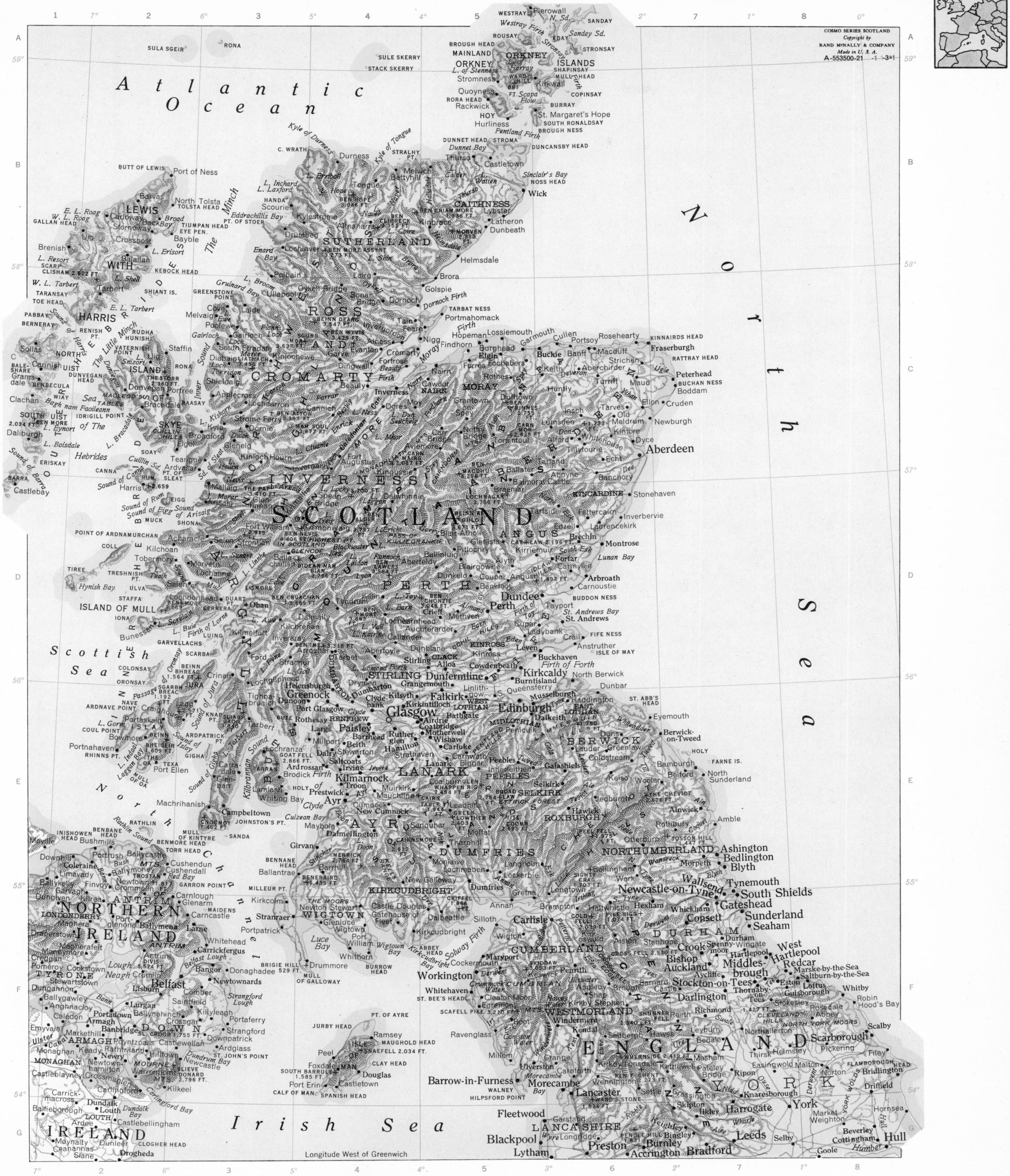

COSMO SERIES SCOTLAND
Copyright by
RAND McNALLY & COMPANY
Made in U. S. A.
A-553500-21 -1 -3-1

Lambert Conformal Conic Projection
SCALE 1 : 2,000,000 1 Inch = 32 Statute Miles

Statute Miles 5 0 5 10 20 30 40 50
Kilometers 5 0 5 10 20 30 40 50 60

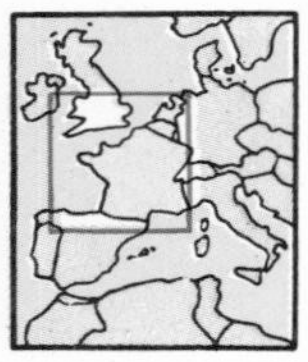

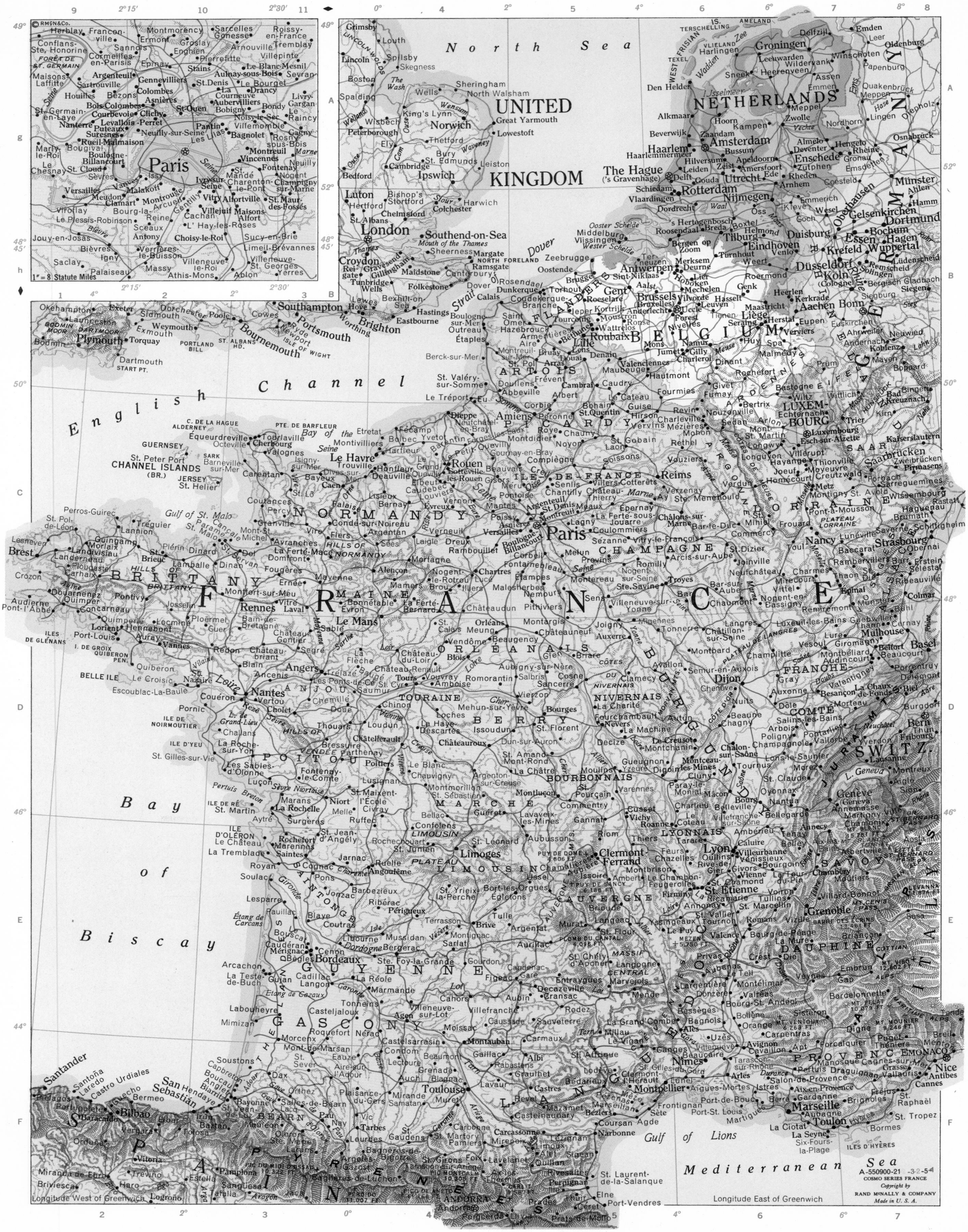

FRANCE AND THE LOW COUNTRIES

Statute Miles

Kilometers

Conic Projection
SCALE 1:4,000,000   1 Inch = 63 Statute Miles

COSMO SERIES BELGIUM NETH.
Copyright by
RAND McNALLY & COMPANY
Made in U. S. A.
A-559199-21 -1 -1 -5°1

Longitude East of Greenwich

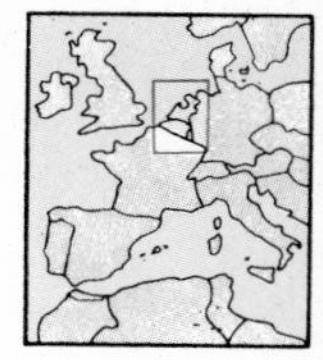

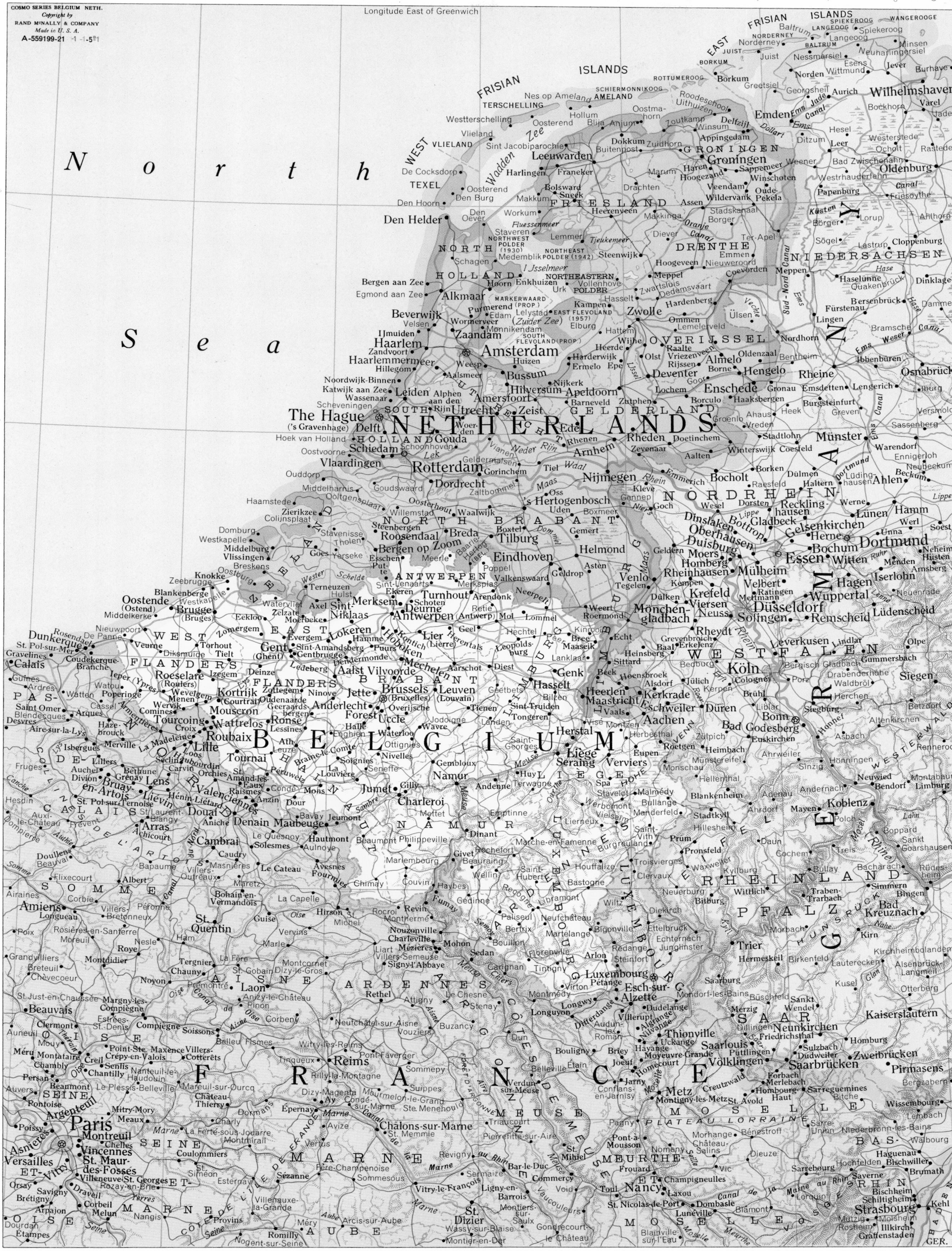

Lambert Conformal Conic Projection
SCALE 1:2,000,000   1 Inch = 32 Statute Miles

Statute Miles   5 0 5 10   20   30   40   50
Kilometers   5 0 5 10   20   30   40   50   60

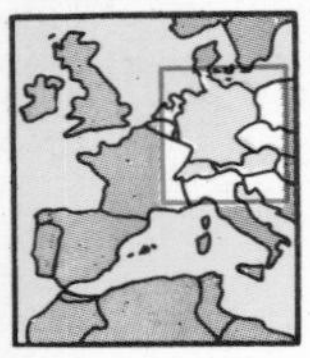

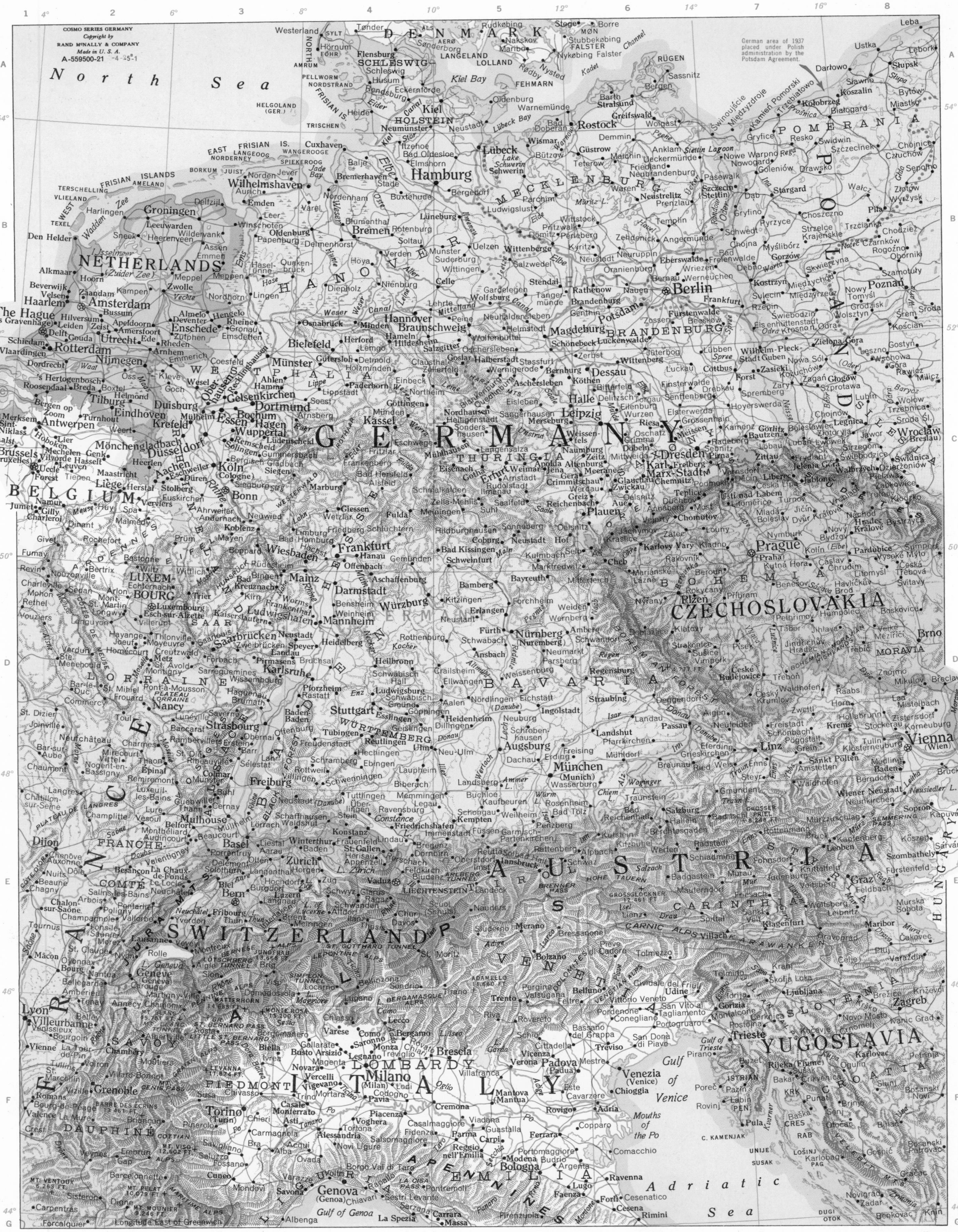

Statute Miles

Kilometers

Conic Projection

SCALE 1:4,000,000   1 Inch = 63 Statute Miles

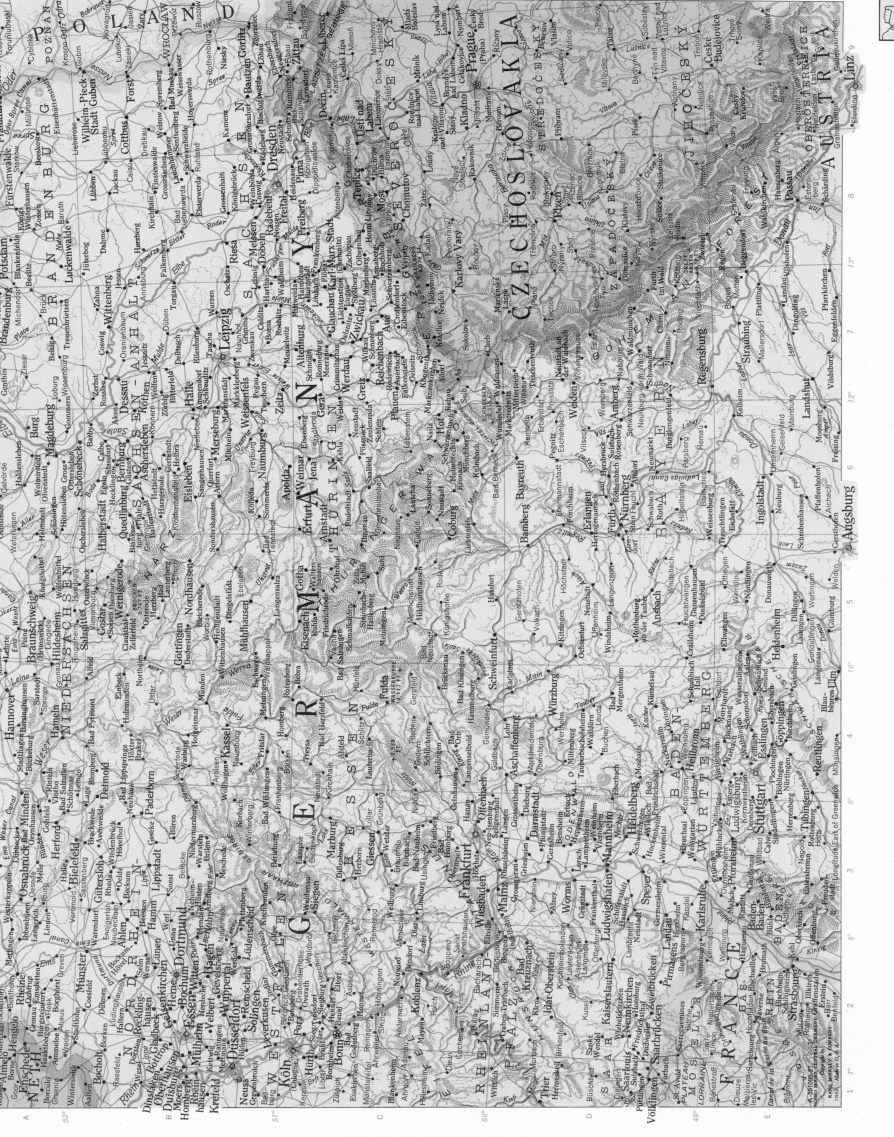

Lambert Conformal Conic Projection

SCALE 1:2,000,000   1 Inch = 32 Statute Miles

Statute Miles   5 0 5 10   20   30   40   50

Kilometers   5 0 5 10 20   30   40   50   60

17

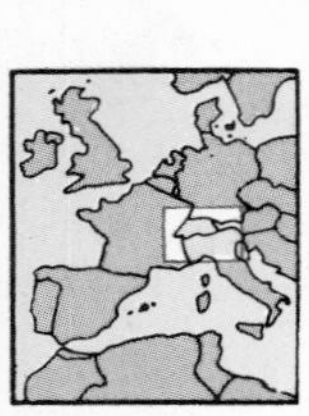

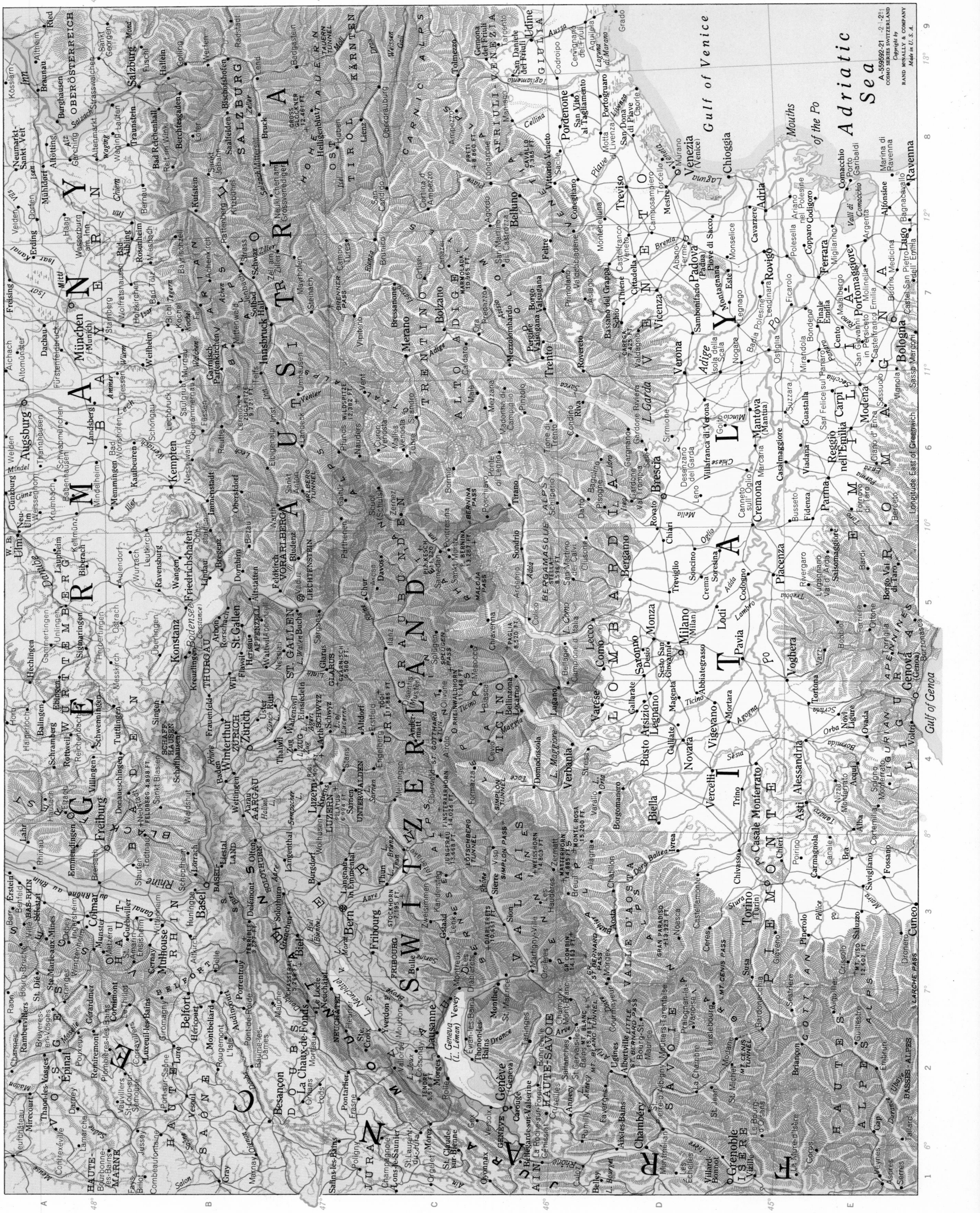

Statute Miles 5 0 5 10 20 30 40 50

Kilometers 5 0 5 10 20 30 40 50 60

Lambert Conformal Conic Projection

SCALE 1:2,000,000   1 Inch = 32 Statute Miles

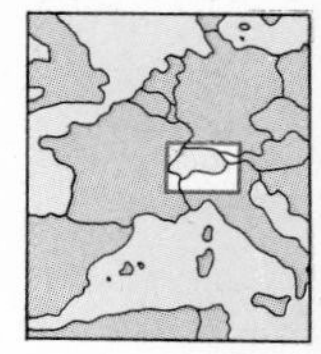

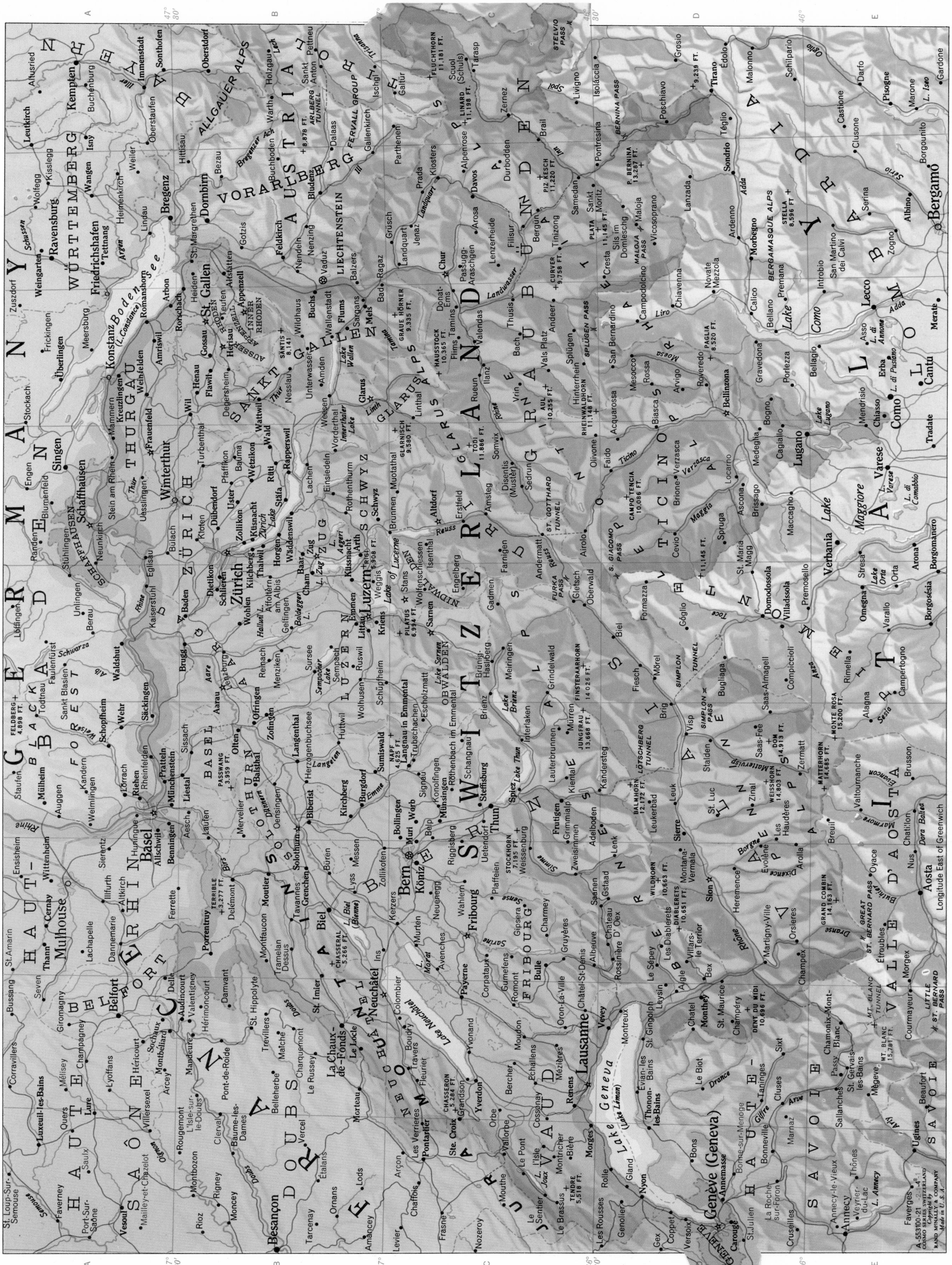

Lambert Conformal Conic Projection

SCALE 1: 1,100,000   1 Inch = 17 Statute Miles

Statute Miles

Kilometers

20

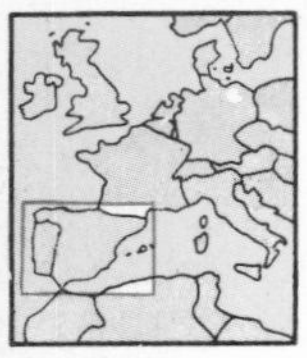

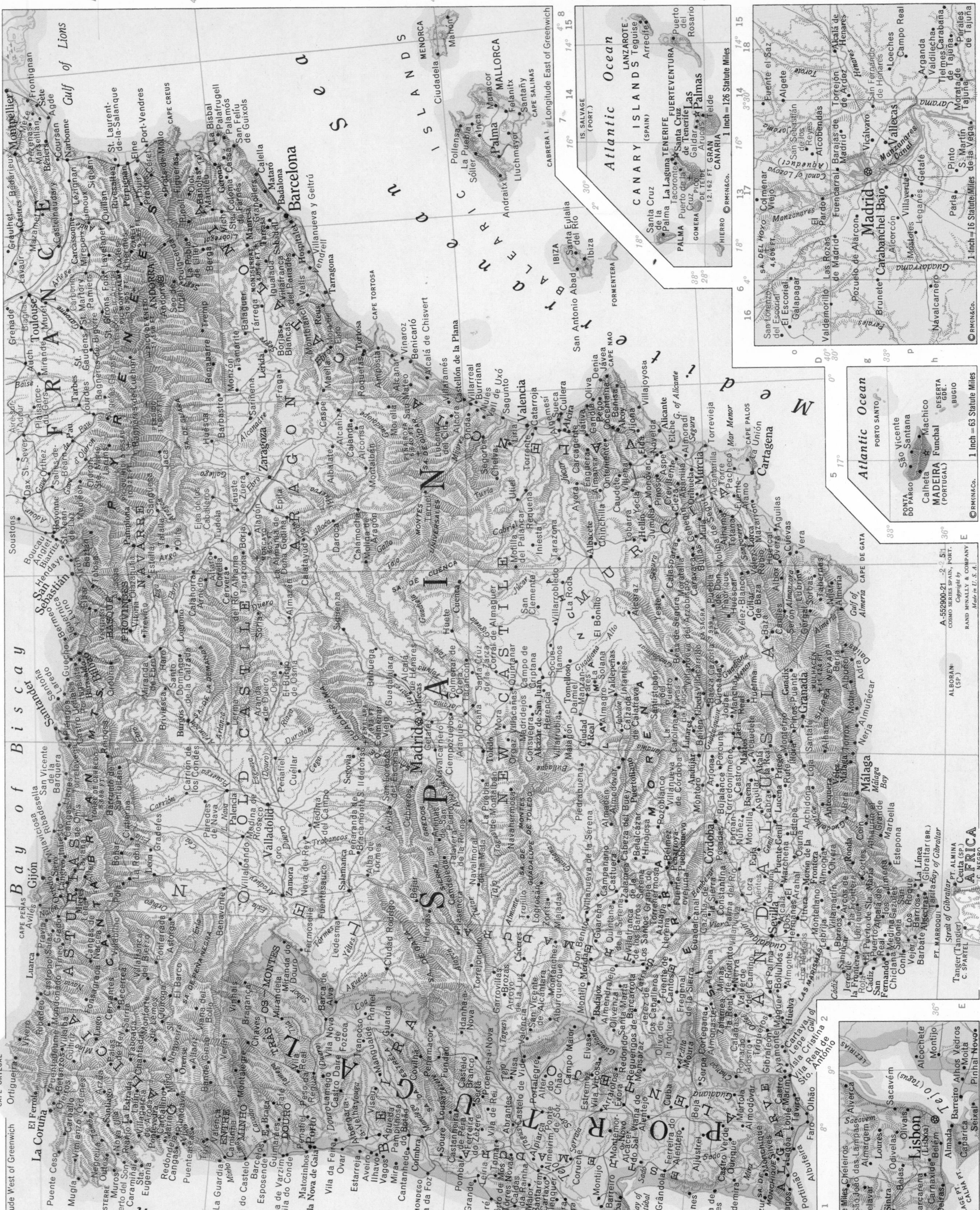

Statute Miles 25 0 25 50 75
Kilometers 25 0 25 50 100

Conic Projection
SCALE 1:4,000,000   1 Inch = 63 Statute Miles

ITALY

Sacrofano · Palombara · Sabina · Lenzona
Manziana · L. Bracciano · Anguillara · Cretone · Sant'Angelo · Vicovaro
Bracciano · Castel Giuliano · Formello · Monterotondo · Romano · Montecelio
Cerveteri · Vecchia (Buxus) · Boccea (Alsium) · Arrone · Mentana · Guidonia · Castel Madama · VILLA ADRIANA
Ladispoli · Palidoro · Castel di Guido · Maccarese · Vatican City · Rome (Roma) · Gallicano nel Lazio · Palestrina
Fregene · Fiumicino · Ostia Antica (RUINS) · Marino · Albano Laziale · Genzano di Roma · Pomezia · Ardea · Aprilia · Cisterna di Latina · Cori · Velletri

1 Inch = 16 Statute Miles

SWITZERLAND · AUSTRIA · YUGOSLAVIA

Ligurian Sea · Tyrrhenian Sea · Adriatic Sea · Mediterranean Sea

LOMBARDY · PIEDMONT · VENETO · EMILIA-ROMAGNA · TUSCANY · UMBRIA · LATIUM · ABRUZZI AND MOLISE · CAMPANIA · APULIA · BASILICATA · CALABRIA

CORSICA · SARDINIA · SICILY

Milano · Torino · Genova · Venezia · Bologna · Firenze · Roma · Napoli · Bari · Palermo · Catania

TUNISIA · Tunis

Longitude East of Greenwich

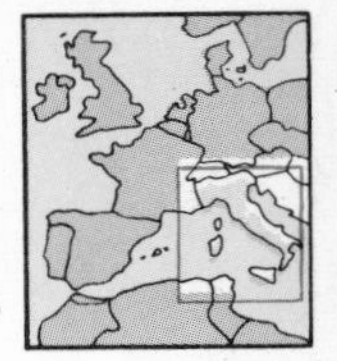

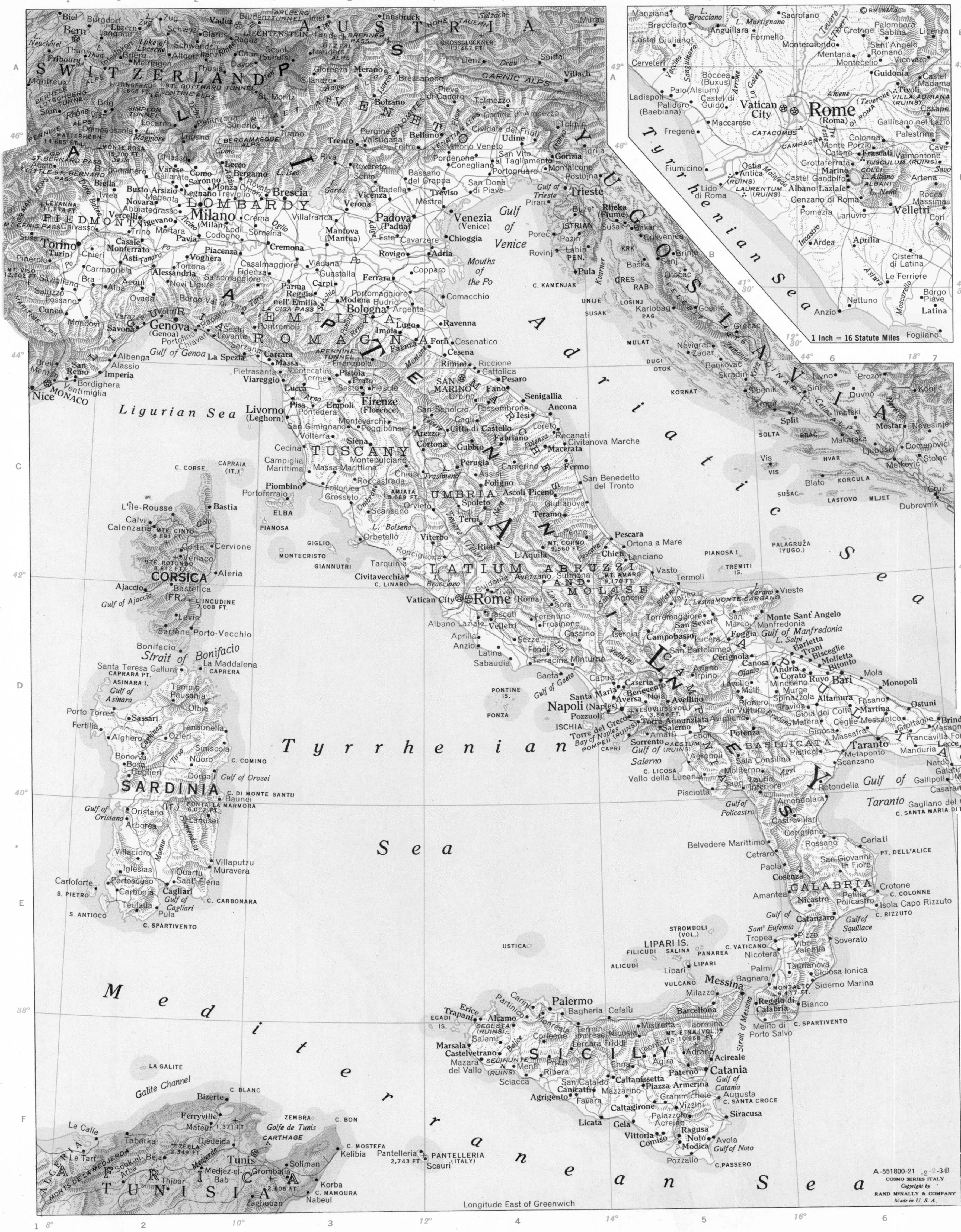

Conic Projection
SCALE 1:4,000,000 1 Inch = 63 Statute Miles

Statute Miles   25 0   25   50   75
Kilometers   25 0 25 50 100

A-551800-21
COSMO SERIES ITALY
Copyright by
RAND McNALLY & COMPANY
Made in U.S.A.

21

YUGOSLAVIA, HUNGARY, ROMANIA AND BULGARIA

22

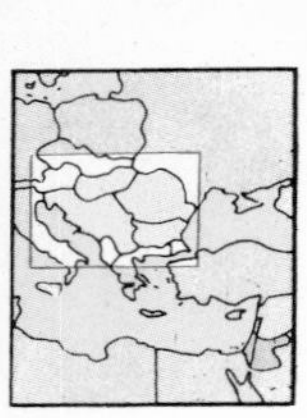

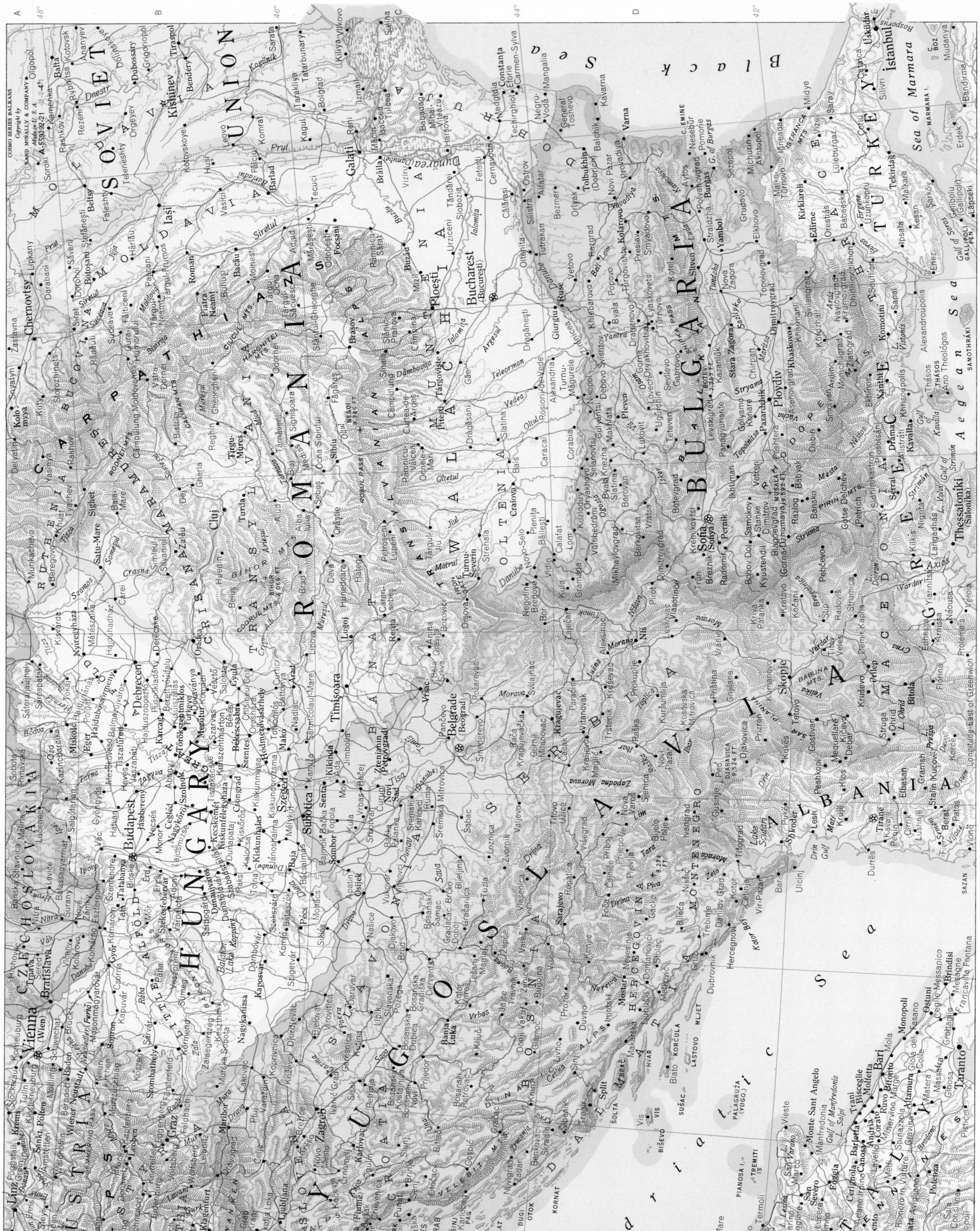

Statute Miles 25 0 25 50 75
Kilometers 25 0 50 100

Conic Projection
SCALE 1:4,000,000   1 Inch = 63 Statute Miles

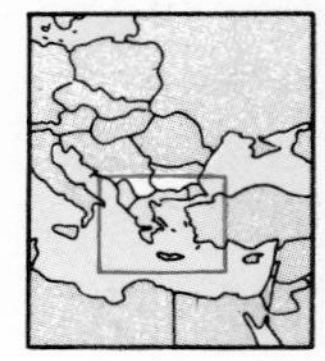

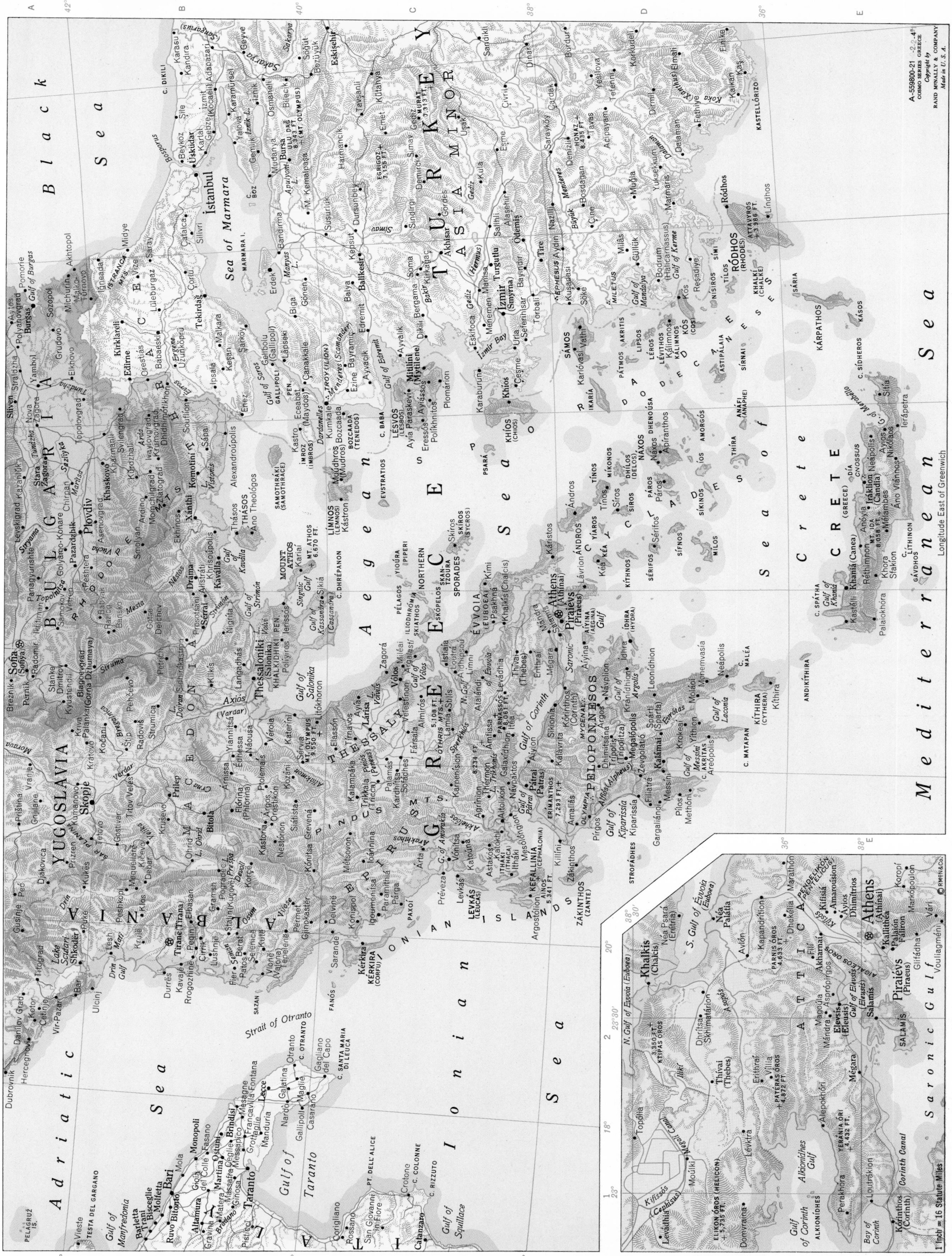

Conic Projection

SCALE 1:4,000,000   1 Inch = 63 Statute Miles

Statute Miles

Kilometers

1 Inch = 16 Statute Miles

A-559800-21
COSMO SERIES, GREECE
Copyright by
RAND McNALLY & COMPANY
Made in U.S.A.

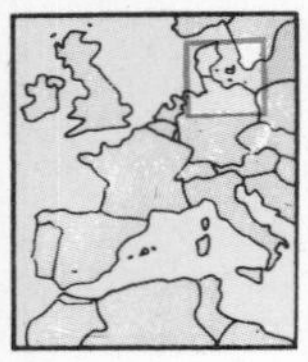

Statute Miles
Kilometers

Lambert Conformal Conic Projection
SCALE 1:2,000,000   1 Inch = 32 Statute Miles

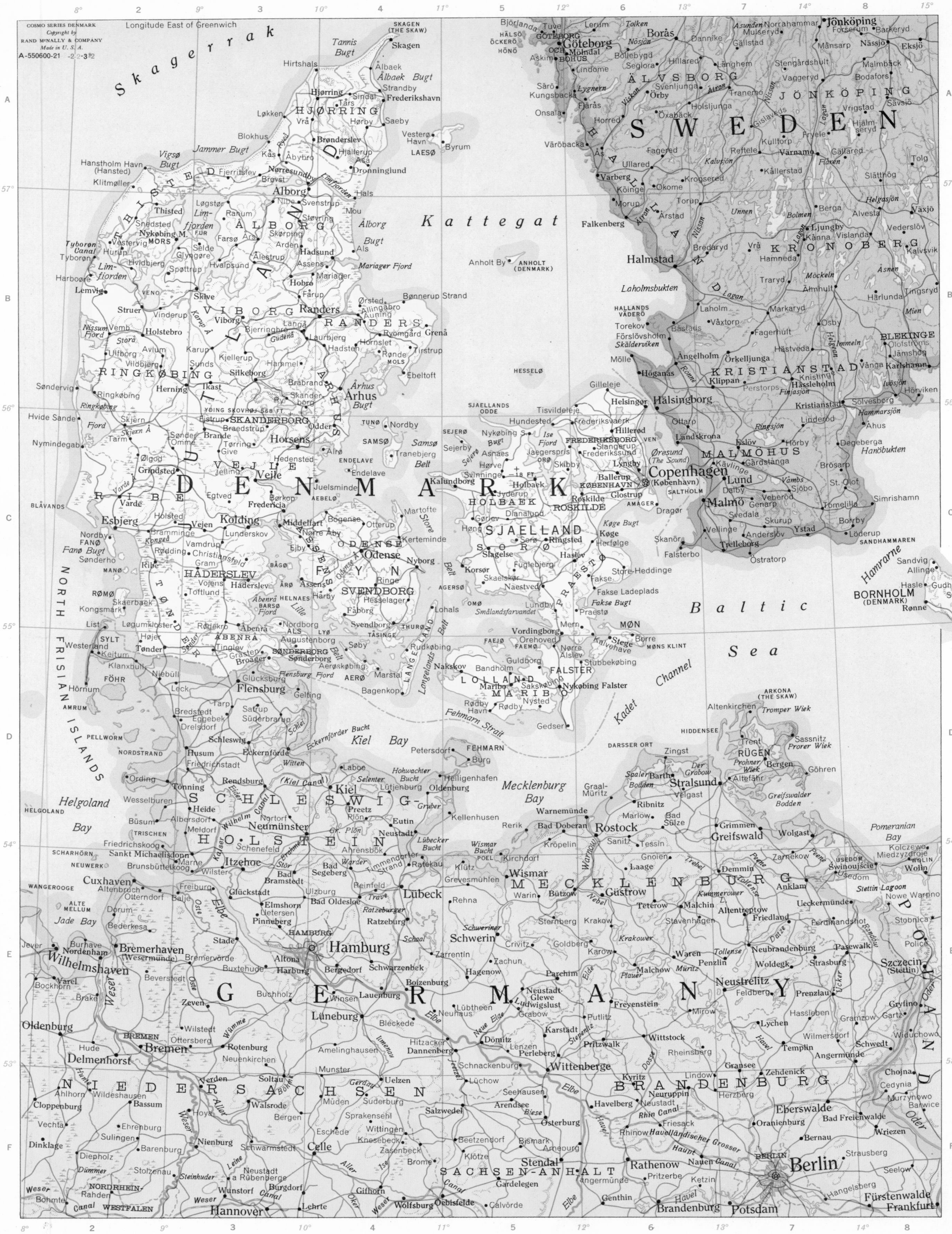

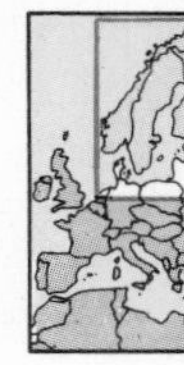

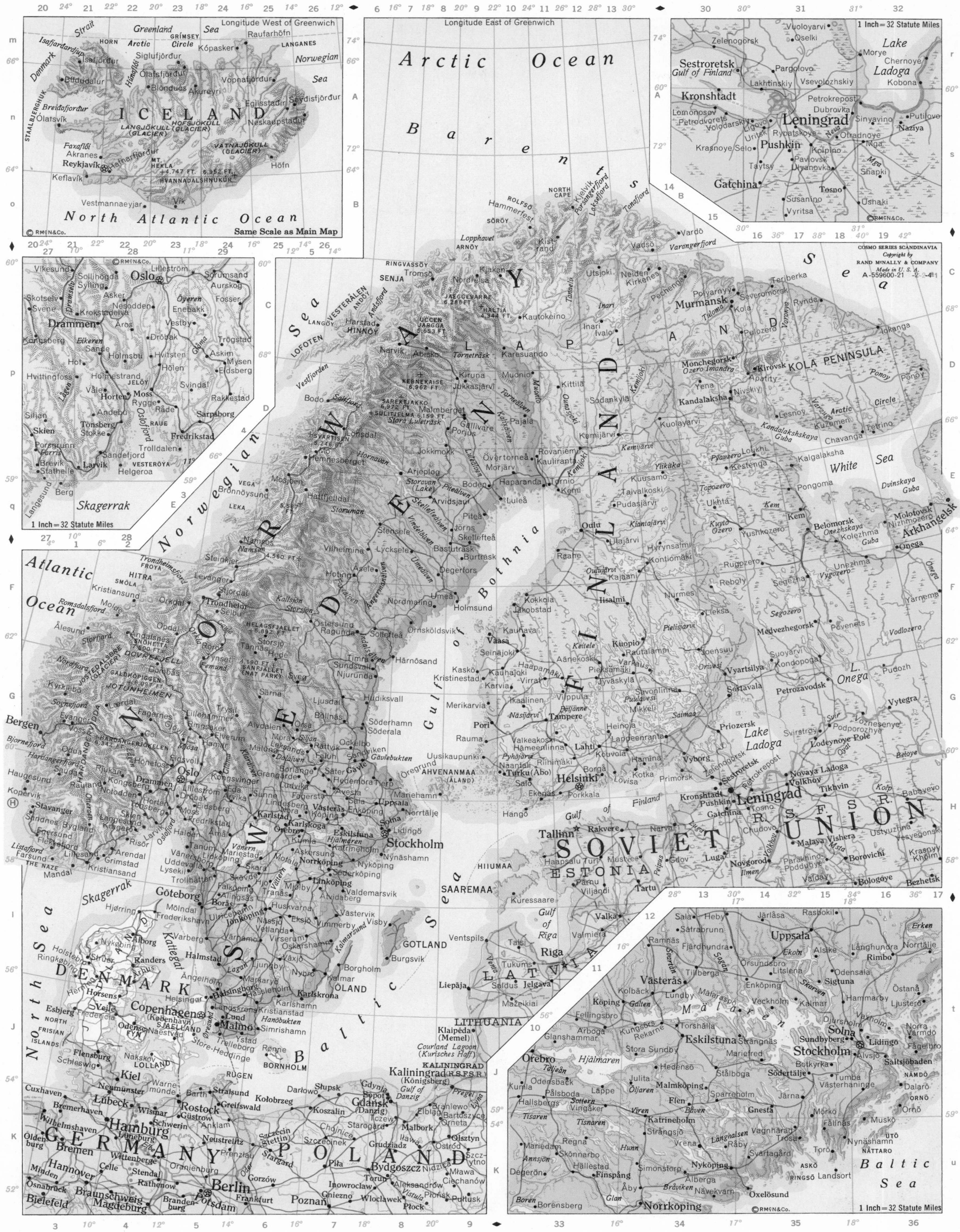

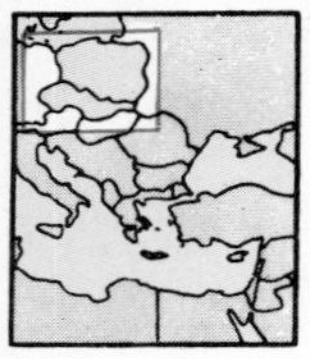

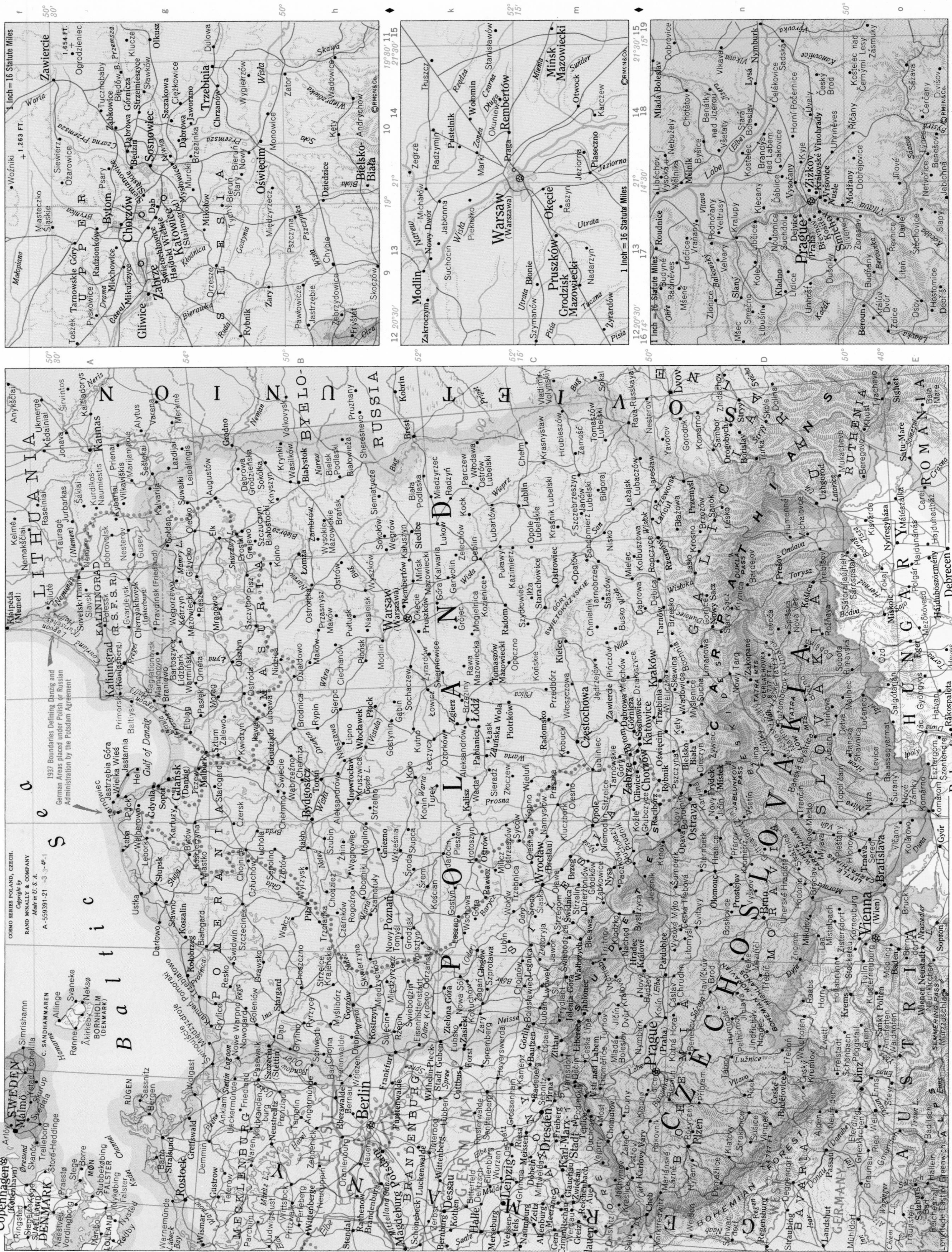

Statute Miles 25 0 25 50 75

Kilometers 25 0 50 100

Conic Projection

SCALE 1:4,000,000   1 Inch = 63 Statute Miles

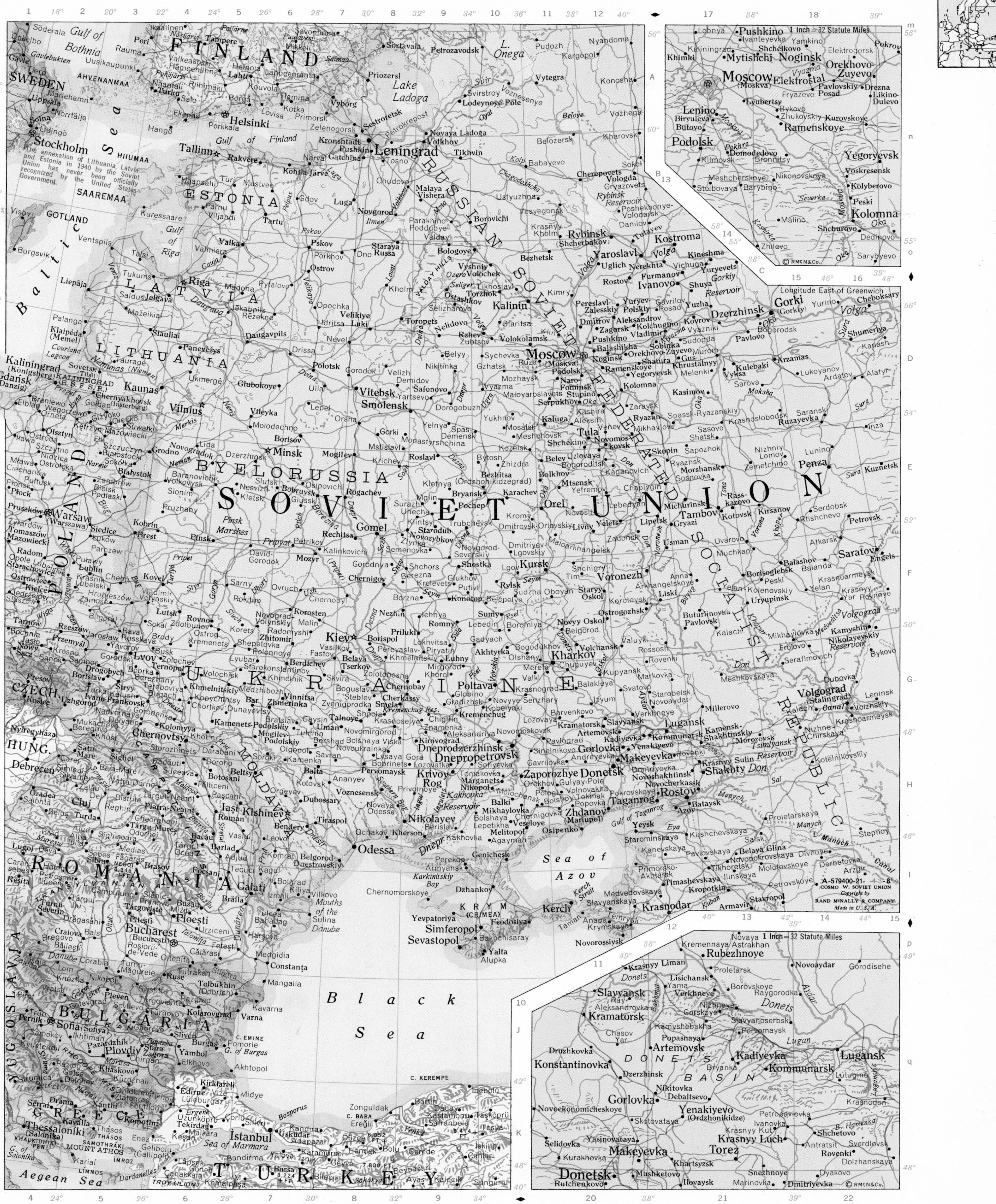

Conic Projection
SCALE 1:8,000,000 1 Inch = 126 Statute Miles

Statute Miles
50   0   50   100   150

Kilometers
50 0 50 100   200

THE SOVIET UNION

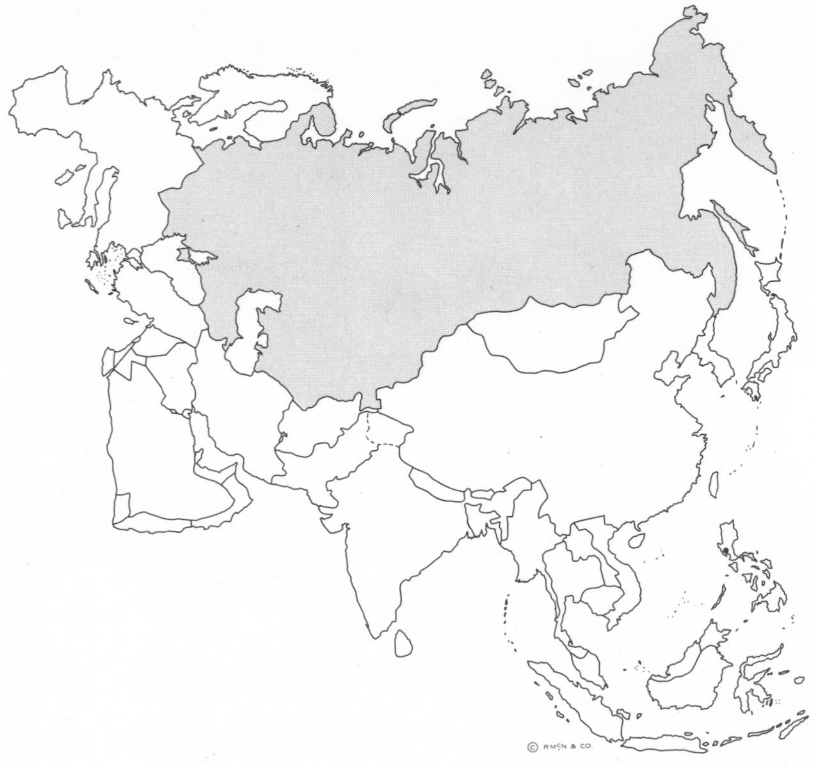

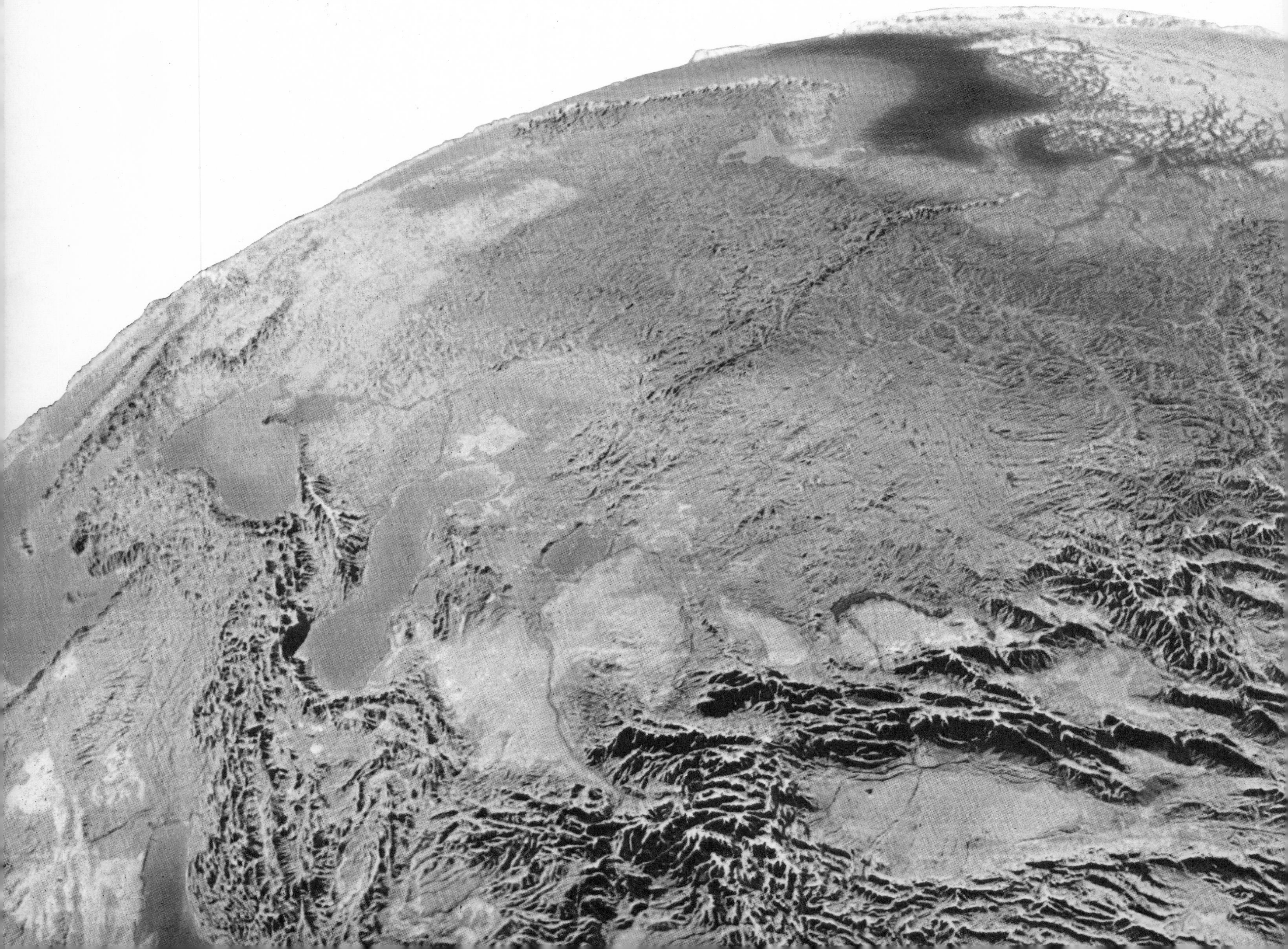

The Soviet Union sprawls almost halfway around the world, through 150° of longitude from Kaliningrad on the Baltic to the Bering Strait. It extends from northern seas, jammed with ice throughout most of the year, to southern mountains, deserts, and steppes. It covers more than 8,500,000 square miles.

This global view of the largest country in the world points up the extreme monotony of its landscape. Only where the southern border dips down to the Black, Caspian, and Aral seas, and to Lake Balkhash, does a change in coloration occur. From the west the relatively flat plains of Northern Europe extend well into the Soviet Union. This unbroken terrain is interrupted only by the low spine of the Urals until it finally merges with the mountainous upland east of the Yenisey River.

East of the Urals masses of cold winter air dominate the interior, and warm, dry summer air spreads over the southwestern steppes. Under the influence of these two climates vast stretches of coniferous forests, the taiga, have developed in the central region, and semiarid grasslands and desert in the south. Together, the two air masses with their extremes of temperature limit the penetration of mild, moist Atlantic air to the interior. Consequently, the Atlantic's influence is felt only in the west, in a wedge-shaped area, its base an imaginary line connecting the Baltic Sea and the Black Sea, and its apex in the midsection of the low Urals.

In this western area which covers a sizable portion of European Russia, man has created the most agriculturally productive tract of the Soviet Union. Today approximately 70 per cent of the Soviet people live in this area which includes the agricultural and industrial Ukraine, the Volga River region, and the northern plain focusing on Moscow. Here, too, is the industrial heart of modern Russia built not only on the agriculture of the area, but also upon the mineral wealth of the Urals and the Donets Basin. The transportation net is heaviest in this region.

Only within the relatively recent past have the Russian people ventured, with authority, into the "virgin lands" of the southeast and the taiga and tundra of the interior. In so doing they have tapped the vast iron deposits of the Urals and Kuznets, the coal reserves of the Kuznets, Karaganda, and Irkutsk, the forests of the taiga, and some of the agricultural potential of the semiarid steppes. As in the past, the severe environment of the interior will continue to limit man's development of the Soviet Union. Under the strict governmental control of economy and people, however, it is likely that the vast resources of Russia will continue to be developed as rapidly as possible to supplement those of the more densely populated western heartland.

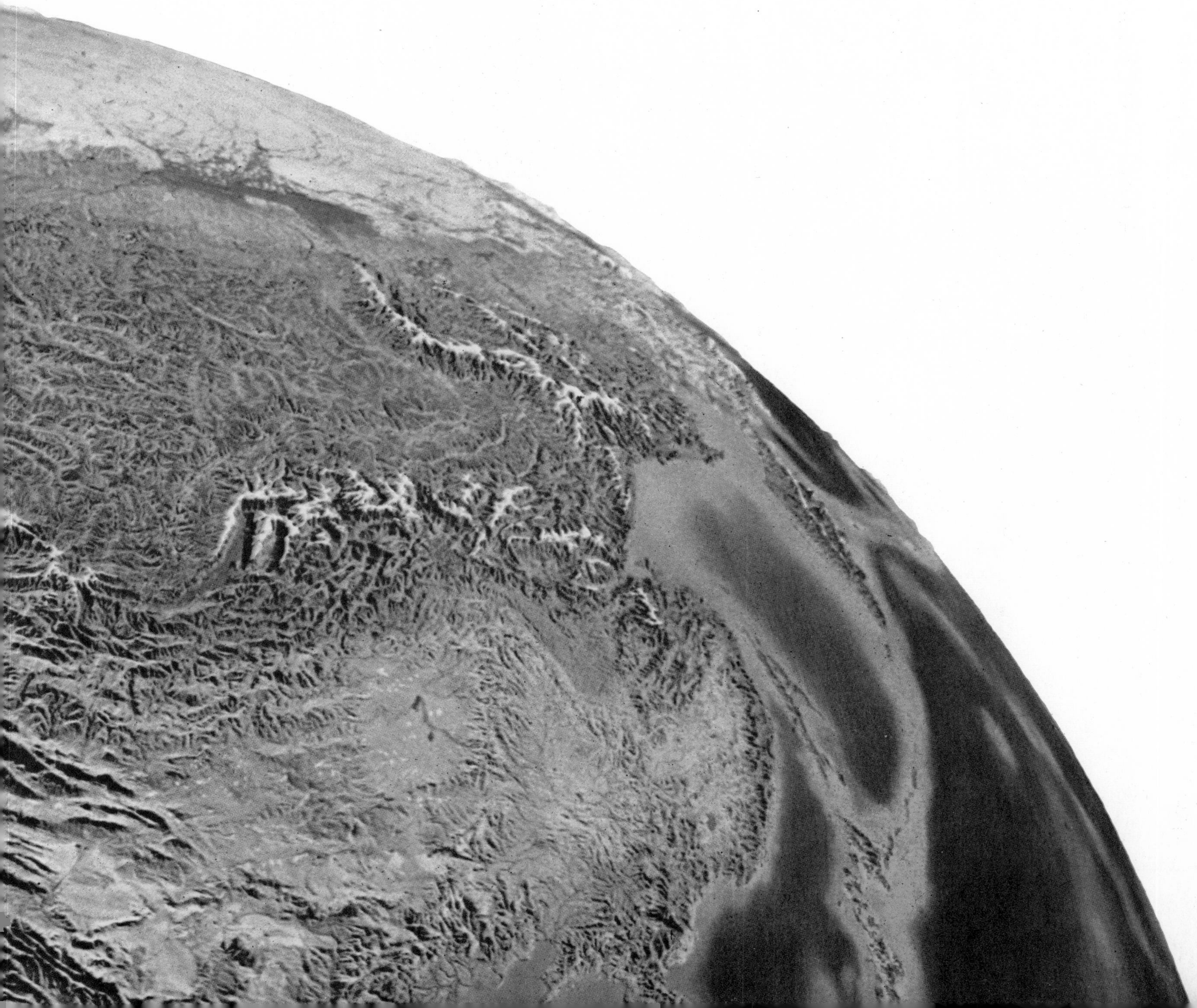

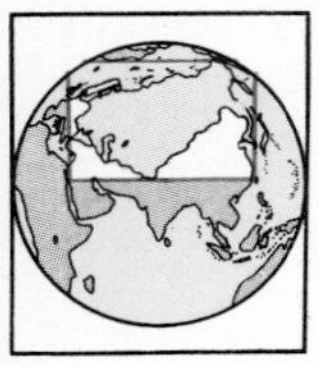

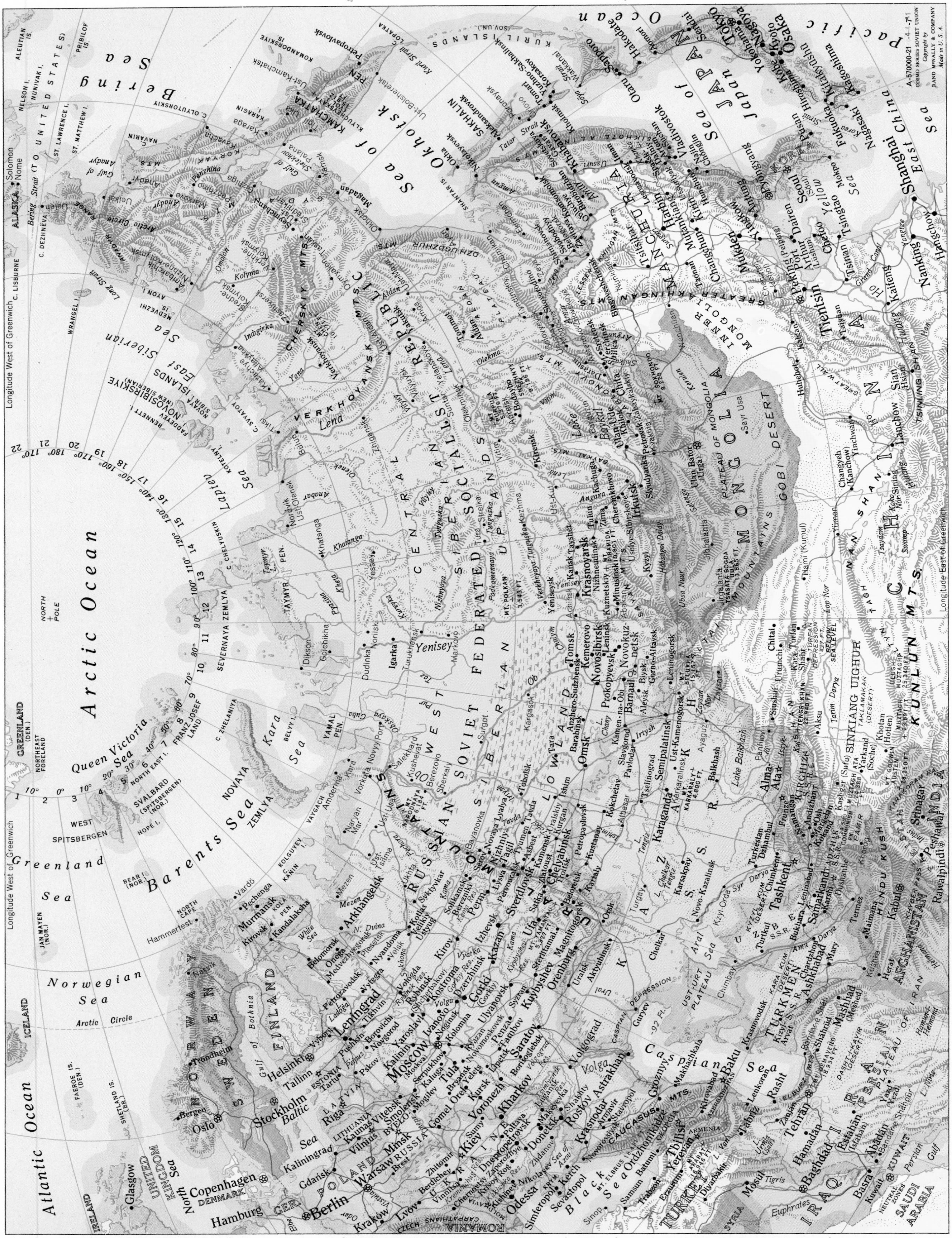

28

Statute Miles

Kilometers

Lambert Azimuthal Equal Area Projection
SCALE 1:28,000,000   1 Inch = 442 Statute Miles

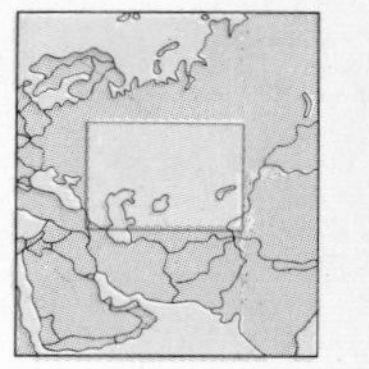

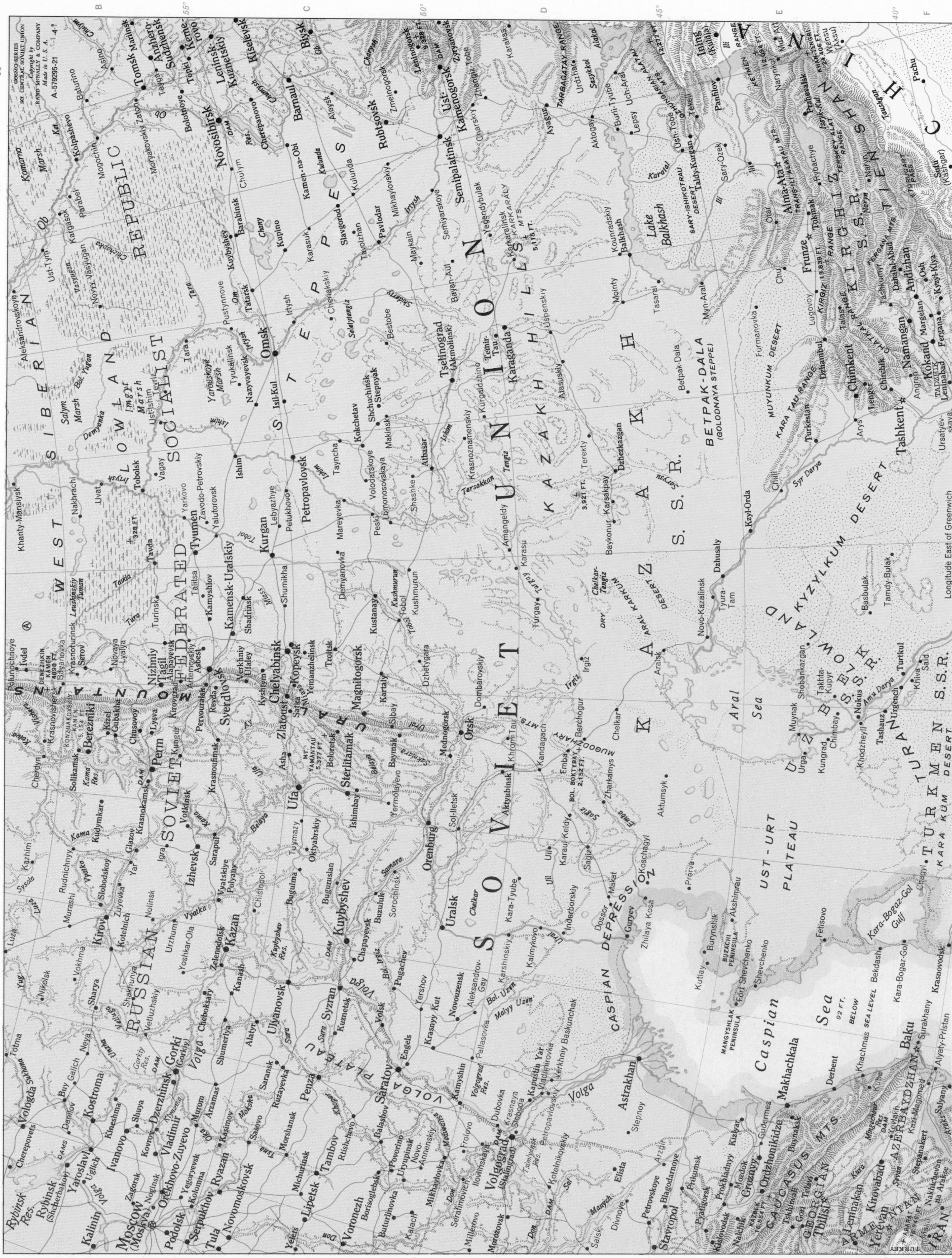

GROSSO SERIES
SO. CENTRAL SOVIET UNION
RAND McNALLY & COMPANY
Made in U.S.A.
A-579295-21 ... 4-1

Sinusoidal Projection

SCALE 1: 11,400,000   1 Inch = 180 Statute Miles

Statute Miles
50 0 50 100 150 200 250

Kilometers
50 0 50 100 150 200 250 300

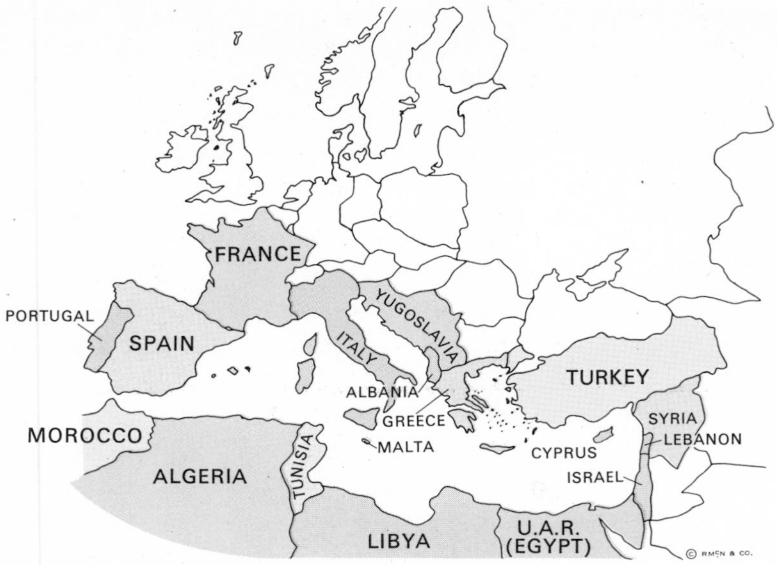

Southern Europe, extreme Southwest Asia, and the rim of North Africa, all integral parts of their respective continents, also belong to another significant world region. As lands that hem in the Mediterranean Sea, the waterway of the ancients, their history began early, and the climate provided by this body of water led to distinctive crops and cultures.

The Mediterranean region curves from the Biblical lands of the Middle East westward 2,500 miles to the Portuguese coast, and back again across the top of Africa to the Sinai Peninsula. Besides the Mediterranean itself, the region includes peninsulas, islands, and a thin, scalloped, often mountainous coastal strip. Both the sea and the general characteristics associated with the region are confined on the west and east by the constrictions at Gibraltar and the Suez. The Pyrenees, Alps, Balkan Mountains, and Black Sea on the north, and the Atlas Mountains and the North African desert on the south form the region's limits.

Although the Iberian, Italian, Balkan, and Anatolian peninsulas are imposing physical features, the Mediterranean Sea itself is the dominant element of the region's landscape. Upon this sea, which nature has segmented into two basins by the boot of Italy

THE
MEDITERRANEAN

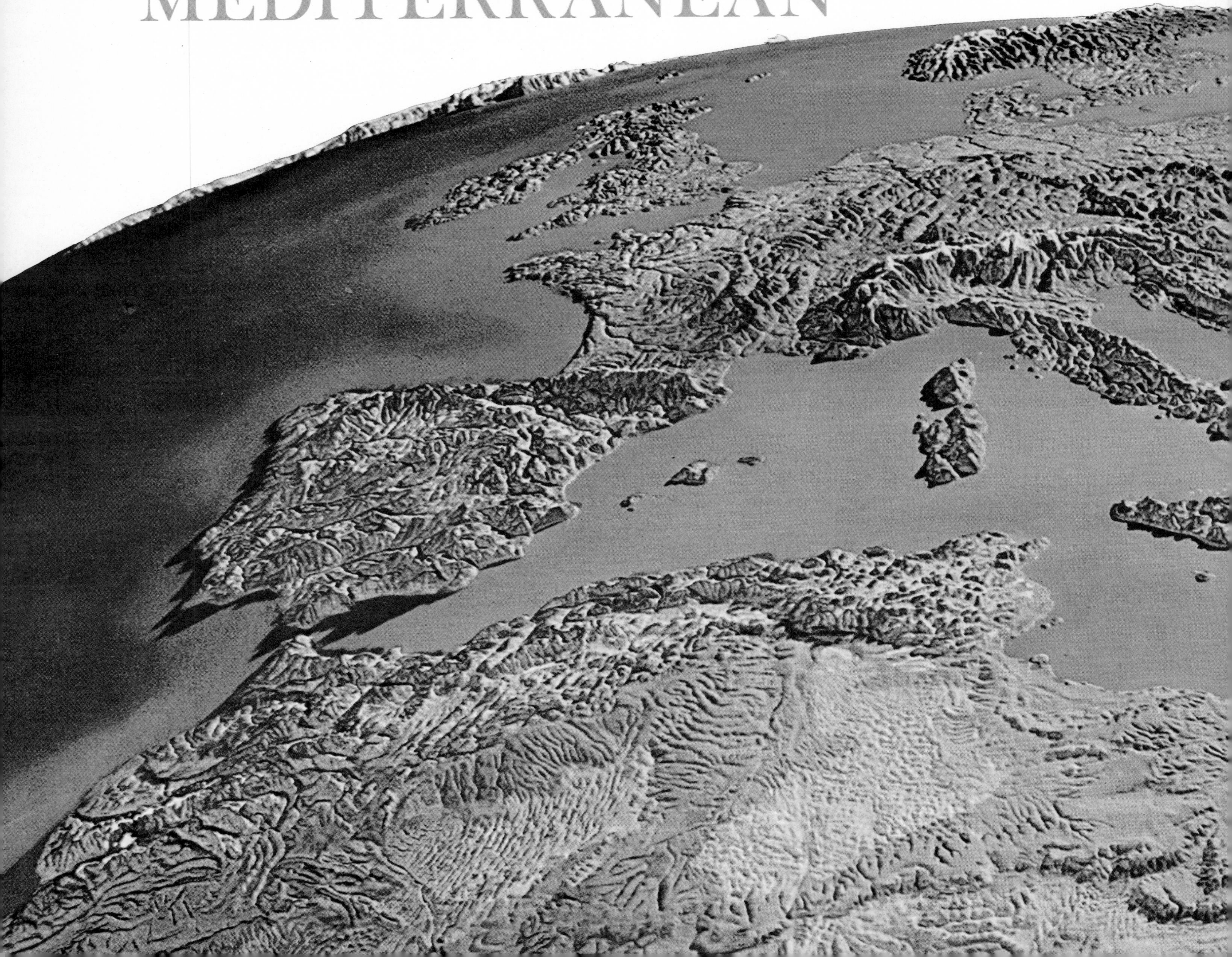

and the island of Sicily, were developed the navigation techniques of the Western World. Over this body of water a commerce of goods and ideas flowed and still flows between Asia, Africa, and Europe. And from it many of the Italian, Spanish, and Portuguese explorers of the 1400's and 1500's sailed to discover and conquer new lands.

The rugged shores of the Mediterranean, insular and peninsular, with hot, dry summers and mild, moist winters have long presented man a challenging landscape from which to extract a living. By growing olive trees and grapevines, whose long roots sustain them through the dry summer, by cultivating barley and wheat, and by grazing sheep where little else can subsist on the rugged terrain, man has met this challenge. The scenic beauty of the azure sky and sea and the mountainous terrain—the Rivieras of France, Spain, and Italy, the Balkan coast and islands—contribute to a long famous and steadily expanding tourist economy.

Though the efforts to conquer the rugged natural elements have been heroic, most of the significant economic development has taken place on the few lowland plains and valleys of the region. The Nile Valley of Egypt, the Languedoc region of France,

the Guadalquivir Valley of Spain, and the Po Plain of Italy are representative. Here milder natural conditions have aided agricultural success. Coupled with what little industrial expansion has taken place, these areas have bolstered the total economy. Still the economy of these few widely separated, thriving pockets is not dynamic enough to absorb immigrants from the fairly dense rural population. In recent years thousands of workers have left for the industries of Northern Europe.

It is difficult to realize that in the rough land of the Mediterranean are buried many of the roots of Western civilization. Here Greek, Roman, and Byzantine cultures flourished and passed on their heritage to the far reaches of the earth. Around the shores of the Mediterranean, too, Christianity and Islam have their roots. Although today the major power centers are removed from the region, strong national feelings still prevail, based in good measure on the fact that each nation has played a role in world history. So, although the Mediterranean lands display similarities in climate, economy, and physical make-up, the variety of individual cultures and strong traditions that exist continue to defy political unification.

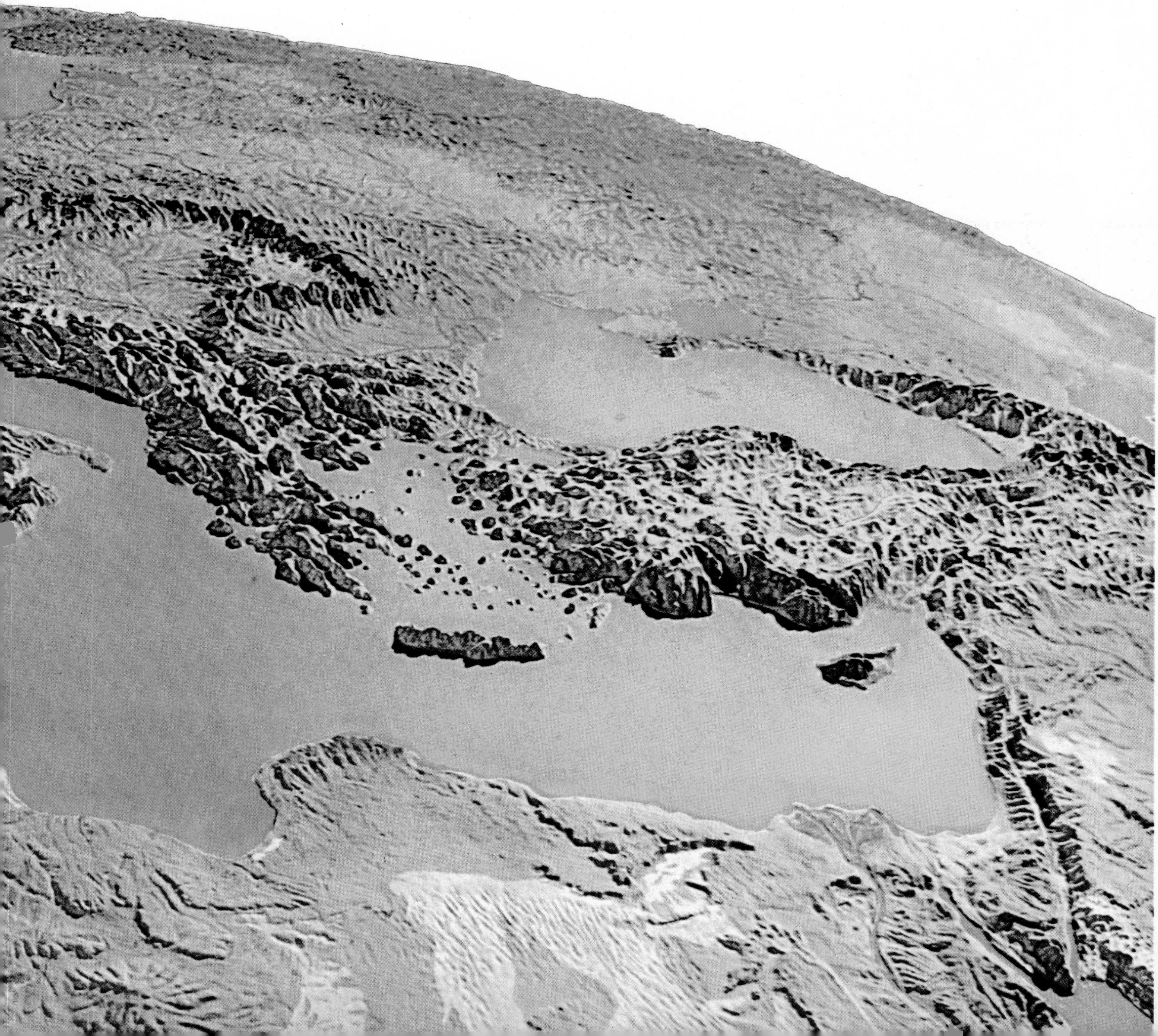

29 B

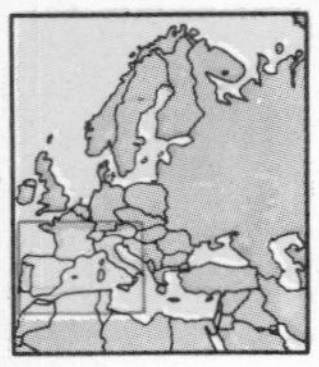

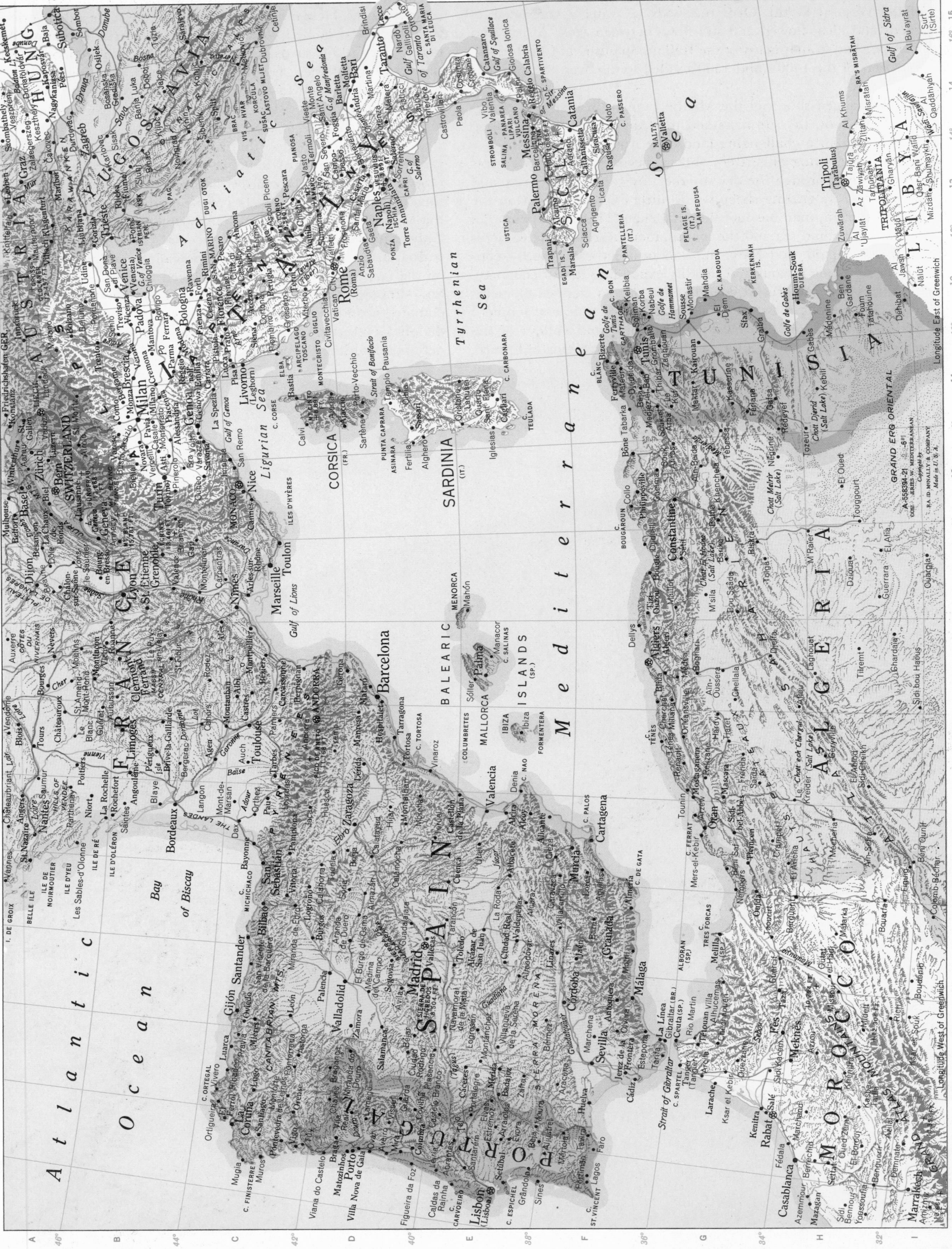

Statute Miles 50 0 50 100 150

Kilometers 50 0 50 100 200

Lambert Conformal Conic Projection
SCALE 1 : 8,000,000   1 Inch = 126 Statute Miles

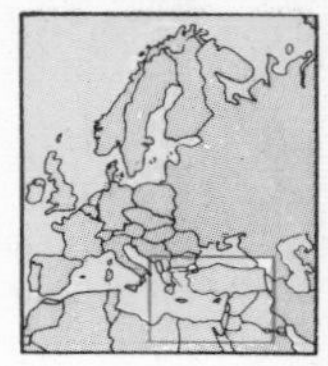

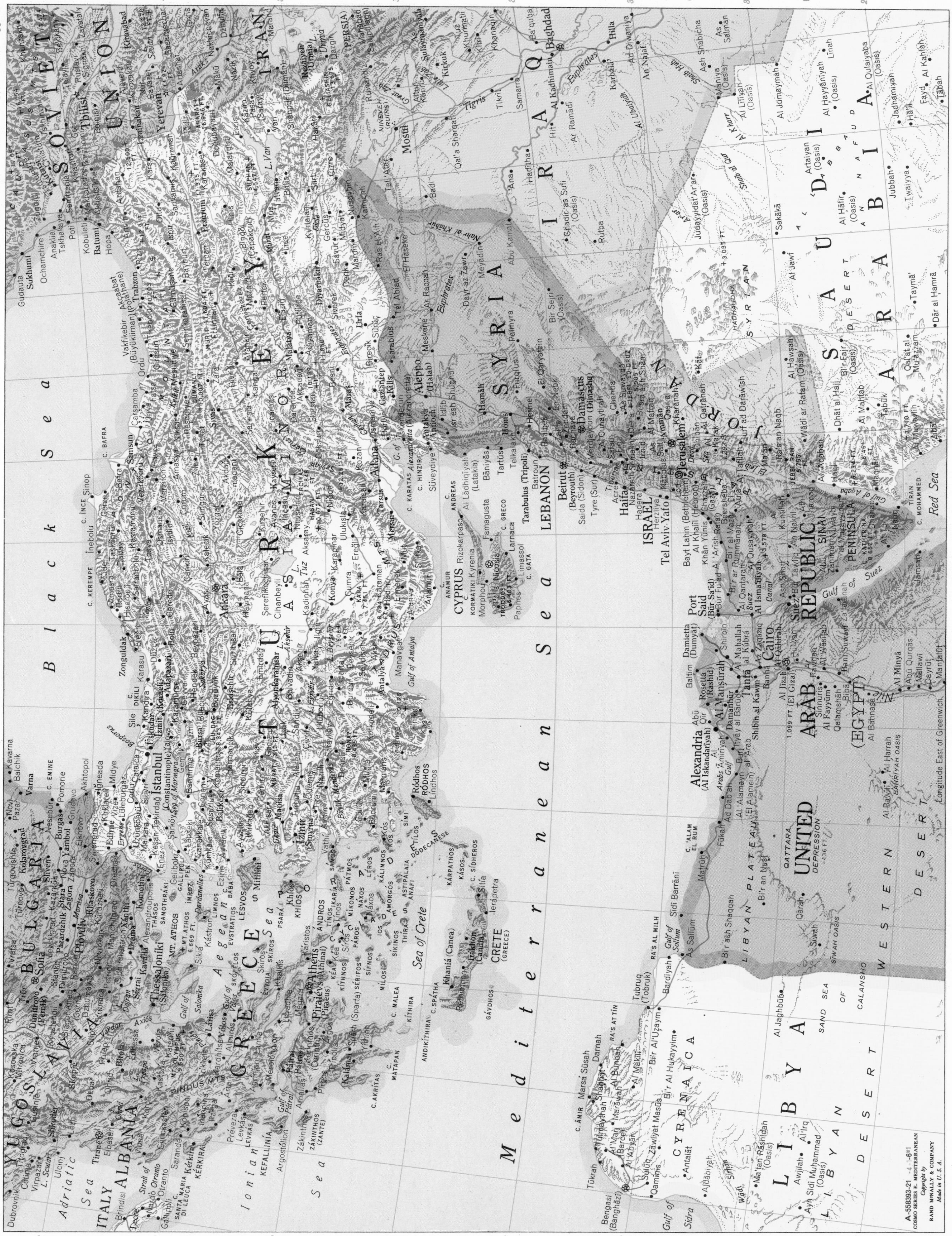

Lambert Conformal Conic Projection

SCALE 1 : 8,000,000   1 Inch = 126 Statute Miles

Statute Miles 50 0 50 100 150

Kilometers 50 0 50 100 200

A-558393-21 -4 -6-1
COSMO SERIES E. MEDITERRANEAN
Copyright by
RAND McNALLY & COMPANY
Made in U.S.A.

ISRAEL AND NORTHERN U.A.R.

JERUSALEM
1 Inch = 1 Statute Mile

Mediterranean Sea

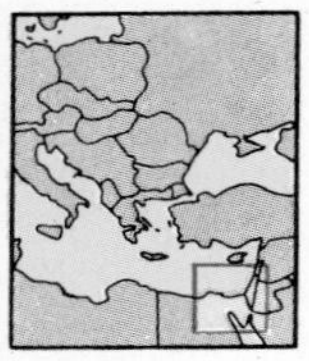

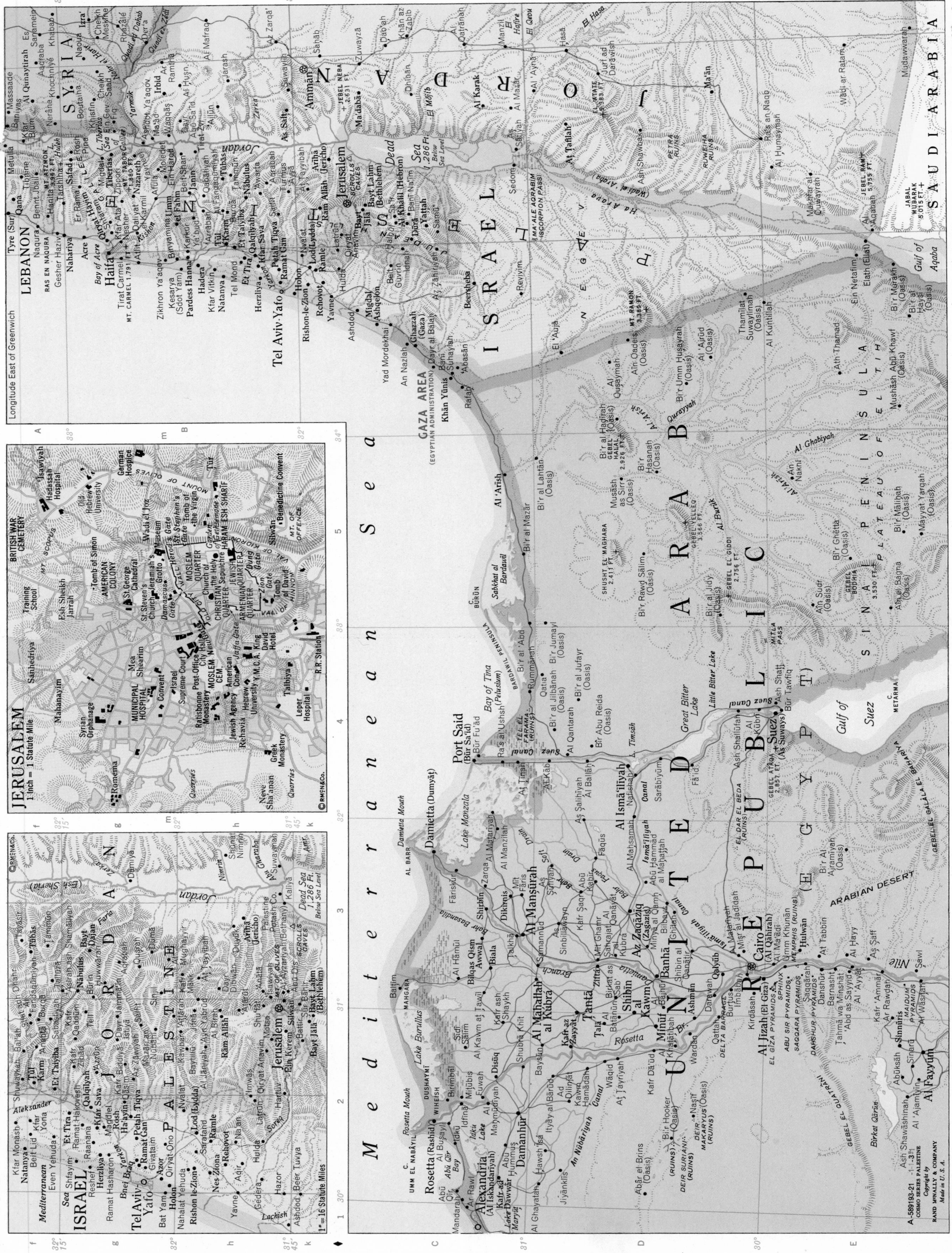

Statute Miles 5 0 5 10 20 30 40 50
Kilometers 5 0 5 10 20 30 40 50 60

Lambert Conformal Conic Projection
SCALE 1:2,000,000   1 Inch = 32 Statute Miles

32

A-59193-21   Copyright by RAND McNALLY & COMPANY   Made in U.S.A.

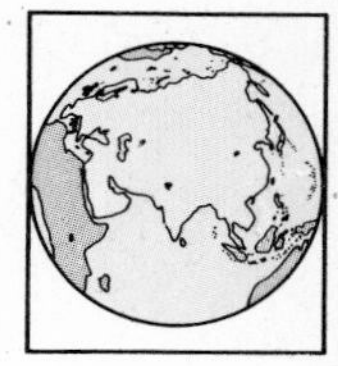

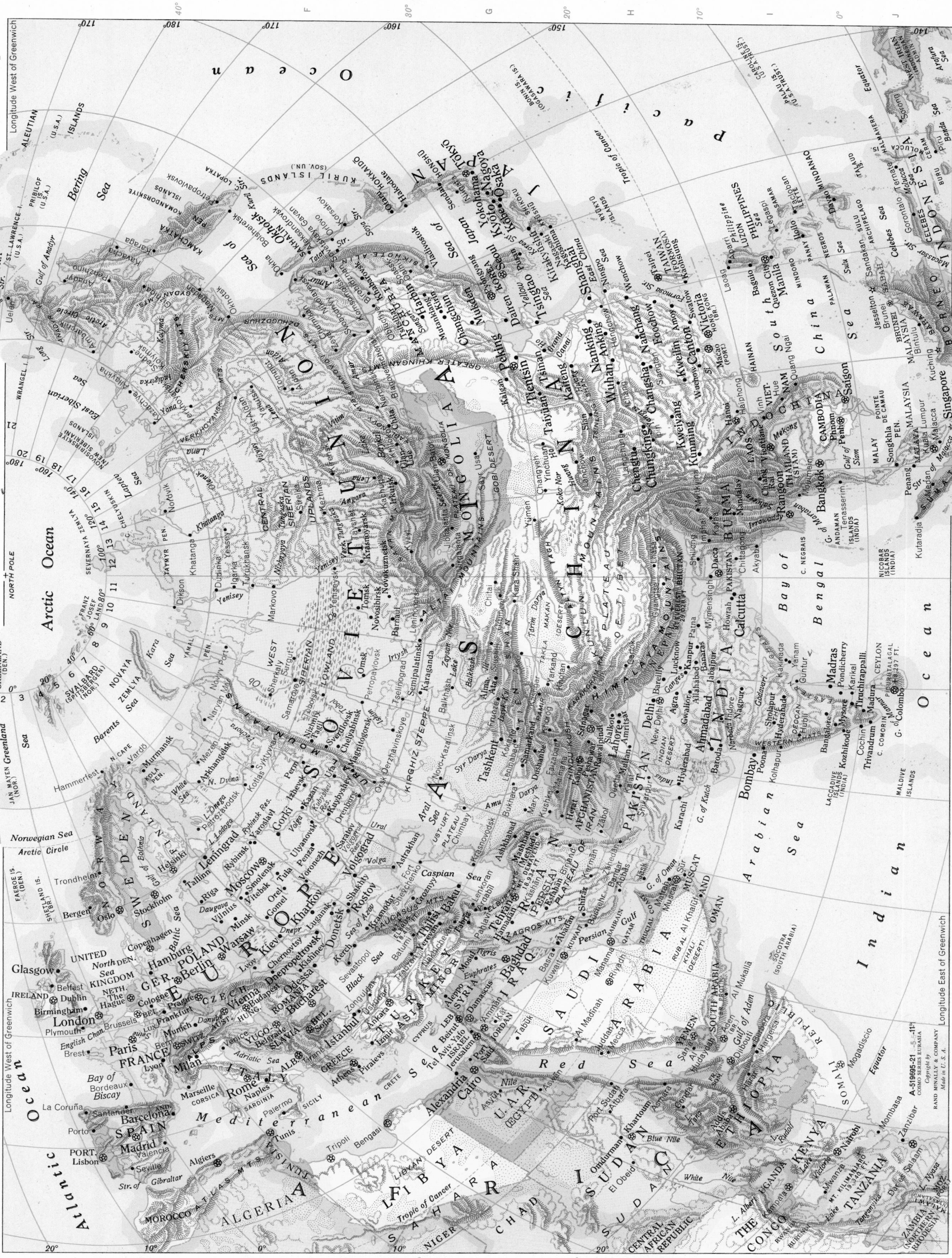

Lambert Azimuthal Equal Area Projection
SCALE 1:42,000,000 1 Inch = 663 Statute Miles

Statute Miles
100 0 100   300   500   700   900

Kilometers
100 0 100 300   700   1100

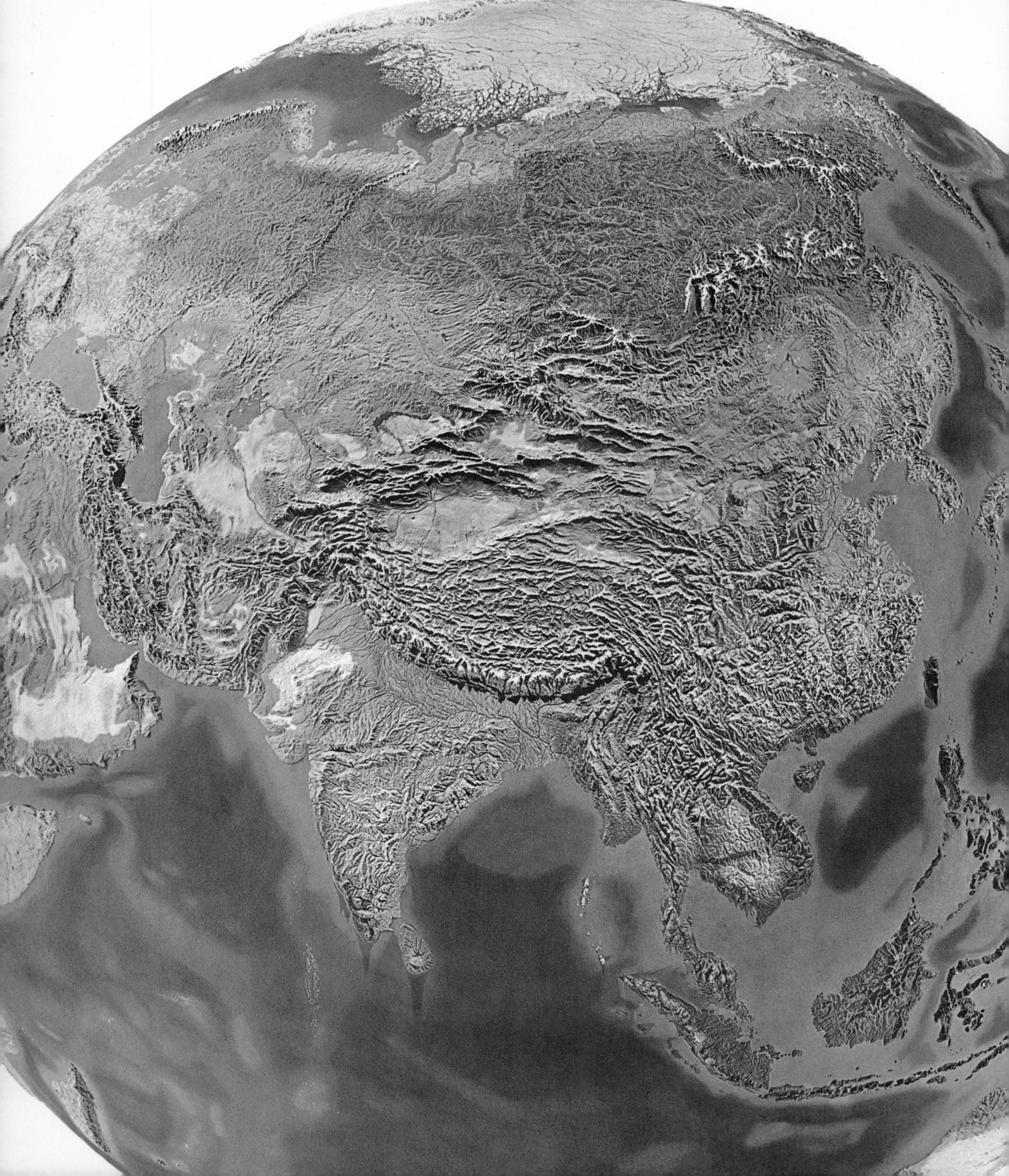

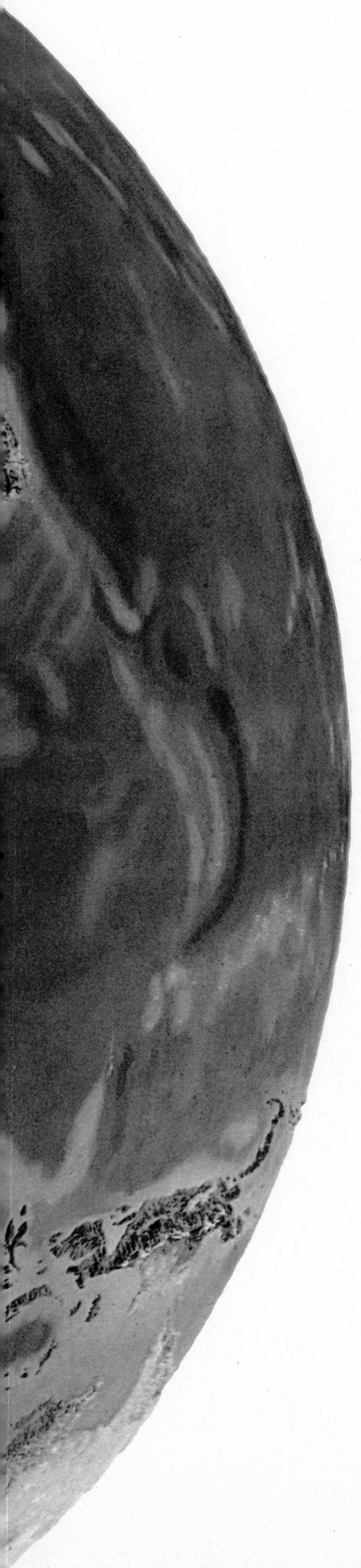

ASIA

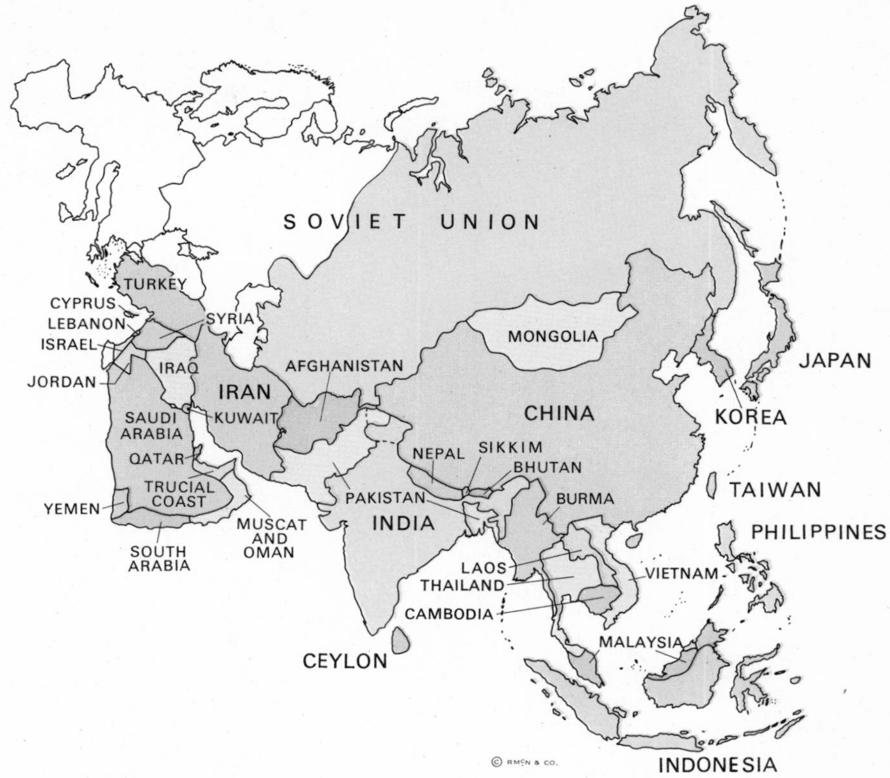

Asia, the massive giant of continents, spreads its 17,000,000 square miles from polar wastes to regions of tropical abundance, and from Oriental to Occidental hearthlands. Much of Asia's vastness, however, is occupied by deserts, steppes, and by frozen and near-frozen wastes. Rugged upland areas stretch from Turkey and Iran, through the two-mile-high Tibetan Plateau, to the Bering Strait, leaving only one-third of Asia suitable for human habitation. These barriers also separate the two dominant, sharply contrasting parts of Asia—the realm made up of Southwest, South, and Southeast Asia from that of "European" Asia.

Rimming the south and east coasts of the continent are the most densely populated regions of the world, each dominated by a life-giving river system—the Tigris-Euphrates, the Indus and Ganges, the Brahmaputra, the Irrawaddy and Salween, the Menam and Mekong, the Yangtze and Hwang Ho, as well as innumerable small river valleys, plains, and islands. Separated from one another by deserts, massifs, and seas these regions account for over one-half of the world's population.

The civilizations associated with this population (where rural densities frequently may exceed 1,000 people per square mile) were developed largely upon the strength of intensive agricultural systems. Today these systems occupy more than 60 per cent of the populace, who manage only to win a bare subsistence. Changeover from subsistence agricultural economic systems to industrialized economies has been successful only in Japan and parts of the U.S.S.R.

North of the great Gobi Desert and the mountain barriers of the interior is the second Asia which, on almost every hand, differs from the southern portion of the continent. In the far north severe climatic elements send temperatures to −90°F., and permanently frozen ground impedes growth of vegetation. Only the scattered settlements next to the Trans-Siberian Railway give the area an indication of development. The activities of most of the populace are clearly directed toward Europe rather than Asia.

These two realms of the Asian continent do share two common characteristics. One is vast, yet generally inaccessible, natural resources—extensive forests, minerals, and hydroelectric potential—and the second is the drive to industrialize in order to "catch up" to the general material well-being of the Western World.

In the future, as the common characteristics, resources and drive, are developed, Asia's two realms may witness a change. A material way of life may result consistent with their heritage and historic contributions to the world.

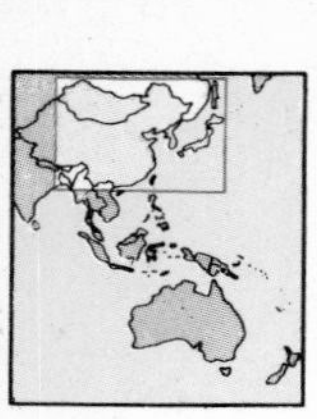

CHINA, MONGOLIA, KOREA, JAPAN and TAIWAN

34

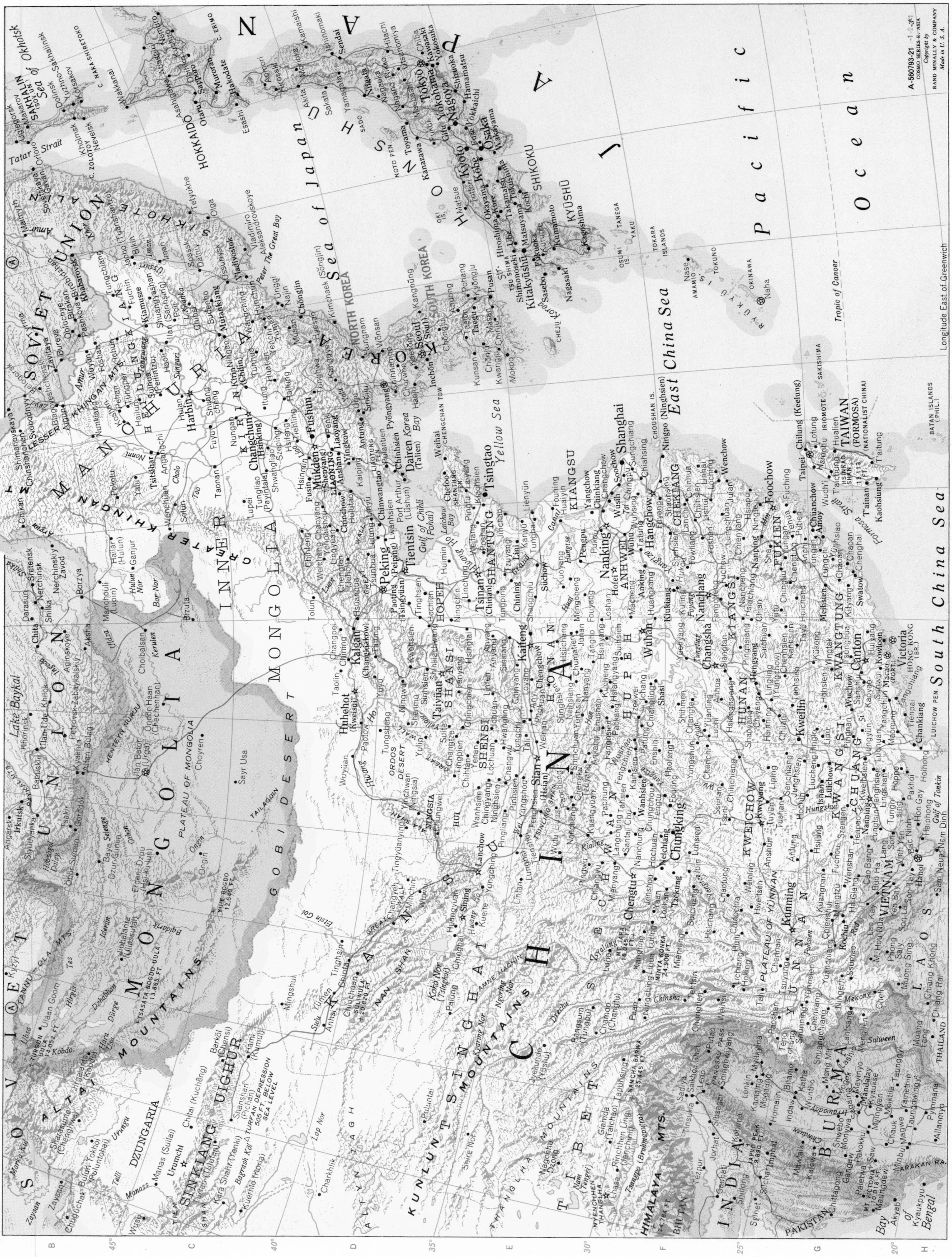

Statute Miles 100 0 100 200 300
Kilometers 100 0 100 200 300 400

Polyconic Projection
SCALE 1:16,000,000   1 Inch = 252 Statute Miles

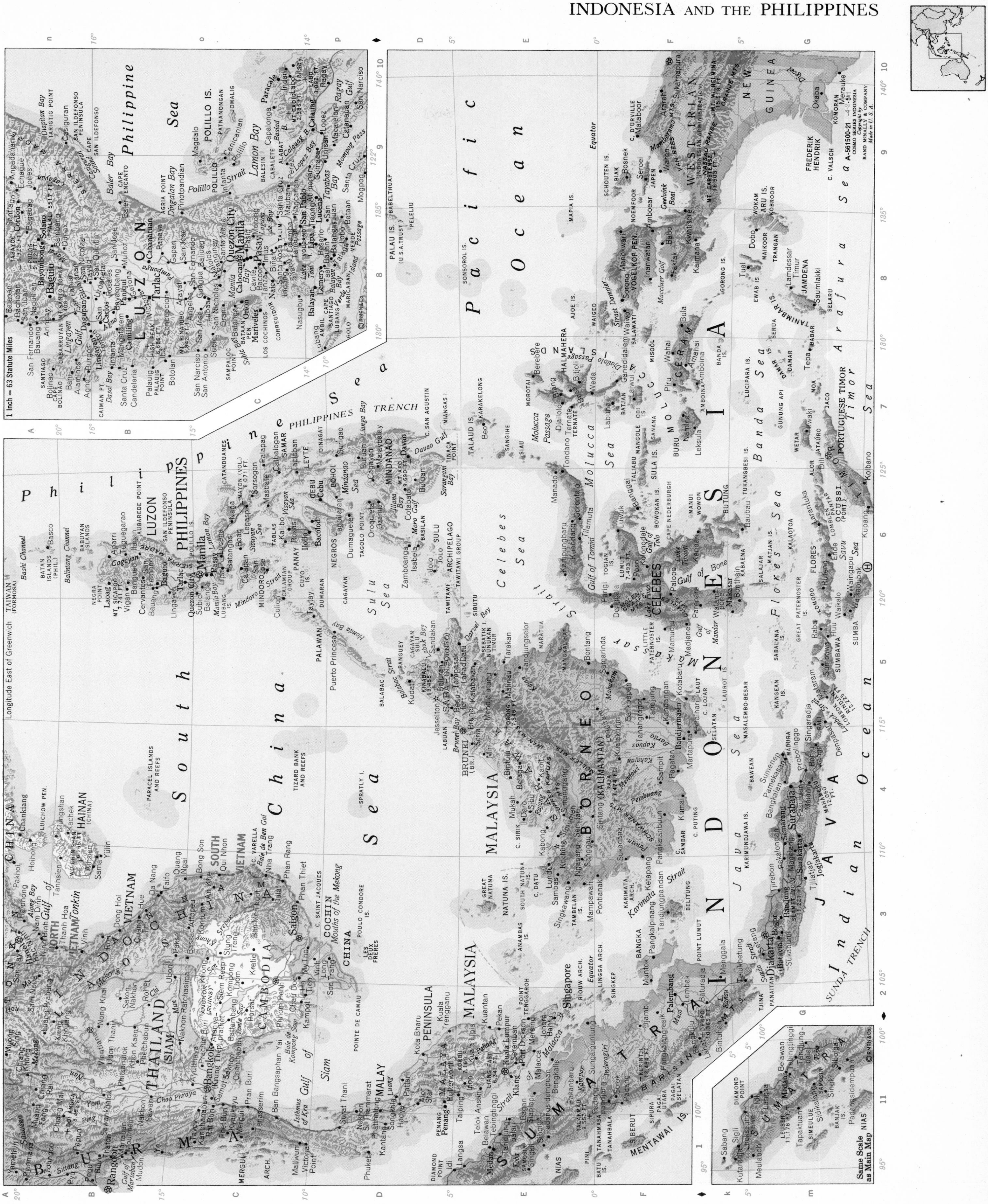

Polyconic Projection
SCALE 1:16,000,000 1 Inch = 252 Statute Miles

Statute Miles 100 0 100 200 300
Kilometers 100 0 100 200 300 400

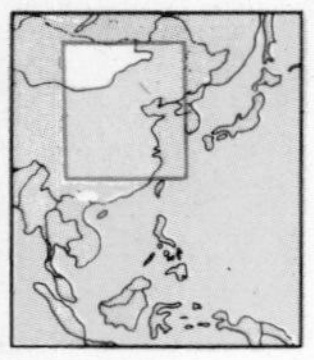

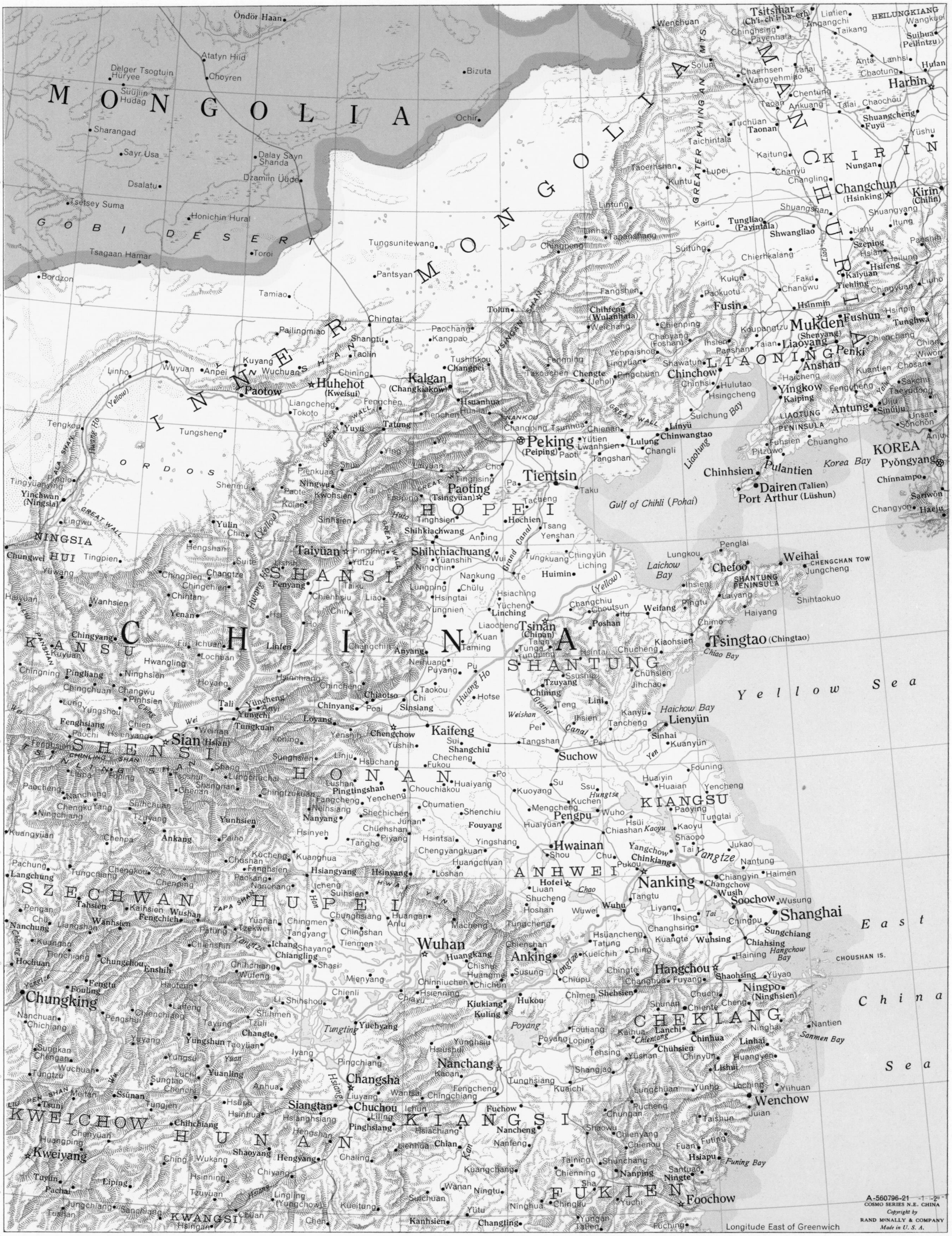

Statute Miles
Kilometers

Lambert Conformal Conic Projection
SCALE 1 : 8,000,000   1 Inch = 126 Statute Miles

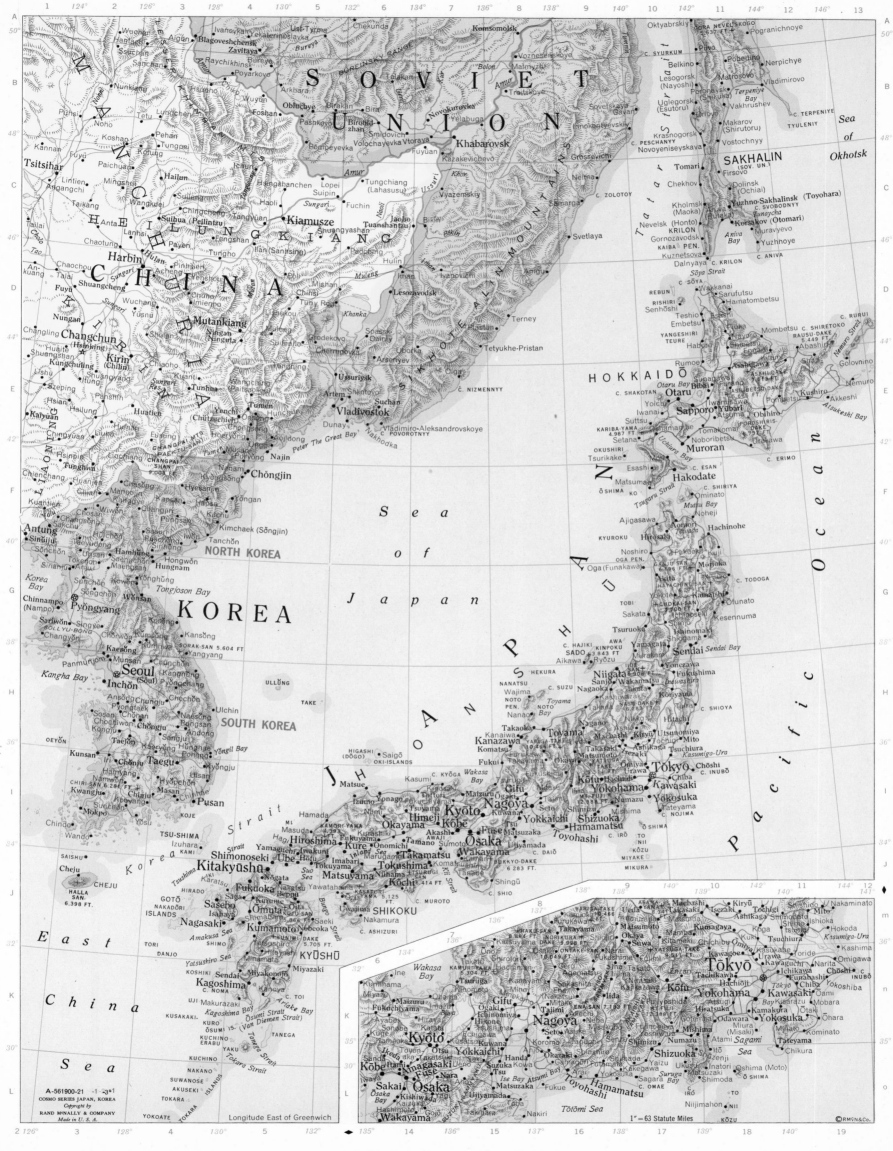

SOVIET UNION

MANCHURIA

CHINA

HEILUNGKIANG

Tsitsihar

Harbin

Changchun

Kirin

LIAONING

Vladivostok

KOREA

NORTH KOREA

SOUTH KOREA

Pyŏngyang

Seoul
Inchŏn

Taegu

Pusan

Korea Strait

TSU-SHIMA

Cheju
CHEJU
HALLA SAN.
6,398 FT.

East China Sea

SAKHALIN

Sea of Okhotsk

HOKKAIDŌ

Sapporo

Muroran
Hakodate

Sea of Japan

HONSHŪ

Sendai

Niigata

SADO

Kanazawa

Kyōto
Kōbe
Osaka
Takamatsu

Kitakyūshū
Fukuoka

Nagasaki

Kumamoto

KYŪSHŪ

Kagoshima

Nagoya

Tōkyō
Yokohama
Kawasaki

SHIKOKU

Pacific Ocean

Tōkyō
Yokohama
Nagoya
Kyōto
Osaka

Longitude East of Greenwich

1" = 63 Statute Miles

©RMcN&Co.

Lambert Conformal Conic Projection
SCALE 1 : 8,000,000   1 Inch = 126 Statute Miles

Statute Miles
50   0   50   100   150

Kilometers
50   0   50   100   200

CAMBODIA, LAOS, VIETNAM, THAILAND AND MALAYSIA

A-561100-21 -2-3-3-2
COSMO SERIES INDOCHINA, THAILAND
Copyright by
RAND MCNALLY & COMPANY
Made in U.S.A.

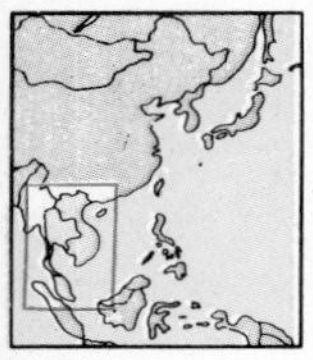

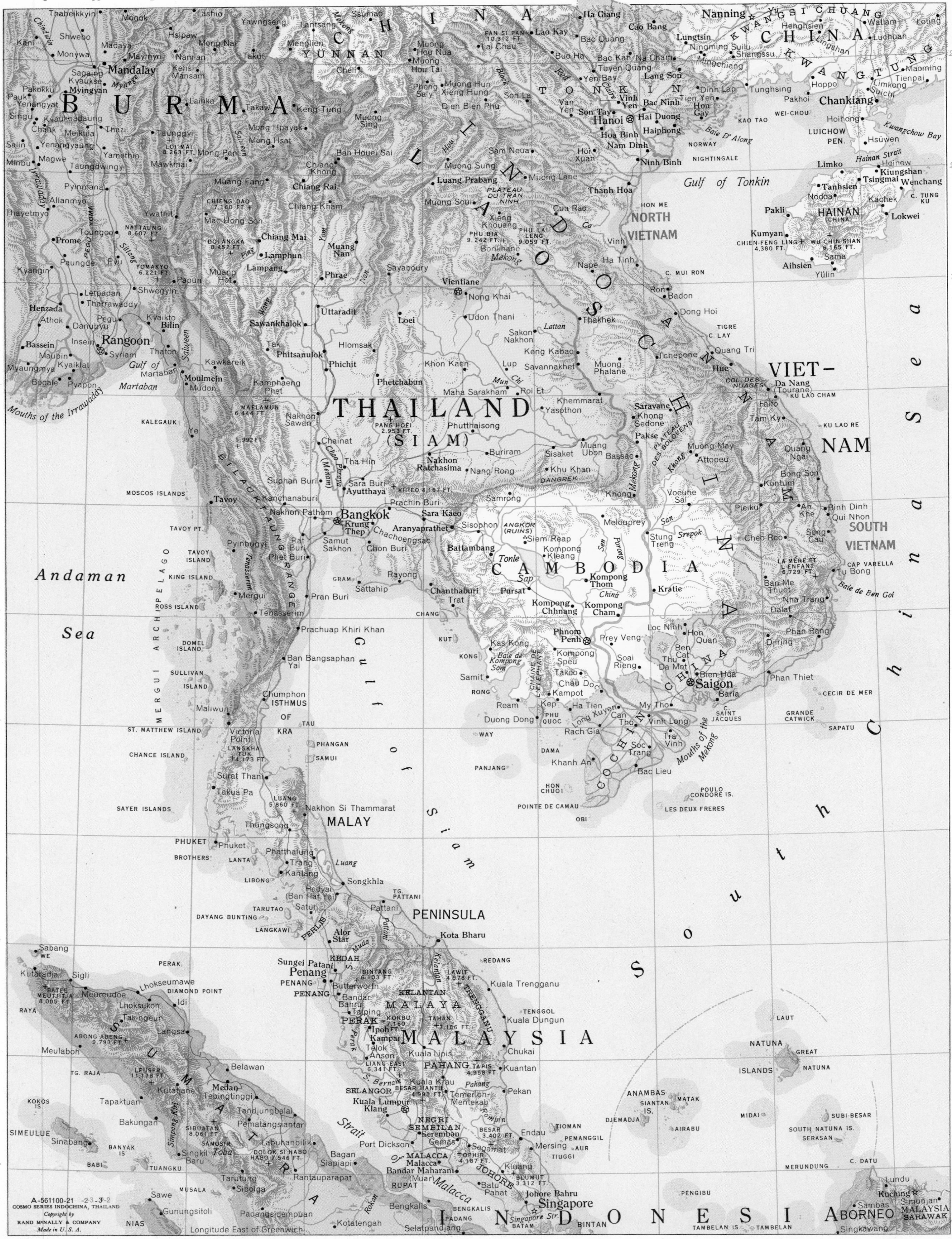

Statute Miles 50 0 50 100 150
Kilometers 50 0 50 100 200

Lambert Conformal Conic Projection
SCALE 1:8,000,000 1 Inch = 126 Statute Miles

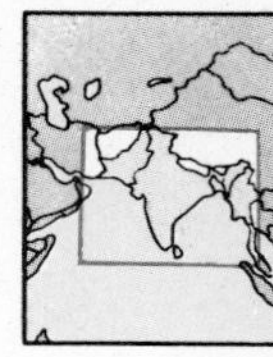

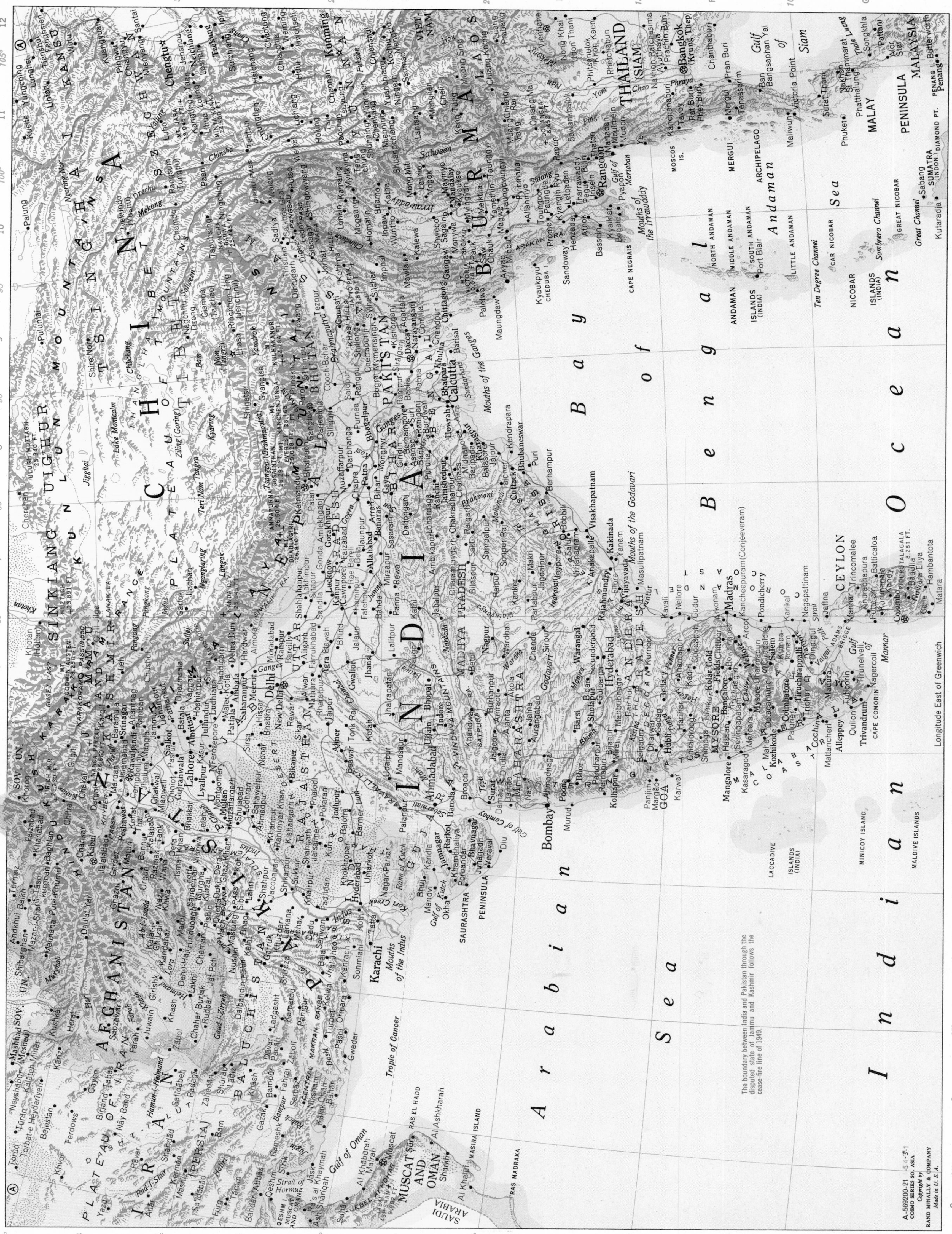

Polyconic Projection
SCALE 1:16,000,000   1 inch = 252 Statute Miles

Statute Miles

Kilometers

The boundary between India and Pakistan through the
disputed state of Jammu and Kashmir follows the
cease-fire line of 1949.

A-569200-21
COSMO SERIES SO. ASIA
Copyright by
RAND McNALLY & COMPANY
Made in U.S.A.

Statute Miles 50 0 50 100 150

Kilometers 50 0 50 100 200

Lambert Conformal Conic Projection

SCALE 1 : 8,000,000 1 Inch = 126 Statute Miles

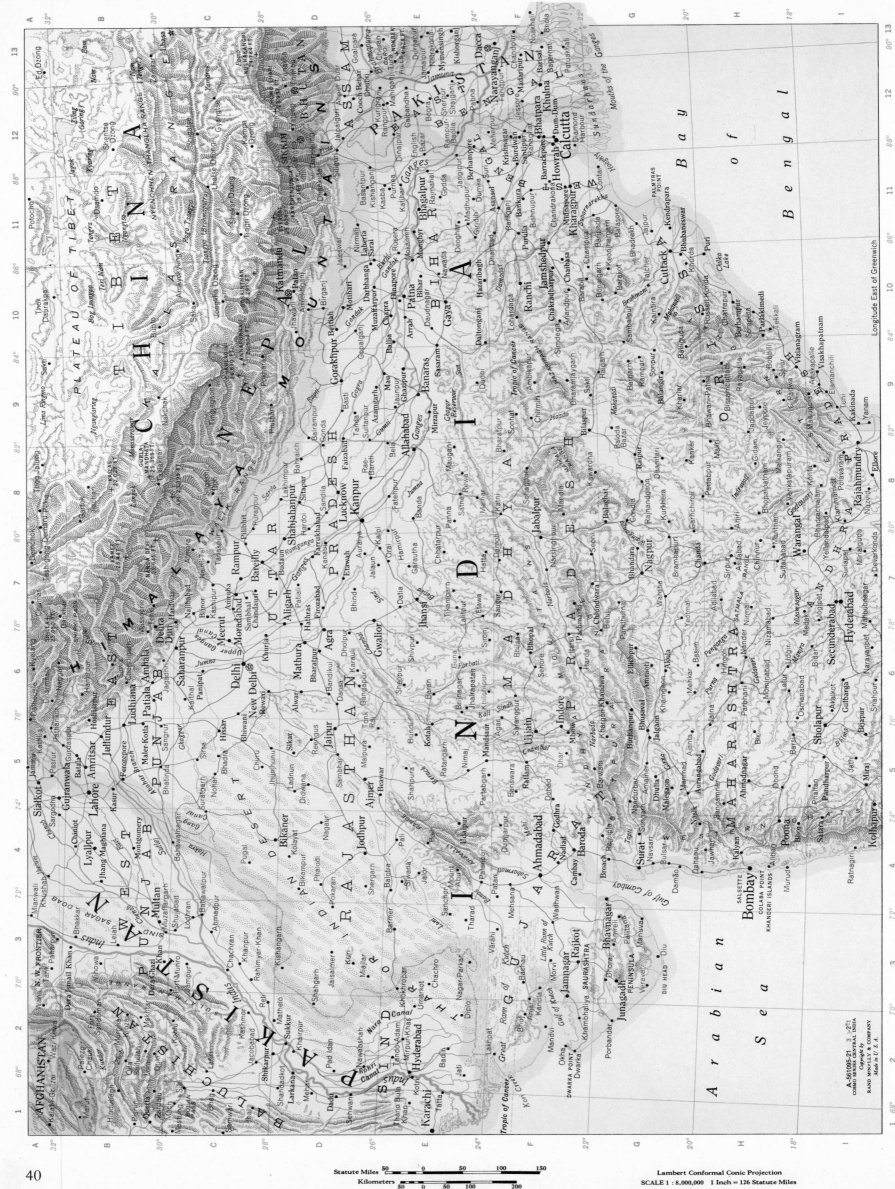

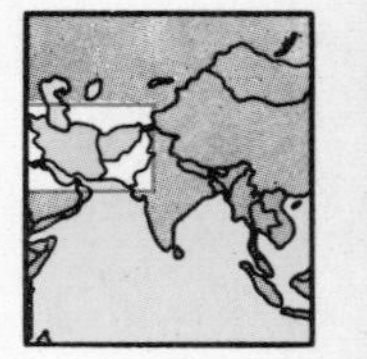

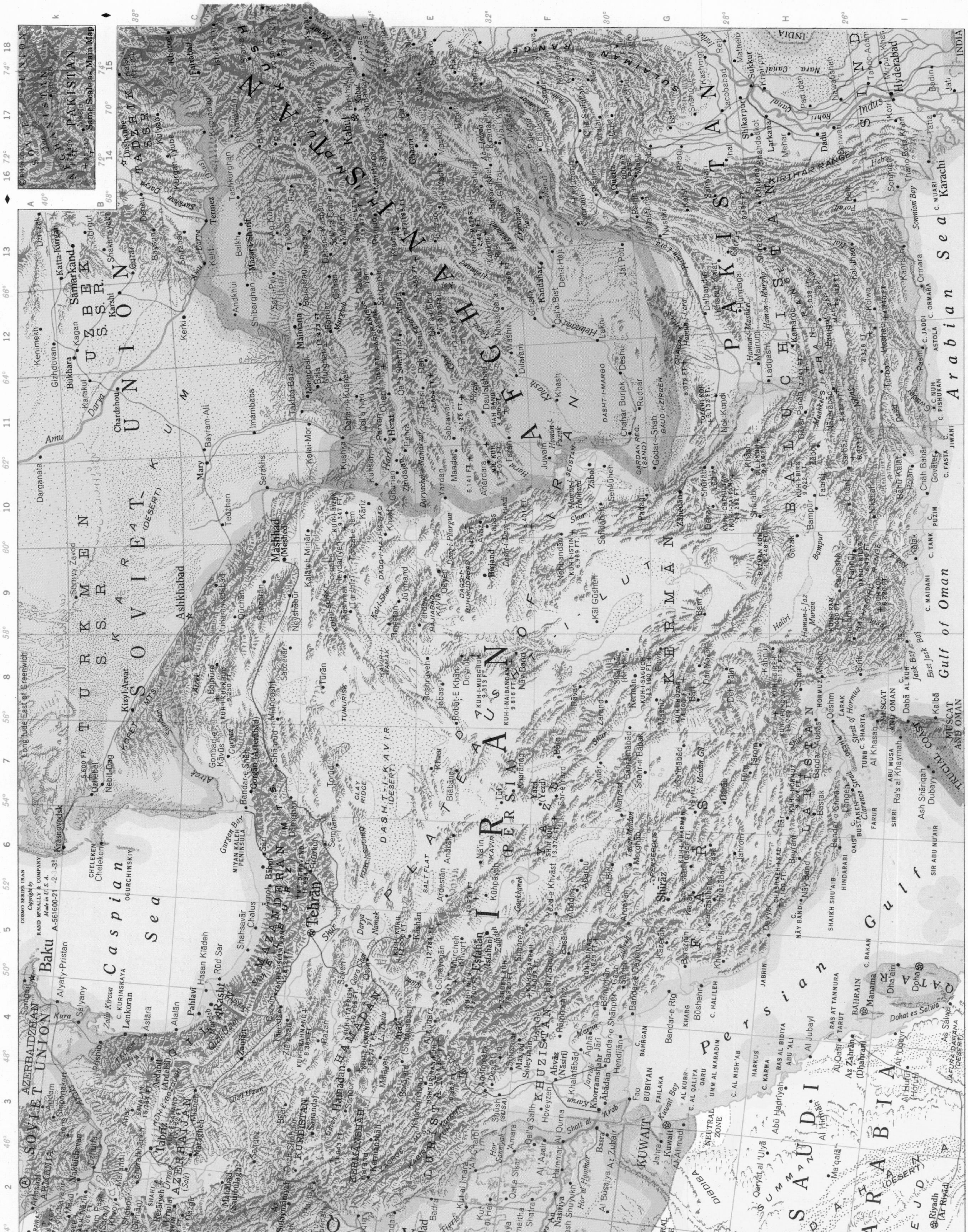

Lambert Conformal Conic Projection
SCALE 1 : 8,000,000 1 Inch = 126 Statute Miles

Statute Miles
Kilometers

41

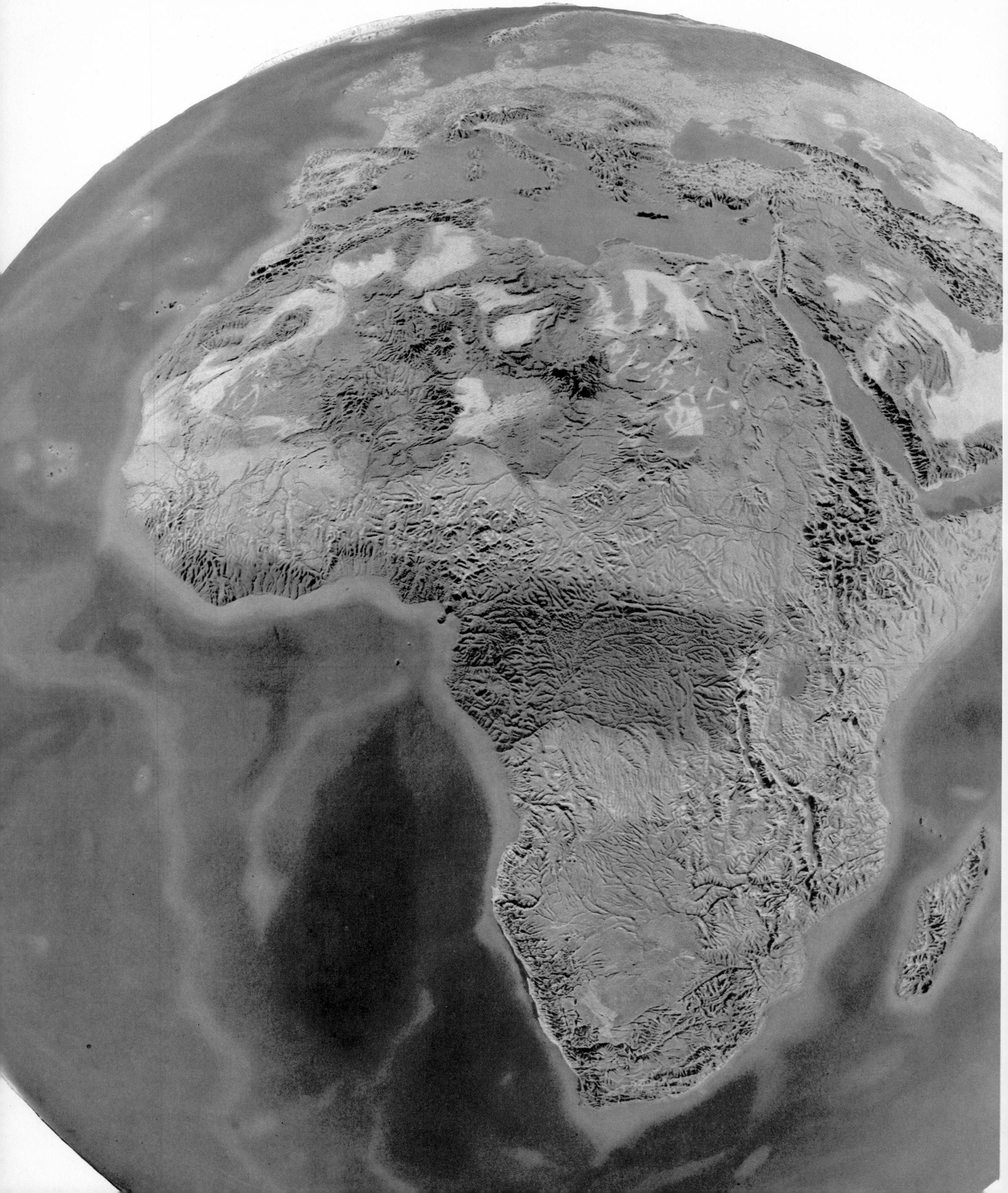

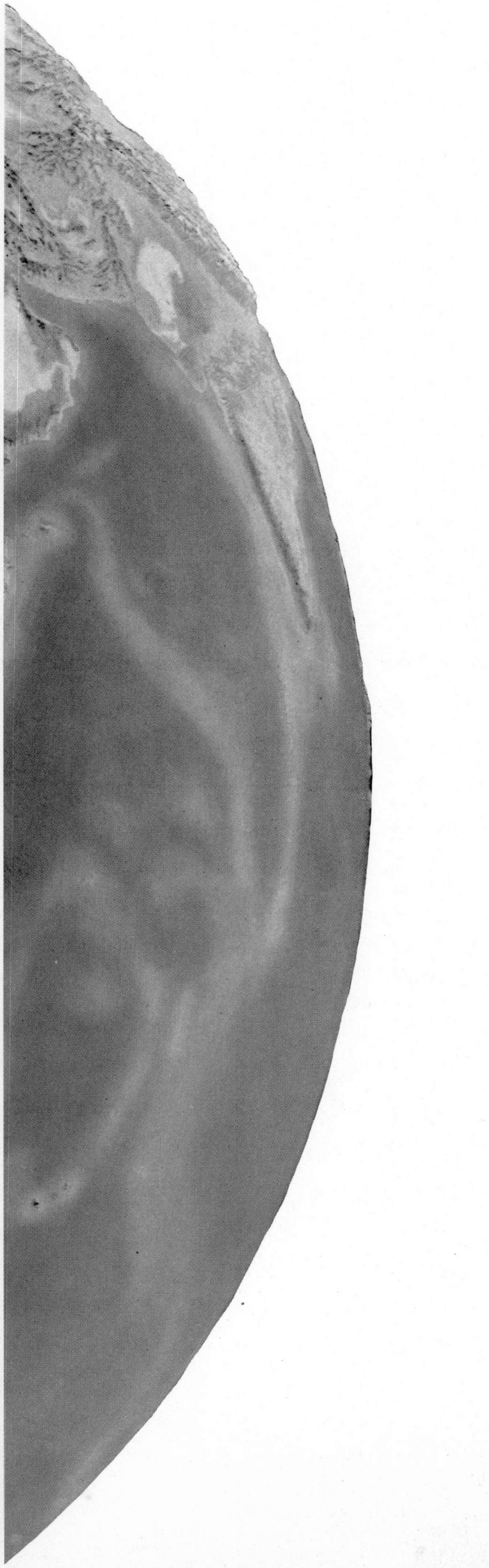

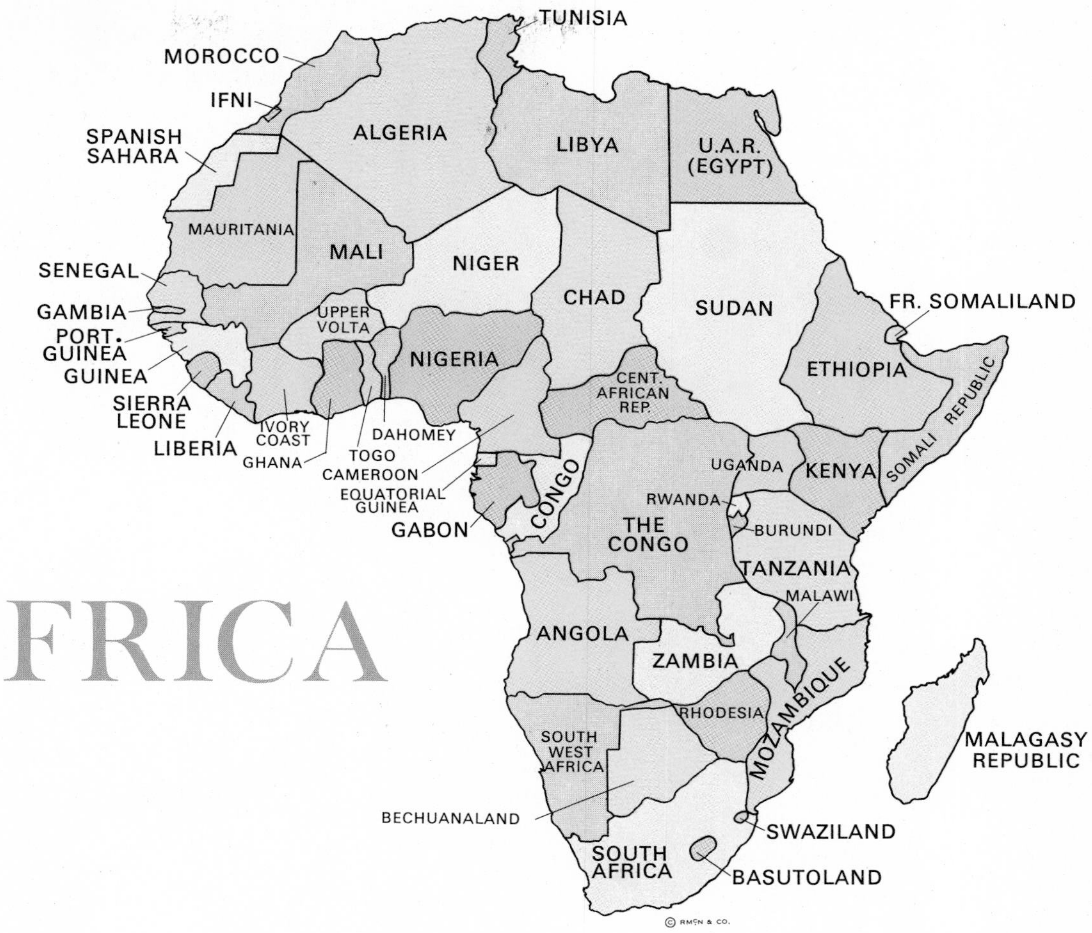

AFRICA

For centuries most of Africa's 11,500,000 square miles was unknown to outsiders. Access by one available avenue, the Nile, was impeded by the cataracts above Aswan. Since much of the interior is upland or plateau, usually dropping off rather sharply near the coasts, most of Africa's great rivers have rapids or falls close to the seaboard and so have not provided convenient routes to the interior. Moreover, the coastline is very regular, with few of the natural harbors of the other continents.

Once penetrated, much of the interior proved inhospitable to man. In the north, the world's largest desert, the immense expanse of the Sahara, blocks Africa's north rim from the central and southern portions. Near the other end of Africa, the Kalahari Desert helps separate the pleasant southernmost portion from the rest of the continent. In the center, the vast Congo Basin, humid, thinly settled, and unattractive, runs from the Atlantic seaboard east to the foot of the rugged highlands of East Africa, marked by the Rift Valley, which can be identified by the string of elongated lakes.

Africa's most important internal boundary is the Sahara. North of it the Mediterranean coastal countries are Moslem in tradition and have had close connections with Europe and the Near East. South of the Sahara are the many rich and varied cultures of Negroid tribal Africa. Unlike in many ways though they are, Mediterranean and Black Africa have until recently shared a common history of domination by non-African colonial powers. As late as 1945 there were only four independent nations in the entire continent. Now, spurred by the forces of nationalism, one new nation after another has emerged.

Past developments in communications, transport, education, and agricultural and industrial techniques, though limited, have formed a legacy from the old colonial powers on which the new African nations can build. Resources of iron ore, gold, oil, copper, timber, and a host of other vital raw materials are available. And there are many areas where climate and soil conditions are conducive to commercial agriculture, particularly for peanuts and cacao.

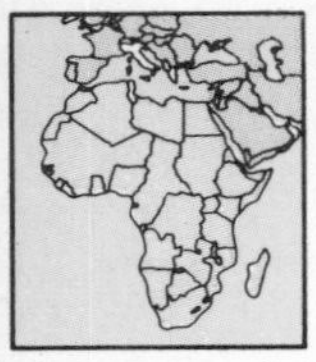

Statute Miles
Kilometers

Sinusoidal Projection
SCALE 1:36,313,000 1 Inch = 565 Statute Miles

A-580000-21 -4 -13⁶
COSMO SERIES AFRICA
Copyright by
RAND McNALLY & COMPANY
Made in U. S. A.

Longitude West of Greenwich   Longitude East of Greenwich

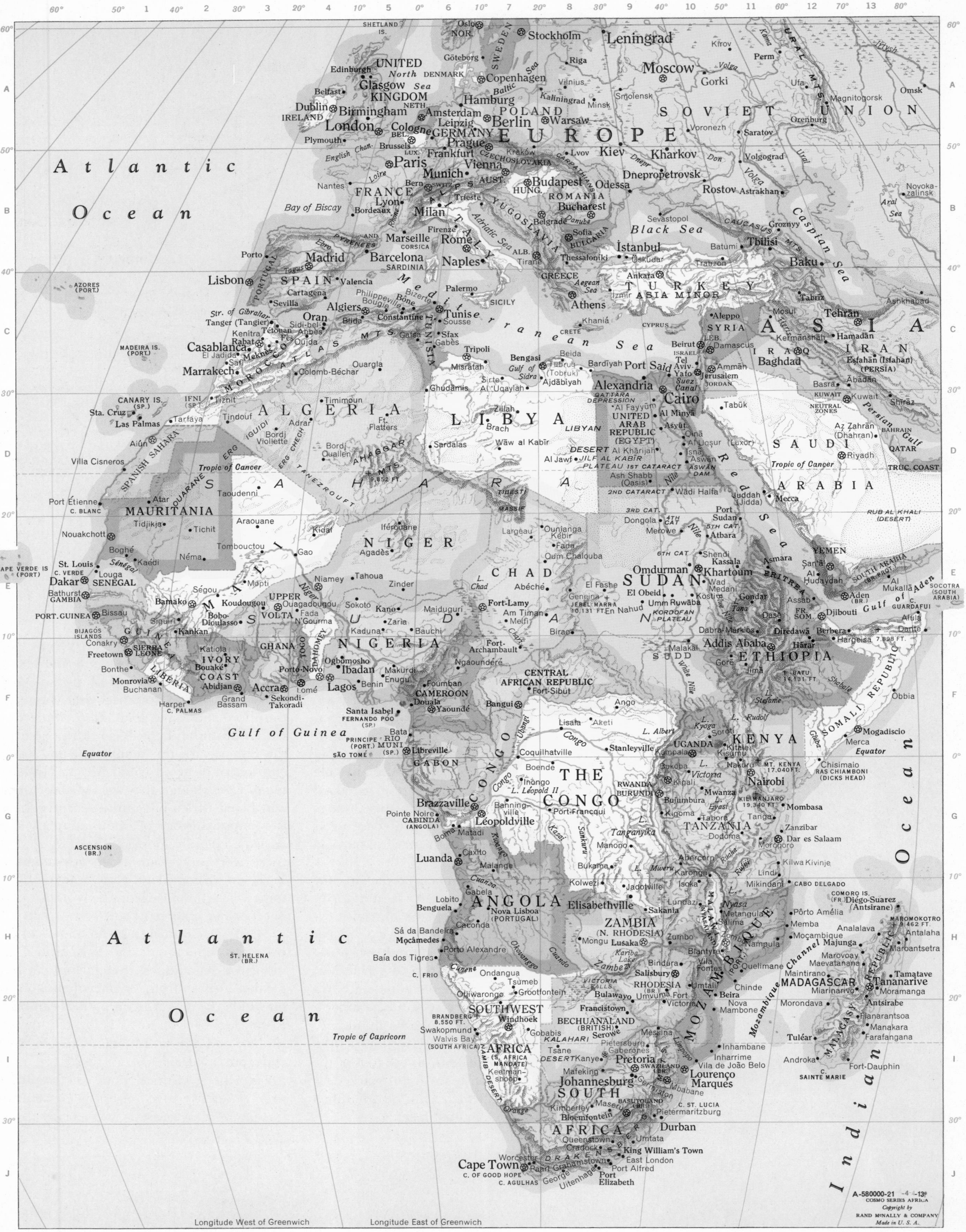

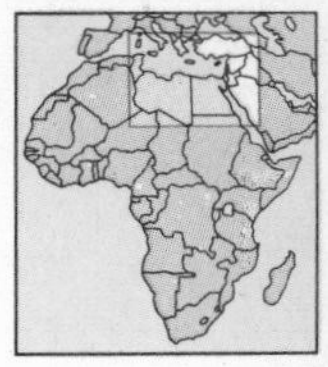

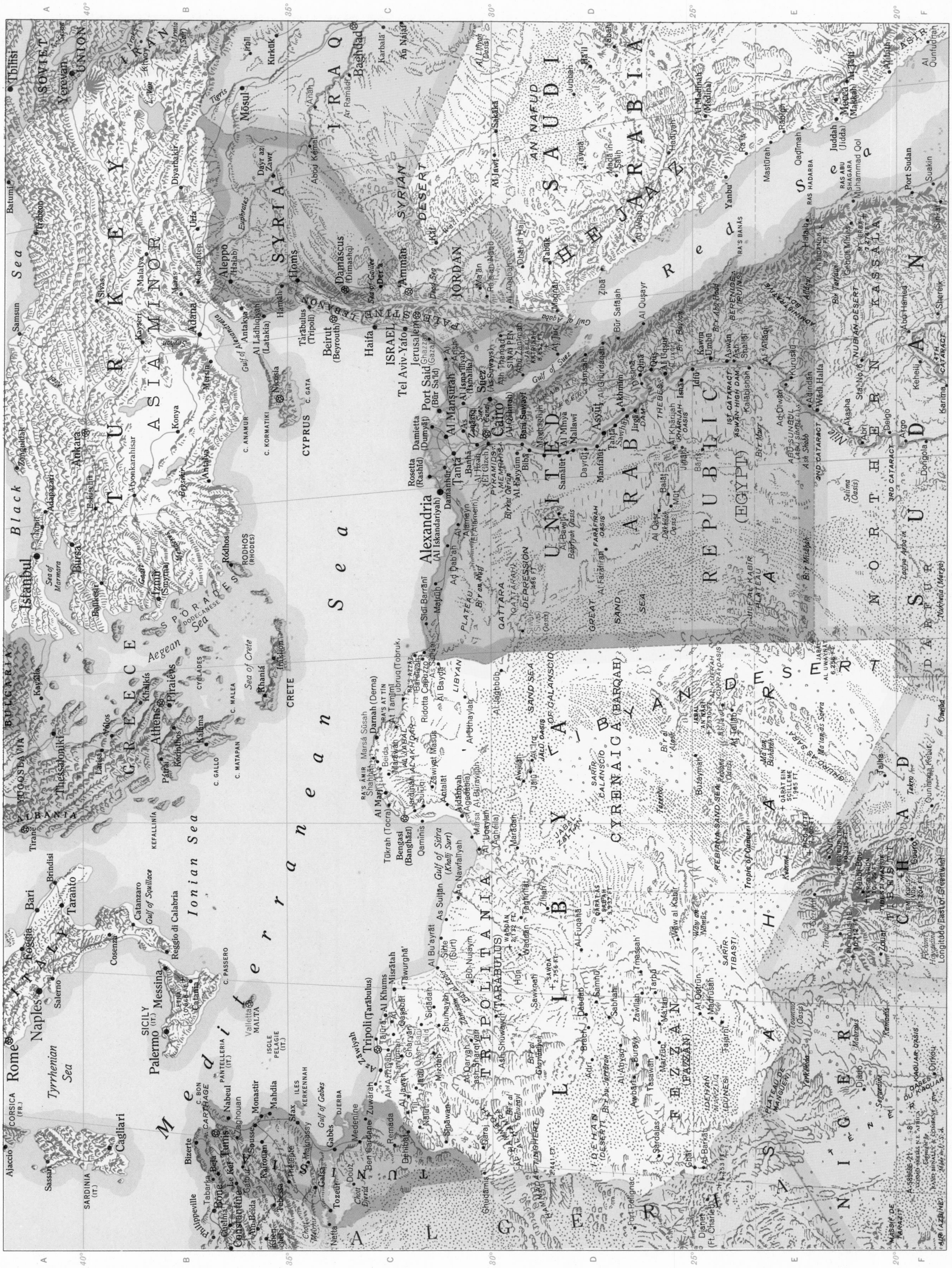

Sinusoidal Projection
SCALE 1 : 11,400,000   1 Inch = 180 Statute Miles

Statute Miles
50 0   50   100   150   200   250
50 0   50   100   150   200   300

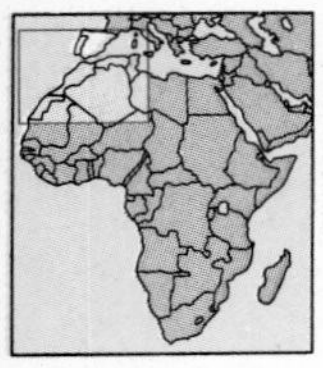

NORTHWEST AFRICA

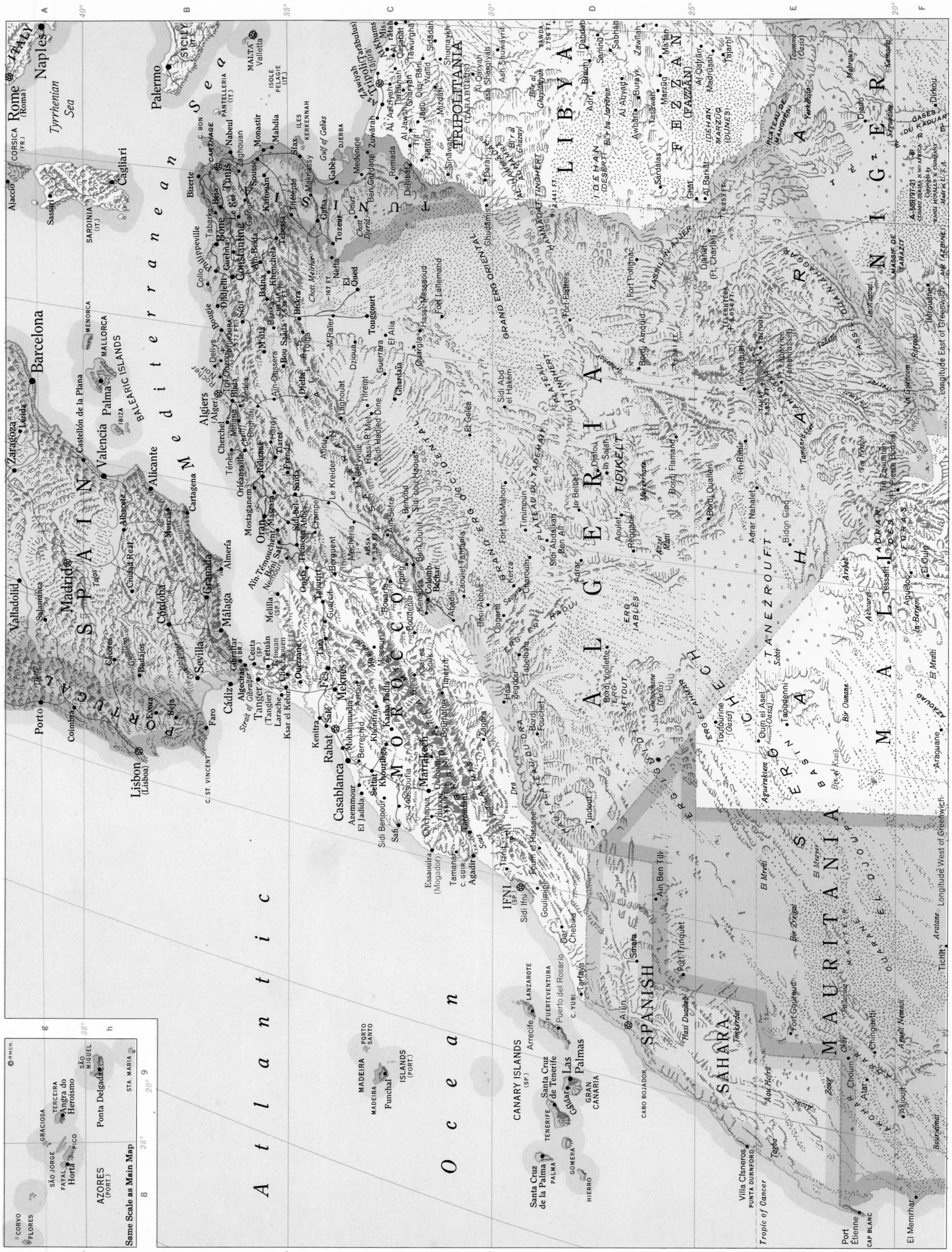

44

Statute Miles

Sinusoidal Projection
SCALE 1 : 11,400,000   1 Inch = 180 Statute Miles

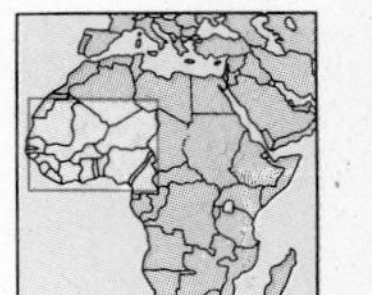

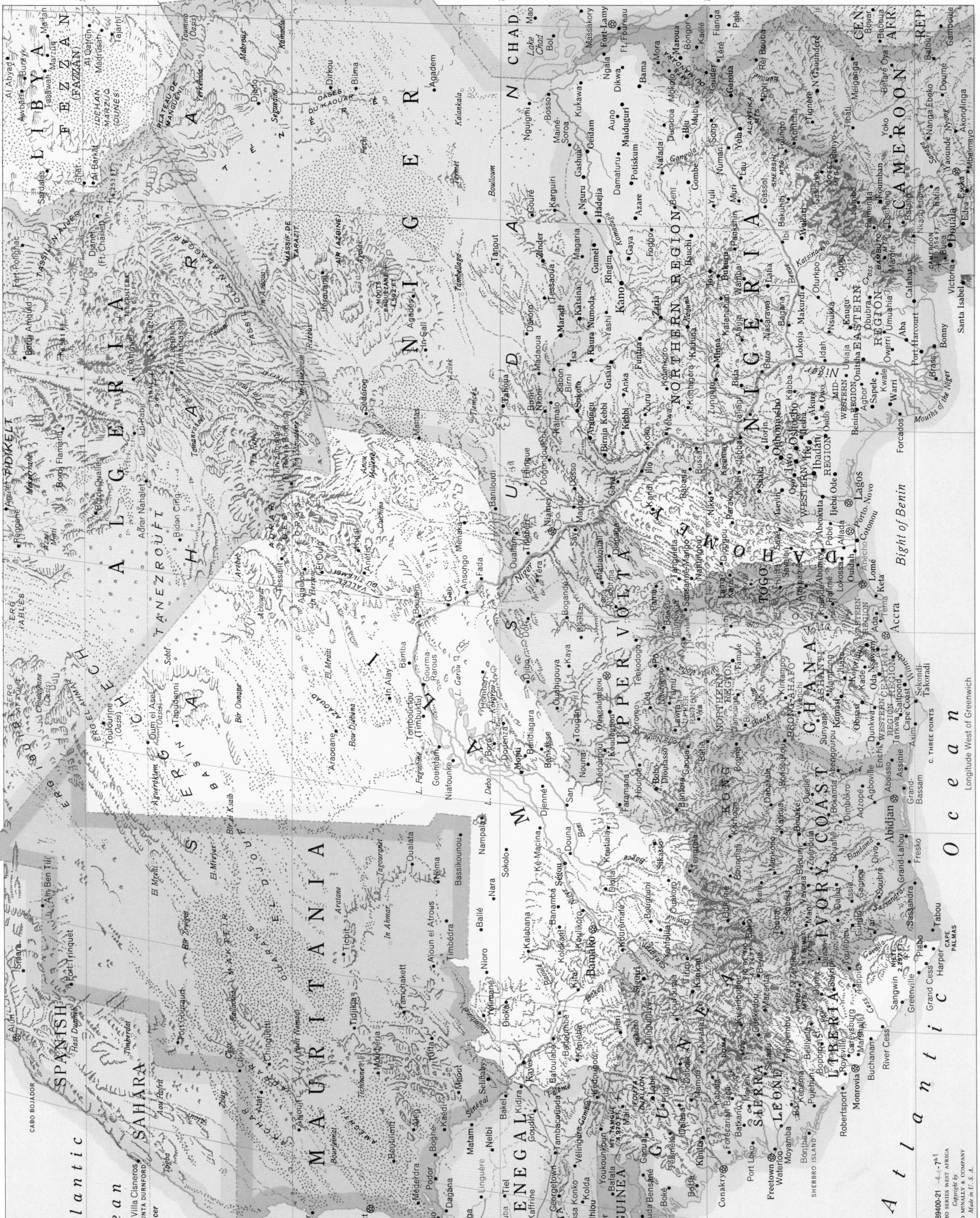

Sinusoidal Projection
SCALE 1: 11,400,000   1 Inch = 180 Statute Miles

Statute Miles
50 25 0   50   100   150   200   250

Kilometers
50 0 50 100 150 200 250 300

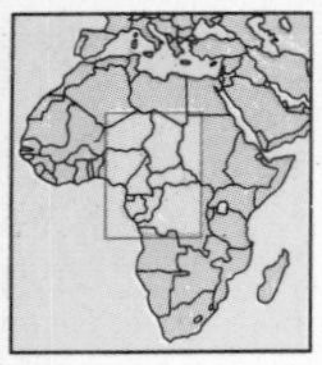

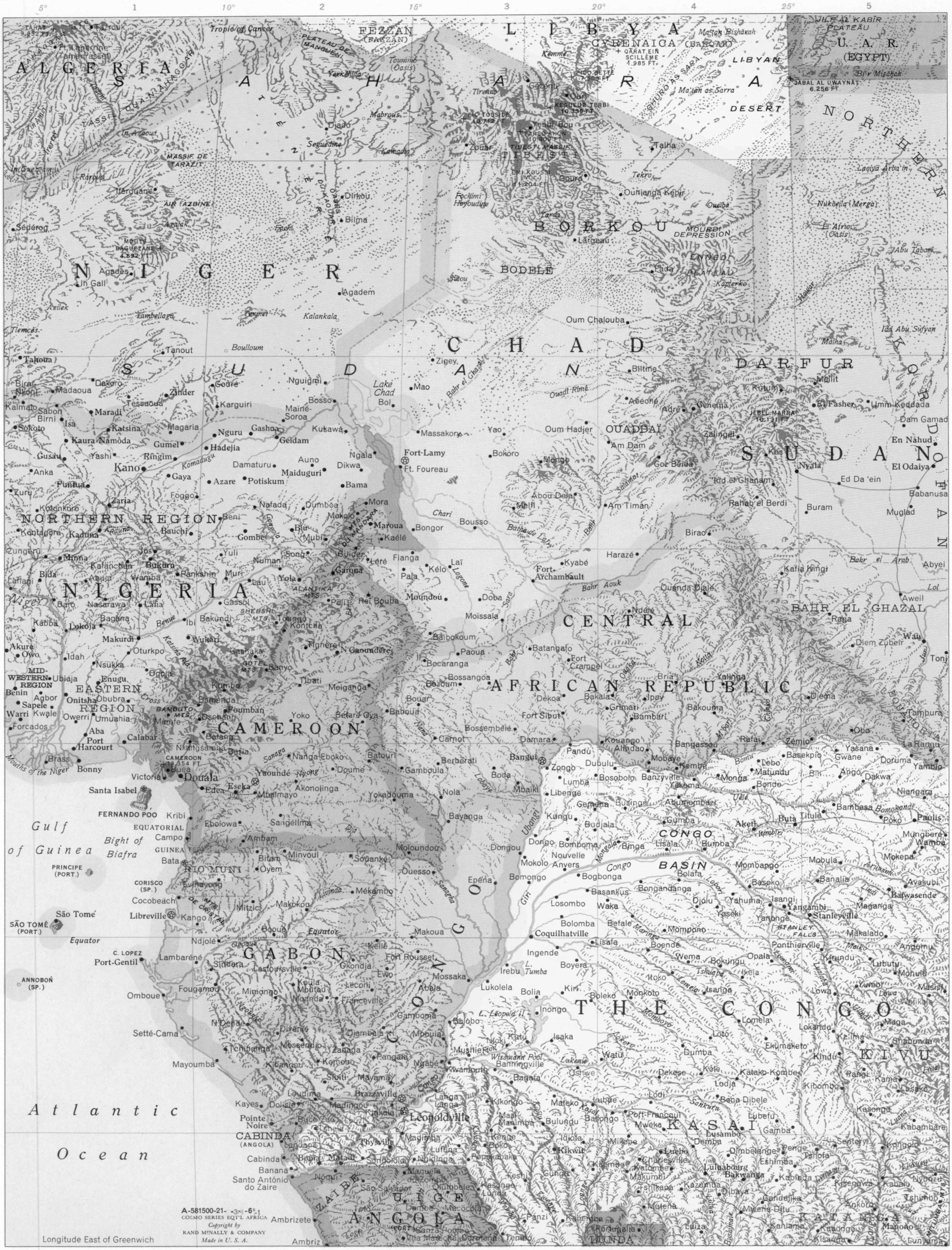

Statute Miles 50 25 0 50 100 150 200 250

50 0 50 100 150 200 250 300

Sinusoidal Projection
SCALE 1:11,400,000   1 Inch = 180 Statute Miles

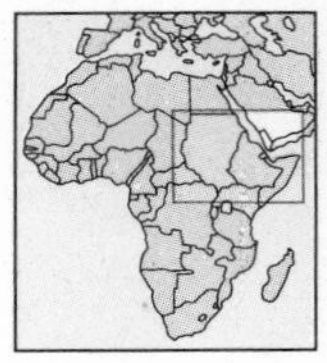

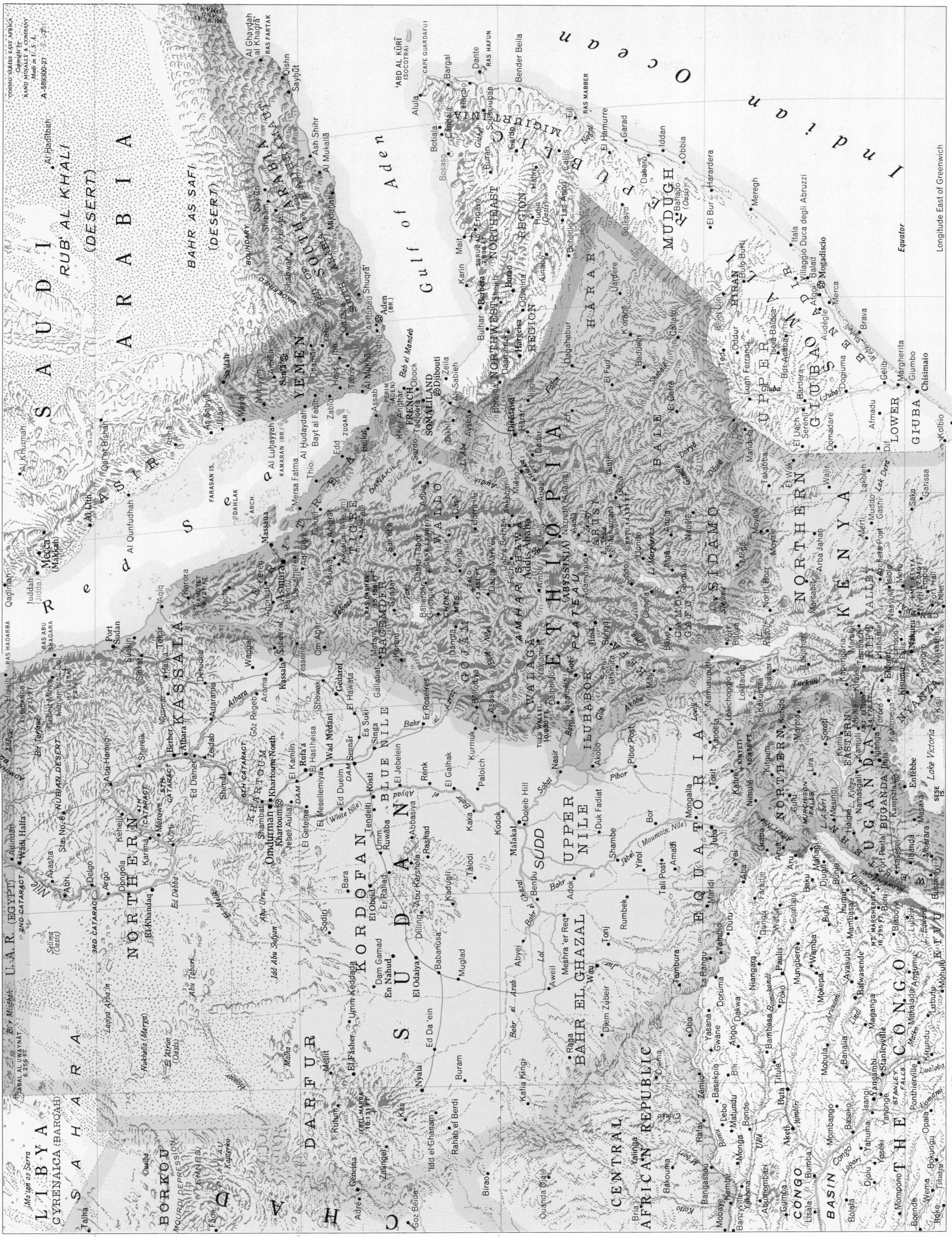

Sinusoidal Projection
SCALE 1 : 11,400,000   1 Inch = 180 Statute Miles

Statute Miles
50 25 0   50   100   150   200   250
Kilometers
50 0 50 100 150 200 250 300

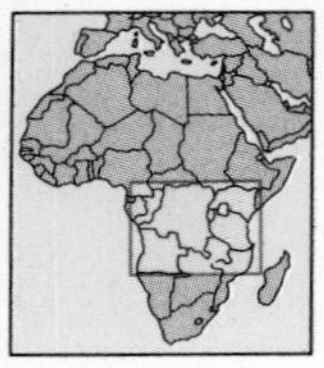

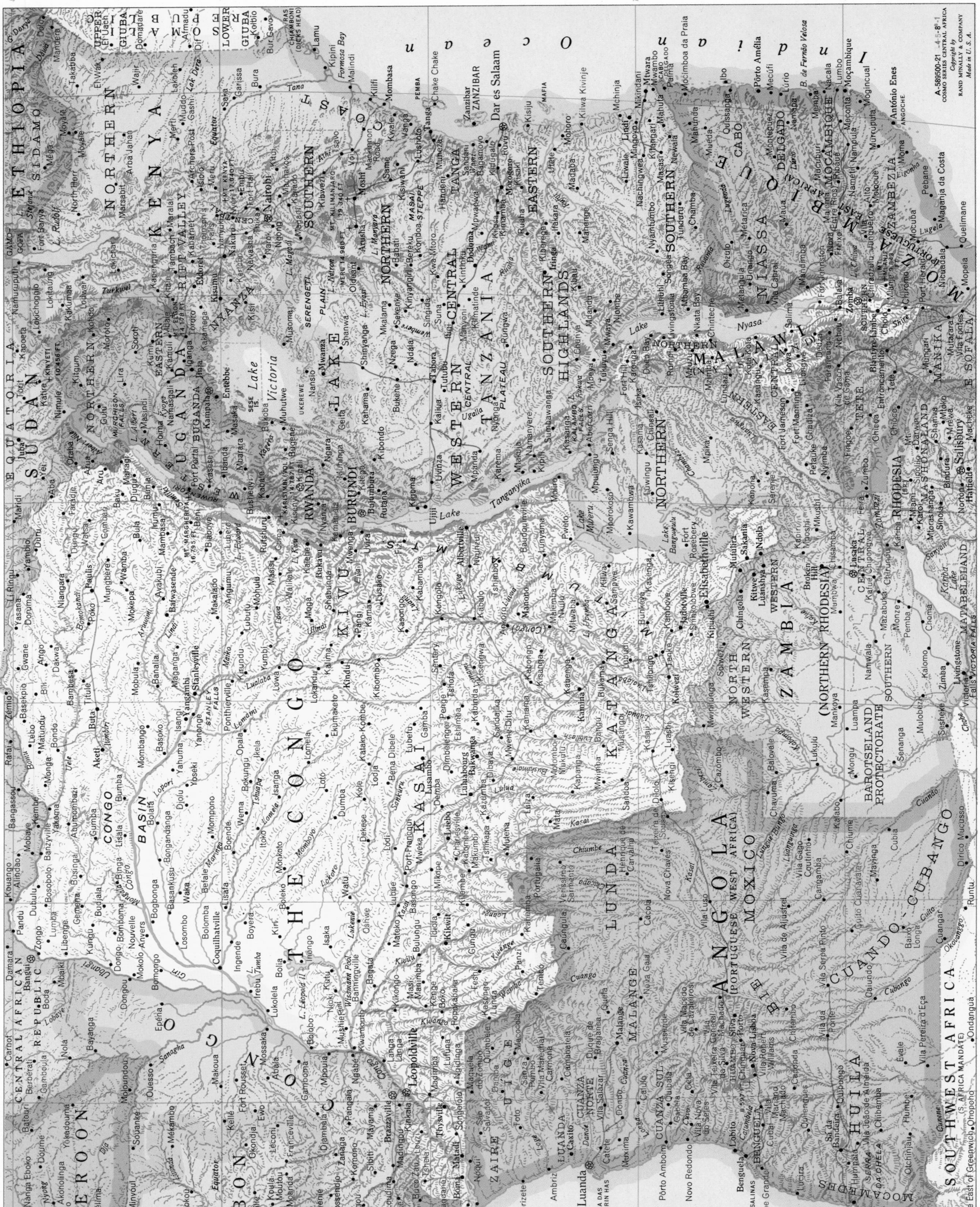

CENTRAL AFRICA

Statute Miles

Sinusoidal Projection

SCALE 1 : 11,400,000   1 Inch = 180 Statute Miles

Same Scale as Main Map

INDIAN OCEAN

MOZAMBIQUE CHANNEL

MALAGASY REP.

MADAGASCAR

MALAGASY REPUBLIC

Indian Ocean

Tropic of Capricorn

ANGOLA

HUILA

MOÇAMBIQUE

ZAMBIA
(NORTHERN RHODESIA)

BAROTSELAND
PROTECTORATE

RHODESIA
(SOUTHERN RHODESIA)

MATABELELAND

BECHUANALAND
(BRITISH PROTECTORATE)

KALAHARI DESERT

SOUTH WEST AFRICA
(S. AFRICA)

NAMIB DESERT

TRANSVAL

ORANGE FREE STATE

BASUTOLAND

SWAZILAND

NATAL

SOUTH AFRICA

CAPE OF GOOD HOPE

GREAT KARROO

Atlantic Ocean

Tropic of Capricorn

Indian Ocean

Longitude East of Greenwich

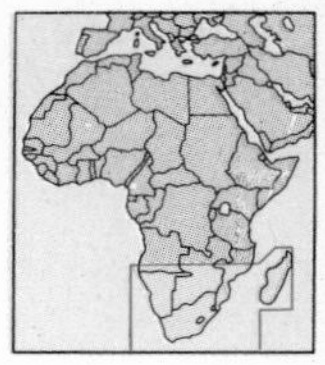

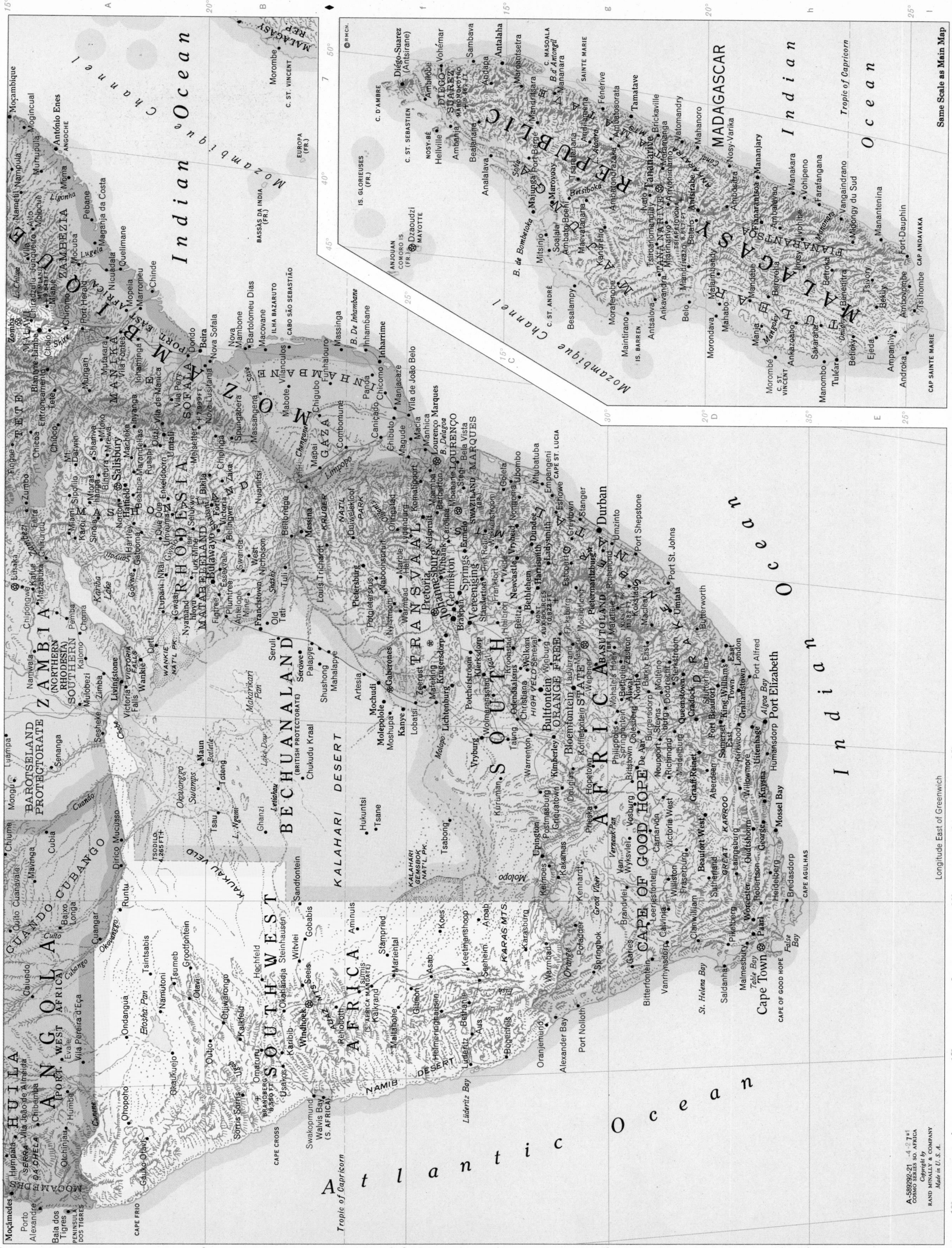

Sinusoidal Projection
SCALE 1:11,400,000   1 Inch = 180 Statute Miles

Statute Miles

Kilometers

49

A-589292-21
Copyright by
RAND McNALLY & COMPANY
Made in U.S.A.
COSMO SERIES SO. AFRICA

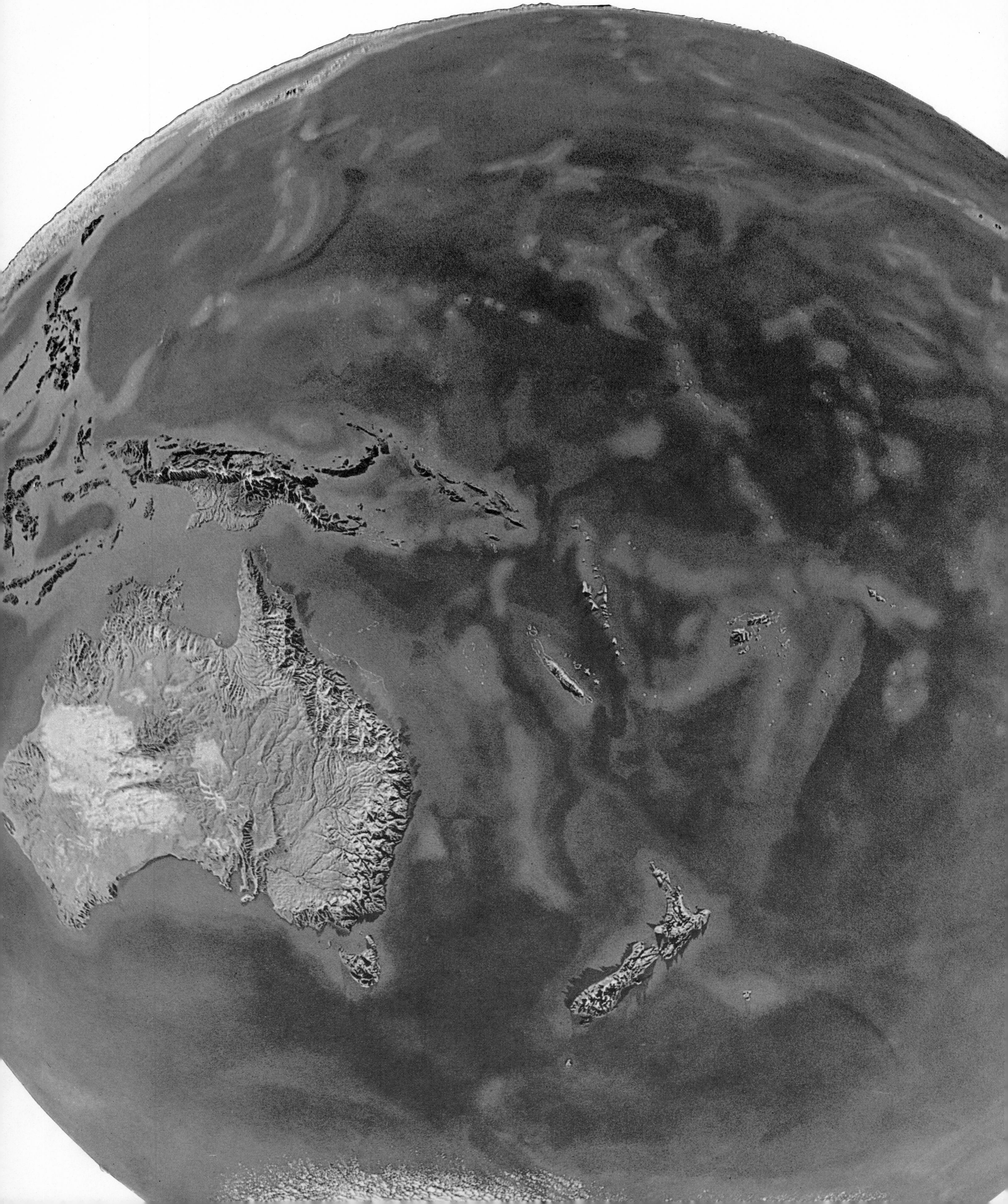

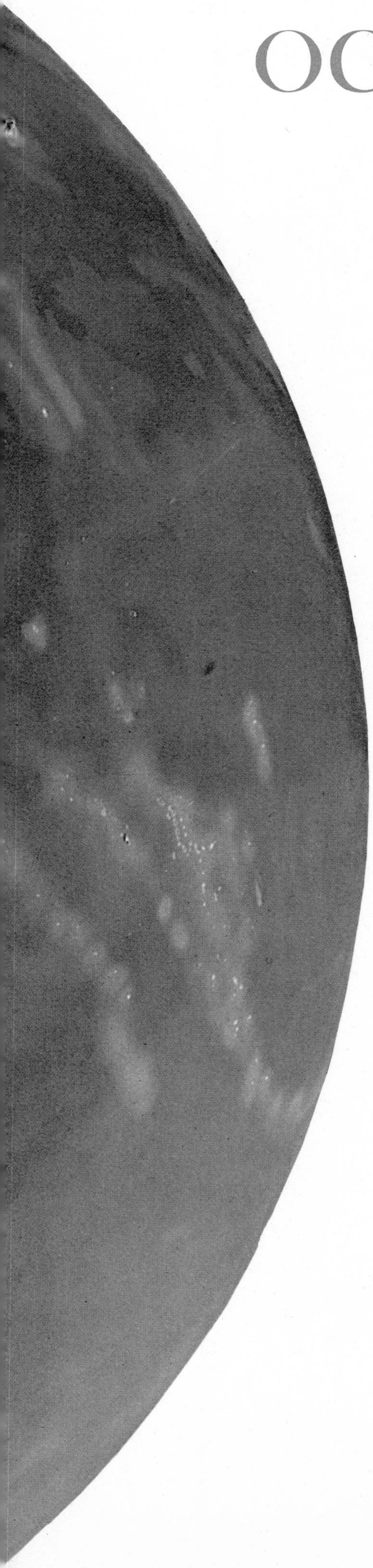

AUSTRALIA AND OCEANIA

This region of the world is composed of the island continent of Australia, the substantial islands of New Zealand and New Guinea, clusters of smaller islands, and the many pinpoint atolls scattered throughout the expanse of the central and southern Pacific. Extreme isolation and their island nature are common characteristics held by these realms, but other similarities are few.

Australia's size compares with that of the forty-eight conterminous United States. Dry air masses sweep across the western interior from the west, creating the largest desert outside of the Sahara. Along the eastern coast higher temperatures and humidity have combined to produce climates conducive to a varied agricultural system, and therefore, the population is concentrated along this favorable coastal strip. The mountains of the east tend to isolate the population in a number of distinct clusters. Sydney, Melbourne, Brisbane, and Adelaide are the four principal centers, acting as chief exporters of the wool and wheat, and the importers, manufacturers, and distributors for the continent.

New Zealand, like Australia, is an enclave of a European settlement in the Pacific. Upon the vegetation of this climatically mild area the descendants of European settlers have established a thriving economy based upon the exportation of butter, beef, and mutton. The mountainous spine running the length of New Zealand provides some magnificent scenery and the gamut of climatic types.

New Guinea is closely related to both Indonesia and Melanesia, and so links Southeast Asia with Oceania. Although much larger, it typifies the larger islands of the Southwestern Pacific. Like New Guinea, these islands have a mountainous core and narrow, alluvial coastal plains. Upon the plains, under tropical heat and humidity, a variety of tropical agricultural products are raised and some of the islands, such as Fiji, have well developed commercial economies.

Unlike New Guinea and the larger islands are the speck-like atolls scattered throughout the central and southern Pacific. These South Sea Islands are famed for isolation, mild climate, and scenic beauty. But their size, limited resources, and small population, keep their economies at a subsistence level.

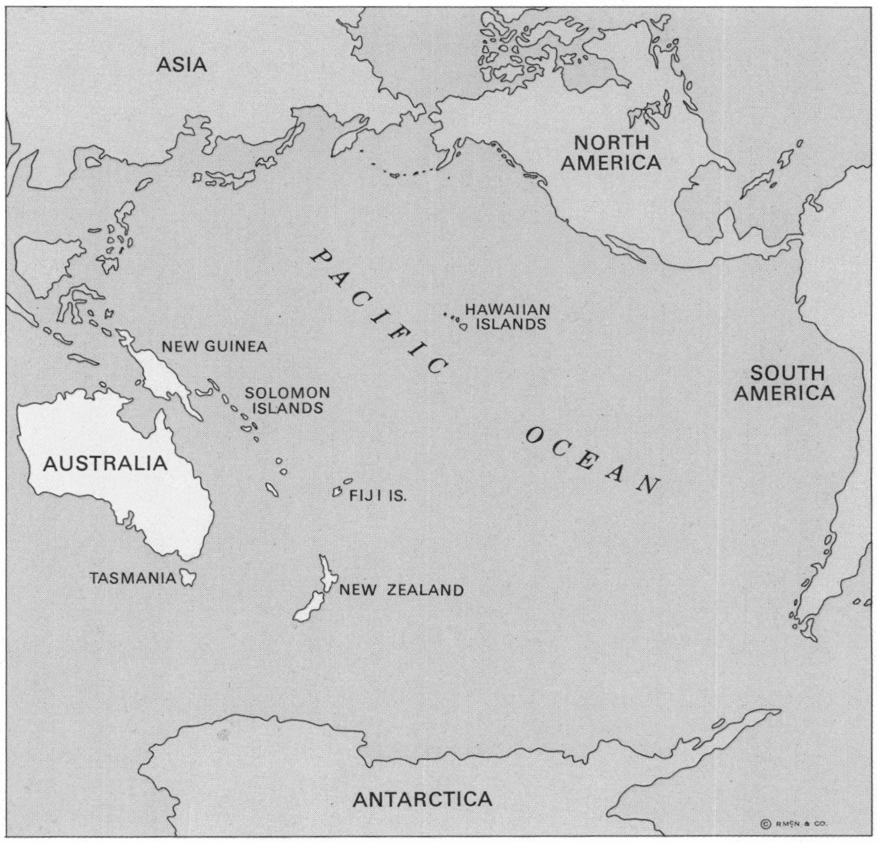

AUSTRALIA

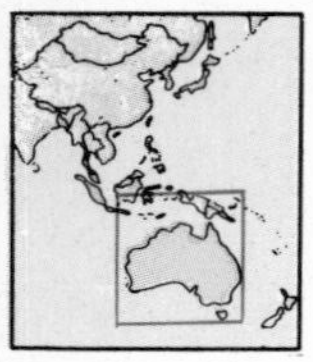

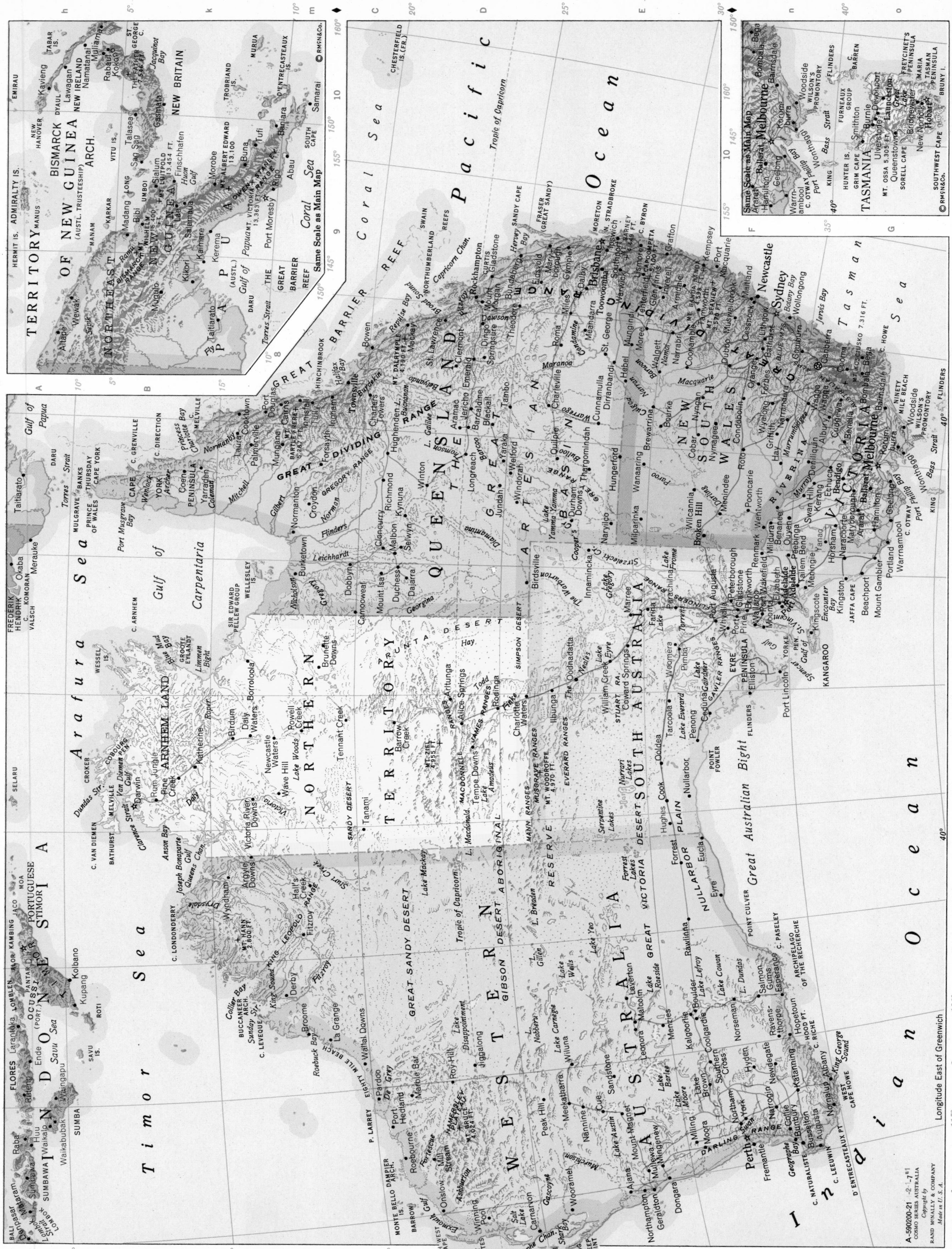

Statute Miles
100   0   100   200   300

Kilometers
100   0   100   200   300   400

Lambert Azimuthal Equal Area Projection
SCALE 1:16,000,000   1 Inch = 252 Statute Miles

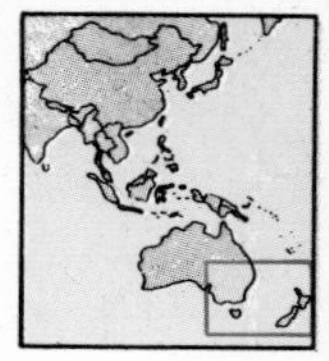

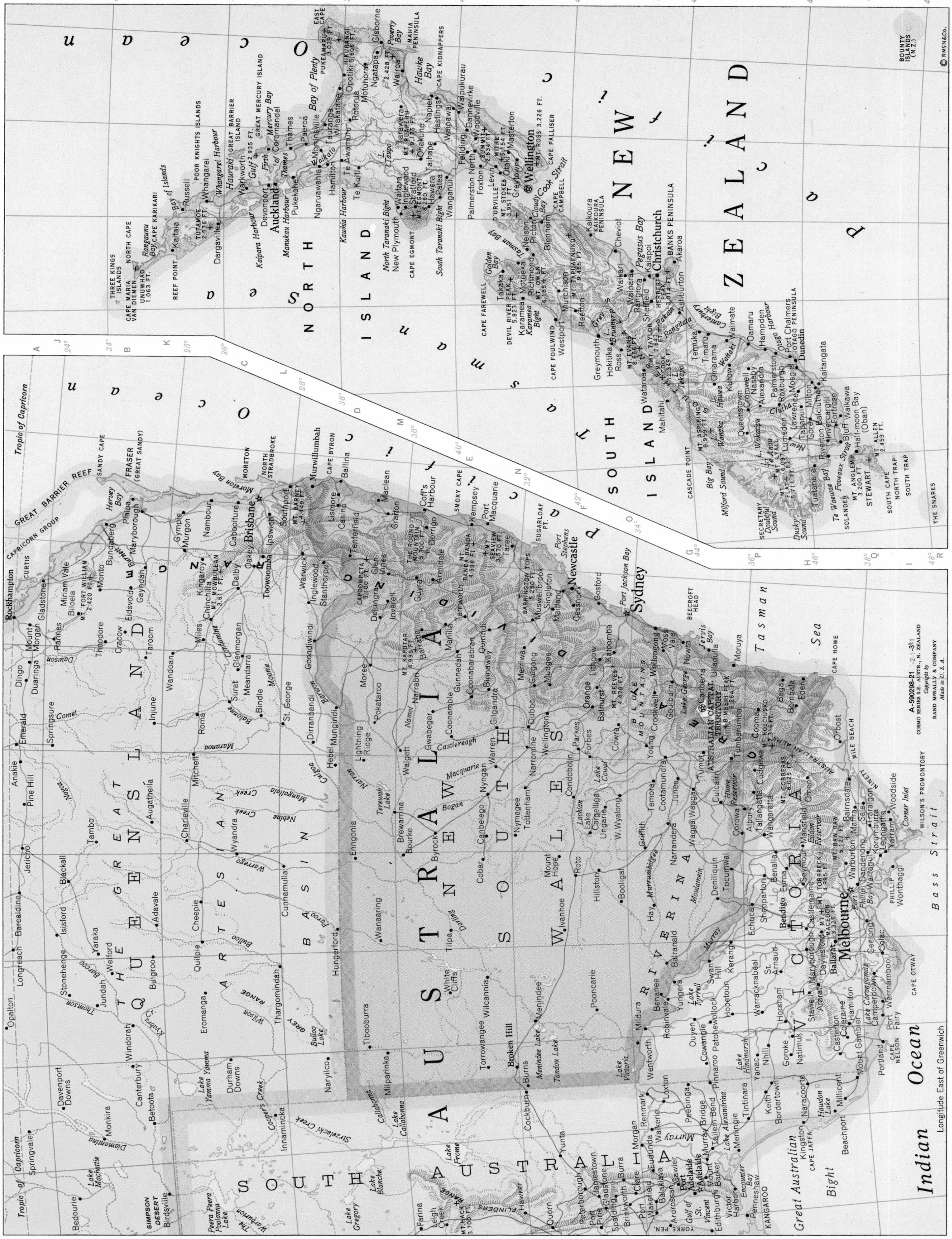

Lambert Conformal Conic Projection
SCALE 1 : 8,000,000   1 Inch = 126 Statute Miles

Statute Miles
Kilometers

166°35′E.
TOKI PT.
PEALE I.
FLIPPER PT.
HEEL PT.
KUKU PT.
WILKES I.
WAKE
Lagoon
ISLAND
(U.S.A.)
19°18′N.
19°18′N.
PEACOCK PT.
STATUTE MILES
0 1 2
©RMcN
166°35′E.

177°20′W.
SAND ISLET
MIDWAY
MIDDLE GROUND
Seward Roads
28°14′N.
Welles Harbor
ISLANDS
(U.S.A.)
28° 14′N.
EASTERN
SAND ISLET
ISLAND
SAND ISLAND
STATUTE MILES
0 1 2 3 4
©RMcN
177°20′W.

COSMO SERIES PACIFIC IS.
Copyright by
RAND McNALLY & COMPANY
Made in U. S. A.
A-592000-21
128°E.
HEDO PT.
Hedo
Uka
Ibu
Ada
Hetona
Kana
IE
Bise
KOURI
Kahira
Masuya
1,650 FT.
Tokuchi
Sesoko
SESOKE
Tsunami
Sakimotobu
Nago
Nakaushi
Kawada
Nago Bay
Tenniya
Teema
26°30′N.
26°30′N.
Onna
Kin
ZAMPA PT.
Ishikawa
Gima
ICHI BANARE
Chibana
Tobaru
TAKA BANARE
HEANZA
HAMAHIKA
Isa
Ujidomai
Awashi
Heshikiya
TSUKAN
Naha
Shuri
Nakagusuku Bay
Yunabaru
Azama
KUTAKA
Iha
Itoman
Kiyan
CHAM PT.
Nazaka
O K I N A W A
(UNDER U.S. ADMINISTRATION)
STATUTE MILES
0 5 10 15 20 25
©RMcN
128°E.

145°45′E.
MARPI PT.
MARPI 832 FT.
15°15′N.
15°15′N.
MANIAGASSA I.
Tanapag
Tanapag Harbor
ATCHUGAU 767 FT.
Inai Fahan
MUTCHO PT.
Garapan
SAIPAN
Garapan Anchorage
TAPOTCHAU 1 554 FT.
Laulau
(U.S.A. TRUST)
KAGMAN 479 FT.
FINA SUSU 294 FT.
Magicienne Bay
AGINGAN PT.
NAFUTAN 404 FT.
USHI PT.
C. OBIAM
Inai Obiam
NAFUTAN PT.
Saipan Channel
FAIBUS SAN HILO PT.
MAGA 456 FT.
ASIGA PT.
LASSO 564 FT.
TINIAN
MASALOG PT.
GURGUAN PT.
15° N.
15°N.
(U.S.A. TRUST.)
Tinian
Tinian Harbor
MARPO PT.
LALO PT.
STATUTE MILES
0 1 2 3 4 5 6
©RMcN
145°45′E.

144°45′E.
RITIDIAN PT.
PAJON PT.
MT. MACHANAO 610 FT.
URUNO PT.
PATI PT.
Tarague
TANGUISSON PT.
ANAO PT.
MT. SANTA ROSA 870 FT.
AMANTES PT.
Dededo
Tumon Bay
Finegayan
CATALINA PT.
Agana Bay
Mogfog
PAGAT PT.
Agana
BARRIGADA HILL 674 FT.
TAGUAN PT.
Apra Harbor
Asan
Toto
Barrigada
Piti
Ordot
Sinajana
Sumay
MT. RECONNAISSANCE 1,125 FT.
FADIAN PT.
IATES PT.
OROTE PEN.
Pago Bay
NEYE I.
Atantano
Yona
PAGO POINT
13°25′N.
13°25′N.
New Agat
TAGACHAN PT.
Agat Bay
Ylig Bay
GUAM
Santa Rita
(U.S.A.)
ANAE I.
MT. ALIFAN 858 FT.
TARTUGUAN PT.
Talofofo
FACPI PT.
Talofofo Bay
JUMULLONG MANGLO 1,274 FT.
Cetti Bay
ASIGA PT.
MT. BOLANOS 1,240 FT.
Umatac Bay
JALAIGAI PT.
Inarajan
SASALAGUAN 1 120 FT.
Inarajan Bay
Agfayan Bay
Port Merizo
Ajayan Bay
COCOS I.
Manell Chan.
STATUTE MILES
0 2 4 6 8
©RMcN
144°45′E.

STATUTE MILES
0 1 2
141°20′E.
KITANO PT.
KANGOKU ROCK
MOTO MTN. 358 FT.
Nishi
Kita
HIRAIWA CAPE
OSAKA MTN. 324 FT.
FURU MTN. 351 FT.
KAMA ROCK
TACHIIWA PT.
NIDAN ROCK 379 FT.
IWO
Minami
(UNDER U.S. ADMINISTRATION)
SURIBACHI MTN 554 FT.
FUTATSUNE
24° 45′N.
24°45′N.
TOBUSHI PT.
©RMcN
141°20′E.

165°10′E.
165°20′E.
165°30′E.
STATUTE MILES
0 2 4 6 8
NAMU I.
YUROCHI I.
ROMURIKKU I.
AOMOEN I.
11° 40′N.
11°40′N.
BOKOBYAADAA I.
BIKINI
(U.S.A. TRUST.)
BIKINI I.
BOKORORYURU I.
OURUKAEN I.
ROCHIKARAI I.
ARRIIKAN I.
CHIEERETE I.
RUKOJI I.
ENYU I.
11°30′N.
11°30′N.
Rukoji Pass
Enyu Channel
AIRUKIIJI
REERE I.
ENIIRIKKU I.
165°10′E.
165°20′E.
©RMcN
165°30′E.

172°W.
Sataua Bay
Safune Bay
Solomea
Fatuvalu
Safune
ALELAI PT.
C. PAPALAULELEI
Puapua
Samata
SAVAII
Safatulafei
C. TUASIVI
Salealua Bay
Siutu
Palauli
Iva
Satupaitea
C. PAEPAEALEIA
C. ASUISUI
Levi
Vailele Bay
Apia Hbr.
Palauli Bay
Apia
Vailele Bay
Saluafata Hbr.
Falefa Hbr.
Satapuala
Fagaloa Bay
Apolima Strait
APOLIMA I.
MANONO
C. FATUOSOFIA
C. MATAFOTUFOTU
UPOLU
Musumusu
C. OLOMONO
14°S.
C. MULITAPUILI
Matautu
Lotofaga
Safata Bay
C. NUUTOI
Sataio
Vaigalu
NAMUA I.
NUUTELE
C. TAPAGA
Falealili Hbr.
14°S.
WESTERN SAMOA
STATUTE MILES
0 10 20 30 40
©RMcN
172°W.
STATUTE MILES
0 1 2
170°40′W.
Leloaloa
Anua
Atuu
Aua
Pago Pago
Pago Pago Hbr.
PAPATELE 1 065 FT.
Fagatogo
GOAT I.
14°17′S.
Utulei
14° 17′S.
Laulii
BREAKER PT.
Fagaalu
Fagamafute
TOWER RK.
©RMcN
170°40′W.
171°W.
TUTUILA
(U.S.A.)
Massacre Bay
Afono Bay
Masefau Bay
C. TAPUTAPU
Pago Pago
C. FOGAUSO
Leone Bay
STEPS PT.
171°W.

158°10′E.
STATUTE MILES
0 2 4 6 8
NANKAPENPARAM REEF
Jokaj Harbor
PARAM I.
Mant Hbr.
Palikir Pass
7°N.
7°N.
JOKAJ
MANT IS
CAPE U
Ponape
Tapak
TAPAK I.
PONAPE
ARU PT.
PALIKER PT.
(U.S.A. TRUST.)
Tamora
MAJIJO PK. 1 129 FT.
Meilap
TOLOCOLME PK.
Palang 2,576 FT.
6°50′N.
6°50′N.
KITI PT.
Ronkiti
Tamoroi
Pok
Lot
Lot Hbr.
Ronkiti Hbr.
ROJ I.
Mutok Hbr.
©RMcN
158°10′E.

©RMcN
151°45′E.
RUAC I.
LAMOIL I.
HOLAP I.
FALALU I.
PIS I.
LAP I.
NORTH EAST IS.
QUOI I.
FALAS I.
MOR I.
YAWATA I.
LELOM REEF
TRUK
FALO I.
ULALU I.
(U.S.A. TRUST)
MOEN I.
TOL I.
UDOT
PARAM
KUTUA PT.
DUBLON I.
Piaanu Pass
ETEN I.
FALA-BEGUETS
TARIK
FEFAN I.
UMAN I.
BERNARD IS.
TSIS I.
7°20′N.
7° 20′N.
OLLAN I.
Ulifauro Pass
FOURUP I.
OTTA I.
UIJEC I.
MESEGON I.
GIVRY I.
HACO I.
KUOP IS. (ROYALISTS IS.)
STATUTE MILES
0 5 10 15
SOUTH I.
151°45′E.

©RMcN
178°E.
180°
178°W.
CAPE UNDU
NGELE LEVU I.
THE GREAT SEA REEF
KIA I.
MALI I.
Visonau
Round Island Passage
Nanduri
Lambasa
RAMBI I.
RINGGOLD ISLES
Ngaloa Bay
Nakalau
VANUA LEVU
Natewa Bay
Passage
YASAWA GROUP
SLEEPY PT.
Rukuruku Bay
NARARU 2 420 FT.
KIOA I.
NANUKU REEF
YASAWA I.
LAUTHALA
WAILANGILALA I.
DUFF REEF
YENDUA I.
Savusavu Bay
NATHOULA I.
Mbya Bay
NGAMEA
Nanuku
AGATA I.
LEKUMBI PT.
Fawn Harbor
TAVEUNI
VUYA PT.
Somosomo Strait
VIWA I.
NAVITI I.
Wainunu Bay
KANATHEA I.
ELD I.
YATHATA I.
VANUA MBALAVU
WAIA
Viti Levu Bay
KORO I.
VATIA PT.
MANGO I.
NATHILAU PT.
Tuvu
TANAVUSO PT.
MAKONGAI
PT. ALDIN
VATU VARA I.
MAMANUTHA ISLANDS
Lautoka
Namoli
TAILEVU PT.
WAKAYA
NAKOROKORO PT.
Sagara
Narata
Levuka
OVALAU
MBATIKI
MAMOLO I.
VITI LEVU
THITHIA I.
TUVUTHA I.
UVERITE PT.
Nasala
Naloto
MOTURIKI I.
NAIRAI
Momi
MONA VATU 3 709 FT.
KAMBA PT.
NAIAU
18°S.
18°S.
Etumba
Mau
Rewa
NGAU
Thuvu
Suva
LAKEMBA I.
Navola
Lakemba Passage
Mbenga Pass
MBENGA
Suva Hbr.
VANUA VATU
AIWA
VATU LEILE
ONEATA
MOALA I.
Fulanga Passage
(BRITISH)
MOTHE
NDRAVUNI
TOVA REEF
MBULIA I.
WANGAVA
YANGASA CLUSTER
KANDAVU
ONO
KAMBARA
Naingoro Pass
TOTOYA I.
ONGEA LEVU
C. WASHINGTON
Ngaloa Harbor
MATUKU I.
FULANGA
LAU OR EASTERN GROUP
FIJI ISLANDS
STATUTE MILES
0 25 50 75
178°E.
180°
178°W.

STATUTE MILES
0 10 20 30 40
134°30′E.
NGARUANGL REEF
KAYANGEL IS.
8°N.
8°N.
KOSSOL REEF
Kossol Passage
CORMORAN REEF
PALAU
Aiyon
Ngardmau
Galap
(U.S.A. TRUST.)
BABELTHUAP I.
Namai Bay
IS.
Mukeru
Melekeiok
ARAKABESAN I.
Garashiyoo
Airai
KOROR I.
ORUKUIZU I.
URUKTHAPEL I.
EIL MALK
NGEMELIS IS.
NGESEBUS I.
GARAKAYO I.
PELELIU I.
7°N.
7°N.
ANGAUR I.
134°30′E.
©RMcN

173°E.
STATUTE MILES
0 2 4 6 8
LEPER COLONY
TARITAI
TARAWA
(BR.)
1°30′N.
1°30′N.
Lagoon
BIKEMAN I.
BITITU I.
EITA
BAIRIKI
©RMcN
173°E.

167°E.
STATUTE MILES
0 10 20 30 40
EBADON I.
OREBA I.
BIGGERANN I.
ONIOTTO I.
ROI I.
NAMUR I.
BIGI I.
EDGIGEN I.
GAGAN I.
TABIK I.
BOGGERIK I.
KWAJALEIN
(U.S.A. TRUST.)
GELLINAM
YABBENOHR I.
9°N.
9°N.
NELL I.
ONEMAK I.
MECK I.
ELLER I.
Ambo Channel
BIGEJ I.
GUGEGWE I.
ENNYLABEGAN I.
South Pass
KWAJALONG I.
©RMcN
167°E.

162°10′E.
STATUTE MILES
0 2 4 6 8 10 12
TEITEIRIPUCCHI
BOGON
ENGEBI
BOGALLUA
RUCHI
RUJIYORU
KIRINIAN
BIIZIRI
AOMON
ISLET
PIIRAI
RUUNITTO
WEST SPIT
11° 30′N.
11° 30′N.
ENIWETOK
(U.S.A. TRUST.)
RIGILI
JAPTAN I.
Deep Entrance
PARRY I.
Passage
GRINEM
LIBIRON
MUI
BOGAN
IGURIN
Wide Passage
ENIWETOK I.
©RMcN
162°10′E.

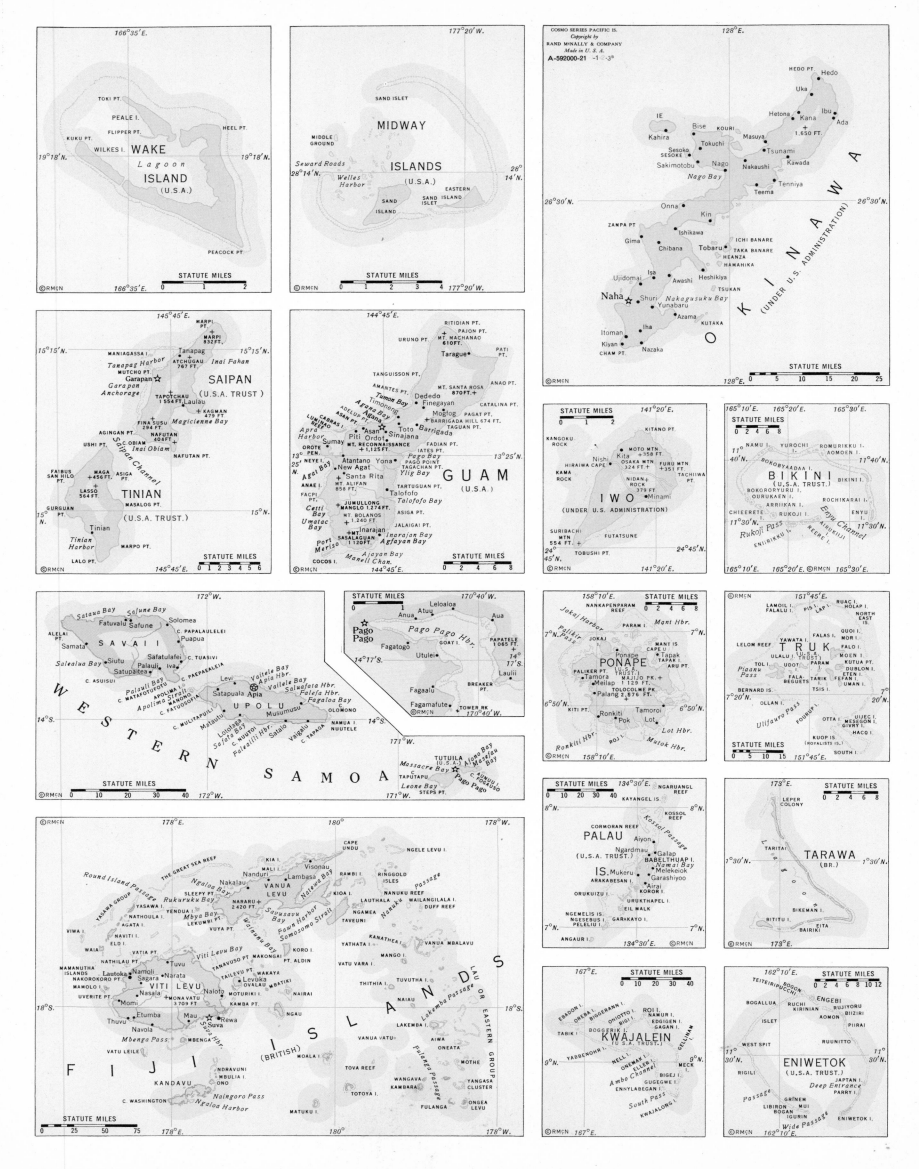

Gulf of Mexico

WEST INDIES

MEXICO

Caribbean Sea

CENTRAL AMERICA

Atlantic Ocean

VENEZUELA

COLOMBIA

BRITISH GUIANA

SURINAM (NETH. GUIANA)

FRENCH GUIANA

Equator

ECUADOR

S E L V A S

B R A Z I L

PERU

BOLIVIA

BRAZILIAN PLATEAU OF MATO GROSSO

HIGHLANDS

Tropic of Capricorn

PARAGUAY

CHACO

Pacific Ocean

Rio de Janeiro

São Paulo

URUGUAY

Buenos Aires

Montevideo

ARGENTINA

PATAGONIA

Atlantic Ocean

FALKLAND ISLANDS (GREAT BRITAIN)

TIERRA DEL FUEGO

CAPE HORN

Longitude West of Greenwich

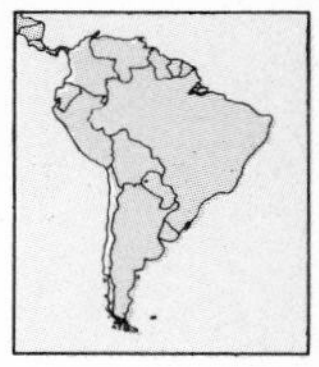

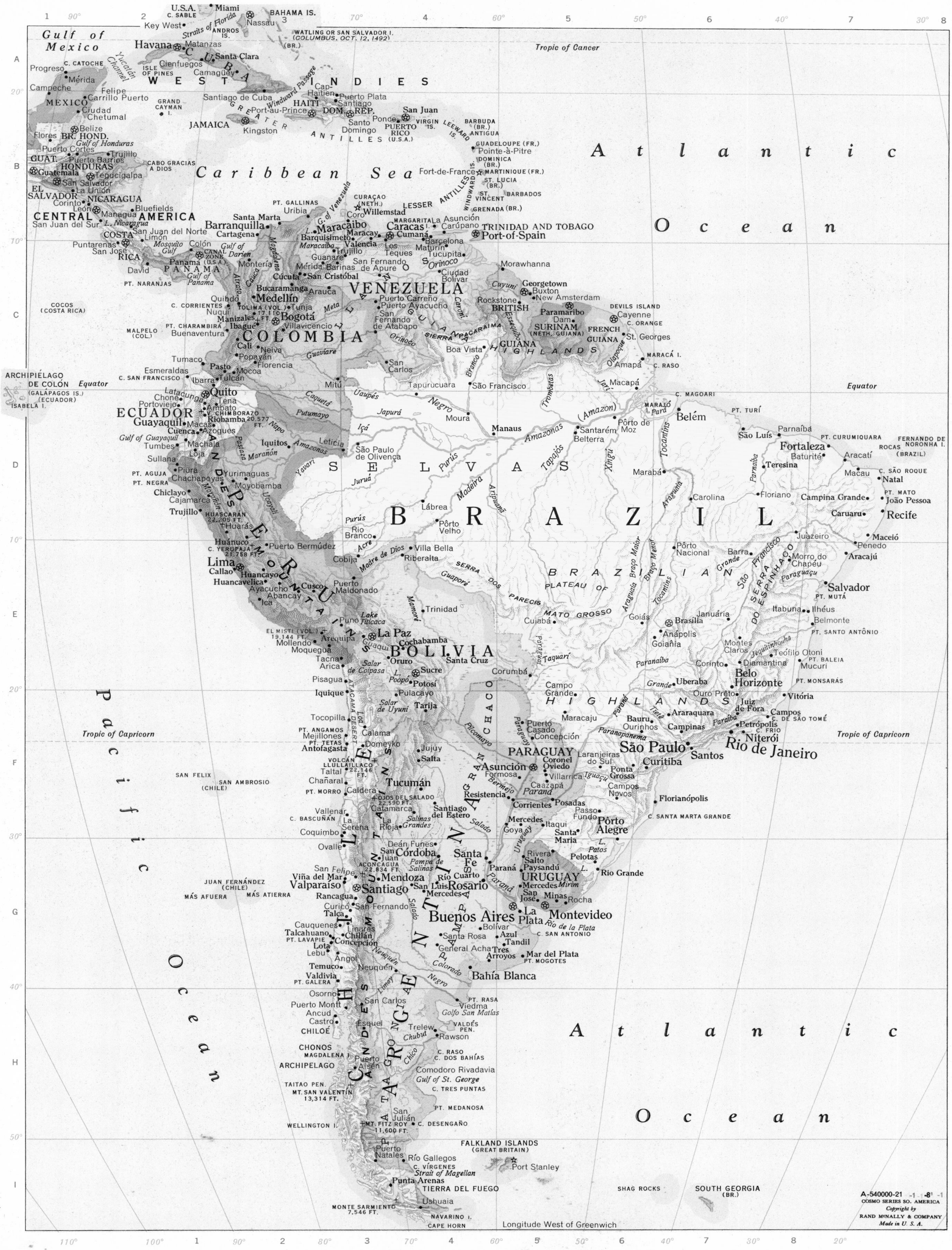

Sinusoidal Projection
SCALE 1: 29,465,000   1 Inch = 465 Statute Miles

Statute Miles
100   0   100   300   500   700

Kilometers
100 0 100   300   500   700   900   1100

A-540000-21   -1 . .-8° -1
COSMO SERIES SO. AMERICA
Copyright by
RAND McNALLY & COMPANY
Made in U.S.A.

53

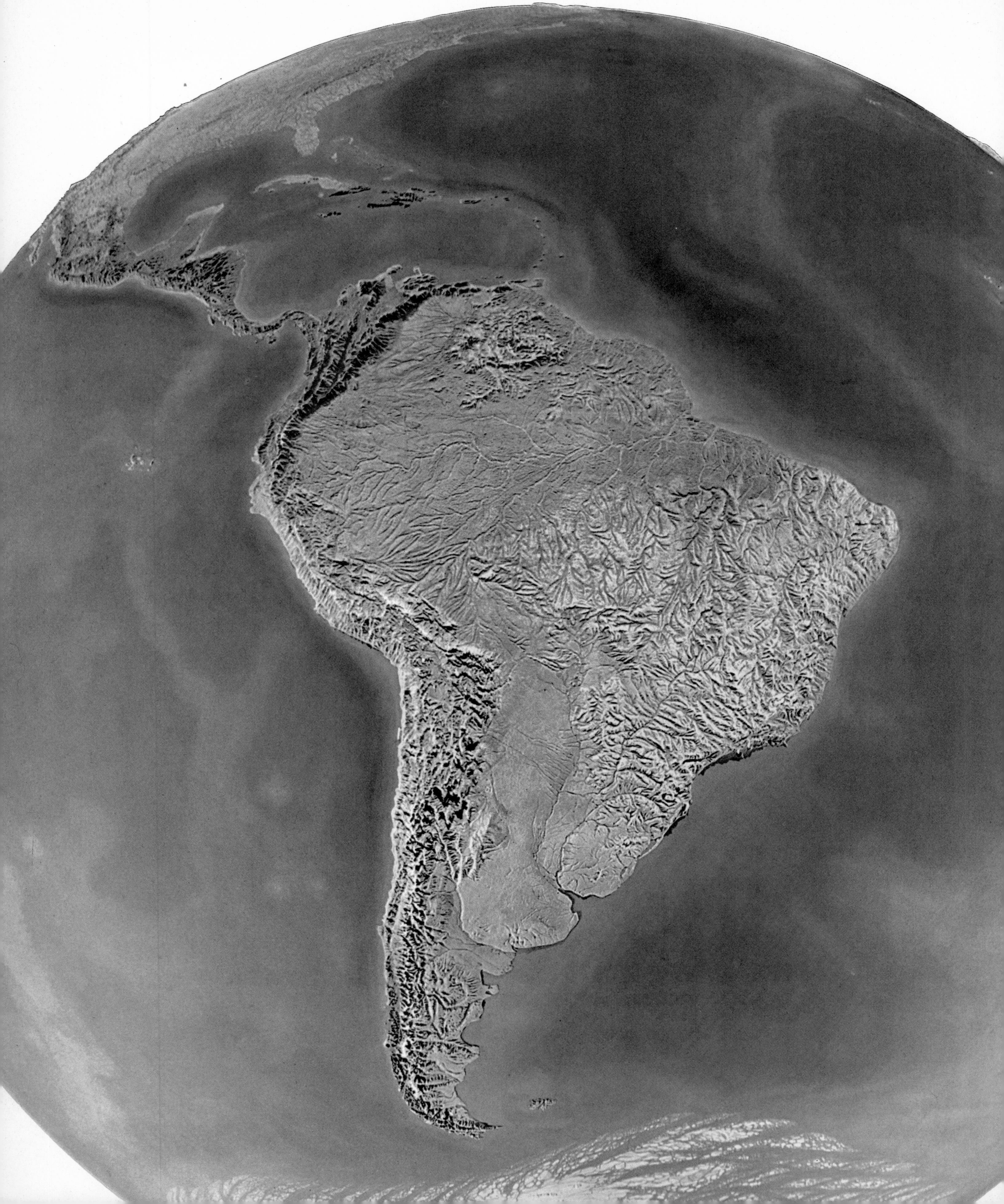

VENEZUELA
BRITISH GUIANA
SURINAM
FRENCH GUIANA
COLOMBIA
ECUADOR
PERU
BRAZIL
BOLIVIA
PARAGUAY
CHILE
ARGENTINA
URUGUAY

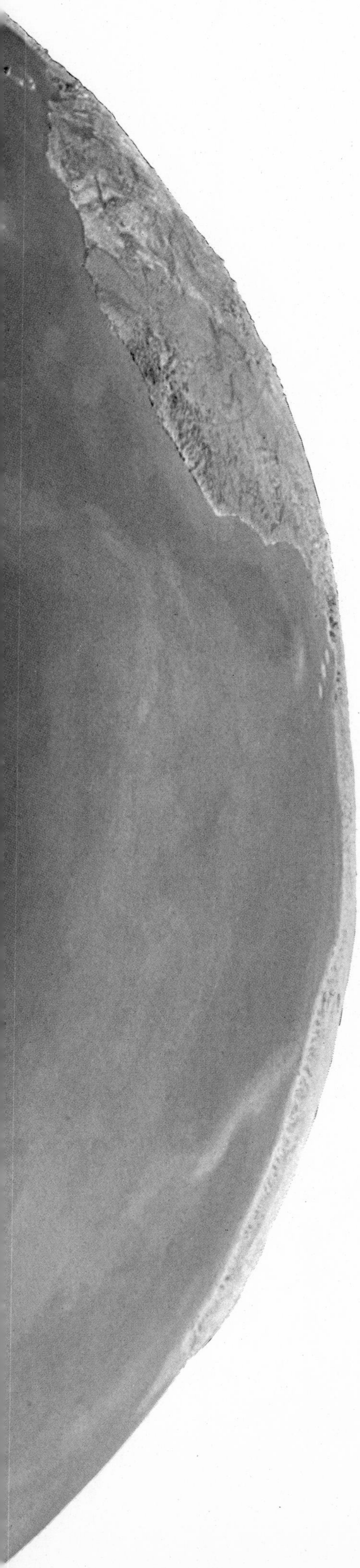

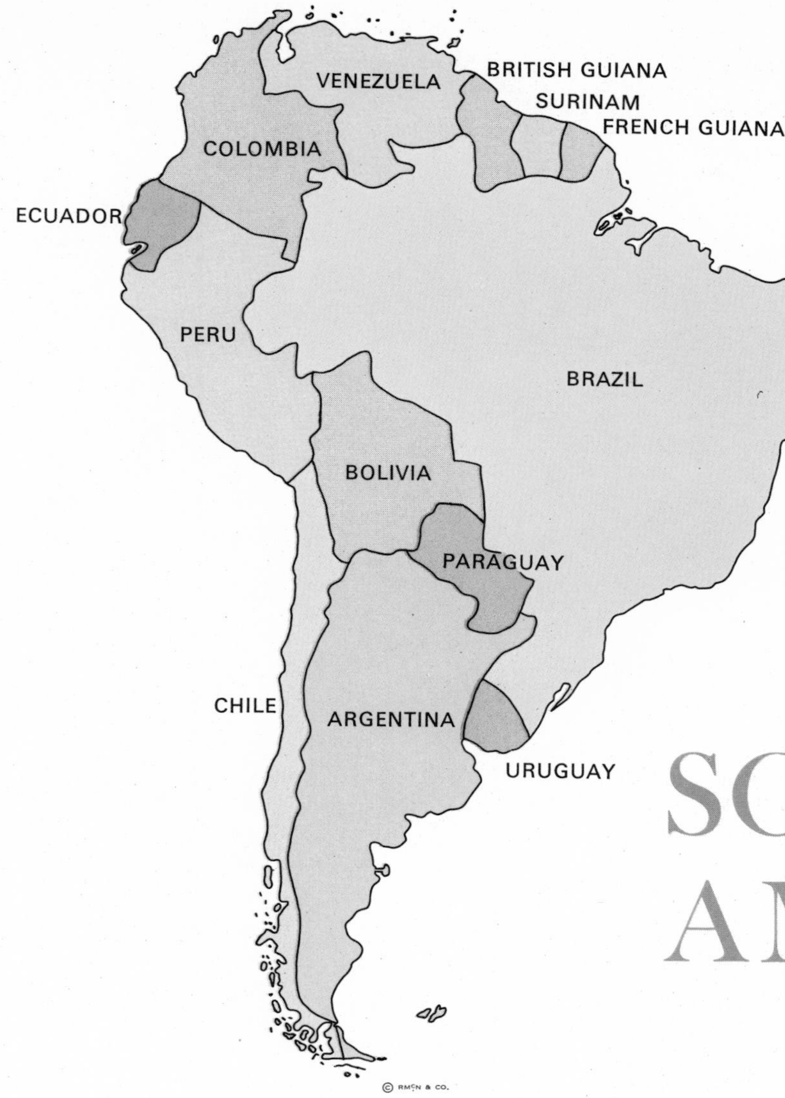

SOUTH AMERICA

Triangularly shaped South America is surrounded by water except at the narrow Isthmus of Panama. No great peninsulas extend into its seas or oceans, and its outlines are more regular than those of most other continents.

The Andes Mountains rise like a wall along the western shores, and this formidable chain runs the entire length of the continent, rising to altitudes of over 20,000 feet. It is the longest continuous mountain chain in the world.

The bulk of the continent slopes eastward from the eastern face of the Andes. From north to south, landforms include plains drained by the Orinoco and the eroded plateau areas of the Guiana and Brazilian highlands, the tropical lowlands of the Amazon Basin, savanna called the Gran Chaco, which is drained by the Paraná-Paraguay-Plata river systems, the pampas, and the plains of Patagonia.

The shape of the continent, its position astride the Equator, the water surrounding it, and the mountainous terrain have resulted in a variety of climates. The area east of the Andes from Venezuela to Northern Argentina, is dominated by moisture-laden air masses of the Atlantic. This two-thirds of the continent has a tropical or subtropical environment. Most of the remaining portion is under the influence of the relatively dry, cool Pacific air masses, which create the driest region in the world—the Atacama Desert of Chile. These cool Pacific air masses, too, on crossing the Andes in the narrow southern portion of the continent, create the Patagonian Desert of Argentina. In the higher altitudes of the mountain chain climates familiar to mid and upper latitudes are found.

Much of the interior of South America is still inaccessible, owing to extensive regions of mountains or jungle. Most of the settlement has been around the periphery of the continent. Spanish and Portuguese settlers, and later Germans and Italians, have developed highly specialized commercial economies in certain of the peripheral areas. Around Buenos Aires, São Paulo, Santiago, Bogotá economies based on agricultural products have been developed—wheat, beef, coffee, citrus fruit to name a few. Exported minerals—oil from Venezuela, tin from Bolivia, and copper from Chile—are economic mainstays of other countries.

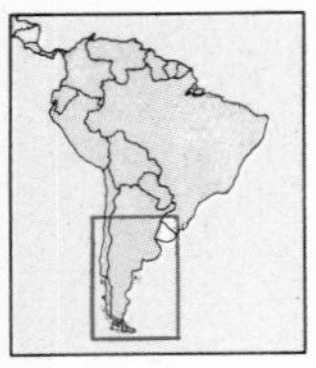

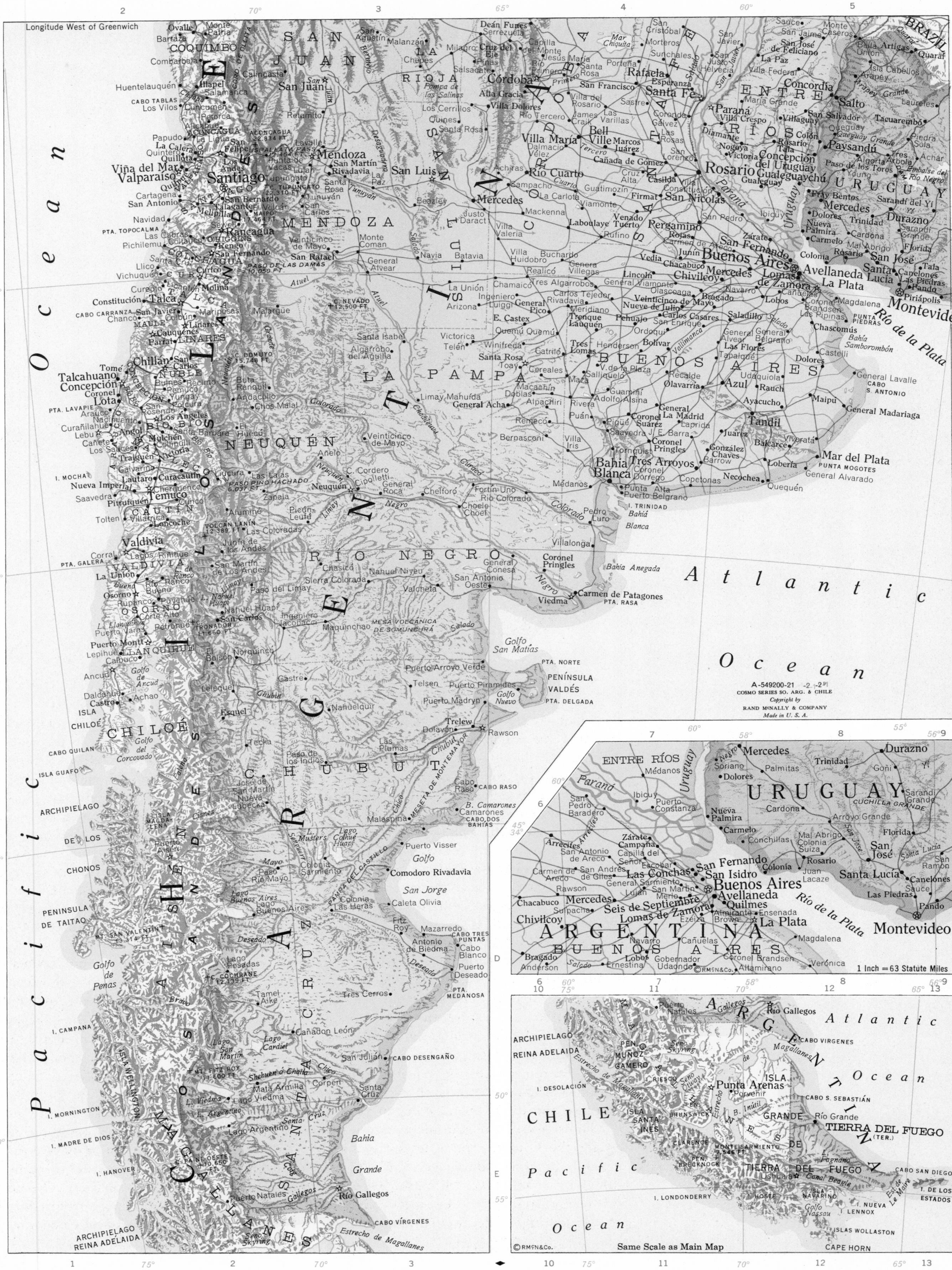

CENTRAL AND SOUTHERN ARGENTINA AND CHILE

Statute Miles

Kilometers

Oblique Conic Conformal Projection
SCALE 1:8,000,000   1 Inch = 126 Statute Miles

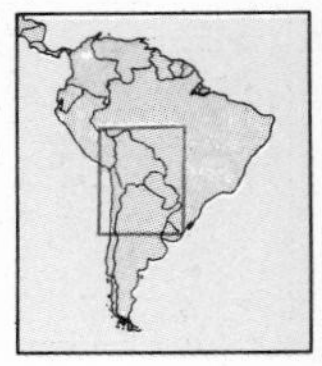

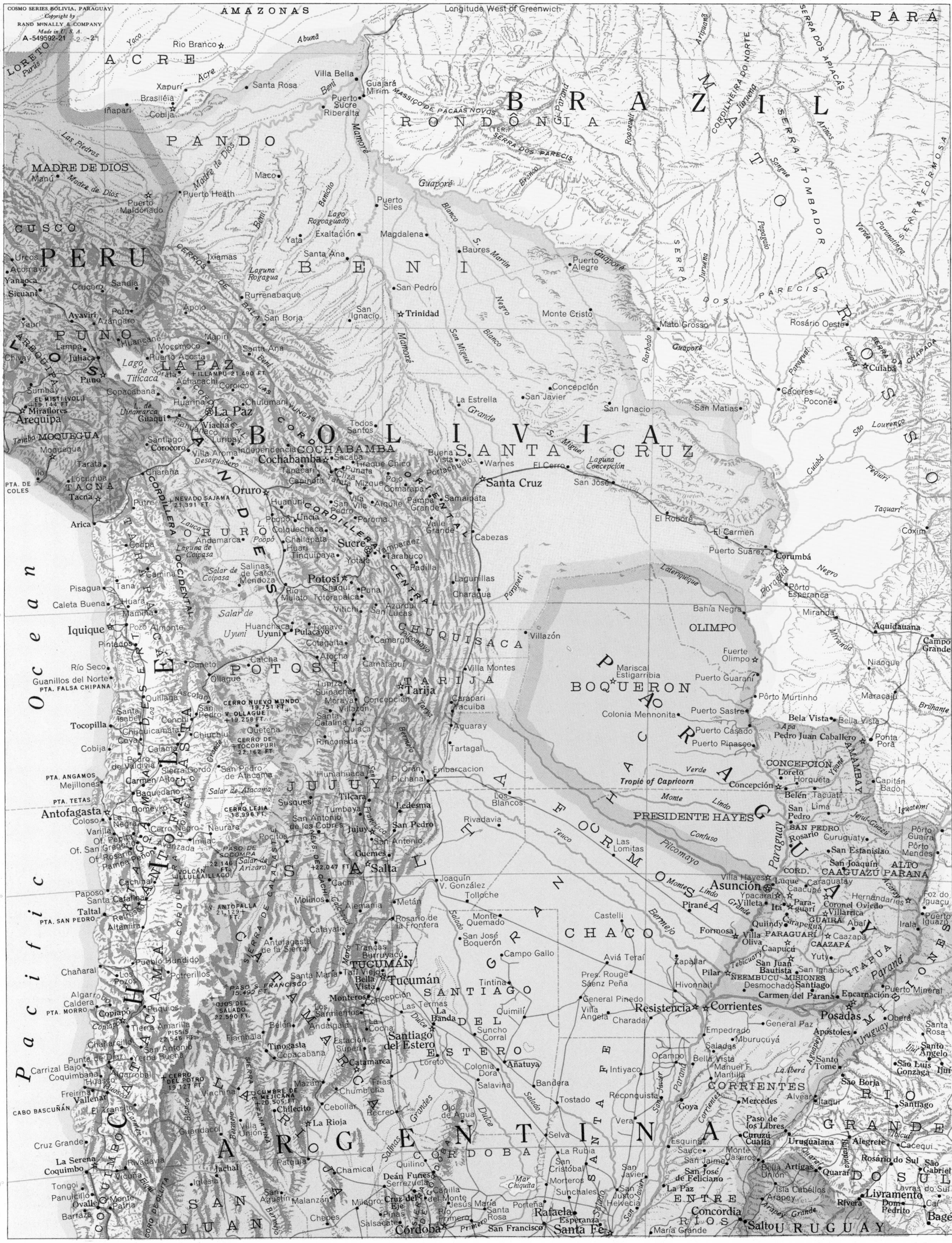

Oblique Conic Conformal Projection
SCALE 1:8,000,000   1 Inch = 126 Statute Miles

Statute Miles
50   0   50   100   150

Kilometers
50   0   50   100   150   200

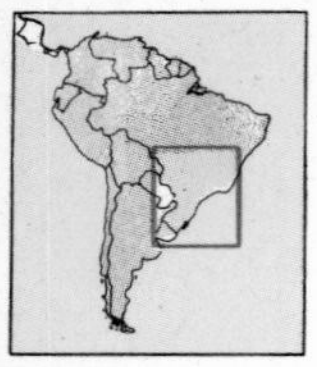

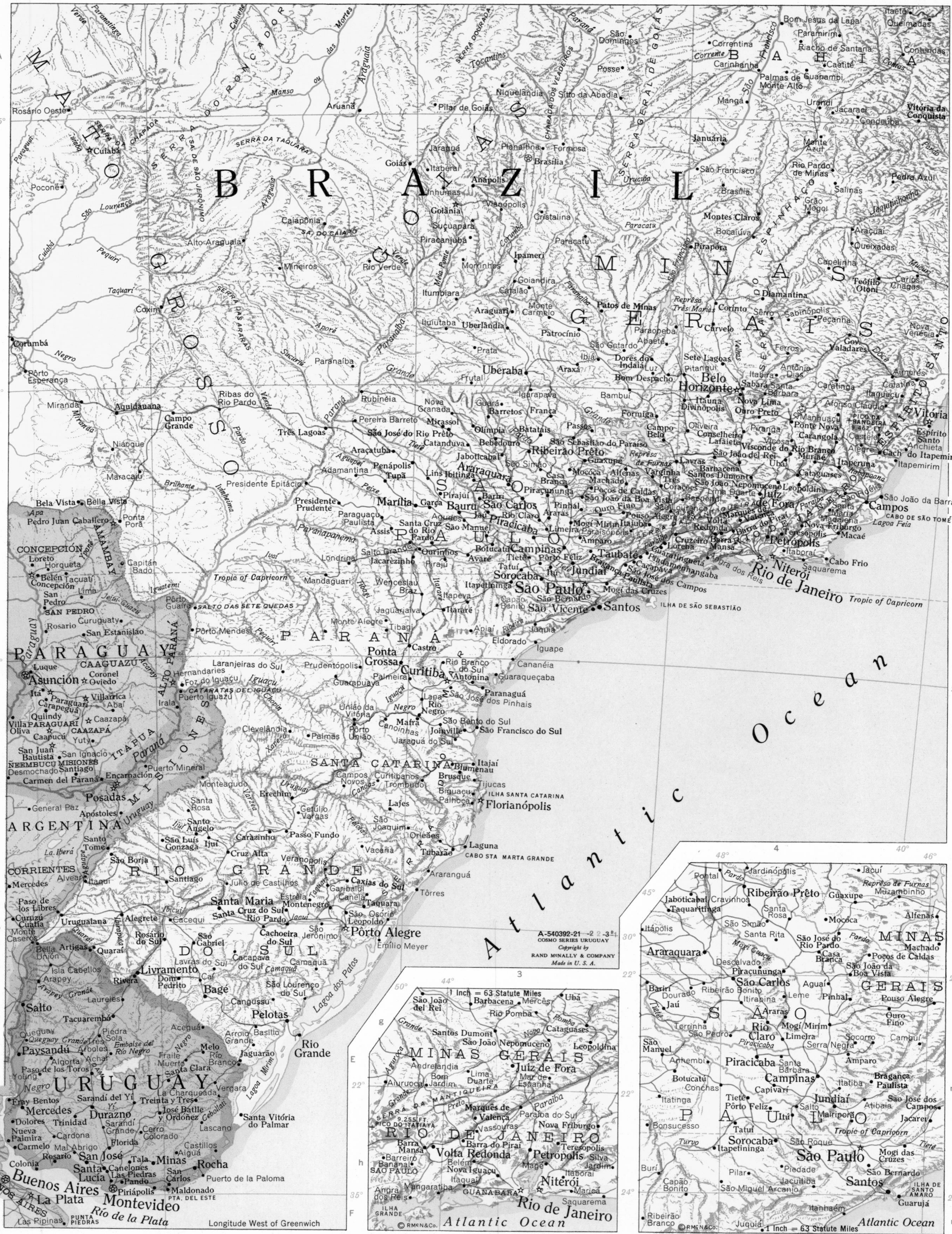

URUGUAY AND SOUTHERN BRAZIL

A-540392-21—2 2 -3⁴⁄
COSMO SERIES URUGUAY
Copyright by
RAND McNALLY & COMPANY
Made in U.S.A.

Oblique Conic Conformal Projection
SCALE 1:8,000,000   1 Inch = 126 Statute Miles

56

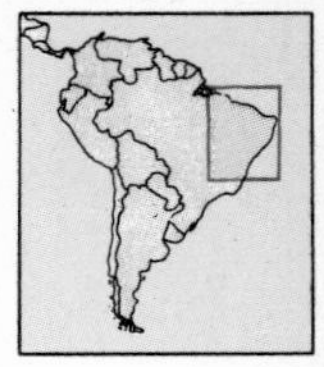

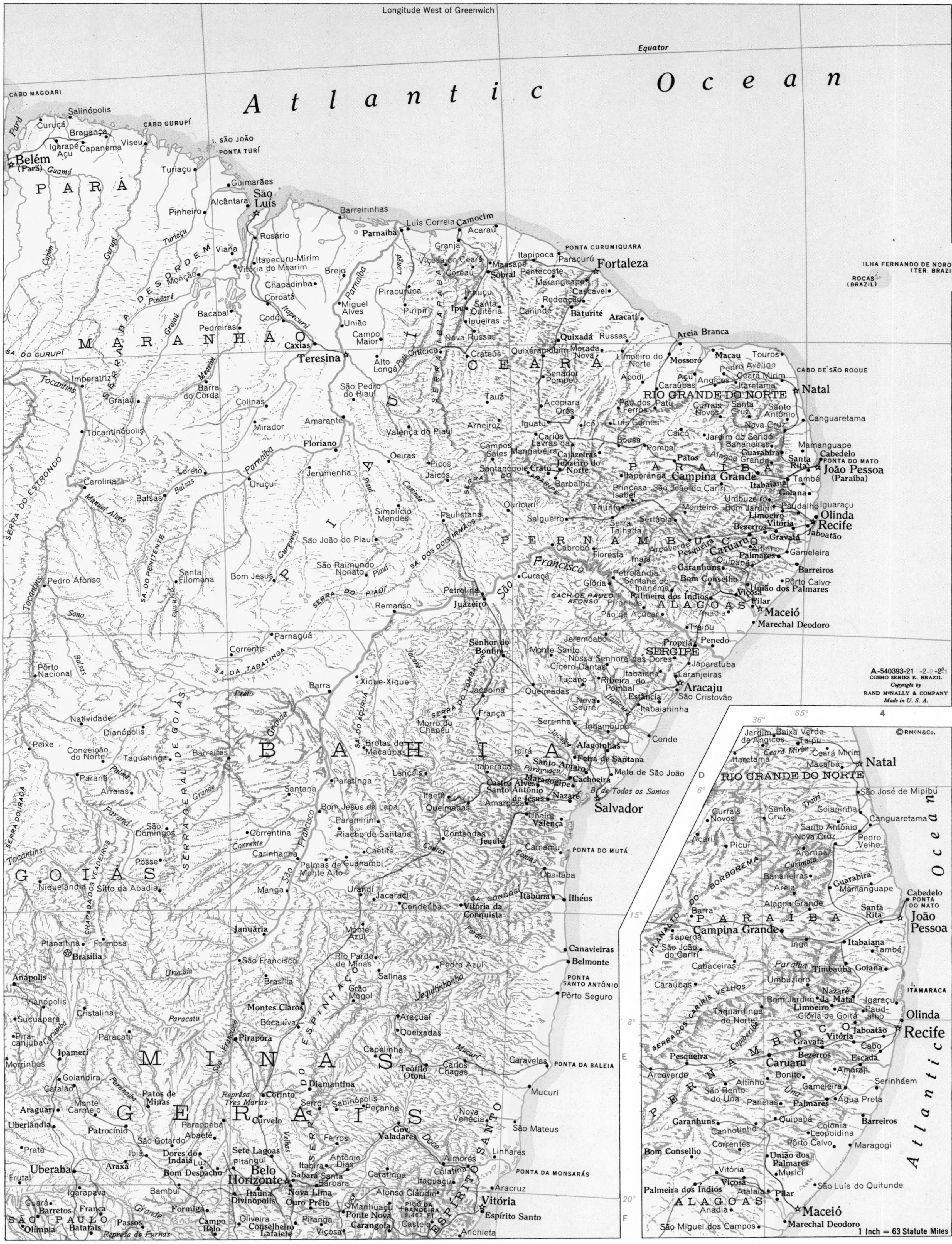

Oblique Conic Conformal Projection
SCALE 1:8,000,000   1 Inch = 126 Statute Miles

Statute Miles   50   0   50   100   150

Kilometers   50   0   50   100   150   200

1 Inch = 63 Statute Miles

PERU AND ECUADOR

Pacific Ocean

Pacific Ocean

Pacific Ocean
I. DARWIN
I. WOLF
I. PINTA
I. MARCHENA
PTA. ALBEMARLE
I. GENOVESA
Equator
C. BERKELEY
B. de Banks
I. SAN SALVADOR (SANTIAGO)
I. FERNANDINA (NARBOROUGH)
I. PINZÓN
B. Elizabeth
BALTRA
I. STA. CRUZ (INDEFATIGABLE)
ISLA ISABELA (ALBEMARLE I.)
I. SAN CRISTÓBAL (CHATHAM)
Villamil
I. STA. FÉ
Puerto Baquerizo
PTA. ESSEX
ARCHIPIELAGO DE COLÓN (GALÁPAGOS IS.) (ECUADOR)
I. STA. MARÍA
I. ESPANOLA

Same Scale as Main Map

A-549400-2
COSMO SERIES PERU, ECUADOR
Copyright by
RAND MCNALLY & COMPANY
Made in U.S.A.

58

COLOMBIA
VAUPÉS
VEN.
CAQUETÁ
AMAZONAS
BRAZIL
ACRE
PANDO
BOLIVIA
BENI
CHILE

ECUADOR
PERU
LORETO

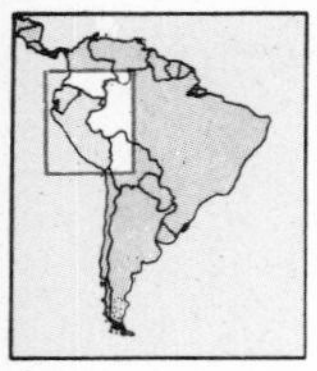

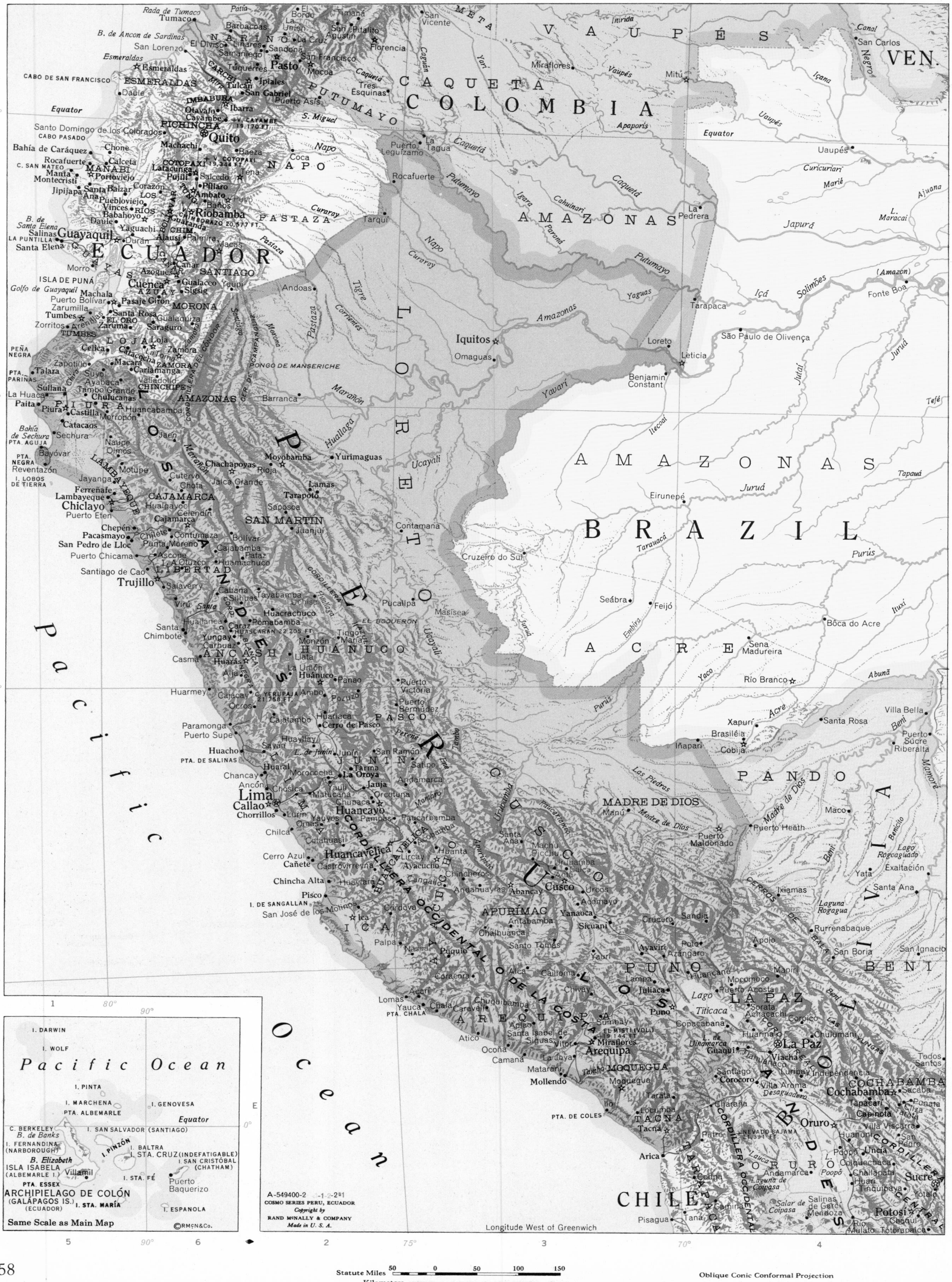

Statute Miles 50 0 50 100 150
Kilometers 50 0 50 100 150 200

Longitude West of Greenwich

Oblique Conic Conformal Projection
SCALE 1:8,000,000   1 Inch = 126 Statute Miles

Longitude West of Greenwich

Atlantic Ocean

VENEZUELA

BOLÍVAR

BRITISH

GUIANA

SURINAM
(NETH. GUIANA)

FRENCH
GUIANA

RIO BRANCO
(TER.)

AMAPÁ
(TER.)

AMAZONAS

BRAZIL

PARÁ

MATO GROSSO

RONDONIA
(TER.)

BOLIVIA

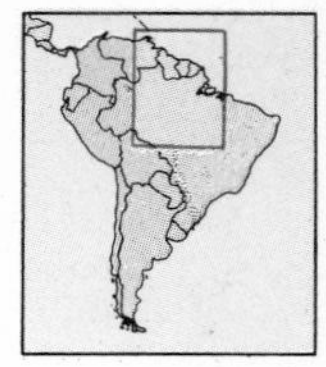

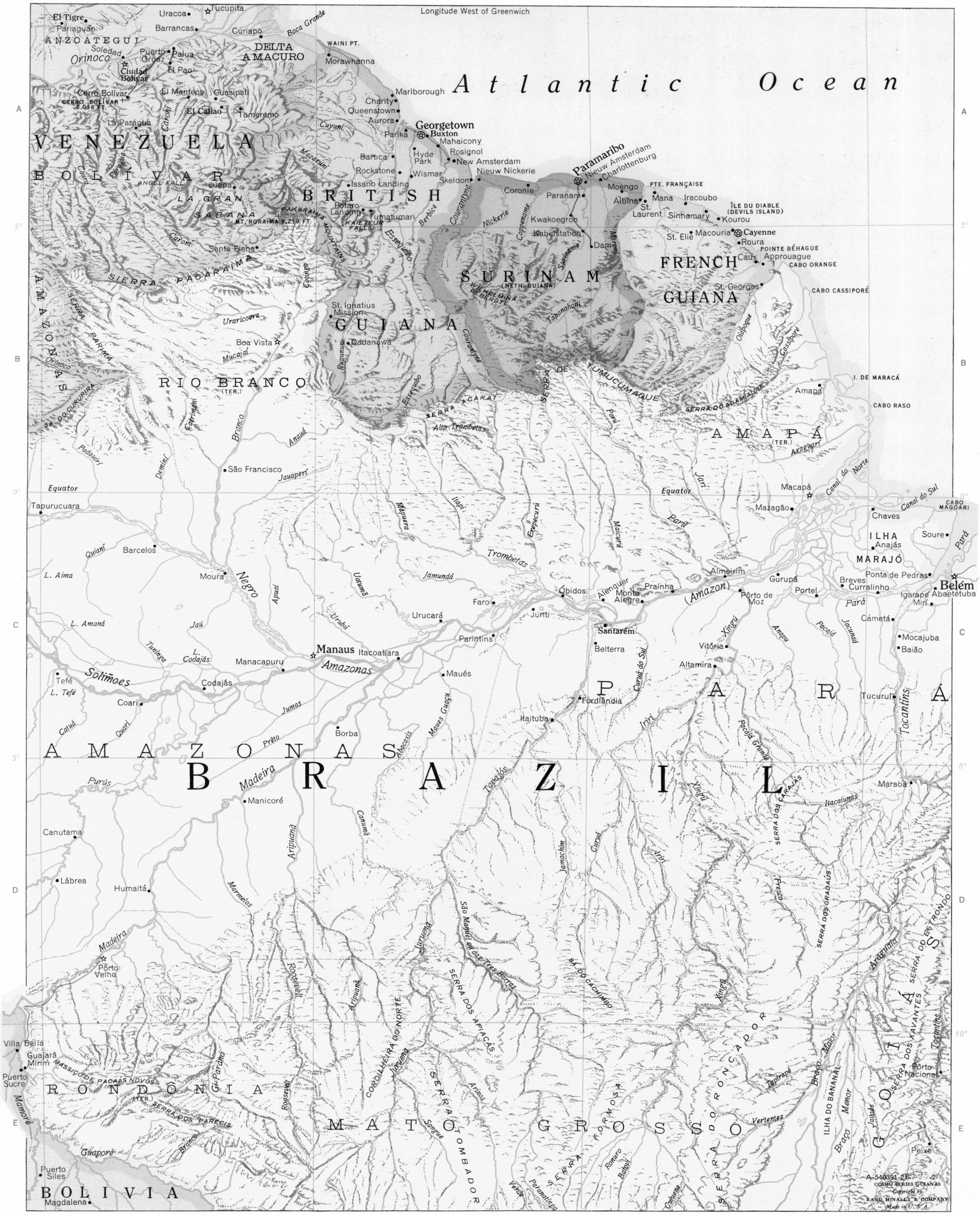

Oblique Conic Conformal Projection
SCALE 1:8,000,000   1 Inch = 126 Statute Miles

Statute Miles

Kilometers

COLOMBIA AND VENEZUELA

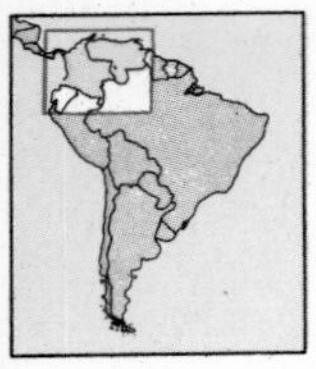

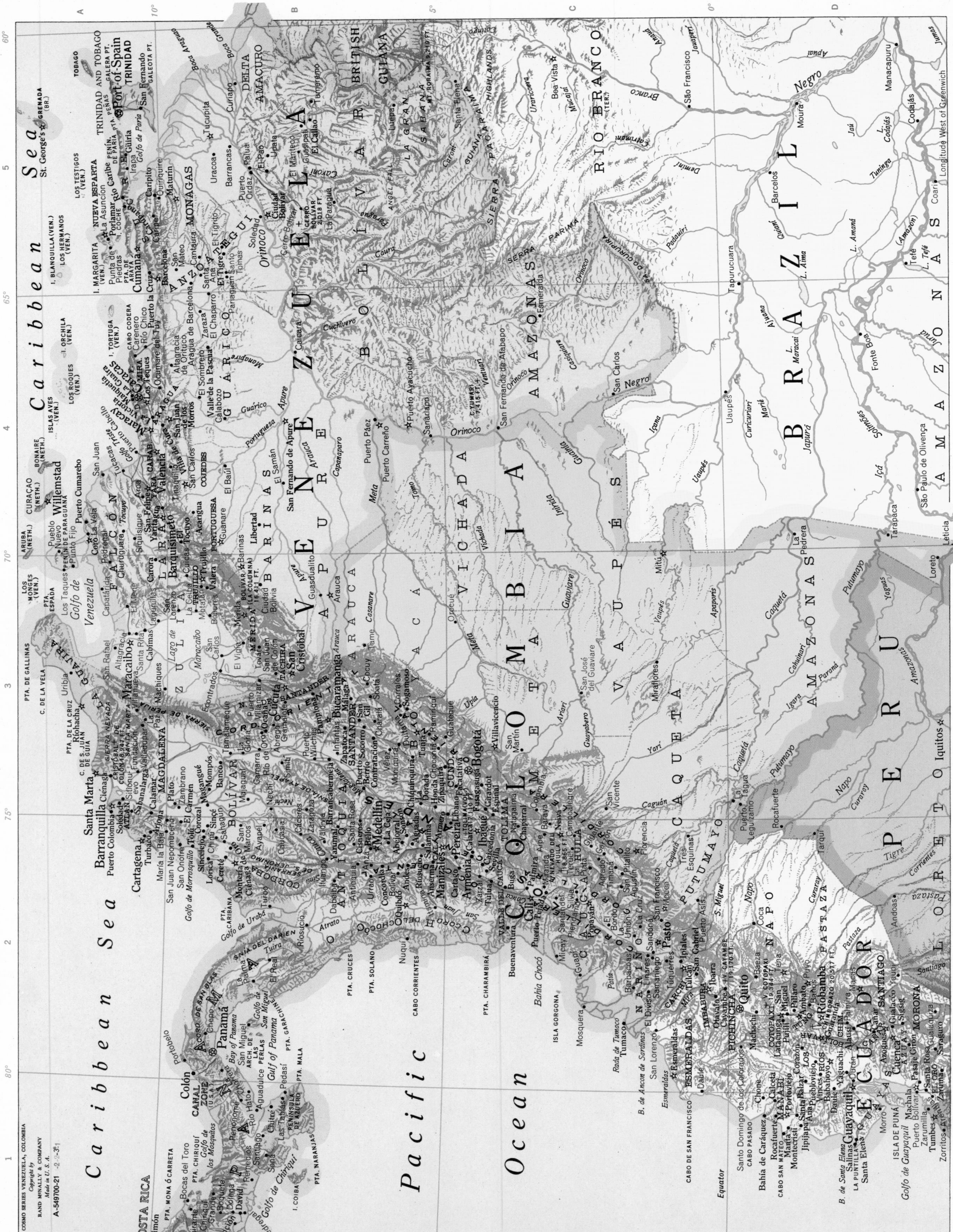

Statute Miles
50   0   50   100   150

Kilometers
50   0   50   100   150   200

Oblique Conic Conformal Projection
SCALE 1:8,000,000 1 Inch = 126 Statute Miles

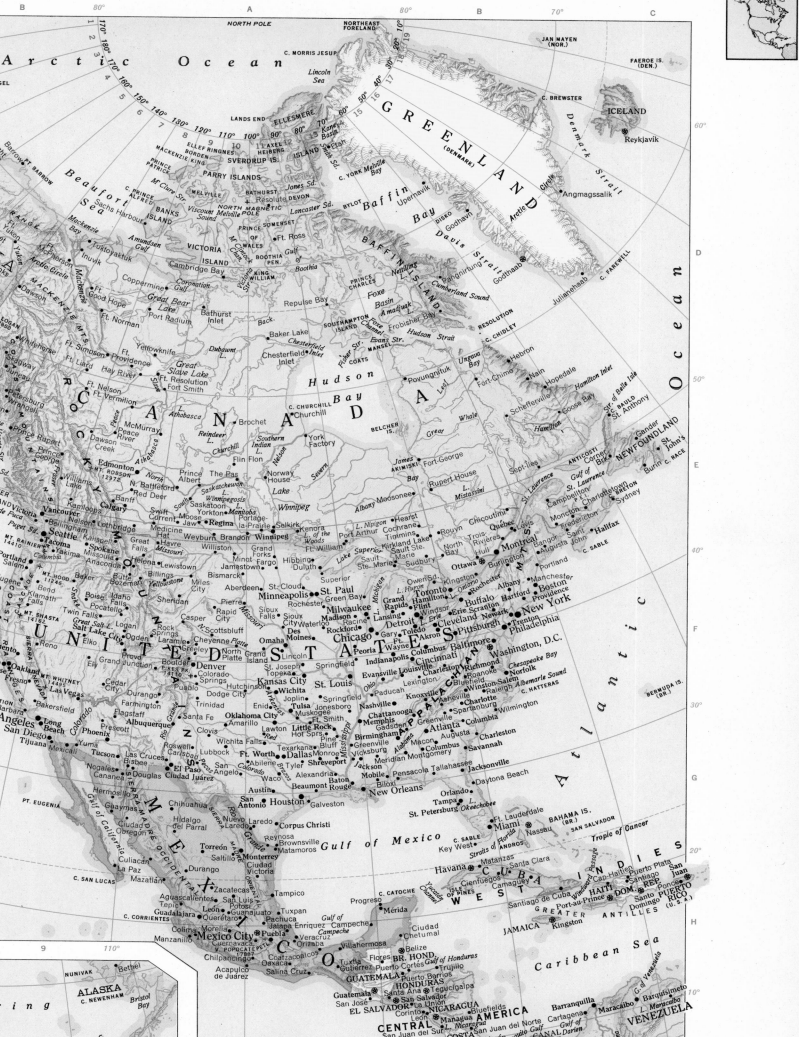

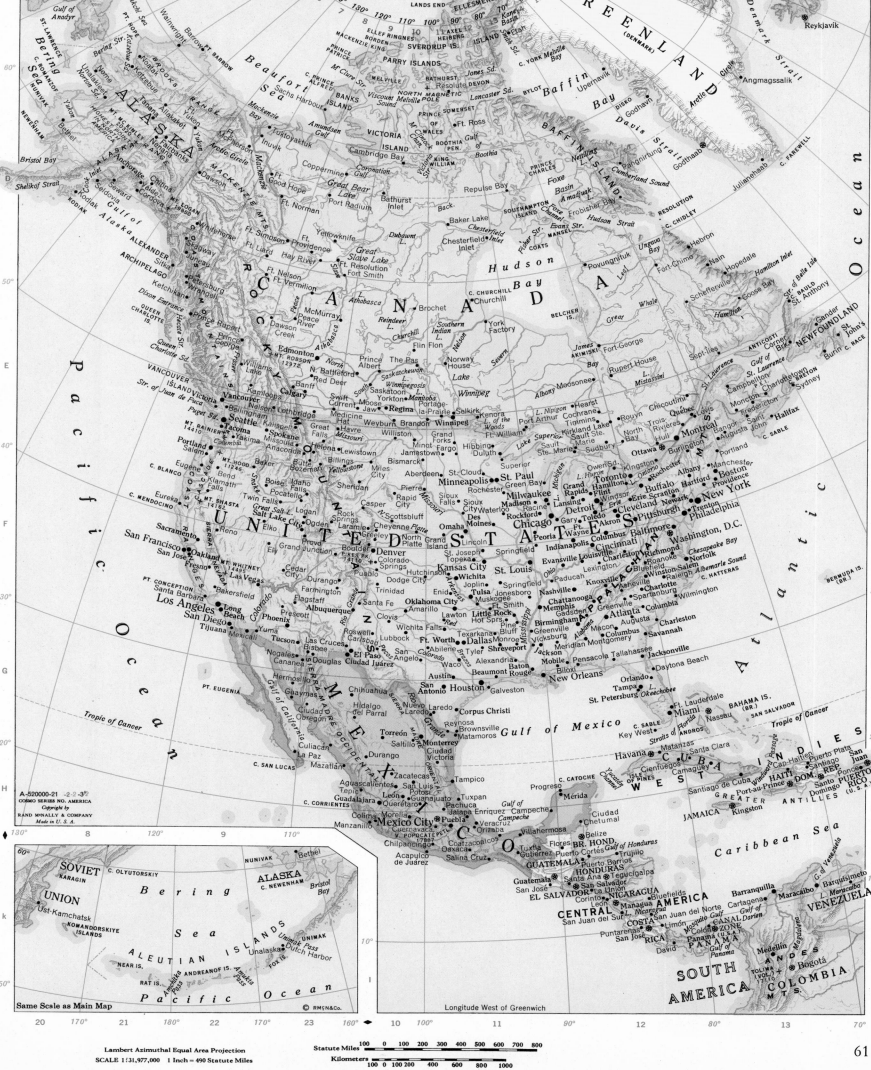

SOVIET UNION
ASIA

Arctic Ocean

NORTH POLE   NORTHEAST FORELAND

C. MORRIS JESUP

GREENLAND
(DENMARK)

JAN MAYEN (NOR.)

FAEROE IS. (DEN.)

ICELAND

Reykjavik

Bering Sea

ALASKA

Beaufort Sea

CANADA

Hudson Bay

Baffin Bay

Davis Strait

Denmark Strait

NEWFOUNDLAND

Pacific Ocean

ROCKY MOUNTAINS

UNITED STATES

APPALACHIAN MTS.

Atlantic Ocean

BERMUDA IS. (BR.)

San Francisco
Los Angeles
San Diego

Denver
Kansas City
St. Louis
Chicago
Detroit
New York
Philadelphia
Washington, D.C.

MEXICO

Mexico City

Gulf of Mexico

CUBA
HAITI
DOM. REP.
PUERTO RICO (U.S.A.)

WEST INDIES
GREATER ANTILLES

JAMAICA

Caribbean Sea

CENTRAL AMERICA

GUATEMALA
HONDURAS
EL SALVADOR
NICARAGUA
COSTA RICA
PANAMA
CANAL ZONE

VENEZUELA
COLOMBIA

SOUTH AMERICA

Tropic of Cancer

Longitude West of Greenwich

A-520000-21 -2-2-3½
COSMO SERIES NO. AMERICA
Copyright by
RAND McNALLY & COMPANY
Made in U.S.A.

SOVIET UNION

Bering Sea

ALASKA

ALEUTIAN ISLANDS

Pacific Ocean

Same Scale as Main Map

Lambert Azimuthal Equal Area Projection
SCALE 1:31,977,000   1 Inch = 490 Statute Miles

Statute Miles 100 0 100 200 300 400 500 600 700 800
Kilometers 100 0 100 200 400 600 800 1000

61

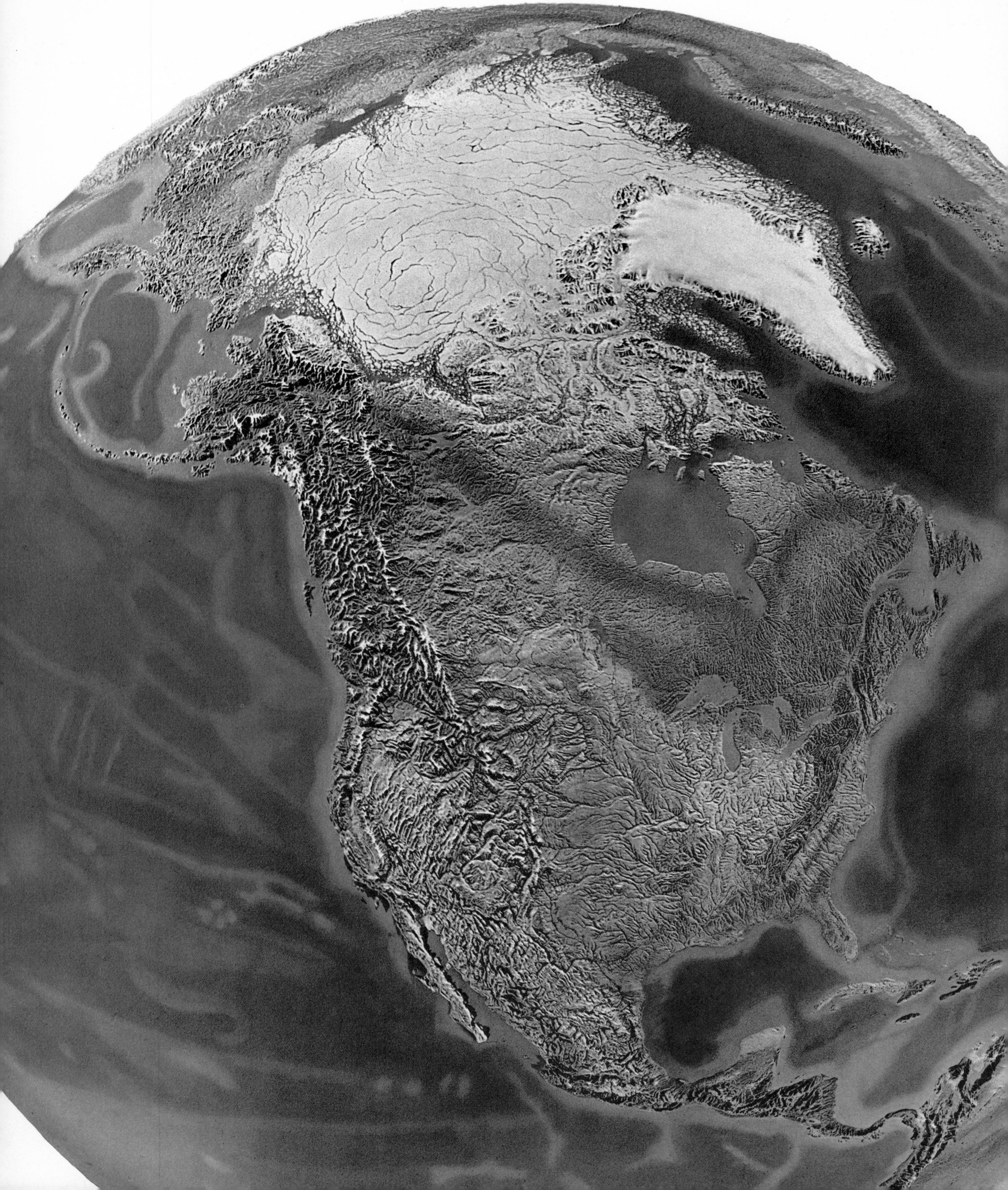

NORTH AMERICA

Physically the North American continent extends from the ice-covered Arctic Ocean in the north to the tropical Isthmus of Panama in the south. North America, like Africa and South America, tapers from north to south. Canada, the United States, and Mexico occupy over 85 per cent of its total area of nearly 9,500,000 square miles. Central America, the West Indies, and Greenland make up the remainder.

Within this vast area, differences, rather than similarities, abound. All major types of climate can be found in North America ranging from the cold, perpetual ice cap of Greenland to the hot, moist tropical rain forests of Central America. Landforms vary from the towering chain of the Rocky Mountains, through the high plateau of Mexico, the relatively low Appalachian Highland, the featureless expanses of the Arctic tundra, the regularity of the Great Plains, and the fertile fields of the interior lowlands and coastal plains. Soils, vegetation, temperature, precipitation—all reflect the differences that can be expected over such an area.

Similarly, the development of agriculture and industry has varied considerably over the North American continent. Modern methods and the extensive use of machinery characterize agriculture in the flat to gently rolling areas of Midwestern United States and the Prairie Provinces of Canada. Stock-grazing is prevalent in the more arid areas of the continent. Agriculture in Middle America is characterized by the extensive use of hand labor. Here subtropical crops are important, for instance, bananas in Central America and sugar cane in the West Indies.

Early settlement, access to raw materials, a well developed transportation network, and a density of population providing both labor and markets have led to a heavy concentration of industrial development in the northeast quarter of the United States and the southeastern rim of Canada. Other industrial development has taken place in scattered locations in southern and western United States and in the largest cities of Middle America.

61 B

CENTRAL AMERICA

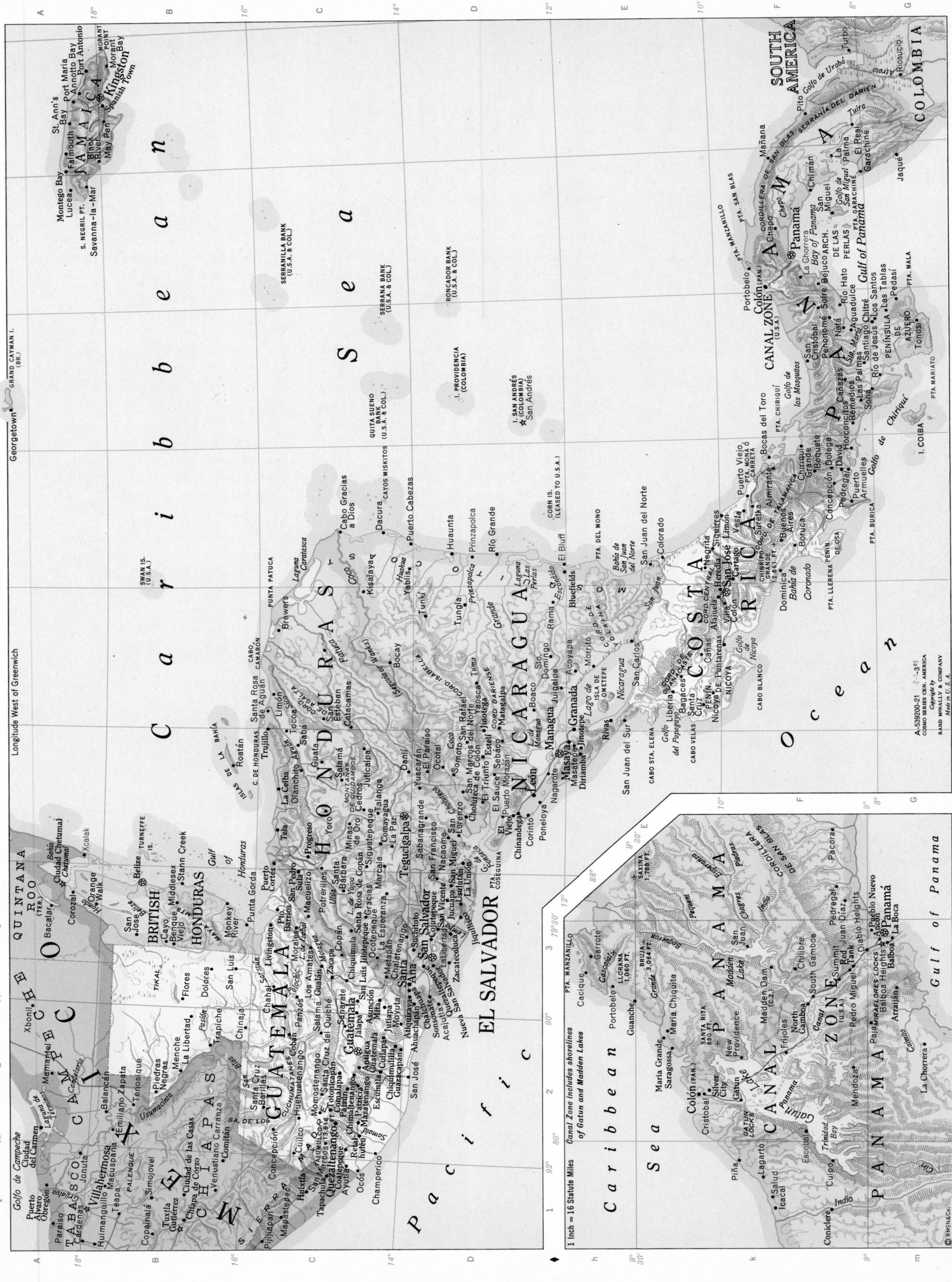

Statute Miles 25 0 25 75 125

Kilometers 25 0 25 75 125 175

Oblique Conic Conformal Projection
SCALE 1:6,000,000 1 Inch = 95 Statute Miles

MEXICO

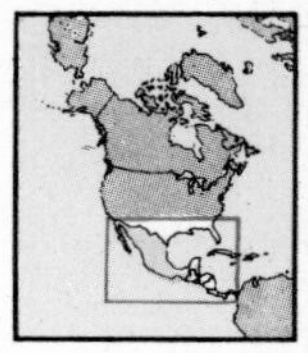

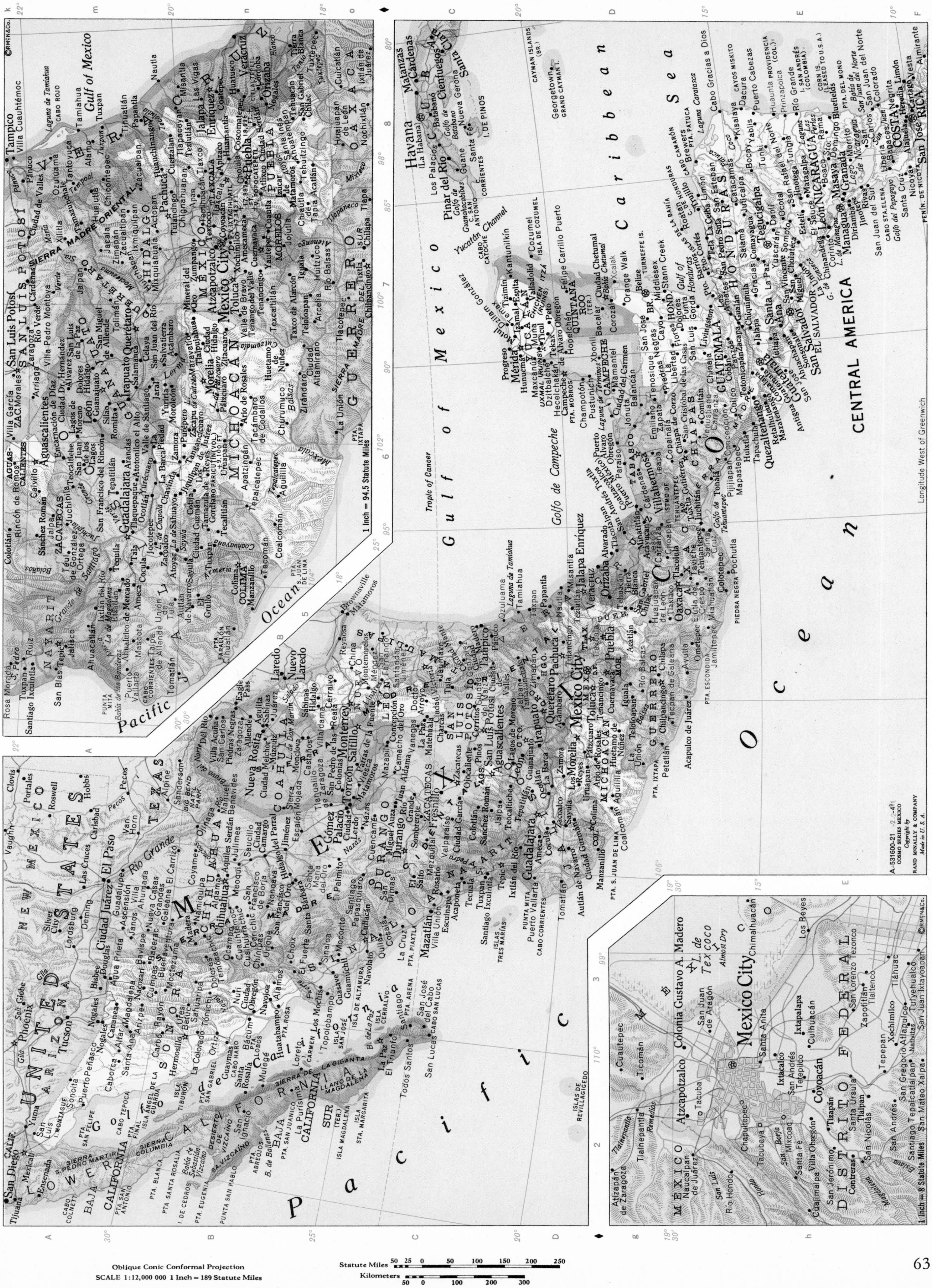

Oblique Conic Conformal Projection
SCALE 1:12,000 000 1 Inch = 189 Statute Miles

Statute Miles 50 25 0   50   100   150   200   250
Kilometers   50 0   100   200   300

63

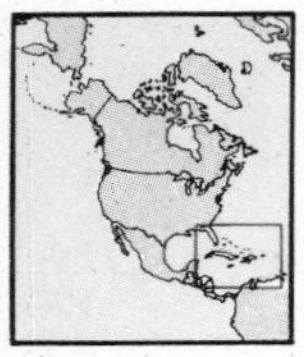

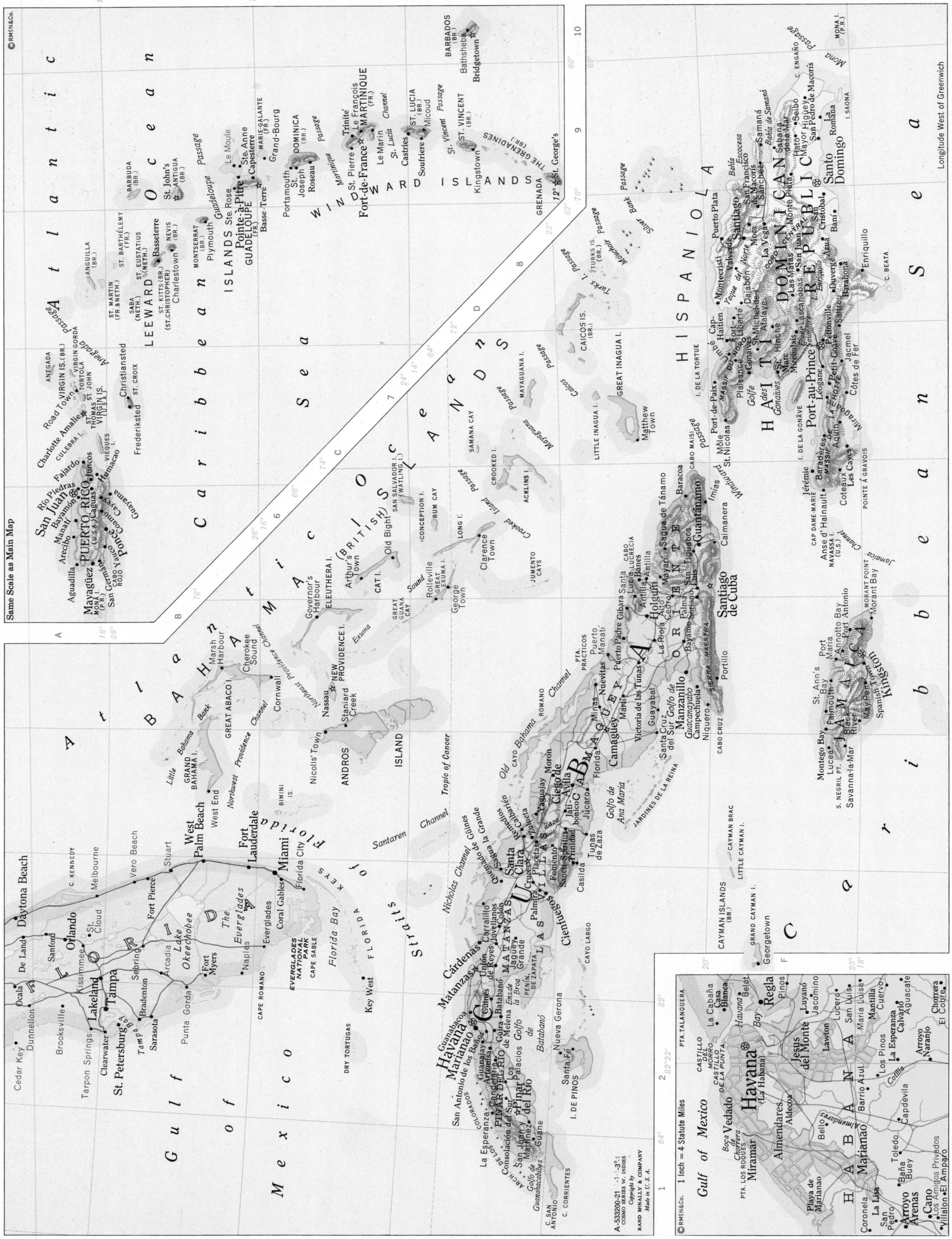

Same Scale as Main Map

Statute Miles

Kilometers

Oblique Conic Conformal Projection
SCALE 1:6,000,000 1 Inch = 95 Statute Miles

1 Inch = 4 Statute Miles

A-532000-21 -1:-3¹₁
COSMO SERIES W. INDIES
Copyright by
RAND McNALLY & COMPANY
Made in U.S.A.

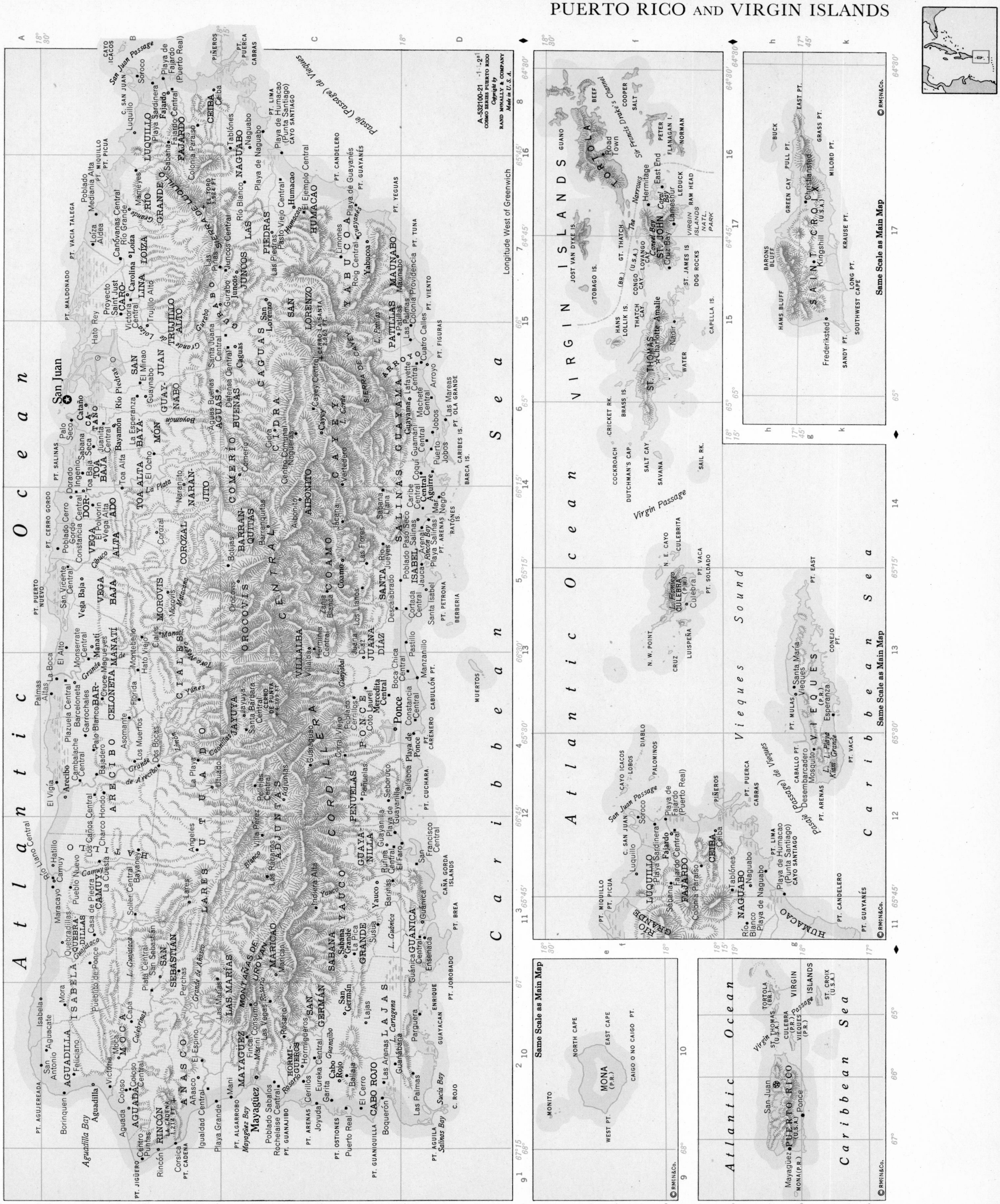

Lambert Conformal Conic Projection
SCALE 1 : 600,000   1 Inch = 9.5 Statute Miles

Statute Miles
Kilometers

65

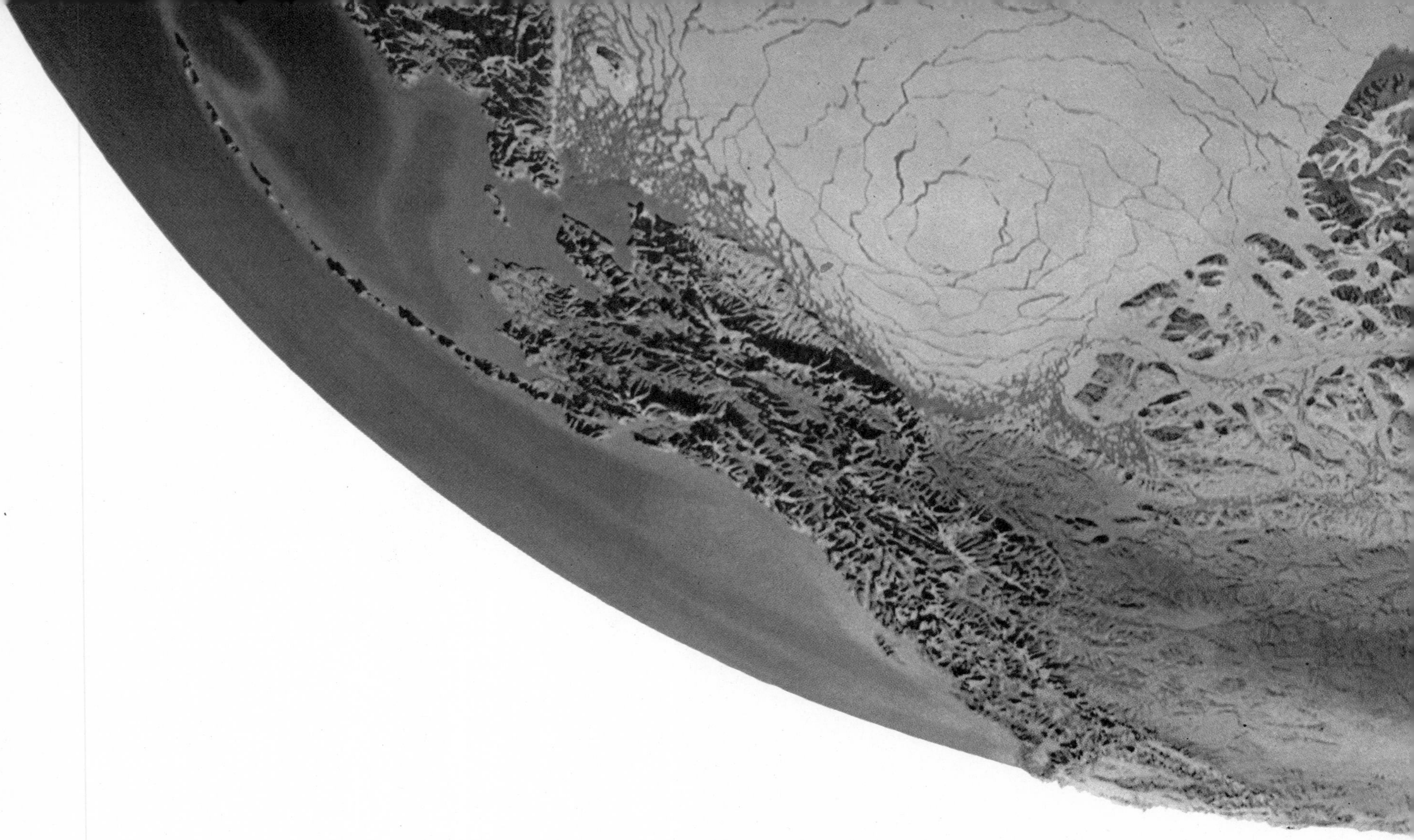

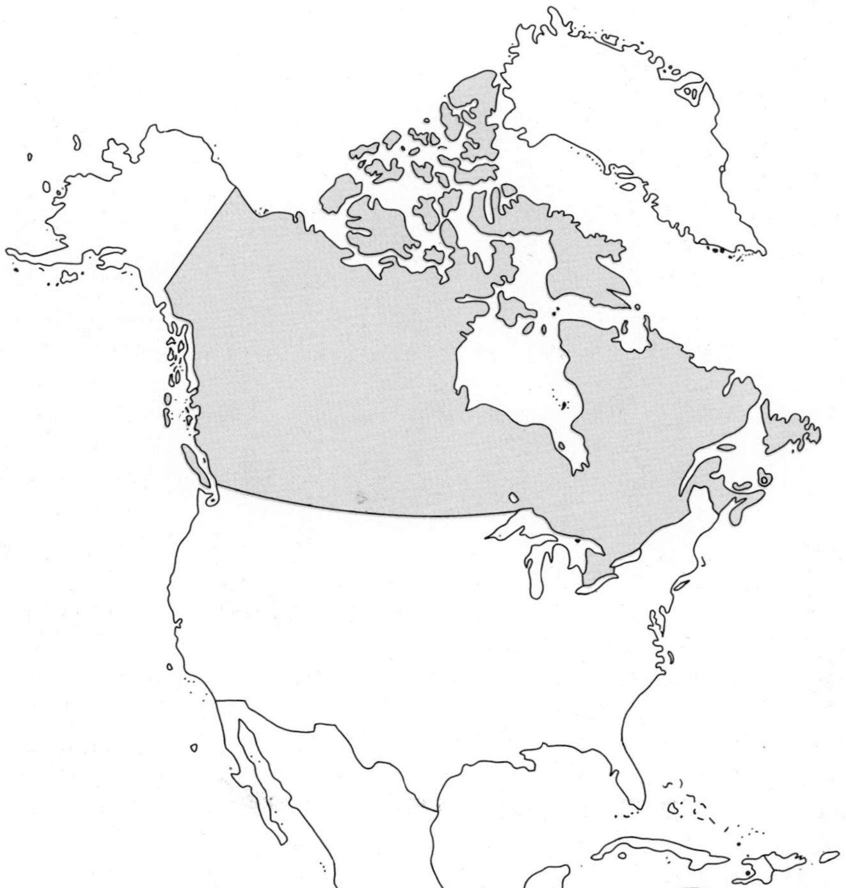

CANADA

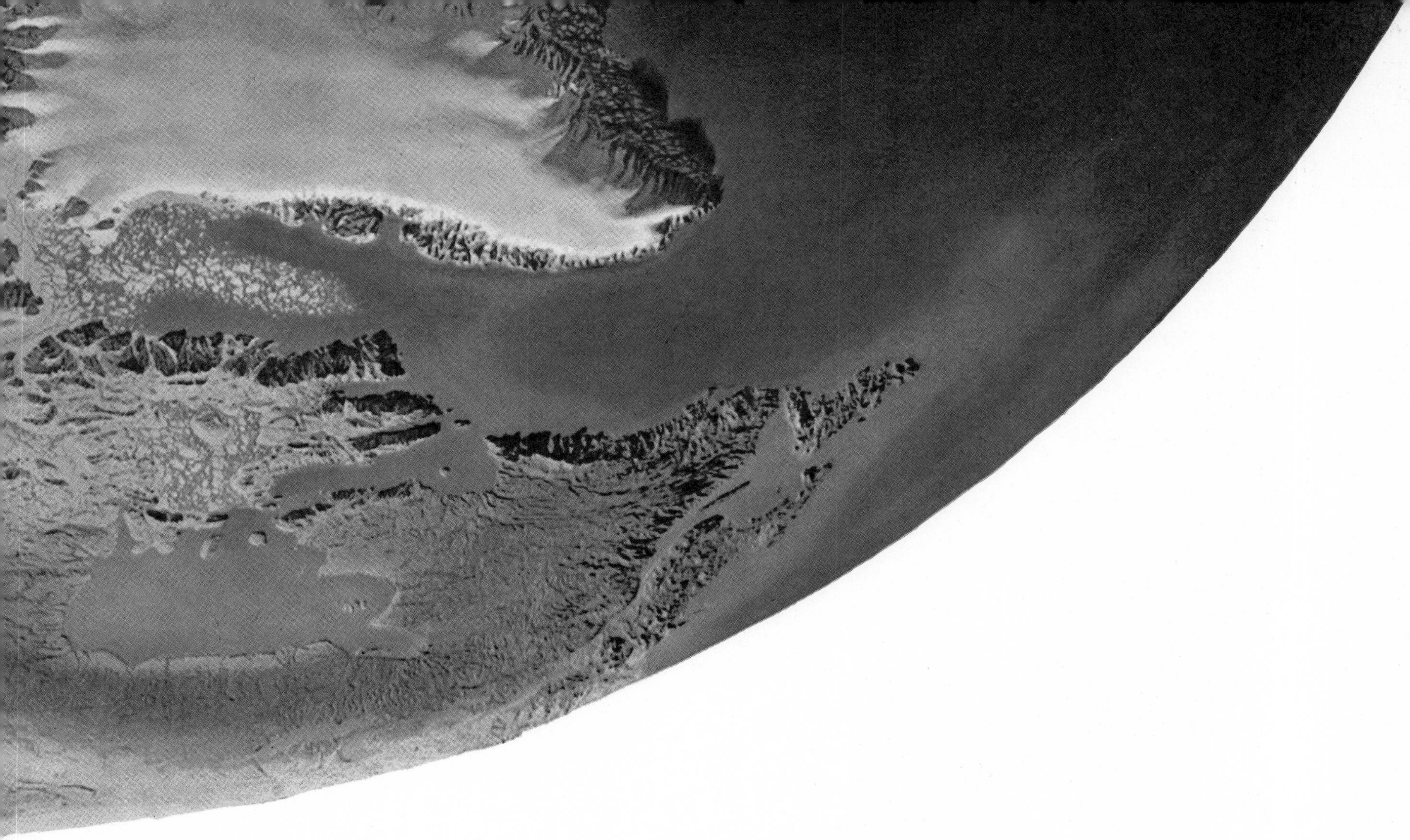

Canada, the largest single political entity in the Western Hemisphere, occupies the great territorial expanse of northern North America. It crosses the breadth of the continent from ocean to ocean and extends from the frozen wastes of the Arctic to the northern bounds of the United States. Although Canada is second only to the Soviet Union in total land area, it does not share the population density of other territorial giants. Only a narrow strip of land adjacent to the boundary of the United States possesses the agricultural and industrial activities to support any substantial concentration of population. Here, within a hundred miles of the United States' northern boundary, 90 per cent of Canada's population is concentrated.

The geographic location of Canada has profoundly influenced the economic development of the country. Proximity to the Polar region has provided the hostile, barren tundra and has placed Canada within the path of the frigid air masses moving southward over North America. The great glacial movements from the north during the Ice Age scoured much of Canada, leaving a shield-shaped region whose broad base lies along the northern lands from Great Bear Lake to the Maritimes and whose apex dips into the State of Minnesota. The Laurentian, or Canadian, Shield occupies more than half of the country's total area. Such was the thoroughness of the glaciers that only in a few places did they leave even a veneer of soil suitable for concentrated agriculture. Today the Interior Plains and the St. Lawrence Valley have adequate soils and climate to be intensively cultivated. The rugged western portion of the North American continent reaches its

greatest heights in British Columbia and the Yukon, also limiting the amount of agricultural activity.

Although the scoured rock of the Canadian Shield, the rugged terrain, and the climate limit Canada's agriculture, these same factors contribute to the vast natural resources of the country. Contained in the ancient glaciated rocks of the Shield and the western mountain chains is much of the mineral wealth of Canada —gold, uranium, iron ore. Under the dry plains lying to the east of the Rocky Mountains are the recently tapped oil reserves of Alberta. And on both the rocks of the Shield and the terrain of the west tracts of coniferous forests flourish, providing the raw material for lumber and wood-pulp industries. In these same areas great hydroelectric potential abounds.

Transportation has proved an impetus to the exploitation of the wilderness frontiers and provided a link between the southeastern urban centers and the outlying trading centers. The completion of the Canadian Pacific Railroad in 1886 bound the Prairie Provinces and British Columbia to the financial, commercial, and industrial centers of Ontario, Quebec, and the Maritime Provinces. The Trans-Canada Highway augmented the ties. Joint development of the St. Lawrence Seaway with the United States has further enhanced the movement of grain and other agricultural products from the interior through the Great Lakes.

British and French influences shaped the early development of the country, but most of modern Canada owes its cultural heritage to Great Britain. Only the Province of Quebec still bears the imprint of its French settlers.

65 B

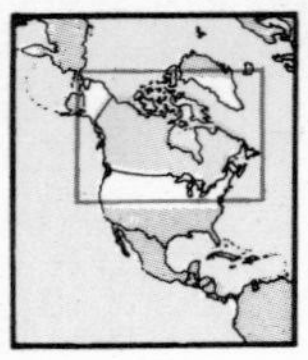

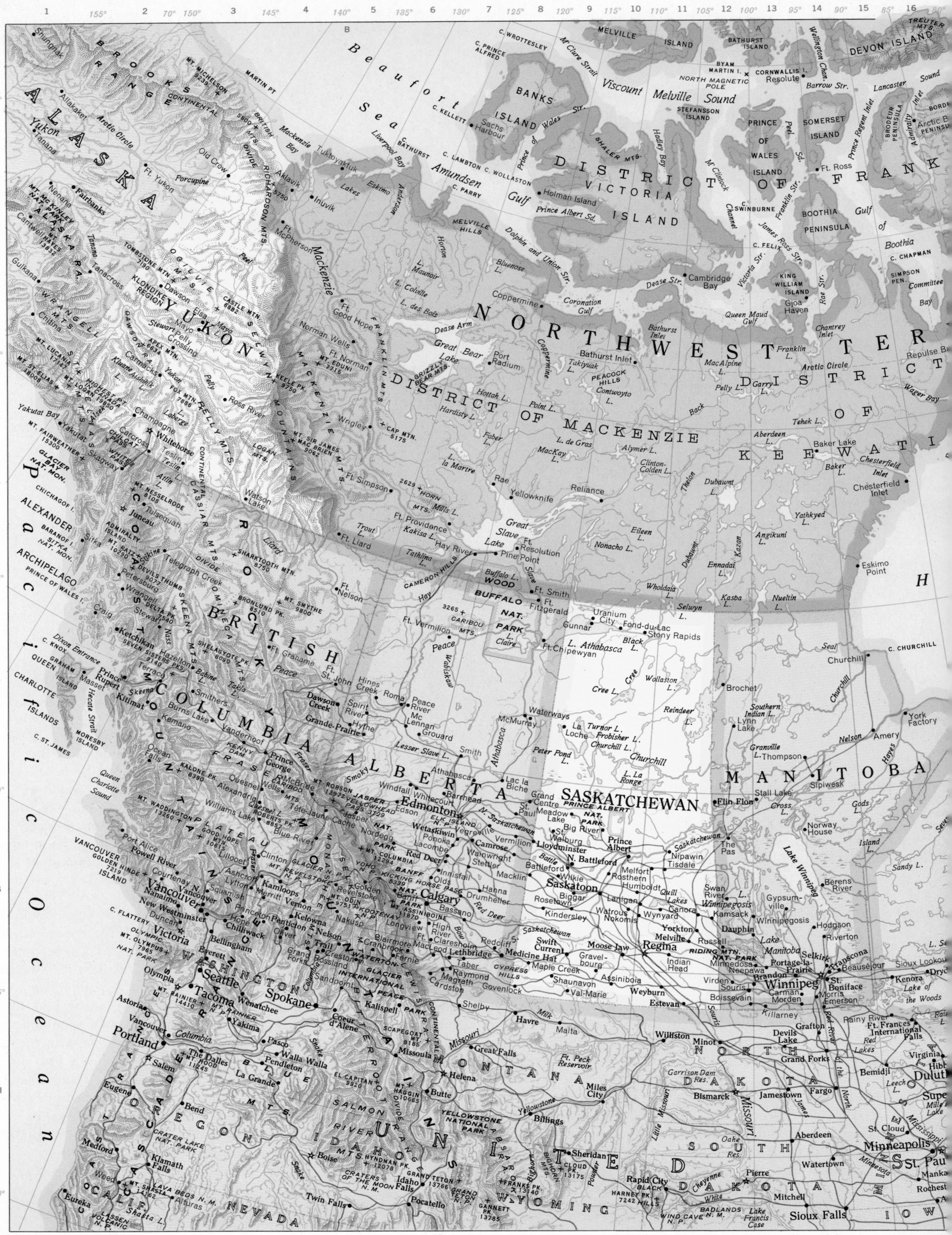

Statute Miles 50 25 0 50 100 150 200 250

Kilometers 50 0 100 200 300

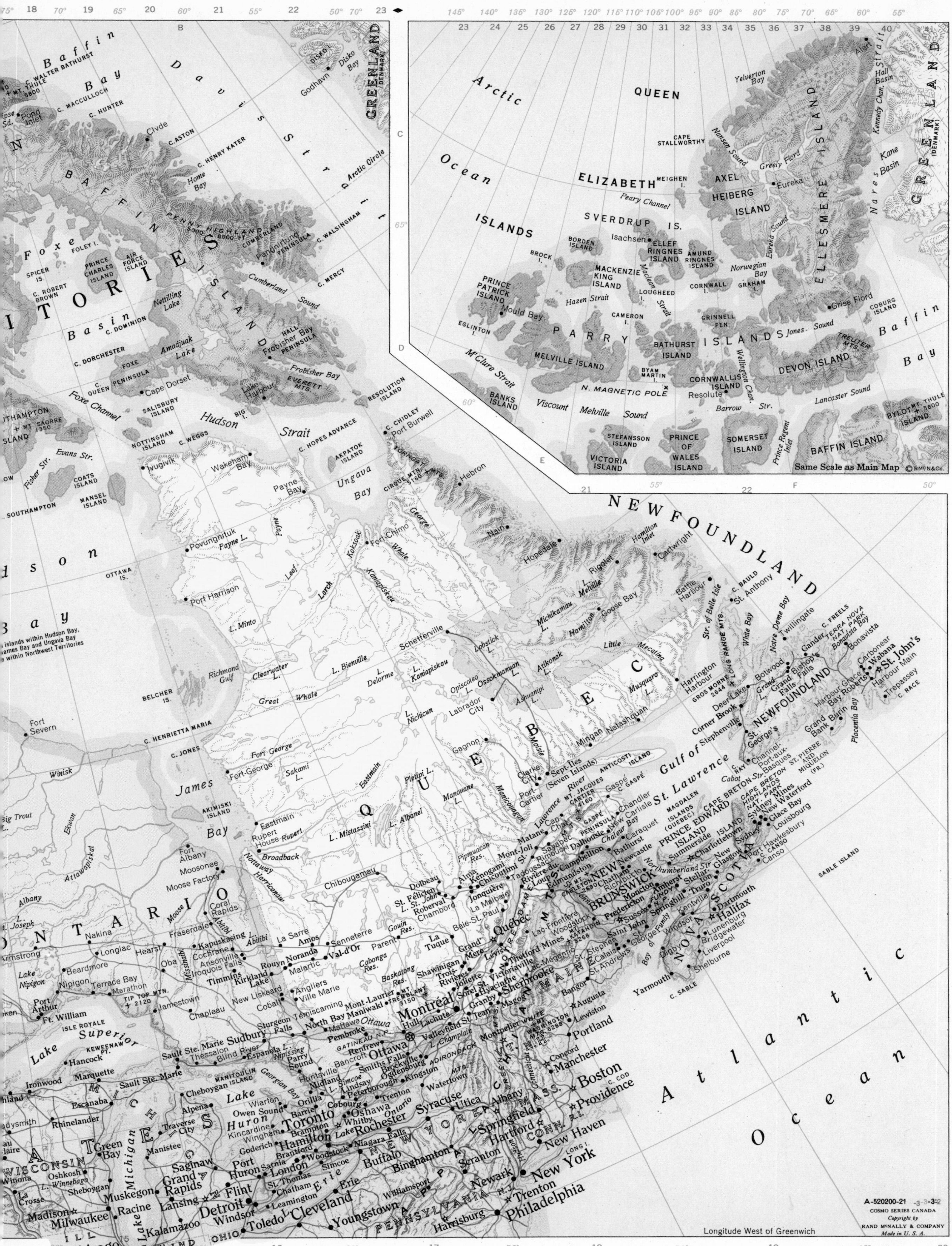

Lambert Conformal Conic Projection
SCALE 1:12,000,000   1 Inch = 189 Statute Miles

67

BRITISH COLUMBIA

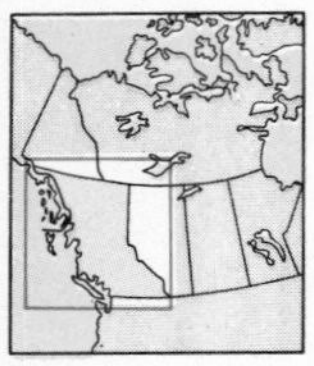

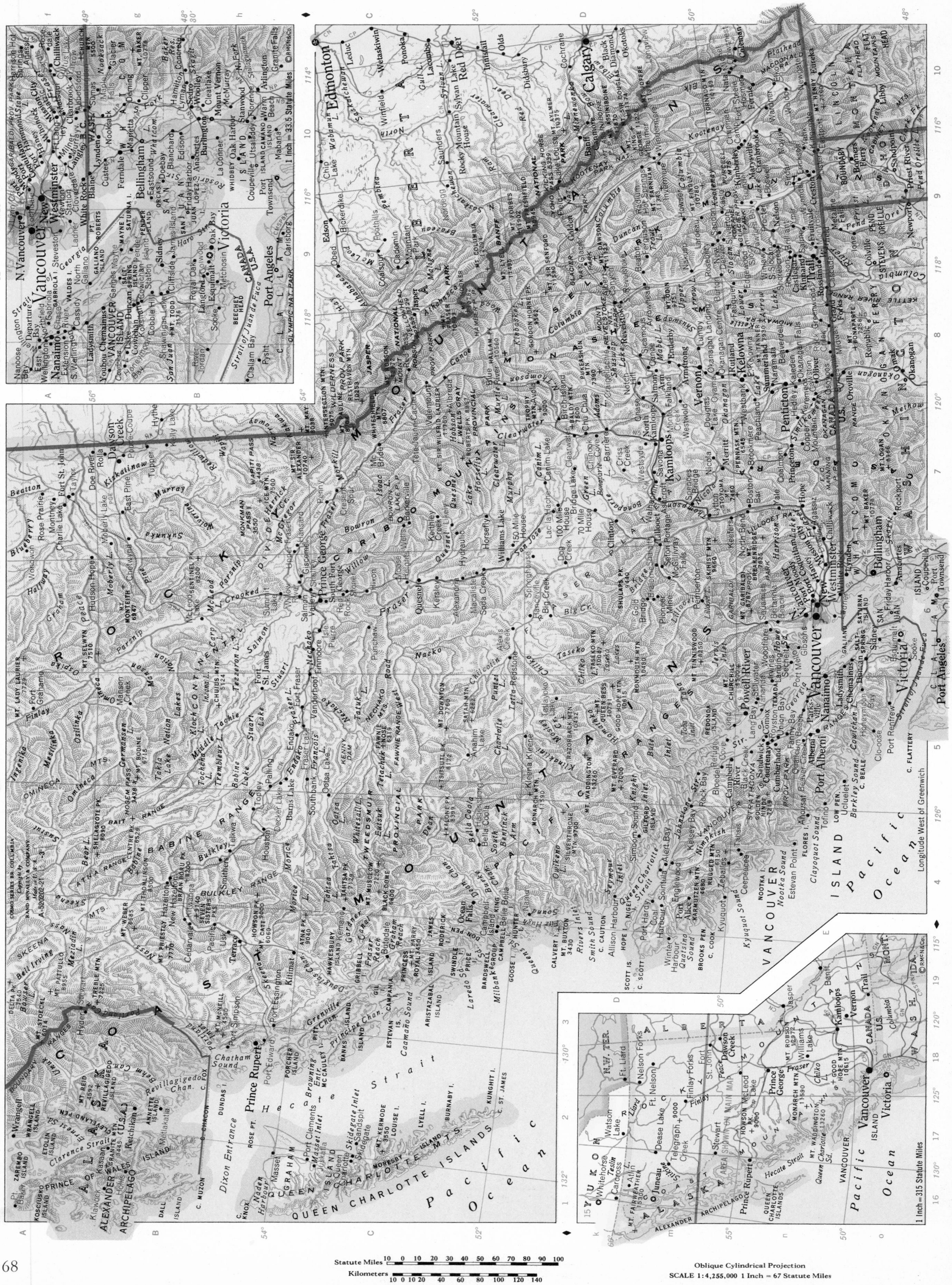

Statute Miles 10 0 10 20 30 40 50 60 70 80 90 100

Kilometers 10 0 10 20 40 60 80 100 120 140

Oblique Cylindrical Projection
SCALE 1:4,255,000 1 Inch = 67 Statute Miles

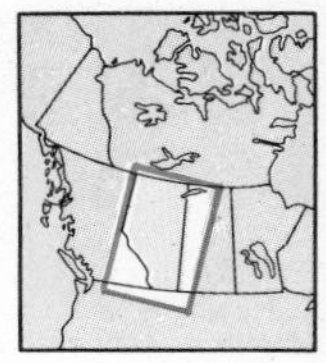

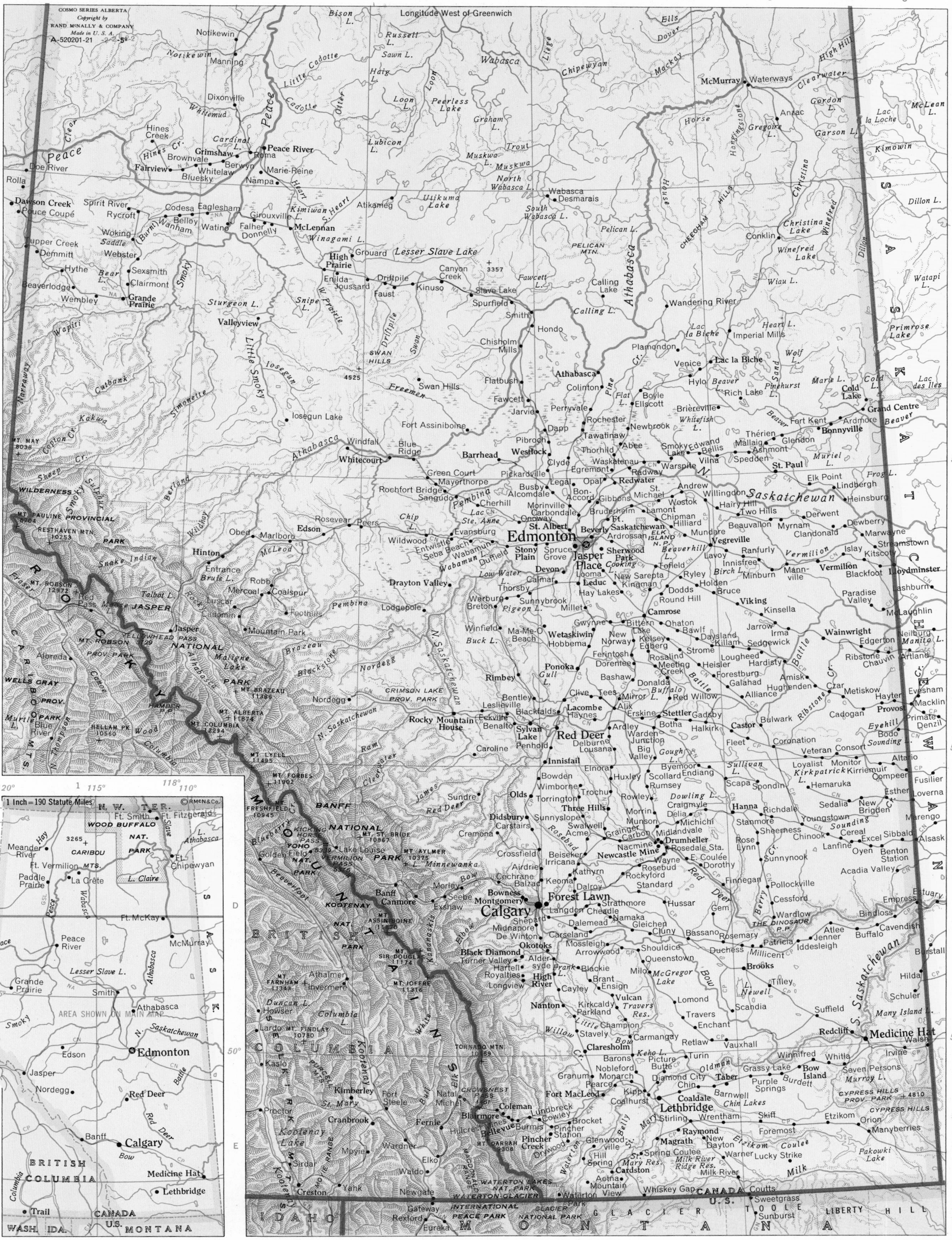

Oblique Cylindrical Projection
SCALE 1:3,110,000 1 Inch = 49 Statute Miles

Statute Miles

Kilometers

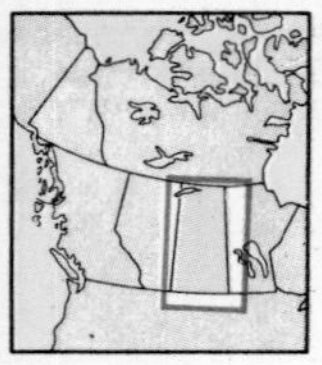

SASKATCHEWAN

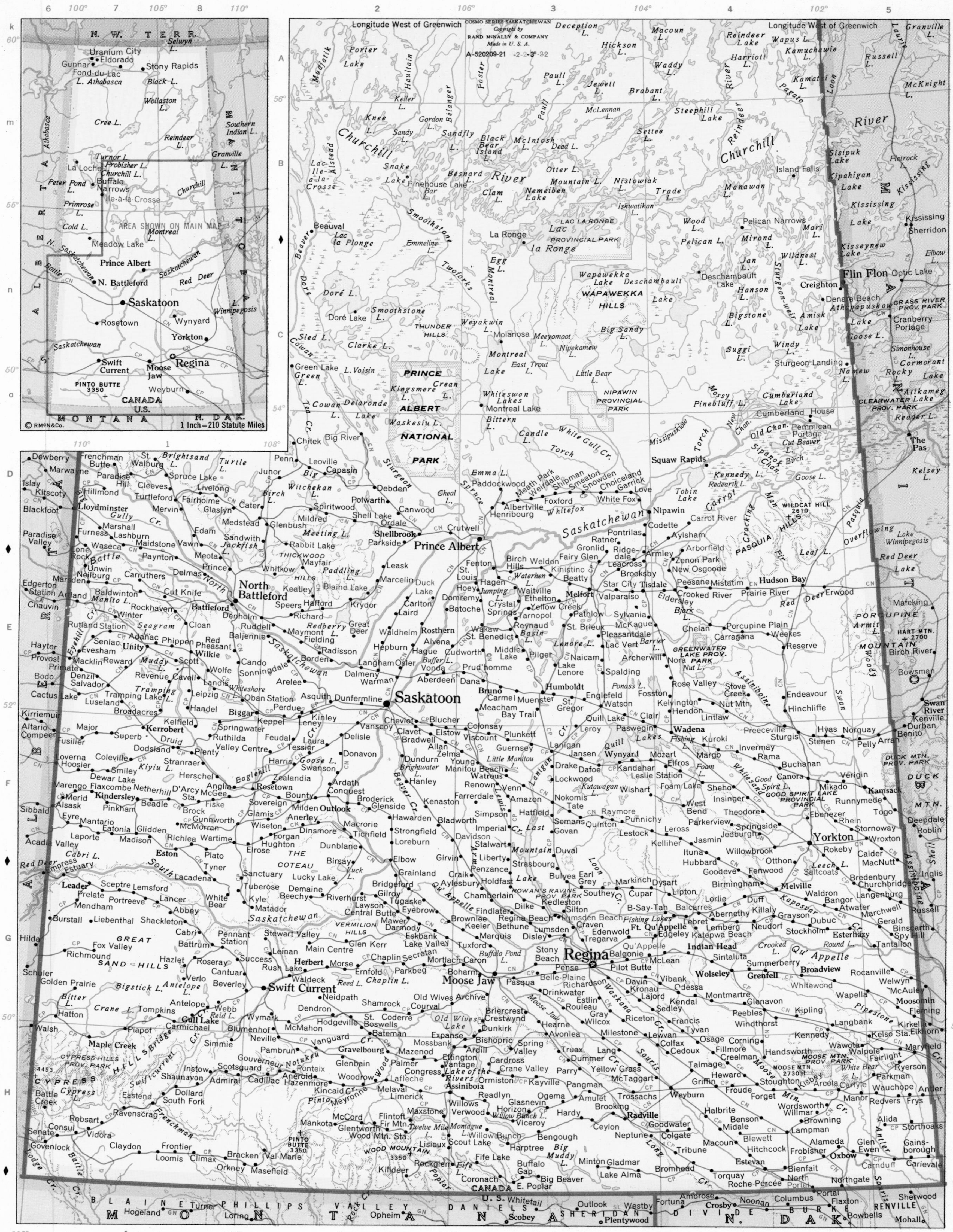

Statute Miles 10 0 10 20 30 40 50 60
Kilometers 10 0 20 40 60 80

Oblique Cylindrical Projection
SCALE 1:2,827,000   1 Inch = 44 Statute Miles

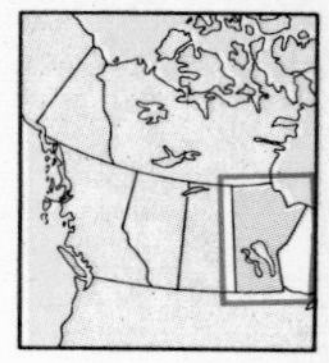

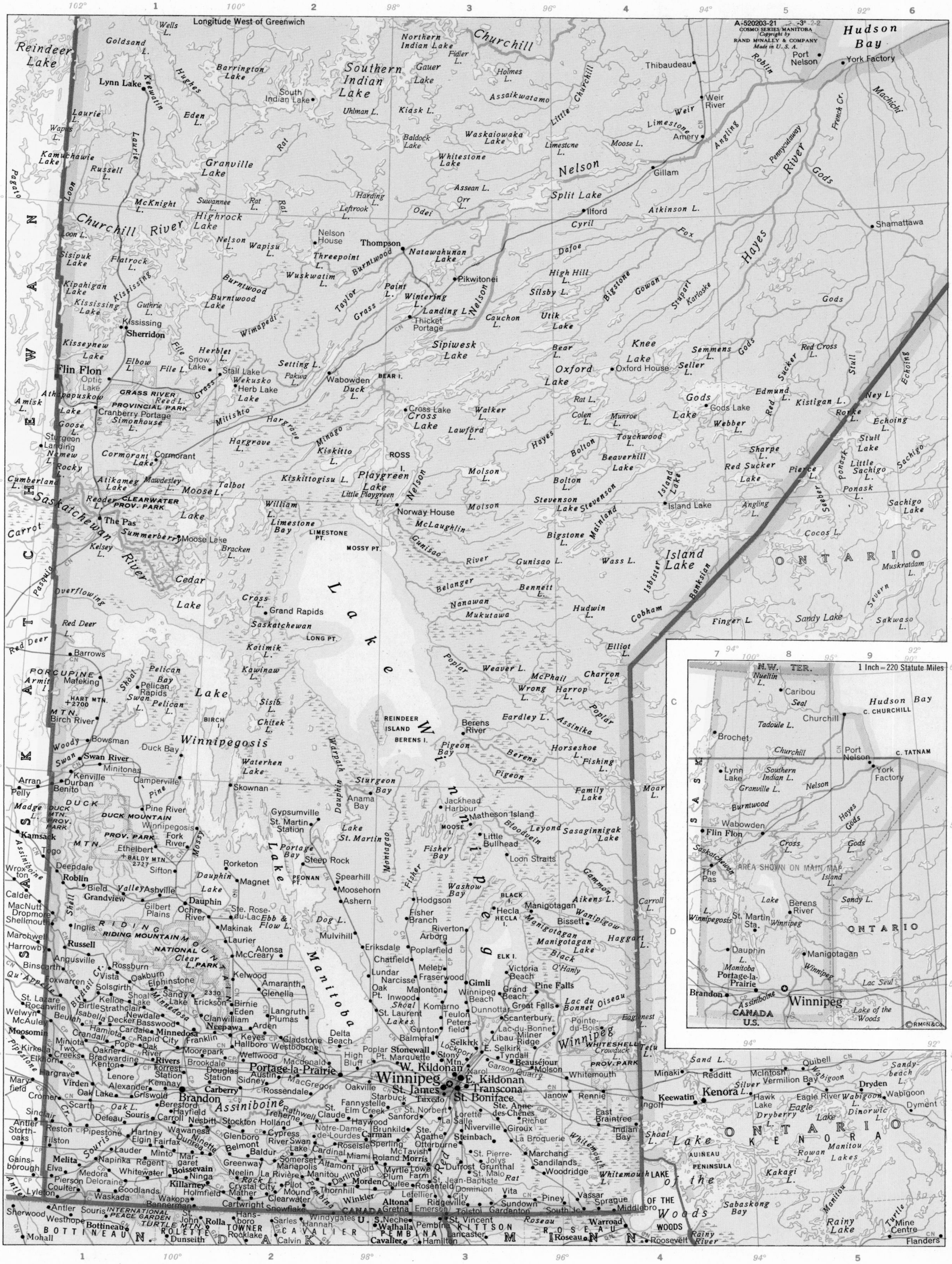

Oblique Cylindrical Projection
SCALE 1:3,167,000 1 Inch = 50 Statute Miles

Statute Miles
10 0 10 20 30 40 50 60 70

Kilometers
10 0 10 20 40 60 80 100

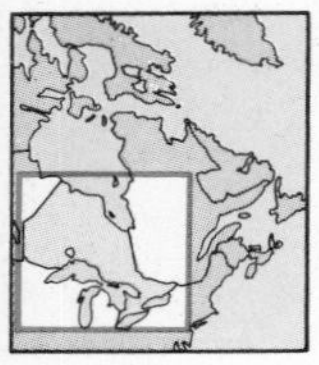

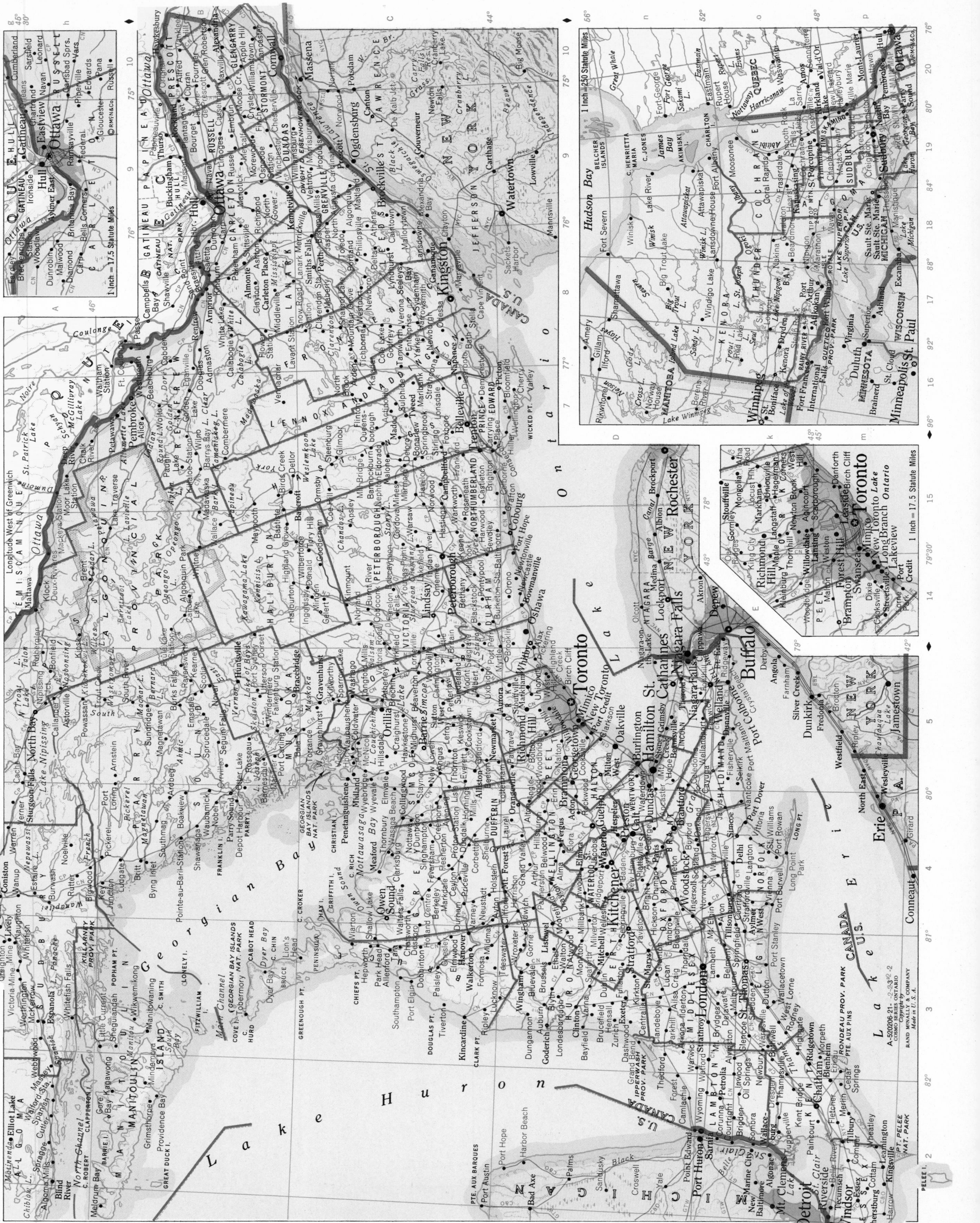

ONTARIO

Statute Miles
Kilometers

Oblique Cylindrical Projection
SCALE 1:2,226,000 1 Inch = 35 Statute Miles

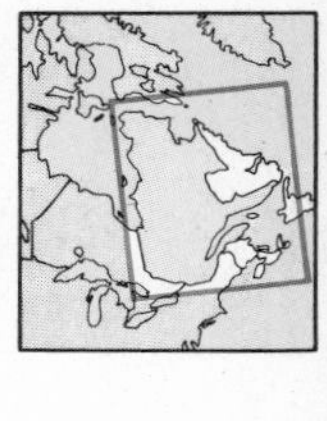

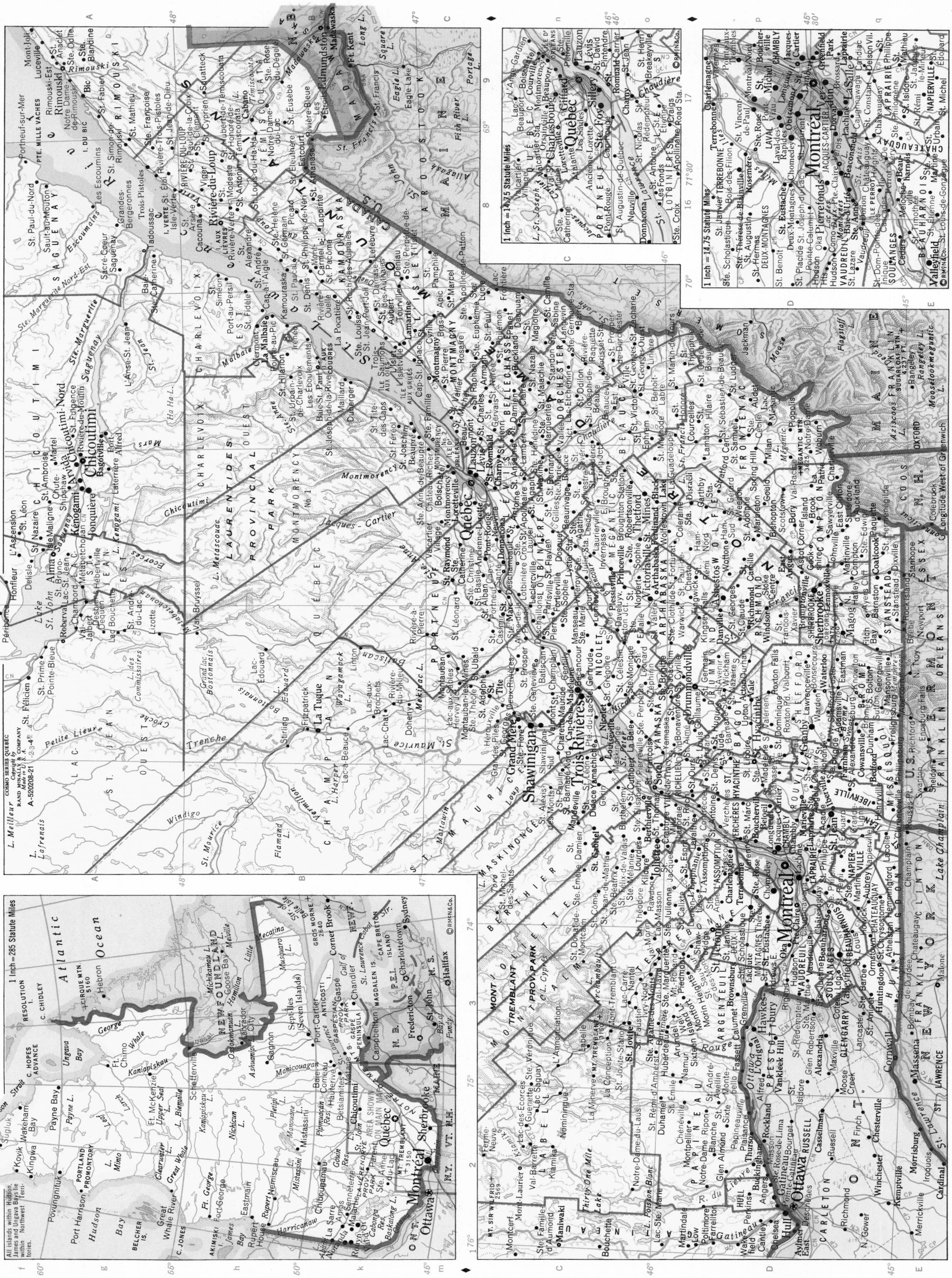

Oblique Cylindrical Projection
SCALE 1:1,929,000 1 Inch = 30.5 Statute Miles

Statute Miles

Kilometers

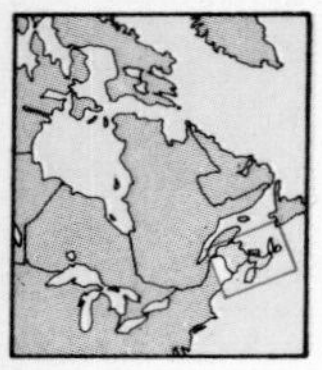

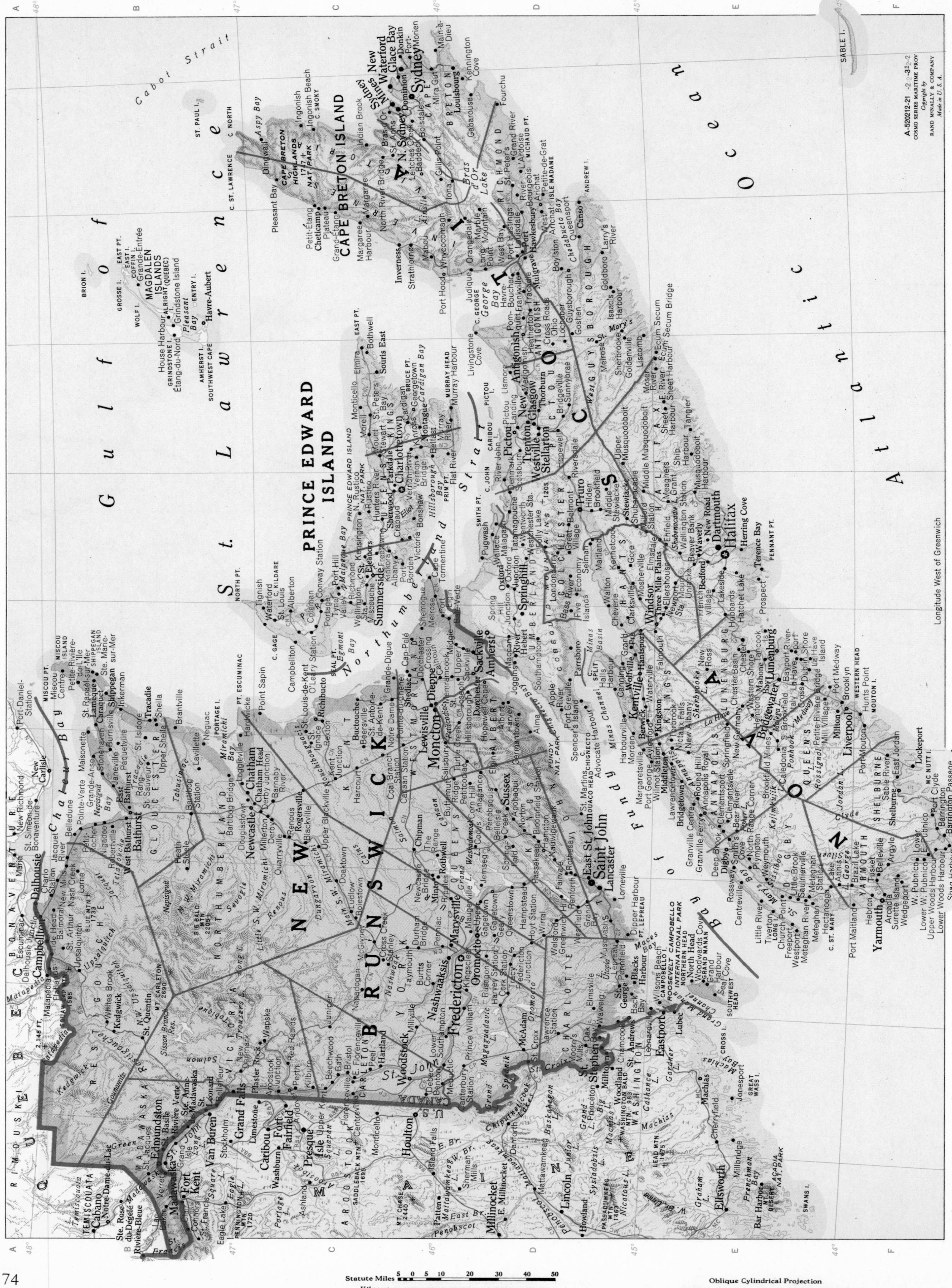

PRINCE EDWARD ISLAND

CAPE BRETON ISLAND

N E W   B R U N S W I C K

Gulf of St. Lawrence

Cabot Strait

Atlantic Ocean

Bay of Fundy

Northumberland Strait

Chaleur Bay

MAGDALEN ISLANDS (QUEBEC)

CANADA
U.S.

Statute Miles
Kilometers

Oblique Cylindrical Projection
SCALE 1:2,312,000   1 Inch = 36.5 Statute Miles

A-500212-21
COSMO SERIES MARITIME PROV
Copyright by
RAND M9NALLY COMPANY
Made in U.S.A.

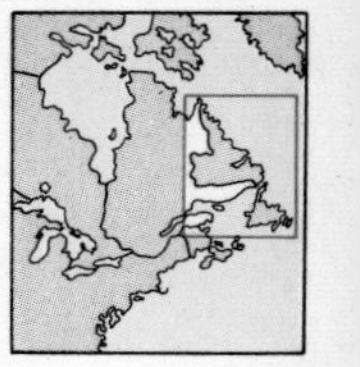

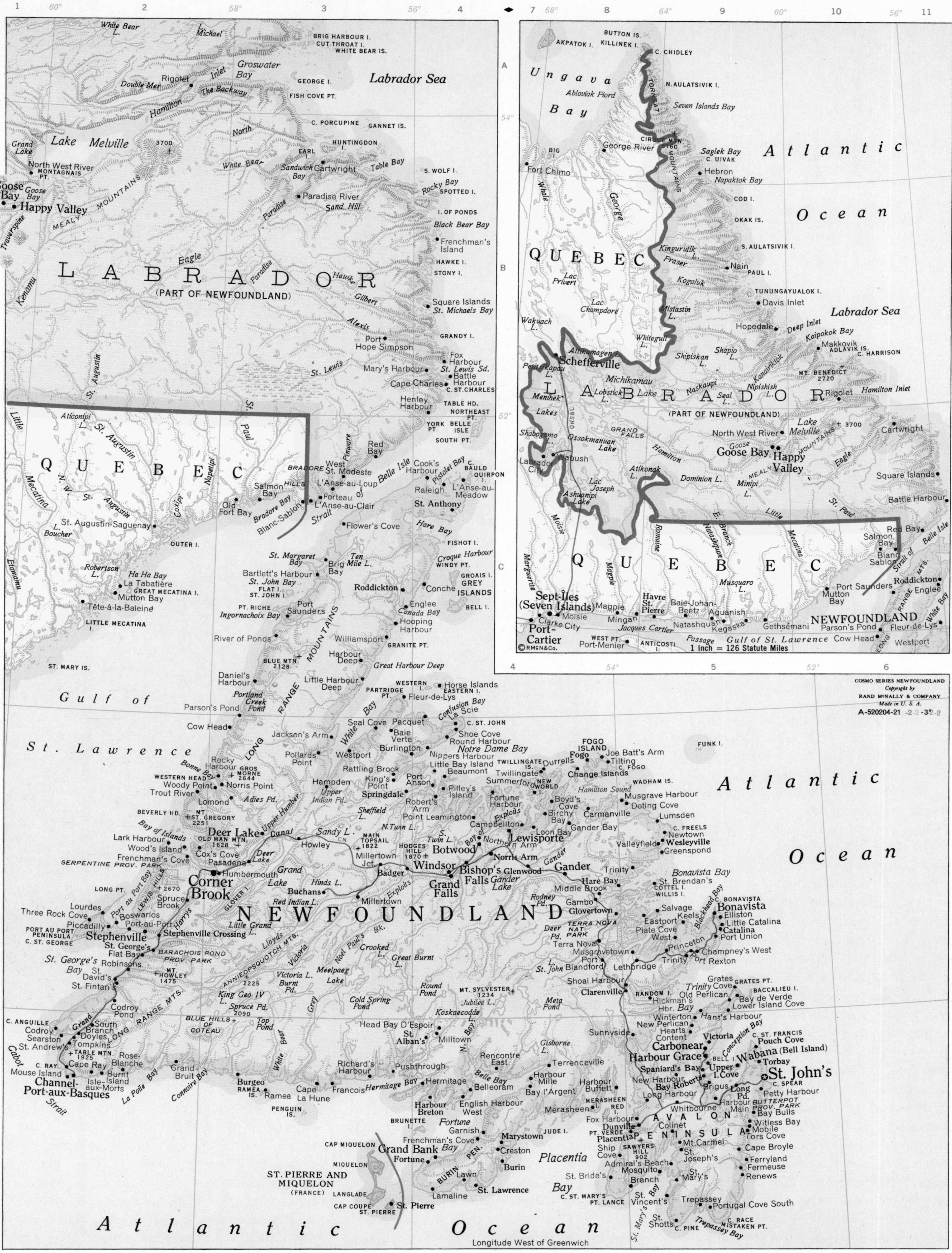

Lambert Conformal Conic Projection
SCALE 1 : 3,000,000 1 Inch = 47 Statute Miles

Statute Miles 5 0 5 10 20 30 40 50 60
Kilometers 5 0 5 10 20 30 40 50 60 70 80

THE UNITED STATES

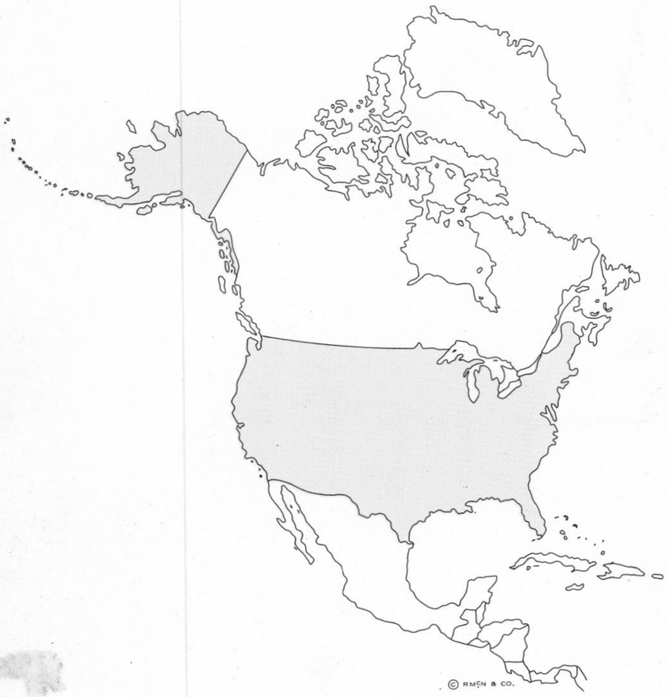

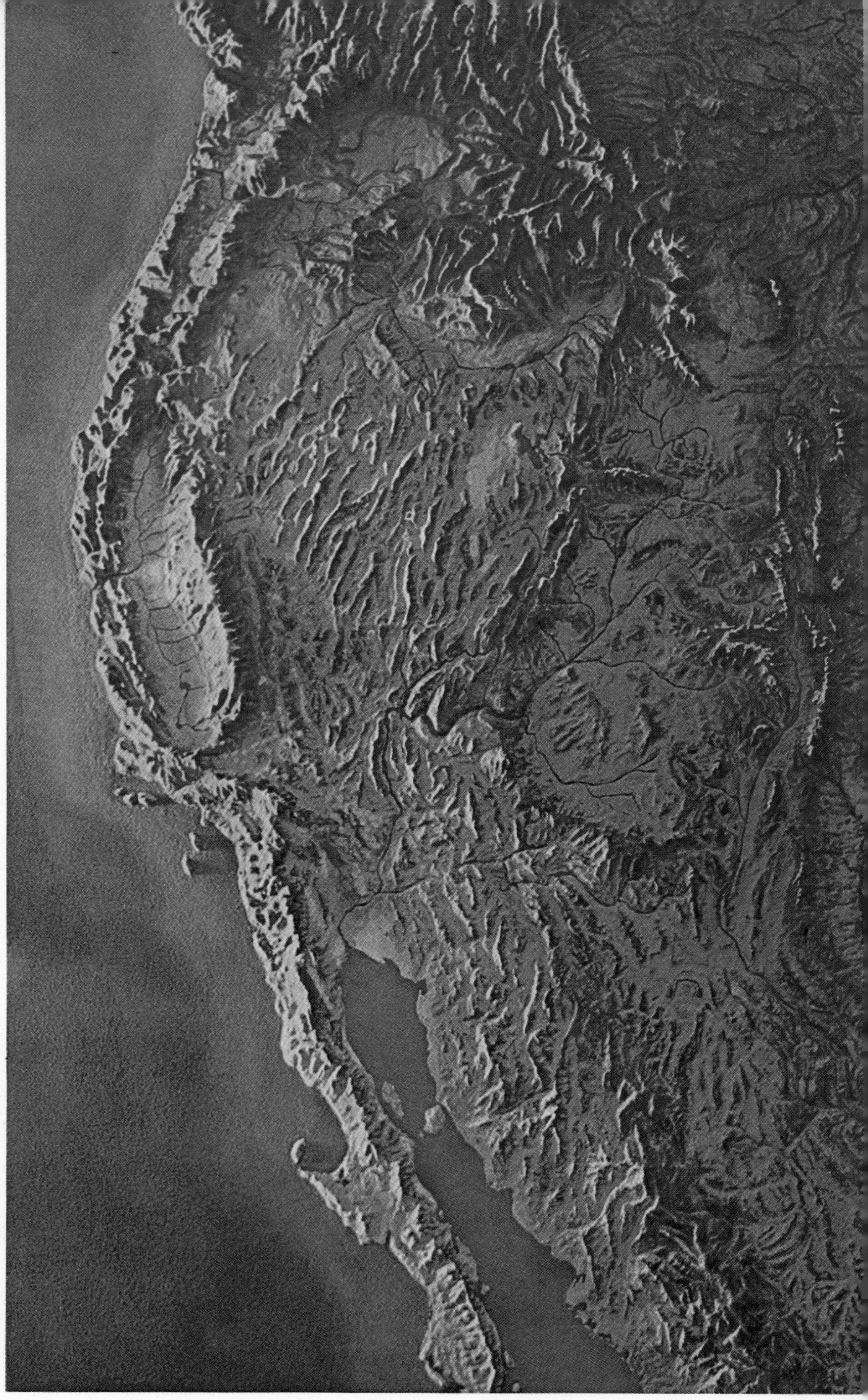

Today the world's strongest and most prosperous major power, the United States, has developed in less than two centuries from a modest group of British colonies huddled along the Atlantic coastline of a new and undeveloped continent. This tremendous expansion in population, area, wealth, and power has had its roots partly in the richness of the natural resources America has had to offer to a new and growing nation. But perhaps equally important have been the human resources of initiative, political stability, and religious faith brought by America's first settlers and augmented by later arrivals from the Old World.

The landscape of the United States today reflects many patterns. First, there is the fundamental pattern of the terrain from east to west—the Atlantic Coastal Plain, the low but rugged Appalachian Highlands, the great interior lowland, drained by the Mississippi and its tributaries and merging on the south into the Gulf Coastal Plain, the long chain of the Rockies, the high and arid Great Basin with its many ranges and plateaus, and finally the Cascades, Sierras, and the other mountains and valleys of the Pacific coast. On this variety of terrain, the forces of climate and natural vegetation have combined to produce different soils. Man, in turn, has developed different kinds of farming in response to the particular conditions of each section—dairying along the northern frontier in the East; corn and livestock on the rich soils of the Midwest; cotton, orchards, or cattle in the South; wheat on the drier lands of the Great Plains; cattle and sheep raising in the more rugged, drier areas of the West; and special fruit and vegetable crops in scattered local areas, but especially in the Far West and the South.

Just as the pattern of American agriculture reflects that of climate and soils, so does that of American manufacturing reflect the distribution of natural resources. Here the

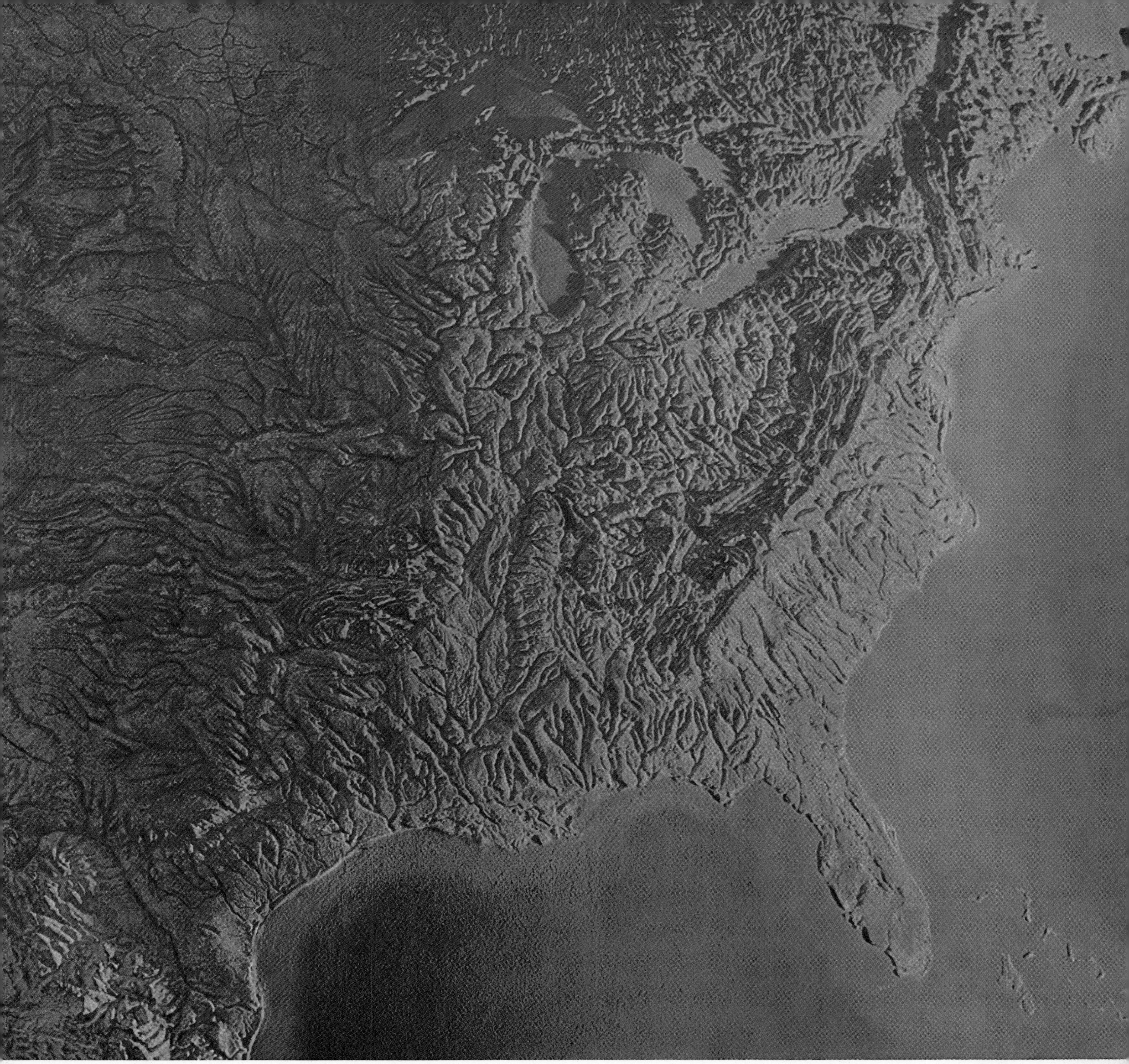

pattern becomes more complex, since industries use many raw materials, and nearness to markets today is more important for many factories than nearness to supplies.

Roughly two-thirds of U.S. manufacturing is concentrated in the northeast quarter of the nation. This degree of localization reflects the interplay of many factors, including the early start of many industries in or near Boston, New York, Philadelphia; resources of water power, coal, and iron ore in the Appalachians-Great Lakes region; accessibility to the major harbors of the Atlantic seaboard and through them contact with Europe; and convenient inland water and rail routes across the Appalachians and Midwest, focusing in New York on the east and Chicago on the west.

Recent times have seen the South and Far West making giant strides in the development of manufacturing, and the gap between these areas and the manufacturing belt has narrowed, especially as their number of consumers has increased.

BRITISH COLUMBIA
ALBERTA
SASKATCHEWAN
MANITOBA
WASHINGTON
OREGON
CALIFORNIA
NEVADA
IDAHO
MONTANA
WYOMING
UTAH
COLORADO
ARIZONA
NEW MEXICO
NORTH DAKOTA
SOUTH DAKOTA
NEBRASKA
KANSAS
OKLAHOMA
TEXAS
SONORA
CHIHUAHUA
COAHUILA
NUEVO LEON
TAMAULIPAS
BAJA CALIFORNIA
Pacific Ocean
Gulf of California
GREAT BASIN
Edmonton
Calgary
Vancouver
Victoria
Seattle
Tacoma
Spokane
Portland
Salem
Boise
Helena
Great Falls
Butte
Billings
Salt Lake City
Ogden
Cheyenne
Denver
Pueblo
Colorado Sprs
Santa Fe
Albuquerque
El Paso
Ciudad Juárez
Phoenix
Tucson
San Diego
Los Angeles
Long Beach
San Bernardino
Sacramento
San Francisco
Oakland
San Jose
Fresno
Reno
Carson City
Las Vegas
Bismarck
Pierre
Lincoln
Omaha
Topeka
Wichita
Oklahoma City
Tulsa
Amarillo
Lubbock
Ft. Worth
Dallas
Austin
San Antonio
Monterrey
Chihuahua
Winnipeg
Regina
Saskatoon
Same Scale as Main Map
HAWAIIAN ISLANDS
Honolulu
Hilo
ALASKA
Anchorage
Fairbanks
Juneau
Bering Sea
Gulf of Alaska
ALEUTIAN ISLANDS
1 inch = 378 Statute Miles
1 inch = 48 Statute Miles
A-520500-21
COSMO SERIES UNITED STATES
Copyright by RAND McNALLY & COMPANY
Made in U. S. A.
Statute Miles
Kilometers

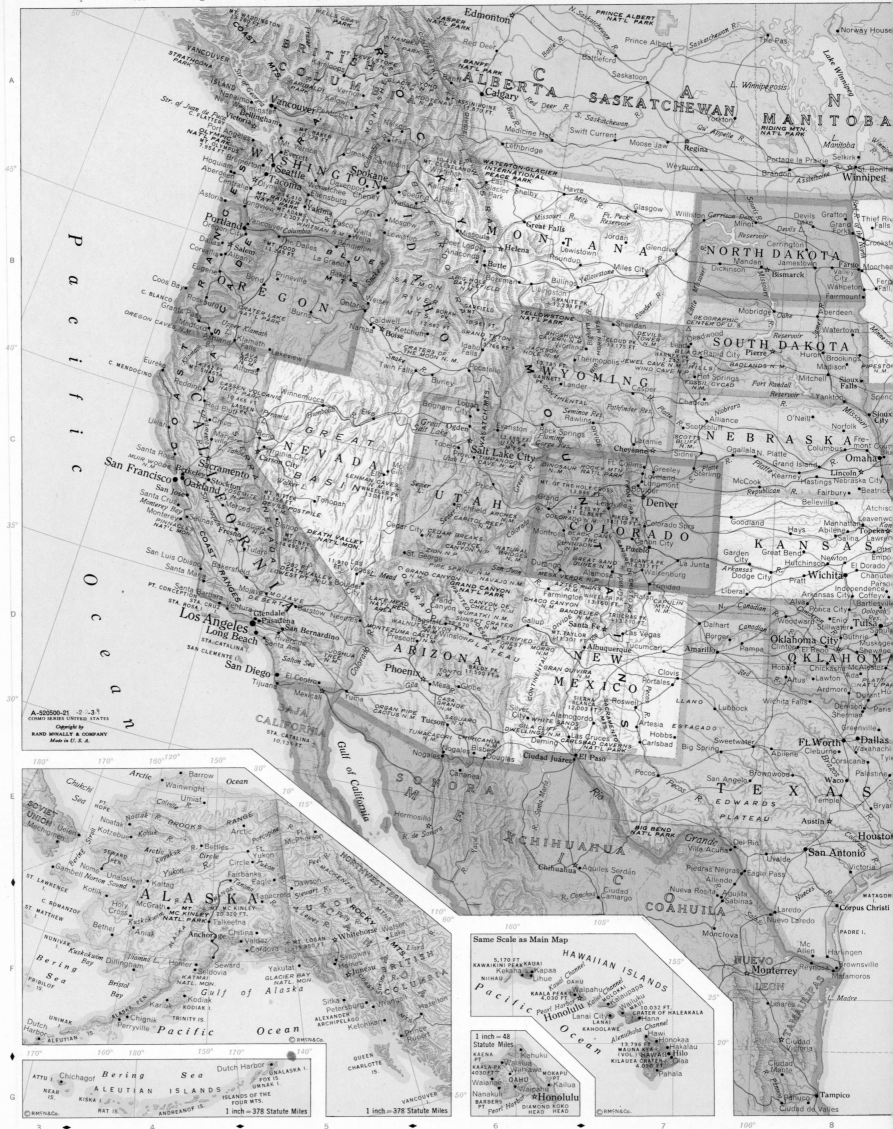

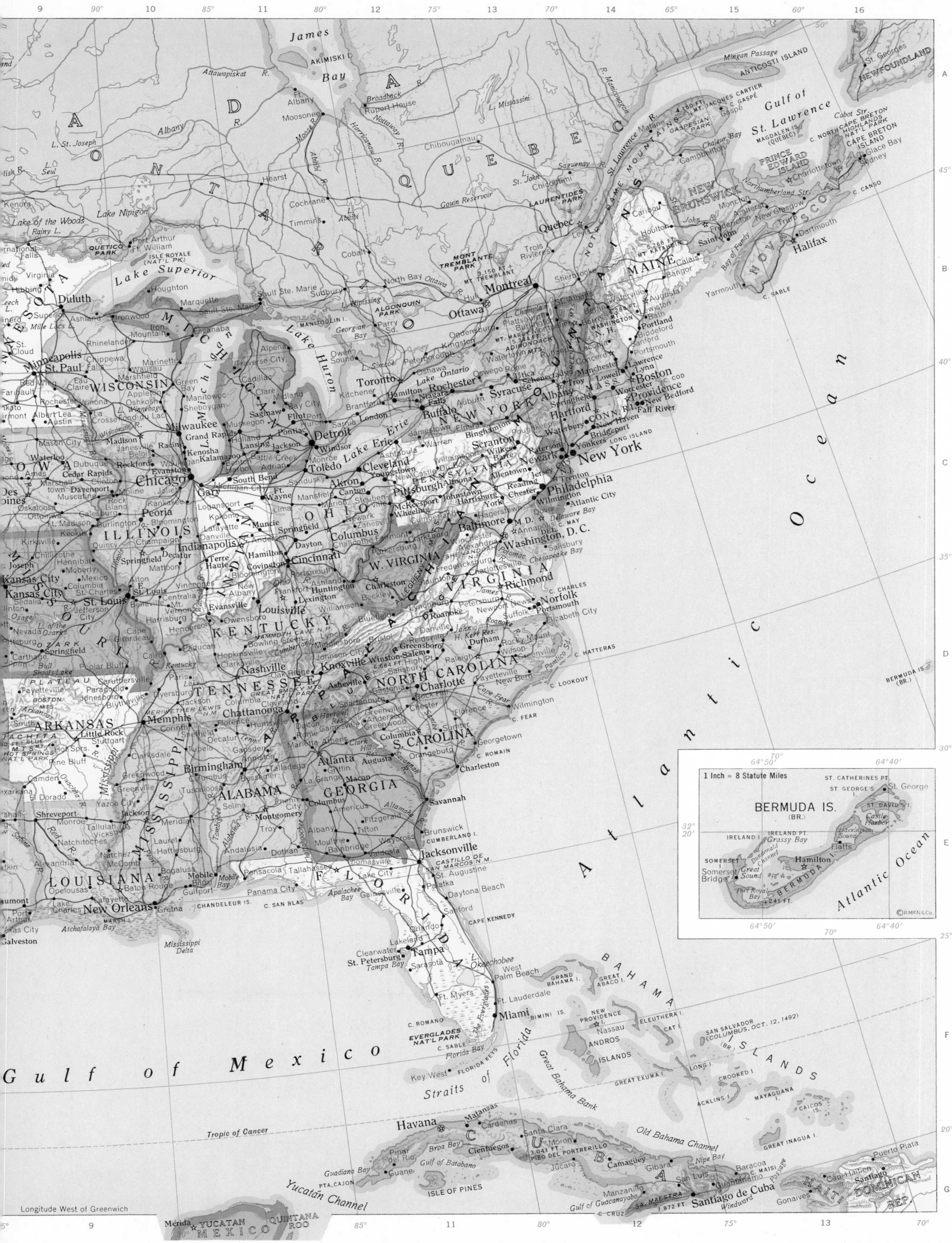

Lambert Conformal Conic Projection
SCALE 1:12,000,000   1 Inch = 189 Statute Miles

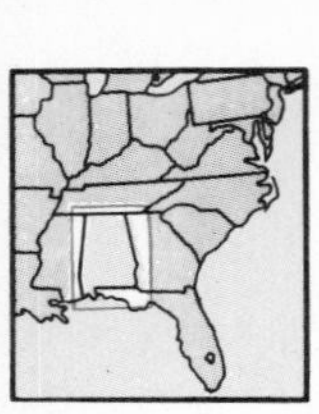

ALABAMA

Gulf of Mexico

Longitude West of Greenwich

A-520501-21 · 34-1-4
COSMO SERIES 34 ALABAMA
Copyright by
RAND McNALLY & COMPANY
Made in U.S.A.

78

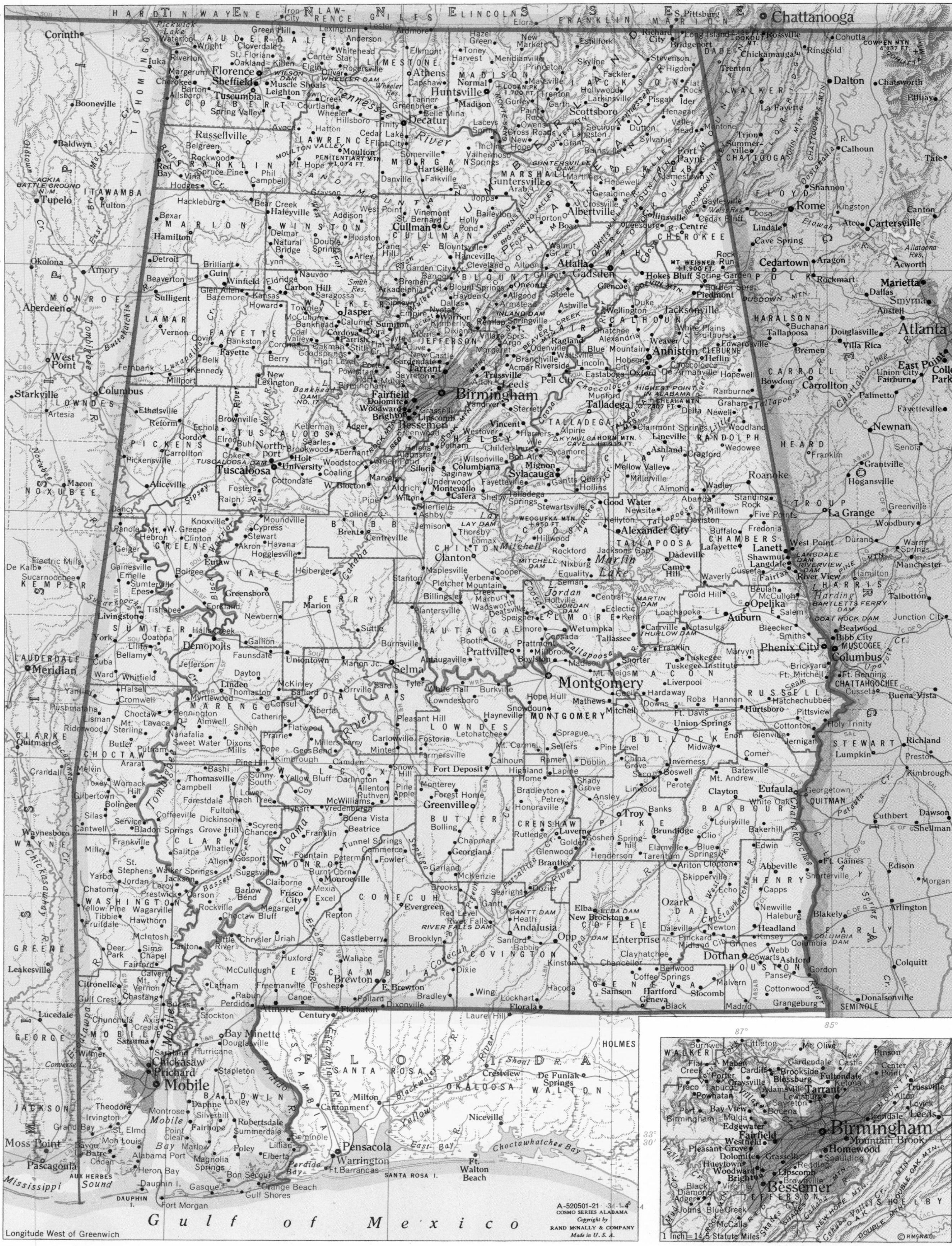

Statute Miles
5 0 5 10   20   30   40

Kilometers
5 0 5   15   25   35   45   55

Lambert Conformal Conic Projection
SCALE 1:1,831,000 1 Inch = 29 Statute Miles

1 Inch = 14.5 Statute Miles

Pacific Ocean

Arctic Ocean

Bering Sea

Gulf of Alaska

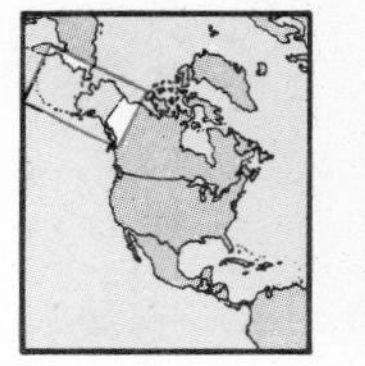

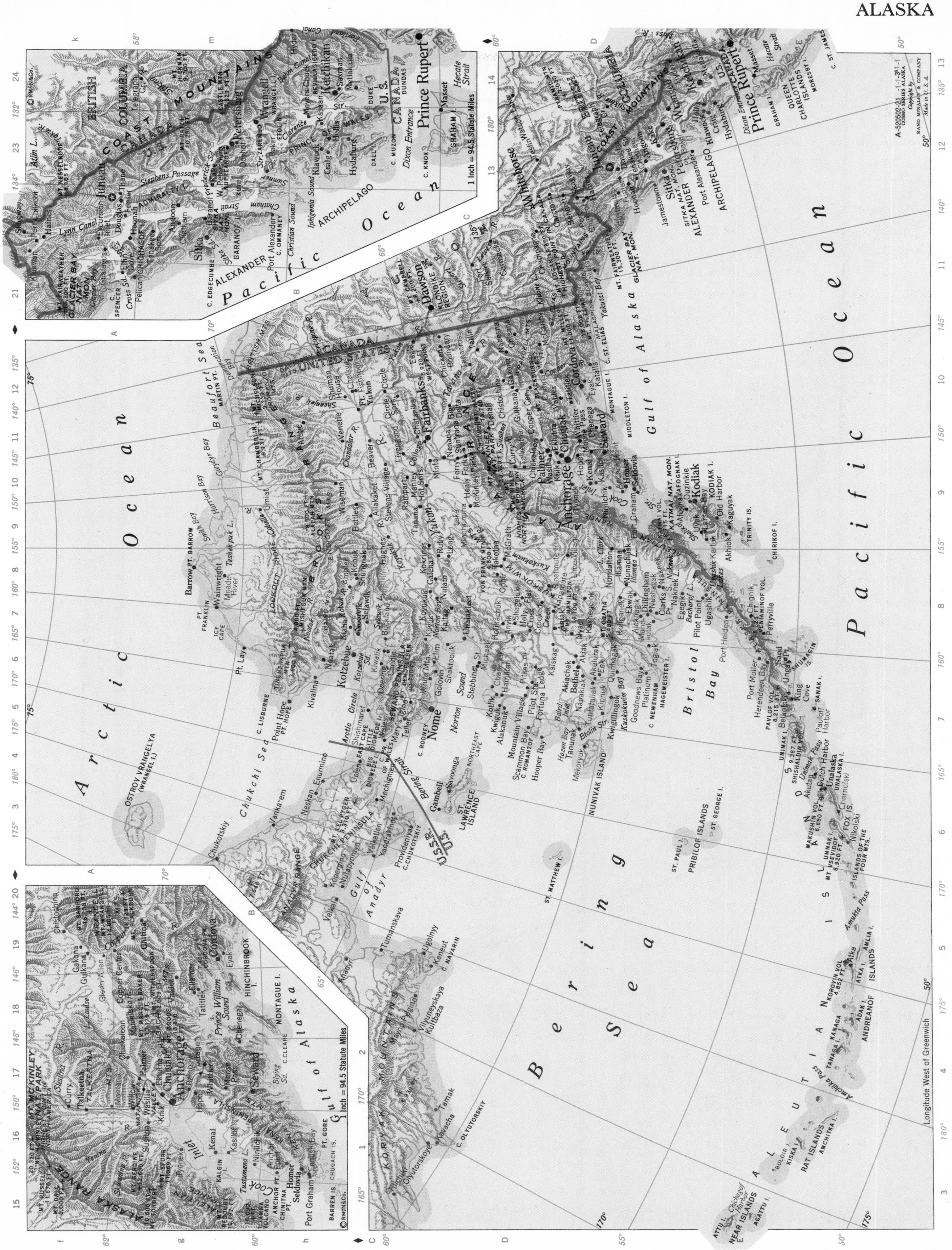

Polyconic Projection
SCALE 1:12,000,000 1 Inch = 189 Statute Miles

Statute Miles 50 25 0   50   100   150   200   250
Kilometers 50   0   100   200   300

Arizona

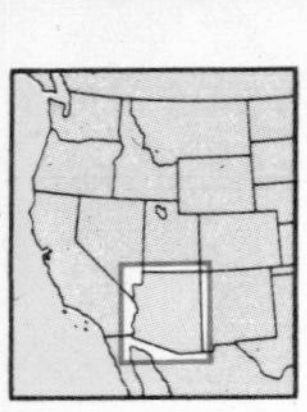

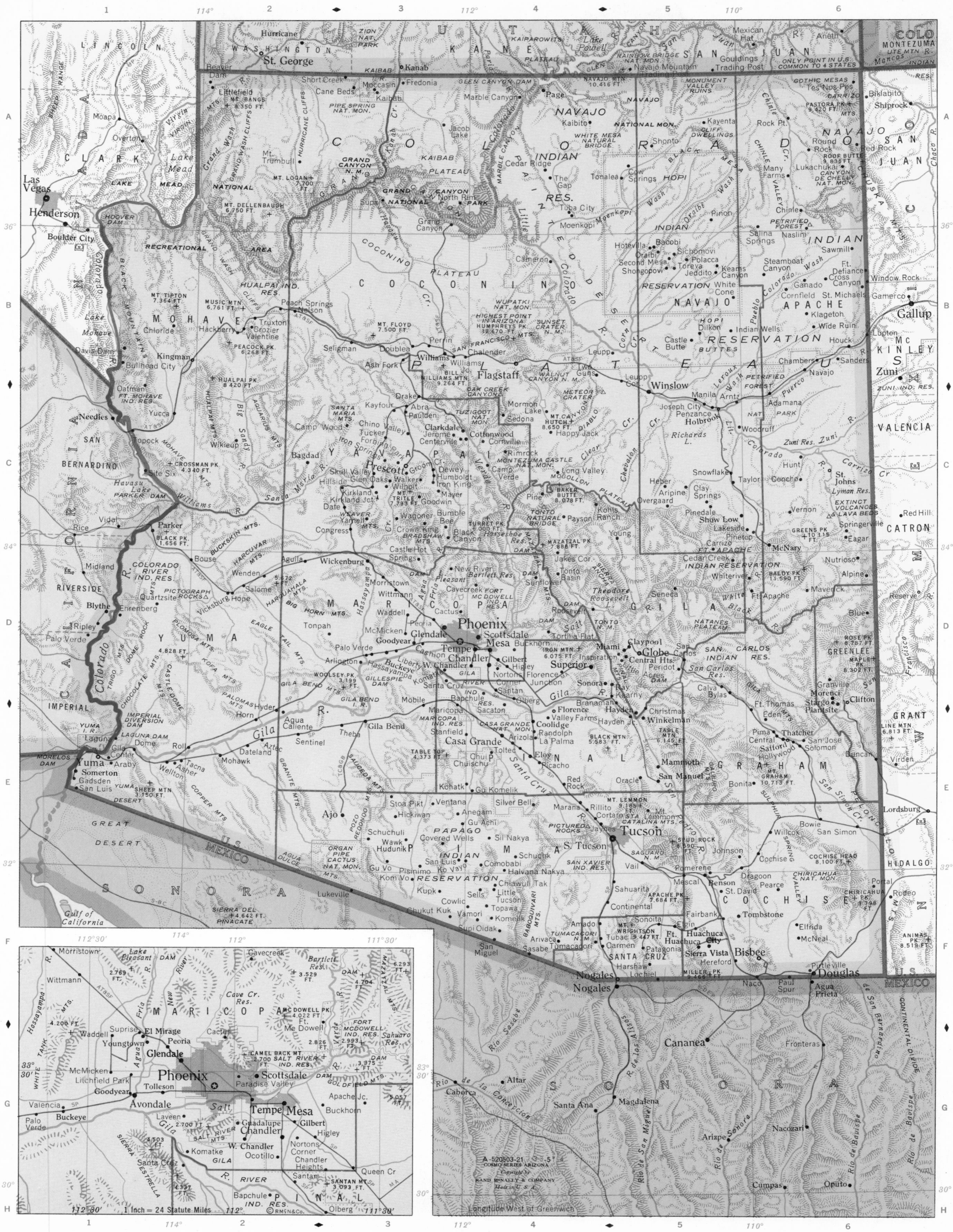

Statute Miles 10 0 10 20 30 40 50 60 70 80 90

Kilometers 10 0 10 20 30 40 50 60 70 80 90 100 120

Lambert Conformal Conic Projection
SCALE 1:2,725,000 1 Inch = 43 Statute Miles

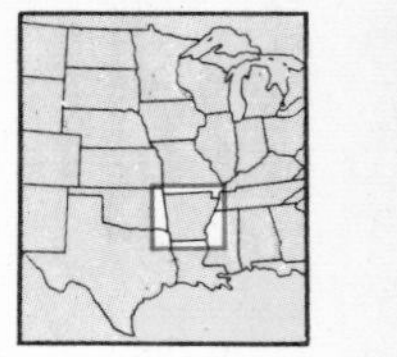

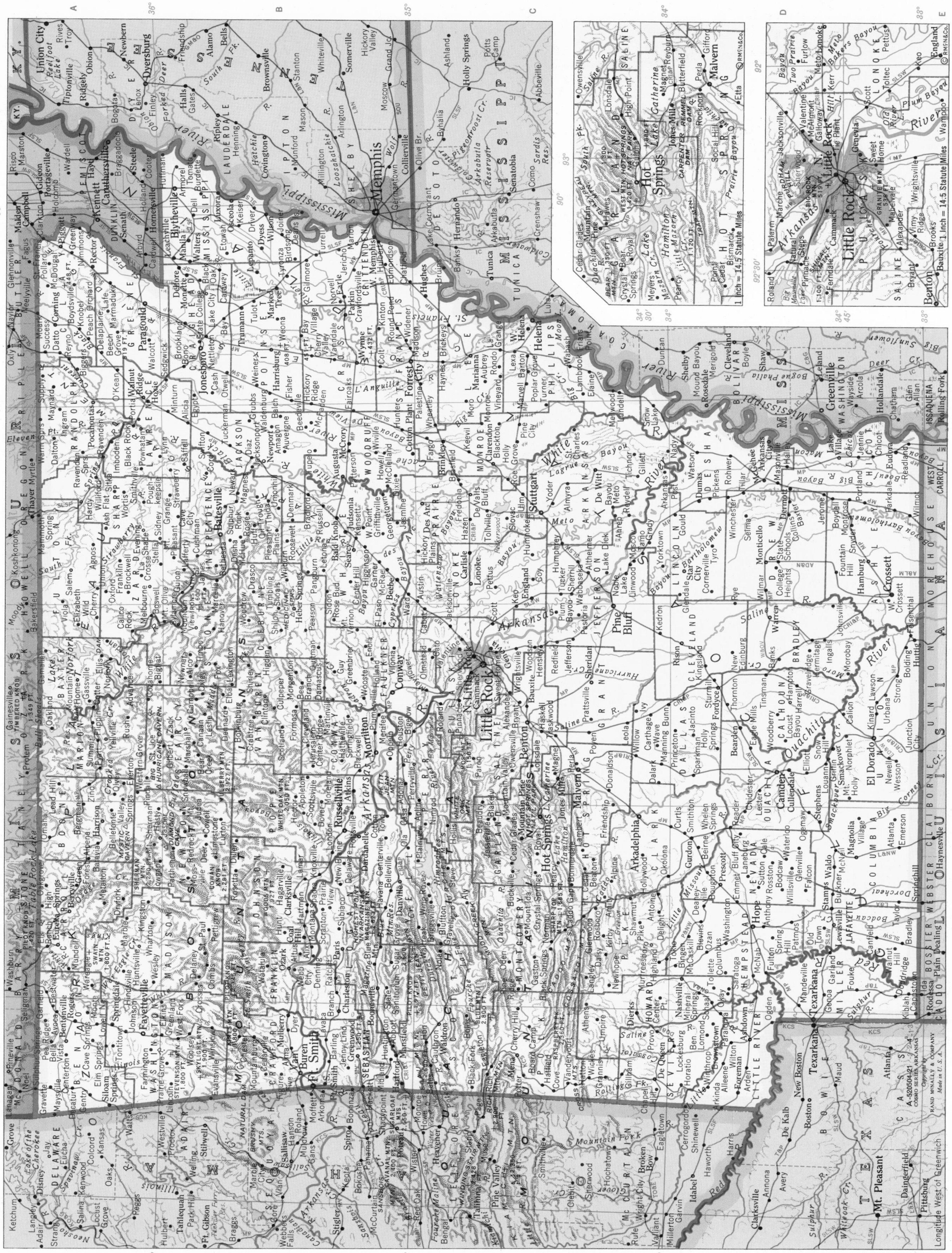

Lambert Conformal Conic Projection
SCALE 1:1,832,000 1 Inch = 29 Statute Miles

Statute Miles
Kilometers

CALIFORNIA

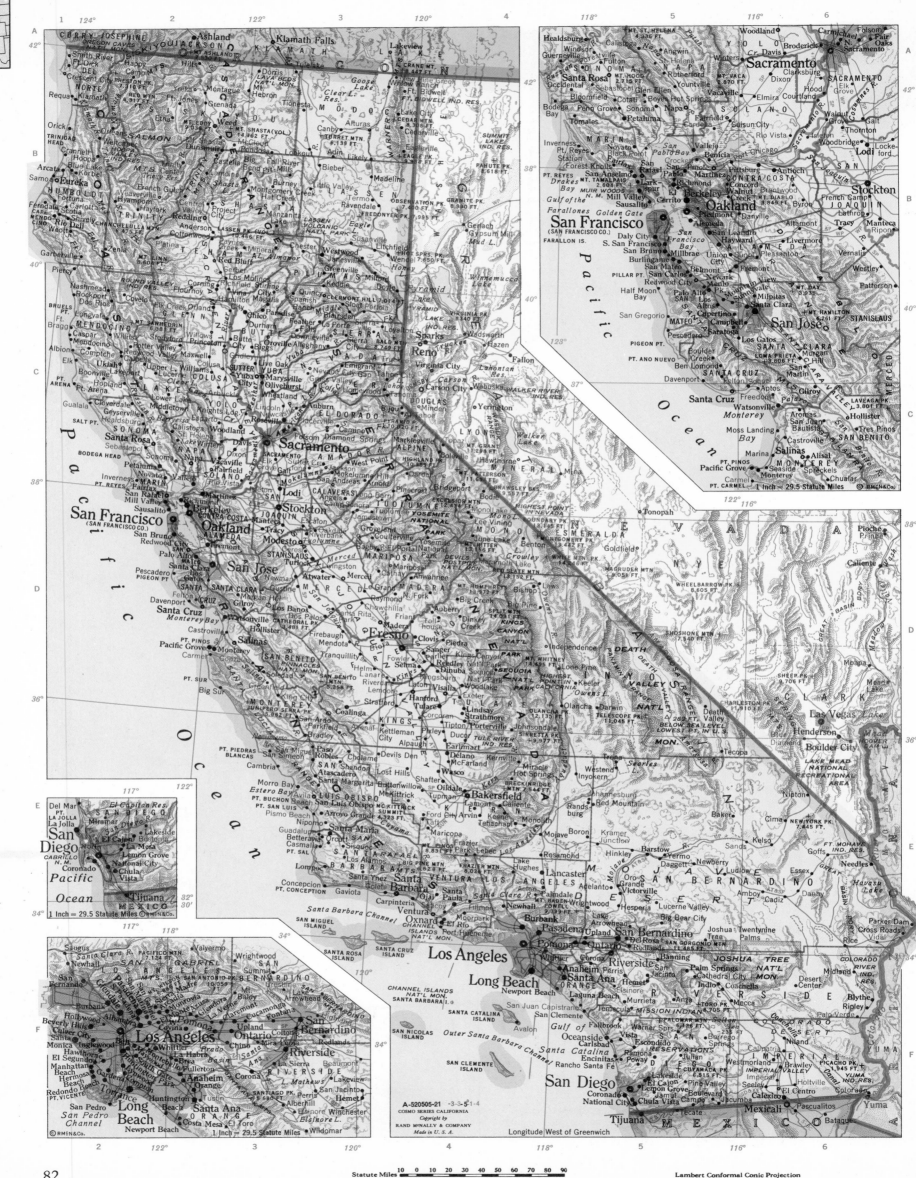

Statute Miles 10 0 10 20 30 40 50 60 70 80 90

Kilometers 10 0 10 20 40 60 80 100 120

Lambert Conformal Conic Projection
SCALE 1:3,733,000 1 Inch = 59 Statute Miles

A-520505-21 -3-3-5-1-4
COSMO SERIES CALIFORNIA
Copyright by
RAND MCNALLY & COMPANY
Made in U.S.A.   Longitude West of Greenwich

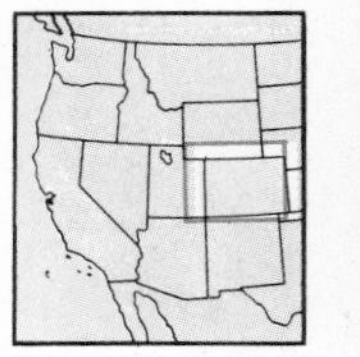

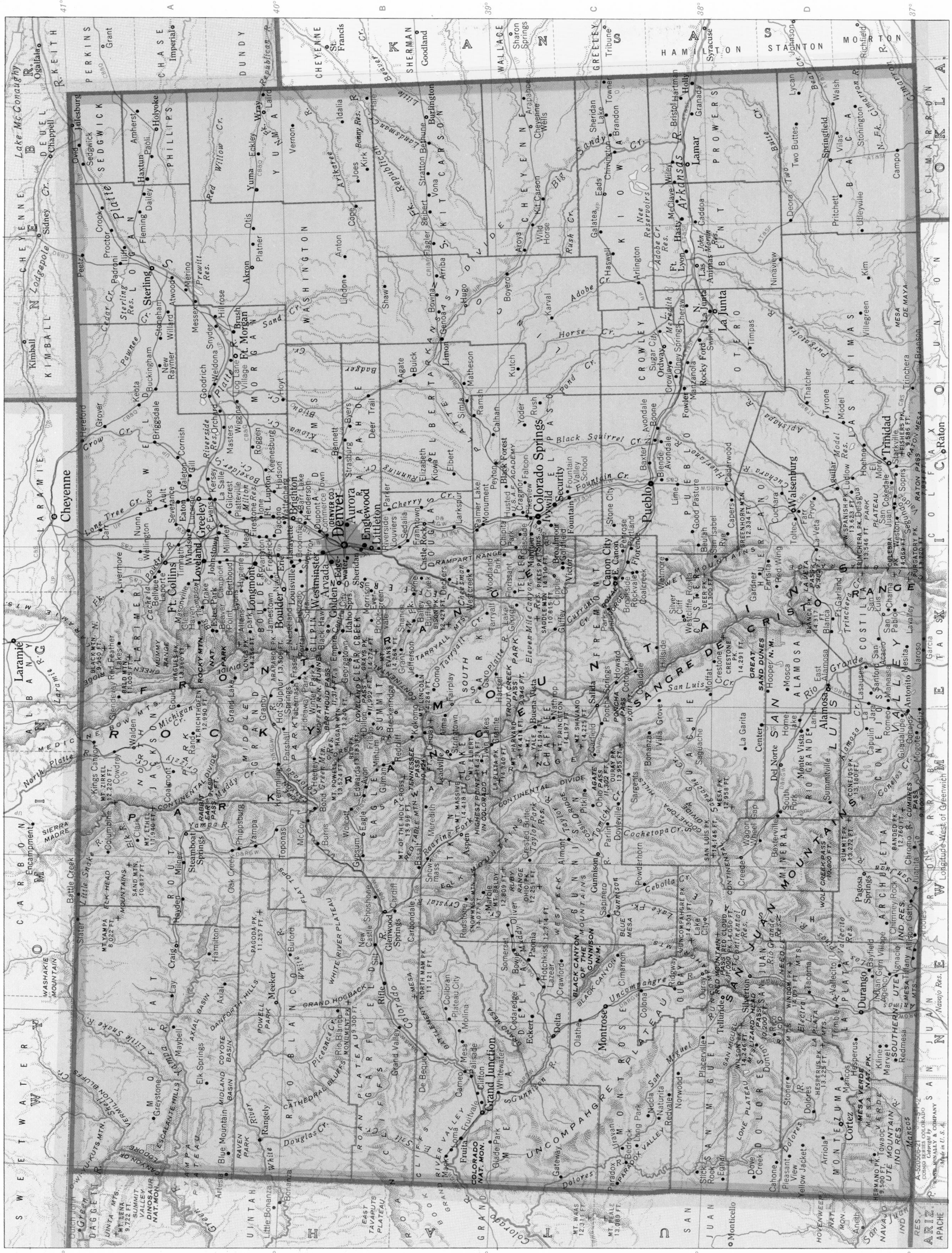

Lambert Conformal Conic Projection
SCALE 1:2,186,000   1 Inch = 34.5 Statute Miles

Statute Miles
Kilometers

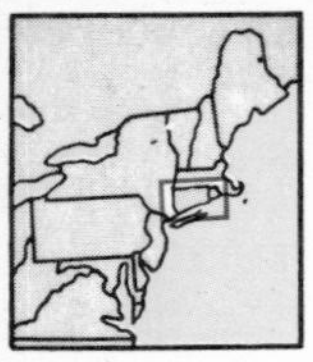

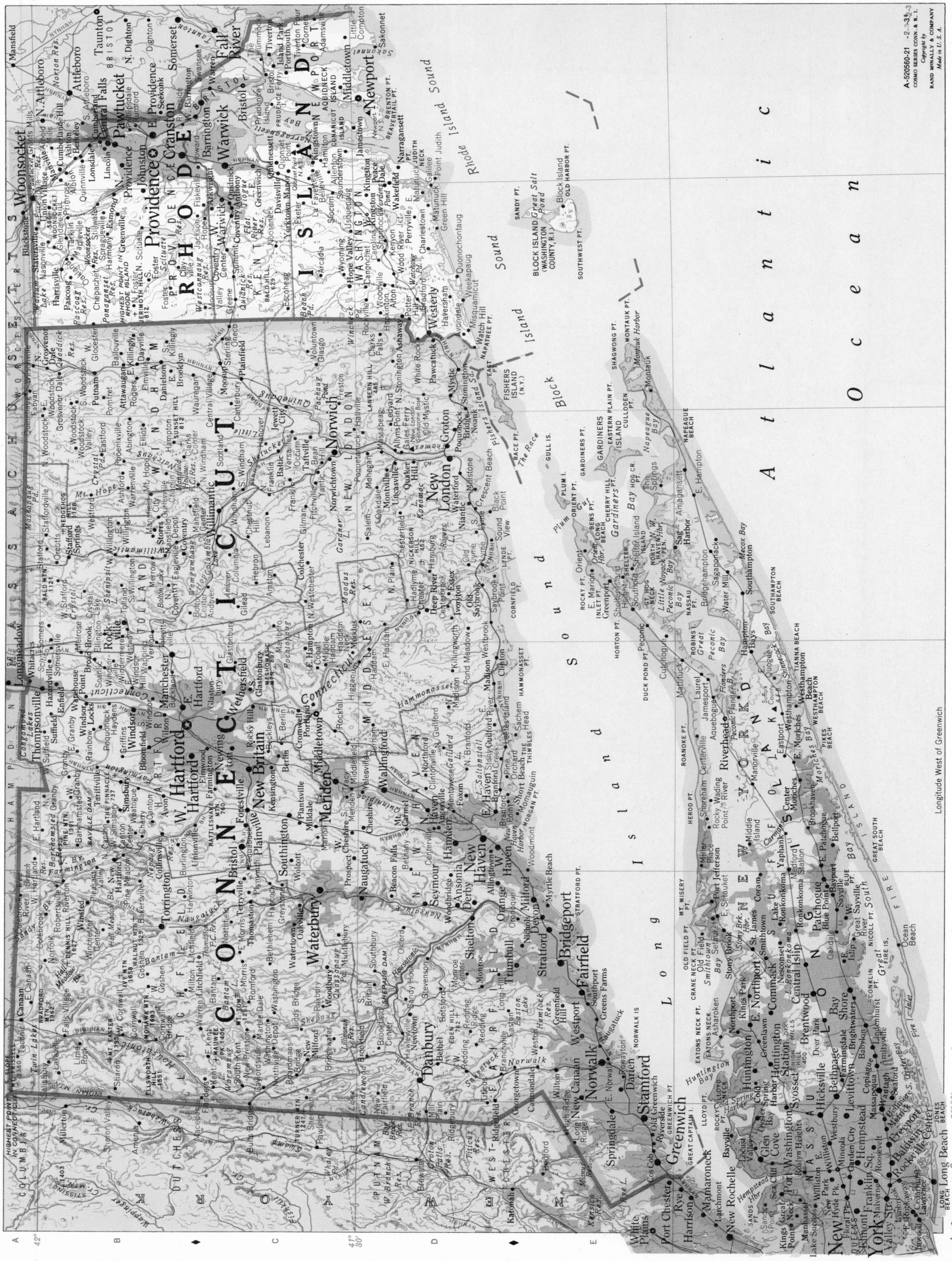

CONNECTICUT AND RHODE ISLAND

Statute Miles

Kilometers

Lambert Conformal Conic Projection
SCALE 1:731.000 1 Inch = 11.5 Statute Miles

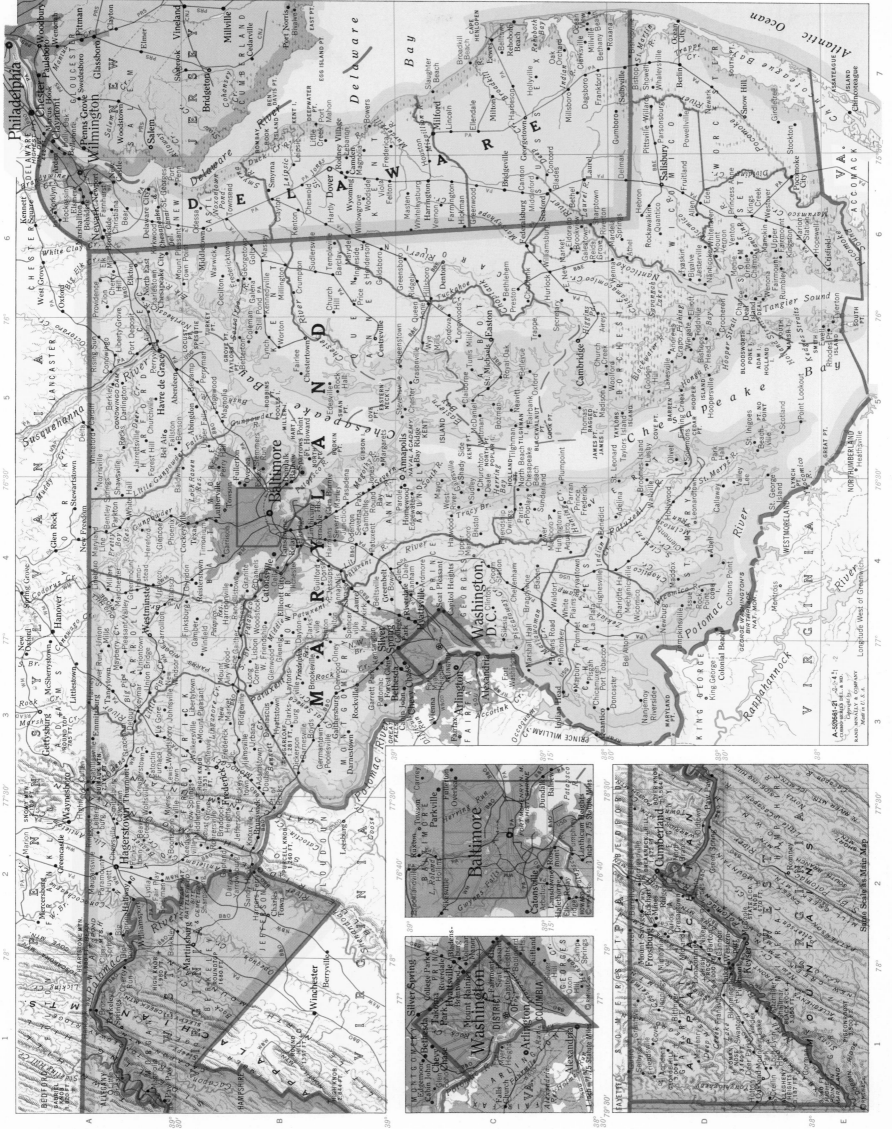

Lambert Conformal Conic Projection
SCALE 1:985,000 1 Inch = 15.5 Statute Miles

Statute Miles
Kilometers

85

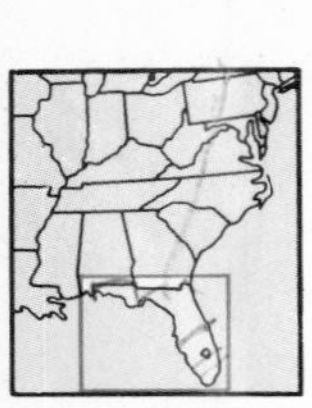

FLORIDA

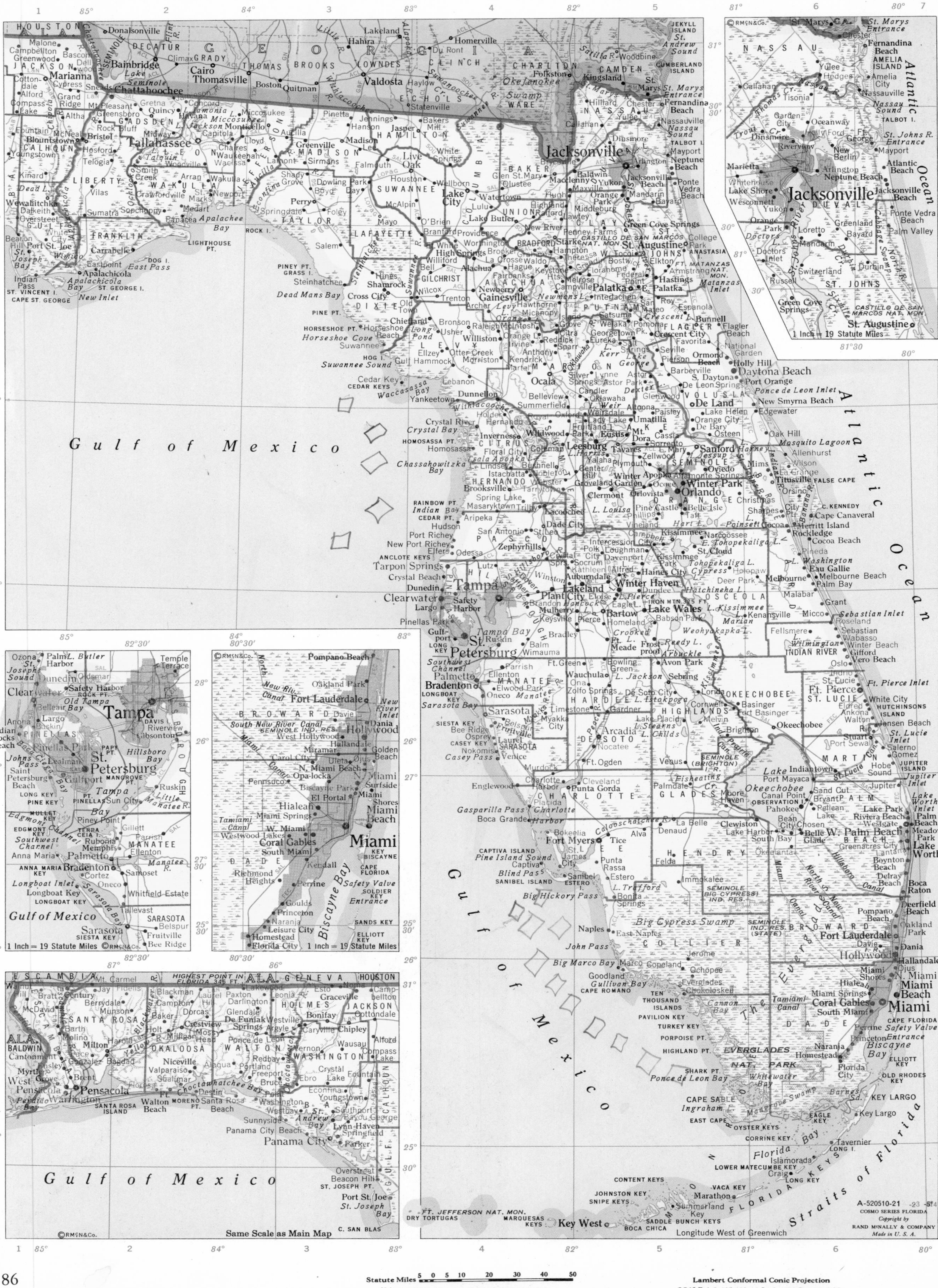

Gulf of Mexico
Atlantic Ocean
Straits of Florida
GEORGIA
ALA.
Jacksonville
St. Augustine
Tallahassee
Pensacola
Panama City
Gainesville
Ocala
Daytona Beach
Orlando
Tampa
St. Petersburg
Clearwater
Lakeland
Sarasota
Fort Myers
Naples
West Palm Beach
Fort Lauderdale
Hollywood
Miami
Miami Beach
Coral Gables
Key West
Lake Okeechobee
EVERGLADES NAT. PARK
Big Cypress Swamp
Florida Bay
FLORIDA KEYS
Same Scale as Main Map
1 Inch = 19 Statute Miles
A-520510-21
COSMO SERIES FLORIDA
Copyright by RAND McNALLY & COMPANY
Made in U. S. A.
Longitude West of Greenwich
Statute Miles
Kilometers
Lambert Conformal Conic Projection
SCALE 1:2,425,000 1 Inch = 38 Statute Miles

ATLANTA

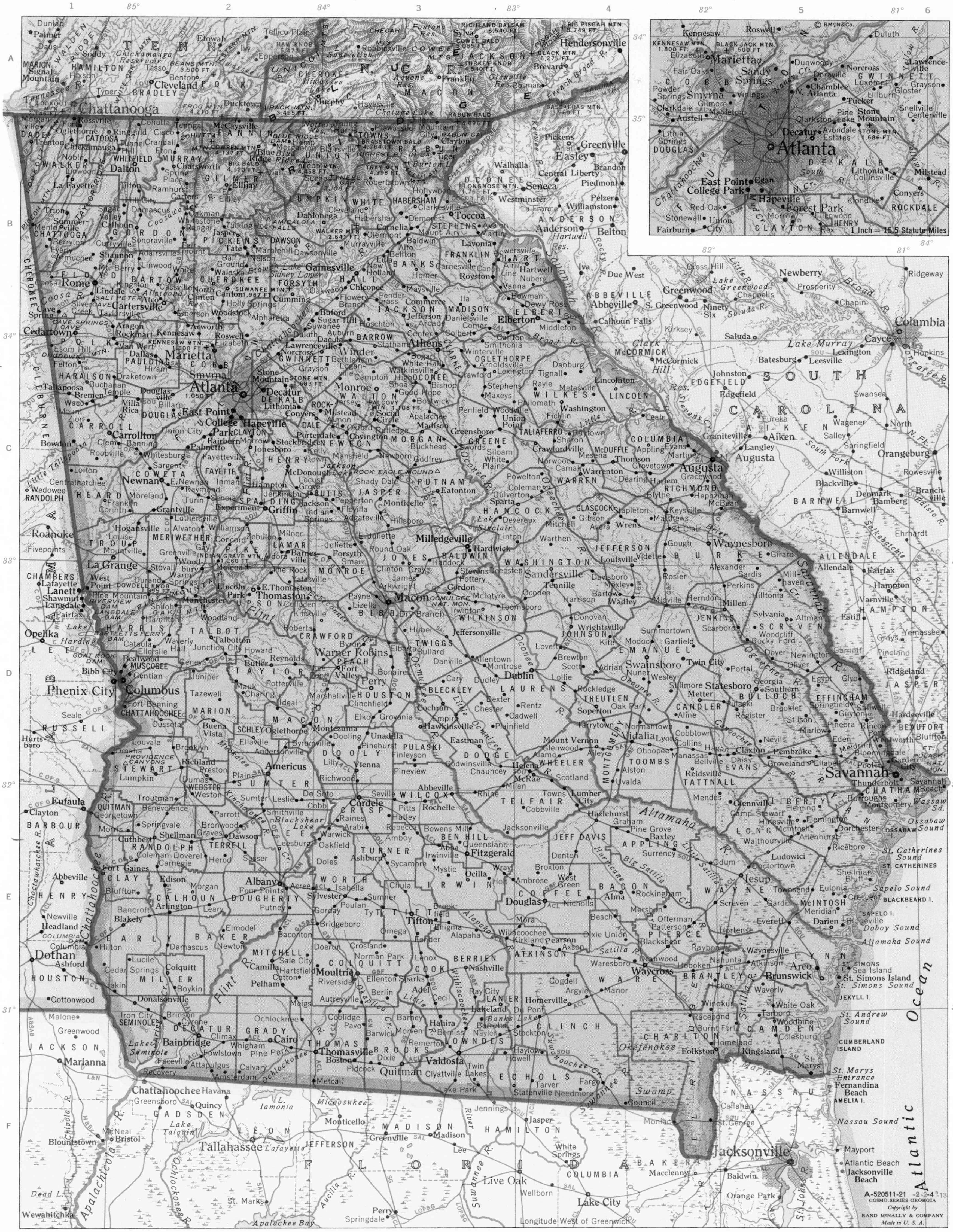

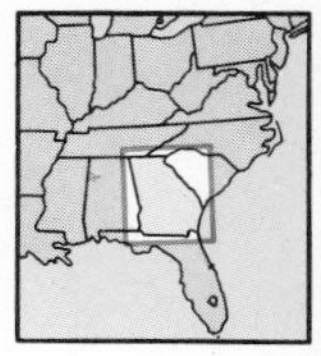

Lambert Conformal Conic Projection
SCALE 1:1,962,000 1 Inch = 31 Statute Miles

Statute Miles
Kilometers

HAWAII

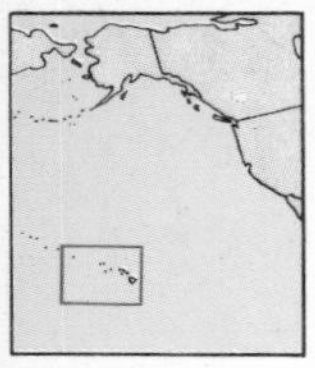

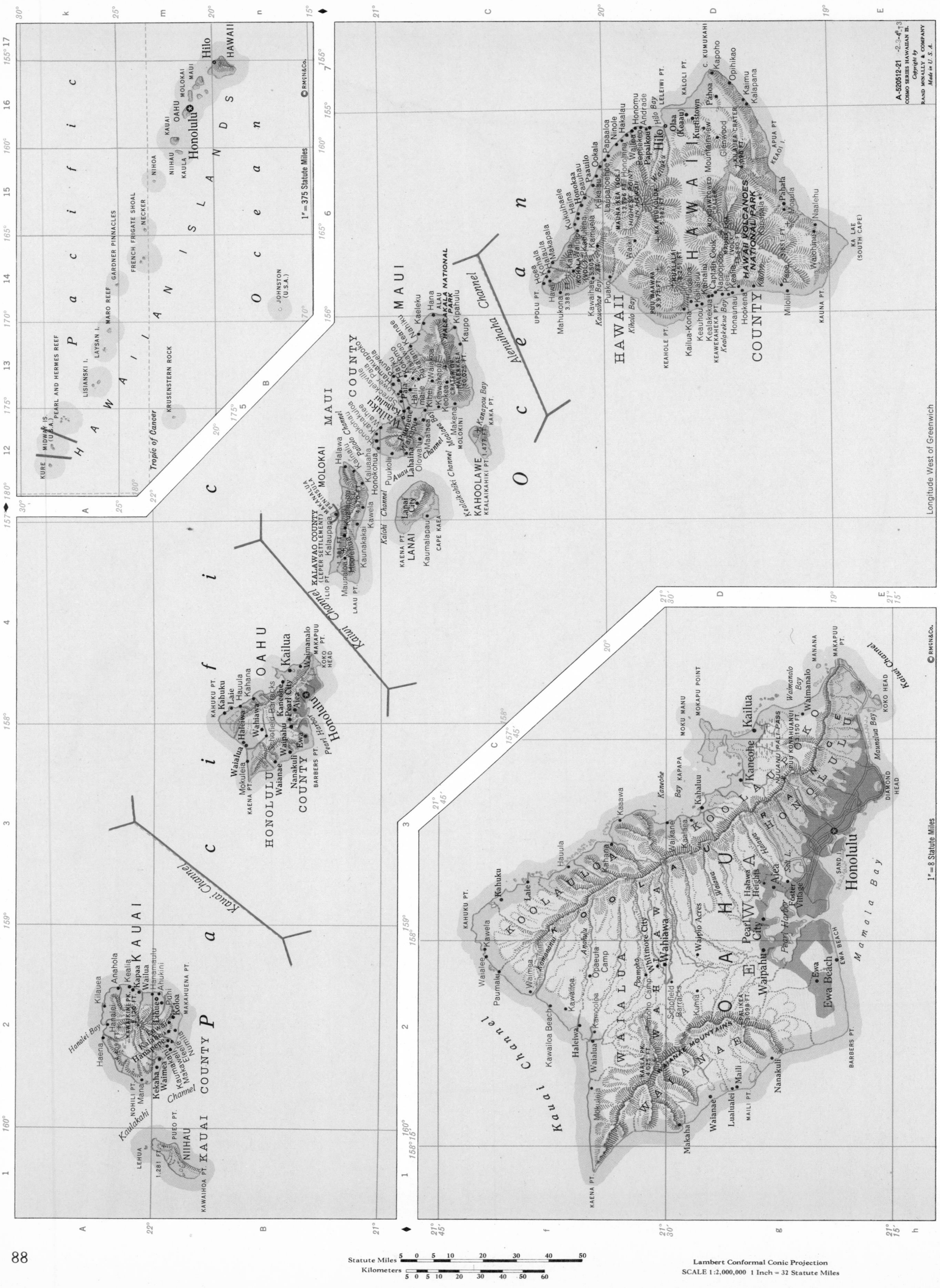

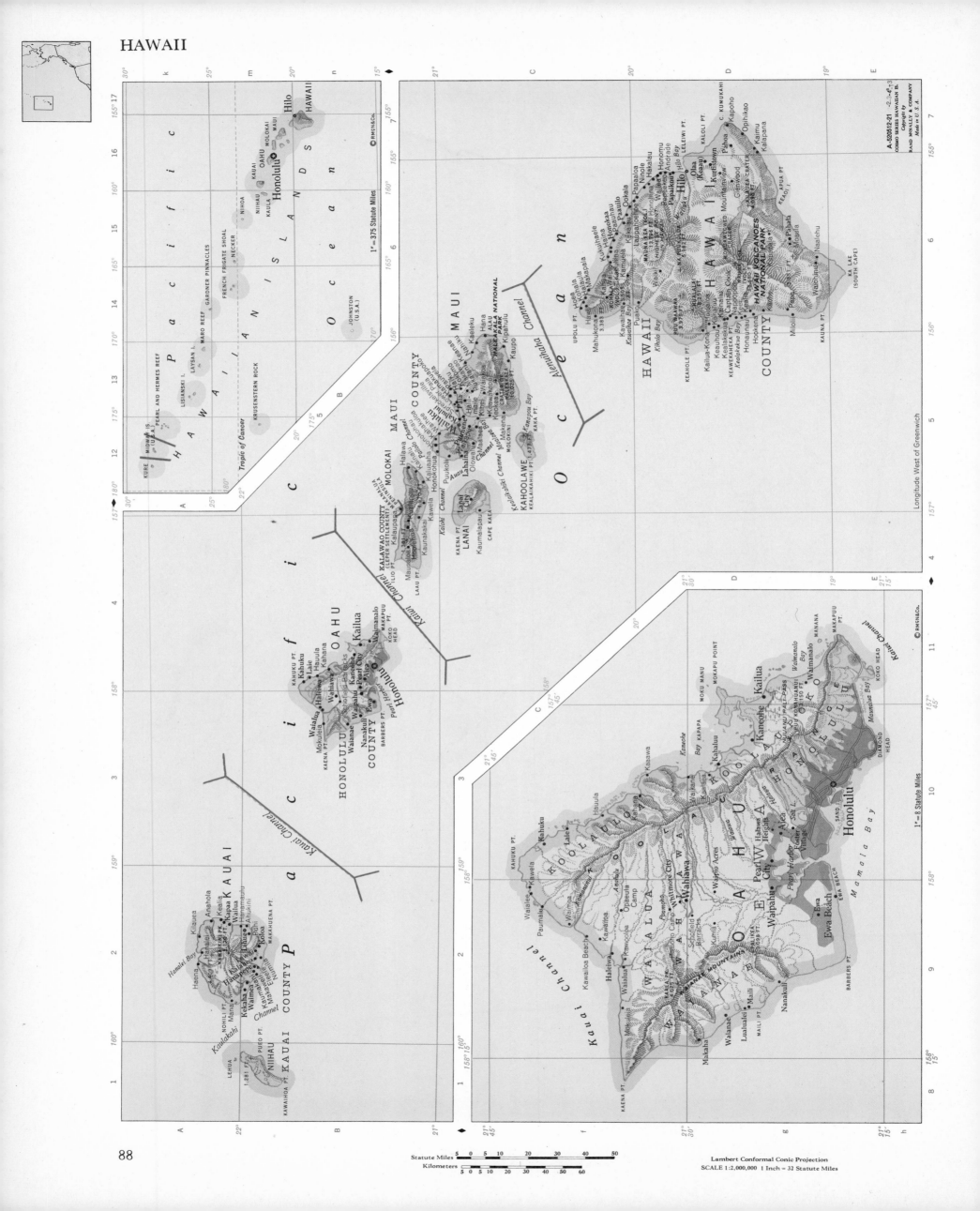

Statute Miles
Kilometers

Lambert Conformal Conic Projection
SCALE 1:2,000,000   1 Inch = 32 Statute Miles

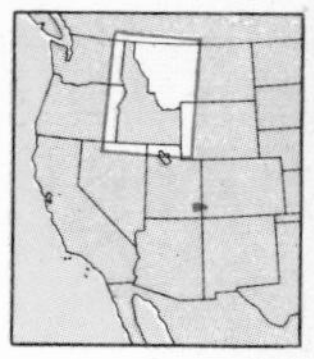

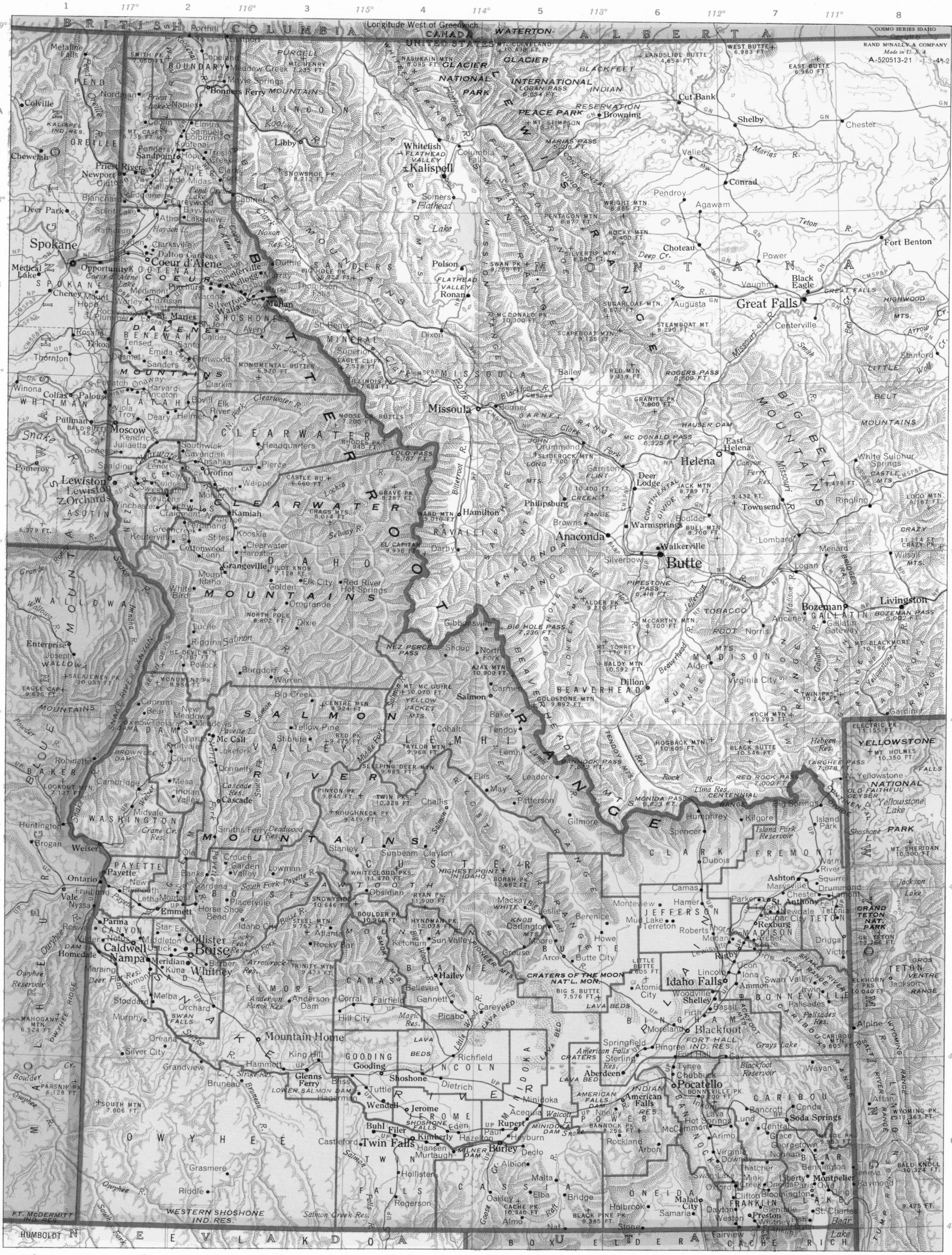

Lambert Conformal Conic Projection
SCALE 1:2,633,000 1 Inch = 41.5 Statute Miles

Statute Miles
5 0 5 10   20   30   40   50   60

Kilometers
5 0 5 15 25 35 45 55 65 75

Statute Miles 5 0 5 10 20 30 40
Kilometers 5 0 5 15 25 35 45 55

Lambert Conformal Conic Projection
SCALE 1:1,997,000   1 Inch = 31.5 Statute Miles

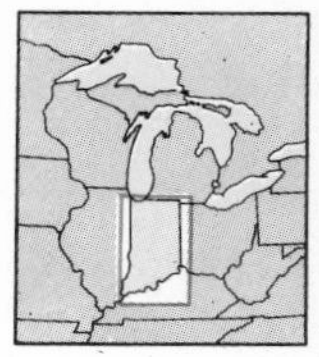

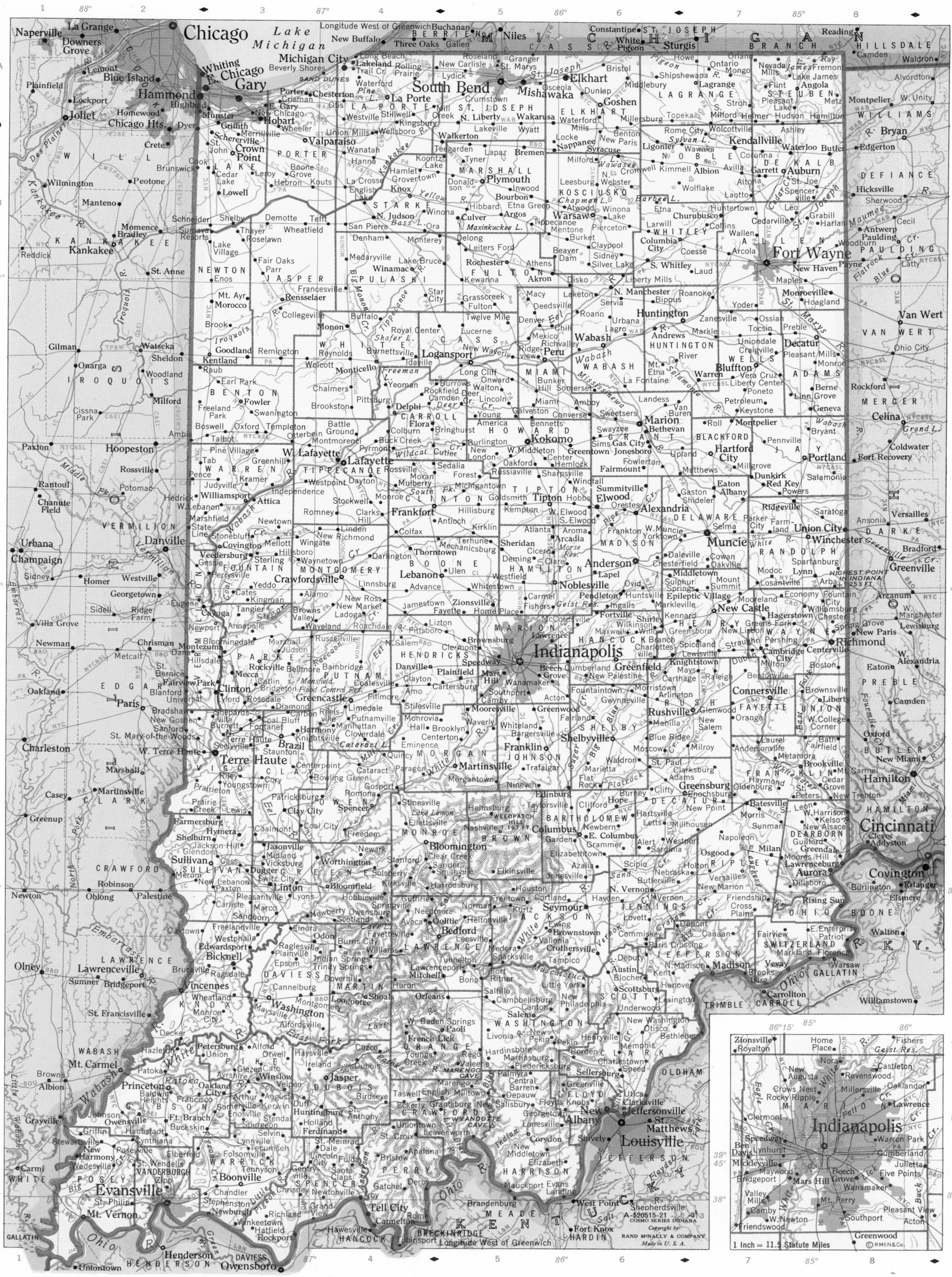

Indianapolis

Lambert Conformal Conic Projection
SCALE 1:1,465,000 1 Inch=23 Statute Miles

Statute Miles

Kilometers

1 Inch = 11.5 Statute Miles

IOWA

Des Moines

Davenport

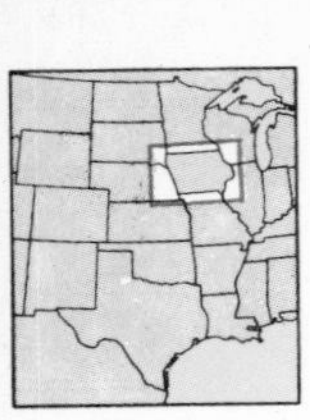

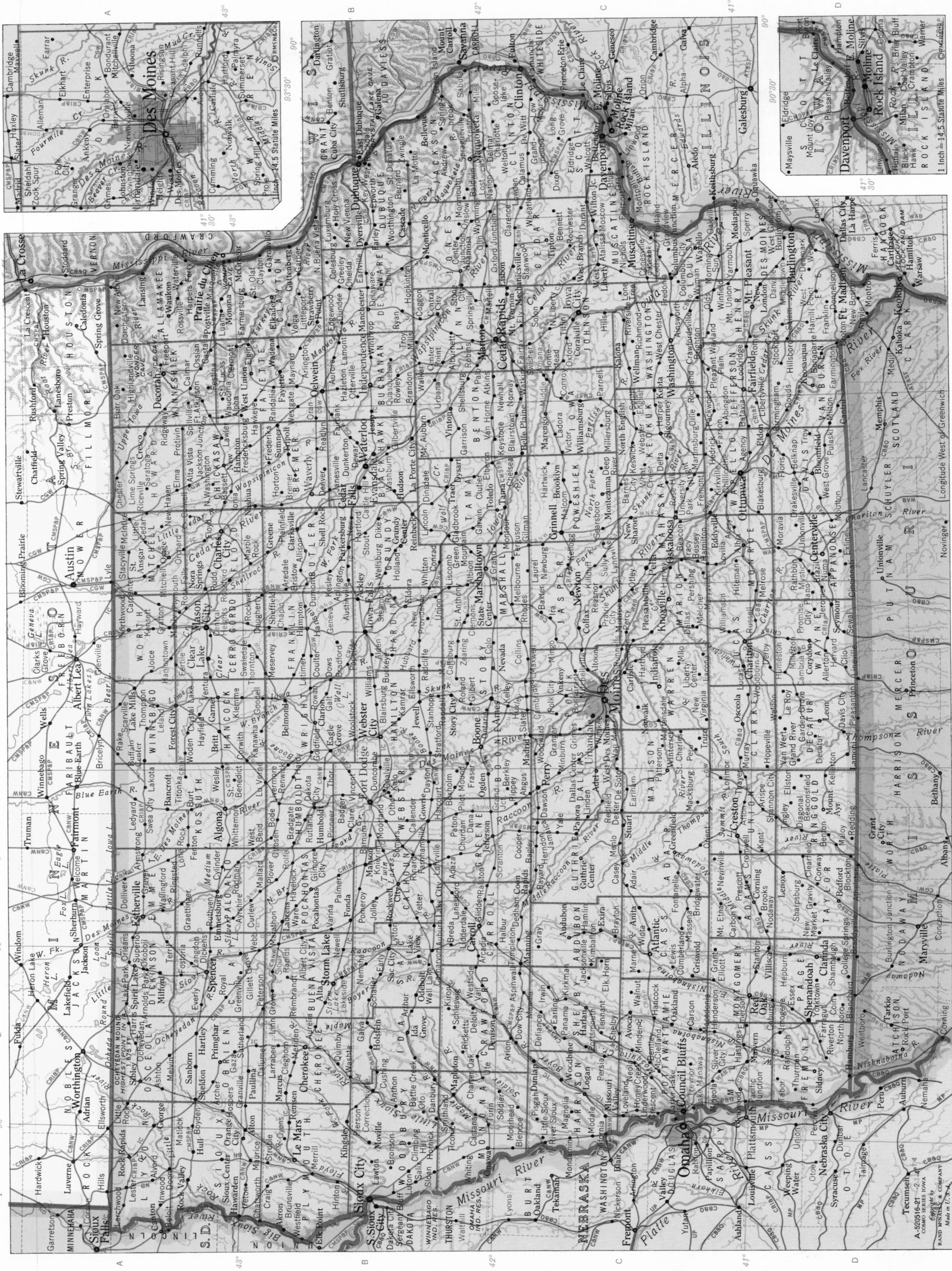

Statute Miles 5 0 5 10 20 30 40

Kilometers 5 0 5 15 25 35 45 55

Lambert Conformal Conic Projection
SCALE 1:1,834,000   1 Inch = 29 Statute Miles

A-520516-21 -2-41
COSMO SERIES IOWA
RAND MCNALLY AND COMPANY
Made in U.S.A.

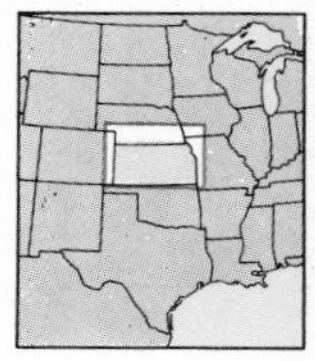

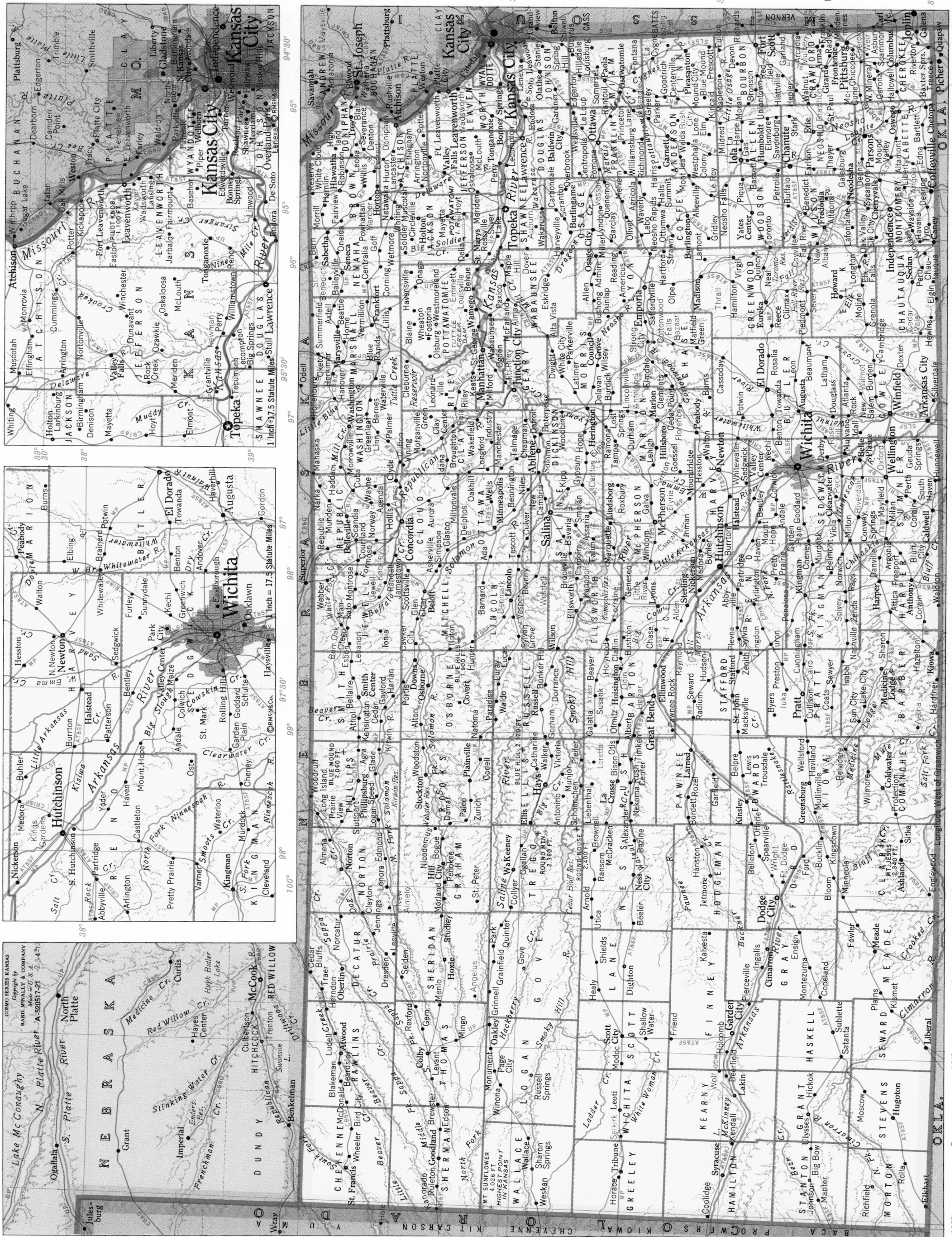

Lambert Conformal Conic Projection
SCALE 1:2,208,000 1 Inch = 35 Statute Miles

Statute Miles
Kilometers

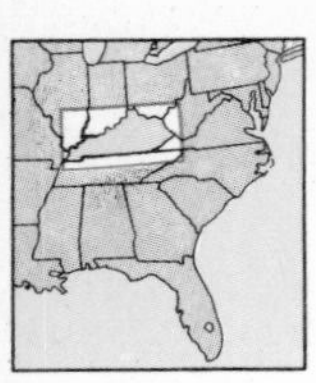

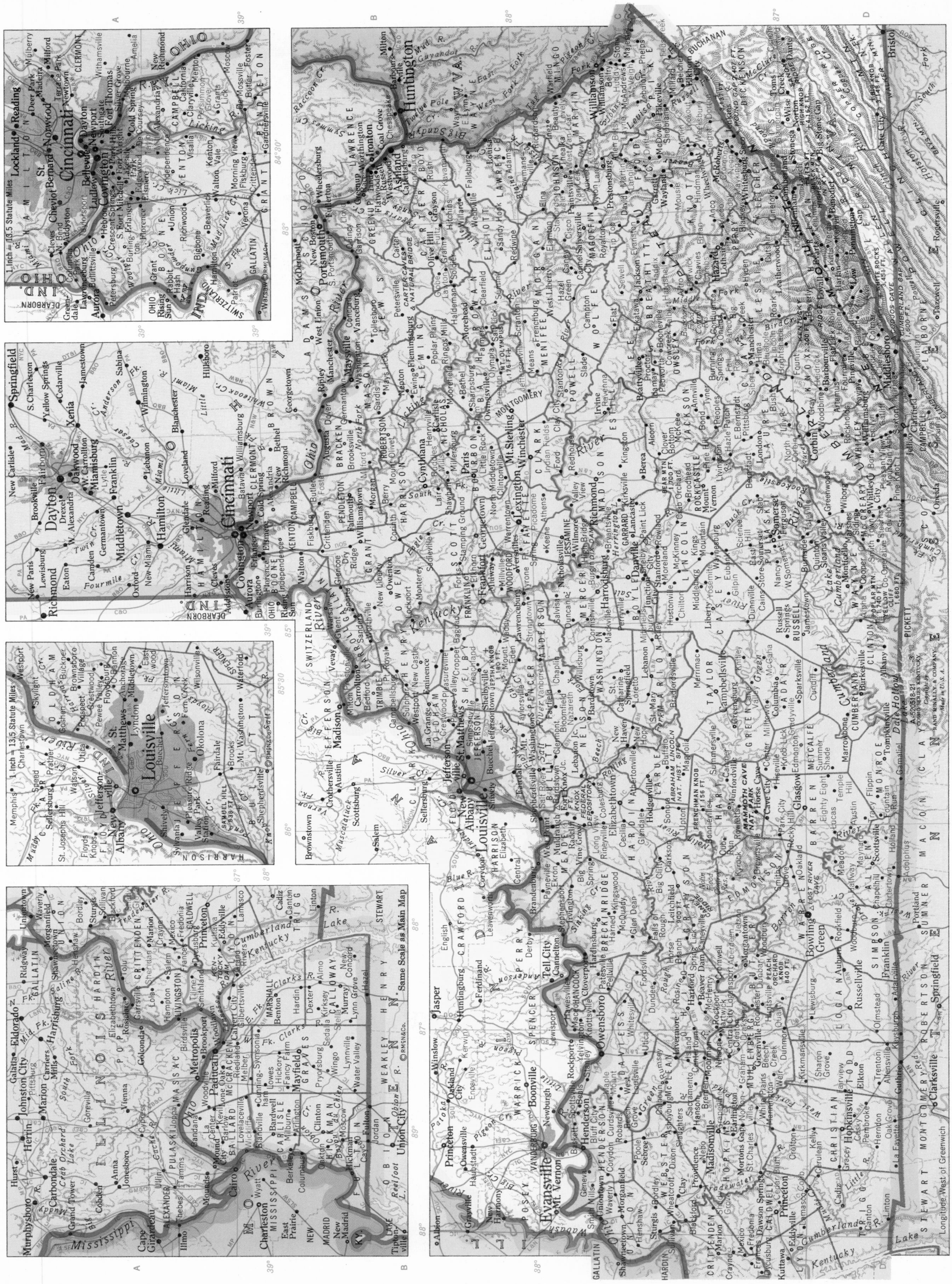

Statute Miles

Kilometers

Lambert Conformal Conic Projection

SCALE 1:1,738,000 1 Inch = 27 Statute Miles

LOUISIANA

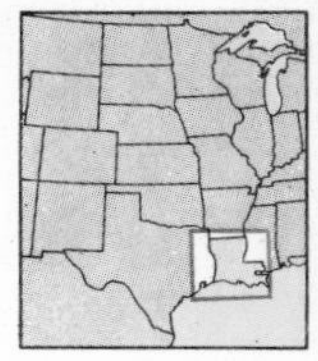

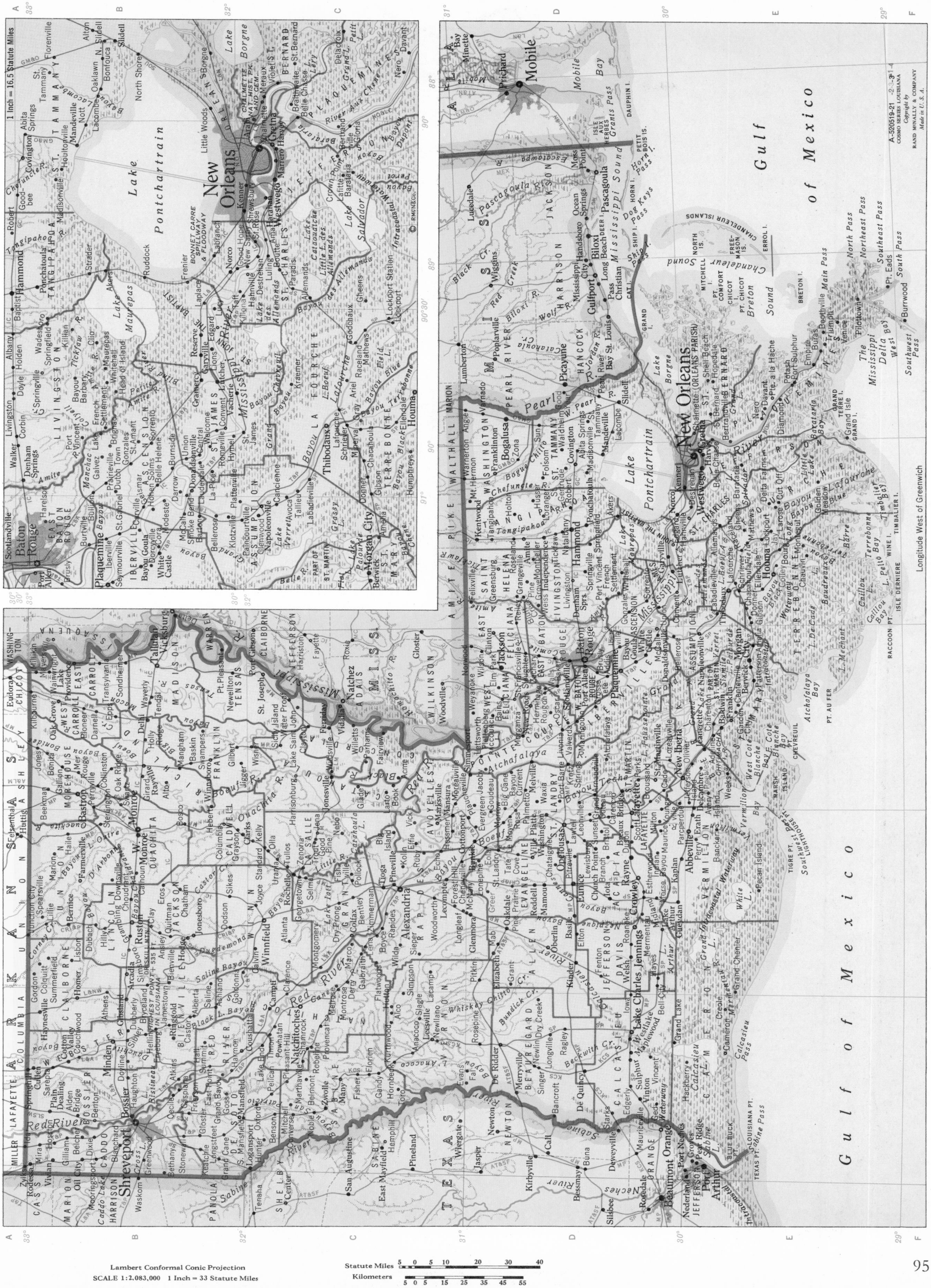

Lambert Conformal Conic Projection
SCALE 1:2.083,000   1 Inch = 33 Statute Miles

Statute Miles

Kilometers

95

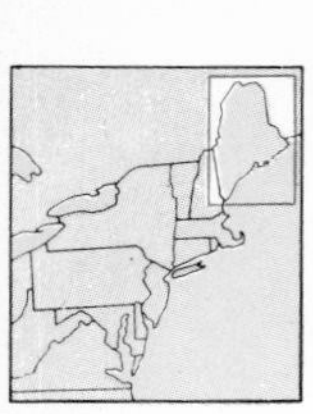

MAINE

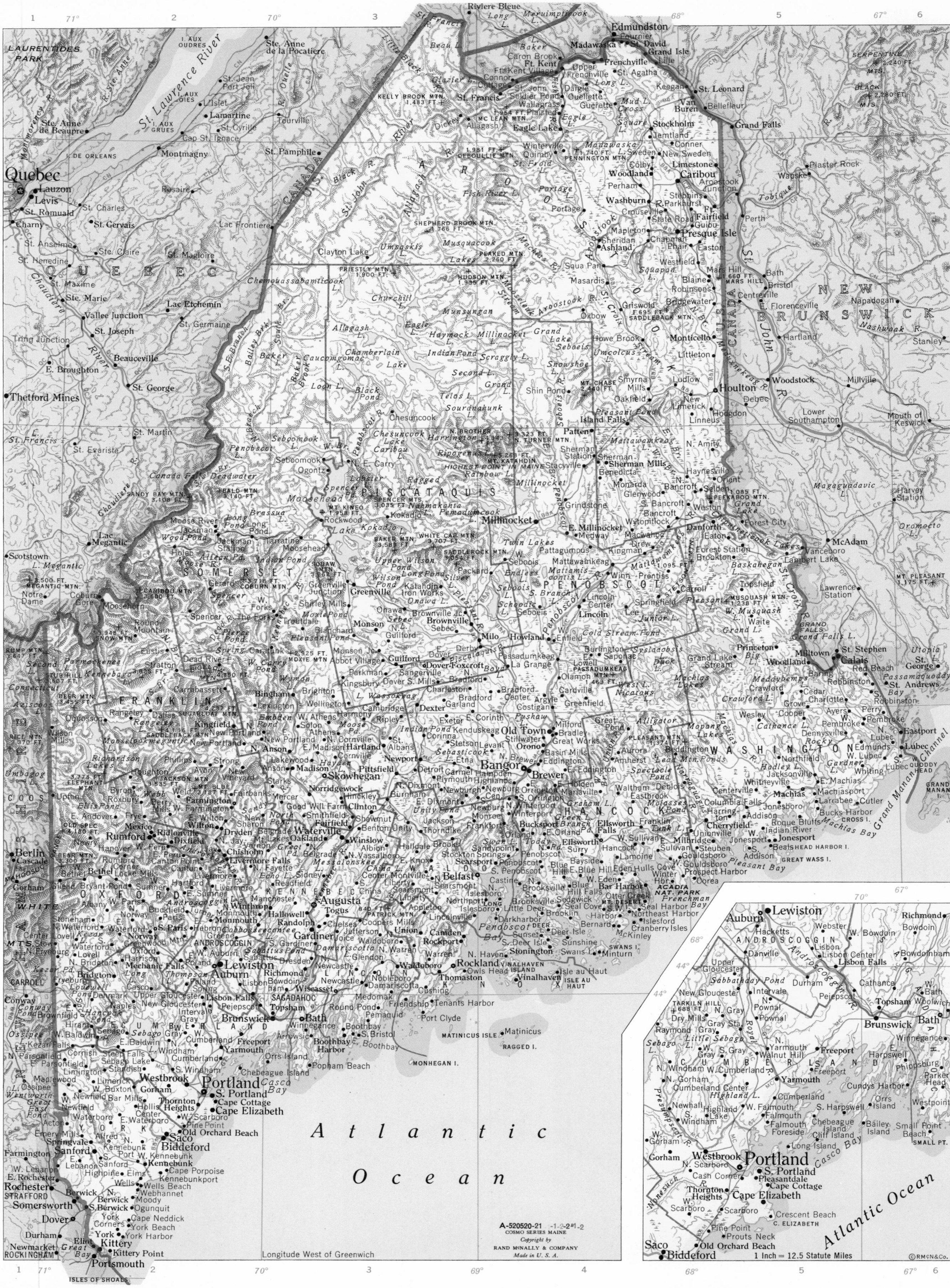

A-520520-21 -1-2-#1-2
COSMO SERIES MAINE
Copyright by
RAND McNALLY & COMPANY
Made in U.S.A.

Statute Miles
Kilometers

Lambert Conformal Conic Projection
SCALE 1:1,581,000 1 Inch = 25 Statute Miles

1 Inch = 12.5 Statute Miles

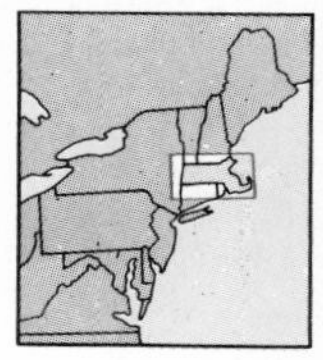

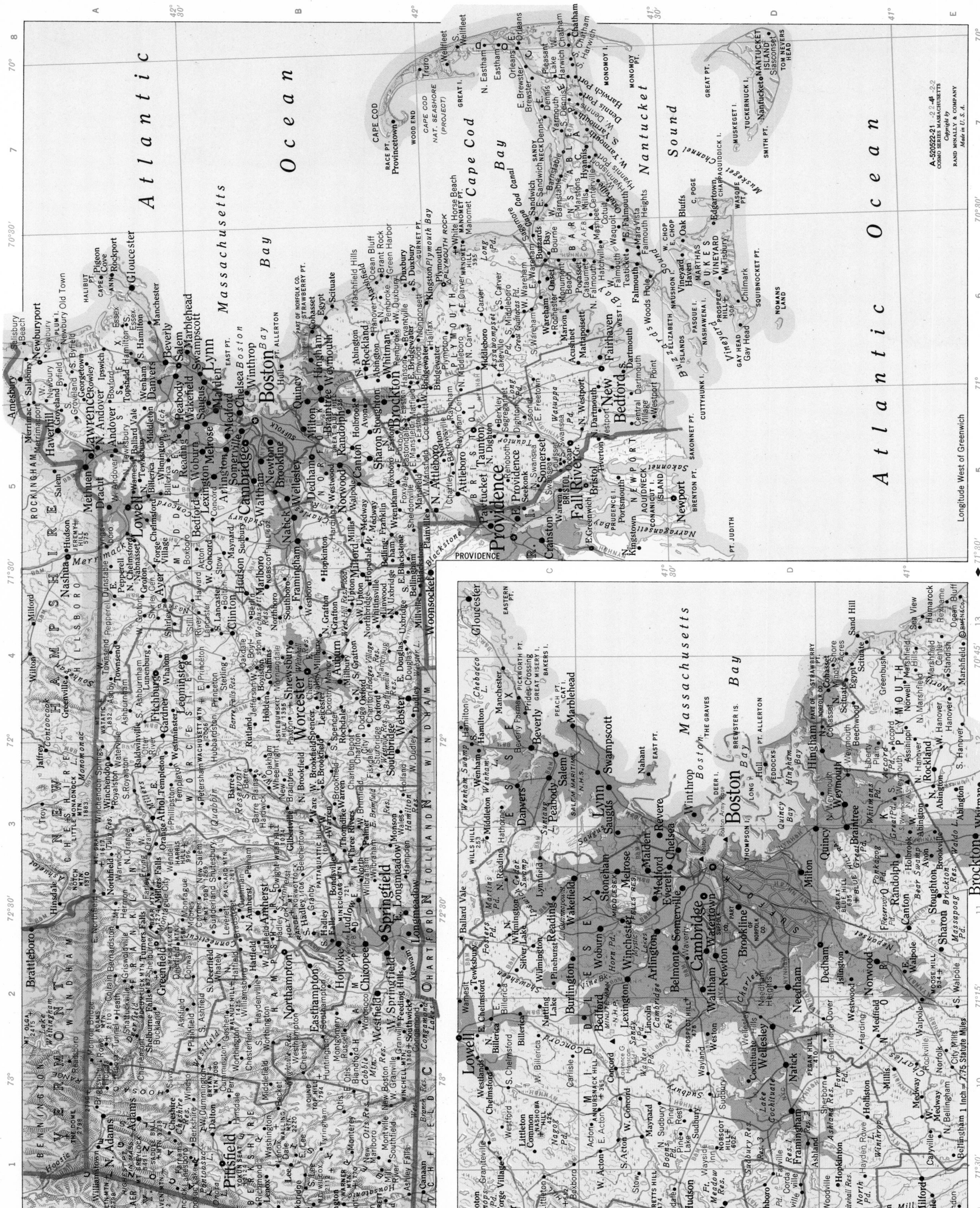

Lambert Conformal Conic Projection
SCALE 1:978,000   1 Inch = 15.5 Statute Miles

Statute Miles

Kilometers

MICHIGAN

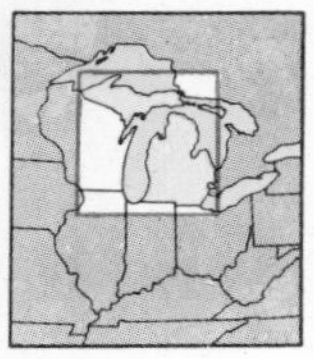

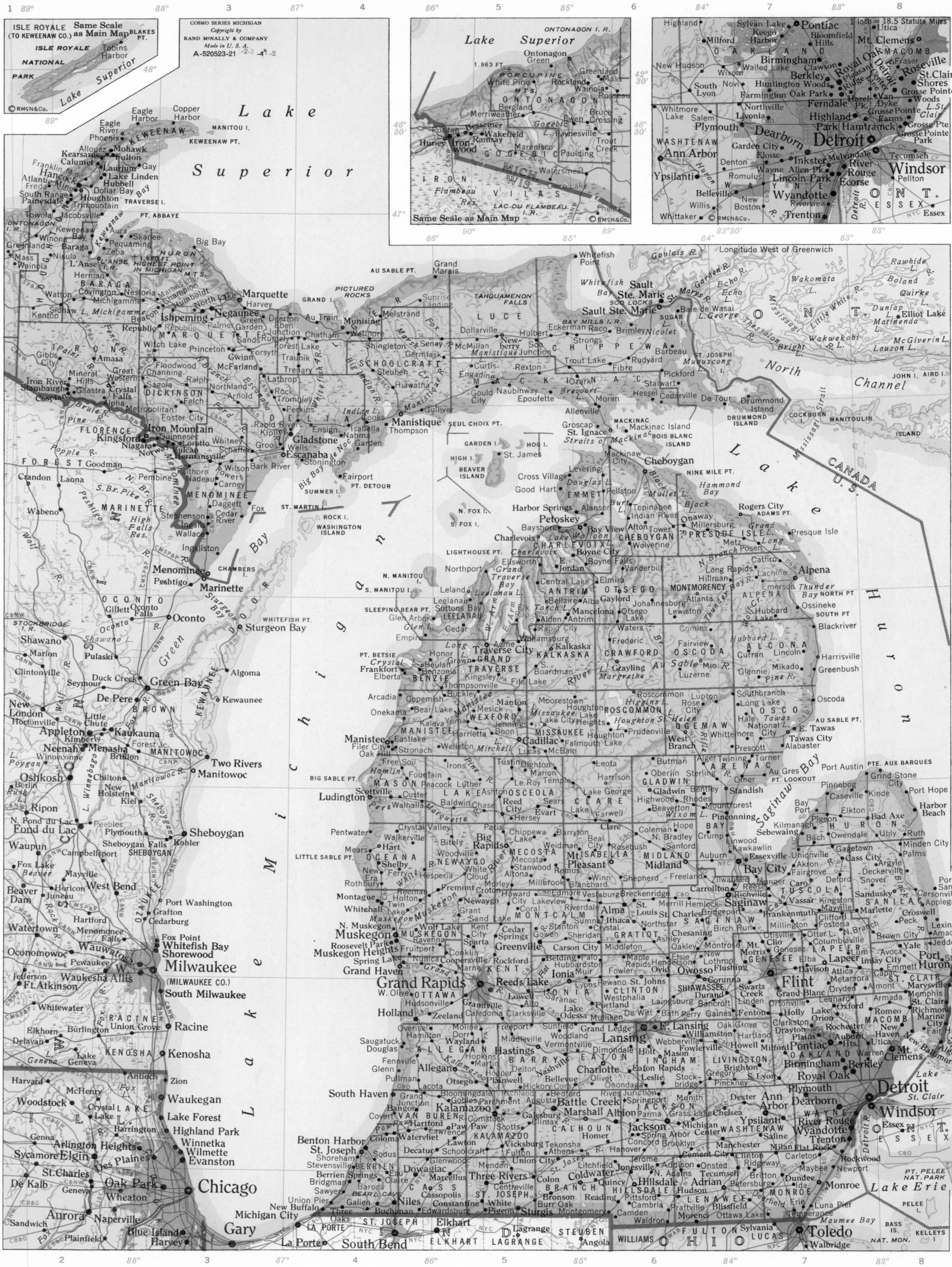

Statute Miles 5 0 5 10   20   30   40   50
Kilometers 5 0 5 15 25 35 45 55 65 75

Lambert Conformal Conic Projection
SCALE 1:2,347,000 1 Inch = 37 Statute Miles

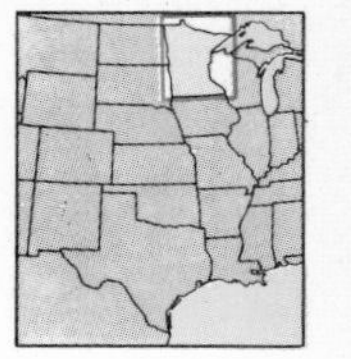

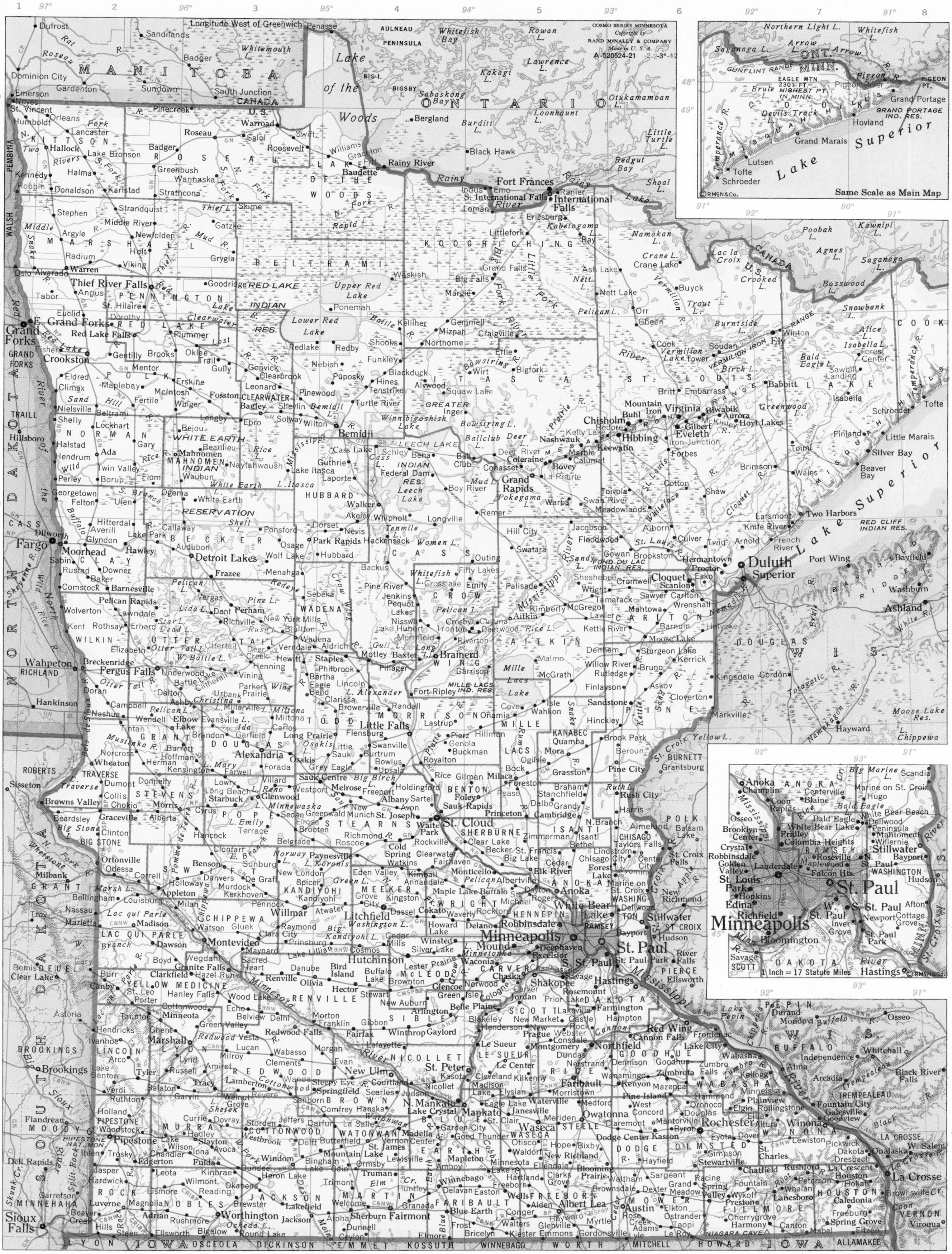

Lambert Conformal Conic Projection
SCALE 1:2,179,000 1 Inch = 34 Statute Miles

Statute Miles 5 0 5 10 20 30 40 50
Kilometers 5 0 5 15 25 35 45 55 65

MISSISSIPPI

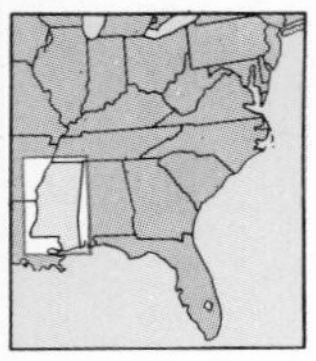

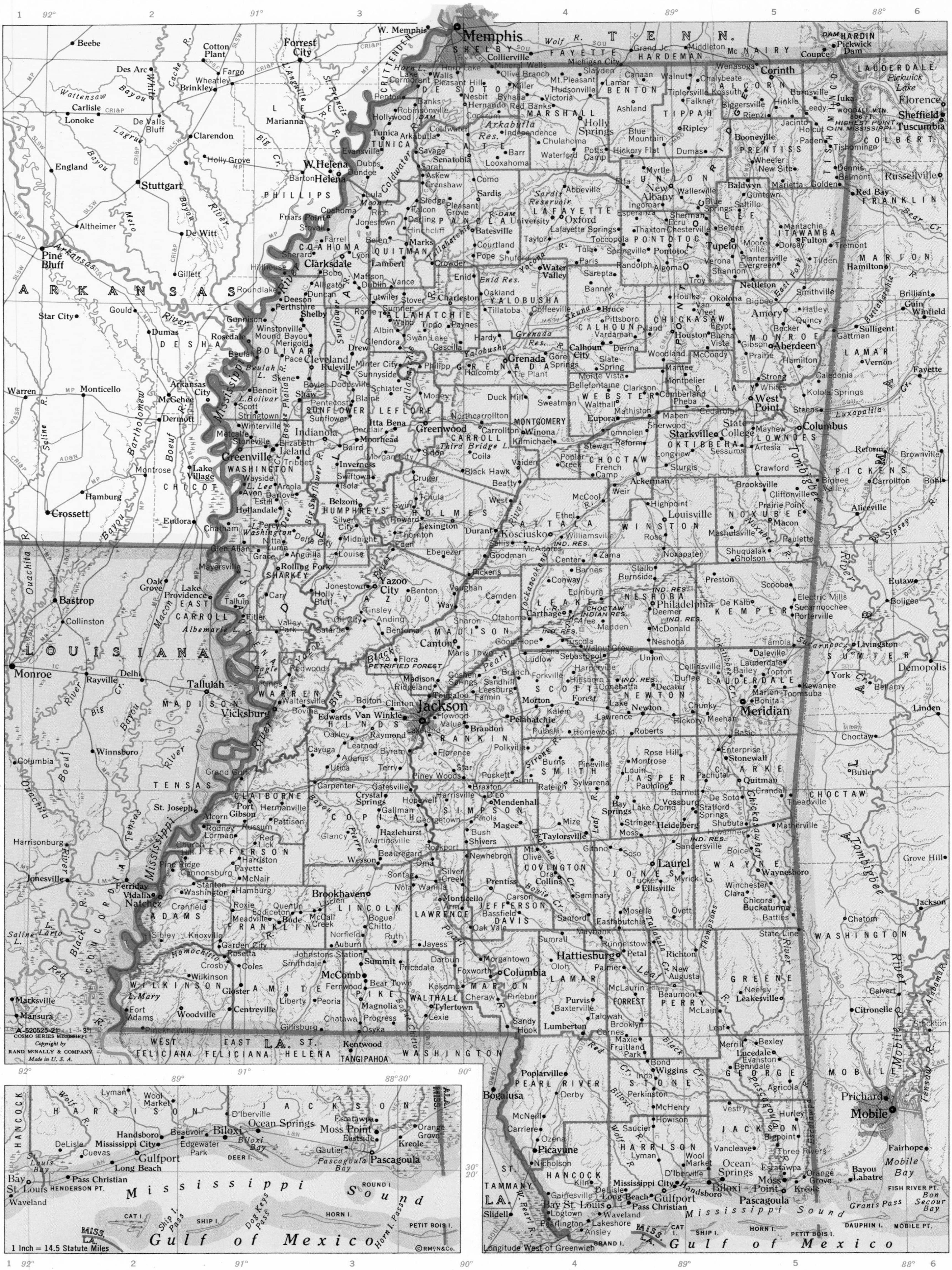

Statute Miles
Kilometers

Lambert Conformal Conic Projection
SCALE 1:1,837,000 1 Inch = 29 Statute Miles

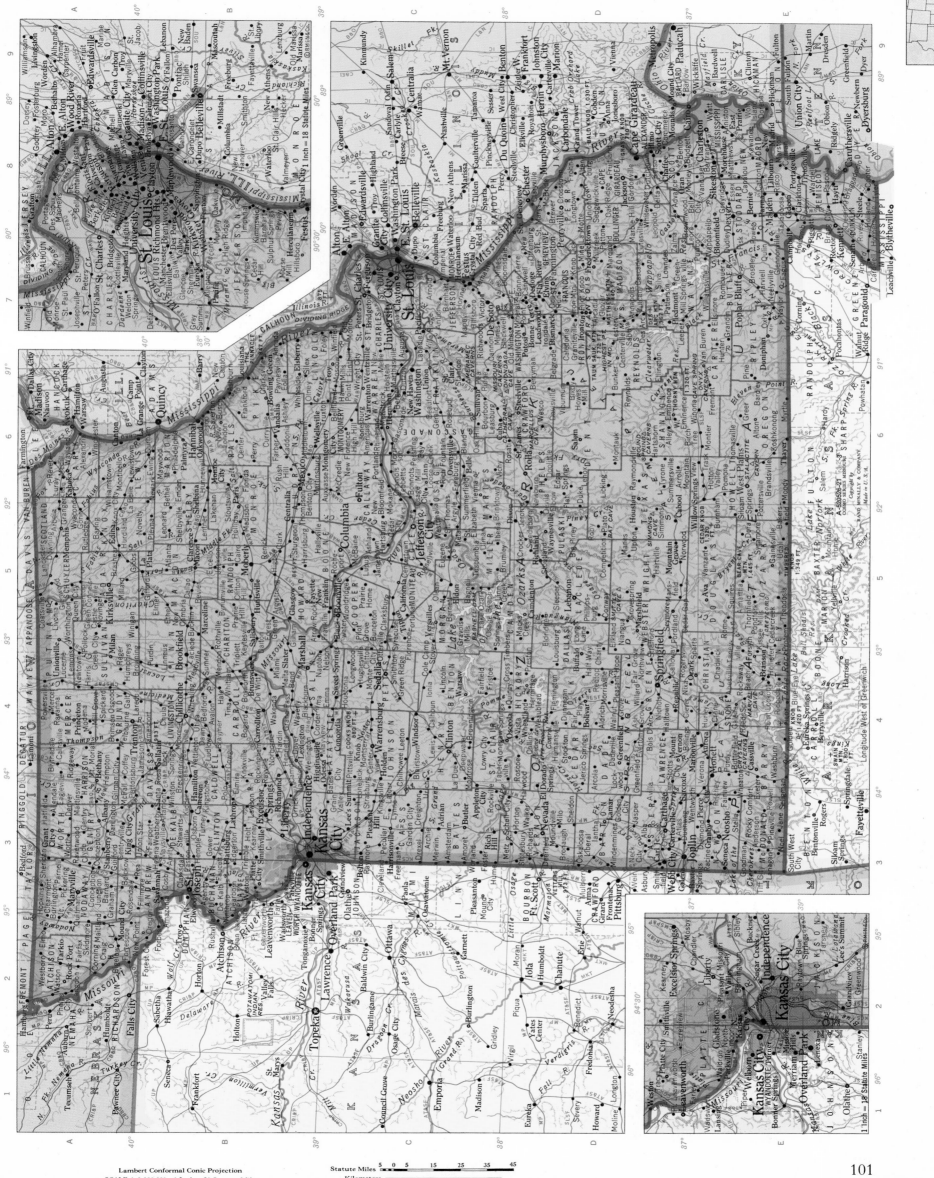

Lambert Conformal Conic Projection
SCALE 1:2,283,000   1 Inch = 36 Statute Miles

Statute Miles 5 0 5 15 25 35 45
Kilometers 5 0 5 15 25 35 45 55 65

101

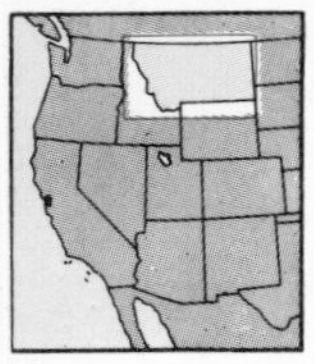

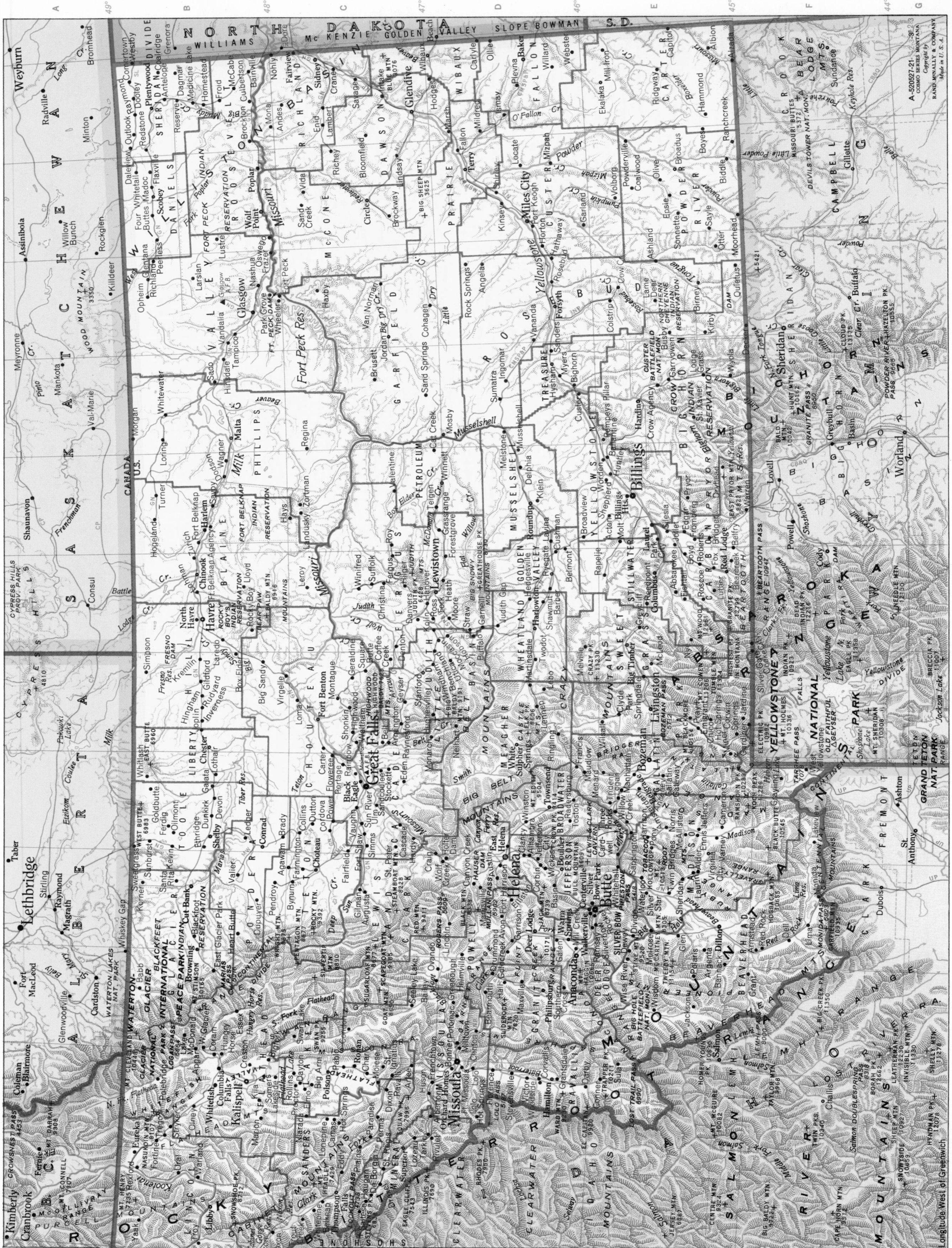

Statute Miles 10 0 10 20 30 40 50 60 70
Kilometers 10 0 10 30 50 70 90

Lambert Conformal Conic Projection
SCALE 1:2,999,000 1 Inch = 47.5 Statute Miles

NEBRASKA

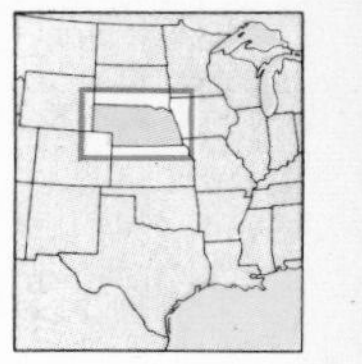

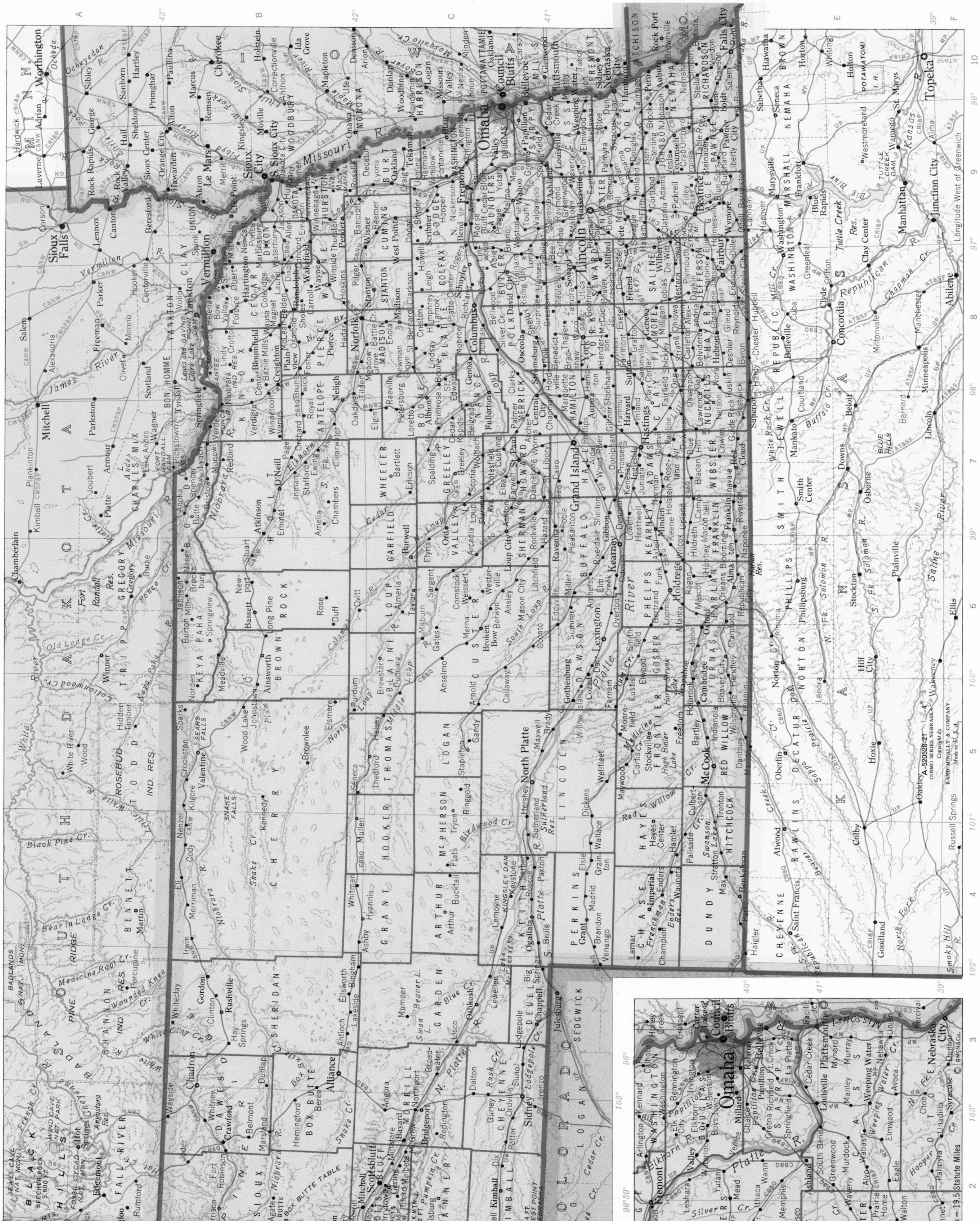

Lambert Conformal Conic Projection
SCALE 1:2,460,000 1 Inch = 39 Statute Miles

Statute Miles
Kilometers

103

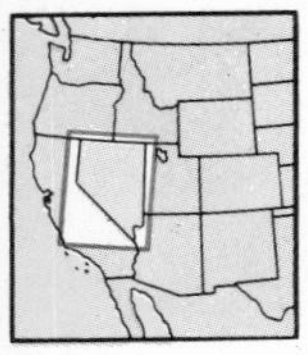

NEVADA

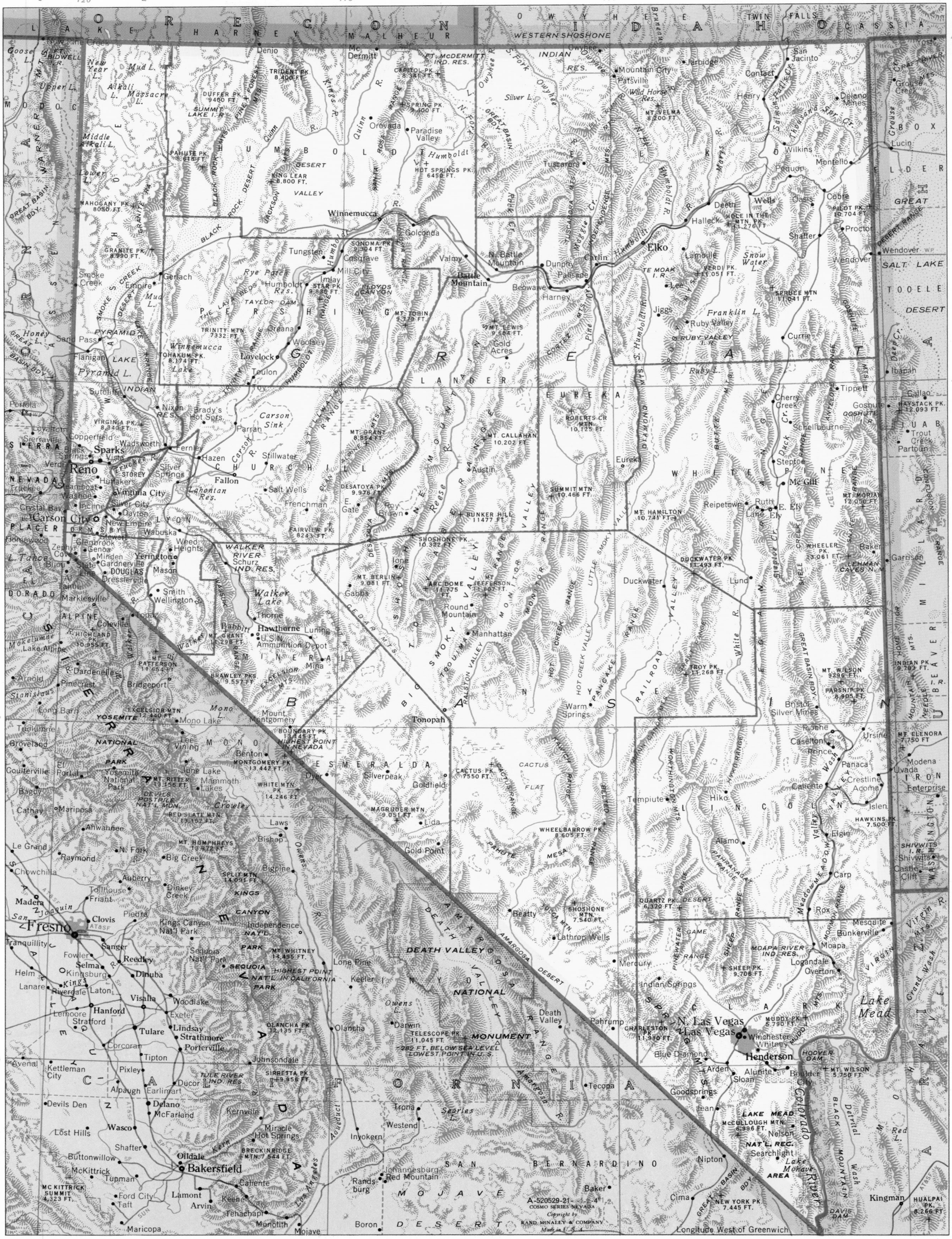

Statute Miles
Kilometers
5 0 5 10 20 30 40 50 60 70 80
5 0 10 20 40 60 80 100 120

Lambert Conformal Conic Projection
SCALE 1:2,630,000 1 Inch = 41.5 Statute Miles

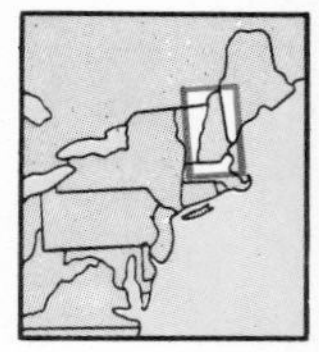

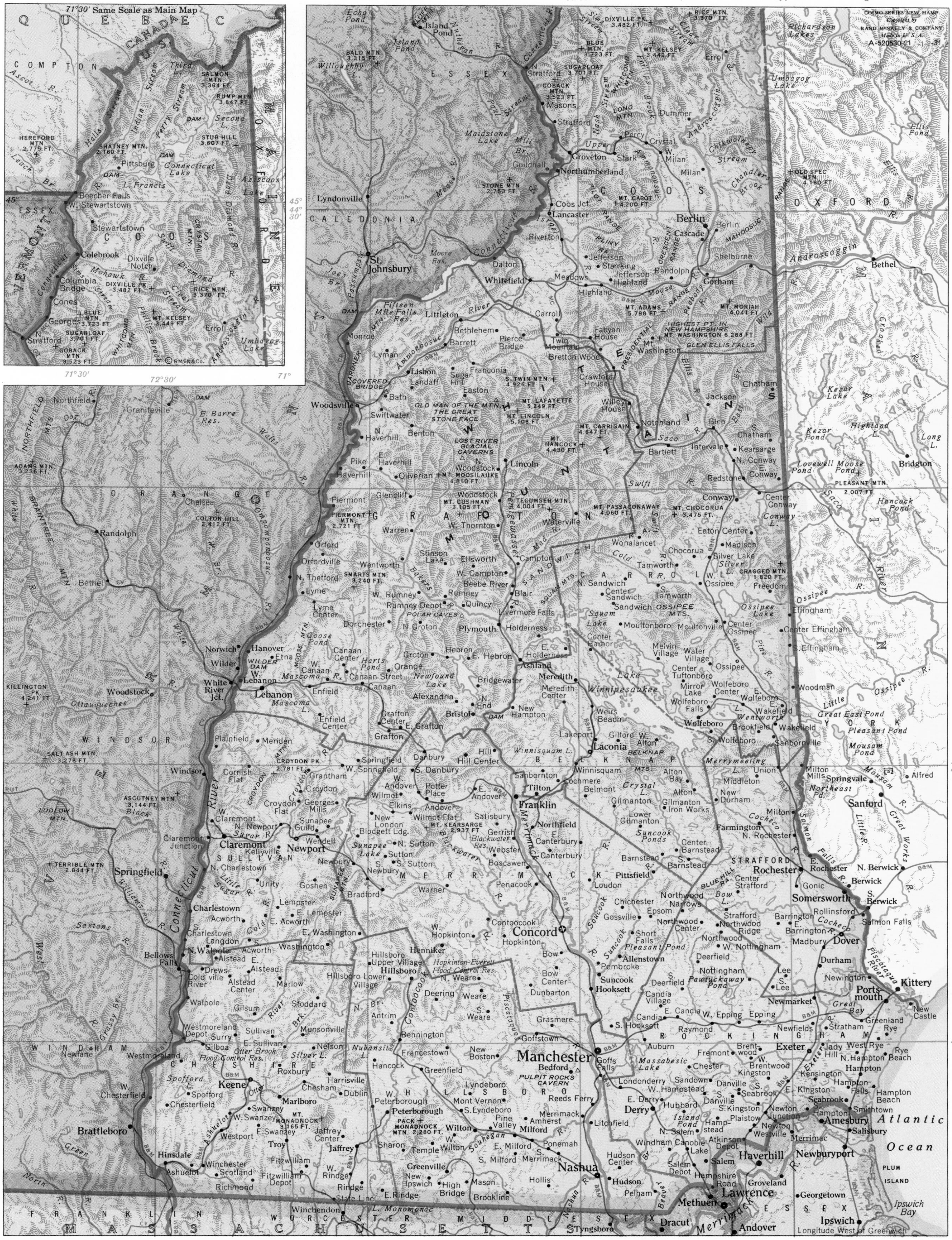

Lambert Conformal Conic Projection
SCALE 1:792,000   1 Inch = 12.75 Statute Miles

Statute Miles

Kilometers

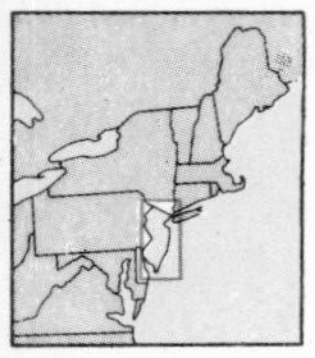

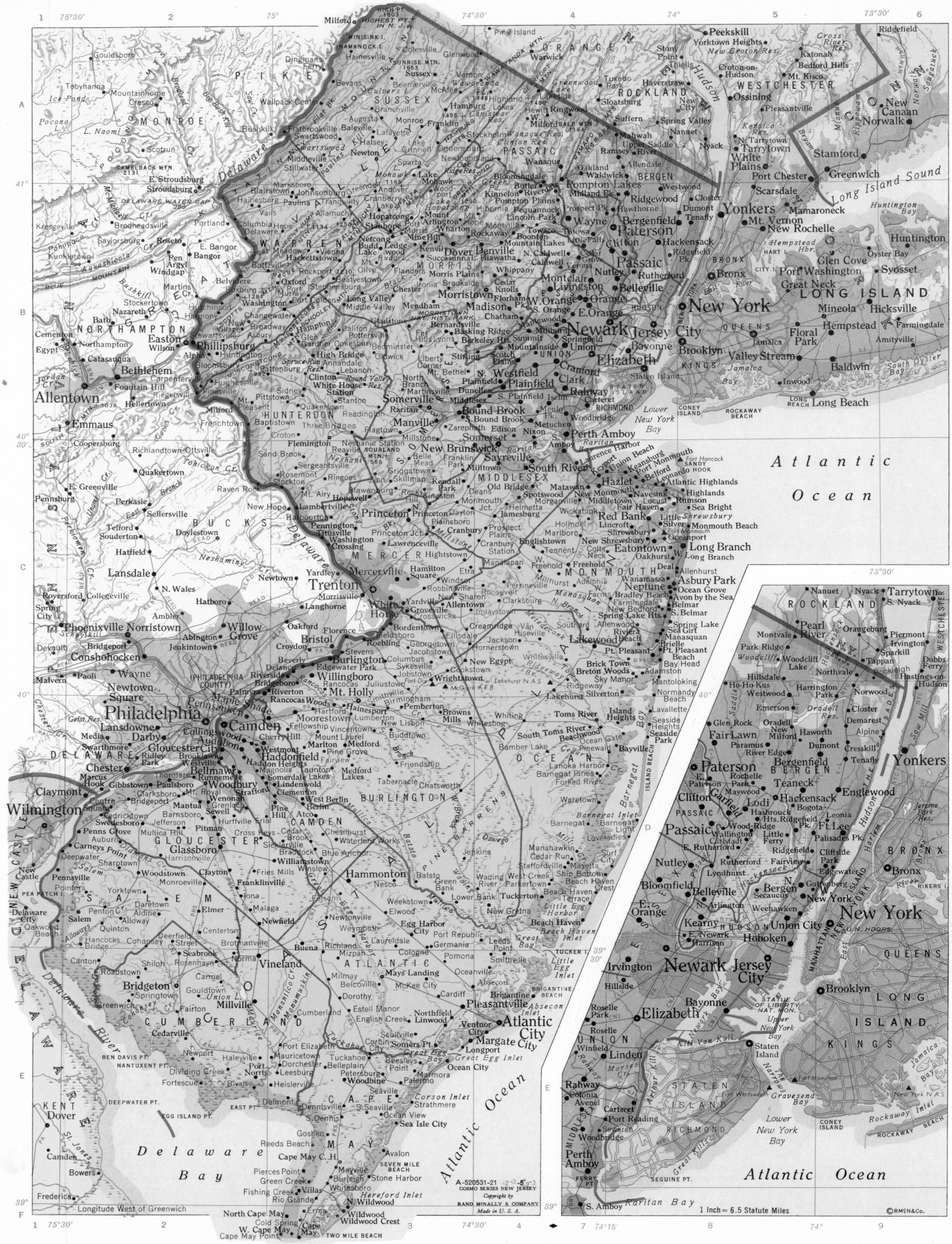

NEW JERSEY

106

Longitude West of Greenwich

A-520531-21
COSMO SERIES NEW JERSEY
Copyright by
RAND McNALLY & COMPANY
Made in U.S.A.

Statute Miles
Kilometers

Lambert Conformal Conic Projection
SCALE 1:849,000   1 Inch = 13 Statute Miles

1 Inch = 6.5 Statute Miles
©RM&N&Co.

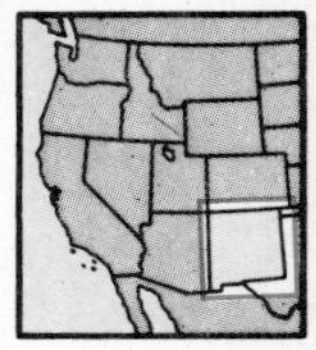

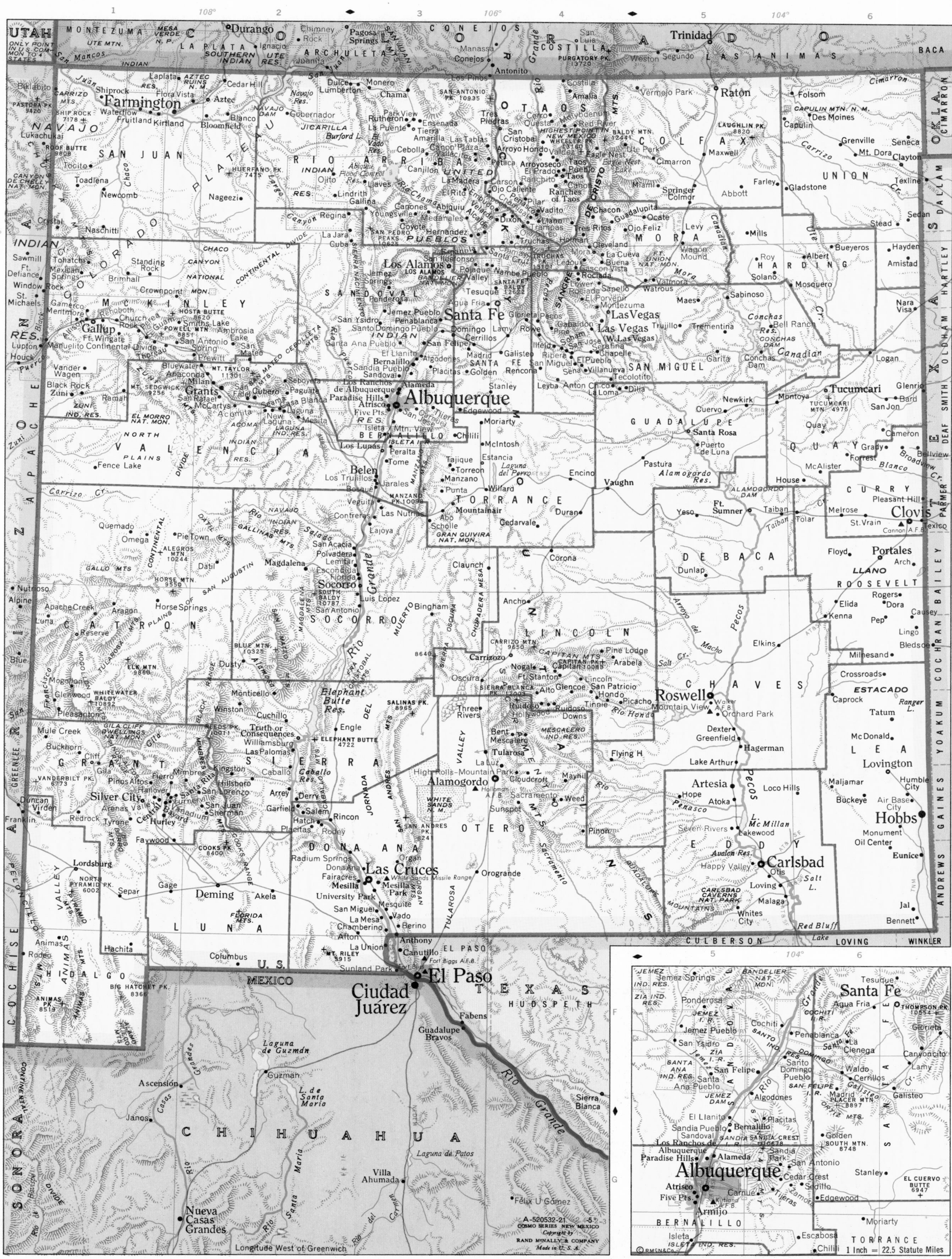

Lambert Conformal Conic Projection
SCALE 1:2,600,000 1 Inch = 41 Statute Miles

Statute Miles

Kilometers

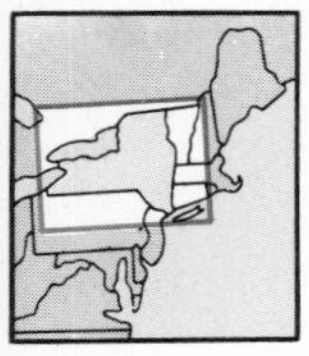

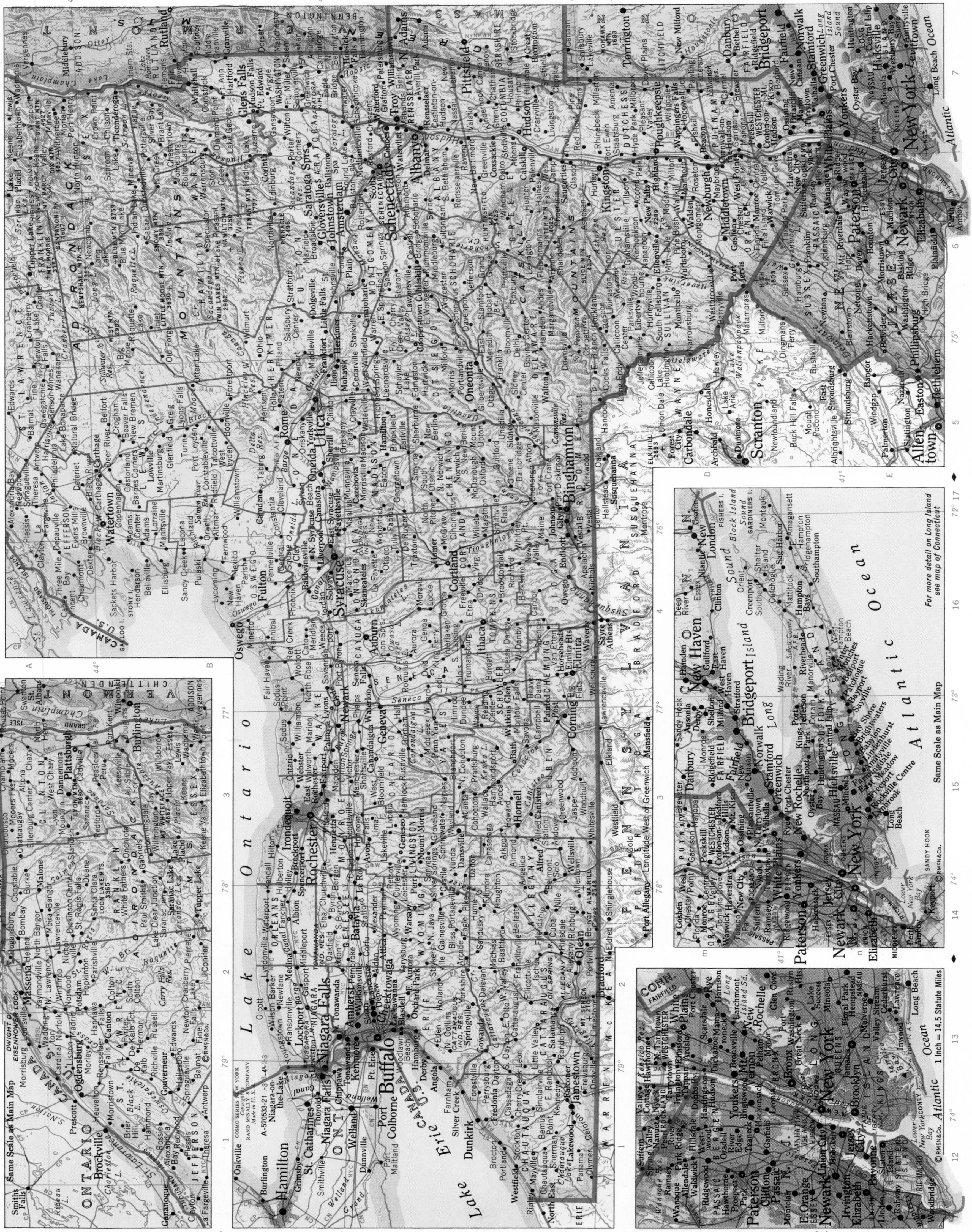

Statute Miles 5 0 5 10   20   30   40

Kilometers 5 0 5 15 25 35 45 55

Lambert Conformal Conic Projection
SCALE 1:1,862,000   1 Inch = 29 Statute Miles

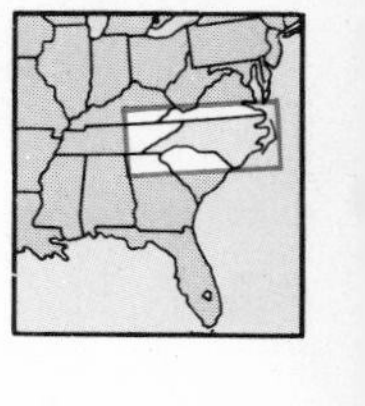

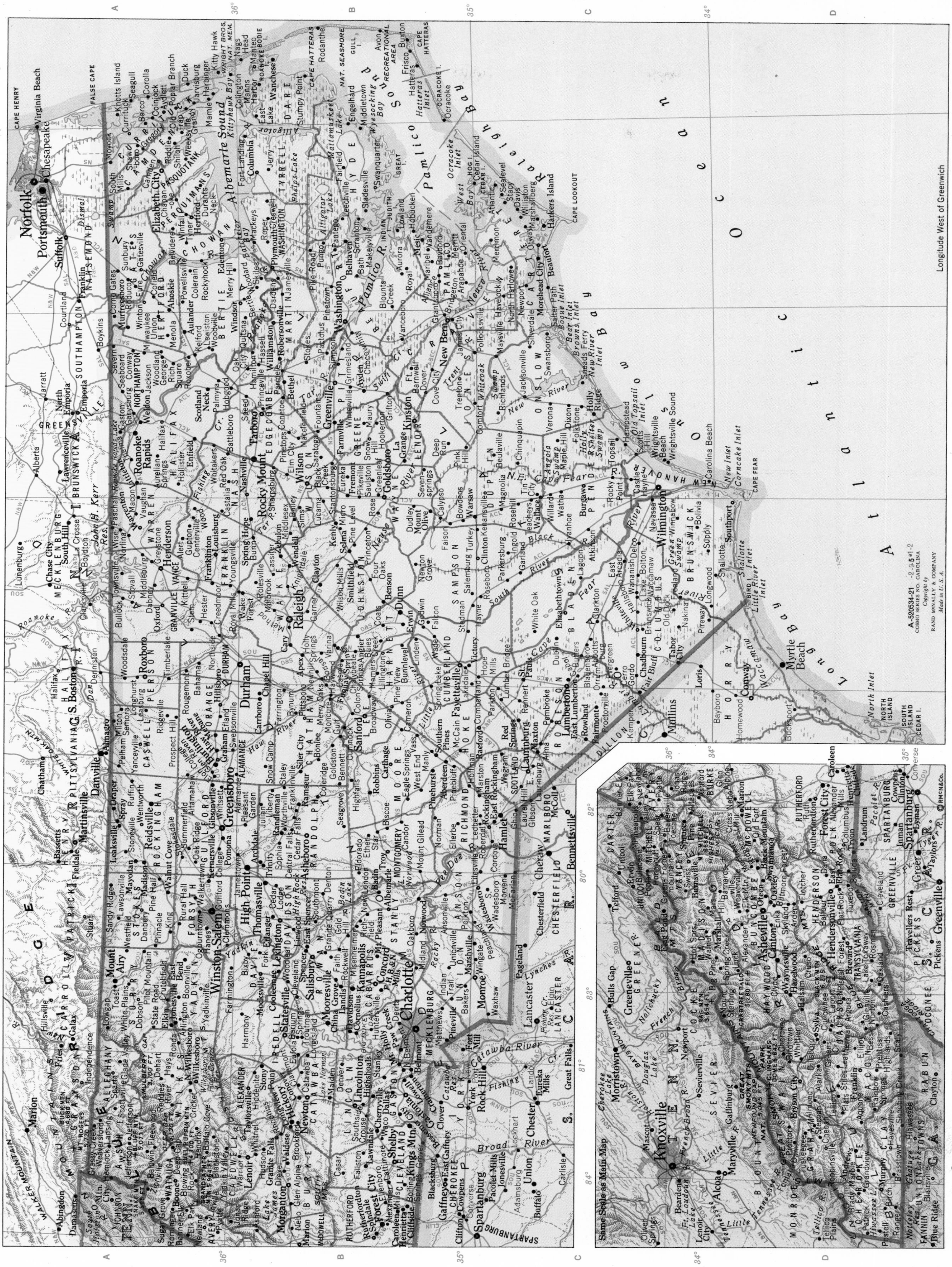

Lambert Conformal Conic Projection
SCALE 1:1,950,000   1 Inch = 31 Statute Miles

Statute Miles
Kilometers

Longitude West of Greenwich

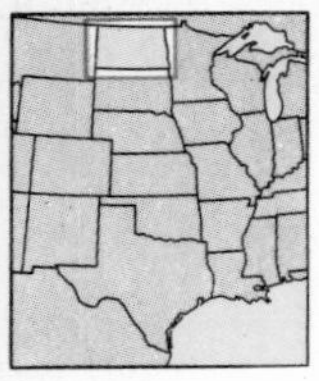

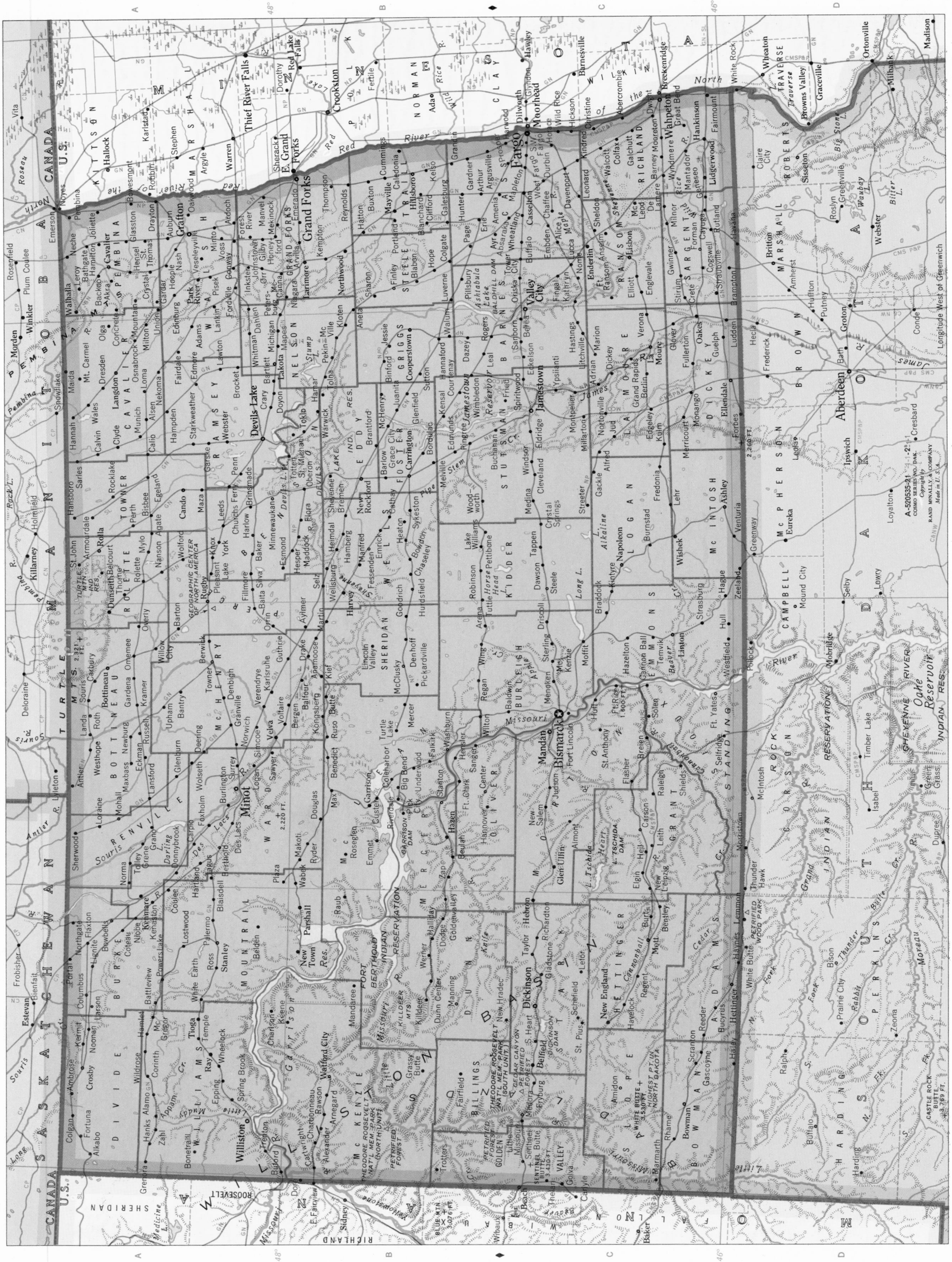

Statute Miles 5 0 5 10 20 30 40 50 60
Kilometers 5 0 5 15 25 35 45 55 65 75

Lambert Conformal Conic Projection
SCALE 1:2,091,000 1 Inch = 33 Statute Miles

OHIO

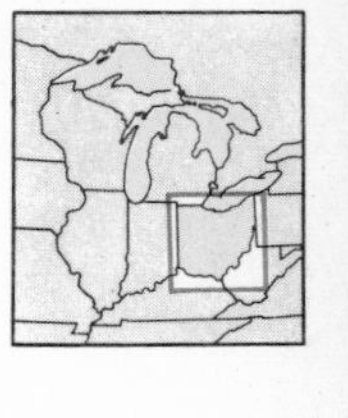

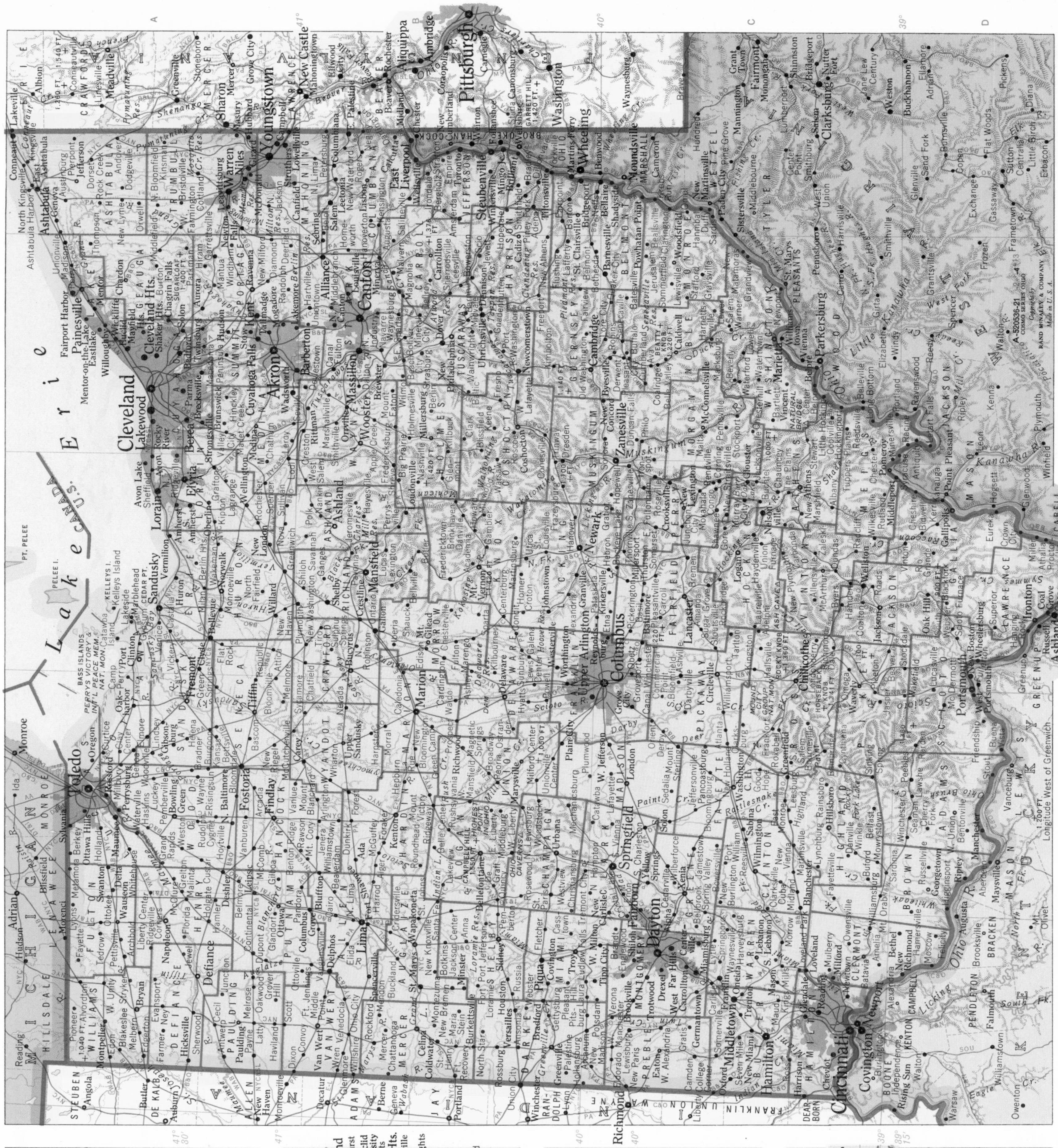

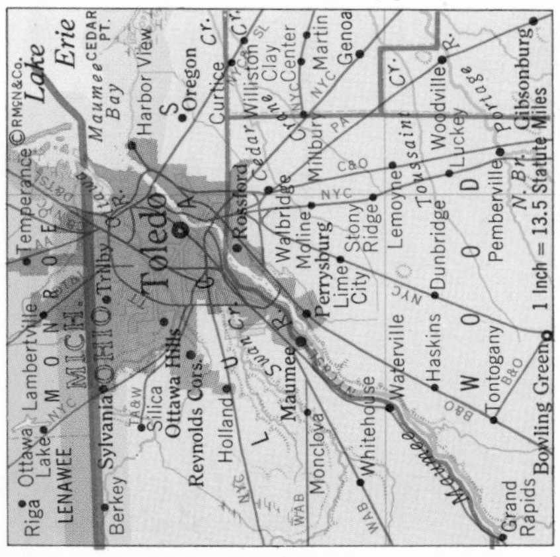

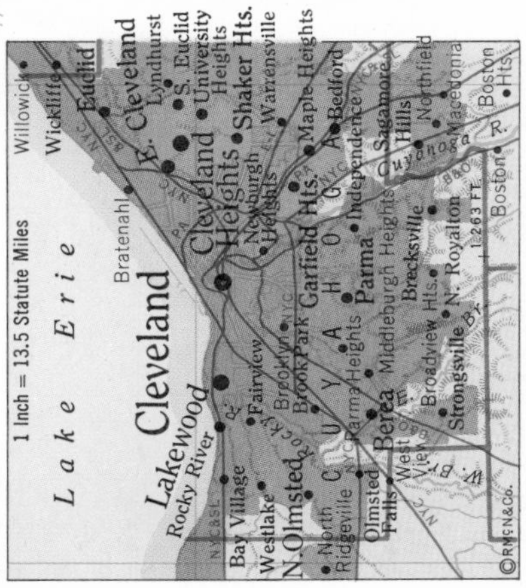

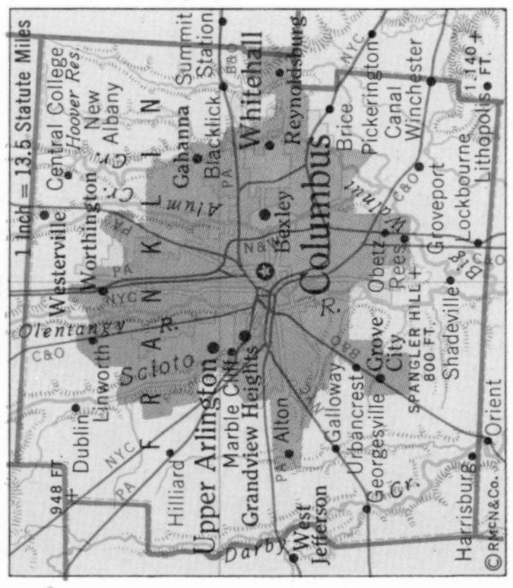

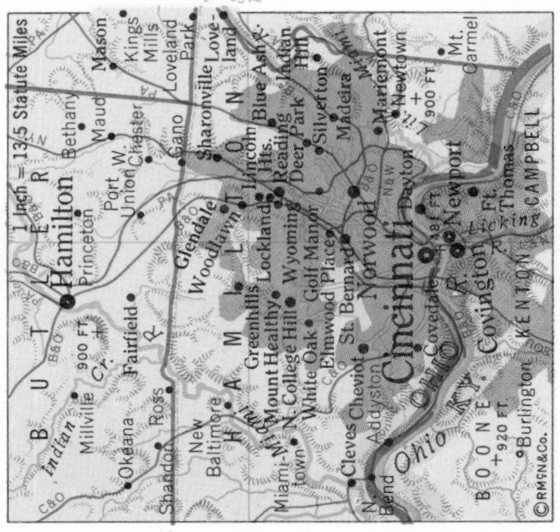

Lambert Conformal Conic Projection
SCALE 1:1,714,000   1 Inch = 27 Statute Miles

Statute Miles

Kilometers

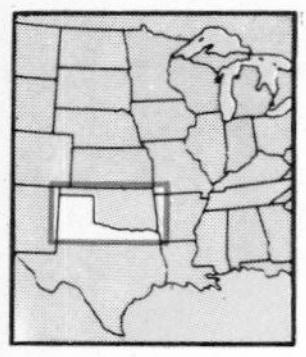

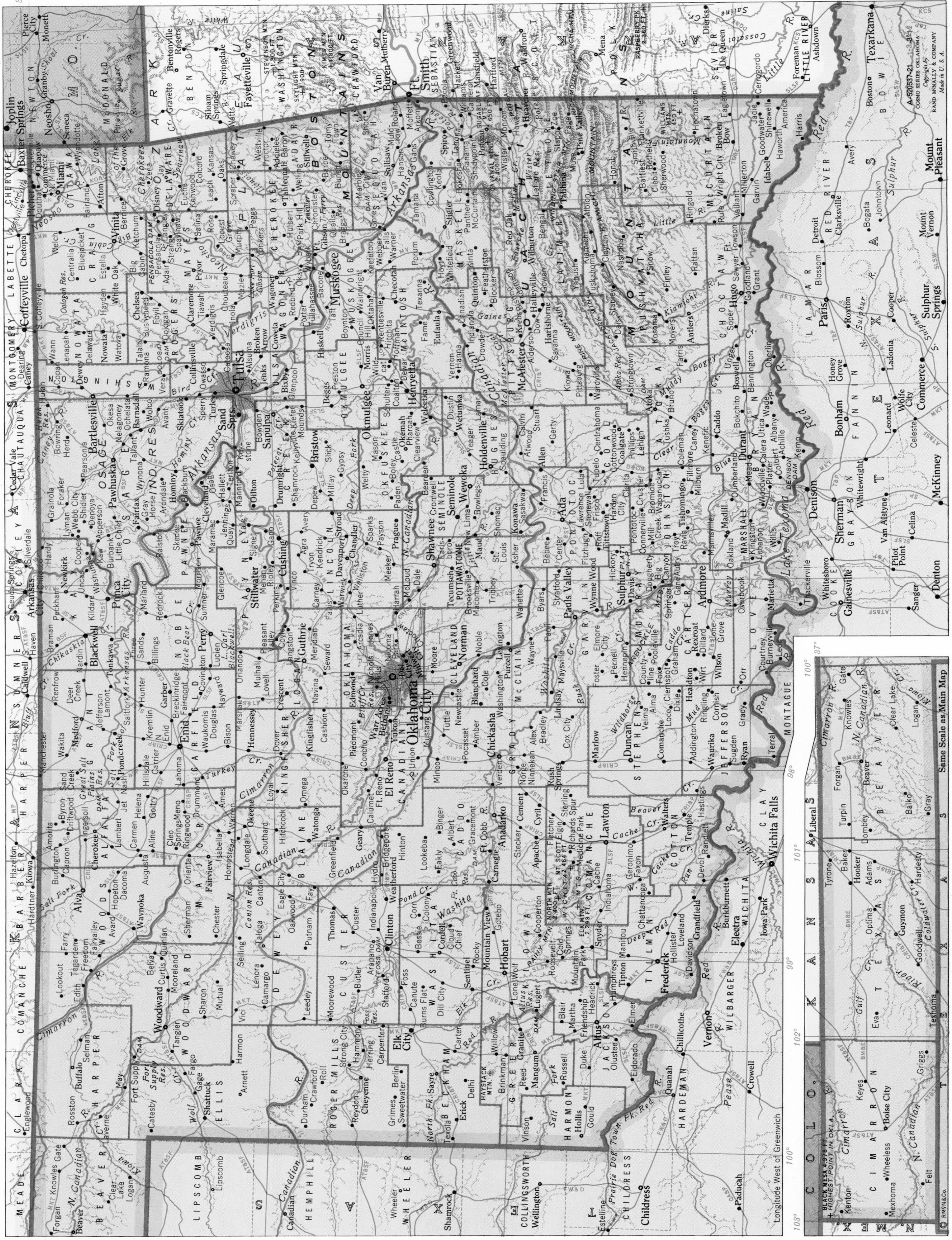

Statute Miles 5 0 5 10 20 30 40
Kilometers 5 0 5 15 25 35 45 55

Lambert Conformal Conic Projection
SCALE 1:1,957,000 1 Inch = 31 Statute Miles

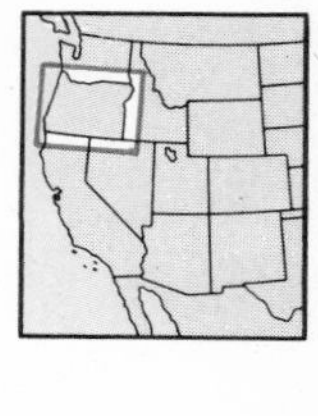

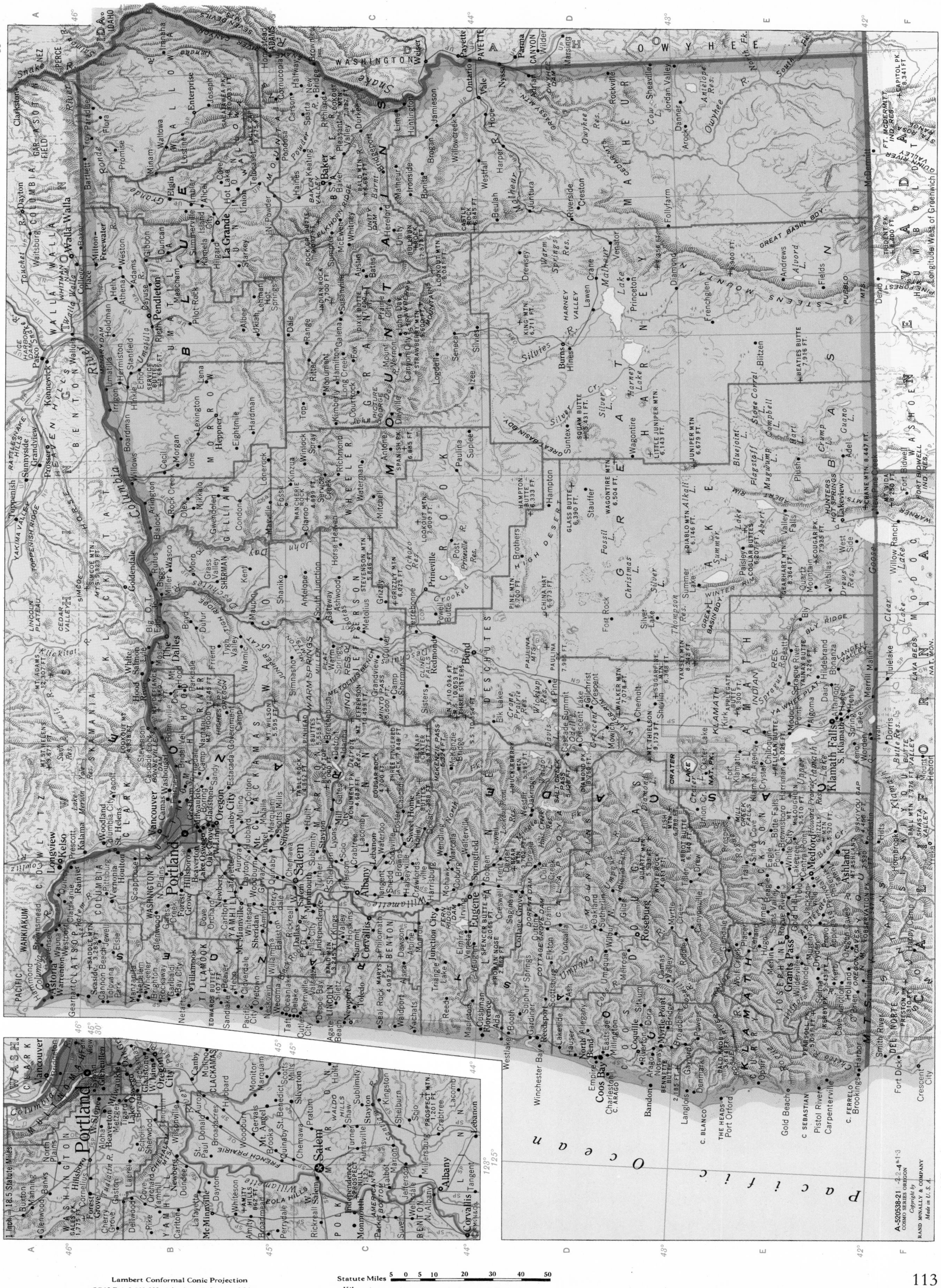

Lambert Conformal Conic Projection
SCALE 1:2,329,000   1 Inch = 37 Statute Miles

Statute Miles 5 0 5 10   20   30   40   50

Kilometers 5 0 5 15 25 35 45 55 65 75

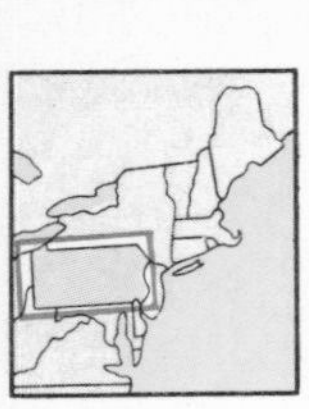

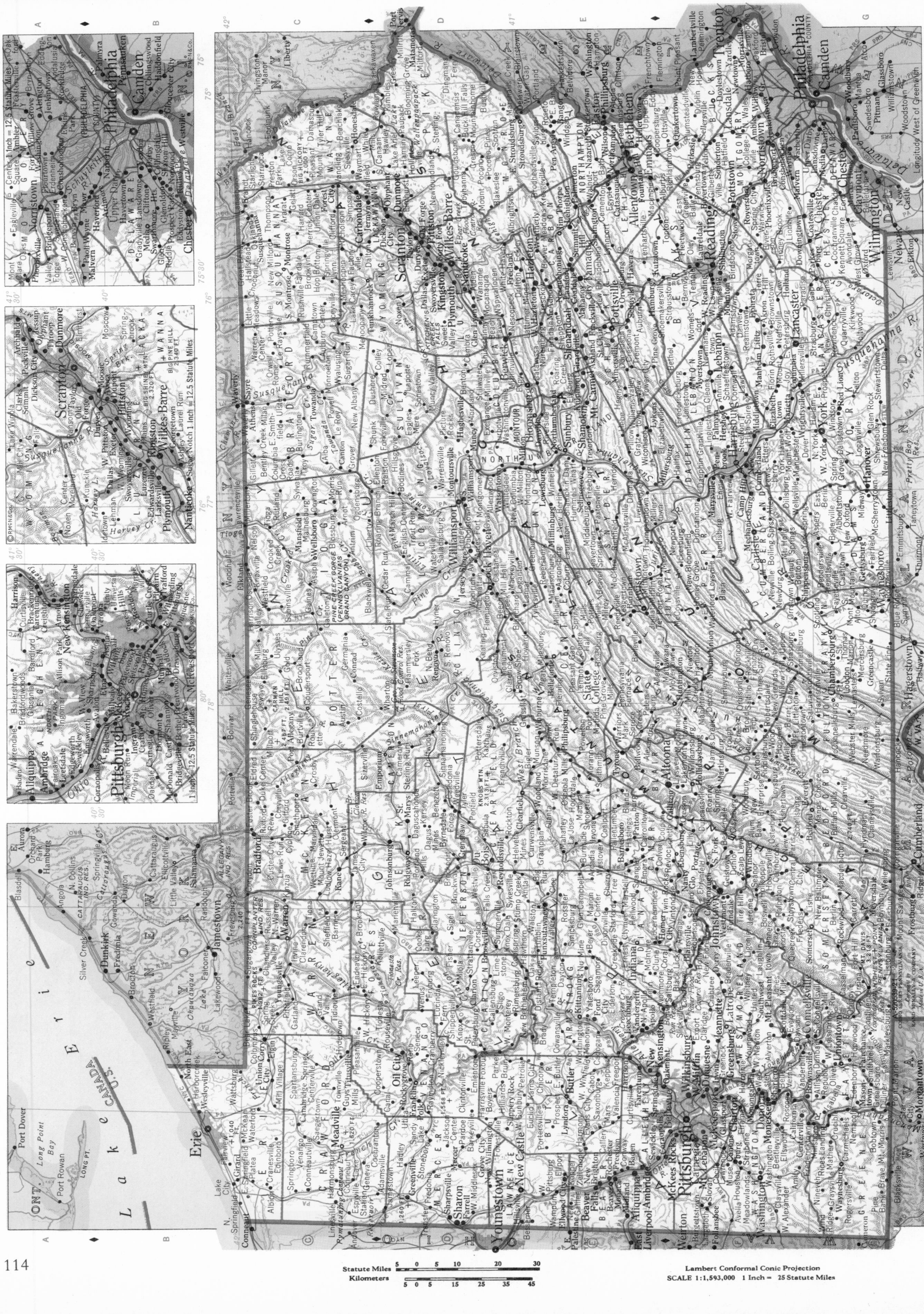

PENNSYLVANIA

Statute Miles

Kilometers

Lambert Conformal Conic Projection
SCALE 1:1,593,000   1 Inch = 25 Statute Miles

A-50561-21
COSMO SERIES SO. CAROLINA
Copyright by
RAND MCNALLY & COMPANY
Made in U.S.A.

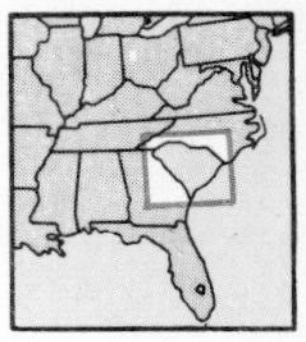

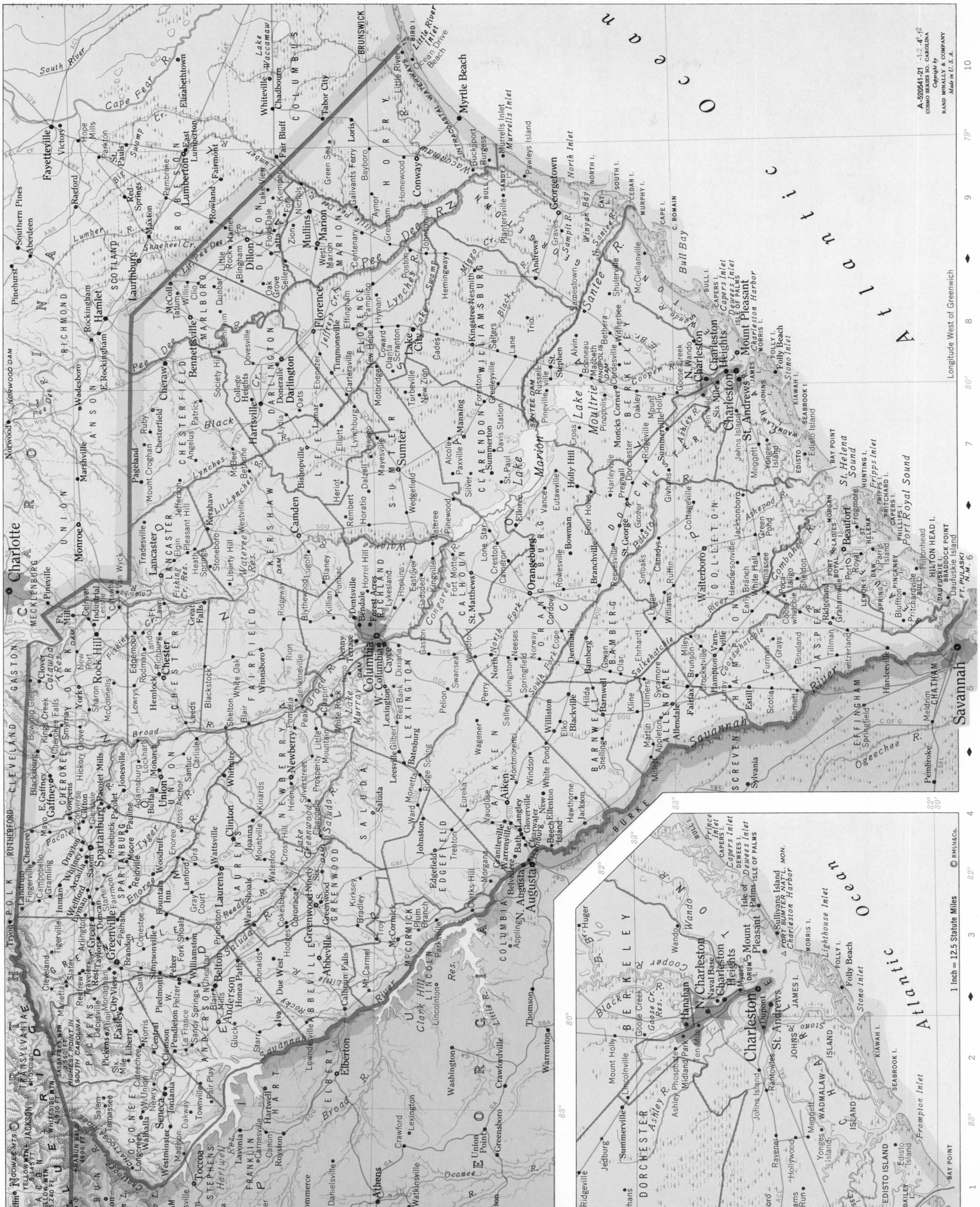

Lambert Conformal Conic Projection
SCALE 1:1,566,000 1 Inch = 25 Statute Miles

Statute Miles

Kilometers

1 Inch = 12.5 Statute Miles

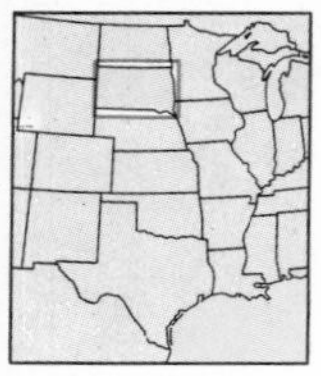

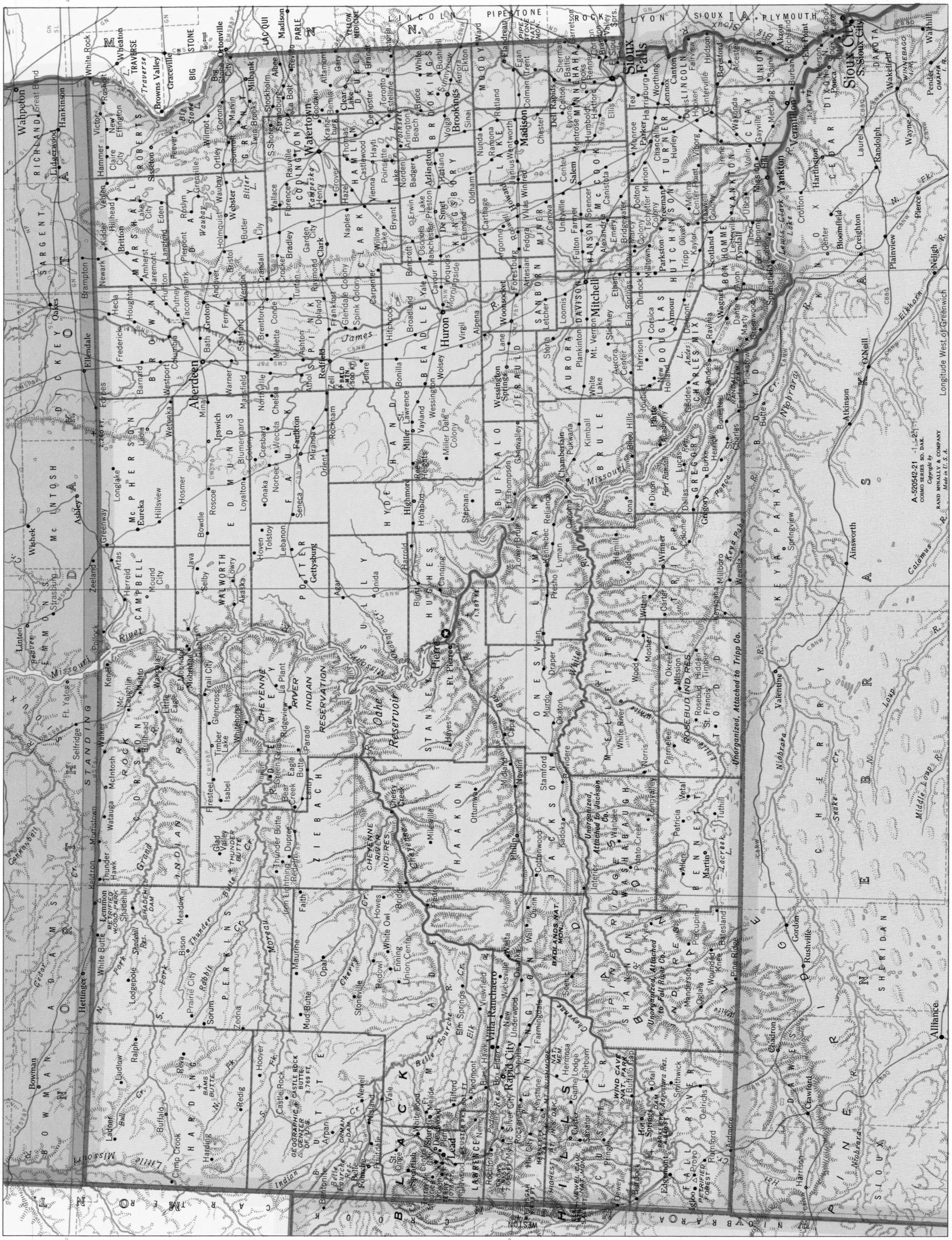

Statute Miles 5 0 5 10 20 30 40 50 60
Kilometers 5 0 5 15 25 35 45 55 65 75

Lambert Conformal Conic Projection
SCALE 1:2,091,000   1 Inch = 33 Statute Miles

A-520542-21
COSMO SERIES SO. DAK.
Rand McNally & Company
Made in U.S.A.

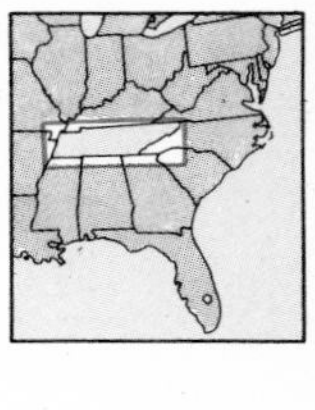

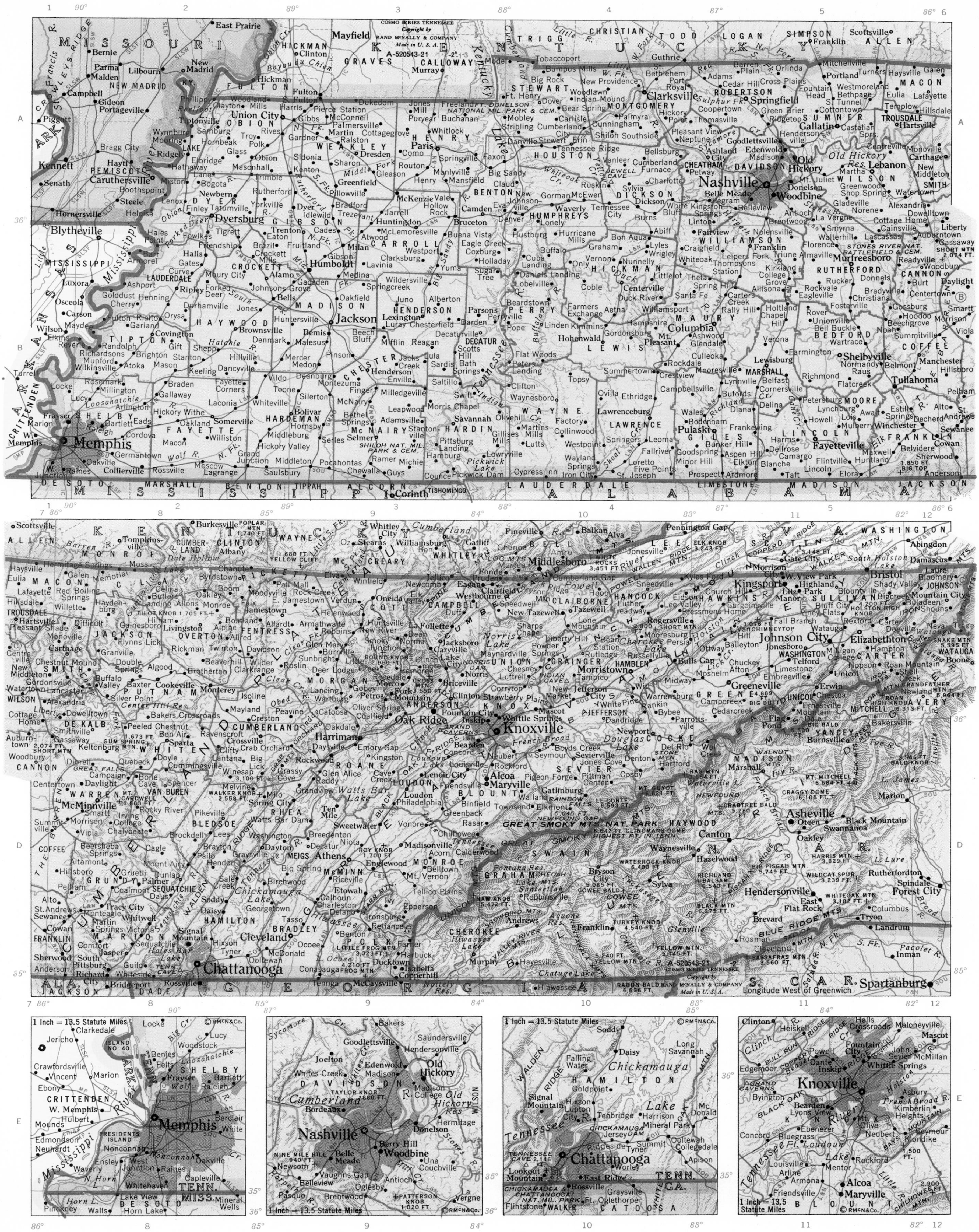

Lambert Conformal Conic Projection
SCALE 1:1,713,000 1 Inch = 27 Statute Miles

Statute Miles
Kilometers

TEXAS

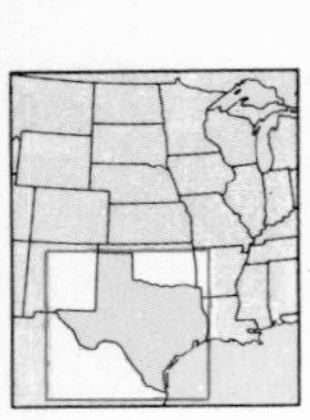

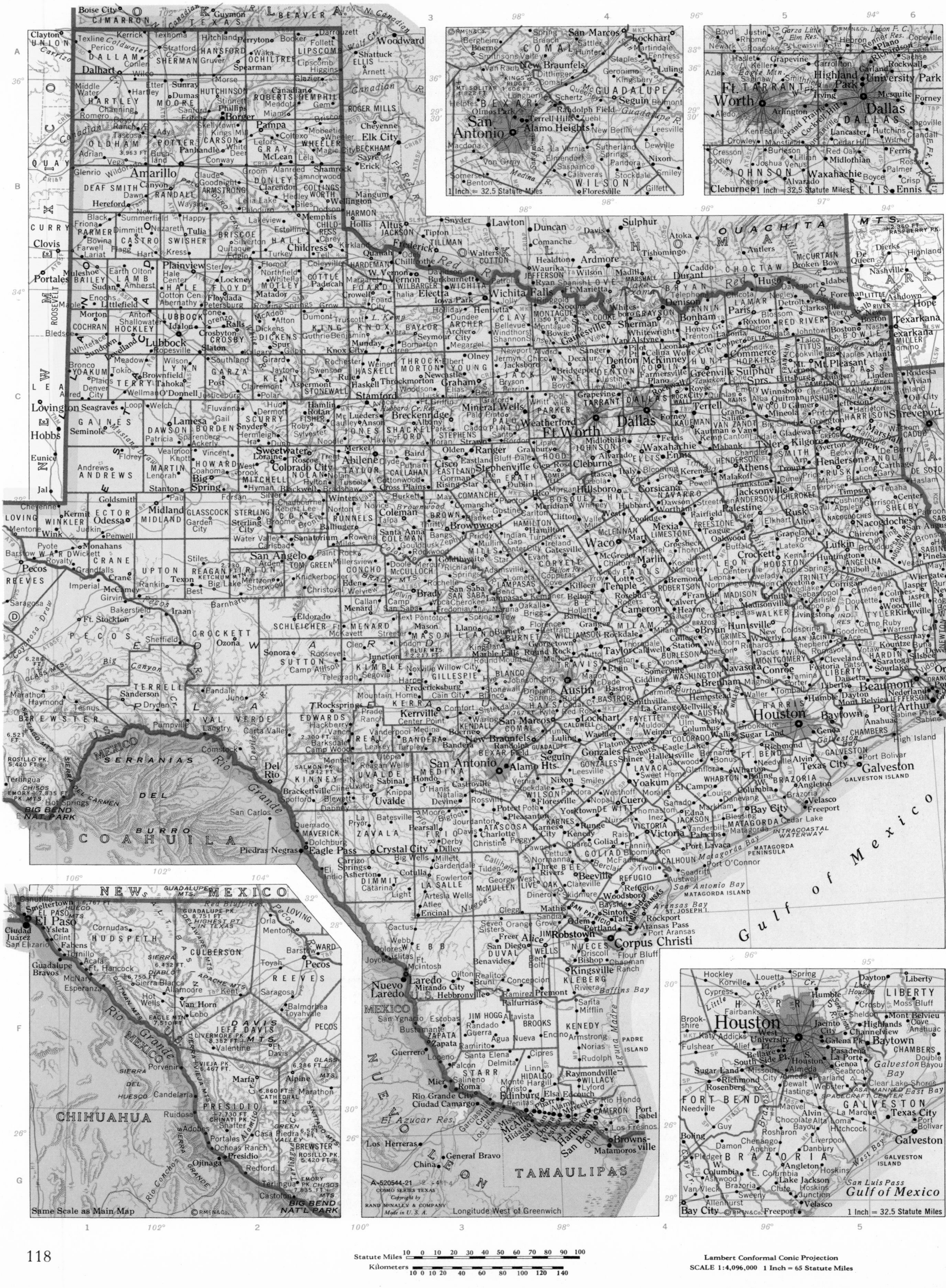

Statute Miles

10 0 10 20 30 40 50 60 70 80 90 100

Kilometers

10 0 10 20 30 40 50 60 80 100 120 140

Lambert Conformal Conic Projection
SCALE 1:4,096,000   1 Inch = 65 Statute Miles

A-520544-21
COSMO SERIES TEXAS
Copyright by
RAND McNALLY & COMPANY
Made in U.S.A.
Longitude West of Greenwich

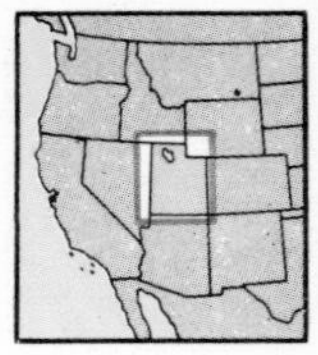

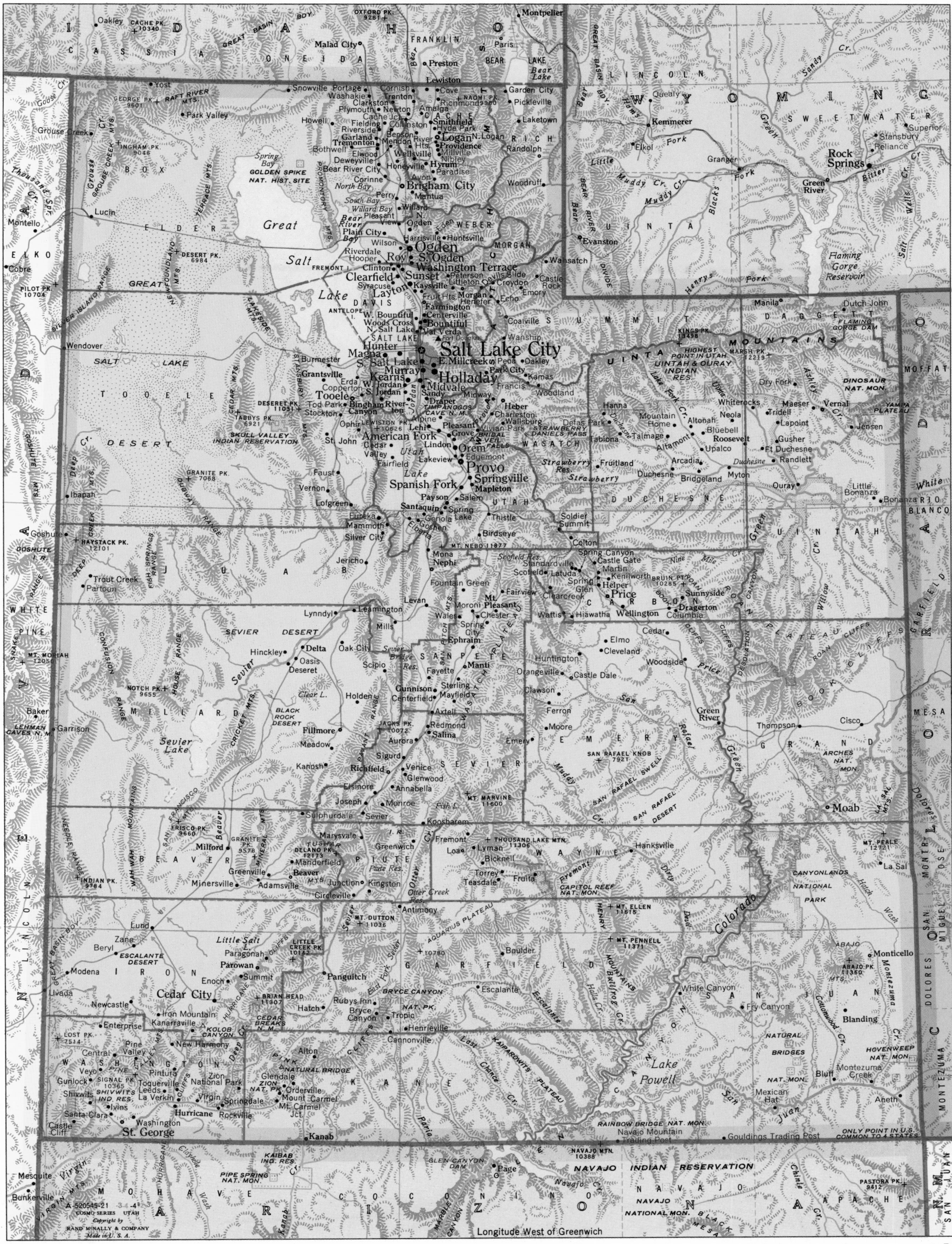

Lambert Conformal Conic Projection
SCALE 1:2,100,000   1 Inch = 33 Statute Miles

Statute Miles
5 0 5 10   20   30   40   50   60

Kilometers
5 0 5   15   25   35   45   55   65   75

Longitude West of Greenwich

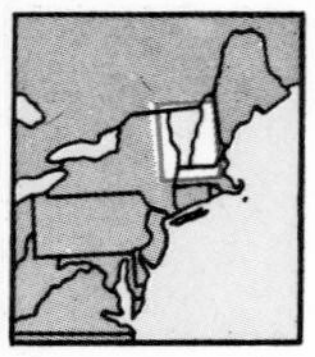

VERMONT

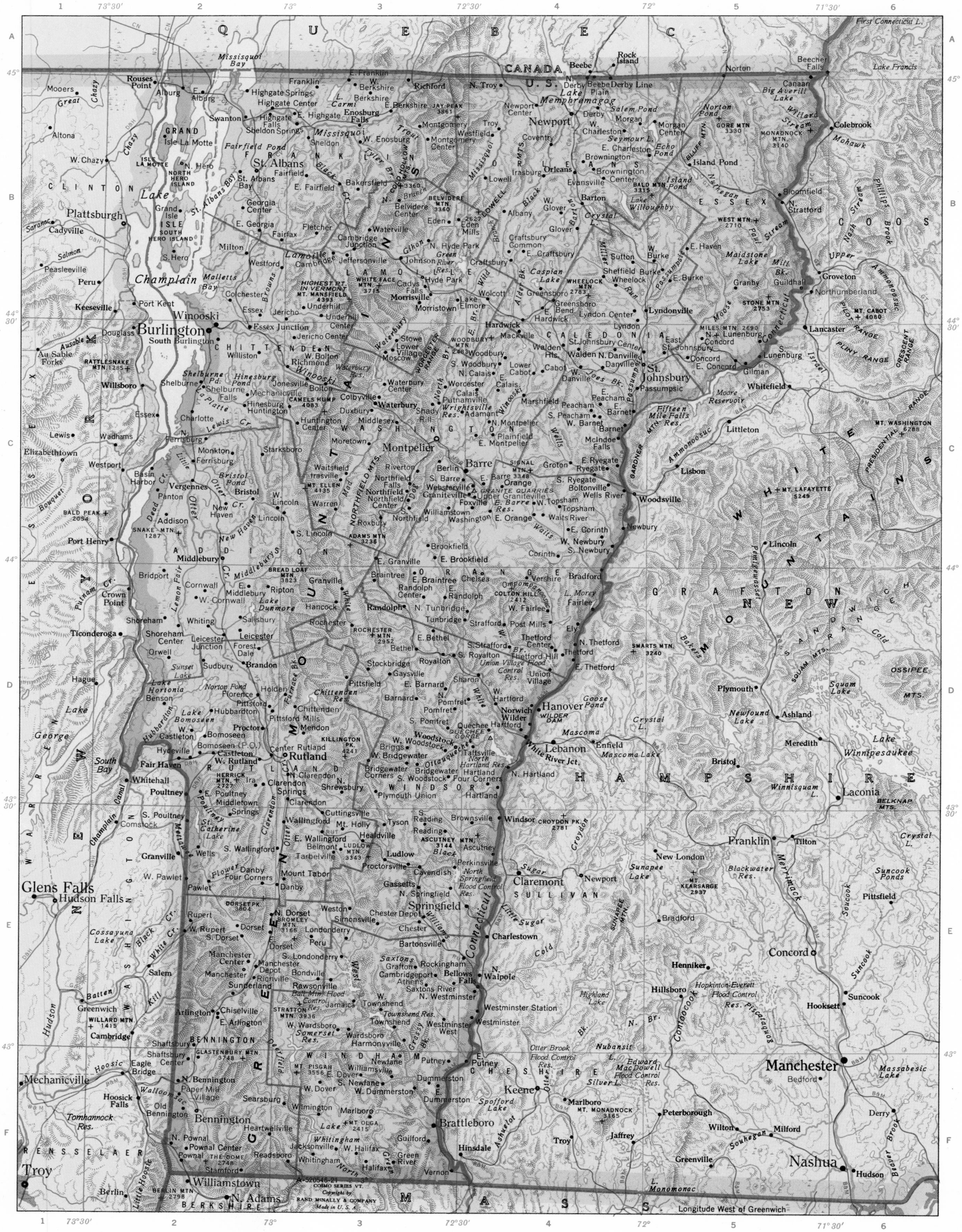

Statute Miles 5 0 5 10 20
Kilometers 5 0 5 10 15 20 25

Lambert Conformal Conic Projection
SCALE 1:903,000 1 Inch = 14.25 Statute Miles

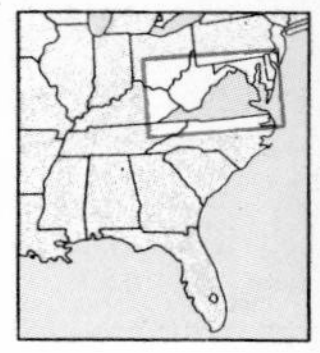

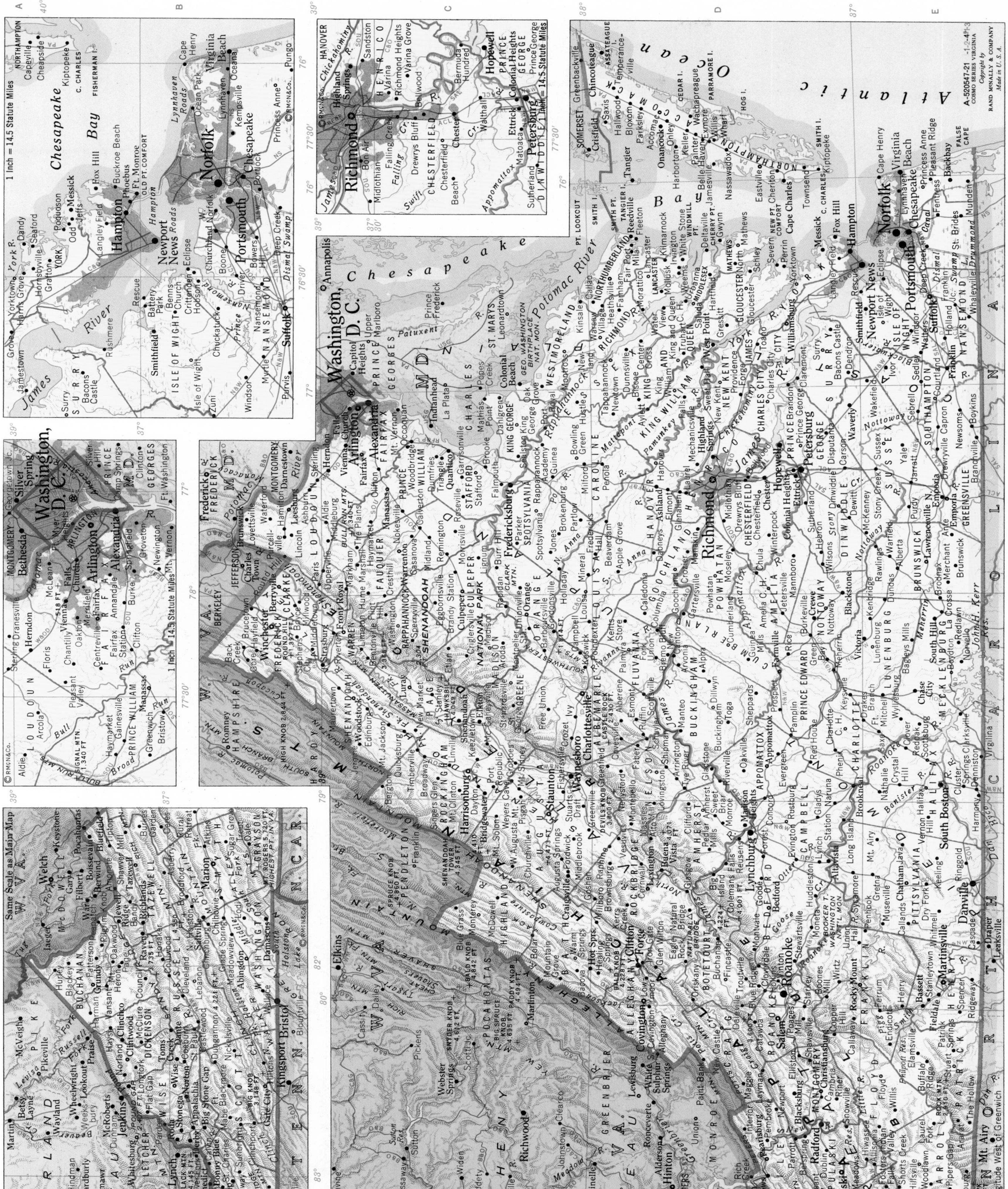

Lambert Conformal Conic Projection
SCALE 1:1,822,000 1 Inch = 29 Statute Miles

Statute Miles
Kilometers

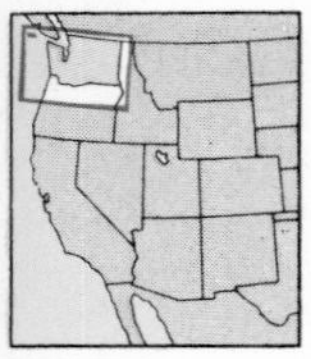

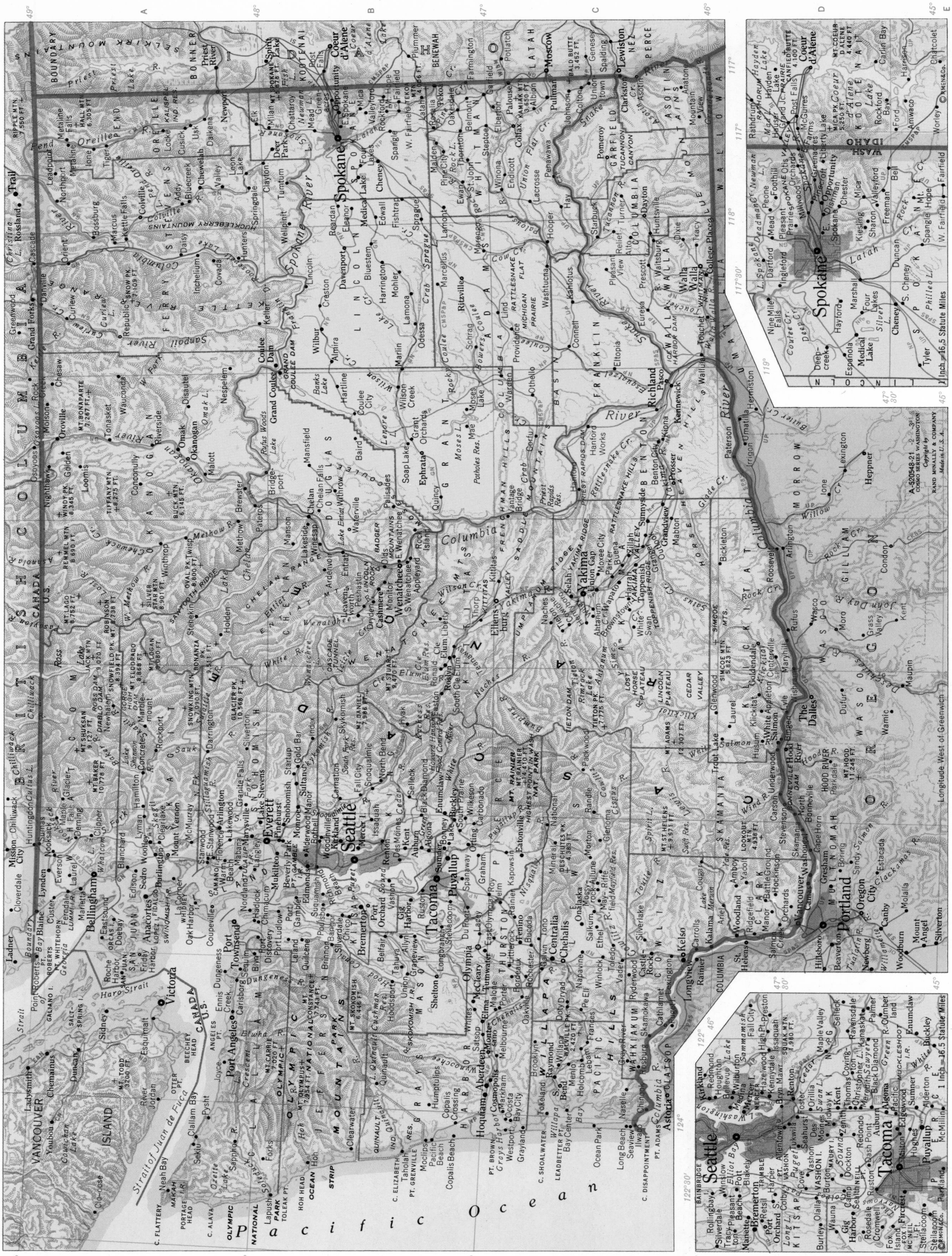

Statute Miles 5 0 5 10 20 30 40 50

Kilometers 5 0 5 15 25 35 45 55 65

Lambert Conformal Conic Projection
SCALE 1:2,068,000 Inch = 33 Statute Miles

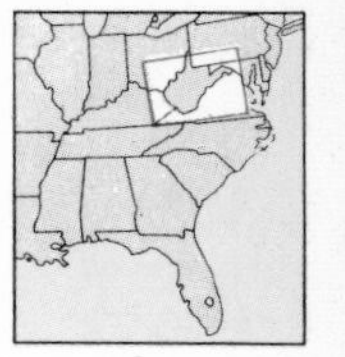

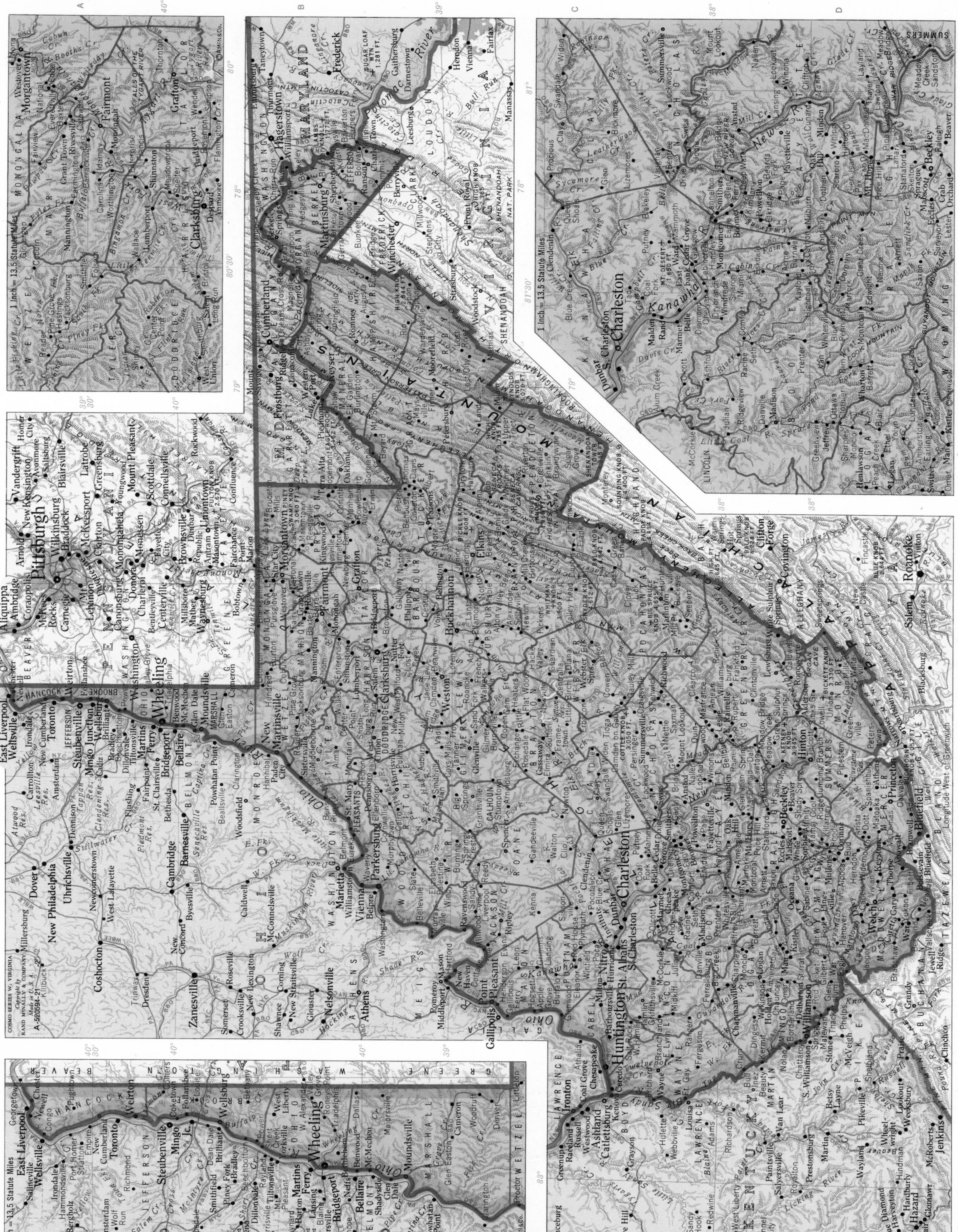

Lambert Conformal Conic Projection
SCALE 1:1,704,000   1 Inch = 27 Statute Miles

Statute Miles   5 0 5   10   20   30   40
Kilometers   5 0 5   15   25   35   45   55

WISCONSIN

Longitude West of Greenwich

1 inch = 16.5 Statute Miles Sheboygan Falls

1 Inch = 16.5 Statute Miles

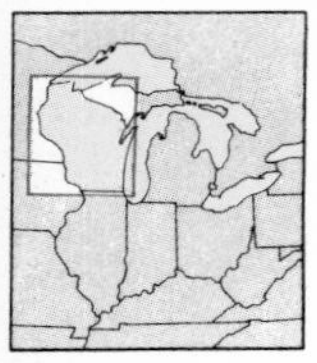

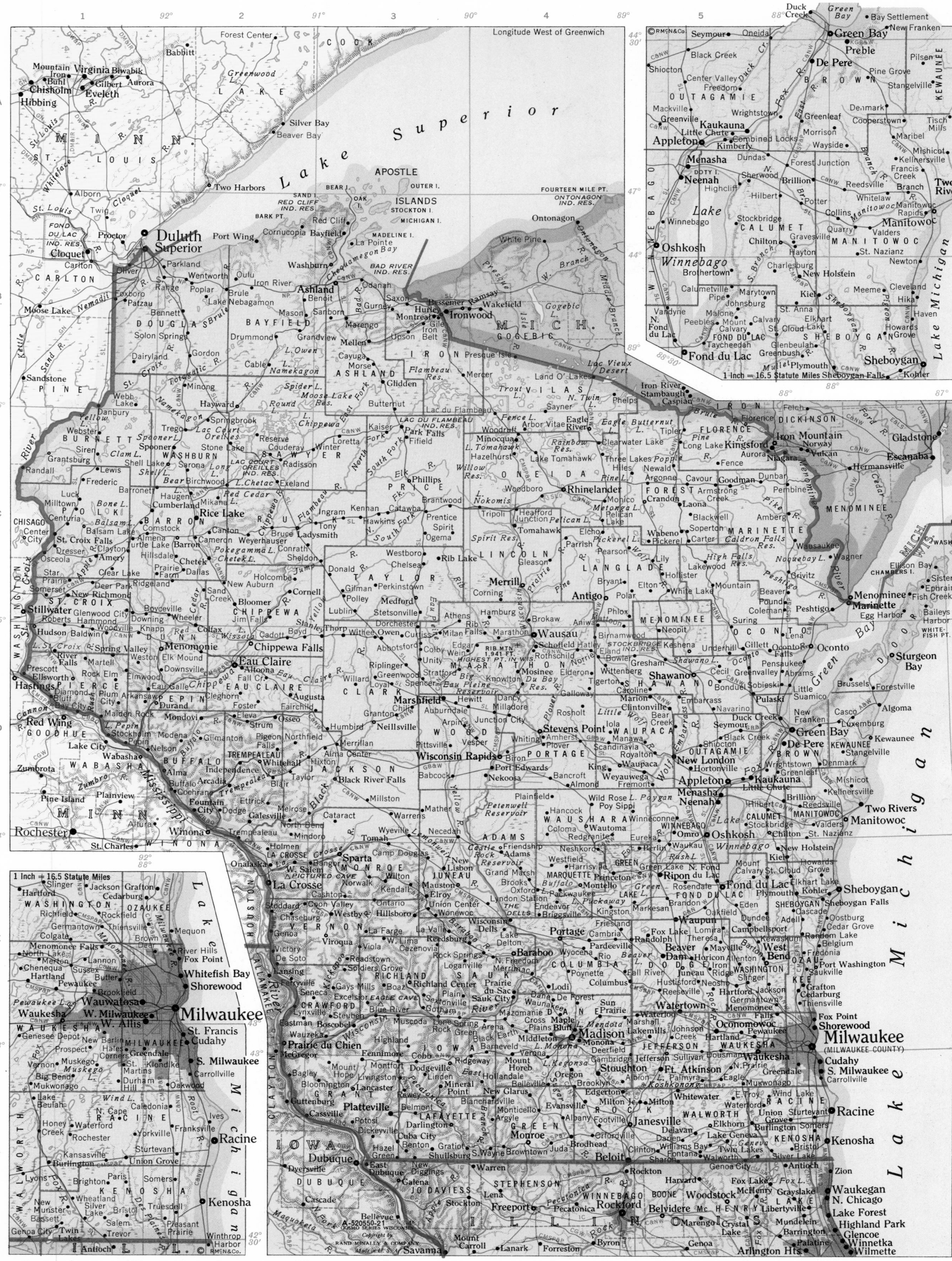

Statute Miles
5 0 5 10 20 30 40

Kilometers
5 0 5 15 25 35 45 55

Lambert Conformal Conic Projection
SCALE 1:2,088,000   1 Inch = 33 Statute Miles

Copyright by
RAND McNALLY & COMPANY
Made in U.S.A.

A-520550-21
COSMO SERIES WISCONSIN

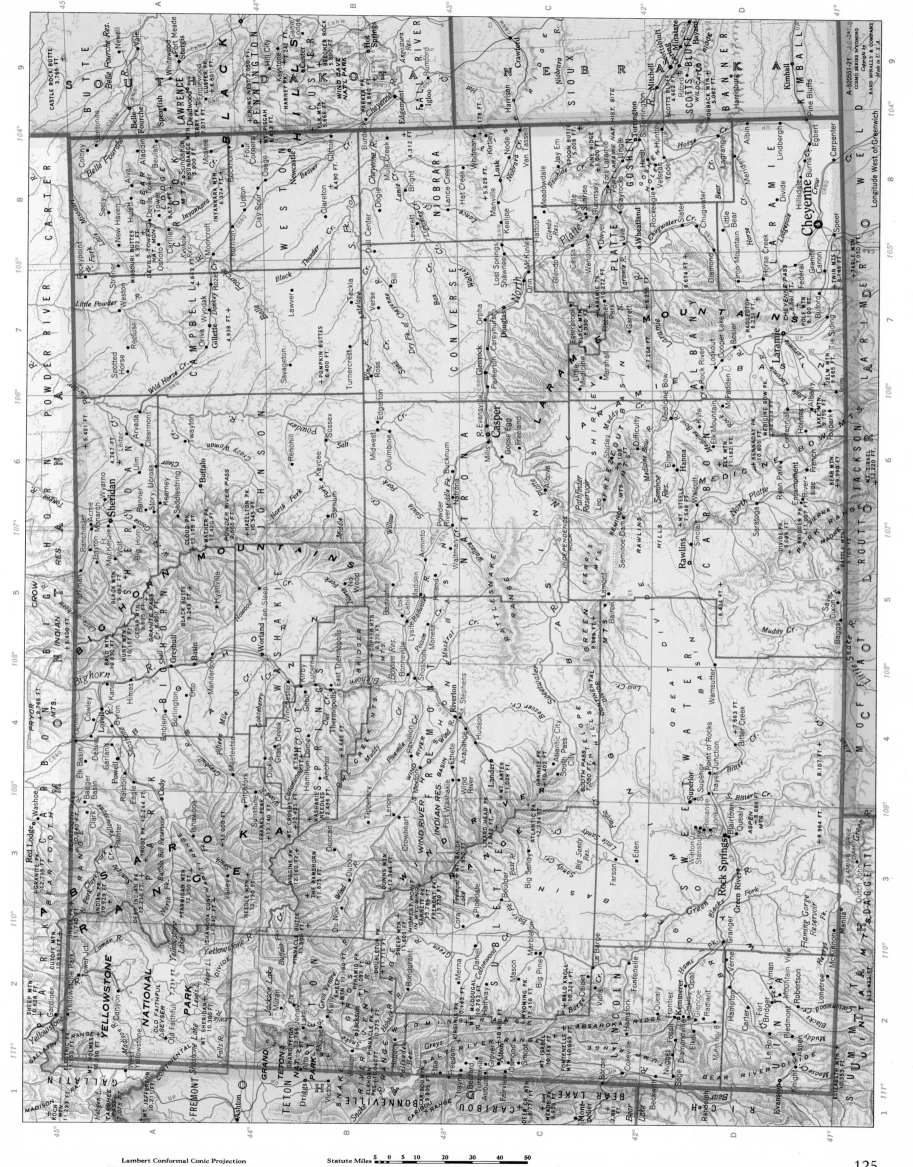

Lambert Conformal Conic Projection
SCALE 1:2,186,000   1 Inch = 34.5 Statute Miles

Statute Miles

Kilometers

THE PHYSICAL WORLD IN MAPS

The maps in the following section cover the world, the continents, Canada, and the United States. Their purpose is to emphasize the Earth's major landforms—mountains, hills, plateaus, valleys, rivers, etc.—and to provide an impression of the depths and contours of the oceans' floors.

To portray the Earth most effectively, the maps have been designed to show both the elevations of features above sea level and also to show the forms of the features. Generalized contour lines indicate the elevation. Multicolored tints, each enclosed by these lines, help differentiate between the elevation zones. (See the opposite page.) These tints become lighter and brighter as the zones increase in elevation, making the higher elevations appear closer to the viewer, creating the illusion of height. A shaded drawing of the Earth's landforms as they might appear when casting a shadow gives the map an additional three-dimensional quality. Superimposed upon the elevation and form information are the major political divisions, their most important cities, and chief transportation routes.

The depths below sea level are pictured conversely to the representation of the land. Shallow water, such as that over continental shelves, is white, and as the oceans assume greater depths, the tints signifying specified depths become darker and darker.

By emphasizing major landforms, these special maps make it possible to gain a broad general impression of the elevation and the forms of the Earth's surface. With this increased understanding of the significant physical features of the Earth, the reader is able to supplement the material contained in the Cosmo Series Maps. The Physical Maps also aid in understanding the relationship of urban development and political boundaries to the Earth's landforms and their elevation.

The symbols used on these maps are described on the opposite page. A diagram of a portion of the Earth's surface shows the way in which it is represented by the maps in this section.

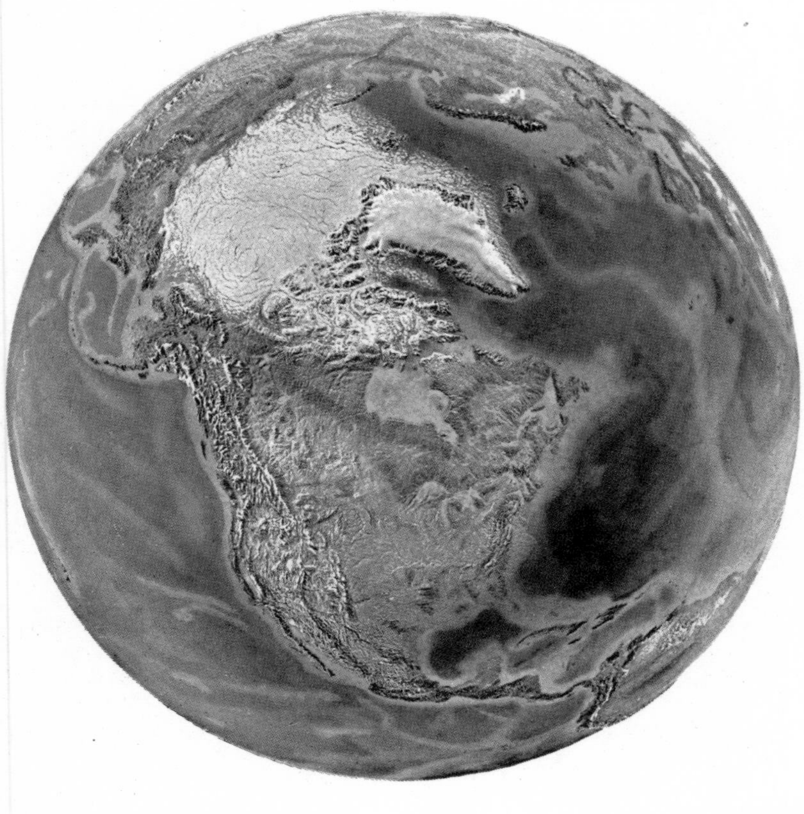

Physical Map Symbols

CULTURAL FEATURES

Political Boundaries

International

Intercolonial

Secondary: State, Provincial, etc.

Disputed or Indefinite

Parks, Indian Reservations

City Limits

Cities, Towns and Villages
(Except for scales of 1:20,000,000 or smaller)

PARIS — 1,000,000 and over

Ufa — 500,000 to 1,000,000

Győr — 50,000 to 500,000

Agadir — 25,000 to 50,000

Moreno — 0 to 25,000

TŌKYŌ — National Capitals

Boise — Secondary Capitals

Transportation

Railroads

Railroad Ferries

Roads

Caravan Routes

Airports

Other Cultural Features

Dams

Pipelines

Pyramids

Ruins

WATER FEATURES

Lakes and Reservoirs

Fresh Water

Fresh Water: Intermittent

Salt Water

Salt Water: Intermittent

Other Water Features

Salt Basins, Flats

Swamps

Ice Caps and Glaciers

Rivers

Canals

Aqueducts

Ship Channels

Falls

Rapids

Springs

Water Depths

Fishing Banks

Sand Bars

Reefs

LAND FEATURES

Peaks, Spot Heights

Passes

Sand

Contours

127

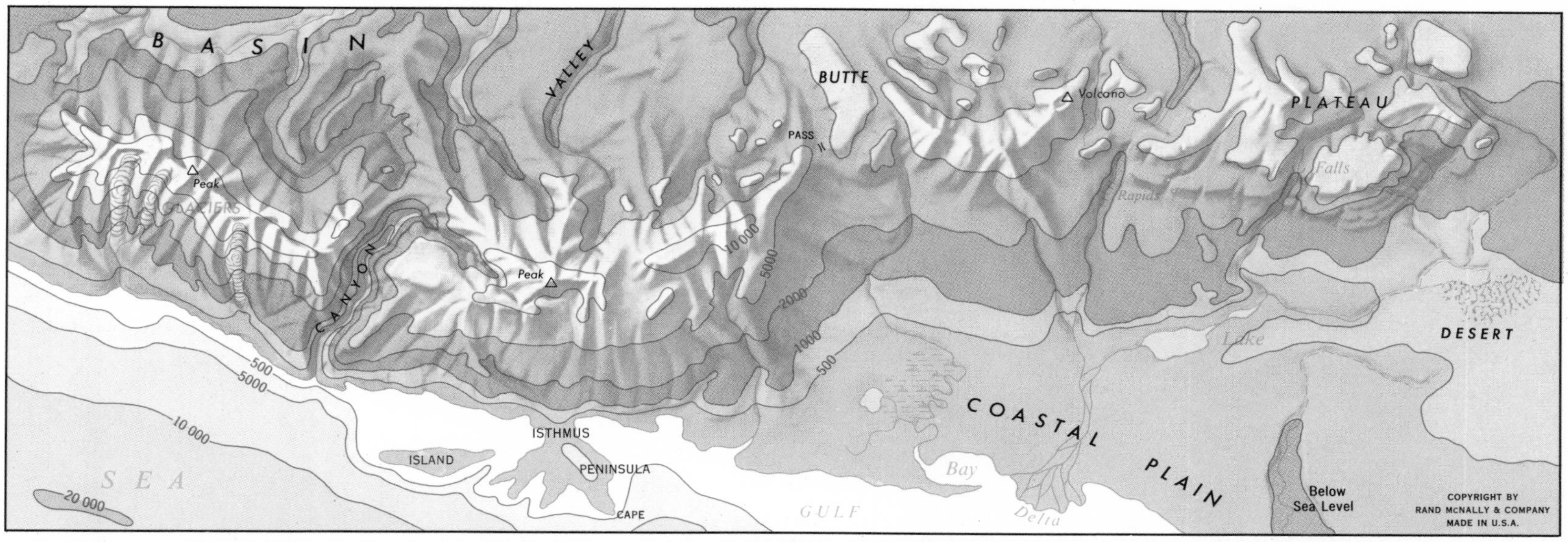

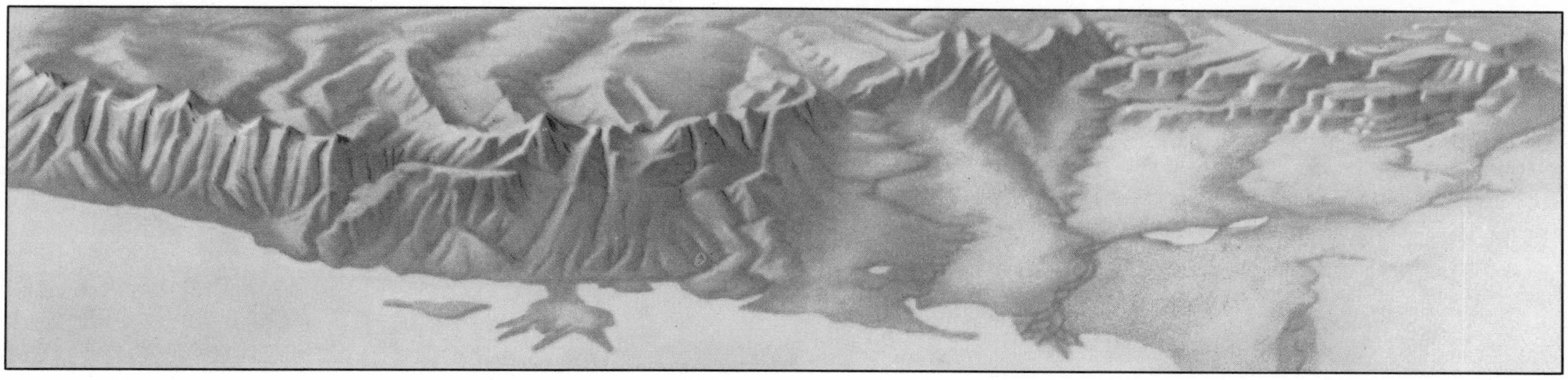

GLOSSARY

Baía, B. (Port.)...............bay
Cabo, C. (Sp.) (Port.).........cape
Cap, C. (Fr.)..................cape
Dar'ya (Turki)................river
Djebel, Dj. (Arab.).......mountain
Erg (Arab.)..........sandy desert
Estrecho, Estr. (Sp.)........strait
Goenoeng, G. (Malay)...mountain
Golfo, G. (Sp.)..................gulf
Gora (Rus.)...............mountain
Guntō (Jap.)............archipelago
Iles, Is. (Fr.).................islands
Ilhas, Is. (Port)..............islands
Islas, Is. (Sp.)...............islands
Istmo (Sp.).................isthmus
Kap (Dan.)......................cape
Kapp (Swe.)....................cape
Khrebet (Rus.)........mtn. range

Note: Abbrev. given may be used on map.

RELIEF

Meters	Feet
3 050	10 000
1 525	5 000
610	2 000
305	1 000
0	0 (SEA L.)
	BELOW SEA LEVEL
152.5	500
3 050	10 000
6 100	20 000

LAND ELEVATIONS

OCEAN DEPTHS

Elevations and depressions

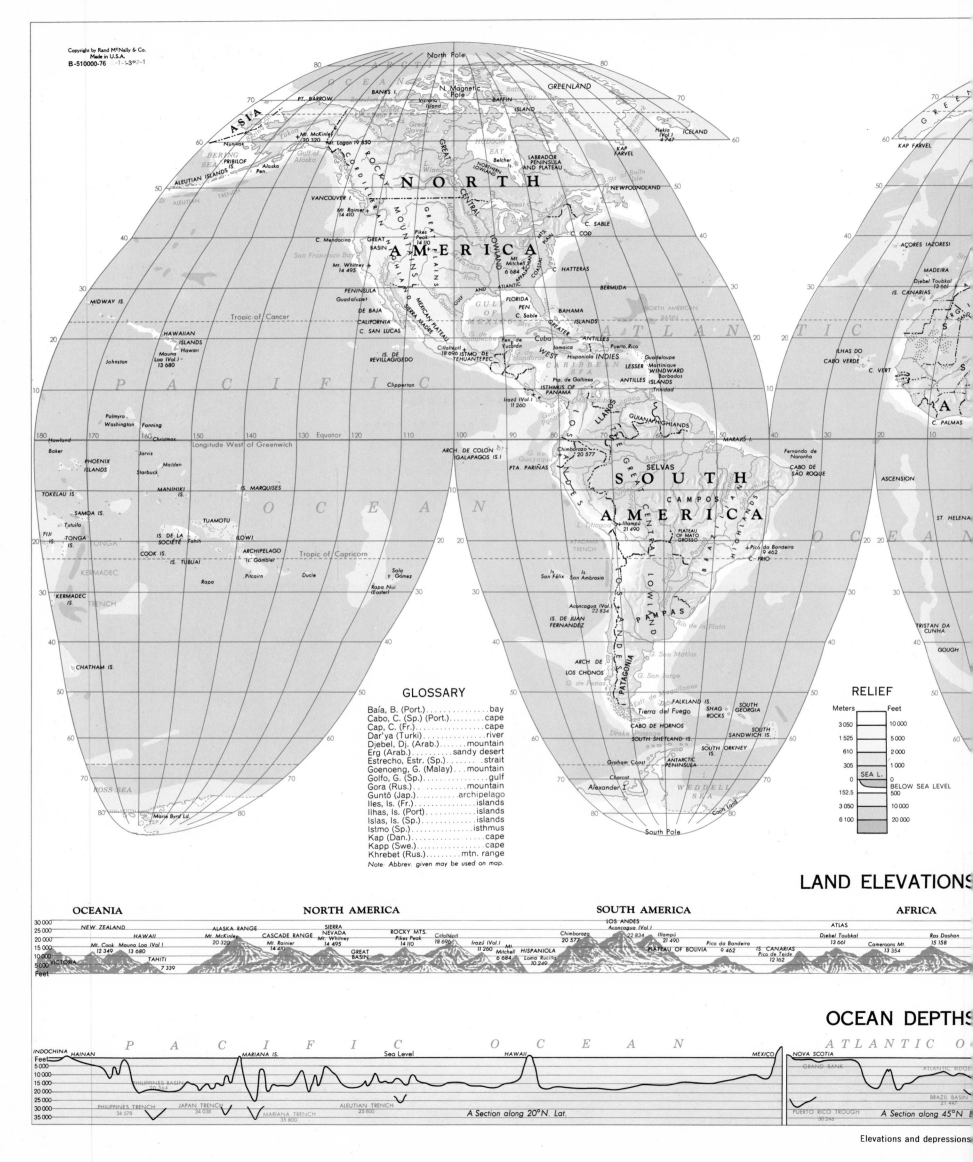

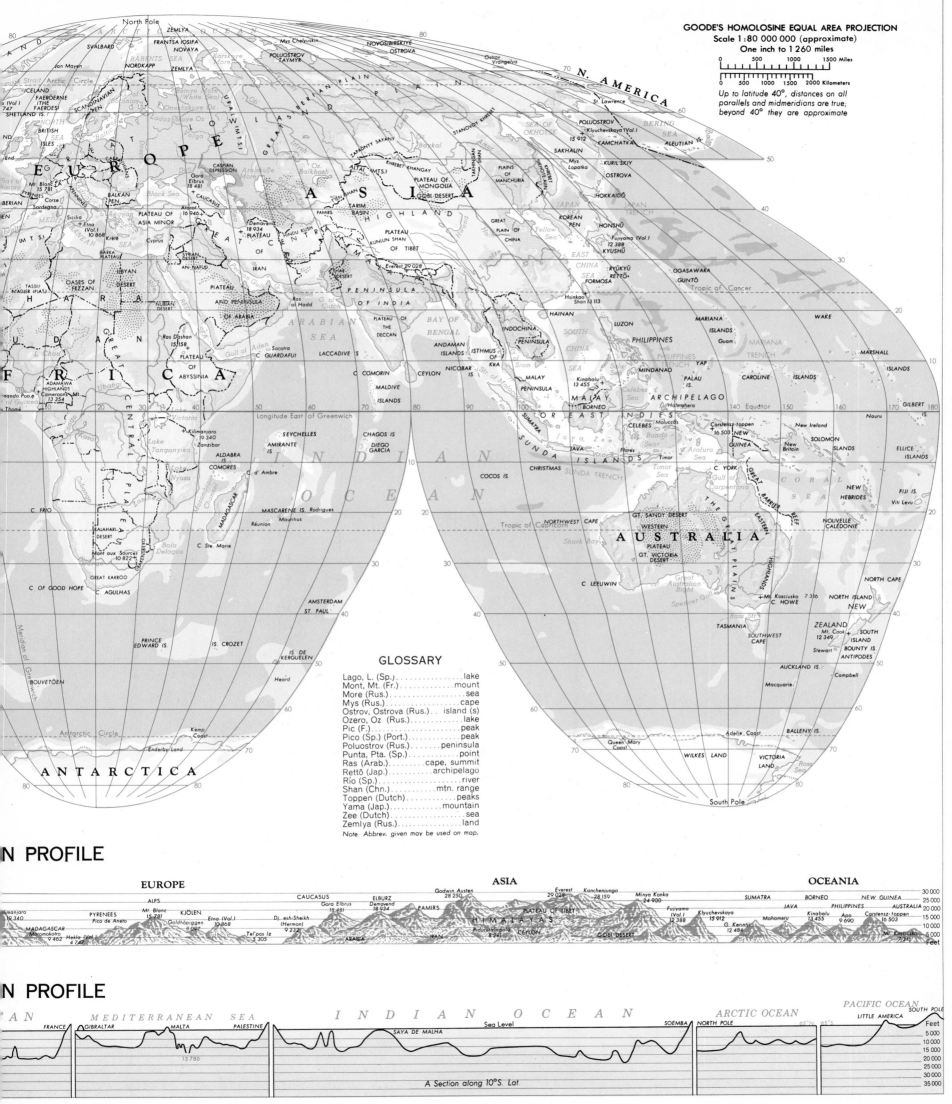

Up to latitude 40°, distances on all parallels and midmeridians are true; beyond 40° they are approximate

GLOSSARY

Lago, L. (Sp.)	lake
Mont, Mt. (Fr.)	mount
More (Rus.)	sea
Mys (Rus.)	cape
Ostrov, Ostrova (Rus.)	island (s)
Ozero, Oz (Rus.)	lake
Pic (F.)	peak
Pico (Sp.) (Port.)	peak
Poluostrov (Rus.)	peninsula
Punta, Pta. (Sp.)	point
Ras (Arab.)	cape, summit
Rettō (Jap.)	archipelago
Río (Sp.)	river
Shan (Chn.)	mtn. range
Toppen (Dutch)	peaks
Yama (Jap.)	mountain
Zee (Dutch)	sea
Zemlya (Rus.)	land

Note. Abbrev. given may be used on map.

N PROFILE

EUROPE ASIA OCEANIA

A Section along 10°S. Lat

e given in feet

EUROPE

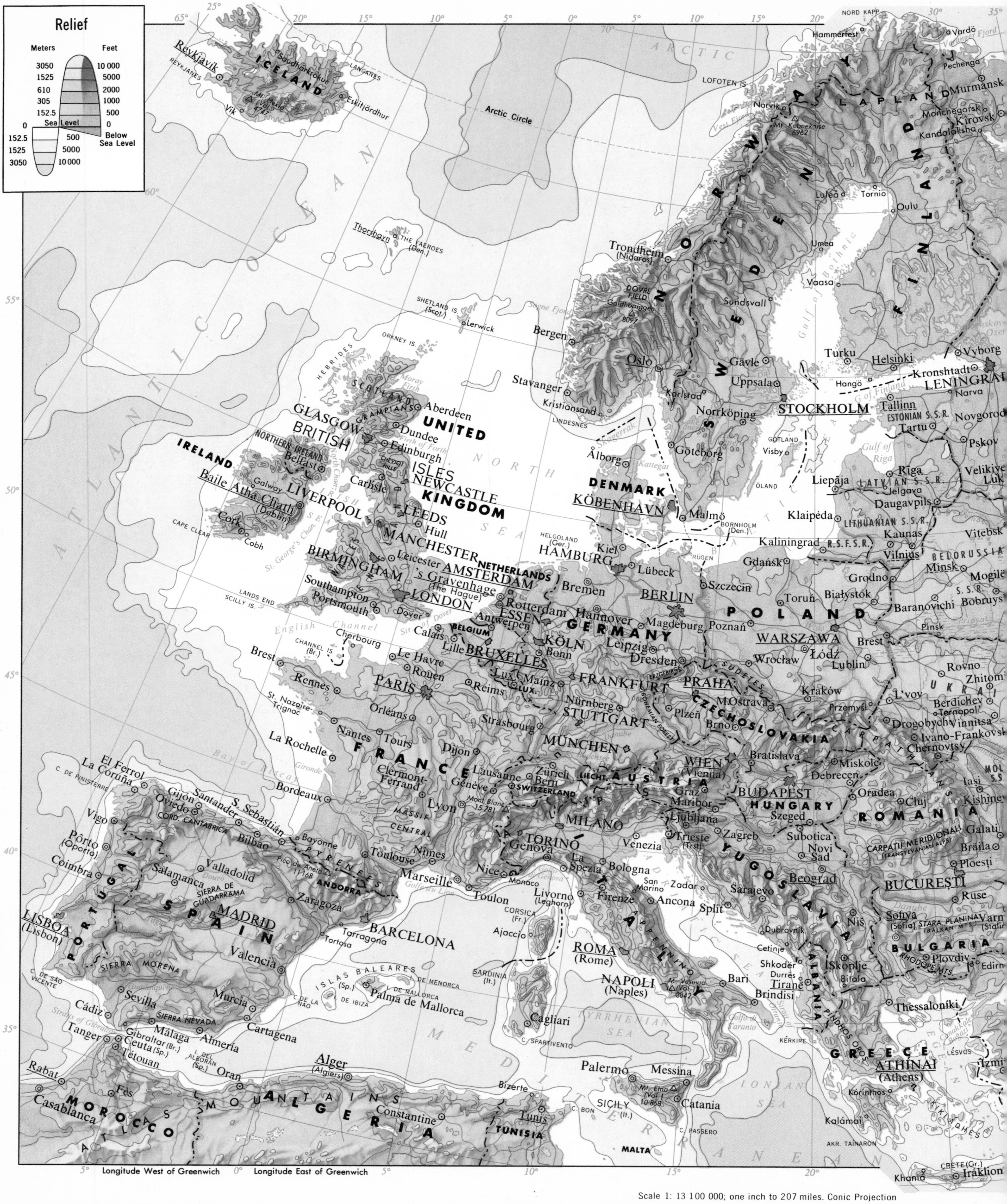

Relief

Meters		Feet
3050		10 000
1525		5000
610		2000
305		1000
152.5		500
0	Sea Level	0
152.5		Below
500		Sea Level
1525	500	
3050	5000	
	10 000	

Scale 1: 13 100 000; one inch to 207 miles. Conic Projection
Elevations and depressions are given in feet

Longitude West of Greenwich   Longitude East of Greenwich

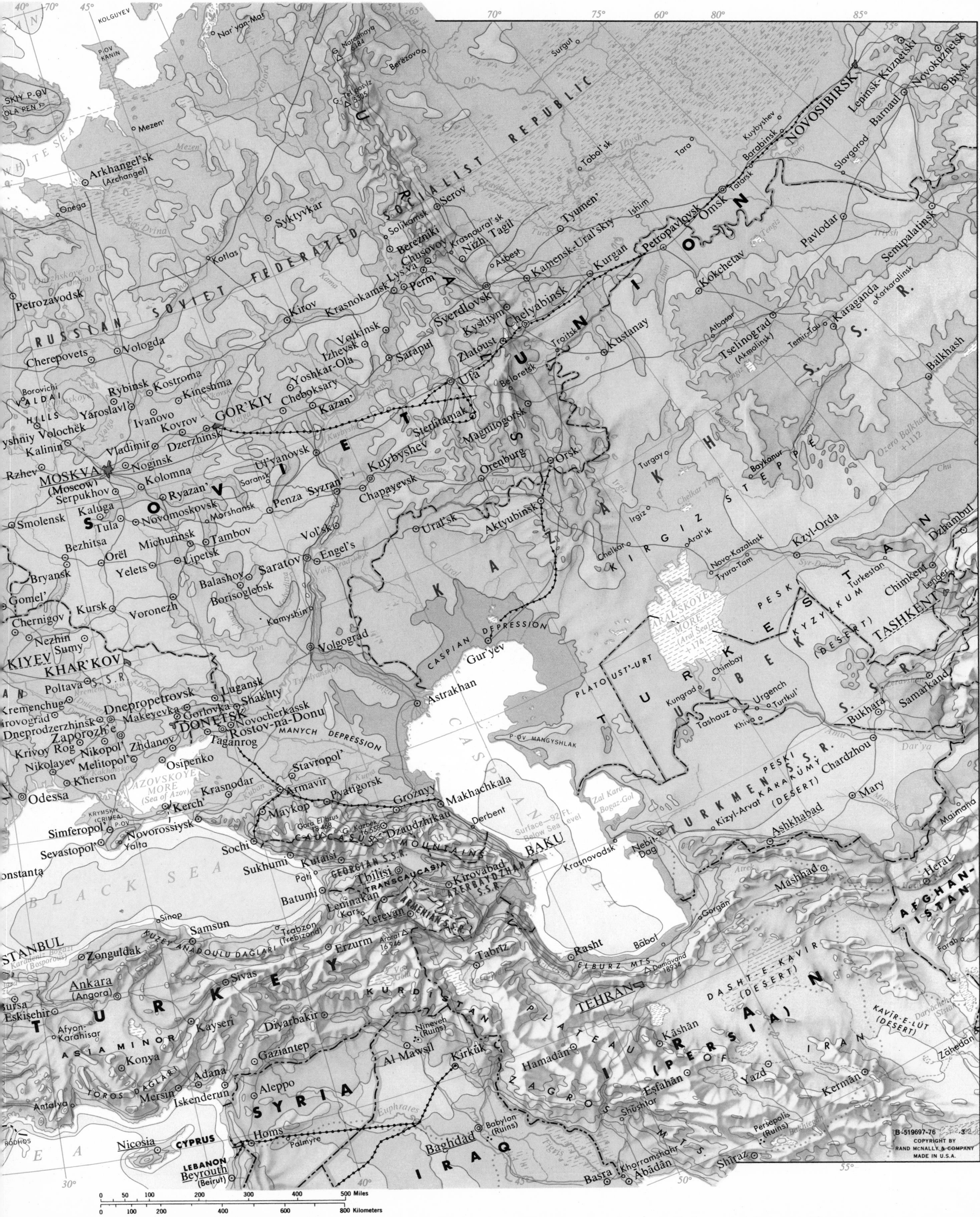
KOLGUYEV
P-OV KANIN
Nar'yan-Mar
G. Narodnaya 6184
G. Tel'posiz 5305
Berëzovo
Surgut
Ob'
WHITE SEA
Mezen'
Arkhangel'sk (Archangel)
Onega
SOVIET FEDERATED SOCIALIST REPUBLIC
RUSSIAN
URAL
Syktyvkar
Solikamsk
Serov
Berezniki
Krasnoural'sk
Nizh. Tagil
Chusovoy
Lys'va
Perm'
Kotlas
Kirov
Krasnokamsk
Asbest
Tobol'sk
Tara
Tyumen'
Ishim
Kamensk-Ural'skiy
Kurgan
Petropavlovsk
Omsk
Tatarsk
Barabinsk
Kuybyshev
NOVOSIBIRSK
Leninsk-Kuznetskiy
Novokuznetsk
Barnaul
Biysk
Slavgorod
Pavlodar
Semipalatinsk
Kokchetav
Sverdlovsk
Chelyabinsk
Kyshtym
Zlatoust
Troitsk
Kustanay
Petrozavodsk
Vologda
Cherepovets
Votkinsk
Izhevsk
Sarapul
Yoshkar-Ola
Cheboksary
Kazan'
Ufa
Beloretsk
Magnitogorsk
Sterlitamak
Borovichi
VALDAI HILLS
Rybinsk
Kostroma
Kineshma
Yaroslavl'
Ivanovo
Kovrov
GOR'KIY
Dzerzhinsk
Vyshniy Volochëk
Kalinin
Vladimir
Noginsk
Rzhev
MOSKVA (Moscow)
Kolomna
Serpukhov
Ryazan'
Saransk
Ul'yanovsk
Kuybyshev
Syzran'
Chapayevsk
Penza
Orenburg
Orsk
Kaluga
Tula
Novomoskovsk
Morshansk
Smolensk
Tambov
Michurinsk
Bezhitsa
Orël
Lipetsk
Yelets
Saratov
Engel's
Vol'sk
Ural'sk
Aktyubinsk
Balashov
Borisoglebsk
Bryansk
Gomel'
Kursk
Voronezh
Chernigov
Kamyshin
Nezhin
Sumy
KIYEV
KHAR'KOV
Volgograd
Poltava
Lugansk
Shakhty
Kremenchug
Kirovograd
Dnepropetrovsk
Dneprodzerzhinsk
Makeyevka
Gorlovka
DONETSK
Novocherkassk
Rostov-na-Donu
Zaporozh'e
Krivoy Rog
Nikopol'
Zhdanov
Taganrog
Nikolayev
Melitopol'
Osipenko
Kherson
Odessa
AZOVSKOYE MORE (Sea of Azov)
Kerch'
Krasnodar
Stavropol'
Armavir
Pyatigorsk
Groznyy
Makhachkala
Maykop
Simferopol'
Novorossiysk
Yalta
Sevastopol'
Sochi
Gora El'brus 18,468
G. Kazbek 16,558
Dzaudzhikau
CAUCASUS MOUNTAINS
Derbent
BAKU
Sukhumi
Kutaisi
Poti
GEORGIAN S.S.R.
Tbilisi
TRANSCAUCASIA
Kirovabad
AZERBAYDZHAN S.S.R.
Batumi
Leninakan
Kars
Yerevan
ARMENIAN S.S.R.
Constanța
BLACK SEA
Sinop
Samsun
Trabzon (Trebizond)
Erzurum
Ararat 16,946
Tabriz
STANBUL
Karadeniz Boğazı (Bosporous)
Zonguldak
KUZEY ANADOLU DAĞLARI
Ankara (Angora)
Sivas
Eskişehir
TURKEY
Afyon-Karahisar
Kayseri
Diyarbakir
KURDISTAN
Nineveh (Ruins)
ASIA MINOR
Konya
Gaziantep
Al Mawsil
Kirkūk
TOROS DAĞLARI
Adana
Mersin
Iskenderun
Aleppo
Antalya
SYRIA
Euphrates
RODHOS
Nicosia
CYPRUS
LEBANON
Beyrouth (Beirut)
Homs
Palmyra
Baghdad
IRAQ
Babylon (Ruins)
Tigris
Basra
Khorramshahr
Ābādān
KAZAKH S.S.R.
SOVIET UNION
TURGAY
Turgay
Irgiz
Chelkar
Aral'sk
KIRGIZ STEPPE
Baykonur
Atbasar
Tselinograd (Akmolinsk)
Temir-Tau
Karaganda
Karkaralinsk
Balkhash
Ozero Balkhash +1112
Chu
Kzyl-Orda
Novo-Kazalinsk
Tyura-Tam
ARAL'SKOYE MORE (Aral Sea) +174
PESKI KYZYLKUM (DESERT)
Turkestan
Chimkent
Lenger
Dzhambul
TASHKENT
UZBEK S.S.R.
CASPIAN DEPRESSION
Gur'yev
Astrakhan
MANYCH DEPRESSION
PLATO UST'-URT
Chimbay
Kungrad
Urgench
Turtkul'
Tashauz
Khiva
Bukhara
Samarkand
P-OV MANGYSHLAK
CASPIAN SEA
Surface—92 Ft. Below Sea Level
Zal Kara Bogaz-Gol
Amu Dar'ya
TURKMEN S.S.R.
PESKI KARAKUMY (DESERT)
Kizyl-Arvat
Chardzhou
Mary
Maimana
Krasnovodsk
Nebit-Dag
Ashkhabad
Atrek
Mashhad
Herat
AFGHANISTAN
Gorgān
Rasht
Bābol
ELBURZ MTS.
Damāvand 18,934
TEHRAN
DASHT-E-KAVIR (DESERT)
KAVĪR-E-LŪT (DESERT)
Farah
Zāhedān
IRAN (PERSIA)
PLATEAU OF IRAN
ZAGROS MTS.
Hamadān
Kāshān
Eşfahān
Yazd
Kermān
Shūshtar
Persepolis (Ruins)
Shīrāz
B-519697-76
COPYRIGHT BY RAND McNALLY & COMPANY MADE IN U.S.A.
0 50 100 200 300 400 500 Miles
0 100 200 400 600 800 Kilometers

EURASIA

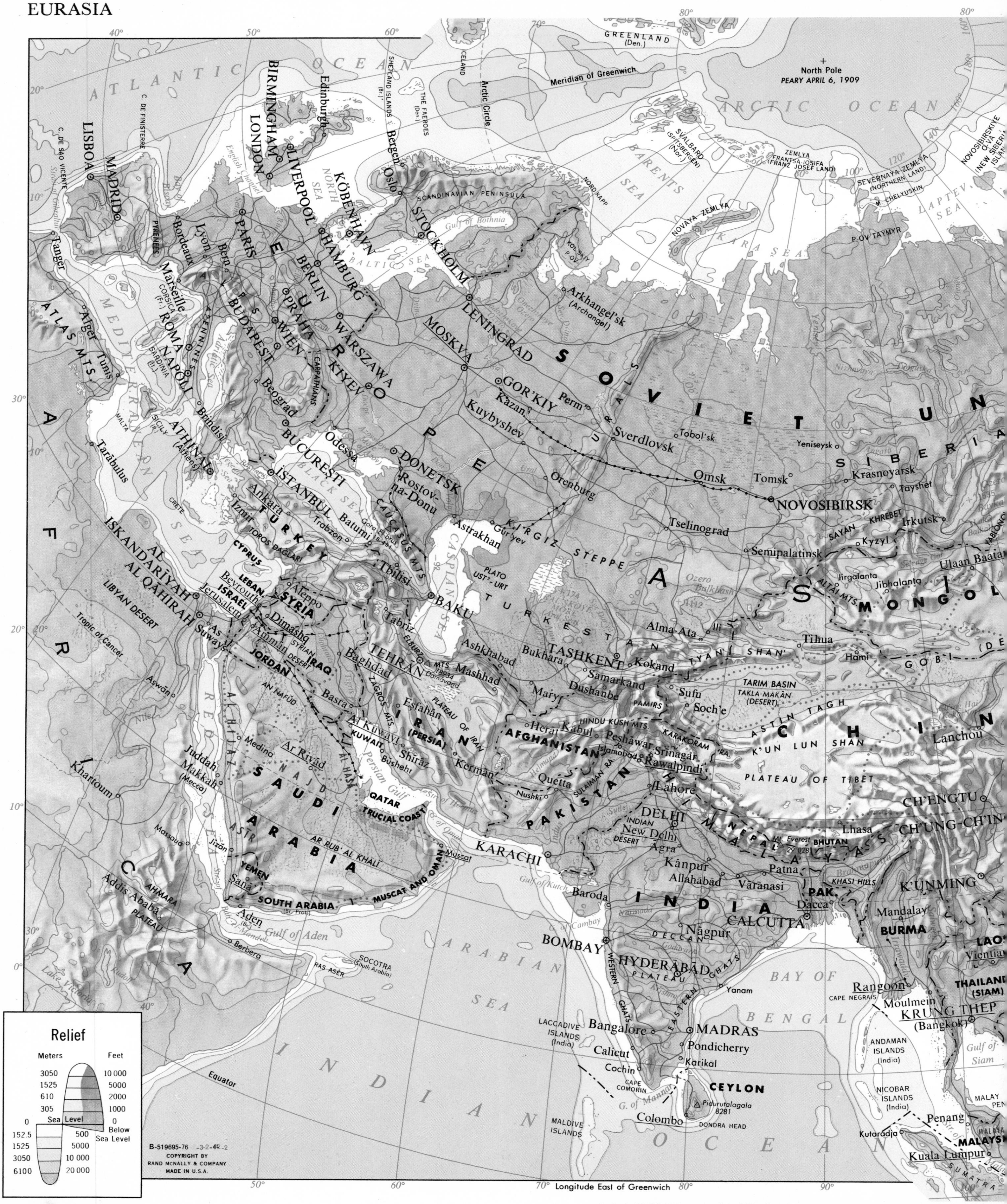

Relief

Meters	Feet
3050	10 000
1525	5000
610	2000
305	1000
0 Sea Level	0
	Below Sea Level
152.5	500
1525	5000
3050	10 000
6100	20 000

B-519695-76   -3-2-4½-2
COPYRIGHT BY
RAND MCNALLY & COMPANY
MADE IN U.S.A.

Scale 1:31 933 000; one inch to 504 miles. Lambert's Azimuthal, Equal Area Projection
Elevations and depressions are given in feet

132

NORTH AMERICA
Bering Str.
M. DEZHNEVA (EAST CAPE)
BERING SEA
ALEUTIAN ISLANDS (U.S.A.)
ALEUTIAN TRENCH
KOMANDORSKIYE OSTROVA (Sov. Union)
Petropavlovsk-Kamchatskiy
Okhotsk
Yakutsk
SEA OF OKHOTSK
KURIL ISLANDS (Sov. Union)
SAKHALIN (Sov. Union)
Komsomolsk
Blagoveshchensk
Sovetskaya Gavan
Khabarovsk
Nerchinsk
MANCHURIA
Vladivostok
Hakodate
HOKKAIDO
JAPAN
Sendai
HONSHU
TOKYO
YOKOHAMA
KYOTO
KOBE
OSAKA
SHIKOKU
KYUSHU
Nagasaki
KITAKYUSHU
HAERHPIN
CH'ANGCH'UN
Chilin
SHENYANG (Mukden)
NORTH KOREA
P'yongyang
SOUTH KOREA
SOUL
LÜTA
TIENTSIN
TSINGTAO
Tsinan
NANKING
SHANGHAI
EAST CHINA SEA
WUHAN
Fuchou
Amoy
Shant'ou
CANTON
HONG KONG (Br.)
VICTORIA
Macau (Port.)
T'AIPEI
TAIWAN (FORMOSA)
RYUKYU IS.
PHILIPPINE SEA
Tropic of Cancer
PACIFIC OCEAN
HAINAN TAO
LUZON
PHILIPPINES
Quezon City
MANILA
MINDORO
SAMAR
LEYTE
PANAY
NEGROS
PALAWAN
MINDANAO
ARCHIPELAGO
PHILIPPINE TRENCH
SULU SEA
SOUTH CHINA SEA
CELEBES SEA
Jesselton
Sandakan
SABAH
SARAWAK
MALAYSIA
Brunei
Kuching
BORNEO
CELEBES
HALMAHERA
NEW GUINEA
Equator
Hué
SAIGON
SINGAPORE
INDONESIA
East Longitude
West Longitude
0 100 200 400 600 800 1000 Miles
0 200 400 800 1200 1600 Kilometers

Longitude 35° East of Greenwich 36°
CYPRUS
Mt. Troodos 6400
OLYMPUS MTS.
Ktima
Pissouri
Limassol
Larnaca
Akrotiri Bay
Episkopi Bay
CAPE GATA
CAPE GRECO
MEDITERRANEAN SEA
T'arabulus (Tripoli)
Halba
Al Qusayr
Al Hirmal
Zagharta
Al Batrun
Amyun
Jubayl (Byblos)
LEBANON
Beyrouth (Beirut)
Juniyah
Ba'labakk
Zahlah
Zabdani
Ad Damur
Sayda (Sidon)
Jazzin
Dimashq (Damascus)
Duma
Rashayya
Kiswah
Sur (Tyre)
Marj 'Uyun
SYRIA
Tibnin
Al Qunaytirah
As Sanamayn
Nahariya
Acre
Safad
Haifa
Tiberias
Nazareth
Gader (Ruins)
Irbid
Dar'a
'Afula
Beit Shean
Hadera
Nathanya
Janin
Tul Karm
Shomron (Ruins)
Nabulus
Jarash
Al Mafraq
Herzlia
Petah Tiqva
Tel Aviv-Jaffa
Rishon le Zion
Rehovoth
Lod
As Salt
Az Zarqa'
Amman
Jerusalem
Ariha (Jericho)
Qumran
Ma'daba
Zuwayza
Migdal Ashkelon
Berekhot Shelomo (Ruins)
Bayt Lahm (Bethlehem)
Ghazzah (Gaza)
Al Khalil (Hebron)
Dhiban
Jad'ah
Khan Yunis
Beersheba
Al Mazra'
Al Karak
Al Qatranah
Al Mazar
Bur Sa'id (Port Said)
Khalig el Tina
Sabkhat al Bardawil
Bi'r al Mazar
Al 'Arish
Rummanah
Tel Sharuhen (Ruins)
Mamshit (Ruins)
Sedom
Shivta (Ruins)
El 'Auja
Al Qantarah
Kom Dafana (Ruins)
Al Isma'iliyah
Al Qusaymah
At Tafilah
Jurf ad Darawish
UNITED ARAB REPUBLIC
(EGYPT)
Ras Abu Quran 3578
GEBEL YI'ALLAR
NEGEV
ISRAEL
JORDAN
Ash Shawbak
Petra (Ruins)
Wadi Musa
Ma'an
As Suways (Suez)
Bur Tawfiq
Ash Shatt
An Nakhl
Al Kuntillah
Ra's an Naqb
Ath Thamad
Aqabat al Hijaziyah
Jabal Ramm 5755
Eilat
Al 'Aqabah
Ar Ramla
Al Mudawwarah
GEBEL EL GALALA EL BAHARIYA
Za'faranah
GEBEL EL TIH
GEBEL EL 'IGMA
Gulf of Suez (Khalig el Suweis)
Gulf of Aqaba
Al Haql
Hallat 'Ammar
Abu Zanimah
Ras el Gineina 5335
GEBEL EL GALALA EL QIBLIYA
Nuwaybi' al Muzayyinah
SAUDI ARABIA
JABAL MAZHAFAH 6232
SINAI
Scale 1:3 200 000
0 10 20 30 40 50 Miles
0 20 40 60 80 Kilometers
©RMCN.

Kuala Lumpur
Klang
Kajang
Bukit Payong 3549
Port Swettenham
Kuala Klawang
SELANGOR
PAHANG
MALAYA
Telok Datok
Bangi
Gunong Telapa 3915
NEGRI SEMBILAN
Bahau
Sepang
Seremban
Rantau
Rompin
Port Dickson
Rembau
Gemas
Tampin
Segamat
Gunong Besar 3402
CAPE RACHADO
Alor Gajah
Jasin
Mt. Ophir 4187
Labis
MALACCA
Panchor
MALAYSIA
Malacca
Paloh
JOHORE
Bandar Maharani
Kluang
Gunong Blumut 3312
MALAY PENINSULA
TANJONG TOHOR
Rengam
Layang Layang
PALAU RUPAT
Telukletjak
Djumrah
Bandar Penggaram
Ayer Hitam
Kota Tinggi
STRAIT OF MALACCA
Puak
Bengkalis
PALAU BENGKALIS
Johore Bahru
Pontian Kechil
SUMATERA (SUMATRA)
Ketamputih
SINGAPORE
TANJONG PIAI
Dedap
PALAU PADANG
Pinggir
Telesung
GREAT KARIMUN
Phillip Channel
Singapore Strait
INDONESIA
BATAM
RIOUW ARCHIPELAGO
PALAU BINTAN
SUMATERA TENGA
PALAU RANGSANG
Tandjungbalai
Tandjungpinang
REMPANG
Gunung-kidjang
Siak Sri Indrapura
PALAU TEBINGTINGGI
KUNDUR
Serangoong
Minas
Buatam
Baranpauh
Endau
TIOMAN
Gunong Kajang 3444
PEMANGGIL
AUR
Mersing
PALAU TINGGI
SOUTH CHINA SEA
Jason Bay
TANJONG RAMUNIA
TANJUNG BERAKIT
Scale 1:3 200 000
0 10 20 30 40 50 Miles
0 20 40 60 80 Kilometers
Longitude East of Greenwich
©RMCN

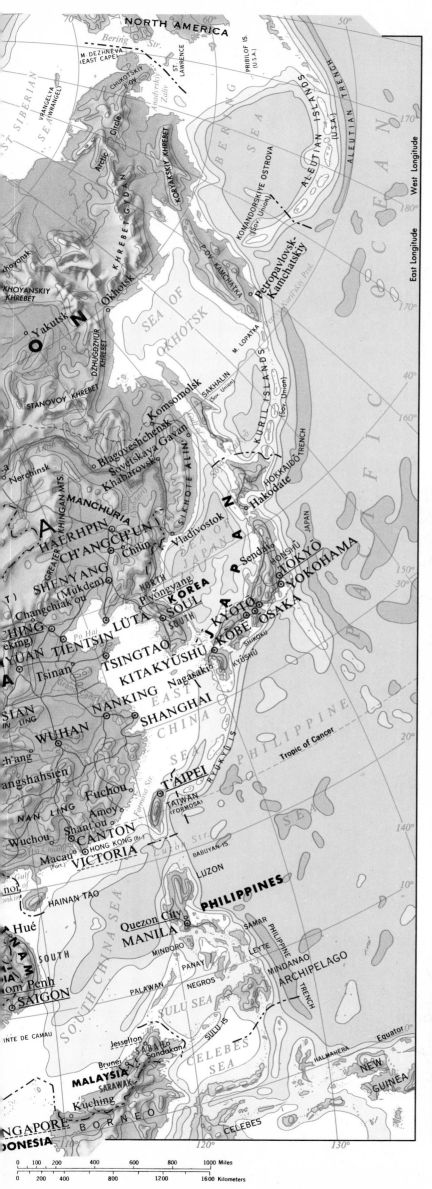

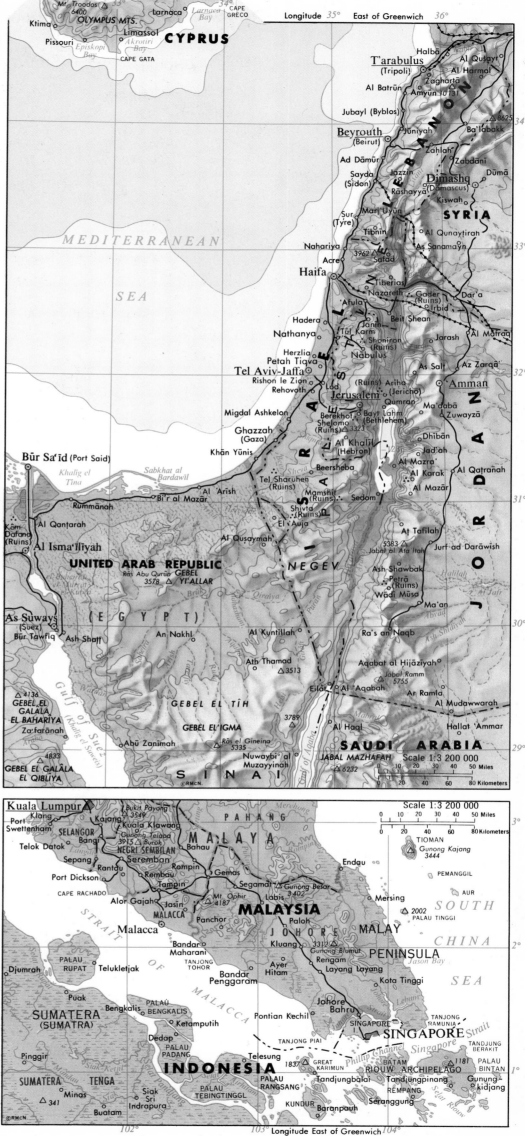

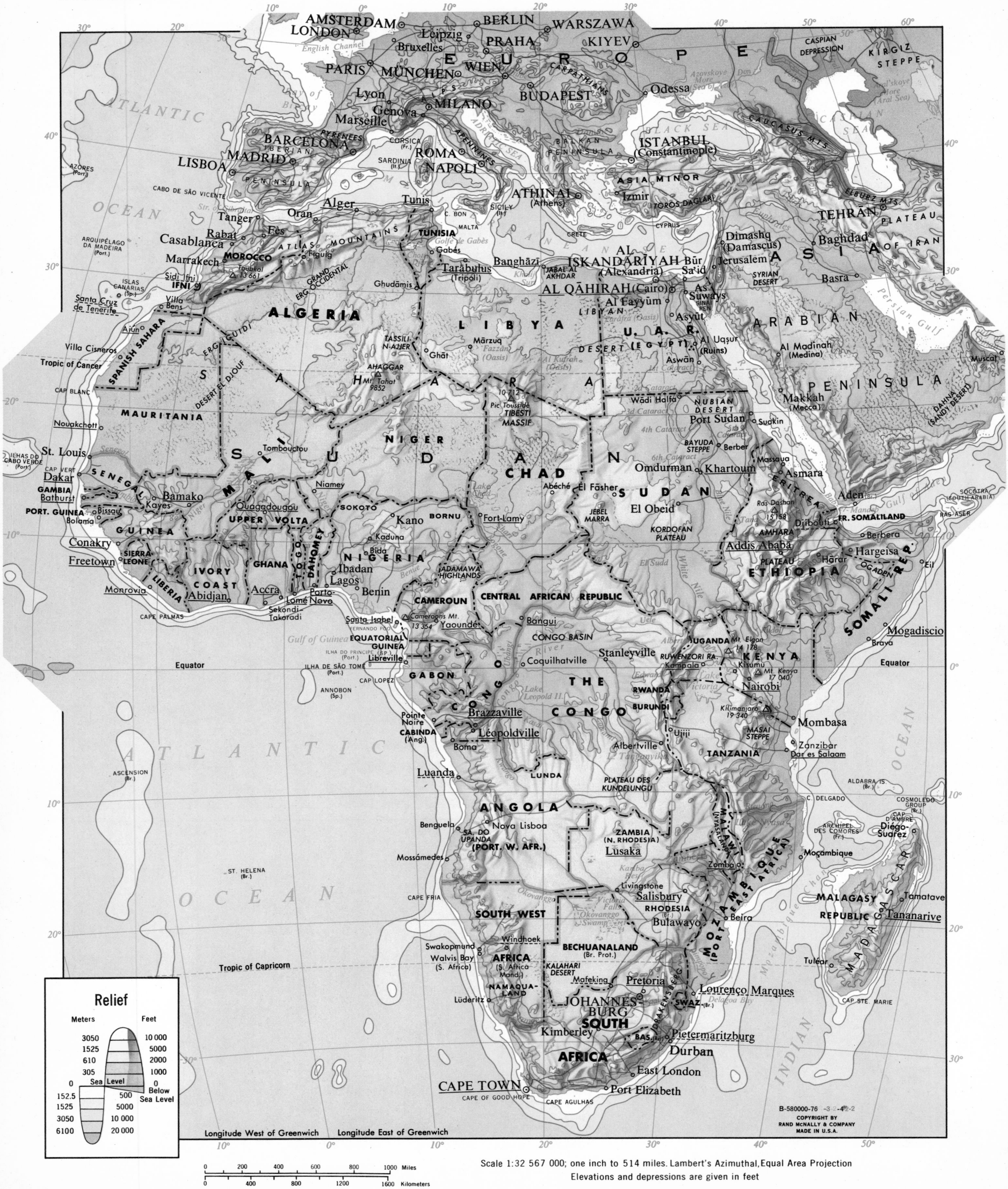

AFRICA

Scale 1:32 567 000; one inch to 514 miles. Lambert's Azimuthal, Equal Area Projection
Elevations and depressions are given in feet

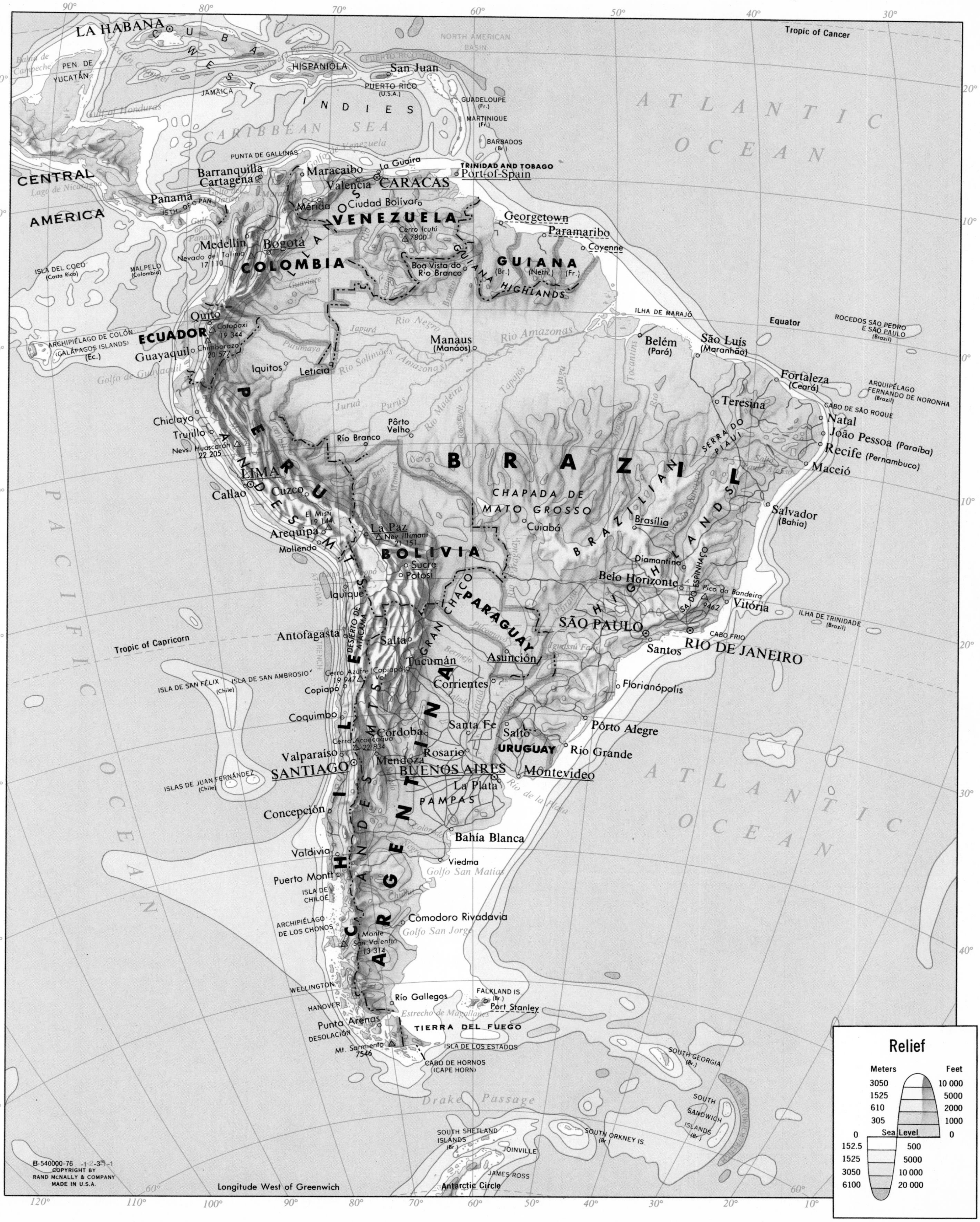

SOUTH AMERICA

Tropic of Cancer

ATLANTIC OCEAN

CENTRAL AMERICA

CARIBBEAN SEA

WEST INDIES

PACIFIC OCEAN

VENEZUELA

COLOMBIA

ECUADOR

PERU

BRAZIL

BOLIVIA

PARAGUAY

CHILE

ARGENTINA

URUGUAY

PAMPAS

Tropic of Capricorn

Equator

GUIANA HIGHLANDS

CHAPADA DE MATO GROSSO

BRAZILIAN HIGHLANDS

TIERRA DEL FUEGO

Longitude West of Greenwich

Antarctic Circle

Scale 1:32 567 000; one inch to 514 miles. Lambert's Azimuthal, Equal Area Projection
Elevations and depressions are given in feet

B-540000-76 -1-2-3-1-1
COPYRIGHT BY
RAND McNALLY & COMPANY
MADE IN U.S.A.

0   200   400   600   800   1000 Miles
0   400   800   1200   1600 Kilometers

Relief

Meters		Feet
3050		10 000
1525		5000
610		2000
305		1000
0	Sea Level	0
152.5		500
1525		5000
3050		10 000
6100		20 000

135

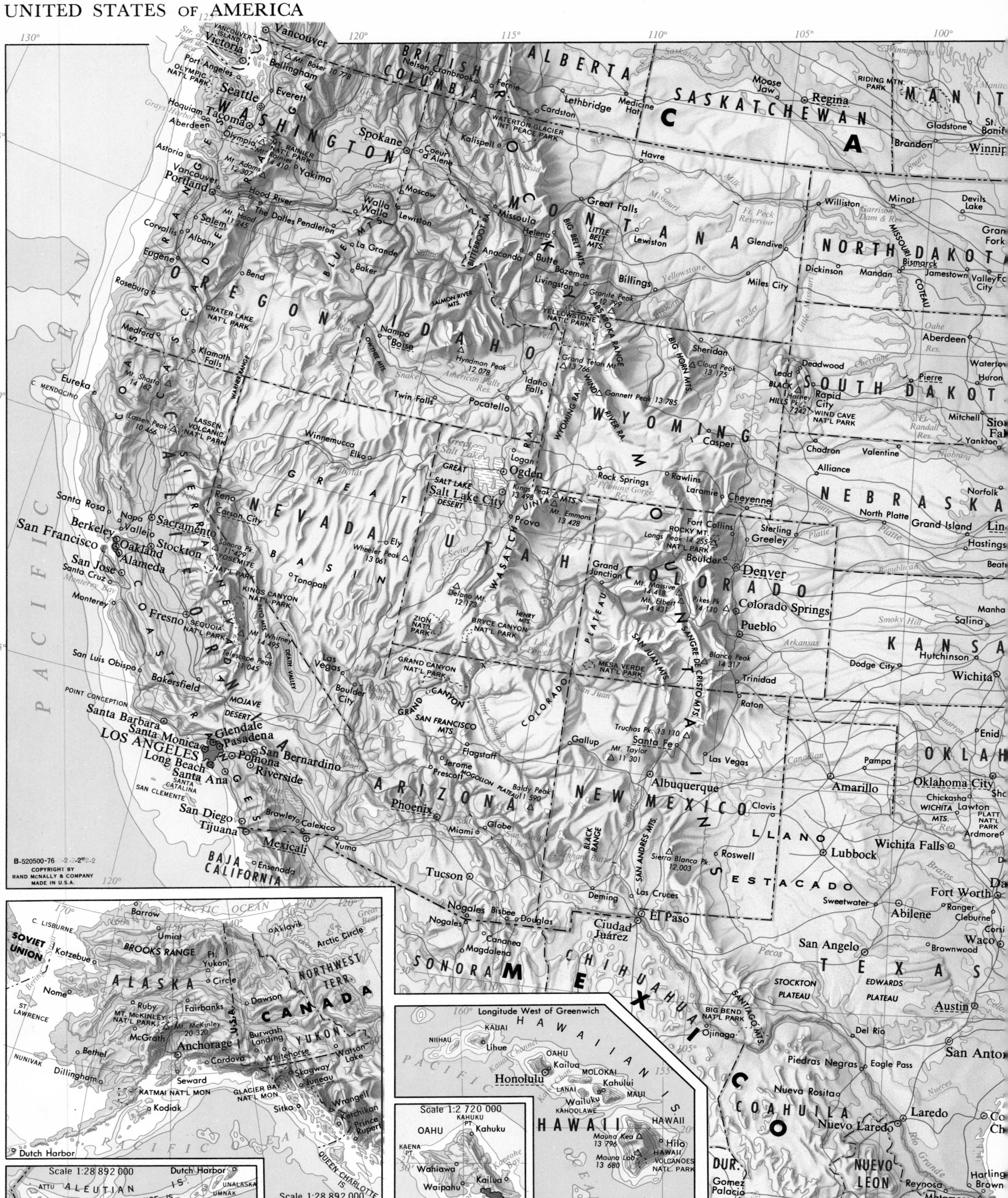

Scale 1:9 631 000; one inch to 152 miles. Polyconic Projection
Elevations and depressions are given in feet

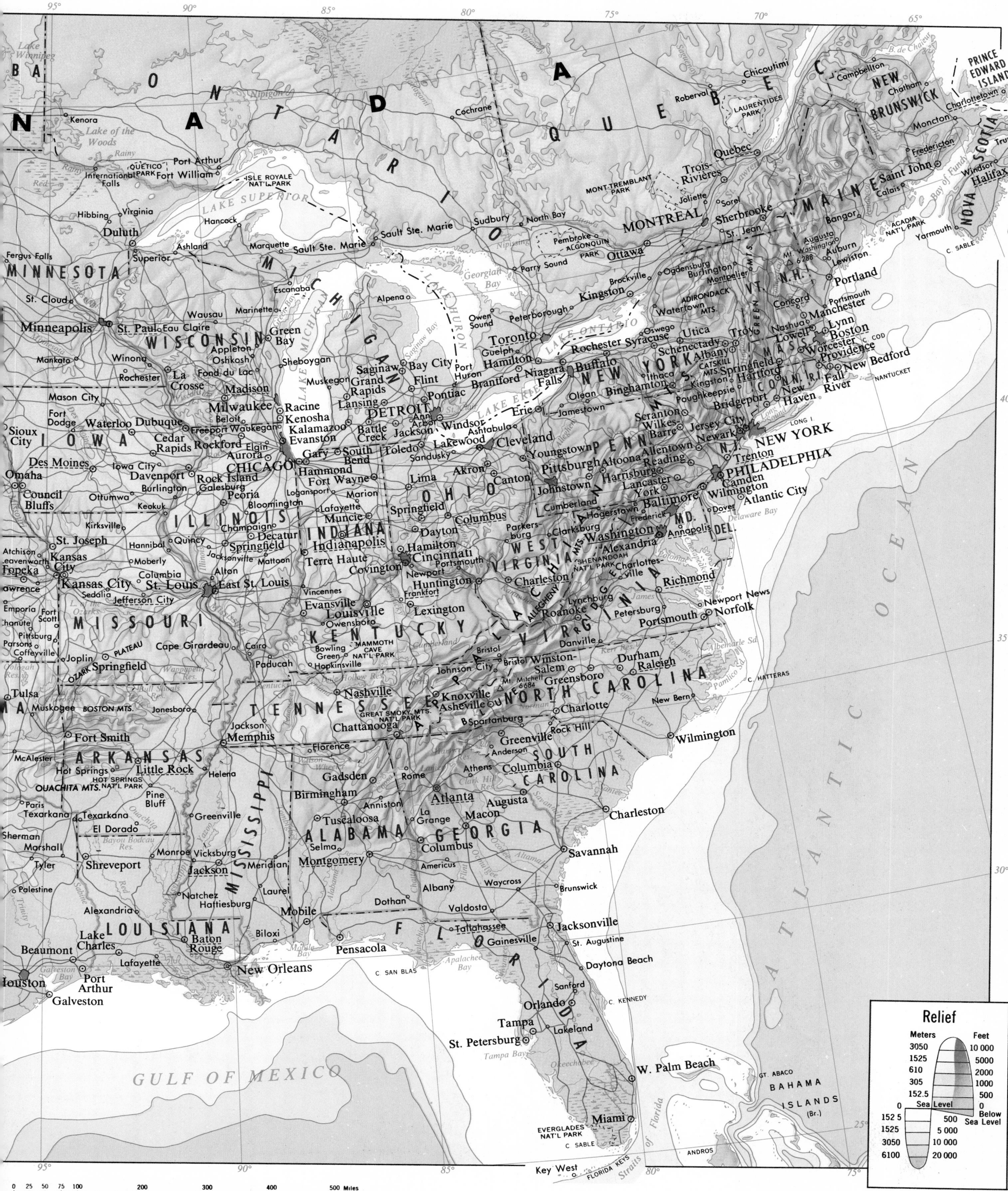

95°
90°
85°
80°
75°
70°
65°
40°
35°
30°
25°
45°
C A N A D A
O N T A R I O
Q U E B E C
NEW BRUNSWICK
PRINCE EDWARD ISLAND
NOVA SCOTIA
Lake Winnipeg
Kenora
Lake of the Woods
Rainy
International Falls
QUETICO PARK
Port Arthur
Fort William
ISLE ROYALE NAT'L PARK
LAKE SUPERIOR
Nipigon
Cochrane
Roberval
Chicoutimi
LAURENTIDES PARK
Campbellton
B. de Chaleur
Chatham
Charlottetown
Moncton
Truro
Fredericton
Saint John
Calais
Bay of Fundy
Windsor
Halifax
Yarmouth
C. SABLE
ACADIA NAT'L PARK
Quebec
Trois-Rivières
MONT-TREMBLANT PARK
Joliette
Sorel
MONTREAL
Sherbrooke
St. Jean
M A I N E
Bangor
Augusta
Mt. Washington 6288
Auburn
Lewiston
Portland
Portsmouth
Sudbury
North Bay
Pembroke
ALGONQUIN PARK
Ottawa
Sault Ste. Marie
Hancock
Marquette
Ashland
Superior
Hibbing
Virginia
Duluth
Fergus Falls
MINNESOTA
St. Cloud
Minneapolis
St. Paul
Mankato
Winona
Rochester
La Crosse
Eau Claire
Wausau
WISCONSIN
Appleton
Oshkosh
Fond du Lac
Madison
Milwaukee
Racine
Kenosha
Green Bay
Marinette
Escanaba
Sheboygan
MICHIGAN
LAKE MICHIGAN
LAKE HURON
Georgian Bay
Parry Sound
Alpena
Owen Sound
Peterborough
Kingston
Brockville
Ogdensburg
Burlington
Montpelier
ADIRONDACK MTS.
GREEN MTS.
VT.
N.H.
Watertown
Concord
Manchester
Nashua
Lowell
Lynn
Boston
C. COD
Worcester
Providence
Fall River
New Bedford
NANTUCKET
MASS.
CONN.
R.I.
Toronto
Guelph
Hamilton
Brantford
Niagara Falls
Buffalo
LAKE ONTARIO
Rochester
Syracuse
Oswego
Utica
Schenectady
Albany
Troy
NEW YORK
Ithaca
Binghamton
CATSKILL MTS.
Kingston
Poughkeepsie
Springfield
Hartford
New Haven
Bridgeport
LONG I.
Saginaw
Bay City
Port Huron
Flint
Grand Rapids
Muskegon
Lansing
Pontiac
DETROIT
Ann Arbor
Windsor
Kalamazoo
Battle Creek
Jackson
LAKE ERIE
Erie
Jamestown
Olean
Ashtabula
Cleveland
Lakewood
Toledo
Sandusky
Youngstown
Scranton
Wilkes Barre
Allentown
Reading
Jersey City
Newark
NEW YORK
N.J.
Trenton
PHILADELPHIA
Camden
Wilmington
Atlantic City
Delaware Bay
Dover
DEL.
PENN.
Pittsburgh
Altoona
Harrisburg
Lancaster
York
Johnstown
Cumberland
Hagerstown
Baltimore
Frederick
MD.
Annapolis
Washington
Alexandria
Mason City
Fort Dodge
Waterloo
Dubuque
Sioux City
I O W A
Cedar Rapids
Des Moines
Iowa City
Davenport
Omaha
Council Bluffs
Ottumwa
Burlington
Keokuk
Beloit
Freeport
Waukegan
Rockford
Elgin
Evanston
Aurora
CHICAGO
Gary
South Bend
Hammond
Fort Wayne
Rock Island
Galesburg
Peoria
Bloomington
ILLINOIS
Logansport
Marion
Lafayette
Muncie
INDIANA
Indianapolis
Champaign
Decatur
Springfield
Quincy
Hannibal
Kirksville
St. Joseph
Atchison
Leavenworth
Kansas City
Topeka
Lawrence
Moberly
Columbia
Jacksonville
Mattoon
Terre Haute
Alton
St. Louis
East St. Louis
Sedalia
Jefferson City
MISSOURI
Emporia
Fort Scott
Chanute
Pittsburg
Parsons
Coffeyville
Joplin
OZARK PLATEAU
Springfield
Cape Girardeau
Cairo
Paducah
Lima
OHIO
Akron
Canton
Springfield
Dayton
Columbus
Hamilton
Cincinnati
Covington
Newport
Portsmouth
Huntington
Parkersburg
Clarksburg
WEST VIRGINIA
Charleston
SHENANDOAH NAT'L PARK
Charlottesville
Richmond
Lynchburg
Roanoke
VIRGINIA
Petersburg
Portsmouth
Norfolk
Newport News
ALLEGHENY MTS.
BLUE RIDGE
APPALACHIAN
Vincennes
Evansville
Louisville
Owensboro
Frankfort
Lexington
KENTUCKY
Bowling Green
MAMMOTH CAVE NAT'L PARK
Hopkinsville
Bristol
Johnson City
Danville
Winston-Salem
Greensboro
Durham
Raleigh
Albemarle Sd
Pamlico Sd
C. HATTERAS
Mt. Mitchell 6684
NORTH CAROLINA
Knoxville
Asheville
New Bern
Nashville
TENNESSEE
GREAT SMOKY MTS. NAT'L PARK
Chattanooga
Charlotte
Spartanburg
Rock Hill
Greenville
Anderson
SOUTH CAROLINA
Columbia
Wilmington
Tulsa
Muskogee
BOSTON MTS.
Jonesboro
Fort Smith
McAlester
ARKANSAS
Hot Springs
HOT SPRINGS NAT'L PARK
OUACHITA MTS.
Little Rock
Pine Bluff
Helena
Jackson
Memphis
Florence
Gadsden
Rome
Birmingham
Anniston
Atlanta
Athens
Augusta
Macon
La Grange
Tuscaloosa
ALABAMA
GEORGIA
Columbus
Selma
Montgomery
Charleston
Savannah
Paris
Texarkana
El Dorado
Greenville
MISSISSIPPI
Sherman
Marshall
Tyler
Shreveport
Monroe
Vicksburg
Jackson
Meridian
Americus
Albany
Waycross
Brunswick
Palestine
Natchez
Hattiesburg
Laurel
Dothan
Valdosta
Alexandria
LOUISIANA
Lake Charles
Beaumont
Baton Rouge
Lafayette
Biloxi
Mobile
Pensacola
Tallahassee
Jacksonville
Gainesville
St. Augustine
FLORIDA
Houston
Port Arthur
Galveston
New Orleans
C. SAN BLAS
Apalachee Bay
Daytona Beach
Sanford
Orlando
C. KENNEDY
Tampa
Lakeland
St. Petersburg
Tampa Bay
Okeechobee
W. Palm Beach
Miami
EVERGLADES NAT'L PARK
C. SABLE
Key West
FLORIDA KEYS
Straits of Florida
GT. ABACO
BAHAMA ISLANDS (Br.)
ANDROS
GULF OF MEXICO
ATLANTIC OCEAN
Relief
Meters
Feet
3050
1525
610
305
152.5
0
Sea Level
10 000
5000
2000
1000
500
0
Below Sea Level
152 5
1525
3050
6100
500
5 000
10 000
20 000
0 25 50 75 100 200 300 400 500 Miles
0 100 200 400 600 800 Kilometers

CANADA

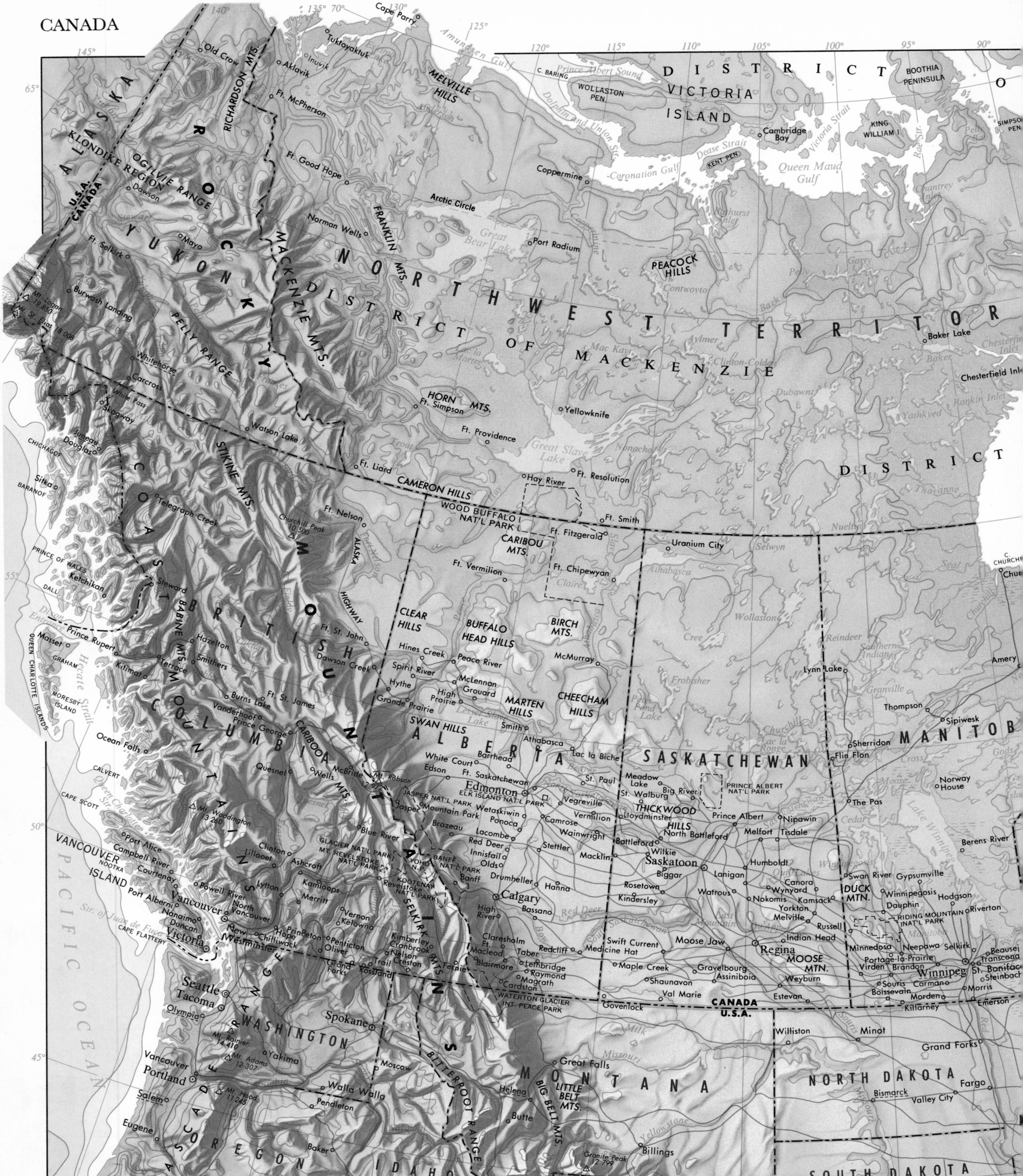

Scale 1:9 631 000; one inch to 152 miles. Polyconic Projection
Elevations and depressions are given in feet

Longitude West of Greenwich

138

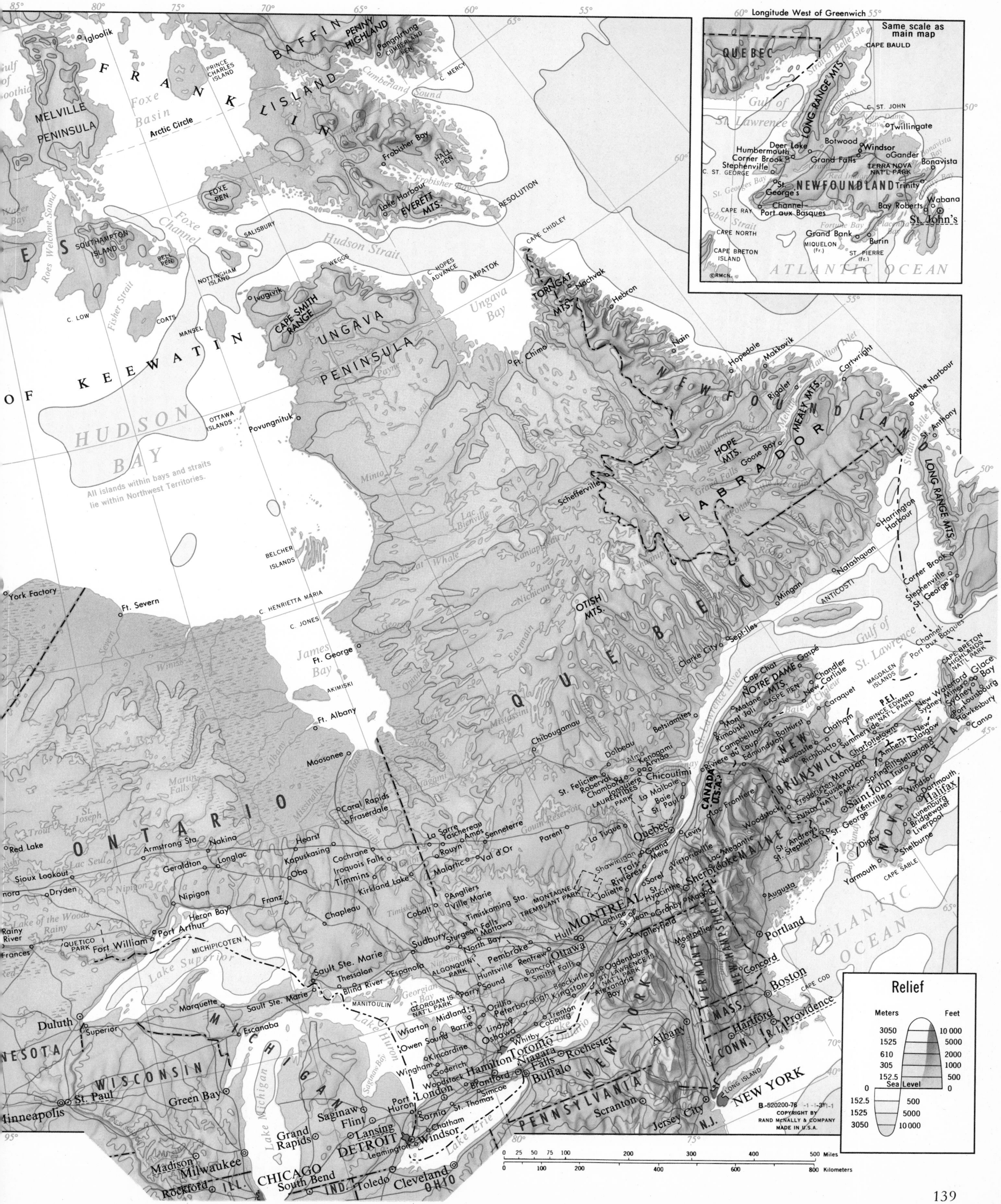
Longitude West of Greenwich
Same scale as main map
QUEBEC
Strait of Belle Isle
CAPE BAULD
LONG RANGE MTS.
Gulf of St. Lawrence
C. ST. JOHN
Twillingate
Deer Lake
Botwood
Humbermouth
Corner Brook
Windsor
Gander
Stephenville
Grand Falls
TERRA NOVA NAT'L PARK
Bonavista
C. ST. GEORGE
St. George's
NEWFOUNDLAND
Trinity
Wabana
CAPE RAY
Channel-Port aux Basques
Bay Roberts
St. John's
Cabot Strait
CAPE NORTH
Grand Bank
Burin
MIQUELON (Fr.)
ST. PIERRE (Fr.)
CAPE BRETON ISLAND
ATLANTIC OCEAN
Igloolik
PENNY HIGHLAND
Pangnirtung
CUMBERLAND PEN.
BAFFIN ISLAND
PRINCE CHARLES ISLAND
C. MERCY
Cumberland Sound
FRANKLIN
Foxe Basin
Arctic Circle
MELVILLE PENINSULA
Frobisher Bay
HALL PEN.
FOXE PEN.
Lake Harbour
EVERETT MTS.
RESOLUTION
Foxe Channel
SALISBURY
SOUTHAMPTON ISLAND
BELL PEN.
Roes Welcome Sound
Hudson Strait
CAPE CHIDLEY
C. WEGGS
C. HOPES ADVANCE
AKPATOK
NOTTINGHAM ISLAND
Ivugivik
CAPE SMITH RANGE
TORNGAT MTS.
Nachvak
Hebron
Ungava Bay
C. LOW
COATS
MANSEL
UNGAVA PENINSULA
Ft. Chimo
Nain
Hopedale
Makkovik
Cartwright
KEEWATIN
Hudson Bay
OTTAWA ISLANDS
Povungnituk
Rigolet
MEALY MTS.
Battle Harbour
NEWFOUNDLAND
LABRADOR
HOPE MTS.
Goose Bay
St. Anthony
All islands within bays and straits lie within Northwest Territories.
Schefferville
Lac Bienville
Harrington Harbour
LONG RANGE MTS.
BELCHER ISLANDS
Natashquan
Corner Brook
Stephenville
St. George's
York Factory
Ft. Severn
C. HENRIETTA MARIA
Mingan
ANTICOSTI
OTISH MTS.
C. JONES
Sept-Iles
Clarke City
Gulf of St. Lawrence
Channel-Port aux Basques
James Bay
Ft. George
AKIMISKI
QUEBEC
Gaspé
Cap Chat
NOTRE DAME MTS.
Chandler
New Carlisle
MAGDALEN ISLANDS
CAPE BRETON HIGHLANDS NAT'L PARK
Glace Bay
Sydney
Port Louisbourg
Ft. Albany
Betsiamites
P.E.I.
PRINCE EDWARD NAT'L PARK
Chibougamau
Dolbeau
Alma
Kenogami
Arvida
Chicoutimi
Moosonee
St. Felicien
Roberval
Chambord
Jonquière
LAURENTIDES PARK
La Malbaie
Baie St. Paul
CANADA
U.S.A.
NEW BRUNSWICK
NOVA SCOTIA
Halifax
Dartmouth
Canso
ONTARIO
Coral Rapids
Fraserdale
Quebec
Levis
La Tuque
Parent
Senneterre
La Sarre
Taschereau
Amos
Rouyn
Val d'Or
Red Lake
Armstrong Sta.
Nakina
Hearst
Kapuskasing
Cochrane
Iroquois Falls
Timmins
Kirkland Lake
Malartic
Geraldton
Longlac
Sioux Lookout
Dryden
Nipigon
Chapleau
Cobalt
Angliers
Ville Marie
Timiskaming Sta.
MONTAGNE TREMBLANT PARK
Joliette
Trois Rivieres
Grand Mere
Shawinigan
Victoriaville
Sherbrooke
Magog
MONTREAL
Lachine
St. Jean
Granby
Valleyfield
Heron Bay
Port Arthur
Fort William
QUETICO PARK
Rainy River
Lake of the Woods
Lake Superior
MICHIPICOTEN I.
Sault Ste. Marie
Thessalon
Blind River
Espanola
Sudbury
Sturgeon Falls
Mattawa
North Bay
ALGONQUIN PARK
Pembroke
Renfrew
Hull
Ottawa
Huntsville
Parry Sound
Bancroft
Smiths Falls
Brockville
Kingston
Ogdensburg
MANITOULIN
GEORGIAN IS. NAT'L PARK
Midland
Orillia
Peterborough
Trenton
Cobourg
Whitby
Oshawa
Lindsay
Barrie
Owen Sound
Wiarton
Kincardine
Goderich
Wingham
Toronto
Hamilton
Niagara Falls
Rochester
Buffalo
Brantford
Woodstock
London
St. Thomas
Simcoe
Port Huron
Sarnia
Chatham
Windsor
DETROIT
Leamington
Lake Erie
Lake Huron
Lake Ontario
Lake Michigan
Marquette
Escanaba
Duluth
Superior
MICHIGAN
WISCONSIN
Green Bay
Minneapolis
St. Paul
Saginaw
Flint
Lansing
Grand Rapids
Madison
Milwaukee
Rockford
CHICAGO
South Bend
Toledo
Cleveland
OHIO
IND.
ILL.
PENNSYLVANIA
Scranton
NEW YORK
Albany
Jersey City
N.J.
LONG ISLAND
VERMONT
NEW HAMPSHIRE
MAINE
Augusta
Portland
Concord
MASS.
Boston
CAPE COD
Hartford
CONN.
R.I.
Providence
Montpelier
Saint John
Fredericton
Moncton
Yarmouth
Digby
Shelburne
Liverpool
Bridgewater
Lunenburg
CAPE SABLE
ATLANTIC OCEAN
Relief
Meters
Feet
3050
1525
610
305
152.5
0
Sea Level
10 000
5000
2000
1000
500
B-520200-76
COPYRIGHT BY RAND McNALLY & COMPANY MADE IN U.S.A.
Miles
Kilometers

NORTH AMERICA

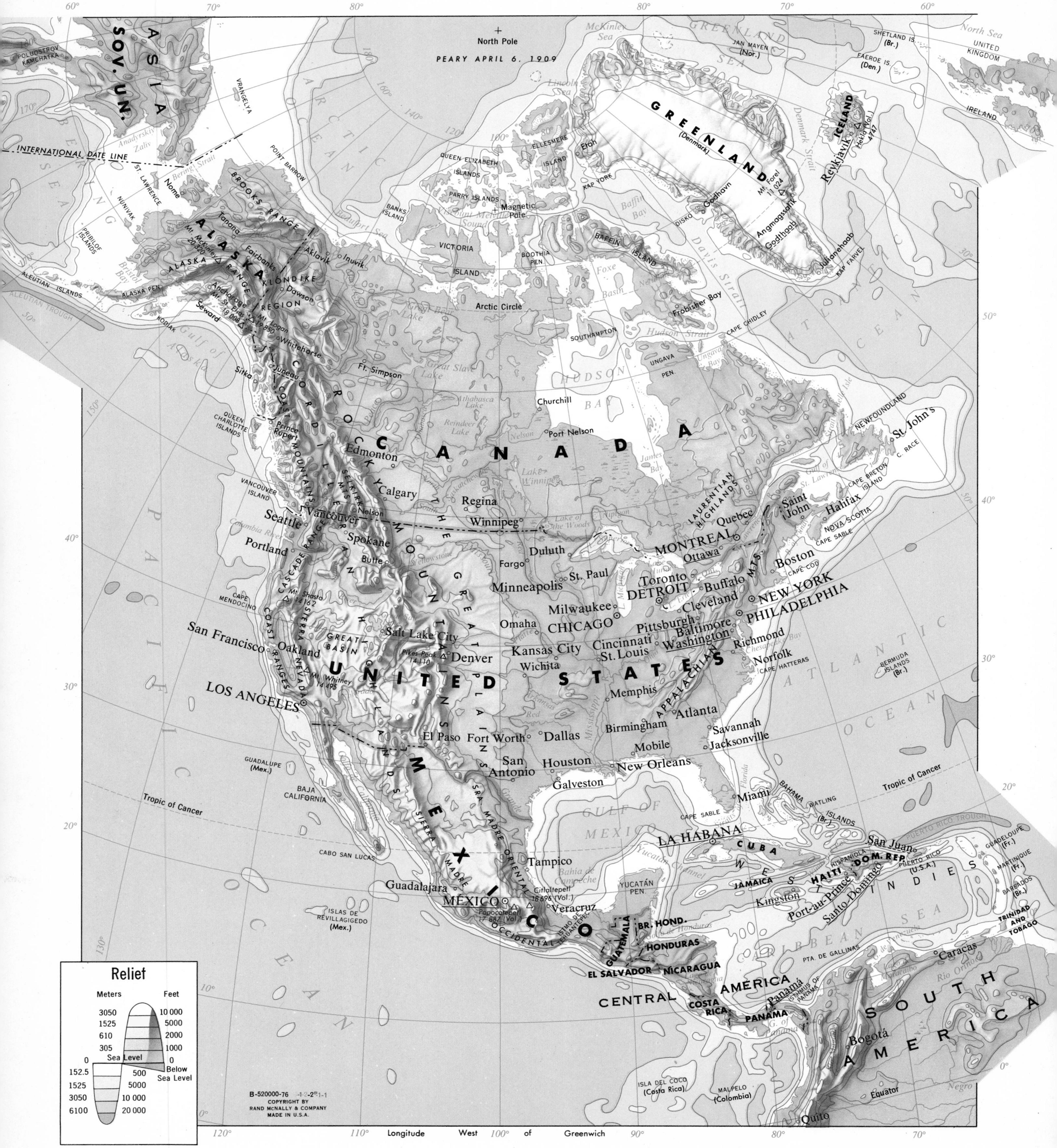

ASIA SOV. UN.

PEARY APRIL 6. 1909
North Pole

INTERNATIONAL DATE LINE

GREENLAND
(Denmark)

ICELAND
Reykjavik

SHETLAND IS.
(Br.)

UNITED KINGDOM

FAEROE IS.
(Den.)

IRELAND

North Sea

ALASKA
Fairbanks
BROOKS RANGE
Aklavik
Inuvik
Nome
Anchorage
Whitehorse
Juneau
Sitka
Seward
Kodiak

QUEEN ELIZABETH ISLANDS
VICTORIA ISLAND
Magnetic Pole
BANKS ISLAND

ELLESMERE ISLAND
Mt. Forel
11 024
Godhavn
Angmagssalik
Godthaab
Julianehaab
Kap Farvel

BAFFIN ISLAND

Arctic Circle

C A N A D A

Ft. Simpson
Great Slave Lake
Churchill
Port Nelson
Reindeer Lake
HUDSON BAY

Edmonton
Calgary
Regina
Winnipeg
Lake Winnipeg

Frobisher Bay
CAPE CHIDLEY
UNGAVA PEN.

NEWFOUNDLAND
St. John's
C. RACE

Vancouver
Seattle
Spokane
Portland
Butte
Duluth
Fargo
Minneapolis
St. Paul

MONTREAL
Ottawa
Quebec
Saint John
Halifax
NOVA SCOTIA
CAPE SABLE
CAPE BRETON ISLAND

San Francisco
Oakland
Salt Lake City
Denver
Omaha
CHICAGO
Milwaukee
DETROIT
Toronto
Buffalo
Cleveland
Boston
NEW YORK
PHILADELPHIA
Pittsburgh
Baltimore
Washington
Richmond
Norfolk

LOS ANGELES
Kansas City
St. Louis
Cincinnati
Wichita
Memphis
APPALACHIAN MTS.

U N I T E D   S T A T E S

El Paso
Fort Worth
Dallas
San Antonio
Houston
Galveston

Birmingham
Atlanta
Savannah
Mobile
New Orleans
Jacksonville

CAPE HATTERAS
BERMUDA ISLANDS
(Br.)

ATLANTIC OCEAN

Tropic of Cancer

GUADALUPE
(Mex.)
BAJA CALIFORNIA
CABO SAN LUCAS

Miami
CAPE SABLE
BAHAMA ISLANDS
WATLING
Tropic of Cancer

M E X I C O
Guadalajara
MÉXICO
Tampico
Veracruz

GULF OF MEXICO
YUCATÁN PEN.

LA HABANA
CUBA
JAMAICA
Kingston
HAITI
Port-au-Prince
DOM. REP.
Santo Domingo
San Juan
PUERTO RICO
(U.S.A.)

GUADELOUPE
(Fr.)
MARTINIQUE
(Fr.)
BARBADOS
(Br.)

WEST INDIES

ISLAS DE REVILLAGIGEDO
(Mex.)

GUATEMALA
BR. HOND.
HONDURAS
EL SALVADOR
NICARAGUA
COSTA RICA
PANAMA

TRINIDAD AND TOBAGO
Caracas

CENTRAL   AMERICA

CARIBBEAN SEA

SOUTH AMERICA
Bogotá

ISLA DEL COCO
(Costa Rica)
MALPELO
(Colombia)

PACIFIC OCEAN

Quito
Equator

B-520000-76 1-2-2⊕1-1
COPYRIGHT BY
RAND McNALLY & COMPANY
MADE IN U.S.A.

Relief

Meters		Feet
3050		10 000
1525		5000
610		2000
305		1000
0	Sea Level	0
152.5		Below Sea Level
		500
1525		5000
3050		10 000
6100		20 000

120° 110° Longitude West 100° of Greenwich 90° 80° 70°

| 0 | 200 | 400 | 600 | 800 | 1000 Miles |

| 0 | 400 | 800 | 1200 | 1600 Kilometers |

Scale 1:32 567 000; one inch to 514 miles. Lambert's Azimuthal, Equal Area Projection
Elevations and depressions are given in feet

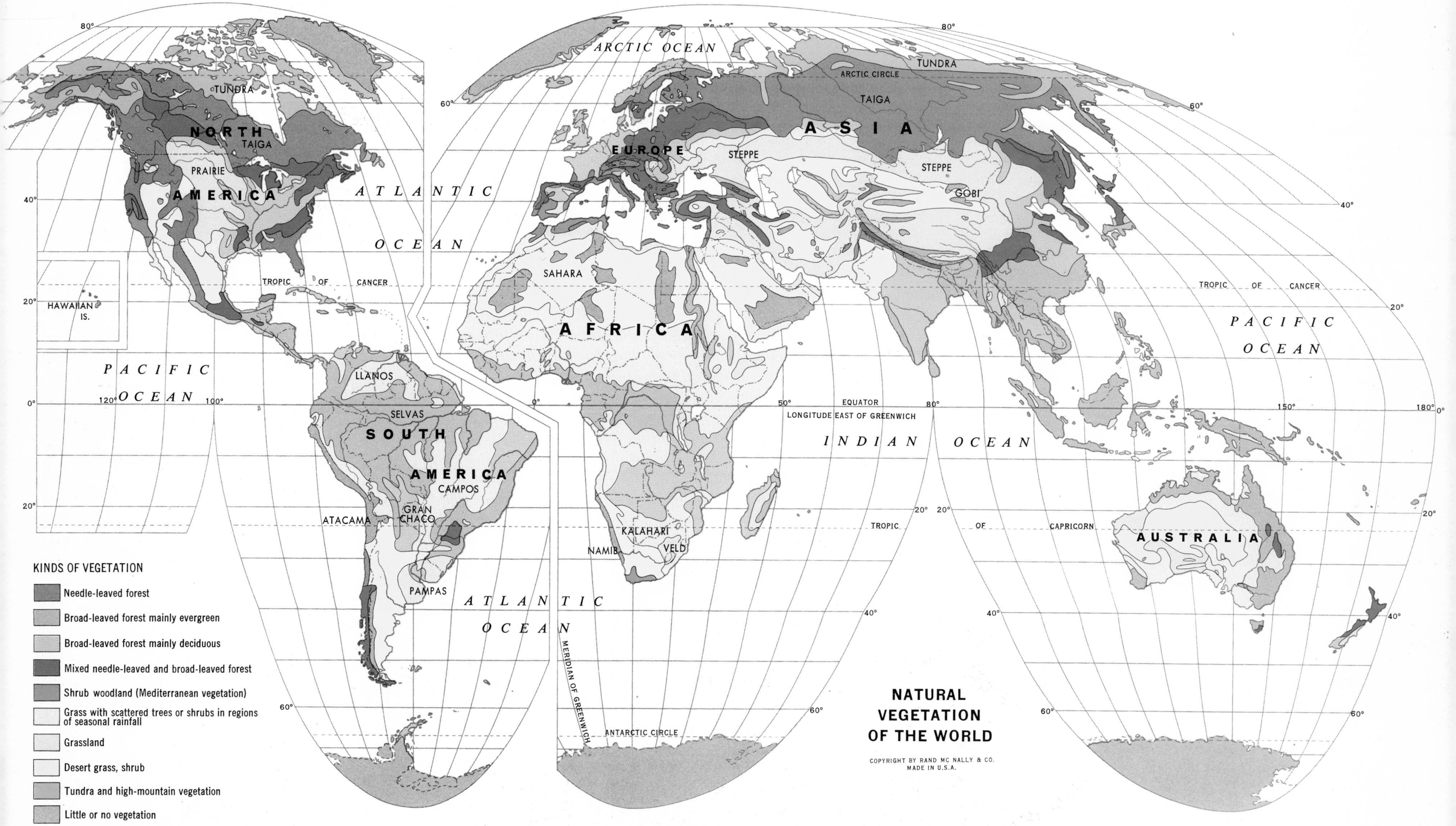

Nearly everywhere on earth some vegetation grows; only the ice caps and the most barren deserts lack vegetation. The most important single control of vegetation is climate, but soil and the altitude of the land also are significant in determining vegetative cover.

The pattern of natural vegetation resembles closely the pattern of world climates. In the rainy lands forests extend for hundreds of miles. Where the climate is too dry or too cold for forests, shrub, grasses, and lichens are found.

In general there are three main forest types, which correspond with low, middle, and high latitude lands. In the humid low latitudes luxuriant evergreen forests of broad-leaved trees predominate. The humid middle latitudes have forests which consist of broad-leaved trees which are deciduous, losing their leaves in winter. Much of the middle latitude forest has been cleared for farm land, and few regions of these hardwood forests remain. High latitude forests occur only in the Northern Hemisphere, and they all but girdle the earth. The northern forest, or taiga, is almost entirely composed of needle-leaved, cone-bearing softwood trees. The southern parts of this great forest region are today the suppliers of the world's lumber and paper.

The moister parts of the semiarid lands where the natural vegetation was grass have in places been plowed to raise small grain. The drier semiarid lands remain in grass and are the world's great grazing regions. Tundra areas, covered with mosses and lichens, are found in polar regions.

NATURAL VEGETATION OF THE WORLD

COPYRIGHT BY RAND McNALLY & CO.
MADE IN U.S.A.

KINDS OF VEGETATION

- Needle-leaved forest
- Broad-leaved forest mainly evergreen
- Broad-leaved forest mainly deciduous
- Mixed needle-leaved and broad-leaved forest
- Shrub woodland (Mediterranean vegetation)
- Grass with scattered trees or shrubs in regions of seasonal rainfall
- Grassland
- Desert grass, shrub
- Tundra and high-mountain vegetation
- Little or no vegetation

143

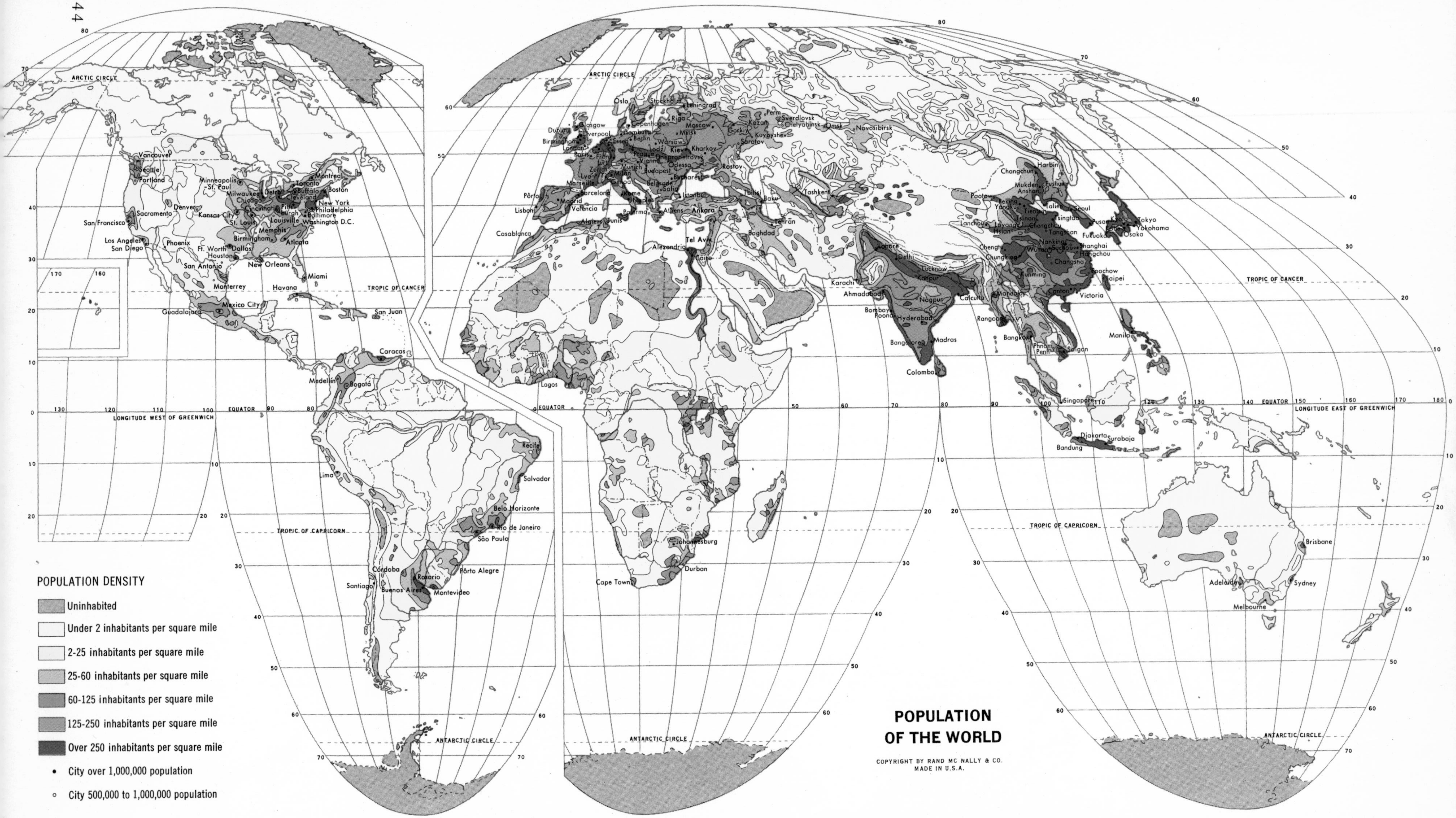

POPULATION OF THE WORLD

COPYRIGHT BY RAND MC NALLY & CO.
MADE IN U.S.A.

POPULATION DENSITY

- Uninhabited
- Under 2 inhabitants per square mile
- 2-25 inhabitants per square mile
- 25-60 inhabitants per square mile
- 60-125 inhabitants per square mile
- 125-250 inhabitants per square mile
- Over 250 inhabitants per square mile
- • City over 1,000,000 population
- ○ City 500,000 to 1,000,000 population

The population of the world is nearly three billion. One hundred and fifty years ago there were only about one-quarter as many people. Yet, today, there is still a square mile for every fifty people in the world. Approximately one-fourth of mankind lives, or at least works, in cities. This population map shows the densest population categories as more than 250 persons per square mile, but this is not the actual extreme. Population densities range from no people at all in parts of desert and polar regions to over 1,000 per square mile in the congested lands of India, China, Egypt, or the Island

of Java. The highest densities anywhere, of course, are in the great cities.

The map above shows three large areas of very dense population, along with numerous small ones. The densest areas are in central eastern Asia, the Indian subcontinent, and Europe. Other than in these three large areas, the rest of the world is very much less densely populated.

The United States shows clusters of dense population in the Northeast and Midwest, but most of the land has no more than the average density and much of the land has a great

deal less. In South America nine-tenths of the population lives around the margin of the continent.

Compare the population map with the climate and vegetation map. Why do people live where they do? Three-fourths of the world's population lives and works on the land producing food, not only for its own needs, but for the rest of humanity. The remaining one-quarter lives mainly in cities and is employed in manufacturing, transportation, and service industries. The cities named on this map are classified by their metropolitan area populations.

144

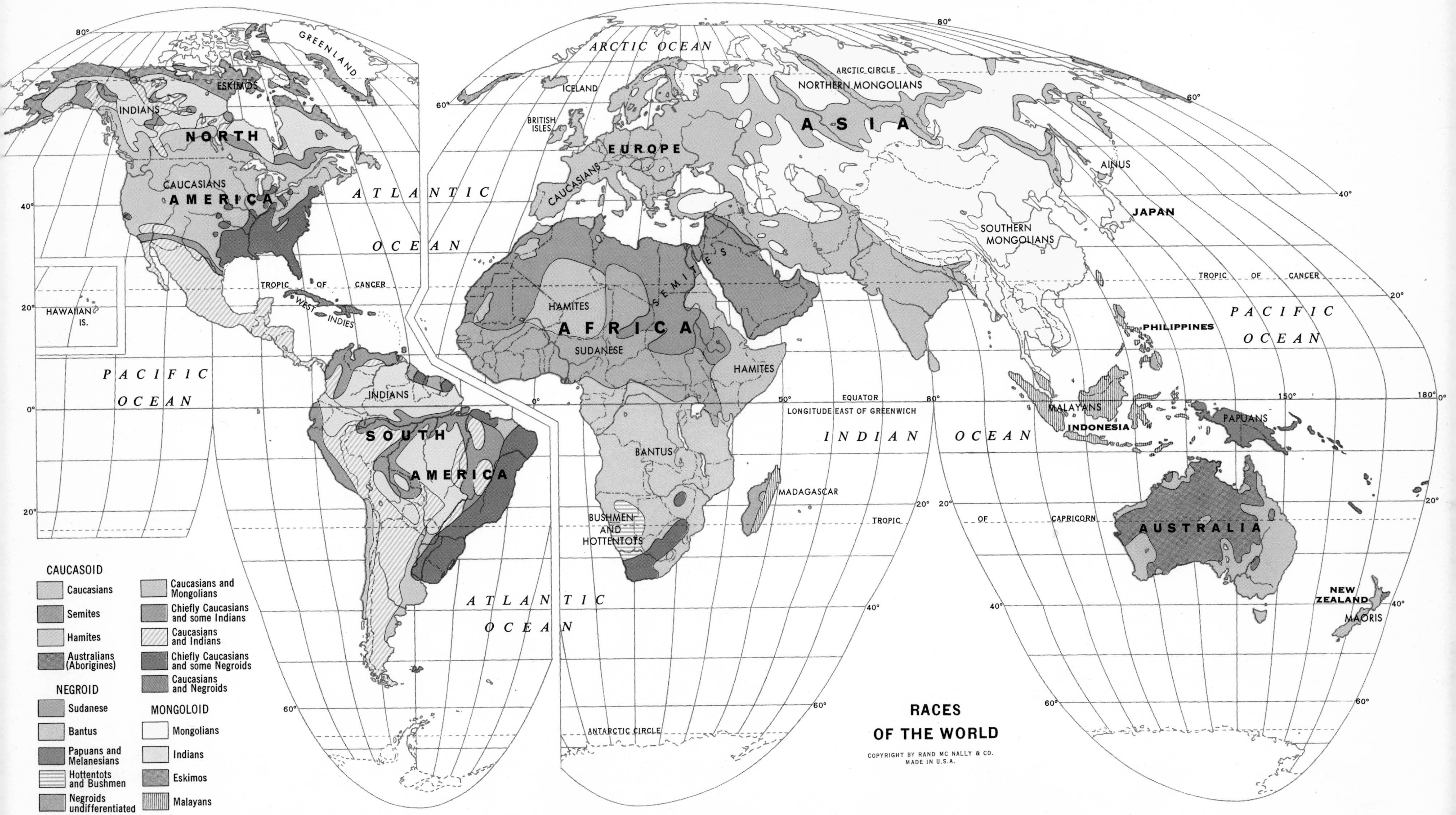

RACES OF THE WORLD

COPYRIGHT BY RAND MC NALLY & CO.
MADE IN U.S.A.

CAUCASOID
- Caucasians
- Semites
- Hamites
- Australians (Aborigines)

NEGROID
- Sudanese
- Bantus
- Papuans and Melanesians
- Hottentots and Bushmen
- Negroids undifferentiated

- Caucasians and Mongolians
- Chiefly Caucasians and some Indians
- Caucasians and Indians
- Chiefly Caucasians and some Negroids
- Caucasians and Negroids

MONGOLOID
- Mongolians
- Indians
- Eskimos
- Malayans

The term race denotes a group of people who have inherited certain physiological characteristics such as shape of the skull, the nose, and chin, skin color, and texture of the hair. Most conspicuous of racial attributes is skin color, although it may cover a wide range even within a single race. There is no "typical person" in any race.

During the course of history the major races of the world have so intermixed and have given rise to so many subgroups that a precise schematic diagram of the human race cannot be achieved. The map above shows what the anthropologists recognize as the predominant racial types in each area.

Every racial group in the world is well represented in the Americas. There are Mongoloids, represented by descendants of the original Indian peoples, and also Negroids, who make up important groups in parts of Brazil, the United States, and especially in the West Indies. In Latin America the Caucasoids, mainly from Spain and Portugal, are mixed in varying degrees with the Negroids and Mongoloids.

The people of Europe are almost all Caucasoid. Today there is only slight evidence in a few areas of the Mongoloid or Negroid races. In Africa south of the Sahara most of the people are Negroid; northward the majority are Caucasoid. The chief race of southwest and west central Asia is Caucasoid with a wide variance of characteristics, depending upon the area. In India there are many people who have hair and facial features of the Caucasoid but are likely to have brown skins, dark brown or black hair, and dark eyes. The rest of Asia is mainly Mongoloid. Nearly all of these people have dark straight hair and dark eyes. Skin color varies from medium brown to very pale yellow.

145

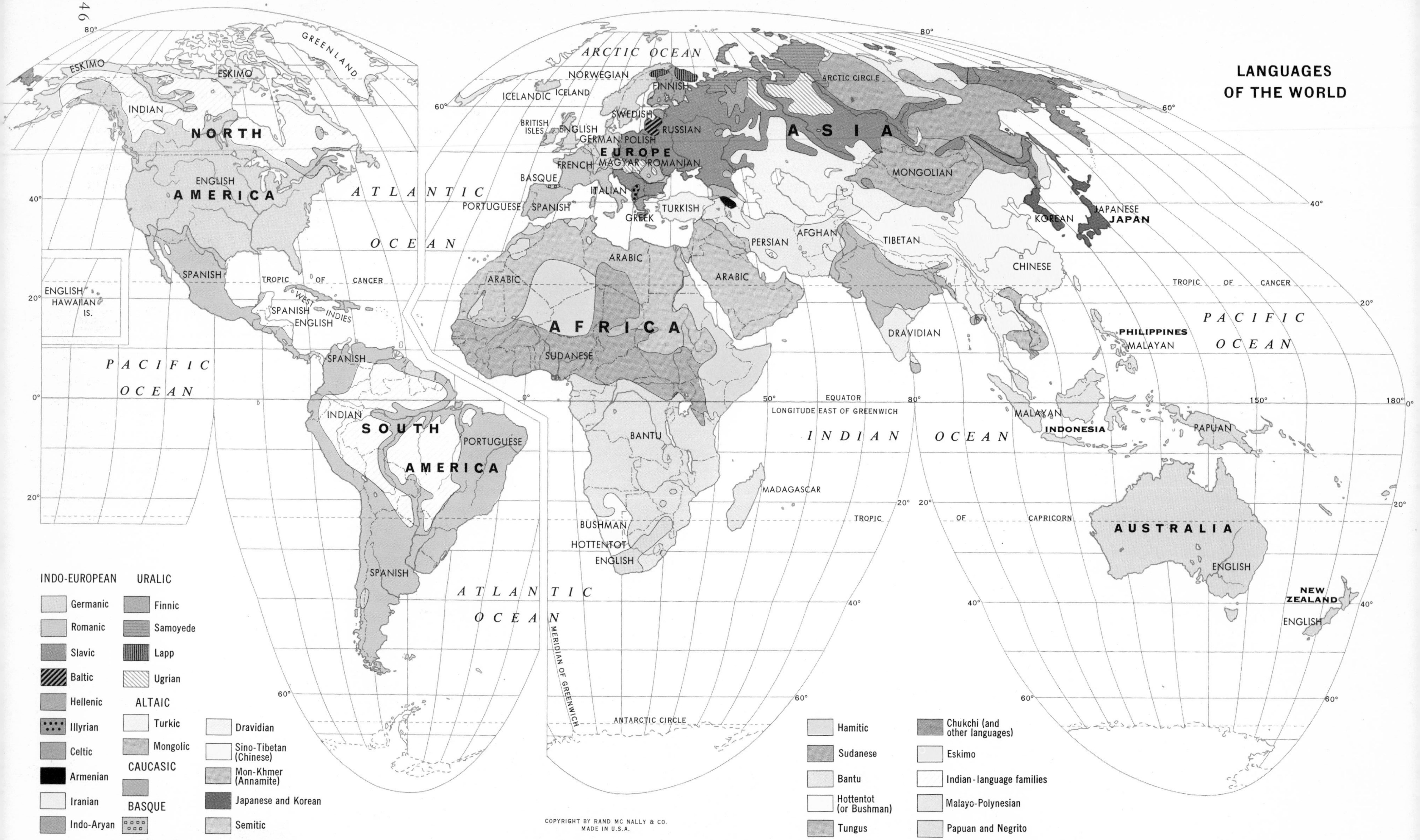

LANGUAGES OF THE WORLD

Language, as we know it today, is of very recent growth and is continually changing, absorbing new words and simplifying older grammatical forms. A world map cannot attempt to show individual areas in which a single language is spoken. This would be an impossible task for it is claimed by linguists that there are some 4,000 distinct languages spoken in the world today and, within them, an almost infinite number of dialects. The languages on the map above are grouped according to relationships determined by language specialists.

Many languages are spoken by only a handful of people while another language, Chinese, if we include all its dialect forms, is spoken by almost one-quarter of the human race. In the area or areas shown on the map in a single color, several different languages may be spoken, and a person speaking one of these languages might understand little or none of the other languages in the group, but since they are related, it would be easier for him to learn them. The Indo-European languages are by far the most important and are spoken by almost two-thirds of the human

race. Significant among these are the Germanic subgroup which includes English, the Romanic with Spanish, French Italian, and others, and Slavic, especially Russian.

Next in importance are the Sino-Tibetan group, mainly Chinese and related languages; the Uralic and Altaic groups which include Finnish, Hungarian, Turkish, and Mongolian; Japanese and Korean; the Semitic languages of the Middle East; and the Sudanese and Bantu languages of Africa. The distribution of these language groups can be related to the spread of cultures in the world.

COPYRIGHT BY RAND MC NALLY & CO.
MADE IN U.S.A.

INDO-EUROPEAN
Germanic
Romanic
Slavic
Baltic
Hellenic
Illyrian
Celtic
Armenian
Iranian
Indo-Aryan

URALIC
Finnic
Samoyede
Lapp
Ugrian

ALTAIC
Turkic
Mongolic

CAUCASIC

BASQUE

Dravidian
Sino-Tibetan (Chinese)
Mon-Khmer (Annamite)
Japanese and Korean
Semitic

Hamitic
Sudanese
Bantu
Hottentot (or Bushman)
Tungus

Chukchi (and other languages)
Eskimo
Indian-language families
Malayo-Polynesian
Papuan and Negrito

146

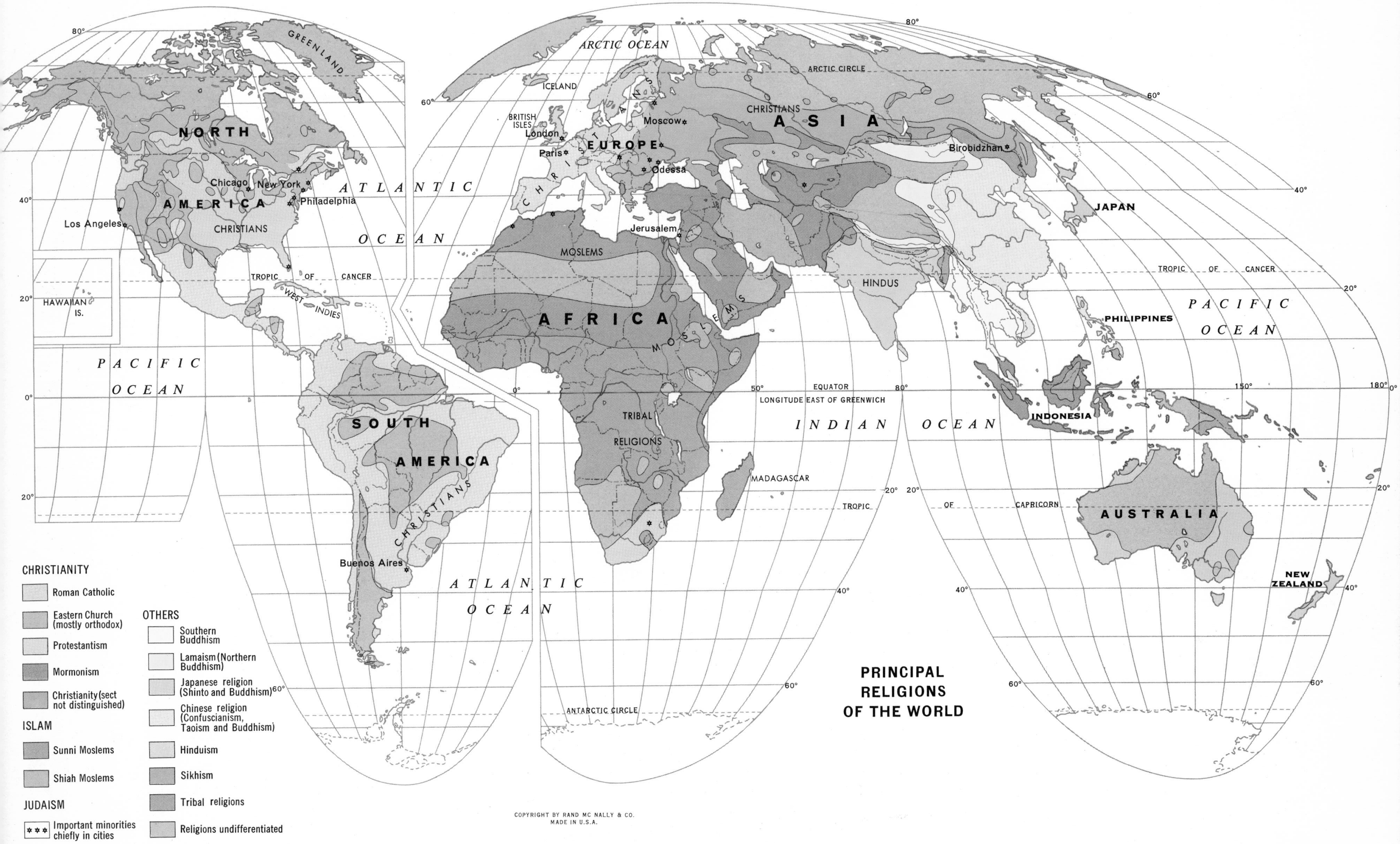

PRINCIPAL RELIGIONS OF THE WORLD

CHRISTIANITY
- Roman Catholic
- Eastern Church (mostly orthodox)
- Protestantism
- Mormonism
- Christianity (sect not distinguished)

ISLAM
- Sunni Moslems
- Shiah Moslems

JUDAISM
- ✳✳✳ Important minorities chiefly in cities

OTHERS
- Southern Buddhism
- Lamaism (Northern Buddhism)
- Japanese religion (Shinto and Buddhism)
- Chinese religion (Confucianism, Taoism and Buddhism)
- Hinduism
- Sikhism
- Tribal religions
- Religions undifferentiated

The distribution of the main religions of the world shows a certain similarity to the language map although in comparison there are fewer religions. The Romanic-speaking world with certain notable exceptions, like Romania, is Roman Catholic; the Arabic world is predominantly Islamic; the Germanic world is heavily Protestant; the Slavic world is chiefly Orthodox or Eastern, and the Chinese world is a blend of Buddhism, Confucianism, and Taoism. Western Christianity was propagated from Rome, the

source also of the Latin language from which the Romance languages derived. Islam was spread by the Arab invasions, and missionaries of the Eastern or Orthodox church played an important role in shaping the Slavic languages and providing them with an alphabet. Protestantism, derived chiefly from the German Reformation, is important in the countries where languages of Germanic origin are widely spoken.

Common religious beliefs have often brought peoples into closer association, but religious differences have at times kept

people apart. Two or more religions may flourish in the same area but on a world map it is often only possible to show the religion of the majority. Because, other than in Israel, the Jewish religion is not concentrated in an area large enough to show by color, symbols have been used to show other areas where there is a large concentration of Jews. In some places people may be members of two or more religious groups, as in Japan. Here the joint practice of Shinto and Buddhism is common and the term Japanese religion is used.

147

THE HABITABLE WORLD
According to Ptolemy, about 150 A.D.

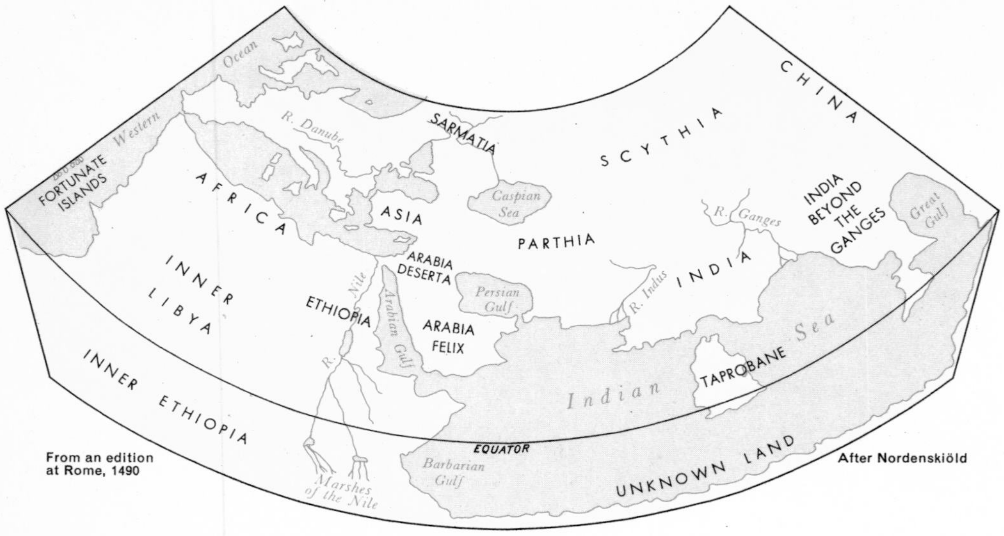

From an edition at Rome, 1490

After Nordenskiöld

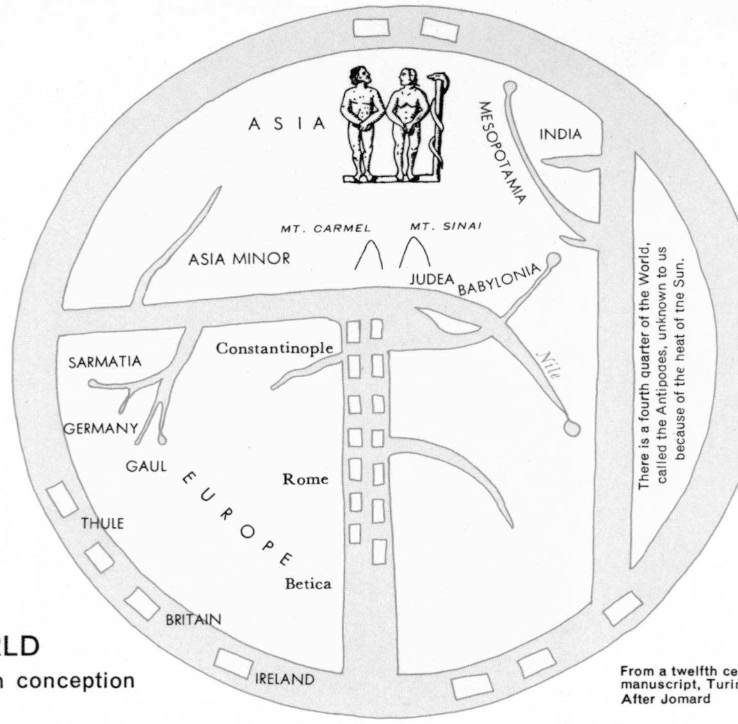

THE WORLD
A medieval European conception

There is a fourth quarter of the World, called the Antipodes, unknown to us because of the heat of the Sun.

From a twelfth century manuscript, Turin
After Jomard

WORLD HISTORY IN MAPS

This world history section of twenty-seven pages is a collection of modern maps illustrating past periods of time, not a collection of old maps made in times past. The maps on this page, however, are drawings of old maps, reproduced here only to show how men at three points in history conceived the world in which they lived.

Centuries of Greek and Near Eastern thought are summarized in the map made by Ptolemy at Alexandria about 150 A.D. He knew that the Earth is a sphere, but he believed about only one-third of the Northern Hemisphere was habitable. His map represents this portion of the globe. He understood the principles of map projection, that is of representing a curved surface on a flat page, and he located places according to longitude and latitude, defining longitude by distance east of the Fortunate Islands (now the Canaries) and latitude by the length of the longest day of the year. His map was defective not in conception but by lack of information.

The sample of a medieval map represents a common form of map in use at this period of time—a diagram rather than a true map. The outer circle represents the

ocean, the vertical radius containing oblong islands in the Mediterranean Sea. The East is at the top and the Holy Land is in the center. A person using this map could get a rough idea of direction, but he would have no idea of distance, size, or proportion.

The Behaim globe, below, represents man's conception of the world at the time of Columbus.

There are forty-eight maps in this section, including insets. Asia is represented at successive periods of its history, and we have given attention to Africa and Latin America, but since this book is mainly for American use, the treatment of North American and European history is given better coverage. The maps both illustrate general ideas and supply particular information. Modern maps differ from old maps in being more exact in projection and in scale.

THE WORLD
According to Behaim, 1492

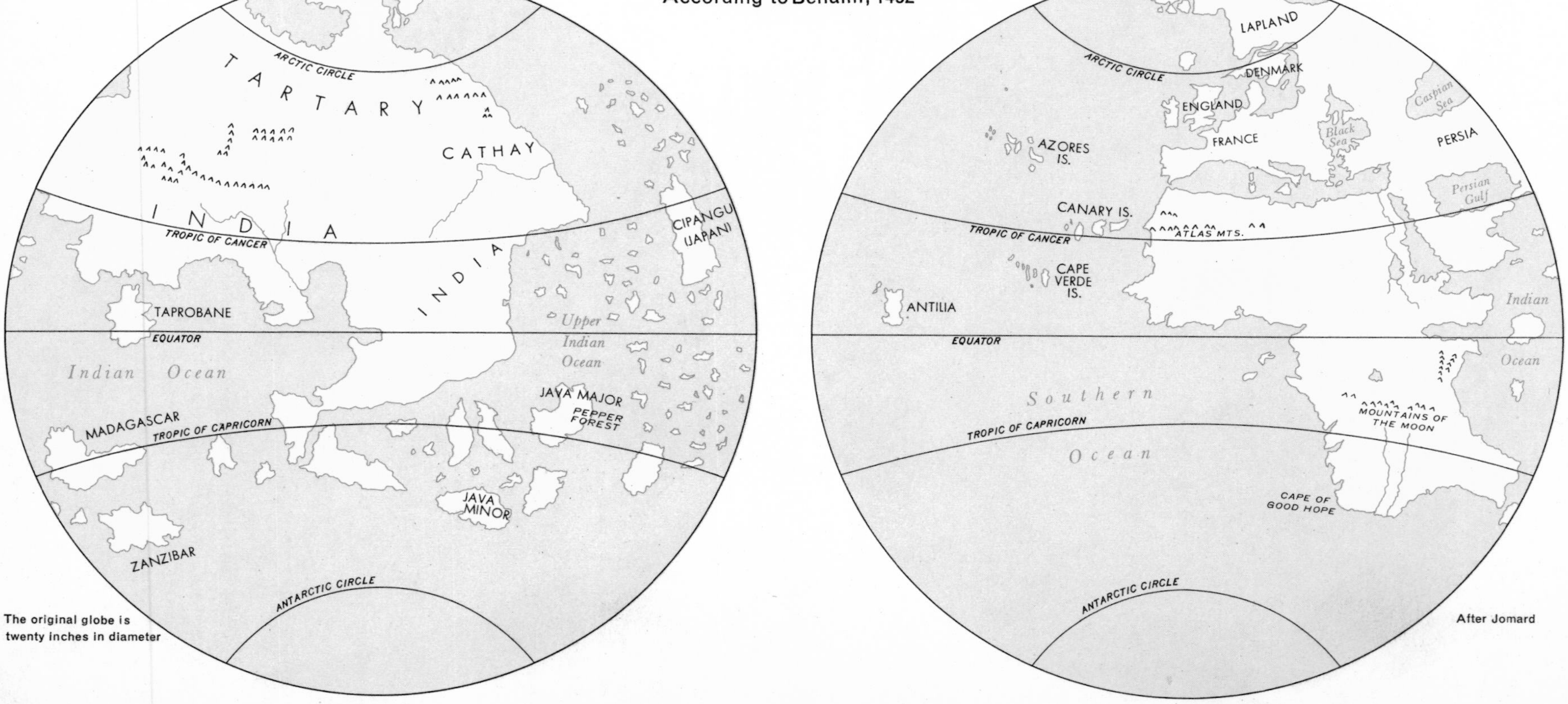

The original globe is twenty inches in diameter

After Jomard

148

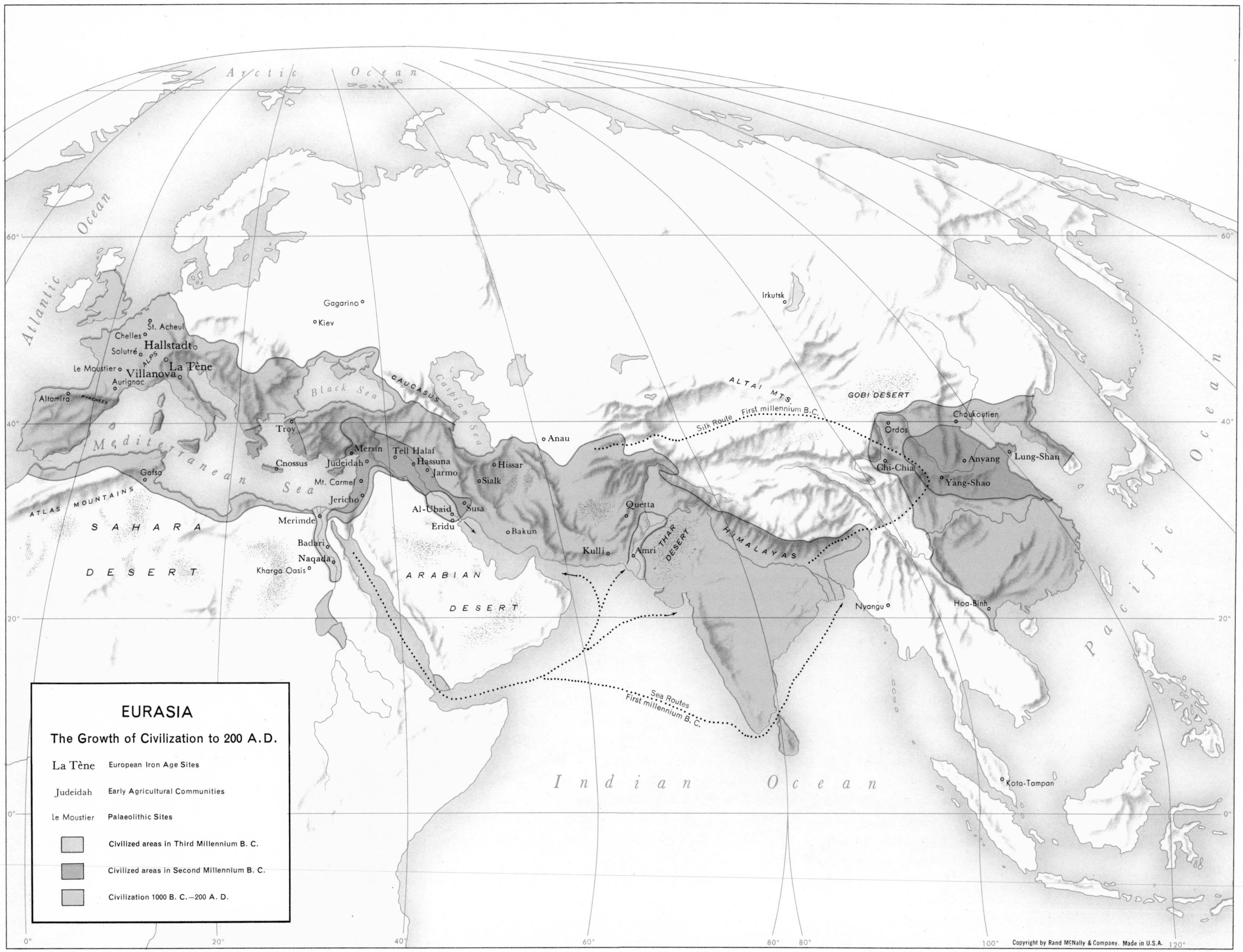

EURASIA

The Growth of Civilization to 200 A. D.

La Tène — European Iron Age Sites

Judeidah — Early Agricultural Communities

le Moustier — Palaeolithic Sites

Civilized areas in Third Millennium B. C.

Civilized areas in Second Millennium B. C.

Civilization 1000 B. C.—200 A. D.

Lung-Shan
Chou-kou-tien
Anvang
Yang-Shao
Ordos
Chi-Chia
Hoa-Binh
Koto-Tampon

GOBI DESERT
ALTAI MTS.
Silk Route First millennium B.C.
Irkunk

HIMALAYAS

Nyangu

THAR DESERT

Sea Routes First millennium B.C.

Indian Ocean

Anau
Quetta
Amri
Kulli
Baluri

ARABIAN DESERT

Caspian Sea
Hissar
Sialk
Susa
Jarmo
Hassuna
Tell Halaf
Al-Ubaid
Eridu

CAUCASUS

Black Sea

Gagarino
Kiev

Mersin
Judeidah
Mt. Carmel
Jericho

Troy
Cnossus

Merimde
Badari
Naqada
Kharga Oasis

Mediterranean Sea

ATLAS MOUNTAINS

SAHARA DESERT

La Tène
Hallstadt
Villanova
Cheilles
St. Acheul
Soluré
Aurignac
le Moustier
Gafsa
Altamira

Arctic Ocean

Atlantic Ocean

Pacific Ocean

Copyright by Rand McNally & Company. Made in U.S.A.

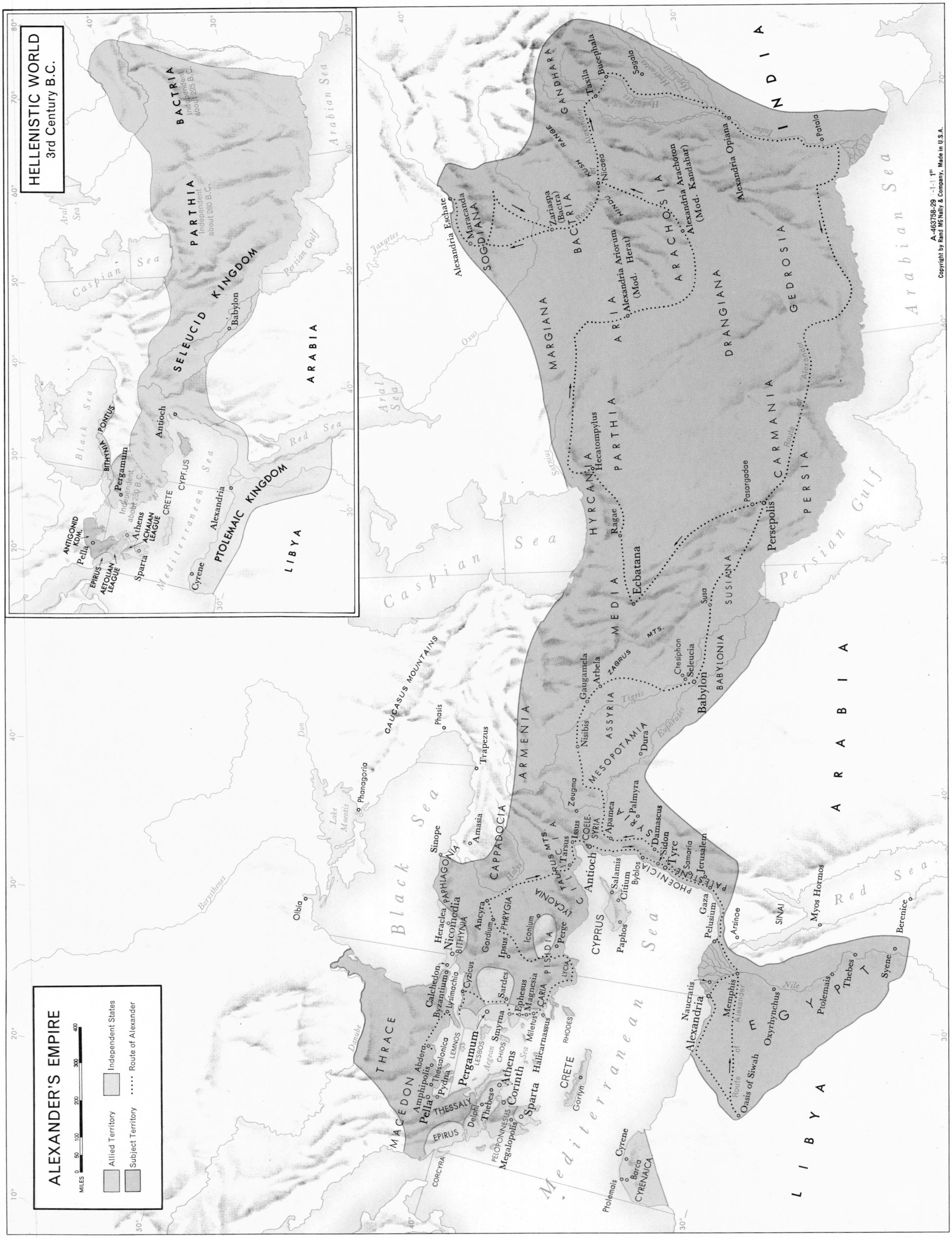

ALEXANDER'S EMPIRE

MILES
0 50 100 200 300 400

Allied Territory
Subject Territory
Independent States
Route of Alexander

HELLENISTIC WORLD
3rd Century B.C.

BACTRIA
independent
about 225 B.C.

PARTHIA
independent
about 250 B.C.

SELEUCID KINGDOM

Babylon

Antioch

PONTUS
BITHYNIA

Pergamum
independent
about 250 B.C.

ANTIGONID
KDM.
Pella
EPIRUS
AETOLIAN
LEAGUE
Athens
Sparta
ACHAEAN
LEAGUE

CYPRUS
CRETE

Alexandria

PTOLEMAIC KINGDOM

Cyrene

LIBYA

ARABIA

Aral
Sea

Caspian
Sea

Black Sea

Persian Gulf

Red Sea

Arabian Sea

Mediterranean Sea

INDIA

Alexandria Eschate
Maracanda
SOGDIANA
Zariaspa (Bactra)
BACTRIA
Nicaea
GANDHARA
Taxila
Bucephala
Sangala
Sogdia
Patala

Alexandria Ariorum
(Mod. Herat)
ARIA
ARACHOSIA
Alexandria Arachoton
Alexandria (Mod. Kandahar)
Alexandria Opiana

MARGIANA

HYRCANIA
Hecatompylus
PARTHIA
DRANGIANA
GEDROSIA
CARMANIA

Ragae
MEDIA
Ecbatana
Passargadae
Persepolis
PERSIA

Gaugamela
Arbela
ZAGRUS MTS.
ASSYRIA
Nisibis
MESOPOTAMIA
Dura
Ctesiphon
Seleucia
Babylon
BABYLONIA
Susa
SUSIANA

ARMENIA

Phasis
Trapezus
CAUCASUS MOUNTAINS

Don

Lake
Maeotis

Phanagoria

Olbia

Sinope
Amasia
PAPHLAGONIA
Heraclea
Nicomedia
BITHYNIA
Calchedon
Byzantium
Lysimachia
Cyzicus
Gordium
PHRYGIA
Ancyra
LYCAONIA
Iconium
Ipsus
PISIDIA
CAPPADOCIA
TAURUS MTS.
CILICIA
Tarsus
Issus
COELE-SYRIA
Antioch
Apamea
SYRIA
Palmyra
Damascus
Sidon
Tyre
PHOENICIA
Byblos
Samaria
Jerusalem
PALESTINE
Gaza
Pelusium

THRACE
MACEDON
Amphipolis
Abdera
Thessalonica
Pella
Pydna
THESSALY
EPIRUS
Delphi
Thebes
Chaeronea
PELOPONNESUS
Megalopolis
Corinth
Sparta
CORCYRA

Pergamum
Lysimachia
Sardes
Smyrna
Ephesus
Magnesia
Miletus
CARIA
Halicarnassus
LYDIA
LYCIA
RHODES

LESBOS
CHIOS
Aegean Sea
Athens

CRETE
Gortyn

CYPRUS
Salamis
Paphos
Citium

SINAI
Arsinoe
Myos Hormos

Naucratis
Alexandria
Memphis
EGYPT
Oasis of Siwah
Oxyrhynchus
Ptolemais
Thebes
Syene
Berenice

Cyrene
Borca
CYRENAICA
Ptolemais

LIBYA

ARABIA

Tigris
Euphrates
Nile

150

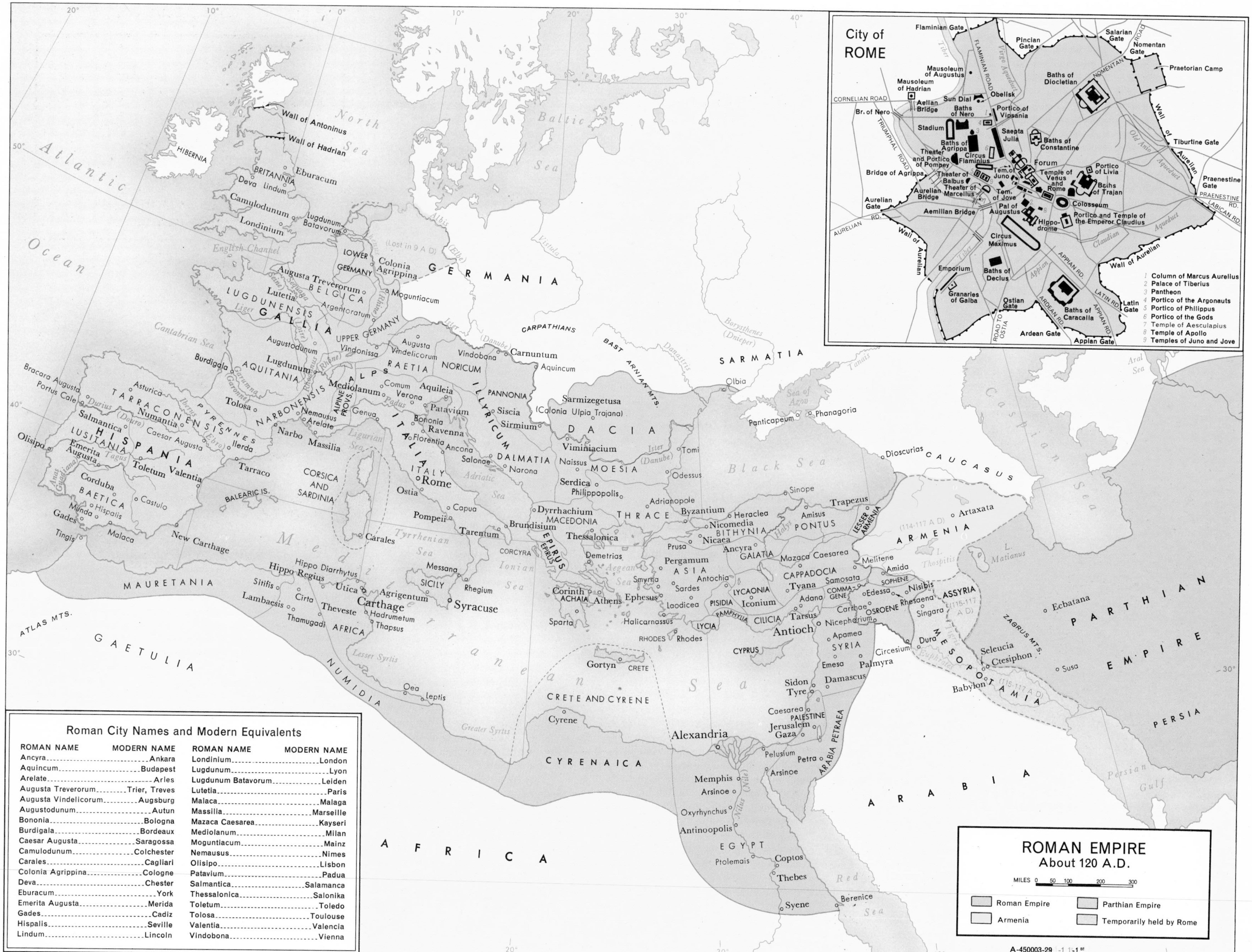

City of ROME

1 Column of Marcus Aurelius
2 Palace of Tiberius
3 Pantheon
4 Portico of the Argonauts
5 Portico of Philippus
6 Portico of the Gods
7 Temple of Aesculapius
8 Temple of Apollo
9 Temples of Juno and Jove

ROMAN EMPIRE
About 120 A.D.

MILES
0   50   100   200   300

Roman Empire
Armenia
Parthian Empire
Temporarily held by Rome

Copyright by Rand McNally & Company, Made in U.S.A.

A-450003-29 -1 -1 st

Roman City Names and Modern Equivalents

ROMAN NAME	MODERN NAME	ROMAN NAME	MODERN NAME
Ancyra	Ankara	Londinium	London
Aquincum	Budapest	Lugdunum	Lyon
Arelate	Arles	Lugdunum Batavorum	Leiden
Augusta Treverorum	Trier, Treves	Lutetia	Paris
Augusta Vindelicorum	Augsburg	Malaca	Malaga
Augustodunum	Autun	Massilia	Marseille
Bononia	Bologna	Mazaca Caesarea	Kayseri
Burdigala	Bordeaux	Mediolanum	Milan
Caesar Augusta	Saragossa	Moguntiacum	Mainz
Camulodunum	Colchester	Nemausus	Nimes
Carales	Cagliari	Olisipo	Lisbon
Colonia Agrippina	Cologne	Patavium	Padua
Deva	Chester	Salmantica	Salamanca
Eburacum	York	Thessalonica	Salonika
Emerita Augusta	Merida	Toletum	Toledo
Gades	Cadiz	Tolosa	Toulouse
Hispalis	Seville	Valentia	Valencia
Lindum	Lincoln	Vindobona	Vienna

151

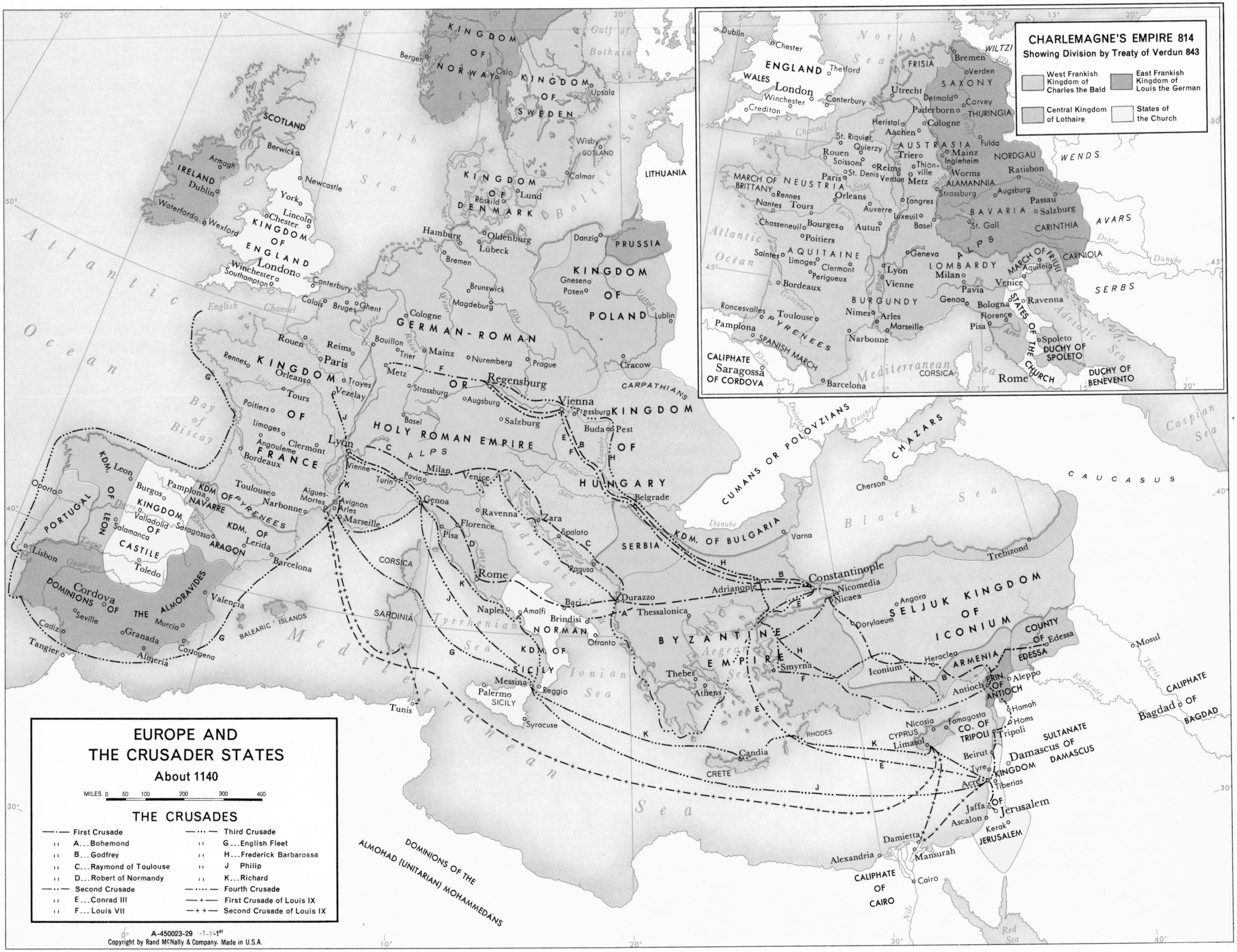

CHARLEMAGNE'S EMPIRE 814
Showing Division by Treaty of Verdun 843

West Frankish
Kingdom of
Charles the Bald

East Frankish
Kingdom of
Louis the German

Central Kingdom
of Lothaire

States of
the Church

EUROPE AND
THE CRUSADER STATES
About 1140

MILES 0 50 100 200 300 400

THE CRUSADES

	First Crusade			Third Crusade
"	A...Bohemond	"	G...English Fleet
"	B...Godfrey	"	H...Frederick Barbarossa
"	C...Raymond of Toulouse	"	J...Philip
"	D...Robert of Normandy	"	K...Richard
	Second Crusade			First Crusade of Louis IX
"	E...Conrad III			Second Crusade of Louis IX
"	F...Louis VII			

A-450023-29 -1.1-1st
Copyright by Rand McNally & Company. Made in U.S.A.

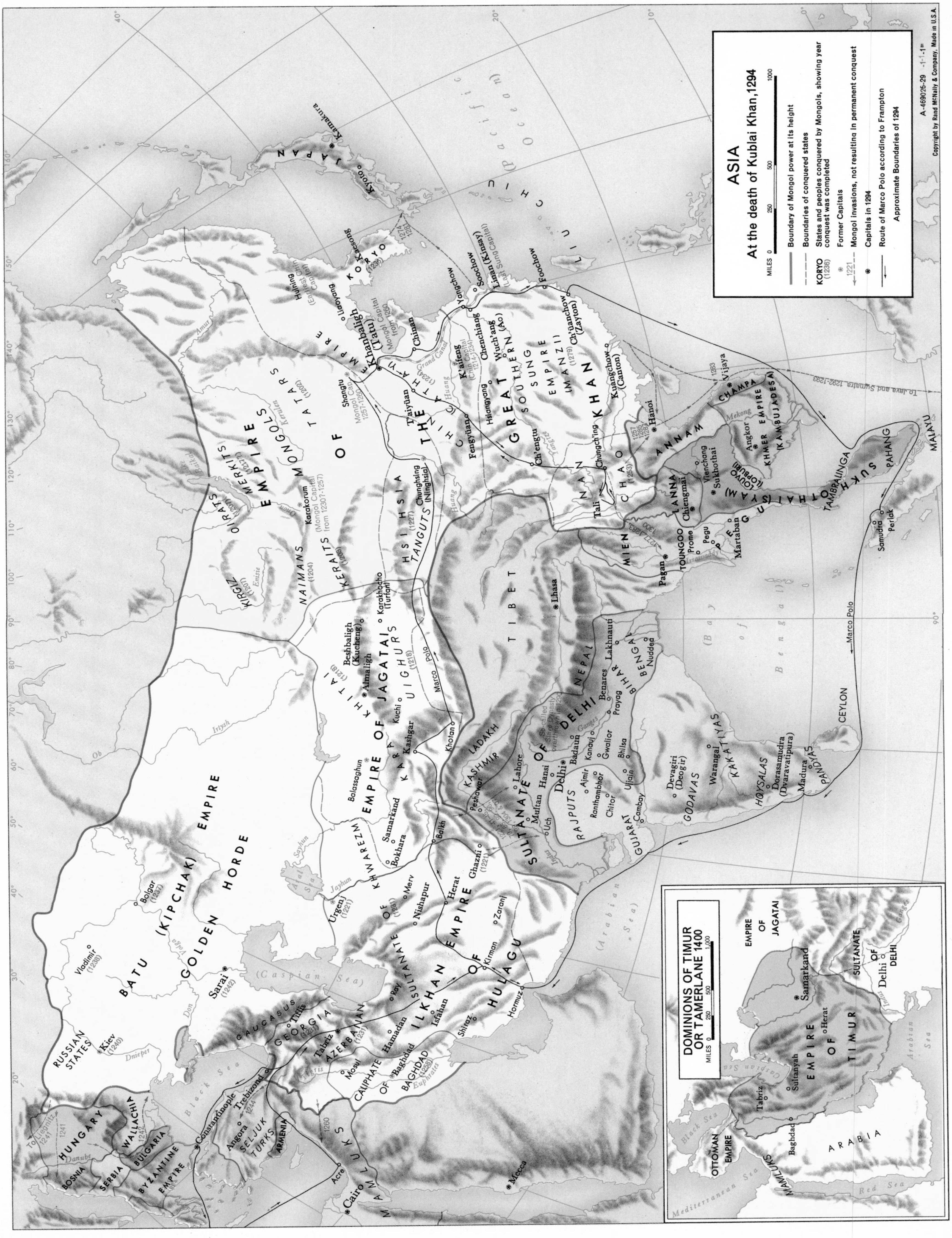

A-469026-29 -1-1-1™

Copyright by Rand McNally & Company, Made in U.S.A.

ASIA
At the death of Kublai Khan, 1294

MILES 0   250   500   1000

———— Boundary of Mongol power at its height

———— Boundaries of conquered states

———— States and peoples conquered by Mongols, showing year
        conquest was completed

KORYO   Former Capitals
(1236)

•   Mongol Capitals

1221 ——— Mongol invasions, not resulting in permanent conquest

✳   Capitals in 1294

————→   Route of Marco Polo according to Frampton

———— Approximate Boundaries of 1294

DOMINIONS OF TIMUR
OR TAMERLANE 1400

MILES 0   250   500   1000

EMPIRE
OF
JAGATAI

SULTANATE
OF
DELHI

Delhi o

OTTOMAN
EMPIRE

Samarkand ✳

EMPIRE
OF
TIMUR

o Herat

MAMLUKS

Tabriz o

Sultaniyah o

Baghdad o

ARABIA

Black Sea

Caspian Sea

Arabian
Sea

Red Sea

Mediterranean Sea

RUSSIAN
STATES

✳ Kiev
(1240)

Vladimir o
(1238)

BATU (KIPCHAKI)

GOLDEN HORDE

Bolgar o
(1237)

Sarai ✳
(1282)

Don

Dnieper

HUNGARY

Tollowitz
1241

1241
1241

BOSNIA

SERBIA

WALLACHIA

BULGARIA

✳ Constantinople

BYZANTINE
EMPIRE

Danube

Trebizond o

Angora o

SELJUK
TURKS

ARMENIA

Acre o

✳ Cairo

MAMLUK

✳ Mecca

GEORGIA

Tiflis o

CAUCASUS

AZERBAIJAN

Tabriz ✳
(1231)

Mosul o

Baghdad o
(1258)

CALIPHATE OF
BAGHDAD

Hamadan o

Isfahan o

Shiraz o

ILKHAN
OF
HULAGU

Kirman o

Hormuz o

Euphrates

(Caspian Sea)

KIRGIZ

Enisei

Irtish

Ob

OIRATS

MERKITS

NAIMANS
(1204)

KERAITS
(1204)

EMPIRE
OF
JAGATAI

Beshbaligh
(Kucheng)
(1209)

Almaligh ✳
(1211)

Kuchi

UIGHURS
(1218)

KARA KHITAI

Balassaghun o

Samarkand o

Bokhara o

Urgenj o
(1221)

SULTANATE OF
KHWAREZM

Merv o

Nishapur o

Balkh o

EMPIRE OF

Herat o

Ghazni o
(1221)

Zaroni o

Syr Daria

Jaxartes

Aral Sea

MONGOLS

EMPIRES
OF THE

Karakorum
(Mongol Capital)
(1230?-1257)

Shang-tu
(Mongol Capital
1257-1260)

Amur

Kerulen

KHANBALIGH
(Tatu)

Kamakura ✳

JAPAN

Kyoto o

(Pacific Ocean)

KOSONG

LIAO-TUNG

Huning
(Eastern Capital)

KORYO
(1236)

Liaoyang o

Peking o

1214
1211
1210

1287

CHINA

THE GREAT KHAN

TANGUTS
(1227)

HSIHSIA

Chunghsing
(Ninghsia)

Karakhocho
(Turfan)

Kashgar o

Kholan o

Yarkand o

LADAKH

KASHMIR

Peshawar o

Lahore ✳

Multan o

Uch o

o Hansi

Delhi ✳

Ajmir o

RAJPUTS

Chitor o

Ronthambhor o

o Badaun

Kanauj o

Gwalior o

o Bhilsa

Ujjain o

SULTANATE OF DELHI

NEPAL

TIBET

Lhasa ✳

Huang
(Yellow)

Lanchow o

Fengt'ian o

Chengtu o

Taiyuan o

YUNNAN

Tali o

Chungching o

Kaifeng
(1214)

Hsiangyang
(1273)

Wuch'ang
(Ao)
(1279)

SOUTHERN SUNG EMPIRE
(MANZI)

Soochow o

Yangchow o

Lin-an (Kinsay)
(Last Sung Capital)

Ch'üanchow
(Zayton)

Foochow o

Kuangchow
(Canton)

Chinan o

Chenchiang o

Grand Canal

Yangtze

MIEN

Pagan o

TOUNGOO ✳

Prome o

Pegu o

Martaban o

LANNA

Chiengmai ✳

Vienchang o

Sukhothai ✳

SUKHOTHAI
(SIAM)

LOUVO
(LOPBURI)

KHMER EMPIRE
(KAMBUJADESA)

Angkor ✳

TAMBRALINGA

PAHANG

MALAYU

ANNAM

Hanoi o
1257
1283

CHAMPA

Vijaya ✳
1283

Mekong

Salween

Mirananotai

Irrawaddy

To Java and Sumatra 1292-1293

Marco Polo

BENGAL

Lakhnauti o

Nuddea o

Benares o

Proyag o

BIHAR

BENGAL

Gangetic

Ganges

Doraganga o

GODAVAS

Warangai o

Doraganga
(Deogir)

KAKATIYAS

Devagiri
(Deogir) o

HOYSALAS

Dorasamudra
(Dvaravatipura) o

Madura o

PANDYAS

CEYLON

Cambay o

Gandhi o

GUJARAT

Bay of Bengal

Arabian Sea

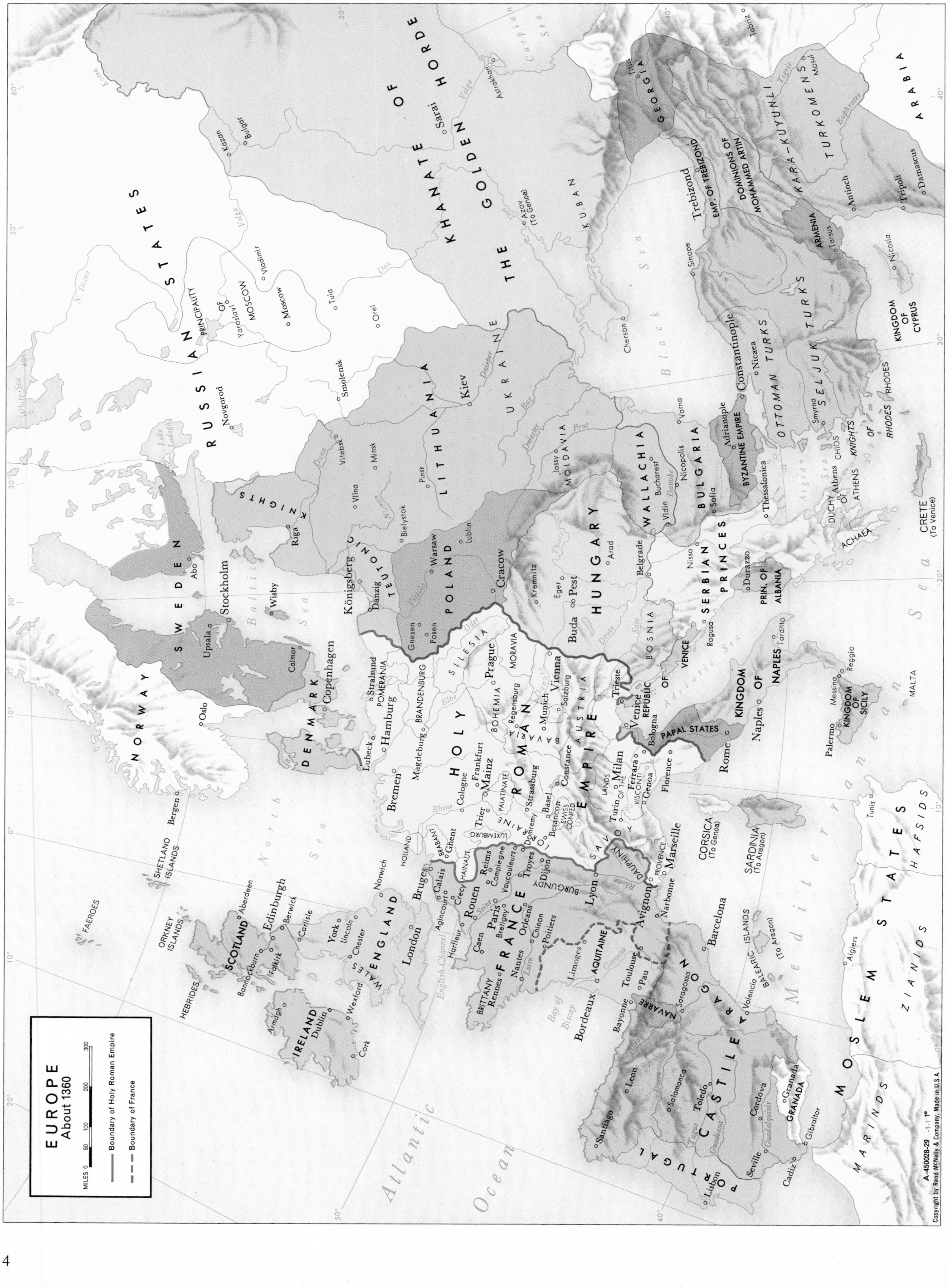

EUROPE
About 1360

MILES 0 50 100 200 300

—— Boundary of Holy Roman Empire
- - - Boundary of France

Copyright by Rand McNally & Company. Made in U.S.A.

A-450028-29 -1-1-Tth

154

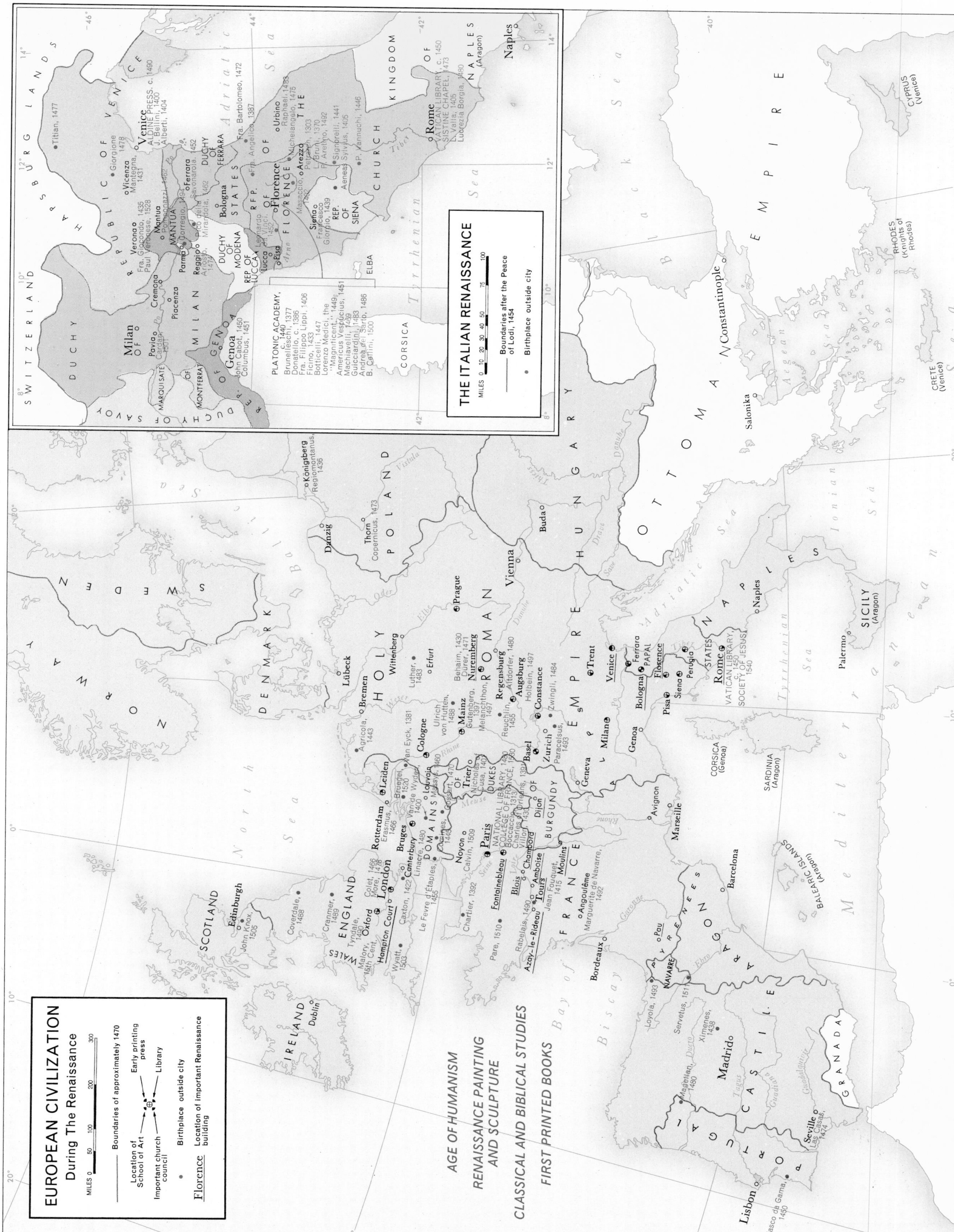

EUROPEAN CIVILIZATION
During The Renaissance

MILES 0   50   100   200   300

— Boundaries of approximately 1470

Location of
School of Art

Early printing
press

Important church
council

Library

● Birthplace outside city

Florence   Location of important Renaissance building

AGE OF HUMANISM
RENAISSANCE PAINTING AND SCULPTURE
CLASSICAL AND BIBLICAL STUDIES
FIRST PRINTED BOOKS

THE ITALIAN RENAISSANCE

MILES 0 10 20 30 40 50   75   100

—— Boundaries after the Peace of Lodi, 1454

● Birthplace outside city

Copyright by Rand McNally & Company. Made in U.S.A.

155

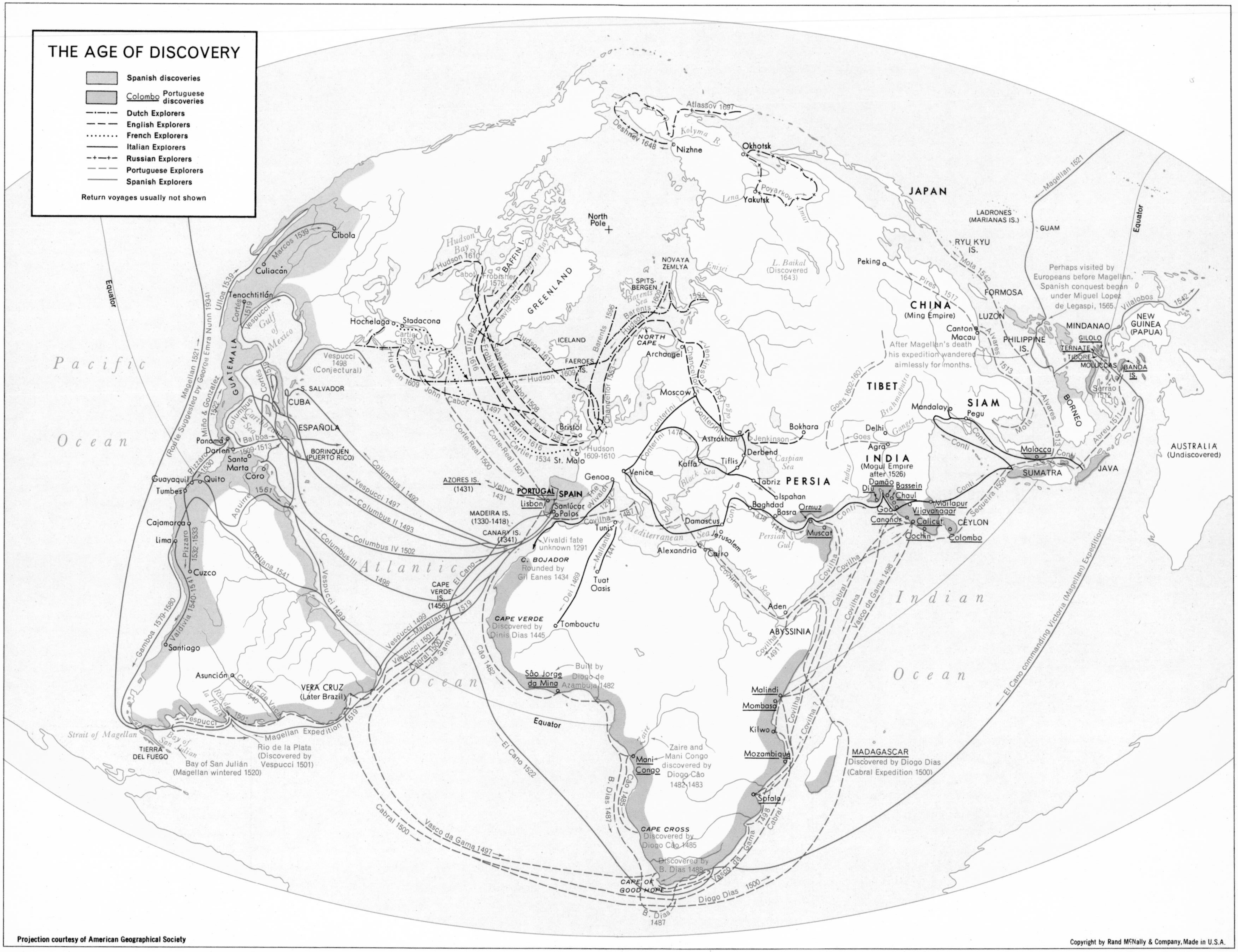

THE AGE OF DISCOVERY

Spanish discoveries
Colombo Portuguese discoveries

- Dutch Explorers
- English Explorers
- French Explorers
- Italian Explorers
- Russian Explorers
- Portuguese Explorers
- Spanish Explorers

Return voyages usually not shown

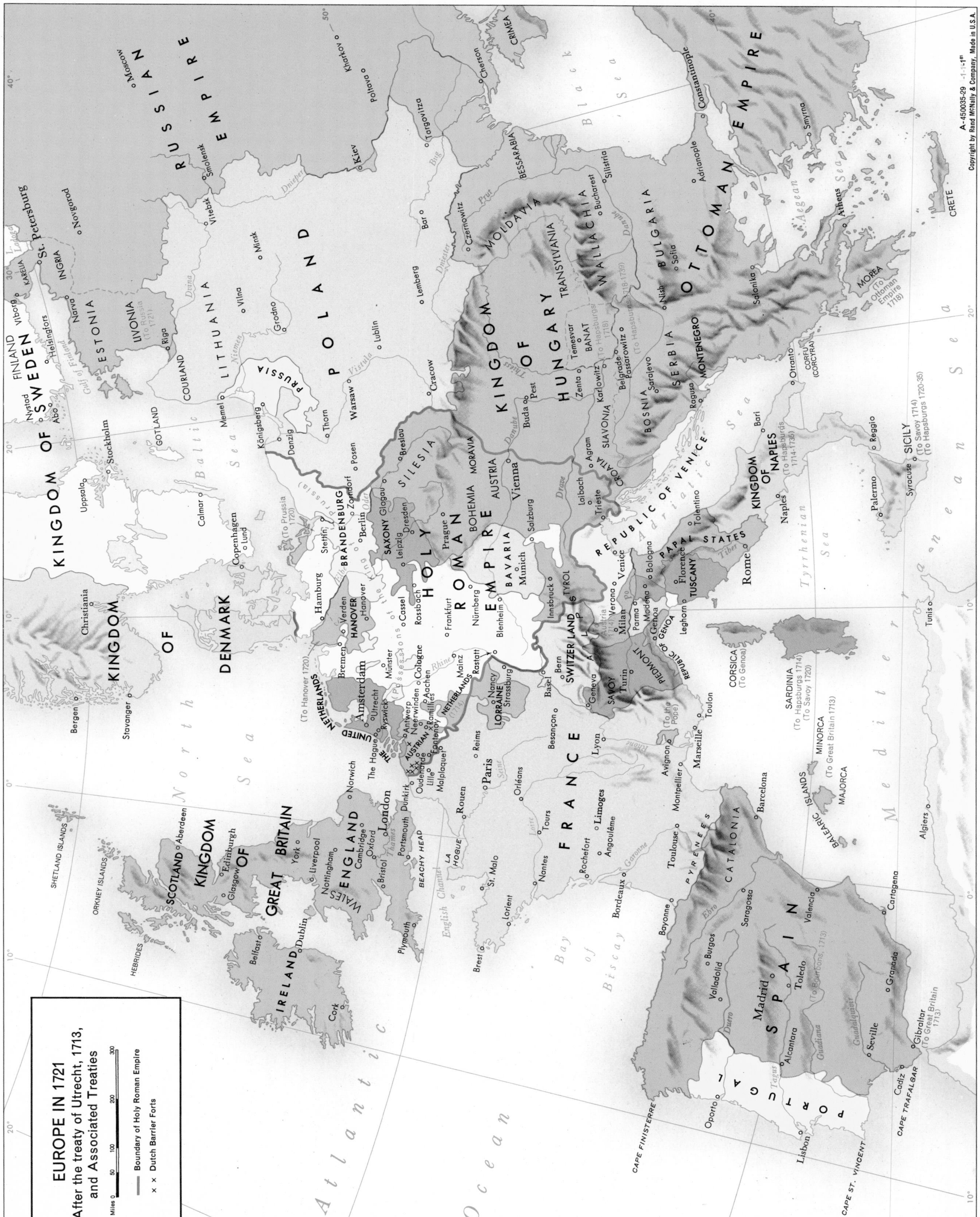

EUROPE IN 1721
After the treaty of Utrecht, 1713,
and Associated Treaties

▬▬▬ Boundary of Holy Roman Empire
x x Dutch Barrier Forts

Miles 0   50 100   200   300

RUSSIAN EMPIRE

Moscow
Khotkov
Poltava
Kiev
Chernov
Kharkov

FINLAND
St. Petersburg
KARELIA
Viborg
INGRIA
Novgorod
Nyslot
Narva
Helsingfors
ESTONIA
LIVONIA (To Russia 1721)
Riga
Abo
COURLAND
Reval
Memel
PRUSSIA
Königsberg
Vilna
LITHUANIA
Grodno
Minsk
Vitebsk
Smolensk

KINGDOM OF SWEDEN
Uppsala
Stockholm
GOTLAND
Calmar

POLAND
Danzig
Thorn
Warsaw
Posen
Lublin
Lemberg
Cracow
Targowitza

CRIMEA
Cherson

OTTOMAN EMPIRE
Constantinople
Adrianople
Silistria
Bucharest
Nicopolis
Sofia
Salonika
Smyrna
Athens
MOREA (To Ottoman Empire 1718)
CRETE
Black Sea
Aegean Sea

BESSARABIA
MOLDAVIA
WALLACHIA
TRANSYLVANIA
BULGARIA
SERBIA
BOSNIA
MONTENEGRO
Belgrade
Sarajevo
Ragusa
Nissa
Passarowitz
Zenta
Karlowitz
Temesvar
BANAT (To Hapsburgs 1718)

KINGDOM OF HUNGARY
Buda
Pest
Agram
SLAVONIA
CROATIA
Laibach
Trieste

KINGDOM OF DENMARK OF NORWAY
Bergen
Stavanger
Christiania
Copenhagen
Lund
Hamburg
Stettin

BRANDENBURG (To Prussia 1720)
Berlin
Stargard
Zwittau
SILESIA
Breslau
Glogau

SAXONY
Leipzig
Dresden
Glatz

HOLY ROMAN EMPIRE
BOHEMIA
Prague
MORAVIA
AUSTRIA
Vienna
Salzburg
BAVARIA
Munich
Nürnberg
Frankfurt
TYROL
Innsbruck
Blenheim
HANOVER
Hanover
Bremen
Verden
Cassel
Rossbach
Hamburg

NETHERLANDS
AUSTRIAN NETHERLANDS
Antwerp
Neerwinden
Cologne
Aachen
Oudenarde
Ramillies
Lille
Malplaquet
Dunkirk

UNITED NETHERLANDS
Amsterdam
Utrecht
The Hague
Ryswick
Münster
Mainz
Rastatt
Strassburg
Nancy
LORRAINE

SWITZERLAND
Basel
Bern
Geneva

REPUBLIC OF VENICE
Venice
Verona
Milan
Parma
Modena
Bologna
Genoa
Leghorn
Florence
TUSCANY
PAPAL STATES
Rome
Tolentino
Ancona

SAVOY
PIEDMONT
Turin
CORSICA (To Genoa)
SARDINIA (To Hapsburgs 1714) (To Savoy 1720)

KINGDOM OF NAPLES
Naples
Bari
Reggio
Palermo
SICILY (To Savoy 1714) (To Hapsburgs 1714-20) (To Hapsburgs 1720-35)
Syracuse

FRANCE
Paris
Reims
Rouen
Orléans
Tours
Nantes
Limoges
Angoulême
Bordeaux
Bayonne
Toulouse
Montpellier
Marseille
Toulon
Avignon (To the Pope)
Lyon
Besançon
Rochefort
La Rochelle
Brest
St. Malo
Lorient

KINGDOM OF GREAT BRITAIN
SCOTLAND
Aberdeen
Edinburgh
Glasgow
ENGLAND
WALES
London
York
Oxford
Cambridge
Liverpool
Nottingham
Norwich
Bristol
Portsmouth
Plymouth
IRELAND
Dublin
Belfast
Cork
SHETLAND ISLANDS
ORKNEY ISLANDS
HEBRIDES
BEACHY HEAD
LA HOGUE

SPAIN
Madrid
Toledo
Burgos
Valladolid
Alcántara
Saragossa
Barcelona
CATALONIA
Valencia
Cartagena
Granada
Seville
Cádiz
Gibraltar (To Great Britain 1713)
BALEARIC ISLANDS
MINORCA (To Great Britain 1713)
MAJORCA

PORTUGAL
Lisbon
Oporto
CAPE ST. VINCENT
CAPE TRAFALGAR
CAPE FINISTERRE

Algiers
Tunis

North Sea
Baltic Sea
Atlantic Ocean
Bay of Biscay
English Channel
Mediterranean Sea
Adriatic Sea
Tyrrhenian Sea

A-450035-29 · -: : 1ª · Made in U.S.A.
Copyright by Rand McNally & Company

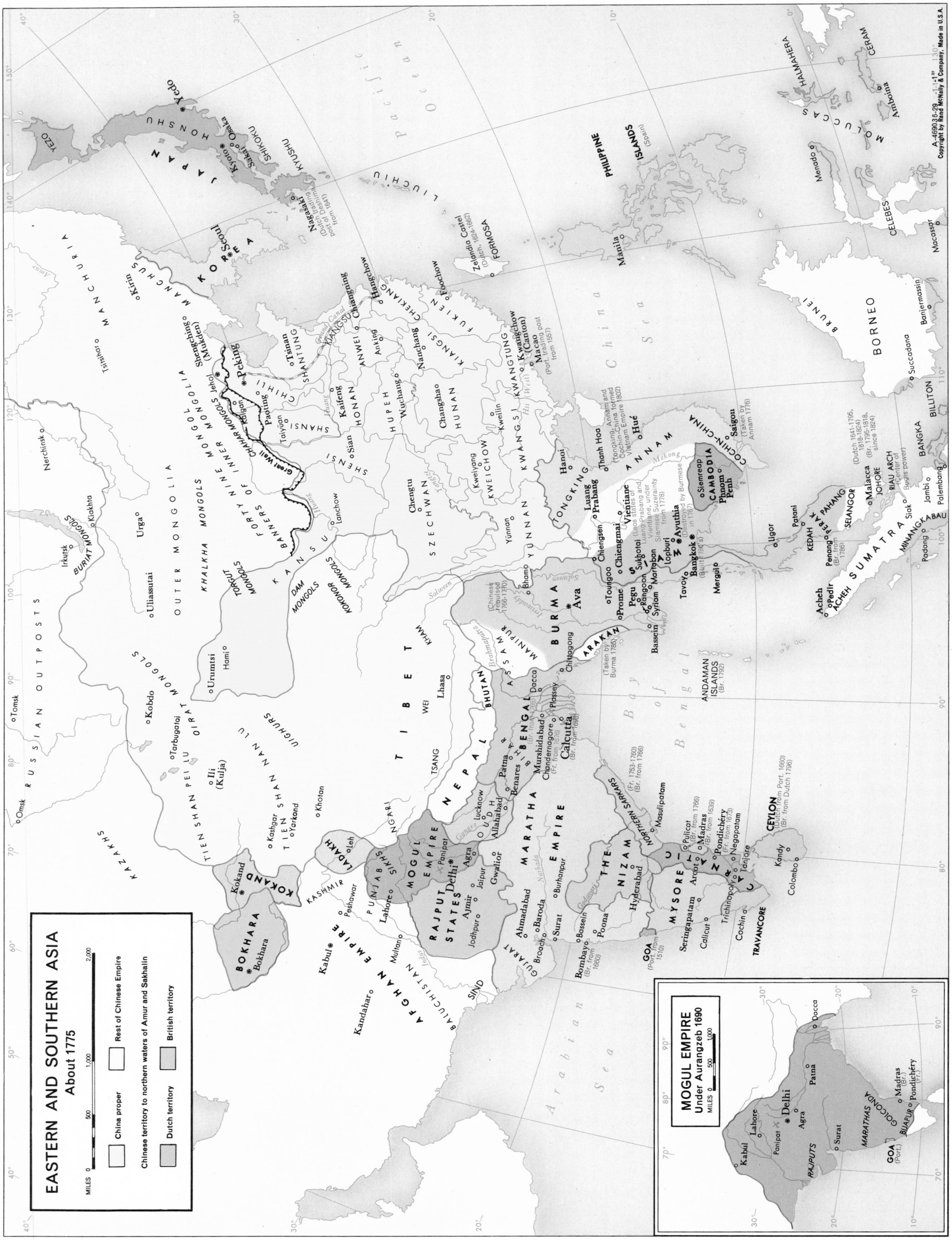

EASTERN AND SOUTHERN ASIA
About 1775

MILES 0   500   1,000   2,000

- China proper
- Rest of Chinese Empire
- Chinese territory to northern waters of Amur and Sakhalin
- Dutch territory
- British territory

MOGUL EMPIRE
Under Aurangzeb 1690

MILES 0   500   1,000

A-46903.6-29 — 1″ × -1 = -1″
Copyright by Rand McNally & Company, Made in U.S.A.

158

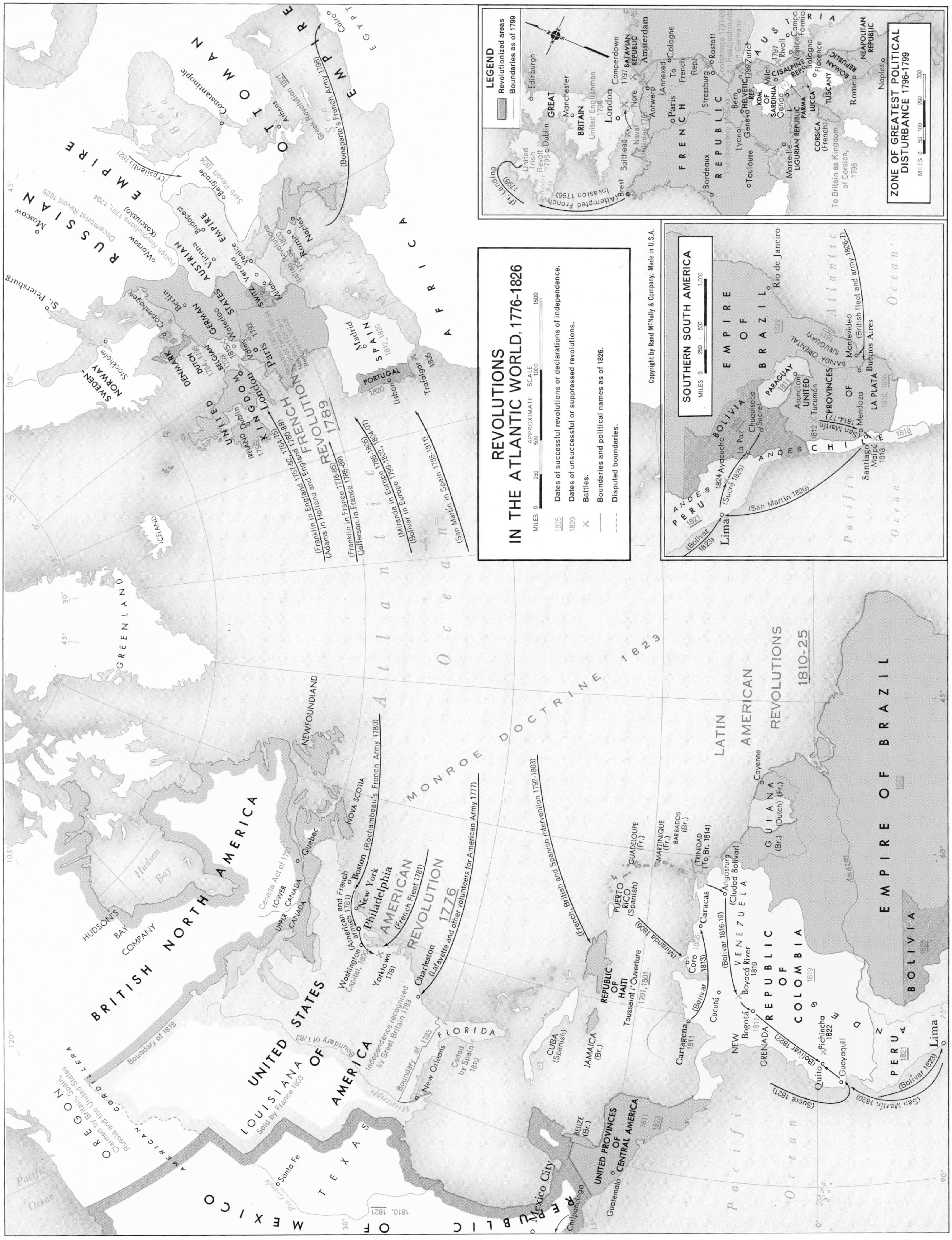
REVOLUTIONS IN THE ATLANTIC WORLD, 1776-1826
MILES 0 250 500 1000 1500
APPROXIMATE SCALE
Dates of successful revolutions or declarations of independence.
Dates of unsuccessful or suppressed revolutions.
Battles.
Boundaries and political names as of 1826.
Disputed boundaries.
Copyright by Rand McNally & Company, Made in U.S.A.
SOUTHERN SOUTH AMERICA
ZONE OF GREATEST POLITICAL DISTURBANCE 1796-1799
LEGEND
Revolutionized areas
Boundaries as of 1799
AMERICAN REVOLUTION 1776
FRENCH REVOLUTION 1789
LATIN AMERICAN REVOLUTIONS 1810-25
MONROE DOCTRINE 1823
BRITISH NORTH AMERICA
UNITED STATES OF AMERICA
REPUBLIC OF MEXICO
UNITED PROVINCES OF CENTRAL AMERICA
REPUBLIC OF COLOMBIA
EMPIRE OF BRAZIL
RUSSIAN EMPIRE
OTTOMAN EMPIRE
AUSTRIAN EMPIRE
UNITED KINGDOM
Atlantic Ocean
Pacific Ocean

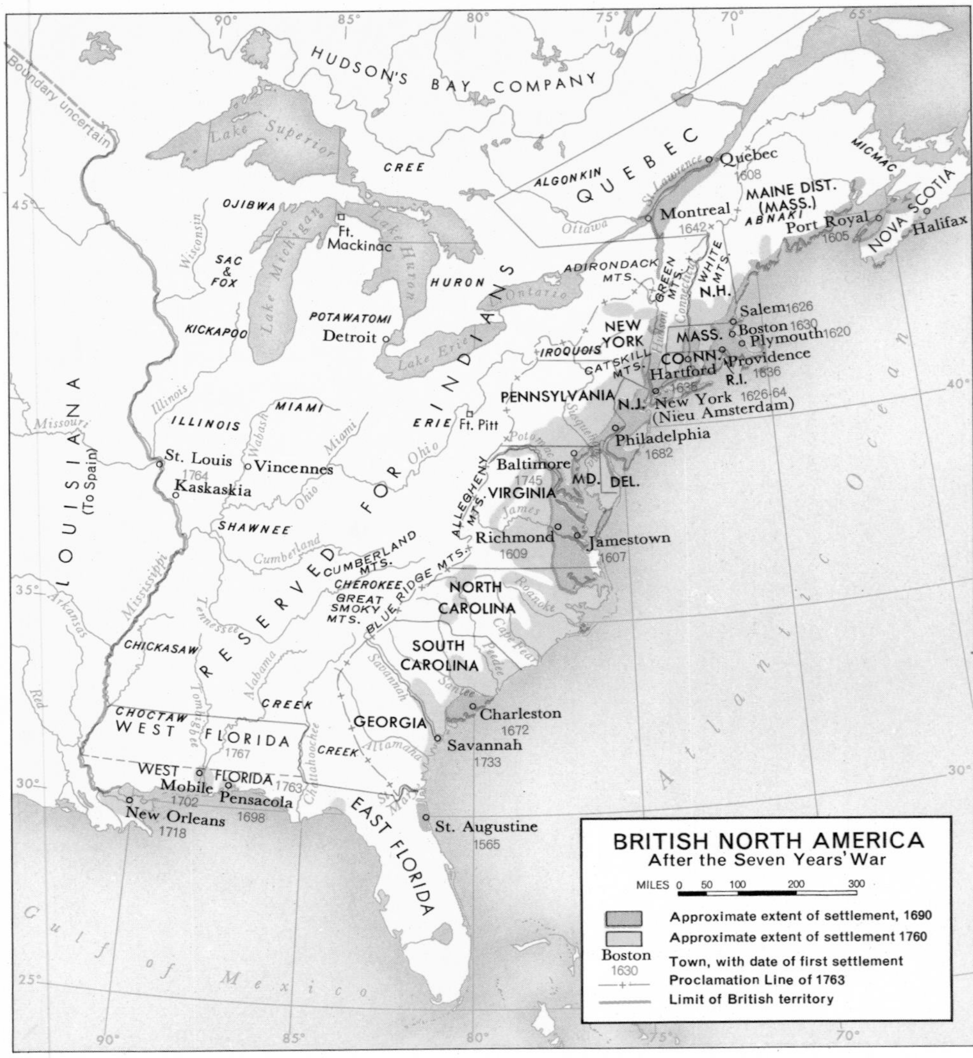

BRITISH NORTH AMERICA
After the Seven Years' War
MILES 0 50 100 200 300
Approximate extent of settlement, 1690
Approximate extent of settlement 1760
Boston 1630 Town, with date of first settlement
Proclamation Line of 1763
Limit of British territory
HUDSON'S BAY COMPANY
QUEBEC
LOUISIANA (To Spain)
RESERVED FOR INDIANS
Boundary uncertain
Lake Superior
Lake Michigan
Lake Huron
Lake Erie
Quebec 1608
Montreal 1642
MAINE DIST. (MASS.)
Port Royal 1605
NOVA SCOTIA
Halifax
N.H.
NEW YORK
MASS.
CONN.
R.I.
Salem 1626
Boston 1630
Plymouth 1620
Providence 1636
Hartford 1635
New York 1626-64 (Nieu Amsterdam)
PENNSYLVANIA
N.J.
Philadelphia 1682
Baltimore 1745
MD.
DEL.
VIRGINIA
Richmond 1609
Jamestown 1607
NORTH CAROLINA
SOUTH CAROLINA
Charleston 1672
GEORGIA
Savannah 1733
WEST FLORIDA 1767
WEST FLORIDA 1763
EAST FLORIDA
Mobile 1702
Pensacola 1698
New Orleans 1718
St. Augustine 1565
St. Louis 1764
Kaskaskia
Vincennes
Detroit
Ft. Mackinac
Ft. Pitt
Gulf of Mexico
Atlantic Ocean

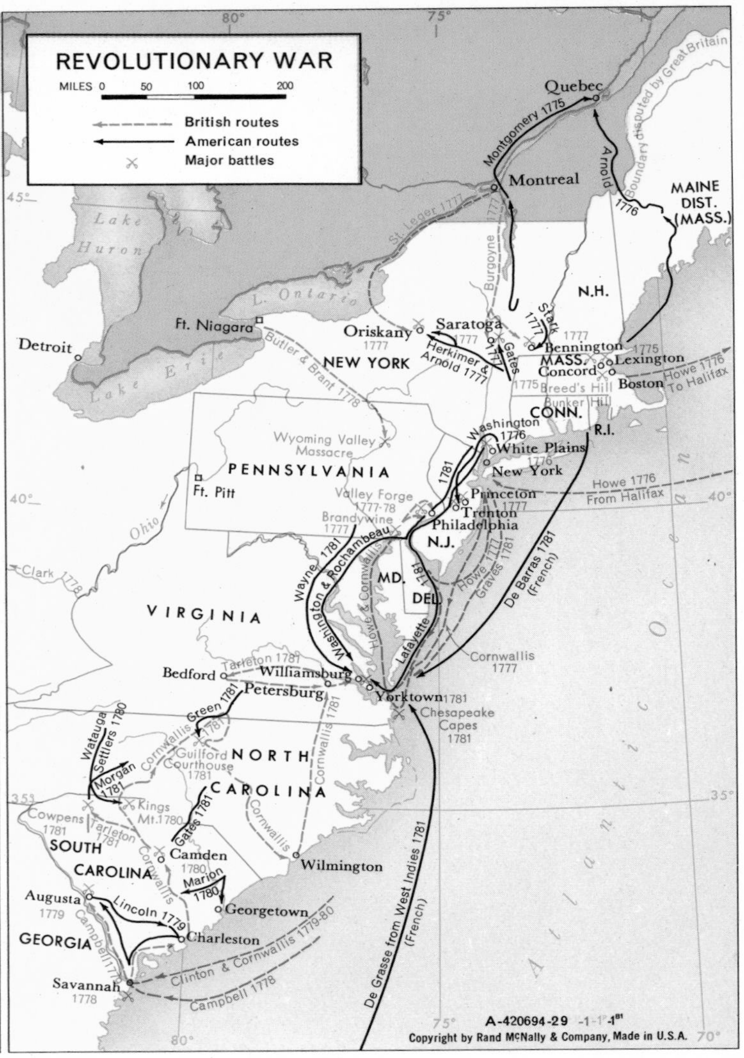

REVOLUTIONARY WAR
MILES 0 50 100 200
British routes
American routes
Major battles
Quebec
Montreal
Montgomery 1775
Arnold 1775
MAINE DIST. (MASS.)
N.H.
Lake Huron
Lake Ontario
Lake Erie
Detroit
Ft. Niagara
Oriskany 1777
Saratoga 1777
Bennington 1777
NEW YORK
MASS.
Concord
Lexington 1775
Boston
CONN.
R.I.
PENNSYLVANIA
Ft. Pitt
Wyoming Valley Massacre
White Plains 1776
New York
Princeton 1777
Trenton 1776
Philadelphia
Valley Forge 1777-78
Brandywine 1777
N.J.
MD.
DEL.
VIRGINIA
Williamsburg
Yorktown 1781
Chesapeake Capes 1781
Petersburg
Bedford
NORTH CAROLINA
Guilford Courthouse 1781
Kings Mt. 1780
Cowpens 1781
SOUTH CAROLINA
Camden 1780
Wilmington
Georgetown
Charleston
Augusta 1779
GEORGIA
Savannah 1778
De Grasse from West Indies 1781 (French)
A-420694-29
Copyright by Rand McNally & Company, Made in U.S.A.

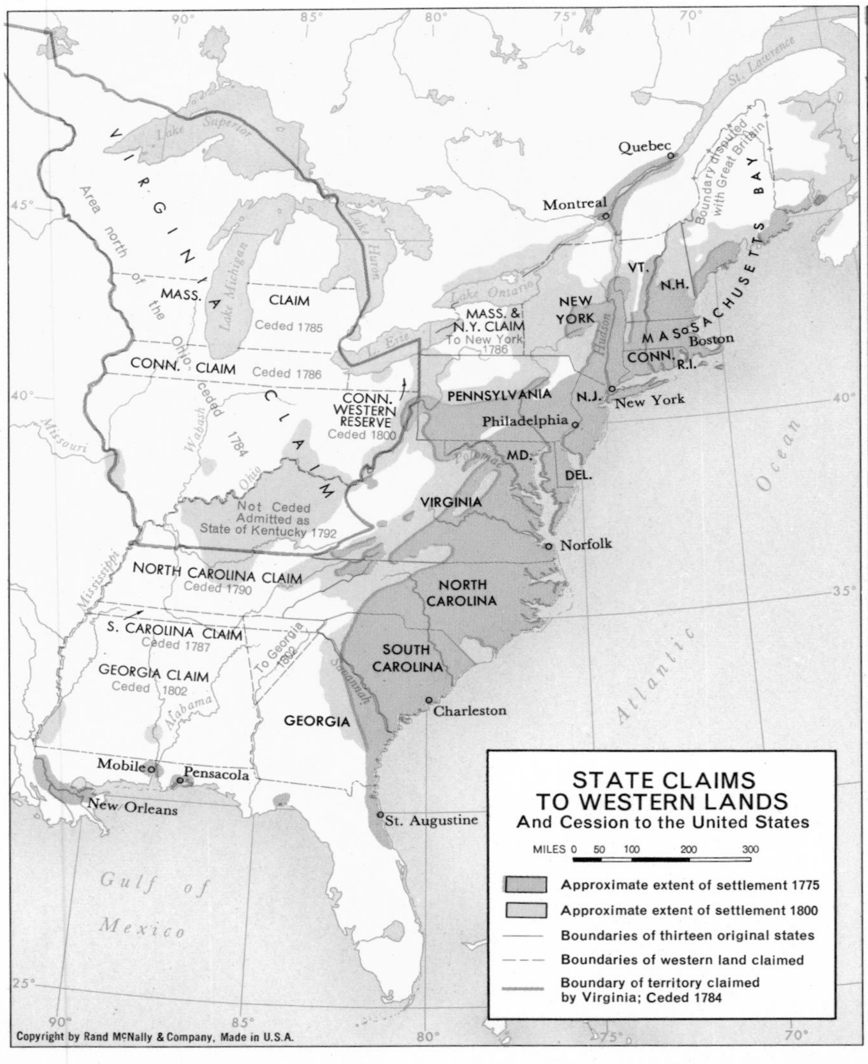

STATE CLAIMS TO WESTERN LANDS
And Cession to the United States
MILES 0 50 100 200 300
Approximate extent of settlement 1775
Approximate extent of settlement 1800
Boundaries of thirteen original states
Boundaries of western land claimed
Boundary of territory claimed by Virginia; Ceded 1784
VIRGINIA CLAIM
Area north of the Ohio ceded 1784
MASS. CLAIM Ceded 1785
CONN. CLAIM Ceded 1786
CONN. WESTERN RESERVE Ceded 1800
MASS. & N.Y. CLAIM To New York 1786
Not Ceded Admitted as State of Kentucky 1792
NORTH CAROLINA CLAIM Ceded 1790
S. CAROLINA CLAIM Ceded 1787
GEORGIA CLAIM Ceded 1802
Quebec
Montreal
Boundary disputed with Great Britain
VT.
N.H.
NEW YORK
MASSACHUSETTS BAY
Boston
CONN.
R.I.
PENNSYLVANIA
Philadelphia
N.J.
New York
MD.
DEL.
VIRGINIA
Norfolk
NORTH CAROLINA
SOUTH CAROLINA
Charleston
GEORGIA
Mobile
Pensacola
New Orleans
St. Augustine
Gulf of Mexico
Atlantic Ocean
Copyright by Rand McNally & Company, Made in U.S.A.

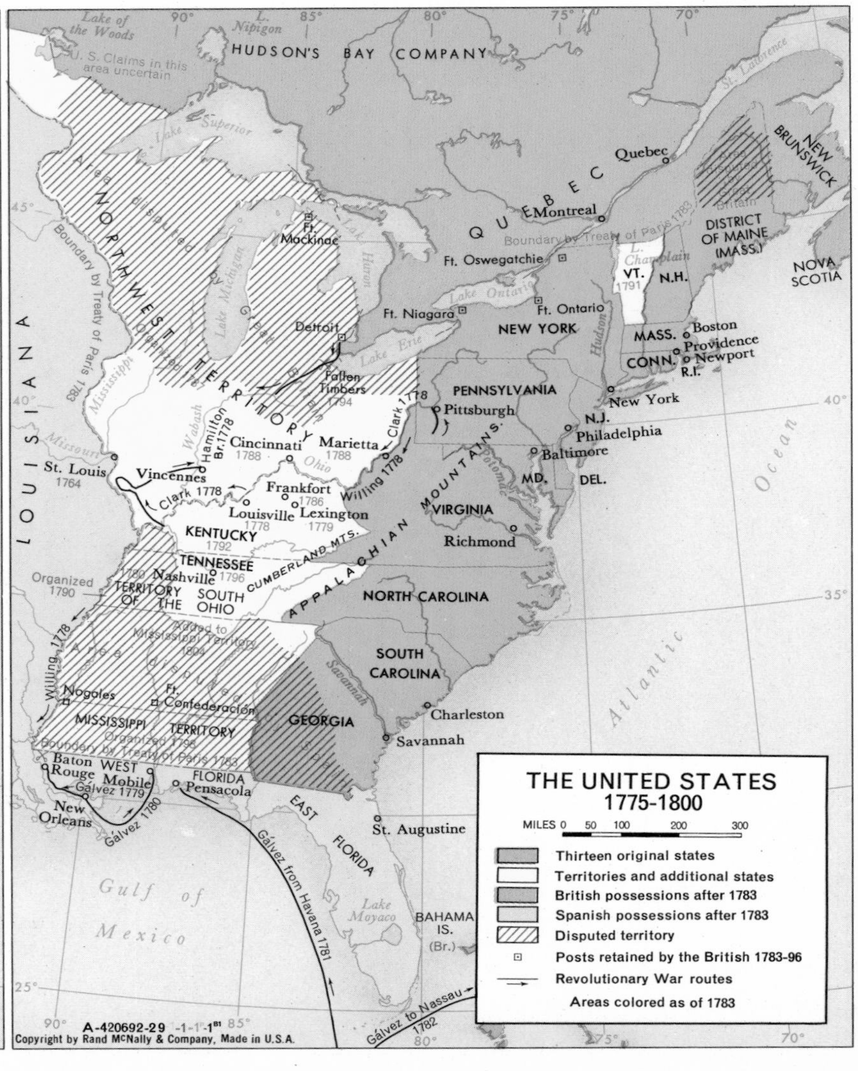

THE UNITED STATES
1775-1800
MILES 0 50 100 200 300
Thirteen original states
Territories and additional states
British possessions after 1783
Spanish possessions after 1783
Disputed territory
Posts retained by the British 1783-96
Revolutionary War routes
Areas colored as of 1783
HUDSON'S BAY COMPANY
U. S. Claims in this area uncertain
QUEBEC
Quebec
Montreal
NEW BRUNSWICK
DISTRICT OF MAINE (MASS.)
NOVA SCOTIA
VT. 1791
N.H.
NORTHWEST TERRITORY
LOUISIANA
Boundary by Treaty of Paris 1783
Ft. Mackinac
Ft. Oswegatchie
Ft. Niagara
Ft. Ontario
Detroit
Fallen Timbers 1794
NEW YORK
Boston
Providence
Newport
MASS.
CONN.
R.I.
PENNSYLVANIA
Pittsburgh
New York
N.J.
Philadelphia
Baltimore
MD.
DEL.
VIRGINIA
Richmond
APPALACHIAN MOUNTAINS
St. Louis 1764
Vincennes
Cincinnati 1788
Marietta 1788
Frankfort 1786
Louisville 1778
Lexington 1779
KENTUCKY 1792
TENNESSEE 1796
Nashville
TERRITORY SOUTH OF THE OHIO
Organized 1790
NORTH CAROLINA
SOUTH CAROLINA
Charleston
Savannah
GEORGIA
MISSISSIPPI TERRITORY
Baton Rouge
WEST FLORIDA
Mobile
Pensacola
New Orleans
EAST FLORIDA
St. Augustine
Gálvez from Havana 1781
Gálvez to Nassau 1782
BAHAMA IS. (Br.)
Gulf of Mexico
Atlantic Ocean
A-420692-29
Copyright by Rand McNally & Company, Made in U.S.A.

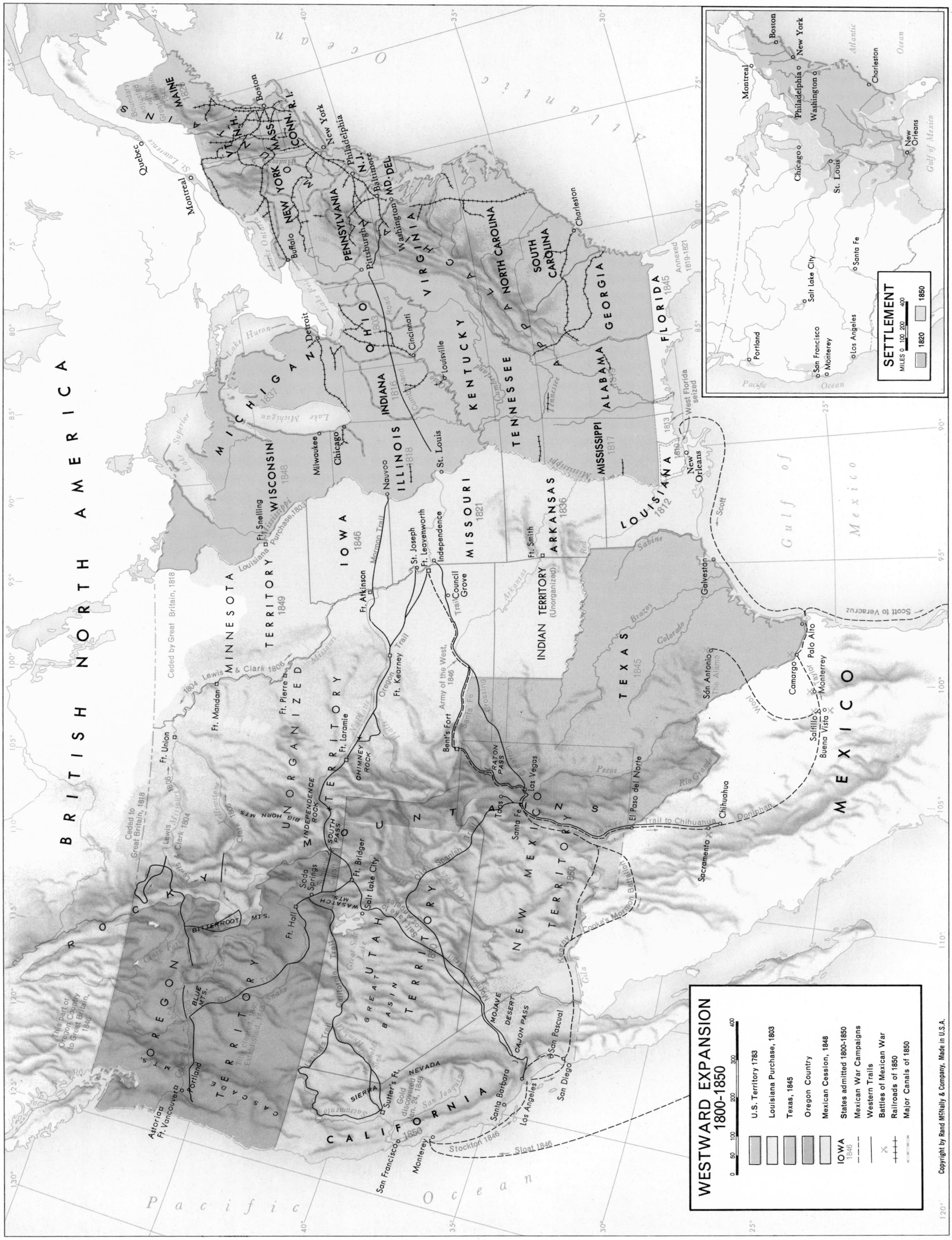

SETTLEMENT

MILES 0 100 200 400

1820   1850

WESTWARD EXPANSION
1800-1850

U.S. Territory 1783
Louisiana Purchase, 1803
Texas, 1845
Oregon Country
Mexican Cession, 1848

IOWA   States admitted 1800-1850

        Mexican War Campaigns
        Western Trails
    X   Battles of Mexican War
        Railroads of 1850
        Major Canals of 1850

MILES 0 100 200 300 400

Copyright by Rand McNally & Company, Made in U.S.A.

BRITISH   NORTH   AMERICA

MEXICO

Pacific   Ocean

Gulf   of   Mexico

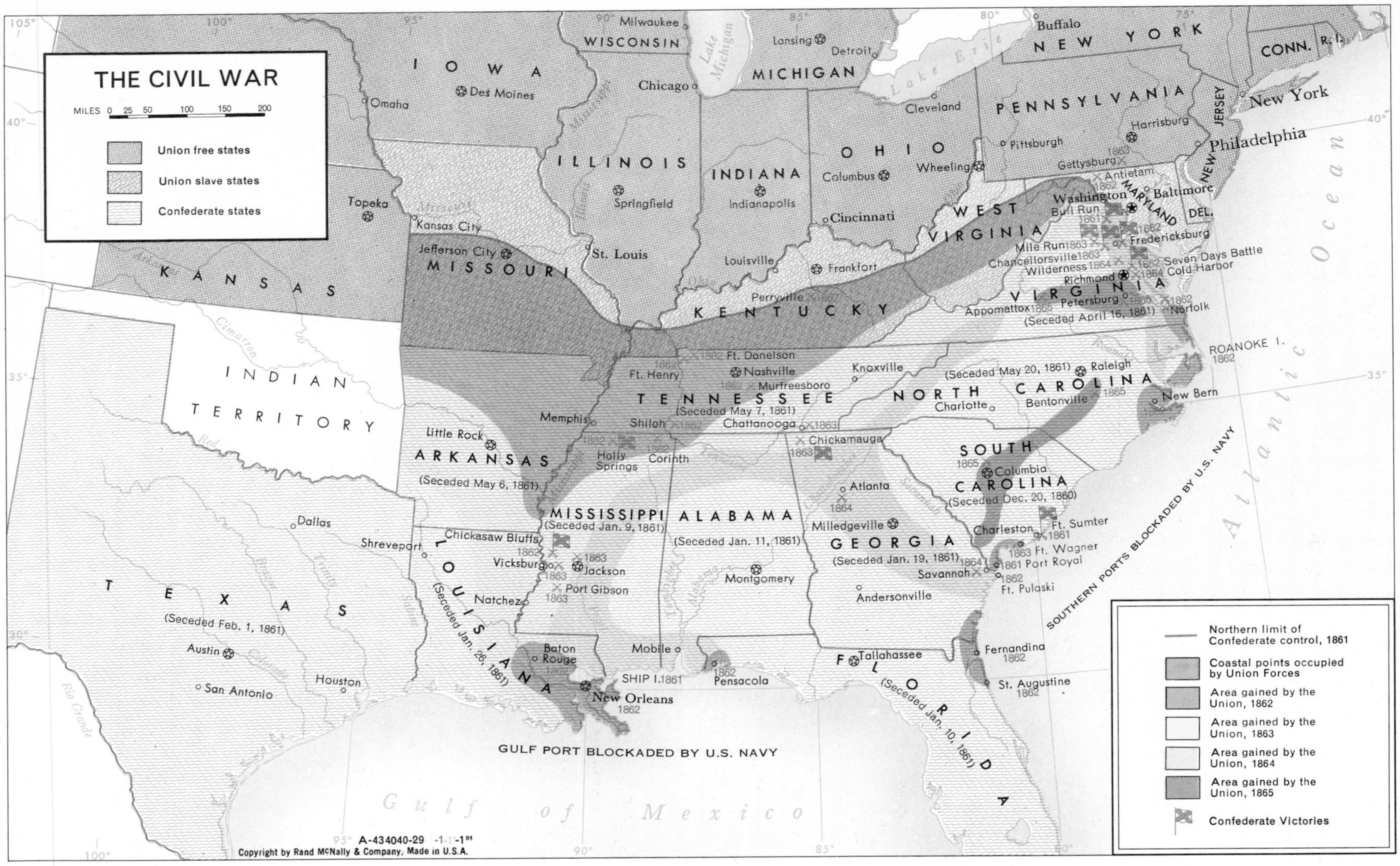

THE CIVIL WAR
MILES 0 25 50 100 150 200
Union free states
Union slave states
Confederate states
Northern limit of Confederate control, 1861
Coastal points occupied by Union Forces
Area gained by the Union, 1862
Area gained by the Union, 1863
Area gained by the Union, 1864
Area gained by the Union, 1865
Confederate Victories
IOWA
Des Moines
Omaha
WISCONSIN
Milwaukee
Chicago
Lake Michigan
MICHIGAN
Lansing
Detroit
Lake Erie
Buffalo
NEW YORK
CONN.
R.I.
New York
PENNSYLVANIA
Cleveland
Pittsburgh
Harrisburg
NEW JERSEY
Philadelphia
ILLINOIS
Springfield
INDIANA
Indianapolis
OHIO
Columbus
Wheeling
Cincinnati
Gettysburg 1863
Antietam 1862
Washington
Baltimore
MARYLAND
DEL.
Bull Run 1861 1862
WEST VIRGINIA
Fredericksburg 1862
Mile Run 1863
Chancellorsville 1863
Wilderness 1864
Seven Days Battle 1862
Cold Harbor 1864
Richmond
Topeka
Kansas City
Jefferson City
MISSOURI
St. Louis
Louisville
Frankfort
KANSAS
Perryville
KENTUCKY
VIRGINIA
Appomattox 1865
Petersburg
(Seceded April 16, 1861)
Norfolk
Ocean
INDIAN TERRITORY
Cimarron
Ft. Donelson 1862
Ft. Henry 1862
Nashville
Murfreesboro 1862
Knoxville
(Seceded May 20, 1861)
Raleigh
ROANOKE I. 1862
NORTH CAROLINA
Bentonville 1865
New Bern
Charlotte
TENNESSEE
(Seceded May 7, 1861)
Memphis
Shiloh 1862
Chattanooga 1863
Chickamauga 1863
Little Rock
ARKANSAS
(Seceded May 6, 1861)
Holly Springs 1862
Corinth 1862
SOUTH CAROLINA
Columbia 1865
(Seceded Dec. 20, 1860)
Atlanta 1864
MISSISSIPPI
(Seceded Jan. 9, 1861)
ALABAMA
(Seceded Jan. 11, 1861)
Milledgeville
Dallas
Shreveport
Chickasaw Bluffs 1862
Vicksburg 1863
Jackson 1863
Port Gibson 1863
Natchez 1863
GEORGIA
(Seceded Jan. 19, 1861)
Charleston
Ft. Sumter 1861
Ft. Wagner 1863
Port Royal 1861
Savannah 1864
Ft. Pulaski 1862
Montgomery
Andersonville
LOUISIANA
(Seceded Jan. 26, 1861)
SOUTHERN PORTS BLOCKADED BY U.S. NAVY
Atlantic
TEXAS
(Seceded Feb. 1, 1861)
Austin
San Antonio
Houston
Rio Grande
Baton Rouge 1862
Mobile
Pensacola 1862
SHIP I. 1861
New Orleans 1862
Tallahassee
FLORIDA
(Seceded Jan. 10, 1861)
Fernandina 1862
St. Augustine 1862
GULF PORT BLOCKADED BY U.S. NAVY
Gulf of Mexico
A-434040-29
Copyright by Rand McNally & Company, Made in U.S.A.

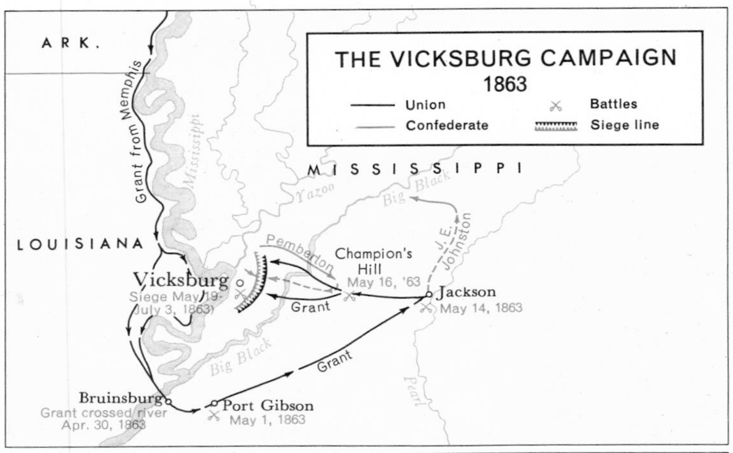

THE VICKSBURG CAMPAIGN
1863
Union
Confederate
Battles
Siege line
ARK.
MISSISSIPPI
LOUISIANA
Grant from Memphis
Mississippi
Yazoo
Big Black
Pemberton
Champion's Hill
May 16, '63
J. E. Johnston
Jackson
May 14, 1863
Vicksburg
Siege May 19-July 3, 1863
Grant
Big Black
Bruinsburg
Grant crossed river
Apr. 30, 1863
Port Gibson
May 1, 1863
Pearl

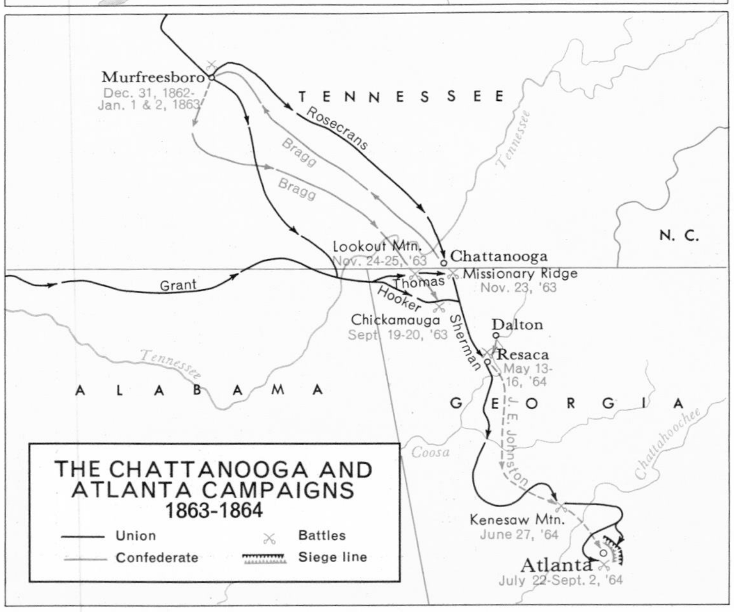

Murfreesboro
Dec. 31, 1862-Jan. 1 & 2, 1863
TENNESSEE
Rosecrans
Bragg
Bragg
Tennessee
Lookout Mtn.
Nov. 24-25, '63
Chattanooga
Missionary Ridge
Nov. 23, '63
N. C.
Grant
Thomas
Hooker
Chickamauga
Sept. 19-20, '63
Sherman
Dalton
Resaca
May 13-16, '64
ALABAMA
GEORGIA
J. E. Johnston
Coosa
Chattahoochee
Kenesaw Mtn.
June 27, '64
Atlanta
July 22-Sept. 2, '64
THE CHATTANOOGA AND ATLANTA CAMPAIGNS
1863-1864
Union
Confederate
Battles
Siege line

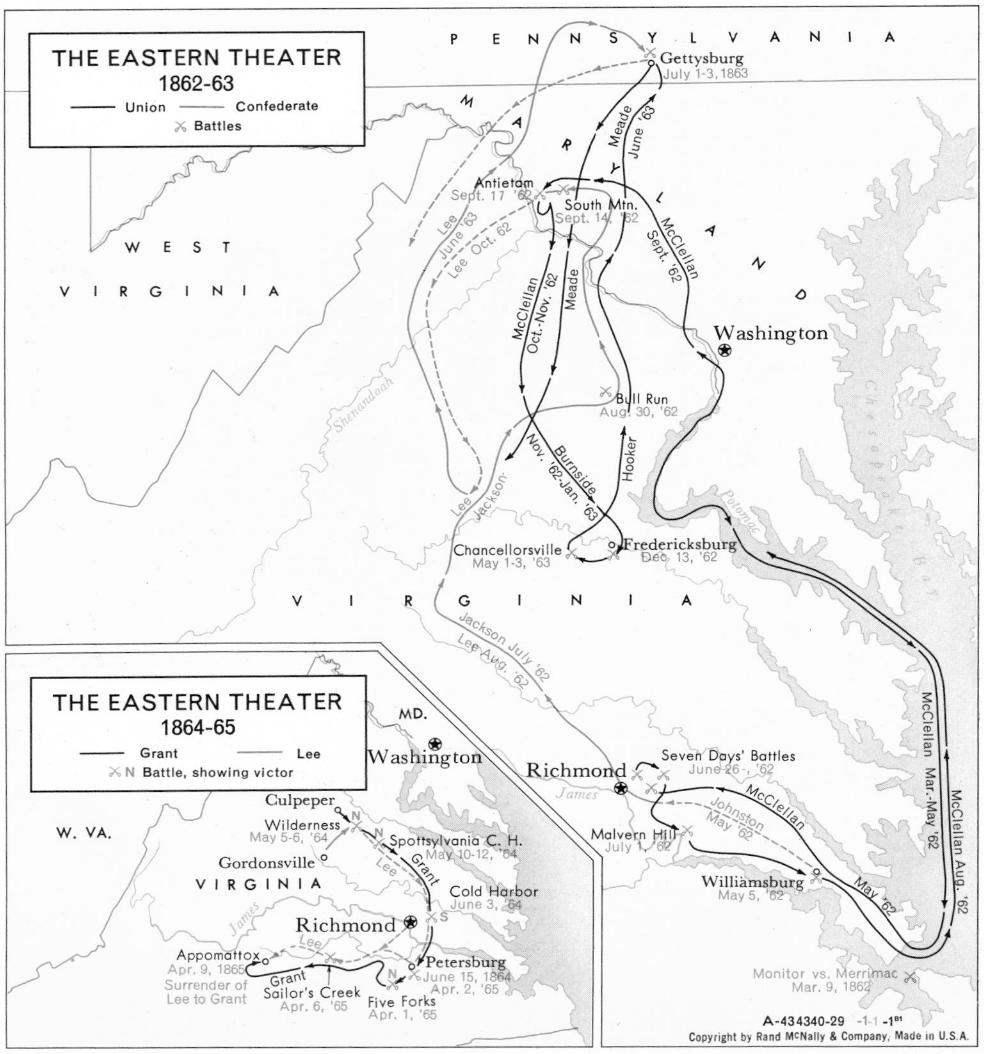

THE EASTERN THEATER
1862-63
Union
Confederate
Battles
PENNSYLVANIA
Gettysburg
July 1-3, 1863
MARYLAND
Meade
June '63
Antietam
Sept. 17 '62
South Mtn.
Sept. 14 '62
McClellan
Sept. '62
Lee June '63
Lee Oct. '62
WEST VIRGINIA
McClellan Oct.-Nov. '62
Meade
Washington
Shenandoah
Bull Run
Aug. 30, '62
Hooker
Burnside Nov. '62-Jan. '63
Lee
Jackson
Potomac
Chancellorsville
May 1-3, '63
Fredericksburg
Dec. 13, '62
VIRGINIA
Jackson July '62
Lee Aug. '62
Richmond
James
Seven Days' Battles
June 26-, '62
McClellan
Johnston May '62
Malvern Hill
July 1, '62
Williamsburg
May 5, '62
May '62
McClellan Mar.-May '62
McClellan Aug. '62
Monitor vs. Merrimac
Mar. 9, 1862
THE EASTERN THEATER
1864-65
Grant
Lee
Battle, showing victor
MD.
Washington
W. VA.
Culpeper
Wilderness
May 5-6, '64
Spottsylvania C. H.
May 10-12, '64
Lee
Grant
Gordonsville
VIRGINIA
Cold Harbor
June 3, '64
James
Richmond
Appomattox
Apr. 9, 1865
Surrender of Lee to Grant
Lee
Grant
Sailor's Creek
Apr. 6, '65
Five Forks
Apr. 1, '65
Petersburg
June 15, 1864-Apr. 2, '65
A-434340-29
Copyright by Rand McNally & Company, Made in U.S.A.

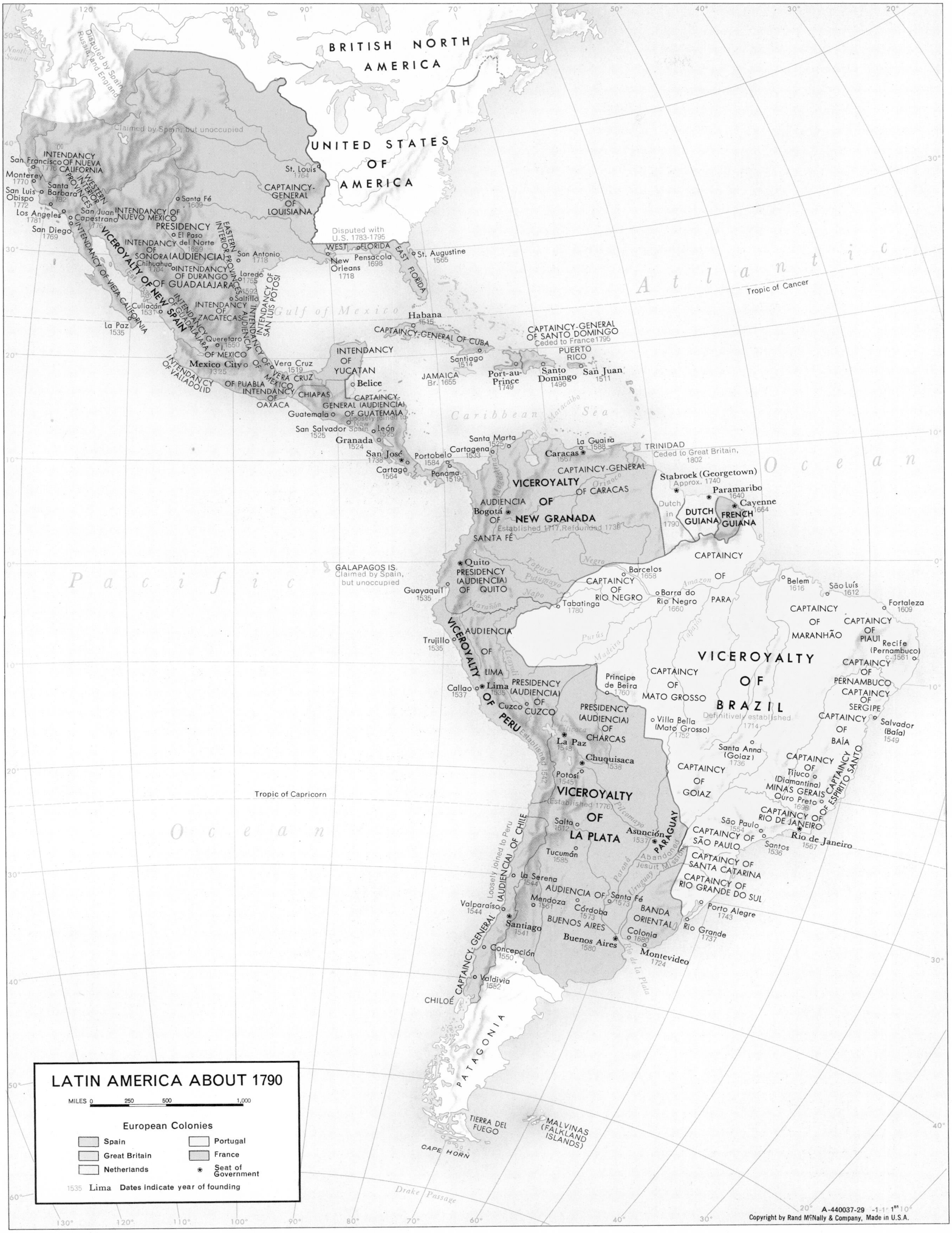

BRITISH NORTH AMERICA

UNITED STATES OF AMERICA

CAPTAINCY-GENERAL OF LOUISIANA

Disputed with U.S. 1783-1795

INTENDANCY OF NUEVA CALIFORNIA
San Francisco 1776
Monterey 1770
Santa Barbara 1782
San Luis Obispo 1772
Los Angeles 1781
San Diego 1769
San Juan Capestrano

VICEROYALTY OF VIEJA CALIFORNIA

La Paz 1535

INTENDANCY OF SONORA
INTENDANCY OF DURANGO
INTENDANCY OF GUADALAJARA
Culiacán 1531
INTENDANCY OF ZACATECAS
INTENDANCY OF MEXICO
Querétaro 1550

PRESIDENCY OF NUEVO MEXICO
El Paso
Chihuahua
INTENDANCY OF SAN LUIS POTOSI
Saltillo
EASTERN INTERIOR PROVINCES
WESTERN INTERIOR PROVINCES
INTENDANCY OF NUEVO MEXICO
Santa Fé 1609
San Antonio 1718
Laredo 1755

St. Louis

VICEROYALTY OF NEW SPAIN

INTENDANCY OF VALLADOLID
Mexico City 1325
Vera Cruz 1519
INTENDANCY OF VERA CRUZ
INTENDANCY OF PUABLA
OAXACA
INTENDANCY OF CHIAPAS

New Orleans 1718
Pensacola 1698
St. Augustine 1565
WEST FLORIDA
EAST FLORIDA

Gulf of Mexico

Habana 1515
CAPTAINCY-GENERAL OF CUBA
Santiago 1514
JAMAICA Br. 1655
Port-au-Prince 1749
CAPTAINCY-GENERAL OF SANTO DOMINGO Ceded to France 1795
Santo Domingo 1496
PUERTO RICO
San Juan 1511

INTENDANCY OF YUCATAN
Belice
CAPTAINCY-GENERAL (AUDIENCIA) OF GUATEMALA
Guatemala 1524
San Salvador 1525
Granada 1524
León
San José 1738
Cartago 1564
Portobelo 1584
Panama 1519

Caribbean Sea

TRINIDAD Ceded to Great Britain, 1802

Santa Marta 1525
Cartagena 1533
La Guaira 1588
Caracas

CAPTAINCY-GENERAL OF CARACAS

VICEROYALTY OF NEW GRANADA
Bogotá
AUDIENCIA OF
SANTA FÉ
Established 1717, Refounded 1739

Atlantic Ocean

Stabroek (Georgetown) Approx. 1740
Paramaribo 1640
Cayenne 1664
DUTCH GUIANA Dutch in 1790
FRENCH GUIANA

GALAPAGOS IS. Claimed by Spain, but unoccupied

Quito
PRESIDENCY (AUDIENCIA) OF QUITO
Guayaquil 1535

CAPTAINCY OF RIO NEGRO
Barcelos 1658
Barra do Rio Negro 1660
Tabatinga 1780

CAPTAINCY OF PARA
Belem 1616
São Luís 1612

Pacific Ocean

Trujillo 1535

VICEROYALTY OF PERU
Lima
Callao 1537
Lima 1535
PRESIDENCY (AUDIENCIA) OF CUZCO
Cuzco 1533

Tropic of Capricorn

CAPTAINCY OF MATO GROSSO
Príncipe de Beira 1760
Villa Bella (Mato Grosso) 1752
PRESIDENCY (AUDIENCIA) OF CHARCAS
La Paz
Chuquisaca 1538
Potosí 1545

VICEROYALTY OF BRAZIL
Definitively established 1714

CAPTAINCY OF MARANHÃO
Fortaleza 1609
CAPTAINCY OF PIAUI
Recife (Pernambuco) 1561
CAPTAINCY OF PERNAMBUCO
CAPTAINCY OF SERGIPE
CAPTAINCY OF BAÍA
Salvador (Baía) 1549

VICEROYALTY OF LA PLATA
(Established 1776)
Salta 1612
Tucumán 1595
CAPTAINCY OF GOIAZ
Santa Anna (Goiaz) 1736
Tijuco (Diamantina)
MINAS GERAIS
Ouro Preto 1698
CAPTAINCY OF ESPIRITO SANTO
CAPTAINCY OF RIO DE JANEIRO
São Paulo 1554
Santos 1536
Rio de Janeiro 1567
CAPTAINCY OF SÃO PAULO

La Serena 1544
Mendoza 1561
Córdoba 1573
Santa Fé 1573
BUENOS AIRES
Buenos Aires 1580
AUDIENCIA OF BUENOS AIRES
Asunción 1537
PARAGUAY
Abandoned Jesuit Missions
BANDA ORIENTAL
Colonia 1680
Rio Grande 1737
Porto Alegre 1743
CAPTAINCY OF RIO GRANDE DO SUL
CAPTAINCY OF SANTA CATARINA

Valparaíso 1544
Santiago 1541
Concepción 1550
CAPTAINCY-GENERAL (AUDIENCIA) OF CHILE
Loosely joined to Peru
Valdivia 1582
CHILOÉ
Montevideo 1724

PATAGONIA

TIERRA DEL FUEGO
MALVINAS (FALKLAND ISLANDS)
CAPE HORN

Drake Passage

LATIN AMERICA ABOUT 1790

MILES 0   250   500   1,000

European Colonies

Spain
Great Britain
Netherlands
Portugal
France
* Seat of Government
1535 Lima Dates indicate year of founding

A-440037-29
Copyright by Rand McNally & Company, Made in U.S.A.

163

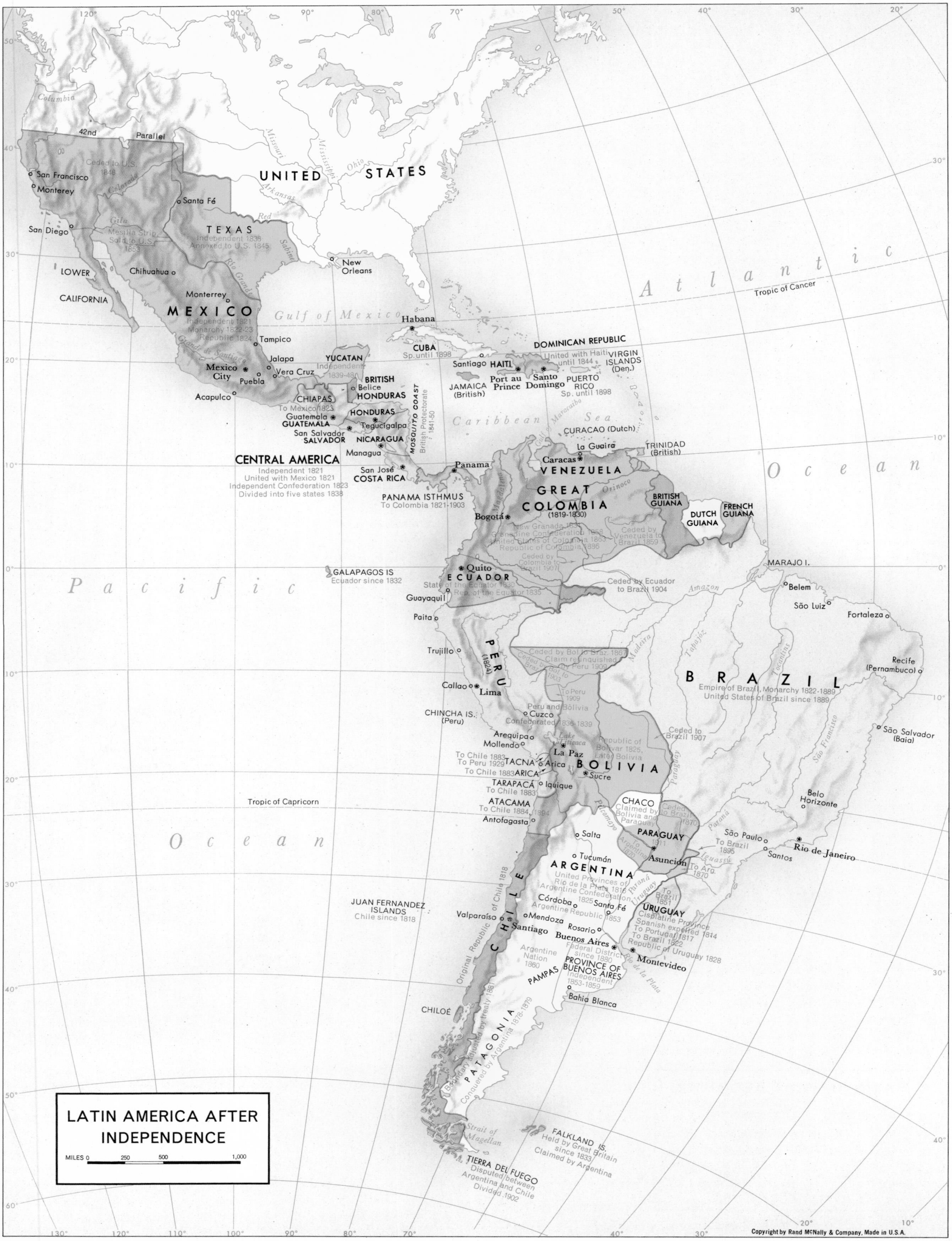

LATIN AMERICA AFTER
INDEPENDENCE

MILES 0   250   500   1,000

UNITED   STATES

Columbia

42nd   Parallel

San Francisco
Monterey

Santa Fé

San Diego

Ceded to U.S.
1846

Mesilla Strip
Sold to U.S.
1853

Gila

Colorado

TEXAS
Independent 1836
Annexed to U.S. 1845

New
Orleans

LOWER

Chihuahua

CALIFORNIA

Rio Grande

Arkansas

Red

Ohio

Missouri

Mississippi

Atlantic

Tropic of Cancer

MEXICO
Independent 1821
Monarchy 1822-23
Republic 1824

Monterrey

Gulf of Mexico

Habana

Tampico

Jalapa

Mexico
City

Vera Cruz

Puebla

YUCATAN
Independent
1839-46

CUBA
Sp. until 1898

Santiago

DOMINICAN REPUBLIC

United with Haiti
until 1844

HAITI

VIRGIN
ISLANDS
(Den.)

Acapulco

CHIAPAS
To Mexico 1823

BRITISH
HONDURAS

Belize

Port au
Prince

Santo
Domingo

PUERTO
RICO
Sp. until 1898

Ocean

Guatemala

GUATEMALA

San Salvador

HONDURAS

Tegucigalpa

JAMAICA
(British)

SALVADOR

NICARAGUA

MOSQUITO COAST

CENTRAL AMERICA
Independent 1821
United with Mexico 1821
Independent Confederation 1823
Divided into five states 1838

Managua

British Protectorate
? 1841-50

Caribbean   Sea

CURACAO (Dutch)

TRINIDAD
(British)

San José

COSTA RICA

PANAMA ISTHMUS
To Colombia 1821-1903

Panama

Caracas

La Guaira

VENEZUELA

Maracaibo

GREAT
COLOMBIA
(1819-1830)

Orinoco

BRITISH
GUIANA

DUTCH
GUIANA

FRENCH
GUIANA

Bogotá

New Granada 1831
Granadine Confederation 1858
United States of Colombia 1863
Republic of Colombia 1886

Ceded by
Venezuela to
Brazil 1859

GALAPAGOS IS
Ecuador since 1832

Quito

ECUADOR

State of the Equator
Free State of the Equator 1835

Ceded by
Colombia to
Brazil 1907

Ceded by Ecuador
to Brazil 1904

MARAJO I.

Belem

Guayaquil

São Luiz

Fortaleza

Amazon

Paita

PERU
(1824)

Ceded by Bol. to Braz. 1867
Claim relinquished by Peru 1909

Pacific

Trujillo

Callao

Lima

To Peru
1909

Madeira

Tapajoz

B R A Z I L
Empire of Brazil, Monarchy 1822-1889
United States of Brazil since 1889

Recife
(Pernambuco)

CHINCHA IS.
(Peru)

Cuzco

Peru and Bolivia
Confederated 1836-1839

Arequipa

Lake
Titicaca

Republic of
Bolivar 1825,
Later Bolivia

São Salvador
(Baia)

São Francisco

Mollendo

La Paz

Ceded to
Brazil 1907

BOLIVIA

To Chile 1883
To Peru 1929

TACNA

Arica

Sucre

To Chile 1883

ARICA

Ocean

TARAPACÁ
To Chile 1883

Iquique

Belo
Horizonte

ATACAMA
To Chile 1884, 1894

CHACO
Claimed by
Bolivia and
Paraguay

Ceded to Braz. 1870

Antofagasta

Tropic of Capricorn

Salta

PARAGUAY

Paraná

Pilcomayo

To Braz.
1895

São Paulo

Santos

Rio de Janeiro

JUAN FERNANDEZ
ISLANDS
Chile since 1818

Tucumán

ARGENTINA
United Provinces of
Rio de la Plata 1816
Argentine Confederation
Argentine Republic 1853

Asunción

To Arg.
1870

Córdoba

Santa Fé

Paraná

Uruguay

To
Brazil
1851

Valparaíso

Mendoza

Rosario

1825

1853

URUGUAY
Cisplatine Province
Spanish expelled 1814
To Portugal 1817
To Brazil 1822
Republic of Uruguay 1828

Santiago

CHILE

Buenos Aires

Federal District
since 1880

Montevideo

Argentine
Nation
1860

PAMPAS

PROVINCE OF
BUENOS AIRES
Independent
1853-1859

Río de la Plata

Original Republic of Chile 1818

Bahía Blanca

CHILOÉ

PATAGONIA
Conquered by Argentina 1878-1879

Eastern half ceded by treaty 1881

Strait of Magellan

FALKLAND IS.
Held by Great Britain
since 1833
Claimed by Argentina

TIERRA DEL FUEGO
Disputed between
Argentina and Chile
Divided 1902

Copyright by Rand McNally & Company, Made in U.S.A.

164

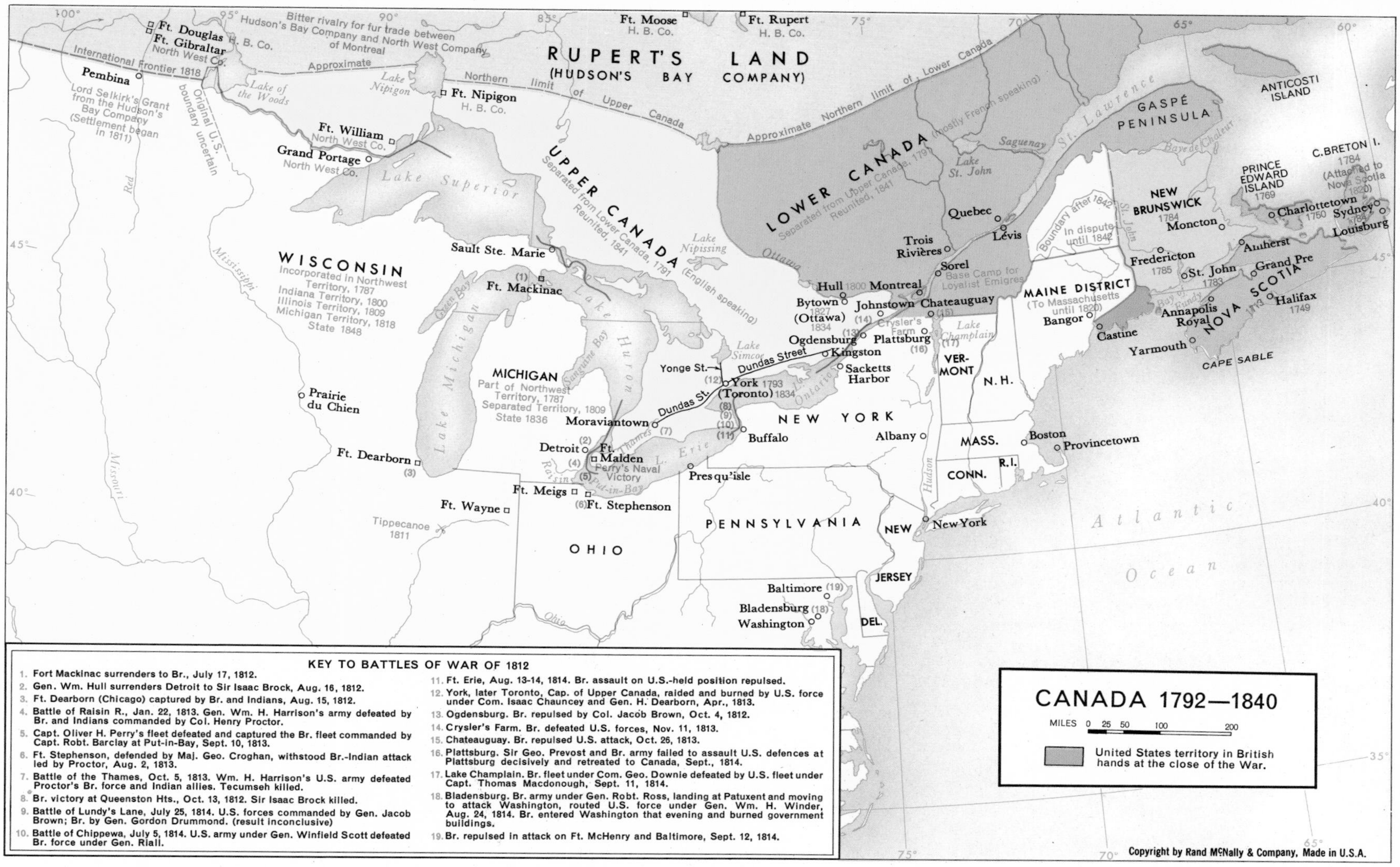

KEY TO BATTLES OF WAR OF 1812

1. Fort Mackinac surrenders to Br., July 17, 1812.
2. Gen. Wm. Hull surrenders Detroit to Sir Isaac Brock, Aug. 16, 1812.
3. Ft. Dearborn (Chicago) captured by Br. and Indians, Aug. 15, 1812.
4. Battle of Raisin R., Jan. 22, 1813. Gen. Wm. H. Harrison's army defeated by Br. and Indians commanded by Col. Henry Proctor.
5. Capt. Oliver H. Perry's fleet defeated and captured the Br. fleet commanded by Capt. Robt. Barclay at Put-in-Bay, Sept. 10, 1813.
6. Ft. Stephenson, defended by Maj. Geo. Croghan, withstood Br.-Indian attack led by Proctor, Aug. 2, 1813.
7. Battle of the Thames, Oct. 5, 1813. Wm. H. Harrison's U.S. army defeated Proctor's Br. force and Indian allies. Tecumseh killed.
8. Br. victory at Queenston Hts., Oct. 13, 1812. Sir Isaac Brock killed.
9. Battle of Lundy's Lane, July 25, 1814. U.S. forces commanded by Gen. Jacob Brown; Br. by Gen. Gordon Drummond. (result inconclusive)
10. Battle of Chippewa, July 5, 1814. U.S. army under Gen. Winfield Scott defeated Br. force under Gen. Riall.

11. Ft. Erie, Aug. 13-14, 1814. Br. assault on U.S.-held position repulsed.
12. York, later Toronto, Cap. of Upper Canada, raided and burned by U.S. force under Com. Isaac Chauncey and Gen. H. Dearborn, Apr., 1813.
13. Ogdensburg. Br. repulsed by Col. Jacob Brown, Oct. 4, 1812.
14. Crysler's Farm. Br. defeated U.S. forces, Nov. 11, 1813.
15. Chateauguay. Br. repulsed U.S. attack, Oct. 26, 1813.
16. Plattsburg. Sir Geo. Prevost and Br. army failed to assault U.S. defences at Plattsburg decisively and retreated to Canada, Sept., 1814.
17. Lake Champlain. Br. fleet under Com. Geo. Downie defeated by U.S. fleet under Capt. Thomas Macdonough, Sept. 11, 1814.
18. Bladensburg. Br. army under Gen. Robt. Ross, landing at Patuxent and moving to attack Washington, routed U.S. force under Gen. Wm. H. Winder, Aug. 24, 1814. Br. entered Washington that evening and burned government buildings.
19. Br. repulsed in attack on Ft. McHenry and Baltimore, Sept. 12, 1814.

CANADA 1792—1840

MILES 0 25 50 100 200

United States territory in British hands at the close of the War.

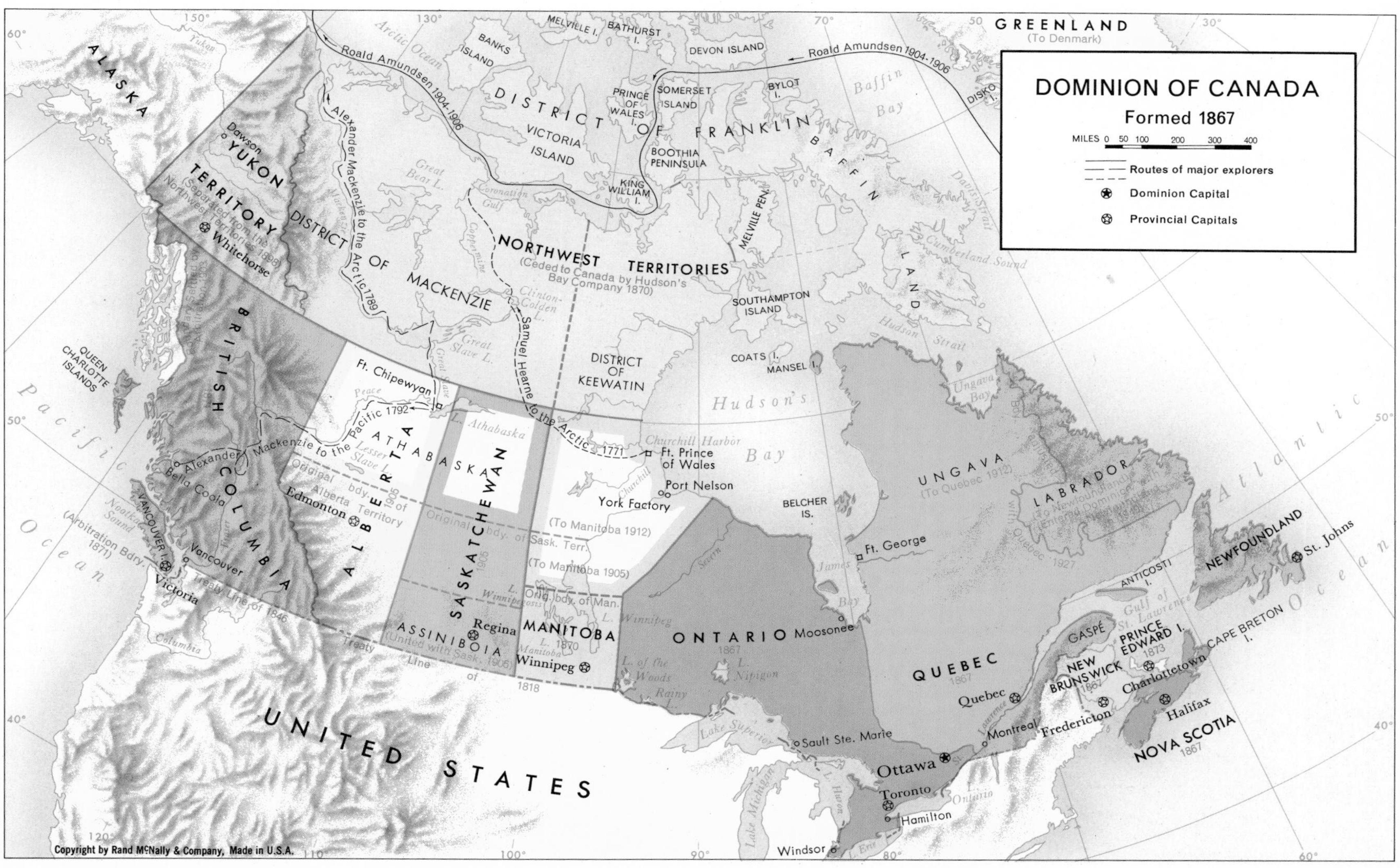

DOMINION OF CANADA
Formed 1867

MILES 0 50 100 200 300 400

— — — Routes of major explorers

✳ Dominion Capital

✿ Provincial Capitals

165

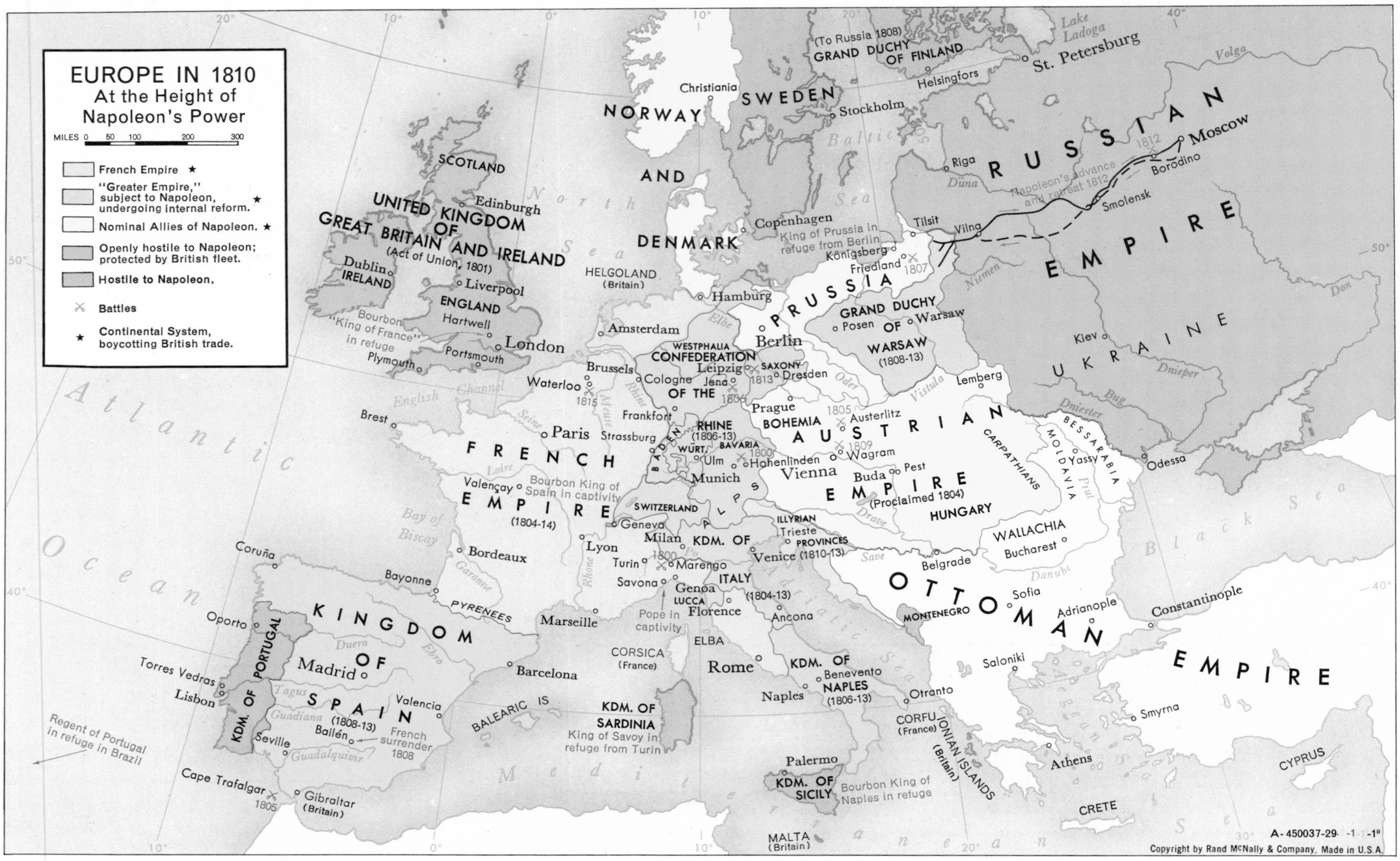
EUROPE IN 1810
At the Height of Napoleon's Power
MILES 0 50 100 200 300
French Empire ★
"Greater Empire," subject to Napoleon, undergoing internal reform. ★
Nominal Allies of Napoleon. ★
Openly hostile to Napoleon; protected by British fleet.
Hostile to Napoleon.
Battles
Continental System, boycotting British trade.
(To Russia 1808) GRAND DUCHY OF FINLAND
St. Petersburg
Helsingfors
Christiania
SWEDEN
Stockholm
NORWAY AND DENMARK
Copenhagen
King of Prussia in refuge from Berlin
Königsberg
Friedland 1807
Tilsit
Vilna
Riga
RUSSIAN EMPIRE
Moscow
Borodino
Smolensk
Napoleon's advance and retreat 1812
SCOTLAND
Edinburgh
UNITED KINGDOM OF GREAT BRITAIN AND IRELAND
(Act of Union, 1801)
Dublin
IRELAND
Liverpool
ENGLAND
Hartwell
London
Portsmouth
Plymouth
Bourbon "King of France" in refuge
HELGOLAND (Britain)
Hamburg
PRUSSIA
Berlin
GRAND DUCHY OF WARSAW (1808-13)
Posen
Warsaw
Amsterdam
WESTPHALIA
CONFEDERATION OF THE RHINE (1806-13)
Leipzig
Jena 1806
SAXONY 1813
Dresden
Brussels
Waterloo 1815
Cologne
Frankfort
Lemberg
Kiev
UKRAINE
Brest
Paris
Strassburg
FRENCH EMPIRE (1804-14)
Valençay
Bourbon King of Spain in captivity
BADEN
WÜRT.
BAVARIA
Ulm
Hohenlinden 1800
Munich
Prague
BOHEMIA
Austerlitz 1805
AUSTRIAN EMPIRE (Proclaimed 1804)
Wagram 1809
Vienna
Buda
Pest
HUNGARY
CARPATHIANS
BESSARABIA
MOLDAVIA
Yassy
Odessa
SWITZERLAND
Geneva
ALPS
ILLYRIAN PROVINCES (1810-13)
Trieste
Lyon
Milan
Turin
Marengo 1800
KDM. OF ITALY (1804-13)
Venice
Savona
Genoa
LUCCA
Florence
Pope in captivity
Ancona
Bordeaux
Bay of Biscay
Coruña
Bayonne
PYRENEES
Marseille
WALLACHIA
Bucharest
Belgrade
Sofia
Adrianople
Constantinople
MONTENEGRO
OTTOMAN EMPIRE
Black Sea
Atlantic Ocean
KINGDOM OF SPAIN (1808-13)
Oporto
KDM. OF PORTUGAL
Madrid
Torres Vedras
Lisbon
Valencia
Bailén
French surrender 1808
Seville
Regent of Portugal in refuge in Brazil
Cape Trafalgar 1805
Gibraltar (Britain)
Barcelona
BALEARIC IS.
CORSICA (France)
ELBA
Rome
KDM. OF SARDINIA
King of Savoy in refuge from Turin
KDM. OF NAPLES (1806-13)
Benevento
Naples
Otranto
CORFU (France)
IONIAN ISLANDS (Britain)
Saloniki
Smyrna
Athens
CYPRUS
CRETE
Palermo
KDM. OF SICILY
Bourbon King of Naples in refuge
MALTA (Britain)
Mediterranean Sea
North Sea
Baltic Sea
A-450037-29
Copyright by Rand McNally & Company, Made in U.S.A.

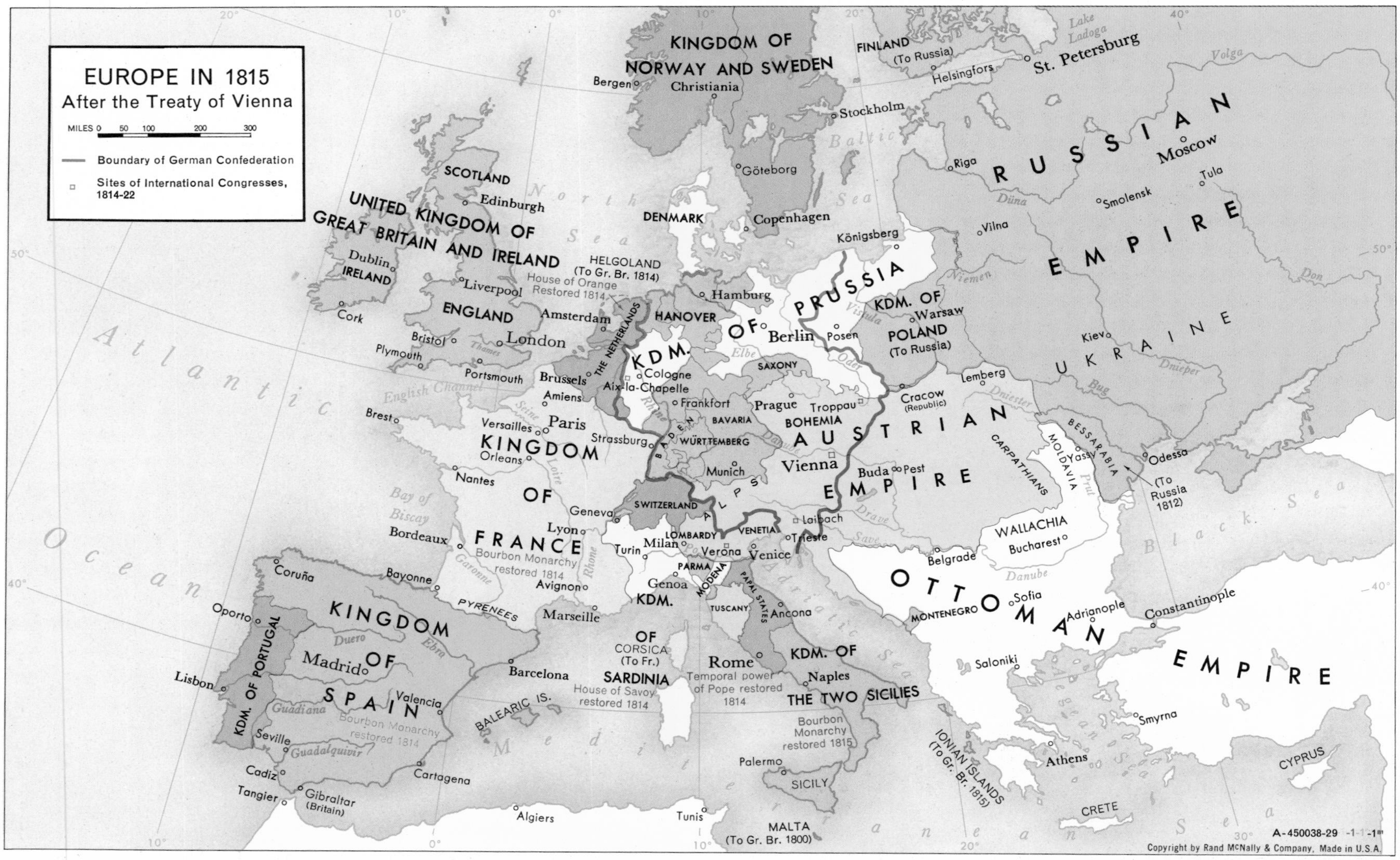
EUROPE IN 1815
After the Treaty of Vienna
MILES 0 50 100 200 300
Boundary of German Confederation
Sites of International Congresses, 1814-22
KINGDOM OF NORWAY AND SWEDEN
Bergen
Christiania
FINLAND (To Russia)
Helsingfors
St. Petersburg
Stockholm
Göteborg
DENMARK
Copenhagen
Königsberg
Riga
Vilna
RUSSIAN EMPIRE
Moscow
Smolensk
Tula
SCOTLAND
Edinburgh
UNITED KINGDOM OF GREAT BRITAIN AND IRELAND
Dublin
IRELAND
Cork
Liverpool
ENGLAND
Bristol
London
Plymouth
Portsmouth
HELGOLAND (To Gr. Br. 1814)
House of Orange Restored 1814
Amsterdam
THE NETHERLANDS
HANOVER
Hamburg
KDM. OF PRUSSIA
Berlin
Posen
KDM. OF POLAND (To Russia)
Warsaw
Kiev
UKRAINE
Brussels
Aix-la-Chapelle
Cologne
SAXONY
Amiens
Frankfort
Prague
Troppau
Cracow (Republic)
Lemberg
Versailles
Paris
BADEN
BAVARIA
WÜRTTEMBERG
BOHEMIA
AUSTRIAN EMPIRE
Strassburg
Munich
Vienna
Buda
Pest
CARPATHIANS
BESSARABIA
MOLDAVIA
Yassy
Odessa
(To Russia 1812)
Brest
KINGDOM OF FRANCE
Orleans
Nantes
Bourbon Monarchy restored 1814
Geneva
SWITZERLAND
ALPS
Laibach
Trieste
VENETIA
LOMBARDY
Milan
Verona
Venice
Lyon
Turin
PARMA
MODENA
Genoa
KDM. OF SARDINIA
TUSCANY
PAPAL STATES
Ancona
Avignon
Bordeaux
Bay of Biscay
Bayonne
PYRENEES
Marseille
WALLACHIA
Bucharest
Belgrade
MONTENEGRO
Sofia
Adrianople
Constantinople
OTTOMAN EMPIRE
Coruña
KINGDOM OF SPAIN
Oporto
KDM. OF PORTUGAL
Madrid
Lisbon
Valencia
Bourbon Monarchy restored 1814
Seville
Cadiz
Tangier
Gibraltar (Britain)
Cartagena
Barcelona
BALEARIC IS.
CORSICA (To Fr.)
House of Savoy restored 1814
Rome
Temporal power of Pope restored 1814
KDM. OF THE TWO SICILIES
Naples
Bourbon Monarchy restored 1815
Palermo
SICILY
IONIAN ISLANDS (To Gr. Br. 1815)
Saloniki
Smyrna
Athens
CYPRUS
CRETE
Algiers
Tunis
MALTA (To Gr. Br. 1800)
Atlantic Ocean
North Sea
Baltic Sea
Black Sea
Mediterranean Sea
A-450038-29
Copyright by Rand McNally & Company, Made in U.S.A.

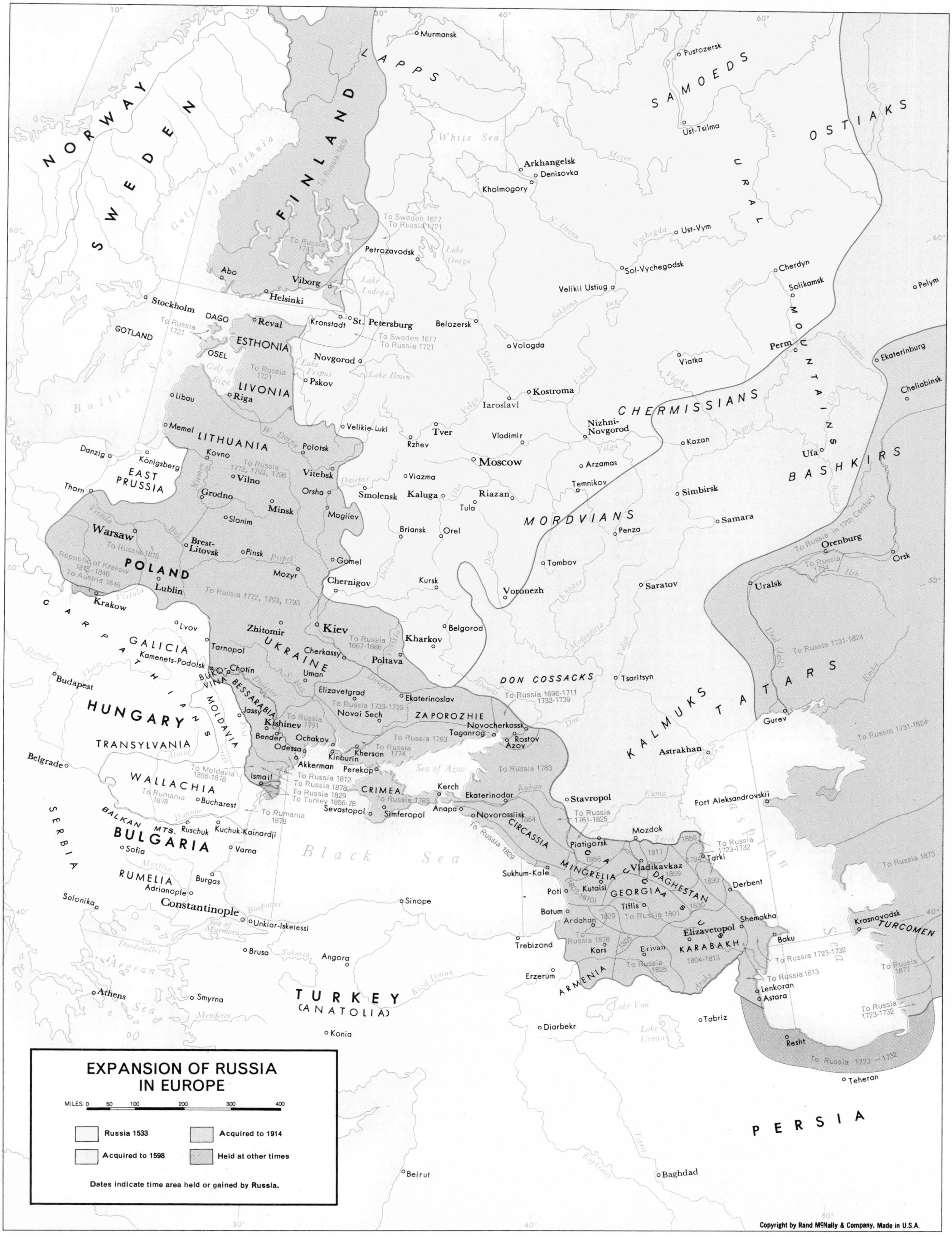

NORWAY

SWEDEN

LAPPS

SAMOEDS

OSTIAKS

○ Murmansk

○ Pustozersk

FINLAND
To Russia 1809

White Sea

○ Ust-Tsilma

URAL

○ Arkhangelsk
○ Denisovka

Mecen

○ Cherdyn
○ Solikamsk

○ Pelym

○ Holmogory

*To Sweden 1617
To Russia 1721*

*To Russia
1743*

○ Abo

○ Petrozavodsk

S. Dvina

○ Sol-Vychegodsk

○ Ekaterinburg

MOUNTAINS

○ Viborg

Lake
Ladoga

○ Velikii Ustiug

Viatka

Perm

○ Cheliabinsk

Sukhona

○ Stockholm

DAGO
To Russia
1721

○ Helsinki

Gulf of Bothnia

Lake
Onega

GOTLAND

○ Reval
ESTHONIA

Kronstadt

St. Petersburg

○ Belozersk

*To Sweden 1617
To Russia 1721*

○ Vologda

Viatka

○ Viatka

BASHKIRS

OSEL

Gulf of
Riga

○ Novgorod

Lake
Peipus

*To Russia
1721*

Pskov

Kostroma

CHERMISSIANS

○ Ufa

Baltic

LIVONIA

Libau

Riga

Lake Ilmen

○ Iaroslavl

Nizhni-
Novgorod

○ Kazan

Kama

Memel

LITHUANIA

○ Velikie Luki

Tver

Vladimir

Danzig

Königsberg

Kovno

Polotsk

Rzhev

Viazma

Moscow

Arzamas

Temnikov

○ Simbirsk

To Russia in 17th Century

EAST
PRUSSIA

Vilno

Vitebsk

Dnieper

Smolensk

Kaluga

Riazan

○ Orenburg

Thorn

Grodno

Minsk

Orsha

Tula

MORDVIANS

Penza

Samara

*To Russia
1731-1824*

Warsaw
To Russia
1815

Slonim

Mogilev

Brianed

Orel

○ Tambov

Orsk

Republic of Krakow
1815-1846
To Austria 1846

POLAND

Brest-
Litovsk

Pinsk

Pripet

Gomel

Chernigov

Kursk

Voronezh

Don

○ Saratov

Uralsk

*To Russia
1794*

Lublin

Mozyr

To Russia 1772, 1793, 1795

○ Krakow

Zhitomir

Kiev

Belgorod

KALMUKS

TATARS

Lvov

GALICIA

Tarnopol

UKRAINE

Cherkassy

To Russia
1667-1686

Kharkov

Tsaritsyn

Kamenets-Podolsk

Chotin

Uman

Poltava

*To Russia
1731-1824*

CARPATHIANS

BUKOVINA

Elizavetgrad

Ekaterinoslav

DON COSSACKS

Gurev

Budapest

BESSARABIA

Novai Sech

ZAPOROZHIE

*To Russia 1696-1711
1733-1739*

Jassy

*To Russia
1733-1739*

Novocherkassk

HUNGARY

MOLDAVIA

Kishinev

Ochakov

*To Russia
1774*

Taganrog

Rostov

Astrakhan

*To Russia
1791*

Bender

Odessa

Azov

TRANSYLVANIA

Kinburin

Perekop

To Russia 1783

Kherson

Akkerman

To Russia 1783

Caspian

Belgrade

*To Moldavia
1856-1878*

Ismail

CRIMEA

Kerch

Kuban

Stavropol

Fort Aleksandrovskii

WALLACHIA

To Moldavia
1878

*To Russia 1812
To Russia 1878
To Russia 1829
To Turkey 1856-78*

Ekaterinodar

Anapa

Novorossiisk

*To Russia
1761-1825*

Mozdok

*To Russia
1723-1732*

SERBIA

Bucharest

To Rumania
1878

Sevastopol

Simferopol

CIRCASSIA

1859

Piatigorsk

Tarki

To Russia 1873

BALKAN
MTS.

Ruschuk

Kuchuk-Kainardji

Sukhum-Kale

MINGRELIA

1859

Vladikavkaz

DAGHESTAN

BULGARIA

Varna

Poti

GEORGIA

1830

Derbent

Sofia

Black

Sea

Kutaisi

Tiflis

To Russia 1801

Shemakha

RUMELIA

Burgas

Batum

Ardahan
1829

Elizavetpol

Baku

Krasnovodsk

TURCOMEN

Adrianople

Trebizond

Kars

Erivan

KARABAKH

To Russia 1723-1732

Constantinople

Bosphorus

Sinope

1878

ARMENIA

1828

1804-1813

To Russia 1813

Unkiar-Iskelessi

Brusa

Erzerum

Lenkoran

Astara

Sea of
Marmara

Angora

*To Russia
1723-1732*

Dardanelles

Athens

Smyrna

Aegean

Sea

Kizil Irmak

TURKEY
(ANATOLIA)

Diarbekr

Lake Van

Lake
Urmia

○ Tabriz

Resht

*To Russia
1723 - 1732*

Konia

○ Teheran

PERSIA

EXPANSION OF RUSSIA IN EUROPE

MILES 0 50 100   200   300   400

☐ Russia 1533   ☐ Acquired to 1914

☐ Acquired to 1598   ☐ Held at other times

Dates indicate time area held or gained by Russia.

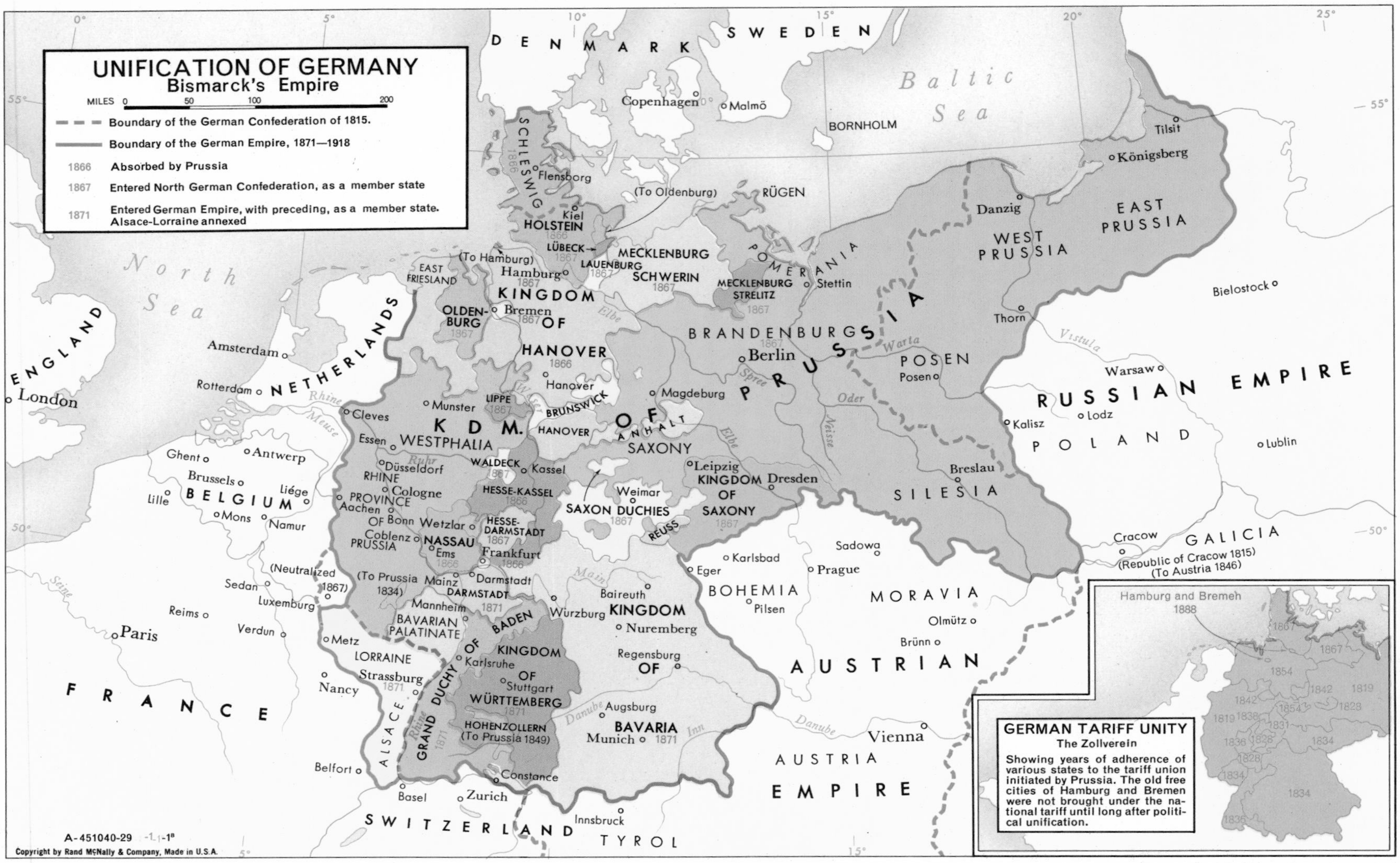

UNIFICATION OF GERMANY
Bismarck's Empire

MILES 0 50 100 200

- – – – Boundary of the German Confederation of 1815.
- ——— Boundary of the German Empire, 1871—1918

1866 Absorbed by Prussia

1867 Entered North German Confederation, as a member state

1871 Entered German Empire, with preceding, as a member state. Alsace-Lorraine annexed

A-451040-29   -1.1-1ᵃ
Copyright by Rand McNally & Company, Made in U.S.A.

GERMAN TARIFF UNITY
The Zollverein
Showing years of adherence of various states to the tariff union initiated by Prussia. The old free cities of Hamburg and Bremen were not brought under the national tariff until long after political unification.

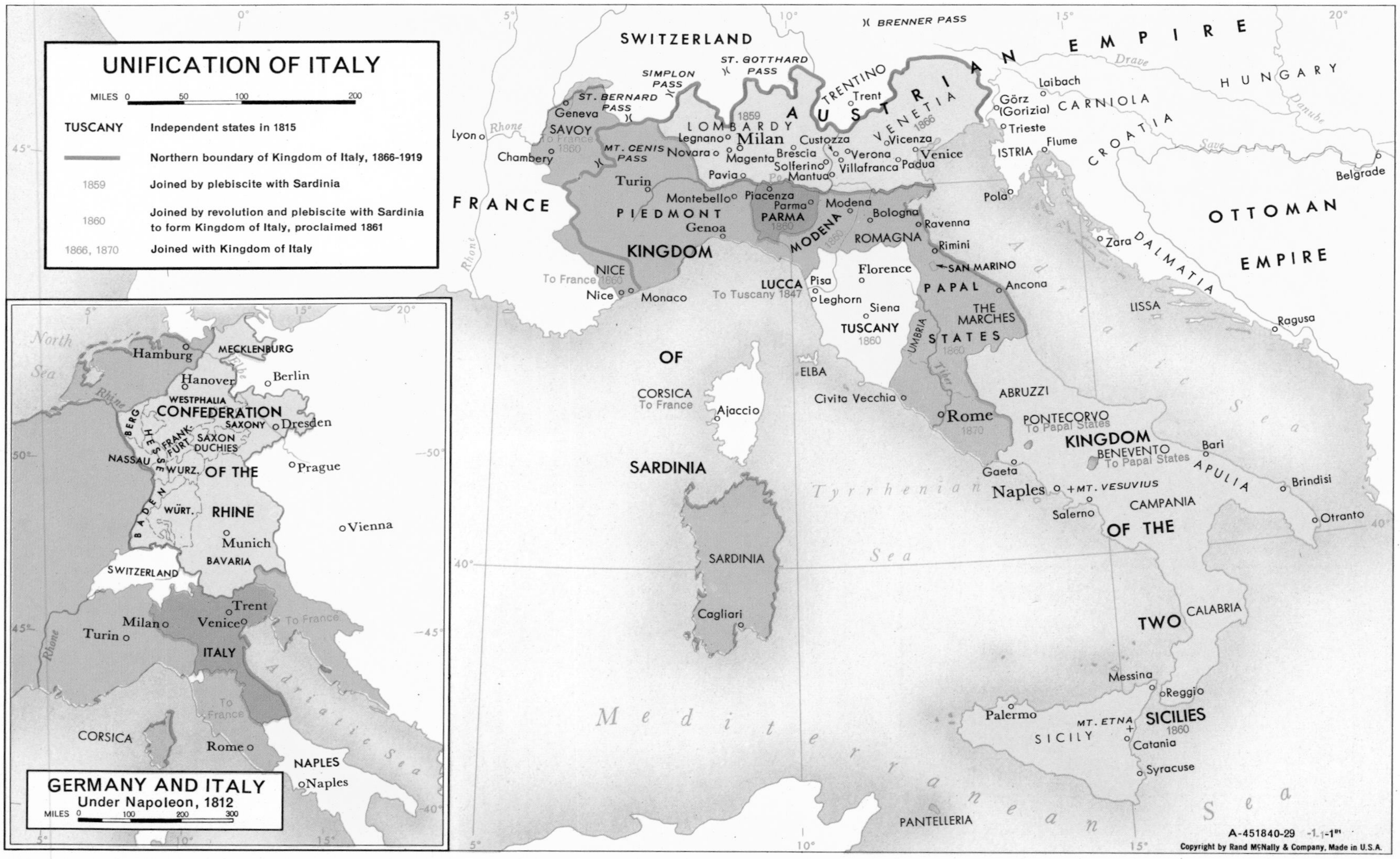

UNIFICATION OF ITALY

MILES 0 50 100 200

TUSCANY Independent states in 1815

——— Northern boundary of Kingdom of Italy, 1866-1919

1859 Joined by plebiscite with Sardinia

1860 Joined by revolution and plebiscite with Sardinia to form Kingdom of Italy, proclaimed 1861

1866, 1870 Joined with Kingdom of Italy

GERMANY AND ITALY
Under Napoleon, 1812
MILES 0 100 200 300

A-451840-29   -1.1-1ᵐ
Copyright by Rand McNally & Company, Made in U.S.A.

168

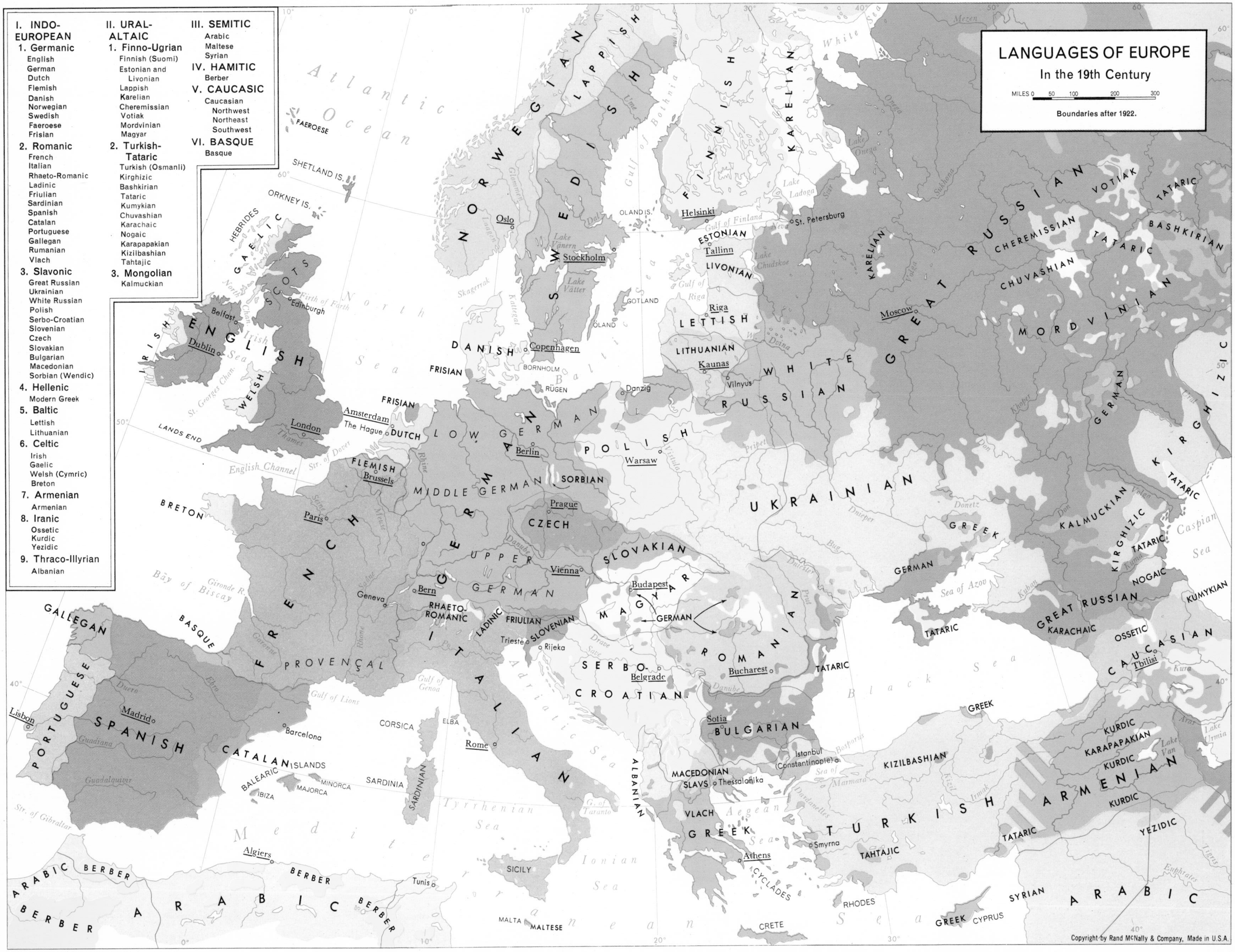

LANGUAGES OF EUROPE
In the 19th Century

MILES 0 50 100 200 300

Boundaries after 1922.

Copyright by Rand McNally & Company. Made in U.S.A.

I. INDO-EUROPEAN
1. Germanic
English
German
Dutch
Flemish
Danish
Norwegian
Swedish
Faeroese
Frisian

2. Romanic
French
Italian
Rhaeto-Romanic
Ladinic
Friulian
Sardinian
Spanish
Catalan
Portuguese
Gallegan
Rumanian
Vlach

3. Slavonic
Great Russian
Ukrainian
White Russian
Polish
Serbo-Croatian
Slovenian
Czech
Slovakian
Bulgarian
Macedonian
Sorbian (Wendic)

4. Hellenic
Modern Greek

5. Baltic
Lettish
Lithuanian

6. Celtic
Irish
Gaelic
Welsh (Cymric)
Breton

7. Armenian
Armenian

8. Iranic
Ossetic
Kurdic
Yezidic

9. Thraco-Illyrian
Albanian

II. URAL-ALTAIC
1. Finno-Ugrian
Finnish (Suomi)
Estonian and
    Livonian
Lappish
Karelian
Cheremissian
Votiak
Mordvinian
Magyar

2. Turkish-Tataric
Turkish (Osmanli)
Kirghizic
Bashkirian
Tataric
Kumykian
Chuvashian
Karachaic
Nogaic
Karapapakian
Kizilbashian
Tahtajic

3. Mongolian
Kalmuckian

III. SEMITIC
Arabic
Maltese
Syrian

IV. HAMITIC
Berber

V. CAUCASIC
Caucasian
    Northwest
    Northwest
    Southwest

VI. BASQUE
Basque

169

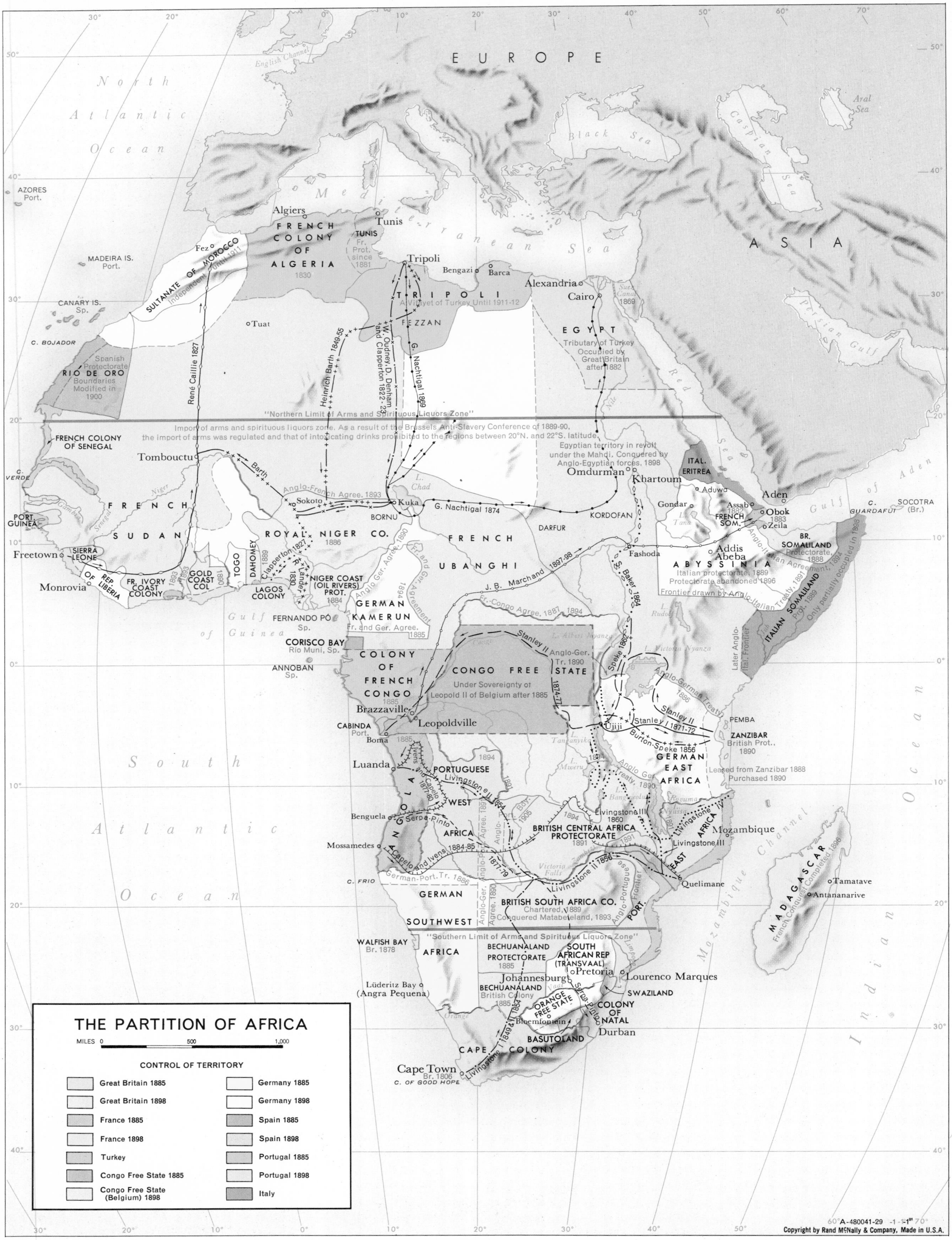

THE PARTITION OF AFRICA

MILES 0   500   1,000

CONTROL OF TERRITORY

Great Britain 1885	Germany 1885
Great Britain 1898	Germany 1898
France 1885	Spain 1885
France 1898	Spain 1898
Turkey	Portugal 1885
Congo Free State 1885	Portugal 1898
Congo Free State (Belgium) 1898	Italy

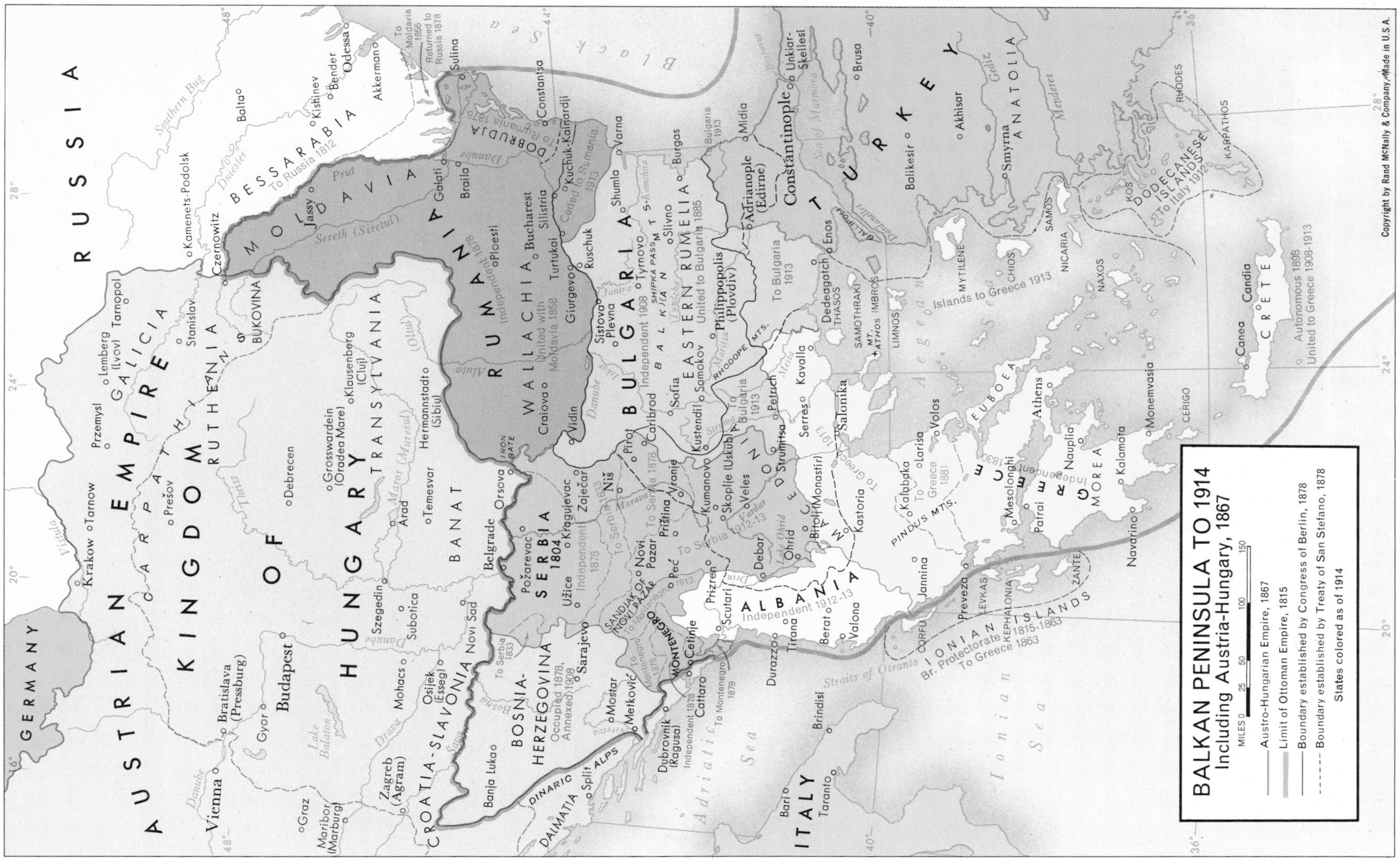

BALKAN PENINSULA TO 1914
Including Austria-Hungary, 1867

MILES 0 25 50 100 150

Austro-Hungarian Empire, 1867
Limit of Ottoman Empire, 1815
Boundary established by Congress of Berlin, 1878
Boundary established by Treaty of San Stefano, 1878
States colored as of 1914

Copyright by Rand McNally & Company, Made in U.S.A.

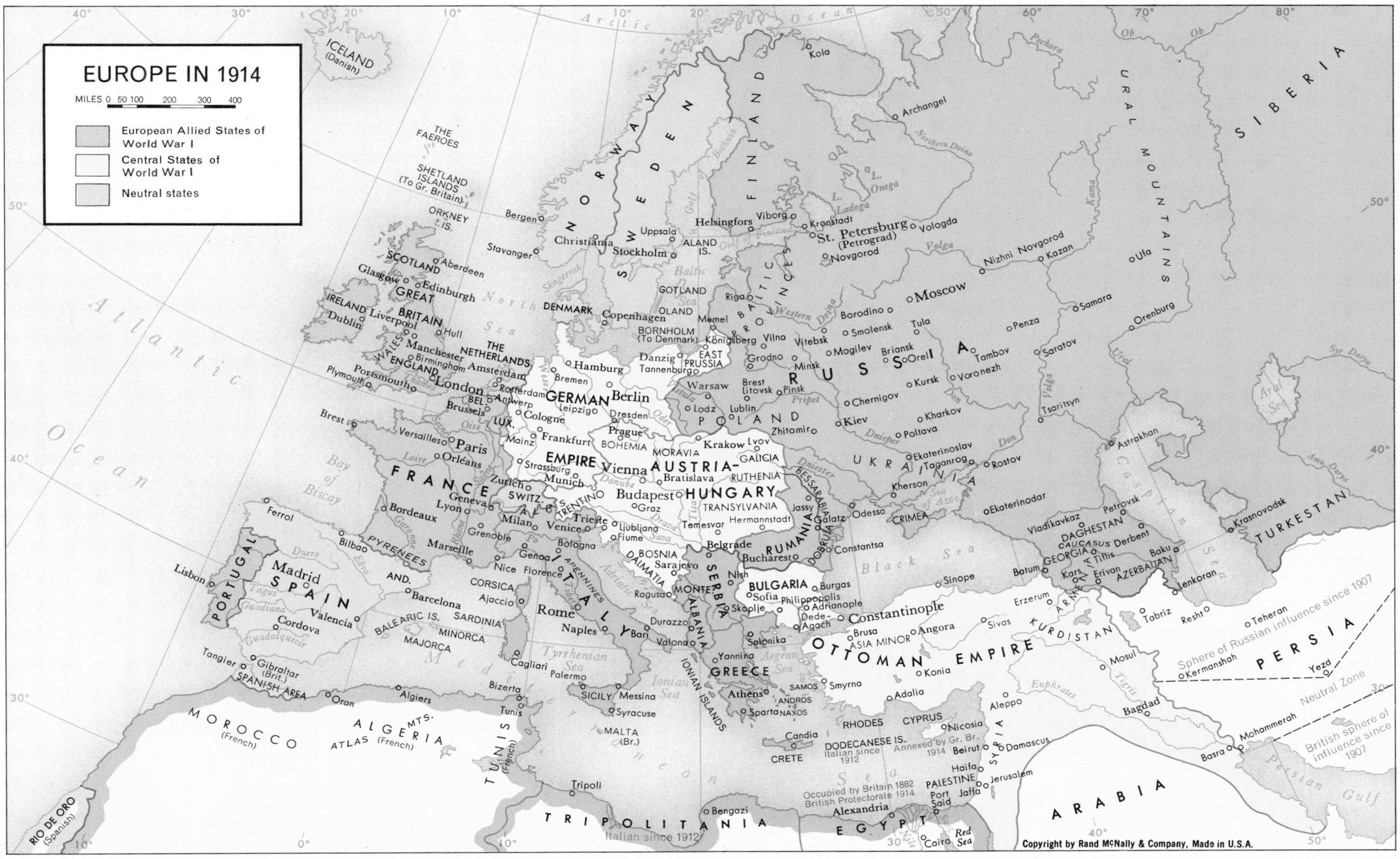

EUROPE IN 1914

MILES 0 50 100 200 300 400

European Allied States of World War I
Central States of World War I
Neutral states

Copyright by Rand McNally & Company, Made in U.S.A.

171

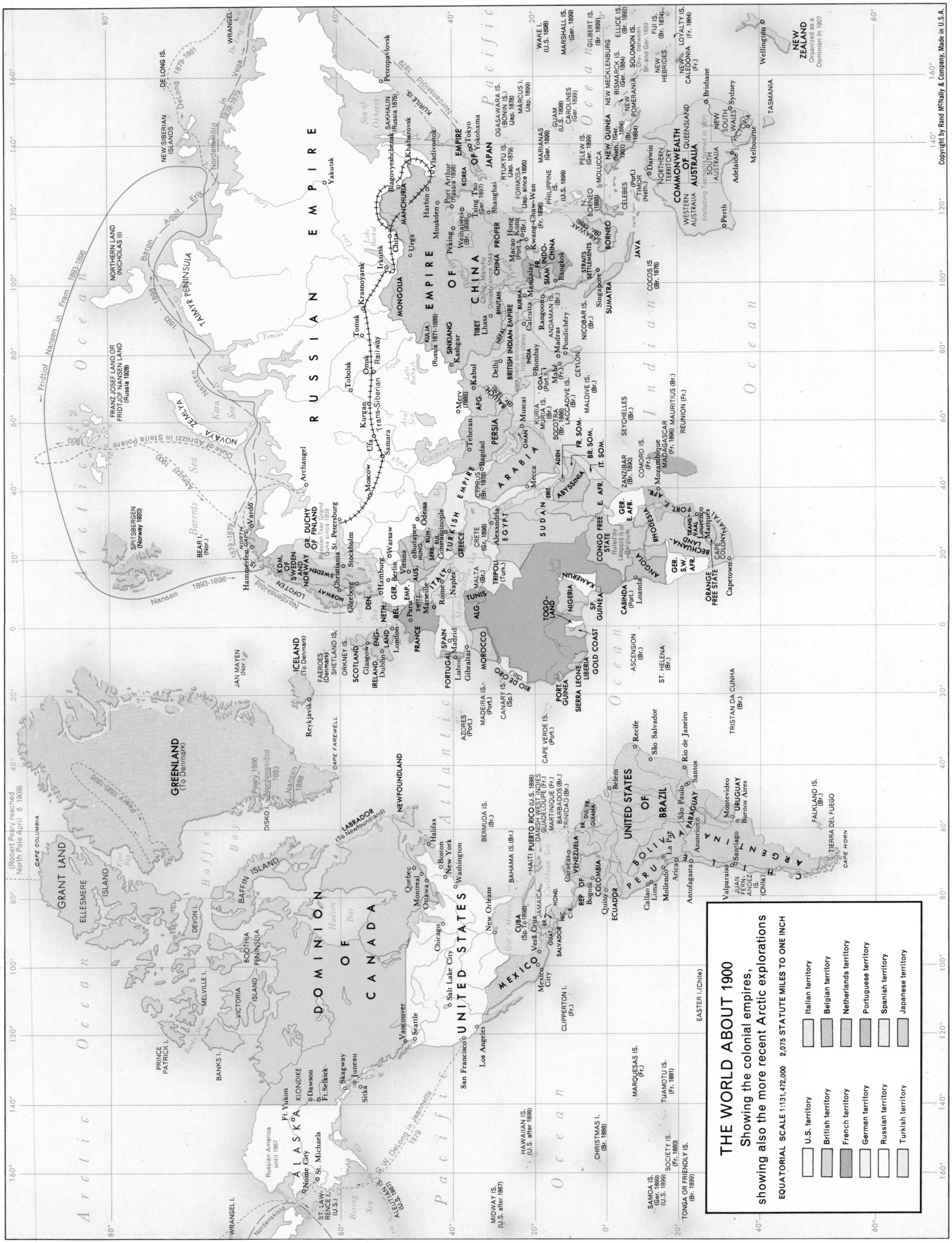

THE WORLD ABOUT 1900
Showing the colonial empires,
showing also the more recent Arctic explorations

EQUATORIAL SCALE 1:131,472,000   2,075 STATUTE MILES TO ONE INCH

U.S. territory		Italian territory
British territory		Belgian territory
French territory		Netherlands territory
German territory		Portuguese territory
Russian territory		Spanish territory
Turkish territory		Japanese territory

172

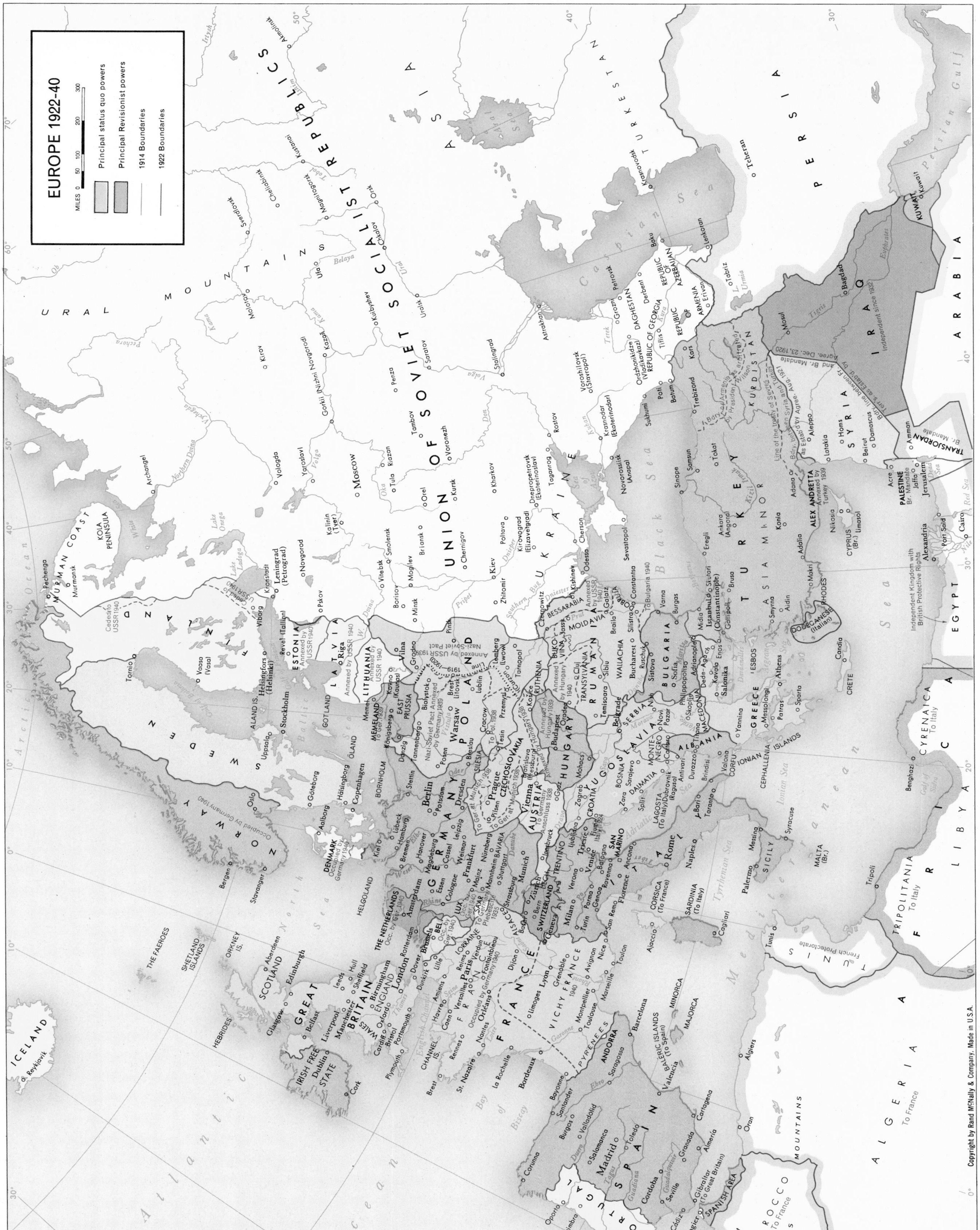

EUROPE 1922–40

MILES 0 50 100 200 300

Principal status quo powers
Principal Revisionist powers
1914 Boundaries
1922 Boundaries

Copyright by Rand McNally & Company. Made in U.S.A.

173

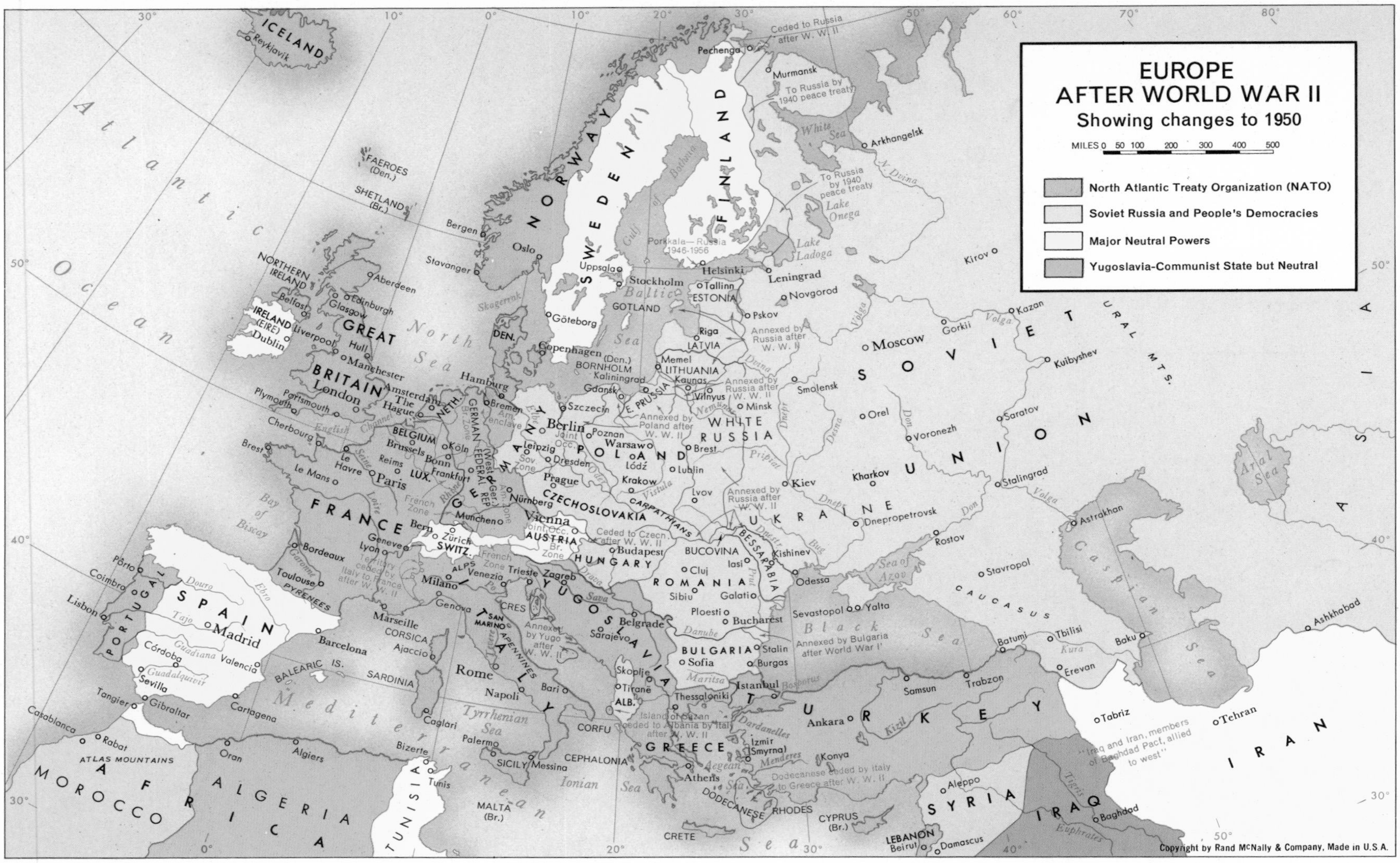

EUROPE
AFTER WORLD WAR II
Showing changes to 1950

MILES 0 50 100   200   300   400   500

- North Atlantic Treaty Organization (NATO)
- Soviet Russia and People's Democracies
- Major Neutral Powers
- Yugoslavia-Communist State but Neutral

Copyright by Rand McNally & Company, Made in U.S.A.

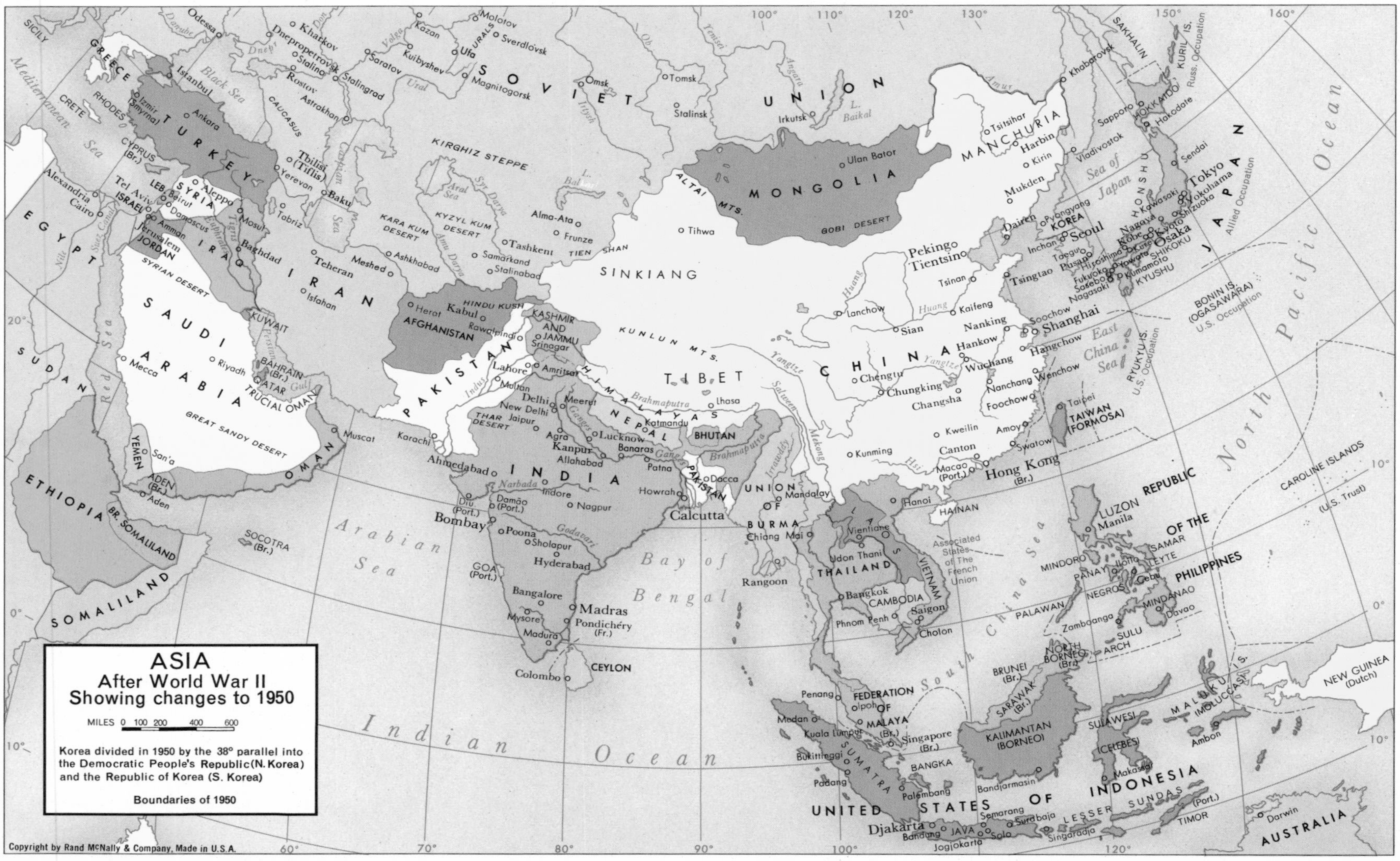

ASIA
After World War II
Showing changes to 1950

MILES 0 100 200   400   600

Korea divided in 1950 by the 38° parallel into
the Democratic People's Republic (N. Korea)
and the Republic of Korea (S. Korea)

Boundaries of 1950

Copyright by Rand McNally & Company, Made in U.S.A.

174

AMERICA'S HERITAGE IN MAPS

Map Selection and Text by
Carl H. Mapes, Ph.D., Senior Map Editor, Rand McNally

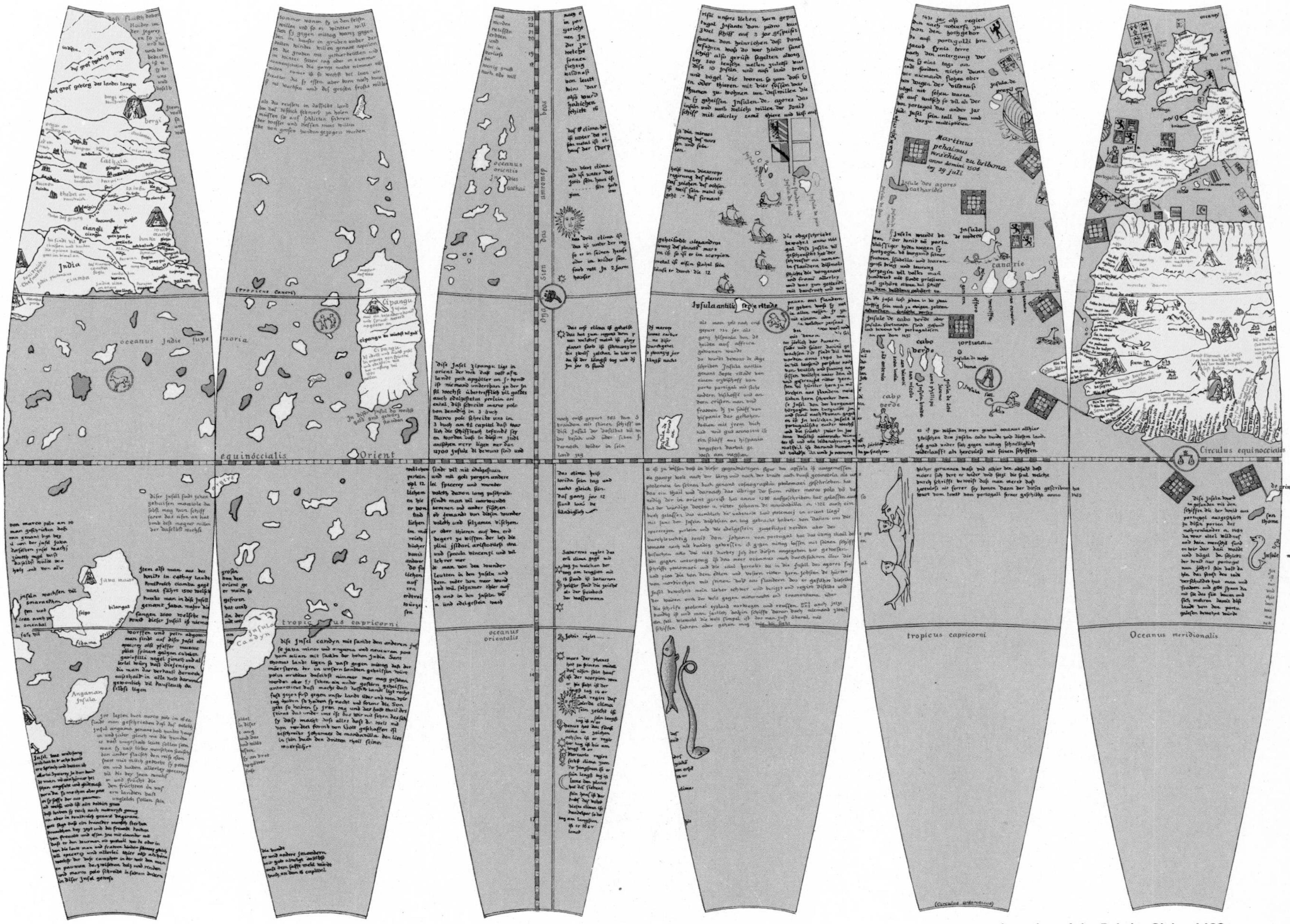

A portion of the Behaim Globe, 1492

Of the two great landmasses of the Earth, Eurasia and Africa as one and North and South America as the other, only the Americas have a history complete in maps. From hundreds of old maps which illustrate the growth of knowledge about North America through discovery, exploration, and settlement, we have here selected ten to highlight the story.

We know that Columbus carried a map of the world along with him on his voyage of discovery into unknown seas. But no such map, nor direct copy of it, is known to exist. In the same year that Columbus set out for the Indies by sailing west, however, another man was at work upon a large globe showing the distribution of the Earth's lands and seas according to the best authorities of the time. Fortunately, the globe of Martin Behaim, produced in 1492 for the citizens of Nuremberg in Germany, has been preserved down through the centuries. It pro-

vides an original contemporary map of the world as conceived by such men as Columbus, Cabot, Vespucci, and others who were destined to place the Americas upon the map.

The reduced reproduction above of half of the Behaim globe shows clearly that Columbus expected to reach the island of *Cipangu* (Japan) by sailing westward from the *Canarie* islands. Halfway along, he might encounter the legendary *Insula Antilia*, shown on Behaim's map as a triangular island near the Tropic of Cancer. The journal that Columbus kept relates that one day he consulted with his captains over maps which showed they were then in the area where *Antilia* should be found. But since it was not, on they went. *Cipangu*, as Behaim shows, became Columbus' next objective. And when he finally coasted the shores of the actual island of Cuba, he was sure it was the fabulous island.

Perhaps Behaim's globe is the oldest terres-

trial globe to survive because it became so badly out of date in a few years that it was put away in storage. In 1500 one of the associates of Columbus, Juan de la Cosa, produced a large manuscript map of the world showing the discoveries of Cabot as well as those of Columbus. In 1507, Martin Waldseemüller constructed both a small globe and a large world map which showed the New World as several long narrow islands "which," he declared, "because Amerigo discovered it, we may call Amerige, the land of Amerigo, so to speak, or America."

Since the maps of La Cosa, Waldseemüller, and others of the early sixteenth century are very large, this story of America in maps begins with the earliest atlas map to show America as a continent. Following are nine other maps showing certain comparative stages in the cartographic history of North America. The full story would require many more.

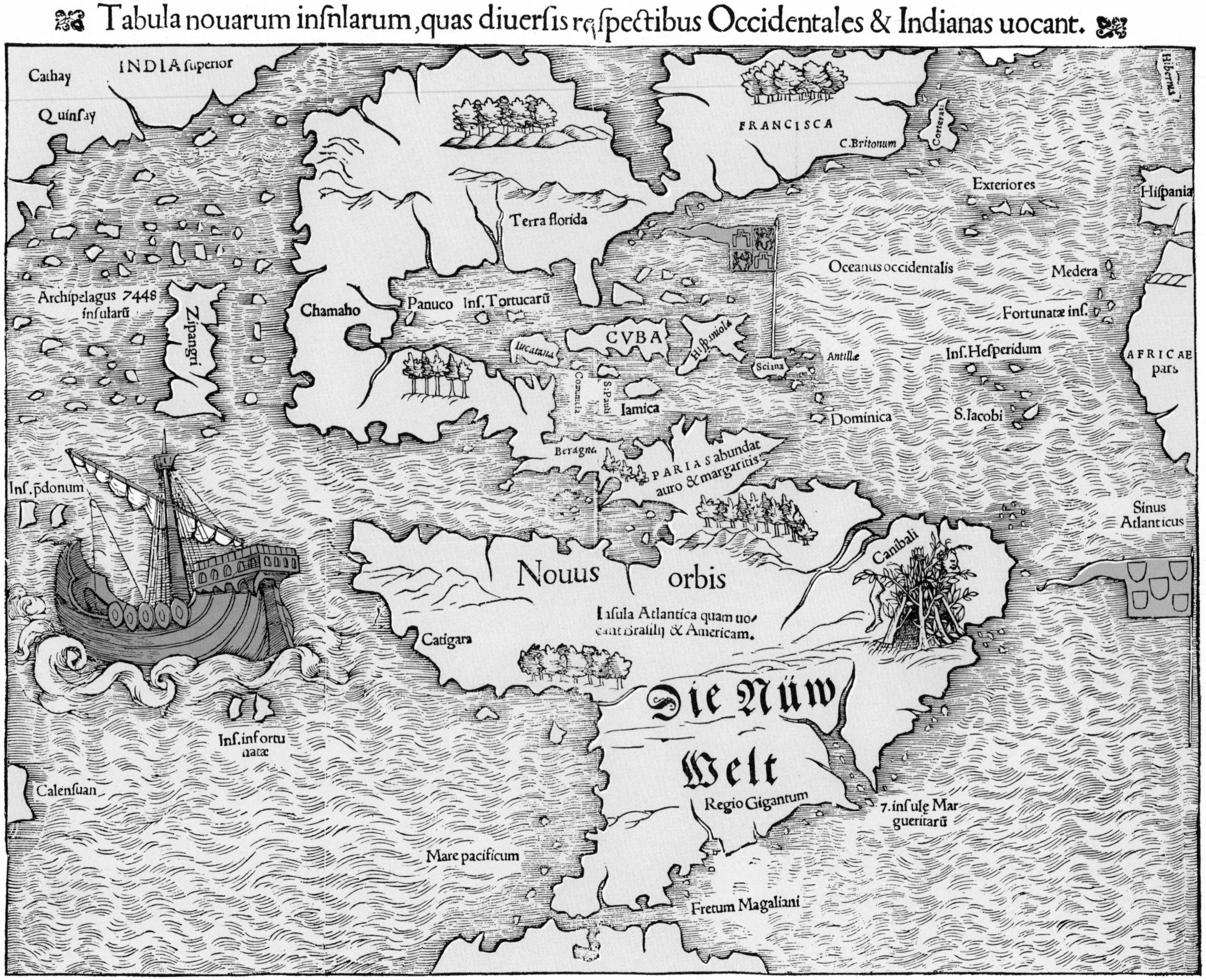

Tabula nouarum infularum, quas diuerfis refpectibus Occidentales & Indianas uocant.

THE NEW WORLD
IN 1540
by Sebastian Munster

This charming woodcut, from Munster's edition of the *Geographia* of Ptolemy, is one of the earliest maps to show America as the fourth great continent. Although crude in some of its details and configurations, it is surprisingly accurate in its delineation of the east coasts of the Americas.

Many of the place-names reflect the major discoveries and explorations of the first half-century after Columbus. *Hispaniola, Cuba,* and *Iamica* recall the voyages of the great admiral himself. *Terra florida, Panuco,* and *Iucatana* reveal the scope of later Spanish explorations in North America during the early decades of the sixteenth century. Farther to the north, the unnamed sea that almost cuts the continent in two bears witness to the French voyage of exploration under Verrazano. And the names *Francisca, C. Britonum,* and *Corterati* show that the English and Portuguese, as well as the French, had been active in this part of the New World.

The ship sailing boldly westward across the *Mare pacificum* can only be that of Magellan, whose discovery of the strait leading into that sea is memorialized by the name *Fretum Magaliani.* And the large island of *Zipangri,* surrounded by the 7,448 islands of the *Archipelagus insularu,* shows familiarity with the book of Marco Polo or the globe of Martin Behaim. Truly indeed, there is history in every map.

Heritage Map Number TWO

NORTH AMERICA
IN 1566
by Bolognino Zaltieri

Here, in an Italian map designed primarily to commemorate recent French explorations, we have one of the earliest maps to portray the triangular shape of North America, and perhaps the first to name the Strait of Anian (*Streto de Anian*), reputed to separate America from Asia.

Translated, the legend of the map reads as follows: "Map of the discovery of New France,

made lately from the most recent voyage of the French to that place, wherein one can see the islands, ports, capes, and inland places there existing. Venice, on copper plates by Zalterius of Bologna, 1566." Such names as *La Nova Franza, Canada Proļvincia], Ochelaga,* and others, indicate some familiarity by the author with the results of Cartier's voyages. Strangely, however,

the name of the St. Lawrence River (*R. S. Lorenzo*) is mislocated, although the river itself is properly placed.

Another area on this map, of interest for its place-names, is the southwest coast and interior. Here, somewhat crudely but indelibly, the exploits of Cortez, Coronado, Cabrillo, and others are perpetuated by such names as *C. del Cortese,*

Y di Cedri, Quivira, Granata, and many more. California, although not named, is distinctly peninsular, and the island of Japan (*Giapan*) has now been moved northward and altered in shape, but is still located in the middle of the Pacific Ocean. Areas in the northwest and northeast labeled *Terra Incognita* show that the northern coasts are entirely hypothetical.

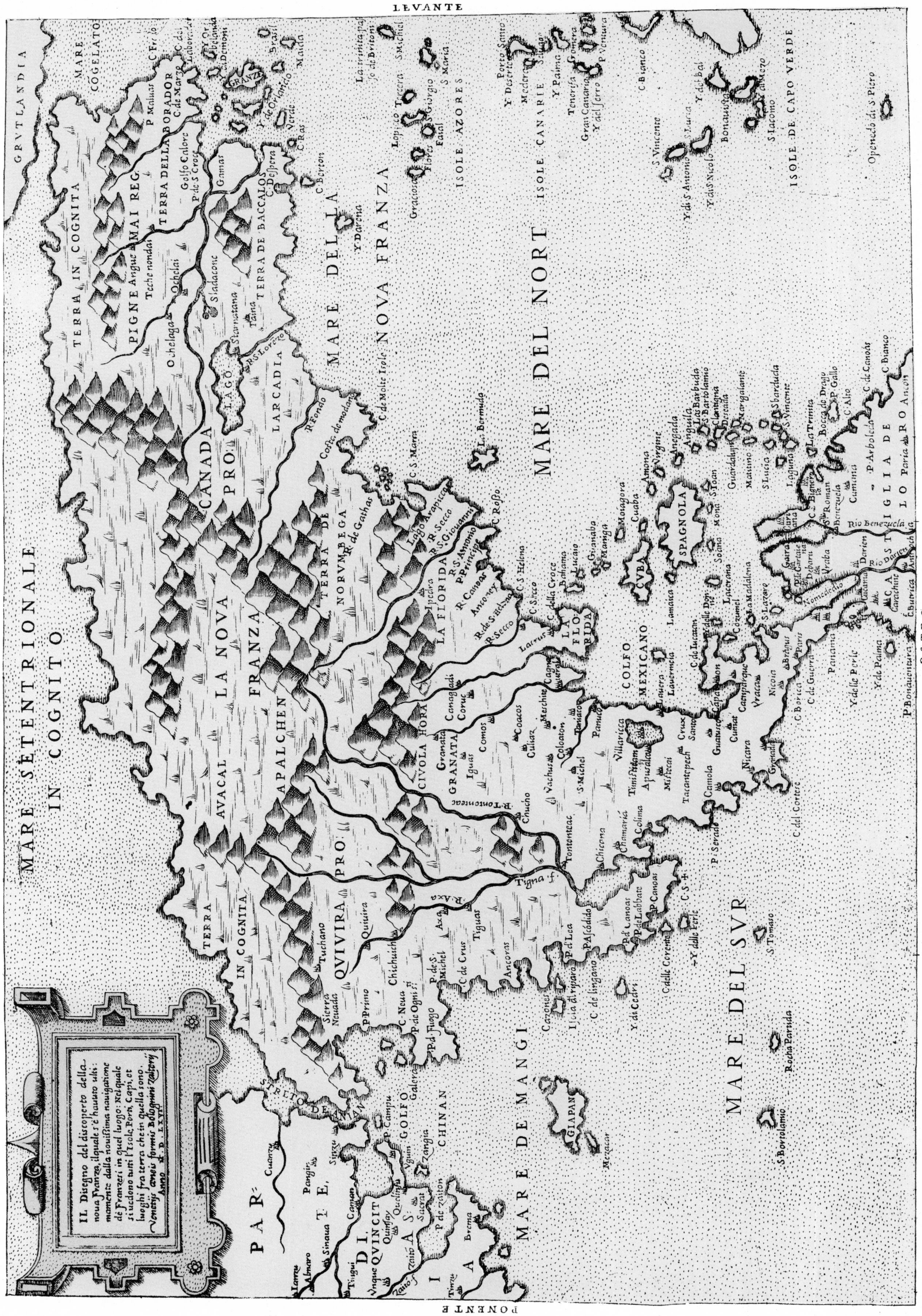
LEVANTE
TRAMONTANA
PONENTE
OSTRO
MARE SETENTRIONALE IN COGNITO
MARE COGELATO
GRVTLANDIA
TERRA IN COGNITA
LA NOVA FRANZA
CANADA
APALCHEN
QVIVIRA
TERRA DE NORVMBEGA
LA FLORIDA
MARE DEL NORT
MARE DEL SVR
MARE DE MANGI
GOLFO MEXICANO
CVBA
SPAGNOLA
GIAPAN
ISOLE AZORES
ISOLE CANARIE
ISOLE DE CAPO VERDE
Il Disegno del discoperto della noua Franza, ilquale s'è hauuto ultimamente dalla nouissima nauigatione de Franzesi in quel luogo: Nel quale si uedono tutti l'Isole, Porti, Capi, et luoghi fra terra che in quella sono.
Venetijs aeneis formis Bolognini Zalterij.
ANNO M.D.LXVI

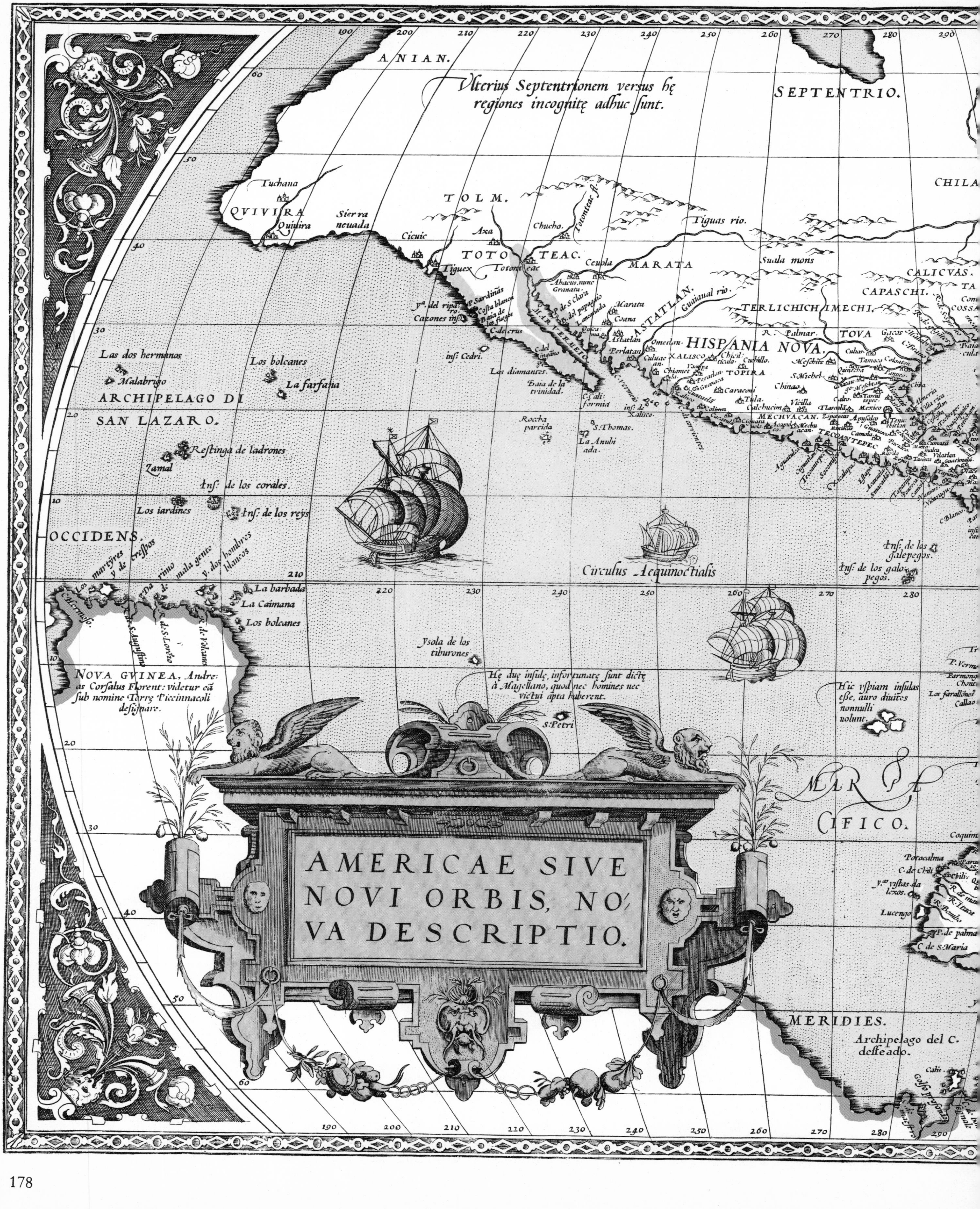

ANIAN.

Vlterius Septentrionem versus hę regiones incognitę adhuc sunt.

SEPTENTRIO.

CHILA

Tuchana

QVIVIRA
Quivira

Sierra neuada

TOLM.

Vremicai fl.

Tiguas rio.

Cicuic

Axa

Chucho.

TOTO TEAC.

Tiguex   Toront eac

Ceupla

MARATA

Suila mons

CALICVAS.

CAPASCHI.

COSSA

TA

Com

TERLICHICH IMECHI.

yⁿ. del riparto
Cazones inſ.

Sardinas
Coſta blanca
Baia de fuegos

de S. clara

Abacus nunc
Granata

del papagio
amollada

Marata
Coana

ASTATLAN.

Guaiaual rio

R. Palmar.

TOVA

inſ. Cedri.

del
mgino

Culuae
an.

Omedan
Perlatan

HISPANIA NOVA.

Culuz

Meschire

Tamacx Colaxos

Las dos hermanas

Los bolcanes

C. del
Engaño

Los diamantes

Baia de la
trinidad.

C. Cali:
formia

Chiametl
Xcopa
Patetlan
Guacana

XALISCO
Chical
ticalo

Cuello.

Chinas

Quinechia

Jabia vica

Malabrigo

La farfana

inſ. de
Xaliſco.

Caraconi

Tula

S. Michel

Vicilla

Calco

Tlarolli

Ameria

Villa rica

ARCHIPELAGO DI

Rocha
parcida

S. Thomas.

La Anuli
ada.

Cali:
formia

Calchucim
aca.

Quecatula
Acapul

Nechu

MEXICO

Tlacopa

Tenu
vitlan

SAN LAZARO.

MECHVACAN.

Escancauo

Apulea

Camella

OCCIDENS

Reſtinga de ladrones.

Zamal

Inſ. de los corales.

Los iardines

Inſ. de los reys

TECOANTEPEC.

Pazalco

Chochoya

Yflarlan

Tauca

Guatmala

Inſ. de los
galepegos.

martyres
y de treſſos

Da rimo
mala gente

V. dos hombres
blancos

Circulus Æquinoctialis

Inſ. de los galo
pegos.

C. Blanco

inſ
car

Hermo:
ſa.

La barbada

La Caimana

Los bolcanes

Ysola de los
tiburones

Hę duę inſulę, infortunatę ſunt dictę
à Magellano, quod nec homines nec
victui apta haberent.

Tr
P. Verm

Parmon
Chonte

Los farallines

Callao

Inſ. maior.
S. Iuan fluu:
R. des Lonſo
R. de Volcanes

S. Petri

Hic vſpiam inſulas
eſſe, auro diuites
nonnulli
volunt.

NOVA GVINEA, Andre:
as Corſalus Florent: videtur eā
ſub nomine Terrę Piccinnacoli
deſignare.

MAR
CIFICO.

Coquim

Porocalma

C. de Chili

Chili.

y.ᵃˢ viſtas da
lexos.

R. de Iaera

R. Bonbo

P. le palma

C. de S. Maria

Lucengo

MERIDIES.

Archipelago del C.
deſſeado.

Cali:

AMERICAE SIVE NOVI ORBIS, NO/ VA DESCRIPTIO.

178

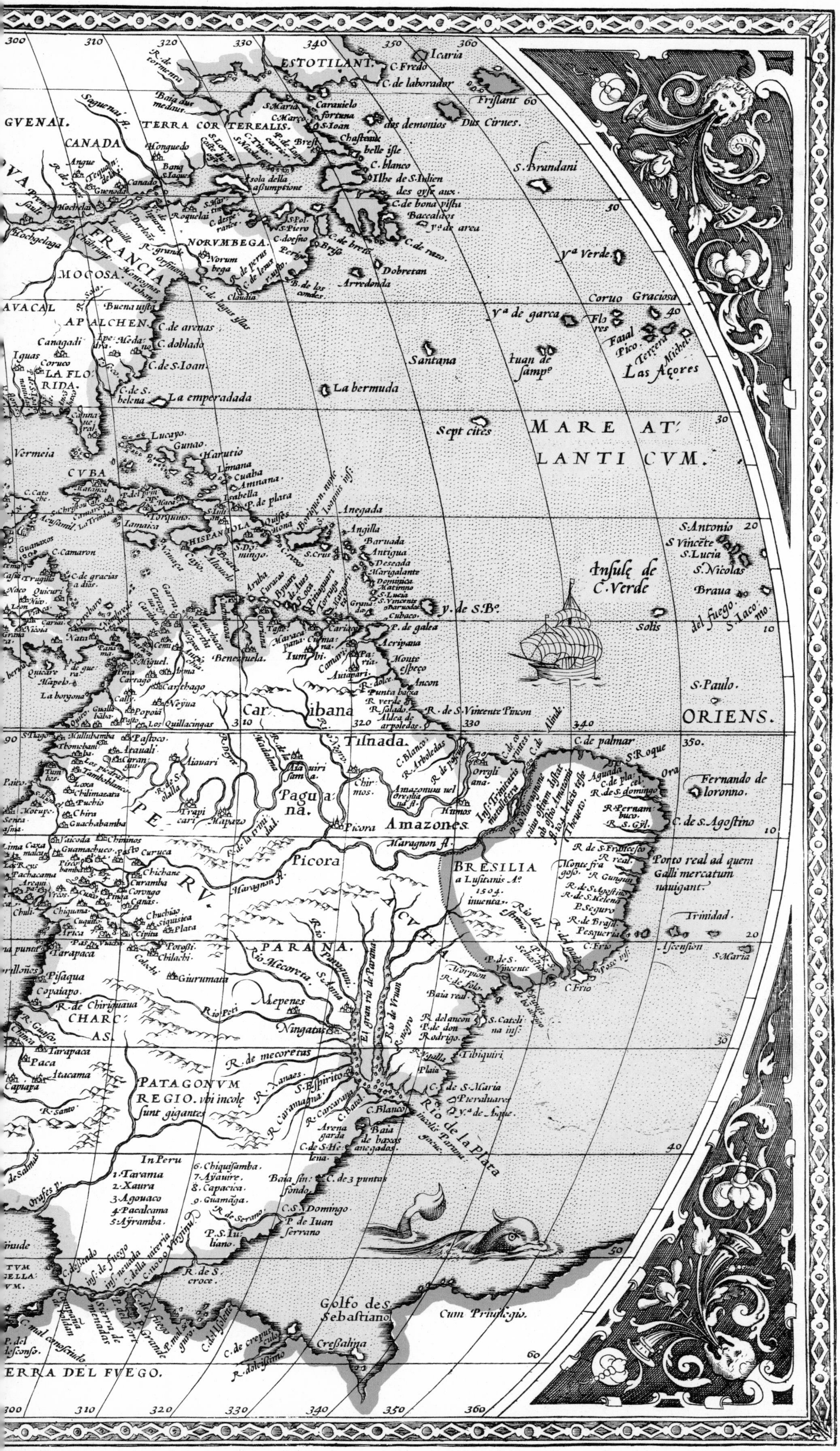

AMERICA IN 1570

by Abraham Ortelius

Although this map of America, or the New World, newly described, was issued by Abraham Ortelius of Antwerp in his *Theatrum Orbis Terrarum*, usually regarded as the first modern atlas, its general contours and details are patterned after the famous world map of Gerard Mercator published in 1569.

In North America, *Nova Francia* in the northeast, and *Hispania Nova* in the southwest, are the two most prominent regional names. Other areas with names of permanent historical significance are *Canada*, *La Flo-rida*, *Iucatan*, *Tecoantepec*, and *Xalisco*. The map, however, is rich in legendary and semimythical place-names. *Estotilant*, in the far northeast, is a name associated with the legendary voyages of the Zeno brothers in the fourteenth century; *Norumbega*, region and city, is believed by some to be of Indian origin; *Quivira*, the golden city sought by Coronado, here appears at the westernmost extension of the continent; while *Tiguex*, *Axa*, *Totonteac*, and *Cevola* are other mythical locations associated with Spanish penetration into the western interior.

A legend in the northwest, as well as the blank area in this part of the map, testifies to the fact that much of the interior of North America was still unknown (*regiones incognite*). In South America, by comparison, the exploration of the Amazon and Paraná river systems had established much more knowledge of the interior.

179

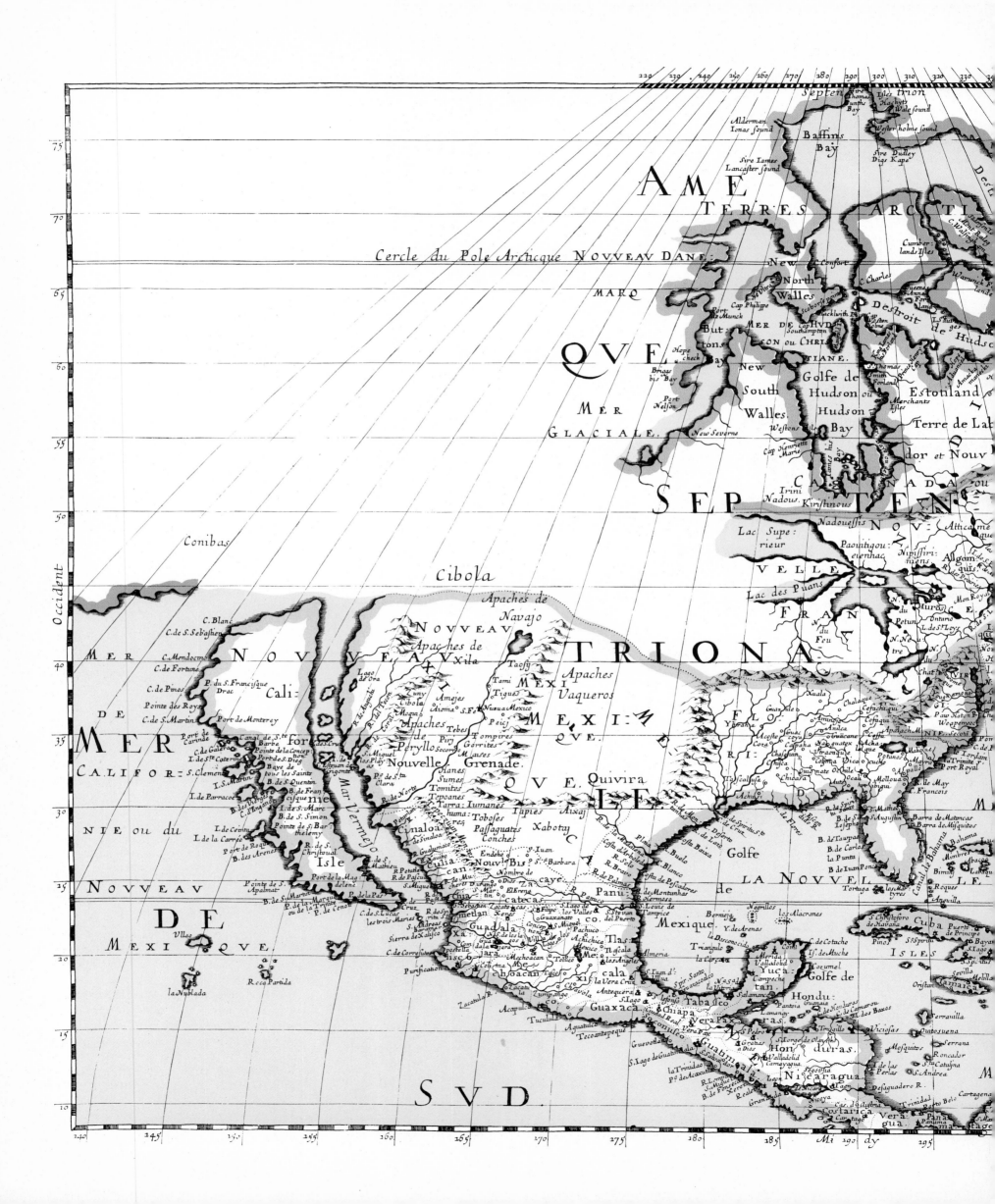

Septen trion
Alderman Ionas found
Baffins Bay
Sire Iames Lancaster sound
AME
TERRES ARCTI
Cercle du Pole Arctique
NOUVEAU DANEMARQ
QUE
MER GLACIALE.
New North Walles
Cap Philippe
Port Nelson
New South Walles
Golfe de Hudson ou Hudson Bay
Destroit de Hudson
Estotiland
Terre de Lab
New Severne
SEP TEN
CANADA ou NOUVELLE FRANCE
Lac Superieur
Lac des Puans
Conibas
Cibola
Apaches de Navajo
NOUVEAU MEXIQUE
Apaches de Xila
Apaches Vaqueros
Quivira
TRIONALE
MER DE CALIFORNIE ou du NOUVEAU MEXIQUE
Isle de Californie
C. Blanc
C. Mendocino
C. de Fortune
Port de Monterey
Mar Vermejo
Nouvelle Grenade
Cinaloa
Culiacan
Nouv.le Biscaye
Zacatecas
Panuco
Guadalajara
Mechoacan
Mexico
Tlascala
Guaxaca
Tabasco
Chiapa
Vera Paz
Guatimala
Honduras
Nicaragua
Costarica
Veragua
Golfe de LA NOUVELLE ESPAGNE
Golfe de Mexique
Yucatan
Golfe de Honduras
Cuba
ISLES
Tortuga
la Florida
MER DE SUD
la Nublada
Roca Partida
Occident
Midy

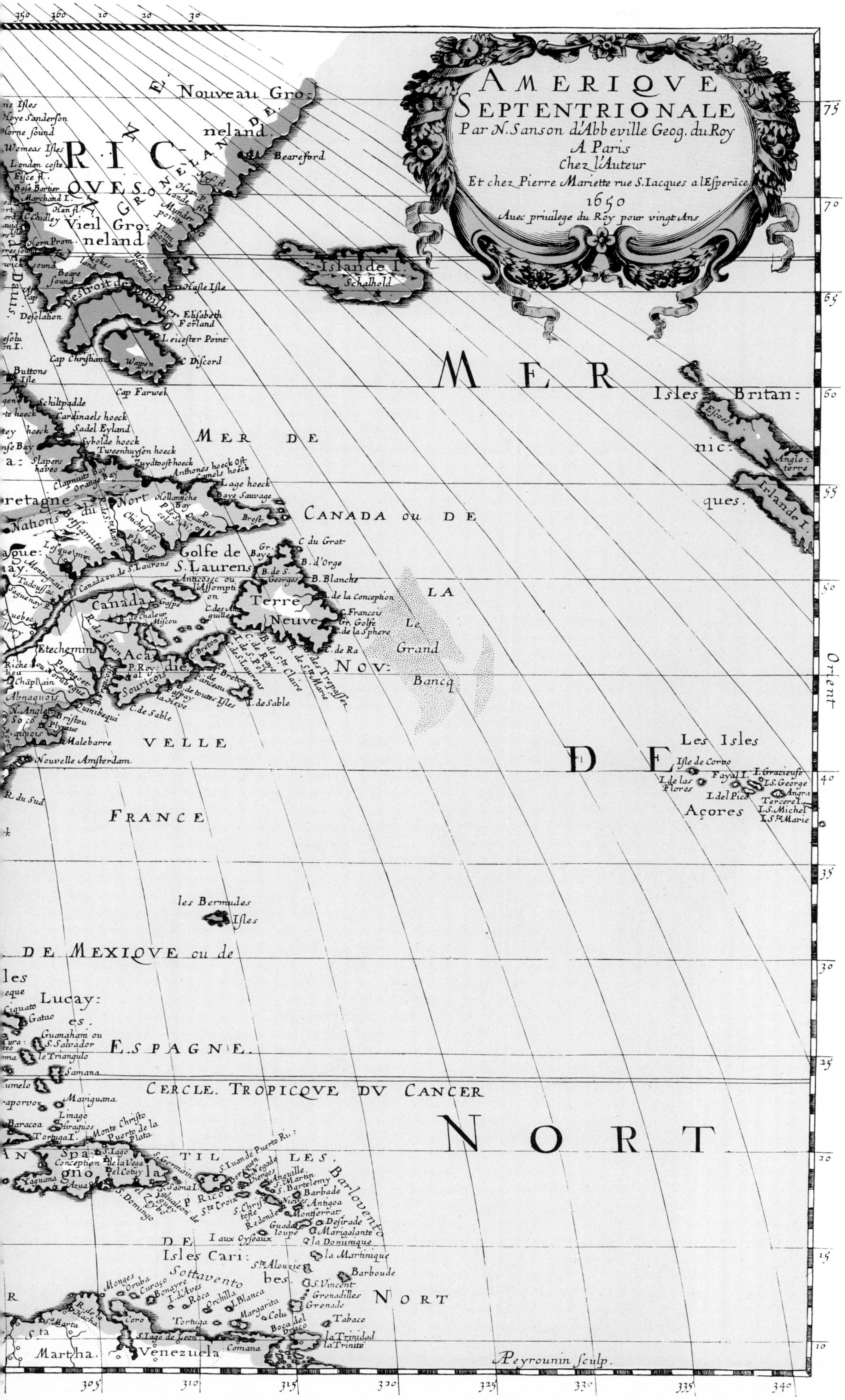

NORTH AMERICA IN 1650

by Nicolas Sanson

In comparison with the preceding map by Ortelius, this map by the first Royal Geographer of France reveals impressively the progress made in the exploration and settlement of North America during the first half of the seventeenth century. Here we have one of the truly great heritage maps of America.

The cartography of every section of the map merits detailed examination, but we can only call attention to a few highlights. Along the middle Atlantic seaboard, the names *Vir- gi- nie and N. Anglet[erre]* identify the recently established English colonies, at this date separated by the *Nouvelle Hol- lande* of the Dutch. Around the *Golfe de Hudson ou Hudson Bay*, such names as *New North Walles, New South Walles, Iames his Bay,* and *Briggs his Bay,* attest to the English penetration into that area. The possibility that the waters of Hudson Bay might link up with those of the great South Sea is entrancingly depicted by open waterways to the west.

Since this is a French map by the Royal Geographer, it is natural to find the St. Lawrence and Great Lakes waterways to be major centers of interest. The omission of any Lake Ontario, and the absence of any western shores to *Lac Supe- rieur* and *Lac des Puans,* show that there were still uncharted areas to entice Frenchmen westward into the interior.

The southwest, too, contains many cartographic features and names that attract interest and repay study. Even without the name *Cali- for- nie Isle,* the belief throughout most of the seventeenth century that California was an island, is here vividly portrayed. And scattered among the multitude of names in this part of the map are many which are familiar today. In California we find *C. Mendocino, P. du S. Francisque Drac, Port de Monterey, Port de S. Dieg, C. de S. Lucas,* and many others. In the interior district of *Nouveau Mexique* there is clear evidence that the Spanish outposts along the *Rio de Norte* (which here flows into the Gulf of California) were practically surrounded by four separate groups of *Apaches.*

Note that legendary *Quivira* has been brought back from the west coast almost into the heart of what is now Texas, while *Cibola* has been moved northward beyond the limits of Spanish America. Farther to the north, the map by Sanson is just as blank as that by Ortelius, although it was drawn almost a hundred years later.

NORTH AMERICA IN 1700

by Guillaume Delisle

With the Delisle map of 1700 we come to the first modern scientific map of North America—at least of those areas occupied by the French, English, and Spanish. Comparison of this map with the Sanson map of 1650 reveals the tremendous progress made in the mapping of North America during the last half of the seventeenth century.

Almost all the major geographical features of eastern North America are recognizable in the map of Delisle. The Atlantic coastline is sufficiently detailed so that its major rivers, bays, and islands may be identified. Seven English colonies are located by their names, from *Nouv. Angleterre* in the north to *Caroline* in the south. The Great Lakes are now five in number, with reasonably good shapes and with their interconnections by straits and rivers clearly shown.

In the Mississippi basin, Delisle has drawn upon the reports and maps of such great explorers as Marquette, Joliet, La Salle, Hennepin, Du Luth, and many others. Although extended too far northward, the *Missisipi R.* is here given its true character as the master stream of the continent. Flowing into it from the east, and thus forming connecting links with the waterways of the Great Lakes, are the *Ouisconsin R.*, the *R. des Ilinois*, the *Ouabache R.*, and the unnamed Ohio. The river to be known later as the Missouri is here called the *Pekitononi*, and is somewhat mixed up with the headwaters of other rivers flowing eastward into the Mississippi.

In its treatment of Spanish America, the Delisle map of 1700 is every bit as fascinating as it is in its portrayal of the French and English areas. The major divisions are *Californie* (once more a peninsula), *Nouveau Mexique* (still dominated by the *Apaches, Peuples vagabonds*), *Nouvelle Espagne* (including most of the present-day Mexico), and the *Isles Antilles*. Almost every modern place-name in the Caribbean can be found in this map, more than 250 years old.

As late as 1700 the vast expanse of North America north of California and New Mexico, and west of the Mississippi and Hudson Bay, was still unknown. Conveniently, the author uses much of this blank area on his map for graphic scales in French, Spanish, Portuguese, and German units of measurements, together with an *Avertissement* of his latest textbook in *Geographie*. But the unkown west was soon to be placed upon the map.

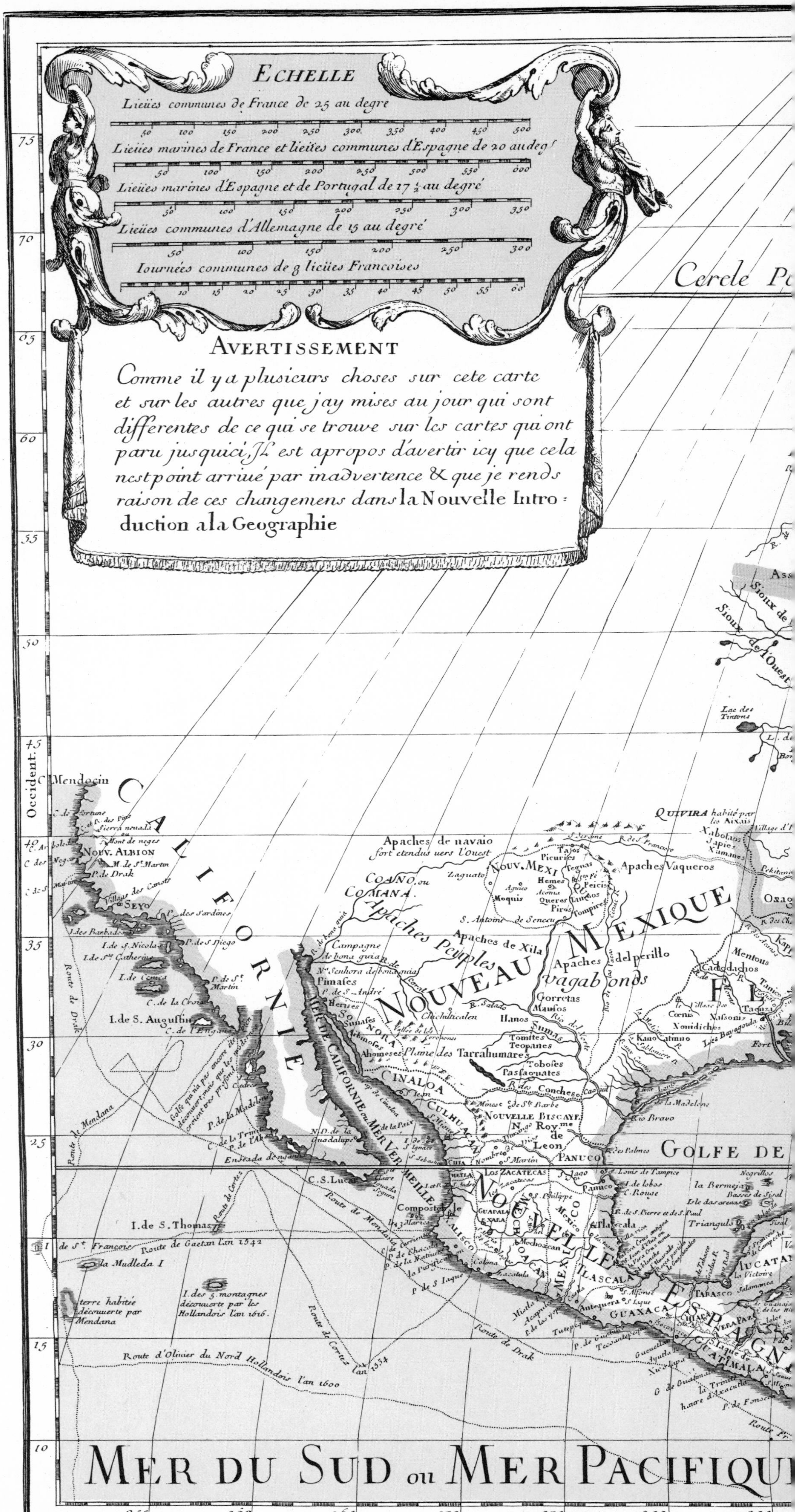

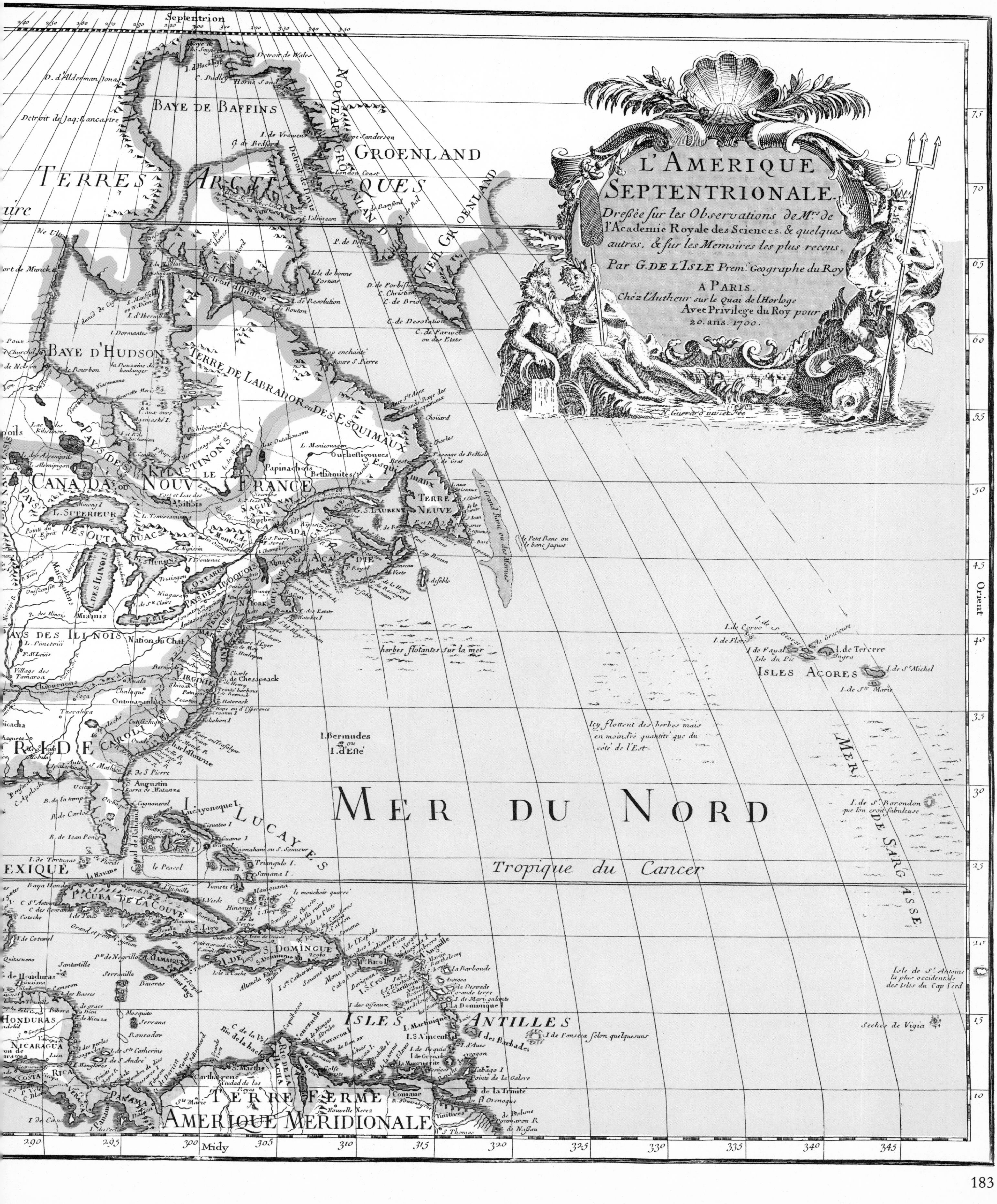

L'AMERIQUE SEPTENTRIONALE.
Dressée sur les Observations de Mrs de l'Academie Royale des Sciences. & quelques autres, & sur les Memoires les plus recens.
Par G. DE L'ISLE Premr. Geographe du Roy
A PARIS.
Chez l'Autheur sur le Quai de l'Horloge
Avec Privilege du Roy pour 20. ans. 1700.
Septentrion
Midy
Orient
BAYE DE BAFFINS
GROENLAND
TERRES ARCTIQUES
NOUVEAU GROENLAND
VIEU GROENLAND
BAYE D'HUDSON
TERRE DE LABRADOR ou DES ESQUIMAUX
CANADA ou NOUV LE FRANCE
L. SUPERIEUR
TERRE NEUVE
ACADIE
VIRGINIE
CAROLINE
I. Bermudes ou I. d'Este
herbes flotantes sur la mer
Icy flottent des herbes mais en moindre quantité que du côté de l'Est
ISLES ACORES
I. de Tercere
I. de St. Michel
MER DE SARGASSE
MER DU NORD
Tropique du Cancer
I. LUCAYES
P. CUBA DE LA COUVE
S. DOMINGUE
ISLES ANTILLES
TERRE FERME
AMERIQUE MERIDIONALE
Seches de Vigia

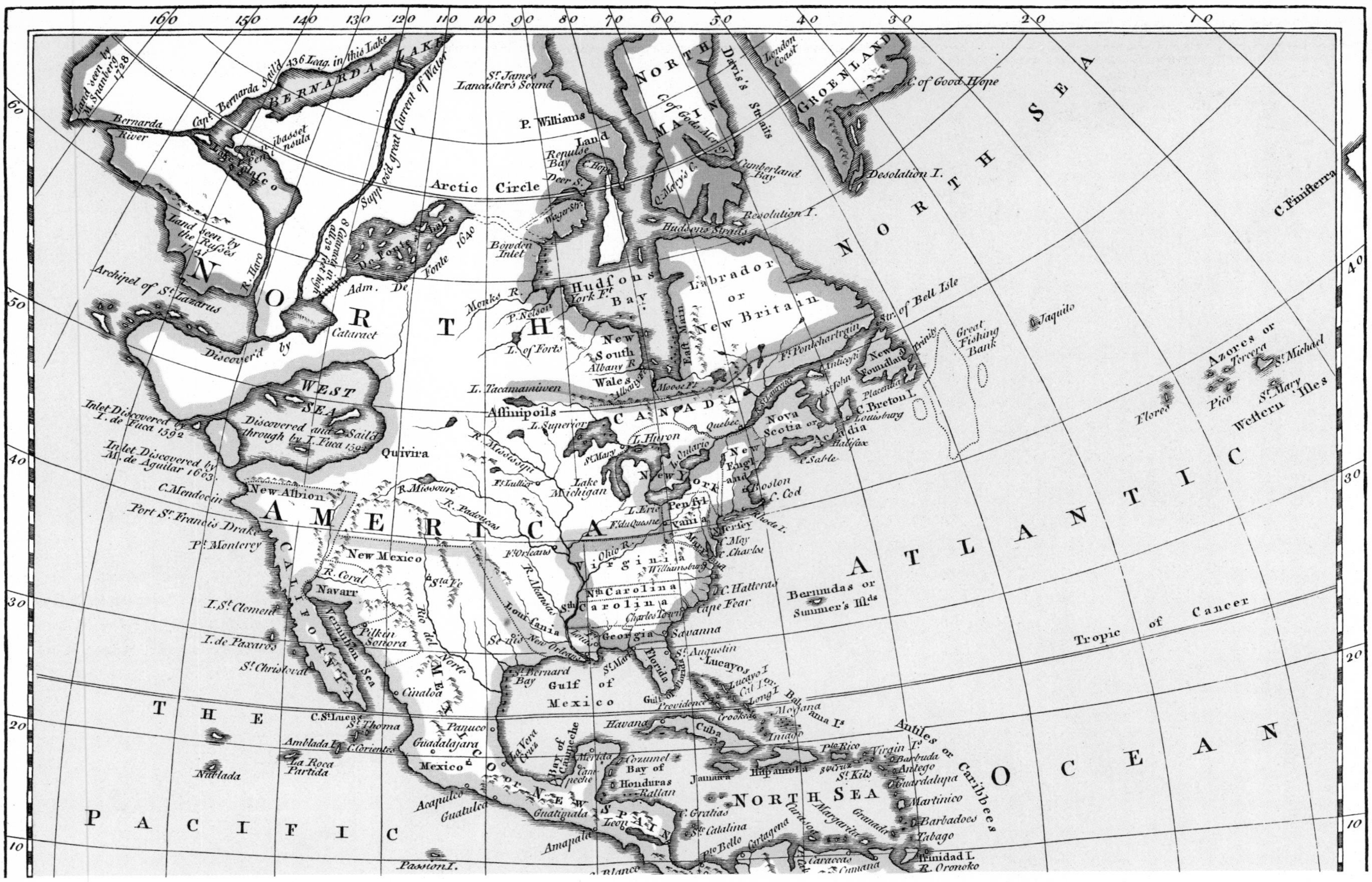

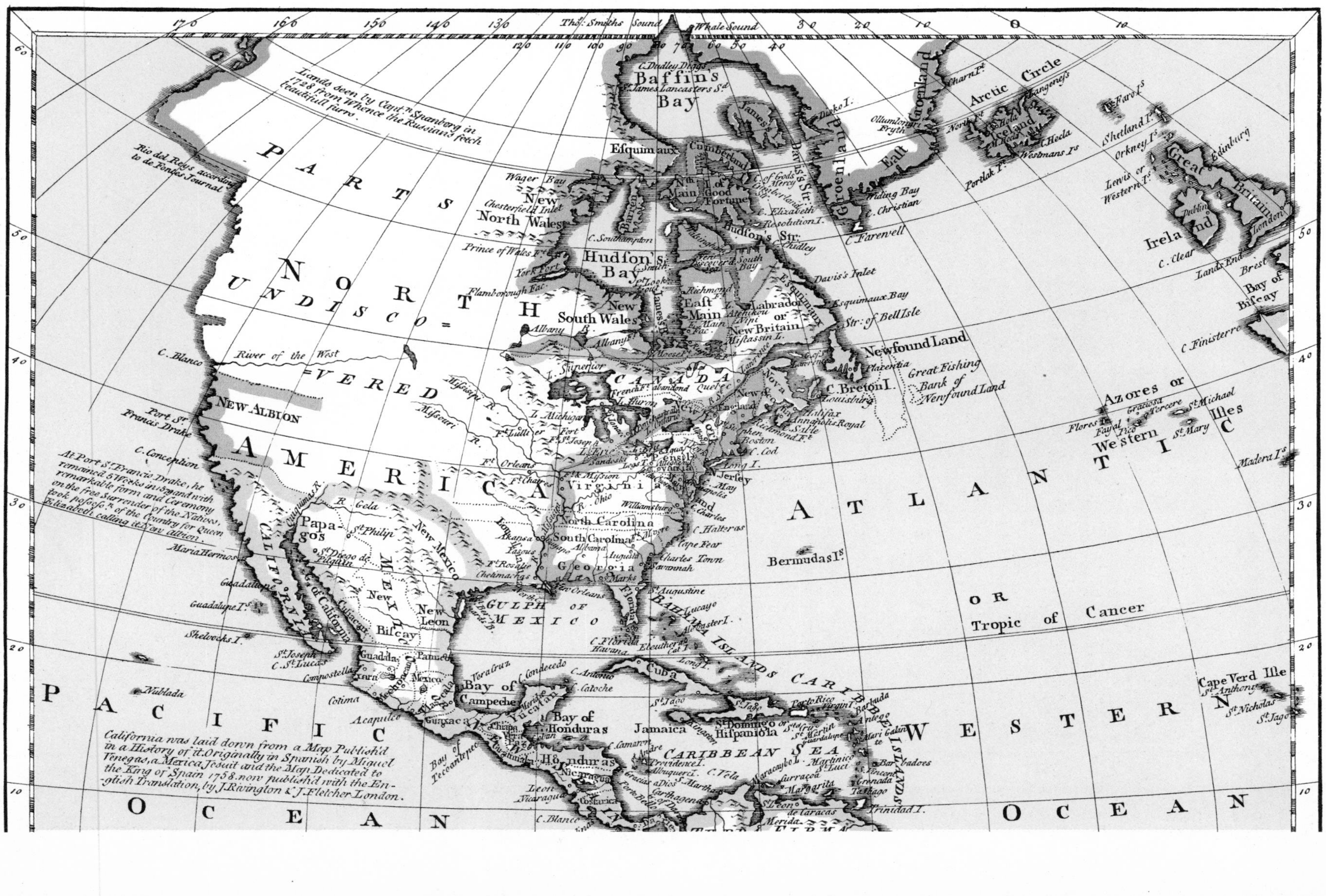

184

AMERICA
IN 1759

by Thomas Kitchin

Not until the last quarter of the eighteenth century did explorations by sea and land provide data which enabled cartographers to fill in the blank areas in the map of North America that extended northward of California. In the meantime legend, fantasy, and rumor gave rise to one cartographic version of the northwest coast and interior which was almost too fantastic to be believed. Yet several of the leading French and English cartographers of the mid-eighteenth century produced maps in which the cartography of northwest North America was similar to that provided here by Thomas Kitchin for inclusion in a popular gazetteer of the time.

Except for the legends—*Inlet Discovered by M. de Aguilar 1603*, *Land seen by the Russes 1741*, and

Land seen by M. Spanberg 1728—all of the cartographic information depicted on Kitchin's map north of *C. Mendocin* is apocryphal. The *Inlet Discovered by I. de Fuca 1592* and the great *West Sea, Discovered and Sail'd through by I. Fuca 1592* represent imaginary cartography based upon the claim of an aged Greek navigator to have made such discoveries when in the service of Spain at the end of the sixteenth century. The cartography of the waterways *Discover'd by Adm. De Fonte 1640* is equally imaginary, and was based upon a literary hoax perpetrated in 1708 which purported to reproduce the letters of one Admiral Bartholomew de Fonte "giving an account . . . on his Discoveries to find out if there was any Northwest Passage from the Atlantic Ocean into the South and Tartarian Sea." The discoveries of the Russians along the northwest coast of America during the first half of the eighteenth century seem to have stimulated English and French research into the historical literature of earlier claims to discoveries in this part of the world, with the result that the legendary voyages of both De Fuca and De Fonte were revived and depicted in numerous maps.

In eastern North America, Kitchin's map is of primary interest for the way in which it shows the overlapping territorial claims of the French and the English. *New York* extends westward into present-day Ontario and Michigan, while *Virginia*, *N'th Carolina*, and *S'th Carolina* extend to the Mississippi. The misspelling of Louisiana—*Louisania*—indicates that mapmakers, too, are human.

NORTH AMERICA
IN 1762

by John Gibson

Both Gibson's and Kitchin's maps portray the cartography of North America during the years of military struggle by the English and French for control of the continent, yet their differences are more striking than their similarities. In the

(Continued on page 188)

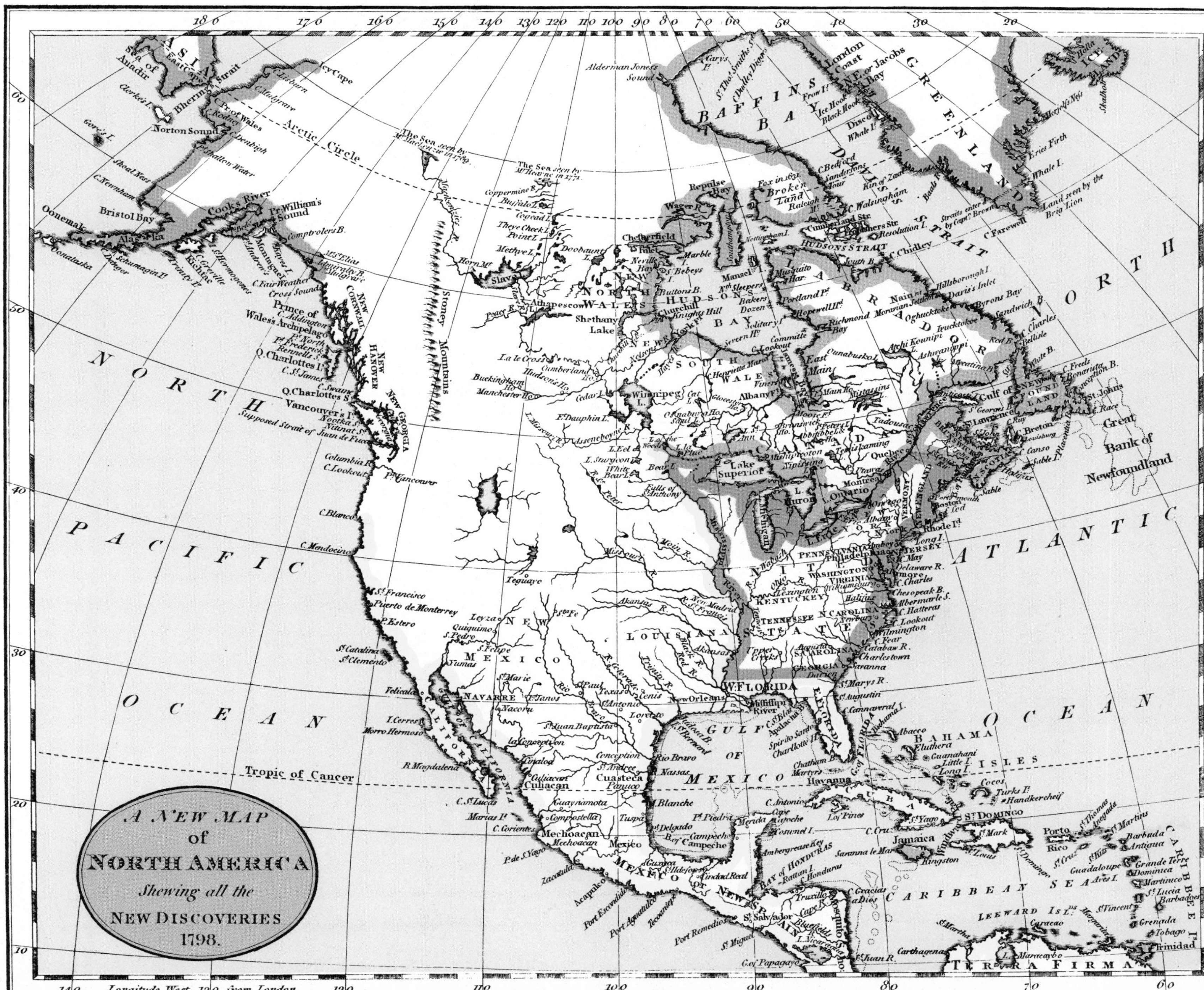

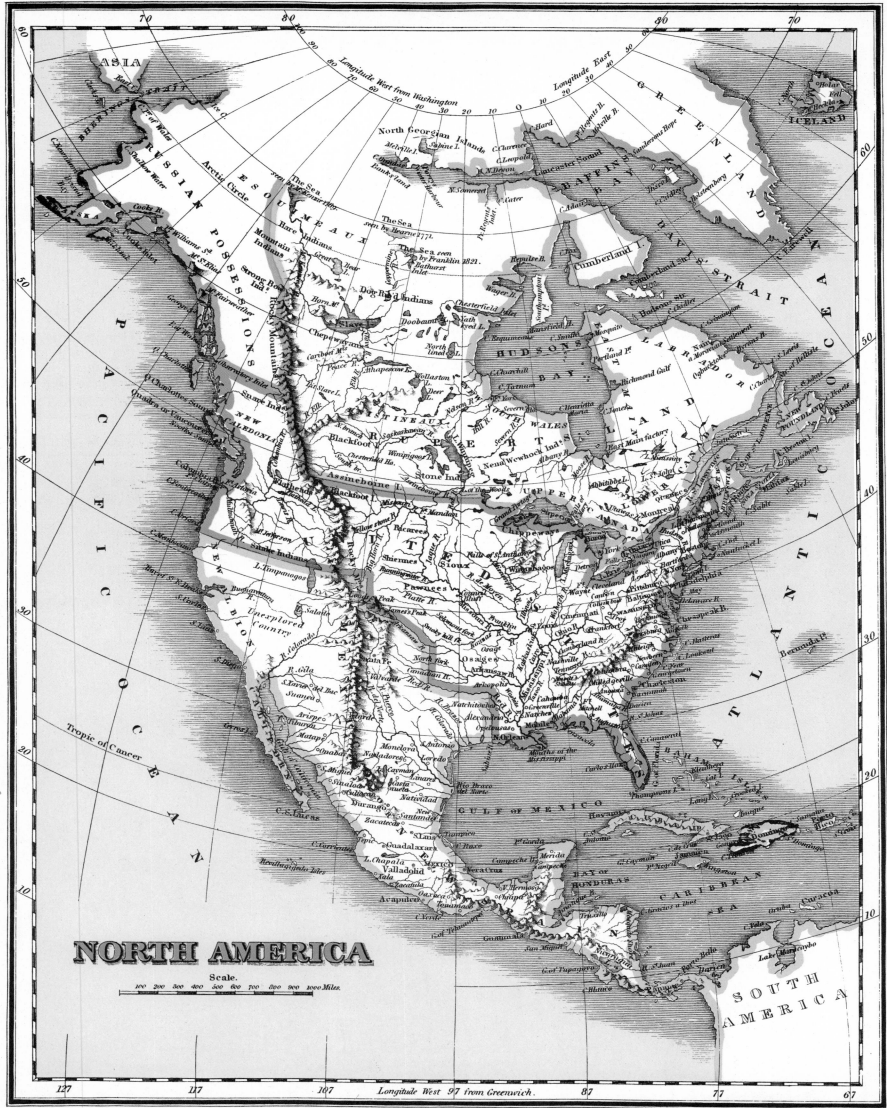

NORTH AMERICA

Scale.

100 200 300 400 500 600 700 800 900 1000 Miles.

Published by A. Finley Philad.ª

Young & Belleker Sc.

Heritage Map Number NINE

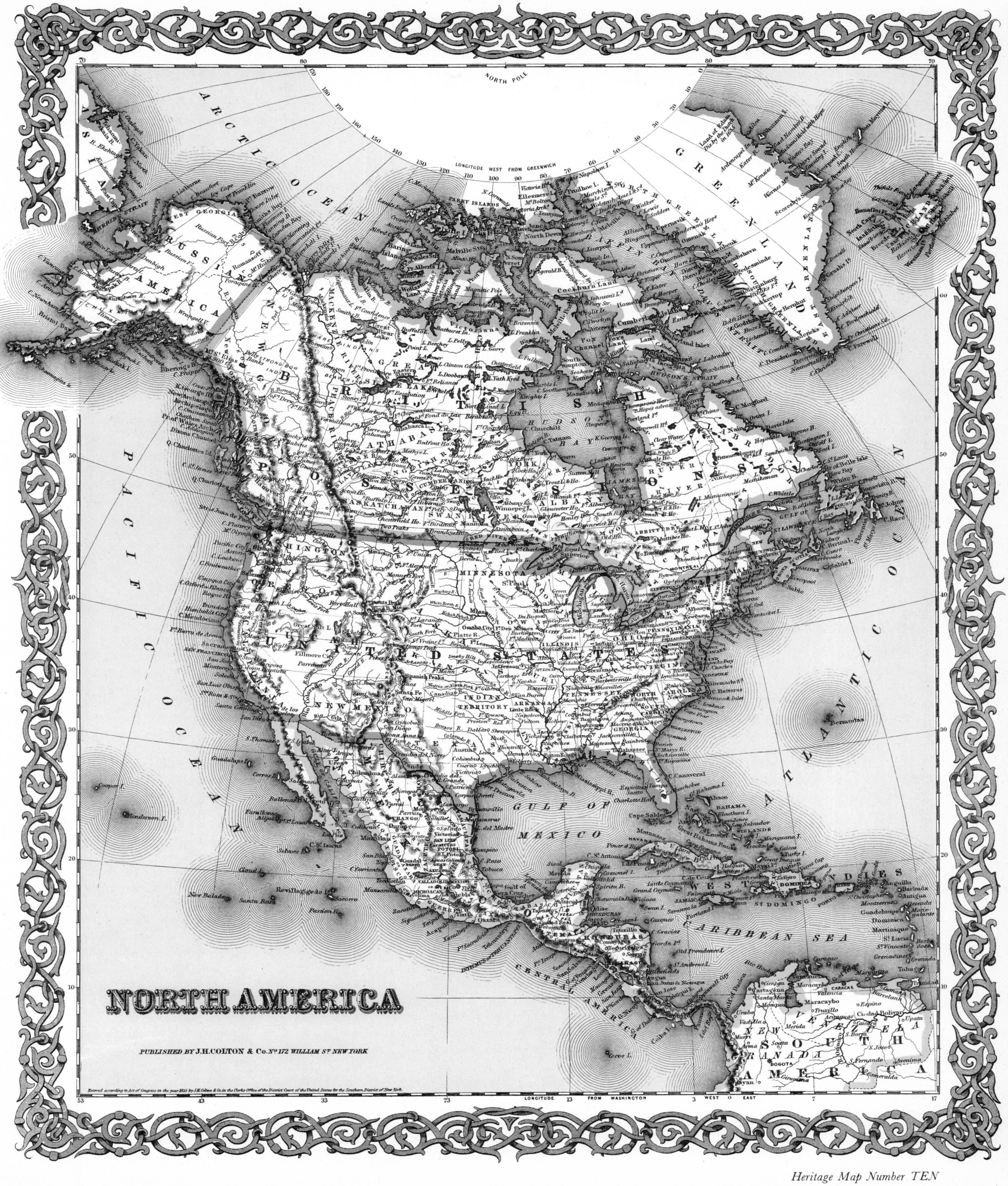
NORTH POLE
LONGITUDE WEST FROM GREENWICH
ARCTIC OCEAN
GREENLAND
RUSSIAN AMERICA
PACIFIC OCEAN
ATLANTIC OCEAN
UNITED STATES
GULF OF MEXICO
WEST INDIES
CARIBBEAN SEA
CENTRAL AMERICA
NORTH AMERICA
PUBLISHED BY J.H.COLTON & Co. No 172 WILLIAM St NEW YORK
LONGITUDE FROM WASHINGTON

west, Gibson labels the interior, *Parts Undiscovered*, but shows a mythical *River of the West* rising in an interior lake and flowing westward to the Pacific at *C. Blanco*. To the north his coastline is broken to indicate that it was hypothetical.

Just south of 50 degrees, the inlet of Juan de Fuca is shown but not named, while near 60 degrees is the legend, *Rio del Reys according to de Fontes Journal*. Strangely enough, he gives credit to Captain Spanberg for Russian discoveries in 1728, but ignores those of Bering and Chirikov in 1741. But even the *American Gazetteer* of 1762, in which Gibson's map appears, fails to include any mention of the Russian discoveries.

Both Kitchin and Gibson were reliable and popular cartographers and their maps (and others like them of the same period) offered encouraging rewards to men like Jonathan Carver, Samuel Hearne, Alexander Mackenzie, Captains James Cook and George Vancouver, and many others who were to clear up much of the mystery in the cartography of northwestern North America during the remaining decades of the eighteenth century.

Heritage Map Number EIGHT

NORTH AMERICA IN 1798

by Jedidiah Morse

In comparison with the two preceding gazetteer maps of Kitchin's (1759) and Gibson's (1762), the map of North America in the London edition of *Morse's American Gazetteer* (1798) reveals at a glance much that has been accomplished in the exploration of North America during the last three decades of the eighteenth century, and much that remained to be done.

In the north, two expeditions from *Slave L.* to the Arctic sea are here recorded. *The Sea seen by Mr. Hearne in 1772* calls attention to a little-known expedition which settled once and for all the question of waterways leading from Hudson Bay to the Pacific Ocean. Similarly, *The Sea seen by Mr. Mackenzie in 1789* provides additional evidence that the Northwest Passage by sea would have to be found north of 70 degrees, if it were to be found at all.

It is along the northwest coast, from *C. Blanco* at 42 degrees to *Icy Cape* beyond 70 degrees, that the map from Morse's gazetteer presents its richest heritage of "new discoveries." Here are names such as *Nootka S'd, Cooks River, Bristol Bay, Alaska*, and many others which are drawn from the extensive explorations of Captain James Cook in 1778 and 1779. Other names, such as *Queen Charlottes I.* and *Columbia R.* come from discoveries made by private fur traders, both English and American. Vancouver's intensive examination of the coastal islands and inlets from the *Supposed Strait of Juan de Fuca* to the *Prince of Wales's Archipelago*, during the summers of 1792 through 1794, is reflected in the detailed coastline of the map, as well as in such names as *New Cornwall, New Hanover, New Georgia*, and *Pt. Vancouver*.

There was a great deal in western North America still to be discovered, however, according to Morse's map of 1798. The fact that the many-tentacled lake, occupying the center of the otherwise blank area between the Missouri and Columbia rivers, is not named is witness by Morse that these are still "parts undiscovered" as labeled by Gibson thirty-five years earlier.

Heritage Map Number NINE

NORTH AMERICA IN 1824

by Anthony Finley

During the first quarter of the nineteenth century, the map of North America began to take its final form. Lewis and Clark provided rough drafts of the Missouri and Columbia river systems; David Thompson mapped the headwaters of the Saskatchewan and the Columbia; Alexander Humboldt drew upon the archives of Mexico to improve the maps of New Spain and New Mexico; Zebulon Pike, Stephen Long, and others filled in the details of the southern plains. These and numerous other explorations and maps are neatly summarized in the ordinary atlas map by Anthony Finley.

There were still some unexplored areas of North America, however, and consequently some open spaces in Finley's map. The far northern interior of Mexico, or New Spain, is labeled *Unexplored Country*. Little is shown in the interior of *New Caledonia*, and still less in the heart of the vast area labeled *Russian Possessions*. *The Sea seen by Franklin 1821* has been added to the notes of similar accomplishments by Hearne and Mackenzie, but the Arctic shorelines remain spotty and disconnected. The gaps are beginning to close, however, as exploration moves northward.

In 1824 the United States consisted of twenty-four states and three territories, the latter being Florida, Arkansas, and Michigan. Frontier settlements shown on Finley's map are *Detroit, St. Louis, Franklin, Arkopolis*, and *Natchitoches*. In the far west, at the mouth of the Columbia River, are *Ft. Clatsop* (Lewis and Clark) and *Ft. Astoria*.

Heritage Map Number TEN

NORTH AMERICA IN 1855

by J. H. Colton

By 1855 both the outline of the continent and the boundaries of the United States have taken final form. The latter now consists of thirty states and eight territories, all of which are named and outlined on Colton's map. In the west, only *California* is a state; *Washington, Oregon, Utah*, and *New Mexico* are territories, all more than twice the size of the states later to bear these names. The territory of *Nebraska*, in 1855, appears to equal the state of *Texas* in size.

The frontier settlements are now *St. Paul* in the north, *Omaha City* and *Independence* on the Missouri, *Preston, Dallas*, and *Austin* in the south. Along the Pacific coast, the map names *Olympia, Salem*, and *Sacramento City* as capitals; *Pacific City, Umpqua City, Humboldt City* as minor seaports; and *San Francisco* as the metropolis (40,000 population). In southern California are the *Pueblo de Los Angelos* and *San Diego*. The only places named in the western interior, besides military forts, are *Gt. Salt L. City, Provo, Fillmore City*, and several other Mormon settlements.

One area still to be explored is the interior of *Russian America* where, on Colton's map, the *R. Youcan* appears to flow northward into the Arctic Ocean.

Geographical Facts, Figures, and Information about the World and the United States

In the fifty-nine pages which follow, the editors of the atlas have provided factual information of geographic interest on the world, the continents, individual foreign countries, and the fifty United States. Presented mainly in tabular form, these pages are designed to supplement the maps with data not readily available from the maps themselves. Here will be found answers to many of the questions raised by atlas users, particularly questions that ask "how large?" "how many?" and "when?"

The first of the tables, and in many ways the most useful of all, is the World Political Information Table. For each political unit listed, this table specifies the 1965 estimated population, area in square miles, population density, capital, largest city, and principal languages. In addition, the table states the precise political or administrative status of the units listed, and classifies them into major types.

Under the heading of World Facts and Comparisons appear the answers to many frequently asked questions. Here are the basic facts about the Earth's movements and measurements, as well as information on the physiographic and temperature extremes found in each of the continents. The population growth of the continents is summarized for the period since the year 1650, and the countries with the largest areas and populations are listed.

Following the World Facts and Comparisons come listings of the major physical features of the world, including mountains, oceans and seas, lakes, rivers, and islands. Each list includes the outstanding features in each category and provides a ready answer to questions about which of two mountains is higher, which of two rivers is longer, and many similar queries.

Next are two tables giving current population figures for the world's major metropolitan areas and cities. The data for metropolitan areas have been especially prepared by Rand McNally to make possible accurate comparisons of size among the world's great urban centers. This summary of population data is followed by a convenient pair of tables giving air and steamship distances between important world cities and ports.

Atlas users frequently encounter a geographical name in their reading that is of historical significance but does not appear on most contemporary maps. The Historical Gazetteer identifies a large number of these places and references, and gives modern names or descriptions to aid the user in locating the feature on today's maps.

Many atlas users will find the list of Principal Discoveries and Explorations among the most fascinating in the entire series. Here are traced the contributions of the long procession of explorers, traders, and soldiers whose voyages successively opened up to civilized man the continents and oceans familiar to us today. That the Age of Discovery has not entirely passed is confirmed by the listing of several recent events in the exploration of Antarctica.

The group of tables relating to the world as a whole closes with a listing of major world cities and their altitudes.

The series of tables relating primarily to the United States begins with a summary of geographical and historical facts about the nation, including extremes of elevation, distance, temperature, and rainfall. The historical growth of the country's territory is charted; so is the course of settlement, as reflected in the steady westward migration of the center of population. The land and water areas and 1960, 1950, and 1940 populations of the fifty states are conveniently summarized, and each state's rankings in area and population are included.

Concise sketches of the topography, climate, and principal products of each of the states comprise the State Climatic and Economic Table, condensing a great volume of information into convenient and readily utilized form.

The U.S. State General Information Table is another that will provide the answers to many questions of atlas users. Besides the capital, largest city, and official state bird, flower, and nickname, the table gives the extremes of length and width, the highest point, and information on the date of entry into the Union. The next tables trace the growth of the population of the nation and the individual states from the small Colonial communities of 1650 down to the present.

Next, U.S. metropolitan areas of 100,000 or more are listed, ranked according to 1965 population. This table and a supplementary table also give populations for the central cities of these metropolitan areas. The table following provides a detailed breakdown of the more than 100,000 named localities in the United States by population size groups.

The special characteristics of the different regions of the country are shown in another way in the list of National Parks, Monuments, and Historical Sites, accompanied by a convenient map. This list and map will, of course, be of special interest to tourists, vacation planners, and armchair travelers.

The Railroad Map of the United States serves to present a bird's-eye view of the entire railroad network, shown in detail on the individual color maps of the states. Supplementing the map is a table of U.S. railroad distances, and immediately following, a table of air distances between principal American cities.

Armchair travelers may find the summary of Places of Interest in the United States the most interesting section of the atlas after the color maps themselves. Here the historical and scenic highlights of each state are presented in convenient alphabetical form, and supplemented with a number of illustrations.

Closing this section and introducing the detailed Index to the maps are a Glossary of Foreign Geographical Terms and a Glossary of Map Terminology. The first will aid the atlas user in understanding and translating the foreign geographical terms found on the maps and in the Index. The Glossary of Map Terminology offers convenient definitions and descriptions of the more frequently found geographical and map terms.

WORLD POLITICAL INFORMATION TABLE

This table lists all countries and dependencies in the world, U.S. States, Canadian provinces, and other important regions and political subdivisions. Besides specifying the form of government for all political areas, the table classifies them into six groups according to their political status. Units labeled **A** are independent sovereign nations. (Several of these are designated as members of the British Commonwealth of Nations.) Units labeled **B** are independent as regards internal affairs, but for purposes of foreign affairs they are also under the protection of another country. Areas under military government are also labeled **B**. Units labeled **C** are colonies, overseas territories, dependencies, etc., of other countries. Together the **A**, **B**, and **C** areas comprise practically the entire inhabited area of the world. The areas labeled **D** are physically separate units, such as groups of islands, which are *not* separate countries, but form part of a nation or dependency. Units labeled **E** are States, provinces, Soviet Republics, or similar major administrative subdivisions of important countries. Units in the table with no letter designation are regions or other areas that do not constitute separate political units by themselves.

Region or Political Division	Area in sq. miles	Estimated Population 1/1/1965	Pop. per sq. mi.	Form of Government and Ruling Power	Capital; Largest City (unless same)	Predominant Languages
Aden	80	250,000	3,125	Colony (U.K.) C	Aden	Arabic, English
Afghanistan†	251,000	15,200,000	60	Monarchy .... A	Kabul	Pushtu (Afghan), Persian
Africa	11,685,000	290,200,000	25		..........; Cairo	....
Alabama	51,609	3,462,000	67	State (U.S.) .... E	Montgomery; Birmingham	
Alaska	586,400	247,000	0.4	State (U.S.) .... E	Juneau; Anchorage	English, Indian, Eskimo
Albania†	11,099	1,846,000	166	People's Republic .... A	Tiranë	Albanian
Alberta	255,285	1,449,000	5.7	Province (Canada) .... E	Edmonton	English
Algeria†	919,595	10,700,000	12	Republic .... A	Algiers (Alger)	Arabic, French
American Samoa	76	21,000	276	Unincorporated Territory (U.S.) C	Pago Pago	Polynesian, English
Andaman & Nicobar Is.	3,215	74,000	23	Territory (India) .... D	Port Blair	Andaman, Nicobar Malay
Andorra	175	12,000	69	Principality .... A	Andorra	Catalan
Angola	481,351	5,125,000	11	Overseas Province (Portugal) C	Luanda	Bantu languages
Antarctica	5,100,000	....	....			English
Antigua (incl. Barbuda)	171	59,000	345	Colony (U.K.) C	St. John's	English
Arabian Peninsula	933,211	14,636,000	16		..........; Mecca	Arabic
Argentina†	1,072,070	22,200,000	21	Federal Republic .... A	Buenos Aires	Spanish
Arizona	113,909	1,635,000	14	State (U.S.) .... E	Phoenix	
Arkansas	53,104	1,889,000	36	State (U.S.) .... E	Little Rock	
Armenia (S.S.R.)	11,500	2,100,000	183	Soviet Socialist Republic (Sov. Un.) .... E	Yerevan	Armenian
Aruba	69	63,000	913	Division of Netherlands Antilles (Neth.) .... D	Oranjestad	Dutch, Spanish, English, Papiamento
Ascension I.	34	400	12	Dependency of St. Helena (U.K.) .... D	Georgetown	English
Asia	17,085,000	1,877,000,000	110		..........; Tōkyō	....
Australia†	2,971,081	11,335,000	3.8	Monarchy (Federal) (Br. Commonwealth of Nations) .... A	Canberra; Sydney	English
Australian Capital Territory	939	86,000	92	Federal Territory (Australia) .... E	Canberra	English
Austria†	32,374	7,235,000	223	Federal Republic .... A	Vienna (Wien)	German
Azerbaidzhan (S.S.R.)	33,450	4,400,000	132	Soviet Socialist Republic (Sov. Un.) .... E	Baku	Turkic languages, Russian, Armenian
Azores Is.	894	332,000	371	Part of Portugal (3 Districts) .... D	..........; Ponta Delgada	Portuguese
Baden-Wurttemberg	13,803	8,245,000	597	State (Germany, West) .... E	Stuttgart	German
Bahama Is.	4,375	136,000	31	Colony (U.K.) C	Nassau	English
Bahrain	231	166,000	719	Sheikdom (U.K. protection) .... B	Manama	Arabic
Balearic Is.	1,936	453,000	234	Part of Spain (Baleares Province) .... D	Palma de Mallorca	Catalan
Baltic Republics	67,200	6,350,000	94	Soviet Union .... E	..........; Riga	Lithuanian, Latvian, Estonian, Russian
Barbados	166	242,000	1,458	Colony (U.K.) C	Bridgetown	English
Basutoland	11,716	740,000	63	Territory (Protectorate) (U.K.) C	Maseru	Kaffir, other Bantu languages
Bavaria (Bayern)	27,239	9,970,000	366	State (Germany, West) .... E	München (Munich)	German
Bechuanaland	275,000	555,000	2.0	Protectorate (U.K.) C	Mafeking, S. Afr.; Kanye	Bechuana, other Bantu languages
Belgium†	11,778	9,400,000	798	Monarchy .... A	Brussels (Bruxelles)	Flemish, French
Benelux	25,726	21,932,000	853		Brussels (Bruxelles)	Dutch, Flemish, French, Luxembourgeois
Berlin, West	186	2,200,000	11,828	State (Germany, West) .... E	Berlin (West)	German
Bermuda	21	60,000	2,857	Colony (U.K.) C	Hamilton	English
Bhutan	19,300	750,000	39	Monarchy (Indian protection) .... B	Thimbu and Paro	Tibetan dialects
Bismarck Archipelago	20,415	193,000	9.5	Part of Australian Trust Ter. of New Guinea (3 Districts) .... D	..........; Rabaul	Malay-Polynesian and Papuan languages
Bolivia†	424,163	3,675,000	8.7	Republic .... A	Sucre and La Paz; La Paz	Spanish, Quechua, Aymará, Guaraní
Bonin Islands	40	200	5.0	U.S. Military Administration .... B		English
Borneo, Indonesian (Kalimantan)	208,286	4,470,000	21	Part of Indonesia (4 Provinces) .... D	..........; Bandjermasin	Bahasa Indonesia (Indonesian)
Brazil†	3,286,478	80,250,000	24	Federal Republic .... A	Brasília; Rio de Janeiro	Portuguese
Bremen	156	732,000	4,692	State (Germany, West) .... E	Bremen	German
British Columbia	366,255	1,770,000	4.8	Province (Canada) .... E	Victoria; Vancouver	English
British Commonwealth of Nations	10,890,827	795,539,000	73		London	....
British Guiana	83,000	631,000	7.6	Colony (U.K.) C	Georgetown	English
British Honduras	8,866	105,000	12	Colony (U.K.) C	Belize	English, Spanish, Indian languages
Brunei	2,226	105,000	47	Protectorate (U.K.) C	Brunei	Malay-Polynesian languages
Bulgaria†	42,829	8,175,000	190	People's Republic .... A	Sofia (Sofiya)	Bulgarian
Burma†	261,789	24,500,000	94	Federal Republic .... A	Rangoon	Burmese, English
Burundi (Urundi)†	10,747	2,775,000	258	Monarchy .... A	Usumbura	Bantu and Hamitic languages
Byelorussia (S.S.R.)†	80,150	8,500,000	106	Soviet Socialist Republic (Sov. Un.) .... E	Minsk	Byelorussian, Polish
California	158,693	18,338,000	116	State (U.S.) .... E	Sacramento; Los Angeles	....
Cambodia†	66,606	6,100,000	92	Monarchy .... A	Phnom Penh	Cambodian (Khmer), French
Cameroon†	183,569	4,750,000	26	Federal Republic .... A	Yaoundé; Douala	Native languages, French
Canada†	3,851,809	19,445,000	5.0	Monarchy (Federal) (Br. Commonwealth of Nations) .... A	Ottawa; Montreal	English, French
Canal Zone	558	50,000	90	Under U.S. Jurisdiction C	Balboa Heights; Rainbow City	Spanish, English
Canary Is.	2,808	1,005,000	358	Part of Spain (2 Provinces) .... D	..........; Las Palmas	Spanish
Canton & Enderbury	27	300	11	U.K.-U.S. Administration C	Canton Island	Malay-Polynesian languages, English
Cape of Good Hope	277,543	5,830,000	21	Province (South Africa) .... E	Cape Town	English, Afrikaans, Bantu languages
Cape Verde Is.	1,538	229,000	149	Overseas Province (Portugal) C	Praia; Mindelo	Portuguese
Caroline Is.	457	62,000	136	Part of U.S. Pacific Is. Trust Ter. (4 Districts) ...... D		Malay-Polynesian languages
Cayman Is.	100	9,000	90	Colony (U.K.) C	Georgetown	English
Celebes (Sulawesi)	72,987	7,700,000	105	Part of Indonesia (2 Provinces) .... D	..........; Makassar	Malay-Polynesian languages
Central African Republic†	238,200	1,350,000	5.7	Republic .... A	Bangui	Bantu languages, French
Central America	200,412	13,800,000	69		..........; Guatemala	Spanish, Indian languages
Central Asia, Soviet	478,150	16,800,000	35	Soviet Union	..........; Tashkent	Uzbek, Russian, Kirghiz, Turkoman, Tadzhik
Ceylon†	25,332	11,000,000	434	Commonwealth (Br. Commonwealth of Nations) ...... A	Colombo	Sinhalese, Tamil, English
Chad†	495,800	2,900,000	5.8	Republic .... A	Fort Lamy	Hamitic languages, Arabic, French
Channel Is. (Guernsey, Jersey, etc.)	75	112,000	1,493		..........; St. Helier	English, French
Chile†	286,397	8,450,000	30	Republic .... A	Santiago	Spanish

†*Member of the United Nations (1964).*

Region or Political Division	Area in sq. miles	Estimated Population 1/1/1965	Pop. per sq. mi.	Form of Government and Ruling Power	Capital; Largest City (unless same)	Predominant Languages
China (excl. Taiwan)	3,691,500	700,000,000	190	People's Republic ... A	Peking (Peiching); Shanghai	Chinese, Mongolian, Turkish, Tungus
China (Nationalist), see Taiwan	...	...	...		...	...
Christmas I. (Indian Ocean)	55	3,500	64	External Territory (Australia) ... C	...	Chinese, Malay, English
Christmas I. (Pacific Ocean)	222	400	1.8	Part of Gilbert & Ellice Is. (U.K.); also claimed by U.S. ...	...	Malay-Polynesian languages, English
Cocos (Keeling) Is.	5	700	140	External Territory (Australia) ... C	...	Malay, English
Colombia†	439,513	15,600,000	35	Republic ... A	Bogotá	Spanish
Colorado	104,247	2,003,000	19	State (U.S.) ... E	Denver	...
Commonwealth of Nations, see Br. Commonwealth of Nations	...	...	...	...	...	...
Comoro Is.	838	192,000	229	Overseas Territory (France) ... C	Dzaoudzi; Moroni	Malagasy, French
Congo (Rep. of Congo; Capital: Brazzaville)†	132,000	1,050,000	8.0	Republic ... A	Brazzaville	Bantu languages, French
Congo, The (Rep. of The Congo; Capital: Léopoldville)†	905,565	15,500,000	17	Republic ... A	Léopoldville	Bantu languages, French
Connecticut	5,009	2,752,000	549	State (U.S.) ... E	Hartford	...
Cook Is.	93	19,000	204	Island Territory (New Zealand) ... C	Avarua	Malay-Polynesian languages
Corsica	3,368	280,000	83	Part of France (Corse Department) ... D	Ajaccio; Bastia	French, Italian
Costa Rica†	19,600	1,425,000	73	Republic ... A	San José	Spanish
Crete	3,219	480,000	149	Part of Greece (4 Prefectures) ... D	...; Iraklion	Greek
Cuba†	44,217	7,100,000	161	Republic ... A	Havana (Habana)	Spanish
Curaçao	173	133,000	769	Division of Netherlands Antilles (Neth.) ... D	Willemstad	Dutch, Spanish, English, Papiamento
Cyprus†	3,572	590,000	165	Republic (Br. Commonwealth of Nations) ... A	Nicosia	Greek, Turkish, English
Czechoslovakia†	49,370	14,100,000	286	People's Republic ... A	Prague (Praha)	Czech, Slovak
Dahomey†	44,696	2,300,000	51	Republic ... A	Porto Novo	Native languages, French
Delaware	2,057	494,000	240	State (U.S.) ... E	Dover; Wilmington	...
Denmark†	16,619	4,740,000	285	Monarchy ... A	Copenhagen (København)	Danish
Denmark and Possessions	857,159	4,817,000	5.6	...	Copenhagen (København)	Danish, Faeroese, Greenlandic
District of Columbia	69	810,000	11,739	District (U.S.) ... E	Washington	...
Dominica	305	65,000	213	Colony (U.K.) ... C	Roseau	English, French
Dominican Republic†	18,704	3,500,000	187	Republic ... A	Santo Domingo	Spanish
Ecuador†	104,506	4,950,000	47	Republic ... A	Quito; Guayaquil	Spanish, Quechua
Egypt, see United Arab Republic	...	...	...	...	...	...
El Salvador†	8,260	2,875,000	348	Republic ... A	San Salvador	Spanish
England (excl. Monmouthshire)	50,327	45,150,000	897	United Kingdom ...	...; London	English
England & Wales	58,344	47,825,000	820	Administrative division of United Kingdom ... E	London	English, Welsh
Equatorial Guinea	10,830	266,000	25	African Province (Spain) ... C	Bata and Santa Isabel; Santa Isabel	Bantu languages, Spanish
Estonia (S.S.R.)	17,400	1,250,000	72	Soviet Socialist Republic (Sov. Un.) ... E	Tallinn	Estonian, Russian
Ethiopia†	457,267	21,500,000	47	Monarchy ... A	Addis Ababa	Amharic and other Semitic languages, English, various Hamitic languages
Eurasia	20,910,000	2,478,900,000	119	...	...; Tōkyō	...
Europe	3,825,000	601,900,000	157	...	...; London	...
Faeroe Is.	540	37,000	69	Self-Governing Territory (Denmark) ... C	Thorshavn	Danish, Faeroese
Falkland Is. (excl. Deps)	4,618	2,200	0.5	Colony (U.K.) ... C	Port Stanley	English
Fernando Poo	785	71,000	90	Part of Equatorial Guinea ... D	...; Santa Isabel	Bantu languages, Spanish
Fiji	7,040	455,000	65	Colony (U.K.) ... C	Suva	Malaya-Polynesian languages, English, Hindi
Finland†	130,119	4,600,000	35	Republic ... A	Helsinki	Finnish, Swedish
Florida	58,560	5,913,000	101	State (U.S.) ... E	Tallahassee; Miami	...
France†	212,822	48,800,000	229	Republic ... A	Paris	French
France and Possessions	276,238	50,366,000	182	...	Paris	...
Franklin	549,253	6,300	0.01	District of Northwest Territories, Canada ... E	...; Cambridge Bay	English, Eskimo, Indian
French Guiana	35,100	36,000	1.0	Overseas Department (France) ... C	Cayenne	French
French Polynesia	1,550	89,000	57	Overseas Territory (France) ... C	Papeete	Malay-Polynesian languages, French
French Somaliland	8,500	80,000	9.4	Overseas Territory (France) ... C	Djibouti	Somali, French
French Southern & Antarctic Ter. (excl. Adélie Coast)	2,917	150	0.05	Overseas Territory (France) ... C	...	French
French West Indies	1,112	620,000	558	...	...; Fort-de-France	French
Gabon†	103,100	465,000	4.5	Republic ... A	Libreville	Bantu languages, French
Galápagos Is.	3,028	2,500	0.8	Province (Ecuador) ... D	Puerto Baquerizo	Spanish
Gambia	4,008	320,000	80	Self-Governing Member (Br. Comm. of Nations) ... A	Bathurst	Mandingo, Fula, English
Georgia (S.S.R.)	26,900	4,460,000	166	Soviet Socialist Republic (Sov. Un.) ... E	Tbilisi	Georgic, Armenian, Russian
Georgia	58 876	4,312,000	73	State (U.S.) ... E	Atlanta	...
Germany (Entire)	137,743	75,800,000	550	...	...; Berlin	German
Germany, East	41,815	17,250,000	413	People's Republic ... A	Berlin (East)	German
Germany, West (incl. West Berlin)	95,928	58,550,000	610	Federal Republic ... A	Bonn; Berlin (West)	German
Ghana†	91,843	7,600,000	83	Republic (Br. Commonwealth of Nations) ... A	Accra	Twi, Fanti, Ewe-Fon, English
Gibraltar	2	25,000	12,500	Colony (U.K.) ... C	Gibraltar	Spanish, English
Gilbert & Ellice Is.	369	51,000	138	Colony (U.K.) ... C	Tarawa	Malay-Polynesian languages
Great Britain & Northern Ireland, see United Kingdom	...	...	...	...	...	...
Greece†	50,547	8,500,000	168	Monarchy ... A	Athens (Athinai)	Greek
Greenland	840,000	40,000	0.05	Overseas Territory (Denmark) ... C	Godthaab	Greenlandic, Danish, Eskimo
Grenada	133	93,000	699	Colony (U.K.) ... C	St. George's	English
Guadeloupe (incl. Dependencies)	687	308,000	448	Overseas Department (France) ... C	Basse-Terre; Pointe-à-Pitre	French
Guam	212	70,000	330	Unincorporated Territory (U.S.) ... C	Agana	English, Chamorro
Guatemala†	42,042	4,375,000	104	Republic ... A	Guatemala	Spanish, Indian languages
Guernsey (incl. Dependencies)	30	49,000	1,633	Bailiwick (U.K.) ... C	St. Peter Port	English, French
Guinea†	94,925	3,500,000	37	Republic ... A	Conakry	Native languages, French
Haiti†	10,714	4,600,000	429	Republic ... A	Port-au-Prince	Creole, French
Hamburg	288	1,860,000	6,458	State (Germany, West) ... E	Hamburg	German
Hawaii	6,424	710,000	111	State (U.S.) ... E	Honolulu	English, Japanese, Hawaiian
Hesse (Hessen)	8,150	5,082,000	624	State (German, West) ... E	Wiesbaden; Frankfurt am Main	German
Hispaniola	29,530	8,100,000	274	...	...; Santo Domingo	French, Spanish
Holland, see Netherlands	...	...	...	...	...	...
Honduras†	43,277	2,125,000	49	Republic ... A	Tegucigalpa	Spanish
Hong Kong	398	3,750,000	9,422	Colony (U.K.) ... C	Victoria	Chinese, English
Hungary†	35,919	10,135,000	282	People's Republic ... A	Budapest	Hungarian
Iceland†	39,800	190,000	4.8	Republic ... A	Reykjavík	Icelandic
Idaho	83,557	702,000	8.4	State (U.S.) ... E	Boise (Boise City)	...
Ifni	580	51,000	88	African Province (Spain) ... C	Sidi Ifni	Spanish, Arabic
Illinois	56,400	10,584,000	188	State (U.S.) ... E	Springfield; Chicago	...
India (incl. part of Kashmir)†	1,227,275	479,000,000	390	Republic (Br. Commonwealth of Nations) ... A	New Delhi; Calcutta	Hindi and other Indo-Aryan languages, Dravidian languages, English
Indiana	36,291	4,914,000	135	State (U.S.) ... E	Indianapolis	...
Indonesia (excl. West Irian)†	574,670	103,350,000	180	Republic ... A	Djakarta	Bahasa Indonesia (Indonesian), Chinese, English
Iowa	56,290	2,783,000	49	State (U.S.) ... E	Des Moines	...
Iran (Persia)†	636,300	23,100,000	36	Monarchy ... A	Tehrān	Persian, Turkish dialects, Kurdish
Iraq†	173 260	7,050,000	41	Republic ... A	Baghdad	Arabic, Kurdish

†*Member of the United Nations (1964).*

Region or Political Division	Area in sq. miles	Estimated Population 1/1/1965	Pop. per sq. mi.	Form of Government and Ruling Power	Capital; Largest City (unless same)	Predominant Languages
Ireland†	27,135	2,855,000	105	Republic.....................................A	Dublin	English, Irish
Isle of Man	227	48,000	211	Possession (U.K.)..........................C	Douglas	English
Israel†	7,993	2,520,000	315	Republic.....................................A	Jerusalem; Tel Aviv	Hebrew, Arabic
Italy†	116,303	50,900,000	438	Republic.....................................A	Rome (Roma)	Italian
Ivory Coast†	124,504	3,775,000	30	Republic.....................................A	Abidjan	French, native languages
Jamaica†	4,411	1,750,000	397	Self-Governing Member (Br. Commonwealth of Nations)...........................A	Kingston	English
Japan†	142,726	97,400,000	682	Monarchy.....................................A	Tōkyō	Japanese
Java (Djawa) (incl. Madura)	51,040	67,000,000	1,313	Part of Indonesia (5 Provinces)..........D	........; Djakarta	Bahasa Indonesia (Indonesian), Chinese, English
Jersey	45	63,000	1,400	Bailiwick (U.K.)............................C	St. Helier	English, French
Jordan†	37,301	1,900,000	51	Monarchy.....................................A	Amman	Arabic
Kansas	82,264	2,251,000	27	State (U.S.)..................................E	Topeka; Wichita	
Kashmir, Jammu &	86,024	4,700,000	55	In dispute (India & Pakistan).............	Srinagar	Kashmiri, Punjabi
Kazakh S.S.R.	1,050,000	11,800,000	11	Soviet Socialist Republic (Sov. Un.).....E	Alma-Ata	Turkic languages, Russian
Keewatin	228,160	2,400	0.01	District of Northwest Territories, Canada...........E	........; Chesterfield Inlet	English, Eskimo, Indian
Kentucky	40,395	3,138,000	77	State (U.S.)..................................E	Frankfort; Louisville	
Kenya†	224,960	9,200,000	41	Republic (Br. Comm. of Nations).........A	Nairobi	Swahili and other Bantu languages, English
Kerguélen	2,700	150	0.06	Part of French Southern & Antarctic Ter. (Fr.)...........D		French
Kirghiz S.S.R.	76,650	2,490,000	32	Soviet Socialist Republic (Sov. Un.).....E	Frunze	Turkic languages, Persian
Korea (Entire)	84,540	39,500,000	467		........; Seoul (Soul)	Korean
Korea, North	46,540	11,500,000	247	People's Republic...........................A	Pyongyang	Korean
Korea South	38,000	28,000,000	737	Republic.....................................A	Seoul (Soul)	Korean
Kuwait†	6,000	405,000	68	Sheikdom....................................A	Kuwait	Arabic
Labrador	112,826	16,000	0.1	Part of Newfoundland Province, Canada...........D	........; Goose Bay	English, Eskimo
Laos†	91,400	2,000,000	22	Monarchy.....................................A	Vientiane	Lao, French
Latin America	7,923,124	237,100,000	30		........; Buenos Aires	
Latvia (S.S.R.)	24,600	2,200,000	89	Soviet Socialist Republic (Sov. Un.).....E	Riga	Latvian, Russian
Lebanon†	4,000	2,265,000	566	Republic.....................................A	Beirut	Arabic, French, English
Liberia†	43,000	1,050,000	24	Republic.....................................A	Monrovia	Native languages, English
Libya†	679,362	1,580,000	2.3	Monarchy.....................................A	Tripoli and Bengasi; Tripoli	Arabic
Liechtenstein	61	18,000	295	Principality..................................A	Vaduz	German
Lithuania (S.S.R.)	25,150	2,900,000	115	Soviet Socialist Republic (Sov. Un.).....E	Vilnius	Lithuanian, Polish, Russian
Louisiana	48,523	3,480,000	72	State (U.S.)..................................E	Baton Rouge; New Orleans	
Lower Saxony (Niedersachsen)	18,294	6,855,000	375	State (Germany, West).......................E	Hannover (Hanover)	German
Luxembourg†	998	332,000	333	Grand Duchy.................................A	Luxembourg	Luxembourgeois, French
Macao	6	175,000	29,167	Overseas Province (Portugal)..............C	Macao	Chinese, Portuguese
Mackenzie	527,490	16,300	0.03	District of Northwest Territories, Canada...........D	........; Yellowknife	English, Eskimo, Indian
Madeira Is.	308	270,000	877	Part of Portugal (Funchal District)......D	Funchal	Portuguese
Maine	33,215	989,000	30	State (U.S.)..................................E	Augusta; Portland	
Malagasy Republic (Madagascar)†	227,800	6,200,000	27	Republic.....................................A	Tananarive	French, Malagasy
Malawi (Nyasaland)†	45,747	3,650,000	80	Self-Governing Member (Br. Comm. of Nations)......A	Zomba; Blantyre-Limbe	Bantu languages
Malaya	50,700	7,950,000	157	Part of Malaysia	Kuala Lumpur	Malay, Chinese, English
Malaysia†	128,655	11,150,000	87	Self-Governing Member (Br. Comm. of Nations)......A	Kuala Lumpur; Singapore	Malay, Chinese, English
Maldive Is.	115	95,000	826	Sultanate (U.K.) protection................B	Malé	Arabic
Mali†	464,874	4,550,000	9.8	Republic.....................................A	Bamako	Native languages, French, Arabic
Malta†	122	325,000	2,664	Self-Governing Member (Br. Comm. of Nations)......A	Valletta	English, Maltese
Manitoba	251,000	963,000	3.8	Province (Canada)..........................E	Winnipeg	English
Mariana Is. (excl. Guam)	154	11,000	71	District of U.S. Pacific Is. Trust Ter.....D	Saipan	Malay-Polynesian languages
Maritime Provinces (excl. Newfoundland)	51,963	1,489,000	29	Canada	........; Halifax	English
Marshall Is.	61	17,000	279	District of U.S. Pacific Is. Trust Ter.....D	Majuro	Malay-Polynesian languages
Martinique	425	312,000	734	Overseas Department (France)..............C	Fort-de-France	French
Maryland	10,577	3,480,000	329	State (U.S.)..................................E	Annapolis; Baltimore	
Massachusetts	8,257	5,387,000	652	State (U.S.)..................................E	Boston	
Mauritania†	419,230	1,000,000	2.4	Republic.....................................A	Nouakchott; Atar	Arabic, French
Mauritius (incl. Dependencies)	808	752,000	931	Colony (U.K.)...............................C	Port Louis	Indo-Aryan languages, French, Creole
Mexico†	761,602	40,250,000	53	Federal Republic............................A	Mexico City	Spanish
Michigan	58,216	8,269,000	142	State (U.S.)..................................E	Lansing; Detroit	
Middle America	1,053,124	76,300,000	72		........; Mexico City	
Midway Is.	2	2,500	1,250	Possession (U.S.)...........................C		English
Minnesota	84,068	3,613,000	43	State (U.S.)..................................E	St. Paul; Minneapolis	
Mississippi	47,716	2,320,000	49	State (U.S.)..................................E	Jackson	
Missouri	69,686	4,446,000	64	State (U.S.)..................................E	Jefferson City; St. Louis	
Moldavia (S.S.R.)	13,000	3,250,000	250	Soviet Socialist Republic (Sov. Un.).....E	Kishinev	Moldavian, Russian, Ukrainian
Monaco	0.8	22,000	27,500	Principality..................................A	Monaco	French, Italian
Mongolia†	592,700	1,079,000	1.8	People's Republic...........................A	Ulan Bator	Mongolian
Montana	147,138	717,000	49	State (U.S.)..................................E	Helena; Great Falls	
Montserrat	32	13,000	406	Colony (U.K.)...............................C	Plymouth	English
Morocco†	171,305	13,150,000	77	Monarchy.....................................A	Rabat; Casablanca	Arabic, Berber, French
Mozambique	297,846	6,900,000	23	Overseas Province (Portugal)..............C	Lourenço Marques	Bantu Languages, Portuguese
Muscat & Oman	82,000	580,000	7.1	Sultanate.....................................A	Muscat; Matrah	Arabic
Natal	35,284	3,270,000	93	Province (South Africa)....................E	Pietermaritzburg; Durban	English, Afrikaans, Bantu languages
Nauru	8	5,000	625	Trust Territory (Austl.-U.K.-N.Z.)........C		Malay-Polynesian languages, Chinese, English
Nebraska	77,227	1,507,000	20	State (U.S.)..................................E	Lincoln; Omaha	
Nepal†	54,362	9,900,000	180	Monarchy.....................................A	Katmandu	Nepali, Tibeto-Burman languages
Netherlands†	12,950	12,200,000	942	Monarchy.....................................A	The Hague (s' Gravenhage) and Amsterdam; Amsterdam	Dutch
Netherlands and Possessions	68,464	12,793,000	187		The Hague and Amsterdam; Amsterdam	
Netherlands Antilles	371	208,000	561	Self-Governing Territory (Netherlands).............C	Willemstad	Dutch, Spanish, English, Papiamento
Netherlands Guiana, see Surinam	....	....	....			
Netherlands New Guinea, see West Irian						
Nevada	110,540	426,000	3.9	State (U.S.)..................................E	Carson City; Las Vegas	
New Brunswick	28,354	620,000	22	Province (Canada)..........................E	Fredericton; Saint John	English, French
New Caledonia (incl. Deps.)	6,531	85,000	13	Overseas Territory (France)................C	Nouméa	Malay-Polynesian languages, French
New England	66,608	11,060,000	166	United States	........; Boston	English
Newfoundland	156,185	495,000	3.2	Province (Canada)..........................E	St. John's	English
Newfoundland (excl. Labrador)	43,359	479,000	11		........; St. John's	English
New Guinea, North-East	69,695	1,320,000	19	Part of Australian Trust Ter. of New Guinea (3 Districts)...........D	........; Lae	Papuan and Negrito languages
New Guinea, Ter. of	94,430	1,575,000	17	Trust Territory (Austl.; administered from Papua).....C	Port Moresby, Papua; Rabaul	Papuan and Negrito languages, English
New Hampshire	9,304	639,000	69	State (U.S.)..................................E	Concord; Manchester	
New Hebrides	5,700	65,000	11	Condominium (France-U.K.)................C	Vila	Malay-Polynesian languages, French
New Jersey	7,836	6,587,000	841	State (U.S.)..................................E	Trenton; Newark	
New Mexico	121,666	1,048,000	8.6	State (U.S.)..................................E	Santa Fe; Albuquerque	

†*Member of the United Nations (1964).*

Region or Political Division	Area in sq. miles	Estimated Population 1/1/1965	Pop. per sq. mi.	Form of Government and Ruling Power	Capital; Largest City (unless same)	Predominant Languages
New South Wales	309,433	4,160,000	13	State (Australia) ....E	Sydney	English
New York	49,576	17,834,000	360	State (U.S.) ....E	Albany; New York	
New Zealand†	103,736	2,625,000	25	Monarchy (Br. Commonwealth of Nations) ....A	Wellington; Auckland	English
Nicaragua†	48,600	1,620,000	33	Republic ....A	Managua	Spanish
Niedersachsen, see Lower Saxony	....	....				
Niger†	458,995	3,275,000	7.1	Republic ....A	Niamey	Hausa, Arabic, French
Nigeria†	356,669	43,200,000	121	Republic (Br. Commonwealth of Nations) ....A	Lagos; Ibadan	Hausa, Ibo, Yoruba, English
Niue	100	5,000	50	Island Territory (New Zealand) C	Alofi	Malay-Polynesian languages, English
Norfolk Island	13	1,000	77	External Territory (Australia) C	Kingston	English
North America	9,420,000	289,700,000	31		.........; New York	
North Borneo, see Sabah	....					
North Carolina	52,712	4,877,000	93	State (U.S.) ....E	Raleigh; Charlotte	
North Dakota	70,665	642,000	9.1	State (U.S.) ....E	Bismarck; Fargo	
Northern Ireland	5,459	1,460,000	267	Administrative division of United Kingdom ....E	Belfast	English
Northern Rhodesia, see Zambia	....					
Northern Territory	523,620	51,000	0.1	Territory (Australia) ....E	Darwin	English, Aboriginal languages
North Polar Regions	....	....				
North Rhine-Westphalia (Nordrhein-Westfalen)	13,119	16,540,000	1,261	State (Germany, West) ....E	Düsseldorf; Köln	German
Northwest Territories	1,304,903	25,000	0.02	Territory (Canada) ....E	Ottawa, Ontario; Yellowknife	English, Eskimo, Indian
Norway†	125,181	3,710,000	30	Monarchy ....A	Oslo	Norwegian (Riksmål and Landsmål)
Nova Scotia	21,425	761,000	36	Province (Canada) ....E	Halifax	English
Nyasaland, see Malawi	....					
Oceania (incl. Australia)	3,295,000	17,400,000	5.3		.........; Sydney	
Ohio	41,222	10,372,000	252	State (U.S.) ....E	Columbus; Cleveland	
Oklahoma	69,919	2,512,000	36	State (U.S.) ....E	Oklahoma City	
Ontario	412,582	6,670,000	16	Province (Canada) ....E	Toronto	English
Orange Free State	49,649	1,580,000	32	Province (South Africa) ....E	Bloemfontein	English, Afrikaans, Bantu languages
Oregon	96,981	1,896,000	20	State (U.S.) ....E	Salem; Portland	
Orkney Is.	376	18,400	49	Part of Scotland, U.K. (Orkney County) ....D	Kirkwall	English
Pacific Islands Trust Territory	672	90,000	134	Trust Territory (U.S.) C	Saipan	Malay-Polynesian languages, English
Pakistan (incl. part of Kashmir)†	399,373	102,700,000	257	Federal Republic (Br. Comm. of Nations) ....A	Rawalpindi and Dacca; Karachi	Urdu, Bengali, English
Pakistan, East	55,134	54,600,000	990	Province (Pakistan) ....D	Dacca	Bengali, English
Pakistan, West (incl. Karachi and part of Kashmir)	344,239	48,100,000	140	Pakistan	.........; Karachi	Urdu, English
Palestine (Gaza Area)	78	400,000	5,128	Military Government (U.A.R.) ....B	Gaza	Arabic
Panama†	29,209	1,225,000	42	Republic ....A	Panamá	Spanish
Papua (excl. New Guinea Ter.)	90,600	560,000	6.2	External Territory (Australia) C	Port Moresby	Papuan and Negrito languages, English
Paraguay†	157,048	1,920,000	12	Republic ....A	Asuncion	Spanish, Guaraní
Pennsylvania	45,333	11,511,000	254	State (U.S.) ....E	Harrisburg; Philadelphia	
Persia, see Iran	....					
Peru†	496,224	11,500,000	23	Republic ....A	Lima	Spanish, Quechua
Philippines†	115,707	31,800,000	275	Republic ....A	Quezon City; Manila	Tagalog and other Malay-Polynesian languages, English
Pitcairn (excl. Dependencies)	2	100	50	Colony (U.K.) C	Adamstown	English
Poland†	120,359	31,350,000	260	People's Republic ....A	Warsaw (Warszawa)	Polish
Portugal†	35,340	9,140,000	259	Republic ....A	Lisbon (Lisboa)	Portuguese
Portugal and Possessions	837,733	22,697,000	27		Lisbon (Lisboa)	
Portuguese Guinea	13,948	525,000	38	Overseas Province (Portugal) C	Bissau	Native languages, Portuguese
Portuguese India (former) (Goa, Damão & Diu; Dadra & Nagar Haveli)	....					
Portuguese Timor	7,332	548,000	75	Overseas Province (Portugal) C	Dili	Malay, Papuan languages, Portuguese
Prairie Provinces	757,985	3,359,000	4.4	Canada	.........; Winnipeg	English
Prince Edward Island	2,184	108,000	49	Province (Canada) ....E	Charlottetown	English
Puerto Rico	3,435	2,600,000	757	Commonwealth (U.S.) C	San Juan	Spanish, English
Qatar	8,500	65,000	7.6	Sheikdom (U.K. protection) ....B	Doha	Arabic
Quebec	594,860	5,620,000	9.4	Province (Canada) ....E	Quebec; Montreal	French, English
Queensland	667,000	1,606,000	2.4	State (Australia) ....E	Brisbane	English
Reunion	969	385,000	397	Overseas Department (France) C	St. Denis	French
Rhineland-Palatinate (Rheinland-Pfalz)	7,657	3,545,000	463	State (Germany, West) ....E	Mainz; Ludwigshafen am Rhein	German
Rhode Island	1,214	897,000	739	State (U.S.) ....E	Providence	
Rhodesia	150,333	4,200,000	28	Self-Governing Colony (U.K.) C	Salisbury	Bantu languges, English
Rhodesia & Nyasaland, Federation of, see Malawi, Rhodesia, and Zambia	....	....			....	
Rio Muni, see Equatorial Guinea	....					
Rodrigues	42	19,000	452	Dependency of Mauritius (U.K.) ....D	Port Mathurin	English, French
Romania†	91,698	19,025,000	207	People's Republic ....A	Bucharest (Bucuresti)	Romanian, Hungarian
Ruanda-Urundi, see Rwanda and Burundi	....				....	
Russian Soviet Federated Socialist Republic	6,592,850	126,300,000	19	Soviet Federated Socialist Republic (Sov. Un.) ...E	Moscow (Moskva)	Russian, Finno-Ugric languages, various Turkic, Iranian, and Mongol languages
Russian S.F.S.R. in Europe	1,919,750	92,900,000	48	Soviet Union	.........; Moscow	Russian, Finno-Ugric languages
Rwanda†	10,169	2,800,000	275	Republic ....A	Kigali	Bantu and Hamitic languages
Ryukyu Is. (Southern)	848	940,000	1,108	U.S. Military Administration ....B	Naha	Japanese
Saar (Saarland)	991	1,116,000	1,126	State (Germany, West) ....E	Saarbrücken	German
Sabah (North Borneo)	29,388	515,000	18	Administrative division of Malaysia ....E	Jesselton; Sandakan	Malay, Chinese
St. Helena (incl. Dependencies)	160	4,600	29	Colony (U.K.) C	Jamestown	English
St. Kitts-Nevis-Anguilla	153	64,000	418	Colony (U.K.) C	Basseterre	English
St. Lucia	238	94,000	395	Colony (U.K.) C	Castries	English
St. Pierre & Miquelon	93	5,000	54	Overseas Territory (France) C	St. Pierre	French
St. Vincent	150	85,000	567	Colony (U.K.) C	Kingstown	English
Samoa (Entire)	1,206	145,000	120		.........; Apia	Malay-Polynesian languages, English
San Marino	23	17,000	739	Republic ....A	San Marino	Italian
Sao Tome & Principe	372	55,000	148	Overseas Province (Portugal) C	São Tomé	Bantu languages, Portuguese
Sarawak	48,250	845,000	18	Administrative division of Malaysia ....E	.........; Kuching	Malay, Chinese, English
Sardinia	9,301	1,440,000	155	Part of Italy (3 Provinces) ....D	.........; Caglairi	Italian
Saskatchewan	251,700	947,000	3.8	Province (Canada) ....E	Regina	English
Saudi Arabia†	617,800	7,000,000	11	Monarchy ....A	Riyadh; Mecca	Arabic
Scandinavia (incl. Finland and Iceland)	510,026	20,952,000	41		.........; Copenhagen (København)	Swedish, Danish, Norwegian, Finnish, Icelandic
Schleswig-Holstein	6,045	2,405,000	398	State (Germany, West) ....E	Kiel	German
Scotland	30,411	5,215,000	171	Administrative division of United Kingdom ....E	Edinburgh; Glasgow	English
Senegal†	76,124	3,480,000	46	Republic ....A	Dakar	Wolof, Poular, French
Seychelles	156	47,000	301	Colony (U.K.) C	Victoria	French, Creole, English

† *Member of the United Nations (1964).*

193

WORLD POLITICAL INFORMATION TABLE (*Continued*)

Region or Political Division	Area in sq. miles	Estimated Population 1/1/1965	Pop. per sq. mi.	Form of Government and Ruling Power	Capital; Largest City (unless same)	Predominant Languages
Shetland Is.	550	17,500	32	Part of Scotland, U.K. (Zetland County) D	Lerwick	English
Siam, see Thailand	...	...	...	...	...	...
Sicily	9,926	4,810,000	485	Part of Italy (Sicilia Autonomous Region) D	Palermo	Italian
Sierra Leone†	27,925	2,250,000	81	Monarchy (Br. Commonwealth of Nations) A	Freetown	Temne, Mende, English
Sikkim	2,744	170,000	62	Monarchy (Indian protection) B	Gangtok	Tibeto-Burman languages
Singapore	224	1,840,000	8,214	Administrative division of Malaysia E	Singapore	Chinese, Malay, English
Solomon Is. (Austl. Trust)	4,320	62,000	14	Part of Australian Trust Ter. of New Guinea (Bougainville District) D	Sohano; Kieta	Malay-Polynesian languages
Solomon Is., British	11,500	133,000	12	Protectorate (U.K.) C	Honiara	Malay-Polynesian languages
Somali Republic†	246,202	2,350,000	9.5	Republic A	Mogadiscio	Somali
South Africa†	472,359	17,700,000	37	Federal Republic A	Pretoria and Cape Town; Johannesburg	English, Afrikaans, Bantu languages
South America	6,870,000	160,800,000	23	...	...; Buenos Aires	...
South Arabia	111,000	1,050,000	9.5	Protectorate (U.K.) C	Aden; Al Mukallā	Arabic
South Australia	380,070	1,042,000	2.7	State (Australia) E	Adelaide	English
South Carolina	31,055	2,524,000	81	State (U.S.) E	Columbia	...
South Dakota	77,047	711,000	9.2	State (U.S.) E	Pierre; Sioux Falls	...
Southern Rhodesia, see Rhodesia	...	...	...	...	...	...
South Georgia	1,450	500	0.3	Dependency of Falkland Is. (U.K.) D	Grytviken	English, Norwegian
South Polar Regions	...	...	...	...	...	...
South-West Africa	317,725	555,000	1.7	Mandate (South Africa) C	Windhoek	Bantu languages, Hottentot, Bushman, Afrikaans, English
Soviet Union (Union of Soviet Socialist Republics)†	8,599,300	229,500,000	27	Federal Soviet Republic A	Moscow (Moskva)	Russian and other Slavic languages, various Finno-Ugric, Turkic, and Mongol languages, Caucasian languages, Persian
Soviet Union in Europe	1,919,750	156,500,000	82	Soviet Union	...; Moscow (Moskva)	Russian, Ruthenian, various Finno-Ugric and Caucasian languages
Spain†	194,884	31,500,000	162	Monarchy (Regency) A	Madrid	Spanish, Catalan, Galician, Basque
Spain and Possessions	309,079	32,020,000	104	...	Madrid	...
Spanish Possessions in North Africa	82	158,000	1,927	Five Possessions (no central government) (Spain) C	...; Melilla	Spanish, Arabic, Berber
Spanish Sahara	102,703	45,000	0.4	African Province (Spain) C	Aiún	Arabic, Spanish
Spitsbergen, see Svalbard	...	...	...	...	...	...
Sudan†	967,500	13,350,000	14	Republic A	Khartoum	Arabic, native languages, English
Sumatra (Sumatera)	182,860	17,150,000	94	Part of Indonesia (6 Provinces) D	...; Medan	Bahasa Indonesia, English, Chinese
Surinam (Neth. Guiana)	55,143	385,000	7.0	Self-Governing Territory (Netherlands) C	Paramaribo	Dutch, Indo-Aryan languages
Svalbard (Spitsbergen)	24,101	No perm. pop.	...	Dependency (Norway) C	Longyearbyen	Norwegian, Russian
Swaziland	6,705	295,000	44	Territory (Protectorate)(U.K.) C	Mbabane	Swazi and other Bantu languages, English
Sweden†	173,666	7,675,000	44	Monarchy A	Stockholm	Swedish
Switzerland	15,941	6,075,000	381	Federal Republic A	Bern (Berne); Zürich	German, French, Italian
Syria†	71,498	5,100,000	71	Republic A	Damascus (Esh Sham)	Arabic
Tadzhik S.S.R.	55,250	2,410,000	44	Soviet Socialist Republic (Sov. Un.) E	Dushanbe	Tadzhik, Turkic languages, Russian
Taiwan (Formosa) (Nationalist China)†	13,884	12,250,000	882	Republic A	Taipei	Chinese
Tanganyika, see Tanzania	...	...	...	...	...	...
Tanzania (Tanganyika & Zanzibar)†	362,820	10,425,000	29	Republic (Br. Comm. of Nations) A	Dar es Salaam	Swahili and other Bantu languages, English Arabic
Tasmania	26,215	371,000	14	State (Australia) E	Hobart	English
Tennessee	42,244	3,737,000	88	State (U.S.) E	Nashville; Memphis	...
Texas	267,339	10,669,000	40	State (U.S.) E	Austin; Houston	...
Thailand (Siam)†	198,500	30,100,000	152	Monarchy A	Bangkok (Krung Thep)	Thai, Chinese
Tibet	471,660	1,300,000	2.8	Autonomous Region (China) E	Lhasa	Tibetan
Togo†	21,850	1,620,000	74	Republic A	Lomé	Native languages, French
Tokelau (Union) Is.	4	2,000	500	Island Territory (New Zealand) C	...; Fakaofo	Malay-Polynesian languages
Tonga	270	72,000	278	Protected Monarchy (U.K.) C	Nukualofa	Malay-Polynesian languages, English
Transcaucasia	71,850	11,000,000	153	Soviet Union	...; Baku	...
Transvaal	110,450	7,020,000	64	Province (South Africa) E	Pretoria; Johannesburg	English, Afrikaans, Bantu languages
Trinidad & Tobago†	1,980	960,000	485	Self-Governing Member (Br. Comm. of Nations) A	Port-of-Spain	English, Spanish
Tristan da Cunha	40	300	7.5	Dependency of St. Helena (UK.) D	Edinburgh	English
Trucial Coast	32,300	120,000	3.7	Seven Sheikdoms (no central government) (U.K. protection) B	...; Dubayy	Arabic
Tunisia†	48,332	4,600,000	95	Republic A	Tunis	Arabic, French
Turkey†	301,381	31,300,000	104	Republic A	Ankara; Istanbul	Turkish
Turkey in Europe	9,121	2,600,000	285	Turkey	...; Istanbul	Turkish
Turkmen S.S.R.	188,450	1,850,000	10	Soviet So alist Republic (Sov. Un.) E	Ashkhabad	Turkic languages, Russian
Turks & Caicos Is.	166	6,000	36	Colony (U.K.) C	Grand Turk	English
Uganda†	92,525	7,450,000	81	Self-Governing Member (Br. Commonwealth of Nations) A	Kampala	Bantu languages
Ukraine (S.S.R.)†	232,050	45,500,000	196	Soviet Socialist Republic (Sov. Un.) E	Kiev	Ukrainian, Russian
Union of Soviet Socialist Republics, see Soviet Union	...	...	...	...	...	...
United Arab Republic (Egypt)†	386,000	29,000,000	75	Republic A	Cairo (Al Qāhirah)	Arabic
United Kingdom of Great Britain & Northern Ireland†	94,214	54,500,000	578	Monarchy (Br. Commonwealth of Nations) A	London	English, Welsh, Gaelic
United Kingdom & Possessions	787,734	69,208,000	88	...	London	...
United States†	*3,675,633	193,850,000	53	Federal Republic A	Washington; New York	English
United States and Possessions	3,680,757	196,723,000	53	...	Washington; New York	English, Spanish
Upper Volta†	105,869	4,775,000	45	Republic A	Ouagadougou	Voltaic and Mande languages, French
Uruguay†	72,172	2,600,000	36	Republic A	Montevideo	Spanish
Utah	84,916	1,008,000	12	State (U.S.) E	Salt Lake City	...
Uzbek S.S.R.	171,900	10,050,000	58	Soviet Socialist Republic (Sov. Un.) E	Tashkent	Turkic languages, Sart, Russian
Vatican City (Holy See)	0.2	1,000	5,000	Ecclesiastical State A	Vatican City	Italian, Latin
Venezuela†	352,143	8,600,000	24	Federal Republic A	Caracas	Spanish
Vermont	9,609	396,000	41	State (U.S.) E	Montpelier; Burlington	...
Victoria	87,884	3,155,000	36	State (Australia) E	Melbourne	English
Vietnam (Entire)	127,574	33,400,000	262	...	...; Saigon	Annamese, Chinese
Vietnam, North	61,294	17,500,000	286	People's Republic A	Hanoi	Annamese, Chinese
Vietnam, South	66,280	15,900,000	240	Republic A	Saigon	Annamese, Chinese
Virgin Is., British	59	8,000	136	Colony (U.K.) C	Road Town	English
Virgin Is. of the U.S.	133	38,000	286	Unincorporated Territory (U.S.) C	Charlotte Amalie	English
Virginia	40,815	4,400,000	108	State (U.S.) E	Richmond; Norfolk	...
Wake I.	3	1,200	400	Possession (U.S.) C	...	English
Wales (incl. Monmouthshire)	8,017	2,675,000	334	United Kingdom	Cardiff	English, Welsh
Wallis & Futuna	106	9,000	85	Overseas Territory (France) C	Mata-Utu	Malay-Polynesian languages
Washington	68,192	3,051,000	45	State (U.S.) E	Olympia; Seattle	...
Western Australia	975,920	814,000	0.8	State (Australia) E	Perth	English
Western Samoa	1,133	124,000	111	Self-Governing Member (Br. Commonwealth of Nations) A	Apia	Malay-Polynesian languages, English
West Indies	91,110	22,250,000	244	...	...; Havana	...
West Irian	160,600	775,000	4.8	Under Indonesian Administration C	Kotabaru (Hollandia)	Various Papuan languages
West Virginia	24,181	1,797,000	74	State (U.S.) E	Charleston; Huntington	...
White Russia, see Byelorussia	...	...	...	...	...	...
Wisconsin	56,154	4,166,000	74	State (U.S.) E	Madison; Milwaukee	...
World	57,280,000	3,237,000,000	57	...	...; New York	...
Wyoming	97,914	355,000	3.6	State (U.S.) E	Cheyenne	...
Yemen†	75,300	5,000,000	66	Republic A	Şan'ā'	Arabic
Yugoslavia†	98,766	19,400,000	196	Socialist Federal Republic A	Belgrade (Beograd)	Serbo-Croatian-Slovenian, Macedonian
Yukon	207,076	17,000	0.08	Territory (Canada) E	Whitehorse	English, Eskimo, Indian
Zambia (Northern Rhodesia)†	290,537	3,650,000	13	Republic A	Lusaka; Kitwe	Bantu languages, English
Zanzibar	1,020	335,000	328	Part of Tanzania D	...; Zanzibar	Arabic, English

†*Member of the United Nations (1964).*
**Total area of the United States includes 3,548,974 square miles of land; 66,237 square miles of inland water; and 60,422 square miles of Great Lakes area, not included in any State.*
‡*Total 1965 estimated population of the United States includes 193,200,000 residents of the 50 States and D.C., and 650,000 armed forces overseas, not included in any State.*

WORLD FACTS AND COMPARISONS

MOVEMENTS OF THE EARTH

The earth makes one complete revolution around the sun every 365 days, 5 hours, 48 minutes, and 46 seconds.

The earth makes one complete rotation on its axis in 23 hours and 56 minutes.

The earth revolves in its orbit around the sun at a speed of 66,700 miles per hour.

The earth rotates on its axis at an equatorial speed of more than 1,000 miles per hour.

MEASUREMENTS OF THE EARTH

Estimated age of the earth, at least 3 billion years.
Equatorial diameter of the earth, 7,926.68 miles.
Polar diameter of the earth, 7,899.99 miles.
Mean diameter of the earth, 7,918.78 miles.
Equatorial circumference of the earth, 24,902.45 miles.
Polar circumference of the earth, 24,818.60 miles.
Difference between equatorial and polar circumference of the earth, 83.85 miles.

Weight of the earth, 6,600,000,000,000,000,000,000 tons, or 6,600 billion billion tons.
Total area of the earth, 196,940,400 square miles.
Total land area of the earth (including inland water and Antarctica), 57,280,000 square miles.

THE EARTH'S INHABITANTS

Total population of the earth is estimated to be 3,237,000,000 (January 1, 1965).
Estimated population density of the earth, 57 per square mile.

THE EARTH'S SURFACE

Highest point on the earth's surface, Mount Everest, China (Tibet)–Nepal, 29,028 feet.
Lowest point on the earth's land surface, shores of the Dead Sea, Israel-Jordan, 1,286 feet below sea level.
Greatest ocean depth, the Marianas Trench, south of Guam, Pacific Ocean, 36,198 feet.

EXTREMES OF TEMPERATURE AND RAINFALL OF THE EARTH

Highest temperature ever recorded, 136.4°F. at Azizia, Libya, Africa, on September 13, 1922.

Lowest temperature ever recorded, −126.9°F. at Vostok, Antarctica, on August 24, 1960.

Highest mean annual temperature, 88°F. at Lugh Ferrandi, Somali Republic.

Lowest mean annual temperature, −67°F at Vostok, Antarctica.

At Baguio, Luzon, in the Philippines, 46 inches of rainfall was reported in a 24-hour period, July 14–15, 1911. This is believed to be the world's record for a 24-hour rainfall.

An authenticated rainfall of 366 inches in 1 month—July, 1861—was reported at Cherrapunji, India. More than 131 inches fell in a period of 7 consecutive days in June, 1931. Average annual rainfall at Cherrapunji is 450 inches.

THE CONTINENTS

CONTINENT	Area (sq. mi.)	Population Estimated Jan. 1, 1965	Population per sq. mi.	Mean Elevation (feet)	Highest Elevation (Feet)	Lowest Elevation (Feet)	Highest Recorded Temperature	Lowest Recorded Temperature
North America	9,420,000	289,700,000	31	2,000	Mt. McKinley, United States (Alaska), 20,320	Death Valley, California, 282 below sea level	Death Valley, California, 134°F.	Snag, Yukon, Canada, −81°F.
South America	6,870,000	160,800,000	23	1,800	Mt. Aconcagua, Argentina, 22,834	Salinas Grandes, Península Valdés, Argentina, 131 below sea level	Rivadavia, Argentina, 120°F.	Sarmiento, Argentina, −27.4°F.
Europe	3,825,000	601,900,000	157	980	Mt. Elbrus, Soviet Union, 18,481	Caspian Sea, Soviet Union—Iran, 92 below sea level	Sevilla (Seville), Spain, 122°F.	Ust-Shchugor, Soviet Union, −67°F.
Asia	17,085,000	1,877,000,000	110	3,000	Mt. Everest, China (Tibet)-Nepal, 29,028	Dead Sea, Israel-Jordan, 1,286 below sea level	Tirat Zvi, Israel, 129.2°F.	Oymyakon, Soviet Union, −89.9°F.
Africa	11,685,000	290,200,000	25	1,900	Mt. Kilimanjaro, Tanganyika, 19,340	Qattara Depression, U.A.R. (Egypt), 436 below sea level	Azizia, Libya, 136.4°F.	Ifrane, Morocco, −11.2°F.
Oceania, incl. Australia	3,295,000	17,400,000	5	.....	Mt. Wilhelm, New Guinea Ter., 15,400	Lake Eyre, South Australia, 39 below sea level	Cloncurry, Queensland, Australia, 127.5°F.	Charlotte Pass, New South Wales, Australia, −8°F.
Australia	2,971,081	11,335,000	4	1,000	Mt. Kosciusko, New South Wales, 7,316	Lake Eyre, South Australia, 39 below sea level	Cloncurry, Queensland, 127.5°F.	Charlotte Pass, New South Wales, −8°F.
Antarctica	5,100,000	Uninhabited	...	6,000	Vinson Massif, 16,864	Sea level	Esperanza (Palmer Peninsula), 58.3°F.	Vostok, −126.9°F.
World	57,280,000	3,237,000,000	57	.....	Mt. Everest, China (Tibet)-Nepal, 29,028	Dead Sea, Israel-Jordan, 1,286 below sea level	Azizia, Libya, 136.4°F.	Vostok, −126.9°F.

APPROXIMATE POPULATION OF THE WORLD, 1650–1965*

AREA	1650	1750	1800	1850	1900	1914	1920	1939	1950	1965
North America	5,000,000	5,000,000	13,000,000	39,000,000	106,000,000	141,000,000	147,000,000	186,000,000	219,000,000	289,700,000
South America	8,000,000	7,000,000	12,000,000	20,000,000	38,000,000	55,000,000	61,000,000	90,000,000	111,000,000	160,800,000
Europe	100,000,000	140,000,000	190,000,000	265,000,000	400,000,000	470,000,000	453,000,000	530,000,000	601,900,000
Asia	335,000,000	476,000,000	593,000,000	754,000,000	932,000,000	1,006,000,000	1,000,000,000	1,247,000,000	1,418,000,000	1,877,000,000
Africa	100,000,000	95,000,000	90,000,000	95,000,000	118,000,000	130,000,000	140,000,000	170,000,000	199,000,000	290,200,000
Oceania, incl. Australia	2,000,000	2,000,000	2,000,000	2,000,000	6,000,000	8,000,000	9,000,000	11,000,000	13,000,000	17,400,000
Australia					4,000,000	5,000,000	6,000,000	7,000,000	8,000,000	11,335,000
World	550,000,000	725,000,000	900,000,000	1,175,000,000	1,600,000,000	1,810,000,000	1,810,000,000	2,230,000,000	2,490,000,000	3,237,000,000

Figures prior to 1965 are rounded to the nearest million.   Figures in italics represent very rough estimates.

LARGEST COUNTRIES OF THE WORLD IN POPULATION

	Population 1/1/1965		Population 1/1/1965		Population 1/1/1965
1 China (excl. Taiwan)	700,000,000	10 United Kingdom of Great Britain & Northern Ireland	54,500,000	17 Poland	31,350,000
2 India (incl. part of Kashmir)	479,000,000	11 Italy	50,900,000	18 Turkey	31,300,000
3 Soviet Union	229,500,000	12 France	48,800,000	19 Thailand	30,100,000
4 United States	193,850,000	13 Nigeria	43,200,000	20 United Arab Republic (Egypt)	29,000,000
5 Indonesia	103,350,000	14 Mexico	40,250,000	21 Korea, South	28,000,000
6 Pakistan (incl. part of Kashmir)	102,700,000	15 Philippines	31,800,000	22 Burma	24,500,000
7 Japan	97,400,000	16 Spain	31,500,000	23 Iran	23,100,000
8 Brazil	80,250,000			24 Argentina	22,200,000
9 Germany, West (incl. West Berlin)	58,550,000			25 Ethiopia	21,500,000

LARGEST COUNTRIES OF THE WORLD IN AREA

	Area (sq. mi.)		Area (sq. mi.)		Area (sq. mi.)
1 Soviet Union	8,599,300	9 Sudan	967,500	18 Indonesia	574,670
2 Canada	3,851,809	10 Algeria	919,595	19 Peru	496,224
3 China (excl. Taiwan)	3,691,500	11 Congo, The (Léopoldville)	905,565	20 Chad	495,800
4 United States	3,675,633	12 Greenland (Den.)	840,000	21 Angola (Port.)	481,351
5 Brazil	3,286,478	13 Mexico	761,602	22 South Africa	472,359
6 Australia	2,971,081	14 Libya	679,362	23 Mali	464,874
7 India (incl. part of Kashmir)	1,227,275	15 Iran	636,300	24 Niger	458,995
8 Argentina	1,072,070	16 Saudi Arabia	617,800	25 Ethiopia	457,267
		17 Mongolia	592,700		

PRINCIPAL MOUNTAINS OF THE WORLD

Height (feet)

NORTH AMERICA

McKinley, △Alaska (△United States;
  △North America)................20,320
Logan, △Canada (△St. Elias Mts.)........19,850
Citlaltépetl (Orizaba), △Mexico.........18,696
St. Elias, Alaska–Canada...............18,008
Popocatepetl, Mexico..................17,887
Foraker, Alaska......................17,395
Ixtacihuatl, Mexico..................17,343
Lucania, Yukon, Canada...............17,150
Whitney, △California.................14,495
Elbert, △Colorado (△Rocky Mts.).......14,431
Massive, Colorado...................14,418
Harvard, Colorado...................14,414
Rainier, △Washington (△Cascade Range)...14,410
Williamson, California...............14,384
Blanca Pk., Colorado
  (△Sangre de Cristo Range)..........14,317
Uncompahgre Pk., Colorado
  (△San Juan Mts.)..................14,301
Grays Pk., Colorado (△Front Range).....14,274
Evans, Colorado.....................14,264
Longs Pk., Colorado.................14,256
Colima, Nevado de, Mexico............14,235
Shasta, California..................14,162
Pikes Peak, Colorado................14,110
Wrangell, Alaska....................14,005
Tajumulco, △Guatemala (△Central America)..13,816
Mauna Kea, △Hawaii (△Hawaii I.)......13,796
Gannett Pk., △Wyoming...............13,785
Grand Teton, Wyoming...............13,766
Mauna Loa, Hawaii..................13,680
Kings Pk., △Utah...................13,498
Waddington, Canada (△Coast Mts.).....13,260
Cloud Pk., Wyoming (△Big Horn Mts.)...13,175
Wheeler Pk., △New Mexico............13,160
Boundary Pk., △Nevada..............13,145
Robson, Canada (△Canadian Rockies)...12,972
Chirripó Grande, △Costa Rica.........12,861
Granite Pk., △Montana..............12,799
Humphreys Pk., △Arizona............12,670
Borah Pk., △Idaho.................12,662
Adams, Washington................12,307
Gunnbjörn, △Greenland.............12,139
San Gorgonio, California
  (△Southern California)............11,485
Chiriquí, △Panama..................11,410
Hood, △Oregon.....................11,245
Lassen Pk., California.............10,466
Duarte, Pico, △Dominican Rep. (△West Indies)..10,417
Haleakala, Hawaii (△Maui)...........10,025
Paricutín, Mexico..................9,100
Selle, Massif de la, △Haiti.........8,793
Guadalupe Pk., △Texas.............8,751
Olympus, Washington (△Olympic Mts.)..7,954
Santa Ana, △El Salvador...........7,812
Blue Mountain Pk., △Jamaica........7,520
Harney Pk., △South Dakota (△Black Hills)..7,242
Mitchell, △North Carolina (△Appalachian Mts.)..6,684
Clingmans Dome, North Carolina–
  △Tennessee (△Great Smoky Mts.).....6,642
Turquino, Pico de, △Cuba...........6,496
Washington, △New Hampshire (△White Mts.)..6,288
Rogers, △Virginia.................5,729
Marcy, △New York (△Adirondack Mts.)..5,344
Katahdin, △Maine.................5,268
Kawaikini, Hawaii (△Kauai)........5,170
Spruce Knob, △West Virginia.......4,860
Pelée, △Martinique...............4,800
Mansfield, △Vermont (△Green Mts.)..4,393
Punta, Cerro de, △Puerto Rico.....4,389
Black Mtn., △Kentucky...........4,145
Kilauea, Hawaii (Hawaii I.).......4,090
Kaala Pk., Hawaii (△Oahu)........4,025

SOUTH AMERICA

Aconcagua, △Argentina (△Andes Mts.;
  △South America).................22,834
Ojos del Salado, Nudos, Argentina–△Chile..22,590
Pissis, Argentina.................22,546
Tupungato, Argentina–Chile........22,310
Mercedario, Argentina............22,211
Huascarán, △Peru................22,205
Llullaillaco, Argentina–Chile......22,146
Yerupaja, Peru..................21,758
Incahuasi, Argentina–Chile.......21,719
Illampu, △Bolivia...............21,490
Ancohuma, Bolivia..............21,489
Sajama, Nevado, Bolivia.........21,391
Illimani, Bolivia...............21,151
Chimborazo, △Ecuador..........20,577
Cotopaxi, Ecuador.............19,344
Misti, El, Peru...............19,144
Cristóbal Colón, △Colombia.....18,947

△ Highest mountain in state, country, range, or region named.

196

Height (feet)

Huila, Colombia (△Cordillera Central)......18,865
Bolívar (La Columna), △Venezuela.........16,411
Fitz Roy, Argentina...................11,600
Bandeira, Pico da, △Brazil.............9,462

EUROPE

Elbrus, Soviet Union (△Caucasus Mts.;
  △Europe).........................18,481
Shkhara, Soviet Union................17,059
Dykh-Tau, Soviet Union...............17,054
Kazbek, Soviet Union.................16,554
Blanc, Mont, △France (△Alps).........15,781
Rosa, Monte (Dufourspitze) △Switzerland..15,200
Rosa, Monte (Grenzgipfel) △Italy–Switzerland..15,194
Weisshorn, Switzerland...............14,803
Matterhorn, Switzerland..............14,685
Finsteraarhorn, Switzerland..........14,026
Jungfrau, Switzerland...............13,668
Gross Glockner, △Austria...........12,461
Teide, Pico de, △Spain (△Canary Is.)..12,162
Mulhacén, △Spain (continental).....11,424
Aneto, Pico de, Spain (△Pyrenees)...11,168
Perdido (Perdu), Spain.............11,007
Etna, Italy (△Sicily)............10,868
Clapier, France-Italy (△Maritime Alps)..10,817
Zugspitze, △Germany.............9,721
Coma Pedrosa, Andorra..........9,665
Musala, △Bulgaria.............9,592
Corno, Italy (△Apennines)......9,560
Olympus, △Greece.............9,550
Triglav, △Yugoslavia.........9,393
Korab, △Albania.............9,068
Cinto, France (△Corsica)......8,891
Gerlachovka, △Czechoslovakia
  (△Carpathian Mts.)............8,737
Negoi, △Romania.............8,346
Rysy Pk., Czechoslovakia......8,212
Galdhöpiggen, △Norway (△Scandinavia)..8,097
Parnassós, Greece............8,061
Idhi (Ida), Greece (△Crete)....8,058
Pico, △Portugal (△Azores Is.)..7,615
Kebnekaise, △Sweden..........6,962
Hvannadalshnúkur, △Iceland.....6,952
Malhão, △Portugal (continental)..6,532
Narodnaya, Soviet Union (△Ural Mts.)..6,184
Marmora, Punta La, Italy (△Sardinia)..6,017
Hekla, Iceland..............4,747
Nevis, Ben, △United Kingdom (△Scotland)..4,406
Haltia, △Finland...........4,344
Vesuvius, Italy............3,842
Snowdon, △Wales...........3,560
Carrantuohill, △Ireland.....3,414
Kekes, △Hungary..........3,330
Scafell Pike, △England......3,210
Stromboli, Italy..........3,038

ASIA

Everest, △China (△Tibet)–△Nepal (△Himalaya
  Mts.; △Asia; △World).............29,028
Godwin Austen (K²), △Pakistan (△Kashmir)
  (△Karakoram Range)...............28,250
Kanchenjunga, Nepal–△Sikkim.........28,168
Makalu, China (Tibet)–Nepal.........27,790
Dhaulagiri, Nepal..................26,810
Nanga Parbat, Pakistan (Kashmir)....26,660
Annapurna, Nepal..................26,504
Gasherbrum, Pakistan (Kashmir)......26,470
Gosainthan, China (Tibet)..........26,291
Nanda Devi, △India...............25,645
Rakaposhi, Pakistan (Kashmir).....25,551
Kamet, India....................25,447
Namcha Barwa, China (Tibet)......25,445
Gurla Mandhata, China (Tibet)....25,355
Ulugh Muztagh, China (△Kunlun Mts.)..25,340
Tirich Mir, Pakistan (△Hindu Kush)..25,230
Minya Konka, China.............24,900
Kangri, △Bhutan..............24,740
Communism Pk., △Soviet Union
  (△Pamir-Alay Mts.).............24,590
Pobeda Pk., China–Soviet Union (△Tien Shan)..24,409
Muztagh Ata, China............24,388
Api, Nepal...................23,398
Lenin Pk., Soviet Union.......23,382
Tengri Khan, Soviet Union.....22,940
Kailas, China (Tibet)........22,028
Hkakabo Razi, △Burma........19,296
Demavend, △Iran............18,934
Ararat, △Turkey............16,946
Carstensz, △West Irian (△New Guinea)..16,503
Klyuchevskaya, Soviet Union (△Kamchatka)..15,912
Wilhelmina, West Irian........15,518

Height (feet)

Tabun Bogdo (Khuitun), △Mongolia (△Altai
  Mts.)..........................15,266
Belukha, Soviet Union...............15,157
Turgun Uula, Mongolia..............14,052
Kinabalu, △Malaysia (△Borneo)......13,455
Hsinkao, China (△Formosa)..........13,113
Erciyas, Turkey...................12,848
Munku-Sardyk, Mongolia–Soviet Union
  (△Sayan Mts.)...................12,821
Kerintji, △Indonesia (△Sumatra)....12,484
Fuji, △Japan (△Honshu)...........12,388
Hadūr Shu'ayb, △Yemen
  (△Arabian Peninsula)............12,336
Rindjani, Indonesia (△Lombok).....12,225
Mahameru, Indonesia (△Java).......12,060
Qalate Qarrāde, △Iraq............12,000
Razih, Jabal, △Saudi Arabia......11,999
Rantemario, Indonesia (△Celebes)..11,286
Qurnet es Sa'uda, △Lebanon.......10,131
Shām, Jabal ash, △Muscat and Oman..9,902
Apo, △Philippines (△Mindanao)....9,690
Pulog, Philippines (△Luzon)......9,612
Phu Bia, △Laos................9,242
Hermon, Lebanon–△Syria.........9,232
Changpai, △Korea.............9,003
Anai Mudi, △India (peninsular)..8,841
Angka, Doi, △Thailand........8,452
Pidurutalagala, △Ceylon.......8,281
Mayon, Philippines (Luzon)....8,071
Asahi, Japan (△Hokkaido).....7,513
Tahan, Gunong, Malaysia (△Malaya)..7,186
Troodos, △Cyprus...........6,403
Kuju-San, Japan (△Kyushu)...5,866
Atzmon, △Israel............3,962
Krakatoa (Rakata), Indonesia...2,667
Carmel, Israel............1,791

AFRICA

Kilimanjaro (Kibo), △Tanzania
  (△Africa).......................19,340
Kenya, △Kenya....................17,040
Margherita, Mt., △Congo L.–△Uganda..16,795
Ras Dashan, △Ethiopia............15,158
Meru, Tanzania..................14,980
Elgon, Kenya–Uganda............14,178
Toubkal, Djebal, △Morocco (△Atlas Mts.)..13,661
Cameroon, △Cameroon..........13,354
Thabantshonyana, △Basutoland (△Southern
  Africa).......................11,425
Emi Koussi, △Chad (△Tibesti Mts.)..11,204
Injasuti, △South Africa.......11,182
Neiges, Piton des, △Reunion....10,069
Tahat, △Algeria (△Ahaggar Mts.)..9,852
Maromokotro, △Malagasy Republic..9,462
Santa Isabel, △Equatorial Guinea
  (△Fernando Poo)...............9,350
Cano, △Cape Verde Is..........9,760
Katrīnah, Jabal, △United Arab Republic
  (Egypt)......................8,652
São Tomé, Pico de, △Sao Tome...6,640

OCEANIA

Wilhelm, △New Guinea Ter........15,400
Bangeta, New Guinea Ter........13,434
Giluwe, △Papua................13,660
Victoria, Papua (△Owen Stanley Range)..13,363
Cook, △New Zealand (△South Island)..12,349
Balbi, △Solomon Is. (△Bougainville)..10,170
Ruapehu, New Zealand (△North Island)..9,175
Egmont, New Zealand...........8,260
Mauga Silisili, △Western Samoa...8,000
Orohena, △Fr. Polynesia (△Tahiti)..7,618
The Father, New Guinea Ter.
  (△Bismarck Archipelago).......7,546
Kosciusko, △Australia (△New South Wales)..7,316
Hombolt, △New Caledonia.......5,380
Panié, New Caledonia.........5,348
Ossa, Australia (△Tasmania)...5,305
Bartle Frere, Australia (△Queensland)..5,287
Woodroffe, Australia (△South Australia)..4,970
Victoria, △Fiji (△Viti Levu)..4,341
Bruce, Australia (△Western Australia)..4,024

ANTARCTICA

Vinson Massif (△Antarctica)......16,864
Kirkpatrick...................14,600
Markham.....................14,275
Andrew Jackson..............13,747
Sidley......................13,717
Wade.......................13,398

GREAT OCEANS AND SEAS OF THE WORLD

OCEANS AND SEAS	Area (sq. mi.)	Average Depth (feet)	Greatest Depth (feet)
Pacific Ocean	63,855,000	14,050	36,198
Atlantic Ocean	31,744,000	12,690	27,498
Indian Ocean	28,371,000	13,000	26,400
Arctic Ocean	5,427,000	5,010	17,880
Mediterranean Sea	967,000	4,780	15,900
South China Sea	895,000	5,420	18,090
Bering Sea	876,000	4,710	16,800
Caribbean Sea	750,000	7,310	24,580
Gulf of Mexico	596,000	4,960	14,360
Okhotsk, Sea of	590,000	2,760	11,400
East China Sea	482,000	620	9,840
Yellow Sea	480,000	150	300
Hudson Bay	476,000	420	850
Japan, Sea of	389,000	4,490	12,280
North Sea	222,000	310	2,170
Black Sea	178,000	3,610	7,360
Red Sea	169,000	1,610	7,370
Baltic Sea	163,000	180	1,440

PRINCIPAL LAKES OF THE WORLD

LAKES	Area (sq. mi.)
Caspian, Soviet Union–Iran (salt)	152,084
Superior, United States–Canada	31,820
Victoria, Kenya–Uganda–Tanzania	26,828
Aral, Soviet Union (salt)	26,518
Huron, United States–Canada	23,010
Michigan, United States	22,400
Great Bear, Canada	12,275
Baykal, Soviet Union	12,159
Great Slave, Canada	10,980
Tanganyika, Congo L.–Tanzania–Burundi–Zambia	10,965
Nyasa, Malawi–Tanzania–Mozambique	10,900
Erie, United States–Canada	9,940
Winnipeg, Canada	9,465
Ontario, United States–Canada	7,540
Ladoga, Soviet Union	7,092
Balkhash, Soviet Union	6,678
Chad, Chad–Nigeria–Cameroon	△6,300
Onega, Soviet Union	3,821
Eyre, Australia (salt)	△3,700
Titicaca, Peru–Bolivia	3,500
Athabasca, Canada	3,120
Nicaragua, Nicaragua	2,972
Rudolf, Kenya–Ethiopia (salt)	2,473
Reindeer, Canada	2,467
Issyk-Kul, Soviet Union	2,393
Urmia, Iran (salt)	△2,229
Torrens, Australia (salt)	△2,200
Albert, Uganda–Congo L.	2,162
Vänern, Sweden	2,156
Winnipegosis, Canada	2,103
Bangweulu, Zambia	△1,900
Nipigon, Canada	1,870
Manitoba, Canada	1,817
Great Salt, United States (salt)	1,700
Koko Nor, China	1,650
Dubawnt, Canada	1,600
Gairdner, Australia (salt)	△1,500
Lake of the Woods, United States–Canada	1,485
Van, Turkey (salt)	1,470

△ Due to seasonal fluctuations in water level, areas of these lakes vary considerably.

PRINCIPAL RIVERS OF THE WORLD

River	Length (miles)
Nile, Africa	4,132
Amazon, South America	3,900
Mississippi–Missouri–Red Rock, North America	3,860
Ob-Irtysh, Asia	3,461
Yangtze, Asia	3,430
Hwang Ho, Asia	2,903
Congo, Africa	2,900
Amur, Asia	2,802
Irtysh, Asia	2,747
Lena, Asia	2,653
Mackenzie, North America	2,635
Mekong, Asia	2,600
Niger, Africa	2,590
Yenisey, Asia	2,566
Missouri, North America	2,466
Paraná, South America	2,450
Mississippi, North America	2,348
Plata-Paraguay, South America	2,300
Volga, Europe	2,293
Madeira, South America	2,060
Indus, Asia	1,980
Purús, South America	1,900
St. Lawrence, North America	1,900
Rio Grande, North America	1,885
Brahmaputra, Asia	1,800
Orinoco, South America	1,800
São Francisco, South America	1,800
Yukon, North America	1,800
Danube, Europe	1,770
Darling, Australia	1,750
Salween, Asia	1,730
Euphrates, Asia	1,675
Syr Darya, Asia	1,653
Zambezi, Africa	1,650
Tocantins, South America	1,640
Araguaia, South America	1,630
Amu Darya, Asia	1,628
Kolyma, Asia	1,615
Murray, Australia	1,600
Ganges, Asia	1,550
Pilcomayo, South America	1,550
Angara, Asia	1,549
Ural, Asia	1,522
Vilyuy, Asia	1,513
Arkansas, North America	1,450
Colorado, North America (U.S.–Mexico)	1,450
Irrawaddy, Asia	1,425
Dnepr, Europe	1,420
Aldan, Asia	1,392
Negro, South America	1,305
Paraguay, South America	1,290
Kama, Europe	1,261
Juruá, South America	1,250
Xingú, South America	1,230
Don, Europe	1,224
Ucayali, South America	1,220
Columbia, North America	1,214
Saskatchewan, North America	1,205
Peace, North America	1,195
Orange, Africa	1,155
Tigris, Asia	1,150
Sungari, Asia	1,140
Pechora, Europe	1,118
Tobol, Asia	1,093
Snake, North America	1,038
Uruguay, South America	1,025
Red, North America	1,018
Churchill, North America	1,000
Marañón, South America	1,000
Ohio, North America	981
Magdalena, South America	950
Roosevelt (River of Doubt), South America	950
Godavari, Asia	930
Si, Asia	930
Oka, Europe	920
Canadian, North America	906
Dnestr, Europe	876
Brazos, North America	870
Salado, South America	870
Fraser, North America	850
Parnaíba, South America	850
Colorado, North America (Texas)	840
Rhine, Europe	820
Narbada, Asia	800
Athabasca, North America	765
Donets, Europe	735
Pecos, North America	735
Green, North America	730
Elbe, Europe	720
James, North America	710
Ottawa, North America	696
White, North America	690
Cumberland, North America	687
Gambia, Africa	680
Yellowstone, North America	671
Tennessee, North America	652
Gila, North America	630
Vistula, Europe	630
Loire, Europe	625
Tagus, Europe	625
North Platte, North America	618
Albany, North America	610
Tisza, Europe	607
Back, North America	605
Ouachita, North America	605
Cimarron, North America	600
Sava, Europe	585
Nemunas (Niemen), Europe	582
Branco, South America	580
Oder, Europe	565

PRINCIPAL ISLANDS OF THE WORLD

Island	Area (sq. mi.)
Greenland, Arctic Region	840,000
New Guinea, Oceania	316,856
Borneo, Indonesia	286,967
Madagascar, Indian Ocean	227,800
Baffin, Canadian Arctic	183,810
Sumatra, Indonesia	182,859
Honshū, Japan	88,930
Great Britain, North Atlantic Ocean	88,756
Ellesmere, Canadian Arctic	82,119
Victoria, Canadian Arctic	81,930
Celebes, Indonesia	72,986
South Island, New Zealand	58,093
Java, Indonesia	50,745
North Island, New Zealand	44,281
Cuba, West Indies	44,217
Newfoundland, North Atlantic Ocean	43,359
Luzon, Philippines	40,814
Iceland, North Atlantic Ocean	39,800
Mindanao, Philippines	36,906
Ireland, North Atlantic Ocean	32,596
Novaya Zemlya, Soviet Arctic	31,390
Hokkaidō, Japan	29,950
Hispaniola, West Indies	29,530
Sakhalin, Soviet Union	29,344
Tasmania, Australia	26,215
Ceylon, Indian Ocean	25,332
Banks, Canadian Arctic	23,230
Devon, Canadian Arctic	20,861
Tierra del Fuego, Argentina-Chile	18,600
Kyūshū, Japan	16,215
Melville, Canadian Arctic	16,141
Southampton, Hudson Bay, Canada	15,700
West Spitsbergen, Arctic Region	15,260
New Britain, Oceania	14,592
Formosa, China Sea	13,884
Hainan, South China Sea	13,127
Timor, Timor Sea	13,094
Prince of Wales, Canadian Arctic	12,830
Vancouver, Canada	12,408
Sicily, Mediterranean Sea	9,926
Somerset, Canadian Arctic	9,370
Sardinia, Mediterranean Sea	9,301
Shikoku, Japan	7,245
North East Land, Svalbard Group	6,350
Ceram, Indonesia	6,046
New Caledonia, Oceania	5,671
Flores, Indonesia	5,513
Samar, Philippines	5,124
Negros, Philippines	4,903
Palawan, Philippines	4,500
Panay, Philippines	4,448
Jamaica, West Indies	4,411
Hawaii, Oceania	4,030
Cape Breton, Canada	3,970
Bougainville, Oceania	3,880
Mindoro, Philippines	3,794
Cyprus, Mediterranean Sea	3,572
Kodiak, Gulf of Alaska	3,569
Puerto Rico, West Indies	3,435
Corsica, Mediterranean Sea	3,367
Crete, Mediterranean Sea	3,238
New Ireland, Oceania	3,205
Leyte, Philippines	3,090
Wrangel, Soviet Arctic	2,819
Guadalcanal, Oceania	2,500
Long Island, United States	1,620

LARGEST METROPOLITAN AREAS AND CITIES OF THE WORLD, 1964

This table lists every metropolitan area in the world with 1,000,000 or more population. For ease of comparison, each metropolitan area has been defined by Rand McNally & Company according to consistent rules. A metropolitan area includes a central city, neighboring communities linked to it by continuous built-up areas, and more distant communities if the bulk of their population is supported by commuters to the central city. All populations are estimates for January 1, 1964. The "city proper" figures refer to the area locally considered to be the city, provided it is under a single municipal government. Some metropolitan areas, such as Tōkyō–Yokohama, have more than one central city; in such cases the "city proper" figure is for the first-named city only.

Rank 1964		Estimated Population, 1/1/1964 Metropolitan Area	City Proper	Rank 1964		Estimated Population, 1/1/1964 Metropolitan Area	City Proper
1	New York, New York	16,325,000	8,085,000	71	Saigon, Vietnam (South)	1,700,000	1,350,000
2	Tōkyō–Yokohama, Japan	15,400,000	8,850,000	72	Donetsk–Makeyevka, Soviet Union	1,700,000	785,000
3	London, England	11,025,000	3,175,000	73	Baltimore, Maryland	1,700,000	930,000
4	Ōsaka–Kōbe, Japan	8,700,000	3,250,000	74	Liverpool, England	1,685,000	738,000
5	Moscow (Moskva), Soviet Union	8,450,000	6,475,000	75	Nanking (Nanching), China	1,650,000	1,650,000
6	Paris, France	8,000,000	2,800,000	76	Sian (Hsian), China	1,600,000	1,600,000
7	Buenos Aires, Argentina	7,700,000	2,950,000	77	Warsaw (Warszawa), Poland	1,575,000	1,210,000
8	Shanghai, China	7,600,000	10,400,000▲	78	Köln (Cologne), Germany (West)	1,550,000	835,000
9	Los Angeles, California	7,475,000	2,660,000	79	Kyōto, Japan	1,550,000	1,330,000
10	Chicago, Illinois	7,090,000	3,575,000	80	Havana (Habana), Cuba	1,550,000	875,000
11	Calcutta, India	6,700,000	3,000,000	81	Minneapolis–St. Paul, Minnesota	1,540,000	470,000
12	Mexico City, Mexico	6,100,000	3,050,000	82	Miami–Fort Lauderdale, Florida	1,500,000	335,000
13	São Paulo, Brazil	5,450,000	4,425,000	83	München (Munich), Germany (West)	1,500,000	1,175,000
14	Rio de Janeiro, Brazil	5,250,000	3,600,000	84	Lahore, Pakistan	1,450,000	1,350,000
15	Essen–Dortmund–Duisburg, Germany (West)	5,200,000	729,000	85	Frankfurt am Main, Germany (West)	1,450,000	695,000
16	Bombay, India	4,700,000	4,500,000	86	Taipei, Taiwan	1,425,000	1,025,000
17	Cairo (Al Qāhirah), United Arab Republic	4,600,000	3,800,000	87	Gorkiy (Gorki), Soviet Union	1,425,000	1,060,000
18	Peking (Peiping), China	4,200,000	7,000,000▲	88	Kitakyūshū–Shimonoseki, Japan	1,425,000	1,065,000
19	Detroit–Windsor, Michigan–Canada	4,170,000	1,610,000	89	Houston, Texas	1,420,000	1,045,000
20	Philadelphia, Pennsylvania	4,150,000	2,040,000	90	Stuttgart, Germany (West)	1,415,000	642,000
21	Berlin, Germany	4,025,000	2,180,000	91	Bucharest (Bucureşti), Romania	1,400,000	1,265,000
22	Leningrad, Soviet Union	4,000,000	3,100,000	92	Kiev (Kiyev), Soviet Union	1,390,000	1,280,000
23	San Francisco–Oakland–San Jose, California	3,730,000	750,000	93	Copenhagen (København), Denmark	1,380,000	705,000
24	Boston, Massachusetts	3,480,000	665,000	94	Ahmadabad, India	1,375,000	1,250,000
25	Tientsin (Tienching), China	3,400,000	3,800,000▲	95	Lisbon (Lisboa), Portugal	1,375,000	825,000
26	Victoria, Hong Kong	3,275,000	725,000	96	Buffalo–Niagara Falls, New York–Canada	1,370,000	515,000
27	Seoul, Korea (South)	3,200,000	3,125,000	97	Leeds–Bradford, England	1,360,000	514,000
28	Djakarta, Indonesia	3,150,000	3,150,000	98	Bogotá, Colombia	1,350,000	1,150,000
29	Manila, Philippines	2,900,000	1,190,000	99	Torino (Turin), Italy	1,350,000	1,110,000
30	Delhi–New Delhi, India	2,900,000	2,575,000	100	Chengtu, China	1,350,000	1,350,000
31	Manchester, England	2,850,000	652,000	101	Hyderabad, India	1,350,000	950,000
32	Milano (Milan), Italy	2,775,000	1,675,000	102	Montevideo, Uruguay	1,335,000	1,180,000
33	Mukden (Shenyang), China	2,650,000	2,650,000	103	Bangalore, India	1,325,000	950,000
34	Birmingham, England	2,640,000	1,115,000	104	Cincinnati, Ohio	1,315,000	495,000
35	Wuhan, China	2,600,000	2,600,000	105	Milwaukee, Wisconsin	1,315,000	760,000
36	Madrid, Spain	2,575,000	2,450,000	106	Pusan, Korea (South)	1,300,000	1,300,000
37	Rome (Roma), Italy	2,500,000	2,340,000	107	Dairen (Talien), China	1,300,000	1,250,000
38	Santiago, Chile	2,400,000	640,000	108	Tsingtao (Chingtao), China	1,300,000	1,300,000
39	Sydney, Australia	2,340,000	168,000	109	Recife (Pernambuco), Brazil	1,250,000	900,000
40	Lima, Peru	2,300,000	1,975,000	110	Taiyüan (Yangkü), China	1,250,000	1,250,000
41	Hamburg, Germany (West)	2,300,000	1,855,000	111	Kharkov, Soviet Union	1,250,000	1,020,000
42	Washington, D.C.	2,265,000	785,000	112	Baku, Soviet Union	1,235,000	710,000
43	Budapest, Hungary	2,265,000	1,920,000	113	Tashkent, Soviet Union	1,205,000	1,055,000
44	Cleveland, Ohio	2,260,000	865,000	114	San Diego–Tijuana, California–Mexico	1,200,000	640,000
45	Montreal, Canada	2,250,000	1,225,000	115	Fushun, China	1,200,000	1,200,000
46	Johannesburg–Germiston, South Africa	2,200,000	575,000	116	Dallas, Texas	1,180,000	750,000
47	Barcelona, Spain	2,175,000	1,650,000	117	Stockholm, Sweden	1,180,000	800,000
48	St. Louis, Missouri	2,155,000	720,000	118	Casablanca, Morocco	1,175,000	1,100,000
49	Nagoya, Japan	2,150,000	1,750,000	119	Mannheim–Ludwigshafen–Heidelberg, Germany (West)	1,170,000	323,000
50	Madras, India	2,150,000	1,825,000	120	Newcastle-on-Tyne, England	1,155,000	262,000
51	Bangkok (Krung Thep), Thailand	2,100,000	1,500,000	121	Changchun (Hsinking), China	1,150,000	1,150,000
52	Karachi, Pakistan	2,100,000	1,550,000	122	Surabaja, Indonesia	1,125,000	1,050,000
53	Melbourne, Australia	2,055,000	75,000	123	Atlanta, Georgia	1,115,000	515,000
54	Chungking (Chungching), China	2,050,000	2,400,000▲	124	Kansas City, Missouri	1,110,000	525,000
55	Canton (Kuangchou), China	2,050,000	2,050,000	125	Prague (Praha), Czechoslovakia	1,110,000	1,011,000
56	Vienna (Wien), Austria	2,025,000	1,660,000	126	Dnepropetrovsk, Soviet Union	1,090,000	755,000
57	Tehrān, Iran	2,000,000	1,900,000	127	Kanpur (Cawnpore), India	1,075,000	950,000
58	Athens (Athínai), Greece	1,975,000	650,000	128	Kuybyshev, Soviet Union	1,075,000	920,000
59	Brussels (Bruxelles), Belgium	1,975,000	169,000	129	Bandung, Indonesia	1,075,000	1,025,000
60	Pittsburgh, Pennsylvania	1,975,000	575,000	130	Novosibirsk, Soviet Union	1,065,000	1,000,000
61	Toronto, Canada	1,960,000	665,000	131	Kunming, China	1,050,000	1,050,000
62	Katowice–Zabrze–Bytom, Poland	1,960,000	285,000	132	Düsseldorf, Germany (West)	1,050,000	704,000
63	Harbin (Haerhpin), China	1,950,000	1,950,000	133	Sverdlovsk, Soviet Union	1,040,000	885,000
64	Istanbul, Turkey	1,950,000	1,625,000	134	Seattle, Washington	1,035,000	565,000
65	Glasgow, Scotland	1,885,000	1,030,000	135	Tsinan (Chinan), China	1,025,000	1,025,000
66	Singapore, Malaysia	1,825,000	1,100,000	136	Denver, Colorado	1,020,000	520,000
67	Napoli (Naples), Italy	1,765,000	1,225,000	137	Antwerpen (Antwerp), Belgium	1,015,000	248,000
68	Caracas, Venezuela	1,750,000	890,000	138	Rotterdam, Netherlands	1,010,000	732,000
69	Amsterdam, Netherlands	1,730,000	866,000	139	Lyon, France	1,000,000	545,000
70	Alexandria (Al Iskandarīyah), United Arab Republic	1,700,000	1,650,000				

▲ Municipal boundaries of Shanghai, Peking, Tientsin, and Chungking now include extensive rural zones, which have been excluded in estimating their metropolitan populations.

PRINCIPAL WORLD CITIES AND POPULATIONS

This table includes all cities with 500,000 or more population, as well as many smaller cities of importance. The populations for all United States cities are estimates for January 1, 1965. The populations for foreign cities listed in the table of World Metropolitan Areas on the preceding page are estimates for January 1, 1964. For other cities, the populations are recent census figures or official estimates. Metropolitan populations are given for as many cities as possible, and identified by a star symbol (*). Some metropolitan areas, such as Minneapolis-St. Paul, include more than one large city. In such cases, the entry for the first named city carries the entire metropolitan population, and other cities in the metropolitan area carry a reference to the first-named city with a star symbol.

Aachen, Germany (West) (*450,000)	174,700
Abidjan, Ivory Coast	180,000
Accra, Ghana	337,800
Addis Ababa, Ethiopia	448,512
Adelaide, Australia (*660,000)	21,300
Aden, Aden (*138,441)	99,285
Agra, India (*508,680)	462,020
Ahmadabad, India (*1,375,000)	1,250,000
Akron, Ohio (*615,000)	298,000
Albany, New York (*605,000)	127,000
Aleppo (Halab), Syria	425,467
Alexandria (Al Iskandarīyah), U.A.R. (*1,700,000)	1,650,000
Algiers (Alger), Algeria (*995,000)	883,879
Allahabad, India (*430,730)	411,955
Alma-Ata, Soviet Union	580,000
'Ammān, Jordan (*246,475)	224,974
Amritsar, India (*398,047)	376,295
Amsterdam, Netherlands (*1,730,000)	866,000
Ankara (Angora), Turkey	650,067
Anshan, China	805,000
Antwerpen (Antwerp), Belgium (*1,015,000)	248,000
Apia, Western Samoa	21,699
Asunción, Paraguay	305,200
Athens (Athínai), Greece (*1,975,000)	650,000
Atlanta, Georgia (*1,230,000)	535,000
Auckland, New Zealand (*499,700)	147,900
Baghdad, Iraq (*650,000)	355,958
Baku, Soviet Union (*1,235,000)	710,000
Baltimore, Maryland (*1,730,000)	925,000
Bamako, Mali	135,000
Banaras (Benares), India (*489,864)	471,258
Bandung, Indonesia (*1,075,000)	1,025,000
Bangalore, India (*1,325,000)	950,000
Bangkok (Krung Thep), Thailand (*2,100,000)	1,500,000
Bangui, Central African Republic	79,600
Barcelona, Spain (*2,175,000)	1,650,000
Barranquilla, Colombia	431,000
Basel (Bâle), Switzerland (*505,000)	211,500
Beirut (Beyrouth), Lebanon	400,000
Belém (Pará), Brazil (*405,000)	359,988
Belfast, Northern Ireland (*580,000)	412,500
Belgrade (Beograd), Yugoslavia	585,234
Belo Horizonte, Brazil (*775,000)	642,912
Bengasi (Banghāzī), Libya	136,600
Berlin, East, Germany (*Berlin)	1,061,200
Berlin, West, Germany (*4,025,000)	2,180,000
Bern (Berne), Switzerland (*225,000)	167,400
Bilbao, Spain (*565,000)	297,942
Birmingham, Alabama (*655,000)	345,000
Birmingham, England (*2,640,000)	1,115,000
Bogotá, Colombia (*1,350,000)	1,150,000
Bologna, Italy	475,700
Bombay, India (*4,700,000)	4,500,000
Bonn, Germany (West) (*285,000)	143,000
Bordeaux, France (*480,000)	249,688
Boston, Massachusetts (*3,540,000)	670,000
Bradford, England (*Leeds)	297,000
Brasília, Brazil	150,000
Brazzaville, Congo	133,700
Bremen, Germany (West)	581,000
Brighton, England (*405,000)	162,900
Brisbane, Australia (*649,500)	619,000
Bristol, England (*605,000)	433,900
Brussels (Bruxelles), Belgium (*1,975,000)	169,000
Bucharest (Bucureşti), Romania (*1,400,000)	1,265,000
Budapest, Hungary (*2,265,000)	1,920,000
Buenos Aires, Argentina (*7,700,000)	2,950,000
Buffalo, New York (*1,370,000)	505,000
Cairo (Al Qāhirah), U.A.R. (*4,600,000)	3,800,000
Calcutta, India (*6,700,000)	3,000,000
Cali, Colombia	591,000
Canberra, Australia	77,644
Canton (Kuangchou), China (*2,050,000)	2,050,000
Cape Town, South Africa (*807,211)	508,341
Caracas, Venezuela (*1,750,000)	890,000
Cardiff, Wales (*605,000)	260,600
Casablanca, Morocco (*1,175,000)	1,100,000
Changchun (Hsinking), China (*1,150,000)	1,150,000
Changsha, China	703,000
Chelyabinsk, Soviet Union (*950,000)	767,000
Chengchow, China	766,000
Chengtu, China (*1,350,000)	1,350,000
Chicago, Illinois (*7,225,000)	3,520,000
Chittagong, Pakistan (364,205)	180,000
Chungking (Chungching), China (2,400,000▲)	*2,050,000
Cincinnati, Ohio (*1,310,000)	495,000
Cleveland, Ohio (*2,250,000)	855,000
Colombo, Ceylon (*800,000)	510,947
Columbus, Ohio (*825,000)	540,000
Conakry, Guinea (*109,500)	43,000
Copenhagen (København), Denmark (*1,380,000)	705,000
Córdoba, Argentina	580,000
Coventry, England (*580,000)	313,900
Dacca, Pakistan (*750,000)	362,006
Dairen (Talien), China (*1,300,000)	1,250,000
Dakar, Senegal (*435,000)	374,700
Dallas, Texas (*1,280,000)	790,000
Damascus (Dimashq), Syria	529,963
Dar es Salaam, Tanzania	128,742
Dayton, Ohio (*720,000)	260,000
Delhi, India (*2,900,000)	2,575,000
Denver, Colorado (*1,035,000)	520,000
Detroit, Michigan (*4,370,000)	1,600,000
Djakarta (Batavia), Indonesia (*3,150,000)	3,150,000
Dnepropetrovsk, Soviet Union (*1,090,000)	755,000
Donetsk (Stalino), Soviet Union (*1,700,000)	785,000
Dortmund, Germany (West) (*Essen)	652,000
Dresden, Germany (East) (*625,000)	494,600
Dublin (Baile Átha Cliath), Ireland (*690,000)	537,448
Duisburg, Germany (West) (*Essen)	497,500
Durban, South Africa (*659,934)	560,010
Düsseldorf, Germany (West) (*1,050,000)	704,000
Edinburgh, Scotland (*615,000)	476,200
Edmonton, Canada (*337,568)	281,027
Elisabethville, The Congo	183,700
El Paso, Texas (*650,000)	309,000
Essen, Germany (West) (*5,200,000)	729,000
Firenze (Florence), Italy (*560,000)	455,000
Foochow, China	616,000
Fortaleza, Brazil (*525,000)	354,942
Fort-Lamy, Chad	91,700
Fort Worth, Texas (*540,000)	360,000
Frankfurt [am Main], Germany, (West) (*1,450,000)	695,000
Freetown, Sierra Leone	128,000
Fukuoka, Japan (*790,000)	647,122
Fushun, China (*1,200,000)	1,200,000
Gdańsk (Danzig), Poland (*550,000)	301,700
Genève (Geneva), Switzerland (*305,000)	174,700
Genova (Genoa), Italy (*865,000)	825,500
Gent (Ghent), Belgium (*330,000)	157,811
Georgetown, British Guiana (*148,402)	79,965
Glasgow, Scotland (*1,885,000)	1,030,000
Gorkiy (Gorki), Soviet Union (*1,425,000)	1,060,000
Göteborg, Sweden (*515,000)	410,700
Guadalajara, Mexico (*830,000)	736,800
Guatemala, Guatemala	417,200
Guayaquil, Ecuador	510,800
Halle [an der Saale], Germany (East) (*425,000)	278,000
Hamburg, Germany (West) (*2,300,000)	1,855,000
Hamilton, Canada (*395,189)	273,991
Hangchow, China	784,000
Hannover (Hanover), Germany (West) (*740,000)	567,400
Hanoi, Vietnam (North) (*643,576)	414,620
Harbin (Haerhpin), China (*1,950,000)	1,950,000
Hartford, Connecticut (*885,000)	158,000
Havana (Habana), Cuba (*1,550,000)	875,000
Helsinki, Finland (*635,000)	476,400
Hiroshima, Japan (*560,000)	431,336
Honolulu, Hawaii (*560,000)	315,000
Houston, Texas (*1,490,000)	1,100,000
Howrah, India (*Calcutta)	512,598
Huhehot (Kweisui), China	314,000
Hull (Kingston-upon-Hull), England (*360,000)	301,000
Hyderabad, India (*1,350,000)	950,000
Hyderabad, Pakistan (*460,000)	416,441
Ibadan, Nigeria	459,196
Inchŏn, Korea (South)	430,100
Indianapolis, Indiana (*900,000)	530,000
Indore, India	394,941
Irkutsk, Soviet Union	390,000
Istanbul, Turkey (*1,950,000)	1,625,000
Ivanovo, Soviet Union	368,000
Izmir (Smyrna), Turkey (*500,000)	360,829
Jabalpur (Jubbulpore), India (*367,014)	295,375
Jacksonville, Florida (*525,000)	198,000
Jaipur, India	403,444
Jamshedpur, India (*328,044)	291,791
Jerusalem, Israel (*260,000)	175,500
Jerusalem, Jordan (*Jerusalem)	60,488
Johannesburg, South Africa (*2,200,000)	575,000
Juddah, Saudi Arabia	147,900
Kabul, Afghanistan	236,000
Kalgan, China	299,300
Kampala, Uganda (*123,332)	46,735
Kanpur (Cawnpore), India (*1,075,000)	950,000
Kansas City, Missouri (*1,140,000)	530,000
Karachi, Pakistan (*2,100,000)	1,550,000
Karaganda, Soviet Union	462,000
Karl-Marx-Stadt (Chemnitz), Germany (East) (*400,000)	287,400
Katmandu, Nepal	122,500
Katowice, Poland (*1,960,000)	285,000
Kaunas, Soviet Union	247,000
Kawasaki, Japan (*Tōkyō)	632,975
Kazan, Soviet Union	725,000
Khabarovsk, Soviet Union	377,000
Kharkov, Soviet Union (*1,250,000)	1,020,000
Khartoum, Sudan (*370,000)	132,000
Kiev (Kiyev), Soviet Union (*1,390,000)	1,280,000
Kigali, Rwanda	4,000
Kingston, Jamaica	421,718
Kirin, China	568,000
Kitakyūshū, Japan (*1,425,000)	1,065,000
Kōbe, Japan (*Ōsaka)	1,113,977
Köln (Cologne), Germany (West) (*1,550,000)	835,000
Kowloon, Hong Kong (*Victoria)	726,976
Kraków (Cracow), Poland	495,600
Krasnoyarsk, Soviet Union	483,000
Krivoy Rog, Soviet Union	448,000
Kuala Lumpur, Malaysia (*400,000)	316,230
Kunming, China (*1,050,000)	1,050,000
Kuwait, Kuwait (*151,247)	96,860
Kuybyshev, Soviet Union (*1,075,000)	920,000
Kweiyang, China	504,000
Kyoto, Japan (*1,550,000)	1,330,000
Lagos, Nigeria	665,246
Lahore, Pakistan (*1,450,000)	1,350,000
Lanchow, China	699,000
La Paz, Bolivia	450,000
La Plata, Argentina (*410,000)	295,000
Leeds, England (*1,360,000)	514,000
Le Havre, France (*223,000)	183,776
Leicester, England (*430,000)	270,400
Leipzig, Germany (East) (*735,000)	587,200
Leningrad, Soviet Union (*4,000,000)	3,100,000
Léopoldville, The Congo	402,500
Libreville, Gabon	31,027
Liège, Belgium (*550,000)	153,240
Lille, France (*865,000)	193,096
Lima, Peru (*2,300,000)	1,975,000
Lisbon (Lisboa), Portugal (*1,375,000)	825,000
Liverpool, England (*1,685,000)	738,000
Łódź, Poland (*875,000)	726,800
Lomé, Togo	80,000
London, England (*11,025,000)	3,175,000
Los Angeles, California (*7,635,000)	2,695,000
Louisville, Kentucky (*795,000)	392,000
Lourenço Marques, Mozambique (*183,800)	78,500
Loyang, China	171,200
Luanda, Angola	225,000
Lucknow, India (*675,000)	595,440
Lusaka, Zambia	114,400
Luxembourg, Luxembourg	73,900
Lvov, Soviet Union	469,000
Lyon (Lyons), France (*1,000,000)	545,000
Macao, Macao (*169,299)	153,630
Madras, India (*2,150,000)	1,825,000
Madrid, Spain (*2,575,000)	2,450,000
Madura, India (*500,000)	424,810
Magdeburg, Germany (East) (*370,000)	265,500
Managua, Nicaragua	234,800
Manchester, England (*2,850,000)	652,000
Manila, Philippines (*2,900,000)	1,190,000
Mannheim, Germany (West) (*1,170,000)	323,000
Maracaibo, Venezuela	432,902
Marseille (Marseilles), France (*870,000)	778,071
Mecca (Makkah), Saudi Arabia	158,900
Medan, Indonesia	466,370
Medellín, Colombia (*750,000)	614,000
Melbourne, Australia (*2,055,000)	75,000
Memphis, Tennessee (*700,000)	525,000
Mexico City, Mexico (*6,100,000)	3,050,000
Miami, Florida (*1,500,000)	325,000
Middlesbrough, England (*545,000)	158,100
Milano (Milan), Italy (*2,775,000)	1,675,000
Milwaukee, Wisconsin (*1,330,000)	765,000
Minneapolis, Minnesota (*1,590,000)	465,000
Minsk, Soviet Union	644,000
Mogadiscio, Somali Rep	90,600
Monrovia, Liberia	81,000
Monterrey, Mexico (*695,000)	596,939
Montevideo, Uruguay (*1,335,000)	1,180,000
Montreal, Canada (*2,250,000)	1,225,000
Moscow (Moskva), Soviet Union (*8,450,000)	6,475,000
Mukden (Shenyang), China (*2,650,000)	2,650,000
München (Munich), Germany (West) (*1,500,000)	1,175,000
Nagasaki, Japan	344,153
Nagoya, Japan (*2,150,000)	1,750,000
Nagpur, India (*700,000)	643,659
Nairobi, Kenya	266,795
Nanchang, China	508,000
Nanking (Nanching), China (*1,650,000)	1,650,000
Napoli (Naples), Italy (*1,765,000)	1,225,000
Nashville, Tennessee (*450,000)	261,000
Newark, New Jersey (*New York)	395,000
Newcastle-on-Tyne, England (*1,155,000)	262,000
New Delhi, India (*Delhi)	261,545
New Orleans, Louisiana (*985,000)	655,000
New York, New York (*16,550,000)	8,080,000
Niamey, Niger	30,030
Nice, France	292,958
Norfolk, Virginia (*655,500)	322,000
Nottingham, England (*630,000)	315,100
Novokuznetsk (Stalinsk), Soviet Union	410,000
Novosibirsk, Soviet Union (*1,065,000)	1,000,000
Nürnberg (Nuremberg), Germany (West) (*675,000)	466,200
Oakland, California (*San Francisco)	378,000
Odessa, Soviet Union	709,000
Oklahoma City, Oklahoma (*585,000)	380,000
Omaha, Nebraska (*495,000)	340,000
Omsk, Soviet Union	674,000
Ōsaka, Japan (*8,700,000)	3,250,000
Oslo, Norway (*635,000)	477,100
Ottawa, Canada (*429,750)	268,206
Ouagadougou, Upper Volta	59,126
Palembang, Indonesia	458,661
Palermo, Italy	614,000
Panamá, Panama (*330,000)	306,000
Paotow, China	400,000
Paris, France (*8,000,000)	2,800,000
Patna, India (*450,000)	363,700
Peking (Peiping), China (7,000,000▲)	*4,200,000
Penang (George Town), Malaysia (*325,000)	234,903
Perm, Soviet Union	722,000
Perth, Australia (*485,000)	95,000
Philadelphia, Pennsylvania (*4,200,000)	2,030,000
Phnom Penh, Cambodia	403,500
Phoenix, Arizona (*810,000)	520,000
Pittsburgh, Pennsylvania (*1,955,000)	560,000
Poona, India (*800,000)	597,562
Port-au-Prince, Haiti	240,000
Portland, Oregon (*795,000)	380,000
Pôrto (Oporto), Portugal (*750,000)	303,424
Pôrto Alegre, Brazil (*850,000)	617,629
Port-of-Spain, Trinidad & Tobago (*170,000)	93,954
Porto Novo, Dahomey	65,000
Port Said (Būr Sa'īd), U.A.R.	245,318
Portsmouth, England (*445,000)	224,900
Poznań, Poland	422,700
Prague (Praha), Czechoslovakia (*1,110,000)	1,011,000
Pretoria, South Africa (*422,590)	303,684
Providence, Rhode Island (*850,000)	195,000
Pusan, Korea (South) (*1,300,000)	1,300,000
Pyŏngyang, Korea (North)	653,100
Quebec, Canada (*357,568)	171,979
Quezon City, Philippines (*Manila)	397,990
Quito, Ecuador	355,200
Rabat, Morocco (*310,000)	227,445
Rangoon, Burma	821,800
Rawalpindi, Pakistan (*340,175)	197,370
Recife (Pernambuco), Brazil (*1,250,000)	900,000
Reykjavík, Iceland (*92,000)	75,000
Richmond, Virginia (*455,000)	223,000
Rīga, Soviet Union	632,000
Rio de Janeiro, Brazil (*5,250,000)	3,600,000
Riyadh (Ar Riyād), Saudi Arabia	169,185
Rochester, New York (*645,000)	305,000
Rome (Roma), Italy (*2,500,000)	2,340,000
Rosario, Argentina	595,000
Rostov [-na-Donu], Soviet Union (*780,000)	689,000
Rotterdam, Netherlands (*1,010,000)	732,000
Sacramento, California (*655,000)	265,000
Saigon, Vietnam (South) (*1,700,000)	1,350,000
St. Louis, Missouri (*2,195,000)	710,000
St. Paul, Minnesota (*Minneapolis)	308,000
St. Petersburg, Florida (*415,000)	200,000
Salisbury, Rhodesia (*315,300)	220,000
Salt Lake City, Utah (*488,000)	195,000
Salvador, Brazil	630,878
Şan'ā', Yemen	89,000
San Antonio, Texas (*790,000)	645,000
San Bernardino, California (*575,000)	102,000
San Diego, California (*1,210,000)	636,000
San Francisco, California (*3,805,000)	745,000
San Jose, California (*San Francisco)	308,000
San José, Costa Rica (*320,000)	101,162
San Juan, Puerto Rico (*660,000)	432,377
San Salvador, Salvador (*360,000)	255,744
Santiago, Chile (*2,400,000)	640,000
Santo Domingo, Dominican Republic	367,053
Santos, Brazil (*400,000)	262,048
São Paulo, Brazil (*5,450,000)	4,425,000
Sapporo, Japan (*615,000)	523,839
Saratov, Soviet Union (*770,000)	644,000
Seattle, Washington (*1,045,000)	565,000
Semarang, Indonesia	487,006
Sendai, Japan (*515,000)	425,272
Seoul, Korea (South) (*3,200,000)	3,125,000
Sevilla (Seville), Spain	442,300
Shanghai, China (10,400,000▲)	*7,600,000
Sheffield, England (*735,000)	495,300
Shihchiachuang, China	598,000
Shizuoka, Japan (*485,000)	323,819
Sian (Hsian), China (*1,600,000)	1,600,000
Singapore, Malaysia (*1,825,000)	1,100,000
Sofia (Sofiya), Bulgaria (*769,700)	695,400
Soochow (Suchou), China	663,000
Southampton, England (*355,000)	207,200
Springfield, Massachusetts (*495,000)	174,000
Srinagar, India (*295,084)	285,257
Stockholm, Sweden (*1,180,000)	800,000
Stoke-on-Trent, England (*440,000)	266,100
Strasbourg, France (*320,000)	228,971
Stuttgart, Germany (West) (*1,415,000)	642,000
Suchow, China	676,000
Sucre, Bolivia	55,000
Suez, U.A.R.	203,610
Surabaja, Indonesia (*1,125,000)	1,050,000
Sverdlovsk, Soviet Union (*1,040,000)	885,000
Sydney, Australia (*2,340,000)	168,000
Syracuse, New York (*485,000)	216,000
Szczecin (Stettin), Poland	286,300
Taegu, Korea (South)	716,600
Taipei, Taiwan (*1,425,000)	1,025,000
Taiyüan (Yangkü), China (*1,250,000)	1,250,000
Tallinn, Soviet Union	311,000
Tampa, Florida (*395,000)	305,000
Tananarive, Malagasy Republic	254,271
Tangier, Morocco	141,714
Tangshan, China	800,000
Tashkent, Soviet Union (*1,205,000)	1,055,000
Tbilisi, Soviet Union (*860,000)	768,000
Tegucigalpa, Honduras	133,887
Tehrān, Iran (*2,000,000)	1,900,000
Tel Aviv [-Jaffa], Israel (*715,000)	392,900
The Hague ('s Gravenhage), Netherlands (*830,000)	602,400
Thessaloniki (Salonika), Greece (*373,635)	250,920
Tientsin (Tienching), China (3,800,000▲)	*3,400,000
Tiranë, Albania	140,300
Tōkyō, Japan (*15,400,000)	8,850,000
Toledo, Ohio (*540,000)	354,000
Torino (Turin), Italy (*1,350,000)	1,110,000
Toronto, Canada (*1,960,000)	665,000
Tripoli (Tarābulus), Libya	212,600
Tsinan (Chinan), China (*1,025,000)	1,025,000
Tsingtao (Chingtao), China (*1,300,000)	1,300,000
Tsitsihar, China	668,000
Tula, Soviet Union	351,000
Tunis, Tunisia	410,000
Ufa, Soviet Union	630,000
Ulan Bator, Mongolia	195,300
Usumbura, Burundi	50,000
Utrecht, Netherlands (*410,000)	264,200
Valencia, Spain (*660,000)	505,066
Valletta, Malta (*208,000)	18,300
Valparaíso, Chile (*440,000)	252,900
Vancouver, Canada (*790,165)	384,522
Venezia (Venice), Italy	355,700
Victoria, Hong Kong (*3,275,000)	725,000
Vienna (Wien), Austria (*2,025,000)	1,660,000
Vientiane, Laos	162,300
Vilnius, Soviet Union	271,000
Vladivostok, Soviet Union	338,000
Volgograd (Stalingrad), Soviet Union (*775,000)	665,000
Voronezh, Soviet Union	535,000
Warsaw (Warszawa), Poland (*1,575,000)	1,210,000
Washington, D.C. (*2,485,000)	810,000
Wellington, New Zealand (*267,400)	125,900
Wiesbaden, Germany (West) (*520,000)	258,200
Winnipeg, Canada (*475,989)	265,429
Wrocław (Breslau), Poland	451,600
Wuhan, China (*2,600,000)	2,600,000
Wuppertal, Germany (West) (*900,000)	421,800
Wusih, China	613,000
Yaoundé, Cameroon	92,600
Yaroslavl, Soviet Union	454,000
Yerevan, Soviet Union	578,000
Yokohama, Japan (*Tōkyō)	1,375,710
Youngstown, Ohio (*490,000)	162,000
Zagreb, Yugoslavia	430,802
Zaporozhye, Soviet Union	507,000
Zürich, Switzerland (*715,000)	440,000

* *Population of metropolitan area, including suburbs. See headnote.*
▲ *Population of entire municipality or district, including rural area. Starred population in these entries refers to urban portion of municipality only.*

	Apia	Azores Islands	Berlin	Bombay	Buenos Aires	Calcutta	Cape Town	Cape Verde Islands	Chicago	Darwin	Denver	Gibraltar	Hong Kong	Honolulu	Istanbul	Juneau	London	Los Angeles	Manila	Melbourne	Mexico City	Moscow
Apia, Western Samoa		9644	9743	8154	6931	7183	9064	10246	6557	3843	5653	10676	5591	2604	10175	5415	9789	4828	4993	3113	5449	9116
Azores Islands	9644		2185	5967	5417	6549	5854	1499	3093	10209	3991	1249	7572	7180	2975	4526	1527	4794	8250	12101	4385	3165
Berlin, Germany	9743	2185		3910	7376	4376	5977	3194	4402	8036	5077	1453	5500	7305	1078	4560	574	5782	6128	9919	6037	996
Bombay, India	8154	5967	3910		9273	1041	5134	6297	8054	4503	8383	4814	2673	8020	2991	6866	4462	8701	3148	6097	9722	3131
Buenos Aires, Argentina	6931	5417	7376	9273		10242	4270	4208	5596	9127	5928	5963	11463	7558	7568	7759	6918	6118	11042	7234	4633	8375
Calcutta, India	7183	6549	4376	1041	10242		6026		7148	3744	8050	5521	1534	7037	3646	6326	4954	8148	2189	5547	9495	3447
Cape Town, South Africa	9064	5854	5977	5134	4270	6026		4509	8449	6947	9327	5076	7372	11532	5219	10330	6005	9969	7525	6412	8511	6294
Cape Verde Islands	10246	1499	3194	6297	4208	7148	4509		4066	10664	4975	1762	8539	8311	3507	5911	2731	5772	9221	10856	4857	3982
Chicago, U.S.A.	6557	3093	4402	8054	5596	7981	8449	4066		9346	920	4258	7790	4244	5476	2305	3950	1745	8128	9668	1673	4984
Darwin, Australia	3843	10209	8036	4503	9127	3744	6947	10664	9346		8557	9265	2642	5355	7390	7105	8598	7835	1979	1964	9081	7046
Denver, U.S.A.	5653	3991	5077	8383	5928	8050	9327	4975	920	8557		5122	7465	3338	6154	1831	4688	831	7661	8759	1434	5485
Gibraltar, Gibraltar	10676	1249	1453	4814	5963	5521	5076	1762	4258	9265	5122		6828	8075	1874	5273	1094	5936	7483	10798	5629	2413
Hong Kong, Asia	5591	7572	5500	2673	11463	1534	7373	8539	7790	2642	7465	6828		5537	4980	5634	5981	7240	693	4607	8776	4439
Honolulu, Hawaii, U.S.A.	2604	7180	7305	8020	7558	7037	11532	8311	4244	5355	3338	8075	5537		8104	2815	7226	2557	5296	5513	3781	7033
Istanbul (Constantinople), Turkey	10175	2975	1078	2991	7568	3646	5219	3507	5476	7390	6154	1874	4980	8104		5498	1551	6843	5659	9088	7102	1088
Juneau, Alaska, U.S.A.	5415	4526	4560	6866	7759	6326	10330	5911	2305	7105	1831	5273	5634	2815	5498		4418	1842	5869	8035	3219	4534
London, United Kingdom	9789	1527	574	4462	6918	4954	6005	2731	3950	8598	4688	1094	5981	7226	1551	4418		5439	6667	10501	5541	1549
Los Angeles, U.S.A.	4828	4794	5782	8701	6118	8148	9969	5772	1745	7835	831	5936	7240	2557	6843	1842	5439		7269	7931	1542	6068
Manila, Philippines	4993	8250	6128	3148	11042	2189	7525	9221	8128	1979	7661	7483	693	5296	5659	5869	6667	7269		3941	8829	5130
Melbourne, Australia	3113	12101	9919	6097	7234	5547	6412	10856	9668	1964	8759	10798	4607	5513	9088	8035	10501	7931	3941		8422	8963
Mexico City, Mexico	5449	4385	6037	9722	4633	9495	8511	4857	1673	9081	1434	5629	8776	3781	7102	3219	5541	1542	8829	8422		6688
Moscow, Soviet Union	9116	3165	996	3131	8375	3447	6294	3982	4984	7046	5485	2413	4439	7033	1088	4534	1549	6068	5130	8963	6688	
New Orleans, U.S.A.	6085	3524	5116	8865	4916	8803	8316	4194	833	9545	1082	4757	8480	4207	6171	2905	4627	1673	8724	9275	934	5756
New York, U.S.A.	7242	2422	3961	7794	5297	7921	7801	3355	713	9959	1631	3627	8051	4959	5009	2854	3459	2451	8493	10355	2085	4662
Nome, Alaska, U.S.A.	5438	4954	4342	5901	8848	5271	10107	6438	3314	6235	2925	5398	4547	3004	5101	1094	4381	2876	4817	7558	4309	4036
Oslo, Norway	9247	2234	515	4130	7613	4459	6494	3444	4040	8022	4653	1791	5337	6784	1518	4045	714	5325	6016	9926	5706	1016
Panamá, Panama	6514	3778	5849	9742	3381	10114	7014	3734	2325	10352	2636	4926	10084	5245	6750	4644	5278	3001	9022	10283	1495	6711
Paris, France	9990	1659	542	4359	6877	4889	5841	2666	4133	8575	4885	964	5956	7434	1401	4628	213	5601	6673	10396	5706	1541
Peking (Peiping), China	5903	6565	4567	2964	11974	2024	8045	7763	6592	3728	6348	6009	1226	5067	4379	4522	5054	6250	1770	5667	7733	3597
Port Said, U.A.R.	10485	3391	1747	2659	7362	3506	4590	3672	6103	7159	6819	2179	4975	8738	693	6215	2154	7528	5619	8658	7671	1710
Quebec, Canada	7406	2240	3583	7371	5680	7481	7857	3355	878	9724	1752	3383	7650	5000	4644	2660	3101	2579	8124	10497	2454	4242
Reykjavik, Iceland	8678	1777	1479	5191	7099	5409	7111	3248	2954	8631	3596	2047	6031	6084	2558	3268	1171	4306	6651	10544	4622	2056
Rio de Janeiro, Brazil	8120	4428	6144	8257	1218	9376	3769	3040	5296	9960	5871	4775	10995	8190	6395	7598	5772	6296	11254	8186	4770	7179
Rome, Italy	10475	2125	734	3843	6929	4496	5249	2772	4808	8190	5561	1034	5768	8022	854	5247	887	6326	6457	9934	6353	1474
San Francisco, U.S.A.	4786	4872	5657	8392	6474	7809	10241	5921	1858	7637	949	5936	6894	2392	6700	1525	5355	347	6963	7854	1885	5868
Seattle, U.S.A.	5222	4501	5041	7741	6913	7224	10199	5714	1737	7619	1021	5462	6471	2678	6063	899	4782	959	6641	8186	2337	5199
Shanghai, China	5399	7229	5215	3133	12197	2112	8059	8443	7053	3142	6698	6646	772	4934	4959	4869	5710	6477	1152	5005	8039	4235
Singapore, Malaysia	5850	8326	6166	2429	9864	1791	6016	8700	9365	2075	9063	7231	1652	6710	5373	7235	6744	8767	1479	3761	10307	5238
Tokyo, Japan	4656	7247	5538	4188	11400	3186	9071	8589	6303	3367	5795	6988	1796	3850	5556	4011	5938	5470	1863	5089	7035	4650
Valparaíso, Chile	6267	5678	7795	10037	761	10993	4998	4649	5268	8961	5452	6408	11607	6793	8172	7271	7263	5527	10930	6998	4053	8792
Washington, D.C., U.S.A.	7066	2667	4167	7988	5216	8088	7894	3486	591	9923	1494	3822	8148	4829	5216	2834	3665	2300	8560	10173	1878	4883
Wellington, New Zealand	2062	11269	11265	7677	6260	7042	7019	10363	8349	3310	7516	12060	5853	4708	10663	7475	11682	6714	5162	1595	6899	10279
Vienna, Austria	10010	2291	328	3718	7368	4259	5671	3147	4694	7974	5383	1386	5429	7626	783	4895	772	6108	6120	9792	6306	1044
Winnipeg, Canada	6283	3389	4286	7644	6297	7424	9054	4556	714	8684	798	4435	7096	3806	5361	1597	3918	1525	7414	9319	2097	4687
Zanzibar, Tanzania	9892	5323	4309	2855	6421	3859	2346	4635	8358	6409	9221	4103	5414	10869	3312	8795	4604	10021	5763	6802	9484	4270

WORLD STEAMSHIP DISTANCE TABLE

	Bombay	Buenos Aires	Cape Town	Colombo	Gibraltar	Halifax	Hamburg	Honolulu	Istanbul	Le Havre	Lisbon	Liverpool	Manila	Melbourne	New Orleans	New York	Panama Roads	Port Said	Rio de Janeiro	San Francisco	Shanghai	Singapore	Valparaiso	Wellington	Yokohama
Bombay, India		9601	5469	1042	5639	8760	7552	9631	4412	7024	6036	7156	4361	6365	10927	9413	14921	3511	8998	11247	5328	2824	11356	7961	6155
Buenos Aires, Argentina	9601		4345	9415	6074	6600	7622	8744	8488	7074	6148	7178	12128	8477	7233	6761	8259		1325	10062	13087	3181	10782	6956	13921
Cape Town, South Africa	5469	4345		5070	5982	7386	7388	11948	7058	6861	5912	7001	7821	6998	9382	7814	7417	6148	3769	11154	8787	6511	6977	7531	9614
Colombo, Ceylon	1042	9415	5070		6227	9278	8090	8594	4920	7563	6577	7717	3399	5380	11489	9941	13919	4010	8839	10289	4370	1825	11073	7058	5151
Gibraltar, Gibraltar	5639	6074	5982	6227		3051	1863	10433	2099	1336	350	1490	9641	11257	5271	3714	5038	2217	4816	8775	10553	8008	9006	12847	11353
Halifax, Canada	8760	6600	7386	9278	3051		3480	8152	5147	3082	2792	2891	12591	11876	2517	686	2718	5257	5332	6456	12707	10196	11592		
Hamburg, Germany	7552	7622	7388	8090	1863	3480		11283	3939	573	1543	1083	16678	13066	5935	4166	5888	4058	6354	9625	12349	9838	8900	13758	14734
Honolulu, Hawaii, U.S.A.	9631	8744	11948	8594	10433	8152	11283		12510	10757	10363	10682	5571	5691	7046	7718	5395	12604	9875	2408	4986	6772	6816	4736	3908
Istanbul, Turkey	4412	8488	7058	4920	2099	5147	3939	12510		3421	2430	3543	8245	9928	7384	5788	7115	910	6897	10884	9210	11020	11540	10037	
Le Havre, France	7024	7074	6861	7563	1336	3082	573	10757	3421		1017	578	10856	12540	5315	3640	5363	3521	5820	9095	11822	9312	8347	12801	12649
Lisbon, Portugal	6036	6148	5912	6577	350	2792	1543	10363	2430	1017		1148	9867	11551	5377	3403	4968	2532	4858	8737	10833	8323	7975	12459	11660
Liverpool, United Kingdom	7156	7178	7001	7717	1490	2891	1083	10682	3543	578	1148		11111	12764	5266	3539	5287	3652	5932	9024	12201	9490	8299	12778	13399
Manila, Philippines	4361	12128	7821	3399	9641	12591	16678	5571	8245	10856	9867	11111		5214	12414	13086	10764	7335	1524	7164	1338	1578	11967	5647	2023

SHOWING GREAT CIRCLE DISTANCES BETWEEN PRINCIPAL CITIES OF THE WORLD IN STATUTE MILES

New Orleans	New York	Nome	Oslo	Panamá	Paris	Peking (Peiping)	Port Said	Quebec	Reykjavik	Rio de Janeiro	Rome	San Francisco	Seattle	Shanghai	Singapore	Tokyo	Valparaiso	Washington, D.C.	Wellington	Vienna	Winnipeg	Zanzibar	
6085	7242	5438	9247	6514	9990	5903	10485	7406	8678	8120	10475	4786	5222	5399	5850	4656	6267	7066	2062	10010	6283	9892	Apia
3524	2422	4954	2234	3778	1659	6565	3391	2240	1777	4428	2125	4872	4501	7229	8326	7247	5678	2667	11269	2291	3389	5323	Azores Islands
5116	3961	4342	515	5849	542	4567	1747	3583	1479	6114	734	5657	5041	5215	6166	5538	7795	4167	11265	328	4286	4309	Berlin
8865	7794	5901	4130	9742	4359	2964	2659	7371	5191	8257	3843	8392	7741	3133	2429	4188	10037	7988	7677	3718	7644	2855	Bombay
4916	5297	8848	7613	3381	6877	11974	7362	5680	7099	1218	6929	6474	6913	12197	9864	11400	761	5216	6260	7368	6297	6421	Buenos Aires
8803	7921	5271	4459	10114	4889	2024	3506	7481	5409	9376	4496	7809	7224	2112	1791	3186	10993	8088	7042	4259	7424	3859	Calcutta
8316	7801	10107	6494	7014	5841	8045	4590	7857	7111	3769	5249	10241	10199	8059	6016	9071	4998	7894	7019	5671	9054	2346	Cape Town
4194	3355	6438	3444	3734	2666	7763	3672	3355	3248	3040	2772	5921	5714	8443	8700	8589	4649	3486	10363	3147	4556	4635	Cape Verde Islands
833	713	3314	4040	2325	4133	6592	6103	878		5296	4808	1858	1737	7053	9365	6303	5268	591	8349	4694	714	8358	Chicago
9545	9959	6235	8022	10352	8575	3728	7159	9724	8631	9960	8190	7637	7619	3142	2075	3367	8961	9923	3310	7974	8684	6409	Darwin
1082	1631	2925	4653	2636	4885	6348	6819	1752	3596	5871	5561	949	1021	6698	9063	5795	5452	1494	7516	5383	798	9221	Denver
4757	3627	5398	1791	4926	964	6009	2179	3383	2047	4775	1034	5936	5462	6646	7231	6988	6408	3822	12060	1386	4435	4103	Gibraltar
8480	8051	4547	5337	10084	5956	1226	4975	7650	6031	10995	5768	6894	6471	772	1652	1796	11607	8148	5853	5429	7096	5414	Hong Kong
4207	4959	3004	6784	5245	7434	5067	8738	5000	6084	8190	8022	2392	2678	4934	6710	3850	6793	4829	4708	7626	3806	10869	Honolulu
6171	5009	5101	1518	6750	1401	4379	693	4644	2558	6395	854	6700	6063	4959	5373	5556	8172	5216	10663	783	5361	3312	Istanbul
2905	2854	1094	4045	4460	4628	4522	6215	2660	3268	7598	5247	1525	899	4869	7235	4011	7271	2834	7475	4895	1597	8795	Juneau
4627	3459	4381	714	5278	213	5054	2154	3101	1171	5772	887	5355	4782	5710	6744	5938	7263	3665	11682	772	3918	4604	London
1673	2451	2876	5325	3001	5601	6250	7528	2579	4306	6326		347	959	6477	8767	5527	5470	2300	6714	6108	1525	10021	Los Angeles
8724	8493	4817	6016	10283	6673	1770	5619	8124	6651	11254	6457	6963	6641	1152	1479	1863	10930	8560	5162	6120	7414	5763	Manila
9275	10355	7558	9926	9022	10396	5667	8658	10497	10544	8186	9934	7854	8186	5005	3761	5089	6998	10173	1595	9792	9319	6802	Melbourne
934	2085	4309	5706	1495	5706	7733	7671	2454	4622	4770	6353	1885	2337	8039	10307	7035	4053	1878	6899	6306	2097	9484	Mexico City
5756	4662	4036	1016	6711	1541	3597	1710	4242	2056	7179	1474	5868	5199	4235	5238	4650	8792	4883	10279	1044	4687	4270	Moscow
	1171	3937	4795	1603	4788	7314	6756	1534	3711	4796	5439	1926	2101	7720	10082	6858	4514	966	7794	5385	1418	8754	New Orleans
1171		3769	3672	2231	3622	6823	5590	439	2576	4820	4273	2571	2408	7357	9630	6735	5094	205	8946	4224	1281	7698	New York
3937	3769		3836	5541	4574	3428	5745	3489	3366	8586	5082	2547	1976	3784	6148	2983	8360	3792	7383	4657	2599	8209	Nome
4795	3672	3836		5691	832	4360	2211	3263	1083	6482	1243	5181	4591	5020	6246	5221	7914	3870	10974	850	3854	4803	Oslo
1603	2231	5541	5691		5382	8906	7146	2659	4706	3294	5903	3322	3651	9324	11687	8423	2943	2080	7433	6026	2998	8245	Panamá
4788	3622	4574	832	5382		5101	1975	3235	1380	5703	682	5441	4993	5752	6671	6033	7251	3828	11791	644	4118	4396	Paris
7314	6823	3428	4360	8906	5101		4584	6423	4903	10768	5047	5902	5396	662	2774	1307	11774	6922	6698	4639	5907	5803	Peking (Peiping)
6756	5590	5745	2211	7146	1975	4584		5250	3227	6244	1317	7394	6759	5132	5088	5842	8088	5796	10249	1429	6032	2729	Port Said
1534	439	3489	3263	2659	3235	6423	5250		2189	5125	3943	2642	2353	6981	9097	6417	5504	610	9228	3858	1199	7443	Quebec
3711	2576	3366	1083	4706	1380	4903	3227	2189		6118	2044	4199	3614	5559	7160	5472	7225	2800	10724	1805	2804	5757	Reykjavik
4796	4820	8586	6482	3294	5703	10768	6244	5125	6118		5684	6619	6891	11340	9774	11535	1855	4797	7349	6136	6010	5589	Rio de Janeiro
5439	4273	5082	1243	5903	682	5047	1317	3943	2044	5684		6240	5659	5677	6232	6124	7420	4435	11524	463	4803	3712	Rome
1926	2571	2547	5181	3322	5441	5902	7394	2642	4199	6619	6240		678	6132	8479	5131	5876	2442	6739	5988	1504	9958	San Francisco
2101	2408	1976	4591	3651	4993	5396	6759	2353	3614	6891	5659	678		5703	8057	4777	6230	2329	7242	5376	1150	9359	Seattle
7720	7357	3784	5020	9324	5752	662	5132	6981	5559	11340	5677	6132	5703		2377	1094	11650	7442	6054	5270	6350	5971	Shanghai
10082	9630	6148	6246	11687	6671	2774	5088	9097	7160	9774	6232	8479	8057	2377		3304	10226	9834	5292	6036	8685	4480	Singapore
6858	6735	2983	5221	8423	6033	1307	5842	6417	5472	11535	6124	5131	4777	1094	3304		10635	6769	5760	5679	5575	7040	Tokyo
4514	5094	8360	7914	2943	7251	11774	8088	5504	7225	1855	7420	5876	6230	11650	10226	10635		4977	5785	7783	5931	7184	Valparaiso
966	205	3792	3870	2080	3828	6922	5796	610	2800	4797	4435	2442	2329	7442	9834	6769	4977		8745	4429	1243	7884	Washington, D.C.
7794	8946	7383	10974	7433	11791	6698	10249	9228	10724	7349	11524	6739	7242	6054	5292	5760	5785	8745		11278	8230	8122	Wellington
5385	4224	4657	850	6026	644	4639	1429	3858	1805	6136	463	5988	5376	5270	6036	5679	7783	4429	11278		4604	3983	Vienna
1418	1281	2599	3854	2998	4118	5907	6032	1199	2804	6010	4803	1504	1150	6350	8685	5575	5931	1243	8230	4604		8416	Winnipeg
8754	7698	8209	4803	8245	4396	5803	2729	7443	5757	5589	3712	9958	9359	5971	4480	7040	7184	7884	8122	3983	8416		Zanzibar

SHOWING STEAMSHIP DISTANCES BETWEEN PRINCIPAL PORTS OF THE WORLD IN STATUTE MILES

	Bombay	Buenos Aires	Cape Town	Colombo	Gibraltar	Halifax	Hamburg	Honolulu	Istanbul	Le Havre	Lisbon	Liverpool	Manila	Melbourne	New Orleans	New York	Panama Roads	Port Said	Rio de Janeiro	San Francisco	Shanghai	Singapore	Valparaiso	Wellington	Yokohama
Melbourne, Australia	6365	8477	6998	5380	11257	11876	13066	5691	9928	12540	11551	12764	5214		10780	11452	9130	9040	9416	8011	6012	4396	7222	1737	5606
New Orleans, U.S.A.	10927	7233	9382	11489	5271	2517	5935	7046	7384	5315	5377	5266	12414	10780		1970	1650	7498	5965	5287	11495	13207	4663	9133	10489
New York, U.S.A.	9413	6761	7814	9941	3714	686	4166	7718	5788	3640	3403	3539	13086	11452	1970		2323	5895	5493	6059	12176	11693	5335	9814	11169
Panama Roads, Canal Zone	14921	6311	7417	13919	5038	2718	5888	5395	7115	5363	4968	5287	10764	9130	1650	2323		7217	5058	3737	9853	12097	3013	7491	8846
Port Said, U.A.R.	3511	8259	6148	4010	2217	5257	4058	12604	910	3521	2532	3652	7335	9040	7498	5895	7217		7006	10986	8301	5791	10225	10630	9128
Rio de Janeiro, Brazil	8998	1325	3769	8839	4816	5332	6354	9875	6897	5820	4858	5932	11524	9416	5965	5493	5058	7006		8794	12490	10179	4191	7915	13317
San Francisco, U.S.A.	11247	10062	11154	10289	8775	6456	9625	2408	10884	9095	8737	9024	7164	8011	5287	6059	3737	10986	8794		6339	8467	5919	6800	5223
Shanghai, China	5328	13087	8787	4370	10553	12707	12349	4986	9210	11822	10833	12201	1338	6012	11495	12176	9853	8301	12490	6339		2545	11806	6184	1199
Singapore, Malaysia	2824	10782	6511	1825	8008	11047	9838	6772	6700	9312	8323	9490	1578	4396	13207	11693	12097	5791	10179	8467	2545		12534	5992	3345
Valparaíso, Chile	11356	3181	6977	11073	9006	5731	8900	6816	11020	8347	7975	8299	11967	7222	4663	5335	3013	10225	4191	5919	11806	12534		5799	10740
Wellington, New Zealand	7961	6956	7531	7058	12847	10196	13758	4736	11540	12801	12459	12778	5647	1737	9133	9814	7491	10630	7915	6800	6184	5992	5799		5736
Yokohama, Japan	6155	13921	9614	5151	11353	11592	14734	3908	10037	12649	11660	13399	2023	5606	10489	11169	8846	9128	13317	5223	1199	3345	10740	5736	

HISTORICAL GAZETTEER

A

A B C Countries. Term applied to three South American countries: Argentina, Brazil, and Chile.

Abraham, Plains of. Battlefield near the city of Quebec where the English under Wolfe defeated the French under Montcalm, 1759.

Abydos. Ancient town on the Hellespont, site of the Bridge of Xerxes. Also an ancient Egyptian town on the Nile below Thebes.

Abyssinia. Former name of Ethiopia.

Acadia. Old French colonial territory bounded by the Atlantic, the river and gulf of St. Lawrence, and a line running north from Penobscot Bay.

Achaia. Separate regions of ancient Greece in southern Thessaly and northern Peloponnesus. Later, a Roman province embracing all but the northern part of modern Greece.

Acropolis. Hill in Athens, Greece, where some of the finest monuments of antiquity now stand.

Actium. Off this promontory at the entrance to the Gulf of Amvrakia in northwestern Greece, Octavius won a naval battle against Antony and Cleopatra, 31 B.C.

Aegospotami. Off the mouth of this river in ancient Thrace, the Spartans crushed the Athenian fleet in 405 B.C., in the final battle of the Peloponnesian War.

Aelia Capitolina. Jerusalem in late Roman times.

Aeolian Islands. Ancient name of the Lipari Islands, off the coast of Sicily.

Aetolia. District of ancient Greece along the north shore of the Gulf of Corinth.

Africa. Roman province corresponding with modern Tunisia. Name was later applied to entire continent.

Agassiz, Lake. Prehistoric lake temporarily created by the withdrawal of glaciers. Covered an area which includes parts of present-day Manitoba, Saskatchewan, Ontario, Minnesota; and North Dakota.

Agincourt. Village near Boulogne, France, where outnumbered English forces under Henry V defeated the French, 1415.

Agrigentum. Prosperous commercial center on the southern coast of Sicily in the fifth century, B.C. The modern Agrigento.

Ai. Old city of the Canaanites near Bethel. It was destroyed by Joshua.

Aix-la-Chapelle. Northern capital and residence of Charlemagne, and coronation site of later German emperors. Now Aachen, Germany.

Akkad. Very ancient land of the Akkadians in north Babylonia at the closest approach of the Tigris and Euphrates. The capital was Agade.

Albania. Ancient country west of the Caspian Sea in the territory roughly corresponding to Soviet Azerbaidzhan. Also the small Adriatic republic.

Albion. Ancient name of Britain.

Alsace-Lorraine. Region in northeastern France seized by Germany in 1871, and returned to France following World War I. The capital was at Strasbourg.

America. Inclusive name of the continents and adjacent islands of North and South America. It is also commonly used when referring to the United States.

Amphipolis. City of ancient Macedonia near the mouth of the Struma River, site of a Spartan victory over Athens in 422 B.C.

Anáhuac. Old Indian term, now applied to the high plateau containing Mexico City.

Anatolia. See Asia Minor.

Anau. Ruins of an ancient city in the desert near Ashkhabad, Soviet Union.

Ancyra. Important city of Phrygia, Asia Minor, and later capital of Galatia. The modern Ankara or Angora, the capital of Turkey.

Andalusia. Region comprising the eight provinces of southern Spain in basin of Guadalquivir River.

Angkor. Extensive ruins of magnificent old city in northern Cambodia.

Antarctic Ocean. Obsolete name for southern part of the Pacific, Atlantic, and Indian Oceans bordering the continent of Antarctica.

Antilles. Collective name for the islands of the West Indies which enclose the Caribbean Sea. They consist of the Greater Antilles (Cuba, Jamaica, Hispaniola, and Puerto Rico) to the north and the Lesser Antilles (which include a number of islands and groups) to the east.

Antioch. Capital of ancient Syria and one of the greatest commercial centers of the time, Antioch later became a stronghold of Christianity. The Roman Antiochia, it is now Antakya, Turkey. It was also a city of Pisidia, Asia Minor, prominent in the journeys of Paul.

Antipodes. Name occasionally applied to New Zealand and Australia, because of their location on the globe diametrically opposite the British Isles.

Apulia. Division of southeastern Italy, containing the important cities of Bari, Taranto, and Foggia.

Aquitania. Originally a region in Transalpine Gaul between the Pyrenees and the Garonne, later extending northward to the Loire.

Arabia. Large Asiatic peninsula extending south of Iraq and Jordan between the Red Sea, the Persian Gulf, and the Arabian Sea on the south.

Arab League. A group of Arab states organized in 1945, with headquarters in Cairo. Original members were Egypt, Iraq, Syria, Lebanon, Transjordan (Jordan), Saudi Arabia, and Yemen. The purpose of the League is to coordinate the foreign policy of the member states for the mutual benefit of all Arab countries.

Aragon. Medieval kingdom in northeastern Spain, whose conquests included the Balearic Islands, Sardinia, and Sicily. Its union with Castile in 1479 created the Spanish kingdom.

Aram. Biblical name of Syria. Also called Aramea.

Ararat. Hebrew name of an ancient kingdom in eastern Armenia. Noah's Ark reputedly came to rest on one of its mountains. The Assyrian Urartu.

Araucania. Old name for the land of the Araucanian Indians in southern Chile, between Concepción and Puerto Montt.

Araxes. Ancient name of the Aras River on the border of Armenia and Media.

Arbela. The modern town of Arbil, Iraq, east of Mozul, where Alexander the Great defeated a huge Persian army, 331 B.C.

Argolis. Region of ancient Greece on the east coast of the Peloponnesus. Its principal cities were Argos and Mycenae.

Ariel. Poetic name of Jerusalem.

Armageddon. Greek name of "The Hill of Megiddo," near an Israelite battlefield. In present usage, the name refers to a final battle between the powers of good and evil.

Armenia. Region of western Asia now roughly comprising northeastern Turkey, Soviet Armenia, and adjacent parts of Soviet and Iranian territory.

Arnon. Biblical name of the Wady Mojib, which flows from Jordan into the Dead Sea.

Ascalon. Also called Ashkelon, an ancient Philistine city on the Mediterranean north of Gaza, Palestine. The present village of Askalan is on its site.

Asculum. Capital of ancient Picenum and site of the original "Pyrrhic victory." Here, in 279 B.C., Pyrrhus of Epirus defeated the Romans, suffering very heavy losses. Asculum is modern Ascoli Piceno, Italy.

Ashdod. Ancient city of the Philistines, later called Azotus. Now it is a village in Israel.

Asia. Roman province comprising western part of Asia Minor. Name was later given to entire continent.

Asia Minor. Name of the peninsula in western Asia bounded by the Black, Aegean, and Mediterranean Seas. The area is nearly identical with Anatolia and contains a large part of Asiatic Turkey.

Asshur. First capital and original name of Assyria. Also Assur and Asur.

Assyria. Very ancient empire which developed on the right bank of the upper Tigris. The empire eventually extended from Elam in the east to Egypt and eastern Asia Minor in the west. Its power ended with the fall of the capital, Nineveh, 612 B.C.

Asturias. Located in northwestern Spain in the early Middle Ages, Asturias was the first Christian kingdom to be established on the Iberian peninsula.

Athos, Mount. Mountain southeast of Salonika (Thessaloniki), Greece, where a community of monks has maintained almost complete autonomy since the early Middle Ages.

Atlantis. Legendary island of great size in the Atlantic Ocean west of the Pillars of Hercules. After reaching an advanced state of civilization, it was supposedly destroyed by a subterranean cataclysm.

Attica. Ancient Greek state southeast of Boeotia. Its capital and chief city was Athens.

Augusta Treverorum. Capital of ancient Belgica; the modern Trier, Germany.

Austerlitz. Town near Brno, Czechoslovakia, where Napoleon defeated armies of Russia and Austria, 1805.

Australasia. That part of the southwest Pacific containing Australia, New Zealand, and the islands of Melanesia. Term is often used to include all Oceania.

Austria-Hungary. Dual monarchy which ruled an empire extending from Bohemia to Transylvania and from Galicia to the Adriatic between 1867 and 1918. Its capital was Vienna.

Axis. Term used to denote first the early understanding between Rome and Berlin and later the military alliance that developed in World War II between Germany, Italy, and their allies.

B

Baalbek. Also Baalbec and the Greek Heliopolis, an ancient city of Syria near headwaters of Litani River, now in Lebanon.

Babel. Biblical name of the city, probably Babylon, where the notorious tower of Babel was located.

Babylon. Capital city of ancient Babylonia on both sides of the lower Euphrates.

Babylonia. Very ancient and powerful kingdom—also called Shinar and Chaldea—in the lower valley of the Tigris and Euphrates. Its capital was Babylon. The Chaldean Empire eventually extended westward to the Mediterranean.

Bactria. Ancient country of central Asia between the Oxus River and the Hindu Kush Mountains. Its capital Bactra is the modern Balkh, Afghanistan.

Baden. Old grand duchy and state of Germany along the right bank of the upper Rhine. Karlsruhe was its capital.

Bad Lands. Name applied to barren, badly eroded areas in the western United States. The best known region is located in western South Dakota.

Balaklava. Town in the Crimea, southeast of Sevastopol. Near here the courageous "Charge of the Light Brigade" took place, 1854. Also Balaclava.

Balkan Peninsula. That part of southeastern Europe south of the Sava and Danube Rivers.

Balkan States. Countries located partly or entirely within the Balkan Peninsula: Yugoslavia, Albania, Greece, Romania, Bulgaria, and European Turkey.

Baltic States. Term used for the former republics of Estonia, Latvia, and Lithuania, bordering Baltic Sea. They were absorbed into Soviet Union in 1940.

Banat, The. Region in Central Europe bounded by the Transylvanian Alps and the Danube, Tisza, and Muresul rivers.

Banda Oriental. Old Spanish name for the "eastern shore" of Plata River, now the country of Uruguay.

Bannockburn. Village south of Stirling, Scotland, where Bruce defeated the English under Edward II, 1314, and assured the independence of Scotland.

Bantam. Seaport, formerly of great commercial importance, west of Djakarta, Java.

Barbary States. Old collective term for the countries of Africa along the "Barbary Coast" of the Mediterranean, between Egypt and the Atlantic Ocean.

Basque Provinces. Region along the Bay of Biscay, extending from the areas around Bilbao and Vitoria, Spain, across the Pyrenees into southwestern France.

Batavia. Latin name for island home of Batavi on lower Rhine, later applied to all the Netherlands.

Behistun. Place near Kermanshah, Iran, where a famous rock carries ancient Assyrian inscriptions on its precipitous face.

Belgica. Northerly region of Transalpine Gaul between the Rhine and Seine. It eventually extended southward to the Rhône-Saône confluence and eastward to include most of Switzerland.

Benelux. Collective term for Belgium, the Netherlands, and Luxembourg.

Beneventum. The modern Benevento, Italy; in antiquity, the battleground for the decisive Roman victory over Pyrrhus of Epirus, 275 B.C.

Bengal. Former province in eastern British India between the Himalayas and the mouths of the Ganges. In 1947, most of the province, except the western part containing Calcutta, was absorbed into the new state of Pakistan.

Berea. Ancient Macedonian town near Mount Olympus, where Paul found willing converts to Christianity. It is now Verria, Greece.

Bessarabia. Region in southeastern Europe between the Prut and the Dnestr rivers. After its cession by Romania, in 1940, it became a part of the Soviet Union.

Bethabara. Site of the baptism of Jesus by John the Baptist. It may have been located at a ford of the Jordan 13 miles south of the Sea of Galilee.

Bethany. Famous village that once stood at the foot of the Mount of Olives, east of Jerusalem. The ascension of Christ took place near by.

Bethel. Shrine city of ancient Israel north of Jerusalem. The modern Beitin.

Beth-horon. Site of the great victory of Joshua over the Canaanites. The battle took place between the present villages of Beit Ur el Foka and Beit Ur el Tahta, midway between Jerusalem and Lydda.

Bethsaida. Ancient town at the north end of the Sea of Galilee where Jesus fed the five thousand.

Bimini. Island or region of West Indian legend where the Fountain of Youth was supposed to be located. The name has been given to an island group in the western Bahamas.

Black Country, The. Mining and manufacturing area in the vicinity of Birmingham, England.

Blarney. Village near Cork, Ireland, where the castle containing the famous Blarney Stone is located.

Boeotia. Ancient district in central Greece northwest of Attica. The chief city and capital was Thebes.

Bohemia. Medieval duchy and kingdom of varying frontiers and later a crownland of Austria-Hungary. After World War I, Bohemia became the western section of the new republic of Czechoslovakia. Its capital is Prague.

Bonneville, Lake. Extinct lake that covered northwestern Utah during the glacial period.

Borodino. Village 70 miles west of Moscow where Napoleon defeated the Russians, 1812.

Bosnia. Mountainous region south of the Sava River in Yugoslavia. It was formerly a medieval kingdom and part of the Austro-Hungarian Empire.

Bosporus. Name of an ancient Greek kingdom encircling the Sea of Azov, Soviet Union. This name was derived from the Cimmerian Bosporus, now called Kerch, or Yenikale Strait. Also name of famous strait at Istanbul, ancient Thracian Bosporus.

Bourbon. Medieval duchy in central France, the early home of the famous royal house. Also the county and province of Bourbonnais. Capital was Moulins.

Brabant. Old duchy containing the cities of Antwerp, Brussels, and Louvain. The territory is now divided between Belgium and the Netherlands.

Brandenburg. Former Prussia, now divided between Germany and Poland. Its capital was Potsdam.

Brandywine. Creek near Philadelphia where British defeated Americans commanded by Washington, 1777.

Britannia. Roman name for island of Great Britain, specifically, the southern part. Now used poetically.

British America. Name usually restricted to Canada.

British East Africa. Old descriptive name for the British territories of Kenya, Uganda, and Zanzibar. Also applied to Tanganyika.

British India. That part of the subcontinent of India before August, 1947, under the direct control of Great Britain. The relatively independent princely states were not considered in this category.

British West Africa. Name occasionally used collectively for the former British colonies in western Africa—Nigeria, Gold Coast, now Ghana, Sierra Leone, Gambia, Togo, and Cameroon.

Brundisium. Ancient Roman port on Adriatic and terminus of famed Appian Way. Now Brindisi, Italy.

Bukovina. Region on the eastern slope of the Carpathians, formerly a part of Austria-Hungary, now divided between the Soviet Ukraine in the north and Romania in the south. Also Bukowina.

Bull Run. Small river east of Manassas, in northern Virginia. Two battles were fought in this vicinity (1861 and 1862) between the armies of the Union and the Confederacy.

Bunker Hill. Famous hill in Charlestown, Mass. The battle of that name was actually fought on nearby Breed's Hill in 1775.

Burgenland. Fertile region along the Austro-Hungarian border. Its chief city is Sopron, Hungary.

Burgundy. Early medieval kingdom in southeastern France largely east of the Rhône and Saône and west of the Alps, including the western half of present-day Switzerland. Later, a duchy in the Seine, Loire, and Saône river basins of northeastern France.

Byblos. Important port in ancient Phoenicia north of Beirut, Lebanon. Called Gebal in Old Testament.

Bytown. Early name of Ottawa, Canada.

Byzantine Empire. Name for the Eastern Roman Empire, established in 330 A.D. Included in the Empire were the territories of modern U.A.R., Israel, Jordan, Syria, Turkey, Greece, and Bulgaria.

Byzantium. Ancient Greek city on the Hellespont. Constantinople was built on its site in 330 A.D. and became the capital of the Byzantine Empire.

C

Caesarea Philippi. Ancient town of northern Palestine at the foot of Mt. Hermon, near the modern Banias, Syria.

Calabria. Roman name for the "heel" of Italy, now applied to the "toe."

Caledonia. Roman name for that part of Scotland lying north of the Firths of Clyde and Forth. The name is now used poetically to include all Scotland.

Calvary. Latin word for "skull," an unidentified place outside Jerusalem where Christ was crucified. Also Golgotha.

Campagna di Roma. Extensive reclaimed lowlands around Rome, Italy, comprising roughly the territory of ancient Latium.

Campania. Division of Italy containing the cities of Naples and Salerno. Roman cities of importance were Capua and Nola.

Camulodunum. Early Roman city in Britannia; now Colchester, England.

Cana. Town where Jesus performed his first miracle. Probably the modern Kefr Kenna, Israel.

Canaan. The biblical land of Canaan lay west of the Jordan and the Dead Sea, and extended from Mount Lebanon to the southern deserts of Palestine.

Cannae. North of this ancient town in Apulia, a Roman army was almost completely destroyed by Hannibal, 216 B.C.

Capernaum. Biblical town on the west shore of the Sea of Galilee. It was often visited by Christ.

Cappadocia. Ancient country in eastern Asia Minor extending originally from Cilicia to the Euxine. Under the Romans, the region comprised the provinces of Cappadocia to the south and Pontus to the north.

Carchemish. Old capital of the Hittites on the Euphrates, at its closest approach to the Mediterranean. It was the site of a decisive Babylonian victory over Egypt, 605 B.C.

Caria. Ancient country south of the Meander River in southwest Asia Minor. The principal cities were Halicarnassus and Miletus.

Caribbees. General name for the Lesser Antilles.

Carinthia. Mountainous province in southern Austria, a former crownland of Austria-Hungary. The capital is Klagenfurt.

Carmel, Mount. Mountain ridge south of the Bay of Acre, prominent in the Old Testament.

Carniola. Medieval duchy, later a crownland of Austria-Hungary, located in what is now the northwestern part of Yugoslavia. Laibach, now called Ljubljana, was the principal city.

203

Carthage. Ancient Phoenician city in northern Africa near Tunis. In 146 B.C., it was destroyed by its great commercial rival, Rome.

Castile. Medieval kingdom in northern and central Spain which united with Aragon in 1479 to form the Spanish monarchy. Old Castile was in the northern part of kingdom and New Castile was in southern part.

Catalonia. Originally an independent state in the northeast corner of the Iberian Peninsula, Catalonia united with Aragon in the twelfth century. Barcelona is chief city of region. Spanish name is Cataluña.

Cathay. Old name for China, used by Marco Polo.

Caucasia. General name for that part of the Soviet Union between the Black and Caspian seas and traversed by the Caucasus Mountains.

Celestial Empire. Once a popular name of China.

Central America. Name applied to that portion of North America south of Mexico and often including Panama. Specifically, the area between the isthmuses of Tehuantepec and Panama.

Central Powers. Collective term formerly used for Germany and Austria-Hungary due to their location in central Europe. In World War I the definition was expanded to include Bulgaria and Turkey, the allies of Germany.

Chaco. Low-lying, swampy region in South America between Paraguay River and the Andes, in Argentina, Paraguay, and Bolivia. Also called Gran Chaco.

Chaeronea. Ancient town in western Boeotia, the site of the victory of Philip over the forces of Thebes and Athens, 338 B.C., which introduced the era of Macedonian supremacy.

Chalcedon. Ancient Greek town on the Bosporus opposite Byzantium.

Chalcidice. Three-armed peninsula of ancient Macedonia containing the cities of Olynthus and Potidaea. It was colonized and named by Euboeans from Chalcis—the modern Khalkis, Greece.

Chaldea. Ancient name for the lowlands at the head of the Persian Gulf, but commonly applied to all of Babylonia. The second and final empire of Babylonia was called the Chaldean Empire.

Champagne. Old province of northeastern France whose capital was at Troyes.

Chancellorsville. Village near Spotsylvania, Virginia, the scene of a victory gained over the Union army by the outnumbered Confederates, 1863.

Chapultepec. Rocky hill southwest of Mexico City, the site of Aztec fortifications and the summer residence of the viceroys and presidents of Mexico.

Charcas. Old Spanish colonial province, a part successively of the viceroyalties of Peru and La Plata. It corresponded roughly to modern Bolivia and extended westward to the Pacific.

Chichén Itzá. Principal city of the Mayas. Its ruins lie in the jungles of eastern Yucatán.

Chinnereth. Sea of Galilee in the Old Testament.

Chosen. Native name of Korea.

Christiania. Former name of Oslo, Norway.

Cibola. Old name given to a region of New Mexico containing seven cities, supposedly rich and powerful. Coronado identified them in 1540 as commonplace Zuni Indian villages.

Cimmeria. Ancient country of the Cimmerians, probably located along northern shores of Black Sea.

Cinnamon, Land of. Old name of the Napo River region in Peru, first explored in the 16th century.

Cinque Ports. In medieval England, a group of coastal towns in Kent and Sussex carrying special royal privileges and responsibilities. Included were the cities of Hastings and Dover.

Cipango, or Cipangu. Name given by Marco Polo to an island group east of Asia, probably Japan.

Circassia. Region in the southern Soviet Union, bordering on Kuban River, Black Sea, and Caucasus Mountains.

Cisalpine Republic. Short-lived state in the valley of the Po between Piedmont and Venetia. In 1802, it was reconstituted as the Italian Republic.

Cisleithania. Old name for the Austrian portion of Austria-Hungary to the west and north of Transleithania. Besides Austria, it included what is now western Czechoslovakia, Galicia, northern Bukovina, and Slovenia. Name is derived from Leitha River, which formed part of the boundary south of Vienna.

Colchis. Ancient country on the eastern shores of the Euxine south of the Caucasus, now part of Soviet Georgia. The legendary land of the Golden Fleece.

Colonia Agrippina. Roman colony on the Rhine; the modern Köln (Cologne), Germany.

Colossae. Early Christian stronghold of Phrygia, Asia Minor, whose people were recipients of Paul's Epistle to the Colossians. Also Colosse.

Columbia. Poetic name of the New World or, more specifically, the United States, in honor of Christopher Columbus.

Constantinople. Old name of Istanbul, Turkey, the ancient Byzantium.

Copais. Ancient lake northwest of Thebes, Boeotia. Recent drainage of the lake and its surrounding marshes has altered the map of central Greece.

Courland. Old Baltic duchy with the capital at Mitau. Most of its territory is now contained in the southern part of Soviet Latvia. Also called Kurland.

Crécy. Small town near Abbeville, France, where an English army badly defeated the French, 1346.

Crimea. Large peninsula of the Soviet Union on the northern coast of the Black Sea. Its chief cities are Simferopol, Sevastopol, and Yalta.

Croatia. Important state on the northwestern coast of the Adriatic in early Middle Ages. More recently it became, with Slavonia, a crownland of Austro-Hungarian Empire. Capital is Zagreb, in Yugoslavia.

Cumae. Ancient city, reputedly the earliest Greek settlement in Italy, 10 miles west of Naples.

Cunaxa. Ancient town of north Babylonia, the site of the Persian victory which precipitated the retreat of the Ten Thousand to Trepezus, 401 B.C.

Cush. Biblical name applied to ancient Ethiopia and also to a land in Mesopotamia. Also called Kush.

Cynoscephalae. Heights in southeastern Thessaly, Greece, the site of a Roman victory over the Macedonians, 197 B.C.

Cyzicus. Ancient name for a city and peninsula on the south coast of the Propontis in Asia Minor. In 410 B.C., near here, the Athenian navy won a victory over Sparta.

D

Dacia. Ancient territory of Rome which lay north of the Danube in an area now occupied in large part by Romania.

Dalmatia. Former crownland of Austria-Hungary along the Adriatic, now part of Yugoslavia.

Dalriada. Kingdom of Scots on southwest coast of Scotland in early Middle Ages. They united with the Picts in ninth century, and combined territories eventually formed the greater part of Scotland.

Dan. Biblical town, originally Laish, in the extreme north of Israel. It is noted for the saying, "from Dan to Beersheba."

Danelaw. That part of northeastern England, from the Tyne to the Thames, under Danish law and control in the early Middle Ages. Also called Danelagh.

Darién. Old name of eastern Panama. The name "Isthmus of Darién," formerly applied to the Isthmus of Panama, now pertains particularly to the isthmus between the gulfs of Darién and San Miguel.

Dark Continent. Name popularly applied to Africa.

Dartmoor. Desolate moorland in south Devonshire, England. Site of the famous prison of the same name.

Dauphiné. A medieval province between the Rhône and the Alps, with its capital at Grenoble. From it was derived the French royal title, "Dauphin."

Deccan. In its broadest sense, the peninsula of India south of the Narbada River. In particular, that part of the peninsula north of the Kistna River.

Decelea. Village in northern Attica used as a Spartan base and giving its name to the final stage of the Peloponnesian War between Sparta and Athens.

Delos. Sacred island of the ancient Greeks, in the Cyclades southwest of Mykonos Island.

Delphi. Ancient city of Phocis, Greece, the site of the Delphic oracle. It is now the village of Kastri.

Deseret. Early Mormon name of Utah.

Dixie. Popular term for the southern states of the United States. It may have stemmed from the ten dollar bills or "Dixies" issued in Louisiana before the Civil War. These bills bore the French word "dix," meaning "ten."

Dobruja. Region bounded on the west and north by the Danube, on the east by the Black Sea, and extending south into Bulgaria. Its chief port and town is Constanta, Romania.

Dodecanese. In Greek, literally "twelve islands." Actually there are about fourteen main islands, with numerous smaller ones belonging to this group. The largest of the islands is Rhodes.

Dogger Bank. Shallow sand bank covering a wide area in central North Sea; valuable fishing ground.

Doris. Small mountainous territory in the central part of ancient Greece; also, a maritime region of Caria colonized by Dorians.

Down Under. A British term for the lands south of the equator; specifically, in the Antipodes.

Drogio. Unidentified island to the south of Estotiland on late medieval maps. Modern Cape Breton Island most nearly answers the description.

Dur Sharrukin. Ancient Assyrian city north of Nineveh. For a short time it was a royal residence.

E

East Anglia. Early medieval kingdom comprising present English counties of Norfolk and Suffolk.

Eastern Archipelago. Name for Malaysia or the Malay Archipelago.

Eastern Empire. Name of the Eastern Roman or Byzantine Empire.

East Indies. Old collective name for southeast Asia including India, Indochina, and Malaysia.

Ebal, Mount. In Old Testament, mountain of the curse, overlooking Shechem (now Nābulus, Jordan).

Eburacum. Old Roman town and military base on site of modern York, England. Also Eboracum.

Ecbatana. Capital of ancient Media; it is now the city of Hamadan, Iran.

Eden. In the Bible, first home of man. Some scholars place it in the valley of the Tigris and Euphrates.

Edessa. Capital of an ancient kingdom in Mesopotamia. The modern Urfa, Turkey.

Edom. In the Old Testament, a mountainous district south of Moab and the Dead Sea. The Roman Idumaea extended westward to include the Negev.

Eire. Official name of Ireland.

Ekron. Important city of the ancient Philistines. The modern Akir, Israel.

Elam. Very ancient kingdom east of the Tigris and north of Persian Gulf, later absorbed into Persian Empire as province of Susiana. Capital city was Susa.

El Dorado. Legendary land of opulence sought by early Spanish explorers in northern South America. The name of the country was taken from its fabled king, El Dorado (the gilded one), who ruled in the golden city of Manoa.

Emerald Isle. Popular name of Ireland.

Emilia. Division of northern Italy between the Po River and the Apennines. Its chief city is Bologna.

Ephesus. Metropolis of ancient Ionia, Asia Minor, important as a center of commerce and Christianity through much of the Roman period. Its ruins are located south of Izmir, Turkey.

Ephraim, Mount. In the Old Testament, the land of the tribe of Ephraim in central Palestine. It contained the village of Ephraim (the Old Testament Ophrah) northeast of Bethel, in Jordan.

Epirus. Ancient country along Ionian Sea in northwestern Greece and southern Albania. Capital was Ambracia, modern Arta.

Eridu. Very ancient city of Sumeria. Originally built on the Euphrates near the Persian Gulf, it has now been placed over one hundred miles inland by the growth of the delta.

Erin. Popular name of Ireland.

Esdraelon. Great plain of northern Israel, famous as a battlefield and surrounded by Mounts Carmel, Gilboa, and Tabor.

Estotiland. Unidentified island on late medieval maps, in the general location of Newfoundland.

Ethiopia. Ancient kingdom of the upper Nile extending south from Nubia. It was known in the Bible as the land of Cush, with successive capitals at Napata and Meroe. Also used in antiquity for all of known Africa, name is now restricted to Empire of Ethiopia.

Etruria. Land of ancient Etruscans, extending from outskirts of Rome northward to include Tuscany.

Eurasia. Continental land mass of Europe and Asia.

Euxine, The. Name for the Black Sea, known in Roman times as Pontus Euxinus.

Eylau. Town southeast of Königsberg, East Prussia (now Kaliningrad, Soviet Union), where the Russians and Prussians met Napoleon in a bloody, inconclusive battle, 1807.

F

Faesulae. Ancient Roman city in northern Etruria; the modern Fiesole, near Florence.

Far East. Collective name for all Asiatic countries east of Iran and Afghanistan, including eastern Siberia, Japan, and the islands of Malaysia.

Farther India. Old name for peninsula of Indochina.

Fertile Crescent. Name for the fertile lands of antiquity, which extended in a great crescent around the Syrian desert from Israel and Jordan through the valley of the Tigris and the Euphrates.

Finger Lakes. Beautiful group of long, narrow lakes in the western part of New York state.

Flanders. Medieval country along the North Sea from the Straits of Dover to the mouth of the Schelde River, containing the cities of Ypres, Ghent, and Bruges. It is now divided between Belgium and France.

Flodden. Field southwest of Berwick, England, where the Scots under James IV were defeated by the English, 1513.

Fontenoy. Village near Tournai, Belgium, the site of the French victory over the English and their allies in the War of the Austrian Succession (1745).

Fortunate Isles. Legendary islands in the western seas, also called the Isles of the Blest and the Happy Isles. When the Canary and Madeira Islands were discovered the name was attached to them.

Francia. Early medieval land of the Franks embracing the kingdoms of Neustria and Austrasia. The name was applied later to a region of varying boundaries in the basins of the Seine and Loire. Also the Italian and Spanish names for France.

Franklin. Short-lived state government organized in eastern Tennessee in 1784. Capital was Jonesboro.

French North Africa. Collective name sometimes used when referring to former possessions of France in North Africa—Algeria, French Morocco, and Tunisia.

French Shore. The western coastal regions of Newfoundland where the French for many years exercised exclusive fishing rights.

Friedland. Former German town southeast of Kaliningrad, Soviet Union, where Napoleon won a great victory over the Russians, 1807. A temporary peace with Russia and Prussia was the consequence.

Friesland. Medieval state which included, at its greatest extent, most of the Netherlands north of the Schelde and Meuse. Now a province of northern Netherlands with its capital at Leeuwarden.

G

Gadara. Ancient city southeast of the Sea of Galilee, which gave its name to the region along the eastern shore. The name has been perpetuated by the biblical account of the Gadarene swine.

Gades. Westernmost colony of the Phoenicians, also called Gadeira. On site is modern city of Cadiz, Spain.

Galatia. Region and later Roman province in central Asia Minor settled by, and named after, the Gauls. Chief city was Ancyra, now Ankara, Turkey.

Galicia. Former Austro-Hungarian crownland to the north of the western Carpathians. Its chief cities were Lvov, now in the Soviet Ukraine, and Krakow, now in Poland. Also a coastal region of northwestern Spain.

Galilee. In the Roman period, the northern part of Palestine containing the towns of Nazareth, Capernaum, and Ptolemais. It was located west of the Jordan between Phoenicia and Samaria.

Gascony. Old duchy and province of southwestern France bordering the Bay of Biscay. Auch was the chief city of the region, which later became a part of the province of Guyenne and Gascogne with its capital at Bordeaux.

Gath. Ancient capital of the Philistines, birthplace of giant Goliath. The modern Tell es Safi, Israel.

Gaul. Ancient name for the land of the Gauls, the Roman Gallia. The greater part, located west of the Rhine and Alps and north of the Pyrenees, was called Transalpine Gaul. That part in the Po Basin of northern Italy was called Cisalpine Gaul.

Gedrosia. Country of ancient Persia along the northern coast of the Arabian Sea. Now part of Pakistan and Iran.

Gehenna. New Testament name for Tophet.

Gennesaret, Lake of. The Sea of Galilee.

Germania. Roman name for the region east of the Rhine, north of the Danube, and west of the Vistula.

German Ocean. Former name of the North Sea.

Germantown. Site of a British victory over the Americans under Washington, 1777. Now a part of residential Philadelphia.

Giant's Causeway. Peninsula northeast of Coleraine, Northern Ireland. Its unusual columns of basalt have given rise to the legend that it was constructed by giants as a causeway to Scotland.

Gilead. Mountainous biblical region east of the Jordan River, now the northwestern part of modern Jordan, between the Parmak and the Mojib rivers.

Gilgal. Camp city of the Israelites near Jericho. It was their base during the conquest of Canaan.

Golgotha. Hebrew word for "skull," and the site of the crucifixion of Christ. Also Calvary.

Goshen. Region of ancient Egypt colonized by the early Israelites. It was located between the Nile delta and the present Suez Canal.

Grand Banks. Extensive submarine plateau east of Newfoundland, noted as a fishing ground.

Great Basin. Extensive region of the western United States between Wasatch Mountains and the Sierra Nevadas. It contains no drainage outlet to the sea except at the northern and southern extremities.

Great Britain. The name of the island containing England, Scotland, and Wales.

Great Lakes. Collective name for Lakes Superior, Michigan, Huron, Erie, and Ontario.

Great Plains. A vast elevated region of North America between the Rockies and the central prairies, and extending from the Mackenzie River south to the Rio Grande. Included in the area are western parts of the Dakotas, Nebraska, Kansas, Oklahoma, and Texas, and the eastern sections of Montana, Wyoming, Colorado, and New Mexico.

Guano Islands. Islands off the Peruvian coast famed for their guano deposits. The most important are the Lobos and Chincha Islands.

Guinea. All lands on west coast of Africa between Sénégal River and the southern boundary of Angola.

H

Halicarnassus. Important seaport of ancient Caria whose site is now occupied by Budrum, Turkey.

Hamelin. German city, commonly Hameln, noted for the legend of the Pied Piper. It is located on the Weser southwest of Hanover.

Haran. Ancient city of Mesopotamia, southeast of Urfa, Turkey. It later became the Roman Carrhae, site of a Parthian victory over the Romans, 53 B.C.

Hatay. District around Iskenderon (Alexandretta), Turkey. It was formerly the Syrian mandated Sanjak of Alexandretta and the short-lived republic of Hatay.

Heartland. The vast center of the Eurasian continent, protected on almost every side by great mountains and seas. The largest portion is the Soviet Union.

Heliopolis. Important city of ancient Egypt whose ruins lie a few miles north of Cairo. The biblical On.

Hellas. Ancient Greece, land of the Hellenes.

Hellespont, The. Ancient name of the Dardanelles.

Helluland. Early Norse name for a desolate land southwest of Greenland, possibly Labrador.

Helvetia. That part of Gaul comprising the western part of Switzerland. The word is used poetically with reference to the entire country.

Heraclea. Name of numerous Greek cities of antiquity, the most important of which was located on the Gulf of Taranto, Italy. In the vicinity, Pyrrhus of Epirus defeated the Romans, 280 B.C., in the first known battle between Greeks and Romans.

Hercegovina. Old duchy in the mountains south of Sarajevo, Bosnia, now absorbed into the republic of Yugoslavia. Also Herzegovina.

Herculaneum. Roman city at the foot of Mt. Vesuvius. Destroyed with Pompeii, 79 A.D.

Hermopolis. City of ancient Egypt midway between Memphis and Thebes. Also called Hermopolis Magna.

Heshbon. Biblical capital of the Amorites near Mt. Nebo, now Hesban in Jordan.

Hesperia. Name given by the Greeks to lesser–known lands in the extreme western Mediterranean.

Hesse. Former grand duchy and state in western Germany with capital at Darmstadt. German Hessen.

Hibernia. Ancient name of Ireland.

Hiddekel. Biblical name of the Tigris River.

Hieromax. Old name of the Wady Varmuk, which flows into the Jordan south of the Sea of Galilee.

Hierosolyma. Greek name of Jerusalem.

Himera. Important seaport founded by the ancient Greeks near the Sicilian city of Termini. It was destroyed by Carthage about 408 B.C.

Hindustan. Old name for predominantly Hindu India north of the Vindhya Mountains, including the upper Ganges Basin and much of the Punjab. In a looser sense, the entire subcontinent.

Hispania. Roman name of the Iberian Peninsula.

Hispaniola. Name of the second largest island in the West Indies, a corruption of the Spanish Española. The island contains Haiti and the Dominican Republic.

Holland. Name of a district along the west coast of the Netherlands; now often applied to entire country.

Holy Alliance. Loose agreement signed in 1815 under which the signatories, Russia, Prussia, and Austria, proposed to conduct their affairs in a Christian manner. The alliance, to which all European states except Great Britain, Turkey, and the Papal States adhered, became reactionary and had lost all its significance by 1848.

Holy Land. Familiar term for Palestine, now a region divided between Israel and Jordan.

Holy Roman Empire. Medieval confederation of Germanic peoples of central Europe ruled by emperors claiming succession to the emperors of Rome. Although the empire lost northern Italy at an early date, it retained close connection with the papacy until the Reformation. The last monarch abdicated in 1806 after a long period of imperial decline.

Hondo. Island of Honshu, Japan.

Hump, The. Nickname given the eastern end of the lofty Himalayas, which lay astride the route of the India-China air transport service in World War II.

Hyrcania. Ancient region on the southeastern shores of the Caspian Sea; now part of northern Iran.

I

Iberia. That part of ancient Europe south of the Pyrenees, now called the Iberian Peninsula. Also an ancient name of Georgia, Soviet Union.

Île-de-France. Old French province whose capital was Paris.

Ilium. Roman name of ancient Troy, Asia Minor.

Illyria. Very ancient region along the Adriatic corresponding to western Yugoslavia. The name Illyricum was later applied by the Romans to western Yugoslavia, northern Albania, Hungary, and eastern Austria. The former Austro-Hungarian kingdom of Illyria included Carinthia, Carniola, and Kustenland.

Indies. Name assigned by early geographers to the newly discovered islands and coasts of America, which they believed to be the Indies of Asia. The islands later became known as the West Indies. The Netherlands East Indies, on the other hand, assumed the official title of Indonesia in 1948.

Indochina. That part of southeast Asia between India and China (i.e., Burma, Thailand, Laos, Cambodia, Vietnam, and Malaya), formerly called Farther India.

Ingermanland. Old name of the region of the Soviet Union south of the Neva and the Gulf of Finland, the ancient Ingria.

Inland Empire. Name of the great white–pine lumber region in the interior basin of the Columbia River. It encompasses northern Idaho, western Montana, and eastern Washington and Oregon.

Ionia. Maritime region of western Asia Minor colonized by the Ionian Greeks. Its chief cities were Ephesus, Miletus, and Smyrna.

Ipsus. Famous Phrygian town where successors of Alexander the Great fought over division of his empire, 301 B.C. It was north of Pisidian Antioch.

Isabela. Name of the first known European settlement in New World. Located on north coast of Hispaniola in 1493 by Columbus, it was soon abandoned.

Israel. Northern kingdom of the Jews. Its territory included Samaria, Galilee, Bashan, and Gilead, and was bounded on the south by Judah. The capital was successively at Shechem, Tirzah, and Samaria. Also, the name of the modern Jewish republic.

Issus. Famous town in ancient Cilicia where Alexander the Great defeated the Persians in battle, 333 B.C. It was located on Turkish Gulf of Iskenderun.

Ithaca. The modern island of Ithake, Greece, the legendary home of Ulysses.

Ivry. Village of Ivry-la-Bataille, south of Rouen, France. Here, in 1590, Henry IV led the Huguenots to victory over forces of the Catholic League.

J

Jamestown. First permanent English settlement in the United States, established on a peninsula on the left bank of the James in 1607. The site is now on Jamestown Island, near Williamsburg, Virginia.

Jaxartes. Ancient name of the Syr Darya River.

Jebus. Early name of Jerusalem—also called Salem, Ariel, Hierosolyma, and Aelia Capitolina.

Jericho. Walled city of biblical fame which once stood in the valley of the Jordan northwest of the Dead Sea. A small village remains.

Judah. Southern kingdom of the Jews, to the south of Israel between the Dead Sea and the Mediterranean. Its chief cities were Hebron, Beersheba, and the capital, Jerusalem.

Judea. Also Judaea, the Roman division of Palestine south of Samaria and west of the Dead Sea. At its greatest extent, the province included Idumaea, Samaria, Galilee, and Peraea.

Jutland. The Danish Jylland, the continental peninsula of Denmark.

K

Kadesh. Southernmost capital of the ancient Hittites near the source of the Orontes.

Kadesh-Barnea. Desert headquarters of Moses and his wandering Israelites near the present border of the U.A.R. and Israel.

Karafuto. Japanese name of the southern half of Sakhalin Island, transferred to Soviet Union in 1945.

Karakorum. Medieval capital of Genghis Khan whose ruins lie along the Orkhon River west of Urga, Mongolia.

Karelia. Old name of district between Lake Ladoga and Gulf of Finland, now part of the Soviet Union.

Kaskaskia. Early French settlement in Illinois on the right bank of the Kaskaskia River near its confluence with the Mississippi.

Kedesh. The present village of Kades, town of Old Testament prominence in northern Palestine near the Waters of Merom.

Kingsmill Islands. The Gilbert Islands.

Kiptchak. Medieval khanate or kingdom ruled by the descendants of the Mongol leader, Genghis Khan. Also called the Kingdom of the Golden Horde, it extended from central Asia to the Black Sea. Its capital was at Sarai on the lower Volga.

Kishon. Famous biblical river, watering plain of Esdraelon in northern Israel.

Kittim. Biblical name of the island of Cyprus, probably derived from its Phoenician port of Citium. The name Chittim also referred to Cyprus, as well as to islands and shores of the eastern Mediterranean.

Klondike. Name of a stream which flows westward into the Yukon River at Dawson, Yukon. Since the gold rush of 1897, name has been applied to entire area of gold fields extending westward into Alaska.

Kurdistan. Land of the Kurds, comprising part of Turkey, Iraq, Iran, and Soviet Armenia.

Kustenland. Old province of Austria-Hungary containing Trieste and the Istrian Peninsula.

L

Laconia. In antiquity, the southeastern division of the Peloponnesus, with its capital at Sparta. Also called Lacedaemon.

Ladrone Islands. Old Spanish name of the Mariana or Marianne Islands. Also called the Ladrones.

Lake District. Picturesque, lake-studded mountain region in England north of Morecambe Bay.

Landes, The. Extensive marshy plain in France along the Bay of Biscay south of the Gironde.

Land of the Midnight Sun. Norway.

Languedoc. Medieval government and province of southern France bordering the Rhône, Mediterranean, and eastern Pyrenees. Its capital was at Toulouse.

Lanka. Ancient name of Ceylon.

Laodicea. Capital of ancient Phrygia and site of one of Paul's seven Asiatic churches. Its ruins now lie near Denizli, Turkey.

Lapland. Country of the Lapps in arctic Europe. This region extends westward from the Kola Peninsula in the Soviet Union through northern Finland, Sweden, and Norway.

Latin America. Collective term for all countries and islands south of the United States where people of Spanish, Portuguese, and French ancestry predominate. It includes Mexico, Central and South America, and most of the West Indies.

Latium. Ancient land of the Latins along the Tyrrhenian Sea. Rome lay in the extreme north.

Laurentian Lakes. Lakes of the glacial period that occupied largely the same area as the present Great Lakes. Huge Lake Algonquin (now divided into lakes Superior, Michigan, and Huron) emptied into Lake Iroquois (now Lake Ontario), which in turn emptied into the Atlantic through the Mohawk and Hudson valleys.

Leeward Islands. General name of the northern group of islands in the Lesser Antilles, extending southeastward from Puerto Rico to include Guadeloupe.

León. Kingdom in northwestern Spain in the early Middle Ages. It absorbed the kingdom of Asturias.

Lepanto. Greek strait between the gulfs of Patras and Corinth, the site of an Italo-Spanish naval victory over Turkey, 1571.

Leuctra. Ancient Greek village near Thebes, Boeotia, where the Thebans destroyed the military power of Sparta, 371 B.C.

Levant, The. Collective name for the lands on the eastern shores of the Mediterranean, including the U.A.R. and Asia Minor. The name was derived from the Latin "levare" (to raise), meaning "the rising

sun" or "the east." It was therefore originally applied to all the Mediterranean lands east of Italy.

Lidice. Small village west of Prague, Czechoslovakia, whose inhabitants were put to death by the Germans in World War II.

Lilybaeum. Fortress city on the western tip of ancient Sicily. The modern Marsala.

Little America. Admiral Byrd's base in Antarctica at 78° 40′ S. and 164° 03′ W.

Little Russia. Name given to an old division of Russia, now in the northern part of the Soviet Ukraine. The region contains the cities of Kharkov, Kiev, Poltava, and Chernigov.

Livonia. Medieval country on the Baltic Sea with its capital at Riga. Its territory is now divided between the Soviet republics of Latvia and Estonia.

Llano Estacado. Vast arid plateau in western Texas and eastern New Mexico, called in English "The Staked Plains."

Lombardy. Early medieval kingdom of the Lombards extending originally from the Alps to southern Italy. It was reduced later to the Po Valley region of northern Italy.

Loochoo Islands. The Ryukyu Islands.

Lorraine. Former kingdom, duchy, and province of varying boundaries in the Meuse and Moselle river basins between France and Germany. The chief city is Metz, France.

Lotharingia. Latin name of the kingdom of Lothaire which extended in the early Middle Ages from the Alps along the left bank of the Rhine to its mouth. It dwindled in size and became duchy of Lorraine.

Louisbourg. Famous French fortress south of Sydney, Nova Scotia, destroyed by the British in 1758. The small port of Louisburg survives near its site.

Louisiana Territory. Name given to the vast frontier region which the United States purchased from France in 1803. It extended roughly from the Mississippi to the Rockies and from Texas to Canada.

Low Countries. Term originally applied to the medieval Netherlands, which then included the present Netherlands, Belgium, and Luxembourg. The term still applies to all three countries.

Lugdunensis. Roman province in central Gaul lying largely between the Seine and Loire rivers and extending westward to the ocean. Its capital city of Lugdunum, the modern Lyon, France, lay in its southeastern extremity.

Lutetia. Roman name of Paris. Also called Lutetia Parisiorum.

Lydia. Powerful kingdom of antiquity extending from the Aegean to the Halys River in Asia Minor. It was conquered by Persia in 546 B.C. and reduced to a small Aegean coastal province. The chief cities were Sardes and Smyrna (now Izmir, Turkey).

M

Macedonia. Also called Macedon. An ancient kingdom, empire, and Roman province of varying boundaries in northern Greece around the head of the Gulf of Salonika. Under Alexander the Great the empire extended from Greece eastward to Egypt and India. The northern part of modern Macedonia is contained within Yugoslavia and Bulgaria.

Maeander. Old name of Menderes River, which flows into the Aegean south of Izmir, Turkey. Its winding course has given rise to the modern word "meander."

Maelström. Also Malström. A strait south of Moskenäsö island in the Lofoten Islands, noted for its dangerous current and whirlpool.

Magna Graecia. Latin name of the southern part of ancient Italy colonized by the Greeks. It extended from the Bay of Naples to the eastern shore of the Gulf of Taranto.

Magnesia. Coast district of ancient Thessaly. It has given its name to magnetic ore which may have been first discovered there.

Maine. Old French province south of Normandy.

Maipo. Chilean river which reaches the Pacific south of Santiago. San Martín's victory over the Spanish here, at the town of Maipú in 1818, assured the independence of Chile.

Malacca. Old name occasionally applied to the Malay Peninsula.

Malaysia. General name for all the islands in the East Indies except New Guinea and including the Philippines. Also called the Malay Archipelago.

Mancha, La. Former province of central Spain southeast of Madrid. Famous in fiction as the home of Don Quixote.

Manche, La. French name of the English Channel.

Manchukuo. State created in Manchuria and part of North China through Japanese intervention in 1932. Its existence ended with the fall of Japan in 1945.

Mantinea. Ancient Arcadian city in the Peloponnesus west of Argos, Greece. It was the site of several ancient battles. Also Mantineia.

Marathon. Famous coastal village and plain of ancient Greece northeast of Athens. Here, in 490 B.C., the Athenian army defeated the Persian invaders.

Mareotis, Lake. Ancient name of the Birket-el-Mariut, a large lake southeast of Alexandria, Egypt.

Maritime Provinces. Historic term for the Canadian provinces of New Brunswick, Nova Scotia, and Prince Edward Island.

Markland. Early Norse name of a region southwest of Greenland, probably Newfoundland.

Mason and Dixon Line. Popular name for the dividing line between North and South prior to the Civil War. Originally, it was the boundary between Maryland and Pennsylvania as surveyed by two English astronomers, 1763-1767.

Massilia. Roman name of Marseilles, France.

Mauretania. Ancient name of northwestern Africa, embracing modern Morocco and part of Algeria. Distinguished from Mauritania, the former French protectorate north of Senegal.

Mayapán. Old capital of the Mayas. Its ruins are located south of Merida, Yucatan.

Mazaca. Capital of ancient Cappadocia. The Roman Caesarea and the modern Kayseri, Turkey.

Mecklenburg. Medieval duchy and later a province of Germany along the Baltic, west of Pomerania. Its chief cities are Schwerin and Rostock.

Media. Ancient country of northwestern Iran with its capital at Ecbatana. Once a powerful empire itself it became in the sixth century, B.C., a part of the empire of Persia.

Megaris. District of ancient Greece on the eastern end of the Isthmus of Corinth. The capital was Megara.

Megiddo. Ancient city on the plain of Esdraelon which gave its name to Armageddon, "the mountain of Megiddo."

Melanesia. Collective name for certain islands in the Southwest Pacific whose inhabitants have similar racial characteristics. They comprise the entire chain of islands from New Guinea to the Fijis, including the Admiralties, the Bismarck Archipelago, the Solomons, New Caledonia, and the New Hebrides.

Melita. Ancient name of Malta.

Memphis. Very ancient capital of Egypt on the left bank of the Nile below Cairo.

Mercia. Early medieval kingdom of central England.

Meroe. Capital of the ancient kingdom of Ethiopia on the Nile below Khartoum.

Merom, Waters of. Biblical name of the small lake in the Jordan valley between Mt. Hermon and the Sea of Galilee. Its modern name is Hula.

Mesopotamia. Old name for the land between the Tigris and Euphrates, the biblical Aram Naharaim. Also a Roman province. It is now a part of Iraq.

Messenia. Ancient country in the southwestern Peloponnesus, Greece. Its chief city was Messene. Now a province of Greece.

Michmash. Site of early Israelite victory over Philistines, now Mukhmas, Jordan, northeast of Jerusalem.

Micronesia. Name applied to an extensive chain of islands in the western Pacific whose races are related. The chief Micronesian groups are the Marianas and Palaus (volcanic), and the Carolines, Marshalls, and Gilberts (coral).

Middle East. Originally, a collective name for the lands between the Near and Far East, including Iraq, Iran, Afghanistan, and the countries of the Arabian peninsula. The name has recently been applied also to the countries of the eastern Mediterranean, from the U.A.R. to Turkey, and east to Iran and is replacing "Near East" in official U.S. State Department usage.

Middle West. Collective name for the lowland states of the north-central United States. West of the Mississippi River it includes Missouri and Kansas and all the states to the north; east of the Mississippi it includes all the states north of the Ohio River.

Miletus. Important seaport of ancient Ionia, Asia Minor, south of Ephesus.

Mizpeh. Mountain meeting-place of the ancient Israelites, northwest of Jerusalem. Also Mizpah.

Mizraim. Hebrew name of Egypt.

Moab. Ancient kingdom between Gilead and Edom on the eastern shores of the Dead Sea. Now it is a part of Jordan.

Moldau. The Vltava River which flows through Prague, Czechoslovakia.

Moldavia. Former principality along the right bank of the Prut River, with its capital at Iasi. In 1861 it united with Walachia to create the kingdom of Romania. Also, the name given to the new Soviet republic in previously Romanian Bessarabia.

Mongolia. Vast land of the Mongols in central Asia between China and the Soviet Union. Outer Mongolia is now the Soviet-dominated People's Republic of Mongolia with its capital at Urga. Inner Mongolia comprises an extensive plateau area in north and northeast China. In the Middle Ages the Mongols ruled an empire which reached to western Russia.

Montenegro. Former principality and kingdom in the mountains northwest of Albania. Now part of Yugoslavia.

Mont-Saint-Michel. Famous island and village west of Avranches, France, containing an historic monastery. It is connected to the mainland by a causeway.

Moon, Mountains of the. Mountain range believed by ancient geographers to lie across central Africa, and to give rise to the headwaters of the Nile.

Moravia. Former Austro-Hungarian crownland in the Morava River valley; now the central province of Czechoslovakia. The capital is Brno.

Morgarten. Mountain slope near Lucerne, Switzerland, where an Austrian army was routed, 1315, and the independence of Switzerland assured.

Moriah, Mount. Hill on the east side of Jerusalem, the site of the Temple of Solomon.

Mount of Olives. This mountain, east of Jerusalem, is frequently mentioned in scripture. It is 2,665 ft. high. Also called Mount Olivet.

Muscovy. Old name of Russia derived from Moscow, the capital of a strong medieval grand duchy.

207

Mutina. Early Roman colony, the modern Italian city of Modena. It was the site of the last resistance of the Cisalpine Gauls to the growing power of Rome, 193 B.C.

Mycale. Promontory east of island of Samos where Greeks destroyed a Persian naval force, 479 B.C.

Mycenae. Very ancient Greek city whose ruins have been of great archaeological interest. It was located in Argolis northeast of Argos.

N

Narbonensis. Roman province extending along the Mediterranean coast of Gaul from the Alps to the Pyrenees. Its important cities were Massilia, Tolosa, and the capital, Narbo Martius (now Narbonne).

Naseby. Village near Northampton in central England; site of the decisive victory of the Parliamentarians under Cromwell over Charles I, 1645.

Naucratis. Ancient Greek trading center on the Nile delta south of Alexandria.

Navarre. Early medieval kingdom in the western Pyrenees. Its capital was at Pamplona, Spain. Most of the kingdom later united with Aragon, while the remainder, on the northern slopes of the Pyrenees, was absorbed by France.

Navigators' Islands. Old name of Samoan Islands.

Neanderthal. Valley between Düsseldorf and Wuppertal, Germany, where the skull of the famed prehistoric man was found.

Near East. Name formerly associated with the Ottoman Empire, and more recently applied to those countries making up the "Middle East."

Nebo (Pisgah), Mount. Mountain of Gilead near the north end of the Dead Sea, with an altitude of 2,631 ft. Now Jebel Neba in Jordan.

Negev. Vast desert region of southern Israel.

New Albion. Name given by Drake to part of the Pacific Coast north of San Francisco Bay.

New Amsterdam. Old name of New York City under the Dutch regime.

New Carthage. Important colony of the Carthaginians; now the city of Cartagena, Spain.

New England. Collective name since the early colonial days for the northeastern part of the United States. It includes the states of Maine, New Hampshire, Vermont, Massachusetts, Connecticut, and Rhode Island.

New France. Old name applied to the French colonies in North America, specifically, those in eastern Canada which were yielded to the British after the capture of Quebec City in 1763.

New Georgia. Old name of Vancouver Island, Canada, and adjacent mainland territory.

New Granada. Old Spanish viceroyalty in that part of Latin America now occupied by the republics of Colombia and Panama.

New Holland. Old name of Australia.

New Netherland. Originally an English land grant to the Duke of York, for lands between the Connecticut and Delaware Rivers. After the English defeat by the Dutch, it became a Dutch colony, roughly comprising much of New Jersey, New York, and Delaware.

New Spain. Early Spanish colony and viceroyalty of varying boundaries, now the republic of Mexico.

New Sweden. Old Swedish colony along the lower Delaware River.

New World. Name first applied in the 15th century to the newly discovered Western Hemisphere.

Nineveh. Capital of the Assyrian Empire and one of the most splendid cities of antiquity. Its ruins lie across the Tigris from Mosul, Iraq. Also called Ninus.

Nippon. Name of the old Japanese Empire, now reduced to the main and adjacent islands of Japan. Name sometimes restricted to Honshu, largest island.

Nod. Unknown land east of Eden to which Cain fled for refuge.

Normandy. Old French duchy and province along the English Channel containing the cities of Rouen (the capital), Le Havre, Caen, and Cherbourg.

Northeast Passage. Maritime passage from the Atlantic to the Pacific Ocean along north coast of Europe and Asia. It is navigable only in summer months.

North Polar Sea. The Arctic Ocean.

North River. Name of Hudson River near mouth.

Northumbria. Powerful kingdom of the early Middle Ages, located in northeastern England between the Humber and the Firth of Forth. Also called the kingdom of Northumberland, it was created by the union of the kingdoms of Bernicia and Deira.

Northwest Passage. A navigable passage from the Atlantic to the Pacific and the Orient, sought for centuries along the northern coast of North America. The Arctic passage finally found proved to be impassable most of the year.

Northwest Territory. Old name of the region west of Pennsylvania bounded by the Mississippi and Ohio rivers and the Great Lakes. It was ceded by England to the United States at close of Revolution, 1783.

North Woods. Popular name for the forest regions of northern Michigan, Wisconsin, and Minnesota.

Norumbega. In early maps of North America, a mysterious city and region on the Atlantic coast. Its existence has never been proven, though speculation has placed it in Massachusetts and Maine.

Notium. Ancient port west of Ephesus in Asia Minor, noted for the Spartan naval victory over Athens in 407 B.C.

Nubia. Name applied since the dawn of history to a region of the upper Nile now lying in the northern Sudan. It was part of the ancient kingdom of Ethiopia.

Numantia. Ancient town near Soria, Spain, famed for resistance to Roman conquest, 143-133 B.C.

Numidia. Ancient kingdom and later Roman province of northern Africa, in the northeastern part of modern Algeria.

O

Oberammergau. Famous resort in the Bavarian Alps, Germany, noted for its decennial "Passion Play."

Occident. The lands toward the setting sun, a general name for Western Europe and the New World in contradistinction to "Orient."

Oceania. Term used for the Pacific island divisions of Melanesia, Micronesia, and Polynesia. Occasionally it includes the islands of Australasia and Malaysia as well. Also called Oceanica.

Oceanus. According to the ancients, a swift and boundless stream flowing around all the known seas and continents.

Old World. Name applied to Eastern Hemisphere, particularly Europe, since discovery of America.

Olivet. Mount of Olives, east of Jerusalem, in Jordan.

Olympia. Valley of ancient Elis, Greece, site of the Olympic games. It was located along the Alfios River in the western Peloponnesus.

Olynthus. City of ancient Chalcidice, the subject of the famed Olynthiac orations of Demosthenes. It was destroyed in 347 B.C.

On. Biblical name of ancient Heliopolis, Egypt.

Ophir. In the Old Testament, a country which supplied Solomon with gold, silver, and other luxuries. It may have been located in India, southern Arabia, or eastern Africa.

Orange. Medieval principality of France, eventually absorbed by the house of Nassau. It has given its name to the royal house of the Netherlands. The capital, Orange, is located north of Avignon.

Orange River Free State. Former independent republic in South Africa with its capital at Bloemfontein. It was defeated by the British in the Boer War (1899-1902) and later became a province of South Africa.

Orient. The lands toward the rising sun; a western term for the countries of Asia and the Far East.

Ormuz. Famous medieval trade emporium on an island at the mouth of the Persian Gulf. Also called Ormus and Hormuz.

Orontes. Chief river of western Syria, the Arabic Nahr el Asi.

Ottoman Empire. Old Turkish Empire which, at its height in the 16th century, embraced parts of three continents: Asia, Europe, and Africa. Turkish power in Europe advanced to the gates of Vienna and nearly encircled the Black Sea. Turkey also ruled Syria and Mesopotamia in Asia and the entire African coast from Egypt to Algeria.

Oxus. Ancient name of the Amu Darya River in central Asia, which flows into the Aral Sea.

P

Paestum. Ancient city of Magna Graecia whose ruins lie on the southern shore of Italy's Gulf of Salerno. An earlier name was Posidonia.

Palatine Hill. One of the "seven hills" of Rome reputedly selected by Romulus as original site of city.

Palmyra. Desert metropolis of ancient Syria which flourished particularly in Roman times. It was the Tadmor of the Bible, and is now a small Syrian village.

Pampas, The. A vast fertile plain of central Argentina extending from the Atlantic and the Paraná in the east to the Andes and from the Gran Chaco in the north to Patagonia.

Panhandle. Name applied to any strip of territory projecting from the main body of a state or territory, for example, northern Texas, Idaho, and West Virginia; western Oklahoma; southeastern Alaska.

Papal States. Formerly an independent country of central Italy ruled by the Papal See. Stretching from coast to coast, it included the cities of Rome, Bologna, and Ancona. The papacy also possessed Venaissin, an enclave at Avignon, France.

Papua. Former name sometimes applied to the entire island of New Guinea, but now restricted to the Australian-owned territory in the southeast.

Paran. Desert wilderness north of Mt. Sinai where the Israelites wandered before reaching Canaan.

Parima. Legendary lake which early explorers vainly sought in northern South America. The name has since been given to a mountain range at the source of the Orinoco.

Parthia. Ancient country southeast of the Caspian Sea containing the city of Hecatompylos. The Parthian Empire extended from the Indus to the Euphrates before its downfall in 226 A.D.

Pas-de-Calais. French name for the Strait of Dover.

Patagonia. That part of South America south of the Argentine Río Negro between Andes and Atlantic.

Patmos. Small Greek island in the Sporades where John the Divine is believed to have experienced the visions of the Apocalypse.

Pella. Capital of ancient Macedonia, west of Salonika (Thessaloniki), Greece.

Peloponnesus. Ancient name of the large peninsula in southern Greece. The modern Morea.

Peraea. In the New Testament, a region east of the Jordan corresponding closely to Gilead.

Pergamum. Also Pergamon and Pergamus, the name of an ancient Greek kingdom and its capital in Mysia, Asia Minor. The city is identified with the biblical Pergamos, site of one of Paul's seven Asiatic churches. The modern Bergama, Turkey.

Persepolis. Capital of the Persian Empire. Its famous ruins are located northeast of Shiraz, Iran.

Persia. Old name of Iran. The original Persia or Persis was a mountainous country on the northeastern shores of the Persian Gulf. It later grew into an empire extending from the Aegean to the Indus.

Petra. The biblical Sela, midway between the Dead Sea and the Gulf of Aqaba; capital of ancient Edom and, later, of Roman province of Arabia Petraea.

Petrograd. The name of Leningrad between 1914 and 1924. Prior to 1914 city was called St. Petersburg.

Pharos. Peninsula near Alexandria, U.A.R. In ancient times it was an island and the site of a great lighthouse that was considered one of the seven wonders of the world.

Pharsalus. City in southern Thessaly near which Caesar defeated Pompey, 48 B.C. The modern Farsala, Greece.

Philadelphia. Ancient Lydian city where Paul established one of his seven Asiatic churches. It is now the town of Alasehir, Turkey. Also an old name of Amman, the capital of Jordan.

Philippi. City of ancient Greece, inland from the present port of Kavalla. Near here, in 42 B.C., Augustus and Antony defeated the Roman Republicans led by Brutus and Cassius. Here also Paul founded the first Christian church in Europe.

Philistia. Ancient country of the Philistines in southwest Palestine. Its chief cities were Gaza, Ashkelon, Ashdod, Ekron, and Gath. The name Palestine was derived from "Philistine."

Phoenicia. The first nation to engage in large-scale Mediterranean commerce and colonization. Its chief cities were Sidon and Tyre, the present ports of Saida and Tyre (Sur), Lebanon.

Phrygia. In the time of Persian power a large country in west-central Asia Minor. Its important cities were Celaenae and, later, Apamea.

Picardy. Old province of northern France with its capital at Amiens.

Pichincha. Lofty volcano west of Quito, Ecuador, in Pichincha province. It is the site of one of the world's highest battlefields. Here, in 1822, Sucre defeated the Spanish and insured the independence of Ecuador.

Piedmont. Originally, a division of northern Italy in the upper basin of the Po, a part of the old duchy of Savoy and kingdom of Sardinia. Now, a name applied to any foothill region, for example, the plateau between the Appalachians and the Atlantic Coastal Plain, extending from Virginia to Alabama.

Pillars of Hercules. Ancient name of the two promontories forming the Strait of Gibraltar.

Pisgah, Mount. The spur of Mount Nebo from which Moses beheld the Promised Land.

Plassey. Indian village north of Calcutta where Clive defeated Bengal army, 1757, assuring British control of lower Ganges basin and, eventually, of all India.

Plataea. Town south of ancient Thebes, Greece, where the Greeks, principally Spartans, decisively defeated an invading Persian army, 479 B.C.

Polish Corridor. Narrow corridor of former German territory assigned to Poland in 1919 to give that country access to the Baltic Sea. As a result of its World War II acquisitions from Germany east and west of corridor, Poland has extensive Baltic frontage.

Polynesia. Collective name of a myriad of islands in the Central and South Pacific inhabited by closely related races. Important in this category are the Hawaiian, Marquesas, Tuamotu, Society, Samoa, Tonga, Ellice, and Phoenix Islands.

Pomerania. Formerly, a Prussian province along the coast of the Baltic Sea. Most of the old province including Stettin, its capital, is now Polish territory. The German Pommern.

Pompeii. Famous Roman city southeast of Naples. Destroyed by the eruption of Mt. Vesuvius in 79 A.D.

Pontine Marshes. Also called Pomptine Marshes. Extensive areas of reclaimed marshland along the southern coast of the Campagna di Roma, Italy.

Pontus. Old kingdom of northeastern Asia Minor, later a Roman province. It took its name from the Euxine, or Pontus Euxinus, on whose shores it lay.

Porto Bello. Famous port for gold shipment in Spanish colonial days. It is now a small Panamanian village (Portobelo) on the Caribbean east of Colón. Also Puerto Bello.

Port Royal. Old French name of Annapolis Royal, Nova Scotia, founded in 1604.

Prairie Provinces. Collective name for the Canadian provinces of Manitoba, Saskatchewan, and Alberta.

Prussia. Medieval duchy on the Baltic around the lower Vistula and Niemen. Under the later kingdom of Prussia it was divided into provinces; East Prussia (capital, Königsberg) and West Prussia (capital, Danzig). The kingdom, around which greater Germany was constructed, extended westward to Rhenish Prussia (capital, Coblenz).

Pteria. Old capital of the Hittites, believed to be the site of a Persian victory over Lydia. Its ruins are near the village of Boghaz-Keui, Turkey.

Punjab. Former province in the lowlands of northwestern British India. In 1947 much of the Punjab including the capital at Lahore became part of the new state of Pakistan.

Puteoli. A leading seaport of ancient Italy; the modern Pozzuoli, west of Naples.

Pydna. Town in ancient Macedonia where the Romans won a final decisive victory over the Macedonians, 168 B.C.

R

Rabbah. Biblical capital of the Ammonites. Later Philadelphia, it is now Amman, capital of Jordan.

Ragae. First capital of ancient Media, on site of modern Tehrān, Iran. Also called Rhagae and Rages.

Ramah. Ancient home of Samuel, north of Jerusalem.

Ramoth-Gilead. Place of biblical importance east of the Jordan River, possibly near Es Salt in Jordan. May be identical with Ramoth-Mizpah.

Ratisbon. A Bavarian city on the Danube northeast of Munich; now called Regensburg. The story of its capture by Napoleon in 1809 is told in Browning's poem "Ratisbon."

Reval. Also Revel, the former name of Tallinn, capital of Soviet Estonia.

Rhaetia. Alpine province of Rome which has given its name to the Rhaetian Alps between Austria and Switzerland. Also called Raetia.

Rhineland. Also called Rhenish Prussia or Rhine Province, in the basin of the German lower Rhine. Important cities are Köln (Cologne) and Düsseldorf.

Rimland. That part of the World Island adjacent to the Heartland but close enough to the temperate seas and oceans to be influenced by sea power. Included are Western Europe, the Middle East, the Far East, and Africa.

Riviera. Popular name for a narrow strip of territory between the mountains and the Mediterranean extending from Hyères, France to La Spezia, Italy. It includes the cities of Nice and Genova (Genoa) and many smaller resorts.

Roman Empire. The greatest empire of ancient times, administered from the city of Rome. The lands under Roman control included entire Mediterranean littoral and extended from Britain to Mesopotamia.

Roncesvalles. Modern French, Roncevaux, a Spanish village near a pass in the Pyrenees northeast of Pamplona; scene of the death of Roland in 778.

Rubicon. Small stream north of Rimini marking the boundary between Cisalpine Gaul and ancient Italy. Caesar crossed the stream in 49 B.C., precipitating a Roman civil war.

Ruhr. Name applied to industrial district in Ruhr River valley of western Germany. Chief city is Essen.

Rumelia. Also Roumelia. Name, loosely used, for the European territory of the Ottoman Empire along the northern shore of the Aegean. It corresponded roughly with ancient Thrace and Macedonia. Eastern Rumelia was annexed by Bulgaria in 1885.

Runnymede. Also Runnimede. A meadow on the right bank of the Thames west of London, where King John signed the Magna Carta, 1215.

Rupert's Land. Also Rupert Land, an early name for the vast area in the basin of Hudson Bay, later known as the Hudson's Bay Territory.

Russia. Popular name of the Union of Soviet Socialist Republics (Soviet Union), formerly the Russian Empire. The name is now applied more properly to two Soviet republics, the Russian Socialist Federated Soviet Republic and White Russia. Soviet Russia is also a popular name of the Soviet Union.

Ruthenia. Land of the Ruthenians in the central Carpathian Mountains. Parts of Ruthenia have at various times been under the control of Poland, Austria-Hungary, Czechoslovakia, and Russia. At the close of World War II, Czechoslovakia ceded that part of Ruthenia south of the Carpathians to the Soviet Union.

Ryswick. Village near the Hague, the Netherlands, where the French signed a treaty with England, the Netherlands, and Spain, 1697; now Rijswijk.

S

Saguntum. Ancient city noted for its valiant resistance to Hannibal, 219 B.C. Later called Murviedro, it is now the town of Sagunto, Spain.

Saikio. Name occasionally given to Kyoto, the old "western capital" of Japan, to distinguish it from Tokio or Tokyo, the present "eastern capital."

Saint Brendan's Island. According to medieval legend, one of several islands in the Atlantic visited by Irish monks and their leader, Saint Brendan.

Saint Petersburg. Name of the former capital of Russia. The name was changed to Petrograd in 1914 and Leningrad in 1924. In 1918, the capital was transferred to Moskva (Moscow).

Salamis. Chief seaport of ancient Cyprus, now a heap of ruins north of Famagusta. Also, an island near Peiraieus (Piraeus), Greece, noted for Athenian naval victory over Persia off its shores, 480 B.C.

Salem. Original name of Jerusalem, still used poetically. Also Shalem.

Salt Sea. One of the biblical names for the Dead Sea, the others being the Sea of the Plain and the East Sea. Known to Romans as Lacus Asphaltites.

Samaria. Name for the capital of the ancient kingdom of Israel, later applied to the entire region between Galilee and Judea. The city of Samaria became the Roman Sebaste and the present village of Sebustieh, northwest of Nābulus, Jordan.

Sandwich Islands. Old name of Hawaiian Islands.

San Juan Hill. Celebrated elevation southeast of Santiago de Cuba, taken by storm by the Americans, 1898, in an engagement in the Spanish-American War. The famous Rough Riders were prominent in the assault.

San Stefano. Small port west of Constantinople, now Istanbul. The treaty signed there, 1878, ended Russo-Turkish War.

Sarai. Capital of the medieval khanate of Kiptchak. Soviet city of Leninsk, east of Volgograd, formerly Stalingrad, now on site.

Sardes. Also Sardis, capital of the early kingdom of Lydia and seat of one of the seven Asiatic churches of Paul. It was located east of what is now Izmir, Turkey.

Sardinia. Old kingdom created in 1720 out of Savoy, Piedmont, Genoa, and the island of Sardinia. The kings of Sardinia passed the royal succession from the dukes of Savoy to the later kings of Italy.

Sargasso Sea. An extensive ocean area northeast of the West Indies, laden with drifting weeds, chiefly Sargassum or gulf weed. Since it is the center of a great elliptical gyration of ocean currents in the North Atlantic, the region is relatively calm.

Satsuma. Formerly a province on Kyushu Island, Japan; famed for its fine porcelain.

Savoy. Old county and duchy in the French and Italian Alps. At its height, the duchy controlled the Piedmont and an outlet to the sea at Nice, France. In 1860, the Nice district and that part of Savoy on the western slopes of the Alps were ceded to France. The early counts of Savoy founded the reigning house of the kingdom of Italy.

Saxony. Early medieval duchy extending from the North Sea almost to Leipzig in the southeast and the Rhine in the southwest. It later became an electorate and a kingdom north of the Erzgebirge (Ore Mountains), with Dresden and Leipzig as the chief cities.

Scandinavia. Sweden, Norway, and Denmark.

Scapa Flow. Large protected bay in southern Orkney Islands. Main anchorage of the British Home (Grand) Fleet. Chief British naval base in World War I and World War II.

Schleswig-Holstein. Old duchy and province north of the Elbe between the North and Baltic Seas, for whose possession Germany and Denmark have contended for centuries. Northern Schleswig (the Danish Slesvig) is now in Danish territory

Scotia. Early medieval name of Ireland, the original home of the Scots. It was later applied poetically to Scotland, the land to which many Scots emigrated.

Scylla. Prominent rock on the Italian side of the Strait of Messina. It was the legendary home of the sea monster, Scylla, across the strait from the whirlpool, Charybdis.

Sea of the Plain. Biblical name of the Dead Sea, also called in scripture the Salt Sea and the East Sea. The Roman name was Lacus Asphaltites.

Sedgemoor. Moor near Bridgwater, England, where the Royalists of James II defeated the Duke of Monmouth in 1685.

Seleucia. Capital of the Seleucid Empire on the Tigris south of Baghdad. This empire extended from the Mediterranean to the Indus before being absorbed by Rome. Also, a Syrian city, the port for ancient Antioch.

Senlac. Hill near Hastings, England, where the invading Normans, led by William the Conqueror, won their great victory over the Saxons, 1066.

Sepharvaim. Biblical name of Sippar, a city north of Babylon.

Serbia. Formerly an independent kingdom, now a part of eastern Yugoslavia. Also called Servia. The capital was Belgrade.

Sharon. Coastal plain in Israel between Jaffa and Mt. Carmel.

Sheba. Biblical name of Saba or Sabea, a wealthy kingdom in southwestern Arabia.

Shechem. Also Sichem, the earliest capital of the kingdom of Israel. The Sychar of the New Testament and the Roman Flavia Neapolis, it is now the city of Nābulus, Jordan.

Shiloh. Early religious center of Israelites between Nābulus and Jerusalem. Also a great battlefield near Pittsburg Landing, Tennessee, in the Civil War.

Shinar. Biblical name of Babylonia or its southern part; also called Chaldea or Sumer.

Shire. In England, a land division or county.

Shushan. Biblical name of Susa.

Siberia. Vast expanse of Soviet territory in Asia extending from the Urals to the Pacific. It is bounded on the south by the Soviet republics of central Asia, and by Sinkiang, Mongolia, and Manchuria, and on the north by the Arctic Ocean.

Sick Man of Europe. Term given to the Ottoman or Turkish Empire in the years prior to World War I, when its control over southeastern Europe and its Arabic and North African empire was beginning to weaken.

Sicyon. Important city of ancient Greece northwest of Corinth. The area surrounding the city was called Sicyonia.

Sidon. Principal port of ancient Phoenicia, also called Zidon. Saida, Lebanon, now occupies its site.

Silesia. Industrial region, largely in the valley of the upper Oder. Formerly a province of Prussia and Germany, it now forms the southwestern part of Poland. The chief city is Wroclaw, formerly Breslau, Germany. Austrian Silesia, in the Moravska Ostrava region, was divided between Czechoslovakia and Poland following World War I. German Schlesin.

Sinai, Mount. Famous biblical mountain where Moses received the Ten Commandments. Many identify it with Ras es Sufsafeh or Jebel Musa, near Jebel Katherina on the U.A.R.'s Sinai Peninsula.

Slavonia. Region between Drava and Sava rivers in north-central Yugoslavia, formerly part of Austro-Hungarian crownland of Croatia and Slavonia.

Slot, The. Name given in World War II to the sound which bisects the Solomon Island chain to the northeast and southwest.

Slovakia. Mountainous province of eastern Czechoslovakia. Capital is Bratislava, the German Pressburg.

Slovenia. Region in northwestern Yugoslavia. The chief city is Ljubljana, formerly called Laibach.

Smyrna. Former Greek name of Izmir, Turkey. One of Paul's seven churches of Asia was located here.

Sofala. Seaport of Mozambique, southwest of Beira, taken from the Arabs by Portugal in 1505.

Southern Ocean. Name formerly applied to the ocean waters between 40° South Latitude and the Antarctic Circle.

South Sea. Old name of the Pacific Ocean. It is now applied to the South Pacific, commonly in the plural form, "South Seas."

Spanish America. Those portions of the New World settled by the Spaniards in the early Colonial period.

Spanish Main. Old name of the mainland of Spanish America; particularly the Caribbean coast of South and Central America, the Spanish Tierra Firme. Popularly, the name has become associated with the entire Caribbean area during the colorful pirate period.

Stonehenge. This mysterious roofless monument stands on Salisbury Plain, near Wiltshire, England. It is formed by huge standing stones, apparently the ruins of a prehistoric sacred enclosure. It is believed to have been erected by men of the Bronze Age.

Straits Settlements. Former crown colony of Great Britain on the Malay Peninsula. The principal settlements were Singapore (the capital), Penang Island, and Malacca.

Straits, The. Name used collectively in referring to the strategic waterway between the Black and the Aegean Seas. It includes the Bosporus, the Sea of Marmara, and the Dardanelles.

Strathclyde. Old Celtic kingdom of northwestern England south of the Clyde, including the districts of Cumbria and Galloway.

Stresa. Resort town on the southwestern shore of Lake Maggiore in northern Italy. It was the site of an important international conference in 1935.

Styria. Crownland of Austria–Hungary located north of the Drava River, largely within the southeastern boundaries of modern Austria.

Sudan. An extensive region south of the Sahara stretching from the horn of Africa on the Atlantic to the southern shores of the Red Sea. Includes most of the independent nation of the same name.

Sudetenland. Strip of territory in northwestern Czechoslovakia across the Erzgebirge (Ore Mountains) from Germany. It contained a majority of Sudeten Germans prior to World War II.

Sumer. That part of ancient Babylonia south of Akkad at the head of the Persian Gulf. Also called Sumeria, Shumer, and the Land of Shinar.

Susa. Capital of ancient Elam or Susiana and royal residence of kings of Persia. Called Shushan in Bible.

Swanee. Musical adaptation by Stephen Foster of the name of the Suwannee River in Georgia and northern Florida.

Sybaris. Wealthy and luxury-loving city of ancient Magna Graecia. Its ruins are now located in northern Calabria near the Gulf of Taranto.

Sychar. The New Testament name of Shechem; now Nābulus, Jordan.

Syrtis. Ancient name applied to two North African gulfs. Syrtis Major, southwest of Bengazi, is now called the Gulf of Sidra. Syrtis Minor, in Tunisia, is now called the Gulf of Gabes.

T

Tabor, Mount. A mountain east of Nazareth, Palestine, prominent in the Old Testament. Its altitude is 1,880 ft.

Tadmor. Biblical name of Palmyra, Syria.

Tanagra. Ancient town in eastern Boeotia, Greece, the site of a Spartan victory over Athens, 457 B.C. Famed also for its terra-cotta figurines.

Tannenberg. Small village south of Ostróda, Poland, formerly within the boundaries of East Prussia. Here, in 1914, a German army surrounded and partially destroyed a large Russian force.

Taprobane. Ancient name of Ceylon. Also, in the domain of the legendary Prester John somewhere in Asia or Africa, a remarkable island containing deposits of pure gold.

Tarraconensis. Largest of the three Roman provinces in Spain, located east of Baetica and north and east of Lusitania. The capital was Tarraco, the modern city of Tarragona.

Tarshish. Biblical name for a region remote from Palestine. It probably refers to the area around Tartessus, a Phoenician city near the mouth of the Guadalquivir in southern Spain.

Tarsus. Town of southeastern Asia Minor, southwest of what is now Adana, Turkey. It is chiefly famous as the birthplace of the Apostle Paul.

Tatary. Old name (commonly, but less correctly, Tartary) of the vast center of the Eurasian continent inhabited by the Tatars. In the Middle Ages, they extended their control from Mongolia westward to the Dnepr River in European Tatary and eastward to the Pacific. An autonomous Tatar republic now exists with its capital at Kazan, Soviet Union.

Tenochtitlán. Capital of the old Aztec Empire, captured by the Spanish in 1521. Modern Mexico City has been built on the same site.

Thapsus. Town southeast of Sousse, Tunisia, where Caesar defeated the followers of Pompey, 46 B.C.

Thebes. Very ancient capital of Egypt on the right bank of the Nile near the present town of Luxor. Also, the chief city of Boeotia, Greece.

Therma. Ancient name for the modern Thessaloniki, or Salonika, Greece.

Thermopylae. Famous pass between the sea marshes and the mountains southeast of Lamia, Greece. It is the site of the heroic stand made by several hundred Spartans against the invading Persians, 480 B.C.

Thessaly. Division of ancient Greece bordering the Aegean Sea and completely surrounded by mountains, including the famous Olympus. The chief city of the region today is Larisa.

Thrace. Region of antiquity bounded by the Danube and the Black and Aegean seas. The subsequent Roman province, Thracia, included only territory south of the Balkan Mountains, what is now southern Bulgaria, European Turkey, and northeastern Greece.

Thule. Ancient name of the most northerly part of the known world, probably Iceland, or Norway, or one of the Shetland Islands. The expression "Ultima Thule" refers to any distant human objective, geographical or otherwise.

Thyatira. City of ancient Lydia, the site of one of Paul's seven churches of Asia. Its ruins lie near Akhisar, Turkey.

Tierra del Fuego. Desolate archipelago at the southern tip of South America, separated from the continent proper by the Strait of Magellan.

Timbuktu. Remote town on the upper Niger in the interior of Mali. The French form is Tombouctou.

Tiphsah. Biblical name of ancient Thapsacus, Syria.

Tippecanoe. River in northwestern Indiana noted for Harrison's victory over the Indians, near its confluence with the Wabash, 1811.

Tipperary. County and city in south-central Ireland, prominent in a popular song of World War I.

Tiryns. Very old city southeast of Argos, Greece. Its ruins are of great archaeological significance.

Tirzah. Early capital of the kingdom of Israel, east of modern Sebustieh in Jordan.

Tolosa. Roman name of Toulouse, France.

Tophet. That part of the Valley of Hinnom south of Jerusalem where the idolatrous Jews of antiquity worshiped their god of fire. Also called Gehenna.

Touraine. Medieval duchy and province of France with its capital at Tours.

Trafalgar. Cape in southern Spain between Cadiz and Gibraltar. Off this promontory, the British fleet under Lord Nelson defeated the combined navies of France and Spain, 1805.

Transcaucasia. That part of the Soviet Union south of the Caucasus Mountains, comprising the republics of Georgia, Azerbaidzhan, and Armenia.

Transleithania. Old name for the Hungarian portion of Austria-Hungary, to the east and south of Cisleithania. It included all of modern Hungary and parts of Yugoslavia, Czechoslovakia, and Romania.

Transylvania. Region in northwestern Romania separated from the rest of the country by the Carpathians and the Transylvanian Alps. A former part of Austria-Hungary, the area has long been a source of conflict between Hungary and Romania. The capital is Cluj.

Trapezus. Ancient name of Trabzon, Turkey.

Trebizond. Medieval empire of the Byzantines along the southeastern coast of the Black Sea. The capital was Trebizond, which is now the city of Trabzon, Turkey.

Tremont. Also Trimontaine, original name of Boston, derived from the three summits of Beacon Hill.

Trinacria. Ancient name of Sicily, so called because of the island's three large promontories to the northeast, southeast, and west.

Troas. Also called the Troad, a region of ancient Asia Minor bordering the Aegean and the Hellespont. Located here was the famous city of Troy or Ilium and the ancient seaport Troas or Alexandria Troas.

Troy. Ancient city of Troas, Asia Minor, destroyed by the Greeks in the Trojan War. The Greek Ilion and the Roman Ilium.

Turkestan. Extensive region in central Asia bounded by the Caspian to the west, Iran and Afghanistan to the south, the Tien Shan Mtns. to the east, and Siberia to the north. It is divided among constituent republics of the Soviet Union.

Tuscany. Medieval duchy in western Italy containing the old cities of Florence and Pisa.

Two Sicilies. United medieval kingdom of Sicily and southern Italy.

Tyrol. Mountainous region which formed, with Vorarlberg, the westernmost crownland in Austria-Hungary. After World War I, the southern part became the Italian Trentino. The capital of the Tyrol, also called Tirol, was Innsbrück, Austria.

U

Ukraine. Formerly, a general name for the lands in the basin of the Dnepr (Dnieper) River of southwestern Russia. In its broadest sense, the name included all of Russia westward to Polish Galicia, and is now applied to a Soviet republic in that area. It has often been called "Little Russia."

Ulster. Northern division of Ireland largely contained within the boundaries of Northern Ireland, a unit of the United Kingdom. The other divisions, Connaught, Leinster, and Munster, are in Eire (Republic of Ireland).

Umbria. Ancient land of the Umbrians in central Italy, probably extending at one time from the Adriatic to the Tyrrhenian Sea. Modern Umbria lies landlocked in the basin of the upper Tiber. Its capital is Perugia.

United Kingdom. Collective name now applied to Great Britain and Northern Ireland. Before 1931, all of Ireland was included.

Ur (Ur of the Chaldees). Capital of a very ancient kingdom in Chaldea. Its ruins, called Mugheir by the Arabs, are located near the left bank of the lower Euphrates.

Urartu. Assyrian name of Ararat.

Utica. After the fall of Carthage, 146 B.C., the capital of the Roman province of Africa. Utica was located northwest of Carthage.

Uxmal. Ruined Maya city in southern Yucatan.

Uz. In the Old Testament, the home of Job, somewhere in northern Arabia.

V

Van Diemen's Land. Former name of Tasmania.

Veii. Ancient Etruscan city which fell to the Romans in 396 B.C. after a ten-year siege. Generally thought to be site of modern Isola Farnese, Italy.

Veld (Veldt). Open plateau country in South Africa. The name is taken from the Dutch word for "field," or "grassland."

Venaissin. Old county and papal possession whose chief city was Avignon. It was ceded to France in 1791.

Venetia. Province of ancient Italy north of the Adriatic and the lower Po. Modern Venetia is divided into three parts: Venetia proper or Veneto (capital, Venice); Venezia Tridentina (capital, Trento); and Venezia Giulia (capital, Trieste), now ceded in part to Yugoslavia.

Vindelicia. Ancient region of north Rhaetia between the Danube and the Alps. Its chief city was Augusta Vindelicorum, now Augsburg, Germany.

Vinland. Name given by Norsemen to an unidentified region, possibly New England, on northeastern coast of North America. In English, Wineland.

W

Wagram. Village northeast of Vienna. It was the site, in 1809, of a Napoleonic victory over Austria.

Wahlstatt. Village in Silesia where the Germans fought the Mongols and checked their westward advance through Europe, 1241.

Walachia. Also Wallachia. That part of southern Romania between the Danube and the Transylvanian Alps. It united with Moldavia in 1861 to form the kingdom of Romania. Chief city is Bucharest.

Waterloo. Belgian village south of Brussels where Napoleon suffered his final defeat, 1815.

Western Reserve. Early name of a vast tract of land on Lake Erie which was claimed by the state of Connecticut. Incorporated in Northwest Territory in 1800, it is now the northeastern corner of Ohio.

Westphalia. Province of northwestern Germany, formerly duchy and kingdom. Capital is Münster.

White Russia. General name of the land of the White Russians in the western Soviet Union and adjacent parts of Poland and Lithuania. The name applies specifically to the Byelorussian (White Russian) Soviet Republic, whose capital is located at Minsk.

Wilderness, The. In the Civil War, a battlefield south of the Rapidan River, Virginia.

Windward Islands. General name of the southern group of islands in the Lesser Antilles, extending from Dominica to Grenada.

World Island. Term used when referring to the combined land mass of Eurasia and Africa.

Wurtemberg. Old kingdom of southern Germany comprising much of medieval Swabia and almost completely encircled by Baden and Bavaria. German name was Württemberg. Capital was Stuttgart.

X

Xanthus. Famous city of western Lycia, destroyed by the Persians in 545 B.C. and the Romans in 43 B.C. Only ruins remain.

Y

Yedo. Also Yeddo, an old name of Tokyo, Japan.

Yellow River. In Chinese, the Hwang Ho, second of the great rivers of China. Rising in Tibet, it flows through Mongolia and China to the Gulf of Pohai, a distance of 2,903 miles. Its periodic floods have earned it the name of "China's sorrow."

Yezo. Former name of island of Hokkaido, Japan.

Z

Zealand. Largest island in Denmark, the Danish Sjaelland. Also, low-lying province of islands in southwestern Netherlands, commonly called Zeeland.

Zela. Ancient town on the site of Zile, Turkey. After defeating the king of Pontus there in 47 B.C., Caesar sent his famous message, "Veni, vidi, vici."

Zidon. Biblical name of Sidon, Phoenicia; the modern Saida, Lebanon.

Zion, Mount. The highest hill in Jerusalem, where the ancient City of David stood. The name "Zion" was later applied to Jerusalem itself and to the Zionist movement. Also called Sion.

Zoar. In early biblical history, the sole Canaanite city on the plain near the Dead Sea which was spared destruction. It stood near Sodom.

Zuider Zee. Inlet of the North Sea which projects into the Netherlands for a distance of 80 miles. The seaward end is enclosed by a dike. It was once a lake but in the 13th century was joined to the sea by a great flood. Since 1920, site of major land reclamation project. Also IJsselmeer.

Zululand. Former native kingdom north of Durban, Natal. Now part of South Africa.

211

PRINCIPAL DISCOVERIES AND EXPLORATIONS

Ancient and Medieval (to the Discovery of America)

DATE	EXPLORER	COUNTRY REPRESENTED	DESCRIPTION
600 B.C.	Phoenician Sailors	Egypt	Reported by Herodotus to have sailed around Africa from east to west in three years, under orders of King Necho.
500-450 B.C.	Himilco	Carthage	Said to have explored the west coast of Europe, possibly reaching Britain.
500 B.C.	Hanno	Carthage	Explored west coast of Africa to Sierra Leone or about 5°N.
450 B.C.	Herodotus	Greece	Visited Black Sea, eastern Mediterranean, and Egypt, and described the world of his time.
334-323 B.C.	Alexander the Great	Macedonia	Explored and conquered all of southwestern Asia from Egypt to the Jaxartes and Indus rivers.
320 B.C.	Pytheas	Marseilles	Visited Britain and northwestern Europe and, possibly, either Iceland or Norway, which he called Thule.
59-44 B.C.	Julius Caesar	Rome	Added information about Gaul, Britain, and Germany to current geographical knowledge.
20 B.C.	Strabo	Rome	Traveled widely throughout Mediterranean lands; compiled most complete geography of ancient times.
570 A.D.	St. Brendan	Ireland	Alleged to have sailed the western seas for seven years in search of tropical islands; may have reached Madeira or West Indies.
690 A.D.	Bishop Arculf	France	Visited Jerusalem and other holy places; described Egypt.
721-31 A.D.	Willibard	England	Visited and described the Holy Land, Constantinople, and Rome.
890 A.D.	Othere	Norway	Sailed around North Cape, along the Lapland coast, and discovered the White Sea.
925-950 A.D.	Al Masudi	Baghdad	Traveled in India, Ceylon, China, Russia, Persia, and Egypt.
982 A.D.	Eric the Red	Norway	Discovered and colonized southern Greenland.
1000 A.D.	Leif Ericson	Norway	Discovered Labrador, Newfoundland, and nearby coasts.
1003-06 A.D.	Thorfinn Karlsefni	Iceland	Explored and attempted to colonize northeast coast of North America.
1099-1154 A.D.	Idrisi	Spain and Sicily	Traveled in north Africa and Asia Minor; compiled a description and map of the world.
1106 A.D.	Daniel of Kiev	Russia	Visited Jaffa, Jerusalem, the Jordan, and Damascus on pilgrimage to the Holy Land.
1160-73 A.D.	Benjamin of Tudela	Spain	Traveled through Egypt, Assyria, Persia, and central Asia, visiting Jewish centers.
1245-47 A.D.	John de Plano Carpini	Italy	Traveled through Poland, Russia, and central Asia to Karakoram, in Mongolia, as legate of the pope.
1253-55 A.D.	William of Rubruck	France	Visited Karakoram, in Mongolia, by way of southern Russia and Turkestan.
1270 A.D.	Lancelot Malocello	Italy	Rediscovered the Fortunate or Canary Islands.
1271-95 A.D.	Marco Polo	Italy	Journeyed to China by way of central Asia; returned by sea by way of Sumatra, Ceylon, India, and Persia; reported existence of Japan and Madagascar.
1281-91 A.D.	Vivaldi Brothers	Italy	Attempted voyage to India by sea along west coast of Africa, but never returned.
1323-28 A.D.	Friar Odoric		Traveled to China by way of India and Malaya; returned through central Asia.
1325-54 A.D.	Ibn Battuta		Visited every Islamic country from Spain to India; traveled widely in Far East, Arabia, and western Africa.
1346 A.D.	Jayme Ferrer	Catalonia	Credited by 14th-century maps with having rounded Cape Bojador on west coast of Africa.
1427-31 A.D.	Diogo de Seville	Portugal	Discovered some of the Azores Islands.
1433-35 A.D.	Gil Eannes	Portugal	Rounded Cape Bojador in exploration of west coast of Africa.
1435-36 A.D.	Affonso Baldaya	Portugal	Landed on coast of Africa in vicinity of Río de Oro.

America (1492-1850) continued

DATE	EXPLORER	COUNTRY REPRESENTED	DESCRIPTION
1577-80	Francis Drake	England	Explored west coast of North America to 46° or 48°N. and named it New Albion; circumnavigated the earth.
1583	Humphrey Gilbert	England	Made first effort to establish an English colony in North America; ship lost returning to England.
1585-87	John Davis	England	Made several voyages in search of Northwest Passage; discovered Davis Strait and Baffin Bay.
1602-03	Sebastian Vizcaino and Martin Aguilar	Spain	Sailed along coast of California to about 42° or 43°N.; discovered Monterey Bay but missed that of San Francisco; Aguilar reported large river near 43°N.
1603-15	Samuel de Champlain	France	Explored and mapped St. Lawrence R., New England coast, Ottawa R., Lake Huron, Lake Ontario; discovered Lake Champlain (1609).
1607-14	John Smith	England	Explored and mapped vicinity of Jamestown, Virginia (1608) and coast of New England (1614).
1609-11	Henry Hudson	Holland and England	Explored Hudson R. to Albany for Holland (1609); discovered and explored Hudson Bay for England (1610-1611).
1612-13	Thomas Button	England	Explored Hudson Bay in search of strait to the Western Ocean.
1615-16	William Baffin	England	Made two voyages in search of Northwest Passage; explored Baffin Bay to 78°N.
1631-32	Luke Foxe and William James	England	Explored northern and southern extensions of Hudson Bay without finding passage westwards.
1634	Jean Nicollet	France	Crossed Lake Huron to Mackinac Strait and Green Bay; reported "Western Sea" three days distant.
1658-59	Pierre Radisson and Sieur des Groseillers	France	Explored upper Mississippi R. and western shores of Lake Superior.
1669-70	John Lederer	England	Crossed the Blue Ridge and explored the Shenandoah Valley.
1669-87	Robert Cavalier, Sieur de la Salle	France	Explored Lake Ontario and upper Ohio R. (1669) and the Great Lakes to head of Lake Michigan (1679); descended Illinois and Mississippi rivers to Gulf of Mexico (1681-82); killed in Texas after failing to locate Mississippi R. by sea (1684-87).
1673	Jacques Marquette and Louis Joliet	France	Descended Mississippi R. from the Wisconsin R. to the Arkansas and returned to the Great Lakes via the Illinois-Chicago portage.
1680	Louis Hennepin	France	Explored upper Mississippi R. from the Illinois R. to the Minnesota.
1688	Louis de la Hontan	France	Explored upper Mississippi region; spread reports of fictitious "Long River" leading to Western Sea.
1699	Pierre le Moyne, Sieur d' Iberville	France	Entered mouth of Mississippi from Gulf of Mexico and explored delta.
1701-02	Eusebio Francisco Kino	Spain	Explored the Gila and lower Colorado rivers; proved that California was not an island.
1718-19	Bernard de la Harpe	France	Explored the Red and Arkansas rivers.
1721	Pierre François Xavier de Charlevoix	France	Visited French settlements in North America from Quebec to New Orleans.
1728-41	Vitus Bering	Russia	Confirmed existence of strait between Asia and America (1728); discovered northwest coast and named Mt. St. Elias (1741).
1730-43	Sieur de La Vérendrye and sons	France	Explored territory northwest of Lake Superior; discovered Lake Winnipeg; sons may have seen Rocky Mountains.
1742	Christopher Middleton	England	Discovered Repulse Bay in search of passage to Western Sea.
1749	Celoron de Bienville	France	Buried plates along the Ohio R., claiming formal possession for France.
1750	Thomas Walker	England	Discovered Cumberland Gap route into Kentucky.
1750	Christopher Gist	England	Explored Ohio R. and Kentucky areas.

Date	Explorer	Country	Accomplishment
1441–46 A.D.	Nuno Tristam	Portugal	Reached the Sénégal R. along west coast of Africa.
1445 A.D.	Dinis Diaz	Portugal	Rounded Cape Verde on west coast of Africa.
1455–57 A.D.	Alvise da Cadamosto	Portugal	Explored the Sénégal and Gambia rivers; discovered Cape Verde Islands.
1472 A.D.	Fernando Póo	Portugal	Discovered island bearing his name in Gulf of Guinea.
1482–86 A.D.	Diogo Cao	Portugal	Discovered mouth of Congo R. (1482), reached Cape Negro at 16° S. (1486).
1487 A.D.	Pedro de Covilhã	Portugal	Traveled to India via Egypt and Arabia; visited east coast of Africa, south to Zambezi R.
1487–88 A.D.	Bartolomeu Dias	Portugal	Discovered Cape of Good Hope; explored coast east to Mossel Bay.

America (1492–1850)

Date	Explorer	Country	Accomplishment
1492–1502	Christopher Columbus	Spain	Discovered the West Indies (1492); in three later voyages explored coasts of northern South America and Central America.
1497–98	John and Sebastian Cabot	England	Discovered shores of Nova Scotia and Newfoundland, and visited southern Greenland.
1499–1500	Amerigo Vespucci, Juan de la Cosa and Alonso de Ojeda	Spain	Discovered and explored northeastern coast of South America.
1499–1500	Vincente Yañez Pinzón	Spain	Discovered mouth of Amazon R.
1500	Pedro Álvares Cabral	Portugal	Discovered or visited coast of Brazil on voyage to India.
1500–01	Gaspar Corte Real	Portugal	Made two voyages to northeastern North America, but never returned.
1501–02	Amerigo Vespucci	Portugal	Explored coast of Brazil to 30° S. or farther.
1513	Juan Ponce de León	Spain	Discovered and explored coasts of Florida.
1513	Vasco Núñez de Balboa	Spain	Crossed Isthmus of Panama and discovered the South Sea (Pacific Ocean).
1515	Juan Diaz de Solis	Spain	Explored mouth of Río de la Plata.
1517	Francisco Fernández de Córdoba	Spain	Discovered Yucatán and evidence of Mayan culture.
1518	Juan de Grijalva	Spain	Explored east coast of Mexico north of Yucatán.
1519	Alvárez Pineda	Spain	Explored Gulf of Mexico and may have discovered mouth of Mississippi R.
1519–22	Ferdinand Magellan	Spain	Discovered Strait of Magellan (1520) during first circumnavigation of the earth.
1519–27	Hernando Cortes	Spain	Explored and conquered Mexico.
1523–41	Francisco Pizarro	Spain	Explored northwestern South America and conquered Peru.
1524	Giovanni da Verrazano	France	Discovered New York Bay and explored coast northward.
1524–25	Estéban Gomez	Spain	Sailed along east coast of North America from Nova Scotia to Florida.
1527–37	Cabeza de Vaca	Spain	Wandered for nine years along and near coast of Gulf of Mexico from Florida to Mexico.
1534–41	Jacques Cartier	France	Explored Gulf of St. Lawrence (1534) and river as far as sites of Quebec and Montreal (1536).
1535–36	Diego de Almagro	Spain	Explored and conquered Chile.
1536–38	Gonzalo Jiménez de Quesada	Spain	Explored and conquered New Granada, and founded Bogotá.
1539	Francisco de Ulloa	Spain	Explored Gulf of California to its head.
1539–43	Hernando de Soto	Spain	Explored southeastern United States from Florida to Tennessee; discovered Mississippi R. (1541).
1540	Hernando de Alarcón	Spain	Sailed up Gulf of California and entered Colorado R.
1540–42	Francisco Vasquez de Coronado	Spain	Led expedition into southwestern United States; explored Great Plains northward to Kansas; Grand Canyon of Colorado R. discovered by one of his party.
1541	Francisco de Orellana	Spain	Crossed the Andes and descended Amazon R. to its mouth.
1542–43	Bartolomé Ferrelo and Juan Rodriguez Cabrillo	Spain	Discovered San Diego Bay and explored California coast to about 42° N. or Cape Mendocino.
1562–65	René de Laudonnière and Jean de Ribaut	France	Failed in effort to establish a permanent colony on coast of South Carolina.
1766–68	Jonathan Carver	England	Explored the upper Mississippi region and reported existence of the Oregon or River of the West.
1769–75	Daniel Boone	England	Explored eastern Kentucky (1769–71) and blazed the famous Wilderness Road (1775).
1769	José Ortega	Spain	Discovered San Francisco Bay during overland expedition into upper California.
1770–72	Samuel Hearne	England	Traced the Coppermine R. to the Northern Ocean and discovered Great Slave Lake.
1774–75	Juan Pérez and Bruno Heceta	Spain	Sent to explore northwest coast, reaching 55° N.; Heceta observed entrance to Columbia R.; Pérez discovered Nootka Sound.
1778–79	James Cook	England	Rediscovered Hawaiian Islands; explored and charted northwest coast from 45° N. to Arctic Ocean.
1788–92	Robert Gray	United States	Explored northwest coast; discovered Grays Harbor; entered and named the Columbia R. (1792).
1789–93	Alexander Mackenzie	England	Traced Mackenzie R. to its mouth (1789); crossed Rocky Mountains via Peace R. and reached Pacific Ocean.
1792–94	George Vancouver	England	Explored and mapped Puget Sound; charted inside passage and inlets along northwest coast.
1804–06	Meriwether Lewis and William Clark	United States	Ascended Missouri R. to its source, crossed Rocky Mountains and descended Columbia R. to Pacific Ocean.
1805–07	Zebulon M. Pike	United States	Explored and mapped upper Mississippi R. (1805); and southwestern section of Louisiana Territory (1806–07).
1807–08	Manuel Lisa and John Colter	United States	Explored Northern Rockies (Yellowstone–Big Horn region) as trappers and fur traders.
1811–12	Wilson Price Hunt (Astorians)	United States	Discovered overland route to Pacific via the Snake and Columbia rivers.
1819–20	Stephen H. Long	United States	Explored the high plains between Platte and Arkansas rivers; called the Great Plains the "Great American Desert."
1821	William Becknell	United States	Opened trade route between Missouri R. and Santa Fe.
1823–29	Jedediah Smith	United States	Located famous South Pass across Rocky Mts.; crossed desert between Colorado R. and California.
1824–28	Peter Skene Ogden	England	Explored upper Snake R. and northern Great Basin; discovered Humboldt R. and Great Salt Lake.
1829–30	Ewing Young and party	United States	Opened up Spanish Trail between Santa Fe and Los Angeles.
1832–33	Nathaniel J. Wyeth	United States	Led first expedition along Oregon Trail to Columbia R.
1833	Joseph E. Walker	United States	Crossed Great Basin between Great Salt Lake and California.
1841	Charles Wilkes	United States	Visited Oregon country and California during official Pacific exploring expedition by sea.
1842–45	John C. Frémont	United States	First official government explorer to re-trace explorations of fur trappers in the Far West.

Africa

Date	Explorer	Country	Accomplishment
1520–27	Francisco Alvarez	Portugal	Visited Ethiopia and described it in detail.
1541	Christopher da Gama	Portugal	Led expedition into Ethiopia.
1578–89	Duarte López	Portugal	Visited the Kingdom of Congo; his reports a chief source of information until 19th century.
1604–22	Pedro Páez	Portugal	First European to visit Ethiopian sources of the Nile R.
1616	Gaspar Boccaro	Portugal	Explored interior from upper Zambezi R. to west coast.
1618–19	George Thompson	England	Explored the Gambia R.
1625–35	Jerome Lobo	Portugal	Lived in Ethiopia as a missionary.
1698–1700	C. J. Poncet	France	Traveled as a physician into Ethiopia to treat the Emperor.
1768–73	James Bruce	England	Explored Ethiopia, especially source of the Blue Nile R.
1777–79	William Patterson	England	Made several trips into the Kaffir country as a naturalist.
1795–1805	Mungo Park	England	Explored the Gambia R. and was first modern European to reach the Niger R.
1797–98	John Barrow	England	Journeyed from Cape of Good Hope to upper Orange R.

PRINCIPAL DISCOVERIES AND EXPLORATIONS (Continued)

Africa continued

DATE	EXPLORER	COUNTRY REPRESENTED	DESCRIPTION
1797–1800	Frederick Hornemann	England	Traveled from Egypt to Marzūq and the Niger R., disguised as an Arab.
1798–99	Francisco de Lacerda	Portugal	Explored southeastern interior north of Zambezi R.
1801	John Trutter and William Somerville	England	Explored Bechuanaland, north of Orange R.
1802–06	Pedro Baptista and A. José	Portugal	Made first recorded crossing of continent eastward from Angola.
1812–14	Johann L. Burckhardt	Switzerland	Traveled up the Nile R. and across to the Red Sea.
1822–25	Dixon Denham and Hugh Clapperton	England	Crossed desert from Tripoli to Lake Chad and westward to the Niger R.
1825–26	Alexander G. Laing	England	Reached Timbuktu from Tripoli, but was murdered on return trip.
1827–28	René Caillé	France	Traveled from Guinea Coast to Fez and Tangier by way of Timbuktu.
1830–34	Richard Lander	England	Explored the lower Niger R. and located its mouth.
1849–73	David Livingstone	England	Discovered Zambezi R. (1851), Victoria Falls (1855), and Lake Nyasa (1859); explored upper Congo tributaries; found by Stanley on Lake Tanganyika in 1871.
1856–59	Richard Burton	England	Discovered Lake Tanganyika and explored surrounding area.
1858–63	John Speke	England	Discovered Victoria Nyanza as source of the Nile R.
1861–69	Samuel Baker	England	Explored upper Nile R.; discovered Lake Albert.
1863–71	Georg A. Schweinfurth	Germany	Explored extensively in the Sudan and equatorial Africa.
1871–90	Henry Stanley	United States	Continued Livingstone's explorations in the lakes region; descended Congo R. to Atlantic Ocean (1877); discovered Stanley Pool and Lake Edward.
1877–86	Serpa Pinto	Portugal	Crossed the continent from Angola to Mozambique.
1879–90	Joseph Thomson	England	Explored new areas in Tanganyika, Kenya, and Uganda.
1888	Samuel Teleki	Hungary	Discovered lakes Rudolph and Stephanie.

Asia

DATE	EXPLORER	COUNTRY REPRESENTED	DESCRIPTION
1497–99	Vasco da Gama	Portugal	Discovered sea route to India by way of South Africa and Indian Ocean.
1502–07	Ludovici di Varthema	Portugal	Traveled as convert to Islam in Arabia, Persia, India, and East Indies.
1511	Mathias Albuquerque	Portugal	Conquered Malacca, East Indian spice center.
1520–21	Thomé Pires	Portugal	Sent to Peking as commercial envoy.
1537–58	Fernão Mendes Pinto	Portugal	Described travels in India, China, and Japan.
1549–51	Francis Xavier	Portugal	Introduced Christianity into Japan.
1561–63	Anthony Jenkinson	England	Visited Persia by overland route from Russia.
1578–1610	Matteo Ricci	Portugal	Established first Christian missions in China.
1603–05	Benedict de Goez	Portugal	Made first overland trip to China after Marco Polo.
1632–68	Jean B. Tavernier	France	Traveled as commercial trader in Persia, India, and East Indies.
1656	Pieter van Goyer and Jacob von Keyser	Holland	Visited Peking by overland route from Canton.
1665–77	John Chardin	France	Described extensive travels in Persia and India.
1683–93	Engelbert Kaempfer	Holland	As physician with Dutch embassy, visited and described Thailand (Siam) and Japan.
1715–47	John Bell	Russia	Traveled as physician with Russian embassies to Persia and through Siberia to China.
1716–21	Ipolito Desideri	Italy	Reached Tibetan city of Lhasa from Kashmir.
1761–64	Carsten Niebuhr	Denmark	Explored Yemen, reaching cities of San'ā and Mocha (Al Mukāh); also visited Oman, Syria, and Palestine.
1795–97	W. R. Broughton	England	Explored coasts of Hokkaido and Korea.

Arctic Regions continued

DATE	EXPLORER	COUNTRY REPRESENTED	DESCRIPTION
1871–74	Julius Payer and Carl Weyprecht	Austria	Discovered Franz Josef Land Archipelago.
1876	Albert H. Markham	England	Reached 83° 20' on northwest coast of Greenland.
1878–79	Nils A. E. Nordenskjöld	Sweden	Completed the Northeast Passage in two seasons in ship Vega.
1879–81	George W. DeLong	United States	Explored Arctic Ocean northwest of Bering Strait; ship Jeannette and most of party lost.
1881–83	Adolphus W. Greely	United States	Explored northern Greenland and Ellesmere Island; party established new record of 83° 24' N.
1888–96	Fridtjof Nansen	Norway	Made first crossing of Greenland (1888); reached record of 86° 14' during drift of ship Fram (1895).
1897	Salomon A. Andrée	Sweden	Attempted balloon flight to North Pole from Spitsbergen (Svalbard); remains of party found in 1930 on White Island.
1898–1902	Otto Sverdrup	Norway	Explored northern Ellesmere Island and discovered Axel Heiberg Island.
1899–1900	Umberto Cagni	Italy	Reached new record at 86° 34' N. by sledge from Franz Josef Land; member of Abruzzi expedition.
1900–09	Robert E. Peary	United States	Made repeated efforts to reach North Pole, succeeding (April 6, 1909) by sledge from Grant Land.
1903–6	Roald Amundsen	Norway	Completed first trip through Northwest Passage from east to west.
1907–9	Frederick A. Cook	United States	Claimed to have reached North Pole on April 20, 1908.
1925–26	Lincoln Ellsworth	United States	Made flight with Amundsen from Spitsbergen (Svalbard) to 87° 43' N. and return; co-leader of dirigible flight over North Pole (1926).
1926	Richard Byrd and Floyd Bennett	United States	Made successful flight from Spitsbergen (Svalbard) to North Pole and return.
1926–28	Umberto Nobile	Italy	Made numerous dirigible flights across arctic region; rescued after Italia crashed on ice in 1928.
1937–38	Otto Schmidt	Russia	Spent nine months with scientific expedition near North Pole.

Antarctic Regions

DATE	EXPLORER	COUNTRY REPRESENTED	DESCRIPTION
1738–39	J.B.C. Bouvet de Lozier	France	Discovered Bouvet Island south of Africa in latitude 54° S.
1768–75	James Cook	England	Established non-existence of southern continent in habitable latitudes; reached record of 71° 10' S.
1771–73	Yves Joseph de Kerguélen-Trémarec	France	Discovered and explored Kerguélen Island in latitude 49° 50' S., longitude 69° 30' E.
1819	William Smith	England	Discovered South Shetland Islands.
1819–21	Fabian von Bellingshausen	Russia	Circumnavigated Antarctica; discovered Alexander I Land.
1821	Nathaniel Palmer	United States	Discovered Palmer Peninsula on sealing expedition.
1823	James Weddell	England	Discovered Weddell Sea; reached 74° 15' S.
1837–40	Jules Dumont d'Urville	France	Discovered Adélie Land south of Tasmania.
1839–40	Charles Wilkes	United States	Sighted Antarctic coast between 108° and 148° E.
1840–43	James Ross	England	Charted coast in neighborhood of Ross Sea; reached record of 78° 9' S.
1902–04	Robert F. Scott	England	Explored coast of Edward VII Land; reached 82° 17' S.
1903–05	Jean B. Charcot	France	Explored Palmer Peninsula; discovered Loubet Coast.
1908–09	Ernest Shackleton	England	Explored head of Ross Sea; reached 88° 23' S.
1910–12	Roald Amundsen	Norway	Discovered Queen Maud Range; reached South Pole Dec. 16, 1911.
1910–12	Robert Scott	England	Reached South Pole January 18, 1912; entire party perished during return.
1911–13	Douglas Mawson	England and Australia	Explored coast from King George V Land to Enderby Land in two expeditions.
1929–31			
1914–17	Ernest Shackleton	England	Discovered Caird coast; ship lost in Weddell Sea, but party rescued after many hardships.

Date	Explorer	Country	Description
1928–30	Hubert Wilkins	England	Made first Antarctic explorations by air.
1928–47	Richard Byrd	United States	Established base at Little America and made first flight over South Pole (1929); second expedition remained through winter of 1934; third expedition (1939–40) made extensive aerial explorations; fourth expedition concentrated on scientific work.
1935–36	Lincoln Ellsworth	United States	Explored by air between Palmer Peninsula and Little America.
1947–48	Finn Ronne	United States	Explored Palmer Peninsula and Weddell Sea by land and air.
1955–58	Vivian Fuchs and Edmund Hillary	United Kingdom and New Zealand	Commonwealth Trans-Antarctic Expedition crossed the Continent through the South Pole from Weddell Sea to McMurdo Sound.
1957–58	I. G. Y. (International Geophysical Year)	Arg.; Austl.; Bel.; Chile; Fr.; Jap.; N.Z.; Nor.; S. Afr.; Sov. Un.; U.K.; U.S.	Established research stations; field expeditions led to new discoveries of physical features, as well as new information on ice conditions; extensive oceanographic surveys and mapping conducted.
1959–61	Australian National Antarctic Expedition	Australia	Gathered data on weather, cosmic rays, geomagnetism, seismology; field explorations and mapping; extensive aerial surveys.

Pacific Ocean and Australia

Date	Explorer	Country	Description
1520–21	Ferdinand Magellan	Spain	Crossed the Pacific from South America to the Philippines during first circumnavigation of the earth.
1542	Lopez de Villalobos	Spain	Sailed from Mexico to the Philippines; discovered Caroline and Palau Islands.
1565	Andrés de Urdaneta	Spain	Discovered northern sailing route from Philippines to Mexico in latitude of the Forties.
1567–95	Alvaro de Mendana	Spain	Discovered Solomon, Marshall, and Ellice Islands (1567); also Marquesas and Santa Cruz (1595).
1578	Francis Drake	England	Crossed the Pacific from California to the East Indies on first English circumnavigation.
1606	Pedro de Quiros	Spain	Discovered Tahiti and New Hebrides Islands.
1606	Luis de Torres	Spain	Sailed through Torres Strait between Australia and New Guinea.
1616	Dirk Hartog	Holland	Explored section of west coast of Australia.
1616	William Van Schouten and Jacob Lemaire	Holland	Rounded Cape Horn and crossed Pacific; discovered Bismarck Archipelago.
1642–44	Abel Tasman	Holland	Discovered Tasmania and part of New Zealand; explored the north coast of Australia.
1699	William Dampier	England	Explored west and northwest coasts of Australia.
1721	Jacob Roggeveen	Holland	Discovered Easter Island and Samoa.
1767–69	Louis de Bougainville	France	Explored South Pacific islands, including Tahiti, Samoa, and the New Hebrides.
1768–79	James Cook	England	Made three voyages into the Pacific; explored coasts of New Zealand and eastern Australia (1769–70); proved non-existence of continental land north of Antarctic Circle (1772–75); discovered Hawaiian Islands and explored northwest coast of North America (1776–79).
1785–88	Jean de La Pérouse	France	Explored North Pacific Ocean, especially coasts of Siberia and Japan; lost at sea.
1798	George Bass	England	Discovered strait separating Tasmania from Australia.
1802–03	Matthew Flinders	England	Explored south coast of Australia and sailed completely around the continent.
1816–22	John Oxley	England	Explored the interior of New South Wales, Australia.
1828–45	Charles Sturt	England	Discovered the Darling R.; descended Murray R. to its mouth; reached center of continent (1845).
1833–35	Charles Darwin	England	Explored South Pacific islands as a naturalist.
1839–41	Edward Eyre	England	Crossed southern Australia from Spencer Gulf to King George Sound.
1844–48	Ludwig Leichhardt	Germany	Explored interior of northern Queensland and Arnhem Land.
1858–62	John Stuart	England	Explored interior of South Australia and made unsuccessful attempt to cross the continent (1860); succeeded (1862).
1860–61	Robert Burke and W. J. Wills	England	Succeeded in crossing Australia from Melbourne to Gulf of Carpentaria.
1873	Peter E. Warburton	England	Crossed western Australia from Alice Springs to the coast, using camels.
1874	John Forrest	England	Crossed desert region of Australia from Perth to Adelaide.
1875–76	Ernest Giles	England	Made trip across desert from Port Augusta to Perth and return.

Date	Explorer	Country	Description
1839–46	Evariste Regis Huc	France	Traveled through interior of China, Mongolia and Tibet.
1851–54	Matthew C. Perry	United States	Opened Japan to foreign trade.
1862–67	Peter Kropotkin	Russia	Made geographical surveys of North Manchuria.
1867–88	Nikolai Przhevalsky	Russia	Led expeditions into Central Asia, Mongolia, and Tibet; rediscovered Lop Nor.
1868–72	Ferdinand Richthofen	Germany	Explored and described most of Chinese Empire.
1869–70	Joseph Halévy	France	Explored interior of southwestern Arabia.
1873	Jean Dupuis	France	Explored Tonkin route into China.
1885–1908	Sven Hedin	Sweden	Traveled extensively in Persia, Turkestan, China, and Tibet.
1886–1904	Francis Younghusband	England	Explored and surveyed in Kashmir, Central Asia, and Tibet.
1889–92	William W. Rockhill	United States	Explored eastern Tibet.
1899–1914	Gertrude Bell	England	Traveled widely in Palestine, Mesopotamia, and inner Arabia.
1899–1926	Aurel Stein	England	Made archaeological explorations in India, Persia, and central Asia.
1901–06	Ellsworth Huntington	United States	Explored upper Euphrates R. and Chinese Turkestan.
1914–29	Roy Chapman Andrews	United States	Explored western China and Mongolia as a naturalist, discovering many animal fossils.
1917–32	St. John Philby	England	Crossed Arabia from sea to sea; explored oases of Nejd.

Arctic Regions

Date	Explorer	Country	Description
1553–54	Hugh Willoughby and Richard Chancellor	England	Attempted exploration of Northeast Passage; Willoughby lost, but Chancellor reached Archangel and opened trade with Russia.
1576–78	Martin Frobisher	England	Made three voyages in search of Northwest Passage; discovered Frobisher Bay.
1580	Arthur Pet and Charles Jackman	England	Reached the Kara Sea, exploring Northeast Passage.
1585–87	John Davis	England	Reached latitude 73° N. in Baffin Bay, exploring Northwest Passage.
1594–97	Willem Barents	Holland	Discovered Spitsbergen (Svalbard) and reached Novaya Zemlya along Northeast Passage.
1607–11	Henry Hudson	England and Holland	Made several voyages in search of both Northeast and Northwest Passages to India; reached 73° N. on east Greenland coast.
1615–16	William Baffin and Robert Bylot	England	Explored Baffin Bay; reached 78° N.
1648	Simon Dezhnev	Russia	Explored northeastern Siberian coast from the Kolyma to Anadyr rivers.
1728	Vitus Bering	Russia	Discovered Bering Strait and the St. Lawrence and Diomede Islands.
1737–42	Dimitri Laptev	Russia	Explored north Siberian coast from Lena R. to Cape Baranov.
1742	T. Chelyuskin	Russia	Discovered northernmost point of Asia by land.
1773	C. J. Phipps	England	Reached 80° 48' north of Spitsbergen (Svalbard).
1818–27	William E. Parry	England	Explored Canadian arctic and Spitsbergen (Svalbard) areas; reached 82° 45' (1827).
1820–22	William Scoresby	England	Discovered Scoresby Sound in eastern Greenland; published standard description of Arctic regions.
1825–28	Frederick W. Beechey	England	Explored arctic coast of North America from Bering Strait to Point Barrow.
1829–49	John and James Ross	England	Discovered Boothia Peninsula and Gulf; James located North Magnetic Pole (1831); both participated in search for Franklin (1848–49).
1845–48	John Franklin	England	Lost two ships and 129 men in attempt to sail through Northwest Passage; reached King William Island.
1850–54	Richard Collinson and Robert McClure	England	Reached Melville Sound from Bering Strait and proved existence of northwest waterway passage.
1853–55	Elisha K. Kane	United States	Explored Smith Sound and Kane Basin; reached 80° 10' N.
1857–58	Francis L. McClintock	England	Discovered McClintock Channel and relics of Franklin expedition on King William Island.
1860–71	Charles F. Hall	United States	On third expedition, explored northern shores of Ellesmere Island and Greenland, reaching 82° 26' N.

ALTITUDES OF SELECTED WORLD CITIES

Abbreviations

Afg. — Afghanistan
Ala. — Alabama
Arg. — Argentina
Ariz. — Arizona
Ark. — Arkansas
Aus. — Austria
Austl. — Australia
Bel. — Belgium
Calif. — California
Colo. — Colorado
Conn. — Connecticut
Con. B. — Congo; Capital: Brazzaville
Con. L. — Congo, The; Capital: Léopoldville
Czech. — Czechoslovakia
D.C. — District of Columbia
Del. — Delaware
Den. — Denmark
Eng. — England
Eth. — Ethiopia
Fla. — Florida
Ga. — Georgia
Guat. — Guatemala
Ill. — Illinois
Ind. — Indiana
Ire. — Ireland
Kans. — Kansas
Ky. — Kentucky
La. — Louisiana
Leb. — Lebanon
Lux. — Luxembourg
Malag. Rep. — Malagasy Republic
Mass. — Massachusetts
Md. — Maryland
Mex. — Mexico
Mich. — Michigan
Minn. — Minnesota
Mo. — Missouri
N. Car. — North Carolina
Nebr. — Nebraska
Neth. — Netherlands
N. H. — New Hampshire
N. J. — New Jersey
N. Mex. — New Mexico
N. Y. — New York
N. Z. — New Zealand
Okla. — Oklahoma
Oreg. — Oregon
Pa. — Pennsylvania
Par. — Paraguay
R. I. — Rhode Island
S. Afr. — South Africa
Sov. Un. — Soviet Union
Switz. — Switzerland
Tenn. — Tennessee
U.A.R. — United Arab Republic (Egypt)
Ur. — Uruguay
U. S. — United States
Va. — Virginia
Ven. — Venezuela
Wash. — Washington
Wis. — Wisconsin
Wyo. — Wyoming

A

City	Height in Feet
Aachen, Germany (West)	580
Addis Ababa, Eth.	7,749
Adelaide, Austl.	40
Aden, Aden	20
Agra, India	545
Aguascalientes, Mex.	6,258
Ahmadabad, India	180
Ajmer, India	1,685
Akron (Ohio), U. S.	875
Albany (N. Y.), U. S.	20
Albuquerque (N. Mex.), U. S.	4,950
Aleppo, Syria	1,290
Alexandria, U.A.R.	25
Algiers (Alger), Algeria	200
Amman, Jordan	2,548
Amritsar, India	760
Amsterdam, Neth.	8
Andorra, Andorra	3,376
Ankara, Turkey	2,250
Antwerpen (Antwerp), Belgium	30
Asheville (N. Car.), U. S.	1,985
Aspen (Colo.), U. S.	7,930
Astrakhan, Sov. Un.	—50
Asunción, Par.	246
Athens (Athínai), Greece	300
Atlanta (Ga.), U. S.	1,050
Augsburg, Germany (West)	1,623

B

Baden-Baden, Germany (West)	594
Badgastein, Aus.	3,323
Baghdad, Iraq	112
Baguio, Philippines	4,640
Baku, Sov. Un.	—40
Baltimore (Md.), U. S.	20
Banff, Canada	4,534
Banaras (Benares), India	250
Bangalore, India	2,950
Bangkok, Thailand	10
Barcelona, Spain	43
Basel, Switz.	1,050
Batavia, see Djakarta, Indonesia.	
Beirut (Beyrouth), Leb.	200
Belém, Brazil.	30
Belfast, N. Ireland	20
Belgrade (Beograd), Yugoslavia	433
Belo Horizonte, Brazil	2,490
Benares, see Banaras, India.	
Beograd, see Belgrade, Yugoslavia.	
Berlin, Germany	115
Bern, Switz	1,876
Beyrouth, see Beirut, Leb.	
Bilbao, Spain	30
Birmingham, Eng.	452
Birmingham (Ala.), U. S.	600
Bogor (Buitenzorg), Indonesia	570
Bogotá, Colombia	8,659
Bologna, Italy	180
Bolton, Eng.	480
Bombay, India	25
Bonn, Germany (West)	197
Bordeaux, France	49
Boston (Mass.), U. S.	21
Bradford, Eng.	635
Brasília, Brazil	3,474
Braunschweig (Brunswick), Germany (West)	230
Brawley (Calif.), U. S.	—109
Brazzaville, Con. B.	1,055
Bremen, Germany (West)	10
Breslau, see Wrocław, Poland.	
Brisbane, Austl.	35
Bristol, Eng.	220
Brno, Czech.	750
Brunswick, see Braunschweig, Germany (West).	
Brussels (Bruxelles), Bel.	190
Bucharest (București), Romania	276
Budapest, Hungary	370
Buenos Aires, Arg.	45
Buffalo (N. Y.), U. S.	585
Bydgoszcz, Poland	233

C

Cairo, U.A.R.	98
Calcutta, India	20
Campinas, Brazil	2,220
Canberra, Austl.	1,875
Canton, China	33
Canton (Ohio), U. S.	1,030
Cape Town, S. Afr.	36
Caracas, Ven.	3,164
Cardiff, Wales	60
Cawnpore, see Kanpur, India.	
Cerro de Pasco, Peru	14,385
Chamonix [-Mont-Blanc], France	3,402
Changchun (Hsinking), China	735
Changsha, China	200
Chattanooga (Tenn.), U. S.	675
Chelyabinsk, Sov. Un.	700
Chemnitz, see Karl-Marx-Stadt, Germany (East).	
Chengteh (Jehol), China	1,630
Chengtu, China	1,195
Chernovtsy, Sov. Un.	1,040
Chicago (Ill.), U. S.	595
Chihuahua, Mex.	4,443
Chita, Sov. Un.	2,300
Chungking, China	787
Cincinnati (Ohio), U. S.	550
Clermont-Ferrand, France	1,316
Cleveland (Ohio), U. S.	580
Cochabamba, Bolivia	8,435
Cody (Wyo.), U. S.	4,980
Cologne, see Köln, Germany (West).	
Colombo, Ceylon	15
Colorado Springs (Colo.), U. S.	5,980
Columbus (Ohio), U. S.	780
Constantine, Algeria	1,670
Constantinople, see Istanbul, Turkey.	
Conway (N. H.), U. S.	465
Copenhagen (København), Den.	45
Córdoba, Arg.	1,240
Cortina d'Ampezzo, Italy	4,003
Croydon, Eng.	325
Cuiabá, Brazil	771
Cusco, Peru	11,440

D

Dacca, Pakistan	26
Dairen, China	80
Dallas (Texas), U. S.	435
Damascus (Dimashq), Syria	2,250
Danzig, see Gdańsk, Poland.	
Darjeeling, India	7,000
Davos, Switz.	5,062
Dayton (Ohio), U. S.	745
Dehra Dun, India	2,282
Delhi, India	770
Denver (Colo.), U. S.	5,280
Des Moines (Iowa), U. S.	805
Detroit (Mich.), U. S.	585
Djakarta (Batavia), Indonesia	16
Dnepropetrovsk, Sov. Un.	250
Dortmund, Germany (West)	249
Dresden, Germany (East)	375
Dublin (Baile Átha Cliath), Ire.	35
Duisburg, Germany (West)	108
Duluth (Minn.), U. S.	610
Durango, Mex.	6,196
Durban, S. Afr.	25
Düsseldorf, Germany (West)	118

E

Edinburgh, Scotland	195
Elisabethville, Con. L.	4,101
El Paso (Texas), U. S.	3,695
Ely (Minn.), U. S.	1,415
Erfurt, Germany (East)	656
Erie (Pa.), U. S.	671
Essen, Germany (West)	269
Evansville (Ind.), U. S.	385

F

Fairbanks, Alaska	512
Fès (Fez), Morocco	1,020
Firenze (Florence), Italy	164
Flagstaff (Ariz.), U. S.	6,890
Flint (Mich.), U. S.	715
Florence, see Firenze, Italy.	
Fort Wayne (Ind.), U. S.	790
Fort Worth (Texas), U. S.	620
Frankfurt [am Main], Germany (West)	312
Fukuoka, Japan	25
Fusan, see Pusan, Korea (South).	

G

Garmisch-Partenkirchen, Germany (West)	2,330
Gartok, Tibet, China	14,240
Gdańsk (Danzig), Poland	49
Genève (Geneva), Switz	1,329
Genova (Genoa), Italy	62
Glasgow, Scotland	45
Gorkiy, Sov. Un.	230
Göteborg, Sweden	45
Granada, Spain	2,265
Grand Rapids (Mich.), U. S.	610
Graz, Aus.	1,170
Greenwich, Eng.	235
Grenoble, France	770
Groningen, Neth.	5
Guadalajara, Mex.	5,180
Guatemala, Guat.	4,850
Guayaquil, Ecuador	30

H

Halle, Germany (East)	328
Hamburg, Germany (West)	20
Hamilton, Canada	323
Hangchow, China	49
Hannover, Germany (West)	180
Hanoi, Vietnam (North)	30
Harbin, China	460
Hartford (Conn.), U. S.	40
Havana (Habana), Cuba	35
Helsinki, Finland	25
Hiroshima, Japan	75
Hong Kong, see Victoria, Hong Kong.	
Honolulu (Hawaii), U.S.	25
Hot Springs (Ark.), U. S.	607
Houston (Texas), U. S.	40
Hull, Eng.	25
Huntington (W. Va.), U. S.	565
Hyderabad, India	1,750

I

Ibadan, Nigeria	768
Indianapolis (Ind.), U. S.	710
Innsbruck, Aus.	1,985
Interlaken, Switz.	1,850
Iquitos, Peru	350
Irkutsk, Sov. Un.	1,400
Istanbul, Turkey	30
Izmir (Smyrna), Turkey	35

J

Jacksonville (Fla.), U. S.	20
Jaipur, India	1,258
Jersey City (N. J.), U. S.	20
Jerusalem, Israel–Jordan	2,618
Jiachan, Tibet, China	15,870
Johannesburg, S. Afr.	5,689
Juf, Switz.	6,975

K

Kabul, Afg.	5,890
Kaifeng, China	670
Kaliningrad (Königsberg), Sov. Un.	75
Kandy, Ceylon	1,602
Kanpur (Cawnpore), India	410
Kansas City (Kans.), U. S.	750
Kansas City (Mo.), U. S.	750
Karachi, Pakistan	60
Karaganda, Sov. Un.	2,000
Karl-Marx-Stadt (Chemnitz), Germany (East)	1,013
Karlsruhe, Germany (West)	377
Kassel, Germany (West)	476
Katmandu, Nepal	4,223
Kaunas, Sov. Un.	255
Kazan, Sov. Un.	290
Kharkov, Sov. Un.	450
Khartoum, Sudan	1,252
Kiel, Germany (West)	46
Kiev (Kiyev), Sov. Un.	450
Kingston, Jamaica	25
Kishinev, Sov. Un.	130
Knoxville (Tenn.), U. S.	890
Kobe, Japan	50
Köln (Cologne), Germany (West)	174
Königsberg, see Kaliningrad, Sov. Un.	
Kraków, Poland	700
Kumamoto, Japan	200
Kunming, China	6,080
Kure, Japan	275
Kuybyshev, Sov. Un.	570
Kyoto, Japan	360

L

Lahore, Pakistan	3,270
Lake Placid (N.Y.), U. S.	1,740
Lanchow, China	5,185
La Paz, Bolivia	12,795
La Plata, Arg.	40
Leadville (Colo.), U. S.	10,152
Leeds, Eng.	245
Leh, India	11,253
Le Havre, France	200
Leipzig, Germany (East)	387
Leningrad, Sov. Un.	33
Léopoldville, Con. L.	1,045
Lhasa, Tibet, China	11,800
Lille, France	69
Lima, Peru	501
Lisbon (Lisboa), Portugal	285
Liverpool, Eng.	130
Łódź, Poland	660
London, Eng.	80
Long Beach (Calif.), U. S.	35
Los Angeles (Calif.), U. S.	340
Louisville (Ky.), U. S.	450
Lourdes, France	1,345
Luanda, Angola	243
Lucknow, India	425
Ludwigshafen, Germany (West)	308
Luxembourg, Lux.	945
Luzern, Switz.	1,634
Lvov, Sov. Un.	980
Lyon, France	555

M

Madras, India	30
Madrid, Spain	2,150
Magdeburg, Germany (East)	164
Mainz, Germany (West)	269
Managua, Nicaragua	195
Manaus, Brazil	141
Manchester, Eng.	275
Manila, Philippines	30
Mannheim, Germany (West)	318
Maracaibo, Ven.	30
Marrakech, Morocco	1,535
Marseille, France	150
Mecca, Saudi Arabia	919
Medellín, Colombia	5,044
Melbourne, Austl.	30
Memphis (Tenn.), U. S.	275
Merano, Italy	1,062
Mérida, Mex.	65
Mérida, Ven.	5,415
Mexico City, Mex.	7,349
Miami (Fla.), U. S.	10
Milano (Milan), Italy	397
Milwaukee (Wis.), U. S.	635
Minneapolis (Minn.), U. S.	815
Minsk, Sov. Un.	690
Monterrey, Mex.	1,765
Montevideo, Ur.	80
Montréal, Canada	104
Mont Tremblant, Canada	745
Moscow (Moskva), Sov. Un.	425
Mosul, Iraq	800
Mukden, China	560
München (Munich), Germany (West)	1,699
Münster, Germany (West)	203

N

Nagasaki, Japan	210
Nagoya, Japan	50
Nagpur, India	1,020
Nairobi, Kenya	5,452
Nancy, France	675
Nanking, China	90
Nantes, France	26
Napoli (Naples), Italy	33
Nashville (Tenn.), U. S.	546
Newark (N. J.), U. S.	55
Newcastle-on-Tyne, Eng.	175
New Orleans (La.), U. S.	5
New York (N. Y.), U. S.	55
Nice, France	94
Niigata, Japan	50
Nikko, Japan	1,746
Norfolk (Va.), U. S.	10
Northampton, Eng.	235
Novosibirsk, Sov. Un.	490
Nürnberg, Germany (West)	1,110

O

Oakland (Calif.), U. S.	25
Odessa, Sov. Un.	165
Oklahoma City (Okla.), U. S.	1,195
Omaha (Neb.), U. S.	1,040
Omsk, Sov. Un.	286
Oran, Algeria	35
Orizaba, Mex.	4,028
Oruro, Bolivia	12,149
Osaka, Japan	40
Oslo, Norway	55
Ottawa, Canada	286

P

Palermo, Italy	46
Panamá, Panama	40
Paris, France	250
Patna, India	170
Peking (Peiping), China	165
Peoria (Ill.), U. S.	470
Perm, Sov. Un.	250
Perth, Austl.	55
Petropavlovsk, Sov. Un.	313
Petrópolis, Brazil	2,800
Philadelphia (Pa.), U. S.	100
Phnom Penh, Cambodia	33
Phoenix (Ariz.), U. S.	1,090
Piraievs (Piraeus), Greece	30
Pittsburgh (Pa.), U. S.	745
Plauen, Germany (East)	1,335
Plzeň, Czech	995
Poona, India	1,720
Port-au-Prince, Haiti	25
Portland (Oreg.), U. S.	75
Pôrto, Portugal	300
Port Said, U.A.R.	30
Portsmouth, Eng.	20
Potosí, Bolivia	13,600
Poznań (Posen), Poland	292
Prague (Praha), Czech	575
Pretoria, S. Afr.	4,472
Providence (R. I.), U. S.	80
Puebla, Mex.	7,091
Puno, Peru	12,648
Pusan (Fusan), Korea (South)	25
Pyongyang, Korea (North)	60

Q

Québec, Canada	19; 305
Quito, Ecuador	9,320

R

Rangoon, Burma	20
Rawalpindi, Pak.	1,726
Recife, Brazil	10
Regensburg, Germany (West)	1,075
Reims, France	280
Reno (Nevada), U. S.	4,490
Richmond (Va.), U. S.	164
Riga, Sov. Un.	30
Rio de Janeiro, Brazil	30
Riyadh, Saudi Arabia	1,897
Rochester (N. Y.), U. S.	510
Rome (Roma), Italy	66
Rosario, Arg.	86
Rostov, Sov. Un.	100
Rotterdam, Neth.	—8; 15
Rouen, France	90

S

Saarbrücken, Germany (West)	625
Sacramento (Calif.), U. S.	30
Saigon, Vietnam (South)	26
St. Étienne, France	1,800
St. Louis (Mo.), U.S.	455
St. Paul (Minn.), U.S.	780
Salisbury, Rhodesia	4,780
Salt Lake City (Utah), U. S.	4,390
Salvador, Brazil	135
Salzburg, Aus.	1,391
San'ā', Yemen	7,700
San Antonio (Texas), U. S.	650
San Francisco (Calif.), U. S.	65
San José, Costa Rica	3,021
San Juan, Puerto Rico	10
Sankt Moritz, Switz	6,037
San Salvador, El Salvador	2,178
Santa Fe (N. Mex.), U. S.	6,950
Santiago, Chile	1,795
Santos, Brazil	30
São Paulo, Brazil	2,545
Sapporo, Japan	245
Saratov, Sov. Un.	250
Scranton (Pa.), U. S.	725
Seattle (Wash.), U. S.	75
Sendai, Japan	250
Seoul, Korea (South)	75
Sevilla (Seville), Spain	39
's Gravenhage, see The Hague, Neth.	
Shanghai, China	20
Sheffield, Eng.	325
Sholapur, India	1,435
Sian (Siking), China	1,364
Simla, India	7,186
Singapore, Malaysia	35
Smyrna, see Izmir, Turkey.	
Sodom, Israel	—1,286
Sofia (Sofiya), Bulgaria	1,700
Soochow, see Wuhsien, China.	
Southampton, Eng.	45
Springfield (Mo.), U. S.	1,200
Spokane (Wash.), U. S.	1,890
Srinagar, India	5,130
Stalingrad, see Volgograd, Sov. Un.	
Stettin, see Szczecin, Pol.	
Stockholm, Sweden	46
Strasbourg, France	450
Stuttgart, Germany (West)	853
Sucre, Bolivia	8,950
Sun Valley (Idaho), U. S.	6,000
Surabaja, Indonesia	25
Sverdlovsk, Sov. Un.	860
Sydney, Austl.	35
Syracuse (N. Y.), U. S.	400
Szczecin (Stettin), Pol	50

T

Tabriz, Iran	5,250
Tacoma (Wash.), U. S.	110
Taipei, Taiwan (Formosa)	26
Tallinn, Sov. Un.	25
Tampa (Fla.), U. S.	15
Tananarive, Malag. Rep.	4,200
Taos (N. Mex.), U. S.	6,985
Tashkent, Sov. Un.	1,500
Taxco [de Alarcón], Mex.	5,756
Tbilisi, Sov. Un.	1,450
Tegucigalpa, Honduras	3,070
Tehran, Iran	3,865
The Hague ('s Gravenhage), Neth.	—4; 25
Tientsin, China	15
Timbuktu, see Tombouctou, Mali.	
Tiranë, Albania	374
Tōkyō, Japan	45
Toledo (Ohio), U. S.	1,799
Tombouctou, Mali	938
Tomsk, Sov. Un.	303
Torino (Turin), Italy	784
Toronto, Canada	356
Toulouse, France	490
Tours, France	160
Trieste, Italy	7
Tripoli, Libya	35
Tsinan, China	125
Tucson (Ariz.), U. S.	2,390
Tucumán, Arg.	1,385
Tulsa (Okla.), U. S.	804
Tunis, Tunisia	30
Turin, see Torino, Italy.	

U

Ulan Bator, Mongolia	4,160

V

Valencia, Spain	49
Valparaíso, Chile	35
Vancouver, Canada	38
Venezia (Venice), Italy	5
Verona, Italy	194
Versailles, France	445
Victoria, Hong Kong	50
Vienna (Wien), Aus.	550
Vilnius, Sov. Un.	500
Vladivostok, Sov. Un.	65
Volgograd (Stalingrad), Sov. Un.	180

W

Wanchuan (Kalgan), China	2,550
Warsaw (Warszawa), Poland	344
Washington (D. C.), U. S.	25
Wellington, N. Z.	415
Whitehorse, Canada	2,083
White Sulphur Springs (W. Va.), U. S.	2,000
Wichita (Kans.), U. S.	1,290
Wien, see Vienna, Aus.	
Wiesbaden, Germany (West)	361
Wilmington (Del.), U. S.	135
Winnipeg, Canada	764
Worcester (Mass.), U. S.	475
Wrocław (Breslau), Poland	390
Wuhan, China	55
Wuhsien (Soochow), China	30
Wuppertal, Germany (West)	1,100

Y

Yakutsk, Sov. Un.	210
Yokohama, Japan	110
Youngstown (Ohio), U. S.	863

Z

Zacatecas, Mex.	8,010
Zagreb, Yugoslavia	515
Zakopane, Poland	2,733
Zaragoza, Spain	820
Zermatt, Switz.	5,279
Zürich, Switz.	1,867
Zwickau, Germany (East)	855

GEOGRAPHICAL FACTS ABOUT THE UNITED STATES

ELEVATION

The highest elevation in the United States is Mount McKinley, Alaska, 20,320 feet.

The lowest elevation in the United States is in Death Valley, California, 282 feet below sea level.

The average elevation of the United States is 2,500 feet.

EXTREMITIES

Direction	Location	Latitude	Longitude
North	Point Barrow, Alaska	71°23′N.	156°29′W.
South	South Cape, Hawaii	18°56′N.	155°41′W.
East	West Quoddy Head, Maine	44°49′N.	66°57′W.
West	Cape Wrangell, Alaska	52°55′N.	172°27′E.

The two places in the United States separated by the greatest distance are Kure Island, Hawaii, and Mangrove Point, Florida. These points are 5,848 miles apart.

LENGTH OF BOUNDARIES

The total length of the Canadian boundary of the United States is 5,525 miles.

The total length of the Mexican boundary of the United States is 2,013 miles.

The total length of the Atlantic coastline of the United States is 2,069 miles.

The total length of the Pacific and Arctic coastline of the United States is 8,683 miles.

The total length of the Gulf of Mexico coastline of the United States is 1,631 miles.

The total length of all coastlines and land boundaries of the United States is 19,921 miles.

The total length of the tidal shoreline and land boundaries of the United States is 96,171 miles.

GEOGRAPHIC CENTERS

The geographic center of the United States (including Alaska and Hawaii) is in Butte County, South Dakota at 44°58′N., 103°46′W.

The geographic center of North America is in North Dakota, a few miles west of Devils Lake, at 48°10′N., 100°10′W.

EXTREMES OF TEMPERATURE

The highest temperature ever recorded in the United States was 134°F., at Greenland Ranch, Death Valley, California, on July 10, 1913.

The lowest temperature ever recorded in the United States was —76°F., at Tanana, Alaska, in January, 1886.

PRECIPITATION

The average annual precipitation for the United States is approximately 29 inches.

Hawaii is the wettest state, with an average annual rainfall of 82.48 inches. Nevada, with an average annual rainfall of 8.81 inches, is the driest state.

The greatest local average annual rainfall in the United States is at Mt. Waialeale, Kauai, Hawaii, 460 inches.

Greatest 24-hour rainfall in the United States, 23.22 inches at New Smyrna, Florida, October 10–11, 1924.

Extreme minimum rainfall records in the United States include a total fall of only 3.93 inches at Bagdad, California, for a period of 5 years, 1909–13, and an annual average of 1.78 inches at Death Valley, California.

Heavy snowfall records include 60 inches at Giant Forest, California, in 1 day; 42 inches at Angola, New York, in 2 days; 87 inches at Giant Forest, California, in 3 days; and 108 inches at Tahoe, California, in 4 days.

Greatest seasonal snowfall, 1,000.3 inches, more than 83 feet, at Paradise Ranger Station, Washington, during the winter of 1955–56.

HISTORICAL FACTS ABOUT THE UNITED STATES

TERRITORIAL ACQUISITIONS

Accession	Date	Area (sq. mi.)	Cost in Dollars
Original territory of the Thirteen States	1790	888,811	....
Purchase of Louisiana Territory, from France	1803	827,192	$11,250,000.00
By treaty with Spain: Florida	1819	58,560	$ 5,000,000.00
Other areas	1819	13,443	
Annexation of Texas	1845	390,144	....
Oregon Territory, by treaty with Great Britain	1846	285,580	....
Mexican Cession	1848	529,017	$15,000,000.00
Gadsden Purchase, from Mexico	1853	29,640	$10,000,000.00
Purchase of Alaska, from Russia	1867	586,400	7,200,000.00
Annexation of Hawaiian Islands	1898	6,424	....
Puerto Rico, by treaty with Spain	1898	3,435	....
Guam, by treaty with Spain	1898	212	....
American Samoa, by treaty with Great Britain and Germany	1900	76	....
Panama Canal Zone, by treaty with Panama	1904	553	*$10,000,000.00
Virgin Islands, by purchase from Denmark	1917	133	$25,000,000.00
Total		3,619,620	$83,450,000.00

Note: The Philippines, ceded by Spain in 1898 for $20,000,000.00, were a territorial possession of the United States from 1898 to 1946. On July 4, 1946 they became the independent republic of the Philippines.

* $25,000,000.00 was also paid to the republic of Colombia, out of whose territory the republic of Panama was created. In addition, an annual payment of $430,000.00 is made to the republic of Panama.

WESTWARD MOVEMENT OF CENTER OF POPULATION

Year	U.S. Population Total at Census	Approximate Location
1790	3,929,214	23 miles east of Baltimore, Md.
1800	5,308,483	18 miles west of Baltimore, Md.
1810	7,239,881	40 miles northwest of Washington, D.C.
1820	9,638,453	16 miles east of Moorefield, W. Va.
1830	12,866,020	19 miles southwest of Moorefield, W. Va.
1840	17,069,453	16 miles south of Clarksburg, W. Va.
1850	23,191,876	23 miles southeast of Parkersburg, W. Va.
1860	31,443,321	20 miles southeast of Chillicothe, Ohio
1870	39,818,449	48 miles northeast of Cincinnati, Ohio
1880	50,155,783	8 miles southwest of Cincinnati, Ohio
1890	62,947,714	20 miles east of Columbus, Ind.
1900	75,994,575	6 miles southeast of Columbus, Ind.
1910	91,972,266	Bloomington, Ind.
1920	105,710,620	8 miles southeast of Spencer, Ind.
1930	122,775,046	3 miles northeast of Linton, Ind.
1940	131,669,275	2 miles southeast of Carlisle, Ind.
1950	150,697,361	8 miles northwest of Olney, Ill.
1960	179,323,175	6 miles northwest of Centralia, Ill.

STATE AREAS AND POPULATIONS

STATE	Land Area (square miles) in 1960	Water Area (square miles) in 1960	Total Area (square miles) in 1960	Rank in Area	Population in 1960	Population Per Square Mile in 1960	Rank in Population in 1960	Population in 1950	Rank in Population in 1950	Population 1940
Alabama	51,060	549	51,609	29	3,266,740	63	19	3,061,743	17	2,832,961
Alaska	571,065	15,335	586,400	1	226,167	0.4	50	128,643	51	72,524‡
Arizona	113,575	334	113,909	6	1,302,161	11	35	749,587	37	499,261
Arkansas	52,499	605	53,104	27	1,786,272	34	31	1,909,511	30	1,949,387
California	156,573	2,120	158,693	3	15,717,204	99	2	10,586,223	2	6,907,387
Colorado	103,884	363	104,247	8	1,753,947	17	33	1,325,089	34	1,123,296
Connecticut	4,899	110	5,009	48	2,535,234	506	25	2,007,280	28	1,709,242
Delaware	1,978	79	2,057	49	446,292	217	46	318,085	47	266,505
District of Columbia†	61	8	69	..	763,956	11,072	..	802,178	..	663,091
Florida	54,252	4,308	58,560	22	4,951,560	85	10	2,771,305	20	1,897,414
Georgia	58,274	602	58,876	21	3,943,116	67	16	3,444,578	13	3,123,723
Hawaii	6,415	9	6,424	47	632,772	99	43	499,794	45	423,330
Idaho	82,708	849	83,557	13	667,191	8.0	42	588,637	43	524,873
Illinois	55,930	470	56,400	24	10,081,158	179	4	8,712,176	4	7,897,241
Indiana	36,185	106	36,291	38	4,662,498	128	11	3,934,224	12	3,427,796
Iowa	56,032	258	56,290	25	2,757,537	49	24	2,621,073	22	2,538,268
Kansas	82,048	216	82,264	14	2,178,611	26	28	1,905,299	31	1,801,028
Kentucky	39,863	532	40,395	37	3,038,156	75	22	2,944,806	19	2,845,627
Louisiana	45,106	3,417	48,523	31	3,257,022	67	20	2,683,516	21	2,363,880
Maine	31,012	2,203	33,215	39	969,265	29	36	913,774	35	847,226
Maryland	9,874	703	10,577	42	3,100,689	293	21	2,343,001	23	1,821,244
Massachusetts	7,867	390	8,257	45	5,148,578	624	9	4,690,514	9	4,316,721
Michigan	57,019	1,197	58,216	23	7,823,194	134	7	6,371,766	7	5,256,106
Minnesota	80,009	4,059	84,068	12	3,413,864	41	18	2,982,483	18	2,792,300
Mississippi	47,223	493	47,716	32	2,178,141	46	29	2,178,914	26	2,183,796
Missouri	69,138	548	69,686	19	4,319,813	62	13	3,954,653	11	3,784,664
Montana	145,736	1,402	147,138	4	674,767	4.6	41	591,024	42	559,456
Nebraska	76,612	615	77,227	15	1,411,330	18	34	1,325,510	33	1,315,834
Nevada	109,788	752	110,540	7	285,278	2.6	49	160,083	49	110,247
New Hampshire	9,014	290	9,304	44	606,921	65	45	533,242	44	491,524
New Jersey	7,521	315	7,836	46	6,066,782	774	8	4,835,329	8	4,160,165
New Mexico	121,510	156	121,666	5	951,023	7.8	37	681,187	39	531,818
New York	47,939	1,637	49,576	30	16,782,304	339	1	14,830,192	1	13,479,142
North Carolina	49,067	3,645	52,712	28	4,556,155	86	12	4,061,929	10	3,571,623
North Dakota	69,457	1,208	70,665	17	632,446	8.9	44	619,636	41	641,935
Ohio	40,972	250	41,222	35	9,706,397	235	5	7,946,627	5	6,907,612
Oklahoma	68,887	1,032	69,919	18	2,328,284	33	27	2,233,351	25	2,336,434
Oregon	96,248	733	96,981	10	1,768,687	18	32	1,521,341	32	1,089,684
Pennsylvania	45,007	326	45,333	33	11,319,366	250	3	10,498,012	3	9,900,180
Rhode Island	1,058	156	1,214	50	859,488	708	39	791,896	36	713,346
South Carolina	30,272	783	31,055	40	2,382,594	77	26	2,117,027	27	1,899,804
South Dakota	76,378	669	77,047	16	680,514	8.8	40	652,740	40	642,961
Tennessee	41,762	482	42,244	34	3,567,089	84	17	3,291,718	16	2,915,841
Texas	262,840	4,499	267,339	2	9,579,677	36	6	7,711,194	6	6,414,824
Utah	82,339	2,577	84,916	11	890,627	10	38	688,862	38	550,310
Vermont	9,276	333	9,609	43	389,881	41	47	377,747	46	359,231
Virginia	39,838	977	40,815	36	3,966,949	97	14	3,318,680	15	2,677,773
Washington	66,709	1,483	68,192	20	2,853,214	42	23	2,378,963	24	1,736,191
West Virginia	24,079	102	24,181	41	1,860,421	77	30	2,005,552	29	1,901,974
Wisconsin	54,705	1,449	56,154	26	3,951,777	70	15	3,434,575	14	3,137,587
Wyoming	97,411	503	97,914	9	330,066	3.4	48	290,529	48	250,742
United States	3,548,974	66,237	3,675,633*	..	179,323,175	49	..	151,325,798	..	132,165,129

† District.   * Includes the United States parts of the Great Lakes (60,422 square miles). These are not included in state figures.   ‡ Census taken in 1939.

217

U.S. STATE CLIMATIC AND ECONOMIC TABLE

State	Topography	Climate Information				Principal Mineral Products	Principal Agricultural Products	Principal Forest and Fishery Products	Principal Manufactures
		Weather Station	Annual Rainfall	January Mean Temp.	July Mean Temp.				
ALABAMA	Mountainous in north and northeast; southward the land gradually slopes to sea level.	Birmingham Mobile	53.52 in., 67.57 in.,	45.2°F., 52.7°F.,	79.6°F. 80.7°F.	Coal, cement, iron ore, stone, lime, sand & gravel, clays, natural gas.	Poultry and eggs, cotton, cattle, dairy products, hogs, peanuts, corn, cottonseed, soybeans, potatoes.	Shortleaf and loblolly pine, longleaf and slash pine, oak, gum, naval stores; shrimp, red snapper.	Steel rolling, textiles, paper products, rubber & plastics, iron & steel products, lumber & wood products.
ALASKA	Very high elevations in E. Broad, rolling, central plateaus, wide river valleys; NE.–W., mountain range sloping gradually to Arctic.	Anchorage Fairbanks	14.27 in., 11.92 in.,	13.0°F., –9.8°F.,	57.3°F. 60.9°F.	Coal, gold, sand & gravel, petroleum, mercury, stone, natural gas, copper, silver, clay.	Dairy products, field crops, poultry & poultry products, vegetables, cattle, sheep, hogs, horses.	Western hemlock, spruce lodgepole pine; salmon, halibut, herring, crabs.	Canned and frozen salmon & other fish products, lumber & wood products, newspapers.
ARIZONA	South—high plains with scattered mountains; north—plateaus, rough mountains, Grand Canyon of Colorado River.	Flagstaff Tucson	18.47 in., 10.66 in.,	25.3°F., 49.7°F.,	65.2°F. 86.2°F.	Copper, sand & gravel, zinc, uranium, molybdenum, stone, gold, silver, lime, lead.	Cotton, cattle, lettuce, dairy products, cottonseed, hay, cantaloups, barley, poultry & eggs.	Ponderosa pine, Douglas fir, true firs, spruce.	Printing & publishing, concrete products, dairy products, lumber & wood products, machinery.
ARKANSAS	Boston Mountains and Ouachita Mountains in northwest, separated by Arkansas River Valley; rest of state slopes southeast to Mississippi River.	Little Rock El Dorado	47.38 in., 51.58 in.,	41.8°F., 47.1°F.,	81.9°F. 82.9°F.	Petroleum, bauxite, stone, sand & gravel, natural gas, natural gas liquids, coal, barite, clays, gypsum, gem stones.	Cotton, poultry & eggs, soybeans, cattle, rice, dairy products, cottonseed, hogs, turkeys, wheat, peaches.	Shortleaf and loblolly pine, oak, gum, hickory, cypress, walnut, cottonwood; buffalofish, catfish.	Lumber & wood products, paper products, chemicals, shoes, primary metals, electrical machinery, clothing, furniture.
CALIFORNIA	Coast Ranges along western edge, bisected by Central Valley; Sierra Nevada inland; low areas in southeast at Death Valley and Imperial Valley.	Los Angeles San Francisco San Diego Sacramento Eureka	14.54 in., 17.43 in., 10.86 in., 16.32 in., 36.15 in.,	55.0°F., 47.9°F., 54.9°F., 45.2°F., 47.2°F.,	72.5°F. 60.4°F. 69.3°F. 75.3°F. 56.4°F.	Petroleum, natural gas, cement, sand & gravel, natural gas liquids, stone.	Cattle, dairy products, cotton, poultry & eggs, grapes, oranges, tomatoes, hay, lettuce, potatoes, turkeys,	Douglas fir, true firs, Ponderosa pine, redwood, sugar pine, lodgepole pine; tuna, sardines, crabs, salmon.	Metal products, electrical machinery, aircraft, machinery, chemicals, printing & publishing, canned & frozen foods.
COLORADO	Great Plains in east rise abruptly westward to high ranges of Rocky Mountains; Colorado Plateau in west central part.	Denver Sterling Pueblo Grand Junction	13.43 in., 14.00 in., 11.87 in., 9.06 in.,	31.4°F., 24.8°F., 29.4°F., 24.0°F.,	73.7°F. 74.2°F. 74.9°F. 78.2°F.	Petroleum, molybdenum, uranium ore, coal, sand & gravel, natural gas, natural gas liquids, zinc.	Cattle, wheat, sugar beets, dairy products, sheep, potatoes, dry edible beans, hay, poultry & eggs, hogs.	Spruce, lodgepole pine, Ponderosa pine, true firs, cottonwood, aspen, Douglas fir.	Machinery, metal products, meat products, dairy products, beverages, newspapers.
CONNECTICUT	Wide central Connecticut Valley; coastal plain rises inland to hills in east, low mountains in west.	Hartford New Haven	40.48 in., 44.99 in.,	27.0°F., 29.1°F.,	73.8°F. 71.2°F.	Stone, sand & gravel, lime, clays, peat, beryllium concentrate, gem stones.	Poultry & eggs, dairy products, tobacco, cattle, potatoes, apples, tomatoes, sweet corn, turkeys.	Oysters, clams, flounders, lobsters, scup or porgy, scallops, shad, cod, swordfish, butterfish, sea bass.	Electrical machinery, rubber & plastics, chemicals, precision instruments, copper rolling, hardware.
DELAWARE	Low plain, swampy along coast; low rolling hills in north.	Dover	46.40 in.,	36.8°F.,	77.2°F.	Sand & gravel, clays, stone.	Poultry & eggs, corn, soybeans, dairy products, potatoes, cattle, lima beans, hogs.	Menhaden, oysters, clams, crabs, sea trout or gray weakfish, flounders, white perch, shad.	Periodicals, chemicals, clothing, metal products, primary metals, rubber & plastics, animal feeds.
FLORIDA	Generally low and flat; many swamps, most extensive in south (The Everglades); many lakes in central part.	Jacksonville Pensacola Tampa Miami	52.08 in., 61.60 in., 49.94 in., 47.20 in.,	55.9°F., 54.0°F., 61.5°F., 68.5°F.,	82.1°F. 81.0°F. 81.7°F. 81.6°F.	Phosphate rock, stone, cement, titanium concentrate, clays, sand & gravel, lime.	Oranges, dairy products, cattle, tomatoes, poultry & eggs, grapefruit, tobacco, potatoes, snap beans.	Naval stores, longleaf and slash pine, cypress, gum; shrimp, mullet, red snapper, catfish and bullheads.	Paper products, canned & frozen food, metal products, concrete & plaster, agricultural chemicals.
GEORGIA	Ridges of the southern Appalachian Mountains in northwest, separated from wide coastal plain by Piedmont.	Atlanta Macon Savannah	49.16 in., 46.31 in., 45.75 in.,	44.6°F., 49.5°F., 51.6°F.,	79.5°F. 82.4°F. 81.2°F.	Clays, stone, cement, sand & gravel, iron ore, mica sheets, talc & soapstone, peat, coal.	Poultry & eggs, cotton, tobacco, hogs, peanuts, cattle, dairy products, corn, pecans, peaches.	Longleaf and slash pine, shortleaf and loblolly pine, gum, oak, cypress, poplars; shrimp, crabs, shad.	Textiles, transportation equipment, paper, clothing, lumber & wood, machinery.
HAWAII	Rugged with young volcanoes, lava slopes, small plains areas.	Honolulu	21.70 in.,	72.2°F.,	78.8°F.	Stone, sand & gravel, pumice, cement.	Pineapples, sugar, poultry & eggs, cattle, coffee, vegetables, hogs.	Sandalwood, ohia, lehua, kukui, koa; tuna, snapper, marlin, big-eye scad.	Sugar products, canned & frozen food, printing, clothing, bakery products.
IDAHO	High Snake River plains in south and west; Bitterroot and other rugged mountain ranges to north, east, and south.	Boise Idaho Falls Lewiston	11.48 in., 7.69 in., 13.12 in.,	27.3°F., 15.7°F., 30.8°F.,	74.8°F. 69.2°F. 75.2°F.	Silver, phosphate rock, lead, zinc, sand & gravel, copper, stone, mercury.	Cattle, potatoes, wheat, dairy products, sugar beets, dry edible beans, sheep, hay, poultry & eggs.	Douglas fir, Ponderosa pine, true firs, sugar and white pines, spruce, lodgepole pines, hemlock.	Lumber & wood products, chemicals, dairy products, frozen fruits & vegetables, printing, machinery.
ILLINOIS	Broad, plain, undulating and ridged in north, hilly in extreme south.	Chicago Rockford Springfield	33.28 in., 36.36 in., 36.65 in.,	27.4°F., 24.0°F., 27.4°F.,	75.2°F. 75.3°F. 76.3°F.	Petroleum, coal, stone, sand & gravel, cement, natural gas, natural gas liquids.	Cattle, hogs, corn, soybeans, dairy products, wheat, poultry & eggs, oats, sheep, hay, turkeys, sweet corn, tomatoes.	Oak, hickory, maple; catfish, buffalofish, carp, chubs.	Electrical machinery, metal products, printing & publishing, primary metals, chemicals, heavy machinery, precision instruments.
INDIANA	Undulating glaciated plains with many lakes in north; sand dunes along Lake Michigan; rocky hill lands in south.	Indianapolis South Bend Evansville	39.69 in., 35.59 in., 41.37 in.,	28.8°F., 24.6°F., 34.7°F.,	76.0°F. 73.4°F. 78.2°F.	Coal, cement, stone, petroleum, sand & gravel, clays.	Hogs, cattle, corn, soybeans, dairy products, poultry & eggs, wheat, turkeys, tomatoes, oats.	Oak, soft maple, hickory, walnut, sugar maple, poplar, gum; buffalofish, carp, catfish.	Steel products, electrical machinery, automobiles & parts, chemicals, machinery, metal products.
IOWA	Land slopes gradually eastward to Mississippi River; undulating to rolling surface.	Des Moines Sioux City Davenport	30.74 in., 24.90 in., 34.27 in.,	22.1°F., 19.1°F., 24.3°F.,	76.2°F. 76.3°F. 77.3°F.	Cement, stone, sand & gravel, gypsum, coal, clays.	Cattle, hogs, corn, dairy products, poultry & eggs, soybeans, turkeys, sheep, oats, hay, wheat.	Oak; catfish, buffalofish, sheepshead.	Meat products, farm machinery, electrical machinery, grain mill products, printing & publishing.
KANSAS	Rolling, valley-cut plain in east; high, gently undulating plain in west. Elevations increase gradually westward.	Topeka Wichita Dodge City	33.28 in., 30.70 in., 20.58 in.,	29.9°F., 32.0°F., 30.3°F.,	80.6°F. 80.9°F. 79.9°F.	Petroleum, natural gas, cement, stone, salt, natural gas liquids, sand & gravel, coal, clays, zinc.	Cattle, wheat, sorghum, dairy products, hogs, poultry & eggs, corn, soybeans, hay, sheep, barley, turkeys.		Aircraft, chemicals, meat products, petroleum refining, machinery, grain mill products.
KENTUCKY	Southeast—Appalachian ridges and valleys; south central—highland rim; north central—Bluegrass plain.	Frankfort Bowling Green	43.55 in., 48.67 in.,	36.6°F., 38.7°F.,	77.7°F. 79.4°F.	Coal, petroleum, stone, natural gas, sand & gravel, fluorspar.	Tobacco, cattle, dairy products, hogs, poultry & eggs, corn, soybeans, wheat, sheep, hay.	Oak, hickory, beech, poplar, shortleaf and loblolly pine, maple, ash, walnut; catfish, buffalofish.	Tobacco, electrical machinery, chemicals, distilled liquor, machinery, metal products.
LOUISIANA	Broad Mississippi Valley on eastern border, with delta at southeast; west undulating to rolling; coastlands marshy.	New Orleans Shreveport	63.54 in., 45.10 in.,	55.9°F., 47.8°F.,	83.1°F. 85.5°F.	Petroleum, natural gas, natural gas liquids, sulfur, salt, sand & gravel, stone.	Cotton, cattle, rice, dairy products, sugarcane, poultry & eggs, soybeans, sweet potatoes.	Shortleaf and loblolly pine, oak, gum, tupelo, hickory, walnut, naval stores; shrimp, menhaden, oysters.	Chemicals, petroleum products, paper, primary metals, lumber & wood products, sugar.
MAINE	Rugged, dissected by numerous stream valleys; coast fringed with promontories and rocky islands.	Portland Farmington	41.78 in., 44.47 in.,	20.7°F., 18.3°F.,	67.8°F. 69.3°F.	Sand & gravel, stone, cement, clay, gem stones.	Poultry & eggs, potatoes, dairy products, cattle, apples, blueberries, hay, oats, hogs, lettuce.	Spruce and balsam fir, red and white pine, birch; shellfish, lobsters, perch, herring, clams, haddock.	Paper, leather, textiles, lumber & wood products, transportation equipment, canned & frozen food.
MARYLAND	Parallel mountain ridges in west; rolling hill lands in central part; coastland lowlands in East, penetrated by Chesapeake Bay.	Baltimore Frederick	42.59 in., 40.23 in.,	34.2°F., 32.7°F.,	76.3°F. 76.7°F.	Stone, sand & gravel, coal, natural gas, clays, gem stones.	Poultry & eggs, dairy products, cattle, tobacco, corn, soybeans, hogs, wheat, tomatoes, apples.	Oak, poplar, gum, pine; shellfish, oysters, crabs, clams, bass, shad, fluke.	Primary metals, chemicals, clothing, communication equipment, machinery, ships, beverages.
MASSACHUSETTS	West—hilly to mountainous, split by Connecticut Valley; Berkshire Hills in far west; rolling lowlands on the coast, with Cape Cod extension.	Boston Springfield New Bedford	38.76 in., 44.87 in., 41.43 in.,	29.1°F., 28.8°F., 31.8°F.,	72.2°F 74.2°F 72.0°F.	Sand & gravel, stone, lime, clay, gem stones.	Dairy products, poultry & eggs, tobacco, cattle, apples, hogs, potatoes, sweet corn, turkeys, hay, tomatoes, carrots, lettuce.	Pine, oak; shellfish, haddock, perch, yellowtail, cod, whiting, lobsters, pollock, clams, blackback, fluke, sole, alewives.	Electrical machinery, machinery, leather products, textiles, printing, paper, clothing, rubber & plastics, transportation equipment.
MICHIGAN	Northern peninsula—hilly, with mountain ranges in west; southern peninsula—rolling, glaciated surface with many moraines.	Detroit Grand Rapids Sault Ste. Marie	31.03 in., 31.50 in., 30.19 in.,	26.2°F., 23.5°F., 13.8°F.,	73.1°F. 71.5°F. 63.9°F.	Iron ore, cement, petroleum, sand & gravel, gypsum, salt, stone, clays, natural gas, peat, copper.	Dairy products, cattle, wheat, poultry & eggs, corn, dry edible beans, hogs, apples, cherries.	Maple, hemlock, pine, fir; chubs, herring, trout, pike, perch, whitefish, smelt.	Automobiles & parts, food products, chemicals, metal working machinery, steel products, paper.
MINNESOTA	Glaciated surface dotted with lakes and swamps; Mesabi and other ranges in northeast.	Minneapolis Duluth Bemidji	24.71 in., 29.72 in., 21.95 in.,	14.6°F., 8.3°F., 4.9°F.,	74.1°F. 66.4°F. 68.5°F.	Iron ore, granite, dolomite, sandstone, sand & gravel, clay, manganiferous ore.	Cattle, dairy products, hogs, poultry & eggs, corn, soybeans, turkeys, wheat, oats, barley.	Cottonwood and aspen, oak, red and white pine, jack pine, spruce and balsam fir; herring, pike.	Machinery, meat products, printing, paper, chemicals, electrical machinery.
MISSISSIPPI	Rolling to hilly, sloping gently to south and west; Yazoo-Mississippi Delta in west.	Jackson Greenville Biloxi	50.86 in., 51.69 in., 57.59 in.,	48.3°F., 47.0°F., 54.2°F.,	82.1°F. 82.4°F. 81.8°F.	Petroleum, natural gas, sand & gravel, clays, natural gas liquids, stone.	Cotton, poultry & eggs, cattle, dairy products, soybeans, cottonseed, hogs, corn, rice, pecans.	Shortleaf and loblolly pine, oak, gum, longleaf and slash pine, hickory, naval stores; shellfish, shrimp.	Forest products, paper, clothing, transportation equipment, lumber & wood products, chemicals.
MISSOURI	Highly dissected Ozark Plateau in south; Missouri River traverses northern hill lands from west to east.	St. Louis Kansas City Springfield	37.86 in., 35.31 in., 41.51 in.,	33.3°F., 30.0°F., 32.7°F.,	80.6°F. 80.9°F. 77.5°F.	Cement, stone, lead, lime, coal, sand & gravel, clays, barite, zinc, copper, natural gas, silver.	Cattle, hogs, dairy products, soybeans, corn, poultry & eggs, cotton, wheat, turkeys, sheep.	Oak, hickory, shortleaf and loblolly pine, walnut, cottonwood, aspen, maple; buffalofish, catfish, carp.	Automobiles, chemicals, printing, leather, machinery, electrical machinery, clothing.
MONTANA	Rockies cover western third; remainder consists of plateaus and undulating plains.	Butte Great Falls Billings	12.67 in., 14.03 in., 13.10 in.,	14.2°F., 22.7°F., 22.9°F.,	62.4°F. 69.6°F. 73.3°F.	Petroleum, copper, sand & gravel, chromium ore & concentrate, silver, zinc, natural gas, manganese ore.	Cattle, wheat, barley, dairy products, sheep, sugar beets, wool, hay, hogs, poultry & eggs.	Douglas fir, Ponderosa pine, lodgepole pine, spruce, sugar and western white pine.	Lumber & wood products, petroleum, printing & publishing, dairy products, sugar, beverages.

Giving the Various Principal Products and Manufactures for Each U.S. State

State	Topography	Climate Information				Principal Mineral Products	Principal Agricultural Products	Principal Forest and Fishery Products	Principal Manufactures
		Weather Station	Annual Rainfall	January Mean Temp.	July Mean Temp.				
NEBRASKA	Platte River flows eastward through undulating sand-and-loess-covered plains; foothills of the Rockies in far west.	Omaha Grand Island Scottsbluff	25.90 in., 22.70 in., 15.00 in.,	23.0°F., 23.0°F., 23.5°F.,	78.5°F. 78.5°F. 74.6°F.	Petroleum, sand & gravel, stone, natural gas liquids, natural gas, clays.	Cattle, corn, wheat, hogs, dairy products, poultry & eggs, sorghum grain, sheep, sugar beets, hay, soybeans.		Packed meat, grain mill products, printing & publishing, metal products, dairy products, machinery.
NEVADA	Broken series of roughly parallel ranges and basins with a north to south orientation. High Sierra Nevada on west.	Carson City Las Vegas Elko	11.50 in., 4.35 in., 9.13 in.,	31.7°F., 44.2°F., 21.9°F.,	69.6°F. 90.5°F. 70.2°F.	Copper, sand & gravel, iron ore, manganese ore, gypsum, gold.	Cattle, dairy products, hay, sheep, wool, cotton, wheat, onions, potatoes, hogs, barley, cottonseed.	Ponderosa pine, true firs.	Concrete & plaster products, newspapers, lumber & wood products, dairy products.
NEW HAMPSHIRE	North central—rugged, culminating in White Mountains; high ridges separate Connecticut and Merrimac river valleys; low coastal plain in southeast.	Concord Berlin	37.23 in., 39.13 in.,	20.1°F., 16.0°F.,	69.0°F. 66.6°F.	Sand & gravel, mica, stone, clays, gem stones, feldspar.	Dairy products, poultry & eggs, apples, cattle, hay, potatoes, turkeys, hogs, maple, snap beans.	Red and white pine, birch, maple, spruce and balsam fir, hemlock; shellfish, lobster, smelt.	Leather footwear, textiles, machinery, paper, electrical machinery, lumber & wood products, printing & publishing, food products.
NEW JERSEY	Southern half—low coastal plain, stream-indented coastline with protecting sand bars; northern half—parallel ridges and valleys.	Trenton Atlantic City	40.06 in., 41.77 in.,	32.6°F., 35.8°F.,	75.3°F. 73.6°F.	Stone, sand & gravel, clays, lime, iron ore, uranium, peat.	Poultry & eggs, dairy products, tomatoes, cattle, asparagus, peaches, potatoes, blueberries, apples, corn, hogs.	Oak, beech, maple, gum, poplar; shellfish, menhaden, clams, flounders, oysters, scup or porgy, bass, shad, perch.	Chemicals, electrical machinery, transportation equipment, machinery, metal products, clothing, primary metals.
NEW MEXICO	Rolling plains & plateaus; scattered mountain ranges running north to south; Rio Grande & Pecos valleys drain southward.	Albuquerque Roswell	8.68 in., 12.07 in.,	33.7°F., 39.6°F.,	79.0°F. 79.0°F.	Petroleum, natural gas, potassium salts, uranium ore, natural gas liquids, copper, sand & gravel.	Cattle, cotton, dairy products, wheat, hay, sorghum grain, sheep, poultry & eggs, cottonseed.	Ponderosa pine, Douglas fir, spruce, true firs, cottonwood, aspen.	Food products, lumber & wood products, petroleum & coal products, newspapers.
NEW YORK	Rolling plateau; Adirondacks in northeast, Catskills in southeast, separated by Mohawk Valley; Hudson-Champlain lowland along eastern border.	New York Buffalo Albany	42.03 in., 32.29 in., 35.81 in.,	32.9°F., 25.5°F., 25.2°F.,	74.6°F. 70.6°F. 73.1°F.	Stone, sand & gravel, iron ore, salt, zinc, abrasive garnet, petroleum, gypsum, clays, natural gas.	Dairy products, poultry & eggs, cattle, potatoes, apples, grapes, wheat, snap beans, dry edible beans, hay, onions, tomatoes.	Maples, beech, white and red pine, hemlock, firs; shellfish, clams, oysters, lobster, whiting, bass.	Clothing, printing & publishing, electrical machinery, machinery, chemicals, transportation equipment, precision instruments.
NORTH CAROLINA	Coastal plain in eastern third; Piedmont Uplands in central; Blue Ridge and Smoky Mountains along western border.	Asheville Raleigh Winston-Salem	37.22 in., 45.05 in., 43.15 in.,	39.4°F., 41.4°F., 39.3°F.,	73.8°F. 78.5°F. 77.5°F.	Stone, sand & gravel, feldspar, mica, clays, asbestos, talc & pyrophyllite, silver.	Tobacco, poultry & eggs, dairy products, hogs, corn, cotton, cattle, peanuts, soybeans, wheat, turkeys.	Shortleaf and loblolly pine, oak, gum, cypress, poplar, hickory, hemlock; menhaden, shellfish, crabs.	Textiles, cigarettes, furniture, chemicals, electrical machinery, clothing, paper products.
NORTH DAKOTA	Red River Valley on eastern border; central section, glaciated plains; west, Missouri Plateau cut by Missouri River system.	Bismarck Grand Forks Williston	15.40 in., 20.05 in., 14.66 in.,	9.2°F., 4.4°F., 10.0°F.,	72.1°F. 70.7°F. 70.9°F.	Petroleum, sand & gravel, coal, natural gas, clays, stone, natural gas liquids.	Wheat, cattle, barley, flaxseed, dairy products, hogs, potatoes, poultry & eggs, oats, sheep, sugar beets.	Bullheads, carp, catfish, suckers, buffalofish, perch, burbot, shovelnose.	Dairy products, newspapers, meat products, concrete products.
OHIO	Nearly level plains in north; rolling glacial plains in west; dissected Allegheny Plateau in southeast.	Cleveland Columbus Cincinnati	32.08 in., 34.36 in., 39.34 in.,	28.5°F., 31.1°F., 34.6°F.,	73.7°F. 75.8°F. 78.1°F.	Coal, cement, stone, sand & gravel, lime, salt, petroleum, clays, natural gas.	Dairy products, hogs, cattle, corn, poultry & eggs, wheat, soybeans, tomatoes, oats, turkeys, sheep, tobacco, apples.	Oak, hickory, maple, beech; pike, perch, catfish, bass, carp, sheepshead, whitefish, suckers, bullheads.	Iron & steel products, transportation equipment, machinery, electrical machinery, metal products, rubber products, chemicals.
OKLAHOMA	Ouachita Mountains in southeast; rolling prairies and high plains rising westward.	Oklahoma City Tulsa Lawton	30.22 in., 37.68 in., 29.68 in.,	37.1°F., 37.4°F., 41.1°F.,	82.1°F. 82.1°F. 83.9°F.	Petroleum, natural gas, natural gas liquids, stone, coal, sand & gravel, helium.	Cattle, wheat, cotton, dairy products, poultry & eggs, hogs, peanuts, pecans, hay, sorghum grain.	Shortleaf and loblolly pine, oak, hickory.	Petroleum refining, aircraft, metal products, oilfield machinery, meat products, glass.
OREGON	Broad Cascade Range separates wide Willamette Valley and Coast Range from lava plateaus and basins in southeast, and from mountains in northeast.	Portland Klamath Falls	39.91 in., 13.94 in.,	39.5°F., 29.2°F.,	68.5°F. 68.7°F.	Stone, sand & gravel, nickel, cement, clays, mercury, gold, pumice, gem stones, copper.	Cattle, wheat, dairy products, poultry & eggs, potatoes, barley, hay, beans, pears, strawberries, sheep, hogs, turkeys.	Douglas fir, Ponderosa pine, true firs, hemlock, sugar and western white pine; salmon, tuna, shellfish, crabs, flounders.	Lumber & wood products, canned & frozen fruits & vegetables, paper, iron & steel products, dairy products, machinery.
PENNSYLVANIA	Rolling piedmont in southeast; folded ranges of Appalachians from northeast to southwest; Allegheny Plateau in north and west.	Pittsburgh Philadelphia Scranton	36.23 in., 41.13 in., 40.49 in.,	33.0°F., 33.2°F., 26.9°F.,	75.4°F. 76.3°F. 72.2°F.	Coal, cement, stone, natural gas, petroleum, sand & gravel, clays, lime, zinc.	Dairy products, poultry & eggs, cattle, corn, hogs, wheat, potatoes, tobacco, apples, turkeys, hay, peaches, tomatoes.	Oak, maple, hemlock, white and red pine.	Iron & steel products heavy machinery, metal products, electrical machinery, chemicals, clothing, glass.
RHODE ISLAND	Glaciated highland in west; Narragansett Bay penetrates rolling eastern lowlands; Block Island lies 10 miles off shore.	Providence	39.63 in.,	28.7°F.,	71.0°F.	Stone, sand & gravel.	Dairy products, poultry & eggs, potatoes, cattle, apples, hogs, tomatoes, sweet corn, turkeys, hay.	Shellfish, clams, scup or porgy, yellowtail, butterfish, fluke, lobster, blackback, menhaden.	Textiles, jewelry, machinery, printing & publishing, metal products, silverware.
SOUTH CAROLINA	Coastal plain occupies three-fifths of state; in remainder, Piedmont Upland rises to Blue Ridge Mountains on northwest border.	Charleston Columbia Greenville	45.99 in., 46.15 in., 47.65 in.,	51.4°F., 47.0°F., 43.0°F.,	81.5°F. 81.4°F. 78.4°F.	Stone, clay, sand & gravel, mica.	Tobacco, cotton, poultry & eggs, dairy products, soybeans, peaches, corn, cottonseed, wheat, oats.	Shortleaf and loblolly pine, gum, oak, cypress, poplar, maple; shellfish, shrimp, oysters, crabs, menhaden.	Textiles, chemicals, clothing, paper, lumber & wood products.
SOUTH DAKOTA	Black Hills and Badlands in southwest; Missouri River Valley separates glaciated plains in east from high, dissected plains of west.	Sioux Falls Aberdeen Rapid City	25.24 in., 19.63 in., 17.10 in.,	14.2°F., 11.0°F., 21.1°F.,	74.8°F. 73.9°F. 72.3°F.	Gold, sand & gravel, stone, cement, uranium ore, feldspar, clays, mica, silver.	Cattle, hogs, wheat, poultry & eggs, dairy products, corn, sheep, oats, flaxseed, wool, barley.	Ponderosa pine, cottonwood and aspen; carp, bullheads, buffalofish, suckers.	Meat products, dairy products, newspapers, wood products.
TENNESSEE	Regions from east to west; Smoky Mountains; parallel valleys; eroded Cumberland Plateau; Nashville Basin; sloping plains to Mississippi River Valley.	Memphis Nashville Chattanooga	46.81 in., 45.03 in., 53.60 in.,	41.9°F., 39.9°F., 41.6°F.,	81.3°F. 80.0°F. 78.3°F.	Stone, cement, zinc, coal, phosphate rock, copper, sand & gravel, clays.	Cotton, cattle, dairy products, tobacco, hogs, poultry & eggs, soybeans, corn, cottonseed, wheat, apples, strawberries, hay.	Oak, hickory, poplar, shortleaf and loblolly pine, gum; catfish, buffalofish, carp, paddlefish.	Chemicals, metal products, plastics, textiles, clothing, paper, printing & publishing, wood products, footwear.
TEXAS	Gulf coastal plain in east; broad, rolling, central plains; high, rolling plateaus in west; mountains extreme southwest.	Houston Dallas Amarillo El Paso San Antonio	45.37 in., 34.42 in., 21.12 in., 7.83 in., 27.93 in.,	53.8°F., 45.7°F., 35.3°F., 43.4°F., 50.6°F.,	83.8°F. 85.5°F. 77.8°F. 81.3°F. 84.2°F.	Petroleum, natural gas, natural gas liquids, cement, sulfur, stone, sand & gravel.	Cotton, cattle, sorghum grain, wheat, cottonseed, rice, hogs, sheep, mohair, wool, peanuts, turkeys.	Shortleaf and loblolly pine, oak, gum, longleaf and slash pine; shellfish, shrimp, menhaden, snapper, trout.	Chemicals, petroleum refining, aircraft & parts, metal products, construction equipment, oilfield machines.
UTAH	High Colorado Plateau in east; basins and ranges in west; Great Salt Lake Plain in northwest; high mountains in northeast.	Salt Lake City Logan Richfield	14.74 in., 17.03 in., 8.19 in.,	26.5°F., 23.6°F., 28.0°F.,	76.6°F. 73.5°F. 71.8°F.	Copper, petroleum, coal, uranium ore, iron ore, gold, asphalt, lead, natural gas.	Cattle, dairy products, poultry & eggs, turkeys, sheep, sugar beets, wheat, hay, wool, potatoes, hogs.	Spruce, lodgepole pine, Ponderosa pine, Douglas fir, true fir, cottonwood and aspen.	Primary metals, petroleum refining, construction machinery, metal products, concrete & plaster products.
VERMONT	The Green Mountains are the main feature; Champlain lowlands in northwest; Connecticut River forms eastern border.	Burlington Rutland	32.22 in., 38.67 in.,	17.9°F., 21.5°F.,	70.4°F. 69.5°F.	Stone, sand & gravel, asbestos, clays, lime, talc, gem stones.	Dairy products, cattle, poultry & eggs, apples, hay, maple, potatoes, hogs, turkeys.	Birch and maple, spruce and balsam, fir, beech, hemlock, white and red pine, oak, walnut.	Machinery & machine tools, paper products, cut stone & stone products, lumber & wood products.
VIRGINIA	Coastal plain merges with Piedmont Upland; Great Valley lies between Blue Ridge and other Appalachian ranges in west.	Richmond Norfolk Roanoke	42.89 in., 43.26 in., 41.58 in.,	38.3°F., 41.5°F., 37.9°F.,	77.5°F. 77.5°F. 75.9°F.	Coal, stone, sand & gravel, lime, zinc, clays, cement, gypsum, gem stones, iron ore.	Dairy products, tobacco, poultry & eggs, cattle, peanuts, hogs, apples, soybeans, turkeys, corn.	Oak, shortleaf and loblolly pine, poplar, gum, hickory, maple and beech, ash, walnut; shellfish, oysters.	Fibers, plastics & rubber, cigarettes, textiles, paper, furniture, chemicals, lumber & wood products.
WASHINGTON	Coast Ranges and Cascade Range, separated by Puget Sound lowland, parallel the west coast; rolling plateau in southeast; Rockies in northeast.	Seattle Spokane Walla Walla	31.92 in., 14.92 in., 15.07 in.,	40.7°F., 24.9°F., 32.0°F.,	65.6°F. 69.6°F. 76.2°F.	Sand & gravel, stone, zinc, uranium ore, lead, coal, barite, pumice, diatomite, clay, peat, gypsum.	Wheat, dairy products, cattle, apples, poultry & eggs, barley, potatoes, hay, hops, sugar beets, green peas, dry field peas.	Douglas fir, western hemlock, true firs, Ponderosa pine, spruce, red alder; salmon, halibut, shellfish, crabs, oysters.	Aircraft, lumber & wood products, pulp & paper, primary metals, chemicals, canned & frozen foods, printing & publishing.
WEST VIRGINIA	Greater portion in Allegheny Plateau; Appalachian ranges and valleys in extreme east.	Charleston Clarksburg	45.00 in., 41.82 in.,	36.4°F., 33.0°F.,	75.4°F. 73.6°F.	Coal, natural gas, natural gas liquids, stone, sand & gravel, salt, clays.	Poultry & eggs, dairy products, cattle, apples, turkeys, sheep, hogs, corn, tobacco.	Oak, maple, birch, beech, yellow poplar, hickory, ash, basswood, walnut, gum, hemlock.	Chemicals, steel rolling & finishing, metal products, electrical machinery, glassware, machinery.
WISCONSIN	Southwest, rough and dissected; remainder, rolling to level glaciated plateau with many lakes and moraines.	Milwaukee Madison Green Bay	27.57 in., 30.71 in., 26.51 in.,	21.9°F., 19.3°F., 16.1°F.,	71.3°F. 73.1°F. 69.9°F.	Sand & gravel, stone, zinc, cement, lime, iron ore, clays.	Dairy products, cattle, hogs, poultry & eggs, corn, potatoes, turkeys, hay, green peas, tobacco, oats, sweet corn, soybeans.	Oak, birch, maple, red and white pine, hemlock, ash, basswood, walnut, cottonwood, aspen; chubs, perch, herring, trout.	Heavy machinery, paper, electrical machinery, automobiles & parts, metal products, dairy products, malt liquors, leather.
WYOMING	Numerous large, high, basins surrounded by high ranges of the Rockies; high plains in northeast quarter.	Cheyenne Sheridan Saratoga Moran	16.25 in., 16.75 in., 9.53 in., 21.21 in.,	25.5°F., 20.1°F., 20.4°F., 10.3°F.,	69.7°F. 70.6°F. 65.8°F. 57.6°F.	Petroleum, uranium ore, natural gas, clays, natural gas liquids, coal, sand & gravel, stone.	Cattle, sheep, wool, wheat, sugar beets, dairy products, dry edible beans, hay, poultry & eggs, hogs.	Lodgepole pine, spruce, Ponderosa pine, Douglas fir.	Petroleum & coal products, food products, stone, clay & glass products, lumber & wood products.

U.S. STATE GENERAL INFORMATION TABLE

STATE	CAPITAL	LARGEST CITY	ENTERED UNION AS STATE — Date of Entry	Rank of Entry	Greatest N-S Measurement (miles)	Greatest E-W Measurement (miles)	HIGHEST POINT — Location	Altitude (feet)	STATE FLOWER	STATE BIRD	STATE NICKNAME
Alabama	Montgomery	Birmingham	Dec. 14, 1819	22	330	200	Cheaha Mountain	2,407	Camellia	Yellowhammer	Cotton
Alaska	Juneau	Anchorage	Jan. 3, 1959	49	1,332	2,250	Mt. McKinley	20,320	Forget-me-not	Willow Ptarmigan	Last Frontier
Arizona	Phoenix	Phoenix	Feb. 14, 1912	48	390	335	Humphreys Peak	12,670	Saguaro Cactus	Cactus Wren	Grand Canyon
Arkansas	Little Rock	Little Rock	June 15, 1836	25	240	275	Magazine Mtn.	2,823	Apple Blossom	Mockingbird	Land of Opportunity
California	Sacramento	Los Angeles	Sept. 9, 1850	31	800	375	Mt. Whitney	14,495	Golden Poppy	California Valley Quail	Golden
Colorado	Denver	Denver	Aug. 1, 1876	38	270	380	Mt. Elbert	14,431	Rocky Mountain Columbine	Lark Bunting	Centennial
Connecticut*	Hartford	Hartford	Jan. 9, 1788	5	75	90	S. slope of Mt. Frissell	2,380	Mountain Laurel	Robin	Constitution
Delaware*	Dover	Wilmington	Dec. 7, 1787	1	95	35	Ebright Road, New Castle Co.	442	Peach Blossom	Blue Hen Chicken	Diamond
District of Columbia†	Washington	Washington	March 3, 1791	..	15	15	Tenleytown	410	American Beauty Rose	....	....
Florida	Tallahassee	Miami	March 3, 1845	27	460	400	N. boundary, Walton Co.	345	Orange Blossom	Mockingbird	Sunshine
Georgia*	Atlanta	Atlanta	Jan. 2, 1788	4	315	250	Brasstown Bald (mtn.)	4,784	Cherokee Rose	Brown Thrasher	Peach State
Hawaii	Honolulu	Honolulu	Aug. 21, 1959	50	...	1,600	Mauna Kea	13,796	Red Hibiscus	Nene (Hawaiian Goose)	The Aloha
Idaho	Boise	Boise	July 3, 1890	43	480	305	Borah Peak	12,662	Syringa	Mountain Bluebird	Gem
Illinois	Springfield	Chicago	Dec. 3, 1818	21	380	205	Charles Mound	1,241	Native Violet	Cardinal	Prairie
Indiana	Indianapolis	Indianapolis	Dec. 11, 1816	19	265	160	Near Spartanburg	1,253	Peony	Cardinal	Hoosier
Iowa	Des Moines	Des Moines	Dec. 28, 1846	29	205	310	Ocheyedan Mound	1,675	Wild Rose	Eastern Goldfinch	Hawkeye
Kansas	Topeka	Wichita	Jan. 29, 1861	34	205	410	Mt. Sunflower	4,026	Sunflower	Western Meadowlark	Sunflower
Kentucky	Frankfort	Louisville	June 1, 1792	15	210	350	Black Mountain	4,145	Goldenrod	Kentucky Cardinal	Bluegrass
Louisiana	Baton Rouge	New Orleans	April 30, 1812	18	275	300	Driskill Mountain	535	Magnolia	Eastern Brown Pelican**	Pelican
Maine	Augusta	Portland	March 15, 1820	23	310	210	Mt. Katahdin	5,268	White Pine Cone and Tassel	Chickadee	Pine Tree
Maryland*	Annapolis	Baltimore	April 28, 1788	7	120	200	Backbone Mountain	3,360	Black-eyed Susan	Baltimore Oriole	Old Line
Massachusetts*	Boston	Boston	Feb. 6, 1788	6	110	190	Mt. Greylock	3,491	Mayflower	Chickadee	Bay
Michigan	Lansing	Detroit	Jan. 26, 1837	26	400	310	N.E. Baraga Co.	1,980	Apple Blossom	Robin	Wolverine
Minnesota	St. Paul	Minneapolis	May 11, 1858	32	400	350	Eagle Mtn.	2,301	Showy Lady's-slipper	Loon	Gopher
Mississippi	Jackson	Jackson	Dec. 10, 1817	20	340	180	Woodall Mountain	806	Magnolia	Mockingbird	Magnolia
Missouri	Jefferson City	St. Louis	Aug. 10, 1821	24	280	300	Taum Sauk Mountain	1,772	Hawthorne	Bluebird	Show Me
Montana	Helena	Great Falls	Nov. 8, 1889	41	315	570	Granite Peak	12,799	Bitterroot	Western Meadowlark	Treasure
Nebraska	Lincoln	Omaha	March 1, 1867	37	210	415	S.W. corner Kimball Co.	5,424	Goldenrod	Western Meadowlark	Cornhusker
Nevada	Carson City	Las Vegas	Oct. 31, 1864	36	485	315	Boundary Peak	13,145	Sagebrush	Mountain Bluebird**	Silver
New Hampshire*	Concord	Manchester	June 21, 1788	9	185	90	Mt. Washington	6,288	Purple Lilac	Purple Finch	Granite
New Jersey*	Trenton	Newark	Dec. 18, 1787	3	166	70	High Point	1,803	Purple Violet	Eastern Goldfinch	Garden
New Mexico	Santa Fe	Albuquerque	Jan. 6, 1912	47	390	350	Wheeler Peak	13,160	Yucca	Road Runner	Land of Enchantment
New York*	Albany	New York	July 26, 1788	11	310	330	Mt. Marcy	5,344	Rose	Bluebird	Empire
North Carolina*	Raleigh	Charlotte	Nov. 21, 1789	12	200	520	Mt. Mitchell	6,684	Dogwood	Cardinal	Tar Heel
North Dakota	Bismarck	Fargo	Nov. 2, 1889	39	210	360	White Butte	3,530	Wild Prairie Rose	Western Meadowlark	Flickertail
Ohio	Columbus	Cleveland	March 1, 1803	17	230	205	Campbell Hill	1,550	Scarlet Carnation	Cardinal	Buckeye
Oklahoma	Oklahoma City	Oklahoma City	Nov. 16, 1907	46	210	460	Black Mesa	4,978	Mistletoe	Scissor-tailed Flycatcher	Sooner
Oregon	Salem	Portland	Feb. 14, 1859	33	290	375	Mt. Hood	11,245	Oregon Grape	Western Meadowlark	Beaver
Pennsylvania*	Harrisburg	Philadelphia	Dec. 12, 1787	2	180	310	Mt. Davis	3,213	Mountain Laurel	Ruffed Grouse	Keystone
Rhode Island*	Providence	Providence	May 29, 1790	13	50	35	Jerimoth Hill	812	Violet**	Rhode Island Red	Little Rhody
South Carolina*	Columbia	Columbia	May 23, 1788	8	215	285	Sassafras Mountain	3,560	Yellow Jessamine	Carolina Wren	Palmetto
South Dakota	Pierre	Sioux Falls	Nov. 2, 1889	40	240	360	Harney Peak	7,242	American Pasque Flower	Ringnecked Pheasant	Coyote
Tennessee	Nashville	Memphis	June 1, 1796	16	120	430	Clingmans Dome	6,642	Iris	Mockingbird	Volunteer
Texas	Austin	Houston	Dec. 29, 1845	28	710	760	Guadalupe Peak	8,751	Bluebonnet	Mockingbird	Lone Star
Utah	Salt Lake City	Salt Lake City	Jan. 4, 1896	45	345	275	Kings Peak	13,498	Sego Lily	Sea Gull	Beehive
Vermont*	Montpelier	Burlington	March 4, 1791	14	155	90	Mt. Mansfield	4,393	Red Clover	Hermit Thrush	Green Mountain
Virginia*	Richmond	Norfolk	June 25, 1788	10	205	425	Mt. Rogers	5,720	American Dogwood	Cardinal	Old Dominion
Washington	Olympia	Seattle	Nov. 11, 1889	42	230	340	Mt. Rainier	14,410	Western Rhododendron	Willow Goldfinch	Evergreen
West Virginia	Charleston	Charleston	June 20, 1863	35	200	225	Spruce Knob	4,860	Big Rhododendron	Cardinal	Mountain
Wisconsin	Madison	Milwaukee	May 29, 1848	30	300	290	Rib Mountain	1,941	Wood Violet	Robin	Badger
Wyoming	Cheyenne	Cheyenne	July 10, 1890	44	275	365	Gannett Peak	13,785	Indian Paint Brush	Meadowlark	Equality
United States	Washington, D.C.	New York	...	...	...	...	Mt. McKinley, Alaska	20,320	....	Bald Eagle	....

*One of the Thirteen Original States.   **Unofficial.   †District.

U.S. POPULATION BY STATE OR COLONY
1650 TO 1960

STATES	1650	1700	1750	1770	1790	1800	1820	1840	1860	1880	1900	1910	1920	1930	1940	1950	1960
Alabama							127,901	590,756	964,201	1,262,505	1,828,697	2,138,093	2,348,174	2,646,248	2,832,961	3,061,743	3,266,740
Alaska										33,426	63,592	64,356	55,036	59,278	72,524	128,643	226,167
Arizona										40,440	122,931	204,354	334,162	435,573	499,261	749,587	1,302,161
Arkansas							14,273	97,574	435,450	802,525	1,311,564	1,574,449	1,752,204	1,854,482	1,949,387	1,909,511	1,786,272
California									379,994	864,694	1,485,053	2,377,549	3,426,861	5,677,251	6,907,387	10,586,223	15,717,204
Colorado									34,277	194,327	539,700	799,024	939,629	1,035,791	1,123,296	1,325,089	1,753,947
Connecticut	4,139	25,970	111,280	183,881	237,946	251,002	275,248	309,978	460,147	622,700	908,420	1,114,756	1,380,631	1,606,903	1,709,242	2,007,280	2,535,234
Delaware	185	2,470	28,704	35,496	59,096	64,273	72,749	78,085	112,216	146,608	184,735	202,322	223,003	238,380	266,505	318,085	446,292
District of Columbia						8,144	23,336	33,745	75,080	177,624	278,718	331,069	437,571	486,869	663,091	802,178	763,956
Florida								54,477	140,424	269,493	528,542	752,619	968,470	1,468,211	1,897,414	2,771,305	4,951,560
Georgia			5,200	23,375	82,548	162,686	340,989	691,392	1,057,286	1,542,180	2,216,331	2,609,121	2,895,832	2,908,506	3,123,723	3,444,578	3,943,116
Hawaii											154,001	191,874	255,881	368,300	422,770	499,794	632,772
Idaho										32,610	161,772	325,594	431,866	445,032	524,873	588,637	667,191
Illinois							55,211	476,183	1,711,951	3,077,871	4,821,550	5,638,591	6,485,280	7,630,654	7,897,241	8,712,176	10,081,158
Indiana						5,641	147,178	685,866	1,350,428	1,978,301	2,516,462	2,700,876	2,930,390	3,238,503	3,427,796	3,934,224	4,662,498
Iowa								43,112	674,913	1,624,615	2,231,853	2,224,771	2,404,021	2,470,939	2,538,268	2,621,073	2,757,537
Kansas									107,206	996,096	1,470,495	1,690,949	1,769,257	1,880,999	1,801,028	1,905,299	2,178,611
Kentucky				15,700	73,677	220,955	564,317	779,828	1,155,684	1,648,690	2,147,174	2,289,905	2,416,630	2,614,589	2,845,627	2,944,806	3,038,156
Louisiana							153,407	352,411	708,002	939,946	1,381,625	1,656,388	1,798,509	2,101,593	2,363,880	2,683,516	3,257,022
Maine[4]				31,257	96,540	151,719	298,335	501,793	628,279	648,936	694,466	742,371	768,014	797,423	847,226	913,774	969,265
Maryland	4,504	29,604	141,073	202,599	319,728	341,548	407,350	470,019	687,049	934,943	1,188,044	1,295,346	1,449,661	1,631,526	1,821,244	2,343,001	3,100,689
Massachusetts[4]	16,603	55,941	188,000	235,308	378,787	422,845	523,287	737,699	1,231,066	1,783,085	2,805,346	3,366,416	3,852,356	4,249,614	4,316,721	4,690,514	5,148,578
Michigan							8,896	212,267	749,113	1,636,937	2,420,982	2,810,173	3,668,412	4,842,325	5,256,106	6,371,766	7,823,194
Minnesota									172,023	780,773	1,751,394	2,075,708	2,387,125	2,563,953	2,792,300	2,982,483	3,413,864
Mississippi						8,850	75,448	375,651	791,305	1,131,597	1,551,270	1,797,114	1,790,618	2,009,821	2,183,796	2,178,914	2,178,141
Missouri							66,586	383,702	1,182,012	2,168,380	3,106,665	3,293,335	3,404,055	3,629,367	3,784,664	3,954,653	4,319,813
Montana										39,159	243,329	376,053	548,889	537,606	559,456	591,024	674,767
Nebraska									28,841	452,402	1,066,300	1,192,214	1,296,372	1,377,963	1,315,834	1,325,510	1,411,330
Nevada									6,857	62,266	42,335	81,875	77,407	91,058	110,247	160,083	285,278
New Hampshire	1,305	4,958	27,505	62,396	141,885	183,858	244,161	284,574	326,073	346,991	411,588	430,572	443,083	465,293	491,524	533,242	606,921
New Jersey		14,010	71,393	117,431	184,139	211,149	277,575	373,306	672,035	1,131,116	1,883,669	2,537,167	3,155,900	4,041,334	4,160,165	4,835,329	6,066,782
New Mexico									93,516	119,565	195,310	327,301	360,350	423,317	531,818	681,187	951,023
New York	4,116	19,107	76,696	162,920	340,120	589,051	1,372,812	2,428,921	3,880,735	5,082,871	7,268,894	9,113,614	10,385,227	12,588,066	13,479,142	14,830,192	16,782,304
North Carolina		10,720	72,984	197,200	393,751	478,103	638,829	753,419	992,622	1,399,750	1,893,810	2,206,287	2,559,123	3,170,276	3,571,623	4,061,929	4,556,155
North Dakota[3]										36,909	319,146	577,056	646,872	680,845	641,935	619,636	632,446
Ohio						45,365	581,434	1,519,467	2,339,511	3,198,062	4,157,545	4,767,121	5,759,394	6,646,697	6,907,612	7,946,627	9,706,397
Oklahoma[5]											790,391	1,657,155	2,028,283	2,396,040	2,336,434	2,233,351	2,328,284
Oregon									52,465	174,768	413,536	672,765	783,389	953,786	1,089,684	1,521,341	1,768,687
Pennsylvania		17,950	119,666	240,057	434,373	602,365	1,049,458	1,724,033	2,906,215	4,282,891	6,302,115	7,665,111	8,720,017	9,631,350	9,900,180	10,498,012	11,319,366
Rhode Island	785	5,894	33,226	58,196	68,825	69,122	83,059	108,830	174,620	276,531	428,556	542,610	604,397	687,497	713,346	791,896	859,488
South Carolina		5,704	64,000	124,244	249,073	345,591	502,741	594,398	703,708	995,577	1,340,316	1,515,400	1,683,724	1,738,765	1,899,804	2,117,027	2,382,594
South Dakota[3]									4,837	98,268	401,570	583,888	636,547	692,849	642,961	652,740	680,514
Tennessee				1,000	35,691	105,602	422,823	829,210	1,109,801	1,542,359	2,020,616	2,184,789	2,337,885	2,616,556	2,915,841	3,291,718	3,567,089
Texas									604,215	1,591,749	3,048,710	3,896,542	4,663,228	5,824,715	6,414,824	7,711,194	9,579,677
Utah									40,273	143,963	276,749	373,351	449,396	507,847	550,310	688,862	890,627
Vermont				10,000	85,425	154,465	235,981	291,948	315,098	332,286	343,641	355,956	352,428	359,611	359,231	377,747	389,881
Virginia[6]	18,731	58,560	231,033	447,016	691,737	807,557	938,261	1,025,227	1,219,630	1,512,565	1,854,184	2,061,612	2,309,187	2,421,851	2,677,773	3,318,680	3,966,949
Washington									11,594	75,116	518,103	1,141,990	1,356,621	1,563,396	1,736,191	2,378,963	2,853,214
West Virginia[6]					55,873	78,592	136,808	224,537	376,688	618,457	958,800	1,221,119	1,463,701	1,729,205	1,901,974	2,005,552	1,860,421
Wisconsin								30,945	775,881	1,315,497	2,069,042	2,333,860	2,632,067	2,939,006	3,137,587	3,434,575	3,951,777
Wyoming										20,789	92,531	145,965	194,402	225,565	250,742	290,529	330,066
Total[1]	50,368	250,888	1,170,760	2,148,076	3,929,214	5,308,483	9,638,453	17,069,453[2]	31,443,321	50,189,209	76,212,168	92,228,496	106,021,537	123,202,624	132,164,569	151,325,798	179,323,175

[1] All figures exclude uncivilized Indians. Figures for 1650 through 1770 include only the British colonies that later became the United States. No areas are included prior to their annexation to the United States. However, many of the figures refer to territories prior to their admission as States. U.S. total includes Alaska from 1880 through 1960 and Hawaii from 1900 through 1960.

[2] U.S. total for 1840 includes 6,100 persons on public ships in service of the United States, not credited to any State.

[3] South Dakota figure for 1860 represents entire Dakota Territory. North and South Dakota figures for 1880 are for the parts of Dakota Territory which later constituted the respective States.

[4] Maine figures for 1770 through 1800 are for that area of Massachusetts which later became the State of Maine in 1820. Massachusetts figures exclude Maine from 1770 through 1800, but include it from 1650 through 1750. Massachusetts figure for 1650 also includes Plymouth, a separate colony until 1691.

[5] Oklahoma figure for 1900 includes population of Indian Territory (392,060).

[6] West Virginia figures for 1790 through 1860 are for that area of Virginia which became West Virginia in 1863. These figures are excluded from the figures for Virginia from 1790 through 1860.

U.S. METRO. AREAS OF 100,000 OR MORE, 1965

To facilitate comparisons, Rand McNally Metro. Areas are defined according to consistent rules, so as to include with each city those neighboring communities linked to it by continuous built-up areas, and more distant communities in the bulk of their population is supported by commuters to the central city. The "city proper" figure always refers to the first-named central city only.

Rank 1965		POPULATION Metro. Area 1/1/1965	4/1/1960	City Proper 1/1/1965	4/1/1960
1	New York, New York	16,550,000	15,408,100	8,080,000	7,781,984
2	Los Angeles, California	7,635,000	6,565,000	2,695,000	2,479,015
3	Chicago, Illinois	7,225,000	6,777,800	3,520,000	3,550,404
4	Philadelphia, Pennsylvania	4,200,000	3,969,500	2,030,000	2,002,512
5	Detroit, Michigan	4,170,000	3,931,500	1,600,000	1,670,144
	incl. part in Canada	*4,370,000*	*4,124,900*		
6	San Francisco–Oakland–San Jose, California	3,805,000	3,275,000	745,000	740,316
7	Boston, Massachusetts*	3,540,000	3,372,800	670,000	697,197
8	Washington, District of Columbia*	2,485,000	2,053,600	810,000	763,956
9	Cleveland, Ohio	2,250,000	2,090,800	855,000	876,050
10	St. Louis, Missouri	2,195,000	2,050,800	710,000	750,026
11	Pittsburgh, Pennsylvania	1,955,000	1,957,700	560,000	604,332
12	Baltimore, Maryland	1,730,000	1,636,500	925,000	939,024
13	Minneapolis–St. Paul,* Minnesota	1,590,000	1,441,700	465,000	482,872
14	Miami–Fort Lauderdale, Florida	1,500,000	1,212,000	325,000	291,688
15	Houston, Texas	1,490,000	1,251,700	1,100,000	938,219
16	Milwaukee, Wisconsin	1,330,000	1,247,100	765,000	741,324
17	Cincinnati, Ohio	1,310,000	1,203,300	495,000	502,550
18	Buffalo–Niagara Falls, New York	1,285,000	1,244,200	505,000	532,759
	incl. part in Canada	*1,370,000*	*1,327,600*		
19	Dallas, Texas	1,280,000	1,022,300	790,000	679,684
20	Atlanta, Georgia*	1,230,000	1,011,100	535,000	487,455
21	Kansas City, Missouri	1,140,000	1,025,900	530,000	475,539
22	Seattle, Washington	1,045,000	938,400	565,000	557,087
23	Denver, Colorado*	1,035,000	858,300	520,000	493,887
24	San Diego, California	1,000,000	890,000	636,000	573,224
	incl. part in Mexico	*1,210,000*	*1,045,000*		
25	New Orleans, Louisiana	985,000	885,200	655,000	627,525
26	Indianapolis, Indiana*	900,000	806,900	530,000	476,258
27	Hartford*–New Britain, Connecticut	885,000	810,300	158,000	162,178
28	Providence*–Pawtucket–Woonsocket, Rhode Island	850,000	816,200	195,000	207,498
29	Columbus, Ohio*	825,000	715,400	540,000	471,316
30	Phoenix, Arizona*	810,000	619,600	520,000	439,170
31	Louisville, Kentucky	795,000	735,800	392,000	390,639
32	Portland, Oregon	795,000	731,200	380,000	372,676
33	San Antonio, Texas	790,000	689,700	645,000	587,718
34	Dayton, Ohio	720,000	648,600	260,000	262,332
35	Memphis, Tennessee	700,000	628,100	525,000	497,524
36	Norfolk–Portsmouth, Virginia	655,500	578,500	322,000	305,872
37	Birmingham, Alabama	655,000	624,000	345,000	340,887
38	Sacramento, California*	655,000	536,000	265,000	191,667
39	Rochester, New York	645,000	594,500	305,000	318,611
40	Akron, Ohio	615,000	573,800	298,000	290,351
41	Albany*–Schenectady–Troy, N.Y.	605,000	588,200	127,000	129,726
42	Oklahoma City, Oklahoma*	585,000	493,000	380,000	324,253
43	San Bernardino–Riverside, Calif.	575,000	460,000	102,000	91,922
44	Honolulu, Hawaii*	560,000	486,400	315,000	294,179
45	Fort Worth, Texas	550,000	505,100	360,000	356,268
46	Toledo, Ohio	540,000	514,200	354,000	318,003
47	Jacksonville, Florida	525,000	456,700	198,000	201,030
48	Omaha, Nebraska–Council Bluffs, Iowa	495,000	434,800	340,000	301,598
49	Springfield–Holyoke, Massachusetts	495,000	470,500	174,000	174,463
50	Youngstown–Warren, Ohio	490,000	467,600	162,000	166,689
51	Salt Lake City, Utah*	488,000	410,200	195,000	189,454
52	Syracuse, New York	485,000	442,300	216,000	216,038
53	Richmond, Virginia*	055,000	409,100	223,000	219,958
54	Nashville, Tennessee*	450,000	411,500	261,000	170,874
55	New Haven–Meriden, Connecticut	449,000	419,100	151,000	152,048
56	Flint, Michigan	415,000	379,900	202,000	196,940
57	St. Petersburg–Clearwater, Florida	415,000	355,200	200,000	181,298
58	Bridgeport, Connecticut	411,000	386,300	156,000	156,748
59	Tulsa, Oklahoma	410,000	387,100	280,000	261,685
60	Grand Rapids, Michigan	395,000	367,300	203,000	177,313
61	Tampa, Florida	395,000	356,200	305,000	274,970
62	Wilmington, Delaware	355,000	318,700	92,500	95,827
63	El Paso, Texas	342,000	306,800	309,000	276,687
	incl. part in Mexico	*650,000*	*570,000*		
64	Wichita, Kansas	342,000	346,200	275,000	254,698
65	Mobile, Alabama	338,000	304,000	222,000	202,779
66	Worcester, Massachusetts	329,000	322,400	180,000	186,587
67	Tacoma, Washington	322,000	298,000	152,000	147,979
68	Albuquerque, New Mexico	317,000	266,300	242,000	201,189
69	Chattanooga, Tennessee	310,000	286,700	127,500	130,009
70	Tucson, Arizona	310,000	243,000	245,000	212,892
71	Charlotte, North Carolina	308,000	272,700	230,000	201,564
72	Knoxville–Oak Ridge, Tennessee	305,000	286,000	181,000	111,827
73	Orlando, Florida	305,000	255,800	93,500	88,135
74	Allentown–Bethlehem, Pennsylvania	302,000	299,700	106,500	108,347
75	Pomona–Ontario, California	300,000	212,000	83,000	67,157
76	Utica–Rome, New York	299,000	284,000	100,000	100,410
77	Trenton, New Jersey*	298,000	279,800	107,000	114,167
78	Canton-Massillon, Ohio	295,000	281,900	110,000	113,631
79	Beaumont–Port Arthur, Texas	287,000	266,600	126,000	119,175
80	Baton Rouge, Louisiana*	280,000	248,700	166,000	152,419
81	Peoria, Illinois	280,000	265,000	100,000	103,162
82	Davenport, Iowa–Rock Island–Moline, Illinois	279,000	260,300	94,500	88,981
83	Des Moines, Iowa*	279,000	261,800	216,000	208,982
84	South Bend, Indiana	274,000	265,100	135,000	132,445
85	Harrisburg, Pennsylvania*	272,000	257,600	75,000	79,697
86	Shreveport, Louisiana	272,000	245,200	171,000	164,372
87	Little Rock, Arkansas*	270,000	238,500	130,500	107,813
88	Spokane, Washington	262,000	252,000	184,000	181,608
89	Fresno, California	260,000	228,000	156,000	133,929
90	Newport News–Hampton, Virginia	260,000	219,200	130,000	113,662
91	Austin, Texas*	246,000	210,000	220,000	186,545
92	Columbia, South Carolina*	242,000	213,400	100,000	97,433
93	Wilkes-Barre, Pennsylvania	240,000	250,700	58,500	63,551
94	Fort Wayne, Indiana	235,000	215,400	172,000	161,776
95	Lansing, Michigan*	235,000	209,100	120,500	107,807
96	Huntington, W. Va.–Ashland, Ky	234,000	231,100	81,500	83,627
97	Binghamton, New York	228,000	212,600	75,000	75,941
98	Charleston, South Carolina	225,000	203,100	79,500	65,925
99	Las Vegas, Nevada	225,000	119,300	110,000	64,405
100	Columbus, Georgia	224,000	201,500	125,000	116,779
101	Jackson, Mississippi*	220,000	191,200	161,000	144,422
102	Erie, Pennsylvania	219,000	218,000	137,500	138,440
103	Charleston, West Virginia*	215,000	213,900	85,000	85,796
104	Rockford, Illinois	210,000	191,100	136,000	126,706
105	Corpus Christi, Texas	208,000	195,200	195,000	167,690
106	Madison, Wisconsin*	208,000	179,200	154,000	126,706
107	Winston-Salem, North Carolina	207,000	185,700	139,000	111,135
108	Scranton, Pennsylvania	206,000	215,600	105,000	111,443
109	Savannah, Georgia	205,000	189,200	141,000	149,245
110	Evansville, Indiana	201,000	200,300	138,500	141,543
111	Reading, Pennsylvania	201,000	192,500	94,500	98,177
112	West Palm Beach, Florida	200,000	157,200	59,000	56,208
113	Macon, Georgia	195,000	170,700	128,000	69,764
114	Pensacola, Florida	190,000	165,400	60,500	56,752
115	Kalamazoo, Michigan	187,000	170,000	86,000	82,089
116	Waterbury, Connecticut	187,000	182,100	106,000	107,130
117	New London–Norwich, Connecticut	186,000	167,600	35,000	34,182
118	Augusta, Georgia	180,000	160,600	67,000	70,626
119	Greensboro, North Carolina	179,000	156,800	136,000	119,574
120	Muskegon, Michigan	178,000	167,400	45,000	46,485
121	Roanoke, Virginia	178,000	160,400	100,500	97,110
122	Saginaw, Michigan	175,000	160,900	99,000	98,265
123	Bakersfield, California	174,000	154,500	65,500	56,848
124	Greenville, South Carolina	174,000	164,500	67,000	66,188
125	Lubbock, Texas	172,000	144,300	152,000	128,691
126	Amarillo, Texas	171,000	142,500	164,000	137,969
127	Stockton, California	170,000	160,000	92,500	86,321
128	Colorado Springs, Colorado	168,000	139,500	82,000	70,194
129	Montgomery, Alabama	167,000	155,200	148,000	134,393
130	Lincoln, Nebraska*	166,000	145,400	149,000	128,521
131	Duluth, Minnesota–Superior, Wis	164,000	165,200	104,000	106,884
132	Ogden, Utah	162,000	141,400	74,500	70,197
133	Ventura–Oxnard, California	162,000	127,200	39,000	29,114
134	Portland, Maine	161,000	156,000	72,000	72,566
135	Fayetteville, North Carolina	153,000	132,000	51,500	47,106
136	Galveston–Texas City, Texas	152,000	138,700	68,000	67,175
137	York, Pennsylvania	152,000	146,600	52,500	54,504
138	Eugene, Oregon	150,000	123,900	70,000	50,977
139	New Bedford, Massachusetts	149,500	149,000	98,500	102,477
140	Raleigh, North Carolina*	147,000	130,200	104,000	93,931
141	Lexington, Kentucky	146,000	124,000	79,000	62,810
142	Topeka, Kansas*	146,000	135,800	127,500	119,484
143	Huntsville, Alabama	145,000	94,800	122,000	72,365
144	Lake Charles, Louisiana	142,000	127,200	65,000	63,392
145	Gulfport–Biloxi, Mississippi	140,000	124,200	33,500	30,204
146	Anderson, Indiana	137,000	131,600	69,500	49,061
147	Appleton, Wisconsin	137,000	123,200	53,000	48,411
148	Atlantic City, New Jersey	136,000	129,800	59,000	59,544
149	Fall River, Massachusetts	136,000	136,900	94,000	99,942
150	Waco, Texas	136,000	129,000	105,000	97,808
151	Wichita Falls, Texas	135,000	116,900	116,000	101,724
152	Cedar Rapids, Iowa	133,000	119,600	103,000	92,035
153	Springfield, Illinois*	131,000	122,700	87,000	83,271
154	Lancaster, Pennsylvania	130,000	125,100	60,000	61,055
155	Jackson, Michigan	128,000	121,400	50,500	50,720
156	Racine, Wisconsin	128,000	115,600	94,500	89,144
157	Manchester, New Hampshire	127,000	121,300	89,500	88,282
158	Poughkeepsie, New York	126,000	112,400	37,000	38,330
159	Johnstown, Pennsylvania	124,000	125,500	48,500	53,949
160	Newburgh, New York	124,000	114,600	29,000	30,979
161	Steubenville–Weirton, Ohio	122,500	121,300	34,500	32,495
162	Waterloo, Iowa	122,000	114,300	74,000	71,755
163	Springfield, Missouri	121,000	108,700	103,500	95,865
164	Wheeling, West Virginia	121,000	126,600	50,000	53,400
165	Pueblo, Colorado	120,000	111,000	98,000	91,181
166	Decatur, Illinois	118,000	111,300	85,000	78,004
167	Durham, North Carolina	117,000	106,200	81,000	78,302
168	Green Bay, Wisconsin	116,000	105,300	82,500	62,888
169	Santa Barbara, California	116,000	92,000	69,500	58,768
170	Springfield, Ohio	116,000	112,100	82,500	82,723
171	Terre Haute, Indiana	116,000	120,900	70,500	72,500
172	Mansfield, Ohio	111,000	101,600	49,000	47,325
173	Petersburg–Hopewell, Virginia	111,000	100,300	37,000	36,750
174	Provo, Utah	111,000	101,000	39,500	36,047
175	Abilene, Texas	110,000	97,400	103,000	90,368
176	Hamilton, Ohio	110,000	103,200	73,000	72,354
177	High Point, North Carolina	109,500	100,600	65,000	62,063
178	Asheville, North Carolina	109,000	105,000	62,000	60,192
179	Reno, Nevada	108,000	81,500	68,000	51,470
180	Battle Creek, Michigan	106,500	107,300	42,500	44,169
181	Altoona, Pennsylvania	106,000	104,500	67,000	69,407
182	Muncie, Indiana	106,000	100,500	70,500	68,603
183	Sioux City, Iowa	104,500	101,500	91,000	89,159
184	Salem, Oregon*	104,000	89,900	63,500	49,142
185	Pittsfield, Massachusetts	102,000	97,400	60,500	57,879
186	Modesto, California	101,000	90,400	44,500	36,585

** National or State capital.*

OTHER CENTRAL CITIES OF METRO. AREAS

These are secondary central cities of Metro. Areas listed in the table on the preceding page.
The Metro. Area in which each is located is designated by the name of its chief central city.

CITY	CHIEF CITY OF METRO. AREA	POPULATION 1/1/1965	4/1/1960
Newark, New Jersey	(*New York)	395,000	405,220
Oakland, California	(*San Francisco)	378,000	367,548
San Jose, California	(*San Francisco)	308,000	204,196
St. Paul, Minnesota	(*Minneapolis)	308,000	313,411
Paterson, New Jersey	(*New York)	144,000	143,663
Riverside, California	(*San Bernardino)	131,000	84,332
Portsmouth, Virginia	(*Norfolk)	118,000	114,773
Fort Lauderdale, Florida	(*Miami)	114,000	83,648
Hampton, Virginia	(*Newport News)	110,000	89,258
Niagara Falls, New York	(*Buffalo)	101,000	102,394
Lowell, Massachusetts	(*Boston)	91,000	92,107
New Britain, Connecticut	(*Hartford)	85,500	82,201
Brockton, Massachusetts	(*Boston)	83,000	72,813
Pawtucket, Rhode Island	(*Providence)	80,500	81,001
Ann Arbor, Michigan	(*Detroit)	80,000	67,340
Schenectady, New York	(*Albany)	78,000	81,682
Bethlehem, Pennsylvania	(*Allentown)	73,000	75,408
Lawrence, Massachusetts	(*Boston)	67,000	70,933
Port Arthur, Texas	(*Beaumont)	67,000	66,676
Troy, New York	(*Albany)	65,500	67,492
Ontario, California	(*Pomona)	63,000	46,617
Warren, Ohio	(*Youngstown)	62,500	59,648
Oxnard, California	(*Ventura)	59,000	40,265
Council Bluffs, Iowa	(*Omaha)	58,500	55,641
Meriden, Connecticut	(*New Haven)	55,000	51,850
Rome, New York	(*Utica)	53,000	51,646
Rock Island, Illinois	(*Davenport)	52,500	51,863
Holyoke, Massachusetts	(*Springfield)	52,000	52,689
Biloxi, Mississippi	(*Gulfport)	46,500	44,053
Woonsocket, Rhode Island	(*Providence)	46,500	47,080
Haverhill, Massachusetts	(*Boston)	46,200	46,346
Moline, Illinois	(*Davenport)	45,500	42,705
Clearwater, Florida	(*St. Petersburg)	42,500	34,653
Norwich, Connecticut	(*New London)	40,000	38,506
Salem, Massachusetts	(*Boston)	39,000	39,211
Texas City, Texas	(*Galveston)	37,000	32,065
Superior, Wisconsin	(*Duluth)	33,000	33,563
Massillon, Ohio	(*Canton)	32,000	31,236
Ashland, Kentucky	(*Huntington)	31,000	31,283
Oak Ridge, Tennessee	(*Knoxville)	30,000	27,169
Weirton, West Virginia	(*Steubenville)	29,500	28,201
Hopewell, Virginia	(*Petersburg)	20,000	17,695

NUMBER OF U.S. COUNTIES, CITIES, TOWNS, AND LOCALITIES BY STATES, 1965

STATES	Number of Counties*	Number of Places Under 1,000 Population	Number of Places 1,000-2,500 Population	Number of Places 2,500-5,000 Population	Number of Places 5,000-10,000 Population	Number of Places 10,000-25,000 Population	Number of Places 25,000-50,000 Population	Number of Places 50,000-100,000 Population	Number of Places Over 100,000 Population	Total Places
Alabama	67	2,604	89	61	28	18	8	2	4	2,814
Alaska†	4	652	17	2	2	2	1	.....	.....	676
Arizona	14	736	42	17	11	5	5	.....	2	818
Arkansas	75	2,300	59	32	19	15	3	3	1	2,432
California	58	3,889	221	179	111	123	64	42	18	4,647
Colorado	63	1,272	58	23	15	11	5	5	1	1,390
Connecticut	8	739	44	22	22	21	13	6	5	872
Delaware	3	346	40	8	2	3	.....	1	.....	400
District of Columbia	1*	107	.....	.....	.....	.....	.....	.....	1	108
Florida	67	1,914	138	114	63	50	15	8	5	2,307
Georgia	159	2,279	140	70	34	26	7	2	4	2,562
Hawaii	5	493	26	14	4	3	2	.....	1	543
Idaho	45*	850	33	17	4	9	2	.....	.....	916
Illinois	102	4,016	288	139	86	81	33	16	3	4,662
Indiana	92	3,199	163	79	39	32	9	5	6	3,532
Iowa	99	1,595	139	45	34	11	7	5	2	1,838
Kansas	105	1,431	104	51	18	23	5	1	3	1,636
Kentucky	120	3,967	111	54	24	16	5	2	1	4,180
Louisiana†	64	1,960	99	46	25	27	5	4	3	2,169
Maine	16	2,839	41	29	13	12	2	1	.....	2,937
Maryland	24*	2,435	115	48	27	24	8	4	1	2,662
Massachusetts	14	1,427	101	58	27	44	30	19	4	1,710
Michigan	83	2,469	173	102	52	41	21	15	6	2,879
Minnesota	87	1,829	144	50	32	29	12	3	3	2,102
Mississippi	82	1,836	70	33	21	11	7	1	1	1,980
Missouri	115*	2,700	133	62	43	30	12	4	3	2,987
Montana	57*	1,012	38	17	6	5	2	2	.....	1,082
Nebraska	93	853	71	19	12	9	1	.....	2	967
Nevada	17	344	12	5	2	2	1	1	1	368
New Hampshire	10	666	33	10	7	6	3	1	.....	726
New Jersey	21	1,789	148	109	102	102	33	9	6	2,298
New Mexico	32	927	32	13	9	8	5	1	1	996
New York	62	4,857	294	167	128	94	36	13	8	5,597
North Carolina	100	2,947	167	63	27	21	9	4	4	3,242
North Dakota	53	782	48	4	4	4	3	1	.....	846
Ohio	88	3,338	237	124	97	89	27	11	8	3,931
Oklahoma	77	1,439	83	37	25	18	8	1	2	1,613
Oregon	36	1,422	55	41	23	18	2	2	1	1,564
Pennsylvania	67	8,009	495	209	178	87	23	10	5	9,016
Rhode Island	5	282	17	11	6	8	2	4	1	331
South Carolina	46	1,313	118	42	29	12	3	2	1	1,520
South Dakota	67	654	38	14	3	7	1	1	.....	718
Tennessee	95	3,212	95	48	24	24	5	.....	4	3,412
Texas	254	4,755	266	127	84	74	19	12	13	5,350
Utah	29	672	47	16	17	12	2	1	1	768
Vermont	14	657	23	5	9	3	1	.....	.....	698
Virginia	130	3,950	102	38	22	23	3	2	9	4,149
Washington	39	1,877	106	51	26	25	8	1	3	2,097
West Virginia	55	3,073	98	32	12	9	4	3	.....	3,231
Wisconsin	72	2,860	137	53	35	29	12	6	2	3,134
Wyoming	24*	472	17	10	4	3	2	.....	.....	508
United States	3,115	102,046	5,365	2,620	1,647	1,359	496	238	150	113,921

* Includes 3,075 counties, parishes, and senatorial districts; the District of Columbia; Baltimore city, Md.; St. Louis city, Mo.; 34 independent cities in Virginia; and the parts of Yellowstone National Park in Idaho, Montana, and Wyoming.
† The divisions of Louisiana are known as parishes. Those shown for Alaska are the at-large senatorial districts.

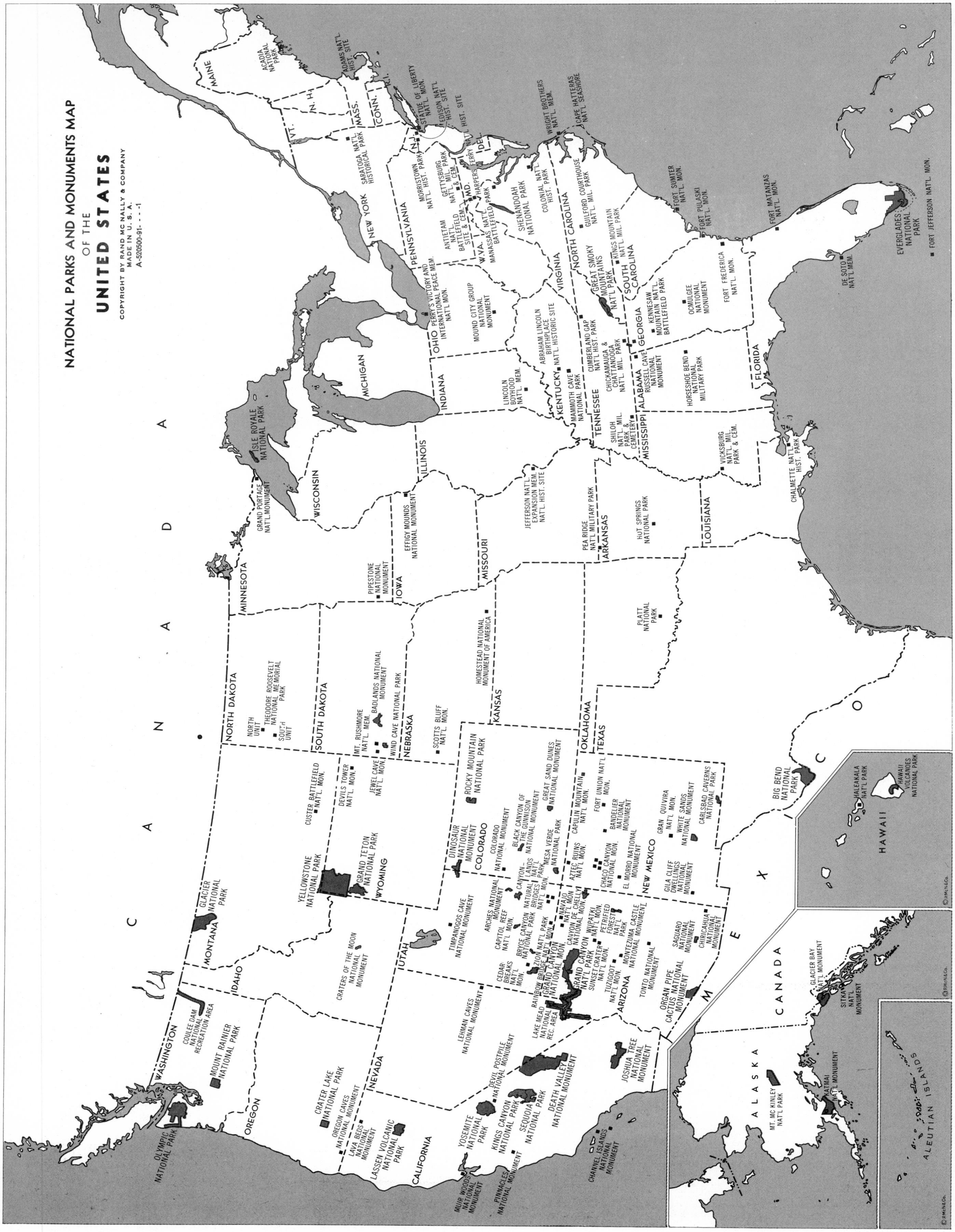

National Parks and Monuments Map
OF THE
UNITED STATES

COPYRIGHT BY RAND MCNALLY & COMPANY
MADE IN U. S. A.
A-520500-91- - - -1

U.S. NATIONAL PARK SYSTEM Showing Parks, Monuments, and Other National Units

Name	Year Estab-lished	Location	Gross Acreage	Description
PARKS				
Acadia	1919	Maine	41,634	Wilderness area on Mount Desert Island, Schoodic Point, and Isle au Haut
Big Bend	1944	Texas	708,221	Spectacular mountains and deserts in bend of Rio Grande
Bryce Canyon	1928	Utah	36,010	Wonderland of colorful rocks and pinnacles
Canyonlands	1964	Utah	257,640	Mesas, canyons, and pinnacles resulting from centuries of erosion
Carlsbad Caverns	1930	N.Mex.	49,448	Immense limestone caverns with brilliantly colored formations
Crater Lake	1902	Oreg.	160,290	High cliffs encircle deep-blue lake in extinct volcano crater
Everglades	1947	Fla.	1,401,693	Subtropical area; mangrove swamps; rare birds and plants
Glacier	1910	Mont.	1,013,129	Part of Waterton-Glacier International Peace Park
Grand Canyon	1919	Ariz.	673,575	Tremendous gorge; ever-changing colors; fantastic rock shapes
Grand Teton	1929	Wyo.	310,350	Majestic, snow-capped peaks, lakes, and evergreen forests
Great Smoky Mountains	1930	N.C.-Tenn.	511,714	Highest eastern mountains; primeval hardwood forests
Haleakala	1961	Hawaii	26,403	One of world's largest dormant volcanoes
Hawaii Volcanoes	1916	Hawaii	220,345	Active volcanoes; tropical forests; tree ferns
Hot Springs	1921	Ark.	1,018	Forty-seven historically famous mineral hot springs
Isle Royale	1940	Mich.	539,339	Forested island in Lake Superior; large moose herd
Kings Canyon	1940	Calif.	454,650	Imposing peaks and canyons; giant sequoias
Lassen Volcanic	1916	Calif.	106,934	Recently active volcano; many lakes and volcanic exhibits
Mammoth Cave	1936	Ky.	51,354	Beautiful limestone caverns, underground rivers, and lakes
Mesa Verde	1906	Colo.	51,334	Well-preserved prehistoric cliff dwellings and pueblo houses
Mount McKinley	1917	Alaska	1,939,493	Highest mountain in N.A.; glaciers; interesting wildlife
Mount Rainier	1899	Wash.	241,782	Glaciers radiating from snow-capped peak; dense forests
Olympic	1938	Wash.	896,599	Mountain wilderness; luxuriant forests of huge evergreens
Petrified Forest	1962	Ariz.	94,189	Spectacular display of petrified wood; part of Painted Desert
Platt	1906	Okla.	912	Cold mineral springs, some of which contain bromides
Rocky Mountain	1915	Colo.	260,018	Magnificent mountain scenery; interesting wildlife
Sequoia	1890	Calif.	386,551	Immense groves of sequoias; Mt. Whitney and other peaks
Shenandoah	1935	Va.	212,304	Blue Ridge Mountains; Skyline Drive
Theodore Roosevelt National Memorial	1947	N.Dak.	70,374	Section of badlands and part of Roosevelt's Elkhorn Ranch
Virgin Islands	1956	Virgin Is.	15,150	A tropical area having historic and prehistoric interest
Wind Cave	1903	S.Dak.	28,059	"Boxwork" limestone caverns in Black Hills; buffalo herd
Yellowstone	1872	Wyo-Mont.-Idaho	2,221,773	World's greatest geyser area; bubbling hot springs and colorful pools; beautiful Yellowstone Falls; wildlife sanctuary
Yosemite	1890	Calif.	760,951	Spectacular gorges, domes, and waterfalls; giant sequoias
Zion	1919	Utah	147,035	Colorful canyon, displaying picturesque rock formations
MONUMENTS				
Arches	1929	Utah	34,010	Giant arches, bridges, windows, spires eroded from sandstone
Aztec Ruins	1923	N.Mex.	27	Ruins of 12th-century prehistoric Indian town
Badlands	1939	S.Dak.	111,530	Deeply eroded hills containing prehistoric animal fossils
Bandelier	1916	N.Mex.	30,703	Prehistoric Indian ruins of the later Pueblo period
Black Canyon of the Gunnison	1933	Colo.	13,548	Remarkably deep, narrow gorge of great geologic interest
Booker T. Washington	1957	Virginia	200	Memorial to the famous educator and reformer
Buck Island Reef	1961	Virgin Is.	850	One of the finest marine gardens in the Caribbean Sea
Cabrillo	1913	Calif.	81	Memorial to Juan Cabrillo, discoverer of San Diego Bay, 1542
Canyon de Chelly	1931	Ariz.	83,840	Prehistoric Indian ruins built in caves; modern Navajo homes
Capitol Reef	1937	Utah	39,173	Twenty-mile-long buttressed cliff of colored sandstone
Capulin Mountain	1916	N.Mex.	680	Large cinder cone of a recently extinct volcano
Casa Grande Ruins	1918	Ariz.	473	Adobe tower built by the Indians 600 years ago
Castillo de San Marcos	1924	Fla.	22	Oldest masonry fort in Continental U.S.—built by Spanish
Castle Clinton	1950	N.Y.	1	Through its door, 1855–90, 7,500,000 people entered America
Cedar Breaks	1933	Utah	6,155	Brilliantly colored amphitheater 2000 feet deep; eroded cliffs
Chaco Canyon	1907	N.Mex.	21,509	Most extensive Indian ruins in the U.S.; shows Pueblo culture
Channel Islands	1938	Calif.	18,167	Sea lion rookery; other interesting wildlife, fossil beds
Chesapeake and Ohio Canal	1961	Md.-W.Va.	4,475	One of the least altered of the older American canals
Chiricahua	1924	Ariz.	10,646	Strange rock shapes depict billion years of geologic history
Colorado	1911	Colo.	17,693	Deep canyons with weirdly eroded red-sandstone walls
Craters of the Moon	1924	Idaho	53,545	Craters, lava flows, caves and other volcanic Phenomena
Custer Battlefield	1946	Mont.	765	Site of battle in which Custer and all his men were killed
Death Valley	1933	Calif.-Nev.	1,907,760	Colorful desert area; lowest point in Western Hemisphere
Devils Postpile	1911	Calif.	798	Sixty-foot basaltic cliff, composed of blue-gray columns
Devils Tower	1906	Wyo.	1,347	Fluted tower of volcanic rock, 865 feet high
Dinosaur	1915	Utah-Colo.	205,136	Well-preserved fossils of many dinosaurs; spectacular canyons
Effigy Mounds	1949	Iowa	1,468	Indian mounds shaped like birds and other animals
El Morro	1906	N.Mex.	1,279	Monolith inscribed by early Spaniards and Americans
Fort Frederica	1945	Ga.	250	Built by Oglethorpe, 1736, as defense against the Spaniards
Fort Jefferson	1935	Fla.	47,125	Huge masonry fortification; notable bird refuge; marine life
Fort McHenry National Monument and Historic Shrine	1939	Md.	43	Its defense, 1814, inspired writing of "Star Spangled Banner"
Fort Matanzas	1924	Fla.	228	Historical Spanish fort built, 1737, to protect St. Augustine
Fort Pulaski	1924	Ga.	5,517	Southern fortress important in the Civil War
Fort Sumter	1948	S.C.	2.4	Scene of first battle of the Civil War
Fort Union	1956	N.Mex.	721	Site of an old fort erecteed to protect the Santa Fe Trail
Geo. Washington Birthplace	1930	Va.	394	Memorial house and gardens on site of Washington's birthplace
Geo. Washington Carver	1951	Mo.	210	Site of birthplace and childhood home of famous scientist
Gila Cliff Dwellings	1907	N.Mex.	533	Remains of dwellings built in face of an overhanging cliff
Glacier Bay	1925	Alaska	2,274,595	Area of receding glaciers and post-glacial forests
Grand Canyon	1932	Ariz.	198,280	Portion of the Grand Canyon, including Toroweap Point
Grand Portage	1960	Minn.	770	Portage on principal route of Indians, explorers, missionaries and fur traders into the Northwest
Gran Quivira	1909	N.Mex.	611	Ruins of 17th-century Spanish mission and Indian pueblo
Great Sand Dunes	1932	Colo.	36,740	Very large and high shifting sand dunes
Homestead	1939	Nebr.	163	First claim under the Homestead Act of 1862
Hovenweep	1923	Utah-Colo.	505	Several groups of cliff dwellings, pueblos, and towers
Jewel Cave	1908	S.Dak.	1,275	Series of limestone rooms incrusted with calcite crystals
Joshua Tree	1936	Calif.	557,992	Desert area containing a fine stand of the rare Joshua tree
Katmai	1918	Alaska	2,697,590	Crater of Katmai Volcano; Valley of Ten Thousand Smokes
Lava Beds	1925	Calif.	46,239	Volcanic formations; scene of Modoc Indian War, 1873
Lehman Caves	1922	Nev.	640	Limestone caverns containing stalactites and other formations
Montezuma Castle	1906	Ariz.	842	Unusually well-preserved, 5-story, 20-room cliff dwelling
Mound City Group	1923	Ohio	68	Prehistoric Indian mounds
Muir Woods	1908	Calif.	503	Virgin forest of Coast redwoods and other interesting plants
Natural Bridges	1908	Utah	7,600	Three bridges carved from sandstone walls by running water
Navajo	1909	Ariz.	360	Three large and elaborate cliff dwellings
Ocmulgee	1936	Ga.	683	Mounds and other remains constructed by Southern mound-builders
Oregon Caves	1909	Oreg.	480	Caverns containing unique limestone formations
Organ Pipe Cactus	1937	Ariz.	330,874	Desert area containing rare cactus species
MONUMENTS *(Continued)*				
Perry's Victory and International Peace Memorial	1936	Ohio	14	Monument to Perry's naval victory and amity with Canada
Pinnacles	1908	Calif.	14,498	Rock spires 500–1200 feet high; caves of volcanic origin
Pipe Spring	1923	Ariz.	40	Historic fort and other Mormon structures
Pipestone	1937	Minn.	283	Quarry from which Indians obtained materials for peace pipes
Rainbow Bridge	1910	Utah	160	Greatest known natural bridge—a rainbow in stone
Russell Cave	1961	Ala.	310	Believed to have been continuously inhabited by stoneage men from 7000 B.C. to 1650 A.D.
Saguaro	1933	Ariz.	78,644	Forest of giant saguaro cactus and other rare desert plants
Scotts Bluff	1919	Nebr.	3,452	High bluff on Oregon Trail—landmark for early wagon trains
Sitka	1910	Alaska	54	Scene of last stand of Kik-Siti Indians against Russians
Statue of Liberty	1924	N.Y.	10	Famous statue on Liberty Island—gift of the French people
Sunset Crater	1930	Ariz.	3,040	Volcanic cone with highly colored rim; ice caves; lava flows
Timpanogos Cave	1922	Utah	250	Brilliantly colored caves on the slope of Mt. Timpanogos
Tonto	1907	Ariz.	1,120	Two 14th-century Pueblo Indian cliff dwellings
Tumacacori	1908	Ariz.	10	Site of historic Spanish mission dating from 1691
Tuzigoot	1939	Ariz.	43	Excavated ruins of large pueblo dating from 1000–1400
Walnut Canyon	1915	Ariz.	1,879	Cliff dwellings built in shallow caves along canyon walls
White Sands	1933	N.Mex.	146,535	Sand dunes 10 to 60 feet high, composed of snow-white gypsum
Wupatki	1924	Ariz.	35,545	Red-sandstone pueblo believed built by ancestors of Hopis
HISTORICAL PARKS, SITES, AND MEMORIALS				
Abraham Lincoln Birthplace	1939	Ky.	117	Log cabin thought to have been Lincoln's birthplace
Adams	1946	Mass.	5	Home of John Adams and John Quincy Adams, U.S. Presidents
Andrew Johnson	1942	Tenn.	16	President Johnson's tailor shop, home, and grave
Appomattox Court House Park	1954	Va.	972	Scene of Robert E. Lee's surrender to Grant in Civil War
Bent's Old Fort	1963	Colo.	178	One of the most significant fur-trading posts of the West
Chalmette Park	1939	La.	136	Part of site of the Battle of New Orleans, War of 1812
City of Refuge Park	1961	Hawaii	182	An area preserving the history of the Polynesian people and early Hawaiian culture
Colonial Park	1936	Va.	9,430	Jamestown Isl., Cape Henry Mem., Yorktown, Williamsburg Parkway
Coronado Mem.	1952	Ariz.	2,745	Place where Coronado entered U.S. (1540–42) to explore southwest
Cumberland Gap Park	1955	Ky.-Tenn.-Va.	20,193	Gap through which passed the main artery of the great trans-Allegheny migration
Custis-Lee Mansion Mem.	1925	Va.	3	Home of the Confederate General Robert E. Lee
De Soto Mem.	1948	Fla.	30	Commemorates landing of De Soto in Florida, 1539
Dutch Reformed (Sleepy Hollow) Church	1962	N.Y.	...	Dutch Colonial church made famous by Washington Irving
Edison	1955	N.J.	18	Glenmont, home of Thomas Alva Edison from 1886 until his death, 1931; also includes his laboratory, stock room and library
Federal Hall Mem.	1939	N.Y.	.45	Subtreasury building; site of first seat of U.S. Government
Fort Caroline Mem.	1950	Fla.	120	Overlooks site of French colony of 1564
Fort Clatsop Mem.	1958	Ore.	125	Commemorates Lewis & Clark's winter camp
Fort Davis	1963	Texas	447	Ruins of Army post used from 1854 to 1891
Fort Laramie	1938	Wyo.	564	Military post on Oregon Trail, famous in covered-wagon days
Fort Raleigh	1941	N.C.	144	Scene of Sir Walter Raleigh's "Lost Colony" settlement
Fort Smith	1963	Ark.	14	One of the first U.S. military posts in the Louisiana Territory
Fort Vancouver	1954	Wash.	90	Site of stockaded fur trading post from 1824 to 1846
General Grant Mem.	1959	N.Y.	1	Memorial to the commander of the Union armies
Hampton	1948	Md.	45	Eighteenth-century Georgian mansion
Harpers Ferry Park	1962	W. Va.-Md.	1,500	Scene of John Brown's famous raid in 1859
Home of Franklin D. Roosevelt	1944	N.Y.	94	Birthplace and home of President F. D. Roosevelt
Hopewell Village	1938	Pa.	848	Ruins of an 18th- and early 19th-century iron-making village
House Where Lincoln Died Mem.	1896	D.C.	.05	Petersen House, where Lincoln was taken after he was shot
Independence Park	1956	Pa.	22	Structures in Philadelphia associated with the founding of the U.S.
Jefferson National Expansion Mem.	1935	Mo.	85	Riverfront area in St. Louis commemorating westward expansion
Lincoln Boyhood Mem	1962	Ind.	200	Site of Lincoln's residence from ages 7 to 21
Lincoln Mem.	1911	D.C.	.61	White-marble structure enclosing seated figure of Lincoln
Lincoln Museum Mem.	1866	D.C.	.18	Site of Ford's Theatre, where Abraham Lincoln was shot
Minute Man Park	1959	Mass.	750	Site of Revolutionary War skirmish
Morristown Park	1933	N.J.	958	Washington's Headquarters, 1779–80, and other historical sites
Mount Rushmore Mem.	1925	S.Dak.	1,278	Features of four great Presidents carved on face of mountain
Sagamore Hill	1963	N.Y.	...	Victorian-style home of Theodore Roosevelt on Long Island
Salem Maritime	1938	Mass.	11	Several buildings important in New England maritime history
San Juan	1949	P.R.	40	16th Century fortifications guarding San Juan Harbor
Saratoga Park	1948	N.Y.	5,500	Scene of the defeat of Burgoyne, British general, in 1777
Theodore Roosevelt Birthplace	1963	N.Y.	...	New York City birthplace of President Roosevelt
Thomas Jefferson Mem.	1934	D.C.	1	Structure in classic style introduced in America by Jefferson
Vanderbilt Mansion	1940	N.Y.	212	Palatial residence of the "Gay Nineties"
Washington Monument Mem.	1848	D.C.	.37	An obelisk 555 feet high—memorial to George Washington
Whitman Mission	1962	Wash.	96	Site of mission where Indians massacred Whitman family
Wright Brothers Mem.	1927	N.C.	425	Commemorates Wright brothers' airplane flight at Kitty Hawk
RECREATION AREAS				
Cape Cod National Seashore	1961	Mass.	26,666	An immense area of historical interest, geological significance, and beaches and dunes for recreation
Cape Hatteras Seashore	Project	N.C.	28,500	Extensive beaches with surf fishing and waterfowl refuge
Coulee Dam	1946	Wash.	98,500	Dam forms Franklin D. Roosevelt Lake extending to Canada
Glen Canyon	1958	Ariz.-Utah	1,429,007	Third highest dam in world—forms Lake Powell
Lake Mead	1936	Ariz.-Nev.	1,951,928	Formed by Hoover Dam across the gorge of the Colorado River
Padre Island Seashore	Project	Texas	...	80 miles of subtropical offshore bar; excellent fishing
Point Reyes Seashore	Project	Calif.	53,000	Peninsular area containing beaches, meadows and timberland
Shadow Mountain	1952	Colo.	18,240	Included is Shadow Mountain Lake and Granby Reservoir

MILITARY PARKS, BATTLEFIELDS, AND CEMETERIES

Antietam (Battlefield and Cemetery)	Md.	**Fredricksburg and Spotsylvania Co. Battlefields Mem.**	Va.	**Moores Creek (Military Park)**	N.C.
Battleground (Cemetery)	D.C.	**Fredricksburg (Cemetery)**	Va.	**Pea Ridge (Military Park)**	Ark.
Big Hole (Battlefield)	Mont.	**Gettysburg (Military Park and Cemetery)**	Pa.	**Petersburg (Battlefield)**	Va.
Brices Cross Roads (Battlefield)	Miss.	**Guilford Courthouse (Military Park)**	N.C.	**Poplar Grove (Cemetery)**	Va.
Chickamauga and Chattanooga (Military Park)	Ga.-Tenn.	**Horseshoe Bend (Military Park)**	Ala.	**Richmond (Battlefield Park)**	Va.
Cowpens (Battlefield)	S.C.	**Kennesaw Mountain (Battlefield Park)**	Ga.	**Shiloh (Military Park and Cemetery)**	Tenn.
Fort Donelson (Military Park and Cemetery)	Tenn.	**Kings Mountain (Military Park)**	S.C.	**Stones River (Battlefield and Cemetery)**	Tenn.
Fort Necessity (Battlefield)	Pa.	**Manassas (Battlefield Park)**	Va.	**Tupelo (Battlefield)**	Miss.
				Vicksburg (Park and Cemetery)	Miss.
				Yorktown (Cemetery)	Va.

RAILROAD MAP OF THE UNITED STATES

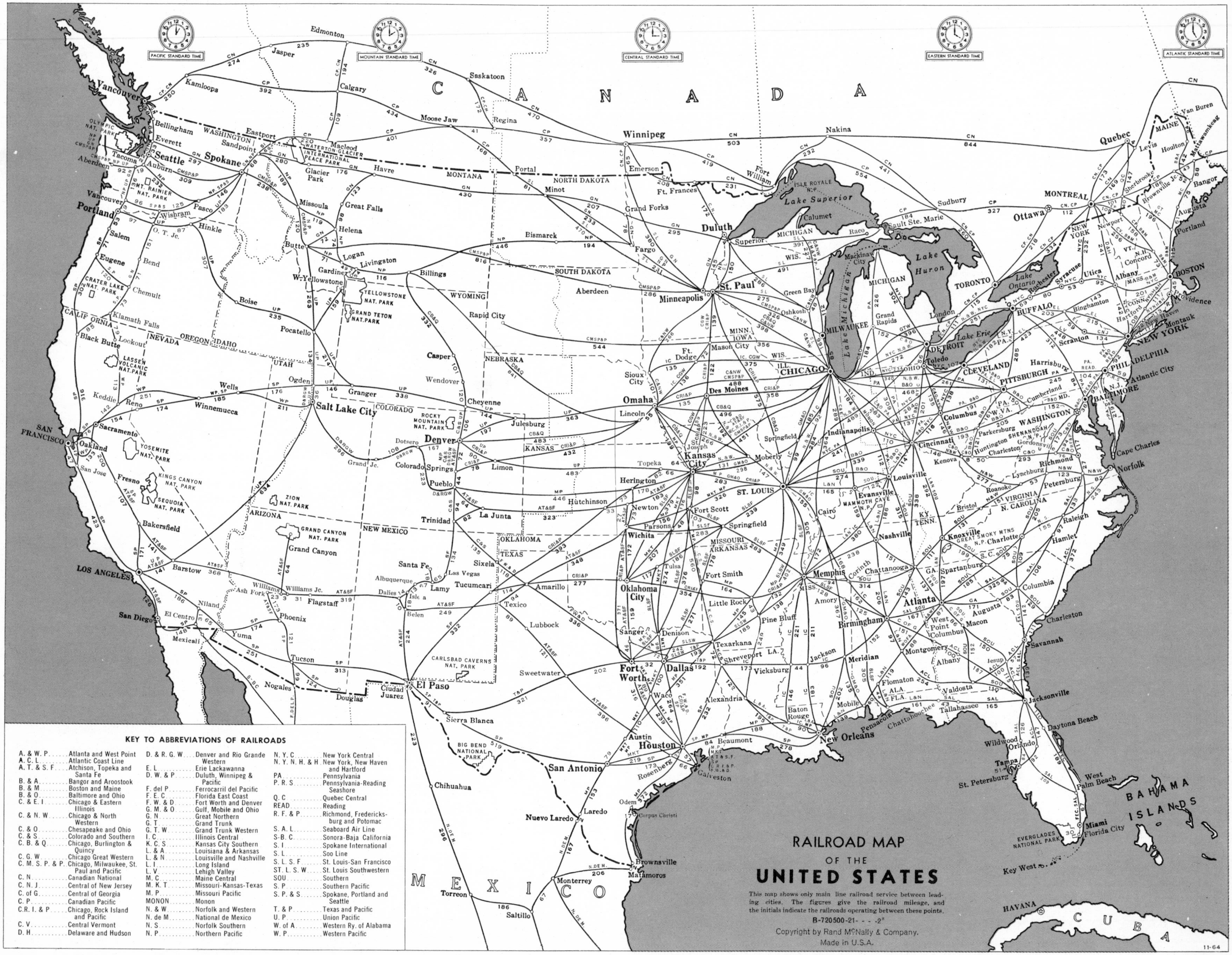

RAILROAD MAP OF THE UNITED STATES

This map shows only main line railroad service between leading cities. The figures give the railroad mileage, and the initials indicate the railroads operating between these points.

B-720500-21- - -.2°

Copyright by Rand McNally & Company.

Made in U.S.A.

KEY TO ABBREVIATIONS OF RAILROADS

A. & W. P.	Atlanta and West Point	N. Y. C.	New York Central
A. C. L.	Atlantic Coast Line	N. Y. N. H. & H.	New York, New Haven and Hartford
A. T. & S. F.	Atchison, Topeka and Santa Fe	P. R. S.	Pennsylvania-Reading Seashore
B. & M.	Bangor and Aroostook	Q. C.	Quebec Central
B. & O.	Baltimore and Ohio	READ	Reading
C. & E. I.	Chicago & Eastern Illinois	R. F. & P.	Richmond, Fredericks- burg and Potomac
C. & N. W.	Chicago & North Western	S. A. L.	Seaboard Air Line
C. & O.	Chesapeake and Ohio	S. B. C.	Sonora-Baja California
C. & S.	Colorado and Southern	S. I.	Spokane International
C. B. & Q.	Chicago, Burlington & Quincy	S. L. S. F.	St. Louis-San Francisco
C. G. W.	Chicago Great Western	S. I. W.	St. Louis Southwestern
C. M. S. P. & P.	Chicago, Milwaukee, St. Paul and Pacific	SOU	Southern
C. N.	Canadian National	S. P.	Southern Pacific
C. N. J.	Central of New Jersey	S. P. & S.	Spokane, Portland and Seattle
C. of G.	Central of Georgia	T. & P.	Texas and Pacific
C. P.	Canadian Pacific	U. P.	Union Pacific
C. R. I. & P.	Chicago, Rock Island and Pacific	W. of A.	Western Ry. of Alabama
C. V.	Central Vermont	W. P.	Western Pacific
D. H.	Delaware and Hudson		
D. & R. G. W.	Denver and Rio Grande Western		
E. L.	Erie Lackawanna		
D. W. & P.	Duluth, Winnipeg & Pacific		
F. del P.	Ferrocarril del Pacific		
F. E. C.	Florida East Coast		
F. W. & D.	Fort Worth and Denver		
G. M. & O.	Gulf, Mobile and Ohio		
G. N.	Great Northern		
G. T. W.	Grand Trunk Western		
I. C.	Illinois Central		
K. C. S.	Kansas City Southern		
L. & A.	Louisiana & Arkansas		
L. & N.	Louisville and Nashville		
L. I.	Long Island		
L. V.	Lehigh Valley		
M. C.	Maine Central		
M. K. T.	Missouri-Kansas-Texas		
M. P.	Missouri Pacific		
MONON	Monon		
N. & W.	Norfolk and Western		
N. de M.	National de Mexico		
N. P.	Northern Pacific		

U.S. RAILROAD DISTANCE TABLE

Showing Travel Distances (Short Line) Between Railroad Centers of the United States in Statute Miles

	Albuquerque, N. Mex.	Amarillo, Tex.	Atlanta, Ga.	Baltimore, Md.	Billings, Mont.	Birmingham, Ala.	Boston, Mass.	Buffalo, N.Y.	Butte, Mont.	Cheyenne, Wyo.	Chicago, Ill.	Cincinnati, Ohio	Cleveland, Ohio	Columbia, S. C.	Dallas, Tex.	Denver, Colo.	Des Moines, Iowa	Detroit, Mich.	Duluth, Minn.	El Paso, Tex.	Fargo, N. Dak.	Houston, Tex.	Indianapolis, Ind.	Jacksonville, Fla.	Kansas City, Mo.
Albuquerque, N. Mex.		374	1554	2102	1133	1388	2356	1862	1369	583	1338	1528	1678	1801	723	477	1108	1610	1515	253	1605	925	1430	1819	887
Amarillo, Tex.	374		1181	1728	1121	1014	2028	1534	1357	571	1010	1154	1339	1434	370	465	780	1282	1191	444	1281	634	1056	1466	559
Atlanta, Ga.	1554	1181		676	1921	167	1091	934	2157	1532	734	490	750	254	825	1526	952	748	1202	1471	1372	856	585	350	890
Baltimore, Md.	2102	1728	676		2085	799	416	395	2305	1791	796	582	459	515	1448	1822	1154	624	1265	2095	1435	1517	691	794	1198
Billings, Mont.	1133	1121	1921	2085		1788	2296	1802	236	550	1278	1559	1618	2142	1491	656	1041	1550	899	1386	640	1755	1462	2226	1051
Birmingham, Ala.	1388	1014	167	799	1788		1215	925	2024	1399	651	481	741	420	658	1373	819	739	1119	1304	1289	718	503	438	737
Boston, Mass.	2356	2028	1091	416	2296	1215		494	2526	2013	1018	938	678	930	1864	2044	1376	746	1486	2414	1656	1933	962	1210	1469
Buffalo, N.Y.	1862	1534	934	395	1802	925	494		2032	1519	524	444	184	910	1418	1550	882	252	992	1920	1162	1554	468	1190	975
Butte, Mont.	1369	1357	2157	2305	236	2024	2526	2032		786	1514	1795	1854	2378	1727	892	1377	1780	1135	1622	876	1991	1692	2462	1287
Cheyenne, Wyo.	583	571	1532	1791	550	1399	2013	1519	786		995	1259	1335	1753	941	106	652	1267	1007	836	1097	1205	1161	1877	702
Chicago, Ill.	1338	1010	734	796	1278	651	1018	524	1514	995		281	340	867	968	1026	358	272	468	1396	638	1205	184	1083	451
Cincinnati, Ohio	1528	1154	490	582	1559	481	938	444	1795	1259	281		260	586	975	1252	639	258	749	1561	919	1110	109	840	616
Cleveland, Ohio	1678	1339	750	459	1618	741	678	184	1854	1335	340	260		846	1234	1366	698	164	808	1736	978	1370	283	1100	791
Columbia, S.C.	1801	1434	254	515	2142	420	930	910	2378	1753	867	586	846		1078	1747	1173	844	1335	1724	1513	1110	681	280	1111
Dallas, Tex.	723	370	825	1448	1491	658	1864	1418	1727	941	968	975	1234	1078		835	738	1200	1149	646	1239	264	951	1096	517
Denver, Colo.	477	465	1526	1822	656	1373	2044	1550	892	106	1026	1252	1366	1747	835		683	1298	1038	730	1128	1099	1154	1811	636
Des Moines, Iowa	1108	780	952	1154	1041	819	1376	882	1377	652	358	639	698	1173	738	683		630	411	1166	501	1002	542	1301	221
Detroit, Mich.	1610	1282	748	624	1550	739	746	252	1780	1267	272	258	164	844	1200	1298	630		740	1668	910	1368	303	1098	723
Duluth, Minn.	1515	1191	1202	1265	899	1119	1486	992	1135	1007	468	749	808	1335	1149	1038	411	740		1577	259	1413	652	1551	632
El Paso, Tex.	253	444	1471	2095	1386	1304	2414	1920	1622	836	1396	1561	1736	1724	646	730	1166	1668	1577		1667	827	1500	1764	945
Fargo, N. Dak.	1605	1281	1372	1435	640	1289	1656	1162	876	1097	638	919	978	1513	1239	1128	501	910	259	1667		1503	822	1721	722
Houston, Tex.	925	634	856	1517	1755	718	1933	1554	1991	1205	1205	1110	1370	1110	264	1099	1002	1368	1413	827	1503		1107	975	781
Indianapolis, Ind.	1430	1056	585	691	1462	503	962	468	1692	1161	184	109	283	681	951	1154	542	303	652	1500	822	1107		935	518
Jacksonville, Fla.	1819	1466	350	794	2226	438	1210	1190	2462	1877	1083	840	1100	280	1096	1811	1301	1098	1551	1764	1721	975	935		1175
Kansas City, Mo.	887	559	890	1198	1051	737	1469	975	1287	702	451	616	791	1111	517	636	221	723	632	945	722	781	518	1175	
Knoxville, Tenn.	1556	1183	197	545	1849	254	961	737	2085	1460	574	296	553	293	903	1454	880	551	1042	1549	1212	972	388	547	818
Los Angeles, Calif.	889	1216	2285	2908	1452	2118	3244	2750	1216	1302	2227	2370	2555	2538	1460	1353	1954	2499	2309	814	2092	1641	2272	2578	1776
Louisville, Ky.	1463	1090	474	696	1583	392	1052	558	1809	1194	295	114	374	581	861	1188	614	372	763	1508	933	996	111	824	552
Memphis, Tenn.	1135	761	420	967	1535	253	1382	938	1771	1186	527	494	754	673	481	1120	645	752	1031	1128	1121	616	491	691	484
Miami, Fla.	2185	1832	716	1160	2592	804	1576	1556	2828	2243	1449	1206	1466	646	1462	2177	1667	1464	1917	2130	2087	1341	1301	366	1541
Mobile, Ala.	1369	1016	353	1029	1958	266	1444	1191	2194	1569	917	747	1007	607	646	1481	988	1005	1374	1292	1464	503	769	472	926
Nashville, Tenn.	1374	1000	288	761	1634	205	1177	745	1870	1245	446	301	561	509	720	1238	664	559	914	1367	1084	855	298	637	602
New Orleans, La.	1229	876	493	1154	1924	355	1569	1280	2160	1447	921	836	1096	747	506	1341	1039	1094	1425	1152	1515	363	858	612	873
New York, N.Y.	2216	1866	862	187	2186	986	229	396	2416	1903	908	755	571	701	1635	1934	1266	648	1376	2310	1546	1703	811	981	1329
Oklahoma City, Okla.	648	274	907	1454	1394	740	1743	1249	1631	845	794	880	1065	1160	236	739	565	1031	976	718	1066	500	782	1178	343
Omaha, Nebr.	1015	754	1025	1284	896	892	1506	1012	1132	507	488	752	828	1246	712	538	145	760	500	1140	590	976	654	1330	195
Philadelphia, Pa.	2124	1775	771	95	2094	894	321	415	2330	1811	816	664	479	610	1543	1842	1174	644	1285	2190	1454	1612	719	890	1237
Pittsburgh, Pa.	1776	1427	806	328	1747	797	668	260	1983	1463	468	316	131	772	1291	1494	826	296	937	1834	1107	1426	371	1052	889
Portland, Oreg.	1849	1837	2798	3030	961	2665	3217	2723	725	1266	2199	2470	2539	3019	2227	1372	1918	2505	1820	2002	1601	2491	2427	3184	1968
Richmond, Va.	2038	1664	579	155	2140	735	570	550	2370	1840	862	581	544	360	1385	1833	1220	708	1330	2031	1500	1435	690	640	1197
St. Louis, Mo.	1190	816	612	920	1310	479	1202	708	1546	921	284	338	523	833	711	914	340	489	726	1223	816	921	240	917	278
St. Paul, Minn.	1363	1039	1130	1193	882	1047	1414	920	1112	855	396	677	736	1263	997	886	259	668	152	1425	242	1261	580	1479	480
Salt Lake City, Utah	985	973	2051	2310	669	1906	2532	2038	433	519	1514	1778	1854	2272	1343	570	1171	1786	1526	1238	1309	1607	1680	2344	1206
San Antonio, Tex.	870	617	1066	1720	1739	928	2125	1631	1975	1189	1208	1247	1447	1320	271	1083	1009	1413	1420	617	1510	210	1164	1185	788
San Francisco, Calif.	1209	1537	2718	3059	1418	2551	3281	2787	1182	1268	2263	2527	2603	2971	1930	1374	1920	2535	2275	1284	2058	2111	2429	2989	1970
Seattle, Wash.	2031	2019	2824	2937	903	2691	3159	2665	667	1448	2141	2422	2481	3045	2394	1554	1944	2413	1762	2184	1503	2656	2325	3129	1954
Spokane, Wash	1726	1714	2514	2628	593	2381	2849	2355	357	1143	1831	2112	2171	2735	2084	1249	1634	2103	1452	1979	1193	2348	2015	2819	1644
Tucson, Ariz.	565	756	1783	2407	1698	1616	2726	2232	1718	1148	1708	1873	2048	2036	958	1042	1478	1980	1889	312	1979	1139	1775	2076	1257
Washington, D.C.	2047	1690	638	38	2043	761	454	434	2273	1759	764	544	427	476	1410	1790	1122	592	1233	2056	1403	1478	653	756	1160
Wichita, Kans.	721	347	986	1401	1236	819	1681	1187	1472	686	663	819	1003	1239	408	580	433	935	844	791	934	672	721	1257	212

	Knoxville, Tenn.	Los Angeles, Calif.	Louisville, Ky.	Memphis, Tenn.	Miami, Fla.	Mobile, Ala.	Nashville, Tenn.	New Orleans, La.	New York, N.Y.	Oklahoma City, Okla.	Omaha, Nebr.	Philadelphia, Pa.	Pittsburgh, Pa.	Portland, Oreg.	Richmond, Va.	St. Louis, Mo.	St. Paul, Minn.	Salt Lake City, Utah	San Antonio, Tex.	San Francisco, Calif.	Seattle, Wash.	Spokane, Wash.	Tucson, Ariz.	Washington, D.C.	Wichita, Kans.
Albuquerque, N. Mex.	1556	889	1463	1135	2185	1369	1374	1229	2216	648	1015	2124	1776	1849	2038	1190	1363	985	870	1209	2031	1726	565	2047	721
Amarillo, Tex.	1183	1216	1090	761	1832	1016	1000	876	1866	274	754	1775	1427	1837	1664	816	1039	973	617	1537	2019	1714	756	1690	347
Atlanta, Ga.	197	2285	474	420	716	353	288	493	862	907	1025	771	806	2798	579	612	1130	2051	1066	2718	2824	2514	1783	638	986
Baltimore, Md.	545	2908	696	967	1160	1029	761	1154	187	1454	1284	95	328	3030	155	920	1193	2310	1720	3059	2937	2628	2407	38	1401
Billings, Mont.	1849	1452	1583	1535	2592	1958	1634	1924	2186	1394	896	2094	1747	961	2140	1310	882	669	1739	1418	903	593	1698	2043	1236
Birmingham, Ala.	254	2118	392	253	804	266	205	355	986	740	892	894	797	2665	735	479	1047	1906	928	2551	2691	2381	1616	761	819
Boston, Mass.	961	3244	1052	1382	1576	1444	1177	1569	229	1743	1506	321	668	3217	570	1202	1414	2532	2125	3281	3159	2849	2726	454	1681
Buffalo, N.Y.	737	2750	558	938	1556	1191	745	1280	396	1249	1012	415	260	2723	550	708	920	2038	1631	2787	2665	2355	2232	434	1187
Butte, Mont.	2085	1216	1809	1771	2828	2194	1870	2160	2416	1631	1132	2330	1983	725	2370	1546	1112	433	1975	1182	667	357	1718	2273	1472
Cheyenne, Wyo.	1460	1302	1194	1186	2243	1569	1245	1447	1903	845	507	1811	1463	1266	1840	921	855	519	1189	1268	1448	1143	1148	1759	686
Chicago, Ill.	574	2227	295	527	1449	917	446	921	908	794	488	816	468	2199	862	284	396	1514	1208	2263	2141	1831	1708	764	663
Cincinnati, Ohio	296	2370	114	494	1206	747	301	836	755	880	752	664	316	2470	581	338	677	1778	1247	2527	2422	2112	1873	544	819
Cleveland, Ohio	553	2555	374	754	1466	1007	561	1096	571	1065	828	479	131	2539	544	523	736	1854	1447	2603	2481	2171	2048	427	1003
Columbia, S.C.	293	2538	581	673	646	607	509	747	701	1160	1246	610	772	3019	360	833	1263	2272	1320	2971	3045	2735	2036	476	1239
Dallas, Tex.	903	1460	861	481	1462	646	720	506	1635	236	712	1543	1291	2227	1385	711	997	1343	271	1930	2394	2084	958	1410	408
Denver, Colo.	1454	1353	1188	1120	2177	1481	1238	1341	1934	739	538	1842	1494	1372	1833	914	886	570	1083	1374	1554	1249	1042	1790	580
Des Moines, Iowa	880	1954	614	645	1667	988	664	1039	1266	565	145	1174	826	1918	1220	340	259	1171	1009	1920	1944	1634	1478	1122	433
Detroit, Mich.	551	2499	372	752	1464	1005	559	1094	648	1031	760	644	296	2505	708	489	668	1786	1413	2535	2413	2103	1980	592	935
Duluth, Minn.	1042	2309	763	1031	1917	1374	914	1425	1376	976	500	1285	937	1820	1330	726	152	1526	1420	2275	1762	1452	1889	1233	844
El Paso, Tex.	1549	814	1508	1128	2130	1292	1367	1152	2310	718	1140	2190	1834	2002	2031	1223	1425	1238	617	1284	2184	1979	312	2056	791
Fargo, N. Dak.	1212	2092	933	1121	2087	1464	1084	1515	1546	1066	590	1454	1107	1601	1500	816	242	1309	1510	2058	1503	1193	1979	1403	934
Houston, Tex.	972	1641	996	616	1341	503	855	363	1703	500	976	1612	1426	2491	1435	921	1261	1607	210	2111	2656	2348	1139	1478	672
Indianapolis, Ind.	388	2272	111	491	1301	769	298	858	811	782	654	719	371	2427	690	240	580	1680	1164	2429	2325	2015	1775	653	721
Jacksonville, Fla.	547	2578	824	691	366	472	637	612	981	1178	1330	890	1052	3148	640	917	1479	2344	1185	2989	3129	2819	2076	756	1257
Kansas City, Mo.	818	1776	552	484	1541	926	602	873	1329	343	195	1237	889	1968	1197	278	480	1206	788	1970	1954	1644	1257	1160	212
Knoxville, Tenn.		2363	277	422	913	520	216	609	732	909	953	640	609	2726	482	540	970	2001	1174	2720	2715	2405	1861	507	988
Los Angeles, Calif.	2363		2306	1942	2944	2106	2181	1966	3082	1490	1809	2991	2643	1188	2845	2032	2157	783	1431	470	1370	1556	502	2906	1563
Louisville, Ky.	277	2306		380	1190	658	187	747	869	867	687	778	430	2460	695	274	691	1713	1133	2462	2486	2176	1820	658	755
Memphis, Tenn.	422	1942	380		1057	384	239	394	1153	487	679	1062	810	2496	903	305	879	1653	753	2298	2438	2128	1440	929	566
Miami, Fla.	913	2944	1190	1057		838	1003	978	1347	1544	1696	1256	1418	3514	1006	1283	1845	2710	1551	3355	3495	3185	2442	1122	1623
Mobile, Ala.	520	2106	658	394	838		471	140	1215	871	1062	1124	1063	2872	932	648	1222	1988	713	2553	2861	2551	1604	991	1053
Nashville, Tenn.	216	2181	187	239	1003	471		560	948	726	738	856	617	2511	697	324	842	1892	992	2537	2537	2227	1679	723	805
New Orleans, La.	609	1966	747	394	978	140	560		1355	742	1068	1264	1152	2732	1072	699	1273	1848	573	2436	2900	2590	1464	1115	913
New York, N.Y.	732	3082	869	1153	1347	1215	948	1355		1592	1396	91	439	3107	341	1051	1304	2422	1906	3171	3049	2739	2586	225	1532
Oklahoma City, Okla.	909	1490	867	487	1544	871	726	742	1592		538	1501	1153	2131	3190	542	824	1247	507	1811	2293	1987	1030	1424	172
Omaha, Nebr.	953	1809	687	679	1696	1062	738	1068	1396	538		1304	956	1773	1333	414	348	1026	983	1775	1799	1489	1452	1252	407
Philadelphia, Pa.	640	2991	778	1062	1256	1124	856	1264	91	1501	1304		348	3015	250	959	1212	2330	1815	3079	2957	2647	2494	133	1440
Pittsburgh, Pa.	609	2643	430	810	1418	1063	617	1152	439	1153	956	348		2668	413	611	865	1982	1535	2731	2610	2300	2146	296	1092
Portland, Oreg.	2726	1188	2460	2496	3514	2872	2511	2732	3107	2131	1773	3015	2668		3095	2187	1803	884	2498	718	182	368	1690	3025	1971
Richmond, Va.	482	2845	695	903	1006	932	697	1072	341	1390	1333	250	413	3095		919	1258	2359	1645	3108	3003	2693	2343	117	1400
St. Louis, Mo.	540	2032	274	305	1283	648	324	699	1051	542	414	959	611	2187	919		574	1440	924	2189	2213	1903	1572	882	481
St. Paul, Minn.	970	2157	691	879	1845	1222	842	1273	1304	824	348	1212	865	1803	1258	574		1374	1268	2123	1745	1435	1737	1161	692
Salt Lake City, Utah	2001	783	1713	1653	2710	1988	1892	1848	2422	1247	1026	2330	1982	884	2359	1440	1374		1614	821	1066	790	1285	2278	1087
San Antonio, Tex.	1174	1431	1133	753	1551	713	992	573	1906	507	983	1815	1535	2498	1645	924	1268	1614		1901	2666	2356	929	1681	679
San Francisco, Calif.	2720	470	2462	2298	3355	2553	2537	2436	3171	1811	1775	3079	2731	718	3108	2189	2123	821	1901		900	1086	972	3028	1884
Seattle, Wash.	2715	1370	2486	2438	3495	2861	2537	2900	3049	2293	1799	2957	2610	182	3003	2213	1745	1066	2666	900		310	1872	2906	2139
Spokane, Wash	2405	1556	2176	2128	3185	2551	2227	2590	2739	1987	1489	2647	2300	368	2693	1903	1435	790	2356	1086	310		2291	2596	1829
Tucson, Ariz.	1861	502	1820	1440	2442	1604	1679	1464	2586	1030	1452	2494	2146	1690	2343	1572	1737	1285	929	972	1872	2291		2368	1103
Washington, D.C.	507	2906	658	929	1122	991	723	1115	225	1424	1252	133	296	3025	117	882	1161	2278	1681	3028	2906	2596	2368		1363
Wichita, Kans.	988	1563	755	566	1623	1053	805	913	1532	172	407	1440	1092	1971	1400	481	692	1087	679	1884	2139	1829	1103	1363	

U.S. AIR DISTANCE TABLE

Showing Great Circle Distances Between Principal Cities of the United States in Statute Miles

	Albuquerque, N. Mex.	Amarillo, Tex.	Atlanta, Ga.	Billings, Mont.	Birmingham, Ala.	Boston, Mass.	Buffalo, N.Y.	Burlington, Vt.	Charleston, S.C.	Charlotte, N.C.	Cheyenne, Wyo.	Chicago, Ill.	Cincinnati, Ohio	Cleveland, Ohio	Dallas, Tex.	Denver, Colo.	Des Moines, Iowa	Detroit, Mich.	El Paso, Tex.	Fargo, N. Dak.	Houston, Tex.	Indianapolis, Ind.	Jacksonville, Fla.	Kansas City, Mo.	Knoxville, Tenn.
Albuquerque, N. Mex.		273	1272	744	1138	1972	1580	1878	1539	1457	429	1129	1251	1421	588	334	837	1364	229	961	754	1169	1488	720	1280
Amarillo, Tex.	273		999	809	866	1722	1338	1640	1266	1185	440	894	992	1173	334	358	626	1124	358	847	533	915	1219	481	1009
Atlanta, Ga.	1272	999		1519	140	937	697	951	267	227	1229	587	369	554	721	1212	739	596	1291	1114	701	426	285	676	155
Billings, Mont.	744	809	1519		1425	1861	1473	1713	1761	1617	370	1073	1304	1369	1092	453	798	1283	973	565	1315	1204	1796	846	1447
Birmingham, Ala.	1138	866	140	1425		1052	776	1049	402	361	1119	578	406	618	581	1095	670	641	1152	1060	567	433	374	579	235
Boston, Mass.	1972	1722	937	1861	1052		400	182	820	721	1735	851	740	551	1551	1769	1159	613	2072	1300	1605	807	1017	1251	818
Buffalo, N.Y.	1580	1338	697	1473	776	400		304	699	538	1335	454	393	173	1198	1370	760	216	1692	919	1286	435	879	861	548
Burlington, Vt.	1878	1640	951	1713	1049	182	304		884	755	1612	749	690	476	1501	1654	1049	516	1995	1149	1580	739	1079	1161	815
Charleston, S.C.	1539	1266	267	1761	402	820	699	884		177	1486	757	506	609	981	1474	967	681	1552	1317	936	594	197	928	316
Charlotte, N.C.	1457	1185	227	1617	361	721	538	755	177		1362	587	335	435	930	1358	819	504	1496	1153	927	428	341	803	180
Cheyenne, Wyo.	429	440	1229	370	1119	1735	1335	1612	1486	1362		891	1082	1199	726	96	583	1125	653	563	947	986	1493	560	1183
Chicago, Ill.	1129	894	587	1073	578	851	454	749	757	587	891		252	308	803	920	309	238	1252	569	940	165	863	414	454
Cincinnati, Ohio	1251	992	369	1304	406	740	393	690	506	335	1082	252		222	814	1094	510	235	1335	820	892	100	626	541	219
Cleveland, Ohio	1421	1173	554	1369	618	551	173	476	609	435	1199	308	222		1025	1227	617	90	1525	835	1114	263	770	700	400
Dallas, Tex.	588	334	721	1092	581	1551	1198	1501	981	930	726	803	814	1025		663	632	999	572	972	225	763	908	451	767
Denver, Colo.	334	358	1212	453	1095	1769	1370	1654	1474	1358	96	920	1094	1227	663		610	1156	557	642	879	1000	1467	558	1178
Des Moines, Iowa	837	626	739	798	670	1159	760	1049	967	819	583	309	510	617	632	610		546	983	397	821	411	1023	180	651
Detroit, Mich.	1364	1124	596	1283	641	613	216	516	681	504	1125	238	235	90	999	1156	546		1479	745	1105	240	831	645	442
El Paso, Tex.	229	358	1291	973	1152	2072	1692	1995	1552	1496	653	1252	1335	1525	572	557	983	1479		1163	676	1264	1473	839	1326
Fargo, N. Dak.	961	847	1114	565	1060	1300	919	1149	1317	1153	563	569	820	835	972	642	397	745	1163		1183	725	1399	549	1004
Houston, Tex.	754	533	701	1315	567	1605	1286	1580	936	927	947	940	892	1114	225	879	821	1105	676	1183		865	821	644	790
Indianapolis, Ind.	1169	915	426	1204	433	807	435	739	594	428	986	165	100	263	763	1000	411	240	1264	725	865		699	453	290
Jacksonville, Fla.	1488	1219	285	1796	374	1017	879	1079	197	341	1493	863	626	770	908	1467	1023	831	1473	1399	821	699		950	410
Kansas City, Mo.	720	481	676	846	579	1251	861	1161	928	803	560	414	541	700	451	558	180	645	839	549	644	453	950		624
Knoxville, Tenn.	1280	1009	155	1447	235	818	548	815	316	180	1183	454	219	400	767	1178	651	442	1326	1004	790	290	410	624	
Little Rock, Ark.	816	543	456	1143	325	1259	913	1214	723	649	813	552	524	740	293	780	478	723	847	869	388	483	690	325	479
Los Angeles, Calif.	664	937	1936	959	1802	2596	2198	2485	2203	2119	882	1745	1897	2049	1240	831	1438	1983	701	1427	1374	1809	2147	1356	1941
Louisville, Ky.	1178	915	319	1275	331	826	483	780	500	343	1033	269	90	311	726	1038	476	316	1254	818	803	107	594	480	188
Memphis, Tenn.	939	667	337	1213	217	1137	803	1100	604	521	902	482	410	630	420	879	485	623	976	882	484	384	590	369	350
Miami, Fla.	1698	1441	604	2085	665	1255	1181	1347	482	652	1763	1188	952	1087	1111	1726	1333	1152	1643	1716	968	1024	326	1241	736
Minneapolis, Minn.	983	812	907	742	862	1123	731	985	1104	939	642	355	605	630	862	700	235	543	1157	214	1056	511	1191	413	792
Nashville, Tenn.	1119	848	214	1309	182	943	627	916	455	340	1032	397	238	459	617	1023	525	470	1169	902	665	251	499	473	161
New Orleans, La.	1029	776	424	1479	312	1359	1086	1361	630	649	1131	833	706	924	443	1082	827	939	983	1222	318	712	504	680	547
New York, N.Y.	1815	1560	748	1760	864	188	292	260	641	533	1604	713	570	405	1374	1631	1022	482	1905	1210	1420	646	838	1097	632
Omaha, Nebr.	721	526	817	703	732	1282	883	1171	1058	918	463	432	622	739	586	488	123	669	878	390	794	525	1098	166	745
Philadelphia, Pa.	1753	1494	666	1727	783	271	279	328	562	451	1556	666	503	360	1299	1579	973	443	1836	1184	1341	585	758	1038	552
Phoenix, Ariz.	330	598	1592	872	1456	2300	1906	2202	1857	1783	663	1453	1581	1749	887	586	1155	1690	346	1225	1017	1499	1794	1049	1607
Pittsburgh, Pa.	1499	1244	521	1479	608	483	178	445	528	362	1298	410	257	115	1070	1320	715	205	1590	949	1137	330	703	781	375
Portland, Oreg.	1107	1304	2172	686	2066	2540	2156	2385	2425	2290	947	1758	1985	2055	1633	982	1475	1969	1286	1239	1836	1885	2439	1497	2115
Raleigh, N.C.	1576	1306	356	1698	491	609	490	665	220	130	1461	642	396	428	1057	1463	902	510	1621	1210	1056	495	414	905	296
St. Louis, Mo.	942	685	467	1057	400	1038	662	966	704	568	795	262	309	492	547	796	273	455	1034	660	679	231	751	238	392
Salt Lake City, Utah	484	668	1583	387	1466	2099	1699	1969	1845	1727	371	1260	1453	1568	999	371	953	1492	689	863	1200	1356	1837	925	1547
San Antonio, Tex.	617	444	882	1252	744	1766	1430	1729	1122	1105	882	1051	1039	1256	252	802	882	1238	503	1207	189	999	1011	702	959
San Francisco, Calif.	896	1157	2139	904	2013	2699	2300	2568	2405	2301	967	1858	2043	2166	1483	949	1550	2091	995	1446	1645	1949	2374	1506	2121
Seattle, Wash.	1184	1359	2182	668	2082	2493	2117	2333	2428	2285	973	1737	1972	2026	1681	1021	1467	1938	1376	1197	1891	1872	2455	1506	2114
Spokane, Wash.	1030	1176	1961	443	1865	2266	1888	2108	2204	2059	768	1508	1744	1796	1489	826	1240	1709	1239	969	1704	1644	2237	1287	1890
Syracuse, N.Y.	1718	1475	781	1600	875	264	138	177	738	595	1472	592	514	303	1326	1508	898	354	1828	1042	1403	567	928	998	641
Tulsa, Okla.	604	335	678	930	552	1398	1023	1327	945	853	588	598	661	853	236	550	396	813	674	741	442	591	921	216	676
Washington, D.C.	1653	1391	543	1669	661	393	292	432	453	330	1477	597	404	306	1185	1494	896	396	1728	1140	1220	494	647	945	430
Wichita, Kans.	549	304	776	801	658	1424	1036	1337	1039	933	465	591	702	873	340	437	334	821	661	634	559	620	1031	177	753

	Little Rock, Ark.	Los Angeles, Calif.	Louisville, Ky.	Memphis, Tenn.	Miami, Fla.	Minneapolis, Minn.	Nashville, Tenn.	New Orleans, La.	New York, N.Y.	Omaha, Nebr.	Philadelphia, Pa.	Phoenix, Ariz.	Pittsburgh, Pa.	Portland, Oreg.	Raleigh, N.C.	St. Louis, Mo.	Salt Lake City, Utah	San Antonio, Tex.	San Francisco, Calif.	Seattle, Wash.	Spokane, Wash.	Syracuse, N.Y.	Tulsa, Okla.	Washington, D.C.	Wichita, Kans.
Albuquerque, N. Mex.	816	664	1178	939	1698	983	1119	1029	1815	721	1753	330	1499	1107	1576	942	484	617	896	1184	1030	1718	604	1653	549
Amarillo, Tex.	543	937	915	667	1441	812	848	776	1560	526	1494	598	1244	1304	1306	685	668	444	1157	1359	1176	1475	335	1391	304
Atlanta, Ga.	456	1936	319	337	604	907	214	424	748	817	666	1592	521	2172	356	467	1583	882	2139	2182	1961	781	678	543	776
Billings, Mont.	1143	959	1275	1213	2085	742	1309	1479	1760	703	1727	872	1479	686	1698	1057	387	1252	904	668	443	1600	930	1669	801
Birmingham, Ala.	325	1802	331	217	665	862	182	312	864	732	783	1456	608	2066	491	400	1466	744	2013	2082	1865	875	552	661	658
Boston, Mass.	1259	2596	826	1137	1255	1123	943	1359	188	1282	271	2300	483	2540	609	1038	2099	1766	2699	2493	2266	264	1398	393	1424
Buffalo, N.Y.	913	2198	483	803	1181	731	627	1086	292	883	279	1906	178	2156	490	662	1699	1430	2300	2117	1888	138	1023	292	1036
Burlington, Vt.	1214	2485	780	1100	1347	985	916	1361	260	1171	328	2202	445	2385	665	966	1969	1729	2568	2333	2108	177	1327	432	1337
Charleston, S.C.	723	2203	500	604	482	1104	455	630	641	1058	562	1857	528	2425	220	704	1845	1122	2405	2428	2204	738	945	453	1039
Charlotte, N.C.	649	2119	343	521	652	939	340	649	533	918	451	1783	362	2290	130	568	1727	1105	2301	2285	2059	595	853	330	933
Cheyenne, Wyo.	813	882	1033	902	1763	642	1032	1131	1604	463	1556	663	1298	947	1461	795	371	882	967	973	768	1472	588	1477	465
Chicago, Ill.	552	1745	269	482	1188	355	397	833	713	432	666	1453	410	1758	642	262	1260	1051	1858	1737	1508	592	598	597	591
Cincinnati, Ohio	524	1897	90	410	952	605	238	706	570	622	503	1581	257	1985	396	309	1453	1039	2043	1972	1744	514	661	404	702
Cleveland, Ohio	740	2049	311	630	1087	630	459	924	405	739	360	1749	115	2055	428	492	1568	1256	2166	2026	1796	303	853	306	873
Dallas, Tex.	293	1240	726	420	1111	862	617	443	1374	586	1299	887	1070	1633	1057	547	999	252	1483	1681	1489	1326	236	1185	340
Denver, Colo.	780	831	1038	879	1726	700	1023	1082	1631	488	1579	586	1320	982	1463	796	371	802	949	1021	826	1508	550	1494	437
Des Moines, Iowa	478	1438	476	485	1333	235	525	827	1022	123	973	1155	715	1475	902	273	953	882	1550	1467	1240	898	396	896	334
Detroit, Mich.	723	1983	316	623	1152	543	470	939	482	669	443	1690	205	1969	510	455	1492	1238	2091	1938	1709	354	813	396	821
El Paso, Tex.	847	701	1254	976	1643	1157	1169	983	1905	878	1836	346	1590	1286	1621	1034	689	503	995	1376	1239	1828	674	1728	661
Fargo, N. Dak.	869	1427	818	882	1716	214	902	1222	1210	390	1184	1225	949	1239	1210	660	863	1207	1446	1197	969	1042	741	1140	634
Houston, Tex.	388	1374	803	484	968	1056	665	318	1420	794	1341	1017	1137	1836	1056	679	1200	189	1645	1891	1704	1403	442	1220	559
Indianapolis, Ind.	483	1809	107	384	1024	511	251	712	646	525	585	1499	330	1885	495	231	1356	999	1949	1872	1644	567	591	494	620
Jacksonville, Fla.	690	2147	594	590	326	1191	499	504	838	1098	758	1794	703	2439	414	751	1837	1011	2374	2455	2237	928	921	647	1031
Kansas City, Mo.	325	1356	480	369	1241	413	473	680	1097	166	1038	1049	781	1497	905	238	925	702	1506	1506	1287	998	216	945	177
Knoxville, Tenn.	479	1941	188	350	736	792	161	547	632	745	552	1607	375	2115	296	392	1547	959	2121	2114	1890	641	676	430	753
Little Rock, Ark.		1480	435	129	949	708	325	355	1081	492	1007	1137	779	1759	774	291	1148	516	1688	1785	1573	1038	231	892	348
Los Angeles, Calif.	1480		1829	1603	2339	1524	1780	1673	2451	1315	2394	357	2136	825	2237	1589	579	1204	347	959	940	2336	1266	2300	1197
Louisville, Ky.	435	1829		320	919	605	154	623	652	580	582	1508	344	1950	429	242	1402	949	1986	1943	1717	603	582	476	633
Memphis, Tenn.	129	1603	320		872	699	197	358	957	529	881	1263	660	1849	645	240	1250	631	1802	1867	1650	923	341	765	442
Miami, Fla.	949	2339	919	872		1511	815	669	1092	1397	1019	1982	1010	2708	695	1061	2089	1148	2594	2734	2520	1212	1176	923	1297
Minneapolis, Minn.	708	1524	605	699	1511		697	1051	1018	290	985	1280	743	1427	996	466	987	1110	1584	1395	1166	861	626	934	546
Nashville, Tenn.	325	1780	154	197	815	697		469	761	607	685	1446	472	1969	457	254	1393	823	1963	1975	1752	739	515	569	594
New Orleans, La.	355	1673	623	358	669	1051	469		1171	847	1089	1316	919	2063	776	598	1434	507	1926	2101	1898	1187	548	966	677
New York, N.Y.	1081	2451	652	957	1092	1018	761	1171		1144	83	2145	317	2445	426	875	1972	1584	2571	2408	2179	194	1231	205	1266
Omaha, Nebr.	492	1315	580	529	1397	290	607	847	1144		1094	1036	836	1371	1008	354	833	828	1429	1369	1146	1021	352	1014	257
Philadelphia, Pa.	1007	2394	582	881	1019	985	685	1089	83	1094		2083	259	2412	345	811	1925	1507	2523	2380	2151	220	1163	123	1204
Phoenix, Ariz.	1137	357	1508	1263	1982	1280	1446	1316	2145	1036	2083		1828	1005	1903	1272	504	849	653	1114	1019	2044	932	1983	879
Pittsburgh, Pa.	779	2136	344	660	1010	743	472	919	317	836	259	1828		2165	330	559	1668	1291	2264	2138	1908	268	917	192	950
Portland, Oreg.	1759	825	1950	1849	2708	1427	1969	2063	2445	1371	2412	1005	2165		2377	1723	636	1720	534	145	290	2281	1531	2354	1411
Raleigh, N.C.	774	2237	429	645	695	996	457	776	426	1008	345	1903	330	2377		667	1829	1235	2410	2367	2139	519	972	233	1044
St. Louis, Mo.	291	1589	242	240	1061	466	254	598	875	354	811	1272	559	1723	667		1162	792	1744	1724	1500	796	361	712	394
Salt Lake City, Utah	1148	579	1402	1250	2089	987	1393	1434	1972	833	1925	504	1668	636	1829	1162		1087	600	701	550	1835	917	1848	808
San Antonio, Tex.	516	1204	949	631	1148	1110	823	507	1584	828	1507	849	1291	1720	1235	792	1087		1490	1787	1614	1553	486	1388	573
San Francisco, Calif.	1688	347	1986	1802	2594	1584	1963	1926	2571	1429	2523	653	2264	534	2410	1744	600	1490		678	727	2435	1461	2442	1369
Seattle, Wash.	1785	959	1943	1867	2734	1395	1975	2101	2408	1369	2380	1114	2138	145	2367	1724	701	1787	678		229	2238	1560	2329	1437
Spokane, Wash.	1573	940	1717	1650	2520	1166	1752	1898	2179	1146	2151	1019	1908	290	2139	1500	550	1614	727	229		2010	1353	2100	1227
Syracuse, N.Y.	1038	2336	603	923	1212	861	739	1187	194	1021	220	2044	268	2281	519	796	1835	1553	2435	2238	2010		1157	290	1173
Tulsa, Okla.	231	1266	582	341	1176	626	515	548	1231	352	1163	932	917	1531	972	361	917	486	1461	1560	1353	1157		1058	130
Washington, D.C.	892	2300	476	765	923	934	569	966	205	1014	123	1983	192	2354	233	712	1848	1388	2442	2329	2100	290	1058		1106
Wichita, Kans.	348	1197	633	442	1297	546	594	677	1266	257	1204	879	950	1411	1044	394	808	573	1369	1437	1227	1173	130	1106	

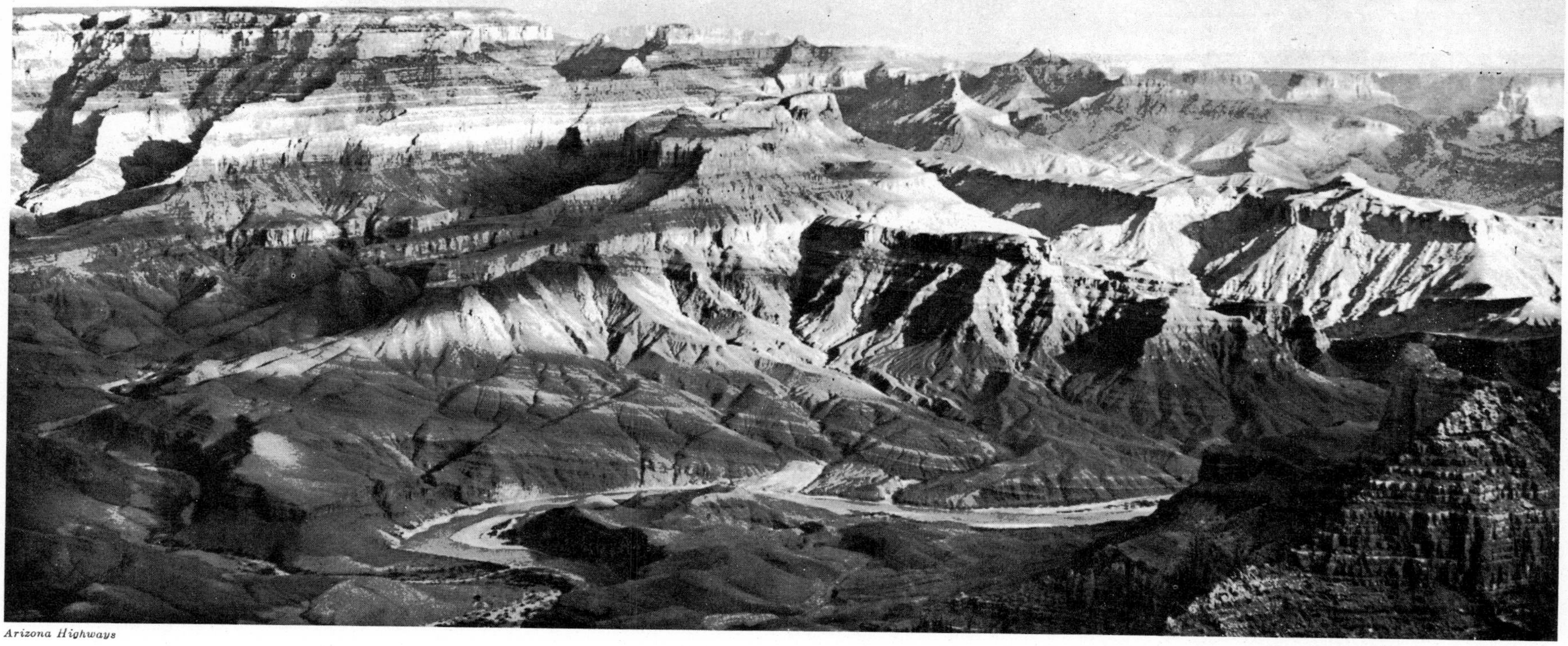

Arizona's Grand Canyon—Mighty Gorge of the Colorado

PLACES OF INTEREST IN THE UNITED STATES

For the state capital, largest city, highest point, and other general information about each state, see the U.S. State General Information Table on page 220. Also see the U.S. National Park System Table and Map, pages 224-225, for additional information about the national parks, monuments, historical parks, and other units under the National Park Service.

ALABAMA

Birmingham. Largest city in Alabama and steel center of the South. On top of Red Mountain, overlooking the city, stands the 53-foot statue of Vulcan on a pedestal 124 feet high. Cast in a Birmingham foundry, from pig iron mined in the area, the statue is second in size only to the Statue of Liberty. Other points of interest are Woodrow Wilson Park, in the city, and Vestavia, on nearby Shades Mountain. Built as a circular residence and patterned after the Roman Temple of Vesta, Vestavia now houses a museum and is surrounded by gardens.

Mobile. Important southern seaport and Alabama's first permanent white settlement, the city is famed for its historic old-colonial homes, a five-day Mardi Gras, and a thirty-five mile Azalea Trail. On this Trail, southwest of the city, are beautiful Bellingrath Gardens, containing many kinds of flowers and shrubs. On Dauphin Island, Alabama's annual Deep Sea Fishing Rodeo is held.

Montgomery. Capital of Alabama and first capital of the southern Confederacy. The Capitol and its grounds, situated on Goat Hill, contain many historic relics and monuments. The first White House of the Confederacy, the Montgomery home of Jefferson Davis, has many war relics, as well as some of Davis' personal belongings.

Mound State Monument. Thirty-four prehistoric Indian mounds. The largest is 58½ feet high and covers one and a quarter acres. A museum near the center of the park contains burial exhibits, tools, pottery, beads, and other relics excavated on the site. The monument is near Moundville.

Muscle Shoals. Site of Wilson Dam and two nitrate plants, construction of which was begun in 1916 as a defense measure and which later was expanded into the vast Tennessee Valley Authority project. Wilson Dam, 137 feet high and nearly a mile long, has two navigation locks that lift boats 89 feet in less than an hour. Fifteen miles up the Tennessee is Wheeler Dam.

ALASKA

Aleutian Islands. A thousand-mile chain of twenty volcanic, treeless islands stretching out from the Alaska Peninsula. Scattered along the archipelago are small native villages peopled by Aleuts.

Anchorage. Largest city in the state and gateway to a fabulous hunting area for bear, mountain sheep and goats, caribou, and moose. Ski areas are nearby. Short trips from the city lead to Portage Glacier and to Matanuska Valley where giant vegetables and fruits are produced.

Barrow. Located on Point Barrow, the northernmost point in the United States. From here the Distant Early Warning (DEW) Line sweeps across the Arctic to the Atlantic Ocean. Here Eskimos hunt polar bear on the ice and harpoon whale.

Fairbanks. Situated on a loop of the Chena River, Alaska's second largest city lies in the heart of a great gold mining region where giant dredges have replaced the early miner's pan. The University of Alaska is at the nearby town of College. Sightseeing trips on the Tanana River can be taken in a "paddlewheeler," and there are air trips to Chena Hot Springs for hunting and fishing.

Glaciers. The best known glaciers are the Columbia, at the head of Columbia Bay, near Valdez; the Mendenhall, the most photographed glacier, available from Juneau; Portage, available from Anchorage; and Glacier Bay National Monument at the uppermost portion of the Panhandle.

Juneau. The State capital nestles on a narrow ledge of land at the foot of the steep slope of Mt. Juneau. A lumbering and fishing center, its early glory is preserved in the Alaska-Juneau Gold Mine.

Ketchikan. Salmon fishing center, noted for its picturesque harbor. Interesting collection of totem poles at Saxman Indian Village.

Mt. McKinley National Park. Twin peaks of Mt. McKinley overlook more than 3,000 square miles, in which ice-capped domes rise above sphagnum growth, and glaciers wait to be explored.

National Monuments. Glacier Bay, west of Juneau; Katmai, on the Alaska Peninsula; Sitka. See U.S. NATIONAL PARK SYSTEM, pages 224-25.

Nome. Metropolis of Seward Peninsula, where gold, silver, and other valuable minerals are mined.

More than 350 varieties of wildflowers bloom in season. Also see King Island ivory carvers.

Pribilof Islands. Breeding grounds for government protected fur seals which arrive each May.

Sitka. Settled in 1799, it became the Russian capital of Alaska in 1802. Points of interest include Alaska Pioneers' Home, St. Michael's Cathedral, the Old Russian Blockhouse, and Sitka National Monument with its eighteen totem poles.

Skagway. Port of entry to Canada at the terminus of the Yukon Railway. White Pass and Chilkoot Pass are points of interest.

Wrangell. Early Russian fur trading post, now lumber and fishing center. Headquarters for the lovely Stikine River trip through a cut in the Coast Range Mountains. Also see the Tlingit Indian Community House and the remarkable totem poles.

ARIZONA

Apache Trail. Now a graveled road, this famous trail winds through rugged mountain scenery.

Bisbee. Center of a rich copper district. Located on the steep upper slopes of Mule Pass Gulch, Bisbee is built in tiers, and many of the houses are reached by steep flights of steps. Sacramento Pit, 435 feet deep and covering 35 acres, is at Bisbee.

Flagstaff. Home of the Lowell Observatory and Arizona State College. Situated near Humphreys Peak, highest point in the state. The city is popular with summer tourists because of its cool climate.

Glen Canyon Dam and Lake Powell. One of the world's largest concrete dams forms the second largest reservoir in the United States. The Glen Canyon Bridge, adjacent to the dam, is the world's highest steel arch bridge.

Grand Canyon National Park. One of nature's most magnificent spectacles, 5,000 feet deep Grand Canyon of the Colorado is lined with rocky towers and pinnacles and is filled with constantly changing colors. Many observation points along the North and South Rims afford excellent views of the Canyon from above, and mule trails lead to the bottom of the gorge. Grand Canyon is from 4 to 18 miles wide and is more than 200 miles long.

Hoover (Boulder) Dam and Lake Mead National Recreation Area. See NEVADA.

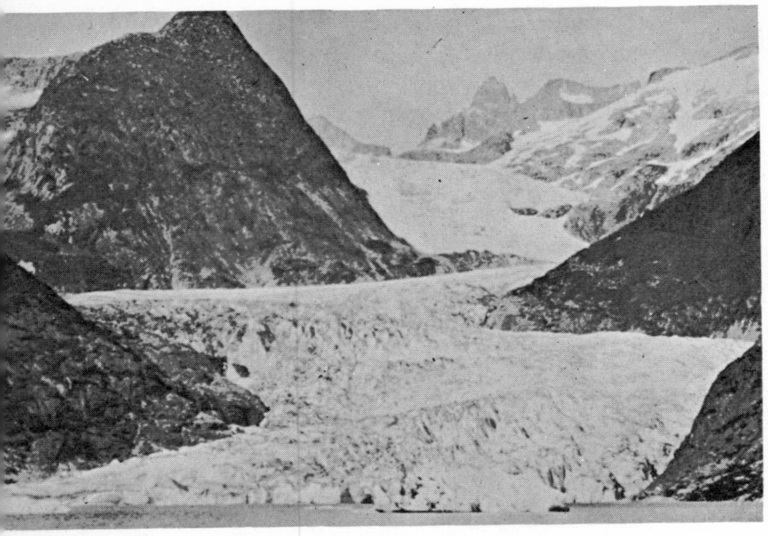

Hole-in-the-Wall Glacier, Near Juneau

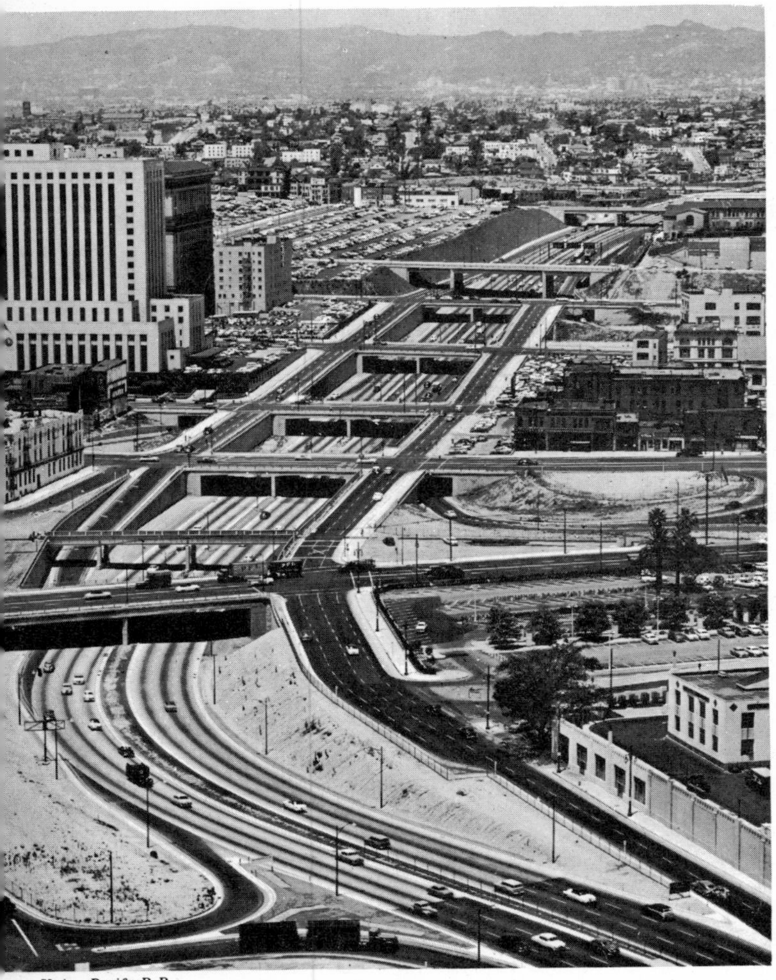

Los Angeles' Fabulous Freeway System

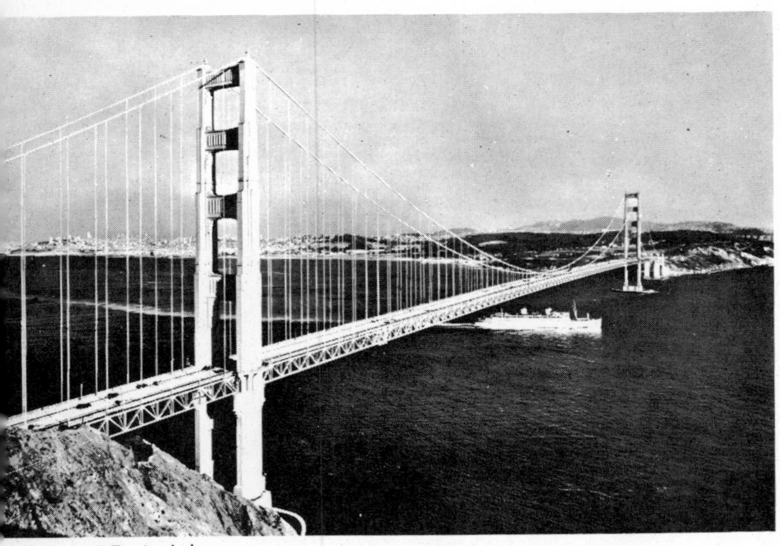

Historic Golden Gate Bridge, San Francisco

Indian Reservations. Located in the northeastern part of the state and completely surrounded by NAVAJO reservations, the HOPI reservation is one of the most interesting of the numerous Indian reservations. Most of its eleven villages are built on the tops of mesas. Oraibi has existed since 1400.

The HAVASUPAI reservation is on the bottom of Cataract Canyon in Grand Canyon National Park, and the HUALPAI is south of Grand Canyon. FORT MOJAVE and COLORADO RIVER reservations, near the California border, are the homes of the Mojave and Southern Paiute Indians. Other reservations are the MARICOPA, south of Phoenix, the PAPAGO, west of Tucson, and the Apache reserves—SAN CARLOS and FORT APACHE—near the New Mexico border.

Meteor Crater. This crater, 600 feet deep and a mile wide, was formed centuries ago by a meteor believed to have displaced between five and six million tons of earth; west of Winslow.

Monument Valley. Colorful valley in the northeastern corner of the state. Its red sandstone pillars and spires resemble huge temple ruins.

National Monuments. There are 15 national monuments in Arizona. CANYON DE CHELLY is in the Navajo Reservation and contains more than 300 cliff-dwelling ruins in an area of nearly 84,000 acres. For other National Monuments, see the U.S. NATIONAL PARK SYSTEM, pages 224-25.

Painted Desert. Three hundred miles of sand, shale, and sandstone formations splashed with brilliant shades of red, amethyst, yellow, and purple that change to other hues in the shifting light.

Petrified Forest National Park. This park includes six forests of petrified wood, much of it in the form of huge logs. The Administration Building contains many fine specimens of the wood, as well as Indian relics and fern fossils.

Phoenix. Capital of Arizona and, because of its semi-tropical climate, a popular winter tourist resort. The city is built on the site of a prehistoric community; not far from the business district is La Ciudad (the city), an excavation of an ancient pueblo. The Heard Museum contains relics from La Ciudad, relics of other Indians, including a collection of blankets. The Arizona Museum is also in Phoenix, as is the South Mountain Park.

San Xavier del Bac. Founded in 1700 by a Jesuit missionary and completed in 1797 by the Franciscans, this mission, one of the best preserved in the Southwest, is still in use. It is near Tucson.

Southwestern Arboretum. Located near Superior, this 120-acre tract of land contains 10,000 varieties of plants, brought from all over the world. Founded by the late William Boyce Thompson.

Tombstone. Roaring mining camp of the 1880's, noted for its gambling houses and gun fights. In Boothill Graveyard are buried many desperadoes and others who died violent deaths. Some of the old buildings still in existence are the Bird Cage Theater, Crystal Palace Saloon, Oriental Bar, Russ House, and office of the *Epitaph*, Tombstone newspaper.

Tucson. Resort and site of the University of Arizona. In the southern city, modern metropolitan sections rub elbows with the remnants of the old Spanish town. Businessmen and cowboys, students and Indians, mingle on the streets and in the stores.

ARKANSAS

Arkansas Post Memorial. Scene of one of the first white settlements in the Mississippi River Valley, made by the French in 1686; also the first capital of Arkansas Territory. The area contains Confederate fortifications and other historical ruins.

Bauxite. Site of numerous bauxite mines and several aluminum refineries. The mines are worked largely by a stripping process.

Devil's Den State Park. A heavily wooded area of more than 4,000 acres in the Boston Mountains, southern section of the Ozarks. Sandstone formations with deep cracks and crevices are a feature.

Diamond Cave. Large, brilliantly colored cave near Jasper, in the Ozark Mountains.

Eureka Springs. A health resort in the Ozarks, northeast of Fayetteville. On steep mountain slopes, town contains many springs and limestone caves.

Fort Smith. Second largest urban center in Arkansas. The old fort, erected to protect the settlers against the Indians, is still standing.

Hot Springs. Famous tourist resort and site of Hot Springs National Park. Containing 1,018 acres the Park includes the mountains around the city.

Little Rock. State capital and largest city. A fascinating blend of ante-bellum homes and modern metropolitan buildings. The restored Territorial Capitol was the scene of the last territorial legislature in 1835. The War Memorial Building, one of the most beautiful buildings in Arkansas, was the state Capitol for three-quarters of a century. The present Capitol faces Capitol Avenue and contains, in addition to the legislative chambers and other state offices, the State History Museum. In MacArthur Park, birthplace of General Douglas MacArthur, is the Old Arsenal, last building of the old army post. It now contains the Arkansas Museum of Natural History and Antiquities.

Mammoth Spring. One of the largest springs in the world and the source of Spring River; located in Fulton County, near the Missouri Line.

Murfreesboro. Scene of the only diamond mine in the United States.

Ozark Mountains. Highlands extending from southern Missouri into northern Arkansas and Oklahoma, famous for rugged scenery.

Petit Jean State Park. Situated on Petit Jean Mountain, a wooded plateau on the edge of the Arkansas Valley, near Morrilton. Attractions include Bear Cave and Cedar Falls.

CALIFORNIA

Catalina Island. Famous resort island where fishing and boating are prime attractions.

Coloma. The site of Sutter's Sawmill, where discovery of gold in 1848 precipitated the California gold rush. Placerville, a few miles south, was a typical "rip-roaring" camp and a station for Pony Express, Overland Mail, and freight. Gold is still mined in the area; dredging is in operation at Chico, to the north.

Death Valley National Monument. Almost 3,000 square miles of desert—salt flats, volcanic craters, hills and valleys and jagged peaks weirdly eroded. Its normal colorings of mauve to red and white to nearly black take on sunset shades as the sunlight changes, with deep shadows of purple and blue. Near Badwater, in the sink of the Amargosa River, is the lowest spot in North America, 282 feet below sea level.

Donner Pass. Six miles above Donner Lake and the spot where the hapless Donner party camped through the winter of 1846.

Hollywood. Part of Los Angeles and world motion picture capital.

Kings Canyon National Park. Established in 1940 and incorporating the old General Grant National Park, as well as Redwood Mountain and Redwood Canyon. Much of this park is a roadless wilderness of mountains, canyons, and sequoia forests. In the southern section a paved automobile road traverses Kings Canyon, whose peaks and crags include Sentinel Dome, North Dome, and Lookout Peak. Famous General Grant Grove Section, containing the General Grant Tree, is at the southwest corner.

Lake Tahoe. This colorful mountain lake is shared by Nevada through most of its length.

Lassen Volcanic National Park. Lassen Peak, a dormant volcano, centers the western half of this region of boiling mudpots, steaming sinks, and weird volcanic formations.

Los Angeles. Spreading for miles inland and along the ocean, this great city is the center of far-flung

orange groves and other agriculture and of an important oil-producing area. It is rich in manufactures, with a fine harbor, and its superb beaches are an unexcelled resort attraction. In the Olvera Street district, the point of the city's origin, Mexican pottery and other wares are made and sold in quaint old shops. Fine residential sections, handsome gardens and parks, flowers in exotic masses of color—for these Los Angeles is famous. Here are the Bernheimer Oriental Gardens and a fine botanic garden at the southern branch of the University of California. (Los Angeles is also home-city for the University of Southern California.) Numerous museums include the Southwest, showing early art, handicraft, and history of the American Indians; the Los Angeles County Museum of History, Science, and Art, containing fossils from La Brea Tar Pits, also here; and Lyons Pony Express Museum, with a fine collection of western relics. The Olympic Stadium and the race track at Santa Anita Park are sports attractions; Great Western Livestock Show is held in December. See HOLLYWOOD, PASADENA, and CATALINA ISLAND.

Missions. In the earliest days of the white man in California, the Spanish missions were the outposts of civilization. A day's journey apart, they made a chain that still reaches from San Diego to Sonoma. Soundly and beautifully built, they contain today many examples of the work of skilled artisans. SAN LUIS REY DE FRANCIA MISSION has changed little since 1798; at SAN JUAN CAPISTRANO beautiful grounds are background for swallows whose regularity of migration is legend; at MISSION SANTA BARBARA, the altar fire has never died since it was first set. The Mission Festival is held in September, at SAN GABRIEL ARCHANGEL.

Monterey and Carmel. South of Monterey Bay, the two towns are at the base of Monterey Peninsula, whose jutting, rocky coast is a series of superb crags, reefs, and white surf. Here are the famous Monterey cypress trees, and the pines. Monterey was the early key-city of the state and its first capital.

Mount Shasta. Famed for its beauty the peak is a favorite of mountain climbers. The region south of it contains Castle Crags State Park, and, farther south, Shasta Lake, with gigantic Shasta Dam.

National Monuments. See DEATH VALLEY NATIONAL MONUMENT, and U. S. NATIONAL PARK SYSTEM, pages 224-25.

Palomar Observatory. Northeast of San Diego: Home of the world's largest reflector telescope.

Pasadena. Home of the famed Rose Bowl. Here each January 1 the Tournament of Roses takes place. Nearby is the Mount Wilson Observatory; and the Huntington Library, Art Gallery, and Gardens are in San Marino to the south.

Redwoods. All along the northern half of California's coast, the redwood forests are spectacular. From Mill Creek Redwoods State Park in the north to the Big Basin Redwoods State Park south of San Francisco, the coastal area is a series of state parks and groves.

Sacramento. California's capital, on the Sacramento River. Sutter's Fort is a faithful restoration of the ranch and fort where Captain John A. Sutter first settled in 1839, and where scores of starving, exhausted pioneers were given succor. The Crocker Art Gallery, partly housed in the Old Crocker Home, is one of the finest in the country.

San Diego. At the southwestern tip of California. San Diego has a huge training station and military base for the United States Marine Corps and a United States Naval Training Center. The ocean drive from Long Beach ends here. Numerous missions are near the highway. Cabrillo National Monument, the Old Spanish Lighthouse, is a half-acre monument. Tijuana is over the line in Old Mexico.

San Francisco. "City of the world, of the hills, and of the sea." The Golden Gate Bridge links it with the mainland to the north; the Bay Bridge connects it with Oakland, across San Francisco Bay; by a narrow neck of land its peninsula joins the mainland. Twin Peaks Scenic Drive offers a superb view of the city, bay, waterfront, and suburban cities across the bay. A scenic highway skirts the ocean along the peninsula's length. Sea-going ships in the harbor, Fisherman's Wharf, the Latin Quarter, and Chinatown's temples and bazaars lend an air of adventure. Beauty spots are the well-preserved Dolores Mission, the Civic Center, and the all-year parks, including the beautiful 1,000-acre Golden Gate Park. Other features of interest are the San Francisco "Symphony Orchestra," the Opera, the M.H. De Young Memorial Museum (art), the California Palace of the Legion of Honor, the Wells Fargo Historical Collection, and the Steinhart Aquarium. Across the bay are **Oakland** and **Berkeley,** site of the University of California; Stanford University is at nearby **Palo Alto.**

San Jose. Key-city of California's prune and apricot industry and world's largest canning center. Lick Observatory is on nearby Mount Hamilton.

Sequoia National Park. Home of the Big Trees. Grove after grove of these gigantic sequoias are the park's greatest attraction. (See also KINGS CANYON and YOSEMITE NATIONAL PARK.) Chief among them is the Giant Forest, where the sequoias are intermingled with white firs, ponderosa pines, sugar pines, and incense cedars. The park rises sharply to the crest of the High Sierras at its eastern border. Here is Mt. Whitney, at 14,495 feet the highest peak in conterminous United States.

Sonoma and Napa Counties. The vineyard of California, one of the greatest grape and wine areas in the world. Luther Burbank conducted his famous experiments here, and his experimental gardens still may be seen at Santa Rosa and Sebastopol. Calistoga, at the northern end of Napa Valley, is a region of mineral springs and geysers.

Yosemite National Park. Yosemite, in California's High Sierras, is a scenic park of mountains, canyons, lakes, streams, waterfalls and mountain parks. Its sights include Yosemite Valley, walled by towering granite cliffs and monoliths such as El Capitan and Half Dome, accented by waterfalls—Yosemite, Bridalveil, Nevada, Vernal; the Mariposa grove of giant sequoia trees (there are two others in the park); and the mule deer and black bear.

COLORADO

Aspen. West of Continental Divide on Roaring Fork River, this early mining camp is now a popular ski center and winter resort, and a summer cultural center. Beautiful Snowmass Mountain, streams, and lakes are in the vicinity.

Black Canyon of the Gunnison National Monument. State road leads to rim of canyon where rock walls drop 2200 feet to Gunnison river. An old trail takes skilled climbers down to the river.

Boulder. Home of the University of Colorado and site of Colorado's first schoolhouse. Boulder Canyon, Roosevelt National Forest, and Rocky Mountain National Park are nearby.

Central City. First town on Gregory Gulch, scene of the first great gold rush to the Rockies and called "the richest square mile on earth." Now the town is partly "ghost."

Colorado National Monument. Near Grand Junction, 17,693 acres of canyons and desert hills are filled with red and yellow sandstone monoliths and columns of fantastic size and shape. There are good views from Serpent's Trail, Rimrock Drive, and Cold Shivers Point. Dinosaur beds are numerous.

Colorado Springs. Famed health and pleasure resort. Here are Pike's Peak, Garden of the Gods, containing many fantastic formations of red and yellow sandstone, Manitou Springs, Cave of the Winds, Cheyenne Canyon, Seven Falls, and Will Rogers Shrine of the Sun on Cheyenne Mountain.

Cripple Creek. In the mining era, one of the richest gold fields in the world.

Denver. The state capital's beautiful Civic Center and Capitol Hill are marked by fine architecture, murals, and statuary. The city park has a color-lighted electric fountain in the center of its lake. Rare western history collections are in the Public Library and the State Museum. Denver is the home

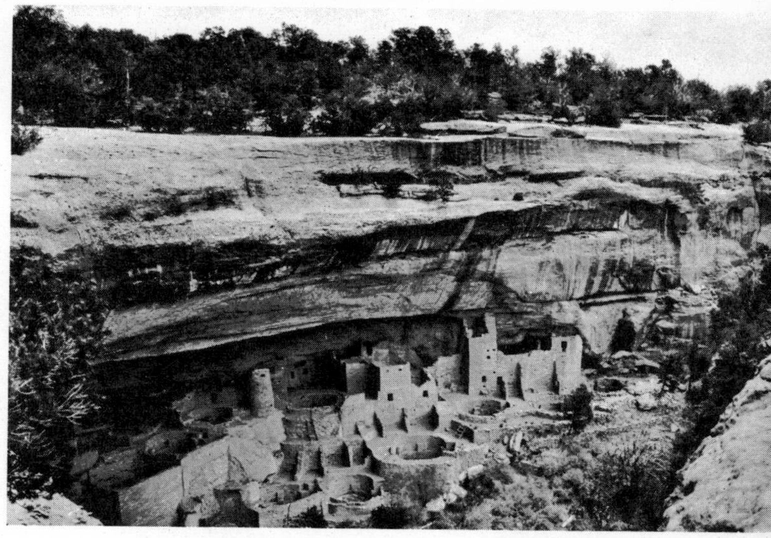

Cliff Palace, Mesa Verde National Park

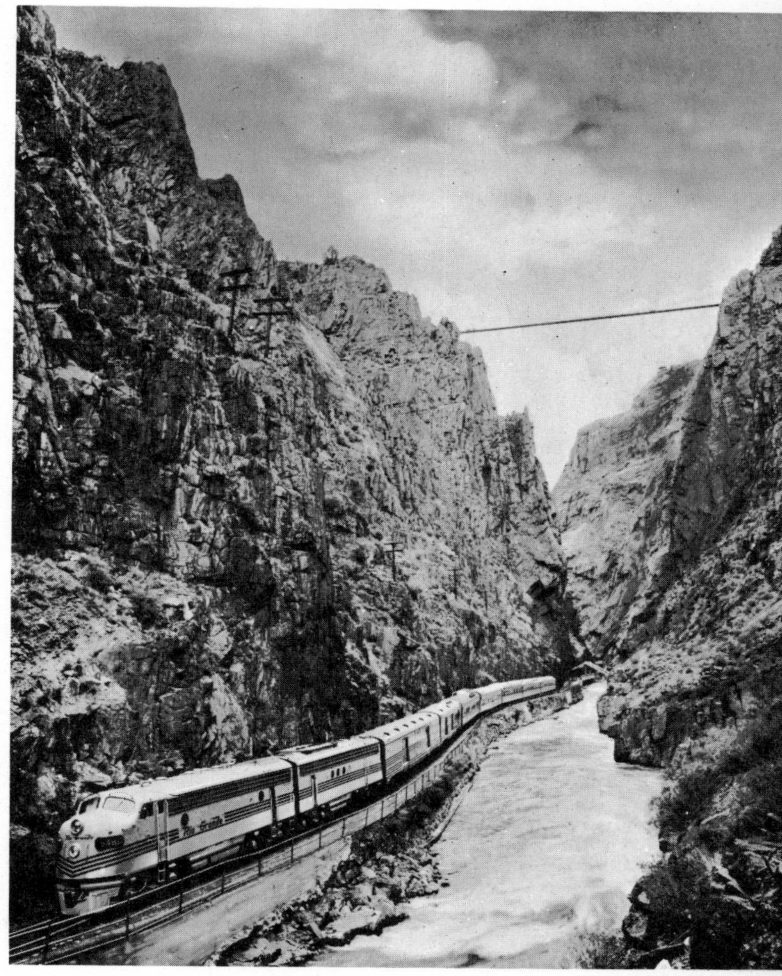

Spectacular Royal Gorge, Colorado D.&R.G.W. R.R.

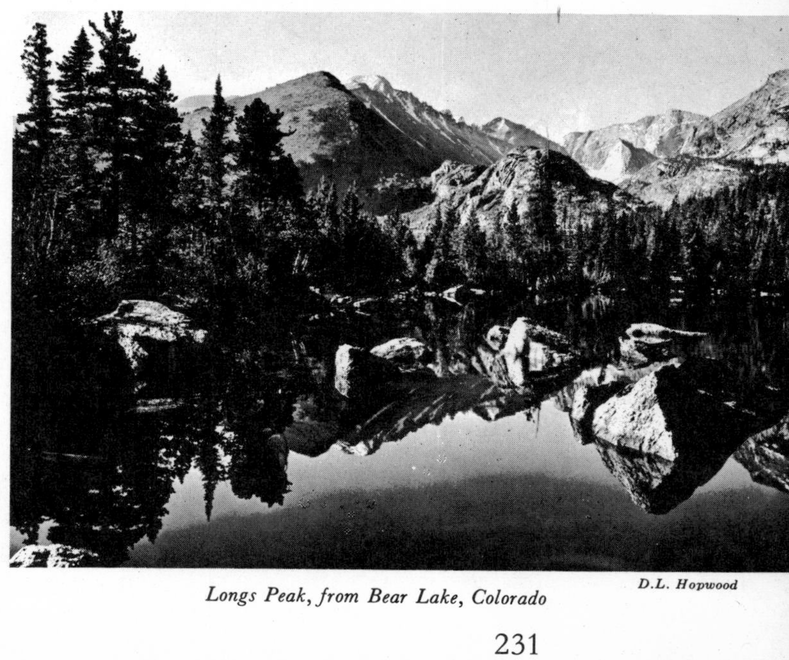

Longs Peak, from Bear Lake, Colorado D.L. Hopwood

231

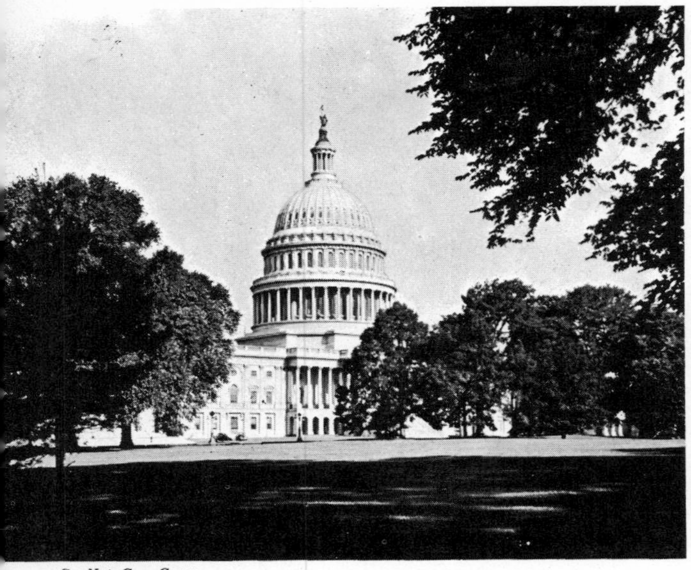

Gr. Nat. Cap. Comm.

Capitol of the United States, Washington, D.C.

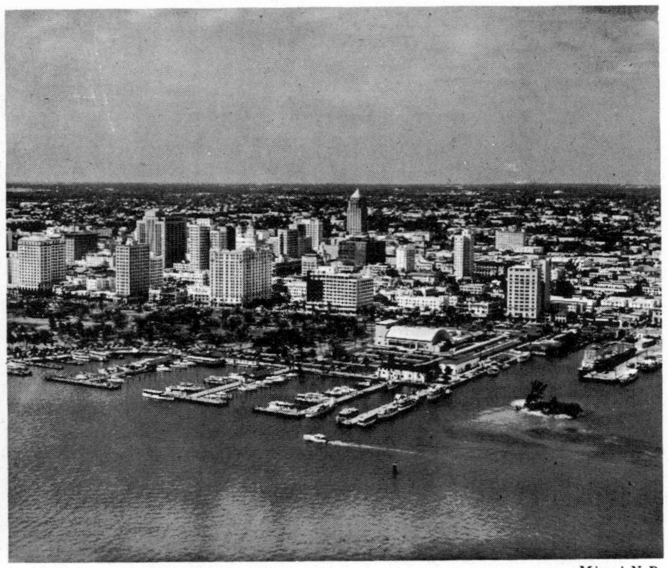

Miami, Florida, City of Sunshine

Miami N.B.

of the first Juvenile Court, the Emily Griffith Opportunity School and the University of Denver. A U.S. Mint is here, and the Denver Union Stockyards. The National Western Stock Show and Rodeo is an annual attraction in January. The Mountain Parks System includes Red Rocks, with its outdoor theater, Echo Lake, Mount Evans, and Lookout Mountain, with Buffalo Bill's grave.

Dinosaur National Monument. Over 205,000 acres of dinosaur beds in Colorado and Utah.

Estes Park. Gateway to Rocky Mountain National Park and headquarters for many vacationers.

Glenwood Springs. Hot mineral springs resort at mouth of Glenwood Canyon of the Colorado River.

Grand Mesa. Flat-topped, high-altitude mountain (10,500 feet) in Grand Mesa National Forest—a land of lakes, fishing, camping, and winter sports. Land's End is a vantage point on the Mesa's rim that offers a panoramic view of hundreds of miles.

Leadville. This highest city in the United States (10,152 feet) has around it the storied gold and silver mines of early-day Colorado. It was the home of the fabulous H. A. W. Tabor and the locale of his mines; it is still the heart of a rich mining region. Nearby Mt. Elbert is the highest peak in Colorado.

Mesa Verde National Park. A great plateau carved by deep canyons, in whose walls are hundreds of prehistoric Indian cliff dwellings. Cliff Palace alone contains more than 200 rooms and a score of kivas. The region is reached by the spectacular Million Dollar Highway, through the most rugged mountains and canyons of the Rockies.

National Monuments. See BLACK CANYON OF THE GUNNISON; COLORADO NATIONAL MONUMENT; DINOSAUR NATIONAL MONUMENT; and U. S. NATIONAL PARK SYSTEM, pages 224-25.

Ouray. Mountain mining town, famous in goldmining history as the home of Thomas F. Walsh and his Camp Bird Mine, which is still in operation, as are others in the region. Footpaths and horseback trails to mountain viewpoints, towering peaks and mountain cataracts, Box Canyon with its falls and cavern, are attractive to tourists. This is the northern terminal of the Million Dollar Highway to the southwestern tip of the state.

Pagosa Springs. Mineral springs and health resort. It is just west of the Continental Divide, crossed by spectacular Wolf Creek Pass.

Pueblo. Colorado's second largest city, notable for its huge smelters and steel plants.

Rocky Mountain National Park. Astride the Continental Divide, here is a land of snow-capped mountain ranges, sparkling lakes, pine and fir and quaking aspen, elk, deer, and bighorn sheep, and much other wildlife. Trail Ridge Road, a wide and beautiful highway, crosses the park and drops down

the west side of the Divide to Grand Lake. Among many other sights, the Mummy Range, the Never Summer Range, Iceberg Lake, and Specimen Mountain are seen from the Trail Ridge Road.

Royal Gorge. Deep and colorful canyon of the Arkansas River, near Canon City. An 880-foot suspension bridge swings across the top of the Gorge, 1,053 feet above the river.

San Luis Valley. Largest mountain park in Colorado, near the head of the Rio Grande, and a fertile and important agricultural area. The state's earliest-settled region, it still retains the atmosphere of the first Spanish and Mexican settlements. Among many scenic attractions, it contains the Great Sand Dunes National Monument.

Uravan. Site of one of the most extensive uranium deposits in the world; in Montrose County.

CONNECTICUT

Bridgeport. Industrial city, famous as the home of the circusman, P. T. Barnum. Among the points of interest are the Tom Thumb House, P. T. Barnum Museum, and Seaside Park, which contains Barnum's statue.

East Haddam. At the cemetery, above the Connecticut River, stands the schoolhouse where Nathan Hale taught. Uniquely furnished Gillette Castle, once the country estate of William Gillette, the famous actor, has become a state park.

Guilford. More than 150 old houses still remain in this well-preserved village, settled in 1639 by Reverend Henry Whitfield. His stone home is now a historical museum.

Hartford. State capital and famous insurance center. The Capitol, on a swelling crest of land, overlooks the other State buildings to the south and Bushnell Park to the north. Several blocks to the northeast stands the Old State House, designed by the colonial architect, Bulfinch, in 1796. Between Main and Prospect Streets are grouped the Wadsworth Athenaeum, Morgan Memorial, Colt Memorial, and Avery Memorial.

Marine Historical Museum. At Mystic, former clipper shipbuilding center. The museum houses an outstanding collection of clipper models.

Newgate Prison. In the countryside near East Granby. The dungeons and leg chains serve as grim reminders of punishments used in Colonial days.

New Haven. Graceful elms edge the streets of the home of Yale University. Noteworthy structures connected with the University are Connecticut Hall (built in 1752), Payne Whitney Gymnasium, Harkness Memorial Tower, Sterling Memorial Library, Gallery of Fine Arts, Sprague Memorial Hall, and the Yale Bowl.

New London. Former whaling town. Among its educational institutions are the U. S. Coast Guard

Academy and Connecticut College. Across the river, north of Groton, lies the U. S. Navy Submarine Base.

DELAWARE

Dover. State capital since 1777. The Georgian-Colonial-style State House, first completed in 1792, has undergone several remodelings and additions. Christ Church dates from 1734.

Lewes. Here the first white men of the Delaware River Region settled in 1630. Early Colonial antiques are exhibited in Zwaanendael House, an adapted model of Town Hall at Hoorn, Holland. Cannons used in War of 1812 stand in Memorial Park. Lewes Beach stretches along Delaware Bay.

Newark. University of Delaware campus cuts through the town. Of special interest are Old College, Elliott Hall, and Mitchell Hall.

New Castle. Colonial appearance is preserved by stately 17th-century homes and buildings. Market and Courthouse Squares comprise The Green, plotted by Peter Stuyvesant. The Old Court House was the State Capitol until 1777. Its central portion was completed in 1704, and its east wing was begun before 1698. Immanuel Church dates from 1710. Town Common, a common land grant of the Dutch era, lies west of the city; this farming tract still yields revenue to the city.

Rehoboth Beach. White sand beaches, fronting Atlantic Ocean, draw vacationers throughout the state and give town the title "Delaware's Summer Capital." Annually, art exhibits line the boardwalk near Virginia Avenue.

Wilmington. Largest city in the state and heavily industrialized. A stone monument, at The Rocks, marks the site of Fort Christina, the original Swedish settlement of 1638. Old Swedes (Holy Trinity) Church, built in 1698, presents a gray-stone facade with a hooded gable roof. The approach from Church Street leads through the cemetery where the earliest legible stone marker bears the date 1719. The Historical Society of Delaware, housed in Old Town Hall (1798), includes in its collection a portion of the eastern terminal stone of the Mason and Dixon Line.

DISTRICT OF COLUMBIA

Washington. Considered by many the most beautiful capital in the world. Washington was planned by George Washington, Thomas Jefferson, and the French engineer, Major Pierre Charles L'Enfant.

Among the government buildings are the Capitol; White House; Library of Congress, largest in the world; the State Treasury, and other department buildings; the Pentagon, home of the Department of Defense; and the United States Supreme Court Building. The Smithsonian Institution administers ten bureaus, including the United States National Museum, the National Zoological Park, the Bureau of American Ethnology, the Freer Gallery of Art, and the National Gallery of Art, home of the Andrew Mellon Collection and others.

The Grecian charm of the Lincoln Memorial, the clean, straight shaft of the 555-foot Washington Monument, and the classic dignity of the Thomas Jefferson Memorial are beauty spots in the capital, which is at its loveliest when the cherry trees blossom in the spring. The Lincoln Museum (Ford's Theatre), containing a great collection of Lincolniana, and the House Where Lincoln Died have been made National Memorials. At Arlington National Cemetery, on the Virginia side of the Potomac, is the grave of President John F. Kennedy and the Tomb of the Unknown Soldier. The Custis-Lee Mansion, on a hillside in the cemetery, is now a National Memorial.

FLORIDA

Cape Kennedy. Home of the astronauts. From here on May 5, 1961, Commander Alan Shepard became our first man in space.

Daytona Beach. World-famous international speedway.

Everglades National Park. Including part of the Florida Keys, the Ten Thousand Islands, and Big

Cypress Swamp, the 2,000 square miles of tropical and sub-tropical wilderness, marsh, and semi-aquatic grasslands comprise America's third largest national park. Here are alligator and otter, raccoon, bobcat, and cougar; snowy egret and white and wood ibis; and tropical trees and other plants found nowhere else in the United States.

Jacksonville. Fourth largest city in Florida and most important commercially on the south Atlantic seaboard. Near the mouth of the St. Johns River, it is a great ship port and yacht harbor. The Oriental Gardens offer an orange grove and lush plantings of Florida flowers.

Key West. At the tip of Florida's long chain of keys, Key West is a tropical city with Latin atmosphere; its most modern note is the superb Overseas Highway that reaches it by traversing the whole chain of keys. Turtle, sponge, and deep-sea fishing are of interest, as are also the quaint old houses built by ships' carpenters. A United States Naval Station has been based there since 1823. Fort Jefferson National Monument is reached by boat or plane.

Lake Okeechobee. Florida's largest fresh-water lake, claiming the country's best black bass fishing.

Miami and Miami Beach. Cosmopolitan Miami, largest city in Florida, is important as a financial, transportation, and recreation center. Sights include the Hialeah Park with its race track, its avenues of royal palms, and its flamingos; the city docks where the fishing fleets unload, and the steamship piers; the International Airport; the Seminole Indian Village. At nearby Coral Gables is the University of Miami. MacArthur and other causeways cross Biscayne Bay to Miami Beach, fashionable resort.

Ocala. Hub of Florida's thriving Brahman cattle industry, center of an important citrus fruit area, and resort town in the north-central lake district, which is studded with lakes and springs, parks and recreational areas. At Silver Springs, the largest of the state's many springs, the flow of water is estimated at from 500,000,000 to 800,000,000 gallons a day; glass-bottomed boats, a jungle tour, and a fine bathing beach are attractions.

Orlando. Citrus center of lake area. Lake Eola Park and Orlando Zoo are natural homes for Florida's native flowers, trees, and animals.

Palm Beach and West Palm Beach. Luxury resorts popular among the socially elect.

Pensacola. Old and historically interesting city, with a definitely Spanish air. Plaza Ferdinand VII is on the site of the city's first fort; many old forts are around the harbor and elsewhere. Old Christ Church was built in 1835. Modern points of interest are the huge Naval Air Station nearby, the picturesque red snapper fleet, and the fine beaches across the bay on Santa Rosa Island.

St. Augustine. Oldest city in the United States. Founded in 1565. The Plaza de la Constitucion was the parade grounds of the first settlement; other landmarks include America's oldest house and oldest schoolhouse; the Spanish Treasury; Zero Milestone where the Spanish trail to California began; the old city gates; Castillo de San Marcos, the oldest masonry fort in the nation, now a National Monument. The Fountain of Youth Gardens have a central fountain where Ponce de León supposedly drank the waters of eternal life.

St. Petersburg. The west coast's important resort, lying on a climatically favorable and sunny peninsula between Tampa Bay and the Gulf of Mexico; numerous causeways and bridges.

Suwannee River. Beautiful river made romantic by the song, "Old Folks at Home." At White Springs is the Stephen Foster Memorial; dioramas in the museum tell his songs' stories.

Tallahassee. The state's capital, of which the grounds are a beautifully wooded park. There are many points of interest, among them Walker Memorial Library, containing Indian relics and pieces of armor dating from De Soto.

Tampa. South Florida's most important commercial city. An early Spanish trading post, it was

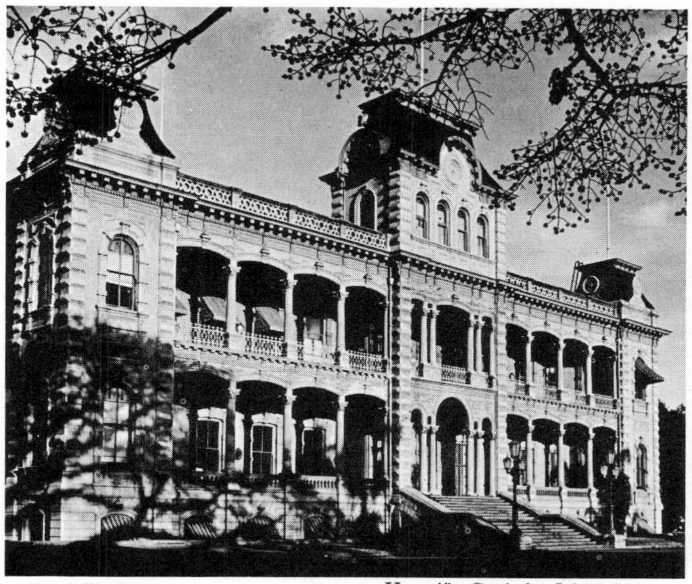

Hawaii's Capitol—Iolani Palace

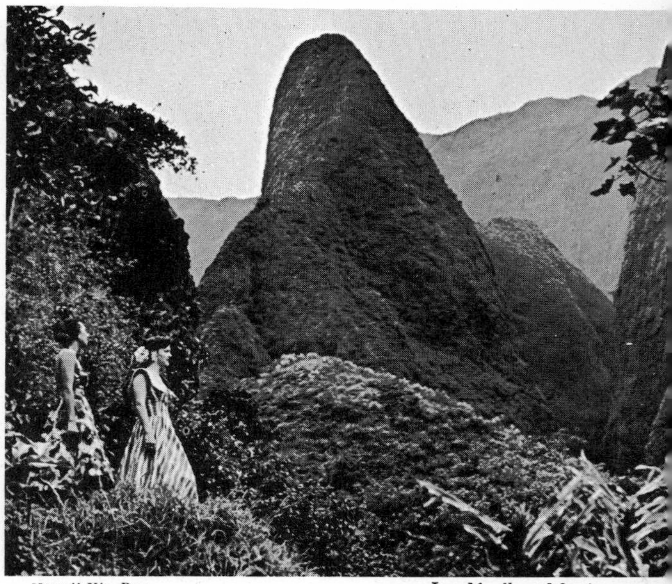

Iao Needle—Maui

later a base for José Gaspar and other west coast pirates. Among important exports, its handmade cigars are famous.

GEORGIA

Andersonville Prison Park. Site of famous Confederate Military Prison. Providence Spring, said to have bubbled forth in answer to prayers of prisoners, is still to be seen.

Athens. Home of the University of Georgia, chartered in 1785, the oldest university in the state. Overlooking Oconee River, Athens retains much of the atmosphere of the old South.

Atlanta. Capital of the state and one of the great railroad and banking centers of the United States. Here is the "Wren's Nest," home of Joel Chandler Harris. In Grant Park stands Fort Walker, historic breastworks of the Battle of Atlanta.

Chickamauga and Chattanooga National Military Park. Battlefields where Confederate and Union armies met in one of the great campaigns of the war.

Fort Benning. Largest infantry school in the United States, located nine miles from Columbus.

Macon. Industrial city in the State's great agricultural belt. A stately city, it is rich in historic tradition. Nearby, at Ocmulgee National Monument, 683 acres of prehistoric mounds disclose homes and relics of six successive Indian cultures.

Okefenokee Swamp. More than 600 square miles of swampland wilderness in southern Georgia and northern Florida. A wonderland of flowers, canopied by forests of gum, pine, bay, and cypress, it is inhabited by deer, bear, panthers, alligators, birds, and great varieties of fish.

Savannah. "Birthplace of Georgia," founded in 1733. Famous resort and great export city, Savannah's traditions are among the earliest in America.

Stone Mountain. Near Atlanta; immense granite dome, rises 800 feet above the surroundings.

HAWAII

Island of Oahu
Honolulu. This romantic south-seas tourist center, home of fabled Waikiki Beach and its sentinel Diamond Head, an extinct volcano, is the capital of the newest state. Iolani Palace, the present capitol, served as the royal palace from the 1880's; its Throne Room is kept as it was during the reign of King Kalakaua. The world-famous Bishop Museum houses Polynesian and royal Hawaiian objects; other museums include Queen Emma Museum and the Royal Mausoleum. Foster Park Botanical Gardens with its orchid displays and Kapiolani Park with both an aquarium of Pacific marine life and a zoo with a tropical bird aviary are well worth a visit. Also see the National Memorial Cemetery of the Pacific and the University of Hawaii.

Kahana Beach. Here breadfruit, bamboo, and mango trees mark the site of a once populous old-Hawaiian settlement.

Kaneohe. Fantastic coral formations may be viewed from glass-bottomed boats.

Koko Head Park. Named for the volcanic mountain which dominates the head of land that juts into the sea. A feature of the area is lovely Hanauma Bay, created by volcanic action 10,000 years ago. At the Blow Hole the mighty sea forces its way through a tiny hole in the lava ledge to form miniature geysers rising high in the air.

Laie. A quiet Samoan village where visitors are charmed by the splendid white Mormon Temple, often called the Taj Mahal of Hawaii.

Nuuanu Pali. Seven miles from Honolulu, at the head of the Nuuanu Valley, lies this scenic mountain pass which separates the windward and leeward sides of the island. Here in 1795, during the wars to unite the islands, Kamehameha the Great forced defeated Oahuan warriors over the precipice to death on the rocks below.

Pearl Harbor. United States Naval base. In the harbor lie the sunken remains of the battleships *Arizona* and *Utah*, which entomb the heroes who went down with their ships on December 7, 1941. A monument was erected over the sunken battleship *Arizona* and was dedicated on Memorial Day in 1962.

Sacred Falls. Off the highway near Hauula a crystal stream leaps from the sheer cliffs to a beautiful pool below.

Island of Hawaii
Hawaii Volcanoes National Park. The Kilauea-Mauna Loa section of the park features volcanoes, lava flows, and luxurious tropical forest with giant fern trees. Mauna Loa, largest single mountain mass in the world, rises 13,680 feet above sea level. A trip to the rim of Kilauea is rewarded with a view of lava activity in the firepit. Kilauea last erupted in 1961 and enlarged the Puna Lava Flow, an area of raw cinder cones and steaming lava.

Hilo. Famous as "Orchid Capital," its daily export of blooms numbers in the thousands. The lovely Japanese gardens and a banyan-tree grove in Liluokalani Park delight visitors, as do the ever changing colors in Rainbow Falls, where the Wailuku River cascades over a volcanic ledge. Another spectacular waterfall, Akaka Falls, lies north of the city. The Lyman Memorial Museum features a collection of ancient Hawaiian relics.

Honaunau. The City of Refuge National Historical Park was established in July 1961. It has 180 acres and contains temple foundations dating from the twelfth century.

Kailua-Kona. Site of the old Hulihee Palace, a reminder that the Islands' monarchy sprang from this island. Here also is the First Christian Church, established by missionaries in 1806.

233

Kalapana Black Sand Beach. A tremendous coco palm grove surrounds a jet-black beach, where the volcanic sands are washed by creamy surf.

Kohala. Birthplace of Kamehameha I, marked by the original of the statue of the king which stands in the Palace Square in Honolulu. Nearby is the scenic Pululu Valley once the site of ancient Hawaiian temples.

Mauna Kea. Its snow-capped majesty marks the highest point in the Islands; 13,796 feet.

Puna Warm Springs. Near Kapoho. Lush tropical vegetation, including green ferns, surround waters warmed by volcanic heat.

Island of Maui

Haleakala National Park. The Park features the enormous Haleakala Crater; its floor measures twenty-five square miles, and the rim extends twenty-one miles around. Along the walls, and in the crater itself, bloom rare silversword plants. Rain clouds, borne by the trade winds, find their way into this crater to form world-famous cloud effects.

Iao Valley. A dense green gorge west of Wauluku, best known for the Iao Needle. This freak formation, a solid mass of volcanic stone, rises 1,200 feet.

Lahaina. Romantic and easy-going, this town was a favorite spot of ancient Hawaiians. Here Kamehameha II established the royal capital. Nineteenth-century whalers, also delighted with the locale, spent their winters here.

Maui Ditch. On the winding highway between Wailuku and Hana, through dense forests of bamboo and ape plant, here and there are glimpses of the water gates and tunnels of this famous ditch, important in the battles between the warriors of Maui and Hawaii.

Island of Kauai

Hanalei Valley. This majestic valley can be viewed from a look-out on the highway which skirts the northern coast of the island.

Waimea Canyon. Volcanic rock, sculptured and plunging to great depths, reflects varied colors as mist and sunshine alternately sweep the great expanse which stretches miles into the interior of the island from the south shore highway.

Wet and Dry Caves of Haena. Situated at the base of a volcanic cliff, these large caverns were the gathering place of Hawaiian chiefs. The dry cave is large enough to drive in an automobile.

IDAHO

American Falls. Dam and reservoir on the Snake River, adjacent to Fort Hall Indian Reservation.

Boise. Idaho's capital and largest city is the center of a rich agricultural and mining region.

Of interest are the Municipal Art Gallery, the Capitol, the Veterans' Hospital, and the Julia Davis Park. East of Boise is Arrowrock Dam; northwest is Black Canyon Dam.

Coeur d'Alene. Lumber, agricultural, and tourist city in noted Coeur d'Alene mining area. In this region are Coeur d'Alene and Pend Oreille lakes.

Craters of the Moon National Monument. Volcanic area of craters, cinder cones, lava flows, and stalactite caves; resembles craters on the moon.

Hells Canyon of the Snake River. Spectacular canyon along the Snake at Oregon boundary. From four to nine miles wide and almost 8,000 feet deep at some points; its walls are red, purple, yellow.

Idaho Falls. Center of rich farming region. Idaho Falls of the Snake and the Lavas are nearby.

Primitive Area. In central Idaho, 1,500,000 acres in Boise, Challis, and Sawtooth National Forests; access is by pack-train only. Rugged mountains, gigantic precipices, and sheer canyons.

Sun Valley. World-famous winter sports resort, popular also with summer tourists. To the northwest is the Lost River Range that includes Borah, Idaho's highest mountain (12,662 feet).

Twin Falls. Center of great irrigated agricultural region. Nearby are the Blue Lakes, the Twin Falls-Jerome Bridge, Twin and Shoshone Falls, and the Thousand Springs.

ILLINOIS

Brookfield Zoo. Chicago Zoological Park, in Brookfield, near Chicago. Most of the lairs are of the natural habitat type, without bars. The zoo contains everything, from insects to elephants.

Cahokia Mounds State Park. Site of Monks Mound, largest Indian mound in United States. A museum exhibits many Indian relics taken from the Cahokia Mounds. The park is near East St. Louis.

Champaign-Urbana. These two cities are the home of the University of Illinois.

Charleston. Scene of fourth Lincoln-Douglas debate and site of the grave of Dennis Hanks. Near town is the Lincoln Log Cabin State Park, containing reconstructed cabin of Lincoln's father, built on the original foundation.

Chicago. Vibrant and noisy, the great metropolis of the Midwest sprawls over a 200-square-mile area at the lower western end of Lake Michigan. It is the greatest railway center in the world and the heart of an arterial system of steel rails, concrete roads, waterways, and airways, radiating in all directions. It is called the Convention City. Outstanding points of interest include the Art Institute,

Chicago Natural History Museum, parks and boulevards, Navy Pier, University of Chicago, Planetarium, Aquarium, Soldier Field, Museum of Science and Industry, Board of Trade, Prudential Building, McCormick Place, Stock Yards, airports, and Chicago Zoological Park in Brookfield, where most of the lairs are of the natural habitat type.

Dickson Mounds State Park. Here 230 Indian remains have been exhumed and left lying in their original postures; located near Havana.

Galena. Scene of famous "lead rush" in first half of the 19th century. Built on terraces cut by the Galena River, Galena's houses are placed like chalets in an Alpine village. The first home of Ulysses S. Grant and the one presented to him after the Civil War are still standing.

Great Lakes Naval Training Center. Only major naval unit in Middle West and one of three naval training centers in the United States.

Lincoln's New Salem State Park. Authentic reproduction of the village, near Springfield, where Lincoln spent six of his early Illinois years.

Peoria. Third largest city of state, on the northwest bank of the Illinois River. Located in the Corn Belt, Peoria distilleries draw a considerable portion of the corn crop of the area.

Rock Island Arsenal. Located on an island in the Mississippi River. Here are stored a portion of the nation's war supplies; War Museum.

Springfield. Capital of Illinois. The Capitol and the Lincoln Home are attractions. The Lincoln Tomb in Oak Ridge Cemetery contains the bodies of Abraham Lincoln, his wife, and three of his children.

Starved Rock State Park. On Starved Rock, rising 140 feet above the Illinois River, La Salle built Fort St. Louis in 1683. Legend has it that a band of Indians starved to death on the rock.

INDIANA

Bedford and Bloomington. In limestone region from which comes stone for world's finest buildings. Visiting parties are taken through quarries.

Brown County State Park. In the heart of Indiana's rolling hills and dense woods, Brown County's scenic beauty is world famous. Nearby Nashville has a world-famous art colony.

Gary. In Gary and nearby cities are northern Indiana's steel and associated industries; most of the large plants have tours for visitors.

Greenfield. Birthplace of James Whitcomb Riley. Riley Memorial Park contains the original "Old Swimmin' Hole," and the old Riley Homestead is an authentic and notable Riley museum.

Indiana Dunes State Park. East of Gary. Three miles of beach and sand dunes on Lake Michigan; wooded inland.

Indianapolis. State capital, Indiana's largest city, and center of a highly developed agricultural area. The city is large and spacious; four great diagonals reach its center, Monument Circle, holding the impressive Soldiers and Sailors Monument. West of the Circle are the Capitol and Indiana University Medical Center for Children, where murals and stained-glass windows illustrate the Riley poems. East of the Circle is the Riley Home. (See also Greenfield.) North are the World War Memorial, Scottish Rite Cathedral with its carillon and gigantic pipe organ, and the Benjamin Harrison Home. At the famous Indianapolis Motor Speedway, Memorial Day races are an annual event.

International Friendship Gardens. A hundred acres of beautifully landscaped gardens of all nations; colorful outdoor theaters. Near Michigan City.

Lincoln Boyhood National Memorial. Located near Gentryville, are the grave of Nancy Hanks Lincoln and site of the Lincoln cabin, the fireplace reconstructed from the original stones. At nearby Rockport is the Lincoln Pioneer Village.

Ky. Dept. of Cons.

Cumberland Falls, Ky. — Scene of the "Moonbow"

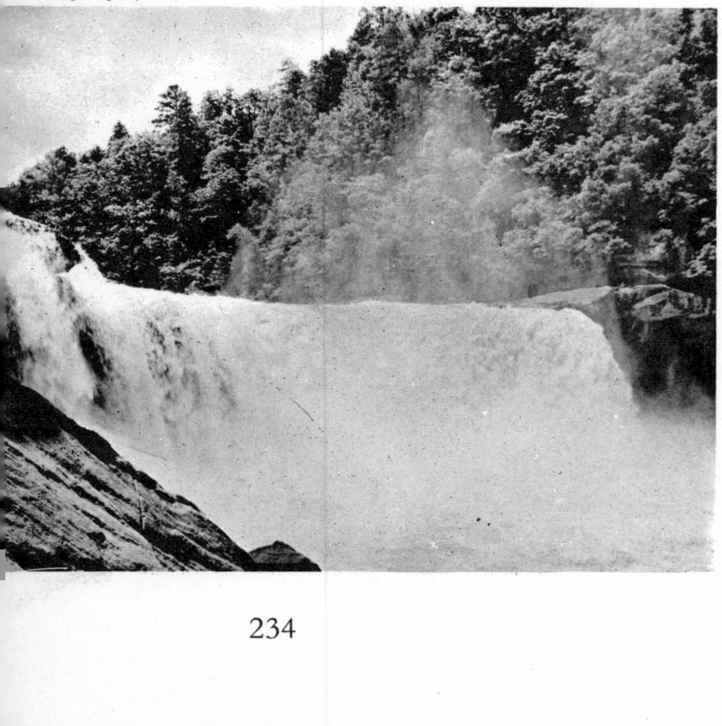

Ewing Galloway

New Orleans' Imposing Jackson Square

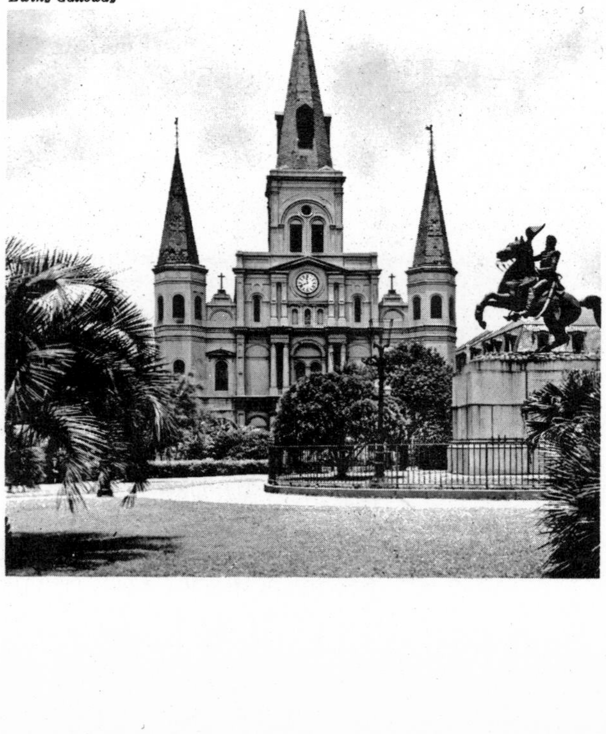

New Harmony. Wabash village founded in 1815 by the Rappites, a religious communal sect. Many of the original stone buildings still remain: Old Rappite Fort, the Community Houses, the Rapp-Maclure Home, the Workingmen's Institute.

South Bend. Home of University of Notre Dame and automobile manufacturing city.

Spring Mill State Park. A pioneer village has been restored around an old stone grist mill, powered by water-wheel. Meal is ground for visitors.

Turkey Run State Park. On picturesque Sugar Creek, famed for its lovely gorges cut deep in sandstone. There is much virgin forest.

Vincennes. Mellow old city on the Wabash River, in the midst of rich orchards and farmlands. First settlement in Indiana, a key city of the old Northwest Territory, and Indiana Territory's capital, Vincennes is rich in history. One of its many fine monuments is the George Rogers Clark Memorial.

Wyandotte Cave. Spectacular caverns, with 20 miles of passages on five levels; near Wyandotte.

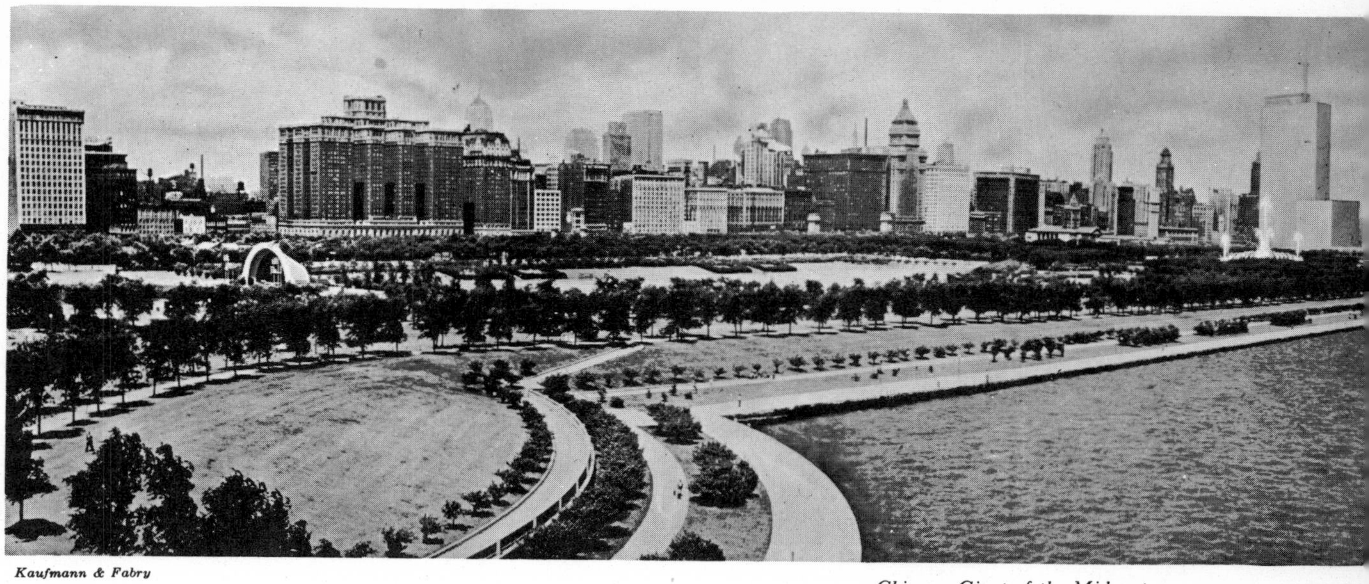

Kaufmann & Fabry

Chicago, Giant of the Midwest

IOWA

Amana Colonies. Seven former communal villages, the first settled in 1855.

Davenport. See nation's largest roller gate dam which operates even when the Mississippi is frozen. Wild Cat Den with old dam and grist mill nearby.

Des Moines. State capital; atop Capitol Hill, the gold-domed Capitol dominates other State buildings clustered on the slopes.

Dubuque. In lead and zinc region, one of the oldest towns in Iowa. Trappist Monastery nearby.

Effigy Mounds National Monument. Near McGregor. Great Indian mounds, some 300 feet long, trace shapes of eagles, bears, and wolves. Nearby are McGregor State Park and Painted Rocks.

Fort Dodge. Vast gypsum fields surround town. In Dolliver Memorial Park, sandstone bluffs edge the Des Moines River.

Iowa City. The University of Iowa campus includes the Old Capitol, of Territorial days.

Maquoketa Caves State Park. Natural bridge, balanced rock, and many limestone caves.

Okoboji Region. Fine resort area including East and West Okoboji and Spirit lakes.

Sioux City. Grand View Park offers a natural amphitheater with outdoor pavilion. At War Eagle Park is the grave of the famous Sioux chief.

KANSAS

Abilene. Famous frontier cow town. Site of the Eisenhower family home and the new Dwight D. Eisenhower Museum.

Council Grove. Historic town on the site of an old Santa Fe Trail campground.

Dodge City. On the Arkansas River, the town was famous as a watering place and shipping point for Texas longhorns. "Boot Hill Cemetery" contains early-day memorials.

Emporia. Birthplace and home of the late William Allen White, noted Kansas journalist. His residence is a show place of the city.

Fort Riley. Military reservation and cavalry post established in 1853 to protect travelers on the Santa Fe Trail from the Indians. The Old Territorial Capitol is nearby.

Fort Scott. On the site of an old army post, of which Carroll Plaza was the parade ground.

Hanover. Near town stands the only original unaltered Pony Express station in the country.

John Brown Memorial Park. This park commemorates the Battle of Osawatomie and includes a museum built around John Brown's cabin, moved from its original site.

Kansas City. Important meat-packing and railroad center. Nearby is Wyandotte County Park and Lake, largest in the state, and also the Old Shawnee Mission.

Lawrence. Scene of the Quantrell raid in 1863; now home of the University of Kansas and Haskell Institute, government Indian school.

Leavenworth. First settlement in Kansas Territory. Nearby Fort Leavenworth, military reservation and officers' training school, was established in 1827. A Federal penitentiary is also at Leavenworth.

Topeka. Capital of Kansas and third largest city. In the Capitol are the "John Brown" murals, by John Steuart Curry. Some of the historical buildings are Constitution Hall, Underground Railroad Station, and the Old Settlers' Memorial Cabin in Gage Park.

Wichita. Largest city in Kansas and important airplane manufacturing and oil refinery center. Points of interest are the Art Museum and the airplane wind tunnel at the University of Wichita campus.

KENTUCKY

Abraham Lincoln Birthplace National Historic Site. At Hodgenville, the birthplace of Abraham Lincoln. Some of the original Lincoln farm is contained within the park. A granite memorial room encloses the birthplace cabin.

Audubon State Park. Near Henderson, once the home of John James Audubon. The museum has superb collection of his bird prints and other Audubonia.

Berea College. Oldest and largest of Kentucky's mountain schools, at Berea; weaving produced by the school is famous throughout America.

Cumberland Falls State Park. Woodland park on the Cumberland River, where a semi-circular cataract makes a "moonbow" under the moon's light.

Cumberland Gap National Historical Park. Daniel Boone blazed a trail into Kentucky through this pass in the Cumberland Mountains. The park is in three states—Kentucky, Tennessee, and Virginia.

Frankfort. Capital of Kentucky. The Capitol and the Governor's Mansion are characteristic of the stately south. The old Capitol now houses the Kentucky Historical Society. Daniel and Rebecca Boone are buried at Frankfort.

Harrodsburg. First white settlement in Kentucky. In Pioneer Memorial State Park is a replica of old Fort Harrod, complete with stockade and blockhouse. The Lincoln Marriage Temple contains the cabin that was the first home of Lincoln's parents.

Kentucky Lake. Man-made lake, formed by Kentucky Dam across the Tennessee River.

Lexington. Home of the University of Kentucky and "Heart of the Bluegrass." Here some of the world's finest race horses have been raised.

Louisville. Kentucky's largest and most important commercial and industrial city; also the famous home of the Kentucky Derby. Points of interest include the Public Library and the Filson Club, with collections of Kentucky history; Iroquois Park; the grave of George Rogers Clark.

Mammoth Cave National Park. In 150 miles of charted passages there are three underground rivers, eight waterfalls, and two lakes, as well as stalactite, stalagmite, and drapery formations.

My Old Kentucky Home State Shrine. The stately old mansion where Stephen Foster was a guest when he wrote the beloved song.

LOUISIANA

Avery Island. Of special interest are the McIlhenny Jungle Gardens and the bird refuges.

Baton Rouge. Winding drives, scenic lakes and bayous, and ante-bellum homes typify the state capital. The present Capitol was built in 1932. The Old Capitol overlooks the Mississippi River.

Grand Isle. Semitropical island in Gulf of Mexico. Once headquarters for the pirate, Lafitte.

New Iberia and St. Martinville. Both on Bayou Teche and settled by French colonists in 18th century. In cemetery at St. Martinville Church the Evangeline Monument marks grave of Emmeline Labiche, supposedly Longfellow's "Evangeline."

New Orleans. Founded in 1718, the "Crescent City" was nearly 100 years old when it became part of the United States. The flavor of its glamorous past has been preserved in the Vieux Carre, or French Quarter. A tour through the Quarter leads along narrow streets, lined with two- and three-story French and Spanish buildings, many with balconies of exquisite iron-lace grill. Views through doorways and porte-cocheres reveal lovely patios and oleander, camellia, and wistaria gardens. Surrounding Jackson Square are St. Louis Cathedral, the Pontalba buildings, the Presbytere, and the Cabildo, home of the Spanish governors. At the French Market foodstuffs are vended in the open. The Mardi Gras, preceding Lent, is one of the most famous annual events.

MAINE

Augusta. State capital on the Kennebec River, which bisects the town. The State House, started in 1829, retains only the graceful portico of Bulfinch's design; the 1911 enlargement demolished the major portion. The James G. Blaine House serves as the Executive Mansion. Fort Western has been restored to its appearance in 1754.

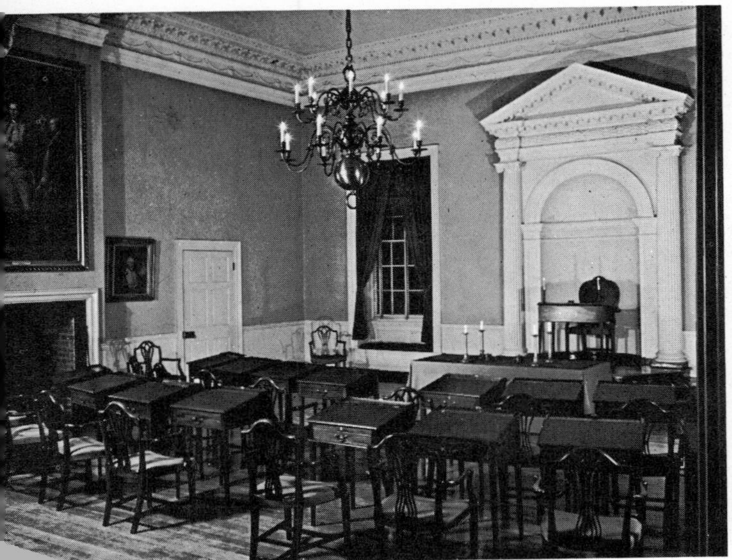

Warren—Md. Dept. Econ. Develop.
Old Senate Chamber, State House, Annapolis

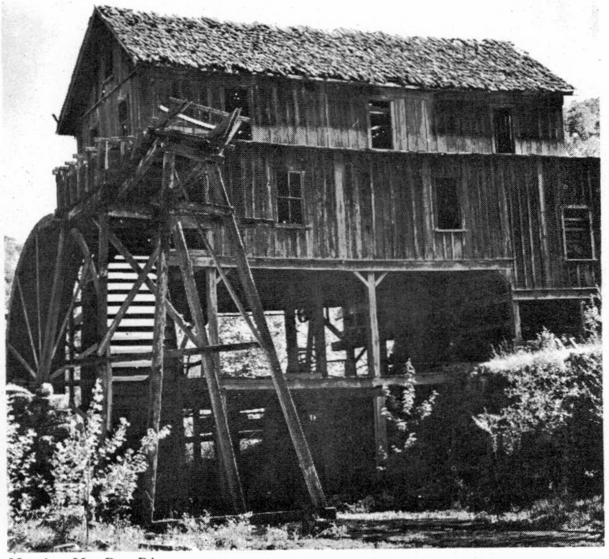

Massie—Mo. Res. Div.
Interesting Old Mill in Shannon County, Mo.

Bar Harbor. Fashionable resort on Mt. Desert Island, gateway to Acadia National Park. The park, a 41,634-acre tract, preserves a section of the magnificent wilderness that was once part of the French grant to Sieur de Monts.

Baxter State Park. More than 160,000 acres of spectacular wilderness. Within area is Mt. Katahdin, highest point in Maine (5,268 feet).

Brunswick. Seat of Bowdoin College. Longfellow stayed at Emmons House while teaching at the college. Harriet Beecher Stowe wrote her famous book "Uncle Tom's Cabin" at the house bearing her name.

Moosehead Lake. Largest lake in state. It is popular with trout and salmon fishermen.

Portland. State's largest city and principal port since colonial days. A monument in Longfellow Square honors Portland's noted citizen. The Wadsworth-Longfellow House, the writer's boyhood home, is open. The Museum of the Maine Historical Society and the Portland Museum of Art, including Sweat Mansion, are among the cultural institutions in the city. Near South Portland, the Portland Head Light, built in 1791, marks the entrance to the Portland Harbor.

MARYLAND

Annapolis. State capital, famous as the seat of the U. S. Naval Academy and St. John's College. In the Old Senate Chamber of the State House, Washington surrendered his commission and (1784) the peace treaty with Great Britain was ratified.

Baltimore. Maryland's largest city, and an important port and industrial center. Products of its diversified industries leave the city through its great harbor on the Patapsco River. Of the many monuments marking the parks and squares, Washington Monument is best known. Among educational and cultural institutions are Johns Hopkins University, the Walters Art Gallery, Maryland Historical Society, and Enoch Pratt Free Library. Outside the city, on a point reaching into the harbor, lies Fort McHenry National Monument, site of the terrible bombardment during the War of 1812, which inspired Francis Scott Key to write "The Star-Spangled Banner."

Frederick. Barbara Fritchie House, reconstructed, contains relics supposedly used by the heroine of Whittier's poem. The home of Roger Brooke Taney, Chief Justice who handed down the Dred Scott decision, preserves his personal effects and those of his brother-in-law, Francis Scott Key.

Hagerstown. In a city park the house of the founder, Jonathan Hager, is maintained. It dates from 1739. Nearby is the Antietam National Battlefield Site.

Ocean City. Important seashore and fishing resort, with marlin ranking highest.

MASSACHUSETTS

Adams National Historic Site. Home of four generations of the John Adams and John Quincy Adams family; near Quincy.

Amherst. Home of Emily Dickinson, Noah Webster, and Robert Frost, and seat of two famous institutions of learning, Amherst College, founded in 1821, and the University of Massachusetts.

Boston. "Hub of the Universe," state capital, leading seaport, industrial and cultural center. Greater Boston, at the mouths of the Mystic and Charles Rivers, includes East Boston, Charlestown, South Boston, Roxbury, Dorchester, Brighton, Hyde Park, and other sections. In the crooked streets and narrow alleys of old Boston it is almost impossible to proceed in any direction without passing a spot of historic significance. The first free public school in America was established at Boston in 1635, followed next year by the founding of Harvard University at Cambridge. In Boston Navy Yard is the reconstructed U.S. frigate *Constitution*, revered by the nation as "Old Ironsides." A tablet marks the spot of the Boston Tea Party. Other points of interest are the Paul Revere House, Old North Church, Battle of Bunker Hill Monument, Boston Athenaeum, Faneuil Hall, King's Chapel, Massachusetts Historical Society Museum, Old South Meeting House, Old State House, The Common and Trinity Church.

Cambridge. Home of Harvard University, Massachusetts Institute of Technology, and Radcliffe College. Among the points of interest are the Botanic Garden, Fogg Museum, the noted glass flower collection at University Museum, and the homes of Longfellow and Lowell.

Concord. Noted for its historic and literary associations, it shares with Lexington the honor of being the "Birthplace of the American Revolution." It was the home of Emerson, Hawthorne, Louisa M. Alcott, Thoreau, and Channing. Hawthorne lived at Old Manse and Wayside, both standing; at Orchard House Miss Alcott wrote *Little Women*.

Gloucester. On the peninsula of Cape Ann, this great fishing port has been dominated by the seafaring tradition for more than 300 years.

Lexington. "Birthplace of American Liberty." It was here that the Minute Men faced the British redcoats and fired "the shot heard 'round the world." In the Common stands a bronze statue of a Minute Man, commemorating the event.

Martha's Vineyard. A large triangular island between Buzzard's Bay and Nantucket Sound, a few miles from the mainland. Its variety of scenery and lively villages have made it a popular summer resort.

Nantucket. Last seaward outpost of New England. With its crooked cobbled streets, quaint comfortable homes, yacht club, artists' colony, beaches, it still retains an atmosphere of the great whaling days. Places of interest are its Whaling Museum; Friends

Meetinghouse; Old Mill, dating from 1746; and Oldest House, built in 1686.

Plymouth. Here is enshrined "the cornerstone of the nation," Plymouth Rock, on which the Pilgrims landed in 1620. There are many fine 17th-century houses and other reminders of the Pilgrim era.

Salem. Witches, clipper ships, privateers, exotic wares from the Indies and China, wharves and docks laden with incoming and outgoing merchandise— all these are conjured up by Salem, historic treasure chest of New England. Nathaniel Hawthorne was born in an old gambrel-roofed house built in 1692; the House of Seven Gables, said to be the setting for his novel of that name, is one of the celebrated structures of Salem. Another is the Witch House.

Woods Hole. Cape Cod port; site of Oceanographic Institute and Marine Biological Laboratory.

MICHIGAN

Ann Arbor. Campus of the University of Michigan extends over half the town. The famous Nichol Arboretum features lilacs and peonies.

Benton Harbor and St. Joseph. Central points in the state's southern fruit belt. Benton Harbor holds an annual Blossom Festival; fruit is marketed wholesale at the Municipal Fruit Market.

Dearborn. Home of Henry Ford. Greenfield Village, model of early American town, exhibits historic buildings moved to this site—Henry Ford's Birthplace; Logan County Courthouse, where Lincoln practiced law; Edison Buildings, including Menlo Park Laboratory; and Luther Burbank's office.

Detroit. "Motor Capital of the World." The Rivera Murals at the Institute of Arts depicts its industrial greatness. In the channel of the Detroit River lies the great amusement park, Belle Isle. In the Detroit Zoological Park, at Royal Oak, animals roam in open areas resembling their natural habitat. Grosse Point, residential section, fronts on Lake St. Clair.

Holland. Dutch settled here in 1847. Now famous for the Annual Tulip Festival, the Netherlands Museum, and the Wooden Shoe Factory.

Isle Royale National Park. This island wilderness lies in Lake Superior fifty miles off the Upper Peninsula. Moose, coyote, mink, beaver, and snowshoe rabbit find a haven here. Wildflowers grow in profusion among the hardwoods and conifers.

Lansing. State capital and important automobile manufacturing center.

Mackinac Island. Boats ferry from Mackinaw City, where automobiles are left behind. Horsedrawn buggies and bicycles provide transportation to Ft. Mackinac, Astor Fur Post, and Arch Rock. Father Marquette is buried at St. Ignace, across the Straits of Mackinac.

Sault Ste. Marie. Michigan's first permanent white settlement. Through the famous "Soo" locks and St. Marys Ship Canal passes America's greatest marine commercial tonnage.

Traverse City. Deep-sea fishing resort in the heart of cherry land. Each May the Blessing of the Cherry Blossoms is held and there is an annual Cherry Festival in mid-July.

MINNESOTA

Alexandria. Resort town in western part of state. The much discussed Kensington Runestone is on exhibit here. Runic inscription on stone tells of visit to this area by Norsemen in year 1362.

Bemidji. Named for Chief Bemidji, leader of a band of Chippewa, whose settlement was located at the present site of the city on the southern end of Lake Bemidji. The legendary stories of Paul Bunyan add to the romantic folklore of Bemidji.

Duluth. Third of Minnesota's cities in size. From the western tip of Lake Superior, the city is 800 feet above the lake level. The Duluth-Superior port is fifth only to New York City in annual tonnage.

Grand Marais. Gateway to the Arrowhead country and the Superior-Quetico canoe country.

Hibbing-Virginia. Two important mining towns in the great Mesabi Iron Range. The largest open pit iron mine in the world is at Hibbing.

Indian Reservations. The WHITE EARTH INDIAN RESERVATION is the largest; authentic Indian customs and language are maintained at the RED LAKE RESERVATION. Chippewas are predominant.

Lake of the Woods. On the Canadian border, this region is a paradise for fishers and hunters.

Minneapolis. Largest city in the state, and one of the largest flour-producing cities in the world. It has a wonderful system of boulevards, lakes, and parks, including the Falls of the Minnehaha, immortalized by Longfellow's "Hiawatha." Minneapolis is the home of the University of Minnesota and the well known Minneapolis Symphony Orchestra.

Pipestone National Monument. Famed quarries of red stone, used by the Plains Indians for material for their ceremonial pipes.

Rochester. Home of famed Mayo Clinic. Health seekers descend on Rochester from every state in the Union and from nearly every country in the world. Transient guests double the official population; because of this unique turnover of inhabitants, the town has an amazing number of apartment buildings, rooming houses, and restaurants.

St. Paul. Capitol and second largest city. The industrial, social, and educational life of the entire state revolves around the hub of St. Paul and its Twin City, Minneapolis, just across the Mississippi River.

Superior National Forest. The nation's largest wilderness park. Only by water, foot, or seaplane can the camper or fisherman traverse much of this area. Hunting is prohibited within the greater portion of its boundaries.

MISSISSIPPI

Biloxi. First permanent settlement in the lower Mississippi River Valley. At nearby Ocean Springs, now a resort, d'Iberville founded Ft. Maurepas in 1699. The Old Lighthouse, built in 1848, still blinks its warning to sailors. Beauvoir, Jefferson Davis' last home, is near the city.

Gulfport. Coastal resort. Fort Massachusetts, used as a Federal prison during the Civil War, is on Ship Island, nearby.

Jackson. State capital. At the Old Capitol the Mississippi Ordinance of Secession was passed and Jefferson Davis made his last public appearance. The State Hall of Fame and the Department of Archives and History are housed in the modern War Memorial Building. Mississippi governors since 1842 have resided at the charming old Governor's Mansion. Manship Home was the Confederate headquarters during the siege of the city.

Natchez. Famous for two annual garden pilgrimages, the town is a virtual museum of ante-bellum mansions. The old Natchez Trail, which terminated at Nashville, Tennessee, started at Natchez.

Pascagoula. Modern shipbuilding center on Pascagoula Bay. Old Spanish Fort, constructed of oyster shells and moss, was built in 1718. Horn Island Light, built on stilts over the water, affords an excellent point for study of marine life. It is eight miles from town.

Vicksburg. Site of the famous Civil-War siege which lasted forty-seven days. The battleground of this campaign is well marked in the Vicksburg National Military Park.

Washington. Second Territorial capital and first capital of the state. Under "Burr Oaks," on the campus of Jefferson Military College, Aaron Burr stood his preliminary trial for treason.

MISSOURI

Arrow Rock State Park. On the Missouri River in the central part of the state. Here is the historic Old Tavern, built in 1834, and the Arrow Rock Academy, furnished with ante-bellum objects.

Hannibal. Important industrial city, and home of Mark Twain. Huck Finn and Tom Sawyer roamed the banks of the Mississippi River in this section. The Mark Twain Museum and Home contains much Mark Twain and Hannibal memorabilia.

Independence. Historic frontier town on the Missouri River, eastern terminal of Santa Fe and Oregon Trails; the Overland Stage started here. Permanent settlers came in 1825; the Jackson County Courthouse, still standing, was erected two years later. Independence is the home of former President Harry S. Truman and here is Truman Museum and Library.

Jefferson City. State capital. In the Capitol, of Carthage marble, are the murals of Thomas Hart Benton—a crowded design of Frankie and Johnny, Huck Finn and Nigger Jim, the James Boys, a political rally, and other subjects.

Kansas City. Second largest city, railroad center, and market place. Kansas City grew out of two frontier towns—Kansas, on the Missouri River, and Westport, four miles south, on the Santa Fe Trail. Incorporated as a city in 1853, it is noted for its packing plants and as one of the nation's largest horse and mule markets. Among the points of interest are William Rockhill Nelson Gallery of Art and Atkins Museum of Fine Arts; the $2,000,000 Liberty Memorial; Union Station, designed by Jarvis Hunt of Chicago; Swope Park, with its Zoological Gardens; and the Kansas City Museum.

Lake of the Ozarks. Large artificial lake, formed by impounding the waters of the Osage River behind Bagnell Dam. The lake is about 130 miles long and has an irregular shoreline of 1,300 miles.

Ste. Genevieve. First permanent settlement in state; noted for 18th-century French buildings.

St. Joseph. Important as a manufacturing, grain, and meat-packing center. Situated on the bluffs above the Missouri River, it was once the focal point of the trade lanes westward. This was the eastern end of the Pony Express route, and the Pony Express stables are still standing.

St. Louis. Largest city in Missouri, situated on the Mississippi River just below its junction with the Missouri. Founded by French fur traders, St. Louis is still an important market for raw furs, as well as a center for grain and the production of stoves, machinery, and other manufactures. Points of interest are the Old Courthouse, historically associated with the Dred Scott case; Wainwright Building, one of the first skyscrapers, completed in 1891; seven bridges across the Mississippi; Missouri Botanical (Shaw's) Garden, containing more than 12,000 species of trees and plants; Forest Park, site of the Louisiana Purchase Exposition in 1904; St. Louis Municipal Opera, an open-air theater seating 10,000; Jefferson Memorial, containing pioneer and Indian relics, trophies and gifts to Charles A. Lindbergh after his 1927 trans-Atlantic flight; St. Louis Zoological Garden; and the Jefferson Expansion National Memorial, commemorating westward expansion.

MONTANA

Anaconda. Smelting point for the ores of copper and zinc that are mined at Butte; the Anaconda smelter has the world's biggest smokestack.

Bear Tooth Mountains. Spectacular high plateau, carved by deep canyons and jutting precipices, in southern Montana and northern Wyoming. A scenic highway travels through the area from Red Lodge to Cooke City, at the northeastern entrance to Yellowstone National Park. One of the many peaks is Granite, highest point in Montana (12,799 feet). Nearby is Grasshopper Glacier, where grasshopper hordes are frozen in the ice.

Butte. Fourth largest city and center of the state's great copper-producing region. Numerous old homes and other structures compete in interest with the nearby mines.

Custer Battlefield National Monument. Within today's Crow Indian Reservation, General George A. Custer, with a command of about 262 men, made his ill-fated stand against overwhelmingly large numbers of Sioux and Cheyenne Indians. Marble slabs mark the spots where the men fell, and the cemetery also holds the graves of many soldiers and civilians removed from other forts of the Northwest.

Flathead Lake. Largest body of fresh water west of the Great Lakes, surrounded by magnificent mountain scenery. To the south is the Flathead Indian Reservation and the National Bison Range.

Fort Peck Dam. The huge earth-fill dam across the Missouri forms a 175-mile-long lake.

Glacier National Park. Almost 1,600 square miles, high at Montana's Canadian border, this park is a glacier-carved Rocky Mountain wonderland. The park has sixty small glaciers, in the process of disappearing, and nearly 200 glacier-formed lakes. Alpine flowers and other vegetation are of interest, as well as animal life, including the white mountain goat, elk, moose, bighorn sheep, deer, bear, and many others. Park is part of Waterton-Glacier International Peace Park.

Helena. Capital of Montana. Its streets still follow the line of gulches, as they did when this mining town was first laid out. Helena's oldest building still stands; the State Historical Library has a collection of Custer and Indian relics; a feature of the State Capitol is the paintings depicting the state's history.

Lewis and Clark Cavern State Park. Largest limestone cavern in the Pacific Northwest.

Virginia City. This colorful early gold mining camp has been restored to the 1865 period.

Minneapolis—Nation's Flour-Milling Center

Minneapolis C. of C.

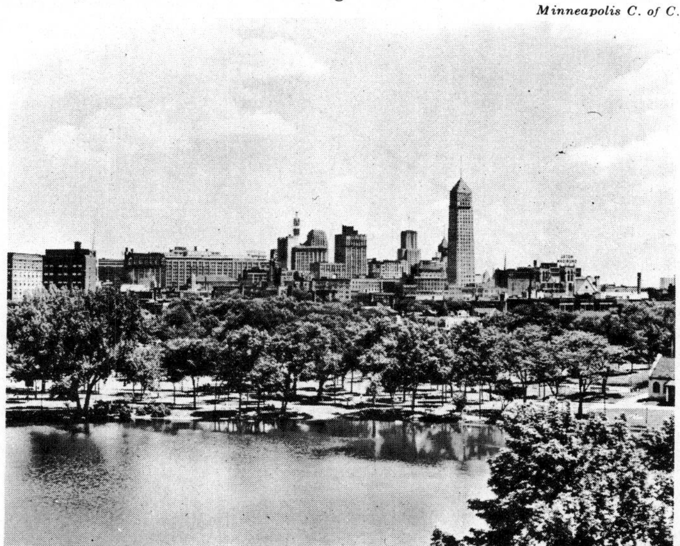

Busy Soo Locks, at Sault Ste. Marie, Michigan

Mich. Tour. Council

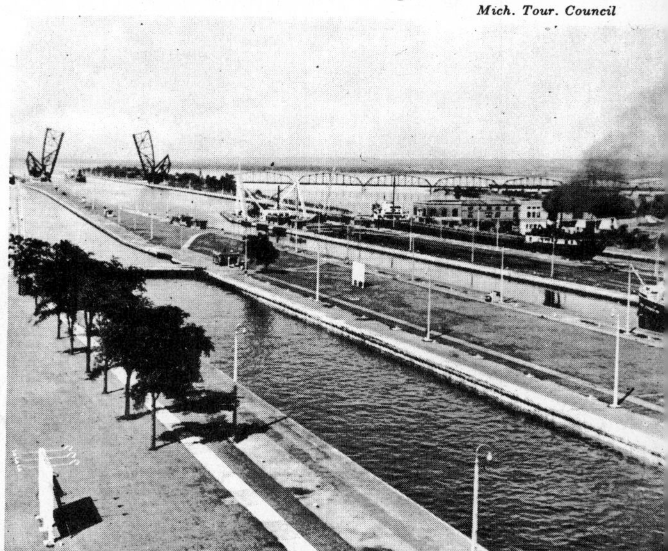

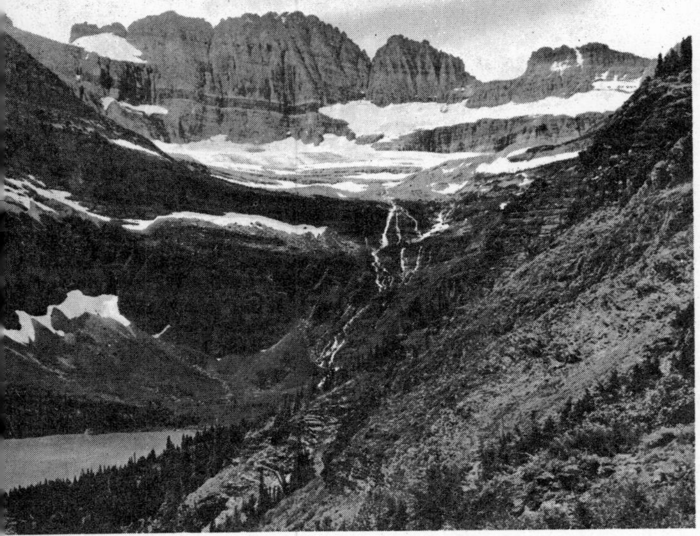

Grinnell Glacier, in Glacier National Park

Glacier Nat. Park

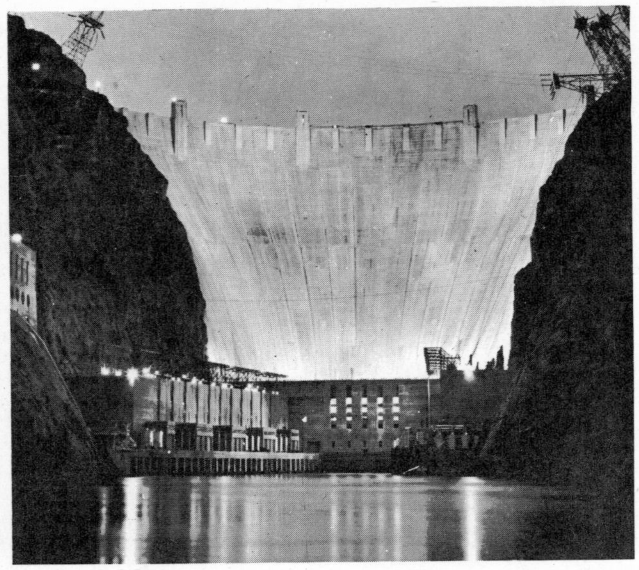

Union Pacific R.R.

Immense Hoover Dam at Night

Yellowstone and Powder Rivers. Heading in Wyoming, but traveling most of its length through Montana and draining the whole southeastern corner of the state, the Yellowstone and its tributaries are closely associated with the state's present agricultural economy and with its eventful Indian and cow-country history. On the Yellowstone are Miles City and Billings, rip-roaring cow towns in the day of cattle empires and still holding the flavor now that the range has taken on the character of irrigated ranches. Here, emptying into the Yellowstone near Miles, is the famous Powder River; from this country still comes some of Montana's best beef.

NEBRASKA

Arbor Lodge State Park. At Nebraska City, home of J. Sterling Morton, sponsor of Arbor Day and a distinguished Secretary of Agriculture. The 52-room mansion has fine pioneer and art collections; the arboretum is a mass of color from spring to fall.

Boys Town. A thousand-acre city, 11 miles from Omaha, founded by Father Flanagan for homeless boys, and managed largely by the boys themselves.

Homestead National Monument of America. Site of first land claimed under the Homestead Act of 1862. Includes Daniel Freeman's pioneer cabin.

Kearney. Near Kearney State Recreation Grounds, site of historic Fort Kearney on the Oregon Trail. Farther west is Gothenburg, where a fur-trading post and Pony Express cabin are preserved; lower 96 Ranch, another Pony Express station, is near Gothenburg.

Kingsley Dam. This earthen dam forms the 23-mile-long Lake McConaughy, which affords excellent boating and fishing; near Ogallala.

Lincoln. Capital of the state and home of the University of Nebraska. From far across Nebraska's prairie, the towering 400-foot shaft of the modern Capitol can be seen.

Omaha. Railroad center of Nebraska and the state's largest city. From here the first transcontinental railway was built across the prairies. Points of interest include the Union Passenger Terminal, the Union Stockyards and meat-packing plants. The Joslyn Memorial, tribute to the founder of the Nebraska Western Newspaper Union, houses an art gallery and a concert hall.

Oregon Trail. Crosses the whole state of Nebraska. All along the course of the wide, shallow Platte River, choked with sand, are markers and monuments showing the path of the white-topped wagons, the Pony Express, and the Overland Stage. Later, the first transcontinental railroad was built along this path. Famous Chimney Rock may be seen along this trail.

Pioneer Village. In Minden a two-block area of twelve museum buildings houses pioneer items.

Scotts Bluff National Monument. Scotts Bluff, a great butte of sandstone and clay in the western part, was an important landmark of the Oregon Trail. Mitchell Pass, a defile through the Bluff, was made passable for wagons in 1852 and used thereafter; the Pony Express and the first transcontinental telegraph went through it. Today's Oregon Trail Museum at its foot contains relics, paintings, and dioramas of the Trail; an automobile road leads to the summit for a view of distant Trail landmarks.

Valentine. Near the junction of the Minnechaduza and Niobrara rivers. Here are dozens of small lakes offering boating, fishing, and camping.

NEVADA

Carson City. Smallest state capital; grown from a Pony Express station and mining-boom town named for Kit Carson. Besides the Capitol, points of interest include the Supreme Court and Library Building, the office of the Carson City *Daily Appeal*, where a newspaper has been published since 1865, the old firehouse, the old mint, the Abe Curry House, and other old homes. The Carson Indian Agency, School, and Museum are nearby.

Hoover (Boulder) Dam. Gigantic dam across the Colorado's Black Canyon, vital to water supply of the whole Colorado River Valley; reservoir is enormous Lake Mead, where water backs up for more than a hundred miles and spreads into tributary canyons. Lake Mead National Recreational Area, surrounding almost entire lake, makes it a vast play center.

Las Vegas. Glamorous winter-summer resort featuring gambling and spectacular shows.

Lehman Caves National Monument. Near Baker; delicate, beautiful stalactites and stalagmites.

Reno. Notorious for gambling and easy divorces, Reno is still a mining town and increasingly an all-year sports center. On the Truckee River in the Sierras, with Lake Tahoe to the south and Pyramid Lake to the north, it has great scenic attraction. The University of Nevada is at Reno.

Ruth. Site of large open-cut copper pits.

Tonopah. Famous old mining town and supply center for Nevada's south-central mining country.

Virginia City. Site of the Comstock Lode, colossal gold and silver lode that made endless millions. Largely "ghost" today, the town preserves many famous old buildings—the Crystal Bar, Piper's Opera House, International Hotel, *Territorial Enterprise* office, where Mark Twain reported and edited.

NEW HAMPSHIRE

Berlin. Northern manufacturing city, split by rushing waters of Androscoggin River, which form Berlin Falls; important ski center.

Concord. State capital. Points of interest include granite quarries, the State House, Historical Society and Museum, Kent House, State Library.

Dixville Notch. Sheer rock prominences rise on each side of a two-mile section of highway.

Franconia Notch. Deep cut between the Kinsman and Franconia ranges. Here is the 40-foot granite profile of the Old Man of the Mountain, made famous by Hawthorne's *The Great Stone Face*. In the vicinity are Indian Head, Echo Lake, Cannon Mountain Aerial Tramway, and the Flume, a deep rift with high granite walls.

Hanover. Seat of Dartmouth College, founded as an Indian school in 1769.

Lake Winnipesaukee. The state's largest lake and well-known New England resort area.

Manchester. Largest city and great industrial center. Located on Merrimack River at Amoskeag Falls, Manchester's industrial growth dates from the development of the Amoskeag Mills in 1810. Points of interest include the Manchester Historic Association Building, Home of General John Stark, Stark Park, St. Anselm's College, the Currier Art Gallery, Weston Observatory, and Massabesic Lake.

Mount Washington. Highest point in New Hampshire; a bald, rocky peak of the Presidential Range, 6,288 feet above sea level. The three-mile cog railway and a motor road lead to the summit.

Portsmouth. Port city for New Hampshire since before the Revolutionary War. Today it is a shipping and service center for the United States Navy Yard situated in the harbor. John Paul Jones' *Ranger* was built here; so was the 74-gun ship *Washington* (1815), as well as the *Kearsarge* of Civil War fame. There are many notable structures in the vicinity, including Old State House, Pitt Tavern, Fort Constitution, Fort Stark, the John Paul Jones House, and the Jackson House.

NEW JERSEY

Atlantic City. Warmed by the Gulf Stream and protected by the New Jersey pine belt, this pleasure resort on the Atlantic Ocean is visited by some 16,000,000 persons annually. It is famous for its boardwalk and five great piers. The Miss America Pageant is held here every year.

Burlington. Settled by Quakers about 1677 and one time capital of the Province of West New Jersey, Burlington is most noted for its historic associations. Among its interesting old buildings are the James Fenimore Cooper House, Thomas Revel House, Friends Meeting-House, and General Grant House.

Delaware Water Gap. On the Pennsylvania border, where the Delaware River cuts through the rocky ridge of the Kittatinny Mountains, the Gap affords a pass for railroads and highways. It is surrounded by a picturesque resort section.

Edison National Historic Site. At West Orange; the prototype for industrial laboratories of today. Established in 1887.

Elizabeth. Settled in 1664, Elizabeth is a residential suburb of the New York and New Jersey metropolitan area, and an important industrial center. Of interest are the Statue of the Minute Man, Boudinot House, Galloping Hill Monument, Nathaniel Bonnell House, Belcher Mansion, and others.

Highlands. Fishing village and summer resort on the Atlantic Ocean. Nearby is the Navesink Lighthouse, which flashes its beam 22 miles at sea. North of Highlands, on Sandy Hook, is the Sandy Hook Lighthouse, 85 feet high and built in 1763.

Jersey City. Situated on the Hudson River, at the western end of the Holland Tunnel, Jersey City is a shipping, manufacturing, and industrial center. Settled about 1630, the city has many reminders of its Dutch forebears, such as the Old Bergen Church and the Statue of Peter Stuyvesant.

Lakehurst. Famous for many years for the U. S. Naval Air Station for lighter-than-air ships.

Morristown National Historical Park. Headquarters for Washington and his men during the winters of 1777 and 1779-80.

Newark. Largest city in the state, active shipping port, and one of the leading manufacturing centers of the country. Newark's airport is one of the busiest in the world. Among the interesting relics of Newark's past are Military Park, used in colonial days as a drill ground; Trinity Episcopal Church built in 1743; John Plume Home, probably erected in 1710; Newark Academy, founded in 1774 and used as barracks by Revolutionary troops.

Paterson. Known as the "Silk City," because the manufacture of silk is one of its leading industries, Paterson is situated on the Passaic River, which supplies power for many manufacturing plants. Paterson Museum contains an excellent mineral exhibit and the first submarine built by John Holland in 1878.

Princeton. Seat of Princeton University, situated on a 1,300-acre campus. Most famous of the many fine buildings is Nassau Hall, built in 1756. The Chapel is the largest university chapel in America.

Trenton. Situated at the headwaters of the Delaware. Important historically, Trenton was the scene of one of the most decisive battles of the Revolution. See the Trenton Battle Monument. The State House is composed of a part of the original structure of 1792; the Annex houses the state museum.

Washington Crossing State Park. Here Washington made his famous crossing of the Delaware. McKonkey Ferry House, restored to its appearance in colonial days, is maintained as a museum.

NEW MEXICO

Acoma Pueblo. On Acoma Rock 60 miles west of the Rio Grande, this fortress-like Indian village is thought to be the oldest community in the United States. Enchanted Mesa is seen from the pueblo.

Albuquerque. Largest city and important financial and transportation center. Old Town section has much of the picturesque Spanish period; the new town is a modern business and residence section. Buildings of the University of New Mexico are in Spanish-Pueblo architecture, as are many fine residences. Of interest are Old Town Plaza, with the Church of San Felipe de Neri (built in 1706); the Sandia Mountain Rim Drive; and Isleta Indian Pueblo.

Bandelier National Monument. In the beautiful Frijoles Canyon where a northern wall is lined with cliff houses and cave rooms. On the floor of the canyon is the Tyuonyi Pueblo, with its ceremonial kivas, excavated 1908-10.

Carlsbad Caverns National Park. Vast limestone caverns, world-famous for size and beauty, are central feature of 49,448-acre park. Many miles have been explored, on three levels; but the actual size of the caverns is still unknown. In the vast chambers open to the public, huge stalactites and stalagmites and massive draperies form King's Palace, Queen's Chamber, Big Room, Giant Dome, Rock of Ages, and many others. In summer several million bats fly from the caverns every evening.

Chaco Canyon National Monument. Prehistoric Indian ruins, the Pueblo Bonito dates back more than 1,000 years and is believed to have housed in four stories 1,200 people.

Fort Sumner. Ruins of old Fort Sumner where Kit Carson held 7,000 Navajos prisoner for four years. Billy the Kid is buried nearby.

Fort Union National Monument. Ruins of an important outpost, and guardian, of the Santa Fe Trail; near Watrous.

Gallup. Coal mining center, once an Overland Stage station; today it attracts nation-wide interest with Intertribal Ceremonial each August, when Navajos, Apaches, and Pueblo Indians gather for tribal dances. The Navajo Reservation and the Zuñi Pueblo Reservation are nearby.

Lincoln. Theater of the famous Lincoln County War of the late 1870's. Lincoln County Courthouse State Monument, branch of the Museum of New Mexico, displays local art and traveling exhibits, and houses much historical and archaeological material.

National Monuments. See BANDELIER, CHACO CANYON, and WHITE SANDS and U.S. NATIONAL PARK SYSTEM, pages 224-25.

Pecos. Ranch town and outfitting point for hunting and fishing on Pecos River. Nearby are ruins of Pecos Pueblo (about 1350) and Apache Canyon where Geronimo, great Apache chief, met defeat.

Santa Fe. Capital of New Mexico and a capital city for 300 years under the flags of Spain, Mexico, the Confederacy, and the United States. Oldest city in the West, it was the terminus of the Santa Fe Trail and was trade and supply center for the whole southwest for many years. Points of interest are the Plaza; the adobe Palace of the Governors, dating from the city's earliest years and housing some of the West's finest historical and archaeological collections; ancient San Miguel Church; Cathedral of St. Francis; art and historical museums; Seton Village.

Taos. Famed artists' and writers' colony. There are three settlements: Taos (Don Fernando de Taos), Spanish town, with the home and grave of Kit Carson; Taos Pueblo, with the ruins of the Mission of San Geronimo de Taos, founded in 1600; and Ranchos de Taos, an old Indian farming center, whose massive adobe church, built in 1772, is one of the most impressive in the southwest. Taos Canyon is nearby.

White Sands National Monument. Desert of glistening white gypsum near Alamogordo. In this vicinity the atom bomb was first tested.

NEW YORK

Adirondack Forest Preserve. Covering almost two-thirds of the state north of the Mohawk River, between Lakes Champlain and Ontario, this park consists of several million acres of private and public land, comprising lakes, mountains, and valley regions. Included is Adirondack Forest Preserve, more than 2,000,000 acres of primitive forest land. Famous Ausable Chasm, three miles from Lake Champlain, is in the preserve; also Lake Placid and Saranac Lake.

Albany. State capital, industrial city, and freight center. Founded in 1614 by the Dutch, it is the second oldest permanent white settlement in the thirteen colonies. Points of interest include the Capitol, costing $25,000,000, and Schuyler Mansion.

Buffalo. On the eastern end of Lake Erie, Buffalo is one of the nation's great ports and grain distributing centers. Among the points of interest are the International Peace Bridge, McKinley Monument, and Albright Art Gallery.

Catskills. Scenic wooded mountain area west of the Hudson. Kingston, the first state capital, and Rip Van Winkle country are nearby.

Finger Lakes Region. In central part of state, it includes the lakes Cayuga, Keuka, Seneca, and Watkins Glen State Park.

Lake George. This beautiful body of water lies between majestic mountains in Adirondack Forest Preserve. At its southern end are the ruins of Fort William Henry; at the northern tip is Fort Ticonderoga, captured from the British in 1775 by Ethan Allen.

Long Island. Extends from the mouth of the Hudson River 125 miles along the Connecticut coast, from which it is separated by Long Island Sound. Considered today as one of America's most important playgrounds, with great country estates, beaches, and resorts, Long Island is rich in historic tradition. The Battle of Long Island was fought here; Captain Kidd is said to have buried his gold on nearby Gardiner's Island; the Whaling Museum and Whaler's Church at Sag Harbor are interesting reminders of whaling days. At the extreme tip is Montauk Point Light.

New York City. Greatest metropolis in the world today, New York City embraces five boroughs—Manhattan, business and financial district; Queens, Brooklyn, and the Bronx, industrial and residential areas; and Richmond (Staten Island), reached by bridge. Flags of all nations may be seen on vessels in the harbor; people of all nationalities are a part of its heterogeneous population. Major among its attractions are Wall Street and the New York Stock Exchange; Central Park and other parks, boulevards, highways, and tunnels; Bronx Zoo; Aquarium; Greenwich Village; the Bowery; Chinatown, Harlem; famous cathedrals and churches; Broadway and Times Square; Metropolitan Opera; Empire State, United Nations Building, and other buildings and skyscrapers; City Hall; great museums and art galleries; General Grant's National Memorial; Statue of Liberty National Monument; Radio City; Columbia University; Brooklyn Navy Yard; Governors Island; Coney Island.

Niagara Falls. Acclaimed one of the seven natural wonders of the world.

Poughkeepsie. Home of Vassar College, founded in 1861 as one of the first institutions in the world to offer women the same educational advantages that universities offered men. Near the city is Hyde Park, estate of the late Franklin D. Roosevelt.

Syracuse. Home of Syracuse University. Once known as "Salt City," because of its production of salt, Syracuse is rich in historic, geologic, and scenic features; Onondaga Indian Reservation nearby.

Thousand Islands. Vacation area of beautiful islands, on the St. Lawrence River.

West Point. Overlooking the Hudson River, West Point is the home of the U. S. Military Academy, established in 1802.

NORTH CAROLINA

Asheville. Mountain resort city and North Carolina's gateway to the Great Smoky Mountains

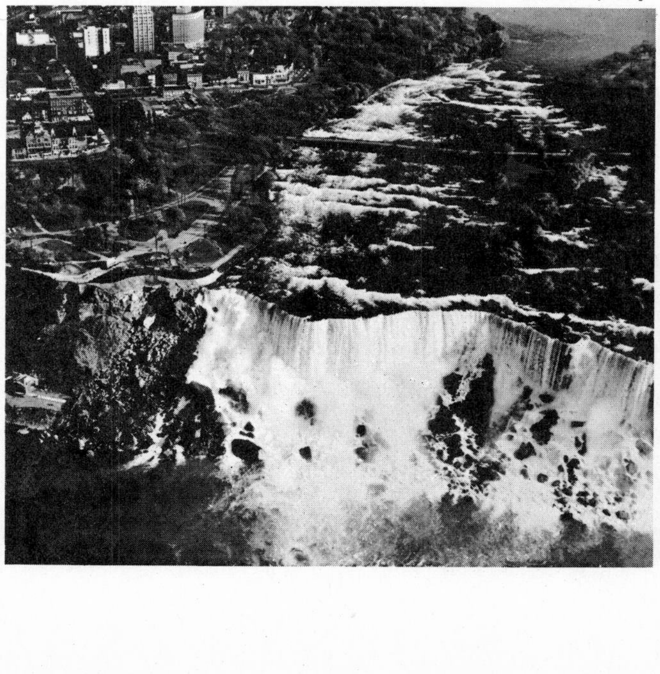
Niagara Falls, Spectacular Source of Power
Bell Aircraft Corp.

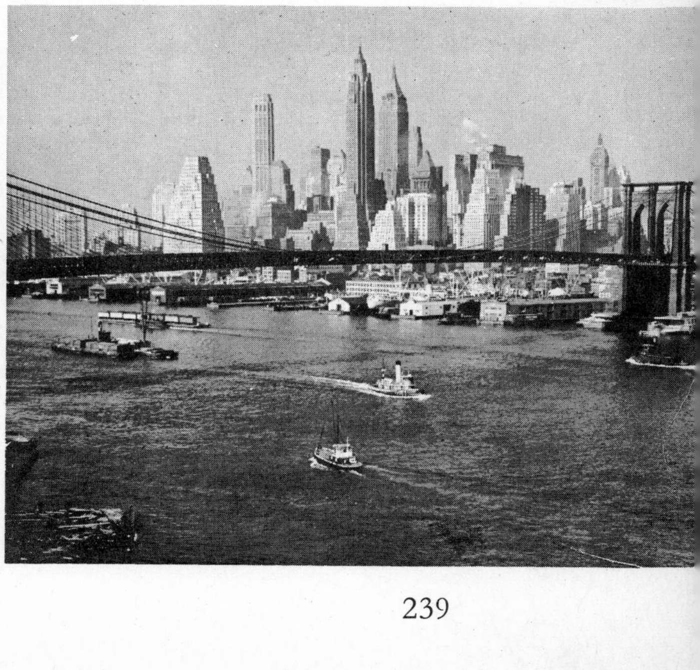
World-famous Brooklyn Bridge, New York
"NYSPIX"

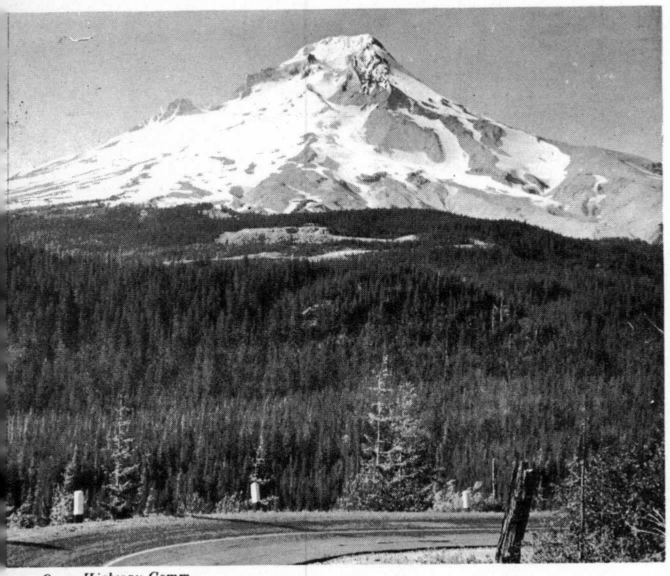

Oreg. Highway Comm.

Mount Hood, Oregon's Highest Mountain

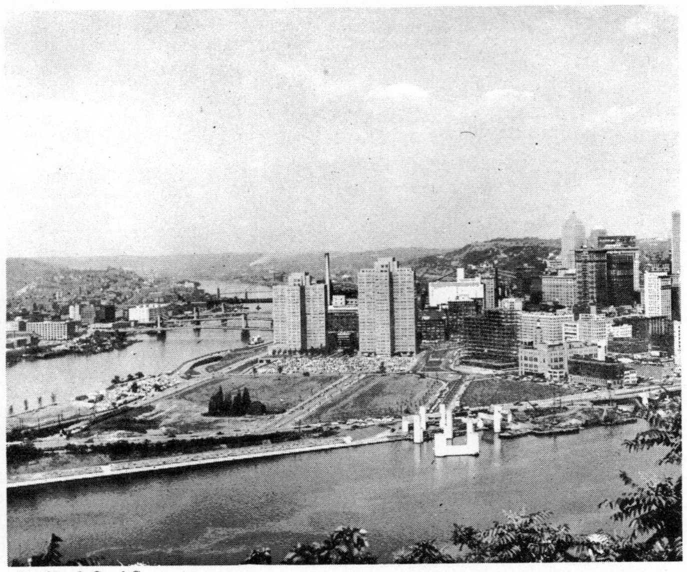

Pittsburgh C. of C.

Pittsburgh's "Golden Triangle"

National Park. The magnificent Biltmore House displays a fortune in art objects. A drive over Elk Mountain Scenic Highway affords an excellent view of the plateau on which the city is located.

Cape Hatteras National Seashore. A 28,500-acre area preserving the flora and fauna, with beach recreational areas. Site of the old lighthouse (built in 1793), is part of the area. Wright Brothers National Memorial is also here.

Fayetteville. Market Hall, once a slave market, then the town hall, now houses the public library. Fort Bragg, a large military reservation is nearby.

Fontana Dam. The highest dam in the TVA system has formed the 30-mile-long Fontana Lake, which is a paradise for fishermen. Fontana Village is the center for this resort area.

Fort Raleigh National Historic Site. Scene, on Roanoke Island, of Sir Walter Raleigh's "lost colony." A facsimile of the setting has been made.

Great Smoky Mountains National Park. Overlaps the Tennessee-North Carolina border. This spur of the Appalachian Range contains many peaks 6,000 feet high. Virgin forest and frontier mountain communities lie in the park. See TENNESSEE.

Raleigh. State capital. The Capitol, a noteworthy example of Greek Revival architecture, is surrounded by statuary of state and national heroes. In the Hall of History, the state historical museum, all phases of North Carolina's history, from the Roanoke Colony to modern transportation, are represented.

Winston-Salem. In 1766 a Moravian group settled Salem. The Moravian Brothers' House, dating from 1769, the Home Moravian Church, and the Moravian Graveyard are reminders of the religious settlers and their influence. In 1913 Winston and Salem were united. At nearby Bethabara (Oldtown), the church and graveyard are all that remain of the original communal settlement of 1753.

NORTH DAKOTA

Badlands. A strange and fantastic region along the Little Missouri River, where the land is carved into a jumble of weirdly colored buttes, domes, ridges, pyramids, and other shapes. The Theodore Roosevelt Memorial National Park encloses the heart of the Badlands area.

Bismarck. State capital; located in the south-central part of the state, on the Missouri River. The 19-story Capitol, replacing the former building which burned in 1930, is an outstanding example of modern architecture. There are interesting Indian and pioneer relics in the Historical Society Museum. The log cabin from Theodore Roosevelt's Elkhorn Ranch stands nearby.

Crow Flies High Butte. From this vantage point the French explorer Verendrye first looked across the Missouri River.

Fargo. Largest city in North Dakota, and the

chief shipping and distributing center. Because of the location there of the North Dakota State University, it is also state agricultural headquarters.

Fort Abraham Lincoln State Park. Lying on the west bluffs of the Missouri River, near Mandan, this park encloses the site of an old Mandan Indian village, now partially restored, and two frontier forts, also restored to show their original appearance.

Garrison Dam. Huge earth-fill dam at Riverdale forms 200-mile-long Garrison Lake.

International Peace Garden. A formal garden, one mile square, on the international border between North Dakota and Manitoba.

OHIO

Akron. The rubber capital of the world. Points of interest include the rubber plants, Goodyear Air Dock, Baptist Temple, and the parks.

Cincinnati. Metropolis of southern Ohio, the city is a cultural center supported by diversified industry.

Cleveland. Largest city, Lake Erie port, iron and steel center. Severance Hall is the home of the symphony, and the white marble Museum of Art houses a collection of Byzantine and European art. The Cultural Gardens are divided into sections in which each nationality presents a representative display.

Columbus. State capital, situated at the confluence of the Scioto and Olentangy rivers. The Doric-style Capitol and the beautiful Civic Center are the show places of the city.

Dayton. Industrial city and home of Wright-Patterson Air Force Base.

Fort Ancient. Prehistoric earthworks enclosing an area of 100 acres; in Warren County.

Marietta. Peaceful trading center of a large farm area. The Campus Martius Museum is built around Rufus Putnam's Block House, where early pioneers took refuge during Indian attacks.

Mound City Group National Monument. Near Chillicothe. Twenty-three prehistoric burial mounds.

Put-In-Bay. Here Commodore Perry defeated the British in the Battle of Lake Erie (1813). The Perry's Victory and International Peace Memorial National Monument commemorates this event and the subsequent peace between Canada and the United States.

Schoenbrunn Village State Memorial. At New Philadelphia. Schoolhouse, church, and cabins of early Moravian village (1772) have been restored.

Serpent Mound State Memorial. In Adams County. Mound extends for a quarter of a mile in the shape of a snake holding an egg in its mouth.

Toledo. Diversified industry supports this city, originally Anthony Wayne's Fort Industry.

OKLAHOMA

Arbuckle Mountains. Located in the south-central part of the state, these aged mountains, worn down to a height of only 700 feet above the surrounding plains, contain a great variety of geological formations of limestone, sandstone, shale, and granite.

Claremore. Rogers County seat, named for Clem Rogers, father of Oklahoma's well-known citizen, Will Rogers. The state erected the Will Rogers Memorial in Claremore on land donated by his widow.

Lake Texoma and Murray. Denison Dam on the Red River, impounds waters to form Lake Texoma, which nudges the southeastern tip of Lake Murray. Both lakes offer water sports.

Muskogee. Once capital of the Five Civilized Tribes—Cherokee, Choctaw, Chickasaw, Creek, and Seminok. The Bacone University for Indians is located here, and Fort Gibson National Cemetery is nearby.

Oklahoma City. State capital and largest city. Settled in the afternoon of April 22, 1889, the date of the "Historic Run." Some of country's largest oil companies have their headquarters here, and there are many oil derricks in the city.

Platt National Park. Well-known for its sulfur, iron, bromide, and fresh water springs. Wild flowers, birds, and small game animals are also abundant.

Sequoyah Shrine. Log cabin of the famous Cherokee Indian statesman and educator. Sequoyah invented the Cherokee syllabary after being intrigued by the white man's language. The Shrine is located near Hulbert and Wagoner.

Tulsa. The state's largest oil refining center. There is a large population of Indians and white people.

Wichita Mountains Wildlife Refuge. Mountainous area lying entirely within Comanche County. Bison, elk, Texas longhorns, wild turkeys and other birds are found in this wildlife sanctuary.

OREGON

Bonneville Dam. This huge dam spans the Columbia River about 42 miles northeast of Portland, supplying electric power over a wide area, and making the Columbia River navigable for seagoing vessels as far as The Dalles. Fish ladders allow the salmon to ascend the Columbia past the dam to their spawning grounds.

Crater Lake National Park. One of the scenic wonders of America, the waters of the lake, 1,996 feet deep, are crystal clear and intensely blue. Hemmed in by steep mountain walls and towering forests, the lake lies 6,000 feet above sea level, in a sunken volcanic crater.

Mount Hood. Oregon's highest mountain, rising 11,245 feet in the Cascade Range east of Portland. Its impressive snow-capped pyramidal peak can be seen from a great distance. Comparatively easy to ascend, by tramway and chairlift, it is a popular recreational area, offering magnificent views from its summit.

Oregon Caves National Monument. A series of caves in Elijah Mountain in the Siskiyou Range, known as "The Marble Halls of Oregon." The mountain is a labyrinth of corridors and caverns of weird beauty, filled with strange and intricate marble formations. The region around the caves has been set aside as a game refuge.

Portland. The largest city of Oregon and one of the leading lumber-shipping ports in the world; also known as "the City of Roses." The annual Rose Festival is held in June. Points of interest include the Portland Art Museum; the Civic Auditorium, which houses the Oregon Historical Society Collection; the Rough Rider Statue of Theodore Roosevelt; the statue of Sacajawea, the "Bird Woman," in Washington Park; the sunken rose gardens in Peninsula Park; and the Forestry Building.

Snake River Canyon. See Idaho.

PENNSYLVANIA

Bethlehem. Steel city and music center; home of the Bach Festival, and of the Moravian College (1742). The log Gemein Haus (1741) is the oldest structure in the city.

Chester. Second oldest city in state, settled by the Swedes in 1644. The Caleb Pusey House, in nearby Upland, is the oldest English-built house in the state (1683). Other old-time houses are the Washington House, where General Washington stayed after the Battle of Brandywine, and the Friends Meetinghouse, erected in 1736.

Delaware Water Gap. A scenic three-mile gorge in the Kittatinny Mountains near Stroudsburg. Northwest are the beautiful Pocono Mountains.

Erie. State's only port on the Great Lakes. Of historic interest are the Wayne Memorial, a reproduction of the blockhouse where "Mad Anthony" Wayne died in 1796; the Old Custom House; and Perry's flagship, the *Niagara*.

Fort Necessity National Battlefield. Reconstructed stockade, scene of opening of French and Indian Wars.

Gettysburg. Scene of the Battle of Gettysburg and site of the Soldiers' National Monument, where Lincoln delivered his immortal Gettysburg Address.

Harrisburg. State capital, on the Susquehanna River. There are six buildings in the Capitol group, including the Capitol, flanked by the George Gray Barnard sculptured group.

Lancaster County. Pennsylvania Dutch country.

Philadelphia. Fourth largest American city, important port, and great industrial center. Here starts the great Pennsylvania Turnpike, a fast four-lane highway that goes to the Ohio border, via Pittsburgh. Founded in 1682 and first capital of the United States, Philadelphia is second to no other city in historic associations. Among its many points of interest are Independence Hall, where the Liberty Bell is exhibited; Carpenters' Hall, where the first Continental Congress assembled in 1774; Benjamin Franklin's grave in the burial ground of Christ Church; Betsy Ross House; William Penn's House; the United States Mint; Bartram's Gardens; Philadelphia Zoological Gardens; Philadelphia Navy Yard; University of Pennsylvania; Philadelphia Museum of Art, and others.

Pittsburgh. Second largest city in the state and one of the greatest steel centers in the world. Pittsburgh is on the Ohio River, at the junction of the Monongahela and Allegheny rivers. The city began as the French Fort Duquesne (1754), which later became the English Fort Pitt. Points of interest are Carnegie Institute and Library; Carnegie Institute of Technology; University of Pittsburgh's Cathedral of Learning, 42-story skyscraper; Schenley Park; Liberty Tunnels, which pierce the bluff of Mount Washington; Fort Pitt Blockhouse; Stephen Collins Foster Memorial Building, Mellon Institute, and many others.

Valley Forge State Park. Here Washington camped in the winter 1777–78. Remains of entrenchments and commemorative buildings are to be seen.

RHODE ISLAND

Block Island. Pear-shaped and studded with low hills and ponds, it lies in the mouth of Long Island Sound. The Great Salt Pond which covers more than 100 acres almost bisects the island.

Charlestown. The Indian Burial Ground and Fort Neck Lot are nearby.

Narragansett. Fine beach; the old casino, the Towers, at the pier is a landmark.

Newport. Famed as an elite summer capital, the city's historic associations are often overlooked. Washington Square is the center of the old city. Nearby are Old Colony House, once the statehouse, and Friends Meeting House. Touro Synagogue, now

a National Historic Site, dates from 1763. The U. S. Naval Base and Goat Island, the Navy's Torpedo Station, are in Newport. The Breakers, Vanderbilt's palatial residence, is open to the public.

Pawtucket. Home of Samuel Slater, the man who built, from memory, the first spinning frame in America, thereby founding the textile industry. The Old Slater Mill, now a memorial, contains some of the original machinery and early relics.

Providence. State capital. Built on three hills, the city was founded by Roger Williams, "Father of Rhode Island," in 1636. Old State House was seat of the General Assembly until 1901. The new Capitol, made of white marble, boasts of a dome which rivals that of St. Peter's in Rome. Rolling woodlands, notable rose gardens, and many lagoons extend throughout Roger Williams Park. Noteworthy collections are found in the Providence Athenaeum and in the libraries at Brown University.

SOUTH CAROLINA

Beaufort. Historic port town on the Intracoastal Waterway. Mellowed residences, surrounded by live oaks, front on narrow, crooked streets. Points of interest are the Oldest House, Tabby Manse, the Beaufort National Cemetery, and Fort Frederick. Parris Island, U. S. Marine base, is nearby.

Charleston. Important city and deep-sea port on the Intracoastal Waterway, six and one-half miles from the ocean. The beautiful harbor with its historic forts spreads before the palmetto-fringed waterfront—"the Battery." In the harbor is Fort Sumter, where the first shots of the Civil War were fired. Charleston gardens and those of nearby plantations have won world acclaim for more than a century. North of the city are the tropical Cypress Gardens, whose moss-laden trees grow in a freshwater lake.

Columbia. State capital. The walls of the gray-granite State House bear scars of Sherman's bombardment. The World War Memorial Building, at the University of South Carolina, houses a historic collection and a shrine to the state's soldiers.

Georgetown. Paper pulp and lumbering center. At the nearby Brookgreen Gardens an outdoor museum of statuary is set among boxwoods, oaks, and flowers. Azaleas and camellias bloom among live oaks at Belle Isle Gardens, also nearby. Myrtle Beach is a little farther up the coast.

Kings Mountain National Military Park. Third largest battlefield park in the United States. In 1780 a Whig force defeated a larger British force entrenched on the summit of the mountain, thus breaking British resistance in the South.

SOUTH DAKOTA

Angostura Dam. This dam impounds the waters of the Cheyenne River, one of the tributaries of the Missouri; near Hot Springs in the southern Black Hills. A reservoir and recreation area are nearby.

Badlands National Monument. Fantastically eroded sedimentary rock formations in many unusual pastel shades. Story book castles and temples seem very real in pink and lavender hues. A weird beauty characterizes this strange land just east of the Black Hills. Numerous fossils and rocks are found among the prickly cactus and wild flowers.

Belle Fourche. Trading center for cattle and sheep empire extending into Montana and Wyoming.

Black Hills. National forest region on the west embracing the highest mountains between the Rockies and the Appalachians. Rising dark against the surrounding colorless plains, the "black" is in reality the brown and green of lofty pines. Popular as a vacation land.

Custer State Park. Features some of the most spectacular scenery in the Black Hills—Needles highway, Sylvan Lake, and Harney Peak (7,242 feet), highest point east of the Rockies. The park covers 128,000 acres and includes a wildlife sanctuary.

Deadwood. Historic mining town and setting for Wild Bill Hickok, Calamity Jane, and other frontier characters. Deadwood Gulch was the center of gold rush of 1876. Adams Memorial Museum houses an excellent collection of pioneer mining devices. In No. 10 Saloon, Wild Bill Hickok was shot in the back holding a poker hand of aces and eights.

Lead. Mile-high city built around the fabulous Homestake Mine, largest gold mine in the Western Hemisphere. Underground shafts go down a mile.

Mt. Rushmore National Memorial. Faces of Washington, Jefferson, Lincoln, and Theodore Roosevelt, carved in granite by Gutzon Borglum, are proportioned to men 465 feet tall. Each head is 60 feet from chin to forehead, twice the height of the Great Sphinx of Egypt. A 500 word history of the United States in letters three feet high is also shown. Three tunnels through adjoining mountains are lined up to focus on Mt. Rushmore.

Pierre. One of the smallest capital cities in the United States. Nearby Ft. Pierre, built in 1817, is the oldest continuous settlement in the state.

Rapid City. Gateway to the Black Hills, it was the supply point for mining camps during the gold rush of 1876. Stratosphere Bowl was the takeoff point for the 72,395-foot balloon flight by General Orvil Anderson and Albert Stevens on Nov. 11, 1935. South Dakota School of Mines and Technology features fossil and mineral exhibits. Dinosaur Park has five prehistoric monsters, molded of cement.

Sioux Falls. Largest city, located on the Big Sioux River. An important processing center for farm products, it is also a cultural and medical center for a large area. Extensive use is made of locally quarried pink quartzite.

Wind Cave National Park. Located in the southern Black Hills, it is a limestone cavern featuring unusual boxwork formations; several miles of lighted routes. The temperature is always 47°F. There is a buffalo herd in the park area.

Great White Throne, Zion National Park

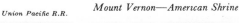
Union Pacific R.R.

Mount Vernon—American Shrine

Va. Dept. of C.&D.

Wash. Adv. Comm.
Grand Coulee Dam, Washington

TENNESSEE

Andrew Johnson National Historic Site. Former president's home and tailor shop; at Greeneville.

Chattanooga. Manufacturing city on the Tennessee River near the Georgia border. Trips from Chattanooga lead to Lookout Mountain (which also may be reached by the Incline Railway) and to Chickamauga and Chattanooga National Military Park. Atop the mountain are the unusual rock formations of Rock City, and Point Park, vantage point for a breath-taking view of Moccasin Bend.

Great Smoky Mountains National Park. Smoky haze hovering about the multi-green mountain tops gives this scenic wonderland its name. The highway from Gatlinburg, headquarters for the Park, passes Mt. Le Conte, Mountaineer Museum, Chimney Tops, and Newfound Gap. At the Gap, trails for mountain climbers wind to the top of Clingman's Dome, highest point in Tennessee. See NORTH CAROLINA.

Knoxville. Industrial center and farm market, especially for tobacco. About 20 miles north is Norris Dam. Oak Ridge, a few miles northwest, features the American Museum of Atomic Energy.

Memphis. Largest city, inland port, and cotton market. The Cotton Exchange is the hub of the city's economy. The annual Cotton Carnival, in May, draws thousands of visitors.

Meriwether Lewis Monument. Honors co-leader of famous western expedition and marks his place of death at Grinder's Inn and his grave.

Nashville. Capital and second largest city. The grounds of the Capitol exhibit statues of Tennessee's prominent people. A replica of Fort Nashborough (1780) is built on its original site; "the Parthenon," a reproduction of the Athenian structure, stands in Centennial Park. Near the city, Andrew Jackson's home, "The Hermitage," remains much as it was when he lived there.

National Military Parks. See U. S. NATIONAL PARK SYSTEM, pages 224-25.

TEXAS

Amarillo. Commercial center of the Panhandle section, Amarillo has developed from a barren prairie to a thriving metropolis. Helium gas is produced in large quantities here. Southeast of Amarillo is the spectacular Palo Duro Canyon.

Austin. State capital, commercial city, and home of the University of Texas. Planned by the founders of the Republic of Texas, Austin was the national

capital until Texas became a state in the United States. Points of interest are the Capitol and grounds, Governor's Mansion, former French Legation, O. Henry Museum, and others.

Big Bend National Park. Vast frontier area located in a picturesque section of Mexican-border wilderness, in the big bend of the Rio Grande. Spectacular mountains, desert, and canyon areas contain a variety of unusual geological formations.

Dallas. Industrial and commercial city, cotton market and oil center. The city is modern in every way, with beautiful parks and highways, theaters and museums. Points of interest are the John Neely Bryan Cabin, reconstructed on the site where the founder of the city built his home in 1843; Dallas Cotton Exchange; Southern Methodist University; Museum of Fine Arts, and others.

El Paso. Opposite Juarez, Mexico, on the Rio Grande, El Paso dates from the time of the Spanish conquistadores. Today it is a thriving commercial center and important port of entry. Noteworthy are Texas Western College; Fort Bliss, once the largest cavalry post in the United States; and International Bridge.

Galveston. One of the largest cotton ports in the world, year-round resort, and commercial city. Galveston lies on the eastern extremity of Galveston Island, which parallels the Texas mainland. Interesting are the sea wall, built to prevent a disaster similar to the Galveston Flood of 1900; the landlocked harbor; the coast-defense forts.

Houston. Largest city and important port, especially for the export of cotton and oil. Although 50 miles inland, Houston is connected with the Gulf Coast by the Houston Ship Channel. Points of interest are the Hermann Park Zoo, Rice University, and museums. The San Jacinto Battlefield and State Park, where the *Texas* is berthed, is nearby.

Kingsville. Home of Texas College of Arts and Industries; headquarters of million-acre King Ranch.

San Antonio. Historic old city and busy industrial community. Among its many interesting places are the Alamo, where 187 Americans made their last stand; San Fernando Cathedral; Spanish Governor's Palace; Mexican quarter; Franciscan Missions; La Villita; Randolph and Kelly fields.

UTAH

Bingham Canyon. Largest open cut copper mine in world; highway leads to observation points from which operations can be seen in the many-tiered pit. Town is a single street, three miles long.

Bryce Canyon National Park. Vast amphitheater filled with pink and white sandstone eroded into myriads of spires, shafts, minarets, and like formations; sharply defined stratification heightens the color. The highway winds along the west rim with frequent short side roads to viewpoints at the very edge, from which are seen such groups as Fairyland, Queen's Gardens, Fairy Castle, Wall of Windows.

Canyonlands National Park. An area of strangely beautiful canyon country. Natural arches, sculptured monoliths, and multicolored pinnacles are the results of centuries of erosion.

Glen Canyon Dam and Lake Powell. See ARIZONA.

National Monuments. See U.S. NATIONAL PARK SYSTEM, pages 224-25.

Salt Lake City. Capital of the state, home of the University of Utah, and one of the most beautiful cities in America. Wide and shaded streets, green lawns of beautiful homes, spacious grounds of the Capitol, are in sharp contrast to the encroaching desert. The Capitol itself holds a masterful exhibit of the resources and the means by which this green empire has been wrested from an arid wasteland. Famous all over the world are the beautiful Mormon Temple and the Tabernacle with its great dome put together with wooden pegs; in its auditorium a 10,000-pipe, hand-built organ is played every noon in public concert. Nearby is Great Salt Lake and the Great Salt Lake Desert.

Zion National Park. An area of awe-inspiring rock formations. Great shafts and temples and sheer walls rise from the bottom of Zion Canyon, where the road winds. Vermilion toward the base, they blend to rose, to pink, and finally to white, adding the glow of red and white fire to majestic line and towering height. Some of the formations are the Temple of Sinawava, Angel's Landing, the Great White Throne, the Great Arch.

VERMONT

Barre. Granite center. Cutting and polishing of granite can be watched at the Granite Sheds, which stretch along the floor of the valley.

Bennington. Textile mills and furniture plants in new section. Old First Church, Walloomsac Inn, the Ethan Allen House and the Tichenor Mansion in old section. On a nearby hill is the 306-foot Bennington Battle Monument.

Burlington. Largest city, lake port, and home of the University of Vermont. Historic points are Battery Park, site of big guns in the War of 1812; Green Mountain Cemetery, where Ethan Allen and other soldiers are buried; Ethan Allen Park.

Grand Isle. Several islands and a peninsula, all in Lake Champlain, comprise this resort isle.

Green Mountains. This magnificent chain of rounded, verdant peaks bisects the state and extends from the Massachusetts line to the Canadian border. The highest point in the range, Mt. Mansfield, is also the highest point in the state. Scenic points near here are Smuggler's Notch, Bingham Falls.

Montpelier. From every approach to the city the golden dome of the State Capitol can be viewed. Museum of Natural History contains the Daye Press.

Mount Equinox. Highest mountain overlooking the Vermont valley; has skyline drive to summit.

Rutland. Industrial center surrounded by great marble fields. Methods of cutting and finishing marble and exhibits are shown at nearby Proctor.

VIRGINIA

Appomattox Court House National Historical Park. Commemorates Lee's surrender to Grant on April 9, 1865. For National Military Parks, Battlefield Parks, etc., see U. S. NATIONAL PARK SYSTEM, pages 224-25.

Arlington National Cemetery. Burial ground of the nation's heroic dead. The Tomb of the Unknown Soldier is here, as is the Custis-Lee Mansion.

Colonial National Historical Park. Park includes Jamestown, first permanent English settlement, which has reconstructed Glasshouse and Jamestown Festival Park; Yorktown, where Cornwallis surrendered; and a parkway between these two places and Williamsburg.

Fredericksburg. Washington's mother's home and Kenmore, his sister's home, are here, as is James Monroe's law office, and the home of John Paul Jones. East of the city, reached by State Route 3, is Stratford Hall, birthplace of Robert E. Lee, built by his family 1725-30.

Monticello. Home of Thomas Jefferson, third president of the United States. His tomb is here.

Mount Vernon. Famous country place of George Washington, standing since 1743 and filled with Washington treasures.

Natural Bridge. Higher than Niagara, it spans the Cedar Creek; near Lexington.

Norfolk and Portsmouth. Location of Naval Station and Navy Yard, respectively. In vicinity are Newport News, site of immense shipbuilding plant, Hampton Roads, and Virginia Beach, popular resort.

Richmond. State capital since 1779 and Confederate capital from 1861 to 1865. The Capitol, designed by Thomas Jefferson, has Houdon's marble figure of Washington. Other points of interest are the Edgar Allan Poe Shrine, St. John's Church,

Chief Justice John Marshall's Home, Confederate Museum, Hall of Delegates.

Shenandoah National Park. Embraces a portion of the Blue Ridge Mountains. Scenic Skyline Drive traverses the Park. Luray Caverns are nearby.

Williamsburg. Home of the College of William and Mary and subject of extensive restoration to the 18th-century days when Williamsburg was the colonial capital of Virginia.

WASHINGTON

Grand Coulee. A 50-mile dry gorge cut 800 feet deep during glacial times by an ice-diverted Columbia River. At mid point is Dry Falls, once the greatest waterfall known to have existed in North America. Grand Coulee Dam, 550 feet high and 4,173 feet long, furnishes electric power to all parts of the state. Surplus power pumps water 300 feet higher into Grand Coulee, where retaining dams create a huge reservoir. From here it spreads south and east into the Columbia Basin, to irrigate, ultimately, a million acres.

Mt. Rainier National Park. Rising from near sea level to over 14,410 feet, Mt. Rainier, dormant if not extinct volcano, is the dominant natural feature of the state. Park has permanent snow fields and glaciers, high meadows and crystal clear lakes, great variety of trees and flowers. Paradise Valley on south side has hotel and camping; Yakima Park on north, cabin camp and picnic grounds. Summit climb of two days starts from Paradise Inn.

Olympia. New capitol buildings on impressive site overlooking Budd Inlet emphasize character of city as state capital. Suburb of Tumwater, first American settlement on Puget Sound (1845). Gateway to famed Olympic Peninsula recreation area.

Olympic National Park. Occupies the heart of rugged Olympic Peninsula between Pacific Ocean and Puget Sound; preserves primeval forests of giant trees and native animal life, zones ranging from temperate rain forests to mountain glaciers.

Puget Sound Islands. These include beautiful Vashon and Bainbridge, island suburbs of Tacoma and Seattle; Whidbey, the largest island, has access to the mainland, via Fidalgo Island, by a bridge across tide-ripped Deception Pass; the San Juan group of nearly 200 habitable islands and hundreds of barren rocks; and scores of others. Protected waters and sheltered coves are a paradise for yachtsman, fisherman, picnicker, and camper.

Seattle. Metropolis of Washington and the Pacific Northwest. Salt water harbor of Elliott Bay rimmed by port facilities for largest ocean going vessels; fresh water harbor via government locks a haven for fishing and pleasure boats. Scenic boulevards link waterfronts with hilltops and provide views of distant mountains. University of Washington, farmers' Public Market, Frozen Fish Museum, Volunteer Park Conservatory, Smith Cove docks, and Lake Washington Bridge are of interest. Industries are varied—lumbering, airplane manufacturing, aluminum fabrication, shipbuilding, and others. Snoqualmie Falls are to the east.

Spokane. Metropolis of the so-called "Inland Empire"—portions of four states between Cascade and Rocky Mountains. Flour mills, lumber mills, and light metal industries are based upon agricultural, timber, and power resources. Spokane Falls in heart of city supplied water-power for original settlement (1871). Nearby lakes and Mt. Spokane provide summer and winter recreation.

Tacoma. Important lumber manufacturing center. Large smelter handles copper ores from all parts of the world. In Point Defiance Park is full size replica of Hudson's Bay Co. Fort Nisqually, first white settlement in the area. Nearby Fort Lewis is one of largest permanent army posts.

Vancouver. River fort and industrial center; dates from Hudson's Bay Co. post of 1825 (Fort Vancouver National Historic Site) when fur-trading and trapping brigades fanned out in all directions. Aluminum industry, based on low-cost power from Bonneville Dam, and wood-processing plants now are major activities.

Walla Walla. Old Fort Walla Walla of fur-trading days was at Wallula; Waiilatpu Mission of Marcus Whitman is now in Whitman National Monument.

WEST VIRGINIA

Berkeley Springs. Historic spa, willed to the state by Lord Fairfax. The Washington Elm, Lovers' Leap, and the Castle are of interest.

Charleston. State capital and state's largest city, near coal, natural gas, and oil fields. The gold-leaf dome of the State Capitol rises 300 feet above the ground. "Stonewall" Jackson Monument and Pioneer Monument are on the Capitol grounds.

Charles Town. In the Eastern Panhandle. The town is named for Charles Washington, brother of George; his home "Mordington" is preserved. John Brown stood trial at the Jefferson County Courthouse and was hanged at Site of John Brown Gallows.

Grave Creek Mound. At Moundsville. It is the largest conical Indian mound in the country.

Harpers Ferry. John Brown Monument marks site of the engine house where the abolitionist made his last stand; "John Brown's Fort," part replica and part reconstruction of the engine house, is on the campus of Storer College. Harpers Ferry National Historical Park includes Federal hillsides surrendered to Jackson, thus permitting his quick juncture with Lee at Antietam.

Huntington. Picturesquely situated on the Ohio, the state's second largest city is an industrial center primarily known for its huge nickel plant.

Monongahela National Forest. A vacation land along the eastern boundary. Points of interest include Spruce Knob, highest point in the state; Blackwater Falls, which drop 63 feet and rush through a 1,000-foot gorge; "Pictured Rocks" at Petersburg Gap, and nearby Smoke Hole Caverns; the eroded, castle-like white sandstone mountain, Seneca Rock, near Mouth of Seneca; and the Sinks, near Osceola, where the Gandy River goes underground.

Wheeling. Industrial center, leading city of the Northern Panhandle. Oglebay Park contains Mansion Museum, Nature Museum, Greenhouse and Conservatory, and recreational facilities.

White Sulphur Springs. A popular spa since the 1800's. The President's Cottage has housed several Chief Executives since the time of Andrew Jackson, and the Robert E. Lee Cottage remains unchanged.

WISCONSIN

Ashland. Center of hunting area; nearby is beautiful Copper Falls State Park. A side trip leads to Bayfield and from here the offshore Apostle Islands in Lake Superior can be visited.

Big Manitou Falls. Highest waterfall in the state. In Pattison State Park, south of Superior, Black River cascades 165 feet down a narrow, rocky gorge.

Devil's Lake State Park. Unusual rock formations and geological curiosities. Of glacial origin, Devil's Lake is hemmed in by towering cliffs 400 to 500 feet high; near West Baraboo.

Green Bay. State's oldest settlement and gateway to Door Peninsula, famed for cherry blossoms.

Lake Geneva. Fashionable summer resort; many fine estates. Sailboat races are popular on lake. World-famous Yerkes observatory, of the University of Chicago, is at Williams Bay.

Lake Winnebago. Largest lake in state and extensive summer-winter vacation area.

Madison. Capital of Wisconsin and site of the University of Wisconsin; on narrow isthmus between Lake Monona and Lake Mendota, with three other lakes close by. The Capitol, second in height only to the National capitol in Washington, has the only granite dome in the United States.

Milwaukee. Largest city in Wisconsin and important center for the manufacture of heavy machinery. It is also noted for its many large breweries, some of which conduct tours for visitors. Has a Lake Michigan harbor and many fine parks. Among the points of interest are the botanical gardens of Mitchell Park; Court of Honor, with its war memorials; Milwaukee Public Library and Museum.

Prairie du Chien. The second oldest settlement in the state, this picturesque little city has numerous reminders of the old fur-trading days.

Rib Mountain. Near Wausau; 1,941 feet above sea level, highest point in Wisconsin; popular winter sports area, with majestic scenic views from summit.

Superior. Sister city to Duluth. *See* MINNESOTA.

Wisconsin Dells. Spectacular rock formations formed by the Wisconsin River as it dashes through eight miles of rocky gorges. Tribal ceremonies by the Winnebago Indians are a summer feature.

WYOMING

Casper. Trading center for rich oil fields (Teapot Dome is to the north) and lively cattle country; on Oregon Trail and rich in frontier history.

Cheyenne. Wyoming's capital; founded as a construction terminus for the building of the first transcontinental railroad, today an important transportation and trade center. Drawing much of its wealth from the cattle industry, it is world-famous for its Cheyenne Frontier Days celebration (July). Points of interest include the Capitol, Ft. Warren, Frontier Park, the State Historical Museum.

Cody. Near entrance of Yellowstone National Park and Shoshone Canyon and Dam; founded by Buffalo Bill Cody; it contains statue and museum of his effects.

Devils Tower National Monument. The first National Monument; of columnar basalt, it rises 865 feet high; northwest of Sundance.

Fort Bridger. Historic trading post established by the famous frontiersman, Jim Bridger.

Fort Laramie National Historic Site. Trade, military, and supply outpost for many years before and during wagon travel on the Oregon Trail; called "Cradle of American civilization in the west." Some original buildings are still standing.

Fort Washakie. Agency for Shoshone Indian Reservation; Sacajawea and Chief Washakie buried here.

Grand Teton National Park. Vistas of shining gray-blue peaks, snow-frosted, reflected in sky-blue lakes amid close ranks of spruce and fir—these are the Tetons. No less typical is the little log Church of the Transfiguration, its altar window framing Grand Teton Peak. Jackson and Jenny are two of several beautiful lakes; adjacent is the famous Jackson Hole country.

Hot Springs State Park. Hot mineral springs. Big Horn Spring is world's largest, flowing 18,000,000 gallons (135°) a day. At Thermopolis.

Independence Rock. On the Sweetwater; famed landmark of Oregon Trail. Called "Register of the Desert" by Father De Smet (1840), it bears 5,000 names scratched by explorers, traders, and emigrants.

Sheridan. Gateway to the Big Horn Mountains; outfitting point for dude and cattle ranches. To the south are sites of Ft. Phil Kearney and Wagon Box Fight, famous turning-point of the Red Cloud War.

Yellowstone National Park. Probably the most famous of all the national parks, the Yellowstone is a fabulous combination of mountains and canyons, lakes and waterfalls, spouting geysers and wildlife that includes moose, buffalo, grizzly bear, and trumpeter swan. Old Faithful Geyser, errupting regularly every hour, is hallmark to the Park. Others that play at more or less regular intervals are Jewel, Daisy, Rocket, and Grotto; the spectacular Grand Geyser performs about every 16 to 20 hours. Many pools, like sparkling blue Morning Glory, terraces like Mammoth Hot Springs, and boiling mud pots are of interest. Yellowstone Canyon and Falls are among the world's most beautiful; from Fishing Bridge almost anyone can catch a trout.

GLOSSARY OF FOREIGN GEOGRAPHICAL TERMS

Arab....Arabic	Kor....Korean
Bantu...Bantu	Lao....Laotian
Bur....Burmese	Lapp....Lappish
Camb...Cambodian	Mal....Malayan
Celt....Celtic	Mong...Mongolian
Chn....Chinese	Nor....Norwegian
Czech...Czech	Per....Persian
Dan....Danish	Pol....Polish
Du....Dutch	Port....Portuguese
Fin....Finnish	Rom....Romanian
Fr.....French	Rus....Russian
Ger....German	Siam...Siamese
Grc....Greek	So. Slav...Southern
Hung...Hungarian	Slavonic
Ice.....Icelandic	Sp.....Spanish
India...India	Swe....Swedish
Indian...American	Tib....Tibetan
Indian	Tur....Turkic
It......Italian	Viet....Vietnamese
Jap....Japanese	

A

å, Dan., Nor...................river
aan, Du.......................at, on
abad, India, Per.........dwelling, town
abu, abou, Arab...............father
ålen, Nor......................spit
alf, elf, Swe.................river
alp, Ger....................mountain
alt, Ger.......................old
alta, -o, It., Port., Sp.........high
altopiano, It.................plateau
älv, älven, Swe...............river
amarillo, Sp.................yellow
arquipélago, Port...........archipelago
arroyo, Sp.....brook, dry bed of stream
as, Dan,. Nor., Swe........hill, ridge
austral, Sp..................southern

B

baai, Du.......................bay
bab, Arab.................gate, strait
bach, Ger..............brook, stream
backe, Swe....................hill
bad, Ger......................bath
bahía, Port., Sp.........bay, gulf
bahr, Arab...............bay, river
baia, It..................bay, gulf
baie, Fr..................bay, gulf
bajo, Sp..............low, lower
bakke, Dan., Nor..............hill
balkan, Tur...........mountain range
ban, Lao, Mal................village
ban, Siam...................house
bana, Jap....................cape
bandar, Per.................harbor
batang, Mal..................river
belyy, belaya, Rus...........white
ben, Celt.......mountain, summit
bender, bandar, Arab., India
................market town, port
beni, bani, Arab......sons of, tribe of
berg, Du., Ger., Nor., Swe..mountain, hill
bir, bi'r, Arab...............well
birkat, Arab.............pool, well
bjeli, -a, -o, So. Slav.........white
bjerğ, bjaerğ, Dan., Nor......mountain
blanc, Fr....................white
blanco, Sp...................white
blau, Ger.....................blue
bleu, Fr......................blue
bodden, Ger..................ground
bogaz, bogazi, Tur...........strait
bois, Fr..............forest, wood
boloto, Rus...................marsh
bolshoy, bolshoye, Rus.......great
boreal, Sp..................northern
borg, Dan., Nor., Swe........castle
borgo, It.....................town
bosch, Du.............forest, wood
bouche, Fr............river, mouth
bourg, Fr...........town, borough
bro, Dan., Nor., Swe.........bridge
brücke, brücken, Ger.....bridge, bridges
brun, Fr.....................brown
bucht, Ger..............bay, bight
bugt, Dan., Nor...........bay, gulf
bukt, bukten, Swe........bay, gulf
bulak, Tur...................spring
būr, Arab.....................port
burg, Du., Ger........castle, town
buri, Siam....................city

burun, burnu, Tur................cape
büyük, Tur......................great
by, Dan., Nor., Swe.......town, village

C

cabeza, Sp...................summit
cabo, Port., Sp...............cape
cairn, carn, Celt........rocky headland
campo, It., Port., Sp..........field
campos, Port. (Brazil)............plains
cañon, Sp...................canyon
cap, Fr.......................cape
capo, It......................cape
casa, It., Port., Sp..........house
castello, It., Port...........castle, fort
castillo, Sp.............castle, fort
catingas, Port. (Brazil)...open brushlands
cayo, Sp...........rock, shoal, islet
central, Fr..................middle
cerro, Sp......................hill
chai, ciai, Tur...............river
champ, Fr....................field
chapada, Port. (Brazil).......hills, hill
chateau, Fr..................castle
cherniy, chernaya, Rus...........black
chin, Chn.............market town
chott, shat, Arab......salt river or lake
chou, Chn..................island
cidade, Port..................city
città, It................town, city
ciudad, Sp..............town, city
col, Fr........................pass
colina, Sp.....................hill
colorado, Sp....................red
cordillera, Sp........mountain chain
costa, It., Port., Sp..........coast
côte, côtes, Fr....coast, hills, peak, ridge
crkva, So. Slav..............church
crni, So. Slav................black
cuchilla, Sp..........mountain range
cumbre, Sp............peak, ridge

D

daal, dal, Du.................valley
dag, Tur....................mountain
dağlari, Tur..........mountains, range
dake, take, Jap..........peak, ridge
dal, Dan., Du., Nor., Swe......valley
dalay, Mong...................lake
dar, Arab............land, country
darya, daria, Per.......river, sea
dasht, Per..........plain, desert
dawḥat, Arab.........bay, inlet
deccan, India.................south
deir, Arab..................convent
denis, -z, Tur........sea, lake
désert, Fr..................desert
deserto, It..................desert
desierto, Sp.................desert
détroit, Fr..................strait
djebel, jebel, Arab.........mountain
dolok, Mal.................mountain
dorf, Ger...................village
dorp, Du....................village
drift, Dan., Ger............current
duinen, Du...................dunes
dun, Celt..............fortified hill
dyk, Du...............dam, dyke
dzong, Tib...fort, administrative capital

E

eau, Fr.......................water
ecuador, Sp.................equator
eiland, Du...................island
elf, älf, Swe.................river
elv, Dan., Nor...............river
erg, Arab......dune, region of dunes
eski, Tur......................old
est, Fr........................east
estado, Sp....................state
este, It., Port., Sp..........east
estrecho, Sp.................strait
étang, Fr..............pond, lake
état, Fr......................state
étroit, Fr...................narrow

F

feld, Ger...............field, plain
fels, Ger......................rock
festung, Ger...................fort
firth, Scotch................estuary
fiume, It.....................river
fjäll, fjället, Swe..........mountain
fjärd, Swe...............bay, inlet
fjeld, Nor.............mountain, hill
fjell, Nor..................mountain
fjord, fjorden, Dan., Nor.....fiord, inlet
fjördhur, Ice..........fiord, inlet
fleuve, Fr....................river
flod, Dan, Swe................river
flói, Ice......................bay
fluss, Ger....................river
foce, It................river mouth
fontein, Du...............a spring
fors, Swe..........waterfall, torrent
forst, Ger...................forest
fos, Dan., Nor..............waterfall
fuente, Sp........spring, fountain
fuerte, Sp.....................fort
furt, Ger......................ford

G

gamla, Swe.....................old
gamle, Dan., Nor...............old
gat, Dan., Nor.......passage, channel
gavan', Rus..................harbor
gebel, Arab................mountain
gebergte, Du........mountain range
gebiet, Ger.........district, territory
gebirge, Ger.......range, mountains
ghat, India..mountain pass, river passage
gobi, Mong..................desert
göl, gölu, Tur................lake
golf, Du., Ger...........gulf, bay
golfe, Fr................gulf, bay
golfo, It., Port., Sp.....gulf, bay
gong, India.................village
gora, Pol., Rus., So. Slav......mountain
gornji, -a, -o, So. Slav.......upper
gorny, Pol...................upper
gorod, grad, Rus., So. Slav......town
grand, grande, Fr......large, great
grande, It., Port., Sp.....large, great
grod, gorod, Pol., Rus........town
grön, Dan....................green
groot, Du....................great
gross, Ger...................great
guba, Rus...............bay, gulf
gunto, Jap.............archipelago

H

haf, Swe.......................sea
hafen, Ger...........port, harbor
haff, Ger.........gulf, inland sea
hai, Chn................sea, lake
hamn, Swe...................harbor
hamun, Per.......swampy lake, plain
haus, hausen, Ger......house, houses
haut, Fr.......high, summit, upper
havet, Nor.....................bay
havn, Dan., Nor.......harbor, port
havre, Fr.............harbor, port
hawr, Arab.............lake, marsh
haz, -a, Hung........house, dwelling of
heim, Ger...................hamlet
hem, Swe....................hamlet
higashi, Jap..................east
hinterland, Ger.........back country
hissar, hisar, Tur.......castle, fort
ho, Chn.......................river
hoch, Ger......................high
hoek, Du.......................cape
hof, Ger.........court, farm house
höfn, Ice...................harbor
hoku, Jap....................north
holm, Dan., Nor., Swe.........island
hora, Czech................mountain
horn, Ger......................peak
hoved, Dan., Nor......cape, headland
hsien, Chn......district, district capital
hügel, Ger.....................hill

I

ile, Fr.......................island
ilha, Port....................island
indre, Dan., Nor..............inner
indsö, Dan., Nor..............lake
inférieur, Fr.................lower
insel, Ger...................island
insjö, Swe....................lake
irmak, Tur...................river
isla, Sp.....................island
isola, It....................island
istmo, It., Sp..............isthmus

J

jabal, Arab.....mountain, plateau, ridge
järvi, Fin....................lake
jebel, djebel, Arab.........mountain
jima, shima, Jap.............island
jökel, jökelen, Nor..........glacier
joki, Fin.....................river
jökull, Ice.......ice-covered mountain
južna, So. Slav.........south, southern

K

kaap, Du......................cape
kafr, kefr, Arab.............village
kaikyo, Jap..................strait
kaise, Lapp................mountain
kala, kalat, Arab., Per
..............castle, fortress, village
kale, Tur.............castle, fort
kamen', Rus...................rock
kang, Chn...................village
kap, Ger......................cape
kapp, Nor.....................cape
kara, Tur....................black
kaupunki, Fin............town, city
kavir, Per..............salt desert
kebir, Arab..................great
kefr, kafr, Arab.............village
ken, Jap..................prefecture
kend, kand, Per.............village
khalīj, Arab.............bay, gulf
khrebet, Rus.........mountain range
ki, Jap................tree, forest
kil, cill, Celt.........church, cell
kirche, Ger.................church
kirchen, Ger.................parish
kio, kyo, Jap........town, capital
kis, Hung.............little, small
klein, Dan., Ger.............small
köbstad, Dan..................city
köl, Mong., Tur.......lake, marsh
kompong, Camb...............village
kong, Chn....................river
kopf, Ger.........head, summit, peak
köping, Swe......market, borough
kraal, Du............native village
krasniy, krasnaya, Rus.
..............beautiful, fair, red
kuala, Mal......junction, river mouth
kuchuk, Tur..................small
kuh, koh, Per..............mountain
kul, Mong., Tur..............lake
kum, qum, Tur...............desert
kuppe, Ger..................summit
küste, Ger...................coast
kyzyl, kizil, Tur.............red

L

laag, Du.......................low
lac, Fr.......................lake
lago, It., Sp.................lake
lâgoa, Port.................lagoon
laguna, It., Port., Sp....lagoon, lake
lahti, Fin.............bay, gulf
län, Swe....................county
landsby, Dan., Nor..........village
lao, Viet....................island
lilla, Swe...................small

GLOSSARY OF FOREIGN GEOGRAPHICAL TERMS *(Continued)*

lille, *Dan., Nor* ... small
liman, *Tur* ... bay, port
ling, *Chn* ... mountain, range
llanos, *Sp* ... prairies, plains
loch, *Celt* ... lake, bay (Scotland)
lough, *Celt* ... lake, bay (Ireland)

M

maha, *India* ... great
malyy, malaya, *Rus* ... small
mar, *Port., Sp* ... sea
mare, *It., Rom* ... sea
mare, *Rom* ... great
mark, *Ger* ... boundary, limit
massif, *Fr* ... mountain range
mato, *Port* ... jungle, copse
medio, *Sp* ... middle
meer, *Du., Ger* ... lake, sea
mer, *Fr* ... sea
mesa, *Sp* ... flat-topped mountain
meseta, *Sp* ... hill
midden, *Du* ... middle
mina, *Port., Sp* ... mine
mittel, *Ger* ... middle
mont, *Fr* ... mount, mountain
montagna, *It* ... mountain
montagna, *Fr* ... mountain
montaña, *Sp* ... mountain
monte, *It., Port., Sp* ... mount, mountain
more, *Rus., So. Slav* ... sea
morro, *Port., Sp* ... hill
moyen, *Fr* ... middle
mühle, *Ger* ... mill
mund, munde, *Ger* ... river mouth
mündung, *Ger* ... river mouth
muong, *Lao* ... town, village
mura, *Jap* ... village
muz, *Tur* ... ice
mys, *Rus* ... cape, point

N

nada, *Jap* ... sea
nadi, *India* ... river, creek
naes, näs, *Dan., Nor., Swe* ... cape
nagar, nagon, *India* ... town, city
nagy, *Hung* ... large, great
naka, *Jap* ... middle
neder, *Du* ... low
nedre, *Nor* ... lower
negro, *It., Port., Sp* ... black
nejd, *Arab* ... highland
neu, *Ger* ... new
nevado, *Sp* ... mountain
nez, *Fr* ... point, cape
nieder, *Ger* ... low, lower
nieuw, *Du* ... new
nizhne, nizhniy, nizhnyaya, *Rus* ... lower
noir, *Fr* ... black
nong, *Siam* ... marsh, pond, lake
noord, *Du* ... north
nor, *Tib* ... lake
nord, *Dan., Fr., Ger., It., Nor* ... north
norr, norra, *Swe* ... north
norte, *Port., Sp* ... north
nos, *Rus* ... cape
nouvelle, *Fr* ... new
novi, -a, -o, *So. Slav* ... new
novo, *Port* ... new
novy, -e, -a, *Czech* ... new
novyy, novyye, novaya, novo, *Rus* ... new
nowa, nowy, Pol ... new
nuevo, *Sp* ... new
nuovo, *It* ... new
nuur, *Mong* ... lake
ny, *Dan., Swe* ... new
nyasa, *Bantu* ... lake

O

o, *Jap* ... great, large
ö, *Dan., Nor., Swe* ... island
ober, *Ger* ... upper
occidental, *Sp* ... western
odde, *Dan., Nor* ... point, cape
oedjoeng, *Mal* ... cape
oeste, *Port., Sp* ... west
ojo, *Sp* ... spring
oost, *Du* ... east
op, *Du* ... on
oriental, *Sp* ... eastern
oro, *Sp* ... gold
óros, *Grc* ... mountain
ost, *Ger., Swe* ... east
öst, öster, östre, *Dan., Nor., Swe.* ... east, eastern
ostrog, *Rus* ... fort
ostrov, *Rus* ... island
ouadi, *Arab* ... intermittent stream
ouest, *Fr* ... west
öy, *Nor* ... island
ozero, *Rus* ... lake

P

paa, *Fin* ... mountain
padang, *Mal* ... plain, field
pampas, *Sp. (Argentina)* ... grassy plains
para, *Indian (Brazil)* ... river
pas, *Fr* ... channel, strait, pass
paso, *Sp* ... mountain pass
passo, *It., Port* ... mountain pass
patam *India* ... city, town
pequeño *Sp* ... small
peresheyek. *Rus* ... isthmus
pertuis, *Fr* ... strait
peski, *Rus* ... desert, sands
petit, petite, *Fr* ... small, little
pic, *Fr* ... mountain peak
piccolo, *It* ... small
pico, *Port., Sp* ... mountain peak
piedra, *Sp* ... stone, rock
pik, *Rus* ... peak
planalto, *Port* ... plateau
plata, *Sp* ... silver
plato, *Rus* ... plateau
playa, *Sp* ... shore, beach
po, *Chn* ... lake
pointe, *Fr* ... point
polder, *Du., Ger* ... reclaimed marsh
polje, *So. Slav* ... field
poluostrov, *Rus* ... peninsula
pont, *Fr* ... bridge
ponta, *Port* ... point, headland
ponte, *It., Port* ... bridge
pore, pur, *India* ... city, town
porto, *It* ... port, harbor
pôrto, *Port* ... port, harbor
prado, *Sp* ... field, meadow
presqu'île, *Fr* ... peninsula
proliv, *Rus* ... strait
pu, *Chn* ... commercial village
pueblo, *Sp* ... town, village
puerto, *Sp* ... port, harbor
pulau, *Mal* ... island
punkt, *Ger* ... point
punt, *Du* ... point
punta, *It., Sp* ... point
pur, pura, *India* ... city, town
puy, *Fr* ... peak

R

rann, *India* ... wasteland
ra's, *Arab* ... cape, summit
reg, *Arab* ... coarse gravel desert
reka, *Rus., So. Slav* ... river
represa, *Port* ... reservoir
retto, *Jap* ... archipelago
ria, *Sp* ... river mouth
ribeira, -ão, *Port* ... stream, river
rio, *It., Port* ... river
río, *Sp* ... river
rivière, *Fr* ... river
roca, *Sp* ... rock
rochedos, *Port. (Brazil)* ... rocks in water
rouge, *Fr* ... red
rud, *Per* ... river

S

saari, *Fin* ... island
sable, *Fr* ... sand
sahra, *Arab* ... desert
sal, *Sp* ... salt
samar, *Mong* ... path, route
san, *Chn., Jap., Kor* ... mountain, hill
san, santa, santo, *It., Port., Sp* ... saint
são, *Port* ... saint
sat, satu, *Rom* ... village
schloss, *Ger* ... castle, fort
sebkha, *Arab* ... salt marsh
see, *Ger* ... lake, sea
sehir, shehr, *Tur* ... town
selat, *Mal* ... channel, strait
selatan, *Mal* ... south, southern
selvas, *Port. (Brazil)* ... tropical rain forests
seno, *Sp* ... bay
serra, *It., Port* ... pass, mountain ridge
serranía, *Sp* ... mountain ridge
seto, *Jap* ... strait, channel
severnaya, *Rus* ... north
shahr, shehr, *Per* ... town
sha'īb, *Arab* ... depression, intermittent stream
shan, *Chn* ... range, mountain, hill
shaṭṭ, chott, *Arab* ... salt river or lake
shima, sima, *Jap* ... island
shimo, *Jap* ... lower
shiu, *Chn., Jap* ... province
shoto, *Jap* ... archipelago
si, *Chn* ... west, western
sierra, *Sp* ... mountain range
sint, *Du* ... saint
sjö, *Nor., Swe* ... lake, sea
sö, *Dan., Nor* ... lake, sea
söder, *Swe* ... south
soengai, sungei, *Mal* ... river
sopka, *Rus* ... extinct volcano
source, *Fr* ... spring
spitze, *Ger* ... summit, point
sredniy, sredne, srednyaya, *Rus* ... middle
staat, *Ger* ... state
stad, *Dan., Du.. Nor., Swe* ... city, town
stadt, *Ger* ... city, town
stari, -a, -o, *So. Slav* ... old
stary, *Czech., Pol* ... old
staryy, staraya, *Rus* ... old
stato, *It* ... state
sten, *Dan., Nor., Swe* ... stone
step, *Rus* ... treeless plain, steppe
stor, *Dan., Nor., Swe* ... great, large
straat, *Du* ... strait
strand, *Dan., Du., Ger., Nor., Swe* ... shore, beach
stretto, *It* ... strait
strom, *Ger* ... stream
ström, *Dan., Nor., Swe* ... river
stroom, *Du* ... stream, river
su, suyu, *Tur* ... water, river
sud, *Fr., Sp* ... south
süd, *Ger* ... south
sul, *Port* ... south, southern
sund, *Dan., Nor., Swe* ... sound
supérieure, *Fr* ... upper
sur, *Fr* ... on
sur, *Sp* ... south
syd, *Dan., Nor., Swe* ... south

T

tafelland, *Du., Ger* ... plateau, tableland
tagh, *Mong., Tur* ... mountain
tai, *Jap* ... large, great
taiga, *Rus* ... northern coniferous forest
take, dake, *Jap* ... peak, ridge
tandjung, tanjong, *Mal* ... cape
tao, -u, *Chn* ... island
targ, targu, *Rom* ... market, town
tash, *Per., Tur* ... rock, stone
tau, *Tur* ... mountain range
tell, tel, *Arab* ... hill
terra, *It* ... land
terre, *Fr* ... earth, land
thal, *Ger* ... valley
tierra, *Sp* ... earth, land
torp, *Swe* ... village, cottage
torre, *It., Port., Sp* ... tower
tsi, *Chn* ... village, borough
tsu, *Jap* ... port
tundra, *Rus* ... marshy arctic plains
tung, *Chn* ... east, eastern
turn, turnu, *Rom* ... tower
tuz, *Tur* ... salt

U

udd, udde, *Swe* ... cape
ufer, *Ger* ... beach, shore, river bank
uj, *Hung* ... new
ulan, *Mong* ... red
umi, *Jap* ... sea, gulf
unter, *Ger* ... lower
ura, *Jap* ... bay, shore, creek
ust, *Rus* ... river mouth
uula, *Mong* ... mountain, range
utara, *Mal* ... north, northern

V

vall, *Swe* ... coast
valle, *Port., Sp* ... valley
vallée, *Fr* ... valley
valli, *It* ... lake, lagoon
var, *Hung* ... fortress
varos, *Hung., So. Slav* ... town
varre, *Lapp* ... mountain
vecchio, *It* ... old
veld, *Du* ... open plain, field
velho, *Port* ... old
velikiy, *Rus., So. Slav* ... great
verde, *It., Port., Sp* ... green
verkhniy, verkhnyaya, *Rus* ... upper, higher
vert, *Fr* ... green
ves, *Czech* ... village
vest, *Dan., Nor., Swe* ... west
viejo, *Sp* ... old
vieux, *Fr* ... old
vik, viken, *Swe* ... bay
villa, *Port., Sp* ... small town
villar, *Sp* ... village, hamlet
ville, *Fr* ... town, city
vinh, *Viet* ... bay
vishni, visni, *Rus* ... high
vostok, *Rus* ... east
volcán, *Sp* ... volcano

W

wadi, wādī, wad, *Arab* ... intermittent stream
wald, *Ger* ... forest, woodland
wan, *Chn., Jap* ... bay, gulf
weiler, *Ger* ... hamlet, village
weiss, *Ger* ... white
westersch, *Du* ... western
wiek, *Ger* ... bay
wüste, *Ger* ... desert

Y

yama, *Jap* ... mountain
yang, *Chn* ... channel
yeni, *Tur* ... new
yokara, *Tur* ... upper
yoma, *Bur* ... mountain range
yug, *Rus* ... south
yuzhno, *Rus* ... south, southern

Z

zaki, saki, *Jap* ... cape
zaliv, *Rus* ... bay, gulf
zapad, zapadnyy, *Rus* ... west
zapadni, -a, -o, *So. Slav* ... west, western
zee, *Du* ... sea
zemlya, *Rus* ... land
zuid, *Du* ... south

GLOSSARY OF MAP TERMINOLOGY

A

Altitude. The height of an object or elevation above a given level.

Analemma. A graphic scale, usually drawn in the form of a figure 8, showing the overhead sun's latitude for every day in the year as well as the difference between sun time and mean time.

Antarctic Circle. The geographic parallel of 66° 33′ S., enclosing the area within which the sun is continuously above the horizon on December 22, and below the horizon on June 21.

Antipodes. Two places on the surface of the globe diametrically opposite to each other, i.e., North Pole and South Pole; England and the Antipodes Is.

Antoeci. Two places on the same meridian and in corresponding latitudes north and south of the Equator.

Aphelion. That point in the earth's orbit which is most distant from the sun, 94,560,000 miles.

Archipelago. A group of islands more or less adjacent to each other and arranged in groups covering portions of the sea.

Arctic Circle. The geographic parallel of 66° 33′ N., enclosing the area within which the sun is continuously above the horizon on June 21, and below the horizon on December 22.

Atlas. A bound collection of maps. First used in this sense by Mercator in the 16th century.

Atmosphere. The ocean of air surrounding the earth.

Atoll. A coral island in the form of a ring, more or less continuous, around an interior lagoon.

Autumnal Equinox. The time when the overhead sun crosses the Equator on its apparent migration from north to south, or about September 23, and the length of day and night is approximately the same in all latitudes.

Axis. The straight line passing through the center of the earth, about which the earth rotates.

Azimuth. A great circle direction, or the angle measured clockwise between any meridian and an intersecting great circle.

Azimuthal Projection. A map projection on which the directions of all lines radiating from a central point or pole are the same as the directions of the corresponding lines on the sphere. When centered on one of the poles, sometimes called a "polar projection."

B

Bank. An elevation of the ocean bottom above which the water is relatively shallow but sufficient for navigation, yet without any island rising from it to the surface.

Bar. A ridge of sand or other substance extending across the mouth of a river or harbor, and which may obstruct navigation.

Barrier Ice. The edge of a great glacier which enters the sea but remains attached to the land.

Basin. The area drained by a river and its tributaries.

Bathymetric Chart. A topographic map of the bed of the ocean showing ocean depth contours.

Bay. A penetration of the sea into the coast, and it is usually very much wider in the middle than at the entrance.

Bayou. A sluggish watercourse, usually the outlet of a lake or of a river through its delta.

Beach. The area between high and low water forming the margin of sea or lake.

Bight. A comparatively slight indentation in the coastline between distant headlands.

Bluff. A cliff or headland with an almost perpendicular face.

Butte. A conspicuous, isolated hill or mountain.

C

Calms, Belt of. A zone on either side of the Trade Winds where calms of long duration prevail.

Canal. An artificial watercourse. Sometimes applied to a natural waterway which has the appearance of an artificial canal.

Canyon. A deep gorge or ravine through which a river flows.

Cape. A point of land projecting into a body of water.

Cartography. The art or science of making maps.

Celestial Globe. A sphere on whose surface is drawn a map or representation of the heavens.

Central Meridian. The vertical meridian of a map projection around which the map is centered.

Chart. A map for use in marine or aeronautical navigation.

Civil Time. Solar time in a day that is considered as beginning at midnight. It may be counted in two series of 12 hours each (A.M. and P.M.) or in a single series of 24 hours beginning at midnight. Civil Time may be either true solar time or mean solar time.

Cliff. Land projecting nearly vertically from the water or from the surrounding land.

Climate. The aggregate weather conditions of a given region over a long period of time.

Co-Latitude. The difference between the latitude of a place and 90°, or its distance in degrees from one of the poles of the earth.

Conformal Projection. A map projection on which all small or elementary figures upon the surface of the earth retain true shape, the meridians and parallels being at right angles to one another.

Conic Projection. A map projection which can be imagined as drawn on the surface of a cone. The meridians appear as straight lines along which the parallels, as concentric circles, may be spaced in such a way as to give some desired quality, such as conformality or equal area.

Continent. One of the main continuous bodies of land on the earth's surface. The number of continents considered to exist varies with usage from five to seven, i.e., America (North and South); Eurasia (Europe and Asia); Africa; Antarctica; and Australia.

Continental Divide. The height of land which separates the streams flowing into one ocean from those flowing into another.

Continental Shelf. The zone of the continental margin extending from the shore line to the depth, usually about 100 fathoms or 200 meters, where there is a marked or rather steep descent toward the ocean depth.

Contour Line. A line drawn on a map to indicate points of the same height or depth.

Coordinates, Geographical. The intersecting lines of latitude and longitude which determine the geographical position of any given place.

Coulee. A dry ravine or gulch originally formed by running water.

Crater. The bowl-shaped cavity at the summit or on the side of a volcano.

Cultural Feature. Any man-made feature of the earth's surface shown on a map.

Cyclone. Technically, an atmospheric movement in which the wind blows spirally around and in toward a center. Popularly used as a synonym for tornado.

Cylindrical Projection. A map projection produced by projecting the geographic meridians and parallels onto a cylinder which is tangent to the surface of a sphere, and then developing the cylinder into a plane.

D

Day. A measure of time based upon one complete rotation of the earth. A solar day is measured from a transit of the sun across a given meridian to its next successive transit across the same meridian. A civil day is a solar day beginning at midnight.

Degree. A unit of measurement equal to 1/360 of a circle. A degree of latitude on the earth's surface is roughly equivalent to 69 statute miles. A degree of longitude varies in length but is always equivalent to about 4 minutes of time.

Delta. The tract of land formed by the deposit of silt at the mouth of a river.

Desert. A region of considerable extent which is almost destitute of vegetation, chiefly because of insufficient moisture.

Doldrums. The equatorial belt of calms and variable winds.

Downs. Certain hilly districts in southern England underlain by chalk and hence unforested.

Downstream. The direction in which a stream is flowing.

E

Eastern Hemisphere. Usually considered in cartography to be half of the earth extending from pole to pole between 20° W. and 160° E., including Old World continents of Eurasia, Africa, and Australia.

Ecliptic. A great circle sometimes shown on a map or globe and representing the apparent annual path of the sun across the surface of the earth.

Elevation. The vertical distance of a point above or below a reference surface, usually mean sea level.

Equal Area Projection. A map projection on which a constant ratio of areas is preserved; that is, any given part of the map bears the same relation to the area on the sphere which it represents, as the whole map bears to the entire area represented.

Equator. The great circle around the earth equidistant from the poles.

Equatorial Current. The westward drift of surface water on either side of the Equator in the Trade Wind belts.

Estuary. The coastal section of a river which is to a greater or lesser extent invaded by the sea and subject to tidal influence.

F

Fathom. A unit of measurement used for soundings, equal to 1.83 meters or 6 feet.

Ferrell's Law. Moving bodies on the earth's surface (such as air and water) are deflected to the right in the Northern Hemisphere and to the left in the Southern Hemisphere, as a result of the earth's rotation.

Firth. A long arm of the sea, partially landlocked.

Fjord. A long, narrow arm of the sea between high lands.

G

Geodesy. The investigation of scientific questions connected with the shape and dimensions of the earth.

Geographical Mile. See Nautical Mile.

Geographic Center. That point on which any area would balance if it were a plate of uniform thickness. The geographic center of the conterminous United States is at latitude 39° 50', longitude 98° 35', in the eastern part of Smith County, Kansas.

Geography. The scientific description and explanation of the earth's regions.

Glacier. A field or body of land-formed ice moving slowly down a mountainside or valley.

Global Geography. Those aspects of the science of geography which are directly related to the spherical shape of the earth.

Globe. A spherical map of the earth or heavens.

Globe Gore. A section of a map so shaped that it may be mounted on a sphere without appreciable stretching or shrinking.

Gnomonic Projection. A perspective map projection on a plane tangent to the surface of a sphere, having the point of projection at the center of the sphere. It is the only map projection on which all great circles represented are straight lines. Chiefly used for navigational charts.

Great Circle. The line of intersection of the surface of a sphere and any plane which passes through the center of the sphere.

Great Circle Direction. The great circle direction of point A from point B is the angle, measured clockwise from true North, formed by the meridian of point B and the great circle passing through points A and B. See Azimuth.

Great Circle Distance. The distance between any two points, measured either in degrees or miles, along the great circle connecting them.

Greenwich Civil Time. Mean solar time for the Greenwich Meridian, counted from midnight.

Greenwich Meridian. See Prime Meridian.

Gulf. A relatively large portion of the sea partly enclosed by land.

Gulf Stream. The warm current which flows out of the Gulf of Mexico through the Straits of Florida and northward through the Atlantic Ocean until it merges with the West Wind Drift.

H

Hachures. Lines used in shading elevations on a map to outline them and to indicate slope.

Hemisphere. Any half of the earth's surface. See Northern, Southern, Eastern, Western, Land, and Water Hemisphere.

Hill. A natural elevation of the earth's surface above surroundings but lower than a mountain.

Horizon. The line at which the earth and sky appear to meet.

Horizon Ring. A graduated ring fitted to a globe in such manner that its plane contains the center of the globe, and it can be adjusted into the plane of the horizon for a given point.

Horse Latitudes. Zones of high atmospheric pressure with calms and variable breezes, which border the polar edges of the Trade Wind areas.

Hurricane. A violent and destructive storm of the cyclonic type, originating in the Tropics.

Hydrography. The science of measuring and studying oceans, seas, rivers, and other waters, with their marginal land areas, especially for the purpose of aiding navigation. As a map feature, the pattern of rivers, lakes, seas, and oceans shown on a map.

Hypsometric Map. A map colored to show variations in elevation above sea level.

I

Iceberg. A mass of land ice which has broken away from its parent formation on the coast, and either floats in the sea or is stranded on a shoal.

Ice Cap. An ice sheet of vast extent covering the topographic features of a continental land mass.

Inch. A unit of lineal measurement; 1/12 of a foot, or 0.0254 of a meter.

Inclination of the Earth. The tilt of the earth's axis in relation to the plane of the earth's orbit. The angle of inclination is 23½° from vertical.

Insolation. The amount of solar radiation or heat received at a given place over a given period of time.

International Date Line. The line extending from pole to pole along the 180th meridian, with local variations, where each new calendar day begins with the passing of the midnight hour. Travelers crossing the line going west must advance their calendar one day, while those going east must retard the calendar one day.

Interrupted Map Projection. A projection in which the pattern of meridians and parallels is interrupted or broken so that certain areas may be centered upon different central meridians. Goode's Interrupted Homolosine Projection is probably the best known example.

Island. A body of land surrounded by water and smaller than a continent.

Isobar. A line on a map connecting places on the earth at which the barometric pressure is the same at a given time or on the average for a given period of time.

Isogonic Lines. Lines drawn so as to connect points on the earth's surface where the magnetic variation is the same.

Isohyet. A line drawn on a map to connect points having equal rainfall during a given period.

Isopleth. Any line on a map connecting points of equal density or value of distribution. A generic term for such lines as isotherms, isobars, isohyets, etc.

Isotherm. A line on a map connecting places on the earth at which the mean temperature is the same.

Isthmus. A narrow strip of land with water on both sides connecting two larger bodies of land.

K

Kilometer. A unit of length; 1,000 meters; 3,280.84 feet; approximately ⅝ of a mile.

L

Lake. A large sheet of water surrounded by land on all sides.

Land Forms. The shapes into which the earth's surface is sculptured by natural forces.

Land Hemisphere. That half of the earth, centered near Nantes, France, which includes the greatest possible land area.

Latitude. The angular distance in degrees of a point on the earth north or south of the Equator.

Lithosphere. The solid mass of the earth.

Longitude. The angular distance (degrees) of a place east or west of the Prime Meridian.

M

Magnetic Declination. From any given place, the angle of magnetic North from true North.

Magnetic Poles. The two locations representing the poles of unlike magnetism belonging to the earth as a magnetized body. The **North Magnetic Pole** is currently located at approximately 73°N. Lat. and 100°W. Long. on Prince of Wales Island. The **South Magnetic Pole** is currently located at approximately 71°S. Lat. and 149°E. Long. in Antarctica.

Map. A graphic representation, on a plane, of certain selected features of a part or the whole of the earth's surface.

Map Grid. The framework of parallels and meridians by means of which map features are located.

Map Projection. A network of lines representing parallels of latitude and meridians of longitude, derived by geometrical construction or mathematical analysis.

Map Scale. The relationship which exists between a distance on a map and the corresponding distance on the earth. It may be expressed as an equivalence, one inch equals 16 statute miles; as a fraction or ratio, 1:1,000,000; or as a bar graph subdivided to show the distance which each of its parts represents on the earth.

Mean Solar Time. Also called Mean Time. Time measured by the daily motion of a fictitious body called the "mean sun." Since the apparent sun travels in the ecliptic with a variable motion, it cannot be used to measure time, and the "mean sun," supposedly moving uniformly in the Celestial Equator, is used.

Mercator Projection. A conformal projection on which the meridians and parallels are shown as parallel straight lines at right angles to one another, the divisions of latitude being expanded north and south of the Equator in the same proportion as the divisions of longitude have been lengthened by projection. On this projection a line of constant bearing, or rhumb line, is represented by a straight line.

Meridian. A great circle on the earth's surface which passes through the terrestrial poles.

Meridian Ring. A graduated ring fitted to a globe in such manner that its plane contains the poles of the globe, and it can be adjusted into the plane of any given meridian of the globe.

Mesa. A flat-topped mountain or hill, usually bounded on at least one side by a steep cliff.

Meter. A unit of length equivalent in the United States to exactly 39.37 inches.

Mile. A unit of distance. See Nautical Mile and Statute Mile.

Monsoon. A periodic, seasonal movement of air from land to water and vice versa.

Moraine. A mound or ridge of unstratified rock material deposited by a glacier.

Mountain. A natural elevation of the earth's surface rising to a great height.

N

Nadir. The point in the heavens diametrically opposite to the Zenith, or the point directly under the observer.

Nautical Mile. A unit commonly used for measuring

distances at sea; the length of a minute of latitude; 1,853 meters or 6,080 feet. Also called Geographical Mile.

Noon. The instant when the sun's rays fall vertically on any given meridian.

North. The direction along any meridian toward the North Pole.

Northern Hemisphere. That half of the earth north of the Equator.

North Pole. The end or pole of the earth's axis pointing toward the star Polaris.

O

Ocean. A vast expanse of salt water bordered by the continents. The oceans are usually considered to be four in number: Pacific, Atlantic, Indian, and Arctic.

Ocean Basin. A large submarine cavity of more or less round or oval form.

Ocean Current. A specific portion of any ocean moving in a definite direction. It may also be called a stream or drift.

Ocean Deep. Smaller areas, within the great ocean basins, whose depths exceed 16,500 feet.

Oceanography. The science of the oceans, their forms, physical features, and phenomena.

Ocean Trench. A long, narrow, oceanic depression with relatively steep sides.

Orbit of the Earth. The curve which the earth describes in the heavens as it revolves around the sun.

P

Parallels. Small circles on the earth's surface, or lines on a map, perpendicular to the axis of the earth and marking latitude north or south of the Equator.

Peninsula. A piece of land nearly surrounded by water.

Perihelion. That point in the orbit of the earth when the earth is nearest to the sun, 91,450,000 miles.

Perioeci. A point in the same latitude but with a difference in longitude of 180°.

Physical Feature. Usually considered to be any natural feature of the earth's surface shown on a map.

Physical Map. A map in which natural regions and physical features are emphasized by the use of different colors.

Plane of the Ecliptic. The plane of the earth's orbit.

Planet. A celestial body revolving around the sun in a nearly circular orbit, such as the earth.

Plateau. An elevated area of comparatively flat or level land.

Polar Ice Pack. The entire area of thick and closely packed polar ice, more than one year old.

Polar Projection. One in which the meridians appear as straight lines radiating from the pole and the parallels of latitude as concentric circles with the pole as center.

Political Map. A map in which political divisions and boundaries are emphasized through the use of color.

Pond. A sheet of shallow water, generally without outlet, located in the interior of the land.

Prime Meridian. The meridian on the earth's surface from which longitude is measured, generally the meridian of Greenwich, England, on modern maps.

Projection. Any method of delineating on a plane surface the whole or a part of the surface of the earth, including parallels of latitude and meridians of longitude. See Azimuthal, Conformal, Conic, Cylindrical, Equal Area, Gnomonic, Mercator, and Polar Projections.

R

Reef. A rocky or coral elevation in the ocean bottom, which may be uncovered at times.

Representative Fraction. The fraction with unity or one as the numerator, denoting the scale of a map. Abbreviated as "R.F."

Revolution. The movement of the earth around the sun. One complete revolution of the earth requires one year, or 365 days, 5 hours, 48 minutes, 46 seconds.

Rhumb Line. A line which makes equal angles with all the meridians it crosses.

Right Bank. The right bank of a river is the one on the right hand when facing downstream; that of a channel, the same, when facing in the direction of the ebb tide.

Roaring Forties. A term used by sailors to describe the stormy regions between 40° and 50° from the Equator in both the northern and southern oceans.

Rotation. The movement of the earth around its axis. One complete rotation determines the length of one day.

S

Savanna. Originally, an extensive treeless plain, but now more frequently used to mean a tropical landscape of scattered trees and extensive grasslands.

Sea. A mass of salt water more or less confined by portions of the continent or by chains of islands, and forming a basin distinct from the great masses of water.

Sea Level. The level of the surface of the sea considered at any moment at a given place.

Small Circle. Any circle on a sphere smaller than a great circle. Thus, all parallels on a globe or map except the Equator.

Solar System. The sun and all celestial bodies revolving around it, together with their satellites.

Solar Time. Also called true solar time. Time measured by the apparent daily motion of the sun.

Solstice. The time at which the overhead sun is at its greatest distance from the Equator. In the Northern Hemisphere the summer solstice occurs about June 21, and the winter solstice about December 22.

South. The direction along any meridian toward the South Pole.

Southern Hemisphere. That half of the earth south of the Equator.

South Pole. The opposite end of the earth's axis from the North Pole.

Standard Parallel. A parallel of latitude which is used as a control line in the computation of a map projection, and is therefore true to scale.

Statute Mile. A unit of distance generally used in measurements on land, and equal to 5,280 feet.

Steppe. The grassy plains of European and Asiatic Russia.

Strait. A relatively narrow waterway between two larger bodies of water.

T

Temperate Zones. The two belts or zones of the earth lying between the Tropics and the Polar Circles.

Time. The measurable aspect of duration based upon the happening of periodic events, such as: the rotation of the earth (day), the revolution of the moon around the earth (month), and the revolution of the earth around the sun (year). See Civil Time, Greenwich Civil Time, Mean Solar Time, Solar Time.

Time Zone. A belt or zone, extending from north to south across a country, which is given a designated time by law. The United States has four standard time zones, namely: Eastern, Central, Mountain, and Pacific.

Topography. The features of the actual surface of the earth, considered collectively as to form. A single feature, such as a mountain or valley, is called a topographic feature.

Torrid Zone. A term formerly used to describe the belt or zone of the earth's surface bounded by the Tropic of Cancer and the Tropic of Capricorn. Better geographical form today is "Tropical Zone."

Trade Winds. The regular easterly winds which prevail over the oceans on either side of the Equator to about 30° north and south latitudes.

Transverse Projection. A map projection which is turned 90° from its usual orientation, and consequently is centered upon some other great circle than a meridian.

Triangulation. The measurement and calculation of a system of triangles connecting stations covering a particular region, for the purpose of fixing and plotting the positions of same on a chart or map.

Tropic. A line on a map or globe, usually broken or dotted, marking the limit reached by the overhead or vertical sun in its apparent annual migration. The northern line is called the **Tropic of Cancer**, and the southern line the **Tropic of Capricorn**. Both are about 23½° from the Equator.

Trough. A long and broad depression in the ocean bottom, with gently sloping sides.

Tundra. The marshy, treeless plains of northern Asia and northern North America.

Twilight. The periods of partial daylight after sunset and before sunrise, when light from the sun is reflected from the atmosphere overhead.

Typhoon. A violent and destructive storm similar to a hurricane, that occurs in the western Pacific Ocean.

V

Vernal Equinox. The date when the overhead sun crosses the Equator on its apparent migration from south to north, or about March 21, and the length of day and night is approximately the same in all latitudes.

Volcano. A more or less conical hill or mountain from which, when active, steam, gasses, ashes, or molten rocks are ejected.

W

Water Hemisphere. That half of the earth centered near New Zealand which includes the greatest possible water area.

Westerlies. The prevailing winds of the middle latitudes, that is, between 30° and 60° in north and south latitudes.

Western Hemisphere. Usually considered in cartography to be that half of the earth extending from pole to pole between 160° E. and 20° W., thus including the Americas and Greenland.

West Wind Drift. A general term applied to the eastward movement of oceanic water under the influence of the westerly winds.

Y

Year. An interval of time based upon the revolution of the earth in its orbit around the sun. It is equal to 365.24220 mean solar days.

Z

Zenith. The point in the celestial sphere directly over a given point on the earth.

Explanation of the Index and Abbreviations

This universal index includes in a single alphabetical list all important names that appear on the reference maps. For ease in index usage and interpretation, two kinds of type are used to distinguish political names from those of physical features and points of interest. All political names (cities, towns, counties, districts, states, provinces, countries, etc.) are set in roman type. Physical features, and points of interest (rivers, mountains, lakes, bays, hills, straits, islands, national parks, etc.) are set in *italic* type. The supplementary descriptive information with each index entry varies with its political or physical classification.

POLITICAL NAMES

The more important names and political divisions shown on the maps are listed in the index. Each place name is followed by its location; the population figure, when available; the map index key; and the page number of the map.

County and State locations are given for all places in the United States. Province and country locations are given for all places in Canada. All other place name entries show only country locations.

The index reference key, always a letter and figure combination, and the map page are the last items in each entry. Because some places are shown on both a main map and an inset map, more than one index key may be given for a single map page. Reference also may be made to more than a single map. In each case, however, the index key *letter and figure* precede the map *page number* to which reference is made. A lower case key letter indicates reference to an inset map which has been keyed separately.

All major and minor political divisions are followed by both a descriptive term (co., dist., reg., prov., dept., state, etc.), indicating political status, and by the country in which they are located. U.S. counties are listed with State locations; all others are given with country references.

POPULATION FIGURES

The populations in the index are based upon the latest available complete census figures and official estimates for each country. In some cases these populations may differ from those for the same places appearing in the tables elsewhere in the atlas. In these tables, all the populations refer to a single date, to facilitate comparisons. In some instances this date may be more recent than the last complete census used for the populations in the index.

For some larger cities a second population figure is given accompanied by a star (★). The second figure indicates the population of the city's entire metropolitan area including suburbs, as: Chicago, 3,550,404 (★6,777,800). A triangular symbol (▲) denotes a population figure for an *entire* township, district, or other minor civil division.

PHYSICAL NAMES AND POINTS OF INTEREST

The more important physical names and points of interest that are shown on the maps are listed in the index. Each entry is followed by a descriptive term (*bay, hill, range, riv., tombs, nat. park, mtn., isl.*, etc.), to indicate its nature.

Country locations are given for each name, except for features entirely within States of the United States or provinces of Canada, in which case these divisions are also given.

Some names are included in the index that were omitted from the maps because of scale size or lack of space. These entries may be identified by an asterisk (*) and reference is given to the approximate location of the place.

A long name may appear on the map in a shortened form, with the full name given in the index. The part of the name not on the map then appears in brackets, thus: St. Gabriel [-de-Brandon].

In the index, when more than one name with the same spelling is shown, including both political and physical names, the order of precedence is as follows: *first*, place names, *second*, political divisions, and *third*, physical features.

ABBREVIATIONS

admin	administered
Afg	Afghanistan
Afr	Africa
Ala	Alabama
Alb	Albania
Alg	Algeria
Alsk	Alaska
Alta	Alberta
Am	American
Am. Sam	American Samoa
And	Andorra
Ang	Angola
Ant	Antarctica
Arc	Arctic
arch	archipelago
Arg	Argentina
Ariz	Arizona
Ark	Arkansas
Atl. O	Atlantic Ocean
Aus	Austria
Austl	Australia, Australian
auton	autonomous
Ba. Is	Bahama Islands
Barb	Barbados
Bas	Basutoland
B.C	British Columbia
Bech	Bechuanaland
Bel	Belgium, Belgian
Bhu	Bhutan
Bis. Arch	Bismarck Archipelago
Bol	Bolivia
Br	British
Braz	Brazil
Br. Gu	British Guiana
Br. Hond	British Honduras
Bru	Brunei
Bul	Bulgaria
Bur	Burma
Calif	California
Cam	Cameroon
Camb	Cambodia
Can	Canada
Can. Is	Canary Islands
Cen. Afr. Rep.	Central African Republic
Cen. Am	Central America
Cey	Ceylon
C.H	Court House
chan	channel
co	county
Col	Colombia
Colo	Colorado
Con. B.	Congo; Capital: Brazzaville
Con. L.	Congo, The; Capital· Léopoldville
Conn	Connecticut
cont	continent
C.R	Costa Rica
C.V. Is	Cape Verde Islands
Cyp	Cyprus
C.Z	Canal Zone
Czech	Czechoslovakia
Dah	Dahomey
Dan	Danish
D.C	District of Columbia
Del	Delaware
Den	Denmark
dept	department
dep	dependency, dependencies
des	desert
dist	district
div	division
Dom. Rep	Dominican Republic
Ec	Ecuador
Eg	Egypt
Eng	England
Equat. Gui	Equatorial Guinea
est	estuary
Eth	Ethiopia
Eur	Europe
Falk. Is	Falkland Islands
Fed	Federation
Fin	Finland
Fla	Florida
Fr	France, French
Fr. Gu	French Guiana
Fr. Som	French Somaliland
Ga	Georgia
Gam	Gambia
Ger	Germany
Gib	Gibraltar
Grc	Greece
Grnld	Greenland
Guad	Guadeloupe
Guat	Guatemala
Hai	Haiti
Haw	Hawaii
hbr	harbor
Hond	Honduras
Hung	Hungary
I	island
I.C	Ivory Coast
Ice	Iceland
Ill	Illinois
incl	includes, including
Ind	Indiana
Indon	Indonesia
Indian res	Indian reservation
I. of Man	Isle of Man
Ire	Ireland
is	islands
isl	island
Isr	Israel
isth	isthmus
It	Italy
Jam	Jamaica
Jap	Japan
Kans	Kansas
Ken	Kenya
Kor	Korea
Kuw	Kuwait
Ky	Kentucky
La	Louisiana
Leb	Lebanon
Le. Is	Leeward Islands
Lib	Liberia
Liech	Liechtenstein
Lux	Luxembourg
Mala	Malaysia
Malag	Malagasy Republic
Man	Manitoba
Mart	Martinique
Mass	Massachusetts
Maur	Mauritania
Md	Maryland
Medit	Mediterranean
Mex	Mexico
Mich	Michigan
Minn	Minnesota
Miss	Mississippi
Mo	Missouri
Mong	Mongolia
Mont	Montana
Mor	Morocco
Moz	Mozambique
mtn	mount, mountain
mts	mountains
mun	municipality
Mus. & Om	Muscat & Oman
N.A	North America
nat. mon	national monument
nat. park	national park
N.B	New Brunswick
N.C	North Carolina
N. Cal	New Caledonia
N. Dak	North Dakota
Nebr	Nebraska
Nep	Nepal
Neth	Netherlands
Nev	Nevada
Newf	Newfoundland
New Hebr	New Hebrides
N. Gui	New Guinea Territory
N.H	New Hampshire
Nic	Nicaragua
Nig	Nigeria
N. Ire	Northern Ireland
N.J	New Jersey
N. Mex	New Mexico
Nor	Norway, Norwegian
N.S	Nova Scotia
N.W. Ter	Northwest Territories
N.Y	New York
N.Z	New Zealand
occ	occupied area
Okla	Oklahoma
Ont	Ontario
Oreg	Oregon
Pa	Pennsylvania
Pac. O	Pacific Ocean
Pak	Pakistan
Pan	Panama
Pap	Papua
Par	Paraguay
par	parish
P.E.I	Prince Edward Island
pen	peninsula
Phil	Philippines
plat	plateau
Pol	Poland
pol. dist	political district
pop	population
Port	Portugal, Portuguese
Port. Gui	Portuguese Guinea
Port. Timor	Portuguese Timor
poss	possession
P.R	Puerto Rico
pref	prefecture
prot	protectorate
prov	province, provincial
pt	point
Que	Quebec
reg	region, regions
rep	republic
res	reservation, reservoir
Rh	Rhodesia
R.I	Rhode Island
riv	river
Rom	Romania
S.A	South America
S. Afr	South Africa
Sal	El Salvador
Sask	Saskatchewan
Sau. Ar	Saudi Arabia
S.C	South Carolina
Scot	Scotland
S. Dak	South Dakota
Sen	Senegal
S.L	Sierra Leone
Sol. Is	Solomon Islands
Som	Somali Republic
Sov. Un	Soviet Union
Sp	Spain, Spanish
St., Ste	Saint, Sainte
Sud	Sudan
Sur	Surinam
S.W. Afr	South West Africa
Swaz	Swaziland
Swe	Sweden
Switz	Switzerland
Syr	Syria
Tan	Tanzania
Tenn	Tennessee
ter	territories, territory
Tex	Texas
Thai	Thailand
Trin	Trinidad & Tobago
Tr. Coast	Trucial Coast
trust	trusteeship
Tun	Tunisia
Tur	Turkey
U.A.R	United Arab Republic
Ug	Uganda
U.K	United Kingdom
Ur	Uruguay
U.S	United States
Va	Virginia
val	valley
Ven	Venezuela
Viet	Vietnam
Vir. Is	Virgin Islands
vol	volcano
Vt	Vermont
Wash	Washington
W.I	West Indies
Win. Is	Windward Islands
Wis	Wisconsin
W. Sam	Western Samoa
W. Va	West Virginia
Wyo	Wyoming
Yugo	Yugoslavia

Index to Political-Physical Maps

Aïoun el Atrous, Maur...C3 45
Aipe, Col., 2,221...C2 60
Aiquile, Bol., 3,465...C2 55
Air (Azbine), reg., Niger...C6 45
Airabu, isl., Indon...K7 38
Airai, Palau Is... 52
Airaines, Fr., 1,673...E9 12
Air Base City, Lea, N. Mex., 200...E6 107
Aird, isl., Ont., Can...B8 98
Aird Bremish, isl., Scot...B1 13
Airdrie, Alta., Can., 524...D3 69
Airdrie, Scot., 33,620...E5 13
Aire, riv., Eng...A6 12
Aire, riv., Fr...E5 15
Aire-sur-l'Adour, Fr., 3,544...F3 14
Aire-sur-la-Lys, Fr., 5,528...D2 15
Aireys, Dorchester, Md., 50...C6 85
Air Force, isl., N.W. Ter., Can...C18 67
Air Line, Hart, Ga., 200...B3 87
Airolo, Switz., 2,023...C6 19
Airukiiji, isl., Bikini... 52
Aisch, riv., Ger...D5 17
Aisén, prov., Chile, 37,085...D2 54
Aishihik, lake, Yukon, Can...D5 66
Aisne, dept., Fr., 512,920...E3 15
Aisne, riv., Fr...C5 14
Aissa, mtn., Alg...C4 44
Aitape, N. Gui...h11 50
Aitkin, Aitkin, Minn., 1,829...D5 99
Aitkin, co., Minn., 12,162...D5 99
Aitolia kai Akarnania (Aetolia and Acarnania), prov., Grc., 237,738...*C3 23
Aitolikon, Grc., 5,959...C3 23
Aiud, Rom., 11,886...B6 22
Aiún, Sp. Sahara, 1,369...D2 44
Aiuruoca, Braz., 1,591...g5 56
Aiwa, isl., Fiji Is... 52
Aix-en-Provence, Fr., 67,943...F6 14
Aix-la-Chapelle, see Aachen, Ger.
Aix-les-Bains, Fr., 18,132...D1 18
Aiyina, Grc., 6,217...D4 23
Aiyina (Aegina), isl., Grc...D4 23
Aiyion, Grc., 17,762...C4 23
Aiyon, Palau Is... 52
Ajaccio, Fr., 41,006...D2 21
Ajaccio, gulf, Fr...D2 21
Ajana, Austl., 80...E1 50
Ajanta, India, 3,560...G6 40
Ajax, Ont., Can., 7,755...D6 72
Ajayan, bay, Guam... 52
Ajdābiyah (Agedábia), Libya, 16,386...C4 43
Ajigasawa, Jap., 8,100...F10 37
'Ajlūn, Jordan, 2,518...B7 32
Ajlune, Lewis, Wash., 100...C3 122
Ajmer, India, 231,240...C5 38, D5 40
Ajmer, state, India, 693,372...*D5 40
Ajo, Pima, Ariz., 7,049...E3 80
Ajoe, is., W. Irian...E8 35
Ajuana, riv., Braz...D4 60
Akaishi-Sammyaku, mts., Jap...n17 37
Akalkot, India, 21,278...I6 40
Akaroa, N.Z., 632...O14 51
Akasha, Sud...A3 47
Akashi, Jap., 129,780...I7 37
Akaska, Walworth, S. Dak., 90...B5 116
Ak-Bulak, Sov. Un., 10,000...E20 9
Akcaabat, Tur., 4,414...B12 31
Akcadag, Tur., 3,540...C11 31
Akdag-madeni, Tur., 4,000...C10 31
Akchar, sand dunes, Maur...B2 45
Akechi, Jap., 4,800...n16 37
Akela, Luna, N. Mex., 10...E2 107
Akeley, Hubbard, Minn., 434...C4 99
Aken, Ger., 12,700...B7 17
Akers, Tangipahoa, La., 150...B7, D5 95
Akershus, co., Nor., 234,500...*H4 25
Aksum (Axum), Eth...C4 47
Aketi, Con. L., 12,100...A3 48
Akhaia (Achaea), prov., Grc., 239,206...C3 23
Akhaltsikhe, Sov. Un., 10,245...B14 31
Akharnai, Grc., 11,290...g11 23
Akhdar, mts., Libya...C4 43
Akheloos, riv., Grc...C3 23
Akhiok, Alsk., 84...D9 79
Akhisar, Tur., 40,000...C6 31
Akhmîm, Eg., U.A.R., 38,000...D6 43
Akhtopol, Bul., 1,052...D8 22
Akhtyrka, Sov. Un., 55,200...F10 27
Aki, Jap., 13,100...J6 37
Akiachak, Alsk., 229...C7 79
Akiak, Alsk., 187...C7 79
Akimiski, isl., N.W. Ter., Can...F16 67
Åkirkeby, Den., 1,461...A3 26
Akita, Jap., 166,000 (203,661▲)...G10 37
Akita, pref., Jap., 1,335,580...*G10 37
Akjoujt, Maur., 2,200...C2 45
Akkeshi, Jap., 16,100...E12 37
Aklan, prov., Phil., 226,500...*D7 35
Aklavik, N.W. Ter., Can., 599...C5 66
Akobo, Sud...D3 47
Akobo, riv., Eth...D3 47
Akola, India, 115,760...D6 39
Akonolinga, Cam...E2 46
Akpatok, isl., N.W. Ter., Can...D19 67
Akra, India...D8 39
Akra, Pembina, N. Dak., 26...A8 110
Akranes, Ice., 3,913...n21 25
Akritas, cape, Grc...D3 23
Akritis, isl., Grc...D6 23
Akron, Hale, Ala, 604...C2 78
Akron, Washington, Colo., 1,890...A7 83
Akron, Fulton, Ind., 958...B5 91
Akron, Plymouth, Iowa, 1,351...B1 92
Akron, Tuscola, Mich., 503...E7 98
Akron, Erie, N.Y., 2,841...B2 108
Akron, Summit, Ohio, 290,351 (*573,800)...A6 111
Akron, Lancaster, Pa., 2,167...F9 114
Aksaray, Tur., 20,000...C10 31
Aksehir, Tur., 20,600...C8 31
Aksehir, lake, Tur...C8 31
Akseki, Tur., 2,700...D8 31
Aksenovo-Zilovskove, Sov. Un., 10,000...D14 28
Akshimrau, Sov. Un...E4 29
Aksu, China...E11 28
Aksuat, Sov. Un., 3,000...E21 9
Aktogay, Sov. Un...D9 29
Aktumsyk, Sov. Un...D5 29
Aktyubinsk, Sov. Un., 116,000...C5 29
Akure, Nig., 38,853...E6 45
Akureyri, Ice., 8,957...n23 25
Akuseki, isl., Jap...L4 37
Akutan, Alsk., 107...E6 79
Akyab, Bur., 42,329...D9 39
Alabama, state, U.S., 3,266,740...D10 77, 78
Alabama, riv., Ala...D2 78
Alabama Port, Mobile, Ala., 200...E1 78
Alabaster, Shelby, Ala., 1,623...B3 78
Alabaster, Iosco, Mich., 125...D7 98
Alabat, isl., Phil...o14 35
Al Abyār, Libya, 150...F3 31
Alachua, Alachua, Fla., 1,974...C4 86
Alachua, co., Fla., 74,074...C4 86
Aladdin, Crook, Wyo., 10...A8 125
Alagna, It., 516...D3 18
Alagoa Grande, Braz., 12,115...C3, h6 57
Alagôas, state, Braz., 1,271,062...C3, k5 57
Alagoinhas, Braz., 38,246...D3 57
Alagón, Sp., 5,270...B5 20
Alagón, riv., Sp...B2 20
Al-Ahmadi, Kuw., 7,205...G4 41
Al 'Ajamīyin, Eg., U.A.R., 2,000...E2 32
Alajuela, C.R., 19,900...E5 62
Alajuela, prov., C.R., 232,000...*E5 62
Alakanuk, Alsk., 278...C7 79
Alakol, lake, Sov. Un...D10 29
Al'Alamayn (El Alamein), Eg., U.A.R...C5 43
Alalān, Iran, 10,000...C4 41
Alamance, Alamance, N.C., 450...B4 109
Alamance, co., N.C., 85,674...B4 109
Alameda, Alameda, Calif., 63,855...B5 82
Alameda, Sask., Can., 312...H4 70
Alameda, Bernalillo, N. Mex., 3,500...B3, k7 107
Alameda, co., Calif., 908,209...D3 82
Alaminos, Phil., 3,014...n12 35
Al 'Āmirīyah, Eg., U.A.R., 10,000...G7 31
Alamito, creek, Tex...F2 118
Alamo, Contra Costa, Calif., 1,791...*B6 82
Alamo, Wheeler, Ga., 822...D4 87
Alamo, Montgomery, Ind., 144...E3 91
Alamo, Mex., 6,375...m15 63
Alamo, Lincoln, Nev., 250...F6 104
Alamo, Williams, N. Dak., 182...A2 110
Alamo, Crockett, Tenn., 1,665...B2 117
Alamo, Hidalgo, Tex., 4,121...F3 118
Alamogordo, Otero, N. Mex., 21,723...E4 107
Alamogordo, res., N. Mex...C5 107
Alamo Heights, Bexar, Tex., 7,552...B4, E3 118
Alamo Hueco, mts., N. Mex...F1 107
Alamos, Mex., 2,872...B3 63
Alamosa, Alamosa, Colo., 6,205...D5 83
Alamosa, co., Colo., 10,000...D5 83
Alamosa, creek, Colo...D4 83
Alamosa, riv., N. Mex...D2 107
Åland (Ahvenanmaa), dept., Fin., 22,787...*G8 25
Alanreed, Gray, Tex. 200...B2 118
Alanson, Emmet, Mich., 290...C6 98
Alantika, mts., Cam...D2 46
Alanya, Tur., 10,100...D9 31
Alaotra, lake, Malag...g9 49
Alapah, mtn., Alsk...B9 79
Alapaha, Berrien, Ga., 631...E3 87
Alapaha, riv., Ga...E3 87
Alapayevsk, Sov. Un., 50,000...B6 29, D21 9
Al 'Aqabah, Jordan, 2,835...E7 32
Alaqua, Walton, Fla., 200...G3 86
Al 'Arish, Eg., U.A.R., 10,791...C6 43
Alarka, Swain, N.C., 300...D2 109
Alasehir, Tur., 13,900...C7 31
Ala Shan, mts., China...D6 34
Al Ashkharah, Mus. & Om...D2 39
Alaska, state, U.S., 226,167...E4 76, 79
Alaska, gulf, Alsk...D10 79
Alaska, pen., Alsk...D8 79
Alaska, range, Alsk...C9 79
Alassio, It., 8,544...C2 21
Alatyr, Sov. Un., 34,700...C3 29
Alau, isl., Haw...C6 88
Alausí, Ec., 4,812...B2 58
Alava, prov., Sp., 138,934...*A4 20
Alava, cape, Wash...A1 122
Alaverdi, Sov. Un., 10,000...B15 31
Al 'Aynā, Jordan 1,000...D7 32
Al 'Ayzarīyah (Bethany), Jordan, 2,000...h12 32
Al 'Azair, Iraq...F3 41
Alba, It., 12,000...B2 21
Alba, Antrim, Mich., 200...D6 98
Alba, Jasper, Mo., 336...D3 101
Alba, Bradford, Pa., 192...C8 114
Alba, Wood, Tex., 742...C5 118
Albacete, Sp., 61,635 (74,417▲)...C5 20
Albacete, prov., Sp., 370,976...*C5 20
Alba de Tormes, Sp., 3,666...B3 20
Ålbaek, Den., 877...A4 24
Ålbaek, bay, Den...A4 24
Alba Iulia, Rom., 14,776...B6 22
Al Bājhūr, Eg., U.A.R., 10,000...D3 32
Albalate [del Arzobispo], Sp., 3,844...B5 20
Al Ballaḥ, Eg., U.A.R., 1,000...D4 32
Albanel, lake, Que., Can...F18 67
Albania, country, Eur., 1,846,000...G13 8, B3 23
Albano, lake, It...h9 21
Albano Laziale, It., 15,300...D4, h9 21
Albany, Austl., 10,526...F2 50
Albany, P.E.I., Can., 226...C6 74
Albany, Dougherty, Ga., 55,890...E2 87
Albany, Whiteside, Ill., 637...B3 90
Albany, Delaware, Ind., 2,132...D7 91
Albany, Clinton, Ky., 1,887...D4 94
Albany, Livingston, La., 557...A6 95
Albany, Stearns, Minn., 1,375...E4 99
Albany, Gentry, Mo., 1,662...A3 101
Albany, Albany, N.Y., 129,726 (*588,200)...C7 108
Albany, Athens, Ohio, 629...C5 111
Albany, Bryan, Okla., 150...D5 112
Albany, Linn, Oreg., 12,926...C1, C3 113
Albany, Shackelford, Tex., 2,174...C3 118
Albany, Orleans, Vt., 169 (560▲)...B4 120
Albany, Green, Wis., 892...F4 124
Albany, Albany, Wyo., 100...D6 125
Albany, co., N.Y., 272,926...C6 108
Albany, co., Wyo., 21,290...D7 125
Albany, riv., Ont., Can...o18 72
Albany South, Dougherty, Ga., 1,200...*E2 87
Al Barkāt, Libya...E2 43
Al Batānūn, Eg., U.A.R., 1,000...D2 32
Al Bawīṭī, Eg., U.A.R...D5 43
Albay, prov., Phil., 516,000...*C6 35
Albee, Grant, S. Dak., 42...B9 116
Albemarle, Stanly, N.C., 12,261...B3 109
Albemarle, co., Va., 30,969...D4 121
Albemarle, sound, N.C...A7 109
Albenga, It., 8,700...B2 21
Alberche, riv., Sp...B3 20
Alberene, Albemarle, Va., 300...D4 121
Alberga, Swe., 267...u34 25
Albergaria-a-Velha, Port...B1 20
Alberhill, Riverside, Calif., 200...F3 82
Alberni, B.C., Can., 4,616...E5 68
Albers, Clinton, Ill., 566...E4 90
Albersdorf, Ger., 2,800...D3 24
Albert, N.B., Can., 522...D5 74
Albert, Fr., 10,247...B5 14
Albert, Barton, Kans., 221...D4 93
Albert, Harding, N. Mex., 5...B6 107
Albert, Caddo, Okla., 135...B3 112
Albert, Tucker, W. Va., 45...B5 123
Albert, co., N.B., Can., 12,485...D5 74
Albert, lake, Ug...A5 48
Alberta, Wilcox, Ala., 225...C2 78
Alberta, Stevens, Minn., 149...E2 99
Alberta, Brunswick, Va., 430...E5 121
Alberta, prov., Can., 1,331,944...F9 66, 69
Alberta, mtn., Alta., Can...C2 69
Alberta Beach, Alta., Can., 135...*C3 69
Albert Canyon, B.C., Can...D9 68
Albert City, Buena Vista, Iowa, 722...B3 92
Albert Lea, Freeborn, Minn., 17,108...G5 99
Albert Markham, mtn., Ant...A28 5
Albert Nile, riv., Ug...A5 48
Alberton, P.E.I., Can., 855...C5 74
Alberton, Mineral, Mont., 356...C2 102
Albertson, Nassau, N.Y., 12,200...*E7 108
Albertville, Marshall, Ala., 8,250...A3 78
Albertville, Con. L., 29,500...C4 48
Albertville, Sask., Can., 100...D3 70
Albertville Fr., 12,159...E7 14
Albertville, Wright, Minn., 279...E5 99
Albeuve, Switz., 601...C3 19
Albi, Fr., 38,709...F5 14
Albia, Monroe, Iowa 4,582...C5 92
Albin, Tallahatchie, Miss., 40...B3 100
Albin, Laramie, Wyo., 172...D8 125
Albina, Sur...A4 59
Albion, Mendocino, Calif., 300...C2 82
Albion, Cassia, Idaho, 415...G5 89
Albion, Edwards, Ill., 2,025...E5 90
Albion, Noble, Ind., 1,325...B7 91
Albion, Marshall, Iowa 588...B5 92
Albion, Kennebec, Maine, 100 (974▲)...D3 96
Albion, Calhoun, Mich., 12,749...F6 98
Albion, Carter, Mont., 5...E12 102
Albion, Boone, Nebr., 1,982...C7 103
Albion, Orleans, N.Y., 5,182...B2 108
Albion, Pushmataha, Okla., 161...C6 112
Albion, Erie, Pa., 1,630...C1 114
Albion, Providence, R.I., 700...B11 84
Albion, Whitman, Wash., 291...C8 122
Albion, Dane, Wis., 150...F4 124
Al Bīrah, Jordan...h11 32
Alborán, isl., Sp...E4 20
Ålborg, Den., 85,800 (*119,063)...A3 24
Ålborg, co., Den., 232,885...B3 24
Ålborg, bay, Den...B4 24
Alborn, St. Louis, Minn., 50...D6 99
Albox, Sp., 9,908...D4 20
Albreda, B.C., Can., 52...C8 68
Albright, Preston, W. Va., 304...*B5 123
Albrightsville, Carbon, Pa., 90...D10 114
Al Bu'ayrāt, Libya...C3 43, I14 30
Albufeira, Port., 3,160...D1 20
Albuñol, Sp., 7,989...D4 20
Albuquerque, Bernalillo, N. Mex., 201,189 (*266,300)...B3, k7 107
Alburg, Grand Isle, Vt., 426 (1,123▲)...B2 120
Alburnett, Linn, Iowa 341...B6 92
Alburquerque, Sp., 9,756...C2 20
Alburtis, Lehigh, Pa., 1,086...E10 114
Albury, Austl., 22,983...H6 51
Al Busaiya, Iraq...F3 41
Al Buṣaylī, Eg., U.A.R., 1,000...C2 32
Alca, Peru, 713...E3 58
Alcabideche, Port., 9,485...f9 20
Alcácer do Sal, Port., 4,040...C1 20
Alcalá de Chisvert, Sp., 4,394...B6 20
Alcalá [de Guadaira], Sp., 25,000 (31,004▲)...D3 20
Alcalá de Henares, Sp., 25,123...B4, p18 20
Alcalá de los Gazules, Sp., 9,693...D3 20
Alcalá la Real, Sp., 9,979...D4 20
Alcalde, Rio Arriba, N. Mex., 650...A3 107
Alcamo, It., 43,000...F4 21
Alcanadre, riv., Sp...B5 20
Alcanar, Sp., 6,944...B6 20
Alcañiz, Sp., 10,035...B5 20
Alcântara, Braz., 1,300...B2 57
Alcantarilla, Sp., 15,748...D5 20
Alcaraz, Sp., 5,864...C4 20
Alcaudete, Sp., 18,442...D3 20
Alcázar de San Juan, Sp., 24,963...C4 20
Alcester, Union, S.Dak., 479...D9 116
Alcira, Sp., 26,669...C5 20
Alco, Stone, Ark., 25...B3 81
Alco, Vernon, La., 40...C2 95
Alcoa, Blount, Tenn., 6,395...D10, E11 117
Alcobendas, Sp., 4,778...o17 20
Alcochete, Port., 6,494...f10 20
Alcolu, Clarendon, S.C., 275...D7 115
Alcomdale, Alta., Can...C4 69
Alcona, co., Mich., 6,352...D7 98
Alcora, Sp., 3,782...B5 20
Alcorcón, Sp., 3,356...p17 20
Alcorisa, Sp., 3,497...B5 20
Alcorn, Jackson, Ky., 5...C5 94
Alcorn, Claiborne, Miss., 1,100...D2 100
Alcorn, co., Miss., 25,282...A5 100
Alcova, Natrona, Wyo., 75...C6 125
Alcovy, mtn., Ga...C3 87
Alcoy, Sp., 51,096...C5 20
Alda, Hall, Nebr., 229...D7 103
Aldama, Mex., 5,194...B3 63
Aldan, Delaware, Pa., 4,324...*G11 114
Aldan, Sov. Un., 10,000...D15 28
Aldan, plat., Sov. Un...D15 28
Aldan, riv., Sov. Un...C16 28
Aldeburgh, Eng., 2,972...B9 12
Aldecoa, Cuba...h11 64
Alden, Jefferson, Ala. (part of Graysville)...E4 78
Alden, McHenry, Ill., 200...A5 90
Alden, Hardin, Iowa, 838...B4 92
Alden, Rice, Kans., 239...D5 87
Alden, Antrim, Mich., 190...D5 98
Alden, Freeborn, Minn., 215...G5 99
Alden, Erie, N.Y., 2,042...C2 108
Alden, Luzerne, Pa., 1,000...D9 114
Alden Bridge, Bossier, La., 200...B2 95
Alder, Madison, Mont., 100...E4 102
Alder, brook, Vt...B4 120
Alder, mtn., Scot...D4 13
Aldergrove, B.C., Can., 520...*E6 68
Alderney, isl., Guernsey...F5 10
Aldershot, Eng., 32,900 (*165,000)...C7 12
Alderson, Pittsburg, Okla., 207...C6 112
Alderson, Greenbrier and Monroe, W. Va., 1,225...D4 123
Aldersyde, Alta., Can., 121...D4 69
Alderwood Manor, Snohomish, Wash., 4,000...B3 122
Aldie, Loudoun, Va., 100...A4, C5 121
Aldin, pt., Fiji Is... 52
Aldine, Salem, N.J., 30...D2 106
Aldora, Lamar, Ga., 535...C2 87
Aldrich, Shelby, Ala., 800...B3 78
Aldrich, Wadena, Minn., 90...D4 99
Aldrich, Polk, Mo., 181...D4 101
Aldridge, Walker, Ala., 100...B2 78
Ale, riv., Scot...E6 13
Aledo, Mercer, Ill., 3,080...B3 90
Aledo, Parker, Tex., 450...B5 118
Alegre, Braz., 7,487...C4 56
Alegrete, Braz., 33,735...D1 56
Alegria, Phil., 2,624...*C6 35
Alegros, mtn., N. Mex...C1 107
Aleknagik, Alsk., 231...D8 79
Aleksander, wadi, Isr...f10 32
Aleksandriya, Sov. Un., 43,300...G9 27
Aleksandrov, Sov. Un., 30,600...C12 27
Aleksandrov-Gay, Sov. Un...C3 29
Aleksandrovskoye, Sov. Un., 12,000...A9 29
Aleksandrovsk [-Sakhalinskiy], Sov. Un., 39,400...D17 28
Aleksandrow, Pol., 7,577...B5 26
Aleksandrow, Pol., 6,926...C5 26
Aleksin, Sov. Un., 50,000...D11 27
Aleksinac, Yugo., 8,741...D5 22
Alelai, pt., W. Sam... 52
Alemania, Arg...E2 55
Alençon, Fr., 25,584...C4 14
Alenquer, Braz., 7,027...C4 59
Alenquer, Port., 2,498...C1 20
Alentejo, reg., Port., 685,300...C2 20
Alepokhori, Grc...g10 23
Aleppo (Halab), Syr., 425,467...D11 31
Aleria, Fr., 907...C2 21
Alert, N.W. Ter., Can...k39 67
Alert, Decatur, Ind., 80...F6 95
Alert, Franklin, N.C...A5 109
Alert Bay, B.C., Can., 825...D4 68
Alès, Fr., 41,360...E6 14
Alessandria, It., 96,100...B2 21
Alestrup, Den., 1,763...B3 24
Ålesund, Nor., 19,200 (*35,000)...F2 25
Alet, Fr., 695...F5 14
Aleutian, is., Alsk...E3 79
Aleutian, range, Alsk...D9 79
Alex, Grady, Okla., 545...C4 112
Alexander, Pulaski and Saline, Ark., 177...C3, D5 81
Alexander, Man., Can., 269...E1 71
Alexander, Burke, Ga., 150...C5 87
Alexander, Morgan, Ill., 300...D3 90
Alexander, Franklin, Iowa, 294...B4 92
Alexander, Rush, Kans., 153...D4 93
Alexander, Genesee, N.Y., 414...C2 108
Alexander, Buncombe, N.C., 75...D3 109
Alexander, McKenzie, N. Dak., 269...B2 110
Alexander, Upshur, W. Va., 25...C4 123
Alexander, co., Ill., 16,061...F4 90
Alexander, co., N.C., 15,625...B2 109
Alexander, arch., Alsk...D12 79
Alexander, isl., Ant...B5 5
Alexander, lake, Minn...D4 99
Alexander Bay, S. Afr., 2,066...C2 49
Alexander City, Tallapoosa, Ala., 13,140...C4 78
Alexander Humboldt, mts., Ant...B14 5
Alexander Mills, Rutherford, N.C., 947...B3, D4 109
Alexandra, N.Z., 2,296...P12 51
Alexandra, isl., Sov. Un...A10 4
Alexandretta, gulf, Tur...D10 31
Alexandria, Calhoun, Ala., 200...B4 78
Alexandria, B.C., Can., 205...C6 68
Alexandria, Ont., Can., 2,597...B10 72
Alexandria (Al Iskandarīyah), Eg., U.A.R., 1,516,234 (*1,575,000)...C5 43
Alexandria, Madison, Ind., 5,582...D6 91
Alexandria, Campbell, Ky., 1,318...A7, B5 94
Alexandria, Rapides, La., 40,279...C3 95
Alexandria, Douglas, Minn., 6,713...E3 99
Alexandria, Clark, Mo., 452...A6 101
Alexandria, Thayer, Nebr., 257...D8 103
Alexandria, Grafton, N.H., 75 (370▲)...C3 105
Alexandria, Licking, Ohio, 452...B5 111
Alexandria, Huntingdon, Pa., 381...E5 114
Alexandria, Rom., 19,294...D7 22
Alexandria, Hanson, S. Dak., 614...D8 116
Alexandria, DeKalb, Tenn., 599...C7 117
Alexandria (Independent City), Va., 91,023...B5, C5 121
Alexandria Bay, Jefferson, N.Y., 1,583...A5, f9 108
Alexandria Southwest, Rapides, La., 2,782...*C3 95
Alexandrina, lake, Austl...G2 51
Alexandroupolis, Grc., 18,712...B5 23
Alexis, Warren and Mercer, Ill., 878...B3 90
Alexis, riv., Newf., Can...B3 75
Alexis Creek, B.C., Can., 134...C6 68
Aley, riv., Sov. Un...E25 9
Aleysk, Sov. Un., 10,000...C10 29
Alfalfa, co., Okla., 8,445...A3 112
Al Fandaqūmīyah, Jordan, 3,000...B7, f11 32
Al Farāfirah, Eg., U.A.R., 749...D5 43
Alfaro, Sp., 8,570...A5 20
Alfatar, Bul., 3,346...D8 22
Al Fayyūm (El Faiyûm), Eg., U.A.R., 102,064...E2 32
Alfeld, Ger., 13,100...B4 17
Alfenas, Braz., 16,051...C3, k9 56
Alfios (Alpheus), riv., Grc...D3 23
Alfonsine, It., 4,606...E8 18
Alford, Eng., 2,134...A8 12
Alford, Jackson, Fla., 380...B1, G3 86
Alford, Pike, Ind., 25...H3 91
Alford, Berkshire, Mass., 45 (256▲)...B1 97
Alford, Scot., 1,248...C6 13
Alfordsville, Daviess, Ind., 121...C4 91
Alfortville, Fr., 32,332...g10 14
Alfred, Ont., Can., 1,195...B10 72
Alfred, York, Maine, 300 (1,201▲)...E2 96
Alfred, Allegany, N.Y., 2,807...C3 108
Alfred, La Moure, N. Dak., 150...C6 110
Alfred Station, Allegany, N.Y., 200...C3 108
Al Fuqaha, Libya...D3 43
Algā, Eth...D4 47
Algarrobal, Chile...E1 55
Algarrobo, Chile...E1 55
Algarrobo del Aguilla, Arg...B3 54
Algarve, prov., Port., 328,231...*D2 20
Algarve, reg., Port., 314,800...D1 20
Algeciras, Sp., 66,317...D3 20
Algemesí, Sp., 19,057...C5 20
Alger, see Algiers, Alg.
Alger, Arenac, Mich., 60...D6 98
Alger, Hardin, Ohio, 1,068...B4 111
Alger, co., Mich., 9,250...B4 98
Algeria, country, Afr., 10,700,000...D5 42, D4 44
Algete, Sp., 1,150...o18 20
Al Ghayatah, Eg., U.A.R., 1,000...D2 32
Alghero, It., 24,000...D2 21
Al Ghurdaqah, Eg., U.A.R., 2,727...D6 43
Algiers (Alger), Alg., 883,879 (*995,000)...F8 30, B5 44
Algoa, bay, S. Afr...D4 49
Algodones, Sandoval, N. Mex., 260...B3, k8 107
Algoma, Pontotoc, Miss., 190...A4 100
Algoma, Kewaunee, Wis., 3,855...D6 124
Algoma, dist., Ont., Can., 111,408...A2 72
Algoma Mills, Ont., Can., 373...A2 72
Algona, Kossuth, Iowa, 5,702...A3 92
Algona, King, Wash., 1,311...B3, D2 122
Algonac, St. Clair, Mich., 3,190...F8 98
Algonquin, Ont., Can., 120...C9 72
Algonquin, McHenry, Ill., 2,692...A5, E2 90
Algonquin, prov. park, Ont., Can...B6 72
Algonquin Park, Ont., Can...B6 72
Algood, Putnam, Tenn., 886...C8 117
Algorta, Ur...E1 56
Algrange, Fr., 9,163...E6 15
Al Ḥāfir (Oasis), Sau. Ar...H13 31
Alhama, Sp., 9,849...D4 20
Alhama, Sp., 6,442...D5 20
Alhambra, Los Angeles, Calif., 54,807...F2 82
Alhambra, Madison, Ill., 537...E4 90
Alhambra, Jefferson, Mont., 60...D5 102
Al Hāmūl, Eg., U.A.R., 2,000...D3 32
Alhaurín el Grande, Sp., 11,525...D3 20
Al Ḥawṣah (Oasis), Jordan...H11 31
Al Ḥayy, Eg., U.A.R., 1,000...E3 32
Al Ḥayyānīyah (Oasis), Sau. Ar...H14 31
Alhos Vedros, Port., 2,509...f9 20
Al Ḥudaydah, Yemen, 40,000...C5 47
Al Hufūf (Hofuf), Sau. Ar., 85,000...I4 41
Al Ḥumaymah, Jordan, 1,000...D7 32
Al Ḥuṣn, Jordan, 1,000...B7 32
Aliakmon, riv., Grc...B3 23
Alibag, India, 9,909...H4 40
Alicahue, Chile...A2 54
Alicante, Sp., 121,527...C5 20
Alicante, prov., Sp., 711,942...*C5 20
Alicante, gulf, Sp...C5 20
Alice, Ont., Can., 97...B7 72
Alice, Cass, N. Dak., 124...C8 110
Alice, Jim Wells, Tex., 20,861...F3 118
Alice, lake, Minn...C7 99
Alicel, Union, Oreg., 35...B9 113
Alice Southwest, Jim Wells, Tex., 1,813...*F3 118
Alice Springs, Austl., 4,648...D5 50
Aliceville, Pickens, Ala., 3,194...B1 78
Aliceville, Coffey, Kans., 100...D8 93
Alicia, Lawrence, Ark., 236...B4 81
Alicudi, isl., It...E5 21
Alida, Sask., Can., 241...H5 70
Alief, Harris, Tex., 300...F4 118
Aligarh, India, 185,020...C6 39
Ali Gharbi, Iraq, 3,377...E3 41
Aligūdarz, Iran, 8,459...E4 41
Alindao, Cen. Afr. Rep...E4 46
Aline, Chandler, Ga., 100...D4 87
Aline, Alfalfa, Okla., 314...A3 112
Alingsås, Swe., 17,500...I5 25
Alipur Duar, India, 17,882...D12 40
Aliquippa, Beaver, Pa., 26,369...A5, E1 114
Alisal, Monterey, Calif., 16,473...C6 82
Al Iskandarīyah, see Alexandria, Eg., U.A.R.
Al Isma 'īlīyah, Eg., U.A.R., 116,302...G9 31, D4 32
Alistrati, Grc., 4,951...B5 23
Aliwal North, S. Afr., 10,706...D4 49
Alix, Franklin, Ark., 350...B2 81
Alix, Alta., Can., 631...C4 69
Al Jaghbūb, Libya, 196...D4 43
Al Jāniyah, Jordan, 1,000...h11 32
Al Jawf (Jauf), Sau. Ar., 10,000...D7 43
Al Jawsh, Libya, 2,680...C2 43
Aljezur, Port., 5,286...D1 20
Al Jīzah (El Gizeh) (El Gîza), Eg., U.A.R., 216,218...C6 43
Aljustrel, Port., 5,844...D1 20
Alkabo, Divide, N. Dak., 70...A2 110
Al Kadhimain, Iraq, 126,443...F15 31
Alkali, creek, Wyo...D4 125
Alkali, lake, Nev...B2 104
Alkali, lake, Oreg...E6 113
Alkaline, lake, N. Dak...C6 110
Al Karak, Jordan, 5,539...C7 32
Al Kawm aṭ Ṭawīl, Eg., U.A.R., 1,000...C3 32
Al Khābūrah, Mus. & Om...D2 39
Al Khalīl (Hebron), Jordan, 37,868...C7 32
Al Khalūf, Mus. & Om...D2 39
Al Khārijah, Eg., U.A.R., 11,155...D6 43
Al Khasab, Mus. & Om...H8 41
Al Khaṭaṭibah, Eg., U.A.R., 1,000...D2 32
Al Khums, Libya, 62,272...C2 43
Al Khurmah, Sau. Ar...A5 47
Alkionidhes, gulf, Grc...g10 23
Alkionidhes, is., Grc...g9 23
Alkmaar, Neth., 46,100 (*75,000)...B4 15
Al Kubr, isl., Kuw...G4 41
Al Kūbrī, Eg., U.A.R., 1,000...D4 32
Al Kufrah (Cufra), oasis, Libya, Eg., U.A.R...D4 43
Al Kuh, cape, Iran...I8 41
Al Kuntillah, Eg., U.A.R., 1,000...E6 32
Allada, Dah., 4,700...E5 45
Al Lādhiqīyah (Latakia), Syr., 67,604...E10 31
Allagash, Aroostook, Maine, 500 (557▲)...A3 96
Allagash, lake, Maine...B3 96
Allagash, riv., Maine...B3 96
Allahabad, India, 411,955 (*430,730)...C7 39, E8 40
Allakaket, Alsk., 115...B9 79
Allamakee, co., Iowa, 15,982...A6 92
Allamoore, Hudspeth, Tex., 20...F2 118
Allamuchy, Warren, N.J., 120...B3 106
Allamuchy, mtn., N.J...B3 106
Allan, Sask., Can., 417...F2 70
Allanmyo, Bur., 15,580...E10 39
Allāqui, wadi, Eg., U.A.R...E6 43
Allardt, Fentress, Tenn., 650...C9 117
Allariz, Sp., 9,403...A2 20
Allaykha, Sov. Un., 800...B36 4
Alleene, Little River, Ark., 120...D1 81
Allegan, Allegan, Mich., 4,827...F5 98
Allegan, co., Mich., 57,729...F4 98
Allegany, Cattaraugus, N.Y., 2,064...C2 108
Allegany, Coos, Oreg., 40...D2 113
Allegany, co., Md., 84,169...A1 85
Allegany, co., N.Y., 43,978...C2 108
Allegany, Indian res., N.Y...C2 108
Alleghany, Sierra, Calif., 200...C3 82
Alleghany, Alleghany, Va., 150...D2 121
Alleghany, co., N.C., 7,734...A2 109
Alleghany, co., Va., 12,128...D3 121
Allegheny, co., Pa., 1,628,587...E2 114
Allegheny, mts., U.S...C11 77
Allegheny, plat., Pa., W. Va...E1 114, C3 123
Allegheny, riv., N.Y., Pa...E2 114
Allegheny Heights, mtn., Md...D1 85
Alleman, Polk, Iowa, 100...A7 92
Allemands, St. Charles, La., 1,167...C6, E5 95
Allen, Clarke, Ala., 50...D2 78
Allen, Lyons, Kans., 205...D7 93
Allen, Floyd, Ky., 400...C7 94
Allen, Wicomico, Md., 175...D6 85
Allen, Dixon, Nebr., 350...B9 103
Allen, Hughes and Pontotoc, Okla., 1,005...C5 112
Allen, Cumberland, Pa., 300...F7 114
Allen, Bennett, S. Dak., 100...D4 116
Allen, co., Ind., 232,196...B7 91
Allen, co., Kans., 16,369...E8 93
Allen, co., Ky., 12,269...D3 94

Allen, co., Ohio, 103,691 B3 111
Allen, par., La., 19,867 D3 95
Allen, lake, Ire C3 11
Allen, mtn., N.Z. Q11 51
Allendale, Wabash, Ill., 465 E6 90
Allendale, Worth, Mo., 136 A3 101
Allendale, Bergen, N.J., 4,092 A4 106
Allendale, Allendale, S.C., 3,114 F5 115
Allendale, co., S.C., 11,362 E5 115
Allende, Mex., 9,938 B4 63
Allenford, Ont., Can., 209 C3 72
Allenhurst, Brevard, Fla., 200 D6 86
Allenhurst, Liberty, Ga., 200 E5 87
Allenhurst, Monmouth, N.J., 795 C5 106
Allenhurst, Matagorda, Tex., 40 G4 118
Allen Park, Wayne, Mich., 37,494 A7 98
Allenport, Washington, Pa., 981 *F2 114
Allenspark, Boulder, Colo., 40 A5 83
Allenstein, see Olsztyn, Pol.
Allenstown, Merrimack, N.H., (1,789▲) D4 105
Allensville, Todd, Ky., 286 D2 94
Allensville, Vinton, Ohio, 100 C5 106
Allensville, Mifflin, Pa., 300 E6 114
Allenton, Wilcox, Ala., 100 B2 78
Allenton, St. Louis, Mo., 350 B7 101
Allenton, Washington, R.I., 900 C11 84
Allenton, Washington, Wis., 350 E5 124
Allentown, Wilkinson, Ga., 225 D3 87
Allentown, Monmouth, N.J., 1,393 C3 106
Allentown, Allegany, N.Y., 500 C2 108
Allentown, Lehigh, Pa., 108,347 (★299,700) E11 114
Allentown, King, Wash., 600 D1 122
Allenville, Moultrie, Ill., 191 D5 90
Allenville, Mackinac, Mich., 35 C6 98
Allenwood, Monmouth, N.J., 500 C4 106
Allenwood, Union, Pa., 300 D8 114
Alleppey, India, 138,834 G6 39
Aller (Cabañaquinta), Sp., 828 A3 20
Aller, riv., Ger A6 17
Allerton, Champaign and Vermilion, Ill., 282 D6 90
Allerton, Wayne, Iowa, 692 D4 92
Allerton, pt., Mass B6 97
Alley Spring, Shannon, Mo., 30 D6 101
Allgood, Blount, Ala., 147 B3 78
Alliance, Alta., Can., 291 C5 69
Alliance, Box Butte, Nebr., 7,845 B3 103
Alliance, Pamlico, N.C., 200 B7 109
Alliance, Stark, Ohio, 28,362 B6 111
Allier, dept., Fr., 380,221 *D5 14
Allier, riv., Fr D5 14
Al Lifiyah (Oasis) Sau. Ar. G14 31
Alligator, Bolivar, Miss., 227 A3 100
Alligator, lake, Maine D4 96
Alligator, lake, N.C B7 109
Alligator, riv., N.C B7 109
Allihies, Ire., 77 F1 11
Allimaso, creek, N. Mex C5 107
Allingåbro, Den., 1,312 B4 24
Allinge, Den., 2,114 C8 24
Allingtown, New Haven, Conn. (part of West Haven) D5 84
Allison, La Plata, Colo., 125 D3 83
Allison, Butler, Iowa, 952 B5 92
Allison, McKinley, N. Mex., 50 B1 107
Allison, Fayette, Pa., 1,285 G2 114
Allisona, Williamson, Tenn., 100 B5 117
Allison Harbour, B.C., Can D4 68
Allisonia, Pulaski, Va., 160 E2 121
Allison Park, Allegheny, Pa., 5,000 A6 114
Alliston, Ont., Can., 2,884 C5 72
Al Līth, Sau. Ar., 10,000 A5 47
Alloa, Scot., 13,895 D5 13
Allons, Overton, Tenn., 270 C8 117
Allouez, Keweenaw, Mich., 175 A2 98
Allouez, Brown, Wis., 9,557 *A5 124
Alloway, Salem, N.J., 850 D2 106
Alloways, creek, N.J D2 106
Allred, Overton, Tenn., 100 C8 117
All-Sabieh, Fr. Som C5 47
Allsboro, Colbert, Ala., 50 A1 78
Allschwil, Switz., 12,875 A4 19
Al Luḩayyah, Yemen, 5,000 B5 47
Allumette, lake, Ont., Can B7 72
Allyns Point, New London, Conn., 75 D8 84
Alma, Crawford, Ark., 1,370 B1 85
Alma, N.B., Can., 476 D5 74
Alma, Ont., Can., 167 D4 72
Alma, Que., Can., 20,124 A6 73
Alma, Park, Colo., 107 B4 83
Alma, Bacon, Ga., 3,515 E4 87
Alma, Marion, Ill., 358 E5 90
Alma, Wabaunsee, Kans., 838 C7 93
Alma, Gratiot, Mich., 8,978 E6 98
Alma, Lafayette, Mo., 390 B4 101
Alma, Harlan, Nebr., 1,342 D6 103
Alma, Robeson, N.C., 60 C4 109
Alma, Stephens, Okla., 120 C4 112
Alma, Tyler, W. Va., 250 B4 123
Alma, Buffalo, Wis., 1,008 D2 124
Alma, hill, N.Y C2 108
Al Ma'ādī, Eg., U.A.R., 4,000 E3 32
Alma-Ata, Sov. Un., 580,000 E9 29
Alma Center, Jackson, Wis., 464 D3 124
Almada, Port., 11,995 C1, f9 20
Almadén, Sp., 13,443 C3 20
Al Madīnah (Medina), Sau. Ar., 60,000 E7 43
Al-Mafraq, Jordan, 1,000 F11 31
Almagro, Sp., 9,681 C4 20
Al Maḩallah al Kubrá, Eg., U.A.R., 178,288 D3 32
Al Maḩmūdīyah, Eg., U.A.R., 1,000 C2 32
Al Maḩsamah, Eg., U.A.R., 1,000 D4 32
Al Maḩtab, Sau. Ar. H11 31
Al Makīlī, Libya F4 31
Almanor, lake, Calif B3 82
Almansa, Sp., 15,391 C5 20
Al Manşūrah, Eg., U.A.R., 151,192 C3 32, C6 43
Al Manzilah, Eg., U.A.R., 2,000 C3 32
Almanzora, riv., Sp D4 20
Almargem [do Bispo], Port., 4,867 f9 20
Al Marj (Barce), Libya, 12,000 C4 43, F3 31
Almartha, Ozark, Mo., 225 E5 101
Al Maţarīyah, Eg., U.A.R., 2,000 C4 32
Almaville, Rutherford, Tenn., 60 B5 117
Almazán, Sp., 3,958 B4 20
Al Mazār, Jordan, 1,000 C7 32
Almeirim, Braz., 2,082 C4 56
Almeirim, Port., 7,104 C1 25
Almelo, Neth., 54,600 B6 15
Almelund, Chisago, Minn., 150 E6 99
Almena, Norton, Kans., 555 C4 93
Almena, Barron, Wis., 398 C1 124
Almendares, Cuba h11 64
Almendralejo, Sp., 21,884 C2 20
Almeria, Loup, Nebr., 18 C6 103
Almería, Sp., 86,808 D4 20
Almería, prov., Sp., 360,777 *D4 20
Almería, gulf, Sp D4 20
Almería, riv., Sp D4 20
Älmhult, Swe., 5,300 B8 24
Al Minyā, Eg., U.A.R., 93,300 D6 43
Almira, Lincoln, Wash., 414 B7 122
Almirante, Pan., 3,521 F6 62
Almirante Brown, Arg g7 54
Almiros, Grc., 7,034 C4 23
Al Mishab, cape, Sau. Ar G4 41
Almo, Cassia, Idaho, 100 G5 89
Almo, Calloway, Ky., 150 B3 94
Almodôvar, Port., 4,390 D1 20
Almodóvar, Sp., 14,633 C3 20
Almogía, Sp., 8,341 D3 20
Almon, Newton, Ga., 300 C3 87
Almonaster, Sp., 4,770 D2 20
Almond, Randolph, Ala., 50 B4 78
Almond, Allegany and Steuben, N.Y., 696 C3 108
Almond, Swain, N.C., 100 D2 109
Almond, Portage, Wis., 391 D4 124
Almond, riv., Scot D5 13
Almonesson, Gloucester, N.J., 2,000 *D2 106
Almont, Gunnison, Colo., 11 C4 83
Almont, Lapeer, Mich., 1,279 F7 98
Almont, Morton, N. Dak., 190 C4 110
Almonte, Marin, Calif., 600 *B5 82
Almonte, Ont., Can., 3,267 B8 72
Almonte, Sp., 11,538 D2 20
Almonte, riv., Sp C3 20
Almora, India, 16,004 C6 39
Almoradí, Sp., 3,998 C5 20
Al Mughaiyir, Jordan, 1,000 g12 32
Al Mukallā, S. Arabia, 25,000 C6 47
Al Mukhā (Mocha) (Mokha), Yemen, 5,000 C5 47
Almuñécar, Sp., 6,235 D4 20
Al Muwayliḩ, Sau. Ar I10 31
Almy, Uinta, Wyo., 25 D2 125
Almyra, Arkansas, Ark., 240 C4 81
Almyville, Windham, Conn., 350 *C9 84
Aln, riv., Eng E7 13
Alness, Scot., 1,019 C4 13
Alnwick, Eng., 7,482 C6 10
Aloha, Washington, Oreg., 4,000 B2 113
Along, bay, Viet B7 38
Alonsa, Man., Can., 133 D2 71
Alor, isl., Indon G6 35
Álora, Sp., 5,960 D3 20
Alor Star, Mala., 52,915 I4 38
Alorton (Fireworks), St. Clair, Ill., 3,282 *E3 90
Alosno, Sp., 5,814 D2 20
Alpachiri, Arg B4 54
Alpaugh, Tulare, Calif., 600 E4 82
Alpbach, Aus., 1,576 E5 16
Alpena, Boone, Ark., 283 A2 81
Alpena, Alpena, Mich., 14,682 C7 98
Alpena, Jerauld, S. Dak., 407 C7 116
Alpena, Randolph, W. Va., 50 C5 123
Alpena, co., Mich., 28,556 C7 98
Alpenrose, Switz C8 19
Alpes-Maritimes, dept., Fr., 618,265 *F7 14
Alpha, Henry, Ill., 637 B3 90
Alpha, Fayette, Iowa, 119 B5 92
Alpha, Clinton, Ky., 100 D4 94
Alpha, Iron, Mich., 317 B2 98
Alpha, Jackson, Minn., 207 G4 99
Alpha, Warren, N.J., 2,406 B2 106
Alpha, Greene, Ohio, 250 C3 111
Alpharetta, Fulton, Ga., 1,349 B2 87
Alphen aan den Rijn, Neth., 24,900 B4 15
Alpheus, see Alfios, riv., Grc.
Alpiarça, Port., 6,680 C1 20
Alpine, Talladega, Ala., 100 B3 78
Alpine, Apache, Ariz., 300 D6 80
Alpine, Clark, Ark., 75 C2 81
Alpine, San Diego, Calif., 1,044 *F5 82
Alpine, Bonneville, Idaho, 50 F7 89
Alpine, Bergen, N.J., 921 h9 106
Alpine, Benton, Oreg., 115 C3 113
Alpine, Overton, Tenn., 65 C8 117
Alpine, Brewster, Tex., 4,740 F2 118
Alpine, Utah, Utah, 775 C4 119
Alpine, co., Calif., 397 C4 82
Alpoca, Wyoming, W. Va., 400 D3 123
Alps, mts., Eur F10 8
Al Qaddāhīyah, Libya, I14 30
Al Qāhirah, see Cairo, Eg., U.A.R.
Al Qanāyāt, Eg., U.A.R., 12,385 D3 32
Al Qanţarah, Eg., U.A.R., 2,000 D4 32
Al Qaryah ash Sharqīyah, Libya C2 43
Al Qaşabāt, Libya, 3,190 C2 43
Al Qaşr, Eg., U.A.R D5 43
Al Qaţīf, Sau. Ar., 5,000 H5 41
Al Qaţrānah, Jordan, 4,000 G11 31
Al Qaţrūn, Libya, 1,674 E2 43
Al Qulaiyaba (Oasis), Sau. Ar H14 31
Al Qunaytirah, Syr., 17,100 F10 31
Al Qurna, Iraq, 3,156 F3 41
Al Quşaymah, Eg., U.A.R., 1,000 D6 32
Al Quşayr, Eg., U.A.R D6 43
Alright, isl., Que., Can B8 74
Alrø, Den C4 24
Als, Den., 685 B4 24
Alsace, former prov., Fr., 1,317,000 C7 14
Alsask, Sask., Can., 230 F1 70
Alsasua, Sp., 5,927 A4 20
Alsdorf, Ger., 31,000 D6 15
Alsea, Benton, Oreg., 200 C3 113
Alsek, riv., Alsk., B.C., Yukon, Can D5 66
Alsen, Cavalier, N. Dak., 228 A7 110
Alsenbrück-Langmeil, Ger., 740 D2 17
Alsey, Scott, Ill., 248 D3 90
Alsfeld, Ger., 9,900 C4 17
Alsike, Swe., 271 t35 25
Alsip, Cook, Ill., 3,770 *F3 90
Alstead, Cheshire, N.H., 325 (843▲) D2 105
Alstead, riv., Sask., Can B2 70
Alstead Center, Cheshire, N.H., 40 D2 105
Alston, Eng., 1,724 F6 13
Alston, Montgomery, Ga., 154 D4 87
Alsuma, Tulsa, Okla., 500 A6 112
Alta, Buena Vista, Iowa, 1,393 B2 92
Alta, Teton, Wyo B2 125
Altadena, Los Angeles, Calif., 40,568 *F2 82
Altaelv, riv., Nor C10 25
Alta Gracia, Arg., 11,570 A4 54
Altagracia, Ven., 14,000 A3 60
Altagracia de Orituco, Ven., 13,860 B4 60
Alta Hill, Nevada, Calif., 1,078 *C3 82
Al Tahoe, El Dorado, Calif., 1,500 C4 82
Altai, mts., Asia B3 34
Alta Loma, San Bernardino, Calif., 850 *F5 82
Alta Loma, Galveston, Tex., 1,020 G5 118
Altamaha, riv., Ga E4 87
Altamaha, sound, Ga E5 87
Altamahaw, Alamance, N.C., 625 A4 109
Altamira, Braz., 2,939 C4 59
Altamira, Chile E2 55
Altamirano, Arg g7 54
Altamont, Alameda, Calif., 20 B6 82
Altamont, Man., Can., 123 E2 71
Altamont, Effingham, Ill., 1,656 D5 90
Altamont, Labetta, Kans., 672 E8 93
Altamont, Daviess, Mo., 190 B3 101
Altamont, Albany, N.Y., 1,365 C6 108
Altamont, Klamath, Oreg., 10,811 E5 113
Altamont, Deuel, S. Dak., 77 C9 116
Altamont, Grundy, Tenn., 552 D8 117
Altamont, Duchesne, Utah, 102 C5 119
Altamonte Springs, Seminole, Fla., 1,212 D5 86
Altamura, It., 43,700 D6 21
Altamura, isl., Mex C3 63
Altapass, Mitchell, N.C., 150 C4 109
Altar, Mex., 1,116 A2 63
Altario, Alta., Can., 72 D5 69
Alta Vista, Chickasaw, Iowa, 276 A5 92
Alta Vista, Wabaunsee, Kans., 400 D7 93
Altavista, Jim Hogg, Tex F3 118
Altavista, Campbell, Va., 3,299 D3 121
Altdorf, Ger., 5,800 D6 17
Altdorf, Switz., 7,477 C6 19
Altefähr, Ger., 11,445 D7 24
Alte Mellum, isl., Ger E2 24
Altenberg, Ger., 1,796 C8 17
Altenbruch, Ger., 4,000 E2 24
Altenburg, Ger., 46,900 C7 17
Altenburg, Perry, Mo., 260 D8 101
Altenkirchen, Ger., 4,500 C2 17
Altenkirchen, Ger., 1,478 D7 24
Altenmarkt, Ger., 2,800 A8 18
Altentreptow, Ger., 8,604 E7 24
Alter do Chão, Port., 4,633 C2 20
Altha, Calhoun, Fla., 413 B1 86
Altheim, Aus., 4,271 A9 18
Altheimer, Jefferson, Ark., 979 C4 81
Altinho, Braz., 3,825 C3, k6 57
Altkirch, Fr., 4,246 B3 18
Altman, Screven, Ga., 100 D5 87
Altmar, Oswego, N.Y., 277 B4 108
Altmühl, riv., Ger E6 17
Altnaharra, Scot B4 13
Alto, Banks and Habersham, Ga., 275 B3 87
Alto, Richland, La., 100 F5 95
Alto, Kent, Mich., 250 F5 98
Alto, Lincoln, N. Mex., 5 D4 107
Alto, Franklin, Tenn., 85 B6 117
Alto, Cherokee, Tex., 869 D5 118
Alto Alentejo, prov., Port., 400,374 *C2 20
Alto Araguaia, Braz., 2,077 B2 56
Alto Cedro, Cuba, 679 E6 64
Alto Cuchumatanes, mts., Guat C2 62
Alto Longá, Braz., 784 C2 57
Alto Molocuè, Moz A6 49
Altomünster, Ger., 1,900 A7 18
Alton, Jefferson, Ala., 350 B3, E5 78
Alton, Ont., Can., 438 D4 72
Alton, Eng., 9,158 C7 12
Alton, Madison, Ill., 43,047 E3 90
Alton, Sioux, Iowa, 1,048 B1 92
Alton, Osborne, Kans., 299 C5 93
Alton, St. Tammany, La., 60 B8 95
Alton, Oregon, Mo., 677 E6 101
Alton, Belknap, N.H., 300 (1,241▲) D4 105
Alton, Franklin, Ohio, 180 C2 111
Alton, Washington, R.I., 300 D10 84
Alton, Kane, Utah, 116 F3 119
Alton, Upshur, W. Va., 70 C4 123
Altona, Man., Can., 2,026 E3 71
Altona, Ger. (part of Hamburg) E3 24
Altona, Knox, Ill., 505 B3 90
Altona, DeKalb, Ind., 313 B7 91
Altona, Mecosta, Mich., 150 E5 98
Altona, Clinton, N.Y., 400 f11 108
Altonah, Duchesne, Utah, 10 C5 119
Alton Bay, Belknap, N.H., 300 (1,241▲) D4 105
Alton North, Madison, Ill., 1,505 *E3 90
Altoona, Etowah, Ala., 744 A3 78
Altoona, Lake, Fla., 200 D5 86
Altoona, Polk, Iowa, 1,458 A7, C4 92
Altoona, Wilson, Kans., 490 E8 93
Altoona, Blair, Pa., 69,407 (▲104,500) E5 114
Altoona, Eau Claire, Wis., 2,114 D2 124
Alto Paraná, dept., Par., 9,531 E5 55
Alto Pass, Union, Ill., 323 F4 90
Alto Trombetas, riv., Braz B3 59
Altötting, Ger., 9,200 A8 18
Altrincham, Eng., 41,300 A5 12
Altro, Breathitt, Ky., 300 C6 94
Altstätten, Switz., 8,751 B8 19
Altun Kopru, Iraq, 3,744 E15 31
Altura, Winona, Minn., 320 F7 99
Alturas, Modoc, Calif., 2,819 B3 82
Altus, Franklin, Ark., 392 B2 81
Altus, Jackson, Okla., 21,225 C2 112
Altus, res., Okla C2 112
Altyn Tagh, mts., China D2 34
Al 'Ujaylāt, Libya H13 32
Alula, Som., 1,300 C7 47
Alum, creek, Ohio C2 111
Alum Bank (Pleasantville), Bedford, Pa., 300 F4 114
Alum Bridge, Lewis, W. Va., 125 B4 123
Alum Creek, Kanawha, W. Va., 500 C5 123
Aluminé, Arg B2 54
Alum Rock, Santa Clara, Calif., 18,942 *D3 82
Alunite, Clark, Nev., 10 H7 104
Alupka, Sov. Un., 21,200 I10 27
Al Uqaylah (Aghéila), Libya C3 43
Al 'Uqayr, Sau. Ar I5 41
Al Uqşur (Luxor), Eg., U.A.R., 30,100 D6 43
Al Uthaylah, Libya C4 43
Alva, Lee, Fla., 300 F5 86
Alva, Harlan, Ky., 700 D6 94
Alva, Woods, Okla., 6,258 A3 112
Alva, Crook, Wyo., 60 A8 125
Alvarado, Mex., 12,424 D5 63
Alvarado, Marshall, Minn., 282 B2 99
Alvarado, Johnson, Tex., 1,907 B5, C4 118
Alvaton, Meriwether, Ga., 24 C2 87
Älvdalen, Swe., 1,771 G6 25
Alvear, Arg., 3,544 E4 55
Alvena, Sask., Can., 220 E2 70
Alverca [do Ribatejo], Port., 4,665 f9 20
Alverton, Westmoreland, Pa., 300 F2 114
Alvesta, Swe., 6,600 B8 24
Alvin, Vermilion, Ill., 281 C6 90
Alvin, Berkeley, S.C., 100 E8 115
Alvin, Brazoria, Tex., 5,643 E5, F5 118
Alvinston, Ont., Can., 660 E3 72
Alviso, Santa Clara, Calif., 1,174 *D2 82
Alvo, Cass, Nebr., 159 D9, E2 103
Alvord, Lyon, Iowa, 238 A1 92
Alvord, Wise, Tex., 694 C4 118
Alvord, lake, Oreg E8 113
Alvordton, Williams, Ohio, 388 A3 111
Älvsborg, co., Swe., 376,500 A6 24
Älvsjö, Swe t36 25
Alvwood, Itasca, Minn., 20 C4 99
Al Wajh, Sau. Ar D7 43
Alwar, India, 72,707 C6 39
Al Wāsiţah, Eg., U.A.R., 4,000 E3 32
Aly, Yell, Ark., 35 C2 81
Alyaty-Pristan, Sov. Un., 500 F3 29
Alymer, lake, N.W. Ter., Can D11 66
Alyth, Scot., 1,862 D5 13
Alytus, Sov. Un., 9,084 A8 26
Alz, riv., Ger D6 16
Alzada, Carter, Mont., 50 E12 102
Alzey, Ger., 11,900 D3 17
Ama, St. Charles, La., 600 C7 95
Amadeus, lake, Austl D5 50
Amadi, Sud D3 47
Amadjuak, lake, N.W. Ter., Can C18 67
Amado, Santa Cruz, Ariz., 30 F4 80
Amador, co., Calif., 9,990 C3 82
Amagansett, Suffolk, N.Y., 1,300 n16 108
Amagasaki, Jap., 405,955 o14 37
Amager, isl., Den C6 24
Amagon, Jackson, Ark., 234 B4 81
Amahai, Indon F7 35
Amakusa, sea, Jap J5 37
Amål, Swe., 9,200 H5 25
Amalfi, It., 5,200 D5 21
Amalga, Cache, Utah, 198 B4 119
Amalia, Taos, N. Mex., 50 A4 107
Amalias, Grc., 15,468 D3 23
Amalner, India, 46,963 G5 40
Amambay, dept., Par., 18,160 D4 55
Amamio (Amami), isl., Ryukyu Is F10 34
Amana, Iowa, Iowa, 465 C6 92
Amanã, lake, Braz D5 60
Amanda, Fairfield, Ohio, 732 C5 111
Amangeldy, Sov. Un C7 29
Amantea, It., 5,822 E6 21
Amantes, pt., Guam 52
Amapá, Braz., 1,591 B4 59
Amapá, ter., Braz., 68,889 B4 59
Amara, Iraq, 44,064 F3 41
Amaraji, Braz., 2,271 k6 57
Amarante, Braz., 3,199 C2 57
Amaranth, Man., Can., 294 D2 71
Amargosa, Braz., 6,059 D3 57
Amargosa, range, Calif D5 82
Amargosa, riv., Calif E5 82
Amarillo, Potter and Randall, Tex., 137,969 (★142,500) B2 118
Amaro, mtn., It C5 21
Amarousion, Grc., 20,135 g11 23
Amasa, Iron, Mich., 500 B2 98
Amasra, Tur., 1,379 B9 31
Amasya (Amasia), Tur., 28,200 B10 31
Amawalk, res., N.Y D2 84
Amazon, Sask., Can F3 70
Amazon, see Solimões, riv., Braz., Peru
Amazon, see Amazonas, riv., S.A.
Amazonas, dept., Peru, 100,527 B2 58
Amazonas, comisaría, Col., 8,120 D3 60
Amazonas, state, Braz., 721,215 B3 58
Amazonas, ter., Ven., 11,757 C4 60
Amazonas (Amazon), riv., S.A D5 47, C3 59
Amazonia, Andrew, Mo., 326 B3 101
Ambala, India, 76,204 (★181,747) B6 40
Ambalavao, Malag., 4,000 h9 49
Ambam, Cam E2 46
Ambanja, Malag f9 49
Ambarchik, Sov. Un., 800 C19 28
Ambato, Ec., 53,700 B2 58
Ambato-Boeni, Malag g9 49
Ambatosorata, Malag g9 49
Amber, Grady, Okla., 300 B4 112
Amberg, Ger., 42,100 D6 17
Amberg, Marinette, Wis., 220 C6 124
Ambérieu [-en-Bugey], Fr., 7,748 E6 14
Amberley, Hamilton, Ohio, 2,951 *D2 111
Amberson, Franklin, Pa., 25 F6 114
Ambert, Fr., 5,604 E5 14
Ambia, Benton, Ind., 351 D2 91
Ambikapur, India, 15,240 F9 40
Ambilobe, Malag f9 49
Amble, Eng., 4,889 E7 13
Ambler, Montgomery, Pa., 6,765 A11, F11 114
Ambo, Eth D4 47
Ambo, chan., Kwajalein 52
Ambo, Peru, 1,243 D2 58
Amboear, W. Irian F8 35
Amboina, Indon., 55,263 F7 35
Amboina, isl., Indon F7 35
Amboise, Fr., 7,953 D4 14
Ambositra, Malag., 4,636 h9 49
Ambovombe, Malag., 2,250 k9 49
Amboy, San Bernardino, Calif., 125 E6 82
Amboy, Turner, Ga., 75 E3 87
Amboy, Lee, Ill., 2,067 B4 90
Amboy, Miami, Ind., 446 C6 91
Amboy, Blue Earth, Minn., 629 G4 99
Amboy, Clark, Wash., 150 D3 122
Ambridge, Beaver, Pa., 13,865 A5, E1 114
Ambridge Heights, Beaver, Pa., 5,106 *A5 114
Ambriz, Ang., 2,196 C1 48
Ambrizete, Ang., 1,147 C1 48
Ambrose, Coffee, Ga., 244 E3 87
Ambrose, Divide, N. Dak., 220 A2 110
Ambrosia Lake, McKinley, N. Mex., 300 B2 107
Amchitka, isl., Alsk E3 79
Amchitka, pass, Alsk E4 79
Am Dam, Chad, 1,299 C4 46
Amden, Switz., 1,270 B7 19
Amderma, Sov. Un., 10,000 C9 28
Ameagle, Raleigh, W. Va., 500 D3, D6 123
Ameca, Mex., 17,396 C4, m11 63
Amecameca, Mex., 12,271 n14 63
Amechtil, sand dunes, Maur C2 45
Ameland, isl., Neth A5 15
Amelia, St. Mary, La., 950 C5, E4 95
Amelia, Holt, Nebr., 50 B7 103
Amelia, Clermont, Ohio, 913 C3 111
Amelia City, Nassau, Fla., 100 B6 86
Amelia, co., Va., 7,815 D4 121
Amelia, isl., Fla B6 86
Amelia Court House, Amelia, Va., 800 D5 121
Amelinghausen, Ger., 920 E4 24
Amendolara, It., 3,297 E6 21
Amenia, Dutchess, N.Y., 900 D7 108
Amenia, Cass, N. Dak., 220 B8 110
American, highland, Ant B21 5
American, riv., Calif C3 82
American Bottom, valley, Oreg C1 113
American Canyon, Napa, Calif., 800 *C2 82
American Falls, Power, Idaho, 2,123 G6 89
American Falls, dam, Idaho G6 89
American Falls, res., Idaho F5 89
American Fork, Utah, Utah, 6,373 C4 119
American Samoa, U.S. dep., Oceania, 21,000 52
Americus, Sumter, Ga., 13,472 D2 87
Americus, Lyon, Kans., 300 D7 93
Amersfoort, Neth., 72,600 (★103,000) B5 15
Amery, Man., Can A4 71
Amery, Polk, Wis., 1,769 C1 124
Amery, ice shelf, Ant C20 5
Ames, Story, Iowa, 27,003 B4 92
Ames, Cloud, Kans., 80 C6 93
Ames, Dodge, Nebr., 65 C9, D2 103
Ames, Major, Okla., 211 A3 112
Amesbury, Essex, Mass., 10,787 A6 97
Amfissa, Grc., 5,546 C4 23
Amga, Sov. Un., 800 C16 28
Amgu, Sov. Un D8 37
Amgun, riv., Sov. Un D16 28
Amhar, plat., Eth D4 47
Amherst, N.S., Can., 10,788 D5 74
Amherst, Phillips, Colo., 106 A8 83
Amherst, Brevard, Fla., 1,500 *D6 86
Amherst, Hancock, Maine, 140 (168▲) D4 96
Amherst, Hampshire, Mass., 14,500 (13,718▲) B2 97
Amherst, Buffalo, Nebr., 220 D6 103
Amherst, Hillsboro, N.H., 500 (2,051▲) E3 105
Amherst (Eggertsville), Erie, N.Y., 52,000 C2 108
Amherst, Lorain, Ohio, 6,750 A5 111
Amherst, Marshall, S. Dak., 75 B8 116
Amherst, Lamb, Tex., 883 B1 118
Amherst, Amherst, Va., 1,200 D3 121
Amherst, Portage, Wis., 596 D4 124
Amherst, co., Va., 22,953 D3 121
Amherst, isl., Que., Can B7 74
Amherstburg, Ont., Can., 4,452 E1 72
Amherstdale, Logan, W. Va., 900 D3, D5 123
Amiata, mtn., It C3 21
Amicalola, falls, Ga B2 87
Amidon, Slope, N. Dak., 82 C2 110
Amiens, Fr., 105,433 C5 14
Aminuis, S.W. Afr B2 49
'Āmir, cape, Libya C4 43
Amirante, is., Indian O G24 3
Amiret, Lyon, Minn., 75 F3 99
Amisk, Alta., Can., 127 C5 69
Amisk, lake, Sask., Can C4 70
Amistad, Union, N. Mex., 25 B6 107
Amite, Tangipahoa, La., 3,316 D5 95
Amite, co., Miss., 15,573 D3 100
Amite, riv., La D5 95
Amity, Clark, Ark., 543 C2 81
Amity, De Kalb, Mo., 111 B3 101
Amity, Yamhill, Oreg., 620 B1, B3 113
Amity, Washington, Pa., 155 F1 114
Amity, hills, Oreg B1 113
Amityville, Suffolk, N.Y., 8,890 E7, n15 108
Amizmiz, Mor., 4,036 I2 30
Amkyokyung, China C11 40
Amlekhganj, Nep D10 40
Amlwch, Wales, 2,910 A3 12
'Ammān, Jordan, 224,974 (★246,475) G10 31
Ammanford, Wales, 6,264 C3 12
Ammeloe, Ger., 7,200 A1 17
Ammendorf, Ger. (part of Halle) B7 17
Ammer, lake, Ger B7 18
Ammon, Bonneville, Idaho, 1,882 F7 89
Ammonoosuc, riv., N.H B3 105
Amne Machin, mts., China E4 34
Amo, Hendricks, Ind., 437 E4 91
Amol, Iran, 14,166 C6 41
Amonate, Tazewell, Va., 875 B3 121
Amoret, Bates, Mo., 261 C3 101
Amorgos, isl., Grc D5 23
Amorita, Alfalfa, Okla., 74 A3 112
Amory, Monroe, Miss., 6,474 B5 100
Amos, Que., Can., 6,080 k11 73
Amoy (Hsiamen), China, 224,300 G8 34
Ampanihy, Malag h8 49
Amparo, Braz., 14,382 C3, m8 56
Amper, riv., Ger E6 17
Ampezzo, It., 2,413 C8 18
Amposta, Sp., 8,444 B6 20
Amqui, Que., Can., 3,659 *k13 73
'Amrān, Yemen, 20,000 B5 47
Amraoti, India, 137,875 (★161,715) G6 40
Amreli, India, 34,699 G3 40
Amriswil, Switz., 6,752 A7 19
Amritsar, India, 376,295 (★398,047) B5 40
Amroha, India, 68,965 C7 40
Amrum, isl., Ger D2 24
Amsteg, Switz C6 19
Amsterdam, Decatur, Ga., 400 F2 87
Amsterdam, Bates, Mo., 118 C3 101
Amsterdam, Gallatin, Mont., 100 E5 102
Amsterdam, Neth., 868,400 (★1,730,000) B4 15
Amsterdam, Montgomery, N.Y., 28,772 C6 108
Amsterdam, Jefferson, Ohio, 931 B7 111
Amsterdam, isl., Indian O I2 2
Amstetten, Aus., 12,086 D7 16
Amston, Tolland, Conn., 300 C7 84
Am Timan, Chad, 1,859 C4 46
Amu Darya, riv., Sov. Un H21 9
Amukta, pass, Alsk E5 79
Amulet, Sask., Can., 47 H3 70
Amund Ringnes, isl., N.W. Ter., Can m32 67
Amundsen, bay, Ant C17 5
Amundsen, gulf, N.W. Ter., Can B7 66
Amundsen, sea, Ant B36 5
Amundsen-Scott Station, U.S. scientific station, Ant A18 5
Amur, riv., Sov. Un E16 28
Amvrakia, gulf, Grc C3 23
Amwaco, Kootenai, Idaho E8 122
'Ana, Iraq, 5,860 E13 31
Anabar, riv., Sov. Un B14 28
Anabta, Jordan, 3,000 f11 32
Anacoco, Vernon, La., 300 C2 95
Anaconda, Deer Lodge, Mont., 12,054 D4 102
Anaconda, Valencia, N. Mex., 100 B2 107
Anaconda, range, Mont E3 102
Anacortes, Skagit, Wash., 8,414 A3 122
Anacostia, riv., Md C1 85
Anadarko, Caddo, Okla., 6,299 B3 112
Anadia, Braz., 2,592 C3, k5 57
Anadyr, Sov. Un., 5,000 C20 28
Anadyr, gulf, Sov. Un C21 28
Anadyr, range, Sov. Un C20 28
Anadyr, riv., Sov. Un C20 28
Anae, isl., Guam 52
Anafi (Anaphe), isl., Grc D5 23
Anagance, N.B., Can., 129 D4 74
Anaheim, Orange, Calif., 104,184 F3, F5 82
Anahim Lake, B.C., Can C5 68
Anahola, Kauai, Haw., 326 A2 88
Anahuac, Chambers, Tex., 1,985 E5, F5 118
Anajás, Braz., 182 C5 59
Anakapalle, India, 46,402 I9 40
Anakie, Austl A6 51
Anaklia, Sov. Un A13 31
Analalava, Malag f9 49
Anama Bay, Man., Can D2 71
Ana Maria, gulf, Cuba E4 64
Anambas, is., Indon E3 35
Anamoose, McHenry, N. Dak., 503 B5 110
Anamosa, Jones, Iowa, 4,616 B6 92
Anamur, Tur., 6,600 D9 31
Anamur, cape, Tur D9 31
Anandale, Rapides, La., 2,827 *C3 95
Anandpur, India F10 40
Anantapur, India, 52,280 F6 39
Anantnag, India, 21,087 B6 39
Ananyev, Sov. Un., 5,000 H7 27
Anao, pt., Guam 52
Anapa, Sov. Un., 32,900 I11 27
Anápolis, Braz., 48,847 E1 57
Anapú, riv., Braz C4 59
Anār, Iran, 15,000 F7 41
Anārak, Iran, 1,270 E6 41
Anardara, Afr., 10,000 E10 41
Añasco, P.R., 2,068 B2 65

Añasco, mun., P.R., 17,200...B2 65
Anastasia, isl., Fla...C5 86
Anata, Jordan, 1,000...h12 32
Anatahan (Anatajan) isl., Mariana Is...E8 7
Anatone, Asotin, Wash., 90...C8 122
Añatuya, Arg., 9,310...E3 55
Anauá, riv., Braz...C5 60
Anawalt, McDowell, W. Va., 1,062...D3 123
Ancash, dept., Peru, 521,661.C2 58
Ancaster, Ont., Can., 1,077...D4 72
Ancell, Scott, Mo. (part of Scott City)...D8 101
Anceney, Gallatin, Mont., 10.E5 102
Ancenis, Fr., 5,095...D3 14
Anchi, China, 6,000...F8 34
Anchieta, Braz., 1,179...F2 57
Ancho, Lincoln, N. Mex., 25.D4 107
Anchor, Brazoria, Tex., 40...G5 118
Anchor, Hot Springs, Wyo...B4 125
Anchorage, Alsk., 44,237 (*80,000)...C10, g17 79
Anchorage, Jefferson, Ky., 1,170...A4 94
Anchor Bay Gardens, Macomb, Mich., 1,830...*A8 98
Anchor Point, Alsk., 171...h16, D9 79
Ancienne Lorette, Que., Can., 3,961...C6, n17 73
Anclote, keys, Fla...D4 86
Anco, Knott, Ky., 350...C6 94
Ancon, C.Z., 1,151...m11 62
Ancón, Peru, 1,097...D2 58
Ancona, It., 103,300...C4 21
Ancud, Chile, 6,410...C2 54
Ancud, gulf, Chile...C2 54
Anda, Phil., 1,612...*D6 35
Andacollo, Arg...B2 54
Andahuaylas, Peru, 2,309...D3 58
Andale, Sedgwick, Kans., 432...B4, E6 93
Andalgalá, Arg., 5,016...E2 55
Andalsnes, Nor., 1,943...F2 25
Andalusia, Covington, Ala., 10,263...D3 78
Andalusia, Rock Island, Ill., 560...B3 90
Andalusia, reg., Sp., 5,893,396...D3 20
Andaman, is., India...F9 39
Andaman, sea, Indian O...F10 39
Andaman and Nicobar Is., ter., India, 74,000...*F9 39
Andamarca, Bol...C2 55
Andamarca, Peru, 1,576...D3 58
Andapa, Malag...f9 49
Andavaka, cape, Malag...k9 49
Andebu, Nor...p28 25
Andeer, Switz., 988...C7 19
Andenne, Bel., 7,829...D5 15
Anderlecht, Bel., 94,677...D4 15
Andermatt, Switz., 1,523...C6 19
Andernach, Ger., 20,800...C2 17
Anderslöv, Swe., 881...C7 24
Anderson, Lauderdale, Ala., 450...A2 78
Anderson, Arg...g6 54
Anderson, Shasta, Calif., 4,492...B2 82
Anderson, Madison, Ind., 49,061 (*131,600)...D6 91
Anderson, McDonald, Mo., 992...E3 101
Anderson, Anderson, S.C., 41,316...B2 115
Anderson, Franklin, Tenn., 40...B6 117
Anderson, Grimes, Tex., 500.D5 118
Anderson, co., Kans., 9,035...D8 93
Anderson, co., Ky., 8,618...C4 94
Anderson, co., S.C., 98,478...B2 115
Anderson, co., Tenn., 60,032.C9 117
Anderson, co., Tex., 28,162...D5 118
Anderson, riv., N.W. Ter., Can...C7 66
Anderson, riv., Ind...H4 91
Anderson Dam, Elmore, Idaho, 35...F3 89
Anderson East Side, Madison, Ind., 3,778...*D6 91
Anderson Ranch, res., Idaho...F3 89
Andersonville, Sumter, Ga., 263...D2 87
Andersonville, Franklin, Ind., 250...F7 91
Andes, Col., 6,905...B2 60
Andes, Richland, Mont...C12 102
Andes, Delaware, N.Y., 399...C6 108
Andes, lake, S. Dak...D7 116
Andes, mts., S.A...D3, H3 53
Andhra Pradesh, state India, 35,983,447...E6 39
Andidanob, mtn., Sud...A4 47
Andikíthira, isl., Grc...E4 23
Andilamena, Malag...g9 49
Andimeshk, Iran., 7,324...E4 41
Anding, Yazoo, Miss., 30...C3 100
Andizhan, Sov. Un., 150,000.E8 29
Andkhui, Afg., 18,438...C12 41
Andoas, Peru, 189...B2 58
Andong, Kor., 48,000 (56,500▲)...H4 37
Andorra, And., 600...A6 20
Andorra, country, Eur., 12,000...G9 8, A6 20
Andover, N.B., Can., 848...C2 74
Andover, Tolland, Conn., 200 (1,771▲)...C7 84
Andover, Eng., 16,974...C6 12
Andover, Henry, Ill., 295...B3 90
Andover, Butler, Kans., 186...B6 93
Andover, Essex, Mass., 10,800 (17,134▲)...A5 97
Andover, Merrimack, N.H., 350 (955▲)...D3 105
Andover, Sussex, N.J., 734...B3 106
Andover, Alleghany, N.Y., 1,247...C3 108
Andover, Ashtabula, Ohio, 1,116...A7 111
Andover, Day, S. Dak., 224...B8 116
Andover (Town of), Windsor, Vt., (215▲)...*E3 120
Andover, lake, Conn...C7 84
Andöy, isl., Nor...C6 25
Andrade, Hawaii, Haw., 130.D6 88
Andraitx, Sp., 5,077...C7 20
Andreanof, is., Alsk...E4 79
Andreas, cape, Cyp...E10 31
Andrelândia, Braz., 4,617...g5 56
Andrew, Alta., Can., 601...C4 69
Andrew, Jackson, Iowa, 349...B7 92
Andrew, co., Mo., 11,062...B3 101
Andrew, isl., N.S., Can...D9 74
Andrew Jackson, mtn., Ant...B6 5
Andrews, Huntington, Ind., 1,132...C6 91
Andrews, Dorchester, Md., 1,404...D5 85
Andrews, Cherokee, N.C., 1,404...D2 109
Andrews, Harney, Oreg., 5...E8 113
Andrews, Georgetown and Williamsburg, S.C., 2,995...E8 115
Andrews, Andrews, Tex., 11,135...C1 118
Andrews, co., Tex., 13,450...C1 118
Andreyevka, Sov. Un., 10,000...G11 27
Andria, It., 72,400...D6 21
Androka, Malag...h8 49
Andros, Grc., 2,238...D5 23
Andros, isl., Ba. Is...C5 64
Andros, isl., Grc...D5 23
Androscoggin, co., Maine, 86,312...D2 96
Androscoggin, lake, Maine...D2 96
Androscoggin, riv., Maine, N.H...B5 90, A4 105
Andrychow, Pol., 5,055...h10 26
Andsfjord, fiord, Nor...C7 25
Andújar, Sp., 26,100...C3 20
Anécho, Togo...E5 45
Anéfis, Mali...C5 45
Anegada, bay, Arg...C4 54
Anegada, isl., Vir. Is. (Br.)...m14 64
Anegada, passage, N.A...m15 64
Anegam, Pima, Ariz., 100...E3 80
Añelo, Arg...B3 54
Anerley, Sask., Can...F2 70
Aneroid, Sask., Can., 279...H2 70
Aneta, Nelson, N. Dak., 451...B8 110
Aneth, San Juan, Utah, 70...F6 119
Aneto, mtn., Sp...A6 20
Angadanan, Phil., 2,510...n13 35
Angamos, pt., Chile...D1 55
Angangchi, China, 12,717...B9 34
Angara, riv., Sov. Un...D13 28
Angarsk, Sov. Un., 160,000...A5 34
Angaur, isl., Palau Is... 52
Angel, fall, Ven...B5 60
Angela, Rosebud, Mont., 5.D10 102
Ángel de la Guarda, is., Mex...B2 63
Angeles, Phil., 57,603...o13 35
Angeles, P.R...B3 65
Angeles, pt., Wash...A2 122
Angelholm, Swe., 12,600...I5 25
Angelica, Allegany, N.Y., 898...C2 108
Angelina, co., Tex., 39,814...D5 118
Angels Camp, Calaveras, Calif., 1,121...C3 82
Angelus, Sheridan, Kans., 70.C3 93
Angelus, Chesterfield, S.C., 65...B7 115
Ångermanälven, riv., Swe...F7 25
Angermünde, Ger., 11,700...B7 16
Angers, Que., Can., 575...D2 73
Angers, Fr., 115,252...D3 14
Angicos, Braz., 1,551...C3 57
Angie, Washington, La., 254.D6 95
Angier, Harnett, N.C., 1,249.B5 109
Angikuni, lake, N.W. Ter., Can...D13 66
Angkor, ruins, Camb...F5 38
Angleim, mtn., N.Z...Q11 51
Anglesey, co., Wales, 51,700.A3 12
Anglesey, is., Wales...D4 10
Anglet, Fr., 16,150...F3 14
Angleton, Brazoria, Tex., 7,312...E5, G5 118
Anglia, Sask., Can., 70...F1 70
Angliers, Que., Can., 488...G17 67
Angling, lake, Man., Can...C5 71
Angling, riv., Man., Can...A5 71
Anglo-Egyptian Sudan, see Sudan, country, Afr.
Angmagssalik, Grnld., 612...C18 4
Ango, Con. L...A4 48
Angoche, isl., Moz...A6 49
Angohrān, Iran, 5,000...H8 41
Angol, Chile, 14,292...B2 54
Angola, Steuben, Ind., 4,746.A8 91
Angola, Labette, Kans., 50...E8 93
Angola, Erie, N.Y., 2,499...C1 108
Angola, Port. dep., Afr., 5,125,000...D2 48, H7 42
Angola, swamp, N.C...C6 109
Angoon, Alsk., 395...D13, m22 79
Angora, Morrill, Nebr., 80...C2 103
Angostura, res., S. Dak...D2 116
Angoulême, Fr., 48,190 (*80,000)...E4 14
Angoumois, former prov., Fr., 292,000...*E4 14
Angra do Heroismo, Port. (Azores), 10,296...g9 44
Angra dos Reis, Braz., 10,634...C4, h5 56
Angren, Sov. Un., 65,000...E7 29
Anguilla, Sharkey, Miss., 580.B3 100
Anguilla, isl., St. Kitts-Nevis-Anguilla...m15 64
Anguillara Sabazia, It., 2,774...g8 21
Anguille, cape, Newf., Can...E2 75
Angumu, Con. L...B4 48
Anguran, Iran...H8 41
Angus, Ont., Can., 1,180...C5 72
Angus, Boone, Iowa, 100...C3 92
Angus, Polk, Minn., 80...B2 99
Angus, co., Scot., 278,370...D5 13
Angusville, Man., Can., 208.D1 71
Angwin, Napa, Calif., 1,400...A5 82
Anhembi, Braz., 505...m7 56
Anholt, isl., Den...B5 24
Anholt By, Den...B5 24
Anhsi, China...C4 34
Anhua, China...J4 36
Anhwei, prov., China, 33,560,000...E8 34
Aniak, Alsk., 308...C8 79
Aniche, Fr., 10,419...D3 15
Aniene, riv., It...h9 21
Animas, Hidalgo, N. Mex., 100...F1 107
Animas, mts., N. Mex...F1 107
Animas, peak, N. Mex...F1 107
Animas, riv., Colo...D3 83
Animas, val., N. Mex...F1 107
Anina, Rom., 11,837...C5 22
Anita, Cass, Iowa, 1,233...C3 92
Anita, Jefferson, Pa., 550...E4 114
Aniva (Rutaka), Sov. Un., 10,000...C11 37
Aniva, bay, Sov. Un...C11 37
Aniva, cape, Sov. Un...C11 37
Aniwa, Shawano, Wis., 247...C4 118
Anizy-le-Château, Fr., 1,526.E3 15
Anjar, India...F3 40
Anjean, Greenbrier, W. Va., 180...C4 123
Anjo, Jap., 33,000 (56,787▲).o16 37
Anjou, Que., Can., 9,511...*D4 73
Anjou, former prov., Fr., 631,000...D3 14
Anjouan, isl., Comoro Is...f8 49
Anju, Kor., 21,861...G2 37
Anjum, Neth., 1,002...A6 15
Ankang, China...H3 36
Anka, Nig...D6 45
Ankara, Tur., 650,067...C9 31
Ankaratra, mts., Malag...g9 49
Ankavandra, Malag...g9 49
Ankazoabo, Malag., 1,800...h8 49
Ankeny, Polk, Iowa, 2,964...A7, C4 92
An Khe, Viet...F8 38
Anking (Hwaining), China, 105,300...I7 36
Anklam, Ger., 19,400...B6 16
Ankobar, Eth...D4 47
Ankona, St. Lucie, Fla., 89...E6 86
Ankoro, Con. L...C4 48
Ankuang, China, 5,000...D1 36
Anlu, China...I5 36
Anlung, China, 9,000...F6 34
Anmoore, Harrison, W. Va., 1,050...B4, B7 123
Ann, cape, Ant...C18 5
Ann, cape, Mass...A6 97
Anna, Union, Ill., 4,280...F4 90
Anna, Shelby, Ohio, 701...B3 111
Anna, Sov. Un., 5,000...F13 27
Annabella, Sevier, Utah, 177.E3 119
Annaberg-Buchholz, Ger., 29,000...C8 17
Annaburg, Ger., 5,184...B8 17
Annada, Pike, Mo., 105...B7 101
An Nafud, des., Sau. Ar...H13 31
An Najaf, Iraq, 74,089...I17 9
An Nakhl, Eg., U.A.R., 3,000...E5 32
Annalee Heights, Fairfax, Va., 2,000...*B5 121
Annam, reg., Viet., 8,000,000...D7 38
Anna Maria, Manatee, Fla., 690...F2 86
Anna Maria, key, Fla...F1 86
Annan, Scot., 5,572...F5 13
Annan, riv., Scot...E5 13
Annandale, Wright, Minn., 984...E4 99
Annandale, Hunterdon, N.J., 600...B3 106
Annandale, Fairfax, Va., 5,000...B5 121
Annapolis, Crawford, Ill., 130...D6 90
Annapolis, Parke, Ind., 100...E3 91
Annapolis, Anne Arundel, Md., 23,385...C5 85
Annapolis, Iron, Mo., 334...D7 101
Annapolis, Kitsap, Wash., 600...D1 122
Annapolis, co., N.S., Can., 22,649...E4 74
Annapolis, riv., N.S., Can...E4 74
Annapolis Junction, Howard, Md., 525...B4 85
Annapolis Naval Academy, Md...C5 85
Annapolis Royal, N.S., Can., 800...E4 74
Annapurna 1, peak, Nep...C9 40
Ann Arbor, Washtenaw, Mich., 67,340...A6, F7 98
An Nāri, mtn., Libya...E4 43
An Nasiriya, Iraq, 25,515...F3 41
Annawan, Henry, Ill., 701...B4 90
An Nawfaliyah, Libya...C3 43
An Nazlah, Gaza Area, 4,000.C6 32
Anne Arundel, co., Md., 206,634...B4 85
Annecy, Fr., 43,255 (*57,500)...E7 14
Annecy-le-Vieux, Fr., 4,681...E1 19
Annemasse, Fr., 13,814...D7 14
Annestown, Ire...E4 11
Annieopsquotch, mts., Newf., Can...D3 75
Anniston, Calhoun, Ala., 33,657...B4 78
Anniston, Mississippi, Mo., 307...E8 101
Annobón, isl., Afr...F1 46
Annonay, Fr., 18,434...E6 14
Annotto Bay, Jam., 3,559...F5 64
Annsjon, lake, Swe...u33 25
Annursnack, hill, Mass...g10 97
Annville, Jackson, Ky., 400...C6 94
Annville, Lebanon, Pa., 4,264...F8 114
Anoka, Anoka, Minn., 10,562...E5, E6 99
Anoka, Boyd, Nebr., 32...B7 103
Anoka, co., Minn., 85,916...E5 99
Anona, Pinellas, Fla., 500...E1 86
Ano Nuevo, pt., Calif...C5 82
Ano Theologos, Grc., 2,320...B5 23
Anou Mellène (Well), Mali...C5 45
Ano Viannos, Grc., 1,961...E5 23
Anoyia, Grc., 3,072...E5 23
Anpei, China, 2,000...D3 36
Anping, China...E6 36
Ansbach, Ger., 32,900...D5 17
Anse d'Hainault, Hai., 1,000.F6 64
Anselm, Ransom, N. Dak., 20...C8 110
Anselmo, Custer, Nebr., 269.C6 103
Anserma, Col., 7,767...B2 60
Anshan, China, 805,000...C9 34, D10 36
Anshun, China, 41,000...F6 34
Ansley, Pike, Ala., 90...D3 78
Ansley, Jackson, La., 400...B3 95
Ansley, Hancock, Miss., 60...E4 100
Ansley, Custer, Nebr., 714...C6 103
Anson, Somerset, Maine, 900 (2,252▲)...D3 96
Anson, Jones, Tex., 2,890...C3 118
Anson, co., N.C., 24,962...B3 109
Ansŏng, Kor., 15,800...H2 37
Ansongo, Mali, 400...C5 45
Ansonia, New Haven, Conn., 19,819...D4 84
Ansonia, Darke, Ohio, 1,002.B3 111
Ansonville, Ont., Can., 3,080...o19 72
Ansonville, Anson, N.C., 558.B3 109
Ansted, Fayette, W. Va., 1,511...C3, D7 123
Anstruther, Scot., 3,400...D6 13
Anta, China, 5,000...C2 37
Anta, Peru, 1,542...D3 58
Antabamba, Peru, 2,127...D3 58
Antakya (Antioch), Tur., 45,674...D11 31
Antalaha, Malag., 10,300...f10 49
Antalāt, Libya...C4 43
Antalya (Adalia), Tur., 50,908...D8 31
Antalya, gulf, Tur...D8 31
Antarctic, pen., Ant...B6 5
Antarctica, cont... 5
Ante, Brunswick, Va., 20...E5 121
Antelope, Sask., Can...G1 70
Antelope, Marion, Kans., 50...D7 93
Antelope, Sheridan, Mont., 100...B12 102
Antelope, Wasco, Oreg., 46...C6 113
Antelope, co., Nebr., 10,176...B7 103
Antelope, creek, Wyo...B7 125
Antelope, hills, Wyo...C4 125
Antelope, isl., Utah...C3 119
Antelope, lake, Sask., Can...G1 70
Antelope, range, Nev...D7 104
Antelope, res., Oreg...E9 113
Antelope Mine, Rh...B4 49
Antequera, Sp., 28,400 (42,327▲)...D3 20
Antes Fort, Lycoming, Pa., 380...D7 114
Anthon, Woodbury, Iowa, 681...B2 92
Anthony, Hempstead, Ark. 120...D2 81
Anthony, Marion, Fla., 500...C4 86
Anthony, Harper, Kans., 2,744...E5 93
Anthony, Dona Ana, N. Mex., 1,000...F3 107
Anthony, Kent, R.I., 3,000.C10 84
Anthony, El Paso, Tex., 1,082...*E3 107
Anthonys, creek, W. Va...D4 123
Anthony Wayne Village, Allen, Ind., 3,000...*B7 91
Anti-Atlas, mts., Mor...C3 44
Antibes, Fr., 35,439...F7 14
Anticosti, isl., Que., Can...k14 73
Antietam, creek, Md...A2 85
Antietam, nat. battlefield site and cemetery, Md...B2 85
Antigo, Langlade, Wis., 9,691.C4 124
Antigonish, N.S., Can., 4,344...D8 74
Antigonish, co., N.S., Can., 14,360...D7 74
Antigua, Br. dep., N.A., 59,000...n16 64
Antigua Guatemala, Guat., 10,996...C2 62
Antilla, Cuba, 5,786...E6 64
Antimony, Garfield, Utah, 161...E4 119
Antioch, Contra Costa, Calif., 17,305...B6 82
Antioch, Lake, Ill., 2,268...A5, D2 90
Antioch, Clinton, Ind., 75...D4 91
Antioch, Sheridan, Nebr., 30.B3 103
Antioch, Davidson, Tenn., 250...A5, E9 117
Antioch, see Antakya, Tur.
Antionia, Jefferson, Mo., 150.C7 101
Antioquia, Col., 3,998...B2 60
Antioquia, dept., Col., 1,747,580...B2 60
Antique, prov., Phil., 239,200...*C6 35
Antiquity, Meigs, Ohio, 150.D6 111
Antler, Sask., Can., 149...H5 70
Antler, Bottineau, N. Dak., 210...A4 110
Antler, riv., Man., Sask., Can...E1 71
Antlers, Pushmataha, Okla., 2,085...C6 112
Antofagasta, Chile, 87,900...D1 55
Antofagasta, prov., Chile, 214,090...D1 55
Antofalla, vol., Arg...E2 55
Antoine, Pike, Ark., 163...C2 81
Anton, Washington, Colo., 50...B7 83
Anton, Hockley, Tex., 1,068.C1 118
Anton Chico, Guadalupe, N. Mex., 450...B4 107
Antongil, bay, Malag...g9 49
Antonina, Braz., 8,520...D3 56
Antonino, Ellis, Kans., 50...D4 93
Antonio de Biedma, Arg...D3 54
Antônio Dias, Braz., 1,338...E2 57
Antônio Enes, Moz., 11,628...A6 49
Antonito, Conejos, Colo., 1,045...D5 83
Antony, Fr., 46,483...g10 14
Antratsit, Sov. Un., 60,000...q22 27
Antrim, Antrim, Mich., 200.D5 98
Antrim, Hillsboro, N.H., 850 (1,121▲)...D3 105
Antrim, N. Ire., 1,448...C5 11
Antrim, Tioga, Pa., 375...C7 114
Antrim, co., Mich., 10,373...C5 98
Antrim, co., N. Ire., 273,923...C5 11
Antrim, mts., N. Ire...C5 11
Antsalova, Malag., 1,000...g8 49
Antsirabe, Malag., 11,332...g9 49
Antsirane, see Diégo-Suarez, Malag.
Antung, China, 360,000...C9 32, F2 37
Antwerp, see Antwerpen, Bel.
Antwerp, Jefferson, N.Y., 881...A5, f9 108
Antwerp, Paulding, Ohio, 1,465...A3 111
Antwerpen (Antwerp) (Anvers), Bel., 253,295 (*1,000,000).C4 15
Antwerpen, prov., Bel., 1,443,355...C4 15
Anua, Am Sam... 52
Anvers, see Antwerpen, Bel.
Anvers, isl., Ant...C6 5
An Uaimh, Ire., 3,998...D5 11
Anuradhapura, Cey., 18,390.G7 39
Anvik, Alsk., 120...C7 79
Anyang, China, 124,900...D7 34
Anyi, China...E7 34
Anyksciai, Sov. Un...A8 26
Anza, Riverside, Calif., 220...F5 82
Anzá, Col., 610...B2 60
Anzac, Alta., Can., 154...A5 69
Anzhero-Sudzhensk, Sov. Un., 120,000...B11 28
Anzin, Fr., 16,275...D3 15
Anzio, It., 14,300...D4, k9 21
Anzoátegui, state, Ven., 382,002...B5 60
Aojidong, Kor., 39,616...E5 37
Aomoen, isl., Bikini... 52
Aomon, isl., Eniwetok... 52
Aomori, Jap., 159,000 (202,211▲)...F10 37
Aomori, pref., Jap., 1,426,606...*F10 37
Aosta, It., 31,700...B1 21
Aoûk, riv., Cen. Afr. Rep...D3 46
Aoulef, Alg...D5 44
Apa, riv., Par...D4 57
Apache, Caddo, Okla., 1,455.C3 112
Apache, co., Ariz., 30,438...B6 80
Apache, mts., Tex...F2 118
Apache, peak, Ariz...F5 80
Apache Creek, Catron, N. Mex., 20...D1 107
Apache Junction, Pinal, Ariz., 1,000...G3 80
Apalachee, Morgan, Ga., 158...C3 87
Apalachee, bay, Fla...B2 86
Apalachicola, Franklin, Fla., 3,099...C2 86
Apalachicola, bay, Fla...C2 86
Apalachicola, riv., Fla...B1 86
Apalachin, Tioga, N.Y., 900.C4 108
Apalona, Perry, Ind...H4 91
Apan, Mex., 8,589...n14 63
Apoporis, riv., Col...C3 60
Aparri, Phil., 14,000 (33,500▲)...B6 35
Apatin, Yugo., 17,203...C4 22
Apatity, Sov. Un...D15 25
Apatzingán, Mex., 19,340...n12 63
Apeldoorn, Neth., 110,500...B5 15
Apennine, tunnel, It...B3 21
Apennines, mts., It...C4 21
Apex, Wake, N.C., 1,368...B5 109
Apex, mtn., Yukon, Can...D5 66
Apgar, Flathead, Mont...B3 102
Api, peak, Nep...C8 40
Apia, W. Sam., 21,699... 52
Apia, hbr., W. Sam... 52
Apiacás, mts., Braz...E3 59
Apiaí, Braz., 2,728...C3 56
Apiranthos, Grc., 2,438...D5 23
Apishapa, riv., Colo...D6 83
Apison, Hamilton, Tenn., 375...E10 117
Apizaco, Mex., 15,622...n14 63
Aplao, Peru, 840...E3 58
Aplin, Perry, Ark., 100...C3 81
Aplington, Butler, Iowa, 840.B5 92
Apo, vol., Phil...D6 35
Apodaca, Rio Arriba, N. Mex., 90...A4 107
Apodi, Braz., 2,512...C3 57
Apohaqui, N.B., Can., 343...D4 74
Apolda, Ger., 29,300...B6 17
Apolima, isl., W. Sam... 52
Apolima, strait, W. Sam... 52
Apollo, Armstrong, Pa., 2,694...E2 114
Apolo, Bol., 1,043...B2 55
Apopka, Orange, Fla., 3,578.D5 86
Aporé, riv., Braz...B2 56
Apostle, is., Wis...A3 124
Apóstoles, Arg., 3,385...E4 55
Appalachia, Wise, Va., 2,456.B2 121
Appalachian, mts., N.A...F12 61
Appam, Williams, N. Dak., 60...A2 110
Appanoose, co., Iowa, 16,015...D5 92
Appenzell, Switz., 5,001...B7 19
Appenzell, canton, Switz., 61,863...B7 19
Apperson, Osage, Okla., 15. A5 112
Appingedam, Neth., 7,800...A6 15
Apple, creek, N. Dak...C5 110
Apple, riv., Ill...F3 124
Apple, riv., Wis...C1 124
Appleby, Eng., 1,751...F6 13
Appleby, Nacogdoches, Tex., 150...D5 118
Apple Creek, Wayne, Ohio, 722...B6 111
Applecross, Scot., 735...C3 13
Applegate, Jackson, Oreg., 350...E3 113
Applegate, Sanilac, Mich., 244...E8 98
Applegate, butte, Oreg...E5 113
Applegate, riv., Oreg...E3 113
Apple Grove, Louisa, Va., 25...D5 121
Apple Grove, Mason, W. Va., 600...C2 123
Apple Hill, Ont., Can., 384...B10 72
Apple River, N.S., Can., 78...D5 74
Apple River, Jo Daviess, Ill., 477...A3 90
Apple Springs, Trinity, Tex., 200...D5 118
Appleton, Pope, Ark., 150...B3 81
Appleton, Knox, Maine, 160 (672▲)...D3 96
Appleton, Swift, Minn., 2,172...E2 99
Appleton, Allendale, S.C., 198...E5 115
Appleton, Lawrence, Tenn., 60...B4 117
Appleton, Klickitat, Wash., 10...D4 122
Appleton, Outagamie, Wis., 48,411 (*123,200)...A5, D5 124
Appleton City, St. Clair, Mo., 1,075...C3 101
Apple Valley, San Bernardino, Calif., 950...*E5 82
Appleyard, Chelan, Wash., 950...B5 122
Appling, Columbia, Ga., 200.C4 87
Appling, co., Ga., 13,246...E4 87
Appomattox, Appomattox, Va., 1,184...D4 121
Appomattox, co., Va., 9,148.D4 121
Appomattox, riv., Va...D5 121
Approuague, Fr. Gu., 856...B4 59
Apra, hbr., Guam... 52
Aprelsk, Sov. Un., 800...D14 28
Aprilia, It...D4, h9 21
Apsheron, pen., Sov. Un...G19 9
Apsley, Ont., Can., 295...C6 72
Apt, Fr., 5,521...F6 14
Aptos, Santa Cruz, Calif., 950...C6 82
Apuai, riv., Braz...D5 60
Apulia, reg., It...D6 21
Apulyont, lake, Tur...B7 23
Apure, state, Ven., 117,577...B3 60
Apure, riv., Ven...B4 60
Apurimac, dept., Peru, 324,338...D3 58
Apurimac, riv., Peru...D3 58
Aqaba, gulf, Afr., Asia...H10 31
'Aqiq, Sud...B4 47
Aqir, Isr., 996...h10 32
Aq Kupruk, Afg., 5,000...C13 41
Aqraba, Jordan, 3,000...B7, g12 32
Aquarius, mts., Ariz...C2 80
Aquarius, plat., Utah...E4 119
Aquasco, Prince Georges, Md., 400...C4 85
Aquashicola, creek, Pa...B2 106
Aquebogue, Suffolk, N.Y., 600...F6 84
Aquidauana, Braz., 11,997...C1 56
Aquidneck, isl., R.I...C11 84
Aquileia, It., 1,400...D9 18
Aquiles Serdán, Mex., 3,927.B3 63
Aquin, Hai...F7 64
Aquone, Macon, N.C., 150...D2 109
Arab, Marshall, Ala., 2,989...A3 78
Arabela, Lincoln, N. Mex., 60...D4 107
Arabi, Crisp, Ga., 303...E3 87
Arabi, St. Bernard, La., 5,000...C7 95
Arabia, see Saudi Arabia, Asia
Arabian, des., Eg., U.A.R...E3 32
Arabian, sea, Asia...H9 33
Arabs, gulf, Eg., U.A.R...G7 31
Araby, Yuma, Ariz., 5...E1 80
Aracaju, Braz., 112,516...D3 57
Aracati, Braz., 11,016...B3 57
Araçatuba, Braz., 53,563...C2 56
Aracena, Sp., 7,737...D2 20
Araçuaí, Braz., 6,763...E2 57
Aracruz, Braz., 413...E2 57
Arad, Rom., 113,500...B5 22
Araduey, riv., Sp...B3 20
Arafura, sea, Indon...G8 35
Arago, Coos, Oreg., 140...D2 113
Arago, cape, Oreg...D2 113
Aragon, Polk, Ga., 1,023...B1 87
Aragon, Catron, N. Mex., 60.D1 107
Aragon, reg., Sp., 1,105,498...B5 20
Aragón, riv., Sp...A5 20
Aragua, state, Ven., 313,274.A4 60
Araguaia, riv., Braz...D6 53
Aragua de Barcelona, Ven., 6,830...B5 60
Araguao, riv. mouth, Ven...B5 60
Araguari, Braz., 35,520...E1 57
Araguari, riv., Braz...B4 59
Arai, Jap., 9,600...o16 37
Arāk (Sultanabad), Iran, 58,998...D4 41
Arakabesan, isl., Palau Is... 52
Arakan, range, Bur...E9 39
Arakhthos, riv., Grc...C3 23
Araks, riv., Asia...B3 41
Aral, sea, Sov. Un...D5 29
Aral Karkum, des., Sov. Un...D6 29
Aralsk, Sov. Un., 18,600...D6 29
Aramac, Austl., 488...D8 50
Aran, isl., Ire...C3 11
Aran, is., Ire...D2 11
Aranda de Duero, Sp., 13,454.B4 20
Arandas, Mex., 17,110...m12 63
Aranjuez, Sp., 27,251...B4 20
Aransas, co., Tex., 7,006...E4 118
Aransas, bay, Tex...E4 118
Aransas Pass, San Patricio and Aransas, Tex., 6,956...F4 118
Aranyaprathet, Thai., 11,601.F5 38
Araouane, Mali...C4 45
Arapaho, Custer, Okla., 351...B3 112
Arapaho, peak, Colo...A5 83
Arapahoe, Cheyenne, Colo., 125...C8 83
Arapahoe, Furnas, Nebr., 1,084...D6 103
Arapahoe, Pamlico, N.C., 274...B7 109
Arapahoe, Fremont, Wyo., 30...C4 125
Arapahoe, co., Colo., 113,426.B6 83
Arapey, Ur...E1 56
Arapey Grande, riv., Ur...E1 56
Arapkir, Tur., 6,900...C12 31
Arar, wadi, Sau. Ar...G13 31
Araranguá, Braz., 7,775...D3 56
Araraquara, Braz., 58,076...C3, k7 56
Araras, Braz., 23,898...C3, m8 56
Araras, mts., Braz...B2 56
Ararat, Choctaw, Ala., 50...D1 78
Ararat, Austl., 7,934...H4 51
Ararat, Susquehanna, Pa., 35...C10 114
Ararat, Patrick, Va., 300...E2 121
Ararat, mtn., Tur...C15 31
Arareh, W. Irian...F9 35
Araripe, mts., Braz...C2 57
Araruna, Braz., 2,261...h6 57
Aratane (Well), Maur...C3 45
Arauca, Col., 2,028...B3 60
Arauca, intendencia, Col., 14,080...B3 60
Arauca, riv., Ven...B4 60
Arauco, Chile, 2,707...B2 54
Arauco, prov., Chile, 89,211.B2 54
Aravaipa, Graham, Ariz...E5 80
Aravalli, range, India...C5 39
Araxá, Braz., 24,041...E1 57
Arayat, Phil., 791...o13 35
Arba, Randolph, Ind., 100...D8 91
Arba Jahan, Ken...A6 48
Arbela, Scotland, Mo., 70...A5 101
Arboga, Swe., 11,100...t33 25
Arbois, Fr., 3,960...D6 14
Arboles, Archuleta, Colo., 100...D3 83
Arbon, Power, Idaho, 10...G6 89
Arbon, Switz., 11,608 (*13,748)...A7 19
Arbor, Middlesex, N.J., 2,800...*B4 106
Arborea, It., 2,681...E2 21
Arborfield, Sask., Can., 579.D4 70
Arborg, Man., Can., 811...D3 71
Arbor Terrace, St. Louis, Mo., 1,225...*C7 101
Arbor Vitae, Vilas, Wis., 150...C4 124
Arbroath, Scot., 19,533...D6 13
Arbuckle, Colusa, Calif., 950...C2 82
Arbuckle, lake, Fla...E5 86
Arbuckle, mts., Okla...C4 112
Arbutus, Baltimore, Md. (part of Halethorpe)...C2 85
Arcachon, Fr., 14,862 (*33,500)...E3 14
Arcade, Jackson, Ga., 108...B3 87
Arcade, Wyoming, N.Y., 1,930...C2 108
Arcadia, Los Angeles, Calif., 41,005...F2 82
Arcadia, N.S., Can., 400...F3 74
Arcadia, De Soto, Fla., 5,889.E5 86
Arcadia, Hamilton, Ind., 1,271...D5 91
Arcadia, Carroll, Iowa, 437...B2 92
Arcadia, Crawford, Kans., 507...E9 93
Arcadia, Bienville, La., 2,547.B3 95
Arcadia, Manistee, Mich., 600...D4 98
Arcadia, Iron, Mo., 489...D7 101
Arcadia, Valley, Nebr., 446...C6 103
Arcadia, Hancock, Ohio, 610.A4 111
Arcadia, Oklahoma, Okla., 400...B4 112
Arcadia, Indiana, Pa., 500...E4 114

Assaikwatamo, riv., Man., Can. . A3 71
Aş Şalihiyah, Eg., U.A.R., 1,000 . . . D3 32
As Sallūm, Eg., U.A.R., 1,011 . . . C5 43
As Salman, Iraq . . . G15 31
As Salţ, Jordan, 15,478 . . . F10 31
As Salwá, Sau. Ar. . . . I5 41
Assam, state, India, 11,872,772 . . . C9 39
Assaria, Saline, Kans., 322 . . . D6 93
Assateague, isl., Va. . . . D7 121
Assawompset, pond, Mass . . . C6 97
Assean, lake, Man., Can . . . A3 71
Assen, Neth., 31,800 . . . B6 15
Assens, Den., 1,236 . . . B4 24
Assens, co., Den., 58,005 . . . C3 24
As Sinbillāwayn, Eg., U.A.R., 23,831 . . . D3 32
Assiniboia, Sask., Can., 2,491 . . . H3 70
Assiniboine, mtn., Alta., B.C., Can . . . D3 69
Assiniboine, riv., Man., Sask., Can . . . F5 70
Assinie, I.C. . . . E4 45
Assinika, riv., Man., Can . . . C4 71
Assinippi, Plymouth, Mass., 200 . . . h12 97
Assis, Braz., 30,207 . . . C2 56
Assisi, It., 5,200 . . . C4 21
Assonet, Bristol, Mass., 550 . . C5 97
Aş Şūfiyah, Eg., U.A.R., 1,000 . . . D3 32
As Sulaymānīyah, Iraq., 35,352 . . . E15 31
As Sulayyil, Sau. Ar. . . . A6 47
As Sultān, Libya . . . C3 43
Assumption, Christian, Ill., 1,439 . . . D4 90
Assumption, par., La., 17,991 . . . E4 95
As Suwaydā', Syr., 18,200 . . F11 31
As Suways, see Suez, Eg., U.A.R.
Astakos, Grc., 2,992 . . . C3 23
Āstārā, Iran, 8,425 . . . B4 41
Asten, Neth., 5,100 . . . C5 15
Asterābād, see Gorgan, Iran
Asti, It., 48,200 (65,300▲) . . . B2 21
Astipalaia, isl., Grc . . . D6 23
Astola, isl., Pak . . . I11 41
Aston, Delaware, Pa., 1,200 . . . *G11 114
Aston, cape, N.W. Ter., Can . . B19 67
Aston Junction, Que., Can., 396 . . . C5 73
Astor, Lake, Fla., 150 . . . C5 86
Astorga, Sp., 10,101 . . . A2 20
Astoria, Fulton, Ill., 1,206 . . C3 90
Astoria, Clatsop, Oreg., 11,239 . . . A3 113
Astoria, Deuel, S. Dak., 176 . . C9 116
Astor Park, Lake, Fla., 85 . . . C5 86
Astorville, Ont., Can., 200 . . . A5 72
Astrakhan, Sov. Un., 324,000 . . . D3 29
Astura, riv., It . . . h9 21
Asturias, reg., Sp., 989,344 . . A2 20
Asuisui, cape, W. Sam . . . 52
Asuke, Jap., 5,700 . . . n16 37
Asunción, Par., 305,300 . . . E4 55
Asuncion, isl., Mariana Is . . . E8 7
Asunción Mita, Guat., 4,014 . C3 62
Asunden, lake, Swe . . . A7 24
Aswān, Eg., U.A.R., 28,400 . E6 43
Aswān High, dam, Eg., U.A.R. . E6 43
Asyūţ, Eg., U.A.R., 127,485 . D6 43
Atacama, prov., Chile, 114,277 . . . E1 55
Atacama, des., Chile . . . D2 55
Atacama, salt flat, Chile . . . D2 55
Atakpamé, Togo, 6,005 . . . E5 45
Atalaia, Braz., 1,844 . . . k6 57
Atalandi, Grc., 4,272 . . . C4 23
Atalante, Que., Can . . . n17 73
Atalissa, Muscatine, Iowa, 212 . . . C6 92
Atami, Jap., 52,163 . . . n18 37
Atantano, Guam . . . 52
Atar, Maur., 9,528 . . . B2 45
Atārūt, Jordan, 1,000 . . . h11 32
Atascadero, San Luis Obispo, Calif., 5,983 . . . E3 82
Atascosa, co., Tex., 18,828 . . E3 118
Atasuskiy, Sov. Un., 2,800 . . D8 29
Atatyn Hiid, Mong . . . A3 36
Ataúro, isl., Port. Timor . . . G7 35
Atbara, Sud., 36,298 . . . B3 47
Atbara, riv., Sud . . . B4 47
Atbasar, Sov. Un., 22,300 . . . C7 29
Atchafalaya, St. Martin, La., 10 . . . D4 95
Atchafalaya, bay, La . . . E4 95
Atchafalaya, riv., La . . . D4 95
Atchison, Atchison, Kans., 12,529 . . . A8, C8 93
Atchison, co., Kans., 20,898 . C8 93
Atchison, co., Mo., 9,213 . . A2 101
Atchugau, mtn., Saipan . . . 52
Atco, Bartow, Ga. (part of Cartersville) . . . B2 87
Atco, Camden, N.J., 1,900 . . D3 106
Atenango, riv., Mex . . . n14 63
Ath, Bel., 10,965 . . . D3 15
Athabasca, Alta., Can., 1,487 . . . B4, g8 69
Athabasca, lake, Alta., Sask., Can . . . m7 70
Athabasca, riv., Alta., Can . . . B4 69
Athalia, Lawrence, Ohio, 341 . . . D5 111
Athalmer, B.C., Can., 304 . . D10 68
Athapapuskow, lake, Man., Can . . . B1 71
Atha Road, Ont., Can., 58 . . k15 72
Athboy, Ire., 680 . . . D4 11
Athel, Wicomico, Md . . . D6 85
Athelstan, Que., Can., 167 . . D3 73
Athelstan, Taylor, Iowa, 72 . . D3 92
Athena, Umatilla, Oreg., 950 . B8 113
Athenry, Ire., 1,266 . . . D3 11
Athens, Limestone, Ala., 9,330 . . . A3 78
Athens, Howard, Ark., 67 . . . C2 81
Athens, Ont., Can., 1,015 . . . C9 72
Athens, Clarke, Ga., 31,355 . . C3 87
Athens (Athinai), Grc., 627,564 (*1,852,709) . . . C4, h11 23
Athens, Menard, Ill., 1,035 . . D4 90
Athens, Fulton, Ind., 100 . . . B5 91
Athens, Fayette, Ky., 225 . . . C5 94
Athens, Claiborne, La., 406 . . B2 95
Athens, Somerset, Maine, 225 (602▲) . . . D3 96
Athens, Calhoun, Mich., 966 . F5 98
Athens, Greene, N.Y., 1,754 . . . C7 108
Athens, Athens, Ohio, 16,470 . C5 111
Athens, Bradford, Pa., 4,515 . . C8 114
Athens, McMinn, Tenn., 12,103 . . . D9 117
Athens, Henderson, Tex., 7,086 . . . C5 118
Athens, Windham, Vt., 100 (142▲) . . . E3 120
Athens, Mercer, W. Va., 1,086 . . . D3 123
Athens, Marathon, Wis., 770 . C3 124
Athens, co., Ohio, 46,998 . . . C5 111
Athensville, Greene, Ill., 40 . . D3 90
Atherley, Ont., Can., 348 . . . C5 72
Atherton, San Mateo, Calif., 7,717 . . . *B5 82
Athertonville, Larue, Ky., 150 . . . C4 94
Athi, riv., Ken . . . B6 48
Athis-Mons, Fr., 24,004 . . . h10 14
Athleague, Ire., 132 . . . D3 11
Athlone, Ire., 9,624 . . . D4 11
Athok, Bur., 4,770 . . . E10 39
Athol, Kootenai, Idaho, 214 . . B2 89
Athol, Smith, Kans., 140 . . . C5 93
Athol, Worcester, Mass., 11,637 . . . A3 97
Athol, Spink, S. Dak., 100 . . B7 116
Athos, mtn., Grc . . . B5 23
Ath Thamad, Eg., U.A.R., 3,000 . . . D6 43
Athy, Ire., 3,842 . . . D5 11
Atibaia, Braz., 8,957 . . . m8 56
Atico, Peru, 373 . . . E3 58
Aticonipi, lake, Que., Can . . . C2 75
Atikameg, Alta., Can., 135 . . B3 69
Atikameg, lake, Man., Can . . . B1 71
Atikokan, Ont., Can., 6,674 . o17 72
Atikonak, lake, Newf., Can . . . h8 75
Atimonan, Phil., 4,027 . . . p13 35
Atiquizaya, Sal., 6,338 . . . D3 62
Atizapán de Zaragoza, Mex., 1,840 . . . g9 63
Atka, Alsk., 119 . . . E5 79
Atka, isl., Alsk . . . E5 79
Atkarsk, Sov. Un., 39,800 . . F15 27
Atkins, Pope, Ark., 1,391 . . . B3 81
Atkins, Benton, Iowa, 527 . . . B6 92
Atkins, Bossier, La . . . B2 95
Atkins, Smyth, Va., 400 . B3, E1 121
Atkinson, Brantley, Ga., 50 . . . E5 87
Atkinson, Henry, Ill., 944 . . . B3 90
Atkinson, Holt, Nebr., 1,324 . B7 103
Atkinson, Pender, N.C., 302 . C5 109
Atkinson, co., Ga., 6,188 . . . E4 87
Atkinson, lake, Man., Can . . . A4 71
Atkinson Depot (Atkinson), Rockingham, N.H., 700 (1,017▲) . . . E4 105
Atlanta, Columbia, Ark., 50 . . . D2 81
Atlanta, Fulton and DeKalb, Ga., 487,455 (*1,011,100) . B5, C2 87
Atlanta, Elmore, Idaho, 50 . . F3 89
Atlanta, Logan, Ill., 1,568 . . . C4 90
Atlanta, Hamilton, Ind., 602 . D5 91
Atlanta, Cowley, Kans., 267 . . E7 93
Atlanta, Winn, La., 300 . . . C3 95
Atlanta, Montmorency, Mich., 450 . . . C6 98
Atlanta, Macon, Mo., 386 . . . B5 101
Atlanta, Phelps, Nebr., 107 . . D6 103
Atlanta, Steuben, N.Y., 700 . . C3 108
Atlanta, Pickaway, Ohio, 160 . . . C4 111
Atlanta, Cass, Tex., 4,076 . . . C5 118
Atlantic, Cass, Iowa, 6,890 . . . C2 92
Atlantic, Carteret, N.C., 850 . C7 109
Atlantic, co., N.J., 160,880 . . E3 106
Atlantic, ocean . . . 6
Atlantic, peak, Wyo . . . C3 125
Atlantic Beach, Duval, Fla., 3,125 . . . B6 86
Atlantic Beach, Nassau, N.Y., 1,025 . . . *G2 84
Atlantic City, Atlantic, N.J., 59,544 (*129,800) . . . E4 106
Atlantic City, Fremont, Wyo., 25 . . . C4 125
Atlantic Highlands, Monmouth, N.J., 4,119 . . . C4 106
Atlantic Mine, Houghton, Mich., 400 . . . A2 98
Atlántico, dept., Col., 514,490 . A2 60
Atlas, Northumberland, Pa., 1,574 . . . *E9 114
Atlas, mts., Afr . . . C5 42
Atlee, Alta., Can . . . D5 69
Atlin, B.C., Can., 150 . . . m16 68
Atlin, lake, B.C., Can . . . E6 66
Atlit, Isr., 1,300 . . . B6 32
Atlixco, Mex., 30,433 . . . n14 63
Atmore, Escambia, Ala., 8,173 . . . D2 78
Atna, peak, B.C., Can . . . C3 68
Atna, range, B.C., Can . . . B4 68
Atocha, Bol . . . D2 55
Atoka, Eddy, N. Mex., 30 . . E5 107
Atoka, Atoka, Okla., 2,877 . . C5 112
Atoka, Tipton, Tenn., 357 . . B2 117
Atoka, co., Okla., 10,352 . . . C5 112
Atoka, res., Okla . . . C5 112
Atomic City, Bingham, Idaho, 143 . . . F6 89
Atotonilco el Alto, Mex., 14,190 . . . m12 63
Atoyac, Mex., 5,324 . . . m12 63
Atoyac, riv., Mex . . . n14 63
Atrato, riv., Col . . . B2 60
Atrek, riv., Iran . . . C8 41
Atrisco, Bernalillo, N. Mex., 4,000 . . . B3, k7 107
Atsugi, Jap., 20,800 . . . n18 37
Atsukeshi, bay, Jap . . . E12 37
Atsuma, Jap . . . E10 37
Atsumi, bay, Jap . . . o16 37
At Tabbīn, Eg., U.A.R., 1,000 . . . E3 32
Aţ Ţafīlah, Jordan, 8,588 . . . D7 32
Aţ Ţā'if, Sau. Ar., 25,000 . . . A5 47
Attala, co., Miss., 21,335 . . B4 100
Attalla, Etowah, Ala., 8,257 . . A3 78
Aţ Ţallāb, Libya . . . E4 43
At Tamīmī, Libya . . . C4 43
Attapulgus, Decatur, Ga., 567 . . . F2 87
Aţţarah, Jordan, 1,000 . . . g11 32
Attavyros, mtn., Grc . . . D6 23
Attawapiskat, Ont., Can . . . n19 72
Attawapiskat, riv., Ont., Can . n18 72
Attawaugan, Windham, Conn., 300 . . . B9 84
Aţ Ţayyibah, Jordan, 2,000 . . . C7, h12 32
Attean, pond, Maine . . . C2 96
Attica, Fountain, Ind., 4,341 . D3 91
Attica, Harper, Kans., 845 . . . E5 93
Attica, Lapeer, Mich., 250 . . . E7 98
Attica, Genesee and Wyoming, N.Y., 2,758 . . . C2 108
Attica, Seneca, Ohio, 965 . . . A5 111
Attica, reg., Grc . . . g11 23
Attica (Attiki), prov., Grc., 2,057,974 . . . *C4 23
Attigny, Fr., 1,525 . . . E4 15
Attikamagen, lake, Newf., Can . . g8 75
Attiki (Attica), prov., Grc., 2,057,974 . . . *C4 23
Aţ Ţīnah, Eg., U.A.R., 1,000 . . . C4 32
Attleboro, Bristol, Mass., 27,118 . . . C5 97
Attleborough, Eng., 2,741 . . . B9 12
Attopeu, Laos . . . E7 38
Attow, mtn., Scot . . . B4 10, C3 13
Attu, isl., Alsk . . . E2 79
Aţ Ţūr, Eg., U.A.R . . . D6 43
Attymon, Ire . . . D3 11
Atuel, riv., Arg . . . B3 54
Atuu, Am. Sam., 186 . . . 52
Atvidaberg, Swe., 7,800 . . . H 25
Atwater, Merced, Calif., 7,318 . . . D3 82
Atwater, Sask., Can., 95 . . . G4 70
Atwater, Kandiyohi, Minn., 899 . . . E4 99
Atwood, Ont., Can., 418 . . . D3 72
Atwood, Logan, Colo., 55 . . . A7 83
Atwood, Piatt and Douglas, Ill., 1,258 . . . D5 90
Atwood, Kosciusko, Ind., 250 . . . B6 91
Atwood, Rawlins, Kans., 1,906 . . . C2 93
Atwood, Hughes, Okla., 200 . C5 112
Atwood, Carroll, Tenn., 461 . B3 117
Atwood, res., Ohio . . . B6 111
Atwood Heights, Cook, Ill., 1,000 . . . *F3 90
Atzcapotzalco (Azcapotzalco), Mex., 63,857 . . . h9, n14 63
Atzmon, mtn., Isr . . . B7 32
Aua, Am. Sam., 505 . . . 52
Auasc, Eth . . . D5 47
Auau, chan., Haw . . . C5 88
Auaz, mts., S.W. Afr . . . B2 49
Aubagne, Fr., 12,612 . . . F6 14
Aube, dept., Fr., 255,099 . . . F4 15
Aube, riv., Fr . . . F4 15
Aubenas, Fr., 5,754 . . . E6 14
Auberry, Fresno, Calif., 400 . D4 82
Aubervilliers, Fr., 70,632 . . . g10 14
Aubière, Fr., 6,820 . . . E5 14
Aubigny-sur-Nère, Fr., 3,244 . . . D5 14
Aubin, Fr., 7,821 . . . E5 14
Aubrey, Lee, Ark., 400 . . . C5 81
Aubrey, Que., Can., 40 . . . D4 73
Aubrey, Denton, Tex., 746 . . . C4 118
Auburn, Lee, Ala., 16,261 . . . C4 78
Auburn, Placer, Calif., 5,586 . C3 82
Auburn, Ont., Can., 216 . . . D3 72
Auburn, Barrow, Ga., 374 . . . B3 87
Auburn, Sangamon, Ill., 2,209 . . . D4 90
Auburn, DeKalb, Ind., 6,350 . B7 91
Auburn, Sac, Iowa, 367 . . . B3 92
Auburn, Shawnee, Kans., 200 . . . D8 93
Auburn, Logan, Ky., 1,013 . . D3 94
Auburn, Androscoggin, Maine, 24,449 . . . D2, D5 96
Auburn, Worcester, Mass., 14,047 . . . B4 97
Auburn, Bay, Mich., 1,497 . . . E6 98
Auburn, Lincoln, Miss., 250 . . D3 100
Auburn, Nemaha, Nebr., 3,229 . . . D10 103
Auburn, Rockingham, N.H., 150 (1 292▲) . . . D4 105
Auburn, Salem, N.J., 175 . . D2 106
Auburn, Cayuga, N.Y., 35,249 . . . C4 108
Auburn, Walsh, N. Dak., 60 . A8 116
Auburn, Schuylkill, Pa., 936 . E9 114
Auburn, King, Wash., 11,933 . . . B3, D2 122
Auburn, Ritchie, W. Va., 139 . . . B4 123
Auburn, Lincoln, Wyo., 100 . C2 125
Auburn Center, Schuylkill, Pa., 30 . . . C9 114
Auburndale, Polk, Fla., 5,595 . . . D5 86
Auburndale, Wood, Wis., 396 . . . D3 124
Auburn Heights, Oakland, Mich., 2,500 . . . F7 98
Auburntown, Cannon, Tenn., 256 . . . B5 117
Aubusson, Fr., 5,669 . . . E5 14
Auch, Fr., 18,918 . . . F4 14
Auchel, Fr., 14,412 . . . D2 15
Auchterarder, Scot., 2,426 . . D5 13
Aucilla, Jefferson, Fla., 240 . . B3 86
Aucilla, riv., Fla . . . B3 86
Auckland, N.Z., 147,900 (*499,700) . . . L15 51
Auckland, is., N.Z. (Pac. O.) . D29 5
Aude, dept., Fr., 269,782 . . *F5 14
Aude, riv., Fr . . . F5 14
Audégle, Som., 2,000 (7,800▲) . . . E5 47
Audet, Que., Can., 110 . . . D7 73
Audierne, Fr., 3,782 . . . D1 14
Audincourt, Fr., 12,433 . . . D1 14
Audrain, co., Mo., 26,079 . . B6 101
Audubon, Audubon, Iowa, 2,928 . . . C3 92
Audubon, Becker, Minn., 245 . . . D3 99
Audubon, Camden, N.J., 10,440 . . . D2 106
Audubon, co., Iowa, 10,919 . . C3 92
Audubon Park, Jefferson, Ky., 1,867 . . . *A4 94
Audubon Park, Camden, N.J., 1,713 . . . *C3 106
Audun-le-Roman, Fr., 2,848 . E5 15
Aue, Ger., 31,200 . . . C7 17
Auerbach, Ger., 19,400 . . . C7 17
Au Fer, pt., La . . . E4 95
Augathella, Austl., 624 . . . B6 51
Aughnacloy, N. Ire., 805 . . . C5 11
Aughrim, Ire., 528 . . . E5 11
Auglaize, co., Ohio, 36,147 . B3 111
Auglaize, riv., Ohio . . . A3 111
Au Gres, Arenac, Mich., 584 . D7 98
Augsburg, Ger., 209,600 (*290,000) . . . E5 17
Augusta, Austl., 142 . . . F2 50
Augusta, Woodruff, Ark., 2,272 . . . B4 81
Augusta, Richmond, Ga., 70,626 (*160,600) . . . C5 87
Augusta, Hancock, Ill., 915 . C3 90
Augusta, Marion, Ind., 200 . . . H3, H7 91
Augusta, It., 27,950 . . . F5 21
Augusta, Butler, Kans., 6,434 . . . B6, E7 93
Augusta, Bracken, Ky., 1,458 . B6 94
Augusta, Kennebec, Maine, 21,680 . . . D3 96
Augusta, Kalamazoo, Mich., 972 . . . F5 98
Augusta, St. Charles, Mo., 206 . . . C7 101
Augusta, Lewis and Clark, Mont., 400 . . . C4 102
Augusta, Sussex, N.J., 150 . . A3 106
Augusta, Carroll, Ohio, 250 . B6 111
Augusta, Eau Claire, Wis., 1,338 . . . D2 124
Augusta, Hampshire, W. Va., 250 . . . B6 123
Augusta, co., Va., 37,363 . . . C3 121
Augusta Springs, Augusta, Va., 300 . . . C3 121
Augustenborg, Den., 1,926 . . D3 24
Augustow, Pol., 12,700 . . . B7 26
Auneau, pen., Ont., Can . . . E4 71
Auja, see Tarkon, riv., Isr.
Aul, mtn., Switz . . . C7 19
Aulander, Bertie, N.C., 1,083 . . . A6 109
Aulendorf, Ger., 5,000 . . . B5 18
Aulnay-sous-Bois, Fr., 47,507 . . . g11 14
Aulne, riv., Fr . . . C1 14
Aulnoye [-Aymeries], Fr., 9,405 (*18,000) . . . D3 15
Ault, Weld, Colo., 799 . . . A6 83
Aumale, Alg., 4,028 . . . F8 30
Aumale, Fr., 1,757 . . . E9 12
Aumsville, Marion, Oreg., 300 . . . C2 113
Auneuil, Fr., 969 . . . E2 15
Auning, Den., 1,314 . . . B4 24
Aunis, former prov., Fr., 167,000 . . . *D3 14
Auno, Nig . . . D7 45
Aunuu, isl., Am. Sam . . . 52
Aur, isl., Mala . . . K6 38
Aura, Baraga, Mich., 40 . . . B2 98
Auraiya, India, 17,463 . . . D7 40
Aurangabad, India, 87,579 (*97,701) . . . E6 39, G5 40
Auray, Fr., 8,118 . . . D2 14
Aurelia, Cherokee, Iowa, 904 . B2 92
Aurelian Springs, Halifax, N.C. 75 . . . A6 109
Aurich, Ger., 13,000 . . . B3 16
Aurillac, Fr., 24,563 . . . E5 14
Aurora, Br. Gu., 290 . . . A3 59
Aurora, Ont., Can., 8,791 . . . D5 72
Aurora, Arapahoe and Adams, Colo., 48,548 . . . B6 83
Aurora, Kane, Ill., 63,715 . . . B5, F1 90
Aurora, Dearborn, Ind., 4,756 . . . F8 91
Aurora, Buchanan, Iowa, 223 . . . B6 92
Aurora, Cloud, Kans., 150 . . . C6 93
Aurora, Hancock, Maine, 70 (75▲) . . . D4 96
Aurora, St. Louis, Minn., 2,799 . . . C6 99
Aurora, Lawrence, Mo., 4,683 . . . E4 101
Aurora, Hamilton, Nebr., 2,576 . . . D7 103
Aurora, Cayuga, N.Y., 834 . . C4 108
Aurora, Beaufort, N.C., 449 . B7 109
Aurora, Portage, Ohio, 4,049 . A6 111
Aurora, Marion, Oreg., 247 . . . B2, B4 113
Aurora, Brookings, S. Dak., 232 . . . C9 116
Aurora, Sevier, Utah, 465 . . E4 119
Aurora, Preston, W. Va., 400 . . . B5 123
Aurora, Florence, Wis . . . C5 124
Aurora, co., S. Dak., 4,749 . . D7 116
Aurora Center, Brookings, S. Dak., 232 . . . D7 116
Aurskog, Nor . . . p29 25
Aus, S. W. Afr., 687 . . . C2 49
Au Sable, pt., Mich . . . B4 98
Au Sable, pt., Mich . . . D7 98
Au Sable, riv., Mich . . . D6 98
Ausable, riv., N.Y . . . f11 108
Au Sable Forks, Clinton and Essex, N.Y., 2,100 . . . f11 108
Aussa, riv., It . . . D9 18
Ausser-Rhoden, sub canton, Switz., 48,920 . . . B7 19
Aust-Agder, co., Nor., 76,900 . . . *H3 25
Austell, Cobb, Ga., 1,867 . . . B4 87
Austin, Lonoke, Ark., 210 . . . C4 81
Austin, Man., Can., 384 . . . E2 71
Austin, Scott, Ind., 3,838 . . . G6 91
Austin, Barren, Ky., 150 . . . D3 94
Austin, Mower, Minn., 27,908 . . . G6 99
Austin, Lewis and Clark, Mont., 40 . . . D4 102
Austin, Lander, Nev., 500 . . . D4 104
Austin, Grant, Oreg., 35 . . . C8 113
Austin, Potter, Pa., 721 . . . C5 114
Austin, Travis, Tex., 186,545 (*210,000) . . . D4 118
Austin, co., Tex., 13,777 . . . E4 118
Austin, lake, Austl . . . E2 50
Austinburg, Ashtabula, Ohio, 300 . . . A7 111
Austin Lake, Kalamazoo, Mich., 3,520 . . . *F5 98
Austintown, Mahoning, Ohio, 5,000 . . . *A7 111
Austinville, Butler, Iowa, 130 . B5 92
Austinville, Wythe, Va., 750 . . . E2 121
Australia, country, Oceania, 11,335,000 . . . H6 2, 50
Australian Alps, mts., Austl . . G8 50
Australian Capital Territory, Austl., 86,000 . . . G7 51
Austria, country, Eur., 7,235,000 . . . F11 8, E6 16
Austwell, Refugio, Tex., 287 . E4 118
Autauga, co., Ala., 18,739 . . . C3 78
Autaugaville, Autauga, Ala., 440 . . . C3 78
Authie, riv., Fr . . . D2 15
Autlán de Navarro, Mex., 17,069 . . . D4, n11 63
Au Train, Alger, Mich., 100 . B4 98
Autreyville, Colquitt, Ga., 50 . E3 87
Autun, Fr., 15,305 . . . D6 14
Auvergne, Jackson, Ark., 100 . B4 81
Auvergne, mts., Fr . . . E5 14
Auvergne, former prov., Fr., 1,298,000 . . . E5 14
Auvers [-sur-Oise], Fr., 3,772 . . . C2 14
Aux Barques, pt., Mich . . . D8 98
Aux Chene, riv., La . . . C7 95
Auxerre, Fr., 31,178 . . . D5 14
Auxier, Floyd, Ky., 800 . . . C7 94
Auxi-le-Château, Fr., 3,135 . D10 12
Auxonne, Fr., 4,084 . . . D6 14
Auxvasse, Callaway, Mo., 534 . . . B6 101
Ava, Jackson, Ill., 665 . . . F4 90
Ava, Douglas, Mo., 1,581 . . . E5 101
Ava, Noble, Ohio, 220 . . . C6 111
Avakubi, Con. L . . . A4 48
Avallon, Fr., 5,976 . . . D5 14
Avalon, Los Angeles, Calif., 1,536 . . . F4 82
Avalon, Stephens, Ga., 194 . . B3 87
Avalon, Livingston, Mo., 65 . B4 101
Avalon, Cape May, N.J., 695 . E3 106
Avalon, Allegheny, Pa., 6,859 . . . A5 114
Avalon, pen., Newf., Can . . . E5 75
Avalon, res., N. Mex . . . E5 107
Avanos, Tur., 5,700 . . . C10 31
Avant, Osage, Okla., 381 . . . A5 112
Avard, Woods, Okla., 56 . . . A3 112
Avaré, Braz., 20,334 . . . C3 56
Āvāz, Iran . . . E10 41
Aveiro, Port., 13,423 . . . B1 20
Avella, Washington, Pa., 1,310 . . . F1 114
Avellaneda, Arg., 329,626 . . . A5, g7 54
Avellino, It., 35,600 (44,400▲) . . . D5 21
Avenal, Kings, Calif., 3,147 . . E3 82
Avenches, Switz., 1,776 . . . C3 19
Avenel, Middlesex, N.J., 10,000 . . . k7 106
Avening, Ont., Can., 51 . . . C4 72
Avenwedde, Ger., 8,500 . . . B3 17
Avera, Jefferson, Ga., 197 . . . C4 87
Averill, Clay, Minn., 54 . . . D2 99
Averill Park, Rensselaer, N.Y., 1,000 . . . C7 108
Aversa, It., 42,300 . . . D5 21
Avery, Shoshone, Idaho, 450 . B3 89
Avery, Monroe, Iowa, 200 . . . C5 92
Avery, Lincoln, Okla., 30 . . . B5 112
Avery, Red River, Tex., 343 . C5 118
Avery, co., N.C., 12,009 . . . A2 109
Avery Island, Iberia, La., 650 . . . E4 95
Aves, is., Ven . . . A4 60
Avesnes [-sur-Helpe], Fr., 6,151 . . . D3 15
Avesta, Swe., 10,900 (*18,500) . . . G7 25
Aveyron, dept., Fr., 290,442 . . . *E5 14
Avezzano, It., 25,000 . . . C4 21
Aviá Terai, Arg . . . E3 55
Aviemore, Scot . . . C5 13
Avigliano, It., 4,554 . . . D5 21
Avignon, Fr., 72,717 . . . F6 14
Avila, San Luis Obispo, Calif., 300 . . . E3 82
Ávila, Sp., 26,807 . . . B3 20
Ávila, prov., Sp., 238,372 . . *B3 20
Avilés, Sp., 48,503 . . . A3 20
Avilla, Noble, Ind., 919 . . . B7 91
Avilla, Jasper, Mo., 135 . . . D3 101
Avinger, Cass, Tex., 730 . . . C5 118
Avis, Clinton, Pa., 1,262 . . . D7 114
Avisio, riv., It . . . C7 18
Avize, Fr., 1,888 . . . F4 15
Avlon, Grc., 2,231 . . . g11 23
Avlum, Den., 1,253 . . . B2 24
Avoca, Lawrence, Ala., 400 . . A2 78
Avoca, Benton, Ark., 90 . . . A1 81
Avoca, Lawrence, Ind., 400 . G4 91
Avoca, Pottawattamie, Iowa, 1,540 . . . C2 92
Avoca, Assumption, La . . . C5 95
Avoca, St. Clair, Mich., 300 . E8 98
Avoca, Murray, Minn., 226 . . G3 99
Avoca, Cass, Nebr., 218 . . . E3 103
Avoca, Steuben, N.Y., 1,086 . . . C3 108
Avoca, Luzerne, Pa., 3,562 . . B9 114
Avoca, Jones, Tex., 200 . . . C3 118
Avola, It., 27,453 . . . F5 21
Avola, B.C., Can., 138 . . . D8 68
Avon, Ont., Can., 97 . . . E4 72
Avon, Eagle, Colo., 5 . . . B4 83
Avon, Hartford, Conn., 2,500 (5,273▲) . . . B5 84
Avon, Fulton, Ill., 996 . . . C3 90
Avon, Polk, Iowa, 25 . . . A7 92
Avon, Franklin, Maine, (436▲) . . . D2 96
Avon, Norfolk, Mass., 4,301 . . . B5, h11 97
Avon, Stearns, Minn., 443 . . . E4 99
Avon, Washington, Miss., 150 . . . B2 100
Avon, Powell, Mont., 200 . . D4 102
Avon, Livingston, N.Y., 2,772 . . . C3 108
Avon, Dare, N.C., 300 . . . B8 109
Avon, Lorain, Ohio, 6,002 . . A5 111
Avon, Lebanon, Pa., 1,212 . . *F9 114
Avon, Bon Homme, S. Dak., 637 . . . E7 116
Avon, Cache, Utah, 60 . . . B4 119
Avon, riv., Eng . . . E6 10, B6 12
Avon, riv., Eng . . . D6 10, B5 12
Avon, riv., Eng . . . C5 12
Avon, riv., Scot . . . C5 13
Avon by the Sea, Monmouth, N.J., 1,707 . . . C4 106
Avondale, Maricopa, Ariz., 6,151 . . . G1 80
Avondale, Newf., Can., 511 . *E5 75
Avondale, Pueblo, Colo., 400 . . . C6 83
Avondale, Prince Georges, Md., 2,000 . . . *C4 85
Avondale, Clay, Mo., 663 . . E2 101
Avondale, Chester, Pa., 1,016 . . . G10 114
Avondale Estates, DeKalb, Ga., 1,646 . . . B5 87
Avondale, Washington, R.I., 200 . . . D9 84
Avon Lake, Lorain, Ohio, 9,403 . . . A5 111
Avonlea, Sask., Can., 354 . . G3 70
Avonmore, Westmoreland, Pa., 1,351 . . . E3 114
Avon Park, Highlands, Fla., 6,073 . . . E5 86
Avoyelles, par., La., 37,606 . . C3 95
Avranches, Fr., 8,854 . . . C3 14
Awa, isl., Jap . . . G9 37
Awaji, isl., Jap . . . I7 37
Awalt, Franklin, Tenn., 40 . . B5 117
Awarta, Jordan, 2,000 . . . B7 32
Awāsh, riv., Eth . . . C5 47
Awashi, Okinawa . . . 52
Awbārī, Libya . . . D2 43
Awe, lake, Scot . . . D3 13
Aweil, Sud., 2,438 . . . D2 47
Awjilah, Libya . . . D4 43
Axel, Neth., 5,200 . . . C3 15
Axel Heiberg, isl., N.W. Ter., Can . . . k33 67
Axial, Moffat, Colo., 5 . . . A3 83
Axial, basin, Colo . . . A2 83
Axim, Ghana, 4,647 . . . F4 45
Axios (Vardar), riv., Grc . . . B4 23
Axis, Mobile, Ala., 300 . . . E1 78
Ax-les-Thermes, Fr., 1,628 . . F4 14
Axson, Atkinson, Ga., 320 . . E4 87
Axtell, Marshall, Kans., 493 . C7 93
Axtell, Kearney, Nebr., 477 . D6 103
Axtell, Sanpete, Utah, 10 . . . D4 119
Ay, Fr., 6,806 . . . C6 14
Ay, riv., Sov. Un . . . B5 29
Ayabaca, Peru, 2,481 . . . B2 58
Ayabe, Jap., 21,500 (51,258▲) . . . n14 37
Ayacucho, Arg., 9,220 . . . B5 54
Ayacucho, Peru, 21,531 . . . D3 58
Ayacucho, dept., Peru, 469,396 . . . D3 58
Ayaguz, Sov. Un., 52,400 . . D10 29
Ayakhta, Sov. Un . . . D28 9
Ayamonte, Sp., 8,908 . . . D2 20
Ayan, Sov. Un., 9,300 . . . D16 28
Ayapel, Col., 2,436 . . . B2 60
Ayapel, mts., Col . . . B3 60
Ayas, Tur., 4,300 . . . B9 31
Ayaviri, Peru, 6,586 . . . D3 58
Aycliffe, Eng., 594 . . . F7 13
Aydar, riv., Sov. Un . . . G13 27
Ayden, Pitt., N.C., 3,108 . . . B6 109
Aydin (Aidin), Tur., 35,700 . D6 31
Aydlett, Currituck, N.C., 100 . . . A8 109
Ayer, Middlesex, Mass., 14,927 . . . A4, f9 97
Ayers, Washington, Maine . . D5 96
Ayers Cliff, Que., Can., 747 . D5 73
Ayía, Grc., 2,823 . . . C4 23
Ayía Paraskeví, Grc., 12,122 . . . C6 23
Ayiassos, Grc., 5,692 . . . C6 23
Ayion Oros (Mount Athos), prov., Grc., 2,687 . . . *B5 23
Ayios Dhimitrios, Grc., 21,365 . . . g11 23
Ayios Nikolaos, Grc., 3,319 . . E5 23
Aylen, lake, Ont., Can . . . B7 72
Aylesbury, Sask., Can., 162 . . G3 70
Aylesbury, Eng., 27,891 . . . C7 12
Aylesford, N.S., Can., 964 . . D5 74
Aylett, King William, Va., 60 . . . D5 121
Aylmer, Pierce, N. Dak., 10 . . B5 110
Aylmer, mtn., Alta., Can . . . D3 69
Aylmer East, Que., Can., 6,286 . . . D2 73
Aylmer West, Ont., Can., 4,705 . . . E4 72
Aylsham, Sask., Can., 251 . . D4 70
Aynor, Horry, S.C., 635 . . . D9 115
Ayn Sīdī Muḩammad (Oasis), Libya . . . H3 31
'Ayn Yabrūd, Jordan, 1,000 . . . h11 32
Ayon, isl., Sov. Un . . . C19 28
Ayora, Sp., 6,634 . . . C5 20
Ayr, Ont., Can., 1,016 . . . D4 72
Ayr, Adams, Nebr., 111 . . . D7 103
Ayr, Cass, N. Dak., 81 . . . B8 110
Ayr, Scot., 45,200 . . . E4 13
Ayr, co., Scot., 342,855 . . . E4 13
Ayr, riv., Scot . . . E4 13
Ayrshire, Pike, Ind., 100 . . . H3 91
Ayrshire, Palo Alto, Iowa, 298 . . . A3 92
Aysén, see Aisén, prov., Chile
Aysha, Eth . . . C5 47
Ayton, Ont., Can., 375 . . . C4 72
Aytos, Bul., 9,972 . . . D8 22
Aytre, Fr., 5,302 . . . D3 14
Ayutla, Guat., 1,653 . . . C1 62
Ayutla [de los Libres], Mex., 2,688 . . . D5 63
Ayutthaya, Thai., 32,368 . . . E4 38
Ayvacik, Tur., 1,900 . . . C6 31
Ayvalik, Tur., 16,100 . . . C6 31
Azalea Park, Orange, Fla., 6,500 . . . *D5 86
Azalia, Bartholomew, Ind., 100 . . . F6 91
Azama, Okinawa . . . 52
Azamgarh, India, 32,391 . . . D9 40
Azángaro, Peru, 2,619 . . . D3 58
Azaouak Assakari, wadi, Mali . C5 45
Azaouad, sand dunes, Mali . . C4 45
Azare, Nig . . . D7 45
Azemmour, Mor., 12,449 . . . C3 44
Azerbaidzhan, (S.S.R.), rep., Sov. Un., 4,400,000 . . . G18 9
Azilal, Mor., 1,340 . . . I3 30
Azilek (Well), Niger . . . C6 45
Aziscoos, lake, Maine . . . C1 96
Azle, Tarrant, Tex., 2 969 . . B5 118
Azogues, Ec., 6,579 . . . B2 58
Azor, Isr., 3,300 . . . g10 32
Azores Islands, reg., Port. (Atl. O.), 327,500 . . . h8 44
Azov, Sov. Un., 39,931 . . . H12 27
Azov, sea, Sov. Un . . . I11 27
Azrou, Mor., 14,143 . . . C3 44
Aztec, Yuma, Ariz., 30 . . . E2 80
Aztec, San Juan, N. Mex., 4,137 . . . A2 107
Aztec Ruins, nat. mon., N. Mex . . . A1 107
Azua, Dom. Rep., 12,350 . . . F8 64
Azuaga, Sp., 17,518 . . . C3 20
Azuay, prov., Ec., 277,772 . . B2 58
Azuero, pen., Pan . . . G7 62
Azul, Arg., 28,609 . . . B5 54
Azul, range, Peru . . . C2 58
Azurdui, Bol., 1,234 . . . C3 55
Azusa, Los Angeles, Calif., 20,497 . . . F3 82
Az Zāhirīyah, Jordan, 4,000 . . C6 32
'Az Zahrān (Dhahran), Sau. Ar., 12,500 . . . H5 41
Az Zaqāzīg, Eg., U.A.R., 124,417 . . . G8 31
Az Zarqā', Jordan, 4,000 . . . B8 32
'Azzās, cape, Libya . . . C5 43
Az Zāwiyah, Jordan, 1,000 . . . g11 32
Az Zawiyah, Libya, 8,428 . . . C2 43
Azzel Matti, lake, Alg . . . D5 44
Az Zubair, Iraq, 23,582 . . . F3 41
Azzun, Jordan, 2,000 . . . g11 32

B

Baagö, isl., Den C3 24
Baal, Ger., 1,850 C6 15
Baalbek, Leb., 9,623 E11 31
Baar, Switz., 9,114 B6 19
Baarle-Hertog, Bel., 2,044 C4 15
Baba, cape, Tur C6 23
Babadag, Rom., 5,549 C9 22
Babaeski, Tur., 11,700 B6 23
Babahoyo, Ec., 9,045 B2 58
Babana, Nig D5 45
Babanusa, Sud C2 47
Babati, Tan B6 48
Babayevo, Sov. Un., 10,000 B11 27
Babb, Glacier, Mont., 50 B3 102
Babb, creek, Pa C7 114
Babbie, Covington, Ala., 60 D3 78
Babbit, Mineral, Nev., 2,159 E3 104
Babbitt, St. Louis, Minn., 2,587 C7 99
Babcock, Wood, Wis., 125 D3 124
Bab el Mandeb, strait, Afr C5 47
Babelthuap, isl., Palau Is 52
Babenhausen, Ger., 3,800 A6 18
Babi, is., Indon K2 38
Babine, lake, B.C., Can B5 68
Babine, range, B.C., Can B4 68
Babine, riv., B.C., Can B4 68
Babo, W. Irian F8 35
Bābol, Iran, 36,194 C6 41
Baboquivari, mts., Ariz F4 80
Baboua, Cen. Afr. Rep D2 46
Babson Park, Polk, Fla., 950 E5 86
Babuna, mts., Yugo E5 22
Babushkin, Sov. Un., 20,000 A6 34
Babuyan, chan., Phil *B6 35
Babuyan, is., Phil B6 35
Babyak, Bul., 6,211 E6 22
Babylon, Suffolk, N.Y., 12,299 n15 108
Baca, co., Colo., 6,310 D8 83
Bacabal, Braz., 4,857 B2 57
Bacalar, Mex., 744 D7 63
Bacarra, Phil., 6,566 *B6 35
Bacău, Rom., 62,900 B8 22
Baccalieu, isl., Newf., Can D5 75
Baccarat, Fr., 6,067 C7 14
Baccaro, pt., N.S., Can F4 74
Baceras, Mex., 1,016 A3 63
Bach, Huron, Mich., 100 E7 98
Bach, Switz C7 19
Bacharach, Ger., 2,000 C2 17
Bachau, India, 4,868 F3 40
Back, Scot B2 13
Back, riv., N.W. Ter., Can C12 66
Backa Palanka, Yugo., 16,487 C4 22
Bac Kan, Viet., 10,000 A6 38
Backa Topola, Yugo., 15,057 B4 22
Back Bay, N.B., Can., 725 D3 74
Backbay, Princess Anne, Va., 500 E6 121
Backbone, mtn., Md D1 85
Back Creek, Frederick, Va B4 121
Backnang, Ger., 23,700 E4 17
Backoo, Pembina, N. Dak., 35 A8 110
Backus, Cass, Minn., 317 D4 99
Backway, The, bay, Newf., Can A2 75
Bac Lieu, Viet., 58,920 H6 38
Bacliff, Galveston, Tex., 1,707 *E5 118
Bac Ninh, Viet., 25,000 B7 38
Bacnotan, Phil., 1,069 n13 35
Bacobi, Navajo, Ariz., 100 B5 80
Bacolod, Phil., 88,854 (119,315▲) C6 35
Bacon, co., Ga., 8,359 E4 87
Bacone, Muskogee, Okla., 250 B6 112
Bacons Castle, Surry, Va B6, D6 121
Baconton, Mitchell, Ga., 564 E2 87
Bacoor, Phil, 6,276 o13 35
Bacova, Bath, Va., 175 C3 121
Bac Quang, Viet A6 38
Bacqueville-en Caux, Fr:, 1,022 E8 12
Bacsalmas, Hung., 7,344 B4 22
Bács-Kiskun, co., Hung., 587,028 *B4 22
Bacuit, Phil., 1,392 *C5 35
Bácum, Mex., 1,509 B2 63
Bad, riv., S. Dak C5 116
Bad, riv., Wis B3 124
Bad Aibling, Ger., 7,400 B8 18
Badajoz, Sp., 80,000 (96,317▲) C2 20
Badajoz, prov., Sp., 834,370 *C2 20
Badalona, Sp., 92,257 B7 20
Bad Axe, Huron, Mich., 2,998 E7 98
Bad Berneck, Ger., 3,300 C6 17
Bad Blankenburg, Ger., 6,601 C6 17
Bad Bramstedt, Ger., 6,200 E3 24
Baddeck, N.S., Can., 825 C9 74
Bad Doberan, Ger., 12,600 A5 16
Baden, Aus., 22,484 D8 16
Baden, Ont., Can., 977 D4 72
Baden, Prince Georges, Md., 12 C4 85
Baden, Beaver, Pa., 6,109 A5, E1 114
Baden, Switz., 14,900 (★52,800) B5 19
Baden, reg., Ger D4 16
Baden-Baden, Ger., 39,800 E3 17
Baden Baden, Bond, Ill. (part of Pierron) E4 90
Baden-Powell, mtn., Calif E5 82
Baden-Württemberg, state, Ger., 8,245,000 D4 17
Bad Freienwalde, Ger., 12,200 B7 16
Bad Friedrichshall, Ger., 8,600 D4 17
Badgastein, Aus., 5,742 B9 18
Badger, Newf., Can., 1,036 D3 75
Badger, Webster, Iowa, 340 B3 92
Badger, Roseau, Minn., 338 B2 99
Badger, Kingsbury, S. Dak., 117 C8 116
Badger, creek, Colo B7 83
Badger, mts., Wash B5 122
Badger Basin, Park, Wyo A3 125
Badger's Quay, Newf., Can., 696 *D5 75
Bad Godesberg, Ger., 67,300 C2 17
Bad Hersfeld, Ger., 23,000 C4 16
Bad Homburg, Ger., 38,300 C3 17
Bad Hönningen, see Hönningen, Ger.
Badi, Iraq E13 31
Badia Polesine, It., 3,825 D7 18
Badin, Stanly, N.C., 1,905 B3 109
Badin, Pak E2 40
Badin, lake, N.C B3 109
Bad Ischl, Aus., 12,703 E6 16
Bad Kissingen, Ger., 12,900 C5 17
Bad Kreuznach, Ger., 36,000 D2 17
Badlands, reg., N. Dak C2 110
Badlands, reg., S. Dak D3 116
Badlands, nat. mon., S. Dak D3 116
Bad Lauterberg, Ger., 10,100 B5 17
Bad Liebenwerda, Ger., 6,472 B8 17
Bad Lippspringe, Ger., 8,800 B3 17
Bad Mergentheim, Ger., 11,600 D4 17
Bad Muskau, Ger., 5,122 B9 17
Bad Nauheim, Ger., 13,400 C3 17
Bad Neustadt, Ger., 8,600 C5 17
Bad Oeynhausen, Ger., 14,100 A3 17
Bad Oldesloe, Ger., 16,000 B5 16
Badon, Viet D7 38
Bad Orb, Ger., 7,300 C4 17
Badoumé, Mali D2 45
Bad Pyrmont, Ger., 14,400 B4 17
Badra, Iraq, 3,638 E2 41
Bad Ragaz, Switz., 2,699 B7 19
Bad Reichenhall, Ger., 13,100 E6 16
Bad River, Indian res., Wis B3 124
Bad Salzuflen, Ger., 16,600 A3 17
Bad Salzungen, Ger., 10,000 C5 17
Bad Schandau, Ger., 5,095 C9 17
Bad Segeberg, Ger., 11,700 E4 24
Bad Sülze, Ger., 3,222 D6 24
Bad Tennstedt, Ger., 4,351 B5 17
Bad Tölz, Ger., 11,700 E5 16
Baduein, Eth D5 47
Badulla, Cey., 17,323 G7 39
Badwater, Natrona, Wyo B5 125
Badwater, riv., Wyo B5 125
Bad Wildungen, Ger., 11,200 B4 17
Bad Wörishofen, Ger., 7,500 A6 18
Bad Zwischenahn, Ger., 16,900 A8 15
Baena, Sp., 17,761 D3 20
Baependi, Braz., 5,109 C4 56
Baeza, Ec B2 58
Baeza, Sp., 15,176 D4 20
Bafang, Cam D2 46
Bafata, Port. Gui D2 45
Bafia, Cam E2 46
Baffin, bay, N.W. Ter., Can B18 67
Baffin, isl., N.W. Ter., Can C18 67
Baffins, bay, Tex F4 118
Bafoulabé, Mali, 2,700 D2 45
Bāfq, Iran, 6,000 F7 41
Bafra, Tur., 20,800 B10 31
Bafra, cape, Tur B11 31
Bāft, Iran, 8,693 G8 41
Bafwasende, Con. L A4 48
Baga, S.L. E2 45
Bagabag, Phil., 2,477 n13 35
Bagaces, C.R., 4,079 E5 62
Bagamoyo, Tan., 3,861 C6 48
Bagana, Nig E6 46
Bagan Siapiapi, Indon., 15,321 E2 35, K4 38
Bagata, Con. L B2 48
Bagby, Mariposa, Calif., 20 D3 82
Bagdad, Yavapai, Ariz., 1,462 C2 80
Bagdad, Santa Rosa, Fla., 900 G2 86
Bagdad, Shelby, Ky., 500 B4 94
Bagé, Braz., 47,930 E2 56
Bagēmder, prov., Eth C4 47
Bagenkop, Den., 705 D4 24
Bagerhat, Pak., 7,431 F12 40
Baggs, Carbon, Wyo., 199 D5 125
Baghdad, Iraq, 355,958 (★650,000) E2 41
Bagheria, It., 35,100 E4 21
Baghlan, Afg., 24,410 C14 41
Baghnam Faoileann, riv., Scot C2 13
Bagley, Guthrie, Iowa, 406 C3 92
Bagley, Clearwater, Minn., 1,385 C3 99
Bagley, Grant, Wis., 275 F2 124
Bagleys Mills, Lunenburg, Va., 10 E4 121
Bagnacavallo, It., 4,693 E7 18
Bagnara [Calabra], It., 10,000 E5 21
Bagnell, Miller, Mo., 62 C5 101
Bagnell, dam, Mo C5 101
Bagnères-de-Bigorre, Fr., 8,996 (10,314▲) F4 14
Bagnères-de-Luchon, Fr., 3,888 F4 14
Bagnolet, Fr., 31,576 g10 14
Bagnols [-sur-Cèze], Fr., 12,905 E6 14
Bagoe, riv., Mali D3 45
Bagolino, It., 5,549 D6 18
Bagot, co., Que., Can., 21,390 D5 73
Bagotville, Que., Can., 5,629 A7 73
Bagrash Kol, lake, China C2 34
Bagrationovsk (Preussisch Eylau), Sov. Un., 5,000 A6 26
Baguezane, mtn., Niger C6 45
Baguio, Phil., 50,436 B6, n13 35
Bahado (Well), Som D6 47
Bahama, Durham, N.C., 200 A5 109
Bahama Islands, Br. dep., N.A., 136,000 C6 64
Bahawalnagar, Pak., 18,373 C4 40
Bahawalpur, Pak., 84,377 C5 39
Bahawalpur, prov., Pak., 1,823,125 *C5 39
Bāherdār-Giyorgis, Eth C4 47
Bahia, see Salvador, Braz.
Bahia, state, Braz., 5,990,605 D2 57
Bahía, is., Hond B4 62
Bahía Blanca, Arg., 136,000 B4 54
Bahía de Caráquez, Ec., 7,993 B1 58
Bahía Negra, Par., 590 D4 55
Bahraich, India, 56,033 D8 40
Bahrain (Bahrein), country, Asia, 166,000 H5 41
Bahrāmābād, Iran, 14,867 F8 41
Bahr el Abyad (White Nile), riv., Sud C3 47
Bahr el Arab, riv., Sud D2 47
Bahr el Azraq (Blue Nile), riv., Sud C3 47
Bahr el Ghazal, reg., Sud., 991,022 D2 47
Bahr el Ghazal, riv., Sud D2 47
Bahr el Je'bel (Mountain Nile), riv., Sud D3 47
Bahrgan, cape, Iran G4 41
Bahrīyah, oasis, Eg., U.A.R D5 43
Bāhū Kalāt, Iran, I10 41
Baia dos Tigres, Ang E1 48
Baia-Mare, Rom., 43,100 B6 22
Baião, Braz., 2,265 C5 59
Baïbokoum, Chad, 3,130 D3 46
Baidarik, riv., Mong B4 34
Baie-Comeau, Que., Can., 7,956 k13 73
Baie de Wasai, Chippewa, Mich., 30 B6 98
Baie-d'Urfé, Que., Can., 3,549 q19 73
Baie-Johan-Beetz, Que., Can., 237 h9 75
Baiersbronn, Ger., 9,200 E3 17
Baie-Ste. Catherine, Que., Can A8 73
Baie-St. Paul, Que., Can., 4,674 B7 73
Baie-Verte, N.B., Can., 133 C5 74
Baie Verte, Newf., Can., 958 D3 75
Baile Átha Cliath, see Dublin, Ire.
Bailén, Sp., 11,245 C4 20
Băileşti, Rom., 15,932 C6 22
Bailey, Park, Colo., 100 B5 83
Bailey, Lauderdale, Miss., 150 *C5 100
Bailey, Powell, Mont C3 102
Bailey, Nash, N.C., 795 B5 109
Bailey, co., Tex., 9,090 B1 118
Bailey, brook, Maine B2 96
Bailey, isl., S.C G1 115
Bailey Island, Cumberland, Maine, 250 E5 96
Baileys Harbor, Door, Wis., 300 C6 124
Baileyton, Cullman, Ala., 100 A3 78
Baileyton, Greene, Tenn., 206 C11 117
Baileyville, Ogle, Ill., 200 A4 90
Baileyville, Nemaha, Kans., 200 C7 93
Bailieborough, Ire., 1,136 D5 11
Bainbridge, Decatur, Ga., 12,714 F2 87
Bainbridge, Putnam, Ind., 603 E4 91
Bainbridge, Chenango, N.Y., 1,712 C5 108
Bainbridge, Ross., Ohio, 1,001 C4 111
Bainbridge, is., Wash C1 122
Bain-de-Bretagne, Fr., 1,734 D3 14
Bains, West Feliciana, La., 85 D4 95
Bainville, Roosevelt, Mont., 285 B12 102
Baird, Sunflower, Miss., 175 B3 100
Baird, Callahan, Tex., 1,633 C3 118
Baird, Douglas, Wash B6 122
Baird, inlet, Alsk C7 79
Baird, mts., Alsk B7 79
Bairdford, Allegheny, Pa., 950 A6 114
Bairiki, isl., Tarawa 52
Bairnsdale, Austl., 7,428 H6 51
Bairoil, Sweetwater, Wyo., 300 C5 125
Baïse, riv., Fr F4 14
Bait, range, B.C., Can B4 68
Baixa Verde, Braz., 3,495 g6 57
Baixo Alentejo, prov., Port., 380,236 *C2 20
Baixo Longa, Ang E2 48
Baja, Hung., 30,355 B4 22
Baja California, state, Mex., 520,913 A1 63
Baja California Sur, ter., Mex., 83,433 B2 63
Bajadero, P.R B4 65
Bajmok, Yugo., 11,716 C4 22
Bakala, Cen. Afr., Rep D4 46
Bakar, Yugo., 2,026 C2 22
Bakel, Sen., 2,300 D2 45
Baker, San Bernardino, Calif., 200 E5 82
Baker, Okaloosa, Fla., 800 G2 86
Baker, Lemhi, Idaho, 200 D5 89
Baker, East Baton Rouge, La., 4,823 *D4 95
Baker, Clay, Minn., 60 D2 99
Baker, Fallon, Mont., 2,365 D12 102
Baker, White Pine, Nev., 30 E7 104
Baker, Benson, N. Dak., 45 A6 110
Baker, Texas, Okla., 70 D3 112
Baker, Baker, Oreg., 9,986 C9 113
Baker, co., Fla., 7,363 B4 86
Baker, co., Ga., 4,543 E2 87
Baker, co., Oreg., 17,295 C9 113
Baker, brook, Maine B3 96
Baker, butte, Ariz C4 80
Baker, isl., Pac. O F11 7
Baker, lake, N.W. Ter., Can D13 66
Baker, lake, Maine B3 96
Baker, mtn., Maine C3 96
Baker, mtn., Wash A4 122
Baker, riv., Wash A4 122
Baker, valley, Oreg C9 113
Bakerhill, Barbour, Ala., 125 D4 78
Baker Lake, N.W. Ter., Can., 386 D13 66
Bakers, Union, N.C., 80 B3 109
Bakers, Davidson, Tenn., 100 E9 117
Bakers, bayou, Ark D6 81
Bakers, isl., Mass f12 97
Bakers, riv., N.H C3 105
Bakersburg, Texas, Okla D3 112
Bakers Crossroads, White, Tenn C8 117
Bakersfield, Kern, Calif., 56,848 (★154,500) E4 82
Bakersfield, Ozark, Mo., 177 E5 101
Bakersfield, Pecos, Tex., 125 D1 118
Bakersfield, Franklin, Vt., 225 (664▲) B3 120
Bakers Mill, Hamilton, Fla., 30 B4 86
Bakerstown, Allegheny, Pa., 700 A6 114
Bakersville, Litchfield, Conn., 350 B4 84
Bakersville, Mitchell, N.C., 393 C4 109
Bakerton, see Elmora, Pa.
Bakerton, Jefferson, W. Va., 300 B7 123
Bakhchisaray, Sov. Un., 17,200 I9 27
Bakhmut, riv., Sov. Un q21 27
Bakir, riv., Tur C6 23
Bāko, Eth D4 47
Bako, I. C E3 45
Bakony Forest, mts., Hung B3 22
Bakouma, Cen. Afr. Rep D4 46
Bakoy, riv., Mali D3 45
Baku, Con. L A5 48
Baku, Sov. Un., 700,000 (★1,210,000) E3 29
Bakundi, Nig E7 45
Bakungan, Indon K2 38
Bakwanga, Con. L., 40,500 C3 48
Bala, Ont., Can., 495 B5 72
Bala, Riley, Kans., 50 C6 93
Bala, Tur., 3,100 C9 31
Bala, Wales, 1,603 B4 12
Bala, mts., Bol B2 55
Balabac, isl., Phil D5 35
Balabac, strait, Phil D5 35
Bala-Cynwyd, Montgomery, Pa., 8,000 *B11 114
Balad, Som E6 47
Balaghat, India, 18,990 G8 40
Balaguer, Sp., 8,342 B6 20
Bal'ah, Jordan, 4,000 f11 32
Balaka, Malawi D6 48
Balakhna, Sov. Un., 31,800 D17 9
Balakhta, Sov. Un D27 9
Balaklava, Austl., 1,301 G2 51
Balakleya, Sov. Un., 5,000 G11 27
Balallan, Scot B2 13
Bala Murghab, Afg., 5,000 D11 41
Balancán, Mex., 1,980 D6 63
Balanda, Sov. Un., 10,000 F15 27
Balanga, Phil., 5,061 C6, o13 35
Balangiga, Phil., 5,264 *C7 35
Balaoan, Phil., 2,376 n13 35
Balashikha, Sov. Un., 64,000 D11 27
Balashov, Sov. Un., 62,000 C2 29
Balasore, India, 33,931 G11 40
Balassagyarmat, Hung., 12,457 A4 22
Balāţ, Eg., U.A.R. D5 43
Balaton, Lyon, Minn., 723 F3 99
Balaton, lake, Hung B3 22
Balayan, Phil., 6,033 p13 35
Balayan, bay, Phil p13 35
Balboa, C.Z., 3,139 m11 62
Balboa, dist., C.Z., 30,623 *m11 62
Balboa Heights, C.Z., 118 m11 62
Balbriggan, Ire., 2,943 D5 11
Balcarce, Arg., 15,210 B5 54
Balcarres, Sask., Can., 710 G4 70
Balch, Jackson, Ark., 100 B4 81
Balchik, Bul., 6,011 D9 22
Balch Springs, Dallas, Tex., 6,821 *A6 118
Balclutha, N.Z., 3,935 Q12 51
Balcones Heights, Bexar, Tex., 950 *E3 118
Bald, hill, R.I C10 84
Bald, mtn., Calif C3 82
Bald, mtn., Colo A5 83
Bald, mtn., Conn B7 84
Bald, mtn., Maine C2 96
Bald, mtn., N.J A4 106
Bald, mtn., Oreg C3 113
Bald, mtn., Oreg C9 113
Bald, mtn., S. Dak C7 116
Bald, mtn., Vt B5 120
Bald, mtn., Wyo A5 125
Bald, mts., N.C C3 109
Bald, mts., Tenn C11 117
Bald Eagle, Ramsey, Minn., 1,200 E7 99
Bald Eagle, lake, Minn C7 99
Bald Eagle, lake, Minn E7 99
Baldegger, lake, Switz B5 19
Baldhill, dam, N. Dak B8 110
Bald Knob, White, Ark., 2,096 B4 81
Bald Knob, mtn., Oreg E2 113
Bald Knob, mtn., Va D3 121
Bald Knob, mtn., W. Va C5 123
Bald Knoll, mtn., Wyo C2 125
Baldock, lake, Man., Can A3 71
Baldur, Man., Can., 370 E2 71
Baldwin, Duval, Fla., 1,272 B5 86
Baldwin, Habersham and Banks, Ga., 698 B3 87
Baldwin, Randolph, Ill., 336 E4 90
Baldwin, Jackson, Iowa, 228 B7 92
Baldwin, St. Mary, La., 1,548 E4 95
Baldwin, Baltimore, Md., 100 B5 85
Baldwin, Lake, Mich., 835 E5 98
Baldwin, Nassau, N.Y., 34,500 G2 84
Baldwin, Ashe, N.C., 50 A2 109
Baldwin, Burleigh, N. Dak., 60 B5 110
Baldwin, Allegheny, Pa., 24,489 *F1 114
Baldwin, St. Croix, Wis., 1,184 C1 24
Baldwin, co., Ala., 49,088 E2 78
Baldwin, co., Ga., 34,064 C3 87
Baldwin City, Douglas, Kans., 1,877 D8 93
Baldwin Heights, Gibson, Ind., 200 H2 91
Baldwin Park, Los Angeles, Calif., 33,951 *F3 82
Baldwinsville, Onondaga, N.Y., 5,985 B4 108
Baldwinton, Sask., Can., 61 E1 70
Baldwinville, Worcester, Mass., 1,700 A3 97
Baldwyn, Lee and Prentiss, Miss., 2,023 A5 100
Baldy, mtn., Calif E5 82
Baldy, mtn., B.C., Can D7 68
Baldy, mtn., Man., Can D1 71
Baldy, mtn., Colo C3 83
Baldy, mtn., Mont B7 102
Baldy, mtn., N. Mex A4 107
Baldy, mtn., Wyo C3 125
Baldy, peak, Ariz D6 80
Bale, prov., Eth D5 47
Baleares (Balearic Islands), prov., Sp., 453,000 *C7 20
Balearic, is., Sp C6 20
Balembangan, isl., Mala *D5 35
Baler, Phil., 2,769 o13 35
Baleshare isl., Scot C1 13
Balesin, isl., Phil o14 35
Baleville, Sussex, N.J., 75 A3 106
Balfour, Henderson, N.C., 1,106 D3 109
Balfour, McHenry, N. Dak., 159 B5 110
Balgonie, Sask., Can., 430 G3 70
Bal Harbour, Dade, Fla., 727 *F3 86
Bali, Cam., 18,277 *E6 45
Bali, India, 9,855 E4 40
Bali, isl., Indon G5 35
Balikesir (Balikisri), Tur., 61,145 C6 23
Balikpapan, Indon., 88,534 F5 35
Balingen, Ger., 11,600 A4 18
Balintang, chan., Phil B6 35
Baliuag, Phil., 3,535 o13 35
Balje, Ger., 1,600 B4 16
Baljennie, Sask., Can E2 70
Balkan, Bell, Ky., 70 D6 94
Balkan, mts., Bul D7 22
Balkh, Afg., 12,466 C13 41
Balkhash, Sov. Un., 65,000 D8 29
Balkhash, lake, Sov. Un D9 29
Balki, Sov. Un., 25,000 H10 27
Balko, Beaver, Okla., 100 D3 112
Balla, Ire., 324 D2 11
Ballachulish, Scot., 2,960 D3 13
Ballagh, Ire E4 11
Ballaghaderreen, Ire., 1,308 D3 11
Ballaja, P.R C2 65
Ballantine, Yellowstone, Mont., 350 E8 102
Ballantrae, Scot., 886 E4 13
Ballarat, Austl., 41,600 (★56,600) H4 51
Ballard, co., Ky., 8,291 A2 94
Ballard Vale, Essex, Mass., 1,000 A5, f11 97
Ballater, Scot., 1,132 C5 13
Ball Club, Itasca, Minn., 100 C5 99
Ballclub, lake, Minn C5 99
Ballé, Mali C3 45
Ballenas, bay, Mex B2 63
Ballenstedt, Ger., 11,000 B6 17
Balleny, is., Ant C29 5
Ballerup, Den., 9,392 C6 24
Ball Ground, Cherokee, Ga., 707 B2 87
Ballia, India, 38,216 E10 40
Balliguda, India G9 40
Ballina, Austl., 4,129 D9 51
Ballina, Ire., 6,027 C2 11
Ballina, Ire., 273 E3 11
Ballinakill, Ire., 315 E4 11
Ballinalack, Ire., 55 D4 11
Ballinamallard, N. Ire., 352 C4 11
Ballinascarthy, Ire F3 11
Ballinasloe, Ire., 5,711 D3 11
Ballindine, Ire., 222 D3 11
Ballineen, Ire., 270 F3 11
Ballingarry, Ire., 360 E3 11
Ballingeary, Ire., 180 F2 11
Ballinger, Runnels, Tex., 5,043 D3 118
Ballinluig, Scot D5 13
Ballinrobe, Ire., 1,165 D2 11
Ballinskelligs, bay, Ire F1 11
Ballintra, Ire., 250 C3 11
Ball Mountain, flood control res., Vt E3 120
Ballouville, Windham, Conn., 400 B9 84
Ballston, Polk, Oreg., 200 B3 113
Ballston Lake, Saratoga, N.Y., 930 C7 108
Ballston Spa, Saratoga, N.Y., 4,991 B7 108
Ballville, Sandusky, Ohio, 1,424 *A4 111
Ballwin, St. Louis, Mo., 5,710 B7 101
Bally, India, 101,159 *F12 40
Bally, Berks, Pa., 1,033 F10 114
Ballybofey, Ire., 1,030 C4 11
Ballybunion, Ire., 1,163 E2 11
Ballycanew, Ire., 168 E5 11
Ballycastle, Ire., 191 C2 11
Ballycastle, N. Ire., 2,643 B5 11
Ballyconneely, Ire D1 11
Ballyconnell, Ire., 542 C4 11
Ballycroy, Ire C2 11
Ballyduff, Ire., 379 E2 11
Ballyduff, Ire., 99 E3 11
Ballyferriter, Ire E1 11
Ballygar, Ire., 315 D3 11
Ballygawley, N. Ire., 427 C4 11
Ballyglunin, Ire D3 11
Ballygorman, Ire B4 11
Ballyhaunis, Ire., 1,174 D3 11
Ballyheige, Ire., 417 E2 11
Ballyheige, bay, Ire E2 11
Ballyhoura, mts., Ire E2 11
Ballyjamesduff, Ire., 581 D4 11
Ballykelly, N. Ire., 367 B4 11
Ballylongford, Ire., 594 E2 11
Ballymahon, Ire., 830 D4 11
Ballymena, N. Ire., 14,740 C5 11
Ballymoe, Ire., 117 D3 11
Ballymoney, N. Ire., 3,409 B5 11
Ballymote, Ire., 965 C3 11
Ballymurray, Ire D3 11
Ballynahinch, N. Ire., 2,038 C6 11
Ballyneety, Ire E3 11
Ballynoe, Ire., 102 E3 11
Ballysadare, Ire., 143 C3 11
Ballyshannon, Ire., 2,322 C3 11
Ballyteige, bay, Ire E5 11
Ballytore, Ire., 269 D5 11
Ballyvaughan, Ire., 152 D2 11
Ballyvourney, Ire., 321 F2 11
Balm, Hillsborough, Fla., 250 E4 86
Balmat, St. Lawrence, N.Y., 100 A5, f9 108
Balmazujvaros, Hung., 16,312 B5 22
Balmhorn, mtn., Switz D4 19
Balmoral, Man., Can., 103 D3 71
Balmoral, N.B., Can., 898 B3 74
Balmoral Castle, Scot C5 13
Balmorhea, Reeves, Tex., 604 F2 118
Balmville, Orange, N.Y., 1,538 *D6 108
Baloda Bazar, India, 7,108 G9 40
Balonne, riv., Austl C7 51
Balotra, India, 12,110 E4 40
Balovale, Zambia, 1,110 D3 48
Balrampur, India, 31,776 D9 40
Balranald, Austl., 1,331 G4 51
Balş, Rom., 6,956 C7 22
Balsam, Jackson, N.C., 300 D3 109
Balsam, lake, Wis C1 124
Balsam, lake, Ont., Can C6 72
Balsam Lake, Polk, Wis., 541 C1 124
Balsas, Braz., 4,690 C1 57
Balsas, riv., Braz C1 57
Balsas, riv., Braz D1 57
Balsas, riv., Mex D4 63
Balsthal, Switz., 5,735 B4 19
Balta, Pierce, N. Dak., 165 A5 110
Balta, Sov. Un., 47,400 H7 27
Baltic, New London, Conn., 1,400 C8 84
Baltic, Tuscarawas, Ohio, 537 B6 111
Baltic, Minnehaha, S. Dak., 278 D9 116
Baltic, sea, Eur I8 25
Balţīm, Eg., U.A.R., 2,000 C3 32
Baltimore, Ont., Can., 220 C6 72
Baltimore, Ire., 188 F2 11
Baltimore (Independent City), Md., 939,024 (★1,636,500) B4, C2 85
Baltimore, Fairfield, Ohio, 2,116 C5 111
Baltimore, co., Md., 492,428 B4 85
Baltimore (Town of), Windsor, Vt. (90▲) *E3 120
Baltinglass, Ire., 806 E5 11
Baltiysk (Pillau), Sov. Un., 30,000 A5 26
Baltra, isl., Ec g5 58
Baltrum, Ger., 770 A7 15
Baltrum, isl., Ger A7 15
Baluchistan, reg., Iran, Pak C4 39
Balya, Tur., 1,700 C6 23
Balzac, Alta., Can D3 69
Balzar, Ec., 3,015 B2 58
Bam, Iran, 13,938 G9 41
Bam, lake, China B9 39
Bama, Nig D7 45
Bamako, Mali, 135,000 D3 45
Bamba, Mali C4 45
Bambang, Phil., 4,225 n13 35
Bambari, Cen. Afr. Rep., 19,700 D4 46
Bamberg, Ger., 73,400 D5 17
Bamberg, Bamberg, S.C., 3,081 E5 109
Bamberg, co., S.C., 16,274 E9 115
Bamber Lake, Ocean, N.J., 100 D4 106
Bambesa, Con. L A4 48
Bambuí, Braz., 8,148 F1 57
Bamburgh, Eng., 438 E7 13
Bambuto, mts., Nig., Cam E6 45
Bamenda [Mankou], Cam., 14,259 E7 45
Bampūr, Iran, 25,000 H10 41
Bampur, riv., Iran H9 41
Bams, butte, S. Dak B2 116
Baña Buey, Cuba k11 64
Banagher, Ire., 1,050 D4 11
Banalia, Con. L A4 48
Banamba, Mali D3 45
Banana, riv., Fla D6 86
Bananal, Braz., 2,189 h5 56
Bananal, isl., Braz E4 59
Bananeiras, Braz., 3,060 C3, h6 57
Banaras (Benares), India, 471,258 (★489,864) C7 39, E9 40
Banās, cape, Eg., U.A.R E6 43
Banas, riv., India F3 39
Banat, prov., Rom., 948,596 *C5 22
Banat, reg., Rom., Yugo C5 22
Ban Bangsaphan Yai, Thai., 3,362 G3 38
Banbridge, N. Ire., 6,115 C5 11
Banbury, Eng., 20,996 B6 12
Banchory, Scot., 1,918 C6 13
Bancker, Vermilion, La E3 95
Banco, Col., 9,636 B3 60
Bancroft, Ont., Can., 2,615 B7 72
Bancroft, Early, Ga., 100 E2 87
Bancroft, Caribou, Idaho, 416 G7 89
Bancroft, Kossuth, Iowa, 1,000 A3 92
Bancroft, Beauregard, La., 100 D2 95
Bancroft, Aroostook, Maine, 50 (94▲) C4 96
Bancroft, Shiawassee, Mich., 636 F6 98
Bancroft, Cuming, Nebr., 496 B9 103
Bancroft, Kingsbury, S. Dak., 86 C8 116
Bancroft, Portage, Wis., 250 D4 124
Banda, India, 37,744 E8 40
Banda, is., Indon F7 35
Banda, sea, Indon G7 35
Bandama, riv., I.C E3 45
Bandana, Ballard, Ky., 400 A2 94
Bandar, Afg., 5,000 D12 41
Bandar 'Abbās, Iran, 14,278 H8 41
Bandar Bahru, Mala., 1,187 J4 38
Bandar-e Chīrū, Iran H6 41
Bandar-e Deylam, Iran, 3,130 F5 41
Bandar-e Rīg, Iran, 2,250 G5 41
Bandar-e Shāh, Iran, 8,284 C7 41
Bandar-e Shāhpūr, Iran F4 41
Bandar Maharani (Muar), Mala., 39,046 K5 38
Bande, Sp., 6,275 A2 20
Banded, peak, Colo D4 83
Bandeira, peak, Braz F2 57
Bandelier, nat. mon., N. Mex B3 107
Bandera, Arg E3 55
Bandera, Bandera, Tex., 950 E3 118
Bandera, co., Tex., 3,892 E3 118
Banderas, bay, Mex m11 63
Bandholm, Den., 712 D5 24
Bandiagara, Mali, 3,800 D4 45
Bandikui, India, 10,638 D6 40
Bandirma, Tur., 28,900 B6 23
Bandjermasin, Indon., 212,683 F4 35
Bandoeng, see Bandung, Indon.
Bandon, Ire., 2,308 F3 11
Bandon, Coos, Oreg., 1,653 D2 113
Bandon, riv., Ire F3 11
Bandung (Bandoeng), Indon., 966,359 (★1,025,000) G3 35
Bandy, Tazewell, Va., 800 B3 121
Banes, Cuba, 20,257 E6 64
Banff, Alta., Can., 3,429 D3, g7 69
Banff, Scot., 3,329 C6 13
Banff, co., Scot., 46,400 C5 13
Banff, nat. park, Alta., Can D2 69
Banfora, Upper Volta, 4,000 D4 45
Bangalore, India, 905,134 (★1,225,000) F6 39
Bangassou, Cen. Afr. Rep E4 46
Banggai, Indon F6 35
Banghāzī, see Bengasi, Libya
Bangka, isl., Indon F3 35
Bangkalan, Indon., 12,359 G4 35
Bangkok (Krung Thep), Thai., 1,299,528 (★1,800,000) F4 38
Bangor, Blount, Ala., 75 B3 78
Bangor, Sask., Can., 109 G4 70
Bangor, Penobscot, Maine, 38,912 D4 96
Bangor, Van Buren, Mich., 2,109 F4 98
Bangor, Franklin, N.Y., 200 f10 108
Bangor, N. Ire., 24,900 C6 11
Bangor, Northampton, Pa., 5,766 E11 114
Bangor, Wales, 13,977 A3 12

Bangor, La Crosse, Wis., 928 .E3 124
Bangor Erris, Ire., 125 ......C2 11
Bangs, Brown, Tex., 967 .....D3 118
Bangs, mtn., Ariz A2 80
Bangued, Phil., 5,663 ....B6 35
Banguey (Banggi), isl., Mala ...D5 35
Bangui, Cen. Afr. Rep., 79,600 ....E3 46
Bangweulu, lake, Zambia D5 48
Banhā, Eg., U.A.R., 42,600 ..D3 32
Ban Hat Yai, see Hadyai, Thai.
Ban Houei Sai, Laos B4 38
Baní, Dom. Rep., 14,472 ....F8 64
Bani, Phil., 2,565 ....n12 35
Bani, riv., Mali D3 45
Baniara, Pap k12 50
Baniloudi, Niger C5 45
Banī Na 'īn, Jordan, 3,000 ...C7 32
Banister, riv., Va E4 121
Bani Suheila, Gaza Area, 3,000 ....C6 32
Banī Suwayf, Eg., U.A.R., 65,600 ....D6 43
Bāniyās, Syr., 8,500 ....E10 31
Baniyas, Syr A7 32
Banjak, is., Indon K2 38
Banja Luka, Yugo., 50,463 ...C3 22
Banjuwangi, Indon., 25,185 ..G4 35
Bankasse, Mali D4 45
Bankfoot, Scot., 2,310 ....D5 13
Bankhead, Walker, Ala., 50 ..B2 78
Bankhead, lake, Ala B2 78
Banks, Pike. Ala., 201 ....D4 78
Banks, Bradley, Ark., 233 ....D3 81
Banks, Boise, Idaho, 50 ......E2 89
Banks, Tunica, Miss., 300 ...A3 100
Banks, Washington, Oreg., 347 ....A1 113
Banks, co., Ga., 6,497 ....B3 87
Banks, bay, Ec g5 58
Banks, isl., Austl B7 50
Banks, isl., B.C., Can C2 68
Banks, isl., N.W. Ter., Can ...B8 66
Banks, lake, Ga F3 87
Banks, pen., N.Z O14 51
Banksian, riv., Man., Can C4 71
Bankston, Fayette, Ala., 120 ..B2 78
Bankura, India, 62,833 ....F11 40
Ban Me Thuot, Viet., 5,000 ...F8 38
Bann, riv., N. Ire B5 11
Bannack, Beaverhead, Mont., 15 ....E3 102
Banner, Calhoun, Miss., 75 ..A4 100
Banner, Sheridan, Wyo., 10 ..A6 125
Banner, co., Nebr., 1,269 ....C2 103
Banner Elk, Avery, N.C., 564 ....A2, C4 109
Banner Hill, Unicoi, Tenn., 1,100 ....*C11 117
Bannerman, Man., Can E2 71
Banner Town, Surry, N.C., 1,096 ....*A3 109
Banning, Riverside, Calif., 10,250 ....F5 82
Banning, Carroll, Ga., 150 ...C2 87
Banningville, Con. L., 4,753 ..B2 48
Bannock, co., Idaho, 49,342 ..G6 89
Bannock, pass, Idaho, Mont E5 89
Bannock, peak, Idaho G6 89
Bannockburn, Ont., Can., 186 ....C7 72
Bannu, Pak., 20,509 (*27,516) B5 39
Bañolas, Sp., 8,075 ....A7 20
Baños, Ec., 2,768 ....B2 58
Banqu, Con. L C3 48
Bansha, Ire., 244 ....E3 11
Banska Bystrica, Czech., 22,600 ....D5 26
Banska Stiavnica, Czech., 9,500 ....D5 26
Bansko, Bul., 6,161 ....E6 22
Banswara, India, 19,566 .....F5 40
Bantam, Litchfield, Conn., 833 ....C4 84
Bantam, lake, Conn C3 84
Bantam, riv., Conn B4 84
Banteer, Ire., 139 ....E3 11
Bantry, Ire., 2,234 ....F2 11
Bantry, McHenry, N. Dak., 93 ....A5 110
Bantry, bay, Ire F2 11
Banyo, Cam D2 46
Banzare, coast, Ant C25 5
Banzyville, Con. L A3 48
Baoulé, riv., Mali D3 45
Baoulé, riv., Mali D3 45
Bapaume, Fr., 3,275 ....D2 15
Bapchule, Pinal, Ariz., 100 ....D4, H2 80
Baptist, Tangipahoa, La A6 95
Baptiste, Ont., Can., 57 ......B6 72
Baptistown, Hunterdon, N.J., 350 ....B2 106
Baquba, Iraq, 13,203 ....F15 31
Baquedano, Chile D2 55
Bar, Sov. Un., 22,100 ....G6 27
Bar, Yugo., 2,163 ....D4 22
Bar, lake, Sask., Can B2 70
Bara, Sud., 4,885 ....C3 47
Barabinsk, Sov. Un., 38,900 ..B9 29
Baraboo, Sauk, Wis., 7,660 ..E4 124
Baraboo, riv., Wis E3 124
Baracaldo, Sp., 77,802 ....A4 20
Barachois Pond, prov. park, Newf., Can D2 75
Baracoa, Cuba, 11,459 ....E6 64
Barada, Richardson, Nebr., 58 ....D10 103
Baradères, Hai F7 64
Baradero, Arg., 10,194 ....f7 54
Baraga, Baraga, Mich., 991 ..B2 98
Baraga, co., Mich., 7,151 .....B2 98
Barahona, Dom. Rep., 20,398 ....F8 64
Barajas de Madrid, Sp., 2,184 (pop. incl. in Madrid) p17 20
Barak Khel, Afg., 5,000 ....E13 41
Barakot, India, 5,000 ....G10 40
Baramula, India, 19,854 ......B5 39
Baran, India, 22,764 ....E6 40
Baranagar, India, 107,837 .*F12 40
Baranof, Alsk., 13 ....m22 79
Baranof, isl., Alsk m22 79
Baranov, cape, Sov. Un C34 4
Baranovichi, Sov. Un., 64,000 ....E5 27
Baranya, co., Hung., 285,316 ....*B4 22
Barataria, Jefferson, La., 900 ....C7, E5 95
Barataria, bay, La E6 95
Barataria, bayou, La C7 95
Baraya, Col., 1,736 ....C2 60
Barbacena, Braz., 41,931 ....C4, g6 56
Barbacoas, Col., 3,349 ....C2 60
Barbado, riv., Braz C3 55
Barbados, Br. dep., N.A., 242,000 ....p17 64
Barbalha, Braz., 6,967 ....C3 57
Barbastro, Sp., 10,227 ....A6 20
Barbate, Sp., 10,720 ....D3 20
Barbeau, Chippewa, Mich., 20 ....B6 98
Barbee, lake, Ind B6 91
Barber, Ada, Idaho, 15 ......F2 89
Barber, Golden Valley, Mont., 10 ....D7 102
Barber, Cherokee, Okla B7 112
Barber, co., Kans., 8,713 .....E5 93
Barberton, Summit, Ohio, 33,805 ....A6 111
Barberton, S. Afr.,11,016 ....C5 49
Barberville, Volusia, Fla., 250 ....C5 86
Barbezieux, Fr., 3,058 ....E4 14
Barbour, co., Ala., 24,700 ...D2 78
Barbour, co., W. Va., 15,474 .B4 123
Barboursville, Orange, Va., 150 ....C4 121
Barboursville, Cabell, W. Va., 2,331 ....C2 123
Barbourville, Knox, Ky., 3,211 ....D6 94
Barbuda, isl., Barb n16 64
Barby, Ger., 7,788 ....B6 17
Barca de Alva, Port B2 20
Barcaldine, Austl., 1,705 .....A5 51
Barcarena, Port., 2,552 ....F9 20
Barcarrota, Sp., 7,898 ....C2 20
Barce, see Al Marj, Libya
Barcellona [Pozzo di Gotto], It., 20,500 (32,138*) E5 21
Barcelona, Sp., 1,557,863 (*2,020,000) B7 20
Barcelona, Ven., 40,773 .....A5 60
Barcelona, prov., Sp., 2,877,966 ....*B7 20
Barceloneta, P.R., 762 ....B4 65
Barceloneta, mun., P.R., 19,334 ....B4 65
Barcelonnette, Fr., 2,432 .....E7 14
Barcelos, Braz., 1,094 ....D5 60
Barcelos, Port., 7,875 ....B1 20
Barclay, Osage, Kans., 50 ...D8 93
Barclay, Queen Annes, Md., 142 ....B6 85
Barco, Currituck, N.C., 250 .A8 109
Barcoo, riv., Austl B4 51
Bard, Quay, N. Mex., 10 .....B6 107
Bardejov, Czech., 6,572 ......D6 26
Bardera, Som., 1,500 (4,900*) E5 47
Bardi, It., 8,159 ....E5 21
Bardiyah, Libya C5 43
Bardley, Ripley, Mo., 50 ......E6 101
Bardolph, McDonough, Ill., 266 ....C3 90
Bardonecchia, It., 2,273 ......D1 20
Bardsey, isl., Wales B3 12
Bardstown, Nelson, Ky., 4,798 ....C4 94
Bardstown Junction, Bullitt, Ky., 50 ....C4 94
Bardswell Group, is., B.C., Can .C3 68
Bardwell, Carlisle, Ky., 1,067 .A2 94
Bare Hill, pond, Mass g9 97
Bareilly, India, 254,409 (*272,828) C7 40
Barelas, Bernalillo, N. Mex., 700 ....*B3 107
Barenburg, Ger., 990 ....F2 24
Barentin, Fr., 7,962 ....C4 14
Barents, isl., Nor B13 4
Barents, sea, Sov. Un B6 28
Barentu, Eth B4 47
Baresville, York, Pa., 1,700 .*G8 114
Barfleur, pt., Fr C3 14
Bargal, Som., 2,200 ....C7 47
Bargarh, India, 15,375 ....G9 40
Barge, canal, N.Y B2 108
Bargersville, Johnson, Ind., 586 ....E5 91
Barguzin, Sov. Un., 5,600 .D13 28
Bar Harbor, Hancock, Maine, 2,444 (3,807*) D4 96
Bari, It., 323,100 ....D6 21
Baria, Viet., 5,000 ....G7 38
Barika, Alg., 2,945 (71,235*) .B6 44
Barinas, P.R C3 65
Barinas, Ven., 25,707 ....B3 60
Barinas, state, Ven., 139,271 .B3 60
Baring, Washington, Maine, 130 ....C5 96
Baring, Knox, Mo., 213 ......A5 101
Baripada, India, 20,301 ......G11 40
Bariri, Braz., 8,403 ....C3, m7 56
Bāris, Eg., U.A.R E6 43
Barisal, Pak., 69,936 ....F13 40
Barisan, mts., Indon F2 35
Barium Springs, Iredell, N.C., 300 ....B3 109
Bark, lake, Ont., Can B7 72
Bark, pt., Wis B2 124
Barker, Niagara, N.Y., 528 ...B2 108
Barkers Point, N.B., Can., 1,451 ....*D3 74
Barkerville, B.C., Can., 62 ...C7 68
Barkeryd, Swe A8 24
Barkeyville, Venango, Pa., 200 ....D2 114
Barkhamsted (Town of), Litchfield, Conn., (1,370*) *B4 84
Barkhamsted, res., Conn B5 84
Barking. Eng., 72,282 ....k13 10
Barkley, sound, B.C., Can E5 68
Barkly East, S. Afr., 3,648 ...D4 49
Barkmere, Que., Can., 56 ...D3 73
Barkol (Chensi), China, 10,000 ....C3 34
Bark River, Delta, Mich., 200 ....C3 98
Barksdale, Edwards, Tex., 150 ....E2 118
Barlad, Rom., 32,043 ....B8 22
Barladul, riv., Rom B8 22
Bar-le-Duc, Fr., 18,346 ......C6 14
Barlee, lake, Austl E2 50
Barletta, It., 69,300 ....D6 21
Barling, Sebastian, Ark., 1,518 ....B1 81
Barlow, Ballard, Ky., 731 ....A2 94
Barlow, Foster, N. Dak., 50 ..B6 110
Barlow Bend, Clarke, Ala., 200 ....D2 78
Barmer, India, 27,600 ....E3 40
Bar Mills, York, Maine, 400 .E2 96
Barmouth, Wales, 2,348 ......B3 12
Barna, Ire., 143 ....D2 11
Barnaby River, N.B., Can., 204 ....C4 74
Barnard, Lincoln, Kans., 205 .C5 93
Barnard, Nodaway, Mo., 237 .A3 101
Barnard, Brown, S. Dak., 82 .B7 116
Barnard, Windsor, Vt., 150 (435*) D3 120
Barnard Castle, Eng., 4,969 ..F6 13
Barnardsville, Buncombe, N.C., 199 ....D3 109
Barnasht, Eg., U.A.R E3 32
Barnaul, Sov. Un., 357,000 .C10 29
Barne, inlet, Ant g40 5
Barnegat, Ocean, N.J., 900 ..D4 106
Barnegat, bay, N.J D4 106
Barnegat, inlet, N.J D4 106
Barnegat Light, Ocean, N.J., 287 ....D4 106
Barnegat Lighthouse, state park, N.J D4 106
Barnegat Pines, Ocean, N.J., 300 ....D4 106
Barnes, Washington, Kans., 247 ....C7 93
Barnes, Leake, Miss., 50 .....C4 100
Barnes, Douglas, Oreg., 5,076 ....*D3 113
Barnes, Warren, Pa., 220 .....C3 114
Barnes, co., N. Dak., 16,719 ..B7 110
Barnes, sound, Fla G6 86
Barnesboro, Cambria, Pa., 3,035 ....E4 114
Barnes City, Mahaska and Poweshiek, Iowa, 273 ......C5 92
Barnes Corners, Lewis, N.Y., 100 ....B5 108
Barnesdale, Ont., Can B5 72
Barnesmore, Ire C4 11
Barneston, Gage, Nebr., 177 .D9 103
Barnesville, Lamar, Ga., 4,919 ....C2 87
Barnesville, Montgomery, Md., 145 ....B3 85
Barnesville, Clay, Minn., 1,632 ....D2 99
Barnesville, Belmont, Ohio, 4,425 ....C6 111
Barnet, Caledonia, Vt., 225 (1,445*) C4 120
Barnett, Morgan, Mo., 200 ...C5 101
Barnette, Clarke, Miss., 40 . D5 100
Barneveld, Neth., 7,400 ....B5 15
Barneveld, Iowa, Wis., 420 ..E4 124
Barneville-sur-Mer, Fr., 656 ..C3 14
Barney, Brooks, Ga., 165 .....E3 87
Barney, Richland, N. Dak., 115 ....C8 110
Barnhart, Jefferson, Mo., 400 ....B8, C7 101
Barnhart, Irion, Tex., 250 ....D5 118
Barnsboro, Gloucester, N.J., 900 ....D2 106
Barnsdall, Osage, Okla., 1,663 ....A5 112
Barnsley, Eng., 75,000 (*193,000) A6 12
Barnstable, Barnstable, Mass., 900 (13,465*) C7 97
Barnstable, co., Mass., 70,286 ....C7 97
Barnstaple, Eng., 15,907 .....C3 12
Barnstaple, bay, Eng C3 12
Barnstead, Belknap, N.H., 200 (850*) D4 105
Barnston, Que., Can., 123 ...D6 73
Barnum, Webster, Iowa 154 B3 92
Barnum, Carlton, Minn., 417 .D6 99
Barnwell, Alta., Can., 190 ...E4 69
Barnwell, Barnwell, S.C., 4,568 ....E3 115
Barnwell, co., S.C., 17,659 ...E5 115
Baro, Nig., 217 ....E6 45
Baro, riv., Eth D3 47
Baroda, India, 295,144 (*298,398) F4 40
Baron, Adair, Okla., 100 .....B7 112
Barons, Alta., Can., 345 ......E4 69
Barotseland Protectorate, prov., Zambia E3 48
Barquisimeto, Ven., 196,557 ..A4 60
Barr, Fr., 4,207 ....C7 14
Barr, Tate, Miss., 275 ....A4 100
Barr, Lauderdale, Tenn B2 117
Barra, Braz., 7,237 ....D2 57
Barra, Braz., 1,539 ....h5 57
Barra, isl., Scot D1 13
Barraba, Austl., 1,469 ....E8 51
Barrack, pt., Ire F2 11
Barrackpore, India, 63,778 ..F12 40
Barrackville, Marion, W. Va., 950 ....A7, B4 123
Barra do Corda, Braz., 3,723 C1 57
Barra do Piraí, Braz., 29,398 ....C4, h6 56
Barra Mansa, Braz., 47,398 ....C4, h5 56
Barranca, Rio Arriba, N. Mex., 50 ....*A3 107
Barranca, Peru, 192 ....B2 58
Barrancabermeja, Col., 25,046 ....B3 60
Barrancas, Ven., 4,034 ....B5 60
Barranquilla, Col., 431,000 ...A3 60
Barranquitas, P.R., 4,684 ....C5 65
Barranquitas, mun., P.R., 18,978 ....C5 65
Barraza, Chile A2 54
Barré, Que., Can C7 73
Barre, Worcester, Mass., 1,100 (3,479*) B3 97
Barre, Washington, Vt., 10,387 ....C4 120
Barre, lake, La E5 95
Barre des Ecrins, mtn., Fr E7 14
Barre Falls, res., Mass B4 97
Barreiras, Braz., 7,175 ....D1 57
Barreirinhas, Braz., 2,184 ....B2 57
Barreiro, Braz., 870 ....h5 56
Barreiro, Port, 22,190 ....C1, f9 20
Barreiros, Braz., 10,402 ..C3, k6 57
Barrellville, Allegany, Md., 300 ....D2 85
Barren, co., Ky., 28,303 .....D4 94
Barren, isl., Alsk h15 79
Barren, is., Malag g8 49
Barren, isl., Md D5 85
Barren, riv., Ky D3 94
Barren Plain, Robertson, Tenn., 100 ....A5 117
Barrens, plat., Tenn B6 117
Barre Plains, Worcester, Mass., 500 ....B3 97
Barretos, Braz., 39,950 ....F1 57
Barrett, Grant, Minn., 345 ...E3 99
Barrett, Grafton, N.H B3 105
Barrett, Harris, Tex., 1,200 .*F5 118
Barrett, Boone, W. Va., 800 ....D3, D6 123
Barretts, Lowndes, Ga., 100 ..F3 87
Barretts, hill, Mass g9 97
Barrhead, Alta., Can., 2,286 ..B3 69
Barrhead, Scot., 14,442 ....E4 13
Barrhill, Scot E4 13
Barrie, Ont., Can., 21,169 ...C5 72
Barrie, isl., Ont., Can B2 72
Barrier, bay, Ant C21 5
Barrier, lake, Sask., Can E4 70
Barrière, B.C., Can., 472 ....D7 68
Barrigada, Guam, 1,729 52
Barrigada, hill, Guam 52
Barrington, N.S., Can., 261 ..F4 74
Barrington, Lake and Cook, Ill., 5,434 ....A5, E2 90
Barrington, Strafford, N.H., 70 (1,036*) D4 105
Barrington, Camden, N.J., 7,943 ....*D2 106
Barrington, Bristol, R.I., 11,200 (13,826*) C11 84
Barrington, lake, Man., Can A1 71
Barrington, mtn., Austl F8 51
Barrington Hills, Cook and Lake, Ill., 1,726 ....*A5 90
Barrington Passage, N.S., Can., 381 ....F4 74
Barrio Azul, Cuba k11 64
Barr Lake, Adams, Colo B6 83
Barron, Barron, Wis., 2,338 . C2 124
Barron, co., Wis., 34,270 ....C2 124
Barronett, Barron, Wis., 100 .C2 124
Barrow, Alsk., 1,314 ....A8 79
Barrow, Arg B4 54
Barrow, co., Ga., 14,485 .....B3 87
Barrow, isl., Austl D2 50
Barrow, pt., Alsk A8 79
Barrow, riv., Ire E5 11
Barrow, strait, N.W. Ter., Can B14 66
Barrow Creek, Austl., 40 ....D5 50
Barrow-in-Furness, Eng., 65,300 ....C5 10
Barrows, Man., Can., 123 ...C1 71
Barrowsville, Bristol, Mass., 500 ....C5 97
Barruelo de Santullán, Sp., 7,770 ....A3 20
Barry, Pike, Ill., 1,422 ....D2 90
Barry, Wales, 42,200 ....C4 12
Barry, co., Mich., 31,738 .....F5 97
Barry, co., Mo., 18,921 ....E4 101
Barrys Bay, Ont., Can., 1,439 .B7 72
Barryton, Mecosta, Mich., 418 ....E5 98
Barryville, Sullivan, N.Y., 500 ....D6 108
Barsi, India, 50,389 ....H5 40
Barsinghausen, Ger., 11,500 ..A4 17
Barsø, isl., Den C3 24
Barstow, San Bernardino, Calif., 11,644 ....E5 82
Barstow, Ward, Tex., 707 ....D1, F2 118
Bar-sur-Aube, Fr., 4,801 .....C6 14
Bar [-sur-Seine], Fr., 2,559 ...C6 14
Bartelso, Clinton, Ill., 370 ...E4 90
Barth, Escambia, Fla., 200 ..G2 86
Barth, Ger., 12,200 ....A6 16
Bartholomew, co., Ind., 48,198 ....F6 91
Bartholomew, bayou, Ark C4 81
Bartibog Bridge, N.B., Can., 214 ....B4 74
Bartibog Station, N.B., Can ..B4 74
Bartica, Br. Gu., 2,352 ....A3 59
Bartin, Tur., 11,700 ....B9 31
Bartlesville, Washington, Okla., 27,893 ....A6 112
Bartlett, Cook, Ill., 1,540 ....E2 90
Bartlett, Labette, Kans., 137 .E8 93
Bartlett, Wheeler, Nebr., 125 .C7 103
Bartlett, Carroll, N.H., 500 (1,013*) D4 105
Bartlett, Ramsey, N. Dak., 39 ....A7 110
Bartlett, Washington, Ohio, 240 ....C6 111
Bartlett, Wallowa, Oreg B9 113
Bartlett, Shelby, Tenn., 508 ....B2, E8 117
Bartlett, Williamson and Bell, Tex., 1,540 ....D4 118
Bartlett, res., Ariz D4, F3 80
Bartletts Ferry, dam, Ala., Ga C4 72, D1 84
Bartlett's Harbour, Newf., Can., 185 ....C3 75
Bartley, Red Willow, Nebr., 309 ....D5 103
Bartolomeu Dias, Moz B6 49
Barton, Colbert, Ala., 300 ...A2 78
Barton, Phillips, Ark., 250 ...C5 81
Barton, Ascension, La., 200 .B5 95
Barton, Allegany, Md., 731 ..B2 85
Barton, Pierce, N. Dak., 80 ..A5 110
Barton, Belmont, Ohio, 975 .B7 111
Barton, Orleans, Vt., 1,169 (3,066*) B4 120
Barton, Washington, Wis., 1,569 ....E5 124
Barton, co., Kans., 32,368 ...D5 93
Barton, co., Mo., 11,113 .....D3 101
Barton, riv., Vt B4 120
Barton-on-Humber, Eng., 6,584 ....A7 12
Bartonsville, Windham, Vt., 100 ....E3 120
Bartonville, Peoria, Ill., 7,253 ....C4 90
Bartonwoods, Dekalb, Ga., 3,000 ....*C2 87
Bartoszyce, Pol., 3,449 ....A6 26
Bartow, Polk, Fla., 12,849 ....E5 86
Bartow, Jefferson, Ga., 366 ..D4 87
Bartow, co., Ga., 28,267 ......B2 87
Baruth, Ger., 2,232 ....A8 17
Barvas, Scot B2 13
Barvenkovo, Sov. Un., 10,000 ....G11 27
Barwani, India, 17,446 ....F5 40
Barwice, Pol., 1,819 ....F8 24
Barwick, Brooks and Thomas, Ga., 400 ....F3 87
Barwick, Breathitt, Ky., 300 .C6 94
Barwon, riv., Austl D7 51
Barybino, Sov. Un n17 27
Barycz, riv., Pol C4 26
Bārz Shovār, Iran F5 41
Basāki, Iran, 10,000 ....F5 41
Basalt, Eagle, Colo., 213 .....B3 83
Basalt, Bingham, Idaho, 275 .F6 89
Basankusu, Con. L., 1,784 ...A2 48
Basantpur, India, 5,000 .....D11 40
Basargechar, Sov. Un B15 31
Basbulak, Sov. Un E6 29
Basco, Hancock, Ill., 199 ....C2 90
Basco, Phil., 804 ....A6 35
Bascom, Jackson, Fla., 250 ..B1 86
Bascom, Seneca, Ohio, 450 ..A4 111
Basehor, Leavenworth, Kans., 315 ....B8 93
Basekpio, Con. L A3 48
Basel, Switz., 211,500 (*505,000) A4 19
Basel, canton, Switz., 373,870 ....B4 19
Basel-Land, sub canton, Switz., 148,282 ....*B4 19
Basel-Stadt, sub canton, Switz., 225,588 ....*A4 19
Bashagird, range, Iran H9 41
Bashaw, Alta., Can., 614 .....C4 69
Bashi, Clarke, Ala., 200 ......D2 78
Basiad, bay, Phil o14 35
Basic, Clarke, Miss., 70 ......C5 100
Basil, Fairfield, Ohio (part of Baltimore) C5 111
Basilan, isl., Phil D6 35
Basildon, see Billericay, Eng.
Basile, Evangeline, La., 1,932 ....D3 95
Basilicata, pol. dist., It., 644,297 ....*D5 21
Basilicata, reg., It D5 21
Basilio, Braz., 305 ....E2 56
Basim, India G6 40
Basin, Jefferson, Mont., 300 ..D4 102
Basin, Big Horn, Wyo., 1,319 ....A4 125
Basin, lake, Sask., Can E3 70
Basinger, Okeechobee, Fla., 150 ....E5 86
Basingstoke, Eng., 25,940 ....C6 12
Basin Harbor, Addison, Vt., 20 ....C2 120
Basin Mills, Penobscot, Maine (part of Orono) D4 96
Baska, Yugo., 1,016 ....C2 22
Baskahegan, lake, Maine C5 96
Baskatong, res., Que., Can G17 67
Baskett, Henderson, Ky., 300 ....C2 94
Baskin, Pinellas, Fla., 500 ....E1 86
Baskin, Franklin, La., 238 ...C2 95
Basking Ridge, Somerset, N.J., 2,600 ....B3 106
Basoko, Con. L A3 48
Basongo, Con. L B3 48
Basque Provinces, reg., Sp., 1,371,654 ....A4 20
Basra, Iraq, 164,623 ....F3 41
Bas-Rhin, dept., Fr., 770,150 ....F7 15, A3 18
Bass, isl., Ohio A4 111
Bass, lake, Ind B4 91
Bass, strait, Austl I5 51
Bassac, Laos, 5,000 ....E6 38
Bassano, Alta., Can., 815 ....D4 69
Bassano del Grappa, It., 23,800 (30,497*) B3 21
Bassein, Bur., 77,905 ....E9 39
Basses-Alpes, dept., Fr., 91,843 ....E2 18
Basses-Pyrénées, dept., Fr., 466,038 ....*F3 14
Basse-Terre, Guad., 13,978 ..o16 64
Basseterre, St. Kitts-Nevis-Anguilla, 15,579 ....n15 64
Bassett, Los Angeles, Calif., 2,000 ....*F3 82
Bassett, Chickasaw, Iowa, 130 ....A5 92
Bassett, Allen, Kans., 67 .....E8 93
Bassett, Rock, Nebr., 1,023 ..B6 103
Bassett, Henry, Va., 3,148 ...E3 121
Bassett, creek, Ala D2 78
Bassfield, Jefferson Davis, Miss., 295 ....D4 100
Bassikounou, Maur C3 45
Bass River, N.S., Can., 447 ..D6 74
Bassum, Ger., 6,550 ....F2 24
Basswood, Man., Can., 121 ..D1 71
Basswood, lake, Ont., Can B7 99
Båstad, Swe., 2,200 ....*B6 24
Bastak, Iran, 7,500 ....H7 41
Bastelica, Fr., 2,188 ....D2 21
Basti, India, 38,403 ....D9 40
Bastia, Fr., 50,117 ....C2 21
Bastian, Bland, Va., 600 .....D1 121
Bastogne, Bel., 5,927 ....D5 15
Bastrop, Morehouse, La., 15,193 ....B4 95
Bastrop, Bastrop, Tex., 3,001 .D4 118
Bastrop, co., Tex., 16,925 ....D4 118
Bastuträsk, Swe., 820 ....E9 25
Basutoland, Br. dep., Afr., 740,000 ....C4 49, I8 42
Basyūn, Eg., U.A.R., 1,000 ..D2 32
Bat, cave, Mo D5 101
Bata, Equat. Gui., 4,000 (27,024*) E1 46
Bataan, Phil., 2,186 ....p13 35
Bataan, prov., Phil., 145,900 ....*C6 35
Bataan, pen., Phil o13 35
Batabanó, Cuba, 3,177 ....D2 64
Batabanó, gulf, Cuba D2 64
Batac, Phil., 6,218 ....*B6 35
Batala, India, 51,300 ....B5 40
Batam, isl., Indon L5 38
Batamay, Sov. Un C2 4
Batan, is., Phil A6 35
Batanes, prov., Phil., 10,300 ....*A6 35
Batangafo, Cen. Afr. Rep D3 46
Batangas, Phil., 15,000 (82,627*) C6, p13 35
Batangas, prov., Phil., 682,900 ....*C6 35
Bataques, Mex., 21 ....F6 82
Bataszek, Hung., 6,235 ....B4 22
Batatais, Braz., 15,266 ....F1 57
Batavia, Arg A3 54
Batavia, Boone, Ark., 40 .....A2 75
Batavia, Kane, Ill., 7,496 ....B5, F1 90
Batavia, see Djakarta, Indon.
Batavia, Jefferson, Iowa, 533 .D5 92
Batavia, Genesee, N.Y., 18,210 ....C2 108
Batavia, Clermont, Ohio, 1,729 ....C3 111
Bataysk, Sov. Un., 72,000 ..H12 27
Batchelor, bay, N.C B7 109
Batchtown, Calhoun, Ill., 248 ....D3 90
Bateman, Sask., Can., 106 ...G2 70
Bates, Scott, Ark., 106 ....C1 81
Bates, Grant, Oreg., 200 .....C8 113
Bates, co., Mo., 15,905 ......C3 101
Batesburg, Lexington and Saluda, S.C., 3,806 ....D4 115
Bates City, Lafayette, Mo., 110 ....B3 101
Batesland, Shannon, S. Dak., 95 ....D3 116
Batesville, Barbour, Ala., 75 ..C4 78
Batesville, Independence, Ark., 6,207 ....B4 81
Batesville, Ripley, Ind., 3,349 ....F7 91
Batesville, Panola, Miss., 3,284 ....A4 100
Batesville, Noble, Ohio, 160 ..C6 111
Batesville, Zavala, Tex., 500 .E3 118
Bath, N.B., Can., 767 ....C2 74
Bath, Ont., Can., 693 ....C8 72
Bath, Eng., 82,600 ....C5 12
Bath, Mason, Ill., 398 ....C3 90
Bath, Franklin, Ind., 100 ....E8 91
Bath, Sagadahoc, Maine, 10,717 ....E3, E6 96
Bath, Clinton, Mich., 500 ....F6 98
Bath, Grafton, N.H., 160 (604*) B3 105
Bath, Steuben, N.Y., 6,166 ..C3 108
Bath, Beaufort, N.C., 346 ....B7 109
Bath, Northampton, Pa., 1,736 ....E11 114
Bath, Aiken, S.C., 1,419 .....D4 115
Bath, Brown, S. Dak., 80 ....B7 116
Bath, co., Ky., 9,114 ....B6 94
Bath, co., Va., 5,335 ....C3 121
Batha de Lairi, riv., Chad C3 46
Bathgate, Pembina, N. Dak., 175 ....A8 110
Bathgate, Scot., 12,686 ......E8 13
Bathsheba, Barb., 850 ....p17 64
Bath Springs, Decatur, Tenn., 50 ....B3 117
Bathurst, Austl., 16,939 .....F7 51
Bathurst, N.B., Can., 5,494 ..B4 74
Bathurst, Gam., 27,800 (*40,000) D1 45
Bathurst, cape, N.W. Ter., Can B7 66
Bathurst, inlet, N.W. Ter., Can C11 66
Bathurst, isl., Austl B4 50
Bathurst, isl., N.W. Ter., Can m31 67
Bathurst Inlet, N.W. Ter., Can C11 66
Batie, Upper Volta E4 45
Batiscan, Que., Can., 231 ....C5 73
Batiscan, riv., Que., Can B5 73
Batkanu, S.L E2 45
Batna, Alg., 14,732 (26,413*) .B6 44
Batoche, Sask., Can E2 70
Baton Rouge, La., East Baton Rouge, La., 152,419 (*248,700) B5, D4 95
Batouri, Cam E2 46
Batovi, riv., Braz E4 59
Batroun, Leb., 5,000 ....E10 31
Batson, Hardin, Tex., 650 ...D5 118
Batsto, Burlington, N.J., 50 ..D3 106
Batsto, riv., N.J D3 106
Battambang, Camb., 38,800 ..F5 38
Batten Kill, riv., Vt E2 120
Battery Park, Isle of Wight, Va., 240 ....B6 121
Batticaloa, Cey., 17,662 ......G7 39
Battiest, McCurtain, Okla., 50 ....C7 112
Battir, Isr., 200 ....k11 32
Battle, creek, Sask., Can H1 70
Battle, creek, Mont B7 102
Battle, mtn., Wyo D5 125
Battle, riv., Alta., Sask., Can ...C5 69
Battle, riv., Minn C4 99
Battleboro, Nash and Edgecombe, N.C., 364 ....A6 109
Battle Creek, Sask., Can H1 70
Battle Creek, Routt, Colo A3 83
Battle Creek, Ida., Iowa, 786 ....B2 92
Battle Creek, Calhoun, Mich., 44,169 (*107,300) F5 98
Battle Creek, Madison, Nebr., 587 ....C8 103
Battleford, Sask., Can., 1,627 ....E1 70
Battle Ground, Tippecanoe, Ind., 804 ....C4 91
Battle Ground, Clark, Wash., 888 ....D3 122
Battle Harbour, Newf., Can., 87 ....B4, h11 75
Battle Lake, Otter Tail, Minn., 733 ....D3 99
Battlement, mesa, Colo B2 83
Battle Mountain, Lander, Nev., 950 ....C5 104
Battles, Wayne, Miss., 100 ...D5 100
Battleview, Burke, N. Dak., 55 ....A3 110
Battonya, Hung., 9,216 ....B5 22
Battrum, Sask., Can G1 70
Batu, is., Indon F1 35
Batu, mtn., Eth D4 47
Batuc, Mex., 1,267 ....B2 63
Batumi, Sov. Un., 91,000 ...B13 31
Batu Pahat, Mala., 39,294 ...L5 38
Baturadja, Indon., 2,955 .....F2 35
Baturino, Sov. Un B11 29
Baturité, Braz., 7,198 ....B3 57
Bat Yam, Isr., 31,338 ....g9 32
Bauan, Phil., 2,975 ....p13 35
Bauang, Phil., 3,188 .....B6, n13 35
Baubau, Indon., 2,493 ....G6 35
Bauchi, Nig., 13,440 ....D6 45
Baudette, Lake of the Woods, Minn., 1,597 ....B4 99
Baudouinville, Con. L C4 48
Bauer, rock, Pa B1 106
Baugé, Fr., 3,363 ....D4 14
Bauld, cape. Newf., Can C4 75
Bauma, Switz., 3,214 ....B6 19
Baume-les-Dames, Fr., 4,038 .B2 18
Baunei, It., 4,033 ....D2 21
Baures, Bol., 592 ....B3 55
Bauru, Braz., 85,237 ....C3 56
Bautzen, Ger., 42,300 ....B9 17
Bauxite, Saline, Ark., 950 ....C3, E5 81
Bavaria, Saline, Kans., 76 ...D6 93
Bavaria, reg., Ger D5 16
Bavarian Alps, mts., Aus., Ger .B7 18
Bavay, Fr., 2,273 ....D3 15
Båven, lake, Swe t34 25
Bavispe, Mex., 923 ....A3 63
Bawcomville, Ouachita, La., 1,500 ....*B3 95
Bawean, isl., Indon G4 35
Bawku, Ghana D4 45
Bawlf, Alta., Can., 203 ......C4 69
Baxley, Appling, Ga., 4,268 ..E4 87
Baxter, Drew, Ark D4 81
Baxter, Jasper, Iowa, 681 ....C4 92
Baxter, Crow Wing, Minn., 1,037 ....D4 99
Baxter, Putnam, Tenn., 853 ..C8 117
Baxter, Marion, W. Va., 600 ....A7, B4 123
Baxter, co., Ark., 9,943 ......A3 81
Baxter Estates, Nassau, N.Y., 932 ....*D2 108
Baxter Springs, Cherokee, Kans., 4,498 ....E9 93
Baxterville, Rio Grande, Colo., 50 ....D4 83
Baxterville, Lamar, Miss., 175 ....D4 100

Bay, Craighead, Ark., 627 ... B5 81
Bay, Gasconade, Mo., 54 ... C6 101
Bay, co., Fla., 67,131 ... G3 86
Bay, co., Mich., 107,042 ... E6 98
Bay, pt., S.C ... G7 115
Bay (Laguna de), lake, Phil ... o13 35
Baya Dzur-Gunen, Mong., 5,000 ... B5 34
Bay al Kabir, riv., Libya ... C2 43
Bayambang, Phil., 3,945 ... o13 35
Bayamo, Cuba., 26,000 ... E5 64
Bayamón, P.R., 15,109 ... B6 65
Bayamón, mun., P.R., 72,221 ... B6 65
Bayamón, riv., P.R ... B6 65
Bayan-Aul, Sov. Un., 2,600 ... C9 29
Bayaney, P.R ... B3 65
Bayanga, Cen. Afr. Rep ... E3 43
Bayanovka, Sov. Un ... A5 29
Bayard, Duval, Fla., 400 ... B5, C6 86
Bayard, Guthrie, Iowa, 597 ... C3 92
Bayard, Morrill, Nebr., 1,519 ... C2 103
Bayard, Grant, N. Mex., 2,327 ... E1 107
Bayard, Grant, W. Va., 484 ... B5 123
Baybay, Phil., 9,500 (51,400▲) ... *C6 35
Bayble, Scot ... B2 13
Bayboro, Pamlico, N.C., 545 ... B7 109
Bayboro, Horry, S.C., 25 ... D9 115
Bay Bulls, Newf., Can., 697 ... E5 75
Bayburt, Tur., 12,000 ... B13 31
Bay Center, Pacific, Wash., 600 ... C2 122
Bay City, Bay, Mich., 53,604 ... E7 98
Bay City, Tillamook, Oreg., 996 ... B3 113
Bay City, Matagorda, Tex., 11,656 ... E5, G4 118
Bay City, Grays Harbor, Wash ... C1 122
Bay City, Pierce, Wis., 327 ... D1 124
Baydarata, bay, Sov. Un ... C8 4
Bay de Verde, Newf., Can., 884 ... D5 75
Bayern, state, Ger., 9,513,900 ... D6 17, A7 18
Bayeux, Fr., 9,678 ... C3 14
Bayfield, Ont., Can., 395 ... D3 72
Bayfield, La Plata, Colo., 322 ... D3 83
Bayfield, Bayfield, Wis., 969 ... B3 124
Bayfield, co., Wis., 11,910 ... B2 124
Bay Harbour Islands, Dade, Fla., 3,249 ... *F3 86
Bay Head, Ocean, N.J., 824 ... C4 106
Bayindir, Tur., 11,300 ... C6 23
Baykal, lake, Sov. Un ... D13 28
Baykal, mts., Sov. Un ... D13 28
Baykonur, Sov. Un ... D7 29
Bay l'Argent, Newf., Can., 431 ... E4 75
Baylis, Pike, Ill., 284 ... D3 90
Baylor, co., Tex., 5,893 ... C3 118
Baymak, Sov. Un ... C5 29
Bay Mills, Indian res., Mich ... B6 98
Bay Minette, Baldwin, Ala., 5,197 ... E2 78
Bayombong, Phil., 6,929 ... n13 35
Bayonne, Fr., 36,941 (*89,000) ... F3 14
Bayonne, Hudson, N.J., 74,215 ... B4, k8 106
Bayou Barbary, Livingston, La ... B6 95
Bayou Cane, Terrebonne, La., 3,173 ... *E5 95
Bayou Current, St. Landry, La. 75 ... D4 95
Bayou George, Bay, Fla., 100 ... G3 86
Bayou Goula, Iberville, La., 750 ... B4, D4 95
Bayou LaBatre, Mobile, Ala., 2,572 ... E1 78
Bayou Meto, Arkansas, Ark., 20 ... C4 81
Bayóvar, Peru ... C1 58
Bay Park, Nassau, N.Y., 2,500 ... *G2 84
Bayport, N.S., Can., 141 ... E5 74
Bay Port, Huron, Mich., 400 ... E7 98
Bayport, Washington, Minn., 3,205 ... E6, E8 99
Bayport, Suffolk, N.Y., 5,800 ... n15 108
Bayram-Ali, Sov. Un., 25,000 ... C11 41
Bayramic, Tur., 4,100 ... C6 23
Bayreuth, Ger., 61,600 ... D6 17
Bay Ridge, Anne Arundel, Md., 750 ... C5 85
Bayrischzell, Ger., 1,700 ... B8 18
Bay Roberts, Newf., Can., 1,328 ... E5 75
Bays, lake, Ont., Can ... B5 72
Bays, mtn., Tenn ... C10 117
Bay St. Louis, Hancock, Miss., 5,073 ... E2, E4 100
Bayshore, San Mateo, Calif., 1,500 ... *D2 82
Bayshore, Charlevoix, Mich., 160 ... C5 98
Bay Shore, Suffolk, N.Y., 32,000 ... E7, n15 108
Bayshore Gardens, Manatee, Fla., 2,297 ... *E4 86
Bayside, Hancock, Maine, 70 ... D4 96
Bayside, Refugio, Tex., 300 ... E4 118
Bayside, Princess Anne, Va., 6,000 ... *B7 121
Bayside, Milwaukee, Wis., 3,181 ... *E6 124
Bay Springs, Jasper, Miss., 1,544 ... D4 100
Baysun, Sov. Un ... B13 41
Bayt Dajan, Jordan, 5,000 ... g12 32
Baytillū, Jordan, 1,000 ... h11 32
Bayt Jālā, Jordan, 5,000 ... C7, k11 32
Bayt Laḥm (Bethlehem), Jordan, 22,453 ... C7, k11 32
Baytown, Harris, Tex., 28,159 ... E5, F6 118
Bay Trail, Sask., Can ... E3 70
Bayview, Jefferson, Ala., 1,081 ... E4 78
Bayview, Humboldt, Calif., 1,800 ... *B1 82
Bayview, Kootenai, Idaho, 250 ... B2 89
Bay View, Emmet, Mich ... C6 98
Bay Village, Cross, Ark., 150 ... B5 81
Bay Village, Cuyahoga, Ohio, 14,489 ... B1 111
Bayville, Ocean, N.J., 1,000 ... D4 106
Bayville, Nassau, N.Y., 3,962 ... F2 84
Baza, Sp., 14,880 ... D4 20
Bazaar, Chase, Kans., 100 ... D7 93
Bazaruto, isl., Moz ... B6 49
Bazemore, Fayette, Ala., 100 ... B2 78
Bazile Mills, Knox, Nebr., 45 ... B8 103
Bazine, Ness, Kans., 429 ... D4 93
Bazman Kuh, mtn., Iran ... G10 41
Baztán, Sp., 1,534 ... A5 20
Beach, Ware, Ga., 53 ... E4 87
Beach (Dunes Park), Lake, Ill., 1,800 ... *A6 90
Beach, Golden Valley, N. Dak., 1,460 ... C1 110
Beach, Chesterfield, Va., 70 ... C7 121
Beach, pond, Conn., R.I ... C9 84
Beachburg, Ont., Can., 542 ... B8 72
Beach City, Stark, Ohio, 1,151 ... B6 111
Beach Haven, Ocean, N.J., 1,041 ... D4 106
Beach Haven, Luzerne, Pa., 500 ... D9 114
Beach Haven, inlet, N.J ... D4 106
Beach Haven Crest, Ocean, N.J., 75 ... D4 106
Beach Haven Terrace, Ocean, N.J., 300 ... D4 106
Beachlake, Wayne, Pa., 250 ... C11 114
Beachport, Austl., 293 ... G7 50
Beachville, Ont., Can., 849 ... D4 72
Beachville, St. Marys, Md., 350 ... D5 85
Beachwood, Ocean, N.J., 2,765 ... D4 106
Beachwood, Cuyahoga, Ohio, 6,089 ... *A6 111
Beachy, head, Eng ... D8 12
Beacon, Mahaska, Iowa, 718 ... C5 92
Beacon, Marquette, Mich. (part of Champion) ... B2 98
Beacon, Dutchess, N.Y., 13,922 ... D7 108
Beacon Falls, New Haven, Conn., 1,500 (2,886▲) ... D4 84
Beacon Hill, Gulf, Fla., 150 ... C1, H3 86
Beacon Hill, Cowlitz, Wash., 1,019 ... *C3 122
Beaconsfield, Que., Can., 10,064 ... q19 73
Beaconsfield, Ringgold, Iowa, 71 ... D3 92
Beadle, Sask., Can ... F1 70
Beadle, co., S. Dak., 21,682 ... C7 116
Beadling, Allegheny, Pa., 1,500 ... *F1 114
Beagle, Miami, Kans., 150 ... D9 93
Bealanana, Malag ... f9 49
Beal City, Isabella, Mich., 150 ... E6 98
Beale, cape, B.C., Can ... E5 68
Beallsville, Monroe, Ohio, 491 ... C6 111
Beals, Henderson, Ky., 100 ... C2 94
Beals, Washington, Maine, 400 (640▲) ... D5 96
Bealwood, Muscogee, Ga. (part of Columbus) ... D2 87
Beamsville, Ont., Can., 2,537 ... D5 72
Bean City, Palm Beach, Fla., 150 ... F6 86
Bean Lake, Platte, Mo., 245 ... B3 101
Bean Station, Grainger, Tenn., 100 ... C10 117
Bear, New Castle, Del., 65 ... A6 85
Bear, Adams, Idaho, 5 ... D2 89
Bear, cave, Mich ... G4 98
Bear, cave, Mo ... E5 101
Bear, creek, Ala ... A1 78
Bear, creek, Colo ... D8 83
Bear, creek, Kans ... E2 93
Bear, creek, Miss ... A5 100
Bear, creek, Oreg ... E4 113
Bear, creek, Wyo ... D8 125
Bear, inlet, N.C ... C6 109
Bear, isl., Ant ... B2 5
Bear, isl., Man., Can ... B2 71
Bear, isl., Ire ... F2 11
Bear, isl., Nor ... B13 4
Bear, isl., Wis ... A3 124
Bear, lake, Alta., Can ... B1 69
Bear, lake, B.C., Can ... A4 68
Bear, lake, Man., Can ... B4 71
Bear, lake, Idaho, Utah ... A4 119
Bear, lake, Wis ... C2 124
Bear, mtn., Ark ... C5 81
Bear, mtn., Ky ... C5 90
Bear, mtn., Maine ... D2 96
Bear, mtn., Mass ... A3 97
Bear, mtn., Oreg ... D4 113
Bear, mtn., Wyo ... D6 125
Bear, riv., Utah, Wyo ... B5 119
Bear, swamp, Mass ... h11 97
Bear Creek, Marion, Ala., 243 ... A2 78
Bearcreek, Carbon, Mont., 61 ... E7 102
Bear Creek, Dewey, S. Dak., 40 ... C4 116
Bear Creek, Outagamie, Wis., 455 ... D5 124
Bear Creek, flood control res., Pa ... D10 114
Bearden, Ouachita, Ark., 1,268 ... D3 81
Bearden, Okfuskee, Okla., 150 ... B5 112
Bearden, Knox, Tenn., 3,600 ... D9, E11 117
Beardmore, Ont., Can., 1,043 ... o18 72
Beardmore, glacier, Ant ... A30 5
Beards Fork, Fayette, W. Va., 800 ... D7 123
Beardsley, Rawlins, Kans., 50 ... C2 93
Beardsley, Big Stone, Minn., 410 ... E2 99
Beardstown, Cass, Ill., 6,294 ... C3 90
Beardstown, Perry, Tenn., 50 ... B4 117
Bearfort, mtn., N.J ... A4 106
Bear Lake, Manistee, Mich., 323 ... D4 98
Bear Lake, Warren, Pa., 260 ... C3 114
Bear Lake, co., Idaho, 7,148 ... G7 89
Bear Lodge, mts., Wyo ... A8 125
Bearmouth, Granite, Mont., 10 ... D3 102
Béarn, former prov., Fr., 275,000 ... F3 14
Bear Paw, mts., Mont ... B7 102
Bear Pond, mts., Md ... A2 85
Bear River, N.S., Can., 830 ... E4 74
Bear River, bay, Utah ... B3 119
Bear River, divide, Wyo ... D2 125
Bear River City, Box Elder, Utah, 447 ... B3 119
Bear Spring, Stewart, Tenn., 50 ... A4 117
Beartooth, pass, Wyo ... A3 125
Beartooth, range, Mont ... E7 102
Bear Town (McComb South), Pike, Miss., 1,865 ... D3 100
Beas de Segura, Sp., 9,251 ... C4 20
Beason, Logan, Ill., 250 ... C4 90
Beata, cape, Dom. Rep ... G8 64
Beaties, butte, Oreg ... E7 113
Beaton, B.C., Can., 50 ... D9 68
Beatrice, Monroe, Ala., 506 ... D2 78
Beatrice, Gage, Nebr., 12,132 ... D9 103
Beatrice, Rh ... A5 49
Beattie, Marshall, Kans., 314 ... C7 93
Beatton, riv., B.C., Can ... A7 68
Beatty, Sask., Can., 143 ... E3 70
Beatty, Carroll, Miss., 50 ... B4 100
Beatty, Nye, Nev., 450 ... G5 104
Beatty, Klamath, Oreg., 200 ... E5 113
Beatty Knob, hill, Ohio ... C6 111
Beattyville, Lee, Ky., 1,048 ... C6 94
Beatyestown, Warren, N.J., 100 ... B3 106
Beau, lake, Maine ... A3 96
Beaucaire, Fr., 8,243 ... F6 14
Beauce, co., Que., Can., 62,264 ... C7 73
Beauceville-Est, Que., Can., 1,920 ... C7 73
Beauceville Ouest, Que., Can., 1,645 ... *C7 73
Beaucourt, Fr., 4,570 ... D7 14
Beaudry, Garland, Ark ... C3 81
Beaufort, Mala., 2,000 ... D5 35
Beaufort, Franklin, Mo., 125 ... C6 101
Beaufort, Carteret, N.C., 2,922 ... C7 109
Beaufort, Beaufort, S.C., 6,298 ... G6 115
Beaufort, co., N.C., 36,014 ... B6 109
Beaufort, co., S.C., 44,187 ... G6 115
Beaufort, sea, N.A ... B7 61
Beaufort West, S. Afr., 16,323 ... D3 49
Beaugency, Fr., 3,493 ... D4 14
Beauharnois, Que., Can., 8,704 ... D4, q19 73
Beauharnois, co., Que., Can., 49,667 ... D3 73
Beaulieu, Mahnomen, Minn., 40 ... C3 99
Beauly, Scot ... C4 13
Beauly, firth, Scot ... C4 13
Beauly, riv., Scot ... C4 13
Beaumaris, Wales, 1,960 ... A3 12
Beaumaris, bay, Wales ... A4 12
Beaumont, Bel., 1,725 ... D4 15
Beaumont, Riverside, Calif., 4,432 ... F4 82
Beaumont, Newf., Can., 340 ... D4 75
Beaumont, Que., Can ... C7 73
Beaumont, Fr., 2,702 ... F4 14
Beaumont, Butler, Kans., 150 ... E7 93
Beaumont, Perry, Miss., 926 ... D5 100
Beaumont, Jefferson, Tex., 119,175 (*266,600) ... D5 118
Beaumont Place, Harris, Tex., 1,500 ... *E5 118
Beaumont [-sur-Oise], Fr., 6,787 ... E2 15
Beaune, Fr., 15,367 ... D6 14
Beauport, Que., Can., 9,192 ... n17 73
Beauport, isl., Ant ... e38 5
Beaupré, Que., Can., 2,587 ... B7 73
Beauraing, Bel., 2,383 ... D4 15
Beauregard, Copiah, Miss., 193 ... D9 100
Beauregard, par., La., 19,191 ... D2 95
Beaurepaire, Que., Can., 2,400 ... *q19 73
Beaurivage, Que., Can., 526 ... C6 73
Beauséjour, Man., Can., 1,770 ... D3 71
Beauty, Martin, Ky., 300 ... C7 88
Beauvais, Fr., 33,995 ... C5 14
Beauval, Sask., Can., 504 ... B2 70
Beauval, Fr., 2,173 ... D2 15
Beauvallon, Alta., Can., 71 ... C5 69
Beauvoir, Harrison, Miss., 50 ... E2 100
Beaver, Alsk., 101 ... B10 79
Beaver, Carroll, Ark., 24 ... A2 81
Beaver, Barton, Kans., 125 ... D5 93
Beaver, Pike, Ohio, 341 ... C5 111
Beaver, Beaver, Okla., 2,087 ... A1, D4 112
Beaver, Tillamook, Oreg., 200 ... B3 113
Beaver, Beaver, Pa., 6,160 ... E1 114
Beaver, Beaver, Utah, 1,548 ... E3 119
Beaver (Glen Hedrick), Raleigh, W. Va., 1,230 ... D3, D7 123
Beaver, Marinette, Wis., 75 ... C5 124
Beaver, co., Okla., 6,965 ... A1 106
Beaver, co., Pa., 206,948 ... E1 114
Beaver, co., Utah, 4,331 ... E2 119
Beaver, brook, N.H ... E4 105
Beaver, creek, Sask., Can ... F2 70
Beaver, creek, Iowa ... A7 92
Beaver, creek, Kans ... C2 93
Beaver, creek, Kans ... C5 93
Beaver, creek, Ky ... C7 94
Beaver, creek, Md ... A2 85
Beaver, creek, Mo ... E5 101
Beaver, creek, Mont ... B9 102
Beaver, creek, Mont ... C12 102
Beaver, creek, Nebr ... C5 103
Beaver, creek, N. Dak ... C5 110
Beaver, creek, Okla ... C3 112
Beaver, creek, Tenn ... E11 117
Beaver, creek, Wyo ... B8 125
Beaver, creek, Wyo ... C4 125
Beaver, isl., Mich ... C5 98
Beaver, lake, Alta., Can ... B5 69
Beaver, lake, Nebr ... C3 103
Beaver, lake, Wis ... E5 124
Beaver, riv., Alta., Sask., Can ... B5 69
Beaver, riv., N.Y ... B6 108
Beaver, riv., Utah ... E2 119
Beaver Bank, N.S., Can., 870 ... E6 74
Beaver Bay, Lake, Minn., 287 ... C7 99
Beaver City, Furnas, Nebr., 818 ... D6 103
Beaver Creek, B.C., Can., 601 ... E5 68
Beaver Creek, Washington, Md., 150 ... A2 85
Beaver Creek, Rock, Minn., 250 ... G2 99
Beaver Creek, mtn., Ala ... B3 78
Beaver Crossing, Seward, Nebr., 439 ... D8 103
Beaverdale, Cambria, Pa., 1,000 ... F4 114
Beaver Dam, Mohave, Ariz., 25 ... A2 80
Beaver Dam, Kosciusko, Ind., 100 ... B5 91
Beaver Dam, Ohio, Ky., 1,648 ... C3 94
Beaverdam, Allen, Ohio, 514 ... B4 111
Beaverdam, Hanover, Va., 50 ... D5 121
Beaver Dam, Dodge, Wis., 13,118 ... E5 124
Beaver Dams, Schuyler, N.Y., 300 ... C4 108
Beaverdell, B.C., Can., 332 ... E8 68
Beaver Falls, Lewis, N.Y., 640 ... B5 108
Beaver Falls, Beaver, Pa., 16,240 ... E1 114
Beaverfoot, riv., B.C., Can ... D2 69
Beaverhead, co., Mont., 7,194 ... E3 102
Beaverhead, mts., Mont ... E3 102
Beaverhead, riv., Mont ... E4 102
Beaverhill, Overton, Tenn ... C8 117
Beaverhill, lake, Alta., Can ... C4 69
Beaverhill, lake, Man., Can ... B4 71
Beaverlick, Boone, Ky., 175 ... A7 94
Beaverlodge, Alta., Can., 897 ... B1 69
Beaver Meadows, Carbon, Pa., 1,392 ... E10 114
Beaver Point, Larimer, Colo., 50 ... A5 83
Beaver Run, res., Pa ... E2 114
Beaver Springs, Snyder, Pa., 750 ... E7 114
Beavertail, pt., R.I ... D11 84
Beaverton, Lamar, Ala., 162 ... B1 78
Beaverton, Ont., Can., 1,217 ... C5 72
Beaverton, Gladwin, Mich., 926 ... E6 98
Beaverton, Washington, Oreg., 5,937 ... B2, B3 113
Beavertown, Snyder, Pa., 738 ... E7 114
Beaverville, Iroquois, Ill., 430 ... C6 90
Beawar, India, 53,931 ... D5 40
Beazley, Arg ... A3 54
Bebedouro, Braz., 18,249 ... C3 56
Bebee, Pontotoc, Okla ... C5 112
Bebra, Ger., 7,500 ... C4 17
Becancour, Que., Can., 320 ... C5 73
Becancour, riv., Que., Can ... C6 73
Beccles, Eng., 7,330 ... B9 12
Bečej, Yugo., 24,853 ... C5 22
Becerreá, Sp., 7,776 ... A2 20
Becharof, lake, Alsk ... D8 79
Bechuanaland, Br. dep., Afr., 555,000 ... B3 49, I8 42
Bechyne, Czech., 2,251 ... D9 17
Beckemeyer, Clinton, Ill., 1,056 ... E4 90
Beckenham, Eng., 77,265 ... m12 10, C7 12
Becker, Sherburne, Minn., 279 ... E5 99
Becker, Monroe, Miss., 141 ... B5 100
Becker, co., Minn., 23,959 ... D3 99
Becket, Berkshire, Mass., 200 (770▲) ... B1 97
Beckham, co., Okla., 17,782 ... B2 112
Beckley, Raleigh, W. Va., 18,642 ... D3, D7 123
Beckum, Ger., 20,600 ... B3 17
Beckville, Panola, Tex., 632 ... C5 118
Beckwith, Lincoln, Wyo ... D2 125
Beckwith, creek, La ... D2 95
Bedale, Eng., 1,115 ... F7 13
Bédarieux, Fr., 7,263 ... F5 14
Bedburg, Ger., 9,100 ... C1 17
Beddington, Washington, Maine, (14▲) ... D4 96
Bederkesa, Ger., 2,900 ... E2 24
Bedford, N.S., Can ... E6 74
Bedford, Que., Can., 2,855 ... D5 73
Bedford, Eng., 65,400 ... B7 12
Bedford, Lawrence, Ind., 13,024 ... G5 91
Bedford, Taylor, Iowa, 1,807 ... D6 92
Bedford, Trimble, Ky., 717 ... B4 94
Bedford, Middlesex, Mass., 10,969 ... B5, g10 97
Bedford, Calhoun, Mich., 150 ... F5 98
Bedford, Livingston, Mo., 15 ... B4 101
Bedford, Hillsboro, N.H., 175 (3,636▲) ... E3 105
Bedford, Westchester, N.Y., 893 ... D7 108
Bedford, Cuyahoga, Ohio, 15,223 ... A6, B2 111
Bedford, Bedford, Pa., 3,696 ... F4 114
Bedford, Tarrant, Tex., 2,706 ... *C4 118
Bedford, Bedford, Va., 5,921 ... D3 121
Bedford, Lincoln, Wyo., 75 ... C2 125
Bedford, co., Eng., 380,704 ... B7 12
Bedford, co., Pa., 42,451 ... G4 114
Bedford, co., Tenn., 23,150 ... B5 117
Bedford, co., Va., 31,028 ... D3 121
Bedford Heights, Cuyahoga, Ohio, 5,275 ... *B2 111
Bedford Hills, Westchester, N.Y., 3,000 ... m15 108
Bedias, Grimes, Tex., 500 ... D5 118
Bédja, prov., Tun., 248,525 ... *B6 44
Bedlington, Eng., 29,373 ... C6 10
Bedminster, Somerset, N.J., 800 ... B3 106
Bedourie, Austl ... B2 51
Bedrock, Montrose, Colo., 5 ... C2 83
Bedzin, Pol., 39,000 ... g10 26
Bee, Seward, Nebr., 149 ... C8 103
Bee, co., Tex., 23,755 ... E4 118
Beebe, White, Ark., 1,697 ... B4 81
Beebe, Que., Can., 1,363 ... D5 73
Beebe Plain, Orleans, Vt., 140 ... B4 120
Beebe River, Grafton, N.H., 250 ... C3 105
Bee Branch, Van Buren, Ark., 63 ... B3 81
Beech, fork, Ky ... C4 94
Beech Bluff, Madison, Tenn., 150 ... B3 117
Beechbottom, Brooke, W. Va., 506 ... A4, B2 123
Beech Creek, Muhlenberg, Ky., 788 ... C2 94
Beech Creek, Clinton, Pa., 634 ... D6 114
Beecher, Will, Ill., 1,367 ... B6 90
Beecher City, Effingham, Ill., 452 ... D5 90
Beecher Falls, Essex, Vt., 400 ... A5 120
Beechey, head, B.C., Can ... h12 68
Beech Grove, Greene, Ark., 60 ... A5 81
Beech Grove, Marion, Ind., 10,973 ... E5, H8 91
Beech Grove, McLean, Ky., 159 ... C2 94
Beechgrove, Coffee, Tenn., 150 ... B5 117
Beech Island, Aiken, S.C., 900 ... E4 115
Beechwood, N.B., Can., 125 ... C2 74
Beechwood, Norfolk, Mass., 300 ... h12 97
Beechwood Village, Jefferson, Ky., 1,903 ... *A4 94
Beechy, Sask., Can., 402 ... G2 70
Beecroft, head, Austl ... G8 51
Beedeville, Jackson, Ark., 150 ... B4 81
Beef, isl., Vir. Is ... f16 65
Beek, Neth., 6,000 ... D5 15
Beekman, Morehouse, La ... B4 95
Beeler, Ness, Kans., 100 ... D4 93
Beelitz, Ger., 5,895 ... A7 17
Beemer, Cuming, Nebr., 667 ... C9 103
Beemerville, Sussex, N.J., 100 ... A3 106
Bee Ridge, Sarasota, Fla., 2,043 ... E4, F2 86
Beersheba, Isr., 51,600 ... C6 32
Beersheba Springs, Grundy, Tenn., 577 ... D8 117
Beersville, N.B., Can., 123 ... C4 74
Beer Tuvya, Isr., 574 ... k9 32
Beeskow, Ger., 7,571 ... A9 17
Beesleys Point, Cape May, N.J., 350 ... E3 106
Beethoven, pen., Ant ... B5 5
Beeton, Ont., Can., 810 ... C5 72
Beetzendorf, Ger., 2,386 ... F5 24
Beeville, Bee, Tex., 13,811 ... E4 118
Befale, Con. L ... A3 48
Beg, lake, N. Ire ... C5 11
Bega, Austl., 3,858 ... H7 51
Beggs, Okmulgee, Okla., 1,114 ... B5 112
Begicheva, isl., Sov. Un ... B3 4
Bègles, Fr., 24,388 ... E3 14
Begovat, Sov. Un., 30,000 ... G22 9
Béhague, pt., Fr. Gu ... B4 59
Behbehān, Iran, 22,610 ... F5 41
Behm, canal, Alsk ... n24 79
Beida, Libya, 12,800 ... C4 43
Beilngries, Ger., 3,300 ... D6 17
Beilul, Eth ... C5 47
Beira, Moz., 40,000 ... A5 49
Beira, reg., Port., 2,039,800 ... B2 20
Beira Alta, prov., Port., 703,231 ... *B2 20
Beira Baixa, prov., Port., 361,191 ... *C2 20
Beira Litoral, prov., Port., 985,135 ... *B1 20
Beirne, Clark, Ark., 300 ... D2 81
Beirut (Beyrouth), Leb., 400,000 ... F10 31
Beiseker, Alta., Can., 360 ... D4 69
Beitbridge, Rh., 395 ... B5 49
Beit Guvrin, Isr ... C6 32
Beith, Scot., 6,908 ... E4 13
Beit Lid, Isr ... f10 32
Beit-Shan, Isr., 9,572 ... B7 32
Beiuş, Rom., 6,467 ... B6 22
Beja, Port., 14,058 ... C2 20
Beja, Tun., 34,645 ... B6 44
Béjar, Sp., 13,522 ... B3 20
Bejestan, Iran ... D9 41
Bejou, Mahnomen, Minn., 164 ... C3 99
Bejuco, Pan., 988 ... F8 62
Bekdash, Sov. Un ... E4 29
Békés, Hung., 17,661 (21,699▲) ... B5 22
Békés, co., Hung., 468,303 ... *B5 22
Bekescsaba, Hung., 42,500 (51,300▲) ... B5 22
Bekily, Malag ... h9 49
Bela, India, 21,397 ... E8 40
Bela, Pak., 3,063 ... C4 39
Bela Crkva, Yugo., 10,749 ... C5 22
Belaga, Mala., 258 ... E4 39
Bel Air, Harford, Md., 4,300 ... A5 85
Bel Aire Estates, New London, Conn., 800 ... *D9 84
Belalcázar, Sp., 8,793 ... C3 20
Bel Alton, Charles, Md., 175 ... D4 85
Belanger, riv., Man., Can ... C3 71
Bélanger, riv., Sask., Can ... B2 70
Belas, Port., 8,514 ... f9 20
Bela Vista, Braz., 8,878 ... C1 56
Bela Vista, Moz ... C5 49
Belawan, Indon ... E1, m11 35
Belaya, riv., Sov. Un ... B4 29
Belaya Glina, Sov. Un., 10,000 ... H13 27
Belaya Tserkov, Sov. Un., 77,000 ... G8 27
Belcamp, Harford, Md., 225 ... B5 85
Belcher, Pike, Ky., 591 ... C7 94
Belcher, Caddo, La., 400 ... B2 95
Belcher, is., N.W. Ter., Can ... E16 67
Belchertown, Hampshire, Mass., 950 (5,186▲) ... B3 97
Belchirag, Afg., 5,000 ... D12 41
Belcourt, Rolette, N. Dak., 200 ... A6 110
Belcoville, Atlantic, N.J., 300 ... E3 106
Belden, Lee, Miss., 250 ... A5 100
Belden, Cedar, Nebr., 157 ... B8 103
Belden, Mountrail, N. Dak., 26 ... A3 110
Belding, Ionia, Mich., 4,887 ... E5 98
Belecke, Ger., 4,500 ... B3 17
Belém (Pará), Braz., 359,988 (*405,000) ... B1 57
Belém, Port., 24,637 ... f9 20
Belén, Arg., 4,342 ... E2 55
Belen, Quitman, Miss., 90 ... A3 100
Belen, Valencia, N. Mex., 5,031 ... C5 107
Belén, Par., 6,647 ... D4 55
Belet Uin, Som., 7,800 ... E6 47
Belev, Sov. Un., 10,000 ... E11 27
Belfair, Mason, Wash., 400 ... B3 122
Belfast, P.E.I., Can ... C7 74
Belfast, Waldo, Maine, 6,140 ... D3 96
Belfast, Allegany, N.Y., 900 ... C2 108
Belfast, N. Ire., 412,500 (*580,000) ... C6 11
Belfast, Highland, Ohio, 100 ... C4 111
Belfast, Marshall, Tenn., 200 ... B5 117
Belfast, bay, N. Ire ... C6 11
Belfield, Stark, N. Dak., 1,064 ... C2 110
Belfodiya, Eth ... C3 47
Belford, Eng., 891 ... E7 13
Belford, Monmouth, N.J., 6,000 ... C4 106
Belfort, Fr., 48,070 (*62,500) ... D7 14
Belfort, Lewis, N.Y., 75 ... B5 108
Belfort, dept., Fr., 109,371 ... B2 18
Belfry, Pike, Ky., 950 ... C7 94
Belfry, Carbon, Mont., 250 ... E7 102
Belgaum, India, 127,885 (*146,790) ... E5 39
Belgica, mts., Ant ... B16 5
Belgium, Vermilion, Ill., 494 ... C6 90
Belgium, Ozaukee, Wis., 643 ... E6 124
Belgium, country, Eur., 9,400,000 ... E9 8, D4 15
Belgorod, Sov. Un., 92,000 ... F11 27
Belgorod-Dnestrovskiy, Sov. Un., 38,600 ... H8 27
Belgrade, Kennebec, Maine, 250 (1,102▲) ... D3 96
Belgrade, Sterns, Minn., 666 ... E4 99
Belgrade, Washington, Mo., 187 ... D7 101
Belgrade, Gallatin, Mont., 1,057 ... E5 102
Belgrade, Nance, Nebr., 224 ... C7 103
Belgrade (Beograd), Yugo., 585,234 ... C5 22
Belgrade Lakes, Kennebec, Maine, 300 ... D3 96
Belgreen, Franklin, Ala., 200 ... A2 78
Belhaven, Beaufort, N.C., 2,386 ... B7 109
Belice, riv., It ... F4 21
Beli Lom, riv., Bul ... D8 22
Belington, Barbour, W. Va., 1,528 ... B5 123
Belingwe, Rh., 1,100 ... B4 49
Belitung, isl., Indon ... F3 35
Belize, Br. Hond., 32,690 ... B3 62
Belize, riv., Br. Hond., Guat ... B3 56
Belk, Fayette, Ala., 150 ... B2 78
Belkino, Sov. Un ... B11 37
Belknap, Johnson, Ill., 203 ... F5 90
Belknap, Davis, Iowa, 85 ... D5 92
Belknap, Sanders, Mont., 5 ... C1 102
Belknap, co., N.H., 28,912 ... C3 105
Belknap, crater, Oreg ... C5 113
Belknap, mts., N.H ... C4 105
Belkofski, Alsk., 57 ... D7 79
Belkovski, isl., Sov. Un ... B1 4
Bell, Los Angeles, Calif., 19,450 ... F2 73
Bell, Gilchrist, Fla., 134 ... C4 86
Bell, Spokane, Wash ... D8 122
Bell, co., Ky., 35,336 ... D6 94
Bell, co., Tex., 94,097 ... D4 118
Bell, isl., Newf., Can ... C4 75
Bell, isl., Newf., Can ... E5 75
Bella Bella, B.C., Can., 40 ... C3 68
Bellac, Fr., 4,022 ... D4 14
Bella Coola, B.C., Can., 345 ... C4 68
Bella Coola, riv., B.C., Can ... C4 68
Bell Acres, Allegheny, Pa., 1,283 ... *E1 114
Bellagio, It., 1,364 ... D5 18
Bellahy, Ire., 727 ... D3 11
Bellaire, Smith, Kans., 50 ... C5 93
Bellaire, Antrim, Mich., 689 ... D5 98
Bellaire, Belmont, Ohio, 11,502 ... C7 111
Bellaire, Harris, Tex., 19,872 ... F5 118
Bellamy, Sumter, Ala., 750 ... C1 78
Bellary, India, 85,673 ... E6 39
Bella Unión, Ur., 2,519 ... E1 56
Bella Vista, Arg., 8,352 ... E2 55
Bella Vista, Arg., 7,922 ... E4 55
Bella Vista, Benton, Ark ... A1 81
Bella Vista, Par., 5,762 ... D4 55
Bellbrook, Greene, Ohio, 941 ... C3 111
Bell Buckle, Bedford, Tenn., 318 ... B5 117
Bellburn, Greenbrier, W. Va., 200 ... C4 123
Bell City, Calcasieu, La., 250 ... D3 95
Bell City, Stoddard, Mo., 409 ... D8 101
Belle, Maries, Mo., 1,016 ... C6 101
Belle, Kanawha, W. Va., 2,559 ... C3, C6 123
Belle, bay, Newf., Can ... E4 75
Belle, isl., Newf., Can ... C4 75
Belle, isl., Fr ... D2 14
Belle, riv., La ... C5 95
Belleair, Pinellas, Fla., 2,456 ... E1 87
Belle Center, Logan, Ohio, 949 ... B4 111
Belle Chasse, Plaquemines, La., 700 ... C7, E5 95
Bellechasse, co., Que., Can., 26,054 ... C7 73
Belledune, N.B., Can., 163 ... B4 74
Belleek, N. Ire., 162 ... C3 11
Bellefleur, N.B., Can., 142 ... B2 74
Bellefont, Ford, Kans., 25 ... E4 93
Bellefontaine, Webster, Miss., 144 ... B4 100
Bellefontaine, Logan, Ohio, 11,424 ... B4 111
Bellefontaine Neighbors, St. Louis, Mo., 13,650 ... *A8 101
Bellefonte, Boone, Ark., 100 ... A2 81
Bellefonte, New Castle, Del., 1,536 ... A7 85
Bellefonte, Centre, Pa., 6,088 ... E6 114
Belle Fourche, Butte, S. Dak., 4,087 ... C2 116
Belle Fourche, res., S. Dak ... C2 116
Belle Fourche, riv., S. Dak., Wyo ... C2 110, A7 125
Bellegarde-sur-Valserine, Fr., 6,588 ... C1 18
Belle Glade, Palm Beach, Fla., 11,273 ... F6 86
Belle Haven, Accomack, Va., 371 ... D7 121
Belle Helene, Ascension, La ... B5 95
Belle Isle, Orange, Fla., 2,344 ... D5 86
Belle Isle, strait, Newf., Can ... C3 75
Belleisle Creek, N.B., Can., 75 ... D4 74
Bellemead, Prince Georges, Md., 1,400 ... *C4 85
Belle Mead, Somerset, N.J., 500 ... C3 106
Belle Meade, Davidson, Tenn., 3,082 ... A5, E9 117
Belle Mina, Limestone, Ala., 250 ... A3 78
Belleoram, Newf., Can., 577 ... E4 75
Belleplain, Cape May, N.J., 400 ... E3 106
Belle-Plaine, Sask., Can., 117 ... G3 70
Belle Plaine, Benton, Iowa, 2,923 ... C5 92
Belle Plaine, Sumner, Kans., 1,579 ... E6 93
Belle Plaine, Scott, Minn., 1,931 ... F5 99
Belle Rive, Jefferson, Ill., 303 ... E5 90
Belle River, Ont., Can., 1,854 ... E2 72
Bellerive Station, Que., Can., 96 ... C3 73

Bellerose, Assumption, La., 300 ... B5, D4 95
Bellerose, Nassau, N.Y., 1,083 ... *E3 108
Belleterre, Que., Can., 638 ... *h11 73
Belleu, Fr., 2,723 ... E3 15
Belle Valley, Noble, Ohio, 438 ... C6 111
Belle Vernon, Fayette, Pa., 1,784 ... F2 114
Belleview, Marion, Fla., 864 ... C4 86
Belleview, Davidson, Tenn., 100 ... A5, E9 117
Belle View, Fairfax, Va., 3,500 ... *B5 121
Belleville, Yell, Ark., 273 ... B2 81
Belleville, N.S., Can., 276 ... F4 74
Belleville, Ont., Can., 30,655 ... C7 72
Belleville, Fr., 3,030 ... E5 15
Belleville, St. Clair, Ill., 37,264 ... E4 90
Belleville, Republic, Kans., 2,940 ... C6 93
Belleville, Wayne, Mich., 1,921 ... A7 98
Belleville, Essex, N.J., 35,005 ... B4, h8 106
Belleville, Jefferson, N.Y., 300 ... B4 108
Belleville, Mifflin, Pa., 1,539 ... E6 114
Belleville, Washington, R.I., 500 ... C11 84
Belleville, Wood, W. Va., 50 ... B3 123
Belleville, Dane and Green, Wis., 844 ... F4 124
Belleville North, Wayne, Mich., 1,128 ... *A7 98
Belleville [-sur-Saône], Fr., 2,976 ... D6 14
Bellevue, Alta., Can., 1,323 ... E3 69
Bellevue, Blaine, Idaho, 384 ... F4 89
Bellevue, Peoria, Ill., 1,561 ... *C4 90
Bellevue, Jackson, Iowa, 2,181 ... B7 92
Bellevue, Campbell, Ky., 9,336 ... A7 94
Bellevue, Talbot, Md., 267 ... C5 85
Bellevue, Eaton, Mich., 1,277 ... F5 98
Bellevue, Sarpy, Nebr., 8,831 ... C9, E3 103
Bellevue, Huron and Sandusky, Ohio, 8,286 ... A5 111
Bellevue, Allegheny, Pa., 11,412 ... B5, F1 114
Bellevue, Clay, Tex., 309 ... C3 118
Bellevue, King, Wash., 12,809 ... D2 122
Belley, Fr., 4,609 ... E6 14
Bellflower, Los Angeles, Calif., 45,909 ... *F2 82
Bellflower, McLean, Ill., 389 ... C5 90
Bellflower, Montgomery, Mo., 245 ... B6 101
Bell Gardens, Los Angeles, Calif., 26,467 ... *F2 82
Bellingham, Eng., 1,242 ... E6 13
Bellingham, Norfolk, Mass., 1,000 (6,774▲) ... B5, h10 97
Bellingham, Lac qui Parle, Minn., 327 ... E2 99
Bellingham, Whatcom, Wash., 34,688 ... A3 122
Bellingshausen, sea, Ant. ... C3 5
Bellinzona, Switz., 13,435 (*17,716) ... D7 19
Bell Irving, riv., B.C., Can. ... A3 68
Bellis, Atla., Can., 98 ... B4 69
Bellivela, Lib. ... E3 45
Bellmawr, Camden, N.J., 11,853 ... D2 106
Bellmead, McLennan, Tex., 5,127 ... *D4 118
Bellmont, Wabash, Ill., 320 ... E6 90
Bellmore, Parke, Ind., 75 ... E3 91
Bellmore, Nassau, N.Y., 14,100 ... G2 84
Bello, Col., 28,398 ... B2 60
Bello, Cuba ... h11 64
Bellows Falls, Windham, Vt., 3,831 ... E4 120
Belloy, Alta., Can. ... B1 69
Bellport, Suffolk, N.Y., 2,707 ... n16 108
Bell Ranch, San Miguel, N. Mex., 25 ... B5 107
Bell River, Ont., Can., 1,854 ... *E2 72
Bells, Crockett, Tenn., 1,232 ... B2 117
Bells, creek, W. Va. ... C6 123
Bellsburg, Dickson, Tenn., 75 ... A4 117
Bells Corners, Ont., Can., 1,900 ... h12 72
Bellton, Hall and Banks, Ga. (part of Lula) ... B3 87
Belltown, Sussex, Del., 300 ... C7 85
Belltown, Monroe, Tenn. ... D9 117
Belluno, It., 23,000 ... A4 21
Bellview, Curry, N. Mex., 20 ... C6 107
Bell Ville, Arg., 15,796 ... A4 54
Bellville, Evans, Ga., 300 ... D5 87
Bellville, Richland, Ohio, 1,621 ... B5 111
Bellville, Austin, Tex., 2,218 ... E4 118
Bellvue, Larimer, Colo., 100 ... A5 83
Bellwood, Geneva, Ala., 273 ... D4 78
Bellwood, Cook, Ill., 20,729 ... F2 90
Bellwood, Butler, Nebr., 361 ... C8 103
Bellwood, Blair, Pa., 2,330 ... E5 114
Belly, riv., Atla., Can. ... E4 69
Belmar, Monmouth, N.J., 5,190 ... C4 106
Bélmez, Sp., 8,068 ... C3 20
Belmond, Wright, Iowa, 2,506 ... B4 92
Belmont, San Mateo, Calif., 15,996 ... B5 82
Belmont, Man., Can., 378 ... E2 71
Belmont, N.S., Can., 307 ... D6 74
Belmont, Ont., Can., 649 ... E3 72
Belmont, Pinellas, Fla., 2,000 ... *E4 86
Belmont, Kingman, Kans., 200 ... E6 93
Belmont, Pointe Coupee, La. ... C2 95
Belmont, Middlesex, Mass., 28,715 ... g11 97
Belmont, Tishomingo, Miss., 901 ... A5 100
Belmont, Golden Valley, Mont., 15 ... D7 102
Belmont, Dawes, Nebr. ... B2 103
Belmont, Belknap, N.H., 600 (1,953▲) ... D4 105
Belmont, Allegany, N.Y., 1,146 ... C2 108
Belmont, Gaston, N.C., 5,007 ... B2 109
Belmont, Belmont, Ohio 563 ... B6 111
Belmont, Coffee, Tenn. ... B5 117
Belmont, Gonzales, Tex., 50 ... B4 118
Belmont, Rutland, Vt., 100 ... E3 120
Belmont, Whitman, Wash., 50 ... B8 122
Belmont, Pleasants, W. Va., 454 ... B3 123
Belmont, Lafayette, Wis., 616 ... F3 124
Belmont, co., Ohio, 83,864 ... C6 111
Belmonte, Braz., 7,897 ... E3 57
Belmore, Putnam, Ohio, 232 ... A4 111
Belmullet, Ire., 724 ... C2 11
Bel-Nor, St. Louis, Mo., 2,388 ... A8 101
Belo, Malag., 3,278 ... g8 49
Beloeil, Que., Can., 6,283 ... D4 73
Belo Horizonte, Braz., 642,912 (*775,000) ... E2 57
Beloit, Lyon, Iowa, 110 ... A1 92
Beloit, Mitchell, Kans., 3,837 ... C5 93
Beloit, Mahoning, Ohio, 877 ... B7 111
Beloit, Rock, Wis., 35,199 ... F4 124
Beloit North (Perrygo Place), Rock, Wis., 4,475 ... *F4 124
Beloit West, Rock, Wis., 2,162 ... *F4 124
Belokany, Sov. Un., 10,000 ... B16 31
Belomorsk, Sov. Un., 17,400 ... E16 25
Belopolye, Sov. Un., 10,000 ... F10 27
Beloretsk, Sov. Un., 62,000 ... C5 29
Belot, Cuba ... h12 64
Belovo, Sov. Un., 118,000 ... E26 9
Beloye, lake, Sov. Un. ... A11 27
Belozersk, Sov. Un., 16,800 ... A11 27
Belp, Switz., 4,922 ... C4 19
Belper, Eng., 15,563 ... A6 12
Belpre, Edwards, Kans., 211 ... E4 93
Belpre, Washington, Ohio, 5,418 ... C6 111
Bel-Ridge, St. Louis, Mo., 4,878 ... *A8 101
Belspring, Pulaski, Va., 400 ... D2 121
Belt, Cascade, Mont., 757 ... C6 102
Belt, creek, Mont. ... C6 102
Belted, range, Nev. ... F5 104
Belterra, Braz., 5,347 ... C4 59
Belton, Cass, Mo., 4,897 ... C3 101
Belton, Anderson, S.C., 5,106 ... B3 115
Belton, Bell, Tex., 8,163 ... D4 118
Belton, res., Tex. ... D7 118
Beltra, Ire. ... C3 11
Beltrami, Polk, Minn., 186 ... C2 99
Beltrami, co., Minn., 23,425 ... B3 99
Beltsville, Prince Georges, Md., 3,500 ... B4 85
Beltsy, Sov. Un., 73,000 ... H6 27
Belturbet, Ire., 1,093 ... C4 11
Belukha, mtn., Sov. Un. ... E11 28
Beluran, Mala., 50 ... D5 35
Belva, Woodward, Okla., 35 ... A2 112
Belvedere, Marin, Calif., 2,148 ... *B5 82
Belvedere, Aiken, S.C., 500 ... D4 115
Belvedere, Fairfax, Va., 1,100 ... *B5 121
Belvedere Marittimo, It., 9,069 ... E5 21
Belvidere, New Castle, Del., 1,000 ... A6 85
Belvidere, Boone, Ill., 11,223 ... A5 90
Belvidere, Kiowa, Kans., 125 ... E4 93
Belvidere, Thayer, Nebr., 185 ... D8 103
Belvidere, Warren, N.J., 2,636 ... B2 106
Belvidere, Perquimans, N.C., 75 ... A7 109
Belvidere, Jackson, S. Dak., 232 ... D4 116
Belvidere, Franklin, Tenn., 125 ... B5 117
Belvidere, mtn., Vt. ... B3 120
Belvidere Center, Lamoille, Vt., 75 (155▲) ... B3 120
Belview, Redwood, Minn., 400 ... F3 99
Belvue, Pottawatomie, Kans., 179 ... C7 93
Belwood, Ont., Can., 117 ... D4 72
Belyando, riv., Austl. ... D8 50
Belyy, Sov. Un., 17,200 ... D9 27
Belyy, isl., Sov. Un. ... B9 28
Belyy Bom, Sov. Un. ... E26 9
Belzig, Ger., 7,597 ... A7 17
Belzoni, Humphreys, Miss., 4,142 ... B3 100
Bembezar, riv., Sp. ... D3 20
Bement, Piatt, Ill., 1,558 ... D5 90
Bemidji, Beltrami, Minn., 9,958 ... C4 99
Bemidji, lake, Minn. ... C4 99
Bemis, Deuel, S. Dak., 50 ... C9 116
Bemis, Madison, Tenn., 3,127 ... B3 117
Bemis, Randolph, W. Va., 85 ... C5 123
Bemiss, Lowndes, Ga., 100 ... F3 87
Bemus Point, Chautauqua, N.Y., 443 ... C1 108
Bena, Cass, Minn., 286 ... C4 99
Benabarre, Sp., 1,231 ... A6 20
Bena Dibele, Con. L. ... B3 48
Benadir, reg., Som. ... E5 47
Benalla, Austl., 8,259 ... H5 51
Benalto, Alta., Can., 147 ... C3 69
Benanee, Austl., 155 ... G4 51
Benares (Banaras), India, 471,258 (*489,864) ... C7 39, E9 40
Benatky nad Jizerou, Czech., 4,266 ... n18 26
Benavente, Sp., 11,080 ... A3 20
Benavides, Duval, Tex., 2,459 ... F3 118
Ben Avon, Allegheny, Pa., 2,553 ... *E1 114
Benbane, head, Ire. ... B5 11
Benbecula, isl., Scot. ... C1 13
Ben Bolt, Jim Wells, Tex., 200 ... F3 118
Benbrook, Tarrant, Tex., 3,254 ... *C4 118
Benbush, Tucker, W. Va., 100 ... B5 123
Ben Cat, Viet. ... G7 38
Benchland, Judith Basin, Mont., 25 ... C6 102
Bend, Deschutes, Oreg., 11,936 ... C5 113
Bend, San Saba, Tex., 25 ... D3 118
Bendale, Richland, S.C., 1,544 ... C5 115
Ben Davis, Marion, Ind., 900 ... H7 91
Ben Davis, pt., N.J. ... E2 106
Bendeleben, mtn., Alsk. ... B7 79
Bender Beila, Som., 1,900 ... D7 47
Bendersville, Adams, Pa., 484 ... G7 114
Bendery, Sov. Un., 38,000 ... H7 27
Bendigo, Austl., 30,900 (*41,600) ... H5 51
Bendorf, Ger., 14,000 ... C2 17
Benedict, Wilson, Kans., 128 ... E8 93
Benedict, Charles, Md., 460 ... C4 85
Benedict, York, Nebr., 170 ... C8 103
Benedict, McLean, N. Dak., 129 ... B4 110
Benedict, Lee, Va., 30 ... B2 121
Benedict, mtn., Newf., Can. ... g10 75
Benedicta, Aroostook, Maine, 50 (200▲) ... C4 96
Benenitra, Malag. ... h9 49
Beneraird, mtn., Scot. ... E4 13
Benesov, Czech., 9,000 ... D3, o18 26
Bénestroff, Fr., 557 ... F6 15
Benevento, It., 40,800 (56,400▲) ... D5 21
Benevolence, Randolph, Ga., 123 ... E2 87
Benewah, co., Idaho, 6,036 ... B2 89
Benezett, Elk, Pa., 200 ... D5 114
Benfeld, Fr., 3,449 ... A3 18
Bengal, Latimer, Okla., 40 ... C6 112
Bengal, reg., India, Pak. ... D8 39
Bengal, bay, India ... F8 39
Ben Gardane, Tun., 2,100 ... C7 44
Bengasi (Banghāzī), Libya, 136,600 ... C4 43
Bengkalis, Indon., 3,291 ... E2 35
Bengkulu, Indon., 16,800 ... F2 35
Ben Goi, bay, Viet. ... F8 38
Bengough, Sask., Can., 613 ... H3 70
Benguela, Ang., 15,399 ... D1 48
Benguela, dist., Ang., 487,871 ... D1 48
Benguerir, Mor., 4,325 ... H3 30
Benham, Harlan, Ky., 1,874 ... D7 94
Ben Hill, co., Ga., 13,633 ... E3 87
Beni, Con. L. ... A4 48
Beni, Nig. ... D7 45
Beni, dept., Bol., 119,770 ... B3 55
Beni, riv., Bol. ... B2 55
Béni Abbès, Alg., 1,427 (12,418▲) ... C4 44
Benicarló, Sp., 10,627 ... B6 20
Benicia, Solano, Calif., 6,070 ... B2 82
Benicito, riv., Bol. ... B2 55
Benin, Nig., 53,753 ... E6 45
Benin, bight, Afr. ... E5 45
Béni Ounif, Alg., 877 ... C4 44
Benisa, Sp., 6,036 ... C6 20
Béni Saf, Alg., 10,934 (21,098▲) ... B4 44
Benito, Man., Can., 427 ... D1 71
Benjamin, Knox, Tex., 338 ... C3 118
Benjamin Constant, Braz., 3,224 ... B3 58
Benjes, Shelby, Tenn. ... E8 117
Benkelman, Dundy, Nebr., 1,400 ... D4 103
Benkovac, Yugo., 1,367 ... C2 22
Benld, Macoupin, Ill., 1,848 ... D4 90
Ben Lomond, Sevier, Ark., 157 ... D1 81
Ben Lomond, Santa Cruz, Calif., 1,814 ... C5 82
Benmore, head, Ire. ... B5 11
Bennane, head, Scot. ... E3 13
Benndale, George, Miss., 450 ... E5 100
Bennet, Lancaster, Nebr., 381 ... D9, F2 103
Bennett, Adams, Colo., 287 ... B6 83
Bennett, Cedar, Iowa, 374 ... C7 92
Bennett, Lea., N. Mex., 30 ... E6 107
Bennett, Chatham, N.C., 222 ... B4 109
Bennett, Douglas, Wis., 50 ... B2 124
Bennett, co., S. Dak., 3,053 ... D4 116
Bennett, creek, Md. ... B3 85
Bennett, isl., Sov. Un. ... B17 28
Bennett, lake, Man., Can. ... C3 71
Bennette, butte, Oreg. ... E2 113
Bennetts, Miami, Ind., 130 ... C5 91
Bennettsbridge, Ire., 325 ... E4 11
Bennettsville, Marlboro, S.C., 6,963 ... B8 115
Bennetsville Southwest, Marlboro, S.C., 1,022 ... *B8 115
Benningen, Switz., 7,864 ... A4 19
Bennington, Bear Lake, Idaho, 100 ... G7 89
Bennington, Ottawa, Kans., 535 ... C6 93
Bennington, Douglas, Nebr., 341 ... D3 103
Bennington, Hillsboro, N.H., 400 (591▲) ... D3 105
Bennington, Bryan, Okla., 226 ... D5 112
Bennington, Bennington, Vt., 8,023 (13,002▲) ... F2 120
Bennington, co., Vt., 25,088 ... E2 120
Bennion, Salt Lake, Utah, 200 ... *C4 119
Benns Church, Isle of Wight, Va. ... B6 121
Bennt Jbail, Leb., 4,000 ... A7 32
Benoit, Bolivar, Miss., 453 ... B2 100
Benoit, Bayfield, Wis., 30 ... B2 124
Benoit's Cove, Newf., Can., 592 ... *D2 75
Benoni, S. Afr., 122,502 ... *C4 49
Bénoué, riv., Cam. ... D2 46
Benque Viejo, Br. Hond., 1,561 ... B3 62
Bens, pt., N.Y. ... E8 84
Bensané, Guinea ... D2 45
Bensberg, Ger., 30,000 ... C2 17
Bensenville, Du Page, Ill., 11,057 ... B6, E2 90
Bensheim, Ger., 24,100 ... D3 17
Benson, Cochise, Ariz., 2,494 ... F5 80
Benson, Sask., Can., 137 ... H4 70
Benson, Woodford, Ill., 427 ... C4 90
Benson, De Soto, La., 100 ... C2 95
Benson, Harford, Md., 325 ... A5 85
Benson, Swift, Minn., 3,678 ... E3 99
Benson, Johnston, N.C., 2,355 ... B5 109
Benson, Somerset, Pa., 350 ... *F4 114
Benson, Cache, Utah, 150 ... B4 119
Benson, Rutland, Vt., 60 (549▲) ... D2 120
Benson, co., N. Dak., 9,435 ... A6 110
Benson Mines, St. Lawrence, N.Y., 40 ... A5 108
Bens Run, Tyler, W. Va., 200 ... B3 123
Bensted Corner, Hartford, Conn., 350 ... *C5 84
Bent, Otero, N. Mex., 10 ... D4 107
Bent, co., Colo., 7,419 ... D7 83
Bentheim, Ger., 6,700 ... A2 17
Bentiu, Sud. ... D2 47
Bentley, Alta., Can., 588 ... C3 69
Bentley, Pottawattamie, Iowa, 50 ... C2 92
Bentley, Sedgwick, Kans., 204 ... B5, E6 93
Bentley, Grant, La., 200 ... C3 95
Bentley, Bay, Mich., 100 ... E6 98
Bentley, Hettinger, N. Dak., 70 ... C3 110
Bentley Creek, Bradford, Pa., 120 ... C8 114
Bentley Springs, Baltimore, Md., 120 ... A4 85
Bentleyville, Washington, Pa., 3,160 ... F1 114
Benton, Saline, Ark., 10,399 ... C3 81
Benton, Mono, Calif., 100 ... D4 82
Benton, N.B., Can., 184 ... D2 74
Benton, Franklin, Ill., 7,023 ... E5 90
Benton, Elkhart, Ind., 250 ... A6 91
Benton, Ringgold, Iowa, 84 ... D3 92
Benton, Butler, Kans., 452 ... B6, E6 93
Benton, Marshall, Ky., 3,074 ... B3 94
Benton, Bossier, La., 1,336 ... B2 95
Benton, Kennebec, Maine, 100 (1,521▲) ... D3 96
Benton, Yazoo, Miss., 100 ... C3 100
Benton, Scott, Mo., 554 ... D8 101
Benton, Grafton, N.H., 35 (172▲) ... B3 105
Benton, Columbia, Pa., 981 ... D9 114
Benton, Polk, Tenn., 638 ... D9 117
Benton, Atascosa, Tex. ... B3 118
Benton, Lafayette, Wis., 837 ... F3 124
Benton, co., Ark., 36,272 ... A1 81
Benton, co., Ind., 11,912 ... C3 91
Benton, co., Iowa, 23,422 ... B5 92
Benton, co., Minn., 17,287 ... E4 99
Benton, co., Miss., 7,723 ... A4 100
Benton, co., Mo., 8,737 ... C4 101
Benton, co., Oreg., 39,165 ... C3 113
Benton, co., Tenn., 10,662 ... A3 117
Benton, co., Wash., 62,070 ... C6 122
Benton City, Audrain, Mo., 155 ... B6 101
Benton City, Benton, Wash., 1,210 ... C6 122
Benton Harbor, Berrien, Mich., 19,136 ... F4 98
Benton Heights, Berrien, Mich., 6,112 ... *F4 98
Bentonia, Yazoo, Miss., 511 ... C3 100
Benton Ridge, Hancock, Ohio, 325 ... A4 111
Benton Station, Alta., Can. ... D5 69
Bentonville, Benton, Ark., 4,015 ... A1 81
Bentonville, Adams, Ohio, 250 ... D4 111
Bentonville, Warren, Va., 350 ... C4 121
Bentree, Nicholas, W. Va. ... C7 123
Benue, riv., Nig. ... E6 45
Benwee, head, Ire. ... C2 11
Benwood, Marshall, W. Va., 2,850 ... A4, B2 123
Benzie, co., Mich., 7,834 ... D4 98
Benzonia, Benzie, Mich., 407 ... D4 98
Beo, Indon. ... E7 35
Beograd, see Belgrade, Yugo.
Béoumi, I.C., 3,200 ... E3 45
Beowawe, Eureka, Nev., 200 ... C5 104
Beppu, Jap., 107,734 ... J5 37
Berach, riv., India ... E5 40
Berat, Alb., 15,700 ... B2 23
Berat, pref., Alb., 176,000 ... *B2 23
Berber, Sud., 10,977 ... B3 47
Berbera, Som., 20,000 ... C6 47
Berbérati, Cen. Afr. Rep. ... E3 46
Berberia, isl., P.R. ... D5 65
Berbice, riv., Br. Gu. ... A3 59
Berceto, It., 6,860 ... E6 18
Bercher, Switz., 407 ... C2 19
Berchogur, Sov. Un. ... D5 29
Berchtesgaden, Ger., 4,800 ... E6 16
Berck-sur-Mer, Fr., 12,877 ... B4 14
Berclair, Leflore, Miss., 75 ... B3 100
Berclair, Shelby, Tenn. (part of Memphis) ... E8 117
Berclair, Goliad, Tex., 280 ... E4 118
Berdichev, Sov. Un., 57,000 ... G7 27
Berdsk, Sov. Un., 30,000 ... E25 9
Berea, Madison, Ky., 4,302 ... C5 94
Berea, Box Butte, Nebr., 23 ... B3 103
Berea, Barnes, N. Dak., 10 ... C7 110
Berea, Cuyahoga, Ohio, 16,592 ... A6 111
Berebere, Indon. ... E7 35
Beregovo, Sov. Un., 5,000 ... G4 27
Bereku, Tan. ... B6 48
Berenice, Butte, Idaho ... F6 89
Berenice, ruins, Eg., U.A.R. ... E7 43
Berens, isl., Man., Can. ... C3 71
Berens, riv., Man., Can. ... C3 71
Berens River, Man., Can., 169 ... C3, g8 71
Beresford, Man., Can. ... E1 71
Beresford, Lincoln and Union, S. Dak., 1,794 ... D9 116
Berettyoujfalu, Hung., 11,377 ... B5 22
Berezhany, Sov. Un., 5,000 ... G5 27
Berezina, riv., Sov. Un. ... E7 27
Berezna, Sov. Un., 10,000 ... F8 27
Berezniki, Sov. Un., 120,000 ... B5 29
Berezovo, Sov. Un. ... C21 9
Berezovskiy, Sov. Un., 28,300 ... D21 9
Berg, Nor. ... q27 25
Berga, Sp., 9,822 ... A6 20
Berga, Swe. ... B8 24
Bergama, Tur., 21,800 ... C6 23
Bergamasque Alps, mts., It. ... C5 18
Bergamo, It., 118,700 (*275,000) ... B2 21
Bergedorf, Ger. (part of Hamburg) ... B5 16
Bergen, see Mons, Bel.
Bergen, Ger., 10,500 ... A6 16
Bergen [bei Celle] (Bergen-Belsen), Ger., 5,300 ... F3 24
Bergen, Genesee, N.Y., 964 ... B3 108
Bergen, McHenry, N. Dak., 52 ... A5 110
Bergen, Nor., 115,900 (*205,000) ... G1 25
Bergen, co., N.J., 780,255 ... A4 106
Bergen aan Zee, Neth., 221 ... B4 15
Bergenfield, Bergen, N.J., 27,203 ... B4, h8 106
Bergen op Zoom, Neth., 35,500 ... C4 15
Berger, Franklin, Mo., 187 ... C6 101
Bergerac, Fr., 21,236 ... E4 14
Bergheim, Kendall, Tex., 25 ... A3 118
Bergholz, Jefferson, Ohio, 955 ... B7 111
Bergisch Gladbach, Ger., 44,900 ... C2 17
Bergland, Ont., Can. ... B4 99
Bergland, Ontonagon, Mich., 600 ... A5 98
Bergman, Boone, Ark., 100 ... A2 81
Bergoo, Webster, W. Va., 460 ... C4 123
Bergton, Rockingham, Va., 100 ... C4 121
Berguent, Mor., 2,607 ... C4 44
Bergün, Switz., 551 ... C8 19
Bergzabern, Ger., 5,300 ... D3 17
Berhampore, India, 76,931 ... E12 40
Berhampur, India, 62,317 ... H10 40
Bering, sea, Alsk., Sov. Un. ... D3 79
Bering, strait, Alsk. ... C5 79
Berino, Dona Ana, N. Mex., 200 ... E3 107
Berislav, Sov. Un., 10,000 ... H9 27
Berja, Sp., 6,425 ... D4 20
Berkeley, Alameda, Calif., 111,268 ... B5, D2 82
Berkeley, Ont., Can., 116 ... C4 72
Berkeley, Cook, Ill., 5,792 ... *F2 90
Berkeley, St. Louis, Mo., 18,676 ... A8 101
Berkeley, Providence, R.I., 2,000 ... B11 84
Berkeley, Berkeley, W. Va., 200 ... B7 123
Berkeley, co., S.C., 38,196 ... E8 115
Berkeley, co., W. Va., 33,791 ... B6 123
Berkeley, cape, Ec. ... g5 58
Berkeley Heights, Union, N.J., 8,721 ... B4 106
Berkeley Springs (Bath), Morgan, W. Va., 1,138 ... B6 123
Berkey, Lucas, Ohio, 257 ... A1, A4 111
Berkley, Boone, Iowa, 58 ... C3 92
Berkley, Harford, Md., 48 ... A5 85
Berkley, Bristol, Mass., 400 (1,609▲) ... C5 97
Berkley, Oakland, Mich., 23,275 ... A7, F7 98
Berkner, isl., Ant. ... B7 5
Berkovitsa, Bul., 6,870 ... D6 22
Berks, co., Pa., 275,414 ... F9 114
Berkshire, Prince Georges, Md., 1,200 ... *C4 85
Berkshire, Berkshire, Mass., 300 ... A1 97
Berkshire, Tioga, N.Y., 350 ... C4 108
Berkshire, Franklin, Vt., 35 (965▲) ... B3 120
Berkshire, co., Eng., 503,357 ... C6 12
Berkshire, co., Mass., 142,135 ... B1 97
Berkshire, hills, Mass. ... B1 97
Berland, riv., Alta., Can. ... C1 69
Berleburg, Ger., 6,400 ... B3 17
Berlengas, is., Port. ... C1 20
Berlin, Hartford, Conn., 3,000 (11,250▲) ... C5 84
Berlin, Colquitt, Ga., 419 ... E3 87
Berlin, Ger., 3,247,400 (*4,025,000) ... B6 16
Berlin, East, Ger., 1,061,200 ... *B6 16
Berlin, West, Ger., 2,186,200 (*4,025,000) ... *B6 16
Berlin, Worcester, Md., 2,046 ... D7 85
Berlin, Worcester, Mass., 500 (1,742▲) ... B4 97
Berlin, Coos, N.H., 17,821 ... B4 105
Berlin, Camden, N.J., 3,578 ... D3 106
Berlin, Rensselaer, N.Y., 800 (1,329▲) ... C7 108
Berlin, La Moure, N. Dak., 78 ... C7 110
Berlin, Holmes, Ohio, 300 ... B6 111
Berlin, Roger Mills, Okla., 50 ... B2 112
Berlin, Somerset, Pa., 1,600 ... G4 114
Berlin, Washington, Vt., 150 (1,306▲) ... C3 120
Berlin, Green Lake and Waushara, Wis., 4,838 ... E5 124
Berlin, mtn., Ant. ... B35 5
Berlin, mtn., Nev. ... E4 104
Berlin, res., Ohio ... A6 111
Berlin Heights, Erie, Ohio, 721 ... A5 111
Bermejo, riv., Arg., Par. ... E4 55
Bermeo, Sp., 13,781 ... A4 20
Bermuda, Br. dep., N.A., 60,000 ... D5 6, E14 77
Bermuda Hundred, Chesterfield, Va., 30 ... C7 121
Bern, Nemaha, Kans., 206 ... C8 93
Bern, Switz., 167,400 (*255,000) ... C3 19
Bern, canton, Switz., 889,523 ... C3 19
Bernalillo, Sandoval, N. Mex., 2,574 ... B3, k7 107
Bernalillo, co., N. Mex., 262,199 ... C3 107
Bernard, Sask., Can. ... G2 70
Bernard, Dubuque, Iowa, 173 ... B7 92
Bernard, Hancock, Maine, 200 ... D4 96
Bernard, isl., Truk ... C2 52
Bernard, lake, Ont., Can. ... B5 72
Bernardston, Franklin, Mass., 500 (1,370▲) ... A2 97
Bernardsville, Somerset, N.J., 5,515 ... B3 106
Bernasconi, Arg., 2,094 ... B4 54
Bernau, Ger., 13,600 ... B6 16
Bernau, Ger., 1,300 ... B8 18
Bernay, Fr., 7,418 ... C4 14
Bernburg, Ger., 44,800 ... B6 17
Berndorf, Aus., 8,992 ... E8 16
Berne, Adams, Ind., 2,644 ... C8 91
Berne, Albany, N.Y., 150 ... C6 108
Berneray, isl., Scot. ... C1 13
Bernese Alps, mts., Switz. ... D3 19
Bernice, Union, La., 1,641 ... B3 95
Bernice, Delaware, Okla., 100 ... A7 112
Bernie, Stoddard, Mo., 1,578 ... E8 101
Bernina, pass, Switz. ... D9 19
Bernina, peak, Switz. ... D8 19
Bernstadt, Laurel, Ky., 425 ... C5 94
Bernville, Berks, Pa., 884 ... F9 114
Beroroha, Malag. ... h9 49
Beroun, Czech., 15,600 ... D3, o17 26
Beroun, Pine, Minn., 100 ... C6 99
Berounka, riv., Czech. ... o17 26
Berre, Fr., 8,677 ... F6 14
Berrechid, Mor., 13,780 ... C3 44
Berrien, co., Ga., 12,038 ... E3 87
Berrien, co., Mich., 149,865 ... G4 98
Berrien Springs, Berrien, Mich., 1,953 ... G4 98
Berry, Fayette, Ala., 645 ... B2 78
Berry, Harrison, Ky., 279 ... B5 94
Berry, former prov., Fr., 464,000 ... D4 14
Berry, creek, Alta., Can. ... D5 69
Berrydale, Santa Rosa, Fla., 25 ... G2 86
Berryessa Lake, res., Calif. ... C2 82
Berry Hill, Davidson, Tenn., 1,551 ... A5 117
Berryman, Crawford, Mo., 150 ... D6 101
Berry Mills, N.B., Can., 318 ... *C5 74
Berry Mills, Franklin, Maine, 75 ... D2 96
Berryton, Chattooga, Ga., 300 ... B1 87
Berryville, Carroll, Ark., 1,999 ... A2 81
Berryville, Clarke, Va., 1,645 ... B5 121
Bersenbrück, Ger., 3,600 ... B3 17
Bershad, Sov. Un., 10,000 ... G7 27
Bertha, Todd, Minn., 562 ... D3 99
Berthier, co., Que., Can., 27,325 ... C4 73
Berthierville, Que., Can., 3,708 ... C4 73
Berthold, Ward, N. Dak., 431 ... A4 110
Berthoud, Larimer, Colo., 1,014 ... A5 83
Berthoud, pass, Colo. ... B5 83
Bertie, Bertie, N.C., 303 ... B7 109
Bertie, co., N.C., 24,350 ... A6 109
Bertraghboy, bay, Ire. ... D2 11
Bertram, Burnet, Tex., 850 ... D3 118
Bertrand, Berrien, Mich., 3,500 ... G4 98
Bertrand, Mississippi, Mo., 465 ... E8 101
Bertrand, Phelps, Nebr., 691 ... D6 103
Bertrandville, Plaquemines, La., 100 ... C7, E5 95
Bertrix, Bel., 4,466 ... E5 15
Berwick, N.S., Can., 1,282 ... D5 74
Berwick, Warren, Ill., 160 ... C3 90
Berwick, Polk, Iowa, 150 ... A7 92
Berwick, St. Mary, La., 3,880 ... C5, E4 95
Berwick, York, Maine, 1,557 (2,738▲) ... E2 96
Berwick, McHenry, N. Dak., 56 ... A5 110
Berwick, Columbia, Pa., 13,353 ... D9 114
Berwick, co., Scot., 22,441 ... E6 13
Berwick-on-Tweed, Eng., 12,100 ... C6 10
Berwind, McDowell, W. Va., 950 ... D3 123
Berwyn, Alta., Can., 347 ... A2 69
Berwyn, Cook, Ill., 54,224 ... F2 90
Berwyn, Custer, Nebr., 104 ... C6 103
Berwyn, Chester, Pa., 5,000 ... A10 114
Berwyn Heights, Prince Georges, Md., 2,376 ... B4 85
Beryl, Iron, Utah, 70 ... F2 119
Besa, Indon. ... E7 35
Besançon, Fr., 95,642 ... D7 14, B2 18
Beskids, mts., Czech., Pol. ... D5 26
Besnard, lake, Sask., Can. ... B2 70
Besalampy, Malag. ... g8 49
Besni, Tur., 11,200 ... D11 31
Bessèges, Fr., 5,770 ... E6 14
Bessemer, Jefferson, Ala., 33,054 ... B3, E4 78
Bessemer, Gogebic, Mich., 3,304 ... A5 98
Bessemer, Lawrence, Pa., 1,491 ... E1 114
Bessemer City, Gaston, N.C., 4,017 ... B2 109
Bessie, Jackson, N.C. ... D3 109
Bessie, Washita, Okla., 226 ... B3 112
Bessmay, Jasper, Tex., 250 ... D6 118
Best, Reagan, Tex., 30 ... D2 118
Bestobe, Sov. Un. ... C8 29
Bestwater, Benton, Ark. ... A1 81
Betafo, Malag. ... g9 49
Betanzos, Sp., 7,561 ... A1 20
Bétaré Oya, Cam. ... D2 46
Bethalto, Madison, Ill., 3,235 ... E3 90
Bethanie, S.W. Afr., 1,053 ... C2 49
Bethany, Man., Can., 80 ... *D2 71
Bethany, Ont., Can., 279 ... C6 72
Bethany, New Haven, Conn., 800 (2,384▲) ... D5 84
Bethany, Moultrie, Ill., 1,118 ... D5 90
Bethany, see Al 'Ayzariyah, Jordan
Bethany, Caddo, La., 160 ... B1 95
Bethany, Harrison, Mo., 2,771 ... A3 101
Bethany, Butler, Ohio, 165 ... C2 111
Bethany, Oklahoma, Okla., 12,342 ... B4 112
Bethany, Brooke, W. Va., 992 ... B2 123
Bethany Beach, Sussex, Del., 170 ... C7 85
Bethayres-Huntingdon Valley, Montgomery, Pa., 2,500 ... *F11 114
Bethel, Alsk., 1,258 ... C7 79
Bethel, Fairfield, Conn., 8,200 ... D3 84
Bethel, Sussex, Del., 236 ... C6 85
Bethel, Bath, Ky., 200 ... B6 94
Bethel, Oxford, Maine, 1,117 (2,408▲) ... D2 96
Bethel, Anoka, Minn., 302 ... E5 99
Bethel, Shelby, Mo., 152 ... B5 101
Bethel, Pitt, N.C., 1,578 ... B6 109
Bethel, Clermont, Ohio, 2,019 ... D3 111
Bethel, McCurtain, Okla., 150 ... C7 112
Bethel, Lane, Oreg., 1,500 ... *C3 113
Bethel (Bethel Park), Allegheny, Pa., 23,650 ... B5 114
Bethel, Berks, Pa., 450 ... F9 114
Bethel, Windsor, Vt., 600 (1,356▲) ... D3 120
Bethel Springs, McNairy, Tenn., 533 ... B3 117
Bethera, Berkeley, S.C., 165 ... E8 115
Bethesda, Independence, Ark., 115 ... B4 81
Bethesda, Montgomery, Md., 56,527 ... C1, C3 85
Bethesda, Belmont, Ohio, 1,178 ... B6 111
Bethesda, Wales, 4,151 ... A3 12
Bethevan, Grant, Ind. ... C6 91
Bethlehem, Litchfield, Conn., 800 (1,486▲) ... C4 84
Bethlehem, Barrow, Ga., 297 ... C3 87
Bethlehem, Clark, Ind., 150 ... G7 91
Bethlehem, see Bayt Laḥm, Jordan
Bethlehem, Caroline, Md., 85 ... C6 85
Bethlehem, Grafton, N.H., 450 (898▲) ... B3 105

Blackall, Austl., 2,217 .... B5 51
Black Bear, bay, Newf., Can ... B4 75
Black Bear, creek, Okla A4 112
Blackbeard, isl., Ga E5 87
Black Bear Island, lake, Sask., Can B3 70
Blackburn, Eng., 105,000 (*230,000) A5 12
Blackburn, Saline, Mo., 310 .. B4 101
Blackburn, Pawnee, Okla., 129 .... A5 112
Blackburn, mtn., Alsk C11 79
Black Canyon, Yavapai, Ariz., 150 .... C3 80
Black Canyon of the Gunnison, nat. mon., Colo C3 83
Black Creek, B.C., Can., 521 . E5 68
Black Creek, Wilson, N.C., 310 .... B6 109
Black Creek, Outagamie, Wis., 707 .... A5, D5 124
Black Diamond, Jefferson, Ala., 250 .... E4 78
Black Diamond, Alta., Can., 1,043 .... D3 69
Black Diamond, King, Wash., 1,026 .... B3, D2 122
Black Dome, mtn., B.C., Can ... C4 68
Blackdown, hills, Eng D4 12
Blackduck, Beltrami, Minn., 765 .... C4 99
Black Eagle, Cascade, Mont., 2,200 .... C5 102
Black Earth, Dane, Wis., 784 . E4 124
Blackey, Buchanan, Va., 200 . B3 121
Blackfalds, Alta., Can., 477 .. C4 69
Blackfeet, Indian res., Mont B3 102
Blackfoot, Alta., Can., 91 ..... C5 69
Blackfoot, Bingham, Idaho, 7,378 .... F6 89
Blackfoot, Glacier, Mont., 50 . B4 102
Blackfoot, res., Idaho G7 89
Blackfoot, riv., Mont C3 102
Blackfoot, mts., Idaho F7 89
Blackford, co., Ind., 14,792 .. D7 91
Black Forest, El Paso, Colo., 1,000 .... C6 83
Black Forest, mts., Ger E3 17
Black Fork, Scott, Ark., 30 .. C1 81
Blackfork, Lawrence, Ohio, 300 .... D5 111
Black Hawk, Ont., Can., 40 .. B5 99
Black Hawk, Gilpin, Colo., 171 .... B5 83
Black Hawk, Carroll, Miss., 100 .... B4 100
Black Hawk, Meade, S. Dak., 200 .... C2 116
Black Hawk, co., Iowa, 122,482 .... B5 92
Blackhead, bay, Newf., Can ... D5 75
Blackie, Alta., Can., 184 .... D4 69
Blackjack, St. Louis, Mo., 215 .... A8 101
Black Jack, mtn., Ga A5 87
Black Lake, Que., Can., 4,180 .... C6 73
Black Lake, Sask., Can., 290 .... *m7 70
Black Lake, bayou, La B2 95
Blacklick, Franklin, Ohio, 200 .... C2 111
Black Lick, Indiana, Pa., 700 .... F3 114
Blackman, Okaloosa, Fla., 50 . G2 86
Blackmore, mtn., Mont E6 102
Black Mountain, Buncombe, N.C., 1,313 .... D4 109
Black Oak, Craighead, Ark., 220 .... B5 81
Black Oak, Lake, Ind., 15,000 .... *A3 91
Black Oak, ridge, Tenn D9 117
Black Pine, peak, Idaho G5 89
Black Point, Marin, Calif., 650 .... B5 82
Black Point, New London, Conn., 60 .... D8 84
Blackpool, Eng., 151,000 (*260,000) A4 12
Black River, Jam., 2,616 ..... F5 64
Blackriver, Alcona, Mich., 90 .... D7 98
Black River, Jefferson, N.Y., 1,237 .... A5 108
Black River Falls, Jackson, Wis., 3,195 .... D3 124
Black Rock, Lawrence, Ark., 554 .... A4 81
Black Rock, McKinley, N. Mex., 150 .... B1 107
Black Rock, des., Nev B3 104
Black Rock, des., Utah D3 119
Black Rock, mts., Nev B3 104
Blacks, fork, Utah, Wyo B5 119
Blacksburg, Cherokee, S.C., 2,174 .... A4 115
Blacksburg, Montgomery, Va., 7,070 .... D2 121
Blacks Harbour, N.B., Can., 1,297 .... D3 74
Blackshear, Pierce, Ga., 2,482 .... E4 87
Blacksod, bay, Ire C1 11
Black Springs, Montgomery, Ark., 75 .... C2 81
Black Springs, Washoe, Nev., 100 .... D2 104
Black Squirrel, creek, Colo C6 83
Blackstairs, mtn., Ire E5 11
Blackstairs, mts., Ire E5 11
Blackstock, Ont., Can., 265 .. C6 72
Blackstock, Chester and Fairfield, S.C., 175 .... B5 115
Blackstone, Worcester, Mass., 2,500 (5,130*) B4 97
Blackstone, Caldwell, N.C. .. A2 109
Blackstone, Nottoway, Va., 3,659 .... D5 121
Blackstone, riv., Alta., Can C2 69
Blackstone Acres, New Haven, Conn., 400 .... *D5 84
Blacksville, Monongalia, W. Va., 211 .... B4 123
Black Thunder, creek, Wyo B8 125
Blackton, Monroe, Ark., 50 .. C4 81
Blackville, N.B., Can., 484 .. C4 74
Blackville, Barnwell, S.C., 1,901 .... E5 115
Black Volta, riv., Ghana E4 45
Black Walnut, pt., Md C5 85
Black Warrior, riv., Ala C2 78
Blackwater, Ire., 216 .... E5 11
Blackwater, Cooper, Mo., 284 .... C5 101
Blackwater, Lee, Va., 50 .... B2 121
Blackwater, res., N.H D3 105
Blackwater, res., Scot D3 13
Blackwater, riv., Eng C8 12
Blackwater, riv., Fla G2 86
Blackwater, riv., Ire E3 11
Blackwater, riv., Md D5 85
Blackwater, riv., N.H D3 105
Blackwater, riv., Va E6 121
Blackwell, Conway, Ark., 750 .... B3 81
Blackwell, St. Francis, Mo., 100 .... C7 101
Blackwell, Kay, Okla., 9,588 . A4 112
Blackwell, Tioga, Pa., 75 ..... C7 114
Blackwell, Nolan, Tex., 314 .. C2 118
Blackwell, Forest, Wis., 100 . C5 124
Blackwood, Camden, N.J., 3,500 .... *D2 106
Bladen, Webster, Nebr., 322 . D7 103
Bladen, co., N.C., 28,881 .... C5 109
Bladenboro, Bladen, N.C., 774 .... C5 109
Bladensburg, Prince Georges, Md., 3,103 .... C2 85
Blades, Sussex, Del., 729 .... C6 85
Bladon Springs, Choctaw, Ala., 150 .... D1 78
Bladworth, Sask., Can., 190 .. F2 70
Blagnac, Fr., 5,320 .... F4 14
Blagodarnoye, Sov. Un., 29,500 .... D2 29
Blagoevgrad (Gorna-Dzhumaya), Bul., 14,066 .... D6 22
Blagoveshchensk, Sov. Un., 104,000 .... D15 28
Blagoveshchensk, Sov. Un., 10,000 .... D20 9
Blain, Fr., 2,009 .... D3 14
Blain, Perry, Pa., 336 ...... F7 114
Blaine, Pottawatomie, Kans., 78 .... C7 93
Blaine, Aroostook, Maine, 375 (945*) B5 96
Blaine, Anoka, Minn., 7,570 .... E7 99
Blaine, Sunflower, Miss., 125 . B3 100
Blaine, Belmont, Ohio, 750 .. B1 111
Blaine, Whatcom, Wash., 1,735 .... A3 122
Blaine, co., Idaho, 4,598 .... F4 89
Blaine, co., Mont., 8,091 .... B7 102
Blaine, co., Nebr., 1,016 .... C6 103
Blaine, co., Okla., 12,077 .... B3 112
Blaine, creek, Ky B7 94
Blaine Lake, Sask., Can., 641 .... E2 70
Blainville-sur-l'Eau, Fr., 4,309 .... F6 15
Blair, Doniphan, Kans., 75 .. C8 93
Blair, Washington, Nebr., 4,931 .... C9 103
Blair, Grafton, N.H., 60 ..... C3 105
Blair, Jackson, Okla., 893 .... C2 112
Blair, Fairfield, S.C., 75 ..... C5 115
Blair, Logan, W. Va., 500 .... D5 123
Blair, Trempealeau, Wis., 909 .... D2 124
Blair, co., Pa., 137,270 ...... E5 114
Blair-Atholl, Scot., 1,868 .... D5 13
Blairgowrie [& Rattray], Scot., 5,168 .... D5 13
Blair Mills, Anderson, S.C., 75 .... B2 115
Blairmore, Alta., Can., 1,980 . E3 69
Blairsburg, Hamilton, Iowa, 287 .... B4 92
Blairsden, Plumas, Calif., 90 . C3 82
Blairstown, Benton, Iowa, 583 .... C5 92
Blairstown Henry, Mo., 177 . C4 101
Blairstown, Warren, N.J., 650 .... B3 106
Blairsville, Union, Ga., 437 .. B3 87
Blairsville, Indiana, Pa., 4,930 .... F3 114
Blairton, Berkeley, W. Va., 200 .... B7 123
Blaisdell, Mountrail, N. Dak., 62 .... A3 110
Blaj, Rom., 8,731 .... B7 22
Blakeley, Scott, Minn., 100 .... F5 99
Blakeley, Kanawha, W. Va., 165 .... C6 123
Blakely, Garland, Ark., 250 .. C2 81
Blakely, Early, Ga., 3,580 .... E2 87
Blakeman, Rawlins, Kans., 12 .... C2 93
Blakes, pt., Mich A2 98
Blakesburg, Wapello, Iowa, 401 .... D5 92
Blakeslee, Williams, Ohio, 156 .... A3 111
Blakeslee, Monroe, Pa., 225 .... D10 114
Blalock, Gilliam, Oreg., 20 .. B6 113
Blâmont, Fr., 1,409 .... F6 15
Blanc, cape, Maur B1 45
Blanc, cape, Tun F11 30
Blanc, mtn., Fr E7 14
Blanca, Costilla, Colo., 233 . D5 83
Blanca, bay, Arg B4 54
Blanca, cape, Oreg E2 113
Blanca, peak, Colo D5 83
Blanca, pt., Mex B2 63
Blanca, range, Peru C2 58
Blanchard, Bonner, Idaho, 100 .... A2 89
Blanchard, Page, Iowa, 174 . D2 92
Blanchard, Caddo, La., 500 . B2 95
Blanchard, Piscataquis, Maine, 10 (57*) C3 96
Blanchard, Isabella, Mich., 275 .... E5 98
Blanchard, Trail, N. Dak., 40 . B8 110
Blanchard, McClain, Okla., 1,377 .... B4 112
Blanchard, Centre, Pa., 600 . D6 114
Blanchard, Skagit, Wash., 200 .... A3 122
Blanchard, riv., Ohio A3 111
Blanchardville, Lafayette, Wis., 632 .... F4 124
Blanche, Que., Can., 95 ..... D2 73
Blanche, Lincoln, Tenn., 200 .... B5 117
Blanche, lake, Austl D2 51
Blanchester, Clinton, Ohio, 2,944 .... C4 111
Blanco, San Juan, N. Mex., 100 .... A2 107
Blanco, Blanco, Tex., 789 .... D3 118
Blanco, co., Tex., 3,657 ...... D3 118
Blanco, cape, C.R F5 62
Blanco, cape, Oreg E2 113
Blanco, creek, N. Mex C6 107
Blanco, riv., Arg E2 55
Blanco, riv., Bol B3 55
Blanco, riv., Mex n15 63
Blanco, riv., P.R C3 65
Blanc-Sablon, Que., Can., 252 .... C3, h10 75
Bland, Gasconade, Mo., 654 .... C6 101
Bland, Bland, Va., 500 ...... D1 121
Bland, co., Va., 5,982 .... D1 121
Blandburg, Cambria, Pa., 900 .... E5 114
Blandford [Forum], Eng., 3,558 .... D5 12
Blandford, Hampden, Mass., 600 (636*) B2 97
Blanding, San Juan, Utah, 1,805 .... F6 119
Blandinsville, McDonough, Ill., 853 .... C3 90
Blandville, Ballard, Ky., 133 . A2 94
Blandy, Baldwin, Ga C3 87
Blaney, Kershaw, S.C., 329 .. C6 115
Blanford, Vermilion, Ind., 800 .... E2 91
Blangy-sur-Bresle, Fr., 2,925 .... E9 12
Blankenberge, Bel., 10,199 .. C3 15
Blankenburg, Ger., 19,500 .. B5 17
Blankenfelde, Ger., 6,667 .... A8 17
Blankenheim, Ger., 1,100 .... C1 17
Blanket, Brown, Tex., 320 .. D3 118
Blantyre-Limbe, Malawi, 62,400 .... E5 48
Blarney, Ire., 995 .... F3 11
Blasdell, Erie., N.Y., 3,909 .. C2 108
Blatna, Czech., 3,209 .... D8 16
Blato, Yugo., 5,140 .... D3 22
Blaubeuren, Ger., 7,800 ..... E4 17
Blauvelt, Rockland, N.Y., 3,500 .... *D6 108
Blawenburg, Somerset, N.J., 250 .... C3 106
Blawnox, Allegheny, Pa., 2,085 .... A6 114
Blaye, Fr., 4,291 .... E3 14
Blazon, Lincoln, Wyo D2 125
Blazowa, Pol., 4,002 .... D7 26
Bleckede, Ger., 4,000 .... E4 24
Bleckley, co., Ga., 9,642 ..... D3 87
Bled-Grad, Yugo., 4,120 ..... B1 22
Bledow, Pol g10 26
Bledsoe, Cochran, Tex., 100 .. C1 118
Bledsoe, co., Tenn., 7,811 .... D8 117
Bleecker, Lee, Ala., 175 ..... C4 78
Bleicherode, Ger., 7,923 ..... B5 17
Blekinge, co., Swe., 145,000 . B8 24
Blencoe, Monona, Iowa, 286 . C1 92
Blende, Pueblo, Colo., 600 ... C6 83
Blendecques, Fr., 3,943 ..... D10 12
Blenheim, Ont., Can., 3,151 .. E3 72
Blenheim, Marlboro, S.C., 185 .... B8 115
Blenheim, N.Z., 11,957 ..... N14 51
Blessing, Matagorda, Tex., 700 .... E4 118
Blessington, Ire., 491 .... D5 11
Blevins, Hempstead, Ark., 198 .... D2 81
Blewett, Sask., Can H4 70
Blewett, Uvalde, Tex., 300 .... E3 118
Blida, Alg., 79,223 (93,246*) . B5 44
Blija, Neth., 784 .... A5 15
Blind, pass, Fla F4 86
Blind, riv., La B6 95
Blind River, Ont., Can., 4,093 .... A2 72
Bliss, Gooding, Idaho, 91 .... G4 89
Bliss, Wyoming, N.Y., 500 ... C2 108
Blissfield, Lenawee, Mich., 2,653 .... G7 98
Blitta, Togo E5 45
Blitzen, Harney, Oreg E7 113
Blocher, Scott, Ind., 250 ..... G6 91
Blocker, Pittsburg, Okla., 85 . B6 112
Block, isl., R.I E10 84
Block Island, Washington, R.I., 400 (486*) E10 84
Block Island, sound, N.Y., R.I. . E9 84
Blockton, Taylor, Iowa 343 . D3 92
Blodgett, Scott, Mo., 203 .... D8 101
Blodgett Landing, Merrimack, N.H., 30 .... D2 105
Bloedel, B.C., Can D5 68
Bloemfontein, S. Afr., 112,606 (*145,273) C4 49
Blois, Fr., 33,838 .... D4 14
Blokhus, Den A3 24
Blomberg, Ger., 7,000 .... B4 17
Blönduós, Ice., 599 .... n22 25
Blonie, Pol., 6,416 .... m13 26
Blood, mtn., Ga B3 87
Bloodsworth, isl., Md D5 85
Bloodvein, riv., Man., Can D3 71
Bloody Foreland, pt., Ire B3 11
Bloom, Ford, Kans., 100 ..... E4 93
Bloomdale, Wood, Ohio, 669 .... A4 111
Bloomer, Chippewa, Wis., 2,834 .... C2 124
Bloomfield, Sonoma, Calif., 200 .... B4 82
Bloomfield, Newf., Can., 537 .... *D5 75
Bloomfield, Ont., Can., 803 .. D7 72
Bloomfield, Hartford, Conn., 4,000 (13,613*) B6 84
Bloomfield, Bibb, Ga., 4,381 .... *D3 87
Bloomfield, Greene, Ind., 2,224 .... F4 91
Bloomfield, Davis, Iowa, 2,771 .... D5 92
Bloomfield, Nelson, Ky., 916 .... C4 94
Bloomfield, Stoddard, Mo., 1,330 .... E8 101
Bloomfield, Dawson, Mont., 40 .... C12 102
Bloomfield, Knox, Nebr., 1,349 .... B8 103
Bloomfield, Essex, N.J., 51,867 .... h8 106
Bloomfield, San Juan, N. Mex., 1,292 .... A2 107
Bloomfield, Essex, Vt., 100 (212*) B5 120
Bloomfield Hills, Oakland, Mich., 2,378 .... A7 98
Bloomfield Station, N.B., Can., 68 .... D4 74
Bloomfield Station, P.E.I., Can., 77 .... *C5 74
Bloomfield Village, Oakland, Mich., 3,500 .... *F7 98
Bloomingburg, Fayette, Ohio, 719 .... C4 111
Bloomingdale, Chatham, Ga., 1,000 .... D5 87
Bloomingdale, Du Page, Ill., 1,262 .... E2 90
Bloomingdale, Parke, Ind., 455 .... E3 91
Bloomingdale, Van Buren, Mich., 471 .... F5 98
Bloomingdale, Passaic, N.J., 5,293 .... A4 106
Bloomingdale, Essex, N.Y., 490 .... f10 108
Blooming Grove, Pike, Pa., 250 .... D11 114
Blooming Grove, Navarro, Tex., 725 .... C4 118
Blooming Grove, Dane, Wis., 8,500 .... *E4 124
Blooming Prairie, Steele, Minn., 1,778 .... G5 99
Bloomington, San Bernardino, Calif., 3,500 .... *F3 82
Bloomington, Bear Lake, Idaho, 254 .... G7 89
Bloomington, McLean, Ill., 36,271 .... C5 90
Bloomington, Monroe, Ind., 31,357 .... F4 91
Bloomington, Garrett, Md., 338 .... D1 85
Bloomington, Hennepin, Minn., 50,498 .... F7 99
Bloomington, Franklin, Nebr., 176 .... D6 103
Bloomington, Victoria, Tex., 1,756 .... E4 118
Bloomington, Grant, Wis., 735 .... F3 124
Bloomsburg, Columbia, Pa., 10,655 .... E9 114
Bloomsbury, Hunterdon, N.J., 838 .... B2 106
Bloomsdale, Ste. Genevieve, Mo., 400 .... C7 101
Bloomville, Delaware, N.Y., 250 .... C6 108
Bloomville, Seneca, Ohio, 836 .... A4 111
Blossburg, Jefferson, Ala., 500 .... E4 78
Blossburg, Tioga, Pa., 1,956 . C7 114
Blosseville, coast, Grnld C17 4
Blossom, Lamar, Tex., 545 ... C5 118
Blossom Hill, Lancaster, Pa., 1,000 .... *F9 114
Blount, co., Ala., 25,449 ..... B3 78
Blount, co., Tenn., 57,525 .. D10 117
Blount Springs, Blount, Ala., 50 .... B3 78
Blounts Creek, Beaufort, N.C., 50 .... B7 109
Blountstown, Calhoun, Fla., 2,375 .... B1 86
Blountsville, Blount, Ala., 672 .... A3 78
Blountville, Sullivan, Tenn., 600 .... C11 117
Blovice, Czech., 2,388 .... D8 17
Blowing Rock, Watauga and Caldwell, N.C., 711 .... A2 109
Bloxom, Accomack, Va., 349 . D7 121
Blucher, Sask., Can E2 70
Bludenz, Aus., 11,127 .... E4 16
Blue, Greenlee, Ariz., 10 .... D6 80
Blue, bayou, La E5 95
Blue, creek, Nebr C3 103
Blue, creek, W. Va C6 123
Blue, glacier, Ant e39 5
Blue, hill, Kans C4 93
Blue, hills, Kans C5 93
Blue, mesa, Colo C3 83
Blue, mound, Kans C4 93
Blue, mtn., Ark C1 81
Blue, mtn., N.B., Can B3 74
Blue, mtn., Newf., Can C3 75
Blue, mtn., Maine D2 96
Blue, mtn., Mont C12 102
Blue, mtn., N.H A4 105
Blue, mtn., N. Mex D2 107
Blue, mtn., N.Y B6 108
Blue, mtn., Pa B1 106
Blue, mtn., Pa F6 114
Blue, mts., Austl F8 50
Blue, mts., Oreg C7 113
Blue, mts., Tex D3 118
Blue, mts., Wash C8 122
Blue, pt., N.Y G4 84
Blue, riv., Ind H5 91
Blue, riv., Mo E2 101
Blue, riv., Okla D5 112
Blue Anchor, Camden, N.J., 450 .... D3 106
Blue Ash, Hamilton, Ohio, 8,341 .... D2 111
Blue Bell, Montgomery, Pa., 1,000 .... *F11 114
Bluebell, Duchesne, Utah, 160 .... C5 119
Blueberry, creek, B.C., Can D2 69
Blueberry, riv., B.C., Can A7 68
Blue Buck, pt., La E2 95
Bluecreek, Stevens, Wash., 45 .... A8 122
Blue Creek, Kanawha, W. Va., 310 .... C3, C6 123
Blue Diamond, Clark, Nev., 300 .... G6 104
Blue Earth, Faribault. Minn., 4,200 .... G4 93
Blue Earth, co., Minn., 44,385 .... G4 99
Blue Earth, riv., Iowa, Minn ... A3 92
Blue Eye, Stone, Mo., 75 .... E4 101
Bluefield, Tazewell, Va., 4,235 .... B3 121
Bluefield, Mercer, W. Va., 19,256 .... D3 123
Bluefields, Nic., 11,900 ..... D6 62
Blue Grass, Scott, Iowa, 568 . C7 92
Bluegrass, Knox, Tenn E10 117
Blue Grass, Highlands, Va., 75 .... C3 121
Blue Hill, Hancock, Maine, 500 (1,270*) D4 96
Blue Hill, Webster, Nebr., 723 .... D7 103
Blue Hill, range, Mass h11 97
Blue Hill, range, N.H D4 105
Blue Hill Falls, Hancock, Maine, 100 .... D4 96
Blue Hills, Hartford, Conn., 6,500 .... *B6 84
Blue Hills of Coteau, hills, Newf., Can E3 75
Bluehole, Clay, Ky., 200 ..... C6 94
Blue Island, Cook, Ill., 19,618 .... B6, F3 90
Bluejacket, Craig, Okla., 245 . A6 112
Bluejoint, lake, Oreg E7 113
Blue Lake, Humboldt, Calif., 1,234 .... B2 82
Blue Mound, Macon, Ill., 1,038 .... D4 90
Blue Mound, Linn, Kans., 319 .... D8 93
Blue Mound, Tarrant, Tex., 1,253 .... *B5 118
Blue Mountain, Calhoun, Ala., 446 .... B4 78
Blue Mountain, Logan, Ark., 94 .... B2 81
Blue Mountain, Moffat, Colo., 30 .... A2 83
Blue Mountain, Tippah, Miss., 741 .... A4 100
Blue Mountain, dam and res., Ark B2 81
Blue Mountain Lake, Hamilton, N.Y., 250 .... B6 108
Blue Mud, bay, Austl B6 50
Blue Nile, reg., Sud., 2,069,646 .... C3 47
Bluenose, lake, N.W. Ter., Can C9 66
Blue Pennant, Boone, W. Va., 300 .... D3, D6 123
Blue Point, Suffolk, N.Y., 2,600 .... G4 84
Blue Rapids, Marshall, Kans., 1,426 .... C7 93
Blue Ridge, Alta., Can., 233 .. B3 69
Blue Ridge, Fannin, Ga., 1,406 .... B2 87
Blue Ridge, Shelby, Ind., 150 .... E6 91
Blue Ridge, Botetourt, Va., 900 .... D3 121
Blue Ridge, dam, Ga B2 87
Blue Ridge, lake, Ga B2 87
Blue Ridge, mts., U.S C11 77
Blue Ridge, reg., N.C D2 109
Blue Ridge Summit, Franklin, Pa., 800 .... G7 114
Blue River, B.C., Can., 390 .. C8 68
Blue River, Grant, Wis., 356 . E3 124
Bluesky, Alta., Can., 108 ..... A1 69
Blue Springs, Barbour, Ala., 94 .... D3 78
Blue Springs, Jackson, Mo., 2,555 .... E2 101
Blue Springs, Union, Miss., 99 .... A5 100
Blue Springs, Gage, Nebr., 509 .... D6 103
Blue Stack, mts., Ire C3 11
Bluestem, Lincoln, Wash B7 122
Bluestone, res., W. Va D4 123
Bluestone, riv., W. Va D3 123
Bluevale, Ont., Can., 148 .... D3 72
Bluewater, Valencia, N. Mex., 500 .... B2 107
Bluff, Fayette, Ill., 160 ...... E4 90
Bluff, N.Z., 3,042 .... Q12 51
Bluff, San Juan, Utah, 200 .. F6 119
Bluff, creek, Kans E4 93
Bluff, creek, Kans E6 93
Bluff, creek, Okla A4 112
Bluff, mtn., N.C A1 109
Bluff, mtn., Vt B5 120
Bluff City, Nevada, Ark., 140 . D2 81
Bluff City, Harper, Kans., 152 .... E6 93
Bluff City, Henderson, Ky., 250 .... C2 94
Bluff City, Sullivan, Tenn., 948 .... C11 117
Bluff Creek, res., Okla B4 112
Bluff Dale, Erath, Tex., 400 .. C3 118
Bluff Park, Jefferson, Ala., 3,000 .... *B3 78
Bluffs, Scott, Ill., 779 .... D3 90
Bluffton, Yell, Ark., 50 .... C2 81
Bluffton, Wells, Ind., 6,238 .. C7 91
Bluffton, Otter Tail, Minn., 211 .... D3 99
Bluffton, Allen, Ohio, 2,591 .. B4 111
Bluffton, Beaufort, S.C., 356 . G6 115
Bluford, Jefferson, Ill., 388 ... E5 90
Blumenau, Braz., 46,591 .... D3 56
Blumengard Colony, Faulk, S. Dak., 70 .... B6 116
Blumenhof, Sask., Can., 79 .. G2 70
Blunt, Hughes, S. Dak., 532 . C6 116
Bly, Riverside, Calif., 1,554 . *F3 82
Bly, Klamath, Oreg., 600 .... E5 113
Bly, ridge, Oreg E5 113
Blying, sound, Alsk h17 79
Blyn, Clallam, Wash., 50 .... A3 122
Blyth, Ont., Can., 724 .... D3 72
Blyth, Eng., 36,400 .... C6 10
Blyth, riv., Eng E7 13
Blythe, Riverside, Calif., 6,023 .... F6 82
Blythe, Richmond and Burke, Ga., 172 .... C4 87
Blythedale, Harrison, Mo., 179 .... A4 101
Blytheville, Mississippi, Ark., 25,883 .... B6 81
Blythewood, Richland, S.C., 300 .... C6 115
Bnei Braq, Isr., 51,700 ...... g10 32
Bo, S.L E2 45
Boac, Phil., 3,262 .... C6 35
Boaco, Nic., 3,078 .... D5 62
Boakview, Ont., Can B4 72
Boalsburg, Centre, Pa., 800 . E6 114
Board Camp, Polk, Ark., 70 .. C1 81
Boardman, Mahoning, Ohio, 20,000 .... *A7 111
Boardman, Morrow, Oreg., 153 .... B7 113
Boardmans Bridge, Litchfield, Conn., 200 .... C3 84
Boatland, Fentress, Tenn C8 117
Boa Vista, Braz., 10,592 ..... C5 60
Boaz, Marshall, Ala., 4,654 .. A3 78
Boaz, Richland, Wis., 117 .... E3 124
Bobbili, India, 25,592 .... H9 40
Bobbio, It., 6,970 .... E5 18
Bobcaygeon, Ont., Can., 1,210 .... C6 72
Bobigny, Fr., 37,010 .... g10 14
Böblingen, Ger., 25,400 ..... E4 17
Bobo, Coahoma, Miss., 150 .. A3 100
Bobo-Dioulasso, Upper Volta, 45,000 .... D4 45
Bobov Dol, Bul., 2,627 .... D6 22
Bobr, riv., Pol C3 26
Bobrawa, riv., Ger B10 17
Bobrinets, Sov. Un., 10,000 .. G9 27
Bobrka, Sov. Un., 10,000 .... G5 27
Bobruysk, Sov. Un., 108,000 . E7 27
Bobtown, Greene, Pa., 1,167 . G2 114
Bobures, Ven., 9,397 .... B3 60
Boca Chica, is., Fla H5 86
Boca Chica Central, P.R D4 65
Boca Ciega, bay, Fla E1 86
Bôca do Acre, Braz., 2,994 .. C4 58
Boca Grande, Lee, Fla., 400 .. F4 86
Bocaiúva, Braz., 5,952 .... E2 57
Bocaranga, Cen. Afr. Rep D3 46
Boca Raton, Palm Beach, Fla., 6,961 .... F6 86
Bocas del Toro, Pan., 2,459 .. F6 62
Bocay, Nic C5 62
Boccea (Buxus), It h8 21
Bochnia, Pol., 11,000 .... D6 26
Bocholt, Ger., 46,300 .... B1 17
Bochov, Czech., 1,084 .... C8 17
Bochum, Ger., 360,000 ...... B2 17
Bock, Mille Lacs, Minn., 91 .. E5 99
Bockhorn, Ger., 7,100 .... E2 24
Bockum-Hövel, Ger., 24,300 .. B2 17
Boda, Cen. Afr. Rep E3 46
Bodafors, Swe., 2,500 .... A8 24
Bodaybo, Sov. Un., 14,700 .... D14 28
Bodcau, creek, Ark D2 81
Bodcaw, Nevada, Ark., 100 .. D2 81
Boddam, Scot C7 13
Bode, Humboldt, Iowa, 430 .. B3 92
Bode, riv., Ger B6 17
Bodega, head, Calif C2 82
Bodele, reg., Afr B3 42
Boden, Mercer, Ill B3 90
Boden, Swe., 13,700 .... E9 25
Bodenham, Giles, Tenn B4 117
Bodensee (Constance), lake, Ger., Switz A7 19
Boderg, lake, Ire D3 11
Bodhia, mtn., Eg., U.A.R E5 32
Bodie, isl., N.C B8 109
Bodine, mtn., B.C., Can B5 68
Bodines, Lycoming, Pa., 90 .... D8 114
Bodkin, pt., Md B5 85
Bodmin, Eng., 6,209 .... D3 12
Bodmin, moor, Eng D3 12
Bodo, Alta., Can., 40 .... C5 69
Bodö, Nor., 12,700 .... D6 25
Bodrog, riv., Hung A5 22
Bodrum (Halicarnassus), Tur., 5,000 .... D6 31
Bodva, riv., Hung A5 22
Boelus (Howard City), Howard, Nebr., 181 .... C7 103
Boende, Con. L B3 48
Boeotia (Voiotia), prov., Grc., 114,256 .... *C4 23
Boerne, Kendall, Tex., 2,169 .... A3, E3 118
Boeuf, bayou, La C3 95
Boeuf, lake, La E5 95
Boeuf, riv., Ark., La .. D4 81, B4 95
Boffa, Guinea, 1,000 .... D2 45
Bogale, Bur., 23,211 .... E10 39
Bogallua, isl., Eniwetok 52
Bogalusa, Washington, La., 21,423 .... D6 95
Bogan, isl., Eniwetok 52
Bogan, riv., Austl E6 51
Bogandé, Upper Volta D4 45
Bogard, Carroll, Mo., 277 .. B4 101
Bogart, Clark and Oconee, Ga., 403 .... C3 87
Bogata, Red River, Tex., 1,112 .... C5 118
Bog Brook, res., N.Y D2 84
Bogatynia, Pol., 2,851 .... C9 17
Bogbonga, Con. L A2 48
Bogen, Ger., 3,200 .... E7 17
Bogenfels, S.W. Afr C2 49
Bogense, Den., 2,968 .... C4 24
Boger City, Lincoln, N.C., 2,200 .... *B2 109
Boggeragh, mts., Ire E3 11
Boggerik, isl., Kwajalein 52
Boghari, Alg., 10,166 (11,518*) B5 44
Boghé, Maur., 1,200 .... C2 45
Bogno, Switz., 145 .... D7 19
Bognor Regis, Eng., 28,144 .. D7 12
Bogo, Phil., 6,371 .... *C6 35
Bogodukhov, Sov. Un., 10,000 .... F10 27
Bogon, isl., Eniwetok 52
Bogor (Buitenzorg), Indon., 146,907 .... G3 35
Bogoroditsk, Sov. Un., 10,000 .... E12 27
Bogorodsk, Sov. Un., 36,200 . C14 27
Bogotá, Col., 1,188,000 (*1,350,000) C3 60
Bogota, Bergen, N.J., 7,965 .. h8 106
Bogota, Dyer, Tenn., 250 .... A2 117
Bogotol, Sov. Un., 25,000 .. D26 9
Bogra, Pak., 25,303 .... E12 40
Boguchany, Sov. Un., 10,000 .... D28 9
Bogue, Graham, Kans., 234 .. C4 93
Bogue Chitto, Lincoln, Miss., 400 .... D3 100
Bogue Chitto, riv., La., Miss D5 95, D3 100
Bogue Phalia, riv., Miss B3 100
Boguslav, Sov. Un., 10,000 .. G8 27
Bohain-en-Vermandois, Fr., 6,726 .... E3 15
Boharm, Sask., Can G3 70
Bohemia, Suffolk, N.Y., 3,000 .... *G4 84
Bohemia (Čechy), reg., Czech., 6,035,500 .... D3 26
Bohemian Forest, mts., Ger D7 17
Bohemian-Moravian, highlands, Czech D3 26
Böhme, riv., Ger F3 24
Bohmte, Ger., 4,000 .... A3 17
Bohodle, Som D6 47
Bohol, prov., Phil., 602,500 . *D6 35
Bohol, isl., Phil D6 35
Boice, Wayne, Miss., 30 ..... D5 100
Boiestown, N.B., Can., 343 .. C3 74
Boiling Springs, Cleveland, N.C., 1,311 .... B2 109
Boiling Springs, Cumberland, Pa., 1,182 .... F7 114
Bois, lake, N.W. Ter., Can C8 66
Bois Blanc, isl., Mich C6 98
Boischatel, Que., Can., 1,576 .... C6, n17 73
Bois-Colombes, Fr., 29,938 .. g10 14
Boisdale, N.S., Can., 179 .... C9 74
Boisdale, inlet, Scot C1 13
Bois D'Arc, Greene, Mo., 152 .... D4 101
Bois-des-Filion, Que., Can., 2,499 .... p19 73
Bois de Sioux, riv., Minn E2 99
Boise, Ada, Idaho, 34,481 .... F2 89
Boise, co., Idaho, 1,646 ...... F3 89
Boise City, Cimarron, Okla., 1,978 .... D2 112
Boise, riv., Idaho F2, F3 89
Boissevain, Man., Can., 1,303 . E1 71
Boissevain, Tazewell, Va., 600 .... B3 121
Boizenburg, Ger., 11,600 .... E4 24
Bojador, cape, Sp. Sahara D1 44
Bojnūrd, Iran, 15,293 .... C8 41
Bokanda, I.C E4 45
Bokchito, Bryan, Okla., 620 .. C5 112
Bokeelia, Lee, Fla., 150 ...... F4 86

Boké, Guinea, 5,400 D2 45
Boko, Con. L C2 48
Bokobyaadaa, isl., Bikini 52
Bokoro, Chad, 1,739 C3 46
Bokororyuru, isl., Bikini 52
Bokoshe, Le Flore, Okla., 431 B7 112
Boksburg, S. Afr., 71,029 *C4 49
Bokungu, Con. L B3 48
Bol, Chad, 1,073 C2 46
Bolafa, Con. L A3 48
Boland, riv., Ont., Can B8 98
Bolanos, mtn., Guam 52
Bolaños, riv., Mex m12 63
Bolar, Bath, Va., 45 C3 121
Bolbec, Fr., 12,212 C4 14
Bolckow, Andrew, Mo., 232 A3 101
Bolding, Union, Ark., 75 D3 81
Bole, Ghana, 1,813 E4 45
Boleko, Con. L B2 48
Boles, Scott, Ark., 120 C1 81
Boles, Otero, N. Mex., 300 *E3 107
Boleslawiec, Pol., 23,000 C3 26
Boley, Okfuskee, Okla., 573 B5 112
Bolgrad, Sov. Un., 10,000 I7 27
Boli, see Bolu, Tur.
Bolia, Con. L B2 48
Boligee, Greene, Ala., 134 C1 78
Bolinao, Phil., 2,041 n12 35
Bolinao, cape, Phil n12 35
Boling, Wharton, Tex., 950 E5, G4 118
Bolinger, Choctaw, Ala., 200 D1 78
Bolívar, Arg., 14,010 B4 54
Bolívar, Col., 6,121 B2 60
Bolivar, Polk, Mo., 3,512 D4 101
Bolivar, Allegany, N.Y., 1,405 C2 108
Bolivar, Tuscarawas, Ohio, 932 B6 111
Bolivar, Westmoreland, Pa., 716 F3 114
Bolívar, Peru C2 58
Bolivar, Hardeman, Tenn., 3,338 B3 117
Bolivar, Jefferson, W. Va., 754 B7 123
Bolivar, co., Miss., 54,464 B3 100
Bolívar, dept., Col., 737,890 B2 60
Bolívar, prov., Ec., 123,205 B2 58
Bolívar, state, Ven., 213,543 B4 60
Bolivar, lake, Miss B2 100
Bolivar (La Columna), peak, Ven B3 60
Bolivia, Brunswick, N.C., 201 C5 109
Bolivia, country, S.A., 3,675,000 E4 53, C2 55
Bolkhov, Sov. Un., 10,000 E11 27
Bollebygd, Swe., 708 A6 24
Bollène, Fr., 9,276 E6 14
Bolling, Butler, Ala., 200 D3 78
Bollingen, Switz., 14,914 C4 19
Bollinger, co., Mo., 9,167 D7 101
Bollnäs, Swe., 10,679 (16,699▲) G7 25
Bollullos, Sp., 10,947 D2 20
Bolmen, lake, Swe B7 24
Bolnisi, Sov. Un., 6,065 B15 31
Bolobo, Con. L B2 48
Bologna, It., 475,700 E7 18, B3 21
Bologoye, Sov. Un., 22,000 C10 27
Bolomba, Con. L A2 48
Bolon, lake, Sov. Un B8 37
Bolotnoye, Sov. Un., 26,500 B10 29
Bolovens, plat., Laos E7 38
Bolsena, lake, It C3 21
Bolshaya Boktybay, mtn., Sov. Un D5 29
Bolshaya Irgiz, riv., Sov. Un C3 29
Bolshaya Lepetikha, Sov. Un., 5,000 H9 27
Bolshaya Uzen, riv., Sov. Un D3 29
Bolshaya Viska, Sov. Un., 10,000 G8 27
Bolshaya Yugan, riv., Sov. Un B8 29
Bolsheretsk, Sov. Un. D35 4
Bolshevik, isl., Sov. Un B4 4
Bolshoya Hamenka, riv., Sov. Un q22 27
Bolshoy Tokmak, Sov. Un., 10,000 H10 27
Bolsward, Neth., 8,300 A5 15
Bolton, Ont., Can., 2,104 D5 72
Bolton, Tolland, Conn., 250 (3,300▲) *B6 84
Bolton, Eng., 159,800 A5 12
Bolton, Worcester, Mass., 175 (1,264▲) B4, g9 97
Bolton, Hinds, Miss., 797 C3 100
Bolton, Columbus, N.C., 617 C5 109
Bolton, Chittenden, Vt., 75 (237▲) C3 120
Bolton, lake, Man., Can B4 71
Bolton, lake, Conn B7 84
Bolton, riv., Man., Can B4 71
Bolton Center, Tolland, Conn., 500 B7 84
Bolton Landing, Warren, N.Y., 900 B7 108
Boltonville, Orange, Vt., 25 C4 120
Bolu, Tur., 13,700 B8 31
Bolus, head, Ire F1 11
Bolvadin, Tur., 16,100 C8 31
Bolzano, It., 93,700 A3 21
Boma, Con. L., 31,500 C1 48
Bomarton, Baylor, Tex., 100 C3 118
Bomba, Libya F4 31
Bombala, Austl., 1,389 H7 51
Bombay, India, 4,152,056 (★4,300,000) E5 39, H4 40
Bombay, Franklin, N.Y., 400 f10 108
Bombay Hook, isl., Del B7 85
Bombetoka, bay, Malag g9 49
Bomboma, Con. L A2 48
Bom Conselho, Braz., 6,840 C3, k5 57
Bom Despacho, Braz., 13,568 E1 57
Bom Jardim, Braz., 1,894 g5 56
Bom Jardim, Braz., 2,500 h6 57
Bom Jesus, Braz., 1,431 C2 57
Bom Jesus da Lapa, Braz., 6,107 D2 57
Bomokandi, riv., Con. L A4 48
Bomongo, Con. L A2 48
Bomoseen, Rutland, Vt., 200 D2 120
Bomoseen (P.O.), Rutland, Vt., 400 D2 120
Bomoseen, lake, Vt D2 120
Bomu, riv., Cen. Afr. Rep., Con. L A3 48
Bon, cape, Tun B7 44
Bonabéri, Cam., 13,268 *E1 46
Bon-Accord, Alta., Can., 175 C4 69
Bonaigarh, India G10 40
Bon Air, Talladega, Ala., 297 B3 78
Bon Air, Delaware, Pa., 1,000 *G11 114
Bon Air, White, Tenn., 200 D8 117
Bon Air, Chesterfield, Va., 1,500 C7 121
Bonaire, Houston, Ga., 200 D3 87
Bonaire, isl., Neth. Antilles A4 60
Bonanza, Sebastian, Ark., 247 B1 81
Bonanza, Saguache, Col., 19 C4 83
Bonanza, Klamath, Oreg., 297 E5 113
Bonanza, Uintah, Utah, 150 C6 119
Bonanza, peak, Wash A5 122
Bonaparte, Van Buren, Iowa, 574 D6 92
Bonaparte, lake, B.C., Can D7 68
Bonaparte, mtn., Wash A6 122
Bonaparte, riv., B.C., Can D7 68
Bon Aqua, Hickman, Tenn., 150 B4 117
Boñar, Sp., 3,682 A3 20
Bonar Bridge, Scot C4 13
Bonarlaw, Ont., Can C7 72
Bonaventure, Que., Can., 804 *k13 73
Bonaventure, co., Que., Can., 42,962 A3 74
Bonavista, Newf., Can., 4,186 D5 75
Bonavista, bay, Newf., Can D5 75
Bonavista, cape, Newf., Can D5 75
Bond, Eagle, Colo., 150 B4 83
Bond, Jackson, Ky., 600 C5 94
Bond, Stone, Miss., 250 E4 100
Bond, co., Ill., 14,060 E4 90
Bondeno, It., 6,000 E7 18
Bondo, Con. L A3 48
Bondoukou, I.C., 5,100 E4 45
Bondsville, Hampden and Hampshire, Mass., 1,000 B3 97
Bonduel, Shawano, Wis., 876 D5 124
Bondurant, Polk, Iowa, 389 A7, C4 92
Bondurant, Sublette, Wyo., 35 B2 125
Bondville, Bennington, Vt., 100 E3 120
Bondy, Fr., 38,039 g10 14
Bône, Alg., 137,716 (164,844▲) F10 30, B6 44
Bone, gulf, Indon F6 35
Bone, lake, Wis C1 124
Bone Cave, Van Buren, Tenn., 50 D8 117
Bone Gap, Edwards, Ill., 245 E5 90
Bonesteel, Gregory, S. Dak., 452 D7 116
Bonetrail, Williams, N. Dak., 7 A2 110
Bonfield, Ont., Can., 714 A5 72
Bonfouca, St. Tammany, La., 60 B8 95
Bongā, Eth D4 47
Bongandanga, Con. L A3 48
Bongor, Chad C3 46
Bong Son, Viet E8 38
Bonham, Fannin, Tex., 7,357 C4 118
Bon Homme, co., S. Dak., 9,229 D8 116
Bon Homme Colony, Bon Homme, S. Dak., 100 E8 116
Bonidee, bayou, La B4 95
Bonifacio, Fr., 1,895 D2 21
Bonifacio, strait, It D2 21
Bonifay, Holmes, Fla., 2,222 G3 86
Bonilla, Beadle, S. Dak., 75 C7 116
Bonin (Ogasawara) Islands, U.S. occ., Asia, 200 E8 7
Bonita, Graham, Ariz., 10 E6 80
Bonita, San Diego, Calif., 2,000 *E2 82
Bonita, Morehouse, La., 574 B4 95
Bonita, Lauderdale, Miss., 500 C5 100
Bonita Springs, Lee, Fla., 356 F5 86
Bonito, Braz., 5,427 k6 57
Bonlee, Chatham, N.C., 300 B4 109
Bonn, Ger., 143,000 (★285,000) C2 17
Bonne, bay, Newf., Can D2 75
Bonneau, Berkeley, S.C., 402 E8 121
Bonner, Missoula, Mont., 400 D3 102
Bonner, co., Idaho, 15,587 A2 89
Bonnerdale, Hot Spring, Ark., 40 C2 81
Bonners Ferry, Boundary, Idaho, 1,921 A2 89
Bonner Springs, Wyandotte, Kans., 3,171 B8, C9 93
Bønnerup Strand, Den B4 24
Bonnétable, Fr., 2,435 C4 14
Bonnet Carre, spillway and floodway, La B7 95
Bonne Terre, St. Francois, Mo., 3,219 D7 101
Bonneville, Fr., 2,913 C2 18
Bonneville, Mulnomah, Oreg., 150 B5 113
Bonneville, Fremont, Wyo., 50 B4 125
Bonneville, co., Idaho, 46,906 F7 89
Bonneville, dam, Oreg., Wash B4 113, D4 122
Bonneville, peak, Idaho G6 89
Bonney Lake, Pierce, Wash., 645 B3 122
Bonnie, Jefferson, Ill., 215 E5 90
Bonnie Doone, Cumberland, N.C., 4,481 *B5 109
Bonnieville, Hart, Ky., 376 C4 94
Bonnots Mill, Osage, Mo., 210 C6 101
Bonny, Nig., 8,690 F6 45
Bonny, res., Colo B8 83
Bonny Blue, Lee, Va., 504 B2 121
Bonnyville, Alta., Can., 1,736 B5 69
Bono, Craighead, Ark., 339 B5 81
Bono, Lawrence, Ind., 75 G5 91
Bono, Lucas, Ohio, 450 A4 111
Bonorva, It., 6,669 D2 21
Bonsal, Wake, N.C., 100 B5 109
Bon Secour, Baldwin, Ala., 600 E2 78
Bonsecours, Que., Can., 224 D5 73
Bonshaw, P.E.I., Can., 214 C6 74
Bonsucesso, Braz m7 56
Bontang, Indon E5 35
Bonthain, Indon, 6,711 G5 35
Bonthe, S.L., 4,404 E2 45
Bontoc, Phil., 4,471 *B6 35
Bon Wier, Newton, Tex., 350 D6 118
Book, Catahoula, La., 20 C4 95
Book, cliffs, Colo B1 83
Book, cliffs, Utah D6 119
Booker, Lipscomb and Ochiltree, Tex., 817 A2 118
Booker T. Washington, nat. mon., Va D13 121
Booligal, Austl., 26 F5 51
Boolyglass, Ire E4 11
Boom, Pickett, Tenn., 50 C8 117
Boomer, Fayette, W. Va., 1,657 C3, D6 123
Boon, Wexford, Mich., 150 D5 98
Boone, Pueblo, Colo., 548 C6 83
Boone, Boone, Iowa, 12,468 B4 92
Boone, Boone, Nebr., 60 C8 103
Boone, Watauga, N.C., 3,686 A2 109
Boone, Norfolk, Va., 30 B6 121
Boone, co., Ark., 16,116 A2 81
Boone, co., Ill., 20,326 A5 90
Boone, co., Ind., 27,543 D4 91
Boone, co., Iowa, 28,037 B9 92
Boone, co., Ky., 21,940 B5 94
Boone, co., Mo., 55,202 B5 101
Boone, co., Nebr., 9,134 C7 103
Boone, co., W. Va., 28,764 C3 123
Boone, riv., Iowa B4 92
Boone Grove, Porter, Ind., 175 B3 91
Boones Mill, Franklin, Va., 371 D3 121
Booneville, Logan, Ark., 2,690 B2 75
Booneville, Owsley, Ky., 143 C6 94
Booneville, Prentiss, Miss., 3,480 A5 100
Boons, pond, Mass g10 97
Boonsboro, Washington, Md., 1,211 A2 85
Boon Terrace, Washington, Pa., 1,100 *F1 114
Boonton, Morris, N.J., 7,981 B4 106
Boonville, Mendocino, Calif., 950 C2 82
Boonville, Warrick, Ind., 4,801 H3 91
Boonville, Cooper, Mo., 7,090 C5 101
Boonville, Oneida, N.Y., 2,403 B5 108
Boonville, Yadkin, N.C., 539 A3 109
Boot, Eng F5 13
Booth, Autauga, Ala., 250 C3 78
Boothbay, Lincoln, Maine, 600 (1,617▲) E3 96
Boothbay Harbor, Lincoln, Maine, 1,850 (2,252▲) E3 96
Boothby, cape, Ant C18 5
Boothia, gulf, N.W. Ter., Can B14 66
Boothia, pen., N.W. Ter., Can B13 66
Booths, creek, W. Va A7 123
Boothspoint, Dyer, Tenn., 30 A2 117
Boothville, Plaquemines, La., 550 E6 95
Boothwyn, Delaware, Pa., 5,000 *G11 114
Bootle, Eng., 83,300 A4 12
Booué, Gabon E2 46
Boporo, Lib E2 45
Boppard, Ger., 8,600 C2 17
Boque, inlet, N.C C6 109
Boquerón, P.R C2 65
Boqueron, dept., Par., 28,082 D3 55
Boqueron, pass, Peru C2 58
Boquerón, riv., Pan k11 62
Boquete, Pan., 2,611 F6 62
Bor, Sov. Un., 31,700 D17 9
Bor, Sud., 1,632 D3 47
Bor, Yugo., 18,612 C6 22
Borah, peak, Idaho E5 89
Borama, Som C5 47
Borama, dist., Som C5 47
Borås, Swe., 68,000 A6 24, I5 25
Borāzjān, Iran, 8,543 G5 46
Borba, Braz., 1,304 C3 59
Borborema, plat., Braz h5 57
Borculo, Neth., 2,596 B6 15
Bordeaux, Fr., 249,688 (★480,000) E3 14
Bordeaux, Davidson, Tenn., 500 E9 117
Bordeaux, Thurston, Wash C2 122
Borden, Sask., Can., 208 E2 70
Borden (New Providence), Clark, Ind., 327 H6 91
Borden, co., Tex., 1,076 C2 118
Borden, isl., N.W. Ter., Can m29 67
Borden, pen., N.W. Ter., Can B16 66
Borden Springs, Cleburne, Ala., 500 B4 78
Bordentown, Burlington, N.J., 4,974 C3 106
Border, Lincoln, Wyo C2 125
Borderland, Mingo, W. Va., 300 D2 123
Bordertown, Austl., 1,546 H3 51
Bordighera, It., 8,621 C1 21
Bordj Amquid, Alg D6 44
Bordj Flamand, Alg D5 44
Bordj Fouchet, Alg D3 44
Bordj-Ménaïel, Alg., 27,920 *B5 44
Bordj Ouallen, Alg E5 44
Bordj Viollette, Alg D4 44
Bordley, Union, Ky., 150 C2 94
Bordulac, Foster, N. Dak., 200 B7 110
Bordzon, Mong C1 36
Boré, Mali C4 45
Boren, lake, Swe u33 25
Borensberg, Swe., 1,230 u33 25
Borg, mtn., Ant B12 5
Borgå, Fin., 11,800 G11 25
Börger, Ger., 1,700 B7 15
Borger, Neth., 1,411 B6 15
Borger, Hutchinson, Tex., 20,911 B2 118
Borgholm, Swe., 2,500 I7 25
Borghorst, Ger., 15,500 A2 17
Borgne, lake, La D6 95
Borgne, riv., Switz D3 19
Borgomanero, It., 7,900 B2 21
Borgo Piave, It k9 21
Borgo Val di Taro, It., 11,809 B2 21
Borgo Valsugana, It., 5,141 C7 18
Borikhane, Laos C5 38
Borinquen, P.R B2 65
Borislav, Sov. Un., 47,500 G4 27
Borisoglebsk, Sov. Un., 57,000 C2 29
Borisov, Sov. Un., 65,000 D7 27
Borispol, Sov. Un., 25,000 F8 27
Borja, Sp., 4,381 B5 20
Borjas Blancas, Sp., 5,082 B6 20
Borken, Ger., 12,300 B1 17
Borken, Ger., 4,300 B4 17
Børkop, Den., 1,051 C3 24
Borkou, reg., Chad B3 46
Borkum, Ger., 5,800 A6 15
Borkum, isl., Ger B3 16
Borlänge, Swe., 26,700 G6 25
Bormes, Fr., 772 F7 14
Bormida, riv., It E4 18
Bormio, It., 3,293 C6 18
Borna, Ger., 17,800 B7 17
Borne, Neth., 9,800 B6 15
Borneo, North, see Sabah, state, Mala.
Borneo (Kalimantan), isl., Asia E4 35
Bornheim, Ger., 12,000 C2 17
Bornholm, co., Den., 48,632 C8 24
Bornholm, isl., Den C8 24
Bor Nor, lake, China B8 34
Bornos, Sp., 8,697 D3 20
Boromlya, Sov. Un., 10,000 F10 27
Boromo, Upper Volta D4 45
Boron, Kern, Calif., 950 E5 82
Borongan, Phil., 2,965 *C7 35
Borovan, Bul., 5,905 D6 22
Borovichi, Sov. Un., 47,100 B9 27
Borovsk, Sov. Un., 31,200 D20 9
Borovskoye, Sov. Un., 5,000 q21 27
Borrby, Swe., 1,139 C8 24
Borre, Den D6 24
Borrego Springs, San Diego, Calif F5 82
Borris, Ire., 413 E5 11
Borrisokane, Ire., 750 E3 11
Borrisoleigh, Ire., 465 E4 11
Borroloola, Austl C6 50
Borsod-Abauj-Zemplen, co., Hung., 583,001 *A5 22
Bort-les-Orgues, Fr., 5,115 E5 14
Boruca, C.R., 682 F6 62
Borūjerd, Iran, 49,186 E4 41
Borup, Norman, Minn., 145 C2 99
Borzhomi, Sov. Un., 8,218 B14 25
Borzna, Sov. Un., 10,000 F9 27
Borzonasca, It., 3,985 E5 18
Bosa, It., 8,169 D2 21
Bosanska Dubica, Yugo., 6,253 C3 22
Bosanska Gradiska, Yugo., 6,373 C3 22
Bosanska Kostajnica, Yugo., 2,037 C3 22
Bosanski Novi, Yugo., 7,082 C3 22
Bosanski Petrovac, Yugo., 3,374 C3 22
Bosanski Samac, Yugo., 3,607 C4 22
Bosaso, Som., 5,200 C6 47
Boscawen, Merrimack, N.H., 350 (2,181▲) D3 105
Bosco, Ouachita, La., 100 B3 95
Boscobel, Grant, Wis., 2,608 E3 124
Bosdagan, Tur., 3,842 D7 23
Boshrūyeh, Iran E8 41
Boskovice, Czech., 6,396 D4 26
Bosler, Albany, Wyo., 75 D7 125
Bosna, riv., Yugo C3 22
Bosnek, W. Irian, 4,500 F9 35
Bosnia, reg., Yugo C3 22
Bosnia-Hercegovina, rep., Yugo., 3,274,886 *C3 22
Bosobolo, Con. L A2 48
Bosporus, strait, Tur B7 31
Bosque, Valencia, N. Mex., 10 C3 107
Bosque, co., Tex., 10,809 D4 118
Bossangoa, Cen. Afr. Rep D3 46
Bossembélé, Cen. Afr. Rep D3 46
Bossier, Bossier, La., 32,776 B2 95
Bossier, par., La., 57,622 B2 95
Bosso, Niger D7 45
Boston, Eng., 25,000 B7 12
Boston, Thomas, Ga., 1,357 F3 87
Boston, Wayne, Ind., 240 E8 91
Boston, Suffolk, Mass., 697,197 (★3,372,800) B5, g11 97
Boston, Summit, Ohio, 400 B2 111
Boston, Allegheny, Pa., 2,300 *F2 114
Boston, bay, Mass B6 97
Boston, mts., Ark B2 81
Boston, mts., Okla B7 112
Boston Bar, B.C., Can., 629 E7 68
Boston Heights, Summit, Ohio, 831 B2 111
Bostonnais, riv., Que., Can B5 73
Bostwick, Putnam, Fla., 400 C5 86
Bostwick, Morgan, Ga., 272 C3 87
Bostwick, Nuckolls, Nebr., 50 D7 103
Boswarlos, Newf., Can., 404 D2 75
Boswell, Izard, Ark., 10 A3 81
Boswell, B.C., Can., 100 E9 68
Boswell, Benton, Ind., 957 C3 91
Boswell, Choctaw, Okla., 753 C6 112
Boswell, Somerset, Pa., 1,508 F3 114
Bosworth, Carroll, Mo., 465 B4 101
Botany, bay, Austl F9 50
Botetourt, co., Va., 16,715 D3 121
Botev, peak, Bul D7 22
Botevgrad, Bul., 5,925 D6 22
Botha, Alta., Can., 112 C4 69
Bothell, King, Wash., 2,237 B3 122
Bothnia, gulf, Eur F9 25
Bothwell, Ont., Can., 819 E3 72
Bothwell, P.E.I., Can., 63 C7 74
Bothwell, Box Elder, Utah, 302 B3 119
Botiala, Som C6 47
Botijas, P.R C5 65
Botkinburg, Van Buren, Ark., 175 B3 81
Botkins, Shelby, Ohio, 854 B3 111
Botkyrka, Swe., 4,348 t35 25
Botlelte, riv., Bech B3 49
Botolan, Phil., 1,963 o13 35
Botoşani, Rom., 29,569 B8 22
Botsford, Fairfield, Conn., 150 D3 84
Bottineau, Bottineau, N. Dak., 2,613 A5 110
Bottineau, co., N. Dak., 11,315 A4 110
Bottrop, Ger., 112,000 B1 17
Botucatu, Braz., 33,878 C3, m7 56
Botwood, Newf., Can., 3,680 D4 75
Bouaflé, I.C., 1,700 E3 45
Bouaké, I.C., 45,000 E3 45
Bouar, Cen. Afr. Rep., 20,700 D3 46
Bouarfa, Mor., 8,775 C4 44
Boucau, Fr., 5,400 F3 14
Boucher, lake, Que., Can C2 75
Boucherville, Que., Can., 8,182 D4, p20 73
Bouches-du-Rhône, dept., Fr., 1,248,355 *F6 14
Bouchette, Que., Can., 464 C2 73
Boudenib, Mor C4 44
Bou Djébena, Mali C4 45
Boudreaux, lake, La E5 95
Boudry, Switz., 3,086 C2 19
Boufarik, Alg., 23,024 *B5 44
Bougainville, isl., Solomon Is G9 7
Bougaroun, cape, Alg F10 30
Bougie, Alg., 62,921 B6 44
Bougival, Fr., 7,296 g9 14
Bougouni, Mali, 3,100 D3 45
Bouillon, Bel., 3,017 E5 15
Boulder, Austl., 5,773 F3 51
Boulder, Boulder, Colo., 37,718 A5 83
Boulder, Jefferson, Mont., 1,394 D4 102
Boulder, Garfield, Utah, 108 F4 119
Boulder, Sublette, Wyo., 30 C3 125
Boulder, co., Colo., 74,254 A5 83
Boulder City, Clark, Nev., 4,059 H7 104
Boulder Creek, Santa Cruz, Calif., 1,306 C5 82
Boulevard, San Diego, Calif., 25 F5 82
Boulevard Heights, Prince Georges, Md., 750 C2 85
Boulloum (Well), Niger C7 45
Boulogne-Billancourt, Fr., 106,641 C5, g9 14
Boulogne-sur-Mer, Fr., 49,281 (★98,000) D9 12, B4 14
Boulsa, Upper Volta D4 45
Boumalne, Mor C3 44
Bouna, I.C., 2,300 E4 45
Boundary, Alsk., 10 C11 79
Boundary, co., Idaho, 5,809 A2 89
Boundary, peak, Nev F3 104
Bound Brook, Somerset, N.J., 10,263 B3 106
Boundiali, I.C., 2,800 E3 45
Bountiful, Davis, Utah, 17,039 C4 119
Bounty, Sask., Can., 87 F2 70
Bounty, is., Pac. O J11 7
Bourbeuse, riv., Mo C6 101
Bourbon, Marshall, Ind., 1,522 B5 91
Bourbon, Crawford, Mo., 779 C6 101
Bourbon, co., Kans., 16,090 E9 93
Bourbon, co., Ky., 18,178 B5 94
Bourbonnais, Kankakee, Ill., 3,336 B6 90
Bourbonnais, former prov., Fr., 318,000 D5 14
Bourbonne-les-Bains, Fr., 2,617 A1 18
Bourem, Mali, 1,700 C4 45
Bourg, Terrebonne, La., 900 E5 95
Bourg-Bruche, Fr., 444 A3 18
Bourg-de-Péage, Fr., 7,804 E6 14
Bourg [-en-Bresse], Fr., 32,596 D6 14
Bourges, Fr., 60,632 D5 14
Bourget, Ont., Can., 769 B9 72
Bourget, lake, Fr D1 18
Bourg-la-Reine, Fr., 17,694 g10 14
Bourgoin, Fr., 9,240 E6 14
Bourg-St.-Andéol, Fr., 3,152 E6 14
Bourg-St. Maurice, Fr., 2,666 D2 18
Bourjeïmat (Well), Maur C1 45
Bourke, Austl., 3,001 E5 51
Bourlamaque, Que., Can., 3,344 *k11 73
Bourne, Eng., 5,339 B7 12
Bourne, Barnstable, Mass., 400 (14,011▲) C6 97
Bournemouth, Eng., 150,700 (★280,000) D6 12
Bourneville, Ross, Ohio, 275 C4 111
Bou Saâda, Alg., 11,661 B5 44
Bouse, Yuma, Ariz., 150 D2 80
Bousso, Chad, 2,573 C3 46
Boutaiha, Syr B7 32
Boutilimit, Maur C2 45
Boutte, St. Charles, La., 155 C6 95
Bouvet, isl., Nor. (Atl. O.) D13 5
Bovey, Itasca, Minn., 1,086 C5 99
Bovill, Latah, Idaho, 357 C2 89
Bovina, Lincoln, Colo., 25 B7 85
Bovina, Warren, Miss., 25 C3 100
Bovina, Parmer, Tex., 1,029 B1 181
Bovina Center, Delaware, N.Y., 250 C6 108
Bow, Merrimack, N.H., 300 (1,340▲) D3 105
Bow, lake, N.H D4 105
Bow, riv., Alta., Can D4 69
Bowbells, Burke, N. Dak., 687 A3 110
Bowden, Alta., Can., 437 D4 69
Bowden, Creek, Okla., 35 A5 112
Bowdens, Duplin, N.C., 300 B5 109
Bowdle, Edmunds, S. Dak., 678 B6 116
Bowdoin, Sagadahoc, Maine, 75 (668▲) D6 96
Bowdoinham, Sagadahoc, Maine, 375 (1,131▲) D3, D6 96
Bowdon, Carroll, Ga., 1,548 C1 87
Bowdon, Wells, N. Dak., 259 B6 110
Bowen, Austl., 5,160 C8 50
Bowen, Hancock, Ill., 559 C2 90
Bowens Mill, Ben Hill, Ga., 25 E3 87
Bowers, Kent, Del., 324 B7 85
Bowers, coulee, Wash B7 122
Bowers Hill, Norfolk, Va., 800 B6 121
Bowerston, Harrison, Ohio, 463 B6 111
Bowersville, Hart, Ga., 293 B3 87
Bowersville, Greene, Ohio, 327 C4 111
Bowesmont, Pembina, N. Dak., 175 A8 110
Bowie, Cochise, Ariz., 500 E6 80
Bowie, Delta, Colo., 100 C3 83
Bowie, Prince Georges, Md., 1,072 B4 85
Bowie, Montague, Tex., 4,566 C4 118
Bowie, co., Tex., 59,971 C5 118
Bowie, creek, Miss D4 100
Bow Island, Alta., Can., 1,122 E5 69
Bowlegs, Seminole, Okla., 200 B5 112
Bowler, Shawano, Wis., 274 D5 124
Bowling Green, Hardee, Fla., 1,171 E5 86
Bowling Green, Clay, Ind., 229 F3 91
Bowling Green, Warren, Ky., 28,338 D3 94
Bowling Green, Pike, Mo., 2,650 B6 101
Bowling Green, Wood, Ohio, 13,574 A2, A4 111
Bowling Green, York, S.C., 700 A5 115
Bowling Green, Caroline, Va., 528 C5 121
Bowlus, Morrison, Minn., 263 E4 99
Bowman, Elbert, Ga., 654 B3 87
Bowman, Bowman, N. Dak., 1,730 C2 110
Bowman, Orangeburg, S.C., 1,106 E6 115
Bowman, co., N. Dak., 4,154 C2 110
Bowman, creek, Pa A7 114
Bowman, isl., Ant C23 5
Bowmanville, Ont., Can., 7,397 D6 72
Bowmont, Canyon, Idaho, 25 F2 89
Bowmore, Scot E2 13
Bowness, Alta., Can., 9,184 D3 69
Bowokan, is., Indon F6 35
Bowring, Osage, Okla., 100 A5 112
Bowringpet, India, 11,360 F6 39
Bowron, riv., B.C., Can C7 68
Bowron Lake, prov. park, B.C., Can C7 68
Bowser, lake, B.C., Can A3 68
Bowsman, Man., Can., 504 C1 71
Bowstring, lake, Minn C5 99
Bowstring, riv., Minn C5 99
Bow Valley, Cedar, Nebr., 75 B8 103
Box, creek, Wyo B7 125
Boxboro, Middlesex, Mass., 150 (744▲) A5, f10 97
Box Butte, co., Nebr., 11,688 B2 103
Box Butte, creek, Nebr B3 103
Box Butte Table, plat., Nebr B2 103
Box Elder, Hill, Mont., 275 B6 102
Box Elder, Pennington, S. Dak., 56 C2 116
Box Elder, co., Utah, 25,061 B2 119
Boxelder, creek, Colo A6 83
Boxelder, creek, Mont E12 102
Box Elder, creek, Mont C8 102
Boxford, Essex, Mass., 300 (2,010▲) A6 97
Boxholm, Boone, Iowa, 250 B3 92
Boxmeer, Neth., 5,600 C5 15
Boxtel, Neth., 11,000 C5 15
Boyacá, dept., Col., 824,700 B3 60
Boyce, Rapides, La., 1,094 C3 95
Boyce, Ellis, Tex., 60 B5 118
Boyce, Clarke, Va., 384 B4 121
Boyceville, Dunn, Wis., 660 C1 124
Boyd, Taylor, Fla., 250 B3 86
Boyd, Lac qui Parle, Minn., 419 F3 99
Boyd, Carbon, Mont., 25 E7 102
Boyd, Wasco, Oreg., 30 B5 113
Boyd, Wise, Tex., 581 A5, C4 118
Boyd, Chippawa, Wis., 622 D2 124
Boyd, co., Ky., 52,163 B7 94
Boyd, co., Nebr., 4,513 B7 103
Boyd, glacier, Ant B34 5
Boyd, lake, Maine C4 96
Boydell, Ashley, Ark., 85 D4 81
Boyden, Sioux, Iowa, 562 A2 92
Boyds, Montgomery, Md., 85 B3 85
Boyd's Cove, Newf., Can., 368 D4 75
Boyds Creek, Sevier, Tenn D10 117
Boydsville, Clay, Ark., 25 A5 81
Boydton, Mecklenburg, Va., 449 E4 121
Boyer, riv., Iowa C2 92
Boyera, Con. L C2 48
Boyer Knob, mtn., Md D3 85
Boyero, Lincoln, Colo., 66 C7 83
Boyers, Butler, Pa., 550 D2 114
Boyertown, Berks, Pa., 4,067 F10 114
Boyes, Carter, Mont., 15 E11 102
Boyes Hot Springs, Sonoma, Calif., 2,462 B5 82
Boykin, Miller, Ga., 601 E2 87
Boykins, Southampton, Va., 710 E5 121
Boyle, Alta., Can., 346 B4 69
Boyle, Ire., 1,739 D3 11
Boyle, Bolivar, Miss., 848 B3 100
Boyle, co., Ky., 21,257 C5 94
Boylston, Montgomery, Ala., 1,300 C3 78
Boylston, N.S., Can., 121 D8 74
Boylston, Worcester, Mass., 600 (2,367▲) B4 97
Boyne, riv., Ire D5 11
Boyne City, Charlevoix, Mich., 2,797 C5 98
Boyne Falls, Charlevoix, Mich., 260 C6 98
Boynton, Muskogee, Okla., 604 B6 112
Boynton, Somerset, Pa., 300 G3 114
Boynton Beach, Palm Beach, Fla., 10,467 F6 86
Boy River, Cass, Minn., 51 C4 99
Boysen, res., Wyo B4 125
Boys Ranch, Oldham, Tex., 350 B1 118
Boys Town, Douglas, Nebr., 997 D3 103
Boz, cape, Tur B7 23
Bozcaada, Tur., 1,800 C6 23
Bozcaada (Tenedos), isl., Tur C6 23
Bozeman, Gallatin, Mont., 13,361 E5 102
Bozeman, pass, Mont E6 102
Bozman, Talbot, Md., 150 C5 85
Bozoum, Cen. Afr. Rep D3 46
Bozovici, Rom., 3,431 C6 22
Bozrah (Town of), New London, Conn. (1,590▲) *C8 84
Bozuyuk, Tur., 9,200 C8 31
Bra., It., 13,100 B1 21
Braband, Den., 5,139 B4 24
Brabant, isl., Ant C6 5
Brabant, lake, Sask., Can A4 70
Brabant, prov., Bel., 1,992,139 D4 15
Brac, isl., Yugo D3 22
Bracadale, Scot., 969 C2 13
Bracadale, bay, Scot C2 13
Bracciano, It., 6,783 g8 21
Bracciano, lake, It C4 21
Bracebridge, Ont., Can., 2,927 B5 72
Braceville, Grundy, Ill., 558 B5 90
Brach, Libya, 3,874 D2 43
Bracken, Sask., Can., 132 H1 70
Bracken, co., Ky., 7,422 B5 94
Bracken, lake, Man., Can C2 71
Brackenridge, Allegheny, Pa., 5,697 A7 114
Brackettville, Kinney, Tex., 1,662 E2 118
Brackley, Eng., 3,202 B6 12
Brackwede, Ger., 26,000 B3 17
Brad, Rom., 9,963 B6 22
Bradano, riv., It D6 21
Bradbury Heights, Prince Georges, Md., 1,100 *C3 85
Braddock, Camden, N.J., 200 D3 106
Braddock, Emmons, N. Dak., 141 C5 110
Braddock, Allegheny, Pa., 12,337 B6 114

BRAD-BROC 15X

Braddock, pt., S.C. ... G6 115
Braddock Heights, Frederick, Md., 600 ... B2 85
Braddock Hills, Allegheny, Pa., 2,414 ... *B5 114
Braddyville, Page, Iowa, 176 ... D2 92
Braden, Fayette, Tenn., 500 ... B2 117
Bradenton, Manatee, Fla., 19,380 ... E4, F2 86
Bradenton Beach, Manatee, Fla., 1,124 ... *E4 86
Bradenville, Westmoreland, Pa., 1,000 ... F3 114
Bradford, White, Ark., 779 ... B4 81
Bradford, Ont., Can., 2,342 ... C5 72
Bradford, Eng., 297,000 ... A4 12
Bradford, Stark, Ill., 857 ... B4 90
Bradford, Franklin, Iowa, 200 ... B4 92
Bradford, Penobscot, Maine, 150 (670▲) ... C4 96
Bradford, Merrimack, N.H., 300 (508▲) ... D6 105
Bradford, Darke and Miami, Ohio, 2,148 ... B3 111
Bradford, McKean, Pa., 15,061 ... C4 114
Bradford, Washington, R.I., 950 ... D10 84
Bradford, Gibson, Tenn., 763 ... A3 117
Bradford, Orange, Vt., 760 (1,619▲) ... D4 120
Bradford, co., Fla., 12,446 ... C4 88
Bradford, co., Pa., 54,925 ... C8 114
Bradford, mtn., Conn ... B3 84
Bradford Center, Penobscot, Maine, 175 ... C4 96
Bradfordsville, Marion, Ky., 387 ... C4 94
Bradfordwoods, Allegheny, Pa., 866 ... A5 114
Bradgate, Humboldt, Iowa, 166 ... B3 92
Bradley, Escambia, Ala., 100 ... D3 78
Bradley, Lafayette, Ark., 712 ... D2 81
Bradley, Monterey, Calif., 60 ... E3 82
Bradley, Polk, Fla., 1,035 ... E5 86
Bradley, Kankakee, Ill., 8,082 ... B6 90
Bradley, Penobscot, Maine, 500 (951▲) ... D4 96
Bradley, Jefferson, Ohio, 500 ... B7 111
Bradley, Grady, Okla., 294 ... C4 112
Bradley, Greenwood, S.C., 135 ... C3 115
Bradley, Clark, S. Dak., 188 ... B8 116
Bradley, co., Ark., 14,029 ... D3 81
Bradley, co., Tenn., 38,324 ... D9 117
Bradley Beach, Monmouth, N.J., 4,204 ... C4 106
Bradley Gardens, Somerset, N.J., 1,500 ... *B3 106
Bradleyton, Crenshaw, Ala., 100 ... D3 78
Bradleyville, New Haven, Conn., 350 ... *C4 84
Bradner, Wood, Ohio, 994 ... A4 111
Bradore, bay, Que., Can ... C3 75
Bradore, hills, Newf., Que., Can ... C3 75
Bradshaw, Vigo, Ind., 150 ... E2 91
Bradshaw, York, Nebr., 306 ... D8 103
Bradshaw, Taylor, Tex., 75 ... C3 118
Bradshaw, McDowell, W. Va., 950 ... D3 123
Bradshaw, mts., Ariz ... C3 80
Bradstreet, Hampshire, Mass., 150 ... B2 97
Bradwardine, Man., Can., 75 ... D1 71
Bradwell, Sask., Can., 115 ... F2 70
Brady, Pondera, Mont., 250 ... B5 102
Brady, Lincoln, Nebr., 273 ... C5 103
Brady, Cherokee, N.C ... D2 109
Brady, McCulloch, Tex., 5,338 ... D3 118
Brady, Lincoln, W. Va ... C2 123
Brady, mts., Tex ... D3 118
Brady's Hot Springs, Churchill, Nev., 5 ... D3 104
Bradyville, Cannon, Tenn., 75 ... B5 117
Braedstrup, Den., 1,619 ... C3 24
Braemar, Scot., 1,291 ... C5 13
Braeside, Ont., Can., 528 ... B8 72
Braga, Port., 40,977 ... B1 57
Bragado, Arg., 16,104 ... B4, g6 54
Bragança, Braz., 12,848 ... B1 57
Bragança, Port., 8,245 ... B2 57
Bragança Paulista, Braz., 27,328 ... C3, m8 56
Braggadocio, Pemiscot, Mo., 450 ... E8 101
Bragg City, Pemiscot, Mo., 274 ... E8 101
Braggs, Muskogee, Okla., 279 ... B6 112
Braham, Isanti, Minn., 728 ... E5 99
Brahmani, riv., India ... G10 40
Brahmaputra, riv., Asia ... C9 39
Brahme, riv., Ger ... D3 24
Braidwood, Will, Ill., 1,944 ... B5 90
Brail, Switz ... C9 19
Brăila, Rom., 113,200 ... C8 22
Brainard, Butler, Nebr., 300 ... C9 103
Braine-le-Comte, Bel., 10,779 ... D4 15
Brainerd, Butler, Kans., 65 ... B6 93
Brainerd, Crow Wing, Minn., 12,898 ... D4 99
Braintree, Norfolk, Mass., 31,069 ... B5, h11 97
Braintree, Orange, Vt., 100 (536▲) ... D3 120
Braithwaite, Plaquemines, La., 375 ... C7 95
Brake, Ger., 15,900 ... E2 24
Brakel, Ger., 6,400 ... B4 17
Brakpan, S. Afr., 77,777 ... C4 49
Bralorne, B.C., Can., 670 ... D6 68
Braman, Kay, Okla., 336 ... A4 112
Bramhapuri, India ... G7 40
Bramminge, Den., 2,900 ... C2 24
Brampton, Ont., Can., 18,467 ... D5, m14 72
Brampton, Eng., 3,130 ... F6 13
Bramtpon, Sargent, N. Dak., 70 ... B8 110
Bramche, Ger., 10,200 ... B3 15
Bramwell, Mercer, W. Va., 1,195 ... D3 123
Branaman, Pinal, Ariz., 4 ... D5 80
Branch, Franklin, Ark., 258 ... B2 81
Branch, Newf., Can., 556 ... E5 75
Branch, Acadia, La., 100 ... D3 95
Branch, Scott, Miss., 30 ... C4 100
Branch, Manitowoc, Wis., 190 ... B6 124
Branch, co., Mich., 34,903 ... G5 98
Branch, pond, Maine ... D4 96
Branch, riv., Wis ... A6 124
Branchland, Lincoln, W. Va., 500 ... C2 123
Branchport, Yates, N.Y., 230 ... C3 108
Branch Village, Providence, R.I., 300 ... *A10 84
Branchville, St. Clair, Ala., 50 ... B3 78
Branchville, Fairfield, Conn., 350 ... D3 84
Branchville, Sussex, N.J., 963 ... A3 106
Branchville, Orangeburg, S.C., 1,182 ... E6 115
Branchville, Southampton, Va., 158 ... E5 121
Branco, riv., Braz ... C5 60
Branco, riv., Braz ... E2 59
Brandberg, mtn., S.W. Afr ... B1 49
Brande, Den., 4,151 ... C3 24
Brandenburg, Ger., 88,000 ... A7 17
Brandenburg, Meade, Ky., 1,542 ... C3 94
Brandenburg, reg., Ger ... B6 16
Brandenburg, former state, Ger., 2,527,492 ... C8 17
Brandon, Man., Can., 28,166 ... E2, h7 71
Brandon, Kiowa, Colo., 75 ... C8 83
Brandon, Hillsborough, Fla., 1,665 ... E4 86
Brandon, Buchanan, Iowa, 322 ... B6 92
Brandon, Douglas, Minn., 353 ... E3 99
Brandon, Rankin, Miss., 2,139 ... C4 100
Brandon, Perkins, Nebr., 35 ... D4 103
Brandon, Greenville, S.C., 1,000 ... B3 115
Brandon, Minnehaha, S. Dak., 200 ... D9 116
Brandon, Rutland, Vt., 1,675 (3,329▲) ... D2 120
Brandon, Prince George, Va ... D6 121
Brandon, Fond du Lac, Wis., 758 ... E5 124
Brandon, head, Ire ... E1 11
Brandon, hill, Ire ... E1 11
Brandsville, Howell, Mo., 128 ... E6 101
Brandt, Miami, Ohio, 450 ... C3 111
Brandt, Susquehanna, Pa., 60 ... C10 114
Brandt, Deuel, S. Dak., 148 ... C9 116
Brandvlei, S. Afr., 1,417 ... D3 49
Brandys nad Labem, Czech., 13,300 ... n18 26
Brandy Station, Culpeper, Va., 200 ... C5 121
Brandywine, Prince Georges, Md., 80 ... C4 85
Brandywine, Pendleton, W. Va., 200 ... C5 123
Brandywine, creek, Del ... A6 85
Branford, New Haven, Conn., 2,371 (16,610▲) ... D5 84
Branford, Suwannee, Fla., 663 ... C4 86
Branford Hills, New Haven, Conn., 400 ... *D5 84
Branford Point, New Haven, Conn., 500 ... D5 84
Braniewo, Pol., 1,373 ... A5 26
Bransfield, strait, Ant ... C6 5
Bransk, Pol., 2,542 ... B7 26
Branson, Las Animas, Colo., 124 ... D7 83
Branson, Taney, Mo., 1,887 ... E4 101
Brant, Alta., Can., 76 ... D4 69
Brant, co., Ont., Can., 83,839 ... D4 72
Brantford, Ont., Can., 55,201 (*56,741) ... D4 72
Brantford, Eddy, N. Dak., 55 ... B7 110
Brant Lake, Warren, N.Y., 800 ... B7 108
Brantley, Crenshaw, Ala., 1,014 ... D3 78
Brantley, co., Ga., 5,891 ... E4 87
Brant Rock, Plymouth, Mass., 350 ... B6 97
Brantville, N.B., Can., 800 ... B5 74
Brantwood, Price, Wis., 40 ... C3 124
Bras-d'Apic, Que., Can., 56 ... C7 73
Bras-d'Or, N.S., Can., 947 ... C9 74
Bras d'Or, lake, N.S., Can ... D9 74
Brasfield, Prairie, Ark., 200 ... C4 81
Brashear, Adair, Mo., 309 ... A5 101
Brasiléia, Braz., 1,852 ... D4 58
Brasília, Braz., 150,000 ... B3 56, E1 57
Brasília, Braz., 3,182 ... E2 57
Braşov, Rom., 129,600 (222,300▲) ... C7 22
Brass, Nig ... F6 45
Brass, is., Vir. Is ... f15 65
Brasstown, Clay, N.C., 200 ... D2 109
Brasstown Bald, mtn., Ga ... B3 87
Brassua, lake, Maine ... C3 96
Bratenahl, Cuyahoga, Ohio, 1,332 ... B2 111
Bratislava, Czech., 252,800 ... D4 26
Bratsk, Sov. Un., 82,000 ... D29 9
Bratslav, Sov. Un., 10,000 ... G7 27
Bratt, Escambia, Fla., 150 ... G1 86
Brattleboro, Windham, Vt., 11,734 ... F3 120
Braunau [am Inn], Aus., 14,449 ... D6 16
Braunfels, Ger., 3,700 ... C3 17
Braunschweig (Brunswick), Ger., 240,400 ... A5 17
Brava, Som., 3,000 (7,000▲) ... E5 47
Brave, Greene, Pa., 400 ... G1 114
Bråviken, lake, Swe ... u34 25
Bravo, riv., Chile ... E2 54
Brawley, Imperial, Calif., 13,752 ... F6 82
Brawsley, peaks, Calif ... C4 82
Braxton, Simpson, Miss., 191 ... C4 100
Braxton, co., W. Va., 15,152 ... C4 123
Bray, Ire., 11,688 ... D5 11
Bray, head, Ire ... D4 11
Bray, head, Ire ... F1 11
Braymer, Caldwell, Mo., 874 ... B4 101
Brayton, Audubon, Iowa, 225 ... C3 92
Brayton, Bledsoe, Tenn ... D8 117
Brazeau, mtn., Alta., Can ... C2 69
Brazeau, riv., Alta., Can ... C2 69
Brazil, Clay, Ind., 8,853 ... E3 91
Brazil, Appanoose, Iowa, 300 ... D5 92
Brazil, Gibson, Tenn., 200 ... B2 117
Brazil, country, S.A., 80,250,000 ... D5 53, C3 56, C2 57
Brazil Lake, N.S., Can., 87 ... F4 74
Brazilton, Crawford, Kans., 80 ... E9 93
Brazoria, Brazoria, Tex., 1,291 ... E5, G4 118
Brazoria, co., Tex., 76,204 ... E5 118
Brazos, co., Tex., 44,895 ... D4 118
Brazos, riv., Tex ... D4 118
Brazzaville, Con. B., 133,700 ... F3 46
Brčko, Yugo., 17,834 ... C4 22
Brda, riv., Pol ... B4 26
Brea, Orange, Calif., 8,487 ... F3 82
Brea, pt., P.R ... D3 65
Breaden, lake, Austl ... E4 51
Bread Loaf, mtn., Vt ... C3 120
Breakenridge, mtn., B.C., Can ... E7 68
Breaker, pt., Am. Sam ... 52
Breakeyville, Que., Can ... o17 73
Breakneck, hill, Md ... D2 85
Breathitt, co., Ky., 15,490 ... C6 94
Breaux Bridge, St. Martin, La., 3,303 ... D4 95
Brechin, Scot., 7,114 ... D6 13
Brechin, Ont., Can., 264 ... C5 72
Breckenridge, Summit, Colo., 393 ... B4 83
Breckenridge, Gratiot, Mich., 1,131 ... E6 98
Breckenridge, Wilkin, Minn., 4,335 ... D2 99
Breckenridge, Caldwell, Mo., 605 ... B4 101
Breckenridge, Stephens, Tex., 6,273 ... C3 118
Breckenridge Hills, St. Louis, Mo., 6,299 ... *A8 101
Breckenridge Station, Que., Can ... h12 72
Breckinridge, Garfield, Okla., 42 ... A4 112
Breckinridge, co., Ky., 14,734 ... C3 94
Breckinridge, mtn., Calif ... E4 84
Brecknock, co., Wales, 55,544 ... C4 12
Brecksville, Cuyahoga, Ohio, 5,435 ... A6, B2 111
Breclav, Czech., 11,800 ... D4 26
Brecon, Wales, 6,466 ... C4 12
Brecon Beacons, mts., Wales ... C4 12
Breda, Carroll, Iowa, 543 ... B3 92
Breda, Neth., 114,900 ... C4 15
Bredaryd, Swe., 723 ... B7 24
Bredasdorp, S. Afr., 4,686 ... D3 49
Bredenbury, Sask., Can., 484 ... G4 70
Bredstedt, Ger., 4,100 ... D2 24
Bredy, Sov. Un., 3,800 ... E21 9
Bree, Bel., 7,031 ... C5 15
Breedenton, Meigs, Tenn ... D9 117
Breese, Clinton, Ill., 2,461 ... E4 90
Bregalnica, riv., Yugo ... E6 22
Bregenz, Aus., 21,428 ... E4 16
Bregovo, Bul., 5,271 ... C6 22
Breid, bay, Ant ... B15 5
Breien, Morton, N. Dak., 14 ... C5 110
Breil [sur Roya], Fr., 1,994 ... F7 14
Breisach, Ger., 4,900 ... A3 18
Breitenbush, Marion, Oreg ... C5 113
Brejo, Braz., 3,084 ... B2 57
Bremen, Cullman, Ala., 65 ... B2 78
Bremen, Haralson, Ga., 3,132 ... C1 87
Bremen, Ger., 581,000 ... B4 16, E2 24
Bremen, Marshall, Ind., 3,062 ... B5 91
Bremen, Muhlenberg, Ky., 328 ... C2 94
Bremen, Wells, N. Dak., 87 ... B6 110
Bremen, Fairfield, Ohio, 1,417 ... C5 111
Bremen, state, Ger., 732,000 ... E2 24
Bremer, co., Iowa, 21,108 ... B5 92
Bremerhaven, Ger., 143,900 ... B4 16, E2 24
Bremerton, Kitsap, Wash., 28,922 ... B3, D1 122
Bremerton East (Enetai), Kitsap, Wash., 2,539 ... *B3 122
Bremervörde, Ger., 9,300 ... E3 24
Bremgarten, Switz., 4,155 ... *B5 19
Bremo Bluff, Fluvanna, Va., 100 ... D4 121
Bremond, Robertson, Tex., 803 ... D4 118
Brendon, hills, Eng ... C4 12
Brenham, Washington, Tex., 7,740 ... D4 118
Brenish, Scot ... B1 13
Brenner, pass, Aus., It ... C7 18
Brent, Bibb, Ala., 1,879 ... C2 78
Brent, Ont., Can., 56 ... A6 72
Brent, Escambia, Fla., 7,000 ... G2 86
Brenta, riv., It ... D7 18
Brentford, Spink, S. Dak., 96 ... B7 116
Brentford [& Chiswick], Eng., 54,832 ... m11 10
Brenton, Wyoming, W. Va., 500 ... *D3 123
Brenton, pt., R.I ... D11 84
Brentwood, Contra Costa, Calif., 2,186 ... B6 82
Brentwood, Prince Georges, Md., 3,693 ... C1 85
Brentwood, St. Louis, Mo., 12,250 ... B8 101
Brentwood, Rockingham, N.H., 75 (1,072▲) ... E4 105
Brentwood, Suffolk, N.Y., 28,500 ... F3 84
Brentwood, Allegheny, Pa., 13,706 ... B6 114
Brentwood, Williamson, Tenn., 350 ... A5, E9 117
Brescia, It., 185,000 ... D6 18, B3 21
Breskens, Neth., 3,700 ... C3 15
Breslau, see Wroclaw, Pol.
Bressanone, It., 9,100 ... A3 21
Bressler, Dauphin, Pa., 1,000 ... *F8 114
Bressuire, Fr., 6,528 ... D3 14
Brest, Fr., 136,104 ... C1 14
Brest, Sov. Un., 82,000 ... E4 27
Breteuil, Fr., 2,748 ... E2 15
Brétigny [-sur-Orge], Fr., 6,830 ... C5 14
Breton, Alta., Can., 428 ... C3 69
Breton, isl., La ... E6 95
Breton, sound, La ... E6 95
Breton, strait, Fr ... D3 14
Breton Woods, Ocean, N.J., 1,200 ... C4 106
Bretton Woods, Eaton, Mich., 1,500 ... *F6 98
Bretton Woods, Coos, N.H., 15 ... B4 105
Breuil, It., 142 ... D3 18
Brevard, Transylvania, N.C., 4,857 ... D3 109
Brevard, co., Fla., 111,435 ... D6 86
Breves, Braz., 2,051 ... C4 59
Brevik, Nor., 2,400 ... p27 25
Brevnov, Czech. (part of Prague) ... n17 26
Brevoort, lake, Mich ... B6 98
Brewarrina, Austl., 1,225 ... D6 51
Brewer, Penobscot, Maine, 9,009 ... D4 96
Brewer, Perry, Mo., 200 ... D8 101
Brewers, Hond ... C5 62
Brewster, Thomas, Kans., 317 ... C2 93
Brewster, Barnstable, Mass., 700 (1,236▲) ... C7 97
Brewster, Nobles, Minn., 500 ... G3 99
Brewster, Blaine, Nebr., 44 ... C6 103
Brewster, Putnam, N.Y., 1,714 ... D7, m15 108
Brewster, Stark, Ohio, 2,025 ... B6 111
Brewster, Okanogan, Wash., 940 ... A6 122
Brewster, co., Tex., 6,434 ... E1 118
Brewster, cape, Grnld ... C17 4
Brewster, isl., Mass ... g12 97
Brewton, Escambia, Ala., 6,309 ... D2 78
Brewton, Laurens, Ga., 100 ... D4 87
Brežice, Yugo., 2,625 ... C2 22
Breznice, Czech., 2,385 ... D8 17
Breznik, Bul., 197 ... D6 22
Brezno [nad Hronom], Czech., 9,900 ... D5 26
Bria, Cen. Afr. Rep ... D4 46
Brian Boru, peak, B.C., Can ... B4 68
Briançon, Fr., 7,570 ... E7 14
Brian Head, mtn., Utah ... F3 119
Briar Bluff, Henry, Ill ... D7 92
Briarcliff, Delaware, Pa., 9,000 ... *G11 114
Briarcliff Manor, Westchester, N.Y., 6,535 ... D7 108
Briare, Fr., 4,114 ... D5 14
Brice, Franklin, Ohio, 180 ... C2 111
Bricelyn, Faribault, Minn., 542 ... G5 99
Briceville, Anderson, Tenn., 1,217 ... C9 117
Brickaville, Malag ... g9 49
Brickeys, Lee, Ark., 62 ... C5 81
Brick Town, Ocean, N.J., 2,000 ... C4 106
Brickyard, Russell, Ala., 100 ... C4 78
Bridal Veil, Multnomah, Oreg., 60 ... B4 113
Bridal Veil, falls, Utah ... C4 119
Bride, riv., Ire ... E3 11
Brideport, Saginaw, Mich., 1,326 ... E7 98
Bridesville, B.C., Can., 112 ... E8 68
Bridge, Cassia, Idaho, 10 ... G5 89
Bridge, Coos, Oreg., 200 ... D3 113
Bridge, creek, Sask., Can ... H1 70
Bridge, riv., B.C., Can ... D6 68
Bridgeboro, Worth, Ga., 200 ... E3 87
Bridgeboro, Burlington, N.J., 1,400 ... C3 106
Bridge City, Jefferson, La., 3,000 ... *C7 95
Bridge City, Orange, Tex., 4,677 ... *D6 118
Bridgedale, Jefferson, La., 15,000 ... *C7 95
Bridgeford, Sask., Can., 66 ... G2 70
Bridgehampton, Suffolk, N.Y., 900 ... n16 108
Bridge Lake, B.C., Can ... D7 68
Bridgeland, Duchesne, Utah, 50 ... C5 119
Bridgend, Wales, 15,156 ... C4 12
Bridgeport, Jackson, Ala., 2,906 ... A4 78
Bridgeport, Mono, Calif., 300 ... C4 82
Bridgeport, Ont., Can., 1,672 ... D4 72
Bridgeport, Fairfield, Conn., 156,748 (*386,300) ... E4 84
Bridgeport, Lawrence, Ill., 2,260 ... E6 90
Bridgeport, Marion, Ind., 700 ... H7 91
Bridgeport, Saginaw, Mich., 1,326 ... E7 98
Bridgeport, Morrill, Nebr., 1,645 ... C2 103
Bridgeport, Gloucester, N.J., 500 ... D2 106
Bridgeport, Belmont, Ohio, 3,824 ... B7 111
Bridgeport, Caddo, Okla., 139 ... B3 112
Bridgeport, Baker, Oreg., 10 ... C9 113
Bridgeport, Montgomery, Pa., 5,306 ... A10, F11 114
Bridgeport, Wise, Tex., 3,218 ... C4 118
Bridgeport, Douglas, Wash., 876 ... B6 122
Bridgeport, Harrison, W. Va., 4,199 ... B4, B7 123
Bridger, Carbon, Mont., 824 ... E8 102
Bridger, Ziebach, S. Dak ... C4 116
Bridger, basin, Wyo ... D3 125
Bridger, mts., Wyo ... B4 125
Bridger, peak, Wyo ... E5 125
Bridger, range, Mont ... E6 102
Bridgeton, Parke, Ind., 350 ... E3 91
Bridgeton, St. Louis, Mo., 7,820 ... A8, C7 101
Bridgeton, Cumberland, N.J., 20,966 ... E2 106
Bridgeton, Craven, N.C., 638 ... B6 109
Bridgeton, Multnomah, Oreg., 300 ... A2 113
Bridgetown, Barb., 11,452 (*110,000) ... p17 64
Bridgetown, N.S., Can., 1,043 ... E4 74
Bridgetown, Hamilton, Ohio, 5,000 ... *D2 111
Bridgeview, Cook, Ill., 7,334 ... *F3 90
Bridgeville, N.S., Can., 162 ... D7 74
Bridgeville, Sussex, Del., 1,469 ... C6 85
Bridgeville, Allegheny, Pa., 7,112 ... B5 114
Bridgewater, Austl., 267 ... o15 50
Bridgewater, N.S., Can., 4,497 ... E5 74
Bridgewater, Litchfield, Conn., 450 (898▲) ... C3 84
Bridgewater, Adair, Iowa, 225 ... C3 92
Bridgewater, Aroostook, Maine, 700 (999▲) ... B5 96
Bridgewater, Plymouth, Mass., 4,500 (10,276▲) ... C6 97
Bridgewater, Grafton, N.H., 40 (293▲) ... C3 105
Bridgewater, McCook, S. Dak., 694 ... D8 116
Bridgewater, Windsor, Vt., 250 (776▲) ... D3 120
Bridgewater, Rockingham, Va., 1,815 ... C4 121
Bridgewater Corners, Windsor, Vt., 100 ... D3 120
Bridgman, Berrien, Mich., 1,454 ... G4 98
Bridgnorth, Eng., 7,552 ... B5 12
Bridgton, Cumberland, Maine, 1,715 (2,707▲) ... D2 96
Bridgwater, Eng., 25,582 ... C5 12
Bridgwater, bay, Eng ... C4 12
Bridlington, Eng., 26,007 ... C6 10
Bridport, Eng., 6,517 ... D5 12
Bridport, Addison, Vt., 135 (653▲) ... D2 120
Brielle, Monmouth, N.J., 2,619 ... C4 106
Brienz, Switz., 2,864 ... C5 19
Brienz, lake, Switz ... C5 19
Brier, creek, Ga ... C5 87
Briercrest, Sask., Can., 175 ... G3 70
Brièreville, Alta., Can ... B5 69
Brierfield, Bibb, Ala., 90 ... B3 78
Brier Hill, St. Lawrence, N.Y., 350 ... f9 108
Brig, Switz., 4,647 ... D4 19
Brigantine, Atlantic, N.J., 4,201 ... E4 106
Brigantine, beach, N.J ... E4 106
Brig Bay, Newf., Can., 157 ... C3 75
Brigden, Ont., Can., 620 ... E2 72
Brigg, Eng., 4,906 ... A7 12
Briggs, Burnet, Tex., 150 ... D4 118
Briggs, Windsor, Vt., 65 ... D3 120
Briggsdale, Weld, Colo., 120 ... A6 83
Briggsville, Yell, Ark., 60 ... C2 81
Briggsville, Berkshire, Mass., 200 ... A1 97
Briggsville, Marquette, Wis., 200 ... E4 124
Brigham City, Box Elder, Utah, 11,728 ... B3 119
Bright Harbour, isl., Newf., Can ... A3 75
Bright, Ont., Can., 301 ... D4 72
Bright, Niobrara, Wyo ... B8 125
Bright, lake, Ont., Can ... B7 98
Brighton, Jefferson, Ala., 2,884 ... B3, E4 78
Brighton, Ont., Can., 2,403 ... C7 72
Brighton, Adams, Colo., 7,055 ... B6 83
Brighton, Eng., 162,900 (*405,000) ... D7 12
Brighton, Highlands, Fla., 50 ... E5 86
Brighton, Macoupin and Jersey, Ill., 1,248 ... D3 90
Brighton, Washington, Iowa, 724 ... C6 92
Brighton, Somerset, Maine, (62▲) ... C3 96
Brighton, Livingston, Mich., 2,282 ... F7 98
Brighton, Monroe, N.Y., 29,898 ... *B3 108
Brighton, Tillamook, Oreg., 110 ... B3 113
Brighton, Tipton, Tenn., 652 ... B2 117
Brighton (Town of), Essex, Vt. (1,545▲) ... *B5 120
Brighton, Kenosha, Wis., 35 ... F1 124
Brightsand, lake, Sask., Can ... D1 70
Brightshade, Clay, Ky., 200 ... C6 94
Brightwater, lake, Sask., Can ... F2 70
Brightwaters, Suffolk, N.Y., 3,389 ... n15 108
Brigie, hill, Scot ... F3 13
Brignac, Ascension, La ... B6 95
Brignoles, Fr., 5,347 ... F7 14
Brigus, Newf., Can., 704 ... E5 75
Brihuega, Sp., 2,229 ... B4 20
Brijnagar, India, 14,643 ... E6 40
Brilhante, riv., Braz ... C2 56
Brilliant, Marion, Ala., 749 ... A2 78
Brilliant, B.C., Can., 590 ... E9 68
Brilliant, Jefferson, Ohio, 2,174 ... B7 111
Brillion, Calumet, Wis., 1,783 ... A6, D5 124
Brilon, Ger., 11,900 ... B3 17
Brimfield, Peoria, Ill., 656 ... C4 90
Brimfield, Hampden, Mass., 400 (1,414▲) ... *B3 97
Brimhall, McKinley, N. Mex., 200 ... B1 107
Brimley, Chippewa, Mich., 400 ... B6 98
Brimson, Grundy, Mo., 107 ... A4 101
Brimson, St. Louis, Minn., 50 ... C7 99
Brindisi, It., 74,100 ... D6 21
Bringhurst, Carroll, Ind., 275 ... C4 91
Brinje, Yugo., 997 ... C2 22
Brinkhaven (Gann), Knox, Ohio, 191 ... B5 111
Brinkley, Monroe, Ark., 4,636 ... C4 81
Brinkman, Greer, Okla., 14 ... B2 112
Brinkworth, Austl., 218 ... F2 51
Brinnon, Jefferson, Wash., 100 ... B3 122
Brinsmade, Benson, N. Dak., 110 ... A6 110
Brinson, Decatur, Ga., 246 ... F2 87
Brion, isl., Que., Can ... B8 74
Brione-Verzasca, Switz., 337 ... D6 19
Brioude, Fr., 6,184 ... E5 14
Brisbane, Austl., 619,000 (*649,500) ... C9 51
Brisbane, San Mateo, Calif., 5,000 ... *B5 82
Briscoe, Wheeler, Tex., 100 ... B2 118
Briscoe, co., Tex., 3,577 ... B2 118
Brissago, Switz., 1,845 ... D6 19
Bristol, N.B., Can., 643 ... C2 74
Bristol, Prowers, Colo., 250 ... C8 83
Bristol, Hartford, Conn., 45,499 ... C5 84
Bristol, Eng., 433,900 (*605,000) ... C5 12
Bristol, Liberty, Fla., 614 ... B2 86
Bristol, Kendall, Ill. (part of Yorkville) ... B5 90
Bristol, Elkhart, Ind., 991 ... A6 91
Bristol, St. Landry, La., 65 ... D3 95
Bristol, Anne Arundel, Md., 16 ... C4 85
Bristol, Grafton, N.H., 1,054 (1,470▲) ... C3 105
Bristol, Bucks, Pa., 12,364 ... F12 114
Bristol, Bristol, R.I., 14,570 ... C12 84
Bristol, Day, S. Dak., 562 ... B8 116
Bristol, Sullivan, Tenn., 17,582 ... C11 117
Bristol, Addison, Vt., 1,421 (2,159▲) ... C2 120
Bristol (Independent City), Va., 17,144 ... B2 121
Bristol, Harrison, W. Va., 300 ... B6 123
Bristol, Kenosha, Wis., 350 ... F1, F5 124
Bristol, co., Mass., 398,488 ... C5 97
Bristol, co., R.I., 37,146 ... C11 84
Bristol, bay, Alsk ... D7 79
Bristol, chan., Eng ... C4 12
Bristol, pond, Vt ... C2 120
Bristol Ferry, Newport, R.I., 150 ... C12 84
Bristol Silver Mines, Lincoln, Nev., 10 ... E7 104
Bristol Terrace No. 2, Bucks, Pa., 1,300 ... *F12 114
Bristolville, Trumbull, Ohio, 400 ... A7 111
Bristow, Perry, Ind., 100 ... H4 91
Bristow, Butler, Iowa, 268 ... B5 92
Bristow, Boyd, Nebr., 153 ... B7 103
Bristow, Creek, Okla., 4,795 ... B5 112
Bristow, Prince William, Va., 50 ... B4 121
Britannia, range, Ant ... B28 5
Britannia Bay, Ont., Can ... h12 72
Britannia Beach, B.C., Can., 775 ... E6 68
British, mts., Yukon, Can ... C4 66
British Columbia, prov., Can., 1,629,082 ... E7 66, 68
British Guiana, dep., S.A., 631,000 ... C5 53, A3 59
British Honduras, dep., N.A., 105,000 ... H12 61, B3 62
British North Borneo, see Sabah, state, Mala.
Britstown, S. Afr., 2,834 ... D3 49
Britt, Ont., Can., 621 ... B4 72
Britt, Hancock, Iowa, 2,042 ... A4 92
Britt, St. Louis, Minn., 5 ... C6 99
Brittany (Bretagne), former prov., Fr., 3,072,000 ... C2 14
Britton, Lenawee, Mich., 622 ... G7 98
Britton, Oklahoma, Okla. (part of Oklahoma City) ... B4 112
Britton, Marshall, S. Dak., 1,442 ... B8 116
Brive [-la-Gaillarde], Fr., 40,175 ... E4 14
Briviesca, Sp., 3,779 ... A4 20
Brixham, Eng., 10,679 ... D4 12
Brno, Czech., 319,900 ... D4 26
Broach, India, 73,639 ... G4 40
Broad, bay, Scot ... B2 13
Broad, riv., Ga ... B4 87
Broad, riv., S.C ... C5 115
Broad, run, Va ... B4 121
Broadacres, Sask., Can., 87 ... E1 70
Broadacres, Marion, Oreg., 65 ... B2 113
Broadalbin, Fulton, N.Y., 1,438 ... B6 108
Broadback, riv., Que., Can ... F17 67
Broadbent, Coos, Oreg., 300 ... D2 113
Broad Brook, Hartford, Conn., 1,500 ... B6 84
Broaddus, San Augustine, Tex., 200 ... D5 118
Broadford, Scot ... C3 13
Broadford, Smyth, Va., 600 ... B3 121
Broad Haven, bay, Ire ... C2 11
Broadhead, creek, Pa ... A2 106
Broadkill, riv., Del ... C7 85
Broadkill Beach, Sussex, Del., 40 ... C7 85
Broadland, Beadle, S. Dak., 33 ... C7 116
Broadlands, Champaign, Ill., 44 ... D5 90
Broad Law, mtn., Scot ... E5 13
Broadmead, Polk and Yamhill, Oreg., 15 ... B1 113
Broadmoor, El Paso, Colo., 2,000 ... C6 83
Broad Top, Huntingdon, Pa., 334 ... F5 114
Broadus, Powder River, Mont., 628 ... E11 102
Broadview, Sask., Can., 1,008 ... G4 70
Broadview, Cook, Ill., 8,588 ... *F2 90
Broadview, Monroe, Ind., 1,865 ... *F4 91
Broadview, Yellowstone, Mont., 160 ... D8 102
Broadview, Curry, N. Mex., 40 ... C6 107
Broadview Heights, Cuyahoga, Ohio, 6,209 ... B2 111
Broadwater, Morrill, Nebr., 235 ... C3 103
Broadwater, co., Mont., 2,804 ... D5 102
Broadway, Warren, N.J., 300 ... B2 106
Broadway, Lee, N.C., 466 ... B4 109
Broadway, Union, Ohio, 300 ... B4 111
Broadway, Rockingham, Va., 646 ... C4 121
Broager, Den., 1,601 ... D3 24
Brochet, Man., Can., 158 ... E12 66
Brock, Sask., Can., 222 ... F1 70
Brock, Nemaha, Nebr., 213 ... D10 103
Brock, isl., N.W. Ter., Can ... m28 67
Brockdell, Bledsoe, Tenn ... D7 117
Brocken, mtn., Ger ... B5 17
Brocket, Alta., Can ... E4 69
Brocket, Ramsey, N. Dak., 153 ... A7 110
Brockport, Monroe, N.Y., 6,058 ... B3 108
Brockport, Elk., Pa., 450 ... D4 114
Brocksburg, Keya Paha, Nebr., 15 ... B6 103
Brockton, Plymouth, Mass., 72,813 ... B5, h11 97
Brockton, Roosevelt, Mont., 367 ... B12 102
Brockton, res., Mass ... h11 97

Bukovina (Bucovina), prov., Rom., 300,751....*B7 22
Bukuru, Nig., 8,450....E6 45
Bula, Indon....F8 35
Bulacan, prov., Phil., 557,700....*C6 35
Bülach, Switz., 8,188....A6 19
Buladean, Mitchell, N.C., 200....C4 109
Buladeen, Carter, Tenn., 100....C12 117
Bulan, Perry, Ky., 500....C6 94
Bulan, Phil., 14,279....*C6 35
Bulawayo, Rh., 180,000 (*212,100)....B4 49
Bulgaria, country, Eur., 8,175,000....G14 8, D7 22
Bulgroo, Austl....B4 51
Bulhar, Som....C5 47
Bulkley, range, B.C., Can....B4 68
Bulkley, riv., B.C., Can....B4 68
Bull, Wayne, W. Va., 150....D2 123
Bull, bay, S.C....F9 115
Bull, creek, S. Dak....B2 116
Bull, isl., S.C....F4, F8 115
Bull, mtn., Mont....D4 102
Bullaque, riv., Sp....C3 20
Bullange, Bel., 2,216....D6 15
Bullard, Twiggs, Ga., 120....D3 87
Bullas, Sp., 8,936....C5 20
Bullay, Ger., 930....C2 17
Bulle, Switz., 5,983....C3 19
Bullfrog, creek, Utah....F5 119
Bullhead, Corson, S. Dak., 200....B4 116
Bullhead City, Mohave, Ariz., 250....B1 80
Bullion, Ascension, La....B5 95
Bullitt, co., Ky., 15,726....C4 94
Bullittsville, Boone, Ky., 100....A6 94
Bulloch, co., Ga., 24,263....D5 87
Bullock, Granville, N.C., 150....A5 109
Bullock, co., Ala., 13,462....C4 78
Bulloo, riv., Austl....C5 51
Bull Ruffin, mtn., N.C....A2 109
Bull Run, mts., Nev....B5 104
Bull Run, mts., Va....C5 121
Bull Run, ridge, Tenn....E11 117
Bull Run, riv., Va....B4 121
Bullrun Rock, mtn., Oreg....C8 113
Bulls Bridge, Litchfield, Conn., 60....C2 84
Bulls Gap, Hawkins, Tenn., 682....C10 117
Bull Shoals, Marion, Ark., 268....*A3 81
Bull Shoals, res., Ark., Mo....A3 81
Bulnes, Chile, 5,147....B2 54
Bulo Burti, Som., 3,300....E6 47
Buloir, is., Alsk....E3 79
Bulsar, India, 25,440....G4 40
Bultfontein, S. Afr....C4 49
Bulu, Con. L....A4 48
Buluan, Phil., 3,296....D6 35
Bulun, Sov. Un., 800....B15 28
Bulungu, Con. L....B2 48
Bulun Tukhoi (Puluntohai), China, 10,000....B2 34
Bulwark, Alta., Can....C5 69
Bulyea, Sask., Can., 193....G3 70
Bumba, Con. L., 3,531....A3 48
Bumble Bee, Yavapai, Ariz., 10....C3 80
Bumping, riv., Wash....C4 122
Bumpus Mills, Stewart, Tenn., 200....A4 117
Buna, Pap....k12 50
Buna, Jasper, Tex., 950....D6 118
Bunbury, Austl., 13,186....F2 50
Bunceton, Cooper, Mo., 468....C5 101
Bunch, Adair, Okla., 80....B7 112
Bunche Park, Dade, Fla., 5,000....*F3 86
Buncombe, Johnson, Ill., 200....F5 90
Buncombe, co., N.C., 130,074....D3 109
Buncrana, Ire., 2,960....B4 11
Bundaberg, Austl., 22,799....B9 51
Bünde, Ger., 10,700....A3 17
Bundi, India, 26,478....E5 40
Bundick, creek, La....D2 95
Bundoran, Ire., 1,326....C3 11
Bunessan, Scot....D2 13
Bungay, Eng., 3,581....B9 12
Bunger, hills, Ant....C23 5
Bungo, strait, Jap....J6 37
Bunia, Con. L., 5,000....A5 48
Bunker, Reynolds, Mo., 250....D6 101
Bunker Hill, Macoupin, Ill., 1,524....D4 90
Bunker Hill, Miami, Ind., 1,049....C5 91
Bunker Hill, Russell, Kans., 200....D5 93
Bunker Hill, Coos, Oreg., 1,655....*D2 113
Bunker Hill, Giles, Tenn., 75....B5 117
Bunker Hill, Harris, Tex., 2,216....*E5 118
Bunker Hill, Berkeley, W. Va., 400....B6 123
Bunker Hill, peak, Nev....D4 104
Bunkerville, Clark, Nev., 210....G7 104
Bunkeya, Con. L....D4 48
Bunkie, Avoyelles, La., 5,188....D3 95
Bunn, Dallas, Ark., 25....C3 81
Bunn, Franklin, N.C., 332....B5 109
Bunnahowen, Ire....C2 11
Bunnell, Flagler, Fla., 1,860....C5 86
Bunnlevel, Hartnett, N.C., 187....B5 109
Bunny Run, Oakland, Mich., 1,058....*F7 98
Bū Nujaym, Libya....C3 43
Buo Ha, Viet., 10,000....A6 38
Buolkalakh, Sov. Un....B2 4
Buor-Khaya, bay, Sov. Un....B1 4
Bupto, China....B10 40
Bura, Ken....B7 48
Bur A'caba, Som., 2,500 (10,600▲)....E5 47
Buram, Sud....C2 47
Buran, Som....C6 47
Burao, Som., 10,000....E6 47
Buras, Plaquemines, La., 4,000....E6 95
Buraydah, Sau. Ar., 50,000....*G7 33
Burayk, Libya, 683....D2 43
Burbank, Los Angeles, Calif., 90,155....E4, F2 82
Burbank, Santa Clara, Calif., 5,000....*B6 82
Burbank, Osage, Okla., 238....A5 112
Burbank, Clay, S. Dak., 112....E9 116
Burchard, Pawnee, Nebr., 132....D9 103
Burdekin, riv., Austl....C8 50
Burden, Cowley, Kans., 580....E7 93
Burdett, Alta., Can., 229....E5 69
Burdett, Pawnee, Kans., 250....D4 93
Burdett, Schuyler, N.Y., 420....C4 108
Burdette, Mississippi, Ark., 115....B6 81
Burdick, Morris, Kans., 100....D7 93
Burditt, lake, Ont., Can....B5 99
Burdock, Fall River, S. Dak., 5....D2 116
Burdur, Tur., 25,400....D8 23
Burdwan, India, 108,224....F11 40
Bureau, Bureau, Ill., 401....B4 90
Bureau, co., Ill., 37,594....B4 90
Bureinsky, range, Sov. Un....B6 37
Büren, Ger., 5,900....B3 17
Büren, Switz., 2,432....B3 19
Bureya, Sov. Un., 5,000....B4 37
Bureya, riv., Sov. Un....A5 37
Burford, Ont., Can., 1,074....D4 72
Burford, lake, N. Mex....A3 107
Burg, Ger., 29,300....A6 17
Burg al'Arab, Eg., U.A.R....G7 31
Burg [auf Fehmarn], Ger., 6,049....D5 24
Burgas, Bul., 72,526....D8 22
Burgas, co., Bul., 629,593....*D8 22
Burgas, gulf, Bul....D8 22
Bur Gavo, Som....F5 47
Burgaw, Pender, N.C., 1,750....C6 109
Burgdorf, Ger., 12,400....F3 24
Burgdorf, Idaho, Idaho....D3 89
Burgdorf, Switz., 13,936 (*16,966)....B4 19
Burgenland, state, Aus., 271,001....*E8 16
Burgeo, Newf., Can., 1,454....E3 75
Burgersdorp, S. Afr., 6,184....D4 49
Burgess, Horry, S.C., 100....D11 115
Burgess Hill, Eng., 13,990....D7 12
Burgettstown, Washington, Pa., 2.383....F1 114
Burghead, Scot., 1,346....C5 13
Burghausen, Ger., 13,200....A8 18
Burgin, Mercer, Ky., 879....C5 94
Burglengenfeld, Ger., 8,100....D7 17
Burgoon, Sandusky, Ohio, 243....A4 111
Burgos, Phil., 1,420....n12 35
Burgos, Sp., 82,177....A4 20
Burgos, prov., Sp., 380,791....*A4 20
Burgreuland, Bel., 1,985....D6 15
Burgstädt, Ger., 17,300....C7 17
Burgsteinfurt, Ger., 12,200....A2 17
Burgsvik, Swe., 378....I8 25
Burgundy (Bourgogne), former prov., Fr., 1,264,000....D6 14
Burhanpur, India, 82,090....G6 40
Burhave, Ger., 2,400....E2 24
Buri, Braz., 1,844....m7 56
Burien, King, Wash., 10,000....*D1 122
Burin, Newf., Can., 1,144....E4 75
Burin, Jordan, 2,000....g12 32
Burin, pen., Newf., Can....E4 75
Buriram, Thai., 12,352....E5 38
Burkburnett, Wichita, Tex., 7,621....B3 118
Burke, Shoshone, Idaho, 300....B3 89
Burke, Franklin, N.Y., 273....f10 108
Burke, Gregory, S. Dak., 811....D6 116
Burke, Caledonia, Vt., 50....B5 120
Burke, Fairfax, Va., 150....B4 121
Burke, co., Ga., 20,596....C4 87
Burke, co., N.C., 52,701....B2 109
Burke, co., N. Dak., 5,886....A3 110
Burke, chan., B.C., Can....C4 68
Burke, isl., Ant....B2 5
Burke City, St. Louis, Mo., 1,500....A8 101
Burkes Garden, Tazewell, Va., 100....B3, D1 121
Burkesville, Cumberland, Ky., 1,688....D4 94
Burket, Kosciusko, Ind., 259....B6 91
Burketon Station, Ont., Can., 152....C6 72
Burketown, Austl., 59....C6 50
Burkett, Coleman, Tex., 150....C3 118
Burkettsville, Mercer and Darke, Ohio, 290....B3 111
Burkeville, Newton, Tex., 300....D6 118
Burkeville, Nottoway, Va., 705....D4 121
Burkley, Carlisle, Ky., 150....B2 94
Burks Falls, Ont., Can., 926....B5 72
Burkville, Lowndes, Ala., 100....C3 78
Burleigh, Cape May, N.J., 550....E3 106
Burleigh, co., N. Dak., 34,016....C5 110
Burleson, Johnson, Tex., 2,345....B5 118
Burleson, co., Tex., 11,177....D4 118
Burley, Cassia, Idaho, 7,508....G5 89
Burley, Kitsap, Wash., 250....D1 122
Burlingame, San Mateo, Calif., 24,036....B5 82
Burlingame, Osage, Kans., 1,151....D8 93
Burlington, Newf., Can., 263....D3 75
Burlington, Ont., Can., 47,008....D5 72
Burlington, Kit Carson, Colo., 2,090....B8 83
Burlington, Hartford, Conn., 700 (2,790▲)....B5 84
Burlington, Kane, Ill., 360....A5 90
Burlington, Carroll, Ind., 500....D5 91
Burlington, Des Moines, Iowa, 32,430....D6 92
Burlington, Coffey, Kans., 2,113....D8 93
Burlington, Boone, Ky., 350....A5, A6 94
Burlington, Penobscot, Maine, 150 (353▲)....C4 96
Burlington, Middlesex, Mass., 12,852....f11 97
Burlington, Burlington, N.J., 12,687....C3 106
Burlington, Alamance, N.C., 33,199....A4 109
Burlington, Ward, N. Dak., 262....A4 110
Burlington, Alfalfa, Okla., 174....A3 112
Burlington, Bradford, Pa., 115....C8 114
Burlington, Chittenden, Vt., 35,531....C2 120
Burlington, Skagit, Wash., 2,968....A3 122
Burlington, Mineral, W. Va., 200....B6 123
Burlington, Racine, Wis., 5,856....F1, F5 124
Burlington, Big Horn, Wyo., 100....A4 125
Burlington, co., N.J., 224,499....D3 106
Burlington Junction, Nodaway, Mo., 650....A2 101
Burli-Tyube, Sov. Un....D9 29
Burlyu-Tobe, Sov. Un., 10,000....F24 9
Burma, country, Asia, 24,500,000....G12 33, D10 39
Burmester, Tooele, Utah, 10....C3 119
Burmis, Alta., Can., 67....E3 69
Burnaby, isl., B.C., Can....C2 68
Burnet, Burnet, Tex., 2,214....D3 118
Burnet, co., Tex., 9,265....D3 118
Burnett, Vigo, Ind., 270....E3 91
Burnett, co., Wis., 9,214....C1 124
Burnett, riv., Austl....B8 51
Burnettsville, White, Ind., 452....C4 91
Burney, Shasta, Calif., 1,294....B3 82
Burney, Decatur, Ind., 250....F6 91
Burneyville, Love, Okla., 30....D4 112
Burnham, Cook, Ill., 2,478....*F3 90
Burnham, Waldo, Maine, 100 (755▲)....D3 96
Burnham, Howell, Mo., 50....E6 101
Burnham, Mifflin, Pa., 2,755....E6 114
Burnham-on-Sea, Eng., 9,850....C5 12
Burnie, Austl., 14,201....o15 50
Burning Springs, Clay, Ky., 350....C6 94
Burning Springs, Wirt, W. Va., 25....C3 123
Burnley, Eng., 80,200 (*165,000)....A5 12
Burns, Austl., 42....F3 51
Burns, Eagle, Colo., 30....B4 83
Burns, Marion, Kans., 314....A6, D7 93
Burns, Smith, Miss., 100....C4 100
Burns, Harney, Oreg., 3,523....D7 113
Burns, Dickson, Tenn., 386....A4 117
Burns, Laramie, Wyo., 225....D8 125
Burns City, Martin, Ind., 180....G4 91
Burns Flat, Washita, Okla., 2,280....B2 112
Burnside, Hancock, Ill., 125....C2 90
Burnside, Pulaski, Ky., 575....D5 94
Burnside, Ascension, La., 20....B5 95
Burnside, Neshoba, Miss., 100....C4 100
Burnside, Clearfield, Pa., 307....E4 114
Burns Lake, B.C., Can., 1,041....B5 68
Burnstad, Logan, N. Dak., 50....C6 110
Burnsville, Dallas, Ala., 250....C3 78
Burnsville, N.B., Can., 209....B4 74
Burnsville, Tishomingo, Miss., 416....A5 100
Burnsville, Yancy, N.C., 1,388....C4 109
Burnsville, Braxton, W. Va., 728....C4 123
Burnt, pond, Newf., Can....D3 75
Burnt, riv., Oreg....C9 113
Burnt Cabins, Fulton, Pa., 150....F6 114
Burnt Corn, Monroe, Ala., 300....D2 78
Burnt Fort, Camden, Ga., 50....F5 87
Burnt Island, Newf., Can., 678....E2 75
Burntisland, Scot., 6,036....D5 13
Burnt Prairie (Liberty), White, Ill., 118....E5 90
Burnt River, Ont., Can., 121....C6 72
Burntroot, lake, Ont., Can....B6 72
Burntside, lake, Minn....C6 99
Burntwood, lake, Man., Can....B1 71
Burntwood, riv., Man., Can....B2 71
Burnwell, Walker, Ala., 500....E4 78
Burnwell, Kanawha, W. Va., 210....D6 123
Burqā, Jordan, 3,000....B7, f11 32
Burr, Yellow Medicine, Minn., 50....F2 99
Burr, Otoe, Nebr., 81....D9 103
Burra, Austl., 1,382....F2 51
Burray, isl., Scot....B6 13
Burr Hill, Orange, Va., 106....C5 121
Burriana, Sp., 15,154....C5 20
Burrillville (Town of), Providence, R.I. (9119▲)....*B10 84
Burro, mts., Mex....E1 118
Burroak, Winneshiek, Iowa, 200....A6 92
Burr Oak, Jewell, Kans., 473....C5 93
Burr Oak, St. Joseph, Mich., 867....G5 98
Burr Oak, lake, Ohio....C5 111
Burroughs, Chatham, Ga., 30....E5 87
Burrow, head, Scot....F4 13
Burrows, Carroll, Ind., 200....C4 91
Burrton, Harvey, Kans., 774....A4, D6 93
Burruyacú, Arg., 3,034....E3 55
Burrville, Morgan, Tenn., 230....C9 117
Burrwood, Plaquemines, La., 400....F6 95
Burry Port, Wales, 5,671....C3 12
Bursa, Tur., 153,866....B7 23
Būr Sa'īd, see Port Said, Eg., U.A.R.
Bursey, mtn., Ant....B35 5
Burstall, Sask., Can., 266....G1 70
Burt, Kossuth, Iowa, 620....A3 92
Burt, Hettinger, N. Dak., 75....C3 110
Burt, Cannon, Tenn., 25....B5 117
Burt, co., Nebr., 10,192....C9 103
Burt, lake, Mich....C6 98
Būr Tawfīq, Eg., U.A.R., 1,000....E4 32
Burton, B.C., Can., 283....D9 68
Burton, Tulare, Calif., 4,635....*D4 82
Burton, Adams, Ill., 50....D2 90
Burton, Keya Paha, Nebr., 17....B6 103
Burton, Geauga, Ohio, 1,085....A6 111
Burton, Washington, Tex., 400....D4 118
Burton, King, Wash., 400....D1 122
Burton, Wetzel, W. Va., 250....B4 123
Burton, lake, Ga....B3 87
Burton-on-Trent, Eng., 50,600....B6 12
Burton Port, Ire., 224....C3 11
Burträsk, Swe., 1,350....E9 25
Burtrum, Todd, Minn., 160....E4 99
Burtts Corner, N.B., Can., 389....C3 74
Burtus, Eg., U.A.R....D3 32
Burtville, Potter, Pa., 50....C5 114
Buru, isl., Indon....F7 35
Burullus, lake, Eg., U.A.R....C2 32
Burūn, cape, Eg., U.A.R....C5 32
Burundi, country, Afr., 2,775,000....B4 48
Burwash, Ont., Can....A4 72
Burwell, Garfield, Nebr., 1,425....C6 103
Bury, Que., Can., 440....D6 73
Bury, Eng., 61,700....A5 12
Burynshik, Sov. Un....D4 29
Bury St. Edmunds, Eng., 22,200....B8 12
Busby, Alta., Can., 85....C4 69
Busby, Big Horn, Mont., 300....E10 102
Busch, Pike, Mo., 50....B6 101
Büschfeld, Ger., 1,200....D1 17
Bush, Laurel, Ky., 20....C5 94
Bush, Simpson, Miss., 50....D4 100
Bush, riv., Md....B5 85
Bush, riv., N. Ire....B5 11
Bush City, Anderson, Kans., 50....D8 93
Būshehr, Iran, 27,317....G5 41
Bushenyi, Ug....B5 48
Bushimoie, riv., Con. L....C3 48
Bushkill, Pike, Pa., 500....D11 114
Bushkill, creek, Pa....B2 106
Bushland, Potter, Tex., 200....B1 118
Bushmills, N. Ire., 935....B5 11
Bushnell, Sumter, Fla., 644....D4 86
Bushnell, McDonough, Ill., 3,710....C3 90
Bushnell, Kimball, Nebr., 266....C2 103
Bushnell, Brookings, S. Dak., 92....C9 116
Bushong, Lyon, Kans., 51....D7 93
Bushton, Rice, Kans., 499....D5 93
Businga, Con. L....A3 48
Busk, Sov. Un., 13,900....G5 27
Buskerud, co., Nor., 168,500....*H4 25
Busko, Pol., 5,975....C6 26
Buşrá ash Shām, Syr....F11 31
Bussa, Nig....D5 45
Busselton, Austl., 3,495....F2 50
Busseto, It., 9,959....E6 18
Bussey, Marion, Iowa, 557....C5 92
Bussum, Neth., 41,500....B5 15
Bustamante, Arg....D3 54
Bustamante, Zapata, Tex., 100....F3 118
Busto Arsizio, It., 68,600 (*340,000)....B2 21
Büsum, Ger., 4,200....D2 24
Buta, Con. L., 11,200....A3 48
Buta Ranquil, Arg....B3 54
Bute, co., Scot., 15,129....E3 13
Bute, inlet, B.C., Can....D5 68
Bute, isl., Scot....E3 13
Butedale, B.C., Can....C3 68
Buthier, riv., It....D3 18
Butkhak, Afg., 10,000....D14 41
Butler, Choctaw, Ala., 1,765....C1 78
Butler, Taylor, Ga., 1,346....D2 87
Butler, Montgomery, Ill., 249....D4 90
Butler, DeKalb, Ind., 2,176....B8 91
Butler, Pendleton, Ky., 450....B5, B7 94
Butler, Bates, Mo., 3,791....C3 101
Butler, Morris, N.J., 5,414....B4 106
Butler, Richland, Ohio, 976....B5 111
Butler, Custer, Okla., 351....B2 112
Butler, Butler, Pa., 20,975....E2 114
Butler, Day, S. Dak., 62....B8 116
Butler, Johnson, Tenn., 608....C12 117
Butler, Waukesha, Wis., 2,274....E1 124
Butler, co., Ala., 24,560....D3 78
Butler, co., Iowa, 17,467....B5 92
Butler, co., Kans., 38,395....E7 93
Butler, co., Ky., 9,586....C3 94
Butler, co., Mo., 34,656....E7 101
Butler, co., Nebr., 10,312....C8 111
Butler, co., Ohio, 199,076....C3 111
Butler, co., Pa., 114,639....E2 114
Butler, lake, Fla....E2 86
Butler's Bridge, Ire., 157....C4 11
Butlers Landing, Clay, Tenn....C8 117
Butlerville, Jennings, Ind., 240....F6 91
Butman, Gladwin, Mich....D6 98
Butner, Granville, N.C., 1,000....*A5 109
Butovo, Sov. Un....n17 27
Buttahatchie, riv., Ala....B1 78
Buttahatchie, riv., Miss....B5 100
Butte, Silver Bow, Mont., 27,877....E4 102
Butte, Boyd, Nebr., 526....B7 103
Butte, McLean, N. Dak., 257....B5 110
Butte, co., Calif., 82,030....C3 82
Butte, co., Idaho, 3,498....F5 89
Butte, co., S. Dak., 8,592....C2 116
Butte, mts., Nev....D6 104
Butte City, Glenn, Calif., 5....C3 82
Butte City, Butte, Idaho, 104....F5 89
Butte Falls, Jackson, Oreg., 384....E4 113
Butterfield, Hot Spring, Ark., 200....D6 81
Butterfield, Watonwan, Minn., 601....G4 99
Butterfield, Barry, Mo., 125....E4 101
Butternut, Ashland, Wis., 499....B3 124
Butternut, lake, Wis....C5 124
Butternut Ridge, N.B., Can., 190....D4 74
Butterpot, prov. park, Newf., Can....E5 75
Butters, Bladen, N.C., 225....C5 109
Butterworth, Mala., 42,504....J4 38
Butterworth, S. Afr., 2,354....D4 49
Buttevant, Ire., 981....E3 11
Butt of Lewis, cape, Scot....B2 13
Button, is., N.W. Ter., Can....f8 75
Buttonwillow, Kern, Calif., 950....E4 82
Butts, co., Ga., 8,976....C3 87
Buttzville, Warren, N.J., 350....B2 106
Butuan, Phil., 34,443....D7 35
Butung, isl., Indon....F6 35
Buturlinovka, Sov. Un., 39,800....C2 29
Butzbach, Ger., 9,900....C3 17
Bützow, Ger., 10,900....B5 16
Buxtehude, Ger., 15,700....B4 16
Buxton, Br. Gu., 5,164....A3 59
Buxton, Eng., 19,400....A6 12
Buxton, Dare, N.C., 500....B8 109
Buxton, Traill, N. Dak., 321....B8 110
Buxton, Washington, Oreg., 110....A1 113
Buxton, mtn., B.C., Can....D3 68
Buy, Sov. Un., 25,500....B2 29
Buyck, St. Louis, Minn., 20....B6 99
Buynaksk, Sov. Un., 27,300....E3 29
Buyukliman, see Vakfikebir, Tur.
Büyük Menderes (Maeander), riv., Tur....D7 23
Buzachi, pen., Sov. Un....G19 9
Buzancy, Fr., 461....E4 15
Buzău, Rom., 52,300....C8 22
Buzau, riv., Rom....C8 22
Buzaymah, Libya....E4 43
Buzet, Yugo., 444....C1 22
Buzuluk, Sov. Un., 57,000....C4 29
Buzzards, bay, Mass....D6 97
Buzzards Bay, Barnstable, Mass., 2,500....C6 97
Byala, Bul., 1,388....D7 22
Byala Slatina, Bul., 9,357....D6 22
Byam Martin, isl., N.W. Ter., Can....m31 67
Byars, McClain, Okla., 256....C4 112
Bybee, Cocke, Tenn., 50....C10 117
Bydgoszcz, Pol., 244,000....B5 26
Byelorussia (S.S.R.) (White Russia), rep., Sov. Un., 8,500,000....E5 27
Byemoor, Alta., Can., 129....D4 69
Byer, Jackson, Ohio, 100....C5 111
Byers, Arapahoe, Colo., 500....B6 83
Byers, Pratt, Kans., 52....E5 93
Byesville, Guernsey, Ohio, 2,447....C6 111
Byfield, Essex, Mass., 850....A6 97
Bygland, Nor....H2 25
Byhalia, Marshall, Miss., 674....A4 100
Byington, Knox, Tenn., 700....E11 117
Bykovo, Sov. Un., 10,000....G15 27
Bykovo, Sov. Un., 1,000....n18 27
Bylas, Graham, Ariz., 700....D5 80
Bylot, isl., N.W. Ter., Can....B17 67
Byng Inlet, Ont., Can....B4 72
Bynum, Teton, Mont., 40....C4 102
Bynum, Chatham, N.C., 400....B4 109
Bynumville, Chariton, Mo., 78....B5 101
Byram, Hinds, Miss., 350....C3 100
Byrd, glacier, Ant....g40 5
Byrd Station, U.S. scientific station, Ant....A36 5
Byrdstown, Pickett, Tenn., 613....C8 117
Byrnedale, Elk, Pa., 500....D4 114
Byrock, Austl., 139....E6 51
Byromville, Dooly, Ga., 349....D3 87
Byron, Contra Costa, Calif., 500....B6 82
Byron, Peach, Ga., 1,138....D3 87
Byron, Ogle, Ill., 1,578....A4 90
Byron, Oxford, Maine, 60 (108▲)....D2 96
Byron, Olmsted, Minn., 660....F6 99
Byron, Thayer, Nebr., 147....D8 103
Byron, Genesee, N.Y., 450....B2 108
Byron, Alfalfa, Okla., 82....A3 112
Byron, Big Horn, Wyo., 417....A4 125
Byron, cape, Austl....D9 51
Byrum, Den., 395....A5 24
Bysice, Czech., 1,170....n18 26
Bystra, riv., Czech....o18 26
Bystrzyca, Pol., 9,564....C4 26
Bytom, Pol., 189,700....C5, g9 26
Bytosh, Sov. Un., 10,000....E10 27
Bytow, Pol., 3,810....A4 23

C

Ca, riv., Viet....C6 38
Caacupé, Par., 15,834....E4 55
Caaguazú, dept., Par., 2,610....E4 55
Caamaño, sound, B.C., Can....C3 68
Caapucú, Par., 6,608....E4 55
Caazapá, Par., 16,588....E4 55
Caazapá, dept., Par., 3,003....E4 55
Cabaceiras, Braz., 581....h5 57
Cabalete, isl., Phil....o13 35
Caballo, Sierra, N. Mex., 10....E2 107
Caballo, mts., N. Mex....E2 107
Caballo, pt., P.R....g12 65
Caballo, res., N. Mex....E2 107
Cabana, Peru, 2,560....C2 58
Cabanaconda, Peru, 2,278....E3 58
Cabanatuan, Phil., 38,379....G6 37, o13 35
Cabano, Que., Can., 2,695....B9 73
Cabarrus, co., N. Car., 68,137....B3 109
Cabarruyan, isl., Phil....n12 35
Cabbage, swamp, Fla....C6 86
Cabedelo, Braz., 10,738....C4, h6 57
Cabell, co., W. Va., 108,202....C2 123
Cabery, Ford and Kankakee, Ill., 293....C5 90
Cabeza del Buey, Sp., 11,737....C3 20
Cabezas, Bol., 298....C3 55
Cabimas, Ven., 93,347....A3 60
Cabin, creek, Okla....A6 112
Cabin, creek, W. Va....D6 123
Cabincreek, Kanawha, W. Va., 800....C3, C6 123
Cabinda, Ang., 1,554....C1 48
Cabinda, dist., Ang., 58,453....C1 48
Cabinet, Bonner, Idaho, 10....A2 89
Cabinet, mts., Mont....B1 102
Cabinet Gorge, res., Mont....B1 102
Cabin John, Montgomery, Md., 2,000....C1, C3 85
Cable, Bayfield, Wis., 262....B2 124
Cabo, Braz., 6,029....k6 57
Cabo Blanco, Arg....D3 54
Cabo Delgado, prov., Moz....D6 48
Cabo Frio, Braz., 13,117....C4 56
Cabo Gracias a Dios, Nic., 590....C6 62
Cabonga, res., Que., Can....k11 73
Cabool, Texas, Mo., 1,284....D5 101
Caboolture, Austl., 1,926....C9 51
Cabo Raso, Arg....C3 54
Caborca, Mex., 9,285....A2 63
Cabo Rojo, P.R., 3,086....C2 65
Cabo Rojo, mun., P.R., 24,868....C2 65
Cabot, Lonoke, Ark., 1,321....C3 81
Cabot, Butler, Pa., 400....E2 114
Cabot, Washington, Vt., 244 (763▲)....C4 120
Cabot, head, Ont., Can....B3 72
Cabot, mtn., N.H....B6 120
Cabot, strait, Newf., N.S., Can....G20 67
Cabra, Sp., 15,995....D3 20
Cabras, isl., Guam.... 52
Cabras, isl., P.R....C8 65
Cabrera, isl., Sp....C7 20
Cabri, Sask., Can., 711....G1 70
Cabri, lake, Sask., Can....F1 70
Cabriel, riv., Sp....C5 20
Cabrillo, nat. mon., Calif....E2 82
Cabrobó, Braz., 2,889....C3 57
Cabullón, pt., P.R....D4 65
Čačak, Yugo., 27,356....D5 22
Caçapava, Braz., 7,987....C3 56
Caçapava do Sul, Braz., 6,712....E2 56
Cacapon, mtn., W. Va....B6 123
Cacequi, Braz., 8,458....D2 56
Cáceres, Braz., 8,246....C4 55
Cáceres, Col., 305....B2 60
Cáceres, Sp., 48,005....C2 20
Cáceres, prov., Sp., 544,407....C2 20
Cachan, Fr., 23,282....g10 14
Cache, Alexander, Ill., 60....F4 90
Cache, Comanche, Okla., 1,003....C3 112
Cache, co., Utah, 35,788....B4 119
Cache, creek, Calif....C2 82
Cache, creek, Okla....C3 112
Cache, peak, Idaho....G5 89
Cache, riv., Ark....B4 81
Cache, riv., Ill....F4 90
Cache Bay, Ont., Can., 810....A5 72
Cache Creek, B.C., Can., 344....*D7 68
Cache Junction, Cache, Utah, 100....B3 119
Cache la Poudre, riv., Colo....A5 83
Cachi, Arg....E2 55
Cachi, mts., Arg....D2 55
Cachimbo, mts., Braz....D4 59
Cachinal, Chile....D2 55
Cachoeira, Braz., 11,415....D3 57
Cachoeira do Sul, Braz., 38,661....E2 56
Cachoeiro do Itapemirim, Braz., 39,470....C4 56
Cacique, Pan., 102....h11 62
Cacola, Ang....D2 48
Caconda, Ang., 4,851....D2 48
Cacouna, Que., Can., 834....B8 73
Cactus, Maricopa, Ariz., 300....D3, G2 80
Cactus, flat, Nev....F5 104
Cactus, Moore, Tex., 900....*A2 118
Cactus, peak, Nev....F5 104
Cactus, range, Nev....F5 104
Cactus Lake, Sask., Can....E1 70
Caddo, Bryan, Okla., 814....C5 112
Caddo, Stephens, Tex., 120....C3 118
Caddo, co., Okla., 28,621....B3 112
Caddo, par., La., 223,859....B2 95
Caddo, creek, Okla....C4 112
Caddo, lake, La., Tex....B1 95
Caddo, mts., Ark....C2 81
Caddo, riv., Ark....C2 81
Caddoa, Bent, Colo., 25....C8 83
Caddo Gap, Montgomery, Ark., 75....C2 81
Cade, St. Martin, La., 500....D4 95
Cadena, mtn., P.R....B2 65
Cadena, pt., P.R....B2 65
Cades, Williamsburg, S. C., 125....D8 115
Cades, Gibson, Tenn., 15....B3 117
Cadig, mtn., Phil....o14 35
Cadillac, Que., Can., 1,077....*h11 73
Cadillac, Sask., Can., 245....H2 70
Cadillac, Fr., 2,324....E3 14
Cadillac, Wexford, Mich., 10,112....D5 98
Cadiz, San Bernardino, Calif., 50....E6 79
Cadiz, Trigg, Ky., 1,980....D2 94
Cadiz, Harrison, Ohio, 3,259....B6 111
Cádiz, Sp., 117,871....D2 20
Cádiz, prov., Sp., 818,847....*D2 20
Cádiz, gulf, Sp....D2 20
Cadogan, Alta., Can., 109....C5 69
Cadogan, Armstrong, Pa., 562....E2 114
Cadomin, Alta., Can., 106....C2 69
Cadott, Chippewa, Wis., 881....D2 124
Cadotte, riv., Alta., Can....A2 69
Cadron, creek, Ark....B3 81
Cadwell, Laurens, Ga., 360....D3 87
Cadys Falls, Lamoille, Vt., 100....B3 120
Cadyville, Clinton, N.Y., 800....f11 108
Caen, Fr., 91,336 (*120,000)....C3 14
Caernarvon, Wales, 8,998....A3 12
Caernarvon, co., Wales, 121,194....A3 12
Caernarvon, bay, Wales....A3 12
Caerphilly, Wales, 36,600....C4 12
Caetité, Braz., 4,823....D2 57
Cafayate, Arg....E2 55
Cagayan, Phil., 34,672....D6 35
Cagayan, prov., Phil., 445,700....*B6 35
Cagayan, is., Phil....D6 35
Cagayan, riv., Phil....B6 35
Cagayan Sulu, isl., Phil....D5 35
Cagiallo, Switz., 319....D6 19
Cagle, Sequatchie, Tenn....D8 117
Cagli, It., 3,235....C4 21
Cagliari, It., 194,000....E2 21
Cagliari, gulf, It....E2 21
Cagnes-sur-Mer, Fr., 15,392....F7 14
Caguán, riv., Col....C3 60
Caguas, P.R., 32,015....C6 65
Caguas, mun., P.R., 65,098....C6 65
Caha, mts., Ire....F2 11
Cahaba, riv., Ala....C2 78
Cahaba Heights, Jefferson, Ala., 2,000....*B3 78
Cahaba Valley, creek, Ala....E5 78
Caherdaniel, Ire., 83....F1 11
Cahir, Ire., 1,662....E4 11
Cahirciveen, Ire., 1,659....F1 11
Cahokia, St. Clair, Ill., 15,829....B8 101
Cahokia, creek, Ill....A8 101
Cahone, Dolores, Colo., 50....D2 83
Cahore, pt., Ire....E5 11
Cahors, Fr., 17,046....E4 14
Cahuinari, riv., Col....D3 60
Caí, Braz., 3,361....E2 56
Caiapó, mts., Braz....B2 56
Caiapônia, Braz., 2,476....B2 56
Caibarién, Cuba, 25,500....D4 64
Caicara, Ven., 3,082....B4 60
Caicedonia, Col., 10,681....C2 60
Caicó, Braz., 15,826....C3 57
Caicos, is., Turks & Caicos Is....E7 64
Caicos, passage, Ba. Is....E7 64
Caigo o no Caigo, pt., P.R....e10 65

Cannon Mines, Washington, Mo., 40 ... C7 101
Cannonsburg, Boyd, Ky., 300 ... B7 94
Cannonsburg, Jefferson, Miss., 25 ... D2 100
Cannonsville, res., N.Y ... C5 108
Cannonville, Garfield, Utah, 153 ... F3 119
Cano, Cuba, 1,258 ... k11 64
Canobie Lake, Rockingham, N.H., 250 ... E4 105
Canoe, Escambia, Ala., 500 ... D2 78
Canoe, B.C., Can., 504 ... D8 68
Canoe, riv., B.C., Can ... C8 68
Canoe Lake, Ont., Can ... B6 72
Canoe Lake, Sask., Can., 117 ... *m7 70
Canoinhas, Braz., 9,252 ... D2 56
Canon, Franklin and Hart, Ga., 626 ... B3 87
Canon, Taos, N. Mex., 500 ... A4 107
Canonchet, Washington, R.I., 100 ... D10 84
Canon City, Fremont, Colo., 8,973 ... C5 83
Canones, Rio Arriba, N. Mex., 100 ... A3 107
Canon Plaza, Rio Arriba, N. Mex., 50 ... A3 107
Canonsburg, Washington, Pa., 11,877 ... F1 114
Canoochee, riv., Ga ... D5 87
Canora, Sask., Can., 2,117 ... F4 70
Canosa, It., 34,015 ... D6 21
Canova, Miner, S. Dak., 247 ... D8 116
Canóvanas Central, P.R ... B7 65
Canso, N.S., Can., 1,151 ... D8 74
Canso, cape, N.S., Can ... G20 67
Cantabrian, mts., Sp ... A3 20
Cantal, dept., Fr., 172,977 ... *E5 14
Cantanhede, Port., 3,133 ... B1 20
Cantaura, Ven., 14,096 ... B5 60
Canterbury, Austl., 114,600 ... B3 51
Canterbury, Windham, Conn., 120 (1,857▲) ... C9 84
Canterbury, Eng., 31,000 ... C9 12
Canterbury, Merrimack, N.H., 100 (674▲) ... D3 105
Canterbury, bight, N.Z ... P13 51
Canterbury Station, N.B., Can., 595 ... D2 74
Can Tho, Viet., 49,310 ... G6 38
Cantilan, Phil., 4,141 ... *D7 35
Cantley, Que., Can., 359 ... D2 73
Canton, China, 1,840,000 ... G7 34
Canton, Hartford, Conn., 800 (4,783▲) ... B5 84
Canton, Cherokee, Ga., 2,411 ... B2 87
Canton, Fulton, Ill., 13,588 ... C3 90
Canton, McPherson, Kans., 784 ... D6 93
Canton, Trigg, Ky., 350 ... D2 94
Canton, Oxford, Maine, 400 (728▲) ... D2 96
Canton, Norfolk, Mass., 12,771 ... B5, h11 97
Canton, Fillmore, Minn., 467 ... G7 99
Canton, Madison, Miss., 9,707 ... C3 100
Canton, Lewis, Mo., 2,562 ... A6 101
Canton, Salem, N.J., 200 ... E2 106
Canton, St. Lawrence, N.Y., 5,046 ... f9 108
Canton, Haywood, N.C., 5,068 ... D3 109
Canton, Stark, Ohio, 113,631 (*281,900) ... B6 111
Canton, Blaine, Okla., 887 ... A3 112
Canton, Bradford, Pa., 2,102 ... C8 114
Canton, Lincoln, S. Dak., 2,511 ... D9 116
Canton, Van Zandt, Tex., 1,114 ... C5 118
Canton, Barron, Wis., 100 ... C2 124
Canton, res., Okla ... A3 112
Canton [& Enderbury], Br. and U.S. dep., Oceania, 300 ... G11 7
Canton Center, Hartford, Conn., 175 ... B5 84
Cantonment, Escambia, Fla., 2,499 ... G2 86
Canton Point, Oxford, Maine ... D2 96
Cantril, Van Buren, Iowa, 299 ... D5 92
Cantuar, Sask., Can ... G1 70
Cantwell, Choctaw, Ala ... D1 78
Cantwell, Alsk., 20 ... C10 79
Cantwell, St. Francois, Mo., 900 ... D7 101
Cañuelas, Arg., 5,614 ... B5, g7 54
Canutama, Braz., 977 ... D2 59
Canute, Washita, Okla., 370 ... B2 112
Canutillo, El Paso, Tex., 1,377 ... E1 118
Canwood, Sask., Can., 311 ... D2 70
Cany, creek, Tex ... G4 118
Cany-Barville, Fr., 1,045 ... E8 12
Canyon, Randall, Tex., 5,864 ... B2 118
Canyon, Yellowstone National Park, Wyo ... A2 125
Canyon, co., Idaho, 57,662 ... F2 89
Canyoncito, Santa Fe, N. Mex., 10 ... h9 107
Canyon City, Grant, Ore., 654 ... C8 113
Canyon Creek, Alta., Can., 267 ... B3 69
Canyon Creek, Lewis and Clark, Mont., 10 ... D4 102
Canyon De Chelly, nat. mon., Ariz ... A6 80
Canyon Ferry, res., Mont ... D5 102
Canyonlands, nat. park, Utah ... E6 119
Canyonville, Douglas, Oreg., 1,089 ... E3 113
Cao Bang, Viet., 25,000 ... A7 38
Caorle, It., 3,207 ... D8 18
Cap, mtn., N.W. Ter., Can ... D8 66
Capa, P.R ... B2 65
Capa, Jones, S. Dak., 39 ... C5 116
Capac, St. Clair, Mich., 1,235 ... F8 98
Cap-à-l'Aigle, Que., Can., 659 ... B7 73
Capalonga, Phil., 1,344 ... o14 35
Capanaparo, riv., Ven ... B4 60
Capanema, Braz., 9,678 ... B1 57
Capão Bonito, Braz., 6,829 ... C3, m7 56
Caparica, Port., 8,575 ... f9 20
Capasin, Sask., Can ... D2 70
Capatárida, Ven., 1,277 ... A3 60
Cap Bon, prov., Tun., 240,350 ... *B7 44
Capbreton, Fr., 3,688 ... F3 14
Cap Chat, Que., Can., 2,035 ... G19 67
Cap-de-la-Madeleine, Que., Can., 26,925 ... C5 73
Capdenac-Gare, Fr., 115 ... E5 14
Capdevila, Cuba ... k11 64
Cape, isl., S.C ... E9 115
Cape Breton, co., N.S., Can., 131,507 ... C9 74
Cape Breton, isl., N.S., Can ... C9 74
Cape Breton Highlands, nat. park, N.S., Can ... C9 74
Cape Broyle, Newf., Can., 630 ... E5 75
Cape Canaveral, Fla., 3,500 ... D6 86
Cape Charles, Newf., Can ... B4 75
Cape Charles, Northampton, Va., 2,041 ... D6 121
Cape Coast, Ghana, 41,200 ... E4 45
Cape Cod, bay, Mass ... C7 97
Cape Cod, canal, Mass ... C6 97
Cape Cod, reg., Mass ... C7 97
Cape Dorset, N.W. Ter., Can., 161 ... D17 67
Cape Elizabeth (The Cape), Cumberland, Maine, 5,505 ... E2, E5 96
Cape Fear, riv., N.C ... C5 109
Cape Girardeau, Cape Girardeau, Mo., 24,947 ... D8 101
Cape Girardeau, co., Mo., 42,020 ... D8 101
Cape Hatteras, nat. seashore recreational area, N.C ... B8 109
Cape Henry, Princess Anne, Va ... B7, E6 121
Cape Horn, Skamania, Wash ... D3 122
Cape La Hune, Newf., Can., 84 ... E3 75
Capelinha, Braz., 3,262 ... E3 57
Capella, is., Vir. Is ... f15 65
Capels, McDowell, W. Va., 800 ... D3 123
Cape May, Cape May, N.J., 4,477 ... F3 106
Cape May, co., N.J., 48,555 ... E3 106
Cape May Court House, Cape May, N.J., 1,900 ... E3 106
Cape May Point, Cape May, N.J., 263 ... F3 106
Cape Neddick, York, Maine, 600 ... E2 96
Cape of Good Hope, prov., S. Afr., 5,830,000 ... D3 49
Cape Porpoise, York, Maine, 400 ... E2 96
Cape Ray, Newf., Can., 207 ... E2 75
Capers, Pueblo, Colo., 25 ... D6 83
Capers, inlet, S.C ... F8 115
Capers, is., S.C ... F8 115
Capers, is., S.C ... G6 115
Cape Sable, isl., N.S., Can ... F4 74
Capesterre, Guad., 3,725 ... n16 64
Capeto, Chile ... D2 55
Cape Tormentine, N.B., Can., 345 ... C6 74
Cape Town, S. Afr., 508,341 (*807,211) ... D2 49
Cape Verde Island, Port. dep., Afr., 229,000 ... E3 42
Cape Verde, is., Atl. O ... E3 42
Capeville, Northampton, Va., 200 ... A7 121
Cape Vincent, Jefferson, N.Y., 770 ... A4 108
Cape York, pen., Austl ... B7 50
Cap-Haïtien, Hai., 24,423 ... F7 64
Capilla del Monte, Arg., 2,522 ... A4 54
Capilla del Señor, Arg., 3,421 ... g7 54
Capinota, Bol., 1,734 ... C2 55
Capistrano Beach, Orange, Calif., 2,026 ... *F5 82
Capital Federal, fed. dist., Arg., 2,966,816 ... *g7 54
Capitan, Lincoln, N. Mex., 552 ... D4 107
Capitan, mts., N. Mex ... D4 107
Capitan, peak, N. Mex ... D4 107
Capitán Bado, Par., 4,104 ... D4 55
Capitol, Carter, Mont., 5 ... E12 104
Capitol, peak, Nev ... B4 102
Capitola, Santa Cruz, Calif., 2,021 ... *C6 82
Capitola, Leon, Fla., 30 ... B2 86
Capitol Heights, Prince Georges, Md., 3,138 ... C2, C4 85
Capitol Reef, nat. mon., Utah ... E4 119
Capivarí, Braz., 10,961 ... m8 56
Capiz, prov., Phil., 314,800 ... *C6 35
Capleville, Shelby, Tenn., 350 ... E8 117
Capon Bridge, Hampshire, W. Va., 198 ... B6 123
Capon Springs, Hampshire, W. Va., 200 ... B6 123
Cap-Pelé, N.B., Can., 859 ... C5 74
Cappoquin, Ire., 806 ... E4 11
Capps, Henry, Ala ... D4 78
Cappstown, Miller, Ark ... D2 81
Capraia, isl., It ... C2 21
Caprara, pt., It ... D2 21
Capreol, Ont., Can., 3,003 ... p19 72
Caprera, isl., It ... D2 21
Capri, isl., It ... D5 21
Capricorn, is., Austl ... J9 51
Caprock, Lea, N. Mex., 5 ... D6 107
Capron, Boone, Ill., 656 ... A5 90
Capron, Woods, Okla., 102 ... A3 112
Capron, Southampton, Va., 327 ... E5 121
Cap-Rouge, Que., Can ... n17 73
Cap-St. Ignace, Que., Can., 1,247 ... B7 73
Cap-Santé, Que., Can., 546 ... C6 73
Capshaw, Limestone, Ala., 250 ... A3 78
Captain Cook, Hawaii, Haw., 1,687 ... D6 88
Captina, creek, Ohio ... B1 111
Captiva, Lee, Fla., 200 ... F4 86
Captiva, isl., Fla ... F4 86
Capua, It., 14,800 ... D5 21
Capulin, Conejos, Colo., 20 ... D4 83
Capulin, Union, N. Mex., 150 ... A6 107
Capulin Mountain, nat. mon., N. Mex ... A6 107
Caputa, Pennington, S. Dak., 40 ... D3 116
Caquetá, intendencia, Col., 63,970 ... C3 60
Caquetá, riv., Col ... D3 60
Carabaña, Sp., 1,947 ... p18 20
Carabanchel Bajo, Sp. (part of Madrid) ... p17 20
Carabobo, state, Ven., 381,636 ... A4 60
Caracal, Rom., 19,082 ... C7 22
Caracas, Ven., 786,710 (*1,550,000) ... A4 60
Carajás, mts., Braz ... D4 59
Carangola, Braz., 11,896 ... F2 57
Caransebes, Rom., 15,195 ... C6 22
Carapari, Bol., 351 ... D3 55
Carapeguá, Par., 23,675 ... E4 55
Caraquet, N.B., Can., 1,214 ... B5 74
Caratinga, Braz., 22,275 ... E2 57
Caratunk, Somerset, Maine, (90▲) ... C3 96
Caraúbas, Braz., 3,066 ... C3 57
Caraúbas, Braz., 285 ... h5 57
Caravaca, Sp., 10,678 ... C5 20
Caravelas, Braz., 3,096 ... E3 57
Caraveli, Peru, 1,177 ... E3 58
Caraway, Craighead, Ark., 821 ... B5 81
Caraz, Peru, 3,065 ... C2 58
Caràzinho, Braz., 18,162 ... D2 56
Carballino, Sp., 9,639 ... A1 20
Carballo, Sp., 3,110 ... A1 20
Carberry, Man., Can., 1,113 ... E2 71
Carbó, Mex., 2,213 ... B2 63
Carbon, Alta., Can., 371 ... D4 69
Carbon, Clay, Ind., 409 ... E3 91
Carbon, Adams, Iowa, 162 ... C3 92
Carbon, Kanawha, W. Va., 400 ... D6 123
Carbon, co., Mont., 8,317 ... E7 102
Carbon, co., Pa., 52,889 ... E10 114
Carbon, co., Utah, 21,135 ... D5 119
Carbon, co., Wyo., 14,937 ... D5 125
Carbonado, Pierce, Wash., 424 ... B3 122
Carbonara, cape, It ... E2 21
Carbon Cliff, Rock Island, Ill., 1,268 ... *B3 90
Carbondale, Alta., Can., 52 ... C4 69
Carbondale, Garfield, Colo., 612 ... B3 83
Carbondale, Jackson, Ill., 14,670 ... F4 90
Carbondale, Osage Kans., 664 ... D8 93
Carbondale, Athens, Ohio, 350 ... C3 111
Carbondale, Lackawanna, Pa., 13,595 ... C10 114
Carbonear, Newf., Can., 4,234 ... E5 75
Carbon Hill, Walker, Ala., 1,944 ... B2 78
Carbonia, It., 34,700 ... E2 21
Carbury, Bottineau, N. Dak., 40 ... A5 110
Carcagente, Sp., 17,937 ... C5 20
Carcans, lagoon, Fr ... E3 14
Carcar, Phil., 5,344 ... *C6 35
Carcassonne, Fr., 40,897 ... F5 14
Carchi, prov., Ec., 84,738 ... A2 58
Carcross, Yukon, Can., 175 ... D6 66
Cardak, Tur., 144 ... D7 23
Cardale, Man., Can., 91 ... D1 71
Cardale, Fayette, Pa., 900 ... *G2 114
Cárdenas, Cuba, 55,000 ... D3 64
Cárdenas, Mex., 12,344 ... k14 63
Cárdenas, Mex., 3,010 ... D6 63
Carderview, Johnson, Tenn ... C12 117
Cardiel, lake, Arg ... D2 54
Cardiff, Jefferson, Ala., 202 ... F4 78
Cardiff, Garfield, Colo., 120 ... B3 83
Cardiff, Harford, Md., 450 ... A5 85
Cardiff, Atlantic, N.J., 200 ... E3 106
Cardiff, Wales, 260,600 (*605,000) ... C4 12
Cardiff-by-the-Sea, San Diego, Calif., 1,500 ... *F5 82
Cardigan, P.E.I., Can., 193 ... C7 74
Cardigan, Wales, 3,780 ... B3 12
Cardigan, co., Wales, 53,564 ... B3 12
Cardigan, bay, P.E.I., Can ... C7 74
Cardigan, bay, Wales ... B3 12
Cardinal, Man., Can., 50 ... E2 71
Cardinal, Ont., Can., 1,944 ... C9 72
Cardinal, lake, Alta., Can ... A2 69
Cardington, Morrow, Ohio, 1,613 ... B3 111
Cardona, Ur ... E1 56
Cardross, Sask., Can ... H3 70
Cardston, Alta., Can., 2,801 ... E4 69
Cardville, Penobscot, Maine, 130 ... C4 96
Cardwell, Dunklin, Mo., 816 ... E7 101
Cardwell, Jefferson, Mont., 40 ... E5 102
Cardwell, mtn., Tenn ... D8 117
Carega, mtn., It ... D7 18
Carei, Rom., 16,780 ... B6 22
Carencro, Lafayette, La., 1,519 ... D3 95
Carenero, Ven ... A4 60
Carentan, Fr., 5,256 ... C3 14
Caretta, McDowell, W. Va., 1,092 ... D3 123
Carey, Blaine, Idaho, 200 ... F5 89
Carey, Wyandot, Ohio, 3,722 ... B4 111
Carey, Childress, Tex., 100 ... B2 118
Careyhurst, Converse, Wyo ... C7 125
Careysburg, Lib ... E2 45
Careywood, Bonner, Idaho, 25 ... A2 89
Carhaix, Fr., 4,032 ... C2 14
Carhuaz, Peru, 2,359 ... C2 58
Cariamanga, Ec., 3,376 ... B2 58
Cariati, It., 5,204 ... E6 21
Caribana, pt., Col ... B2 60
Caribbean, sea, N.A ... H13 61
Caribe Central, P.R ... D5 65
Caribes, is., P.R ... D6 65
Cariboo, mts., B.C., Can ... C7 68
Caribou, Man., Can ... f8 71
Caribou, Aroostook, Maine, 8,305 (12,464▲) ... B5 96
Caribou, co., Idaho, 5,976 ... G7 89
Caribou, isl., N.S., Can ... D7 74
Caribou, lake, Maine ... C3 96
Caribou, mts., Alta., Can ... f7 69
Caribou, mtn., Idaho ... F7 89
Caribou, mtn., Maine ... C2 96
Caribou, range, Idaho ... F7 89
Carichic, Mex., 965 ... B3 63
Carievale, Sask., Can., 264 ... H5 70
Carignan, Fr., 3,403 ... E5 15
Carinhanha, Braz., 2,163 ... D2 57
Carini, It., 16,723 ... E4 21
Carinish, Scot ... C1 13
Carinthia, reg., Aus ... E6 16
Caripe, Ven., 3,651 ... A5 60
Caripito, Ven., 19,003 ... A5 60
Cariris Velhos, mts., Braz ... h5 57
Cariús, Braz., 1,523 ... C3 57
Carl Blackwell, lake, Okla ... A4 112
Carle Place, Nassau, N.Y., 7,300 ... *G2 84
Carleton, Monroe, Mich., 1,379 ... F7 98
Carleton, Thayer, Nebr., 207 ... D8 103
Carleton, co., N.B., Can., 23,507 ... C2 74
Carleton, co., Ont., Can., 352,932 ... B9 72
Carleton, mtn., N.B., Can ... B3 74
Carleton Place, Ont., Can., 4,796 ... B8 72
Carlile, Crook, Wyo., 5 ... A8 125
Carlin, Elko, Nev., 1,023 ... C5 104
Carlin Bay, Kootenai, Idaho ... B8 122
Carlingford, Ire., 471 ... C5 11
Carlingford, bay, Ire., N. Ire ... C5 11
Carlinville, Macoupin, Ill., 5,440 ... D4 90
Carlisle, Lonoke, Ark., 1,514 ... C4 81
Carlisle, Eng., 71,000 ... C5 10
Carlisle, Sullivan, Ind., 755 ... G3 91
Carlisle, Warren, Iowa, 1,317 ... A7, C4 92
Carlisle, Nicholas, Ky., 1,601 ... B5 94
Carlisle, Middlesex, Mass., 350 (1,488▲) ... f10 97
Carlisle, Warren, Ohio, 671 ... C3 111
Carlisle, Cumberland, Pa., 16,623 ... F7 114
Carlisle, Union, S.C., 390 ... B5 115
Carlisle, Stewart, Tenn., 100 ... A4 117
Carlisle, Trinity, Tex., 35 ... D5 118
Carlisle, co., Ky., 5,608 ... B2 94
Carl Junction, Jasper, Mo., 1,220 ... D3 101
Carlock, McLean, Ill., 318 ... C4 90
Carloforte, It., 7,275 ... E2 21
Carlos, Allegany, Md., 135 ... D2 85
Carlos, Douglas, Minn., 262 ... E3 99
Carlos Casares, Arg., 7,558 ... B4 54
Carlos Chagas, Braz., 6,383 ... E2 57
Carlos Tejedor, Arg., 2,897 ... B4 54
Carlow, Ire., 7,708 ... E5 11
Carlow, co., Ire., 33,342 ... E4 11
Carloway, Scot ... B2 13
Carlowville, Dallas, Ala., 250 ... C2 78
Carlsbad, San Diego, Calif., 9,253 ... F5 82
Carlsbad, Eddy, N. Mex., 25,541 ... E5 107
Carlsbad, Tom Green, Tex., 350 ... D2 118
Carlsbad Caverns, nat. park, N. Mex ... E5 107
Carlsbad Springs, Ont., Can., 256 ... h13 72
Carlsborg, Clallam, Wash., 250 ... A2 122
Carlstadt, Bergen, N.J., 6,042 ... h8 106
Carlton, Clarke, Ala., 200 ... D2 78
Carlton, Sask., Can., 67 ... E2 70
Carlton, Eng., 38,790 ... B6 12
Carlton, Madison, Ga., 321 ... B3 87
Carlton, Dickinson, Kans., 78 ... D6 93
Carlton, Carlton, Minn., 862 ... D6 99
Carlton, Yamhill, Oreg., 959 ... B1, B3 113
Carlton, Hamilton, Tex., 220 ... D3 118
Carlton, co., Minn., 27,932 ... D6 99
Carluke, Scot., 11,415 ... E5 13
Carlyle, Sask., Can., 982 ... H4 70
Carlyle, Clinton, Ill., 2,903 ... E4 90
Carlyle, Wibaux, Mont., 15 ... D12 102
Carmacks, Yukon, Can., 218 ... D5 66
Carmagnola, It., 4,800 ... B1 21
Carman, Man., Can., 1,930 ... E2 71
Carman, hill, Pa ... C6 114
Carmangay, Alta., Can., 297 ... D4 69
Carmans, riv., N.Y ... F5 84
Carmanville, Newf., Can., 855 ... D4 75
Carmarthen, Wales, 13,249 ... C3 12
Carmarthen, co., Wales, 167,736 ... C3 12
Carmarthen, bay, Wales ... C3 12
Carmaux, Fr., 14,565 ... E5 14
Carmel, Monterey, Calif., 4,580 ... C6, D3 82
Carmel, Sask., Can., 106 ... E3 70
Carmel, Hamilton, Ind., 1,442 ... E5 91
Carmel, Penobscot, Maine, 650 (1,206▲) ... D3 96
Carmel, Cumberland, N.J., 400 ... E2 106
Carmel, Putnam, N.Y., 800 ... D7 108
Carmel, mtn., Isr ... B7 32
Carmel, pt., Calif ... C5 82
Carmelo, Ur., 11,800 ... E1 56
Carmel Valley, Monterey, Calif., 1,143 ... *D3 82
Carmel Woods, Monterey, Calif., 1,043 ... *D3 82
Carmen, Santa Cruz, Ariz., 100 ... F4 80
Carmen, Lemhi, Idaho, 10 ... D5 89
Carmen, Alfalfa, Okla., 533 ... A3 112
Carmen, isl., Mex ... B2 63
Carmen Alto, Chile ... D2 55
Carmen de Areco, Arg., 4,411 ... A5, g7 54
Carmen del Paraná, Par., 10,699 ... E4 55
Carmen de Patagones, Arg., 5,243 ... C4 54
Carmen-Sylva, Rom., 3,286 ... C9 22
Carmi, White, Ill., 6,152 ... E5 90
Carmi, lake, Vt ... B3 120
Carmichael, Sacramento, Calif., 20,455 ... A6 82
Carmichael, Sask., Can., 53 ... G1 70
Carmichaels, Greene, Pa., 788 ... G2 114
Carmine, Fayette, Tex., 500 ... E4 118
Carmona, Sp., 28,216 ... D3 20
Carmyllie, Scot., 665 ... D6 13
Carnarvon, Austl., 1,809 ... D1 50
Carnarvon, Sac, Iowa, 100 ... B2 92
Carnarvon, S. Afr., 3,762 ... D3 49
Carnation, King, Wash., 490 ... B4 122
Carnaxide, Port., 20,136 ... f9 20
Carncastle, N. Ire ... C6 11
Carndonagh, Ire., 1,016 ... B4 11
Carnduff, Sask., Can., 957 ... H5 70
Carnegie, Randolph, Ga., 113 ... E2 86
Carnegie, Caddo, Okla., 1,500 ... B3 112
Carnegie, Allegheny, Pa., 11,887 ... B5, F1 114
Carneiro, Ellsworth, Kans., 56 ... D5 93
Carnes, Forrest, Miss., 30 ... E4 100
Carnesville, Franklin, Ga., 481 ... B3 87
Carnew, Ire., 551 ... E5 11
Carney, Menominee, Mich., 250 ... C3 98
Carney, Lincoln, Okla., 227 ... B4 112
Carneys Point, Salem, N.J., 3,000 ... D2 106
Carnforth, Eng., 4,113 ... F6 13
Carnic Alps, mts., Aus ... E6 16
Car Nicobar, isl., India ... G9 39
Carnlough, N. Ire., 585 ... C6 11
Carn Mairg, mtn., Scot ... C4 13
Carnmor, mtn., Scot ... C5 13
Carnot, Cen. Afr. Rep ... D3 46
Carnoustie, Scot., 5,511 ... D6 13
Carnsore, pt., Ire ... E5 11
Carnuel, Bernalillo, N. Mex., 200 ... B3, k8 107
Carnwath, Scot., 6,160 ... E5 13
Caro, Tuscola, Mich., 3,534 ... E7 98
Carol City, Dade, Fla., 21,749 ... E3 86
Caroleen, Rutherford, N.C., 1,168 ... B2 109
Carolina, Braz., 8,137 ... C1 57
Carolina, P.R., 3,075 ... B7 65
Carolina, mun., P.R., 40,923 ... B7 65
Carolina, Washington, R.I., 500 ... D10 84
Carolina, S. Afr., 4,336 ... C5 49
Carolina, Marion, W. Va., 700 ... A7 123
Carolina Beach, New Hanover, N.C., 1,192 ... C6 109
Caroline, Alta., Can., 321 ... C3 69
Caroline, Shawano, Wis., 350 ... D5 124
Caroline, co., Md., 19,462 ... C6 85
Caroline, co., Va., 12,725 ... D5 121
Caroline, atoll, Pac. O ... G13 7
Caroline, is., Pac. O ... F8 7
Caron, Sask., Can., 105 ... G3 70
Carona, Cherokee, Kans., 175 ... E9 93
Caron Brook, N.B., Can., 149 ... A4 96
Caroní, riv., Ven ... B5 60
Carora, Ven., 22,251 ... A3 60
Carouge, Switz., 12,760 ... D1 19
Carp, Ont., Can., 498 ... B8, h11 72
Carp, Lincoln, Nev., 25 ... F7 104
Carp, lake, B.C., Can ... B6 68
Carpathians, mts., Czech., Pol., Rom ... D6, B7 22
Carpentaria, gulf, Austl ... B6 50
Carpenter, Madison, Ill., 125 ... A9 101
Carpenter, Mitchell, Iowa, 177 ... A4 92
Carpenter, Copiah, Miss., 15 ... C3 100
Carpenter, Roger Mills, Okla ... B2 112
Carpenter, Clark, S. Dak., 75 ... C8 116
Carpenter, Laramie, Wyo., 100 ... D8 125
Carpenter, dam, Ark ... D6 81
Carpentersville, Kane, Ill., 17,424 ... E2 90
Carpenterville, Warren, N.J., 30 ... B2 106
Carpenterville, Curry, Oreg., 25 ... E2 113
Carpentras, Fr., 14,169 ... E6 14
Carpi, It., 21,000 (45,208▲) ... B3 21
Carpinteria, Santa Barbara, Calif., 4,998 ... E4 82
Carpio, Ward, N. Dak., 199 ... A4 110
Carr, Weld, Colo., 90 ... A6 83
Carr, lake, Ind ... G4 91
Carrabasset, Franklin, Maine, 45 ... C2 96
Carrabelle, Franklin, Fla., 1,146 ... C2 86
Carradale, Scot ... E3 13
Carragana, Sask., Can., 257 ... E4 70
Carrantuohill, mtn., Ire ... E2 11
Carranza, cape, Chile ... B2 54
Carrara, It., 65,900 ... B3 21
Carrboro, Orange, N.C., 1,997 ... B4 109
Carr Bridge, Scot ... C5 13
Carrickfergus, N. Ire., 10,211 ... C6 11
Carrickmacross, Ire., 1,940 ... D5 11
Carrick-on-Shannon, Ire., 1,497 ... D4 11
Carrick-on-Suir, Ire., 4,672 ... E4 11
Carrie, mtn., Wash ... B2 122
Carrier, Que., Can ... o17 73
Carrier, Garfield, Okla., 150 ... A3 112
Carriere, Pearl River, Miss., 700 ... E4 100
Carriers Mills, Saline, Ill., 2,006 ... F5 90
Carrigahorig, Ire ... D3 11
Carrigain, mtn., N.H ... B4 105
Carrigaline, Ire., 688 ... F3 11
Carrigan, head, Ire ... C3 11
Carrington, Foster, N. Dak., 2,438 ... B6 110
Carrión, riv., Sp ... A3 20
Carrión de los Condes, Sp., 3,414 ... A3 20
Carrizal Bajo, Chile ... E1 55
Carrizo, Navajo, Ariz ... C5 80
Carrizo, creek, Ariz., N. Mex ... C6 80
Carrizo, creek, N. Mex., Tex ... A6 107
Carrizo, mtn., N. Mex ... D4 107
Carrizo, mts., Ariz., N. Mex ... A1 107
Carrizo Springs, Dimmit, Tex., 5,699 ... E3 118
Carrizozo, Lincoln, N. Mex., 1,546 ... D4 107
Carroll, Man., Can., 40 ... E1 71
Carroll, Carroll, Iowa, 7,682 ... B3 92
Carroll, Penobscot, Maine, 25 (147▲) ... C4 96
Carroll, Wayne, Nebr., 220 ... B8 103
Carroll, Coos, N.H., 115 (295▲) ... B3 105
Carroll, Fairfield, Ohio, 444 ... C5 111
Carroll, co., Ark., 11,284 ... A2 81
Carroll, co., Ga., 36,451 ... C1 87
Carroll, co., Ill., 19,507 ... A4 90
Carroll, co., Ind., 16,934 ... C4 91
Carroll, co., Iowa, 23,431 ... B3 92
Carroll, co., Ky., 7,978 ... B4 94
Carroll, co., Md., 52,785 ... A3 85
Carroll, co., Miss., 11,177 ... B4 100
Carroll, co., Mo., 13,847 ... B4 101
Carroll, co., N.H., 15,829 ... C4 105
Carroll, co., Ohio, 20,857 ... B6 111
Carroll, co., Tenn., 23,476 ... B3 117
Carroll, co., Va., 23,178 ... E2 121
Carroll, lake, Man., Ont., Can ... D4 71
Carrolls, Cowlitz, Wash., 150 ... C3 122
Carrollton, Pickens, Ala., 894 ... B1 78
Carrollton, Carroll, Ga., 10,973 ... C1 87
Carrollton, Greene, Ill., 2,558 ... D3 90
Carrollton, Carroll, Ky., 3,218 ... B4 94
Carrollton (P.O.), Carroll, Md., 75 ... A4 85
Carrollton, Prince Georges, Md., 3,385 ... *C4 85
Carrollton, Saginaw, Mich., 6,718 ... E7 98
Carrollton, Carroll, Miss., 343 ... B4 100
Carrollton, Carroll, Mo., 4,554 ... B4 101
Carrollton, Carroll, Ohio, 2,786 ... B6 111
Carrollton, Dallas, Tex., 4,242 ... B5 118
Carrolltown, Cambria, Pa., 1,525 ... E4 114
Carrollville, Milwaukee, Wis. (part of Oak Creek) ... F2, F6 124
Carron, inlet, Scot ... B4 10
Carron, riv., Scot ... C3 13
Carrot, riv., Man., Sask., Can ... D4 70
Carrot River, Sask., Can., 930 ... D4 70
Carrowkeel, Ire., 109 ... B4 11
Carrowmore, lake, Ire ... C2 11
Carrsville, Ky., 166 ... A3 94
Carruthers, Sask., Can ... E1 70
Carrville, Tallapoosa, Ala., 1,081 ... C4 78
Carry Falls, res., N.Y ... f10 108
Carrying Place, Ont., Can., 197 ... C7 72
Çarşamba, Tur., 14,800 ... B11 31
Carseland, Alta., Can., 117 ... D4 69
Carshalton, Eng., 61,000 ... m12 10
Carson, Washington, Ala., 20 ... D2 78
Carson (N. Wilmington), Los Angeles, Calif., 38,059 ... *F2 82
Carson, Pottawattamie, Iowa, 583 ... C2 92
Carson, Jefferson Davis, Miss., 250 ... D4 100
Carson, Taos, N. Mex., 30 ... A4 107
Carson, Grant, N. Dak., 501 ... C4 110
Carson, Baker, Oreg., 30 ... C9 113
Carson, Dinwiddie, Va., 160 ... D5 121
Carson, Skamania, Wash., 250 ... D4 122
Carson, co., Tex., 7,781 ... B2 118
Carson, riv., Nev ... D3 104
Carson sink, Nev ... D3 104
Carson City, Montcalm, Mich., 1,201 ... E5 98
Carson City, Ormsby, Nev., 5,163 ... D2 104
Carsonville, Sanilac, Mich., 502 ... E8 98
Carsonville, St. Louis, Mo., 4,500 ... *A8 101
Carstairs, Alta., Can., 665 ... D3 69
Carstensz, mtn., W. Irian ... F9 35
Carswell, McDowell, W. Va., 500 ... *D3 123
Cartagena, Chile, 2,384 ... A2 54
Cartagena, Col., 152,380 ... A2 60
Cartagena, Sp., 100,000 (123,630▲) ... D5 20
Cartagena, lake, P.R ... C2 65
Cartago, Col., 49,000 ... C2 60
Cartago, C.R., 18,900 ... F6 62
Cartago, prov., C.R., 154,200 ... *F6 62
Carta Valley, Edwards, Tex., 15 ... E2 118
Cartaxo, Port., 5,920 ... C1 20
Cartaya, Sp., 9,002 ... D2 20
Carter, Carter, Ky., 122 ... B6 94
Carter, Chouteau, Mont., 120 ... C6 102
Carter, Beckham, Okla., 364 ... B2 112
Carter, Tripp, S. Dak., 18 ... D5 116
Carter, Carter, Tenn., 200 ... C11 117
Carter, Forest, Wis., 100 ... C5 124
Carter, Uinta, Wyo., 85 ... D2 125
Carter, co., Ky., 20,817 ... B6 94
Carter, co., Mo., 3,973 ... E7 101
Carter, co., Mont., 2,493 ... E12 102
Carter, co., Okla., 39,044 ... C4 112
Carter, co., Tenn., 41,578 ... C11 117
Carter, caves and natural bridge, Ky ... B6 94
Carteret, Middlesex, N.J., 20,502 ... B4, k8 106
Carteret, co., N.C., 30,940 ... C7 109
Carter Lake, Pottawattamie, Iowa, 2,287 ... C2 92
Carters, Murray, Ga., 100 ... B2 87
Cartersburg, Hendricks, Ind., 300 ... E5 91
Carters Creek, Maury, Tenn ... B5 117
Cartersville, Bartow, Ga., 8,668 ... B2 87
Cartersville, Florence. S.C., 96 ... C7 115
Cartersville, Cumberland, Va., 85 ... D4 121
Cartertown, Allen, Ky., 100 ... D3 94
Carterville, Williamson, Ill., 2,643 ... F4 90
Carterville, Jasper, Mo., 1,443 ... D3 101
Carthage, Dallas, Ark., 528 ... C3 81
Carthage, Hancock, Ill., 3,325 ... C2 90
Carthage, Rush, Ind., 1,043 ... E6 91
Carthage, Leake, Miss., 2,442 ... C4 100
Carthage, Jasper, Mo., 11,264 ... D3 101
Carthage, Jefferson, N.Y., 4,216 ... B5 108
Carthage, Moore, N.C., 1,190 ... B4 109
Carthage, Miner, S. Dak., 368 ... C8 116
Carthage, Smith, Tenn., 2,021 ... C8 117
Carthage, Panola, Tex., 5,262 ... C5 118
Carthage, Tun., 4,873 ... *F12 30
Carthage, ruins, Tun ... F12 30
Cartwright, Man., Can., 482 ... E2 71
Cartwright, Newf., Can., 493 ... B3, h10 75
Cartwright, McKenzie, N. Dak., 45 ... B2 110
Caruaru, Braz., 64,471 ... C3, k6 57
Carúpano, Ven., 38,210 ... A5 60
Caruthersville, Pemiscot, Mo., 8,643 ... E8 101

Center Point, Turner and Yankton, S. Dak., 20...D8 116
Center Point, Kerr, Tex., 1,000...E3 118
Center Point, Doddridge, W. Va., 125...A6, B4 123
Centerport, Suffolk, N.Y., 4,600...*n15 108
Center Ridge, Conway, Ark., 100...B3 81
Center Rutland, Rutland, Vt., 500...D2 120
Center Sandwich, Carroll, N.H., 250...C4 105
Center Square, Montgomery, Pa., 900...A11 114
Center Stafford, Stafford, N.H., 40...D4 105
Center Star, Lauderdale, Ala., 200...A2 78
Centerton, Benton, Ark., 177..A1 81
Centerton, Morgan, Ind., 500...E5 91
Centerton, Salem, N.J., 100..D2 106
Centertown, Ohio, Ky., 327..C3 94
Centertown, Cole, Mo., 190..C5 101
Centertown, Warren, Tenn., 169...D8 117
Center Tuftonboro, Carroll, N.H., 100...C4 105
Center Valley, Outagamie, Wis., 25...A5 124
Centerview, Johnson, Mo., 208...C4 101
Centerville, Yavapai, Ariz., 25...C3 80
Centerville, Yell, Ark., 200..B2 81
Centerville, Gwinnett, Ga..B6 87
Centerville, St. Clair, Ill., 12,769...E3 90
Centerville, Wayne, Ind., 2,378...E8 91
Centerville, Appanoose, Iowa, 6,629...D5 92
Centerville, Linn, Kans., 250...D8 93
Centerville, St. Mary, La., 537...E4 95
Centerville, Washington, Maine, 40 (47▲)... D5 96
Centerville, Barnstable, Mass., 700...C7 97
Centerville, Anoka, Minn., 338...E7 99
Centerville, Reynolds, Mo., 163...D7 101
Centerville, Silver Bow, Mont., 1,800...D4 102
Centerville, Suffolk, N.Y...F6 84
Centerville, Franklin, N.C., 300...A5 109
Centerville, Montgomery, Ohio, 3,490...C3 111
Centerville, Crawford, Pa., 238...C2 114
Centerville, Washington, Pa., 5,088...F2 114
Centerville, Turner, S. Dak., 887...D9 116
Centerville, Hickman, Tenn., 1,678...B4 117
Centerville, Leon, Tex., 836.D5 118
Centerville, Davis, Utah, 2,361...C4 119
Centerville, Klickitat, Wash., 100...D5 122
Cento, It., 7,700...E7 18
Centrahoma, Coal, Okla., 148...C5 112
Central, Elmore, Ala., 40...C3 78
Central, Graham, Ariz., 110..E6 80
Central, Caribou, Idaho, 10..G7 89
Central, St. James, La...B5 95
Central, Grant, N. Mex., 1,075...E1 107
Central, Pickens, S.C., 1,473..B2 115
Central, Washington, Utah, 21...F2 119
Central, dept., Par., 174,789...*E4 55
Central, prov., Malawi...D5 48
Central, prov., Zambia...E4 48
Central, reg., Ghana...E4 45
Central, reg., Ken...B6 48
Central, reg., Tan., 886,306..C6 48
Central, plat., Tan...C5 48
Central, range, Dom. Rep...F8 64
Central African Republic, country, Afr., 1,350,000...D4 46, F8 42
Central Aguirre, P.R., 1,689..D6 65
Central America, reg., N.A., 13,800,000...H12 61, 62
Central Avenue Park, Lucas, Ohio, 900...*A2 105
Central Barren, Harrison, Ind., 100...H5 91
Central Bridge, Schoharie, N.Y., 500...C6 108
Central Butte, Sask., Can., 459...G2 70
Central City, Gilpin, Colo., 250...B5 83
Central City, Marion, Ill., 1,422...E4 90
Central City, Linn, Iowa, 1,087...B6 92
Central City, Muhlenberg, Ky., 3,694...C2 94
Central City, Merrick, Nebr., 2,406...C8 103
Central City, Somerset, Pa., 1,604...F4 114
Central City, Lawrence, S. Dak., 247...C2 116
Central College, Franklin, Ohio, 120...B2 111
Central Falls, Randolph, N.C., 400...B4 109
Central Falls, Providence, R.I., 19,858...B11 84
Centralhatchee, Heard, Ga., 174...C1 87
Central Heights, Gila, Ariz., 2,486...D5 80
Central Heights, Cerro Gordo, Iowa, 900...A4 92
Centralia, Ont., Can., 179...D3 72
Centralia, Clinton and Marion, Ill., 13,904...E4 90
Centralia, Nemaha, Kans., 527...C7 93
Centralia, Boone, Mo., 3,200...B5 101
Centralia, Craig, Okla., 80..A6 112
Centralia, Columbia, Pa., 1,435...*E9 114
Centralia, Lewis, Wash., 8,586...C3 122
Centralia, Braxton, W. Va., 145...C4 123
Central Islip, Suffolk, N.Y., 24,000...E7, n15 108
Central Java, see Java, isl., Indon.
Central Lake, Antrim, Mich., 692...C5 98
Central Makran, range, Iran, Pak...C3 39
Central Nyack, Rockland, N.Y., 1,300...*D7 108
Central Park, Vermilion, Ill., 2,676...*C6 90
Central Park, Grays Harbor, Wash., 1,622...*C2 122
Central Point, Jackson, Oreg., 2,289...E4 113
Central Provinces, see Madhya Pradesh, state, India
Central Siberian, uplands, Sov. Un...C13 28
Central Square, Oswego, N.Y., 935...B4 108
Central Sumatra, see Sumatra, isl., Indon.
Central Valley, Shasta, Calif., 2,854...B2 82
Central Valley, Orange, N.Y., 900...D6, m14 108
Central Village, Windham, Conn., 900...C9 84
Central Village, Bristol, Mass., 300...C5 97
Centre, Cherokee, Ala., 2,392...A4 78
Centre, co., Pa., 78,580...E6 114
Centre, mtn., Idaho...D3 89
Centre, peak, B.C., Can...B4 68
Centre Hall, Centre, Pa., 1,109...E6 114
Centre Square, Gloucester, N.J., 75...D2 106
Centreville, Bibb, Ala., 1,981.C2 78
Centreville, St. Joseph, Mich., 971...G5 98
Centreville, N.B., Can., 352..C2 74
Centreville, N.S., Can., 304..E3 74
Centreville, Queen Annes, Md., 1,863...B5 85
Centreville, St. Joseph, Mich., 971...*G5 98
Centreville, Amite and Wilkinson, Miss., 1,737...D2 100
Centreville, Wilson, Tenn., 50...A5 117
Centreville, Fairfax, Va., 600.B4 121
Centro Comunal Nogueras, P.R...C6 65
Centropolis, Franklin, Kans., 100...D8 93
Centro Puntas, P.R...B1 65
Centuria, Polk, Wis., 551...C1 124
Century, Escambia, Fla., 2,046...G2 86
Century, Barbour, W. Va., 700...B4 123
Ceram, isl., Indon...F7 35
Cercany, Czech., 1,261...o18 26
Cereal, Alta., Can., 195...D5 69
Cereales, Arg...B4 54
Ceredo, Wayne, W. Va., 1,387...C2 123
Ceres, Stanislaus, Calif., 4,406...D3 82
Ceres, It., 562...D3 18
Ceres, Allegany, N.Y., 300...C2 108
Ceres, Bland, Va., 75...B3, D1 121
Ceresco, Saunders, Nebr., 429...C9, E2 103
Ceres Northwest, Stanislaus, Calif., 1,126...*D3 82
Céret, Fr., 4,548...F5 14
Cereté, Col., 6,161...B2 60
Cerignola, It., 47,400...D5 21
Cerillos, P.R...C2 65
Cerknica, Yugo., 1,404...C2 24
Cernavodă, Rom., 8,802...C8 22
Cernay, Fr., 8,372...D7 14
Cerralvo, Mex., 3,050...B5 63
Cerralvo, isl., Mex...C3 63
Cerrillos, Santa Fe, N. Mex., 200...B3, k8 107
Cerritos, Mex., 9,849...C4 63
Cerro, Taos, N. Mex., 50...A4 107
Cerro Azul, Peru, 1,372...D2 58
Cerro Bolívar, Ven...B5 60
Cerro Colorado, Ur...E1 56
Cerro de Pasco, Peru, 5,700...D2 58
Cerro de Punta, peak, P.R...C4 65
Cerrogordo, Little River, Ark...D1 81
Cerro Gordo, Piatt, Ill., 1,067...D5 90
Cerro Gordo, Columbus, N.C., 306...C5 109
Cerrogordo, McCurtain, Okla., 60...D7 112
Cerro Gordo, co., Iowa, 49,894...A4 102
Cerro Largo, dept., Ur., 67,500...*E2 56
Cerro Negro, Chile...E2 56
Cerulean, Trigg, Ky., 206...D2 94
Cervantes, Phil., 682...B6 35
Cervantes, Sp., 7,011...A2 20
Cervera del Río Alhama, Sp., 7,101...A5 20
Cerveteri, It., 3,759...g8 21
Cervignano del Friuli, It., 7,729...D9 18
Cervione, Fr., 1,162...C2 21
Cesena, It., 39,000 (81,800▲).B4 21
Cesenatico, It., 5,935...B4 21
Ceská Kamenice, Czech., 4,885...C9 17
Ceska Lipa, Czech., 14,000...C3 26
Ceska Trebova, Czech., 13,000...D4 26
České Budějovice, Czech., 65,900...D3 26
Cesky Brod, Czech., 5,754..n18 26
Cesky Krumlov, Czech., 8,900...D3 26
Cesme, Tur., 3,700...C6 23
Cess, riv., Lib...E3 45
Cessford, Alta., Can...D5 69
Cessnock, Austl., 35,282...F8 51
Cetina, riv., Yugo...D3 22
Cetinje, Yugo., 9,345...D4 22
Cetraro, It., 9,366...E5 21
Cetti, bay, Guam...52
Ceuta, Sp., dep., Afr., 73,182...B3 44, G4 30
Cévennes, mts., Fr...E5 14
Cevio, Switz., 504...D6 19
Ceyhan, riv., Tur...D11 31
Ceylon, Ont., Can., 95...C4 72
Ceylon, Sask., Can., 288...H3 70
Ceylon, Martin, Minn., 554..G4 99
Ceylon, country, Asia, 11,000,000...I11 33, G7 39
Cezma, riv., Yugo...C3 22
Chabarovice, Czech., 3,388..C8 17
Chacabuco, Arg., 12,530.A4, g6 54
Chacahoula, Terrebonne, La., 50...C5, E5 95
Chachapoyas, Peru, 6,480...C2 58
Chachoengsao, Thai., 19,849.F4 38
Chachran, Pak., 2,954...C3 40
Chachro, Pak...E3 40
Chaco, prov., Arg., 62,377...E3 55
Chaco, riv., N. Mex...A1 107
Chaco Canyon, nat. mon., N. Mex.B2 107
Chacon, Mora, N. Mex., 10..A4 107
Chad, country, Afr., 2,900,000...B3 46, E7 42
Chad, lake, Chad...C2 46
Chadbourn, Columbus, N.C., 2,323...C5 109
Chadds Ford, Delaware, Pa., 140...G10 114
Chadiza, Zambia...D5 48
Chadron, Dawes, Nebr., 5,079...B3 103
Chadwick, Carroll, Ill., 602..A4 90
Chadwick, Christian, Mo., 175...E4 101
Chadwicks, Oneida, N.Y., 1,000...*B5 108
Chaerhsen, China...A9 36
Chaffee, Scott, Mo., 2,862...D8 101
Chaffee, Cass, N. Dak., 106..C8 110
Chaffee, co., Colo., 8,298...C4 83
Chaffins, Worcester, Mass., 3,000...B4 97
Chagny, Fr., 4,065...D6 14
Chagadoshcha, riv., Sov. Un..B10 27
Chagos, is., Indian O...G1 2
Chagres, riv., Pan...k12 62
Chagrin Falls, Cuyahoga, Ohio, 3,458...A6 111
Chagyl, Sov. Un...E5 29
Chahal, Guat., 329...C3 62
Chahar Burjak, Afg., 5,000..F11 41
Chahba, Syr., 2,700...F11 31
Chāh Bahār, Iran, 5,189...I10 41
Chaibasa, India, 22,019...D8 39
Chainat, Thai., 4,431...E4 38
Chaires, Leon, Fla., 85...B2 86
Chakai, Pak...A5 39
Chake Chake, Tan., 7,167...C6 48
Chakradharpur, India, 20,260 (*30,906)...D8 39
Chakwal, Pak., 13,319...B5 39
Chala, Peru, 721...E3 58
Chalatenango, Sal., 5,183...C3 62
Chalchuapa, Sal., 13,680...D3 62
Chalcidice (Khalkidhiki), prov., Grc., 79,849...*B4 23
Chalco, Sarpy, Nebr...D2 103
Chalender, Coconino, Ariz., 20...B3 80
Chaleur, bay, N.B., Que., Can..B4 74
Chalfant, Allegheny, Pa., 1,414...*F2 114
Chalfont, Bucks, Pa., 1,410..F11 114
Chalhuanca, Peru, 2,538...D3 58
Chaling, China...K5 36
Chalk River, Ont., Can., 1,135...A7 72
Chalkville, Jefferson, Ala., 1,000...*E4 78
Chalkyitsik, Alsk., 57...B11 79
Challans, Fr., 2,915...D3 14
Challapata, Bol., 2,529...C2 55
Challis, Custer, Idaho, 732...E4 89
Chalmers, White, Ind., 548..C4 91
Chalmette, St. Bernard, La., 10,000...C7, E6 95
Chalmette, nat. hist. park and cem., La...C7 95
Châlons-sur-Marne, Fr., 41,705...C6 14
Chalon-sur-Saône, Fr., 43,655...D6 14
Chalus, Iran...C5 41
Chalybeate, Tippah, Miss., 199...A5 100
Chalybeate, Van Buren, Tenn...D8 117
Chalybeate Springs, Harnett, N.C., 200...B5 109
Cham, Ger., 9,200...D7 17
Cham, Switz., 6,483...B5 19
Cham, pt., Okinawa...52
Chama, Costilla, Colo., 350..D5 83
Chama, Rio Arriba, N. Mex., 1,000...A3 107
Chamaicó, Arg...B4 54
Chamalières, Fr., 14,700...E5 14
Chaman, Pak., 7,161...B4 39
Chamba, Tan...D6 48
Chamberino, Dona Ana, N. Mex., 50...E3 107
Chamberlain, Sask., Can., 162...G3 70
Chamberlain, Brule, S. Dak., 2,598...D6 116
Chamberlain, lake, Maine...B3 96
Chamberlain's, Newf., Can., 667...*E5 75
Chamberlayne Heights, Henrico, Va., 1,000...*D5 121
Chamberlin, mtn., Alsk...B10 79
Chambers, Apache, Ariz., 200...B6 80
Chambers, Holt, Nebr., 396..B7 103
Chambers, co., Ala., 37,828..C4 78
Chambers, co., Tex., 10,379..E5 118
Chambers, isl., Wis...C6 124
Chambersburg, Franklin, Pa., 17,670...G6 114
Chambéry, Fr., 44,246 (*57,000)...E6 14
Chambezi, riv., Zambia...D5 48
Chamblee, DeKalb, Ga., 6,635...A5 87
Chambly, Que., Can., 3,737...D4 73
Chambly, Fr., 5,331...E2 15
Chambly, co., Que., Can., 146,745...D4 73
Chambord, Que., Can., 1,188...A5 73
Chamcook, N.B., Can., 327..D2 74
Chamdo (Changtu), China...E4 34
Chamical, Arg., 2,702...F2 55
Chamisal, Taos, N. Mex., 500...A4 107
Chamois, Osage, Mo., 658..C6 101
Chamonix-Mont-Blanc, Fr., 3,164...E7 14, D2 18
Champ, Somerset, Md., 100.D6 85
Champagne, Yukon, Can., 56...D5 66
Champagne, former prov., Fr., 1,504,000...C5 14
Champagnole, Fr., 7,531...D6 14
Champaign, Champaign, Ill., 49,583...C5 90
Champaign, co, Ill., 132,436..C5 90
Champaign, co., Ohio, 29,714...B4 111
Champdoré, lake, Que., Can...g8 75
Champerico, Guat., 982...C2 62
Champéry, Switz., 810...D3 19
Champex, Switz...D3 19
Champigneulles, Fr., 5,854...F6 15
Champigny-sur-Marne, Fr., 57,876...g11 14
Champion, Alta., Can., 419..D4 69
Champion, Marquette, Mich., 750...B3 98
Champion, Chase, Nebr., 140...D4 103
Champion (Champion Heights), Trumbull, Ohio, 2,500...*A7 111
Champlain, Que., Can., 750...C5 73
Champlain, Clinton, N.Y., 1,549...f11 108
Champlain, co., Que., Can., 111,953...B5 73
Champlain, lake, Can., U.S...B13 77
Champlin, Hennepin, Minn., 1,271...E6 99
Champlitte, Fr., 1,423...D6 14
Champney's West, Newf., Can., 266...D5 75
Champotón, Mex., 2,853...D6 63
Champua, India, 5,000...F10 40
Chana, Ogle, Ill., 200...B4 90
Chañaral, Chile, 2,980...E1 55
Chanārān, Iran,...C9 41
Chañarcillo, Chile...E1 55
Chanca, riv., Port...D2 20
Chancay, Peru, 2,761...D2 58
Chance, Clarke, Ala., 400...D2 78
Chance, Somerset, Md., 275.D6 85
Chancellor, Geneva, Ala., 150...D4 78
Chancellor, Turner, S. Dak., 214...D8 116
Chanchelulla, mtn., Calif...B2 82
Chanco, Chile, 1,931...B2 54
Chanda, India, 51,484...E6 39
Chandalar, riv., Alsk...B10 79
Chandausi, India, 48,557...C7 40
Chandeleur, is., La...E7 95
Chandeleur, sound, La...E6 95
Chandernagore, India, 67,105...*F12 40
Chandigarh, India, 89,321 (*99,262)...B6 39, B6 40
Chandler, Maricopa, Ariz., 9,531...D4, G2 80
Chandler, Que., Can., 3,406...k14 73
Chandler, Warrick, Ind., 1,784...H3 91
Chandler, Murray, Minn., 388...G3 99
Chandler, Clay, Mo...E2 101
Chandler, Lincoln, Okla., 2,524...B5 112
Chandler, Henderson, Tex., 500...C5 118
Chandler Heights, Maricopa, Ariz., 400...G3 80
Chandlers, brook, N.H...A4 105
Chandlers Valley, Warren, Pa...C8 114
Chandlerville, Cass, Ill., 718.C3 90
Chandos, lake, Ont., Can...C6 72
Chandpur, Pak., 32,048...D9 39
Chandrakona, India, 7,383..F11 40
Chaneliak, Alsk., 25...C7 79
Chaneysville, Bedford, Pa., 50...G5 114
Chānf, Iran...H10 41
Chang, riv., China...C11 39
Changchih, China, 97,800...F5 36
Changchiu, China...F7 36
Changchow, China, 296,500..E8 34
Changchun (Hsinking), China, 975,000...C10 34, E2 37
Change Islands, Newf., Can., 747...D4 75
Changewater, Warren, N.J., 100...B3 106
Changhsing, China, 12,000...I8 36
Changhua, China, 6,000...I8 36
Changhua, Taiwan, 52,340..*G9 34
Changjin, Kor., 5,000...F3 37
Changkiakow, see Kalgan, China
Changli, China...E8 36
Changling, China, 5,000...D1 37
Chang-pai (Paektu-san), mts., China...E3 37
Changpa Shan, peak, Kor...F4 37
Changpei, China...C7 34
Changping, China...D7 36
Changsha, China, 703,000...F7 34, J5 36
Changsŏng, Kor., 17,661...F2 37
Changte, China, 94,800...F7 34
Changting, China, 27,000...F8 34
Changtu, see Chamdo, China
Changtze, China...D6 34
Changwu, China, 8,000...C10 36
Changwu, China, 10,000...D6 36
Changyeh, China...D5 34
Changyon, Kor., 18,072...G2 37
Chanhassen, Carver, Minn., 244...F5 99
Chankiang, China, 166,000..G7 34
Channahon, Will, Ill., 400...B5 90
Channel, is., Eur...F5 10
Channel Islands, nat. mon., Calif...E4 82
Channel Lake, Lake, Ill., 1,969...*D2 90
Channel-Port-aux-Basques, Newf., Can., 4,141...E2 75
Channelview, Harris, Tex., 7,500...F5 118
Channing, Dickinson, Mich., 600...B2 98
Channing, Hartley, Tex., 351...B1 118
Chantada, Sp., 2,262...A2 20
Chanthaburi, Thai., 10,649..F5 38
Chantilly, Fr., 8,197...C5 14
Chantilly, Fairfax, Va., 400..B4 121
Chantrey, inlet, N.W. Ter., Can...C13 66
Chanute, Neosho, Kans., 10,849...E8 93
Chanute, Pickett, Tenn., 25..C8 117
Chany, lake, Sov. Un...D24 9
Chanyu, China...B10 36
Chao, lake, China...I7 36
Chaochen (Chaochow), China, 101,300...G8 34
Chaoan, China, 23,000...G8 34
Chaochou, China, 5,000...D2 37
Chao Phraya (Menam), riv., Thai...E4 38
Chaotung, China...C2 37
Chaotung, China...F5 34
Chaoyang, China, 66,000...*G8 34
Chaoyang, China, 16,000...C9 34
Chapada, mts., Braz...B1 56
Chapadinha, Braz., 3,698...B2 57
Chapala, lake, Mex...m12 63
Chapanoke, Perquimans, N.C., 50...A7 109
Chaparral, Col., 11,705...C2 60
Chapayevsk, Sov. Un., 85,000...C5 29
Chapel Arm, Newf., Can., 561...*E5 75
Chapel Hill, Sevier, Ark...C1 81
Chapelhill, Allen, Ky., 300..D3 94
Chapel Hill, Orange, N.C., 12,573...B4 109
Chapel Hill, Marshall, Tenn., 630...B5 117
Chapelle, San Miguel, N. Mex., 35...B4 107
Chapin, Morgan, Ill., 477...D3 90
Chapin, Franklin, Iowa, 200..B4 92
Chapin, Lexington, S.C., 358.C5 115
Chapleau, Ont., Can., 3,350.p19 72
Chaplin, Sask., Can., 479...G2 70
Chaplin, Windham, Conn., 115 (1,230▲)...B8 84
Chaplin, Nelson, Ky., 350...C4 94
Chaplin, lake, Sask., Can...G2 70
Chaplygin, Sov. Un., 10,000.E12 27
Chapman, Butler, Ala., 617..D3 78
Chapman, Dickinson, Kans., 1,095...D6 93
Chapman, Aroostook, Maine, 40 (376▲)...B4 96
Chapman, Merrick, Nebr., 303...C7 103
Chapman, cape, N.W. Ter., Can...C15 66
Chapman, lake, Ind...B6 91
Chapman Camp, B.C., Can., 649...E10 68
Chapman Ranch, Nueces, Tex., 200...F4 118
Chapmanville, Logan, W. Va., 1,241...D2 119
Chappaqua, Westchester, N.Y., 4,500...*D7 108
Chappaquiddick, isl., Mass...D7 97
Chappell, Deuel, Nebr., 1,280...C3 103
Chappells, Newberry, S.C., 128...C4 115
Chapra, India, 75,580 (*88,264)...C7 39, E10 40
Chaptico, creek, Md...D4 85
Chaqui, Bol., 291...C2 55
Char (Well), Maur...B2 45
Charadai, Arg...E4 55
Charagua, Bol., 1,185...C3 55
Charalá, Col., 3,309...B3 60
Charaña, Bol., 794...C2 55
Charcas, Mex., 9,058...C4 63
Charco, Goliad, Tex., 50...E4 118
Charco Hondo, P.R...B4 65
Charcot, isl., Ant...C5 5
Chard, Eng., 5,778...D5 12
Chardon, Geauga, Ohio, 3,154...A6 111
Chardzhou, Sov. Un., 75,000...H21 9
Charente, dept., Fr., 327,658...*E4 14
Charente, riv., Fr...E3 14
Charente-Maritime, dept., Fr., 470,897...*D3 14
Charenton, St. Mary, La., 650...E4 95
Charenton-le-Pont, Fr., 22,530...g10 14
Charette, Que., Can., 583...C5 73
Chargoggagoggmanchauggagogg-chaubunagungamaugg, lake, Mass...*B4 97
Chari, riv., Chad...C3 46
Charikar, Afg., 21,070...D14 41
Charing, Taylor, Ga., 100...D2 87
Chariton, Lucas, Iowa, 5,042...C4 92
Chariton, co., Mo., 12,720..B4 101
Chariton, riv., Iowa, Mo...A5 101
Charity, Br. Gu., 838...A3 59
Charity, Dallas, Mo...D4 101
Charkhlik, China, 5,000...D2 34
Charlack, St. Louis, Mo., 1,493...*A8 101
Charlemagne, Que., Can., 3,068...D4, p19 73
Charlemont, Franklin, Mass., 500 (897▲)...A2 97
Charleroi, Bel., 26,175 (*375,000)...D4 15
Charleroi, Washington, Pa., 8,148...F2 114
Charles, co., Md., 32,572...C3 85
Charles, cape, Va...D6 121
Charles, mound, Ill...A3 90
Charles, riv., Mass...B5 97
Charlesbourg, Que., Can., 14,308...n17 73
Charlesburg, Calumet, Wis., 100...B5 124
Charles City, Floyd, Iowa, 9,964...A5 92
Charles City, Charles City, Va., 20...D5 121
Charles City, co., Va., 5,492.D5 121
Charles Mill, res., Ohio...B5 111
Charles Mix, co., S. Dak., 11,785...D7 116
Charleston, Franklin, Ark., 1,036...B1 81
Charleston, Coles, Ill., 10,505...D5 90
Charleston, Penobscot, Maine, 175 (750▲)...C3 96
Charleston, Tallahatchie, Miss., 2,528...A3 100
Charleston, Mississippi, Mo., 5,911...E8 101
Charleston, Coos, Oreg., 500...D2 113
Charleston, Charleston, S.C., 65,925 (*203,100)...F3, F8 115
Charleston, Bradley, Tenn., 764...D9 117
Charleston, Wasatch, Utah, 223...C4 119
Charleston (Town of), Orleans, Vt. (668▲)...*B4 120
Charleston, Kanawha, W. Va., 85,796 (*213,900)...C3, C6 123
Charleston, co., S.C., 216,382...F8 115
Charleston, harbor, S.C...F8 115
Charleston, peak, Nev...G6 104
Charleston Heights, Charleston, S.C., 25,000...F2 115
Charlestown, Clark, Ind., 5,726...H6 91
Charlestown, Ire., 727...D3 11
Charlestown, St. Kitts-Nevis-Anguilla, 1,852...n15 64
Charlestown, Cecil, Md., 711...A6 85
Charlestown, Sullivan, N.H., 1,173 (2,576▲)...D2 105
Charlestown, Washington, R.I., 600 (1,966▲)...D10 84
Charles Town, Jefferson, W. Va., 3,329...B7 123
Charlesville, Con. L...C3 48
Charleville, Austl., 5,154...C6 51
Charleville, Fr., 24,668 (*56,000)...C6 14
Charlevoix, Charlevoix, Mich., 2,751...C5 98
Charlevoix, co., Mich., 13,421...C5 98
Charlevoix, lake, Mich...C5 98
Charlevoix-Est, co., Que., Can., 16,450...B7 73
Charlevoix-Ouest, co., Que., Can., 14,562...B7 73
Charlie Lake, B.C., Can., 104...A7 68
Charlieu, Fr., 4,911...D6 14
Charlo, Lake, Mont., 150...C2 102
Charlo Station, N.B., Can., 409...B3 74
Charlotte, Clinton, Iowa, 417...C7 92
Charlotte, Washington, Maine, (260▲)...C5 96
Charlotte, Eaton, Mich., 7,657...F6 98
Charlotte, Mecklenburg, N.C., 201,564 (*272,700)...B3 109
Charlotte, Dickson, Tenn., 551...A4 117
Charlotte, Atascosa, Tex., 1,465...E3 118
Charlotte, Chittenden, Vt., 200 (1,271▲)...C2 120
Charlotte, co., N.B., Can., 23,285...D2 74
Charlotte, co., Fla., 12,594...F4 86
Charlotte, co., Va., 13,368...D4 121
Charlotte, harbor, Fla...F4 86
Charlotte, lake, B.C., Can...C5 68
Charlotte Amalie, Vir. Is. (U.S.), 12,880...m14 64, f15 65
Charlotte Court House, Charlotte, Va., 555...D4 121
Charlotte Hall, St. Marys, Md., 83...D4 85
Charlotte Harbor, Charlotte, Fla., 500...F4 86
Charlottenburg, Ger...A8 17
Charlottenburg, Sur...A4 59
Charlottesville, Hancock, Ind., 500...E6 91
Charlottesville (Independent City), Va., 29,427...C4 121
Charlottetown, P.E.I., Can., 18,318...C6 74
Charlotte Waters, Austl...E5 50
Charlson, McKenzie, N. Dak., 15...A3 110
Charlton, Worcester, Mass., 500 (3,685▲)...B4 97
Charlton, co., Ga., 5,313...F4 87
Charlton City, Worcester, Mass., 900...B4 97
Charlton Depot, Worcester, Mass., 250...B4 97
Charmco, Greenbrier, W. Va., 700...*D4 123
Charmes, Fr., 5,177...C7 14
Charmey, Switz., 1,144...C3 19
Charny, Que., Can., 4,189...C6, o17 73
Charouîn, Alg...D4 44
Charron, lake, Man., Can...C4 71
Charskiy, Sov. Un...D10 29
Charter Oak, Los Angeles, Calif., 4,000...*F3 82
Charter Oak, Crawford, Iowa, 665...B2 92
Charters Towers, Austl., 7,633...D8 50
Chartierville, Que., Can., 188...D6 73
Chartley, Bristol, Mass., 700.C5 97
Chartrand, Ont., Can...h13 72
Chartres, Fr., 31,495 (*48,000)...C4 14
Charysh, riv., Sov. Un...C10 29
Chascomús, Arg., 9,105...B5 55
Chase, B.C., Can., 990...D8 68
Chase, Rice, Kans., 922...D5 93
Chase, Lake, Mich., 185...E5 98
Chase, co., Kans., 3,921...D7 93
Chase, co., Nebr., 4,317...D4 103
Chase, mtn., Maine...B4 96
Chaseburg, Vernon, Wis., 242...E2 124
Chase City, Mecklenburg, Va., 3,207...E4 121
Chaseley, Wells, N. Dak., 72.B6 110
Chase River, B.C., Can., 603...f12 68
Chasicó, Arg...C3 54
Chaska, Carver, Minn., 2,501...F5 99
Chasong, Kor., 5,000...F3 37
Chasov Yar, Sov. Un., 10,000...q20 27
Chassahowitzka, bay, Fla...D4 86
Chasseral, mtn., Switz...B2 19
Chasseron, mtn., Switz...C2 19
Chastang, Mobile, Ala., 200..D1 78
Chataignier, Evangeline, La., 550...D3 95
Chatanika, Alsk., 14...B10 79
Chatawa, Pike, Miss., 100...D3 100
Chatcolet, Benewah, Idaho, 101...B2 89
Châteaubriant, Fr., 10,852...D3 14
Chateau d'Oex, Switz., 3,378...D3 19
Château-du-Loir, Fr., 4,707..D4 14
Châteaudun, Fr., 11,982...C4 14
Chateaugay, Franklin, N.Y., 1,097...f10 108
Château-Gontier, Fr., 7,065..D3 14
Châteauguay, Que., Can., 7,570...D4, q19 73
Châteauguay, co., Que., Can., 34,042...D4 73
Châteauguay Centre, Que., Can., 7,591...*D4 73

22X CHAT-CHIN

Châteauguay Heights, Que., Can., 1,231 q19 73
Châteauneuf [-sur-Loire], Fr., 4,350 D5 14
Château-Renault, Fr., 4,238 D4 14
Château-Richer, Que., Can., 1,837 C6 73
Châteauroux, Fr., 45,063 D4 14
Château-Salins, Fr., 2,174 F6 15
Château-Thierry, Fr., 10,006 C5 14
Châtellerault, Fr., 27,079 D4 14
Châtel-St.-Denis, Switz., 2,666 C2 19
Chatfield, Crittenden, Ark., 100 B5 81
Chatfield, Man., Can., 158 D3 71
Chatfield, Fillmore and Olmstead, Minn., 1,841 G6 99
Chatfield, Crawford, Ohio, 263 B5 111
Chatham, Alsk., 5 m22, D12 79
Chatham, N.B., Can., 7,109 B4 74
Chatham, Ont., Can., 29,826 E2 72
Chatham, Eng., 50,200 (*200,000) C8 12
Chatham, Sangamon, Ill., 1,069 D4 90
Chatham, Jackson, La., 758 B3 95
Chatham, Barnstable, Mass., 1,580 (3,273▲) C8 97
Chatham, Alger, Mich., 175 B4 98
Chatham, Washington, Miss., 50 B2 100
Chatham, Carroll, N.H., 30 (150▲) B4 105
Chatham, Morris, N.J., 9,517 B4 106
Chatham, Columbia, N.Y., 2,426 C7 108
Chatham, Medina, Ohio, 200 A5 111
Chatham, Pittsylvania, Va., 1,822 E3 121
Chatham, co., Ga., 188,299 E5 87
Chatham, co., N.C., 26,785 B4 109
Chatham, is., Pac. O I11 7
Chatham, sound, B.C., Can B2 68
Chatham, strait, Alsk m22 79
Chatham Head, N.B., Can., 1,610 C4 74
Chatillon, It., 2,335 D3 18
Châtillon-sur-Seine, Fr., 5,518 D6 14
Chatkal, range, Sov. Un E8 29
Chatom, Washington, Ala., 993 D1 78
Chatrapur, India, 7,835 H10 40
Chatsworth, Ont., Can., 419 C4 72
Chatsworth, Murray, Ga., 1,184 B2 87
Chatsworth, Livingston, Ill., 1,330 C5 90
Chatsworth, Sioux, Iowa, 84 B1 92
Chatsworth, Burlington, N.J., 400 D3 106
Chattahoochee, Gadsden, Fla., 9,699 B2 86
Chattahoochee, Fulton, Ga. (part of Atlanta) B5, C2 87
Chattahoochee, co., Ga., 13,011 D2 87
Chattahoochee, riv., U.S D10 77
Chattanooga, Mercer, Ohio, 150 B3 111
Chattanooga, Comanche, Okla., 356 C3 112
Chattanooga, Hamilton, Tenn., 130,009 (*286,700) D8, E10 117
Chattaroy, Spokane, Wash., 150 B8 122
Chattaroy, Mingo, W. Va., 950 D2 123
Chatteris, Eng., 5,490 B8 12
Chattooga, co., Ga., 19,954 B1 87
Chattooga, ridge, S.C B1 115
Chattooga, riv., S.C B1 115
Chatuge, lake, N.C D2 109
Chatwood, Chester, Pa., 3,621 *G10 114
Chaudière, riv., Que., Can C7 73
Chau Doc, Viet., 5,000 G6 38
Chaudrant, bayou, La B3 95
Chauk, Bur., 24,466 D9 39
Chaumont, Fr., 21,717 C6 14
Chaumont, Jefferson, N.Y., 523 A4 108
Chaun, bay, Sov. Un B34 4
Chauncey, Dodge, Ga., 330 D3 87
Chauncey, Athens, Ohio, 996 C5 111
Chauncey, Logan, W. Va., 300 D3 123
Chauncy, pond, Mass g9 97
Chauny, Fr., 12,626 C5 14
Chautauqua, Chautauqua, Kans., 205 E7 93
Chautauqua, Chautauqua, N.Y., 500 C1 108
Chautauqua, co., Kans., 5,956 E7 93
Chautauqua, co., N.Y., 145,377 C1 108
Chautauqua, lake, N.Y C1 108
Chauvigny, Fr., 4,024 D4 14
Chauvin, Alta., Can., 395 C5 69
Chauvin, Terrebonne, La., 950 E5 95
Chavanga, Sov. Un D17 25
Chaves, Braz., 428 C5 59
Chaves, Port., 11,286 B2 20
Chaves, co., N. Mex., 57,649 D5 107
Chavies, Perry, Ky., 250 C6 94
Chavinda, Mex., 5,418 m12 63
Chavuma, Zambia D3 48
Chazelles [-sur-Lyon], Fr., 5,076 E6 14
Chazy, Clinton, N.Y., 800 f11 108
Cheadle, Alta., Can D4 69
Cheaha, mtn., Ala B4 78
Cheal, lake, Sask., Can D2 70
Cheapside, Northampton, Va., 150 A7 121
Cheat, mtn., W. Va C5 123
Cheat, riv., W. Va B5 123
Cheatham, co., Tenn., 9,428 A4 117
Cheb, Czech., 20,600 C2 26
Chebacco, lake, Mass f12 97
Chebanse, Iroquois and Kankakee, Ill., 995 C6 90
Chebeague Island, Cumberland, Maine, 300 E2, E5 96
Cheboksary, Sov. Un., 142,000 B3 29
Cheboygan, Cheboygan, Mich., 5,859 C6 98
Cheboygan, co., Mich., 14,550 C6 98
Chech, sand dunes, Alg., Mali E4 44
Chechaouen, Mor., 13,712 B3 44
Checheng, China G6 36
Chechon, Kor., 24,600 H4 37
Checotah, McIntosh, Okla., 2,614 B6 112
Chedabucto, bay, N.S., Can D8 74
Cheddar, Eng., 2,600 C5 12
Cheddar, Anderson, S.C., 500 B3 115
Cheduba, isl., Bur E9 39
Cheecham, hills, Alta., Can B4 69
Cheektowaga, Erie, N.Y., 80,500 C2 108
Cheepie, Austl., 60 C5 51
Cheesman, lake, Colo B5 83
Chefoo, China, 116,000 F9 36
Chefuncte, riv., La D5 95
Chehalem, mts., Oreg B1 113
Chehalis, Lewis, Wash., 5,199 C3 122
Chehalis, riv., Wash C2 122
Cheikh Meskine, Syr., B8 32
Cheikh Saad, Syr., B7 32
Cheju, Kor., 37,000 (73,400▲) J3 37
Cheju, isl., Kor J3 37
Chekhov, Sov. Un., 10,000 C10 37
Chekiang, prov., China, 25,280,000 F9 34
Chekunda, Sov. Un A6 37
Chela, mts., Ang E1 48
Chelan, Sask., Can., 115 E4 70
Chelan, Chelan, Wash., 2,402 B6 122
Chelan, co., Wash., 40,744 B5 122
Chelan, lake, Wash A5 122
Chelan, range, Wash B5 122
Chelan Falls, Chelan, Wash., 150 B6 122
Cheleiros, Port., 1,253 f9 20
Cheleken, Sov. Un B6 41
Cheleken, isl., Sov. Un B6 41
Chelforó, Arg B3 54
Cheli, China G5 34
Chelia, mtn., Alg B6 44
Chéliff, riv., Alg B5 44
Chelkar, Sov. Un., 19,300 D5 29
Chelkar, lake, Sov. Un E19 9
Chelkar Tengiz, lake, Sov. Un F21 9
Chellala, Alg., 2,899 G8 30
Chelles, Fr., 28,382 F2 15
Chełm [Lubelski], Pol., 27,000 C7 26
Chełmno, Pol., 14,400 B5 26
Chelmsford, Ont., Can., 2,559 *A3 72
Chelmsford, Eng., 52,200 C8 12
Chelmsford, Middlesex, Mass., 4,000 (15,130▲) A5, f10 97
Chelmża, Pol., 12,200 B5 26
Chelsea, Que., Can., 327 D2 73
Chelsea, Tama, Iowa, 453 C5 92
Chelsea, Kennebec, Maine, 125 (1,893▲) D3 96
Chelsea, Suffolk, Mass., 33,749 B5, g11 97
Chelsea, Washtenaw, Mich., 3,355 F6 98
Chelsea, Rogers, Okla., 1,541 A6 112
Chelsea, Faulk, S. Dak., 53 B7 116
Chelsea, Orange, Vt., 500 (957▲) D4 120
Chelsea, Taylor, Wis., 110 C3 124
Cheltenham, Eng., 74,300 C5 12
Cheltenham, Prince Georges, Md., 500 C4 85
Cheltenham, Montgomery, Pa., 7,000 *A12 114
Chelva, Sp., 4,400 C5 20
Chelyabinsk, Sov. Un., 767,000 (*950,000) B6 29
Chelyan, Kanawha, W. Va., 500 C3, C6 117
Chelyuskin, cape, Sov. Un B13 28
Chelyuskintsy, ice tongue, Ant C21 5
Chemainus, B.C., Can., 1,518 E6, g12 68
Chemal, Sov. Un E26 9
Chemawa, Marion, Oreg C1, C4 113
Chemillé, Fr., 3,109 D3 14
Chemnitz, see Karl-Marx-Stadt, Ger.
Chemquassabamticook, lake, Maine B3 96
Chemult, Klamath, Oreg., 150 D5 113
Chemung, McHenry, Ill., 150 A5 90
Chemung, co., N.Y., 98,706 C4 108
Chemung, lake, Ont., Can C6 72
Chen, mtn., Sov. Un C17 28
Chenab, riv., Pak B5 39
Chenachane (Oasis), Alg D4 44
Chenan, China H3 36
Chenango, Brazoria, Tex G5 118
Chenango, co., N.Y., 43,243 C5 108
Chenango, riv., N.Y C5 108
Chenango Bridge, Broome, N.Y., 3,500 *C5 108
Chenango Forks, Broome, N.Y., 500 C5 108
Chenchi, China, 2,000 K4 34
Chene, bayou, La C5 95
Chenega, Alsk., 20 C10, g17 79
Chenequa, Waukesha, Wis., 445 E1 124
Chénéville, Que., Can., 746 D2 73
Cheney, Sedgwick, Kans., 1,101 B4, E6 93
Cheney, Spokane, Wash., 3,173 B8, D7 122
Cheneyville, Rapides, La., 1,037 C3 95
Cheng, China J9 36
Chengan, China, 14,000 J2 36
Chengane, riv., Moz B5 49
Chengchan Tow, pt., China D9 34
Chengchow, China, 766,000 G5 36
Chenghai, China, 33,000 G8 34
Chenghsien, see Chengchow, China
Chenghwa, see Sharasume, China
Chengkou, China, 13,000 I3 36
Chengku, China, 10,000 H2 36
Chengteh (Jehol), China, 92,900 C8 34, D7 36
Chengtu, China, 1,107,000 E5 34
Chengyangkuan, China H6 36
Chenhsien, China F7 34
Chenkang, China G4 34
Chennan, China, 5,000 F5 34
Chenoa, McLean, Ill., 1,523 C5 90
Chenôve, Fr., 5,517 D6 14
Chenpa, China, 3,000 H2 36
Chenping, China I3 36
Chensi, see Barkol, China
Chentung, China, 5,000 B10 36
Chenyuan, China, 11,000 K3 36
Cheoah, Graham, N.C D2 109
Cheo Reo, Viet F8 38
Chepachet, Providence, R.I., 900 B10 84
Chepén, Peru, 8,214 C2 58
Chepes, Arg., 2,131 A3 54
Chepo, Pan., 1,664 F8 62
Chepstow, Wales, 6,041 C5 12
Cheptsa, riv., Sov. Un D19 9
Chequamegon, bay, Wis B3 124
Cher, dept., Fr., 293,514 *D5 14
Cher, riv., Fr D4 14
Cheran, India, 5,000 E13 40
Cheraw, Otero, Colo., 173 C7 83
Cheraw, Marion, Miss., 50 D4 100
Cheraw, Chesterfield, S.C., 5,171 B8 115
Cherbourg, Fr., 37,486 (*70,000) C3 14
Cherchel, Alg., 7,805 B5 44
Cherchen, China, 5,000 A8 39
Cherdyn, Sov. Un A5 29
Cheremkhovo, Sov. Un., 140,000 D13 28
Cherepanovo, Sov. Un., 23,100 C10 29
Cherepovets, Sov. Un., 124,000 B1 29
Cherhill, Alta., Can., 72 C3 69
Cheriton, Northampton, Va., 761 D7 121
Cherkassy, Sov. Un., 103,000 G9 27
Cherkessk, Sov. Un., 49,000 G17 9
Cherlakskiy, Sov. Un C8 29
Chernigov, Sov. Un., 113,000 F8 27
Chernigovka, Sov. Un., 3,300 H11 27
Chernikovsk, Sov. Un., 206,000 *E20 9
Chernobay, Sov. Un., 25,000 G9 27
Chernobyl, Sov. Un., 10,000 F8 27
Chernofski, Alsk., 5 E6 79
Chernogor, Sov. Un., 30,000 E27 9
Chernomorskoye, Sov. Un., 3,800 I9 27
Chernovtsy, Sov. Un., 152,000 A7 22, G5 27
Chernoye, Sov. Un r32 25
Chernyakhovsk (Insterburg), Sov. Un., 33,000 D3 27
Cherokee, Colbert, Ala., 1,349 A2 78
Cherokee, Cherokee, Iowa, 7,724 B2 92
Cherokee, Crawford, Kans., 797 E9 93
Cherokee, Swain, N.C., 500 D3 109
Cherokee, Alfalfa, Okla., 2,410 A3 112
Cherokee, San Saba, Tex., 150 D3 118
Cherokee, co., Ala., 16,303 A4 78
Cherokee, co., Ga., 23,001 B2 87
Cherokee, co., Iowa, 18,598 B2 92
Cherokee, co., Kans., 22,279 E9 93
Cherokee, co., N.C., 16,335 D2 109
Cherokee, co., Okla., 17,762 B6 112
Cherokee, co., S.C., 35,205 A4 115
Cherokee, co., Tex., 33,120 D5 118
Cherokee, Indian res., Tenn C10 117
Cherokee Falls, Cherokee, S.C., 350 A5 115
Cherokee, lake, Okla A7 112
Cherokee, lake, Tenn C10 117
Cherokee Ranch, Berks, Pa., 1,200 *F10 114
Cherokee Sound, Ba. Is., 320 B5 64
Cherquenco, Chile, 1,677 B2 54
Cherrapunji, India C9 39
Cherry, Bureau, Ill., 501 B4 90
Cherry, Lauderdale, Tenn., 75 B2 117
Cherry, co., Nebr., 8,218 B4 103
Cherry, creek, Colo B6 83
Cherry, creek, S. Dak C3 116
Cherry, pt., Va D6 121
Cherry Creek, White Pine, Nev., 50 D7 104
Cherry Creek, Chautauqua, N.Y., 649 C1 108
Cherry Creek, Ziebach, S. Dak., 150 C4 116
Cherryfield, Washington, Maine, 750 (780▲) D5 96
Cherry Fork, Adams, Ohio, 185 D4 111
Cherrygrove, Fillmore, Minn., 60 G6 99
Cherry Grove, Hamilton, Ohio, 2,000 *C3 111
Cherry Grove, Washington, Oreg., 300 B1 113
Cherry Hill, Polk, Ark., 150 C1 81
Cherry Hill, Cecil, Md., 150 A6 85
Cherry Hill, Camden, N.J., 31,522 D2 106
Cherry Hill, pt., N.Y E8 84
Cherry Hills Village, Arapahoe, Colo., 1,931 *B6 83
Cherry Run, Morgan, W. Va., 100 B6 123
Cherry Tree, Indiana, Pa., 469 E4 114
Cherryvale, Montgomery, Kans., 2,783 E8 93
Cherry Valley, Cross, Ark., 455 B5 81
Cherry Valley, Ont., Can., 272 D7 72
Cherry Valley, Winnebago, Ill., 875 A5 90
Cherry Valley, Worcester, Mass., 1,800 B4 97
Cherry Valley, Otsego, N.Y., 668 C6 108
Cherryville, Gaston, N.C., 3,607 B2 109
Cherskiy, mts., Sov. Un C17 28
Chesaning, Saginaw, Mich., 2,770 E6 98
Chesapeake, Lawrence, Ohio, 1,396 D5 111
Chesapeake (Independent City), Va., 73,647 E6, B7 121
Chesapeake, Kanawha, W. Va., 2,699 C3 123
Chesapeake, bay, U.S C12 77
Chesapeake Beach, Calvert, Md., 731 C4 85
Chesapeake City, Cecil, Md., 1,104 A6 85
Chesapeake and Delaware, canal, Del A6 85
Chesaw, Okanogan, Wash., 50 A6 122
Chesha, bay, Sov. Un C10 4
Chesham, Cheshire, N.H., 150 E2 105
Cheshire, New Haven, Conn., 3,500 (13,383▲) D5 84
Cheshire, Berkshire, Mass., 1,150 (2,472▲) A1 97
Cheshire, Gallia, Ohio, 369 D5 111
Cheshire, co., Eng., 1,367,860 A5 12
Cheshire, co., N.H., 43,342 E2 105
Cheshire, res., Mass A1 97
Cheshskaya, bay, Sov. Un B18 9
Chesilhurst, Camden, N.J., 384 D3 106
Chesley, Ont., Can., 1,697 C3 72
Chesnee, Spartanburg, S.C., 1,045 A4 115
Chesney, Union, Tenn C10 117
Chesnokovka, Sov. Un., 20,000 E25 9
Chester, Crawford, Ark., 99 B1 81
Chester, Plumas, Calif., 1,553 B3 82
Chester, N.S., Can., 990 E5 74
Chester, Middlesex, Conn., 1,500 (2,520▲) D7 84
Chester, Eng., 59,400 A5 12
Chester, Nassau, Fla., 100 B5, B6 86
Chester, Dodge, Ga., 377 D3 87
Chester, Freemont, Idaho, 100 F7 89
Chester, Randolph, Ill., 4,460 F4 90
Chester, Wayne, Ind., 130 E8 91
Chester, Howard, Iowa, 211 A5 92
Chester, Queen Annes, Md., 900 C5 85
Chester, Hampden, Mass., 750 (1,155▲) B2 97
Chester, Liberty, Mont., 1,158 B6 102
Chester, Thayer, Nebr., 480 D8 103
Chester, Rockingham, N.H., 400 (1,053▲) E4 105
Chester, Morris, N.J., 1,074 B3 106
Chester, Orange, N.Y., 1,492 D6, m14 108
Chester, Meigs, Ohio, 200 C6 111
Chester, Major, Okla., 150 A3 112
Chester, Delaware, Pa., 63,658 B10, G11 114
Chester, Chester, S.C., 6,906 B5 115
Chester, Lake, S. Dak., 200 D9 116
Chester, Sanpete, Utah, 5 D5 119
Chester, Windsor, Vt., 923 (2,318▲) E3 120
Chester, Chesterfield, Va., 2,000 C7, D5 121
Chester, Spokane, Wash D8 122
Chester, Hancock, W. Va., 3,787 A2, A4 123
Chester, co., Pa., 210,608 G10 114
Chester, co., S.C., 30,888 B5 115
Chester, co., Tenn., 9,569 B3 117
Chester, creek, Pa D1 106
Chester, riv., Md B5 85
Chester Basin, N.S., Can., 490 E5 74
Chester Depot, Windsor, Vt., 350 E3 120
Chesterfield, New London, Conn., 150 D8 84
Chesterfield, Eng., 68,200 (*129,000) A6 12
Chesterfield, Macoupin, Ill., 280 D3 90
Chesterfield, Madison, Ind., 2,588 D6 91
Chesterfield, Hampshire, Mass., 200 (556▲) B2 97
Chesterfield, Cheshire, N.H., 90 (1,405▲) E2 105
Chesterfield, Chesterfield, S.C., 1,532 B7 115
Chesterfield, Henderson, Tenn., 200 B3 117
Chesterfield, Chesterfield, Va., 135 C7, D5 121
Chesterfield, co., S.C., 33,717 B7 115
Chesterfield, co., Va., 71,197 D5 121
Chesterfield, inlet, N.W. Ter., Can D14 66
Chesterfield, is., Pac. O H9 7
Chesterfield Inlet, N.W. Ter., Can., 146 D14 66
Chesterhill, Morgan, Ohio, 876 C6 111
Chesterton, Porter, Ind., 4,335 A3 91
Chestertown, Kent, Md., 3,602 B5 85
Chestertown, Warren, N.Y., 500 B7 108
Chesterville, Ont., Can., 1,248 B9 72
Chesterville, Pontotoc, Miss A5 100
Chesterville, Morrow, Ohio, 275 B5 111
Chestnut, Logan, Ill., 300 C4 90
Chestnut Hill, New London, Conn., 150 C8 84
Chestnut Mound, Smith, Tenn., 125 C8 117
Chestoa, Unicoi, Tenn., 150 C11 117
Chesuncook, Piscataquis, Maine, 10 B3 96
Chesuncook, lake, Maine C3 96
Cheswick, Allegheny, Pa., 2,734 A6 114
Cheswold, Kent, Del., 281 B6 85
Chetac, lake, Wis C2 124
Chetco, riv., Oreg E2 113
Chetek, Barron, Wis., 1,729 C2 124
Chetek, lake, Wis C2 124
Chéticamp, N.S., Can., 1,223 C8 74
Chetopa, Labette, Kans., 1,538 E8 93
Chetumal, bay, Mex D7 63
Chetwynd, B.C., Can., 1,020 B7 68
Chevalon, creek, Ariz C5 80
Chèverie, N.S., Can., 195 D5 74
Cheverly, Prince Georges, Md., 5,223 *C1 85
Cheviot, Sask., Can E2 70
Cheviot, N.Z., 440 O14 51
Cheviot, Hamilton, Ohio, 10,701 C3, D2 111
Cheviot, hills, Scot., Eng E6 13
Chevreuil, bayou, La C6 95
Chevreuil, pt., La E4 95
Chevy Chase, Montgomery, Md., 2,405 C1, C3 85
Chevy Chase Heights, Indiana, Pa., 1,160 *E3 114
Chevy Chase Lake, Montgomery, Md., 2,500 *C3 85
Chevy Chase Section Four, Montgomery, Md., 2,243 *C3 85
Chevy Chase View, Montgomery, Md., 1,000 *C3 85
Chewack, creek, Wash A5 122
Chewalla, McNairy, Tenn., 150 B3 117
Chewelah, Stevens, Wash., 1,525 A8 122
Chewey, Adair, Okla., 30 A7 112
Chewsville, Washington, Md., 250 A2 85
Cheyenne, Roger Mills, Okla., 930 B2 112
Cheyenne, Winkler, Tex., 15 D1 118
Cheyenne, Laramie, Wyo., 43,505 D8 125
Cheyenne, co., Colo., 2,789 C8 83
Cheyenne, co., Kans., 4,708 C2 93
Cheyenne, co., Nebr., 14,828 C2 103
Cheyenne, pass, Wyo D7 125
Cheyenne, riv., S. Dak., Wyo C4 116
Cheyenne Agency, Dewey, S. Dak C5 116
Cheyenne River, Indian res., S. Dak B5 116
Cheyenne Wells, Cheyenne, Colo., 1,020 C8 83
Chhatarpur, India, 22,146 E7 40
Chhindwara, India, 37,244 F7 40
Chi, China G6 36
Chia, China E4 36
Chiahsing, China, 78,300 I9 36
Chiai, Taiwan, 96,500 (191,100▲) *G9 34
Chialing, riv., China J2 36
Chiamboni (Dicks Head), cape, Ken B7 48
Chiamussu, see Kiamusze, China
Chian, China F3 37
Chian, China, 52,800 K6 36
Chianghua, China *F7 34
Chiang Kham, Thai C4 38
Chiang Khong, Thai., 3,320 B4 38
Chiangling, China, 15,000 I5 36
Chiang Mai, Thai., 65,736 C3 38
Chiang Rai, Thai., 13,494 C3 38
Chiangyin, China, 57,000 I9 36
Chiangyu, China, 15,000 E5 34
Chiaochia, China, 13,000 F5 34
Chiaoho, China, 5,000 E3 37
Chiaotso, China G5 36
Chiapa de Corzo, Mex., 6,972 D6 63
Chiapas, state, Mex., 1,215,475 D6 63
Chiari, It., 9,000 B2 21
Chiashan, China H8 36
Chiasso, Switz., 7,377 (*12,216) E7 19
Chiatura, Sov. Un., 20,000 A14 31
Chiautla de Tapia, Mex., 3,554 n14 63
Chiavari, It., 24,603 B2 21
Chiavenna, It., 6,211 C5 18
Chiawuli Tak, Pima, Ariz., 100 F4 80
Chiayu, China, 18,000 J5 60
Chiba, Jap., 241,615 I10, n19 37
Chiba, pref., Jap., 2,306,010 *I10 37
Chibana, Okinawa 52
Chibemba, Ang., 354 E1 48
Chiblow, lake, Ont., Can A1 72
Chibougamau, Que., Can., 4,765 k12 73
Chibuto, Moz B5 49
Chicago, Cook, Ill., 3,550,404 (*6,777,800) B6, F3 90
Chicago Heights, Cook, Ill., 34,331 B6, F3 90
Chicago Ridge, Cook, Ill., 5,748 *F3 90
Chicago Sanitary and Ship, canal, Ill F2 90
Chicamacomico, creek, Md D6 85
Chicamuxen, Charles, Md C3 85
Chicapa, riv., Ang C3 48
Chichagof, hbr., Alsk E2 79
Chichagof, isl., Alsk k22 79
Chichaoua, Mor C3 44
Chichen-Itzá, ruins, Mex C7 63
Chichester, Eng., 19,600 D7 12
Chichester, Merrimack, N.H., 130 (821▲) D4 99
Chichiang, China., 20,000 J2 36
Chichibu, Jap., 43,700 (59,796▲) n18 37
Ch'i-ch'i-ha-erh, see Tsitsihar, China
Chichun, China, 32,000 I6 36
Chickahominy, riv., Va D5 121
Chickaloon, Alsk., 43 C10, g17 79
Chickamauga, Walker, Ga., 1,824 B1 87
Chickamauga, dam, Tenn E10 117
Chickamauga, lake, Tenn D8 117
Chickasaw, Mobile, Ala., 10,002 E1 78
Chickasaw, co., Iowa, 15,034 A5 92
Chickasaw, co., Miss., 16,891 B5 100
Chickasawhay, riv., Miss D5 100
Chickasha, Grady, Okla., 14,866 B4 112
Chicken, Alsk., 23 C11 79
Chiclana, Sp., 21,524 D2 20
Chiclayo, Peru, 86,900 C2 58
Chico, riv., Arg C3 54
Chico, Butte, Calif., 14,757 C3 82
Chico Hot Springs, Park, Mont., 5 E6 102
Chico, Wise, Tex., 654 C4 118
Chico, Kitsap, Wash., 300 B3 122
Chicoa, Moz A5 49
Chicomo, Moz B5 49
Chicontepec, Mex., 2,859 m14 63
Chicopee, Hall, Ga., 900 B3 88
Chicopee, Crawford, Kans., 200 E9 93
Chicopee, Hampden, Mass., 61,553 B2 97
Chicora, Wayne, Miss., 100 D5 100
Chicora (Millerstown), Butler, Pa., 1,156 E2 114
Chicot, Chicot, Ark., 25 D4 81
Chicot, co., Ark., 18,990 D4 81
Chicot, isl., La E6 95
Chicot, lake, Ark D4 81
Chicot, pt., La E6 95
Chicota, Lamar, Tex., 370 C5 118
Chicoutimi, Que., Can., 31,657 (*105,009) A6, k12 73
Chicoutimi, co., Que., Can., 157,196 A6 73
Chicoutimi, riv., Que., Can A6 73
Chicoutimi-Nord, Que., Can., 11,229 A6 73
Chico Vecino, Butte, Calif., 4,688 *C3 82
Chidester, Ouachita, Ark., 348 D2 81
Chidley, cape, N.W. Ter., Can f8 75
Chieerete, isl., Bikini 52
Chiefland, Levy, Fla., 1,459 C4 86
Chiefs, pt., Ont., Can C3 72
Chiehhsiu, China F4 36
Chiem, lake, Ger E6 16
Chien, China G3 36
Chienan, China D8 36
Chienchang, China F2 37
Chienchiang, China, 11,000 J3 36
Chienli, China, 20,000 J5 36
Chienning, China, 8,000 K7 36
Chienou, China, 12,000 K8 36
Chienping, China D8 36
Chienshan, China I7 36
Chienshih, China, 15,000 I3 36
Chienshui, China, 28,000 G5 34
Chientang, riv., China J8 36
Chiente, China, 12,000 J8 36
Chienyang, China, 12,000 F8 34
Chierhkalang, China C10 36
Chieri, It., 11,900 B1 21
Chiers, riv., Fr E5 15
Chiese, riv., It D6 18
Chieti, It., 36,800 (48,900▲) C5 21
Chigirin, Sov. Un., 10,000 G9 27
Chignahuapan, Mex., 3,873 n14 63
Chignecto, bay, N.B., N.S., Can D5 74
Chignecto, cape, N.S., Can D5 74
Chignik, Alsk D8 79
Chigubo, Moz B5 49
Chigwell, Eng., 62,200 k13 10
Chihchiang, China F6 34
Chihchiang, China, 19,000 I4 36
Chihfeng, China, 40,000 C8 36
Chihli (Pohai), gulf, China D8 34
Chihsi, China, 50,000 B11 34
Chihtan, China D6 34
Chihuahua, Mex., 150,430 B3 63
Chihuahua, state, Mex., 1,235,891 B3 63
Chiili, Sov. Un E7 29
Chikan, China A9 34
Chikaskia, creek, Okla A4 112
Chikaskia, riv., Kans E6 93
Chiko, China B4 37
Chikura, Jap., 10,900 o18 37
Chikwolnepy, stream, N.H A4 105
Chilapa, Mex., 7,105 D5, o14 63
Chilca, Peru, 1,341 D2 58
Chilcat, pass, B.C., Can E5 66
Chilcotin, riv., B.C., Can C5 68
Childersburg, Talladega, Ala., 4,884 B3 78
Childress, Childress, Tex., 6,399 B2 118
Childress, co., Tex., 8,421 B2 118
Childs, lake, Fla E5 86
Chile, country, S.A., 8,450,000 G3 53, B2 54, E2 55
Chilecito, Arg., 6,121 E2 55
Chilete, Peru, 476 C2 58
Chilhowee, Johnson, Mo., 339 C4 101
Chilhowee, Blount, Tenn D9 117
Chilhowee, mtn., Tenn E12 117
Chilhowie, Smyth, Va., 1,169 B3 121
Chili, Miami, Ind., 145 C5 91
Chili, Rio Arriba, N. Mex., 100 *A3 107
Chili, Clark, Wis., 225 D3 124
Chilibre, Pan., 1,220 k11 62
Chilili, Bernalillo, N. Mex., 50 C3, m8 107
Chilin, see Kirin, China
Chilka, lake, India H10 40
Chilko, lake, B.C., Can D5 68
Chilko, riv., B.C., Can D6 68
Chillán, Chile, 59,100 B2 54
Chillicothe, Peoria, Ill., 3,054 C4 90
Chillicothe, Wapello, Iowa, 148 C5 92
Chillicothe, Livingston, Mo., 9,236 B4 101
Chillicothe, Ross, Ohio, 24,957 C5 111
Chillicothe, Hardeman, Tex., 1,161 B3 118
Chilliwack, B.C., Can., 8,259 E7, f14 68
Chilliwack, lake, B.C., Can A4 122
Chilliwack, riv., B.C., Can A4 122
Chillum, Prince Georges, Md., 10,000 *C3 85
Chilmark, Dukes, Mass., 130 (238▲) D6 97
Chilocco, Kay, Okla., 80 A4 112
Chiloé, prov., Chile, 98,662 C2 54
Chiloé, isl., Chile C2 54
Chiloquin, Klamath, Oreg., 945 E5 113
Chilpancingo [de los Bravos], Mex., 18,022 D5, o14 63
Chilson, Essex, N.Y., 50 B7 108
Chilton, Casey, Ky., 65 C5 94
Chilton, Falls, Tex., 400 D4 118
Chilton, Calumet, Wis., 2,578 B5, D5 124
Chilton, co., Ala., 25,693 C3 78
Chilung (Keelung), Taiwan, 193,500 (248,800▲) F9 34
Chilwa, lake, Malawi, Moz E6 48
Chimacum, Jefferson, Wash., 100 A3 122
Chimalhuacán, Mex., 2,433 h10 63
Chimaltenango, Guat., 6,138 C2 62
Chimán, Pan., 535 F8 62
Chimay, Bel., 3,180 D4 15
Chimayo, Rio Arriba, N. Mex., 600 A4 107
Chimbay, Sov. Un., 16,100 E5 29
Chimborazo, prov., Ec., 241,258 B2 58
Chimborazo, vol., Ec B2 58
Chimbote, Peru, 64,000 C2 58
Chimen, China J7 36
Chimkent, Sov. Un., 185,000 E7 29
Chimney Rock, Archuleta, Colo., 5 D3 83
Chimney Top, mtn., Tenn C11 117
Chimo, China F9 36
Chin, Alta., Can E4 69
Chin, China F5 36
Chin, cape, Ont., Can B3 72
Chin, lakes, Alta., Can E4 69
Chin, riv., China G5 36
China, Mex., 2,496 B5 63
China (excl. Taiwan), country, Asia, 700,000,000 F12 33, E5 34
China, lake, Maine D3 96
China Grove, Pike, Ala., 50 C4 78
China Grove, Rowan, N.C., 1,500 B3 109
China Hat, mtn., Oreg D5 113
Chinaja, Guat B2 62
Chinan, see Tsinan, China
Chinandega, Nic., 19,800 D4 62

24X CLAR-COGN

Clarksville, Johnson, Ark., 3,919 ... B2 81
Clarksville, N.S., Can ... D6 74
Clarksville, Sussex, Del., 200 ... C7 85
Clarksville, Kootenai, Idaho, 44 ... B2 89
Clarksville, Clark, Ind., 8,088 ... H6 91
Clarksville, Butler, Iowa, 1,328 ... B5 92
Clarksville, Howard, Md., 180 ... B4 85
Clarksville, Ionia, Mich., 371 ... F5 98
Clarksville, Pike, Mo., 638 ... B7 101
Clarksville, Clinton, Ohio, 583 ... C4 111
Clarksville, Montgomery, Tenn., 22,021 ... A4 117
Clarksville, Red River, Tex., 3,851 ... C5 118
Clarksville, Mecklenburg, Va., 1,530 ... E4 121
Clarkton, Dunklin, Mo., 1,049 ... E8 101
Clarkton, Bladen, N.C., 662 ... C5 109
Clarno, Wheeler, Oreg ... C6 113
Claryville, Campbell, Ky., 20 ... A7 94
Claryville, Perry, Mo., 30 ... D8 101
Clashmore, Ire., 175 ... E4 11
Clatonia, Gage, Nebr., 203 ... D9 103
Clatskanie, Columbia, Oreg., 797 ... A3 113
Clatsop, co., Oreg., 27,380 ... A3 113
Claude, Armstrong, Tex., 895 ... B2 118
Claudy, N. Ire., 286 ... C4 11
Claunch, Socorro, N. Mex., 15 ... C3 107
Clausthal-Zellerfeld, Ger., 15,200 ... B5 17
Claveria, Phil., 5,046 ... *B6 35
Clavet, Sask., Can ... F2 70
Clawson, Oakland, Mich., 14,795 ... A7 98
Clawson, Emery, Utah, 130 ... D4 119
Claxton, Evans, Ga., 2,672 ... D5 87
Clay, Webster, Ky., 1,343 ... C2 94
Clay, Onondaga, N.Y., 100 ... B4 108
Clay, Burleson, Tex., 250 ... D4 118
Clay, Clay, W. Va., 486 ... C3, C7 123
Clay, co., Ala., 12,400 ... B4 78
Clay, co., Ark., 21,258 ... A5 81
Clay, co., Fla., 19,535 ... B5 86
Clay, co., Ga., 4,551 ... E2 87
Clay, co., Ill., 15,815 ... E5 90
Clay, co., Ind., 24,207 ... F3 91
Clay, co., Iowa, 18,504 ... A2 92
Clay, co., Kans., 10,675 ... C6 93
Clay, co., Ky., 20,748 ... C6 94
Clay, co., Minn., 39,080 ... D2 99
Clay, co., Miss., 18,933 ... B5 100
Clay, co., Mo., 87,474 ... B3 101
Clay, co., Nebr., 8,717 ... D7 103
Clay, co., N.C., 5,526 ... D2 109
Clay, co., S. Dak., 10,810 ... E8 116
Clay, co., Tenn., 7,289 ... C8 117
Clay, co., Tex., 8,351 ... C3 118
Clay, co., W. Va., 11,942 ... C3 123
Clay Center, Clay, Kans., 4,613 ... C6 93
Clay Center, Clay, Nebr., 792 ... D7 103
Clay Center, Ottawa, Ohio, 446 ... A2, A4 111
Clay City, Clay, Ill., 1,144 ... E5 90
Clay City, Clay, Ind., 950 ... F3 91
Clay City, Powell, Ky., 764 ... C6 94
Claycomo, Clay, Mo., 1,423 ... *B3 101
Clay Cross, Eng., 9,173 ... A6 12
Claydon, Sask., Can ... H1 70
Clayhatchee, Dale, Ala., 300 ... D4 78
Clayhole, wash, Utah ... G2 119
Claymont, New Castle, Del., 10,000 ... A7 85
Clayoquot, sound, B.C., Can ... E4 68
Claypool, Gila, Ariz., 1,800 ... D5 80
Claypool, Kosciusko, Ind., 452 ... B6 91
Claysburg, Blair, Pa., 1,439 ... F5 114
Clay Springs, Navajo, Ariz., 200 ... C1 80
Clay Spur, Weston, Wyo., 15 ... A8 125
Claysville, Washington, Pa., 986 ... F1 114
Clayton, Barbour, Ala., 1,313 ... D4 78
Clayton, Ont., Can., 84 ... B8 72
Clayton, Kent, Del., 1,028 ... B6 85
Clayton, Rabun, Ga., 1,507 ... B3 87
Clayton, Custer, Idaho, 125 ... E3 89
Clayton, Adams, Ill., 774 ... C3 90
Clayton, Hendricks, Ind., 653 ... E4 91
Clayton, Clayton, Iowa, 130 ... B6 92
Clayton, Norton and Decatur, Kans., 161 ... C3 93
Clayton, Concordia, La., 882 ... C4 95
Clayton, St. Louis, Mo., 15,245 ... B8, C7 101
Clayton, Gloucester, N.J., 4,711 ... D2 106
Clayton, Union, N. Mex., 3,314 ... A6 107
Clayton, Jefferson, N.Y., 1,996 ... A4, f8 108
Clayton, Johnston, N.C., 3,302 ... B5 109
Clayton, Pushmataha, Okla., 615 ... C6 112
Clayton, Obion, Tenn., 45 ... A2 117
Clayton, Stevens, Wash., 240 ... B8 122
Clayton, Polk, Wis., 324 ... C1 124
Clayton, co., Ga., 46,365 ... C2 87
Clayton, co., Iowa, 21,962 ... B6 92
Clayton Lake, Aroostook, Maine ... B3 96
Clayville, Oneida, N.Y., 686 ... C5 108
Clayville, Providence, R.I., 200 ... B10 84
Clear, cape, Alsk ... h18 79
Clear, cape, Ire ... F2 11
Clear, creek, Ariz ... C4 80
Clear, creek, Tenn ... C9 117
Clear, creek, Wyo ... A6 125
Clear, fork, Ohio ... B5 111
Clear, fork, Tenn ... C9 117
Clear, fork, W. Va ... D3 123
Clear, fork, W. Va ... D6 123
Clear, isl., Ire ... F2 11
Clear, lake, Calif ... C2 82
Clear, lake, Man., Can ... D1 71
Clear, lake, Ont., Can ... B7 72
Clear, lake, Iowa ... A4 92
Clear, lake, Utah ... D3 119
Clear, riv., Alta., Can ... A1 69
Clear, stream, N.H ... A4 105
Clear Boggy, creek, Okla ... C5 112
Clearbrook, B.C., Can., 1,964 ... f13 68
Clearbrook, Clearwater, Minn., 650 ... C3 99
Clearco, Greenbrier, W. Va., 35 ... C4 123
Clear Creek, Monroe, Ind., 250 ... F4 91
Clearcreek, Carbon, Utah, 100 ... D4 119
Clear Creek, Raleigh, W. Va., 400 ... D6 123
Clear Creek, co., Colo., 2,793 ... B5 83
Clearfield, Taylor and Ringgold, Iowa, 504 ... D3 92
Clearfield, Rowan, Ky., 550 ... B6 94
Clearfield, Clearfield, Pa., 9,270 ... D5 114
Clearfield, Davis, Utah, 8,833 ... B3 119
Clearfield, co., Pa., 81,534 ... D5 114
Clear Fork, Wyoming, W. Va., 210 ... D3 123
Clear Lake, Cerro Gordo, Iowa, 6,158 ... A4 92
Clear Lake, Sherburne, Minn., 316 ... E5 99
Clear Lake, Beaver, Okla., 112 ... A1, D4 122
Clear Lake, Deuel, S. Dak., 1,137 ... C9 116
Clearlake, Skagit, Wash., 600 ... A3 122
Clear Lake, Polk, Wis., 724 ... C1 124
Clear Lake, res., Calif ... B3 82
Clear Lake Shores, Tex., 700 ... F5 118
Clearmont, Nodaway, Mo., 292 ... A2 101
Clearmont, Sheridan, Wyo., 154 ... A6 125
Clear Spring, Washington, Md., 488 ... A2 85
Clearview, Okfuskee, Okla., 500 ... B5 112
Clearville, Bedford, Pa., 140 ... G5 114
Clearwater, B.C., Can., 204 ... D7 68
Clearwater, Man., Can., 121 ... E2 71
Clearwater, Pinellas, Fla., 34,653 ... E1, E4 86
Clearwater, Idaho, Idaho, 40 ... C3 89
Clearwater, Sedgwick, Kans., 1,073 ... E6 93
Clearwater, Wright, Minn., 274 ... E4 99
Clearwater, Antelope, Nebr., 416 ... B7 103
Clearwater, Aiken, S.C., 1,450 ... E4 115
Clearwater, Jefferson, Wash., 70 ... B1 122
Clearwater, co., Idaho, 8,548 ... C3 89
Clearwater, co., Minn., 8,864 ... C3 99
Clearwater, creek, Kans ... B4 93
Clearwater, lake, B.C., Can ... C7 68
Clearwater, lake, Que., Can ... g11 73
Clearwater, mts., Idaho ... C2 89
Clearwater, prov. park, Man., Can ... C1 71
Clearwater, res., Mo ... D7 101
Clearwater, riv., Alta., Can ... A5 69
Clearwater, riv., Alta., Can ... D3 69
Clearwater, riv., B.C., Can ... C7 68
Clearwater, riv., Idaho ... C2 89
Clearwater, riv., Minn ... C3 99
Clearwater Lake, Oneida, Wis., 200 ... C4 124
Cleaton, Muhlenberg, Ky., 700 ... C2 94
Cleator Moor, Eng., 6,411 ... F5 13
Clebit, McCurtain, Okla., 250 ... C7 112
Cleburne, Riley, Kans., 150 ... C7 93
Cleburne, Johnson, Tex., 15,381 ... B5, C4 118
Cleburne, co., Ala., 10,911 ... B4 78
Cleburne, co., Ark., 9,059 ... B3 81
Cle Elum, Kittitas, Wash., 1,814 ... B5 122
Cle Elum, res., Wash ... B4 122
Cle Elum, riv., Wash ... B4 122
Cleethorpes, Eng., 32,705 ... A7 12
Cleeves, Sask., Can ... D1 70
Clegg, Live Oak, Tex ... E3 118
Cleggan, Ire ... D1 11
Cleghorn, Cherokee, Iowa, 228 ... B2 92
Cleghorn, Eau Claire, Wis., 80 ... D2 124
Clem, Carroll, Ga., 180 ... C1 87
Clementon, Camden, N.J., 3,766 ... D3 106
Clements, Chase, Kans., 50 ... D7 93
Clements, St. Marys, Md., 150 ... D4 85
Clements, Redwood, Minn., 269 ... F3 99
Clementsport, N.S., Can., 519 ... E4 74
Clementsvale, N.S., Can., 266 ... E4 74
Clemmons, Forsyth, N.C., 700 ... A3 109
Clemons, Marshall, Iowa, 198 ... B4 92
Clemons, Washington, N.Y., 100 ... B7 108
Clemscot, Carter, Okla., 250 ... C4 112
Clemson, Pickens, S.C., 1,587 ... *B2 115
Clemson College, Oconee, S.C., 3,500 ... *B2 115
Clendenin, Kanawha, W. Va., 1,510 ... C3, C6 123
Clendening, res., Ohio ... B6 111
Cleo, Kimble, Tex., 30 ... D3 118
Cleona, Lebanon, Pa., 1,988 ... F9 114
Cleo Springs, Major, Okla., 236 ... A3 112
Clermont, Austl., 1,737 ... D8 51
Clermont, Que., Can., 3,114 ... B7 73
Clermont, Lake, Fla., 3,313 ... D5 86
Clermont, Fr., 7,509 ... E2 15
Clermont, Hall, Ga., 268 ... B3 87
Clermont, Marion, Ind., 1,058 ... E5, H7 91
Clermont, Fayette, Iowa, 570 ... A6 92
Clermont, Bullitt, Ky., 100 ... C4 94
Clermont, McKean, Pa., 250 ... C5 114
Clermont, co., Ohio, 80,530 ... C3 111
Clermont, hill, Calif ... C3 82
Clermont-Ferrand, Fr., 127,684 (*160,000) ... E5 14
Clermont-l'Hérault, Fr., 5,538 ... F5 14
Clervaux, Lux., 1,459 ... D6 15
Cleve, see Kleve, Ger.
Clevedon, Eng., 9,700 ... C5 12
Cleveland, Blount, Ala., 500 ... A3 78
Cleveland, Conway, Ark., 79 ... B3 81
Cleveland, Charlotte, Fla., 200 ... F5 86
Cleveland, White, Ga., 657 ... B3 87
Cleveland, Kingman, Kans ... B3 93
Cleveland, Le Sueur, Minn., 389 ... F5 99
Cleveland, Bolivar, Miss., 10,172 ... B3 100
Cleveland, Cass, Mo., 216 ... C3 101
Cleveland, Mora, N. Mex., 200 ... A4 107
Cleveland, Oswego, N.Y., 732 ... B5 108
Cleveland, Rowan, N.C., 594 ... B3 109
Cleveland, Stutsman, N. Dak., 169 ... C6 110
Cleveland, Cuyahoga, Ohio, 876,050 (*2,090,800) ... A6, B2 111
Cleveland, Pawnee, Okla., 2,519 ... A5 112
Cleveland, Greenville, S.C., 250 ... A2 115
Cleveland, Bradley, Tenn., 16,196 ... D9 117
Cleveland, Liberty, Tex., 5,838 ... D5 118
Cleveland, Emery, Utah, 261 ... D5 119
Cleveland, Russell, Va., 415 ... B3 121
Cleveland, Maitowoc, Wis., 687 ... B6 124
Cleveland, co., Ark., 6,944 ... D3 81
Cleveland, co., N.C., 66,048 ... B2 109
Cleveland, co., Okla., 47,600 ... B4 112
Cleveland, hills, Eng ... F7 13
Cleveland, mtn., Mont ... B3 102
Cleveland Heights, Cuyahoga, Ohio, 61,813 ... A6, B2 111
Clevelândia, Braz., 1,671 ... D2 56
Clever, Christian, Mo., 283 ... D4 101
Cleves, Hamilton, Ohio, 2,076 ... *C3 111
Clew, bay, Ire ... D2 11
Clewiston, Hendry, Fla., 3,114 ... F6 86
Clibreck, mtn., Scot ... B4 13
Clichy [-la-Garenne], Fr., 56,316 ... g10 14
Clifden, Ire., 986 ... D1 11
Cliff, Grant, N. Mex., 100 ... E1 107
Cliff Dwellings, ruins, Ariz ... A5 80
Clifford, Ont., Can., 542 ... D4 72
Clifford, Bartholomew, Ind., 241 ... F6 91
Clifford, Lapeer, Mich., 389 ... E7 98
Clifford, Traill, N. Dak., 109 ... B8 110
Clifford, Susquehanna, Pa., 250 ... C10 114
Clifford, Amherst, Va., 135 ... D3 121
Cliffside, B.C., Can ... g12 68
Cliffside, Rutherford, N.C., 1,275 ... B2, D4 109
Cliffside Park, Bergen, N.J., 17,642 ... h9 106
Clifftop, Fayette, W. Va., 300 ... D7 123
Cliffwood, Monmouth, N.J., 1,500 ... *C4 106
Cliffwood Beach, Middlesex and Monmouth, N.J., 3,500 ... *C4 106
Clifton, Greenlee, Ariz., 4,191 ... D6 80
Clifton, Mesa, Colo., 300 ... B2 83
Clifton, Franklin, Idaho, 150 ... G7 89
Clifton, Iroquois, Ill., 1,018 ... C6 90
Clifton, Washington and Clay, Kans., 746 ... C6 93
Clifton, Passaic, N.J., 82,084 ... B4, h8 106
Clifton, Spartanburg, S.C., 1,249 ... B4 115
Clifton, Wayne, Tenn., 708 ... B4 117
Clifton, Bosque, Tex., 2,335 ... D4 118
Clifton, Fairfax, Va., 230 ... B4, C5 121
Clifton, Weston, Wyo ... B8 125
Clifton City, Cooper, Mo., 125 ... C4 101
Clifton Forge (Independent City), Va., 5,268 ... D3 121
Clifton Heights, Delaware, Pa., 8,005 ... B11 114
Clifton Hill, Randolph, Mo., 207 ... B5 101
Clifton Springs, Ontario, N.Y., 1,953 ... C3 108
Cliftonville, Noxubee, Miss., 250 ... B5 100
Clifty, Decatur, Ind., 197 ... F6 91
Clifty White and Cumberland, Tenn., 75 ... D8 117
Climax, Sask., Can., 425 ... H1 70
Climax, Lake, Colo., 1,609 ... B4 83
Climax, Decatur, Ga., 329 ... F2 87
Climax, Greenwood, Kans., 81 ... E7 93
Climax, Kalamazoo, Mich., 587 ... F5 98
Climax, Polk, Minn., 310 ... C2 99
Climax Springs, Camden, Mo., 93 ... C4 101
Climbing Hill, Woodbury, Iowa, 100 ... B1 92
Clinch, co., Ga., 6,545 ... F4 87
Clinch, mtn., Va ... B2 121
Clinch, mts., Tenn ... C10 117
Clinch, riv., Tenn ... D9 117
Clinch, riv., Va ... B2 121
Clinchburg, Washington, Va., 450 ... B3 121
Clincho, Dickenson, Va., 975 ... B2 121
Clinchfield, Houston, Ga., 250 ... D3 87
Clinchfield, McDowell, N.C., 950 ... *D4 109
Clinchmore, Campbell, Tenn., 250 ... C9 117
Clinchport, Scott, Va., 302 ... B2 121
Cline, Uvalde, Tex., 50 ... E2 11
Cline, falls, Oreg ... C5 113
Clingmans Dome, mtn., Tenn ... D10 117
Clint, El Paso, Tex., 800 ... F1 118
Clinton, Greene, Ala., 150 ... C1 78
Clinton, Van Buren, Ark., 744 ... B3 81
Clinton, B.C., Can., 1,011 ... D7 68
Clinton, Ont., Can., 3,491 ... D3 72
Clinton, Middlesex, Conn., 4,166 ... D6 84
Clinton, Jones, Ga ... C3 87
Clinton, DeWitt, Ill., 7,355 ... C5 90
Clinton, Vermillion, Ind., 5,843 ... E3 91
Clinton, Clinton, Iowa, 33,589 ... C7 92
Clinton, Hickman, Ky., 1,647 ... B2 94
Clinton, East Feliciana, La., 1,568 ... D4 94
Clinton, Kennebec, Maine, 800 (1,729▲) ... D3 96
Clinton, Prince Georges, Md., 1,578 ... C4 85
Clinton, Worcester, Mass., 12,848 ... B4 97
Clinton, Lenawee, Mich., 1,481 ... F7 98
Clinton, Big Stone, Minn., 565 ... E2 98
Clinton, Hinds, Miss., 3,438 ... C3 100
Clinton, Henry, Mo., 6,925 ... C4 101
Clinton, Missoula, Mont., 160 ... D3 102
Clinton, Sheridan, Nebr., 46 ... B3 103
Clinton, Hunterdon, N.J., 1,158 ... B3 106
Clinton, Oneida, N.Y., 1,855 ... B5 108
Clinton, Sampson, N.C., 7,461 ... C5 109
Clinton, Summit, Ohio, 924 ... *B6 111
Clinton, Custer, Okla., 9,617 ... B3 112
Clinton, Laurens, S.C., 7,937 ... C4 115
Clinton, Anderson, Tenn., 4,943 ... C9, E11 117
Clinton, Davis, Utah, 1,025 ... B3 119
Clinton, Rock, Wis., 1,274 ... F5 124
Clinton, co., Ill., 24,029 ... E4 90
Clinton, co., Ind., 30,765 ... D4 91
Clinton, co., Iowa, 55,060 ... C7 92
Clinton, co., Ky., 8,886 ... D4 94
Clinton, co., Mich., 37,969 ... F6 98
Clinton, co., Mo., 11,588 ... B3 101
Clinton, co., N.Y., 72,722 ... f11 108
Clinton, co., Ohio, 30,004 ... C4 111
Clinton, co., Pa., 37,619 ... D6 114
Clinton, res., N.J ... A4 106
Clinton-Colden, lake, N.W. Ter., Can ... D11 66
Clintonville, New Haven, Conn. (part of North Haven) ... D5 84
Clintonville, Bourbon, Ky., 200 ... B5 94
Clintonville, Venango, Pa., 311 ... D2 114
Clintonville, Greenbrier, W. Va., 25 ... D4 123
Clintonville, Waupaca, Wis., 4,778 ... D5 124
Clintwood, Dickenson, Va., 1,400 ... B2 121
Clio, Barbour, Ala., 929 ... D4 78
Clio, Wayne, Iowa, 120 ... D4 92
Clio, Livingston, La ... B6 95
Clio, Genesee, Mich., 2,212 ... E7 98
Clio, Marlboro, S.C., 847 ... B8 115
Clio, Roane, W. Va., 300 ... C3 123
Clipper, Whatcom, Wash., 65 ... A3 122
Clipperton, isl., Pac. O ... F15 7
Clisham, mtn., Scot ... C1 13
Clitherall, Ottertail, Minn., 138 ... D3 99
Clive, Alta., Can., 251 ... C4 69
Cliza, Bol., 3,121 ... C2 55
Cloan, Sask., Can ... E1 70
Cloe, Jefferson, Pa., 500 ... E4 114
Cloghan, Ire ... D4 11
Cloghan, Ire., 303 ... D4 11
Cloghane, Ire., 75 ... E1 11
Clogheen, Ire., 576 ... E3 11
Clogher, head, Ire ... D5 11
Clonakilty, Ire., 2,417 ... F3 11
Clonakilty, bay, Ire ... F3 11
Cloncurry, Austl., 2,438 ... D7 50
Clonegall, Ire., 158 ... E5 11
Clones, Ire., 2,107 ... C4 11
Clonmany, Ire., 238 ... B4 11
Clonmel, Ire., 10,640 ... E4 11
Clonmellon, Ire., 271 ... D4 11
Clontarf, Swift, Minn., 139 ... E3 99
Cloone, Ire., 106 ... D4 11
Clo-oose, B.C., Can ... E5 68
Cloppenburg, Ger., 15,200 ... F2 24
Clopton, Dale, Ala., 125 ... D4 78
Cloquet, Carlton, Minn., 9,013 ... D6 99
Cloquet, riv., Minn ... C6 99
Closter, Bergen, N.J., 7,767 ... B5, h9 106
Clothier, Logan, W. Va., 500 ... D5 123
Cloud, co., Kans., 14,407 ... C6 93
Cloud, peak, Wyo ... A5 125
Cloud Chief, Washita, Okla., 75 ... B3 112
Cloudcroft, Otero, N. Mex., 464 ... E4 107
Cloud Lake, Palm Beach, Fla., 148 ... *F6 86
Cloudy, bay, N.Z ... N15 51
Clover, York, S.C., 3,500 ... A5 115
Clover, Halifax, Va., 261 ... C4 121
Clover Botton, Jackson, Ky., 190 ... C5 94
Cloverdale, Lauderdale, Ala., 800 ... A2 78
Cloverdale, Sonoma, Calif., 2,848 ... C2 82
Cloverdale, B.C., Can., 650 ... f13 68
Cloverdale, Du Page, Ill., 40 ... F2 90
Cloverdale, Putnam, Ind., 741 ... E4 91
Cloverdale, Tillamook, Oreg., 200 ... B3 113
Cloverdale, Botetourt, Va., 500 ... D3 121
Cloverleaf, Harris, Tex., 3,000 ... *E5 118
Clover Lick, Pocahontas, W. Va., 200 ... C5 123
Cloverport, Breckinridge, Ky., 1,334 ... C3 94
Cloverton, Pine, Minn., 150 ... D6 99
Clovis, Fresno, Calif., 7,704 ... D4 82
Clovis, Curry, N. Mex., 23,713 ... C6 107
Cloyne, Ire., 612 ... F3 11
Cluanie, lake, Scot ... C3 13
Cluj, Rom., 163,200 (201,000▲) ... B6 22
Clune, Indiana, Pa., 400 ... E3 114
Cluny, Alta., Can., 174 ... D4 69
Cluny, Fr., 4,032 ... D6 14
Clusone, It., 6,832 ... D5 18
Cluster Springs, Halifax, Va., 150 ... E4 121
Clute, Brazoria, Tex., 4,501 ... G5 116
Clutier, Tama, Iowa, 292 ... B5 92
Clyattville, Lowndes, Ga., 150 ... F3 87
Clyde, Alta., Can., 259 ... B4 69
Clyde, N.W. Ter., Can ... B19 67
Clyde, Cloud, Kans., 1,025 ... C6 93
Clyde, Nodaway, Mo., 90 ... A3 101
Clyde, Wayne, N.Y., 2,693 ... B4 108
Clyde, Haywood, N.C., 680 ... D3 109
Clyde, Cavalier, N. Dak., 100 ... A7 110
Clyde, Sandusky, Ohio, 4,826 ... A5 111
Clyde, Callahan, Tex., 1,116 ... C3 118
Clyde, firth, Scot ... E4 13
Clyde, riv., N.S., Can ... E4 74
Clyde, riv., Scot ... E4 13
Clydebank, Scot., 50,200 ... E4 13
Clyde Hill, King, Wash., 1,871 ... *D2 122
Clyde Park, Park, Mont., 253 ... E6 102
Clymer, Chautauqua, N.Y., 500 ... C1 108
Clymer, Indiana, Pa., 2,251 ... E3 114
Clyo, Effingham, Ga., 250 ... D5 87
Cnocmoy, mtn., Scot ... E3 13
Cnossus, ruins, Grc ... E5 23
Coachella, Riverside, Calif., 4,854 ... F4 82
Coachella, canal, Calif ... F12 82
Coachford, Ire., 275 ... F3 11
Coahoma, Coahoma, Miss., 300 ... A3 100
Coahoma, Howard, Tex., 1,239 ... C2 118
Coahoma, co., Miss., 46,212 ... A3 100
Coahuila, state, Mex., 896,509 ... B4 63
Coal, co., Okla., 5,546 ... C5 112
Coal, creek, Ind ... D3 91
Coal, creek, Okla ... B6 112
Coal, fork, W. Va ... D6 123
Coal, lake, W. Va ... C3 123
Coal, riv., W. Va ... C3 123
Coal Bluff, Vigo, Ind., 100 ... E3 91
Coal Branch Station, N.B., Can., 142 ... C4 74
Coalburn, Scot ... E5 13
Coal City, Grundy, Ill., 2,852 ... B5 90
Coal City, Owen, Ind., 235 ... F3 91
Coalcoman, Mex., 7,371 ... D4, h12 63
Coalcreek, Fremont, Colo., 206 ... C5 83
Coaldale, Alta., Can., 2,592 ... E4 69
Coaldale, Fremont, Colo., 15 ... C5 83
Coaldale, Schuylkill, Pa., 3,949 ... E10 114
Coalfield, Morgan, Tenn., 250 ... C9 117
Coal Fork, Kanawha, W. Va., 1,000 ... C3, C6 123
Coalgate, Coal, Okla., 1,689 ... C5 112
Coalgood, Harlan, Ky 800 ... D6 94
Coal Grove, Lawrence, Ohio, 2,961 ... D5 111
Coal Harbour, B.C., Can., 137 ... D4 68
Coal Hill, Johnson, Ark., 704 ... B2 81
Coalhurst, Alta., Can., 190 ... E4 69
Coaling, Tuscaloosa, Ala., 200 ... B2 78
Coalinga, Fresno, Calif., 5,965 ... D3 82
Coalmont, B.C., Can., 66 ... E7 68
Coalmont, Jackson, Colo., 8 ... A4 83
Coalmont, Clay, Ind., 500 ... F3 91
Coalmont, Grundy, Tenn., 458 ... D8 117
Coalport, Clearfield, Pa., 821 ... E4 114
Coalridge, Sheridan, Mont., 15 ... B12 102
Coalridge, Noble, Ohio, 70 ... C6 111
Coalspur, Alta., Can ... C2 69
Coalton, Montgomery, Ill., 352 ... D4 90
Coalton, Jackson, Ohio, 648 ... B4 111
Coalton, Okmulgee, Okla., 150 ... B6 112
Coaltown, Lawrence, Pa., 1,033 ... *D1 114
Coal Valley, Walker, Ala., 653 ... B2 78
Coal Valley, Rock Island, Ill., 435 ... D7 92
Coalville, Eng., 26,159 ... B6 12
Coalville, Webster, Iowa, 300 ... B3 92
Coalville, Summit, Utah, 907 ... C4 119
Coalwood, Powder River, Mont., 5 ... E11 102
Coalwood, McDowell, W. Va., 1,199 ... *D3 123
Coamo, P.R., 12,146 ... C5 65
Coamo, mun., P.R., 26,082 ... C5 65
Coari, Braz., 5,908 ... D5 60
Coast, reg., Ken ... B6 48
Coast, mts., Alsk., B.C., Can ... E6 66
Coast, ranges, U.S ... B3 76
Coastal, plain, U.S ... C5 109, E2 106
Coatbridge, Scot., 54,800 ... E4 13
Coatepec, Mex., 18,081 ... n15 63
Coatepeque, Guat., 6,281 ... C2 62
Coatesville, Hendricks, Ind., 497 ... E4 91
Coatesville, Chester, Pa., 12,971 ... G10 114
Coaticook, Que., Can., 6,906 ... D6 73
Coatopa, Sumter, Ala., 20 ... C1 78
Coats, Pratt, Kans., 152 ... E5 93
Coats, Harnett, N.C., 1,049 ... B5 109
Coats, isl., N.W. Ter., Can ... D16 67
Coats Land, reg., Ant ... B9 5
Coatsville, Schuyler, Mo., 100 ... A5 101
Coatzacoalcos (Puerto México), Mex., 36,989 ... D6 63
Cobalt, Ont., Can., 2,209 ... p19 72
Cobalt, Middlesex, Conn., 200 ... C6 84
Cobalt, Lemhi, Idaho, 250 ... E4 89
Cobán, Guat., 7,911 ... C2 62
Cobar, Austl., 2,178 ... E5 51
Cobb, Sumter, Ga., 90 ... E3 87
Cobb, Caldwell, Ky., 75 ... D2 94
Cobb, Iowa, Wis., 387 ... F3 124
Cobb, co., Ga., 114,174 ... C2 87
Cobb, isl., Md ... D4 85
Cobb, riv., Minn ... G5 99
Cobble Hill, B.C., Can., 97 ... g12 68
Cobble Mountain, res., Mass ... B2 97
Cobbosseecontee, lake, Maine ... D3 96
Cobbtown, Tattnall, Ga., 280 ... D4 87
Cobbville, Telfair, Ga ... E4 87
Cobden, Ont., Can., 942 ... B8 72
Cobden, Union, Ill., 918 ... F4 90
Cobequid, mts., N.S., Can ... D5 74
Cobh, Ire., 5,266 ... F3 11
Cobham, riv., Man., Can ... C4 71
Cobija, Bol., 1,726 ... B2 55
Cobija, Chile ... D1 55
Coble, Hickman, Tenn., 100 ... B4 117
Cobleskill, Schoharie, N.Y., 3,471 ... C6 108
Coboconk, Ont., Can., 506 ... C6 72
Cobourg, Ont., Can., 10,646 ... D6 72
Cobourg, pen., Austl ... B5 50
Cobre, Elko, Nev., 25 ... B7 98
Cobun, creek, W. Va ... A7 123
Coburg, Ger., 42,900 ... C5 17
Coburg, Montgomery, Iowa, 54 ... D2 92
Coburg, Lane, Oreg., 754 ... C3 113
Coburg, isl., N.W. Ter., Can ... m36 67
Coburn, Centre, Pa., 280 ... E7 114
Coburn, Wetzel, W. Va., 125 ... A6, B4 123
Coburn, mtn., Maine ... C2 96
Coburn Gore, Franklin, Maine, 80 ... C2 96
Coca, Ec ... B2 58
Cocanada, see Kakinada, India
Cocentaina, Sp., 8,108 ... C5 20
Cochabamba, Bol., 90,000 ... C2 55
Cochabamba, dept., Bol., 490,475 ... C2 55
Coche, isl., Ven ... A5 60
Cocheco, riv., N.H ... D4 105
Cochem, Ger., 6,900 ... D7 15
Cochesett, Plymouth, Mass., 500 ... B5 97
Cochetopa, creek, Colo ... C4 83
Cochetopa, hills, Colo ... C4 83
Cochin, India, 35,076 (*300,000) ... G6 39
Cochin China, reg., Viet., 6,500,000 ... G7 38
Cochise, Cochise, Ariz., 90 ... E6 80
Cochise, co., Ariz., 55,039 ... F5 80
Cochise Head, mtn., Ariz ... E6 80
Cochiti, Sandoval, N. Mex., 150 ... h8 107
Cochiti, Indian res., N. Mex ... h8 107
Cochituate, Middlesex, Mass., 5,200 ... g10 97
Cochituate, lake, Mass ... g10 97
Cochran, Bleckley, Ga., 4,714 ... D3 87
Cochran, co., Tex., 6,417 ... C1 118
Cochrane, Alta., Can., 857 ... D3 69
Cochrane, Ont., Can., 4,521 ... o19 72
Cochrane, Buffalo, Wis., 455 ... D2 124
Cochrane, dist., Ont., Can., 95,666 ... o18 72
Cochrane, mtn., Arg ... D2 54
Cochranton, Crawford, Pa., 1,139 ... C1 114
Cochranville, Chester, Pa., 350 ... G10 114
Cockburn, Austl., 101 ... F3 51
Cockburn, isl., Ont., Can ... C7 98
Cocke, co., Tenn , 23,390 ... D10 117
Cockermouth, Eng., 5,823 ... F5 13
Cockeysville, Baltimore, Md., 2,582 ... B4 85
Cockrell Hill, Dallas, Tex., 3,104 ... B5 118
Cockroach, isl., Vir. Is ... f14 65
Cockrum, De Soto Miss., 150 ... A4 100
Coco, riv., Nic ... C6 62
Cocoa, Brevard, Fla., 12,294 ... D6 86
Cocoa Beach, Brevard, Fla., 3,475 ... D6 86
Cocoa West, Brevard, Fla., 3,975 ... *D6 86
Cocobeach, Gabon ... E2 46
Cocolalla, Bonner, Idaho, 20 ... A2 89
Coconino, co., Ariz., 41,857 ... B3 80
Coconino, plat., Ariz ... B3 80
Cocos, isl., Guam ... 52
Cocos, lake, Ont., Can ... C5 71
Cocos (Keeling) Is., Austl. dep., Oceania, 700 ... G3 2
Cocula, Mex., 10,148 ... C4, m12 63
Cocuy, Col., 2,973 ... B3 60
Cod, cape, Mass ... B7 97
Cod, isl., Newf., Can ... g9 75
Codajás, Braz., 1,505 ... D5 60
Codajás, lake, Braz ... D5 60
Codell, Rooks, Kans., 100 ... C4 93
Coden, Mobile, Ala., 950 ... E1 78
Coderre, Sask., Can., 229 ... G2 70
Codesa, Alta., Can ... B1 69
Codette, Sask., Can., 186 ... D3 70
Codigoro, It., 6,631 ... E8 18
Codington, co., S. Dak., 20,220 ... C8 116
Codó, Braz., 11,089 ... B2 57
Codogno, It., 10,500 ... B2 21
Codpa, Chile ... C2 55
Codroipo, It., 4,305 ... D8 15
Codroy, Newf., Can., 258 ... E2 75
Codroy Pond, Newf., Can., 40 ... D2 75
Codrul, mts., Rom ... B6 22
Cody, Cherry, Nebr., 230 ... B4 103
Cody, Park, Wyo., 4,838 ... A3 125
Codys, N.B., Can., 40 ... D4 74
Coeburn, Wise, Va., 2,471 ... B2 121
Coe Hill, Ont., Can., 239 ... C7 72
Coen, Austl., 77 ... B7 50
Coesfeld, Ger., 20,300 ... B2 17
Coesse, Whitley, Ind., 225 ... B7 91
Coeur d'Alene, Kootenai, Idaho, 14,291 ... B2 89
Coeur d'Alene, lake, Idaho ... B2 89
Coeur d'Alene, mtn., Idaho ... D9 122
Coeur d'Alene, mts., Idaho ... B2 89
Coevorden, Neth., 5,800 ... B6 15
Coffee, co., Ala., 30,583 ... D3 78
Coffee, co., Ga., 21,953 ... E4 87
Coffee, co., Tenn., 28,603 ... B5 117
Coffee Creek, Fergus, Mont., 55 ... C6 102
Coffeen, Montgomery, Ill., 502 ... D4 90
Coffee Springs, Geneva, Ala., 205 ... D4 78
Coffeeville, Clarke, Ala., 250 ... D1 78
Coffeeville, Yalobusha, Miss., 813 ... B4 100
Coffey, Daviess, Mo., 190 ... A3 110
Coffey, co., Kans., 8,403 ... D8 93
Coffeyville, Montgomery, Kans., 17,382 ... E8 93
Coffin, isl., Que., Can ... B8 74
Coff's Harbour, Austl., 7,185 ... E9 51
Cofield, Hertford, N.C., 350 ... A7 109
Cogdell, Clinch, Ga., 210 ... E4 87
Coggon, Linn, Iowa, 672 ... B6 92
Coghinas, riv., It ... D2 21
Coglar, buttes, Oreg ... E6 113
Cognac, Fr., 20,798 ... E3 14

COGS-CONN 25X

Cogswell, Sargent, N. Dak., 305..........C8 110
Cohagen, Garfield, Mont., 25..........C10 102
Cohansey, Cumberland and Salem, N.J., 100..........D2 106
Cohansey, creek, N.J...........E2 106
Cohasset, Norfork, Mass., 3,000 (5,840▲)..........B6, h12 97
Cohasset, Itasca, Minn., 605..C5 99
Cohocton, Steuben, N.Y., 929..........C3 108
Cohocton, riv., N.Y...........C3 108
Cohoes, Albany, N.Y., 20,129..........C7 108
Cohutta, Whitfield, Ga., 325..B2 87
Cohutta, mtn., Ga...........B2 87
Coila, Carroll, Miss., 200....B4 100
Coimbatore, India, 286,305 (*410,000)..........F6 39
Coimbra, Port., 46,313..........B1 20
Coin, Page, Iowa, 346..........D2 92
Coín, Sp., 11,828..........D3 20
Coinjock, Currituck, N.C., 150..........A8 109
Coipasa, lake, Bol...........C2 55
Coipasa, salt flat, Bol...........C2 55
Coire, riv., Scot...........B4 13
Cojedes, state, Ven., 72,652..B4 60
Cojutepeque, Sal., 11,617....D3 62
Cokato, Wright, Minn., 1,356..........E4 99
Coke, co., Tex., 3,589..........D2 118
Cokeburg, Washington, Pa., 989..........*F1 114
Cokedale, Las Animas, Colo., 219..........D6 83
Coker, Tuscaloosa, Ala., 400..B2 78
Cokesbury, Hunterdon, N.J., 100..........B3 106
Cokesbury, Greenwood, S.C. C3 115
Coketon, Brooke, W. Va., 140..........B2 123
Coketon, Tucker, W. Va., 130..........B5 123
Cokeville, Lincoln, Wyo., 545..........C2 125
Colac, Austl., 9,257..........I4 51
Colares, Port., 4,976..........f9 20
Colatina, Braz., 26,757..........E2 57
Colbeck, cape, Ant...........B33 5
Colbert, Madison, Ga., 425..B3 87
Colbert, Bryan, Okla., 671...D5 112
Colbert, co., Ala., 46,506....A2 78
Colborne, Ont., Can., 1,336. D7 72
Colbún, Chile..........B2 54
Colburn, Bonner, Idaho, 50..A2 89
Colburn, Tippecanoe, Ind., 280..........C4 91
Colby, Thomas, Kans., 4,210..........C2 93
Colby, Aroostook, Maine, 200..........B4 96
Colby, Marathon and Clark, Wis., 1,085..........D3 124
Colbyville, Washington, Vt., 110..........C3 120
Colchagua, prov., Chile, 158,024..........A2 54
Colchester, New London, Conn., 2,260 (4,648▲)....C7 84
Colchester, Eng., 67,400....C8 12
Colchester, McDonough, Ill., 1,495..........C3 90
Colchester, Chittenden, Vt., 350 (4,718▲)..........B2 120
Colchester, co., N.S., Can., 34,307..........D6 74
Colcord, Delaware, Okla., 173..........A7 112
Cold, lake, Alta., Sask., Can.....B5 69
Cold, riv., N.H...........C4 105
Cold, riv., N.H...........D2 105
Cold Fell, mtn., Eng...........F6 13
Cold Hollow, mts., Vt...........B3 120
Colditz, Ger., 6,971..........B7 17
Cold Lake, Alta., Can., 1,307..........B5 69
Cold River, Cheshire, N.H., 50..........D2 105
Cold Spring, Campbell, Ky., 1,095..........A7, B5 94
Cold Spring, Stearns, Minn., 1,760..........E4 99
Cold Spring, Cape May, N.J., 700..........F3 106
Cold Spring, Putnam, N.Y., 2,083..........*D7 108
Coldspring, San Jacinto, Tex., 500..........D5 118
Cold Spring, hbr., N.Y...........F3 84
Cold Spring, pond, Newf., Can...D3 75
Cold Spring Harbor, Suffolk, N.Y., 1,800..........F3 84
Cold Springs, Kiowa, Okla., 75..........C3 112
Coldstream, Scot., 1,227....E6 13
Cold Stream, pond, Maine.....C4 96
Coldwater, Ont., Can., 726..C5 72
Coldwater, Comanche, Kans., 1 164..........E4 93
Coldwater, Branch, Mich., 8,880..........G5 98
Coldwater, Tate, Miss., 1,264..........A4 100
Coldwater, Mercer, Ohio, 2,766..........B3 111
Coldwater, creek, Okla...........D3 112
Coldwater, creek, Tex...........A1 118
Coldwater, riv., Miss...........A3 100
Cole, McClain, Okla., 100....B4 112
Cole, co., Mo., 40,761..........C5 101
Colebrook, Litchfield, Conn., 60 (791▲)..........B4 84
Colebrook, Coos, N.H., 1,550 (2,389▲)..........B1 105
Cole Camp, Benton, Mo., 853..........C4 101
Coleharbor, McLean, N. Dak., 210..........B4 110
Cole Lake, Ont., Can.....C8 72
Coleman, Alta., Can., 1,713..E3 69
Coleman, P.E.I., Can., 160..C5 74
Coleman, Sumter, Fla., 921..D4 86
Coleman, Randolph, Ga., 220..........E2 87
Coleman, Hancock, Ga.....C4 87
Coleman, Kent, Md., 275....B5 85
Coleman, Midland, Mich., 1,264..........E6 98
Coleman, Johnston, Okla., 150..........C5 112
Coleman, Coleman, Tex., 6,371..........D3 118
Coleman, Marinette, Wis., 718..........C5 124
Coleman, co., Tex., 12,458..D3 118
Coleman, riv., Austl...........B7 50
Colemans Falls, Bedford, Va., 180..........D3 121
Colen, lake, Man., Can.........B4 71
Colerain, Bertie, N.C., 340...A7 109
Coleraine, Austl., 1,503.....H3 51
Coleraine, N. Ire., 11,912....B5 11
Coleraine, Itasca, Minn., 1,346..........C5 99
Coleridge, Cedar, Nebr., 604. B8 103
Coleridge, Randolph, N.C., 500..........B4 109
Coles, Amite, Miss., 150......D2 100
Coles, co., Ill., 42,860.......D5 90
Colesberg, S. Afr., 4,855.....D4 49
Colesburg, Camden, Ga., 75..F5 87
Colesburg, Delaware, Iowa, 365..........B6 92
Colesburg, Hardin, Ky., 150.C4 94
Colestin, Jackson, Oreg.......E4 113
Colesville, Sussex, N.J., 100..A3 106
Coleta, Whiteside, Ill., 197...B4 90
Coleville, Sask., Can., 503...F1 70
Coleville, Mono, Calif., 275..C4 82
Coley's Point South, Newf., Can., 628..........*E5 75
Coleyville, Cottle, Tex., 100..B2 118
Colfax, Placer, Calif., 915....C3 82
Colfax, Sask., Can., 69.......H4 70
Colfax, McLean, Ill., 894....C5 90
Colfax, Clinton, Ind., 725....D4 91
Colfax, Jasper, Iowa, 2,331..C4 92
Colfax, Grant, La., 1,934....C3 95
Colfax, Richland, N. Dak., 98..........C9 110
Colfax, Whitman, Wash., 2,860..........C8 122
Colfax, Dunn, Wis., 885.....D2 124
Colfax, co., Nebr., 9,595.....C8 103
Colfax, co., N. Mex., 13,806. A5 107
Colgan, Divide, N. Dak., 22..A2 110
Colgate, Sask., Can., 101....H4 70
Colgate, Steele, N. Dak., 60..B8 110
Colgate, Washington, Wis., 60..........E1 124
Colico, It., 4,475..........C5 18
Colijnsplaat, Neth., 1,686....C3 15
Colima, Mex., 43,518...D4, n12 63
Colima, state, Mex., 157,338..........D4, n12 63
Colinas, Braz., 2,972.......*C2 57
Colinet, Newf., Can., 261....E5 75
Colington, Dare, N.C., 140..A8 109
Colinton, Alta., Can., 114....B4 69
Coll, isl., Scot...........D2 13
Collbran, Mesa, Colo., 310...B3 83
College, Alsk., 1,755..........C10 79
College Corner, Preble and Butler, Ohio, 439..........C3 111
Collegedale, Hamilton, Tenn., 1,500..........E10 117
College Gardens, Stanislaus, Calif., 4,132..........*D3 82
College Grove, Williamson, Tenn., 200..........B5 117
College Heights, Drew, Ark., 1,000..........D4 81
College Heights, Darlington, S.C., 1,330..........C7 115
College Park, St. Johns, Fla., 950..........C5 86
College Park, Fulton and Clayton, Ga., 23,469...B5, C2 87
College Park, Prince Georges, Md., 18,482..........C2, C4 85
College Place, Richland, S.C. C5 115
College Place, Walla Walla, Wash., 4,031..........C7 122
College Springs, Page, Iowa, 290..........D2 92
College Station, Brazos, Tex., 11,396..........D4 118
College View, Arapahoe, Colo., 1,800..........*B6 83
Collegeville, Saline, Ark., 30. D5 81
Collegeville, Jasper, Ind., 1,400..........C3 91
Collegeville (P.O.), Stearns, Minn., 1,600..........*E4 99
Collegeville, Montgomery, Pa., 2,254..........F11 114
Colleton, co., S.C., 27,816...F6 115
Colley, Sullivan, Pa., 75.....C9 114
Colleyville, Tarrant, Tex., 1,491..........*B5 118
Collie, Austl., 7,547..........F2 50
Collier, co., Fla., 15,753......F5 86
Collier, bay, Austl...........C3 50
Colliers, Brooke, W. Va., 900. A2 123
Collierville, Shelby, Tenn., 2,020..........B2 117
Collin, co., Tex., 41,247.....C4 118
Collingdale, Delaware, Pa., 10,268..........B11 114
Collingswood, Camden, N.J., 17,370..........D2 106
Collingsworth, co., Tex., 6,276..........B2 118
Collingwood, Ont., Can., 8,385..........C4 72
Collins, Drew, Ark., 107.....D4 81
Collins, Tattnall, Ga., 565...D4 87
Collins, Whitley, Ind., 95....B7 91
Collins, Story, Iowa, 435.....C4 92
Collins, Covington, Miss., 1,537..........D4 100
Collins, St. Clair, Mo., 177..D4 101
Collins, Teton, Mont., 25....C5 102
Collins, Manitowoc, Wis., 190..........B6 124
Collins Park, New Castle, Del., 2,500..........*A6 85
Collinston, Morehouse, La., 497..........B4 95
Collinston, Box Elder, Utah, 60..........B3 119
Collins View, Multnomah, Oreg., 1,500..........*B4 113
Collinsville, DeKalb, Ala., 1,199..........A4 78
Collinsville, Hartford, Conn., 1,700..........B5 84
Collinsville, DeKalb, Ga., 120..........B5 87
Collinsville, Madison and St. Clair, Ill., 14,217..........E4 90
Collinsville, Lauderdale, Miss., 400..........C5 100
Collinsville, Tulsa, Okla., 2,526..........A6 112
Collinsville, Henry, Va., 3,586..........*E6 121
Collinwood, Wayne, Tenn., 596..........B4 117
Collipulli, Chile, 4,057.......B2 54
Collis, Traverse, Minn., 30...E2 99
Collister, Ada, Idaho, 5,436..F2 89
Collo, Alg., 4,518 (6,960▲)...B6 44
Collooney, Ire., 553..........C3 11
Collyer, Trego, Kans., 253...C3 93
Colman, Moody, S. Dak., 505..........D9 116
Colmar, Fr., 52,355..C7 14, A3 18
Colmar, Bell, Ky., 500......D6 94
Colmar Manor, Prince Georges, Md., 1,772..........C2 85
Colmenar de Oreja, Sp., 5,547..........B4 20
Colmenar Viejo, Sp., 8,375..........B4, o17 20
Colmesneil, Tyler, Tex., 500..........D5 118
Colmor, Colfax, N. Mex., 25..........A5 107
Colo, Story, Iowa 574........B4 92
Cologne, see Köln, Ger.
Cologne, Carver, Minn., 454. F5 99
Cologne, Atlantic, N.J., 600..........D3 106
Coloma, Berrien, Mich., 1,473..........F4 98
Coloma, Waushara, Wis., 312..........D4 124
Colomb-Béchar, Alg., 18,090 (43,250▲)..........C4 44
Colombes, Fr., 76,918.......g10 14
Colombia, Col., 1,217........C3 60
Colombia, country, S.A., 15,600,000..........C3 53, C3 60
Colombier, Switz., 2,652.....C2 19
Colombo, Cey., 510,947 (*800,000)..........G6 39
Colome, Tripp, S. Dak., 398..........D6 116
Colón, Arg., 8,335..........A5 54
Colón, Cuba, 15,755..........D3 64
Colon, St. Joseph, Mich., 1,055..........G5 98
Colon, Saunders, Nebr., 110..D2 103
Colon, Lee, N.C., 350........B4 109
Colón, Pan., 59,598 (*69,000)..........F8, k11 62
Colón, Archipielago de (Galápagos Is.), prov., Ec., 2,500..........g5 58
Colona, Ouray, Colo., 75....C3 83
Colonia, Middlesex, N.J., 18,500..........k7 106
Colonia, Ur., 7,500..........E1 56
Colonia, dept., Ur., 95,400..........*E1 56
Colonia Dora, Arg., 2,183...E3 55
Colonia Gustavo A. Madero, Mex., 102,602..........h9 63
Colonia Las Heras, Arg.....D3 54
Colonial Beach, Westmoreland, Va., 1,769..........C6 121
Colônia Leopoldina, Braz., 1,694..........k6 57
Colonial Heights, Sullivan, Tenn., 2,312..........*C11 118
Colonial Heights (Independent City), Va., 9,587....C7, D5 121
Colonial Manor, Gloucester, N.J., 1,000..........*D2 106
Colonial Park, Dauphin, Pa., 2,500..........*F8 114
Colonia Mennonita, Par., 2,247..........D4 55
Colonia Paraíso, P.R.....B8, f12 65
Colonia Providencia, P.R.....D6 65
Colonia Sarmiento, Arg., 3,648..........D3 54
Colonia Suiza, Ur., 4,307....g8 54
Colonie, Albany, N.Y., 6,992..........*C7 108
Colonna, It., 1,695..........h9 21
Colonne, cape, It...........E6 21
Colonsay, Sask., Can., 278...F3 70
Colonsay, isl., Scot...........D2 13
Colony, Anderson, Kans., 419..........D8 93
Colony, Washita, Okla., 200. B3 112
Colony, Crook, Wyo..........A8 125
Colorado, C.R..........E6 62
Colorado, state, U.S., 1,753,947..........C6 76, 83
Colorado, co., Tex., 18,463..E4 118
Colorado, desert, Calif...........F6 82
Colorado, nat. mon., Colo.....B2 83
Colorado, plat., Ariz...........A3 80
Colorado, plat., N. Mex......B1 107
Colorado, riv., Arg...........B3 54
Colorado, riv., Tex...........D3 118
Colorado, riv., U.S...........D5 76
Colorado City, Mitchell, Tex., 6,457..........C2 118
Colorado River, Indian res., Ariz. D1 80
Colorados, arch., Cuba.......D1 64
Colorado Springs, El Paso, Colo., 70,194 (*139,500).. C6 83
Colored Hill, Mercer, W. Va., 1,115..........*D3 123
Coloso, Chile..........D1 55
Coloso, P.R..........B2 65
Coloso Central, P.R..........B2 65
Colotepec, Mex., 455........D5 63
Colotlán, Mex., 6,281...C4, k12 63
Colquechaca, Bol., 1,070....C2 55
Colquitt, Miller, Ga., 1,556..E2 87
Colquitt, Claiborne, La., 40..B3 95
Colquitt, co., Ga., 34,048.....E3 87
Colrain, Franklin, Mass., 155 (1,426▲)..........A2 97
Colstrip, Rosebud, Mont., 75..........E10 102
Colt, St. Francis, Ark., 394..B5 81
Coltauco, Chile..........A2 54
Colton, San Bernardino, Calif., 18,666..........F3 82
Colton, St. Lawrence, N.Y., 400..........f10 108
Colton, Clackamas, Oreg., 150..........B4 113
Colton, Minnehaha, S. Dak., 593..........D9 116
Colton, Utah, Utah, 5........D5 119
Colton, Whitman, Wash., 253..........C8 122
Colton, hill, Vt...........D4 120
Coltons Point, St. Marys, Md., 118..........D4 85
Colts Neck, Monmouth, N.J., 500..........C4 106
Colulli, Eth..........C5 47
Columbia, Houston, Ala., 783..........D4 78
Columbia, Tolland, Conn., 200 (2,163▲)..........C7 84
Columbia, Monroe, Ill., 3,174..........E3 90
Columbia, Adair, Ky., 2,255.C4 94
Columbia, Caldwell, La., 1,021..........B3 95
Columbia, Marion, Miss., 7,117..........D4 100
Columbia, Boone, Mo., 36,650..........C5 101
Columbia, Warren, N.J., 350..........B2 106
Columbia, Tyrrell, N.C., 1,099..........B7 108
Columbia, Lancaster, Pa., 12,075..........F9 114
Columbia, Richland, S.C., 97,433 (*213,400)..........D5 115
Columbia, Brown, S. Dak., 272..........B7 116
Columbia, Maury, Tenn., 17,624..........B4 117
Columbia, Carbon, Utah, 400..........D5 119
Columbia, Fluvanna, Va., 86..........D4 121
Columbia, co., Ark., 26,400..D2 81
Columbia, co., Fla., 20,077..B4 86
Columbia, co., Ga., 13,423...C4 87
Columbia, co., N.Y., 47,322..C7 108
Columbia, co., Oreg., 22,379.B3 113
Columbia, co., Pa., 53,489...D9 114
Columbia, co., Wash., 4,569..C7 122
Columbia, co., Wis., 36,708..E4 124
Columbia, basin, Wash........C6 122
Columbia, cape, N.W. Ter., Can...........A22 4
Columbia, dam, Ala., Ga.......E1 87
Columbia, lake, B.C., Can.....D10 68
Columbia, lake, Conn.........C7 84
Columbia, mtn., Alta., Can.....C2 69
Columbia, mts., Mex...........B2 63
Columbia, riv., Can., U.S........G9 66
Columbia Bridge, Coos, N.H.B1 105
Columbia City, Whitley, Ind., 4,803..........B7 91
Columbia City, Columbia, Oreg., 423..........B4 113
Columbia Cross Roads, Bradford, Pa., 200........C8 114
Columbia Falls, Washington, Maine, 300 (442▲)........D5 96
Columbia Falls, Flathead, Mont., 2,132..........B2 102
Columbia Heights, Anoka, Minn., 17,533..........E7 99
Columbia Heights, Cowlitz, Wash., 2,227..........*C3 122
Columbiana, Shelby, Ala., 2,264..........B3 78
Columbiana, Columbiana, Ohio, 4,164..........B7 111
Columbiana, co., Ohio, 107,004..........B7 111
Columbia Park (Pittsburg East), Contra Costa, Calif., 1,977..........*B5 82
Columbia Park, Hamilton, Ohio..........A6 111
Columbia Station, Lorain, Ohio, 1,000..........*A5 111
Columbiaville, Lapeer, Mich., 878..........E7 98
Columbine, Routt, Colo., 4...A4 83
Columbine, Natrona, Wyo., 20..........B6 125
Columbus, Hempstead, Ark., 275..........D2 81
Columbus, Muscogee, Ga., 116,779 (*201,500)........D2 87
Columbus, Bartholomew, Ind., 20,778..........F6 91
Columbus, Cherokee, Kans., 3,395..........E9 93
Columbus, Hickman, Ky., 357..........B2 94
Columbus, Lowndes, Miss., 24,771..........B5 100
Columbus, Stillwater, Mont., 1,281..........E7 102
Columbus, Platte, Nebr., 12,476..........C8 103
Columbus, Burlington, N.J., 600..........C3 106
Columbus, Luna, N. Mex., 307..........F2 107
Columbus, Polk, N.C., 725..D4 109
Columbus, Burke, N. Dak., 672..........A3 110
Columbus, Franklin, Ohio, 471,316 (*715,400)...C2, C5 111
Columbus, Warren, Pa., 500..........C2 114
Columbus, Colorado, Tex., 3,656..........E4 118
Columbus, Columbus, Wis., 3,467..........E4 124
Columbus, co., N.C., 48,973. C5 109
Columbus City, Louisa, Iowa, 327..........C6 92
Columbus Grove, Putnam, Ohio, 2,104..........B3 111
Columbus Junction, Louisa, Iowa, 1,016..........C6 92
Columbus Manor, Cook, Ill., 2,500..........*B6 90
Colusa, Colusa, Calif., 3,518..C2 82
Colusa, co., Calif., 12,075....C2 82
Colver, Cambria, Pa., 1,261..E4 114
Colville, Stevens, Wash., 3,806..........A8 122
Colville, lake, N.W. Ter., Can...C7 66
Colville, lake, Wash...........B7 122
Colville, riv., Alsk...........B9 79
Colville, riv., Wash...........A8 122
Colvin, mtn., Ala...........B4 78
Colvos, pass, Wash...........D1 122
Colwich, Sedgwick, Kans., 703..........B5, E6 93
Colwood, B.C., Can., 863....h12 68
Colwyn, Delaware, Pa., 3,074..........*G11 114
Colwyn Bay, Wales, 23,090..A4 12
Colyell, creek, La...........B6 95
Comacchio, It., 10,200......B4 21
Comal, Comal, Tex., 25......B4 118
Comal, co., Tex., 19,844.....E3 118
Comalapa, Guat., 7,404.....C2 62
Comalcalco, Mex., 4,282...D6 63
Coman, mtn., Ant...........B6 5
Comanche, Stephens, Okla., 2,082..........C4 112
Comanche, Comanche, Tex., 3,415..........D3 118
Comanche, co., Kans., 3,271. E4 93
Comanche, co., Okla., 90,803..........C3 112
Comanche, co., Tex., 11,865..........C3 118
Comarapa, Bol., 1,096.......C3 55
Comayagua, Hond., 4,828....C4 62
Combahee, riv., S.C...........F6 115
Combarbalá, Chile, 2,112....A2 54
Combeaufontaine, Fr., 412...B1 18
Comber, Ont., Can., 601.....E2 72
Comber, N. Ire., 3,980.......C6 11
Combermere, Ont., Can., 82..........B7 72
Combined Locks, Outagamie, Wis., 1,421..........A5 124
Comboumune, Moz..........B5 49
Combs, Madison, Ark., 200..B2 81
Combs, Perry, Ky., 900......C6 94
Comer, Barbour, Ala., 100...C4 78
Comer, Madison, Ga., 882...B3 87
Comeragh, mts., Ire...........E4 11
Comerío, P.R., 5,232..........C6 65
Comerío, mun., P.R., 18,583..........C6 65
Comertown, Sheridan, Mont..........B12 102
Comfort, Jones, N.C., 400....B6 109
Comfort, Marion, Tenn., 35..........D8 117
Comfort, Kendall, Tex., 950..........E3 118
Comfort, Boone, W. Va., 250..........C3, D6 123
Comfort, pt., La...........E6 95
Comfrey, Brown, Minn., 616..........F4 99
Comilla, Pak., 54,504........D9 39
Comines, Bel., 8,373..........D2 15
Comins, Oscoda, Mich., 80..D6 98
Comiso, It., 25,904..........F5 21
Comitán, Mex., 15,378.......D6 63
Comite, riv., La...........D4 95
Commack, Suffolk, N.Y., 19,200..........F3 84
Commentry, Fr., 9,711.......D5 14
Commerce, Conecuh, Ala....D3 78
Commerce, Los Angeles, Calif., 9,555..........*F2 82
Commerce, Jackson, Ga., 3,551..........B3 87
Commerce, Oakland, Mich., 1,200..........*A7 98
Commerce, Scott, Mo., 247..D8 101
Commerce, Ottawa, Okla., 2,378..........A7 112
Commerce, Hunt, Tex., 5,789..........C5 118
Commerce Town, Adams, Colo., 8,970..........B6 83
Commercial Point, Pickaway, Ohio, 308..........C4 111
Commercy, Fr., 7,043........C6 14
Commiskey, Jennings, Ind., 100..........G6 91
Committee, bay, N.W. Ter., Can...........C15 66
Common Fence Point, Newport, R.I., 350........*C12 84
Commonwealth, bay, Ant.......C27 5
Commonwealth, range, Ant.....A30 5
Communism, peak, Sov. Un.....H23 9
Como, Que., Can., 807........q18 73
Como, It., 85,100 (*130,000). B2 21
Como, Panola, Miss., 789....A4 100
Como, Hertford, N.C., 150...A6 109
Como, Henry, Tenn., 160....A3 117
Como, lake, It...........B2 21
Comobab, Pima, Ariz., 75...E4 80
Comodoro Rivadavia, Arg., 25,651..........D3 54
Comoé, riv., I.C...........E3 45
Comoro, is., Afr...........f9 49
Comoro Islands, Fr. dep., Afr., 192,000..........f9 49
Comox, B.C., Can., 1,756....E5 68
Compass Lake, Jackson, Fla., 300..........B1, G3 86
Compeer, Alta., Can., 55.....D5 69
Competition, Laclede, Mo., 80..........D5 101
Compiègne, Fr., 24,427 (*32,500)..........C5 14
Comptche, Mendocino, Calif., 175..........C2 82
Compton, Los Angeles, Calif., 71,812..........F2 82
Compton, Que., Can., 543...D6 73
Compton, co., Que., Can., 24,410..........D6 73
Compton, Lee, Ill., 366......B4 90
Comstock, Kalamazoo, Mich., 3,000..........F5 98
Comstock, Clay, Minn., 138. D2 99
Comstock, Custer, Nebr., 235..........C6 103
Comstock, Washington, N.Y., 300..........B7 108
Comstock, Val Verde, Tex., 300..........E2 118
Comstock, Barron, Wis., 60..C1 124
Comstock Park, Kent, Mich., 2,500..........*E5 98
Conakry, Guinea, 43,000 (*109,500)..........E2 45
Conanicut, isl., R.I...........C11 84
Conasauga, Polk, Tenn., 150.D9 117
Concarneau, Fr., 11,691......D2 14
Conceição do Norte, Braz., 245..........D1 57
Concepción, Arg., 12,338....E2 55
Concepción, Bol., 1,056.....C3 55
Concepción, Bol., 860.......D3 55
Concepcion, Santa Barbara, Calif..........E3 82
Concepción, Chile, 148,100 (*295,000)..........B2 54
Concepción, Guat., 1,855....C2 62
Concepción, Pan., 6,532.....F6 62
Concepción, Par., 18,000.....D4 55
Concepcion, Phil., 3,014....o13 35
Concepcion, Duval, Tex., 150..........F3 118
Concepción, dept., Par., 14,640..........D4 55
Concepción, prov., Chile, 537,711..........B2 54
Concepción del Oro, Mex., 8,379..........C4 63
Concepción del Uruguay, Arg., 31,498..........A5 54
Conception, Nodaway, Mo., 450..........A3 101
Conception, bay, Newf., Can.....E5 75
Conception, pt., Calif...........E3 82
Conception Harbour, Newf., Can., 585..........*E5 75
Conception Junction, Nodaway, Mo., 253..........A3 101
Conchas, Braz., 2,519.......m7 56
Conchas, res., N. Mex........B5 107
Conchas Dam, San Miguel, N. Mex., 100..........B5 107
Conche, Newf., Can., 498....C4 75
Conchi, Chile..........D2 55
Conchillas, Ur..........g7 54
Concho, Apache, Ariz., 150..C6 80
Concho, Canadian, Okla., 500..........B4 112
Concho, co., Tex., 3,672....D3 118
Conconully, Okanogan, Wash., 108..........A6 122
Concord, Contra Costa, Calif., 36,208..........B5 82
Concord, Sussex, Del., 400...C6 85
Concord, Gadsden, Fla., 80..B2 86
Concord, Pike, Ga., 333.....C2 87
Concord, Morgan, Ill., 210..D3 90
Concord, Lewis, Ky., 83.....B6 94
Concord, Middlesex, Mass., 5,000 (12,517▲)........B5, g10 97
Concord, Jackson, Mich., 990..........F6 98
Concord, Dixon, Nebr., 150..B9 103
Concord, Merrimack, N.H., 28,991..........D3 105
Concord, Cabarrus, N.C., 17,799..........B3 109
Concord, Franklin, Pa., 175..F6 114
Concord, Knox, Tenn., 250..........D9, E11 117
Concord, Essex, Vt., 389 (956▲)..........C5 120
Concord, Campbell, Va., 400..........D4 121
Concord, riv., Mass...........A5 97
Concordia, Arg., 64,000.....A5 54
Concordia, Col., 3,906.......B2 60
Concordia, Cloud, Kans., 7,022..........C6 93
Concordia, Lafayette, Mo., 1,471..........C4 101
Concordia, par., La., 20,467.C4 95
Concord North, Cabarrus, N.C., 2,199..........B3 109
Concrete, Cavalier, N. Dak., 125..........A8 110
Concrete, Skagit, Wash., 840.A4 122
Conda, Caribou, Idaho, 200.G7 89
Conde, Braz., 4,190..........D3 57
Conde, Spink, S. Dak., 388..B7 116
Condé [-sur-l'Escaut], Fr., 14,066..........D3 15
Condé-sur-Marne, Fr., 528..........E4 15
Condé-sur-Noireau, Fr., 6,231..........C3 14
Condeúba, Braz., 1,628......D2 57
Condino, It., 1,297..........D6 18
Condit, Delaware, Ohio, 35..B5 111
Condobolin, Austl., 3,147....F6 51
Condom, Fr., 4,473..........F4 14
Condon, Missoula, Mont., 10.C3 102
Condon, Gilliam, Oreg., 1,149..........B6 113
Condor, range, Peru..........B2 58
Cone, Crosby, Tex., 120.....C2 118
Conecuh, co., Ala., 17,762...D2 78
Conecuh, riv., Ala...........D3 78
Conegliano, It., 11,300......B4 21
Conehatta, Newton, Miss., 60..........C4 100
Conejos, Conejos, Colo., 175.D4 83
Conejos, co., Colo., 8,428....D4 83
Conejos, creek, Colo...........D4 83
Conejos, peak, Colo...........D4 83
Conemaugh, Cambria, Pa., 3,334..........F4 114
Conemaugh River, flood control res., Pa...........F3 114
Cones, Coos, N.H..........B1 105
Conestee, Greenville, S.C., 750..........B3 115
Conesville, Muscatine, Iowa, 248..........C6 92
Conesville, Coshocton, Ohio, 451..........B6 111
Conetoe, Edgecomb, N.C., 147..........B6 109
Coney, isl., N.Y...........k13 108
Conflans-en-Jarnisy, Fr., 2,802..........E5 15
Conflans-Ste. Honorine, Fr., 21,874..........g9 14
Confluence, Leslie, Ky., 175..C6 94
Confluence, Somerset, Pa., 938..........G3 114
Confolens, Fr., 2,462........D4 14
Confusion, bay, Newf., Can.....C4 75
Confusion, range, Utah.......D2 119
Cong, Ire., 178..........D2 11
Congamond, Hampden, Mass., 800..........B2 97
Congamond, lakes, Conn., Mass. B2 97
Congaree, riv., S.C...........D6 115
Conger, Freeborn, Minn., 694..........G5 99
Congers, Rockland, N.Y., 3,500..........*D7 108
Congleton, Eng., 16,802.....A5 12
Congo, Perry, Ohio, 100.....C5 111
Congo, Hancock, W. Va., 50.A2 123
Congo (Brazzaville), country, Afr., 1,050,000...B2 48, G7 42
Congo, The (Léopoldville), country, Afr., 15,500,000.......B3 48, G8 42
Congo, basin, Con. L...........A3 48
Congo, riv., Afr...........G7 42
Congress, Yavapai, Ariz., 150.C3 80
Congress, Sask., Can., 86....H2 70
Coniclere, Pan..........k10 62
Conifer, St. Lawrence, N.Y., 100..........A6, f10 108
Conil, Sp., 9,002..........D2 20
Coniston, Ont., Can., 2,692..........A4, p19 72
Coniston Water, lake, Eng......F5 13
Conjeeveram, see Kancheepuram, India
Conklin, Alta., Can., 69.....B5 69
Conklin, Ottawa, Mich., 270.E5 98
Conklin, pt., N.Y...........G3 84
Conlen, Dallam, Tex., 35....A1 118
Conn, lake, Ire...........C2 11
Connacht, prov., Ire., 419,465..........D2 11
Conneaut, Ashtabula, Ohio, 10,557..........A7 111
Conneaut, creek, Ohio.........A7 111
Conneaut Lake, Crawford, Pa., 700..........C1 114
Conneautville, Crawford, Pa., 1,100..........C1 114
Connecticut, state, U.S., 2,535,234..........B13 77, 84
Connecticut, lake, N.H........A2 105
Connecticut, riv., U.S........B2 97
Connell, Franklin, Wash., 906..........C7 122
Connell, mtn., B.C., Can.......A1 102
Connellsville, Fayette, Pa., 12,814..........F2 114
Connelsville, Adair, Mo., 80..........A5 101
Connemara, mts., Ire..........D2 11
Conner, Aroostook, Maine, 180..........B4 96
Conner, Ravalli, Mont., 5...E2 102
Connersville, Fayette, Ind., 17,698..........E7 91
Connerville, Johnston, Okla., 200..........C5 112
Conning Towers, Conn., 3,457..........*D8 84

COUR-CRYS 27X

Courbevoie, Fr., 59,491 .... g10 14
Courcelles, Que., Can., 773 .. D7 73
Courland (Kurisches Haff), lagoon, Sov. Un. A6 26
Courmayeur, It., 719 .... D2 18
Coursan, Fr., 3,212 .... F5 14
Courtenay, B.C., Can., 3,485 .... E5 68
Courtenay, Stutsman, N. Dak., 168 .... B7 110
Courtland, Lawrence, Ala., 495 .... A2 78
Courtland, Sacramento, Calif., 550 .... B6 82
Courtland, Ont., Can., 605 .. E4 72
Courtland, Republic, Kans., 384 .... C6 93
Courtland, Nicollet, Minn., 239 .... F4 99
Courtland, Panola, Miss., 242 .... A4 100
Courtland, Southampton, Va., 855 .... E5 121
Courtmacsherry, Ire., 205 .. F3 11
Courtney, Love, Okla., 40 .. D4 112
Courtrai, see Kortrijk, Bel.
Courtright, Ont., Can., 532 .. E2 72
Courtrock, Grant, Oreg C7 113
Courval, Sask., Can., 108 .. G2 70
Courville, Que., Can., 4,670 .... n17 73
Coushatta, Red River, La., 1,663 .... B2 95
Coutances, Fr., 7,806 .... C3 14
Coutras, Fr., 3,688 .... E3 14
Coutts, Alta., Can., 469 .... E5 69
Couvin, Bel., 3,840 .... D4 15
Covada, Perry, Wash A7 122
Cove, Polk, Ark., 320 .... C1 81
Cove, Garrett, Md D1 85
Cove, Mille Lacs, Minn., 45 .. D5 99
Cove, Union, Oreg., 311 .... B9 113
Cove, Scot C3 13
Cove, Chambers, Tex., 25 .. F5 118
Cove, Cache, Utah, 50 .... B4 119
Cove, King, Wash., 150 .... D1 122
Cove, isl., Ont., Can B3 72
Cove, pt., Md D5 85
Cove City, Craven, N.C., 551 .... B6 109
Cove City, Orange, Tex., 1,749 .... *D6 118
Covedale, Hamilton, Ohio, 10,000 .... D2 111
Covelo, Mendocino, Calif., 600 .... C2 82
Coventry, Tolland, Conn., 3,700 (6,356▲) B7 84
Coventry, Eng., 313,900 (*580,000) B6 12
Coventry, Kent, R.I., 5,000 (15,432▲) C10 84
Coventry, Orleans, Vt., 200 (458▲) B4 120
Coventry Center, Kent, R.I., 200 .... C10 84
Cove Orchard, Yamhill, Oreg B1, B3 113
Covered Bridge, N.H B3 105
Covert, Osborne, Kans., 50 .. C5 93
Covert, Van Buren, Mich., 500 .... F4 98
Covesville, Albemarle, Va., 150 .... D4 121
Covilhã, Port., 20,423 .... B2 20
Covin, Fayette, Ala., 100 .... B2 78
Covina, Los Angeles, Calif., 20,124 .... *F3 82
Covington, Newton, Ga., 8,167 .... C3 87
Covington, Fountain, Ind., 2,759 .... D3 91
Covington, Kenton, Ky., 60,376 .... A5, A7 94
Covington, St. Tammany, La., 6,754 .... B7, D5 95
Covington, Baraga, Mich., 200 .... B2 98
Covington, Miami, Ohio, 2,473 .... B3 111
Covington, Garfield, Okla., 687 .... A4 112
Covington, Tioga, Pa., 673 .. C7 114
Covington, Tipton, Tenn., 5,298 .... B2 117
Covington (Independent City), Va., 11,062 .... D3 121
Covington, King, Wash., 50 .. D2 122
Covington, co., Ala., 35,631 .. D3 78
Covington, co., Miss., 13,637 . D4 100
Cow, creek, Wash C7 122
Cow, lake, Oreg D9 113
Cowal, lake, Austl F6 51
Cowan, Delaware, Ind., 250 .... D7 91
Cowan, Franklin, Tenn., 1,979 .... B5 117
Cowan, lake, Austl F3 50
Cowan, lake, Sask., Can C2 70
Cowan, riv., Sask., Can C2 70
Cowangie, Austl., 159 .... G3 51
Cowan Knob, mtn., Ark B2 81
Cowansville, Que., Can., 7,050 .... D5 73
Cowansville, Armstrong, Pa., 400 .... E2 114
Coward, Florence, S.C., 150 .. D8 115
Coward Springs, Austl E6 50
Cowarts, Houston, Ala., 200 . D4 78
Cowcreek, Owsley, Ky C6 94
Cow Creek, Rosebud, Mont E10 102
Cowden, Shelby, Ill., 575 .... D5 90
Cowdenbeath, Scot., 11,918 .. D5 13
Cowdrey, Jackson, Colo., 100 .... A4 83
Cowell, Newton, Ark., 35 .... B2 81
Cowen, Webster, W. Va., 475 .... D4 123
Cowen, mtn., Mont E6 102
Cowes, Eng., 17,100 .... D6 12
Coweta, Wagoner, Okla., 1,858 .... B6 112
Coweta, co., Ga., 28,893 .... C2 87
Cowgill, Caldwell, Mo., 259 .. B4 101
Cow Head, Newf., Can., 544 .... D3, k10 75
Cowichan, lake, B.C., Can E5 68
Cowichan Station, B.C., Can., 97 .... g12 68
Cowiche, Kakima, Wash., 175 .... C5 122
Cowles, Webster, Neb., 55 .. D7 103
Cowley, Alta., Can., 127 .... E3 69
Cowley, Big Horn, Wyo., 459 . A3 125
Cowley, co., Kans., 37,861 .. E7 93
Cowlic, Pima, Ariz., 80 .... F4 80
Cowlington, LeFlore, Okla., 74 .... B7 112
Cowlitz, co., Wash., 57,801 .. C3 122
Cowlitz, riv., Wash C3 122
Cowpasture, riv., Va C3 121
Cowpen mtn., Ga B2 87
Cowpens, Spartanburg, S.C., 2,038 .... A4 115
Cowra, Austl., 6,289 .... F7 51
Cowskin, creek, Kans B5 93
Cow Springs, Coconino, Ariz., 3 .... A5 80
Coxburg, Benton, Tenn B3 117
Cox City, Grady, Okla., 150 . C4 112
Coxim, Braz., 1,371 .... B2 56
Coxipi, riv., Que., Can C2 75
Coxsackie, Greene, N.Y., 2,849 .... C7 108
Cox's Cove, Newf., Can., 630 .... D2 75
Coxs Mills, Gilmer, W. Va., 75 .... B4 123
Coy, Wilcox, Ala., 100 .... D2 78
Coy, Lonoke, Ark., 206 .... C4 81
Coya, Chile D2 55
Coyame, Mex., 790 .... B3 63
Coyanosa, draw, Tex D1 118
Coyle, Logan, Okla., 292 .... B4 112
Coyoacán, Mex., 54,866 . h9, n14 63
Coyote, Rio Arriba, N. Mex., 50 .... A3 107
Coyote, basin, Colo A2 83
Coyville, Wilson, Kans., 133 . E8 93
Cozad, Dawson, Nebr., 3,184 . D6 103
Cozahome, Searcy, Ark., 50 .. A3 81
Cozumel, Mex., 2,330 .... C7 63
Cozumel, isl., Mex C7 63
Crab, creek, Wash B7 122
Crab, creek, Wash C6 122
Crab Orchard, Lincoln, Ky., 808 .... C5 94
Crab Orchard, Johnson, Nebr., 103 .... D9 103
Crab Orchard, Cumberland, Tenn., 700 .... D9 117
Crab Orchard, Raleigh, W. Va., 1,953 .... D7 123
Crab Orchard, lake, Ill F5 90
Crab Orchard, mts., Tenn D9 117
Crabtree, Van Buren, Ark .. B3 81
Crabtree, Linn, Oreg., 250 .... C2, C4 113
Crabtree, Westmoreland, Pa., 950 .... F3 114
Crabtree Bald, mtn., N.C D3 109
Crabtree Mills, Que., Can., 1,313 .... D4 73
Cracking, riv., Sask., Can D4 70
Cracow, Austl., 417 .... B8 51
Cracow (Kraków), Pol., 495,600 .... C5 26
Cradock, S. Afr., 19,476 .... D4 49
Crafton, Allegheny, Pa., 8,418 .... B5 114
Craftsbury, Orleans, Vt., 120 (674▲) B4 120
Craftsbury Common, Orleans, Vt., 80 .... B4 120
Cragford, Clay, Ala., 100 .... B4 78
Cragged, mtn., N.H C4 105
Cragmor, El Paso, Colo. (part of Ivywild) C6 83
Crags, mts., Idaho C3 89
Craig, Alsk., 273 .... D13, n23 79
Craig, Moffat, Colo., 3,984 .. A3 83
Craig, Monroe, Fla., 50 .... H6 86
Craig, Plymouth, Iowa, 117 .. B1 92
Craig, Holt, Mo., 488 .... A2 101
Craig, Lewis and Clark, Mont., 50 .... C4 102
Craig, Burt, Nebr., 378 .... C9 103
Craig, co., Okla., 16,303 .... A6 112
Craig, co., Va., 3,356 .... D2 121
Craig, creek, Va D2 121
Craig Beach, Mahoning, Ohio, 1,139 .... *A7 111
Craigellachie, B.C., Can., 51 . D8 68
Craigfield, Williamson, Tenn B4 117
Craighead, co., Ark., 47,253 .. B5 81
Craighouse, Scot E3 13
Craighurst, Ont., Can., 56 .. C5 72
Craigmont, Lewis, Idaho, 703 .... C2 89
Craigmyle, Alta., Can., 107 .. D4 69
Craigs Road Station, Que., Can o17 73
Craigsville, Augusta, Va., 978 .... C3 121
Craigsville, Nicholas, W. Va., 250 .... C4 123
Craigville, Wells, Ind., 190 .. C7 91
Craigville, Koochiching, Minn., 35 .... C5 99
Crail, Sask., Can., 606 .... F3 70
Crail, Scot., 1,066 .... D6 13
Crailsheim, Ger., 14,400 .... D5 17
Craiova, Rom., 112,400 .... C6 22
Cramerton, Gaston, N.C., 3,123 .... B2 109
Crampel, Alg., 161 .... C4 44
Crampton, Henry, Ill D7 92
Cranberry, Venango, Pa., 275 .... D2 114
Cranberry, lake, N.Y A6 108
Cranberry Isles, Hancock, Maine, 135 (181▲) D4 96
Cranberry Lake, Sussex, N.J., 500 .... B3 106
Cranberry Lake, St. Lawrence, N.Y., 300 .... A6, f10 108
Cranberry Portage, Man., Can., 838 .... B1 71
Cranbrook, B.C., Can., 5,549 .... E10 68
Cranbury, Middlesex, N.J., 1,300 .... C3 106
Cranbury Station, Middlesex, N.J., 40 .... C4 106
Crandall, Man., Can., 105 .. D1 71
Crandall, Murray, Ga., 208 .. B2 87
Crandall, Clarke, Miss., 75 .. D5 100
Crandall, Day, S. Dak., 30 .. B8 116
Crandall, Kaufman, Tex., 640 . B6 118
Crandon, Forest, Wis., 1,679 . C5 124
Crane, Stone, Mo., 954 .... E4 101
Crane, Richland, Mont., 60 . C12 102
Crane, Harney, Oreg., 75 .. D8 113
Crane, Crane, Tex., 3,796 .. D1 118
Crane, co., Tex., 4,699 .... D1 118
Crane, creek, Ohio e7 111
Crane, lake, Sask., Can G1 70
Crane, lake, Ill C3 90
Crane, lake, Minn B6 99
Crane, mtn., Oreg E6 113
Crane Creek, res., Idaho E2 89
Crane Hill, Cullman, Ala., 90 .... A2 78
Crane Lake, St. Louis, Minn., 100 .... B6 99
Crane Neck, pt., N.Y F4 84
Crane Prairie, res., Oreg D5 113
Cranesville, Erie, Pa., 575 .. C1 114
Crane Valley, Sask., Can., 113 .... H3 70
Cranfield, Adams, Miss., 100 . D2 100
Cranford, Union, N.J., 26,424 .... B4 106
Crannell, Fresno, Calif B1 82
Cransac, Fr., 4,765 .... E5 14
Cranston, Providence, R.I., 66,766 .... B11 84
Cranstown, cape, Grnld B20 4
Crapaud, P.E.I., Can., 201 .. C6 74
Crapo, Dorchester, Md., 40 .. D5 85
Crary, Ramsey, N. Dak., 195 . A7 110
Craryville, Columbia, N.Y., 200 .... C7 108
Crasna, riv., Rom B6 22
Crater, lake, Oreg E4 113
Crater Lake, Klamath, Oreg., 50 .... E4 113
Crater Lake, nat. park, Oreg E4 113
Craters of the Moon, nat. mon., Idaho F5 89
Crateús, Braz., 14,572 .... C3 57
Crato, Braz., 27,649 .... C3 57
Craughwell, Ire., 159 .... D3 11
Craven, Sask., Can., 147 .... G3 70
Craven, co., N.C., 58,773 .... B6 109
Cravinhos, Braz., 6,294 .... k8 56
Crawford, Delta, Colo., 147 .. C3 83
Crawford, Oglethorpe, Ga., 541 .... C3 87
Crawford, Washington, Maine (83▲) C5 96
Crawford, Lowndes, Miss., 317 .... B5 100
Crawford, Dawes, Nebr., 1,588 .... B2 103
Crawford, Roger Mills, Okla., 50 .... B2 112
Crawford, co., Ark., 21,318 .. B1 81
Crawford, co., Ga., 5,816 .... D3 87
Crawford, co., Ill., 20,751 .... D6 90
Crawford, co., Ind., 8,379 .... H4 91
Crawford, co., Iowa, 18,569 .. B2 92
Crawford, co., Kans., 37,032 . E9 93
Crawford, co., Mich., 4,971 .. D6 98
Crawford, co., Mo., 12,647 .. D6 101
Crawford, co., Ohio, 46,775 .. B5 111
Crawford, co., Pa., 77,956 .... C1 114
Crawford, co., Wis., 16,351 .. E3 124
Crawford, lake, Maine C5 96
Crawford Bay, B.C., Can., 284 .... E9 68
Crawford House, Coos, N.H., 10 .... B4 105
Crawfordsville, Crittenden, Ark., 744 .... B5 81
Crawfordsville, Montgomery, Ind., 14,231 .... D4 91
Crawfordsville, Washington, Iowa, 317 .... C6 92
Crawfordsville, Linn, Oreg., 170 .... C4 113
Crawfordville, Wakulla, Fla., 650 .... B2 86
Crawfordville, Taliaferro, Ga., 786 .... C4 87
Crayne, Crittenden, Ky., 125 . A3 94
Crazy, mts., Mont D6 102
Crazy, peak, Mont D6 102
Crazy Woman, creek, Wyo A6 125
Creagerstown, Frederick, Md., 75 .... A3 85
Creal Springs, Williamson and Marion, Ill., 784 .... F5 90
Creamridge, Monmouth, N.J., 75 .... C3 106
Crean, lake, Sask., Can C2 70
Crediton, Eng., 4,422 .... D4 12
Cree, lake, Sask., Can m7 70
Cree, riv., Sask., Can E11 66
Creede, Mineral, Colo., 350 .. D4 83
Creedmoor, Granville, N.C., 862 .... A5 109
Creek, co., Okla., 40,495 .... B5 112
Creekside, Indiana, Pa., 482 .. E3 114
Creelman, Sask., Can., 196 .. H4 70
Creemore, Ont., Can., 850 .. C4 72
Creggan, N. Ire C4 11
Cregganbaun, Ire D2 11
Creighton, Sask., Can., 1,729 .... C5 70
Creighton, Cass, Mo., 228 .. C3 101
Creighton, Knox, Nebr., 1,388 .... B8 103
Creighton, Allegheny, Pa., 2,865 .... A6 114
Creighton Mine, Ont., Can., 1,727 .... A3, p19 72
Creil, Fr., 19,235 (*48,000) .. C5 14
Crellin, Garrett, Md., 425 .. D1 85
Crema, It., 30,035 .... B2 21
Cremona, Alta., Can., 221 .. D3 69
Cremona, It., 76,900 .... B3 21
Crenshaw, Panola, Miss., 1,382 .... A3 100
Crenshaw, Jefferson, Pa., 350 . D4 114
Crenshaw, co., Ala., 14,909 .. D3 78
Creola, Mobile, Ala., 500 .... E1 78
Creole, Cameron, La., 150 .. E2 95
Crépy-en-Valois, Fr., 7,379 .. E2 15
Cres, isl., Yugo C2 22
Cresaptown, Allegany, Md., 1,680 .... D2 85
Cresbard, Faulk, S. Dak., 229 .... B7 116
Crescent, McIntosh, Ga., 80 .... E5 87
Crescent, Pottawattamie, Iowa, 296 .... C2 92
Crescent, St. Louis, Mo., 300 . B7 101
Crescent, Saratoga, N.Y., 500 .... C7 108
Crescent, Logan, Okla., 1,264 .... B4 112
Crescent, Klamath, Oreg., 350 .... D5 113
Crescent, lake, Fla C5 86
Crescent, lake, Oreg D5 113
Crescent, lake, Wash A2 122
Crescent, range, N.H B4 105
Crescent Beach, New London, Conn. (part of Niantic) D8 84
Crescent Beach, Cumberland, Maine (part of Cape Elizabeth) E5 96
Crescent City, Del Norte, Calif., 2,958 .... B1 82
Crescent City, Putnam, Fla., 1,629 .... C5 86
Crescent City, Iroquois, Ill., 393 .... C6 90
Crescent City Northwest, Del Norte, Calif., 3,086 .... *B1 82
Crescent Lake, Klamath, Oreg., 175 .... D5 113
Crescent Springs, Kenton, Ky., 946 .... A7 94
Cresco, Howard, Iowa, 3,809 . A5 92
Cresco, Monroe, Pa., 500 .. D11 114
Cresent Spur, B.C., Can., 221 .... C7 68
Crespo, see Villa Crespo, Arg.
Cresskill, Bergen, N.J., 7,290 . h9 106
Cresson, Cambria, Pa., 2,659 . F4 114
Cresson, Hood, Tex., 300 .... B5 118
Cressona, Schuylkill, Pa., 1,854 .... E9 114
Crest, Fr., 4,494 .... E6 14
Cresta, Switz D8 19
Crested Butte, Gunnison, Colo., 289 .... C4 83
Crest Hill, Will, Ill., 5,887 .. *F2 90
Cresthill, Fauquier, Va., 50 .. C5 121
Crestline, San Bernardino, Calif., 1,290 .... F3 82
Crestline, Lincoln, Nev., 15 .. F7 104
Crestline, Crawford, Ohio, 5,521 .... B5 111
Crestmont, Montgomery, Pa., 2,000 .... *F11 114
Crestmore, San Bernardino and Riverside, Calif., 2,000 .. *E5 82
Creston, B.C., Can., 2,460 .. E9 68
Creston, Newf., Can., 837 .... E4 75
Creston, Ogle, Ill., 454 .... B5 90
Creston, Union, Iowa, 7,667 . C3 92
Creston, Flathead, Mont., 25 . B2 102
Creston, Platte, Nebr., 177 .. C8 103
Creston, Wayne, Ohio, 1,522 . B6 111
Creston, Malheur, Oreg D8 113
Creston, Calhoun, S.C., 250 .. D6 115
Creston, Cumberland, Tenn., 25 .... C8 117
Creston, Lincoln, Wash., 317 . B7 122
Creston, Wirt, W. Va., 75 .. C3 123
Crestone, Saguache, Colo., 51 .... D5 83
Crestone, peak, Colo D5 83
Crestview, Okaloosa, Fla., 7,467 .... G2 86
Crestview, Lawrence, Tenn .. B4 117
Crestwood, Cook, Ill., 3,918 . *B6 90
Crestwood, Oldham, Ky., 600 .... A4, B4 94
Crestwood, St. Louis, Mo., 11,106 .... *B8 101
Crestwood, Norfolk, Va., 2,200 .... *E6 121
Crestwynd, Sask., Can G3 70
Creswell, Washington, N.C., 402 .... B7 109
Creswell, Lane, Oreg., 760 .. D3 113
Crete, Will, Ill., 3,463 .... B6 90
Crete, Saline, Nebr., 3,546 .. D9 103
Crete, Sargent, N. Dak., 200 . C8 110
Crete, isl., Grc E5 23
Crete, sea, Grc D5 23
Cretone, It., 374 .... g9 21
Creuse, dept., Fr., 163,515 .. *D4 14
Creuse, riv., Fr D4 14
Creutzwald, Fr., 13,649 .... C7 14
Crevasse Valley, glacier, Ant B34 5
Creve Coeur, Tazewell, Ill., 6,684 .... C4 90
Creve Coeur, St. Louis, Mo., 5,122 .... *C7 101
Crevillente, Sp., 14,047 .... C5 20
Crewe, Eng., 53,200 .... A5 12
Crewe, Nottoway, Va., 2,012 . D4 121
Crewkerne, Eng., 4,215 .... D5 12
Criam More, mtn., Scot B5 13
Cricket, Wilkes, N.C., 950 .. A2 109
Cricket, mts., Utah E3 119
Cridersville, Auglaize, Ohio, 1,053 .... B3 111
Crieff, Scot., 5,773 .... D5 13
Criffel, mtn., Scot F5 13
Criglersville, Madison, Va., 45 .... C4 121
Crikvenica, Yugo., 3,637 .... C2 22
Crimea, see Krym, Sov. Un.
Crimmitschau, Ger., 31,300 . C7 17
Crimson Lake, prov. park, Alta., Can C3 69
Crinan, Scot D3 13
Cripple Creek, Teller, Colo., 614 .... C5 83
Cripple Creek, Wythe, Va., 300 .... E1 121
Crisana-Maramures, prov., Rom., 1,391,672 .... *B6 22
Crisfield, Somerset, Md., 3,540 .... E6 85
Crisman, Porter, Ind. (part of Portage) A3 91
Crisp, Ellis, Tex B6 118
Crisp, co., Ga., 17,768 .... E3 87
Crisp Creek, B.C., Can D7 68
Crissolo, It., 701 .... E3 18
Cristal, mts., Gabon E2 46
Cristalina, Braz., 3,810 .... E1 57
Cristobal, C.Z., 817 .... k11 62
Cristobal, dist., C.Z., 11,499 .... *k11 62
Cristóbal Colón, mtn., Col A3 60
Crisul Alb, riv., Rom B5 22
Crittenden, Grant, Ky., 287 .... B5, B7 94
Crittenden, Nansemond, Va., 250 .... B6 121
Crittenden, co., Ark., 47,564 . B5 81
Crittenden, co., Ky., 8,648 .. A3 94
Crivitz, Ger., 5,879 .... E5 24
Crivitz, Marinette, Wis., 650 .... C6 124
Crna, riv., Yugo E5 22
Crna Gora (Montenegro), rep., Yugo., 419,625 .... *D4 22
Crnomelj, Yugo., 2,326 .... C2 22
Croatia, rep., Yugo., 4,148,122 .... *C2 22
Croatia, reg., Yugo C2 22
Croche, riv., Que., Can A5 73
Crocheron, Dorchester, Md., 125 .... D5 85
Crocker, Pulaski, Mo., 821 .. D5 101
Crocker, Clark, S. Dak., 77 .. B8 116
Crockett, Contra Costa, Calif., 4,500 .... B5 82
Crockett, Houston, Tex., 5,356 .... D5 118
Crockett, co., Tenn., 14,594 .. B2 117
Crockett, co., Tex., 4,209 .... D2 118
Crockett Mills, Crockett, Tenn., 125 .... B2 117
Crocketville, Hampton, S.C., 75 .... F5 115
Crofton, Christian, Ky., 892 .. F5 94
Crofton, Knox, Nebr., 604 .... B8 103
Croghan, Lewis, N.Y., 821 .... B5 108
Crohy, head, Ire C3 11
Croix, Fr., 20,081 .... D5 14
Croker, cape, Ont., Can C4 72
Croker, isl., Austl B5 50
Crolly, Ire B3 11
Cromarty, Scot., 605 .... C4 13
Cromer, Man., Can., 71 .... E1 71
Cromer, Eng., 4,895 .... B9 12
Cromona (Haymond), Letcher, Ky., 950 .... C7 94
Cromwell, Choctaw, Ala., 150 .... C1 78
Cromwell, Middlesex, Conn., 6,780 .... C6 84
Cromwell, Noble, Ind., 451 . B6 91
Cromwell, Union, Iowa, 138 . C3 92
Cromwell, Ohio, Ky., 200 .... C3 94
Cromwell, Carlton, Minn., 187 .... D6 99
Cromwell, N.Z., 942 .... P12 51
Cromwell, Seminole, Okla., 269 .... B5 112
Cromwell, Pierce, Wash D1 122
Crook, Logan, Colo., 209 .... A8 83
Crook, Eng., 25,218 .... F7 13
Crook, co., Oreg., 9,430 .... C6 113
Crook, co., Wyo., 4,691 .... A8 125
Crooked, creek, Ark A3 81
Crooked, creek, Kans B7 93
Crooked, creek, Kans E3 93
Crooked, creek, Pa C7 114
Crooked, isl., Ba. Is D6 64
Crooked, lake, Newf., Can D3 75
Crooked, lake, Sask., Can G4 70
Crooked, lake, Fla E5 86
Crooked, lake, Minn B7 99
Crooked, riv., B.C., Can B6 68
Crooked, riv., Oreg C6 113
Crooked Creek, Alsk., 92 .... C8 79
Crooked Creek, Tioga, Pa., 90 .... C7 114
Crooked Creek, res., Pa E3 114
Crooked River, Sask., Can., 163 .... E4 70
Crooks, Minnehaha, S. Dak., 135 .... D9 116
Crookston, Polk, Minn., 8,546 .... C2 99
Crookston, Cherry, Nebr., 139 .... B5 103
Crookstown, Ire., 124 .... F3 11
Crooksville, Perry, Ohio, 2,958 .... C5 111
Crookwell, Austl., 2,340 .... G7 51
Croom, Ire., 720 .... E3 11
Croom Station, Prince Georges, Md C4 85
Cropper, Shelby, Ky., 250 .. B4 94
Cropsey, McLean, Ill., 170 .. C5 90
Croque, hbr., Newf., Can C4 75
Crosby, Crow Wing, Minn., 2,629 .... D5 99
Crosby, Amite, and Wilkinson, Miss., 705 .... D2 100
Crosby, Divide, N. Dak., 1,759 .... A2 110
Crosby, McKean, Pa., 350 .. C5 114
Crosby, Harris, Tex., 1,200 .. F5 118
Crosby, co., Tex., 10,347 .... C2 118
Crosby, mtn., Wyo B3 125
Crosbyton, Crosby, Tex., 2,088 .... C2 118
Crosland, Colquitt, Ga., 95 .. E3 87
Cross, Berkeley, S.C., 100 .... E7 115
Cross, Grimes, Tex., 25 .... D2 118
Cross, co., Ark., 19,551 .... B5 81
Cross, cape, S.W. Afr B1 49
Cross, creek, W. Va B2 123
Cross, isl., Maine D5 96
Cross, lake, Man., Can g8 71
Cross, lake, Man., Can C2 71
Cross, lake, La B2 95
Cross, lake, Maine A4 96
Cross, mtn., Tenn C9 117
Cross, mts., Ark C1 81
Cross, riv., Nig E6 45
Cross, sound, Alsk k21 79
Cross Anchor, Spartanburg, S.C., 500 .... B4 115
Crossbost, Scot B2 13
Cross Canyon, Apache, Ariz .. B6 80
Cross City, Dixie, Fla., 1,857 . C3 86
Cross Creek, N.B., Can., 252 . C3 74
Cross Creek, Brooke, W. Va . *A4 123
Crossdoney, Ire D4 11
Crosses, Madison, Ark B2 81
Crossett, Ashley, Ark., 5,370 . D4 81
Cross Fell, mtn., Eng F6 13
Crossfell Edge, mts., Eng F6 13
Crossfield, Alta., Can 593 .. D3 69
Crossgar, N. Ire., 843 .... C6 11
Crosshaven, Ire., 858 .... F3 11
Cross Hill, Laurens, S.C., 441 .... C4 115
Cross Keys, Bibb, Ga., 1,000 .... *D3 87
Cross Keys, Gloucester, N.J., 140 .... D2 106
Cross Lake, Man., Can., 164 .... B3 71
Crosslake, Crow Wing, Minn., 165 .... D4 99
Crossmaglen, N. Ire., 932 .... C5 11
Cross Mill, McDowell, N.C., 700 .... D4 109
Crossmolina, Ire., 777 .... C2 11
Cross Plains, Ripley, Ind., 160 .... G7 91
Cross Plains, Robertson, Tenn., 200 .... A5 117
Cross Plains, Callahan, Tex., 1,168 .... C3 118
Cross Plains, Dane, Wis., 1,066 .... E4 124
Cross Roads, San Bernardino, Calif., 150 .... E6 82
Crossroads, Lea, N. Mex., 30 . D6 107
Cross Roads Ohio, N.S., Can., 143 .... D7 74
Cross Timbers, Hickory, Mo., 186 .... C4 101
Crosstown, Perry, Mo., 83 .. D8 101
Cross Village, Emmet, Mich., 50 .... C5 98
Crossville, DeKalb, Ala., 579 .... A4 78
Crossville, White, Ill., 874 .. E5 90
Crossville, Cumberland, Tenn., 4,668 .... D8 117
Crosswicks, Burlington, N.J., 550 .... C3 106
Croswell, Sanilac, Mich., 1,817 .... E8 98
Crothersville, Jackson, Ind., 1,449 .... G6 91
Croton, Lee, Iowa, 60 .... D6 92
Croton, Newaygo, Mich E5 98
Croton, Hunterdon, N.J., 75 . B3 106
Croton (Hartford), Licking, Ohio, 397 .... B5 111
Crotone, It., 44,800 .... E6 21
Croton Falls, Westchester, N.Y., 900 .... *D7 108
Croton Falls, res., N.Y D2 84
Croton-on-Hudson, Westchester, N.Y., 6,812 . D7, m15 108
Crottendorf, Ger., 5,562 .... C7 17
Crouch, Boise, Idaho, 89 .... E3 89
Crouse, Lincoln, N.C., 901 .. B2 109
Crouseville, Aroostook, Maine, 230 .... B4 96
Crow, creek, Colo A6 83
Crow, creek, Wyo D8 125
Crow, Indian res., Mont E9 102
Crow, peak, Mont D5 102
Crow, riv., Minn F5 99
Crow Agency, Big Horn, Mont., 600 .... E9 102
Crowder, Panola and Quitman, Miss., 528 .... A3 100
Crowder, Pittsburg, Okla., 254 .... B6 112
Crowduck, lake, Man., Can D4 71
Crowell, Foard, Tex., 1,703 .. C3 118
Crowheart, Fremont, Wyo., 5 .... B3 125
Crowley, Crowley, Colo., 265 .... C7 83
Crowley, Acadia, La., 15,617 . D3 95
Crowley, Tarrant, Tex., 583 .. B5 118
Crowley, co., Colo., 3,978 .... C7 83
Crowley, lake, Calif D4 82
Crowleys, ridge, Ark., Mo E7 101
Crown City, Gallia, Ohio, 323 .... D5 111
Crown King, Yavapai, Ariz., 50 .... C3 80
Crown Point, Lake, Ind., 8,443 .... B3 91
Crown Point, Jefferson, La., 175 .... C7 95
Crownpoint, McKinley, N. Mex., 475 .... B1 107
Crown Point, Essex, N.Y., 800 .... B7 108
Crowsnest, B.C., Can., 40 .. E10 68
Crows Nest, Marion, Ind., 122 .... H8 91
Crows Nest, mtn., S. Dak C2 116
Crowsnest, pass, Alta., B.C., Can E3 69
Crow Wing, co., Minn., 32,134 .... D4 99
Crow Wing, riv., Minn D4 99
Croydon, Austl., 86 .... C7 50
Croydon, Eng., 252,387 .... C7 12, E6, m12 10
Croydon, Sullivan, N.H., 100 (312▲) D2 105
Croydon, Bucks, Pa., 9,000 .. F12 114
Croydon, Morgan, Utah, 80 .. B4 119
Croydon, mtn., N.H D2 105
Croydon, peak, N.H D2 105
Croydon, riv., N.H D2 105
Croydon Flat, Sullivan, N.H., 130 .... D2 105
Crozet, Albemarle, Va., 900 .. C4 121
Crozet, is., Indian O J24 3
Crozier, Mohave, Ariz., 10 .. B2 80
Crozier, Goochland, Va., 100 . D2 121
Crozon, Fr., 2,130 .... C1 14
Cruachan, mtn., Scot D3 13
Cruagh, isl., Ire D1 11
Cruce Magueyes, P.R B4 65
Crucero, Peru, 226 .... D3 58
Cruces, Cuba, 10,704 .... D3 64
Crucible, Greene, Pa., 1,064 . G1 114
Cruden, Scot., 2,294 .... C7 13
Cruger, Holmes, Miss., 362 .. B3 100
Crum, Wayne, W. Va., 500 .. D2 123
Crumlin, N. Ire., 822 .... C5 11
Crum Lynne, Delaware, Pa., 3,500 .... *B10 114
Crummock Water, lake, Eng F5 13
Crump, Bay, Mich., 50 .... E6 98
Crump, lake, Oreg E7 113
Crumpton, Queen Annes, Md., 300 .... B6 85
Crumstown, St. Joseph, Ind., 250 .... A5 91
Cruseilles, Fr., 865 .... C2 18
Crusheen, Ire., 97 .... E3 11
Cruso, Haywood, N.C., 175 .. D3 109
Crutchfield, Surry, N.C A3 109
Crutwell, Sask., Can., 115 .. D2 70
Cruz, cape, Cuba F5 64
Cruz Alta, Arg., 4,196 .... A4 54
Cruz Alta, Braz., 33,190 .... D2 56
Cruz Bay, Vir. Is., 200 .... f15 65
Cruz del Eje, Arg., 15,563 .. A4 54
Cruzeiro, Braz., 27,005 .... C4 56
Cruzeiro do Sul, Braz., 4,807 . C3 58
Cruz Grande, Chile E1 55
Crysler, Ont., Can., 498 .... B9 72
Crystal, Montcalm, Mich., 400 .... E6 98
Crystal, Hennepin, Minn., 24,283 .... E6 99
Crystal, Coos, N.H., 40 .... A4 105
Crystal, San Juan, N. Mex., 75 .... A1 107
Crystal, Pembina, N. Dak., 372 .... A8 110
Crystal, Klamath, Oreg E4 113
Crystal, bay, Fla D4 86
Crystal, caverns, Mo E4 101
Crystal, lake, Conn B7 84
Crystal, lake, Mich D4 98
Crystal, lake, N.H D4 105
Crystal, lake, Vt B4 120
Crystal, mtn., N.H B2 105
Crystal, pond, Conn B8 84
Crystal, riv., Colo B3 83
Crystal Bay, Washoe, Nev., 500 .... D2 104
Crystal Beach, Ont., Can., 1,886 .... E5 72
Crystal Beach, Pinellas, Fla., 1,000 .... D4 86
Crystal City, Man., Can., 542 .... E2 71
Crystal City, Jefferson, Mo., 3,678 .... B8, C7 101
Crystal City, Zavala, Tex., 9,101 .... E3 118
Crystal Falls, Iron, Mich., 2,203 .... B2 98
Crystal Hill, Halifax, Va., 150 .... E4 121
Crystal Lake, Tolland, Conn., 250 .... B7 84
Crystal Lake, Washington, Fla., 100 .... G3 86
Crystal Lake, McHenry, Ill., 8,314 .... A5, E1 90
Crystal Lake, Hancock, Iowa, 267 .... A4 92
Crystal Lake, cave, Iowa B7 92
Crystal Lakes, Clark, Ohio, 1,569 .... C3 111

28X CRYS-DANS

Crystal River, Citrus, Fla., 1,423 .... D4 86
Crystal Springs, Garland, Ark., 100 .... C2, C5 81
Crystal Springs, Sask., Can., 113 .... E3 70
Crystal Springs, Pasco, Fla., 350 .... D4 86
Crystal Springs, Copiah, Miss., 4,496 .... D3 100
Crystal Springs, Kidder, N. Dak., 30 .... C6 110
Crystal Valley, Oceana, Mich., 100 .... E4 98
Csongrad, Hung., 16,801 (20,690*) B5 22
Csongrad, co., Hung., 335,565 .... *B5 22
Csorna, Hung., 9,208 .... B3 22
Cuajimalpa, Mex., 3,504 .... h9 63
Cuando, riv., Ang., Zambia E3 48
Cuando Cubango, dist., Ang., 113,400 .... E2 48
Cuangar, Ang., 136 .... E2 48
Cuango, riv., Ang C2 48
Cuanza, riv., Ang C2 48
Cuanza Norte, dist., Ang., 263,101 .... C1 48
Cuanza Sul, dist., Ang., 405,012 .... D1 48
Cua Rao, Viet C6 38
Cuarto, riv., Arg A4 54
Cuatro Calles, P.R. (part of Arrayo) D6 65
Cuauhtémoc, Mex., 14,639 .... B3 63
Cuautepec, Mex., 5,122 .... g9 63
Cuautla [Morelos], Mex., 11,847 .... n14 63
Cuba, Sumter, Ala., 390 .... C1 78
Cuba, Fulton, Ill., 1,380 .... C3 90
Cuba, Republic, Kans., 336 .... C6 93
Cuba, Crawford, Mo., 1,672 .... C6 101
Cuba, Sandoval, N. Mex., 700 .... A3 107
Cuba, Allegany, N.Y., 1,949 .... C2 108
Cuba, Clinton, Ohio, 150 .... C4 111
Cuba, Port., 4,394 .... C2 20
Cuba, country, N.A., 7,100,000 .... G13 61, E4 64
Cuba City, Grant, Wis., 1,673 .... F3 124
Cubal, Ang D1 48
Cuba Landing, Humphreys, Tenn B4 117
Cubango, riv., Ang E2 48
Cubero, Valencia, N. Mex., 100 .... B2 107
Cubia, Ang E3 48
Cub Run, Hart, Ky., 250 .... C3 94
Cucamonga, San Bernardino, Calif., 2,500 .... F3 82
Cuchara, Huerfano, Colo., 20 .... D6 83
Cuchillo, Sierra, N. Mex., 70 .... D2 107
Cuchivero, riv., Ven B4 60
Cuchora, riv., Colo D6 83
Cuckfield, Eng., 20,113 .... C7 12
Cúcuta, Col., 101,000 (137,000*) B3 60
Cudahy, Los Angeles, Calif., 12,000 .... *F2 82
Cudahy, Milwaukee, Wis., 17,975 .... E2, F6 124
Cuddalore, India, 79,168 .... F6 39
Cuddapah, India, 49,027 .... F6 39
Cuddy, Allegheny, Pa., 1,400 .... *B5 114
Cudgewa, Austl., 192 .... H6 51
Cudjos, cave, Ky., Va D6 94
Cudworth, Sask., Can., 628 .... E3 70
Cue, Austl., 511 .... E2 50
Cuéllar, Sp., 7,514 .... B3 20
Cuenca, Ec., 46,428 .... B2 58
Cuenca, Sp., 27,007 .... B4 20
Cuenca, prov., Sp., 315,433 .... *B4 20
Cuenca, mts., Sp B4 20
Cuencamé [de Ceniceros], Mex., 2,321 .... C4 63
Cuernavaca, Mex., 37,144 .... D5, n14 63
Cuero, DeWitt, Tex., 7,338 .... E4 118
Cuervo, Cuba k12 64
Cuervo, Guadalupe, N. Mex., 25 .... B5 107
Cuetzalan [del Progreso], Mex., 4,006 .... m15 63
Cuevas, Harrison, Miss., 500 .... E2 100
Cuevas, Sp., 9,530 .... D5 20
Cuglieri, It., 4,435 .... D2 21
Cuiabá, Braz., 43,112 .... B1 56
Cuiabá, riv., Braz B1 56
Cuicas, Ven., 963 .... B3 60
Cuicatlán, Mex., 1,986 .... o15 63
Cuilapa, Guat., 2,746 .... C2 62
Cuilcagh, mtn., Ire C4 11
Cuilco, Guat., 519 .... C2 62
Cuillin, hills, Scot C2 13
Cuillin, sound, Scot C2 13
Cuipo, Pan., 99 .... k10 62
Cuito, riv., Ang E2 48
Cuito Cuanavale, Ang E2 48
Cuitzéo, lake, Mex n13 63
Cuivre, riv., Mo B6 101
Culberson, co., Tex., 2,794 .... F2 118
Culbertson, Roosevelt, Mont., 919 .... B12 102
Culbertson, Hitchcock, Nebr., 803 .... D5 103
Culcairn, Austl G6 51
Culdaff, bay, Ire B4 11
Culdesac, Nez Perce, Idaho, 209 .... C2 89
Culebra, P.R., 498 .... f13 65
Culebra, mun., P.R., 573 .... f13 65
Culebra, isl., P.R f13 65
Culebra, peak, Colo D5 83
Culebrinas, riv., P.R B2 65
Culebrita, isl., P.R f14 65
Culhuacán, Mex., 2,087 .... h9 63
Culiacán, Mex., 85,024 .... C3 63
Culion, Phil., 3,279 .... C6 35
Cúllar de Baza, Sp., 9,502 .... D4 20
Cullen, Webster, La., 2,194 .... B2 95
Cullen, Frederick, Md., 550 .... A3 85
Cullen, Scot., 1,327 .... C6 13
Culleoka, Maury, Tenn., 300 .... B4 117
Cullera, Sp., 14,103 .... C5 20
Cullion, N. Ire C4 11
Cullison, Pratt, Kans., 129 .... E5 93
Cullman, Cullman, Ala., 10,883 .... A3 78
Cullman, co., Ala., 45,572 .... A3 78
Culloden, Monroe, Ga., 260 .... D2 87
Culloden, Cabell, W. Va., 700 .... *C2 123
Culloden, pt., N.Y E9 84
Cullom, Livingston, Ill., 555 .... C5 90
Cullowhee, Jackson, N.C., 1,500 .... D3 109
Culmore, Fairfax, Va., 1,700 .... *B5 121
Culoz, Fr., 2,317 .... D1 18
Culp Creek, Lane, Oreg., 100 .... D4 113
Culpeper, Van Buren, Ark B3 81
Culpeper, Culpeper, Va., 2,412 .... C4 121
Culpeper, co., Va., 15,088 .... C5 121
Cultus Lake, B.C., Can., 674 .... f14 68
Culuene, riv., Braz A2 56
Culver, Marshall, Ind., 1,558 .... B5 91
Culver, Ottawa, Kans., 200 .... D6 93
Culver, St. Louis, Minn., 60 .... D6 99
Culver, Jefferson, Oreg., 301 .... C5 113
Culver City, Los Angeles, Calif., 32,163 .... F2 82
Culvers, lake, N.J A3 106
Culverton, Hancock, Ga C4 87
Culzean, bay, Scot E3 13
Cumaná, Ven., 71,563 .... A5 60
Cumberland, B.C., Can., 1,303 .... E5 68
Cumberland, Ont., Can., 360 .... g13 72
Cumberland, Marion, Ind., 872 .... E6, H8 91
Cumberland, Cass, Iowa, 425 .... C3 92
Cumberland, Harlan, Ky., 4,271 .... D7 94
Cumberland, Cumberland, Maine, 600 (2,765*) E2, E5 96
Cumberland, Allegany, Md., 33,415 .... D2 85
Cumberland, Webster, Miss., 145 .... B4 100
Cumberland, Cumberland, N.J., 200 .... E3 106
Cumberland, Cumberland, N.C., 500 .... B5 109
Cumberland, Guernsey, Ohio, 493 .... C6 111
Cumberland, Marshall, Okla., 250 .... C5 112
Cumberland, Providence, R.I., 5,800 (18,792*) B11 84
Cumberland, Cumberland, Va., 250 .... D4 121
Cumberland, King, Wash., 160 .... D2 122
Cumberland, Barron, Wis., 1,860 .... C1 124
Cumberland, co., N.S., Can., 37,767 .... D5 74
Cumberland, co., Eng., 294,162 .... *C5 10
Cumberland, co., Ill., 9,936 .... D5 90
Cumberland, co., Ky., 7,835 .... D4 94
Cumberland, co., Maine, 182,751 .... E2 96
Cumberland, co., N.J., 106,850 .... E2 106
Cumberland, co., N.C., 148,418 .... B5 109
Cumberland, co., Pa., 124,816 .... F7 114
Cumberland, co., Tenn., 19,135 .... D8 117
Cumberland, co., Va., 6,360 .... D4 121
Cumberland, isl., Ga F5 87
Cumberland, lake, Sask., Can C4 70
Cumberland, lake, Ky D4 94
Cumberland, mts., Ky., Tenn C9 117
Cumberland, pen., N.W. Ter., Can C19 67
Cumberland, plat., Ala., Ky., Tenn A3 78, C6 94, D7 117
Cumberland, riv., U.S C11 77
Cumberland, sound, N.W. Ter., Can C19 67
Cumberland Center, Cumberland, Maine, 600 (2,765*) E5 96
Cumberland, City, Stewart, Tenn., 314 .... A4 117
Cumberland Furnace, Dickson, Tenn., 250 .... A4 117
Cumberland Gap, Claiborne, Tenn., 291 .... C10 117
Cumberland Hill, Providence, R.I., 2,000 .... B11 84
Cumberland House, Sask., Can., 486 .... D4 70
Cumbres, pass, Colo D4 83
Cumbrian, mts., Eng F5 13
Cuming, co., Nebr., 12,435 .... C9 103
Cumming, Forsyth, Ga., 1,561 .... B2 87
Cumming, Warren, Iowa, 148 .... A7 92
Cummings, Atchison, Kans., 50 .... A7 93
Cummings, Traill, N. Dak., 51 .... B8 110
Cummingsville, Van Buren, Tenn D8 117
Cummington, Hampshire, Mass., 150 (550*) B2 97
Cumnock, Lee, N C., 200 .... B4 109
Cumnock, Scot., 5,403 .... E4 13
Cumpas, Mex., 2,314 .... A3 63
Cumra, Tur., 7,100 .... D9 31
Cunard, Fayette, W. Va., 450 .... D7 123
Cunco, Chile, 2,728 .... B2 54
Cuncumen, Chile A2 54
Cundiff, Adair, Ky., 125 .... D4 94
Cundinamarca, dept., Col., 1,840,890 .... C3 60
Cundiyo, Santa Fe, N. Mex., 50 .... *B4 107
Cundys Harbor, Cumberland, Maine, 125 .... E6 96
Cunene, riv., Ang., S.W. Afr A1 49
Cuneo, It., 35,800 (48,400*) B1 21
Cuney, Cherokee, Tex., 220 .... C5 118
Cunnamulla, Austl., 2,234 .... D5 52
Cunningham, Kingman, Kans., 618 .... E5 93
Cunningham, Carlisle, Ky., 300 .... A2 94
Cunningham, Montgomery, Tenn., 40 .... A4 117
Cupar, Sask., Can., 578 .... G3 70
Cupar, Scot., 5,495 .... D6 13
Cupertino, Santa Clara, Calif., 3,664 .... C5 82
Cuprum, Adams, Idaho, 20 .... D2 89
Curacá, Braz., 1,264 .... C3 57
Curaçao, isl., Neth. Antilles A4 60
Curacautín, Chile, 9,201 .... B2 54
Curacó, riv., Arg B3 54
Curañilahue, Chile, 3,995 .... B2 54
Curaray, riv., Ec., Peru B2 58
Curdsville, Daviess, Ky., 175 .... C2 94
Curepto, Chile, 1,739 .... B2 54
Curiapo, Ven., 374 .... B5 60
Curicó, Chile, 35,000 .... A2 54
Curicó, prov., Chile, 107,160 .... A2 54
Curicuriari, riv., Braz D4 60
Curimata, riv., Braz h6 57
Curitiba, Braz., 344,560 .... D3 56
Curitibanos, Braz., 8,339 .... D2 56
Curlew, Palo Alto, Iowa, 134 .... B3 92
Curlew, Ferry, Wash., 100 .... A7 122
Curlew, creek, Wash A7 122
Curlew, lake, Wash A7 122
Curon Venosta, It., 2,970 .... C6 18
Currais Novos, Braz., 7,782 .... C3, h5 57
Curralinho, Braz., 361 .... C5 59
Curran, Ont., Can., 113 .... B10 72
Curran, Alcona, Mich., 50 .... D7 98
Currans, Ire E2 11
Currant, creek, Colo C5 83
Curreeny, Ire E3 11
Current, riv., Ark., Mo D6 101
Currie, Murray, Minn., 438 .... F3 99
Currie, Elko, Nev., 25 .... C7 104
Currituck, Currituck, N.C., 250 .... A7 109
Currituck, co., N.C., 6,601 .... A7 109
Curry, Alsk., 20 .... C10, f17 79
Curry, co., N. Mex., 32,691 .... C6 107
Curry, co., Oreg., 13,983 .... E2 113
Curryville, Gordon, Ga., 40 .... B1 87
Curryville, Pike, Mo., 287 .... B6 101
Curtea-de-Arges, Rom., 10,764 .... C7 22
Curtice, Lucas and Ottawa, Ohio, 500 .... A2, A4 111
Curtici, Rom., 8,050 .... B5 22
Curtin, Douglas, Oreg., 40 .... D3 113
Curtis, Clark, Ark., 350 .... D2 81
Curtis, Mackinac, Mich., 40 .... B5 98
Curtis, Frontier, Nebr., 868 .... D5 103
Curtis, Woodward, Okla., 25 .... A2 112
Curtis, isl., Austl A8 51
Curtiss, Clark, Wis., 147 .... D3 124
Curtisville, Allegheny, Pa., 1,376 .... A6, E2 114
Curuá, riv., Braz D4 59
Curuá do Sul, riv., Braz C4 59
Curuçá, Braz., 3,871 .... B1 57
Curug, Yugo., 9,457 .... C5 22
Curuguaty, Par., 2,342 .... D4 55
Curupira, mts., Ven C5 60
Curuzú Cuatia, Arg., 15,440 .... E4 55
Curve, Lauderdale, Tenn., 40 .... B2 117
Curvelo, Braz., 21,772 .... E2 57
Curver, mtn., Switz C7 19
Curwensville, Clearfield, Pa., 3,231 .... E4 114
Cusco, Peru, 78,300 .... D3 58
Cusco, dept., Peru, 649,643 .... D3 58
Cushendall, N. Ire., 618 .... B5 11
Cushendunn, N. Ire B5 11
Cushing, Woodbury, Iowa, 261 .... B2 92
Cushing, Knox, Maine, 130 (479*) D3 96
Cushing, Howard, Nebr., 56 .... C7 103
Cushing, Payne, Okla., 8,619 .... B5 112
Cushing, Nacogdoches, Tex., 388 .... D5 118
Cushman, Independence, Ark., 241 .... B4 81
Cushman, Hampshire, Mass., 200 .... B3 97
Cushman, Golden Valley, Mont., 5 .... D7 102
Cushman, Lane, Oreg., 150 .... D2 113
Cushman, mtn., N.H C3 105
Cushman, res., Wash B2 122
Cusick, Pend Oreille, Wash., 299 .... A8 122
Cusihuiriachic, Mex., 380 .... B3 63
Cusset, Fr., 11,468 .... D5 14
Cusseta, Chambers, Ala., 180 .... C4 78
Cusseta, Chattahoochee, Ga., 768 .... D2 87
Custar, Wood, Ohio, 246 .... A4 111
Custer, Mason, Mich., 365 .... E4 98
Custer, Yellowstone, Mont., 350 .... D9 102
Custer, McLean, N. Dak., 20 .... B4 110
Custer, Custer, Okla., 448 .... B3 112
Custer, Custer, S. Dak., 2,105 .... D2 116
Custer, Whatcom, Wash., 400 .... A3 122
Custer, co., Colo., 1,305 .... C5 83
Custer, co., Idaho, 2,996 .... E4 89
Custer, co., Mont., 13,227 .... D11 102
Custer, co., Nebr., 16,517 .... C6 103
Custer, co., Okla., 21,040 .... B2 112
Custer, co., S. Dak., 4,906 .... D2 116
Custer, peak, S. Dak C2 116
Custer Battlefield, nat. mon., Mont E9 102
Custer City, McKean, Pa., 400 .... C4 114
Cut Bank, Glacier, Mont., 4,539 .... B4 102
Cutbank, riv., Alta., Can B1 69
Cut Beaver, lake, Sask., Can D4 70
Cutchogue, Suffolk, N.Y., 350 .... m16 108
Cutervo, Peru, 3,481 .... C2 58
Cuthbert, Randolph, Ga., 4,300 .... E2 87
Cut Knife, Sask., Can., 487 .... E1 70
Cutler, Tulare, Calif., 2,191 .... *D4 82
Cutler, Ont., Can A2 72
Cutler, Carroll, Ind., 200 .... D4 91
Cutler, Washington, Maine, 200 (654*) D5 96
Cutler City, Lincoln, Oreg., 525 .... C3 113
Cutler Ridge, Dade, Fla., 7,005 .... *G6 86
Cut Off, Lafourche, La., 700 .... E5 95
Cutshin, Leslie, Ky., 450 .... C6 94
Cuttack, India, 146,308 .... D8 38, G10 40
Cutten, Humboldt, Calif., 1,572 .... *B1 82
Cut Throat, isl., Newf., Can A3 75
Cuttingsville, Rutland, Vt., 120 .... E3 120
Cuttyhunk, isl., Mass D6 97
Cutzamala, riv., Mex n13 63
Cuvo, riv., Ang D1 48
Cuxhaven, Ger., 45,400 .... B4 16
Cuyahoga, co., Ohio, 1,647,895 .... A6 111
Cuyahoga, riv., Ohio A6 111
Cuyahoga Falls, Summit, Ohio, 47,922 .... A6 111
Cuyama, riv., Calif E4 82
Cuyamaca, peak, Calif F5 82
Cuyamungue, Santa Fe, N. Mex., 50 .... *B4 107
Cuylerville, Livingston, N.Y., 280 .... C3 108
Cuyo, Phil., 2,326 .... *C6 35
Cuyo, is., Phil C6 35
Cuyuna, Crow Wing, Minn., 86 .... D5 99
Cuyuni, riv., Br. Gu A3 59
Cuzco, Dubois, Ind., 30 .... H4 91
Cwmamman, Wales, 4,272 .... C4 12
Cybinka, Pol., 1,025 .... A9 17
Cyclades (Kiklades), prov., Grc., 99,959 .... *D5 23
Cyclades, is., Grc D5 23
Cyclone, McKean, Pa., 450 .... C4 114
Cygnet, Wood, Ohio, 593 .... A4 111
Cylinder, Palo Alto, Iowa, 161 .... A3 92
Cynthiana, Posey, Ind., 663 .... H2 91
Cynthiana, Harrison, Ky., 5,641 .... B5 94
Cynthiana, Pike, Ohio, 150 .... C4 111
Cyprès, lake, Que., Can C3 73
Cypress, Hale, Ala., 125 .... C2 78
Cypress, Orange, Calif., 1,753 .... *F2 82
Cypress, Jackson, Fla., 260 .... B1 86
Cypress, Johnson, Ill., 264 .... F4 90
Cypress, Harris, Tex., 25 .... F4 118
Cypress, bayou, Ark B4 81
Cypress, hills, Alta., Sask., Can G10 66
Cypress, lake, Alta., Sask., Can H1 70
Cypress, lake, Fla D5 86
Cypress Hills, prov. park, Alta., Can E5 69
Cypress Hills, prov. park, Sask., Can H1 70
Cypress Inn, Wayne, Tenn., 250 .... B4 117
Cypress River, Man., Can., 288 .... E2 71
Cyprus, country, Asia, 590,000 .... E9 31
Cyrenaica, prov., Libya, 291,328 .... D4 43
Cyrene, Decatur, Ga., 200 .... F2 87
Cyril, Caddo, Okla., 1,284 .... C3 112
Cyril, riv., Man., Can B4 71
Cyrus, Pope, Minn., 362 .... E3 99
Czar, Alta., Can., 196 .... C5 69
Czarna, riv., Pol k14 26
Czarna Przemsza, riv., Pol g10 26
Czarnkow, Pol., 4,394 .... B4 26
Czechoslovakia, country, Eur., 14,100,000 .... F12 8, D4 26
Czersk, Pol., 7,092 .... B4 26
Częstochowa, Pol., 169,400 .... C5 26
Czluchow, Pol., 3,711 .... B4 26

D

Daaquam, Que., Can., 195 .... C7 73
Daarburuk, Som D5 47
Dab, Pol., 9,096 .... B3 26
Dab, Pol., 13,666 .... g9 26
Dabā, Tr. Coast I8 41
Dab'ah, Jordan C8 32
Dabakala, I.C., 900 .... E4 45
Dabaro, Som B6 44
Dabdab, Libya D2 43
Dabeiba, Col., 2,832 .... B2 60
Dablice, Czech., 5,378 .... n18 26
Dabney, Vance, N.C., 25 .... A5 109
Dabneys, Louisa, Va., 15 .... D5 121
Dabola, Guinea, 3,700 .... D2 45
Dabra-Berhām, Eth D4 47
Dabra-Mārk'os, Eth C4 47
Dabra-Tābor, Eth C4 47
Dabrowa, Pol., 4,520 .... C6 26
Dabrowa Gornicza, Pol., 58,400 .... C5, g10 26
Dabrowa Grodzienska, Pol., 3,026 .... B7 26
Dacca, Pak., 362,006 (*750,000) D9 39, F13 40
Dachau, Ger., 29,100 .... D5 16
Dacoma, Woods, Okla., 219 .... A3 112
Dacono, Weld, Colo., 302 .... A6 83
Dacula, Gwinnett, Ga., 440 .... C3 87
Dacura, Nic C6 62
Dacus, Montgomery, Tex D5 118
Dacusville, Pickens, S.C., 175 .... B2 115
Dadanawa, Br. Gu B3 59
Dadar, Eth D5 47
Daday, Tur., 1,600 .... B9 31
Daddy, creek, Tenn C9 117
Dade, co., Fla., 935,047 .... G6 86
Dade, co., Ga., 8,666 .... B1 87
Dade, co., Mo., 7,577 .... D4 101
Dade City, Pasco, Fla., 4,759 .... D4 86
Dadeville, Tallapoosa, Ala., 2,940 .... C4 78
Dadeville, Dade, Mo., 142 .... D4 101
Dadu, Pak., 13,716 .... D1 40
Daet, Phil., 20,000 (35,600*) *C6 35
Dafoe, Sask., Can., 79 .... F3 70
Dafoe, riv., Man., Can B4 71
Dagahabur, Eth D5 47
Dagana, Sen., 4,000 .... C1 45
Daggett, San Bernardino, Calif., 400 .... E5 82
Daggett, Menominee, Mich., 296 .... C3 98
Daggett, co., Utah, 1,164 .... C6 119
Dagmar, Sheridan, Mont., 70 .... B12 102
Dagsboro, Sussex, Del., 477 .... C7 85
Dagupan, Phil, 34,484 .... n13 35
Daguscahonda, Elk, Pa., 150 .... D4 114
Dagus Mines, Elk, Pa., 450 .... D4 114
Dahan-i-Kashan, Afg., 5,000 .... D13 41
Dahan-i-Kusnak, Afg., 5,000 .... D11 41
Dahanu, India, 9,648 .... H4 40
Dahinda, Knox, Ill., 225 .... C3 90
Dahlen, Nelson, N. Dak., 100 .... A8 110
Dahlgren, Hamilton, Ill., 480 .... E5 90
Dahlgren, King George, Va., 475 .... C5 121
Dahlonega, Lumpkin, Ga., 2,604 .... B3 87
Dahme, Ger., 6,391 .... B8 17
Dahomey, country, Afr., 2,300,000 .... F6 42, E5 45
Dahshūr, Eg., U.A.R E3 32
Daigle, Aroostook, Maine, 150 .... A4 96
Daigleville, Terrebonne, La., 5,906 .... *E6 95
Dailey, Logan, Colo., 10 .... A8 83
Dailey, Randolph, W. Va., 800 .... C5 123
Daimiel, Sp., 19,625 .... C4 20
Daingean, Ire., 679 .... D4 11
Daingerfield, Morris, Tex., 3,133 .... C5 118
Dairen (Talien), China, 950,000 .... D9 34
Dairy, Klamath, Oreg., 50 .... E5 113
Dairyland, Douglas, Wis., 25 .... B1 124
Dairy Valley, Los Angeles, Calif., 3,508 .... *F2 82
Daisetta, Liberty, Tex., 1,500 .... D5 118
Daisy, Pike, Ark., 86 .... C2 81
Daisy, Evans, Ga., 229 .... D5 87
Daisy, Atoka, Okla., 25 .... C6 112
Daisy (Melville), Hamilton, Tenn., 1,508 .... D8, E10 117
Daisy, Stevens, Wash., 30 .... A7 122
Daisytown, Washington, Pa., 1,396 .... *F2 114
Dajabón, Dom. Rep., 3,230 .... E8 64
Dajarra, Austl., 182 .... D6 50
Dakar, Sen., 374,700 (*435,000) D1 45
Dakhilah, oasis, Eg., U.A.R D5 43
Dakoro, Niger D6 45
Dakota, Stephenson, Ill., 363 .... A4 90
Dakota, Winona, Minn., 339 .... G7 99
Dakota, co., Minn., 78,303 .... F5 99
Dakota, co., Nebr., 12,168 .... B9 103
Dakota City, Humboldt, Iowa, 706 .... B3 92
Dakota City, Dakota, Nebr., 928 .... B9 103
Dakwa, Con. L A4 48
Dalaba, Guinea, 5,500 .... D2 45
Dalälven, riv., Swe G6 25
Dalaman, Tur D7 23
Dalaman, riv., Tur D7 23
Dalark, Dallas, Ark., 123 .... C3 81
Dalarö, Swe., 523 .... t36 25
Dalat, Viet, 48,840 .... G8 38
Dalay Sayn Shanda, Mong B4 36
Dalbandin, Pak C3 39
Dalbeattie, Scot., 3,104 .... F5 13
Dalbo, Isanti, Minn., 60 .... E5 99
Dalby, Austl., 7,400 .... C8 51
Dalby, Swe., 1,461 .... C7 24
Dalcahue, Chile C2 54
Dale, Hamilton, Ill., 140 .... F5 90
Dale, Spencer, Ind., 900 .... H4 91
Dale, Pottawatomie, Okla., 400 .... B4 112
Dale, Grant, Oreg., 5 .... C8 113
Dale, Cambria, Pa., 2,807 .... *F4 114
Dale, co., Ala., 31,066 .... D4 78
Dale Hollow, lake, Tenn C8 117
Dalemead, Alta., Can D4 69
Daleview, Sheridan, Mont B12 102
Daleville, Dale, Ala., 693 .... D4 78
Daleville, Delaware, Ind., 1,548 .... D6 91
Daleville, Lauderdale, Miss., 125 .... C5 100
Dalhart, Dallam and Hartley, Tex., 5,160 .... A1 118
Dalhousie, N.B., Can., 5,856 .... A3 74
Dalhousie, India, 2,739 .... A5 40
Dalhousie Junction, N.B., Can., 172 .... A3 74
Dalías, Sp., 3,540 .... D4 20
Daliburgh, Scot C1 13
Daliyat-el Karmil, Isr., 3,144 .... B7 32
Dalkeith, Gulf, Fla., 35 .... B1 86
Dalkeith, Scot., 8,864 .... E5 13
Dalkena, Pend Oreille, Wash., 30 .... A8 122
Dalkey, Ire D5 11
Dall, isl., Alsk n23 79
Dall, mtn., Alsk f15 79
Dallam, co., Tex., 6,302 .... A1 118
Dallas, Blount, Ala., 150 .... B3 78
Dallas, Paulding, Ga., 2,065 .... C2 87
Dallas, Franklin, Maine, 50 (77*) D2 96
Dallas, Gaston, N.C., 3,270 .... B2 109
Dallas, Polk, Oreg., 5,072 .... C3 113
Dallas, Luzerne, Pa., 2,586 .... B8, D10 114
Dallas, Gregory, S. Dak., 212 .... D6 116
Dallas, Dallas, Tex., 679,684 (*1,022,300) B5, C4 118
Dallas, Marshall, W. Va., 100 .... B2 123
Dallas, Barron, Wis., 401 .... C2 124
Dallas, co., Ala., 56,667 .... C2 78
Dallas, co., Ark., 10,522 .... D3 81
Dallas, co., Iowa, 24,123 .... C3 92
Dallas, co., Mo., 9,314 .... D4 101
Dallas, co., Tex., 951,527 .... C4 118
Dallas Center, Dallas, Iowa, 1,083 .... C4 92
Dallas City, Hancock and Henderson, Ill., 1,276 .... C2 90
Dallas Mine, Dallas, Iowa, 165 .... A7 92
Dallastown, York, Pa., 3,615 .... G8 114
Dalmacio Vélez, Arg A4 54
Dalmally, Scot., 876 .... D4 13
Dalmatia, Northumberland, Pa., 600 .... E8 114
Dalmatia, reg., Yugo D3 22
Dalmellington, Scot., 4,702 .... E4 13
Dalmeny, Sask., Can., 415 .... E2 70
Dalnyaya, Sov. Un., 10,000 .... D10 37
Daloa, I.C., 13,000 .... E3 45
Dalroy, Alta, Can D4 69
Dalry, Scot., 6,764 .... E4 13
Dalrymple, mtn., Austl D8 50
Dalton, Randolph, Ark., 25 .... A4 81
Dalton, Whitfield, Ga., 17,868 .... B2 87
Dalton, Berkshire, Mass., 6,436 .... B1 97
Dalton, Otter Tail, Minn., 239 .... D3 99
Dalton, Chariton, Mo., 197 .... B5 101
Dalton, Cheyenne, Nebr., 503 .... C3 103
Dalton, Coos, N.H., 50 (567*) B3 105
Dalton, Livingston, N.Y., 500 .... C3 108
Dalton, Wayne, Ohio, 1,067 .... B6 111
Dalton, Lackawanna, Pa., 1,229 .... C10 114
Dalton, iceberg tongue, Ant C25 5
Dalton City, Moultrie, Ill., 386 .... D5 90
Daltonganj, India, 25,270 .... E10 40
Dalton Gardens, Kootenai, Idaho, 1,083 .... B2 89
Dalwhinnie, Scot D4 13
Daly, riv., Austl B5 50
Daly City, San Mateo, Calif., 44,791 .... B5 82
Daly Waters, Austl C5 50
Dalzell, Sumter, S.C., 80 .... C7 115
Dam, Sur B3 59
Dama, is., Viet H6 38
Damanhūr, Eg., U.A.R., 126,600 .... C6 43
Damão, India, 10,000 .... G4 40
Damar, Rooks, Kans., 361 .... C4 93
Damar, isl., Indon G7 35
Damar, is., Indon G7 35
Damara, Cen. Afr. Rep D3 46
Damariscotta, Lincoln, Maine, 800 (1,093*) D3 96
Damariscotta, lake, Maine D3 96
Damas, pass, Arg A2 54
Damascus, Faulkner, Ark., 400 .... B3 81
Damascus, Early, Ga., 297 .... E2 87
Damascus, Gordon, Ga., 200 .... B2 87
Damascus, Montgomery, Md., 1,500 .... B3 85
Damascus, Wayne, Pa., 250 .... C11 114
Damascus (Dimashq), Syr., 529,963 .... F11 31
Damascus, Washington, Va., 1,485 .... B3 121
Damaturu, Nig., 2,379 .... D7 45
Damba, Ang., 1,367 .... C2 48
Dambidolo, Eth D3 47
Dambovita, riv., Rom C7 22
D'Ambre, cape, Malag f9 49
Dame-Marie, cape, Hai F6 64
Dam Gamad, Sud C2 47
Damghan, Iran, 12,235 .... C7 41
Damietta (Dumyāṭ), Eg., U.A.R., 63,100 .... C6 43
Damietta, riv. mouth, Eg., U.A.R C3 32
Damietta Branch, riv., Eg., U.A.R D3 32
Dāmiyā, Jordan, 1,000 .... g13 32
Damme, Ger., 9,300 .... B8 15
Dam No. 17, Ala B2 78
Damodar, riv., India F10 40
Damoh, India, 46,656 .... F7 40
Damon, Brazoria, Tex., 750 .... G4 118
Damongo, Ghana E4 45
Dampier, strait, W. Irian F8 35
Dan, riv., N.C., Va A4 103, E4 121
Dana, Sask., Can E3 70
Dana, LaSalle, Ill., 240 .... C5 90
Dana, Vermillion, Ind., 811 .... E2 91
Dana, Greene, Iowa, 123 .... B3 92
Dana, Henderson, N.C., 200 .... D4 109
Danakil, depression, Eth C5 47
Danané, I.C., 4,000 .... E3 45
Da Nang (Tourane), Viet., S., 109,000 .... D8 38
Dana Point, Orange, Calif., 1,186 .... *F5 82
Danburg, Wilkes, Ga., 108 .... C4 87
Danbury, Fairfield, Conn., 22,928 (39,382*) D3 84
Danbury, Woodbury, Iowa, 510 .... B2 92
Danbury, Red Willow, Nebr., 185 .... D5 103
Danbury, Merrimack, N.H., 200 (435*) C3 105
Danbury, Stokes, N.C., 175 .... A3 109
Danbury, Brazoria, Tex., 600 .... G5 118
Danbury, Burnett, Wis., 300 .... C1 124
Danby, San Bernardino, Calif., 20 .... E6 82
Danby, Tompkins, N.Y., 100 .... C4 108
Danby, Rutland, Vt., 250 (891*) E3 120
Danby Four Corners, Rutland, Vt., 40 .... E2 120
Dancy, Pickens, Ala., 100 .... B1 78
Dancy, Marathon, Wis., 100 .... D4 124
Dancyville, Haywood, Tenn., 50 .... B2 117
Dande, riv., Ang C1 48
Dandenong, Austl., 24,914 .... H5 51
Dandridge, Jefferson, Tenn., 829 .... C10 117
Dandy, York, Va., 400 .... A6 121
Dane, Dane, Wis., 394 .... E4 124
Dane, co., Wis., 222,095 .... E4 124
Danevang, Wharton, Tex., 300 .... E4 118
Danforth, Ont., Can m15 72
Danforth, Iroquois, Ill., 394 .... C6 90
Danforth, Washington, Maine, 800 (821*) C5 96
Danforth, hills, Colo A2 83
Dānglā Eth C4 47
Dangrek, mts., Thai E6 38
Dania, Broward, Fla., 7,065 .... E3, F6 86
Daniel, Sublette, Wyo., 110 .... C2 125
Daniel, mtn., Wash B4 122
Daniels, Howard, Md., 750 .... B4 85
Daniels, co., Mont., 3,755 .... B11 102
Daniel's Harbour, Newf., Can., 403 .... C3 75
Daniels Landing, Perry, Tenn B4 117
Danielson, Windham, Conn., 4,642 .... B9 84
Danielsville, Madison, Ga., 362 .... B3 87
Danilov, Sov. Un., 16,600 .... B2 29
Danilov Grad, Yugo., 1,373 .... D4 22
Danjo, isl., Jap J4 37
Dankhar, India B7 40
Danlí, Hond., 3,757 .... C4 62
Dannebrog, Howard, Nebr., 277 .... C7 103
Dannemora, Clinton, N.Y., 4,835 .... f11 108
Dannenberg, Ger., 3,500 .... E5 24
Danner, Malheur, Oreg E9 113
Dannevirke, N.Z., 5,508 .... N16 51
Dannike, Swe., 218 .... A7 24
Danripple, Halifax, Va E3 121
Dans, mtn., Md D2 85

Dansalan, Phil., 4,882......*D6 35
Dansville, Livingston, N.Y., 5,460......C3 108
Dante, Som......C7 47
Dante, Charles Mix, S. Dak., 102......D7 116
Dante, Knox, Tenn., 600...E11 117
Dante, Russell, Va., 1,436...B2 121
Danube, Renville, Minn., 494......F3 99
Danube, riv., Eur......G14 8
Danube, riv. mouths, Eur......F14 8
Danubyu, Bur., 10,000......D1 38
Danvers, McLean, Ill., 783..C4 90
Danvers, Essex, Mass., 21,926......A6, f12 97
Danvers, Swift, Minn., 132..E3 99
Danvers, Fergus, Mont., 20..C7 102
Danville, Morgan, Ala., 140......A2 78
Danville, Yell, Ark., 955......B2 81
Danville, Contra Costa, Calif., 3,585......B6 82
Danville, Que., Can., 2,562..D5 73
Danville, Twiggs and Wilkinson, Ga., 459......D3 87
Danville, Vermilion, Ill., 41,856......C6 90
Danville, Hendricks, Ind., 3,287......E3 91
Danville, Des Moines, Iowa, 579......D6 92
Danville, Harper, Kans., 118.E6 93
Danville, Boyle, Ky., 9,010..C5 94
Danville, Rockingham, N.H., 175 (605▲)......E4 105
Danville, Highland, Ohio, 50......C4 111
Danville, Knox, Ohio, 926...B5 111
Danville, Montour, Pa., 6,889......E8 114
Danville, Houston, Tenn....A4 117
Danville, Caledonia, Vt., 400 (1,368▲)......C4 120
Danville (Independent City), Va., 46,577......E3 121
Danville, Ferry, Wash., 80...A7 122
Danville Boone, W. Va., 507......C3, D5 123
Danville East (Mechanicsville), Montour, Pa., 1,758....*E8 114
Danzig, see Gdańsk, Pol.
Danzig, gulf, Pol......A5 26
Daosa, India, 14,612......D6 40
Daphne, Baldwin, Ala., 1,527......E2 78
Dapp, Alta., Can., 71......B4 69
Dārāb, Iran, 7,403......G7 41
Darabani, Rom., 11,379.....A8 22
Daraj, Libya......C2 43
Dār al Ḩamrā, Sau. Ar......I12 31
Darasun, Sov. Un., 18,000..D14 28
Darawah, Eg., U.A.R......D3 32
Darbhanga, India, 103,016......C8 39, D10 40
D'Abronne, bayou, La......B3 95
Darbun, Marion, & Walthall, Miss., 150......D3 100
Darby, Ravalli, Mont., 398..D2 102
Darby, Delaware, Pa., 14,059......B11, G11 114
Darby, creek, Ohio......C4 111
Darbyville, Pickaway, Ohio, 213......C4 111
Dar Chebika, Mor......D2 44
D'Arcy Station, Sask., Can., 65......F1 70
Dardanelle, Yell, Ark., 2,098.B2 81
Dardanelle, Tuolumne, Calif......C4 82
Dardanelles, strait, Tur......B6 23
Darden, Henderson, Tenn., 250......B3 117
Dardenne, creek, Mo......A7 101
Dardens, Martin, N.C., 175..B7 109
Dare, co., N.C., 5,936......B8 109
Darende, Tur., 6,900......C11 31
Dar es Salaam, Tan., 128,742......C6 48
Daretown, Salem, N.J., 150..D2 106
Darfo, It., 8,711......D6 18
Darfur, Watonwan, Minn., 191......F4 99
Darfur, reg., Sud., 1,328,765..C1 47
Dargai, Pak......B5 39
Dargan, Washington, Md., 150......B2 85
Darganata, Sov. Un......A11 41
Dargaville, N.Z., 3,733......K14 51
Darien, Fairfield, Conn., 18,437......E3 84
Darien, McIntosh, Ga., 1,569......E5 87
Darien, Walworth, Wis., 805......F5 124
Darien, mts., Pan......F9 62
Dariense, mts., Nic......D5 62
Darjeeling, India, 40,651...D12 40
Dark Cove, Newf., Can., 955......*D4 75
Darke, co., Ohio, 45,612.....B3 111
Darkesville, Berkeley, W. Va., 200......*B7 123
Darkharbor, Waldo, Maine, 100......D4 96
Darling, Quitman, Miss., 250......A3 100
Darling, lake, N. Dak......A4 110
Darling, range, Austl......F2 50
Darling, riv., Austl......E5 51
Darlingford, Man., Can., 189......E2 71
Darlington, Wilcox, Ala., 100......D2 78
Darlington, Eng., 84,200...C6 10
Darlington, Walton, Fla., 1,100......G3 86
Darlington Butte, Idaho, 10......F5 89
Darlington, Montgomery, Ind., 668......D4 91
Darlington, Harford, Md., 250......A5 85
Darlington, Gentry, Mo., 169......A3 101
Darlington, Darlington, S.C., 6,710......C8 115
Darlington, Lafayette, Wis., 2,349......F3 124
Darlington, co., S.C., 52,928.C8 115
Darlove, Washington, Miss., 50......B3 100
Darłowo, Pol., 5,262......A4 26
Dar Mazar, Iran......G8 41
Darmody, Sask., Can., 48...G2 70
Darmstadt, Ger., 139,100 (*220 000)......D3 17
Darnah (Derna), Libya, 15,891......C4 43
Darnell, West Carroll, La., 65......B4 95
Darnestown, Montgomery, Md., 150......B3 85
Darney, Fr., 1,810......A2 18
Darnley, cape, Ant......C19 5
Daro, Mala......E4 35
Daroca, Sp., 3,378......B5 20
Darr, Dawson, Nebr., 11....D6 103
Darrah, mtn., Alta., B.C., Can.E3 69
Darrington, Snohomish, Wash., 1,272......A4 122
Darrouzett, Lipscomb, Tex., 375......A2 118
Darrow, Ascension, La., 400..B5 95
Darsser, pt., Ger......D6 24
Dart, cape, Ant......B36 5
Dart, riv., Eng......D4 12
Dartford, Spokane, Wash., 30......D7 122
Dartmoor, moor, Eng......D4 12
Dartmouth, N.S., Can., 46,966......E6 74
Dartmouth, Eng., 5,757.....D4 12
Dartmouth, Bristol, Mass., 200 (14,607▲)......C5 97
Dartry, mts., Ire......C3 11
Daru, isl., Pap......k11 50
Daruvar, Yugo., 6,280......C3 22
Darvel, bay, Mala......E5 35
Darwin, Austl., 13,500......B5 50
Darwin, Inyo, Calif., 450....D5 82
Darwin, glacier, Ant......f41 5
Darwin, isl., Ec......f5 58
Daryacheh-i-Namakzar, salt lake, Iran......E10 41
Darya yi Namak, salt lake, Iran......D5 41
Dasē, Eth., 40,000......C4 47
Dash Point, Pierce, Wash., 300......D1 122
Dasht, riv., Pak......C3 39
Dasht-i-Daqq-i-Tundi, salt lake, Afg......E10 41
Dasht-i-Kavir, salt plain, Iran..D7 41
Dasht-i-Lut, plain, Iran......E8 41
Dasht-i-Margo, des., Afg......F11 41
Dashwood, Ont., Can., 433..D3 72
Dasol, bay, Phil......o12 35
Dassel, Meeker, Minn., 863..E4 99
Date, Yavapai, Ariz., 25.....C3 80
Dateland, Yuma, Ariz., 30...E2 80
Datia, India, 29,430......E7 40
Datil, Catron, N. Mex., 60...C2 107
Datil, mts., N. Mex......C2 107
Datto, Clay, Ark., 167......A5 81
Datu, cape, Indon., Mala......K8 38
Datze, riv., Ger......E7 24
Dauchite, bayou, La......B2 95
Daudnagar, India, 13,320......E10 40
Daufuskie, isl., S.C.......G6 115
Daufuskie Island, Beaufort, S.C., 225......G6 115
Daugava (Dvina), riv., Sov. Un.C5 27
Daugavpils, Sov. Un., 74,000.D6 27
Daulatabad; Afg., 5,000....E11 41
Daulat, Yar Afg., 5,000....D12 41
Daule, Ec......A2 58
Daule, Ec., 4,697......B2 58
Daun, Ger., 3,400......C1 17
Dauphin, Man., Can., 7,374......D1, g7 71
Dauphin, Dauphin, Pa., 638..F8 114
Dauphin, co., Pa., 220,255...F8 114
Dauphin, isl., Ala......E1 78
Dauphin, lake, Man., Can......D2 71
Dauphin, riv., Man., Can......D2 71
Dauphiné, former prov., Fr., 1,016,000......E6 14
Daus, Sequatchie, Tenn., 250......D8 117
Davant, Plaquemines, La., 415......C8, E6 95
Davao, Phil., 93,104......D7 35
Davao, prov., Phil., 903,200.*D7 35
Davao, gulf, Phil......D7 35
Dāvar Panāh, Iran, 10,000.H11 41
Daveluyville, Que., Can., 733......C5 73
Davenport, Santa Cruz, Calif., 500......C5, D2 82
Davenport, Polk, Fla., 1,209.D5 86
Davenport, Scott, Iowa, 88,981 (*260,300)....C7, D7 92
Davenport, Thayer, Nebr., 416......D8 103
Davenport, Delaware, N.Y., 260......C6 108
Davenport, Cass, N. Dak., 143......C8 110
Davenport, Lincoln, Okla., 813......B5 112
Davenport, Red River, Tex..C5 118
Davenport, Lincoln, Wash., 1,494......B7 122
Davenport Downs, Austl.....B3 51
Davenport, Eng., 5,846......B6 12
Davey, Lancaster, Nebr., 121.E2 103
David, Floyd, Ky., 600......C7 94
David, Pan., 22,924......F6 62
David City, Butler, Nebr., 2,304......C8 103
David-Gorodok, Sov. Un., 10,000......E6 27
Davidson, Sask., Can., 928...F3 70
Davidson, Mecklenburg, N.C., 2,573......B3 109
Davidson, Tillman, Okla., 429......C2 112
Davidson, Fentress, Tenn., 200......C8 117
Davidson, co., N.C., 79,493..B3 109
Davidson, co., Tenn., 399,743......A5 117
Davidson, mts., Alsk......B11 79
Davie, Broward, Fla., 1,500......E3, F6 86
Davie, co., N.C., 16,728.....B3 109
Daviess, co., Ind., 26,636....G3 91
Daviess, co., Ky., 70,588....C2 94
Daviess, co., Mo., 9,502.....B3 101
Davin, Sask., Can., 60......G3 70
Davis, Yolo, Calif., 8,910.A6, C3 82
Davis, Stephenson, Ill., 404..A4 90
Davis, Carteret, N.C., 500...C7 109
Davis, Murray, Okla., 2,203..C4 112
Davis, Turner, S. Dak., 124..D9 116
Davis, Atascosa, Tex......E3 118
Davis, Tucker, W. Va., 898..B5 123
Davis, co., Iowa, 9,199......D5 92
Davis, co., Utah, 64,760.....C3 119
Davis, bay, Ant......C26 5
Davis, creek, W. Va......C6 123
Davis, dam, Nev......H7 104
Davis, isl., Fla......E2 86
Davis, lake, Oreg......D5 113
Davis, mtn., Pa......G3 114
Davis, mts., Tex......F2 118
Davis, sea, Ant......C22 5
Davis, strait, N. W. Ter., Can......B20 67
Davisboro, Washington, Ga., 417......D4 87
Davis City, Decatur, Iowa, 337......D4 92
Davis Dam, Mohave, Ariz., 200......B1 80
Davis Inlet, Newf., Can., 98..g9 75
Davis Junction, Ogle, Ill., 250......A4 90
Davison, Genesee, Mich., 3,761......E7 98
Davison, co., S. Dak., 16,681.D7 116
Davis Station, Clarendon, S.C., 60......D7 115
Daviston, Tallapoosa, Ala., 129......C4 78
Davisville, Crawford, Mo., 100......D6 101
Davisville, Washington, R.I., 1,800......C11 84
Davle, Czech., 1,490......o17 26
Davos, Switz., 11,400......C8 19
Davy, McDowell, W. Va., 1,331......D3 123
Dāwā, riv., Eth......E5 47
Dawes, co., Nebr., 9,536.....B2 103
Dawley, Eng., 9,553......B5 12
Dawn, Livingston, Mo., 200..B4 101
Dawn, Deaf Smith, Tex., 60..B1 118
Dawros, head, Ire......C3 11
Dawson, Yukon, Can., 881....D5 66
Dawson, Terrell, Ga., 5,062..E2 87
Dawson, Dallas, Iowa, 257...C3 92
Dawson, Lac qui Parle, Minn., 1,766......F2 99
Dawson, Richardson, Nebr., 263......D10 103
Dawson, Kidder, N. Dak., 206......C6 110
Dawson, Fayette, Pa., 707...F2 114
Dawson, Navarro, Tex., 911......D4 118
Dawson, co., Ga., 3,590......B2 87
Dawson, co., Mont., 12,314.C11 102
Dawson, co., Nebr., 19,405...D6 103
Dawson, co., Tex., 19,185....C1 118
Dawson, mtn., B.C., Can......D9 68
Dawson, range, Yukon, Can......D5 66
Dawson, riv., Austl......D8 50
Dawson Creek, B.C., Can., 10,946......B7, m18 68
Dawson-Lambton, glacier, Ant..B10 5
Dawson Springs, Hopkins, Ky., 3,002......*C2 94
Dawsonville, Dawson, Ga., 307......B2 87
Dax, Fr., 17,051......F3 14
Day, Lafayette, Fla., 125....B3 86
Day, co., S. Dak., 10,516....B8 116
Day, mtn., Calif......B6 82
Dayang, Bunting, isl., Thai....I3 38
Daykin, Jefferson, Nebr., 144.D8 103
Daylesford, Austl., 2,776....H5 51
Daylight, Warren, Tenn., 20......D8 117
Dayr Abū Saʻīd, Jordan, 1,000......B7 32
Dayr al Balaḩ, Gaza Area, 3,000......C6 32
Dayr az Zawr, Syr., 42,036.E13 31
Dayr Dibwān, Jordan, 3,000.h12 32
Dayr Istiyā, Jordan, 2,000...g11 32
Dayrūţ, Eg., U.A.R., 5,000..D6 43
Daysland, Alta., Can., 539...C4 69
Daysville, Cumberland, Tenn., 100......D9 117
Dayton, Marengo, Ala., 99...C2 78
Dayton, Franklin, Idaho, 212......G7 89
Dayton, Tippecanoe, Ind., 700......D4 91
Dayton, Webster, Iowa, 820..B3 92
Dayton, Campbell, Ky., 9,050......A7 94
Dayton, Howard, Md., 200....B4 85
Dayton, Hennepin and Wright, Minn., 456......E5 99
Dayton, Lake, Mont., 50.....C2 102
Dayton, Lyon, Nev., 150.....D2 104
Dayton, Middlesex, N.J., 500.C3 106
Dayton, Cattaraugus, N.Y., 100......C2 108
Dayton, Montgomery, Ohio, 262,332 (*648,600)......C3 111
Dayton, Yamhill, Oreg., 673......B1, B3 113
Dayton, Armstrong, Pa., 769.E3 114
Dayton, Rhea, Tenn., 3,500..D8 117
Dayton, Liberty, Tex., 3,367......D5, F5 118
Dayton, Rockingham, Va., 930......C4 121
Dayton, Columbia, Wash., 2,913......C8 122
Dayton, Sheridan, Wyo., 333.A5 125
Daytona Beach, Volusia, Fla., 37,395......C5 86
Daytona Beach Shores (South Peninsula), Volusia, Fla., 3,741......*C6 86
Dayville, Windham, Conn., 950......B9 84
Dayville, Grant, Oreg., 234..C7 113
Dazey, Barnes, N. Dak., 226..B7 110
Dazgir, Iran......C2 41
De Aar, S. Afr., 14,357......D3 49
Dead, creek, Vt......C2 120
Dead, lake, Sask., Can......B3 70
Dead, lake, Fla......B1 86
Dead, lake, Minn......D3 99
Dead, riv., Maine......C2 96
Dead, sea, Isr., Jordan......C7 32
Dead Diamond, riv., N.H......A2 105
Dead Indian, peak, Wyo......A3 125
Deadman, creek, Wash......D7 122
Deadmans, bay, Fla......C3 86
Dead River, Somerset, Maine......C2 96
Deadwood, Lawrence, S. Dak., 3,045......C2 116
Deadwood, res., Idaho......E3 89
Deaf Smith, co., Tex., 13,187.B1 118
Deakin, bay, Ant......C28 5
Deal, Eng., 24,791......C9 12
Deal, Monmouth, N.J., 1,889.C4 106
Deal, isl., Md......D6 85
Deale, Anne Arundel, Md., 900......C4 85
Deal Island, Somerset, Md., 600......D6 85
Dean, Scott, Tenn., 50......C9 117
Dean, chan., B.C., Can......C4 68
Dean, riv., B.C., Can......C4 68
Deanburg, Chester, Tenn., 60.B3 117
Dean Dale, Jefferson, Ohio (part of Mingo Junction)......B2 123
Deaneyville, Hempstead, Ark......D2 81
Deán Funes, Arg., 13,840....A4 54
Deans, Middlesex, N.J., 400..C3 106
Deans Island, Mississippi, Ark......B5 81
Deanville, Lewis, W. Va., 350......B4 123
Deanwood, Ware, Ga., 2,758.E4 87
Dearborn, Wayne, Mich., 112,007......A7, F7 98
Dearborn, Platte, Mo., 444...B3 101
Dearborn, co., Ind., 28,674...F8 91
Dearborn Heights, Cook, Ill., 1,300......*B6 90
Dearg, mtn., Scot......C4 13
Dearing, McDuffie, Ga., 403.C4 87
Dearing, Montgomery, Kans., 249......E8 93
DeArmanville, Calhoun, Ala., 250......B4 78
Deary, Latah, Idaho, 349....C2 89
Dease, arm, N.W. Ter., Can..C8 66
Dease, strait, N.W. Ter., Can..C11 66
Dease Lake, B.C., Can......m17 68
Death, val., Calif......D5 82
Death Valley, Inyo, Calif., 75......D5 82
Death Valley, nat. mon., Calif...D5 82
Deatsville, Elmore, Ala., 200.C3 78
Deauville, Fr., 5,051......C4 14
Deaver, Big Horn, Wyo., 121.A4 125
De Baca, co., N. Mex., 2,991.C5 107
Debaltsevo, Sov. Un., 33,800......q21 27
Debar, Yugo., 6,341......E5 22
DeBary, Volusia, Fla., 2,362......D5 86
Debden, Sask., Can., 402....D2 70
Debec, N.B., Can., 236......C2 74
De Beque, Mesa, Colo., 172..B2 83
De Berry, Panola, Tex., 250..C5 118
Debica, Pol., 19,000......C6 26
Debin, Bul., 2,745......E7 22
Deblin, Pol., 1,000......C6 26
Deblois, Washington, Maine, 20 (26▲)......D4 96
Debno, Pol., 3,341......B3 26
Debo, lake, Mali......C4 45
De Borgia, Mineral, Mont., 75......C1 102
Deboullie, mtn., Maine......B4 96
Debovo, Bul., 2,028......D7 22
Debrecen, Hung., 139,600....B5 22
De Cade, lake, La......E5 95
Decamere, Eth......B4 47
Decatur, Morgan, Ala., 29,217......A3 78
Decatur, Benton, Ark., 415...A1 81
Decatur, De Kalb, Ga., 22,026......B5, C2 87
Decatur, Macon, Ill., 78,004 (*111,300)......D5 90
Decatur, Adams, Ind., 8,327......C8 91
Decatur, Decatur, Iowa, 203.D4 92
Decatur, Van Buren, Mich., 1,827......F5 98
Decatur, Newton, Miss., 1,340......C4 100
Decatur, Burt, Nebr., 786....B9 103
Decatur, Meigs, Tenn., 681..D9 117
Decatur, Wise, Tex., 3,563...C4 118
Decatur, co., Ga., 25,203....F2 87
Decatur, co., Ind., 20,019....F6 91
Decatur, co., Iowa, 10,539...D4 92
Decatur, co., Kans., 5,778...C3 93
Decatur, co., Tenn., 8,324...B3 117
Decatur, lake, Ill......D5 90
Decaturville, Decatur, Tenn., 571......B3 117
Decazeville, Fr., 11,855......E5 14
Deccan, reg., India......E6 39
Deception, lake, Sask., Can...A3 70
Decherd, Franklin, Tenn., 1,704......B5 117
Decin, Czech., 40,200......C3 26
Decize, Fr., 6,594......D5 14
Decker, Man., Can., 67......D1 71
Decker, Knox, Ind., 317......G3 91
Decker, Big Horn, Mont., 5.E10 102
Decker Lake, B.C., Can., 235......B5 68
Deckers, Douglas, Colo., 50..B5 83
Deckerville, Sanilac, Mich., 798......E8 98
Declo, Cassia, Idaho, 237....G5 89
De Cocksdorp, Neth., 347....A4 15
Decorah, Winneshiek, Iowa, 6,435......A6 92
Decota, Kanawha, W. Va., 500......D6 123
De Coursey, Kenton, Ky., 200......A7 94
Dededo, Guam, 2,247......52
Dedemsvaart, Neth., 5,800....B6 15
Dedham, Carroll, Iowa, 322..C3 92
Dedham, Norfolk, Mass., 23,869......B5, h11 97
Dedinovo, Sov. Un., 5,000....n19 27
Dédougou, Upper Volta, 2,900......D4 45
Dedza, Malawi, 2,325......D5 48
Dee, Hood River, Oreg., 50..B5 113
Dee, riv., Eng......A5 10
Dee, riv., Scot......C6 13
Dee, riv., Wales......D5 10
Deedsville, Miami, Ind., 120.C5 91
Deel, riv., Ire......E3 11
Deemer, Neshoba, Miss., 100.C4 100
Deep, creek, Del......C6 85
Deep, creek, Mont......C4 102
Deep, creek, Utah......C2 119
Deep, creek, Utah......F3 119
Deep, creek, Wash......D7 122
Deep, entrance, Eniwetok......52
Deep, fork, Okla......B5 112
Deep, inlet, Newf., Can......g10 75
Deep Bay, Malawi......D5 48
Deep Brook, N.S., Can., 462.E4 74
Deep Creek, Norfolk, Va., 350......B6, E6 121
Deepcreek, Spokane, Wash., 100......D7 122
Deep Creek, lake, Md......D1 85
Deep Creek, mts., Utah......D2 119
Deepdale, Man., Can......D1 71
Deep Gap, Watauga, N.C., 130......A2 109
Deep Gap, mtn., N.C......A2 109
Deephaven, Hennepin, Minn., 3,286......*F3 99
Deep Red, run, Okla......C3 112
Deep River, Ont., Can., 5,377......A7 72
Deep River, Middlesex, Conn., 2,200 (2,968▲)......D7 84
Deep River, Poweshiek, Iowa, 329......C5 92
Deep Run, Lenoir, N.C., 183.B6 109
Deepstep, Washington, Ga., 139......C4 87
Deepwater, Henry, Mo., 712.C4 101
Deepwater, Salem, N.J., 700......D2 106
Deep Water, Fayette, W. Va., 900......D6 123
Deepwater, pt., Del......B7 85
Deer, Newton, Ark., 150.....B2 81
Deer, creek, Ind......C5 91
Deer, creek, Md......A5 85
Deer, creek, Miss......B3 100
Deer, creek, Ohio......C4 111
Deer, isl., Maine......D4 96
Deer, isl., Mass......g12 97
Deer, isl., Miss......E2 100
Deer, lake, Newf., Can......D3 75
Deer, lake, Minn......C5 99
Deer, mtn., Maine......C2 96
Deer, peak, Colo......C5 83
Deer, pond, Newf., Can......D4 75
Deer Creek, Tazewell and Woodford, Ill., 583......C4 90
Deer Creek, Carroll, Ind., 200......C5 91
Deer Creek, Otter Trail, Minn., 312......D3 99
Deer Creek, Grant, Okla., 215......A4 112
Deerfield, Lake, Ill., 11,786......A6, E2 90
Deerfield, Kearny, Kans., 442......E2 93
Deerfield, Franklin, Mass., 500 (3,338▲)......A2 97
Deerfield, Lenawee, Mich., 866......G7 98
Deerfield, Vernon, Mo., 200..D3 101
Deerfield, Rockingham, N.H., 75 (714▲)......D4 105
Deerfield, Portage, Ohio, 700.A6 111
Deerfield, Dane, Wis., 795...E4 124
Deerfield, riv., Mass., Vt......F3 120
Deerfield Beach, Broward, Fla., 9,573......F6 86
Deerfield Street, Cumberland, N.J., 400......D2 106
Deer Flat, res., Idaho......F2 89
Deer Grove, Whiteside, Ill., 86......B4 90
Deering, Alsk., 95......B7 79
Deering, Pemiscot, Mo., 122.E8 101
Deering, Hillsboro, N.H., 30 (345▲)......D3 105
Deering, McHenry, N. Dak., 117......A4 110
Deer Isle, Hancock, Maine, 600 (1,129▲)......D4 96
Deer Lake, Newf., Can., 3,998......D3 75
Deer Lodge, Powell, Mont., 4,681......D4 102
Deer Lodge, Morgan, Tenn., 250......C9 117
Deer Lodge, co., Mont., 18,640......E3 120
Deer Park, Washington, Ala., 200......D1 78
Deer Park, Osceola, Fla., 100.D6 86
Deer Park, Garrett, Md., 379.D1 85
Deer Park, Suffolk, N.Y., 23,500......G3 84
Deer Park, Hamilton, Ohio, 8,423......D2 111
Deer Park, Harris, Tex., 4,865......*E5 118
Deer Park, Spokane, Wash., 1,333......B8 122
Deer Park, St. Croix, Wis., 221......C1 124
Deer River, Itasca, Minn., 992......C5 99
Deer River, Lewis, N.Y., 200.B5 108
Deerton, Alger, Mich., 50....B3 98
Deer Trail, Arapahoe, Colo., 764......B6 83
Deerwood, Crow Wing, Minn., 527......D5 99
Deeson, Bolivar, Miss., 100...A3 100
Deeth, Elko, Nev., 75......B6 104
Defas Park, Duchesne, Utah, 20......C5 119
Defensa Central, P.R. (part of Aguas)......C6 65
Defense Highway, Prince Georges, Md., 1,000.....*C4 85
Deferiet, Jefferson, N.Y., 470.A5 108
Defiance, Shelby, Iowa, 386..C2 92
Defiance, St. Charles, Mo., 110......B7 101
Defiance, Defiance, Ohio, 14,553......A3 111
Defiance, co., Ohio, 31,508..A3 111
Defiance, mtn., Oreg......B5 113
Deford, Tuscola, Mich., 150..E7 98
De Forest, Dane, Wis., 1,223......E4 124
De Funiak Springs, Walton, Fla., 5,282......G3 86
Degeberga, Swe., 590......C8 24
Degerfors, Swe., 9,500......E8 25
Degerön, Swe......u33 25
Degersheim, Switz., 3,221....B7 19
Deggendorf, Ger., 17,100....E7 17
De Graff, Swift, Minn., 196..E3 99
Degraff, Logan, Ohio, 996....B4 111
Dehak, Iran, 5,000......G10 41
Dehart, Wilkes, N.C......A2 109
Deh Bid, Iran, 10,000......F6 41
Dehibat, Tun., 1,579......C7 44
Deh-i-Haji, Afg......F12 41
Deh Pāin, Iran, 10,000......G8 41
Dehra Dun, India, 126,918 (*156,341)......B6 39, B7 40
Deh Titan, Afg., 5,000......E11 41
Deinze, Bel., 6,004......D3 15
Dej, Rom., 19,281......B6 22
Dejvice, Czech. (part of Prague)......n17 26
De Kalb, De Kalb, Ill., 18,486......B5 90
De Kalb, Kemper, Miss., 880......C5 100
De Kalb, Buchanan, Mo., 304......B3 101
De Kalb, St. Lawrence, N.Y., 100......f9 108
De Kalb, Bowie, Tex., 2,042......C5 118
De Kalb, co., Ala., 41,417....A4 78
De Kalb, co., Ga., 256,782....C2 87
De Kalb, co., Ill., 51,714.....B5 90
De Kalb, co., Ind., 28,271....B7 91
De Kalb, co., Mo., 7,226.....B3 101
De Kalb, co., Tenn., 10,174..D8 117
De Kalb Junction, St. Lawrence, N.Y., 400.....f9 108
Dekese, Con. L......B3 48
Dekoa, Cen. Afr. Rep......D3 46
Delacroix, St. Bernard, La., 650......C8 95
Delafield, Waukesha, Wis., 2,334......*E5 124
Delagoa, bay, Moz......C5 49
Delagua, Las Animas, Colo..D6 83
Del Aire, Los Angeles, Calif., 5,000......*F2 82
Delake, Lincoln, Oreg., 803..C3 113
De Lamere, Sargent, N. Dak., 170......C8 110
Delanco, Burlington, N.J., 4,011......C3 106
De Land, Volusia, Fla., 10,775......C5 86
De Land, Piatt, Ill., 422.....C5 90
Delaney, Madison, Ark., 75..B2 81
Delano, Kern, Calif., 11,913..E4 82
Delano, Wright, Minn., 1,612......E5 99
Delano, Polk, Tenn., 200....D9 117
Delano, peak, Utah......E3 119
Delano Mines, Elko, Nev., 5..B7 104
Delanson, Schenectady, N.Y., 398......C6 108
Delaplaine, Greene, Ark., 186......A5 81
Delaronde, lake, Sask., Can...C2 70
Delavan, Tazewell, Ill., 1,377......C4 90
Delavan, Morris, Kans., 200......D7 93
Delavan, Faribault, Minn., 322......G4 99
Delavan, Walworth, Wis., 4,846......F5 124
Delavan Lake, Walworth, Wis., 1,884......*F5 124
Delaware, Logan, Ark., 300..B2 81
Delaware, Ont., Can., 466...E3 72
Delaware, Delaware, Iowa, 167......B6 92
Delaware, Warren, N.J., 325......B2 106
Delaware, Delaware, Ohio, 13,282......B4 111
Delaware, Nowata, Okla., 540......A6 112
Delaware, co., Ind., 110,938.D7 91
Delaware, co., Iowa, 18,483..B6 92
Delaware, co., N.Y., 43,540..C5 108
Delaware, co., Ohio, 36,107..B4 111
Delaware, co., Okla., 13,198.A7 112
Delaware, co., Pa., 553,154......G11 114
Delaware, state, U.S., 446,292......C12 77, 85
Delaware, bay, Del......C7 85
Delaware, bay, N.J......E2 106
Delaware, mts., Tex......F2 118
Delaware, res., Ohio......B4 111
Delaware, riv., U.S......C3 106
Delaware, riv., Kans......A7 93
Delaware City, New Castle, Del., 1,658......A6 85
Delaware Water Gap, Monroe, Pa., 554......E11 114
Delaware Water Gap, N.J., Pa......B2 106
Delbarton, Mingo, W. Va., 1,122......D2 123
Delburne, Alta., Can., 450...C4 69
Delcambre, Vermilion and Iberia, La., 1,857......E4 95
Del City, Oklahoma, Okla., 12,934......B4 112
Delco, Columbus, N.C., 466..C5 109
Deleau, Man., Can......E1 71
Delémont, Switz., 9,542......B3 19
De Leon, Comanche, Tex., 2,022......C3 118
De Leon Springs, Volusia, Fla., 900......C5 86
De Léry, Que., Can., 1,957..q19 73
Delevan, Cattaraugus, N.Y., 777......C2 108
Delfore, Craighead, Ark.....B5 81
Delft, Cottonwood, Minn., 125......G3 99
Delft, Neth., 76,000......B4 15
Delfzijl, Neth., 16,600......A6 15
Delgado, cape, Moz......D7 48
Delger Tsogtuin Huryee, Mong......A2 36
Delgo, Sud......A3 47
Delhi, Merced, Calif., 1,175.*D3 82
Delhi, Ont., Can., 3,427......E4 72
Delhi, India, 2,061,758 (*2,658,612)......C6 36, C6 40
Delhi, Delaware, Iowa, 464..B6 92
Delhi, Richland, La., 2,514..B4 95
Delhi, Redwood, Minn., 124.F3 99
Delhi, Delaware, N.Y., 2,307.C6 108
Delhi, Beckham, Okla., 50...B2 112
Delhi, ter., India, 2,658,612......*C6 40
Delhi Hills, Hamilton, Ohio, 5,000......*D2 111
Delia, Alta., Can., 287......D4 69
Delia, Jackson, Kans., 163...C8 93
Delight, Pike, Ark., 446......C2 81
Delina, Marshall, Tenn......B5 117
Delisle, Que., Can., 1,302...A6 73
Delisle, Sask., Can., 508.....F2 70
DeLisle, Harrison, Miss., 800......E2, E4 100
Delitzsch, Ger., 22,900......B7 17
Dell, Mississippi, Ark., 383..B5 81
Dell, Beaverhead, Mont., 35..F4 102
Dell, Fr., 5,189......B3 18
Dellenbaugh, mtn., Ariz......A2 80
Dell Rapids, Minnehaha, S. Dak., 1,863......D9 116
Dellrose, Lincoln, Tenn., 175.B5 117
Dellroy, Carroll, Ohio, 391...B6 111
Dells, gorge, Wis......E4 124
Dellwood, Jackson, Fla., 100.B1 86
Dellwood, Washington, Minn., 310......E6, E7 99
Dellwood, St. Louis, Mo., 4,720......*C7 101
Dellwood, Yamhill, Oreg....B1 113
Dellys, Alg., 5,774 (21,591▲).B5 44
Delmar, Winston, Ala., 100..A2 78
Del Mar, San Diego, Calif., 3,124......E2 82
Delmar, Sussex, Del., 934...D6 85
Delmar, Clinton, Iowa, 556..C7 92
Delmar, Wicomico, Md., 1,291......D6 85
Delmar, Albany, N.Y., 7,300......C7 108
Del Mar-Heights (Marro Beach), San Luis Obispo, Calif., 1,907......*E3 82
Delmas, Sask., Can., 234....E1 70
Delmenhorst, Ger., 59,900...B4 16

Delmita, Starr, Tex., 70....F3 118
Delmont, Cumberland, N.J., 370....E3 106
Delmont, Westmoreland, Pa., 1,313....*F2 114
Delmont, Douglas, S. Dak., 363....D7 116
Del Monte Heights, Monterey, Calif., 1,174....*C6 82
Del Monte Park, Monterey, Calif., 2,177....*D3 82
Del Norte, Rio Grande, Colo., 1,856....D4 83
Del Norte, co., Calif., 17,771....B2 82
Deloit, Crawford, Iowa, 222..B2 92
Delong, Fulton, Ind., 130....B5 91
De Long, is., Sov. Un.....B35 4
Deloraine, Man., Can., 916..E1 71
Delorme, lake, Que., Can.....F18 67
Deloro, Ont., Can., 157....C7 72
Del Paso Heights, Sacramento, Calif., 11,495....*A6 82
Delphi, Carroll, Ind., 2,517..C4 91
Delphia, Musselshell, Mont., 10....D8 102
Delphos, Ottawa, Kans., 619....C6 93
Delphos, Allen, Ohio, 6,961..B3 111
Delray Beach, Palm Beach, Fla., 12,230....F6 86
Del Ray Oaks, Monterey, Calif., 1,831....*C6 82
Del Rio, Cocke, Tenn., 25..D10 117
Del Rio, Val Verde, Tex., 18,612....E2 118
Del Rosa, San Bernardino, Calif., 6,000....*E5 82
Delson Village, Que., Can., 2,075....q19 73
Delta, Clay, Ala., 150....B4 78
Delta, Ont., Can., 417....C8 72
Delta, Delta, Colo., 3,832....C2 83
Delta, Keokuk, Iowa, 514....C5 92
Delta, Madison, La., 111....B5 95
Delta, Cape Girardeau, Mo., 416....D8 101
Delta, Fulton, Ohio, 2,376...A4 111
Delta, York, Pa., 822....G9 114
Delta, Millard, Utah, 1,576..D3 119
Delta, co., Colo., 15,602....C3 83
Delta, co., Mich., 34,298....C4 98
Delta, co., Tex., 5,860....C5 118
Delta, peak, B.C., Can.....A3 68
Delta, res., N.Y.....B5 108
Delta Amacuro, ter., Ven., 33,979....B5 60
Delta Beach, Man., Can., 74....D2 71
Delta City, Sharkey, Miss., 300....B3 100
Delta Farms, Lafourche, La..E5 95
Deltaville, Middlesex, Va., 800....D6 121
Delton, Barry, Mich., 250....F5 98
Delungra, Austl., 585....D8 51
Delvin, Ire., 346....D4 11
Delvine, Alb., 3,207....C3 23
Delyatin, Sov. Un., 14,000..G5 27
Demaine, Sask., Can., 166...G2 70
Demarcation, bay, Alsk.....B11 79
Demarest, Bergen, N.J., 4,231....h9 106
Demavend, mtn., Iran....D6 41
Demba, Con. L....C3 48
Demchok, China, 5,000....A7 40
Demidov, Sov. Un., 10,000..D8 27
Deming, Hamilton, Ind., 50....D5 91
Deming, Luna, N. Mex., 6,764....E2 107
Deming, Whatcom, Wash., 250....A3 122
Demirci, Tur., 8,700....C7 23
Demir Kapija, Yugo....E6 22
Demmin, Ger., 16,400....B6 16
Demmitt, Alta., Can....B1 69
Demnate, Mor., 6,223....C3 44
Demopolis, Marengo, Ala., 7,377....C2 78
Demorest, Habersham, Ga., 1,029....B3 87
Demorestville, Ont., Can., 120....C7 72
DeMossville, Pendleton, Ky., 90....B7 94
Demotte, Jasper, Ind., 700...B3 91
Dempster, Hamlin, S. Dak., 95....C9 116
Demyanka, riv., Sov. Un.....B8 29
Demyanovka, Sov. Un....C7 29
Denain, Fr., 29,467 (*65,500)....D3 15
Denali, Alsk., 3....C10 79
Denare Beach, Sask., Can., 128....C4 70
Denau, Sov. Un., 15,000...B13 41
Denaud, Hendry, Fla., 120...F5 86
Denbigh, McHenry, N. Dak., 25....A5 110
Denbigh, Wales, 8,044....A4 12
Denbigh, co., Wales, 173,843....A4 12
Den Burg, Neth., 2,888....A4 15
Dendermonde, Bel., 9,815...C4 15
Dendron, Sask., Can....G2 70
Dendron, Surry, Va., 403...D6 121
Denezhkin Kamen, mtn., Sov. Un.....A5 29
Denham, Pulaski, Ind., 180..B4 91
Denham, Pine, Minn., 71...D6 99
Denham Springs, Livingston, La., 5,991....A5, D5 95
Den Helder, Neth., 52,900...B4 15
Denhoff, Sheridan, N. Dak., 164....B5 110
Denholm, Sask., Can., 72....E1 70
Den Hoorn, Neth., 454....A4 15
Denia, Sp., 7,876....C6 20
Deniau, Que., Can....B8 73
Deniliquin, Austl., 5,574....G5 51
Denio, Humboldt, Nev., 30..B3 104
Denison, Crawford, Iowa, 4,930....B2 92
Denison, Jackson, Kans., 184....A7 93
Denison, Grayson, Tex., 22,748....C4 118
Denison, dam, Okla.....D5 112
Denizli, Tur., 48,925....D7 23
Denman, Buffalo, Nebr., 25..D7 103
Denman, glacier, Ant.....C22 5
Denmark, Jackson, Ark....B4 81
Denmark, N.S., Can., 40....D6 74
Denmark, Lee, Iowa, 235....D6 92
Denmark, Lincoln, Kans., 50....C5 93
Denmark, Oxford, Maine, 160 (376▲)....E2 96
Denmark, Curry, Oreg., 25..E2 113
Denmark, Bamberg, S.C., 3,221....E5 115
Denmark, Madison, Tenn., 58....B2 117
Denmark, Brown, Wis., 1,106....A6, D6 124
Denmark, country, Eur., 4,740,000....D10 8, 24
Denmark, strait, Grnld., Ice...C17 4
Dennard, Van Buren, Ark., 100....B3 81
Denning, Franklin, Ark., 227.B2 81
Denning, San Augustine, Tex. D5 118
Dennis, Labette, Kans., 150..E8 93
Dennis, Barnstable, Mass., 600 (3,727▲)....C7 97
Dennis, Tishomingo, Miss., 125....A5 100
Dennis, hill, Conn.....B4 84
Dennis Port, Barnstable, Mass., 1,300....C7 97
Dennison, Goodhue and Rice, Minn., 179....F5 99
Dennison, Tuscarawas, Ohio, 4,158....B6 111
Denniston, Halifax, Va., 50..E4 121
Dennisville, Cape May, N.J., 500....E3 106
Dennysville, Washington, Maine, 250 (303▲)....D5 96
Denny Terrace, Richland, S.C., 3,000....C5 115
Den Oever, Neth., 1,497....B5 15
Denoya, Osage, Okla....A5 112
Denpasar, Indon., 16,639....G5 35
Dent, Otter Tail, Minn., 176.D3 99
Dent, co., Mo., 10,445....D6 101
Dent du Midi, mtn., Switz.....D2 19
Denton, Jeff Davis, Ga., 255....E4 87
Denton, Doniphan, Kans., 161....C8 93
Denton, Caroline, Md., 1,938....C6 85
Denton, Wayne, Mich., 200..A7 98
Denton, Fergus, Mont., 410...C7 102
Denton, Lancaster, Nebr., 94....D9 103
Denton, Davidson, N.C., 852....B3 109
Denton, Cocke, Tenn., 100..D10 117
Denton, Denton, Tex., 26,844....C4 118
Denton, co., Tex., 47,432....C4 118
Denton, creek, Tex.....A5 118
D'Entrecasteaux, pt., Austl.....F2 50
D'Entrecasteaux, is., Pap.....k13 50
Dentsville, Richland, S.C., 1,500....C6 115
Denver, Denver, Colo., 493,887 (*858,300)....B6 83
Denver, Hancock, Ill., 120...C2 90
Denver, Miami, Ind., 565....C5 91
Denver, Bremer, Iowa, 831..B5 92
Denver, Worth, Mo., 116....A3 101
Denver, Lincoln, N.C., 113..B2 109
Denver, Lancaster, Pa., 1,875....F9 114
Denver, Humphreys, Tenn., 100....A4 117
Denver, Marshall, W. Va., 45.C2 123
Denver, Preston, W. Va., 50.B5 123
Denver, co., Colo., 493,887...B6 83
Denver City, Yoakum, Tex., 4,302....C1 118
Denville, Morris, N.J., 10,632....B4 106
Denzil, Sask., Can., 328....E1 70
Deoghar, India, 30,813....E11 40
Deora, Baca, Colo., 5....D8 83
De Panne, Bel., 6,407....C2 15
Departure Bay, B.C., Can., 1,235....f12 68
Depauville, Jefferson, N.Y., 330....A4 108
Depauw, Harrison, Ind., 120....H5 91
De Pere, Brown, Wis., 10,045....A6, D5 124
Depew, Erie, N.Y., 13,580...C2 108
Depew, Creek, Okla., 686...B5 112
Depoe Bay, Lincoln, Oreg., 750....C3 113
Deport, Lamar and Red River, Tex., 639....C5 118
Deposit, Broome and Delaware, N.Y., 2,025....C5 108
Depot Harbour, Ont., Can...B4 72
Depue, Bureau, Ill., 1,920...B4 90
Deputy, Jefferson, Ind., 300..G6 91
DeQueen, Sevier, Ark., 2,859....C1 81
Dequen, Que., Can., 267....A5 73
DeQuincy, Calcasieu, La., 3,928....D2 95
Der'a, Syr., 15,635....F11 31
Dera Ghazi Khan, Pak., 47,105....B5 39, B3 40
Dera Ismail Khan, Pak., 44,319 (*46,140)....B3 40
Derbent, Sov. Un., 52,000....E3 29, G18 9
Derbetovka, Sov. Un., 10,000....I14 27
Derby, Austl., 326....C3 50
Derby, N.B., Can., 111....C4 74
Derby, Adams, Colo., 10,124....*B6 83
Derby, New Haven, Conn., 12,132....D4 84
Derby, Eng., 131,600 (*265,000)....B6 12
Derby, Perry, Ind., 60....H4 91
Derby, Lucas, Iowa, 151....D4 92
Derby, Sedgwick, Kans., 6,458....E6 93
Derby, Piscataquis, Maine, 500....C4 96
Derby, Pearl River, Miss., 200....E4 100
Derby, Erie, N.Y., 3,000....C2 108
Derby, Pickaway, Ohio, 365.C4 111
Derby, Frio, Tex., 40....E3 118
Derby, Orleans, Vt., 433 (2,506▲)....B4 120
Derby, Wise, Va., 800....B2 121
Derby, co., Eng., 877,548...A6 12
Derby Junction, N.B., Can., 146....C4 74
Derby Line, Orleans, Vt., 849....B4 120
Derecske, Hung., 9,970....B5 22
Derg, lake, Ire.....E3 11
De Ridder, Beauregard, La., 7,188....D2 95
Derik, Tur., 3,586....D13 31
Derita, Mecklenburg, N.C., 1,500....B3 109
Derma, Calhoun, Miss., 578.B4 100
Dermott, Chicot, Ark., 3,665.D4 81
Dermott, Scurry, Tex., 40....C2 118
Derna, see Darnah, Libya
Derniere, isl., La.....E5 95
Derravaragh, lake, Ire.....D4 11
Derry, Natchitoches, La., 75....C3 95
Derry, Rockingham, N.H., 4,468 (6,987▲)....E4 105
Derry, Sierra, N. Mex., 10...E2 107
Derry, Westmoreland, Pa., 3,426....F3 114
Derrybrien, Ire....D3 11
Derudeb, Sud....B4 47
De Ruyter, Madison, N.Y., 627....C5 108
Derventa, Yugo., 9,795....C3 22
Derwent, Alta., Can., 281...C5 69
Derwent, Guernsey, Ohio, 225....C6 111
Derwent, riv., Eng.....F5 13
Derwent, riv., Eng.....F6 13
Derwent, riv., Eng.....F8 13
Derwood, Montgomery, Md., 110....B3 85
Derzhavinskoye, Sov. Un...E22 9
Desaguadero, riv., Arg.....A3 54
Desaguadero, riv., Bol.....C2 55
Des Allemands, bayou, La.....C6 95
Des Allemands, lake, La.....E5 95
Des Arc, Prairie, Ark., 1,482.C4 81
Des Arc, Iron, Mo., 275....D7 101
Des Arc, bayou, Ark.....B4 81
Des Arc, mtn., Mo.....D7 101
Desatoya, mts., Nev.....D4 104
Desatoya, peak, Nev.....D4 104
Desbiens, Que., Can., 1,970..A6 73
Desboro, Ont., Can., 160....C3 72
Descalabrado, P.R....C5 65
Descalvado, Braz., 7,220....k8 56
Deschaillons, Que., Can. 415....C5 73
Deschaillons sur St. Laurent, Que., Can., 1,283....*C5 73
Deschambault, Que., Can., 1,056....C6 73
Deschambault, lake, Sask., Can...C4 70
Deschambault Lake, Sask., Can., 198....C4 70
Deschênes, Que., Can., 2,090....D2 73
Deschutes, co., Oreg., 23,100.D5 113
Deschutes, peak, Wash.....C3 122
Deschutes, riv., Oreg.....B6 113
Desembarcadero Mosquito, P.R., 4....g12 65
Desengaño, cape, Arg.....D3 54
Desenzano del Garda, It., 6,500....D6 18
Deseret, Millard, Utah, 250.D3 119
Deseret, peak, Utah....C3 119
Deseronto, Ont., Can., 1,797....C7 72
Desert, game range, Nev.....G6 104
Desert, mtn., W. Va.....C6 123
Desert, peak, Utah....B2 119
Desert, val., Nev.....B3 104
Deserta Grande, isl., Port. (Madeira Is.)....h12 20
Desert Center, Riverside, Calif., 200....F6 82
Desert Hot Springs, Riverside, Calif., 1,472....*F5 82
Desha, Independence, Ark., 350....B4 81
Desha, co., Ark., 20,770....D4 81
Deshler, Thayer, Nebr., 956.D8 103
Deshler, Henry, Ohio, 1,824.A4 111
Deshu, Afg., 5,000....F11 41
Desio, It., 23,750....D5 18
Des Lacs, Ward, N. Dak., 185....A4 110
Des Lacs, riv., N. Dak.....A4 110
Desloge, St. Francois, Mo., 2,308....D7 101
Desmarais, Alta., Can., 303..B4 69
Desmet, Benewah, Idaho, 100....B2 89
De Smet, Kingsbury, S. Dak., 1,324....C8 116
Desmochado, Par., 2,398....E4 55
Des Moines, Polk, Iowa, 208,982 (*261,800)...A7, C4 92
Des Moines, Union, N. Mex., 207....A6 107
Des Moines, King, Wash., 1,987....B3, D1 122
Des Moines, co., Iowa, 44,605....D6 92
Des Moines, riv., U.S.....B9 77
Desna, riv., Sov. Un.....F8 27
Desolation, canyon, Utah....D5 119
Desolacion, isl., Chile....h11 54
De Soto, Sumter, Ga., 282....E2 87
De Soto, Jackson, Ill., 723...F4 90
De Soto, Dallas, Iowa, 273..C3 92
De Soto, Johnson, Kans., 1,271....B8, D9 93
De Soto, Clarke, Miss., 240..D5 100
De Soto, Jefferson, Mo., 5,804....C7 101
De Soto, Dallas, Tex., 1,969*C4 118
De Soto, Crawford and Vernon, Wis., 357....E2 124
De Soto, co., Fla., 11,683....E5 86
De Soto, co., Miss., 23,891...A3 100
De Soto, par., La., 24,248...B2 95
De Soto City, Highlands, Fla., 245....E5 86
Despard, Harrison, W. Va., 1,763....B7 123
Desperes, St. Louis, Mo., 4,362....B8 101
Des Plaines, Cook, Ill., 41,209....A6, E2 90
Des Plaines, riv., Ill., Wis.....B5 90, F2 124
Dessau, Ger., 95,200....B7 17
Destin, Okaloosa, Fla., 900...G2 86
Destrehan, St. Charles, La., 330....C7, E5 95
Desvres, Fr., 5,518....D9 12
Detlor, Ont., Can., 65....B7 72
Detmold, Ger., 30,200....B3 17
Detour, Chippewa, Mich., 669....C7 98
Detour, pt., Mich.....C4 98
Detroit, Lamar, Ala., 113....A1 78
Detroit, Dickinson, Kans., 100....D6 93
Detroit, Somerset, Maine, 250 (564▲)....D3 96
Detroit, Wayne, Mich., 1,670,144 (*3,931,500)....A8, F7 98
Detroit, Marion, Oreg., 206..C4 113
Detroit, Red River, Tex., 576....C5 118
Detroit, res., Oreg.....C4 113
Detroit, riv., Ont., Can., Mich...F7 98
Detroit Beach, Monroe, Mich., 1,571....*G7 98
Detroit Lakes, Becker, Minn., 5,633....D3 99
Dett, Rh., 820....A4 49
Detva, Czech., 7,786....D5 26
Deuel, co., Nebr., 3,125....C3 103
Deuel, co., S. Dak., 6,782....C9 116
Deurne, Bel., 68,703....C4 15
Deux Frères, isl., Viet....H7 38
Deux-Montagnes, Que., Can., 7,274....p19 73
Deux-Montagnes, co., Que., Can., 32,837....D3 73
Deux-Rivières, Ont., Can....A6 72
Deux Rivières, Que., Can., 590....C5 73
Deux-Sèvres, dept., Fr., 321,118....*D3 14
Deva, Rom., 16,879....C6 22
De Valls Bluff, Prairie, Ark., 654....C4 81
Devarkonda, India, 8,311....I7 40
Devavanya, Hung., 10,828...B5 22
Deventer, Neth., 58,400....B6 15
Devereux, Hancock, Ga., 200....C3 87
Deveron, riv., Scot.....C6 13
De View, bayou, Ark.....B4 81
Devil River, peak, N.Z.....N14 51
Devils, isl., Fr. Gu.....A4 59
Devils, lake, N. Dak.....A6 110
Devils, riv., Tex.....E2 118
Devils Den, Kern, Calif., 150....E4 82
Devils Elbow, Pulaski, Mo., 150....D5 101
Devils Knob, mtn., Va.....C3 121
Devils Lake, Ramsey, N. Dak., 6,299....B7 110
Devils Lake, Indian res., N. Dak.....B6 110
Devils Postpile, nat. mon., Calif...D4 82
Devils Slide, Morgan, Utah, 150....B4 119
Devils Thumb, mtn., Alsk., B.C., Can.....E6 66
Devils Tower, Crook, Wyo., 10....A8 125
Devils Tower, nat. mon., Wyo...A8 125
Devils Track, lake, Minn.....B7 99
Devine, Medina, Tex., 2,522.E3 118
Devizes, Eng., 8,497....C6 12
Devol, Cotton, Okla., 117....C3 112
Devoll, riv., Alb.....B3 23
Devon, Alta., Can., 1,418....C4 69
Devon, New Haven, Conn. (part of Milford)....E4 84
Devon, Bourbon, Kans., 100..E9 93
Devon, Toole, Mont., 60....B5 102
Devon, Chester, Pa., 1,500.*G11 114
Devon, co., Eng., 822,906....D4 12
Devon, isl., N.W. Ter., Can...A15 66
Devonport, Austl., 13,068...o15 50
Devonport, N.Z., 10,976....L15 51
Dewalt, Fort Bend, Tex., 100....F5 118
Dewar, Black Hawk, Iowa, 68....B5 92
Dewar, Okmulgee, Okla., 817....B6 112
Dewar Lake, Sask., Can....F1 70
Dewberry, Alta., Can., 179..C5 69
Dewdney, B.C., Can., 553...E6 68
Dewees, inlet, S.C.....F8 115
Dewees, isl., S.C.....F4 115
Deweese, Clay, Nebr., 100....D7 103
Dewey, Yavapai, Ariz., 50...C3 80
Dewey, Beaverhead, Mont., 30....E4 102
Dewey, Washington, Okla., 3,994....A6 112
Dewey, Custer, S. Dak., 55..D1 116
Dewey, co., Okla., 6,051....B2 112
Dewey, co., S. Dak., 5,257...B4 116
Dewey, res., Ky.....C7 94
Deweyville, Newton, Tex., 750....D6 118
Deweyville, Box Elder, Utah, 265....B3 119
De Winton, Alta., Can., 51..D3 69
DeWitt, Arkansas, Ark., 3,019....C4 81
DeWitt, DeWitt, Ill., 245....C5 90
DeWitt, Clinton, Iowa, 3,224.C7 92
DeWitt, Clinton, Mich., 1,238....F6 98
DeWitt, Carroll, Mo., 174....B4 101
DeWitt, Saline, Nebr., 504..D9 103
DeWitt, Onondaga, N.Y., 7,000....*B4 108
Dewitt, Dinwiddie, Va., 100.D5 121
DeWitt, co., Ill., 17,253....C5 90
DeWitt, co., Tex., 20,683....E4 118
Dewsbury, Eng., 53,800 (*153,000)....A6 12
Dewy Rose, Elbert, Ga., 150.B4 87
Dexter, Laurens, Ga., 355...D3 87
Dexter, Dallas, Iowa, 670....C3 92
Dexter, Cowley, Kans., 291..E7 93
Dexter, Calloway, Ky., 250..B3 94
Dexter, Penobscot, Maine, 2,720 (3,951▲)....C3 96
Dexter, Washtenaw, Mich., 1,702....F7 98
Dexter, Mower, Minn., 313..G6 99
Dexter, Stoddard, Mo., 5,519.E8 101
Dexter, Chaves, N. Mex., 885....D5 107
Dexter, Jefferson, N.Y., 1,009....A4 108
Dexter, Lane, Oreg., 200....D4 113
Dexter, lake, Fla.....C5 86
Deyhuk, Iran, 10,000....E8 41
Deyyer, Iran, 5,000....H5 41
Dezfūl, Iran, 52,121....E4 41
Dezhnev, cape, Sov. Un.....C21 28
Dezh Shāhpūr, Iran....D3 41
Dhaain, Sau. Ar....I5 41
Dhahran, see Aẓ Ẓahrān, Sau. Ar.
Dhamtari, India, 31,552....G8 40
Dhanbad, India, 46,756 (*125,000)....F11 40
Dhankuta, Nep., 4,194....D11 40
D'Hanis, Medina, Tex., 850..E3 118
Dhar, India, 28,325....F5 40
Dharamjaygarh, India, 5,000.F9 40
Dharmapuri, India, 28,031...F6 39
Dharmsala, India, 10,255....A6 40
Dharwar, India, 77,163....E6 39
Dhāt al Ḩajj, Sau. Ar....H11 31
Dhaulagiri, peak, Nep.....C9 40
Dhekelia, Grc., 388....g11 23
Dhenousa, isl., Grc.....D5 23
Dhībān, Jordan, 2,000....G10 31
Dhidhimotikhon, Grc., 8,111.B6 23
Dhílos (Delos), isl., Grc.....D5 23
Dhimitsana, Grc., 1,710....D4 23
Dhodekanisos, prov., Grc., 123,021....*D6 23
Dholpur, India, 27,412....D6 40
Dhond, India, 9,947 (*18,849)....H5 40
Dhoraji, India, 48,951....g11 40
Dhritsa, Grc., 696....g11 23
Dhubri, India, 28,355....E12 40
Dhulia, India, 98,893....G5 40
Dia, isl., Grc.....E5 23
Diablerets, mtn., Switz.....D3 19
Diablo, Contra Costa, Calif., 2,096....*D2 82
Diablo, canyon, Ariz.....C4 80
Diablo, dam, Wash.....A4 122
Diablo, isl., P.R.....f12 65
Diablo, mtn., Calif.....h9 82
Diablo, mtn., Oreg.....E6 113
Diablo, range, Calif.....D3 82
Diablo Heights, C.Z., 1,647.k11 62
Diagonal, Ringgold, Iowa, 443....D3 92
Dial, Fannin, Ga., 25....B2 87
Diamante, Arg., 13,600....A4 54
Diamantina, Braz., 14,252...E2 57
Diamantina, riv., Austl.....D7 50
Diamond, Ont., Can....h11 72
Diamond, Parke, Ind., 45....E3 91
Diamond, Plaquemines, La., 200....E6 95
Diamond, Newton, Mo., 453.E3 101
Diamond, Portage, Ohio, 280....A6 111
Diamond, Harney, Oreg., 10.D8 113
Diamond, Kanawha, W. Va., 600....C6 123
Diamond, Platte, Wyo., 398..D8 125
Diamond, cave, Ark.....B2 81
Diamond, head, Haw.....g10 88
Diamond, lake, Oreg.....D4 113
Diamond, mts., Nev.....D6 104
Diamond, peak, Oreg.....D4 113
Diamond, pt., Indon.....k11 35
Diamond Bluff, Pierce, Wis., 150....D1 124
Diamond City, Alta., Can., 78....E4 69
Diamond Harbour, India, 10,135....F12 40
Diamond Hill, Providence, R.I., 800....*B11 84
Diamond Lake, Lake, Ill., 700....E2 90
Diamond Point, Warren, N.Y., 400....B7 108
Diamond Springs, Eldorado, Calif., 617....C3 82
Diamond Springs, Princess Anne, Va., 1,500....*E6 121
Diamondville, Lincoln, Wyo., 398....D6 125
Diana, Giles, Tenn., 100....B5 117
Diana, Webster, W. Va., 250.C4 123
Dianalund, Den., 2,145....C5 24
Dianópolis, Braz., 2,145....D1 57
Diapaga, Upper Volta....D5 45
Diapitan, bay, Phil.....n14 35
Diarbekr (Diyarbakir), Tur., 80,600....D3 31
Diaz, Jackson, Ark., 348....B4 81
Dibaya, Con. L....C3 48
Di Monte Santu, cape, It.....D2 21
Dinagat, isl., Phil.....C7 35
Dibble, iceberg tongue, Ant....C26 5
Diber (Dibra), pref., Alb., 96,000....*B3 23
D'Iberville, Harrison & Jackson, Miss., 3,005..E2, E5 100
Diboll, Angelina, Tex., 2,506.D5 118
Dibra (Diber), pref., Alb., 96,000....*B3 23
Dibrell, Warren, Tenn., 90..D8 117
Dibrugarh, India, 58,480....C9 39
Dickens, Clay, Iowa, 241....A2 92
Dickens, Lincoln, Nebr., 25..D5 103
Dickens, Dickens, Tex., 302..C2 118
Dickens, co., Tex., 4,963....C2 118
Dickenson, co., Va., 20,211..B2 121
Dickerson, Montgomery, Md., 246....B3 85
Dickey, Aroostook, Maine....A4 96
Dickey, La Moure, N. Dak., 143....C7 110
Dickey, co., N. Dak., 8,147..C7 110
Dickeyville, Grant, Wis., 671 F3 124
Dickie, Hot Springs, Wyo., 15....B4 125
Dickinson, Clarke, Ala., 250 D2 78
Dickinson, Stark, N. Dak., 9,971....C3 110
Dickinson, Galveston, Tex., 4,715....*F5 118
Dickinson, co., Iowa, 12,574.A2 92
Dickinson, co., Kans., 21,572.D6 93
Dickinson, co., Mich., 23,917.B3 98
Dickinson, dam, N. Dak.....C2 110
Dickinson Center, Franklin, N.Y., 240....f10 108
Dickson, Dickson, Tenn., 5,028....A4 117
Dickson, co., Tenn., 18,839..A4 117
Dickson City, Lackawanna, Pa., 7,738....A9, D10 114
Dicle, riv., Tur.....D13 31
Didsbury, Alta., Can., 1,254.D3 69
Didwana, India, 13,547....D5 40
Die, Fr., 2,824....E6 14
Dieburg, Ger., 9,500....D3 17
Diégo-Suarez (Antsirane), Malag., 29,887....f9 49
Diégo-Suarez, prov., Malag...f9 49
Diekirch, Lux., 4,397....E6 15
Diemel, riv., Ger.....B3 17
Diem Zubeir, Sud....D2 47
Dien Bien Phu, Viet....B5 38
Diepholz, Ger., 10,900....B4 16
Dieppe, N.B., Can., 4,032....C5 74
Dieppe, Fr., 29,967....C4 14
Dierks, Howard, Ark., 1,276.C1 81
Diessen, Ger., 5,000....B7 18
Diest, Bel., 9,816....D5 15
Dieterich, Effingham, Ill., 591....D5 90
Dietikon, Switz., 14,920....B5 19
Dietrich, Lincoln, Idaho, 118....G4 89
Dieuze, Fr., 3,431....F6 15
Diever, Neth., 857....B6 15
Diez, Ger., 9,600....C3 17
Dif, Som....E5 47
Differdange, Lux., 17,637....E5 15
Difficult, Smith, Tenn., 150..C8 117
Difficulty, Carbon, Wyo....C6 125
Digby, N.S., Can., 2,308....E4 74
Digby, co., N.S., Can., 20,216....E4 74
Dighton, Lane, Kans., 1,526.D3 93
Dighton, Bristol, Mass., 700 (3,769▲)....C5 97
Dighton, Osceola, Mich., 75....D5 98
Digne, Fr., 10,299....E7 14
Digoel, riv., W. Irian....G10 35
Digoin, Fr., 8,253....D5 14
Digos, Phil., 21,455....*D7 35
Dijon, Fr., 135,694 ($155,000)....D6 14
Dike, Grundy, Iowa, 630....B5 92
Dikhil, Fr. Som., 500....C5 47
Dikili, Tur., 6,100....C6 23
Dikili, cape, Tur.....B8 23
Dikirnis, Eg., U.A.R., 5,000....C3 32
Diksmuide, Bel., 3,812....C2 15
Dikson, Sov. Un., 10,000...B10 28
Dikwa, Nig., 5,242....D7 45
Dilaram, Afg., 5,000....E11 41
Dildo, Newf., Can., 687....*D5 75
Dili (Dilli), Port. Timor, 52,200....G7 35
Dilia, Guadalupe, N. Mex., 60....B4 107
Dilke, Sask., Can., 187....G3 70
Dilkon, Navajo, Ariz....B5 80
Dillard, Rabun, Ga., 204....B3 87
Dillard, Carter, Okla., 125..C4 112
Dill City, Washita, Okla., 623....B2 112
Dille, Clay, W. Va., 250....C4 123
Dillen, Johnson, Ark....B2 81
Dillenburg, Ger., 10,700....C3 17
Diller, Jefferson, Nebr., 286..D9 103
Dilley, Frio, Tex., 2,118....E3 118
Dilli (Dili), Port. Timor, 1,795....G7 35
Dilliner, Greene, Pa., 100....F2 114
Dilling, Sud., 5,295....C2 47
Dillingen [an der Donau], Ger., 11,200....E5 17
Dillingen, Ger., 17,700....D1 17
Dillingham, Alsk., 424....D8 79
Dillon, Summit, Colo., 814..B4 83
Dillon, Beaverhead, Mont., 3,690....E4 102
Dillon, Dillon, S.C., 6,173....C9 115
Dillon, co., S.C., 30,584....C9 115
Dillon, lake, Sask., Can.....B6 69
Dillon, riv., Alta., Can.....B5 69
Dillonvale, Jefferson, Ohio, 1,232....B7 111
Dillsboro, Dearborn, Ind., 745....F7 91
Dillsboro, Jackson, N.C., 140....D3 109
Dillsburg, York, Pa., 1,322...F7 114
Dillwyn, Buckingham, Va., 515....D4 121
Dilolo, Con. L....D3 48
Dilworth, Clay, Minn., 2,102.D2 99
Dimashq, see Damascus, Syr.
Dimbelenge, Con. L....C3 48
Dimbokro, I.C., 3,800....E4 45
Dimitrovgrad, Bul., 34,162..D7 22
Dimitrovgrad, Yugo., 3,669..D6 22
Dimmit, co., Tex., 10,095....E3 118
Dimmitt, Castro, Tex., 2,935....B1 118
Dimock, Hutchinson, S. Dak., 150....D8 116
Dimondale, Eaton, Mich., 866....F6 98
Dinajpur, Pak., 37,711....E12 40
Dinan, Fr., 12,847....C3 14
Dinant, Bel., 6,851....E4 15
Dinapore, India, 35,159....E10 40
Dinar, Tur., 9,400....C8 23
Dinard [-St. Enogat], Fr., 9,270....C2 14
Dinaric Alps, mts., Yugo.....D3 22
Dindigul, India, 92,947....F6 39
Dinero, Live Oak, Tex., 75..E4 118
Dines, Sweetwater, Wyo....D3 125
Dingalan, bay, Phil.....o13 35
Dingelstädt, Ger., 5,602....B5 17
Dingess, Mingo, W. Va., 400.D2 123
Dingle, Bear Lake, Idaho, 100....G7 89
Dingle, Ire., 1,460....E1 11
Dingle, Phil., 1,328....*C6 35
Dingle, bay, Ire.....E1 11
Dingmans Ferry, Pike, Pa., 300....D12 114
Dingo, Austl., 102....A7 51
Dingolfing, Ger., 10,500....E7 17
Dinguiraye, Guinea, 2,900...D2 45
Dingwall, N.S., Can., 269...C9 74
Dingwall, Scot., 3,752....C4 13
Dinh Lap, Viet., 10,000....B7 38
Dinkelsbühl, Ger., 7,900....D5 17
Dinkey Creek, Fresno, Calif., 300....D4 82
Dinklage, Ger., 7,300....F2 24
Dinorwic, lake, Ont., Can.....E5 71
Dinosaur, nat. mon., Colo., Utah....A1 83
Dinosaur, the prov. park, Alta., Can.....D5 69
Dinsdale, Tama, Iowa, 80....B5 92
Dinslaken, Ger., 47,800....B1 17
Dinsmore, Sask., Can., 433..F2 70
Dinsmore, Duval, Fla., 2,000....B5 86
Dinuba, Tulare, Calif., 6,103....D4 82
Dinwiddie, Dinwiddie, Va., 200....D5 121
Dinwiddie, co., Va., 22,183..D5 121
Dioïla, Mali....D3 45
Dioka, Mali....D2 45
Diomede, is., Alsk.....C31 4
Diourbel, Sen., 20,600....D1 45
Diphu, pass, China, India....C10 39
Diplo, Pak....E2 40
Dipolog, Phil., 8,770....*D6 35
Dipper Harbour, N.B., Can., 150....D3 74
Dippoldiswalde, Ger., 5,937..C8 17
Diredawa, Eth., 30,000....D5 47
Diriamba, Nic., 13,100....E4 62
Dirico, Ang....E3 48
Dirk Hartog, isl., Austl.....E1 50
Dirkou, Niger....C7 45
Dirmil, Tur., 602....D7 23
Dirranbandi, Austl., 514....D7 51
Dirty Devil, riv., Utah....E5 119
Disappointment, cape, Ant....D9 5
Disappointment, cape, Wash....C1 122
Disappointment, lake, Austl....D3 50
Disautel, Okanogan, Wash., 50....A6 122
Discovery, mtn., Ant.....f39 5
Disentis (Mustèr), Switz., 2,376....C6 19
Dishman, Spokane, Wash., 5,000....D7 122

Dishnā, Eg., U.A.R., 16,336....D6 43
Disko, Fulton, Ind., 140....B6 91
Disko, isl., Grnld....C20 4
Disley, Sask., Can., 62....G3 70
Dismal, swamp, N.C., Va....A7 107
Disney, Mayes, Okla., 224...A6 112
Disputanta, Prince George, Va., 350....D5 121
Disraëli, Que., Can., 3,079..D6 73
Diss, Eng., 3,682....B9 12
Distant, Armstrong, Pa., 600.E3 114
District Heights, Prince Georges, Md., 7,534....*C4 85
District of Columbia, U.S., 763,956....C12 77, C7 85
Distrito Federal, fed. dist., Braz., 141,742....*B3 56
Distrito Federal, fed. dist., Mex., 4,829,402....D5 63
Distrito Federal, fed. dist., Ven., 1,257,515....A4 60
Disūq, Eg., U.A.R., 36,600..C2 43
Dittlinger, Comal, Tex., 100..B4 118
Ditzum, Ger., 820....A7 15
Diu, India, 4,856....G3 40
Divénié, Con. B....F2 46
Divernon, Sangamon, Ill., 997....D4 90
Dives-sur-Mer, Fr., 6,258....C4 14
Divide, Silver Bow, Mont., 145....E4 102
Divide, co., N. Dak., 5,566..A2 110
Divide, peak, Wyo....D5 125
Dividing, creek, Md....D6 85
Dividing Creek, Cumberland, N.J., 500....E2 106
Divinópolis, Braz., 41,544....F2 57
Divion, Fr., 11,300....D2 15
Divisov, Czech., 904....o18 26
Divnoye, Sov. Un., 17,300...D2 29
Divo, I.C., 4,800....E3 45
Divrigi, Tur., 8,900....C12 31
Dix, Jefferson, Ill., 181....E5 90
Dix, Kimball, Nebr., 420....C2 103
Dix, dam, Ky....C5 94
Dix, hills, N.Y....F3 84
Dix, mtn., N.Y....A7 108
Dix, riv., Ky....C5 94
Dixence, riv., Switz....D3 19
Dixfield, Oxford, Maine, 1,298 (2,323▲)....D2 96
Dixiana, Jefferson, Ala. 500..B3 78
Dixiana, Lexington, S.C., 150....D5 115
Dixie, Escambia, Ala., 100...D3 78
Dixie, Woodruff, Ark., 40....B4 81
Dixie, Ont., Can....m14 72
Dixie, Brooks, Ga., 220....F3 87
Dixie, Idaho, Idaho, 25....D3 89
Dixie, Caddo, La., 250....B2 95
Dixie, Stephens, Okla....C4 112
Dixie, Walla Walla, Wash., 250....C7 122
Dixie, Nicholas, W. Va., 650....C3, C7 123
Dixie, co., Fla., 4,479....C3 86
Dixie, butte, Oreg....C8 113
Dixie Union, Ware, Ga., 100.E4 87
Dixmoor, Cook, Ill., 3,076..*F3 90
Dixon, Solano, Calif., 2,970....A6, C3 82
Dixon, Lee, Ill., 19,565....B4 90
Dixon, Scott, Iowa, 280....C7 92
Dixon, Webster, Ky., 541....C2 94
Dixon, Pulaski, Mo., 1,473..D5 101
Dixon, Sanders, Mont., 170..C2 102
Dixon, Dixon, Nebr., 139....B9 103
Dixon, Rio Arriba, N. Mex., 500....A4 107
Dixon, Onslow, N.C....C6 109
Dixon, Van Wert, Ohio, 80..B3 111
Dixon, Gregory, S. Dak., 26.D6 116
Dixon, Carbon, Wyo., 108...D5 125
Dixon, co., Nebr., 8,106....B9 103
Dixon, entrance, Alsk., B.C., Can....B1 68
Dixons Mills, Marengo, Ala., 50....C2 78
Dixon Springs, Pope, Ill., 40.F5 90
Dixonville, Escambia, Ala., 200....D2 78
Dixonville, Alta., Can., 104..A2 69
Dixonville, Indiana, Pa., 900....E4 114
Dixville, Que., Can., 521....D6 74
Dixville, peak, N.H....A4, B1 105
Dixville Notch, Coos, N.H., 10....B1 105
Diyarbakir, Tur., 79,888...D13 31
Dizy-le-Gros, Fr., 1,057....E4 15
Dizy-Magenta, Fr., 2,079....E3 15
Dja, riv., Cam....E2 46
Djado, Niger....B7 45
Djafou, Alg....D5 44
Djailolo, Indon....E7 35
Djakarta (Jakarta, Batavia), Indon., 2,922,000....G3 35
Djakovica, Yugo., 20,741....D5 22
Djakovo, Yugo., 12,069....C4 22
Djambala, Con. B....F2 46
Djambi, Indon., 108,834....F2 35
Djanet (Ft. Charlet), Alg., 74.E6 44
Djaravica, peak, Yugo....D5 22
Djedeida, Tun....F11 30
Djelfa, Alg., 10,070 (110,681▲)....C5 44
Djema, Cen. Afr. Rep....D5 46
Djemadja, isl., Indon....K6 38
Djenné, Mali, 5,000....D4 45
Djerba, isl., Tun....C7 44, H12 30
Djerid, salt lake, Tun....C6 44
Djibo, Upper Volta....D4 45
Djibouti, Fr. Som., 31,500...C5 47
Djidjelli, Alg., 31,580....B6 44
Djiring, Viet....G8 38
Djolu, Con. L....A3 48
Djouf, basin, Maur....B3 45
Djougou, Dah., 4,900....E5 45
Djugu, Con L....A5 48
Djurdjevac, Yugo., 6,408....B3 22
Djurjura, mtn., Alg....B5 44
Djursholm, Swe., 7,400....t36 25
D'Lo, Simpson, Miss., 428...D4 100
Dmitriyevka, Sov. Un., 10,000....H12, r21 27
Dmitriyev-Lgovskiy, Sov. Un., 10,000....E10 27
Dmitrov, Sov. Un., 10,000..C11 27
Dmitrovsk-Orlovskiy, Sov. Un., 10,000....E10 27
Dnepr, riv., Sov. Un....H9 27
Dneprodzerzhinsk, Sov. Un., 207,000....G10 27
Dnepropetrovsk, Sov. Un., 738,000 (★1,065,000)....G10 27
Dnestr, riv., Sov. Un....H7 27
Dno, Sov. Un., 10,000....C7 27
Doaktown, N.B., Can., 595...C3 74
Doba, Chad, 7,375....D3 46
Dobbinton, Ont., Can....C3 72
Dobbs Ferry, Westchester, N.Y., 9,260....g13 108
Dobbyn, Austl., 109....C6 50
Döbeln, Ger., 28,900....B8 17
Doblas, Arg....B4 54
Dobo, Indon....G8 35
Doboj., Yugo., 13,445....C4 22
Doboy, sound, Ga....E5 87
Dobrejovice, Czech., 2,188...o18 26
Dobrich, see Tolbukhin, Bul.
Dobris, Czech., 4,130....o17 26
Dobrogea, prov., Rom., 503,217....*C9 22
Dobrovice, Czech., 2,137...n18 26
Dobrovolsk, Sov. Un....A7 26
Dobruja, reg., Bul., Rom....C9 22
Dobsina, Czech., 4,215....D6 26
Dobson, Surry, N.C., 684....A3 109
Doce, riv., Braz....E2 57
Docena, Jefferson, Ala., 1,400....*E4 78
Dock Junction, Glynn, Ga., 3,920....*E5 87
Dockton, King, Wash., 400..D1 122
Doctor Arroyo, Mex., 3,055..C4 63
Doctors, lake, Fla....C6 86
Doctors Inlet, Clay, Fla., 600.C6 86
Doctortown, Wayne, Ga., 200....E5 87
Doddridge, Miller, Ark., 500.D2 81
Doddridge, co., W. Va., 6,970....B4 123
Dodds, Alta., Can....C4 69
Doddsville, Sunflower, Miss., 190....D3 100
Dodecanese, prov., Grc., 123,021....D6 23
Dodecanese, is., Grc....D6 23
Dodge, Worcester, Mass., 200.B4 97
Dodge, Dodge, Nebr., 649....C9 103
Dodge, Dunn, N. Dak., 226..B3 110
Dodge, Trempealeau, Wis., 130....D2 124
Dodge, co., Ga., 16,483....D3 87
Dodge, co., Minn., 13,259....G6 99
Dodge, co., Nebr., 32,471....C9 103
Dodge, co., Wis., 63,170....E5 124
Dodge Center, Dodge, Minn., 1,441....F6 99
Dodge City, Ford, Kans., 13,520....E3 93
Dodgeville, Ashtabula, Ohio, 150....A7 111
Dodgeville, Iowa, Wis., 2,911....F3 124
Dodoma, Tan., 13,435....C6 48
Dodsland, Sask., Can., 365...F1 70
Dodson, Winn, La., 512....B3 95
Dodson, Phillips, Mont., 313.B8 102
Dodson, Collingsworth, Tex., 308....B2 118
Dodson, pen., Ant....B6 5
Doebay, San Juan, Wash., 85....A3 122
Doe River, B.C., Can....A7 68
Doerun, Colquitt, Ga., 1,037.E3 87
Doe Run, St. Francois, Mo., 600....D7 101
Doetinchem, Neth., 17,500...C6 15
Doeville, Johnson, Tenn....C12 117
Dog, isl., Fla....C2 86
Dog, lake, Man., Can....D2 71
Dog, riv., Vt....C3 120
Dog, rocks, Vir. Is....f15 65
Dog Creek, B.C., Can., 59...D6 68
Dogie, Niobrara, Wyo....B8 125
Dogiuma, Som....E5 47
Dog Keys, pass, Miss....E3 100
Dogondoutchi, Niger, 4,000..D5 45
Dogubayazit, Tur., 6,800...C15 31
Doha, Qatar, 35,000....I5 41
Dohad, India, 35,483....F5 40
Dohat es Salwa, bay, Sau. Ar...I5 41
Doheny, Que., Can., 40....B5 73
Doi Angka, mtn., Thai....C3 38
Doire, riv., It....D2 18
Dois Irmãos, mts., Braz....C2 57
Dojran, lake, Yugo....E6 22
Dokkum, Neth., 7,400....A6 15
Doksy, Czech., 3,061....C9 17
Doland, Spink, S. Dak., 481.C7 116
Dolavón, Arg....C3 54
Dolbeau, Que., Can., 6,052.G18 67
Dolchburg, Maverick, Tex...E2 118
Dol [-de-Bretagne], Fr., 4,130....C3 14
Dôle, Fr., 24,525....D6 14
Dolega, Pan., 831....F6 62
Doleib Hill, Sud....D3 47
Doles, Worth, Ga., 60....E3 87
Dolgelley, Wales, 2,267....B4 12
Dolgeville, Fulton and Herkimer, N.Y., 3,058....B6 108
Dolina, Sov. Un., 5,000....D8 26
Dolinsk (Ochiai), Sov. Un., 30,000....C11 37
Dolinskoye, Sov. Un....B9 22
Dolisie, Con. B....F2 46
Dollar Bay, Houghton, Mich., 500....A2 98
Dollard, Sask., Can., 165....H1 70
Dollart, bay, Neth....A7 15
Dollarville, Luce, Mich., 100....B5 98
Dolliver, Emmet, Iowa, 122..A3 92
Dolo, Eth....E5 47
Dolomite, Jefferson, Ala., 1,300....B3, E4 78
Dolomites, mts., It....C7 18
Dolores, Arg., 14,438....B5 54
Dolores, Montezuma, Colo., 805....D2 83
Dolores, Guat., 512....B3 62
Dolores, Mex., 137....B3 63
Dolores, Webb, Tex....F3 118
Dolores, Ur., 13,300....E1 56
Dolores, co., Colo., 2,196....D2 83
Dolores, riv., Colo., Utah....E7 119
Dolores Hidalgo, Mex., 11,733....m13 63
Dolphin and Union, straits, N.W. Ter., Can....C9 66
Dolton, Cook, Ill., 18,746....F3 90
Dolton, Turner, S. Dak., 71...D8 116
Dolzhanskaya, Sov. Un., 5,000....q22 27
Dom, mtn., Switz....D4 19
Domadare, Som....E5 47
Domanovici, Yugo., 1,900....D3 22
Domazlice, Czech., 8,500....D2 26
Dombarovskiy, Sov. Un....C5 29
Dombås, Nor., 502....F3 25
Dombasle [-sur-Meurthe], Fr., 9,367....F6 15
Dombe Grande, Ang....D1 48
Dombey, Beaver, Okla....B4 112
Dombóvár, Hung., 15,355...B4 22
Domburg, Neth., 1,400....C3 15
Dome, Yuma, Ariz., 50....E1 80
Dome, The, mtn., Vt....F2 120
Dome Rock, mts., Ariz....D1 80
Domeyko, Chile, 1,517....D2 55
Domeyko, range, Chile....D2 55
Domfront, Fr., 2,653....C3 14
Domingo, Sandoval, N. Mex., 50....B3 107
Dominguez, Los Angeles, Calif., 6,000....*F2 82
Dominica, C.R....F6 62
Dominica, Br. dep., N.A., 65,000....o16 64
Dominican Republic, country, N.A., 3,500,000..H13 61, F8 64
Dominion, N.S., Can., 2,999....C9 74
Dominion, cape, N.W. Ter., Can....C18 67
Dominion, lake, Newf., Can...h9 75
Dominion City, Man., Can., 534....E3 71
Domino, Cass, Tex....C5 118
Dömitz, Ger., 4,585....B5 16
Dommel, riv., Neth....C5 15
Domodedovo, Sov. Un., 17,600....n17 27
Domodossola, It., 16,728....C4 18
Dom Pedrito, Braz., 15,429..E2 56
Dompierre [-sur-Authie], Fr., 324....D9 12
Domremy, Sask., Can., 234..E3 70
Domuyo, mtn., Arg....B2 54
Domvraina, Grc., 1,993....g9 23
Don, pen., B.C., Can....C3 68
Don, riv., Scot....C6 13
Don, riv., Sov. Un....C1 29
Dona Ana, Dona Ana, N. Mex., 200....E3 107
Dona Ana, co., N. Mex., 59,948....E2 107
Donaghadee, N. Ire., 3,226..C6 11
Donald, Ont., Can., 86....C6 72
Donald, Marion, Oreg., 201..B2 113
Donald, Taylor, Wis....C3 124
Donalda, Alta., Can., 289...C4 69
Donalds, Abbeville, S.C., 416....C3 115
Donaldson, Hot Spring, Ark., 500....C3 81
Donaldson, Marshall, Ind., 120....B5 91
Donaldson, Kittson, Minn., 64....B2 99
Donaldson, Schuylkill, Pa., 637....E9 114
Donaldsonville, Ascension, La., 6,082....B5, D4 95
Donaldsonville, Seminole, Ga., 2,621....E2 87
Donard, Ire., 175....D5 11
Donat-Ems, Switz., 2,694....C7 19
Donau (Danube), riv., Ger....E6 17
Donaueschingen, Ger., 10,700....B4 18
Donauwörth, Ger., 10,200....E5 17
Donavon, Sask., Can., 40....F2 70
Don Benito, Sp., 25,248....C3 20
Doncaster, Eng., 86,900 (★150,000)....A6 12
Doncaster, Charles, Md., 250....D3 85
Dondo, Ang., 645....C1 48
Dondo, Moz....A5 49
Donegal, Ire., 1,458....C3 11
Donegal, co., Ire., 113,842...C3 11
Donegal, bay, Ire....C3 11
Donegal, mts., Ire....C3 11
Donegal, pt., Ire....E2 11
Donelson, Davidson, Tenn., 17,195....A5, E9 117
Doneraile, Darlington, S.C., 1,043....C8 115
Donets, riv., Sov. Un....G13 27
Donetsk, Sov. Un., 774,000 (★1,675,000)....H11, r28 27
Dongara, Austl., 269....E1 50
Donggala, Indon., 3,821....F5 35
Dong Hoi, Viet., 10,000....D7 38
Dongo, Con. L....A2 48
Dongola, Sud., 3,350....B3 47
Dongola, Union, Ill., 757....F4 90
Dongou, Con. B....E3 46
Donington, Eng., 1,917....B7 12
Doniphan, Doniphan, Kans., 150....C8 93
Doniphan, Ripley, Mo., 1,421....E7 101
Doniphan, Hall, Nebr., 390..D7 103
Doniphan, co., Kans., 9,574....C8 93
Donji Vakuf, Yugo., 3,756...C3 22
Donkey, creek, Wyo....A7 125
Donkin, N.S., Can., 1,010...C10 74
Donley, co., Tex., 4,449....B2 118
Don Martin, lake, Mex....B4 63
Donna, Hidalgo, Tex., 7,522.F3 118
Donnacona, Que., Can., 4,812....C6, o16 73
Donnellson, Montgomery and Bond, Ill., 292....D4 90
Donnellson, Lee, Iowa, 709..D6 92
Donnelly, Alta., Can., 289...B2 69
Donnelly, Valley, Idaho, 161....E2 89
Donnelly, Stevens, Minn., 358....E2 99
Donnels, Rutherford, Tenn...B5 117
Donner, Terrebonne, La., 300....C5, E5 95
Donnybrook, Ward, N. Dak., 196....A4 110
Donora, Washington, Pa., 11,131....F2 114
Donovan, Johnson, Ga., 100.D4 87
Donovan, Iroquois, Ill., 320..C6 90
Donzère, Fr., 1,544....E6 14
Dooagh, Ire., 387....D1 11
Doogort, Ire....C1 11
Doole, McCulloch, Tex., 55..D3 118
Dooley, Sheridan, Mont....B12 102
Doolittle, Phelps, Mo., 449..D6 101
Dooly, co., Ga., 11,474....D3 87
Doon, Lyon, Iowa, 436....A1 92
Doon, lake, Scot....E4 13
Doon, riv., Scot....E4 13
Doonbeg, Ire., 224....E2 11
Door, co., Wis., 20,685....D6 124
Dora, Walker, Ala., 1,776...B2 78
Dora, Ozark, Mo., 100....E5 101
Dora, Roosevelt, N. Mex., 200....D7 107
Dora, Coos, Oreg., 100....D3 113
Dora Baltea, riv., It....B1 21
Dorado, P.R., 2,120....B5 65
Dorado, mun., P.R., 13,460..B5 65
Doran, Wilkin, Minn., 136...D2 99
Doraville, DeKalb, Ga., 4,437....A5 87
Dorcas, Okaloosa, Fla., 100..G2 86
Dorcheat, creek, Ark....D2 81
Dorchester, N.B., Can., 1,779....D5 74
Dorchester, Eng., 12,266....D5 12
Dorchester, Liberty, Ga., 50..E2 87
Dorchester, Allamakee, Iowa, 97....A6 92
Dorchester, Saline, Nebr., 460....D8 103
Dorchester, Grafton, N.H., 10 (91▲)....C3 105
Dorchester, Cumberland, N.J., 500....E3 106
Dorchester, Dorchester, S.C., 400....E7 115
Dorchester, Clark, Wis., 504.D3 124
Dorchester, co., Que., Can., 34,711....C7 73
Dorchester, co., Md., 29,666.D5 85
Dorchester, co., S.C., 24,383..E7 115
Dorchester, cape, N.W. Ter., Can....C17 67
Dorchester Crossing, N.B., Can., 569....C5 74
Dorcyville, Iberville, La., 400....B5 95
Dordogne, dept., Fr., 375,455....*E4 14
Dordogne, riv., Fr....E3 14
Dordrecht, Neth., 86,400 (★141,000)....C4 15
Dordrecht, S. Afr., 4,019....D4 49
Dore, McKenzie, N. Dak., 15.B2 110
Doré, lake, Ont., Can....B7 72
Doré, lake, Sask., Can....C2 70
Doré, riv., Sask., Can....C2 70
Doré Lake, Sask., Can., 104....C2 70
Dorena, Mississippi, Mo., 400....E8 101
Dorena, Lane, Oreg., 225...D4 113
Dorena, dam, Oreg....D3 113
Dorenlee, Alta., Can....C4 69
Dores, Scot., 607....C4 13
Dores do Indaiá, Braz., 10,354....E1 57
Dorfen, Ger., 4,200....A8 18
Dorgali, It., 7,189....D2 21
Dori, Upper Volta, 3,500....D4 45
Dorion, Que., Can., 4,996..q18 73
Dormans, Fr., 1,530....E3 15
Dormont, Allegheny, Pa., 13,098....B5 114
Dornbirn, Aus., 28,075....B5 18
Dornie, Scot....C3 13
Dornoch, Scot., 933....C4 13
Dornoch, firth, Scot....C5 13
Dorogobuzh, Sov. Un., 17,900....D9 27
Dorohoi, Rom., 14,771....B8 22
Dorothy, Alta., Can....D4 69
Dorothy, Red Lake, Minn., 60.C2 99
Dorothy, Atlantic, N.J., 500..E3 106
Dorothy, Raleigh, W. Va., 350....D6 123
Dorothy Manor, Worcester, Mass., 600....B4 97
Dorr, Allegan, Mich., 275...F5 98
Dorrance, Russell, Kans., 331....D5 93
Dorrigo, Austl., 1,027....E9 51
Dorris, Siskiyou, Calif., 973..B3 82
Dorset, Ont., Can., 220....B6 72
Dorset, Hubbard, Minn., 50.D4 99
Dorset, Ashtabula, Ohio, 350.A7 111
Dorset, Bennington, Vt., 300 (1,150▲)....E2 120
Dorset, co., Eng., 309,176...D5 12
Dorset, peak, Vt....E2 120
Dorsey, Madison, Ill., 100...A8 101
Dorsey, Anne Arundel and Howard, Md., 500....B4 85
Dorsey, Itawamba, Miss., 130....A5 100
Dorsten, Ger., 36,300....B1 17
Dortmund, Ger., 652,000....B2 17
Dortmund Ems, canal, Ger....B2 17
Dorton, Pike, Ky., 700....C7 94
Dortyol, Tur., 10,200....D11 31
Dorum, Ger., 2,900....E2 24
Doruma, Con. L....A4 48
Dorval, Que., Can., 18,592..q19 73
Dorya, riv., Eth....D5 47
Dos Bahias, cape, Arg....C3 54
Dos Bocas, P.R....B4 65
Dos Hermanas, Sp., 22,700...D3 20
Doshi, Afg., 10,000....D14 41
Dos Palos, Merced, Calif., 2,373....D3 82
Dosquet, Que., Can., 394....C6 73
Dos Rios, Mendocino, Calif., 18....C2 82
Dosse, riv., Ger....E6 24
Dosso, Niger, 2,500....D5 45
Dothan, Houston, Ala., 31,440....D4 78
Dothan, Fayette, W. Va., 400....D7 123
Doting Cove, Newf., Can., 640....D5 75
Dott, Mercer, W. Va., 250...D3 123
Doty, Lewis, Wash., 260....C2 122
Doty, isl., Wis....A5 124
Douai, Fr., 47,639 (★135,000)....B5 14
Douala (Duala), Cam., 127,800....E1 46
Douarnenez, Fr., 19,887....C1 14
Double, mtn., Ala....E5 78
Double Bayou, Chambers, Tex., 120....F5 118
Double Mer, lake, Newf., Can..A2 75
Double Oak, mtn., Ala....E5 78
Double Springs, Winston, Ala., 811....A2 78
Double Springs, Putnam, Tenn., 100....C8 117
Doubletop, peak, Wyo....B2 125
Doubs, Frederick, Md., 200..B3 85
Doubs, dept., Fr., 384,881...B2 18
Doubs, riv., Fr., Switz....B2 19, D7 14
Doubtful, sound, N.Z....P11 51
Doucette, Tyler, Tex., 500...D5 118
Douds, Van Buren, Iowa, 250....D5 92
Doué [-la-Fontaine], Fr., 3,895....D3 14
Douentza, Mali, 2,250....D4 45
Dougherty, Cerro Gordo, Iowa, 398....B4 92
Dougherty, Murray, Okla., 294....C4 112
Dougherty, co., Ga., 75,680..E2 87
Douglas, Alsk., 1,042..D13, k22 79
Douglas, Cochise, Ariz., 11,925....F6 80
Douglas, Ont., Can., 365....B8 72
Douglas, Coffee, Ga., 8,736..E4 87
Douglas, I. of Man, 18,837..C4 10
Douglas, Worcester, Mass., 300 (2,559▲)....B4 97
Douglas, Allegan, Mich., 602....F4 98
Douglas, Olmsted, Minn., 126....F6 99
Douglas, Otoe, Nebr., 197...D9 103
Douglas, Ward, N. Dak., 210.B4 110
Douglas, Garfield, Okla., 74.A4 112
Douglas, S. Afr., 3,974....C3 49
Douglas, Converse, Wyo., 2,822....C7 125
Douglas, co., Colo., 4,816....B6 83
Douglas, co., Ga., 16,741....C2 87
Douglas, co., Ill., 19,243....D5 90
Douglas, co., Kans., 43,720..D8 93
Douglas, co., Minn., 21,313..E3 99
Douglas, co., Mo., 9,653....E5 101
Douglas, co., Nebr., 343,490.C9 103
Douglas, co., Nev., 3,481....E2 104
Douglas, co., Oreg., 68,458..D3 113
Douglas, co., S. Dak., 5,113..D7 116
Douglas, co., Wash., 14,890..B6 122
Douglas, co., Wis., 45,008...B2 124
Douglas, chan., B.C., Can....C3 68
Douglas, creek, Colo....B2 83
Douglas, lake, Mich....C6 98
Douglas, lake, Tenn....D10 117
Douglas, pt., Ont., Can....C3 72
Douglas Lake, B.C., Can., 166....D7 68
Douglass, Butler, Kans., 1,058....E7 93
Douglass, Essex, N.Y., 25....f11 108
Douglas Station, Man., Can., 289....E2 71
Douglastown, N.B., Can., 615....B4 74
Douglasville, Baldwin, Ala...E2 78
Douglasville, Douglas, Ga., 4,462....C2 87
Doullens, Fr., 6,321....B5 14
Doulus, head, Ire....F1 11
Doumé, Cam....E2 46
Douna, Mali....D3 45
Dour, Bel., 10,785....D3 15
Dourada, mts., Braz....D1 57
Dourado, Braz., 10,757....m7 56
Dourdan, Fr., 4,293....F2 15
Douro (Duero), riv., Port....B1 20
Douro Litoral, prov., Port., 1,240,149....*B1 20
Dousman, Waukesha, Wis., 410....E5 124
Douthat, Ottawa, Okla., 250....A7 112
Douz, Tun., 4,993....C6 44
Dove Creek, Dolores, Colo., 986....D2 83
Dover, Pope, Ark., 525....B2 81
Dover, Kent, Del., 7,250....B6 85
Dover, Eng., 36,200....C9 12
Dover, Hillsborough, Fla., 800....D4 86
Dover, Screven, Ga., 150....D5 87
Dover, Bonner, Idaho, 250..A2 89
Dover, Shawnee, Kans., 150....D8 93
Dover, Mason, Ky., 718....B6 94
Dover, Norfolk, Mass., 600 (2,846▲)....h10 97
Dover, Olmsted, Minn., 312.G6 99
Dover, Lafayette, Mo., 172..B4 101
Dover, Stafford, N.H., 19,131....D5 105
Dover, Morris, N.J., 13,034..B3 106
Dover, Craven, N.C., 651....B6 109
Dover, Tuscarawas, Ohio, 11,300....B6 111
Dover, Kingfisher, Okla., 350....B4 112
Dover, York, Pa., 975....F8 114
Dover, Stewart, Tenn., 736..A4 117
Dover, riv., Alta., Can....A4 69
Dover, strait, Eng....E7 10
Doverel, Terrell, Ga., 25....E2 87
Dover-Foxcroft, Piscataquis, Maine, 2,481 (4,173▲)....C3 96
Doverhill, Martin, Ind., 100....G4 91
Dover Plains, Dutchess, N.Y., 1,000....D7 108
Dover South Mills, Piscataquis, Maine....C3 96
Dovesville, Darlington, S.C., 100....C8 115
Dovray, Murray, Minn., 113....F3 99
Dovrefjell, mts., Nor....F3 25
Dow, Pittsburg, Okla., 300..C6 112
Dow, Jersey, Ill., 150....D3 90
Dow, lake, Bech....B3 49
Dowa, Malawi, 1,085....D5 49
Dowagiac, Cass, Mich., 7,208....G4 98
Dow City, Crawford, Iowa, 531....C2 92
Dowdell Knob, mtn., Ga....D2 87
Dowell, Jackson, Ill., 453....F4 90
Dowelltown, De Kalb, Tenn., 279....C8 117
Dowling, lake, Alta., Can....D4 69
Dowling Park, Suwannee, Fla., 150....B3 86
Down, co., N. Ire., 267,013..C5 11
Downer, Clay, Minn., 100...D2 99
Downers Grove, Du Page, Ill., 21,154....F2 90
Downey, Los Angeles, Calif., 82,505....*F2 82
Downey, Bannock, Idaho, 726....G6 89
Downham Market, Eng., 2,650....B8 12
Downhill, N. Ire....B5 11
Downieville, Sierra, Calif., 400....C3 82
Downing, Schuyler, Mo., 463....A5 101
Downing, Dunn, Wis., 241..C1 124
Downingtown, Chester, Pa., 5,598....F10 114
Downpatrick, N. Ire., 4,219..C6 11
Downpatrick, head, Ire....C2 11
Downs, Macon, Ala., 30....C4 78
Downs, McLean, Ill., 654....C5 90
Downs, Osborne, Kans., 1,206....C5 93
Downs, mtn., Wyo....B3 125
Downsville, Union, La., 150..B3 95
Downsville, Delaware, N.Y., 600....C5 108
Downsville, Dunn, Wis., 275.D2 124
Downton, mtn., B.C., Can....C5 68
Dows, Wright and Franklin, Iowa, 882....B4 92
Doyle, Lassen, Calif., 150....B3 82
Doyle, Livingston, La. (part of Livingston)....A6 95
Doyle, White, Tenn., 500...D8 117
Doyle, creek, Kans....A6 93
Doyles, Newf., Can., 210....E2 75
Doylestown, Wayne, Ohio, 1,873....B6 111
Doylestown, Bucks, Pa., 5,917....F11 114
Doyleville, Gunnison, Colo., 35....C4 83
Doyline, Webster, La., 1,061.B2 95
Doyon, Ramsey, N. Dak., 90.A7 110
Dozier, Crenshaw, Ala., 335.D3 78
Dra, plat., Alg....D3 44
Dra, wadi, Mor....D3 44
Drabenderhöhe, Ger., 8,738.C2 17
Drachten, Neth., 9,249....A6 15
Dracut, Middlesex, Mass., 11,500 (13,674▲)....A5 97
Draganeşti, Rom., 3,965....C7 22
Draganovo, Bul., 5,465....D7 22
Drăgăsani, Rom., 9,963....C7 22
Dragerton, Carbon, Utah, 2,400....D5 119
Dragoon, Cochise, Ariz., 100.E5 80
Dragoon, creek, Kans....D8 93
Dragør, Den., 6,986....C6 24
Draguignan, Fr., 11,814....F7 14
Drain, Douglas, Oreg., 1,052.D3 113
Drake, Yavapai, Ariz., 20...C3 80
Drake, Sask., Can., 215....F3 70
Drake, Larimer, Colo., 40...A5 83
Drake, McHenry, N. Dak., 752....B5 110
Drake, creek, Ky....D3 94
Drake Passage, Ant....D6 5
Drakensberg, mts., S. Afr....J8 42
Drakes, bay, Calif....B5 82
Drakesboro, Muhlenberg, Ky., 832....C2 94
Drakes Branch, Charlotte, Va., 759....E4 121
Drakesville, Davis, Iowa, 197.D5 92
Draketown, Haralson, Ga., 100....C1 87
Drama, Grc., 32,195....B5 23
Drama, prov., Grc., 121,006.*B5 23
Drama, riv., Pol....g9 26
Drammen, Nor., 31,300 (★57,500)....H4, p28 25
Dramselv, riv., Nor....p27 25
Drance, riv., Fr....C2 18
Drancy, Fr., 65,890....g10 14
Dranesville, Fairfax, Va....A4 121
Draper, Rockingham, N.C., 3,382....A4 109
Draper, Jones, S. Dak., 215..D5 116
Draper, Salt Lake, Utah, 1,700....C4 119
Draperstown, N. Ire., 592....C5 11
Drasco, Cleburne, Ark., 75...B4 81
Drau, riv., Aus....E6 16
Drava, riv., Yugo....B4 22
Draveil, Fr., 18,124....F2 15
Dravograd, Yugo., 2,131....B2 22
Dravosburg, Allegheny, Pa., 3,458....F2 114
Drawenburg, see Drawsko, Pol.
Drawsko, Pol., 3,504....B3 26
Drayton, Ont., Can., 646....D4 72
Drayton, Pembina, N. Dak., 940....A8 110
Drayton, Spartanburg, S.C., 1,128....B4 115
Drayton Plains, Oakland, Mich., 6,000....F7 98
Drayton Valley, Alta., Can., 3,854....C3 69
Drebkau, Ger., 2,518....B9 17
Drelsdorf, Ger., 910....D3 24
Drenthe, prov., Neth., 314,400....B6 15
Dresbach, Winona, Minn., 350....G7 99
Dresden, Ont., Can., 2,346..E2 72
Dresden, Ger., 494,600 (★625,000)....B8 17
Dresden, Decatur, Kans., 134....C3 93
Dresden, Sagadahoc, Maine.D3 96
Dresden, Cavalier, N. Dak., 65....A7 110
Dresden, Muskingum, Ohio, 1,338....B5 111
Dresden, Weakley, Tenn., 1,510....A3 117
Dresden Village, Macomb, Mich., 5,500....*F7 98
Dresser, Polk, Wis., 498....C1 124
Dresslerville, Douglas, Nev., 150....E2 104
Dreux, Fr., 21,588....C4 14
Drew, Penobscot, Maine, (43▲)....C4 96
Drew, Sunflower, Miss., 2,143....B3 100
Drew, Douglas, Oreg., 25....E4 113
Drew, co., Ark., 15,213....D4 81
Drewrys Bluff, Chesterfield, Va., 250....C7, D5 121
Drewryville, Southampton, Va., 200....E5 121
Drews, res., Oreg....E6 113
Drewsey, Harney, Oreg., 39..D8 113
Drewsville, Cheshire, N.H., 100....D2 105
Drexel, Cass, Mo., 651....C3 101
Drexel, Mineral, Mont....C1 102
Drexel, Burke, N.C., 1,146...B2 109
Drexel, Montgomery, Ohio, 2,500....C3 111
Drexel Gardens, Marion, Ind., 1,000....*E5 91
Drexel Hill, Delaware, Pa., 39,000....*B11 114
Drezna, Sov. Un....n18 27
Driffield, Eng., 6,890....F8 13
Drift, Floyd, Ky., 800....C7 94
Drifton, Luzerne, Pa., 900. D10 114
Driftpile, Alta., Can., 40....B3 69
Driftpile, riv., Alta., Can....B3 69
Driftwood, Alfalfa, Okla., 32.A3 112
Driftwood, Cameron, Pa., 203....D5 114
Driftwood, creek, Kans....C3 93
Driftwood, creek, Nebr....B3 93
Driggs, Teton, Idaho, 824...F7 89
Drimoleague, Ire., 369....F2 11
Drin, gulf, Alb....B2 23
Drina, riv., Yugo....C4 22
Drinkwater, Sask., Can., 138.G3 70
Dripping Springs, Hays, Tex., 150....D3 118
Driscoll, Burleigh, N. Dak., 220....C5 110

E

EAST-ECKV 33X

East (Delaware, riv.), branch, N.Y. C5 108
East (Lamoille, riv.), branch, Vt. C4 120
East, brook, N.H. B4 105
East, butte, Mont B5 102
East, cape, Fla. G5 86
East, cape, N.Z. L17 51
East, cape, P.R. e10 65
East (Sevier, riv.), fork, Utah F3 119
East, isl., Que., Can B8 74
East, pass, Fla C2 87
East, pt., P.E.I., Can C8 74
East, pt., Que., Can B8 74
East, pt., Mass B6 97
East, pt., N.J. E2 106
East, pt., N.Y. D9 84
East, riv., Ont., Can B5 72
East, riv., N.Y. k13 108
East, riv., Wis A6 124
East, riv., Wyo C3 125
Eastaboga, Talladega, Ala., 125 B3 78
Eastabutchie, Jones, Miss., 105 D4 100
East Acton, Middlesex, Mass., 400 g10 97
East Acworth, Sullivan, N.H. D2 105
East Alamosa, Alamosa, Colo., 800 D5 83
East Alburg, Grand Isle, Vt., 75 B2 120
East Alliance, Mahoning, Ohio, 1,275 *B6 111
East Alstead, Cheshire, N.H., 75 D2 105
East Alton, Madison, Ill., 7,630 E3 90
East Andover, Oxford, Maine, 150 D2 96
East Andover, Merrimack, N H., 250 D3 105
East Angus, Que., Can., 4,756 D6 73
East Arcadia, Bladen, N.C. C5 109
East Arlington, Bennington, Vt., 600 E2 120
East Ashtabula, Ashtabula, Ohio, 4,179 A7 111
East Aurora, Erie, N.Y., 6,791 C2 108
East Baldwin, Cumberland, Maine, 150 E2 96
East Bangor, Northampton, Pa., 970 E11 114
East Bank, Kanawha, W. Va., 1,023 C6 123
East Barnard, Windsor, Vt., 45 D3 120
East Barnet, Eng., 40,599 k12 10
East Barnet, Caledonia, Vt., 110 C4 120
East Barre, Washington, Vt., 700 C4 120
East Barre, res., Vt C4 120
East Barrington, Strafford, N.H., 100 B4 105
East Bathurst, N.B., Can., 1,876 B4 74
East Baton Rouge, par., La., 230,058 D4 95
East Bend, Yadkin, N.C., 446 A3 109
East Bengal, reg., Pak E12 40
East Berkshire, Franklin, Vt., 200 B3 120
East Berlin, Hartford, Conn., 950 C6 84
East Berlin, Worcester, Mass., 200 g9 97
East Berlin, Adams, Pa., 1,037 G8 114
East Bernard, Wharton, Tex., 900 E4 118
East Bernstadt, Laurel, Ky., 594 C5 94
East Bethel, Anoka, Minn., 1,408 *E5 99
East Bethel, Windsor, Vt., 100 D3 120
East Billerica, Middlesex, Mass., 900 f11 97
East Blackstone, Worcester, Mass., 2,000 B4 97
East Blue Hill, Hancock, Maine, 200 D4 96
East Bonne Terre, St. Francois, Mo., 150 D7 101
East Boothbay, Lincoln, Maine, 500 E3 96
Eastborough, Sedgwick, Kans., 1,001 B5 93
Eastbourne, Eng., 62,000 D8 12
East Brady, Clarion, Pa., 1,282 E2 114
East Braintree, Man., Can E4 71
East Braintree, Orange, Vt., 50 D3 120
East Branch, Delaware, N.Y., 350 D5 108
East Branch, res., N.Y D2 84
East Branch Clarion River, res., Pa C4 114
East Brewster, Barnstable, Mass., 600 C7 97
East Brewton, Escambia, Ala., 2,511 D2 78
East Bridgewater, Plymouth, Mass., 3,000 (6,139▲) B6 97
East Brimfield, res., Mass B3 97
Eastbrook, Hancock, Maine, 100 (167▲) D4 96
East Brookfield, Worcester, Mass., 1,300 (1,533▲) B3 97
East Brookfield, Orange, Vt., 40 C3 120
East Brooklyn, Windham, Conn., 1,213 B9 84
East Broughton Station, Que., Can., 1,136 C6 73
East Brownfield, Oxford, Maine, 200 E2 96
East Brunswick, Middlesex, N.J., 16,000 *C4 106
East Burke, Caledonia, Vt., 125 B5 120
East Butler, Butler, Pa., 1,007 E2 114
East Calais, Washington, Vt., 110 C4 120
East Canaan, Litchfield, Conn., 570 A3 84
East Candia, Rockingham, N.H., 200 D4 105
East Canon, Fremont, Colo., 1,101 C5 83
East Canterbury, Merrimack, N.H D3 105
East Canton, Stark, Ohio, 1,521 *B6 111
East Carondelet, St. Clair, Ill., 463 B8 101
East Carroll, par., La., 14,433 B4 95
East Carver, Plymouth, Mass., 250 C6 97
East Charleston, Orleans, Vt., 60 (668▲) B5 120
East Chelmsford, Middlesex, Mass., 1,000 f10 97
Eastchester, Westchester, N.Y., 13,000 *E7 108
East Chicago, Lake, Ind., 57,669 A3 91
East Chicago Heights, Cook, Ill., 4,295 *F3 90
East China, sea, China F9 34
East Chop, pt., Mass D6 97
East Cleveland, Cuyahoga, Ohio, 37,991 B2 111
East Clifton, Que., Can D6 73
East Coleman, Alta., Can., 567 *E3 69
East Columbia, Brazoria, Tex., 125 G4 118
East Columbus, Bartholomew, Ind., 1,912 F6 91
East Concord, Essex, Vt., 225 C5 120
East Conemaugh (Conemaugh), Cambria, Pa., 3,334 F4 114
East Conway, Carroll, N.H., 100 B4 105
East Corinth, Penobscot, Maine, 250 D3 96
East Corinth, Orange, Vt., 115 C4 120
East Cote Blanche, bay, La E4 95
East Coulée, Alta., Can., 683 D4 69
East Craftsbury, Orleans, Vt., 60 B4 120
East Dennis, Barnstable, Mass., 400 C7 97
East Dereham, Eng., 7,197 B8 12
East Derry, Rockingham, N.H., 200 E4 105
East Des Moines, riv., Iowa A3 92
East Detroit, Macomb, Mich., 45,756 A8 98
East Dixmont, Penobscot, Maine, 100 D3 96
East Dorset, Bennington, Vt., 285 E2 120
East Douglas, Worcester, Mass., 1,695 B4 97
East Dover, Piscataquis, Maine, 70 C3 96
East Dover, Windham, Vt., 55 F3 120
East Dublin, Laurens, Ga., 1,677 *D4 87
East Dubuque, Jo Daviess, Ill., 2,082 A3 90
East Dummerston, Windham, Vt., 150 F3 120
East Dundee, Kane, Ill., 2,221 *A5 90
East Eddington, Penobscot, Maine, 300 D4 96
East Ellijay, Gilmer, Ga., 501 B2 87
East Ely, White Pine, Nev., 1,796 D7 104
Eastend, Sask., Can., 767 H1 70
East End, Vir. Is f16 65
East Enterprise, Switzerland, Ind., 300 G8 91
Easter, isl., see Rapa Nui, isl., Pac. O.
Easter, mtn., Conn B3 84
Eastern, prov., Zambia D5 48
Eastern, reg., Ghana E4 45
Eastern, reg., Nig., 7,218,000 E6 45
Eastern, reg., Tan., 1,084,484 C6 48
Eastern, reg., Ug A5 48
Eastern, bay, Md C5 85
Eastern, isl., Newf., Can C4 75
Eastern, isl., Midway Is 52
Eastern, pt., Mass f13 97
Eastern Ghats, range, India E7 39
Eastern Neck, isl., Md B5 85
Eastern Plain, pt., N.Y E8 84
Eastern Valley, Jefferson, Ala., 1,000 *E4 78
East Fairfield, Franklin, Vt., 150 B3 120
East Fairview, McKenzie, N. Dak., 200 B1 110
East Falmouth, Barnstable, Mass., 1,700 C6 97
East Farmington Heights, Hartford, Conn., 1,600 *C6 84
East Farms, Spokane, Wash D8 122
East Faxon, Lycoming, Pa., 3,641 *D8 114
East Fayetteville, Cumberland, N.C., 2,797 *B5 109
East Feliciana, par., La., 20,198 D4 95
East Flanders, prov., Bel., 1,272,005 C3 15
East Flat Rock, Henderson, N.C., 1,700 D3 109
East Flevoland Polder, reg., Neth B5 15
East Florenceville, N.B., Can., 443 C2 74
Eastford, Windham, Conn., 500 (746▲) B8 84
East Foxboro, Norfolk, Mass., 700 B5 97
East Franklin, Franklin, Vt., 80 B3 120
East Freetown, Bristol, Mass., 300 C6 97
East Frisian, is., Ger A7 15
East Fultonham, Muskingum, Ohio, 500 C5 111
East Gaffney, Cherokee, S.C., 4,779 A4 115
East Galesburg, Knox, Ill., 660 C3 90
East Gary, Lake, Ind., 9,309 A3 91
East Gastonia, Gaston, N.C., 3,326 *B2 109
East Gate, Churchill, Nev., 10 D4 104
Eastgate, King, Wash., 3,000 *B3 122
East Georgia, Franklin, Vt., 40 B2 120
East Glacier Park, Glacier, Mont., 400 B3 102
East Glastonbury, Hartford, Conn., 300 C6 84
East Glenville, Schenectady, N.Y., 8,000 *C7 108
East Grafton, Grafton, N.H., 100 C3 105
East Granby, Hartford, Conn., 250 (2,434▲) B6 84
East Grand Forks, Polk, Minn., 6,998 C2 99
East Granville, Addison, Vt., 65 C3 120
East Greenbush, Rensselaer, N.Y., 1,325 *C7 108
East Greenville, Montgomery, Pa., 1,931 F10 114
East Greenwich, Kent, R.I., 6,100 C11 84
East Grinstead, Eng., 15,421 C7 12
East Haddam, Middlesex, Conn., 500 (3,637▲) D7 84
East Ham, Eng., 105,359 k13 10
Eastham, Barnstable, Mass., 350 (1,200▲) C8 97
East Hampden, Penobscot, Maine, 1,500 *D4 96
East Hampton, Middlesex, Conn., 3,200 (5,403▲) C6 84
Easthampton, Hampshire, Mass., 12,326 B2 97
East Hampton, Suffolk, N.Y., 1,772 n16 108
East Hardwick, Caledonia, Vt., 200 B4 120
East Harpswell, Cumberland, Maine, 50 E5 96
East Hartford, Hartford, Conn., 43,977 B6 84
East Hartland, Hartford, Conn., 350 B5 84
East Haven, New Haven, Conn., 21,388 D5 84
East Haven, Essex, Vt., 30 (164▲) B5 120
East Haverhill, Grafton, N.H., 75 B3 105
East Hazelcrest, Cook, Ill., 1,457 *F3 90
East Hebron, Oxford, Maine, D2 96
East Hebron, Grafton, N.H., 60 C3 105
East Helena, Lewis and Clark, Mont., 1,490 D5 102
East Herkimer, Herkimer, N.Y., 1,068 *B6 108
East Hickory, Forest, Pa., 200 C3 114
East Highgate, Franklin, Vt., 110 B3 120
East Hills, Nassau, N.Y., 7,184 *E3 108
East Holden, Penobscot, Maine, 200 D4 96
East Holderness, Grafton, N.H., 85 C3 105
East Islip, Suffolk, N.Y., 11,000 G4 84
East Jamestown, Fentress, Tenn C9 117
East Java, see Java, isl., Indon.
East Jordan, N.S., Can., 97 F4 74
East Jordan, Charlevoix, Mich., 1,919 C5 98
East Juliette, Jones, Ga., 201 C3 87
East Keansburg, Monmouth, N.J., 3,500 *C4 106
East Kelowna, B.C., Can., 403 E8 68
East Kent, Litchfield, Conn C3 84
East Kildonan, Man., Can., 27,305 E3 71
East Killingly, Windham, Conn., 700 B9 84
East Kingsford, Dickinson, Mich., 1,063 *C2 98
East Kingston, Rockingham, N.H., 300 (574▲) E4 105
East Knox, Waldo, Maine D3 96
Eastlake, Manistee, Mich., 436 D4 98
East Lake, Dare, N.C., 90 B8 109
Eastlake, Lake, Ohio, 12,467 A6 111
Eastland, Eastland, Tex., 3,292 C3 118
Eastland, co., Tex., 19,526 C3 118
East Lansdowne, Delaware, Pa., 3,224 *G11 114
East Lansing, Ingham, Mich., 30,198 F6 98
East Laport, Jackson, N.C., 50 D3 109
East Laurinburg, Scotland, N.C., 695 C4 109
Eastlawn, Washtenaw, Mich., 2,500 *F7 98
East Layton, Davis, Utah, 444 *B4 119
East Lebanon, York, Maine, 40 E2 96
East Lee, Berkshire, Mass., 200 B1 97
Eastleigh, Eng., 36,577 D6 12
East Lempster, Sullivan, N.H., 150 D2 105
East Liberty, Logan, Ohio, 385 B4 111
East Litchfield, Litchfield, Conn., 150 B4 84
East Livermore, Androscoggin, Maine, 150 D2 96
East Liverpool, Columbiana, Ohio, 22,306 B7 111
East London, S. Afr., 113,746 (*115,677) D4 49
East Longmeadow, Hampden, Mass., 10,294 B2 97
East Los Angeles, Los Angeles, Calif., 98,000 *E4 82
East Lothian, co., Scot., 52,653 E6 13
East Lowell, Penobscot, Maine C4 96
East Lumberton, Robeson, N.C. (part of Lumberton) C5 109
East Lyme, New London, Conn., 700 (6,782▲) *D7 84
East Lynn, Wayne, W. Va., 250 C2 123
East Lynne, Cass, Mo., 243 C3 101
East Machias, Washington, Maine, 700 (1,198▲) D5 96
East McKeesport, Allegheny, Pa., 3,470 F2 114
East Madison, Somerset, Maine, 250 D3 96
Eastmain, riv., Que., Can F18 67
Eastman, Que., Can., 637 D5 73
Eastman, Dodge, Ga., 5,118 D3 87
Eastman, Crawford, Wis., 348 E2 124
East Mansfield, Bristol, Mass., 225 B5 97
East Marion, Plymouth, Mass., 400 *C6 97
East Marion, Suffolk, N.Y., 450 E7 84
East Marion, McDowell, N.C., 2,442 *D2 109
East Matunuck, Washington, R.I., 270 D10 84
East Meadow, Nassau, N.Y., 47,500 n15 108
East Meredith, Delaware, N.Y., 130 C6 108
East Middlebury, Addison, Vt., 500 D2 120
East Milford, Hillsboro, N.H. (part of Milford) E3 105
East Millbury, Worcester, Mass., 1,500 B4 97
East Millcreek, Salt Lake, Utah, 23,000 C4 119
East Millinocket, Penobscot, Maine, 2,392 C4 96
East Millstone, Somerset, N.J., 800 *B3 106
East Missoula, Missoula, Mont., 450 *D2 102
East Mobridge, Walworth, S. Dak. (part of Mobridge) B5 116
East Moline, Rock Island, Ill., 16,732 B3 90
East Monroe, Highland, Ohio, 100 C4 111
East Montpelier, Washington, Vt., 100 (1,200▲) C4 120
East Moriches, Suffolk, N.Y., 1,500 F5 84
East Morris, Litchfield, Conn C4 84
East Naples, Collier, Fla., 1,500 F5 86
East Newark, Hudson, N.J., 1,872 k8 106
East New Market, Dorchester, Md., 225 C6 85
East Newnan, Coweta, Ga., 500 C2 87
East Nishnabotna, riv., Iowa C2 92
East Northfield, Franklin, Mass., 500 A3 97
East Northport, Suffolk, N.Y., 17,500 F3 84
East Norwalk, Fairfield, Conn. (part of Norwalk) E3 84
East Norwich, Nassau, N.Y., 3,200 *F2 84
East Olympia, Thurston, Wash., 500 C3 122
East Omaha, Douglas, Nebr., 684 *D3 103
Easton, Fresno, Calif., 2,500 *D4 82
Easton, Fairfield, Conn., 400 (3,407▲) D3 84
Easton, Mason, Ill., 361 C4 90
Easton, Leavenworth, Kans., 320 B8 93
Easton, Aroostook, Maine, 550 (1,389▲) B5 96
Easton, Talbot, Md., 6,337 C5 85
Easton, Bristol, Mass., 250 (9,078▲) B5 97
Easton, Faribault, Minn., 411 G5 99
Easton, Buchanan, Mo., 198 B3 101
Easton, Grafton, N.H., 50 (740▲) B3 105
Easton, Northampton, Pa., 31,955 E11 114
Easton, Kittitas, Wash., 250 B4 122
Easton, lake, Conn E3 84
Eastondale, Bristol, Mass., 600 B5 97
East Orange, Essex, N.J., 77,259 B4, h8 106
East Orange, Orange, Vt., 60 C4 120
East Orland, Hancock, Maine, 140 D4 96
East Orleans, Barnstable, Mass., 700 C8 97
East Orrington, Penobscot, Maine, 600 D4 96
East Otis, Berkshire, Mass., 100 B1 97
East Otto, Cattaraugus, N.Y., 135 C2 108
Eastover, Richland, S.C., 713 D6 115
East Pakistan, prov., Pak., 50,835,721 *D9 39
East Palatka, Putnam, Fla., 1,133 C5 86
East Palestine, Columbiana, Ohio, 5,232 B7 111
East Palo Alto, San Mateo, Calif., 12,000 *B5 82
East Parsonfield, York, Maine, 100 E2 96
East Patchogue, Suffolk, N.Y., 8,800 G5 84
East Paterson, Bergen, N.J., 19,344 h8 106
East Peacham, Caledonia, Vt., 30 C4 120
East Pea Ridge, Cabell, W. Va., 1,500 *C2 123
East Peoria, Tazewell, Ill., 12,310 C4 90
East Pepperell, Middlesex, Mass., 2,000 A4 97
East Peru, Oxford, Maine, 75 D2 96
East Petersburg, Lancaster, Pa., 2,053 F9 114
East Pine, B.C., Can., 98 B7 68
East Pines, Prince Georges, Md., 1,800 *C4 85
East Pittsburgh, Allegheny, Pa., 4,122 F2 114
Eastpoint, Franklin, Fla., 700 C2 86
East Point, Fulton, Ga., 35,633 B5, C2 87
East Point, Red River, La., 100 B2 95
East Poland, Androscoggin, Maine, 100 D2 96
East Poplar, Sask., Can H3 70
Eastport, Newf., Can., 438 D5 75
Eastport, Boundary, Idaho, 100 A2 89
Eastport, Washington, Maine, 2,537 D6 96
Eastport, Suffolk, N.Y., 1,200 n16 108
East Portal, Gilpin, Colo., 30 B5 83
East Porterville, Tulare, Calif., 2,000 *D4 82
East Poultney, Rutland, Vt., 400 D2 120
East Prairie, Mississippi, Mo., 3,449 E8 101
East Princeton, Worcester, Mass., 150 B4 97
East Prospect, York, Pa., 623 G8 114
East Providence, Providence, R.I., 41,955 B11 84
East Pryor, mtn., Mont E8 102
East Punjab, state, India, 16,000,000 B6 40
East Putney, Windham, Vt., 50 F4 120
East Quincy, Plumas, Calif., 1,020 *C3 82
East Quogue, Suffolk, N.Y., 800 F6 84
East Rainelle, Greenbrier, W. Va., 1,244 D4 123
East Randolph, Cattaraugus, N.Y., 594 C2 108
East Randolph, Orange, Vt., 150 D3 120
East Retford, Eng., 17,788 A7 12
East Richmond, Contra Costa, Calif., 4,000 *B5 82
East Ridge, Hamilton, Tenn., 19,570 E10 117
East Riding, Yorkshire, see York, co., Eng.
East Rindge, Cheshire, N.H., 225 E3 105
East River, New Haven, Conn., 200 D6 84
East River, mtn., Va D1 121
East River Sheet Harbour, N.S., Can., 104 E7 74
East Rochester, Strafford, N.H. (part of Rochester) D5 105
East Rochester, Monroe, N.Y., 8,347 B3 108
East Rockaway, Nassau, N.Y., 10,721 G2 84
East Rockingham, Richmond, N.C., 3,211 C4 109
East Rockwood, Wayne, Mich., 1,000 *F7 98
East Rutherford, Bergen, N.J., 7,769 h8 106
East Ryegate, Caledonia, Vt., 250 C4 120
East St. John, N.B., Can., 4,466 D4 74
East St. Johnsbury, Caledonia, Vt., 150 C5 120
East St. Louis, St. Clair, Ill., 81,712 E3 90
East Salt, creek, Colo B2 83
East Sandwich, Barnstable, Mass., 250 C7 97
East Sebago, Cumberland, Maine, 75 E2 96
East Selkirk, Man., Can., 401 D3 71
East Setauket, Suffolk, N.Y., 1,300 F4 84
East Siberian, sea, Sov. Un B18 28
Eastside, Jackson, Miss., 4,318 E3 100
Eastside, Coos, Oreg., 1,380 D2 113
Eastside Galesburg, Knox, Ill., 1,147 *C3 90
East Sioux Falls, Minnehaha, S. Dak., 45 D9 116
East Smithfield, Bradford, Pa., 350 C8 114
East Somerset, Pulaski, Ky., 3,645 C5 94
Eastsound, San Juan, Wash., 150 A3 122
East Sparta, Stark, Ohio, 961 B6 111
East Spencer, Rowan, N.C., 2,171 B3 109
East Spokane, Spokane, Wash., 6,000 B8, D7 122
East Springfield, Otsego, N.Y., 80 C6 108
East Springfield, Erie, Pa., 511 C1 114
East Stanwood, Snohomish, Wash. (part of Stanwood) A3 122
East Stoneham, Oxford, Maine, 160 D2 96
East Stroudsburg, Monroe, Pa., 7,674 D11 114
East Sudbury, Middlesex, Mass., 900 g10 97
East Sullivan, Hancock, Maine, 250 D4 96
East Sullivan, Cheshire, N.H., 75 E2 105
East Sumner, Oxford, Maine, 100 D2 96
East Swamp, creek, Pa C2 106
East Swanzey, Cheshire, N.H., 250 E2 105
East Syracuse, Onondaga, N.Y., 4,708 B4 108
East Tawas, Iosco, Mich., 2,462 D7 98
East Templeton, Worcester, Mass., 1,000 A3 97
East Thermopolis, Hot Springs, Wyo., 281 B4 125
East Thetford, Orange, Vt., 135 D4 120
East Thomaston, Upson, Ga., 2,237 D2 87
East Tirol, reg., Aus C8 18
East Tohopekaliga, lake, Fla D5 86
East Towanda, Bradford, Pa., 200 C9 114
East Trout, lake, Sask., Can C3 70
East Troy, Walworth, Wis., 1,455 F5 114
East Tulare, Tulare, Calif., 1,342 *D4 82
East Uniontown, Fayette, Pa., 2,424 *G2 114
East Vandergrift, Westmoreland, Pa., 1,388 *E2 114
Eastview, Ont., Can., 24,555 h12 72
Eastville, Northampton, Va., 261 D7 121
East Wakefield, Carroll, N.H., 50 C4 105
East Walker, riv., Nev E2 104
East Wallingford, Rutland, Vt., 200 E3 120
East Walpole, Norfolk, Mass., 3,000 h11 97
East Wareham, Plymouth, Mass., 900 C6 97
East Washington, Sullivan, N.H., 100 D2 105
East Washington, Washington, Pa., 2,483 F1 114
East Waterboro, York, Maine, 180 E2 96
East Waterford, Oxford, Maine, 75 D2 96
East Waterford, Juniata, Pa., 200 F6 114
East Wellington, B.C., Can f11 68
East Wenatchee, Douglas, Wash., 383 B5 122
East Wenatchee Beach, Douglas, Wash., 2,327 *B5 122
East Weymouth, Norfolk, Mass. (part of Weymouth) h12 97
East Whittier, Los Angeles, Calif., 19,884 *F4 82
East Willington, Tolland, Conn., 40 B7 84
East Williston, Nassau, N.Y., 2,940 G2 84
East Wilmington, New Hanover, N.C., 5,520 *C6 109
East Wilton, Franklin, Maine, 250 D2 96
East Windsor (Town of), Hartford, Conn. (7,500▲) *B6 84
East Windsor Hill, Hartford, Conn., 500 B6 84
East Wolfeboro, Carroll, N.H., 340 C4 105
Eastwood, Jefferson, Ky., 250 A4 94
Eastwood, Kalamazoo, Mich., 6,000 *E5 98
East Woodstock, Windham, Conn., 350 B9 84
East Worcester, Otsego, N.Y., 325 C6 108
East York, York, Pa., 1,800 *G8 114
Eaton, Weld, Colo., 1,267 A6 83
Eaton, Crawford, Ill., 100 D6 90
Eaton, Delaware, Ind., 1,529 D7 91
Eaton, Washington, Maine, 75 C5 96
Eaton, Madison, N.Y., 350 C5 108
Eaton, Preble, Ohio, 5,034 C3 111
Eaton, Gibson, Tenn., 125 B2 117
Eaton, co., Mich., 49,684 F6 98
Eaton Center, Carroll, N.H., 75 (151▲) C4 105
Eatonia, Sask., Can., 609 F1 70
Eaton Rapids, Eaton, Mich., 4,052 F6 98
Eatons, neck, N.Y F3 84
Eatons Neck, pt., N.Y F3 84
Eatonton, Putnam, Ga., 3,612 C3 87
Eatontown, Monmouth, N.J., 10,334 C4 106
Eatonville, Pierce, Wash., 896 C3 122
Eau Claire, Berrien, Mich., 562 G4 98
Eau Claire, Chippewa and Eau Claire, Wis., 37,987 D2 124
Eau Claire, co., Wis., 58,300 D2 124
Eau Claire, riv., Wis D3 124
Eau Galle, Dunn, Wis., 235 D2 124
Eau Gallie, Brevard, Fla., 12,300 D6 86
Eau Pleine, riv., Wis D3 124
Eauze, Fr., 1,823 F4 14
Ebadon, isl., Kwajalein
Ebb, Madison, Fla., 40 B3 86
Ebb and Flow, lake, Man., Can D2 71
Ebbw Vale, Wales, 28,631 C4 12
Ebeleben, Ger., 2,535 B5 17
Ebeltoft, Den., 2,227 B4 24
Ebenezer, Sask., Can., 137 F4 70
Ebenezer, Holmes, Miss., 75 C3 100
Ebenezer, Knox, Tenn E11 117
Eben Junction, Alger, Mich., 75 B4 98
Ebensburg, Cambria, Pa., 4,111 F4 114
Ebermannstadt, Ger., 2,600 D6 17
Ebersbach, Ger., 11,100 B9 17
Ebersbach, Ger., 9,200 E4 17
Eberswalde, Ger., 32,100 B6 16
Ebingen, Ger., 21,100 D4 16
Eboli, It., 20,500 (25,634▲) D5 21
Ebolowa, Cam., 1,200 E2 46
Ebony, Crittenden, Ark E8 81
Ebro, Washington, Fla., 125 G3 86
Ebro, Clearwater, Minn., 75 C3 99
Ebro, riv., Sp B6 20
Eccles, Raleigh, W. Va., 1,145 D3, D6 123
Eceabat, (Maydos), Tur., 2,800 B6 23
Echague, Phil., 2,568 n13 35
Echallens, Switz., 1,428 C2 19
Echeconnee, creek, Ga D3 87
Echigawa, Jap., 3,400 n15 37
Echo, Dale, Ala., 100 D4 78
Echo, Rapides, La., 350 C3 95
Echo, Yellow Medicine, Minn., 459 F3 99
Echo, Umatilla, Oreg., 456 B7 113
Echo, Summit, Utah, 85 C4 119
Echo, lake, Ont., Can G4 71
Echo, lake, Maine D2 96
Echo, pond, Vt B5 120
Echo, riv., Ont., Can B7 98
Echoing, lake, Ont., Can B5 71
Echoing, riv., Man., Ont., Can B6 71
Echola, Tuscaloosa, Ala., 100 B2 78
Echols, co., Ga., 1,876 F4 87
Echt, Neth., 4,700 C5 15
Echt, Scot., 1,027 C6 13
Echternach, Lux., 3,389 E6 15
Echuca, Austl., 6,443 H5 51
Écija, Sp., 29,262 (49,762▲) D3 20
Eckelson, Barnes, N. Dak., 90 C7 110
Eckerman, Chippewa, Mich., 200 B5 98
Eckernförde, Ger., 19,500 A4 16
Eckernförder Bucht, bay, Ger D4 24
Eckert (Orchard City), Delta, Colo., 1,021 C3 83
Eckerty, Crawford, Ind., 150 H4 91
Eckhart, Allegany, Md., 900 D3 85
Eckley, Yuma, Colo., 207 A8 83
Eckley, Luzerne, Pa., 340 E10 114
Eckman, Bottineau, N. Dak., 5 A4 110
Eckman, McDowell, W. Va., 1,125 *D3 123
Eckville, Alta., Can., 580 C3 69

Eclectic, Elmore, Ala., 926 . . . C3 78
Eclipse, Nansemond, Va., 290 . . . B6, E6 121
Eclipse, sound, N.W. Ter. Can. . . . B17 67
E. C. Manning, prov. park, B.C., Can. . . . E7 68
Econfina, Bay, Fla., 130 . . . G3 86
Econfina, riv., Fla. . . . B3 86
Economy, N.S., Can., 142 . . . D6 74
Economy, Wayne, Ind., 280 . . . E7 91
Economy, Beaver, Pa., 5,925 . . . *E1 114
Ecorces, riv., Que., Can. . . . A6 73
Ecorse, Wayne, Mich., 17,328 . . . A7 98
Ecru, Pontotoc, Miss., 442 . . . A4 100
Ector, co., Tex., 90,995 . . . D1 118
Ecuador, country, S.A., 4,950,000 . . . D3 53, 58
Ecum Secum, N.S., Can., 243 . . . E7 74
Ecum Secum Bridge, N.S., Can., 222 . . . E7 74
Eda, Swe., 6,344 . . . H5 25
Edam, Sask., Can., 277 . . . D1 70
Edam, Neth. . . . B5 15
Eday, isl., Scot. . . . A6 13
Edberg, Alta., Can., 179 . . . C4 69
Edcouch, Hidalgo, Tex., 2,814 . . . F4 118
Edd, Eth. . . . C5 47
Ed Da'ein, Sud. . . . C2 47
Ed Damer, Sud., 5,458 . . . B3 47
Ed Debba (Well), Sud. . . . B3 47
Eddiceton, Franklin, Miss., 300 . . . D3 100
Eddington, Penobscot, Maine, 130 (958▲) . . . D4 96
Eddington, Bucks, Pa. (part of Cornwells Heights) . . . A12 114
Ed Dueim, Sud., 12,319 . . . C3 47
Eddy, Sanders, Mont. . . . C1 102
Eddy, co., N. Mex., 50,783 . . . E5 107
Eddy, co., N. Dak., 4,936 . . . B7 110
Eddy, mtn., Calif. . . . B2 82
Eddystone, Delaware, Pa., 3,006 . . . B10 114
Eddystone Rocks, reef, English Chan. . . . E4 10
Eddyville, Pope, Ill., 125 . . . F5 90
Eddyville, Wapello and Mahaska, Iowa, 1,014 . . . C5 92
Eddyville, Lyon, Ky., 1,858 . . . A3 94
Eddyville, Dawson, Nebr., 119 . . . C6 103
Ed Dzong, China, 1,000 . . . A13 40
Ede, Neth., 31,800 (63,500▲) . B5 15
Ede, Nig., 44,808 . . . *E5 45
Edea, Cam. . . . E2 46
Eden, Graham, Ariz., 65 . . . E6 80
Eden, Austl., 1,246 . . . H7 51
Eden, Man., Can., 146 . . . D2 71
Eden, Effingham, Ga., 400 . . . D5 87
Eden, Jerome, Idaho, 426 . . . G4 89
Eden, Hancock, Maine, 140 . . . D4 96
Eden, Somerset, Md., 105 . . . D6 85
Eden, Yazoo, Miss., 218 . . . C3 100
Eden, Cascade, Mont. . . . C5 102
Eden, Erie, N.Y., 2,400 . . . C2 108
Eden, Marshall, S. Dak., 136 . . . B8 116
Eden, Concho, Tex., 1,486 . . . D3 118
Eden, Weber, Utah, 100 . . . B4 119
Eden, Lamoille, Vt., 100 (430▲) . . . B3 120
Eden, Fond du Lac, Wis., 312 . . . E5 124
Eden, Sweetwater, Wyo., 220 . . . C3 125
Eden, hill, Conn. . . . D3 84
Eden, lake, Man., Can. . . . A1 71
Eden, riv., Eng. . . . C5 10
Eden, riv., Scot. . . . D5 13
Edenberry, Ire., 2,996 . . . D4 13
Edenborn, Fayette, Pa., 800 . . . G2 114
Eden Mills, Lamoille, Vt., 60 . . . B3 120
Edenton, Chowan, N.C., 4,458 . . . A7 109
Eden Valley, Meeker and Stearns, Minn., 793 . . . E4 99
Edenwold, Sask., Can., 165 . . . G3 70
Edenwold, Davidson, Tenn., 500 . . . A5, E9 117
Eder, riv., Ger. . . . B4 17
Edesville, Kent, Md., 210 . . . B5 85
Edgar, Carbon, Mont., 130 . . . E8 102
Edgar, Clay, Nebr., 730 . . . D8 103
Edgar, Marathon, Wis., 803 . . . D4 120
Edgar, co., Ill., 22,550 . . . D6 90
Edgard, St. John the Baptist, La., 750 . . . B6, D5 95
Edgar Springs, Phelps, Mo., 150 . . . D6 101
Edgartown, Dukes, Mass., 1,200 (1,474▲) . . . D6 97
Edge, isl., Nor. . . . B12 4
Edgecombe, co., N.C., 54,226 . . . B6 109
Edgecumbe, cape, Alsk. . . . m22 79
Edgefield, Edgefield, S.C., 2,876 . . . D4 115
Edgefield, co., S.C., 15,735 . . D4 115
Edgeley, Sask., Can., 67 . . . G4 70
Edgeley, La Moure, N. Dak., 992 . . . C7 110
Edgely, Bucks, Pa., 950 . . . *F12 114
Edgemere, Bonner, Idaho, 10 . . . A2 89
Edgemere, Baltimore, Md., 2,200 . . . *B5 85
Edgemont, Cleburne, Ark., 40 . . . B3 81
Edgemont, Riverside, Calif., 1,628 . . . *F5 82
Edgemont, Jefferson, Colo., 1,500 . . . *B5 83
Edgemont, Fall River, S. Dak., 1,772 . . . D2 116
Edgemont, Utah, Utah, 900 . . C4 119
Edgemont, chan., Fla. . . . F1 86
Edgemont, key, Fla. . . . F1 86
Edgemoor, Montgomery, Md. (part of Bethesda) . . . C1 85
Edgemoor, Chester, S.C., 275 . . . B5 115
Edgemoor, Anderson, Tenn., 50 . . . E11 117
Edgerly, Calcasieu, La., 350 . . . D2 95
Edgerton, Alta., Can., 295 . . . C5 69
Edgerton, Johnson, Kans., 414 . . . D8 93
Edgerton, Pipestone, Minn., 1,019 . . . G2 99
Edgerton, Platte, Mo., 449 . . B3 101
Edgerton, Williams, Ohio, 1,566 . . . A3 111
Edgerton, Rock, Wis., 4,000 . . F4 124
Edgerton, Natrona, Wyo., 512 . . . B6 125
Edgewater, Jefferson, Ala., 1,200 . . . E7 78
Edgewater, Jefferson, Colo., 4,314 . . . B5 83
Edgewater, Volusia, Fla., 2,051 . . . D6 86
Edgewater, Anne Arundel, Md., 3,000 . . . C4 85
Edgewater, Bergen, N.J., 4,113 . . . h9 106
Edgewater Gulf Beach, Bay, Fla., 70 . . . *G3 86
Edgewater Park, Harrison, Miss., 750 . . . E2 100
Edgewater Park, Burlington, N.J., 2,866 . . . C3 106
Edgewood, B.C., Can., 325 . . E8 68
Edgewood, Effingham, Ill., 515 . . . E5 90
Edgewood, Madison, Ind., 2,119 . . . *D6 91
Edgewood, Clayton and Delaware, Iowa, 767 . . . B6 92
Edgewood, Kenton, Ky., 1,100 . . . A7 94
Edgewood, Harford, Md., 2,240 . . . B5 85
Edgewood, Santa Fe, N. Mex., 40 . . . B3, k8 107
Edgewood, Allegheny, Pa., 5,124 . . . F2 114
Edgewood, Northumberland, Pa., 3,399 . . . *E8 114
Edgewood, Pierce, Wash., 100 . . . D2 122
Edgeworth, Allegheny, Pa., 2,030 . . . A5 114
Edgigen, isl., Kwajalein . . . 52
Edgin, Briscoe, Tex. . . . B2 118
Edgmoor, Chester, S.C. . . . B5 115
Edgware, Eng. (part of Hendon) . . . k11 10
Edhessa, Grc., 15,534 . . . B4 23
Edina, Hennepin, Minn., 28,501 . . . E6 99
Edina, Knox, Mo., 1,457 . . . A5 101
Edinboro, Erie, Pa., 1,703 . . C1 114
Edinburg, Christian, Ill., 1,003 . . . D4 90
Edinburg, Johnson, Ind., 3,664 . . . F6 91
Edinburg, Leake, Miss., 200 . . . C4 100
Edinburg, Mercer, N.J., 100 . . . *C3 106
Edinburg, Saratoga, N.Y., 200 . . . B6 108
Edinburg, Walsh, N. Dak., 330 . . . A8 110
Edinburg, Hidalgo, Tex., 18,706 . . . F3 118
Edinburg, Shenandoah, Va., 517 . . . C4 121
Edinburgh, Scot., 476,200 (*615,000) . . . E5 13
Edirne, Tur., 39,410 . . . B6 23
Edison, Calhoun, Ga., 1,232 . E2 87
Edison, Furnas, Nebr., 249 . . D6 103
Edison, Middlesex, N.J., 9,500 (44,799▲) . . . B4 106
Edison, Morrow, Ohio, 559 . . B5 111
Edison, Skagit, Wash., 150 . . A3 122
Edisto, isl., S.C. . . . F7 115
Edisto, riv., S.C. . . . E6 115
Edisto Island, Charleston, S.C., 240 . . . F7, G1 115
Edith, Woods, Okla. . . . A2 112
Edith, mtn., Mont. . . . D5 102
Edithburgh, Austl., 477 . . . G1 51
Edith Ronne Land, reg., Ant. . . . A5 5
Edmeston, Otsego, N.Y., 800 . C5 108
Edmond, Norton, Kans., 91 . . C4 93
Edmond, Oklahoma, Okla., 8,577 . . . B4 112
Edmonds, Snohomish, Wash., 8,016 . . . B3 122
Edmondson, Crittenden, Ark., 288 . . . B5 81
Edmonson, co., Ky., 8,085 . . . C3 94
Edmonston, Prince Georges, Md., 1,197 . . . *C1 85
Edmonton, Alta., Can., 281,027 (*337,568) . . C4, g8 69
Edmonton, Eng., 92,062 . . . k12 10
Edmonton, Metcalfe, Ky., 749 . . . C4 94
Edmore, Montcalm, Mich., 1,234 . . . E5 98
Edmore, Ramsey, N. Dak., 405 . . . A7 110
Edmund, lake, Man., Can. . . . B5 71
Edmunds, Washington, Maine, 35 . . . D5 96
Edmunds, Stutsman, N. Dak., 50 . . . B7 110
Edmunds, co., S. Dak., 6,079 . B6 116
Edmundson, St. Louis, Mo., 1,428 . . . *C7 101
Edmundston, N.B., Can., 12,791 . . . B1 74
Edna, Labette, Kans., 442 . . . E8 93
Edna, Jackson, Tex., 5,038 . . . E4 118
Edna, Monongalia, W. Va., 150 . . . A7 123
Edon, Williams, Ohio, 757 . . . A3 111
Edouard, lake, Que., Can. . . . B5 73
Edremit, Tur., 22,200 . . . C6 23
Edremit, gulf, Tur. . . . C6 23
Edsel Ford, ranges, Ant. . . . B34 5
Edson, Alta., Can., 3,198 . . . C2, g7 69
Edson, Sherman, Kans., 64 . . C2 93
Eduardo Castex, Arg., 4,020 . B4 54
Eduni, mtn., N.W. Ter., Can. . . D7 66
Edwall, Lincoln, Wash., 165 . . B8 122
Edwand, Alta., Can. . . . B4 69
Edward, lake, Con. L. . . . B4 48
Edward VII, pen., Ant. . . . B33 5
Edward VIII, bay, Ant. . . . C18 5
Edwards, Ont., Can., 61 . . . h13 72
Edwards, Eagle, Colo., 10 . . . B4 83
Edwards, Peoria, Ill., 175 . . . C4 90
Edwards, Hinds, Miss., 1,206 . C3 100
Edwards, St. Lawrence, N.Y., 658 . . . A5, f9 108
Edwards, co., Ill., 7,940 . . . E5 90
Edwards, co., Kans., 5,118 . . . E4 93
Edwards, co., Tex., 2,317 . . . E2 118
Edwards, butte, Oreg. . . . B3 113
Edwards, plat., Tex. . . . D2 118
Edwardsburg, Cass, Mich., 902 . . . G4 98
Edwardsport, Knox, Ind., 533 . . . G3 91
Edwardsville, Cleburne, Ala., 168 . . . B4 78
Edwardsville, Madison, Ill., 9,996 . . . E4 90
Edwardsville, Wyandotte, Kans., 513 . . . B8 93
Edwardsville, Luzerne, Pa., 5,711 . . . B8 114
Edwight, Raleigh, W. Va., 70 . . . D6 123
Edwin, Henry, Ala., 100 . . . D4 78
Edzell, Scot., 946 . . . D6 13
Eek, Alsk., 200 . . . C7 79
Eekloo, Bel., 18,510 . . . C3 15
Eel, riv., Calif. . . . B2 82
Eel, riv., Ind. . . . C5 91
Eel, riv., Ind. . . . F3 91
Eferding, Aus., 3,151 . . . D7 16
Effie, Avoyelles, La., 100 . . . C3 95
Effie, Itasca, Minn., 195 . . . C5 99
Effingham, Effingham, Ill., 8,172 . . . D5 90
Effingham, Atchison, Kans., 564 . . . C8, A7 93
Effingham, Carroll, N.H., 40 (329▲) . . . C4 105
Effingham, Florence, S.C., 100 . . . C8 115
Effingham, co., Ga., 10,144 . D5 87
Effingham, co., Ill., 23,107 . . D5 90
Efland, Orange, N.C., 500 . . . A4 109
Eforie, Rom., 428 . . . C9 22
Ega, riv., Sp. . . . A4 20
Egadi, is., It. . . . F4 21
Egan, Fulton, Ga. (part of East Point) . . . B5 87
Egan, Moody, S. Dak., 310 . . D9 116
Egan, range, Nev. . . . E7 104
Eganville, Ont., Can., 1,549 . B7 72
Egbert, Laramie, Wyo. . . . D9 125
Egegik, Alsk., 150 . . . D8 79
Egeland, Towner, N. Dak., 190 . . . A6 110
Egeln, Ger., 7,650 . . . B6 17
Eger, Hung., 35,375 . . . B5 22
Egersund, Nor., 3,900 . . . H2 25
Egerton, mtn., Ant. . . . A28 5
Egg, lake, Sask., Can. . . . B3 70
Eggbornsville, Culpeper, Va. C4 121
Eggebek, Ger., 1,850 . . . D3 24
Eggenfelden, Ger., 5,800 . . . E7 17
Egg Harbor, Door, Wis., 150 . . . C6 124
Egg Harbor City, Atlantic, N.J., 4,416 . . . D3 106
Egg Island, pt., N.J. . . . E2 106
Egilsstadir, Ice., 83 . . . n25 25
Égletons, Fr., 3,201 . . . E4 14
Eglinton, isl., N.W. Ter., Can. . . . m28 67
Eglisau, Switz., 1,911 . . . A6 19
Egmond aan Zee, Neth., 4,200 . . . B4 15
Egmont, bay, P.E.I., Can. . . . C5 74
Egmont, cape, N.Z. . . . M14 51
Egmont, mtn., N.Z. . . . M15 51
Egnar, San Miguel, Colo., 15 . . . D2 83
Egremont, Alta., Can., 119 . . . B4 69
Egremont, Eng., 6,213 . . . F5 13
Egremont (Town of), Berkshire, Mass. (895▲) . . . *B1 97
Egridir, Tur., 7,100 . . . D8 31
Egridir, lake, Tur. . . . C8 31
Egtved, Den., 1,012 . . . C3 24
Egypt, Craighead, Ark., 225 . . B5 81
Egypt, Effingham, Ga., 100 . . D5 87
Egypt, Plymouth, Mass., 1,300 . . . B6, h12 97
Egypt, Chickasaw, Miss., 110 . . . B5 100
Egypt, Lehigh, Pa., 1,500 . . . E10 114
Egypt, see United Arab Republic, country, Afr.
Ehime, pref., Jap., 1,500,687 . . . *J6 37
Ehrenberg, Yuma, Ariz., 250 . . . D1 80
Ehrenburg, Ger., 160 . . . F2 24
Ehrenfeld, Cambria, Pa., 566 . . . F4 114
Ehrhardt, Bamberg, S.C., 482 . . . E5 115
Éibar, Sp., 31,725 . . . A4 20
Eibau, Ger., 5,394 . . . C9 17
Eibenstock, Ger., 8,250 . . . C7 17
Eichstätt, Ger., 10,600 . . . E6 17
Eider, riv., Ger. . . . A4 16
Eidsberg, Nor., 233 . . . H4, p29 25
Eidson, Hawkins, Tenn., 30 . . . C10 117
Eidsvold, Austl., 487 . . . B8 51
Eidsvoll, Nor. . . . G4 25
Eifel, mts., Ger. . . . C1 17
Eigg, isl., Scot. . . . D2 13
Eightmile, Morrow, Oreg. . . . B7 113
Eights, coast, Ant. . . . B3 5
Eighty Eight, Barren, Ky., 150 . . . D4 94
Eighty Mile, beach, Austl. . . . C3 50
Eikeren, lake, Nor. . . . p27 25
Eil, Som., 2,000 . . . D6 47
Eil, lake, Scot. . . . D3 13
Eildon, res., Austl. . . . H6 51
Eileen, lake, N.W. Ter., Can. . . D11 66
Eilenburg, Ger., 19,400 . . . B7 17
Eiler Rasmussen, cape, Grnld. . A16 4
Eil Malk, isl., Palau Is. . . . 52
Einbeck, Ger., 18,600 . . . B4 17
Eindhoven, Neth., 175,400 (*260,000) . . . C5 15
Ein Gev, Isr., 494 . . . B7 32
Ein Harod, Isr., 1,478 . . . B7 32
Ein Kerem, Isr. (part of Jerusalem) . . . h11 32
Ein Netafim, Isr. . . . E6 32
Ein Scilleme, mtn., Libya . . . E4 43
Einsiedeln, Switz., 8,792 . . . B6 19
Eirunepé, Braz., 3,023 . . . C4 58
Eisenach, Ger., 47,600 . . . C5 17
Eisenberg, Ger., 13,800 . . . C6 17
Eisenhüttenstadt, Ger., 34,600 . . . A9 17
Eisfeld, Ger., 5,586 . . . C5 17
Eisleben, Ger., 34,500 . . . B6 17
Eita, isl., Tarawa . . . 52
Eitorf, Ger., 12,800 . . . C2 17
Eitzen, Houston, Minn., 181 . G7 99
Ejby, Den., 1,309 . . . C3 24
Ejeade los Caballeros, Sp., 8,438 . . . A5 20
Ejeda, Malag. . . . h8 49
Ejstrup, Den., 913 . . . C3 24
Ejutla de Crespo, Mex., 4,288 . . . D5 63
Ekalaka, Carter, Mont., 738 . . . E12 102
Ekenäs, Fin., 5,500 . . . G10 25
Ekeren, Bel., 21,452 . . . C4 15
Ekhinos, Grc., 4,005 . . . B5 23
Ekimchan, Sov. Un., 700 . . . D16 28
Eklutna, Alsk., 50 . . . C10, g17 79
Ekoln, lake, Swe. . . . t35 25
Ekron, Meade, Ky., 205 . . . C3 94
Eksjö, Swe., 10,100 . . . I6 25
Ekumaketo, Con. L. . . . B3 48
Ekwan, riv., Ont., Can. . . . F15 67
Ekwok, Alsk., 105 . . . D8 79
El-Abiod Sidi Cheikh, Alg. . . H7 30
Elaine, Phillips, Ark., 898 . . . C5 81
El Alamein, see Al 'Alamayn, Eg., U.A.R.
El Alia, Alg. . . . C6 44
El Alto, P.R. . . . B5 65
Elamanchili, India, 13,556 . . . I9 40
El Amparo, Cuba . . . k11 64
Elamsville, Patrick, Va. . . . E2 121
Elamton, Morgan, Ky., 200 . . C6 94
Elamville, Barbour, Ala., 140 . . . D4 78
Eland, Shawano, Wis., 213 . . . D4 124
El Arahal, Sp., 17,361 . . . D3 20
El Aricha, Alg. . . . G6 30
Elasson, Grc., 5,658 . . . C4 23
El Atate, mtn., Jordan . . . D7 32
El 'Atrun (Oasis), Sud. . . . B2 47
Elath (Eilat), Isr. . . . E6 32
El Auja, Isr. . . . D6 32
Elazig, Tur., 60,289 . . . C12 31
El Azucar, res., Mex. . . . F3 118
Elba, Coffee, Ala., 4,321 . . . D3 78
Elba, Van Buren, Ark., 11 . . . B3 81
Elba, Cassia, Idaho, 70 . . . G5 89
Elba, Lapeer, Mich. . . . E7 98
Elba, Winona, Minn., 152 . . . F6 99
Elba, Howard, Nebr., 184 . . . C7 103
Elba, Genesee, N.Y., 739 . . . B2 108
Elba, dam, Ala. . . . D3 78
Elba, isl., It. . . . C3 21
El Barco, Sp., 7,041 . . . A2 20
Elbasan, Alb., 29,787 . . . B3 23
Elbasan, pref., Alb., 115,000 . . . *B3 23
El Baúl, Ven., 1,522 . . . B4 60
Elbe, riv., Ger. . . . B8 17
Elberfeld, Warrick, Ind., 485 . H3 91
Elberon, Tama, Iowa, 211 . . . B5 92
Elbert, Elbert, Colo., 250 . . . B6 83
Elbert, Throckmorton, Tex., 50 . . . C3 118
Elbert, McDowell, W. Va., 950 . . . *D3 123
Elbert, co., Colo., 3,708 . . . B6 83
Elbert, co., Ga., 17,835 . . . B4 87
Elbert, mtn., Colo. . . . B4 83
Elberta, Baldwin, Ala., 384 . . E2 78
Elberta, Houston, Ga., 644 . . D3 87
Elberta, Benzie, Mich., 552 . . D4 98
Elberta, Utah, Utah, 100 . . . D4 119
Elberton, Elbert, Ga., 7,107 . . . B4 87
Elberton, Whitman, Wash., 66 . . . C8 122
Elbeuf, Fr., 18,988 (*43,000) . . . C4 14
Elbigenalp, Aus., 589 . . . B6 18
Elbing, Butler, Kans., 105 . . . A6 93
Elbing, see Elblag, Pol.
Elbistan, Tur., 10,300 . . . C11 31
Elblag, Pol. 81,400 . . . A5 26
El Bolsón, Arg. . . . C2 54
El Bonillo, Sp., 5,286 . . . C4 20
El Bordo, Col., 1,475 . . . C2 60
El Borouj, Mor., 3,955 . . . H3 30
Elbow, Sask., Can., 401 . . . F2 70
Elbow, lake, Man., Can. . . . B1 71
Elbow, riv., Alta., Can. . . . D3 69
Elbow Lake, Grant, Minn., 1,521 . . . E3 99
Elbridge, Obion, Tenn., 65 . . A2 117
Elbrus, mtn., Sov. Un. . . . G17 9
El Bur, Som., 2,300 . . . E6 47
Elburg, Neth., 3,600 . . . B5 15
El Burgo de Osma, Sp., 3,842 . . . B4 20
Elburn, Kane, Ill., 960 . . . B5 90
Elburz, mts., Iran . . . C5 41
El Cajon, San Diego, Calif., 37,618 . . . E2, F5 82
El Callao, Ven., 3,276 . . . B5 60
El Campo, Wharton, Tex., 7,700 . . . E4 118
El Campo North, Wharton, Tex., 1,086 . . . *E4 118
El Campo South, Wharton, Tex., 1,884 . . . *E4 118
El Capitan, mtn., Mont. . . . D2 102
El Capitan, res., Calif. . . . E2 82
El Carmen, Bol. . . . C4 55
El Carmen, Col., 9,647 . . . B2 60
El Carre, Eth. . . . D5 47
El Carrizo, Mex., 163 . . . B3 63
El Centro, Imperial, Calif., 18,340 . . . F6 82
El Cerrito, Contra Costa, Calif., 25,437 . . . B5 82
El Cerro, Bol., 117 . . . C3 55
El Cerro, P.R. . . . C2 65
El Chaparro, Ven., 913 . . . B4 60
Elche, Sp., 49,000 (73,320▲) . C5 20
Elcho, Langlade, Wis., 525 . . C4 124
Elco, Alexander, Ill., 150 . . . F4 90
El Cobre, Cuba . . . k12 64
El Cuervo, butte, N. Mex. . . . k9 107
Eld, isl., Fiji Is. . . . 52
Elda, Sp., 28,151 . . . C5 20
El Dar el Beda, ruins, Eg., U.A.R. . . . D3 32
Elde, riv., Ger. . . . B5 16
Elderon, Marathon, Wis., 177 . . . D4 124
Eldersley, Sask., Can., 40 . . . E4 70
Elderton, Armstrong, Pa., 387 . . . E3 114
El Diviso, Col. . . . C2 60
El Djem, Tun., 5,122 . . . G12 30
Eldon, Wapello, Iowa, 1,386 . . . D5 92
Eldon, Miller, Mo., 3,158 . . . C5 101
Eldora, Hardin, Iowa, 3,225 . . . B4 92
El Dorado, Union, Ark., 25,292 . . . D3 81
Eldorado, Braz., 1,524 . . . C3 56
Eldorado, Ont., Can., 80 . . . C7 72
Eldorado, Sask., Can., 526 . . m7 70
Eldorado, Saline, Ill., 3,573 . . F5 90
El Dorado, Butler, Kans., 12,523 . . . B6, E7 93
Eldorado, Dorchester, Md., 80 . . . C6 85
Eldorado, Montgomery, N.C., 150 . . . B4 109
Eldorado, Preble, Ohio, 449 . . C3 111
Eldorado, Jackson, Okla., 708 . . . C2 112
Eldorado, Schleicher, Tex., 1,815 . . . D2 118
El Dorado, co., Calif., 29,390 . C3 82
Eldorado, mtn., Wash. . . . A4 122
Eldorado Springs, Boulder, Colo., 150 . . . B5 83
El Dorado Springs, Cedar, Mo., 2,864 . . . D3 101
Eldoret, Ken., 8,193 . . . A6 48
Eldred, St. Lucie, Fla., 100 . . E6 86
Eldred, Greene, Ill., 302 . . . D3 90
Eldred, Polk, Minn., 30 . . . C2 99
Eldred, McKean, Pa., 1,107 . . C5 114
Eldridge, Walker, Ala., 350 . . B2 78
Eldridge, Scott, Iowa, 583 . . . C7, D7 92
Eldridge, Laclede, Mo., 100 . D5 101
Eldridge, Stutsman, N. Dak., 67 . . . C7 110
Eleanor, Putnam, W. Va., 700 . . . C3 123
Electra, Wichita, Tex., 4,759 . B3 118
Electra, lake, Colo. . . . D3 83
Electric, peak, Mont., Wyo. . . . A2 125
Electric City, Grant, Wash., 404 . . . B6 122
Electric Mills, Kemper, Miss., 100 . . . C5 100
Eleele, Kauai, Haw., 950 . . . B2 88
El Ejemplo Central, P.R. . . . C7 65
Elektrogorsk, Sov. Un., 18,900 . . . n18 27
Elektrostal, Sov. Un., 105,000 . . . n18 27
Elephant, butte, N. Mex. . . . D2 107
Elephant, isl., Ant. . . . C7 5
Elephant, mtn., Maine . . . D2 96
Elephant, range, Camb. . . . G5 38
Elephant Butte, res., N. Mex. . . D2 107
El Escorial, Sp., 3,763 . . . o16 20
El Espino, P.R. . . . B2 65
Eleuthera, isl., Ba. Is. . . . C5 64
Eleva, Trempealeau, Wis., 548 . . . D2 124
Eleven Mile Canyon, res., Colo. . C5 83
Eleven Point, riv., Mo. . . . F6 101
Elevsís (Eleusis), Grc., 15,527 . . . g11 23
Elevsís, gulf, Grc. . . . g11 23
El Faiyum (Al Fayyūm), Eg., U.A.R., 84,800 . . . E2 32
El Faro, P.R. . . . C3 65
El Fasher, Sud., 26,161 . . . C2 47
El Ferrol, Sp., 74,799 . . . A1 20
Elfers, Pasco, Fla., 450 . . . D4 86
Elfin Cove, Alsk., 20 . . . k21 79
Elfrida, Cochise, Ariz., 200 . . F6 80
Elfros, Sask., Can., 289 . . . F4 70
El Fud, Eth. . . . D5 47
El Fuerte, Mex., 5,183 . . . B3 63
El Galhak, Sud. . . . C3 47
El Geteina, Sud. . . . C3 47
Elgin, Lauderdale, Ala., 150 . . . A2 78
Elgin, Santa Cruz, Ariz., 25 . . F5 80
Elgin, Man., Can., 259 . . . E1 71
Elgin, N.B., Can., 315 . . . D4 74
Elgin, Cook and Kane, Ill., 49,447 . . . A5, E2 90
Elgin, Fayette, Iowa, 644 . . . B6 92
Elgin, Chautauqua, Kans., 148 . . . E7 93
Elgin, Wabasha, Minn., 521 . . F6 99
Elgin, Antelope, Nebr., 881 . . C7 103
Elgin, Lincoln, Nev., 25 . . . F7 104
Elgin, Grant, N. Dak., 944 . . . C4 110
Elgin, Comanche, Okla., 540 . . . C3 112
Elgin, Union, Oreg., 1,315 . . . B7 113
Elgin, Erie, Pa., 218 . . . C2 114
Elgin, Scot., 11,971 . . . C5 13
Elgin, Lancaster, S.C., 300 . . B6 115
Elgin, Bastrop, Tex., 3,511 . . D4 118
Elgin, co., Ont., Can., 62,862 . . . E3 72
El Gîza (Al Jīzah) (El Gizeh) Eg., U.A.R., 98,000 . . . C6 43
El Gizeh, see Al Jīzah, Eg., U.A.R.
Elgol, Scot. . . . C2 13
El Goléa, Alg., 7,452 (12,486▲) . . . C5 44
Elgon, mtn., Ug. . . . A5 48
El Grullo, Mex., 9,028 . . . n11 63
El Hamurre, Som. . . . D6 47
El Haseke, Syr. 18,900 . . . D13 31
El Hasīheisa, Sud., 6,600 . . . C3 47
El Hawata, Sud., 3,921 . . . C3 47
El Huecu, Arg. . . . B2 54
Eli, Cherry, Nebr., 15 . . . B4 103
Eliasville, Young, Tex., 750 . C3 118
Elida, Roosevelt, N. Mex., 534 . . . D6 107
Elida, Allen, Ohio, 1,215 . . . B3 111
Elikon (Helicon), mtn., Grc. . . . g9 23
Elila, riv., Con. L. . . . B4 48
Elim, Alsk., 145 . . . C7 79
Elim, Cambria, Pa., 1,000 . . *F4 114
El Indio, Maverick, Tex., 120 . . . E2 118
Eliot, York, Maine, 1,730 (3,133▲) . . . E2 96
Eliot, riv., P.E.I., Can. . . . C6 74
Elis (Ilia), prov., Grc., 188,861 . . . *D3 23
Elisabethville, Con. L., 183,000 . . . D4 48
Elista, Sov. Un., 29,000 . . . D2 29
Elizabeth, Fulton, Ark., 20 . . A3 81
Elizabeth, Austl., 33,400 . . . F6 50
Elizabeth, Elbert, Colo., 326 . B6 83
Elizabeth, Cobb, Ga., 1,620 . . . A4, C2 87
Elizabeth, Jo Daviess, Ill., 729 . . . A3 90
Elizabeth, Harrison, Ind., 214 . . . H6 91
Elizabeth, Allen, La., 1,030 . . D3 95
Elizabeth, Otter Tail, Minn., 168 . . . D2 99
Elizabeth, Washington, Miss., 300 . . . B3 100
Elizabeth, Union, N.J., 107,698 . . . B4, k8 106
Elizabeth, Allegheny, Pa., 2,597 . . . *F2 114
Elizabeth, Wirt, W. Va., 727 . B3 123
Elizabeth, bay, Ec. . . . g5 58
Elizabeth, cape, Maine . . . E5 96
Elizabeth, cape, Wash. . . . B1 122
Elizabeth, is., Mass. . . . D6 97
Elizabeth City, Pasquotank, N.C., 14,062 . . . A7 109
Elizabeth Lake Estates, Oakland, Mich., 2,000 . . *F7 98
Elizabethton, Carter, Tenn., 10,896 . . . C11 117
Elizabethtown, Hardin, Ill., 524 . . . F5 90
Elizabethtown, Bartholomew, Ind., 417 . . . F6 91
Elizabethtown, Hardin, Ky., 9,641 . . . C4 94
Elizabethtown, Essex, N.Y., 779 . . . A7, f11 108
Elizabethtown, Bladen, N.C., 1,625 . . . C5 109
Elizabethtown, Lancaster, Pa., 6,780 . . . F8 114
Elizabethville, Dauphin, Pa., 1,455 . . . E8 114
El Jadida, Mor., 40,302 . . . C3 44
El Jebelein, Sud. . . . C3 47
El Jeib, wadi, Jordan . . . D7 32
Elk, Mendocino, Calif., 175 . . C2 82
Elk, Pol., 16,900 . . . B7 26
Elk, Spokane, Wash., 75 . . . A8 122
Elk, Teton, Wyo., 15 . . . B2 125
Elk, co., Kans., 5,048 . . . E7 93
Elk, co., Pa., 37,328 . . . D4 114
Elk, creek, Okla. . . . B2 112
Elk, creek, S. Dak. . . . C3 116
Elk, isl., Man., Can. . . . D3 71
Elk, mtn., N. Mex. . . . D1 107
Elk, mtn., Okla. . . . C3 112
Elk, mtn., S. Dak. . . . D1 116
Elk, mtn., Wyo. . . . D6 125
Elk, mts., Colo. . . . B3 83
Elk, peak, Mont. . . . D6 102
Elk, riv., B.C., Can. . . . D10 68
Elk, riv., Colo. . . . A4 83
Elk, riv., Kans. . . . E7 93
Elk, riv., Md. . . . A6 85
Elk, riv., Tenn. . . . B5 117
Elk, riv., W. Va. . . . C3 123
Elk, riv., Wis. . . . C3 124
Elkader, Clayton, Iowa, 1,526 . . . B6 92
El Kamlin, Sud., 4,341 . . . B3 47
Elkatawa, Breathitt, Ky., 200 . . . C6 94
Elk Basin, Park, Wyo. . . . A4 125
Elk City, Idaho, Idaho, 300 . . D3 89
Elk City, Montgomery, Kans., 498 . . . E8 93
Elk City, Douglas, Nebr., 48 . D2 103
Elk City, Beckham, Okla., 8,196 . . . B2 112
Elk Creek, Glenn, Calif., 300 . C2 82
Elk Creek, Johnson, Nebr., 170 . . . D9 103
Elk Creek, Grayson, Va., 100 . E1 121
Elk Falls, Elk, Kans., 179 . . . E7 93
Elk Garden, Mineral, W. Va., 329 . . . B5 123
Elk Grove, Sacramento, Calif., 2,205 . . . A6, C3 82
Elk Grove Village, Cook, Ill., 4,771 . . . *A6 90
El Khandaq, Sud., 11,995 . . . B3 47
Elkhart, Logan, Ill., 418 . . . C4 90
Elkhart, Elkhart, Ind., 40,274 . . . A6 91
Elkhart, Polk, Iowa, 260 . . . A7 92
Elkhart, Morton, Kans., 1,780 . . . E2 93
Elkhart, Anderson, Tex., 780 . . . D5 118
Elkhart, co., Ind., 106,790 . . A6 91
Elkhart Lake, Sheboygan, Wis., 651 . . . B5, E5 124
Elk Head, mts., Colo. . . . A3 83
Elkhorn, Man., Can., 666 . . . E1 71
Elk Horn, Shelby, Iowa, 679 . C2 92
Elkhorn, Douglas, Nebr., 749 . D2 103
Elkhorn, McDowell, W. Va., 900 . . . *D3 123
Elkhorn, Walworth, Wis., 3,586 . . . F5 124
Elkhorn, peaks, Idaho . . . F7 89
Elkhorn, ridge, Oreg. . . . C8 113
Elkhorn, riv., Nebr. . . . B7 103
Elkhorn City, Pike, Ky., 1,085 . . . C7 94
Elkhovo, Bul., 6,749 . . . D8 22
Elkin, Surry, N.C., 2,868 . . . A3 109
Elkins, Washington, Ark., 250 . . . B1 81
Elkins, Merrimack, N.H., 165 . D3 105
Elkins, Chaves, N. Mex., 25 . . D5 107
Elkins, Randolph, W. Va., 8,307 . . . C5 123
Elkins Park, Montgomery, Pa., 12,000 . . . A11 114
Elkinsville, Brown, Ind. . . . F5 91
Elk Island, nat. park, Alta., Can. . C4 69
Elk Lake, Deschutes, Oreg. . . D5 113
Elkland, Webster, Mo., 200 . . D4 101
Elkland, Tioga, Pa., 2,189 . . . C7 114
Elk Mills, Cecil, Md., 500 . . . A6 85
Elkmont, Limestone, Ala., 169 . . . A3 78
Elkmont, Sevier, Tenn., 50 . D10 117
Elk Mound, Dunn, Wis., 379 . D2 124
Elk Mountain, Buncombe, N.C., 300 . . . D3 109
Elk Mountain, Carbon, Wyo., 190 . . . D6 125
Elko, B.C., Can., 117 . . . E10 68
Elko, Houston, Ga., 165 . . . D3 87
Elko, Elko, Nev., 6,298 . . . C6 104
Elko, Barnwell, S.C., 194 . . . E5 115
Elko, co., Nev., 12,011 . . . B6 104
Elkol, Lincoln, Wyo., 25 . . . D2 125
Elk Park, Avery, N.C., 460 . . . A2, C4 109
Elk Point, Alta., Can., 692 . . C5 69
Elk Point, Union, S. Dak., 1,378 . . . E9 116
Elk Ranch, Carroll, Ark., 35 . A2 81
Elk Rapids, Antrim, Mich., 1,015 . . . D5 98
Elkridge, Howard, Md., 2,000 . . . B4, C2 85
Elkridge, Fayette, W. Va., 400 . . . D6 123
Elk River, Clearwater, Idaho, 382 . . . C2 89
Elk River, Sherburne, Minn., 1,763 . . . E5 99
Elk Run Heights, Black Hawk, Iowa, 1,124 . . . *B5 92
Elk Springs, Moffat, Colo., 6 . A2 83
Elkton, St. Johns, Fla., 400 . . C5 86
Elkton, Todd, Ky., 1,448 . . . D2 94
Elkton, Cecil, Md., 5,989 . . . A6 85
Elkton, Huron, Mich., 1,014 . . . E7 98
Elkton, Mower, Minn., 147 . . G5 99
Elkton, Douglas, Oreg., 146 . . D3 113
Elkton, Brookings, S. Dak., 621 . . . C9 116
Elkton, Giles, Tenn., 199 . . . B5 117
Elkton, Rockingham, Va., 1,506 . . . C4 121
Elk Valley, Campbell, Tenn., 250 . . . C9 117

Elkville, Jackson, Ill., 743....F4 90
Ellabell, Bryan, Ga., 175.....D5 87
Ellamar, Alsk., 20.........g18 79
Ellamore, Randolph, W. Va., 450..........C4 123
Ellaville, Schley, Ga., 905...D2 87
Ellef Ringnes, isl., N.W. Ter., Can........m31 67
Ellen, mtn., Utah........E5 119
Ellen, mtn., Vt...........C3 120
Ellenboro, Rutherford, N.C., 492........B2 109
Ellenboro, Ritchie, W. Va., 340.........B3 123
Ellenburg Center, Clinton, N.Y., 300.........f11 108
Ellendale, Sussex, Del., 370..C7 85
Ellendale, Terrebonne, La., 300..........C6, E5 95
Ellendale, Steele, Minn., 501.G5 99
Ellendale, Dickey, N. Dak., 1,800.........C7 110
Ellendale, Shelby, Tenn., 1,000........*B1 117
Ellensburg, Kittitas, Wash., 8,625.........C5 122
Ellenton, Manatee, Fla., 950.........E4, F2 86
Ellenton, Colquitt, Ga., 385..E3 87
Ellenton, Lycoming, Pa., 40..C8 114
Ellenville, Ulster, N.Y., 5,003........D6 108
Ellenwood, Clayton, Ga., 220.B5 87
Eller, isl., Kwajalein........ 52
Ellerbe, Richmond, N.C., 843........B4 109
Ellershouse, N.S., Can., 397..E6 74
Ellerslie, Harris, Ga., 350...D2 87
Ellerslie, Allegany, Md., 560.D2 85
Ellesmere, isl., N.W. Ter., Can.........m35 67
Ellersmere Port, Eng., 47,100.A5 12
Ellettsville, Monroe, Ind., 1,222..........F4 91
Ellice, is., Gilbert & Ellice Is..G10 7
Ellichpur, India, 36,538 (*54,028)........G6 40
Ellicott City, Howard and Baltimore, Md., 2,000....B4 85
Ellicottville, Cattaraugus, N.Y., 1,150..........C2 108
Ellijay, Gilmer, Ga., 1,320..B2 87
Ellijoy, Macon, N.C.........D3 109
Ellington, Tolland, Conn., 600 (5,580▲)........B7 84
Ellington, Reynolds, Mo., 812.........D7 101
Ellinwood, Barton, Kans., 2,729........D5 93
Elliot, Windham, Conn.....B8 84
Elliot, lake, Man., Can.....C4 71
Elliot Lake, Ont., Can., 9,950.........A2 72
Elliott, Ouachita, Ark., 100..D3 81
Elliott, Ford, Ill., 343......C5 90
Elliott, Montgomery, Iowa, 459........C2 92
Elliott, Dorchester, Md., 150.........D5 85
Elliott, Grenada, Miss., 250..B4 100
Elliott, Ransom, N. Dak., 62.........C8 110
Elliott, Lee, S.C., 270.......C7 115
Elliott, co., Ky., 6,330......B6 94
Elliott, bay, Wash........D1 122
Elliott, key, Fla.........G6 86
Ellis, Baxter, Ark., 250......A3 81
Ellis, Lemhi, Idaho........E4 89
Ellis, Ellis, Kans., 2,218....D4 93
Ellis, Gage, Nebr., 75.......D9 103
Ellis, Minnehaha, S. Dak., 75..........D9 116
Ellis, co., Kans., 21,270....D4 93
Ellis, co., Okla., 5,457.....A2 112
Ellis, co., Tex., 43,395.....C4 118
Ellis, pond, Maine.........D2 96
Ellis, riv., N.H..........B4 105
Ellisburg, Jefferson, N.Y., 328..........B4 108
Ellisburg, Potter, Pa., 40....C6 114
Ellisdale, Burlington and Monmouth, N.J., 50......C3 106
Ellisgrove, Randolph, Ill., 218.........E4 90
Ellison Bay, Door, Wis., 150........C5 124
Elliston, Austl.. 127........F5 50
Elliston, Newf., Can., 678...D5 75
Elliston, Powell, Mont., 200..D4 102
Elliston, Montgomery, Va., 600.........D2 121
Ellisville, Jones, Miss., 4,592..D4 100
Ellisville, St. Louis, Mo., 2,732.........B7 101
El Llanito, Sandoval, N. Mex., 150.......B3, k7 107
Ellon, Scot., 1,456.........C6 13
Ellore, India, 108,321.........E7 39, I8 40
Elloree, Orangeburg, S.C., 1,031.........D6 115
Ellport, Lawrence, Pa., 1,458.........E1 114
Ellrich, Ger., 5,302........B5 17
Ells, riv., Alta., Can......A4 69
Ellscott, Alta., Can........B4 69
Ellsinore, Carter, Mo., 311...E7 101
Ellston, Ringgold, Iowa, 116..........D3 92
Ellsworth, McLean, Ill., 224..........C5 90
Ellsworth, Hamilton, Iowa, 493..........B4 92
Ellsworth, Ellsworth, Kans., 2,361.........D5 93
Ellsworth, Hancock, Maine, 4,444.........D4 96
Ellsworth, Antrim, Mich., 386..........C5 98
Ellsworth, Nobles, Minn., 634.........G3 99
Ellsworth, Sheridan, Nebr., 11..........B3 103
Ellsworth, Grafton, N.H., (3▲)..........C3 105
Ellsworth, Washington, Pa., 1,456.........F1 114
Ellsworth, Pierce, Wis., 1,701.........D1 124
Ellsworth, co., Kans., 7,677..D5 93
Ellsworth, hill, Conn.......B3 84
Ellsworth, mtn., Ant.......B4 5
Ellwangen, Ger., 12,500.....E5 17
Ellwood City, Beaver and Lawrence, Pa., 12,413.....E1 114
Ellzey, Levy, Fla., 25.......C4 86
Elm, creek, Minn.........G4 99
Elm, creek, Tex..........A5 118
Elma, Howard, Iowa, 706...A5 92
Elma, Erie, N.Y., 1,000....*C2 108
Elma, Grays Harbor, Wash., 1,811.........B2 122
Elmali, Tur., 7,800........D7 23
El Manteco, Ven., 899......B5 60
Elm City, Wilson, N.C., 729..B6 109
Elm Creek, Man., Can., 337..E3 71
Elm Creek, Buffalo, Nebr., 778..........D6 103
Elmcrest, Genesee, Mich., 1,000..........*E7 98
Elmdale, Chase, Kans., 114..D7 93
El Melik, riv., Sud........B2 47
El Memrhar, Maur.........C1 45
Elmendorf, Bexar, Tex., 500..B4 118
El Mene, Ven., 3,160.......A3 60
Elmer, Macon, Mo., 266....B5 101
Elmer, Salem, N.J., 1,505...D2 106
Elmer, Jackson, Okla., 120...C2 112
Elmer City, Okanogan, Wash., 265..........B7 122
El Mesellemiya, Sud., 3,131..C3 47
Elm Grove, Waukesha, Wis., 4,994.........*E5 124
Elmhurst, DuPage, Ill., 40,329.........B6, F2 90
Elmhurst, Lakawanna, Pa., 788..........A9, D10 114
El Minao, P.R.........B6 65
Elmira, Solano, Calif., 200...B6 82
Elmira, P.E.I., Can., 149....C7 74
Elmira, Ont., Can., 3,337...D4 72
Elmira, Bonner, Idaho, 20...A2 89
Elmira, Otsego, Mich., 145...C6 98
Elmira, Ray, Mo., 123.......B3 101
Elmira, Chemung, N.Y., 46,517.........C4 108
Elmira, Lane, Oreg., 500....C3 113
Elmira, Braxton, W. Va., 74..C4 123
Elmira Heights, Chemung, N.Y., 5,157.........C4 108
El Mirage, Maricopa, Ariz., 1,723.........G1 80
Elmo, Dickinson, Kans., 50..D6 93
Elmo, Nodaway, Mo., 213...A2 101
Elmo, Lake, Mont., 75.......C2 102
Elmo, Emery, Utah, 175.....D5 119
Elmo, Carbon, Wyo., 91.....D6 125
Elmodel, Baker, Ga., 100....E2 87
El Modeno, Orange, Calif., 1,000..........*F5 82
Elmont, Shawnee, Kans., 75..B6 93
Elmont, Nassau, N.Y., 36,500.........G2 84
Elmont, Hanover, Va., 150...D5 121
El Monte, Contra Costa, Calif., 4,186.........*B5 82
El Monte, Los Angeles, Calif., 13,163.........F3 82
Elmora (Bakerton), Cambria, Pa., 1,057.........E4 114
Elmore, Elmore, Ala., 200...C3 78
Elmore, Faribault, Minn., 1,078.........G4 99
Elmore, Ottawa, Ohio, 1,302.........A4 111
Elmore (Town of), Lamoille, Vt. (237▲).........*B3 120
Elmore, co., Ala., 30,524....C3 78
Elmore, co., Idaho, 16,719...F3 89
Elmore City, Garvin, Okla., 982..........C4 112
El Moro, Las Animas, Colo., 20.........D6 83
El Morro, nat. mon., N. Mex...C1 107
Elm Park, West Feliciana, La..........D4 95
El Mraïti (Well), Mali......C4 45
El Mreïti (Well), Maur......B3 45
El Mreyer (Well), Maur.....B3 45
Elms, York, Maine.........E2 96
Elmsdale, N.S., Can., 535....E6 74
Elmsford, Westchester, N.Y., 3,795.........g13 108
Elmshorn, Ger., 35,000......B4 16
Elm Springs, Washington, Ark., 238..........A1 81
Elm Springs, Meade, S. Dak., 20..........C3 116
Elm Springs Colony, Hutchinson, S. Dak., 100.........D8 116
Elmsville, N.B., Can., 94....D3 74
Elmvale, Ont., Can., 957....C5 72
Elmville, Windham, Conn., 350.........B9 84
Elmwood, Ont., Can., 357...C3 72
Elmwood, Hartford, Conn. (part of West Hartford)...C6 84
Elmwood, Peoria, Ill., 1,882..C4 90
Elmwood, Plymouth, Mass., 500.........B6 97
Elmwood, Cass, Nebr., 481.........D9, E2 103
Elmwood, Pierce, Wis., 776..D1 124
Elmwood Park, Cook, Ill., 23,866.........F2 90
Elmwood Place, Hamilton, Ohio, 3,813.........D2 111
Elna, Johnson and Morgan, Ky., 150.........C7 94
Elne, Fr., 4,458..........F5 14
Elnora, Alta., Can., 214....D4 69
Elnora, Daviess, Ind., 824...G3 91
El Obeid, Sud., 59,000......C3 47
El Ocho, P.R.........B6 65
El Odaiya, Sud., 11,913.....C2 47
Eloise, Polk, Fla., 3,256.....E5 86
Eloise, Wayne, Mich........A7 98
Elon College, Alamance, N.C., 1,284.........A4 109
Elora, Ont., Can., 1,486....D4 72
Elora, Lincoln, Tenn., 300...B5 117
El Oro, prov., Ec., 103,950...B2 58
El Oued, Alg., 13,001 (86,092▲).........C6 44
El Ouig, Mali.........C3 45
Eloy, Pinal, Ariz., 4,899....E4 80
El Palmito, Mex., 640.......B3 63
El Pao, Ven..........B5 60
El Paraíso, Hond., 1,617....D4 62
El Pardo, Sp., 3,902 (part of Madrid)..........o17 20
El Paso, White, Ark., 120....B3 81
El Paso, Woodford, Ill., 1,964.........C4 90
El Paso, El Paso, Tex., 276,687 (*306,800).........o12 118
El Paso, co., Colo., 143,742...C6 83
El Paso, co., Tex., 314,070....E1 118
Elphin, Ire., 494.........D3 11
Elphinstone, Man., Can., 386.........D1 71
El Polvorín, P.R.........B5 65
El Portal, Mariposa, Calif., 200..........D7 82
El Portal, Dade, Fla., 2,079..G6 86
El Porto Beach, Los Angeles, Calif., 1,200.........*F2 82
El Porvenir, San Miguel, N. Mex., 250.........B4 107
El Prado, Taos, N. Mex., 350.A4 107
El Pueblo, San Miguel, N. Mex., 135.........B4 107
El Puerto de Santa María, Sp., 35,505.........D2 20
El Qaryatein, Syr.........E11 31
Elqui, riv., Chile.........F1 55
Elrama, Washington, Pa., 800..........F2 114
El Real, Pan., 1,071........F8 62
El Reno, Canadian, Okla., 11,015.........B4 112
El Rio, Ventura, Calif., 6,966.........E4 82
El Rito, Rio Arriba, N. Mex., 100.........A3 107
El Roboré, Bol., 3,715......C4 55
Elrod, Tuscaloosa, Ala., 200..B2 78
Elrosa, Stearns, Minn., 205..E4 99
Elrose, Sask., Can., 585......F1 70
Elroy, Juneau, Wis., 1,505....E3 124
Elsa, Hidalgo, Tex., 3,847....F3 118
Elsa, Yukon, Can., 395......D5 66
Elsah, Jersey, Ill., 507.......A8 101
El Salto, Mex., 5,926.......C3 63
El Salvador, country, N.A., 2,875,000.......H12 55, D3 62
El Samán, Ven., 1,154......B4 60
El Sauce, Nic., 1,781.......D4 62
Elsberry, Lincoln, Mo., 1,491.B6 101
El Segundo, Los Angeles Calif., 14,219.........F2 82
Elsie, Clinton, Mich., 933....E6 98
Elsie, Perkins, Nebr., 198....D4 103
Elsie, Clatsop, Oreg., 25.....B3 113
Elsinore, Riverside, Calif., 2,432.........F3, F5 82
Elsinore, Sevier, Utah., 483..E3 119
Elsinore, lake, Calif.......F3 82
Elsmere, New Castle, Del., 7,319.........A6 85
Elsmere, Kenton, Ky., 4,607.........A7, B5 94
Elsmere, Cherry, Nebr., 10...B5 103
Elsmore, Allen, Kans., 128...E8 93
El Sobrante, Contra Costa, Calif., 15,000.........*B5 82
El Sombrero, Ven., 5,592....B4 60
Elsterwerda, Ger., 9,749......B8 17
Elstow, Sask., Can., 98.......F2 70
Eltham, Eng. (part of London).........*m13 10
El Tigre, Ven., 41,550......B5 60
El Tigrito, Ven., 19,658.....B5 60
El Tocuyo, Ven., 14,803......B4 60
Elton, Jefferson Davis, La., 1,595.........D3 95
Elton, Langlade, Wis., 50....C5 124
Eltopia, Franklin, Wash., 70..C6 122
El Toro, Orange, Calif., 300..F3 82
El Transito, Chile.........E1 55
El Triunfo, Hond., 893......D4 62
El Triunfo, Mex., 520........C2 63
Eltville, Ger., 6,878.........C3 17
El Uaoh, Som.........E5 47
Elva, Man., Can., 58........E1 71
Elva, Scott, Tenn., 40.......C9 117
El Vado, res., N. Mex.......A3 107
El Valle, Taos, N. Mex., 80..*A4 107
Elvas, Port., 10,821........C2 20
Elvaston, Hancock, Ill., 232...C2 90
El Verano, Sonoma, Calif., 1,236.........*C2 82
Elverson, Chester, Pa., 472..F10 114
Elverum, Nor., 3,595.......G4 25
El Viejo, Nic., 8,900.......D4 62
El Vigía, P.R., (part of Arecibo) 520.........B4 65
El Vigía, Ven., 8,515.......B3 60
Elvins, Francois, Mo., 1,818..D7 101
El Vista, Peoria, Ill., 2,000..*C4 90
El Volcán, Chile.........A2 54
El Wak, Ken.........A7 48
Elwha, riv., Wash........A2 122
Elwood, Will, Ill., 746.......B5 90
Elwood, Madison, Ind., 11,793.........D6 91
Elwood, Doniphan, Kans., 1,191.........C9 93
Elwood, Gosper, Nebr., 581...D6 103
Elwood, Atlantic, N.J., 700..D3 106
Elwood, Suffolk, N.Y., 8,000..........*F3 84
Elwood, Box Elder, Utah, 345.B3 119
Elwood Park, Manatee, Fla., 450.........E4 86
Elwyn, Delaware, Pa., 1,500.........*G10 114
Ely, Eng., 9,815.........B8 12
Ely, Linn, Iowa, 226.......C6 92
Ely, St. Louis, Minn., 5,438..C7 99
Ely, White Pine, Nev., 4,018.D7 104
Ely, Orange, Vt., 50........D4 120
Elyria, McPherson, Kans., 60..........D6 93
Elyria, Valley, Nebr., 89....C6 103
Elyria, Lorain, Ohio, 43,782.A5 111
Elysburg, Northumberland, Pa., 1,100..........E8 114
Elysian, Le Sueur, Minn., 382.........F5 99
Elzach, Ger., 2,400.........A4 18
Emanuel, co., Ga., 17,815...D4 87
Emba, Sov. Un., 2,900.......D5 29
Emba, riv., Sov. Un.........F20 9
Embarcación, Arg., 3,303....D3 55
Embarrass, St. Louis, Minn., 210.........C6 99
Embarrass, Waupaca, Wis., 306.........D5 124
Embarrass, riv., Ill.........E6 90
Embarrass, riv., Wis........D5 124
Embden, pond, Maine........E3 96
Embden, Cass, N. Dak., 61..C8 110
Embetsu, Jap., 3,000.......D10 37
Embira, riv., Braz..........C3 58
Emblem, Big Horn, Wyo., 5..A4 125
Embree, Newf., Can., 698..*D4 75
Embreeville, Washington, Tenn., 50.........C11 117
Embreeville Junction, Washington, Tenn., 1,204.........*C11 117
Embro, Ont., Can., 552......D4 72
Embrun, Ont., Can., 1,112...B9 72
Embrun, Fr., 3,850..........E7 14
Embu, Ken.........B6 48
Embudo, Rio Arriba, N. Mex., 5..........A4 107
Emden, Ger., 45,900........B3 16
Emden, Logan, Ill., 502......C4 90
Emden, Shelby, Mo., 200....B6 101
Emelle, Sumter, Ala., 318....C1 78
Emerado, Grand Forks, N. Dak., 328.........B8 110
Emerald, Austl., 2,029.......A7 51
Emerson, Columbia, Ark., 350..........D2 81
Emerson, Man., Can., 932....E3 71
Emerson, Bartow, Ga., 666...B2 87
Emerson, Mills, Iowa, 521....C2 92
Emerson, Dakota, Nebr., 803.B9 103
Emerson, Bergen, N.J., 6,849.h8 106
Emery, Hanson, S. Dak., 502.D8 116
Emery, Emery, Utah, 326....E4 119
Emery, co., Utah, 5,546......E5 119
Emery Mills, York, Maine, 100..........E2 96
Emeryville, Alameda, Calif., 2,686..........*B5 82
Emet, Tur., 4,100.........C7 23
Emida, Benewah, Idaho, 125.B2 89
Emigrant, Park, Mont., 25...E6 102
Emigrant Gap, Placer, Calif., 50..........C3 82
Emi Koussi, vol., Chad.......B3 46
Emil, riv., China..........F25 9
Emilia-Romagna, pol. dist., It., 3,666,680.........E6 18
Emilia, reg., It.........B3 21
Emiliano Zapata, Mex., 7,483.........D6 63
Emílio Meyer, Braz., 944....E2 56
Emily, Crow Wing, Minn., 351.........D5 99
Emily, lake, Minn.........E3 99
Emine, cape, Bul..........D9 22
Eminence, Morgan, Ind., 200.E4 91
Eminence, Henry, Ky., 1,958.........B4 94
Eminence, Shannon, Mo., 516.........D6 101
Emington, Livingston, Ill., 133.........C5 90
Emirau, isl., Bis. Arch.......h13 50
Emirdag, Tur., 10,000.......C8 31
Emlenton, Venango, Pa., 844.........D2 114
Emlyn, Whitley, Ky., 600...D5 94
Emma, Lafayette and Saline, Mo., 202.........C4 101
Emma, lake, Sask., Can.......D3 70
Emmaus, Lehigh, Pa., 10,262.........E11 114
Emme, riv., Switz.........B4 19
Emmeline, lake, Sask., Can......C2 70
Emmen, Neth., 17,900 (71,200▲).........B6 15
Emmen, Switz., 16,856......B5 19
Emmendingen, Ger., 13,200..A3 18
Emmerich, Ger., 16,800......C3 16
Emmet, Nevada, Ark., 474...D2 81
Emmet, Holt, Nebr., 66......B7 103
Emmet, McLean, N. Dak., 10..........B4 110
Emmet, co., Iowa, 14,871....A3 92
Emmet, co., Mich., 15,904...C6 98
Emmett, Gem, Idaho, 3,769..F2 89
Emmett, Pottawatomie, Kans., 128.........C7 93
Emmett, St. Clair, Mich., 283.F8 98
Emmetsburg, Palo Alto, Iowa, 3,887.........A3 92
Emmitsburg, Frederick, Md., 1,369.........A3 85
Emmons, Freeborn, Minn., 408.........G5 99
Emmons, co., N. Dak., 8,462.........C5 110
Emory, Rains, Tex., 559.....C5 118
Emory, Summit, Utah, 5.....B4 119
Emory, peak, Tex..........G2 118
Emory Gap, Roane, Tenn., 500.........D9 117
Emory University, De Kalb, Ga., 4,200.........*B5 87
Empangeni, S. Afr., 6,572....C5 49
Empedrado, Arg., 3,715....E4 55
Empire, Walker, Ala., 400...B2 78
Empire, Stanislaus, Calif., 1,635.........*D3 82
Empire, Clear Creek, Colo., 110.........B5 83
Empire, Dodge, Ga., 125....D3 87
Empire, Plaquemines, La., 450.........E6 95
Empire, Leelanau, Mich., 448.........D4 98
Empire, Washoe, Nev., 650..C2 104
Empire, Jefferson, Ohio, 551..B7 111
Empire, Coos, Oreg., 3,781...D2 113
Empoli, It., 28,500.........C3 21
Emporia, Lyon, Kans., 18,190.........D7 93
Emporia, Greensville, Va., 5,535.........E5 121
Emporium, Cameron, Pa., 3,397.........C5 114
Empress, Alta, Can., 405....D5 69
Emptinne, Bel., 715.........D5 15
Emrick, Wells, N. Dak., 20..B6 110
Ems, riv., Ger..........A2 17
Emsdale, Ont., Can., 149....B5 72
Emsdetten, Ger., 25,000.....A2 17
Ems-Jade, canal, Ger........A7 15
Ems-Weser, canal, Ger.......A3 17
Emsworth, Allegheny, Pa., 3,341.........A5 114
Emyvale, Ire., 255.........C5 11
Ena (Nakatsu), Jap., 14,700.n16 37
Enard, bay, Scot..........B3 13
Ena-San, peak, Jap.........n16 37
Encampment, Carbon, Wyo., 333.........D6 125
Encanto, cape, Phil.........o13 35
Encarnación, Par., 18,500....E4 55
Encarnación de Díaz, Mex., 8,638.........m12 63
Enchant, Alta., Can., 97....D4 69
Enchi, Ghana, 2,064........E4 45
Encinal, Valencia, N. Mex., 200.........*C2 107
Encinal, LaSalle, Tex., 800.........E3 118
Encinitas, San Diego, Calif., 2,786.........F5 82
Encino, Torrance, N. Mex., 346.........C4 107
Encino, Brooks, Tex., 400....F3 118
Encontrados, Ven., 9,565....B3 60
Encounter, bay, Austl........G2 51
Endako, B.C., Can., 109.....B5 68
Endako, riv., B.C., Can......B5 68
Endau, Mala., 2,675........K5 38
Ende, Indon., 7,226.........G6 35
Endeavor, Forest, Pa., 200...C3 114
Endeavor, Marquette, Wis., 280.........E4 124
Endeavour, Sask., Can., 215..E4 70
Endelave, Den.........C4 24
Endelave, isl., Den.........C4 24
Enderby, B.C., Can., 1,075..D8 68
Enderby Land, reg., Ant......C18 5
Enderlin, Ransom, N. Dak., 1,596.........C8 110
Enders, Chase, Nebr., 100...D4 103
Enders, res., Kans..........B2 93
Endiang, Alta., Can., 40....D4 69
Endicott, Jefferson, Nebr., 166.........D8 103
Endicott, Broome, N.Y., 17,704.........C4 108
Endicott, Franklin, Va., 300..E2 121
Endicott, Whitman, Wash., 369.........C8 122
Endicott, mts., Alsk.........B9 79
Endless, lake, Maine........C4 96
Endwell, Broome, N.Y., 14,000.........*C4 108
Ene, riv., Peru..........D3 58
Enebakk, Nor.........p29 25
Enez, Tur., 566.........B6 23
Enfield, N.S., Can., 258.....E6 74
Enfield, Hartford, Conn., 3,100 (31,464▲).........B6 84
Enfield, Eng., 109,524......C7 12
Enfield, White, Ill., 791......E5 90
Enfield, Grafton, N.H., 1,121 (1,867▲).........C2 105
Enfield, Tompkins, N.Y., 150.........*C4 108
Enfield, Halifax, N.C., 2,978.A6 109
Enfield Center, Grafton, N.H., 200.........C2 105
Engadine, Mackinac, Mich., 240.........B5 98
Engaru, Jap., 11,000.......D11 37
Engebi, isl., Eniwetok........ 52
Engelberg, Switz., 2,646.....C5 19
Engelhard, Hyde, N.C., 600.........B8 109
Engels, Sov. Un., 106,000...C3 29
Enghien, Bel., 4,225.........D4 15
Enghien, Fr., 12,504.........g10 14
England, Lonoke, Ark., 2,861.........C4, E6 81
England, reg., U.K., 45,150,000.........D6 10, B6 12
Engle, Sierra, N. Mex., 30...D3 107
Englee, Newf., Can., 802.C3, h10 75
Englefeld, Sask., Can., 187...E3 70
Englevale, Ransom, N. Dak., 85.........C8 110
Englewood, B.C., Can., 121..D4 68
Englewood, Arapahoe, Colo., 33,398.........B6 83
Englewood, Duval, Fla., 5,000.........*B5 86
Englewood, Sarasota, Fla., 2,877.........F4 86
Englewood, Lawrence, Ind., 1,232.........*G5 91
Englewood, Clark, Kans., 243.........E7 93
Englewood, Bergen, N.J., 26,057.........h9 106
Englewood, Montgomery, Ohio, 1,515.........C3 111
Englewood, Coos, Oreg., 1,382.........*D2 113
Englewood, Lawrence, S. Dak., 10.........C2 116
Englewood, McMinn, Tenn., 1,574.........D9 117
Englewood Cliffs, Bergen, N.J., 2,913.........*B5 106
English, Crawford, Ind., 698.H5 91
English, chan., Eng.........F4 10
English, riv., Iowa........C5, C6 92
English Bazar, India, 45,900.........E12 40
English Bay, Alsk., 78..h16, D9 79
English Center, Lycoming, Pa., 100.........D7 114
English Creek, Atlantic, N.J., 400.........E3 106
English Harbour West, Newf., Can., 371.........E4 75
English Lake, Starke, Ind., 200.........B4 91
Englishtown, Monmouth, N.J., 1,143.........C4 106
Enguera, Sp., 5,663.........C5 20
Enhaut, Dauphin, Pa., 2,000.........*F8 114
Enid, Tallahatchie, Miss., 128.........A4 100
Enid, Richland, Mont., 5...C12 102
Enid, Garfield, Okla., 38,859.A4 112
Enid, res., Miss..........A4 100
Enigma, Berrien, Ga., 525...E3 87
Eniirikku, isl., Bikini........ 52
Enilda, Alta., Can., 106.....B2 69
Eniwetok, isl., Marshall Is...... 52
Enka, Buncombe, N.C., 1,400.D3 109
Enkeldoorn, Rh., 800........A5 49
Enkhuizen, Neth., 10,500....B5 15
Enköping, Swe., 13,200.H7, t35 25
Enna, It., 28,600.........F5 21
En Nahud, Sud., 16,499.....C2 47
En Naqura, Leb., 3,000.....A7 32
En Nebk, Syr., 10,400.......E11 31
Ennadai, lake, N.W. Ter., Can.........D12 66
Ennedi, plat., Chad.........B4 46
Ennell, lake, Ire..........D4 11
Enngonia, Austl., 78........D5 51
Ennigerloh, Ger., 8,900.....B3 17
Enning, Meade, S. Dak., 17..C3 116
Ennis, Ire., 5,699 (*8,410)....E3 11
Ennis, Madison, Mont., 525..E5 102
Ennis, Ellis, Tex., 9,347..B6, C4 118
Enniscorthy, Ire., 5,754.....E5 11
Ennis Creek, Clallam, Wash..A2 122
Enniskillen, N. Ire., 7,438..C4 11
Ennistymon, Ire., 1,145.....E2 11
Enns, Aus., 8,919.........D7 16
Enns, riv., Aus..........D7 16
Ennylabegan, isl., Kwajalein...... 52
Enoch, Iron, Utah, 60.......F3 119
Enochs, Bailey, Tex., 220....C1 118
Enochsburg, Franklin, Ind., 80.........F7 91
Enola, Faulkner, Ark., 100...B3 81
Enola, Madison, Nebr., 20....C8 103
Enola, Cumberland, Pa., 4,500.........F8 114
Enon, Bullock, Ala., 125.....C4 78
Enon, Clark, Ohio, 1,227....C4 111
Enoree, Spartanburg, S.C., 950.........B4 115
Enoree, riv., S.C..........B3 115
Enos, Newton, Ind.........B3 91
Enosburg (Town of), Franklin, Vt. (1,966▲).........*B3 120
Enosburg Falls, Franklin, Vt., 1,321.........B3 120
Enrich, riv., Scot.........C4 13
Enriquillo, Dom. Rep., 3,485.........G8 64
Enriquillo, lake, Dom. Rep......F8 64
Enschede, Neth., 131,800....B6 15
Ensenada, Arg., 24,925......g8 54
Ensenada, Mex., 42,561......A1 63
Ensenada, Rio Arriba, N. Mex., 300.........A3 107
Ensenada, P.R., 3,299.......D3 65
Enshih, China, 16,000.......E6 34
Ensign, Alta., Can., 51......D4 69
Ensign, Gray, Kans., 255....E3 93
Ensign, Delta, Mich., 50.....C4 98
Ensisheim, Fr., 4,498.......B3 18
Ensley, Escambia, Fla., 1,836.........G2 86
Ensley, Shelby, Tenn.......E8 117
Entebbe, Ug., 10,941.......A5 48
Enterprise, Coffee, Ala., 11,410.........D4 78
Enterprise, Shasta, Calif., 4,946.........*B2 82
Enterprise, Ont., Can., 222..C8 72
Enterprise, Polk, Iowa, 26...A7 92
Enterprise, Dickinson, Kans., 1,015.........D6 93
Enterprise, Clarke, Miss., 532.C5 100
Enterprise, Wallowa, Oreg., 1,932.........B9 113
Enterprise, Washington, Utah, 859.........F2 119
Enterprise, Harrison, W. Va., 900.........A7, B4 123
Entiat, Chelan, Wash., 357...B5 122
Entiat, mts., Wash.........B5 122
Entiat, riv., Wash..........B5 122
Entrance, Alta., Can., 87....C2 69
Entraygues, Fr., 917.......E5 14
Entre Minho e Douro, reg., Port., 2,067,900.........B1 20
Entre Ríos, prov., Arg., 803,505.........A5, f7 54
Entroncamento, Moz.......A5 49
Entry, isl., Que., Can........B8 74
Entwistle, Alta., Can., 411...C3 69
Enugu, Nig., 62,764........E6 45
Enumclaw, King, Wash., 3,269.........B4 122
Envermeu, Fr., 795.........E9 12
Enville, Chester, Tenn., 250..B3 117
Enyu, chan., Bikini......... 52
Enyu, isl., Bikini........... 52
Enz, riv., Ger..........E3 17
Enza, riv., It..........E6 18
Enzan, Jap., 12,500.......n17 37
Eola, Avoyelles, La., 250....D3 95
Eola, hills, Oreg..........C1 113
Eolia, Pike, Mo., 400.......B6 101
Eoline, Bibb, Ala., 250......C2 78
Epe, Neth., 4,700.........B5 15
Epéna, Con. B.........E3 46
Epernay, Fr., 21,882.......C5 14
Epes, Sumter, Ala., 337.....C1 78
Ephesus, ruins, Tur........D6 23
Ephraim, Sanpete, Utah, 1,801.........D4 119
Ephraim, Door, Wis., 221....C6 124
Ephrata, Lancaster, Pa., 7,688.........F9 114
Ephrata, Grant, Wash., 6,548.B6 122
Épila, Sp., 5,072.........B5 20
Epileptic Village, Henry, Ind.E7 91
Épinal, Fr., 30,313 (*43,000)........A2 18, C7 14
Épinay [-sur-Seine], Fr., 34,167.........g10 14
Epirus, reg., Grc.........C3 23
Epoufette, Mackinac, Mich., 50.........B5 98
Epping, Rockingham, N.H., 980 (2,006▲).........D4 105
Epping, Williams, N. Dak., 151.........A2 110
Eppingen, Ger., 5,500.......D3 17
Epps, West Carroll, La., 411..B4 95
Epsie, Powder River, Mont., 5.........E11 102
Epsom, Daviess, Ind., 60....G3 91
Epsom, Merrimack, N.H., 35 (1,002▲).........D4 105
Epsom [& Ewell], Eng., 70,700.........C7 12
Epworth, Dubuque, Iowa, 698.........B7 92
Equality, Coosa, Ala., 160....C3 78
Equality, Gallatin, Ill., 665...F5 90
Equatoria, reg., Sud., 903,503.........D3 47
Equatorial Guinea, Sp. dep., Afr., 266,000.....F6 42, E2 46
Équeurdreville, Fr., 9,624...C3 14
Equinunk, Wayne, Pa., 150.C11 114
Erath, Vermilion, La., 2,019.........E3 95
Erath, co., Tex., 16,236.....C3 118
Erba, mtn., Sud..........A4 47
Erbach, Ger., 400.........D3 17
Erbacon, Webster, W. Va., 200.........C4 123
Erbendorf, Ger., 3,200......D7 17
Ercis, Tur., 9,900.........C14 31
Erciyas, mtn., Tur.........C10 31
Ercsi, Hung., 6,296........B4 22
Érd, Hung., 23,177........B4 22
Erda, Tooele, Utah, 100....C3 119
Erdek, Tur., 6,700.........B6 23
Erdenheim, Montgomery, Pa., 3,700.........A11 114
Erdeni Dzuu, Mong.........B5 34
Erding, Ger., 11,300........D5 17
Erebus, mtn., Ant.........B29 5
Erechim, Braz., 24,941......D2 56
Eregli, Tur., 6,360.........B8 31
Eregli, Tur., 32,100........D10 31
Erepecurú, riv., Braz.......C3 59
Eressós, Grc., 3,301........C5 23
Eretria, see Nea Psara, Grc.
Erft, riv., Ger..........D6 15
Erfurt, Ger., 188,500.......C6 17
Ergene, riv., Tur.........B6 23
Erhard, Otter Tail, Minn., 150.........D2 99
Eria, riv., Sp..........A2 20
Erial, Camden, N.J., 900....D2 106
Eriboll, bay, Scot.........B4 13
Erice, It., 18,021.........E4 21
Ericht, riv., Scot.........D4 13
Erick, Beckham, Okla., 1,342.B2 112
Erickson, B.C., Can., 912....E9 68
Erickson, Man., Can., 531...D2 71
Ericsburg, Koochiching, Minn., 140.........B5 99
Ericson, Wheeler, Nebr., 157.C7 103
Erie, Weld, Colo., 875.......A5 83
Erie, Whiteside, Ill., 1,215...B3 90
Erie, Neosho, Kans., 1,309....E8 93
Erie, Monroe, Mich., 500....G7 98
Erie, Cass, N. Dak., 150.....B8 110
Erie, Erie, Pa., 138,440 (*218,000).........B1 114
Erie, co., N.Y., 1,064,688....C2 108
Erie, co., Ohio, 68,000.......A5 111
Erie, co., Pa., 250,682.......C1 114
Erie, lake, U.S. and Can........B11 77
Ericau, Ont., Can., 497......E3 72
Erigavo, Som.........C6 47

Erigavo, dist., Som....C6 47
Eriksdale, Man., Can., 242..D2 71
Erimanthos, mtn., Grc....D3 23
Erimo, cape, Jap....F11 37
Erin, Ont., Can., 1,005....D4 72
Erin, Houston, Tenn., 1,097..A4 117
Eriskay, isl., Scot....C1 13
Erisort, bay, Scot....B2 13
Erithrai, Grc., 3,495....C4, g10 23
Eritrea, prov., Eth....B4 47
Erkelenz, Ger., 11,700....C6 15
Erken, lake, Swe....t36 25
Erlangen, Ger., 74,200....D6 17
Erlanger, Kenton, Ky., 7,072....A5, A7 94
Erma, Cape May, N.J., 800...F3 106
Ermelo, Neth., 6,100....B5 15
Ermelo, S. Afr., 16,894....C5 49
Ermenek, Tur., 7,500....D9 31
Ermont, Fr., 19,263....g10 14
Ernakulam, India, 117,253..*G6 40
Erne, lake, N. Ire....C4 11
Ernée, Fr., 3,901....C3 14
Ernest, Indiana, Pa., 950....E3 114
Ernestina, Arg....g7 54
Ernestville, Unicoi, Tenn., 40....C11 117
Ernfold, Sask., Can., 133....G2 70
Eromanga, Austl., 31....C4 51
Eros, Jackson, La., 176....B3 95
Er Rahad, Sud., 6,706....C3 47
Er Rama, Isr., 2,621....B7 32
Errigal, mtn., Ire....B3 11
Erris, head, Ire....C1 11
Errol, Coos, N.H., 130 (220▲).B2 105
Errol, isl., La....E7 95
Errol Heights, Multnomah, Oreg., 10,000....*B4 113
Er Roseires, Sud., 3,927....C3 47
Erskine, Alta., Can., 208....C4 69
Erskine, Polk, Minn., 614....C3 99
Erstein, Fr., 6,165....C7 14
Erstfeld, Switz., 4,126....C6 19
Erving, Franklin, Mass., 400 (1,272▲)....A3 97
Erwin, Harnett, N.C., 3,183..B5 109
Erwin, Kingsbury, S. Dak., 157....C8 116
Erwin, Unicoi, Tenn., 3,210.C11 117
Erwin, Preston, W. Va., 100..B5 123
Erwood, Sask., Can., 125....E4 70
Erzgebirge (Ore), mts., Czech., Ger....C8 17
Erzincan (Erzinjan), Tur., 36,500....C12 31
Erzurum, Tur., 90,069....C13 31
Esan, cape, Jap....F10 37
Esashi, Jap., 7,700....D11 37
Esashi, Jap., 9,700....F10 37
Esbjerg, Den., 55,171....C2 24
Esbon, Jewell, Kans., 237...C5 93
Escabosa, Bernalillo, N. Mex., 25....m8 107
Escada, Braz., 13,761....k6 57
Escalante, Garfield, Utah, 702....F4 119
Escalante, des., Utah....F2 119
Escalante, hills, Colo....A2 83
Escalante, riv., Utah....F4 119
Escalon, San Joaquin, Calif., 1,763....D3 82
Escalón, Mex., 1,270....B4 63
Escambia, co., Ala., 33,511..D2 78
Escambia, co., Fla., 173,829..G1 86
Escambia, riv., Ala., Fla....D2 78
Escanaba, Delta, Mich., 15,391....C3 98
Escanaba, riv., Mich....B3 98
Escatawpa, Jackson, Miss., 1,464....E3, E5 100
Escatawpa, riv., Ala., Miss....E5 100
Eschede, Ger., 3,600....F4 24
Eschenbach, Ger., 3,200....D6 17
Escholzmatt, Switz., 3,257...C4 19
Esch-sur-Alzette, Lux., 27,954 (★68,000)....E5 15
Eschwege, Ger., 24,100....B5 17
Eschweiler, Ger., 40,200....C3 16
Escobal, C.Z., 580....k11 62
Escobar, Arg., 3,693....g7 54
Escobas, Zapata, Tex., 250...F3 118
Escoheag, Kent, R.I., 35....C9 84
Escondida, Socorro, N. Mex., 100....C3 107
Escondida, pt., Mex....D5 63
Escondido, San Diego, Calif., 16,377....F5 82
Escondido, riv., Nic....D6 62
Escoublac-La-Baule, Fr., 13,004....D2 14
Escoumains, riv., Que., Can....A8 73
Escuinapa, Mex., 9,875....C3 63
Escuintla, Guat., 9,760....C2 62
Escuminac, pt., N.B., Can....B5 74
Eséka, Cam....E2 46
Esens, Ger., 4,500....A7 15
Eşfahān (Isfahan), Iran, 254,708....E5 41
Esgueva, riv., Sp....B3 20
Eshimba, Con. L....C3 48
Eshowe, S. Afr., 4,919....C5 49
Esh Sheikh Jarrah, Jordan..m14 32
Esh Shobek, Jordan, 1,000..D7 32
Esk, riv., Eng....F5 13
Esk, riv., Scot....E6 13
Eskbank, Sask., Can....G2 70
Eskdale, Kanawha, W. Va., 800....C3, D6 123
Eske, lake, Ire....C3 11
Eskifoca, Tur....C6 23
Eskilstuna, Swe., 60,300.t34, H7 25
Eskimo, lakes, N.W. Ter., Can..C6 66
Eskimo Point, N.W. Ter., Can., 168....D14 66
Eskisehir, Tur., 153,096....C8 23
Esko, Carlton, Minn., 240...D6 99
Eskridge, Wabaunsee, Kans., 519....D7 93
Esla, riv., Sp....B3 20
Eslarn, Ger., 2,800....D7 17
Eslava, riv., Mex....h9 63
Eslöv, Swe., 9,700....C7 24
Esme, Tur., 4,900....C7 23
Esmeralda, Ven....C4 60
Esmeralda, co., Nev., 619...F4 104
Esmeraldas, Ec., 14,046....A2 58
Esmeraldas, prov., Ec., 87,870....A2 58
Esmeraldas, riv., Ec....A2 58
Esmond, DeKalb, Ill., 85....A5 90
Esmond, Benson, N. Dak., 420....A6 110
Esmond, Providence, R.I., 4,500....B10 84
Esmond, Kingbury, S. Dak., 19....C8 116
Esmont, Albemarle, Va., 100.D4 121
Esom Hill, Polk, Ga., 200...C1 87
Esopus, Ulster, N.Y., 175...*D7 108
Espada, pt., Col....A3 60
Espanola, Ont., Can., 5,353..A3 72
Espanola, Flagler, Fla., 80...C5 86
Espanola, Rio Arriba and Santa Fe, N. Mex., 1,976..B3 107
Espanola, Spokane, Wash., 25....D7 122
Española, isl., Ec....g6 58
Esparto, Yolo, Calif., 300....C2 82
Esperance, Austl., 1,111....F3 50
Esperanza, Arg., 10,035....A4 54
Esperanza, Pontotoc, Miss., 250....A4 100
Esperanza, Hudspeth, Tex., 40....F1 118
Esperanza, P.R....g13 65
Espichel, cape, Port....C1 20
Espinal, Col., 9,389....C3 60
Espinhaço, mts., Braz....E2 57
Espírito Santo, Braz., 31,027.F2 57
Espírito Santo, state, Braz., 1,188,665....C4 56
Espiritu Santo, isl., New Hebr.H10 7
Espita, Mex., 5,089....C7 63
Esposende, Port., 1,760....B1 20
Espy, Columbia, Pa., 1,375..D9 114
Espyville Station, Crawford, Pa., 200....C1 114
Esquatzel Coulee, creek, Wash...C6 122
Esquel, Arg., 5,584....C2 54
Esquimalt, B.C., Can., 12,048....E6, h12 68
Esquina, Arg., 5,878....F4 55
Es Sanamein, Syr....A8 32
Essaouira (Mogador), Mor., 26,392....C3 44
Esschen, Bel., 9,850....C4 15
Essen, Ger., 728,800 (★5,200,000)....B2 17
Essequibo, riv., Br. Gu....B3 59
Essex, San Bernardino, Calif., 52....E6 82
Essex, Ont., Can., 3,428....E2 72
Essex, Middlesex, Conn., 1,600 (4,057▲)....D7 84
Essex, Kankakee, Ill., 328...B5 90
Essex, Page, Iowa, 767....D2 92
Essex, Baltimore, Md., 35,205.B5 85
Essex, Essex, Mass., 700 (2,238▲)....A6 97
Essex, Stoddard, Mo., 511...E8 101
Essex, Flathead, Mont., 70...B3 102
Essex, Essex, N.Y., 250....f11 108
Essex (Essex Center), Chittenden, Vt., 300 (7,090▲)....B2 120
Essex, co., Ont., Can., 258,218....E2 72
Essex, co., Eng., 2,286,970...C8 12
Essex, co., Mass., 568,831....A5 97
Essex, co., N.J., 923,545....B4 106
Essex, co., N.Y., 35,300....B7 108
Essex, co., Vt., 6,083....B5 120
Essex, co., Va., 6,690....D6 121
Essex Falls, Essex, Mass., 400....*A6 97
Essex Fells, Essex, N.J., 2,174....*B4 106
Essex Junction, Chittenden, Vt., 5,340....C2 120
Essexvale, Rh....B4 49
Essexville, Bay, Mich., 4,590....E7 98
Essington, Delaware, Pa., 3,300....*B11 114
Esslingen, Ger., 82,900....E4 17
Es Suki, Sud., 7,388....C3 47
Estacada, Clackamas, Oreg., 957....B4 113
Estación Superi, Arg....E2 55
Estados, isl., Arg....h13 54
Estaire, Ont., Can....A4 72
Estância, Braz., 16,106....D3 57
Estancia, Torrance, N. Mex., 797....C3 107
Estarreja, Port., 2,450....B1 20
Estcourt, Que., Can., 737....B8 73
Estcourt, S. Afr., 8,959....C4 49
Este, It., 10,600....B3 21
Estelí, Nic., 8,500....D4 62
Estella, Craig, Okla....A6 112
Estella, Sp., 8,236....A4 20
Estell Manor, Atlantic, N.J., 496....E3 106
Estelline, Hamlin, S. Dak., 722....C9 116
Estelline, Hall, Tex., 346....B2 118
Estepa, Sp., 9,476....D3 20
Estepona, Sp., 10,935....D3 20
Esterbrook, Albany, Wyo....C7 125
Esterhazy, Sask., Can., 1,114.G4 70
Esternay, Fr., 691....F3 15
Esternberg, Aus., 2,203....E8 17
Estero, Lee, Fla., 300....F5 86
Estero, bay, Calif....E3 82
Estero, isl., Fla....F5 86
Estes Park, Larimer, Colo., 1,175....A5 83
Estevan, Sask., Can., 7,728..H4 70
Estevan, is., B.C., Can....C3 68
Estevan Point, B.C., Can....E4 68
Esther, Alta., Can....D5 69
Esther, St. Francois, Mo., 1,033....*D7 101
Estherville, Emmet, Iowa, 7,927....A3 92
Estherwood, Acadia, La., 639....D3 95
Estill, Washington, Miss., 75.B3 100
Estill, Hampton, S.C., 1,865..F5 115
Estill, co., Ky., 12,466....C6 94
Estillfork, Jackson, Ala., 100.A3 78
Estill Springs, Franklin, Tenn., 734....B5 117
Estlin, Sask., Can....G3 70
Esto, Holmes, Fla., 148....G3 86
Eston, Sask., Can., 1,695....F1 70
Eston, Eng., 37,160....F7 13
Estonia (S.S.R.), rep., Sov. Un., 1,250,000....D5 28
Estrées-St.-Denis, Fr., 1,658..E2 15
Estrêla, Braz., 5,795....D2 56
Estrêla, mts., Port....B2 20
Estremadura, prov., Port., 1,592,858....*C1 20
Estremadura, reg., Port., 2,626,400....C1 20
Estremadura, reg., Sp., 1,378,777....C2 20
Estremoz, Port., 7,057....C2 20
Estrondo, mts., Braz..C1 57, D5 59
Estuary, Sask., Can., 40....G1 70
Esztergom, Hung., 24,700...B4 22
Etah, Grnld....B22 4
Étain, Fr., 3,764....E5 15
Etamamu, riv., Que., Can....C1 75
Étampes, Fr., 13,515....C5 14
Étang-du-Nord, Que., Can., 1,090....B8 74
Étang Saumatre, lake, Haiti....F7 64
Étaples, Fr., 8,628....B4 14
Etawa, India, 69,681....E7 40
Etawah, India, 59,986....C6 39, D7 40
Eten, isl., Truk.... 52
Eternity, range, Ant....C6 5
Ethan, Davison, S. Dak., 297....D8 116
Ethel, Ont., Can., 134....D3 72
Ethel, Attala, Miss., 566....B4 100
Ethel, Macon, Mo., 149....B5 101
Ethel, Lewis, Wash., 90....C3 122
Ethel, Logan, W. Va., 650...D5 123
Ethel, mtn., Colo....A4 83
Ethelbert, Man., Can., 556..D1 71
Ethelsville, Pickens, Ala., 62....B1 78
Ethelton, Sask., Can., 56....E3 70
Ether, Montgomery, N.C., 150....B4 109
Ethete, Fremont, Wyo....B4 125
Ethiopia (Abyssinia), country, Afr., 21,500,000..D4 47, F9 42
Ethridge, Toole, Mont., 30...B5 102
Ethridge, Lawrence, Tenn., 550....B4 117
Etive, inlet, Scot....D3 13
Etlan, Madison, Va., 100....C4 121
Etna, Whitley, Ind., 125....B6 91
Etna, Penobscot, Maine, 175 (486▲)....D3 96
Etna, Grafton, N.H., 150....C2 105
Etna, Tompkins, N.Y., 450...C4 108
Etna, Licking, Ohio, 365....C5 111
Etna, Allegheny, Pa., 5,519..A6 114
Etna, Lincoln, Wyo., 100....B2 125
Etna, vol., It....F5 21
Etna Green, Kosciusko, Ind., 483....B5 91
Etolin, isl., Alsk....m23 79
Etolin, strait, Alsk....C6 79
Eton, Murray, Ga., 275....B2 87
Etosha, lake, S.W. Afr....A2 49
Etowah, Mississippi, Ark., 100....B5 81
Etowah, McMinn., Tenn., 3,223....D9 117
Etowah, co., Ala., 96,980....A3 78
Etowah, riv., Ga....B2 87
Etra, Mercer, N.J., 50....C3 106
Etretat, Fr., 1,565....C4 14
Etsin Gol, riv., China....C5 34
Etta, Union, Miss., 75....A4 100
Et Taiyiba, Isr., 7,601...B7, f11 32
Ettelbruck, Lux., 4,452....E6 15
Etter, Moore, Tex., 50....A1 118
Etters (Goldsboro), York, Pa., 542....F8 114
Ettington, Sask., Can....H2 70
Et Tira, Isr., 4,154....B6, g10 32
Ettlingen, Ger., 19,400....E3 17
Ettrick, Chesterfield, Va., 2,998....C7, D5 121
Ettrick, Trempealeau, Wis., 479....D2 124
Ettrick, forest, Scot....E5 13
Etumba, Fiji Is.... 52
Etzatlán, Mex., 8,752....m11 63
Etzikom, Alta., Can., 101....E5 69
Etzikom Coulee, riv., Alta., Can..E5 69
Eu, Fr., 7,029....B4 14
Euboea (Evvoia), prov., Grc., 166,097....*C4 23
Eucha, Delaware, Okla., 150.A7 112
Eucla, Austl....F4 50
Euclid, Polk, Minn., 200....C2 99
Euclid, Cuyahoga, Ohio, 62,998....A6, B2 111
Euclid, Butler, Pa., 150....E2 114
Euclid Center, Berrien, Mich., 2,343....*F4 98
Euclid Heights, Garland, Ark., 2,030....*C2 81
Eudora, Chicot, Ark., 3,598..D4 81
Eudora, Douglas, Kans., 1,526....B8, D8 93
Eudora, De Soto, Miss....A3 100
Eudunda, Austl., 735....G2 51
Eufaula, Barbour, Ala., 8,357.D4 78
Eufaula, McIntosh, Okla., 2,382....B6 112
Eufola, Iredell, N.C., 35....B3 109
Eugene, Vermillion, Ind., 300....E3 91
Eugene, Cole, Mo., 151....C5 101
Eugene, Lane, Oreg., 50,977 (★123,900)....C3 113
Eugenia, pt., Mex....B1 63
Euless, Tarrant, Tex., 2,062.*B5 118
Eulia, Macon, Tenn....C7 117
Eulonia, McIntosh, Ga., 200....E5 87
Eunice, St. Landry, La., 11,326....D3 95
Eunice, Lea, N. Mex., 3,531..E6 107
Eupen, Bel., 14,445....D6 15
Euphrates, riv., Asia...I18 9, F2 41
Eupora, Webster, Miss., 1,468....B4 100
Eure, Gates, N.C., 200....A7 109
Enre, dept., Fr., 361,904...*C4 14
Eure, riv., Fr....C4 14
Eure-et-Loir, dept., Fr., 277,546....*C4 14
Eureka, Humboldt, Calif., 28,137....B1 82
Eureka, N.W. Ter., Can....m35 67
Eureka, Marion, Fla., 50....C5 86
Eureka, Woodford, Ill., 2,538....C4 90
Eureka, Greenwood, Kans., 4,055....E7 93
Eureka, St. Louis, Mo., 1,134....B7 101
Eureka, Lincoln, Mont., 1,229....B1 102
Eureka, Eureka, Nev., 500...D6 104
Eureka, Wayne, N.C., 246...B6 109
Eureka (Chambersburg), Gallia, Ohio, 205....D5 111
Eureka, Aiken, S.C., 75....D4 115
Eureka, McPherson, S. Dak., 1,555....B6 116
Eureka, Juab, Utah, 771....D3 119
Eureka, Pleasants, W. Va., 100....B3 123
Eureka, Winnebago, Wis., 300....D5 124
Eureka, co., Nev., 767....D5 104
Eureka, sound, N.W. Ter., Can....m34 67
Eureka Central, P.R....C2 65
Eureka East (Ryans Slough), Humboldt, Calif., 3,634..*B1 82
Eureka Springs, Carroll, Ark., 1,437....A2 81
Euroa, Austl., 3,040....H5 51
Europe, cont., 601,900,000....C22 3, 8
Euros, riv., Tur....B6 31
Euskirchen, Ger., 20,300....C1 17
Eustis, Lake, Fla., 6,189....D5 86
Eustin, Franklin, Maine, 100 (666▲)....C2 96
Eustis, Frontier, Nebr., 386..D5 103
Eutaw, Greene, Ala., 2,784...C2 78
Eutawville, Orangeburg, S.C., 468....E7 115
Eutin, Ger., 16,900....D4 24
Eutsuk, lake, B.C., Can....C4 68
Eva, Morgan, Ala., 150....A3 78
Eva, Texas, Okla., 10....D2 112
Eva, Benton, Tenn., 200....A3 117
Evadale, Jasper, Texas, 900.*D5 118
Evale, Ang....E2 48
Evan, Brown, Minn., 153....F4 99
Evangeline, par., La., 31,639.D3 95
Evanger, Nor., 139....G2 25
Evans, Weld, Colo., 1,453...A6 83
Evans, Columbia, Ga., 600..C4 87
Evans, Vernon, La., 100....D2 95
Evans, Jackson, W. Va., 200.C3 123
Evans, co., Ga., 6,952....D5 87
Evans, lake, Que., Can....o20 72
Evans, mtn., Colo....B5 83
Evans, mtn., N.Z....O13 51
Evans, strait, N.W. Ter., Can.D16 67
Evansburg, Alta., Can., 452..C3 69
Evans City (Evansburg), Butler, Pa., 1,825....E1 114
Evansdale, Black Hawk, Iowa, 5,738....B5 92
Evans Landing, Harrison, Ind....H6 91
Evans Mills, Jefferson, N.Y., 618....A5 108
Evansport, Defiance, Ohio, 290....A3 111
Evanston, Weld, Colo., 200..A6 83
Evanston, Cook, Ill., 79,283....A6, E3 90
Evanston, Breathitt, Ky., 300.C6 94
Evanston, Uinta, Wyo., 4,901....D2 125
Evansville, Washington, Ark., 25....B1 81
Evansville, Randolph, Ill., 846....E4 90
Evansville, Vanderburgh, Ind., 141,543 (★200,300)....I2 91
Evansville, Douglas, Minn., 411....D3 99
Evansville, Tunica, Miss., 15..A3 100
Evansville, Orleans, Vt., 60..B4 120
Evansville, Rock, Wis., 2,858.F4 124
Evansville, Natrona, Wyo., 678....C6 125
Evant, Coryell, Tex., 700....D3 118
Evanton, Scot....C4 12
Evart, Osceola, Mich., 1,775.E5 98
Evarts, Harlan, Ky., 1,473...D6 94
Eveleth, St. Louis, Minn., 5,721....C6 99
Evening Shade, Sharp, Ark., 232....A4 81
Even Yehuda, Isr., 2,549....f10 32
Everard, lake, Austl....F5 50
Everard, mtn., B.C., Can....D5 68
Everard, ranges, Austl....E5 50
Everest, Brown, Kans., 348..C8 93
Everest, peak, Nep....D11 40
Everett, Ont., Can., 426....C5 72
Everett, Middlesex, Mass., 43,544....g11 97
Everett, Bedford, Pa., 2,279..F5 114
Everett, Snohomish, Wash., 40,304....B3 122
Everett, mtn., Mass....B1 97
Everett, mts., N.W. Ter., Can....D19 67
Everett, Glynn, Ga., 250....E5 87
Everettville, Monongalia, W. Va., 300....A7 123
Evergem, Bel., 11,332....C3 15
Everglades, Collier, Fla., 552.G5 86
Everglades, nat. park, Fla....G6 86
Everglades, swamp, Fla....G6 86
Evergreen, Conecuh, Ala., 3,703....D3 78
Evergreen, Jefferson, Colo., 950....B5 83
Evergreen, Avoyelles, La., 325....D3 95
Evergreen, Itawamba, Miss., 100....A5 100
Evergreen, Columbus, N.C., 300....C5 109
Evergreen, Appomattox, Va., 150....D4 121
Evergreen Park, Cook, Ill., 25,284....F3 90
Everly, Clay, Iowa, 668....A2 92
Everman, Tarrant, Tex., 1,076....*B5 118
Everson, Fayette, Pa., 1,304..F2 114
Everson, Whatcom, Wash., 431....A3 122
Everton, Boone, Ark., 118...A3 81
Everton, Dade, Mo., 261....D4 101
Evesham, Sask., Can., 96....E1 70
Evesham, Eng., 12,608....B6 12
Évian-les-Bains, Fr., 3,738...C2 18
Evinayong, Equat. Gui., 870.E1 46
Evington, Campbell, Va., 200....D3 121
Evolène, Switz., 1,786....D3 19
Evora, Port., 25,678....C2 20
Évreux, Fr., 23,647....C4 14
Evritania, prov., Grc., 39,716....*C3 23
Évron, Fr., 2,648....C3 14
Évros, prov., Grc., 157,760..*B5 23
Évros, riv., Grc....B6 23
Evrotas, riv., Grc....D4 23
Evstratios, isl., Grc....C5 23
Evvoia (Euboea), prov., Grc., 166,097....*C4 23
Evvoia (Northern), gulf, Grc....C4 23
Evvoia (Southern), gulf, Grc...g11 23
Evvoia (Eugoea), isl., Grc....C4 23
Ewa, Honolulu, Haw., 3,257....B3, g9 88
Ewa, beach, Haw....g9 87
Ewab, is., Indon....G8 35
Ewa Beach, Honolulu, Haw., 2,459....g9 88
Ewan, Whitman, Wash., 70..B8 122
Ewe, bay, Scot....C3 13
Ewell, Somerset, Md., 380...E5 85
Ewen, Ontonagon, Mich., 500....A6 98
Ewing, Franklin, Ill., 250....E5 90
Ewing, Jackson, Ind., 500...G5 91
Ewing, Fleming, Ky., 375...B6 94
Ewing, Lewis, Mo., 324....A5 101
Ewing, Holt, Nebr., 583....B7 103
Ewing, Lee, Va., 500....B1 121
Ewing Township (West Trenton), Mercer, N.J., 26,628....*C3 106
Ewo, Con. B....F2 46
Exaltación, Bol., 405....B2 55
Excel, Monroe, Ala., 313....D2 78
Excel, Alta., Can....D5 69
Excello, Macon, Mo., 100...B5 101
Excelsior, Hennepin, Minn., 2,020....F5 99
Excelsior, Richland, Wis., 150....E3 124
Excelsior, mtn., Calif....C4 82
Excelsior, mts., Nev....E3 104
Excelsior Springs, Clay and Ray, Mo., 6,473....B3, D2 101
Exchange, Montour, Pa., 150.D8 114
Exchange, Braxton, W. Va., 100....C4 123
Excocesa, bay, Dom. Rep....F9 64
Excursion Inlet, Alsk....k22 79
Exe, riv., Eng....D4 12
Executive Committee, range, Ant....B36 5
Exeland, Sawyer, Wis., 214..C4 124
Exeter, Tulare, Calif., 4,264..D4 82
Exeter, Ont., Can., 3,047....D3 72
Exeter, Eng., 79,700....D4 12
Exeter, Penobscot, Maine, 130 (707▲)....D3 96
Exeter, Barry, Mo., 294....E4 101
Exeter, Fillmore, Nebr., 745..D8 103
Exeter, Rockingham, N.H., 7,243....E5 105
Exeter, Luzerne, Pa., 4,747....B8, D10 114
Exeter, Washington, R.I., 100 (2,298▲)....C10 84
Exeter, riv., N.H....E5 105
Exira, Audubon, Iowa, 1,111....C3 92
Exline, Appanoose, Iowa, 223....D5 92
Exmoor, moor, Eng....C4 12
Exmore, Northampton, Va., 1,566....D7 121
Exmouth, Eng., 19,740....D4 12
Exmouth, gulf, Austl....D1 50
Expanse, Sask., Can....H3 70
Experiment, Spalding, Ga., 2,497....C2 87
Exploits, bay, Newf., Can....D4 75
Exploits, riv., Newf., Can....D3 75
Export, Westmoreland, Pa., 1,518....F2 114
Exshaw, Alta., Can., 678....D3 69
Extension, B.C., Can., 171...f12 68
Extinct Volcanoes and Lava Beds, Ariz....C7 80
Exuma, sound, Ba. Is....C5 64
Eya, riv., Sov. Un....H12 27
Eyak, Alsk., 20....C10, g19 79
Eyasi, lake, Tan....B5 48
Eye, pen., Scot....B2 13
Eyebrow, Sask., Can., 285...G2 70
Eyehill, creek, Alta., Sask., Can..C5 69
Eyemouth, Scot., 2,160....E6 13
Eynort, inlet, Scot....C1 13
Eyota, Olmsted, Minn., 558..G6 99
Eyre, Austl....F4 50
Eyre, Sask., Can....F1 70
Eyre, lake, Austl....E6 50
Eyre, pen., Austl....F6 50
Eyrecourt, Ire., 355....D3 11
Ezeiza, Arg....g7 56
Ezine, Tur., 7,500....C6 23

F

Faaborg, Den., 5,135....C4 24
Fabens, El Paso, Tex., 3,134....F1 118
Faber, Nelson, Va., 80....D4 121
Faber, lake, N.W. Ter., Can....D9 66
Fabius, Onondaga, N.Y., 378....C5 108
Fabius San Hilo, pt., Tinian.... 52
Fabriano, It., 12,700....C4 21
Fabrica, Phil., 8,397....*C6 35
Fabyan, Windham, Conn., 250....A9 84
Fabyan House, Coos, N.H., 25....B4 105
Facatativá, Col., 13,479....C3 60
Faceville, Decatur, Ga., 100..F2 87
Fachi (Well), Niger....C7 45
Fackler, Jackson, Ala., 300...A4 78
Facpi, pt., Guam.... 52
Factory, Wayne, Tenn....B4 117
Factoryville, Wyoming, Pa., 991....C10 114
Fada, Chad....B4 46
Fada, Mali....C4 45
Fada-N'Gourma, Upper Volta, 5,200....D5 45
Faddeya, gulf, Sov. Un....B3 4
Faddeyev, isl., Sov. Un....B17 28
Fadian, pt., Guam.... 52
Faejø, isl., Den....D5 24
Faemø, isl., Den....D5 24
Faenza, It., 27,200 (52,400▲).B3 17
Faeroe Is., Dan. dep., Eur., 37,000....C7 8
Fafan, riv., Eth....D5 47
Fafe, Port., 5,855....B1 20
Fagaalu, Am. Sam., 531.... 52
Fagaloa, bay, W. Sam.... 52
Fagamafute, Am. Sam.... 52
Făgăras, Rom., 17,256....C7 22
Fagatogo, Am. Sam., 1,344.... 52
Fågelbro, Swe....t36 25
Fagered, Swe....A6 24
Fagerhult, Swe., 471....B7 24
Fagernes, Nor., 982....G3 25
Fagersta, Swe., 15,500....G6 25
Fagnano, lake, Arg....h12 54
Faguibine, lake, Mali....C4 47
Fagus, Butler, Mo., 90....E7 101
Fahan, Ire., 322....B4 11
Fahan, inlet, Saipan.... 52
Fahraj, Iran, 2,245....H10 41
Fā'id, Eg., U.A.R., 1,000....D4 32
Faido, Switz., 1,441....D6 19
Faifo, Viet., 5,000....E8 38
Failaka, isl., Kuw....G4 41
Fairacres, Dona Ana, N. Mex., 50....E3 107
Fairbank, Cochise, Ariz., 50..F5 80
Fairbank, Buchanan and Fayette, Iowa, 650....B5 92
Fairbank, Talbot, Md., 175..C5 85
Fairbanks, Alsk., 13,311....C10 79
Fairbanks, Alachua, Fla., 70..C4 86
Fairbanks, Franklin, Maine, 50....D2 96
Fair Bluff, Columbus, N.C., 1,030....C4 109
Fairborn, Greene, Ohio, 19,453....C3 111
Fairburn, Fulton, Ga., 2,470....B4, C2 87
Fairburn, Custer, S. Dak., 47.D2 116
Fairbury, Livingston, Ill., 2,937....C5 90
Fairbury, Jefferson, Nebr., 5,572....D8 103
Fairchance, Fayette, Pa., 2,120....G2 114
Fairchild, Eau Claire, Wis., 594....D3 124
Fairdale, Wyandotte, Kans., 2,100....B8, C9 93
Fairdale, Jefferson, Ky., 6,000....A4 94
Fairdale, Walsh, N. Dak., 126....A7 110
Fairdale, Susquehanna, Pa., 40....C10 114
Fairfax, Chambers, Ala., 3,107....C4 78
Fairfax, Marin, Calif., 5,813....B5, D2 82
Fairfax, Man., Can....E1 71
Fairfax, New Castle, Del., 1,000....*A6 85
Fairfax, Linn, Iowa, 528....C6 92
Fairfax, Renville, Minn., 1,489....F4 99
Fairfax, Atchison, Mo., 736..A2 101
Fairfax, Hamilton, Ohio, 2,430....*C3 111
Fairfax, Osage, Okla., 2,076..A5 112
Fairfax, Allendale, S.C., 1,814....F5 115
Fairfax, Gregory, S. Dak., 253....D7 116
Fairfax, Franklin, Vt., 400 (1,244▲)....B2 120
Fairfax, Fairfax, Va., 13,585....B4, C5 121
Fairfax, co., Va., 262,482....C5 121
Fairfax Station, Fairfax, Va., 175....B4 121
Fairfield, Jefferson, Ala., 15,816....B3, E4 78
Fairfield, Solano, Calif., 14,968....B5, C2 82
Fairfield, Fairfield, Conn., 46,183....E3 84
Fairfield, Camas, Idaho, 474....F4 89
Fairfield, Wayne, Ill., 6,362..E5 90
Fairfield, Franklin, Ind., 175.E8 91
Fairfield, Jefferson, Iowa, 8,054....C6 92
Fairfield, Nelson, Ky., 290...C4 94
Fairfield, Somerset, Maine, 3,766 (5,829▲)....D3 96
Fairfield, Benton, Mo., 46...C4 101
Fairfield, Teton, Mont., 752..C5 102
Fairfield, Clay, Nebr., 495...D7 103
Fairfield, Essex, N.J., 3,310..*B4 106
Fairfield, Hyde, N.C., 250....B7 109
Fairfield, Billings, N. Dak., 6..B2 110
Fairfield, Butler, Ohio, 9,734.C2 111
Fairfield, Lane, Oreg., 2,000....*C3 113
Fairfield, Adams, Pa., 519...G7 114
Fairfield, Freestone, Tex., 1,781....D4 118
Fairfield, Utah, Utah, 75....C3 119
Fairfield, Franklin, Vt., 100 (1,225▲)....B3 120
Fairfield, Spokane, Wash., 367....B8 122
Fairfield, co., Conn., 653,589.D3 84
Fairfield, co., Ohio, 63,912..C5 111
Fairfield, co., S.C., 20,713...C5 115
Fairfield, pond, Vt....B2 120
Fairfield Highland, Jefferson, Ala., 4,500....*B3 78
Fairford, Washington, Ala., 40....D1 78
Fairford, Eng., 2,439....C6 12
Fairgrove, Tuscola, Mich., 609....E7 98
Fair Grove, Greene, Mo., 275....D4 101
Fair Grove, Davidson, N.C., 1,500....*B3 111
Fairhaven, Bristol, Mass., 14,339....C6 97
Fair Haven, St. Clair, Mich., 225....F8 98
Fairhaven, Stearns, Minn., 125....E4 99
Fair Haven, Monmouth, N.J., 5,678....C4 106
Fair Haven, Cayuga, N.Y., 764....B4 108
Fair Haven, Rutland, Vt., 2,378....D2 120
Fairholme, Sask., Can., 58...D1 70
Fairhope, Baldwin, Ala., 4,858....E2 78
Fairhope, Fayette, Pa., 1,700....*F2 114
Fairland, Shelby, Ind., 750..E6 91
Fairland, Ottawa, Okla., 646.A7 112
Fair Lawn, Bergen, N.J., 36,421....h8 106
Fairlawn, Pulaski, Va., 1,325....*D2 121
Fair Lawn Heights, Summit, Ohio, 2,000....*A6 111
Fairlee, Kent, Md., 200....B5 85
Fairlee, Orange, Vt., 400 (569▲)....D4 120
Fairless Hills, Bucks, Pa., 8,000....*F12 114
Fairlight, Sask., Can., 193...H5 70
Fairmont, Will, Ill., 2,000..*F2 90
Fairmont, Martin, Minn., 9,745....G4 99
Fairmont, Fillmore, Nebr., 829....D8 103
Fairmont, Robeson, N.C., 2,286....C4 109
Fairmont, Garfield, Okla., 115....A4 112
Fairmont, Spartanburg, S.C., 300....B3 115
Fairmont, Snohomish, Wash., 1,227....*B3 122
Fairmont, Marion, W. Va., 27,477....A7, B4 123
Fairmont, City, St. Clair, Ill., 2,688....B8 90
Fairmont Heights, Prince Georges, Md., 2,308....C2 85

Fairmount, Gordon, Ga., 619 ... B2 87
Fairmount, Vermilion, Ill., 725 ... C6 90
Fairmount, Grant, Ind., 3,080 ... D6 91
Fairmount, Leavenworth, Kans., 20 ... B8 93
Fairmount, Somerset, Md., 800 ... D6 85
Fairmount, Onondaga, N.Y., 7,000 ... *B4 108
Fairmount, Richland, N. Dak., 503 ... C9 110
Fairoaks, Cross, Ark., 150 ... B4 81
Fair Oaks, Sacramento, Calif., 9,000 ... A6 82
Fair Oaks, San Luis Obispo, Calif., 1,622 ... *E3 76
Fair Oaks, Cobb, Ga., 7,969 ... A5 87
Fair Oaks, Jasper, Ind., 200 ... B3 91
Fairoaks, Allegheny, Pa., 1,239 ... A5 114
Fair Plain, Berrien, Mich., 7,998 ... *F4 98
Fairplay, Park, Colo., 404 ... B5 83
Fair Play, Washington, Md., 420 ... A2 85
Fair Play, Polk, Mo., 335 ... D4 101
Fair Play, Oconee, S.C., 240 ... B2 115
Fairpoint, Belmont, Ohio, 600 ... B7 111
Fairport, Muscatine, Iowa, 150 ... C7 92
Fairport, Delta, Mich., 150 ... C4 98
Fairport, De Kalb, Mo., 88 ... B3 101
Fairport, Monroe, N.Y., 5,748 ... B3 108
Fair Port, Northumberland, Va., 650 ... D6 121
Fairport Harbor, Lake, Ohio, 4,267 ... A6 111
Fairton, Cumberland, N.J., 900 ... E2 106
Fairvale, N.B., Can., 759 ... D4 74
Fairvalley, Woods, Okla ... A2 112
Fairview, Atla., Can., 1,506 ... A1 69
Fairview, Walker, Ga., 2,000 ... *B1 87
Fairview, Fulton, Ill., 544 ... C3 90
Fairview, St. Clair, Ill., 850 ... *E3 90
Fairview, Switzerland, Ind., 35 ... G7 91
Fairview, Brown, Kans., 272 ... C8 93
Fairview, Christian & Todd, Ky., 275 ... D2 94
Fairview, Concordia, La ... C4 95
Fairview, Oscoda, Mich., 250 ... D6 98
Fairview, Newton, Mo., 249 ... E3 101
Fairview, Richland, Mont., 1,006 ... C12 102
Fairview, Bergen, N.J., 9,399 ... h8 106
Fairview, Burlington, N.J., 35 ... D3 106
Fairview, Monmouth, N.J., 5,000 ... *C4 106
Fairview, Dutchess, N.Y., 8,626 ... *D7 108
Fairview, Cuyahoga, Ohio, 14,624 ... B2 111
Fairview, Belmont and Guernsey, Ohio, 166 ... B6 111
Fairview, Major, Okla., 2,213 ... A3 112
Fairview, Multnomah, Oreg., 578 ... B4 113
Fairview, Erie, Pa., 1,399 ... B1 114
Fairview, Northampton, Pa., 1,146 ... *E11 114
Fairview, Northumberland, Pa., 2,100 ... *E8 114
Fairview, Lincoln, S. Dak., 101 ... D9 116
Fairview, Williamson, Tenn., 1,017 ... B4 117
Fairview, Sanpete, Utah, 655 ... D4 119
Fairview, Yakima, Wash., 2,758 ... *C5 122
Fairview, Marion, W. Va., 653 ... A7, B4 123
Fairview, Lincoln, Wyo., 100 ... C2 125
Fairview, peak, Nev ... D3 104
Fairview Park, Vermillion, Ind., 1,039 ... E3 91
Fairview Park, Cuyahoga, Ohio, 14,624 ... *A6 111
Fairview Shores, Orange, Fla., 900 ... *D5 86
Fairvilla, Orange, Fla., 1,000 ... *D5 86
Fairway, Johnson, Kans., 5,398 ... D9 93
Fairweather, mtn., Alsk., B.C., Can ... D12 79
Fairy Glen, Sask., Can., 53 ... D3 70
Fairyland, Walker, Ga., 1,000 ... *B1 87
Faison, Duplin, N.C., 666 ... B5 109
Faith, Rowan, N.C., 494 ... B3 109
Faith, Meade, S. Dak., 591 ... B3 116
Faithorn, Menominee, Mich., 35 ... C3 98
Faix, Pickett, Tenn ... C8 117
Faizabad, Afg., 30,000 ... C15 41
Faizabad, India, 83,717 (*88,296) ... C7 38, D9 40
Fajardo, P.R., 12,409 ... B8, f12 65
Fajardo, mun., P.R., 18,321 ... B8, f12 65
Fajardo Central, P.R ... B8, f12 65
Fakenham, Eng., 2,933 ... B8 12
Fakfak, W. Irian, 1,800 ... F8 35
Fakse, Den., 2,002 ... C6 24
Fakse, bay, Den ... C6 24
Fakse Ladeplads, Den., 1,579 ... C6 24
Faku, China ... C10 36
Fal, Vernon, La ... D2 95
Fal, riv., Eng ... D3 12
Falabequets, isl., Truk ... 52
Falaise, Fr., 6,325 ... C3 14
Falalu, isl., Truk ... 52
Falas, isl., Truk ... 52
Fălciu, Rom., 5,124 ... B9 22
Falcon, Nevada, Ark., 25 ... D2 81
Falcon, Quitman, Miss., 200 ... A3 100
Falcon, El Paso, Colo., 75 ... C6 83
Falcon, Cumberland, N.C., 235 ... B5 109
Falcon, Zapata, Tex., 150 ... F3 118
Falcón, state, Ven., 340,450 ... A3 60
Falconer, Chautauqua, N.Y., 3,343 ... C1 108
Falcon Heights, Ramsey, Minn., 5,927 ... E7 99
Falconwood, Erie, N.Y., 2,100 ... *C2 108
Falealili, hbr., W. Sam ... 52
Falefa, hbr., W. Sam ... 52
Falémé, riv., Mali, Sen ... D2 45
Faleshty, Sov. Un., 5,000 ... B8 22
Falfurrias, Brooks, Tex., 6,515 ... F3 118
Falher, Alta., Can., 741 ... B2 69
Falkenberg, Ger., 7,831 ... B8 17
Falkenberg, Swe., 11,000 ... B6 24
Falkenburg Station, Ont., Can ... B5 72
Falkenstein, Ger., 14,900 ... C7 17
Falkirk, McLean, N. Dak., 15 ... B4 110
Falkirk, Scot., 37,900 ... D5 13
Falkland, B.C., Can., 408 ... D8 68
Falkland Islands, Br. dep., S.A., 2,200 ... I4 53
Falkner, Tippah, Miss., 200 ... A5 100
Falköping, Swe., 14,400 ... H5 25
Falkville, Morgan, Ala., 682 ... A3 78
Fall, Ger ... B7 18
Fall, riv., Kans ... E7 93
Fall Branch, Washington, Tenn., 950 ... C11 117
Fallbrook, San Diego, Calif., 4,814 ... F5 82
Fall City, King, Wash., 560 ... B4, D2 122
Fall Creek, Eau Claire, Wis., 710 ... D2 124
Fallentimber, Cambria, Pa., 200 ... E5 114
Falling, creek, Va ... C7 121
Falling, creek, W. Va ... C6 123
Falling Creek, Chesterfield, Va ... C7 121
Falling Water, Hamilton, Tenn., 500 ... E10 117
Falling Waters, Berkeley, W. Va., 200 ... B6 123
Fallis, Lincoln, Okla., 42 ... B4 112
Fall Mountain Lake, Litchfield, Conn., 700 ... *C4 84
Fällnäs, Swe ... u35 25
Fallon, Prairie, Mont., 280 ... D11 102
Fallon, Churchill, Nev., 2,734 ... D3 104
Fallon, co., Mont., 3,997 ... D12 102
Fall River, Greenwood, Kans., 226 ... E7 93
Fall River, Bristol, Mass., 99,942 (*136,900) ... C5 97
Fallriver, Lawrence, Tenn., 40 ... B4 117
Fall River, Columbia, Wis., 584 ... E4 124
Fall River, co., S. Dak., 10,688 ... D2 116
Fall River Mills, Shasta, Calif., 500 ... B3 82
Fall River, res., Kans ... E7 93
Fall Rock, Clay, Ky., 500 ... C6 94
Falls, Wyoming, Pa., 500 ... A8 114
Falls, co., Tex., 21,263 ... D4 118
Falls, riv., Wyo ... A2 125
Fallsburg, Lawrence, Ky., 200 ... B7 94
Falls Church (Independent City), Va., 10,192 ... B5 121
Falls City, Richardson, Nebr., 5,598 ... D10 103
Falls City, Polk, Oreg., 653 ... C3 113
Falls Creek, Clearfield and Jefferson, Pa., 1,344 ... D4 114
Fallsington, Bucks, Pa., 1,000 ... *F12 114
Falls of Rough, Grayson, Ky., 40 ... C4 94
Fallston, Harford, Md., 100 ... A5 85
Fallston, Cleveland, N.C., 500 ... B2 109
Falls Village, Litchfield, Conn., 650 ... B3 84
Falmouth, N.S., Can., 831 ... E5 74
Falmouth, Eng., 17,400 ... D2 12
Falmouth, Suwannee, Fla., 25 ... B3 86
Falmouth, Jam., 4,126 ... F5 64
Falmouth, Pendleton, Ky., 2,568 ... B5 94
Falmouth, Cumberland, Maine, 5,976 ... E5 96
Falmouth, Barnstable, Mass., 3,500 (13,037▲) ... C6 97
Falmouth, Missaukee, Mich., 250 ... D5 98
Falmouth, Stafford, Va., 1,478 ... C5 121
Falmouth, bay, Eng ... D2 12
Falmouth Foreside, Cumberland, Maine (part of Falmouth) ... E5 96
Falmouth Heights, Barnstable, Mass., 800 ... C6 97
Falo, isl., Truk ... 52
Falsa Chipana, pt., Chile ... D1 55
False, bay, S. Afr ... D2 49
False, cape, Fla ... D6 86
False, cape, Va ... E7 121
Falster, isl., Den ... D5 24
Falsterbo, Swe., 392 ... C6 24
Fălticeni, Rom., 13,305 ... B8 22
Falun, Saline, Kans., 100 ... D6 93
Falun, Swe., 18,700 ... G6 25
Famagusta, Cyp., 26,763 ... E9 31
Famatina, mts., Arg ... E2 55
Fame, McIntosh, Okla., 100 ... B6 112
Family, lake, Man., Can ... D4 71
Fancher, Orleans, N.Y., 200 ... B2 108
Fancy Farm, Graves, Ky., 375 ... B2 94
Fangcheng, China ... H5 36
Fanghsien, China, 12,000 ... E7 34
Fangshen, China ... C8 36
Fannettsburg, Franklin, Pa., 400 ... F6 114
Fannin, Rankin, Miss., 40 ... C4 100
Fannin, Goliad, Texas, 130 ... E4 118
Fannin, co., Ga., 13,620 ... B2 87
Fannin, co., Tex., 23,880 ... C4 118
Fanning, isl., Pac. O ... F12 7
Fannūj, Iran ... H9 41
Fanny Bay, B.C., Can., 132 ... E5 68
Fannystelle, Man., Can., 153 ... E3 71
Fano, It., 23,600 (43,600▲) ... C4 21
Fanø, bay, Den ... C2 24
Fanø, isl., Den ... C2 24
Fanwood, Union, N.J., 7,963 ... *B4 106
Fao, Iraq, 2,916 ... G4 41
Fâqûs, Eg., U.A.R., 2,000 ... D3 32
Faradje, Con. L ... A4 48
Farafangana, Malag., 7,300 ... h9 49
Farāfirah, oasis, Eg., U.A.R ... D5 43
Farah, Afg., 12,000 ... E11 41
Farallon, isl., Calif ... B4 82
Farallón, pt., Mex ... n11 63
Farallones, gulf, Calif ... B4 82
Faramana, Upper Volta ... D4 45
Faranah, Guinea, 2,250 ... D2 45
Farber, Audrain, Mo., 451 ... B6 101
Fareham, Eng., 65,300 ... D6 12
Farewell, cape, Grnld ... D19 4
Farewell, cape, N.Z ... N14 51
Fargo, Monroe, Ark., 100 ... C4 81
Fargo, Clinch, Ga., 900 ... F4 87
Fargo, Cass, N. Dak., 46,662 ... C9 110
Fargo, Ellis, Okla., 291 ... A2 112
Far Hills, Somerset, N.J., 702 ... B3 106
Fari, Mali ... D2 45
Faria, riv., Jordan ... g12 32
Faribault, Rice, Minn., 16,926 ... F5 99
Faribault, co., Minn., 23,685 ... G5 99
Faridpur, Pak., 25,556 ... F12 40
Farilhoes, is., Port ... C1 20
Farina, Austl., 55 ... E2 51
Farina, Fayette, Ill., 692 ... E5 90
Farisita, Huerfano, Colo., 5 ... D5 83
Fāriskūr, Eg., U.A.R., 2,000 ... C3 32
Farley, Dubuque, Iowa, 920 ... B6 92
Farley, Franklin, Mass., 150 ... A3 97
Farley, Platte, Mo., 120 ... B3 101
Farley, Colfax, N. Mex., 40 ... A5 107
Farm, pond, Mass ... h10 97
Farmer, Defiance, Ohio, 120 ... A3 111
Farmer, Hanson, S. Dak., 95 ... D8 116
Farmer City, De Witt, Ill., 1,838 ... C5 90
Farmers, Rowan, Ky., 236 ... B6 94
Farmersburg, Sullivan, Ind., 1,027 ... F3 91
Farmersburg, Clayton, Iowa, 200 ... B6 92
Farmers Exchange, Hickman, Tenn., 15 ... B4 117
Farmersville, Lowndes, Ala., 80 ... C3 78
Farmersville, Tulare, Calif., 3,101 ... *D4 82
Farmersville, Montgomery, Ill., 495 ... D4 90
Farmersville, Collins, Tex., 2,021 ... C4 118
Farmerville, Union, La., 2,727 ... B3 95
Farmingdale, Monmouth, N.J., 959 ... C4 106
Farmingdale, Nassau, N.Y., 6,128 ... n15 108
Farmingdale, Pennington, S. Dak., 30 ... D3 116
Farmington, Washington, Ark., 216 ... A1 81
Farmington, Hartford, Conn., 2,000 (10,813▲) ... C5 84
Farmington, Kent, Del., 142 ... C6 85
Farmington, Fulton, Ill., 2,831 ... C3 90
Farmington, Van Buren, Iowa, 902 ... D6 92
Farmington, Franklin, Maine, 2,749 (5,001▲) ... D2 96
Farmington, Oakland, Mich., 6,881 ... A7 98
Farmington, Dakota, Minn., 2,300 ... F5 99
Farmington, St. Francois, Mo., 5,618 ... D7 101
Farmington, Teton, Mont., 15 ... C4 102
Farmington, Stafford, N.H., 2,241 (3,287▲) ... D4 105
Farmington, San Juan, N. Mex., 23,786 ... A1 107
Farmington, Davie, N.C., 300 ... A3 109
Farmington, Fayette, Pa., 200 ... G2 114
Farmington, Marshall, Tenn., 100 ... B5 117
Farmington, Davis, Utah, 1,951 ... C4 119
Farmington, Whitman, Wash., 176 ... B8 122
Farmington, Marion, W. Va., 709 ... A7 123
Farmington, riv., Conn ... B5 84
Farmingville, Suffolk, N.Y., 595 ... *n16 108
Farmland, Randolph, Ind., 1,102 ... D7 91
Farmville, Pitt, N.C., 3,997 ... B6 109
Farmville, Prince Edward, Va., 4,293 ... D4 121
Farnam, Dawson, Nebr., 258 ... D5 103
Farnams, Berkshire, Mass., 130 ... A1 97
Farnborough, Eng., 31,437 ... C7 12
Farne, is., Eng ... C6 10
Farner, Polk, Tenn., 150 ... D9 117
Farnham, Que., Can., 6,354 ... D5 73
Farnham, Erie, N.Y., 422 ... C1 108
Farnham, mtn., B.C., Can ... D9 68
Farnhamville, Calhoun, Iowa, 409 ... B3 92
Farnham, Richmond, Va., 300 ... D6 121
Farnhurst, New Castle, Del., 60 ... A6 85
Farnigen, Switz ... C6 19
Faro, Braz., 1,434 ... C5 59
Faro, Port., 17,631 ... D2 20
Farragut, Fremont, Iowa, 495 ... D2 92
Farrar, Polk, Iowa, 50 ... A8 92
Farrar, riv., Scot ... C4 13
Farrāshband, Iran ... G6 41
Farrel, Coahoma, Miss., 150 ... A3 100
Farrell, Mercer, Pa., 13,793 ... D1 114
Farrellton, Quebec, Can., 368 ... D2 73
Farrerdale, Sask., Can ... F3 70
Farrington, Chatham, N.C ... B4 109
Farris, Atoka, Okla., 25 ... C6 112
Farris, lake, Nor ... p27 25
Farrukhabad, India, 87,793 (*94,591) ... C6 39, D7 40
Farry, Woods, Okla ... A2 112
Farsala, Grc., 5,771 ... C4 23
Farsi, Afg., 10,000 ... E11 41
Farsø, Den., 1,581 ... B3 24
Farson, Sweetwater, Wyo., 20 ... C3 125
Farsund, Nor., 2,200 ... H2 25
Fårup, Den., 506 ... B3 24
Farwell, Clare, Mich., 737 ... E6 98
Farwell, Pope, Minn., 106 ... E3 99
Farwell (Fardale), Howard, Nebr., 137 ... C7 103
Farwell, Parmer, Tex., 1,009 ... B1 118
Fasā, Iran, 9,907 ... G6 41
Fasano, It., 16,100 ... D6 21
Fassett, Que., Can., 434 ... D3 73
Fastov, Sov. Un., 10,000 ... F7 27
Fatehpur, India, 28,232 ... C7 39
Fatsa, Tur., 6,800 ... B11 31
Fatuosofia, cape, W. Sam ... 52
Fatuvalu, W. Sam., 117 ... 52
Faucett, Buchanan, Mo., 150 ... B3 101
Faulk, co., S. Dak., 4,397 ... B6 116
Faulkner, co., Ark., 24,303 ... B3 81
Faulkton, Faulk, S. Dak., 1,051 ... B6 116
Fault, bluff, Ant ... f41 5
Faunsdale, Marengo, Ala., 124 ... C2 78
Fauquembergues, Fr., 842 ... D10 12
Fauquier, B.C., Can., 114 ... E8 68
Fauquier, co., Va., 24,066 ... C5 121
Faussepoint, lake, La ... D4 95
Faust, Alta., Can., 763 ... B3 69
Faust, Tooele, Utah, 15 ... C3 119
Favara, It., 27,909 ... F4 21
Faverges, Fr., 2,329 ... D1 18
Faversham, Eng., 12,983 ... C8 12
Favorita, Flagler, Fla., 70 ... C5 86
Faw, hbr., Fiji Is ... 52
Fawcett, Alta., Can., 179 ... B3 69
Fawcett, lake, Alta., Can ... B4 69
Fawn, lake, Ont., Can ... F15 67
Fawnie, range, B.C., Can ... C5 68
Fawnie Nose, mtn., B.C., Can ... C5 68
Faxaflói, bay, Ice ... n21 25
Faxon, Comanche, Okla., 137 ... C3 112
Faxon, Lycoming, Pa., 1,841 ... *D8 114
Faxon, Benton, Tenn., 100 ... A3 117
Fay, Dewey, Okla., 150 ... B3 112
Fayd, Sau. Ar ... I14 31
Fayal, isl., Port. (Azores) ... g8 44
Fayette, Fayette, Ala., 4,227 ... B2 78
Fayette, Boone, Ind., 80 ... E5 91
Fayette, Fayette, Iowa, 1,597 ... B6 92
Fayette, Jefferson, Miss., 1,626 ... D2 100
Fayette, Howard, Mo., 3,294 ... B5 101
Fayette, Fulton, Ohio, 1,090 ... A3 111
Fayette, Sanpete, Utah, 161 ... D4 119
Fayette, co., Ala., 16,148 ... B2 78
Fayette, co., Ga., 8,199 ... C2 87
Fayette, co., Ill., 21,946 ... E5 90
Fayette, co., Ind., 24,454 ... E7 91
Fayette, co., Iowa, 28,581 ... B6 92
Fayette, co., Ky., 131,906 ... C5 94
Fayette, co., Ohio, 24,775 ... C4 111
Fayette, co., Pa., 169,340 ... G2 114
Fayette, co., Tenn., 24,557 ... B2 117
Fayette, co., Tex., 20,384 ... E4 118
Fayette, co., W. Va., 61,731 ... C3 123
Fayette City, Fayette, Pa., 1,159 ... *F2 114
Fayette Corners, Fayette, Tenn ... B2 117
Fayetteville, Talladega, Ala., 200 ... B3 78
Fayetteville, Washington, Ark., 22,887 ... A1 81
Fayetteville, Fayette, Ga., 1,389 ... C2 87
Fayetteville, St. Clair, Ill., 294 ... B9 101
Fayetteville, Lawrence, Ind., 150 ... G4 91
Fayetteville, Onondaga, N.Y., 4,702 ... B5 108
Fayetteville, Cumberland, N.C., 47,106 (*132,000) ... B5 109
Fayetteville, Brown, Ohio, 389 ... C4 111
Fayetteville, Franklin, Pa., 950 ... G6 114
Fayetteville, Lincoln, Tenn., 6,804 ... B5 117
Fayetteville, Fayette, W. Va., 1,848 ... C3, D7 123
Fayetteville North, Cumberland, N.C., 3,071 ... *B5 109
Fays-Billot, Fr., 1,409 ... B1 18
Fayston (Town of), Washington, Vt. (158▲) ... *C3 120
Fayville, Worcester, Mass., 900 ... g9 97
Faywood, Grant, N. Mex., 25 ... E1 107
Fear, cape, N.C ... D6 109
Fearn, Scot., 1,317 ... C5 13
Feasterville, Bucks, Pa., 6,000 ... A12 114
Feather, mtn., Ant ... e40 5
Feather, riv., Calif ... C3 82
Feather Falls, Butte, Calif., 900 ... C3 82
Featherston, Pittsburg, Okla., 50 ... B6 112
Fécamp, Fr., 19,491 ... C4 14
Fechē, Eth ... D4 47
Federal, Ont., Can ... h12 72
Federal, Laramie, Wyo., 10 ... D7 125
Federal Dam, Cass, Minn., 185 ... C4 99
Federal Point, Putnam, Fla., 275 ... C5 86
Federalsburg, Caroline, Md., 2,060 ... C6 85
Federal Way, King, Wash., 7,000 ... *B3 122
Fedora, Miner, S. Dak., 150 ... C8 116
Fedscreek, Pike, Ky., 500 ... C7 94
Feeding Hills, Hampden, Mass., 4,500 ... B2 97
Fefan, isl., Truk ... 52
Fehmarn, isl., Ger ... D5 24
Feijó, Braz., 1,628 ... C3 58
Feilding, N.Z., 8,172 ... N15 51
Feira, Zambia ... E5 48
Feira de Santana, Braz., 61,612 ... D3 57
Fejer, co., Hung., 300,119 ... *B4 22
Felanitx, Sp., 11,759 ... C7 20
Felch, Dickinson, Mich., 150 ... B3 98
Felda, Hendry, Fla., 200 ... F5 86
Feldbach, Aus., 3,687 ... E7 16
Feldberg, Ger., 2,862 ... E7 24
Feldberg, mtn., Ger ... B3 18
Feldkirch, Aus., 17,343 ... E4 16
Feliciano, P.R ... B2 65
Felicity, Clermont, Ohio, 878 ... D3 111
Felipe Carrillo Puerto, Mex., 595 ... D7 63
Felix, cape, N.W. Ter., Can ... B13 66
Felixstowe, Eng., 17,254 ... C9 12
Félix U Gómez, Mex., 92 ... G4 107
Felixville, East Feliciana, La., 35 ... D5 95
Fellbach, Ger., 26,000 ... E4 17
Fellingsbro, Swe., 5,348 ... t33 25
Fellows, Kern, Calif., 700 ... E4 82
Fellowship, Burlington, N.J., 140 ... D3 106
Fellsmere, Indian River, Fla., 732 ... E6 86
Felsenthal, Union, Ark., 250 ... D3 81
Felt, Teton, Idaho, 20 ... F7 89
Felt, Cimarron, Okla., 70 ... D1 112
Felton, Santa Cruz, Calif., 1,380 ... D2 82
Felton, Kent, Del., 422 ... D6 85
Felton, Haralson, Ga., 160 ... C1 87
Felton, Clay, Minn., 201 ... C2 99
Felton, York, Pa., 430 ... G8 114
Feltre, It., 8,500 ... A3 21
Femund, lake, Nor ... F4 25
Fence, Florence, Wis., 250 ... C5 124
Fence, lake, Wis ... C4 124
Fence, riv., Mich ... B2 98
Fence Lake, Valencia, N. Mex., 20 ... C1 107
Fender, Tift, Ga., 150 ... E3 87
Fenelon Falls, Ont., Can., 1,359 ... C6 72
Fénérive, Malag ... g9 49
Fengchen, China, 35,000 ... D5 36
Fengcheng, China, 21,000 ... J6 36
Fengchieh, China, 25,000 ... I3 36
Fenghsiang, China, 10,000 ... G2 36
Fenghsien, China, 12,000 ... E6 34
Fengning, China ... D7 36
Fengshan, China, 1,000 ... C4 37
Fengshan, For., 5,000 ... *G9 34
Fengtu, China, 14,000 ... J2 36
Fenick, isl., S.C ... G1 115
Fenn, Idaho, Idaho, 25 ... D2 89
Fennimore, Grant, Wis., 1,747 ... F3 124
Fennville, Allegan, Mich., 705 ... F4 98
Fenton, Sask., Can ... D3 70
Fenton, Kossuth, Iowa, 440 ... A3 90
Fenton, Jefferson Davis, La., 429 ... D3 95
Fenton, Genesee, Mich., 6,142 ... F7 98
Fenton, St. Louis, Mo., 1,059 ... B8 101
Fentress, Caldwell, Tex., 350 ... A4 118
Fentress, Norfolk, Va., 350 ... E6 121
Fentress, co., Tenn., 13,288 ... C9 117
Fenwick, Ont., Can., 685 ... D5 72
Fenwick, Nicholas, W. Va., 505 ... C4 123
Fenwood, Sask., Can., 157 ... F4 70
Fenyang, China, 30,000 ... D7 34, F4 36
Feodosiya, Sov., Un., 51,000 ... I10 27
Ferbane, Ire., 896 ... D4 11
Ferdig, Toole, Mont., 20 ... B5 102
Ferdinand, Idaho, Idaho, 176 ... C2 89
Ferdinand, Dubois, Ind., 1,427 ... H4 91
Ferdinand (Town of), Essex, Vt. (16▲) ... *B5 120
Ferdinandshof, Ger., 2,490 ... E7 24
Ferdows, Iran ... E9 41
Fère-Champenoise, Fr., 2,146 ... F4 15
Ferentino, It., 16,836 ... D4 21
Fergana, Sov. Un., 87,000 ... E8 29
Fergana, mts., Sov. Un ... E8 29
Fergus, Ont., Can., 3,831 ... D4 72
Fergus, Fergus, Mont., 10 ... C7 102
Fergus, co., Mont., 14,018 ... C7 102
Fergus Falls, Otter Tail, Minn., 13,733 ... D2 99
Ferguson, B.C., Can. ... D9 68
Ferguson, Marshall, Iowa, 186 ... C5 92
Ferguson, Pulaski, Ky., 468 ... C5 94
Ferguson, St. Louis, Mo., 22,149 ... A8, C7 101
Ferguson, Wayne, W.Va., 100 ... C2 123
Ferguson Creek, Pike, Ky., 300 ... *C7 94
Fériana, Tun., 4,192 ... G11 30
Ferintosh, Alta., Can., 174 ... C4 69
Fermanagh, co., N. Ire., 51,613 ... C4 11
Ferme-Neuve, Que., Can., 1,971 ... C2 73
Fermeuse, Newf., Can., 311 ... E5 75
Fermo, It., 11,400 ... C4 21
Fermoselle, Sp., 3,885 ... B2 20
Fermoy, Ire., 3,241 ... E3 11
Fern, Clarion, Pa., 50 ... D2 114
Fern, creek, Ky ... A4 94
Fernandina Beach, Nassau, Fla., 7,276 ... B5, B6 86
Fernandina (Narborough), isl., Ec ... g5 58
Fernando de Noronha, ter., Braz., 1,389 ... B4 57
Fernando de Noronha, isl., Braz ... B4 57
Fernando Póo, reg., Equat. Gui., 71,000 ... F6 42, E1 46
Fernando Póo, isl., Equat. Gui ... E1 46
Fernán-Núñez, Sp., 12,225 ... D3 20
Fernão Veloso, bay, Moz ... D7 48
Fernbank, Lamar, Ala., 80 ... B1 78
Fern Creek, Jefferson, Ky., 1,500 ... A5 94
Fern Crest Village, Broward, Fla., 93 ... *F6 86
Ferndale, Pulaski, Ark., 60 ... D5 81
Ferndale, Humboldt, Calif., 1,371 ... B1 82
Ferndale, Bell, Ky., 200 ... D6 94
Ferndale, Anne Arundel, Md., 2,500 ... B4 85
Ferndale, Oakland, Mich., 31,347 ... A7 98
Ferndale, Cambria, Pa., 2,717 ... F4 114
Ferndale, Northumberland, Pa., 1,900 ... *D8 114
Ferndale, Schuylkill, Pa., 40 ... E9 114
Ferndale, Whatcom, Wash., 1,442 ... A3 122
Ferney, Brown, S. Dak., 100 ... B7 116
Fernie, B.C., Can., 2,661 ... E10 68
Fernley, Lyon, Nev., 500 ... D2 104
Fern Ridge, dam, Oreg ... C3 113
Ferns, Ire., 557 ... E5 11
Fernwood, Benewah, Idaho, 250 ... B2 89
Fernwood, Pike, Miss., 600 ... D3 100
Fernwood, Oswego, N.Y., 170 ... B4 108
Ferozepore, India, 47,060 (*97,932) ... B5 40
Ferrara, It., 102,000 (156,900▲) ... E7 18, B3 21
Ferreira do Alentejo, Port., 5,205 ... C1 20
Ferreira do Zêzere, Port., 2,503 ... C1 20
Ferrellsburg, Lincoln, W. Va., 150 ... C2 123
Ferrelo, cape, Oreg ... E2 113
Ferreñafe, Peru, 8,812 ... C2 58
Ferriday, Concordia, La., 4,563 ... C4 95
Ferriere, It., 6,433 ... E5 18
Ferris, Ont., Can., 3,004 ... *A5 72
Ferris, Hancock, Ill., 208 ... C2 90
Ferris, Ellis, Tex., 1,807 ... C4, B6 118
Ferris, mts., Wyo ... C5 125
Ferrisburg, Addison, Vt., 170 (1,426▲) ... C2 120
Ferron, Emery, Utah, 386 ... D4 119
Ferros, Braz., 2,456 ... E2 57
Ferrum, Franklin, Va., 400 ... E2 121
Ferry, Oceana, Mich., 100 ... E4 98
Ferry, co., Wash., 3,889 ... A7 122
Ferry, pt., N.J ... k7 106
Ferryland, Newf., Can., 713 ... E5 75
Ferrysburg, Ottawa, Mich., 2,590 ... *E4 98
Ferryville, Tun., 29,353 ... F11 30
Ferryville, Crawford, Wis., 194 ... E2 124
Fertile, Worth, Iowa, 386 ... A4 92
Fertile, Polk, Minn., 968 ... C2 99
Fertilia, It ... D2 21
Fès (Fez), Mor., 216,133 ... C3 44, G4 30
Feshi, Con. L ... C2 48
Fessenden, Wells, N. Dak., 920 ... B6 110
Festina, Winneshiek, Iowa, 150 ... A6 92
Festus, Jefferson, Mo., 7,021 ... B8, C7 101
Feteşti, Rom., 15,383 ... C8 22
Fethard, Ire., 962 ... E4 11
Fethiye, Tur., 7,700 ... D7 23
Fetisovo, Sov. Un ... E4 29
Fettercairn, Scot., 1,323 ... D6 13
Fetters Hot Springs, Sonoma, Calif., 750 ... *B5 82
Feucht, Ger., 7,300 ... D6 17
Feuchtwangen, Ger., 4,500 ... D5 17
Feudal, Sask., Can ... F2 70
Feurs, Fr., 6,252 ... E6 14
Feversham, Ont., Can., 151 ... C4 72
Fez (Fès), Mor., 216,133 ... C3 44, G4 30
Fezzan (Fazzān), prov., Libya, 54,438 ... D2 43
Ffestiniog, Wales, 6,923 ... B4 12
Fiambala, Arg ... E2 55
Fianarantsoa, Malag., 36,189 ... h9 49
Fianarantsoa, prov., Malag ... h9 49
Fianga, Chad, 1,952 ... D3 46
Fibre, Chippewa, Mich., 20 ... B6 98
Ficarolo, It., 4,821 ... E7 18
Fich, Eth., ... D5 47
Fichtel Gebirge, mts., Ger ... C6 17
Ficklin, Wilkes, Ga., 100 ... C4 87
Ficksburg, S. Afr., 7,778 ... C4 49
Fidalgo, isl., Wash ... A3 122
Fidelis, Santa Rosa, Fla., 150 ... G2 86
Fidenza, It., 9,800 ... B3 21
Fidler, lake, Man., Can ... A3 71
Field, B.C., Can ... D9 68
Field, lake, La ... E5 95
Fieldale, Henry, Va., 1,499 ... E3 121
Field Crest Estates, New London, Conn., 1,000 ... *D9 84
Fielding, Sask., Can., 82 ... E2 70
Fielding, Box Elder, Utah, 270 ... B3 119
Fieldon, Jersey, Ill., 239 ... D3 90
Fields, Harney, Oreg., 10 ... E8 113
Fieldsboro, Burlington, N.J., 583 ... C3 106
Fier, Alb., 11,000 ... B2 23
Fierro, Grant, N. Mex., 150 ... E1 107
Fiesch, Switz., 567 ... D5 19
Fiesole, It., 5,200 ... C3 21
Fife, Pierce, Wash., 1,463 ... *B3 122
Fife, co., Scot., 320,541 ... D5 13
Fife, lake, Sask., Can ... H3 70
Fife Lake, Sask., Can., 144 ... H3 70
Fife Lake, Grand Traverse, Mich., 218 ... D5 98
Fife Ness, cape, Scot ... D6 13
Fifield, Price, Wis., 300 ... C3 124
Fifteen Mile, creek, Wyo ... A4 125
Fifteen Mile Falls, res., N.H. and Vt ... B3 105
5th. Cataract (Nile River), Sud ... B3 47
Fifty Lakes, Crow Wing, Minn., 143 ... D4 99
Figeac, Fr., 6,933 ... E4 14
Figtree, Rh ... B4 49
Figueira da Foz, Port., 10,486 ... B1 20
Figueras, Sp., 17,548 ... A7 20
Figuig, Mor., 12,108 ... C4 44
Figure Five, Crawford, Ark., 50 ... B1 81
Fiji, Br. dep., Oceania, 455,000 ... H11 7, 52
Filbert, McDowell, W. Va., 950 ... D3 123
Filchner, ice shelf, Ant ... B6 5
File, lake, Man., Can ... B1 71
File, riv., Man., Can ... B1 71
Filer, Twin Falls, Idaho, 1,249 ... G4 89
Filer City, Manistee, Mich., 500 ... D4 98
Filey, Eng., 4,705 ... F8 13
Fili, Grc., 1,748 ... g11 23
Filiatra, Grc., 9,209 ... D3 23
Filicudi, isl., It ... E5 21
Filingue, Niger ... D5 45
Filisur, Switz., 318 ... C8 19
Filley, Gage, Nebr., 149 ... D9 103
Fillmore, Ventura, Calif., 4,725 ... E4 82
Fillmore, Sask., Can., 340 ... H4 70
Fillmore, Montgomery, Ill., 360 ... D4 90
Fillmore, Putnam, Ind., 550 ... E4 91
Fillmore, Andrew, Mo., 254 ... A3 101
Fillmore, Allegany, N.Y., 522 ... C2 108
Fillmore, Benson, N. Dak., 125 ... A6 110
Fillmore, Johnston, Okla., 100 ... C5 112

Fillmore, Millard, Utah, 1,602 ... E3 119
Fillmore, co., Minn., 23,768 ... G6 99
Fillmore, co., Nebr., 9,425 ... D8 103
Fimi, riv., Con. L ... B2 48
Finale Emilia, It., 6,157 ... E7 18
Fina Susu, mtn., Saipan ... 52
Finca Marini, P.R ... C2 65
Fincastle, Botetourt, Va., 403 ... D3 121
Finch, Ont., Can., 386 ... B9 72
Finchley, Eng., 69,311 ... k12 10
Finderne, Somerset, N.J., 2,000 ... *B3 106
Findhorn, Scot ... C5 13
Findhorn, riv., Scot ... C5 13
Findlater, Sask., Can., 128 ... G3 70
Findlay, Shelby, Ill., 759 ... D5 90
Findlay, Hancock, Ohio, 30,344 ... A4 111
Findlay, mtn., B.C., Can ... D9 68
Fine, St. Lawrence, N.Y., 300 ... A5, f9 108
Finegayan, Guam ... 52
Finesville, Warren, N.J., 300 ... B2 106
Fingal, Barnes, N. Dak., 190 ... C8 110
Finger, McNairy, Tenn., 150 ... B3 117
Fingerville, Spartanburg, S.C., 350 ... A3 115
Finges, lake, Ont., Can ... C4 71
Fingoe, Moz ... A5 49
Finike, Tur., 2,900 ... D8 23
Finistère, dept., Fr., 727,847 ... *C2 14
Finisterre, cape, Sp ... A1 20
Finjasjon, lake, Swe ... B7 24
Finke, riv., Austl ... E5 50
Finksburg, Carroll, Md., 385 ... B4 85
Finland, Lake, Minn., 200 ... C7 99
Finland, country, Eur., 4,600,000 ... C14 8, E12 25
Finland, gulf, Fin., Sov. Un ... H11 25
Finlay, riv., B.C., Can ... A5 68
Finlay Forks, B.C., Can ... m17 68
Finlayson, Pine, Minn., 213 ... D6 99
Finley, Steele, N. Dak., 808 ... B8 110
Finley, Pushmataha, Okla., 250 ... C6 112
Finley, Dyer, Tenn., 600 ... A2 117
Finleyson, Pulaski, Ga., 82 ... D3 87
Finmoore, B.C., Can., 135 ... C6 68
Finnegan, Alta., Can ... D4 69
Finney, co., Kans., 16,093 ... D3 93
Finneytown, Hamilton, Ohio, 5,000 ... *C3 111
Finnmark, co., Nor., 72,000 ... *B13 25
Finschhafen, N. Gui ... k12 50
Finspång, Swe., 15,200 ... u33 25
Finsteraarhorn, mtn., Switz ... C5 19
Finsterwalde, Ger., 20,700 ... B8 17
Fintona, N. Ire., 1,266 ... C4 11
Fintown, Ire ... C3 11
Finvoy, N. Ire., 1,026 ... B5 11
Finzel, Garrett, Md ... D2 85
Fionn, bay, Scot ... C3 13
Fiq, Syr., 1,494 ... F10 31
Fir, riv., Sask., Can ... D4 70
Firecrest, Pierce, Wash., 3,565 ... B3 122
Fire, isl., N.Y ... G4 84
Fire, is., N.Y ... G4 84
Firebaugh, Fresno, Calif., 2,627 ... D3 82
Fire Island, inlet, N.Y ... G3 84
Firenze (Florence), It., 455,000 (*560,000) ... C3 21
Firenzuola, It., 743 ... B3 21
Firesteel, Dewey, S. Dak., 150 ... B4 116
Firestone, Weld, Colo., 276 ... A6 83
Firmat, Arg., 4,051 ... A4 54
Firminy, Fr., 26,065 ... E6 14
Fir Mountain, Sask., Can., 74 ... H2 70
Firozabad, India, 98,611 ... D7 40
Firsovo, Sov. Un ... C11 37
1st. Cataract (Nile River), Eg., U.A.R ... E6 43
Firth, Bingham, Idaho, 322 ... F6 89
Firth, Lancaster, Nebr., 277 ... D9 103
Fīrūzābād, Iran, 23,382 ... G6 41
Fīrūzkūh, Iran, 5,874 ... D6 41
Fish, creek, W. Va ... C2 123
Fish, lake, Utah ... E4 119
Fish, mtn., Oreg ... D4 131
Fish, riv., Maine ... A4 96
Fish, riv., S.W. Afr ... C2 49
Fish Cove, pt., Newf., Can ... A3 75
Fish Creek, Door, Wis., 180 ... C5 124
Fisheating, creek, Fla ... F5 86
Fisher, Poinsett, Ark., 303 ... B5 81
Fisher, Champaign, Ill., 1,155 ... C5 90
Fisher, Polk, Minn., 326 ... C2 99
Fisher, Clarion, Pa., 150 ... D3 114
Fisher, Hardy, W. Va., 20 ... B5 123
Fisher, co., Tex., 7,865 ... C2 118
Fisher, bay, Man., Can ... D3 71
Fisher, glacier, Ant ... B19 5
Fisher, lake, N.S., Can ... E4 74
Fisher, peak, Va ... E2 121
Fisher, riv., Man., Can ... D3 71
Fisher, strait, N.W. Ter., Can ... D16 67
Fisher Branch, Man., Can., 369 ... D3 71
Fisherman, isl., Va ... B7 121
Fishers, Hamilton, Ind., 344 ... E5, G8 91
Fishers, isl., N.Y ... m16 108
Fishers, peak, Colo ... D6 83
Fishers Island, sound, Conn ... D8 84
Fishersville, Augusta, Va., 700 ... C4 121
Fishertown, Bedford, Pa., 250 ... F4 114
Fisherville, Ont., Can., 234 ... E5 72
Fishguard, Wales, 4,898 ... C3 12
Fish Haven, Bear Lake, Idaho, 130 ... G7 89
Fishing, bay, Md ... D5 85
Fishing, creek, N.C ... A6 109
Fishing, creek, S.C ... B5 115
Fishing, creek, W. Va ... B4 123
Fishing, lake, Man., Can ... C4 71
Fishing, lake, Sask., Can ... F4 70
Fishing, lakes, Sask., Can ... G3 70
Fishing Creek, Dorchester, Md., 544 ... D5 81
Fishing Creek, Cape May, N.J., 100 ... E3 106
Fishing Creek, res., S.C ... B6 115
Fishkill, Dutchess, N.Y., 1,033 ... D7 108
Fishkill, creek, N.Y ... C2 84
Fishot, isl., Newf., Can ... C4 75
Fish River, lake, Maine ... B4 96
Fish Springs, range, Utah ... D2 119
Fishtail, Stillwater, Mont., 80 ... E7 102
Fishtail, pt., Ant ... f39 5
Fishtrap, Lincoln, Wash ... B8 122
Fishville, Grant, La., 150 ... C3 95
Fisk Butler, Mo., 498 ... E7 101
Fiskburg, Kenton, Ky., 40 ... B5, A7 94
Fiskdale, Worcester, Mass., 850 ... B3 97
Fiske, Sask., Can., 117 ... F1 70
Fiskeville, Providence, R.I. (part of Cranston) ... C10 84
Fismes, Fr., 3,222 ... E3 15
Fitch Bay, Que., Can., 189 ... D5 73
Fitchburg, Worcester, Mass., 43,021 ... A4 97
Fitchville, New London, Conn., 700 ... C8 84
Fithian, Vermilion, Ill., 495 ... C6 90
Fitler, Issaquena, Miss., 150 ... C2 100
Fittstown, Pontotoc, Okla., 200 ... B5 112
Fitzgerald, Ben Hill, Ga., 8,781 ... E3 87
Fitzhugh, Pontotoc, Okla., 150 ... C5 112
Fitz Hugh, sound, B.C., Can ... D4 68
Fitzpatrick, Que., Can., 40 ... B5 73
Fitz Roy, Arg ... D3 54
Fitzroy, Austl., 88 ... C4 50
Fitz Roy, mtn., Arg ... D2 54
Fitzroy, riv., Austl ... C3 50
Fitzroy, riv., Austl ... D8 50
Fitzroy Harbour, Ont., Can., 253 ... B8 72
Fitzwilliam, Cheshire, N.H., 300 (966▲) ... E2 105
Fitzwilliam, isl., Ont., Can ... B3 72
Fitzwilliam Depot, Cheshire, N.H., 200 ... E2 105
Fiume, see Rijeka, Yugo.
Fiumicino, It., 1,121 ... h8 21
Five Islands, N.S., Can., 194 ... D5 74
Fivemile, creek, Wyo ... B4 125
Fivemiletown, N. Ire., 777 ... C4 11
Five Points, Chambers, Ala., 285 ... B4 78
Five Points, Los Angeles, Calif., 15,000 ... *F3 82
Five Points, Marion, Ind., 200 ... H8 91
Five Points, Bernalillo, N. Mex., 3,000 ... B3, k7 107
Five Points, Lawrence, Tenn., 115 ... B4 117
Fizi, Con. L ... B4 48
Fjärås, Swe ... A6 24
Fjärdhundra, Swe., 320 ... t34 25
Fjerritslev, Den., 1,925 ... A3 24
Flagg, Castro, Tex ... B1 118
Flagler, Kit Carson, Colo., 693 ... B7 83
Flagler, co., Fla., 4,566 ... C5 86
Flagler Beach, Flagler, Fla., 970 ... C5 86
Flag Pond, Unicoi, Tenn., 75 ... C11 117
Flagstaff, Coconino, Ariz., 18,214 ... B4 80
Flagstaff, lake, Oreg ... E7 113
Flagtown, Somerset, N.J., 650 ... B3 106
Flamand, lake, Que., Can ... B4 73
Flambeau, res., Wis ... B3 124
Flambeau, riv., Wis ... C2 124
Flamborough, head, Eng ... C6 10
Flaming Gorge, dam, Utah ... C6 119
Flaming Gorge, res., Utah, Wyo ... B6 119
Flanagan, Livingston, Ill., 841 ... C5 90
Flanders, Ont., Can., 40 ... E5 71
Flanders, Litchfield, Conn., 60 ... B3 84
Flanders, Morris, N.J., 560 ... B3 106
Flanders, Suffolk, N.Y., 2,000 ... F6 84
Flanders, see East Flanders and West Flanders, provs., Bel.
Flanders (Flandre), former prov., Fr., 2,099,000 ... B5 14
Flanders, bay, N.Y ... F6 84
Flandreau, Moody, S. Dak., 2,129 ... C9 116
Flanigan, Washoe, Nev., 5 ... C2 104
Flannan, is., Scot ... A3 10
Flasher, Morton, N. Dak., 515 ... C4 110
Flat, Alsk., 14 ... C8 79
Flat, Wolfe, Ky., 74 ... C6 94
Flat, Phelps, Mo., 75 ... D6 101
Flat, brook, N.J ... A3 106
Flat, isl., Newf., Can ... C3 75
Flat, lake, Alta., Can ... B4 69
Flat, lake, La ... C5 95
Flat, riv., Mich ... E5 98
Flat Bay, Newf., Can., 388 ... D2 75
Flatbrookville, Sussex, N.J., 25 ... A3 106
Flatbush, Alta., Can., 91 ... B3 69
Flat Creek, Walker, Ala., 800 ... B2, E4 78
Flatcreek, Bedford, Tenn., 100 ... B5 117
Flat Gap, Wise, Va ... B2 121
Flathead, co., Mont., 32,965 ... B2 102
Flathead, lake, Mont ... C2 102
Flathead, mts., Mont ... B2 102
Flathead, riv., B.C., Can., Mont ... E10 68
Flathead, val., Mont ... C2 102
Flatlands, N.B., Can., 282 ... B3 74
Flat Lick, Knox, Ky., 500 ... D6 94
Flatonia, Fayette, Tex., 1,009 ... E4 118
Flat River, P.E.I., Can., 118 ... C7 74
Flat River, St. Francois, Mo., 4,515 ... D7 101
Flat River, res., R.I ... C10 84
Flat Rock, Jackson, Ala., 600 ... A4 78
Flat Rock, Newf., Can., 632 ... *E5 75
Flat Rock, Crawford, Ill., 497 ... E6 90
Flat Rock, Shelby, Ind., 250 ... F6 91
Flat Rock, Wayne, Mich., 4,696 ... F7 98
Flat Rock, Henderson, N.C., 1,808 ... D3 109
Flat Rock, Seneca, Ohio, 400 ... A5 111
Flatrock, creek, Ind ... F6 91
Flatrock, lake, Man., Can ... B1 71
Flats, McPherson, Nebr., 4 ... C4 103
Flats, Macon, N.C ... D2 109
Flattery, cape, Wash ... A1 122
Flattop, Platte, Wyo ... C8 125
Flat Tops, plat., Colo ... B3 83
Flatts, Bermuda ... E14 77
Flat Willow, creek, Mont ... D7 102
Flatwood, Wilcox, Ala., 300 ... C2 78
Flatwoods, Greenup, Ky., 3,741 ... B7 94
Flatwoods, Rapides, La., 150 ... C3 95
Flat Woods, Perry, Tenn., 150 ... B4 117
Flat Woods, Braxton, W. Va., 248 ... C4 123
Flawil, Switz., 7,256 ... B7 19
Flaxcombe, Sask., Can., 123 ... F1 70
Flaxton, Burke, N. Dak., 375 ... A3 110
Flaxville, Daniels, Mont., 262 ... B11 102
Fleet, Alta., Can., 79 ... C5 69
Fleet, Eng., 13,672 ... C7 12
Fleeton, Northumberland, Va., 200 ... D6 121
Fleetwing Estates, Bucks, Pa., 1,100 ... *F12 114
Fleetwood, Eng., 27,760 ... G5 13
Fleetwood, Ashe, N.C., 70 ... A2 109
Fleetwood, Berks, Pa., 2,647 ... F10 114
Fleischmanns, Delaware, N.Y., 450 ... C6 108
Flekkefjord, Nor., 3,200 ... H2 25
Fleming, Sask., Can., 187 ... G5 70
Fleming, Logan, Colo., 384 ... A8 83
Fleming, Liberty, Ga., 150 ... E5 87
Fleming (Unionville), Centre, Pa., 371 ... E6 114
Fleming, co., Ky., 10,890 ... B6 94
Flemingsburg, Fleming, Ky., 2,067 ... B6 94
Flemington, Liberty, Ga., 149 ... E5 87
Flemington, Polk, Mo., 142 ... D4 101
Flemington, Hunterdon, N.J., 3,232 ... B3 106
Flemington, Clinton, Pa., 1,608 ... D7 114
Flemington, Taylor, W. Va., 478 ... B7 123
Flen, Swe., 5,700 ... t34 25
Flensburg, Ger., 96,900 ... A4 16, D3 24
Flensburg, Morrison, Minn., 280 ... E4 99
Flensburg, fjord, Den ... D3 24
Flers, Fr., 14,634 ... C3 14
Flesherton, Ont., Can., 515 ... C4 72
Fletcher, Ont., Can., 109 ... E2 72
Fletcher, Henderson, N.C., 800 ... D3 109
Fletcher, Miami, Ohio, 569 ... B3 111
Fletcher, Comanche, Okla., 884 ... C3 112
Fletcher, Franklin, Vt., 125 (399▲) ... B3 120
Fletcher, is., Ant ... B3 5
Fletcher Park, Albany, Wyo ... C7 125
Fleur-de-Lys, Newf., Can., 457 ... C3, h10 75
Fleurier, Switz., 3,814 ... C2 19
Flieden, Ger., 3,400 ... C4 17
Flims, Switz., 1,444 ... C7 19
Flinders, is., Austl ... F5 50
Flinders, isl., Austl ... n15 50
Flinders, range, Austl ... F6 50
Flinders, riv., Austl ... C7 50
Flin Flon, Man., Can., 11,104 ... B1, g7 71
Flint, Morgan, Ala., 432 ... A3 78
Flint, Steuben, Ind., 60 ... A7 91
Flint, Genesee, Mich., 196,940 (*379,900) ... E7 98
Flint, Wales, 13,690 ... A4 12
Flint, co., Wales, 149,888 ... A4 12
Flint, isl., Pac. O ... G12 7
Flint, riv., Ga ... D2 87
Flint, riv., Mich ... E5 98
Flint, run, W. Va ... A6 123
Flint Creek, range, Mont ... D3 102
Flinthill, St. Charles, Mo., 200 ... C7 101
Flint Hill, Rappahannock, Va., 200 ... C4 121
Flintridge, Los Angeles, Calif., 5,000 ... *F2 82
Flintoft, Sask., Can ... H2 70
Flinton, Ont., Can., 182 ... C7 72
Flintstone, Allegany, Md., 125 ... D2 85
Flintville, Lincoln, Tenn., 175 ... B5 117
Flipper, pt., Wake Isl ... 52
Flippin, Marion, Ark., 433 ... A3 81
Flippin, Monroe, Ky., 150 ... D4 94
Flixecourt, Fr., 3,285 ... D2 15
Flöha, Ger., 6,876 ... C8 17
Flom, Norman, Minn., 75 ... C2 99
Flomaton, Escambia, Ala., 1,454 ... D2 78
Flomot, Motley, Tex., 475 ... B2 118
Floodwood, Dickinson, Mich ... B2 98
Floodwood, St. Louis, Minn., 677 ... D6 99
Flora, Clay, Ill., 5,331 ... E5 90
Flora, Carroll, Ind., 1,742 ... C4 91
Flora, Madison, Miss., 743 ... C3 100
Flora, Benson N. Dak., 38 ... B6 110
Flora, Wallowa, Oreg., 75 ... B9 113
Florahome, Putnam, Fla., 400 ... C5 86
Florala, Covington, Ala., 3,011 ... D3 78
Floral City, Citrus, Fla., 900 ... D4 86
Floral Park, Silver Bow, Mont., 4,079 ... *D4 102
Floral Park, Nassau, N.Y., 17,499 ... k13 108
Flora Vista, San Juan, N. Mex., 400 ... A1 107
Flordell Hills, St. Louis, Mo., 1,119 ... *A8 101
Florence, Lauderdale, Ala., 31,649 ... A2 78
Florence, Pinal, Ariz., 2,143 ... E4 80
Florence, Los Angeles, Calif., 38,164 ... *E4 82
Florence, Fremont, Colo., 2,821 ... C5 83
Florence, Switzerland, Ind., 150 ... G8 91
Florence, see Firenze, It.
Florence, Marion, Kans., 853 ... D7 93
Florence, Boone, Ky., 5,837 ... A5, A7 94
Florence, Rankin, Miss., 360 ... C3 100
Florence, Morgan, Mo., 65 ... C5 101
Florence, Ravalli, Mont., 150 ... D2 102
Florence, Burlington, N.J., 4,000 ... C3 106
Florence, Lane, Oreg., 1,642 ... *D2 113
Florence, Florence, S.C., 24,722 ... C8 115
Florence, Codington, S. Dak., 216 ... B8 116
Florence, Rutherford, Tenn ... B5 117
Florence, Williamson, Tex., 610 ... D4 118
Florence, Rutland, Vt., 100 ... D2 120
Florence, Snohomish, Wash., 45 ... A3 122
Florence, Florence, Wis., 700 ... C5 124
Florence, co., S.C., 84,438 ... C8 115
Florence, co., Wis., 3,437 ... C5 124
Florence Junction, Pinal, Ariz., 25 ... D4 80
Florenceville, N.B., Can., 229 ... C2 74
Florencia, Col., 8,119 ... C2 60
Florenville, Bel., 2,378 ... E5 15
Florenville, St. Tammany, La ... B8 95
Flores, Guat., 1,596 ... B3 62
Flores, dept., Ur., 22,900 ... *E1 56
Flores, isl., B.C., Can ... E4 68
Flores, isl., Indon ... G6 35
Flores, isl., Port. (Azores) ... g8 44
Flores, sea, Indon ... G6 35
Floresta, Braz., 2,377 ... C3 57
Floresville, Wilson, Tex., 2,126 ... E3, B4 118
Florey, Andrews, Tex., 50 ... C1 118
Florham Park, Morris, N.J., 7,222 ... B4 106
Floriano, Braz., 16,063 ... C2 57
Florianópolis, Braz., 74,323 ... D3 56
Florida, Cuba, 21,159 ... E4 64
Florida, Berkshire, Mass., 25 (569▲) ... A1 97
Florida, Monroe, Mo., 55 ... B6 101
Florida, Socorro, N. Mex., 100 ... C3 107
Florida, Orange, N.Y., 1,550 ... D6, m14 108
Florida, Henry, Ohio, 290 ... A3 111
Florida [Adentro], P.R., 2,955 ... B4 65
Florida, Ur., 15,500 ... E1 56
Florida, dept., Ur., 61,200 ... *E1 56
Florida, state, U.S., 4,951,560 ... E11 77, 86
Florida, bay, Fla ... H6 86
Florida, cape, Fla ... G6 86
Florida, keys, Fla ... H6 86
Florida, mts., N. Mex ... E2 107
Florida, straits, Fla ... H6 86
Florida City, Dade, Fla., 4,114 ... F3, G6 86
Florien, Sabine, La., 496 ... C2 95
Florin, Lancaster, Pa., 1,518 ... F8 114
Florina, Grc., 11,933 ... B3 23
Florina, prov., Grc., 67,356 ... *B3 23
Floris, Davis, Iowa, 187 ... D5 92
Floris, Fairfax, Va., 75 ... B4 121
Florissant, Teller, Colo., 40 ... C5 83
Florissant, St. Louis, Mo., 38,166 ... A8 101
Florosa, Okaloosa, Fla., 150 ... G2 86
Flossmoor, Cook, Ill., 4,624 ... F3 90
Flour Bluff, Nueces, Tex., 3,500 ... *F4 118
Flournoy, Tehama, Calif., 50 ... C2 82
Flourtown, Montgomery, Pa., 4,000 ... A11 114
Flovilla, Butts, Ga., 284 ... C3 87
Flower, riv., Vt ... E2 120
Floweree, Chouteau, Mont., 50 ... C5 102
Flower Hill, Nassau, N.Y., 4,594 ... *E7 108
Flower's Cove, Newf., Can., 312 ... C3 75
Flower Station, Ont., Can., 74 ... B8 72
Flower Village, Kern, Calif., 5,000 ... *E4 82
Flowery Branch, Hall, Ga., 741 ... B3 87
Flowood, Rankin, Miss., 486 ... C3 100
Floyd, Floyd, Iowa, 401 ... A5 92
Floyd, Roosevelt, N. Mex., 200 ... C6 107
Floyd, Floyd, Va., 487 ... E2 121
Floyd, co., Ga., 69,130 ... B1 87
Floyd, co., Ind., 51,397 ... H6 91
Floyd, co., Iowa, 21,102 ... A5 92
Floyd, co., Ky., 41,642 ... C7 94
Floyd, co., Tex., 12,369 ... B2 118
Floyd, co., Va., 10,462 ... E2 121
Floyd, mtn., Ariz ... B3 80
Floyd, riv., Iowa ... B1 92
Floydada, Floyd, Tex., 3,769 ... C2 118
Floyd Dale, Dillon, S.C., 125 ... C9 115
Floyds, canyon, Nev ... C4 104
Floyds, fork, Ky ... B4 94
Floydsburg, Oldham, Ky., 75 ... A4 94
Floyds Knobs, Floyd, Ind., 300 ... H6 91
Fluchthorn, mtn., Ger., Switz ... C9 19
Fluessenmeer, lake, Neth ... B5 15
Flumendosa, riv., It ... E2 21
Flums, Switz., 4,462 ... B7 19
Flushing, Genesee, Mich., 3,761 ... E7 98
Flushing, Belmont, Ohio, 1,189 ... B6 111
Fluvanna, Scurry, Tex., 300 ... C2 118
Fluvanna, co., Va., 7,227 ... D4 121
Fly Creek, Otsego, N.Y., 300 ... C6 108
Flying H, Chaves, N. Mex., 40 ... D4 107
Flynns Lick, Jackson, Tenn., 50 ... C8 117
Foam, lake, Sask., Can ... F4 70
Foam Lake, Sask., Can., 933 ... F4 70
Foard, co., Tex., 3,125 ... B3 118
Foard City, Foard, Tex ... C3 118
Foča, Yugo., 6,762 ... D4 22
Fochabers, Scot ... C5 13
Fochimi Hoyoudine, well, Chad ... B3 46
Focşani, Rom., 28,244 ... C8 22
Fogauso, cape, Am. Sam ... 52
Foggia, It., 124,500 ... D5 21
Foggo, Nig ... D6 45
Fogliano, It ... k9 21
Fogo, Newf., Can., 1,152 ... D4 75
Fogo, cape, Newf., Can ... D5 75
Fogo, isl., C.V. Is ... *E4 42
Fogo, isl., Newf., Can ... D4 75
Fohnsdorf, Aus., 11,517 ... E7 16
Föhr, isl., Ger ... A4 16
Foix, Fr., 7,164 ... F4 14
Foix, former prov., Fr., 81,000 ... *F4 14
Fokis (Phocis), prov., Grc., 47,842 ... *C4 23
Folcroft, Delaware, Pa., 7,013 ... *G11 114
Foley, Baldwin, Ala., 2,889 ... E2 78
Foley, Taylor, Fla., 200 ... B3 86
Foley, Benton, Minn., 1,112 ... E5 99
Foley, Lincoln, Mo., 183 ... B7 101
Foley, isl., N.W. Ter., Can ... C17 67
Foligno, It., 32,400 ... C4 21
Folkestone, Eng., 43,600 ... C9 12
Folkston, Charlton, Ga., 1,810 ... F4 87
Folkstone, Onslow, N.C., 75 ... C6 109
Follansbee, Brooke, W. Va., 4,052 ... A4, B2 123
Follett, Lipscomb, Tex., 466 ... A2 118
Follonica, It., 7,147 ... C3 21
Folly, isl., S.C ... F8 115
Folly Beach, Charleston, S.C., 1,137 ... F18, G3 115
Follyfarm, Malheur, Oreg ... D8 113
Folly Lake, N.S., Can., 40 ... D6 74
Folsom, Sacramento, Calif., 3,925 ... A6, C3 82
Folsom, St. Tammany, La., 225 ... D5 95
Folsom, Atlantic, N.J., 482 ... D3 106
Folsom, Union, N. Mex., 142 ... A6 107
Folsom, Delaware, Pa., 5,000 ... *B11 114
Folsom, Wetzel, W. Va., 450 ... A6, B4 123
Folsomville, Warrick, Ind., 130 ... H3 91
Fomento, Cuba, 6,038 ... D4 64
Fonda, Pocahontas, Iowa, 1,026 ... B3 92
Fonda, Montgomery, N.Y., 1,004 ... C6 108
Fond-du-Lac, Sask., Can., 253 ... m7 70
Fond du Lac, Fond du Lac, Wis., 32,719 ... B5, E5 124
Fond du Lac, co., Wis., 75,085 ... E5 124
Fond du Lac, Indian res., Minn ... D6 99
Fonde, Bell, Ky., 200 ... D6 94
Fondi, It., 13,700 ... D4 21
Fonsagrada, Sp., 950 ... A2 20
Fonseca, gulf, Cen. Am ... D4 62
Fontainebleau, Fr., 20,583 (*28,000) ... C5 14
Fontana, San Bernardino, Calif., 14,659 ... F3 82
Fontana, Miami, Kans., 138 ... D9 93
Fontana, Walworth, Wis., 1,326 ... F5 124
Fontana Dam, Graham, N.C., 250 ... D2 109
Fontanelle, Adair, Iowa, 729 ... C3 92
Fontanelle, Washington, Nebr., 50 ... C9 103
Fontanet, Vigo, Ind., 200 ... E3 91
Fonte Boa, Braz., 1,154 ... D4 60
Fontenay-le-Comte, Fr., 10,109 ... D3 14
Fontenay [-sous-Bois], Fr., 37,484 ... g10 14
Fontenelle, Lincoln, Wyo ... C2 125
Fontenelle, mtn., Wyo ... C2 125
Fonthill, Ont., Can., 2,324 ... D5 72
Foochow (Minhow), China, 616,000 ... F8 34
Foosland, Champaign, Ill., 150 ... C5 90
Foothill, Spokane, Wash ... D8 122
Foothills, Alta., Can ... C2 69
Footville, Rock, Wis., 675 ... F4 124
Foping, China, 500 ... H2 36
Forada, Douglas, Minn., 98 ... E3 99
Foraker, Hardin, Ohio, 160 ... B4 111
Foraker, Osage, Okla., 74 ... A5 112
Forbach, Fr., 21,704 (*58,000) ... C7 14
Forbes, Austl., 6,826 ... F7 51
Forbes, St. Louis, Minn., 25 ... C6 99
Forbes, Holt, Mo., 100 ... B2 101
Forbes, Mitchell, N.C., 100 ... C4 109
Forbes, Dickey, N. Dak., 138 ... D7 110
Forbes, mtn., Alta., Can ... D2 69
Forbing Park, Yavapai, Ariz., 300 ... C3 80
Forcados, Nig., 3,001 ... E6 45
Forcalquier, Fr., 2,050 ... F6 14
Force, Elk, Pa., 400 ... D4 114
Forchheim, Ger., 20,900 ... D6 17
Ford, Kootenai, Idaho ... E8 89
Ford, Ford, Kans., 252 ... E4 93
Ford, Clark, Ky., 250 ... C5 94
Ford, Scot ... D3 13
Ford, co., Ill., 16,606 ... C5 90
Ford, co., Kans., 20,938 ... E4 93
Ford, riv., Mich ... C3 98
Ford City, Kern, Calif., 3,926 ... E4 82
Ford City, Armstrong, Pa., 5,440 ... E2 114
Fordland, Webster, Mo., 338 ... D5 101
Fordlândia, Braz ... C3 59
Fords, Middlesex, N.J., 12,500 ... *B4 106
Fords Prairie, Lewis, Wash., 1,404 ... *C3 122
Fordsville, Ohio, Ky., 524 ... C3 94
Fordville, Wash., N. Dak., 367 ... A8 110
Fordwich, Ont., Can., 267 ... D3 72
Fordwick, Augusta, Va., 150 ... C3 121
Fordyce, Dallas, Ark., 3,890 ... D3 81
Fordyce, Cedar, Nebr., 143 ... B8 103
Forécariah, Guinea, 5,300 ... E2 45
Foreman (New Rocky Comfort), Little River, Ark., 1,001 ... D1 81
Foremost, Alta., Can., 561 ... E5 69
Forest, Bel., 51,503 ... D4 15
Forest, Ont., Can., 2,188 ... D2 72
Forest, Livingston, Ill., 1,040 ... C5 90
Forest, Clinton, Ind., 400 ... D5 91
Forest, Scott, Miss., 3,917 ... C4 100
Forest, Hardin, Ohio, 1,314 ... B4 111
Forest, Cherokee, Tex., 100 ... D5 118
Forest, Bedford, Va., 250 ... D3 121
Forest, co., Pa., 4,485 ... C3 114
Forest, co., Wis., 7,542 ... C5 124
Forest Acres, Richland, S.C., 3,842 ... *D6 115
Forestburg, Alta., Can., 677 ... C4 69
Forestburg, Sanborn, S. Dak., 150 ... C8 116
Forest Center, Lake, Minn., 150 ... C7 99
Forest City, Mason, Ill., 249 ... C4 90
Forest City, Winnebago, Iowa, 2,930 ... A4 92
Forest City, Washington, Maine, 25 ... C5 96
Forest City, Holt, Mo., 435 ... B2 101
Forest City, Rutherford, N.C., 6,556 ... B2, D4 109
Forest City, Susquehanna, Pa., 2,651 ... C11 114
Forestdale, Clarke, Ala ... D2 78
Forestdale, Providence, R.I., 750 ... B10 84
Forest Dale, Rutland, Vt., 450 ... D2 120
Forester, Scott, Ark ... C2 81
Forest Glen, Montgomery, Md., 215 ... B3 85
Forest Green, Chariton, Mo., 100 ... B5 101
Forestgrove, Fergus, Mont., 20 ... D7 102
Forest Grove, Washington, Oreg., 5,628 ... B1, B3 113
Forest Heights, Prince Georges, Md., 3,524 ... *C1 85
Forest Hill, Ont., Can., 20,489 ... m15 72
Forest Hill, Rapides, La., 302 ... C3 95
Forest Hill, Harford, Md., 200 ... A5 85
Forest Hill, Tarrant, Tex., 3,221 ... *C4 118
Forest Hills, N.B., Can., 715 ... *D4 74
Forest Hills, Allegheny, Pa., 8,796 ... F2 114
Forest Hills, Davidson, Tenn., 2,101 ... *A5 117
Forest Home, Butler, Ala., 200 ... D3 78
Forest Homes, Madison, Ill., 2,025 ... *E3 90
Forest Junction, Calumet, Wis., 200 ... A6 124
Forest Knolls, Marin, Calif., 800 ... B5 82
Forest Lake, Alger, Mich., 60 ... B4 98
Forest Lake, Washington, Minn., 2,347 ... E6 99
Forest Lawn, Alta., Can., 12,263 ... D4 69
Foreston, Mille Lacs, Minn., 266 ... E5 99
Foreston, Clarendon, S.C., 210 ... D7 115
Forest Park, Clayton, Ga., 14,201 ... B5, C2 87
Forest Park, Cook, Ill., 14,452 ... F2 90
Forestport, Oneida, N.Y., 300 ... B5 108
Forest River, Walsh, N. Dak., 191 ... A8 110
Forest Station, Washington, Maine, 35 ... C5 96
Forest View, Cook, Ill., 1,042 ... *F3 90
Forest View, Greenville, S.C., 1,000 ... *B3 115
Forestville, Que., Can., 1,529 ... *B2 73
Forestville, Hartford, Conn. (part of Bristol) ... C5 84
Forestville, Prince Georges, Md., 1,500 ... *C4 85
Forestville, Chautauqua, N.Y., 905 ... C1 108
Forestville, Butler, Pa., 300 ... D1 114
Forestville, Door, Wis., 300 ... D6 124
Forfar, Scot., 10,252 ... D6 13
Forgan, Sask., Can., 93 ... F2 70
Forgan, Beaver, Okla., 532 ... A1, D4 112
Forges-les-Eaux, Fr., 2,914 ... C4 14
Forget, Sask., Can., 220 ... H4 70
Forge Village, Middlesex, Mass., 1,400 ... A5, f10 97
Fork, Davie, N.C., 85 ... B3 109
Fork, Dillon, S.C., 168 ... C9 115
Fork, creek, W. Va ... D5 123
Forked Deer, Haywood, Tenn., 100 ... B2 117
Forked Deer, riv, Tenn ... B2 117
Forked River, Ocean, N.J., 900 ... D4 106
Forkland, Greene, Ala., 125 ... C2 78
Fork Mountain, Anderson, Tenn., 150 ... C9 117
Fork Ridge, Claiborne, Tenn., 200 ... C10 117
Fork River, Man., Can., 174 ... D1 71
Forks, Clallam, Wash., 1,156 ... B1 122
Fork Shoals, Greenville, S.C., 200 ... B3 115
Forks of Elkhorn, Franklin, Ky., 172 ... B5 94
Forksville, Sullivan, Pa., 131 ... D8 114
Fork Union, Fluvanna, Va., 200 ... D4 121
Forkville, Scott, Miss., 100 ... *C4 100
Forli, It., 62,700 (96,800▲) ... B4 21
Forman, Sargent, N. Dak., 530 ... C8 110
Formazza, It., 570 ... C4 18
Formby, Eng., 11,730 ... A4 12
Formello, It., 2,067 ... g8 21
Formentera, isl., Sp ... C6 20
Formiga, Braz., 18,763 ... F1 57
Formosa, Arg., 16,506 ... E4 55
Formosa, Van Buren, Ark., 190 ... B3 81
Formosa, Braz., 9,449 ... E1 57
Formosa, Ont., Can., 370 ... C3 72
Formosa, prov., Arg., 178,458 ... E4 55
Formosa, see Taiwan, country, Asia.
Formosa, bay, Ken ... B7 48
Formosa, strait, China ... G8 34
Formoso, Jewell, Kans., 192 ... C6 93
Forney, Kaufman, Tex., 1,544 ... B6, C4 118
Fornovo di Taro, It., 6,920 ... E6 18
Forres, Scot., 4,780 ... C5 13
Forrest, Austl., 20 ... F4 50
Forrest, Livingston, Ill., 1,220 ... C5 90
Forrest, Quay, N. Mex., 50 ... C6 107
Forrest, co., Miss., 52,722 ... D4 100
Forrest City, St. Francis, Ark., 10,544 ... B5 81
Forreston, Ogle, Ill., 1,153 ... A4 90
Forrest Station, Man., Can ... E2 71

Forsan, Howard, Tex., 300 C2 118
Forsayth, Austl., 100 C7 50
Forserum, Swe., 1,786 A8 24
Förslövsholm, Swe., 747 B6 24
Forst, Ger., 28,700 B7 17
Forsyth, Monroe, Ga., 3,697 C3 87
Forsyth, Macon, Ill., 424 D5 90
Forsyth, Marquette, Mich., 200 B3 98
Forsyth, Taney, Mo., 489 E4 101
Forsyth, Rosebud, Mont., 1,879 D10 102
Forsyth, co., Ga., 12,170 B2 87
Forsyth, co., N.C., 189,428 A3 109
Fort Adams, Wilkinson, Miss., 100 D2 100
Fort Albany, Ont., Can. n19 72
Fortaleza, Braz., 354,942 (*525,000) B3 57
Fort Ann, Washington, N.Y., 453 B7 108
Fort Apache, Navajo, Ariz., 60 D6 80
Fort Apache, Indian res., Ariz. C5 80
Fort-Archambault, Chad, 22,228 D3 46
Fort Ashby, Mineral, W. Va., 900 B6 123
Fort Assiniboine, Alta., Can., 216 B3 69
Fort Atkinson, Winneshiek, Iowa, 353 A6 92
Fort Atkinson, Jefferson, Wis., 7,908 F5 124
Fort Augustus, Scot. C4 13
Fort Banya, Ken. A6 48
Fort Barnwell, Craven, N.C., 300 B6 109
Fort Basinger, Highlands, Fla., 140 E5 86
Fort Beaufort, S. Afr., 9,748 D4 49
Fort Belfontaine, St. Louis, Mo., 40 A8 101
Fort Belknap, Blaine, Mont., 200 B8 102
Fort Belknap, Indian res., Mont. B8 102
Fort Belknap Agency, Blaine, Mont., 100 B8 102
Fort Bend, co., Tex., 40,527 E5 118
Fort Benning, Chattahoochee, Ga. D2 87
Fort Benton, Chouteau, Mont., 1,887 C6 102
Fort Berthold, Indian res., N. Dak. B3 110
Fort Bidwell, Modoc, Calif., 300 B3 82
Fort Bidwell, Indian res., Calif. B3 82
Fort Blackmore, Scott, Va., 250 B2 121
Fort Bragg, Mendocino, Calif., 4,433 C2 82
Fort Branch, Gibson, Ind., 1,983 H2 91
Fort Bridger, Uinta, Wyo., 150 D2 125
Fort Calhoun, Washington, Nebr., 458 C9 103
Fort Chadbourne, Coke, Tex. D2 118
Fort Chambly, Que., Can., 1,987 *D4 73
Fort Charlet, see Djanet, Alg.
Fort Chimo, Que., Can., 480 g13 73
Fort Chipewyan, Alta., Can., 717 f8 69
Fort Clark, Oliver, N. Dak., 30 B4 110
Fort Cobb, Caddo, Okla., 687 B3 112
Fort Cobb, res., Okla. B3 112
Fort Collins, Larimer, Colo., 25,027 A5 83
Fort Collins West, Larimer, Colo., 1,569 *A5 83
Fort Coulonge, Que., Can., 1,823 B8 72
Fort Covington, Franklin, N.Y., 976 f10 108
Fort Crampel, Cen. Afr. Rep. D3 46
Fort Crook, Sarpy, Nebr., 75 E3 103
Fort-Dauphin, Malag., 7,253 h9 49
Fort Davis, Macon, Ala., 350 C4 78
Fort Davis, Jeff Davis, Tex., 900 F2 118
Fort Defiance, Apache, Ariz., 750 B6 80
Fort-de-France, Mart., 84,811 o16 64
Fort Deposit, Lowndes, Ala., 1,466 D3 78
Fort Dick, Del Norte, Calif., 150 B1 82
Fort Dodge, Webster, Iowa, 28,399 B3 92
Fort Dodge, Ford, Kans. E4 93
Fort Donelson, nat. military park and cemetery, Tenn. A4 117
Fort Duchesne, Uintah, Utah, 100 C6 119
Forteau, Newf., Can., 232 C3 75
Fort Edward, Washington, N.Y., 3,737 B7 108
Fort Erie, Ont., Can., 9,027 E6 72
Fortescue, Holt, Mo., 78 A2 101
Fortescue, Cumberland, N.J., 100 E2 106
Fortescue, riv., Austl. D2 50
Fort Fairfield, Aroostook, Maine, 3,082 (5,876▲) B5 96
Fort Fitzgerald, Alta., Can., 149 f8 69
Fort Flatters, Alg. D6 44
Fort Foureau, Cam., 1,004 C2 46
Fort Frances, Ont., Can., 9,481 o16 72
Fort Fraser, B.C., Can., 311 B5 68
Fort Gaines, Clay, Ga., 1,320 E1 87
Fort Garland, Costilla, Colo., 500 D5 83
Fort Gay, Wayne, W. Va., 739 C2 123
Fort-George, Que., Can., 1,074 h11 73
Fort George, Duval Fla., 250 B6 86
Fort George, riv., Que., Can. h11 73
Fort Gibson, Muskogee, Okla., 1,407 B6 112
Fort Good Hope, N.W. Ter., Can., 292 C7 66
Fort-Gouraud, Maur. B2 45
Fort Grahame, B.C., Can. A5 68
Fort Green, Hardee, Fla., 50 E5 86
Fort Griffin, Shackelford, Tex. C3 118
Forth, firth, Scot. D6 13
Forth, riv., Scot. D4 13
Fort Hall, Bingham, Idaho, 700 F6 89
Fort Hall, Ken. B6 48
Fort Hall, Indian res., Idaho F6 89
Fort Hancock, Hudspeth, Tex., 600 F1 118
Fort Harrison, Lewis and Clark, Mont. D4 102
Fort Henry, Stewart, Tenn., 50 A3 117, 85
Fort Hill, Malawi C5 48
Fort Hill, Somerset, Pa., 150 G3 114
Fort Howard, Baltimore, Md., 375 B5 85
Fort Huachuca, Cochise, Ariz. F5 80
Fortierville, Que., Can., 558 C5 73
Fortín Uno, Arg. B3 54
Fortine, Lincoln, Mont., 100 B2 102
Fort Jameson, Zambia, 3,500 D5 48
Fort Jefferson, nat. mon., Fla. H4 86
Fort Jennings, Putnam, Ohio, 436 B3 111
Fort Johnston, Malawi, 950 D6 48
Fort Jones, Siskiyou, Calif., 483 B2 82
Fort Kent, Aroostook, Maine, 2,787 (4,761▲) A4 96
Fort Kent, Alta., Can., 148 B5 69
Fort Kent Village, Aroostook, Maine (part of Fort Kent) A4 96
Fort Keogh, Custer, Mont. D11 102
Fort Klamath, Klamath, Oreg., 400 E5 113
Fort Knox, Hardin, Ky. C4 94
Fort Lallemand, Alg. C6 44
Fort-Lamy, Chad, 91,700 C3 46
Fort Landing, Tyrrell, N.C. B7 109
Fort Langley, B.C., Can., 962 f13 68
Fort Laperrine (Tamanrasset), Alg., 1,714 (10,089▲) E6 44
Fort Laramie, Goshen, Wyo., 233 C8 125
Fort Laramie, nat. historic site, Wyo. C8 125
Fort Lauderdale, Broward, Fla., 83,648 E3, F6 86
Fort Lawn, Chester, S.C., 192 B6 115
Fort Leavenworth, Leavenworth, Kans. B8, C9 93
Fort Lee, Bergen, N.J., 21,815 h9 106
Fort Liard, N.W., Ter., Can., 154 D8 66
Fort-Liberté, Hai., 1,900 F8 64
Fort Lincoln, Burleigh, N. Dak., 150 C5 110
Fort Littleton, Fulton, Pa., 100 F6 114
Fort Loramie, Shelby, Ohio, 687 B3 111
Fort Loudon, Franklin, Pa., 500 G6 114
Fort Loudon, lake, Tenn. D9 117
Fort Lupton, Weld., Colo., 2,194 A6 83
Fort Lyon, Bent, Colo., 260 C7 83
Fort McDermitt, Indian res., Nev. B4 104
Fort McDowell, Maricopa, Ariz., 150 F2 80
Fort McDowell, Indian res., Ariz. D4, F3 80
Fort McHenry, nat. mon. and historical shrine, Md. C2 85
Fort McIntosh, Webb, Tex. (part of Laredo) F3 118
Fort McKavett, Menard, Tex., 150 D2 118
Fort McKay, Alta., Can., 187 f8 69
Fort McKenzie, Que., Can. g13 73
Fort McKinley, Montgomery, Ohio, 1,000 *C3 111
Fort Macleod, Alta., Can., 2,490 E4 69
Fort MacMahon, Alg. D5 44
Fort McPherson, N.W. Ter., Can., 509 C6 66
Fort Madison, Lee, Iowa, 15,247 D6 92
Fort Manning, Malawi D5 48
Fort Matanzas, nat. mon., Fla. C5 86
Fort Meade, Polk, Fla., 4,014 E5 86
Fort Meade, Meade, S. Dak., 250 C2 116
Fort Meadow, res., Mass. g9 97
Fort Mill, York, S.C., 3,315 A6 115
Fort Miller, Washington, N.Y., 200 B7 108
Fort Missoula, Missoula, Mont. D2 102
Fort Mitchell, Russell, Ala., 25 C4 78
Fort Mitchell, Lunenburg, Va., 150 E4 121
Fort Mohave, Indian res., Ariz. C1 80
Fort Morgan, Baldwin, Ala., 100 E1 78
Fort Morgan, Morgan, Colo., 7,379 A7 83
Fort Motte, Calhoun, S.C., 386 D6 115
Fort Munro, Pak. C2 40
Fort Myers, Lee, Fla., 22,523 F5 86
Fort Myers Beach, Lee, Fla., 2,463 F5 86
Fort Nelson, B.C., Can., 1,607 m18 68
Fort Norman, N.W. Ter., Can., 189 D7 66
Fort Odgen, DeSoto, Fla., 150 E5 86
Fort Oglethorpe, Catoosa and Walker, Ga., 2,251 B1 87
Fort Payne, DeKalb, Ala., 7,029 A4 78
Fort Peck, Valley, Mont., 650 B10 102
Fort Peck, dam, Mont. B10 102
Fort Peck, Indian res., Mont. B11 102
Fort Peck, res., Mont. C10 102
Fort Pierce, St. Lucie, Fla., 25,256 E6 86
Fort Pierce, inlet, Fla. E6 86
Fort Pierre, Stanley, S. Dak., 2,649 C5 116
Fort Pierre Bordes, see Tin Zaouatén, Alg.
Fort Plain, Montgomery, N.Y., 2,809 C6 108
Fort Polignac, Alg. D6 44
Fort Portal, Ug., 8,317 A5 48
Fort Providence, N.W. Ter., Can., 402 D9 66
Fort Pulaski, nat. mon., Ga. D6 87, G6 115
Fort Qu'Appelle, Sask., Can., 1,521 G4 70
Fort Randall, dam., S. Dak. D7 116
Fort Randall, res., S. Dak. D6 116
Fort Ransom, Ransom, N. Dak., 200 C8 110
Fort Recovery, Mercer, Ohio, 1,336 B3 111
Fort Reno, Canadian, Okla., 50 B3 112
Fort Resolution, N.W. Ter., Can., 485 D10 66
Fort Rice, Morton, N. Dak., 15 C5 110
For Riley, Geary, Kans. C7 93
Fort Ripley, Crow Wing, Minn., 55 D4 99
Fort Ritner, Lawrence, Ind., 120 G5 91
Fort Robinson, Dawes, Nebr., 40 B2 103
Fort Robinson, Sullivan, Tenn., 2,000 *C5 117
Fort Rock, Lake, Oreg., 15 D5 113
Fortrose, N.Z., 136 Q12 51
Fortrose, Scot., 902 C4 13
Fort Rosebery, Zambia, 2,600 D4 48
Fort Ross, N.W. Ter., Can. B14 66
Fort Rousset, Con. B F3 46
Fort St. James, B.C., Can., 1,081 B5 68
Fort St. John, B.C., Can., 3,619 A7, m18 68
Fort Sandeman, Pak., 6,001 B4 39
Fort Saskatchewan, Alta., Can, 2,972 C4 69
Fort Scott, Bourbon, Kans., 9,410 E9 93
Fort Severn, Ont., Can. n18 72
Fort Shaw, Cascade, Mont., 100 C5 102
Fort Shawnee, Allen, Ohio, 4,000 B3 111
Fort Sheridan, Lake, Ill. A6, E2 90
Fort Shevchenko, Sov. Un., 18,800 E4 29
Fort-Sibut, Cen. Afr. Rep. D3 46
Fort Simpson, N.W. Ter., Can., 563 D8 66
Fort Smith, Sebastian, Ark., 63,309 B1 81
Fort Smith, N.W. Ter., Can., 1,591 D10 66
Fort Smith, lake, Ark. B1 81
Fort Spring, Fayette, Ky., 60 B5 94
Fort Stanton, Lincoln, N. Mex. D4 107
Fort Steele, B.C., Can., 125 E10 68
Fort Steilacoom, Pierce, Wash. D1 122
Fort Stockton, Pecos, Tex., 6,373 D1 118
Fort Sumner, De Baca, N. Mex., 1,809 C5 107
Fort Sumter, nat. mon., S.C. F3 115
Fort Supply, Woodward, Okla., 394 A2 112
Fort Supply, res. and dam, Okla. A2 112
Fort Thomas, Graham, Ariz., 200 D6 80
Fort Thomas, Campbell, Ky., 14,896 A7 94
Fort Thompson, Buffalo, S. Dak., 150 C6 116
Fort Totten, Benson, N. Dak., 200 A7 110
Fort Towson, Choctaw, Okla., 474 C6 112
Fort Trinquet, Maur. A2 45
Fortuna, Humboldt, Calif., 3,523 B1 82
Fortuna, Moniteau, Mo., 155 C5 101
Fortuna, Divide, N. Dak., 185 A2 110
Fortuna Ledge, Alsk., 71 C7 79
Fortune, Newf., Can., 1,360 E4 75
Fortune, bay, Newf., Can. E4 75
Fortune Harbour, Newf., Can., 156 D4 75
Fort Valley, Peach, Ga., 8,310 D3 87
Fort Vermilion, Alta., Can., 768 f7 69
Fort Victoria, Rh., 12,300 B5 49
Fortville, Hancock, Ind., 2,209 E6 91
Fort Walton Beach, Okaloosa, Fla., 12,147 G2 86
Fort Washakie, Fremont, Wyo., 130 B4 125
Fort Washington, Prince Georges, Md. C3 85
Fort Washington Montgomery, Pa., 2,500 A11 114
Fort Wayne, Allen, Ind., 161,776 (*215,400) B7 91
Fort White, Columbia, Fla., 425 C4 86
Fort William, Ont., Can., 45,214 (*93,251) o17 72
Fort William, Scot., 2,715 D3 13
Fort William, mtn., Austl. B8 51
Fort Wingate, McKinley, N. Mex., 50 B1 107
Fort Worth, Tarrant, Tex., 356,268 (*505,100) B5, C4 118
Fort Wright, Kenton, Ky., 2,184 A7 94
Fort Yates, Sioux, N. Dak., 900 C5 110
Forty Fort, Luzerne, Pa., 6,431 D10 114
Fort Yukon, Alsk., 701 B10 79
Foshan, China, 5,000 B11 34
Foshee, Escambia, Ala. D2 78
Foss, Washita, Okla., 289 B2 112
Foss, dam, Okla. B2 112
Fossano, It., 11,000 B1 21
Fosser, Nor., 113 p29 25
Fossil, Wheeler, Oreg., 672 B6 113
Fossil, Lincoln, Wyo. E2 125
Fossil, Tarrant, Tex. n9 118
Fossil, lake, Oreg. D6 113
Fossil, ridge, Colo. C4 83
Fossombrone, It., 4,659 C4 21
Fosston, Sask., Can., 117 E4 70
Fosston, Polk, Minn., 1,704 C3 99
Foster, Que., Can., 453 D5 73
Foster, Bracken, Ky., 114 B5 94
Foster, Bates, Mo., 153 C3 101
Foster, Pierce, Nebr., 60 B8 103
Foster, Garvin, Okla., 25 C4 112
Foster, Linn, Oreg., 250 C4 113
Foster, Providence, R.I., 125 (2,097▲) B10 84
Foster, Eau Claire, Wis., 80 D2 124
Foster, co., N. Dak., 5,361 B6 110
Foster, riv., Sask., Can. A3 70
Foster Brook, McKean, Pa., 950 C4 114
Fosterburg, Madison, Ill., 100 A8 90
Foster City, Dickinson, Mich., 200 C3 98
Fosters, Tuscaloosa, Ala., 100 B2 78
Fosters, pond, Mass. f11 97
Fosters Falls, Wythe, Va., 200 E2 121
Foster Village, Honolulu, Haw., 2,300 g10 88
Fosterville, Rutherford, Tenn., 150 B5 117
Fostoria, Lowndes, Ala., 200 C3 78
Fostoria, Clay, Iowa, 167 A2 92
Fostoria, Pottawatomie, Kans., 90 C7 93
Fostoria, Tuscola, Mich., 300 E7 98
Fostoria, Seneca and Hancock, Ohio, 15,732 A4 111
Fostoria, Montgomery, Tex., 666 D5 118
Fougamou, Gabon F2 46
Fougères, Fr., 24,279 C3 14
Fouke, Miller, Ark., 394 D2 81
Foula, isl., Scot. g9 10
Fouliang, China, 92,000 J7 36
Fouling, China, 32,000 F6 34
Foulness, isl., Eng. C8 12
Foulwind, cape, N.Z. N13 51
Foumban, Cam., 18,000 D2 46
Foum el Hassane, Mor. D3 44
Founing, China, 85,000 E8 34
Fount, Knox, Ky., 25 D6 94
Fountain, Monroe, Ala., 150 D2 78
Fountain, El Paso, Colo., 1,602 C6 83
Fountain, Bay, Fla., 195 B1, G3 86
Fountain, Mason, Mich., 194 D4 98
Fountain, Fillmore, Minn., 297 G6 99
Fountain, co., Ind., 18,706 D3 91
Fountain, creek, Colo. C6 83
Fountain City, Wayne, Ind., 833 E8 91
Fountain City, Knox, Tenn., 10,365 C10, E11 117
Fountain City, Buffalo, Wis., 934 D2 124
Fountain Green, Sanpete, Utah, 544 D4 119
Fountain Head, Washington, Md., 950 *A2 85
Fountain Head, Sumner, Tenn., 200 A5 117
Fountain Hill, Ashley, Ark., 230 D4 81
Fountain Hill, Lehigh, Pa., 5,428 E11 114
Fountain Inn, Greenville, S.C., 2,385 B3 115
Fountain Place, Easton Baton Rouge, La., 5,000 *D4 95
Fountain Run, Monroe, Ky., 298 D4 94
Fountains, Pitt, N.C., 496 B6 109
Fountaintown, Shelby, Ind., 300 E6 91
Fountain Valley, Orange, Calif., 2,068 *F5 82
Fountain Valley School, El Paso, Colo., 150 C6 83
Fouping, China E6 36
Four Buttes, Daniels, Mont., 35 B11 102
Fourchambault, Fr., 6,240 D5 14
Fourche, riv., Ark. D5 81
Fourche LaFave, riv., Ark. C2 81
Fourche Maline, creek, Okla. C6 112
Fourchu, N.S., Can. D9 74
Four Corners, Marion, Oreg., 4,743 *C4 113
Four Corners, Weston, Wyo., 5 B8 125
Four Holes, Orangeburg, S.C., 300 E7 115
Four Lakes, Spokane, Wash., 250 B8, D7 122
Fourmies, Fr., 14,508 B6 14
Fourmile, Bell, Ky., 500 D6 94
Four Mile, creek, Iowa A7 92
Four Mountains, is., Alsk. E6 79
Fournier, Ont., Can., 227 B10 72
Fournier, Aroostook, Maine, 100 A4 96
Four Oakes, Johnston, N.C., 1,010 B5 109
Four Points, Dougherty, Ga., 1,500 E2 87
4th. Cataract (Nile River), Sud. B3 47
Fourup, isl., Truk 52
Fouta Djallon, mts., Guinea D2 45
Fouyang, China, 65,000 H6 36
Foveaux, strait, N.Z. O12 51
Fowey, Eng., 2,237 D3 12
Fowler, Conecuh, Ala. D2 78
Fowler, Fresno, Calif., 1,892 D4 82
Fowler, Otero, Colo., 1,240 C6 83
Fowler, Adams, Ill., 160 C2 90
Fowler, Benton, Ind., 2,491 C3 91
Fowler, Meade, Kans., 717 E3 93
Fowler, Clinton, Mich., 854 E6 98
Fowlerton, Grant, Ind., 297 D6 91
Fowlerton, LaSalle, Tex., 270 E3 118
Fowlerville, Livingston, Mich., 1,674 F6 98
Fowliang (Kingtehchen), China, 92,000 F8 34
Fowlkes, Dyer, Tenn., 250 B2 117
Fowlstown, Decatur, Ga., 400 F2 87
Fox, Stone, Ark., 100 B3 81
Fox, Menominee, Mich. C3 98
Fox, Carbon, Mont., 10 E7 102
Fox, Carter, Okla., 400 C4 112
Fox, Grant, Oreg., 10 C7 113
Fox, isl., Wash. D1 122
Fox, is., Alsk. E5 79
Fox, lake, Ill. A5 90
Fox, mtn., Yukon, Can. D6 66
Fox, riv., Man., Can. B4 71
Fox, riv., Ill. B5 90
Fox, riv., Iowa D5 92
Fox, riv., Mich. B5 98
Fox, riv., Mo. A6 101
Fox, riv., Wis. D5 124
Foxboro, Ont., Can., 494 C7 72
Foxboro, Norfolk, Mass., 6,000 (10,136) B5 97
Foxboro, Douglas, Wis., 150 B1 124
Foxburg, Clarion, Pa., 383 D2 114
Fox Chapel, Allegheny, Pa., 3,302 *F2 114
Foxdale, I. of Man. F4 13
Foxe, basin, N.W. Ter., Can. C17 67
Foxe, chan., N.W. Ter., Can. D16 67
Foxe, pen., N.W., Ter., Can. C17 67
Fox Farm, Laramie, Wyo., 1,371 *D8 124
Foxford, Sask., Can., 50 D3 70
Foxford, Ire., 876 D2 11
Fox Harbour, Newf., Can., 232 B4 75
Fox Harbour, Newf., Can., 746 E5 75
Fox Hill (part of Hampton), Va. B7, D6 121
Foxholm, Ward, N. Dak., 200 A4 110
Fox Island, Pierce, Wash., 150 D1 122
Fox Lake, Lake, Ill., 3,700 A5, E2 90
Fox Lake, Dodge, Wis., 1,181 E5 124
Foxon, New Haven, Conn. (part of East Haven) D5 84
Foxpark, Albany, Wyo., 150 D6 125
Fox Point, Miwaukee, Wis., 7,315 E2, E6 124
Fox River Grove, McHenry, Ill., 1,866 E2 90
Fox River Heights, Kane, Ill., 700 *E2 90
Foxton, N.Z., 2,628 N15 51
Foxvale, Norfolk, Mass., 500 B5 97
Fox Valley, Sask., Can., 479 G1 70
Foxville, Orange, Vt., 200 C4 120
Foxwarren, Man., Can., 272 D1 71
Foxworth, Marion, Miss., 950 D4 100
Foyil, Rogers, Okla., 127 A6 112
Foyle, bay, N. Ire. B4 11
Foyle, riv., N. Ire. C4 11
Foynes, Ire., 686 E2 11
Foz do Iguaçu, Braz., 7,407 D2 56
Frackville, Schuylkill, Pa., 5,654 E9 114
Fra Cristobal, mts., N. Mex. D3 107
Fraga, Sp., 8,691 B6 20
Fraile Muerto, Ur., 1,876 E2 56
Frametown, Braxton, W. Va., 500 C4 123
Framingham, Middlesex, Mass., 44,526 B5, g10 97
Framnes, mts., Ant. C19 5
França, Braz., 646 D2 57
Franca, Braz., 47,244 F1 57
Francavilla Fontana, It., 27,000 (30,300▲) D6 21
France, country, Eur., 48,800,000 F9 8, 14
Frances, Crittenden, Ky., 200 A3 94
Frances, Pacific, Wash., 100 C2 122
Francestown, Hillsboro, N.H., 180 (495▲) E3 105
Francesville, Pulaski, Ind., 1,002 C4 91
Franceville, Gabon F2 46
Franche-Comté, former prov., Fr., 757,000 D6 14
Francis, Sask., Can., 150 G4 70
Francis, Gallatin, Mont., 15 D5 102
Francis, Pontotoc, Okla., 286 C5 112
Francis, Summit, Utah, 252 C4 119
Francis, Harrison, W. Va., 20 B4 123
Francis, lake, N.H. A1 105
Francisco, Gibson, Ind., 565 H3 91
Francis Creek, Manitowoc, Wis., 400 A6 124
Francistown, Bech., 10,000 B4 49
Francois, Newf., Can., 341 E3 75
Francois, lake, B.C., Can. C5 68
Franconia, Grafton, N.H., 300 (419▲) B3 105
Franconia, Fairfax, Va., 3,000 *C5 121
Franconville, Fr., 11,185 g9 14
Franeker, Neth., 9,400 A5 15
Frank, Alta., Can., 223 *E3 69
Frank, Pocahontas, W. Va., 200 C5 123
Frank, lake, Alta., Can. D4 69
Frankenberg, Ger., 8,100 B3 17
Frankenberg, Ger., 15,400 C8 17
Frankenmuth, Saginaw, Mich., 1,728 E7 98
Frankenthal, Ger., 33,900 D3 17
Frankewing, Giles, Tenn., 100 B5 117
Frankford, Ont., Can., 1,642 C7 72
Frankford, Sussex, Del., 558 C7 85
Frankford, Pike, Mo., 474 B6 101
Frankford, Greenbrier, W. Va. 125 D4 123
Frankfort, Will, Ill., 1,135 F2 90
Frankfort, Clinton, Ind., 15,302 D4 91
Frankfort, Marshall, Kans., 1,106 C7 93
Frankfort, Franklin, Ky., 18,365 B5 94
Frankfort, Waldo, Maine, 300 (692▲) D4 96
Frankfort, Benzie, Mich., 1,690 D4 98
Frankfort, Herkimer, N.Y., 3,872 B5 108
Frankfort, Ross, Ohio, 871 C4 111
Frankfort, Spink, S. Dak., 240 C7 116
Frankfort, S. Afr., 4,787 C4 49
Frankfurt [am Main], Ger., 692,100 (*1,450,000) C4 16, C3 17
Frankfurt [an der Oder], Ger., 57,700 A9 17
Frankische Saale, riv., Ger. C4 17
Franklin, Macon, Ala. C4 78
Franklin, Monroe, Ala., 100 D2 78
Franklin, Izard, Ark., 75 A4 80
Franklin, Man., Can., 73 D2 71
Franklin, New London, Conn., 85 (974▲) C8 84
Franklin, Heard, Ga., 603 C1 87
Franklin, Ada, Idaho, 7,222 *F2 89
Franklin, Franklin, Idaho, 446 G7 89
Franklin, Morgan, Ill., 500 D3 90
Franklin, Johnson, Ind., 9,453 F5 91
Franklin, Lee, Iowa, 174 D6 92
Franklin, Crawford, Kans., 620 E9 93
Franklin, Simpson, Ky., 5,319 D3 94
Franklin, St. Mary, La., 8,673 E4 95
Franklin, Hancock, Maine, 300 (627▲) D4 96
Franklin, Allegany, Md. D1 85
Franklin, Norfolk, Mass., 8,000 (10,530▲) B5 97
Franklin, Oakland, Mich., 2,262 *F7 98
Franklin, Renville, Minn., 548 F4 99
Franklin, Howard, Mo., 355 B5 101
Franklin, Franklin, Nebr., 1,194 D7 103
Franklin, Merrimack, N.H., 6,742 D3 105
Franklin, Sussex, N.J., 3,624 A3 106
Fanklin, Delaware, N.Y., 525 C5 108
Franklin, Macon, N.C., 2,173 D3 109
Franklin, Warren, Ohio, 7,917 C3 111
Franklin, Cambria, Pa., 1,352 *F4 114
Franklin, Venango, Pa., 9,586 D2 114
Franklin, Williamson, Tenn., 6,977 B5 117
Franklin, Robertson, Tex., 1,065 D4 118
Franklin, Franklin, Vt., 170 (796▲) B3 120
Franklin (Independent City), Va., 7,264 E6 121
Franklin, Pendleton, W. Va., 758 C5 123
Franklin, Milwaukee, Wis., 10,006 *F1 124
Franklin, co., Ala., 21,988 A4 78
Franklin, co., Ark., 10,213 B2 81
Franklin, co., Fla., 6,576 C2 86
Franklin, co., Ga., 13,274 B3 87
Franklin, co., Idaho, 8,457 G7 89
Franklin, co., Ill., 39,281 E5 90
Franklin, co., Ind., 17,015 F7 91
Franklin, co., Iowa, 15,472 B4 92
Franklin, co., Kans., 19,548 D8 93
Franklin, co., Ky., 29,421 B5 94
Franklin, co., Maine, 20,069 C2 96
Franklin, co., Mass., 54,864 A2 97
Franklin, co., Miss., 9,286 D3 100
Franklin, co., Mo., 44,566 C6 101
Franklin, co., Nebr., 5,449 D7 103
Franklin, co., N.Y., 44,742 A6 108
Franklin, co., N.C., 28,755 A5 109
Franklin, co., Ohio, 682,962 B4 111
Franklin, co., Pa., 88,172 G6 114
Franklin, co., Tenn., 25,528 B5 117
Franklin, co., Tex., 5,101 C5 118
Franklin, co., Vt., 29,474 B2 120
Franklin, co., Va., 25,925 E3 121
Franklin, co., Wash., 23,342 C7 122
Franklin, dist., N.W. Ter., Can., 5,758 B9 66
Franklin, par., La., 26,088 B4 95
Franklin, isl., Ont., Can. B4 72
Franklin, lake, N.W. Ter., Can. C13 66
Franklin, lake, Nev. C6 104
Franklin, mts., N.W. Ter., Can. C7 66
Franklin, pt., Alsk. A8 79
Franklin, strait, N.W. Ter., Can. B13 66
Franklin D. Roosevelt, lake, Wash. A7 122
Franklin Grove, Lee, Ill., 773 B4 90
Franklin, Hartsell, Brown and Norcot Mills (West Concord), Cabarrus, N.C. 5,510 B3 109
Franklin Lakes, Bergen, N.J., 3,316 *B4 106
Franklin Mine, Houghton, Mich., 150 A2 98
Franklin Park, Cook, Ill., 18,322 E2 90
Franklin Park, Somerset, N.J., 900 C3 106
Franklin Park, Fairfax, Va., 1,300 *C5 121
Franklin Square, Nassau, N.Y., 33,000 G2 84
Franklinton, Washington, La., 3,141 D5 95
Franklinton, Franklin, N.C., 1,513 A5 109
Franklinville, Gloucester, N.J., 1,000 D2 106
Franklinville, Cattaraugus, N.Y., 2,124 C2 108
Franklinville, Randolph, N.C., 686 B4 109
Franks, peak, Wyo. B3 125
Frankston, Anderson, Tex., 953 C5 118
Franksville, Racine, Wis., 400 F2 124
Frankton, Madison, Ind., 1,445 D6 91
Franktown, Douglas, Colo., 50 B6 83
Frankville, Washington, Ala., 500 D1 78
Frankville, Garrett, Md. D1 85
Frankville, N.S., Can., 245 D8 74
Frannie, Park, Wyo., 171 A4 125
Franz Josef Land, arch., Sov. Un. A8 4
Frascati, It., 11,500 D4, h9 21
Fraser, Grand, Colo., 253 B5 83
Fraser, Boone, Iowa, 134 B4 92
Fraser, Macomb, Mich., 7,027 A8 98
Fraser (Great Sandy), isl., Austl. B9 51
Fraser, lake, B.C., Can. B5 68
Fraser, mtn., B.C., Can. C8 68
Fraser, plat., B.C., Can. D6 68
Fraser, riv., B.C., Can. C6 68
Fraser, riv., Newf., Can. g9 75
Fraserburg, S. Afr., 2,359 D3 49
Fraserburgh, Scot., 10,462 C6 13
Fraserdale, Ont., Can., 215 o19 72
Fraser Lake, B.C., Can., 149 B5 68
Fraser Mills, B.C., Can., 165 *E6 68
Fraser Reach, chan., B.C., Can. C3 68
Fraserwood, Man., Can., 78 D3 71
Frasne, Fr., 1,367 C2 18
Frauenfeld, Switz., 14,702 A6 19
Fray Bentos, Ur., 12,900 E1 56
Frazee, Becker, Minn., 1,083 D3 99
Frazer, Valley, Mont., 425 B10 102
Frazeysburg, Muskingum, Ohio, 842 B5 111
Frazier, mtn., Calif. E4 82
Frazier Park, Kern, Calif., 250 E4 82
Frederic, Crawford, Mich., 400 D6 98
Frederic, Polk, Wis., 857 C1 124
Frederica, Kent, Del., 863 B7 85
Fredericia, Den., 29,870 C3 24
Frederick, Weld, Colo., 595 A6 83
Frederick, Schuyler, Ill., 175 C3 90
Frederick, Frederick, Md., 21,744 B3 85

Gallatin Gateway, Gallatin, Mont., 200 ....E5 102
Gallaway, Fayette, Tenn., 100 ....B2 117
Galle, Cey., 55,848 ....G7 39
Gallego, riv., Sp A5 20
Gallegos, riv., Arg E2 54
Galley, head, Ire F3 11
Gallia, co., Ohio, 26,120 ....D5 111
Galliate, It., 12,549 ....D4 18
Gallicano nel Lazio, It., 2,024 ....h9 21
Gallina, Rio Arriba, N. Mex., 100 ....A3 107
Gallinas, mts., N. Mex C2 107
Gallinas, pt., Col A3 60
Gallion, Hale, Ala., 150 ....C2 78
Gallion, Morehouse, La., 75 ..B4 95
Gallipoli, It., 16,196 ....D6 21
Gallipoli, see Gelibolu, Tur.
Gallipoli, pen., Tur B6 23
Gallipolis, Gallia, Ohio, 8,775 ....D5 111
Gallipolis Ferry, Mason, W. Va., 400 ....C2 123
Gallitzin, Cambria, Pa., 2,783 ....F4 114
Gällivare, Swe., 25,363 ......D9 25
Gallman, Copiah, Miss., 100 .D3 100
Gallneukirchen, Aus., 2,742 ..E9 17
Gallo, mts., N. Mex C1 107
Gallo, riv., Sp B5 20
Galloo, isl., N.Y B4 108
Galloway, Greene, Mo., 200 D4 101
Galloway, Franklin, Ohio, 250 ....C2 111
Galloway, Barbour, W. Va., 300 ....B4 123
Galloway, Marathon, Wis., 100 ....D4 124
Galloway Mull, head, Scot F4 13
Gallstad, Swe., 362 ....A7 24
Gallup, McKinley, N. Mex., 14,089 ....B1 107
Galt, Sacramento, Calif., 1,868 ....B6, C3 82
Galt, Ont., Can., 27,830 ....D4 72
Galt, Wright, Iowa, 75 ....B4 92
Galt, Grundy, Mo., 373 ......A4 101
Galten, lake, Swe t34 25
Galtür, Aus., 523 ....C6 18
Galty, mts., Ire E3 11
Galva, Henry, Ill., 3,060 .....B3 90
Galva, Ida, Iowa, 469 ....B2 92
Galva, McPherson, Kans., 442 ....D6 93
Galvarino, Chile, 1,209 ......B2 54
Galveston, Cass, Ind., 1,111 ..C5 91
Galveston, Galveston, Tex., 67,175 (*138,700) E5, G5 118
Galveston, co., Tex., 140,364 .E5 118
Galveston, bay, Tsx E5 118
Galveston, isl., Tex E5 118
Gálvez, Arg., 7,891 ....A5 54
Galvin, Lewis, Wash., 200 ..C2 122
Galway, Ire., 22,028 ....D2 11
Galway, co., Ire., 149,887 .D2, 3 11
Galway, bay, Ire D2 11
Gamaches, Fr., 3,194 ....E9 12
Gamagori, Jap., 55,926 .....o16 37
Gamaliel, Baxter, Ark., 150 ..A3 81
Gamaliel, Monroe, Ky., 868 .D4 94
Gamarra, Col., 2,576 ....B3 60
Gamba, Con. L B3 48
Gambaga, Ghana, 1,952 ....D4 45
Gambēlā, Eth D3 47
Gambell, Alsk., 358 ....C5 79
Gamber, Carroll, Md., 180 ..B4 85
Gambia, country, Afr., 320,000 ....D1 45, E4 42
Gambia, riv., Sen D2 45
Gambier, Knox, Ohio, 1,148 .B5 111
Gambier, is., Fr. Polynesia ...*H14 7
Gambo, Newf., Can., 480 ...D4 75
Gamboma, Con. B F3 46
Gamboula, Cen. Afr. Rep ...E3 46
Gambrills, Anne Arundel, Md., 600 ....B4 85
Game Lodge, Custer, S. Dak., 85 ....D2 116
Gameleira, Braz., 5,078 ..C3, k6 57
Gamerco, McKinley, N. Mex., 350 ....B1 107
Gamina, Chile C2 55
Gammertingen, Ger., 2,000 ..A5 18
Gammon, riv., Man., Can D4 71
Gamo-Gofa, prov., Eth., 900,000 ....D4 47
Ganado, Jackson, Tex., 1,626 .E4 118
Ganālē, riv., Eth D5 47
Gananoque, Ont., Can., 5,096 ....C8 72
Gand, see Gent, Bel.
Gandajika, Con. L C3 48
Gandamak, Afg., 10,000 ....D15 41
Gandeeville, Roane, W. Va., 400 ....C3 123
Gander, Newf., Can., 5,725 ..D4 75
Gander, lake, Newf., Can D4 75
Gander, riv., Newf., Can D4 75
Gander Bay, Newf., Can D4 75
Gandía, Sp., 15,812 ....C5 20
Gandy, Logan, Nebr., 41 ....C5 103
Ganedidalem, Indon F7 35
Gang, canal, India C4 40
Gangapur, India, 22,591 ....D6 40
Gangaw, Bur., 3,800 ....D9 39
Ganges, B.C., Can., 400 ....g12 68
Ganges, Fr., 4,262 ....F5 14
Ganges, Richland, Ohio, 100 ....B5 111
Ganges, riv., India, Pak D8 39
Ganges, riv. mouths, Pak G12 40
Gangtok, Sikkim, 6,848 ....D12 40
Ganjur, China B8 34
Ganju-San, peak, Jap G10 37
Gannat, Fr., 5,376 ....D5 14
Gannet, is., Newf., Can B3 74
Gannett, Blaine, Idaho, 20 ...F4 89
Gannett, peak, Wyo B3 125
Gannon, Allegany, Md., 450 ....D2 85
Gannvalley, Buffalo, S. Dak., 100 ....C7 116
Gano, Butler, Ohio, 150 .....C2 111
Gano, Payne, Okla A5 112
Gans, Sequoyah, Okla., 234 .B7 112
Gansevoort, Saratoga, N.Y., 325 ....B7 108
Ganta, Lib E3 45
Gantt, Covington, Ala., 375 ..D3 78
Gantt, Greenville, S.C., 900 .B2 115
Gantt, dam, Ala D3 78
Gantts Quarry, Talladega, Ala., 238 ....B3 78
Gao, Mali, 6,500 ....C5 45
Gaoua, Upper Volta, 4,300 ..D4 45
Gaoual, Guinea, 4,600 ......D2 45
Gap, Fr., 20,478 ....E7 14
Gap, Lancaster, Pa., 800 ....G9 114
Gapan, Phil., 7,842 ....o13 35
Gapland, Washington, Md., 200 ....B2 85
Gap Mills, Monroe, W. Va., 95 ....D4 123
Gara, lake, Ire D3 11
Garachiné, Pan., 1,326 ......F8 62
Garad, Som D6 47
Garakayo, isl., Palau Is 52
Garanhuns, Braz., 34,050 .C3, k5 57
Garapan, Saipan, 2,977 52
Garapan, anchorage, Saipan 52
Garashiyoo, Palau Is 52
Garautha, India E7 40
Garber, Clayton, Iowa, 148 .B6 92
Garber, Garfield, Okla., 905 ....A4 112
Garberville, Humboldt, Calif., 900 ....B2 82
Garça, Braz., 18,155 ....C3 57
Garching, Ger., 4,900 ......A8 18
Garcia, Costilla, Colo., 160 ..D5 83
Garciasville, Starr, Tex., 900 ....F3 118
Gard, dept., Fr., 435,482 ...*F6 14
Gard, riv., Fr F6 14
Garda, lake, It B3 21
Gardanne, Fr., 4,164 ......F6 14
Gardar, Pembina, N. Dak., 92 ....A8 110
Gardelegen, Ger., 12,400 ....B5 16
Garden, Bartholomew, Ind., 250 ....F6 91
Garden, Delta, Mich., 380 ...C4 98
Garden, co., Nebr., 3,472 ...C3 103
Garden, isl., Mich C5 98
Garden, riv., Ont., Can B6 98
Gardena, Los Angeles, Calif., 35,943 ....*F2 82
Gardena, Boise, Idaho, 25 ...F2 89
Gardena, Tazewell, Ill., 500 .C4 90
Gardena, Bottineau, N. Dak., 113 ....A5 110
Garden City, Cullman, Ala., 536 ....A3 78
Garden City, Duval, Fla., 800 ....B6 86
Garden City (Chatham City), Chatham, Ga., 5,451 ....*D5 87
Garden City, Ada, Idaho, 1,681 ....*F2 89
Garden City, Finney, Kans., 11,811 ....E3 93
Garden City, St. Mary, La., 300 ....E4 95
Garden City, Wayne, Mich., 38,017 ....A7 98
Garden City, Blue Earth, Minn., 300 ....F4 99
Garden City, Franklin, Miss., 40 ....D2 100
Garden City, Cass, Mo., 600 .C3 101
Garden City, Nassau, N.Y., 23,948 ....G2 84
Garden City, Delaware, Pa., 2,000 ....*G11 114
Garden City, Clark, S. Dak., 226 ....C8 116
Garden City, Glasscock, Tex., 325 ....D2 118
Garden City, Rich, Utah, 168 ....B4 119
Garden City Park, Nassau, N.Y., 6,600 ....*G2 84
Gardendale, Jefferson, Ala., 4,712 ....B3, E4 78
Gardendale, La Salle, Tex., 40 ....E3 118
Garden Grove, Orange, Calif., 84,238 ....*F3 82
Garden Grove, Decatur, Iowa, 335 ....D4 92
Garden Home, Washington, Oreg., 2,000 ....*B2 113
Garden Lakes, Floyd, Ga., 1,300 ....*B1 87
Garden Plain, Sedgwick, Kans., 560 ....B4, E6 93
Garden Prairie, Boone, Ill., 300 ....A5 90
Gardenton, Man., Can., 104 ..E3 71
Garden Valley, Boise, Idaho, 10 ....E3 89
Garden View, Lycoming, Pa., 2,418 ....*D7 114
Gardez, Afg., 17,540 ....E14 41
Gardi, Wayne, Ga., 250 .....E5 87
Gardiner, Kennebec, Maine, 6,897 ....D3 96
Gardiner, Park, Mont., 650 ...E6 102
Gardiner, Douglas, Oreg., 550 ....D2 113
Gardiners, bay, N.Y E8 84
Gardiners, isl., N.Y m16 108
Gardiners, pt., N.Y E8 84
Gardner, Huerfano, Colo., 200 ....D5 83
Gardner, Hardee, Fla., 80 ...E5 86
Gardner, Grundy, Ill., 1,041 ..B5 90
Gardner, Johnson, Kans., 1,619 ....D9 93
Gardner, Worcester, Mass., 19,038 ....A4 97
Gardner, Cass, N. Dak., 107 ..B9 110
Gardner, Weakley, Tenn., 40 ....A3 117
Gardner, canal, B.C., Can C3 68
Gardner, lake, Conn C8 84
Gardner, lake, Maine D5 96
Gardner, mtn., N.H B2 105
Gardner Pinnacles, isl., Haw k14 88
Gardnersville, Pendleton, Ky .B7 94
Gardnerville, Douglas, Nev., 800 ....E2 104
Gardo, Som D6 47
Gardone Riviera, It., 1,259 ...D6 18
Gardone Val Trompia, It., 8,330 ....B3 18
Gårdstånga, Swe C7 24
Gardulā, Eth D4 47
Garesnica, Yugo., 2,332 ......C3 22
Garfield, Benton, Ark., 48 ...A2 81
Garfield, Chaffee, Colo., 20 ..C4 83
Garfield, Emanuel, Ga., 225 .D4 87
Garfield, Pawnee, Kans., 278 ....D4 93
Garfield, Douglas, Minn., 240 ....E3 99
Garfield, Bergen, N.J., 29,253 ....h8 106
Garfield, Dona Ana, N. Mex., 300 ....E2 107
Garfield, Whitman, Wash., 607 ....B8 122
Garfield, co., Colo., 12,017 ...B2 83
Garfield, co., Mont., 1,981 ...C9 102
Garfield, co., Nebr., 2,699 ...C6 103
Garfield, co., Okla., 52,975 ...A4 112
Garfield, co., Utah, 3,577 ....F4 119
Garfield, co., Wash., 2,976 ...C8 122
Garfield, mtn., Mont F4 102
Garfield Heights, Cuyahoga, Ohio, 38,455 ....B2 111
Gargalianoi, Grc., 7,658 ....D3 23
Gargzdai, Sov. Un A6 26
Gargnano, It., 4,092 ....D6 18
Garhchiroli, India E6 40
Garibaldi, Braz., 3,635 ......D2 56
Garibaldi, Tillamook, Oreg., 1,163 ....B3 113
Garibaldi, mtn., B.C., Can E6 68
Garibaldi, prov. park, B.C., Can D6 68
Garies, S. Afr., 1,103 ......D2 49
Garissa, Ken B6 48
Garita, San Miguel, N. Mex., 60 ....B5 107
Garita, P.R C2 65
Garland, Miller, Ark., 377 ...D2 81
Garland, Bourbon, Kans., 250 ....E9 93
Garland, Penobscot, Maine, 200 (568▲) C3 96
Garland, Anne Arundel, Md., 1,200 ....*B4 85
Garland, Custer, Mont D11 102
Garland, Seward, Nebr., 198 .D9 103
Garland, Sampson, N.C., 642 ....C5 109
Garland, Warren, Pa., 450 ...C3 114
Garland, Tipton, Tenn., 168 .B2 117
Garland, Dallas, Tex., 38,501 ....B6 118
Garland, Box Elder, Utah, 1,119 ....B3 119
Garland, Park, Wyo., 50 ....A4 125
Garland, co., Ark., 46,697 ...C2 81
Garm, Sov. Un H23 9
Garmisch-Partenkirchen, Ger., 26,800 ....E5 16
Garmouth, Scot C5 13
Garnavillo, Clayton, Iowa, 662 ....B6 92
Garneill, Fergus, Mont., 30 ..D7 102
Garner, White, Ark., 120 ....B4 81
Garner, Hancock, Iowa, 1,990 ....A4 92
Garner, Wake, N.C., 3,451 ...B5 109
Garnet, range, Mont D3 102
Garnett, Anderson, Kans., 3,034 ....D8 93
Garnett, Hampton, S.C., 100 .F5 115
Garnish, Newf., Can., 500 ...E4 75
Garo, Park, Colo B5 83
Garonne, riv., Fr E3 14
Garou, lake, Mali C4 45
Garoua, Cam D2 46
Garrard, co., Ky., 9,747 .....C5 94
Garretson, Minnehaha, S. Dak., 850 ....D9 116
Garrett, Douglas, Ill., 249 ....D5 90
Garrett, DeKalb, Ind., 4,364 .B7 91
Garrett, Floyd, Ky., 800 .....C7 94
Garrett, Somerset, Pa., 617 ...G3 114
Garrett, Albany, Wyo., 5 .....C7 125
Garrett, co., Md., 20,420 ....D1 85
Garrett Park, Montgomery, Md., 965 ....B3 85
Garrett Park Estates, Montgomery, Md., 2,000 ....*B3 85
Garrettsville, Portage, Ohio, 1,662 ....A6 111
Garrick, Sask., Can., 114 ....D3 70
Garrison, Benton, Iowa, 421 ..B5 92
Garrison, Lewis, Ky., 350 ....B6 94
Garrison, Baltimore, Md., 500 ....B4 85
Garrison, Crow Wing, Minn., 118 ....D5 99
Garrison, Powell, Mont., 200 ....D4 102
Garrison, Putnam, N.Y., 400 ....D7, m15 108
Garrison, McLean, N. Dak., 1,794 ....B4 110
Garrison, Nacogdoches, Tex., 951 ....D5 118
Garrison, Millard, Utah, 60 ..E1 119
Garrison, dam, N. Dak B4 110
Garrison, res., N. Dak A2, B3 110
Garrisonville, Stafford, Va., 200 ....C5 121
Garristown, Ire., 121 ....D5 11
Garrochales, P.R B4 65
Garrote, Pan., 166 ....h11 62
Garrovillas, Sp., 5,764 ......C2 20
Garruchos, Arg C4 55
Garry, lake, N.W., Ter., Can .C13 66
Garry, riv., Scot D5 13
Garryowen, Big Horn, Mont., 5 ....E9 102
Garske, Ramsey, N. Dak., 50 .A7 110
Garson, Ont., Can., 3,786 .*p19 72
Garson, lake, Alta., Sask., Can A5 69
Garson Quarry, Man., Can., 330 ....D3 71
Garstang, Eng., 1,439 ......G6 13
Garth, Jackson, Ala., 100 ....A3 78
Garthby Station, Que., Can., 505 ....D6 73
Gartok, China, 5,000 ....B7 39
Gartz, Ger., 3,672 ....E8 24
Garvagh, N. Ire., 550 ....C5 11
Garve, Scot C4 13
Garvellachs, isl., Scot D3 13
Garvin, Lyon, Minn., 205 ....F3 99
Garvin, McCurtain, Okla., 138 ....D7 112
Garvin, co., Okla., 28,290 ...C4 112
Garwin, Tama, Iowa, 546 ....B5 92
Garwolin, Pol., 5,315 ....C6 26
Garwood, Union, N.J., 5,426 ....*B4 106
Garwood, Colorado, Tex., 580 ....E4 118
Gary, Lake, Ind., 178,320 ....A3 91
Gary, Norman, Minn., 262 ...C2 99
Gary, Deuel, S. Dak., 471 ...C9 116
Gary, Panola, Tex., 200 ......C5 118
Gary, McDowell, W. Va., 1,393 ....D3 123
Garysburg, Northampton, N.C., 181 ....A6 109
Garyville, St. John the Baptist, La., 2,389 ....B6, D5 95
Garza, co., Tex., 6,611 ......C2 118
Garza Little Elm, res., Tex A5 118
Garzón, Col., 5,750 ....C2 60
Gas, Allen, Kans., 342 ......E8 93
Gas City, Grant, Ind., 4,469 .D6 91
Gascon, Mora, N. Mex., 60 ..B4 107
Gasconade, Gasconade, Mo., 333 ....C6 101
Gasconade, co., Mo., 12,195 .C6 101
Gasconade, riv., Mo C6 101
Gascons, Que., Can., 207 ..*k13 73
Gascony (Gascogne), former prov., Fr., 996,000 ....E3 14
Gascoyne, Bowman, N. Dak., 50 ....C2 110
Gashaka, Cam., 1,088 ....E7 45
Gashua, Nig D7 45
Gasmata, New Britain I k13 50
Gasparilla, pass, Fla F4 86
Gaspé, Que., Can., 2,603 ...k14 73
Gaspé, cape, Que., Can G20 67
Gaspé, pen., Que., Can k13 73
Gaspe East, co., Que., Can., 41,333 ....*k14 73
Gaspésian, prov. park, Que., Can k13 73
Gaspe West, co., Que., Can., 20,529 ....*k13 73
Gasport, Niagara, N.Y., 900 .B2 108
Gasque, Baldwin, Ala., 100 ..E2 78
Gassaway, Cannon, Tenn., 70 ....B5 117
Gassaway, Braxton, W. Va., 1,223 ....C4 123
Gassetts, Windsor, Vt., 50 ...E3 120
Gassol, Nig E7 45
Gassville, Baxter, Ark., 233 .A3 81
Gaston, Delaware, Ind., 801 .D6 91
Gaston, Northampton, N.C., 1,214 ....A6 109
Gaston, Washington, Oreg., 320 ....B1 113
Gaston, Lexington, S.C., 175 .D5 115
Gaston, co., N.C., 127,074 ...B2 109
Gastonia, Gaston, N.C., 37,276 ....B2 109
Gastre, Arg C3 54
Gata, cape, Sp D4 20
Gata, mts., Sp B2 20
Gatchel, Perry, Ind H4 91
Gatchina, Sov. Un., 47,900 ....B8 27, s31 25
Gate, Beaver, Okla., 130 .A1, D4 112
Gate City, Scott, Va., 2,142 .B2 121
Gatehouse of Fleet, Scot. 820 .F4 13
Gates, Custer, Nebr., 14 .....C6 103
Gates, Monroe, N.Y., 16,405 ....*B3 108
Gates, Gates, N.C., 350 .....A7 109
Gates, Lauderdale, Tenn., 291 ....B2 117
Gates, co., N.C., 9,254 .....A7 109
Gateshead, Eng., 102,600 ....C6 10
Gates Mills, Cuyahoga, Ohio, 1,588 ....*A6 111
Gatesville, Gates, N.C., 460 ..A7 109
Gatesville, Coryell, Tex., 4,626 ....D4 118
Gateway, Mesa, Colo., 110 ..C2 83
Gateway, Jefferson, Oreg C5 113
Gatineau, Que., Can., 13,022 ....D2 73
Gatineau, co., Que., Can., 44,308 ....C2 73
Gatineau, nat. park, Que., Can .B8 72
Gatineau, riv., Que., Can D2 73
Gatliff, Whitely, Ky., 225 ....D5 94
Gatlinburg, Sevier, Tenn., 1,764 ....D10 117
Gato, Archuleta, Colo., 20 ...D3 83
Gatooma, Rh., 13,500 ......A4 49
Gattman, Monroe, Miss., 145 ....B5 100
Gatun, C.Z., 692 ....k11 62
Gatun, lake, C.Z k11 62
Gatzke, Marshall, Minn., 45 .B3 99
Gauer, lake, Man., Can A3 71
Gauhati, India, 100,707 .....C9 39
Gauja, riv., Sov. Un C5 27
Gauko-Otavi, S.W. Afr A1 49
Gaula, riv., Nor F4 25
Gauley, riv., W. Va C4 123
Gauley Bridge, Fayette, W. Va., 950 ....C3, D7 123
Gauley Mills, Webster, W. Va., 180 ....C4 123
Gause, Milam, Tex., 500 ....D4 118
Gautier, Jackson, Miss., 800 ..E3 100
Gavāter, Iran I10 41
Gavdhos, isl., Grc E5 23
Gave de Pau, riv., Fr F3 14
Gave d'Oloron, riv., Fr F3 14
Gaviota, Santa Barbara, Calif., 50 ....E3 82
Gavins Point, dam, Nebr B8 103
Gävle, Swe., 57,000 ....G7 25
Gävleborg, co., Swe., 294,300 ....*G7 25
Gävlebukten, bay, Swe G7 25
Gavrilov Posad, Sov. Un C13 27
Gavrilovka, Sov. Un., 10,000 ....G11 27
Gawler, Austl., 5,639 ....G2 51
Gawler, ranges, Austl F6 50
Gay, Meriwether, Ga., 194 ...C2 87
Gay, Keweenaw, Mich., 240 .A2 98
Gay, head, Mass D6 97
Gaya, Niger, 3,100 ....D5 45
Gaya, India, 151,105 ....D7 39, E10 40
Gaya, Nig., 12,996 ....F6 45
Gay Head, Dukes, Mass., 80 (103▲) D6 97
Gaylesville, Cherokee, Ala., 144 ....A4 78
Gaylord, Smith, Kans., 239 ..C5 93
Gaylord, Otsego, Mich., 2,568 ....C6 98
Gaylord, Sibley, Minn., 1,631 .F4 99
Gaylord, Coos, Oreg., 25 .....E2 113
Gaylordsville, Litchfield, Conn., 500 ....C3 84
Gayndah, Austl., 1,805 ......B8 51
Gays, Moultrie, Ill., 263 .....D5 90
Gaysin, Sov. Un., 10,000 .....G7 27
Gays Mills, Crawford, Wis., 634 ....E3 118
Gaysville, Windsor, Vt., 100 ..D3 120
Gayville, Yankton, S. Dak., 261 ....E8 116
Gaza, O'Brien, Iowa, 100 ...A2 92
Gaza, see Ghazzah, Gaza Area.
Gaza, prov., Moz B5 49
Gaza Area, Eg. occ., Asia, 377,000 ....C6 32
Gazak, Iran H9 41
Gaziantep, Tur., 124,097 ...D11 31
Gdańsk (Danzig), Pol., 301,700 (*550,000) A5 26
Gdov, Sov. Un, 7,900 ....B6 27
Gdynia, Pol., 156,200 ......A5 26
Gearhart, Clatsop, Oreg., 725 ....A3 113
Gearhart, mtn., Oreg E6 113
Geary, N.B., Can., 938 ......D3 74
Geary, Canadian and Blaine, Okla., 1,416 ....B3 112
Geary, co., Kans., 28,779 ....D7 93
Geauga, co., Ohio, 47,573 ...A6 111
Gebeit Mines, Sud A5 47
Gebo, Hot Springs, Wyo., 80 ....B4 125
Gebze, Tur., 7,900 ....B7 23
Ged, Calcasieu, La., 30 ......D2 95
Gedaref, Sud., 17,537 ....C4 47
Geddes, Charles Mix, S. Dak., 380 ....D7 116
Gedera, Isr., 4,000 ....h10 32
Gedern, Ger., 3,000 ....C4 17
Gedinne, Bel., 940 ....E4 15
Gediz, Tur., 7,300 ....C7 23
Gediz (Hermus), riv., Tur C6 23
Gedser, Den., 1,262 ....D5 24
Geel, Bel., 27,007 ....C5 15
Geelong, Austl., 18,200 (*110,000) I5 51
Geelvink, bay, W. Irian F9 35
Geeraardsbergen, Bel., 9,582 ....D3 15
Gees Bend (Boykin), Wilcox, Ala., 100 ....C2 78
Geetbets, Bel., 3,187 ....D5 15
Geff (Jeffersonville), Wayne, Ill., 330 ....E5 90
Geidam, Nig., 11,032 ....D7 45
Geiger, Sumter, Ala., 104 ....C1 78
Geisenfeld, Ger., 2,800 ......E6 17
Geislingen, Ger., 25,800 ......E4 17
Geismar, Ascension, La., 100 .B5 95
Geist, res., Ind E6 91
Geistown, Cambria, Pa., 3,186 ....F4 114
Geita, Tan, 365 ....B5 48
Gela, It., 58,400 ....F5 21
Gelatt, Susquehanna, Pa., 60 ....C10 114
Gelderland, prov., Neth., 1,287,800 ....B5 15
Geldermalsen, Neth., 1,752 ..C5 15
Geldern, Ger., 10,200 ....C6 15
Geldrop, Neth., 19,400 ......C5 15
Gelert, Ont., Can C6 72
Gelfingen, Switz., 493 ......B5 19
Gelib, Som., 3,000 (10,000▲) ..E5 47
Gelibolu (Gallipoli), Tur., 12,945 ....B6 23
Gelligaer, Wales, 34,572 ....C4 12
Gellinam, isl., Kwajalein 52
Gelnhausen, Ger., 7,800 .....C4 17
Gelsenkirchen, Ger., 379,300 .B2 17
Gelting, Ger., 1,600 ....D3 24
Gem, Alta., Can D4 69
Gem, Shoshone, Idaho, 350 ..B3 89
Gem, Thomas, Kans., 116 ....C3 93
Gem, Braxton, W. Va., 30 ....C4 123
Gem, co., Idaho, 9,127 ......E2 89
Gemas, Mala., 4,841 ....k5 38
Gembloux, Bel., 5,875 ....D4 15
Gemena, Con. L A2 48
Gemert, Neth., 7,300 ....C5 15
Gemlik, Tur., 12,700 ....B7 23
Gemmell, Koochiching, Minn., 60 ....C4 99
Gemona, del Friuli, It., 6,772 .C9 18
Gemünden, Ger., 4,200 ......C4 17
Gem Village, La Plata, Colo., 95 ....D3 83
Genarp, Swe., 808 ....C7 24
Gene Autry, Carter, Okla., 110 ....C4 112
Geneina, Sud., 11,817 ....C1 47
General Acha, Arg., 4,709 ..B4 54
General Alvarado, Arg B5 54
General Alvear, Arg., 2,548 ..B4 54
General Alvear, Arg A3 54
General Belgrano, Arg., 3,789 .B5 54
General Bravo, Mex., 1,225 ..G3 118
General Conesa, Arg C4 54
General La Madrid, Arg., 3,572 ....B4 54
General Lavalle, Arg B5 54
General Madariaga, Arg., 7,073 ....B5 54
General Paz, Arg E4 55
General Pico, Arg., 11,121 ...B4 54
General Pinedo, Arg., 2,198 ..E3 55
General Roca, Arg., 7,449 ....B3 54
General San Martín (San Martín), Arg., 269,514 .....g7 54
General Sarmiento, Arg g7 54
General Toshevo, Bul., 2,102 .D9 22
General Viamonte, Arg., 5,324 ....B4 54
General Villegas, Arg., 4,738 .A4 54
Genesee, Latah, Idaho, 535 ..C2 89
Genesee, Genesee, Mich., 700 ....E7 98
Genesee, Potter, Pa., 400 ....C6 114
Genesee, co., Mich., 374,313 ..E7 98
Genesee, co., N.Y., 53,994 ...B2 108
Genesee, riv., N.Y C2 108
Genesee Depot, Waukesha, Wis., 160 ....E1 124
Geneseo, Henry, Ill., 5,169 ...B3 90
Geneseo, Rice, Kans., 558 ....D5 93
Geneseo, Livingston, N.Y., 3,284 ....C3 108
Geneseo, Sargent, N. Dak., 106 ....C8 112
Geneva, Geneva, Ala., 3,840 .D4 78
Geneva, Talbot, Ga., 261 ....D2 87
Geneva, Bearlake, Idaho, 551 ....G7 89
Geneva, Kane, Ill., 7,646 .B5, F1 90
Geneva, Adams, Ind., 1,053 ..C8 91
Geneva, Franklin, Iowa, 219 ..B4 92
Geneva, Henderson, Ky., 150 .C2 94
Geneva, Fillmore, Nebr., 2,352 ....D8 103
Geneva, Ontario, N.Y., 17,286 ....C4 108
Geneva, Ashtabula, Ohio, 5,677 ....A7 111
Geneva, Crawford, Pa., 250 ..C1 114
Geneva, co., Ala., 22,310 .....D4 78
Geneva, see Léman, lake, Switz.
Geneva, lake, Wis F5 124
Genève (Geneva), Switz., 174,700 (*305,000) D1 19
Genève, canton, Switz., 259,234 ....D1 19
Genevia, Pulaski, Ark., 6,000 ....C3, D6 81
Genichesk, Sov. Un., 25,000 .H10 27
Genil, riv., Sp D3 20
Génissiat, Fr., 322 ....C1 18
Genk, Bel., 47,416 ....D5 15
Gennep, Neth., 5,400 ....C5 15
Gennevilliers, Fr., 42,595 ...g10 14
Geno, Harris, Tex E5, F5 118
Genoa, Lincoln, Colo., 185 ...B7 83
Genoa, DeKalb, Ill., 2,330 ...A5 90
Genoa, see Genova, It.
Genoa, Nance, Nebr., 1,009 ..C8 103
Genoa, Douglas, Nev., 115 ...E2 104
Genoa, Cayuga, N.Y., 310 ...C4 108
Genoa, Ottawa, Ohio, 1,957 ....A2, A4 111
Genoa, Stark, Ohio, 1,000 ..*B6 111
Genoa, Harris, Tex., 200 ..E5, F5 118
Genoa, Vernon, Wis., 325 ...E2 124
Genoa, gulf, It B2 21
Genoa City, Walworth, Wis., 1,005 ....F1, F5 124
Genola, Morrison, Minn., 108 ....E4 99
Genola, Utah, Utah, 380 ....D4 119
Genolier, Switz., 286 ....D1 19
Genova (Genoa), It., 825,500 (*865,000) E4 18, B2 21
Genovesa, isl., Ec f6 58
Gent (Gand) (Ghent), Bel., 157,811 (*330,000) C3 15
Gentbrugge, Bel., 22,222 ....C3 15
Genthin, Ger., 15,200 ....A7 17
Gentian, Muscogee, Ga., 800 ....D2 87
Gentilly, Que., Can., 677 ....C5 73
Gentilly, Fr., 19,211 ....g10 14
Gentilly, Polk, Minn., 100 ...C2 99
Gentry, Benton, Ark., 686 ...A1 81
Gentry, Gentry, Mo., 98 .....A3 101
Gentry, co., Mo., 8,793 .....A3 101
Gentryville, Spencer, Ind., 297 ....H3 91
Gentryville, Gentry, Mo., 80 .A3 101
Genzano di Roma, It., 12,727 .h9 21
Geographe, bay, Austl F2 50
Geographe, chan., Austl D1 50
Geographical Society, isl., Grnld .B17 4
Geographic Center of North America, N. Dak A6 110
Geographic Center of United States, S. Dak B7 76
Geokchay, Sov. Un., 10,000 .G18 9
George, Lyon, Iowa, 1,200 ...A2 92
George, Northampton, N.C., 250 ....A6 109
George, S. Afr., 14,505 ......D3 49
George, co., Miss., 11,098 ...E5 100
George, bay, N.S., Can D8 74
George, cape, N.S., Can D8 74
George, hill, Md D1 85
George, isl., Newf., Can A3 75
George, isl., Sov. Un B10 4
George, lake, Austl G7 51
George, lake, N.S., Can E3 74
George, lake, Ont., Can B6 98
George, lake, Fla C5 86
George, lake, N.Y B7 108
George, peak, Utah B2 119
George, riv., Que., Can E19 67
George B. Stevenson, flood control res., Pa D5 114
George V, coast, Ant C28 5
George VI, sound, Ant B6 5
George River, Que., Can., 144 .f8 75
Georges, Mills, Sullivan, N.H., 100 ....B1 105
Georgesville, Franklin, Ohio, 200 ....C1 111
Georgetown, White, Ark., 200 ....B4 81
George Town, Ba. Is., 445 ...D6 64
Georgetown, Br. Gu., 72,965 (*148,402) A3 59
Georgetown, Ont., Can., 10,298 ....D5 72
Georgetown, P.E.I., Can., 744 ....C7 74
Georgetown, Cayman Is., 2,573 ....F3 64
Georgetown, Clear Creek, Colo., 307 ....B5 83
Georgetown, Fairfield, Conn., 1,200 ....E3 84
Georgetown, Sussex, Del., 1,765 ....C7 85
Georgetown, Putnam, Fla., 500 ....C5 86
Georgetown, Gam D2 45
Georgetown, Quitman, Ga., 554 ....E1 87
Georgetown, Bear Lake, Idaho, 551 ....G7 89
Georgetown, Vermilion, Ill., 3,544 ....D6 90
Georgetown, Floyd, Ind., 643 ....H6 91
Georgetown, Scott, Ky., 6,986 ....B5 94
Georgetown, Grant, La., 321 ....C3 95
Georgetown, Kent, Md., 50 ..B6 85
Georgetown, Essex, Mass., 2,300 (3,755▲) A6 97
Georgetown, Clay, Minn., 178 ....C2 99
Georgetown, Copiah, Miss., 285 ....D3 100
Georgetown, Burlington, N.J., 50 ....C3 106
Georgetown, Madison, N.Y., 250 ....C5 108
Georgetown, Brown, Ohio, 2,674 ....D4 111
Georgetown, Beaver, Pa., 246 ....A2 123
Georgetown, Georgetown, S.C., 12,261 ....E9 115
Georgetown, Hamilton, Tenn., 75 ....D9 117
Georgetown, Williamson, Tex., 5,218 ....D4 118
Georgetown, co., S.C., 34,798 ....D9 115
Georgeville, Que., Can., 102 .D5 73
George Washington Birthplace, nat. mon., Va C6 121
George West, Live Oak, Tex., 1,878 ....E3 118
Georgia (Georgian S.S.R.), rep., Sov. Un., 4,460,000 ....G17 9
Georgia, state, U.S., 3,943,116 ....D11 77, 87
Georgia, strait, B.C., Can E5 68
Georgia Center, Franklin, Vt., 100 (1,079▲) B2 120
Georgian S.S.R. (Georgia), rep., Sov. Un., 4,460,000 ....G17 9
Georgian, bay, Ont., Can B3 72
Georgiana, Butler, Ala., 2,093 ....D3 78
Georgian Bay Island, nat. park, Ont., Can B3, C4 72
Georgia Southern, Bulloch, Ga., 1,400 ....D5 87
Georgina, riv., Austl D6 50
Georgiyevsk, Sov. Un., 10,000 ....G17 9
Georgsheil, Ger., 99 ....A7 15
Gera, Ger., 103,000 ....C7 17
Gerald, Sask., Can., 131 ....G5 70
Gerald, Franklin, Mo., 474 ..C6 101
Geraldine, De Kalb, Ala., 340 ....A4 78
Geraldine, Chouteau, Mont., 364 ....C6 102

Geraldton, Austl., 10,894....E1 50
Geraldton, Ont., Can., 3,375....o18 72
Gerard, Somerset, Maine....C2 96
Gérardmer, Fr., 8,970....A2 18
Gerber, Tehama, Calif., 700..B2 82
Gerbstedt, Ger., 6,326....B6 17
Gercüs, Tur., 2,300....D13 31
Gerdau, riv., Ger....F4 24
Gerdine, mtn., Alsk....g15 79
Gerede, Tur., 5,400....B9 31
Gérgal, Sp., 3,934....D4 20
Gérin, Que., Can....C4 73
Gering, Scotts Bluff, Nebr., 4,585....C2 103
Gerlach, Washoe, Nev., 170..C2 104
Gerlachovka, mtn., Czech....D6 26
Germania, Atlantic, N.J., 100....D3 106
Germania, Potter, Pa., 150...C6 114
Germansen, lake, B.C., Can....B5 68
Germantown, N.B., Can., 75 .D5 74
Germantown, Fairfield, Conn., 2,893....*D3 84
Germantown, Clinton, Ill., 983....E4 90
Germantown, Bracken and Mason, Ky., 251....B6 94
Germantown, Montgomery, Md., 125....B3 85
Germantown, Montgomery, Ohio, 3,399....C3 111
Germantown, Shelby, Tenn., 1,104....B2 117
Germantown, Washington, Wis., 622....E1, E5 124
German Valley, Stephenson, Ill., 224....A4 90
Germany, reg., Eur....E11 8, 16
Germany, East, country, Eur., 17,250,000....B6 16
Germany, West, country, Eur., 58,550,000....C4 16
Germersheim, Ger., 7,500...D3 17
Germfask, Schoolcraft, Mich., 125....B5 98
Germiston, S. Afr., 148,102..C4 49
Gernrode, Ger., 6,033....B6 17
Gernsheim, Ger., 7,100....D3 17
Gero, Jap, 16,163....n16 37
Gerolzhofen, Ger., 5,500....D5 17
Gerona, Phil., 2,471....o13 35
Gerona, Sp., 32,784....B7 20
Gerona, prov., Sp., 351,369.*B7 20
Geronimo, Comanche, Okla., 199....C3 112
Geronimo, Guadalupe, Tex., 110....B4 118
Gerrardstown, Berkeley, W. Va., 240....B6 123
Gerrish, Merrimack, N.H., 30....D3 105
Gers, dept., Fr., 182,264...*F4 14
Gersfeld, Ger., 2,100....C4 17
Gersthofen, Ger., 10,800....E5 17
Gerty, Hughes, Okla., 135...C5 112
Gervais, Marion, Oreg., 438....B2, B4 113
Géryville, Alg., 7,614 (62,408▲)....C5 44
Gerze, Tur., 4,272....B10 31
Geseke, Ger., 11,400....B3 17
Gesher Haziv, Isr....A7 32
Gessie, Vermillion, Ind., 130.D3 91
Getafe, Sp., 21,895....B4, p17 20
Gethsémani, Que., Can., 147.h9 75
Gettysburg, Darke, Ohio, 443....B3 111
Gettysburg, Adams, Pa., 7,960....G7 114
Gettysburg, Potter, S. Dak., 1,950....C6 122
Getúlio Vargas, Braz., 5,705.D2 56
Getz, ice shelf, Ant....B36 5
Geuda Springs, Sumner and Cowley, Kans., 223....E6 93
Gevelsberg, Ger., 31,700....B2 17
Gex, Fr., 1,295....C2 18
Geyser, Judith Basin, Mont., 300....C6 102
Geyserville, Sonoma, Calif., 225....C2 82
Geyve, Tur., 3,700....B8 23
Gézenti, Chad, 106....A3 46
Ghadir, as Sufi (Oasis), Iraq....F13 31
Ghagar, res., India....E9 40
Ghaggar, riv., India....C5 40
Ghana, country, Afr., 7,600,000....F5 42, E4 45
Ghanzi, Bech....B3 49
Ghardaïa, Alg., 14,046 (48,080▲)....C5 44
Ghardaïa, reg., Alg....C5 44
Gharyān, Libya, 2,796....C2 43
Ghāt, Libya, 1,508....E2 43
Ghats, mts., India....E5, E7 39
Ghazal, riv., Chad....C3 46
Ghazipur, India, 37,147....E9 40
Ghazni, Afg., 27,084....E14 41
Ghazzah (Gaza), Gaza Area, 100,000....C6 32
Gheen, St. Louis, Minn., 50..C6 99
Gheens, Lafourche, La., 100....C6, E5 95
Ghent, see Gent, Bel.
Ghent, Carroll, Ky., 342....B4 94
Ghent, Lyon, Minn., 326....F3 99
Ghent, Columbia, N.Y., 550....C7 108
Gheorgheni, Rom., 11,969..B7 22
Gherla, Rom., 7,617....B6 22
Ghimir, see Ginir, Eth.
Ghio, Richmond, N.C....C4 109
Ghītah, Eg., U.A.R., 1,000..D3 32
Ghizao, Afg., 5,000....E13 41
Gholson, Noxubee, Miss., 50....C5 100
Ghor, riv., Afg....E11 41
Ghudāmis, Libya....C1 43
Ghurian, Afg., 10,000....D10 41
Giahel, riv., Som....C6 47
Giamda (Taichao), China...E3 34
Giannutri, isl., It....C3 21
Giant, mtn., N.Y....A7 108
Giants Neck, New London, Conn., 500....*D8 84
Giaveno, It., 9,692....D3 18
Gibara, Cuba, 8,045....E5 64
Gibbon, Sibley, Minn., 896..F4 99
Gibbon, Buffalo, Nebr., 1,083....D7 103
Gibbon, Umatilla, Oreg., 80.B8 113
Gibbons, Alta., Can., 192...C4 69
Gibbonsville, Lemhi, Idaho, 125....D5 89
Gibbs, Adair, Mo., 158....A5 101
Gibbs, Obion, Tenn., 100...A3 117
Gibbs City, Iron, Mich....B2 98
Gibbstown, Gloucester, N.J., 4,065....D2 106
Gibeon, S.W. Afr., 485....C2 49
Gibraleón, Sp., 8,865....D2 20
Gibraltar, Gib., 24,502 (*101,000)....D3 20
Gibraltar, Br. dep., Eur., 25,000....*D3 20
Gibraltar, Wayne, Mich., 2,196....*F7 98
Gibraltar, bay, Sp....D3 20
Gibraltar, pt., Eng....A8 12
Gibraltar, strait, Afr., Eur....G4 30
Gibsland, Bienville, La., 1,150....B2 95
Gibson, Glascock, Ga., 479..C4 87
Gibson, Terrebonne, La., 280....C5, E5 95
Gibson, Monroe, Miss., 50...B5 100
Gibson,Dunklin, Mo., 100...E8 101
Gibson, Scotland, N.C., 501..C4 109
Gibson, Gibson, Tenn., 297..B3 117
Gibson, co., Ind., 29,949....H2 91
Gibson, co., Tenn., 44,699...A3 117
Gibson, des., Austl....D3 50
Gibson, isl., Md....B5 85
Gibsonburg, Sandusky, Ohio, 2,540....A2, A4 111
Gibson City, Ford, Ill., 3,453....C5 90
Gibsonia, Allegheny, Pa., 1,150....A6 114
Gibsons, B.C., Can., 1,091...E6 68
Gibsonton, Hillsborough, Fla., 1,673....E2 86
Gibsonville, Guilford and Alamance, N.C., 1,784....A4 109
Gidam, India....H8 40
Giddings, Lee, Tex., 2,821...D4 118
Gideon, New Madrid, Mo., 1,411....E8 101
Gien, Fr., 8,812....D5 14
Giessen, Ger., 70,000 (*105,000)....C3 17
Giffard, Que., Can., 10,129 .n17 73
Gifford, Hot Spring, Ark., 150....D6 81
Gifford, Indian River, Fla., 3,509....E6 86
Gifford, Nez Perce, Idaho, 50.C2 89
Gifford, Champaign, Ill., 609....C5 90
Gifford, McKean, Pa., 430...C4 114
Gifhorn, Ger., 17,700....F4 24
Gift, Tipton, Tenn., 40....B2 117
Gifu, Jap., 304,492....I8, n15 37
Gifu, pref., Jap., 1,638,399..*I8 37
Giganta, mts., Mex....B2 63
Gigante, Col., 2,607....C2 60
Gigha, isl., Scot....E3 13
Gigha, sound, Scot....E3 13
Gig Harbor, Pierce, Wash., 1,094....B3, D1 122
Giglio, isl., It....C3 21
Giguela, riv., Sp....C4 20
Gihon, riv., Vt....B3 120
Gijón, Sp., 124,714....A3 20
Gil, isl., B.C., Can....C3 68
Gila, Grant, N. Mex., 150...E1 107
Gila, co., Ariz., 25,745....D5 80
Gila, mts., Ariz....D6 80
Gila, riv., Ariz., N. Mex....E2 80
Gila, riv., Eth....D3 47
Gila Bend, Maricopa, Ariz., 2,132....E3 80
Gila Bend, Indian res., Ariz....D3 80
Gila Bend, mts., Ariz....D2 80
Gila Center, Yuma, Ariz., 5..E1 80
Gila Cliff Dwellings, nat. mon., N. Mex....D1 107
Gila River, Indian res., Ariz....D4 80
Gilbert, Maricopa, Ariz., 1,833....D4, G2 80
Gilbert, Searcy, Ark., 52....B3 81
Gilbert, Story, Iowa, 318....B4 92
Gilbert, Franklin, La., 472..B4 95
Gilbert, St. Louis, Minn., 2,591....C6 99
Gilbert, Lexington, S.C., 171....D5 115
Gilbert, Mingo, W. Va., 874....D3 123
Gilbert, is., Gilbert & Ellice Is.G 7 10
Gilbert, riv., Austl....C7 50
Gilbert, riv., Newf., Can....B3 75
Gilbert & Ellice Islands, Br. dep., Oceania, 51,000....G10 7
Gilbert Plains, Man., Can., 849....D1 71
Gilberton, Schuylkill, Pa., 1,712....*E9 114
Gilbertown, Choctaw, Ala., 270....D1 78
Gilbertsville, Marshall, Ky., 231....A3 94
Gilbertsville, Otsego, N.Y., 522....C5 108
Gilbertsville, Montgomery, Pa., 750....F10 114
Gilbertville, Black Hawk, Iowa, 533....B5 92
Gilbertville, Worcester, Mass., 1,250....B3 97
Gilboa, Cheshire, N.H., 60..E2 105
Gilboa, Putnam, Ohio, 207..A4 111
Gilby, Grand Forks, N. Dak., 281....A8 110
Gilchrist, Klamath, Oreg., 500....D5 113
Gilchrist, co., Fla., 2,868....C4 86
Gilcrest, Weld, Colo., 357...A6 83
Gildford, Hill, Mont., 340...B6 102
Gilead, Tolland, Conn., 50..C7 84
Gilead, Oxford, Maine, 75 (136▲)....D2 96
Gilead, Thayer, Nebr., 79...D8 103
Giles, Donley, Tex., 25....B2 118
Giles, co., Tenn., 22,410....B4 117
Giles, co., Va., 17,219....D2 121
Gilford, Balknap, N.H., 165 (2,043▲)....C4 105
Gilford, N. Ire....C5 11
Gilford, isl., B.C., Can....D4 68
Gilford Park, Ocean, N.J., 1,400....*D4 106
Gilgandra, Austl., 2,245....E7 51
Gilgit, Pak., 4,671....A5 39
Gill, Weld, Colo., 150....A6 83
Gill (Town of), Franklin, Mass., (1,203▲)....*A2 97
Gill, lake, Ire....C3 11
Gillam, Man., Can., 332...A4 71
Gilleleje, Den., 2,219....B6 24
Gillen, lake, Austl....E3 50
Gillespie, Macoupin, Ill., 3,569....D4 90
Gillespie, co., Tex., 10,048...D3 118
Gillespie, dam, Ariz....D3 80
Gillett, Arkansas, Ark., 674..C4 81
Gillett, Manatee, Fla., 200...F2 86
Gillett, Bradford, Pa., 200...C8 114
Gillett, Karnes, Tex., 100....B4 118
Gillett, Oconto, Wis., 1,374..D5 124
Gillette, Campbell, Wyo., 3,580....A7 125
Gillett Grove, Clay, Iowa, 185....A2 92
Gillham, Sevier, Ark., 177...C1 81
Gilliam, Caddo, La., 300....B2 95
Gilliam, Saline, Mo., 249....B4 101
Gilliam, co., Oreg., 3,069....B6 113
Gillingham, Eng., 75,800....C8 12
Gillisburg, Amite, Miss., 75..D3 100
Gillises Mills, Hardin, Tenn....B3 117
Gillis Point, N.S., Can....C9 74
Gilly, Bel., 23,858....D4 15
Gilman, Eagle, Colo., 356...B4 83
Gilman, New London, Conn., 300....C8 84
Gilman, Iroquois, Ill., 1,704 .C5 90
Gilman, Marshall, Iowa, 491 .C5 92
Gilman, Benton, Minn., 146 .E5 99
Gilman, Lewis and Clark, Mont., 30....C4 102
Gilman, Sandoval, N. Mex., 100....*B3 107
Gilman, Essex, Vt., 400....C5 120
Gilman, Taylor, Wis., 379...C3 124
Gilman City, Harrison, Mo., 379....A4 101
Gilmanton, Belknap, N.H., 185 (736▲)....D4 105
Gilmanton, Buffalo, Wis., 200....D2 124
Gilmanton Iron Works, Belknap, N.H., 150....D4 105
Gilmer, Upshur, Tex., 4,312....C5 118
Gilmer, Gilmer, W. Va., 150.C4 123
Gilmer, co., Ga., 8,922....B2 87
Gilmer, co., W. Va., 8,050...C4 123
Gilmore, Crittenden, Ark., 438....B5 81
Gilmore, Lemhi, Idaho, 5...E5 89
Gilmore City, Humboldt, Iowa, 688....B3 92
Gilmour, Ont., Can., 69....C7 72
Gilpin, Casly, Ky., 50....C5 94
Gilpin, co., Colo., 685....B5 83
Gilpin, Dickens, Tex....C2 118
Gilroy, Santa Clara, Calif., 7,348....C6, D3 82
Gilroy, Sask., Can....G2 70
Gilson, Knox, Ill., 200....C3 90
Gilsum, Cheshire, N.H., 175 (528▲)....D2 105
Giltner, Hamilton, Nebr., 293....D7 103
Gima, Okinawa....52
Gimli, Man., Can., 1,841....D3 71
Gingoog, Phil., 9,331....*D6 35
Ginir, Eth....D5 47
Ginosa, It., 17,800....D6 21
Ginzo, Sp., 9,130....A2 20
Gioia del Colle, It., 24,000..D6 21
Gioiosa Ionica, It., 5,002...E6 21
Gi-Paraná, riv., Braz....E2 59
Gipsera, Switz....C3 19
Girard, Burke, Ga., 248....C5 87
Girard, Macoupin, Ill., 1,734.D4 90
Girard, Crawford, Kans., 2,350....E9 93
Girard, Richland, La., 100...B4 95
Girard, Trumbull, Ohio, 12,997....A7 111
Girard, Erie, Pa., 2,451....C1 114
Girard, Kent, Tex., 100....C2 118
Girardot, Col., 49,000....C3 60
Girardville, Schuylkill, Pa., 2,958....E9 114
Girdletree, Worcester, Md., 300....D7 85
Giresun (Kerasund), Tur., 19,900....B12 31
Giri, riv., Con. L....A2 48
Giridih, India, 36,881....E11 40
Girishk, Afg., 5,000....F12 41
Girna, riv., India....G5 40
Giromagny, Fr., 3,181....D7 14
Girón, Ec., 1,623....B2 58
Gironde, dept., Fr., 935,448.*E3 14
Gironde, riv., Fr....E3 14
Giroux, Man., Can., 51....E3 71
Girouxville, Alta., Can., 318.B2 69
Girvan, Scot., 6,159....E4 13
Girvin, Sask., Can., 143....F3 70
Girvin, Pecos, Tex., 35....D1 118
Gisborne, N.Z., 21,769 (*25,065)....M17 51
Gisborne, lake, Newf., Can....E4 75
Giscome, B.C., Can., 646....B6 68
Gislaveds, Swe., 6,900....A7 24
Gisors, Fr., 6,398....C4 14
Gitano, Jones, Miss., 40....D4 100
Giuba (Juba), riv., Som....E5 47
Giulianova, It., 9,100....C4 21
Giumbo, Som....F5 47
Giurgiu, Rom., 34,400....D7 22
Givataim, Isr., 30,822....g10 32
Give, Den., 1,800....C3 24
Givet, Fr., 7,444....B6 14
Givhans, Dorchester, S.C., 200....E1, E7 115
Givors, Fr., 17,066 (*27,000)....E6 14
Givry, isl., Turk....52
Gizhduvan, Sov. Un., 15,000....A12 41
Gizhiga, Sov. Un....C19 28
Gizycho, Pol., 12,400....A6 26
Gjinokaster, Alb., 13,100....B3 23
Gjinokaster, pref., Alb., 168,000....*B3 23
Gjoa Haven, N.W. Ter., Can., 98....C13 66
Gjövik, Nor., 7,900....G4 25
Glace Bay, N.S., Can., 24,186 (*43,800)....C10 74
Glacier, B.C., Can....D9 68
Glacier, Whatcom, Wash., 50....A4 122
Glacier, co., Mont., 11,565...B2 102
Glacier, bay, Alsk....k21 79
Glacier, nat. park, B.C., Can....D9 68
Glacier, nat. park, Mont....B2 102
Glacier Bay, nat. mon., Alsk...D12 79
Glacier, peak, Wash....A4 122
Gladbeck, Ger., 83,400....B1 17
Gladbrook, Tama, Iowa, 949.B5 92
Glade, Phillips, Kans., 133...C4 93
Glade, Catahoula, La....C4 95
Glade, creek, Wash....C6 122
Glade, creek, W. Va....D7 123
Glade Park, Mesa, Colo., 5..B2 83
Glades, co., Fla., 2,950....F5 86
Glade Spring, Washington, Va., 1,407....B3 121
Glade Valley, Alleghany, N.C., 100....A2 109
Gladeville, Wilson, Tenn., 120....A5 117
Gladewater, Gregg and Upshur, Tex., 5,742....C5 118
Gladmar, Sask., Can., 107...H3 70
Gladsakse, Den., 64,693....*C6 24
Gladstone, Austl., 7,181....A8 51
Gladstone, Austl., 1,063....F2 51
Gladstone, Man., Can., 944..D2 71
Gladstone, Henderson, Ill., 356....C3 90
Gladstone, Delta, Mich., 5,267....C3 98
Gladstone, Clay, Mo., 14,502....*B3 101
Gladstone, Jefferson, Nebr., 55....D8 103
Gladstone (Peapack-Gladstone), Somerset, N.J., 1,804....B3 106
Gladstone, Union, N. Mex., 5....A6 107
Gladstone, Stark, N. Dak., 185....C3 110
Gladstone, Clackamas, Oreg., 3,854....B2, B4 113
Gladstone, Nelson, Va., 150..D4 121
Glad Valley, Ziebach, S. Dak., 30....B4 116
Gladwin, Gladwin, Mich., 2,226....E6 98
Gladwin, co., Mich., 10,769..D6 98
Gladwyne, Montgomery, Pa., 2,500....*A11 114
Glady, Randolph, W. Va., 100....C5 123
Gladys, Campbell, Va., 180..D3 121
Glåma, riv., Nor....G5, p29 25
Glamis, Sask., Can....F2 70
Glamoč, Yugo., 986....C3 22
Glamorgan, co., Wales, 1,227,828....C4 12
Glan, Phil., 856....*D7 35
Glan, lake, Swe....u33 25
Glan, riv., Ger....D2 17
Glancy, Copiah, Miss., 30...D3 100
Gland, Switz., 1,545....D1 19
Glandorf, Putnam, Ohio, 747.A3 111
Glanshammar, Swe., 234....t33 25
Glarnisch, mtn., Switz....C6 19
Glarus, Switz., 5,852....B7 19
Glarus, canton, Switz., 40,148.C7 19
Glarus Alps, mts., Switz....C6 19
Glasco, Cloud, Kans., 812...C6 93
Glasco, Ulster, N.Y., 800....C7 108
Glascock, co., Ga., 2,672....C4 87
Glasford, Peoria, Ill., 1,012..C4 90
Glasgo, New London, Conn., 200....C9 84
Glasgow, Barren Ky., 10,069 .C4 94
Glasgow, Howard, Mo., 1,200....B5 101
Glasgow, Valley, Mont., 6,398....B10 102
Glasgow, Scot., 1,036,300 (*1,885,000)....E4 13
Glasgow, Rockbridge, Va., 1,091....D3 121
Glasgow, Kanawha, W. Va., 914....C6 123
Glaslyn, Sask., Can., 269....D1 70
Glasnevin, Sask., Can....H3 70
Glass, butte, Oreg....D6 113
Glass, Obion, Tenn., 50....A2 117
Glass, mts., Tex....D1 118
Glassboro, Gloucester, N.J., 10,253....D2 106
Glasscock, co., Tex., 1,118...D2 118
Glasson, Ire., 95....D4 11
Glassport, Allegheny, Pa., 8,418....F2 114
Glasston, Pembina, N. Dak., 60....A8 110
Glastenbury, mtn., Vt....F2 120
Glastonbury, Hartford, Conn., 6,000 (14,497▲)....C6 84
Glastonbury, Eng., 5,796....C5 12
Glauchau, Ger., 33,700....C7 17
Glazier, Hemphill, Tex., 55..A2 118
Glazier, lake, Maine....A3 96
Glazov, Sov. Un., 62,000....B4 29
Glazypeau, mtn., Ark....C5 81
Gleason, Weakley, Tenn., 900....A3 117
Gleason, Lincoln, Wis., 200..C4 114
Gleasondale, Middlesex, Mass., 650....g9 97
Gleichen, Alta., Can., 426...D4 69
Glen, Beaverhead, Mont., 50 .E4 102
Glen, Sioux, Nebr., 50....B2 103
Glen, Carroll, N.H., 190....B4 105
Glen, Clay, W. Va., 45..C3, C6 123
Glen, canyon, Utah....G4 119
Glen, lake, Mich....D4 98
Glenada, Lane, Oreg., 75....D2 113
Glenade, Ire....C3 11
Glen Alice, Roane, Tenn....D9 117
Glen Allan, Washington, Miss., 400....B2 100
Glen Allen, Fayette, Ala., 131....B2 78
Glenallen, Henrico, Va., 500.D5 121
Glen Almond, Que., Can....D2 73
Glen Alpine, Burke, N.C., 734....B2, D4 109
Glenalum, Mingo, W. Va., 250....D3 123
Glenamoy, Ire....C2 11
Glénans, is., Fr....D1 14
Glen Arbor, Leelanau, Mich., 500....D4 98
Glenarden, Prince Georges, Md., 1,336....*C4 85
Glenarm, N. Ire., 591....C6 11
Glenavon, Sask., Can., 377..G4 70
Glen Avon Heights, Riverside, Calif., 3,416....*F5 82
Glenbain, Sask., Can., 60...H2 70
Glenbarr, Scot....E3 13
Glenbeigh, Ire., 150....E2 11
Glenbeulah, Sheboygan, Wis., 428....B6 124
Glenboro, Man., Can., 797...E2 71
Glenbrook, Douglas, Nev., 20.D2 104
Glenburn, Renville, N. Dak., 363....A4 110
Glen Burnie, Anne Arundel, Md., 15,000....B4 85
Glenbush, Sask., Can., 56....D2 70
Glen Campbell, Indiana, Pa., 400....E4 114
Glen Canyon, Kane, Utah, 300....*F3 119
Glen Canyon, dam, Ariz....A4 80
Glencar, Ire....E2 11
Glen Carbon, Madison, Ill., 1,241....E4 90
Glencliff, Grafton, N.H., 70..C3 105
Glencliff, Davidson, Tenn., 3,000....*A5 117
Glencoe, Etowah, Ala., 2,592.B4 78
Glencoe, Ont., Can., 1,156..E3 72
Glencoe, Cook, Ill., 10,472...E3 90
Glencoe, Gallatin, Ky., 500..B5 94
Glencoe, Baltimore, Md., 200....A4 85
Glencoe, McLeod, Minn., 3,216....F4 99
Glencoe, St. Louis, Mo., 300.A7 101
Glencoe, Lincoln, N. Mex., 25....D4 107
Glencoe, Belmont, Ohio, 380.B1 123
Glencoe, Payne, Okla., 284..A5 112
Glencoe, val., Scot....D4 13
Glencolumbkille, Ire., 95....C3 11
Glen Cove, Nassau, N.Y., 23,817....h13 108
Glencross, Dewey, S. Dak., 45.B5 116
Glencullen, Multnomah, Oreg., 1,000....B2 113
Glendale, Maricopa, Ariz., 15,696....D3, G2 80
Glendale, Lincoln, Ark., 40..D4 81
Glendale, Los Angeles, Calif., 119,442....F2 82
Glendale, Walton, Fla., 100..G3 86
Glendale, Franklin, Idaho, 30....G7 89
Glendale, Hardin, Ky., 300. C4 94
Glendale, Berkshire, Mass., 350....*B1 97
Glendale, St. Louis, Mo., 7,048....*C7 101
Glendale, Hamilton, Ohio, 2,823....C3, D2 111
Glendale, Douglas, Oreg., 748....E3 113
Glendale, Providence, R.I., 500....B10 84
Glendale, Spartanburg, S.C., 600....B4 115
Glendale, Davidson, Tenn., 9,000....*A5 117
Glendale, Maury, Tenn., 50..B5 117
Glendale, Kane, Utah, 223..F3 119
Glen Dale, Marshall, W. Va., 1,905....B4 123
Glendale, Milwaukee, Wis., 10,432....*E6 124
Glendale Colony, Spink, S. Dak., 100....C7 116
Glen Dean, Breckinridge, Ky., 150....C3 94
Glendevey, Larimer, Colo., 30....A5 83
Glendive, Dawson, Mont., 7,058....C12 102
Glendo, Platte, Wyo., 292...C8 125
Glendo, res., Wyo....C8 125
Glendon, Alta., Can., 315....B5 69
Glendon, Lincoln, Maine, 50....D3 96
Glendora, Los Angeles, Calif., 20,752....F3 82
Glendora, Tallahatchie, Miss., 147....B3 100
Glendora, Camden, N.J., 5,000....*D2 106
Glendowan, Ire....C4 11
Glen Easton, Marshall, W. Va., 85....B4, C2 123
Glen Echo, Montgomery, Md., 310....C1 85
Glen Echo Heights, Montgomery, Md., 700....*C3 85
Glen Elder, Mitchell, Kans., 444....C5 93
Glenelg, Howard, Md., 200..B4 85
Glenelg, Scot., 1,486....C3 13
Glenella, Man., Can., 219...D2 71
Glen Ellen, Sonoma, Calif., 700....B5 82
Glen Ellis, falls, N.H....B4 105
Glen Ellyn, DuPage, Ill., 15,972....F2 90
Glen Ewen, Sask., Can., 289.H4 70
Glengarriff, Ire., 392....F2 11
Glen Ferris, Fayette, W. Va., 300....D7 123
Glenfield, Lewis, N.Y., 300..B5 108
Glenfield, Foster, N. Dak., 129....B7 110
Glenfinnan, Scot....D3 13
Glenflora, Wharton, Tex., 350....E4 118
Glen Gardner, Hunterdon, N.J., 787....B3 106
Glengarriff, Ire., 392....F2 11
Glengarry, co., Ont., Can., 19,217....B10 72
Glenham, Walworth, S. Dak., 171....B5 116
Glen Haven, Larimer, Colo., 25....A5 83
Glen Haven, De Kalb, Ga., 2,000....*C2 87
Glen Head, Nassau, N.Y., 4,400....*F2 84
Glen Innes, Austl., 5,769....D8 51
Glenisla, Scot., 440....D5 13
Glen Jean, Fayette, W. Va., 900....D3, D7 123
Glen Kerr, Sask., Can....G2 70
Glen Lake, B.C., Can., 663.*E6 68
Glenluce, Scot., 1,919....F4 13
Glen Lyon, Luzerne, Pa., 4,173....D9 114
Glen Mary, Scott, Tenn., 175....C9 117
Glenmont, Holmes, Ohio, 283....B5 111
Glen Moore, Lancaster, Pa., 1,700....*G10 114
Glenmora, Rapides, La., 1,447....D3 95
Glenmore, Van Wert, Ohio, 60....B3 111
Glenmorgan, Austl., 127....C7 51
Glenn, Allegan, Mich., 200 .F4 98
Glenn, co., Calif., 17,245....C2 82
Glenn Allen, Alsk., 169....F19 79
Glennamaddy, Ire., 234....D3 11
Glenn Dale, Prince Georges, Md., 205....C4 85
Glennie, Alcona, Mich., 90..D7 98
Glennonville, Dunklin, Mo., 100....E7 101
Glenns Ferry, Elmore, Idaho, 1,374....G3 89
Glennville, Tattnall, Ga., 2,791....E5 87
Glen Oak Acres, Cook, Ill., 1,500....*A6 90
Glen Oaks, Yavapai, Ariz., 20.C3 80
Glenolden, Delaware, Pa., 7,249....B11 114
Glenoma, Lewis, Wash., 50...C3 122
Glenpool, Tulsa, Okla., 353 .B5 112
Glen Raven, Alamance, N.C., 2,418....A4 109
Glen Riddle, Delaware, Pa., 800....B10 114
Glen Ridge, Palm Beach, Fla., 226....*F6 86
Glenridge, Marion, Ill....E4 90
Glenridge, Norfolk, Mass., 100....h10 97
Glenrio, Quay, N. Mex., 60....B6 107
Glenrio, Deaf Smith, Tex., 25....B1 118
Glen Robertson, Ont., Can., 409....B10 72
Glen Rock, Bergen, N.J., 12,896....h8 106
Glen Rock, York, Pa., 1,546.G8 114
Glenrock, Converse, Wyo., 1,584....C7 125
Glen Rose, Somervell, Tex., 1,422....C4 118
Glen St. Mary, Baker, Fla., 329....B4 86
Glens Falls, Warren, N.Y., 18,580....B7 108
Glenshaw, Allegheny, Pa., 24,939....*B6 114
Glenside, Sask., Can., 143...F2 70
Glenside, Montgomery, Pa., 22,500....*A11 114
Glentana, Valley, Mont., 65....B10 102
Glenties, Ire., 828....C3 11
Glentworth, Sask., Can., 150.H2 70
Glen Ullin, Morton, N. Dak., 1,210....C4 110
Glenview, Cook, Ill., 18,132..E2 90
Glenview Countryside, Cook, Ill., 2,000....*E2 90
Glenvil, Clay, Nebr., 323....D7 103
Glenville, Russell, Ala., 100..C4 78
Glenville, Nevada, Ark....D2 81
Glenville, Ire., 146....E3 11
Glenville, Freeborn, Minn., 643....G5 99
Glenville, Jackson, N.C., 250.D3 109
Glenville, Gilmer, W. Va., 1,828....C4 123
Glen White, Raliegh, W. Va., 800....D3 123
Glenwillard, Allegheny, Pa., 1,100....*A5 114
Glen Wilton, Botetourt, Va., 300....D3 121
Glenwood, Grenshaw, Ala., 416....D3 78
Glenwood, Pike, Ark., 840...C2 81
Glenwood, Newf., Can., 1,130....D4 75
Glenwood, Volusia, Fla., 200.C5 86
Glenwood, Wheeler, Ga., 682.D4 87
Glenwood, Fayette, Ind., 382....E7 91
Glenwood, Mills, Iowa, 4,783....C2 92
Glenwood, Aroostook, Maine, (30▲)....C4 96
Glenwood, Howard, Md., 25.B3 85
Glenwood, Cass, Mich., 115 .F4 98
Glenwood, Pope, Minn., 2,631....E3 99
Glenwood, Schuyler, Mo., 242....A5 101
Glenwood, Sussex, N.J., 400..A4 106
Glenwood, Catron, N. Mex., 150....D1 107
Glenwood, Washington, Oreg., 500....A1, B3 113
Glenwood, Sevier, Utah, 277....E4 119
Glenwood, Klickitat, Wash., 300....C4 122
Glenwood, Mason, W. Va., 250....C2 123
Glenwood City, St. Croix, Wis., 835....C1 124
Glenwood Landing, Nassau, N.Y., 4,000....*F2 84
Glenwood Park, Orange, N.Y., 1,317....*D6 108
Glenwood Springs, Garfield, Colo., 3,637....B3 83
Glenwoodville, Alta., Can., 274....E4 69
Gletsch, Switz....C5 19
Glezen, Pike, Ind., 180....H3 91
Glidden, Sask., Can., 145...F1 70
Glidden, Carroll, Iowa, 993..B3 92
Glidden, Ashland, Wis., 700....B3 124
Glide, Douglas, Oreg., 200...D3 113
Glien Albyn, mtn., Scot....D3 13
Glifadha, Grc., 12,361....h11 23
Glin, Ire., 763....E2 11
Gliwice, Pol., 143,500....C5, g9 26
Globe, Gila, Ariz., 6,217....D5 80
Globe, Carter, Ky., 300....B6 94
Globino, Sov. Un., 10,000...G9 27
Glocester (Town of), Providence, R.I., (3,397▲)....*B10 84
Głogów, Pol., 1,681....C3 26
Glorenza, It., 792....A3 21
Glória, Braz., 1,062....C3 57
Glória, Plaquemines, La....C7 95
Glória de Goitá, Braz., 1,959..k6 57
Glorieta, Santa Fe, N. Mex., 200....B4, h9 107
Glorieuses, is., Afr....f9 49
Glossop, Eng., 17,490....A6 12
Glossopteris, mtn., Ant....A1 5
Gloster, Gwinnett, Ga., 60...A5 87
Gloster, De Soto, La., 250...B2 95
Gloster, Amite, Miss., 1,369..D2 100
Glostrup, Den., 21,845....C6 24
Gloucester, Ont., Can....h12 72
Gloucester, Eng., 70,800 (*104,000)....C5 12
Gloucester, Essex, Mass., 25,789....A6, f13 97
Gloucester, Gloucester, Va., 500....D6 121
Gloucester, co., N.B., Can., 66,343....B4 74
Gloucester, co., Eng., 1,000,493....C5 12
Gloucester, co., N.J., 134,840 .D2 106
Gloucester, co., Va., 11,919..D6 121
Gloucester City, Camden, N.J., 15,511....D2 106
Glouster, Athens, Ohio, 2,255....C5 111
Glover, Iron, Mo., 400....D7 101
Glover, Dickey, N. Dak., 75..C7 110

Glover, Orleans, Vt., 230 (683▲)...B4 120
Glover, isl., Newf., Can...D3 75
Glovergap, Marion, W. Va., 125...A6 123
Gloversville, Fulton, N.Y., 21,741...B6 108
Glovertown, Newf., Can., 1,197...D4 75
Glovertown South, Newf., Can., 663...*D5 75
Gloverville, Aiken, S.C., 1,551...E4 115
Glubczyce, Pol., 5,020...C4 26
Glubokoye, Sov. Un., 25,000...D6 27
Glucholazy, Pol., 7,658...C4 26
Gluck, Anderson, S.C. (part of Anderson)...C2 115
Glücksburg, Ger., 5,800...D3 24
Glückstadt, Ger., 12,200...E3 24
Gluek, Chippewa, Minn., 60...E3 99
Glukhov, Sov. Un., 10,000...F9 27
Glussk, Sov. Un., 10,000...E7 27
Glyndon, Baltimore, Md., 915...B4 85
Glyndon, Clay, Minn., 489...D2 99
Glyngøre, Den., 930...B2 24
Glynn, co., Ga., 41,954...E5 87
Gmünd, see Schwäbisch Gmünd, Ger.
Gmunden, Aus., 12,518...E6 16
Gnadenhutten, Tuscarawas, Ohio, 1,257...B6 111
Gnesta, Swe., 3,200...t35 25
Gniezno, Pol., 45,600...B4 26
Gnjilane, Yugo., 12,508...D5 22
Gnoien, Ger., 5,368...E6 24
Goa, Damão, and Diu, ter., India, 684,941...D5, E5 39
Goalpara, India, 13,692...D13 40
Goat, isl., Am. Sam... 52
Goat, mtn., Mont...C3 102
Goat Fell, mtn., Scot...E3 13
Goat Rock, dam, Ala...C4 78
Goat Rock, dam, Ga...D1 87
Goba, Eth...D5 47
Gobabis, S.W. Afr., 1,997...B2 49
Goback, mtn., N.H...A3, B1 105
Gobernador Udaondo, Arg...g7 54
Gobernador, Rio Arriba, N. Mex., 100...A2 107
Gobey, Morgan, Tenn., 95...C9 117
Gobi, des., China, Mong...C5 34
Gobles, Van Buren, Mich., 816...F5 98
Goch, Ger., 15,200...C3 16
Godar-i-Shah, Afg., 5,000...G10 41
Godavari, riv., India...E6 39
Godchaux, Lafourche, La...C6 95
Godda, India, 7,500...E11 40
Goddard, Sedgwick, Kans., 533...B5, E6 93
Goderich, Ont., Can., 6,411...D3 72
Godfrey, Ont., Can...C8 72
Godfrey, Morgan, Ga., 181...C3 87
Godfrey, Madison, Ill., 1,231...E3 90
Godhavn, Grnld., 584...C20 4
Godhra, India, 52,167...F4 40
Godley, Johnson, Tex., 401...B5 118
Gods, lake, Man., Can...B4 71
Gods, riv., Man., Can...A5 71
Gods Lake, Man., Can., 40...B4 71
Godthåb, Grnld., 3,181...C20 4
Godwin, Cumberland, N.C., 149...B5 109
Godwin Austen, peak, Pak...A6 39
Godwinsville, Dodge, Ga., 150...D3 87
Goehner, Seward, Nebr., 106...D8 103
Goes, Neth., 15,200...C3 15
Goessel, Marion, Kans., 327...D6 93
Goff, Nemaha, Kans., 259...C8 93
Goffs, San Bernardino, Calif., 25...E6 82
Goffs Falls, Hillsboro, N.H. (part of Manchester)...E4 105
Goffstown, Hillsboro, N.H., 1,052 (7,230▲)...D3 105
Gogebic, co., Mich., 24,370...A5 98
Gogebic, lake, Mich...A5 98
Gohfeld, Ger., 14,400...A3 17
Göhren, Ger., 2,624...D7 24
Goiana, Braz., 19,026...C4, h6 57
Goiandira, Braz., 3,169...E1 57
Goianinha, Braz., 1,427...h6 57
Goiás, Braz., 7,121...B2 56
Goiás, state, Braz., 1,954,862...D1 57
Goito, It., 9,630...D6 18
Gojām, prov., Eth...C4 47
Gojo, Jap., 18,800...o14 37
Göksun, Tur., 3,700...C11 31
Gokwe, Rh...A4 49
Gol, Nor...G3 25
Gola, isl., Ire...B3 11
Golam, head, Ire...D2 11
Golchikha, Sov. Un., 1,300...B11 28
Golconda, Pope, Ill., 864...F5 90
Golconda, Humboldt, Nev., 225...C4 104
Gold, Potter, Pa., 40...C6 114
Gold Acres, Lander, Nev., 60...C5 104
Goldap, Pol., 632...A7 26
Goldbach, Ger., 6,600...C4 17
Gold Bar, Snohomish, Wash., 315...B4 122
Gold Beach, Curry, Oreg., 1,765...E2 113
Goldberg, Ger., 5,507...E6 24
Goldboro, N.S., Can., 142...D8 74
Gold Bridge, B.C., Can., 153...D6 68
Goldbutte, Toole, Mont...B5 102
Gold Coast, see Ghana, country, Afr.
Goldcreek, Powell, Mont., 60...D4 102
Golddust, Lauderdale, Tenn., 25...B2 117
Golden, Crenshaw, Ala...D3 78
Golden, B.C., Can., 1,776...D9 68
Golden, Jefferson, Colo., 7,118...B5 83
Golden, Idaho, Idaho, 50...D3 89
Golden, Adams, Ill., 491...C2 90
Golden, Ire., 153...E4 11
Golden, Tishomingo, Miss., 121...A5 100
Golden, Barry, Mo., 50...E4 101
Golden, Santa Fe, N. Mex., 25...B3, k8 107
Golden, Okanogan, Wash...A6 122
Golden, lake, Ont., Can...B7 72
Golden Acres, New Haven, Conn., 350...*D5 84
Golden Acres, Harris, Tex., 2,500...*F5 118
Golden Beach, Dade, Fla., 413...E3 86
Golden City, Barton, Mo., 714...D3 101
Goldendale, Klickitat, Wash., 2,536...D5 122
Goldengate, Wayne, Ill., 156...E5 90
Golden Gate, entrance, Calif...B5 82
Golden Glades, Dade, Fla., 3,000...*F3 86
Golden Hill, Dorchester, Md., 300...D5 85
Golden Hill, Olmstead, Minn., 2,190...*F6 99
Golden Hinde, mtn., B.C., Can...E5 68
Golden Lake, Ont., Can., 254...B7 72
Golden Meadow, Lafourche, La., 3,097...E5 95
Golden Prairie, Sask., Can., 206...G1 70
Golden Spike, nat. historical site, Utah...B3 119
Golden Valley, Hennepin, Minn., 14,559...E3 99
Goldenvalley, Mercer, N. Dak., 286...B3 110
Golden Valley, co., Mont., 1,203...D7 102
Golden Valley, co., N. Dak., 3,100...B2 110
Goldenville, N.S., Can., 68...D7 74
Goldfield, Teller, Colo., 75...C5 83
Goldfield, Wright, Iowa, 682...B4 92
Goldfield, Esmeralda, Nev., 300...F4 104
Goldfield, mts., Ariz...G3 80
Gold Hill, Lee, Ala., 195...C4 78
Gold Hill, Rowan, N.C., 249...B3 109
Gold Hill, Jackson, Oreg., 608...E3 113
Goldonna, Natchitoches, La., 292...B3 95
Gold Point, Esmeralda, Nev., 40...F4 104
Goldpoint, Hamilton, Tenn...E10 117
Goldsand, lake, Man., Can...A1 71
Goldsboro, Caroline, Md., 204...B6 85
Goldsboro, Wayne, N.C., 28,873...B6 109
Goldschmidt, cape, Ant...g40 5
Goldsmith, Tipton, Ind., 200...D5 91
Goldsmith, Ector, Tex., 670...D1 118
Goldston, Chatham, N.C., 374...B4 109
Goldstone, mtn., Idaho...D5 89
Goldthwaite, Mills, Tex., 1,383...D3 118
Goleen, Ire., 68...F2 11
Golela, S. Afr...C5 49
Goleniow, Pol., 1,713...B3 26
Goleta, Santa Barbara, Calif., 4,000...E4 82
Golf, Cook, Ill., 409...*E3 90
Golf Manor, Hamilton, Ohio, 4,648...D2 111
Golfview, Palm Beach, Fla., 131...*F6 86
Golfview Heights, Palm Beach, Fla., 1,500...*F6 86
Goliad, Goliad, Tex., 1,782...E4 118
Goliad, co., Tex., 5,429...E4 118
Golling, Aus., 2,845...B9 18
Golovin, Alsk., 22...C7 79
Golovnino, Kur. Is., Sov. Un...E12 37
Golpāyegān, Iran, 20,844...E5 41
Golspie, Scot., 1,323...C5 13
Goltry, Alfalfa, Okla., 313...A3 112
Golts, Kent, Md., 100...B6 85
Golva, Golden Valley, N. Dak., 162...C2 110
Golyamo Konare, Bul., 7,153...D7 22
Goma, Con. L...B4 48
Gombari, Con. L...A4 48
Gombe, Nig., 18,483...D7 45
Gomel, Sov. Un., 199,000...E8 27
Gomera, isl., Sp. (Can. Is.)...D1 44
Gomez, Martin, Fla., 250...E6 86
Gómez Palacio, Mex., 61,174...B4 63
Gommern, Ger., 6,227...A6 17
Gonaïves, Hai., 13,534...F7 64
Gonbad-e Kāvūs, Iran, 9,637...C7 41
Gonda, India, 43,496...C7 39
Gondar, Eth., 25,000...C4 47
Gondia, India, 56,320...G8 40
Gondrecourt-le-Château, Fr., 1,088...F5 15
Gönen, Tur., 10,800...B6 23
Gonesse, Fr., 8,517...g10 14
Gongola, riv., Nig...D7 45
Gonic, Strafford, N.H. (part of Rochester)...D5 105
Gonvick, Clearwater, Minn., 363...C3 99
Gonzales, Monterey, Calif., 2,138...D3 82
Gonzales, Ascension, La., 3,252...B5, D5 95
Gonzales, Gonzales, Tex., 5,829...E4 118
Gonzales, co., Tex., 17,845...E4 118
Gonzalez, Escambia, Fla., 300...G2 86
González, Mex., 1,913...C5 63
González Chaves, Arg., 4,718...B4 54
Goochland, Goochland, Va., 200...D5 121
Goochland, co., Va., 9,206...D5 121
Goodbee, St. Tammany, La...B7 95
Goode, Bedford, Va., 250...D3 121
Goodell, Hancock, Iowa, 231...B4 92
Gooderham, Ont., Can., 275...C6 72
Goodeve, Sask., Can., 212...F4 70
Goodfield, Woodford, Ill., 286...C4 90
Good Hart, Emmet, Mich., 50...C5 98
Good Hope, Walton, Ga., 165...C3 87
Good Hope, McDonough, Ill., 394...C3 90
Good Hope, St. Charles, La. (part of Norco)...C7 95
Good Hope, Leake, Miss., 125...C4 100
Good Hope, Fayette, Ohio, 300...C4 111
Good Hope, cape, S. Afr...D2 49
Good Hope, mtn., B.C., Can...D5 68
Goodhue, Goodhue, Minn., 566...F6 99
Goodhue, co., Minn., 33,035...F6 99
Gooding, Gooding, Idaho, 2,750...G4 89
Gooding, co., Idaho, 9,544...F4 89
Goodland, Collier, Fla., 100...G5 86
Goodland, Newton, Ind., 1,202...C3 91
Goodland, Sherman, Kans., 4,459...C2 93
Goodland, Choctaw, Okla., 50...D6 112
Goodlands, Man., Can., 138...E1 71
Goodlettsville, Davidson, Tenn., 3,163...A5, E9 117
Goodman, Holmes, Miss., 932...C4 100
Goodman, McDonald, Mo., 540...E3 101
Goodman, Marinette, Wis., 550...C5 124
Goodnews Bay, Alsk., 154...D7 79
Goodnight, Armstrong, Tex., 125...B2 118
Good Pasture, Pueblo, Colo...C6 83
Good Pine, La Salle, La., 600...C3 95
Goodrich, Morgan, Colo., 10...A6 83
Goodrich, Linn, Kans., 35...D9 93
Goodrich, Sheridan, N. Dak., 392...B5 110
Goodrich, Polk, Tex., 800...D5 118
Goodridge, Pennington, Minn., 134...B3 99
Goodsoil, Sask., Can., 246...*n7 70
Goodspeeds, Middlesex, Conn...D7 84
Good Spirit, lake, Sask., Can...F4 70
Good Spirit Lake, prov. park, Sask., Can...F4 70
Goodspring, Giles, Tenn., 25...B4 117
Goodsprings, Walker, Ala., 900...B2 78
Goodsprings, Clark, Nev...H6 104
Good Thunder, Blue Earth, Minn., 468...F4 99
Goodview, Winona, Minn., 1,348...F7 99
Good Water, Coosa, Ala., 2,023...B3 78
Goodwater, Sask., Can., 87...H4 70
Goodwater, McCurtain, Okla., 100...D7 112
Goodwell, Texas, Okla., 771...D7 112
Good Will Farm, Somerset, Maine, 100...D3 96
Goodwin, Yavapai, Ariz., 20...C3 80
Goodwin, Deuel, S. Dak., 113...C3 116
Goodyear, Maricopa, Ariz., 1,654...G1 80
Goole, Eng., 18,875...A7 12
Goondiwindi, Austl., 3,274...D8 51
Goor, Neth., 7,600...B6 15
Goose, bay, Newf., Can...B1 75
Goose, creek, Idaho...G5 89
Goose, creek, Utah...B1 119
Goose, creek, Va...D3 121
Goose, creek, Wyo...A6 125
Goose, isl., B.C., Can...D3 68
Goose, lake, Calif...B3 82
Goose, lake, Man., Can...B1 71
Goose, lake, Sask., Can...D4 70
Goose, lake, Sask., Can...F2 70
Goose, lake, Oreg...E6 113
Goose, pond, N.H...C2 105
Goose, river, Newf., Can...h9 75
Goose Bay, Newf., Can., 3,040...B1, h9 75
Gooseberry, creek, Wyo...A4 125
Goose Creek, Berkeley, S.C., 830...E2, F7 115
Goose Creek, res., S.C...E2 115
Goose Egg, Natrona, Wyo...C6 125
Gooselake, Clinton, Iowa, 191...C7 92
Goosport, Calcasieu, La., 16,778...*D2 95
Gopalganj, India, 14,090...D10 40
Goplo, lake, Pol...B5 26
Göppingen, Ger., 48,100...E4 17
Gora, Pol., 3,526...C4 26
Gora Kalwaria, Pol., 3,687...C6 26
Gorakhpur, India, 180,255...C7 39, D9 40
Gorday, Worth, Ga...E3 87
Gordes, Tur., 5,300...C7 23
Gordo, Pickens, Ala., 1,714...B2 78
Gordon, Houston, Ala., 222...D4 78
Gordon, Wilkinson, Ga., 1,793...D3 87
Gordon, Butler, Kans., 100...B6 93
Gordon, Claiborne, La...B3 95
Gordon, Sheridan, Nebr., 2,223...B3 103
Gordon, Schuylkill, Pa., 888...*E9 114
Gordon, Palo Pinto, Tex., 349...C3 118
Gordon, Douglas, Wis., 350...B2 124
Gordon, co., Ga., 19,228...B2 87
Gordon, lake, Alta., Can...A5 69
Gordon, lake, Sask., Can...B2 70
Gordon Horne, peak, B.C., Can...D8 68
Gordonsburg, Lewis, Tenn., 315...B4 117
Gordonsville, Freeborn, Minn., 100...G5 99
Gordonsville, Smith, Tenn., 249...C8 117
Gordonsville, Orange, Va., 1,109...C4 121
Gordonville, Cape Girardeau, Mo., 92...D8 101
Gore, N.S., Can., 144...D6 74
Gorē, Eth., 10,000...D4 47
Gore, N.Z., 7,270...Q12 51
Gore, Hocking, Ohio, 200...C5 111
Gore, Sequoyah, Okla., 334...B6 112
Gore, Frederick, Va., 200...B4 121
Gore, canyon, Colo...B4 83
Gore, mtn., Vt...B5 120
Gore, pt., Alsk...h16 79
Gore, range, Colo...B4 83
Gore Bay, Ont., Can., 716...B2 72
Goree, Knox, Tex., 543...C3 118
Gore Springs, Grenada, Miss., 100...B4 100
Goreville, Johnson, Ill., 625...F5 90
Gorey, Ire., 2,671...E5 11
Gorgān (Asterābād), Iran, 28,380...C7 41
Gorgas, Walker, Ala., 950...B2 78
Gorge High, dam, Wash...A4 122
Gorgona, isl., Col...C2 60
Gorham, Jackson, Ill., 378...F4 90
Gorham, Russell, Kans., 429...D4 93
Gorham, Cumberland, Maine, 2,322 (5,767▲)...E2, E4 96
Gorham, Coos, N.H., 1,945 (3,039▲)...B4 105
Gorham, Ontario, N.Y., 800...C3 108
Gori, Sov. Un., 33,000...E2 29
Gorin, Scotland, Mo., 410...A5 101
Gorinchem, Neth., 21,600...C5 15
Goris, Sov. Un., 4,660...C16 31
Gorizia, It., 43,400...B4 21
Gorki, Sov. Un., 10,000...D8 27
Gorki (Gorkiy), Sov. Un., 1,042,000 (★1,400,000)...B2 29
Gorkiy, res., Sov. Un...B2 29
Gørlev, Den., 1,379...C5 24
Gorlice, Pol., 6,100...D6 26
Görlitz, Ger., 89,300...B9 17
Gorlovka, Sov. Un., 309,000...G12, q21 27
Gorm, lake, Scot...E2 13
Gorman, Garrett, Md., 83...D1 85
Gorman, Humphreys, Tenn., 50...A4 117
Gorman, Eastland, Tex., 1,142...C3 118
Gormania, Grant, W. Va., 150...B5 123
Gormley, Ont., Can., 108...k15 72
Gorna Dzhumaya, see Blagoevgrad, Bul.
Gorna-Oryakhovitsa, Bul., 10,303...D7 22
Gornji Milanovac, Yugo., 4,493...C5 22
Gorno-Altaysk, Sov. Un., 30,000...E26 9
Gornozavodsk, Sov. Un., 20,000...C10 37
Gorodenka, Sov. Un., 10,000...G5 27
Gorodets, Sov. Un., 30,000...D17 9
Gorodishche, Sov. Un., 10,000...q22 27
Gorodnya, Sov. Un., 10,000...F8 27
Gorodok, Sov. Un...A5 34
Gorodok, Sov. Un., 10,000...G4 27
Gorodok, Sov. Un., 10,000...D7 27
Goroke, Austl., 379...H3 51
Gorong, is., Indon...F8 35
Gorontalo, Indon., 71,232...E6 35
Gorrie, Ont., Can., 319...D3 72
Gorskoye, Sov. Un., 10,000...q21 27
Gort, Ire., 1,044...D3 11
Gortahork, Ire...B3 11
Gorumna, isl., Ire...D2 11
Goryn, riv., Sov. Un...F6 27
Gorzow [Wielkopolski], Pol., 62,800...B3 26
Gosainthan, peak, Nep...C10 40
Gosford, Austl., 7,317...F8 51
Goshen, Pike, Ala., 260...D3 78
Goshen, Tulare, Calif., 1,061...*D4 82
Goshen, N.S., Can., 199...D8 74
Goshen, Litchfield, Conn., 300 (1,288▲)...B4 84
Goshen, Elkhart, Ind., 13,718...A6 91
Goshen, Oldham, Ky., 50...A4 94
Goshen, Hampshire, Mass., 300 (385▲)...B2 97
Goshen, Sullivan, N.H., 125 (351▲)...D2 105
Goshen, Cape May, N.J., 500...E3 106
Goshen, Orange, N.Y., 3,906...D6, m14 108
Goshen, Lane, Oreg., 300...D4 113
Goshen, Utah, Utah, 426...D4 119
Goshen, Rockbridge, Va., 99...D3 121
Goshen, co., Wyo., 11,941...C8 125
Goshen Hole, sink, Wyo...D8 125
Goshen Springs, Rankin, Miss., 50...C4 100
Goshute, Juab, Utah, 75...D2 119
Goshute, Indian res., Utah...D2 119
Goshute, mts., Nev...C7 104
Goslar, Ger., 40,900...B5 17
Gosnold (Town of), Dukes, Mass., (66▲)...*D6 97
Gosper, co., Nebr., 2,489...D6 103
Gospic, Yugo., 6,857...C2 22
Gosport, Clarke, Ala., 25...D2 78
Gosport, Eng., 69,900...D6 12
Gosport, Owen, Ind., 646...F4 91
Goss, De Soto, La...B2 95
Goss, Marion, Miss., 30...D4 100
Gossau, Switz., 9,731...B7 19
Gossburg, Coffee, Tenn., 100...B5 117
Gossville, Merrimack, N.H., 155...D4 105
Gostivar, Yugo., 12,776...E5 22
Gostyn, Pol., 8,021...C4 26
Gostynia, riv., Pol...g9 26
Gostynin, Pol., 7,357...B5 26
Gotebo, Kiowa, Okla., 538...B3 112
Göteborg, Swe., 410,700 (★515,000)...A5 24, I4 25
Göteborg och Bohus, co., Swe., 633,000...A5 24
Gotel, mts., Cam...E7 45
Gotemba, Jap., 28,700...n17 37
Gotha, Ger., 56,300...C5 17
Gotham, Richland, Wis., 250...E3 124
Gothenburg, Dawson, Nebr., 3,050...D5 103
Gothic, mesas, Ariz...A6 80
Gotland, co., Swe., 53,700...*I8 25
Gotland, isl., Swe...I8 25
Gotō, is., Jap...J4 37
Gotse Delchev, Bul., 11,061...E6 22
Göttingen, Ger., 82,600 (★115,000)...B4 17
Gottwaldov (Zlin), Czech., 55,600...D4 26
Gouda, Neth., 44,000...B4 15
Goudeau, Avoyelles, La., 130...D3 95
Goudiri, Sen...D2 45
Goudswaard, Neth., 730...C4 15
Gough, Burke, Ga., 300...C4 87
Gough, isl., Atl., O...I9 6
Gough, lake, Alta., Can...C4 69
Gouin, res., Que., Can...k12 73
Goulais, riv., Ont., Can...B6 98
Goulburn, Austl., 20,544...G7 51
Gould, Lincoln, Ark., 1,210...D4 81
Gould, Que., Can., 55...D6 73
Gould, Jackson, Colo., 60...A4 83
Gould, Harmon, Okla., 241...C2 112
Gouldbusk, Coleman, Tex., 75...D3 118
Gould City, Mackinac, Mich., 100...B5 98
Goulding, Escambia, Fla., 900...*G1 86
Gouldings Trading Post, San Juan, Utah, 10...F5 119
Goulds, Dade, Fla., 5,121...F3 86
Gouldsboro, Hancock, Maine, 280 (1,100▲)...D4 96
Gouldsboro, Wayne, Pa., 450...D11 114
Gouldtown, Cumberland, N.J., 300...E2 106
Goulimine, Mor., 8,015...D2 44
Gounamitz, riv., N.B., Can...B2 74
Goundam, Mali, 6,600...C4 45
Gouré, Niger, 1,000...D7 45
Gourma-Rarous, Mali...C4 45
Gournay-en-Bray, Fr., 3,195...C4 14
Gouro, Chad...B3 46
Gouverneur, Sask., Can...H2 70
Gouverneur, St. Lawrence, N.Y., 4,946...f9 108
Govan, Sask., Can., 380...F3 70
Govan, Bamberg, S.C., 138...E5 115
Gove, Gove, Kans., 228...D3 93
Gove, co., Kans., 4,107...D3 93
Govenlock, Sask., Can...H1 70
Governador Valadares, Braz., 70,494...E2 57
Government Camp, Clackamas, Oreg., 40...B5 113
Government Village, Flathead, Mont., 150...*B2 102
Governor Generoso, Phil., 1,659...*D7 35
Governor's Harbour, Ba. Is., 516...C5 64
Gowan, St. Louis, Minn., 15...D6 99
Gowan, riv., Man., Can...B4 71
Gowanda, Cattaraugus and Erie, N.Y., 3,352...C2 108
Gowen, Montcalm, Mich., 200...E5 98
Gowen, Latimer, Okla., 350...C6 112
Gower, Clinton, Mo., 406...B3 101
Gowk, Iran, 6,285...G8 41
Gowna, lake, Ire...D4 11
Gowrie, Webster, Iowa, 1,127...B3 92
Goya, Arg., 20,804...E4 55
Goz Béïda, Chad, 1,250...C4 46
Gōz Regeb, Sud...B4 47
Graaff-Reinet, S. Afr., 16,703...D3 49
Graal-Müritz, Ger., 3,875...D6 24
Graasten, Den., 2,308...D3 24
Grabill, Allen, Ind., 495...B8 91
Grabow, Ger., 8,708...E5 24
Grabow, bay, Ger...D6 24
Gračac, Yugo., 2,831...C2 22
Gračanica, Yugo., 7,668...C4 22
Grace, Caribou, Idaho, 725...G7 89
Grace, Issaquena, Miss., 300...C3 100
Grace, mtn., Mass...A3 97
Grace City, Foster, N. Dak., 100...B7 110
Graceham, Frederick, Md., 165...A3 85
Gracemont, Caddo, Okla., 306...B3 112
Grace Park, Delaware, Pa., 2,000...*B10 114
Graceton, Lake of the Woods, Minn., 45...B4 99
Graceville, Jackson, Fla., 2,307...G3 86
Graceville, Big Stone, Minn., 823...E2 99
Gracewood, Richmond, Ga., 500...C4 87
Gracey, Christian, Ky., 234...D2 94
Gracias, Hond., 1,521...C3 62
Gracias a Dios, prov., Hond...*C5 62
Graciosa, isl., Port. (Azores)...g8 44
Gradačac, Yugo., 5,897...C4 22
Gradaús, mts., Braz...D4 59
Gradefes, Sp., 4,597...A3 20
Gradizhsk, Sov. Un., 10,000...G9 27
Grado, It., 9,666...D9 18
Grado, Sp., 3,671...A2 20
Grady, Lincoln, Ark., 622...C4 81
Grady, Curry, N. Mex., 100...C6 107
Grady, Jefferson, Okla., 25...C4 112
Grady, co., Ga., 18,015...F2 87
Grady, co., Okla., 29,590...C4 112
Gradyville, Adair, Ky., 150...C4 94
Gradyville, Delaware, Pa., 80...B10 114
Graehl, Alsk., 1,200...*C10 79
Graettinger, Palo Alto, Iowa, 879...A3 92
Grafenau, Ger., 2,460...E8 17
Graford, Palo Pinto, Tex., 448...C3 118
Grafton, Austl., 15,526...D9 51
Grafton, Ont., Can., 348...D6 72
Grafton, Jersey, Ill., 1,084...E3 90
Grafton, Worth, Iowa, 273...A4 92
Grafton, Worcester, Mass., 2,000 (10,627▲)...B4 97
Grafton, Fillmore, Nebr., 171...D8 103
Grafton, Grafton, N.H., 75 (348▲)...C3 105
Grafton, Rensselaer, N.Y., 300...C7 108
Grafton, Walsh, N. Dak., 5,885...A8 110
Grafton, Lorain, Ohio, 1,683...A5 111
Grafton, Windham, Vt., 250 (426▲)...E3 120
Grafton, York, Va., 200...B6 121
Grafton, Taylor, W. Va., 5,791...B4, B7 123
Grafton, Ozaukee, Wis., 3,748...E2, E6 124
Grafton, co., N.H., 48,857...C3 105
Grafton Center, Grafton, N.H., 40...C3 105
Graham, Randolph, Ala., 50...B4 78
Graham, Bradford, Fla., 120...C4 86
Graham, Appling, Ga., 130...E4 87
Graham, Muhlenberg, Ky., 550...C2 94
Graham, Nodaway, Mo., 215...A2 101
Graham, Alamance, N.C., 7,723...A4 109
Graham, Carter, Okla., 350...C4 112
Graham, Hickman, Tenn., 35...B4 117
Graham, Young, Tex., 8,505...C3 118
Graham, Pierce, Wash., 75...B3 122
Graham, co., Ariz., 14,045...E5 80
Graham, co., Kans., 5,586...C4 93
Graham, co., N.C., 6,432...D2 109
Graham, creek, Ind...G6 91
Graham, isl., B.C., Can...C1 68
Graham, isl., N.W., Ter., Can...m33 67
Graham, lake, Alta., Can...A3 69
Graham, lake, Maine...D4 96
Graham, mtn., Ariz...E6 80
Graham, riv., B.C., Can...A6 68
Graham Bell, isl., Sov. Un...A8 4
Graham Land, reg., Ant...C6 5
Graham Reach, chan., B.C., Can...C3 68
Grahamstown, S. Afr., 32,611...D4 49
Grahamsville, Sullivan, N.Y., 300...D6 108
Grahamville, Jasper, S.C., 200...G6 115
Grahn, Carter, Ky., 400...B6 94
Graian Alps, mts., Fr., It...D3 18
Graiba, Tun...G12 26
Grainfield, Gove, Kans., 389...C3 93
Grainger, Alta., Can...D4 69
Grainger, co., Tenn., 12,506...C10 117
Grainland, Sask., Can...F2 70
Grainola, Osage, Okla., 67...A5 112
Grainton, Perkins, Nebr., 35...D4 103
Grain Valley, Jackson, Mo., 552...B3 101
Grajaú, Braz., 2,539...C1 57
Grajaú, riv., Braz...B1 57
Grajewo, Pol., 6,171...B7 26
Gram, Den., 1,801...C3 24
Gram, isl., Thai...F4 38
Gramada, Bul., 4,662...D6 22
Gramalote, Col., 2,776...B3 60
Gramastetten, Aus., 2,443...E9 17
Grambling, Lincoln, La., 3,144...B3 95
Gramercy, St. James, La., 2,094...B6 95
Gramling, Spartanburg, S.C., 200...A3 115
Grammer, Bartholomew, Ind., 200...F6 91
Grammichele, It., 14,486...F5 21
Grampian, Clearfield, Pa., 529...E4 114
Grampian, mts., Scot...D4 13
Gramsdale, Scot...C1 13
Gramsh, Alb., 650...B3 23
Gramzow, Ger., 2,152...E8 24
Gran, mtn., Ant...B28 5
Granada, Prowers, Colo., 593...C8 83
Granada, Martin, Minn., 418...G4 99
Granada, Nic., 28,500...E5 62
Granada, Sp., 157,178...D4 20
Granada, prov., Sp., 769,408...*D4 20
Granard, Ire., 1,044...D4 11
Granbury, Hood, Tex., 2,227...C4 118
Granby, Que., Can., 31,463...D5 73
Granby, Grand, Colo., 503...A5 83
Granby, Hartford, Conn., 700 (4,968▲)...B5 84
Granby, Hampshire, Mass., 250 (4,221▲)...B2 97
Granby, Newton, Mo., 1,808...E3 101
Granby, Essex, Vt., 20 (56▲)...B5 120
Gran Canaria, isl., Sp. (Can. Is.)...D1 44
Gran Chaco, plain, Arg., Par...F4 55
Grand, co., Colo., 3,537...A4 83
Grand, co., Utah, 6,345...E6 119
Grand, bayou, La...B5 95
Grand, bayou, La...C6 95
Grand, canal, China...G7 36
Grand, canal, Ire...D4 11
Grand, canyon, Ariz...A3 80
Grand, caverns, Tenn...D9 117
Grand, falls, Newf., Can...h8 75
Grand, falls, Maine...C5 96
Grand, isl., La...D6 95
Grand, isl., La...E6 95
Grand, isl., Mich...B4 98
Grand, lake, N.B., Can...D2 74
Grand, lake, N.B., Can...D3 74
Grand, lake, Newf., Can...B1 75
Grand, lake, Newf., Can...D3 75
Grand, lake, La...E3 95
Grand, lake, La...E4 95
Grand, lake, La...E6 95
Grand, lake, Maine...C5 96
Grand, lake, Mich...C7 98
Grand, lake, Ohio...B3 111
Grand, mesa, Colo...C2 83
Grand, riv., Newf., Can...E2 75
Grand, riv., Ont., Can...D4 72
Grand, riv., La...D4 95
Grand, riv., Mich...E4 98
Grand, riv., Mo...B4 101
Grand, riv., Ohio...A7 111
Grand, riv., S. Dak...B4 116
Grand Atlas, mts., Mor...C3 44
Grand Bahama, isl., Ba. Is...B4 64
Grand Bank, Newf., Can., 2,703...E4 75
Grand Banks, shoals, Newf., Can...C17 3
Grand-Bassam, I.C., 13,000...E4 45
Grand Bay, Mobile, Ala., 600...E1 78
Grand Bay, N.B., Can., 725...D3 74
Grand Bayou, Red River, La...B2 95
Grand Beach, Man., Can., 74...D3 71
Grand Bend, Ont., Can., 928...D3 72
Grand Blanc, Genesee, Mich., 1,565...F7 98
Grand Bostonnais, lake, Que., Can...B5 73
Grand-Bourg, Guad., 13,833...o16 64
Grand Bruit, Newf., Can., 132...E2 75
Grand Cane, De Soto, La., 322...B2 95
Grand Canyon, Coconino, Ariz., 900...A3 80
Grand Canyon, nat. mon. and park, Ariz...A3 80
Grand Cayman, isl., Cayman Is...F3 64
Grand Centre, Alta., Can., 1,493...B5 69
Grand Cess, Lib...F3 45
Grand Chenier, Cameron, La., 200...E3 95
Grand Combin, mtn., Switz...E3 19
Grand Coteau, St. Landry, La., 1,165...D3 95
Grand Coulee, Grant, Wash., 1,058...B6 122
Grand Coulee, canyon, Wash...B6 122
Grand Coulee, dam, Wash...B6 122
Grande, bay, Arg...E3 54
Grande, hills, Ur...f8 54
Grande, isl., Braz...h5 56
Grande, mts., Mex...G2 118
Grande, riv., Arg...B3 54
Grande, riv., Bol...C3 55
Grande, riv., Braz...B2 56

Greenock, Allegheny, Pa., 1,500 ... F2 114
Greenock, Scot., 74,700 (*108,000) ... E4 13
Greenough, Missoula, Mont., 15 ... D3 102
Greenough, pt., Ont., Can ... C3 72
Green Pond, Bibb, Ala., 500 . B2 78
Green Pond, Colleton, S.C., 285 ... F6 115
Green Pond, mtn., N.J. ... B3 106
Greenport, Suffolk, N.Y., 2,608 ... m16 108
Green Ridge, Pettis, Mo., 375 ... C4 101
Green Ridge, Delaware, Pa., 3,500 ... *G11 114
Green River, Emery and Grand, Utah, 1,075 ... D5 119
Green River, Windham, Vt., 30 ... F3 120
Green River, Sweetwater, Wyo., 3,497 ... D3 125
Green River, res., Vt ... B3 120
Green Rock, Henry, Ill., 2,677 ... *B3 90
Greens, peak, Ariz ... C6 80
Greensboro, Hale, Ala., 3,081 ... C2 78
Greensboro, Gadsden, Fla., 709 ... B2 86
Greensboro, Greene, Ga., 2,773 ... C3 87
Greensboro, Henry, Ind., 232 ... E7 91
Greensboro, Caroline, Md., 1,160 ... C6 85
Greensboro, Guilford, N.C., 119,574 (*156,800) ... A4 109
Greensboro, Greene, Pa., 505 . F2 114
Greensboro, Orleans, Vt., 200 (600▲) ... B4 120
Greensboro Bend, Orleans, Vt., 130 ... B4 120
Greensburg, Decatur, Ind., 7,492 ... F7 91
Greensburg, Kiowa, Kans., 1,988 ... E4 93
Greensburg, Green, Ky., 2,334 ... C4 94
Greensburg, St. Helena, La., 512 ... D5 95
Greensburg, Westmoreland, Pa., 17,383 ... F2 114
Greens Creek, Jackson, N.C. . D3 109
Green Sea, Horry, S.C., 100 ... C10 115
Greens Farms, Fairfield, Conn., 335 (part of Westport) ... E3 84
Greens Fork, Wayne, Ind., 474 ... E7 91
Green's Harbour, Newf., Can., 713 ... *E5 75
Greenspond, Newf., Can., 728 ... D5 75
Green Spring, Hampshire, W. Va., 120 ... B6 123
Green Springs, Sandusky and Seneca, Ohio, 1,262 ... A4 111
Green Sulphur Springs, Summers, W. Va., 350 ... D4 123
Greensville, co., Va., 16,155 . E5 121
Greentop, Schuyler, Mo., 311 ... A5 101
Greentown, Howard, Ind., 1,266 ... D6 91
Greentree, Allegheny, Pa., 5,226 ... *F1 114
Greenup, Cumberland, Ill., 1,477 ... D5 90
Greenup, Greenup, Ky., 1,240 ... B7 94
Greenup, co., Ky., 29,238 ... B7 94
Greenvale, Nassau, N.Y., 1,220 ... *F2 84
Green Valley, Tazewell, Ill., 552 ... C4 90
Green Valley, Lyon, Minn., 130 ... F3 99
Greenvalley, Shawano, Wis., 100 ... D5 124
Greenview, Menard, Ill., 796 ... C4 90
Greenview, Boone, W. Va., 250 ... D5 123
Greenville, Butler, Ala., 6,894 ... D3 78
Greenville, Plumas, Calif., 1,140 ... B3 82
Greenville, Madison, Fla., 1,318 ... B3 86
Greenville, Meriwether, Ga., 726 ... C2 87
Greenville, Bond, Ill., 4,569 .. E4 90
Greenville, Floyd, Ind., 453 .. H6 91
Greenville, Clay, Iowa, 173 .. A2 92
Greenville, Muhlenberg, Ky., 3,198 ... C2 94
Greenville, Lib ... F3 45
Greenville, Piscataquis, Maine, 1,400 (2,025▲) ... C3 96
Greenville, Worcester, Mass., 325 ... *B4 97
Greenville, Montcalm, Mich., 7,440 ... E5 98
Greenville, Washington, Miss., 41,502 ... B2 100
Greenville, Wayne, Mo., 282 ... D7 101
Greenville, Hillsboro, N.H., 1,251 (1,385▲) ... E3 105
Greenville, Greene, N.Y., 300 ... C6 108
Greenville, Westchester, N.Y., 2,800 ... *h13 108
Greenville, Pitt, N.C., 22,860 . B6 109
Greenville, Darke, Ohio, 10,585 ... B3 111
Greenville, Mercer, Pa., 8,765 ... D1 114
Greenville, Providence, R.I., 3,000 ... B10 84
Greenville, Greenville, S.C., 66,188 (*164,500) ... B3 115
Greenville, Hunt, Tex., 19,087 ... C4 118
Greenville, Beaver, Utah, 125 ... E3 119
Greenville, Monroe, W. Va., 200 ... D4 123
Greenville, Outagamie, Wis., 200 ... A5 124
Greenville, co., S.C., 209,776 . B3 115
Greenville, creek, Ohio ... B3 111
Greenville Junction, Piscataquis, Maine, 500 ... C3 96
Greenwald, Stearns, Minn., 266 ... E4 99
Greenwater Lake, prov. park, Sask., Can ... E4 70
Greenway, Clay, Ark., 179 ... A5 81
Greenway, Man., Can ... E2 71
Greenway, McPherson, S. Dak., 101 ... B6 116
Greenwich, Fairfield, Conn., 53,793 ... E2 84
Greenwich, Eng., 85,585 (part of London) ... C7 12, m12 10
Greenwich, Sedgwick, Kans., 55 ... B5 93
Greenwich, Cumberland, N.J., 500 ... E2 106
Greenwich, Washington, N.Y., 2,263 ... B7 108
Greenwich, Huron, Ohio, 1,371 ... A5 111
Greenwich, Piute, Utah, 30 ... E4 119
Greenwich, Prince William, Va., 100 ... B4 121
Greenwich, pt., Conn ... E2 84
Greenwich Hill, N.B., Can., 73 ... D3 74
Greenwood, Jefferson, Ala., 400 ... B3 78
Greenwood, Sebastian, Ark., 1,558 ... B1 81
Greenwood, B.C., Can., 932 . E8 68
Greenwood, Sussex, Del., 768 . C6 85
Greenwood, Jackson, Fla., 427 ... B1 86
Greenwood, Johnson, Ind., 7,169 ... E5, I8 91
Greenwood, McCreary, Ky., 200 ... D5 94
Greenwood, Caddo, La., 500 ... B2 95
Greenwood, Leflore, Miss., 20,436 ... B3 100
Greenwood, Jackson, Mo., 488 ... E2 101
Greenwood, Cass, Nebr., 403 ... D9, E2 103
Greenwood, Steuben, N.Y., 450 ... C3 108
Greenwood, Blair, Pa., 1,500 . F5 114
Greenwood, Greenwood, S.C., 16,644 ... C3 115
Greenwood, Charles Mix, S. Dak., 120 ... E7 116
Greenwood, Wilson, Tenn ... A5 117
Greenwood, Clark, Wis., 1,041 ... D3 124
Greenwood, co., Kans., 11,253 ... E7 93
Greenwood, co., S.C., 44,346 . C3 115
Greenwood, lake, Minn ... C7 99
Greenwood, lake, N.J., N.Y ... A4 106
Greenwood, lake, S.C ... C4 115
Greenwood Lake, Orange, N.Y., 1,236 ... *D6 108
Greenwood Mountain, Oxford, Maine, 200 ... D2 96
Greer, Clearwater, Idaho, 70 . C2 89
Greer, Oregon, Mo., 40 ... E6 101
Greer, Greenville and Spartanburg, S.C., 8,967 ... B3 115
Greer, co., Okla., 8,877 ... C2 112
Greetsiel, Ger., 1,400 ... A7 15
Gregg, co., Tex., 69,436 ... C5 118
Gregoire, lake, Alta., Can ... A5 69
Gregory, Livingston, Mich., 300 ... F6 98
Gregory, Currituck, N.C., 50 . A7 109
Gregory, Gregory, S. Dak., 1,478 ... D6 116
Gregory, San Patricio, Tex., 1,970 ... *F4 118
Gregory, co., S. Dak., 7,399 . D6 116
Gregory, lake, Austl ... E6 50
Gregory, range, Austl ... C7 50
Gregory, riv., Austl ... C6 50
Greifenhagen, see Gryfino, Pol.
Greifswald, Ger., 47,200 ... A6 16
Greifswalder, bay, Ger ... D7 24
Greig, Lewis, N.Y., 150 ... B5 108
Grein, Aus., 2,518 ... D7 16
Greinwich Terrace, Calcasieu, La., 2,000 ... *D2 95
Greiz, Ger., 39,100 ... C7 17
Grelton, Henry, Ohio, 150 .. A4 111
Gremyachinsk, Sov. Un., 30,000 ... D20 9
Grenaa, Den., 9,088 ... B4 24
Grenada, Siskiyou, Calif., 300 ... B2 82
Grenada, Grenada, Miss., 7,914 ... B4 100
Grenada, co., Miss., 18,409 .. B4 100
Grenada, Br. dep., N.A., 93,000 ... p16 64
Grenada, res., Miss ... B4 100
Grenade [-sur-Garonne], Fr., 2,112 ... F4 14
Grenadines, The, is., N.A ... p16 64
Grenagh, Ire ... E3 11
Grenay, Fr., 8,730 ... D2 15
Grenchen, Switz., 18,000 ... B3 19
Grene, Renville, N. Dak., 15 .. A4 110
Grenfell, Sask., Can., 1,256 . G4 70
Grenloch, Camden and Gloucester, N.J., 550 ... D2 106
Grenoble, Fr., 156,707 (*235,000) ... E6 14
Grenola, Elk, Kans., 349 ... E7 93
Grenora, Williams, N. Dak., 448 ... A2 110
Grenville, Que., Can., 1,330 . D3 73
Grenville, Union, N. Mex., 55 ... A6 107
Grenville, Day, S. Dak., 151 . B8 116
Grenville, co., Ont., Can., 22,864 ... C9 72
Grenville, cape, Austl ... B7 50
Grenville, chan., B.C., Can ... C3 68
Grenville, pt., Wash ... B1 122
Gresham, Marion, S.C., 150 . D9 115
Gresham, York, Nebr., 239 ... C8 103
Gresham, Multnomah, Oreg., 3,944 ... B4 113
Gresham, Shawano, Wis., 458 ... D5 124
Gressitt, King and Queen, Va., 300 ... D6 121
Gretna, Man., Can., 575 ... E3 71
Gretna, Gadsden, Fla., 647 . B2 86
Gretna, Jefferson, La., 21,967 ... C7, E5 95
Gretna, Sarpy, Nebr., 745 ... C9, E2 103
Gretna, Scot., 3,037 ... F5 13
Gretna, Pittsylvania, Va., 900 ... E3 121
Greven, Ger., 23,000 ... A2 17
Grevena, Grc., 4,779 ... B3 23
Grevenbroich, Ger., 22,000 ... B1 17
Grevesmühlen, Ger., 11,100 .. E5 24
Grey, co., Ont., Can., 62,005 . C4 72
Grey, is., Newf., Can ... C4 75
Grey, riv., Newf., Can ... D3 75
Grey, riv., N.Z ... O13 51
Greybull, Big Horn, Wyo., 2,286 ... A4 125
Greybull, riv., Wyo ... A4 125
Greycliff, Sweet Grass, Mont., 75 ... E7 102
Grey Eagle, Todd, Minn., 372 . E4 99
Greylock, mtn., Mass ... A1 97
Greymouth, N.Z., 8,881 ... O13 51
Greys, riv., Wyo ... B2 125
Greystone, Moffat, Colo., 2 .. A2 83
Greystone, Litchfield, Conn., 250 ... C4 84
Greystone, Vance, N.C., 60 .. A5 109
Greytown, N.Z., 1,580 ... N15 51
Greytown, S. Afr., 7,737 ... C5 49
Gribbell, isl., B.C., Can ... C3 68
Gridley, Butte, Calif., 3,343 .. C3 82
Gridley, McLean, Ill., 889 ... C5 90
Gridley, Coffey, Kans., 321 . D8 93
Griesheim, Ger., 13,700 ... D3 17
Grieskirchen, Aus., 4,137 ... D6 16
Griffin, Union, Ark., 20 ... D3 81
Griffin, Sask., Can., 140 ... H4 70
Griffin, Spalding, Ga., 21,735 ... C2 87
Griffin, Posey, Ind., 212 ... H2 91
Griffing Park, Jefferson, Tex., 2,267 ... *E5 118
Griffins, Hartford, Conn ... B6 84
Griffith, Austl., 7,700 ... G6 51
Griffith, Lake, Ind., 9,483 ... A3 91
Griffith, isl., Ont., Can ... C4 72
Griffithsville, Lincoln, W. Va., 500 ... C3 123
Griffithville, White, Ark., 172 ... B4 81
Grifton, Pitt, N.C., 1,816 ... B6 109
Griggs, Cimarron, Okla., 15 .. D2 112
Griggs, co., N. Dak., 5,023 ... B7 110
Griggstown, Somerset, N.J., 300 ... C3 106
Griggsville, Pike, Ill., 1,240 .. D3 90
Grigoriopol, Sov. Un ... B9 22
Grim, cape, Austl ... o14 50
Grimari, Cen. Afr. Rep ... D4 46
Grimes, Dale, Ala., 50 ... D4 78
Grimes, Polk, Iowa, 697 . A7, C4 92
Grimes, Roger Mills, Okla., 15 ... B2 112
Grimes, co., Tex., 12,709 ... D5 118
Grimesland, Pitt, N.C., 362 . B6 109
Grimma, Ger., 16,100 ... B7 17
Grimmen, Ger., 11,000 ... D7 24
Grimmialp, Switz ... C4 19
Grimms Landing, Mason, W. Va., 300 ... C3 123
Grimsby, Ont., Can., 5,148 .. D5 72
Grimsby, Eng., 96,700 (*138,000) ... A7 12
Grimsey, isl., Ice ... m23 25
Grimshaw, Alta., Can., 1,095 . A2 69
Grimstad, Nor., 2,600 ... H3 25
Grimsthorpe, Ont., Can ... B2 72
Grindelwald, Switz., 3,244 ... C5 19
Grindsted, Den., 5,289 ... C2 24
Grindstone, Penobscot, Maine, 60 ... C4 96
Grindstone, isl., Que., Can ... B8 74
Grind Stone City, Huron, Mich ... D8 98
Grindstone Island, Que., Can., 761 ... B8 74
Grinem, isl., Eniwetok ... 52
Grinnell, Poweshiek, Iowa, 7,367 ... C5 92
Grinnell, Gove, Kans., 396 .. C3 93
Grinnell, pen., N.W. Ter., Can ... m32 67
Griquatown, S. Afr., 2,524 .. C3 49
Grise Fiord, N.W. Ter., Can., 70 ... m35 67
Gris Nez, cape, Fr ... D9 12
Griswold, Man., Can., 137 ... E1 71
Griswold (Town of), New London, Conn. (6,472▲) . *C9 84
Griswold, Cass, Iowa, 1,207 .. C2 92
Griswold, Aroostook, Maine .. B4 96
Griswoldville, Franklin, Mass., 300 ... A2 97
Grizzly, Jefferson, Oreg ... C6 113
Grizzly, creek, Colo ... A4 83
Grizzly, mtn., Oreg ... C6 113
Grizzly, mtn., Oreg ... E4 113
Grizzly Bear, mts., N.W. Ter., Can ... C8 66
Groais, isl., Newf., Can ... C4 75
Grodekovo, Sov. Un., 5,000 .. D5 37
Grodkow, Pol., 2,953 ... C4 26
Grodno, Sov. Un., 88,000 ... E4 27
Grodzisk, Pol., 6,015 ... B4 26
Grodzisk Mazowiecki, Pol., 17,800 ... m13 26
Groenlo, Neth., 6,600 ... B6 15
Groesbeck, Hamilton, Ohio, 9,000 ... *C3 111
Groesbeck, Limestone, Tex., 2,498 ... D4 118
Groix, isl., Fr ... D2 14
Grojec, Pol., 6,841 ... C6 26
Grombalia, Tun., 5,043 ... F12 30
Gronau, Ger., 25,600 ... A2 17
Gronau, Ger., 5,300 ... A4 17
Groningen, Neth., 151,100 (*175,000) ... A6 15
Groningen, prov., Neth., 477,700 ... A6 15
Gronlid, Sask., Can., 152 ... D3 70
Groom, Carson, Tex., 679 ... B2 118
Groom Creek, Yavapai, Ariz., 150 ... C3 80
Groos, Delta, Mich ... C3 98
Groote Eylandt, isl., Austl ... B6 50
Grootfontein, S.W. Afr., 1,525 ... A2 49
Groot Vloer, lake, S. Afr ... C3 49
Groscap, Mackinac, Mich .. C6 98
Groslay, Fr., 4,744 ... g10 14
Gros-Morne, Que., Can., 577 ... *k13 73
Gros Morne, mtn., Newf., Can . D3 75
Gross, Boyd, Nebr., 17 ... B7 103
Grossbreitenbach, Ger., 4,361 ... C6 17
Grosse, isl., Que., Can ... B8 74
Grosse Ile, Wayne, Mich., 6,318 ... *B7 98
Grossenhain, Ger., 19,500 ... B8 17
Grosse Pointe, Wayne, Mich., 6,631 ... A8 98
Grosse Pointe Farms, Wayne, Mich., 12,172 ... A8 98
Grosse Pointe Park, Wayne, Mich., 15,457 ... A8 98
Grosse Pointe Shores, Macomb and Wayne, Mich., 2,301 . *F8 98
Grosse Pointe Woods, Macomb and Wayne, Mich., 18,580 . F8 98
Grosser Plön, lake, Ger ... D4 24
Grosser Priel, peak, Aus ... E7 16
Grosse Tete, Iberville, La., 768 ... D4 95
Grosseto, It., 38,200 (54,300▲) ... C3 21
Grossevichi, Sov. Un ... C9 37
Grossgerau, Ger., 12,200 ... D3 17
Grossglockner, mtn., Aus ... B8 18
Grossmont, San Diego, Calif., 1,000 ... *F5 82
Grossotheim, Ger., 6,900 ... D4 17
Grössraschen, Ger., 12,100 .. B9 17
Grossrörsdorf, Ger., 8,285 ... B9 17
Grosvenor Dale, Windham, Conn., 600 ... B9 84
Gros Ventre, range, Wyo ... B2 125
Gros Ventre, riv., Wyo ... B2 125
Groswater, bay, Newf., Can ... A3 75
Groton, New London, Conn., 10,111 (29,937▲) ... D8 84
Groton, Middlesex, Mass., 1,250 (3,904▲) ... A4, f9 97
Groton, Grafton, N.H., 80 (99▲) ... C3 105
Groton, Tompkins, N.Y., 2,123 ... C4 108
Groton, Brown, S. Dak., 1,063 ... B7 116
Groton, Caledonia, Vt., 387 (631▲) ... C4 120
Groton Long Point, New London, Conn., 400 ... *D8 84
Grottaferrata, It., 5,377 ... h9 21
Grottaglie, It., 23,223 ... D6 21
Grottoes, Rockingham, Va., 969 ... C4 121
Grouard, Alta., Can., 303 ... B2 69
Grouse (Lost River), Custer, Idaho, 58 ... F5 89
Grouse, creek, Kans ... E7 93
Grouse, creek, Utah ... B2 119
Grouse Creek, Box Elder, Utah, 60 ... B2 119
Grouse Creek, mts., Utah ... B2 119
Grovania, Houston, Ga., 186 ... D3 88
Grove, Washington, Maine, 35 ... C5 96
Grove, Delaware, Okla., 975 . A7 112
Grove, York, Va ... A6 121
Grove, pt., Md ... B5 85
Grove City, Meeker, Minn., 466 ... E4 99
Grove City, Franklin, Ohio, 8,107 ... C2, C3 111
Grove City, Mercer, Pa., 8,368 ... D1 114
Grove Hill, Clarke, Ala., 1,834 ... D2 78
Groveland, Tuolumne, Calif., 350 ... D3 82
Groveland, Lake, Fla., 1,747 . D5 86
Groveland, Bryan, Ga., 100 . D5 87
Groveland, Essex, Mass., 1,800 (3,297▲) ... A5 97
Groveland, Livingston, N.Y., 350 ... C3 108
Grove Nunataks, peaks, Ant ... B20 5
Groveport, Franklin, Ohio, 2,043 ... C2, C5 111
Grover, Weld, Colo., 133 ... A6 83
Grover, Cleveland, N.C., 538 ... B2 109
Grover, Bradford, Pa., 160 ... C8 114
Grover, Dorchester, S.C., 300 ... E6 115
Grover, Codington, S. Dak., 35 ... C8 116
Grover, Lincoln, Wyo., 120 .. C2 125
Grover City, San Luis Obispo, Calif., 5,210 ... *E3 82
Grover Hill, Paulding, Ohio, 547 ... A3 111
Grovertown, Starke, Ind., 175 ... B4 91
Groves, Jefferson, Tex., 17,304 ... E6 118
Grovespring, Wright, Mo., 92 ... D5 101
Groveton, Coos, N.H., 2,004 . A3 105
Groveton, Allegheny, Pa., 1,300 ... *B5 114
Groveton, Trinity, Tex., 1,148 ... D5 118
Groveton, Fairfax, Va., 900 .. B5 121
Grovetown, Columbia, Ga., 1,396 ... C4 87
Groveville, Mercer, N.J., 2,500 ... C3 106
Grow, King, Tex ... C2 118
Groznyy, Sov. Un., 300,000 . E3 29
Grubbs, Jackson, Ark., 360 .. B4 81
Gruber, lake, Ger ... D4 24
Grudovo, Bul., 3,928 ... D8 22
Grudziadz, Pol., 68,000 ... B5 26
Gruetli, Grundy, Tenn., 400 . D8 117
Gruinard, bay, Scot ... C3 13
Grulla, Starr, Tex., 1,436 ... F3 118
Grünberg, Ger., 3,900 ... C3 17
Grundy, Buchanan, Va., 2,287 ... B3 121
Grundy, co., Ill., 22,350 ... B5 90
Grundy, co., Iowa, 14,132 ... B5 92
Grundy, co., Mo., 12,220 ... A4 101
Grundy, co., Tenn., 11,512 .. D8 117
Grundy Center, Grundy, Iowa, 2,403 ... B5 92
Grünstadt, Ger., 7,800 ... D3 17
Grunthal, Man., Can., 287 .. E3 71
Grüsch, Switz., 729 ... E8 19
Gruver, Hansford, Tex., 1030 . A2 118
Gruyères, Switz., 1,349 ... C3 19
Gruz, Yugo., 10,000 ... D4 22
Gryazi, Sov. Un., 10,000 ... E12 27
Gryazovets, Sov. Un., 12,500 . B13 27
Gryfice, Pol., 10,100 ... B3 26
Gryfino, Pol., 1,347 ... B3 26
Grygla, Marshall, Minn., 192 . B3 99
Gstaad, Switz ... D3 19
Guacanayabo, gulf, Cuba ... E5 64
Gu Achi, Pima, Ariz., 250 ... E3 80
Guachupangue, Rio Arriba, N. Mex., 150 ... *B3 107
Guadalajara, Mexico, 736,800 (*830,000) ... C4, m12 63
Guadalajara, Sp., 21,230 ... B4 20
Guadalajara, prov., Sp., 183,545 ... *B4 20
Guadalcanal, Sp., 6,931 ... C3 20
Guadalcanal, isl., Sol. Is ... G9 7
Guadalhorce, riv., Sp ... D3 20
Guadalimar, riv., Sp ... C4 20
Guadalope, riv., Sp ... B5 20
Guadalquivir, riv., Sp ... D2 20
Guadalupe, Maricopa, Ariz., 1,200 ... G2 80
Guadalupe, Santa Barbara, Calif., 2,614 ... E3 82
Guadalupe, Conejos, Colo., 150 ... D4 83
Guadalupe, co., N. Mex., 5,610 ... C5 107
Guadalupe, co., Tex., 29,017 . E4 118
Guadalupe, isl., Pac. O ... E14 7
Guadalupe, mts., N. Mex ... E5 107
Guadalupe, mts., Sp ... C3 20
Guadalupe, peak, Tex ... E2 118
Guadalupe, riv., Tex ... B4 118
Guadalupe [Bravos], Mex., 1,214 ... A3 63
Guadalupita, Mora, N. Mex., 290 ... A4 107
Guadarrama, mts., Sp ... B4 20
Guadarrama, riv., Sp ... p17 20
Guadeloupe, Fr. dep., N.A., 308,000 ... n16 64
Guadeloupe, passage, N.A ... n16 64
Guadiana, riv., Port ... D2 20
Guadiana Alto, riv., Sp ... C4 20
Guadiana Menor, riv., Sp ... D4 20
Guadiela, riv., Sp ... B4 20
Guadix, Sp., 18,500 ... D4 20
Guafo, isl., Chile ... C2 54
Guagua, Phil., 5,914 ... o13 35
Guainia, riv., Col ... C4 60
Guairá, dept., Par., 100,446 .. E4 55
Guajará Mirim, Braz., 7,115 . B2 55
Guajataca, lake, P.R ... B3 69
Guajataca, riv., P.R ... B3 65
Gualaceo, Ec., 2,735 ... B2 58
Gualala, Mendocino, Calif., 400 ... C2 82
Gualán, Guat., 2,898 ... C3 62
Gualaquiza, Ec., 259 ... B2 58
Gualeguay, Arg., 23,517 ... A5 54
Gualeguaychú, Arg., 37,109 .. A5 54
Guam, U.S. dep., Oceania, 70,000 ... 52
Guamá, riv., Braz ... B1 57
Guamaní Central, P.R ... D6 65
Guaminí, Arg., 2,273 ... B4 54
Guamúchil, Mex., 5,865 ... B3 63
Guanabacoa, Cuba, 55,000 .. D2 64
Guanabana, P.R ... C2 65
Guanabara, state, Brazil, 3,307,163 ... h6 56
Guanacaste, prov., C.R., 146,600 ... *E5 62
Guanacaste, mts., C.R ... E5 62
Guanahacabibes, gulf, Cuba .. D1 64
Guanajay, Cuba, 12,908 ... D2 64
Guanajibo, pt., P.R ... C2 65
Guanajibo, riv., P.R ... C2 65
Guanajuato, Mex., 28,212 ... C4, m13 63
Guanajuato, state, Mex., 1,728,358 ... C4 63
Guanambi, Braz., 5,268 ... D2 57
Guanare, Ven., 16,935 ... B4 60
Guanche, Pan., 30 ... h11 62
Guandacol, Arg ... E2 55
Guane, Cuba, 2,248 ... D1 64
Guánica, P.R., 4,100 ... D3 65
Guánica, mun., P.R., 13,767 . D3 65
Guánica, lake, P.R ... C3 65
Guanillos del Norte, Chile ... D1 55
Guaniquilla, pt., P.R ... C2 65
Guano, isl., Vir. Is ... f16 65
Guano, lake, Oreg ... E7 113
Guanoco, Ven ... A5 60
Guantánamo, Cuba, 82,000 .. E6 64
Guapí, Col., 1,882 ... C2 60
Guaporé, riv., Bol ... B3 55
Guaporé, riv., Braz ... E2 59
Guaqui, Bol., 2,266 ... C2 55
Guará, Braz., 5,652 ... F1 57
Guara, mts., Sp ... A5 20
Guarabira, Braz., 15,848 . C3, h6 57
Guaraguao, P.R ... C4 65
Guaranda, Ec., 7,287 ... B2 58
Guarapuava, Braz., 13,546 ... D2 56
Guaraqueçaba, Braz., 741 ... D3 56
Guaratinguetá, Braz., 38,293 . C3 56
Guarda, Port., 7,704 ... B2 20
Guardafui, cape, Som ... C7 47
Guardian, Webster, W. Va., 200 ... C4 123
Guareña, Sp., 9,742 ... C2 20
Guárico, riv., Ven ... B4 60
Guárico, state, Ven., 244,966 . B4 60
Guarujá, Braz., 8,506 ... n8 56
Guasave, Mex., 8,505 ... B3 63
Guasdualito, Ven., 4,549 ... B3 60
Guasipati, Ven., 3,382 ... B5 60
Guastalla, It., 6,416 ... E6 18
Guata, Hond., 497 ... C4 62
Guatemala, Guat., 417,200 ... C2 62
Guatemala, country, N.A., 4,375,000 ... H11 61, C2 62
Guateque, Col., 2,408 ... C3 60
Guatimozín, Arg ... A4 54
Guaviare, riv., Col ... C3 60
Guaxupé, Braz., 14,168 ... C3, k8 56
Guayabal, Cuba, 569 ... E5 64
Guayabal, lake, P.R ... C4 65
Guayabero, riv., Col ... C3 57
Guayama, P.R., 19,183 ... D6 65
Guayama, mun., P.R., 33,678 ... D6 65
Guayanés, riv., P.R ... C7 65
Guayanilla, P.R., 3,067 ... C3 65
Guayanilla, mun., P.R., 17,396 ... C3 65
Guayaquil, gulf, Ec ... B1 58
Guayaquil, Ec., 510,800 ... B2 58
Guayas, prov., Ec., 663,516 . B1 58
Guaymas, Mex., 34,865 ... B2 63
Guaynabo, P.R., 3,343 ... B6 65
Guaynabo, mun., P.R., 39,718 ... B6 65
Guazacapán, Guat., 3,383 ... C2 62
Gubakha, Sov. Un., 53,800 ... B5 29
Gubat, Phil., 9,045 ... *C6 35
Gubbio, It., 8,600 ... C4 21
Gubin, Pol., 3,040 ... B9 17
Gúdar, mts., Sp ... B5 20
Gudauta, Sov. Un., 4,379 . A13 31
Gudenå, Den ... B3 24
Gudenaa, riv., Den ... B3 24
Gudermes, Sov. Un ... E3 29
Gudur, India, 25,618 ... F6 39
Guebwiller, Fr., 10,568 ... D7 14
Guecho, Sp., 22,951 ... A4 20
Guékédou, Guinea, 1,400 .. E2 45
Guelma, Alg., 17,225 (21,587▲) ... B6 44
Guelph, Ont., Can., 39,838 (*41,767) ... D4 72
Guelph, Dickey, N. Dak., 300 . C7 110
Güemes, Arg., 5,688 ... D2 55
Guénette, Que., Can., 151 ... C2 73
Guercif, Mor., 5,579 ... C4 44
Guéret, Fr., 11,384 ... D4 14
Guerette, Aroostook, Maine, 160 ... A4 96
Guerneville, Sonoma, Calif., 900 ... A4 82
Guernica [y Luno], Sp., 3,381 . A4 20
Guernsey, Sask., Can., 79 ... F3 70
Guernsey, Platte, Wyo., 800 .. C8 125
Guernsey, co., Ohio, 38,579 .. B6 111
Guernsey, Br. dep., Eur., 49,000 ... F5 10
Guerra, Jim Hogg, Tex., 50 .. F3 118
Guerrara, Alg ... C5 44
Guerrero, Mex., 1,786 ... F3 118
Guerrero, state, Mex., 1,189,085 ... D5 63
Guest, isl., Ant ... B34 5
Gueugnon, Fr., 8,374 ... D5 14
Gueydan, Vermilion, La., 2,156 ... D3 95
Guffey, Park, Colo., 15 ... C5 83
Guge, mtn., Eth ... D4 47
Gugegwe, isl., Kwajalein ... 52
Guiana, British, see British Guiana, dep., S.A.
Guiana, French, see French Guiana, dep., S.A.
Guiana, Netherlands, see Surinam, Neth. dep., S.A.
Guiana, highlands, Ven ... C5 60
Guider, Cam ... D2 46
Guide Rock, Webster, Nebr., 441 ... D7 103
Guidonia, It., 22,205 ... D4, h9 21
Guiglo, I.C., 2,700 ... E3 45
Guild, Sullivan, N.H., 250 .. D2 105
Guild, Marion, Tenn., 400 .. D8 117
Guildford, Eng., 54,300 ... C7 12
Guildhall, Essex, Vt., 100 (248▲) ... B5 120
Guilford, New Haven, Conn., 2,600 (7,913▲) ... D6 84
Guilford, Dearborn, Ind., 250 ... F8 91
Guilford, Piscataquis, Maine, 1,372 (1,880▲) ... C3 96
Guilford, Howard, Md., 175 .. B4 85
Guilford, Nodaway, Mo., 125 . A3 101
Guilford, Chenango, N.Y., 450 ... C5 108
Guilford, Guilford, N.C., 1,000 ... *A4 109
Guilford, Windham, Vt., 100 (823▲) ... F3 120
Guilford, co., N.C., 246,520 .. A4 109
Guilford College, Guilford, N.C., 1,700 ... A4 109
Guillestre, Fr., 913 ... E2 18
Guimarães, Braz., 1,512 ... B2 57
Guimarães, Port., 18,294 ... B1 20
Guin, Marion, Ala., 1,462 ... B2 78
Guinea, Caroline, Va., 75 ... C5 121
Guinea, country, Afr., 3,500,000 ... E4 42, D2 45
Guinea, Portuguese, see Portuguese Guinea, dep., Afr.
Guinea, gulf, Afr ... F6 42
Guinea Mills, Cumberland, Va ... D4 121
Güines, Cuba, 36,000 ... D2 64
Guines, Fr., 3,481 ... D1 15
Guingamp, Fr., 8,912 ... C2 14
Guion, Izard, Ark., 222 ... B4 81
Guipúzcoa, prov., Sp., 478,337 ... *A4 20
Guir, cape, Mor ... C3 44
Güira de Melena, Cuba, 13,715 ... D2 64
Güiria, Ven., 10,724 ... A5 60
Guisachan, B.C., Can., 171 . *E8 68
Guisborough, Eng., 12,079 ... F7 13
Guise, Fr., 6,284 ... C5 14
Guists, creek, Ky ... B4 94
Guitiriz, Sp., 1,006 ... A2 20
Guiuan, Phil., 7,222 ... *C7 35
Gujan [-Mestras], Fr., 3,776 . E3 14
Gujarat, state, India, 20,633,350 ... D5 39
Gujranwala, Pak., 196,154 ... A5 40, B5 39
Gu Komelik, Pinal, Ariz., 30 . E4 80
Gulbarga, India, 97,069 ... E6 39, I6 40
Guldborg, Den., 598 ... D5 24
Gulf, Chatham, N.C., 180 ... B4 109
Gulf, co., Fla., 9,937 ... C1 86
Gulf creek, Okla ... D2 112
Gulf Coastal, plain, Ark ... C4 81
Gulf Crest, Mobile, Ala., 75 ... D1 78
Gulf Hammock, Levy, Fla., 350 ... C4 86
Gulfport, Pinellas, Fla., 9,730 ... E4, F2 86
Gulfport, Henderson, Ill., 214 ... C2 90
Gulfport, Harrison, Miss., 30,204 (*124,200) ... E2, E4 100
Gulf Shores, Baldwin, Ala., 356 ... E2 78
Gulf Stream, Palm Beach, Fla., 176 ... *F6 86
Gulgong, Austl., 1,399 ... F7 51
Gulkana, Alsk., 51 ... C10, f19 79
Gull, isl., N.Y ... E8 84
Gull, isl., N.C ... B8 109
Gull, lake, Alta., Can ... C4 69
Gull, lake, Minn ... D4 99
Gullivan, bay, Fla ... G5 86
Gulliver, Schoolcraft, Mich., 75 ... C3 98
Gull Lake, Sask., Can., 1,038 . G1 70
Gulluk, Tur., 826 ... D6 23
Gully, Polk, Minn., 168 ... C3 99
Gulu, Ug., 4,770 ... A5 48
Gulyantsi, Bul., 4,741 ... D7 22
Gulyay-Pole, Sov. Un., 10,000 ... H11 27
Gumaca, Phil., 6,461 ... p14 35
Gumba, Con. L ... A3 48
Gumboro, Sussex, Del., 150 . D7 85
Gumefens, Switz., 330 ... C3 19
Gumel, Nig., 10,406 ... D6 45
Gumma, pref., Jap., 1,578,476 ... *H9 37
Gummersbach, Ger., 32,000 . B2 17
Gum Spring, mtn., Tenn ... D8 117
Gümüşane (Gumush-Khaneh), Tur., 5,400 ... B12 31
Guna, Eth ... C4 47
Guna, India, 31,031 ... E6 40
Guna, mtn., Eth ... C4 47
Gundelfingen, Ger., 5,100 ... E5 17
Gunflint, range, Minn ... A7 99
Gungu, Con. L ... C2 48
Gunisao, lake, Man., Can ... C3 71
Gunisao, riv., Man., Can ... C3 71
Gunlock, Washington, Utah, 85 ... F2 119
Gunn, Smith, Miss., 50 ... C4 100

Gunnar, Sask., Can., 795 m7 70
Gunnedah, Austl., 6,546 E8 51
Gunningsville, N.B., Can., 1,254 *C5 74
Gunnison, Gunnison, Colo., 3,477 C4 83
Gunnison, Bolivar, Miss., 448 B2 100
Gunnison, Sanpete, Utah, 1,059 D4 119
Gunnison, co., Colo., 5,477 C3 83
Gunnison, riv., Colo C2 83
Gunnworth, Sask., Can F1 70
Gunpowder, creek, Ky A6 94
Gunpowder, riv., Md B5 85
Gunpowder Falls, riv., Md A4 85
Gunter, mtn., Ala A3 78
Guntersville, Marshall, Ala., 6,592 A3 78
Guntersville, dam, Ala A3 78
Gunton, Man., Can., 88 D3 71
Guntown, Lee, Miss., 269 A5 100
Guntur, India, 187,122 E7 39
Gunung Api, vol., Indon G7 35
Gunungsitoli, Indon., 3,124 L2 38
Gunz, riv., Ger A6 18
Günzburg, Ger., 11,800 E5 17
Gunzenhausen, Ger., 9,300 D5 17
Gurabo, P.R., 3,957 B7 65
Gurabo, mun., P.R., 16,603 B7 65
Gurabo, riv., P.R B6 65
Gura-Humorului, Rom., 7,216 B7 22
Gurdaspur, India, 27,665 A5 40
Gurdon, Clark, Ark., 2,166 D2 81
Gurgan, bay, Iran C6 41
Gurgan, riv., Iran C7 41
Gurguan, pt., Tinian 52
Gurgueia, riv., Braz C2 57
Gurk, riv., Aus E7 16
Gurla Mandhata, peak, China B8 40
Gurley, Madison, Ala., 850 A3 78
Gurley, Cheyenne, Nebr., 329 C3 103
Gurleyville, Tolland, Conn., 150 B8 84
Gurnee, Lake, Ill., 1,831 E2 90
Gurnet, pt., Mass B6 97
Gurney, Iron, Wis., 100 B3 124
Gurupá, Braz., 912 C4 59
Gurupí, cape, Braz B1 57
Gurupí, mts., Braz B1 57
Gurupí, riv., Braz B1 57
Gurvevsk, Sov. Un., 30,000 E26 9
Guryev, Sov. Un., 91,000 D4 29
Gusau, Nig., 40,202 D6 45
Gusev (Gumbinnen), Sov. Un., 25,000 A7 26
Gusher, Uintah, Utah, 160 C6 119
Gusinje, Yugo., 2,757 D4 22
Gus-Khrustalnyy, Sov. Un., 59,000 D13 27
Gustavus, Alsk., 107 k22, D12 79
Güsten, Ger., 8,160 B6 17
Gustine, Merced, Calif., 2,300 D3 82
Gustine, Comanche, Tex., 380 D3 118
Güstrow, Ger., 38,000 B6 16
Gutau, Aus., 2,292 E9 17
Gütersloh, Ger., 53,400 B3 17
Guthrie, Lawrence, Ind., 25 G4 91
Guthrie, Todd, Ky., 1,211 D2 94
Guthrie, Hubbard, Minn., 90 C4 99
Guthrie, McHenry, N. Dak., 38 A5 110
Guthrie, Logan, Okla., 9,502 B4 112
Guthrie, King, Tex., 250 C2 118
Guthrie, co., Iowa, 13,607 C3 92
Guthrie, lake, Man., Can B1 71
Guthrie Center, Guthrie, Iowa, 2,071 C3 92
Guttenberg, Clayton, Iowa, 2,087 B6 92
Guttenberg, Hudson, N.J., 5,118 h8 106
Gu Vo, Pima, Ariz., 100 E3 80
Guy, Faulkner, Ark., 300 B3 81
Guy, Fort Bend, Tex., 100 G4 118
Guyandot, mtn., W. Va D6 123
Guyandot, riv., W. Va C2 123
Guyenne, former prov., Fr., 2,061,000 E4 14
Guymon, Texas, Okla., 5,768 D3 112
Guyot, mtn., Tenn D10 117
Guyra, Austl., 1,628 E8 51
Guys, McNairy, Tenn., 100 B3 117
Guysborough, N.S., Can., 490 D8 74
Guysborough, co., N.S., Can., 13,274 D7 74
Guys Mills, Crawford, Pa., 350 C2 114
Guyton, Effingham, Ga., 670 D5 87
Guzman, Mex F2 107
Gvardeysk, Sov. Un., 5,000 A6 26
Gwa, Bur., 5,000 E9 39
Gwaai, Rh A4 49
Gwabegar, Austl E7 51
Gwadar (Gwadur), Pak C3 39
Gwalior, India, 300,587 C6 39, D7 40
Gwanda, Rh., 1,600 B4 49
Gwane, Con. L A4 48
Gweebarra, bay, Ire C3 11
Gweesalia, Ire C2 11
Gwelo, Rh., 32,200 (★39,200) A4 49
Gwin, Holmes, Miss., 150 B3 100
Gwinn, Marquette, Mich., 1,009 B3 98
Gwinner, Sargent, N. Dak., 242 C8 110
Gwinnett, co., Ga., 43,541 C2 87
Gwydyr, bay, Alsk A10 79
Gwynn, Mathews, Va., 400 D6 121
Gwynne, Alta., Can., 109 C4 69
Gwynneville, Shelby, Ind., 300 E6 91
Gwynns Falls, riv., Md C2 85
Gyangtse, China, 10,000 C8 39
Gydan, mts., Sov. Un C18 28
Gympie, Austl., 11,094 C9 51
Gyongyos, Hung., 28,668 B4 22
Gyor, Hung., 75,300 B3 22
Gyor-Sopron, co., Hung., 391,734 *B3 22
Gypsum, Eagle, Colo., 358 B4 83
Gypsum, Saline, Kans., 593 D6 93
Gypsum, Ottawa, Ohio, 400 A5 111
Gypsumville, Man., Can., 235 D2 71
Gypsy, Creek, Okla B5 112
Gyula, Hung., 19,990 (24,609▲) B5 22
Gzhatsk, Sov. Un., 16,000 D10 27

H

Haag, Ger., 2,300 A8 18
Haakon, co., S. Dak., 3,303 C4 116
Haaksbergen, Neth., 6,100 B6 15
Haamstede, Neth., 1,601 C3 15
Haapamäki, Fin., 2,200 F11 25
Haapsalu, Sov. Un., 10,000 B4 27
Ha Arava (Wadi el Araba), depression, Isr., Jordan D7 32
Haarlem, Neth., 172,000 B4 15
Haarlemmermeer, Neth., 5,400 (48,300▲) B4 15
Hab, riv., Pak I13 41
Habana (Havana), prov., Cuba, 1,538,803 h11 64
Habermehl, peak, Ant B13 5
Habersham, Habersham, Ga., 400 B3 87
Habersham, co., Ga., 18,116 B3 87
Haboro, Jap., 19,800 D10 37
Hachiman, Jap., 11,700 n15 37
Hachinohe, Jap., 131,000 (174,348▲) F10 37
Hachioji, Jap., 158,443 I9, n18 37
Hachita, Grant, N. Mex., 100 F1 107
Hacienda, Broward, Fla., 125 *F6 86
Hack, mtn., Austl E2 51
Hackamore, Modoc, Calif., 20 B3 82
Hackberry, Mahave, Ariz., 75 B2 80
Hackberry, Cameron, La., 800 E2 95
Hackberry, Edwards, Tex E2 118
Hackberry, creek, Kans C3 93
Hackensack, Cass, Minn., 204 D4 99
Hackensack, Bergen, N.J., 30,521 B4, h8 106
Hackensack, riv., N.J h8 106
Hacker Valley, Webster, W. Va., 200 C4 115
Hacketstown, Ire., 509 E5 11
Hackett, Sebastian, Ark., 328 B1 81
Hackettstown, Warren, N.J., 5,276 B3 106
Hackleburg, Marion, Ala., 527 A2 78
Haco, isl., Truk 52
Hacoda, Geneva, Ala., 50 D3 78
Hadar, Pierce, Nebr., 100 B8 103
Hadarba, cape, Eg., U.A.R., Sud A4 47
Haddam, Middlesex, Conn., 500 (3,466▲) D7 84
Haddam, Washington, Kans., 311 C6 93
Haddam Neck, Middlesex, Conn., 150 C6 84
Haddington, Scot., 5,506 E6 13
Haddock, Jones, Ga., 600 C3 87
Haddonfield, Camden, N.J., 13,201 D2 106
Haddon Heights, Camden, N.J., 9,260 D2 106
Hadejia, Nig., 10,453 D7 45
Hadera, Isr., 25,358 B6 32
Haderslev, Den., 19,735 C3 24
Haderslev, co., Den., 71,715 C3 24
Hadhramaut, reg., Aden C6 47
Hadim, Tur., 2,584 D9 31
Haditha, Iraq, 5,434 E14 31
Hadleigh, Eng., 3,460 B8 12
Hadley, Hampshire, Mass., 800 (3,099▲) B2 97
Hadley, Murray, Minn., 151 F3 99
Hadley, Saratoga, N.Y., 500 B7 108
Hadley, Mercer, Pa., 250 D1 114
Hadley, bay, N.W. Ter., Can B11 66
Hadley, lake, Maine D5 96
Hadlock, Jefferson, Wash., 300 A3 122
Hadlyme, New London, Conn., 350 D7 84
Hadsten, Den., 2,525 B4 24
Hadsund, Den., 3,424 B4 24
Hadyai (Ban Hat Yai), Thai., 35,504 I4 38
Haeju, Kor., 82,135 G2 37
Haena, Kauai, Haw., 76 A2 86
Hafford, Sask., Can., 511 E2 70
Hafnarfjördur, Ice., 7,310 n22 25
Haft Gal, Iran E4 41
Hafun, cape, Som C7 47
Hagaman, Montgomery, N.Y., 1,292 *C6 108
Hagan, Evans, Ga., 552 D5 87
Hagar, mtn., Colo B5 83
Hagari, riv., India F6 39
Hagar Shores (Lake Michigan Beach), Berrien, Mich., 1,092 *F4 98
Hagarville, Johnson, Ark., 150 B2 81
Hagemeister, isl., Alsk D7 79
Hagen, Sask., Can., 62 E3 70
Hagen, Ger., 198,900 B2 17
Hagenow, Ger., 10,300 E5 24
Hagensborg, B.C., Can., 413 C4 68
Hagerman, Gooding, Idaho, 430 G4 89
Hagerman, Chaves, N. Mex., 1,144 D5 107
Hagerman Corners, Ont., Can., 218 k15 72
Hagerstown, Wayne, Ind., 1,730 E7 91
Hagerstown, Washington, Md., 36,660 A2 85
Hagersville, Ont., Can., 2,075 E4 72
Haggart, lake, Ont., Can D4 71
Haggin, mtn., Mont D3 102
Hagginwood, Sacramento, Calif., 11,469 *A6 82
Hagi, Jap., 41,002 (56,831▲) I5 37
Ha Giang, Viet., 25,000 A6 38
Hags, head, Ire E2 11
Hague, Sask., Can., 430 E2 70
Hague, Alachua, Fla., 75 C4 86
Hague, The ('s Gravenhage), see The Hague, Neth.
Hague, Warren, N.Y., 300 B7 108
Hague, Emmons, N. Dak., 197 C3 110
Hague, cape, Fr C3 14
Haguenau, Fr., 20,457 C7 14
Hagues, peak, Colo A5 83
Ha Ha, bay, Que., Can C2 75
Ha Ha, lake, Que., Can A7 73
Hahira, Lowndes, Ga., 1,297 F3 87
Hahnville, St. Charles, La., 1,297 C6, E5 95
Haicheng, China, 80,000 D10 36
Haichow, bay, China G8 36
Hai Duong, Viet., 25,000 B7 32
Haifa, Isr., 191,200 (★300,000) B6 32
Haig, lake, Alta., Can A3 69
Haigerloch, Ger., 1,800 A4 18
Haigler, Dundy, Nebr., 268 D4 103
Haiku, Maui, Haw., 800 C5 88
Ḩā'il, Sau. Ar., 15,000 I14 31
Hailar (Hulun), China, 43,200 B8 34
Haile, Union, La., 160 B3 95
Hailesboro, St. Lawrence, N.Y., 300 f9 108
Hailey, Blaine, Idaho, 1,185 F4 89
Haileybury, Ont., Can., 2,638 p20 72
Haileyville, Pittsburg, Okla., 922 C6 112
Hailun, China, 47,684 B10 34
Hailung, China, 20,000 C10 34
Haimen, China, 95,000 I9 36
Haina, Hawaii, Haw., 670 C6 88
Hainan, isl., China C8 38
Hainan, strait, China B9 38
Hainaut, prov., Bel., 1,248,854 D3 15
Haines, Alsk., 392 D12, k22 79
Haines, Baker, Oreg., 331 C9 113
Hainesburg, Warren, N.J., 100 B2 106
Haines City, Polk, Fla., 9,135 D5 86
Haines Falls, Greene, N.Y., 700 C6 108
Hainesport, Burlington, N.J., 1,500 D3 106
Hainesville, Sussex, N.J., 85 A3 106
Hainichen, Ger., 11,200 C8 17
Haining, China, 5,000 I9 36
Haiphong, Viet., 182,496 B7 38
Hairy Hill., Alta., Can., 173 C5 69
Haiti, country, N.A., 4,600,000 H13 61, F7 64
Haiya, Sud B4 47
Haiyang, China F9 36
Haiyuan, China F1 36
Hajdu-Bihar, co., Hung., 393,332 *B5 22
Hajdúböszörmény, Hung., 26,918 (32,214▲) B5 22
Hajduhadhaz, Hung., 11,221 B5 22
Hajduki Weilkie, Pol g9 26
Hajdunanas, Hung., 14,003 (18,413▲) B5 22
Hajduszoboszlo, Hung., 16,709 (23,885▲) B5 22
Hajiabad Kavir, salt flats, Iran E9 41
Hajiki, cape, Jap G9 37
Hakalau, Hawaii, Haw., 800 D6 88
Hakari, Tur., 2,664 D14 31
Hakodate, Jap., 243,010 F10 37
Haku-San, peak, Jap m15 37
Halabja, Iraq D2 41
Halaib, Eg., U.A.R E7 43
Halal, mtn., Eg., U.A.R D5 32
Halaula, Hawaii, Haw., 600 C6 88
Halawa, Maui, Haw., 25 B5 88
Halawa, riv., Haw g10 88
Halawa Heights, Honolulu, Haw., 2,000 G10 88
Halberstadt, Ger., 45,700 B6 17
Halbrite, Sask., Can., 180 H4 70
Halbur, Carroll, Iowa, 214 B3 92
Haldeman, Rowan, Ky., 170 B6 94
Halden, Nor., 10,000 H4 25
Haldimand, co., Ont., Can., 28,197 E5 72
Hale, Yuma, Colo., 5 B8 83
Hale, Iosco, Mich., 450 D7 98
Hale, Carroll, Mo., 504 B4 101
Hale, co., Ala., 19,537 C2 78
Hale, co., Tex., 36,798 B2 118
Haleakala, crater, Haw C5 88
Haleburg, Henry, Ala., 75 D4 78
Hale Center, Hale, Tex., 2,196 B2 118
Haledon, Passaic, N.J., 6,161 *B4 106
Haleiwa, Honolulu, Haw., 2,504 B3, f9 88
Hales Bar, lake, Tenn D8 117
Hales Corners, Milwaukee, Wis., 5,549 F1 124
Halesite, Suffolk, N.Y., 3,200 *n15 108
Halesowen, Eng., 45,100 B5 12
Hales Point, Lauderdale, Tenn B2 117
Halesworth, Eng., 2,252 B9 12
Halethorpe, Baltimore, Md., 22,402 C2 85
Haley, Bowman, N. Dak., 112 D2 110
Haleyville, Winston, Ala., 3,740 A2 78
Haleyville, Cumberland, N.J., 175 E2 106
Hal Flood, range, Ant B35 5
Half Moon, Flathead, Mont., 50 *B2 102
Half Moon Bay, San Mateo, Calif., 1,957 B5 82
Half-moon Bay (Oban), N.Z., 281 Q12 51
Halfway, Washington Md., 4,256 A2 85
Half Way, Polk, Mo., 150 D4 101
Halfway, Baker, Oreg., 505 C9 113
Halfway, Sublette, Wyo C2 125
Halfway, riv., B.C., Can A6 68
Halfway Nunatak, peak, Ant f40 5
Ḩalḩūl, Jordan, 4,000 C7 32
Haliburton, Ont., Can., 853 B6 72
Haliburton, co., Ont., Can., 8,928 B6 72
Halibut, pt., Mass A6 97
Halicarnassus, see Bodrum, Tur.
Halifax, N.S., Can., 92,511 (★183,946) E6 74
Halifax, Eng., 95,900 (★168,000) A6 12
Halifax, Plymouth, Mass., 600 (1,599▲) C6 97
Halifax, Halifax, N.C., 370 A6 109
Halifax, Dauphin, Pa., 824 F8 114
Halifax, Windham, Vt., 100 (268▲) F3 120
Halifax, Halifax, Va., 792 E4 121
Halifax, co., N.S., Can., 225,723 E6 74
Halifax, co., N.C., 58,956 A6 109
Halifax, co., Va., 33,637 E4 121
Halifax, bay, Austl C8 50
Haliimaile, Maui, Haw., 600 C5 88
Halileh, cape, Iran G5 41
Halin, Som D6 47
Haliri, riv., Iran H9 41
Halkirk, Alta., Can., 172 C4 69
Hall, Aus., 10,016 E5 16
Hall, Morgan, Ind., 120 E4 91
Hall, Granite, Mont., 90 D3 102
Hall, Ontario, N.Y., 210 C3 108
Hall, co., Ga., 49,739 B3 87
Hall, co., Nebr., 35,757 D7 103
Hall, co., Tex., 7,322 B2 118
Hall, basin, N.W. Ter., Can k39 67
Hall, mtn., Wash A8 122
Hall, pen., N.W. Ter., Can D19 67
Halladale, riv., Scot B5 13
Hallam, Lancaster, Nebr., 264 D9 103
Hallam, peak, B.C., Can C8 68
Halland, co., Swe., 171,200 B6 24
Hallandale, Broward, Fla., 10,483 E3, G6 86
Hallands Väderö, isl., Swe B6 24
Halla San, peak, Kor J3 37
Hallboro, Man., Can D2 71
Halldale, Waldo, Maine D3 96
Halle, Bel., 19,339 D4 15
Halle, Ger., 278,000 (★425,000) B6 17
Halle, Ger., 7,500 A3 17
Halleck, Elko, Nev., 10 C6 104
Hallein, Aus., 13,329 E6 16
Hällestad, Swe., 380 u33 25
Hallett, Pawnee, Okla., 132 A5 112
Hallett, cape, Ant B30 5
Hallettsville, Lavaca, Tex., 2,808 E4 118
Halley, Desha, Ark., 213 D4 81
Halley Bay, Br. scientific station, Ant B10 5
Halliday, Dunn., N. Dak., 509 B3 110
Hall Meadow, brook, Conn B4 84
Hall Meadow Brook, res., Conn B4 84
Hallock, Kittson, Minn., 1,527 B2 99
Hallowell, Cherokee, Kans., 160 E9 93
Hallowell, Kennebeck, Maine, 3,169 D3 96
Halls, Lauderdale, Tenn., 1,890 B2 117
Halls, creek, Utah F5 119
Halls, stream, N.H A1 105
Hallsbergs, Swe., 6,000 t33 25
Hallsboro, Columbus, N.C., 250 C5 109
Halls Creek, Sumter, Ala C2 78
Hall's Creek, Austl., 50 C4 50
Halls Crossroads, Knox, Tenn., 500 E11 117
Halls Harbour, N.S., Can., 98 D5 74
Hallson, Pembina, N. Dak., 4 A8 110
Halls Summit, Coffey, Kans., 40 D8 93
Hallstead, Susquehanna, Pa., 1,580 C10 114
Hall Summit, Red River, La., 170 B2 95
Hallsville, Boone, Mo., 363 B5 101
Hallsville, Ross, Ohio, 250 C5 111
Hallsville, Harrison, Tex., 684 C5 118
Hallton, Elk, Pa., 45 D4 114
Halltown, Lawrence, Mo., 86 D4 101
Hallville, New London, Conn., 150 D8 84
Hallwil, lake, Switz B5 19
Hallwood, Accomack, Va., 269 D7 121
Hallwood, Mason, W. Va C2 123
Halma, Kittson, Minn., 115 B2 99
Halmahera, isl., Indon E7 35
Halmstad, Swe., 40,100 B6 24
Hals, Den., 1,563 B4 24
Halsell, Choctaw, Ala., 200 C1 78
Halsey, Thomas, Nebr., 111 C5 103
Halsey, Sussex, N.J., 75 A3 106
Halsey, Linn, Oreg., 404 C3 113
Hälsingborg, Swe., 77,600 B6 24, I5 25
Halsö, isl., Swe A5 24
Halstad, Norman, Minn., 639 C2 99
Halstead, Eng., 6,465 C8 12
Halstead, Harvey, Kans., 1,598 A5, D6 93
Haltern, Ger., 14,700 B2 17
Haltia, mtn., Fin., Nor C9 25
Halton, co., Ont., Can., 106,967 D4 72
Halton City, Tarrant, Tex., 23,133 *C4 118
Haltwhistle, Eng., 3,745 F6 13
Ham, Fr., 4,204 E3 15
Hama, Okinawa 52
Hamada, Jap., 33,200 I6 37
Hamadān, Iran, 99,909 D4 46
Hamāh, Syr., 97,390 E11 31
Hamahika, isl., Okinawa 52
Hamakuapoko, Maui, Haw., 335 C5 88
Hamamatsu, Jap., 333,009 I8, o16 37
Hamar, Eddy, N. Dak., 84 B7 110
Hamar, Nor., 13,500 G4 25
Hamatombetsu, Jap., 4,700 D11 37
Hambantota, Cey., 4,345 G7 39
Hamber, prov. park, B.C., Can C8 68
Hamberg, Wells, N. Dak., 64 B6 110
Hamblen, co., Tenn., 33,092 C10 117
Hamburg, Ashley, Ark., 2,904 D4 81
Hamburg, New London, Conn., 100 D7 84
Hamburg, Ger., 1,854,600 (★2,300,000) B5 16, E4 24
Hamburg, state, Ger., 1,860,000 E4 24
Hamburg, Calhoun, Ill., 264 D3 90
Hamburg, Fremont, Iowa, 1,647 D2 92
Hamburg, Franklin, Miss., 60 D2 100
Hamburg, Sussex, N.J., 1,532 A3 106
Hamburg, Erie, N.Y., 9,145 C2 108
Hamburg, Berks, Pa., 3,747 E10 114
Hamburg, Aiken, S.C., 150 E4 115
Hamburg, Hardin, Tenn B3 117
Hamburg, Marathon, Wis., 200 C4 124
Hamburg, mts., N.J A3 106
Hamden, New Haven, Conn., 41,056 D5 84
Hamden, Delaware, N.Y., 200 C6 108
Hamden, Vinton, Ohio, 1,035 B5 111
Häme, dept., Fin., 519,015 *G11 25
Hämeenlinna, Fin., 28,300 G11 25
Hamel, Madison, Ill., 362 A9 101
Hamel (Medina), Hennepin, Minn., 1,472 *E5 99
Hameln, Ger., 49,200 A4 17
Hamer, Jefferson, Idaho, 144 F6 89
Hamer, Dillon, S.C., 170 C9 115
Hamersley, plat., Austl D2 50
Hamersville, Brown, Ohio, 224 D4 111
Hamhŭng, Kor., 112,184 G3 37
Hami (Kumul) (Qomul), China, 30,000 C3 34
Hamill, Tripp, S. Dak., 40 D6 116
Hamilton, Marion, Ala., 1,934 A2 78
Hamilton, Alsk., 35 C7 79
Hamilton, Austl., 9,498 H4 51
Hamilton, Bermuda, 2,878 (★15,371) E14 77
Hamilton, Glenn, Calif., 700 C2 82
Hamilton, Ont., Can., 273,991 (★395,189) D5 72
Hamilton, Moffat, Colo., 22 A3 83
Hamilton, Harris, Ga., 396 D2 87
Hamilton, Hancock, Ill., 2,228 C2 90
Hamilton, Steuben, Ind., 380 A8 91
Hamilton, Marion, Iowa, 197 C5 92
Hamilton, Greenwood, Kans., 400 E7 93
Hamilton, Boone, Ky A6 94
Hamilton, Essex, Mass., 900 (5,488▲) A6, f12 97
Hamilton, Allegan, Mich., 700 F4 98
Hamilton, Monroe, Miss., 115 B5 100
Hamilton, Caldwell, Mo., 1,701 B3 101
Hamilton, Ravalli, Mont., 2,475 D2 102
Hamilton, Mercer, N.J., (65,035▲) *C3 106
Hamilton, Madison, N.Y., 3,348 C5 108
Hamilton, N.Z., 57,500 (★57,800) L15 51
Hamilton, Martin, N.C., 565 B6 109
Hamilton, Pembina, N. Dak., 217 A8 110
Hamilton, Butler, Ohio, 72,354 (★103,200) C2, C3 111
Hamilton, Grant, Oreg., 20 C7 113
Hamilton, Washington, R.I., 900 C11 84
Hamilton, Scot., 43,100 E4 13
Hamilton, Hamilton, Tex., 3,106 D3 118
Hamilton, Loudoun, Va., 403 B5 121
Hamilton, Skagit, Wash., 271 A4 122
Hamilton, co., Fla., 7,705 B3 86
Hamilton, co., Ill., 10,010 E5 90
Hamilton, co., Ind., 40,132 D5 91
Hamilton, co., Iowa, 20,032 B4 92
Hamilton, co., Kans., 3,144 E2 93
Hamilton, co., Nebr., 8,714 D7 103
Hamilton, co., N.Y., 4,267 B6 108
Hamilton, co., Ohio, 864, 121 C3 111
Hamilton, co., Tenn., 237,905 D8 117
Hamilton, co., Tex., 8,488 D3 118
Hamilton, inlet, Newf., Can A2 75
Hamilton, lake, Ark C2 81
Hamilton, mtn., Alsk C8 79
Hamilton, mtn., Calif C6 82
Hamilton, mtn., Nev D6 104
Hamilton, mtn., N.Y B6 108
Hamilton, res., Mass B3 97
Hamilton, riv., Newf., Can h9 75
Hamilton, sound, Newf., Can D4 75
Hamilton Acres, Alsk., 960 *C10 79
Hamilton Dome, Hot Springs, Wyo., 150 B4 125
Hamilton Park, Lancaster, Pa., 3,500 *F9 114
Hamilton Square, Mercer, N.J., 8,500 C3 106
Hamina, Fin., 9,800 G12 25
Hamiota, Man., Can., 779 D1 71
Hamirpur, India, 10,000 C7 39
Hamirpur, India, 10,921 B6 40
Hamler, Henry, Ohio, 588 A3 111
Hamlet, Starke, Ind., 688 B4 91
Hamlet, Hayes, Nebr., 113 D4 103
Hamlet, Richmond, N.C., 4,460 C4 109
Hamlet, Williams, N. Dak., 20 A2 110
Hamletsburg, Pope, Ill., 107 F5 90
Hamlin, Audubon, Iowa, 150 C3 92
Hamlin, Brown, Kans., 99 C8 93
Hamlin, Wayne, Pa., 275 D11 114
Hamlin, Jones and Fisher, Tex., 3,791 C2 118
Hamlin, Lincoln, W. Va., 850 C2 123
Hamlin, co., S. Dak., 6,303 C8 116
Hamlin, lake, Mich D4 98
Hammamet, gulf, Tun F12 30
Hammam Lif, Tun., 22,060 *B7 44
Hammar, Iraq F3 41
Hammarby, Swe t35 25
Hammarsjön, lake, Swe C8 24
Hamme, Bel., 16,794 C4 15
Hammel, Den., 2,162 B3 24
Hammelburg, Ger., 6,000 C4 17
Hammer, Roberts, S. Dak., 65 B8 116
Hammerfest, Nor., 5,900 B10 25
Hammersley Fork, Clinton, Pa., 15 D6 114
Hammett, Elmore, Idaho, 75 G3 89
Hamm [in Westfalen], Ger., 71,200 (★160,000) B2 17
Hammon, Roger Mills, Okla., 656 B2 112
Hammonasset, pt., Conn E6 84
Hammonasset, riv., Conn D6 84
Hammond, Piatt, Ill., 471 D5 90
Hammond, Lake, Ind., 111,698 A2 91
Hammond, Tangipahoa, La., 10,563 A6, D5 95
Hammond, Wabasha, Minn., 205 F6 99
Hammond, Carter, Mont., 10 E12 102
Hammond, St. Lawrence, N.Y., 314 f9 108
Hammond, Clatsop, Oreg., 480 A3 113
Hammond, St. Croix, Wis., 645 D1 124
Hammond, bay, Mich C6 98
Hammond East, Tangipahoa, La., 1,462 *A6 95
Hammondsport, Steuben, N.Y., 1,176 C3 108
Hammondsville, Jefferson, Ohio, 475 A1 123
Hammonton, Atlantic, N.J., 9,854 D3 106
Hamneda, Swe., 168 B7 24
Ham-Nord, Que., Can., 573 D6 73
Hamoyet, mtn., Eth B4 47
Hampden, Newf., Can., 682 D3 75
Hampden, Hampden, Mass., 400 (2,345▲) B3 97
Hampden, N.Z., 303 P13 51
Hampden, Ramsey, N. Dak., 159 A7 110
Hampden, co., Mass., 429,353 B2 97
Hampden, Highlands, Penobscot, Maine, 1,000 (4,583▲) D4 96
Hampshire, Kane, Ill., 1,309 A5 90
Hampshire, Maury, Tenn., 150 B11 117
Hampshire (Southampton), co., Eng., 1,336,084 C6 12
Hampshire, co., Mass., 103,229 B2 97
Hampshire, co., W. Va., 11,705 B6 123
Hampshire Road, Rockingham, N.H E4 105
Hampstead, N.B., Can., 116 D3 74
Hampstead, Que., Can., 4,557 *D8 73
Hampstead, Carroll, Md., 696 A4 85
Hampstead, Rockingham, N.H., 300 (1,261▲) E4 105
Hampstead, Pender, N.C., 350 C6 109
Hampton, Calhoun, Ark., 1,011 D3 81
Hampton, N.B., Can., 571 D4 74
Hampton, Windham, Conn., 320 (934▲) B8 84
Hampton, Bradford, Fla., 340 C4 86
Hampton, Henry, Ga., 1,253 C2 87
Hampton, Rock Island, Ill., 742 D7 92
Hampton, Franklin, Iowa, 4,501 B4 92
Hampton, Livingston, Ky., 100 A3 94
Hampton, Dakota, Minn., 305 F6 99
Hampton, Washington, Miss B2 100
Hampton, Hamilton, Nebr., 331 D8 103
Hampton, Rockingham, N.H., 3,281 (5,379▲) E5 105
Hampton, Hunterdon, N.J., 1,135 B3 106
Hampton, Washington, N.Y., 200 B7 108
Hampton, Deschutes, Oreg., 10 D6 113
Hampton, Hampton, S.C., 2,486 F5 115
Hampton, Carter, Tenn., 1,048 C11 117
Hampton (Independent City), Va., 89,258 B6, D6 121
Hampton, Uinta, Wyo D2 125
Hampton, co., S.C., 17,425 F5 115
Hampton, butte, Oreg D6 113
Hampton Bays, Suffolk, N.Y., 2,550 n16 108
Hampton Beach, Rockingham, N.H., 700 E2 105
Hampton Falls, Rockingham, N.H., 400 (885▲) E5 105
Hampton Roads, harbor, Va B6 121
Hamrā, plat., Libya D2 43
Hamrarne, strait, Swe C8 24
Hams, bluff, Vir. Is h17 65
Hams, fork, Wyo D2 125
Hamsfork, Lincoln, Wyo C2 125
Ham-Sud, Que., Can., 59 D6 73
Hamtramck, Wayne, Mich., 34,137 A8 98
Hamun-i-Mashkel, lake, Pak J21 9
Hamun-i-Murgho, lake, Pak H12 41
Hamyang, Kor., 10,300 I3 37
Han, riv., China E7 34
Hana, Maui, Haw., 547 C2 88
Hanahan, Berkeley, S.C., 4,000 F2 115
Hanalei, Kauai, Haw., 364 A2 88
Hanalei, bay, Haw A2 88
Hanamaulu, Kauai, Haw., 950 B2 88
Hanapepe, Kauai, Haw., 1,383 B2 88
Hanau, Ger., 48,900 C3 17
Hanceville, Cullman, Ala., 1,174 A3 77
Hanceville, B.C., Can., 54 D6 68
Hancock, Litchfield, Conn., 40 C4 84
Hancock, Pottawattamie, Iowa, 252 C2 92
Hancock, Hancock, Maine, 350 (806▲) D4 96
Hancock, Washington, Md., 2,004 A1 85
Hancock, Berkshire, Mass., 150 (455▲) A1 97
Hancock, Houghton, Mich., 5,022 A2 98
Hancock, Stevens, Minn., 942 E3 99
Hancock, Hillsboro, N.H., 300 (722▲) E3 105
Hancock, Delaware, N.Y., 1,830 D5 108
Hancock, Addison, Vt., 160 (323▲) D3 120

Hancock, Morgan, W. Va., 100....B6 123
Hancock, Waushara, Wis., 367....D4 124
Hancock, co., Ga., 9,979....C3 87
Hancock, co., Ill., 24,574....C2 90
Hancock, co., Ind., 26,665....E6 91
Hancock, co., Iowa, 14,604....A4 92
Hancock, co., Ky., 5,330....C3 94
Hancock, co., Maine, 32,293....D4 96
Hancock, co., Miss., 14,039....E4 100
Hancock, co., Ohio, 53,686....A4 111
Hancock, co., Tenn., 7,757....C10 117
Hancock, co., W. Va., 39,615....A4 123
Hancock, lake, Fla....E5 86
Hancock, mtn., N.H....B3 105
Hancock, pond, Maine....E2 96
Hancocks Bridge, Salem, N.J., 450....D2 106
Hand, co., S. Dak., 6,712....C6 116
Handa, Jap., 71,380....o15 37
Handa, isl., Scot....B3 13
Handel, Sask., Can., 100....E1 70
Handeni, Tan....C6 48
Handley, Kanawha, W. Va., 900....C6 123
Handsboro, Harrison, Miss., 1,577....E2, E4 100
Handsworth, Sask., Can....H4 70
Haney, B.C., Can., 2,117....E6, f13 68
Hanford, Kings, Calif., 10,133....D4 82
Hanford, Benton, Wash....C6 122
Hanford Northwest, Kings, Calif., 1,364....*D4 82
Hangchow, China, 784,000....E9 34, I9 36
Hangchow, bay, China....I9 36
Hangelsberg, Ger., 976....A8 17
Hanging Rock, Lawrence, Ohio, 352....D5 111
Hangingstone, riv., Alta., Can....A5 69
Hangö, Fin., 8,200....H10 25
Hanita, Isr....A7 32
Hankinson, Claiborne, Miss....C3 100
Hankinson, Richland, N. Dak., 1,285....C9 110
Hanks, Williams, N. Dak., 78....A2 110
Hanksville, Wayne, Utah, 150....E5 119
Hanley, Sask., Can., 455....F2 70
Hanley Falls, Yellow Medicine, Minn., 334....F3 99
Hanley Hills, St. Louis, Mo., 3,308....*A8 101
Hanlontown, Worth, Iowa, 193....A4 92
Hann, mtn., Austl....C4 50
Hanna, Alta., Can., 2,645....D5 69
Hanna, LaPorte, Ind., 500....B4 91
Hanna, McIntosh, Okla., 233....B6 112
Hanna, Duchesne, Utah, 100....C5 119
Hanna, Carbon, Wyo., 625....D6 125
Hanna City, Peoria, Ill., 1,056....C4 90
Hannaford, Griggs, N. Dak., 277....B7 110
Hannagan, Greenlee, Ariz....D6 80
Hannah, Cavalier, N. Dak., 253....A7 110
Hannawa Falls, St. Lawrence, N.Y., 400....f10 108
Hannibal, Marion and Ralls, Mo., 20,028....B6 101
Hannibal, Oswego, N.Y., 611....B4 108
Hannibal, Monroe, Ohio, 525....C7 111
Hannon, Macon, Ala., 50....C4 77
Hannover (Hanover), Ger., 567,400 (*740,000)....A4 17
Hannover, Oliver, N. Dak., 25....B4 110
Hannoversch Münden, see Münden, Ger.
Hanöbukten, bay, Swe....J6 25
Hanoi, Viet., 414,620 (*643,576)....B6 38
Hanover, Stone, Ark., 10....B3 81
Hanover, Ont., Can., 4,401....C3 72
Hanover, New London, Conn., 300....C8 84
Hanover (Hannover), Ger., 567,400 (*740,000)....A4 17
Hanover, Jo Daviess, Ill., 1,396....A3 90
Hanover, Jefferson, Ind., 1,170....G7 91
Hanover, Washington, Kans., 773....C7 93
Hanover, Oxford, Maine, 170 (240▲)....D2 96
Hanover, Plymouth, Mass., 700 (5,923▲)....B6, h12 97
Hanover, Jackson, Mich., 449....F6 98
Hanover, Fergus, Mont., 25....C7 102
Hanover, Grafton, N.H., 5,649 (7,329▲)....C2 105
Hanover, Grant, N. Mex., 450....E1 107
Hanover, Licking, Ohio, 267....B5 111
Hanover, York, Pa., 15,538....G8 114
Hanover, Hanover, Va., 250....D5 121
Hanover, Wyoming, W. Va., 100....D3 123
Hanover, co., Va., 27,550....D5 121
Hanover, reg., Ger....B4 16
Hanover, isl., Chile....E2 54
Hanover Center, Plymouth, Mass., 400....*B6 97
Hanover Green, Luzerne, Pa., 1,000....*D10 114
Hanoverton, Columbiana, Ohio, 442....B7 111
Hansard, B.C., Can., 40....B7 68
Hansboro, Towner, N. Dak., 143....A6 110
Hansell, Franklin, Iowa, 168....B4 92
Hansen, Twin Falls, Idaho, 427....G4 89
Hansford, co., Tex., 6,208....A2 118
Hanska, Brown, Minn., 491....F4 99
Hans Lollik, is., Vir. Is....f15 65
Hanson, Madison, Fla., 40....B3 86
Hanson, Hopkins, Ky., 376....C2 94
Hanson, Plymouth, Mass., 700 (4,370▲)....B6 97
Hanson, Sequoyah, Okla....B7 112
Hanson, co., S. Dak., 4,584....D8 116
Hanson, lake, Sask., Can....C4 70
Hansted, see Hanstholm Havn, Den.
Hansthom Havn (Hansted), Den....A2 24
Hanston, Hodgeman, Kans., 279....D4 93
Hantachi, China....A3 37
Hants, co., N.S., Can., 26,444....D6 74
Hant's Harbour, Newf., Can., 487....D5 75
Hantsport, N.S., Can., 1,381....D5 74
Haofeng, China, 10,000....J3 36
Haoli, China, 90,000....B10 34
Haparanda, Swe., 3,400....E11 25
Hapeville, Fulton, Ga., 10,082....B5, C2 87
Happy, Randall and Swisher, Tex., 624....B2 118
Happy Camp, Siskiyou, Calif., 500....B2 82
Happy Jack, Coconino, Ariz., 350....C4 80
Happy Valley, Newf., Can., 2,861....B1, h9 75
Happy Valley, Eddy, N. Mex., 700....E5 107
Hapsu, Kor....F4 37
Haql, Sau. Ar....H10 31
Haque, Alachua, Fla., 120....C4 86
Harahan, Jefferson, La., 9,275....C7 95
Harald, isl., Sov. Un....B32 4
Haralson, co., Ga., 14,543....C1 87
Härar, Eth., 25,000....D5 47
Härar, prov., Eth....D5 47
Harardera, Som., 500....E6 47
Hara Usa, lake, Mong....B3 34
Harazé, Chad, 742....D4 46
Harbeson, Sussex, Del., 142....C7 85
Harbin, China, 1,814,000....B10 34, D3 37
Harbinger, Currituck, N.C., 100....A8 109
Harboøre, Den., 1,028....B2 24
Harbor, Curry, Oreg., 40....E2 113
Harbor Beach, Huron, Mich., 2,282....E7 98
Harborcreek, Erie, Pa., 800....B2 114
Harbor Isle, Nassau, N.Y., 1,300....*n15 108
Harbor Springs, Emmet, Mich., 1,433....C5 98
Harborton, Accomack, Va., 350....D7 121
Harbor View, Lucas, Ohio, 273....A2 111
Harbour Breton, Newf., Can., 1,076....E4 75
Harbour Buffet, Newf., Can., 285....E4 75
Harbour Deep, Newf., Can....C3 75
Harbour Grace, Newf., Can., 2,650....E5 75
Harbour Main, Newf., Can., 469....E5 75
Harbour Mille, Newf., Can., 345....E4 75
Harbourton, Mercer, N.J., 50....C3 106
Harbourville, N.S., Can., 191....D5 74
Harbuck, Polk, Tenn., 50....D9 117
Harby, Den., 1,225....C4 24
Harcourt, N.B., Can., 231....C4 74
Harcourt, Webster, Iowa, 268....B3 92
Harcuvar, Yuma, Ariz....D2 80
Harcuvar, mts., Ariz....D2 80
Harda, India, 22,279....F6 40
Hardangerfjord, fjord, Nor....H1 25
Hardangerjökelen, mtn., Nor....G2 25
Hardangervidda, mts., Nor....G2 25
Hardaway, Macon, Ala., 100....C4 78
Hardburly, Perry, Ky., 650....C6 94
Hardee, Issaquena, Miss., 40....C3 100
Hardee, co., Fla., 12,370....E5 86
Hardeeville, Beaufort and Jasper, S.C., 700....G5 115
Hardeman, co., Tenn., 21,517....B2 117
Hardeman, co., Tex., 8,275....B3 118
Hardenberg, Neth., 1,957....B6 15
Harden City, Pontotoc, Okla., 150....C5 112
Harderwijk, Neth., 17,700....B5 15
Hardesty, Texas, Okla., 187....D3 112
Hardin, Calhoun, Ill., 1,040....D3 90
Hardin, Marshall, Ky., 458....B3 94
Hardin, Ray, Mo., 727....B4 101
Hardin, Big Horn, Mont., 2,789....E9 102
Hardin, co., Ill., 5,879....F5 90
Hardin, co., Iowa, 22,533....B4 92
Hardin, co., Ky., 67,789....C4 94
Hardin, co., Ohio, 29,633....B4 111
Hardin, co., Tenn., 17,397....B3 117
Hardin, co., Tex., 24,629....D5 118
Harding, Norfolk, Mass., 250....B5, h10 97
Harding, Harding, S. Dak., 15....B2 116
Harding, Randolph, W. Va., 175....C5 123
Harding, co., N. Mex., 1,874....B5 107
Harding, co., S. Dak., 2,371....B2 116
Harding, lake, Ala., Ga....C4 78
Harding, lake, Man., Can....A2 71
Hardinsburg, Washington, Ind., 218....H5 91
Hardinsburg, Breckinridge, Ky., 1,377....C3 94
Hardisty, Alta., Can., 582....C5 69
Hardisty, lake, N.W. Ter., Can....D9 66
Hardman, Morrow, Oreg., 30....B7 113
Hardoi, India, 36,725....D8 40
Hardtner, Barber, Kans., 372....E5 93
Hardwar, India, 58,513 (*59,960)....C7 40
Hardwick, Baldwin, Ga., 3,500....C3 87
Hardwick, Worcester, Mass., 450 (2,340▲)....B3 97
Hardwick, Rock, Minn., 328....G2 99
Hardwick, Caledonia, Vt., 1,521 (2,349▲)....B4 120
Hardwicke, N.B., Can....B5 74
Hardy, Alg., 1,002....B5 44
Hardy, Sharp, Ark., 555....A4 81
Hardy, Sask., Can., 76....H3 70
Hardy, Pike, Ky., 854....C7 94
Hardy, Grenada, Miss., 125....B4 100
Hardy, Cascade, Mont....C5 102
Hardy, Nuckolls, Nebr., 285....D8 103
Hardy, Kay, Okla., 6....A5 111
Hardy, co., W. Va., 9,308....B6 123
Hare, bay, Newf., Can....C4 75
Hare Bay, Newf., Can., 1,467....D4 75
Hareford, inlet, N.J....E3 106
Harelson, East Baton Rouge, La., 150....B5 95
Haren, Neth., 3,787....A6 15
Harfleur, Fr., 10,514....C4 14
Harford, Susquehanna, Pa., 230....C10 114
Harford, co., Md., 76,722....A5 85
Hargeisa, Som., 53,000....D5 47
Hargeisa, dist., Som....D6 47
Harghitei, mts., Rom....B7 22
Hargill, Hidalgo, Tex., 750....F3 118
Hargrave, Man., Can., 40....E1 71
Hargrave, lake, Man., Can....B2 71
Hargrave, riv., Man., Can....B2 71
Hari, riv., Afg....D10 41
Harihar, India, 22,829....F6 39
Harkers Island, Carteret, N.C., 1,362....C7 109
Harkus, isl., Sau. Ar....H4 41
Harlan, Allen, Ind., 500....B8 91
Harlan, Shelby, Iowa, 4,350....C2 92
Harlan, Smith, Kans., 125....C5 93
Harlan, Harlan, Ky., 4,177....D6 94
Harlan, co., Ky., 51,107....D6 94
Harlan, co., Nebr., 5,081....D6 103
Harlan, res., Nebr....D6 103
Harlau, Rom., 4,172....B8 22
Harlech, Wales....B3 12
Harlem, Hendry, Fla., 1,256....*F6 86
Harlem, Columbia, Ga., 1,423....C4 87
Harlem, Blaine, Mont., 1,267....B8 102
Harlem, riv., N.Y....D5 106
Harleton, Harrison, Tex., 150....C5 118
Harleyville, Dorchester, S.C., 561....E7 115
Harlingen, Neth., 12,000....A5 15
Harlingen, Cameron, Tex., 41,207....F4 118
Harlow, Eng., 61,100....C8 12
Harlow, Benson, N. Dak., 90....A6 110
Harlowton, Wheatland, Mont., 1,734....D7 102
Härlunda, Swe....B8 24
Harman, Randolph, W. Va., 128....C5 123
Harmancik, Tur....C7 31
Harmans, Anne Arundel, Md., 300....B4 103
Harmarville, Allegheny, Pa., 2,000....A6 114
Harmon, Lee, Ill., 214....B4 90
Harmon, Red River, La., 80....B2 95
Harmon, Ellis, Okla., 15....A2 112
Harmon, co., Okla., 5,852....C2 112
Harmon, creek, W. Va....A2 123
Harmonsburg, Crawford, Pa., 300....C1 114
Harmony, Clay, Ind., 700....E3 91
Harmony, Somerset, Maine, 350 (712▲)....D3 96
Harmony, Fillmore, Minn., 1,214....G6 99
Harmony, Warren, N.J., 550....B2 106
Harmony, Iredell, N.C., 322....B3 109
Harmony, Butler, Pa., 1,142....E1 114
Harmony, Providence, R.I., 800....B10 84
Harmony, Halifax, Va., 40....E4 121
Harmonyville, Windham, Vt., 30....E3 120
Harms, Lincoln, Tenn., 65....B5 117
Harned, Breckinridge, Ky., 375....C3 94
Harnett, co., N.C., 48,236....B5 109
Harney, Carroll, Md., 200....B3 85
Harney, co., Oreg., 6,744....D7 113
Harney, lake, Fla....D6 86
Harney, lake, Oreg....D7 113
Harney, peak, S. Dak....D2 116
Harney, valley, Oreg....D8 113
Härnösand, Swe., 17,200....F8 25
Haro, Sp., 8,554....A4 20
Haro, cape, Mex....B2 63
Haro, strait, B.C., Can....g12 68
Harold, Santa Rosa, Fla., 200....G2 86
Harper, Keokuk, Iowa, 177....C5 92
Harper, Harper, Kans., 1,899....E5 93
Harper, Lib., 5,000....F3 45
Harper, Malheur, Oreg., 100....D9 113
Harper, Gillespie, Tex., 300....D3 118
Harper, Kitsap, Wash., 500....D1 122
Harper, co., Kans., 9,541....E5 93
Harper, co., Okla., 5,956....A2 112
Harper, lake, Que., Can....B4 73
Harpers Ferry, Allamakee, Iowa, 211....A6 92
Harpers Ferry, Jefferson, W. Va., 572....B7 123
Harpersville, Shelby, Ala., 667....B3 78
Harperville, Scott, Miss., 250....C4 100
Harper Woods, Wayne, Mich., 19,995....*A8 98
Harpeth, riv., Tenn....A5 117
Harpster, Idaho, Idaho....D3 89
Harpster, Wyandot, Ohio, 302....B4 111
Harptree, Sask., Can....H3 70
Harquahala, mts., Ariz....D2 80
Harrah, Oklahoma, Okla., 934....B4 112
Harrah, Yakima, Wash., 284....C5 122
Harray, bay, Scot....A5 13
Harrell, Calhoun, Ark., 267....D3 81
Harricanaw, riv., Ont., Que., Can....F17 67
Harrietta, Wexford, Mich., 119....D5 98
Harriettsville, Noble, Ohio, 100....C6 111
Harriman, Klamath, Oreg....E4 113
Harriman, Roane, Tenn., 5,931....D9 117
Harrington, Kent, Del., 2,495....C6 85
Harrington, Washington, Maine, 500 (717▲)....D5 96
Harrington, Lincoln, Wash., 575....B7 122
Harrington, lake, Maine....C3 96
Harrington, sound, Bermuda....E14 77
Harrington Harbour, Que., Can., 457....F21 67
Harrington Park, Bergen, N.J., 3,581....h9 106
Harriott, lake, Sask., Can....A4 70
Harris, Sask., Can., 305....F2 70
Harris, Osceola, Iowa, 258....A2 92
Harris, Anderson, Kans., 36....D8 93
Harris, Chisago, Minn., 552....E6 99
Harris, Sullivan, Mo., 171....A4 101
Harris, McCurtain, Okla., 110....D7 112
Harris, Kent, R.I., 1,500....*C10 84
Harris, Scot....D2 13
Harris, Obion, Tenn., 120....A3 117
Harris, co., Ga., 11,167....D2 87
Harris, co., Tex., 1,243,158....E5 118
Harris, hill, Mass....A3 97
Harris, lake, Fla....D5 86
Harris, sound, Scot....C1 13
Harrisburg, Poinsett, Ark., 1,907....B5 81
Harrisburg, Saline, Ill., 9,171....F5 90
Harrisburg, Boone, Mo., 124....B5 101
Harrisburg, Banner, Nebr., 100....C2 103
Harrisburg, Pickaway and Franklin, Ohio, 359....C2 111
Harrisburg, Linn, Oreg., 939....C3 113
Harrisburg, Dauphin, Pa., 79,697 (*257,600)....F8 114
Harrisburg, Lincoln, S. Dak., 313....G9 116
Harris Grove, York, Va., 100....A6 121
Harris Hill, Erie, N.Y., 5,000....*C2 108
Harrismith, S. Afr., 13,753....C4 49
Harrison, Boone, Ark., 6,580....A2 81
Harrison, Washington, Ga., 209....D4 87
Harrison, Kootenai, Idaho, 249....B2 89
Harrison, Cumberland, Maine, 550 (1,014▲)....D2 96
Harrison, Clare, Mich., 1,072....D6 98
Harrison, Madison, Mont., 151....E5 102
Harrison, Sioux, Nebr., 448....B2 103
Harrison, Hudson, N.J., 11,743....k8 106
Harrison, Westchester, N.Y., 13,200....h13 108
Harrison, Hamilton, Ohio, 3,878....C3 111
Harrison [Township] (Natrona Heights), Allegheny, Pa., 15,710....A7, E2 114
Harrison, Douglas, S. Dak., 80....D7 116
Harrison, Hamilton, Tenn., 200....E10 117
Harrison, co., Ind., 19,207....H5 91
Harrison, co., Iowa, 17,600....C2 92
Harrison, co., Ky., 13,704....B5 94
Harrison, co., Miss., 119,489....E4 100
Harrison, co., Mo., 11,603....A3 101
Harrison, co., Ohio, 17,995....B6 111
Harrison, co., Tex., 45,594....C5 118
Harrison, co., W. Va., 77,856....B4 123
Harrison, bay, Alsk....A9 79
Harrison, cape, Newf., Can....g10 75
Harrison, lake, B.C., Can....E7 68
Harrisonburg, Catahoula, La., 594....C4 95
Harrisonburg (Independent City), Va., 11,916....C4 121
Harrison Hot Springs, B.C., Can., 475....f14 68
Harrison Valley, Potter, Pa., 375....C6 114
Harrisonville, Monroe, Ill., 100....E3 90
Harrisonville, Baltimore, Md., 180....B4 85
Harrisonville, Cass, Mo., 3,510....C3 101
Harrisonville, Gloucester, N.J., 150....D2 106
Harrisonville, Fulton, Pa., 30....G5 114
Harriston, Ont., Can., 1,631....D4 72
Harriston, Jefferson, Miss., 300....D2 100
Harrisville, Alcona, Mich., 487....D7 98
Harrisville, Simpson, Miss., 165....D3 100
Harrisville, Cheshire, N.H., 250 (459▲)....E2 105
Harrisville, Lewis, N.Y., 842....A5 108
Harrisville, Harrison, Ohio, 343....B1 123
Harrisville, Butler, Pa., 896....D1 114
Harrisville, Providence, R.I., 1,400....B10 84
Harrisville, Weber, Utah, 600....B4 119
Harrisville, Ritchie, W. Va., 1,428....B3 123
Harrisville, Marquette, Wis., 100....E4 124
Harrisville Heights, Weber, Utah, 250....*B3 119
Harrod, Allen, Ohio, 563....B4 111
Harrods, creek, Ky....A4 94
Harrodsburg, Monroe, Ind., 500....F4 91
Harrodsburg, Mercer, Ky., 6,061....C5 94
Harrogate, Eng., 57,500....D6 10
Harrold, Hughes, S. Dak., 255....C6 116
Harrop, lake, Man., Can....C4 71
Harrow, Ont., Can., 1,787....E2 72
Harrow, Eng., 208,963....C7 12
Harrowby, Man., Can....D1 71
Harrowsmith, Ont., Can., 469....C8 72
Harrys, riv., Newf., Can....D2 75
Harshaw, Santa Cruz, Ariz....F5 80
Harșova, Rom., 4,761....C8 22
Harstad, Nor., 3,900....C7 25
Hart, Oceana, Mich., 1,990....E4 98
Hart, Castro, Tex., 577....B1 118
Hart, co., Ga., 15,229....B4 87
Hart, co., Ky., 14,119....C4 94
Hart, isl., Md....B5 85
Hart, isl., N.Y....B5 106
Hart, lake, Fla....D5 86
Hart, lake, Oreg....E7 113
Hart, mtn., Man., Can....C1 71
Hartell, Alta., Can....D3 69
Hartfield, Middlesex, Va., 200....D6 121
Hartford, Geneva, Ala., 1,956....D4 78
Hartford, Sebastian, Ark., 531....B1 81
Hartford, Hartford, Conn., 162,178 (*810,300)....B6 84
Hartford, Madison, Ill., 2,355....E3 90
Hartford, Warren, Iowa, 271....B7, C4 92
Hartford, Lyon, Kans., 337....D8 93
Hartford, Ohio, Ky., 1,618....C3 94
Hartford, Oxford, Maine, 50 (325▲)....D2 96
Hartford, Van Buren, Mich., 2,305....F4 98
Hartford, Burlington, N.J., 325....D3 106
Hartford, Washington, N.Y., 140....B7 108
Hartford, Minnehaha, S. Dak., 688....D9 116
Hartford, Cocke, Tenn., 100....D10 117
Hartford, Windsor, Vt., 450 (6,355▲)....D4 120
Hartford, Mason, W. Va., 376....C3 123
Hartford, Washington, Wis., 5,627....E1, E5 124
Hartford, co., Conn., 689,555....B5 84
Hartford City, Blackford, Ind., 8,053....D7 91
Hartha, Ger., 8,522....B7 17
Hartington, Cedar, Nebr., 1,648....B8 103
Hartland, N.B., Can., 1,025....C2 74
Hartland (Town of), Hartford, Conn. (1,040▲)....*B5 84
Hartland, Somerset, Maine, 1,016 (1,447▲)....D3 96
Hartland, Livingston, Mich., 200....F7 98
Hartland, Freeborn, Minn., 330....G5 99
Hartland, Ward, N. Dak., 35....A4 110
Hartland, Windsor, Vt., 300 (1,592▲)....D4 120
Harland, Waukesha, Wis., 2,088....E1, E5 124
Hartland, pt., Eng....C3 12
Hartland Four Corners, Windsor, Vt., 125....D4 120
Hartlepool, Eng., 17,674....C6 10
Hartley, O'Brien, Iowa, 1,738....A2 92
Hartley, Rh., 2,900....A5 49
Hartley, Hartley, Tex., 185....B1 118
Hartley, co., Tex., 2,171....B1 118
Hartline, Grant, Wash., 206....B6 122
Hartly, Kent, Del., 164....B6 85
Hartman, Johnson, Ark., 299....B2 81
Hartman, Prowers, Colo., 164....C8 83
Hartney, Man., Can., 592....E1 71
Harts, pond, N.H....C2 105
Hartsburg, Logan, Ill., 300....C4 90
Hartsburg, Boone, Mo., 158....C5 101
Hartsdale, Westchester, N.Y., 11,500....*D7 108
Hartsel, Park, Colo., 30....B5 83
Hartselle, Morgan, Ala., 5,000....A3 78
Hartsfield, Colquitt, Ga., 75....E3 87
Hartshorn, Texas, Mo., 135....D6 101
Hartshorne, Pittsburg, Okla., 1,903....C6 112
Hartsville, Bartholomew, Ind., 399....F6 91
Hartsville, Berkshire, Mass., 60....*B1 97
Hartsville, Darlington, S.C., 6,392....C7 115
Hartsville, Trousdale, Tenn., 1,712....A5 117
Hartuv, Isr....h11 32
Hartville, Stark, Ohio, 1,353....B6 111
Hartville, Wright, Mo., 486....D5 101
Hartville, Platte, Wyo., 177....C8 125
Hartwell, Hart, Ga., 4,599....B4 87
Hartwell, dam, Ga., S.C....B4 87, C2 115
Hartwell, res., Ga., S.C....B3 87, B1 115
Hartwick, Poweshiek, Iowa, 126....C5 92
Hartwick, Otsego, N.Y., 600....C5 108
Harty, Ont., Can., 110....*o17 72
Harut, riv., Afg....E10 41
Harvard, McHenry, Ill., 4,248....A5 90
Harvard, Wayne, Iowa, 150....D4 92
Harvard, Worcester, Mass., 65 (2,563▲)....B4, f9 97
Harvard, Clay, Nebr., 1,261....D7 103
Harvard, mtn., Colo....C4 83
Harvel, Montgomery and Christian, Ill., 285....D4 90
Harvest, Madison, Ala., 300....A3 78
Harvey, N.B., Can., 142....D5 74
Harvey, Cook, Ill., 29,071....B6, F3 90
Harvey, Marion, Iowa, 270....C5 92
Harvey, Jefferson, La., 10,000....C7, E5 95
Harvey, Marquette, Mich., 350....B3 98
Harvey, Wells, N. Dak., 2,365....B6 110
Harvey, co., Kans., 25,865....D6 93
Harvey, creek, Pa....B5 114
Harvey, lake, Pa....A7 114
Harvey, mtn., Mass....B1 97
Harveysburg, Warren, Ohio, 514....C1 111
Harvey Station, N.B., Can., 323....D3 74
Harveyton, Perry, Ky., 300....C6 94
Harveyville, Wabaunsee, Kans., 204....D8 93
Harviell, Butler, Mo., 177....E7 101
Harwich, Eng., 13,569....C9 12
Harwich, Barnstable, Mass., 850 (3,747▲)....C7 97
Harwich Port, Barnstable, Mass., 1,000....C7 97
Harwick, Allegheny, Pa., 1,500....*A6 114
Harwinton, Litchfield, Conn., 700 (3,344▲)....B4 84
Harwood, Ont., Can., 185....C6 72
Harwood, Anne Arundel, Md., 125....C4 85
Harwood, Vernon, Mo., 89....D3 101
Harwood, Cass, N. Dak., 100....C9 110
Harwood Heights, Cook, Ill., 5,688....*B6 90
Harz, mts., Ger....B5 17
Harzgerode, Ger., 6,202....B6 17
Ḥasā, Jordan, 1,000....D7 32
Ḥasa, reg., Sau. Ar....*H4 41
Ḥasan Kiādeh, Iran....C4 41
Hasbrouck Heights, Bergen, N.J., 13,046....h8 106
Hasdo, riv., India....F9 40
Hase, riv., Ger....B3 16
Haselünne, Ger., 5,200....B3 16
Hashimoto, Jap., 16,700....o14 37
Hasi Zegdou, Alg....D4 44
Haskell, Saline, Ark., 215....C3 81
Haskell, Musogee, Okla., 1,887....B6 112
Haskell, Haskell, Tex., 4,016....C3 118
Haskell, co., Kans., 2,990....E3 93
Haskell, co., Okla., 9,121....B6 112
Haskell, co., Tex., 11,174....C3 118
Haskins, Wood, Ohio, 521....A2, A4 111
Haskins, Benton, Oreg....C3 113
Haslach, Aus., 2,565....E9 17
Haslam, Shelby, Tex., 100....D5 118
Hasle, Den., 1,487....C8 24
Haslemere, Eng., 12,528....C7 12
Haslet, Tarrant, Tex., 200....A5 118
Haslett, Ingham, Mich., 1,500....*F6 98
Haslev, Den., 6,155....C6 24
Hassan, India, 32,172....F6 39
Hassayampa, Maricopa, Ariz., 10....D3 80
Hassayampa, creek, Ariz....D3 80
Hassayampa, riv., Ariz....F1 80
Hassell, Martin, N.C., 147....B6 109
Hasselt, Bel., 36,618....D5 15
Hasselt, Neth., 2,800....B6 15
Hassfurt, Ger., 6,800....C5 17
Hassleben, Ger., 624....E7 24
Hässleholm, Swe., 13,500....I5 25
Hassloch, Ger., 15,400....D3 17
Hastings, Ont., Can., 897....C7 72
Hastings, Eng., 66,600....D8 12
Hastings, St. Johns, Fla., 617....C5 86
Hastings, Mills, Iowa, 260....C2 92
Hastings, Barry, Mich., 6,375....F5 98
Hastings, Dakota and Washington, Minn., 8,965....F6, F7 99
Hastings, Adams, Nebr., 21,412....D7 103
Hastings, N.Z., 26,200 (*36,200)....M16 51
Hastings, Barnes, N. Dak., 106....C7 110
Hastings, Jefferson, Okla., 200....C3 112
Hastings, Cambria, Pa., 1,751....E4 114
Hastings, Brazoria, Tex., 350....F5 118
Hastings, Wetzel, W. Va., 175....A6 123
Hastings, co., Ont., Can., 93,377....C7 72
Hastings-on-Hudson, Westchester, N.Y., 8,979....h13 108
Hästveda, Swe., 1,109....B7 24
Hasty, Newton, Ark., 65....A2 81
Hasty, Bent, Colo., 180....C8 83
Haswell, Kiowa, Colo., 169....C7 83
Hatboro, Montgomery, Pa., 7,315....F11 114
Hatch, Dona Ana, N. Mex., 888....E2 107
Hatch, Garfield, Utah, 198....F3 119
Hatch, wash, Utah....E6 119
Hatchechubbee, Russell, Ala., 250....C4 78
Hatchet, creek, Ala....C3 78
Hatchet Lake, N.S., Can., 585....E6 74
Hatchie, riv., Tenn....B2 117
Hatchineha, lake, Fla....D5 86
Hatchville, Barnstable, Mass., 200....C6 97
Hat Creek, Shasta, Calif....B3 82
Hat Creek, Niobrara, Wyo., 5....C8 121
Hateg, Rom., 3,853....C6 22
Hatfield, Polk, Ark., 337....C1 81
Hatfield, Sask., Can., 15....F3 70
Hatfield, Spencer, Ind., 500....I3 91
Hatfield, Hampshire, Mass., 1,400 (2,350▲)....B2 97
Hatfield, Harrison, Mo., 75....A3 101
Hatfield, Montgomery, Pa., 1,941....F11 114
Hatfield, Rh., 8,500....A5 49
Hathaway, Rosebud, Mont., 30....D10 102
Hathaway, Lake, Tenn....A2 117
Hathorn, Marion, Miss....D4 100
Hathorne, Essex, Mass. (part of Danvers)....f12 97
Hathras, India, 64,045....D7 40
Ha Tien, Viet., 5,000....G6 38
Hatillo, P.R., 2,582....B3 65
Hatillo, mun., P.R., 20,238....B3 65
Ha Tinh, Viet., 5,000....C6 38
Hatley, Crisp, Ga., 60....E3 87
Hatley, Marathon, Wis., 306....D4 124
Hato Mayor, Dom. Rep., 5,775....F9 64
Hato Rey, P.R. (part of San Juan)....B6 65
Hato Viejo, P.R....B5 65
Hatta, India, 9,117....E7 40
Hattem, Neth., 5,300....B6 15
Hatteras, Dare, N.C., 700....B8 109
Hatteras, cape, N.C....B8 109
Hatteras, inlet, N.C....B8 109
Hattfjelldal, Nor., 159....E5 25
Hattiesburg, Forrest, Miss., 34,989....D4 100
Hattieville, Conway, Ark., 120....B3 81
Hatton, Lawrence, Ala., 250....A2 78
Hatton, Polk, Ark., 100....C1 81
Hatton, Sask., Can., 40....G1 70
Hatton, Traill, N. Dak., 856....B8 110
Hatton Fields, Monterey, Calif., 2,362....*D3 82
Hatvan, Hung., 19,952....B4 22
Hatzic, B.C., Can., 724....f13 68
Haubourdin, Fr., 12,610....D2 15
Haubstadt, Gibson, Ind., 1,029....H2 91
Haugan, Mineral, Mont., 40....C1 102
Haugen, Barron, Wis., 265....C2 124

48X **HAUG-HERM**

Haugesund, Nor., 27,100...H1 25
Haughton, Bossier, La., 611...B2 95
Haultain, riv., Sask., Can...A2 70
Hauppauge, Suffolk, N.Y., 5,500...*D3 108
Hauraki, gulf, N.Z...L15 51
Hausach, Ger., 3,600...A4 18
Hauser, Coos, Oreg., 250...D2 113
Hauser, dam, Mont...D4 102
Hausstock, mtn., Switz...C7 19
Haut, isl., Maine...D4 96
Haute-Garonne, dept., Fr., 594,633...*F4 14
Haute-Loire, dept., Fr., 211,036...*E5 14
Haute-Marne, dept., Fr., 208,446...B1 18
Hauterive, Que., Can., 5,980...k13 73
Hautes-Alpes, dept., Fr., 85,436...E2 18
Haute-Saône, dept., Fr., 208,440...B2 18
Haute-Savoie, dept., Fr., 329,230...D2 18
Hautes-Pyrénées, dept., Fr., 211,433...*F4 14
Haute-Vienne, dept., Fr., 332,514...*E4 14
Hautmont, Fr., 18,594...B6 14
Haut-Rhin, dept., Fr., 547,920...A3 18
Hauula, Honolulu, Haw., 950...B4, f10 88
Hauzenberg, Ger., 2,700...E8 17
Havana, Hale, Ala., 100...C2 78
Havana, Yell, Ark., 277...B2 81
Havana (La Habana), Cuba, 978,400 (*1,635,000)...D2, h11 64
Havana, Gadsden, Fla., 2,090...B2 86
Havana, Mason, Ill., 4,363...C3 90
Havana, Montgomery, Kans., 162...E8 93
Havana, Sargent, N. Dak., 206...D8 110
Havana, bay, Cuba...h12 64
Havasu, creek, Ariz...A3 80
Havasu, lake, Ariz., Calif...B1 80, E6 82
Havel, riv., Ger...A7 17
Havelberg, Ger., 7,027...F6 24
Havelländischer Grosser Haupt, canal, Ger...F6 24
Havelock, Ont., Can., 1,260...C7 72
Havelock, Pocahontas, Iowa, 289...B3 92
Havelock, Craven, N.C., 2,433...C7 109
Havelock, Hettinger, N. Dak., 50...C3 110
Haven, Reno, Kans., 982...B4 93
Haven, Sheboygan, Wis., 50...B6 124
Havensville, Pottawatomie, Kans., 166...C7 93
Haverford, Delaware and Montgomery, Pa., 5,000...*B11 114
Haverfordwest, Wales, 8,872...C3 12
Haverhill, Eng., 5,446...B8 12
Haverhill, Palm Beach, Fla., 442...*F6 86
Haverhill, Butler, Kans., 25...B6 93
Haverhill, Essex, Mass., 46,346...A5 97
Haverhill, Grafton, N.H., 300 (3,127▲)...B2 105
Haversham, Washington, R.I., 175...D10 84
Haverstraw, Rockland, N.Y., 5,959...D7, m15 108
Havertown (Llanerch), Delaware, Pa., 35,000...B11 114
Haviland, Kiowa, Kans., 725...E4 93
Haviland, Paulding, Ohio, 235...A3 111
Havlickuv Brod, Czech., 14,900...D3 26
Havre, see Le Havre, Fr.
Havre, Hill, Mont., 10,740...B7 102
Havre-Aubert, Que., Can., 494...B8 74
Havre-Boucher, N.S., Can., 504...D8 74
Havre de Grace, Harford, Md., 8,510...A5 85
Havre St. Pierre, Que., Can., 2,407...h9 75
Havza, Tur., 4,539...B10 31
Haw, riv., N.C...B4 109
Hawaii, co., Haw., 61,332...D6 82
Hawaii, state, U.S., 632,772...F7 76, 88
Hawaiian Gardens, Los Angeles, Calif., 15,000...*F4 82
Hawarden, Sask., Can., 268...F2 70
Hawarden, Sioux, Iowa, 2,544...A1 92
Hawdon, lake, Austl...H2 51
Hawea, lake, N.Z...P12 51
Hawera, N.Z., 7,542...M15 51
Hawes, Garland, Ark., 100...C5 81
Hawes, Eng., 1,196...F6 13
Hawesville, Hancock, Ky., 882...C3 94
Hawes Water, lake, Eng...F6 13
Hawi, Hawaii, Haw., 800...C6 88
Hawick, Scot., 16,204...E6 13
Hawke, bay, N.Z...M16 51
Hawke, isl., Newf., Can...B4 75
Hawke, riv., Newf., Can...B3 75
Hawker, Austl., 368...E2 51
Hawkes, mtn., Ant...A8 5
Hawkesbury, Ont., Can., 8,661...B10 72
Hawkesbury, isl., B.C., Can...C3 68
Hawkestone, Ont., Can., 202...C5 72
Hawkeye, Fayette, Iowa, 516...B6 92
Hawkins, Bannock, Idaho...G6 89
Hawkins, Rusk, Wis., 402...C3 124
Hawkins, co., Tenn., 30,468...C10 117
Hawkinsville, Pulaski, Ga., 3,967...D3 87
Hawk Point, Lincoln, Mo., 270...C6 101
Hawk Run, Clearfield, Pa., 850...E3 114
Hawksbill, mtn., Va...C4 121
Hawkshaw, N.B., Can., 67...*D2 74
Hawley, Franklin, Mass., 70 (251▲)...*A2 97
Hawley, Clay, Minn., 1,270...D2 99
Hawley, Wayne, Pa., 1,433...D11 114
Hawley, Jones, Tex., 200...C3 118
Hawleyville, Fairfield, Conn., 300...D3 84
Haworth, Bergen, N.J., 3,215...h9 106
Haworth, McCurtain, Okla., 351...D7 112
Haw River, Alamance, N.C., 1,410...A4 109
Hawsh 'Isá, Eg. U.A.R., 1,000...D2 32
Hawthorn, Washington, Ala., 35...D1 78
Hawthorn, Clarion, Pa., 612...D3 114
Hawthorne, Los Angeles, Calif., 33,035...F2 82
Hawthorne, Alachua, Fla., 1,167...C4 86
Hawthorne, Mineral, Nev., 2,838...E3 104
Hawthorne, Passaic, N.J., 17,735...B4 106
Hawthorne, Westchester, N.Y., 5,000...g13 108
Haxby, Garfield, Mont...C10 102
Haxtun, Phillips, Colo., 990...A8 83
Hay, Austl., 3,133...G5 51
Hay, Wales, 1,321...B4 12
Hay, Whitman, Wash., 75...C8 122
Hay, isl., Ont., Can...C4 72
Hay, riv., Austl...D6 50
Hay, riv., Can...E9 66
Hayange, Fr., 11,009...C7 14
Hayden, Blount, Ala., 187...B3 78
Hayden, Gila, Ariz., 1,760...E5 80
Hayden, Routt, Colo., 764...A3 83
Hayden, Jennings, Ind., 275...G6 91
Hayden, Union, N. Mex., 10...B6 107
Hayden, lake, Idaho...B2 89
Hayden, lake, Maine...D3 96
Haydenburg, Jackson, Tenn., 50...C8 117
Hayden Junction, Pinal, Ariz., 55...E5 80
Hayden Lake, Kootenai, Idaho, 247...B2 89
Hayden Rowe, Middlesex, Mass., 200...h9 97
Haydens, Hartford, Conn., 100...B6 84
Haydenville, Hampshire, Mass., 750...B2 97
Haydenville, Hocking, Ohio, 800...C3 111
Hayes, Calcasieu, La., 800...D3 95
Hayes, Stanley, S. Dak., 21...C4 116
Hayes, co., Nebr., 1,919...D4 103
Hayes, mtn., Alsk...C10 79
Hayes, riv., Man., Can...B5 71
Hayes Center, Hayes, Nebr., 283...D4 103
Hayesville, Clay, N.C., 428...D2 109
Hayesville, Ashland, Ohio, 435...B5 111
Hayesville, Marion, Oregon, 4,568...*C4 113
Hayfield, Man., Can...E1 71
Hayfield, Hancock, Iowa, 150...A4 92
Hayfield, Dodge, Minn., 889...G6 99
Hayfield, Frederick, Va., 150...B4 121
Hayford, Spokane, Wash., 350...D7 122
Hayfork, Trinity, Calif., 400...B2 82
Hay Lakes, Alta., Can., 233...C4 69
Haylow, Echols, Ga., 100...F4 87
Haymana, Tur., 2,791...C9 31
Haymarket, Prince William, Va., 257...B4, C5 121
Haymock, lake, Maine...B3 96
Haymond, Franklin, Ind., 120...F7 91
Haymond, Brewster, Tex...D1 118
Haynau, see Chojnow, Pol.
Haynes, Lee, Ark., 200...C5 81
Haynes, Alta., Can...C4 69
Haynes, Sampson, N.C...B5 103
Haynes, Adams, N. Dak., 111...D3 110
Haynesville, Claiborne, La., 3,031...B2 95
Haynesville, Aroostook, Maine, 100 (187▲)...C5 96
Haynesville, Lowndes, Ala., 900...C3 78
Hay River, N.W. Ter., Can., 1,338...D9 66
Hays, Ellis, Kans., 11,947...D4 93
Hays, Blaine, Mont., 600...C8 102
Hays, Wilkes, N.C., 200...A2 109
Hays, co., Tex., 19,934...D3 118
Haysi, Dickenson, Va., 485...B2 122
Hay Springs, Sheridan, Nebr., 823...B3 103
Haystack, mtn., Okla...B2 112
Haystack, peak, Utah...D2 119
Haysville, Dubois, Ind., 500...H4 91
Haysville, Sedgwick, Kans., 5,836...B5 93
Haysville, Macon, Tenn., 100...C7 117
Hayter, Alta., Can., 50...C5 69
Hayti, Pemiscot, Mo., 3,737...E8 101
Hayti, Hamlin, S. Dak., 425...C8 116
Hayton, Calumet, Wis., 95...B6 124
Hayward, Alameda, Calif., 72,700...B5 82
Hayward, Freedom, Minn., 258...G5 99
Hayward, Garfield, Okla., 40...A4 112
Hayward, Sawyer, Wis., 1,540...B2 124
Haywood, Man., Can., 146...E2 71
Haywood, Chatham, N.C., 713...B4 109
Haywood, co., N.C., 39,711...D3 109
Haywood, co., Tenn., 23,393...B2 117
Hazard, Perry, Ky., 5,958...C6 94
Hazard, Sherman, Nebr., 104...C6 103
Hazardville, Hartford, Conn., 4,000...B6 84
Hazaribagh, India, 40,958...E10 40
Hazaribagh, range, India...F9 40
Hazebrouck, Fr., 17,446...B5 14
Hazel, Calloway, Ky., 342...B3 94
Hazel, Hamlin, S. Dak., 128...C8 116
Hazel Crest, Cook, Ill., 6,205...F3 90
Hazel Dell, Cumberland, Ill., 130...D5 90
Hazel Dell, Clark, Washington, 2,500...*D3 122
Hazel Green, Madison, Ala., 125...A3 78
Hazel Green, Wolfe, Ky., 259...C6 94
Hazel Green, Grant, Wis., 807...F3 124
Hazel Hurst, McKean, Pa., 500...C4 114
Hazelhurst, Oneida, Wis., 225...C4 124
Hazel Park, Oakland, Mich., 25,631...F7 98
Hazelridge, Man., Can., 70...*E3 71
Hazel Run, Yellow Medicine, Minn., 115...F3 99
Hazelton, B.C., Can., 410...B4 68
Hazelton, Jerome, Idaho, 433...G4 89
Hazelton, Barber, Kans., 246...E5 93
Hazelton, Emmons, N. Dak., 451...C5 111
Hazelton, peak, Wyo...A5 125
Hazelwood, St. Louis, Mo., 6,045...*C7 101
Hazelwood, Haywood, N.C., 1,925...D3 109
Hazelwood, King, Wash...D2 122
Hazen, Prairie, Ark., 1,456...C4 81
Hazen, Churchill, Nev., 50...D2 104
Hazen, Mercer, N. Dak., 1,222...B4 110
Hazen, bay, Alsk...C6 79
Hazen, strait, N.W. Ter., Can...m29 67
Hazenmore, Sask., Can., 149...H2 70
Hazlehurst, Jeff Davis, Ga., 3,699...E4 87
Hazlehurst, Copiah, Miss., 3,400...D3 100
Hazle Patch, Laurel, Ky., 200...C5 94
Hazlet, Sask., Can., 202...G1 70
Hazlet, Monmouth, N.J., 12,400...C4 106
Hazleton, Gibson, Ind., 507...H2 91
Hazleton, Buchanan, Iowa, 665...B6 92
Hazleton, Luzerne, Pa., 32,056...E10 114
Hazor, Isr., 423...h9 32
Hazy, Raleigh, W. Va...D6 123
Head Bay D'Espoir, Newf., Can., 413...E4 75
Headford, Ire., 567...D2 11
Head Harbor, isl. Maine...D5 96
Headland, Henry, Ala., 2,650...D4 78
Headley, mtn., Mont...C1 102
Headlight, Clinch, Ga., 6...F4 87
Head of Island, Livingston, La., 150...B6 95
Headquarters, Clearwater, Idaho, 300...C3 89
Headrick, Jackson, Okla., 152...C2 112
Heads, cape, Oreg...E2 113
Heafford Junction, Lincoln, Wis., 100...C4 124
Healdsburg, Sonoma, Calif., 4,816...A4, C2 82
Healdton, Carter, Okla., 2,898...C4 112
Healdville, Rutland, Vt., 60...E3 120
Healing Springs, Bath, Va., 200...D3 121
Healy, Lane, Kans., 228...D3 93
Healy Fork, Alsk., 20...C10 79
Heanza, isl., Okinawa...52
Heard, co., Ga., 5,333...C1 87
Heard, isl., Indian O...J1 2
Heardmont, Elbert, Ga., 175...B4 87
Hearne, Sask., Can., 53...G3 70
Hearne, Robertson, Tex., 5,072...D4 118
Hearst, Ont., Can., 2,373...o19 72
Hearst, isl., Ant...C6 5
Heart, lake, Alta., Can...B5 69
Heart, lake, Wyo...A2 125
Heart, riv., Alta., Can...B2 69
Heart, riv., N. Dak...C4 110
Heart Butte, Pondera, Mont., 250...B4 102
Hearts Content, Newf., Can., 607...E5 75
Heart's Delight, Newf., Can., 631...*E5 75
Heartstone, mtn., Md...A2 85
Heartwell, Kearney, Nebr., 113...D7 103
Heartwellville, Bennington, Vt., 50...F2 120
Heaters, Braxton, W. Va., 90...C4 123
Heath, Franklin, Mass., 45 (304▲)...A2 97
Heath, Fergus, Mont...D7 102
Heath, Licking, Ohio, 2,426...*B5 111
Heatherton, N.S., Can., 236...D8 74
Heath Springs, Lancaster, S.C., 832...B6 115
Heath Steele, N.B., Can...B3 74
Heathsville, Northumberland, Va., 225...D6 121
Heaton, Avery, N.C., 250...A2, C4 109
Heaton, Wells, N. Dak., 100...B6 110
Heavener, LeFlore, Okla., 1,891...C7 112
Hebardville, Ware, Ga., 2,758...E4 87
Hebbronville, Jim Hogg, Tex., 3,987...F3 118
Hebel, Austl., 81...D6 51
Heber, Navajo, Ariz., 400...C5 80
Heber, Wasatch, Utah, 2,936...C4 119
Heber Springs, Cleburne, Ark., 2,265...B3 81
Hebert, Caldwell, La., 70...B3 95
Hébertville, Que., Can., 1,604...A6 73
Hebertville Station, Que., Can., 1,257...*A6 73
Hebgen, lake, Mont...F5 102
Hebo, Tillamook, Oreg., 200...B3 113
Hebrides, is., Scot...D15 4
Hebrides, sea, Scot...C2 13
Hebron, Newf., Can., 189...f9 75
Hebron, N.S., Can., 449...F3 74
Hebron, Tolland, Conn., 250 (1,819▲)...C7 84
Hebron, McHenry, Ill., 701...A5 90
Hebron, Porter, Ind., 1,401...B3 91
Hebron, see Al Khalil, Jordan
Hebron, Boone, Ky., 300...A7 94
Hebron, Wicomico, Md., 754...D6 85
Hebron, Thayer, Nebr., 1,920...D8 103
Hebron, Grafton, N.H., 30 (153▲)...C3 105
Hebron, Morton, N. Dak., 1,340...C3 110
Hebron, Licking, Ohio, 1,260...C5 111
Hebron, Denton, Tex., 80...A5 118
Hebron, Dinwiddie, Va., 20...D5 121
Hebron, Pleasants, W. Va., 100...B3 123
Heby, Swe., 2,151...t34 25
Hecate, strait, B.C., Can...C2 68
Hecelchakán, Mex., 3,399...C6 63
Hechingen, Ger., 9,600...D4 16
Hechtel, Bel., 4,016...C5 15
Hecker, Monroe, Ill., 313...E3 90
Hecklingen, Ger., 6,845...B6 17
Hecla, Hooker, Nebr., 4...B4 103
Hecla, Brown, S. Dak., 444...B7 116
Hecla, Man., Can., 66...D3 71
Hecla, isl., Man., Can...D3 71
Hectanooga, N.S., Can., 120...E3 74
Hector, Pope, Ark., 200...B3 81
Hector, Renville, Minn., 1,297...F4 99
Hede, Swe., 385...F5 25
Hedemora, Swe., 6,000...G6 25
Hedensö, Swe...t34 25
Hedensted, Den., 1,717...C3 24
He Devil, mtn., Idaho...D2 89
Hedgehog, hill, Conn...B8 84
Hedgesville, Wheatland, Mont., 10...D7 102
Hedgesville, Berkeley, W. Va., 342...B7 123
Hedley, B.C., Can., 425...E7 68
Hedley, Donley, Tex., 494...B2 118
Hedmark, co., Nor., 177,200...*G4 25
Hedo, Okinawa...52
Hedo, pt., Okinawa...52
Hedon, Eng., 2,238...A7 12
Hedrick, Warren, Ind., 60...D2 91
Hedrick, Keokuk, Iowa, 762...C5 92
Hedwig Village, Harris, Tex., 1,182...*E5 118
Heek, Ger., 3,500...A2 17
Heel, pt., Wake Isl...52
Heeney, Summit, Colo...B4 83
Heerde, Neth., 2,232...B6 15
Heerenveen, Neth., 8,400 (25,900▲)...B5 15
Heerlen, Neth., 75,300 (*252,000)...D5 15
Heessen, Ger., 17,100...B2 17
Heflin, Cleburne, Ala., 2,400...B4 78
Heflin, Webster, La., 289...B2 95
Hegeler, Vermilion, Ill., 1,640...*C6 90
Hegins, Schuylkill, Pa., 800...E9 114
Heglar, Cassia, Idaho...G5 89
Heiberger, Perry, Ala., 50...C2 78
Heide, Ger., 20,000...A4 16
Heidelberg, Ger., 125,600...D4 16
Heidelberg, Jasper, Miss., 1,049...D5 100
Heidelberg, Allegheny, Pa., 2,118...*F1 114
Heidelberg, S. Afr., 9,292...D3 49
Heiden, Switz., 3,158...B9 19
Heidenau, Ger., 19,400...C8 17
Heidenheim, Ger., 50,000...E5 17
Heil, Grant, N. Dak., 100...C4 110
Heilbron, S. Afr., 7,182...C4 49
Heilbronn, Ger., 92,800 (*128,000)...D4 17
Heiligenblut, Aus., 1,195...B8 18
Heiligenhafen, Ger., 8,900...D4 24
Heiligenstadt, Ger., 12,500...B5 17
Heilsberg, see Lidzbark Warminski, Pol.
Heilungkiang, prov., China, 14,860,000...B10 34
Heilwood, Indiana, Pa., 600...E4 114
Heimbach, Ger., 2,000...D6 15
Heimdal, Wells, N. Dak., 130...B6 110
Heinola, Fin., 11,000...G12 25
Heinsberg, Ger., 4,700...C6 15
Heinsburg, Alta., Can., 135...C5 69
Heiskell, Knox, Tenn., 175...E11 117
Heisler, Alta., Can., 214...C4 69
Heislerville, Cumberland, N.J., 600...E3 106
Heizer, Barton, Kans., 90...D5 93
Hejaz, pol. div., Sau. Ar., 2,000,000...D7 43
Hekla, peak, Ice...n23 25
Hekura, isl., Jap...H8 37
Hel, Pol., 1,400...A5 26
Helagsfjaelet, mtn., Swe...F5 25
Helbra, Ger., 9,500...B6 17
Heldt, Goshen, Wyo...D8 125
Helena, Shelby, Ala., 523...B3 78
Helena, Phillips, Ark., 11,500...C5 81
Helena, Telfair, Ga., 1,290...D4 87
Helena, Jackson, Miss...E3 100
Helena, Andrew, Mo., 166...B3 101
Helena, Lewis and Clark, Mont., 20,227...D4 102
Helena, St. Lawrence, N.Y., 350...f10 108
Helena, Sandusky, Ohio, 281...A4 111
Helena, Alfalfa, Okla., 580...A3 112
Helena, Newberry, S.C., 497...C4 115
Helensburgh, Scot., 9,605...D4 13
Helenwood, Scott, Tenn., 300...C9 117
Helgasjön, lake, Swe...B8 24
Helgean, riv., Swe...B8 24
Helgeroa, Nor., 331...p28 25
Helgoland, bay, Ger...D2 24
Helgoland, isl., Ger...D1 24
Helix, Umatilla, Oreg., 148...B8 113
Hellam, York, Pa., 1,234...G8 114
Hellam, peak, B.C., Can...C1 69
Hellenthal, Ger., 4,900...D6 15
Hellertown, Northampton, Pa., 6,716...E11 114
Hellier, Pike, Ky., 104...C7 94
Hellín, Sp., 12,900...C5 20
Hellville, Malag., 9,321...f9 49
Helm, Fresno, Calif., 125...D3 82
Helm, Washington, Miss...B3 100
Helmand, riv., Afg...F12 41
Helmbrechts, Ger., 8,300...C6 17
Helmer, Latah, Idaho, 30...C2 89
Helmer, Steuben, Ind., 110...A7 91
Helmeringhausen, S.W. Afr...C2 49
Helmetta, Middlesex, N.J., 779...C4 106
Helmond, Neth., 44,600...C5 15
Helmsburg, Brown, Ind., 180...F5 91
Helmsdale, Scot...B5 13
Helmsdale, riv., Scot...B5 13
Helmsley, Eng., 1,292...F7 13
Helmstedt, Ger., 29,600...A5 17
Helmville, Powell, Mont., 75...D4 102
Helnaes, isl., Den...C3 24
Heloise, Dyer, Tenn...A2 117
Helotes, Bexar, Tex., 300...E3 118
Helper, Carbon, Utah, 2,459...D5 119
Helsingfors, see Helsinki, Fin.
Helsingør, Den., 26,658 (*32,636)...B6 24
Helsinki, Fin., 476,400 (*635,000)...G11 25
Helston, Eng., 7,085...D1 12
Heltonville, Lawrence, Ind., 400...G5 91
Helvecia, Arg., 3,390...A4 54
Helvetia Mines, Clearfield, Pa., 160...D4 114
Helvick, head, Ire...E4 11
Hemaruka, Alta., Can...D5 69
Hematite, Jefferson, Mo., 204...C7 101
Hemau, Ger., 2,600...D6 17
Hemel Hempstead, Eng., 60,500...C7 12
Hemet, Riverside, Calif., 5,416...F4, F5 82
Hemet East, Riverside, Calif., 1,936...*F5 82
Hemford, N.S., Can., 248...E5 74
Hemingford, Box Butte, Nebr., 904...B2 103
Hemingway, Williamsburg, S.C., 951...D1 115
Hemlock, Howard, Ind...D5 91
Hemlock, Saginaw, Mich., 900...E6 98
Hemlock, Livingston, N.Y., 400...C3 108
Hemlock, Ashe, N.C...A2 109
Hemlock (Eureka), Chester, S.C., 1,423...B5 115
Hemlock, res., Conn...E3 84
Hemmingford, Que., Can., 778...D4 73
Hemnesberget, Nor., 1,212...D5 25
Hemp, Fannin, Ga., 40...B2 87
Hemphill, Sabine, Tex., 913...D6 118
Hemphill, co., Tex., 3,185...B2 118
Hemple, Clinton, Mo., 100...B3 101
Hempstead, Nassau, N.Y., 34,641...k13 108
Hempstead, Waller, Tex., 1,505...D4 118
Hempstead, co., Ark., 19,661...D2 81
Hempstead, hbr., N.Y...F2 84
Henager, De Kalb, Ala., 300...A4 78
Henares, riv., Sp...B4 20
Henau, Switz., 7,828...B7 19
Hendaye, Fr., 7,204...F3 14
Hendek, Tur., 9,900...B8 31
Henderson, Pike, Ala., 60...D3 78
Henderson, Arg., 3,928...B4 54
Henderson, Adams, Colo., 280...B6 83
Henderson, Mills, Iowa, 191...C2 92
Henderson, Henderson, Ky., 16,892...C2 94
Henderson, Caroline, Md., 129...B6 85
Henderson, Shiawassee, Mich., 250...E6 98
Henderson, Sibley, Minn., 728...F5 99
Henderson, York, Nebr., 730...D8 103
Henderson, Clark, Nev., 12,525...H7 104
Henderson, Jefferson, N.Y., 257...B4 108
Henderson, Vance, N.C., 12,740...A5 109
Henderson, Chester, Tenn., 2,691...B3 117
Henderson, Rusk, Tex., 9,666...C5 118
Henderson, Mason, W. Va., 601...C2 123
Henderson, co., Ky., 33,519...C2 94
Henderson, co., Ill., 8,237...C3 90
Henderson, co., N.C., 36,163...f10 109
Henderson, co., Tenn., 16,115...B3 117
Henderson, co., Tex., 21,786...C5 118
Henderson, pt., Miss...E2 100
Hendersonville, Henderson, N.C., 5,911...D3 109
Hendersonville, Colleton, S.C., 200...F6 115
Hendersonville, Sumner, Tenn., 950...A5, E9 117
Hendon, Sask., Can., 111...E4 70
Hendon, Eng., 151,500...k12 10, C7 12
Hendon, Bledsoe, Tenn...D8 117
Hendricks, Lincoln, Minn., 797...F2 99
Hendricks, Wilkes, N.C...A2 109
Hendricks, co., Ind., 40,896...E4 91
Hendrum, Norman, Minn., 305...C2 99
Hendry, co., Fla., 8,119...F5 86
Henefer, Summit, Utah, 408...C4 119
Hengchun, Taiwan, 5,000...*G9 34
Hengelo, Neth., 64,800...B6 15
Henghsien, China, 18,000...G6 36
Hengshan, China...F3 36
Hengshan, China...K5 36
Hengyang, China, 235,000...K5 36
Hénin-Liétard, Fr., 25,527...D2 15
Henley Harbour, Newf., Can., 80...B4 75
Henley-on-Thames, Eng., 9,131...C7 12
Henlopen, cape, Del...C7 85
Hennebont, Fr., 7,623...D2 14
Hennef, Ger., 13,200...C2 17
Hennepin, Putnam, Ill., 391...B4 90
Hennepin, Garvin, Okla., 325...C4 112
Hennepin, co., Minn., 842,854...E5 99
Hennessey, Kingfisher, Okla., 1,228...A4 112
Henniker, Merrimack, N.H., 850 (1,636▲)...D3 105
Henning, Vermilion, Ill., 271...C6 90
Henning, Otter Trail, Minn., 980...D3 99
Henning, Lauderdale, Tenn., 466...B2 117
Henribourg, Sask., Can., 73...D3 70
Henrico, co., Va., 117,339...D5 121
Henrietta, Ray, Mo., 497...B4 101
Henrietta, Monroe, N.Y., 7,500...B3 108
Henrietta, Rutherford, N.C., 950...B2, D4 109
Henrietta, Clay, Tex., 3,062...C3 118
Henrietta, isl., Sov. Un...B35 4
Henrietta Maria, cape, Ont., Can...n19 72
Henrieville, Garfield, Utah, 152...F4 119
Henrique de Carvalho, Ang...C3 48
Henry, Marshall, Ill., 2,278...B4 90
Henry, Scotts Bluff, Nebr., 138...C1 103
Henry, Elko, Nev., 8...B7 104
Henry, Codington, S. Dak., 276...C8 116
Henry, Henry, Tenn., 178...A3 117
Henry, Franklin, Va., 125...E3 121
Henry, Grant, W. Va...B5 123
Henry, co., Ala., 75,286...D4 78
Henry, co., Ga., 17,619...C2 87
Henry, co., Ill., 49,317...B3 90
Henry, co., Ind., 48,899...E7 91
Henry, co., Iowa, 18,187...C6 92
Henry, co., Ky., 10,987...B4 94
Henry, co., Mo., 19,226...C4 101
Henry, co., Ohio, 25,392...A3 111
Henry, co., Tenn., 22,275...A3 117
Henry, co., Va., 40,335...E3 121
Henry, mtn., Mont...B1 102
Henry, mts., Utah...E5 119
Henryetta, Okmulgee, Okla., 7,987...B6 112
Henry Kater, cape, N.W. Ter., Can...C19 67
Henrys, fork, Utah, Wyo...B5 119
Henryville, Que., Can., 711...D4 73
Henryville, Clark, Ind., 400...G6 91
Henryville, Nicholas, Ky., 125...B5 94
Hensall, Ont., Can., 926...D3 72
Hensel (Canton), Pembina, N. Dak., 130...A8 110
Henshaw, Union, Ky., 200...C1 94
Hensler, Oliver, N. Dak., 35...B4 110
Hensley, Pulaski, Ark., 350...C3 81
Henson, creek, Md...C1 85
Henteyn Nuruu, mts., Mong...B6 34
Henzada, Bur., 61,972...E10 39
Hepburn, Sask., Can., 294...E2 70
Hepburn, Page, Iowa, 49...D2 92
Hepburn, Hardin, Ohio, 175...B4 111
Hephzibah, Richmond, Ga., 676...C4 87
Hepler, Crawford, Kans., 178...E9 93
Heppenheim, Ger., 13,900...D3 17
Heppner, Morrow, Oreg., 1,661...B7 113
Hepworth, Ont., Can., 358...C3 72
Herald, isl., Sov. Un...B32 4
Herat, Afg., 100,000...D11 41
Hérault, dept., Fr., 516,658...*F5 14
Herbert, Sask., Can., 1,008...G2 70
Herbert, peak, N.Z...O14 51
Herbertingen, Ger., 2,000...A5 18
Herbesthal (Lontzen), Bel., 2,353...D5 15
Herb Lake, Man., Can., 40...B2 71
Herblay, Fr., 10,220...g9 14
Herblet, lake, Man., Can...B2 71
Herborn, Ger., 10,100...C3 17
Hercegnovi, Yugo., 2,536...D4 22
Hercegovina, reg., Yugo...D4 22
Herchen, Ger., 4,800...C2 17
Herculaneum, Jefferson, Mo., 1,767...B8, C7 101
Herd, Osage, Okla., 100...A5 112
Herdecke, Ger., 17,300...B2 17
Heredia, C.R., 19,000...E5 62
Heredia, prov., C.R., 77,300...*F5 62
Hereford, Cochise, Ariz., 150...F5 80
Hereford, Weld, Colo., 50...A6 83
Hereford, Eng., 42,400...B5 12
Hereford, Baltimore, Md., 380...A4 85
Hereford, Baker, Oreg., 35...C8 113
Hereford, Deaf Smith, Tex., 7,652...B1 118
Hereford, co., Eng., 130,919...B5 12
Hérémence, Switz., 1,868...D3 19
Herencia, Sp., 8,606...C4 20
Herendeen Bay, Alsk., 22...D7 79
Herentals, Bel., 17,451...C4 15
Herford, Ger., 55,600 (*91,000)...A3 17
Herfølge, Den., 1,138...C6 24
Héricourt, Fr., 7,160...B2 18
Herington, Dickinson, Kans., 3,702...D7 93
Heriot, Lee., S.C., 105...C7 115
Herisau, Switz., 14,361...B7 19
Heritage, range, Ant...B4 5
Herkimer, Marshall, Kans., 110...C7 39
Herkimer, Herkimer, N.Y., 9,396...B6 108
Herkimer, co., N.Y., 66,370...B5 108
Herman, Baraga, Mich., 55...B2 98
Herman, Grant, Minn., 764...E2 99
Herman, Washington, Nebr., 335...C9 103
Hermann, Gasconade, Mo., 2,536...C6 101
Hermano, peak, Colo...D2 83
Hermanos, is., Ven...A5 60
Hermansville, Menominee, Mich., 750...C3 98
Hermantown, St. Louis, Minn., 1,000...D6 99
Hermanville, Claiborne, Miss., 200...D3 100
Hermel, Leb...E11 31
Hermeskeil, Ger., 4,500...D1 17
Herminia, Central, P.R...C5 65
Herminie, Westmoreland, Pa., 1,571...F2 114
Hermiston, Umatilla, Oreg., 4,402...B7 113
Hermit, is., N. Gui...h12 50
Hermitage, Bradley, Ark., 379...D3 81
Hermitage, Newf., Can., 417...E4 75

Hermitage, Point Coupee, La., 75....D4 95
Hermitage, Hickory, Mo., 328....D4 101
Hermitage, Davidson, Tenn., 100....E9 117
Hermitage, Vir. Is....f16 65
Hermitage, bay, Newf., Can....E3 75
Hermitage Springs, Clay, Tenn., 150....C8 117
Hermleigh, Scurry, Tex., 650....C2 118
Hermon, St. Lawrence, N.Y., 612....f9 108
Hermosa, Custer, S. Dak., 126....D2 116
Hermosa Beach, Los Angeles, Calif., 16,115....F2 82
Hermosillo, Mex., 95,978....B2 63
Hernad, riv., Hung....A5 22
Hernandaries, Par....E5 55
Hernandez, Rio Arriba, N. Mex., 250....A3 107
Hernando, Citrus, Fla., 301..D4 86
Hernando, De Soto, Miss., 1,898....A4 100
Hernando, co., Fla., 11,205..D4 86
Herndon, Jenkins, Ga., 50..D4 87
Herndon, Guthrie, Iowa, 125....C3 92
Herndon, Rawlins, Kans., 339....C3 93
Herndon, Christian, Ky., 150....D2 94
Herndon, Northumberland, Pa., 622....E8 114
Herndon, Fairfax, Va., 1,960....A4, C5 121
Herndon, Wyoming, W. Va., 200....D3 123
Herne, Ger., 110,500....B2 17
Herning, Den., 24,790....B2 24
Herod, Terrell, Ga., 100....E2 87
Herod, pt., N.Y....F5 84
Heron, Sanders, Mont., 25..B1 102
Heron Bay, Ont., Can., 167.E8 72
Heron Lake, Jackson, Minn., 852....G3 99
Hérouxville, Que., Can., 591.C5 73
Herreid, Campbell, S. Dak., 767....B5 110
Herrenberg, Ger., 8,800....E3 17
Herrick, Shelby, Ill., 440....D5 90
Herrick, Gregory, S. Dak., 160....D6 116
Herrick Center, Susquehanna, Pa., 80....C10 114
Herrick, creek, B.C., Can....B7 68
Herrick, mtn., Vt....D2 120
Herriman, Salt Lake, Utah, 300....*C3 119
Herrin, Williamson, Ill., 9,474....F4 90
Herring, Roger Mills, Okla..B2 112
Herring, bay, Md....C4 85
Herring, run, Md....C2 85
Herring Cove, N.S., Can., 1,368....E6 74
Herrington, LaCross, Wis., 2,405....*E2 124
Herrington, lake, Ky....C5 94
Hersbruck, Ger., 8,300....D6 17
Herschel, Sask., Can., 188..F1 70
Herscher, Kankakee, Ill., 658....B5 90
Hersey, Osceola, Mich., 246..E5 98
Hershey, Lincoln, Nebr., 504.C5 103
Hershey, Dauphin, Pa., 6,851....F8 114
Herstal, Bel., 29,606....D5 15
Herten, Ger., 52,400....*C7 15
Hertford, Eng., 15,734....C7 12
Hertford, Perquimans, N.C., 2,068....A7 109
Hertford, co., Eng., 832,088.C7 12
Hertford, co., N.C., 22,718..A6 109
Hervás, Sp., 4,352....B3 20
Hervey, bay, Austl....B9 51
Hervey Junction, Que., Can., 342....C5 73
Herxheim, Ger., 6,700....D3 17
Herzberg, Ger., 11,100....B5 17
Herzberg, Ger., 6,635....B8 17
Herzberg, Ger., 1,275....F6 24
Herzliya, Isr., 26,809..B6, g10 32
Hezogenaurach, Ger., 9,900.D5 17
Herzogenbuchsee, Switz., 4,641....B4 19
Hesdin, Fr., 3,200....D10 12
Hesel, Ger., 2,100....A7 15
Heshikiya, Okinawa....52
Hespeler, Ont., Can., 4,519.D4 72
Hesper, Benson, N. Dak., 25.B6 110
Hesperia, San Bernardino, Calif., 950....E5 82
Hesperia, Newaygo and Oceana, Mich., 822....E4 98
Hesperus, La Plata, Colo., 47....D2 83
Hesperus, peak, Colo....D2 83
Hesse, reg., Ger....C4 16
Hessel, Mackinac, Mich., 240....B6 98
Hesselager, Den....C4 24
Hesselø, isl., Den....B5 24
Hessen, state, Ger., 5,082,000 C3 17
Hessmer, Avoyelles, La., 433.C3 95
Hesston, Harvey, Kans., 1,103....A5, D6 93
Hester, Granville, N.C....A5 109
Hetland, Kingsbury, S. Dak., 107....C8 116
Hetona, Okinawa....52
Hettick, Macoupin, Ill., 253..D3 90
Hettinger, Adams, N. Dak., 1,769....C3 110
Hettinger, co., N. Dak., 6,317....C3 110
Hettstedt, Ger., 17,000....B6 17
Heuvelton, St. Lawrence, N.Y., 810....f9 108
Heves, Hung., 9,923....B5 22
Heves, co., Hung., 348,756..*B5 22
Heward, Sask., Can., 136..H4 70
Hewins, Chautauqua, Kans., 110....E7 93
Hewitt, Todd, Minn., 267..D3 99
Hewitt, Passaic, N.J., 750..A4 106
Hewitt, Wood, Wis., 150..D3 124
Hewlett, Nassau, N.Y., 7,500....*G2 84
Hexham, Eng., 9,897....F6 13
Hext, Menard, Tex., 40....D3 118
Heyburn, Minidoka, Idaho, 829....G5 89
Heyworth, McLean, Ill., 1,196....C5 90
Hialeah, Dade, Fla., 66,972....G6, F3 86
Hialeah Gardens, Dade, Fla., 172....*G6 86
Hiattville, Bourbon, Kans., 125....E9 93
Hiawassee, Towns, Ga., 455.B3 87
Hiawatha, Linn, Iowa, 1,336....*C6 92
Hiawatha, Brown, Kans., 3,391....C8 93
Hiawatha, Schoolcraft, Mich.B4 98
Hiawatha, Carbon and Emery, Utah, 439....D5 119
Hibbard, Navajo, Ariz....C5 80
Hibbard, Madison, Idaho....f7 89
Hibbard, Marshall, Ind., 150.B5 91
Hibbing, St. Louis, Minn., 17,731....C6 99
Hibernia, Morris, N.J., 250..B4 106
Hickiwan, Pima, Ariz., 100..E3 80
Hickman, Kent, Del., 100..C6 85
Hickman, Fulton, Ky., 1,537....B2 94
Hickman, Lancaster, Nebr., 288....D9 103
Hickman, co., Ky., 6,747....B2 94
Hickman, co., Tenn., 11,862....B4 117
Hickman's Harbour, Newf., Can., 419....D5 75
Hickok, Grant, Kans., 45....E2 93
Hickory, Graves, Ky., 170..B2 94
Hickory, Newton, Miss., 539.C4 100
Hickory, Catawba, N.C., 19,328....B2 109
Hickory, Murray, Okla., 112.C5 112
Hickory, co., Mo., 4,516....D4 101
Hickory Corners, Barry, Mich., 200....F5 98
Hickory East, Catawba, N.C., 3,274....*B2 109
Hickory Flat, Benton, Miss., 344....A4 100
Hickory Grove, York, S.C., 287....B5 115
Hickory Hills, Cook, Ill., 2,707....*F2 90
Hickory Plains, Prairie, Ark., 300....C4 81
Hickory Point, Montgomery, Tenn....A4 117
Hickory Ridge, Cross, Ark., 364....B5 81
Hickory Valley, Hardeman, Tenn., 179....B2 117
Hickory Withe, Fayette, Tenn., 100....B2 117
Hickox, Brantley, Ga., 71....E4 87
Hickson, Ont., Can., 151....D4 72
Hickson, lake, Sask., Can....A3 70
Hicksville, Nassau, N.Y., 53,000....E7, n15 108
Hicksville, Defiance, Ohio, 3,116....A3 111
Hico, Hamilton, Tex., 1,020.D3 118
Hicoria, Highlands, Fla....E5 86
Hidalgo, Jasper, Ill., 126....D5 90
Hidalgo, Hidalgo, Tex., 1,078....*F3 118
Hidalgo, co., N. Mex., 4,961....F1 107
Hidalgo, co., Tex., 180,904.F3 118
Hidalgo, state, Mex., 983,161....C5, m14 63
Hidalgo del Parral, Mex., 41,474....B3 63
Hiddenite, Alexander, N.C., 500....B2 109
Hiddensee, isl., Ger....D7 24
Hidden Timber, Todd, S. Dak., 15....D5 116
Hideaway Park, Grand, Colo., 200....B5 83
Hierro, isl., Sp. (Can. Is.)....n13 20
Higashi (Dōgo), isl., Jap....H6 37
Higbee, Randolph, Mo., 646....B5 101
Higby, Roane, W. Va., 158..C3 123
Higdon, Cleburne, Ark., 40..B3 81
Higdon, Jackson, Ala., 200..A4 78
Higganum, Middlesex, Conn., 650....D6 84
Higgins, Lipscomb, Tex., 711.A2 118
Higgins, pond, Md....C6 85
Higgins Lake, Roscommon, Mich., 100....D6 98
Higginson, White, Ark., 183..B4 81
Higginsport, Brown, Ohio, 412....D4 111
Higginsville, Lafayette, Mo., 403....B4 101
High, Carroll, Ark....A2 81
High, des, Oreg....D6 113
High, hill, N.Y....F3 84
High, isl., Mich....C5 98
High, peak, Phil....o13 35
High Bluff, Man., Can., 77..D2 71
High Bridge, Jessamine, Ky., 250....C5 94
High Bridge, Hillsboro, N.H., 125....E2 105
High Bridge, Hunterdon, N.J., 2,148....B3 106
Highcoal, Boone, W. Va., 15....D6 123
Highest Point in Ala....B4 78
Highest Point in Alsk....C9 79
Highest Point in Ariz....B4 80
Highest Point in Ark....B2 81
Highest Point in Calif....D4 82
Highest Point in Can....D4 66
Highest Point in Colo....B4 83
Highest Point in Conn....A3 84
Highest Point in Del....A6 85
Highest Point in Fla....G3 86
Highest Point in Ga....B3 87
Highest Point in Haw....D6 88
Highest Point in Idaho....E5 89
Highest Point in Ill....A3 90
Highest Point in Ind....D8 91
Highest Point in Iowa....A2 92
Highest Point in Kans....C2 93
Highest Point in Ky....D7 94
Highest Point in La....B3 95
Highest Point in Maine....C4 96
Highest Point in Md....D1 85
Highest Point in Mass....A1 97
Highest Point in Mich....B2 98
Highest Point in Minn....B7 99
Highest Point in Miss....A5 100
Highest Point in Mo....D7 101
Highest Point in Mont....E7 102
Highest Point in Nebr....C1 103
Highest Point in Nev....F3 104
Highest Point in N.H.....B3 105
Highest Point in N.J....A3 106
Highest Point in N. Mex....A5 107
Highest Point in N.Y....A7 108
Highest Point in N.A....C9 79
Highest Point in N.C....D4 109
Highest Point in N. Dak....C2 110
Highest Point in Ohio....B4 111
Highest Point in Okla....D1 112
Highest Point in Oreg....B5 113
Highest Point in Pa....G3 114
Highest Point in R.I.....B9 84
Highest Point in S.C....A2 115
Highest Point in S. Dak....D2 116
Highest Point in Tenn....D10 117
Highest Point in Tex....E2 118
Highest Point in U.S....C9 79
Highest Point in Utah....C5 119
Highest Point in Vt....B3 120
Highest Point in Va....B3 121
Highest Point in Wash....C4 122
Highest Point in W. Va....C5 123
Highest Point in Wis....D4 124
Highest Point in Wyo....B3 125
Highfalls, Moore, N.C., 200.B4 109
High Falls, res., Wis....C5 124
Highfield, Washington, Md., 500....A3 85
Highgate, Ont., Can., 374....E3 72
Highgate Center (Highgate), Franklin, Vt., 300 (1,608▲).B2 120
Highgate Falls, Franklin, Vt., 200....B2 120
Highgate Springs, Franklin, Vt., 200....B2 120
Highgrove, Riverside, Calif., 2,000....*F5 82
High Hill, Montgomery, Mo., 173....C6 101
High Hill, lake, Man., Can....B4 71
High Hill, riv., Alta., Can....A5 69
High Island, Galveston, Tex., 800....E5 118
High Knob, mtn., Md....B3 85
High Knob, mtn., Va....B4 121
High Knob, mtn., W. Va....C5 123
High Knob, mtn., W. Va....B6 123
Highland, Pike, Ark., 50....C2 81
Highland, San Bernardino, Calif., 7,000....F3 82
Highland, Clay, Fla., 100....B4 86
Highland, Madison, Ill., 4,943....E4 90
Highland, Lake, Ind., 16,284.A3 91
Highland, Doniphan, Kans., 755....C8 93
Highland, Oakland, Mich., 375....A7 98
Highland, Ulster, N.Y., 2,931....D7 108
Highland, Highland, Ohio, 265....C4 111
Highland, Iowa, Wis., 741....E3 124
Highland, co., Ohio, 29,716.C4 111
Highland, co., Va., 3,221....C3 121
Highland, lake, Maine....E5 96
Highland, peak, Calif....C4 82
Highland, pt., Fla....G5 86
Highland Beach, Palm Beach, Fla., 65....*F6 86
Highlandale, Leflore, Miss..B3 100
Highland City, Polk, Fla., 1,020....*E5 86
Highland Creek, Ont., Can.D5 72
Highland Crest, Wyandotte, Kans., 4,000....*B8 93
Highland Falls, Orange, N.Y., 4,469....*D7 108
Highland Grove, Ont., Can., 84....B6 72
Highland Heights, Campbell, Ky., 3,491....*A5 94
Highland Heights, Cuyahoga, Ohio, 2,929....*A6 111
Highland Home, Crenshaw, Ala., 200....D3 78
Highland Lake, Cumberland, Maine (part of Westbrook).E5 96
Highland Lakes, Sussex, N.J., 250....A4 106
Highland Park, Lake, Ill., 25,532....A6, E2 90
Highland Park, Wayne, Mich., 38,063....A8 98
Highland Park, Middlesex, N.J., 11,049....*C4 106
Highland Park, Mifflin, Pa., 1,534....*E6 114
Highland Park, Sullivan, Tenn. (part of Kingsport).C11 117
Highland Park, Dallas, Tex., 10,411....B5 118
Highland Park, Norfolk, Va., 2,500....*E6 121
Highlands, Broward, Fla., 5,000....*F6 86
Highlands, Coos, N.H....B4 105
Highlands, Monmouth, N.J., 3,536....C5 106
Highlands, Macon, N.C., 597.D3 109
Highlands, Harris, Tex., 4,336....F5 118
Highlands, co., Fla., 21,338..E5 86
Highland Springs, Henrico, Va., 5,000....C7, D5 121
Highlandville, Winneshiek, Iowa, 57....A6 92
Highmore, Hyde, S. Dak., 1,078....C6 116
Highpine, York, Maine....E2 96
High Point, Garland, Ark....C6 81
Highpoint, Winston, Miss., 75....B4 100
High Point, Guilford, N.C., 62,063 (*100,600)....B3 109
High Point, King, Wash., 100.D2 122
High Point, mtn., N.J....A3 106
High Point, mtn., W. Va....C4 123
High Prairie, Alta., Can., 1,756....B2 69
High Ridge, Fairfield, Conn. (part of Stamford)....E2 84
High Ridge, Jefferson, Mo., 250....B7 101
High River, Alta., Can., 2,276....D4 69
Highrock, York, Pa....G9 114
Highrock, lake, Man., Can....B1 71
High Rock, mtn., Md....D1 85
High Rock, res., N.C....B3 109
High Rolls-Mountain Park, Otero, N. Mex., 400....E4 107
High Shoals, Morgan and Oconee, Ga., 217....C3 87
Highshoals, Gaston, N.C., 900....B2 109
Highspire, Dauphin, Pa., 2,999....F8 114
Highsplint, Harlan, Ky., 500....D6 94
High Springs, Alachua, Fla., 2,329....C4 86
Hightstown, Mercer, N.J., 4,317....C3 106
High Veld, plain, S. Afr....C4 49
Highway City, Fresno, Calif., 1,381....*D4 82
Highway Village, Nueces, Tex., 1,927....*F4 118
Highwood, Lake, Ill., 4,499....A6, E2 90
Highwood, Gladwin, Mich..E6 98
Highwood, Chouteau, Mont., 200....C6 102
Highwood, mts., Mont....C6 102
Highwood Baldy, peak, Mont C6 102
High Wycombe, Eng., 53,400....E6 10, C7 12
Higley, Maricopa, Ariz., 100....D4, G2 80
Higüey, Dom. Rep., 10,084..F9 64
Hiiumaa, isl., Sov. Un....B4 27
Hijo, Phil., 3,606....*D7 35
Hika, Manitowoc, Wis., 150..B6 124
Hiko, Lincoln, Nev., 15....F6 104
Hikone, Jap., 41,400 (60,864▲)....n15 37
Hikurangi, mtn., N.Z....L17 51
Hiland, Natrona, Wyo., 10..C5 125
Hilbert, Calumet, Wis., 736....B5, D5 124
Hilda, Alta., Can., 194....D5 69
Hilda, Barnwell, S.C., 259..E5 115
Hildburghausen, Ger., 7,870.C5 17
Hildebrand, Klamath, Oreg..E5 113
Hilden, N.S., Can., 554....D6 74
Hilden, Ger., 40,800....B1 17
Hildesheim, Ger., 99,200....A4 17
Hildreth, Franklin, Nebr., 305....D6 103
Hiles, Forest, Wis., 125....C5 124
Hilgard, Union, Oreg., 15..B8 113
Hilger, Fergus, Mont., 45..C7 102
Hilham, Overton, Tenn., 164....C8 117
Hill, Merrimack, N.H., 190 (396▲)....C3 105
Hill, co., Mont., 18,653....B6 102
Hill, co., Tex., 23,650....D4 118
Hill, lake, Ark....D6 81
Hilla (Hillah), Iraq, 46,441....I17 9, E2 41
Hillared, Swe., 323....A7 24
Hillburn, Rockland, N.Y., 1,068....*D6 108
Hill Center, Merrimack, N.H.C3 105
Hill City, Camas, Idaho, 30..F3 89
Hill City, Graham, Kans., 2,421....C4 93
Hill City, Aitkin, Minn., 429.D5 99
Hill City, Pennington, S. Dak., 419....D2 116
Hillcrest, Warren, N.J., 1,922....*B2 106
Hillcrest, Broome, N.Y., 1,500....*C5 108
Hillcrest, Rockland, N.Y., 3,000....*g12 108
Hillcrest Center, Kern, Calif., 15,000....*E4 82
Hillcrest Heights, Prince Georges, Md., 15,295....*C3 85
Hillcrest Mines, Alta., Can., 618....E3 69
Hillegom, Neth., 12,400....B4 15
Hiller, Fayette, Pa., 1,746..*F2 114
Hillerød, Den., 11,605 (*18,147)....C6 24
Hillesheim, Ger., 1,443....C1 17
Hillgrove, Los Angeles, Calif., 3,500....*F3 82
Hillhead, Marshall, S. Dak., 20....B8 116
Hilliard, Alta., Can., 85....C4 69
Hilliard, Nassau, Fla., 1,075.B5 86
Hilliards, Franklin, Ohio, 5,633....C2 111
Hilliards, Butler, Pa., 200..D2 114
Hillier, Ont., Can., 77....D7 72
Hillisburg, Clinton, Ind., 245....D5 91
Hillman, Montmorency, Mich., 445....C7 98
Hillman, Morrison, Minn., 80....D5 99
Hillmond, Sask., Can....D1 70
Hillrose, Morgan, Colo., 157.A7 83
Hills, Johnson, Iowa, 310....C6 92
Hills, Rock, Minn., 516....G2 99
Hillsboro, Lawrence, Ala., 218....A2 78
Hillsboro, Jasper, Ga., 150..C3 87
Hillsboro, Montgomery, Ill., 4,232....D4 90
Hillsboro, Fountain, Ind., 517....D3 91
Hillsboro, Henry, Iowa, 218....D6 92
Hillsboro, Marion, Kans., 2,441....D6 93
Hillsboro, Caroline, Md., 201....C6 85
Hillsboro, Scott, Miss., 100..C4 100
Hillsboro, Jefferson, Mo., 457....B7, C7 101
Hillsboro, Hillsboro, N.H., 1,645 (2,310▲)....D3 105
Hillsboro, Sierra, N. Mex., 150....E2 107
Hillsboro, Orange, N.C., 1,349....A4 109
Hillsboro, Traill, N. Dak., 1,278....B8 110
Hillsboro, Highland, Ohio, 5,474....C4 111
Hillsboro, Washington, Oreg., 8,232....B1, B3 113
Hillsboro, Coffee, Tenn., 200....B6 117
Hillsboro, Hill, Tex., 7,402..C4 118
Hillsboro, Pocahontas, W. Va., 210....C4 123
Hillsboro, Vernon, Wis., 1,366....E3 124
Hillsboro, co., N.H., 178,161....E3 105
Hillsboro, canal, Fla....F6 86
Hillsboro, riv., Fla....D4 86
Hillsboro Beach, Broward, Fla., 437....*F6 86
Hillsboro Lower Village, Hillsboro, N.H., 100....D3 105
Hillsboro Upper Village, Hillsboro, N.H., 75....D3 105
Hillsborough, San Mateo, Calif., 7,554....*B5 82
Hillsborough, N.B., Can., 679....D5 74
Hillsborough, co., Fla., 397,788....E4 86
Hillsborough, bay, P.E.I., Can.C6 74
Hillsborough, bay, Fla....E2 86
Hillsburgh, Ont., Can., 440..D4 72
Hills Creek, res., Oreg....D4 113
Hillsdale, Ont., Can., 255....C5 72
Hillsdale, Rock Island, Ill., 490....B3 90
Hillsdale, Vermillion, Ind., 250....E3 91
Hillsdale, Miami, Kans., 142....D9 93
Hillsdale, Hillsdale, Mich., 7,629....G6 98
Hillsdale, St. Louis, Mo., 2,788....*A8 101
Hillsdale, Pearl River, Miss..E4 100
Hillsdale, Bergen, N.J., 8,734....g8 106
Hillsdale, Columbia, N.Y., 365....C7 108
Hillsdale, Garfield, Okla., 60....A4 112
Hillsdale, Macon, Tenn., 25....C7 117
Hillsdale, Barron, Wis., 125.C2 124
Hillsdale, Laramie, Wyo., 100....D8 125
Hillsdale, co., Mich., 34,742....G6 98
Hillsgrove, Sullivan, Pa., 200....D8 114
Hillside, Fremont, Colo., 5....C5 83
Hillside, Cook, Ill., 7,794..*F2 90
Hillside, Union, N.J., 22,304....k8 106
Hillside Manor, Nassau, N.Y., 14,000....*G2 84
Hill Spring, Alta., Can., 243.E4 69
Hillston, Austl....F5 51
Hillsview, McPherson, S. Dak., 44....B6 116
Hillsville, Lawrence, Pa., 950....D1 114
Hillsville, Carroll, Va., 905.E2 121
Hilltonia, Screven, Ga., 353..D5 87
Hilltop, Cochise, Ariz....F6 80
Hilltop, Camden, N.J., 1,500....*D2 106
Hilltop, Fayette, W. Va., 765....D7 123
Hilltown, N. Ire., 209....C5 11
Hillview, Greene, Ill., 305..D3 90
Hillville, Haywood, Tenn., 30....B2 117
Hillwood, Coosa, Ala....C3 78
Hillwood, Fairfax, Va., 1,400....*B5 121
Hilly, Lincoln, La....B3 95
Hilo, Hawaii, Haw., 25,966....D6, n16 88
Hilo, bay, Haw....D6 88
Hilpoltstein, Ger., 3,900....D6 17
Hilpsford, pt., Eng....F5 13
Hilton, Early, Ga., 90....E1 87
Hilton, Monroe, N.Y., 1,800....B3 108
Hiltonhead, Beaufort, S.C., 300....G6 115
Hilton Head, isl., S.C....G6 115
Hiltons, Scott, Va., 250....B2 121
Hilts, Siskiyou, Calif., 500..B2 82
Hilversum, Neth., 103,400....B5 15
Hima, Clay, Ky., 500....C6 94
Himachal Pradesh, ter., India, 1,351,144....*B6 40
Himalaya, mts., Asia....G11 33
Himeji, Jap., 328,689....I7 37
Himes, Big Horn, Wyo....A4 125
Himrod, Yates, N.Y., 165..C4 108
Hinche, Hai., 4,511....F7 64
Hinchinbrook, isl., Alsk....g18 79
Hinchinbrook, isl., Austl....C8 50
Hinchliffe, Sask., Can....E4 70
Hinckley, Eng., 42,000....B6 12
Hinckley, DeKalb, Ill., 940..B5 90
Hinckley, Somerset, Maine, 175....D3 96
Hinckley, Pine, Minn., 851..D6 99
Hinckley, Medina, Ohio, 300.A6 111
Hinckley, Millard, Utah, 397.D3 119
Hinckley, res., N.Y....B5 108
Hindarabi, isl., Iran....H6 41
Hindian, Iran, 2,000....F4 41
Hindman, Knott, Ky., 793..C7 94
Hindmarsh, lake, Austl....G3 51
Hinds, co., Miss., 187,045..C3 100
Hinds, lake, Newf., Can....D3 75
Hindsboro, Douglas, Ill., 376.D5 90
Hindsville, Madison, Ark., 150....A2 81
Hindubagh, Pak....B4 39
Hindu Kush, mts., Afg....D14 41
Hines, Dixie, Fla., 30....C3 86
Hines, Beltrami, Minn., 75..C4 99
Hines, Harney, Oreg., 1,207.D7 113
Hines, creek, Alta., Can....A1 69
Hinesburg, Chittenden, Vt., 250 (1,180▲)....C2 120
Hinesburg, pond, Vt....C2 120
Hines Creek, Alta., Can., 398....A1 69
Hinesville, Liberty, Ga., 3,174....E5 87
Hingham, Plymouth, Mass., 12,500 (15,378▲)....B6, h12 97
Hingham, Hill, Mont., 254..B6 102
Hingham, bay, Mass....g12 97
Hingham Center, Plymouth, Mass....D3 97
Hingoli, India, 23,407....H6 40
Hinis, Tur., 2,511....C13 31
Hinkle, Alcorn, Miss., 75....A5 100
Hinkley, San Bernardino, Calif., 75....E5 82
Hinnom, val., Isr., Jordan....m14 32
Hinnöy, isl., Nor....C6 25
Hinojosa [del Duque], Sp., 14,767....C3 20
Hinsdale, Du Page and Cook, Ill., 12,859....F2 90
Hinsdale, Berkshire, Mass., 900 (1,414▲)....B1 97
Hinsdale, Valley, Mont., 400.B9 102
Hinsdale, Cheshire, N.H., 1,235 (2,187▲)....E2 105
Hinsdale, Cattaraugus, N.Y., 350....C2 108
Hinsdale, co., Colo., 208....D3 83
Hinterrhein, Switz., 86....C7 19
Hinton, Alta., Can., 3,529..C2 69
Hinton, Plymouth, Iowa, 403.B1 92
Hinton, Caddo, Okla., 907..B3 112
Hinton, Summers, W. Va., 5,197....D4 123
Hintonville, Perry, Miss., 150....D5 100
Hinze, Winston, Miss....B4 100
Hinzir, cape, Tur....D10 31
Hirado, isl., Jap....J4 37
Hiraiwa, cape, Iwo....52
Hiram, Paulding, Ga., 358..C2 87
Hiram, Oxford, Maine, 110 (699▲)....E2 96
Hiram, Portage, Ohio, 1,011.A6 111
Hirara, Ryukyu Is., 28,504.*G10 34
Hiratsuka, Jap., 108,279.I9, n18 37
Hiraya, Jap....n14 37
Hire, Cherry, Nebr....B4 103
Hirosaki, Jap., 80,000 (152,132▲)....F10 37
Hiroshima, Jap., 431,336 (*560,000)....I6 37
Hiroshima, pref., Jap., 2,184,043....*I6 37
Hirson, Fr., 11,715....C5 14
Hirtshals, Den., 4,177....A3 24
Hisaronu, Tur., 6,586....B9 31
Hiseville, Barren, Ky., 196..C4 94
Hissar, India, 60,222....C6 39
Hit, Iraq, 4,830....F14 31
Hita, Jap., 37,200....*J5 37
Hitachi, Jap., 161,226....H10 37
Hitchcock, Sask., Can., 66..H4 70
Hitchcock, Blaine, Okla., 134....B3 112
Hitchcock, Beadle, S. Dak., 193....C7 116
Hitchcock, Galveston, Tex., 5,216....G5 118
Hitchcock, co., Nebr., 4,829..D4 103
Hitchcock Lake, New Haven, Conn., 1,500....*C5 84
Hitchin, Eng., 24,243....C7 12
Hitchins, Carter, Ky., 600....B7 94
Hitchita, McIntosh, Okla., 120....B6 112
Hitchland, Hansford, Tex., 25....A2 118
Hiteman, Monroe, Iowa, 200.C5 92
Hitoyoshi, Jap., 27,200....J5 37
Hitra, isl., Nor....F3 25
Hitterdal, Clay, Minn., 235..D2 99
Hitzacker, Ger., 3,800....E5 24
Hivonnait, Arg....E4 55
Hiwassee, Pulaski, Va., 400..E2 121
Hiwassee, lake, N.C....D2 109
Hiwassee, riv., Tenn....D9 117
Hixon, B.C., Can., 308....C6 68
Hixson, Hamilton, Tenn., 1,500....D8, E10 117
Hixton, Jackson, Wis., 310..D2 124
Hjallerup, Den., 1,241....A4 24
Hjälmaren (Hjalmar), lake, Swe....H7 25
Hjälmseryd, Swe....A8 24
Hjo, Swe., 4,600....H6 25
Hjørring, Den., 15,038....A3 24
Hjørring, co., Den., 173,233.A3 24
Hlohovec, Czech., 12,700....D4 26
Hlomsak, Thai, 7,906....D4 38
Ho, China....F4 36
Hoa Binh, Viet., 25,000....B6 38
Hoagland, Allen, Ind., 500...C8 91
Hoagland, Logan, Nebr....C5 103
Hoback, Teton, Wyo....B2 121
Hoback, riv., Wyo....B2 125
Hoban Heights, Wyoming, Pa....A8, D10 114
Hobart, Austl., 53,700 (*121,300)....o15 50
Hobart, Lake, Ind., 18,680...A3 91
Hobart, Delaware, N.Y., 585.C6 108
Hobart, Kiowa, Okla., 5,132....B2 112
Hobbema, Alta., Can., 40....C4 69
Hobbies, Bernalillo, N. Mex., 75....*B3 107
Hobbieville, Greene, Ind., 150....G4 91
Hobbs, Tipton, Ind., 250....D6 91
Hobbs, Lea, N. Mex., 26,275....E6 107
Hobbs Island, Madison, Ala..A3 78
Hobe Sound, Martin, Fla., 900....E6 86
Hobgood, Halifax, N.C., 630.A6 109
Hoboken, Bel., 30,557....C4 15
Hoboken, Brantley, Ga., 552....E4 87
Hoboken, Hudson, N.J., 48,441....k8 106
Hobro, Den., 8,208....B3 24
Hobsogol Dalay, lake, Mong..A5 34
Hobson, Navajo, Ariz....C5 80
Hobson, Judith Basin, Mont., 207....D7 102
Hobson, White Pine, Nev....C6 104
Hobson, Nansemond, Va., 250....B6 121
Hobson, lake, B.C., Can....C7 68
Hobson City, Calhoun, Ala., 770....B4 78
Hobucken, Pamlico, N.C., 500....B7 109
Hochatown, McCurtain, Okla., 100....C7 112
Hochfeld, S.W. Afr....B2 49
Hochfelden, Fr., 2,755....F7 15
Hochien, China....E7 36
Hochih, China....G6 34
Höchst, Ger....C3 17
Höchstadt, Ger., 3,400....D5 17
Hochuan, China, 50,000....I2 36
Hockenheim, Ger., 13,200....D3 17
Hockerville, Ottawa, Okla., 300....A7 112
Hockessin, New Castle, Del., 305....A6 85
Hocking, co., Ohio, 20,168..C5 111
Hocking, riv., Ohio....C5 111
Hockingport, Athens, Ohio, 150....C6 111
Hockinson, Clark, Wash., 50.D3 122
Hockley, Harris, Tex., 200..F4 118
Hockley, co., Tex., 22,340....C1 118
Hodgdon, Aroostook, Maine, 225 (926▲)....B5 96
Hodge, Jackson, La., 875....B3 95
Hodgeman, co., Kans., 3,115.D4 93
Hodgenville, Larue, Ky., 1,985....C4 94
Hodges, Franklin, Ala., 194..A2 78
Hodges, Dawson, Mont., 25....D12 102
Hodges, Greenwood, S.C., 209....C3 115
Hodges, hill, Newf., Can....D4 75
Hodges Village, res., Mass....B4 97
Hodgeville, Sask., Can., 388.G2 70
Hodgkins, Cook, Ill., 1,126..*F2 90
Hodgson, Man., Can., 222....D3 71
Hodmezovasarhely, Hung., 40,000 (52,900▲)....B5 22
Hodna, lake, Alg....G9 30
Hodonín, Czech., 18,000....D4 26
Hoea, Hawaii, Haw., 170....C6 88
Hoehne, Las Animas, Colo., 290....D6 83
Hoek Nederburgh, pt., Indon..F6 35
Hoek van Holland, Neth., 2,245 (part of Rotterdam).C4 15

Housatonic, riv., Conn., Mass. D7 108
House, Quay, N. Mex., 150 C6 107
House, range, Utah D2 119
House, riv., Alta., Can A4 69
House Harbour, Que., Can B8 74
House Rock, Mohave, Ariz A3 80
House Springs, Jefferson, Mo., 375 B7 101
Houston, Perry, Ark., 206 B3 81
Houston, B.C., Can., 699 B4 68
Houston, Kent, Del., 421 C6 85
Houston, Suwannee, Fla., 50 B4 86
Houston, Jackson, Ind., 40 F5 91
Houston, Houston, Minn., 1,082 G7 99
Houston, Chickasaw, Miss., 2,577 B5 100
Houston, Texas, Mo., 1,660 D6 101
Houston, Shelby, Ohio, 95 B3 111
Houston, Washington, Pa., 1,865 F1 114
Houston, Harris, Tex., 938,219 (*1,251,700) E5, F5 118
Houston, co., Ala., 50,718 D4 78
Houston, co., Ga., 39,154 D3 87
Houston, co., Minn., 16,588 G7 99
Houston, co., Tenn., 4,794 A4 117
Houston, co., Tex., 19,376 D5 118
Houston, lake, Tex F5 118
Houstonia, Pettis, Mo., 261 C4 101
Houtzdale, Clearfield, Pa., 1,239 E5 114
Hove, Eng., 72,000 D7 12
Hövelhof, Ger., 7,900 B3 17
Hoven, Potter, S. Dak., 568 B6 116
Hovenweep, nat. mon., Colo., Utah F6 119
Hoveyzeh, Iran F4 41
Hovland, Cook, Minn., 150 B7 99
Howar, riv., Sud B2 47
Howard, Fayette, Ala., 100 B2 78
Howard, Fremont, Colo., 43 C5 83
Howard, Dade, Fla F3 86
Howard, Taylor, Ga., 200 D2 87
Howard, Elk, Kans., 1,017 E7 93
Howard, Holmes, Miss., 100 B3 100
Howard, Steuben, N.Y., 100 C3 108
Howard, Knox, Ohio, 400 B5 111
Howard, Centre, Pa., 770 D6 114
Howard, Providence, R.I. (part of Cranston) C11 84
Howard, Miner, S. Dak., 1,208 C8 116
Howard, Brown, Wis., 3,485 *D5 124
Howard, co., Ark., 10,878 C2 81
Howard, co., Ind., 69,509 C5 91
Howard, co., Iowa, 12,734 A5 92
Howard, co., Md., 36,152 B4 85
Howard, co., Mo., 10,859 B5 101
Howard, co., Nebr., 6,541 C7 103
Howard, co., Tex., 40,139 C2 118
Howard City, Montcalm, Mich., 1,004 E5 98
Howard Hanson, flood control res., Wash B3 102
Howard Lake, Wright, Minn., 1,007 E4 99
Howard Prairie, res., Oreg E4 113
Howards Grove, Sheboygan, Wis., 350 B6, E6 124
Howe, Butte, Idaho, 25 F6 89
Howe, Lagrange, Ind., 550 A7 91
Howe, LeFlore, Okla., 390 C7 112
Howe, cape, Austl H7 51
Howe, sound, B.C., Can E6 68
Howe Brook, Aroostook, Maine, 25 B4 96
Howell, Woodruff, Ark., 200 B4 81
Howell, Echols, Ga., 141 F3 87
Howell, Livingston, Mich., 4,861 F7 98
Howell, Lincoln, Tenn., 125 B5 117
Howell, Box Elder, Utah, 188 B3 119
Howell, co., Mo., 22,027 E6 101
Howells, Colfax, Nebr., 694 C8 103
Howes, Meade, S. Dak., 2 C2 116
Howes Mill, Dent, Mo D6 101
Howesville, Preston, W. Va., 100 B5 123
Howick, Que., Can., 647 D4 73
Howison, Harrison, Miss E4 100
Howland, Penobscot, Maine, 1,362 C4 96
Howland, isl., Pac. O F11 7
Howley, Newf., Can., 452 D3 75
Howley, mtn., Newf., Can D2 75
Howrah, India, 512,598 D8 39, F12 40
Howser, B.C., Can D9 68
Howson, peak, B.C., Can B4 68
Howth, Ire., 4,832 D5 11
Hoxie, Lawrence, Ark., 1,886 A5 81
Hoxie, Sheridan, Kans., 1,289 C3 93
Höxter, Ger., 15,200 B4 17
Hoy, isl., Scot B5 13
Hoya, Ger., 4,300 B4 16
Hoyang, China G4 36
Hoyerswerda, Ger., 24,500 B9 17
Hoylake, Eng., 32,268 A4 12
Hoyleton, Washington, Ill., 475 E4 90
Hoyo, mtn., Sp o17 20
Hoyt, Morgan, Colo., 5 B6 83
Hoyt, Jackson, Kans., 283 C8 93
Hoyt, Haskell, Okla., 320 B6 112
Hoyt Lakes, St. Louis, Minn., 3,186 *C6 99
Hoyt Station, N.B., Can., 327 D3 74
Hoytville, Wood, Ohio, 334 A4 111
Hoytville, Tioga, Pa C7 114
Hradec Kralove, Czech., 57,100 C3 26
Hranice, Czech., 10,800 D4 26
Hrinova, Czech., 6,831 D5 26
Hron, riv., Czech D5 26
Hrubieszow, Pol., 11,300 C7 26
Hsi, China F4 26
Hsiachiang, China, 5,000 K6 36
Hsiaching, China, 4,000 F6 36
Hsiamen, see Amoy, China
Hsian, China, 5,000 E2 37
Hsian, see Sian, China
Hsiang, riv., China J5 36
Hsianghsiang, China, 3,000 K5 36
Hsiangyang, China, 18,000 H5 36
Hsiapu, China, 13,000 K9 36
Hsichang (Sichang), China, 50,000 F5 34
Hsienning, China, 4,000 J6 36
Hsienyang, China G3 36
Hsifeng, China, 33,886 C11 36
Hsilung, China G6 34
Hsinchiang, China G4 36
Hsinchu, Taiwan, 114,000 (160,600▲) G9 34
Hsinfeng, China, 16,000 B3 37
Hsingan, mtn., China D7 36
Hsingcheng, China D9 36
Hsingshanchen, China C5 37
Hsingtai, China, 70,000 F6 36
Hsinhua, China K6 36
Hsining, see Sining, China
Hsinkao, mtn., Taiwan G9 34
Hsinking, see Changchun, China
Hsinmin, China, 35,000 C9 34, C10 36
Hsinning, China F7 34
Hsinpin, China F2 37
Hsintai, China G7 36
Hsintsai, China H6 36
Hsinyang, China, 50,000 H6 36
Hsinyeh, China H5 36
Hsipaw, Bur., 5,000 A2 38
Hsiushui, China, 10,000 J6 36
Hsuancheng, China I8 36
Hsuanhua, China, 114,100 C8 34, D6 36
Hsuchang, China, 58,000 G5 36
Hsui, China H8 36
Hsunho, China B4 37
Hsupu, China K4 36
Hsuwen, China, 15,000 B9 38
Huacho, Peru, 16,039 D2 58
Huachuca City, Cochise, Ariz., 1,330 F5 80
Huacrachuco, Peru, 723 C2 58
Huahua, riv., Nic C6 62
Huai, riv., China E7 34
Huaian, China, 35,000 H8 36
Huailai, China D6 36
Huaite, China, 1,000 E2 37
Huaiyang, China H6 36
Huaiyin, China, 77,000 H8 36
Huaiyuan, China H7 36
Huajuapan de León, Mex., 8,415 D5, o15 63
Hualalai, mtn., Haw D6 88
Hualgayoc, Peru, 1,173 C2 58
Hualien, Taiwan, 32,230 G9 34
Huallaga, riv., Peru C2 58
Huallanca, Peru C2 58
Hualpai, Indian res., Ariz B2 80
Hualpai, mts., Airz C2 80
Hualpai, peak, Ariz B2 80
Huamachuco, Peru, 2,324 C2 58
Huamantla, Mex., 9,811 n15 63
Huambo, dist., Ang., 598,545 D2 48
Huancabamba, Peru, 2,443 C2 58
Huancané, Peru, 2,236 E4 58
Huancavelica, Peru, 9,594 D2 58
Huancavelica, dept., Peru, 305,619 D2 58
Huancayo, Peru, 46,000 D2 58
Huanchaca, Bol D2 55
Huangan, China, 31,000 I6 36
Huangchuan, China H6 36
Huangkang, China, 53,000 I6 36
Huangmei, China, 21,000 I6 36
Huangping, China, 4,000 K2 36
Huangyen, China, 21,000 J9 36
Huangyuan, China D5 34
Huanjen, China, 5,000 F2 37
Huanta, Peru, 4,439 D3 58
Huánuco, Peru, 15,180 C2 58
Huánuco, dept., Peru, 315,025 C2 58
Huanuni, Bol., 5,696 C2 55
Huara, Chile, 1,794 C2 55
Huaral, Peru, 5,012 D2 58
Huarás, Peru, 14,250 C2 58
Huari, Bol., 1,070 C2 55
Huariaca, Peru, 1,593 D2 58
Huarina, Bol., 1,151 C2 55
Huarmey, Peru, 1,333 D2 58
Huasco, Chile, 1,537 E1 55
Huatabampo, Mex., 10,030 B3 63
Huatien, China, 35,000 C10 34
Huatusco, Mex., 8,673 n15 63
Huauchinango, Mex., 12,053 m14 63
Huaunta, Nic D6 62
Huayllay, Peru, 593 D2 58
Huaytará, Peru, 718 D2 58
Hubbard, Sask., Can., 169 F4 70
Hubbard, Hardin, Iowa, 806 B4 92
Hubbard, Hubbard, Minn., 100 D4 99
Hubbard, Rockingham, N.H E4 105
Hubbard, Trumbull, Ohio, 7,137 A7 111
Hubbard, Marion, Oreg., 526 B2, B4 113
Hubbard, Hill, Tex., 1,628 D4 118
Hubbard, co., Minn., 9,962 C4 99
Hubbard, lake, Mich D7 98
Hubbard Creek, res., Tex C3 118
Hubbard Lake, Alpena, Mich., 150 D7 98
Hubbards, N.S., Can., 525 E5 74
Hubbardston, Worcester, Mass., 300 (1,217▲) B3 97
Hubbardston, Ionia and Clinton, Mich., 381 E5 98
Hubbardton, Rutland, Vt., 25 (238▲) D2 120
Hubbardton, riv., Vt D2 120
Hubbell, Houghton, Mich., 1,429 A2 98
Hubbell, Thayer, Nebr., 126 D8 103
Huben, Aus C8 18
Huberdeau, Que., Can., 605 D3 73
Huber Heights, Montgomery, Ohio, 5,000 C3 111
Hubli, India, 171,326 E6 39
Huckleberry, mtn., Oreg D4 113
Huckleberry, mts., Wash A8 122
Huckleberry Hill, Hartford, Conn., 350 *B5 84
Hud, Scurry, Tex C2 118
Huddersfield, Eng., 131,800 (*205,000) A6 12
Huddleston, Bedford, Va., 85 D3 121
Hude, Ger., 7,900 E2 24
Hudiksvall, Swe., 12,000 G7 25
Hudin (Well), Som D6 47
Hudson, Ont., Can., 65 D5 71
Hudson, Que., Can., 1,671 D3, q18 73
Hudson, Weld, Colo., 430 A6 83
Hudson, Pasco, Fla., 800 D4 86
Hudson, McLean, Ill., 493 C5 90
Hudson, Steuben, Ind., 428 A7 91
Hudson, Black Hawk, Iowa, 1,085 B5 92
Hudson, Stafford, Kans., 201 D5 93
Hudson, Middlesex, Mass., 9,666 B4, g9 97
Hudson, Lenawee, Mich., 2,546 G6 98
Hudson, Hillsboro, N.H., 3,561 (5,876▲) E4 105
Hudson, Columbia, N.Y., 11,075 C7 108
Hudson, Caldwell, N.C., 1,536 B2 109
Hudson, Summit, Ohio, 2,438 A6 111
Hudson, Luzerne, Pa., 900 *B8 114
Hudson, Lincoln, S. Dak., 455 D9 116
Hudson, St. Croix, Wis., 4,325 D1 124
Hudson, Fremont, Wyo., 369 C4 125
Hudson, co., N.J., 610,734 B4 106
Hudson, bay, Can D15 66
Hudson, mtn., Maine B3 96
Hudson, mts., Ant B3 5
Hudson, riv., N.J., N.Y E7 108
Hudson, strait, Can D18 67
Hudson Bay, Sask., Can., 1,601 E4 70
Hudson Center, Hillsboro, N.H., 35 E4 105
Hudson Falls, Washington, N.Y., 7,752 B7 108
Hudson Heights, Que., Can., 1,540 q18 73
Hudson Hope, B.C., Can., 66 A6 68
Hudsonville, Ottawa, Mich., 2,649 F5 98
Hudsonville, Marshall, Miss., 40 A4 100
Hudspeth, co., Tex., 3,343 F1 118
Hudwin, lake, Man., Can C4 71
Hue, Viet., 105,800 D7 38
Hueco, mts., Tex E1 118
Huedin, Rom., 5,134 B6 22
Huehuetenango, Guat., 6,187 C2 62
Huejutla, Mex., 3,682 m14 63
Huelma, Sp., 7,739 D4 20
Huelva, Sp., 74,384 D2 20
Huelva, prov., Sp., 399,934 *D2 20
Huentelauquén, Chile A2 54
Huércal-Overa, Sp., 13,016 D5 20
Huerfano, co., Colo., 7,867 D5 83
Huerfano, peak, N. Mex A2 107
Huerfano, riv., Colo D6 83
Huerva, riv., Sp B5 20
Huesca, Sp., 24,377 A5 20
Huesca, prov., Sp., 233,543 *A5 20
Huéscar, Sp., 5,499 D4 20
Huesco, mts., Mex F1 118
Huetamo de Núñez, Mex., 6,195 D4, n13 63
Huete, Sp., 3,209 B4 20
Hueysville, Floyd, Ky., 100 C7 94
Hueytown, Jefferson, Ala., 5,997 E4 78
Huff, Independence, Ark., 70 B4 81
Huff, Morton, N. Dak., 55 C5 110
Huffakers, Washoe, Nev., 150 D2 104
Huffman, Mississippi, Ark., 200 B6 81
Huffton, Brown, S. Dak., 10 B7 116
Huger, Berkeley, S.C., 500 E3 115
Huggins, mtn., Ant B29 5
Hugh Butler Lake, res., Nebr D5 103
Hughenden, Austl., 2,329 D7 50
Hughenden, Alta., Can., 294 C5 69
Hughes, Alsk., 69 B9 79
Hughes, St. Francis, Ark., 1,960 C5 81
Hughes, Austl F4 50
Hughes, co., Okla., 15,144 B5 112
Hughes, co., S. Dak., 12,725 C5 116
Hughes, riv., Man., Can A1 71
Hughes, riv., W. Va B3 123
Hughes Springs, Cass, Tex., 1,813 *C5 118
Hughestown, Luzerne, Pa., 1,615 *D10 114
Hughesville, Charles, Md., 160 C4 85
Hughesville, Pettis, Mo., 134 C4 101
Hughesville, Judith Basin, Mont., 5 C6 102
Hughesville, Hunterdon, N.J., 50 B2 106
Hughesville, Lycoming, Pa., 2,218 D8 114
Hughson, Stanislaus, Calif., 1,898 *D3 82
Hughton, Sask., Can., 86 F2 70
Hugo, Lincoln, Colo., 811 B7 83
Hugo, Washington, Minn., 538 E7 99
Hugo, Choctaw, Okla., 6,287 C6 112
Hugo, Josephine, Oreg E3 113
Hugoton, Stevens, Kans., 2,912 E2 93
Huguley (Southwest Lanett), Chambers, Ala., 2,189 *C4 78
Huhehot (Kweisui), China, 314,000 C7 34, D4 36
Huichang, China, 11,000 F8 34
Huichapan, Mex., 2,197 m14 63
Huichon, Kor., 14,619 F3 37
Huila, dist., Ang., 592,451 E1 48
Huila, dept., Col., 330,270 C2 60
Huili, China F5 34
Huimin, China F7 36
Huinan, China, 1,000 E3 37
Huitzuco, Mex., 6,267 n14 63
Huixtla, Mex., 12,344 D6 63
Huiyang, China, 35,000 G7 34
Huizen, Neth., 17,100 B5 15
Hukou, China, 5,000 J7 36
Hukuntsi, Bech., 1,423 B3 49
Hula (Huleh), lake, Isr A7 32
Hulah, Osage, Okla., 50 A5 112
Hulah, res., Okla A5 112
Hulan, China, 60,000 B10 34
Hulbert, Crittenden, Ark., 500 B5 81
Hulbert, Chippewa, Mich., 300 B5 98
Hulbert, Cherokee, Okla., 500 B6 112
Hulberton, Orleans, N.Y., 300 B2 108
Hulda, Isr., 332 C6, h10 32
Huleh (Hula), lake, Isr A7 32
Hulett, Crook, Wyo., 335 A8 125
Hulin, China, 1,000 D6 37
Hull, Tuscaloosa, Ala B2 78
Hull, Que., Can., 56,929 D2 73
Hull, Eng., 301,000 (*360,000) A7 12
Hull, Pike, Ill., 535 D2 90
Hull, Sioux, Iowa, 1,289 A1 92
Hull, Plymouth, Mass., 7,055 B6, g12 97
Hull, Emmons, N. Dak., 28 C5 110
Hull, co., Que., Can., 84,803 D2 73
Hull, riv., Eng G8 13
Hulls Cove, Hancock, Maine, 350 D4 96
Hullt, Marion, Oreg C2, C4 113
Hulmeville, Bucks, Pa., 968 *F12 114
Hulst, Neth., 5,200 C4 15
Hulun, see Hailar, China.
Hulun Nor, lake, China B8 34
Hulutao, China, 30,000 D9 36
Hulwān, Eg., U.A.R., 8,000 E3 32
Humacao, P.R., 8,005 C7 65
Humacao, mun., P.R., 33,381 C7, g11 65
Humahuaca, Arg., 2,094 D2 55
Humaitá, Braz., 1,192 D1 59
Humansdorp, S. Afr., 3,117 D3 49
Humansville, Polk, Mo., 745 D4 101
Humarock, Plymouth, Mass., 200 h13 97
Humbe, Ang E1 48
Humber, riv., Eng A7 12
Humbermouth, Newf., Can D3 75
Humbird, Clark, Wis., 300 D3 124
Humble, Harris, Tex., 1,711 E5, F5 118
Humble City, Lea, N. Mex., 25 E6 107
Humboldt, Yavapai, Ariz., 450 C3 80
Humboldt, Sask., Can., 3,245 E3 70
Humboldt, Coles, Ill., 342 D5 90
Humboldt, Humboldt, Iowa, 4,031 B3 92
Humboldt, Allen, Kans., 2,285 E8 93
Humboldt, Marquette, Mich B3 98
Humboldt, Kittson, Minn., 169 B1 99
Humboldt, Richardson, Nebr., 1,322 D10 103
Humboldt, Pershing, Nev., 20 C3 104
Humboldt, Minnehaha, S. Dak., 446 D8 116
Humboldt, Gibson, Tenn., 8,482 B3 117
Humboldt, co., Calif., 104,892 B2 82
Humboldt, co., Iowa, 13,156 B3 92
Humboldt, co., Nev., 5,708 B3 104
Humboldt, range, Nev C3 104
Humboldt, riv., Nev C3 104
Hume, res., Austl G6 51
Hume, Edgar, Ill., 449 D6 90
Hume, Bates, Mo., 369 C3 101
Hume, Allegany, N.Y., 300 C2 108
Hume, Fauquier, Va., 130 C5 121
Humenné, Czech., 11,100 D6 26
Humeston, Wayne, Iowa, 638 D4 92
Hummelstown, Dauphin, Pa., 4,474 *F8 114
Hummels Wharf, Snyder, Pa., 700 E8 114
Humnoke, Lonoke, Ark., 319 C4 81
Humpata, Ang., 490 E1 48
Humphrey, Arkansas and Jefferson, Ark., 649 C4 81
Humphrey, Clark, Idaho, 25 E6 89
Humphrey, Platte, Nebr., 801 C8 103
Humphreys, Terrebonne, La C5 95
Humphreys, Sullivan, Mo., 163 A4 101
Humphreys, Jackson, Okla., 50 C2 112
Humphreys, co., Miss., 19,093 B3 100
Humphreys, co., Tenn., 11,511 A4 117
Humphreys, mtn., Calif D4 82
Humphreys, peak, Ariz B4 80
Humpolec, Czech., 5,083 D3 26
Humptulips, Grays Harbor, Wash., 110 B2 122
Humuula, Hawaii, Haw D6 88
Hūn, Libya D3 43
Hunan, prov., China, 36,220,000 F7 34
Hunchun, China, 25,000 C11 34
Hundested, Den., 3,473 C5 24
Hundred, Wetzel, W. Va., 475 B4 123
Hunedoara, Rom., 51,200 C6 22
Hünfeld, Ger., 6,000 C4 17
Hungary, country, Eur., 10,135,000 F12 8, B4 22
Hungerford, Austl., 80 D5 51
Hunghae, Kor H4 37
Hungnam, Kor., 143,600 G3 37
Hungry Horse, Flathead, Mont., 500 B2 102
Hungry Horse, res., Mont B3 102
Hungshui, riv., China G6 34
Huningue, Fr., 4,963 B3 18
Hunnewell, Sumner, Kans., 83 E6 93
Hunnewell, Shelby, Mo., 284 B6 101
Hunsrück, mts., Ger D2 17
Hunstanton, Eng., 4,843 B8 12
Hunt, Apache, Ariz C6 80
Hunt, Johnson, Ark., 50 B2 81
Hunt, co., Tex., 39,399 C4 118
Hunt, mtn., Wyo A5 125
Hunte, riv., Ger B4 16
Hunter, Montgomery, Ala., 1,500 *C3 78
Hunter, Woodruff, Ark., 202 B4 81
Hunter, Mitchell, Kans., 229 C5 93
Hunter, De Soto, La C2 95
Hunter, Carter, Mo., 105 E7 101
Hunter, Greene, N.Y., 457 C6 108
Hunter, Cass, N. Dak., 446 B8 110
Hunter, Garfield, Okla., 203 A4 112
Hunter, Comal, Tex., 50 A4, E3 118
Hunter, Salt Lake, Utah, 5,300 C3 119
Hunter, cape, N.W. Ter., Can B18 67
Hunter, is., Austl o14 50
Hunter, isl., B.C., Can D3 68
Hunter, mtn., N.Y C6 108
Hunterdon, co., N.J., 54,107 B3 106
Hunters, Stevens, Wash., 220 A7 122
Hunters, hot springs, Oreg E6 113
Huntersfield, mtn., N.Y C6 108
Hunters Creek, Harris, Tex., 2,478 *E5 118
Hunters River, P.E.I., Can., 236 C6 74
Huntersville, Mecklenburg, N.C., 1,004 B3 109
Huntersville, Madison, Tenn B3 117
Huntersville, Pocahontas, W. Va., 80 C4 119
Huntertown, Allen, Ind., 400 B7 91
Hunting, creek, Md C4 85
Hunting, isl., S.C G7 115
Huntingburg, Dubois, Ind., 4,146 H4 91
Huntingdon, B.C., Can., 122 f13 68
Huntingdon, Que., Can., 3,134 D3 73
Huntingdon, Eng., 8,812 B7 12
Huntingdon, Huntingdon, Pa., 7,234 F5 114
Huntingdon, Carroll, Tenn., 2,119 A3 117
Huntingdon, co., Que., Can., 14,752 D3 73
Huntingdon, co., Eng., 79,879 B7 12
Huntingdon, co., Pa., 39,457 F5 114
Huntingdon, isl., Newf., Can B3 75
Huntington, Sebastian, Ark., 560 B1 81
Huntington, Huntington, Ind., 16,185 C7 91
Huntington, Hampshire, Mass., 950 (1,392▲) B2 97
Huntington, Warren, N.J., 700 B2 106
Huntington, Suffolk, N.Y., 12,500 E7, n15 108
Huntington, Baker, Oreg., 689 C9 113
Huntington, Angelina, Tex., 1,009 D5 118
Huntington, Emery, Utah, 787 D5 119
Huntington, Chittenden, Vt., 120 (518▲) C3 120
Huntington, Cabell and Wayne, W. Va., 83,627 (*231,100) C2 123
Huntington, co., Ind., 33,814 C6 91
Huntington, bay, N.Y F3 84
Huntington Bay, Suffolk, N.Y., 1,267 *n15 108
Huntington Beach, Orange, Calif., 11,492 F3 82
Huntington Center, Chittenden, Vt., 150 C3 120
Huntington Park, Los Angeles, Calif., 29,920 F2 82
Huntington Station, Suffolk, N.Y., 26,000 F3 84
Huntington Woods, Oakland, Mich., 8,746 A7 98
Huntingtown, Calvert, Md., 165 C4 85
Huntland, Franklin, Tenn., 500 B5 117
Huntley, McHenry, Ill., 1,143 A5 90
Huntley, Faribault, Minn., 136 G4 99
Huntley, Yellowstone, Mont., 250 E8 102
Huntley, Harlan, Nebr., 91 D6 103
Huntley, Goshen, Wyo., 75 D8 125
Huntly, Scot., 3,952 C6 13
Hunts Point, N.S., Can., 169 F5 74
Huntsville, Madison, Ala., 72,365 (*94,800) A3 78
Huntsville, Madison, Ark., 1,050 A2 81
Huntsville, Ont., Can., 3,189 B5 72
Huntsville, Madison, Ind., 300 E6 91
Huntsville, Butler, Ky., 150 C3 94
Huntsville, Randolph, Mo., 1,526 B5 101
Huntsville, Scott, Tenn., 500 C9 117
Huntsville, Walker, Tex., 11,999 D5 118
Huntsville, Weber, Utah, 552 B4 119
Huntsville, Columbia, Wash., 100 C7 122
Hunucmá, Mex., 6,604 C7 63
Huon, gulf, N. Gui k12 50
Hupeh (Hupei), prov., China, 30,790,000 E7 34
Hurd, cape, Ont., Can B3 72
Hurdland, Knox, Mo., 205 A5 101
Hurdsfield, Wells, N. Dak., 183 B6 110
Hurffville, Gloucester, N.J., 500 D2 106
Hurley, Jackson, Miss., 400 E5 100
Hurley, Stone, Mo., 117 E4 101
Hurley, Grant, N. Mex., 1,851 E1 107
Hurley, Ulster, N.Y., 900 D6 108
Hurley, Turner, S. Dak., 450 D8 116
Hurley, Buchanan, Va., 400 B3 121
Hurley, Iron, Wis., 2,763 B3 124
Hurleyville, Sullivan, N.Y., 900 D6 108
Hurliness, Scot B5 13
Hurlock, Dorchester, Md., 1,035 C6 85
Hurmagai, Pak G12 40
Huron, Fresno, Calif., 1,269 *D3 82
Huron, Lawrence, Ind., 225 G4 91
Huron, Atchison, Kans., 119 C8 93
Huron, Erie, Ohio, 5,197 A5 111
Huron, Beadle, S. Dak., 14,180 C7 116
Huron, co., Ont., Can., 53,805 D3 72
Huron, co., Mich., 34,006 E7 98
Huron, co., Ohio, 47,326 A5 111
Huron, lake, Can., U.S B11 77
Huron, mts., Mich B3 98
Huron, riv., Mich A6 98
Huron, riv., Ohio A5 111
Hurricane, Washington, Utah, 1,251 F2 119
Hurricane, Putnam, W. Va., 1,970 C2 123
Hurricane, cliffs, Ariz., Utah G2 119
Hurricane, creek, Ark C3 81
Hurricane, creek, Ga E4 87
Hurricane Mills, Humphreys, Tenn., 15 B4 117
Hurst, Williamson, Ill., 863 F4 90
Hurst, Tarrant, Tex., 10,165 *C4 118
Hürth, Ger., 47,700 C1 17
Hurtsboro, Russell, Ala., 1,056 C4 78
Hurup, Den., 2,160 B2 24
Huși, Rom., 18,055 B9 22
Huskerville, Lancaster, Nebr., 550 *D9 103
Huskvarna, Swe., 13,800 I6 25
Huson, Missoula, Mont., 5 C2 102
Hussar, Alta., Can., 213 D4 69
Husser, Tangipahoa, La., 35 D5 95
Hussein-Dey, Alg., 62,134 *B5 44
Hustburg, Humphreys, Tenn., 150 B4 117
Hustisford, Dodge, Wis., 708 E5 124
Hustle, Essex, Va., 65 C5 121
Hustontown, Fulton, Pa., 150 F5 114
Hustonville, Lincoln, Ky., 387 C5 94
Husum, Ger., 23,800 A4 16
Husum, Klickitat, Wash., 15 D4 122
Hutch, isl., S.C G1 115
Hutch, mtn., Ariz C4 80
Hutchins, Dallas, Tex., 1,100 B5 118
Hutchinson, Reno, Kans., 37,574 A4, D6 93
Hutchinson, McLeod, Minn., 6,207 F4 99
Hutchinson, Warren, N.J., 40 B2 106
Hutchinson, co., S. Dak., 11,085 D8 116
Hutchinson, co., Tex., 34,419 B2 118
Hutchinsons, isl., Fla E6 86
Hutsonville, Crawford, Ill., 583 D6 90
Huttig, Union, Ark., 936 D3 81
Hutto, Williamson, Tex., 442 D4 118
Hutton, Vernon, La., 50 C2 95
Hutton, Garrett, Md., 175 D1 85
Huttonsville, Randolph, W. Va., 242 C5 123
Hutton Valley, Howell, Mo., 125 E6 101
Huttwil, Switz., 4,664 B4 19
Huu, Indon G5 35
Huwwārah, Jordan, 2,000 g12 32
Huxford, Escambia, Ala., 100 D2 78
Huxley, Alta., Can., 102 D4 69
Huxley, Story, Iowa, 486 C4 92
Huy, Bel., 13,447 D5 15
Huyett, Washington, Md A2 85
Hvalpsund, Den., 821 B3 24
Hvidbjerg, Den., 978 B2 24
Hvide Sande, Den., 1,514 C2 24
Hvidovre, Den., 38,411 *C6 24
Hvitsten, Nor., 188 p28 25
Hvittingfoss, Nor., 576 p28 25
Hwainan, China, 286,900 H7 36
Hwaining, see Anking, China
Hwang Ho (Yellow), riv., China D8 34, F4 36
Hwangling, China D6 34
Hweitseh, China F5 34
Hyak, Kittitas, Wash., 30 B4 122
Hyampom, Trinity, Calif., 30 B2 82
Hyannis, Barnstable, Mass., 5,700 C7 97
Hyannis, Grant, Nebr., 373 B4 103
Hyannis Port, Barnstable, Mass., 500 C7 97
Hyas, Sask., Can., 246 F4 70
Hyatts, Delaware, Ohio, 100 B4 111
Hyattstown, Montgomery, Md., 120 B3 85
Hyattsville, Prince Georges, Md., 15,168 C1, C4 85
Hyattville, Big Horn, Wyo., 50 A5 125
Hybart, Monroe, Ala., 150 D2 78
Hybla Valley, Fairfax, Va., 1,500 *C5 121
Hyco, riv., Va E4 121
Hydaburg, Alsk., 251 D13, n23 79
Hyde, co., N.C., 5,765 B7 109
Hyde, co., S. Dak., 2,602 C6 116
Hyden, Austl., 200 F2 50
Hyden, Leslie, Ky., 348 C6 94
Hyde Park, Br. Gu A3 59
Hyde Park, Dutchess, N.Y., 2,800 D7 108
Hyde Park, Berks, Pa., 2,500 *F10 114
Hyde Park, Cache, Utah, 696 B4 119
Hyde Park, Lamoille, Vt., 474 (1,219▲) B3 120
Hyder, Alsk., 32 D13, n24 79
Hyder, Yuma, Ariz E2 80
Hyderabad, India, 931,082 (*1,300,000) E6 39, I7 40
Hyderabad, Pak., 416,441 (*460,000) C4 39, E2 40
Hydetown, Crawford, Pa., 679 C2 114
Hyde Villa, Berks, Pa., 1,300 *F10 114
Hydeville, Rutland, Vt., 350 D2 120
Hydraulic, B.C., Can C7 68
Hydro, Caddo, Okla., 697 B3 112
Hye, Blanco, Tex., 25 D3 118
Hyères, Fr., 18,671 F7 14
Hyères, is., Fr F7 14
Hyesanjin, Kor F4 37
Hygiene, Boulder, Colo., 125 A5 83
Hylo, Alta., Can B4 69
Hylton, Nolan, Tex C2 118
Hyman, Florence, S.C., 40 D8 115
Hyman, Mitchell, Tex C2 118
Hymel, St. James, La., 250 B6 95
Hymera, Sullivan, Ind., 1,015 F3 91
Hyndman, Bedford, Pa., 1,124 G4 114
Hyndman, peak, Idaho F4 89
Hyner, Clinton, Pa., 75 D6 114
Hyogo, pref., Jap., 3,906,487 *I7 37
Hyopchon, Kor., 7,000 I4 37
Hyrum, Cache, Utah, 1,728 B4 119
Hyrynsalmi, Fin., 1,300 E13 25
Hysham, Treasure, Mont., 494 D9 102
Hythe, Alta., Can., 449 B1 69
Hythe, Eng., 10,026 C9 12

I

Iablès, dunes, Alg D4 44
Iaeger, McDowell, W. Va., 930 D3 123
Ialomita, riv., Rom C8 22
Iamonia, lake, Fla B2 86
Iantha, Barton, Mo., 147 D3 101
Iaşi (Jassy), Rom., 124,700 B8 22
Iatan, Platte, Mo., 95 B3 101
Iates, pt., Guam 52
Iatt, lake, La C3 95
Iba, Phil., 3,064 o12 35
Ibadan, Nig., 459,196 E5 45
Ibagué, Col., 76,000 (138,000▲) C2 60
Ibanda, Ug B5 48
Ibapah, Tooele, Utah, 25 C2 119
Ibar, riv., Yugo D5 22

Ibaraki, pref., Jap., 2,047,024 *H10 37
Ibarra, Ec., 14,221 A2 58
Ibbenbüren, Ger., 15,700 A2 17
Ibera, lake, Arg E4 55
Iberia, Miller, Mo., 694 C5 101
Iberia, Morrow, Ohio, 200 B5 111
Iberia, par., La., 51,657 E4 95
Iberville, Que., Can., 7,588 D4 73
Iberville, Iberville, La., 150 B5, D4 95
Iberville, co., Que., Can., 18,080 D4 73
Iberville, par., La., 29,939 D4 95
Ibi, Nig., 6,183 E6 45
Ibiá, Braz., 6,999 E1 57
Ibiapaba, mts., Braz B2 57
Ibicuí, riv., Braz D2 56
Ibicuy, Arg A5, f7 54
Ibirapuitã, riv., Braz E1 56
Ibitinga, Braz., 8,881 C3 56
Ibiza, Sp., 11,259 C6 20
Ibiza, isl., Sp C6 20
Ibo, Moz., 5,000 D7 48
Ibu, Okinawa 52
Iburg, Ger., 3,200 A3 17
Ica, Peru, 38,300 D2 58
Ica, dept., Peru, 158,783 D2 58
Içá, riv., Braz D4 60
Icacal, Pan., 86 k10 62
Icacos, isl., P.R B8 65
Içana, riv., Braz C4 60
Ice, cave, Iowa A6 92
Ice, mtn., B.C., Can B7 68
Ice, mtn., W. Va B6 123
Ice, pond, Pa A1 106
Ice Harbor, dam, Wash C7 122
Iceland, country, Eur., 190,000 C5 8, n23 25
Icemorlee, Union, N.C. B3 109
Ichang, China, 81,000 I4 36
Icheng, China, 15,000 I5 36
Ichi Banare, isl., Okinawa 52
Ichikawa, Jap., 157,301 n18 37
Ichinomiya, Jap., 182,984 n15 37
Ichinoseki, Jap., 25,700 (57,585▲) G10 37
Ichnya, Sov. Un., 10,000 F9 27
Ichuan, China F4 36
Ichun, China, 60,000 B11 34
Ichun, China, 19,000 K6 36
Icicle, creek, Wash B5 122
Ickesburg, Perry, Pa., 300 F7 114
Icó, Braz., 5,586 C3 57
Icy, cape, Alsk A7 79
Icy, strait, Alsk k22 79
Ida, Caddo, La., 300 A2 95
Ida, Monroe, Mich., 700 G7 98
Ida, co., Iowa, 10,269 B2 92
Ida, lake, Minn E3 99
Ida, mtn., Grc E5 29
Idabel, McCurtain, Okla., 4,967 D7 112
Ida Grove, Ida, Iowa, 2,265 B2 92
Idah, Nig., 7,334 E6 45
Idaho, co., Idaho, 13,542 D3 89
Idaho, state, U.S., 667,191 B5 76, 89
Idaho City, Boise, Idaho, 188 F3 89
Idaho Falls, Bonneville, Idaho, 33,161 F6 89
Idaho Springs, Clear Creek, Colo., 1,480 B5 83
Idalia, Yuma, Colo., 75 B8 83
Idalou, Lubbock, Tex., 1,274 C2 118
Idamay, Lee, Ky., 100 C6 94
Idana, Clay, Kans., 100 C6 93
Idanha, Marion, Oreg., 295 C4 113
Idanha-a-Nova, Port., 4,459 C2 20
Idar-Oberstein, Ger., 30,200 D2 17
Idaville, White, Ind., 600 C4 91
Idd Abu Sufyan (Well), Sud B2 47
Iddan, Som D6 47
'Iddel Ghanam, Sud C1 47
Iddesleigh, Alta., Can D5 69
Ideal, Macon, Ga., 432 D2 87
Ideal, Tripp, S. Dak., 30 D6 116
Idehan, des., Libya D2 43
Idehan Marzūq, dunes, Libya E2 43
Ider, DeKalb, Ala., 140 A4 78
Idetown, Luzerne, Pa., 200 B7 114
Idfīnā, Eg., U.A.R., 1,000 C2 32
Idfū, Eg., U.A.R., 20,700 E6 43
Idhra, Grc., 2,786 D7 23
Ídhra (Hydra), isl., Grc D4 23
Idi, Indon E1, m11 35
Idiofa, Con. L E2 48
Idkū, Eg., U.A.R., 1,000 C2 32
Idlewild, Gibson, Tenn., 100 A3 117
Idleyld Park, Douglas, Oreg., 100 D4 113
Idlib, Syr., 23,700 E11 31
Idnah, Jordan, 3,000 C6 32
Idrigill, pt., Scot C2 13
Idrija, Yugo., 6,024 B2 22
Idrinskoye, Sov. Un E27 9
Idritsa, Sov. Un., 7,000 C7 27
Idro, lake, It D6 18
Ie, isl., Okinawa 52
Ieper, Bel., 18,121 D2 15
Ierapetra, Grc., 5,521 E5 23
Ierissos, Grc., 2,768 B4 23
Iesi, It., 21,900 C4 21
Ifakara, Tan C4 48
Ife, Nig., 110,790 E5 45
Iférouane, Niger C6 45
Ifni (city), see Sidi Ifni, Ifni
Ifni, Sp. dep., Afr., 51,000 D2 44
Iganga, Ug A5 48
Igaraçu, Braz., 2,116 h6 57
Igara Paraná, riv., Col D3 60
Igarapava, Braz., 9,083 F1 57
Igarape Açu, Braz., 4,195 B1 57
Igarapé Miri, Braz., 2,591 C5 59
Igarka, Sov. Un., 14,300 C11 28
Igdir, Tur., 12,700 C15 31
Iglesias, It., 28,004 E2 21
Igloo, Fall River, S. Dak., 750 D2 116
Igloolik, N.W. Ter., Can., 133 C23 4
Ignace, Ont., Can., 517 *E7 72
Ignacio, LaPlata, Colo., 609 D3 83
Igneada, Tur., 713 B6 23
Igny, Fr., 4,931 h9 14
Igoumenitsa, Grc., 2,448 C3 23
Igra, Sov. Un B4 29
Iguaçu, cataracts, Braz D2 56
Iguaçu, riv., Braz D2 56
Iguala, Mex., 28,814 D4, n14 63
Igualada, Sp., 19,866 B6 20
Igualdad Central, P.R B2 65
Iguape, Braz., 5,465 C3 56
Iguatemi, riv., Braz C2 56
Iguatu, Braz., 16,540 C3 57
Iguidi, sand dunes, Alg., Maur D3 44
Igurin, isl., Eniwetok 52
Iha, Okinawa 52
Ihlen, Pipestone, Minn., 111 G2 99
Ihosy, Malag L7 49
Ihsien, China D9 36
Ihsien, China F8 36
Ihsien, China G7 36
Ihsing, China, 93,000 I8 36
Iida, Jap., 44,300 (67,555▲) I8, n16 37
Iide-San, peak, Jap H9 37
Iijima, Jap., 3,200 n16 37
Iisalmi, Fin., 6,000 F12 25
Iizuka, Jap., 60,431 (*120,000) *J5 37
Ijamsville, Frederick, Md., 120 B3 85
Ijebu Ode, Nig., 27,558 E5 45
IJmuiden, Neth., 67,300 B4 15
IJssel, riv., Neth B6 15
IJsselmeer (Zuider Zee), sea, Neth B5 15
Ijuí, Braz., 19,671 D2 56
Ijuí, riv., Braz D2 56
Ikaalinen, Fin., 700 G10 25
Ikaria, isl., Grc D6 23
Ikast, Den., 5,797 B3 24
Ikeda, Jap., 59,688 o14 37
Ikela, Con. L B3 48
Ikerre, Nig., 35,584 *E6 45
Ikhtiman, Bul., 6,516 D6 22
Iki, isl., Jap J4 37
Ila, Madison, Ga., 216 B3 87
Ilagan, Phil., 7,436 B6 35
Ilan, Taiwan, 38,910 *G9 34
Ilan (Sanhsing), China, 40,000 B10 34
Ilanz, Switz., 1,843 C7 19
Ilawa, Pol., 2,220 B5 26
Ilbunga, Austl E6 51
Ilchester, Howard, Md., 60 B4 85
Ilderton, Ont., Can., 289 D3 72
Île-à-la-Crosse, Sask., Can., 570 m7 70
Ile-a-la-Crosse, lake, Sask., Can B1 70
Île aux Coudres, isl., Que., Can B7 73
Île aux Grues, isl., Que., Can B7 73
Île aux Lièvres, isl., Que., Can B8 73
Île aux Oies, isl., Que., Can B7 73
Ile-de-France, former prov., Fr., 7,733,000 C5 14
Ile de France, hills, Fr F3 15
Île d' Orléans, isl., Que., Can C6 73
Île du Bic, isl., Que., Can A9 73
Île-Perrot, Que., Can., 3,106 q19 73
Ilesha, Nig., 72,029 E5 45
Ilfeld, San Miguel, N. Mex., 175 B4 107
Ilford, Man., Can., 165 A4 71
Ilford, Eng., 178,210 k13 10, C8 12
Ilfracombe, Eng., 8,701 C3 12
Ilgin, Tur., 3,100 C8 31
Ílhavo, Port., 6,969 B1 20
Ilhéus, Braz., 45,712 D3 57
Ili, Sov. Un E9 29
Ili, riv., Sov. Un G24 9
Ilia (Elis), prov., Grc., 188,861 *D3 23
Iliamna (Newhalen), Alsk., 110 D8 79
Iliamna, lake, Alsk D8 79
Iliamna, vol., Alsk g15 79
Iliff, Logan, Colo., 204 A7 83
Iligan, Phil., 14,281 (58,433▲) *D6 35
Iliki, lake, Grc g10 23
Ilinskaya, Sov. Un., 10,000 I13 27
Iliodhromia, isl., Grc C4 23
Ilion, Herkimer, N.Y., 10,199 B5 108
Ilkeston, Eng., 34,672 B6 12
Ilkley, Eng., 18,519 G7 13
Ill, riv., Aus E4 16
Illampu, mtn., Bol C2 55
Illana, bay, Phil D6 35
Illapel, Chile, 8,266 A2 54
Ille-et-Vilaine, dept., Fr., 614,268 *C3 14
Iller, riv., Ger C5 17
Ille [-sur-la-Têt], Fr., 3,957 F5 14
Illianna, lake, Alsk D8 79
Illiers, Fr., 2,174 C4 14
Illinois, state, U.S., 10,081,158 B10 77, 90
Illinois, bayou, Ark B2 81
Illinois, peak, Idaho, Mont B3 89
Illinois, riv., Ill B5 90
Illinois, riv., Ark., Okla B6 112
Illinois, riv., Oreg E3 113
Illinois City, Rock Island, Ill., 200 B3 90
Illiopolis, Sangamon, Ill., 995 D4 90
Illkirch-Graffenstaden, Fr., 9,607 F7 15
Illmo, Scott, Mo., 1,174 D8 101
Illo, Nig D5 45
Illora, Sp., 13,458 D4 20
Ilmen, lake, Sov. Un B8 27
Ilmenau, Ger., 17,700 C5 17
Ilmenau, riv., Ger B5 17
Ilo, Peru, 1,043 E3 58
Ilobu, Nig., 38,322 *E5 45
Ilocos Norte, prov., Phil., 287,000 *B6 35
Ilocos Sur, prov., Phil., 338,600 *B6 35
Iloilo, Phil., 151,266 C6 35
Iloilo, prov., Phil., 966,100 *C6 35
Ilorin, Nig., 40,994 E5 45
Ilovaysk, Sov. Un., 10,000 r21 27
Ilovlinskaya, Sov. Un D2 29
Ilsenburg, Ger., 6,713 B5 17
Ilubabor, prov., Eth D3 47
Ilwaco, Pacific, Wash., 518 C1 122
Ilwaki, Indon G7 35
Ilza, Pol., 3,813 C6 26
Imabari, Jap., 81,000 (100,082▲) I6 37
Imambaba, Sov. Un C11 41
Im Amguel, Alg E6 44
Iman, Sov. Un., 18,000 E16 28
Iman, riv., Sov. Un D7 37
Imathia, prov., Grc., 114,515 *B4 23
Imazu, Jap., 4,300 n15 37
Imbābah, Eg., U.A.R., 136,429 *C6 43
Imbabura, prov., Ec., 157,356 A2 58
Imbler, Union, Oreg., 137 B9 113
Imboden, Lawrence, Ark., 400 A4 81
Ime, mt., Scot D3 13
Imgyt, marsh, Sov. Un B8 29
Imias, Cuba E6 64
Imienpo, China, 1,000 D4 37
Imilac, Chile D2 55
Imlay, Pershing, Nev., 100 C3 104
Imlay City, Lapeer, Mich., 1,968 E7 98
Imlaystown, Monmouth, N.J., 240 C3 106
Immeln, lake, Swe B8 24
Immenstadt, Ger., 10,000 E5 16
Immokalee, Collier, Fla., 3,224 F5 86
Imnaha, Wallowa, Oreg., 30 B10 113
Imnaha, riv., Oreg B10 113
Imogene, Fremont, Iowa, 264 D2 92
Imola, It., 29,000 (53,400▲) B3 21
Imotski, Yugo., 3,785 D3 23
Imperatriz, Braz., 9,004 C1 57
Imperia, It., 36,500 C1 21
Imperial, Imperial, Calif., 3,007 F6 82
Imperial, Sask., Can., 557 F3 70
Imperial, Jefferson, Mo., 250 B8, C7 101
Imperial, Chase, Nebr., 1,423 D4 103
Imperial, Allegheny, Pa., 2,000 B5 114
Imperial, Pecos, Tex., 750 D1 118
Imperial, co., Calif., 72,105 F6 82
Imperial, diversion dam, Ariz E1 80
Imperial, val., Calif F5 82
Imperial Beach, San Diego, Calif., 17,773 *E2 82
Imperial Mills, Alta., Can., 211 B5 69
Imphal, India, 67,717 D9 39
Imroz, isl., Tur B5 23
Imst, Aus., 5,074 E5 16
Imus, Phil., 3,715 o13 35
'Imwās, Jordan, 2,000 h10 32
Ina, Jap., 18,300 n16 37
Ina, Jefferson, Ill., 332 E5 90
Ina, riv., Pol B3 26
In Ahmar (Well), Maur C3 45
Inajá, Braz., 1,079 C3 57
In Alay, Mali C4 45
Inanwatan, W. Irian F8 35
Iñapari, Peru, 131 D4 58
Inarajan, Guam, 761 52
Inarajan, bay, Guam 52
Inari, Fin., 300 C12 25
Inari, lake, Fin C12 25
Inatori, Jap., 9,100 o18 37
Inavale, Webster, Nebr., 150 D7 103
Inawashiro, lake, Jap H10 37
In Azaoua (Oasis), Niger B6 45
In Belbel, Alg D5 44
In Beriem (Well), Mali C4 45
Inca, Sp., 13,816 C7 20
Incastro, riv., It h9 21
Ince, cape, Tur A10 31
Incesu, Tur., 5,900 C10 31
Inch, Ire E2 11
Inchard, bay, Scot B3 13
Inchelium, Ferry, Wash., 100 A7 122
Inchon, Kor., 430,100 H3 37
Indaal, inlet, Scot E2 13
Indalsälven, riv., Swe F7 25
Indan, Phil o14 35
Indang, Phil., 2,747 o13 35
Indaw, Bur., 2,138 D10 39
Independence, Inyo, Calif., 950 D4 82
Independence, Warren, Ind., 170 D3 91
Independence, Buchanan, Iowa, 5,498 B6 92
Independence, Montgomery, Kans., 11,222 E8 93
Independence, Kenton, Ky., 309 A7, B5 94
Independence, Tangipahoa, La., 1,941 D5 95
Independence, Hennepin, Minn., 1,446 *F5 99
Independence, Tate, Miss., 159 A4 100
Independence, Jackson, Mo., 62,328 B3, E2 101
Independence, Cuyahoga, Ohio, 6,868 B2 111
Independence, Polk, Oreg., 1,930 C1, C3 113
Independence, Grayson, Va., 679 E1 121
Independence, Trempealeau, Wis., 954 D2 124
Independence, co., Ark., 20,048 B4 81
Independence, mts., Nev C5 104
Independence, riv., N.Y B5 108
Independence, rock, Wyo D5 125
Indepedence Hill, Lake, Ind., 1,824 *B3 91
Independencia, Bol., 1,742 C2 55
Inderagiri, riv., Indon F2 35
Inderborskiy, Sov. Un D4 29
Index, peak, Wyo A3 125
India, country, Asia, 479,000,000 D6 39, G10 33
India, Portuguese, see Goa, Damão, and Diu, ter., India
Indiahoma, Comanche, Okla., 378 C3 112
Indialantic, Brevard, Fla., 1,653 *D6 86
Indian, bay, Fla D4 86
Indian, cave, Tenn C10 117
Indian, creek, Ind H5 91
Indian, creek, Md C4 85
Indian, creek, Ohio C3 111
Indian, creek, S. Dak B3 116
Indian, creek, Tenn B3 117
Indian, creek, W. Va D4 123
Indian, isl., N.C B6 109
Indian, lake, Mich C4 98
Indian, lake, N.Y B6 108
Indian, lake, Ohio B4 111
Indian, mtn., Conn B3 84
Indian, ocean, World G2 2
Indian, peak, Utah E2 119
Indian, peak, Wyo A3 125
Indian, pond, Maine B3 96
Indian, pond, Maine C3 96
Indian, pond, Maine D3 96
Indian, riv., Ont., Can B7 72
Indian, riv., Del C7 85
Indian, riv., Fla D6 86
Indian, riv., N.Y A5 108
Indian, rock, Oreg C8 113
Indian, stream, N.H A1 105
Indiana, Indiana, Pa., 13,005 E3 114
Indiana, co., Pa., 75,366 E3 114
Indiana, state, U.S., 4,662,498 B10 77, 91
Indian Agency, La Plata, Colo., 180 D3 83
Indianapolis, Marion, Ind., 476,258 (*806,900) E5, H8 91
Indianapolis, Custer, Okla B3 112
Indian Bay, Man., Can E4 71
Indian Bayou, Vermilion, La D3 95
Indian Brook, N.S., Can., 66 C9 74
Indian Cove, Owyhee, Idaho G3 89
Indian Creek, Dade, Fla., 60 *G6 86
Indian Gap, Hamilton, Tex., 40 D3 118
Indian Grave, mtn., Ga C2 87
Indian Head, Sask., Can., 1,802 G4 70
Indian Head, Charles, Md., 780 C3 85
Indian Hill, Hamilton, Ohio, 4,526 D2 111
Indian Lake, Hamilton, N.Y., 500 B6 108
Indian Mound, Stewart, Tenn., 325 A4 117
Indian Mound Beach, Plymouth, Mass., 600 *C6 97
Indianola, Vermilion, Ill., 295 D6 90
Indianola, Warren, Iowa, 7,062 B7, C4 92
Indianola, Sunflower, Miss., 6,714 B3 100
Indianola, Red Willow, Nebr., 754 D5 103
Indianola, Pittsburg, Okla., 234 B6 112
Indianola, Allegheny, Pa., 1,000 *E2 114
Indian Pass, Gulf, Fla., 50 C1 86
Indian Prairie, canal, Fla E5 86
Indian River, Ont., Can., 130 C6 72
Indian River (village), Washington, Maine, 100 D5 96
Indian River, Cheboygan, Mich., 300 C6 98
Indian River, co., Fla., 25,309 E6 86
Indian Rocks Beach, Pinellas, Fla., 1,940 E1 86
Indian Springs, Butts, Ga., 250 C3 87
Indian Springs, Martin, Ind., 120 G4 91
Indian Springs, Clark, Nev., 450 G6 104
Indian Town, Martin, Fla., 1,411 E6 87
Indian Trail, Union, N.C., 364 B3 109
Indian Valley, Adams, Idaho, 30 E2 89
Indian Valley, Floyd, Va., 75 E2 121
Indian Wells, Navajo, Ariz., 5 B5 80
Indiera Alta, P.R C3 65
Indiga, Sov. Un., 800 B18 9
Indigirka, riv., Sov. Un C17 28
Indio, Riverside, Calif., 9,745 F5 82
Indio, riv., Pan k10 62
Indio, riv., Pan k12 62
Indochina, reg., Asia D6 38, H13 33
Indonesia, country, Asia, 103,350,000 F6 35, J15 33
Indore, India, 394,941 D6 39, F5 40
Indravati, riv., India H8 40
Indre, dept., Fr., 251,432 *D4 14
Indre-et-Loire, dept., Fr., 395,210 *D4 14
Indus, Koochiching, Minn., 10 B5 99
Indus, riv., Pak C4 39
Indus, riv., mouths, Pak D4 39
Industrial, York, S.C., 1,000 B6 115
Industrial City, Jefferson, Ala., 1,000 *E4 78
Industry, McDonough, Ill., 514 C3 90
Industry, Clay and Dickinson, Kans., 7 C6 93
Industry, Beaver, Pa., 2,338 *E1 114
Ine, Jap., 2,500 n14 37
Inebolu, Tur., 5,900 B9 31
Inez, Martin, Ky., 566 C7 94
Inez, Victoria, Tex., 400 E4 118
Infanta, Phil., 957 o12 35
Infanta, Phil., 2,412 o14 35
Infantas, Col B3 60
Infantes, Sp., 9,909 C4 20
Infiesto, Sp., 1,650 A3 20
Ingá, Braz., 6,383 h6 57
In Gall, Niger C6 45
Ingalls, Bradley, Ark., 100 D3 81
Ingalls, Madison, Ind., 873 E6 91
Ingalls, Gray, Kans., 174 E3 93
Ingalls, Menominee, Mich., 200 C3 98
Ingalls Park, Will, Ill., 6,840 *B5 114
Ingallston, Menominee, Mich C3 98
Ingelheim, Ger., 15,800 D3 17
Ingende, Con. L B2 48
Ingeniero Jacobacci, Arg., 2,257 C3 54
Ingeniero Luiggi, Arg B4 54
Ingenika, riv., B.C., Can A5 68
Ingenio, P.R B6 65
Inger, Itasca, Minn., 135 C5 99
Ingersheim, Fr., 3,006 A3 18
Ingersoll, Ont., Can., 6,874 D4 72
Ingersoll, Alfalfa, Okla., 30 A3 112
Ingham, Austl., 4,790 C8 50
Ingham, Lincoln, Nebr D5 103
Ingham, co., Mich., 211,296 F6 98
Ingham, peak, Utah B2 119
Ingleford, Spokane, Wash D7 122
Ingleside, Queen Annes, Md., 110 B6 85
Ingleside, Adams, Nebr., 400 D7 103
Ingleside, San Patricio, Tex., 3,022 F4 118
Inglewood, Austl., 1,058 D8 51
Inglewood, Los Angeles, Calif., 63,390 F2 82
Inglewood, Ont., Can., 419 D5 72
Inglewood, N.Z., 1,901 M15 52
Inglewood, Davidson, Tenn., 26,527 *A5 117
Inglis, Man., Can., 295 D1 71
Ingold, Sampson, N.C., 100 C5 109
Ingoldsby, Ont., Can., 106 C6 72
Ingolf, Ont., Can., 90 E4 71
Ingolstadt, Ger., 65,400 E6 17
Ingomar, Union, Miss., 262 A4 100
Ingomar, Rosebud, Mont., 65 D9 102
Ingomar, Allegheny, Pa., 1,500 A5 114
Ingonish, N.S., Can., 375 C9 74
Ingonish Beach, N.S., Can., 658 C9 74
Ingornachoix, bay, Newf., Can C3 75
Ingraham, lake, Fla G5 86
Ingram, Randolph, Ark A4 81
Ingram, Allegheny, Pa., 4,730 B5 114
Ingram, Kerr, Tex., 950 *D3 118
Ingram, Rusk, Wis., 99 C3 124
Ingramport, N.S., Can., 107 *E6 74
Ingrid Christensen, coast, Ant C20 5
In Guezzam (Oasis), Alg., 3 F5 44
Ingul, riv., Sov. Un H9 27
Ingulets, riv., Sov. Un H9 27
Inhambane, Moz B5 49
Inhambane, prov., Moz B5 49
Inhambane, bay, Moz B6 49
Inhambupe, Braz., 3,811 D3 57
Inhaminga, Moz A6 49
Inharrime, Moz., 10,000 B6 49
Inhuçu, Braz., 938 B2 57
Inhumas, Braz., 8,298 B3 56
Iniesta, Sp., 4,694 C5 20
Ining (Kuldja), China, 108,200 E10 29
Inírida, riv., Col C4 60
Inishark, isl., Ire D1 11
Inishbofin, isl., Ire D1 11
Inishcrone, Ire., 533 C2 11
Inisheer, isl., Ire D2 11
Inishkea, is., Ire C1 11
Inishmaan, isl., Ire D2 11
Inishmore, isl., Ire D2 11
Inishmurray, isl., Ire C3 11
Inishowen, head, Ire B5 11
Inishtioge, Ire., 292 E4 11
Inishtooskert, isl., Ire E1 11
Inishtrahull, isl., Ire B4 11
Inishturk, isl., Ire D1 11
Inishvickillane, isl., Ire E1 11
Injasuti, peak, Bas., S. Afr D4 49
Injune, Austl., 322 B7 52
Inkerman, N.B., Can., 468 B5 74
Inkerman, Luzerne, Pa., 1,000 *B8 114
Inkom, Bannock, Idaho, 528 G6 89
Inkster, Wayne, Mich., 39,097 F7 98
Inkster, Grand Forks, N. Dak., 282 A8 110
Inland, sea, Jap I6 37
Inlet, Hamilton, N.Y., 300 B6 108
Inlet, pt., N.Y E7 84
Inman, Fayette, Ga., 175 C2 87
Inman, McPherson, Kans., 729 D6 93
Inman, Holt, Nebr., 192 B7 103
Inman, Spartanburg, S.C., 1,714 A3 115
Inman Mills, Spartanburg, S.C., 1,769 *A3 115
Inn, riv., Aus., Ger., Switz E8 17, D6 16
Innamincka, Austl., 25 E7 50
Inner, sound, Scot C3 13
Inner Hebrides, is., Scot D2 13
Innerleithen, Scot., 2,299 E5 13
Inner Mongolia, prov., China, 9,200,000 C8 34
Inner-Rhoden, sub canton, Switz., 12,943 B7 19
Innerthaler, lake, Switz B6 19
Innisfail, Austl., 6,917 C8 50
Innisfail, Alta., Can., 2,270 C4 69
Innisfree, Alta., Can., 291 C5 69
Innokentyevskiy, Sov. Un B10 37
Innsbruck, Aus., 104,900 E5 16
Inny, riv., Ire D4 11
Inola, Rogers, Okla., 584 A6 112
Inongo, Con. L., 2,061 B2 48
Inowroclaw, Pol., 49,300 B5 26
I-n-Rabir, Alg E5 44
Ins, Switz., 2,486 B3 19
In Salah, Alg., 330 (17,511▲) D5 44
Insch, Scot., 1,421 C6 13
Insein, Bur., 27,030 E10 39
Insinger, Sask., Can., 129 F4 70
Inspiration, Gila, Ariz., 500 D5 80
Institute, Kanawha, W. Va., 2,500 C3 123
Instow, Sask., Can H1 70
Intake, Dawson, Mont., 14 C12 102
Intercession City, Osceola, Fla., 500 D5 86
Intercity, Snohomish, Wash., 1,475 *B3 122
Interior, Jackson, S. Dak., 179 D4 116
Interior, Giles, Va., 40 D2 121
Interlachen, Putnam, Fla., 349 C5 86
Interlaken, Berkshire, Mass., 300 *B1 97
Interlaken, Monmouth, N.J., 1,168 *C4 106
Interlaken, Seneca, N.Y., 780 C4 108
Interlaken, Switz., 4,738 C4 19
International Falls, Koochiching, Minn., 6,778 B5 99
International Peace Garden, park, Man., Can., N. Dak E1 71
Intersection, mtn., B.C., Can C7 68
Intervale, Cumberland, Maine E2, E5 96
Intervale, Carroll, N.H., 200 B4 105
Intiyaco, Arg E3 55
Intracoastal, waterway, La., Tex E3 95, E5 118
Inubo, cape, Jap I10 37
Inútil, bay, Chile h12 54
Inuvik, N.W. Ter., Can., 1,248 C6 66
Inver, bay, Ire C3 11
Inveraray, Scot., 501 D3 13
Inverbervie, Scot., 921 D6 13
Invercargill, N.Z., 42,500 (*44,900) Q12 51
Inverell, Austl., 8,208 D8 51
Invergarry, Scot C4 13
Invergordon, Scot., 1,640 C4 13
Inver Grove, Dakota, Minn., 713 E7 99
Invermay, Sask., Can., 395 F4 70
Invermere, B.C., Can., 744 D9 68
Inverness, Bullock, Ala., 100 D4 78
Inverness, Marin, Calif., 450 B4, C2 82
Inverness, N.S., Can., 2,109 C8 74
Inverness, Que., Can., 296 C6 73
Inverness, Citrus, Fla., 1,878 D4 86
Inverness, Cook, Ill., 1,110 *E2 90
Inverness, Sunflower, Miss., 1,039 B3 100
Inverness, Hill, Mont., 200 B6 102
Inverness, Scot., 30,000 C4 13
Inverness, co., N.S., Can., 18,718 C8 74
Inverness, co., Scot., 83,425 C3 13
Inwood, Ont., Can., 201 E3 72
Inwood, Man., Can., 183 D3 71
Inwood, Marshall, Ind., 165 B5 91
Inwood, Lyons, Iowa, 638 A1 92
Inwood, Nassau, N.Y., 9,500 k13 108
Inwood, Berkeley, W. Va., 425 B6 123
Inyanga, Rh A5 49
Inyankara, creek, Wyo A8 125
Inyankara, mtn., Wyo A8 125
Inyo, co., Calif., 11,684 D5 82
Inyokern, Kern, Calif., 450 E5 82
Inza, Sov. Un., 2,000 E16 27
Inzana, lake, B.C., Can B5 68
Ioannina, Grc., 34,997 C3 23
Ioannina, prov., Grc., 155,326 *C3 23
Iola, Clay, Ill., 155 E5 90
Iola, Allen, Kans., 6,885 E8 93
Iola, Waupaca, Wis., 831 D4 124
Iona, N.S., Can., 179 D9 74
Iona, Bonneville, Idaho, 702 F7 89
Iona, Murray, Minn., 328 G3 99
Iona, Gloucester, N.J., 350 D2 106
Iona, Lyman, S. Dak., 25 D6 116
Iona, isl., Scot D2 13
Ione, Amador, Calif., 1,118 C3 82
Ione, Weld, Colo., 100 A6 83
Ione, Nye, Nev., 10 E4 104
Ione, Morrow, Oreg., 350 B7 113
Ione, Pend Oreille, Wash., 648 A8 122
Ionia, Chickasaw, Iowa, 265 A5 92
Ionia, Jewell, Kans., 100 C5 93
Ionia, Ionia, Mich., 6,754 F5 98
Ionia, Benton, Mo., 114 G4 101
Ionia, co., Mich., 43,132 F5 98
Ionian, is., Grc C3 23
Ionian, sea, Grc C2 23
Ios, isl., Grc D5 23
Iosco, co., Mich., 16,505 D7 98
Iosegun, riv., Alta., Can B2 69
Iosegun Lake, Alta., Can., 144 B2 69
Iota, Acadia, La., 1,245 D3 95
Iowa, Calcasieu, La., 1,857 D2 95
Iowa, co., Iowa, 16,396 C5 92
Iowa, co., Wis., 19,631 E3 124
Iowa, state, U.S., 2,757,537 B9 77, 92
Iowa, lake, Iowa A3 92
Iowa, riv., Iowa C5 92
Iowa City, Johnson, Iowa, 33,443 C6 92
Iowa Falls, Hardin, Iowa, 5,565 B4 92
Iowa Park, Wichita, Tex., 3,295 C3 118
Ipameri, Braz., 8,987 E1 57
Ipava, Fulton, Ill., 623 C3 90
Ipel, riv., Czech D5 26
Iphigenia, sound, Alsk n23 79
Ipiales, Col., 11,569 C2 60
Ipin, China, 177,500 F5 34
Ipirá, Braz., 3,807 D3 57
Ipoh, Mala., 125,770 J4 38
Ipoly, riv., Hung B4 24
Ipperwash, prov. park, Ont., Can *C3 72
Ippy, Cen. Afr. Rep D4 46
Ipsala, Tur., 6,000 B6 23
Ipswich, Austl., 51,000 C9 51
Ipswich, Essex, Mass., 5,400 (8,544▲) A6 97
Ipswich, Eng., 119,400 B9 12
Ipswich, Edmunds, S. Dak., 1,131 B6 116
Ipswich, riv., Mass A5 97
Ipu, Braz., 7,724 B2 57
Ipueiras, Braz., 3,173 B2 57
Iquique, Chile, 50,700 D2 55
Iquitos, Peru, 55,700 B3 58
Ira, Jasper, Iowa, 95 C4 92
Ira, Scurry, Tex., 250 C2 118
Ira, Rutland, Vt., 50 (220▲) D2 120
Iraan, Pecos, Tex., 1,255 D2 118
Iracoubo, Fr. Gu., 1,109 A4 59
Iraklion, Grc., 63,458 E5 23
Iraklion, prov., Grc., 208,374 *E5 23
Irala, Par., 1,174 E5 55
Iran (Persia), country, Asia, 23,100,000 F8 33, 41
Iran, mts., Indon., Mala E4 35
Iran, plat., Iran E7 41
Irapa, Ven., 3,657 A5 60
Irapuato, Mex., 83,768 C4, m13 63
Iraq, country, Asia, 7,050,000 F14 31, E2 41
Irasburg, Orleans, Vt., 200 (711▲) B4 120
Irasville, Washington, Vt., 125 C3 120
Irbid, Jordan, 44,685 B7 32
Irbil, Iraq, 34,313 D15 31
Irbit, Sov. Un., 41,200 D21 9
Irebu, Con. L B2 48
Iredell, co., N.C., 62,526 B3 109
Ireland, Dubois, Ind., 340 H3 91
Ireland, Coryell, Tex., 60 D4 118
Ireland (Eire), country, Eur., 2,855,000 E7 8, D3 10
Ireland, isl., Bermuda E13 77
Ireland, pt., Bermuda E13 77
Irene, Clay, S. Dak., 399 D8 116
Irerrer, riv., Alg E6 44
Ireton, Sioux, Iowa, 510 B1 62
Irgiz, Sov. Un., 1,900 D6 29
Irgiz, riv., Sov. Un F21 9
Irharhar, riv., Alg D6 44
Iri, Kor., 55,000 (68,000▲) I3 37
Iringa, Tan., 9,587 C6 48
Iriomote, isl., Ryukyu Is G9 34
Irion, co., Tex., 1,183 D2 118
Iriri, riv., Braz C4 59
Irish, sea, Eur D4 10
Irkutsk, Sov. Un., 390,000 D13 28
Irma, Alta., Can., 425 C5 69
Irmo, Lexington, S.C., 359 C5 115
Iron, St. Louis, Minn., 187 C6 99
Iron, co., Mich., 17,184 B2 98

Iron, co., Mo., 8,041 ... D7 101
Iron, co., Utah, 10,795 ... F2 119
Iron, co., Wis., 7,830 ... B3 124
Iron, mtn., Ariz ... D4 80
Iron, mtn., Fla ... E5 86
Iron, mts., Ire ... C4 11
Iron, mts., Tenn., Va ... C12 117, E1 121
Iron Belt, Iron, Wis., 550 ... B3 124
Iron City, Seminole, Ga., 298 ... F2 87
Iron City, Lawrence, Tenn., 700 ... B4 117
Irondale, Jefferson, Ala., 3,501 ... E5 78
Irondale, Washington, Mo., 335 ... D7 101
Irondale, Jefferson, Ohio, 705 ... B7 111
Irondequoit, Monroe, N.Y., 60,704 ... B3 108
Iron Gate, Alleghany, Va., 716 ... D3 121
Iron Gate, gorge, Rom., Yugo ... C6 22
Ironia, Morris, N.J., 900 ... B3 106
Iron Lightning, Ziebach, S. Dak., 60 ... B4 116
Iron Mountain, Dickinson, Mich., 9,299 ... C2 98
Iron Mountain, St. Francois, Mo., 300 ... D7 101
Iron Mountain, Iron, Utah ... F2 119
Iron Mountain, Laramie, Wyo., 15 ... D7 125
Iron Ridge, Dodge, Wis., 419 ... E5 124
Iron River, Iron, Mich., 3,754 ... B2 98
Iron River, Bayfield, Wis., 900 ... B2 124
Irons, Lake, Mich., 30 ... D5 98
Irons, mtn., Ark ... B3 81
Ironsburg, Monroe, Tenn ... D9 117
Ironside, Que., Can., 359 ... h12 72
Ironside, Malheur, Oreg., 30 ... C9 113
Ironspot, Muskingum, Ohio, 100 ... C5 111
Iron Springs, Yavapai, Ariz., 5 ... C3 80
Ironton, Crow Wing, Minn., 724 ... D5 99
Ironton, Iron, Mo., 1,310 ... D7 101
Ironton, Lawrence, Ohio, 15,745 ... D5 111
Ironwood, Gogebic, Mich., 10,265 ... A5 98
Iroquois, N.B., Can., 818 ... *B1 74
Iroquois, Ont., Can., 1,136 ... C9 72
Iroquois, Iroquois, Ill., 231 ... C6 90
Iroquois, Beadle and Kingsbury, S. Dak., 385 ... C8 116
Iroquois, co., Ill., 33,562 ... C6 90
Iroquois, riv., Ind ... C3 91
Iroquois Falls, Ont., Can., 1,681 ... G16 67
Irosin, Phil., 7,394 ... *C6 35
Irrawaddy, riv., Bur ... D10 39
Irricana, Alta., Can., 167 ... D4 69
Irrigon, Morrow, Oreg., 232 ... B7 113
Irt, riv., Eng ... F5 13
Irthing, Eng ... F6 13
Irtysh, Sov. Un ... C8 29
Irtysh, riv., Sov. Un ... E24 9
Irumu, Con. L ... A4 48
Irún, Sp., 29,814 ... A5 20
Irvine, Alta., Can., 240 ... E5 69
Irvine, Marion, Fla., 200 ... C4 86
Irvine, Estill, Ky., 2,955 ... C6 94
Irvine, Warren, Pa., 300 ... C3 114
Irvine, Scot., 16,910 ... E4 13
Irvine, riv., Scot ... E4 13
Irvines Landing, B.C., Can., 83 ... E5 68
Irving, Montgomery, Ill., 570 ... D4 90
Irving, Lane, Oreg., 200 ... C3 113
Irving, Dallas, Tex., 45,985 ... B5 118
Irving College, Warren, Tenn ... D8 117
Irvington, Mobile, Ala., 350 ... E1 78
Irvington, Washington, Ill., 387 ... E4 90
Irvington, Breckinridge, Ky., 1,190 ... D3 94
Irvington, Douglas, Nebr., 150 ... D3 103
Irvington, Essex, N.J., 59,379 ... k8 106
Irvington, Westchester, N.Y., 5,494 ... g13 108
Irvington, Lancaster, Va., 570 ... D6 121
Irvona, Clearfield, Pa., 781 ... E4 114
Irwin, Bonneville, Idaho, 30 ... F7 89
Irwin, Shelby, Iowa, 425 ... C2 92
Irwin, Cherry, Nebr ... B4 103
Irwin, Westmoreland, Pa., 4,270 ... F2 114
Irwin, Lancaster, S.C., 1,113 ... *B6 115
Irwin, co., Ga., 9,211 ... E3 87
Irwindale, Los Angeles, Calif., 1,518 ... *E4 82
Irwinton, Wilkinson, Ga., 673 ... D3 87
Irwinville, Irwin, Ga., 300 ... E3 87
Isa, Nig ... D6 45
Isa, Okinawa ... 52
Isaac, lake, B.C., Can ... C7 68
Isaac's Harbour, N.S., Can., 139 ... D8 74
Isabel, Barber, Kans., 181 ... E5 93
Isabel, Dewey, S. Dak., 488 ... B4 116
Isabel, mtn., Wyo ... C2 125
Isabela (Basilan), Phil., 11,715 (155,712▲) ... D6 35
Isabela, P.R., 7,302 ... A2 65
Isabela, mun., P.R., 28,754 ... B2 65
Isabela, prov., Phil., 442,800 ... *B6 35
Isabela (Albemarle), isl., Ec ... g5 58
Isabella, Man., Can., 52 ... D1 71
Isabella, Worth, Ga., 100 ... E3 87
Isabella, Delta, Mich ... C4 98
Isabella, Lake, Minn., 50 ... C7 99
Isabella, Major, Okla., 100 ... A3 112
Isabella, Fayette, Pa., 900 ... G2 114
Isabella, Polk, Tenn., 415 ... D9 117
Isabella, co., Mich., 35,348 ... E6 98
Isabella, lake, Minn ... C7 99
Isabella, mts., Nic ... D5 62
Isaccea, Rom., 5,203 ... C9 22
Isachsen, N.W. Ter., Can ... m31 67
Isafjördur, Ice., 2,694 ... m21 25
Isahaya, Jap., 31,900 (64,506▲) ... J5 37
Isaka, Con. L ... B2 48
Isanga, Con. L ... B3 48
Isangi, Con. L ... A3 48
Isanti, Isanti, Minn., 521 ... E5 99
Isanti, co., Minn., 13,530 ... E5 99
Isar, riv., Ger ... E7 17
Isarco, riv., It ... A3 21
'Isawīyah, Jordan ... h12, m14 32
Isbergues, Fr., 4,277 ... D2 15
Isbister, riv., Man., Can ... C4 71
Ischia, isl., It ... D4 21
Ischua, Cattaraugus, N.Y., 200 ... C2 108
Iscia Baidoa (Isha Baidoa), Som., 11,000 (13,200▲) ... E5 47
Ise, riv., Ger ... F4 24
Isel, riv., Aus ... E6 16
Iselin, Middlesex, N.J., 17,000 ... B4 106
Iselin, Indiana, Pa., 500 ... E3 114
Isen, riv., Ger ... A8 18
Isenthal, Switz., 556 ... C6 19
Iseo, lake, It ... B3 21
Isère, dept., Fr., 729,789 ... D1 21
Isère, riv., Fr ... E6 14
Iserlohn, Ger., 56,600 (★97,000) ... B2 17
Isernia, It., 8,600 ... D5 21
Iseyin, Nig., 49,680 ... E5 45
Isezaki, Jap., 54,500 (84,250▲) ... H9, m18 37
Isfahan, see Eşfahān, Iran
Isha Baidoa (Iscia Baidoa), Som., 11,000 (13,200▲) ... E5 47
Ishan, China ... G6 38
Ishawooa, Park, Wyo ... A3 125
Ishawooa Cone, mtn., Wyo ... A3 125
Ishikawa, Okinawa ... 52
Ishikawa, pref., Jap., 973,418 ... *H8 37
Ishim, Sov. Un., 39,000 ... B7 29
Ishim, riv., Sov. Un ... D23 9
Ishimbay, Sov. Un., 53,500 ... C5 29
Ishinomaki, Jap., 83,947 ... G10 37
Ishioka, Jap., 17,800 ... m19 37
Ishkashim, Afg., 5,000 ... C15 41
Ishpeming, Marquette, Mich., 8,857 ... B3 98
Isigny-sur-Mer, Fr., 2,391 ... C3 14
Isil-Kul, Sov. Un ... C8 29
Isiolo, Ken ... A6 48
Isisford, Austl., 294 ... B5 51
Iskenderun (Alexandretta), Tur., 62,061 ... D11 31
Isker, riv., Bul ... D6 22
Iskilip, Tur., 12,300 ... B10 31
Iskitim, Sov. Un., 30,000 ... E25 9
Iskwatikan, lake, Sask., Can ... B3 70
Isla Cabellos, Ur., 1,485 ... E1 56
Isla Cristina, Sp., 8,276 ... D2 20
Islamorada, Monroe, Fla., 700 ... H6 86
Island, McLean, Ky., 462 ... C2 94
Island, co., Wash., 19,638 ... A3 122
Island, beach, N.J ... D4 106
Island, dam, Ala ... B3 78
Island, lake, Man., Can ... C4 71
Island, pond, N.H ... E4 105
Island, pond, Vt ... B5 120
Island Brook, Que., Can ... D6 73
Island City, Union, Oreg., 158 ... B8 113
Island Creek, Plymouth, Mass., 400 ... *B6 97
Island Falls, Sask., Can., 185 ... B4 70
Island Falls, Aroostook, Maine, 800 (1,018▲) ... B4 96
Island Grove, Alachua, Fla., 175 ... C4 86
Island Heights, Ocean, N.J., 1,150 ... D4 106
Island Lake, Man., Can ... C4 71
Island Lake, Lake and McHenry, Ill., 1,639 ... *E2 90
Island Lake, riv., Man., Can ... B4 71
Island No. 40, isl., Tenn ... E8 117
Island Park, Fremont, Idaho, 53 ... E7 89
Island Park, Nassau, N.Y., 3,846 ... *E7 108
Island Park, Newport, R.I., 1,147 ... C12 84
Island Park, res., Idaho ... E7 89
Island Pond, Essex, Vt., 1,319 ... B5 120
Islands, bay, Newf., Can ... D2 75
Islay, Alta., Can., 107 ... C5 69
Islay, isl., Scot ... E2 13
Isle, Mille Lacs, Minn., 529 ... D5 99
Isle, riv., Fr ... E4 14
Isle au Haut, Knox, Maine, 60 (68▲) ... D4 96
Isle-aux-Morts, Newf., Can., 884 ... E2 75
Isle La Motte, Grand Isle, Vt., 180 (238▲) ... B2 120
Isle Maligne (part of Alma), Que., Can ... A6 73
Isle of Ely, co., Eng., 89,112 ... *D7 10
Isle of Hope, Chatham, Ga., 1,500 ... *D6 87
Isle of Man, Br. dep., Eur., 48,000 ... C7 11
Isle of Palms, Charleston, S.C., 1,186 ... F3 115
Isle of Wight, Isle of Wight, Va., 60 ... B6, E6 121
Isle of Wight, co., Eng., 95,479 ... D6 12
Isle of Wight, co., Va., 17,164 ... E6 121
Isle of Wight, isl., Eng ... E6 10
Isle Pierre, B.C., Can., 63 ... C6 68
Isle Royale, isl., Mich ... A2 98
Isle Royale, nat. park, Mich ... A2 98
Islesboro, Waldo, Maine, 150 (444▲) ... D4 96
Islesford, Hancock, Maine, 100 ... D4 96
Islet, isl., Eniwetok ... 52
Isleta, Bernalillo, N. Mex., 800 ... C3, m7 107
Isleta, Indian res., N. Mex ... C3 107
Isleton, Sacramento, Calif., 1,039 ... B6, C3 82
Isle-Verte, Que., Can., 1,517 ... A8 73
Islington, Norfolk, Mass., 3,800 ... h11 97
Islip, Suffolk, N.Y., 12,000 ... *G4 84
Islip Terrace, Suffolk, N.Y., 3,600 ... *G4 84
Islitas, Webb, Tex ... F3 118
Ismā'iliah, canal, Eg., U.A.R ... D3 32
Ismay, Custer, Mont., 59 ... D12 102
Isnā, Eg., U.A.R., 27,900 ... D6 43
Isoka, Zambia ... D5 48
Isola, Humphreys, Miss., 532 ... B3 100
Isola Capo Rizzuto, It., 9,218 ... E6 21
Isola della Scala, It., 9,693 ... D7 18
Isole Pelagie, isl., It ... B2 43
Isoline, Cumberland, Tenn ... C8 117
Isparta, Tur., 36,200 ... D8 31
Ispir, Tur., 2,000 ... B13 31
Israel, country, Asia, 2,520,000 ... F6 33, 32
Israel, riv., N.H ... B3 105
Issano Landing, Br. Gu., 353 ... A3 59
Issaquah, King, Wash., 1,870 ... B3, D2 122
Issaquena, co., Miss., 3,576 ... C2 100
Issia, I.C., 1,800 ... E3 45
Issoire, Fr., 10,454 ... E5 14
Issoudun, Fr., 13,900 ... D4 14
Issue, Charles, Md., 35 ... D4 85
Issyk-kul, lake, Sov. Un ... G24 9
Issy-[les-Moulineaux], Fr., 51,776 ... g10 14
Istachatta, Hernando, Fla., 150 ... D4 86
Istanbul (Constantinople), Tur., 1,466,535 (★1,725,000) ... B7 23, B7 31
Istiaia, Grc., 5,147 ... C4 23
Istokpoga, lake, Fla ... E5 86
Istonio, see Vasto, It.
Istranca, mts., Tur ... B6 23
Istres, Fr., 6,426 ... F6 14
Istrian, pen., Yugo ... C2 22
Itá, Par., 18,777 ... E4 55
Itabaiana, Braz., 11,847 ... C3, h6 57
Itabaiana, Braz., 11,050 ... D3 57
Itabaianinha, Braz., 2,907 ... D3 57
Itabapoana, riv., Braz ... C4 56
Itaberaba, Braz., 8,555 ... D2 57
Itaberaí, Braz., 4,632 ... B3 56
Itabira, Braz., 15,539 ... E2 57
Itaboraí, Braz., 4,930 ... C4, h6 56
Itabuna, Braz., 54,268 ... D3 57
Itacaiunas, riv., Braz ... D4 59
Itacoatiara, Braz., 8,818 ... C3 59
Itaetê, Braz., 1,168 ... D2 57
Itaguaçu, Braz., 1,892 ... E2 57
Itaituba, Braz., 1,187 ... C3 59
Itajaí, Braz., 38,889 ... D3 57
Itajubá, Braz., 31,262 ... C3 57
Itala, Som., 800 ... E6 47
Italia, Nassau, Fla ... B6 86
Italy, Ellis, Tex., 1,183 ... C4 118
Italy, country, Eur., 50,900,000 ... G11 8, 21
Italy Cross, N.S., Can., 158 ... E5 74
Itamaraca, isl., Braz ... h6 57
Itami, Jap., 86,455 ... o14 37
Itanhaém, Braz., 5,376 ... n8 56
Itapecurú, riv., Braz ... B2 57
Itapecuru-Mirim, Braz., 3,385 ... B2 57
Itapemirim, Braz., 4,095 ... C4 56
Itaperuna, Braz., 18,095 ... C4 56
Itapetininga, Braz., 29,468 ... C3, m7 56
Itapeva, Braz., 13,510 ... C3 56
Itapi, riv., Braz ... C3 59
Itapicurú, riv., Braz ... D3 57
Itapipoca, Braz., 7,186 ... B3 57
Itápolis, Braz., 7,430 ... k7 56
Itaporanga, Braz., 5,328 ... C3 57
Itapúa, dept., Par., 111,424 ... E4 55
Itaqui, Braz., 13,223 ... D1 56
Itararé, Braz., 12,812 ... C3 56
Itararé, riv., Braz ... C3 56
Itaretama, Braz., 1,559 ... C3, g5 57
Itarsi, India, 33,611 ... F6 40
Itasca, DuPage, Ill., 3,564 ... E2 88
Itasca, Hill, Tex., 1,383 ... C4 118
Itasca, co., Minn., 38,006 ... C5 99
Itasca, lake, Minn ... C3 99
Itatiaya, peak, Braz ... h5 56
Itatiba, Braz., 12,336 ... m8 56
Itatinga, Braz., 1,628 ... m7 56
Itaúna, Braz., 22,319 ... F2 57
Itawamba, co., Miss., 15,080 ... A5 100
Itea, Grc., 2,532 ... C3 23
Itecoaí, riv., Braz ... C3 58
Ithaca, Gratiot, Mich., 2,611 ... E6 98
Ithaca, Saunders, Nebr., 126 ... E2 103
Ithaca, Tompkins, N.Y., 28,799 ... C4 108
Ithaki, Grc., 2,632 ... C3 23
Itháki (Ithaca), isl., Grc ... C3 23
Itigi, Tan ... C5 48
Itimbiri, riv., Con. L ... A3 48
Itirapina, Braz., 2,730 ... m8 56
Ito, Jap., 43,600 (54,564▲) ... o18 37
Itoko, Con. L ... B3 48
Itoman, Okinawa, 6,872 ... 52
Itsmina, Col., 2,755 ... B2 60
Itta Bena, Leflore, Miss., 1,914 ... B3 100
Itu, Braz., 23,435 ... C3, m8 56
Itu, China ... F8 36
Ituango, Col., 2,673 ... B2 60
Ituiutaba, Braz., 29,724 ... B3 56
Itumbiara, Braz., 12,575 ... B3 56
Ituna, Sask., Can., 837 ... F4 70
Itung, China ... C10 34
Ituxi, riv., Braz ... C4 58
Ityāy al Bārūd, Eg., U.A.R., 1,000 ... D2 32
Itzehoe, Ger., 36,100 ... B4 16
Iuka, Marion, Ill., 378 ... E5 90
Iuka, Pratt, Kans., 225 ... E5 93
Iuka, Tishomingo, Miss., 2,010 ... A5 100
Iva, W. Sam., 623 ... 52
Iva, Anderson, S.C., 1,357 ... C2 115
Ivaí, riv., Braz ... C2 56
Ivalo, Fin., 2,600 ... C12 25
Ivangrad, Yugo., 7,020 ... D4 22
Ivanhoe, Austl., 351 ... F5 51
Ivanhoe, Tulare, Calif., 1,616 ... *D4 82
Ivanhoe, Lincoln, Minn., 719 ... F2 99
Ivanhoe, Sampson, N.C., 40 ... C5 109
Ivanhoe, Wythe, Va., 800 ... E2 121
Ivanić Grad, Yugo., 1,111 ... C3 22
Ivanovichi, Sov. Un ... D7 37
Ivano-Frankovsk, Sov. Un., 78,000 ... G5 27
Ivanovka, Sov. Un., 5,000 ... p21 27
Ivanovka, Sov. Un., 1,000 ... A4 37
Ivanovo, Sov. Un., 368,000 ... B2 29
Ivanteyevka, Sov. Un., 10,000 ... n17 27
Ivato, Malag ... g9 49
Ivaton, Lincoln, W. Va ... C5 123
Ivaylovgrad, Bul., 2,419 ... E8 22
Ivdel, Sov. Un., 40,000 ... A6 29
Ivesdale, Champaign and Piatt, Ill., 360 ... D5 90
Ivigtut, Grnld., 123 ... C19 4
Ivinheima, riv., Braz ... C2 57
Ivins, Washington, Utah, 77 ... F2 119
Ivohibe, Malag., 642 ... h9 49
Ivor, Southampton, Va., 398 ... E6 121
Ivory Coast, country, Afr., 3,775,000 ... F5 42, E3 45
Ivoryton, Middlesex, Conn., 1,000 ... D7 84
Ivösjön, lake, Swe ... B8 24
Ivrea, It., 23,723 ... B1 21
Ivry-Nord, Que., Can ... C3 73
Ivry-sur-Seine, Fr., 53,406 ... g10 14
Ivugivik, Que., Can ... D17 67
Ivy, Dallas, Ark., 150 ... C3 81
Ivy, Monroe, Tenn ... D9 117
Ivy, Albemarle, Va., 250 ... C4 121
Ivy, mtn., Conn ... B4 84
Ivyton, Magoffin, Ky., 500 ... C7 94
Ivywild, El Paso, Colo., 11,065 ... C6 83
Iwakuni, Jap., 100,346 ... I6 37
Iwamisawa, Jap., 37,800 (60,650▲) ... E10 37
Iwamurada, Jap., 7,600 ... m17 37
Iwanai, Jap., 21,100 ... E10 37
Iwate, pref., Jap., 1,448,517 ... *G10 37
Iwaya, Jap., 13,700 ... o14 37
Iwo, Nig., 100,006 ... E5 45
Iwo (Iō), isl., Pac. O ... 52
Iwon, Kor ... F4 37
Ixiamas, Bol., 292 ... B2 55
Ixmiquilpan, Mex., 1,739 ... m14 63
Ixmiquilpan, lake, Mex ... m14 63
Ixtacalco, Mex., 10,896 ... h9 63
Ixtapalapa, Mex., 17,372 ... h9 63
Ixtlán de Juárez, Mex., 1,108 ... o15 63
Ixtlán del Rió, Mex., 8,282 ... C4, m11 63
Iyanbito, McKinley, N. Mex., 150 ... *B1 107
Iyang, China, 80,000 ... J5 36
Izabal, lake, Guat ... C3 62
Izamal, Mex., º,675 ... C7 63
Izard, co., Ark., 6,766 ... A4 81
Izberbash, Sov. Un., 25,000 ... G18 9
Izee, Grant, Oreg ... C7 113
Izegem, Bel., 17,095 ... D3 15
Izhevsk, Sov. Un., 330,000 ... B4 29
Izhma, riv., Sov. Un ... C19 9
Izmail, Sov. Un., 55,000 ... I7 27
Izmir (Smyrna), Tur., 360,829 (★500,000) ... C6 23, C6 31
Izmir, bay, Tur ... C6 23
Izmit (Kocaeli), Tur., 73,488 ... B7 23
İznik, Tur., 6,300 ... B7 23
Iznik, lake, Tur ... B7 23
Izra', Syr., 2,900 ... B8 32
Izu, isl., Pac. O ... D8 7
Izúcar de Matamoros, Mex., 16,175 ... n14 63
Izuhara, Jap., 15,300 ... I4 37
Izumo, Jap., 34,400 (69,219▲) ... I6 37
Izyum, Sov. Un., 34,000 ... G11 27

J

Jabal Al'Uwaynat, mtn., Sud ... A2 47
Jabal Ash Sham, mtn., Mus. & Om ... D2 39
Jabalón, riv., Sp ... C4 20
Jabalpur (Jubbulpore), India, 295,375 (★367,014) ... D6 39, F7 40
Jablonec [nad Nisou], Czech., 27,800 ... C3 26
Jablonna, Czech., 219 ... o17 26
Jablonna, Pol., 2,000 ... k13 26
Jablunkov, pass, Czech ... D5 26
Jaboatão, Braz., 33,963 ... C4, k6 57
Jaboticabal, Braz., 20,231 ... C3, k7 56
Jabrin, isl., Iran ... H5 41
Jaca, Sp., 9,856 ... A5 20
Jacala [de Ledesma], Mex., 1,612 ... m14 63
Jácana, P.R ... C5 65
Jacaraci, Braz., 650 ... D2 57
Jacaré, riv., Braz ... D2 57
Jacareí, Braz., 28,131 ... m9 56
Jacarèzinho, Braz., 14,813 ... C3 56
Jachal, Arg., 4,278 ... F2 55
Jachymov, Czech., 6,806 ... C2 26
Jacinto, Dallas, Ark ... D3 81
Jacinto, Alcorn, Miss., 75 ... A5 100
Jacinto City, Harris, Tex., 9,547 ... F5 118
Jack, co., Tex., 7,418 ... C3 118
Jack, mtn., Mont ... D4 102
Jack, mtn., Va ... C3 121
Jack, mtn., Wash ... A5 122
Jackfish, lake, Sask., Can ... D1 70
Jackfork, mtn., Okla ... C6 112
Jackhead Harbour, Man., Can ... D3 71
Jackman, Somerset, Maine, 300 (984▲) ... C2 96
Jackman Station, Somerset, Maine, 500 ... C2 96
Jacks, peak, Utah ... E3 119
Jacksboro, Campbell, Tenn., 800 ... C9 117
Jacksboro, Jack, Tex., 3,816 ... C3 118
Jacks Creek, Chester, Tenn., 150 ... B3 117
Jackson, Clarke, Ala., 4,959 ... D2 78
Jackson, Amador, Calif., 1,852 ... C3 82
Jackson, Butts, Ga., 2,545 ... C3 87
Jackson, Breathitt, Ky., 1,852 ... C6 94
Jackson, Calcasieu, La., 1,824 ... D4 95
Jackson, Waldo, Maine, 65 (220▲) ... D3 96
Jackson, Jackson, Mich., 50,720 (★121,400) ... F6 98
Jackson, Jackson, Minn., 3,370 ... G4 99
Jackson, Hinds, Miss., 144,422 (★191,200) ... C3 100
Jackson, Cape Girardeau, Mo., 4,875 ... D8 101
Jackson, Beaverhead, Mont., 60 ... E3 102
Jackson, Dakota, Nebr., 224 ... B9 103
Jackson, Carroll, N.H., 200 (315▲) ... B4 105
Jackson, Ocean, N.J., 600 ... C4 106
Jackson, Northampton, N.C., 765 ... A6 109
Jackson, Jackson, Ohio, 6,980 ... C5 111
Jackson, Providence, R.I., 140 ... C10 84
Jackson, Aiken, S.C., 1,746 ... E4 115
Jackson, Madison, Tenn., 34,376 ... B3 117
Jackson, Washington, Wis., 458 ... E1, E5 124
Jackson, Teton, Wyo., 1,437 ... B2 125
Jackson, co., Ala., 36,681 ... A3 78
Jackson, co., Ark., 22,843 ... B4 81
Jackson, co., Colo., 1,758 ... A4 83
Jackson, co., Fla., 36,208 ... B1 86
Jackson, co., Ga., 18,499 ... B3 87
Jackson, co., Ill., 42,151 ... F4 90
Jackson, co., Ind., 30,556 ... G5 91
Jackson, co., Iowa, 20,754 ... B7 92
Jackson, co., Kans., 10,309 ... C8 93
Jackson, co., Ky., 10,677 ... C5 94
Jackson, co., Mich., 131,994 ... F6 98
Jackson, co., Minn., 15,501 ... G3 99
Jackson, co., Miss., 55,522 ... E5 100
Jackson, co., Mo., 622,732 ... C3 101
Jackson, co., N.C., 17,780 ... D3 109
Jackson, co., Ohio, 29,372 ... C5 111
Jackson, co., Okla., 29,736 ... C2 112
Jackson, co., Oreg., 73,962 ... E4 113
Jackson, co., S. Dak., 1,985 ... D4 116
Jackson, co., Tenn., 9,233 ... C8 117
Jackson, co., Tex., 14,040 ... E4 118
Jackson, co., W. Va., 18,541 ... C3 123
Jackson, co., Wis., 15,151 ... D3 124
Jackson, par., La., 15,828 ... B3 95
Jackson, lake, Fla ... B2 86
Jackson, lake, Fla ... E5 86
Jackson, lake, Ga ... C3 87
Jackson, lake, Wyo ... B2 125
Jackson, mtn., Maine ... D2 96
Jackson, mts., Nev ... B3 104
Jackson, riv., Va ... D3 121
Jacksonboro, Colleton, S.C., 400 ... F1, F7 115
Jacksonburg, Wetzel, W. Va., 300 ... A6, B4 123
Jackson Center, Shelby, Ohio, 980 ... B3 111
Jackson Center, Mercer, Pa., 292 ... D1 114
Jackson Hill, Sullivan, Ind., 150 ... F3 91
Jackson Junction, Winneshiek, Iowa, 89 ... A5 92
Jacksonport, Jackson, Ark., 271 ... B4 81
Jackson's Arm, Newf., Can., 422 ... D3 75
Jacksons Gap, Tallapoosa, Ala., 500 ... C4 78
Jacksonville, Calhoun, Ala., 5,678 ... B4 78
Jacksonville, Pulaski, Ark., 14,488 ... C3, D6 81
Jacksonville, Duval, Fla., 201,030 (★456,700) ... B5, B6 86
Jacksonville, Telfair, Ga., 236 ... E3 87
Jacksonville, Morgan, Ill., 21,690 ... D3 90
Jacksonville, Shelby, Iowa, 150 ... C2 92
Jacksonville, Washington, Maine, 250 ... D5 96
Jacksonville, Randolph, Mo., 153 ... B5 101
Jacksonville, Onslow, N.C., 13,491 ... C6 109
Jacksonville, Athens, Ohio, 580 ... C5 111
Jacksonville, Jackson, Oreg., 1,172 ... E4 113
Jacksonville, Cherokee, Tex., 9,590 ... D5 118
Jacksonville, Windham, Vt., 240 ... F3 120
Jacksonville Beach, Duval, Fla., 12,049 ... B5, B6 86
Jacmel, Hai., 8,545 ... F7 64
Jaco, isl., Indon ... G7 35
Jacob Lake, Coconino, Ariz., 125 ... A3 80
Jacobabad, Pak., 22,835 ... C2 40
Jacobina, Braz., 12,373 ... D2 57
Jacobson, Aitkin, Minn., 85 ... C5 99
Jacobstown, Burlington, N.J., 225 ... C3 106
Jacobsville, Houghton, Mich., 100 ... B2 98
Jacoby, Pointe Coupee, La., 290 ... D4 95
Jacomino, Cuba, 6,121 ... h12 64
Jacques-Cartier, Que., Can., 40,807 ... D4, p20 73
Jacques-Cartier, co., Que., Can., 1,747,696 ... q19 73
Jacques Cartier, mtn., Que., Can ... G19 67
Jacques Cartier, pass., Que., Can ... h8 75
Jacques-Cartier, riv., Que., Can ... B6 73
Jacquet, riv., N.B., Can ... B3 74
Jacquet River, N.B., Can., 500 ... B4 74
Jacuí, Braz., 1,372 ... k8 56
Jacuí, riv., Braz ... D2 56
Jacuípe, riv., Braz ... D3 57
Jacuitiba, Braz ... m8 57
Jacumba, San Diego, Calif., 650 ... F5 82
Jacundá, riv., Braz ... C4 59
Jaddi, cape, Pak ... I11 41
Jade, Ger., 3,600 ... A8 15
Jade, bay, Ger ... E2 24
Jadhamiyah, Sau. Ar ... I14 31
Jadotville, Con. L., 74,500 ... D4 48
Jādū, Libya, 960 ... C2 43
Jaegerspris, Den., 1,254 ... C5 24
Jaeggevarre, mtn., Nor ... C8 25
Jaén, Peru, 510 ... C2 58
Jaén, Sp., 64,917 ... D4 20
Jaén, prov., Sp., 736,391 ... *D4 20
Jaffa, see Tel Aviv-Yafo, Isr.
Jaffa, cape, Austl ... H2 51
Jaffna, Cey., 77,181 ... G7 39
Jaffrey, Cheshire, N.H., 1,648 ... E2 105
Jaffrey Center, Cheshire, N.H., 300 ... E2 105
Jafura Dahana, des., Sau. Ar ... I4 41
Jagadhri, India, 32,637 (★84,337) ... B6 40
Jagdalpur, India, 20,412 ... H9 40
Jagin, riv., Iran ... H9 41
Jagok, lake, China ... B12 40
Jagst, riv., Ger ... D4 17
Jaguarão, Braz., 12,336 ... E2 56
Jaguariaíva, Braz., 6,465 ... C3 56
Jagüey Grande, Cuba, 4,374 ... D3 64
Jahrom, Iran, 23,390 ... G6 41
Jahra, Kuw ... G3 41
Jaicós, Braz., 1,308 ... C2 57
Jaipur, India, 403,444 ... C6 39, D5 40
Jaisalmer, India, 8,362 ... D3 40
Jajce, Yugo., 6,839 ... C3 22
Jajpur, India, 13,802 ... G11 40
Jakarta, see Djakarta, Indon.
Jakes Corner, Gila, Ariz., 15 ... C4 80
Jakin, Early, Ga., 176 ... E2 87
Jakobstad (Pietersaari), Fin., 7,378 ... F10 25
Jal, Lea, N. Mex., 3,051 ... E6 107
Jalaigai, pt., Guam ... 52
Jalalabad, Afg., 14,756 ... D15 41
Jalapa, Guat., 6,610 ... C2 62
Jalapa Enríquez (Jalapa), Mex., 66,269 ... D5, n15 63
Jalaun, India, 14,101 ... D7 40
Jalca Grande Amazonas, Peru, 1,189 ... C2 58
Jaleswar, India, 10,000 ... D10 40
Jalgaon, India, 80,351 ... G5 40
Jalisco, Mex., 3,154 ... m11 63
Jalisco, state, Mex., 2,402,884 ... C4, m12 63
Jalna, India, 67,158 ... H5 40
Jalón, riv., Sp ... B5 20
Jalor, India, 12,882 ... E4 40
Jalpa, Mex., 6,204 ... C4, m12 63
Jalpaiguri, India, 48,738 ... D12 40
Jalpan, Mex., 1,009 ... C5, m14 63
Jalu, Libya, 80 ... D4 43
Jālū, oasis, Libya ... D4 43
Jamachim, riv., Braz ... D3 59
Jamaica, Guthrie, Iowa, 256 ... C3 92
Jamaica, Queens, N.Y. (part of New York City) ... k13 108
Jamaica, Windham, Vt., 300 (496▲) ... E3 120
Jamaica, country, N.A., 1,750,000 ... F5 64
Jamaica, bay, N.Y ... k13 108
Jamaica, chan., W.I ... G6 64
Jamalpur, Pak., 57,039 ... E12 40
Jamdena, isl., Indon ... G8 35
James, Jones, Ga., 150 ... D3 87
James, bay, Ont., Can ... F16 67
James, isl., B.C., Can ... C3 68
James, isl., Md ... C5 85
James, isl., S.C ... F8 115
James, lake, Ind ... A7 91
James, lake, N.C ... B2 109
James, pt., Md ... C5 85
James, range, Austl ... D5 50
James, riv., Alta., Can ... D3 69
James, riv., Mo ... E4 101
James, riv., N. Dak ... C7 110
James, riv., S. Dak ... C7 116
James, riv., Va ... D5 121
Jamesburg, Middlesex, N.J., 2,853 ... C4 106
James City, Craven, N.C., 1,474 ... B6 109
James City, Elk, Pa., 450 ... C4 114
James City, co., Va., 11,539 ... D6 121
James Craik, Arg., 2,409 ... A4 54
James Creek (Marklesburg), Huntingdon, Pa., 197 ... E5 114
James Island, B.C., Can., 163 ... g12 68
Jameson, Daviess, Mo., 177 ... A3 101
Jamesport, Daviess, Mo., 622 ... B4 101
Jamesport, Suffolk, N.Y., 260 ... F6 84
James Ross, isl., Ant ... C7 5
James Ross, strait, N.W. Ter., Can ... C13 66
Jamestown, Cherokee, Ala., 150 ... A4 78
Jamestown, Austl., 1,304 ... F2 51
Jamestown, Tuolumne, Calif., 900 ... D3 82
Jamestown, Boulder, Colo., 107 ... A5 83
Jamestown, Clinton, Ill., 80 ... E4 90
Jamestown, Boone, Ind., 827 ... E4 91
Jamestown, Ire., 162 ... D3 11
Jamestown, Cloud, Kans., 422 ... C6 93
Jamestown, Russell, Ky., 792 ... D4 94
Jamestown, Bienville, La., 140 ... B2 91
Jamestown, Montieau, Mo., 216 ... C5 101
Jamestown, Chautauqua, N.Y., 41,818 ... C1 108
Jamestown, Guilford, N.C., 1,247 ... B4 109
Jamestown, Stutsman, N. Dak., 15,163 ... C7 110
Jamestown, Greene, Ohio, 1,730 ... C4 111
Jamestown, Mercer, Pa., 897 ... D1 114
Jamestown, Newport, R.I., 2,267 ... D11 84
Jamestown, Berkeley, S.C., 184 ... E8 115
Jamestown, Fentress, Tenn., 1,727 ... C9 117
Jamestown, James City, Va., 5 ... A6 121
Jamestown, res., N. Dak ... B7 110
Jamesville, Onondaga, N.Y., 1,000 ... *C4 108
Jamesville, Martin, N.C., 538 ... B7 109
Jamesville, Northampton, Va., 300 ... D7 121
Jamieson, Gadsden, Fla., 100 ... B2 86
Jamieson, Maheur, Oreg., 10 ... C9 113
Jamiltepec, Mex., 2,029 ... D5 63
Jamison, Keya Paha, Nebr., 200 ... B6 103
Jammain, Jordan, 2,000 ... g11 32
Jammer Bugt, bay, Den ... A3 24
Jammu, India, 102,738 (★108,257) ... A5 40, B5 39
Jammu and Kashmir, disputed reg., India, Pak., 4,700,000 ... B6 39
Jamnagar, India, 139,692 (★148,572) ... D5 39, F3 40
Jampur, Pak., 13,235 ... C3 40
Jamsah, Eg., U.A.R ... D6 43
Jamshedpur, India, 291,791 (★328,044) ... D8 39, F11 40
Jämshög, Swe., 1,024 ... B8 24
Jämtland, co., Swe., 137,600 ... *F6 25

Judyville, Warren, Ind., 70..D3 91
Juelsminde, Den., 950......C4 24
Juian, China, 36,000.........K9 36
Juigalpa, Nic., 5,600.......D5 62
Juist, Ger., 2,300............A6 15
Juist, isl., Ger...............B3 16
Juiz de Fora, Braz., 124,979...........C4, g6 56
Jujuy, Arg., 31,091..........D2 55
Jujuy, prov., Arg., 239,783..D2 55
Jukao, China, 80,000.........H9 36
Jukkasjärvi, Swe., 540.......D9 25
Julesburg, Sedgwick, Colo., 1,840...........A8 83
Juliaca, Peru, 7,002........E3 58
Juliaetta, Latah, Idaho, 368..C2 89
Julian, San Diego, Calif., 400..........F5 82
Julian, Nemaha, Nebr., 131.D10 103
Julian, Randolph and Guilford, N.C., 200..........B4 109
Julian, Boone, W. Va., 300..........C3, D5 123
Julian Alps, mts., Yugo.......C2 22
Julianehåb, Grnld., 1,741...C19 4
Jülich, Ger., 14,700.........D6 15
Julietta, Marion, Ind........H8 91
Juliette, Monroe, Ga., 550...C3 87
Julimes, Mex., 1,209.........B3 63
Júlio de Castilhos, Braz., 6,438.........D2 56
Julita, Swe., 266...........t34 25
Juliustown, Burlington, N.J., 400.........C3 106
Jullundur, India, 222,569 (★265,030).B5 40, B6 39
Jumas, riv., Braz..........C2 59
Jumento, is., Ba. Is.........D6 64
Jumet, Bel., 28,713.........D4 15
Jumilla, Sp., 16,199........C5 20
Jumna, riv., India..........E8 40
Jump, riv., Wis.............C2 124
Jumping, lake, Sask., Can.....E3 70
Jumping Branch, Summers, W. Va., 100..........D4 123
Jumullong Manglo, mtn., Guam.... 52
Junagadh, India, 74,298.........D5 39, G3 40
Junan, China, 30,000.......H6 36
Juncos, P.R., 6,247.........C7 65
Juncos, mun., P.R., 21,496..C7 65
Juncos Central, P.R.........C7 65
Junction, Gallatin, Ill., 238..F5 90
Junction, Paulding, Ohio, 40..........A3 111
Junction, Kimble, Tex., 2,441..........D3 118
Junction, Piute, Utah, 219...E3 119
Junction City, Union, Ark., 749..........D3 81
Junction City, Talbot, Ga., 226..........D2 87
Junction City, Geary, Kans., 17,700........C7 93
Junction City, Boyle, Ky., 1,047..........C5 94
Junction City, Union, La., 639..........B3 95
Junction City, Perry, Ohio, 763..........C5 111
Junction City, Lane, Oreg., 1,614..........C3 113
Junction City, Portage, Wis., 381..........D4 124
Jundah, Austl., 122.........B4 51
Jundiaí, Braz., 79,536...C3, m8 56
Juneau, Alsk., 6,797...D13, k22 79
Juneau, Dodge, Wis., 1,718..........E5 124
Juneau, co., Wis., 17,490....E3 124
Junee, Austl., 3,980.........G6 51
June Lake, Mono, Calif., 25..D4 82
Jungcheng, China..........F10 36
Jungchiang, China, 10,000...L3 36
Jungfrau, mtn., Switz........C4 19
Junghsien, China, 15,000....F6 34
Junglinster, Lux., 1,802......E6 15
Jungyun, China.............G7 34
Juniata, Adams, Nebr., 422..D7 103
Juniata, co., Pa., 15,874.....E7 114
Juniata, riv., Pa............E7 114
Juniata Terrace, Mifflin, Pa., 1,130..........E6 114
Junín, Arg., 36,149.........A4 54
Junín, Peru, 3,058..........D2 58
Junín, dept., Peru, 431,082..D2 58
Junín, lake, Peru...........D2 58
Junín de los Andes, Arg.....B2 54
Junior, Barbour, W. Va., 552..........C5 123
Junior, lake, Maine.........C4 96
Juniper, N.B., Can., 691.....C2 74
Juniper, Talbot, Ga., 100...D2 87
Juniper, flat, Oreg.........B5 113
Juniper, mtn., Oreg.........E7 113
Junipero Serra, peak, Calif......D3 82
Junius, Lake, S. Dak., 50...C8 116
Juno, Henderson, Tenn.......B3 117
Juno, Val Verde, Tex., 30...D2 118
Juno Beach, Palm Beach, Fla., 249..........*F6 86
Junor, Sask., Can...........D2 70
Juntura, Malheur, Oreg., 98..........D8 113
Jupiter, Palm Beach, Fla., 1,058..........F6 86
Jupiter, inlet, Fla..........F6 86
Jupiter, isl., Fla...........E6 86
Juquiá, Braz., 2,573.....C3, n8 56
Jur, riv., Sud.............D2 47
Jura, dept., Fr., 225,682....C1 18
Jura, isl., Scot............D3 13
Jura, mts., Switz., Fr........C1 19
Jura, sound, Scot...........E3 13
Jurbarkas, Sov. Un., 5,000...A7 26
Jurby, head, I. of Man.......F4 13
Jurf ad Darāwish, Jordan, 1,000..........D7 32
Juriti, Braz., 1,868.........C3 59
Juruá, riv., Braz............C4 58
Juruena, riv., Braz.........D3 59
Juskatla, B.C., Can., 214....C1 68
Jussey, Fr., 2,235...........B1 18
Justice, Cook, Ill., 2,803....*F2 90
Justiceburg, Garza, Tex., 50..........C2 118
Justin, Denton, Tex., 622..........A5, C4 118
Justo Daract, Arg., 4,663....A3 54
Jutaí, riv., Braz............B4 58
Jüterbog, Ger., 13,500.......B8 17
Jutiapa, Guat., 5,162........C3 62
Juticalpa, Hond., 3,372.....C4 62
Jutland, pen., Den..........B3 24
Juwain, Afg., 5,000.........F10 41
Jüymand, Iran..............D9 41
Južna Morava, riv., Yugo.....D5 22
Jyderup, Den., 2,305.........C5 24
Jyekundo (Yushu), China....E4 34
Jyväskylä, Fin., 43,600.....F11 25

K

Kaaawa, Honolulu, Haw., 450..........f10 88
Kaala, peak, Haw............f9 88
Kaalaea, Honolulu, Haw., 300..........g10 88
Kabaena, isl., Indon.........G6 35
Kabala, S.L................E2 45
Kabale, Ug., 10,919.........B5 48
Kabalo, Con. L.............C4 48
Kabambare, Con. L..........B4 48
Kabarnet, Ken..............A6 48
Kabba, Nig.................E6 45
Kabelstation, Sur...........B3 59
Kabenga, Con. L............C4 48
Kabetogama, lake, Minn.......B5 99
Kabinda, Con. L............C3 48
Kabir Kuh, mts., Iran........E3 41
Kabompo, riv., Zambia.......D3 48
Kabong, Mala., 1,957........E4 35
Kabongo, Con. L............C4 48
Kaboudia, cape, Tun.......G12 30
Kabul, Afg., 236,000.......D14 41
Kabul, riv., Afg............D14 41
Kacak, riv., Czech..........n17 26
Kachek, China..............C9 38
Kachess, res., Wash.........B4 122
Kachuga, Sov. Un., 53,500..D13 28
Kackley, Republic, Kans., 50..........C6 93
Kadan, Czech., 5,062.......C8 17
Kade, Ghana, 2,077.........E4 45
Kadet, chan., Ger..........D6 24
Kadinhan, Tur., 4,338.......C9 31
Kadiri, India, 24,307........F6 39
Kadiyevka, Sov. Un., 192,000.........G12, q21 27
Kadoka, Jackson, S. Dak., 840..........D4 116
Kadugli, Sud., 4,716........C2 47
Kaduna, Nig., 22,511 (★38,794)..........D6 45
Kaduna, riv., Nig...........D6 45
Kaea, cape, Haw............C5 88
Kaédi, Maur., 8,500.........C2 45
Kaélé, Cam., 619............C2 46
Kaeleku, Maui, Haw., 5......C5 88
Kaena, pt., Haw.............C4 88
Kaena, pt., Haw...........B3, f8 88
Kaeryong, Kor., 6,200.......H4 37
Kaesong, Kor., 100,000 (139,900▲)..........H3 37
Kāf, Sau. Ar., 10,000.......C7 43
Kafanchan, Nig., 7,016......E6 45
Kaffrine, Sen...............D1 45
Kafia Kingi, Sud............D1 47
Kafr ad Dawwār, Eg., U.A.R., 10,000..........C2 32
Kafr 'Ammār, Eg. U.A.R....E3 32
Kafr ash Shaykh, Eg., U.A.R., 3,000..........C2 32
Kafr az Zayyāt, Eg., U.A.R., 25,100..........D2 32
Kafr Dā'ūd, Eg., U.A.R....D2 32
Kafr Malik, Jordan, 2,000...h12 32
Kafr Qaddum, Jordan, 2,000.g11 32
Kafr Qasim, Isr.............g10 32
Kafr Şaqr, Eg., U.A.R., 1,000..........D3 32
Kafr Zibad, Jordan, 2,000...g11 32
Kafue, Zambia, 2,100.......E4 48
Kafue, riv., Zambia..........D4 48
Kagan, Sov. Un., 30,000...B12 41
Kaganovich, Sov. Un., 10,000..........E12 27
Kagawa, pref., Jap., 918,867.*I7 37
Kagawong, Ont., Can., 58....B2 72
Kagera, riv., Tan............B5 48
Kagizman, Tur., 7,200.......B14 31
Kagman, mtn., Saipan.......... 52
Kagoshima, Jap., 296,003...K5 37
Kagoshima, pref., Jap., 1,963,104..........*K5 37
Kagoshima, bay, Jap.........K5 37
Kagul, Sov. Un., 20,000.....C9 22
Kaguyak, Alsk., 36..........D9 79
Kahajan, riv., Indon........F4 35
Kahakuloa, Maui, Haw., 35..B5 88
Kahaluu, Hawaii, Haw., 50..D6 88
Kahaluu, Honolulu, Haw., 1,125..........g10 88
Kahama, Tan., 1,866.........B5 48
Kahana, Honolulu, Haw., 375..........B4, f10 88
Kahemba, Con. L............C2 48
Kahira, Okinawa............ 52
Kahla, Ger., 9,342..........C6 17
Kahnūj, Iran...............H8 41
Kahlotus, Franklin, Wash., 131..........C7 122
Kahoka, Clark, Mo., 2,160.*A6 101
Kahoolawe, isl., Haw.........C5 88
Kahua, Hawaii, Haw., 81....C6 88
Kahuku, Oahu, Haw., 1,238..........B4, f10 88
Kahuku, pt., Haw...........B4 88
Kahului, Maui, Haw., 4,223..........C5 88
Kaiama, Nig................E5 45
Kaiapoi, N.Z., 3,110........O14 51
Kaiba, isl., Sov. Un.........C10 37
Kaibab, Mohave, Ariz., 40..A3 80
Kaibab, Indian res., Ariz......A3 80
Kaibab, plat., Ariz..........A3 80
Kaibito, Coconino, Ariz., 65.A4 80
Kaieteur, falls, Br. Gu........A3 59
Kaifeng, China, 299,100.....G6 36
Kaihsien, China, 21,000.....E6 36
Kaihua, China, 6,000........J8 36
Kaikoura, N.Z., 1,328.......O14 51
Kailas, range, China........C11 40
Kailu, China...............C9 36
Kailua, Honolulu, Haw., 25,622..........g11 88
Kailua-Kona, Hawaii, Haw., 600..........D6 88
Kaimana, W. Irian, 800......F8 35
Kaimare, Pap...............k11 50
Kaimu, Hawaii, Haw., 16...D7 88
Kainaliu, Hawaii, Haw., 510.D6 88
Kainalu, Maui, Haw., 60....B5 88
Kainan, Jap., 42,100 (52,532▲)..........I7 37
Kaintira, India, 5,000.......G10 40
Kaiparowits, plat., Utah.......F4 119
Kaiping, China, 40,000.....D10 36
Kaipokok, bay, Newf., Can.....g10 75
Kairouan, Tun., 33,968......B7 44
Kairouan, prov., Tun., 205,039..........*B7 44
Kaiser, Price, Wis..........C3 124
Kaiserslautern, Ger., 86,800..D2 17
Kaiserstuhl, Switz., 398......A5 19
Kaiser Wilhelm (Kiel), canal, Ger..........D3 24
Kaisiadorys, Sov. Un........A8 26
Kaitaia, N.Z., 2,706........K14 51
Kaitangata, N.Z., 1,249....Q12 51
Kaithal, India, 34,890.......C6 40
Kaitung, China.............B10 36
Kaiwi, chan., Haw...........B4 88
Kaiyuan, China, 25,000.....E2 37
Kaizuka, Jap., 61,067......o14 37
Kajaani, Fin., 14,700.......E12 25
Kajakai, res., Afg...........E12 41
Kajan, riv., Indon...........E5 35
Kajiado, Ken...............B6 48
Kajikazawa, Jap., 4,500.....n17 37
Kaka, Sud..................C3 47
Kakagi, lake, Ont., Can......E5 71
Kakamas, S. Afr.............C3 49
Kakamega, Ken..............A5 48
Kake, Alsk., 455.......D13, m23 79
Kakegawa, Jap., 27,600 (59,762▲)..........O17 37
Kakhovka, Sov. Un., 30,000.H9 27
Kakhovka, res., Sov. Un......H9 27
Kakinada, India, 122,865..........E7 39, I9 40
Kakisa, lake, N.W. Ter., Can..D9 66
Kakogawa, Jap., 57,800 (89,539▲)..........*I7 37
Kakumaa, Ken..............A5 48
Kakwa, riv., Alta., B.C., Can..B7 68
Kalabagh, Pak., 10,523.....B5 38
Kalabakan, Mala............E5 35
Kalabana, Mali.............D3 45
Kalābishah, Eg., U.A.R.....E6 43
Kalabo, Zambia, 1,710......D3 48
Kalach, Sov. Un., 16,900....C2 29
Kalach [-na-Donu], Sov. Un., 16,700..........G14 27
Kaladar, Ont., Can., 251....C7 72
Ka Lae (South Cape), cape, Haw.E6 88
Kalahari, des., Bech.........B3 49
Kalahari Gemsbok, nat. park, S. Afr..........C3 49
Kalaheo, Kauai, Haw., 1,185.B2 88
Kalai-Khumb, Sov. Un.....B15 41
Kalai-Mor, Sov. Un.........D11 41
Kalak, Iran.................I9 41
Kalama, Cowlitz, Wash., 1,088..........C3 122
Kalamai (Kalamata), Grc., 38,211..........D4 23
Kalamazoo, Kalamazoo, Mich., 82,089 (★170,000)..F5 98
Kalamazoo, co., Mich., 169,712..........F5 98
Kalamazoo, riv., Mich........F5 98
Kalambo, falls, Tan., Zambia..C5 48
Kalampaka, Grc., 4,043......C3 23
Kalankala (Well), Niger......C7 45
Kalaotoa, isl., Indon........G6 35
Kalapana, Hawaii, Haw., 60..........D7 88
Kalat, Pak., 2,009..........C4 39
Kalāteh Minār, Iran........D10 41
Kalat-i-Ghilzai, Afg., 5,000.E13 41
Kalaupapa, Maui, Haw., 270..........B5 88
Kalavrita, Grc., 2,189.......C4 23
Kalecik, Tur., 4,100........B9 31
Kaleden, B.C., Can., 350....E8 68
Kalehe, Con. L.............B4 48
Kalem, Scott, Miss., 40......C4 100
Kaleva, Manistee, Mich., 348..........D4 98
Kalewa, Bur., 2,263.........D9 39
Kalgalaksha, Sov. Un......E16 25
Kalgan (Changkiakow), China, 229,300..........C7 34
Kalgary, Crosby, Tex........C2 118
Kalgin, isl., Alsk...........g16 79
Kalgoorlie, Austl., 9,800 (★22,000)..........F3 50
Kāl Gūsheh, Iran...........F9 41
Kalibo, Phil., 6,025.........C6 35
Kalima, Con. L.............B4 48
Kalimnos, Grc., 10,211......D6 23
Kalimnos, isl., Grc..........D6 23
Kalinin, Sov. Un., 292,000..B1 29
Kaliningrad (Königsberg), Sov. Un., 238,000.A6 26, D3 27
Kaliningrad, Sov. Un., 76,000..........n17 27
Kaliningrad, reg., Sov. Un..A6 26
Kalinkovichi, Sov. Un., 10,000..........E7 27
Kali Sindh, riv., India.......E6 40
Kalispel, Indian res., Wash....A8 122
Kalispell, Flathead, Mont., 10,151..........B2 102
Kalisz, Pol., 72,400.........C5 26
Kaliua, Tan................C5 48
Kalixälven, riv., Swe........D10 25
Kalīyā, Jordan.............h12 32
Kalkan, Tur., 474..........D7 23
Kalkaska, Kalkaska, Mich., 1,321..........D5 98
Kalkaska, co., Mich., 4,382..D5 98
Kalkfeld, S.W. Afr., 835....B2 49
Kalkrand, S.W. Afr..........B2 49
Källerstad, Swe............A7 24
Kallithea, Grc., 54,720.....h11 23
Kallsjön, lake, Swe..........F5 25
Kalmalo, Nig...............D6 45
Kalmar, Swe., 31,600........I7 25
Kalmar, Swe...............t35 25
Kalmar, co., Swe., 234,800..*I7 25
Kalmarsund, sound, Swe.......I7 25
Kalmykovo, Sov. Un.........D4 29
Kalo, Webster, Iowa, 150....B3 92
Kalocsa, Hung., 13,663......B4 22
Kalohi, chan., Haw..........C5 88
Kalomo, Zambia, 1,185.......E4 48
Kalona, Washington, Iowa, 1,235..........C6 92
Kalone, peak, B.C., Can.......C4 68
Kalpi, India, 17,278.........D7 40
Kalskag, Alsk., 147.........C7 79
Kaltag, Alsk., 165..........C8 79
Kaluaaha, Maui, Haw., 50...B5 88
Kaluga, Sov. Un., 157,000..D11 27
Kalundborg, Den., 9,763.....C5 24
Kalush, Sov. Un., 10,000....G5 27
Kaluszyn, Pol., 2,554........B6 26
Kalvehave, Den., 454........C6 24
Kalvesta, Finney, Kans., 52..D3 93
Kalvsjön, lake, Swe..........A7 24
Kalyan, India, 73,482 (★194,334)..........H4 40
Kama, Con. L...............B4 48
Kama, res., Sov. Un..........B5 29
Kama, riv., Sov. Un.........D19 9
Kama, rock, Iwo............ 52
Kamadia (Well), Niger.......B7 45
Kamaing, Bur., 608..........C10 39
Kamaishi, Jap., 87,511......G10 37
Kamakura, Jap., 98,617.....n18 37
Kamananui, riv., Haw........f9 88
Kamaniskeg, lake, Ont., Can...B7 72
Kamaran, isl., Asia..........B5 47
Kamarhati, India, 125,457.*F12 40
Kamarod, Pak..............C3 39
Kamas, Summit, Utah, 749..C4 119
Kamatsi, lake, Sask., Can.....A4 70
Kamba, pt., Fiji Is........... 52
Kambara, isl., Fiji Is......... 52
Kambove, Con. L...........D4 48
Kamchatka, pen., Sov. Un.....D18 28
Kamela, Union, Oreg., 10...B8 113
Kamenets-Podolskiy, Sov. Un., 40,299..........G6 27
Kamenjak, cape, Yugo........C1 22
Kamenka, Sov. Un., 3,700...G7 27
Kamen na Obi, Sov. Un., 37,000..........C10 29
Kamensk-Shakhtinskiy, Sov. Un., 62,000..........G13 27
Kamensk-Uralskiy, Sov. Un., 152,000..........B6 29
Kamenz, Ger., 14,900........B9 17
Kameoka, Jap., 17,300......o14 37
Kamet, peak, India...........B7 40
Kami, isl., Jap..............I4 37
Kamiah, Lewis, Idaho, 1,245.C2 89
Kamiak, mtn., Wash.........C8 122
Kamichli, Syr., 34,200.....D13 31
Kamien Pomorski, Pol., 1,576..........A3 26
Kamina, Con. L., 32,100....C4 48
Kamioka, Jap., 20,100.....m16 37
Kamloops, B.C., Can., 10,076..........D7, n19 68
Kamooloa, Honolulu, Haw., 150..........f9 76
Kamori-Yama, peak, Jap.......I6 37
Kamouraska, Que., Can., 518..........B8 73
Kamouraska, co., Que., Can., 27,138..........B8 73
Kampa Dzong, China, 5,000..........C12 40
Kampala, Ug., 46,735 (★123,332)..........A5 48
Kampar, Mala., 24,602.......J4 38
Kampar, riv., Indon..........E2 35
Kampen, Neth., 27,200.......B5 15
Kampeska, lake, S. Dak.......C8 116
Kamphaeng Phet, Thai., 7,045..........D3 38
Kampot, Camb., 5,000.......G6 38
Kampsville, Calhoun, Ill., 453..........D4 90
Kampungbaru, Indon.......E6 35
Kamrar, Hamilton, Iowa, 268..........B4 92
Kamsack, Sask., Can., 2,968..F5 70
Kamuchawie, lake, Man., Sask., Can..........A4 70
Kamuela, Hawaii, Haw., 950..........C6 88
Kamuli, Ug.................A5 48
Kamyshebakha, Sov. Un., 10,000..........q21 27
Kamyshin, Sov. Un., 65,000.C3 29
Kamyshlov, Sov. Un., 25,700..........B6 29
Kan, riv., China.............K6 36
Kana, Okinawa.............. 52
Kanab, Kane, Utah, 1,645...F3 119
Kanab, creek, Ariz., Utah......A3 80
Kanabec, co., Minn., 9,007..E5 99
Kanaga, isl., Alsk...........E4 79
Kanagawa, pref., Jap., 3,443,176..........*I9 37
Kanairiktok, riv., Newf., Can...g9 75
Kananaskis, riv., Alta., Can....D3 69
Kanapou, bay, Haw...........C5 88
Kanarraville, Iron, Utah, 236..........F2 119
Kanash, Sov. Un., 29,000....B3 29
Kanaskat, King, Wash., 100.D2 122
Kanathea, isl., Fiji Is......... 52
Kanauga, Gillia, Ohio, 350..D5 111
Kanauj, India, 24,646.......D7 40
Kanawha, Hancock, Iowa, 735..........B4 92
Kanawha, co., W. Va., 252,925..........C3 123
Kanawha, riv., W. Va........C3 123
Kanayama, Jap., 5,000.....n16 37
Kanazawa, Jap., 298,972....H8 37
Kanchanaburi, Thai., 13,357.E3 38
Kancheepuram (Conjeeveram), India, 92,714..........F7 39
Kanchenjunga, peak, Nep.....D12 40
Kandagach, Sov. Un........D5 29
Kandahar, Afg., 100,000....F12 41
Kandahar, Sask., Can., 111..F3 70
Kandalaksha, Sov. Un., 37,045..........D15 25
Kandalakshskaya, bay, Sov. Un..........D15 25
Kandangan, Indon., 9,774...F5 35
Kandavu, isl., Fiji Is........ 52
Kandel, Ger., 5,700.........D3 17
Kandersteg, Switz., 937.....D4 19
Kandi, Dah., 5,200..........D5 45
Kandira, Tur., 4,900........B8 23
Kandiyohi, Kandiyohi, Minn., 312..........E4 99
Kandiyohi, co., Minn., 29,987..........E3 99
Kandla, India...............F3 40
Kandreho, Malag., 180......g9 49
Kandy, Cey., 57,200.........G7 39
Kane, Greene, Ill., 469......D3 90
Kane, McKean, Pa., 5,380..C4 114
Kane, Big Horn, Wyo., 20..A4 125
Kane, co., Ill., 208,246......B5 90
Kane, co., Utah, 2,667.......F3 119
Kane, basin, N.W. Ter., Can., Grnld..........m38 67
Kaneohe, Honolulu, Haw., 14,414..........B4, g10 88
Kaneohe, bay, Haw...........f10 88
Kanevskaya, Sov. Un., 10,000..........H12 27
Kangal, Tur., 3,700.........C11 31
Kangaroo, isl., Austl........G6 50
Kangean, is., Indon..........G5 35
Kanggye, Kor., 30,013......F3 37
Kangha, bay, Kor............H3 37
Kangley, La Salle, Ill., 267..B5 90
Kangnung, Kor., 36,000 (56,600▲)..........H4 37
Kango, Gabon...............E2 46
Kangoku, rock, Iwo........... 52
Kangpao, China.............D6 36
Kangting, China, 30,000.....E5 34
Kanhsien, China, 98,600.....F7 34
Kani, Bur...................A1 38
Kani, I.C....................E3 45
Kaniama, Con. L............C3 48
Kaniapiskau, lake, Que., Can..h12 73
Kaniapiskau, riv., Que., Can...g13 73
Kanin, cape, Sov. Un.........B17 9
Kanjiža, Yugo., 10,709......B5 22
Kankakee, Kankakee, Ill., 27,666..........B6 90
Kankakee, co., Ill., 92,063...B6 90
Kankakee, riv., Ill., Ind..........B5 90, B4 91
Kankan, Guinea, 29,000.....D3 45
Kanker, India, 6,437.......G8 40
Kånna, Swe................B7 24
Kannan, China, 5,000.......C1 37
Kannapolis, Cabarrus, N.C., 34,647..........B3 109
Kano, Nig., 93,016 (★130,173)..........D6 45
Kanona, Zambia............D5 48
Kanopolis, Ellsworth, Kans., 732..........D5 93
Kanopolis, res., Kans.........D5 93
Kanorado, Sherman, Kans., 245..........C1 93
Kanosh, Millard, Utah, 499..E3 119
Kanovnice, riv., Czech........n18 26
Kanoya, Jap., 31,700 (72,498▲)..........K5 37
Kanpur, India, 881,177 (★1,000,000).....C7 39, D8 40
Kanrach, Pak...............C4 39
Kansas, Walker, Ala., 211...B2 78
Kansas, Edgar, Ill., 815.....D6 90
Kansas, Seneca, Ohio, 375...A4 111
Kansas, Delaware, Okla., 300..........A7 112
Kansas, state, U.S., 2,178,611..........C8 76, 93
Kansas, riv., Kans............C7 93
Kansas City, Wyandotte, Kans., 121,901........B9, C9 93
Kansas City, Jackson, Mo., 475,539 (★1,025,900)..B3, E2 95
Kansasville, Racine, Wis., 100..........F1 124
Kansk, Sov. Un., 90,000...D12 28
Kansong, Kor., 5,000.......G4 37
Kansu, prov., China, 12,800,000..........D5 34
Kantang, Thai., 5,177......I3 38
Kantunilkín, Mex., 872......C7 63
Kanturk, Ire., 1,985........E3 11
Kanye, Bech., 22,922.......B4 49
Kanyü, China, 5,000.......G8 36
Kaoan, China, 10,000.......J6 36
Kaohe, Hawaii, Haw., 35....D6 88
Kaohsiung, (Takao), Taiwan, 390,000 (515,200▲)..........G9 34
Kaolack, Sen., 69,600.......D1 45
Kao Tao, is., Viet...........B7 38
Kaouar, oases, Niger.........C7 45
Kaoyao, China, 49,000......G7 34
Kaoyu, China, 65,000......H8 36
Kaoyu, lake, China..........H8 36
Kapaa, Kauai, Haw., 3,439..A2 88
Kapal, Sov. Un., 10,000.....F24 9
Kapandrition, Grc., 1,462...g11 23
Kapanga, Con. L............C3 48
Kapapa, isl., Haw...........g10 88
Kapapala, Hawaii, Haw., 65.D6 88
Kapenguria, Ken............A6 48
Kapfenberg, Aus., 23,859...E7 16
Kapiri Mposhi, Zambia, 184.D4 48
Kapit, Mala., 1,398..........E4 35
Kaplan, Vermilion, La., 5,267..........D3 95
Kaplice, Czech., 1,588.......E9 17
Kapoeta, Sud...............E3 47
Kapoho, Hawaii, Haw., 250.D7 88
Kaposvar, Hung., 47,300....B3 22
Kaposvar, creek, Sask., Can....G4 70
Kapsan, Kor................F4 37
Kapterko (Well), Chad......B4 46
Kapuas, riv., Indon..........F4 35
Kapulena, Hawaii, Haw., 100..........C6 88
Kapuskasing, Ont., Can., 8,888..........o19 72
Kapustin Yar, Sov. Un......D3 29
Kaputar, mtn., Austl.........E8 51
Kapuvár, Hung., 10,902.....B3 22
Kara, Sov. Un.............B21 9
Kara, mtn., Tur.............D9 31
Kara, sea, Sov. Un...........B9 28
Karabash, Sov. Un., 24,300..........D21 9
Kara-Bogaz-Gol, Sov. Un...E4 29
Kara-Bogaz-Gol, gulf, Sov. Un..E4 29
Karaburun, Tur., 782.......C6 23
Karachev, Sov. Un., 10,000.E10 27
Karachi, Pak., 1,447,419 (★1,912,598)..........D4 39
Karaga, Sov. Un., 10,000..D19 28
Karaganda, Sov. Un., 462,000..........D8 29
Karagin, isl., Sov. Un.......D19 28
Karaisali, Tur., 1,051.......D10 31
Karakas, Sov. Un...........D10 29
Karakelong, isl., Indon.......E7 35
Karakoram, pass, India, Pak...A6 39
Karakoram, range, Asia.......A6 39
Karakose, Tur., 19,800.....C14 31
Karakul, Sov. Un...........B11 41
Karakum, des., Sov. Un.......E5 29
Karaman, Tur., 21,700.....D9 31
Karamea, N.Z., 220.......N14 51
Karamea, bight, N.Z........N13 51
Karamursel, Tur., 6,200.....B7 23
Karand, Iran, 15,000.......D3 41
Karapinar, Tur., 10,800.....D9 31
Karas, mts., S.W. Afr........C2 49
Karasburg, S.W. Afr., 2,233.C2 49
Kara Shahr (Yenki), China, 10,000..........C2 34
Karasu, Sov. Un............C6 29
Karasu, Tur., 2,906.........B8 23
Karasuk, Sov. Un., 17,300...C9 29
Karatal, riv., Sov. Un........D9 29
Karatas, cape, Tur..........D10 31
Kara Tau, range, Sov. Un.....E7 29
Karatsu, Jap., 55,000 (77,825▲)..........J4 37
Kara-Tyube, Sov. Un.......D4 29
Karauli, India, 23,696......D6 40
Karaul Keldy, Sov. Un......D5 29
Karawanken, mts., Aus., Yugo..........E7 16, B2 22
Karbalā', Iraq, 44,600.....F15 31
Karcag, Hung., 20,803 (26,098▲)..........B5 22
Karczew, Pol., 3,000.......m14 26
Kardhitsa, Grc., 23,708......C3 23
Kardhitsa, prov., Grc., 152,543..........*C3 23
Karelia (Karelo-Finnish S.S.R.), former rep., Sov. Un.....*C6 28
Karema, Tan., 882..........C5 48
Karesuando, Swe., 405.....C10 25
Kargasok, Sov. Un., 900....B10 29
Kargat, Sov. Un., 10,000...D25 9
Kargil, India, 5,000.........B6 39
Kargopol, Sov. Un., 5,000..A12 27
Karguiri, Niger.............D7 45
Kariai, Grc., 305...........B5 23
Kariba, Rh., 6,170.........*A4 49
Kariba, lake, Rh., Zambia.....A4 49
Karibib, S.W. Afr., 1,395....B2 49
Karikal, India, 22,252.......F6 39
Karikari, cape, N.Z.........K14 51
Karima, Sud., 5,989........B3 47
Karimata, arch., Indon........F3 35
Karimundjawa, is., Indon......G4 35
Karin, Som.................C6 47
Karisimbi, vol., Con. L., Rwanda.B4 48
Karistos, Grc., 3,118........C5 23
Kārīz, Iran................D10 41
Karkar, isl., N. Gui.........h12 50
Karkaralinsk, Sov. Un., 12,200..........D9 29
Karkaraly, mts., Sov. Un......D9 29
Karkaraly, peak, Sov. Un.....F24 9
Karkinitskiy, bay, Sov. Un......I9 27
Karkur, Isr., 3,200..........B6 32
Karla, lake, Grc.............C4 23
Karl-Marx-Stadt (Chemnitz), Ger., 287,400 (★400,000)..C7 17
Karlobag, Yugo., 403.......C2 22
Karloske, riv., Man., Can......B4 71
Karlovac, Yugo., 38,803.....C2 22
Karlovasi, Grc., 5,024.......D6 23
Karlovy Vary, Czech., 43,100..........C2 26
Karlsbad, see Karlovy Vary, Czech.
Karlshamn, Swe., 11,700.....I6 25
Karlskoga, Swe., 36,100.....H6 25
Karlskrona, Swe., 33,300.....I6 25
Karlsruhe, Ger., 249,900 (★350,000)..........D3 17
Karlsruhe, McHenry, N. Dak., 221..........A5 110
Karlstad, Kittson, Minn., 720..........B2 99
Karlstad, Swe., 44,700......H5 25
Karlstadt, Ger., 6,000.......D4 17
Karluk, Alsk., 129..........D9 79
Karmutzen, mtn., B.C., Can....D4 68
Karnak, Pulaski, Ill., 667....F4 90
Karnes, co., Tex., 14,995....E4 118
Karnes City, Karnes, Tex., 2,693..........E4 118
Karns City, Butler, Pa., 404..E2 114
Kärnten (Carinthia), state, Aus., 495,226..........C9 18
Karoi, Rh...................A4 49
Karonga, Malawi...........C5 48
Karora, Sud................B4 47
Karow, Ger., 1,043.........E6 24
Karpathos, isl., Grc..........E6 23
Karpenision, Grc., 3,693....C3 23
Karpinsk, Sov. Un., 49,000.D21 9
Kars, Tur., 32,141.........B14 31
Karsakpay, Sov. Un., 12,000..........D7 29
Karshi, Sov. Un., 19,000...H22 9
Karshinskiy, Sov. Un.......D4 29
Karstädt, Ger., 1,872.......E5 24
Kartal, Tur., 10,800........B7 23
Kartaly, Sov. Un., 33,400...C6 29
Karthaus, Clearfield, Pa., 500..........D5 114
Kartuzy, Pol., 5,991........A5 26
Karup, Den., 1,137.........B3 24
Karup Å, riv., Den...........B3 24
Karval, Lincoln, Colo., 80...C7 83
Karvia, Fin., 350..........F10 25
Karviná, Czech., 56,600.....D5 26
Karwar, India, 12,134.......F5 39
Kås, Den., 1,005............A3 24
Kas, Sud...................C1 47
Kaş, Tur., 1,500............D7 31
Kasaan, Alsk., 20..........n23 79
Kasai, prov., Con. L., 2,119,500..........B3 48
Kasai, riv., Afr.............G8 42
Kasaji, Con. L.............D3 48
Kasama, Zambia, 3,700.....D5 48
Kasanga, Tan., 5,369.......C5 48
Kasaragod, India, 27,635....F6 39
Kasba, India, 13,051.......E11 40
Kasba, lake, N.W. Ter., Can..D12 66
Kasba Tadla, Mor., 11,733..C3 44
Kasempa, Zambia, 225......C4 48
Kasenga, Con. L............D4 48
Kasese, Ug.................A5 48
Kāshān, Iran, 45,955.......E5 41
Kashegelok, Alsk., 5........C8 79
Kashgar (Sufu), China, 91,000..........H24 9
Kashima, Jap., 3,800.......n19 37
Kashipur, India, 24,258.....C7 40
Kashira, Sov. Un., 10,000...D12 27
Kashirka, riv., Sov. Un.......n18 27
Kashiwazaki, Jap., 39,800 (74,139▲)..........H9 37
Kāshmar, Iran, 12,052......D9 40
Kashmir, see Jammu and Kashmir, state, India
Kashmor, Pak..............C2 40
Kasilof, Alsk., 89.......C9, g16 79
Kasimov, Sov. Un., 33,500...C2 29
Kaskaskia, Randolph, Ill., 97..........F4 90
Kaskaskia, riv., Ill...........D5 90
Kaskö, Fin., 1,500..........F9 25
Kas Kong, Camb...........G5 38
Kaslo, B.C., Can., 646......E9 68
Kasongo, Con. L............B4 48
Kasongo-Lunda, Con. L.....C2 48
Kasos, isl., Grc.............E6 23
Kasota, LeSueur, Minn., 649.F5 99
Kassala, Sud., 35,621.......B4 47
Kassala, reg., Sud., 941,039..B4 47
Kassandra, gulf, Grc.........B4 23
Kassel, Ger., 212,200 (★285,000)..........B4 17
Kasserine, Tun., 5,825.....G11 30
Kassol, passage, Palau Is..........52
Kasson, Dodge, Minn., 1,732..........F6 99
Kastamonu (Kastamuni), Tur., 19,500..........B9 31
Kastelli, Grc., 1,882........E4 23
Kastellorizo, isl., Grc.........D7 23
Kastoria, Grc., 10,162.......B3 23
Kastoria, prov., Grc., 47,487..........*B3 23
Kastro, Tur................B5 23
Kastron, Grc., 3,493........C5 23
Kasugai, Jap., 49,200 (77,174▲)..........*n15 37
Kasukabe, Jap., 18,500.....n18 37
Kasumi, Jap., 12,100........I7 37
Kasumiga-Ura, bay, Jap.....H10 37
Kasungu, Malawi...........D5 48
Kasur, Pak., 74,546.B5 39, B5 40

56X KATA-KHAL

Katada, Jap., 6,900........n14 37
Katahdin, mtn., Maine........C4 96
Katako-Kombe, Con. L......B3 48
Katalla, Alsk., 12..........C11 79
Katanga, prov., Con. L., 1,664,200..............C3 48
Katanning, Austl., 3,360.....F2 50
Katepwa Beach, Sask., Can., 31..........G4 70
Katerini, Grc., 28,046.......B4 23
Katha, Bur., 7,714........D10 39
Katherine, Austl., 314.......B5 50
Kathleen, Polk, Fla., 650...D4 86
Kathryn, Alta., Can........D4 69
Kathryn, Barnes, N. Dak., 142........C8 110
Kathua, India, 9,647.......A5 40
Kathwood, Lexington, S.C., 2,000.........*D4 115
Katia Kingi, Sud...........D1 47
Katihar, India, 46,837 (*59,344)..........E11 40
Katimik, lake, Man., Can......C2 71
Katiola, I.C., 7,900.........E3 45
Katire, Sud., 699...........E3 47
Katmai, nat. mon., Alsk.........D9 79
Katmai, vol., Alsk...........D9 79
Katmandu, Nep., 122,500..D10 40
Katni (Murwara), India, 46,169 (*60,472).........F8 40
Katokhi, Grc., 1,750........C3 23
Katombe, Con. L...........C3 48
Katonah, Westchester, N.Y., 2,500............A5 106
Katoomba (Blue Mountains), Austl., 28,119............F8 51
Katouna, Grc., 3,176........C3 23
Katowice (Stalinograd), Pol., 279,200 (*1,930,000).C5, g10 26
Katrinah, mtn., Eg., U.A.R....D6 43
Katrine, lake, Scot............D4 13
Katrineholm, Swe., 19,000..........H7, u34 25
Katsina, Nig., 52,672........D6 45
Katsina Ala, riv., Nig.........E6 45
Katsuyama, Jap., 19,300....m15 37
Katta-Kurgan, Sov. Un., 47,500..........H22 9
Kattegat, chan., Eur...........I4 25
Katun, riv., Sov. Un........E26 9
Katwijk aan Zee, Neth., 25,200 (30,000▲)........B4 15
Katy, Fort Bend, Harris and Waller, Tex., 1,569........F4 118
Kauai, co., Haw., 28,176....B2 82
Kauai, chan., Haw..........B3 88
Kauai, isl., Haw............A2 88
Kaufbeuren, Ger., 34,700....E5 16
Kaufman, Kaufman, Tex., 3,087...............C4 118
Kaufman, co., Tex., 29,931..C4 118
Kauhajoki, Fin., 1,700.....F10 25
Kauhava, Fin., 2,100.......F10 25
Kaukau Veld, plain, Bech., S. W. Afr...............B3 49
Kaukauna, Outagamie, Wis., 10,096.........A5, D5 124
Kaulakahi, chan., Haw.........A2 88
Kauliranta, Fin., 700.......D10 25
Kaumakani, Kauai, Haw., 950..............B2 88
Kaumalapau, Maui, Haw., 100..............C5 88
Kauna, pt., Haw............D6 88
Kaunakakai, Maui, Haw., 900..............B4 88
Kaunas, Sov. Un., 247,000.........A7 26, D4 27
Kaupo, Maui, Haw., 20.....C5 88
Kaura Namoda, Nig., 19,146.D6 45
Kautokeino, Nor., 284......C10 25
Kavacha, Sov. Un.........C19 28
Kavaje, Alb., 13,700........B2 23
Kavali, India, 20,544........F6 39
Kavála, Grc., 44,517.......B5 23
Kavála, gulf, Grc............B5 23
Kavála, prov., Grc., 140,751..............*B5 23
Kavanaugh, Boyd, Ky., 25...B7 94
Kavar, Iran...............G6 41
Kavarna, Bul., 5,625........D9 22
Kavieng, Bis. Arch., 190....h13 50
Kävlinge, Swe., 3,500........C7 24
Kavrina, Czech., 33,905.....D5 26
Kaw, Kay, Okla., 457........A5 111
Kawada, Okinawa...............52
Kawagama, lake, Ont., Can....B6 72
Kawagoe, Jap., 70,000 (107,523▲)...........n18 37
Kawaguchi, Jap., 170,066...n18 37
Kawaihae, Hawaii, Haw., 100.............C6 88
Kawainae, bay, Haw..........C6 88
Kawaihoa, pt., Haw...........B1 88
Kawaikini, peak, Haw.........A2 88
Kawailoa, Honolulu, Haw., 300..............f9 88
Kawailoa Beach, Honolulu, Haw., 400...........f9 88
Kawambwa, Zambia, 610....C4 48
Kawardha, India............F8 40
Kawasaki, Jap., 632,975.I9, n18 37
Kawayan, Phil., 2,084......*C6 35
Kawbar, Jordan, 2,000.......h11 32
Kawela, Maui, Haw., 20.....B5 88
Kawhia, hbr., N.Z.........M15 51
Kawich, range, Nev..........F5 104
Kawinaw, lake, Man., Can......C2 71
Kawkareik, Bur., 10,000.....D3 38
Kawkawlin, Bay, Mich., 300.E7 98
Kawm, Ḥamādah, Eg. U.A.R., 1,000.............D2 43
Kawm Umbū, Eg., U.A.R., 41,200..............E6 43
Kawnipi, lake, Ont., Can......B7 99
Kay, co., Okla., 51,042......A4 112
Kaya, Upper Volta, 4,000....D4 45
Kayangel, is., Palau Is..........52
Kayenta, Navajo, Ariz., 200..A5 80
Kayes, Con. B..............F2 46
Kayes, Mali, 28,500.........D2 45
Kayford, Kanawha, W. Va., 400..........C3, D6 123
Kayjay, Knox, Ky., 150.....D6 94
Kaylor, Hutchinson, S. Dak., 165...........D8 116
Kayseri, Tur., 102,596......C10 31
Kaysville, Davis, Utah, 3,608.B4 119
Kayville, Sask., Can., 152....H3 70
Kazachye, Sov. Un., 900...B16 28
Kazakevichevo, Sov. Un., 1,000..............B7 37
Kazakh S.S.R., rep., Sov. Un., 11,800,000.....F19 9
Kazakh, hills, Sov. Un........D7 29
Kazalinsk, Sov. Un., 62,000.F21 9
Kazan, Sov. Un., 725,000....B3 29
Kazan, riv., N.W. Ter., Can..D12 66
Kazanlŭk, Bul., 19,386......D7 22
Kazan-retto (Volcano), is., Pac. O..........E8 7
Kazbek, mtn., Sov. Un........E2 29
Kāzerūn, Iran, 30,641.......G5 41
Kazhim, Sov. Un.............A4 29
Kazi-Magomed, Sov. Un....E3 29
Kazimierz, Pol., 2,929......C6 26
Kazim Pasa (Saray), Tur., 3,486..............C15 31
Kazincbarcika, Hung., 15,285..............A5 22
Kazumba, Con. L...........C3 48
Kazym, riv., Sov. Un........C22 9
Kdyne, Czech., 2,177........D8 17
Kea, Grc., 2,200.............D5 23
Kea, isl., Grc..............D5 23
Keady, N. Ire., 1,638........C5 11
Keahole, pt., Haw............D5 88
Kealaikahiki, chan., Haw......C5 88
Kealakekua, Hawaii, Haw., 325..............D6 88
Kealakekua, bay, Haw........D6 88
Kealia, Hawaii, Haw., 100..D6 88
Kealia, Kauai, Haw., 655....A2 88
Keams Canyon, Navajo, Ariz...............B5 80
Keanae, Maui, Haw., 54....C5 88
Keansburg, Monmouth, N.J., 6,854............C4 106
Keaoi, isl., Haw.............D6 88
Kearney, Ont., Can., 365....B5 72
Kearney, Clay, Mo., 678 B3, D2 101
Kearney, Buffalo, Nebr., 14,210..............D6 103
Kearney, Johnson, Wyo.......A6 125
Kearney, co., Nebr., 6,580...D7 103
Kearneyville, Jefferson, W. Va., 600...........B7 123
Kearns, Salt Lake, Utah, 21,000..............C3 119
Kearny, Pinal, Ariz., 902...D4 80
Kearny, Hudson, N.J., 37,472..............h8 106
Kearny, co., Kans., 3,108...D2 93
Kearsarge, Houghton, Mich., 400...............A2 98
Kearsarge, Carroll, N.H., 150..............B4 105
Kearsarge, mtn., N.H..........D3 105
Keasbey, Middlesex, N.J., 1,500............*B4 106
Keatchie, De Soto, La., 345..B2 95
Keating, Baker, Oreg., 10...C9 113
Keating, Clinton, Pa., 35....D6 114
Keatley, Sask., Can.........E2 70
Keats, Riley, Kans., 85......C7 93
Keauhou, Hawaii, Haw., 250...............D6 88
Keawakapu, Maui, Haw., 100...............C5 88
Keawekaheka, pt., Haw........D6 88
Kebbi, Nig...............D5 45
Kebili, Tun..............H11 30
Kebnekaise, mtn., Swe........D8 25
Kebock, head, Scot...........B2 13
Kechi, Sedgwick, Kans., 245................B5, E6 93
Kecskemet, Hung., 48,600 (70,800▲)............B4 22
Kedah, state, Mala., 701,964.I4 38
Kedainiai, Sov. Un., 8,602..A7 26
Keddie, Plumas, Calif., 300..B3 82
Kedges, straits, Md...........D5 85
Kedgwick, N.B., Can., 1,095..............B2 74
Kedgwick, riv., N.B., Que., Can..............B2 74
Kedleston, Sask., Can.......G3 70
Kédougou, Sen., 1,200.......D2 45
Kedron, Cleveland, Ark., 30.C3 81
Keedysville, Washington, Md., 433..............B2 85
Keefers, B.C., Can..........D7 68
Keefeton, Muskogee, Okla., 80..............B6 112
Keegan, Aroostook, Maine, 800................A5 96
Keego Harbor, Oakland, Mich., 2,761.............A7 98
Keei, Hawaii, Haw., 100....D6 88
Keele, peak, Yukon, Can......D6 66
Keeler, Sask., Can., 82......G3 70
Keeler, Inyo, Calif., 200....D5 82
Keeline, Niobrara, Wyo., 30.C8 125
Keeling, Haywood, Tenn., 25...............B2 117
Keeling, Pittsylvania, Va., 30................E3 121
Keels, Newf., Can., 185.....D5 75
Keelung, see Chilung, Taiwan
Keene, Kern, Calif., 120.....E4 82
Keene, Ont., Can., 324......C6 72
Keene, Jessamine, Ky., 500..C5 94
Keene, Kearney, Nebr., 25..D6 103
Keene, Cheshire, N.H., 17,562..............E2 105
Keene, Essex, N.Y., 400.A7, f11 108
Keene, McKenzie, N. Dak., 100...............B3 110
Keene, Coshocton, Ohio, 150.B6 111
Keene, Johnson, Tex., 1,532.E8 118
Keenesburg, Weld, Colo., 409...............A6 83
Keene Valley, Essex, N.Y., 400...............f11 108
Keeney Knob, mtn., W. Va.....D4 123
Keensburg, Wabash, Ill., 263.E6 90
Keeper, hill, Ire..............E3 11
Keeseville, Clinton and Essex, N.Y., 2,213............f11 108
Keetmanshoop, S.W. Afr., 4,410..............C2 49
Keewatin, Ont., Can., 2,197..E4 71
Keewatin, Itasca, Minn., 1,651...............C5 99
Keewatin, dist., N.W. Ter., Can., 2,345..........C12 66
Keewatin, riv., Man., Can.....A1 71
Keezletown, Rockingham, Va., 175..............C4 121
Kefa, prov., Eth...........D4 47
Kefallinia, prov., Grc., 47,314..............*C3 23
Kefallinia (Cephalonia), isl., Grc.C3 23
Keflavik, Ice., 4,852.......o21 25
Kegaska, Que., Can., 93.....h9 75
Kegonsa, lake, Wis...........F4 124
Kegueur Terbi, mtn., Chad......43 46
Keheili, Sud..............B3 47
Kehl, Ger., 13,100..........E3 17
Keho, lake, Alta., Can........E4 69
Kehsi Mansam, Bur.........B2 38
Keighley, Eng., 56,700......D6 10
Keimoes, S. Afr., 2,995......C3 49
Keiser, Mississippi, Ark., 516.B5 81
Keiser (Marion Heights), Northumberland, Pa., 1,132...............*E8 108
Keitele, lake, Fin............F11 25
Keith, Austl..............H3 51
Keith, Scot., 4,208.........C6 13
Keith, co., Nebr., 7,958.....C4 103
Keithley Creek, B.C., Can...C7 68
Keithsburg, Mercer, Ill., 963..................B3 90
Keitum, Ger..............D2 24
Keizer, Marion, Oregon, 5,288...............*C4 113
Kejimkujik, lake, N.S., Can....E4 74
Kekaha, Kauai, Haw., 2,082...............B2 88
Kelantan, state, Mala., 505,522..............I5 38
Kelantan, riv., Mala..........J5 38
Keldron, Corson, S. Dak., 23.B4 116
Kelfield, Sask., Can., 32......F1 70
Kelford, Bertie, N.C., 362...A6 109
Kelheim, Ger., 11,900.......E6 17
Kelibia, Tun..............F12 30
Kelif, Sov. Un...........C13 41
Kelilberg, mtn., Czech.........C8 17
Kelkit, riv., Tur............B11 31
Kell, Marion, Ill., 194.......E5 90
Kellé, Con. B..............F2 46
Kellenhusen, Ger., 1,100....D5 24
Keller, Tarrant, Tex., 827...B5 118
Keller, Accomack, Va., 263..D7 121
Keller, Ferry, Wash., 25.....A7 122
Keller, lake, Sask., Can.......A2 70
Kellerman, Tuscaloosa, Ala., 500................B2 78
Kellerton, Ringgold, Iowa, 341................D3 92
Kellerville, Adams, Ill., 20...D3 90
Kellet, cape, N.W. Ter., Can...B7 66
Kellettville, Forest, Pa., 30...C3 114
Kelley, Story, Iowa, 239.....C4 92
Kelleys, isl., Ohio...........A5 111
Kelleys Island, Erie, Ohio, 171...............A5 111
Kelliher, Sask., Can., 461....F4 70
Kelliher, Beltrami, Minn., 297...............C4 99
Kellmünz, Ger., 1,100.......A6 18
Kellnersville, Manitowoc, Wis., 350..........A6, D6 124
Kelloe, Man., Can..........D1 71
Kellogg, Shoshone, Idaho, 5,061..............B2 89
Kellogg, Jasper, Iowa, 623...C5 92
Kellogg, Wabasha, Minn., 446...............F6 99
Kells, range, Scot...........E4 13
Kelly, Christian, Ky., 175....D2 94
Kelly, Caldwell, La., 450....C3 95
Kelly, Teton, Wyo., 20.......B2 125
Kelly Brook, mtn., Maine......A3 96
Kelly Lake, B.C., Can., 177..B7 68
Kelly Lake, St. Louis, Minn., 900................C5 99
Kellyton, Coosa, Ala., 450....C3 78
Kellytown, Henry, Ga., 200..C2 87
Kellyville, Sullivan, N.H., 140................D2 105
Kellyville, Creek, Okla., 501.B5 106
Kelme, Sov. Un.............A7 26
Kélo, Chad, 6,067..........D3 46
Kelowna, B.C., Can., 13,188.E8 68
Kelsey, Alta., Can., 40......C4 69
Kelsey, lake, Man., Can.......C1 71
Kelsey, mtn., N.H............A4 105
Kelsey Bay, B.C., Can., 307..D4 68
Kelso, San Bernardino, Calif., 100..............E6 82
Kelso, Dearborn, Ind., 150...F8 91
Kelso, Scott, Mo., 258......D8 101
Kelso, Traill, N. Dak., 27.....B8 110
Kelso, Scot., 3,964..........E6 13
Kelso, Cowlitz, Wash., 8,379................C3 122
Kelso Station, Sask., Can....H5 70
Keltie, mtn., Ant............f40 5
Keltonburg, De Kalb, Tenn., 60................D8 117
Keltys, Angelina, Tex., 1,056...............*D5 118
Kelvington, Sask., Can., 885.E4 70
Kelwood, Man., Can., 323....D2 71
Kem, Sov. Un., 10,000......E16 25
Kem, riv., Sov. Un..........E15 25
Ké-Macina, Mali, 1,200......D3 45
Kemah, Galveston, Tex., 950...............*F5 118
Kemano, B.C., Can., 255....C4 68
Kembé, Cen. Afr. Rep.......E4 46
Kemerovo, Sov. Un., 298,000...............B11 29
Kemi, Fin., 28,800..........E11 25
Kemijärvi, Fin., 5,000.......D12 25
Kemijärvi, lake, Fin..........D12 25
Kemijoki, riv., Fin...........D11 25
Kemme, Libya.............E3 43
Kemmerer, Lincoln, Wyo., 2,028..............D2 125
Kemnath, Ger., 3,000.......D6 17
Kemnay, Man., Can., 81.....E1 71
Kemp, Bryan, Okla., 153....D5 112
Kemp, Kaufman, Tex., 816...............C4 118
Kemp, coast, Ant............C18 5
Kemp, lake, Tex.............C3 118
Kemp, pen., Ant.............B6 5
Kempen, Ger., 12,900.......C6 16
Kemper, Dillon, S.C., 40....C9 115
Kemper, co., Miss., 12,277...C5 100
Kempner, Lampasas, Tex., 250...............D3 118
Kempsey, Austl., 8,016.......E9 51
Kempshall, mtn., N.Y.........A6 108
Kempsville, Princess, Anne, Va., 500................B7 121
Kempten, Ger., 43,800.......E5 16
Kempton, Ford, Ill., 252.....C5 90
Kempton, Tipton, Ind., 480..D5 91
Kempton, Grand Forks, N. Dak., 58..............B8 110
Kemptville, Ont., Can., 1,959.................B9 72
Kenadsa, Alg.............C4 44
Kenai, Alsk., 778........C9, g16 79
Kenai, mts., Alsk...........h16 79
Kenai, pen., Alsk...........h15 79
Kenamu, riv., Newf., Can.......B1 75
Kenansville, Osceola, Fla., 250...............E6 86
Kenansville, Duplin, N.C., 724................C6 109
Kenaston, Sask., Can., 423...F2 70
Kenaston, Ward, N. Dak., 30.A3 110
Kenbridge, Lunenburg, Va., 1,188..............E4 121
Kendal, Sask., Can., 161....G4 70
Kendal, Eng., 18,595........C5 10
Kendall, Dade, Fla., 3,000...F3 86
Kendall, Hamilton, Kans., 250...............E2 93
Kendall, Orleans, N.Y., 300..B2 108
Kendall, Monroe, Wis., 528.E3 124
Kendall, co., Ill., 17,540......B5 90
Kendall, co., Tex., 5,889.....E3 118
Kendall Park, Middlesex, N.J., 4,000...............C3 106
Kendallville, Noble, Ind., 6,765...............B7 91
Kendari, Indon.............F6 35
Kendrapara, India, 15,830..G11 40
Kendrick, Marion, Fla., 500..C4 86
Kendrick, Latah, Idaho, 443.C2 89
Kendrick, Lincoln, Okla., 155...............B5 112
Kenduskeag, Penobscot, Maine, 300 (584▲)........D4 96
Kenedy, Karnes, Tex., 4,301.E4 118
Kenedy, co., Tex., 884.......F4 118
Kenefic, Bryan, Okla., 125...C5 112
Kenel, Corson, S. Dak., 75...B5 116
Kenema, S.L.............E2 45
Kenesaw, Adams, Nebr., 546...............D7 103
Kenge, Con. L.............B2 48
Keng Kabao, Laos..........D6 38
Keng Tung, Bur., 5,508.....D10 39
Kenhardt, S. Afr., 2,832.....C3 49
Kenhorst, Berks, Pa., 2,815...............*F10 114
Kéniéba, Mali.............D2 45
Kenilworth, Eng., 14,427....B6 12
Kenilworth, Cook, Ill., 2,959...............E3 90
Kenilworth, Union, N.J., 8,379.................*B4 106
Kenilworth, Carbon, Utah, 400...............D5 119
Kenimekh, Sov. Un.........A12 41
Kenitra, Mor., 86,775........C3 44
Kenly, Johnston, N.C., 1,147...............B5 109
Kenmare, Ire., 1,046.........F2 11
Kenmare, Ward, N. Dak., 2,463...............A3 110
Kenmare, riv., Ire............F2 11
Kenmawr, Allegheny, Pa., 3,000..............*F1 114
Kenmore, Erie, N.Y., 21,261.C2 108
Kenmore, King, Wash., 1,000...............*B3 122
Kenna, Roosevelt, N. Mex., 30.............D6 107
Kenna, Jackson, W. Va., 200.C3 123
Kenneday, peak, Wyo.........D6 125
Kennan, Price, Wis., 162....C3 124
Kennard, Henry, Ind., 466..E6 91
Kennard, Washington, Nebr., 331...............C9, D2 103
Kennard, Houston, Tex., 400.............D5 118
Kennebago, lake, Maine.......C2 96
Kennebec, Lyman, S. Dak., 372...............D6 116
Kennebec, co., Maine, 83,881...............D3 96
Kennebec, riv., Maine.........D3 96
Kennebunk, York, Maine, 2,804 (4,551▲)..........E2 96
Kennebunkport, York, Maine, 700 (1,851▲)......E2 96
Kennedale, Tarrant, Tex., 1,521..............B5 118
Kennedy, Lamar, Ala., 379..B2 78
Kennedy, Sask., Can., 274...G4 70
Kennedy, Kittson, Minn., 458...............B2 99
Kennedy, Cherry, Nebr., 11..B5 103
Kennedy, Chautauqua, N.Y., 600...............C1 108
Kennedy (Canaveral), cape, Fla.D6 86
Kennedy, chan., N.W. Ter., Can...............k38 67
Kennedy, lake, Sask., Can......D4 70
Kennedyville, Kent, Md., 350..............B6 85
Kenner, Jefferson, La., 17,037...............C7, E5 95
Kennesaw, Cobb, Ga., 1,507..............A4, B2 87
Kennesaw, mtn., Ga...........C2 87
Kennet, riv., Eng...........C6 12
Kennetcook, N.S., Can., 375.D6 74
Kenneth City, Pinellas, Fla., 2,114..............*E4 86
Kennett, Dunklin, Mo., 9,098.................E7 101
Kennett Square, Chester, Pa., 4,355...............G10 114
Kennewick, Benton, Wash., 14,244...............C6 122
Kenney, De Witt, Ill., 400...C4 90
Kennington Cove, N.S., Can., 97...............D9 74
Kennisis, lake, Ont., Can......B6 72
Kennydale, King, Wash., 3,500...............D2 122
Keno, Klamath, Oreg., 175..E5 113
Kénogami, Que., Can., 11,816...............A6 73
Kenogami, lake, Que., Can.....A6 73
Kenora, Ont., Can., 10,904.o16 72
Kenora, dist., Ont., Can., 51,474...............o16 72
Kenosha, Kenosha, Wis., 67,899...............F2, F6 124
Kenosha, co., Wis., 100,615..F5 124
Kenova, Wayne, W. Va., 4,577...............C2 123
Kensal, Stutsman, N. Dak., 334...............B7 110
Kensett, White, Ark., 905...B4 81
Kensett, Worth, Iowa, 409...A4 92
Kensico, res., N.Y............g13 108
Kensington, Contra Costa, Calif., 6,161...........*B5 82
Kensington, P.E.I., Can., 884...............C6 74
Kensington, Hartford, Conn., 5,600...............C5 84
Kensington, Smith, Kans., 619...............C4 93
Kensington, Montgomery, Md., 2,175..............B3 85
Kensington, Douglas, Minn., 324..............E3 99
Kensington, Rockingham, N.H., 50 (708▲)..........E5 105
Kensington, Nassau, N.Y., 1,166..............*E3 108
Kensington, Columbiana, Ohio, 350..............B7 111
Kensington Estates, Montgomery, Md., 1,600..........*B3 85
Kensington Park, Sarasota, Fla., 2,969............*E4 86
Kensington Park, Chatham, Ga., 1,000..............*D6 87
Kent, Elmore, Ala., 500.....C4 78
Kent, Litchfield, Conn., 500 (1,686▲)...........C3 84
Kent, Jefferson, Ind., 65.....G6 91
Kent, Union, Iowa, 94.......D3 92
Kent, Wilkin, Minn., 134....D2 99
Kent, Portage, Ohio, 17,836.A6 111
Kent, Sherman, Oreg., 65...B6 113
Kent, Culberson, Tex., 50...F2 118
Kent, King, Wash., 9,017..............B3, D2 122
Kent, co., N.B., Can., 26,667...............C4 74
Kent, co., Ont., Can., 89,427...............E2 72
Kent, co., Del., 65,651.....B6 85
Kent, co., Eng., 1,701,083...C8 12
Kent, co., Md., 15,481.......B5 85
Kent, co., Mich., 363,187....E5 98
Kent, co., R.I., 112,619.....C10 84
Kent, co., Tex., 1,727.......C2 118
Kent, isl., Del..............B7 85
Kent, isl., Md..............C5 85
Kent, pt., Md...............C5 85
Kent, riv., Eng..............F6 13
Kent Bridge, Ont., Can., 118.E2 72
Kent City, Kent, Mich., 617.E5 98
Kentfield, Marin, Calif., 5,000...............*B5 82
Kent Junction, N.B., Can., 182...............C4 74
Kentland, Newton, Ind., 1,783...............C3 91
Kentland, Prince Georges, Md., 1,800.............*C4 85
Kenton, Man., Can., 222.....E1 71
Kenton, Kent, Del., 249.....B6 85
Kenton, Kenton, Ky., 240....A7 94
Kenton, Houghton, Mich., 200................B2 98
Kenton, Hardin, Ohio, 8,747.B4 111
Kenton, Cimarron, Okla., 100...............D1 112
Kenton, Obion and Gibson, Tenn., 1,095.............A2 117
Kenton, co., Ky., 120,700....B5 94
Kents Store, Fluvanna, Va., 20...............D4 121
Kentucky, state, U.S., 3,038,156...........C11 77, 94
Kentucky, dam, Ky...........A3 94
Kentucky, lake, Ky., Tenn......D1 94
Kentucky, ridge, Ky...........D6 94
Kentucky, riv., Ky...........B5 94
Kent Village, Prince Georges, Md., 2,500.............*C4 86
Kentville, N.S., Can., 4,612..D5 74
Kentwood, Tangipahoa, La., 2,607...............D5 95
Kenvil, Morris, N.J., 2,000..B3 106
Kenville, Man., Can., 144...D1 71
Kenvir, Harlan, Ky., 950....D6 94
Kenwood, Hamilton, Ohio, 2,000..............*C3 111
Kenwood, Delaware, Okla., 75................A7 112
Kenya, country, Afr., 9,200,000......F9 42, A6 48
Kenya, mtn., Ken............B6 48
Kenyon, Goodhue, Minn., 1,624...............F6 99
Kenyon, Washington, R.I., 250..............D10 84
Keo, Lonoke, Ark., 237..C4, E6 81
Keokea, Maui, Haw.........C5 88
Keokuk, Lee, Iowa, 16,316..D6 92
Keokuk, co., Iowa, 15,492....C5 92
Keokuk, lock and dam, Iowa....D6 92
Keoma, Alta., Can...........D4 69
Keonjhargarh, India, 12,624...............G10 40
Keosauqua, Van Buren, Iowa, 1,023...............D6 92
Keota, Weld, Colo., 13......A6 83
Keota, Keokuk, Iowa, 1,096.C6 92
Keota, Haskell, Okla., 579...B7 114
Kep, Camb..............G6 38
Kepno, Pol., 7,810...........C5 26
Keppel, Sask., Can..........E2 70
Kepples, Butler, Pa..........E2 114
Kepsut, Tur., 4,000.........C6 23
Kerala, state, India, 16,903,715..............F6 39
Kerang, Austl., 3,727.......G4 51
Kerasund (Giresun), Tur., 19,900..............B12 31
Kerby, Josephine, Oreg., 600.E3 113
Kerby, peak, Oreg...........E3 113
Kerch, Sov. Un., 107,000....I11 27
Kerch, strait, Sov. Un.........I11 27
Kerchemya, Sov. Un.........C19 9
Kerema, Pap..............k12 50
Keremeos, B.C., Can., 563...E8 68
Kerempe, cape, Tur...........A9 31
Keren, Eth., 2,700..........B4 47
Kerens, Navarro, Tex., 1,123.C4 118
Kerguelen, isl., Indian O........J1 2
Kerhonkson, Ulster, N.Y., 750..............D6 108
Kericho, Ken.............B6 48
Kerintji, mtn., Indon..........F2 35
Kerkennah, is., Tun...........C7 44
Kerkhoven, Swift, Minn., 645................E3 99
Kerki, Sov. Un., 21,600.....H22 9
Kerkira, Grc., 26,991.......C2 23
Kerkira, prov., Grc., 101,770..............*C2 23
Kerkira (Corfu), isl., Grc.....C2 23
Kerkrade, Neth., 50,800.....D6 15
Kermadec, is., Pac. O..........I11 7
Kerman, Fresno, Calif., 1,970...............*D4 82
Kermān, Iran, 62,157.......F8 41
Kermānshāh, Iran, 125,439..D3 41
Kermit, Divide, N. Dak., 23..A2 110
Kermit, Winkler, Tex., 10,465..............D1 118
Kermit, Mingo, W. Va., 743.D2 123
Kermode, mtn., B.C., Can......C2 68
Kern, co., Calif., 291,984....E4 82
Kern, riv., Calif.............E4 82
Kernersville, Forsyth, N.C., 2,942...............A3 109
Kernville, Kern, Calif., 600...E4 82
Kernville, Lincoln, Oreg., 15...............C3 113
Kerpen, Ger., 7,200.........C1 17
Kerr, Lonoke, Ark..........D6 81
Kerr, Gallia, Ohio, 30.......D5 111
Kerr, co., Tex., 16,800.....D3 118
Kerr, lake, Fla..............C5 86
Kerr, John H., res., N.C., Va........A5 109, E4 121
Kerrera, isl., Scot...........D3 13
Kerrick, Pine, Minn., 110...D6 99
Kerrick, Dallam, Tex., 50...A1 118
Kerrobert, Sask., Can., 1,220.F1 70
Kerrs Creek, Rockbridge, Va...............D3 121
Kerrville, Kerr, Tex., 8,901..D3 118
Kerry, co., Ire., 116,458.....E2 11
Kerrykeel, Ire.............B4 11
Kersey, Weld, Colo., 378....A6 83
Kersey, Elk, Pa., 600.......D4 114
Kershaw, Kershaw and Lancaster, S.C., 1,567.....B6 115
Kershaw, co., S.C., 33,585...C6 115
Kersley, B.C., Can., 182.....C6 68
Kerteminde, Den., 4,024....C4 24
Kerulen, riv., Mong...........B7 34
Kerza, Alg...............D4 44
Kerzers, Switz., 2,228.......C3 19
Kesan, Tur., 15,100........B6 23
Kesarya (Sdot Yam), Isr., 458................B6 32
Kesch, peak, Switz...........C8 19
Kesennuma, Jap., 37,200 (57,106▲)...........G10 37
Kesh, N. Ire., 202..........C4 11
Keshena, Shawano, Wis., 500.D5 124
Kesley, Butler, Iowa, 115....B5 92
Kestenga, Sov. Un..........E14 25
Kesteven, Lincolnshire, see Lincoln, co., Eng.
Keswick, Ont., Can., 699....C5 72
Keswick, Eng., 4,752........F5 13
Keswick, Keokuk, Iowa, 265.C5 92
Keswick, Albermarle, Va., 300................C4 121
Keszthely, Hung., 14,854....B3 22
Ket, riv., Sov. Un..........D26 9
Keta, Ghana, 11,380.........E5 45
Ketapang, Indon., 4,385.....F3 35
Ketchikan, Alsk., 6,483...............D13, n24 79
Ketchum, Blaine, Idaho, 746................F4 89
Ketchum, Craig, Okla., 255..A6 111
Ketchum, mtn., Tex...........D2 118
Ketona, Jefferson, Ala., 900................E5 78
Ketrzyn Mazowiecki, Pol., 13,900...............A6 26
Kettering, Eng., 38,800......B7 12
Kettering, Montgomery, Ohio, 54,462..............*C3 111
Kettle, creek, Pa............C6 114
Kettle, riv., B.C., Can., Wash..............E8 68
Kettle, riv., Minn............D6 99
Kettle Falls, Stevens, Wash., 905...............A7 122
Kettleman City, Kings, Calif., 400................E4 82
Kettle River, Carlton, Minn., 234...............D6 99
Kettle River, range, Wash......A7 122
Kettlewell, Eng., 304........F6 13
Kettwig, Ger., 17,100.......B1 17
Kety, Pol., 6,581.........D5, h10 26
Ketzin, Ger., 5,107.........A7 17
Keuka, lake, N.Y............C3 108
Keuterville, Idaho, Idaho, 30.C2 89
Kevil, Ballard, Ky., 231.....A2 94
Kevin, Toole, Mont., 375....B5 102
Kew, Eng. (part of Richmond)..............m11 10
Kewanee, Henry, Ill., 16,324...............B4 90
Kewanee, Lauderdale, Miss., 225...............C5 100
Kewanee, New Madrid, Mo., 200...............E8 101
Kewanna, Fulton, Ind., 683..B5 91
Kewaskum, Washington, Wis., 1,572..............E5 124
Kewaunee, Kewaunee, Wis., 2,772...............D6 124
Kewaunee, co., Wis., 18,282.D6 124
Keweenaw, co., Mich., 2,417.A2 98
Keweenaw, bay, Mich..........B2 98
Keweenaw, pt., Mich..........A3 98
Keweenaw Bay, Baraga, Mich., 75...............B2 98
Key, lake, Ire..............C3 11
Keyapaha, Tripp, S. Dak., 19................E6 116
Keya Paha, co., Nebr., 1,672.B6 103
Keya Paha, riv., Nebr., S. Dak..D6 116
Key Biscayne, Dade, Fla., 2,500.............*G6 86
Keyes, Stanislaus, Calif., 1,546...............*D4 82
Keyes, Man., Can...........D2 71
Keyes, Cimarron, Okla., 627.D2 112
Keyesport, Clinton and Bond, Ill., 412...........E4 90
Keyhole, res., Wyo...........A8 125
Key Junction, Ont., Can.....B4 72
Key Largo, Monroe, Fla., 900................G6 86
Keymar, Carroll, Md., 150..A3 85
Keynsham, Eng., 15,144.....C5 12
Keyport, Monmouth, N.J., 6,440...............C4 106
Keysburgh, Logan, Ky., 100.D2 94
Keyser, Mineral, W. Va., 6,192...............B6 123
Keystone, Wells, Ind., 260...C7 91
Keystone, Benton, Iowa, 522.C5 92
Keystone, Keith, Nebr., 50..C4 103
Keystone, White Pine, Nev..D7 104
Keystone, Tulsa, Okla., 151..A5 114
Keystone, Pennington, S. Dak., 500...............D2 116
Keystone, McDowell, W. Va., 1,457...............D3 123
Keystone Heights, Clay, Fla., 655...............C5 86
Keysville, Hillsborough, Fla., 500...............E4 86
Keysville, Burke, Ga., 250...C4 87
Keysville, Charlotte, Va., 733...............D4 121
Keytesville, Chariton, Mo., 644...............B5 101
Key West, Monroe, Fla., 33,956...............H5 86
Key West, Dubuque, Iowa, 85...............B7 92
Kezar, lake, Maine...........D2 96
Kezar, pond, Maine...........D2 96
Kezar Falls, York, Maine, 600...............E2 96
Kezhma, Sov. Un., 3,000...D13 28
Kezmarok, Czech., 7,372....D6 26
Kfar Ata, Isr., 14,245........B7 32
Kfar Blum, Isr.............A7 32
Kfar Monash, Isr., 232.......f10 32
Kfar Saba, Isr., 18,635......g10 32
Kfar Vitkin, Isr., 1,094.....B6 32
Kfar Yona, Isr., 3,500.......f10 32
Khabab, Syr..............A8 32
Khabarovsk, Sov. Un., 377,000...........E16 26, B7 37
Khachmas, Sov. Un.........E3 29
Khadar Khel, Afg., 5,000...E14 41
Khairpur, Pak., 18,186......D2 40
Khalafābād, Iran...........F4 41

KHAL-KISS 57X

Khalij Surt, see Sidra, gulf, Libya.
Khalkí (Chalke), isl., Grc. D6 23
Khalkidhikí (Chalcidice), prov., Grc., 79,849 *B4 23
Khalkidhikí, pen., Grc. B4 23
Khalkis, Grc., 24,745 C4, g11 23
Khambhaliya, India, 20,064 D5 39
Khamgaon, India, 44,432 G6 40
Khanabad, Afg., 30,000 C14 41
Khanaqin, Iraq, 10,090 D2 41
Khān az Zabīb, Jordan, 1,000 C8 32
Khanderi, is., India H4 40
Khandwa, India, 63,505 G6 40
Khanh An, Viet H6 38
Khania, Grc., 38,467 E4 23
Khania, prov., Grc., 131,061 *E4 23
Khania, gulf, Grc E4 23
Khanka, lake, China, Sov. Un. D6 37
Khanpur, Pak., 13,484 C5 39
Khanty-Mansiysk, Sov. Un., 19,000 A7 29
Khan Yunis, Gaza Area, 10,000 C6 32
Kharagpur, India, 147,253 D8 38, F11 40
Kharānaq, Iran E7 41
Kharan Kalat, Pak., 2,589 G12 41
Kharg, isl., Iran G5 41
Khargone, India, 30,652 G5 40
Khariar, India, 7,873 G9 40
Kharijah, oasis, Eg., U.A.R. D6 43
Kharkov, Sov. Un., 1,006,000 (*1,230,000) G11 27
Kharmanli, Bul., 9,240 E7 22
Kharovsk, Sov. Un., 5,000 B13 27
Kharr, wadi, Sau. Ar G14 31
Khartoum, Sud., 132,000 (*370,000) B3 47
Khartoum, reg., Sud., 504,923 B3 47
Khartoum North, Sud., 56,000 B3 47
Khartsyzsk, Sov. Un., 10,000 q21 27
Khasavyurt, Sov. Un., 30,000 G18 9
Khash, Afg., 5,000 F11 41
Khāsh, Iran, 9,291 G10 41
Khashuri, Sov. Un., 5,347 A14 31
Khasi, hills, India C9 39
Khaskovo, Bul., 27,394 E7 22
Khatanga, Sov. Un., 10,000 B13 28
Khatanga, riv., Sov. Un B13 28
Khedive, Sask., Can., 123 *H3 70
Khemmarat, Thai., 8,194 D6 38
Khenchela, Alg., 11,051 (12,196▲) B6 44
Khénifra, Mor., 18,503 C3 44
Kherson, Sov. Un., 192,000 H9 27
Kheta, riv., Sov. Un B12 28
Khilchipur, India, 6,970 E6 40
Khilok, Sov. Un., 18,600 D14 28
Khimki, Sov. Un., 51,000 n17 27
Khios, Grc., 24,053 C6 23
Khios (Chios), prov., Grc., 62,223 *C6 23
Khíos (Chios), isl., Grc C6 23
Khisfin, Syr B7 32
Khiva, Sov. Un., 19,000 E6 29
Khlebarovo, Bul., 5,829 D8 22
Khmelnik, Sov. Un., 10,000 G6 27
Khmelnitskiy, Sov. Un., 72,000 G6 27
Khochniye, Syr A7 32
Khodzheyli, Sov. Un., 15,000 E5 29
Khokhropar, Pak E3 40
Kholm, Sov. Un., 10,000 C8 27
Kholmsk (Maoka), Sov. Un., 33,000 E17 28
Khonak, Afg., 5,000 D13 41
Khong, Laos, 10,000 E6 38
Khong, riv., Laos E7 38
Khong Sedone, Laos, 10,000 E6 38
Khon Kaen, Thai., 17,952 D5 38
Khoper, riv., Sov. Un C2 29
Khor, riv., Sov. Un C7 37
Khor al Kalba, Mus. & Om. I8 41
Khor-Anghar, Fr. Som C5 47
Khora Sfakion, Grc., 377 E5 23
Khorinsk, Sov. Un A6 34
Khorog, Sov. Un., 9,000 H23 9
Khorol, Sov. Un., 10,000 G9 27
Khorramābād, Iran, 38,676 E4 41
Khorramshahr, Iran, 43,850 F4 41
Khotan (Hotien), China, 50,000 A6 39
Khotan, riv., China A7 39
Khotin, Sov. Un., 10,000 G6 27
Khouribga, Mor., 40,838 *C3 44
Khrisoupolis, Grc., 5,037 B5 23
Khrom-Tau, Sov. Un C5 29
Khu Khan, Thai E6 38
Khulna, Pak., 80,917 (*127,970) D9 39
Khunzakh, Sov. Un A16 31
Khurda, India, 12,497 G10 40
Khurja, India, 41,491 C6 40
Khushab, Pak., 20,476 A4 40
Khust, Sov. Un., 10,000 G4 27
Khuzdar, Pak C4 39
Khvāf, Iran D10 41
Khvor, Iran E7 41
Khvormūj, Iran, 2,500 G5 41
Khvoy, Iran, 34,491 B2 41
Khyber, pass, Afg., Pak D15 41
Kia, isl., Fiji Is 52
Kialing, riv., China E6 34
Kiamichi, Pushmataha, Okla., 75 C6 114
Kiamichi, mtn., Okla C7 114
Kiamichi, riv., Okla C6 114
Kiamika, Que., Can., 168 C2 73
Kiamika, riv., Que., Can C2 73
Kiamusze (Chiamussu), China, 146,000 B11 34
Kiana, Alsk., 253 B7 79
Kiangsi, prov., China, 18,610,000 F9 34
Kiangsu, prov., China, 42,630,000 E8 34
Kiani, lake, P.R. g12 65
Kiantajärvi, lake, Fin E13 25
Kiaohsien, China, 75,000 F9 36
Kiask, lake, Man., Can A3 71
Kiawah, isl., S.C. F7 115
Kibangou, Con. B F2 46
Kibau, Tan C6 48
Kiberege, Tan C6 48
Kiblah, Miller, Ark., 195 D2 81
Kibombo, Con. L B4 48
Kibondo, Tan B5 48
Kibwezi, Ken B6 48
Kičevo, Yugo., 10,273 E5 22
Kickapoo, Leavenworth, Kans., 30 A8 93
Kickapoo, Polk, Tex D5 118
Kickapoo, creek, Ill C4 90
Kickapoo, riv., Wis E3 124
Kicking Horse, pass, Alta., B.C., Can D9 68
Kidal, Mali, 750 C5 45
Kidder, Caldwell, Mo., 224 B3 101
Kidder, Marshall, S. Dak., 142 B8 116
Kidder, co., N. Dak., 5,386 B6 110
Kidderminster, Eng., 43,100 B5 12
Kidira, Sen D2 45
Kidnappers, cape, N.Z. M16 51
Kidron, val., Jordan m14 32
Kidsgrove, Eng., 19,726 A5 12
Kidugalo, Tan C6 48
Kidwelly, Wales, 2,879 C3 12
Kief, McHenry, N. Dak., 97 B5 110
Kiefer, Creek, Okla., 489 B5 112
Kiel, Ger., 270,900 A5 16, D4 24
Kiel, Calumet and Manitowoc, Wis., 2,524 B5, E5 124
Kiel, bay, Ger A5 16
Kiel (Kaiser Wilhelm), canal, Ger D3 24
Kielce, Pol., 95,300 C6 26
Kiental, Switz C4 19
Kiesling, Spokane, Wash D7 122
Kiester, Faribault, Minn., 741 G5 99
Kiev (Kiyev), Sov. Un., 1,248,000 (*1,375,000) F8 27
Kifisia, Grc., 14,193 g11 23
Kifisos, riv., Grc g11 23
Kifissos (Cephisus), riv., Grc g9 23
Kifri, Iraq, 4,760 D2 41
Kifta, Maur., 1,300 C2 45
Kigali, Rwanda, 4,000 B5 48
Kigi, Tur., 1,072 C13 31
Kigoma, Tan., 4,244 B4 48
Kihei, Maui, Haw., 95 C5 88
Kiholo, bay, Haw D6 88
Kii, strait, Jap I7 37
Kikinda, Yugo., 33,906 C5 22
Kikládhes (Cyclades), prov., Grc., 99,959 *D5 23
Kikongo, Con. L B2 48
Kikori, Pap k11 50
Kikwit, Con. L., 11,000 C2 48
Kila, Flathead, Mont., 50 B2 102
Kilauea, Kauai, Haw., 800 A2 88
Kilauea, crater, Haw D6 88
Kilbaha, Ire E2 11
Kilbeggan, Ire., 799 D4 11
Kilbourne, Mason, Ill., 352 C3 90
Kilbourne, West Carroll, La., 227 B4 95
Kilbourne, Delaware, Ohio, 220 B5 111
Kilbrannan, sound, Scot E3 13
Kilbride, Newf., Can., 607 *E5 75
Kilburn, N.B., Can., 137 C2 74
Kilcar, Ire., 229 C3 11
Kilchberg, Switz., 6,784 B6 19
Kilchoan, Scot., 948 B2 13
Kilchreest, Ire D3 11
Kilchrenan, Scot., 349 D3 13
Kilchu, Kor., 30,026 F4 37
Kilcock, Ire., 739 D5 11
Kilcolgan, Ire., 113 D3 11
Kilconnell, Ire., 113 D3 11
Kilcoole, Ire., 549 D5 11
Kilcormac, Ire., 1,018 D4 11
Kilcullen, Ire., 637 D5 11
Kildare, Que., Can C4 73
Kildare, Ire., 2,551 D5 11
Kildare, Kay, Okla., 124 A4 110
Kildare, co., Ire., 64,420 D5 11
Kildare, cape, P.E.I., Can C6 74
Kildorrery, Ire., 228 E3 11
Kilembe, Con. L C2 48
Kilfenora, Ire., 135 E2 11
Kilfinnane, Ire., 565 E3 11
Kilgarvan, Ire., 183 F2 11
Kilgore, Clark, Idaho, 20 E7 89
Kilgore, Cherry, Nebr., 157 B5 103
Kilgore, Gregg, Tex., 10,092 C5 118
Kilifi, Ken B6 48
Kilimanjaro, mtn., Tan B6 48
Kilis (Killis), Tur., 33,300 D11 31
Kiliya, Sov. Un., 10,000 I7 27
Kilkee, Ire., 1,392 E2 11
Kilkeel, N. Ire., 2,490 C5 11
Kilkenny, Ire., 1,159 E4 11
Kilkenny, LeSueur, Minn., 221 F5 99
Kilkenny, co., Ire., 61,668 E4 11
Kilkerrin, Ire., 199 D3 11
Kilkieran, Ire., 153 D2 11
Kilkieran, bay, Ire D2 11
Kilkis, Grc., 10,963 B4 23
Kilkis, prov., Grc., 102,812 *B4 23
Kill, Ire., 186 D5 11
Killadoon, Ire D2 11
Killadysert, Ire., 295 E2 11
Killala, Ire., 337 C2 11
Killala, bay, Ire C2 11
Killaloe, Ire., 835 E3 11
Killaloe Station, Ont., Can., 932 B7 72
Killaly, Sask., Can., 212 G4 70
Killam, Alta., Can., 552 C5 69
Killarney, Man., Can., 1,729 E2 71
Killarney, Ire., 6,825 E2 11
Killarney, Raleigh, W. Va., 200 D3 123
Killarney, prov. park, Ont., Can A3 72
Killashandra, Ire., 397 C4 11
Killavally, Ire D2 11
Killbuck, Holmes, Ohio, 865 B6 111
Killdeer, Sask., Can., 52 H2 70
Killdeer, Dunn, N. Dak., 765 B3 110
Killdeer, mts., N. Dak B3 110
Killduff, Jasper, Iowa, 150 C5 92
Killeen, Bell, Tex., 23,377 D4 118
Killen, Lauderdale, Ala., 620 A2 78
Killenaule, Ire., 531 E4 11
Killeter, N. Ire C4 11
Killian, Livingstone, La., 22 B6 95
Killian, Richland, S.C., 800 C6 115
Killiecrankie, pass, Scot D4 13
Killimor, Ire., 195 D3 11
Killin, Scot., 1,199 D4 13
Killinek, isl., N.W. Ter., Can f8 75
Killingly (Town of), Windham, Conn. (11,298▲) *B9 84
Killington, peak, Vt D3 120
Killingworth, Middlesex, Conn., 100 (1,098▲) D6 84
Killini, Grc., 744 D3 23
Killis (Kilis), Tur., 33,300 D11 31
Killona, St. Charles, La., 650 C6 95
Killorglin, Ire., 1,100 E2 11
Killucan, Ire., 314 D4 11
Killybegs, Ire., 1,065 C3 11
Killyleagh, N. Ire., 1,876 C6 11
Kilmacthomas, Ire., 446 E4 11
Kilmaine, Ire., 94 D2 11
Kilmallie, Scot D3 13
Kilmallock, Ire., 1,159 E3 11
Kilmanagh, Huron, Mich., 50 E7 98
Kilmarnock, Scot., 48,000 E4 13
Kilmarnock, Lancaster and Northumberland, Va., 927 D6 121
Kilmatinde, Tan C5 48
Kilmelfort, Scot., 279 D3 13
Kilmichael, Montgomery, Miss., 532 B4 100
Kilmonivaig, Scot D3 13
Kiln, Hancock, Miss., 300 E4 100
Kilosa, Tan., 3,743 C6 48
Kilrea, N. Ire., 954 C5 11
Kilrush, Ire., 2,861 E2 11
Kilsyth, Scot., 9,831 E4 13
Kiltamagh, Ire., 980 D3 11
Kiltoom, Ire D3 11
Kilwa, Con. L C4 48
Kilwa Kivinje, Tan C6 48
Kilworthy, Ont., Can C5 72
Kim, Las Animas, Colo., 400 D7 83
Kimamba, Tan., 1,330 C6 48
Kimball, Stearns, Minn., 535 E4 99
Kimball, Kimball, Nebr., 4,384 C2 103
Kimball, Brule, S. Dak., 912 D7 116
Kimball, McDowell, W. Va., 1,175 *D3 123
Kimball, co., Nebr., 7,975 C2 103
Kimballton, Audubon, Iowa, 380 C2 92
Kimberley, B.C., Can., 6,013 E9 68
Kimberley, S. Afr., 75,376 (*79,031) C3 49
Kimberlin Heights, Knox, Tenn., 275 E12 117
Kimberly, Jefferson, Ala., 763 B3 78
Kimberly, Twin Falls, Idaho, 1,298 G4 89
Kimberly, Aitkin, Minn., 22 D5 99
Kimberly, White Pine, Nev D6 104
Kimberly, Grant, Oreg., 10 C7 113
Kimberly, Fayette, W. Va., 900 D6 123
Kimberly, Outagamie, Wis., 5,322 A5 124
Kimble, co., Tex., 3,943 D3 118
Kimbles, Pike, Pa., 30 D11 114
Kimbolton, Guernsey, Ohio, 218 B6 111
Kimbrough, Wilcox, Ala., 150 C2 78
Kimchaek (Sŏngjin), Kor., 67,778 F4 37
Kimi, Grc., 4,071 C5 23
Kimiwan, lake, Alta., Can B2 69
Kimmell, Noble, Ind., 350 B6 91
Kimmins, Lewis, Tenn., 50 B4 117
Kimmswick, Jefferson, Mo., 303 B8 101
Kimowin, riv., Sask., Can A6 69
Kimry, Sov. Un., 40,000 C11 27
Kin, Okinawa 52
Kinabalu, mtn., Mala D5 35
Kinard, Calhoun, Fla., 150 B1 86
Kinards, Laurens and Newberry, S.C., 234 C4 115
Kinbasket, lake, B.C., Can D8 68
Kinbrace, Scot B5 13
Kinbrae, Nobles, Minn., 55 G3 99
Kinburn, Ont., Can., 172 B8 72
Kincaid, Sask., Can., 310 H2 70
Kincaid, Christian, Ill., 1,544 D4 90
Kincaid, Anderson, Kans., 220 D8 93
Kincardine, Ont., Can., 2,841 C3 72
Kincardine, co., Scot., 25,556 D6 13
Kinchafonee, riv., Ga E2 87
Kinde, Huron, Mich., 624 E8 98
Kinder, Allen, La., 2,299 D3 95
Kinderhook, Pike, Ill., 276 D2 90
Kinderhook, Columbia, N.Y., 1,078 C7 108
Kindersley, Sask., Can., 2,990 F1 70
Kindia, Guinea, 13,000 D2 45
Kindred, Cass, N. Dak., 580 C8 110
Kindu [-Port Empain], Con. L., 14,200 B4 48
Kineo, mtn., Maine C3 96
Kineshma, Sov. Un., 91,000 B2 29
King, Stokes, N.C., 950 A3 109
King, Waupaca, Wis., 500 D4 124
King, co., Tex., 640 C2 118
King, co., Wash., 935,014 B4 117
King, isl., Austl G7, n14 50
King, isl., Bur F3 38
King, isl., B.C., Can C4 68
King, mtn., Oreg D8 113
King, sound, Austl C3 50
King and Queen C. H., King and Queen, Va., 65 D6 121
King and Queen, co., Va., 5,889 D6 121
Kingaroy, Austl., 4,914 C8 51
Kingarrow, Ire C3 11
King Christian IX Land, reg., Grnld C18 4
King Christian X Land, reg., Grnld B17 4
King City, Monterey, Calif., 2,937 D3 82
King City, Ont., Can., 1,864 k14 72
King City, Gentry, Mo., 1,009 A3 101
King Cove, Alsk., 290 E7 79
King Ferry, Cayuga, N.Y., 400 C4 108
Kingfield, Franklin, Maine, 700 (864▲) D2 96
Kingfisher, Kingfisher, Okla., 3,249 B4 112
Kingfisher, co., Okla., 10,635 B4 112
King Frederik VI Coast, reg., Grnld C19 4
King Frederik VIII Land, reg., Grnld B17 4
King George, King George, Va., 240 C5 121
King George, co., Va., 7,243 C5 121
King Goerge, isl., Ant C7 5
King George, mtn., B.C., Can D10 68
King George, sound, Austl F2 50
King George IV, lake, Newf., Can D3 75
King Hill, Elmore, Idaho, 200 F3 89
King Lear, peak, Nev B3 104
King Leopold, range, Austl C4 50
Kingman, Mohave, Ariz., 4,525 B1 80
Kingman, Alta., Can., 108 C4 69
Kingman, Fountain, Ind., 461 E3 91
Kingman, Kingman, Kans., 3,582 B3, E5 93
Kingman, Penobscot, Maine, 250 C4 96
Kingman, co., Kans., 9,958 E5 93
King of Prussia, Montgomery, Pa., 6,000 *F11 114
Kings, Ogle, Ill., 225 A4 90
Kings, Warren, Miss., 65 B3 100
Kings, co., Calif., 49,954 D4 82
Kings, co., N.B., Can., 25,908 D4 74
Kings, co., N.S., Can., 41,747 E5 74
Kings, co., P.E.I., Can., 17,893 C7 74
Kings, co., (Brooklyn borough) N.Y. (part of New York City), 2,627,319 E7 108
Kings, peak, Utah C5 119
Kings, ridge, Tex A3 118
Kings, riv., Ark A2 81
Kings, riv., Calif D4 82
Kings, riv., Ire E4 11
Kings, riv., Nev B3 104
Kingsbridge, Eng., 3,283 D4 12
Kingsburg, Fresno, Calif., 3,093 D4 82
Kingsbury, LaPorte, Ind., 281 A4 91
Kingsbury, Piscataquis, Maine, 5 (80▲) C3 96
Kingsbury, Guadalupe, Tex., 300 B4 118
Kingsbury, co., S. Dak., 9,227 C8 116
Kings Canyon, Jackson, Colo., 10 A4 83
Kings Canyon, nat. park, Calif D4 82
Kingsclear, N.B., Can., 200 D3 74
Kingscote, Austl., 534 G6 50
Kings Creek, Somerset, Md D6 85
Kings Creek, Cherokee, S.C., 200 A5 116
Kingsdale, Pine, Minn., 60 D6 99
Kingsdown, Ford, Kans., 100 E4 93
Kingsey Falls, Que., Can., 531 D5 73
Kingsford, Dickinson, Mich., 5,084 C2 98
Kingsford Heights, La Porte, Ind., 1,276 *B4 91
Kings Gardens, Reno, Kans., 400 A4 93
Kingsgate, B.C., Can., 71 E9 68
Kingshill, Vir. Is k17 65
Kingsland, Cleveland, Ark., 249 D3 81
Kingsland, Camden, Ga., 1,536 F5 87
Kingsland, Llano, Tex., 150 D3 118
Kingsley, Plymouth, Iowa, 1,044 B2 92
Kingsley, Grand Traverse, Mich., 586 D5 98
Kingsley, dam, Nebr C4 103
King's Lynn, Eng., 27,500 B8 12
Kingsmere, lake, Sask., Can C2 70
Kings Mill, Gray, Tex., 75 B2 118
Kings Mills, Warren, Ohio, 700 C2, C3 111
Kings Mountain, Lincoln, Ky., 500 C5 94
Kings Mountain, Cleveland, N.C., 8,008 B2 109
Kings Park, Suffolk, N.Y., 7,000 n15 108
King's Point, Newf., Can., 546 D3 75
Kings Point, Nassau, N.Y., 5,410 F1 84
Kingsport, Sullivan, Tenn., 26,314 C11 117
Kingston, Madison, Ark., 150 A2 81
Kingston, Austl., 806 H2 51
Kingston, N.S., Can., 1,210 E5 74
Kingston, Ont., Can., 53,526 (*63,419) C8 72
Kingston, Bartow, Ga., 695 B2 87
Kingston, Shoshone, Idaho, 200 B2 89
Kingston, De Kalb, Ill., 406 A5 90
Kingston, Jam., 421,718 F5 64
Kingston, Madison, Ky., 200 C5 94
Kingston, Somerset, Md., 5 D6 85
Kingston, Plymouth, Mass., 1,500 (4,302▲) C6 97
Kingston, Tuscola, Mich., 456 E7 98
Kingston, Meeker, Minn., 125 E4 99
Kingston, Caldwell, Mo., 311 B3 101
Kingston, Rockingham, N.H., 600 (1,672▲) E4 105
Kingston, Middlesex and Somerset, N.J., 900 C3 106
Kingston, Sierra, N. Mex., 50 E2 107
Kingston, Ulster, N.Y., 29,260 D6 108
Kingston, Ross, Ohio, 1,066 C5 111
Kingston, Marshall, Okla., 639 D5 112
Kingston, Luzerne, Pa., 20,261 B8, D10 114
Kingston, Washington, R.I., 3,500 D10 84
Kingston, Roane, Tenn., 2,010 D9 117
Kingston, Piute, Utah, 143 E3 119
Kingston, Fayette, W. Va., 400 D3, D6 123
Kingston, Green Lake, Wis., 343 E4 124
Kingston-on-Thames, Eng., 36,450 m11 10
Kingston Springs, Cheatham, Tenn., 400 A4 117
Kingstown, St. Vincent, 4,308 (*16,300) p16 64
Kingstree, Williamsburg, S.C., 3,847 D8 115
Kings Valley, Benton, Oreg., 250 C3 113
Kingsville, Ont., Can., 3,041 E2 72
Kingsville, Johnson, Mo., 225 C4 101
Kingsville, Ashtabula, Ohio, 950 A7 111
Kingsville, Kleberg, Tex., 25,297 F4 118
Kingswood, Breckinridge, Ky., 248 C3 94
Kingtehchen, see Fowliang, China.
Kington, Eng., 1,861 B4 12
Kingurutik, lake, Newf., Can g9 75
Kingussie, Scot., 1,079 C4 13
Kingwa, Que., Can f11 73
King William, King William, Va., 40 D5 121
King William, co., Va., 7,563 D5 121
King William, isl., N.W. Ter., Can C13 66
King William's Town, S. Afr., 14,646 D4 49
Kingwood, Preston, W. Va., 2,530 B5 123
Kinistino, Sask., Can., 764 E3 70
Kinkala, Con. B F2 46
Kinkora, P.E.I., Can., 271 C6 74
Kinley, Sask., Can., 119 E2 70
Kinloch, St. Louis, Mo., 6,501 A8 101
Kinlochewe, Scot C3 13
Kinloch Hourn, Scot C3 13
Kinmount, Ont., Can., 256 C6 72
Kinmundy, Marion, Ill., 813 E5 90
Kinnaird, B.C., Can., 2,123 E9 68
Kinnairds, head, Scot C7 13
Kinnelon, Morris, N.J., 4,431 B4 106
Kinney, co., Tex., 2,452 E2 118
Kinomoto, Jap., 5,600 n15 37
Kinosaki, Jap., 4,400 I7 37
Kinpoku, peak, Jap G9 37
Kinrooi, Bel., 2,022 C5 15
Kinross, P.E.I., Can., 66 C7 74
Kinross, Scot., 2,365 D5 13
Kinross, co., Scot., 6,704 D5 13
Kinsale, Ire., 1,587 F3 11
Kinsale, Westmoreland, Va., 250 C6 121
Kinsella, Alta., Can., 91 C5 69
Kinsey, Houston, Ala., 283 D4 78
Kinsey, Custer, Mont., 25 D11 102
Kinsley, Edwards, Kans., 2,263 E4 93
Kinsman, Trumbull, Ohio, 900 A7 111
Kinston, Coffee, Ala., 470 D3 78
Kinston, Lenoir, N.C., 24,819 B6 109
Kinta, Haskell, Okla., 233 B6 109
Kintampo, Ghana, 2,829 E4 45
Kintinku, Tan C6 48
Kinton, St. Francis, Ark B5 81
Kintore, Scot., 749 C6 13
Kintyre, Emmons, N. Dak., 102 C6 110
Kinuso, Alta., Can., 323 B3 69
Kinvara, Ire., 338 D3 11
Kinwood, Harris, Tex., 2,500 *F5 118
Kinyangiri, Tan., 1,540 B5 48
Kinyeti, mtn., Sud E3 47
Kinzig, riv., Ger C4 17
Kinzig, riv., Ger E2 17
Kinzua, Wheeler, Oreg., 300 C6 113
Kinzua, Warren, Pa., 420 C4 114
Kioa, isl., Fiji Is 52
Kioshkokwi, lake, Ont., Can A6 72
Kiosk, Ont., Can., 350 A6 72
Kiowa, Elbert, Colo., 195 B6 83
Kiowa, Barber, Kans., 1,674 E5 93
Kiowa, Pittsburg, Okla., 607 C6 112
Kiowa, co., Colo., 2,425 C8 83
Kiowa, co., Kans., 4,626 E4 93
Kiowa, co., Okla., 14,825 C3 112
Kiowa, creek, Colo B6 83
Kiowa, creek, Okla A1 112
Kipahigan, lake, Man., Sask., Can B1 71
Kipahulu, Maui, Haw., 25 C5 88
Kiparissia, Grc., 5,027 D3 23
Kiparissia, gulf, Grc D3 23
Kipili, Tan C5 48
Kipini, Ken B7 48
Kipling, Sask., Can., 773 G4 70
Kipling, Delta, Mich., 400 C3 98
Kipnuk, Alsk., 221 C7 79
Kipp, Alta., Can E4 69
Kipp, Saline, Kans., 80 D6 93
Kippens, Newf., Can., 1,079 *D2 75
Kipton, Lorain, Ohio, 353 A5 111
Kiptopeke, Northampton, Va B7 121
Kipushi, Con. L., 15,100 D4 48
Kirby, Pike, Ark., 300 C2 81
Kirby, Big Horn, Mont., 5 E10 102
Kirby (Town of), Caledonia, Vt., (235▲) *C5 120
Kirby, Hot Springs, Wyo., 82 B4 125
Kirbyville, Jasper, Tex., 1,680 D6 118
Kirchberg, Switz., 3,304 B4 19
Kirchdorf, Ger., 783 D5 24
Kirchhain [im Bezirk Kassel], Ger., 5,500 C3 17
Kirchhain [Niederlausitz], Ger., 7,636 B8 17
Kirchheim [unter Teck], Ger., 25,000 E4 17
Kirchheimbolanden, Ger., 5,200 D3 17
Kirchhundem, Ger., 10,500 B3 17
Kirdāsah, Eg., U.A.R., 1,000 D3 32
Kirensk, Sov. Un., 12,500 D13 28
Kirghiz, steppe, Sov. Un E9 33
Kirghiz S.S.R., rep., Sov. Un., 2,490,000 G23 9
Kirgiz, range, Sov. Un E8 29
Kiri, Con. L B2 48
Kirin (Chilin), China, 568,000 C10 34
Kirin, prov., China, 12,550,000 C10 34
Kirinian, isl., Eniwetok 52
Kirk, Yuma, Colo., 75 B3 83
Kirk, Klamath, Oreg., 20 E5 113
Kirkagac, Tur., 11,300 C6 23
Kirkby Lonsdale, Eng., 1,240 F6 13
Kirkby Stephen, Eng., 1,718 F6 13
Kirkcaldy, Alta., Can D4 69
Kirkcaldy, Scot., 52,600 D5 13
Kirkcolm, Scot., 1,635 F3 13
Kirkcudbright, Scot., 2,448 F4 13
Kirkcudbright, co., Scot., 28,877 E4 13
Kirkcudbright, bay, Scot F4 13
Kirkella, Man., Can D1 71
Kirkella, Sask., Can., 80 G5 70
Kirkenes, Nor., 3,596 C14 25
Kirkersville, Licking, Ohio, 417 C5 111
Kirkfield, Ont., Can., 211 C5 72
Kirkintilloch, Scot., 18,257 E4 13
Kirkland, Yavapai, Ariz., 20 C3 80
Kirkland, Atkinson, Ga., 150 E4 87
Kirkland, DeKalb, Ill., 928 A5 90
Kirkland, Oneida, N.Y., 100 *B5 108
Kirkland, Williamson, Tenn., 50 B5 117
Kirkland, Childress, Tex., 300 B2 118
Kirkland, King, Wash., 6,025 B3, D2 122
Kirkland Junction, Yavapai, Ariz., 10 C3 80
Kirkland Lake, Ont., Can., 15,366 o20 72
Kirklareli, Tur., 20,200 B6 23
Kirklin, Clinton, Ind., 767 D5 91
Kirkman, Shelby, Iowa, 92 C2 92
Kirkmansville, Todd, Ky., 150 D2 94
Kirkoswald, Eng., 528 F6 13
Kirkpatrick, lake, Alta., Can D5 69
Kirkpatrick, mtn., Ant A29 5
Kirksey, Calloway, Ky., 180 B3 94
Kirksey, Greenwood, S.C., 60 C3 115
Kirksville, Monroe, Ind., 20 F4 91
Kirksville, Madison, Ky., 100 C5 94
Kirksville, Adair, Mo., 13,125 A5 101
Kirkton, Ont., Can., 182 D3 72
Kirkuk, Iraq, 120,593 D2 41
Kirkville, Wapello, Iowa, 203 C5 92
Kirkwall, Scot., 4,315 B6 13
Kirkwood, New Castle, Del., 430 A6 85
Kirkwood, Warren, Ill., 771 C3 90
Kirkwood, Prince Georges, Md., 2,500 *C3 85
Kirkwood, St. Louis, Mo., 29,421 B7 101
Kirkwood, Broome, N.Y., 425 C5 108
Kirkwood, Lancaster, Pa., 100 G9 114
Kirkwood, S. Afr., 5,055 D4 49
Kirn, Ger., 9,600 D2 17
Kiron, Crawford, Iowa, 271 B2 92
Kirov, Sov. Un., 284,000 B3 29
Kirova, bay, Sov. Un B4 41
Kirovabad, Sov. Un., 126,000 E3 29
Kirovabad, Sov. Un., 123,000 H22 9
Kirovakan, Sov. Un., 60,000 B15 31
Kirovgrad, Sov. Un., 21,500 B6 29
Kirovograd, Sov. Un., 142,000 G9 27
Kirovsk, Sov. Un., 52,800 D15 25
Kirriemuir, Alta., Can., 40 D5 69
Kirriemuir, Scot., 3,485 D5 13
Kirsanov, Sov. Un., 10,000 E14 27
Kirsehir (Kir-Shehr), Tur., 20,200 C10 31
Kirther, range, Pak C4 39
Kirtland, San Juan, N. Mex., 900 A1 107
Kirtland, Lake, Ohio, 1,500 *A6 111
Kirtley, Niobrara, Wyo C8 125
Kiruna, Swe., 20,100 (27,600▲) D9 25
Kirundu, Con. L B4 48
Kirwin, Phillips, Kans., 356 C4 93
Kirwin, res., Kans C4 93
Kiryu, Jap., 123,010 H9, m18 37
Kisaki, Tan C6 48
Kisalaya, Nic C5 62
Kisanga, Con. L C4 48
Kisarazu, Jap., 29,200 (52,689▲) n18 37
Kisbey, Sask., Can., 254 H4 70
Kiselevsk, Sov. Un., 142,000 C11 29
Kisengi, Con. L D3 48
Kisengwa, Con. L C4 48
Kisenyi, Rwanda, 2,800 B5 48
Kishanganj, India, 27,002 D11 40
Kishangarh, India, 25,244 C5 39
Kishi, Nig E5 45
Kishinev, Sov. Un., 254,000 B9 22, H7 27
Kishiwada, Jap., 120,265 o14 37
Kishon, riv., Isr B7 32
Kishorganj, Pak., 19,067 D9 39
Kishorn, inlet, Scot C3 13
Kisii, Ken B5 48
Kisiju, Tan C6 48
Kisiwa, creek, Kans A4 93
Kisiwani, Tan B6 48
Kiska, isl., Alsk E3 79
Kiskatinaw, riv., B.C., Can B7 68
Kiskitto, lake, Man., Can B2 71
Kiskittogisu, lake, Man., Can B2 71
Kiskoros, Hung., 9,972 B4 22
Kiskundorozsma, Hung., 8,705 B5 22
Kiskunfelegyhaza, Hung., 22,925 (33,187▲) B4 22
Kiskunhalas, Hung., 18,314 (26,461▲) B4 22
Kiskunmajsa, Hung., 7,611 B4 22
Kislovodsk, Sov. Un., 83,000 E2 29
Kismayu [Chisimaio], Som., 8,000 (9,800▲) F5 47
Kismet, Seward, Kans., 150 E3 93
Kiso-Sammyaku, mts., Jap n16 37
Kissee Mills, Taney, Mo., 38 E4 101
Kisseynew, lake, Man., Can B1 71
Kissidougou, Guinea, 5,000 E2 45
Kissimmee, Osceola, Fla., 6,845 D5 86
Kissimmee, lake, Fla E5 86
Kissimmee, riv., Fla E5 86
Kissimmee Park, Osceola, Fla., 100 D5 86
Kississing, Man., Can., 183 B1 71
Kississing, lake, Man., Can B1 71

Kississing, riv., Man., Can B1 71
Kistigan, lake, Man., Can B5 71
Kistler, Logan, W. Va., 1,084 D3, D5 123
Kistna, riv., India E6 39
Kistrand, Nor B11 25
Kisujszallas, Hung., 11,304 (13,790▲) B5 22
Kisumu, Ken., 10,899 B5 48
Kisvarda, Hung., 13,284 A6 22
Kita, Iwo 52
Kita, Mali, 5,100 D3 45
Kita Iwo, isl., Pac. O E8 7
Kitakyūshū, Jap., 986,401 (★1,335,000) J5 37
Kitale, Ken., 6,338 A5 48
Kitamaki, Jap m17 37
Kitami, Jap., 38,200 E11 37
Kitangari, Tan D6 48
Kitano, pt., Iwo 52
Kita-Shiretoko, cape, Sov. Un B12 37
Kit Carson, Cheyenne, Colo., 356 C8 83
Kit Carson, co., Colo., 6,957 B8 83
Kitchener, Ont., Can., 74,485 (★154,864) D4 72
Kitchen's Creek, falls, Pa D9 114
Kite, Johnson, Ga., 424 D4 87
Kitega, Burundi, 5,000 B5 48
Kitgum, Ug A5 48
Kithira, Grc., 1,002 D4 23
Kíthira (Cythera), isl., Grc D4 23
Kithnos, isl., Grc D5 23
Kiti, pt., Ponape 52
Kitimat, B.C., Can., 8,217 B3 68
Kitsap, co., Wash., 84,176 B3 122
Kitscoty, Alta., Can., 326 C5 69
Kittanning, Armstrong, Pa., 6,793 E2 114
Kittatinny, mts., N.J B2 106
Kittery, York, Maine, 8,051 (10,689▲) E2 96
Kittery Point, York, Maine, 1,259 E2 96
Kittilä, Fin., 1,700 D11 25
Kittitas, Kittitas, Wash., 536 C5 122
Kittitas, co., Wash., 20,467 B5 122
Kittitas, val., Wash B5 122
Kittrell, Vance, N.C., 121 A5 109
Kitts, Harlan, Ky., 950 D6 94
Kittson, co., Minn., 8,343 B2 99
Kitty Hawk, Dare, N.C., 300 A8 109
Kitty Hawk, bay, N.C A8 109
Kitui, Ken B6 48
Kitwanga, B.C., Can., 167 B3 68
Kitwe, Zambia, 115,000 D4 48
Kityang, China, 54,000 G8 34
Kitzbühel, Aus., 7,744 E6 16
Kitzingen, Ger., 17,800 D5 17
Kitzmiller, Garrett, Md., 535 D1 85
Kiukiang, China, 64,600 F8 34
Kiungshan (Chiungshan), China C9 38
Kivalina, Alsk., 142 B7 79
Kivu, prov., Con. L., 2,205,000 B4 48
Kivu, lake, Con. L B4 48
Kiwalik, Alsk B7 79
Kiya, riv., Sov. Un D26 29
Kiyan, Okinawa 52
Kiyev (Kiev), Sov. Un., 1,248,000 (★1,375,000) F8 27
Kiyiu, lake, Sask., Can F1 70
Kizel, Sov. Un., 60,000 B5 29
Kizil, riv., Tur B10 29
Kizlyar, Sov. Un., 33,200 E3 29
Kizyl-Arvat, Sov. Un., 26,000 H20 9
Kjakan, Nor C10 25
Kjelvik, Nor B12 25
Kjellerup, Den B3 24
Kladno, Czech., 50,800 C3, n17 26
Klagenfurt, Aus., 69,218 E7 16
Klagetoh, Apache, Ariz., 200 B6 80
Klaipeda (Memel), Sov. Un., 105,000 D3 27
Klamath, Del Norte, Calif., 300 B2 82
Klamath, co., Oreg., 47,475 E5 113
Klamath, Indian res., Oreg E5 113
Klamath, mts., Oreg E2 113
Klamath, riv., Calif., Oreg B2 82
Klamath Agency, Klamath, Oreg., 200 E5 113
Klamath Falls, Klamath, Oreg., 16,949 E5 113
Klang, Mala., 75,649 K4 38
Klanxbüll, Ger., 520 D2 24
Klarälven, riv., Swe G5 25
Klatovy, Czech., 14,000 D2 26
Klawock, Alsk., 251 D13, n23 79
Kleberg, Dallas, Tex., 3,572 *B6 118
Kleberg, co., Tex., 30,052 F4 118
Klecany, Czech., 1,700 n17 26
Kleena Kleene, B.C., Can D5 68
Klein, Musselshell, Mont., 300 D8 102
Kleinburg, Ont., Can., 275 k14 72
Klemme, Hancock, Iowa, 615 A4 92
Klerksdorp, S. Afr., 43,726 C4 49
Kletnya, Sov. Un., 10,000 E9 27
Kletsk, Sov. Un., 10,000 E6 27
Kleve, Ger., 21,100 C6 15
Klickitat, Klickitat, Wash., 850 D4 122
Klickitat, co., Wash., 13,455 D5 122
Klickitat, creek, Wash D5 122
Klickitat, riv., Wash C4 122
Klimovsk, Sov. Un., 30,000 n17 27
Klin, Sov. Un., 60,000 C11 27
Klinaklini, riv., B.C., Can D5 68
Kline, La Plata, Colo., 35 D2 83
Kline, Barnwell, S.C., 213 E5 115
Klingenthal, Ger., 15,500 C7 17
Klintsy, Sov. Un., 42,033 E9 27
Klippan, Swe., 8,300 B7 24
Klitmøller, Den., 471 A2 24
Ključ, Yugo., 2,322 C3 22
Klobuck, Pol., 6,533 C5 26
Kloch, lake, B.C., Can B5 68
Klock, Ont., Can A6 72
Klodnica, riv., Pol g9 26
Klodzko, Pol., 20,200 C4 26
Klondike, DeKalb, Ga B5 87
Klondike, Lake, Ill., 400 A5 90
Klondike, Delta, Tex., 20 C5 118
Klondike, Milwaukee, Wis F2 124
Klondike, reg., Yukon, Can D4 66
Klostermansfeld, Ger., 5,957 B6 17
Klosterneuburg, Aus., 22,787 D8 16
Klosters, Switz., 3,181 C8 19
Kloten, Nelson, N. Dak., 120 B7 110
Kloten, Switz., 8,446 B6 19
Klötze, Ger., 6,255 F5 24
Klotzsche, Ger., 9,848 B8 17
Klotzville, Assumption, La., 300 B5 95
Kluane, lake, Yukon, Can D5 66
Kluang, Mala., 31,181 K5 38
Kluczbork, Pol., 11,800 C5 26
Klucze, Pol g11 26
Klukwan, Alsk., 112 k22 79
Klütz, Ger., 3,179 E5 24
Klyazma, riv., Sov. Un B2 29
Klyuchevskaya, vol., Sov. Un D18 28
Knap, pt., Scot E3 13
Knapp, Dunn, Wis., 374 D1 124
Knaresborough, Eng., 9,311 F7 13
Knee, lake, Man., Can B4 71
Knee, lake, Sask., Can B2 70
Knesebeck, Ger., 2,500 F4 24
Knezha, Bul., 13,133 D7 22
Knickerbocker, Tom Green, Tex., 150 D2 118
Knierim, Calhoun, Iowa, 153 B3 92
Knife, riv., N. Dak B3 110
Knife River, Lake, Minn., 350 D7 99
Knifley, Adair, Ky., 250 C4 94
Knight, Uinta, Wyo D2 125
Knight, inlet, B.C., Can D5 68
Knightdale, Wake, N.C., 622 B5 109
Knighton, Wales, 1,817 B4 12
Knights Landing, Yolo, Calif., 725 C3 82
Knightstown, Henry, Ind., 2,496 E6 91
Knight's Town, Ire., 337 F1 11
Knightsville, Clay, Ind., 722 E3 91
Knightsville, res., Mass B2 97
Knik, Alsk., 15 C10, g17 79
Knin, Yugo., 5,112 C3 22
Knippa, Uvalde, Tex., 350 E3 118
Knislinge, Swe., 2,145 B8 24
Knittelfeld, Aus., 14,259 E7 16
Knob, creek, Ky A4 94
Knobel, Clay, Ark., 339 A5 81
Knob Lick, Metcalfe, Ky., 100 C4 94
Knob Lick, St. Francois, Mo., 150 D7 101
Knobly, mtn., W. Va B5 123
Knob Noster, Johnson, Mo., 2,292 C4 101
Knobs, mtn., Pa D5 114
Knobsville, Fulton, Pa., 150 F6 114
Knock, Ire E2 11
Knockadoon, head, Ire F4 11
Knockanefune, mtn., Ire E2 11
Knocklong, Ire E3 11
Knockmealdown, mts., Ire D3 10
Knokke, Bel., 13,649 C3 15
Knollwood, Middlesex, Conn., 700 *D7 84
Knollwood, Greene, Ohio, 2,500 *C3 111
Knollwood Park, Jackson, Mich., 2,100 *F6 98
Knops, pond, Mass f9 97
Knott, Howard, Tex., 100 C2 118
Knott, co., Ky., 17,362 C6 94
Knotts Island, Currituck, N.C., 140 A8 109
Knottsville, Daviess, Ky., 350 C3 94
Knowles, Beaver, Okla., 62 A1, D4 112
Knowlton, Que., Can., 1,396 D5 73
Knowlton, Marathon, Wis., 75 D4 124
Knox, Knox, Ill C3 90
Knox, Starke, Ind., 3,458 B4 91
Knox, Benson, N. Dak., 122 A6 110
Knox, Clarion, Pa., 1,247 D2 114
Knox, co., Ill., 61,280 B3 90
Knox, co., Ind., 41,561 G3 91
Knox, co., Ky., 25,258 D6 94
Knox, co., Maine, 28,575 D4 96
Knox, co., Mo., 6,558 A5 101
Knox, co., Nebr., 13,300 B8 103
Knox, co., Ohio, 38,808 B5 111
Knox, co., Tenn., 250,523 C10 117
Knox, co., Tex., 7,857 C3 118
Knox, cape, B.C., Can B1 68
Knox, coast, Ant C23 5
Knox, creek, Ky., Va., W. Va D2 123
Knox City, Knox, Mo., 330 A5 101
Knox City, Knox, Tex., 1,805 C3 118
Knox Dale, Jefferson, Pa., 350 D3 114
Knoxville, Greene, Ala., 100 C2 78
Knoxville, Johnson, Ark., 300 B2 81
Knoxville, Crawford, Ga., 200 D3 87
Knoxville, Knox, Ill., 2,560 C3 90
Knoxville, Marion, Iowa, 7,817 C4 92
Knoxville, Frederick, Md., 400 B2 85
Knoxville, Franklin, Miss., 150 D2 100
Knoxville, Ray, Mo., 103 B3 101
Knoxville, Tioga, Pa., 694 C7 114
Knoxville, Knox, Tenn., 111,827 (★286,000) D10, E11 117
Knysna, S. Afr., 11,085 D3 49
Knyszyn, Pol., 2,780 B7 26
Kobdo, riv., Mong B3 34
Kobe, Jap., 1,113,977 I7, o14 37
Kobelyaki, Sov. Un., 10,000 G10 27
København (Copenhagen), co., Den., 1,269,366 C6 24
Koblenz, Ger., 101,400 (★170,000) C2 17
Kobona, Sov. Un r32 25
Kobrin, Sov. Un., 25,000 E5 27
Kobroor, isl., Indon G8 35
Kobuk, Alsk., 54 B8 79
Kobuk, riv., Alsk B8 79
Kobuleti, Sov. Un., 10,000 B13 31
Koca (Xanthus), riv., Tur D7 23
Kocaba, riv., Czech o17 26
Kočani, Yugo., 10,986 E6 22
Kočevje, Yugo., 5,760 C2 22
Koch, peak, Mont E5 102
Kochel, Ger., 3,900 B7 18
Kochel, lake, Ger B7 18
Kocher, riv., Ger D4 17
Kochi, Jap., 196,288 J6 37
Kochi, pref., Jap., 854,595 *J6 37
Kochiu, China, 159,700 G5 34
Kock, Pol., 2,381 C7 26
Kodak, Perry, Ky., 500 C6 94
Kodiak, Alsk., 2,628 D9 79
Kodiak, isl., Alsk D9 79
Kodok, Sud D3 47
Koepang, Indon., 7,171 H6 35
Koes, S.W. Afr., 422 C2 49
Koetaradja, Indon., 10,724 k11 35
Koetatjane, Indon K2 38
Koettlitz, glacier, Ant f39 5
Kofa, mts., Ariz D2 80
Koffiefontein, S. Afr., 2,985 C4 49
Koforidua, Ghana, 34,900 E4 45
Kofu, Jap., 160,963 I9, n17 37
Koga, Jap., 42,474 m18 37
Kogaluk, riv., Newf., Can g9 75
Køge, Den., 12,294 C6 24
Køge, bay, Den C6 24
Kogilnik, riv., Sov. Un B9 22
Kohala, Hawaii, Haw., 950 C6 88
Kohat, Pak., 30,016 (★49,854) B5 39
Kohatk, Pinal, Ariz., 50 E3 80
Kohima, India, 7,246 C9 39
Kohler, Sheboygan, Wis., 1,524 B6, E6 124
Kohls Ranch, Gila, Ariz C4 80
Kohlu, Pak C4 39
Kohtla-Jarve, Sov. Un., 60,000 B6 27
Koinge, Swe A6 24
Koje, isl., Kor I4 37
Kokadjo, Piscataquis, Maine, 10 C3 96
Kokadjo, lake, Maine C3 96
Kokai, see Kanggye, Kor.
Kokand, Sov. Un., 117,000 E8 29
Kokanee Glacier, prov. park, B.C., Can E9 68
Kokchetav, Sov. Un., 67,000 C7 29
Kokkola, Fin., 16,200 F10 25
Koko, Nig., 7,624 D5 45
Koko, head, Haw B4 88
Kokomo (Recen), Summit, Colo., 14 B4 83
Kokomo, Maui, Haw., 250 C5 88
Kokomo, Howard, Ind., 47,197 D5 91
Kokomo, Marion, Miss., 250 D3 100
Koko-Nor (Tsinghai), lake, China D4 34
Kokopo, Bis. Arch., 220 h13 50
Kokos, is., Indon K1 38
Kokosing, riv., Ohio B5 111
Kokrines, Alsk., 20 C9 79
Koksilah, B.C., Can., 382 g12 68
Koksoak, riv., Que., Can E19 67
Kokstad, S. Afr., 7,984 D4 49
Kola, Sov. Un C15 25
Kola, pen., Sov. Un D17 25
Kolan, China E4 36
Kolar Gold Fields, India, 146,811 F6 39
Kolarovo, Bul., 31,169 D8 22
Kolarovo, Czech., 10,800 E4 26
Kolbäck, Swe., 1,871 t34 25
Kolbano, Indon H6 35
Kolbio, Som F5 47
Kolbuszowa, Pol., 2,124 C6 26
Kolchugino, Sov., Un., 40,000 C12 27
Kolczewo, Pol., 2,000 E8 24
Kolda, Sen., 4,300 D2 45
Koldewey, isl., Grnld B16 4
Kolding, Den., 35,101 C3 24
Kole, Con. L B3 48
Kolec, Czech., 974 n17 26
Koleno, Sov. Un., 10,000 F13 27
Kolezhma, Sov. Un., 500 E16 25
Kolgueyv, isl., Sov. Un B18 9
Kolhapur, India, 187,442 (★193,186) E5 39, I5 40
Kolliganek, Alsk., 100 D8 79
Kolimbine, riv., Maur C2 45
Kolin, Czech., 23,200 C3 26
Kolin, Rapides, La., 50 C3 95
Kolin, Judith Basin, Mont., 10 C7 102
Kölleda, Ger., 7,672 B6 17
Köln (Cologne), Ger., 835,900 (★1,550,000) C1 17
Kolno, Pol., 3,295 B6 26
Kolo, Pol., 10,600 B5 26
Koloa, Kauai, Haw., 1,426 B2 88
Kolob, canyon, Utah F2 119
Kolobrzeg, Pol., 2,816 A3 26
Kolokani, Mali D3 45
Kolola Springs, Lowndes, Miss., 40 B5 100
Kolomna, Sov. Un., 125,000 B1 29
Kolomyya, Sov. Un., 45,000 G5 27
Kolonodale, Indon F6 35
Kolp, riv., Sov. Un B11 27
Kolpashevo, Sov Un., 32,100 B10 29
Kolpino, Sov. Un., 50,000 s31 25
Kolva, riv., Sov. Un A5 29
Kolwa, Pak C3 39
Kolwezi, Con. L., 48,000 D4 48
Kolyberovo, Sov. Un., 10,000 n18 27
Kolyma, riv., Sov. Un C18 28
Komádi, Hung., 7,362 B5 22
Komadugu, riv., Nig D6 45
Komandorski Village, Alameda, Calif., 1,000 *B6 82
Komandorskiye, is., Sov. Un D19 28
Komarno, Man., Can., 101 D3 71
Komarno, Czech., 24,000 E5 26
Komarno, Sov. Un., 5,000 D7 26
Komarno, marsh, Sov. Un B10 29
Komarom, Hung., 9,862 B4 22
Komárom, co., Hung., 270,208 *B4 22
Komatipoort, S. Afr., 2,031 C5 49
Komatsu, Jap., 54,900 (89,085▲) H8 37
Komatsushima, Jap., 25,100 I7 37
Komelik, Pima, Ariz., 65 F4 80
Komlo, Hung., 24,850 B4 22
Kommunarsk, Sov. Un., 110,000 G12, q21 27
Kominato, Jap., 9,700 n19 37
Komodo, isl., Indon G5 35
Komono, Con. B F2 46
Komoran, isl., W. Irian G9 35
Komotiní (Komotine), Grc., 32,906 B5 23
Kompong Cham, Camb., 25,000 F6 38
Kompong Chhnang, Camb., 25,000 F6 38
Kompong Kleang, Camb., 10,000 F6 38
Kompong Som, bay, Camb G5 38
Kompong Speu, Camb., 5,000 G6 38
Kompong Thom, Camb., 25,000 F6 38
Komrat, Sov. Un., 10,000 H7 27
Komsomolets, isl., Sov. Un A4 4
Komsomolsk [-na Amure], Sov. Un., 192,000 D16 28
Komvo, Pima, Ariz., 50 F3 80
Konawa, Seminole, Okla., 1,555 C5 111
Kondoa, Tan., 2,816 B6 48
Kondopoga, Sov. Un., 5,000 F16 25
Kong, reg., I.C E4 45
Kong, isl., Camb G5 38
Kongeå, riv., Den C2 24
Kongju, Kor., 23,400 H3 37
Kongolo, Con. L., 2,842 C4 48
Kongsberg, McHenry, N. Dak., 20 B5 110
Kongsberg, Nor., 9,700 H3, p27 25
Kongsmark, Den C2 24
Kongsvinger, Nor., 2,300 G5 25
Königsbrück, Ger., 5,100 B8 17
Königshofen, Ger., 3,200 C5 17
Königslutter, Ger., 8,600 A5 17
Königstein, Ger., 5,139 C9 17
Königs Wusterhausen, Ger., 6,614 A8 17
Konin, Pol., 13,500 B5 26
Konispol, Alb., 4,169 C3 23
Konitsa, Grc., 2,313 B3 23
Köniz, Switz., 27,243 C3 19
Konjic, Yugo., 5,891 D3 22
Könnern, Ger., 6,053 B6 17
Konolfingen, Switz., 3,964 C4 19
Konomoc, lake, Conn D8 84
Konosha, Sov. Un., 10,000 A13 27
Konotop, Sov. Un., 56,000 F9 27
Konskie, Pol., 7,386 C6 26
Konstantinovka, Sov. Un., 94,000 q20 27
Konstanz, Ger., 55,400 E4 16
Konta, India, 5,000 I8 40
Kontagora, Nig., 5,665 D6 45
Kontcha, Cam D2 46
Kontich, Bel., 10,923 C4 15
Kontiomäki, Fin., 850 E13 25
Kontum, Viet., 10,000 E8 38
Konya, Tur., 119,841 D9 31
Konyang, Kor., 2,000 I3 37
Konzhakovskiy Kamen, mtn., Sov. Un B5 29
Koochiching, co., Minn., 18,190 B4 99
Koolau, range, Haw g10 88
Koontz Lake, Starke, Ind., 900 B5 91
Koosharem Sevier, Utah, 148 E4 119
Kooskia, Idaho, Idaho, 801 C3 89
Kootenai, Bonner, Idaho, 180 A2 89
Kootenai, co., Idaho, 29,556 B2 89
Kootenai, riv., Mont B1 102
Kootenay, lake, B.C., Can E9 68
Kootenay, nat. park, B.C., Can D9 68
Kootenay, riv., B.C., Can D10 68
Kópasker, Ice., 83 m24 25
Kopervik, Nor., 1,800 H1 25
Kopet, mts., Sov. Un B7 41
Kopeysk, Sov. Un., 168,000 B6 29
Köping, Swe., 17,700 H6, t33 25
Köppany, riv., Hung B4 22
Kopparberg, co., Swe., 286,600 *G6 25
Koppel, Beaver, Pa., 1,389 E1 114
Koprivnica, Yugo., 1,329 B3 22
Kopychintsy, Sov. Un., 10,000 G5 27
K'orāhē, Eth D6 47
Koram, Eth C4 47
Korarou, lake, Mali C4 45
Korba, Tun F12 30
Korbach, Ger., 15,100 B3 17
Korbu, mtn., Mala J4 38
Korçë, Alb., 39,386 B3 23
Korçë, pref., Alb., 175,000 *B3 23
Korcula, isl., Yugo D3 22
Kordofan, reg., Sud., 1,761,968 C2 47
Korea, reg., Asia F15 33, 37
Korea, North, country, Asia, 11,500,000 F4 37
Korea, South, country, Asia, 28,000,000 H3 37
Korea, bay, China D9 34
Korea, strait, Kor I4 37
Korets, Sov. Un., 10,000 F6 27
Korhogo, I.C., 14,000 E3 45
Kori, creek, Pak D4 39, F2 40
Korinthia (Corinthia), prov., Grc., 112,505 *D4 23
Korinthos (Corinth), Grc., 15,892 D4, h9 23
Koriyama, Jap., 102,636 H10 37
Korkino, Sov. Un., 87,000 D21 9
Kormatiki, cape, Cyp E9 31
Kormend, Hung., 7,581 B3 22
Kornat, isl., Yugo D2 22
Korner, Glacier, Mont B4 102
Korneuburg, Aus., 8,276 D8 16
Kornwestheim, Ger., 26,300 E4 17
Koro, isl., Fiji Is 52
Koromo, Jap., 46,822 n16 37
Koronis, lake, Minn E4 99
Koropi, Grc., 7,128 h11 23
Koror, isl., Palau Is 52
Korosten, Sov. Un., 33,800 F7 27
Korotoyak, Sov. Un., 11,500 F12 27
Korovin, vol., Alsk E5 79
Korsakov (Otomari), Sov. Un., 43,800 C11 37
Korsør, Den., 14,276 C5 24
Kõrti, Sud B3 47
Kortrijk, Bel., 43,606 (★90,000) D3 15
Korumburra, Austl., 3,237 I5 51
Korville, Harris, Texas, 75 F4 118
Koryak, mts., Sov. Un C19 28
Kos, Grc., 8,844 D6 23
Kos, isl., Grc D6 23
Koschagyl, Sov. Un D4 29
Koscian, Pol., 12,900 B4 26
Koscierzyna, Pol., 7,820 A4 26
Kosciusko, Attala, Miss., 6,800 B4 100
Kosciusko, co., Ind., 40,373 B6 91
Kosciusko, mtn., Austl H7 51
Koshan, China, 25,000 B10 34
Koshiki, isl., Jap K4 37
Koshkonong, Oregon, Mo., 478 E6 101
Koshkonong, lake, Wis F5 124
Kosi, riv., India C8 39
Košice, Czech., 88,300 D6 26
Koskaecodde, lake, Newf., Can D4 75
Koslan, Sov. Un., 1,000 C18 9
Kosong, Kor., 14,842 G4 37
Kosove (Kosovo), pref., Alb., 53,000 *A3 23
Kosovska Mitrovica, Yugo., 26,620 D5 22
Kospash, Sov. Un., 30,000 D20 9
Kosse, Limestone, Tex., 354 D4 118
Kösslarn, Ger., 900 A9 18
Kossol, reef, Palau Is 52
Kossuth, Alcorn, Miss., 178 A5 100
Kossuth, co., Iowa, 25,314 A3 92
Kostelec, Czech., 2,704 n18 26
Kostelec nad Cernymi Lesy, Czech., 3,341 o18 26
Kosti, Sud., 22,688 C3 47
Kostroma, Sov. Un., 193,000 B2 29
Kostrzyn, Pol., 23,000 B3 26
Koszalin, Pol., 48,000 A4 26
Koszeg, Hung., 9,818 B3 22
Kotabaru, Indon., 38,075 F5 35
Kota Bharu, Mala., 38,103 I5 38
Kotah, India, 120,345 E5 40
Kota Kota, Malawi D5 48
Kotatengah, Indon L4 38
Kotel, Bul., 3,671 D8 22
Kotelnich, Sov. Un., 27,000 B3 29
Kotelnikovskiy, Sov. Un D2 29
Kotelny, isl., Sov. Un B16 28
Köthen, Ger., 37,600 B7 17
Kotido, Ug A5 48
Kotka, Fin., 30,300 G12 25
Kotlas, Sov. Un., 56,000 C18 9
Kotlik, Alsk., 57 C7 79
Kotonkoro, Nig D6 45
Kotor, Yugo., 4,833 D4 22
Kotor, bay, Yugo D4 22
Kotor Varos, Yugo., 2,898 C3 22
Kotovsk, Sov. Un., 30,000 E13 27
Kotovsk, Sov. Un., 10,000 H7 27
Kotovskoye, Sov. Un B9 22
Kotri, Pak., 15,154 E2 40
Kottas, mts., Ant B11 5
Kotung, China, 5,000 B3 37
Kotzebue, Alsk., 1,290 B7 79
Kotzebue, sound, Alsk B7 79
Kötzting, Ger., 3,200 D7 17
Kouango, Cen. Afr. Rep D4 46
Kouba, Alg., 21,183 *B5 44
Kouchibouguacis, riv., N.B., Can C4 74
Koudougou, Upper Volta, 8,000 D4 45
Koula-Moutou, Gabon F2 46
Koulikoro, Mali, 4,350 D3 45
Kounradskiy, Sov. Un D9 28
Kountze, Hardin, Tex., 1,768 D5 118
Koupangtzu, China D9 36
Kourémalé, Mali D3 45
Kouri, isl., Okinawa 52
Kourou, Fr. Gu., 582 A4 59
Kouroussa, Guinea, 6,500 D3 45
Koutiala, Mali, 4,100 D3 45
Kouts, Porter, Ind., 1,007 B3 91
Kouvola, Fin., 18,200 G12 25
Ko Vayo, Pima, Ariz., 50 E4 80
Kovel, Sov. Un., 42,600 F5 27
Kovik, Que., Can f11 73
Kovrov, Sov. Un., 105,000 B2 29
Kowa, Jap., 10,300 o15 37
Kowloon, Hong Kong, 726,976 G7 34
Kowon, Kor., 5,000 G3 37
Koyuk, Alsk., 20 C7 79
Koyukuk, Alsk., 128 C8 79
Koyukuk, riv., Alsk B9 79
Kozan, Tur., 15,200 D10 31
Kozani, Grc., 21,537 B3 23
Kozani, prov., Grc., 190,835 *B3 23
Kozelsk, Sov. Un., 12,600 D10 27
Kozhikode, India, 192,521 (★248,548) F6 39
Kozhva, Sov. Un., 800 B20 9
Kozienice, Pol., 4,099 C6 26
Kozle, Pol., 8,277 C5 26
Kozloduy, Bul., 7,422 D6 22
Kozu, isl., Jap I9 37
Kozuchow, Pol., 8,782 C3 26
Kpandu, Ghana, 4,040 E5 45
Kra, isth., Thai G3 38
Kraemer, La Fourche, La., 450 C6 95
Kragerö, Nor., 4,600 H3 25
Kragujevac, Yugo., 52,491 D5 22
Krakow, Ger., 3,553 E6 24
Kraków (Cracow), Pol., 495,600 C5 26
Krakower, lake, Ger E6 24
Kraljevo, Yugo., 20,409 D5 22
Kralupy [nad Vltavou], Czech., 11,100 n17 26
Kraluv, Dvur, Czech., 3,390 o17 26
Kramatorsk, Sov. Un., 126,000 G11, q20 27
Kramer, Warren, Ind., 150 D3 91
Kramer, Bottineau, N. Dak., 175 A5 110
Kramer Junction, San Bernardino, Calif., 70 E5 82
Kranidhion, Grc., 4,381 D4 23
Kranj, Yugo., 21,354 B2 22
Kranzburg, Codington, S. Dak., 156 C9 116
Kraslice, Czech., 6,294 C2 26
Krasnaya Sloboda, Sov. Un D2 29
Krasnik, Lubelski, Pol., 9,158 C7 26
Krasnoarmeysk, Sov. Un., 54,000 F15 27
Krasnoarmeysk, Sov. Un., 2,000 G15 27
Krasnodar, Sov. Un., 368,000 I12 27
Krasnodon, Sov. Un., 60,000 q22 27
Krasnogorsk, Sov. Un., 25,000 B11 37
Krasnograd, Sov. Un., 10,000 G10 27
Krasnokamsk, Sov. Un., 56,000 B5 29
Krasnoselkup, Sov. Un B25 9
Krasnoselye, Sov. Un., 10,000 G9 27
Krasnoslobodsk, Sov. Un., 5,000 D14 27
Krasnoturinsk, Sov. Un., 64,000 B5 29
Krasnoufimsk, Sov. Un., 31,300 B5 29
Krasnouralsk, Sov. Un., 36,400 D21 9
Krasnovishersk, Sov. Un., 28,300 A5 29
Krasnovodsk, Sov. Un., 39,272 E4 29
Krasnoyarsk, Sov. Un., 483,000 D27 9, D12 28
Krasnoye Selo, Sov. Un s31 25
Krasnoznamenskiy, Sov. Un C7 29
Krasnystaw, Pol., 10,300 C7 26
Krasnyy Kholm, Sov. Un., 11,700 B11 27
Krasnyy Kut, Sov. Un C3 29
Krasnyy Liman, Sov. Un., 10,000 q20 27
Krasnyy Luch, Sov. Un., 98,000 q21 27
Krasnyy Sulin, Sov. Un., 66,600 H13 27
Krasnyy Yar, Sov. Un., 10,000 F15 27
Kratie, Camb., 25,000 F7 38
Kratovo, Yugo., 2,401 D6 22
Kraul, mts., Ant B11 5
Krause, pt., Vir. Is k17 65
Krebs, Pittsburg, Okla., 1,342 C6 112
Krefeld, Ger., 217,200 (★370,000) B1 17
Kremenchug, Sov. Un., 100,000 G9 27
Kremenchug, res., Sov. Un G9 27
Kremenets, Sov. Un., 10,000 F5 27
Kremennaya, Sov. Un., 5,000 p21 27
Kremlin, Hill, Mont., 200 B6 102
Kremlin, Garfield, Okla., 128 A4 112
Kremmling, Grand, Colo., 576 A4 83
Krems, Aus., 21,046 D7 16
Kreole, Jackson, Miss., 1,870 E3, E5 100
Kresgeville, Monroe, Pa., 300 E10 114
Kress, Swisher, Tex., 438 B2 118
Kreuzlingen, Switz., 12,597 A7 19
Kribi, Cam., 3,055 E1 46
Krichev, Sov. Un., 5,000 E8 27
Kriens, Switz., 14,029 B5 19
Krilon, cape, Sov. Un D11 37
Krilon, pen., Sov. Un C11 37
Krishnagar, India, 70,440 F12 40
Krishnagiri, India, 19,774 F6 39
Kristiansand, Nor., 27,900 (★40,000) H2 25
Kristianstad, Swe., 26,100 I6 25
Kristianstad, co., Swe., 256,600 B7 24
Kristiansund, Nor., 17,200 F2 25
Kristinestad, Fin., 2,700 F9 25
Kriva Palanka, Yugo., 2,848 D6 22
Krivoy Rog, Sov. Un., 448,000 H9 27
Križevci, Yugo., 6,498 B3 22
Krk, isl., Yugo C2 22
Krka, riv., Yugo D2 22
Krnov, Czech., 21,600 C4 26
Krogsered, Swe A6 24
Krokeai, Grc., 3,012 D4 23
Krokstadelva, Nor., 2,490 p28 25
Krolevets, Sov. Un., 10,000 F9 27
Kromeriz, Czech., 20,600 D4 26
Kromy, Sov. Un., 10,000 E10 27
Kronach, Ger., 10,200 C6 17
Kronau, Sask., Can., 53 G3 70
Kronoberg, co., Swe., 159,100 B8 24
Kronshtadt, Sov. Un., 40,000 B7 27
Kroonstad, S. Afr., 42,438 C4 49
Kröpelin, Ger., 4,839 D5 24
Kropotkin, Sov. Un., 59,000 I13 27
Krosno, Pol., 20,000 D6 26
Krosno Odrzanskie, Pol., 5,841 B3 26
Krotoszyn, Pol., 16,300 C4 26
Krotz Springs, St. Landry, La., 1,057 D4 95
Krsko, Yugo., 629 C2 22
Kruger, nat. park, S. Afr B5 49
Krugersdorp, S. Afr., 89,947 C4 49
Krujë, Alb., 5,107 B2 23
Krumbach, Ger., 7,900 A6 18
Krumovgrad, Bul., 1,249 E7 22
Krumroy, Summit, Ohio, 1,400 *A6 111
Krusenstern Rock, reef, Haw m12 88
Kruševac, Yugo., 22,140 D5 22
Kruševo, Yugo., 4,099 E6 22
Kruszwica, Pol., 4,822 B5 26
Krydor, Sask., Can., 184 E2 70
Krym (Crimea), pen., Sov. Un I10 27
Krymskaya, Sov. Un., 10,000 I11 27
Krynica, Pol., 2,649 D6 26
Krynki, Pol., 5,290 B7 26
Ksar el Kebir, Mor., 34,035 B3 44
Ksar es Souk, Mor., 6,554 C4 44
Ktipas, mtn., Grc g10 23
Kuala Dungun, Mala., 12,515 J5 38
Kuala Krau, Mala., 1,271 K5 38
Kualakurun, Indon F4 35
Kuala Lipis, Mala., 8,753 J5 38
Kuala Lumpur, Mala., 316,230 (★400,000) K4 38
Kualapuu, Maui, Haw., 607 B4 88
Kuala Trengganu, Mala., 29,446 J5 38
Kuan, China F6 36
Kuandang, Indon E6 35
Kuangan, China, 18,000 I2 36
Kuangchang, China, 10,000 K7 36
Kuanghua, China, 29,000 H4 36
Kuangnan, China G6 34
Kuangte, China I8 36
Kuangyuan, China, 31,000 H1 36
Kuantan, Mala., 23,034 K5 38
Kuanti, China E4 37
Kuantien, China, 5,000 F2 37
Kuanyün, China, 65,000 G8 36
Kuba, Sov. Un E3 29
Kuban, riv., Sov. Un F16 9
Kuchen, China H7 36
Kucheng, China, 20,000 H4 36
Kuching, Mala., 50,579 E4 35
Kuchino, isl., Jap L4 37
Kuchino Erabu, isl., Jap K5 37
Kudat, Mala., 3,660 D5 35
Kudymkar, Sov. Un., 20,000 B4 29
Kueichi, China, 6,000 J7 36
Kueichih, China I7 36
Kueisui, see Huhehot, China
Kueite, China D5 34
Kuerhlo (Korla), China, 10,000 C2 34
Kufstein, Aus., 11,215 E6 16
Kuge, Jap n14 37
Kuh, cape, Iran I8 41
Kuh-e-Bozqūsh, mts., Iran C3 41
Kuh-e-Sahand, mtn., Iran C3 41
Kuhi-Alwand, mtn., Iran D4 41
Kuh-i-Birg, mtn., Iran H10 41
Kuh-i-Birak, mtn., Iran D10 41
Kuh-i-Furgun, mtn., Iran H8 41
Kuh-i-Garrah, mts., Iran F5 41
Kuh-i-Gireh, mtn., Iran H8 41
Kuh-i-Gugird, mts., Iran D6 41
Kuh-i-Hormuz, mtn., Iran H7 41
Kuh-i-Huzar, mtn., Iran G8 41
Kuh-i-Istin, mtn., Iran F10 41
Kuh-i-Kharman, mtn., Iran G6 41

Kuh-i-Kurkhud, mtn., Iran.....C8 41
Kuh-i-Kuru, mtn., Iran.....D5 41
Kuh-i-Mazar, mtn., Afg.....E13 41
Kuh-i-Murghum, mtn., Iran....E8 41
Kuh-i-Naibandan, mtn., Iran....E8 41
Kuh-i-Nila, mtn., Iran.....E5 41
Kuh-i-Rahmand, mtn., Iran.....D4 41
Kuh-i-Ran, mtn., Iran.....H9 41
Kuh-i-Saguch, mtn., Iran.....F8 41
Kuh-i-Surkh, mts., Iran.....D9 41
Kuh-i-Tafrish, mtn., Iran.....D5 41
Kūhpāyeh, Iran.....E6 41
Kuhsan, Afg., 10,000.....D10 41
Kuji, Jap., 14,750.....F10 37
Kuju-San, peak, Jap.....J5 37
Kukaiau, Hawaii, Haw., 80..C6 88
Kukawa, Nig.....D7 45
Kukës, Alb., 3,896.....A3 23
Kuki, Jap., 11,300.....m18 37
Kukong, China, 81,700.....G7 34
Kuku, pt., Wake Isl..... 52
Kukuihaele, Hawaii, Haw., 375.....C6 88
Kula, Bul., 5,566.....D6 22
Kula, Tur., 9,180.....C7 23
Kula, Yugo., 13,612.....C4 22
Ku Lao Cham, isl., Viet.....E8 38
Ku Lao Re, isl., Viet.....E8 38
Kulebaki, Sov. Un., 34,000.D14 27
Kulhakangri, peak, China.....C13 40
Kuling, China, 5,000.....J7 36
Kulltorp, Swe., 231.....A7 24
Kulm, La Moure, N. Dak., 664.....C7 110
Kulmbach, Ger., 23,500.....C6 17
Kulpmont, Northumberland, Pa., 4,288.....E9 114
Kulu, isl., Alsk.....m22 79
Kulun, China.....C9 36
Kulunda, Sov. Un., 800.....C9 29
Kulunda, lake, Sov. Un.....C9 29
Kulyab, Sov. Un., 15,000..H22 9
Kuma, riv., Sov. Un.....F18 9
Kumagaya, Jap., 60,100 (98,168▲).....m18 37
Kumai, Indon.....F4 35
Kumamoto, Jap., 373,922.....J5 37
Kumamoto, pref., Jap., 1,856,192.....*J5 37
Kumanovo, Yugo., 30,734...D5 22
Kumasi, Ghana, 180,600.....E4 45
Kumba, Cam., 11,672.....*F6 45
Kumbakonam, India, 92,581 (*96,746).....F6 39
Kumhwa, Kor., 1,400.....G3 37
Kumi, Ug.....A5 48
Kumihama, Jap., 4,800.....n14 37
Kumkale, Tur., 404.....C6 23
Kumla, Swe., 10,000....H6, t33 25
Kummerower, lake, Ger.....E6 24
Kumsong, Kor., 5,000.....G3 37
Kumukahi, cape, Haw.....D7 88
Kuna, Ada, Idaho, 516.....F2 89
Kunar, Afg., 5,000.....D15 41
Kunar, riv., Pak., Afg.....A5 39, D15 41
Kunckle, Luzerne, Pa., 250..A8 114
Kundar, riv., Pak.....B2 40
Kungchuling, China, 25,000.E2 36
Kunghit, isl., B.C., Can.....C2 68
Kungrad, Sov. Un.....E5 29
Kungsbacka, Swe., 5,000.....A6 24
Kungsörs, Swe., 4,500.....t34 25
Kungu, Con. L.....A2 48
Kungur, Sov. Un., 67,000..D20 9
Kunia, Honolulu, Haw., 570.g9 88
Kunkletown, Monroe, Pa., 400.....B2 106
Kunlun, mts., China.....D3 34
Kunming (Yunnanfu), China, 880,000.....F5 34, C11 39
Kunsan, Kor., 92,200.....I3 37
Kunszentmarton, Hung., 8,783.....B5 22
Kuntu, China.....B9 36
Künzelsau, Ger., 7,800.....D4 17
Kuolayarvi, Sov. Un., 10,000.....D13 25
Kuop (Royalists), is., Truk..... 52
Kuopio, Fin., 47,700.....F12 25
Kuopio, dept., Fin., 453,881.....*F12 25
Kuoyang, China.....H7 36
Kupa, riv., Yugo.....C2 22
Kupang, Indon., 7,171.....H6 35
Kupino, Sov. Un., 20,600...C9 29
Kupk, Pima, Ariz., 25.....F3 80
Kupyansk, Sov. Un., 32,400.G11 27
Kupreanof, isl., Alsk.....m23 79
Kur, riv., Sov. Un.....B7 37
Kura, riv., Sov. Un.....G17 9
Kurakhovka, Sov. Un., 5,000.....q20 27
Kurashiki, Jap., 90,000 (125,097▲).....I6 37
Kuray, Sov. Un.....E26 9
Kurdikos-Naumiestis, Sov. Un.....A7 26
Kurdzhali, Bul., 10,480.....E7 22
Kure, Jap., 210,032.....I6 37
Kure, isl., Haw.....k12 88
Kuressaare, Sov. Un., 10,000.B4 27
Kureyka, riv., Sov. Un.....C12 28
Kurgaldzhina, Sov. Un.....C8 29
Kurgan, Sov. Un., 182,000...B7 29
Kurgannaya, Sov. Un., 10,000.....G17 9
Kurgan-Tyube, Sov. Un., 20,000.....H22 9
Kuri, India, 10,000.....D3 40
Kurigram, Pak., 8,063.....E12 40
Kuril, is., Sov. Un.....E18 28
Kuril, strait, Sov. Un.....D18 28
Kurinskaya, cape, Sov. Un....H18 9
Kurkhera, India.....G8 40
Kurmuk, Sud., 1,647.....C3 47
Kurnool, India, 100,815.....E6 38
Kuro, isl., Jap.....K4 37
Kuroki, Sask., Can., 158.....F4 70
Kurovskoye, Sov. Un., 27,600.....n18 27
Kurow, N.Z., 512.....P13 51
Kursk, Sov. Un., 233,000....F11 27
Kuršumlija, Yugo., 3,392....D5 22
Kurtalan, Tur., 1,591.....D13 23
Kurthwood, Vernon, La., 70 C2 95
Kurtistown, Hawaii, Haw., 1,025.....D6 88
Kurtz, Jackson, Ind., 200...G5 91
Kuruman, S. Afr., 6,386.....C3 49
Kurume, Jap., 155,041.....J5 37
Kurunegala, Cey., 13,510.....G7 39
Kurusku, Eg., U.A.R., 483...E6 43
Kusadasi, Tur., 5,442.....D6 23
Kusakaki, isl., Jap.....K4 37
Kusatsu, Jap., 17,800.....n14 37
Kusel, Ger., 5,500.....D2 17
Kushchevskaya, Sov. Un., 10,000.....H12 27
Kushevat, Sov. Un., 1,000..B22 9
Kushiro, Jap., 150,624.....E12 37
Kushka, Sov. Un.....H21 9
Kushmurun, Sov. Un.....C6 29
Kushmurun, lake, Sov. Un.....C6 29
Kuskokwim, bay, Alsk.....D7 79
Kuskokwim, mts., Alsk.....C8 79
Kuskokwim, riv., Alsk.....C8 79
Küsnacht, Switz., 11,984.....B6 19
Küssnacht, Switz., 6,287.....B5 19
Kustanay, Sov. Un., 105,000.C6 29
Küsten, canal, Ger.....A7 15
Küstrin, see Kostrzyn, Pol.
Kut, isl., Thai.....G5 38
Kutahya (Kutaiah), Tur., 39,900.....C7 23
Kutaisi, Sov. Un., 141,000.....G17 9, A14 31
Kutaka, isl., Okinawa..... 52
Kut al Hai, Iraq, 10,199.....E3 46
Kut al Imara, Iraq, 16,237..E2 46
Kutaradja, Indon., 34,207...k11 35
Kutatjane, Indon.....K2 38
Kutawagan, lake, Sask., Can....F3 70
Kutch, Elbert, Colo., 5.....C7 83
Kutch, gulf, India.....D4 39
Kute, Alb.....B2 23
Kutina, Yugo., 7,132.....C3 22
Kutlay, Sov. Un.....D4 29
Kutna Hora, Czech., 16,900.D3 26
Kutno, Pol., 26,000.....B5 26
Kuttawa, Lyon, Ky., 635....A3 94
Kutu, Con. L.....B2 48
Kutua, pt., Truk..... 52
Kutum, Sud., 7,708.....C1 47
Kuty, Sov. Un.....A7 22
Kutztown, Berks, Pa., 3,312.....E10 114
Kuusamo, Fin., 3,200.....E13 25
Kuvandyk, Sov. Un., 21,500.E20 9
Kuwait, Kuw., 96,860 (*151,247).....G4 41
Kuwait, country, Asia, 405,000.....G7 33, G3 41
Kuwana, Jap., 69,391...I8, n15 37
Kuyang, Mong.....D4 36
Kuybyshev, Sov. Un., 26,500.....B9 29
Kuybyshev, Sov. Un., 901,000 (*1,050,000).....C4 29
Kuybyshev, res., Sov. Un.....D8 28
Kuybyshevka-Vostochnaya, Sov. Un., 50,000.....D15 28
Kuyto Ozero, lake, Sov. Un....E14 25
Kuyuan, China.....G2 36
Kuznetsk, Sov. Un., 64,000.....C3 29
Kuznetsk Alatau, mts., Sov. Un.B11 29
Kuznetsk Basin, reg., Sov. Un. E26 9
Kuznetsova, Sov. Un.....C10 37
Kuzomen, Sov. Un.....D17 25
Kvarner, gulf, Yugo.....C2 22
Kvitoya, isl., Nor.....A11 4
Kwajalein, atoll, Marshall Is..... 52
Kwajalong, isl., Kwajalein..... 52
Kwakoegron, Sur.....A3 59
Kwale, Ken.....B6 48
Kwale, Nig.....E6 45
Kwamouth, Con. L.....B2 48
Kwa Mtoro, Tan.....C6 48
Kwangchow, bay, China.....B9 38
Kwangju, Kor., 245,000 (313,300▲).....I3 37
Kwango, riv., Con. L.....C2 48
Kwangsi Chuang, auton. reg., China, 19,390,000.....F7 34
Kwangtung, prov., China, 37,960,000.....G7 34
Kwatisore, W. Irian.....F8 35
Kweichow, prov., China, 16,890,000.....F6 34
Kweichu, see Kweiyang, China
Kweihsien, China.....G6 34
Kweilin, China, 145,100.....F7 34
Kweisui, see Huhehot, China
Kweiyang, China, 504,000...F6 34
Kwenge, riv., Con. L.....C2 48
Kwidzyn, Pol., 20,000.....B5 26
Kwigillingok, Alsk., 344.....D7 79
Kwiguk, Alsk., 358.....C7 79
Kwilu, riv., Con. L.....B2 48
Kwohsien, China.....D7 34
Kyabé, Chad, 2,918.....D3 46
Kyabra Creek, riv., Austl.....B4 51
Kyaiklat, Bur., 15,781.....E10 39
Kyaikto, Bur., 10,000.....D2 38
Kyakhta, Sov. Un., 21,700..D13 28
Kyangin, Bur., 6,073.....E10 39
Kyaring, lake, China.....B8 39
Kyaring, lake, China.....E4 34
Kyaukpadaung, Bur., 5,000..C1 38
Kyaukpyu, Bur., 7,335.....E9 39
Kyaukse, Bur., 8,659.....B2 38
Kybartai, Sov. Un., 7,274...A7 26
Kyelang, India.....A6 40
Kyje, Czech., 5,836....D9, n18 26
Kyle, Sask., Can., 535.....G1 70
Kyle, Scot., 1,718.....C4 13
Kyle, Shannon, S. Dak., 100.D3 116
Kyle, Hays, Tex., 1,023.....E4 118
Kyles Ford, Hancock, Tenn., 75.....C10 117
Kylestrome, Scot.....B3 13
Kyll, riv., Ger.....D1 17
Kyllburg, Ger., 1,250.....D6 15
Kymes, mtn., Ark.....B1 81
Kymi, dept., Fin., 247,913.*G12 25
Kymulga, cove, Ala.....B3 78
Kynlyn, New Castle, Del., 1,600.....*A6 85
Kynuna, Austl., 32.....D7 50
Kyoga, cape, Jap.....I7 37
Kyoga, lake, Ug.....A5 48
Kyŏngju, Kor., 44,000 (79,500▲).....I4 37
Kyongsong, Kor., 25,925.....F4 37
Kyoto, Jap., 1,284,818 (*1,490,000).....I7, n14 37
Kyoto, pref., Jap., 1,993,403.....*I7 37
Kyrenia, Cyp., 3,680.....E9 31
Kyritz, Ger., 8,679.....B6 16
Kyrkjebö, Nor., 139.....G1 25
Kyrock, Edmonson, Ky., 150.C3 94
Kyshtovka, Sov. Un.....D24 9
Kyshtym, Sov. Un., 31,100...B6 29
Kyuquot, B.C., Can., 184....D4 68
Kyuquot, sound, B.C., Can.....E4 68
Kyuroku, isl., Jap.....F9 37
Kyūshū, isl., Jap.....J5 37
Kyustendil, Bul., 19,309.....D6 22
Kyzyl, Sov. Un., 40,000....D12 28
Kyzyl-Kiya, Sov. Un., 28,600.....E8 29
Kyzyl-Kum, des., Sov. Un.....E6 29
Kzyl-Orda, Sov. Un., 78,000.....E7 29

L

Laa, Aus., 4,925.....D8 16
Laaber, riv., Ger.....E7 17
Laage, Ger., 3,824.....E6 24
La Almunia de Doña Godina, Sp., 4,337.....B5 20
Laasphe, Ger., 5,600.....C3 17
La Asunción, Ven., 5,541....A5 63
Laau, pt., Haw.....B4 88
Labadie, Franklin, Mo., 250.C7 101
Labadieville, Assumption, La., 650.....C5, E5 95
La Baie, Que., Can., 558.....C5 73
La Baie Shawinigan, Que., Can., 1,085.....*C5 73
La Banda, Arg., 16,953.....E5 55
La Barca, Mex., 16,330.C4, m12 63
La Barge, Lincoln, Wyo., 700.C2 125
La Barge, creek, Wyo.....C2 125
Labé, Guinea, 11,800.....D2 45
Labe (Elbe), riv., Czech.....C3 26
Labelle, Que., Can., 1,224...C3 73
Labelle, co., Que., Can., 29,084.....C2 73
La Belle, Hendry, Fla., 1,262.F5 86
La Belle, Lewis, Mo., 866....A6 101
Laber, riv., Ger.....D6 17
Laberge, lake, Yukon, Can.....D5 66
Labette, Labette, Kans., 114.....E8 93
Labette, co., Kans., 26,805...E8 93
Labette, creek, Kans.....E8 93
Labin, Yugo., 6,152.....C2 22
La Bisbal, Sp., 5,275.....B7 20
Labo, Phil., 3,322.....o14 35
Labo, mtn., Phil.....p14 35
La Boca, C.Z.,48.....m11 62
La Boca, P.R.....B4 65
Laboe, Ger., 3,600.....D4 24
La Bolt, Grant, S. Dak., 125..B9 116
Labouheyre, Fr., 2,169.....E3 14
Laboulaye, Arg., 9,032.....A4 54
Labrador, reg., Newf., Can....g8 75
Labrador, sea, Newf., Can.....A3 75
Labrador City, Newf., Can., 386.....h8 75
Lábrea, Braz., 2,080.....D2 59
La Broquerie, Man., Can., 321.....E3 71
Labuan, isl., Mala.....D5 35
Labuco, Jefferson, Ala., 400..E4 78
Labuha, Indon.....F7 35
Labuhanbilik, Indon.....K4 38
Labuk, bay, Mala.....D5 35
Laburnum Manor, Henrico, Va., 2,500.....*D5 121
La Cabaña, Cuba.....h12 64
Lac-à-Beauce, Que., Can....B5 63
Lacadena, Sask., Can., 142..G1 70
L'Acadie, Que., Can., 327....D4 73
Lacamp, Vernon, La., 50.....C3 92
La Canada, Los Angeles, Calif., 13,340.....*F2 85
La Capelle, Fr., 2,019.....E3 15
La Carlota, Arg., 4,501.....A4 54
La Carlota, Phil., 7,213....*C6 35
La Carolina, Sp., 12,138.....C4 20
Lac au Saumon, Que., Can., 1,548.....*k13 73
Lac-aux-Brochets, Que., Can.....B5 73
Lac-aux-Sables, Que., Can., 857.....C5 73
Lac-Baker, N.B., Can., 338..B1 74
Lac-Beauport, Que., Can....n17 73
Lac-Bouchette, Que., Can., 911.....A5 73
Laccadive, Minicoy and Amindivi Is., ter., India, 24,108.....*F5 39
Laccadive, is., India.....F5 39
Lac-Carré, Que., Can., 687..C3 73
Lac Champdoré, lake, Que., Can.g8 75
Lac Chat, Que., Can.....B5 73
Lac Court Oreilles, lake, Wis...C2 124
Lac Court Oreilles, Indian res., Wis.....C2 124
Lac de Gras, lake, N.W. Ter., Can.....D10 66
Lac des Bois, lake, N.W. Ter., Can.....C8 66
Lac des Commissaires, lake, Que., Can.....A5 73
Lac des Duex-Montagnes, lake, Que., Can.....q18 73
Lac-des-Écorces, Que., Can., 653.....C2 73
Lac des Iles, lake, Sask., Can...B6 69
Lac du Bonnet, Man., Can., 569.....D3 71
Lac du Bonnet, lake, Man., Can.D4 71
Lac Du Flambeau, Vilas, Wis., 700.....C4 124
Lac Du Flambeau, Indian res., Wis.....C3 124
Lac-Édouard, Que., Can.....B5 73
La Ceiba, Ven., 197.....B3 60
La Ceiba, Hond., 24,868.....C4 62
La Ceja, Col., 5,075.....B2 60
La Center, Ballard, Ky., 882.....A2 94
Lac-Etchemin, Que., Can., 2,297.....C7 73
Lacey, Thurston, Wash., 6,630.....B3 122
Lacey Park, Bucks, Pa., 4,000.....*F11 114
Laceys Spring, Morgan, Ala., 500.....A3 78
Lac-Frontière, Que., Can., 264.....C7 73
La Chambre, Fr., 773.....D2 18
La Charité, Fr., 5,747.....D5 14
La Charqueada, Ur., 1,189.....E2 56
La Châtre, Fr., 4,025.....D5 14
La Chaux-de-Fonds, Switz., 41,300.....B2 19
Lachen, Switz., 3,913.....B6 19
Lachine, Que., Can., 38,630.....D4, q19 73
Lachine, Alpena, Mich., 120.....C7 98
Lachlan, riv., Austl.....F6 51
La Chorrera, Pan., 8,626.....F8, m11 62
Lachute, Que., Can., 7,560..D3 73
La Cienega, Santa Fe, N. Mex., 50.....h8 107
La Ciotat, Fr., 18,827.....F6 14
La Cisa, pass., It.....B3 21
Lackawanna, Erie, N.Y., 29,564.....C2 108
Lackawanna, co., Pa., 234,531.....D10 114
Lackawaxen, Pike, Pa., 250.....D12 114
Lac la Biche, Alta., Can., 1,314.....B5 69
Lac la Biche, lake, Alta., Can...B4 69
Lac la Croix, lake, Minn.....B6 99
Lac la Hache, B.C., Can., 775.....D7 68
Lac la Loche, lake, Sask., Can..A6 69
Lac la Martre, lake, N.W. Ter., Can.....D9 66
Lac la Plonge, lake, Sask., Can..B2 70
Lac la Ronge, lake, Sask., Can...B3 70
Lac la Ronge, prov. park, Sask., Can.....B3 70
Laclede, Bonner, Idaho, 428.A2 89
La Clede, Fayette, Ill., 140..E5 90
Laclede, Linn, Mo., 428.....B4 101
Laclede, co., Mo., 18,991.....D4 101
Lac Masson, Que., Can.....C3 73
Lac-Mégantic, Que., Can., 7,015.....D7 73
Lacolle, Que., Can., 1,187...D4 73
La Colorado, Mex., 561.....B2 63
Lacomb, Linn, Oreg., 100.....C2, C4 113
Lacombe, Alta., Can., 3,029..C4 69
Lacombe, St. Tammany, La., 650.....B7, D6 95
Lacombe, bayou, La.....B8 95
Lacon, Marshall, Ill., 2,175..B4 90
Lacona, Warren, Iowa, 396..C4 92
Lacona, Oswego, N.Y., 556..B4 108
La Conception, Que., Can., 128.....C3 73
Laconia, Belknap, N.H., 15,288.....C4 105
Laconia, Fayette, Tenn., 40..B2 117
Laconia (Lakonia), prov., Grc., 118,661.....*D4 23
Laconia, gulf, Grc.....D4 23
La Conner, Skagit, Wash., 638.....A3 122
Lacoochee, Pasco, Fla., 1,523.....D4 86
La Coruña, Sp., 177,502.....A1 20
La Coruña, prov., Sp., 971,641.....*A1 20
Lacota, Van Buren, Mich., 135.....F4 98
La Courneuve, Fr., 25,792..g10 14
Lac Privert, lake, Que., Can.....g8 75
Lac qui Parle, co., Minn., 13,330.....F2 99
Lac qui Parle, lake, Minn.....E2 99
Lac qui Parle, riv., Minn.....F2 99
Lacreek, lake, S. Dak.....D4 116
La Crescent, Houston, Minn., 2,624.....G7 99
La Crescenta, Los Angeles, Calif., 12,000.....*F2 82
La Cresta Village, Kern, Calif., 10,000.....*E4 82
La Crête, Alta., Can., 277.....f7 69
La Crosse, Izard, Ark., 30...A4 81
La Crosse, Alachua, Fla., 165.....C4 86
La Crosse, La Porte, Ind., 632.....B4 91
La Crosse, Rush, Kans., 1,767.....D4 93
La Crosse, Mecklenburg, Va., 726.....E4 121
Lacrosse, Whitman, Wash., 463.....C8 122
La Crosse, La Crosse, Wis., 47,575.....E2 124
La Crosse, co., Wis., 72,465..E2 124
La Crosse, riv., Wis.....E3 124
La Cruz, Col., 2,745.....C2 60
La Cruz, Mex., 2,151.....C3 63
Lac-Saguay, Que., Can., 187.....C2 73
Lac-St. Jean-Est, co., Que., Can., 43,920.....A6 73
Lac-St. Jean-Ouest, co., Que., Can., 61,310.....A5 73
Lac-Ste. Marie, Que., Can., 232.....D2 73
Lac Seul, lake, Ont., Can.....g9 71
La Cueva, Mora, N. Mex., 50.B4 107
Lac Vert, Sask., Can., 122...E3 70
La Cygne, Linn, Kans., 810..D9 93
Lacy-Lakeview, McLennan, Tex., 2,272.....*D4 118
Ladd, Bureau, Ill., 1,255.....B4 90
Ladder, creek, Kans.....D2 93
Laddonia, Audrain, Mo., 671.....B6 101
Ladera Heights, Los Angeles, Calif., 1,500.....*F2 82
Ladgasht, Pak.....C3 39
Ladies, isl., S.C.....G6 115
Ladispoli, It., 464.....h8 21
Lādīz, Iran, 10,000.....G10 41
Ladner, B.C., Can., 5,000.....E6, f12 68
Ladner, Harding, S. Dak., 10.B2 116
Ladoga, Montgomery, Ind., 974.....E4 91
Ladoga, lake, Sov. Un.....A8 27
Ladonia, Fannin, Tex., 890..C5 118
Ladora, Iowa, Iowa, 307.....C5 92
La Dorado, Col., 14,577.....B3 60
La Due, Henry Mo., 175.....C4 101
Ladue, St. Louis, Mo., 9,466.....*C7 101
Ladybank, Scot., 1,207.....D5 13
Ladybrand, S. Afr., 7,045.....C4 49
Lady Lake, Lake, Fla., 335..D5 86
Lady Laurier, mtn., B.C., Can..A6 68
Ladysmith, B.C., Can., 2,173.....E6, g12 68
Ladysmith, S. Afr., 22,955...C4 49
Ladysmith, Rusk, Wis., 3,584.....C2 124
Lae, N. Gui., 948.....k12 50
Laerdal, Nor.....G2 25
Laesø, isl., Den.....A4 24
La Esperanza, Cuba.....k12 64
La Esperanza, Cuba, 1,038..D2 64
La Esperanza, Hond., 1,327..C3 62
La Esperanza, P.R.....B6 65
La Estrada, Sp., 2,540.....A1 20
La Estrella, Bol.....C3 55
La Farge, Vernon, Wis., 833..E3 124
La Fargeville, Jefferson, N.Y., 500.....A5, f9 108
Lafayette, Chambers, Ala., 2,605.....C4 78
Lafayette, Contra Costa, Calif., 7,114.....*B5 28
Lafayette, Boulder, Colo., 2,612.....B5 83
La Fayette, Walker, Ga., 5,588.....B1 87
La Fayette, Stark, Ill., 269...B4 90
Lafayette, Tippecanoe, Ind., 42,330.....D4 91
La Fayette, Christian, Ky., 196.....D2 94
Lafayette, Lafayette, La., 40,400.....D3 95
Lafayette, Nicollet, Minn., 516.....F4 99
Lafayette, Sussex, N.J., 200..A3 106
Lafayette, Onondaga, N.Y., 290.....C4 108
Lafayette, Madison, Ohio, 150.....C4 111
Lafayette, Yamhill, Oreg., 553.....B1, B3 113
La Fayette, Washington, R.I., 900.....C11 84
Lafayette, Macon, Tenn., 1,590.....C7 117
Lafayette, co., Ark., 11,030..D2 81
Lafayette, co., Fla., 2,889....C3 86
Lafayette, co., Miss., 21,355..A4 100
Lafayette, co., Mo., 25,274...B4 101
Lafayette, co., Wis., 18,142..F3 124
Lafayette, par., La., 84,656..D3 95
Lafayette, mtn., N.H.....B3 105
Lafayette Central, P.R.....D6 65
Lafayette Hill, Montgomery, Pa., 3,500.....*A11 114
Lafayette Southwest, Lafayette, La., 6,682.....*D3 95
Lafayette Springs, Lafayette, Miss., 151.....A4 100
Lafe, Greene, Ark., 150.....A5 81
La Fère, Fr., 3,161.....E3 15
La Feria, Cameron, Tex., 3,047.....F4 118
La Ferté-Bernard, Fr., 5,979..C4 14
La Ferté-Macé, Fr., 4,109...C3 14
La Ferté-sous-Jouarre, Fr., 4,077.....C5 14
Lafferty, Izard, Ark.....B4 81
Lafferty, Belmont, Ohio, 950.....B6 111
Lafia, Nig.....E6 45
Lafiagi, Nig.....E6 45
Lafitte, Jefferson, La., 257...C7 95
Laflèche (Mackayville), Que., Can., 10,984.....*D4 73
Laflèche, Sask., Can., 749...H2 70
La Flèche, Fr., 9,439.....D3 14
La Follette, Campbell, Tenn., 6,204.....C9 117
La Fontaine, Wabash, Ind., 779.....C6 91
Lafontaine, Wilson, Kans., 100.....E8 93
Lafourche, Lafourche, La., 500.....C6, E5 95
Lafourche, par., La., 55,381..E3 95
Lafourche, bayou, La.....E5 95
La France, Anderson, S.C., 900.....B2 115
Lafrenais, lake, Que., Can.....A4 73
La Garita, Saguache, Colo., 10.....D4 83
Lagarto, Pan., 306.....k10 62
Lage, Ger., 12,900.....B3 17
Lågen, riv., Nor.....G3, p27 25
Lagg, Scot.....E3 13
Laggan, bay, Scot.....E2 13
Laggan, lake, Scot.....D4 13
Laghouat, Alg., 11,058 (43,220▲).....C5 44
La Gloria, Col., 1,277.....B3 60
Lagny, Fr., 11,945.....C5 14
Lago, mtn., Wash.....A5 122
Lagoa, Port., 2,249.....D1 20
Lago Argentino, Arg.....E2 54
Lago Buenos Aires, Arg.....D2 54
Lagoon, Bladen, N.C.....C5 109
Lago Posadas, Arg.....D2 54
Lagos, Chile, 2,106.....B2 54
Lagos, Nig., 665,246.....E5 45
Lagos, fed. reg., Nig., 272,000.....*E5 45
Lagos, Port., 7,143.....D1 20
Lagos de Moreno, Mex., 23,298.....C4, m13 63
Lago Viedma, Arg.....D2 54
La Grand' Combe, Fr., 14,440 (*22,000).....E5 14
La Grande, Union, Oreg., 9,014.....B8 113
La Grange, Lee, Ark., 300....C5 81
La Grange, Austl.....C3 50
La Grange, Brevard, Fla., 300.....D6 86
La Grange, Troup, Ga., 23,632.....C1 87
La Grange, Cook, Ill., 16,326.....B6, F2 90
Lagrange, Lagrange, Ind., 1,990.....A7 91
La Grange, Oldham, Ky., 2,168.....B4 94
La Grange, Penobscot, Maine, 300 (424▲).....C4 96
La Grange, Lewis, Mo., 1,347.....A6 101
La Grange, Lenoir, N.C., 2,133.....B6 109
Lagrange, Lorain, Ohio, 1,007.....A5 111
Lagrange, Fayette, Tenn., 217.....B2 117
La Grange, Fayette, Tex., 3,623.....E4 118
Lagrange, Goshen, Wyo., 176.....D8 125
Lagrange, co., Ind., 17,380....A7 91
La Grange Highlands, Cook, Ill., 5,000.....*F2 90
La Grange Park, Cook, Ill., 13,793.....F2 90
La Guadeloupe, Que., Can., 1,728.....D7 73
La Guaira, Ven., 20,275.....A4 60
La Guajira, intendencia, Col., 112,100.....A3 60
La Guardia, Sp., 9,311.....B1 20
Laguna, Yuma, Ariz., 30....E1 80
Laguna, Braz., 17,451.....D3 56
Laguna, Valencia, N. Mex., 550.....B2 107
Laguna, prov., Phil., 472,200.....*C6 35
Laguna, dam, Ariz.....E1 80
Laguna, Indian res., N. Mex...C2 107
Laguna Beach, Orange, Calif., 9,288.....F5 82
Laguna del Perro, lake, N. Mex.C4 107
Laguna Madre, lagoon, Tex.....F4 118
Laguna Shores, Nueces, Tex., 1,500.....*F4 118
Lagunillas, Bol., 840.....C3 55
Lagunillas, Ven., 67,869.....A3 60
Lagrue, bayou, Ark.....C4 81
La Habana, see Havana, Cuba
La Habra, Orange, Calif., 25,136.....F3 82
LaHabra Heights, Los Angeles, Calif., 1,500.....*F3 82
Lahad Datu, Mala., 600.....L5 35
Lahaina, Maui, Haw., 3,423.....C5 88
La Harpe, Hancock, Ill., 1,322.....C3 90
La Harpe, Allen, Kans., 529..E8 93
Lahat, Indon.....F2 35
La Have, N.S., Can., 248....E5 74
La Have, riv., N.S., Can.....E5 74
La Have Island, N.S., Can., 200.....E5 74
La Haye-Descartes, Fr., 1,679.....D4 14
Laheria Sarai, India.....D10 40
Laḥij, S. Arabia, 10,000.....C5 47
Lahinch, Ire., 389.....E2 11
Lahn, riv., Ger.....C3 17
Laholm, Swe., 3,500.....B7 24
Laholmsbukten, bay, Swe.....B6 24
Lahoma, Garfield, Okla., 160.....A3 112
Lahontan, res., Nev.....D2 104
Lahore, Pak., 1,227,996 (*1,325,000).....B5 39, B5 40
Lahr, Ger., 22,600.....D3 16
Lahri, Pak.....C2 40
Lahti, Fin., 72,200.....G11 25
La Huaca, Peru, 2,012.....B1 58
Laï, Chad, 4,787.....D3 46
Lai Chau, Viet.....A5 38
Laichow, bay, China.....F8 36
Laide, Scot.....C3 13
Laidon, lake, Scot.....D4 13
Laie, Honolulu, Haw., 1,767.....B4, f10 88
Laifeng, China, 14,000.....J3 36
Laigle, Fr., 5,520.....C4 14
Laihka, Bur.....B2 38
Laingsburg, Shiawassee, Mich., 1,057.....F6 98
Laingsburg, S. Afr., 2,815...D3 49
Lair, Harrison, Ky., 102.....B5 94
Laird, Sask., Can., 278.....E2 70
Laird, Yuma, Colo., 156.....A8 83
Lairg, Scot., 962.....B4 13
Laiwui, Indon.....F7 35
Laiyang, China, 40,000.....F9 36
Laiyuan, China.....E6 36
La Jara, Conejos, Colo., 724..D5 83
La Jara, Sandoval, N. Mex., 75.....A3 107
Lajas, P.R., 914.....C2 65
Lajas, mun., P.R., 15,375.....C2 65
Lajes, Braz., 35,112.....D2 56
Lajolla, pt., Calif.....E2 82
Lajord, Sask., Can., 135.....G3 70
La Jose (Newburg), Clearfield, Pa., 150.....E8 114
Lajosmizse, Hung., 4,735.....B4 22
Lajoya, Socorro, N. Mex., 150.....C3 107
La Joya, Peru.....E3 58
La Junta, Otero, Colo., 8,026.....D7 83
Lak, riv., Ken.....A7 48
Lake, Ascension, La.....B6 95
Lake, Clare, Mich., 90.....E5 98
Lake, Scott, Miss., 297.....C4 100
Lake, co., Calif., 13,786.....C2 82
Lake, co., Colo., 7,101.....B4 83
Lake, co., Fla., 57,383.....D5 86
Lake, co., Ill., 293,656.....A6 90
Lake, co., Ind., 513,269.....B3 91
Lake, co., Mich., 5,338.....E5 98
Lake, co., Minn., 13,702.....C7 99
Lake, co., Mont., 13,104.....C2 102
Lake, co., Ohio, 148,700.....A6 111
Lake, co., Oreg., 7,158.....E6 113
Lake, co., S. Dak., 11,764...C8 116
Lake, co., Tenn., 9,572.....A2 117
Lake, reg., Tan., 3,330,206..B5 48
Lake, creek, Wash.....B7 122
Lake, district, Eng.....C5 10
Lake, fork, Colo.....C3 83
Lake, mtn., Wyo.....D6 125
Lake, range, Nev.....C2 104
Lake, swamp, S.C.....D8 115
Lake Alfred, Polk, Fla., 2,191.....D5 86
Lake Alma, Sask., Can., 171.....H3 70
Lake Andes, Charles Mix, S. Dak., 1,097.....D7 116
Lake Annis, N.S., Can.....E4 74
Lake Ariel, Wayne, Pa., 400.....D11 114
Lake Arrowhead, San Bernardino, Calif., 500.E5, F3 82
Lake Arthur, Jefferson Davis, La., 3,541.....D3 95
Lake Arthur, Chaves, N. Mex., 387.....D5 107
Lake Barcroft, Fairfax, Va., 1,800.....*B5 121
Lake Benton, Lincoln, Minn., 905.....F2 99
Lake Beseck, Middlesex, Conn., 500.....*B6 84
Lake Beulah, Walworth, Wis., 80.....F1 124
Lake Bluff, Lake, Ill., 3,494.....A6, E2 90
Lake Bonaparte, Lewis, N.Y., 30.....A5 108
Lake Bronson, Kittson, Minn., 421.....B2 99
Lake Brown, Austl., 170.....F2 50
Lake Bruce, Pulaski, Ind., 100.....B5 91
Lake Burien Heights, King, Wash., 2,000.....*B3 122
Lake Butler, Union, Fla., 1,311.....B4 86
Lake Carey, Wyoming, Pa., 30.....C10 114
Lake Cargelligo, Austl., 1,118.....F6 51
Lake Chance, creek, Utah.....F4 119
Lake Charles, Calcasieu, La., 63,392 (*127,200).....D2 95
Lake City, Craighead, Ark., 850.....B5 81
Lake City, Modoc, Calif., 80..B3 82
Lake City, Hinsdale, Colo., 106.....C3 83
Lake City, Columbia, Fla., 9,465.....B4 86

Leeds, Jefferson and St. Clair, Ala., 6,162 C3, E5 78
Leeds, Eng., 513,800 (★1,355,000) A6 12
Leeds, Benson, N. Dak., 797 A6 110
Leeds, Chester, S.C., 120 B5 115
Leeds, Washington, Utah, 109 F2 119
Leeds, co., Ont., Can., 46,889 C8 72
Leeds Point, Atlantic, N.J., 200 D4 106
Leeds Village, Que., Can C6 73
Leedy, Tishomingo, Miss., 40 A5 100
Leek, Eng., 19,173 A5 12
Leelanau, Leelanau, Mich D5 98
Leelanau, co., Mich., 9,321 D5 98
Leelanau, lake, Mich C5 98
Leenane, Ire., 123 D2 11
Lee Park, Luzerne, Pa., 3,500 *D10 114
Leeper, Wayne, Mo., 350 D7 101
Leeper, Clarion, Pa., 250 D3 114
Lee Pope, Crawford, Ga., 30 D3 87
Leer, Ger., 20,500 B3 16
Lees, Bledsoe, Tenn., 50 D8 117
Leesburg, Cherokee, Ala., 150 A4 78
Leesburg, Lake, Fla., 11,172 D5 86
Leesburg, Lee, Ga., 774 E2 87
Leesburg, Kosciusko, Ind., 427 B6 91
Leesburg, Rankin, Miss C4 100
Leesburg, Cumberland, N.J., 700 E3 106
Leesburg, Highland, Ohio, 932 C4 111
Leesburg, Loudoun, Va., 2,869 B5 121
Lees Ferry, Mohave, Ariz A4 80
Leesport, Berks, Pa., 1,138 *F9 114
Lee's Summit, Jackson, Mo., 8,267 C3, E2 101
Leesville, Lawrence, Ind., 40 G5 91
Leesville, Vernon, La., 4,689 C2 95
Leesville, Carroll, Ohio, 287 B6 111
Leesville, Lexington, S.C., 1,619 D4 115
Leesville, Gonzales, Tex., 150 B4, E4 118
Leetes Island, New Haven, Conn., 400 D6 84
Leeton, Johnson, Mo., 371 C4 101
Leetonia, Columbiana, Ohio, 2,543 B7 111
Leetsdale, Allegheny, Pa., 2,153 A5 114
Leeuwarden, Neth., 85,700 A5 15
Leeuwin, cape, Austl F2 50
Lee Valley, Hawkins, Tenn C10 117
Lee Vining, Mono, Calif., 350 D4 82
Leeward Islands, see Antigua, Montserrat, St. Kitts-Nevis-Anguilla, and Virgin Is. (Br.), Br. dep., N.A.
Lefebvre, Que., Can B8 73
Le Ferriere, It., 1,000 h9 21
Leffingwell, New London, Conn., 350 *C8 84
Leflore, Le Flore, Okla., 250 C7 112
Leflore, co., Miss., 47,142 B3 100
Le Flore, co., Okla., 29,106 C7 112
Lefor, Stark, N. Dak., 175 C3 110
Lefors, Gray, Tex., 864 B2 118
Le François, Mart., 2,189 o16 64
Lefroy, Ont., Can., 366 C5 72
Lefroy, lake, Austl F3 50
Leftrook, lake, Man., Can A2 71
Legal, Alta., Can., 524 C4 69
Leganés, Sp., 8,539 p17 20
Legaspi, Phil., 36,374 (60,593▲) C6 35
Legau, Ger., 2,500 E5 16
Leghorn, see Livorno, It.
Legion, Kerr, Tex., 1,691 *E3 118
Legnago, It., 7,500 D7 18
Legnano, It., 43,800 B2 21
Legnica, Pol., 68,000 C4 26
Le Gore, Frederick, Md., 80 A3 85
Le Grand, Merced, Calif., 900 D3 82
Le Grand, Marshall, Iowa, 465 B5 92
Le Grand-Quevilly, Fr., 18,727 C4 14
Leh, India, 3,720 B6 39
Le Havre, Fr., 183,776 (★223,000) C3 20
Lehi, Utah, Utah, 4,377 C4 119
Lehigh, Webster, Iowa, 846 B3 92
Lehigh, Marion, Kans., 178 D6 93
Lehigh, Coal, Okla., 296 C5 112
Lehigh, co., Pa., 227,536 E10 114
Lehigh, riv., Pa D10 114
Lehighton, Carbon, Pa., 6,318 E10 114
Lehman, Luzerne, Pa., 200 B7 114
Lehman Caves, nat. mon., Nev E7 104
Lehman Hot Springs, Umatilla, Oreg B8 113
Lehr, Logan, N. Dak., 381 C6 110
Lehrte, Ger., 21,300 A4 17
Lehua, isl., Haw A1 88
Leiah, Pak., 14,914 B5 39
Leibnitz, Aus., 6,356 E7 16
Leicester, Eng., 270,400 (★430,000) D6 10, B6 12
Leicester, Worcester, Mass., 1,850 (8,177▲) B4 97
Leicester, Livingston, N.Y., 365 C3 108
Leicester, Addison, Vt., 30 (551▲) D2 120
Leicester, co., Eng., 682,196 B6 12
Leicester Junction, Addison, Vt., 100 D2 120
Leichhardt, riv., Austl C7 50
Leiden, Neth., 98,800 (★121,000) B4 15
Leigh, Colfax, Nebr., 502 C8 103
Leigh Creek, Austl., 1,020 E2 51
Leighlinbridge, Ire., 457 E5 11
Leighton, Colbert, Ala., 1,158 A2 78
Leinan, Sask., Can G2 70
Leine, riv., Ger A4 17
Leinster, prov., Ire., 1,332,149 D4 11
Leinster, mtn., Ire E5 11
Leipalingis, Sov. Un A7 26
Leipers Fork, Williamson, Tenn., 250 B5 117
Leipsic, Kent, Del., 281 B6 85
Leipsic, Putnam, Ohio, 1,802 A4 111
Leipsic, riv., Del B6 85
Leipzig, Sask., Can., 106 E1 70
Leipzig, Ger., 587,200 (★735,000) B7 17
Leiria, Port., 7,123 C1 20
Leisnig, Ger., 9,500 B7 17
Leiston, Eng., 4,119 B9 12
Leisure City, Dade, Fla., 3,001 F3 86
Leitches Creek, N.S., Can., 94 C9 74
Leitchfield, Grayson, Ky., 2,982 C3 94
Leiter, Sheridan, Wyo., 5 A6 125
Leitersburg, Washington, Md A2 85
Leiters Ford, Fulton, Ind., 250 B5 91
Leith, Grant, N. Dak., 100 C4 110
Leith, Fayette, Pa., 1,622 *G2 114
Leitha, riv., Aus E8 16
Leitrim, co., Ire., 33,470 C3 11
Leixlip, Ire., 915 D5 11
Lejunior, Harlan, Ky., 900 D6 94
Lek, riv., Neth C4 15
Leka, isl., Nor E4 25
Le Kef, Tun., 14,743 B6 44
Le Kef, prov. Tun., 265,502 *B6 44
Le Kreider, Alg C5 44
Leksands, Swe., 1,800 G6 25
Leksula, Indon F7 35
Lekumbi, pt., Fiji Is 52
Lela, Wheeler, Tex., 100 B2 118
Leland, La Salle, Ill., 642 B5 90
Leland, Winnebago, Iowa, 209 A4 92
Leland, Leelanau, Mich., 400 C5 98
Leland, Washington, Miss., 6,295 B3 100
Leland, Josephine, Oreg., 75 E3 113
Leland, Jefferson, Wash., 30 B3 122
Leland Grove, Sangamon, Ill., 1,731 *D4 90
Leleiwi, pt., Haw D6 88
Leleque, Arg C2 54
Lelia Lake, Donley, Tex., 150 B2 118
Leloaloa, Am. Sam., 249 52
Le Locle, Switz., 13,762 B2 25
Lelom, reef, Truk 52
Le Loup, Franklin, Kans., 110 D8 93
Lelystad, Neth., 300 B5 15
Léman (*Geneva*), *lake, Switz* D1 19
Le Mans, Fr., 132,181 D4 14
Le Marin, Mart., 4,912 o16 64
Le Mars, Plymouth, Iowa, 6,767 B1 92
Lemasters, Franklin, Pa., 280 G6 114
Lemay (Luxemburg), St. Louis, Mo., 15,000 *C7 95
Lembach, Fr., 1,602 F7 15
Lembak, Indon F2 35
Lemberg, Sask., Can., 468 G4 70
Leme, Braz., 11,785 m8 56
Lemelerveld, Neth., 1,210 B6 15
Lemery, Phil., 6,050 p13 35
Lemeta, Alsk., 1,227 *C10 79
Lemgo, Ger., 21,400 A3 17
Lemhi, Lemhi, Idaho, 4 E5 89
Lemhi, co., Idaho, 5,816 E4 89
Lemhi, pass, Mont F3 102
Lemhi, range, Idaho E5 89
Lemhi, riv., Idaho E5 89
Lemieux, Que., Can., 129 C5 73
Lemitar, Socorro, N. Mex., 200 C3 107
Lemmer, Neth., 4,237 B5 15
Lemmon, Perkins, S. Dak., 2,412 B3 116
Lemmon, mtn., Ariz E5 80
Lemon, isl., S.C G6 125
Lemon Fair, riv., Vt D2 120
Lemon Grove, San Diego, Calif., 19,348 E2, E5 82
Lemons, Putnam, Mo., 140 A4 101
Lemont, Cook, Ill., 3,397 B5, F2 90
Lemont, Centre, Pa., 1,153 E6 114
Lemonweir, riv., Wis E3 124
Lemoore, Kings, Calif., 2,561 D4 82
Le Moule (Moule), Guad., 5,284 n16 64
Le Moyen, St. Landry, La., 200 D3 95
Le Moyne, Que., Can., 8,057 *D4 73
Lemoyne, Keith, Nebr., 60 C4 103
Lemoyne, Wood, Ohio, 200 A2 111
Lemoyne, Cumberland, Pa., 4,662 *F8 114
Lempster, Sullivan, N.H., 75 (272▲) D2 105
Lemsford, Sask., Can., 63 G1 70
Lemvig, Den., 5,783 B2 24
Lena, Stephenson, Ill., 1,552 A4 90
Lena, Rapides, La., 200 C3 95
Lena, Leake, Miss., 307 C4 100
Lena, Morrow, Oreg B7 113
Lena, Sp., 2,252 A3 20
Lena, Oconto, Wis., 506 D5 124
Lena, riv., Sov. Un C15 28
Lenapah, Nowata, Okla., 322 A6 112
Lenawee, co., Mich., 77,789 G6 98
Lençóis, Braz., 2,483 D2 57
Lend, Aus., 2,175 B9 18
Lendinara, It., 16,673 D7 18
Lenexa, Johnson, Kans., 2,487 B8, D9 93
Leney, Sask., Can., 35 E2 70
Lengby, Polk, Minn., 181 C3 99
Lengede, Ger., 3,600 A5 17
Lengeh, Iran, 9,617 H7 41
Lenger, Sov. Un., 40,000 E7 29
Lengerich, Ger., 21,000 A2 17
Lenhartsville, Berks, Pa., 209 E10 114
Leninabad, Sov. Un., 86,000 E7 29
Leninakan, Sov. Un., 117,000 E2 29
Leningrad, Sov. Un., 3,180,000 (★3,950,000) H14, s31 25, B8 27
Lenino, Sov. Un., 19,500 n17 27
Leninogorsk, Sov. Un., 69,000 C10 29
Leninsk, Sov. Un., 5,000 G15 27
Leninsk-Kuznetskiy, Sov. Un., 140,000 C11 29
Lenk, Switz., 1,900 D3 19
Lenkoran, Sov. Un., 30,000 H18 9
Lenne, riv., Ger B2 17
Lennep, Meagher, Mont., 25 D6 102
Lennox, Los Angeles, Calif., 31,224 *F2 82
Lennox, Lincoln, S. Dak., 1,353 D9 116
Lennox, isl., Chile k12 54
Lennox and Addington, co., Ont., Can., 23,717 C7 72
Lennoxville, Que., Can., 3,699 D6 73
Leno, It., 4,550 D6 18
Lenoir, Caldwell, N.C., 10,257 B2 109
Lenoir, co., N.C., 55,276 B6 109
Lenoir City, Loudon, Tenn., 4,979 D9 117
Lenora, Norton, Kans., 512 C4 93
Lenora, Dewey, Okla., 20 A2 112
Lenorah, Martin, Tex., 75 C2 118
Lenore, Man., Can., 98 E1 71
Lenore, Nez Perce, Idaho, 40 C2 89
Lenore, Fremont, Wyo B3 125
Lenore, lake, Sask., Can E3 70
Lenore, lake, Wash B6 122
Lenox, Cook, Ga., 802 E3 87
Lenox, Taylor, Iowa, 1,178 D3 92
Lenox, Berkshire, Mass., 1,750 (4,253▲) B1 97
Lenox, Dent, Mo., 225 D6 101
Lenox, Dyer, Tenn., 250 A2 117
Lenox, Princess Anne, Va., 1,520 *B7 121
Lenox Dale, Berkshire, Mass., 600 B1 97
Lenox Avenue (Center Mills), Chemung, N.Y., 1,400 *C4 108
Lens, Fr., 42,590 (★260,000) B5 14
Lentner, Shelby, Mo., 100 B5 101
Lenwood, San Bernardino, Calif., 2,407 *E5 82
Lenzburg, St. Clair, Ill., 420 B9 101
Lenzburg, Switz., 6,378 B5 19
Lenzen, Ger., 3,480 E5 24
Lenzerheide, Switz C8 19
Léo, Upper Volta, 2,100 D4 45
Leo, Allen, Ind., 600 B7 91
Leo, Carbon, Wyo C6 125
Leoben, Aus., 36,257 E7 16
Léogane, Hai., 3,608 F7 64
Leola, Grant, Ark., 321 C3 81
Leola, McPherson, S. Dak., 833 B7 116
Leoma, Lawrence, Tenn., 150 B4 117
Leominster, Eng., 6,403 B5 12
Leominster, Worcester, Mass., 27,929 A4 97
Leon, Decatur, Iowa, 2,004 D4 92
Leon, Butler, Kans., 541 E7 93
León (León de los Aldamas), Mex., 209,870 C4, m13 63
Leon, Cattaraugus, N.Y., 200 C1 108
León, Nic., 44,100 D4 62
Leon, Love, Okla., 109 D4 112
León, Sp., 73,483 A3 20
Leon, Mason, W. Va., 236 C3 123
Leon, co., Fla., 74,225 B2 86
Leon, co., Tex., 9,951 D5 118
León, prov., Sp., 584,594 *A3 20
León, reg., Sp., 1,291,452 B3 20
Leona, Doniphan, Kans., 110 C8 93
Leona, Leon, Tex., 150 D5 118
Leonard, Ont., Can., 62 h13 72
Leonard, Oakland, Mich., 359 F7 98
Leonard, Clearwater, Minn., 70 C3 99
Leonard, Shelby, Mo., 142 B5 101
Leonard, Cass, N. Dak., 232 C8 110
Leonard, Fannin, Tex., 1,117 C4 118
Leonardo, Monmouth, N.J., 3,000 C4 106
Leonardtown, St. Marys, Md., 1,281 D4 85
Leonardville, N.B., Can., 256 E3 74
Leonardville, Riley, Kans., 378 C7 93
Leonardsville, Madison, N.Y., 350 C5 108
Leonberg, Ger., 20,300 E4 17
Leone, bay, Am. Sam 52
Leonfelden, Aus., 2,546 E9 17
Leonforte, It., 17,927 F5 21
Leongatha, Austl., 2,753 I5 51
Leonia, Holmes, Fla., 225 G3 86
Leonia, Bergen, N.J., 8,384 h9 106
Leonidhion, Grc., 3,356 D4 23
Leonora, Austl., 452 E3 50
Leonville, St. Landry, La., 526 D3 95
Leopold, Bollinger, Mo., 140 D8 101
Léopold II, lake, Con. L B2 48
Leopold and Astrid, coast, Ant C21 5
Leopoldina, Braz., 17,726 C4, g6 56
Leopoldsburg, Bel., 9,375 C5 15
Léopoldville, Con. L., 402,500 B2 48
Leora, Stoddard, Mo., 75 D7 101
Leota, Clare, Mich D6 98
Leota, Nobles, Minn., 275 G3 99
Leoti, Witchita, Kans., 1,401 D2 93
Leoville, Sask., Can., 416 D2 70
Leoville, Decatur, Kans., 90 C3 93
Leovo, Sov. Un., 10,000 H7 27
Lepanto, Poinsett, Ark., 1,585 B5 81
Lepe, Sp., 10,038 D2 20
Lepel, Sov. Un., 10,000 D7 27
Le Petit-Quevilly, Fr., 21,098 C4 14
Lepihué, Chile C2 54
L'Épiphanie, Que., Can., 2,663 D4 73
Le Plessis-Belleville, Fr., 1,016 E2 15
Le Plessis-Robinson, Fr., 18,449 g10 14
LePont, Switz C1 19
Lepontine Alps, mts., Switz D6 19
Le Portel, Fr., 11,198 D9 12
Lepreau, N.B., Can., 94 D3 74
Lepreau, pt., N.B., Can D3 74
Lepsinsk, Sov. Un F25 9
Lepsy, Sov. Un D9 29
Le Puy [-en-Velay], Fr., 25,125 E5 14
Le Quesnoy, Fr., 4,570 D3 15
Le Raincy, Fr., 14,908 g11 14
Le Raysville, Bradford, Pa., 371 C9 114
Lercara Friddi, It., 11,872 F4 21
Léré, Chad, 3,617 D2 46
Lérida, Sp., 50,047 (63,850▲) B6 20
Lérida, prov., Sp., 333,765 *B6 20
Lerma, Sp., 2,605 A4 20
Lerma, riv., Mex m13 63
Lermoos, Aus., 768 B6 18
Lerna, Coles, Ill., 296 D5 90
Leros, isl., Grc D6 23
Leross, Sask., Can., 117 F4 70
Leroux, wash, Ariz B5 80
Leroy, Washington, Ala., 100 D2 78
Leroy, Sask., Can., 515 F3 70
Le Roy, McLean, Ill., 2,088 C5 90
Leroy, Lake, Ind., 350 B3 91
Le Roy, Decatur, Iowa, 70 D8 92
Le Roy, Coffey, Kans., 601 D8 93
Le Roy, Osceola, Mich., 267 D5 98
Le Roy, Mower, Minn., 971 G6 99
Leroy, Blaine, Mont., 5 C7 102
Le Roy, Genesee, N.Y., 4,662 C3 108
Leroy, Pembina, N. Dak., 100 A8 110
Leroy, Medina, Ohio, 504 A6 105
Le Roy, Bradford, Pa., 150 C8 114
Le Roy, Uinta, Wyo D2 125
Lerum, Swe., 6,504 A6 24
Lerwick, Scot., 5,906 g10 10
Lery, lake, La C8 95
Lesbos (Lesvos), prov., Grc., 140,251 *C6 23
Les Cayes, Hai., 11,835 F7 64
Les Diablerets, Switz D3 19
Les Éboulements, Que., Can., 619 B7 73
Les Échelles, Fr., 863 D1 18
Le Sentier, Switz C1 19
Le Sépey, Switz D3 19
Les Escoumins, Que., Can A8 73
Les Étroits, Que., Can., 291 B9 73
Les Fonds, Que., Can., 195 o16 73
Lesh, Alb., 1,609 B2 23
Leshara, Saunders, Nebr., 103 D2 103
Les Haudères, Switz D3 19
Lesina, lake, It D5 21
Lesko, Pol., 2,129 D7 26
Leskovac, Yugo., 33,941 D5 22
Leslie, Searcy, Ark., 506 B3 81
Leslie, Sumter, Ga., 494 E2 87
Leslie, Custer, Idaho, 20 F5 89
Leslie, Ingham, Mich., 1,807 F6 98
Leslie, Greenbrier, W. Va., 500 C4 123
Leslie, co., Ky., 10,941 C6 94
Leslie Station, Sask., Can., 113 F4 70
Leslieville, Alta., Can., 178 C3 69
Les Lilas, Fr., 17,721 g10 14
Lesneven, Fr., 4,581 C1 14
Lesogorsk (Nayoshi), Sov. Un B11 37
Lesozavodsk, Sov. Un., 18,800 D6 37
Lesparre [-Médoc], Fr., 2,372 E3 14
Les Ponts-de-Cé, Fr., 2,786 D3 14
Les Sables-d'Olonne, Fr., 18,401 D3 14
Les Saules, Que., Can., 4,098 n17 73
Lesser Antilles, is., W.I B4 53
Lesser Khingan, mts., China B10 34
Lesser Slave, lake, Alta., Can B3 69
Lessines, Bel., 9,242 D3 15
Lesslie, York, S.C., 250 B6 115
Lester, Limestone, Ala., 250 A2 78
Lester, Ouachita, Ark D3 81
Lester, Lyon, Iowa, 239 A1 92
Lester, Delaware, Pa., 2,000 *B11 114
Lester, Raleigh, W. Va., 626 D6 123
Lester Prairie, McLeod, Minn., 966 F4 99
Lesterville, Reynolds, Mo., 196 D7 101
Lesterville, Yankton, S. Dak., 173 D8 116
Lestock, Sask., Can., 412 F3 70
Le Sueur, Le Sueur, Minn., 3,310 F5 99
Le Sueur, co., Minn., 19,906 F5 99
Les Verrières, Switz., 1,084 C1 19
Lesvos (Lesbos), prov., Grc., 140,251 *C6 23
Lésvos (*Lesbos*), *isl., Grc* C6 23
Leszno, Pol., 29,000 C4 26
Le Tarf, Alg F2 21
Letart Falls, Meigs, Ohio, 300 D6 111
Letcher, Sanborn, S. Dak., 296 D7 116
Letcher, co., Ky., 30,102 C7 94
Letchworth, Eng., 26,500 *C7 12
Le Teil, Fr., 8,236 E6 14
Letellier, Man., Can., 266 E3 71
Letha, Gem, Idaho, 100 F2 89
Lethbridge, Alta., Can., 35,454 E4, h8 69
Lethbridge, Newf., Can., 532 D5 75
Le Thillot, Fr., 2,994 B2 18
Letiahau, riv., Bech B3 49
Leticia, Col., 1,898 D4 60
Letohatchee, Lowndes, Ala., 250 C3 78
Letona, White, Ark., 141 B4 81
Le Touquet-Paris-Plage, Fr., 4,064 D9 12
Letpadan, Bur., 15,896 D1 38
Le Tréport, Fr., 6,136 B4 14
Letterfrack, Ire., 236 D2 11
Letterkenny, Ire., 4,329 C4 11
Lettermullen, Ire D2 11
Letts, Decatur, Ind., 150 F6 91
Letts, Louisa, Iowa, 392 C6 92
Lettsworth, Pointe Coupee, La., 175 D4 95
Leucadia, San Diego, Calif., 5,665 *F5 82
Leucas (Levkas), prov., Grc., 28,980 *C3 23
Leuk, Switz., 2,546 D4 19
Leukerbad, Switz., 619 D4 19
Leupp, Coconino, Ariz., 25 B5 80
Leupp Corners, Coconino, Ariz., 5 B5 80
Leushinskiy Tuman, lake, Sov. Un B6 29
Leutkirch, Ger., 7,200 B6 18
Leuven, Bel., 32,524 (★85,000) D4 15
Leuze, Bel., 7,002 D3 15
Levack, Ont., Can., 3,178 *A3 72
Levadhia, Grc., 12,609 C4, g9 23
Levallois-Perret, Fr., 61,804 g10 14
Levan, Juab, Utah, 421 D4 119
Levanger, Nor., 1,700 F4 25
Levanna, mtn., It B1 21
Levant, Thomas, Kans., 125 C2 93
Levant, Penobscot, Maine, 250 (765▲) D4 96
Level Green, Westmoreland, Pa., 1,500 *B7 114
Levelland, Hockley, Tex., 10,153 C1 118
Leven, Scot., 8,872 D5 13
Leveque, cape, Austl C3 50
Leverett, Franklin, Mass., 100 (914▲) B2 97
Leverett, Niobrara, Wyo B8 125
Leverett, glacier, Ant A32 5
Levering, Emmet, Mich., 300 C6 98
Leverkusen, Ger., 100,000 B1 17
Levey, Polk, Iowa, 100 A7 92
Levi, W. Sam., 2,152 52
Levi, Braxton, W. Va C4 123
Levice, Czech., 13,800 D5 26
Levick, mtn., Ant B29 5
Levie, Fr., 3,409 D2 21
Le Vigan, Fr., 3,110 E5 14
Levin, N.Z., 7,934 N15 51
Lévis, Que., Can., 15,112 C6, n17 73
Lévis, co., Que., Can., 51,842 C6 73
Levisa, fork, Ky C7 94
Levithos, isl., Grc D6 23
Levittown, Nassau, N.Y., 65,276 E7 108
Levittown, Bucks, Pa., 58,000 *F12 114
Levkas, Grc., 6,577 C3 23
Levkas (Leucas), prov., Grc., 28,980 *C3 23
Levkás (*Leucas*), *isl., Grc* C3 23
Levktra, Grc., 1,202 g10 23
Levoca, Czech., 7,584 D6 26
Levskigrad, Bul., 8,862 D7 22
Levuka, Fiji Is., 1,944 52
Levy, Mora, N. Mex., 15 A5 107
Levy, co., Fla., 10,364 C4 86
Levy, lake, Fla C4 86
Lewellen, Garden, Nebr., 411 C3 103
Lewes, Sussex, Del., 3,025 C7 85
Lewes, Eng., 13,637 D8 12
Lewis, Vigo, Ind., 600 F3 91
Lewis, Cass, Iowa, 501 C2 92
Lewis, Edwards, Kans., 486 E4 93
Lewis, Essex, N.Y., 300 A7, f11 108
Lewis, Polk, Wis., 250 C1 124
Lewis, co., Idaho, 4,423 C2 89
Lewis, co., Ky., 13,115 B6 94
Lewis, co., Mo., 10,984 A6 101
Lewis, co., N.Y., 23,249 B5 108
Lewis, co., Tenn., 6,269 B4 117
Lewis, co., Wash., 41,858 C3 122
Lewis, co., W. Va., 19,711 C4 123
Lewis, creek, Sask., Can F3 70
Lewis, creek, Vt C2 120
Lewis, hill, Newf., Can D2 75
Lewis, lake, Wyo A2 125
Lewis, mtn., Nev C5 104
Lewis, range, Can., U.S G10 66
Lewis, riv., Wash C3 122
Lewis, riv., Wyo A2 125
Lewis and Clark, co., Mont., 28,006 C4 102
Lewis and Clark, cavern, Mont D5 102
Lewis and Clark, res., Nebr B8 103
Lewisberry, York, Pa., 314 F8 114
Lewisburg, Jefferson, Ala E4 78
Lewisburg, Logan, Ky., 512 D3 94
Lewisburg, St. Landry, La., 150 D3 95
Lewisburg, Preble, Ohio, 1,415 C3 111
Lewisburg, Union, Pa., 5,523 E8 114
Lewisburg, Marshall, Tenn., 6,338 B5 117
Lewisburg, Greenbrier, W. Va., 2,259 D4 123
Lewis Center, Delaware, Ohio, 220 B4 111
Lewis-Clark, lake, S. Dak E8 116
Lewisdale, Prince George, Md., 5,000 *C3 85
Lewis Gardens, Henrico, Va., 1,380 *D5 121
Lewisport, Hancock, Ky., 610 C3 94
Lewisporte, Newf., Can., 2,702 D4 75
Lewis Run, McKean, Pa., 714 C4 114
Lewis Station, Henry, Mo C4 97
Lewiston, Nez Perce, Idaho, 12,691 C2 89
Lewiston, Androscoggin, Maine, 40,804 D2, D5 96
Lewiston, Montmorency, Mich., 400 D6 98
Lewiston, Winona, Minn., 890 G7 99
Lewiston, Niagara, N.Y., 3,320 B1 108
Lewiston, Bertie, N.C., 360 A8 109
Lewiston, Cache, Utah, 1,336 B4 119
Lewiston, peak, Utah C3 119
Lewiston Orchards, Nez Perce, Idaho, 9,680 C2 89
Lewistown, Fulton, Ill., 2,603 C3 90
Lewistown, Frederick, Md., 350 A3 85
Lewistown, Lewis, Mo., 454 A6 101
Lewistown, Fergus, Mont., 7,408 C7 102
Lewistown, Mifflin, Pa., 12,640 E6 114
Lewisville, Lafayette, Ark., 1,373 D2 81
Lewisville, N.B., Can., 3,094 C5 74
Lewisville, Jefferson, Idaho, 385 F6 89
Lewisville, Henry, Ind., 592 E7 91
Lewisville, Watonwan, Minn., 375 G4 99
Lewisville, Monroe, Ohio, 193 C6 111
Lewisville, Chester, Pa., 200 G10 114
Lewisville, Denton, Tex., 3,956 A5, C4 118
Lewis with Harris, isl., Scot B2 13
Lewvan, Sask., Can., 40 G3 70
Lexa, Phillips, Ark., 400 C5 81
Lexie, Walthall, Miss., 150 D3 100
Lexington, Lauderdale, Ala., 315 A2 78
Lexington, Stone, Ark., 60 B3 81
Lexington, Oglethorpe, Ga., 376 C3 87
Lexington, McLean, Ill., 1,244 C5 90
Lexington, Scott, Ind., 350 G6 91
Lexington, Fayette, Ky., 62,810 (★124,000) B5 94
Lexington, Somerset, Maine C2 96
Lexington, Middlesex, Mass., 27,691 B5, g11 97
Lexington, Sanilac, Mich., 722 E8 98
Lexington, Anoka, Minn., 1,457 *E5 99
Lexington, Holmes, Miss., 2,839 B3 100
Lexington, Lafayette, Mo., 4,845 B4 101
Lexington, Dawson, Nebr., 5,572 D6 103
Lexington, Greene, N.Y., 200 C6 108
Lexington, Davidson, N.C., 16,093 B3 109
Lexington, Richland, Ohio, 1,311 B5 111
Lexington, Cleveland, Okla., 1,216 B4 112
Lexington, Morrow, Oreg., 240 B7 113
Lexington, Lexington, S.C., 1,127 D5 115
Lexington, Henderson, Tenn., 3,943 B3 117
Lexington, Lee, Tex., 711 D4 118
Lexington, Rockbridge, Va., 7,537 D3 121
Lexington, Cowlitz, Wash., 110 C3 122
Lexington, co., S.C., 60,726 D5 115
Lexington Park, St. Marys, Md., 7,039 D5 85
Leyba, San Miguel, N. Mex., 20 B4 107
Leyburn, Eng., 1,281 F7 13
Leyden (Town of), Franklin, Mass. (343▲) *A2 97
Leyond, riv., Man., Can D3 71
Leysdown, Eng., 347 C8 12
Leysin, Switz., 4,241 D2 19
Leyte, prov., Phil., 1,177,400 *C6 35
Leyte, isl., Phil C6 35
Leyton, Eng., 93,857 k12 10
Lezajsk, Pol., 4,957 C7 26
Lézignan, Fr., 6,939 F5 14
Lezirias, reg., Port f10 20
Lgov, Sov. Un., 10,000 F10 27
Lhasa, China, 50,000 F3 34
Lhatse Dzong, China, 5,000 C11 40
L'Hay-les-Roses, Fr., 17,968 g10 14
Lhokseumawe, Indon J2 38
Lhoksukon, Indon J2 38
Li, China J4 36
Lianga, Phil., 3,173 *D7 35
Lianga, bay, Phil D7 35
Liancheng, China, 13,000 D5 36
Liang East, mtn., Mala K4 38
Liangshan, China, 18,000 I2 36
Liao, China F5 36
Liao, riv., China C10 36
Liaocheng, China F6 36
Liaoning, prov., China, 24,090,000 C9 34
Liaotung, bay, China D9 36
Liaotung, pen., China E10 36
Liaoyang, China, 135,000 D10 36
Liard, riv., B.C., N.W. Ter., Can E7 66
Liart, Fr., 668 E4 15
Liathac, mtn., Scot C3 13
Líbano, Col., 12,019 C3 60
Libau, Man., Can., 84 D3 71
Libby, Lincoln, Mont., 2,828 B1 102
Libcice, Czech., 3,121 n17 26
Libechov, Czech., 1,092 n17 26
Libenge, Con. L., 2,747 A2 48
Liberal, Seward, Kans., 13,813 E3 93
Liberal, Barton, Mo., 612 D3 101
Liberec, Czech., 66,400 C3 26
Liberia, C.R., 7,000 E5 62
Liberia, country, Afr., 1,050,000 E2 45, F4 42
Libertad, Ven., 1,171 B4 60
Liberty, Sask., Can., 157 F3 70
Liberty, Bear Lake, Idaho, 60 G7 89
Liberty, Adams, Ill., 325 D2 90
Liberty, Union, Ind., 1,745 E8 91
Liberty, Montgomery, Kans., 233 E8 93
Liberty, Casey, Ky., 1,578 C5 94
Liberty, Waldo, Maine, 150 (458▲) D3 96
Liberty, Amite, Miss., 642 D3 100
Liberty, Clay, Mo., 8,909 B3, E2 101
Liberty, Gage, Nebr., 174 D9 103
Liberty, Sullivan, N.Y., 4,704 D6 108
Liberty, Randolph, N.C., 1,438 B4 109
Liberty, Allegheny, Pa., 3,624 *F2 114
Liberty, Tioga, Pa., 269 C7 114
Liberty, Pickens, S.C., 2,657 B2 115
Liberty, De Kalb, Tenn., 293 C8 117
Liberty, Liberty, Tex., 6,127 D5, F5 118
Liberty, Kittitas, Wash., 30 B5 122
Liberty, co., Fla., 3,138 B2 86
Liberty, co., Ga., 14,487 E5 87
Liberty, co., Mont., 2,624 B5 102
Liberty, co., Tex., 31,595 D5 118
Liberty Acres, Los Angeles, Calif., 5,200 *F2 82
Liberty Center, Wells, Ind., 275 C7 91
Liberty Center, Warren, Iowa, 120 C4 92
Liberty Center, Henry, Ohio, 867 A3 111
Liberty Corner, Somerset, N.J., 800 B3 106
Liberty Grove, Cecil, Md., 55 A5 85
Liberty Hill, Kershaw, S.C., 350 C6 115
Liberty Hill, Grainger, Tenn., 50 C10 117
Liberty Lake, Spokane, Wash., 800 D8 122
Liberty Mills, Wabash, Ind., 300 B6 91
Liberty Plain, Plymouth, Mass., 900 h12 97
Libertytown, Frederick, Md., 650 B3 85
Libertyville, Lake, Ill., 8,560 A6, E2 90
Libertyville, Jefferson, Iowa, 368 D5 92

64X LITT-LORE

Little York, P.E.I., Can., 185 *C6 74
Little York, Warren, Ill., 329 B3 90
Little York, Washington, Ind., 180 G6 91
Little York, Hunterdon, N.J., 135 *B2 106
Little Zab, riv., Iraq E15 31
Lituhi, Tan D5 48
Litz Manor, Sullivan, Tenn. (part of Kingsport) C11 117
Liuan, China I7 36
Liucheng, China G6 34
Liucura, Chile, 1,094 B2 54
Liuho, China, 5,000 E2 37
Liupa, China, 1,000 E6 32
Liu Panshan, mts., China G2 36
Liu Pen Shan, mts., China K2 36
Liuyang, China J5 36
Livelong, Sask., Can., 140 D1 70
Lively, Ont., Can., 3,211 A3 72
Livengood, Alsk., 20 B10 79
Livenza, riv., It D8 18
Live Oak, Sutter, Calif., 2,276 C3 82
Live Oak, Suwannee, Fla., 6,544 B4 86
Live Oak, co., Tex., 7,846 E3 118
Livermore, Alameda, Calif., 16,058 B6 82
Livermore, Larimer, Colo., 20 A5 83
Livermore, Humboldt, Iowa, 545 B3 92
Livermore, McLean, Ky., 1,506 C2 94
Livermore, Androscoggin, Maine, 200 (1,363▲) D2 96
Livermore, peak, Tex F2 118
Livermore Falls, Androscoggin, Maine, 2,882 (3,343▲) D2 96
Livermore Falls, Grafton, N.H., 75 C3 105
Liverpool, Macon, Ala C4 78
Liverpool, N.S., Can., 3,712 E5 74
Liverpool, Eng., 739,700 (*1,680,000) A5 12
Liverpool, Onondaga, N.Y., 3,487 B4 108
Liverpool, Perry, Pa., 894 E7 114
Liverpool, Brazoria, Tex., 90 G5 118
Liverpool, Jackson, W. Va., 75 C3 123
Liverpool, bay, N.W. Ter., Can B6 66
Liverpool, bay, Eng A4 12
Livinda, riv., Gabon, Con. B E2 46
Livingston, Sumter, Ala., 1,544 C1 78
Livingston, Merced, Calif., 2,188 D3 82
Livingston, Guat., 2,606 C3 62
Livingston, Madison, Ill., 964 E4 90
Livingston, Rockcastle, Ky., 419 C5 94
Livingston, Livingston, La., 1,183 A6, D5 95
Livingston, Park, Mont., 8,229 E6 102
Livingston, Essex, N.J., 23,124 B4 106
Livingston, Columbia, N.Y., 190 C7 108
Livingston, Orangeburg, S.C., 208 D5 115
Livingston, Overton, Tenn., 2,817 C8 117
Livingston, Polk, Tex., 3,398 D5 118
Livingston, Grant and Iowa, Wis., 488 F3 124
Livingston, co., Ill., 40,341 C5 90
Livingston, co., Ky., 7,029 A3 94
Livingston, co., Mich., 38,233 F6 98
Livingston, co., Mo., 15,771 B4 101
Livingston, co., N.Y., 44,053 C3 108
Livingston, par., La., 26,974 D5 95
Livingston, isl., Ant C6 5
Livingstone, Zambia, 33,600 E4 48
Livingstone Cove, N.S., Can., 54 D8 74
Livingstonia, Malawi D5 48
Livingston Manor, Sullivan, N.Y., 2,080 D6 108
Livno, Yugo., 5,170 D3 22
Livny, Sov. Un., 10,000 E11 27
Livonia, Washington, Ind., 150 G5 91
Livonia, Pointe Coupee, La., 430 D4 95
Livonia, Wayne, Mich., 66,702 F7 98
Livonia, Putnam, Mo., 154 A5 101
Livonia, Livingston, N.Y., 946 C3 108
Livorno (Leghorn), It., 165,800 C3 21
Livramento, Braz., 37,666 E1 56
Livry-Gargan, Fr., 29,679 g11 14
Liwale, Tan., 2,898 C6 48
Liyang, China, 21,000 I8 36
Lizard, creek, Iowa B3 92
Lizard, pt., Eng E2 12
Lizard Head, pass, Colo D3 83
Lizard Head, peak, Wyo C3 125
Lizella, Bibb, Ga., 450 D3 87
Lizemores, Clay, W. Va., 50 C3, C7 123
Lizotte, Que., Can A5 73
Lizton, Hendricks, Ind., 366 E4 91
Ljubljana, Yugo., 134,169 B2 22
Ljubuski, Yugo., 2,181 D3 22
Ljungby, Swe., 9,300 I5 25
Ljusdal, Swe., 4,400 G7 25
Ljusterö, Swe., 1,132 t36 25
Llandilo, Wales, 1,906 C4 12
Llandovery, Wales, 1,898 C4 12
Llandrindod Wells, Wales, 3,248 B4 12
Llandudno, Wales, 17,200 A4 12
Llanelly, Wales, 29,500 C3 12
Llanerch, see Havertown, Pa.
Llanes, Sp., 20,421 A3 20
Llanfyllin, Wales, 1,251 B4 12
Llangefni, Wales, 3,209 A3 12
Llangollen, Wales, 3,050 B4 12
Llangynog, Wales, 394 B4 12
Llanidloes, Wales, 2,375 B4 12
Llano, Llano, Tex., 2,656 D3 118
Llano, Taos, N. Mex., 60 A4 107
Llano, co., Tex., 5,240 D3 118
Llano Estacado, plain, N. Mex., Tex C1 118
Llanos, plains, Col., Ven C4 53
Llanquihue, lake, Chile C2 54
Llanquihue, prov., Chile, 165,959 C2 54
Llanrwst, Wales, 2,571 A4 12
Llata, Peru, 1,741 C2 58
Llaves, Rio Arriba, N. Mex., 5 A3 107
Llerena, Sp., 8,217 C2 20
Llerena, pt., C.R F6 62
Lleyn, pen., Wales B3 12
Llico, Chile A2 54
Llivia, Sp., 637 F4 14
Llobregat, riv., Sp B6 20
Llorana, mtn., Pan h11 62
Lloyd, Jefferson, Fla., 300 B2 86
Lloyd, Greenup, Ky., 600 B7 94
Lloyd, Blaine, Mont., 5 B7 102
Lloyd, neck, N.Y F3 84
Lloyd, pt., N.Y F3 84
Lloyd Harbor, Suffolk, N.Y., 2,879 *F3 84
Lloydminster, Alta. and Sask., Can., 5,667 D1 70
Lloyd Place, Nansemond, Va., 2,282 *E6 121
Lloyds, riv., Newf., Can D3 75
Lluchmayor, Sp., 10,664 C7 20
Llullaillaco, vol., Chile D2 55
Llyswen, Blair, Pa. (part of Altoona) F5 114
Loa, riv., Chile D2 55
Loa, Wayne, Utah, 359 E4 119
Loachapoka, Lee, Ala., 200 C4 78
Loami, Sangamon, Ill., 450 D4 90
Loan, lake, Maine B3 96
Loange, riv., Con. L C3 48
Lobatsi, Bech C4 49
Löbau, Ger., 16,800 B9 17
Lobaye, riv., Cen. Afr. Rep E3 46
Lobelville, Perry, Tenn., 449 B4 117
Lobenstein, Ger., 4,194 C6 17
Lobería, Arg., 7,916 B5 54
Lobito, Ang., 31,630 D1 48
Lobnya, Sov. Un., 1,000 m17 27
Lobo, Phil., 843 p13 35
Lobo, Culberson, Tex., 30 F2 118
Lobos, Arg., 8,372 B5, g7 54
Lobos, isl., P.R f12 65
Lobos de Tierra, isl., Peru C1 58
Lobster, lake, Maine C3 96
Lobstick, lake, Newf., Can g8 75
Loburg, Ger., 4,051 A7 17
Locarno, Switz., 10,500 (*17,700) D6 19
Locate, Custer, Mont., 10 D11 102
Lochaber, N.S., Can., 68 D7 74
Lochaline, Scot D3 13
Lochbroom, Scot B4 10
Lochcarron, Scot., 822 C3 13
Lochdale, B.C., Can f12 68
Lochdonhead, Scot D3 13
Lochearn, Baltimore, Md., 2,000 *B4 85
Lochearnhead, Scot D4 13
Lochem, Neth., 6,600 B6 15
Loches, Fr., 5,902 D4 14
Lochgilphead, Scot., 1,208 D3 13
Lochiel, Santa Cruz, Ariz., 40 F5 80
Loching, China, 10,000 J9 36
Lochinver, Scot B3 13
Loch Lynn Heights, Garrett, Md., 476 D1 85
Lochmaben, Scot., 1,279 E5 13
Loch Maree, lake, Scot C3 13
Lochmere, Belknap, N.H., 225 D3 105
Lochnagar, mtn., Scot D5 13
Lochranza, Scot E3 13
Loch Raven, Baltimore, Md., 23,278 *B4 85
Loch Raven, res., Md B4 85
Lochsa, riv., Idaho C3 89
Loch Torridon, lake, Scot C3 13
Lochuan, China G3 36
Lochy, lake, Scot D4 13
Lockbourne, Franklin, Ohio, 460 C2 111
Locke, Elkhart, Ind., 80 B5 91
Locke, Cayuga, N.Y., 500 C4 108
Locke, Shelby, Tenn., 50 B1, E8 117
Locke, Pend Oreille, Wash A8 122
Lockeford, San Joaquin, Calif., 900 B6 82
Locke Mills, Oxford, Maine, 160 D2 96
Lockeport, N.S., Can., 1,231 F4 74
Lockerbie, Scot., 2,826 E5 13
Lockesburg, Sevier, Ark., 511 D1 81
Lockhart, Covington, Ala., 799 D3 78
Lockhart, Orange, Fla., 1,500 *D5 86
Lockhart, Norman, Minn., 70 C2 99
Lockhart, Union, S.C., 128 B5 115
Lockhart, Caldwell, Tex., 6,084 A4, E5 118
Lock Haven, Clinton, Pa., 11,748 D7 114
Lockland, Hamilton, Ohio, 5,292 A7 94
Lockney, Floyd, Tex., 2,141 B2 118
Lockport, Man., Can., 405 D3 71
Lockport, Will, Ill., 7,560 B5, F2 90
Lockport, Henry, Ky., 82 B5 94
Lockport, Lafourche, La., 2,221 C6, E5 95
Lockport, Niagara, N.Y., 26,443 B2 108
Lockport Station, Lafourche, La., 2,221 C6 95
Lockridge, Jefferson, Iowa, 206 C6 92
Lock Springs, Daviess, Mo., 117 B4 101
Lockwood, Sask., Can., 109 F3 70
Lockwood, Dade, Mo., 835 D4 101
Lockwood, Nicholas, W. Va., 912 C3, C7 123
Locminé, Fr., 1,898 D2 14
Loc Ninh, Viet G7 38
Loco, Stephens, Okla., 268 C4 112
Loco Hills, Eddy, N. Mex., 350 E6 107
Locumba, Peru, 634 E3 58
Locust, Monmouth, N.J., 800 C4 106
Locust, creek, Mo B4 101
Locust, fork, Ala B3 78
Locust, pt., Md B5 85
Locust Bayou, Calhoun, Ark., 150 D3 81
Locust Grove, Henry, Ga., 369 C2 87
Locust Grove, Washington, Md., 150 B2 85
Locust Grove, Mayes, Okla., 828 A6 112
Locust Hill, Ont., Can., 57 k15 72
Locust Valley, Nassau, N.Y., 3,400 F2 84
Lod (Lydda), Isr., 21,000 C6, h10 32
Loda, Iroquois, Ill., 585 C5 90
Löderup, Swe., 598 C8 24
Lodève, Fr., 6,869 F5 14
Lodeynoye Pole, Sov. Un., 10,000 A9 27
Lodge, Colleton, S.C., 181 E6 115
Lodge, creek, Can., Mont B7 102
Lodge Grass, Big Horn, Mont., 687 E9 102
Lodgepole, Alta., Can., 508 C3 69
Lodgepole, Cheyenne, Nebr., 492 C3 103
Lodgepole, Perkins, S. Dak., 35 B3 116
Lodgepole, creek, Nebr., Wyo C3 103, D8 125
Lodhran, Pak., 4,890 C3 40
Lodi, San Joaquin, Calif., 22,229 B6, C3 82
Lodi, Con. L B3 48
Lodi, It., 39,900 B2 21
Lodi, Bergen, N.J., 23,502 h8 106
Lodi, Seneca, N.Y., 396 C4 108
Lodi, Medina, Ohio, 2,213 A5 111
Lodi, Washington, Va., 35 B3 121
Lodi, Columbia, Wis., 1,620 E4 124
Lodja, Con. L C3 48
Lodore, canyon, Colo A2 83
Lods, Fr., 342 B2 18
Lodwar, Ken A6 48
Łódź, Pol., 726,800 (*875,000) C5 26
Loeches, Sp., 1,719 p18 20
Loei, Thai., 7,700 D4 38
Loelli (Well), Sud D3 47
Loeriesfontein, S. Afr., 2,192 D2 49
Lofer, Aus., 1,519 B8 18
Lofgreen, Tooele, Utah C3 119
Lofoten, is., Nor C5 25
Lofton, Heard, Ga., 200 C1 87
Loftus, Eng., 8,111 F8 13
Logan (Hanaford), Franklin, Ill., 289 F5 90
Logan, Harrison, Iowa, 1,605 C2 92
Logan, Phillips, Kans., 846 C4 93
Logan, Gallatin, Mont., 200 E5 102
Logan, Quay, N. Mex., 400 B6 107
Logan, Ward, N. Dak., 35 A4 110
Logan, Hocking, Ohio, 6,417 C5 111
Logan, Beaver, Okla., 10 A1, D4 112
Logan, Cache, Utah, 18,731 B4 119
Logan, Logan, W. Va., 4,185 D3, D5 123
Logan, co., Ark., 15,957 B2 81
Logan, co., Colo., 20,302 A7 83
Logan, co., Ill., 33,656 C4 90
Logan, co., Kans., 4,036 D2 93
Logan, co., Ky., 20,896 D3 94
Logan, co., Nebr., 1,108 C5 103
Logan, co., N. Dak., 5,369 C6 110
Logan, co., Ohio, 34,803 B4 111
Logan, co., Okla., 18,662 B4 112
Logan, co., W. Va., 61,570 D3 123
Logan, creek, Nebr B9 103
Logan, mtn., Ariz A8 80
Logan, mtn., Yukon, Can D4 66
Logan, mtn., Wash A5 122
Logan, mts., Yukon, Can D7 66
Logan, pass, Mont B3 102
Logan, peak, Ala A3 78
Logandale, Clark, Nev., 360 G7 104
Logansport, Cass, Ind., 21,106 C5 91
Logansport, Butler, Ky., 125 C3 94
Logansport, De Soto, La., 1,371 C2 95
Loganton, Clinton, Pa., 383 D7 114
Loganville, Gwinnett and Walton, Ga., 926 C3 87
Loganville, York, Pa., 742 G8 114
Loganville, Sauk, Wis., 220 E3 124
Logdell, Grant, Oreg C7 113
Loge, riv., Ang C1 48
Loggieville, N.B., Can., 691 B4 74
Log Lane Village, Morgan, Colo., 310 A7 83
Logone, riv., Chad D3 46
Logroño, Sp., 61,292 A4 20
Logroño, prov., Sp., 229,852 *A4 20
Logrosán, Sp., 6,595 C3 20
Løgstør, Den., 3,435 B3 24
Logtown, Hancock, Miss., 250 E4 100
Løgumkloster, Den., 1,907 C2 24
Lohals, Den., 640 C4 24
Lohardaga, India, 13,203 F10 40
Lohman, Blaine, Mont., 30 B7 102
Lohr, Ger., 11,100 D4 17
Lohrville, Calhoun, Iowa, 653 B3 92
Loi Mai, mtn., Bur B2 38
Loire, dept., Fr., *696,348 E6 14
Loire, riv., Fr D3 14
Loire-Atlantique, dept., Fr., 803,372 *D3 14
Loiret, dept., Fr., 389,854 *D4 14
Loir-et-Cher, dept., Fr., 250,741 *D4 14
Lois, Moore, Tenn B5 117
Loíza, P.R., 3,097 B7 65
Loíza, mun., P.R., 28,131 B7 65
Loíza Aldea, P.R., 2,330 B7 65
Loja, Ec., 18,200 B2 58
Loja, Sp., 12,439 D3 20
Loja, prov., Ec., 252,737 B2 58
Lojar, cape, Indon F5 35
Lokandu, Con. L B4 48
Lokeren, Bel., 25,819 C3 15
Lokhvitsa, Sov. Un., 10,000 F9 27
Lokichar, Ken A6 48
Lokichoggio, Ken A5 48
Lokitaung, Ken A6 48
Løkken, Den., 1,506 A3 24
Lokoja, Nig., 12,606 E6 45
Lokoro, riv., Con. L B3 48
Lokossa, Dah E5 45
Lokwei, China C9 38
Lol, riv., Sud D2 47
Lola, Livingston, Ky., 400 A3 94
Lolland, isl., Den D5 24
Lollar, Ger., 4,500 C3 17
Lollie (Minter), Laurens, Ga., 147 D4 87
Lolo, Missoula, Mont., 100 D2 102
Lolo, pass, Idaho, Mont C4 89
Lolo Hot Springs, Missoula, Mont., 10 D2 102
Lom, Bul., 15,182 D6 22
Loma, Mesa, Colo., 100 B2 83
Loma, Chouteau, Mont., 125 C6 102
Loma, Butler, Nebr., 60 C9 103
Loma, Cavalier, N. Dak., 20 A7 110
Loma, mts., Guinea, S.L E2 45
Loma Linda, San Bernardino, Calif., 6,000 *F3 82
Lomami, riv., Con. L B3 48
Loman, Koochiching, Minn., 60 B5 99
Loma Prieta, mtn., Calif C6 82
Lomas, Peru, 500 E3 58
Lomas de Zamora, Arg., 275,219 A5, g7 54
Lomax, Chilton, Ala., 200 C3 78
Lomax, Henderson, Ill., 535 C2 90
Lombard, Du Page, Ill., 25,296 F2 90
Lombardia, pol. dist., It, 7,406,152 *B2 21
Lombardy, reg., It B2 21
Lomblen, isl., Indon G6 35
Lombok, isl., Indon G5 35
Lombok strait, Indon G5 35
Lomé, Togo, 80,000 E5 45
Lomela, Con. L B3 48
Lomela, riv., Con. L B3 48
Lometa, Lampasas, Tex., 817 D3 118
Lomira, Dodge, Wis., 807 E5 124
Lomita, Los Angeles, Calif., 14,983 *F2 82
Lommel, Bel., 17,923 C5 15
Lomond, Alta., Can., 244 D4 69
Lomond, Newf., Can., 77 D3 75
Lomond, lake, Scot D4 13
Lomonosov, Sov. Un., 30,000 s30 25
Lomonosovskaya, Sov. Un C7 29
Lompoc, Santa Barbara, Calif., 14,415 E3 82
Lomza, Pol., 20,000 B7 26
Lonaconing, Allegany, Md., 2,077 D2 85
Loncoche, Chile, 5,061 B2 54
Londesborough, Ont., Can., 113 D3 72
London, Pope, Ark., 282 B2 81
London, Ont., Can., 169,569 (*181,283) E3 72
London, Eng., 3,178,900 (*10,975,000) E6, k12 10, D7 12
London, Laurel, Ky., 4,035 C5 94
London, Madison, Ohio, 6,379 C4 111
London, Kimble, Tex., 200 D3 118
London, Kanawha, W. Va., 500 *C5 123
London, co., Eng., 3,195,114 *E6 10
Londonbridge, Princess Anne, Va., 1,061 *E6 121
Londonderry, N.S., Can., 170 D6 74
Londonderry, N. Ire., 55,000 C4 11
Londonderry, Rockingham, N. H., 500 (2,457▲) E4 105
Londonderry, Ross, Ohio, 225 C5 111
Londonderry, Windham, Vt., 200 (898▲) E3 120
Londonderry, co., N. Ire., 111,565 C4 11
Londonderry, cape, Austl B4 50
Londonderry, isl., Chile k11 54
London Mills, Fulton and Knox, Ill., 617 C3 90
Londrina, Braz., 74,110 C2 56
Lone, plat., Colo D2 83
Lone Elm, Anderson, Kans., 69 D8 93
Lone Grove, Carter, Okla., 500 C4 112
Lonejack, Jackson, Mo., 180 C3 101
Lonely, Humphreys, Tenn., 150 A4 117
Lonely, isl., Ont., Can B3 72
Lone Mountain, Claiborne, Tenn., 200 C10 117
Loneoak, McCracken, Ky., 2,104 A2 94
Lone Oak, Hunt, Tex., 495 C5 118
Lone Pine, Inyo, Calif., 1,310 D4 82
Lonepine, Evangeline, La D3 95
Lonepine, Sanders, Mont., 10 C2 102
Lone Rock, Sask., Can., 191 D1 70
Lone Rock, Kossuth, Iowa, 185 A3 92
Lonerock, Gilliam, Oreg., 31 B7 113
Lone Rock, Richland, Wis., 563 E3 124
Lone Star, Calhoun, S.C., 350 D6 115
Lone Star, Morris, Tex., 1,513 *C5 118
Lone Tree, Johnson, Iowa, 717 C6 92
Lonetree, Uinta, Wyo., 5 D2 125
Lone Tree, creek, Colo A6 83
Lone Wolf, Kiowa, Okla., 617 C2 112
Long, co., Ga., 3,874 E5 87
Long, bay, N.C D5 109
Long, beach, N.Y E7 84
Long, beach, N.Y G2 84
Long, creek, Sask., Can H3 70
Long, isl., Ba. Is D6 64
Long, isl., N.S., Can E3 74
Long, isl., Fla H6 86
Long, isl., Maine D4 96
Long, isl., Mass g12 97
Long, isl., N. Gui k12 50
Long, isl., N.Y G3 84
Long, key, Fla E4 86
Long, key, Fla H6 86
Long, lake, N.B., Can B3 74
Long, lake, La E5 95
Long, lake, Maine A4 96
Long, lake, Maine D2 96
Long, lake, Mich C7 98
Long, lake, Mich D5 98
Long, lake, Minn D4 99
Long, lake, N.Y B6 108
Long, lake, N. Dak C6 110
Long, lake, Wash D1 122
Long, lake, Wis C2 124
Long, mtn., N.H A4 105
Long, pt., Man., Can C2 71
Long, pt., Newf., Can D2 75
Long, pt., Ont., Can E4 72
Long, pond, Fla C4 86
Long, pond, Maine C2 96
Long, pond, Maine C3 96
Long, pond, Mass C6 97
Long, pond, Mass C6 97
Long, strait, Sov. Un B20 28
Longa, riv., Ang D1 48
Longá, riv., Braz B2 57
Longarone, It., 4,727 C8 18
Long Barn, Tuolumne, Calif., 200 C3 82
Long Beach, Los Angeles, Calif., 344,168 F2, F4 82
Longbeach, Manatee, Fla., 1,000 F2 86
Long Beach, La Porte, Ind., 2,007 A4 91
Long Beach, Pope, Minn., 236 E3 99
Long Beach, Harrison, Miss., 4,770 E2, E4 100
Long Beach, Nassau, N.Y., 28,490 E7, n15 108
Long Beach, Pacific, Wash., 665 C1 122
Long Beach Resort, Bay, Fla., 66 *G3 86
Longbenton, Eng., 47,900 *E7 13
Longboat, inlet, Fla F1 86
Longboat, key, Fla E4 86
Longboat Key, Manatee and Sarasota, Fla., 1,000 *E4 86
Long Bottom, Meigs, Ohio, 135 C6 111
Long Branch, Ont., Can., 11,039 m14 72
Long Branch, Monmouth, N.J., 26,228 C5 106
Long Branch, Panola, Tex., 20 C5 118
Longbranch, Pierce, Wash., 150 B3 122
Long Cliff, Cass, Ind C5 91
Long Corner, Howard, Md., 150 B3 85
Long Creek, Grant, Oreg., 295 C7 113
Longcreek, Oconee, S.C., 200 B1 115
Longdale, Blaine, Okla., 218 A3 112
Long Eaton, Eng., 30,464 B6 12
Long Eddy, Sullivan, N.Y., 200 D5 108
Longeten, riv., Switz B4 19
Longford, Ire., 3,558 D4 11
Longford, Clay, Kans., 146 C6 93
Longford, co., Ire., 30,643 D4 11
Longford Mills, Ont., Can C5 72
Longfork, Dickenson, Va B2 121
Long Grove, Scott, Iowa, 182 C7 92
Long Harbour, Newf., Can., 356 E5 75
Long Hill, Fairfield, Conn. (part of Trumbull) D4 84
Longhorn, Bexar, Tex B4 118
Longhurst, Person, N.C., 1,546 A5 109
Longiram, Indon., 5,000 F5 35
Long Island, Jackson, Ala., 500 A4 78
Long Island, Phillips, Kans., 229 C4 93
Long Island, Cumberland, Maine (part of Portland) E5 96
Longisland, Catawba, N.C., 250 B3 109
Long Island, Campbell, Va., 75 D3 121
Long Island, sound, Conn., N.Y E4 84
Longlac, Ont., Can., 1,125 G15 67
Long Lake, Lake, Ill., 3,502 *E2 90
Long Lake, Iosco, Mich., 125 D7 98
Long Lake, Hennepin, Minn., 996 *F5 99
Long Lake, Hamilton, N.Y., 700 B6 108
Longlake, McPherson, S. Dak., 109 B6 116
Long Lake, Florence, Wis., 175 C5 124
Long Lane, Dallas, Mo., 110 D5 101
Long Leaf, Rapides, La., 600 C3 95
Long Leaf Park (South Wilmington), New Hanover, N.C., 2,238 *C3 109
Longmeadow, Hampden, Mass., 10,565 B2 97
Longmont, Boulder, Colo., 11,489 A5 83
Long Park, Montrose, Colo., 25 C2 83
Long Pine, Brown, Nebr., 487 B6 103
Long Point, N.S., Can., 179 D8 74
Long Point, Livingston, Ill., 307 B5 90
Long Point Park, Ont., Can., 120 E4 72
Long Pond, Newf., Can., 1,244 E5 75
Long Pond, Somerset, Maine, 70 C2 96
Longport, Atlantic, N.J., 1,077 E3 106
Long Prairie, Todd, Minn., 2,414 E4 99
Long Range, mts., Newf., Can D3 75
Long Rapids, Alpena, Mich., 90 C7 98
Longreach, Austl., 3,806 D7 51
Long Ridge, Fairfield, Conn. (part of Stamford) E2 84
Longridge, Eng., 4,677 G6 13
Long Run, Doddridge, W. Va., 100 B4, B6 123
Longs, creek, Ark A2 81
Longs, peak, Colo A5 83
Long Savannah, Hamilton, Tenn E10 117
Longstreet, DeSoto, La., 283 B2 95
Longton, Elk, Kans., 401 E7 93
Longtown, Eng., 2,577 E6 13
Longtown, Perry, Mo., 113 D8 101
Longueau, Fr., 5,316 E2 15
Longueuil, Que., Can., 24,131 D4, p19 73
Longuyon, Fr., 8,266 C6 14
Longvale, Mendocino, Calif., 130 C2 82
Long Valley, Coconino, Ariz C4 80
Long Valley, Morris, N.J., 1,220 B3 106
Longvalley, Washabaugh, S. Dak., 10 D4 116
Longview, Alta., Can., 246 D3 69
Longview, Champaign, Ill., 270 D5 90
Long View, Hardin, Ky., 500 C4 94
Longview, Oktibbeha, Miss., 227 B5 100
Longview, Catawba, N.C., 2,997 B2 109
Longview, Gregg, Tex., 40,050 C5 118
Longview, Cowlitz, Wash., 23,349 C3 122
Longville, Beauregard, La., 140 D2 95
Longville, Cass, Minn., 159 C4 99
Longwood, Seminole, Fla., 1,689 *D5 86
Longwood, Pettis, Mo., 35 C4 101
Longwood, Brunswick, N.C., 250 C5 109
Longwoods, Talbot, Md., 70 C5 85
Longwy, Fr., 21,939 (*75,000) C6 14
Long Xuyen, Viet., 5,000 G6 38
Loning, China G4 36
Lonkin, Bur., 5,000 C10 39
Lonoke, Lonoke, Ark., 2,359 C4, D6 81
Lonoke, co., Ark., 24,551 C4 81
Lonsdal, Nor D6 25
Lonsdale, Garland, Ark., 95 C3, C6 81
Lonsdale, Ont., Can C7 72
Lonsdale, Rice, Minn., 541 F5 99
Lonsdale, Providence, R.I., 5,000 (part of Cumberland and Lincoln) B11 84
Lons-le-Saunier, Fr., 15,924 D6 14
Looe, Eng., 3,878 D3 12
Loogootee, Martin, Ind., 2,858 G4 91
Lookeba, Caddo, Okla., 158 B3 112
Lookout, Modoc, Calif B3 82
Lookout, Pike, Ky., 900 C7 94
Lookout, Woods, Okla., 5 A2 112
Lookout, Fayette, W. Va., 600 C4, D7 123
Lookout, Albany, Wyo., 20 D7 125
Lookout, cape, N.C C7 109
Lookout, mtn., Oreg C6 113
Lookout, mtn., Oreg C8 113
Lookout, mtn., Oreg C9 113
Lookout, mtn., Tenn E10 117
Lookout, mtn., Wash D3 122
Lookout, pass, Mont C1 102
Lookout, pt., Mich D7 98
Lookout, ridge, Alsk B8 79
Lookout Mountain, Hamilton, Tenn., 1,817 E10 117
Lookout Mountain, ridge, Ala., Ga., Tenn A4 78
Lookout Point, res., Oreg D4 113
Looma, Alta., Can C4 69
Loomis, Sask., Can H1 70
Loomis, Phelps, Nebr., 299 D6 103
Loomis, Davison, S. Dak., 75 D7 116
Loomis, Okanogan, Wash., 190 A6 122
Loon, creek, Sask., Can F3 70
Loon, lake, Alta., Can A3 69
Loon, lake, Man., Can B1 71
Loon, riv., Alta., Can A3 69
Loon, riv., Man., Can A1 71
Loon Bay, Newf., Can., 144 D4 75
Loonhaunt, lake, Ont., Can B5 99
Loon Lake, Sask., Can., 350 *n7 70
Loon Lake, Stevens, Wash., 50 A8 122
Loon Lake, mts., N.Y f10 108
Loon Straits, Man., Can., 119 D3 71
Loop, Gaines, Tex., 100 C1 118
Loop, creek, W. Va D6 123
Loop, head, Ire E2 11
Loos, Fr., 18,367 D3 15
Loosahatchie, riv., Tenn B2 117
Loose Creek, Osage, Mo., 200 C6 101
Looxahoma, Tate, Miss., 80 A4 100
Lopatka, cape, Sov. Un D18 28
Lopei, China, 5,000 C5 37
Lopeno, Zapata, Tex., 10 F3 118
Lopez, Sullivan, Pa., 500 F9 114
Lopez, Phil., 3,644 p14 35
Lopez, cape, Gabon F1 46
Lopez, isl., Wash A3 122
Loping, China, 18,000 J7 36
Lop Nor, lake, China D3 34
Lopori, riv., Con. L A3 48
Lopphavet, sea, Nor B9 25
Lora, Sp., 11,864 D3 20
Lora, riv., Afg B3 39
Lorado, Logan, W. Va., 700 D3, D6 123
Lorain, Lorain, Ohio, 68,932 A5 111
Lorain, co., Ohio, 217,500 A5 111
Lorain, Cambria, Pa., 1,324 *F4 114
Loraine, Adams, Ill., 303 C2 90
Loraine, Renville, N. Dak., 54 A4 110
Loraine, Mitchell, Tex., 837 C2 118
Loralai, Pak., 4,437 B2 40
Loramie, res., Ohio B3 111
Loranger, Tangipahoa, La., 60 D5 95
Lorca, Sp., 21,000 (58,641▲) D5 20
Lord Howe, is., Pac. O I9 7
Lordsburg, Hidalgo, N. Mex., 3,436 E1 107
Loreauville, Iberia, La., 655 D4 95
Loreburn, Sask., Can., 302 F2 70
Lore City, Guernsey, Ohio, 458 C6 111
Loree Estates, Santa Clara, Calif., 925 *C5 82
Lorena, Braz., 26,068 C3 56
Lorenz, Upshur, W. Va., 200 B4 123
Lorenzo, Jefferson, Idaho, 200 F7 89
Lorenzo, Cheyenne, Nebr., 100 C2 103
Lorenzo, Crosby, Tex., 1,188 C2 118
Loreto, Arg E3 55
Loreto, Braz., 783 C1 57
Loreto, Col D3 60
Loreto, It., 4,600 C4 21
Loreto, Mex., 1,409 B2 63
Loreto, Par., 11,321 D4 55
Loreto, dept., Peru, 350,306 C3 58
Loretta, Rush, Kans., 60 D4 93
Loretta, Sawyer, Wis., 110 C3 124
Lorette, Man., Can E3 71
Loretteville, Que., Can., 6,522 C6, n17 73
Loretto, Duval, Fla., 200 C6 86
Loretto, Marion, Ky., 500 C4 94
Loretto, Dickinson, Mich., 250 C3 98

Loretto, Boone, Nebr., 100....C7 103
Loretto, Cambria, Pa., 1,338.E4 114
Loretto, Lawrence, Tenn., 929....B4 117
Lorica, Col. 8,420....B2 60
Lorida, Highlands, Fla., 300.E5 86
Lorient, Fr., 60,566 (*77,000)....D2 14
L'Orignal, Ont., Can., 1,189....B10 72
Lorimor, Union, Iowa, 460..C3 92
Loring, Phillips, Mont., 50...B9 102
Loris, Horry, S.C., 1,702...C10 115
Lorlie, Sask., Can., 56....G4 70
Lorman, Jefferson, Miss., 200....D2 100
Lorne, N.B., Can., 890....B3 74
Lorne, firth, Scot....D3 13
Lorne Park, Ont., Can....m14 72
Lorneville, N.B., Can., 666..D3 74
Lorneville, Ont., Can., 51...C5 72
Lörrach, Ger., 30,500....E3 16
Lorraine, Ellsworth, Kans., 157....D5 93
Lorraine, Jefferson, N.Y., 150....B5 108
Lorraine, plat., Fr....F6 15
Lorraine, former prov., Fr., 1,956,000....C6 14
Lorsch, Ger., 8,900....D3 17
Lorton, Otoe, Nebr., 58....D9 103
Lorup, Ger., 1,800....B7 15
Los Alamitos, Orange, Calif., 4,312....*F2 82
Los Alamos, Santa Barbara, Calif., 500....E3 82
Los Alamos, Los Alamos, N. Mex., 13,037....B3 107
Los Alamos, co., N. Mex., 13,037....B3 107
Los Altos, Santa Clara, Calif., 19,696....C5 82
Los Altos Hills, Santa Clara, Calif., 3,412....*C5 82
Los Amates, Guat., 628....C3 62
Los Amigos Privados, Cuba..k11 64
Los Andes, Chile, 19,162....A2 54
Los Angeles, Los Angeles, Calif., 2,479,015 (*6,565,000)....E4, F2 82
Los Angeles, Chile, 33,000...B2 54
Los Angeles, co., Calif., 6,038,771....E4, F2 82
Los Angeles, aqueduct, Calif....E4 82
Losantville (Bronson), Randolph, Ind., 251....D7 91
Los Banos, Merced, Calif., 6,090....D3 82
Los Barrios, Sp., 3,583....D3 20
Los Blancos, Arg....D3 55
Los Caños Central, P.R....B4 65
Los Cerrillos, Arg....A3 54
Los Ebanos, Hidalgo, Tex., 750....F3 118
Los Fresnos, Cameron, Tex., 1,289....F4 118
Los Gatos, Santa Clara, Calif., 9,036....C5, D3 82
Loshan, China, 32,000....F5 34
Loshan, China, 5,000....H6 36
Los Herreras, Mex., 1,421...G3 118
Losinj, isl., Yugo....C2 22
Los Llanos, P.R....C5 65
Los Lunas, Valencia, N. Mex., 1,186....C3 107
Los Mochis, Mex., 37,682...B3 63
Los Molinos, Tehama, Calif., 900....B2 82
Los Muertos, P.R....B4 65
Los Nietos, Los Angeles, Calif., 9,000....*F2 82
Losombo, Con. L....A2 48
Los Padillas, Bernalillo, N. Mex., 1,000....*B3 107
Los Palacios, Cuba, 4,008...D2 64
Los Palacios, Sp., 12,524...D3 20
Los Pinos, Cuba....k11 64
Los Pinos, Rio Arriba, N. Mex., 150....A3 107
Los Pinos, riv., Colo....D3 83
Los Pozos, Chile....E1 55
Los Rábanos, P.R....C3 65
Los Ranchos de Albuquerque, Bernalillo, N. Mex., 2,500....B3, k7 107
Los Reyes, Mex., 9,777.D4, n12 63
Los Reyes [la Paz], Mex., 2,171....h10 63
Los Ríos, prov., Ec., 174,335.B2 58
Los Santos, Pan., 3,165....G7 62
Los Santos, Sp., 9,565....C2 20
Los Sarmientos, Arg....E2 55
Los Sauces, Chile, 2,158....B2 54
Lossiemouth, Scot., 5,855...C5 13
Lössnitz, Ger., 7,786....C7 17
Lost, creek, Wyo....C4 125
Lost, peak, Utah....F2 119
Lost, riv., Ind....G4 91
Lost, riv., Minn....C3 99
Lost, riv., Wash....A5 122
Lost, riv., W. Va....B6 123
Lostant, La Salle, Ill., 460...B4 90
Los Taques, Ven., 8,505....A3 60
Lost Cabin, Fremont, Wyo., 47....B5 125
Lost City, Hardy, W. Va., 75.C6 123
Lost Creek, Harrison, W. Va., 678....B4 123
Los Teques, Ven., 34,874....A4 60
Lost Hills, Kern, Calif., 200.E4 82
Lost Horse, plat., Wash....C4 122
Lostine, Wallowa, Oreg., 240.B9 113
Lost Nation, Clinton, Iowa, 567....C7 92
Lost River, Hardy, W. Va., 30....C6 123
Lost River, cave, Ky....D3 94
Lost River, range, Idaho....E5 89
Lost River Glacial, caverns, N.H.B3 105
Lost Springs, Marion, Kans., 139....D7 93
Lost Springs, Converse, Wyo., 5....C7 125
Lost Trail, pass, Mont....E3 102
Los Trujillos, Valencia, N. Mex., 400....C3 107
Lostwood, Mountrail, N. Dak., 34....A3 110
Los Vigiles, San Miguel, N. Mex., 70....*B5 107
Los Vilos, Chile, 1,305....A2 54
Lot, Ponape....52
Lot, dept., Fr., 149,929....*E4 14
Lot, hbr., Ponape....52
Lot, riv., Fr....E4 14
Lota, Chile, 27,700....B2 54
Lotawana, lake, Mo....B2 101
Lotbinière, Que., Can., 561...C6 73
Lotbinière, co., Que., Can., 30,234....C6 73
Lot-et-Garonne, dept., Fr., 275,028....*E4 14
Lothair, Perry, Ky., 1,082...C6 94
Lothair, Liberty, Mont., 40...B5 102
Loting, China, 10,000....A9 38
Loto, Con. L....B3 48
Lotofaga, W. Sam., 418....52
Lötschberg, tunnel, Switz....D4 19
Lott, Falls, Tex., 924....D4 118
Lotung, Taiwan....G9 34
Lotus Point, Lake, Ill., 1,000....*A5 90
Louann, Ouachita, Ark., 261.D3 81
Loudima, Con. B....F2 46
Loudon, Merrimack, N.H., 350 (1,194▲)....D4 105
Loudon, Loudon, Tenn., 3,812....D9 117
Loudon, co., Tenn., 23,757...D9 117
Loudonville, Albany, N.Y., 7,000....*C7 108
Loudonville, Ashland, Ohio, 2,611....B5 111
Loudoun, co., Va., 24,549...B5 121
Loudun, Fr., 5,587....D4 14
Louetta, Harris, Tex....F5 118
Louga, Sen., 13,200....C1 45
Loughborough, Eng., 38,621.B6 12
Lougheed, Alta., Can., 217...C5 69
Lougheed, isl., N.W. Ter., Can....m31 67
Loughman, Polk, Fla., 250...D5 86
Loughrea, Ire., 2,784....D3 11
Loughros More, bay, Ire....C3 11
Loughton, Eng. (part of Chigwell)....k13 10
Louin, Jasper, Miss., 389....C4 100
Louisa, Lawrence, Ky., 2,071....B7 94
Louisa, Louisa, Va., 576....C5 121
Louisa, co., Iowa, 10,290....C6 92
Louisa, co., Va., 12,959....D5 121
Louisa, lake, Fla....D5 86
Louisbourg, N.S., Can., 1,417....D10 74
Louisburg, Miami, Kans., 862....D9 93
Louisburg, Lac qui Parle, Minn., 91....E2 99
Louisburg, Dallas, Mo., 176...D4 101
Louisburg, Franklin, N.C., 2,862....A5 109
Louisburgh, Ire., 346....D2 11
Louisdale, N.S., Can., 793...D8 74
Louise, Troup, Ga., 120....C2 87
Louise, Humphreys, Miss., 481....B3 100
Louise, Wharton, Tex., 900...E4 118
Louise, Brooke, W. Va., 75...B2 123
Louise, isl., B.C., Can....C2 68
Louise, lake, Alsk....f18 79
Louisiade, arch., Sol. Is....G9 7
Louisiana, Pike, Mo., 4,286.B6 101
Louisiana, state, U.S., 3,257,022....D9 77, 95
Louisiana, pt., La....E2 95
Louis Trichardt, S. Afr., 9,703....B4 49
Louisville, Barbour, Ala., 890....D4 78
Louisville, Que., Can., 4,138.C5 73
Louisville, Boulder, Colo., 2,073....B5 83
Louisville, Jefferson, Ga., 2,413....C4 87
Louisville, Clay, Ill., 906....E5 90
Louisville, Pottawatomie, Kans., 204....C7 93
Louisville, Jefferson, Ky., 390,639 (*735,800)..A4, B4 94
Louisville, Winston, Miss., 5,066....B4 100
Louisville, Cass, Nebr., 1,194....D9, E3 103
Louisville, St. Lawrence, N.Y., 400....f9 108
Louisville, Stark, Ohio, 5,116....B6 111
Louisville, Blount, Tenn., 200....D9, E11 117
Loukhi, Sov. Un....D15 25
Loulé, Port., 6,479....D1 20
Louny, Czech., 12,300....C2 26
Loup, co., Nebr., 1,097....C6 103
Loup, riv., Que., Can....C4 73
Loup, riv., Nebr....C8 103
Loup City, Sherman, Nebr., 1,415....C7 103
Lourdes, Newf., Can., 975...D2 75
Lourdes, Que., Can....C4 73
Lourdes, Que., Can., 174....C6 73
Lourdes, Fr., 16,023....F4 14
Lourenço Marques, Moz., 78,500 (*183,800)....C5 49
Lourenço Marques, prov., Moz....C5 49
Loures, Port., 6,089....f9 20
Lousã, Port., 8,922....B1 20
Lousana, Alta., Can., 74....C4 69
Louth, Eng., 11,556....A8 12
Louth, Ire., 207....D5 11
Louth, co., Ire., 67,378....D5 11
Loutra Aidhipsou, Grc., 5,028....C4 23
Loutrákion (Loutrákion-Perakhóra), Grc., 6,168....h9 23
L'Outre, bayou, La....B3 95
Louvain, see Leuven, Bel.
Louvale, Stewart, Ga., 300...D2 87
Louviers, Douglas, Colo., 500.B6 83
Louviers, Fr., 13,160....C4 14
Louzi, Con. L....B1 48
Lovat, riv., Sov. Un....C8 27
Love, Sask., Can., 155....D3 70
Love, co., Okla., 5,862....D4 112
Love, pt., Md....B5 85
Lovech, Bul., 11,730....D7 22
Lovejoy, St. Clair, Ill., 1,922....*E3 90
Lovelaceville, Ballard, Ky., 200....A2 94
Loveladies, Ocean, N.J., 75.D4 106
Lovelady, Houston, Tex., 466....D5 118
Loveland, Larimer, Colo., 9,734....A5 83
Loveland, Pottawattamie, Iowa, 100....C2 92
Loveland, Hamilton, Warren and Clermont, Ohio, 5,008....C3, D2 111
Loveland, Tillman, Okla., 90....C3 112
Loveland, pass, Colo....B5 83
Loveland Park, Warren, Ohio, 1,000....C2, C3 111
Lovell, Oxford, Maine, 65 (588▲)....D2 96
Lovell, Logan, Okla., 27....A4 112
Lovell, Big Horn, Wyo., 2,451....A4 125
Lovelock, Pershing, Nev., 1,948....C3 104
Lovely, Martin, Ky., 600....C7 94
Loverna, Sask., Can., 145....F1 70
Loves Park, Winnebago, Ill., 9,086....A4 90
Lovett, Laurens, Ga., 61....D4 87
Lovett, Jennings, Ind., 40...G6 91
Lovettsville, Loudoun, Va., 217....B5 121
Lovewell, pond, Maine....D2 96
Lovick, Jefferson, Ala., 250...E5 78
Lovilia, Monroe, Iowa, 630...C5 92
Loving, Eddy, N. Mex., 1,646....E5 107
Loving, co., Tex., 226....D1 118
Lovingston, Nelson, Va., 375.D4 121
Lovington, Moultrie, Ill., 1,200....D5 90
Lovington, Polk, Iowa, 800...A7 92
Lovington, Lea, N. Mex., 9,660....E6 107
Lovisa, Fin., 6,600....G12 25
Lovosice, Czech., 4,962....C9 17
Low, Que., Can., 422....D2 73
Low, cape, N.W. Ter., Can...D15 67
Low, pen., B.C., Can....E5 68
Lowa, Con. L....B4 48
Lowa, riv., Con. L....B4 48
Lowden, Cedar, Iowa, 641...C7 92
Lowe Farm, Man., Can., 310.E3 71
Lowell, Benton, Ark., 277....A1 81
Lowell, Lake, Ind., 2,270....B3 91
Lowell, Middlesex, Mass., 92,107....A5, f10 97
Lowell, Kent, Mich., 2,545...F5 98
Lowell, Kearney, Nebr., 84...D7 103
Lowell, Gaston, N.C., 2,784...B2 109
Lowell, Washington, Ohio, 783....C6 111
Lowell, Lane, Oreg., 503....D4 113
Lowell, Orleans, Vt., 175 (617▲)....B4 120
Lowell, Snohomish, Wash., 1,086....*B3 122
Lowell, Summers, W. Va., 100....D4 123
Lowell, mts., Vt....B4 120
Lowell Thomas, mts., Ant....B5 5
Lowellville, Mahoning, Ohio, 2,055....A7 111
Lower, lake, Nev....B2 104
Lower Arrow, lake, B.C., Can.E8 68
Lower Bank, Burlington, N.J., 200....D3 106
Lower Brule, Lyman, S. Dak., 150....C6 116
Lower Burrell, Westmoreland, Pa., 11,952....*E2 114
Lower Cabot, Washington, Vt., 65....C4 120
Lower California, pen., Mex....B2 63
Lower Caraquet, N.B., Can., 807....*B5 74
Lower East Pubnico, N.S., Can., 114....F4 74
Lower Gilmanton, Belknap, N.H....D4 105
Lower Giuba, dist., Som....E5 47
Lower Hutt, N.Z., 55,900..*N15 51
Lower Island Cove, Newf., Can., 494....D5 75
Lower Lake, Lake, Calif., 550....C2 82
Lower Marlboro, Calvert, Md., 75....C4 85
Lower Matecumbe, key, Fla....H6 86
Lower New York, bay, N.Y..k12 108
Lower Paia, Maui, Haw., 950....C5 88
Lower Peach Tree, Wilcox, Ala., 250....D2 78
Lower Red, lake, Minn....C3 99
Lower Rociada, San Miguel, N. Mex., 50....B4 107
Lower Salem, Washington, Ohio, 143....C6 111
Lower Salmon, dam, Idaho....G4 89
Lower Saxony (Niedersachsen), state, Ger., 6,855,000....A4 17
Lower Southampton, N.B., Can., 40....D2 74
Lower Village, Lamoille, Vt., 100....C3 120
Lower West Pubnico, N.S., Can., 618....F4 74
Lower Woods Harbour, N.S., Can., 574....F4 74
Lowes, Graves, Ky., 200....A2 88
Lowestoft, Eng., 47,100....B9 12
Lowgap, Newton, Ark., 10...A2 81
Lowgap, Surry, N.C., 250....A3 109
Lowicz, Pol., 14,400....B5 26
Lowland, Pamlico, N.C., 500.B7 109
Lowman, Boise, Idaho, 100...E3 89
Lowmansville, Lawrence, Ky., 300....C7 94
Low Moor, Clinton, Iowa, 343....C7 92
Lowmoor, Alleghany, Va.,....D3 121
Lowndes, Wayne, Mo., 150...D7 101
Lowndes, co., Ala., 15,417...C3 78
Lowndes, co., Ga., 49,270....F3 87
Lowndes, co., Miss., 46,639..B5 100
Lowndesboro, Lowndes, Ala., 250....C3 78
Lowndesville, Abbeville, S.C., 274....C2 115
Lowry, Pope, Minn., 294....E3 99
Lowry, Walworth, S. Dak., 44....B6 116
Lowry City, St. Clair, Mo., 437....C4 101
Lowrys, Chester, S.C., 298...B5 115
Lowryville, Hardin, Tenn....B3 117
Low Tatra, mts., Czech....D5 26
Lowville, Lewis, N.Y., 3,616.B5 108
Low Water, lake, Alta., Can....C3 69
Loxley, Baldwin, Ala., 831....E2 78
Loxton, Austl., 2,321....G3 51
Loyal, Kingfisher, Okla., 87..B3 112
Loyal, Clark, Wis., 1,146....D3 124
Loyalhanna, Westmoreland, Pa., 1,000....*F3 114
Loyalist, Alta., Can....D5 69
Loyall, Harlan, Ky., 1,260...D6 94
Loyalsock, creek, Pa....D8 114
Loyalton, Sierra, Calif., 936...C3 82
Loyalton, Edmunds, S. Dak., 34....B6 116
Loyalty, is., Pac. O....H10 7
Loyang, China, 171,200....G5 36
Loysburg, Bedford, Pa., 200...F5 114
Loysville, Perry, Pa., 500....F7 114
Lozeau, Mineral, Mont., 15...C2 102
Lozère, dept., Fr., 81,868....*E5 14
Loznica, Yugo., 10,611....C4 22
Lozva, riv., Sov. Un....C21 9
Lozovatka, Sov. Un., 10,000.G9 27
Lozovaya, Sov. Un., 10,000.G11 27
Lozoya, canal, Sp....o17 20
Lualaba (Congo), riv., Con. L....B4 48
Lualualei, Honolulu, Haw., 2,100....g9 88
Luama, riv., Con. L....B4 48
Luampa, Zambia....E3 48
Luan, riv., China....C8 34
Luana, Clayton, Iowa, 276...A6 92
Luanda, Ang., 225,000....C1 48
Luanda, dist., Ang., 347,173.C1 48
Luang Prabang, Laos, 25,000....C5 38
Luanguinga, riv., Ang., Zambia....D3 48
Luangwa, riv., Zambia....D5 48
Luanshya, Zambia, 72,100...D4 48
Luarca, Sp., 4,233....A2 20
Luashi, Con. L....D3 48
Lubaczow, Pol., 4,986....C7 26
Luban, Pol., 11,100....C3 26
Lubang, Phil., 3,149....p13 35
Lubang, is., Phil....C6 35
Lubao, Phil., 1,810....o13 35
Lubartow, Pol., 5,542....C7 26
Lubawa, Pol., 4,679....B5 26
Lübbecke, Ger., 10,500....A3 17
Lübben, Ger., 9,433....B8 17
Lübbenau, Ger., 12,000....B8 17
Lubbock, Lubbock, Tex., 128,691 (*144,300)....C2 118
Lubbock, co., Tex., 156,271.C2 118
Lubec, Washington, Maine, 1,289 (2,684▲)....D6 96
Lübeck, Ger., 237,500....B5 16, E4 24
Lübeck, bay, Ger....B5 16
Lubefu, Con. L....B3 48
Lubero, Con. L....B4 48
Lubicon, lake, Alta., Can....A3 69
Lubilash, riv., Con. L....C3 48
Lubin, Pol., 1,769....C4 26
Lublin, Pol., 192,600....C7 26
Lublin, Taylor, Wis., 160....C3 124
Lubliniec, Pol., 12,400....C5 26
Lubny, Sov. Un., 10,000....F9 27
Lubrín, Sp., 5,417....D4 20
Lubsko, Pol., 10,700....C3 26
Lübtheen, Ger., 5,707....E5 24
Lubudi, Con. L., 7,900....C4 48
Lubudi, riv., Con. L....D3 48
Lubue, Con. L....B2 48
Lubutu, Con. L....B4 48
Lucama, Wilson, N.C., 498...B5 109
Lucan, Ont., Can., 986....D3 72
Lucan, Ire., 1,657....D5 11
Lucan, Redwood, Minn., 216....F3 99
Lucania, see Basilicata, reg., It.
Lucania, mtn., Yukon, Can....D4 66
Lucas, Lucas, Iowa, 357....C4 92
Lucas, Russell, Kans., 559...C5 93
Lucas, Barren, Ky., 150....D3 94
Lucas, Missaukee, Mich., 100....D5 98
Lucas, Richland, Ohio, 719...B5 111
Lucas, Gregory, S. Dak., 24...D6 116
Lucas, co., Iowa, 10,923....C4 92
Lucas, co., Ohio, 456,931....A4 111
Lucasville, Scioto, Ohio, 1,277....D3 111
Lucca, It., 89,500....C3 21
Lucca, Barnes, N. Dak., 37...C8 110
Lucé, Fr., 6,555....C4 14
Luce, co., Mich., 7,827....B5 98
Luce, bay, Scot....F4 13
Lucea, Jam., 2,798....F4 64
Lucedale, George, Miss., 1,977....E5 100
Lucena, Phil., 40,652 (49,264▲)....C6, p13 35
Lucena, Sp., 19,400....D3 20
Lucena del Cid, Sp., 3,585...B5 20
Lucenec, Czech., 16,100....D5 26
Lucera, It., 24,500 (28,409▲)....D5 21
Lucerne, Lake, Calif., 402...C4 82
Lucerne, Weld, Colo., 75....A6 83
Lucerne, Cass, Ind., 215....C5 91
Lucerne, Putnam, Mo., 157...A4 101
Lucerne, see Luzern, Switz.
Lucerne, Hot Springs, Wyo., 25....B4 125
Lucerne, lake, Switz....B5 19
Lucernemines, Indiana, Pa., 1,524....E3 114
Lucerne Valley, San Bernardino, Calif., 900....E5 82
Lucero, Cuba....h12 64
Luceville, Que., Can., 1,419....A9 73
Luchi, China, 10,000....J4 36
Lüchow, Ger., 5,900....F5 24
Luchuan, China, 5,000....G7 34
Lucien, Franklin, Miss., 150....D3 100
Lucien, Noble, Okla., 100...A4 112
Lucile, Miller, Ga., 60....E2 87
Lucile, Idaho, Idaho, 20....D2 89
Lucin, Box Elder, Utah, 15...B2 119
Lucinda, Clarion, Pa., 300...D3 114
Lucipara, is., Indon....G7 35
Lucira, Ang....D1 48
Luck, Madison, N.C., 100...D3 109
Luck, Polk, Wis., 853....C1 124
Luck, lake, Sask., Can....F2 70
Luckau, Ger., 6,145....B8 17
Luckenwalde, Ger., 28,600...A8 17
Luckey, Wood, Ohio, 946....A2, A4 111
Lucknow, Ont., Can., 1,031....D3 72
Lucknow, India, 595,440 (*675,000)....C7 39, D8 40
Lucknow, Dauphin, Pa., 900....*F8 114
Lucky Lake, Sask., Can., 426....G2 70
Lucky Peak, res., Idaho....F2 89
Lucky Strike, Alta., Can....E5 69
Luçon, Fr., 7,599....D3 14
Lucy, St. John the Baptist, La., 725....B6 95
Lucy, Shelby, Tenn., 130....B2, E8 117
Luda Kamchiya, riv., Bul....D8 22
Ludden, Dickey, N. Dak., 59....C7 110
Ludell, Rawlins, Kans., 105.C3 93
Lüdenscheid, Ger., 58,700...B2 17
Lüderitz, S.W. Afr., 2,836...C2 49
Lüderitz, bay, S.W. Afr....C1 49
Ludgate, Ont., Can....B4 72
Ludhiana, India, 244,032....B6 39, B5 40
Lüdinghausen, Ger., 9,500...B2 17
Ludington, Mason, Mich., 9,421....E4 98
Ludlam, Dade, Fla., 20,000.*G6 86
Ludlow, San Bernardino, Calif., 250....E5 82
Ludlow, N.B., Can., 240....C3 74
Ludlow, Las Animas, Colo., 20....D6 83
Ludlow, Eng., 6,774....B5 12
Ludlow, Champaign, Ill., 460.C5 90
Ludlow, Kenton, Ky., 6,233...A7 94
Ludlow, Aroostook, Maine, 25 (274▲)....B4 96
Ludlow, Hampden, Mass., 11,500 (13,805▲)....B3 97
Ludlow, Scott, Miss., 40....C4 100
Ludlow, Livingston, Mo., 235....B4 101
Ludlow, McKean, Pa., 800...C4 114
Ludlow, Harding, S. Dak., 10.B2 116
Ludlow, Windsor, Vt., 1,658 (2,386▲)....E3 120
Ludlow, mtn., Vt....E3 120
Ludlow Center, Hampden, Mass., 400....*B3 97
Ludlow Falls, Miami, Ohio, 273....C3 111
Ludowici, Long, Ga., 1,578...E5 87
Ludvika, Swe., 12,300 (*18,000)....G6 25
Ludwigs, canal, Ger....D6 17
Ludwigsburg, Ger., 75,000...E4 17
Ludwigshafen, Ger., 172,100.D3 17
Ludwigslust, Ger., 12,000...B5 16
Luebo, Con. L....C3 48
Lueders, Jones, Tex., 654....C3 118
Luepa, Ven....B5 60
Lufkin, Angelina, Tex., 17,641....D5 118
Lufuna, Con. L....C2 48
Luga, Sov. Un., 43,000....B7 27
Luga, riv., Sov. Un....B7 27
Lugagnano Val d'Arda, It., 6,240....E5 18
Lugan, riv., Sov. Un....q22 27
Luganchik, riv., Sov. Un....q22 27
Lugano, Switz., 18,300 (*42,400)....D6 19
Lugano, lake, Switz....E6 19
Lugansk, Sov. Un., 314,000....G12, q22 27
Lugau, Ger., 10,600....C7 17
Lugela, riv., Moz....A6 49
Lugenda, riv., Moz....D6 48
Lugert, Kiowa, Okla., 20....C2 112
Lugh Ferrandi, Som., 2,800...E5 47
Lugnaquilla, mtn., Ire....E5 11
Lugo, It., 12,800....B3 21
Lugo, Sp., 45,497 (58,264▲).A2 20
Lugo, prov., Sp., 479,530...*A2 20
Lugoff, Kershaw, S.C., 200...C6 115
Lugoj, Rom., 30,258....C5 22
Lugovoy, Sov. Un....E8 29
Luho, China....E5 34
Luhsien, China, 289,000....F6 34
Luichow, China, 158,800....G6 34
Luichow, pen., China....G6 34
Luing, isl., Scot....D3 13
Luis Correia, Braz., 1,523...B2 57
Luis Gomes, Braz., 1,480....C3 57
Luis Lopez, Socorro, N. Mex., 100....D3 107
Luitpold, mtn., N. Gui....k12 50
Luiza, Con. L....C3 48
Luján, Arg., 19,001....g7 54
Luján [de Cuyo], Arg., 3,542.A3 54
Lukachukai, Apache, Ariz., 20....A6 80
Luke, Allegany, Md., 587....D1 85
Lukenie, riv., Con. L....B2 48
Lukeville, Pima, Ariz., 30....F3 80
Lukolela, Con. L....B2 48
Lukovit, Bul., 7,755....D7 22
Lukow, Pol., 8,513....C7 26
Lukoyanov, Sov. Un., 5,000.D15 27
Lukuga, riv., Con. L....C4 48
Lukulu, Zambia....D3 48
Lula, Hall, Ga., 557....B3 87
Lula, Coahoma, Miss., 484...A3 100
Lula, Pontotoc, Okla., 55....C5 112
Lula, Chester, Tenn....B3 117
Luleå, Swe., 32,300....E10 25
Luleälven, riv., Swe....D9 25
Luling, St. Charles, La., 2,122....C7 95
Luling, Caldwell, Tex., 4,412....B4, E4 118
Lulu, Columbia, Fla., 152....B4 86
Lulua, riv., Con. L....C3 48
Luluabourg, Con. L., 115,000....C3 48
Lulung, China....E8 36
Lum, Lapeer, Mich., 265....E7 98
Lumba, Con. L....A2 48
Lumber, Darlington, S.C....C8 115
Lumber, riv., N.C....C5 109
Lumber Bridge, Robeson, N.C., 100....C4 109
Lumber City, Telfair, Ga., 1,360....E4 87
Lumberport, Harrison, W. Va., 1,031....A6, B4 123
Lumberton, Lamar, Miss., 2,108....D4 100
Lumberton, Burlington, N.J., 700....D3 106
Lumberton, Rio Arriba, N. Mex., 190....A3 107
Lumberton, Robeson, N.C., 15,305....C5 109
Lumbo, Moz....D7 48
Lumby, B.C., Can., 842....D8 68
Luminao, reef, Guam....52
Lummi, Indian res., Wash....A3 122
Lumpkin, Stewart, Ga., 1,348.D2 87
Lumpkin, co., Ga., 7,241....B2 87
Lumsden, Newf., Can., 269.D5 75
Lumsden, Sask., Can., 685...G3 70
Lumsden, N.Z., 666....P12 51
Lumsden, Scot....C6 13
Lumsden Beach, Sask., Can., 9....G3 70
Lumut, mtn., Indon....F6 35
Lumut, pt., Indon....F3 35
Luna, Catron, N. Mex., 250.D1 107
Luna, co., N. Mex., 9,839....E2 107
Lunan, bay, Scot....D6 13
Luna Pier (Lakewood), Monroe, Mich., 1,815....G7 98
Lund, B.C., Can., 198....D5 68
Lund, Caribou, Idaho, 10....G7 89
Lund, White Pine, Nev., 375.E6 104
Lund, Swe., 41,700....J5 25
Lund, Iron, Utah, 25....E2 119
Lunda, dist., Ang., 247,449.C2 48
Lundale, Logan, W. Va., 500....D3, D5 123
Lundar, Man., Can., 713....D2 71
Lundazi, Zambia....D5 48
Lundbreck, Alta., Can., 112..E3 69
Lundby, Den., 549....C5 24
Lundby, Swe....t34 25
Lundell, Phillips, Ark., 150..C5 81
Lunderskov, Den., 1,181....C3 24
Lundu, Mala., 768....E3 35
Lundy, isl., Eng....C3 12
Lune, riv., Eng....F6 13
Lüneburg, Ger., 60,800....B5 16
Lunel, Fr., 7,758....F6 14
Lünen, Ger., 72,200....B2 17
Lunenburg, N.S., Can., 3,056....E5 74
Lunenburg, Worcester, Mass., 1,000 (6,334▲)....A4 97
Lunenburg, Essex, Vt., 200 (1,237▲)....C5 120
Lunenburg, Lunenburg, Va., 40....E5 121
Lunenburg, co., N.S., Can., 34,998....E5 74
Lunenburg, co., Va., 12,523.E4 121
Lunéville, Fr., 21,618....C7 14
Lung, China....G2 36
Lungchen, China, 1,000....B3 37
Lungchi, China, 81,200....G8 34
Lungchuan, China, 12,000..J8 36
Lungchuchai, China....H4 36
Lungshi, China....E5 34
Lungkou, China....F9 36
Lungping, China....F6 36
Lungtsin, China....G6 34
Lungué-Bungo, riv., Ang., Zambia....D3 48
Luni, riv., India....E3 40
Lunino, Sov. Un., 10,000..E15 27
Luning, Mineral, Nev., 55....E3 104
Lunyama, Con. L....C4 48
Lup, Thai., 6,940....D5 38
Lupani, Rh....A4 49
Lupei, China, 1,000....B9 36
Lupeni, Rom., 21,188....C6 22
Lupin, see Manchouli, China.
Lupton, Apache, Ariz., 250..B6 80
Lupton, Ogemaw, Mich., 100....D6 98
Lupton City, Hamilton, Tenn., 250....E10 117
Lupus, Moniteau, Mo., 75..C5 101
Luque, Par., 22,469....E4 55
Luquillo, P.R., 2,107....B8, f12 65
Luquillo, mun., P.R., 8,582....B8, f12 65
Luquillo, mts., P.R....B7 65
Luray, Russell, Kans., 328..C5 93
Luray, Clark, Mo., 154....A6 101
Luray, Hampton, S.C., 102..F5 115
Luray, Henderson, Tenn., 100....B3 117
Luray, Page, Va., 3,014....C4 121
Lure, Fr., 6,408....D7 14
Lurgan, N. Ire., 17,873....C5 11
Luribay, Bol., 392....C2 55
Lurín, Peru, 2,141....D2 58
Lúrio, Moz....D7 48
Lurio, riv., Moz....D6 48
Lurton, Newton, Ark., 100..B2 81
Lusaka, Zambia, 114,400....E4 48
Lusambo, Con. L., 9,800....B3 48
Lusby, Calvert, Md., 75....D5 85
Luscar, Alta., Can....C2 69
Luseland, Sask., Can., 665..E1 70
Lushan, China....H5 36
Lushnje, Alb., 8,585....*B3 23
Lushoto, Tan., 1,270....B6 48
Lushton, York, Nebr., 45....D8 103
Lushun, see Port Arthur, China
Lusignan, Fr., 1,376....D4 14
Lusk, Throckmorton, Tex....C3 118
Lusk, Niobrara, Wyo., 1,890.C8 125
Lustre, Valley, Mont., 10....B11 102
Lutcher, St. James, La., 3,274....B6, D5 95
Lutesville, Bollinger, Mo., 658....D8 101
Luther, Lake, Mich., 325....D5 98
Luther, Carbon, Mont., 15....E7 102
Luther, Oklahoma, Okla., 517....B4 112
Luther, Hancock, Tenn....C10 117
Luthersville, Meriwether, Ga., 282....C2 87
Lutherville, Baltimore, Md., 12,265....B4 85
Luting, China....F5 34
Lütjenburg, Ger., 4,400....D4 24
Luton, Eng., 136,400 (*180,000)....C7 12
Luton, Woodbury, Iowa, 130.B1 92
Lutsen, Cook, Minn., 30....B6 99
Lutsk, Sov. Un., 69,000....F5 27
Luttrell, Union, Tenn., 600.C10 117
Lutts, Wayne, Tenn., 350....B4 117
Lutugino, Sov. Un., 5,000...q22 27
Lutz, Hillsborough, Fla., 700....D4 86
Lützow-Holm, bay, Ant....C16 5
Luverne, Crenshaw, Ala., 2,238....D3 78
Lu Verne, Kossuth and Humboldt, Iowa, 468....B3 92
Luverne, Rock, Minn., 4,249.G2 99
Luverne, Steele, N. Dak., 109.B8 110
Luvua, riv., Con. L....C4 48
Luwingu, Zambia, 540....D5 48
Luwuk, Indon....F6 35
Luxapalila, creek, Ala....B2 78
Luxembourg, Lux., 73,900..E6 15
Luxembourg, country, Eur., 332,000....F10 8, E6 15
Luxembourg, prov., Bel., 216,848....E5 15
Luxemburg, Dubuque, Iowa, 159....B6 92
Luxemburg, Kewaunee, Wis., 730....D6 124
Luxeuil-les-Bains, Fr., 8,161.D7 14
Luxomni, Gwinnett, Ga., 180....A5 87
Luxor, see Al Uqṣur, Eg., U.A.R.
Luxora, Mississippi, Ark., 1,236....B6 81
Luyanó, Cuba....h12 64
Luz, Braz., 5,633....E1 51
Luza, riv., Sov. Un....A3 29
Luzern, Switz., 72,600 (*139,000)....B5 19
Luzern, canton, Switz., 253,446....B5 19
Luzerne, Oscoda, Mich., 75..D6 98
Luzerne, Luzerne, Pa., 5,118.B8 114
Luzerne, co., Pa., 346,972..D9 114
Luznice, riv., Czech....D3 26
Luzon, isl., Phil....B6, O13 35
Lvov, Sov. Un., 469,000....D8 24, G5 27
Lwanhsien, China....E8 34

Lwow, see Lvov, Sov. Un.
Lwowek Slaskie, Pol., 3,364..C3 26
Lyakhov, is., Sov. Un.....B36 4
Lyall, mtn., N.Z.....P11 51
Lyallpur, Pak., 425,248.....B5 38, B4 40
Lyaskovets, Bul., 5,560.....D7 22
Lybster, Scot.....B5 13
Lychen, Ger., 3,649.....E7 24
Lycksele, Swe., 5,800.....E8 25
Lycoming, Oswego, N.Y., 180.....B4 108
Lycoming, co., Pa., 109,367..D7 114
Lycoming, creek, Pa.....D7 114
Lydenburg, S. Afr., 7,393.....C5 49
Lydia, Washington, Md.....A2 85
Lydia, Darlington, S.C., 200.C7 115
Lydia Mills, Laurens, S.C., 1,177.....*C4 115
Lydick, St. Joseph, Ind., 1,217.....A5 91
Lyell, isl., B.C., Can.....C2 68
Lyell, mtn., Alta., B.C., Can...D2 69
Lyerly, Chattooga, Ga., 409..B1 87
Lyford, Parke, Ind., 400.....E3 91
Lyford, Willacy, Tex., 1,554.F4 118
Lygnern, lake, Swe.....A6 24
Lykens, Dauphin, Pa., 2,527..E8 114
Lykesland, Richland, S.C., 35.....D6 115
Lyle, Mower, Minn., 607.....G6 99
Lyle, Klickitat, Wash., 400..D4 122
Lyles, Hickman, Tenn., 500..B4 117
Lyleton, Man., Can., 123.....E1 71
Lyman, Harrison, Miss., 225.....E2, E4 100
Lyman, Scotts Bluff, Nebr., 626.....C1 103
Lyman, Grafton, N.H., 25 (201▲).....B3 105
Lyman, Osage, Okla., 30.....A5 112
Lyman, Spartanburg, S.C., 1,261.....B3 115
Lyman, Lyman, S. Dak., 18..D6 116
Lyman, Wayne, Utah, 170...E4 119
Lyman, Skagit, Wash., 400..A3 122
Lyman, Uinta, Wyo., 425...D2 125
Lyman, co., S. Dak., 4,428..D6 116
Lyman, res., Ariz.....C6 80
Lyme, New London, Conn., 500.....D7 84
Lyme (Town of), New London, Conn. (1,183▲).....*D7 84
Lyme, Grafton, N.H., 250 (1,026▲).....C2 105
Lyme, bay, Eng.....D4 12
Lyme Center, Grafton, N.H., 75.....C2 105
Lymington, Eng., 28,642.....D6 12
Lyna, riv., Pol., Sov. Un.....B6 26
Lynas, pt., Wales.....A3 12
Lynbrook, Nassau, N.Y., 19,881.....G2 84
Lynch, Harlan, Ky., 3,810...D7 94
Lynch, Kent, Md., 150.....B5 85
Lynch, Boyd, Nebr., 409.....B7 103
Lynchburg, Highland, Ohio, 1,022.....C4 111
Lynchburg, Lee, S.C., 544...C7 115
Lynchburg, Moore, Tenn., 396.....B5 117
Lynchburg (Independent City), Va., 54,790.....D3 121
Lynches, riv., S.C.....D8 115
Lynch Station, Campbell, Va., 400.....D3 121
Lynd, Lyon, Minn., 259.....F3 99
Lynde, pt., Conn.....D7 84
Lyndeboro, Hillsboro, N.H., 25 (594▲).....E3 105
Lynden, Ont., Can., 532...*D4 72
Lynden, Whatcom, Wash., 2,542.....A3 122
Lyndhurst, Ont., Can., 192..C8 72
Lyndhurst, Bergen, N.J., 21,867.....h8 106
Lyndhurst, Cuyahoga, Ohio, 16,805.....B2 111
Lyndon, Whiteside, Ill., 677..B4 90
Lyndon, Osage, Kans., 953..D8 93
Lyndon, Jefferson, Ky., 5,000.....A4 94
Lyndon, Caledonia, Vt., 350 (3,425▲).....B4 120
Lyndon Center, Caledonia, Vt., 274.....B4 120
Lyndon Station, Juneau, Wis., 335.....E4 124
Lyndonville, Orleans, N.Y., 755.....B2 108
Lyndonville, Caledonia, Vt., 1,477.....B5 120
Lyndora, Butler, Pa., 5,700..E2 114
Lyngby, Den., 63,712.....C6 24
Lynhurst, Marion, Ind., 183.H7 91
Lynn, Winston, Ala., 531.....A2 78
Lynn, Lawrence, Ark., 200..A4 81
Lynn, Randolph, Ind., 1,260.D8 91
Lynn, Essex, Mass., 94,478.....B6, g12 97
Lynn, Susquehanna, Pa., 75.....C10 114
Lynn, co., Tex., 10,914.....C2 119
Lynn, canal, Alsk.....k22 79
Lynn, lake, W. Va.....B5 123
Lynn Creek, B.C., Can.....f12 68
Lynndyl, Millard, Utah, 145.D3 119
Lynne, Marion, Fla., 200.....C5 86
Lynnfield, Essex, Mass., 8,398.....f11 97
Lynn Garden, Sullivan, Tenn., 5,261.....*C11 117
Lynn Grove, Calloway, Ky., 200.....B3 94
Lynn Haven, Bay, Fla., 3,078.....G3 86
Lynnhaven, Princess Anne, Va., 350.....B7, E6 121
Lynnhaven Roads, hbr., Va.....B7 121
Lynn Lake, Man., Can., 1,881.....A1, f7 71
Lynnport, Lehigh, Pa., 100.E10 114
Lynnview, Jefferson, Ky., 1,711.....*B4 94
Lynnville, Warrick, Ind., 409.....H3 91
Lynnville, Jasper, Iowa, 411..C5 92
Lynnville, Graves, Ky., 130..B2 94
Lynnville, Giles, Tenn., 362..B5 117
Lynton, Eng., 1,198.....C4 12
Lynnwood, Fayette, Pa., 2,230.....*F2 114
Lynnwood, Luzerne, Pa., 1,200.....*D10 114
Lynnwood, Snohomish, Wash., 7,207.....*B3 122
Lynwood, Los Angeles, Calif., 31,614.....F2 82
Lynxville, Crawford, Wis., 183.....E2 124
Lyø, isl., Den.....C4 24
Lyon (Lyons), Fr., 528,535 (*920,000).....E6 14
Lyon, Coahoma, Miss., 393..A3 100
Lyon, co., Iowa, 14,468.....A1 92
Lyon, co., Kans., 26,928.....D7 93
Lyon, co., Ky., 5,924.....C1 94
Lyon, co., Minn., 22,655.....F3 99
Lyon, co., Nev., 6,143.....D2 104
Lyon, mtn., N.Y.....f11 108
Lyon, riv., Scot.....D4 13
Lyon Mountain, Clinton, N.Y., 900.....f11 108
Lyonnais, former prov., Fr., 1,621,000.....E6 14
Lyons, Boulder, Colo., 706...A5 83
Lyons (Lyon), Fr., 528,535 (*920,000).....E6 14
Lyons, Toombs, Ga., 3,219..D4 87
Lyons, Cook, Ill., 9,936.....F3 90
Lyons, Greene, Ind., 651.....G3 91
Lyons, Rice, Kans., 4,592.....D5 93
Lyons, Ionia, Mich., 687.....F6 98
Lyons, Burt, Nebr., 972.....C9 103
Lyons, Somerset, N.J., 200...B3 106
Lyons, Wayne, N.Y., 4,673.....B3 108
Lyons, Fulton, Ohio, 590.....A3 111
Lyons, Linn, Oreg., 463.....C4 113
Lyons, Minnehaha, S. Dak., 95.....D9 116
Lyons, Burleson, Tex., 500...D4 118
Lyons, Walworth, Wis., 400..F1 124
Lyons, creek, Kans.....D7 93
Lyons Falls, Lewis, N.Y., 887.....B5 108
Lyons Plains, Fairfield, Conn., 800.....*E3 84
Lyracrompane, Ire.....E2 11
Lys, riv., Bel., Fr.....D2, D3 15
Lysa, Czech., 6,500.....n18 26
Lysaya Gora, Sov. Un., 10,000.....G8 27
Lysekil, Swe., 7,800.....H4 25
Lysite, Fremont, Wyo., 70.....B5 125
Lysogory, mts., Pol.....C6 26
Lyss, Switz., 5,616.....B3 19
Lyster Station, Que., Can., 912.....C6 73
Lysva, Sov. Un., 76,000.....B5 29
Lytham, Eng., 36,222.....A5 12
Lytle, Atascosa, Tex., 798.....E3 118
Lytton, B.C., Can., 422.....D7 68
Lytton, Sac and Calhoun, Iowa, 376.....B3 92
Lyubar, Sov. Un., 10,000...G6 27
Lyubertsy, Sov. Un., 100,000.....n17 27

M

Ma'ād, Jordan, 1,000.....B7 32
Maalaea, Maui, Haw., 200...C5 88
Maalaea, bay, Haw.....C5 88
Ma'ale Aqrabim (Scorpion Pass), pass, Isr.....D7 32
Maam Cross, Ire.....D2 11
Ma'ān, Jordan, 4,509.....G10 31
Maas, Ire.....C3 11
Maas, riv., Neth.....C5 15
Maaseik, Bel., 8,068.....C5 15
Maastricht, Neth., 94,200 (*122,000).....D5 15
Mab, Allen, La.....D3 95
Mabana, Island, Wash., 75..A3 122
Mabank, Kaufman, Tex., 944.....C4 118
Mabber, cape, Som.....D6 47
Mabe, Scott, Va.....B2 121
Mabel, Fillmore, Minn., 815.....G7 99
Mabel, lake, B.C., Can.....D8 68
Mabelvale, Pulaski, Ark., 550.....D5 81
Maben, Jefferson, Ala., 25.....E4 78
Maben, Oktibbeha and Webster, Miss., 696.....B4 100
Maberly, Ont., Can., 91.....C8 72
Mabie, Randolph, W. Va., 400.....C5 123
Mablethorpe, Eng., 5,389.....A8 12
Mableton, Cobb, Ga., 7,127..A4 87
Mabote, Moz.....B5 49
Mabou, N.S., Can., 293.....C8 74
Mabrous (Well), Niger.....B7 45
Mabscott, Raleigh, W. Va., 1,591.....D3, D7 123
Mabton, Yakima, Wash., 958.C5 122
Macachín, Arg.....B4 54
McAdam, N.B., Can., 2,472..D2 74
McAdams, Attala, Miss., 200.....B4 100
McAdenville, Gaston, N.C., 748.....*B2 109
McAdoo, Schuylkill, Pa., 3,560.....E9 114
McAdoo, Dickens, Tex., 100.C2 118
Macaé, Braz., 19,830.....C4 56
McAfee, De Kalb, Ga., 3,000.....*C2 87
McAfee, Leake, Miss., 100...C4 100
McAfee, Sussex, N.J., 250.....A3 106
Macaíba, Braz., 7,472.....g6 57
Macalelon, Phil., 2,018.....p14 35
McAlester, Pittsburg, Okla., 17,419.....C6 112
McAlester, lake, Okla.....B6 112
Macalister, B.C., Can., 175..C6 68
McAlister, Quay, N. Mex., 10.....C6 107
McAlisterville, Juniata, Pa., 600.....E7 114
McAllen, Hidalgo, Tex., 32,728.....F3 118
McAllister, Madison, Mont., 10.....E5 102
McAlmont, Pulaski, Ark.....D6 81
McAlpin, Suwannee, Fla., 50.....B4 86
MacAlpine, lake, N.W. Ter., Can.....C12 66
Macamic, Que., Can., 1,614.....*h12 73
McAndrews, Pike, Ky., 600..C7 94
Macao, Macao, 153,630 (*169,299).....G7 34
Macao, Port. dep., Asia, 175,000.....G7 34
Macapá, Braz., 27,585.....B4 59
Macará, Ec., 2,702.....B2 58
McArthur, Vinton, Ohio, 1,529.....C5 111
MacArthur (Ormoc), Phil., 13,640 (62,764▲).....*C6 50
Macas, Ec., 1,079.....B2 58
Macassar (Makasar), Indon., 367,882.....G5 35
Macau, Braz., 11,876.....C3 57
McAuley, Man., Can., 199...D1 71
McBain, Missaukee, Mich., 551.....D5 98
McBaine, Boone, Mo., 40.....C5 101
McBean, Richmond, Ga., 100.....C5 87
McBee, Chesterfield, S.C., 512.....C7 115
Macbeth, Berkeley, S.C., 80..E8 115
McBride, B.C., Can., 590.....C7 68
McBride, Perry, Mo., 90.....D8 101
McCabe, Roosevelt, Mont., 30.....B12 102
McCain, Hoke, N.C.....B4 109
McCall, Valley, Idaho, 1,423.E2 89
McCall, Ascension, La., 130.....B5, D4 95
McCalla, Jefferson, Ala., 800.E4 78
McCall Creek, Franklin, Miss., 169.....D3 100
McCallsburg, Story, Iowa, 272.....B4 92
McCamey, Upton, Tex., 3,375.....D1 118
McCammon, Bannock, Idaho, 557.....G6 89
Maccan, N.S., Can., 300.....D5 74
McCanna, Grand Forks, N Dak., 80.....A8 110
Maccarese, It., 4,000.....h8 21
McCarthy, Alsk., 12.....C11 79
McCartney, mtn., Mont.....E4 102
McCartys, Valencia, N. Mex., 200.....B2 107
McCaskill, Hempstead, Ark., 62.....D2 81
McCauley, isl., B.C., Can.....C2 68
McCauley, Fisher, Tex., 125.C2 118
McCaysville, Fannin, Ga., 1,871.....B2 87
McChesneytown, Westmoreland, Pa., 1,140.....*F3 114
McClain, co., Okla., 12,740..B4 112
McClave, Bent, Colo., 90.....C8 83
McCleary, Grays Harbor, Wash., 1,115.....B2 122
McClelland, Woodruff, Ark., 65.....B4 81
McClelland, Pottawattamie, Iowa, 150.....C2 92
McClellanville, Charleston, S.C., 354.....F9 115
Macclenny, Baker, Fla., 2,671.....B4 86
Macclesfield, Eng., 38,000.....A5 12
Macclesfield, Edgecombe, N.C., 473.....B6 109
M'Clintock, chan., N.W. Ter., Can.....B12 66
McClintock, mtn., Ant.....A28 5
McCloud, Suskiyou, Calif., 2,140.....B2 82
Maccluer, gulf, W. Irian.....F8 35
McClure, Alexander, Ill., 400.....F4 90
McClure, Henry, Ohio, 651..A4 111
McClure, Snyder, Pa., 1,001..E7 114
McClure, Dickenson, Va., 500.....B2 121
M'Clure, strait, N.W. Ter., Can.....B9 66
McClusky, Sheridan, N. Dak., 751.....B5 110
McColl, Marlboro, S.C., 2,479.....B8 115
McComas, Mercer, W. Va., 950.....D3 123
McComb, Pike, Miss., 12,020.....D3 100
McComb, Hancock, Ohio, 1,176.....A4 111
McConaughy, lake, Nebr.....C4 103
McCondy, Chickasaw, Miss., 125.....B5 100
McCone, co., Mont., 3,321..C11 102
McConnell, Stephenson, Ill., 225.....A4 90
McConnell, Obion, Tenn., 50.....A3 117
McConnells, York, S.C., 266.B5 115
McConnellsburg, Fulton, Pa., 1,245.....G6 114
McConnellstown, Huntington, Pa., 325.....F5 114
McConnelsville, Morgan, Ohio, 2,257.....C6 111
McCook, Red Willow, Nebr., 8,301.....D5 103
McCook, co., S. Dak., 8,268..D8 116
McCook Lake, Union, S. Dak., 500.....E9 116
McCool, Attala, Miss., 211...B4 100
McCoole, Allegany, Md., 368.....D2 85
McCool Junction, York, Nebr., 246.....D8 103
McCord, Sask., Can., 135.....H2 70
McCordsville, Hancock, Ind., 350.....E6 91
McCorkle, Lincoln, W. Va., 300.....C3, C5 123
McCormick, McCormick, S.C., 1,998.....D3 115
McCormick, co., S.C., 8,629.....D3 115
McCoy, Eagle, Colo., 25.....B4 83
McCoysville, Juniata, Pa., 100.....F6 114
McCracken, Rush, Kans., 406.....D4 93
McCracken, co., Ky., 57,306.A2 94
McCreary, Man., Can., 579..D2 71
McCreary, co., Ky., 12,463..D5 94
McCredie, Callaway, Mo., 90.....C6 101
McCrory, Woodruff, Ark., 1,053.....B4 81
McCulloch, co., Tex., 8,815.....D3 118
MacCulloch, cape, N.W. Ter., Can.....B18 67
McCulloh, Lee, Ala., 100.....C4 78
McCullom Lake, McHenry, Ill., 759.....*A5 90
McCullough, Escambia, Ala., 200.....D2 78
McCullough, mtn., Nev.....H6 104
McCullum, Walker, Ala., 125.....B2 78
McCune, Crawford, Kans., 433.....E8 93
McCurtain, Haskell, Okla., 528.....B7 112
McCurtain, co., Okla., 25,851.....C7 112
McCutchenville, Wyandot and Seneca, Ohio, 300.....B4 111
McDade, Bastrop, Tex., 500..D4 118
McDaniel, Talbot, Md., 50...C5 85
McDavid, Escambia, Fla., 500.....G2 86
McDermitt, Humboldt, Nev., 100.....B4 104
McDermott, Scioto, Ohio, 900.....D4 111
Macdhui, mtn., Scot.....C5 13
Macdona, Bexar, Tex., 300...B3 118
Macdonald, Man., Can., 118.D2 71
McDonald, Rawlins, Kans., 323.....C2 93
McDonald, Neshoba, Miss., 75.....C4 100
McDonald, Lea, N. Mex., 5..D6 107
McDonald, Trumbull, Ohio, 2,727.....A7 111
McDonald, Washington and Allegheny, Pa., 3,141.....B5 114
McDonald, Bradley, Tenn., 125.....D9, E11 117
MacDonald, Fayette, W. Va., 300.....D3, D7 123
McDonald, co., Mo., 11,798..E3 101
McDonald, creek, Mont.....C8 102
McDonald, isl., Indian O.....J1 2
Macdonald, lake, Austl.....D4 50
MacDonald, range, B.C., Can..E10 68
Macdonaldton, Somerset, Pa., 200.....G4 114
MacDonnell, ranges, Austl.....D5 50
McDonough, Henry, Ga., 2,224.....C2 87
McDonough, Chenango, N.Y., 250.....C5 108
McDonough, co., Ill., 28,928.....C3 90
McDougal, Clay, Ark., 200...A5 81
McDougal, mtn., Wyo.....C2 125
McDowell, Floyd, Ky., 500...C7 94
McDowell, Highland, Va., 127.....C3 121
McDowell, co., N.C., 26,742.D4 109
McDowell, co., W. Va., 71,359.....D3 123
McDowell, mtn., Ariz.....F2 80
Macduff, Scot., 3,479.....C6 13
McDuffie, co., Ga., 12,627...C4 87
Macedon, Wayne, N.Y., 645.B3 108
Macedonia, Litchfield, Conn., 100.....C3 84
Macedonia, Pottawattamie, Iowa, 290.....C2 92
Macedonia, Summit, Ohio, 400.....A6, B2 111
Macedonia, reg., Yugo., Grc.B4 23
Macedonia, rep., Yugo., 1,404,883.....*D5 22
Maceió, Braz., 153,305....C3, k6 57
McElhattan, Clinton, Pa., 480.....D7 114
McElroy, creek, W. Va.....A6 123
Macenta, Guinea, 5,000.....E3 45
Maceo, Daviess, Ky., 200.....C2 94
Macerata, It., 24,800.....C4 21
Maces, bay, N.B., Can.....D3 74
McEwen, Baker, Oreg.....C8 113
McEwen, Humphreys, Tenn., 979.....A4 117
McFadden, Jackson, Ark.....B4 81
McFadden, Carbon, Wyo., 150.....D6 125
McFaddin, Victoria, Tex., 300.....E4 118
McFall, Gentry, Mo., 206.....A3 101
McFarlan, Anson, N.C., 161.....C3 109
Macfarlan, Ritchie, W. Va., 150.....B3 123
McFarland, Kern, Calif., 3,686.....E4 82
McFarland, Wabaunsee, Kans., 256.....C7 93
McFarland, Marquette, Mich., 80.....B3 98
McFarland, Dane, Wis., 1,272.....E4 124
McGaha, Adair, Ky., 200.....C4 94
McGaheysville, Rockingham, Va., 250.....C4 121
McGee, Sask., Can., 40.....F1 70
McGehee, Desha, Ark., 4,448.....D4 81
McGill, White Pine, Nev., 2,195.....D7 104
MacGillicuddy's Reeks, mts., Ire..F2 11
McGillivray, lake, Que., Can.....A7 72
McGillivray Falls, B.C., Can.....D6 68
McGiverin, lake, Ont., Can.....B8 98
McGivney, N.B., Can., 235..C3 74
McGrann, Armstrong, Pa., 800.....*E2 114
McGrath, Alsk., 241.....C8 79
McGrath, Aitkin, Minn., 96.....D5 99
McGraw, Cortland, N.Y., 1,276.....C4 108
McGraws, Wyoming, W. Va., 300.....D3 123
Mac Gregor, Man., Can., 642.....E2 71
McGregor, Clayton, Iowa, 1,040.....A6 92
McGregor, Aitkin, Minn., 283.....D5 99
McGregor, Williams, N. Dak., 125.....A3 110
McGregor, McLennan, Tex., 4,642.....D4 118
McGregor, lake, Alta., Can.....D4 69
McGregor, riv., B.C., Can.....B7 68
McGrew, Scotts Bluff, Nebr., 90.....C2 103
McGuffey, Hardin, Ohio, 647.....B4 111
McGuire, mtn., Idaho.....D4 89
McGuires, Kootenai, Idaho..B2 89
Mach, Pak., 3,211.....C1 40
Machachi, Ec., 2,582.....B2 58
Machado, Braz., 8,373...C3, k9 56
Machakos, Ken.....B6 48
Machala, Ec., 7,491.....B2 58
Machanao, mtn., Guam..... 52
Machar, lake, Ont., Can.....B5 72
Macheke, Rh.....A5 49
Macheng, China, 30,000.....I6 36
McHenry, McHenry, Ill., 3,336.....A5, E2 90
McHenry, Ohio, Ky., 446.....C3 94
McHenry, Garrett, Md., 60..D1 85
McHenry, Stone, Miss., 600..E4 100
McHenry, Foster, N. Dak., 155.....B7 110
McHenry, co., Ill., 84,210.....A5 90
McHenry, co., N. Dak., 11,099.....A4 110
Machens, St. Charles, Mo., 101.....A8 101
Machete Central, P.R.....D6 65
Machias, Washington, Maine, 1,523 (2,614▲).....D5 96
Machias, Cattaraugus, N.Y., 400.....C2 108
Machias, bay, Maine.....D5 96
Machias, lakes, Maine.....C4 96
Machias, riv., Maine.....B4 96
Machias, riv., Maine.....D5 96
Machiasport, Washington, Maine, 280 (980▲).....D5 96
Machichi, riv., Man., Can.....A6 71
Machico, Port. (Madeira Is.), 4,734.....h12 20
Machida, Jap., 48,600.....*I9 37
Machiques, Ven., 13,685.....A3 60
Machrihanish, Scot.....E3 13
McHue, Independence, Ark., 25.....B4 81
Machu Picchu, Peru.....D3 58
Machynlleth, Wales, 1,903...B4 12
Macia, Moz.....C5 49
Măcin, Rom., 6,533.....C9 22
McIndoe Falls, Caledonia, Vt., 175.....C4 120
McIntire, Mitchell, Iowa, 270.....A5 92
McIntosh, Washington, Ala., 500.....D1 78
McIntosh, Ont., Can., 110...E5 71
McIntosh, Marion, Fla., 258.....C4 86
McIntosh, Liberty, Ga., 150..E5 87
McIntosh, Polk, Minn., 785..C3 99
McIntosh, Torrance, N. Mex., 15.....C3 107
McIntosh, Corson, S. Dak., 568.....B4 116
McIntosh, co., Ga., 6,364.....E5 87
McIntosh, co., N. Dak., 6,702.....C6 110
McIntosh, co., Okla., 12,371..B6 112
McIntosh, lake, Sask., Can.....B3 70
McIntosh, run, Md.....D4 85
McIntyre, Wilkinson, Ga., 316.....D3 87
McIntyre, Indiana, Pa., 425..E3 114
McIntyre, creek, Ohio.....B1 123
Mack, Mesa, Colo., 150.....B2 83
Mack, Hamilton, Ohio, 3,500.....D2 111
McKague, Sask., Can., 132...E4 70
Mackay, Austl., 16,809.....D8 50
Mackay, Custer, Idaho, 652..F5 89
Mackay, lake, Austl.....D4 50
MacKay, lake, N.W. Ter., Can.....D10 66
MacKay, riv., Alta., Can.....A4 69
McKean, Erie, Pa., 442.....C1 114
McKean, co., Pa., 54,517.....C4 114
McKee, Jackson, Ky., 234...C6 94
McKee City, Atlantic, N.J., 500.....E3 106
McKeesport, Allegheny, Pa., 45,489.....B6, F2 114
McKees Rocks, Allegheny, Pa., 13,185.....B5, F1 114
Mackenna, Arg.....A4 54
McKenney, Dinwiddie, Va., 519.....E5 121
McKenzie, Butler, Ala., 558..D3 78
McKenzie, Burleigh, N. Dak., 100.....C5 110
McKenzie, Carroll and Weakley, Tenn., 3,780.....A3 117
McKenzie, co., N. Dak., 7,296.....B2 110
Mackenzie, dist., N.W. Ter., Can., 14,895.....D8 66
MacKenzie, bay, Ant.....C20 5
Mackenzie, bay, N.W. Ter., Yukon, Can.....C5 66
Mackenzie, mts., N.W. Ter., Can.....D7 66
McKenzie, pass, Oreg.....C4 113
Mackenzie, riv., N.W. Ter., Can.....C6 66
McKenzie Bridge, Lane, Oreg., 315.....C4 113
Mackenzie King, isl., N.W. Ter., Can.....m30 67
McKerrow, Ont., Can., 221..A3 72
Mackey, Gibson, Ind., 92.....*H3 91
Mackeys, Washington, N.C., 200.....B7 109
Mackeys Station, Ont., Can..A7 72
Mackeyville, Clinton, Pa., 250.....D7 114
Mackinac, co., Mich., 10,853.B5 98
Mackinac, isl., Mich.....C6 98
Mackinac, straits, Mich.....C6 98
Mackinac Island, Mackinac, Mich., 942.....C6 98
Mackinaw, Tazewell, Ill., 1,163.....C4 90
Mackinaw, riv., Ill.....C4 90
Mackinaw City, Cheboygan and Emmet, Mich., 934...C6 98
McKinley, Marengo, Ala., 100.....C2 78
McKinley, Hancock, Maine, 300.....D4 96
McKinley, St. Louis, Minn., 408.....C6 99
McKinley, Converse, Wyo., 35.....C7 125
McKinley, co., N. Mex., 37,209.....B1 107
McKinley, mtn., Alsk.....C9 79
McKinley Heights, Trumbull, Ohio, 1,500.....*A7 111
McKinley Park, Alsk., 59...C10 79
McKinleyville, Humboldt, Calif., 950.....*B1 82
McKinney, Lincoln, Ky., 300.....C5 94
McKinney, Collin, Tex., 13,763.....C4 118
McKinney, lake, Kans.....E2 93
McKinnon, Sweetwater, Wyo., 10.....D3 125
Mackinnon Road, Ken.....B6 48
McKittrick, Kern, Calif., 135.E4 82
McKittrick, Montgomery, Mo., 97.....C6 101
McKittrick Summit, mtn., Calif..E4 82
Macklin, Sask., Can., 690.....E1 70
McKnight, Allegheny, Pa., 15,000.....A5 114
McKnight, lake, Man., Can.....A1 71
McKownville, Albany, N.Y., 2,000.....*C7 108
Macksburg, Madison, Iowa, 174.....C3 92
Macksburg, Washington, Ohio, 314.....C6 111
Macks Creek, Camden, Mo., 123.....D5 101
Macksville, Stafford, Kans., 546.....E5 93
Macksville, Washington, Ky., 400.....C4 94
Mackville, Caledonia, Vt., 60.....C4 120
Mackville, Outagamie, Wis., 50.....A5 124
McLain, Greene, Miss., 600..D5 100
McLaughlin, Alta., Can., 52.C5 69
McLaughlin, Corson, S. Dak., 983.....B5 116
McLaughlin, mtn., Oreg.....E4 113
McLaughlin, riv., Man., Can...C3 71
McLaurin, Forrest, Miss., 350.....D4 100
Maclean, Austl., 1,804.....D9 51
McLean, Sask., Can., 202.....G3 70
McLean, McLean, Ill., 758...C4 90
McLean, Pierce, Nebr., 73.....B8 103
McLean, Gray, Tex., 1,330...B2 124
McLean, Fairfax, Va., 2,000.A5 121
McLean, co., Ill., 83,877.....C5 90
McLean, co., Ky., 9,355.....C2 94
McLean, co., N. Dak., 14,030.....B4 110
McLean, lake, Sask., Can.....A6 69
McLean, mtn., Maine.....A4 96
Maclean, strait, N.W. Ter., Can.....m31 67
McLeansboro, Hamilton, Ill., 2,951.....E5 90
Maclear, S. Afr., 3,542.....D4 49
McLemoresville, Carroll, Tenn., 285.....B3 117
McLennan, Alta., Can., 1,078.....B2 69
McLennan, co., Tex., 150,091.....D4 118
McLennan, lake, Sask., Can.....B3 70
McLeod, Sweet Grass, Mont., 15.....E6 102
McLeod, Ransom, N. Dak., 300.....C8 110
McLeod, co., Minn., 24,401..F4 99
McLeod, lake, B.C., Can.....B6 68
McLeod, riv., Alta., Can.....C2 69
MacLeod Lake, B.C., Can., 123.....B6, n18 68
Macleods, isl., Scot.....C2 13
McLoud, Pottawatomie, Okla., 837.....B4 112
McLoughlin, mtn., Oreg.....E4 113
McLouth, Jefferson, Kans., 494.....B7, C8 93
McMahon, Sask., Can., 62...G2 70
McMasterville, Que., Can., 2,075.....*D4 73
McMechen, Marshall, W. Va., 2,999.....B2, B4 123
McMichael, creek, Pa.....B2 106
McMillan, Luce, Mich., 300..B5 98
McMillan, Knox, Tenn.....E12 117
McMillan, lake, N. Mex.....E5 107
McMillan Manor, Ventura, Calif., 1,193.....*E4 82
McMinn, co., Tenn., 33,662..D9 117
McMinnville, Yamhill, Oreg., 7,656.....B1, B3 113
McMinnville, Warren, Tenn., 9,013.....D8 117
McMorran, Sask., Can.....F1 70
McMullen, co., Tex., 1,116..E3 118
McMurdo, sound, Ant.....B29 5
McMurdo, U.S. scientific station, Ant.....B29 5
McMurray, Alta., Can., 1,186.....A5, f8 69
McMurray, Skagit, Wash., 75.....A3 122
McNab, Hempstead, Ark., 142.....D2 81
McNair, Jefferson, Miss., 50..D2 100
McNair, Harris, Tex., 1,880.*F5 118
McNairy, McNairy, Tenn., 100.....B3 117
McNairy, co., Tenn., 18,085..B3 117
McNary, Apache, Ariz., 1,608.....C6 80
McNary, Rapides, La., 250..D3 95
McNary, Umatilla, Oreg., 350.....B7 113
McNary, Hudspeth, Tex., 50.F1 124
McNeal, Cochise, Ariz., 50...F6 80
McNeal, Calhoun, Fla., 150..B1 86
McNeil, Columbia, Ark., 746.D2 81
McNeil, Travis, Tex., 200.....D4 124
McNeil, isl., Wash.....D1 122
McNeill, Pearl River, Miss., 450.....E4 100
McNeill, mtn., B.C., Can.....B2 68
MacNutt, Sask., Can., 211...F5 70
McNutt, isl., N.S., Can.....F4 74
Maco, Bol.....B2 55
Macocola, Ang.....C2 48
Macomb, McDonough, Ill., 12,135.....C3 90
Macomb, Pottawatomie, Okla., 76.....B4 112
Macomb, co., Mich., 405,804.F8 98
Mâcon, Fr., 25,714.....D6 14
Macon, Bibb, Ga., 69,764 (*170,700).....D3 87
Macon, Macon, Ill., 1,229...D5 90
Macon, Noxubee, Miss., 2,432.....B5 100
Macon, Macon, Mo., 4,547...B5 101
Macon, Franklin, Nebr., 25..D7 103
Macon, Warren, N.C., 187...A5 109
Macon, Fayette, Tenn., 50...B2 117
Macon, co., Ala., 26,717.....C4 78
Macon, co., Ga., 13,170.....D2 87
Macon, co., Ill., 118,257.....D5 90
Macon, co., Mo., 16,473.....B5 101
Macon, co., N.C., 14,935.....D2 109
Macon, co., Tenn.. 12,197...C7 117
Macon, bayou, La.....B4 95
Macoun, Sask., Can., 193...H4 70
Macoun, lake, Sask., Can.....A4 70
Macoupin, co., Ill., 43,524..D4 90
Macouria, Fr. Gu., 597.....B4 59
Macovane, Moz.....B6 49
McPhail, riv., Man., Can.....C3 71
McPherson, McPherson, Kans., 9,996.....D6 93
McPherson, co., Kans., 24,285.....D6 93
McPherson, co., Nebr., 735...C4 103

MCPH-MANC 67X

McPherson, co., S. Dak., 5,821........B6 116
McQuady, Breckinridge, Ky., 100........C3 94
Macquarie, isl., Oceania........J7 2
Macquarie, riv., Austl........E6 51
McQueeney, Guadalupe, Tex., 900........B4 118
McRae, White, Ark., 428........B4 81
McRae, Telfair, Ga., 2,738........D4 87
McRoberts, Letcher, Ky., 1,363........C7 94
Mac-Robertson, coast, Ant........C19 5
Macroom, Ire., 2,169........F3 11
Macrorie, Sask., Can., 182........F2 70
McSherrystown, Adams, Pa., 2,839........G7 114
McTaggart, Sask., Can., 93........H3 70
McTavish, Man., Can........E3 71
MacTier, Ont., Can., 851........B5 72
Macuelizo, Hond., 879........C3 62
Macungie, Lehigh, Pa., 1,266........E10 114
McVeigh, Pike, Ky., 800........C7 94
McVeytown, Mifflin, Pa., 488........F6 114
McVille, Nelson, N. Dak., 551........B7 110
Macwahoc, Aroostook, Maine, 100 (165▲)........C4 96
McWilliams, Wilcox, Ala., 225........D2 78
Macy, Miami, Ind., 328........C5 91
Macy, Thurston, Nebr., 203........B2 103
Mad, creek, Ga........B5 87
Mad, lake, Idaho........D8 122
Mad, riv., Calif........B2 82
Mad, riv., N.H........C3 105
Mad, riv., Ohio........C4 111
Mad, riv., Vt........C3 120
Ma'dabā, Jordan, 8,545........C7 32
Madaba, Tan........C6 48
Madagascar, isl., Afr........g9 49
Madame, isl., N.S., Can........D9 74
Madang, N. Gui., 379........k12 50
Madaoua, Niger, 2,100........D6 45
Madaripur, Pak., 21,693........F13 40
Madawaska, Ont., Can., 429........B7 72
Madawaska, Aroostook, Maine, 4,035 (5,507▲)........A4 96
Madawaska, co., N.B., Can., 38,983........B1 74
Madawaska, lake, Maine........B4 96
Madawaska, riv., N.B., Que., Can........B1 74
Madawaska, riv., Ont., Can........B7 72
Madaya, Bur........A2 38
Madbury, Strafford, N.H., 35 (556▲)........D5 105
Madden, Leake, Miss., 130........C4 100
Madden, Natrona, Wyo........B5 125
Madden, lake, Pan........k11 62
Madden Dam, C.Z........k11 62
Maddock, Benson, N. Dak., 740........B6 110
Maddox, St. Marys, Md., 5........D4 85
Madeira, Hamilton, Ohio, 6,744........D2 111
Madeira, riv., Braz........D2 59
Madeira Islands, reg., Port. (Atl. O.) 270,000........h11 20, C1 44
Madelia, Watonwan, Minn., 2,190........F4 99
Madeline, Lassen, Calif., 60........B3 82
Madeline, isl., Wis........B3 124
Madera, Madera, Calif., 14,430........D3 82
Madera, Mex., 7,327........B3 63
Madera, Clearfield, Pa., 900........E4 114
Madera, co., Calif., 40,468........D4 82
Madge, lake, Sask., Can........D1 71
Madhupur, India, 19,519........E11 40
Madhya Pradesh, state, India, 32,372,408........D6 39
Madill, Marshall, Okla., 3,084........C5 112
Madimba, Con. L........C2 48
Madingou, Con. B........F2 46
Madison, Madison, Ala., 1,435........A3 78
Madison, Montgomery, Ala., 900........C3 78
Madison, St. Francis, Ark., 750........B5 81
Madison, Sask., Can., 101........F1 70
Madison, New Haven, Conn., 1,500 (4,567▲)........D6 84
Madison, Madison, Fla., 3,239........B3 86
Madison, Morgan, Ga., 2,680........C3 87
Madison, Madison, Ill., 6,861........E3 90
Madison, Jefferson, Ind., 10,488........G7 91
Madison, Greenwood, Kans., 1,105........D7 93
Madison, Somerset, Maine, 2,761 (3,935▲)........D3 96
Madison, Dorchester, Md., 200........C5 85
Madison, Lac qui Parle, Minn., 2,380........E2 99
Madison, Madison, Miss., 703........C3 100
Madison, Monroe, Mo., 528........B5 101
Madison, Madison, Nebr., 1,513........C8 103
Madison, Carroll, N.H., 130 (429▲)........C4 105
Madison, Morris, N.J., 15,122........B4 106
Madison, Madison, N.Y., 327........C5 108
Madison, Rockingham, N.C., 1,912........A4 109
Madison, Lake, Ohio, 1,347........A6 111
Madison, Oconee, S.C., 300........B1 115
Madison, Lake, S. Dak., 5,420........C8 116
Madison, Davidson, Tenn., 13,583........A5, E9 117
Madison, Madison, Va., 301........C4 121
Madison, Boone, W. Va., 2,215........C3, D5 123
Madison, Dane, Wis., 126,706 (*179,200)........E4 124
Madison, co., Ala., 117,348........A3 78
Madison, co., Ark., 9,068........B2 81
Madison, co., Fla., 14,154........B3 86
Madison, co., Ga., 11,246........B3 87
Madison, co., Idaho, 9,417........F7 89
Madison, co., Ill., 224,689........E4 90
Madison, co., Ind., 125,819........D6 91
Madison, co., Iowa, 12,295........C3 92
Madison, co., Ky., 33,482........C5 94
Madison, co., Miss., 32,904........C4 100
Madison, co., Mo., 9,366........D7 101
Madison, co., Mont., 5,211........E4 102
Madison, co., Nebr., 25,145........C8 103
Madison, co., N.Y., 54,635........C5 108
Madison, co., N.C., 17,217........f10 109
Madison, co., Ohio, 26,454........C4 111
Madison, co., Tenn., 60,655........B3 117
Madison, co., Tex., 6,749........D5 118
Madison, co., Va., 8,187........C4 121
Madison, par., La., 16,444........B4 95
Madison, range, Mont........E5 102
Madison, riv., Mont........E5 102
Madison, riv., Wyo........A2 125
Madisonburg, Centre, Pa., 150........E6 114
Madison College, Davidson, Tenn., 700........E9 117
Madison Heights, Oakland, Mich., 33,343........*F7 98
Madison Heights, Amherst, Va., 3,000........D3 121
Madison Lake, Blue Earth, Minn., 477........F5 99
Madisonville, Hopkins, Ky., 13,110........C2 94
Madisonville, St. Tammany, La., 860........B7, D5 95
Madisonville, Monroe, Tenn., 1,812........D9 117
Madisonville, Madison, Tex., 2,324........D5 118
Madiun, Indon., 122,801........*G4 35
Madjene, Indon........F5 35
Madoc, Ont., Can., 1,347........C7 72
Madoc, Daniels, Mont., 15........B11 102
Madon, riv., Fr........A2 18
Madona, Sov. Un., 5,000........C6 27
Madonna di Campiglio, It., 245........C6 18
Madras, India, 1,729,141 (*2,000,000)........F7 39
Madras, Jefferson, Oreg., 1,515........C5 113
Madras, state, India, 33,686,953........F6 39
Madre, mts., Guat........C2 62
Madre, mts., Mex........C5 63
Madre, mts., Phil........B6 35
Madre de Dios, dept., Peru, 26,116........D3 58
Madre de Dios, isl., Chile........E1 54
Madre de Dios, riv., Bol., Peru........B2 55
Madre del Sur, mts., Mex........o13 63
Madre Occidental, mts., Mex........C3 63
Madre Oriental, mts., Mex........C5 63
Madrid, Houston, Ala., 245........D4 78
Madrid, Boone, Iowa, 2,286........A7, C4 92
Madrid, Perkins, Nebr., 271........D4 103
Madrid, Santa Fe, N. Mex., 15........B3, k8 107
Madrid, St. Lawrence, N.Y., 700........f9 108
Madrid, Sp., 2,259,931 (*2,360,000)........B4, p17 20
Madrid, prov., Sp., 2,606,254........*B4, p17 20
Madridejos, Phil., 3,041........*C6 35
Madridejos, Sp., 9,795........C4 20
Madrūsah, Libya........E2 43
Madugula, India, 7,688........I9 40
Madura, India, 424,810 (*500,000)........G6 39
Madura, isl., Indon........G4 36
Mae, Grant, Wash........B6 122
Maebashi, Jap., 135,000 (181,937▲)........H9, m18 37
Mae Hong Son, Thai., 3,315........C3 38
Maelamun, mtn., Thai........E3 38
Maella, Sp., 2,638........B6 20
Maengsan, Kor........G3 37
Maes, San Miguel, N. Mex., 25........B5 107
Maeser, Uintah, Utah, 929........C6 119
Maesteg, Wales, 21,652........C4 12
Maestra, mts., Cuba........E5 64
Maevatanana, Malag., 6,660........g9 49
Mafeking, Man., Can., 385........C1 71
Mafeking, S. Afr., 8,279........C4 49
Maffra, Austl., 3,404........H6 51
Mafra, Braz., 12,981........D3 56
Mafra, Port., 3,096........C1 20
Maga, mtn., Tinian........52
Magadan, Sov. Un., 72,000........D18 28
Magadi, Ken........B6 48
Magadi, lake, Ken........B6 48
Magaguadavic, lake, N.B., Can........D2 74
Magalia, Butte, Calif., 125........C3 82
Magallanes, see Punta Arenas, Chile
Magallanes, prov., Chile, 73,037........E2, h11 54
Magallanes, strait, Chile........h11 54
Maganga, Con. L........A4 48
Magangué, Col., 17,114........B3 60
Maganjada Costa, Moz........E6 48
Magaria, Niger........D6 45
Magat, riv., Phil........n13 35
Magazine, Logan, Ark., 463........B2 81
Magazine, mtn., Ark........B2 81
Magdalen, is., Que., Can........B8 74
Magdalena, Arg., 4,114........B5, g8 54
Magdalena, Bol., 1,724........B3 55
Magdalena, Mex., 9,413........A2 63
Magdalena, Socorro, N. Mex., 1,211........C2 107
Magdalena, dept., Col., 450,920........A3 60
Magdalena, isl., Chile........C2 54
Magdalena, isl., Mex........C2 63
Magdalena, lake, Mex........m11 63
Magdalena, mts., N. Mex........D2 107
Magdalena, plain, Mex........C2 63
Magdalena, riv., Col........B3 60
Magdalena, riv., Mex........h9 63
Magdalen Islands (Îles-de-la-Madeleine), co., Que., Can., 12,479........B8 74
Magdalo, Phil........o13 35
Magdeburg, Ger., 265,500 (*370,000)........A6 17
Magdiel, Isr., 5,400........g10 32
Magé, Braz., 10,712........h6 56
Magee, Simpson, Miss., 2,039........D4 100
Magelang, Indon., 91,636........G4 36
Mageney, Ire........E5 11
Magenta, It., 18,417........B2 18
Maggia, riv., Switz........D6 19
Maggie, Craig, Va., 25........D2 121
Maggie, creek, Nev........C5 104
Maggiore, lake, It. and Switz........C4 18
Maghāghah, Eg., U.A.R., 23,400........D6 43
Maghera, N. Ire., 1,613........C5 11
Magherafelt, N. Ire., 2,460........C5 11
Maghery, Ire........C3 11
Magic, res., Idaho........F4 89
Magic City, Wheeler, Tex........B2 118
Magicienne, bay, Saipan........52
Magilligan, pt., Ire........B5 11
Maglaj, Yugo., 4,579........C4 22
Maglic, Yugo., 2,182........D5 22
Maglie, It., 13,028........D7 21
Magna, Salt Lake, Utah, 7,300........C3 119
Magness, Independence, Ark., 140........B4 81
Magnet, Hot Spring, Ark., 200........C3, D6 81
Magnet, Man., Can........D2 71
Magnet, Cedar, Nebr., 116........B8 103
Magnetawan, Ont., Can., 205........B5 72
Magnetawan, riv., Ont., Can........B4 72
Magnetic Springs, Union, Ohio, 344........B4 111
Magnisia, prov., Grc., 162,285........*C4 23
Magnitogorsk, Sov. Un., 333,000........C5 29
Magnolia, Columbia, Ark., 10,651........D2 81
Magnolia, Kent, Del., 310........B7 85
Magnolia, Putnam, Ill., 245........B4 90
Magnolia, Harrison, Iowa, 215........C2 92
Magnolia, Larue, Ky., 300........C4 94
Magnolia, Harford, Md., 450........B5 85
Magnolia, Rock, Minn., 280........G2 99
Magnolia, Pike, Miss., 2,083........D3 100
Magnolia, Camden, N.J., 4,199........D2 106
Magnolia, Duplin, N.C., 629........C5 109
Magnolia, Carroll and Stark, Ohio, 1,596........B6 111
Magnolia, Montgomery, Tex., 800........D5 118
Magnolia Springs, Baldwin, Ala., 350........E2 78
Magoari, cape, Braz........B1 57
Magoffin, co., Ky., 11,156........C6 94
Magog, Que., Can., 13,139........D5 73
Magothy, riv., Md........B4 85
Magou, Niger........D5 45
Magoula, Grc., 458........g11 23
Magpie, Que., Can., 359........h8 75
Magpie, riv., Que., Can........h8 75
Magrath, Alta., Can., 1,338........E4 69
Magruder, mtn., Nev........F4 104
Magude, Moz........B5 49
Magwe, Bur., 13,270........D9 39
Mahābād, Iran, 12,858........C2 41
Mahaffey, Clearfield, Pa., 582........E4 114
Mahagi, Con. L........A5 48
Mahaicony, Br. Gu., 1,179........A3 59
Mahakam, riv., Indon........F5 35
Mahalapye, Bech., 2,453........B4 49
Mahameru, mtn., Indon........G4 35
Mahanadi, riv., India........G10 40
Mahanayim, Isr., 188........m14 32
Mahanoro, Malag., 3,436........g9 49
Mahanoy City, Schuylkill, Pa., 8,536........E9 114
Maharashtra, state, India, 39,553,718........D5 39
Maha Sarakham, Thai., 15,709........D5 38
Mahaska, Washington, Kans., 160........C6 93
Mahaska, co., Iowa, 23,602........C5 92
Mahbubnagar, India, 35,588........I6 40
Mahdia, Tun., 10,880........B7 44
Mahe, India, 7,951........F6 39
Mahenge, Tan., 1,180........C6 48
Mahgara, isl., Eg., U.A.R........C2 32
Mahi, riv., India........F4 40
Mahia, pen., N.Z........M16 51
Mahiganj, Pak........E12 40
Mahitahi, N.Z., 19........O12 51
Mahnomen, Mahnomen, Minn., 1,462........C3 99
Mahnomen, co., Minn., 6,341........C3 99
Mahogany, peak, Nev........B2 104
Mahomet, Champaign, Ill., 1,367........C5 90
Mahón, Sp., 16,619........C8 20
Mahone Bay, N.S., Can., 1,103........E5 74
Mahoning, co., Ohio, 300,480........B7 111
Mahoning, riv., Ohio........A7 111
Mahoosuc, range, Maine, N.H........D1 96, B4 105
Mahopac, Putnam, N.Y., 1,500........D7, m15 108
Mahopac, lake, N.Y........D1 84
Mahto, Corson, S. Dak., 3........B5 116
Mahtomedi, Washington, Minn., 2,127........E7 99
Mahtowa, Carlton, Minn., 100........D6 99
Mahukona, Hawaii, Haw., 100........C6 88
Mahunda, Moz........D6 48
Mahuta, Tan........D6 48
Mahuva, India, 32,732........G3 40
Mahwah, Bergen, N.J., 4,500........A4 106
Maîche, Fr., 3,361........B2 21
Maicurú, riv., Braz........C4 59
Maida, Cavalier, N. Dak., 30........A7 110
Maidani, cape, Iran........I9 41
Maiden, Catawba, N.C., 2,039........B2 109
Maidenhead, Eng., 35,374........C7 12
Maiden Rock, Pierce, Wis., 189........D1 124
Maidens, isl., Ire........C6 11
Maidstone, Sask., Can., 577........D1 70
Maidstone, Eng., 61,300........C8 12
Maidstone (Town of), Essex, Vt........*B5 120
Maidstone, lake, Vt........B5 120
Maidsville, Monongalia, W. Va., 200........B5 123
Maiduguri, Nig., 54,646........D7 45
Maihar, India........E8 40
Maikala, range, India........F8 40
Maiko, riv., Con. L........B4 48
Maikoor, isl., Indon........G8 35
Maili, pt., Haw........g9 88
Maillard, Que., Can........B7 73
Mailot, Alg., 215........F9 30
Maimana, Afg., 30,000........D12 41
Main, chan., Ont., Can........B3 72
Main, pass, La........E6 95
Main, riv., Ger........C3, D4 17
Main, riv., Ire........C5 11
Main-a-Dieu, N.S., Can., 382........C10 74
Mainburg, Ger., 5,400........E6 17
Main Centre, Sask., Can., 66........G2 70
Maine, Broome, N.Y., 500........C4 108
Maine, former prov., Fr., 682,000........C3 14
Maine, state, U.S., 969,265........A14 77, 96
Maine-et-Loire, dept., Fr., 556,272........*D3 14
Mainesburg, Tioga, Pa., 175........C7 114
Maïné-Soroa, Niger........D7 45
Mainland, see Pomona, isl., Scot.
Mainland, isl., Scot........g10 10
Mainland, riv., Man., Can........C4 71
Main South West Miramichi, riv., N.B., Can........C3 74
Maintirano, Malag., 2,594........g8 49
Main Topsail, mtn., Newf., Can........D3 75
Mainz, Ger., 139,700........D3 17
Maio, isl., C.V. Is........*E3 42
Maipó, vol., Arg., Chile........A2 54
Maipú, Arg., 5,469........B5 54
Maiquetía, Ven., 73,015........A4 60
Maira, riv., It........E3 18
Maire, strait, Arg........h12 54
Mairhofen, Aus., 2,351........B7 18
Mairiporã, Braz., 9,368........m8 56
Mairum, Pak........G11 46
Maisi, cape, Cuba........D6 64
Maison-Carrée, Alg., 55,144........*B5 44
Maisonette, N.B., Can., 627........B4 74
Maisons-Alfort, Fr., 51,186........g10 14
Maisons-Laffitte, Fr., 19,132........g9 14
Mait, Som........C6 47
Maitland, Austl., 27,351........F8 51
Maitland, N.S., Can., 233........D6 74
Maitland, Ont., Can., 335........C9 72
Maitland (Lake Maitland), Orange, Fla., 3,570........*D5 86
Maitland, Holt, Mo., 427........A2 101
Maize, Sedgwick, Kans., 623........B5 93
Maizuru, Jap., 73,200 (99,615▲)........I7, n14 37
Majagual, Col., 1,516........B3 60
Majé, see Magé, Braz.
Majestic, Pike, Ky., 503........C7 94
Māji, Eth........D4 47
Majijo, peak, Ponape........52
Major, Sask., Can., 179........F1 70
Major, co., Okla., 7,808........A3 112
Majorsville, Marshall, W. Va., 40........B2 123
Majra, Afg., 5,000........D12 46
Majunga, Malag., 38,042........g9 49
Majunga, prov., Malag........g9 49
Makah, Indian res., Wash........A1 122
Makaha, Honolulu, Haw., 2,720........G9 88
Makalado, Con. L........B4 48
Mak'alē, Eth........C4 47
Makanalua, pen., Haw........B4 88
Makanda, Jackson, Ill., 164........F4 90
Makapala, Hawaii, Haw., 100........C6 88
Makapuu, pt., Haw........B4 88
Makarikari Pan, lake, Bech........B4 49
Makarov (Shirutoru), Sov. Un., 5,000........B11 37
Makarska, Yugo., 3,637........D3 22
Makasar (Macassar), Indon., 367,882........G5 35
Makassar (Macassar), strait, Indon........F5 35
Makat, Sov. Un., 3,500........D4 29
Makatea, isl., Fr. Polynesia........*H13 7
Makati, Phil., 114,540........*C6 35
Makawao, Maui, Haw., 950........C5 88
Makaweli, Kauai, Haw., 600........B2 88
Mak'dalā, Eth........C4 47
Makelyville, Hyde, N.C........B7 109
Makena, Maui, Haw., 30........C5 88
Makeni, S.L........E2 45
Makenzen, see Orlyak, Bul.
Makeyevka, Sov. Un., 381,000........G11, 20 27
Makhachkala, Sov. Un., 140,000........E3 29
Makharadze, Sov. Un., 10,000........B14 31
Makhfar al Quwayrah, Jordan, 1,000........E7 32
Makhlata, Bul., 6,537........D7 22
Makin, isl., Gilbert Is........F10 7
Makinak, Man., Can., 68........D2 71
Makinsk, Sov. Un........C8 29
Makkah, see Mecca, Sau. Ar.
Makkinga, Neth., 443........B6 15
Makkovik, Newf., Can., 168........g10 75
Makkum, Neth., 2,086........A5 15
Mako, Hung., 29,935........B5 22
Makokou, Gabon........E2 46
Makongai, isl., Fiji Is........52
Makoti, Ward, N. Dak., 214........B4 110
Makoua, Con. B........F3 46
Makow, Pol., 2,642........B6 26
Makran, range, Pak........H12 41
Makri, India, 5,000........H8 40
Maktar, Tun........G11 30
Makteir, sand dunes, Maur........B3 45
Mākū, Iran, 10,687........B2 41
Makumbi, Con. L........C3 48
Makurazaki, Jap., 15,600........K5 37
Makurdi, Nig., 16,713........E6 45
Makushin, vol., Alsk........E6 79
Mal, bay, Ire........E2 11
Malabang, Phil., 2,377........*D6 35
Malabar, Brevard, Fla., 640........E6 86
Malabar, coast, India........F5 39
Malabon, Phil., 76,438........*C6 35
Mal Abrigo, Ur........E1 56
Malacca, Mala., 69,848........K5 38
Malacca, state, Mala., 291,211........K5 38
Malacca, strait, Asia........K4 38
Malad City, Oneida, Idaho, 2,274........G6 89
Malafede, riv., It........h8 21
Málaga, Col., 6,022........B3 60
Malaga, Gloucester, N.J., 800........D2 106
Malaga, Eddy, N. Mex., 180........E5 107
Málaga, Sp., 301,048........D3 20
Málaga, prov., Sp., 775,167........*D3 20
Málaga, bay, Sp........D3 20
Malagash, N.S., Can., 69........D6 74
Malagasy Republic, country, Afr., 6,200,000........h9 49, I10 42
Malagón, Sp., 9,833........C4 20
Malaimbandy, Malag........h9 49
Malaita, is., Solomon Is........G9 7
Malakal, Sud., 9,680........D3 47
Malakoff, Fr., 33,603........g10 14
Malakoff, Henderson, Tex., 1,657........C4 118
Malalbergo, It., 6,351........E7 18
Malang, Indon., 332,023........G4 35
Malange, Ang., 12,815........C2 48
Malange, dist., Ang., 451,719........C2 48
Malanzán, Arg........A3 54
Malar (Mälaren), lake, Swe........t34 25
Mälaraspö, Swe........t35 25
Mälaren (Malar), lake, Swe........t34 25
Malargüe, Arg........B3 54
Malartic, Que., Can., 6,998........k11 73
Malaspina, glacier, Alsk........D11 79
Malaspina, Arg........C3 54
Malatya, Tur., 83,692........C12 31
Malawi (Nyasaland), country, Afr., 3,650,000........D5 48
Malay, pen., Asia........I11 33
Malaya, r g., Mala., 7,950,000........J4 38
Malaya Uzen', riv., Sov. Un........F18 9
Malaya Vishera, Sov. Un., 25,000........B9 27
Malaybalay, Phil., 2,267........D7 35
Malāyer, Iran, 32,357........D4 41
Malaysia, country, Asia, 11,150,000........E2, E4 35, J5 38
Malazgirt, Tur., 5,100........C14 31
Malbaie, riv., Que., Can........B7 73
Malbon, Austl., 73........D7 50
Malbork, Pol., 26,500........A5 26
Malchin, Ger., 6,825........B6 16
Malchow, Ger., 8,049........E6 24
Malcolm, Austl........E3 50
Malcolm, Lancaster, Nebr., 116........D9 103
Malcolm, Poweshiek, Iowa, 416........C5 92
Malden, Middlesex, Mass., 57,676........B5, g11 97
Malden, Dunklin, Mo., 5,007........E8 101
Malden, Whitman, Wash., 292........B8 122
Malden, Kanawha, W. Va., 1,000........C6 123
Malden, isl., Pac. O........G12 7
Maldive Islands, country, Asia, 95,000........I10 33
Maldon, Eng., 10,507........C8 12
Maldonado, Ur., 12,100........E2 56
Maldonado, dept., Ur., 52,600........*E2 56
Malè, It., 2,841........C6 18
Malé, Maldive Is., 8,431........*I10 33
Malea, cape, Grc........D4 23
Malegaon, India, 121,408........G5 40
Malema (Entre Rios), Moz........D6 48
Malemba-Nkulu, Con. L........C4 48
Maler-Lotla, India, 32,575........B5 40
Malesherbes, Fr., 2,029........C5 14
Malesus, Madison, Tenn., 350........B3 117
Malha (Well), Sud........B2 47
Malheur, Malheur, Oreg........C9 113
Malheur, co., Oreg., 22,764........D9 113
Malheur, lake, Oreg........D8 113
Malheur, riv., Oreg........D9 113
Mali, Guinea........D2 45
Mali, country, Afr., 4,550,000........C4 45, E5 42
Mali, isl., Fiji Is........52
Malibu, Los Angeles, Calif., 2,000........*E4 82
Maligne, lake, Alta., Can........C2 69
Malin, Ire., 164........B4 11
Malin, Klamath, Oreg., 568........E5 113
Malin, Sov. Un., 10,000........F7 27
Malin, head, Ire........B4 11
Malinau, Indon........E5 35
Malin Beg, Ire........C3 11
Malindi, Ken., 3,292........B7 48
Malinec, Czech., 6,551........D5 26
Malinmore, head, Ire........C3 11
Malino, Sov. Un........n18 27
Malinta, Henry, Ohio, 339........A3 111
Malita, Phil., 5,125........*D7 35
Maliwun, Bur., 1,000........G3 38
Maljamar, Lea, N. Mex., 450........E6 107
Malkangiri, India, 5,000........H8 40
Malkara, Tur., 9,300........B6 23
Malko Turnovo, Bul., 3,489........E8 22
Mallaig, Alta., Can., 205........B5 69
Mallard, Palo Alto, Iowa, 431........B3 92
Mallawī, Eg., U.A.R., 43,200........D6 43
Malleco, prov., Chile, 174,185........B2 54
Mallersdorf, Ger., 2,200........E7 17
Malles Venosta, It., 4,171........C6 18
Mallet Creek, Medina, Ohio, 150........A6 111
Malletts, bay, Vt........B2 120
Mallorca, is., Sp........C7 20
Mallory, Logan, W. Va., 1,133........*D3 123
Mallorytown, Ont., Can., 335........C9 72
Mallow, Ire., 5,545........E4 11
Malmbäck, Swe., 1,145........A4 24
Malmberget, Swe., 9,057........D9 25
Malmédy, Bel., 6,355........D6 15
Malmesbury, S. Afr., 8,206........D2 49
Malmköping, Swe., 1,861........t34 25
Malmo, Aitkin, Minn., 40........D5 99
Malmo, Saunders, Nebr., 135........C9, D1 103
Malmö, Swe., 237,500........C7 24, J5 25
Malmöhus, co., Swe., 632,200........C7 24
Maloarkhangelsk, Sov. Un., 10,000........E11 27
Maloja, Switz........D8 19
Maloja, pass, Switz........D8 19
Malolos, Phil., 3,500 (49,300▲)........o13 35
Malone, Ont., Can........C7 72
Malone, Jackson, Fla., 661........B1 86
Malone, Franklin, N.Y., 8,737........f10 108
Malone, Grays Harbor, Wash., 250........C2 122
Malone, Fond du Lac, Wis., 50........B5 124
Maloneyville, Knox, Tenn., 250........E11 117
Malonton, Man., Can........D3 71
Malott, Okanogan, Wash., 350........A6 122
Maloy, Ringgold, Iowa, 68........D3 92
Maloyaroslavets, Sov. Un., 25,000........D11 27
Malpeque, bay, P.E.I., Can........C6 74
Malpura, India, 10,622........D5 40
Malsch, Ger., 7,800........E3 17
Malshaya Uzen, riv., Sov. Un........D1 28
Malta, Cassia, Idaho, 250........G5 89
Malta, De Kalb, Ill., 782........B5 90
Malta, Phillips, Mont., 2,239........B9 102
Malta, Morgan, Ohio, 983........C6 111
Malta, country, Eur., 325,000........G14 30
Malta Bend, Saline, Mo., 338........B4 101
Maltahohe, S.W. Afr., 1,044........B2 49
Malton, Ont., Can., 2,148........D5, m14 72
Malton, Eng., 4,430........C6 10
Malung, Swe., 5,500........G5 25
Malvern, Geneva, Ala., 213........D4 78
Malvern, Hot Spring, Ark., 9,566........C3, D6 81
Malvern, Eng., 27,400........B5 12
Malvern, Mills, Iowa, 1,193........C2 92
Malvern, Carroll, Ohio, 1,320........B6 111
Malvern, Chester, Pa., 2,268........A10, F10 114
Malverne, Nassau, N.Y., 9,968........G2 84
Malwood, Ont., Can........h11 72
Malyye Karmakuly, Sov. Un........B9 4
Mamala, bay, Haw........g10 88
Mamamutha, is., Fiji Is........52
Mamanguape, Braz., 8,512........C3, h6 57
Mamantel, Mex., 89........D6 63
Mamaroneck, Westchester, N.Y., 17,673........h13 108
Mamba, Jap., 1,700........m17 37
Mambasa, Con. L........A4 48
Mamberamo, riv., W. Irian........F9 35
Ma-Me-O Beach, Alta., Can., 142........C4 69
Mamers, Fr., 4,869........C4 14
Mamers, Harnett, N.C., 150........B5 109
Mameyes, P.R........B7 65
Mamfe, Cam., 5,107........E6 45
Mamie, Currituck, N.C., 100........A8 109
Mamiña, Chile........D2 65
Mammern, Switz., 424........A6 19
Mammoth, Pinal, Ariz., 1,913........E5 80
Mammoth, Juab, Utah, 55........D3 119
Mammoth, Kanawha, W. Va., 800........C3, C6 123
Mammoth Cave, nat. park, Ky........C3 94
Mammoth Lakes, Mono, Calif., 300........D4 82
Mammoth Spring, Fulton, Ark., 825........A4 81
Mamolo, isl., Fiji Is........52
Mamoré, riv., Bol., Braz........B2 55
Mamou, Guinea, 5,100........D2 45
Mamou, Evangeline, La., 2,928........D3 95
Mampawah, Indon........E3 35
Mampong, Ghana, 3,948........E4 45
Mamry, lake, Pol........A6 26
Mam Soul, mtn., Scot........C3 13
Mamudju, Indon........F5 35
Man., I.C., 17,000........E3 45
Man, Logan, W. Va., 1,486........D3, D5 123
Man, Isle of, see Isle of Man, Br. dep., Eur.
Man, riv., Sask., Can........D4 70
Mana, Fr. Gu., 1,443........A4 59
Mana, Kauai, Haw., 225........A2 88
Manabí, prov., Ec., 477,503........B1 58
Manabo, Malag........h8 49
Manacapuru, Braz., 2,584........D5 60
Manacor, Sp., 19,224........C7 20
Manado, Indon., 127,614........E6 35
Managua, Nic., 234,800........D4 62
Managua, lake, Nic........D4 62
Manahawkin, Ocean, N.J., 800........D4 106
Manakara, Malag., 6,200........h9 49
Manakin, Goochland, Va., 330........D5 121
Manalapan, Monmouth, N.J., 50........C4 106
Manam, isl., N. Gui........h12 50
Manama, Bahrain, 55,541 (*100,000)........G8 33
Mañana, Pan........F8 62
Manana, isl., Haw........g11 88
Mananara, Malag., 2,852........g9 49
Mananara, riv., Malag........h9 49
Mananjary, Malag., 11,269........h9 49
Manantenina, Malag., 750........h9 49
Manantico, creek, N.J........E3 106
Manapire, riv., Ven........B4 60
Manas (Suilai), China, 10,000........C2 34
Manasarowar, lake, China........B9 40
Manasquan, Monmouth, N.J., 4,022........C4 106
Manasquan, riv., N.J........C4 106
Manass, riv., China........C2 34
Manassa, Conejos, Colo., 831........D5 83
Manassas, Tattnall, Ga., 154........D4 87
Manassas, Prince William, Va., 3,555........B4, C5 121
Manassas Park, Prince William, Va., 5,342........*C5 121
Manatee, co., Fla., 69,168........E4 86
Manatee, riv., Fla........E4 86
Manatí, P.R., 9,682........B5 65
Manatí, mun., P.R., 29,354........B5 65
Manaus, Braz., 154,040........C2 59
Manavgat, Tur., 3,200........D8 31
Manawa, Waupaca, Wis., 1,037........D5 124
Manawan, lake, Sask., Can........B4 70
Mancelona, Antrim, Mich., 1,141........D5 98
Mancha, reg., Sp........C4 20
Manchac, bayou, La........B5 95
Mancha Real, Sp., 7,855........D4 20
Manchaug, Worcester, Mass., 900........B4 97
Manche, dept., Fr., 446,878........*C3 14
Manchester, Hartford, Conn., 42,102........B6 84
Manchester, Eng., 654,700 (*2,850,000)........D5, 10, A5 12
Manchester, Meriwether and Talbot, Ga., 4,115........D2 87
Manchester, Scott, Ill., 282........D3 90
Manchester, Delaware, Iowa, 4,402........B6 92
Manchester, Dickinson, Kans., 153........C6 93
Manchester, Clay, Ky., 1,868........C6 94
Manchester, Kennebec, Maine, 300 (1,068▲)........D3 96
Manchester, Carroll, Md., 1,108........A4 85
Manchester, Essex, Mass., 3,932........A6, f12 97
Manchester, Washtenaw, Mich., 1,568........F6 98
Manchester, St Louis, Mo., 2,021........B7 101
Manchester, Hillsboro, N.H., 88,282 (*121,300)........E4 105
Manchester, Ontario, N.Y., 1,344........C3 108
Manchester, Adams, Ohio, 2,172........D4 111
Manchester, Grant, Okla., 162........A3 112

Manchester, York, Pa., 1,454....F8 114
Manchester, Kingsbury, S. Dak., 70....C8 116
Manchester, Coffee, Tenn., 3,930....B5 117
Manchester, Bennington, Vt., 403 (2,470▲)....E2 120
Manchester Center, Bennington, Vt., 770....E2 120
Manchester Depot, Bennington, Vt., 620....E2 120
Manchouli (Lupin), China, 25,000....B8 34
Manchuria, reg., China....B10 34
Mancos, Montezuma, Colo., 832....D2 83
Mancos, riv., Colo....D2 83
Mandabe, Malag....h8 49
Mandaguari, Braz., 8,210....C2 56
Mandal, Afg., 10,000....E10 41
Mandal, Nor., 5,200....H2 25
Mandalay, Bur., 195,000....B2 38, D10 39
Mandalaya, gulf, Tur....D6 23
Mandali, Iraq, 9,722....E2 41
Mandaluyong, Phil., 71,619....*C6 35
Mandan, Morton, N. Dak., 10,525....C5 110
Mandar, gulf, Indon....F5 35
Mandara, mts., Cam....C2 46
Mandarah, Eg., U.A.R., 2,000....C2 32
Mandaree, McKenzie, N. Dak., 135....B3 110
Mandarin, Duval, Fla., 900....B5, C6 86
Mandera, Ken....A7 48
Manderfeld, Bel., 1,344....D6 15
Manderfield, Beaver, Utah, 70....E3 119
Manderson, Shannon, S. Dak., 55....D3 116
Manderson, Big Horn, Wyo., 167....A5 125
Mandeville, Miller, Ark., 350....D2 81
Mandeville, Que., Can....C4 73
Mandeville, St. Tammany, La., 1,740....B7, D5 95
Mandimba, Moz....D6 48
Mandla, India, 19,416....F8 40
Mandra, Grc., 3,594....C4, g11 23
Mandritsara, Malag....g9 49
Mandsaur, India, 41,876....E5 40
Manduria, It., 22,500....D6 21
Mandvi, India, 29,305....F2 40
Manell, chan., Guam....52
Manes, Wright, Mo., 65....D5 71
Manfalūţ, Eg., U.A.R., 23,900....D6 43
Manfred, Wells, N. Dak., 79..B6 110
Manfredonia, It., 35,200 (40,100▲)....D5 21
Manfredonia, gulf, It....D6 21
Manga, Braz., 2,000....D2 57
Mangalia, Rom., 4,792....D9 22
Mangalore, India, 142,669 (★170,253)....F5 39
Mangaratiba, Braz., 2,741...h5 56
Mangatarem, Phil., 2,392...o13 35
Mañgero, Phil., 254....*C6 35
Mangerton, mtn., Ire....F2 11
Mangham, Richland, La., 521....B4 95
Mangla, Pak....B5 39
Mango, isl., Fiji Is....52
Mangoky, riv., Malag....h8 49
Mangole, isl., Indon....F7 35
Mangonia Park, Palm Beach, Fla., 594....*F6 86
Mangotsfield, Eng., 24,092...C5 12
Mangrove, pt., Fla....F2 86
Mangrove, swamp, Fla....G6 86
Mangualde, Port., 3,093....B2 20
Manguéni, plat., Niger....B7 45
Mangum, Greer, Okla., 3,950....C2 112
Mangyshlak, pen., Sov. Un....E4 29
Manhasset, Nassau, N.Y., 9,000....F2 84
Manhattan, Will, Ill., 1,117....*B6 90
Manhattan, Putnam, Ind., 50....E4 91
Manhattan, Riley, Kans., 22,993....C7 93
Manhattan, Gallatin, Mont., 889....E5 102
Manhattan, Nye, Nev., 25...E4 104
Manhattan, borough (New York co.), N.Y., 1,698,281 (part of New York City)....*k8 106
Manhattan, isl., N.Y....k8 106
Manhattan Beach, Los Angeles, Calif., 34,513....F2 82
Manheim, Lancaster, Pa., 4,790....F9 114
Manheim, Preston, W. Va., 150....B5 123
Manhica, Moz....C5 49
Manhuaçu, Braz., 10,546....F7 56
Mani, P.R....C2 65
Maniagassa, isl., Saipan....52
Maniago, It., 7,518....C8 18
Manica e Sofala, prov., Moz.A5 49
Manicoré, Braz., 2,268....D2 59
Manicouagan, riv., Que., Can..h13 73
Manigotagan, Man., Can., 213....D3, g8 71
Manigotagan, lake, Man., Can.D4 71
Manigotagan, riv., Man., Can..D3 71
Manihiki, is., Pac. O....G12 7
Manika E Sofala, prov., Moz....A5 49
Manila, Navajo, Ariz., 40...C5 80
Manila, Mississippi, Ark., 1,753....B5 81
Manila, Phil., 1,138,611 (★2,500,000)....C6, o13 35
Manila, Daggett, Utah, 329..C6 119
Manila, bay, Phil....C6, o13 35
Manilla, Austl., 1,914....E8 51
Manilla, Rush, Ind., 400....E6 91
Manilla, Crawford, Iowa, 939....C2 92
Manipur, ter., India, 780,037....*D9 39
Manisa, Tur., 59,675....C6 23
Manistee, Manistee, Mich., 8,324....D4 98
Manistee, co., Mich., 19,042.D4 98
Manistee, riv., Mich....D5 98
Manistique, Schoolcraft, Mich., 4,875....C4 98
Manistique, lake, Mich....B5 98
Manistique, riv., Mich....B4 98
Manito, Mason, Ill., 1,093...C4 90
Manito, lake, Sask., Can....E1 70
Manitoba, prov., Can., 921,686....E13 66, 71
Manitoba, lake, Man., Can..D2 71
Manitou, Man., Can., 863....E2 71
Manitou, Tillman, Okla., 269....C3 112
Manitou, isl., Mich....A3 98
Manitou, lake, Ont., Can....B3 72
Manitou, lakes, Ont., Can....E5 71
Manitou, riv., Ont., Can....E5 71
Manitou Beach, Sask., Can., 159....F3 70
Manitou Beach, Lenawee, Mich., 1,544....*G6 98
Manitoulin, dist., Ont., Can., 11,176....B2 72
Manitoulin, isl., Ont., Can....B2 72
Manitou Springs, El Paso, Colo., 3,626....C6 83
Manitowaning, Ont., Can., 400....B3 72
Manitowoc, Manitowoc, Wis., 32,275....B6, D6 124
Manitowoc, co., Wis., 75,215....D6 124
Manitowoc, riv., Wis....B6 124
Manitowoc Rapids, Manitowoc, Wis., 400....B6 124
Maniwaki, Que., Can., 6,349....C2 73
Maniya (Oasis), Iraq....G14 31
Manizales, Col., 166,000....B2 60
Manja, Malag., 2,253....h8 49
Manjra, riv., India....E6 39
Mankato, Jewell, Kans., 1,231....C5 93
Mankato, Blue Earth, Minn., 23,797....F5 99
Mankono, I.C., 4,200....E3 45
Mankota, Sask., Can., 477...H2 70
Mankoya, Zambia, 2,500....D3 48
Manley, Cass, Nebr., 113....E3 103
Manley, Hot Springs, Alsk., 72....B9 79
Manlius, Bureau, Ill., 374....B4 90
Manlius, Onondaga, N.Y., 2,781....C5 108
Manlléu, Sp., 9,410....A7 20
Manly, Worth, Iowa, 1,425..A4 92
Manly, Moore, N.C., 239....B4 109
Manlyville, Henry, Tenn., 40.A3 117
Manmad, India, 31,551....G5 40
Mann, ranges, Austl....E5 50
Mannar, Cey., 5,190....G6 39
Mannar, gulf, India....G6 39
Mannboro, Amelia, Va., 25..D5 121
Mannford, Creek, Okla., 358....A5 112
Mannheim, Ger., 321,100 (★1,170,000)....D3 17
Manning, Dallas, Ark., 300...C3 81
Manning, Alta., Can., 896...A2 69
Manning, Carroll, Iowa, 1,676....C2 92
Manning, Dunn, N. Dak., 50.B3 110
Manning, Washington, Oreg., 40....A1 113
Manning, Clarendon, S.C., 3,917....D7 115
Mannington, Christian, Ky., 500....C2 94
Mannington, Marion, W. Va., 2,996....A7, B4 123
Manns, creek, W. Va....D7 123
Manns Choice, Bedford, Pa., 351....G4 114
Manns Harbor, Dare, N.C., 300....B8 109
Mannsville, Jefferson, N.Y., 446....B4 108
Mannsville, Johnston, Okla., 297....C5 112
Mannu, riv., It....E2 21
Manville, Alta., Can., 632...C5 69
Manø, isl., Den....C2 24
Manokin, Somerset, Md., 80.D6 85
Manokin, riv., Md....D6 85
Manokotak, Alsk., 149....D8 79
Manokwari, W. Irian....F8 35
Manombo, Malag....h8 49
Manomet, Plymouth, Mass., 500....C6 97
Manomet, hill, Mass....C6 97
Manomet, pt., Mass....C6 97
Manono, Con. L., 28,465....C4 48
Manono, isl., W. Sam....52
Manor, Sask., Can., 357....H4 70
Manor, Ware, Ga., 500....E4 87
Manor, Westmoreland, Pa., 1,136....*F2 114
Manor, Travis, Tex., 766....D4 118
Manorhamilton, Ire., 920....C3 11
Manorhaven, Nassau, N.Y., 3,566....*G2 84
Manorville, Suffolk, N.Y., 150....n16 108
Manorville, Armstrong, Pa., 557....E2 114
Manosque, Fr., 7,454....F6 14
Manotick, Ont., Can., 434...B9 72
Manouane, lake, Que., Can....h12 73
Manpojin, Kor., 1,000....F3 37
Manresa, Sp., 52,216....B6 20
Mansalay, Phil., 1,294....*C6 35
Månsarp, Swe., 378....A8 24
Manseau, Que., Can., 837....C5 73
Mansel, isl., N.W. Ter., Can..D16 67
Mansfield, Scott and Sebastian, Ark., 881....B1 81
Mansfield, Austl., 1,944....H6 51
Mansfield, Eng., 54,100 (★190,000)....A6 12
Mansfield, Newton, Ga., 394....C3 87
Mansfield, Piatt, Ill., 743....C5 90
Mansfield, De Soto, La., 5,839....B2 95
Mansfield, Bristol, Mass., 5,000 (7,773▲)....B5 97
Mansfield, Wright, Mo., 949.D5 101
Mansfield, Richland, Ohio, 47,325 (★101,600)....B3 111
Mansfield, Tioga, Pa., 2,678..C7 114
Mansfield, Spink, S. Dak., 250....B7 116
Mansfield, Henry, Tenn., 110....A3 117
Mansfield, Tarrant, Tex., 1,375....B5 118
Mansfield, Douglas, Wash., 335....B6 122
Mansfield, flood control res., Ind..E3 91
Mansfield, mtn., Vt....B3 120
Mansfield Center, Tolland, Conn., 600 (14,638▲)....B8 84
Mansfield City, Tolland, Conn., 30....B7 84
Mansfield Depot, Tolland, Conn., 100....B7 84
Mansfield Hallow, flood control res., Conn....B8 84
Mansfield Southeast, Richland, Ohio, 2,961....*B5 111
Manson, Calhoun, Iowa, 1,789....B3 92
Manson, Chelan, Wash., 350....B5 122
Manson, riv., B.C., Can....B5 68
Manson Creek, B.C., Can....B5 68
Mansonville, Que., Can., 481....D5 73
Manso ou das Mortes, riv., Braz....A2 56
Mansura, Avoyelles, La., 1,579....C3 95
Mant, hbr., Ponape....52
Mant, is., Ponape....52
Manta, Ec., 19,021....B1 58
Mantachie, Itawamba, Miss., 246....A5 100
Mantador, Richland, N. Dak., 98....C9 110
Mantagao, riv., Man., Can....D3 71
Mantario, Sask., Can., 108...F1 70
Mantaro, riv., Peru....D3 58
Mantas, Niger....C5 45
Manteca, San Joaquin, Calif., 8,242....D3, B6 82
Mantee, Webster, Miss., 166..B4 100
Manteno, Kankakee, Ill., 2,225....B6 90
Manteo, Dare, N.C., 587....B8 109
Manteo, Buckingham, Va., 25....C4 121
Manter, Stanton, Kans., 183.E2 93
Mantes [-la-Jolie], Fr., 18,902 (★35,000)....C4 14
Manthani, India, 7,779....H7 40
Manti, Sanpete, Utah, 1,739.D4 119
Mantilla, Cuba, 892....k12 64
Mantiqueira, mts., Braz....C4 56
Mantoloking, Ocean, N.J., 160....C4 106
Manton, Wexford, Mich., 1,050....D5 98
Mantorville, Dodge, Minn., 498....F6 99
Mantova, It., 63,700.D6 18, B3 21
Mantua, Gloucester, N.J., 2,000....D2 106
Mantua, Portage, Ohio, 1,194....A6 111
Mantua, Box Elder, Utah, 275....B4 119
Manú, Peru....D3 58
Manucan, Phil., 5,965....*D6 35
Manuel Alves, riv., Braz....C1 57
Manuel Benavides, Mex., 798.B4 63
Manuelito, McKinley, N. Mex., 15....B1 107
Manuels, Newf., Can., 724..*E5 75
Manui, isl., Indon....F6 35
Manukau, hbr., N.Z....L15 51
Manulla, riv., Ire....D2 11
Manumuskin, riv., N.J....E3 106
Manvel, Grand Forks, N. Dak., 313....A8 110
Manvel, Brazoria, Tex., 50...F5 118
Manville, Somerset, N.J., 10,995....B3 106
Manville, Providence, R.I., 3,600....B11 84
Manville, Niobrara, Wyo., 124....C8 125
Many, Sabine, La., 3,164....C2 95
Manyara, lake, Tan....B6 48
Manyas, lake, Tur....B6 23
Manyberries, Alta., Can., 103....E5 69
Manych, canal, Sov. Un....H14 27
Manych, lake, Sov. Un....H14 27
Manych, riv., Sov. Un....F17 9
Many Farms, Apache, Ariz..A6 80
Many Island, lake, Alta., Can.D5 69
Manyoni, Tan., 1,388....C5 48
Manzala, lake, Eg., U.A.R....C3 32
Manzanares, Sp., 17,847....C4 20
Manzanares, canal, Sp....p17 20
Manzanares, riv., Sp....o17 20
Manzanillo, Cuba, 52,000....E5 64
Manzanillo, Mex., 16,591....D4, n11 63
Manzanillo, P.R....D4 65
Manzanita, Tillamook, Oreg., 363....B3 113
Manzanita Lake, Shasta, Calif., 5....B3 82
Manzano, Torrance, N. Mex., 150....C3 107
Manzano, mts., N. Mex....C3 107
Manzano, peak, N. Mex....C3 107
Manzanola, Otero, Colo., 562....C7 83
Manziana, It., 2,229....g8 21
Manzil, Jordan, 1,000....C8 32
Mao, Chad, 2,349....C3 46
Maoming, China, 14,000...G7 34
Mapai, Moz....B5 49
Mapastepec, Mex., 3,580....D6 63
Mapaville, Jefferson, Mo., 300....C7 101
Mapes, Nelson, N. Dak., 50..A7 110
Mapia, is., W. Irian....E8 35
Mapiri, Bol., 289....C2 55
Maple, Ont., Can., 1,552...k14 72
Maple, Bailey, Tex., 50....C1 118
Maple, peak, Ariz....D6 80
Maple, riv., Iowa....B2 92
Maple, riv., N. Dak....C8 110
Maplebay, Polk, Minn., 75...C2 99
Maple Bluff, Dane, Wis., 1,565....*E4 124
Maple Creek, Sask., Can., 2,291....H1 70
Maple Grove, Hennepin, Minn., 2,213....*E5 99
Maple Heights, Cuyahoga, Ohio, 31,667....B2 111
Maple Hill, Wabaunsee, Kans., 244....C7 93
Maple Hill, Pender, N.C., 200....C6 109
Maple Lake, Wright, Minn., 1,018....E5 99
Maple Lane, St. Joseph, Ind., 2,500....*A5 91
Maple Mount, Daviess, Ky., 500....C2 94
Maple Rapids, Clinton, Mich., 683....E6 98
Maples, Allen, Ind., 125....B8 91
Maple Shade, Burlington, N.J., 12,947....D2 106
Maplesville, Clinton, Ala., 679....C3 78
Mapleton, Monona, Iowa, 1,686....B2 92
Mapleton, Bourbon, Kans., 127....D9 93
Mapleton, Aroostook, Maine, 900 (1,514▲)....B4 96
Mapleton, Blue Earth, Minn., 1,107....G5 99
Mapleton, Cass, N. Dak., 180....C8 110
Mapleton, Lane, Oreg., 700....C3 113
Mapleton, Utah, Utah, 1,516....C4 119
Mapleton Depot, Huntingdon, Pa., 666....E6 114
Maple Valley, King, Wash., 800....D2 122
Mapleville, Providence, R.I., 800....B10 84
Maplewood, Calcasieu, La., 2,432....D2 95
Maplewood, York, Maine, 60....E2 96
Maplewood, Ramsey, Minn., 18,519....E5 99
Maplewood, St. Louis, Mo., 12,552....B8 101
Maplewood, Essex, N.J., 23,977....B4 106
Maplewood, Albany, N.Y., 650....*C7 108
Maplewood, Multnomah, Oreg., 2,000....*B4 113
Maplewood Park, St. Clair, Ill. (part of Cahokia)....B8 101
Maplewood Park, Delaware, Pa., 1,800....*G11 114
Mapuera, riv., Braz....C3 53
Maqalā', Sau. Ar....H3 41
Maqnāh, Sau. Ar....H10 31
Maquela do Zombo, Ang., 1,103....C2 48
Maquinchao, Arg....C3 54
Maquoketa, Jackson, Iowa, 5,909....B7 92
Maquoketa, riv., Iowa....B7 92
Maquon, Knox, Ill., 386....C3 90
Mar, mts., Braz....D3 56
Marabá, Braz., 8,533....D6 59
Maracá, isl., Braz....B4 59
Maracai, lake, Braz....D4 60
Maracaibo, Ven., 432,902....A3 60
Maracaibo, lake, Ven....B3 60
Maracaju, Braz., 1,848....C1 56
Maracay, Ven., 134,123....A4 60
Maracayo, P.R....B3 65
Marādah, Libya, 1,299....D3 43
Maradi, Niger, 10,100....D6 45
Marāgheh, Iran, 36,551....C3 41
Maragogi, Braz., 1,031....k6 57
Maragogipe, Braz., 12,575...D3 57
Marais des Cygnes (Osage), riv., Kans....D8 93
Marajó, isl., Braz....C5 59
Maralal, Ken....A6 48
Maramec, Pawnee, Okla., 169....A5 112
Marana, Pima, Ariz., 500....E4 80
Marand, Iran, 13,945....B2 41
Marandellas, Rh., 6,700....A5 49
Maranguape, Braz., 8,715....B3 57
Maranhão, state, Braz., 2,492,139....B1 57
Marano, lagoon, It....D9 18
Maranoa, riv., Austl....C7 51
Marañón, riv., Peru....B2 58
Marans, Fr., 2,456....D3 14
Maraş (Marash), Tur., 54,447....D11 31
Mărăşeşti, Rom., 5,604....C8 22
Marash (Maras), Tur., 54,447....D11 31
Marathon, Ont., Can., 2,568....o18 72
Marathon, Monroe, Fla., 950....H5 86
Marathon, Grc., 2,515....g11 23
Marathon, Buena Vista, Iowa, 516....B3 92
Marathon, Cortland, N.Y., 1,079....C4 108
Marathon, Brewster, Tex., 800....D1, F2 118
Marathon, Marathon, Wis., 1,022....D4 124
Marathon, co., Wis., 88,874..D4 124
Maratua, isl., Indon....E5 35
Maravatío, Mex., 5,182....n13 63
Mara Vista, Barnstable, Mass., 800....C6 97
Marāwah, Libya, 1,430....F3 31
Marbach, Ger., 9,500....E4 11
Marbella, Sp., 8,982....D3 20
Marble, Madison, Ark., 150..A2 81
Marble, Gunnison, Colo., 5...B3 83
Marble, Itasca, Minn., 879...C5 99
Marble, Cherokee, N.C., 356.D2 109
Marble, canyon, Ariz....A4 80
Marble Bar, Austl., 224....D2 50
Marble Canyon, Coconino, Ariz., 25....A4 80
Marble City, Sequoyah, Okla., 271....B7 112
Marble Cliff, Franklin, Ohio, 622....C2 111
Marble Dale, Litchfield Conn., 200....C3 84
Marble Falls, Burnet, Tex., 2,161....D3 118
Marble Hall, S. Afr., 1,218..B4 49
Marblehead, Adams, Ill., 160....D2 90
Marblehead, Essex, Mass., 18,521....B6, f12 97
Marblehead, Ottawa, Ohio, 858....A5 111
Marblehill, Pickens, Ga., 450.B2 87
Marble Hill, Bollinger, Mo., 497....D8 101
Marblemount, Skagit, Wash., 300....A4 122
Marble Mountain, N.S., Can., 59....D8 74
Marble Rock, Floyd, Iowa, 442....B5 92
Marbleton, Que., Can., 661..D6 73
Marbleton, Sublette, Wyo., 189....C2 125
Marburg, Ger., 47,600....C3 18
Marbury, Autauga, Ala., 150....C3 78
Marbury, Charles, Md., 500..C3 85
Marcala, Hond., 1,611....C4 62
Marcaria, It., 1,090....D6 18
Marcelin, Sask., Can., 280..E2 70
Marceline, Adams, Ill., 100..C2 90
Marceline, Linn, Mo., 2,872..B5 101
Marcella, Stone, Ark., 75....B4 81
Marcellus, Cass, Mich., 1,073.G5 98
Marcellus, Onondaga, N.Y., 1,697....C4 108
Marcellus, cave, Mo....D6 101
March, Eng., 13,119....B8 12
Marchand, Man., Can., 99...E3 71
Marchand, Mor....H3 30
Marche, Pulaski, Ark., 200...D5 81
Marche, pol. dist., It., 1,347,489....*C4 21
Marche, former prov., Fr., 222,000....D4 14
Marche-en-Famenne, Bel., 4,360....D5 15
Marchena, Sp., 17,030....D3 20
Marchena, isl., Ec....f5 58
Marches, reg., It....C4 21
Marchwell, Sask., Can., 146..G5 70
Marco, Collier, Fla., 250....G5 86
Marco, Greene, Ind., 215....G3 91
Marco, Natchitoches, La., 100....C3 95
Marcola, Lane, Oreg., 500...C4 113
Marcos Juárez, Arg., 9,556...A4 54
Marcus, Cherokee, Iowa, 1,307....B2 92
Marcus, Stevens, Wash., 126.A7 122
Marcus Baker, mtn., Alsk....g18 79
Marcus Hook, Delaware, Pa., 3,299....G11 114
Marcy Colony, Hutchinson, S. Dak., 45....D8 116
Marcy, mtn., N.Y....A7 108
Mardan, Pak., 73,246 (★77,932)....B5 39
Mar de Espanha, Braz., 3,661.g6 56
Mardela Springs, Wicomico, Md., 380....D6 85
Mar del Plata, Arg., 203,000..B5 54
Mardin, Tur., 27,400....D13 31
Marechal Deodoro, Braz., 5,269....C3, k6 57
Marengo, Sask., Can., 163....F1 70
Marengo, McHenry, Ill., 3,568....A5 90
Marengo, Crawford, Ind., 803....H5 91
Marengo, Iowa, Iowa, 2,264.C5 92
Marengo, Morrow, Ohio, 321....B5 111
Marengo, Ashland, Wis., 90..B3 124
Marengo, co., Ala., 27,098...C2 78
Marengo, cave, Ind....H5 91
Marenisco, Gogebic, Mich., 900....A5 98
Marennes, Fr., 3,332....E3 14
Maretz, Fr., 1,747....D3 15
Mareuil-sur-Ourcq, Fr., 447..E3 15
Mareyevka, Sov. Un....C7 29
Marfa, Presidio, Tex., 2,799..F2 118
Marfork, Raleigh, W. Va., 200....D3, D6 123
Marfrance, Greenbrier, W. Va., 400....C4 123
Marganets, Sov. Un., 30,000....H10 27
Margão, Goa, 17,175....E5 39
Margaree, N.S., Can., 206...C8 74
Margaree Harbour, N.S., Can., 112....C8 74
Margaret, St. Clair, Ala., 715....B3 78
Margaret, Man., Can., 78....E2 71
Margaret, Foard, Tex., 40....B3 118
Margaretsville, N.S., Can., 172....D4 74
Margaretville, Delaware, N.Y., 833....C6 108
Margarita, isl., Ven....A5 60
Margate, Eng., 45,400....C9 12
Margate, Broward, Fla., 2,646....*F6 86
Margate City, Atlantic, N.J., 9,474....E3 106
Margelan, Sov. Un., 80,000..E8 29
Margerum, Colbert, Ala., 150....A1 78
Marggrabowa, see Olecko, Pol.
Margherita, Som....E5 47
Margherita, lake, Eth....D4 47
Margherita, mtn., Con. L., Ug..A5 48
Marghi, Afg., 5,000....D13 41
Margie, Koochiching, Minn., 100....B5 99
Margny-lès-Compiègne, Fr., 5,870....E2 15
Margo, Sask., Can., 235....F4 70
Margrethe, lake, Mich....D6 98
Marguerite, bay, Ant....C6 5
Marguerite, riv., Que., Can....h8 75
Mari, lake, Sask., Can....B4 70
Maria, Que., Can....A3 74
Maria, isl., Austl....o15 50
Maria, riv., Arg....E2 55
Maria Chiquita, Pan., 229...k11 62
Mariager, Den., 1,500....B3 24
Mariager, fjord, Den....B4 24
Maria Grande, Arg., 3,400...A5 54
Maria Grande, Pan., 4....K11 62
María la Baja, Col., 4,182....A2 60
Maria Luisa, Cuba....k12 64
Marian, lake, Fla....E5 86
Mariana, is., Pac. O....E8 7
Marianao, Cuba, 325,000....k11 64
Marianna, Lee, Ark., 5,134..C5 81
Marianna, Jackson, Fla., 7,152....B1 86
Marianna, Washington, Pa., 1,088....*F3 114
Marianske Lazne, Czech., 12,600....D2 26
Mariapolis, Man., Can., 258..E2 71
Marias, pass, Mont....B3 102
Marias, riv., Mont....B4 102
Maria Stein, Mercer, Ohio, 230....B3 111
Mariato, pt., Pan....G7 62
Maria Van Diemen, cape, N.Z.K14 51
Mariaville, Hancock, Maine, (144▲)....D4 96
Maribel, Pamlico, N.C., 250..B7 109
Maribel, Manitowoc, Wis., 250....A6 124
Maribo, Den., 5,235....D5 24
Maribo, co., Den., 133,870...D5 24
Maribor, Yugo., 82,387....B2 22
Maricá, Braz., 2,200....h6 56
Maricaban, isl., Phil....p13 35
Maricao, P.R., 1,475....C3 65
Maricao, mun., P.R., 6,990...C3 65
Maricopa, Pinal, Ariz., 400..D3 80
Maricopa, Kern, Calif., 648..E4 82
Maricopa, co., Ariz., 663,510.D3 80
Maricopa, Indian res., Ariz....E3 80
Maridi, Sud., 839....E2 47
Marie, lake, Alta., Can....B5 69
Marié, riv., Braz....D4 60
Marie Byrd Land, reg., Ant...B34 5
Mariedam, Swe., 232....u33 25
Mariefred, Swe., 1,673....t35 25
Marie-Galante, isl., Guad....o16 64
Mariehamn, Fin., 6,700....G8 25
Mariembourg, Bel., 1,684....D4 15
Mariemont, Hamilton, Ohio, 4,120....C3 111
Marienberg, Ger., 8,281....C8 17
Mariental, S.W. Afr., 1,803...B2 49
Marienville, Forest, Pa., 800.D3 114
Marie-Reine, Alta., Can., 124....A2 69
Maries, co., Mo., 7,282....C6 101
Mariestad, Swe., 11,900....H5 25
Marietta, Duval, Fla....B6 86
Marietta, Cobb, Ga., 25,565....A5, C2 87
Marietta, Shelby, Ind., 300..F6 91
Marietta, Lac qui Parle, Minn., 327....E2 99
Marietta, Prentiss, Miss., 160.A5 100
Marietta, Washington, Ohio, 16,847....C4 111
Marietta, Love, Okla., 1,933.D4 112
Marietta, Lancaster, Pa., 2,385....F8 114
Marietta, Greenville, S.C., 900....A2 115
Marietta, Whatcom, Wash., 300....A3 122
Marietta East, Cobb, Ga., 4,535....*C2 87
Marieville, Que., Can., 3,809....D4 73
Mariinsk, Sov. Un., 36,000..B11 29
Mariinskiy, Sov. Un., 10,000.E23 9
Marijampole, Sov. Un., 15,652....A7 26
Marília, Braz., 51,789....C3 56
Marín, Sp., 7,261....A1 20
Marin, co., Calif., 146,820...C2 82
Marina, Monterey, Calif., 3,310....C6 82
Marina de Ravenna, It....E8 18
Marin City, Marin, Calif., 2,500....*B5 82
Marinduque, prov., Phil., 114,900....*C6 35
Marine, Madison, Ill., 813...E4 90
Marine City, St. Clair, Mich., 4,404....F8 98
Marine on St. Croix, Washington, Minn., 454....E6, E8 99
Marinette, Marinette, Wis., 13,329....C5 124
Marinette, co., Wis., 34,660.C5 124
Maringa, riv., Con. L....A3 48
Maringouin, Iberville, La., 1,168....D4 95
Marinha Grande, Port., 4,698.C1 20
Marino, It., 9,700....h9 21
Marinovka, Sov. Un....r21 27
Marion, Perry, Ala., 3,807....C2 78
Marion, Crittenden, Ark., 881....B5 81
Marion, Austl., 61,400....*G2 51
Marion, Hartford, Conn., 600....C5 84
Marion, Williamson, Ill., 11,274....F5 90
Marion, Grant, Ind., 37,854..C6 91
Marion, Linn, Iowa, 10,882..B6 92
Marion, Marion, Kans., 2,169....D6 93
Marion, Crittenden, Ky., 2,468....A3 94
Marion, Union, La., 685....B3 95
Marion, Plymouth, Mass., 1,300 (2,881▲)....C6 97
Marion, Osceola, Mich., 898.D5 98
Marion, Lauderdale, Miss., 500....C5 100
Marion, Flathead, Mont., 40.B2 102
Marion, Red Willow, Nebr., 172....D5 103
Marion, Wayne, N.Y., 850...B3 108
Marion, McDowell, N.C., 3,345....B2, D4 109
Marion, LaMoure, N. Dak., 309....C7 110
Marion, Marion, Ohio, 37,079....B4 111
Marion, Marion, Oreg., 250...C4 113
Marion, Franklin, Pa., 650...G6 114
Marion, Marion, S.C., 7,174.C9 115
Marion, Turner, S Dak., 843....D8 116
Marion, Smyth, Va., 8,385...B3 121
Marion, Waupaca, Wis., 1,200....D5 124
Marion, co., Ala., 21,837....A2 78
Marion, co., Ark., 6,041....A3 81
Marion, co., Fla., 51,616....C4 86
Marion, co., Ga., 5,477....D2 87
Marion, co., Ill., 39,349....E5 90
Marion, co., Ind., 697,567...E5 91
Marion, co., Iowa, 25,886...C4 92
Marion, co., Kans., 15,143...D6 93
Marion, co., Ky., 16,887....C4 94
Marion, co., Miss., 23,293...D4 100
Marion, co., Mo., 29,522....B6 101
Marion, co., Ohio, 60,221....B4 111
Marion, co., Oreg., 120,888..C4 113
Marion, co., S.C., 32,014.....C9 115
Marion, co., Tenn., 21,036...D8 117
Marion, co., Tex., 8,049.....C5 118
Marion, co., W. Va., 63,717..B4 123
Marion, lake, S.C....E7 115
Marion Center, Indiana, Pa., 407....E3 114
Marion Junction, Dallas, Ala., 350....B2 78
Marion Station, Somerset, Md., 200....D6 85
Marionville, Lawrence, Mo., 1,251....D4 101
Mariposa, Mariposa, Calif., 550....D4 82
Mariposa, co., Calif., 5,064...D3 82
Mariposas, Chile....B2 54
Marismas, marshes, Sp....D2 20
Marissa, St. Clair, Ill., 1,722.E4 90
Mariscal Estigarribia, Par...D3 55
Maris Town, Madison, Miss., 500....C3 100
Maritime Alps, mts., Fr., It....E7 14
Maritsa, riv., Bul....D7 22
Mariupol, see Zhdanov, Sov. Un.
Marivales, Phil., 1,828......o13 35
Mark, Putnam, Ill., 445.....B4 90
Markaryd, Swe., 2,502.......I5 25
Markdale, Ont., Can., 1,090.C4 72
Marked Tree, Poinsett, Ark., 3,216....B5 101
Markerwaard Polder, reg., Neth....B5 15
Markesan, Green Lake, Wis., 1,060....E5 124
Market Drayton, Eng., 5,853....B5 12

Market Harborough, Eng., 11,556....B7 12
Markethill, N. Ire., 813....C5 11
Market Rasen, Eng., 2,257...A7 12
Market Weighton, Eng., 2,080....G8 13
Markham, Ont., Can., 4,294....D5, k15 72
Markham, Cook, Ill., 11,704.F3 90
Markham, Matagorda, Tex., 800....E4 118
Markham, Fauquier, Va., 100....C5 121
Markham, Grays Harbor, Wash....C2 122
Markham, mtn., Ant....A29 5
Markhana, Afg., 5,000....D13 41
Marki, Pol....k14 26
Markinch, Sask., Can., 117..G3 70
Markkleeberg, Ger., 20,500..B7 17
Markland, Switzerland, Ind., 75....G8 91
Markle, Huntington and Wells, Ind., 789....C7 91
Markleeville, Alpine, Calif., 50....C4 82
Markleville, Madison, Ind., 402....E6 91
Markleysburg, Fayette, Pa., 345....G3 114
Markneukirchen, Ger., 8,903.C7 17
Markopoulon, Grc., 5,094..h11 23
Markovka, Sov. Un., 5,000..G12 27
Markovo, Sov. Un....C20 28
Markovo, Sov. Un....C6 4
Markranstädt, Ger., 10,300...B7 17
Marks, Quitman, Miss., 2,572....A3 100
Marksboro, Warren, N.J., 150....B3 106
Markstay, Ont., Can., 306.*p19 72
Marksville, Avoyelles, La., 4,257....C3 95
Marktheidenfeld, Ger., 4,800.D4 17
Marktredwitz, Ger., 15,500..D7 17
Markville, Pine, Minn., 100..D6 99
Marl, Ger., 73,800....*C3 16
Marland, Noble, Okla., 191..A4 112
Marlbank, Ont., Can., 237...C7 72
Marlboro, Alta., Can., 289...C2 69
Marlboro, Hartford, Conn., 900 (1,961▲)....C7 84
Marlboro, Middlesex, Mass., 18,819....B4, g9 97
Marlboro, Cheshire, N.H., 1,097 (1,612▲)....E2 105
Marlboro, Monmouth, N.J., 600....C4 106
Marlboro, Ulster, N.Y., 1,733....D6 108
Marlboro, Windham, Vt., 30 (347▲)....F3 120
Marlboro, co., S.C., 28,529...B8 115
Marlborough, Br. Gu....A3 59
Marlborough, Eng., 4,843....C6 12
Marle, Fr., 2,912....E3 15
Marlene Village, Washington, Oreg., 1,100....*B3 113
Marlette Sanilac, Mich., 1,640....E7 98
Marley, Anne Arundel, Md., 1,500....B4 85
Marlin, Falls, Tex., 6,918....D4 118
Marlin (Krupp), Grant, Wash., 99....B7 122
Marlinton, Pocahontas, W. Va., 1,586....C4 123
Marlow, Baldwin, Ala., 100...E2 78
Marlow, Effingham, Ga., 100....D5 87
Marlow, Ger., 2,855....D6 24
Marlow, Cheshire, N.H., 250 (350▲)....D2 105
Marlow, Stephens, Okla., 4,027....C4 112
Marlowe, Berkeley, W. Va., 700....B7 123
Marlton, Burlington, N.J., 3,000....D3 106
Marly-le-Roi, Fr., 10,193....g9 14
Marmaduke, Greene, Ark., 657....A5 81
Marmande, Fr., 10,199....E4 14
Marmara, isl., Tur....B6 23
Marmaris, Tur., 3,400....D7 23
Marmarth, Slope, N. Dak., 319....C2 110
Marmelos, riv., Braz....D2 59
Mar Menor, lagoon, Sp....D5 20
Marmet, Kanawha, W. Va., 2,500....C3, C6 123
Marmolada, mtn., It....C7 18
Marmora, Ont., Can., 1,381..C7 72
Marmora, Cape May, N.J., 500....E3 106
Marmora, peak, It....D2 21
Marmora, sea, Tur....B7 31
Marnay, Fr., 869....B1 18
Marne, Ger., 5,000....E3 24
Marne, Cass, Iowa, 205....C2 92
Marne, Ottawa, Mich., 450..E5 98
Marne, canal, Fr....F4 15
Marne, dept., Fr., 442,195....F4 15
Marne, riv., Fr....C5 14
Marne, au Rhin, canal, Fr....F6 15
Mar Negro, P.R....D5 65
Maro, reef, Haw....k13 89
Maroa, Macon, Ill., 1,235....C5 90
Maroantsetra, Malag., 4,412..g9 49
Maromokotro, mtn., Malag....f9 49
Maroni, riv., Sur....B4 60
Maroua, Cam....C2 46
Marovoay, Malag., 7,217....g9 49
Marpi, mtn., Saipan.... 52
Marpi, pt., Saipan.... 52
Marpo, pt., Tinian.... 52
Marquam, Clackamas, Oreg....B2, B4 113
Marquand, Madison, Mo., 392....D7 101
Marquesas, is., Fr. Polynesia..G13 7
Marquesas, keys, Fla....H4 86
Marquês de Valença, Braz., 18,935....C4, h6 56
Marquette, Man., Can., 87...D3 71
Marquette, Clayton, Iowa, 572....A6 92
Marquette, McPherson, Kans., 607....D6 93
Marquette, Marquette, Mich., 19,824....B3 98
Marquette, Hamilton, Nebr., 210....D8 103
Marquette, co., Mich., 56,154....B3 98
Marquette, co., Wis., 8,516...E4 124
Marquette Heights, Tazewell, Ill., 2,517....*C4 90
Marquez, Leon, Tex., 194....D4 118
Marquis, Sask., Can., 170....G3 70
Marquise, Fr., 4,802....D9 12
Marrakech, Mor., 243,134....C3 44, I3 20
Marree, Austl., 190....E6 50
Marrero, Jefferson, La., 19,000....C7 95
Marrickville, Austl., 74,800.*F8 51
Marriott, Weber, Utah, 100.*B3 119
Marromeu, Moz., 5,000....A6 49
Marroqui, pt., Sp....D3 20
Marrowbone, Cumberland, Ky., 200....D4 94
Mars, Butler, Pa., 1,522....E1 114
Mars, hill, Maine....B5 96
Mars, riv., Que., Can....A7 73
Marsá Al Burayqah, Libya...C3 43
Marsabit, Ken....A6 48
Marsala, It., 39,600....F4 21
Marsá Sūsah, Libya.C4 43, F4 31
Marsden, Sask., Can., 208....E1 70
Marseillan, Fr., 3,394....F5 14
Marseille (Marseilles), Fr., 778,071 (*870,000)....F6 14
Marseilles (Marseille), Fr., 778,071 (*870,000)....F6 14
Marseilles, La Salle, Ill., 4,347....B5 90
Marsh, Dawson, Mont., 25..D12 102
Marsh, creek, Mich....B4 98
Marsh, fork, W. Va....D6 123
Marsh, isl., La....E4 95
Marsh, lake, Minn....E2 99
Marsh, peak, Utah....C6 119
Marshall, Searcy, Ark., 1,095....B3 81
Marshall, Sask., Can., 161...D1 70
Marshall, Clark, Ill., 3,270..D6 90
Marshall, Parke, Ind., 360...E3 91
Marshall, Lib....E2 45
Marshall, Calhoun, Mich., 6,736....F6 98
Marshall, Lyon, Minn., 6,681....F3 99
Marshall, Saline, Mo., 9,572.B4 101
Marshall, Madison, N.C., 926....D3 109
Marshall, Logan, Okla., 363..A4 10
Marshall, Harrison, Tex., 23,846....C5 118
Marshall, Fauquier, Va., 500.C5 121
Marshall, Spokane, Wash., 100....D7 122
Marshall, Dane, Wis., 736...E4 124
Marshall, Albany, Wyo....C7 125
Marshall, co., Ala., 48,018...A3 78
Marshall, co., Ill., 13,334....B4 90
Marshall, co., Ind., 32,443...B5 91
Marshall, co., Iowa, 37,984..C4 92
Marshall, co., Kans., 15,598..C7 93
Marshall, co., Ky., 16,736....A3 94
Marshall, co., Minn., 14,262..B2 99
Marshall, co., Miss., 24,503..A4 100
Marshall, co., Okla., 7,263....C5 112
Marshall, co., S. Dak., 6,663..B8 116
Marshall, co., Tenn., 16,859..B5 117
Marshall, co., W. Va., 38,041.B4 123
Marshall, is., Pac. O....F10 7
Marshallberg, Carteret, N.C., 600....C7 109
Marshall Hall, Charles, Md., 20....C3 85
Marshall Northeast, Harrison, Tex., 1,192....*C5 118
Marshalls Creek, Monroe, Pa., 250....D11 114
Marshallton, New Castle, Del., 1,800....A6 85
Marshallton, Northumberland, Pa., 2,316....*E8 114
Marshalltown, Marshall, Iowa, 22,521....B5 92
Marshallville, Macon, Ga., 1,308....D3 87
Marshallville, Wayne, Ohio, 611....B6 111
Marshes Siding, McCreary, Ky., 500....D5 94
Marshfield, Warren, Ind., 100....D3 91
Marshfield, Plymouth, Mass., 1,500 (6,748▲)....B6, h13 97
Marshfield, Webster, Mo., 2,221....D5 101
Marshfield, Washington, Vt., 313 (891▲)....C4 120
Marshfield, Wood, Wis., 14,153....D3 124
Marshfield Center, Plymouth, Mass., 130....h13 97
Marshfield Hills, Plymouth, Mass., 900....B6, h13 97
Marsh Harbour, Ba. Is., 289..B5 64
Marsh Hill, Lycoming, Pa., 100....D8 114
Mars Hill, Marion, Ind., 1,000....E5, H7 91
Mars Hill, Aroostook, Maine, 1,458 (2,062▲)....B5 96
Mars Hill, Madison, N.C., 1,574....D3 109
Marshville, Union, N.C., 1,360....B3 109
Marshyhope, creek, Del., Md...C6 85
Marsing, Owyhee, Idaho, 555....F2 89
Marske-by-the Sea, Eng. (part of Saltburn and Marske-by-the-Sea)....F8 13
Marsland, Dawes, Nebr., 39..B2 103
Marstal, Den., 1,986 (*2,900)....D4 24
Marsteller, Cambria, Pa., 450.E4 114
Marston, New Madrid, Mo., 631....E8 101
Marston, Richmond, N.C., 75....C4 109
Marstons Mills, Barnstable, Mass., 500....C7 97
Mart, McLennan, Tex., 2,197....D4 118
Martaban, Bur., 5,639....E10 39
Martaban, gulf, Bur....E10 39
Martapura, Indon....F4 35
Martel, Que., Can., 1,009....A6 73
Martel, Marion, Fla., 100....C4 86
Martelange, Bel., 1,583....E5 15
Martell, Lancaster, Nebr., 104....D9 103
Martell, Pierce, Wis., 150...D1 124
Martelle, Jones, Iowa, 247....B6 92
Martensdale, Warren, Iowa, 316....B7, C4 92
Martha, Jackson, Okla., 243.C2 112
Martha, Wilson, Tenn., 35..A5 117
Marthasville, Warren, Mo., 339....C6 101
Marthas Vineyard, isl., Mass...D6 97
Marthaville, Natchitoches, La., 181....C2 95
Martí, Cuba, 652....E5 64
Martignano, lake, It....g8 21
Martigny-Ville, Switz., 5,239....D3 19
Martigues, Fr., 9,852....F6 14
Martin, Stephens, Ga., 209..B3 87
Martin, Floyd, Ky., 992....C7 96
Martin, Allegan, Mich., 483..F5 98
Martin, Sherman, N. Dak., 146....B5 110
Martin, Ottawa, Ohio, 220...A2 111
Martin, Allendale, S.C., 80...E5 115
Martin, Bennett, S. Dak., 1,184....D4 116
Martin, Weakley, Tenn., 4,750....A3 117
Martin, Carbon, Utah, 100..D5 119
Martin, co., Fla., 16,932....E6 86
Martin, co., Ind., 10,602....G4 91
Martin, co., Ky., 10,201....C7 94
Martin, co., Minn., 26,986..G4 99
Martin, co., N.C., 27,139....B6 109
Martin, co., Tex., 5,068....C2 118
Martin, dam, Ala....C4 78
Martin, lake, Ala....C4 78
Martin, pen., Ant....B1 5
Martin, pt., Alsk....B29 4
Martina [Franca], It., 25,500....D6 21
Martin City, Flathead, Mont., 400....*B2 102
Martindale, Que., Can....D2 73
Martindale, Caldwell, Tex., 500....A4 118
Martinez, Contra Costa, Calif., 9,604....B5, C2 82
Martínez, Cuba....D2 64
Martinez, Columbia and Richmond, Ga., 2,000....C4 87
Martinique, Fr. dep., N.A., 312,000....o16 64
Martinique, passage, N.A....o16 64
Martins, pond, Mass....f11 97
Martinsburg, Washington, Ind., 100....H5 91
Martinsburg, Keokuk, Iowa, 172....C5 92
Martinsburg, Audrian, Mo., 330....B6 101
Martinsburg, Dixon, Nebr., 68....B9 103
Martinsburg, Lewis N.Y., 200....B5 108
Martinsburg, Knox, Ohio, 228....B5 111
Martinsburg, Blair, Pa., 1,772....F5 114
Martinsburg, Berkeley, W. Va., 15,179....B6 123
Martins Creek, Northampton, Pa., 900....B2 106
Martinsdale, Meagher, Mont., 200....D6 102
Martins Ferry, Belmont, Ohio, 11,919....B7 111
Martins Mills, Wayne, Tenn..B4 117
Martin Springs, Marion, Tenn....D8 117
Martinsville, Clark, Ill., 1,351....D6 90
Martinsville, Morgan, Ind., 7,525....F5 91
Martinsville, Copiah, Miss., 75....D3 100
Martinsville, Harrison, Mo., 79....A3 101
Martinsville, Somerset, N.J., 800....B3 106
Martinsville, Clinton, Ohio, 488....C4 111
Martinsville (Independent City), Va., 18,798....E3 121
Martinton, Iroquois, Ill., 314....C6 90
Martinville, Faulkner, Ark., 25....B3 81
Martinville, Que., Can., 168....D6 73
Martling, Marshall, Ala., 125....A3 78
Martofte, Den....C4 24
Martos, Sp., 16,900....D4 20
Martwick, Muhlenberg, Ky., 200....C2 94
Marty, Charles Mix, S. Dak., 50....E7 116
Maruchak, Afg., 5,000....D11 41
Maruf, Afg., 5,000....F13 41
Marugame, Jap., 39,500 (61,403▲)....I6 37
Marum, Neth., 1,264....A6 15
Marumsco, creek, Md....D6 85
Marun, riv., Iran....F7 41
Marvast, Iran....F7 41
Marvejols, Fr., 3,934....E5 14
Marvel, Bibb, Ala., 250....B2 78
Marvel, La Plata, Colo., 100.D2 82
Marvel, cave, Mo....E4 101
Marvell, Phillips, Ark., 1,690.C5 81
Marvin, Grant, S. Dak., 93...B9 116
Marvindale, McKean, Pa., 40....C4 114
Marvine, mtn., Utah....E4 119
Marvin Terrace, St. Louis, Mo., 1,260....*C7 101
Marvyn, Lee, Ala., 100....C4 78
Marwayne, Alta., Can., 379..C5 69
Mary, Sov. Un., 54,000....H21 9
Mary, lake, Minn....E3 99
Mary, lake, Miss....D2 100
Maryborough, Austl., 7,235..H4 51
Maryborough, Austl., 19,126.B9 51
Marydel, Caroline, Md., 130.B6 85
Mary Esther, Okaloosa, Fla., 780....*G2 86
Maryfield, Sask., Can., 476..H5 70
Maryland, state, U.S., 3,100,689....C12 77, 85
Maryland, pt., Md....D3 85
Maryland Heights, St. Louis, Mo., 2,000....A8 101
Maryland Line, Baltimore, Md., 165....A4 85
Maryland Park, Prince Georges, Md., 1,000....*C4 85
Maryport, Eng., 12,334....C5 10
Marys, peak, Oreg....C3 113
Marys, riv., Nev....A6 104
Mary's Harbour, Newf., Can., 264....B4 75
Mary's Igloo, Alsk., 8....B6 79
Marystown, Newf., Can., 1,691....E4 75
Marysvale, Piute, Utah, 354..E3 119
Marysville, Yuba, Calif., 9,553....C3 82
Marysville, B.C., Can., 1,057....E10 68
Marysville, N.B., Can., 3,233....D3 74
Marysville, Ont., Can., 380..C8 72
Marysville, Fremont, Idaho, 201....E7 89
Marysville, Marion, Iowa, 113....C5 92
Marysville, Marshall, Kans., 4,143....C7 93
Marysville, St. Clair, Mich., 4,065....F8 98
Marysville, Lewis and Clark, Mont., 45....D4 102
Marysville, Union, Ohio, 4,952....B4 111
Marysville, Perry, Pa., 2,580..F8 114
Marysville, Snohomish, Wash., 3,117....A3 122
Marytown, McDowell, W. Va., 100....D3 123
Marytown, Fond du Lac, Wis., 130....B5 124
Maryvale, Maricopa, Ariz., 2,000....*D3 80
Maryville, Madison, Ill., 675....A9 101
Maryville, Nodaway, Mo., 7,807....A3 101
Maryville, Blount, Tenn., 10,348....D10, E11 117
Marzūq, Libya, 2,853....D2 43
Masai Steppe, plat., Tan....B6 48
Masaka, Ug., 4,782....B5 48
Masalembo-Besar, isl., Indon...G5 35
Masalog, pt., Tinian.... 52
Masan, Kor., 152,400....I4 35
Masardis, Aroostook, Maine, 250 (408▲)....B4 96
Masaryktown, Hernando, Fla., 450....D4 86
Masash el Sirr (Oasis), Eg., U.A.R....D5 32
Masasi, Tan., 2,720....D6 48
Masatepe, Nic., 6,600....E4 62
Masaya, Nic., 32,100....E4 62
Masbate, Phil., 7,500 (31,600▲)....C6 35
Masbate, prov., Phil., 336,700....*C6 35
Mascara, Alg., 46,209 (*52,897).B5 44, G7 30
Mascarene, is., Indian O....H24 3
Mascoma, lake, N.H....C2 105
Mascoma, riv., N.H....C2 105
Mascot, Harlan, Nebr., 35...D6 103
Mascot, Knox, Tenn., 1,000....C10, E12 117
Mascota, Mex., 5,214....m11 63
Mascouche, Que., Can., 1,152....D4 73
Mascoutah, St. Clair, Ill., 3,625....E4 90
Masefau, bay, Am. Sam.... 52
Masefield, Sask., Can....H2 70
Maseru, Bas., 9,000....C5 49
Mashaki, Afg., 5,000....E14 41
Masham, Eng., 894....F7 13
Mashapaug, pond, Conn....A8 84
Mashhad (Meshed), Iran, 241,989....C9 40
Mashīz, Iran....G8 41
Mashkel, riv., Iran....H11 41
Mashonaland, reg., Rh....A5 49
Mashpee, Barnstable, Mass., 300 (867▲)....C7 97
Mashulaville, Noxubee, Miss., 150....B5 100
Masi Manimba, Con. L....B2 48
Masindi, Ug....A5 48
Masira, isl., Mus. & Om....D2 39
Masisea, Peru, 1,742....C3 58
Masisi, Con. L....B4 48
Masjed Soleymān, Iran., 44,651....F4 41
Mask, lake, Ire....D2 11
Maskell, Dixon, Nebr., 54...B9 103
Maskinongé, Que., Can., 893....C4 73
Maskinongé, co., Que., Can., 21,274....C4 73
Masnières, Fr., 2,399....D3 15
Mason, Effingham, Ill., 332..E5 90
Mason, Ingham, Mich., 4,522....F6 98
Mason, Lyon, Nev., 350....E2 104
Mason, Hillsboro, N.H., 50 (349▲)....F4 105
Mason, Warren, Ohio, 4,727....C2, C3 111
Mason, Okfuskee, Okla., 50..B5 112
Mason, Tipton, Tenn., 407..B2 117
Mason, Mason, Tex., 1,910..D3 118
Mason, Mason, W. Va., 1,005....B2 123
Mason, Bayfield, Wis., 100...B2 124
Mason, Sublette, Wyo....C2 125
Mason, co., Ill., 15,193....C4 90
Mason, co., Ky., 18,454....B6 94
Mason, co., Mich., 21,929....D4 98
Mason, co., Tex., 3,780....D3 118
Mason, co., Wash., 16,251...B2 122
Mason, co., W. Va., 24,459...C3 123
Mason, bayou, Ark....D4 81
Mason City, Mason, Ill., 2,160....C4 90
Mason City, Cerro Gordo, Iowa, 30,642....A4 92
Mason City, Custer, Nebr., 277....C6 103
Masonhall, Obion, Tenn., 200....A2 117
Masons, Coos, N.H....A3 105
Masontown, Fayette, Pa., 4,730....F2 114
Masontown, Preston, W. Va., 841....B5 123
Masonville, Desha, Ark., 50..D4 81
Masonville, Larimer, Colo., 200....A5 83
Masonville, Delaware, N.Y., 250....C5 108
Mass, Ontonagon, Mich., 300....A6 98
Massa, It., 59,200 (*132,000)....B3 21
Massaade, Syr....A7 32
Massabesic, lake, N.H....E4 105
Massabielle, Que., Can., 415....*D6 73
Massac, co., Ill., 14,341....F5 90
Massachusetts, state, U.S., 5,148,578....B13 77, 97
Massachusetts, bay, Mass....B6 97
Massacre, bay, Am. Sam.... 52
Massacre, lake, Nev....B2 104
Massaemett, mtn., Mass....A2 97
Massafra, It., 20,005....D6 21
Massakory, Chad, 1,033....C3 46
Massa Marittima, It., 5,700..C3 21
Massangena, Moz....B5 49
Massanutten, mtn., Va....C4 121
Massapê, Braz., 4,760....B2 57
Massapeag, New London, Conn., 300....D8 84
Massapequa, Nassau, N.Y., 36,000....G3 84
Massapequa Park, Nassau, N.Y., 19,904....*G3 84
Massapoag, pond, Mass....h11 97
Massaua, Eth., 25,000....B4 47
Massena, Cass, Iowa, 456....C3 92
Massena, St. Lawrence, N.Y., 15,478....f10 108
Masset, B.C., Can., 547....C1 68
Masset, inlet, B.C., Can....C1 68
Massey, Ont., Can., 1,324...A2 72
Massey, Kent, Md., 75....B6 85
Massif Central, mts., Fr....E5 14
Massif de Tarazit, plat., Niger..B6 45
Massillon, Stark, Ohio, 31,236....B6 111
Massinga, Moz....B6 49
Massive, mtn., Colo....B4 83
Masson, Que., Can., 1,933...D2 73
Masson, isl., Ant....C22 5
Massy, Fr., 19,137....h10 14
Masten, Kent, Del., 30....C6 85
Mastergeehy, Ire....F1 11
Masters, Weld, Colo., 3....A6 83
Masterton, N.Z., 15,128....N15 51
Mastic, Suffolk, N.Y., 3,000.*F5 84
Mastic Beach, Suffolk, N.Y., 4,000....*G5 84
Mastuj, Pak....k17 41
Mastung, Pak., 2,792....C1 40
Mastūrah, Sau. Ar....A4 47
Masuda, Jap., 27,400 (56,053▲)....I5 37
Masulipatnam, India, 101,417....E7 39
Masuria, reg., Pol....B6 26
Masury, Trumbull, Ohio, 5,900....A7 111
Masuya, Okinawa.... 52
Mata, Con. L....C3 48
Mata Armilla, Arg....D2 54
Matabeleland, reg., Rh....A4 49
Mataboor, W. Irian....F9 35
Matachewan, Ont., Can., 923....p19 72
Mata de São João, Braz., 8,117....D3 57
Matadi, Con. L., 59,000....C1 48
Matador, Sask., Can., 40....G2 70
Matador, Motley, Tex., 1,217....B2 118
Matafotufotu, cape, W. Sam.... 52
Matagalpa, Nic., 15,900....D5 62
Matagorda, Matagorda, Tex., 500....E5 118
Matagorda, co., Tex., 25,744.E5 118
Matagorda, bay, Tex....E4 118
Matagorda, isl., Tex....E4 118
Matagorda, pen., Tex....E5 118
Matak, isl., Indon....K7 38
Matam, Sen., 2,600....C2 45
Matamā, Eth....C4 47
Matamoras, Pike, Pa., 2,087....D12 114
Matamoros, Mex., 92,327....B5 63
Matamoros [de la Laguna], Mex., 13,572....B4 63
Ma'tan, Libya....D2 43
Ma'tan as Sarra (Well), Libya....E4 43
Ma'tan Bishārah (Well), Libya....E4 43
Matane, Que., Can., 9,190..k13 73
Matane, co., Que., Can., 35,078....*k13 73
Ma'tan Rāshidah, Libya....H3 31
Matanuska, riv., Alsk....g18 79
Matanuska, val., Alsk....g17 79
Matanzas, Cuba, 80,000....D3 64
Matanzas, prov., Cuba, 395,780....D3 64
Matanzas, inlet, Fla....C5 86
Matapan, cape, Grc....D4 23
Matapédia, Que., Can., 596.B3 74
Matapedia, co., Que., Can., 35,586....*k13 73
Matapedia, riv., Que., Can....A2 74
Matara, Cey., 27,735....G7 39
Mataram, Indon....G5 35
Matarani, Peru....E3 58
Matarka, Mor....H5 30
Mataró, Sp., 41,128....B7 20
Matatiele, S. Afr., 3,237....D4 49
Matautu, W. Sam., 392.... 52
Matawan, Monmouth, N.J., 5,097....C4 106
Matehuala, Mex., 19,738....C4 63
Mateko, Con. L....B2 48
Matera, It., 39,900....D6 21
Mateszalka, Hung., 11,249...B6 22
Mateur, Tun., 12,714....F11 30
Matewan, Mingo, W. Va., 896....D2 123
Matfield, Plymouth, Mass., 900....B6 97
Matfield Green, Chase, Kans., 95....D7 93
Mathelo, Pak....D2 40
Mather, Man., Can., 125....E2 71
Mather, Greene, Pa., 1,033..G1 114
Mather, Juneau, Wis., 65....D3 124
Mather, peak, Wyo....A5 125
Matherville, Mercer, Ill., 612.B3 90
Matherville, Wayne, Miss., 100....D5 100
Matheson, Elbert, Colo., 150.B7 83
Matheson Island, Man., Can., 176....D3 71
Mathews, Montgomery, Ala., 10....C3 78
Mathews, Lafourche, La., 200....C6, E5 95
Mathews, Mathews, Va., 500....C6 121
Mathews, co., Va., 7,121....D6 121
Mathews, lake, Calif....F3 82
Mathias, Hardy, W. Va., 300....C6 123
Mathias Point, King George, Va....C5 121
Mathis, San Patricio, Tex., 6,075....E4 118
Mathiston, Webster and Choctaw, Miss., 597....B4 100
Mathura, India, 116,959 (*125,258)....C6 39, D6 40
Mati, Phil., 2,899....*D7 35
Matiakoali, Upper Volta...D5 45
Matinenda, lake, Ont., Can....A2 72
Matinicus, Knox, Maine, 75 (100▲)....E4 96
Matinicus, isl., Maine....E4 96
Matjan, is., Indon....G6 35
Matlock, Eng., 19,200....A6 12
Matlock, Sioux, Iowa, 103...A2 92
Matoaca, Chesterfield, Va., 2,000....C7 121
Matoaka, Mercer, W. Va., 613....D3 123
Mato Grosso, Braz., 520....B4 55
Mato Grosso, state, Braz., 910,262....B1 56
Matopiana, riv., Pol....f9 26
Matozinhos, Port., 37,694....B1 20
Maṭraḥ, Mus. & Om., 14,000....D2 39
Matrosovo, Sov. Un....B11 37
Maṭrūḥ, Eg., U.A.R., 3,047 .G6 31
Matsqui, B.C., Can., 275....f13 68
Matsudo, Jap., 57,900 (86,372▲)....*n18 37
Matsue, Jap., 78,000 (106,476▲)....I6 37
Matsuida, Jap., 9,300....m17 37
Matsumae, Jap., 19,534....F10 37
Matsumoto, Jap., 108,000 (148,710▲)....H9, m16 37
Matsuyama, Jap., 238,604...J6 37
Matsuzaka, Jap., 57,600 (98,441▲)....I8, o15 37
Matsuzaki, Jap., 5,708....o17 37
Mattamiscontis, lake, Maine....C4 96
Mattamuskeet, lake, N.C....B7 109
Mattancheri, India, 83,896..G6 39
Mattapoisett, Plymouth, Mass., 1,800 (3,117▲)....C6 97
Mattaponi, riv., Va....D5 121
Mattawa, Ont., Can., 3,314....A6, p20 72
Mattawamkeag, Penobscot, Maine, 750 (945▲)....C4 96
Mattawamkeag, lake, Maine....C4 96
Mattawamkeag, riv., Maine....C4 96
Mattawana, Mifflin, Pa., 250....F6 114
Mattawin, riv., Que., Can....C4 73
Mattawoman, creek, Md....C3 85
Matterhorn, mtn., Switz....E4 19
Matterson, inlet, Ant....g40 5
Mattervisy, riv., Switz....D4 19
Matteson, Cook, Ill., 3,225...F3 90
Matthews, Jefferson, Ga., 106....C4 87
Matthews, Grant, Ind., 627..D7 91
Matthews, New Madrid, Mo., 450....E8 101
Matthews, Mecklenburg, N.C., 609....B3 109
Matthews, mtn., Mo....D7 101
Matthew Town, Ba. Is., 994..E7 64
Mattituck, Suffolk, N.Y., 1,500....n16 108
Mattoax, Amelia, Va....D5 121
Mattoon, Coles, Ill., 19,088..D5 90
Mattoon, Shawano, Wis., 435....D4 124
Mattson, Coahoma, Miss., 250....A3 100
Mattydale, Onondaga, N.Y., 10,500....*B4 108
Matucana, Peru, 1,746....D2 60
Matuku, isl., Fiji Is.... 52
Matun, Afg., 5,000....E14 41
Matundu, Con. L....A3 48
Matunuck, Washington, R.I., 100....D10 84
Maturín, Ven., 53,445....B5 60
Mau, Fiji Is.... 52
Mau, India, 48,785....E9 40
Maúa, Moz....D6 48
Mauban, Phil., 4,051....o13 35
Maubeuge, Fr., 27,214 (*64,000)....B5 14
Maubin, Bur., 22,130....D1 38
Mauch Chunk, see Jim Thorpe, Pa.
Mauchline, Scot., 4,160....E4 13
Mauckport, Harrison, Ind., 107....H5 91
Maud, Butler, Ohio, 600....C2, C3 111
Maud, Pottawatomie and Seminole, Okla., 1,137....B5 112
Maud, Scot....C6 13
Maud, Bowie, Tex., 951....C5 118
Maudlow, Gallatin, Mont., 20....D5 102
Maués, Braz., 4,161....C3 59
Maues Guaçu, riv., Braz....C3 59
Mauganj, India, 1,000....E8 40
Maugansville, Washington, Md., 625....A2 85
Maugerville, N.B., Can., 631.D3 74
Maughold, head, I. of Man....F4 13
Maui (incl. Kalawao), co., Haw., 42,855....B5 88
Maui, isl., Haw....C5 88
Mauk, Taylor, Ga., 100....D2 87
Mauldin, Greenville, S.C., 1,462....*B3 115
Maule, prov., Chile, 79,304..B2 54
Mauléon, Fr., 3,705....F3 14
Maumakeogh, mtn., Ire....C2 11
Maumee, Lucas, Ohio, 12,063....A2, A4 111
Maumee, bay, Ohio....A2 111
Maumee, riv., Ind., Ohio....B8 91, A4 111
Maun, Bech., 500....A3 49
Maunabo, P.R., 1,027....C7 65
Maunabo, mun., P.R., 10,785....C7 65
Mauna Kea, vol., Haw....D6 88
Maunaloa, Maui, Haw., 950....B4 88
Mauna Loa, vol., Haw....D6 88
Maunalua, bay, Haw....g11 88
Maungdaw, Bur., 3,846....D9 39
Maunie, White, Ill., 363....E5 90
Maunoir, lake, N.W. Ter., Can.C8 66
Maupin, Wasco, Oreg., 381..B5 113
Maurepas, Livingston, La., 50....B6 95
Maurepas, lake, La....D5 95
Maurertown, Shenandoah, Va., 225....C4 121
Maurice, Sioux, Iowa, 237...B1 92
Maurice, Vermilion, La., 411....D3 95
Maurice, Lawrence, S. Dak., 25....C2 116
Maurice, riv., N.J....E2 106
Mauricetown, Cumberland, N.J., 400....E3 106
Mauriceville, Orange, Tex., 750....D2 95
Maurine, Meade, S. Dak., 10.B3 116
Mauritania, country, Afr., 1,000,000....C2 45, D4 42
Mauritius, Br. dep., Afr., 752,000....H24 3

Maury, Greene, N.C., 285...B6 109
Maury, co., Tenn., 41,699...B4 117
Maury, isl., Wash..........D1 122
Maury City, Crockett, Tenn., 624..............B2 117
Mauston, Juneau, Wis., 3,531..................E3 124
Mauterndorf, Aus., 1,615....E6 16
Mauwee, peak, Conn..........C3 84
Maverick, Apache, Ariz., 50.D6 80
Maverick, co., Tex., 14,508..E2 118
Mavinga, Ang..............E3 48
Mawdesley, lake, Man., Can...B1 71
Mawer, Sask., Can., 72......G2 70
Mawkmai, Bur..............D2 38
Mawlaik, Bur., 3,042.......D9 39
Mawson, escarpment, Ant.....B19 5
Mawson, glacier, Ant........e40 5
Mawson, pen., Ant..........C28 5
Max, Dundy, Nebr., 150...D4 103
Max, McLean, N. Dak., 410.B4 110
Maxbass, Bottineau, N. Dak., 218.....................A4 110
Maxcanú, Mex., 5,127.......C6 63
Maxeys, Oglethorpe, Ga., 149........................C3 87
Maxie, Forrest, Miss., 60....E4 100
Maxinkuckee, lake, Ind........B5 91
Max Meadows, Wythe, Va., 900........................E2 121
Maxstone, Sask., Can.......H2 70
Maxton, Robeson, N.C., 1,755......................C4 109
Maxville, Ont., Can., 804...B10 72
Maxville, Duval, Fla., 250...B4 86
Maxville, Granite, Mont., 80.D3 102
Maxwell, Colusa, Calif., 700..C2 82
Maxwell, Hancock, Ind., 280........................E6 91
Maxwell, Story, Iowa, 773..............A8, C4 92
Maxwell, Lincoln, Nebr., 324........................C5 103
Maxwell, Colfax, N. Mex., 392........................A5 107
Maxwell, Franklin, Tenn., 50..........................B5 117
Maxwell Colony, Hutchinson, S. Dak., 200............D8 116
May, Lemhi, Idaho, 60......E5 89
May, Harper, Okla., 114....A2 112
May, Brown, Tex., 400......D3 118
May, cape, N.J...........C13 77
May, isl., Scot.............D6 13
May, mtn., Alta., Can.......B1 69
Maya, mts., Br. Hond.......B3 62
Mayaguana, isl., Ba. Is......D7 64
Mayaguana, passage, Ba. Is....D7 64
Mayagüez, P.R., 50,147......C2 65
Mayagüez, mun., P.R., 83,850........................C2 65
Mayagüez, bay, P.R..........C2 65
Mayama, Con. B.............F2 46
Mayarí, Cuba, 4,519.........E6 64
Maybank, Forrest, Miss., 50.D4 100
Maybee, Monroe, Mich., 459.F7 98
Maybell, Moffat, Colo., 100..A2 83
Mayberry, Carroll, Md., 100.A3 85
Maybeury, McDowell, W. Va., 900..............*D3 123
Maybole, Scot., 4,677.......E4 13
Maybrook, Orange, N.Y., 1,348......................D6 108
Maydee, Lauderdale, Tenn..B2 117
Maydi, Yemen...............B5 47
Mayen, Ger., 17,300.........C2 17
Mayenne, Fr., 10,270.......C3 14
Mayenne, dept., Fr., 250,030..................*C3 14
Mayenne, riv., Fr..........D3 14
Mayer, Yavapai, Ariz., 300..C3 80
Mayersville, Issaquena, Miss., 450........................C2 100
Mayerthorpe, Alta., Can., 663........................C3 69
Mayes, co., Okla., 20,073....A6 112
Mayesville, Sumter, S.C., 750........................D7 115
Mayetta, Jackson, Kans., 218........................B6 93
Mayetta, Ocean, N.J., 150...D4 106
Mayfair, Sask., Can., 95.....E2 70
Mayfair, Greenville, S.C., 5,000....................*B3 115
Mayfield, Sumner, Kans., 119........................E6 93
Mayfield, Graves, Ky., 10 762........................B2 94
Mayfield, Fulton, N.Y., 818..B6 108
Mayfield, Butler, Ohio, 2,747......................*C3 111
Mayfield, Cuyahoga, Ohio, 1,977......................*A6 111
Mayfield, Lackawanna, Pa., 1,996.......................C10 114
Mayfield, Sanpete, Utah, 329........................D4 119
Mayfield, Lewis, Wash., 45..C3 122
Mayfield, res., Wash..........C3 122
Mayfield Heights, Cuyahoga, Ohio, 13,478................A6 111
Mayflower, Faulkner, Ark., 355........................C3 81
Mayflower, Newton, Tex., 100........................D6 118
Mayhew, Lowndes, Miss., 300........................B5 100
Mayhill, Otero, N. Mex., 100........................E4 107
Maykain, Sov. Un..........C9 29
Mayking, Letcher, Ky., 750..C7 94
Maykop, Sov. Un., 95,000..G17 9
Mayland, Cumberland, Tenn., 450........................C8 117
Maymont, Sask., Can., 239...E2 70
Maymyo, Bur., 22,287.......D10 39
Maynard, Randolph, Ark., 201........................A5 81
Maynard, Fayette, Iowa, 515........................B6 92
Maynard, Allen, Ky., 50....D3 94
Maynard, Middlesex, Mass., 7,695..............B5, g10 97
Maynard, Chippewa, Minn., 429........................F3 99
Maynard, Belmont, Ohio, 600........................B1 123
Maynardville, Union, Tenn., 620........................C10 117
Mayne, B.C., Can., 139.....g12 68
Mayne, isl., B.C., Can.......g12 68
Maynooth, Ont., Can.........B7 72
Maynooth, Ire., 1,753.......D5 11
Mayo, Yukon, Can., 342....D5 66
Mayo, Lafayette, Fla., 687...B3 86
Mayo, Anne Arundel, Md., 500........................C4 85
Mayo, Spartanburg, S.C., 500........................A4 115
Mayo, co., Ire., 123,330.....D2 11
Mayo, lake, Yukon, Can.......D6 66
Mayo, mts., Ire..............C2 11
Mayo, riv., Arg..............D2 54
Mayodan, Rockingham, N.C., 2,366.......................A4 109
Mayon, vol., Phil.............C6 35
Mayotte, isl., Comoro Is.........f9 49
Mayoumba, Gabon...........F2 46
May Pen, Jam., 14,214.......G5 64
Mayport, Duval, Fla., 450................B5, B6 86
Mays, Rush, Ind., 200........E7 91
Mays Landing, Atlantic, N.J., 1,500........................E3 106
Mays Lick, Mason, Ky., 400..B6 94
Maysville, Madison, Ala., 400........................A3 78
Maysville, Benton, Ark., 200.A1 81
Maysville, Banks, and Jackson, Ga., 553..............B3 87
Maysville, Daviess, Ind.....G3 91
Maysville, Scott, Iowa, 126..D7 92
Maysville, Mason, Ky., 8,484........................B6 94
Maysville, DeKalb, Mo., 942........................B3 101
Maysville, Jones, N.C., 892...C6 109
Maysville, Garvin, Okla., 1,530.......................C4 112
Maysville, Grant, W. Va., 120........................B5 123
Maytown, Jefferson, Ala., 297......................*B2 78
Mayuram, India, 51,393....*F6 39
May Valley, Prowers, Colo...C8 83
Mayview, Lafayette, Mo., 270........................B4 101
Mayville, Tuscola, Mich., 896........................E7 98
Mayville, Cape May, N.J., 550........................E3 106
Mayville, Chautauqua, N.Y., 1,619.......................C1 108
Mayville, Traill, N. Dak., 2,168.......................B8 110
Mayville, Gilliam, Oreg., 50..B6 113
Mayville, Dodge, Wis., 3,607.E5 124
Maywood, Los Angeles, Calif., 14,588......................F2 82
Maywood, Cook, Ill., 27,330......................F2 90
Maywood, Marion, Ind., 400........................H7 91
Maywood, Lewis, Mo., 158...B6 101
Maywood, Frontier, Nebr., 337........................D5 103
Maywood, Bergen, N.J., 11,460......................h8 106
Maywood, Albany, N.Y., 3,000......................*C7 108
Mayyat Yarqah (Oasis), Eg., U.A.R..................E5 32
Maza, Arg..................B4 54
Maza, Towner, N. Dak., 31..A6 110
Mazabuka, Zambia, 4,400....E4 48
Mazagão, Braz., 919.........C4 59
Mazamet, Fr., 14,863.......F5 14
Mazán, Arg.................E2 55
Mazapil, Mex., 1,742.......C4 63
Mazara del Vallo, It., 36,827......................F4 21
Mazāri 'an Nūbāni, Jordan, 2,000......................g11 32
Mazar-i-Sharif, Afg., 70,000......................C13 41
Mazarn, creek, Ark...........C5 81
Mazarredo, Arg.............D3 54
Mazarrón, Sp., 11,569.......D5 20
Mazaruni, riv., Br. Gu........A2 59
Mazatenango, Guat., 11,067.C2 62
Mazatlán, Mex., 75,751.....C3 63
Mazatzal, mts., Ariz......C4, F3 80
Mazatzal, peak, Ariz..........C4 80
Mažeikiai, Sov. Un., 8,900...C4 27
Mazenod, Sask., Can., 121...H2 70
Mazeppa, Wabasha, Minn., 444........................F6 99
Mazie, Mayes, Okla., 100....A6 112
Mazgirt, Tur., 1,500.......C12 31
Mazomanie, Dane, Wis., 1,069......................E4 124
Mazon, Grundy, Ill., 683....B5 90
Mazzarino, It., 17,789.......F5 21
Mbabane, Swaz., 8,400.......C5 49
Mbaïki, Cen. Afr. Rep......E3 46
Mbale, Ug., 13,569.........A5 48
Mbalmayo, Cam.............E2 46
Mbamba Bay, Tan...........B5 48
Mbarara, Ug................B5 48
M'bari, riv., Cen. Afr. Rep.....D4 46
Mbatiki, isl., Fiji Is..............52
Mbenga, isl., Fiji Is..............52
Mbenga, pass, Fiji Is............52
Mbeya, Tan., 6,932..........C5 48
M'Bour, Sen., 8,800.........D1 45
Mbout, Maur................C2 45
Mbulia, isl., Fiji Is...............52
Mburucuyá, Arg., 2,555.....E4 55
Mbya, bay, Fiji Is...............52
Mchinja, Tan...............C6 48
Mdandu, Tan................C5 48
Meacham, Sask., Can., 245..E3 70
Meacham, Umatilla, Oreg., 120........................B8 113
Meacham Park, St. Louis, Mo., 1,800......................*C7 101
Mead, Weld, Colo., 192......A6 83
Mead, Saunders, Nebr., 428..................C9, D2 103
Mead, Bryan, Okla., 250....D5 112
Mead, Spokane, Wash., 800..................B8, D7 122
Mead, lake, Nev..............G7 104
Meade, Meade, Kans., 2,019......................E3 93
Meade, co., Kans., 5,505....E3 93
Meade, co., Ky., 18,938.....C3 94
Meade, co., S. Dak., 12,044..C3 116
Meade, peak, Idaho...........G7 89
Meade River, Alsk., 5.......A8 79
Meaderville, Silver Bow, Mont., 600.................*D4 102
Meador, Allen, Ky., 40......D3 94
Meadow, Sarpy, Nebr........E3 103
Meadow, Perkins, S. Dak., 35........................B3 116
Meadow, Terry, Tex., 484...C1 118
Meadow, Millard, Utah, 244........................E3 119
Meadow, creek, W. Va........D7 123
Meadow, mtn., Md............D1 85
Meadow, riv., W. Va..........C4 123
Meadow, val., Nev............F7 104
Meadow Bridge, Fayette, W. Va., 426..........D4, D7 123
Meadowbrook, Allen, Ind., 1,500......................*B7 91
Meadowbrook, Montgomery, Pa., 1,500...............*F11 114
Meadowbrook, Harrison, W. Va., 500...............A7 123
Meadow Creek, Boundary, Idaho, 15....................A2 89
Meadow Creek, Summers, W. Va., 325...........D4, D7 123
Meadowdale, Platte, Wyo...C8 125
Meadow Grove, Madison, Nebr., 430.................B8 103
Meadow Lake, Sask., Can., 2,803......................n7 70
Meadowlands, St. Louis, Minn., 176.................C6 99
Meadow Lands, Washington, Pa., 1,967..................F1 114
Meadowlands, S. Afr., 59,000......................*C4 49
Meadow Park, Palm Beach, Fla., 3,500..................F6 86
Meadows, Adams, Idaho, 250........................E2 89
Meadows, Coos, N.H., 40....B4 105
Meadow Valley, wash, Nev.....F7 104
Meadowview, Washington, Va., 750.....................B3 121
Meadville, Franklin, Miss., 611........................D3 100
Meadville, Linn, Mo., 447...B4 101
Meadville, Keya Paha, Nebr., 29........................B6 103
Meadville, Crawford, Pa., 16,671......................C1 114
Meaford, Ont., Can., 3,834......................C4 72
Meagher, co., Mont., 2,616..D6 102
Meaghers Grant, N.S., Can., 127........................E6 74
Mealy, mts., Newf., Can.......B2 75
Meandarra, Austl., 274......C7 51
Meander River, Alta., Can., 244........................f7 69
Means, Menifee, Ky., 160...C6 94
Mearim, riv., Braz............C1 57
Mears, Oceana, Mich., 250..E4 98
Mea Shearim, Isr. (part of Jerusalem)..................m14 32
Meath, co., Ire., 65,122.....D5 11
Meathas Truim, Ire., 624...D4 11
Meath Park, Sask., Can., 184........................D3 70
Meaux, Fr., 22,251..........C5 14
Mebane, Alamance and Orange, N.C., 2,364.......A4 109
Mecca, Riverside, Calif., 300........................F5 82
Mecca, Parke, Ind., 500.....E3 91
Mecca (Makkah), Sau. Ar., 158,900......................A4 47
Mechanic Falls, Androscoggin, Maine, 2,195...............D2 96
Mechanicsburg, Boone, Ind., 120........................D5 91
Mechanicsburg, Champaign, Ohio, 1,810................B4 111
Mechanicsburg, Cumberland, Pa., 8,123....................F7 114
Mechanicsville, Cedar, Iowa, 1,010......................C6 92
Mechanicsville, St. Marys, Md., 175......................D4 85
Mechanicsville, Hanover, Va., 500.....................D5 121
Mechanicville, Saratoga, N.Y., 6,831......................C7 108
Mechanicville, Chittenden, Vt., 150.....................C2 120
Mechant, lake, La............E4 95
Mechelen, Bel., 64,772......C4 15
Mecheria, Alg., 5,290 (39,347*).................C4 44
Meck, isl., Kwajalein.............52
Mecklenburg, co., N.C., 272,111......................B3 109
Mecklenburg, co., Va., 31,428......................E4 121
Mecklenburg, reg., Ger.......B6 16
Mecklenburg, state, Sov. Zone, Ger., 2,139,640.......E5 24
Mecklenburg, bay, Ger.........D5 24
Meckling, Clay, S. Dak., 93........................E8 116
Meconta, Moz...............D6 48
Mecosta, Mecosta, Mich., 303........................E5 98
Mecosta, co., Mich., 21,051..E5 98
Mecox, bay, N.Y..............F7 84
Mecúfi, Moz................D7 48
Medak, India, 15,891.......H7 40
Medan, Indon., 466,370.....E1, m11 33, K3 38
Medanales, Rio Arriba, N. Mex., 150..............A3 107
Médanos, Arg., 2,229.....B4, f7 54
Medanosa, pt., Arg............D3 54
Medart, Wakulla, Fla., 100..B2 86
Medaryville, Pulaski, Ind., 758........................B4 91
Meddybemps, lake, Maine......C5 96
Médéa, Alg., 7,638 (26,350*).....................B5 44
Medeglia, Switz., 304.......D6 19
Medellín, Col., 614,000 (*750,000)...................B2 60
Medemblik, Neth., 5,100....B5 15
Médenine, Tun., 5,350......C7 44
Médenine, prov., Tun., 173,001....................*C7 44
Méderdra, Maur.............C1 45
Medfield, Norfolk, Mass., 2,900 (6,021*)...........h10 97
Medford, Middlesex, Mass., 64,971..............B5, g11 97
Medford, Steele, Minn., 567.F5 99
Medford, Burlington, N.J., 1,600......................D3 106
Medford, Grant, Okla., 1,223......................A4 112
Medford, Jackson, Oreg., 24,425......................E4 113
Medford, Taylor, Wis., 3,260......................C3 124
Medford Lakes, Burlington, N.J., 2,876..................D3 106
Medford Station, Suffolk, N.Y., 2,500..................F5 84
Medgidia, Rom., 17,943.....C9 22
Media, Henderson, Ill., 165..C3 90
Media, Delaware, Pa., 5,803..............B10, G11 114
Mediapolis, Des Moines, Iowa, 1,040..................C6 92
Medias, Rom., 32,503.......B7 22
Medical Lake, Spokane, Wash., 4,765..........B8, D7 122
Medicina, It., 3,881.........E7 18
Medicine, creek, Mo..........A4 101
Medicine, creek, Nebr.........D5 103
Medicine Bow, Carbon, Wyo., 392........................D6 125
Medicine Bow, mts., Colo. and Wyo..............A4 77, D6 125
Medicine Bow, peak, Wyo......D6 125
Medicine Bow, riv., Wyo.......D6 125
Medicine Hat, Alta., Can., 24,484.................D5, g8 69
Medicine Lake, Sheridan, Mont., 452...................B12 102
Medicine Lodge, Barber, Kans., 3,072.................E5 93
Medicine Lodge, riv., Kans.....E5 93
Medicine Park, Comanche, Okla., 800....................C3 112
Medill, Clark, Mo., 140......A6 101
Medimont, Kootenai, Idaho, 50........................B2 89
Medina, Orleans, N.Y., 6,681......................B2 108
Medina, Stutsman, N. Dak., 545........................C6 110
Medina, Medina, Ohio, 8,235......................A6 111
Medina, see Al Madīnah, Sau. Ar.
Medina, Gibson, Tenn., 722..B3 117
Medina, Bandera, Tex., 350..F3 118
Medina, King, Wash., 2,285......................D2 122
Medina, co., Ohio, 65,315....A6 111
Medina, co., Tex., 18,904....E3 118
Medina, riv., Tex.............B4 18
Medina del Campo, Sp., 14,327......................B3 20
Medina de Ríoseco, Sp., 5,011......................B3 20
Medinah, Du Page, Ill., 1,500......................*B5 90
Medina Sidonia, Sp., 8,704...D3 20
Mediterranean, sea.........D22 3, E10 28, E6 31
Medium, lake, Iowa............A3 92
Medjerda, riv., Tun. and Alg...................F11, G10 30
Medjez-el-Bab, Tun., 3,340.F11 30
Medley, Dade, Fla., 112...*G6 86
Mednogorsk, Sov. Un., 32,400......................C5 29
Medomak, Lincoln, Maine, 125........................D3 96
Medon, Madison, Tenn., 97........................B3 117
Medora, Man., Can., 90.....E1 71
Medora, Macoupin, Ill., 447........................D3 90
Medora, Jackson, Ind., 716..G5 91
Medora, Reno, Kans., 75...................A4, D6 93
Medora, Billings, N. Dak., 133........................C2 110
Medstead, Sask., Can., 199..D1 70
Meductic, N.B., Can., 232...D2 74
Meduxnekeag, riv., Maine......B5 96
Medveditsa, riv., Sov. Un.......C2 29
Medvedovskaya, Sov. Un., 10,000......................F16 9
Medvezhi, is., Sov. Un.........B19 28
Medvezhyegorsk, Sov. Un., 19,200......................F16 25
Medway, Penobscot, Maine, 150 (1,266*)..............C4 96
Medway, Norfolk, Mass., 1,800 (5,168*).........B5, h10 97
Medway, riv., N.S., Can........E5 74
Medzhibozh, Sov. Un., 10,000......................G6 27
Meehan, Lauderdale, Miss., 200........................C5 100
Meekatharra, Austl., 524....E2 50
Meeker, Rio Blanco, Colo., 1,655......................A3 83
Meeker, Lincoln, Okla., 664..B5 112
Meeker, co., Minn., 18,887...E4 99
Meelpaeg, lake, Newf., Can.....D3 75
Meeme, Manitowoc, Wis.....B6 124
Meerane, Ger., 24,500.......C7 17
Meerle, Bel., 2,666..........C4 15
Meerut, India, 200,470 (*283,997).............C6 38, C6 40
Meerut Cantonment, India, 75,334......................*C6 40
Meeteetse, Park, Wyo., 514..A4 125
Meeting, lake, Sask., Can......D2 70
Meeting Creek, Alta., Can., 71........................C4 69
Meeyomoot, lake, Sask., Can....C3 70
Mega, Eth...................E4 47
Megali, canal, Grc............g10 23
Megalopolis, Grc., 2,882.....D4 23
Mégantic, co., Que., Can., 57,400......................C6 73
Mégantic, lake, Que., Can.....D7 73
Mégantic, mtn., Que., Can.....D6 73
Megara, Grc., 15,450....C4, g10 23
Megargel, Monroe, Ala., 115........................D2 78
Megargel, Archer, Tex., 417..C3 118
Meggett, Charleston, S.C., 188.....................F1, F7 115
Mehan, Payne, Okla.........A5 112
Mehar, Pak.................C4 39
Meherpur, Pak., 7,174.......F12 40
Meherrin, Lunenburg, Va., 300........................D4 121
Meherrin, riv., Va............E4 121
Mehkar, India, 11,872.......G6 40
Mehoopany, Wyoming, Pa., 250........................C9 114
Mehsana, India, 32,577......F4 40
Mehun-sur-Yèvre, Fr., 4,735.D5 14
Meiganga, Cam..............D2 46
Meighen, isl., N.W. Ter., Can.k32 67
Meigs, Thomas and Mitchell, Ga., 1,236......................F2 87
Meigs, co., Ohio, 22,159.....C5 111
Meigs, co., Tenn., 5,160.....D9 117
Meihsien, China, 85,000.....G8 34
Meiktila, Bur., 25,180.......D10 39
Meilap, Ponape..................52
Meilen, Switz., 8,203.......*B6 19
Meilleur, lake, Que., Can......A4 73
Meiners Oaks, Ventura, Calif., 3,513......................*E4 82
Meiningen, Ger., 23,700.....C5 17
Meiringen, Switz., 3,749.....C5 19
Meissen, Ger., 47,800.......B8 17
Meitan, China, 4,000........K2 36
Meizican, mtn., Arg...........E2 55
Mejillones, Chile, 1,056.....D1 55
Mékambo, Gabon.............E2 46
Mekerrhane, lake, Alg..........D5 44
Mekhtar, Pak................B2 40
Mekinac, lake, Que., Can......B5 73
Mekinock, Grand Forks, N. Dak., 100...................A8 110
Meknès, Mor., 175,943.........C3 44, H4 30
Mekong, riv., Asia...E6 38, B10 39
Mekoryuk, Alsk., 242........C6 79
Melambes, Grc., 1,414.......E5 23
Melaval, Sask., Can., 113...H2 70
Melba, Canyon, Idaho, 197..F2 89
Melber, McCracken, Ky., 219........................A2 94
Melbern, Williams, Ohio, 145........................A3 111
Melbeta, Scotts Bluff, Nebr., 118........................C2 103
Melbourne, Izard, Ark., 571........................A4 81
Melbourne, Austl., 75,900 (*2,035,000)..................H5 51
Melbourne, Ont., Can., 333..E3 72
Melbourne, Brevard, Fla., 11,982......................D6 86
Melbourne, Marshall, Iowa, 517........................C4 92
Melbourne, Campbell, Ky., 250........................A7 94
Melbourne, Harrison, Mo., 70........................A4 101
Melbourne, Grays Harbor, Wash., 50....................C2 122
Melbourne Beach, Brevard, Fla., 1,004..................D6 86
Melcher, Marion, Iowa, 867........................C4 92
Meldorf, Ger., 8,000.........D3 24
Meldrim, Effingham, Ga., 220........................D5 87
Meldrum Bay, Ont., Can., 74........................B1 72
Meleb, Man., Can............D3 71
Melekeiok, Palau................52
Melekess, Sov. Un., 56,000..E18 9
Melenki, Sov. Un., 24,200..D13 27
Melfi, Chad, 1,497...........C3 46
Melfi, It., 18,208............D5 21
Melfort, Sask., Can., 4,039...E3 70
Melilla, Sp. dep., Afr., 79,056......................B4 44
Melipilla, Chile, 11,525......A2 54
Melita, Man., Can., 1,038...E1 71
Melitopol, Sov. Un., 104,000......................H10 27
Melito di Porto Salvo, It., 8,880......................F5 21
Mella, riv., It...............D6 18
Melle, Fr., 3,762............D3 14
Melle, Ger., 9,300...........A3 17
Mellen, Ashland, Wis., 1,182......................B3 124
Mellette, Spink, S. Dak., 208........................B7 116
Mellette, co., S. Dak., 2,664..D4 116
Mellit, Sud..................C2 47
Mellor, glacier, Ant............B19 5
Mellott, Fountain, Ind., 312..D3 91
Mellow Valley, Clay, Ala., 120........................B4 78
Mellrichstadt, Ger., 4,000....C5 17
Mellwood, Phillips, Ark., 300........................C5 81
Melmore, Seneca, Ohio, 300.A4 111
Melnik, Czech., 13,100.....n18 26
Melo, Ur., 27,100............E2 56
Melocheville, Que., Can., 1,666......................q19 73
Meloupre, Camb., 10,000..F6 38
Melrose, N.B., Can., 178.....C6 74
Melrose, N.S., Can., 40......D7 74
Melrose, Hartford, Conn., 100........................B6 84
Melrose, Alachua, Fla., 180..C4 86
Melrose, Monroe, Iowa, 214........................D4 92
Melrose, Natchitoches, La., 200........................C3 95
Melrose, Middlesex, Mass., 29,619................B5, g11 97
Melrose, Stearns, Minn., 2,135......................E4 99
Melrose, Silver Bow, Mont., 200........................E4 102
Melrose, Curry, N. Mex., 698........................C6 107
Melrose, Paulding, Ohio, 260........................A3 111
Melrose, Douglas, Oreg......D3 113
Melrose, Jackson, Wis., 516..D2 124
Melrose Park, Broward, Fla., 4,000......................*F6 86
Melrose Park, Cook, Ill., 22,291......................F2 90
Melrose Park, Montgomery, Pa., 6,000..................*G11 114
Mels, Switz., 5,254..........B7 19
Melsetter, Rh., 400..........A5 49
Melstone, Musselshell, Mont., 266........................D9 102
Melstrand, Alger, Mich., 100........................B4 98
Melsungen, Ger., 8,200.......B4 17
Melton Mowbray, Eng., 15,913......................B7 12
Melun, Fr., 26,873 (*45,000).C5 14
Melvaig, Scot...............C3 13
Melvern, Osage, Kans., 376..D8 93
Melvich, Scot...............B5 13
Melville, Sask., Can., 5,191..G4 70
Melville, St. Landry, La., 1,939......................D4 95
Melville, Sweet Grass, Mont., 15....................D7 102
Melville, Foster, N. Dak., 40........................B6 110
Melville, bay, Grnld..........B21 4
Melville, cape, Austl..........B7 50
Melville, hills, N.W. Ter., Can.C8 66
Melville, isl., Austl...........B5 50
Melville, isl., N.W. Ter., Can........................m29 67
Melville, lake, Newf., Can.....B2 75
Melville, pen., N.W. Ter., Can........................C16 66
Melvin, Choctaw, Ala., 300........................D1 78
Melvin, Ford, Ill., 559........C5 90
Melvin, Osceola, Iowa, 364..A2 92
Melvin, Floyd, Ky, 750......C7 94
Melvin, McCulloch, Tex., 401........................D3 118
Melvin, lake, Ire.............C3 11
Melvindale, Wayne, Mich., 13,089......................A7 98
Melvine, Bledsoe, Tenn., 60........................D8 117
Melvin Village, Carroll, N.H., 270....................C4 105
Melykut, Hung., 6,514.......B4 22
Memba, Moz.................D7 48
Memel, see Klaipeda, Sov. Un.
Memmingen, Ger., 29,800....E5 16
Memorial, Clay, Tenn.......C8 117
Memphis, Manatee, Fla., 2,647......................F2 86
Memphis, Clark, Ind., 200..H6 91
Memphis, Macomb and St. Clair, Mich., 996..........F8 98
Memphis, Scotland, Mo., 2,106......................A5 101
Memphis, Saunders, Nebr., 77........................E2 103
Memphis, Shelby, Tenn., 497,524 (*628,100)....B1, E8 117
Memphis, Hall, Tex., 3,332..B2 118
Memphis, ruins, Eg., U.A.R....D6 43
Memphremagog, lake, Que., Can., Vt....................B4 120
Memramcook, N.B., Can., 402........................C5 74
Memramcook East, N.B., Can., 720....................*C5 74
Mena, Polk, Ark., 4,388.....C1 81
Menahga, Wadena, Minn., 799........................D3 99
Menai, strait, Wales..........A3 12
Ménaka, Mali, 400............C5 45
Menam, see Chao Phraya, riv., Thai.
Menan, Jefferson, Idaho, 496........................F7 89
Menands, Albany, N.Y., 2,702......................C7 108
Menard, Gallatin, Mont.....E5 102
Menard, Menard, Tex., 1,914......................D3 118
Menard, co., Ill., 9,248......C4 90
Menard, co., Tex., 2,964.....D3 118
Menasha, Winnebago, Wis., 14,647...................A5, D5 124
Menche, Guat...............B2 62
Mendawi, riv., Indon..........F4 35
Mende, Fr., 8,337............E5 14
Menden, Ger., 27,500........B2 17
Mendenhall, Simpson, Miss., 1,946......................D4 100
Menderes (Scamander), riv., Tur..........................C6 23
Mendes, Tattnall, Ga., 150..F5 87
Méndez, Mex., 207..........B5 63
Mendham, Sask., Can., 231..G1 70
Mendham, Morris, N.J., 2,371......................B3 106
Mendip, hills, Eng............C5 12
Mendjalutung, Indon.........E5 35
Mendocino, Mendocino, Calif., 900....................C2 82
Mendocino, co., Calif., 51,059......................C2 82
Mendon, Adams, Ill., 784....C2 90
Mendon, Worcester, Mass., 900 (2,068*)................h9 97
Mendon, St. Joseph, Mich., 867........................F5 98
Mendon, Chariton, Mo., 287.B4 101
Mendon, Mercer, Ohio, 663..B3 111
Mendon, Cache, Utah, 345...B4 119
Mendon, Rutland, Vt., 35 (461*).....................D3 120
Mendota, Fresno, Calif., 3,086......................D3 82
Mendota, La Salle, Ill., 6,154......................B4 90
Mendota, Hemphill, Tex....B2 118
Mendota, lake, Wis...........E4 124
Mendota Heights, Dakota, Minn., 5,028..................*F5 99
Mendoza, Arg., 109,149 (*280,000).....................A3 54
Mendoza, prov., Arg., 825,535......................A3 54
Mendoza, Pan., 212..........k11 62
Mendrisio, Switz., 5,109.....E6 19
Menemen, Tur., 15,100.......C6 23
Menen, Bel..................C2 15
Menfi, It., 12,492.............F4 21
Mengcheng, China, 5,000...H7 36
Menggala, Indon.............F2 35
Menglien, China..............G4 34
Mengtzu, China, 9,000.......G5 34
Menifee, Conway, Ark., 300..B3 81
Menifee, co., Ky., 4,276.....C6 94
Menihek, lakes, Newf., Can.....g8 75
Menindee, Austl., 373.......F4 51
Menindee, lake, Austl..........F4 51
Meningie, Austl., 376........G2 51
Menlo, Chattooga, Ga., 466........................B1 87
Menlo, Guthrie, Iowa, 421..C3 92
Menlo, Thomas, Kans., 99...C3 93
Menlo, Pacific, Wash., 100...C2 122
Menlo Park, San Mateo, Calif., 26,957................B5 82
Menlo Park, Middlesex, N.J., 1,630......................B4 106
Menlo Park Terrace, Middlesex, N.J., 2,800............*B4 106
Menno, Hutchinson, S. Dak., 837........................D8 116
Meno, Major, Okla., 118....A3 112
Menoken, Burleigh, N. Dak., 60........................C5 110
Menola, Hertford, N.C., 35..A6 109
Menominee, Menominee, Mich., 11,289..................C3 98
Menominee, co., Mich., 24,685......................C3 98
Menominee, co., Wis., 2,600.C5 124
Menominee, Indian res., Wis....C5 124
Menominee, riv., Mich., Wis..........C3 92, C6 124
Menomonee, riv., Wis..........E1 124
Menomonee Falls, Waukesha, Wis., 18,276..........E1, E5 124
Menomonie, Dunn, Wis., 8,624......................D2 124
Menorca, isl., Sp..............B7 20
Mentana, It., 5,489...........g9 21
Mentawai, is., Indon..........F1 35
Mentmore, McKinley, N. Mex., 70................B1 107
Menton, Fr., 19,904 (*26,500)......................F7 14
Mentone, DeKalb, Ala., 250.A4 78
Mentone, San Bernardino, Calif., 2,000................*F3 82
Mentone, Kosciusko, Ind., 813........................B5 91
Mentone, Loving, Tex., 50..................D1, F2 118
Mentor, Campbell, Ky., 350........................A7 94
Mentor, Polk, Minn., 281....C2 99
Mentor, Lake, Ohio, 4,354...A6 111
Mentor, Blount, Tenn., 350.E11 117
Mentor Headlands, Lake, Ohio, 1,500..................*A6 111
Mentor-on-the-Lake, Lake, Ohio, 3,290..................A6 111
Menzel-Bourguiba, Tun., 34,842......................*B6 44
Menzies, Austl., 217.........E3 50
Menzies, mtn., Ant...........B19 5
Menziken, Switz., 4,060.....B5 19
Meoqui, Mex., 10,298.......B3 63
Meota, Sask., Can., 281.....D1 70
Meppel, Neth., 17,700.......B6 15

Meppen, Ger., 14,900......B3 16
Mequellarë, Alb., 650.......B3 23
Mequon, Ozaukee, Wis., 8,543..........E2 124
Merabello, gulf, Grc.........E5 23
Meramec, caverns, Mo.........C6 101
Meramec, riv., Mo..........C7 101
Merano, It., 31,400..........A3 21
Merasheen, Newf., Can., 291.E4 75
Merasheen, isl., Newf., Can.....E4 75
Merauke, W. Irian, 3,600...G10 35
Meraux, St. Bernard, La., 500..........C7 95
Merca, Som., 15,000 (59,000▲)..........E5 47
Mercara, India, 14,453......F6 39
Merced, Merced, Calif., 20,068..........D3 82
Merced, co., Calif., 90,446...D3 82
Merced, riv., Calif..........D3 82
Mercedes, Arg., 25,912......A3 54
Mercedes, Arg., 16,932...A5, g7 54
Mercedes, Arg., 14,813.......E4 55
Mercedes, Hidalgo, Tex., 10,943..........F3 118
Mercedes, Ur., 25,400.......E1 56
Mercedita Cantral, P.R.....C4 65
Mercer, Somerset, Maine, 140 (272▲)..........D3 96
Mercer, Mercer, Mo., 368...A4 101
Mercer, McLean, N. Dak., 154..........B5 110
Mercer, Mercer, Ohio, 90...B3 111
Mercer, Mercer, Pa., 2,800..D1 114
Mercer, Madison, Tenn., 400..........B2 117
Mercer, Iron, Wis., 700.....B3 124
Mercer, co., Ill., 17,149.....B3 90
Mercer, co., Ky., 14.596.....C5 94
Mercer, co., Mo., 5,750.....A4 101
Mercer, co., N.J., 266,392...C3 106
Mercer, co., N. Dak., 6,805..B4 110
Mercer, co., Ohio, 32,559...B3 101
Mercer, co., Pa., 127,519....D1 114
Mercer, co, W. Va., 68,206..D3 123
Mercer, isl., Wash..........D2 122
Mercer Island, King, Wash., 1,700..........B3, D2 122
Mercersburg, Franklin, Pa., 1,759..........G6 114
Mercerville, Mercer, N.J., 15,500..........C3 106
Mercês, Braz., 2,897.........g6 56
Merchant, Brunswick, Va....E5 121
Merchantville, Camden, N.J., 4,075..........*D2 106
Mercier, Brown, Kans., 50...C8 93
Mercoal, Alta., Can.........C2 69
Mercury, Nye, Nev., 300....G5 104
Mercury, McCulloch, Tex., 100..........D3 118
Mercury, bay, N.Z.........L15 51
Mercy, cape, N.W. Ter., Can.D20 67
Merdjayoun, Leb..........F1 31
Meredith, Pitkin, Colo., 30...B4 83
Meredith, Belknap, N.H., 950 (2,434▲)..........C3 105
Meredith, King, Wash.......D2 122
Meredith, lake, Colo..........C7 83
Meredith Center, Belknap, N.H., 100..........C3 105
Meredosia, Morgan, Ill., 1,034..........D3 90
Merefa, Sov. Un., 10,000...G11 31
Meregh, Som..........E6 47
Mergui, Bur., 33,697.........F10 39
Mergui, arch., Bur..........F10 39
Merid, Sask., Can..........F1 70
Mérida, Mex., 170,834.......C7 63
Mérida, Sp., 34,297.........C2 20
Mérida, Ven., 40,404........B3 60
Mérida, state, Ven., 270,668..B3 60
Meriden, New Haven, Conn., 51,850..........C5 84
Meriden, Cherokee, Iowa, 192..........B2 90
Meriden, Jefferson, Kans., 402..........B7, C8 93
Meriden, Steele, Minn., 115..F5 99
Meriden, Sullivan, N.H., 175..........C2 105
Meriden, Laramie, Wyo., 5..D8 125
Meridian, McIntosh, Ga., 150..........E5 87
Meridian, Ada, Idaho, 2,081..........F2 89
Meridian, Lauderdale, Miss., 49,374..........C5 100
Meridian, Cayuga, N.Y., 379..........B4 108
Meridian, Logan, Okla., 160..B4 112
Meridian, Butler, Pa., 1,649..*E2 114
Meridian, Bosque, Tex., 993..........D4 118
Meridian Hills, Marion, Ind., 1,807..........*E5 91
Meridiano, Arg..........B4 54
Meridianville, Madison, Ala., 250..........A3 79
Mérignac, Fr., 25,874.......E3 14
Merigold, Bolivar, Miss., 602..........B3 100
Merigomish, N.S., Can., 203..........D7 74
Merikarvia, Fin., 2,100......G9 25
Merino, Logan, Colo., 268...A7 83
Merioneth, co., Wales, 39,007..........B4 11
Merion Park, Montgomery, Pa., 1,000..........*F11 114
Merion Station, Montgomery, Pa., 5,500..........*B11 114
Merir, salt lake, Alg.........C6 44
Meriso, port, Guam.......... 52
Meriwether, co., Ga., 19,756..C2 87
Merkel, Taylor, Tex., 2,312...C2 118
Merkine, Sov. Un..........A8 26
Merkis, riv., Sov. Un.........D5 27
Merksem, Bel., 36,098.......C4 15
Merksplas, Bel., 4,912.......C4 15
Merlebach, Fr., 8,715........E7 15
Merlin, Ont., Can., 595.....E2 72
Merlin, Josephine, Oreg., 300..........E3 113
Merlo, Arg., 8,385..........g7 54
Mermentau, Acadia, La., 716..........D3 95
Mermentau, riv., La.........E2 95
Mern, Den., 516..........C6 24
Merna, Custer, Nebr., 349...C6 103
Merna, Sublette, Wyo........C2 125
Merom, Sullivan, Ind., 352..F2 91
Merowe, Sud., 1,620.........B3 47
Merriam, Johnson, Kans., 5,084..........B8 93
Merrick, Nassau, N.Y., 22,500..........G2 84
Merrick, co., Nebr., 8,363...C7 103
Merrick, mtn., Scot.........E4 13
Merrickville, Ont., Can., 947..........C9 72
Merricourt, Dickey, N. Dak., 66..........C7 110
Merrifield, Crow Wings, Minn., 250..........D4 99
Merrifield, Fairfax, Va., 1 000..........B5 121
Merrill, Plymouth, Iowa, 645.B1 92
Merrill, Saginaw, Mich., 963..........E6 98
Merrill, George, Miss., 150..E5 100
Merrill, Klamath, Oreg., 804..........E5 113
Merrill, Lincoln, Wis., 9,451.C4 124
Merrillan, Jackson, Wis., 591..........D3 124
Merrillville, Lake, Ind., 3,120.B3 91
Merrimac, Taylor, Ky., 250..C4 94
Merrimac, Essex, Mass., 2,000 (3,261▲)..........A5 97
Merrimac, Sauk, Wis., 297...E4 124
Merrimack, Hillsboro, N.H., 500 (2,989▲)..........E4 105
Merrimack, co., N.H., 67,785..........D3 101
Merrimack, riv., Mass., N.H...A5 97
Merrimacport, Essex, Mass., 350..........A6 97
Merriman, Cherry, Nebr., 285..........B4 103
Merrimon, Carteret, N.C., 200..........C7 109
Merrionette Park, Cook, Ill., 2,354..........*F3 90
Merritt, B.C., Can., 3,039...D7 68
Merritt, Pamlico, N.C., 100..B7 109
Merritt Island, Brevard, Fla., 3,554..........D6 86
Merritt-Peck Colonies, Fresno, Calif., 1,299..........*D4 82
Merriwa, Austl., 1,073.......F8 51
Merriweather, Ontonagon, Mich., 90..........A5 98
Mer Rouge, Morehouse, La., 853..........B4 95
Merrow, Tolland, Conn., 300.B7 84
Merry Hill, Bertie, N.C., 75..........A7 109
Merrymeeting, lake, N.H.......D4 105
Merry Oaks, Chatham, N.C., 77..........B4 109
Merryville, Beauregard, La., 1,232..........D2 95
Mersa Fatma, Eth..........B5 47
Merseburg, Ger., 50,800.....B6 17
Mers-el-Kebir, Alg., 3,977...C6 30
Mersey, riv., Eng..........A5 12
Mershon, Pierce, Ga., 300...E4 87
Mersin, Tur., 68,485.......D10 31
Mersing, Mala., 7,228.......K5 38
Merthyr Tydfil, Wales, 58,700..........C4 12
Merti, Ken..........A6 48
Mértola, Port., 6,439........D2 20
Merton, Waukesha, Wis., 407..........E1 124
Mertz, glacier, Ant..........C27 5
Mertzon, Irion, Tex., 584...D2 118
Méru, Fr., 5,435..........C5 14
Meru, Ken..........A6 48
Meru, mtn., Tan..........B6 48
Merundung, isl., Indon.........K8 38
Mervelier, Switz., 548.......B4 19
Merville, Fr., 4,936.........D2 15
Mervin, Sask., Can., 193....D1 70
Merwin, Bates, Mo., 76......C3 101
Méry [-sur-Seine], Fr., 1,135..........F3 15
Merzifon, Tur., 22,200......B10 31
Merzig, Ger., 12,100........C3 15
Mesa, Maricopa, Ariz., 33,772..........D4, G2 80
Mesa, Mesa, Colo..........B2 83
Mesa, Adams, Idaho, 30.....E2 89
Mesa, co., Colo., 50,715.....B2 83
Mesa, mts., Colo..........D3 83
Mesa, peak, Colo..........D4 83
Mesabi, iron range, Minn......C5 99
Mesa De Maya, plat., Colo......D7 83
Mesagne, It., 23,000........D6 21
Mesa Verde, nat. park, Colo....D2 83
Mesa Verde, plat., Colo........D2 83
Mescal, Pima, Ariz..........F5 80
Mescalero, Otero, N. Mex., ...D4 107
Mescalero, Indian res., N. Mex.D4 107
Meschede, Ger., 12,600......B3 17
Mesegon, isl., Truk.......... 52
Mesena, Warren, Ga., 200...C4 87
Meservey, Cerro Gordo, Iowa, 331..........B4 92
Meshcherskoye, Sov. Un.....n17 27
Meshchovsk, Sov. Un., 6,800..........D10 27
Meshed, see Mashhad, Iran
Meshkovskiy, Sov. Un., 5,000..........G13 27
Meshomasic, mtn., Conn.......C6 84
Meshoppen, Wyoming, Pa., 470..........C9 114
Meshra'er Req, Sud.........D2 47
Mesic, Pamlico, N.C., 350...B7 109
Mesick, Wexford, Mich., 304.D5 98
Mesilinka, riv., B.C., Can.....A5 68
Mesilla, Dona Ana, N. Mex., 1,264..........E3 107
Mesilla Park, Dona Ana, N. Mex., 1,500..........E3 107
Mesita, Costilla, Colo., 50..D5 83
Mesita, Valencia, N. Mex., 200..........C2 107
Meskéné, Syr..........D12 31
Mesocco, Switz., 1,324......D7 19
Mesologion, Grc., 11,266....C3 23
Mesquita, Braz., 58,835....*C4 56
Mesquite, Clark, Nev., 600..G7 104
Mesquite, Dona Ana, N. Mex., 300..........E3 107
Mesquite, Dallas, Tex., 27,526..........B6 118
Messalonskee, lake, Maine.....D3 96
Messen, Switz., 682.........B3 19
Messenia (Messinia), prov., Grc., 211,970..........*D4 23
Messex, Washington, Colo., 20..........A7 83
Messina, It., 259,700.......E5 21
Messina, S. Afr., 10,225....B5 49
Messina, strait, It.........E5 21
Messini, Grc., 7,725........D3 23
Messini, gulf, Grc.........D4 23
Messinia (Messenia), prov., Grc., 211,970..........*D4 23
Messkirch, Ger., 3,800.......B5 18
Mesta, riv., Bul..........E6 22
Mestre, It., 73,435.........B4 21
Mesudiye, Tur., 2,500......B11 31
Meta, Osage, Mo., 360.......C5 101
Meta, dept., Col., 74,780....C3 60
Meta, pond, Newf., Can.......D4 75
Meta, riv., Ven..........B4 60
Métabetchouan, Que., Can., 1,962..........A6 73
Métabetchouan, riv., Que., Can..A5 73
Metairie, Jefferson, La., 65,000..........*C7 95
Metaline, Pend Oreille, Wash., 299..........A8 122
Metaline Falls, Pend Oreille, Wash., 469..........A8 122
Metalton, Carroll, Ark., 25..A2 81
Metamora, Woodford, Ill., 1,808..........C4 90
Metamora, Franklin, Ind., 400..........F7 91
Metamora, Lapeer, Mich., 452..........F9 98
Metamora, Fulton, Ohio, 598..........A4 111
Metán, Arg., 6,915..........E3 55
Metangula, Moz..........D5 48
Metapán, Sal., 4,073........C3 62
Metaponto, It., 445.........D6 21
Metarica, Moz..........D6 48
Metarma, cape, Eg., U.A.R....E4 32
Metascouac, lake, Que., Can....B6 73
Metasville, Wilkes, Ga., 73..C4 87
Metcalf, Thomas, Ga., 241...F3 87
Metcalf, Edgar, Ill., 278.....D6 90
Metcalfe, Ont., Can., 385....B9 72
Metcalfe, Washington, Miss., 500..........B2 100
Metcalfe, co., Ky., 8,367.....D4 94
Metchosin, B.C., Can., 370..h12 68
Metedeconk, riv., N.J.........C4 106
Meteghan, N.S., Can., 925...E3 74
Meteghan River, N.S., Can., 423..........E3 74
Meteghan Station, N.S., Can., 327..........E3 74
Meteor, crater, Ariz..........C4 80
Method, Wake, N.C. (part of Raleigh)..........B5 109
Methoni, Grc., 2,087........D3 23
Methow, Okanogan, Wash., 75..........A5 121
Methuen, Essex, Mass., 28,114..........A5 97
Methven, Scot., 1,671.......D5 13
Metiskow, Alta., Can., 99...C5 69
Metkovič, Yugo., 4,488......D3 22
Metlakatla, Alsk., 798..D13, n14 79
Meto, Lonoke, Ark..........D6 81
Meto, bayou, Ark..........C4 81
Metolius, Jefferson, Oreg., 270..........C5 113
Metolius, bench, Oreg.........C5 113
Metonga, lake, Wis..........C4 124
Metropolis, Massac, Ill., 7,339..........F4 90
Metropolitan, Dickinson, Mich., 100..........C3 98
Metsovon, Grc., 2,773.......C3 23
Mettewee, riv., Vt..........E2 120
Metten, Ger., 2,800..........E7 17
Meeter, Candler, Ga., 2,362..........D4 87
Mettet, Bel., 3,160..........D4 15
Mettingen, Ger., 9,100......A2 17
Mettmann, Ger., 24,600.....B1 17
Metuchen, Middlesex, N.J., 14,041..........B4 106
Metulla, Isr., 178..........A7 32
Metz, Fr., 102,771 (*150,000)..........C7 14
Metz, Steuben, Ind., 200....A8 91
Metz, Presque Isle, Mich., 60..........C7 98
Metz, Vernon, Mo., 137.....C3 101
Metzeral, Fr., 1,104........A3 18
Metzger, Washington, Oreg. (part of Tigard)..........B2 113
Meudon, Fr., 34,878........g9 14
Meulaboh, Indon., 2,575.....J2 38
Meung [-sur-Loire], Fr., 521..........D4 14
Meureudoe, Indon..........J2 38
Meurthe, riv., Fr..........F6 15
Meurthe-et-Moselle, dept., Fr., 678,078..........F6 15
Meuse, dept., Fr., 215,985..F51 15
Meuse, hills, Fr..........C6 14
Meuse, riv., Bel., Fr......C6 14, D5 15, A1 18
Meuselwitz, Ger., 10,500....B7 17
Mew, isl., Ire..........C6 11
Mexcala, riv., Mex.........n12 63
Mexhoma, Cimarron, Okla..D1 112
Mexia, Monroe, Ala., 100...D2 78
Mexia, Limestone, Tex., 6,121..........D4 118
Mexicali, Mex., 174,540.....A1 63
Mexican Hat, San Juan, Utah, 300..........F6 119
Mexican Springs, McKinley, N. Mex., 30..........B1 107
Mexico, Miami, Ind., 600...C5 91
Mexico, Crittenden, Ky., 200..........A3 94
Mexico, Oxford, Maine, 5,043..........D2 96
Mexico, Audrain, Mo., 12,889..........B6 101
Mexico, Oswego, N.Y., 1,465..........B4 108
Mexico, Juniata, Pa., 400....E7 114
Mexico, country, N.A., 40,250,000..........G10 61, 63
México, state, Mex., 1,883,291..........D5, n14 63
Mexico, gulf, N.A..........G12 61
Mexico City, Mex., 2,832,133 (*5,215,000).....D5, h9, n14 63
Meyādīn, Syr., 7,200........E13 31
Meyers, Garland, Ark., 75...C5 81
Meyers Chuck, Alsk., 27.....n23 79
Meyersdale, Somerset, Pa., 2,901..........G3 114
Meyronne, Sask., Can., 161..........H2 70
Mèze, Fr., 4,546..........F5 14
Mezen, Sov. Un., 7,300.....B17 9
Mézenc, mtn., Fr..........E6 14
Mezenskaya, bay, Sov. Un......B17 9
Mezhdurechensk, Sov. Un., 64,000..........*D11 28
Meziadin, lake, B.C., Can......A3 68
Mézières, Fr., 11,799.......C6 14
Mézières, Switz., 504.......C2 19
Mezokovesd, Hung., 18,640..B5 22
Mezotur, Hung., 18,337 (23,632▲)..........B5 22
Mezotur, Hung., 16,000.....B5 22
Mezquital, Mex., 832........C4 63
Mezzana, It., 1,055.........C6 18
Mezzolombardo, It., 4,873...C7 18
Mga, Sov. Un..........s32 25
Mga, riv., Sov. Un..........s32 25
Mglin, Sov. Un., 10,000.....E9 27
Mhor, lake, Scot..........C4 13
Mhow, India, 48,032.........F5 40
Miahuatlán, Mex., 7,420.....D5 63
Miajadas, Sp., 8,632........C3 20
Miajlar, India, 5,000........D3 40
Miami, Gila, Ariz., 3,350....D5 80
Miami, Man., Can., 349.....E2 71
Miami, Dade, Fla., 291,688 (*1,212,000)..F3, G6 86
Miami, Miami, Ind., 300....C5 91
Miami, Saline, Mo., 156.....B4 101
Miami, Colfax, N. Mex., 150..........A5 107
Miami, Ottawa, Okla., 12,869..........A7 113
Miami, Rh..........A4 49
Miami, Roberts, Tex., 656...B2 118
Miami, Kanawha, W. Va., 500..........D6 123
Miami, co., Ind., 38,000.....C5 91
Miami, co., Kans., 19,884...D9 93
Miami, co., Ohio, 72,901....B3 111
Miami, canal, Fla..........F6 86
Miami, riv., Ohio..........C3 111
Miami Beach, Dade, Fla., 63,145..........F3, G6 86
Miamisburg, Montgomery, Ohio, 9,893..........C3 111
Miami Shores, Dade, Fla., 8,865..........F3, G6 86
Miami Shores, Montgomery, Ohio, 1,200..........*C3 111
Miami Springs, Dade, Fla., 11,229..........F3, G6 86
Miamitown, Hamilton, Ohio, 500..........D2 111
Miāndasht, Iran..........C8 41
Miandrivazo, Malag., 1,505...g9 49
Miāneh, Iran, 14,758.......C3 41
Mianus, res., Conn..........E2 84
Mianwali, Pak., 23,341.....A3 40
Miaoli, For., 5,000........*G9 34
Miarinarivo, Malag..........g9 49
Miass, Sov. Un., 109,000....C6 29
Miass, riv., Sov. Un..........B6 29
Miasteczko Slaskie, Pol., 2,212..........f9 26
Miastko, Pol., 3,417.......A4 26
Mica, Spokane, Wash., 75..........B8, D8 122
Mica, peak, Idaho..........D8 122
Mica, riv., Rom..........B7 22
Micanopy, Alachua, Fla., 658..........C4 86
Micay, Col..........C2 60
Micco, Brevard, Fla., 200....E6 86
Miccosukee, Leon, Fla., 120..B2 86
Miccosukee, lake, Fla.........B2 86
Michael, lake, Newf., Can......A2 75
Michalovce, Czech., 16,300..D6 26
Michalow, Pol., 1,000.......k13 26
Michaud, pt., N.S., Can.......D9 74
Michaudville, Que., Can., 95..........*D4 73
Michel, B.C., Can., 417....E10 68
Michelson, mtn., Alsk.........B11 79
Michendorf, Ger., 3,055......A8 17
Michiana Shores, La Porte, Ind., 229..........*A4 91
Michichi, Alta., Can., 52....D4 69
Michie, McNairy, Tenn., 200..........B3 117
Michigamme, Marquette, Mich..........B2 98
Michigamme, lake, Mich........B2 98
Michigan, Nelson, N. Dak., 551..........A7 110
Michigan, state, U.S., 7,823,194..........B11 77, 98
Michigan, creek, Colo.........A4 83
Michigan, isl., Wis..........B3 124
Michigan, lake, U.S..........B10 77
Michigan, prairie, Wash........C7 122
Michigan Center, Jackson, Mich., 4,611..........F6 98
Michigan City, La Porte, Ind., 36,653..........A4 91
Michigan City, Benton, Miss., 50..........A4 100
Michigantown, Clinton, Ind., 513..........D5 91
Michikamau, lake, Newf., Can..g8 75
Michoacán, state, Mex., 1,862,568..........D4, n13 63
Michurin, Bul., 1,896.......D8 22
Michurinsk, Sov. Un., 85,000..........C2 29
Mickleyville, Marion, Ind., 900..........H7 91
Micoud, St. Lucia, 1,300...p16 64
Micro, Johnston, N.C., 350..B5 109
Midai, isl., Indon..........K7 38
Midale, Sask., Can., 645....H4 70
Midas, Bonner, Idaho, 50....A2 89
Middelburg, Neth., 23,400...C2 15
Middelburg, S. Afr., 8,711...B4 49
Middelfart, Den., 8,801 (*11,701)..........C3 24
Middelharnis, Neth., 5,100..C4 15
Middelkerke, Bel., 4,610....C2 15
Middle, riv., B.C., Can........B5 68
Middle, riv., Iowa..........C3 92
Middle, riv., Minn..........B2 99
Middle Alkali, lake, Nev.......B2 104
Middle Amana, Iowa, Iowa, 250..........C6 92
Middle Andaman, isl., India....F9 39
Middleboro, Plymouth, Mass., 6,300 (11,065▲)..........C6 97
Middlebourne, Tyler, W. Va., 711..........B4 123
Middlebranch, Holt, Nebr...B7 103
Middlebranch, Stark, Ohio, 600..........B6 111
Middlebro, Man., Can., 147..E4 71
Middle Brook, Newf., Can., 744..........D4 75
Middlebrook, Augusta, Va., 140..........C3 121
Middleburg, Clay, Fla., 750..........B5 86
Middleburg, Casey, Ky., 150..........C5 94
Middleburg, Schoharie, N.Y., 1,317..........C6 108
Middleburg, Vance, N.C., 170..........A5 109
Middleburg, Logan, Ohio, 300..........B4 111
Middleburg, Snyder, Pa., 1,366..........E7 114
Middleburg, Hardeman, Tenn., 25..........B2 117
Middleburg, Loudoun, Va., 761..........C5 121
Middleburgh Heights, Cuyahoga, Ohio, 7,282...B2 111
Middlebury, New Haven, Conn., 500 (4,785▲)..........C4 84
Middlebury, Elkhart, Ind., 917..........A6 91
Middlebury, Addison, Vt., 3,688 (5,305▲)..........C2 120
Middlebury, riv., Vt..........D2 120
Middle Bushkill, creek, Pa.....A2 106
Middle Caraquet, N.B., Can., 895..........*B5 74
Middlefield, Middlesex, Conn., 600 (3,255▲)..........C6 84
Middlefield, Hampshire, Mass., 100 (315▲)..........B1 97
Middlefield, Geauga, Ohio, 1,467..........A6 111
Middleford, Sussex, Del., 50..C6 85
Middle Granville, Washington, N.Y., 600..........B7 108
Middle Ground, isl., Midway Is... 52
Middle Haddam, Middlesex, Conn., 500..........C6 84
Middle Island, Suffolk, N.Y., 950..........F5 84
Middle Island, creek, W. Va...B4 123
Middle Lake, Sask., Can., 238..........E3 70
Middle Loup, riv., Nebr........C6 103
Middle Musquodoboit, N.S., Can., 741..........D6 74
Middle Nodaway, riv., Iowa.....C3 92
Middle Park, basin, Colo........A4 83
Middle Patuxent, riv., Md......B4 85
Middle Point, Van Wert, Ohio, 571..........B3 111
Middleport, Niagara, N.Y., 1,882..........B2 108
Middleport, Meigs, Ohio, 3,373..........C5 111
Middle Raccoon, riv., Iowa.....C3 92
Middle River, Baltimore, Md., 10,825..........*B5 85
Middle River, Marshall, Minn., 414..........B2 99
Middlesboro, Bell, Ky., 12,607..........D6 94
Middlesbrough, Eng., 158,100 (*545,000)..........C6 10
Middlesex, Br. Hond., 207...B3 62
Middlesex, Middlesex, N.J., 10,520..........B4 106
Middlesex, Yates, N.Y., 300..........C3 108
Middlesex, Nash, N.C., 588..........B5 109
Middlesex, Washington, Vt., 100 (770▲)..........C3 120
Middlesex, co., Ont., Can., 221,422..........D3 72
Middlesex, co., Conn., 88,865..........D6 84
Middlesex, co., Eng., 2,230,093..........C7 11
Middlesex, co., Mass., 1,238,742..........A5 97
Middlesex, co., N.J., 433,856..........C4 106
Middlesex, co., Va., 6,319...D6 121
Middlesex Fells, res., Mass.....g11 97
Middle Stewiacke, N.S., Can., 217..........D6 74
Middleton, N.S., Can., 1,921..........E4 74
Middleton, Eng., 58,900....*A5 12
Middleton, Elbert, Ga., 106..........B4 87
Middleton, Canyon, Idaho, 541..........F2 89
Middleton, Essex, Mass., 3,718..........A5, f11 97
Middleton, Gratiot, Mich., 550..........E6 98
Middleton, Strafford, N.H., 100 (349▲)..........D4 105
Middleton, Hardeman, Tenn., 461..........B3 117
Middleton, Dane, Wis., 4,410..........E4 124
Middleton, isl., Alsk..........D10 79
Middletown, Lake, Calif., 450..........C2 82
Middletown, Middlesex, Conn., 33,250..........C6 84
Middletown, New Castle, Del., 2,191..........B6 85
Middletown, Logan and Menard, Ill., 543..........C4 90
Middletown, Henry, Ind., 2,033..........D6 91
Middletown, Des Moines, Iowa, 245..........D6 92
Middletown, Jefferson, Ky., 2,764..........A4 94
Middletown, Frederick, Md., 1,036..........B2 85
Middletown, Montgomery, Mo., 199..........B6 101
Middletown, Monmouth, N.J., 8,000 (39,675▲)..........C4 106
Middletown, Orange, N.Y., 23,475..........D6 108
Middletown, Hyde, N.C., 200..........B7 109
Middletown, Butler, Ohio, 42,115..........C3 111
Middletown, Dauphin, Pa., 11,182..........F8 114
Middletown, Newport, R.I., 12,675..........C12 84
Middletown, Frederick, Va., 378..........B4 121
Middletown Heights, Delaware, Pa., 1,000..........*G11 114
Middletown Springs, Rutland, Vt., 230 (381▲)..........E2 120
Middle Valley, Morris, N.J., 100..........B3 106
Middleville, Ont., Can., 84...B8 72
Middleville, Barry, Mich., 1,196..........F6 98
Middleville, Sussex, N.J., 75..........A3 106
Middleville, Herkimer, N.Y., 648..........B6 108
Middle Water, Hartley, Tex., 20..........B1 118
Midelt, Mor., 6,504.........H4 30
Midfield, Jefferson, Ala., 3,556..........*E4 78
Midgic, N.B., Can., 284.....D5 74
Midhurst, Ont., Can., 340....C5 72
Midkiff, Lincoln, W. Va., 300..........C2 123
Midland, Sebastian, Ark., 261..........B1 75
Midland, Riverside, Calif., 500..........F6 82
Midland, Ont., Can., 8,656..........C5 72
Midland, Greene, Ind., 475...F3 91
Midland, Acadia, La., 500...D3 95
Midland, Allegany, Md., 737..........D2 85
Midland, Midland, Mich., 27,779..........E6 98
Midland, Cabarrus, N.C., 750..........B3 109
Midland, Clinton, Ohio, 367..........C4 111
Midland, Beaver, Pa., 6,425..E1 114
Midland, Washington, Pa., 1,317..........*F1 108
Midland, Haakon, S. Dak., 401..........C4 116
Midland, Midland, Tex., 62,625..........D1 118
Midland, Fauquier, Va., 100..........C5 121
Midland, Clark, Wash., 900..........*D3 122
Midland, Pierce, Wash., 4,000..........*B3 122
Midland, co., Mich., 51,450..E6 98
Midland, co., Tex., 67,717...D1 118
Midland, basin, Colo..........A2 83
Midland City, Dale, Ala., 854..........D4 78
Midland Park, Bergen, N.J., 7,543..........B4 106
Midland Park, Charleston, S.C., 800..........F2 115
Midlandvale, Alta., Can., 449..........D4 69
Midleton, Ire., 2,772........F3 11
Midlothian, Cook, Ill., 8,749..........F3 90
Midlothian, Allegany, Md., 525..........D2 85
Midlothian, Ellis, Tex., 1,521..........B5, C4 118
Midlothian, Chesterfield, Va., 400..........C6, D5 121
Midlothian, co., Scot., 580,332..........E5 13
Midnapore, Alta., Can., 399..........D3 69
Midnapore, India, 59,532...F11 40
Midnight, Humphreys, Miss., 150..........B3 100
Midongy du Sud, Malag......h9 49
Midstate Mill (Amerotron Mill), Robeson, N.C., 1,090....*C4 109
Midvale, Washington, Idaho, 211..........E2 89
Midvale, Tuscarawas, Ohio, 683..........B6 111
Midvale, Salt Lake, Utah, 5,802..........C4 119
Midville, Burke, Ga., 676....D4 87
Midway, Bullock, Ala., 594..C4 78
Midway, B.C., Can., 391.....E8 68
Midway, Gadsden, Fla., 200..B2 86
Midway, Woodford, Ky., 1,044..........B5 94
Midway, Multnomah, Oreg., 19,000..........*B4 113
Midway, Adams, Pa., 1,568..........G7 114
Midway, Greene, Tenn., 225..........C11 117
Midway, Wasatch, Utah, 713..........C4 119
Midway, King, Wash., 1,000..........D2 122
Midway, range, B.C., Can.....E8 68
Midway City, Orange, Calif., 2,500..........*F3 82
Midway Islands, U.S. dep., Oceania, 2,500.......... 52
Midway Park, Onslow, N.C., 4,164..........*C6 109
Midway Village, Oklahoma, Okla., 2,292..........*B4 110
Midwest, Natrona, Wyo., 900..........B6 125
Midwest City, Oklahoma, Okla., 36,058..........B4 112
Mid-Western, reg., Nig......E6 45
Midyat, Tur., 9,600........D13 31
Midye, Tur., 1,318..........B7 31
Mie, pref., Jap., 1,485,054..*I8 37
Miechow, Pol., 6,878.......C6 26
Miechowice, Pol., 13,831.....g9 26
Miedzychod, Pol., 4,632.....B3 26
Miedzyrzec, Pol., 8,696.....C7 26
Miedzyrzecz, Pol., 4,385.....B3 26
Miedzyrzecz, Pol..........g10 26
Miedzyzdroje, Pol., 1,949....A3 26
Mielec, Pol., 22,000.........C6 26
Mien, lake, Swe..........B8 24
Mienia, riv., Pol..........m14 26
Mienning, China, 11,000....F5 34
Mienyang, China, 28,000....I5 36
Mier, Mex., 1,018..........F2 118
Mieres, Sp., 19,308 (70,871▲).A3 20
Miesbach, Ger., 5,200.......B7 18
Miēso, Eth..........D5 47
Mifflin, Juniata, Pa., 745....E7 114
Mifflin, Chester, Tenn., 50...B3 117
Mifflin, Kenedy, Tex........F4 118
Mifflin, co., Pa., 44,348.....E6 114
Mifflinburg, Union, Pa., 2,476..........E7 114
Mifflintown, Juniata, Pa., 887..........E7 114
Mifflinville, Columbia, Pa., 1,027..........D7 114
Migdal, Isr., 295..........B7 32
Migdal Ashqelon, Isr., 28,400..........C6 32
Migennes, Fr., 6,352........D5 14
Migiurtinia, dist., Som......D6 47
Migliarino, It., 3,062........E7 18
Mignon, Talladega, Ala., 2,271..........B3 78
Miguel Alves, Braz., 1,537...B2 57
Miguel Auza, Mex., 7,140...C4 63
Mihai-Viteazu, Rom., 2,598..........C9 22
Mihara, Jap., 71,000 (80,395▲)..........*I6 37
Mijares, riv., Sp..........B5 20
Mijdahah, S. Arabia........C6 47
Mikado, Sask., Can., 115....F4 70
Mikado, Alcona, Mich., 125..D7 92
Mikana, Barron, Wis., 120...C2 118
Mikasa, Jap., 56,196......*E10 37
Mikhaylov, Sov. Un., 23,600..........D12 27
Mikhaylov, cape, Ant........C24 5
Mikhaylovgrad, Bul., 8,067..D6 22
Mikhaylovka, Sov. Un., 31,000..........C2 29
Mikhaylovka, Sov. Un., 10,000..........H10 27

Mikhaylovskiy, Sov. Un. C9 29
Mikindani, Tan., 4,807 D7 48
Mikkalo, Gilliam, Oreg., 15 B6 113
Mikkeli, Fin., 19,800 G12 25
Mikkeli, dept., Fin., 235,403 *G12 25
Mikolow, Pol., 16,100 g9 26
Mikonos, isl., Grc D5 23
Mikope, Con. L. C3 48
Mikulczyce, Pol. g9 26
Mikulov, Czech., 5,220 D4 26
Mikura, isl., Jap J9 37
Mila, Northumberland, Va., 25 D6 121
Milaca, Mille Lacs, Minn., 1,821 E5 99
Milagro, Arg A3 54
Milam, Hardy, W. Va., 65 C5 123
Milam, co., Texas, 22,263 D4 118
Milan, Que., Can., 129 D6 73
Milan, Telfair and Dodge, Ga., 786 D3 87
Milan, Rock Island, Ill., 3,065 B3 90
Milan, Ripley, Ind., 1,174 F7 91
Milan, Sumner, Kans., 144 E7 93
Milan, Monroe and Washtenaw, Mich., 3,616 F7 98
Milan, Chippewa, Minn., 482 E3 99
Milan, Sullivan, Mo., 1,670 A4 101
Milan, Coos, N.H., 100 (661▲) A4 105
Milan, Valencia, N. Mex., 2,658 B2 107
Milan, Erie, Ohio, 1,309 A5 111
Milan, Bradford, Pa., 180 C8 114
Milan, Gibson, Tenn., 5,208 B3 117
Milan, Spokane, Wash., 70 B8 122
Milan, Marathon, Wis., 150 D3 124
Milano, It., 1,657,600 (*2,800,000) D5 18, B2 21
Milano, Milam, Tex., 600 D4 118
Milas, Tur., 11,700 D5 23
Milazzo, It., 12,900 E5 21
Milbank, Grant, S. Dak., 3,500 B9 116
Milbanke, sound, B.C., Can C3 68
Milbridge, Washington, Maine, 675 (1,101▲) D5 96
Milburn, Carlisle, Ky., 400 B2 94
Milburn, Custer, Nebr., 16 C6 103
Milburn, Johnston, Okla., 228 C5 112
Milburn, Fayette, W. Va., 200 D6 123
Milden, Sask., Can., 388 F2 70
Mildenhall, Eng., 6,742 B8 12
Mildmay, Ont., Can., 847 C3 72
Mildred, Sask., Can. D2 70
Mildred, Allen, Kans., 60 D8 93
Mildred, Prairie, Mont., 50 D12 102
Mildred, Sullivan, Pa., 800 D9 114
Mildura, Austl., 12,279 G4 51
Mileai, Grc., 1,983 C4 23
Miles, Austl., 1,457 C8 51
Miles, Jackson, Iowa, 376 B7 92
Miles, Runnels, Tex., 626 D2 118
Miles, mtn., Vt. C5 120
Milesburg, Centre, Pa., 1,158 E6 114
Miles City, Custer, Mont., 9,665 D11 102
Milestone, Sask., Can., 465 G3 70
Milesville, Haakon, S. Dak., 20 C4 116
Miletus, ruins, Tur D6 23
Milevsko, Czech., 3,182 D3 17
Miley, Hampton, S.C., 450 F5 115
Milfay, Creek, Okla., 130 B5 111
Milford, Lassen, Calif., 5 B3 82
Milford, New Haven, Conn., 41,662 E4 84
Milford, Sussex and Kent, Del., 5,795 C7 85
Milford, Iroquois, Ill., 1,699 C6 90
Milford, Kosciusko, Ind., 1,167 B6 91
Milford, Dickinson, Iowa, 1,476 A2 92
Milford, Geary, Kans., 318 C7 93
Milford, Bracken, Ky., 100 B5 94
Milford, Penobscot, Maine, 800 (1,572▲) D4 96
Milford, Worcester, Mass., 15,749 B4, h9 97
Milford, Oakland, Mich., 4,323 A6, F7 98
Milford, Seward, Nebr., 1,462 D8 103
Milford, Hillsboro, N.H., 3,916 (4,863▲) E3 105
Milford, Hunterdon, N.J., 1,114 B2 106
Milford, Otsego, N.Y., 548 C6 108
Milford, Hamilton and Clermont, Ohio, 4,131 C3 111
Milford, Pike, Pa., 1,198 D12 114
Milford, Beaver, Utah, 1,471 E2 119
Milford, Caroline, Va., 250 C5 121
Milford Center, Union, Ohio, 794 B4 111
Milford Haven, Wales, 12,802 C2 12
Milford Mills, Baltimore, Md., 5,000 *B4 85
Milford Station, N.S., Can., 528 D6 74
Miliana, Alg., 5,983 (15,666▲) B5 44
Milicz, Pol., 2,929 C4 26
Miling, Austl., 230 F2 50
Milk, riv., Alta., Can., Mont G11 66
Milk River, Alta., Can., 801 E4 69
Milk River Ridge, res., Alta., Can E4 69
Mil Kuh, mtn., Afg E10 41
Mill, brook, Vt B3 120
Mill, creek, Ind F4 91
Mill, creek, Kans C6 93
Mill, creek, Kans D7 93
Mill, creek, N.J. D4 106
Mill, creek, Ohio B4 111
Mill, creek, Tenn E9 117
Mill, creek, W. Va C3 91
Mill, isl., Ant C23 5
Mill, riv., Mass h9 97
Milladore, Wood, Wis., 239 D4 124
Millard, Pike, Ky., 10 C7 94
Millard, Adair, Mo., 250 A5 101
Millard, Douglas, Nebr., 1,014 D3 103
Millard, co., Utah, 7,866 D2 119
Millarton, Stutsman, N. Dak., 40 C7 110
Millau, Fr., 21,229 E5 14
Millbank, Ont., Can., 235 D4 72
Millboro, Tripp, S. Dak., 34 D6 116
Millboro, Bath, Va., 300 D3 121
Millbrae, San Mateo, Calif., 15,873 B5 82
Mill Bridge, Ont., Can., 40 C7 72
Millbrook, Elmore, Ala., 900 C3 78
Millbrook, Ont., Can., 891 C6 72
Millbrook, Mecosta, Mich., 100 E5 98
Millbrook, Morris, N.J., 1,500 *B3 106
Millbrook, Dutchess, N.Y., 1,717 D7 108
Millbrook, Wake, N.C., 75 B5 109
Millburn, Lake, Ill., 125 D2 90
Millburn, Essex, N.J., 18,799 B4 106
Millbury, Worcester, Mass., 5,500 (9,623▲) B4 97
Millbury, Wood, Ohio, 730 A2, A4 111
Mill City, Pershing, Nev., 10 C3 104
Mill City, Marion, Oreg., 1,289 C4 113
Mill City, Wyoming, Pa., 200 A8 114
Millcreek, Union, Ill., 102 F4 90
Mill Creek, La Porte, Ind., 150 A4 91
Millcreek, Madison, Mo., 100 D7 101
Mill Creek, Deer Lodge, Mont., 110 D4 102
Mill Creek, Johnston, Okla., 287 C5 111
Mill Creek, Huntingdon, Pa., 400 E6 114
Mill Creek, Randolph, W. Va., 817 C5 123
Mill Creek, falls, Oreg E4 113
Milldale, Hartford, Conn., 1,000 C5 84
Milledgeville, Baldwin, Ga., 11,117 C3 87
Milledgeville, Carroll, Ill., 1,208 B4 90
Milledgeville, McNairy, Tenn., 300 B3 117
Mille lac, Indian res., Minn D5 99
Mille Lacs, co., Minn., 14,560 E5 99
Mille Lacs, lake, Minn D5 99
Millen, Jenkins, Ga., 3,633 D5 87
Miller, Lyon, Kans., 75 D8 93
Miller, De Soto, Miss., 150 A4 100
Miller, Buffalo, Nebr., 137 D6 103
Miller, Lawrence, Ohio, 180 D5 111
Miller, Sherman, Oreg B6 113
Miller, Hand, S. Dak., 2,081 C7 116
Miller, co., Ark., 31,686 D2 81
Miller, co., Ga., 6,908 E2 87
Miller, co., Mo., 13,800 C5 101
Miller, flat, Oreg C5 113
Miller, isl., Md B5 86
Miller, peak, Alsk C11 79
Miller, peak, Ariz F5 80
Miller, run, Vt. E4 120
Miller Dale Colony, Hand, S. Dak., 50 C6 116
Miller Heights, Northampton, Pa., 1,500 *E11 114
Millerovo, Sov. Un., 32,400 D2 29
Miller Place, Suffolk, N.Y., 1,350 F5 84
Millers, Carroll, Md., 160 A4 85
Millers, riv., Mass A3 97
Millersburg, Elkhart, Ind., 489 A6 91
Millersburg, Iowa, Iowa, 186 C5 92
Millersburg, Bourbon, Ky., 913 B5 94
Millersburg, Presque Isle, Mich., 280 C6 98
Millersburg, Holmes, Ohio, 3,101 B6 111
Millersburg, Linn, Oreg C1 113
Millersburg, Dauphin, Pa., 2,984 E8 114
Millers Falls, Franklin, Mass., 1,199 A3 97
Millers Ferry, Wilcox, Ala., 250 C2 78
Millersport, Fairfield, Ohio, 752 C5 111
Millerstown, Perry, Pa., 675 E7 114
Millersview, Concho, Tex., 200 D3 118
Millersville, Marion, Ind., 65 H8 91
Millersville, Lancaster, Pa., 3,883 F9 114
Millerton, N.B., Can., 232 C4 74
Millerton, Wayne, Iowa, 90 D4 92
Millerton, Dutchess, N.Y., 1,027 D7 108
Millerton, McCurtain, Okla., 150 D6 112
Millerton, Tioga, Pa., 400 C8 114
Millertown, Newf., Can., 365 D3 75
Millertown Junction, Newf., Can., 186 D3 75
Millerville, Clay, Ala., 100 B4 78
Millerville, Douglas, Minn., 119 D3 99
Milles Iles, riv., Que., Can p19 73
Millet, Alta., Can., 403 C4 69
Millett, Allendale, S.C., 50 E4 115
Millett, La Salle, Tex., 150 E3 118
Mille Vaches, pt., Que., Can A8 73
Millgrove, Blackford, Ind., 130 D7 91
Mill Grove, Mercer, Mo., 139 A4 101
Mill Hall, Clinton, Pa., 1,891 D7 114
Millhaven, Screven, Ga., 60 D5 87
Millheim, Centre, Pa., 780 E7 114
Millhousen, Decatur, Ind., 212 F7 91
Millhurst, Monmouth, N.J., 100 C4 106
Millicent, Austl., 3,401 H3 51
Millicent, Alta., Can. D5 69
Milligan, Okaloosa, Fla., 800 G2 86
Milligan, Fillmore, Nebr., 323 D8 103
Milligan College, Carter, Tenn., 200 C11 117
Milliken, Weld, Colo., 630 A6 83
Millikin, East Carroll, La., 100 B4 95
Millington, Kent and Queen Annes, Md., 408 B6 85
Millington, Tuscola, Mich., 1,159 E7 98
Millington, Morris, N.J., 1,300 *B3 106
Millington, Coos, Oreg., 300 D2 113
Millington, Shelby, Tenn., 6,059 B2 117
Millinocket, Penobscot, Maine, 7,453 C4 96
Millinocket, lake, Maine B4 96
Millinocket, lake, Maine C4 96
Mill Iron, Carter, Mont., 5 E12 102
Millis, Norfolk, Mass., 2,900 (4,374▲) B5, h10 97
Millom, Eng., 7,116 F5 13
Mill Plain, Fairfield, Conn. (part of Danbury) D2 84
Mill Point, Pocahontas, W. Va., 50 C4 123
Millport, Lamar, Ala., 943 B1 78
Millport, Potter, Pa., 125 C5 114
Millport, Scot., 1,592 E4 13
Millrift, Pike, Pa., 110 D12 114
Mill River, Berkshire, Mass., 300 B1 97
Mill Run, Fayette, Pa., 300 G3 114
Millry, Washington, Ala., 645 D1 78
Mills, Keya Paha, Nebr., 37 B6 103
Mills, Harding, N. Mex., 25 A5 107
Mills, Potter, Pa., 150 C6 114
Mills, Juab, Utah, 25 D3 119
Mills, Natrona, Wyo., 1,477 C6 125
Mills, co., Iowa, 13,050 C2 92
Mills, co., Tex., 4,467 D3 118
Mills, lake, N.W. Ter., Can D9 66
Millsboro, Sussex, Del., 536 C6 85
Millsboro, Washington, Pa., 1,179 G1 114
Mill Shoals, White, Ill., 322 E5 90
Millside, New Castle, Del., 1,000 *A6 85
Mill Spring, Wayne, Mo., 226 D7 101
Millstadt, St. Clair, Ill., 1,830 E3 90
Millston, Jackson, Wis., 200 D3 124
Millstone, New London, Conn., 150 D8 84
Millstone, Somerset, N.J., 409 B3 106
Millstone, riv., N.J. C3 106
Mill Stream, Austl D2 50
Millstreet, Ire., 1,283 E2 11
Milltown, Chambers, Ala., 45 B4 78
Milltown, N.B., Can., 1,892 D2 74
Milltown, Newf., Can., 438 E4 75
Milltown, Crawford and Harrison, Ind., 793 H5 91
Milltown, Adair, Ky., 150 C4 94
Milltown, Washington, Maine (part of Calais) C5 96
Mill Town, Madison, Miss., 300 *C3 100
Milltown, Missoula, Mont., 750 D3 102
Milltown, Middlesex, N.J., 5,435 C4 106
Milltown, Hutchinson, S. Dak., 52 D8 116
Milltown, Polk, Wis., 608 C1 124
Millvale, Allegheny, Pa., 6,624 B6 114
Mill Valley, Marin, Calif., 10,411 D2 82
Mill Village, N.S., Can., 249 E5 74
Mill Village, Erie, Pa., 336 C2 114
Millville, N.B., Can., 390 C2 74
Millville, Sussex, Del., 231 C7 85
Millville, Woodford, Ky B5 94
Millville, Worcester, Mass., 1,567 B4 97
Millville, Cumberland, N.J., 19,096 E2 106
Millville, Butler, Ohio, 676 C2 111
Millville, Columbia, Pa., 952 D9 114
Millville, Cache, Utah, 364 B4 119
Millville, Jefferson, W. Va., 350 B7 123
Millwood, Clarke, Va., 400 B4 121
Millwood, Spokane, Wash., 1,776 D8 122
Millwood, Jackson, W. Va., 75 C3 123
Milmay, Atlantic, N.J., 200 E3 106
Milmont Park, Delaware, Pa., 2,000 *B11 114
Milner, B.C., Can., 324 f13 68
Milner, Routt, Colo., 100 A3 83
Milner, Lamar, Ga., 305 C2 87
Milner, dam, Idaho G5 89
Milner Ridge, Man., Can., 40 D3 71
Milnesand, Roosevelt, N. Mex., 10 D6 107
Milnor, Sargent, N. Dak., 658 C8 110
Milo, Alta., Can., 167 D4 69
Milo, Warren, Iowa, 468 C4 92
Milo, Piscataquis, Maine, 1,802 (2,756▲) C4 96
Milo, Vernon, Mo., 108 D3 101
Milo, Bledsoe, Tenn D9 117
Milolii, Hawaii, Haw., 95 D6 88
Milos, isl., Grc D5 23
Milparinka, Austl., 83 D3 51
Milpitas, Santa Clara, Calif., 6,572 B6 82
Milroy, Rush, Ind., 690 F7 91
Milroy, Redwood, Minn., 268 F3 99
Milroy, Mifflin, Pa., 1,666 E6 114
Milstead, Rockdale, Ga., 1,047 B6, C3 87
Miltenberg, Ger., 8,100 D4 17
Milton, N.S., Can., 1,121 E5 74
Milton, Litchfield, Conn., 100 B3 84
Milton, Sussex, Del., 1,617 C7 85
Milton, Santa Rosa, Fla., 4,108 G2 86
Milton, Madison, Ill. (part of Alton) A8 101
Milton, Pike, Ill., 309 D3 90
Milton, Wayne, Ind., 700 E7 91
Milton, Van Buren, Iowa, 609 D5 92
Milton, Sumner, Kans., 100 E6 93
Milton, Trimble, Ky., 365 B4 94
Milton, Lafayette, La., 150 D3 95
Milton, Norfolk, Mass., 26,375 B5, g11 97
Milton, Strafford, N.H., 650 (1,418▲) D5 105
Milton, Ulster, N.Y., 800 D7 108
Milton, N.Z., 1,922 Q12 51
Milton, Caswell, N.C., 235 A4 109
Milton, Cavalier, N. Dak., 264 A7 110
Milton, Northumberland, Pa., 7,972 D8 114
Milton, Chittenden, Vt., 817 (2,022▲) B2 120
Milton, Pierce, Wash., 2,218 D1 122
Milton, Cabell, W. Va., 1,714 C2 123
Milton, Rock, Wis., 1,671 F5 124
Milton, res., Colo A6 83
Milton, res., Ohio A7 111
Miltona, Douglas, Minn., 163 D3 99
Miltona, lake, Minn D3 99
Milton-Freewater, Umatilla, Oreg., 4,110 B8 113
Milton Junction, Rock, Wis., 1,433 F5 124
Milton Mills, Strafford, N.H., 275 D5 105
Milton Station, P.E.I., Can., 120 *C6 74
Miltonvale, Cloud, Kans., 814 C6 93
Milton West, Ont., Can., 5,629 D5 72
Miltown Malbay, Ire., 700 E2 11
Milverton, Ont., Can., 1,111 D4 72
Milwaukee, Northampton, N.C., 311 A6 109
Milwaukee, Milwaukee, Wis., 741,324 (*1,247,100) E2, E6 124
Milwaukee, co., Wis., 1,036,041 E5 124
Milwaukee, riv., Wis E2 124
Milwaukie, Clackamas, Oreg., 9,099 B2, B4 113
Mimbres, Grant, N. Mex., 25 E1 107
Mimbres, mts., N. Mex D2 107
Mimico, Ont., Can., 18,212 D5, m15 72
Mimizan, Fr., 855 E3 14
Mimon, Czech., 4,605 C9 17
Mimongo, Gabon C2 46
Mims, Brevard, Fla., 1,307 D6 86
Min, riv., China F8 34
Mina, Mineral, Nev., 300 E3 104
Mina, Edmunds, S. Dak., 50 B7 116
Mināb, Iran H8 41
Minago, riv., Man., Can B2 71
Minaki, Ont., Can., 207 E4 71
Minam, Wallowa, Oreg., 75 B9 113
Minamata, Jap., 30,400 J5 37
Minami, Iwo 52
Minami-Iwo, isl., Pac. O E8 7
Minas, Cuba, 3,305 E5 74
Minas, Ur., 24,400 E1 56
Minas, basin, N.S., Can D5 74
Minas, chan., N.S., Can D5 74
Minas de Oro, Hond., 1,407 C4 62
Minas de Ríotinto, Sp., 9,060 D2 20
Minas Gerais, state, Braz., 9,798,880 B4, g3, k4 56
Minatare, Scotts Bluff, Nebr., 894 C2 103
Minatitlán, Mex., 34,980 D6 63
Minato, see Nakaminato, Jap.
Minato, Jap., 7,100 n18 37
Minbu, Bur., 9,096 D9 39
Minburn, Alta., Can., 164 C5 69
Minburn, Dallas, Iowa, 357 C3 92
Minch, chan., Scot B3 13
Minchin, China D5 34
Mincio, riv., It D6 18
Minco, Grady, Okla., 1,021 B4 112
Mindanao, isl., Phil D7 35
Mindanao, sea, Phil D6 35
Mindel, riv., Ger A6 18
Mindelheim, Ger., 8,500 A6 18
Mindelo, C.V.Is., 18,400 *E3 42
Mindemoya, Ont., Can., 356 B2 72
Minden, Ont., Can., 658 C6 72
Minden, Ger., 49,200 (*87,000) A3 17
Minden, Pottawattamie, Iowa, 355 C2 92
Minden, Webster, La., 12,785 B2 95
Minden, Kearney, Nebr., 2,383 D7 103
Minden, Douglas, Nev., 400 E2 104
Minden, Fayette, W. Va., 1,114 D3, D7 123
Minden City, Sanilac, Mich., 369 E8 98
Mindenmines, Barton, Mo., 356 D3 101
Mindoro, La Crosse, Wis., 200 D2 124
Mindoro, isl., Phil C6 35
Mindoro, strait, Phil C6 35
Mine Centre, Ont., Can., 88 E5 71
Minechoag, mtn., Mass B3 97
Minehead, Eng., 7,674 C4 12
Mine Hill, Morris, N.J., 3,362 B3 106
Mineiros, Braz., 5,105 B2 56
Mine La Motte, Madison, Mo., 100 D7 101
Mineola, Mills, Iowa, 150 C2 92
Mineola, Clark, Kans., 679 E3 93
Mineola, Nassau, N.Y., 20,519 E7, n15 108
Mineola, Wood, Tex., 3,810 C5 118
Miner, Scott, Mo., 548 E8 101
Miner, Park, Mont., 5 E6 102
Miner, co., S. Dak., 5,398 D8 116
Mineral, Bureau, Ill., 330 B4 90
Mineral, Louisa, Va., 366 C5 121
Mineral, Lewis, Wash., 400 C3 122
Mineral, co., Colo., 424 D4 83
Mineral, co., Mont., 3,037 C1 102
Mineral, co., Nev., 6,329 E3 104
Mineral, co., W. Va., 22,354 B6 123
Mineral, mtn., Ariz D2 80
Mineral, mts., Utah E3 119
Mineral City, Tuscarawas, Ohio, 917 B6 111
Mineral del Oro, Mex., 4,283 n13 63
Mineral Hills, Iron, Mich., 311 B2 98
Mineral Park, Bradley, Tenn., 25 E10 117
Mineral Point, Washington, Mo., 332 D7 101
Mineral Point, Iowa, Wis., 2,385 F3 124
Mineral Ridge, Mahoning and Trumbull, Ohio, 2,000 *A7 111
Mineral Springs, Howard, Ark., 616 D2 81
Mineral Wells, De Soto, Miss., 210 A4 100
Mineral Wells, Palo Pinto, Tex., 11,053 C3 118
Minersville, Meigs, Ohio, 350 C6 111
Minersville, Schuylkill, Pa., 6,606 E9 114
Minersville, Beaver, Utah, 580 E3 119
Minerva, Terrebonne, La C6 95
Minerva, Essex, N.Y., 200 B7 108
Minerva, Carroll and Stark, Ohio, 3,833 B6 111
Minerva Park, Franklin, Ohio, 1,169 *C5 111
Minervino Murge, It., 18,427 D6 21
Minetto, Oswego, N.Y., 800 B4 108
Mineville, Essex, N.Y., 1,181 A7 108
Mingan, Que., Can. h8 75
Mingchiang, China A7 38
Mingechaur, Sov. Un., 30,000 G18 9
Mingechaur, res., Sov. Un E3 29
Mingenew, Austl., 317 E2 50
Mingo, Jasper, Iowa, 260 C4 92
Mingo, Thomas, Kans., 10 C3 93
Mingo, co., W. Va., 39,742 D2 123
Mingo, creek, S.C. D9 115
Mingo Junction, Jefferson, Ohio, 4,987 B7 111
Mingoyo, Tan D6 48
Mingshui, China, 5,000 C2 37
Mingshui, China C4 34
Minho, prov., Port., 825,788 *B1 20
Minho, riv., Port B1 20
Minhow, see Foochow, China
Minicoy, isl., India G5 39
Minidoka, Minidoka, Idaho, 154 G5 89
Minidoka, co., Idaho, 14,394 G5 89
Minidoka, dam, Idaho G5 89
Minier, Tazewell, Ill., 847 C4 90
Miniota, Man., Can., 248 D1 71
Minipi, lake, Newf., Can h9 75
Minisink, isl., N.J. A3 106
Minitonas, Man., Can., 606 C1 71
Mink Creek, Franklin, Idaho, 109 G7 89
Minna, Nig., 12,810 E6 45
Minna, bluff, Ant B29 5
Minneapolis, Ottawa, Kans., 2,024 C6 93
Minneapolis, Hennepin, Minn., 482,872 (*1,441,700) E7, F5 99
Minneapolis, Avery, N.C., 200 C4 103
Minnedosa, Man., Can., 2,211 D2 71
Minnedosa, riv., Man., Can D1 71
Minnehaha, Clark, Wash., 2,000 *D3 122
Minnehaha, co., S. Dak., 86,575 D6 116
Minneiska, Wabasha, Minn., 110 F7 99
Minneota, Lyon Minn., 1,297 F3 99
Mineral, Tehama, Calif., 125 B3 82
Minnesota, state, U.S., 3,413,864 A9 77, 99
Minnesota, riv., Minn F3 99
Minnesota Lake, Faribault, Minn., 697 G5 99
Minnetonka, Hennepin, Minn., 25,037 *F5 99
Minnetonka, lake, Minn F5 99
Minnetrista, Hennepin, Minn., 2,076 *E5 99
Minnewanka, lake, Alta., Can D3 69
Minnewaska, lake, Minn E3 99
Minnewaukan, Benson, N. Dak., 420 A6 110
Mino, Jap., 18,700 n15 37
Miño, riv., Sp A1 20
Minoa, Onondaga, N.Y., 1,838 *B4 108
Minocqua, Oneida, Wis., 700 C4 124
Minokamo [Ota], Jap., 36,700 (62,600▲) n15 37
Minong, Washburn, Wis., 348 B2 124
Minonk, Woodford, Ill., 2,001 C4 90
Minooka, Grundy, Ill., 539 B5 90
Minor Hill, Giles, Tenn., 400 B11 117
Minot, Plymouth, Mass., 250 h12 97
Minot, Ward, N. Dak., 33,477 A4 110
Minquadale, New Castle, Del., 1,200 *A6 85
Minsen, Ger., 2,100 A7 15
Minsk, Sov. Un., 644,000 E6 27
Minsk, Mazowiecki, Pol., 20,000 B6, m15 26
Minster, Auglaize, Ohio, 2,193 *B3 111
Minstra, mts., Sp B4 20
Minster, Dallas, Ala., 50 C2 78
Minter City, Leflore, Miss., 250 B3 100
Minto, Alsk., 161 C10 79
Minto, Man., Can., 171 E1 71
Minto, N.B., Can., 1,319 C3 74
Minto, Walsh, N. Dak., 642 A8 110
Minto, lake, Que., Can g11 73
Minto, pass, Oreg C5 113
Minton, Sask., Can., 208 H3 70
Minton Corner, Brevard, Fla., 2,400 *D6 86
Minturn, Lawrence, Ark., 61 B4 81
Minturn, Eagle, Colo., 662 B4 83
Minturn, Hancock, Maine, 120 D4 96
Minturno, It., 3,125 D4 21
Minūf, Eg., U.A.R., 36,900 D3 32
Minusinsk, Sov. Un., 44,600 E27 9
Minute Man, nat. historical park, Mass g10 97
Minvoul, Gabon E2 46
Minya al Qamḥ, Eg., U.A.R., 1,000 D3 32
Minya Konka, peak, China F5 34
Mio, Oscoda, Mich., 500 D6 98
Miola, Clarion, Pa., 15 D3 114
Miquelon, cape, St. Pierre & Miquelon E3 75
Miquelon, isl., St. Pierre & Miquelon E3 75
Mira, Caddo, La., 75 B2 95
Mira, Port., 2,258 B2 20
Mira, riv., Port D1 20
Miracle Hot Springs, Kern, Calif., 40 E4 80
Mirador, Braz., 818 C2 57
Miraflores, Col., 2,456 C3 60
Miraflores, Peru, 16,146 E3 58
Miraflores, locks, C.Z. m11 62
Miragoâne, Hai., 2,499 F7 64
Mira Gut, N.S., Can., 99 C10 74
Miraj, India, 53,345 I5 40
Miraleste, Los Angeles, Calif., 1,800 *E4 82
Mira Loma, Riverside, Calif., 3,982 F3 82
Miramar, San Diego, Calif., 75 E2 82
Miramar, Cuba h11 64
Miramar, Broward, Fla., 5,485 E3 86
Miramichi, bay, N.B., Can B4 74
Miranda, Braz., 2,075 C1 56
Miranda, Col., 4,082 C2 60
Miranda, Faulk, S. Dak., 65 F7 116
Miranda, state, Ven., 492,349 A4 60
Miranda, riv., Braz C1 56
Miranda de Ebro, Sp., 27,881 A4 20
Miranda do Douro, Port., 1,331 B2 20
Mirande, Fr., 3,024 F4 14
Mirandela, Port., 3,418 B2 20
Mirando City, Webb, Tex., 600 F3 118
Mirandola, It., 8,000 E7 18
Mirassol, Braz., 13,674 C3 56
Mirebalais, Hai., 5,200 F7 64
Mirecourt, Fr., 8,572 C7 14
Mirepoix, Fr., 2,477 F4 14
Mirgorod, Sov. Un., 10,000 G9 27
Miri, Mala., 13,350 E4 35
Mirialguda, India, 10,024 I7 40
Miriam Vale, Austl., 297 B8 51
Mirnyy, U.S.S.R. scientific station, Ant C22 5
Mirond, lake, Sask., Can B4 70
Mirow, Ger., 3,801 E6 24
Mirpur-Khas, Pak., 60,861 E2 40
Mirror, Alta., Can., 577 C4 69
Mirror Lake, Carroll, N.H., 60 C4 105
Mirzapur, India, 100,097 C7 39, E9 40
Misakubo, Jap., 5,000 n16 37
Misamis Occidental, prov., Phil., 251,100 *D6 35
Misamis Oriental, prov., Phil., 387,800 *D6 35
Misantla, Mex., 9,078 D5, n15 63
Misawa, Jap., 36,570 *F10 37
Misburg, Ger., 14,400 A4 17
Miscoe, hill, Mass h9 97
Miscou, isl., N.B., Can B5 74
Miscou, pt., N.B., Can A5 74
Miscou Centre, N.B., Can B5 74
Miscouche, P.E.I., Can., 676 C6 74
Misenheimer, Stanly, N.C., 850 B3 108
Mishan, China, 5,000 D6 37
Mishawaka, St. Joseph, Ind., 33,361 A5 91
Mishicot, Manitowoc, Wis., 762 A7, D6 124
Mishima, Jap., 62,966 I9, n17 37
Misiones, prov., Arg., 331,000 E4 55
Misiones, dept., Par., 43,449 E4 55
Miskitos, is., Nic C5 62
Miskolc, Hung., 159,800 A5 22
Misoöl, isl., W. Irian F7 35
Mispillion, riv., Del C7 85
Misquah, hills, Minn B7 99
Misquamicut, Washington, R.I., 60 D9 84
Miṣr al Jadīdah, Eg., U.A.R. D3 32
Misrātah, Libya, 59,902 C3 43
Misratah, cape, Libya H14 30
Missaukee, co., Mich., 6,784 D5 98
Missaukee, lake, Mich D5 98
Missinaibi, riv., Ont., Can G16 67
Mission, Johnson, Kans., 4,626 *B9 93
Mission, Todd, S. Dak., 611 D5 116
Mission, Hidalgo, Tex., 14,081 F3 118
Mission, Indian res., Calif F5 82
Mission, range, Mont C3 102
Mission City, B.C., Can., 3,251 E6, f13 68
Mission Hill, Yankton, S. Dak., 165 E8 116
Mission Hills, Johnson, Kans., 3,621 D9 93
Missipuskiow, riv., Sask., Can D4 70
Missisquoi, co., Que., Can., 29,526 D4 73
Missisquoi, bay, Vt A2 120
Missisquoi, riv., Vt B3 120
Mississagi, riv., Ont., Can B7 98
Mississagi, strait, Ont., Can C7 98
Mississinewa, riv., Ind C6 91
Mississippi, co., Ark., 70,174 B5 81
Mississippi, co., Mo., 20,695 E8 101
Mississippi, state, U.S., 2,178,141 D10 77, 100
Mississippi, delta, La E6 95
Mississippi, lake, Ont., Can B8 72
Mississippi, riv., U.S D9 77
Mississippi, sound, Miss E5 100
Mississippi City, Harrison, Miss., 4,169 E2, E4 100
Missoula, Missoula, Mont., 27,090 D2 102
Missoula, co., Mont., 44,663 D2 102
Missoula Southwest, Missoula, Mont., 3,900 *D2 102
Missour, Mor C4 44
Missouri, state, U.S., 4,319,813 C9 77, 101
Missouri, buttes, Wyo A8 125

Missouri, caverns, Mo........C6 101
Missouri, riv., U.S..........B8 77
Missouri City, Clay, Mo., 404..............E2 101
Missouri City, Fort Bend, Tex., 604..............F5 118
Missouri Valley, Harrison, Iowa, 3,567..............C2 92
Mistaken, pt., Newf., Can.....E5 75
Mistassini, Que., Can., 3,461..............h12 73
Mistassini, lake, Que., Can....h12 73
Mistastin, lake, Newf., Can....g9 75
Mistatim, Sask., Can., 207...E4 70
Mistelbach [an der Zaya], Aus., 5,434..............D8 16
Misti, vol., Peru..........E3 58
Miston, Dyer, Tenn., 100....A2 117
Mistretta, It., 9,979........F5 21
Mita, pt., Mex..............C3 63
Mitaka, Jap., 98,038.........*I9 37
Mitake, Jap., 8,200.....I8, n16 37
Mitcham, Eng., 63,653.....m12 10
Mitchell, Bullock, Ala., 25...C4 78
Mitchell, Austl., 1,822........C6 52
Mitchell, Ont., Can., 2,247..D3 72
Mitchell, Glascock, Ga., 184..............C4 87
Mitchell, Madison, Ill., 150..A8 101
Mitchell, Lawrence, Ind., 3,552..............G5 91
Mitchell, Mitchell, Iowa, 237..............A5 92
Mitchell, Sabine, La., 300....C2 95
Mitchell, Scotts Bluff, Nebr., 1,920..............C2 103
Mitchell, Wheeler, Oreg., 236..............C6 113
Mitchell, Davison, S. Dak., 12,555..............D7 116
Mitchell, co., Ga., 19,652....E2 87
Mitchell, co., Iowa, 14,043..A5 92
Mitchell, co., Kans., 8,866..C5 93
Mitchell, co., N.C., 13,906..C4 109
Mitchell, co., Tex., 11,255..C2 118
Mitchell, dam, Ala..........C3 78
Mitchell, isl., La............E6 95
Mitchell, lake, Ala...........C3 78
Mitchell, lake, Mich..........D5 98
Mitchell, mtn., N.C...........D4 109
Mitchell, riv., Austl..........C7 50
Mitchellsberg, Boyle, Ky., 500..............C5 94
Mitchellville, Polk, Iowa, 957..............A8, C4 92
Mitchellville, Sumner, Tenn., 184..............A5 117
Mitchelstown, Ire., 2,655....E3 11
Mit Fāris, Eg., U.A.R., 1,000..............C3 32
Mit Ghamr, Eg., U.A.R., 34,400..............D3 32
Mitilini (Mytilene), Grc., 25,758..............C6 23
Mitishto, riv., Man., Can.....B2 71
Mitla, pass, Eg., U.A.R.......D4 32
Mito, Jap., 110,000 (139,389▲)........H10, m19 37
Mitre, mtn., N.Z.............N15 51
Mitsinjo, Malag..............g9 49
Mittelland, canal, Ger........B5 16
Mittenwald, Ger., 8,500......B7 18
Mittersill, Aus., 3,502........B8 18
Mitterteich, Ger., 6,500.....D7 17
Mittl Isar, canal, Ger........A7 18
Mittweida, Ger., 20,900......C7 17
Mitú, Col., 211..............C3 60
Mițūbis, Eg., U.A.R., 1,000..C2 32
Mitumba, mts., Con. L........C4 48
Mitwaba, Con. L..............C4 48
Mitzic, Gabon................E2 46
Miura (Misaki), Jap., 19,334..............n18 37
Mixcoac, Mex. (part of Mexico City)..............h9 63
Mixquiahuala, Mex., 7,184..............m14 63
Mixteco, riv., Mex...........o14 63
Miyagi, pref., Jap., 1,743,195..............*G10 37
Miyake, isl., Jap..............I9 37
Miyako, Jap., 37,400 (55,385▲)..............G10 37
Miyakonojo, Jap., 54,600 (92,230▲)..............K5 37
Miyan Kaleh, pen., Iran......C6 41
Miyata, Jap., 51,200.......*J5 37
Miyazaki, Jap., 115,000 (158,328▲)..............K5 37
Miyazaki, pref., Jap., 1,134,590..............*K5 37
Miyazu, Jap., 21,800........n14 37
Mizdah, Libya................C2 43
Mize, Smith, Miss., 371.....D4 100
Mizen, head, Ire..............F2 11
Mizil, Rom., 7,460............C8 22
Mizpah, Koochiching, Minn., 140..............C4 99
Mizpah, Custer, Mont......D11 102
Mizpah, Atlantic, N.J., 400..E3 106
Mizpah, creek, Mont.........E11 102
Mizque, Bol., 870.............C2 55
Mjölby, Swe., 10,700........H6 25
Mjösa, lake, Nor..............G4 25
Mkalama, Tan................B5 48
M. Kemalpasa, see Mustafa Kemalpasa, Tur.
Mkushi, Zambia...............C4 48
Mlada Boleslav, Czech., 25,700..............C3, n18 26
Mlanje, Malawi...............E6 48
Mlanje, mtn., Malawi.........E6 48
Mlawa, Pol., 14,100..........B6 26
Mljet, isl., Yugo..............D3 22
Mnichovo Hradiste, Czech., 3,733..............C9 17
Mo, Nor., 8,300..............D6 25
Moa, isl., Indon...............G7 35
Moab, Grand, Utah, 4,682..E6 119
Moala, isl., Fiji Is...................52
Moamba, Moz................C5 49
Moanda, Gabon...............F2 46
Moapa, Clark, Nev., 20......G7 104
Moapa River, Indian res., Nev..G7 104
Moar, lake, Man., Can.........C4 71
Moark, Clay, Ark., 130.......A5 81
Moate, Ire., 1,261............D4 11
Moaula, Hawaii, Haw., 65...D6 88
Mobara, Jap., 19,300........n19 37
Mobaye, Cen. Afr. Rep.......E4 46
Mobeetie, Wheeler, Tex., 450..............B2 118
Moberly, Randolph, Mo., 13,170..............B5 101
Moberly, lake, B.C., Can.......B7 68
Moberly Lake, B.C., Can., 150..............B7 68
Mobile, Mobile, Ala., 202,779 (*304,000)..............E1 78
Mobile, Maricopa, Ariz., 35..D3 80
Mobile, Newf., Can., 80.....E5 75
Mobile, co., Ala., 314,301...E1 78
Mobile, bay, Ala..............E1 78
Mobile, riv., Ala..............E1 78
Mobley, Stewart, Tenn.......A3 117
Mobridge, Walworth, S. Dak., 4,391..............B5 116
Mobula, Con. L...............A4 48
Moca, Dom. Rep., 13,829....F8 64
Moca, P.R., 1,938............B2 65
Moca, mun., P.R., 21,990...B2 65
Moçajuba, Braz., 1,352.......C5 59
Moçambique, Moz., 12,500..A7 49
Moçambique, prov., Moz....D6 48
Moçâmedes, Ang., 7,185.....E1 48
Moçâmedes, dist., Ang., 43,393..............E1 48
Mocanaqua, Luzerne, Pa., 1,104..............D9 114
Moccasin, Mohave, Ariz., 65..A3 80
Moccasin, Judith Basin, Mont., 225..............C7 102
Mocha (Mokha) (Al Mukhā), Yemen, 5,000..............C5 47
Mocha, isl., Chile.............B2 54
Mochudi, Bech., 11,767......B4 49
Mocimboa da Praia, Moz....D7 48
Möchlen, lake, Swe...........B8 24
Mocksville, Davie, N.C., 2,379..............B3 109
Moclips, Grays Harbor, Wash., 500..............B1 122
Mocoa, Col., 1,698............C2 60
Mococa, Braz., 14,306....C3, k8 56
Mocomoco, Bol., 977.........C2 55
Mocorito, Mex., 2,472.......B3 63
Moctezuma, Mex., 2,151.....B3 63
Moctezuma, riv., Mex.........m14 63
Mocuba, Moz., 1,000.........A6 49
Modale, Harrison, Iowa, 276..............C2 92
Modane, Fr., 4,735...........D2 18
Mode, Shelby, Ill., 125.......D5 90
Model, Las Animas, Colo., 25..............D6 83
Model, Stewart, Tenn., 100..A4 117
Model, res., Colo.............D6 83
Modena, It., 149,800..........E6 19, B3 21
Modena, Mercer, Mo., 66.....A4 101
Modena, Ulster, N.Y., 600...D6 108
Modena, Iron, Utah, 35.......F2 119
Modena, Buffalo, Wis., 125..D2 124
Modeste, Ascension, La., 250..............B5 95
Modesto, Stanislaus, Calif., 36,585 (*90,400)..........D3 82
Modesto, Macoupin, Ill., 228..............D4 90
Modica, It., 30,200 (*44,300)..............F5 21
Modjokerto, Indon., 50,308.*G4 36
Modlin, Pol..............B6, k13 26
Mödling, Aus., 17,274.......D8 16
Modoc, Emanuel, Ga., 33....D4 87
Modoc, Randolph, Ind., 238.D7 91
Modoc, Scott, Kans., 73.....D2 93
Modoc, co., Calif., 8,308.....B3 82
Modoc Point, Klamath, Oreg., 75..............E5 113
Modrany, Czech., 10,100....n17 26
Moe, Austl., 16,300 (*52,200)..............*I6 51
Moecherville, Kane, Ill., 1,200..............*B5 90
Moen, isl., Truk...................52
Moengo, Sur..................A4 59
Moenkopi, Coconino, Ariz., 500..............A4 80
Moenkopi, wash., Ariz.........A5 80
Moerbeke, Bel., 5,164........C3 15
Moers, Ger., 48,400..........B1 17
Moesa, riv., Switz.............D7 19
Moesala, isl., Indon...........L3 38
Moesi, riv., Indon.............F2 36
Moeskroen, see Mouscron, Bel.
Moffat, Saguache, Colo., 104.C5 83
Moffat, co., Colo., 7,061......A2 83
Moffat, Scot., 1,917..........E5 13
Moffat, railroad tunnel, Colo..B5 83
Moffett, Sequoyah, Okla., 357..............B7 112
Moffit, Burleigh, N. Dak., 97.C5 110
Moga, Con. L.................B4 48
Mogadiscio, Som., 90,600....E6 47
Mogador, see Essaouira, Mor.
Mogadore, Portage and Summit, Ohio, 3,851..............A6 111
Mogaung, Bur., 2,940.......C10 39
Mogfog, Guam....................52
Mogi das Cruzes, Braz., 63,748..............C3, m8 56
Mogielnica, Pol., 4,667.......C6 26
Mogi Guaçu, riv., Braz........k8 56
Mogilev, Sov. Un., 145,000...E8 27
Mogilev-Podolskiy, Sov. Un., 46,300..............G6 27
Mogilno, Pol., 5,193..........B4 26
Mogi-Mirim, Braz., 18,345...m8 56
Mogincual, Moz..............A7 49
Mogocha, Sov. Un., 18,000.D14 28
Mogochin, Sov. Un., 3,500..B10 29
Mogok, Bur., 8,369..........D10 39
Mogollon, Catron, N. Mex., 25..............D1 107
Mogollon, mts., N. Mex.......D1 107
Mogollon, plat., Ariz..........C4 80
Mogote, Conejos, Colo., 30...D4 83
Mogotes, pt., Arg..............B5 54
Mogpog, Phil., 1,331.........p13 35
Moguer, Sp., 7,222...........D2 20
Mohacs, Hung., 15,860 (18,045▲)..............C4 22
Mohales Hoek, Bas............D4 49
Mohall, Renville, N. Dak., 956..............A4 110
Mohammadia, Mor., 35,010..............C3 44
Mohammed, cape, Eg., U.A.R..I10 31
Mohave, co., Ariz., 7,736.....B1 80
Mohave, lake, Ariz............B1 80
Mohave, mts., Ariz............C1 80
Mohawk, Yuma, Ariz., 20....E2 80
Mohawk, Keweenaw, Mich., 600..............A2 98
Mohawk, Herkimer, N.Y., 3,533..............C5 108
Mohawk, Lane, Oreg., 100...C4 113
Mohawk, lake, N.J.............A3 106
Mohawk, mtn., Conn...........B3 84
Mohawk, riv., N.H.............B1 105
Mohawk, riv., N.Y.............C6 108
Mohegan, New London, Conn., 800..............D8 84
Mohegan Lake, Westchester, N.Y., 2,000..............*D7 108
Mohican, riv., Ohio...........B5 111
Mohill, Ire., 905..............D4 11
Mohler, Lewis, Idaho, 20....C2 89
Mohler, Lincoln, Wash., 30...B7 122
Mohnton, Berks, Pa., 2,223..F10 114
Mohon, Fr., 9,043............C6 14
Mohoro, Tan., 1,160..........C6 48
Mohulu, Con. L...............B4 48
Moiese, Lake, Mont., 5.......C2 102
Moineşti, Rom., 12,934......B8 22
Mointy, Sov. Un..............D8 29
Moio, Eth....................D4 47
Moira, Franklin, N.Y., 400..f10 108
Moisie, Que., Can., 511.......h8 75
Moisie, riv., Que., Can.......h8 75
Moissac, Fr., 4,770...........E4 14
Moïssala, Chad, 3,203........D3 46
Moita, Port., 3,797...........f10 20
Mojave, Kern, Calif., 1,845...E4 82
Mojave, desert, Calif..........E5 82
Mojave, riv., Calif.............E5 82
Mokameh, India, 35,743.....E10 40
Mokane, Callaway, Mo., 419.C6 101
Mokapu, pt., Haw.............g11 88
Mokelumne, riv., Calif.........C3 82
Mokelumne Hill, Calaveras, Calif., 425..............C3 82
Mokena, Will, Ill., 1,332......F2 90
Mokepa, Con. L...............A4 48
Mokha (Mocha) (Al Mukhā), Yemen, 5,000..............C5 47
Mokhotlong, Bas..............C4 49
Mokmine, Tun., 17,699.......*B7 44
Mokolo, Cam..................C2 46
Mokolo, Con. L...............B2 48
Mokpo, Kor., 142,600.........I3 37
Moksha, riv., Sov. Un.........C2 29
Mokuaweoweo, crater, Haw.....D6 88
Mokuleia, Honolulu, Haw., 200..............B3, f9 88
Moku Manu, isl., Haw..........g11 88
Mol, Bel., 24,794.............C5 15
Mol, Yugo., 8,079.............C5 22
Mola di Bari, It., 22,852.....D6 21
Molalla, Clackamas, Oreg., 1,501..............B4 113
Molanosa, Sask., Can., 144..C3 70
Moláoi, Grc., 3,018...........D4 23
Molasses, pond, Maine........D4 96
Mold, Wales, 6,857............A4 12
Moldavia (Moldova), prov., Rom., 3,250,000..............*B8 22
Moldavia, reg., Rom..........B8 22
Moldavia (S.S.R.), rep., Sov. Un., 3,040,000...E5 28
Molde, Nor., 8,100............F2 25
Moldova (Moldavia), prov., Rom., 3,250,000..............*B8 22
Moldova, riv., Rom............B8 22
Moledet, Isr., 315............B7 32
Molega, lake, N.S., Can.......E5 74
Moleña, Pike, Ga., 279.......D2 87
Molenbeek-St. Jean, Bel., 63,528..............*D4 15
Molengraaff, mts., Indon......F5 35
Molepolole, Bech., 14,805....B5 49
Môle St. Nicolas, Hai., 1,700..............F7 64
Molfetta, It., 63,100..........D6 21
Molina, Chile, 6,123..........B2 54
Molina, Mesa, Colo., 10......B2 83
Molina de Aragón, Sp., 3,181..............B5 20
Molina de Segura, Sp., 8,578..............C5 20
Moline, Rock Island, Ill., 42,705..............B3 90
Moline, Elk, Kans., 698.......E7 93
Moline, Allegan, Mich., 550..F5 98
Moline, Wood, Ohio, 350.....A2 111
Moline Acres, St. Louis, Mo., 3,132..............*C7 101
Molinella, It., 2,950..........E7 18
Molino, Escambia, Fla., 800.G2 86
Molinos, Arg.................E2 55
Moliro, Con. L...............C5 48
Moliterno, It., 5,657.........D5 21
Möll, riv., Aus.................C9 18
Mölle, Swe., 480..............B6 24
Mollendo, Peru, 14,893.......E3 58
Mollusk, Lancaster, Va., 325..............D6 121
Mölndal, Swe., 26,500.......I5 25
Molochansk, Sov. Un., 10,000..............H10 27
Molodechno, Sov. Un., 26,000..............D6 27
Molokai, isl., Haw.............B5 88
Molokini, isl., Haw............C5 88
Molopo, riv., Bech., S. Afr....C3 49
Molotovsk, Sov. Un., 97,000..............E18 25
Molotovskoye, Sov. Un., 10,000..............I13 27
Moloundou, Cam..............E3 46
Mols, isl., Den.................B4 24
Molsheim, Fr., 4,955..........F7 15
Molson, Man., Can., 51.......D3 71
Molson, Okanogan, Wash., 80..............A6 122
Molson, lake, Man., Can.......B3 71
Molson, riv., Man., Can........B3 71
Molt, Stillwater, Mont., 20..E8 102
Molteno, S. Afr., 4,377.......D4 49
Molucca, is., Indon............F7 35
Molucca, passage, Indon.......E7 35
Molucca, sea, Indon...........E7 35
Molus, Harlan, Ky., 500.....D6 94
Molybdenum, Taos, N. Mex., 50..............A4 107
Moma, Moz...................A6 49
Momauguin, New Haven, Conn. (part of East Haven).......E5 84
Mombango, Con. L............A3 48
Mombasa, Ken., 179,575.....B6 48
Mombetsu, Jap., 28,200.....D11 37
Momboyo, riv., Con. L.........B3 48
Momchilgrad, Bul., 3,150....E7 22
Momence, Kankakee, Ill., 2,949..............B6 90
Momi, Fiji Is., 691...................52
Momostenango, Guat., 5,002.C2 62
Mompano, Con. L.............A3 48
Mompog, pass, Phil...........p14 37
Mompós, Col., 9,192..........B3 60
Møn, isl., Den..................D6 24
Mona, Richland, Mont.......B12 102
Mona, Juab, Utah, 347.......D4 119
Mona (Granville), Monongalia, W. Va., 806..............A7 123
Mona, isl., P.R................e10 65
Mona, passage, W.I............F9 64
Monaca, Beaver, Pa., 8,394...E1 114
Monaco, Monaco, 22,000 (*37,500)..............F7 14
Monaco, country, Eur., 22,000..............F7 14
Monadhliath, mts., Scot.......C4 13
Monadnock, mtn., N.H.........E2 105
Monadnock, mtn., Vt...........B5 120
Monagas, state, Ven., 246,217..............B5 60
Monaghan, Ire., 4,013........C5 11
Monaghan, Greenville, S.C., 1,200..............B2 115
Monaghan, co., Ire., 47,088..C4 11
Monahans, Ward, Tex., 8,567..............D1 118
Monamolin, Ire...............E5 11
Monango, Dickey, N. Dak., 133..............C7 110
Mona ó Carreta, pt., C.R......F6 62
Monarch, Alta., Can., 109....E4 69
Monarch, Cascade, Mont., 20..............C6 102
Monarch (Monarch Mills), Union, S.C., 1,990.......B4 115
Monarch, Sheridan, Wyo....A5 125
Monarch, mtn., B.C., Can......D5 68
Monarda, Aroostook, Maine, 50..............C4 96
Monashee, mts., B.C., Can.....D8 68
Monastir, Tun................B7 44
Monastyrshchina, Sov. Un., 5,300..............D8 27
Mona Vatu, mtn., Fiji Is..............52
Monaville, Logan, W. Va., 825..............*D5 123
Monção, Braz., 1,132.........B1 57
Moncayo, mtn., Sp............B5 20
Monchegorsk, Sov. Un., 30,000..............D15 25
Mönchengladbach, Ger., 153,600 (*335,000).........C3 16, C6 15
Monchique, Port., 2,169.....D1 20
Monchique, mts., Port..........D1 20
Moncks Corner, Berkeley, S.C., 2,030..............E7 115
Monclo, Logan, W. Va., 60..............D3, D5 123
Monclova, Mex., 43,077.....B4 63
Monclova, Lucas, Ohio, 125..A1 111
Moncton, N.B., Can., 43,840 (*55,768)..............C5 74
Moncure, Chatham, N.C., 400..............B4 109
Mond, lake, Ger................B9 18
Mondamin, Harrison, Iowa, 436..............C1 92
Mondego, cape, Port...........B1 20
Mondego, riv., Port............B1 20
Mondoñedo, Sp., 9,153.......A2 20
Mondorf-les-Bains, Lux., 1,757..............E6 15
Mondovì, It., 8,800 (*13,000)..............B1 21
Mondovi, Buffalo, Wis., 2,320..............D2 124
Monee, Will, Ill., 646........B6 90
Monegaw Springs, St. Clair, Mo., 53..............C4 101
Monemvasia, Grc., 638.......D4 23
Monero, Rio Arriba, N. Mex., 130..............A3 107
Monessen, Westmoreland, Pa., 18,424..............F2 114
Moneta, Bedford, Va., 170...D3 121
Moneta, Fremont, Wyo., 10..B6 125
Monett, Barry and Lawrence, Mo., 5,359..............E4 100
Monetta, Aiken and Saluda, S.C., 242..............D4 115
Monette, Craighead, Ark., 981..............B5 81
Money, Leflore, Miss., 100...B3 100
Moneymore, N. Ire., 807......C5 11
Monfalcone, Italy, 26,818....B4 21
Monforte de Lemos, Sp., 13,502..............A2 20
Monfort Heights, Hamilton, Ohio, 6,000..............*D2 111
Monga, Con. L................A3 48
Mongala, riv., Con. L..........A3 48
Mongalla, Sud.................D3 47
Monges, is., Ven...............A3 60
Mong Hpayak, Bur............B3 38
Mong Hsat, Bur...............B3 38
Monghyr, India, 89,768 (*146,807)........C8 38, E11 40
Mong Mit, Bur., 5,000......D10 39
Mong Nai, Bur................A3 38
Mongo, Chad, 2,721...........C3 46
Mongo, Lagrange, Ind., 225..A7 91
Mongolia, Ont., Can.........k15 72
Mongolia, country, Asia, 1,079,000........E13 31, B5 34
Mongolia, plat., Mong..........B6 34
Mong Pan, Bur................B3 38
Mongu, Zambia, 3,000........E3 48
Monhegan, isl., Maine.........E3 96
Moniaive, Scot., 1,219........E5 13
Monico, Oneida, Wis., 150...C4 120
Monida, Beaverhead, Mont., 30..............F4 102
Monida, pass, Idaho, Mont.....F4 102
Monie, Somerset, Md., 70....D6 85
Moniquirá, Col., 3,230.........B3 60
Moniteau, co., Mo., 10,500...C5 101
Monito, isl., P.R...............e10 65
Monitor, Alta., Can., 86.....D5 69
Monitor, Marion, Oreg., 100..............B2 113
Monitor, Chelan, Wash., 400.B5 122
Monitor, range, Nev............E5 104
Monitor, val., Nev..............E5 104
Monivea, Ire., 222.............D3 11
Monkey River, Br. Hond., 407..............B3 62
Monkira, Austl.................B3 51
Monkman, pass, B.C., Can......B7 68
Monkoto, Con. L..............B3 48
Monkton, Ont., Can., 422...D3 72
Monkton, Addison, Vt., 130 (551▲)..............C2 120
MonLouis, Mobile, Ala., 300.E1 78
Monmouth, Warren, Ill., 10,372..............C3 90
Monmouth, Jackson, Iowa, 271..............B7 92
Monmouth, Kennebec, Maine, 500 (1,884▲)..............D2 96
Monmouth, Polk, Oreg., 2,229..............C1, C3 113
Monmouth, Wales, 5,432......C5 12
Monmouth, co., Wales, 443,689..............C5 12
Monmouth, co., N. J., 334,401..............C4 106
Monmouth, mtn., B.C., Can.....D6 68
Monmouth Beach, Monmouth, N.J., 1,363..............C5 106
Monmouth Junction, Middlesex, N.J., 900.......C3 106
Monnikendam, Neth., 3,800..B5 15
Monnow, riv., Eng..............C5 12
Mono, co., Calif., 2,213......D4 82
Mono, lake, Calif...............D4 82
Mono, pt., Nic..................E6 62
Monocacy, riv., Md.............B3 85
Mono Lake, Mono, Calif., 150..............C4 82
Monolith, Kern, Calif., 450...E4 82
Monomonac, lake, Mass........A3 97
Monomoy, isl., Mass...........C8 97
Monomoy, pt., Mass............C7 97
Monon, White, Ind., 1,417....C4 91
Monona, Clayton, Iowa, 1,346..............A6 92
Monona, Dane, Wis., 8,178...E4 118
Monona, co., Iowa, 13,916...B1 92
Monona, lake, Wis..............E4 124
Monongah, Marion, W. Va., 1,321..............A7, B4 123
Monongahela, Washington, Pa., 8,388..............F2 114
Monongahela, riv., Pa., W. Va..B5 123
Monongalia, co., W. Va., 55,617..............B4 123
Monopoli, It., 24,000.........D6 21
Monor, Hung., 14,830........B4 22
Monóvar, Sp., 9,933..........C5 20
Monoville, Smith, Tenn., 65..C8 117
Monowi, Boyd, Nebr., 40.....B7 103
Monowice, Pol................g10 26
Monponsett, Plymouth, Mass., 600..............B6 97
Monreale, It., 18,500.........E4 21
Monroe, Monroe, Ark., 150...C4 81
Monroe, Fairfield, Conn., 950 (6,402▲)..............D4 84
Monroe, Walton, Ga., 6,826..C3 87
Monroe, Adams, Ind., 499....C8 91
Monroe, Tippecanoe, Ind., 30..............D4 91
Monroe, Jasper, Iowa, 1,366..............C4 92
Monroe, Ouachita, La., 52,219..............B3 95
Monroe, Waldo, Maine, 180 (497▲)..............D3 96
Monroe (Town of), Franklin, Mass. (210▲)..............*A2 97
Monroe, Monroe, Mich., 22,968..............G7 98
Monroe, Platte, Nebr., 261...C8 103
Monroe, Grafton, N.H., 185 (421▲)..............B2 105
Monroe, Sussex, N.J., 150....A3 106
Monroe, Orange, N.Y., 3,323..............D6, m14 108
Monroe, Union, N.C., 10,882..............C3 109
Monroe, Butler, Ohio, 1,475..............*C3 111
Monroe, Le Flore, Okla., 135..............C7 112
Monroe, Benton, Oreg., 374..C3 113
Monroe, Turner, S. Dak., 156..............D8 116
Monroe, Overton, Tenn., 69.G8 117
Monroe, Sevier, Utah, 955...E3 119
Monroe, Amherst, Va., 800..............D3 121
Monroe, Snohomish, Wash., 1,901..............B4 122
Monroe, Greene, Wis., 8,050..............F4 124
Monroe, co., Ala., 22,372....D2 78
Monroe, co., Ark., 17,327....C4 81
Monroe, co., Fla., 47,921....H5 86
Monroe, co., Ga., 10,495.....D3 87
Monroe, co., Ill., 15,507......E4 90
Monroe, co., Ind., 59,225....F4 91
Monroe, co., Iowa, 10,463...C5 92
Monroe, co., Ky., 11,799.....D4 94
Monroe, co., Mich., 101,120..............G7 98
Monroe, co., Miss., 33,953...B5 100
Monroe, co., Mo., 10,688.....B5 101
Monroe, co., N.Y., 625,018...B3 108
Monroe, co., Ohio, 15,268....C6 111
Monroe, co., Pa., 39,567.....D11 114
Monroe, co., Tenn., 23,316...D9 117
Monroe, co., W. Va., 11,584.D4 123
Monroe, co., Wis., 31,241....E3 124
Monroe Bridge, Franklin, Mass., 150..............A2 97
Monroe Center, Fairfield, Conn., 500..............D4 84
Monroe Center, Ogle, Ill., 300..............A5 90
Monroe City, Knox, Ind., 505..............G3 91
Monroe City, Monroe and Marion, Mo., 2,337.......B6 101
Monroeton, Bradford, Pa., 502..............C9 114
Monroeville, Monroe, Ala., 3,632..............D2 78
Monroeville, Allen, Ind., 1,294..............C8 91
Monroeville, Salem, N.J., 250..............D2 106
Monroeville, Huron, Ohio, 1,371..............A5 111
Monroeville, Allegheny, Pa., 22,446..............*B6 114
Monrovia, Los Angeles, Calif., 27,079..............F3 82
Monrovia, Morgan, Ind., 450..............E5 91
Monrovia, Atchison, Kans., 20..............A7 93
Monrovia, Lib., 81,000.......E2 45
Mons, Bel., 26,973 (*45,000).D3 15
Monsanto, St. Clair, Ill., 324..............B8 101
Monschau, Ger., 2,500.......D6 15
Monselice, It., 6,610..........D7 18
Monserrate Central, P.R......B4 65
Monsey, Rockland, N.Y., 5,000..............*D6 108
Møns Klint, isl., Den...........D6 24
Monson, Piscataquis, Maine, 700 (852▲)..............C3 96
Monson, Hampden, Mass., 2,500 (6,712▲)..............B3 97
Monson Junction, Piscataquis, Maine..............C3 96
Montabaur, Ger., 6,200.......C2 17
Montagnais, pt., Newf., Can....B2 75
Montagnana, It., 5,237.......D7 18
Montague, Siskiyou, Calif., 782..............B2 82
Montague, P.E.I., Can., 1,126..............C7 74
Montague, Franklin, Mass., 600 (7,836▲)..............A2 97
Montague, Muskegon, Mich., 2,366..............E4 98
Montague, Chouteau, Mont., 15..............C6 102
Montague, Montague, Tex., 400..............C4 118
Montague, co., Tex., 14,893..C4 118
Montague, isl., Alsk...........D10 79
Montague, isl., Mex............A2 63
Montague, lake, Sask., Can.....H3 70
Montague City, Franklin, Mass., 600..............A2 97
Montalbán, Sp., 2,200........B5 20
Montalegre, Port., 1,799.....B2 20
Mont Alto, Franklin, Pa., 1,039..............G6 114
Montalto, mtn., It..............E5 20
Montalvo, Ventura, Calif., 2,028..............*E4 82
Montana, Alsk., 39...........f17 76
Montana, Johnson, Ark., 25..B2 81
Montana, state, U.S., 674,767..............A5 76, 102
Montana-Vermala, Switz., 1,543..............D3 19
Montánchez, Sp., 4,190......C2 20
Montandon, Northumberland, Pa., 350..............E8 114
Montargis, Fr., 15,996 (*35,000)..............D5 14
Montataire, Fr., 9,630.......E2 15
Montauban, Que., Can., 623..............C5 73
Montauban, Fr., 30,242 (41,022▲)..............E4 14
Montauban-les-Mines, Que., Can., 318..............C5 73
Montauk, Dent, Mo., 60.....D6 101
Montauk, Suffolk, N.Y., 600..............m17 108
Montauk, hbr., N.Y.............E9 84
Montauk, pt., N.Y..............E9 84
Monta Vista, Santa Clara, Calif., 2,000..............*B5 82
Montbard, Fr., 6,386.........D6 14
Montbéliard, Fr., 21,699 (*96,000)..............D7 14
Mont Belvieu, Chambers, Tex., 950..............E5, F5 118
Montblanch, Sp., 4,598......B6 20
Montbrison, Fr., 9,051.......E5 14
Montcalm, co., Que., Can., 18,766..............C3 73
Montcalm, co., Mich., 35,795..............E5 98
Montcalm, peak, Fr............F4 14
Mont.-Carmel, Que., Can., 895..............B8 73
Montceau-les-Mines, Fr., 29,364 (*51,000)..........D6 14
Mont Cenis, pass, Fr., It.......D2 18
Mont Cenis, tunnel, Fr., It.....D2 18
Montcerf, Que., Can., 216...C1 73
Montchanin [-les-Mines], Fr., 6,405..............D6 14
Montclair (Monte Vista), San Bernardino, Calif., 13,546..F3 82
Montclair, Essex, N.J., 43,129..............B4 106
Mont Clare, Montgomery, Pa., 1,124..............A10 114
Montcoal, Raleigh, W. Va., 275..............D3, D6 123
Montcornet, Fr., 1,439.......E4 15
Mont-de-Marsan, Fr., 20,203..............F3 14
Montdidier, Fr., 5,430.......C5 14
Monteagle, Grundy and Marion, Tenn., 700.......D8 117
Monteagudo, Arg..............D2 56
Monte Alegre, Braz...........C2 56
Monte Alegre, Braz., 3,911...C4 59
Monte Azul, Braz., 4,860.....E2 57
Montebello, Los Angeles, Calif., 32,097..............F2 82
Montebello, Que., Can., 1,486..............D3 73
Montebello, P.R..............B4 65
Montebello, Nelson, Va., 50..D3 121
Monte Bello, is., Austl.........D2 50
Montebelluna, It., 5,348.....D8 18
Monte Carlo, Monaco, 9,516 (part of Monaco).........*F7 14
Monte Carmelo, Braz., 10,016..............E1 57
Monte Caseros, Arg., 11,409..A5 54
Montecatini Terme, It., 18,600..............C3 21
Montecelio, It., 5,000........g9 21
Montecito, Santa Barbara, Calif., 5,000..............*E4 82
Monte Coman, Arg............A3 54
Monte Creek, B.C., Can., 53.D8 68
Montecristi, Dom. Rep., 4,600..............F8 64
Montecristi, Ec., 1,872.......B1 58
Monte Cristo, Bol.............B3 55
Montecristo, isl., It............C3 21
Montefrío, Sp., 5,137.........D4 20
Monte Gargano, pen., It........D5 20
Montego Bay, Jam., 23,471...F5 64
Montegut, Terrebonne, La., 588..............E5 95
Monteiro, Braz., 6,028.......C3 57
Monteith, mtn., B.C., Can......B6 68
Montelavar, Port., 5,373......F9 20
Montélimar, Fr., 15,914......E6 14
Montell, Uvalde, Tex., 50....E2 118
Montellano, Sp., 9,334.......D3 20
Montello, Elko, Nev., 150....B7 104
Montello, Marquette, Wis., 1,021..............E4 124
Montemorelos, Mex., 11,525..............B5 63
Montemor-o-Novo, Port., 5,047..............C1 20
Monte Ne, Benton, Ark., 200.A1 81
Montenegro, Braz., 14,491...D2 56
Montenegro, reg., Yugo.......D4 22
Montenegro (Crna Gora), rep., Yugo., 471,433......*D4 22
Monte Patria, Chile..........A2 54
Monte Plata, Dom. Rep., 2,202..............F9 64
Monte Porzio Catone, It., 3,203..............h9 21
Montepuez, Moz..............D6 48
Montepulciano, It., 17,552..C3 21
Monte Quemado, Arg., 2,512..............E3 55
Montereau, Fr., 14,121.......C5 14
Monterey, Butler, Ala., 25...D3 78
Monterey, Monterey, Calif., 22,618..............C6, D3 82
Monterey, Pulaski, Ind., 278..............B4 91
Monterey, Owen, Ky., 211...B5 94
Monterey, Berkshire, Mass., 150 (480▲)..............B1 97
Monterey, Hamilton, Ohio, 1,500..............*D2 111
Monterey, Putnam, Tenn., 2,069..............C8 117
Monterey, Highland, Va., 270..............C3 121
Monterey, co., Calif., 198,351..............D3 82
Monterey, bay, Calif...........D3 82

74X MONT-MORS

Monterey Park, Los Angeles, Calif., 37,821 ... F2 82
Montería, Col., 31,000 (99,000▲) ... B2 60
Monteros, Arg., 7,745 ... E2 55
Monterotondo, It., 9,340 ... g9 21
Monterrey, Mex., 596,939 (★695,000) ... B4 63
Montesano, Grays Harbor, Wash., 2,486 ... C2 122
Monte Sano, mts., Ala ... A3 78
Monte Sant'Angelo, It., 21,601 ... D5 21
Monte Santo, Braz., 1,607 ... D3 57
Montes Claros, Braz., 40,545 ... E2 57
Monte Serena, Santa Clara, Calif., 1,506 ... *D3 82
Montevallo, Shelby, Ala., 2,755 ... B3 78
Montevarchi, It., 9,100 ... C3 21
Montevideo, Chippewa, Minn., 5,693 ... F3 99
Montevideo, Ur., 1,173,100 (★1,325,000) ... E1 56
Montevideo, dept., Ur., 954,700 ... *E1 56
Monteview, Jefferson, Idaho, 10 ... F6 89
Monte Vista, Rio Grande, Colo., 3,385 ... D4 83
Monte Vista, Webster, Miss., 50 ... B4 100
Monte Vista, Pierce, Wash., 1,500 ... *B3 122
Montevue, Frederick, Md., 100 ... B3 85
Montezuma, Macon, Ga., 3,744 ... D2 87
Montezuma, Parke, Ind., 1,231 ... E3 91
Montezuma, Poweshiek, Iowa, 1,416 ... C5 92
Montezuma, Gray, Kans., 543 ... E3 93
Montezuma, San Miguel, N. Mex., 125 ... B4 107
Montezuma, Mercer, Ohio, 287 ... B3 111
Montezuma, Chester, Tenn., 100 ... B3 117
Montezuma, co., Colo., 14,024 ... D2 83
Montezuma, creek, Utah ... F6 119
Montezuma Castle, nat. mon., Ariz ... C4 80
Montezuma Creek, San Juan, Utah, 200 ... F6 119
Montfaucon, Switz., 524 ... B3 19
Montfort, Que., Can., 76 ... D3 73
Montfort, Grant, Wis., 538 ... F3 124
Montfort-sur-Meu, Fr., 2,031 ... C3 14
Montgomery, Montgomery, Ala., 134,393 (★155,200) ... C3 78
Montgomery, Alta., Can., 5,077 ... D3 69
Montgomery, Chatham, Ga., 350 ... E5 87
Montgomery, Kane, Ill., 2,122 ... F1 90
Montgomery, Daviess, Ind., 446 ... G3 91
Montgomery, Grant, La., 866 ... C3 95
Montgomery, Hampden, Mass., 100 (333▲) ... B2 97
Montgomery, Hillsdale, Mich., 362 ... G6 98
Montgomery, Le Sueur, Minn., 2,118 ... F5 99
Montgomery, Orange, N.Y., 1,312 ... D6 108
Montgomery, Hamilton, Ohio, 3,075 ... *C3 111
Montgomery, Pak., 75,180 ... B4 40
Montgomery, Lycoming, Pa., 2,150 ... D8 114
Montgomery, Franklin, Vt., 200 (876▲) ... B3 120
Montgomery, Wales, 970 ... B4 12
Montgomery, Fayette and Kanawha, W. Va., 3,000 ... C3, C6 123
Montgomery, co., Ala., 169,210 ... C3 78
Montgomery, co., Ark., 5,370 ... C2 81
Montgomery, co., Ga., 6,284 ... D4 87
Montgomery, co., Ill., 31,244 ... D4 90
Montgomery, co., Ind., 32,089 ... D4 91
Montgomery, co., Iowa, 14,467 ... C2 92
Montgomery, co., Kans., 45,007 ... E8 93
Montgomery, co., Ky., 13,461 ... B6 94
Montgomery, co., Md., 340,928 ... B3 85
Montgomery, co., Miss., 13,320 ... B4 100
Montgomery, co., Mo., 11,097 ... C6 101
Montgomery, co., N.Y., 57,240 ... C6 108
Montgomery, co., N.C., 18,408 ... B4 109
Montgomery, co., Ohio, 527,080 ... C3 111
Montgomery, co., Pa., 516,682 ... F10 114
Montgomery, co., Tenn., 55,645 ... A4 117
Montgomery, co., Tex., 26,839 ... D5 118
Montgomery, co., Va., 32,923 ... D2 121
Montgomery, co., Wales, 44,228 ... B4 12
Montgomery, peak, Calif ... D4 82
Montgomery Center, Franklin, Vt., 300 ... B3 120
Montgomery City, Montgomery, Mo., 1,918 ... C4 101
Montgomery Creek, Shasta, Calif., 150 ... B3 82
Monthermé, Fr., 2,995 ... E4 15
Monthey, Switz., 6,834 ... D2 19
Monticello, Drew, Ark., 4,412 ... D4 81
Monticello, P.E.I., Can., 85 ... C7 74
Monticello, Jefferson, Fla., 2,490 ... B3 86
Monticello, Jasper, Ga., 1,931 ... C3 87
Monticello, Piatt, Ill., 3,219 ... C5 90
Monticello, White, Ind., 4,035 ... C4 91
Monticello, Jones, Iowa, 3,190 ... B6 92
Monticello, Wayne, Ky., 2,940 ... D5 94
Monticello, Aroostook, Maine, 625 (1,109▲) ... B5 96
Monticello, Wright, Minn., 1,477 ... E5 99
Monticello, Lawrence, Miss., 1,432 ... D3 100
Monticello, Lewis, Mo., 159 ... A6 101
Monticello, Sierra, N. Mex., 150 ... D2 107
Monticello, Sullivan, N.Y., 5,222 ... D6 108
Monticello, San Juan, Utah, 1,845 ... F6 119
Monticello, Green, Wis., 789 ... F4 124
Mont Ida, Anderson, Kans., 50 ... D8 93
Montier, Shannon, Mo., 61 ... E6 101
Montier-en-Der, Fr., 1,808 ... F4 15
Montiers-sur-Saulx, Fr., 514 ... F5 15
Montigny-lès-Metz, Fr., 22,388 ... E6 15
Montijo, Port., 13,306 ... C1, f10 20
Montijo, Sp., 14,961 ... C2 20
Montilla, Sp., 19,755 ... D3 20
Montivilliers, Fr., 8,427 ... C3 14
Mont-Joli, Que., Can., 6,178 ... A9 73
Mont-Laurier, Que., Can., 5,859 ... C2 73
Montluçon, Fr., 55,184 ... D5 14
Montmagny, Que., Can., 6,850 ... C7 73
Montmagny, co., Que., Can., 26,450 ... C7 73
Montmartre, Sask., Can., 482 ... G4 70
Montmédy, Fr., 2,061 ... E5 15
Montmélian, Fr., 1,583 ... D2 18
Montmirail, Fr., 1,909 ... F3 15
Montmorenci, Tippecanoe, Ind., 100 ... D3 91
Montmorenci, Aiken, S.C., 150 ... D4 115
Montmorency, Que., Can., 5,985 ... C6, n17 73
Montmorency, Fr., 16,369 ... g10 14
Montmorency, co., Mich., 4,424 ... C6 98
Montmorency No. 1, co., Que., Can., 20,734 ... B6 73
Montmorency No. 2, co., Que., Can., 4,974 ... C6 73
Montmorency, riv., Que., Can ... B6 73
Montmorillon, Fr., 4,766 ... D4 14
Montney, B.C., Can ... A7 68
Monto, Austl., 1,795 ... B8 51
Montone, riv., It ... B3 21
Montoro, Sp., 14,950 ... C3 20
Montour, Gem, Idaho, 75 ... F2 89
Montour, Tama, Iowa, 452 ... C5 92
Montour, co., Pa., 16,730 ... D8 114
Montour Falls, Schuyler, N.Y., 1,533 ... C4 108
Montoursville, Lycoming, Pa., 5,211 ... D8 114
Montowese, New Haven, Conn. (part of North Haven) ... D5 84
Montoya, Quay, N. Mex., 35 ... B5 107
Montpelier, Bear Lake, Idaho, 3,146 ... G7 89
Montpelier, Blackford, Ind., 1,954 ... C7 91
Montpelier, Muscatine, Iowa, 105 ... C7 92
Montpelier, St. Helena, La., 197 ... D5 95
Montpelier, Clay, Miss., 230 ... B4 100
Montpelier, Stutsman, N. Dak., 97 ... C7 110
Montpelier, Williams, Ohio, 4,131 ... A3 111
Montpelier, Washington, Vt., 8,782 ... C3 120
Montpelier Station, Orange, Va., 150 ... C4 121
Montpellier, Que., Can., 318 ... D2 73
Montpellier, Fr., 118,864 ... F5 14
Montréal, Que., Can., 1,201,116 (★2,109,509) ... D4, q19 73
Montreal, Iron, Wis., 1,361 ... B3 124
Montreal, lake, Sask., Can ... C3 70
Montreal, riv., Sask., Can ... C3 70
Montréal-Est, Que., Can., 5,884 ... *D4 73
Montreal Lake, Sask., Can., 69 ... C3 70
Montréal-Nord, Que., Can., 48,433 ... p19 73
Montréal West, Que., Can., 6,446 ... *D4 73
Montreat, Buncombe, N.C., 500 ... D4 109
Montreuil, Fr., 92,222 ... C5, g10 14, F2 15
Montreuil-sur-Mer, Fr., 3,253 ... B4 14
Montreux, Switz., 19,000 ... D2 19
Montricher, Switz., 543 ... C1 19
Mont-Rolland, Que., Can., 1,457 ... D3 73
Montrose, Baldwin, Ala., 500 ... E2 78
Montrose, Ashley, Ark., 399 ... D4 81
Montrose, Los Angeles, Calif., 6,000 ... *E4 82
Montrose, B.C., Can., 862 ... E9 68
Montrose, Montrose, Colo., 5,044 ... C3 83
Montrose, Laurens, Ga., 236 ... D3 87
Montrose, Effingham, Ill., 320 ... D5 90
Montrose, Lee, Iowa, 632 ... D6 92
Montrose, Jewell, Kans., 105 ... C5 93
Montrose, Natchitoches, La ... C2 95
Montrose, Genesee, Mich., 1,466 ... E7 98
Montrose, Jasper, Miss., 169 ... C4 100
Montrose, Henry, Mo., 526 ... C4 101
Montrose, Westchester, N.Y., 2,200 ... *D7 108
Montrose, Berks, Pa., 1,100 ... *F10 114
Montrose, Susquehanna, Pa., 2,363 ... C10 114
Montrose, Scot., 10,702 ... D6 13
Montrose, McCook, S. Dak., 430 ... D8 116
Montrose, co., Colo., 18,286 ... C2 83
Montrose Hill, Allegheny, Pa., 2,000 ... *E2 114
Montross, Westmoreland, Va., 394 ... C6 121
Mont-Royal, Que., Can., 21,182 ... *D4 73
Montrouge, Fr., 45,260 ... g10 14
Mont-St. Martin, Fr., 7,016 ... C6 14
Mont-St. Michel, Fr., 268 ... C3 14
Montserrat, Johnson, Mo., 150 ... C4 101
Montserrat, Br. dep., N.A., 13,000 ... n15 64
Montserrat, peak, Sp ... B6 20
Montserrat Island, ter., W.I. Fed., 12,157 ... n15 64
Mont-Tremblant, Que., Can., 303 ... C3 73
Mont Tremblant, prov. park, Que., Can ... C3 73
Montvale, Bergen, N.J., 3,699 ... g8 106
Montvale, Bedford, Va., 500 ... D3 121
Mont Vernon, Hillsboro, N.H., 150 (585▲) ... E3 105
Montville, New London, Conn., 1,060 (7,759▲) ... D8 84
Montville, Berkshire, Mass., 40 ... B1 97
Montville, Morris, N.J., 800 ... B4 106
Montzen, Bel., 2,499 ... D5 15
Monument, El Paso, Colo., 204 ... B6 83
Monument, Logan, Kans., 150 ... C2 93
Monument, Lea, N. Mex., 50 ... E6 107
Monument, Grant, Oreg., 214 ... C7 113
Monument, Centre, Pa., 200 ... D6 114
Monument, peak, Colo ... B3 83
Monument, peak, Idaho ... D2 89
Monument, peak, Oreg ... C4 113
Monumental, buttes, Idaho ... B3 89
Monument Beach, Barnstable, Mass., 900 ... C6 97
Monument Valley, ruins, Ariz ... A5 80
Monywa, Bur., 26,172 ... D10 39
Monza, It., 89,000 ... D5 18, B2 21
Monze, Zambia, 1,800 ... E4 48
Monzón, Peru, 514 ... C2 58
Monzón, Sp., 9,020 ... B6 20
Moodus, Middlesex, Conn., 1,300 ... D7 84
Moodus, res., Conn ... C7 84
Moody, York, Maine, 200 ... E2 96
Moody, Howell, Mo., 61 ... E6 101
Moody, McLennan, Tex., 1,074 ... D4 118
Moody, co., S. Dak., 8,810 ... C9 116
Moodyville, Pickett, Tenn ... C8 117
Mooers, Clinton, N.Y., 543 ... f11 108
Mooers Forks, Clinton, N.Y., 175 ... f11 108
Moon, lake, Miss ... A3 100
Moonachie, Bergen, N.J., 3,052 ... *B4 106
Moon Crest, Allegheny, Pa., 1,500 ... *E1 114
Moon Run, Allegheny, Pa., 650 ... B5 114
Moonta, Austl., 1,151 ... F6 50
Moora, Austl., 1,145 ... F2 50
Moorabbin, Austl., 100,100 ... *H5 51
Moorcroft, Crook, Wyo., 826 ... A8 125
Moore, Butte, Idaho, 358 ... F5 89
Moore, Fergus, Mont., 216 ... D7 102
Moore, Cleveland, Ohio, 1,783 ... B4 112
Moore, Spartanburg, S.C., 150 ... B4 115
Moore, Frio, Tex., 600 ... E3 118
Moore, Emery, Utah, 20 ... E4 119
Moore, Tucker, W. Va., 40 ... B3 123
Moore, co., N.C., 36,733 ... B4 109
Moore, co., Tenn., 3,454 ... B5 117
Moore, co., Tex., 14,773 ... B2 118
Moore, res., N.H., Vt ... C5 120
Moorefield, Ont., Can., 253 ... D4 72
Moorefield, Nicholas, Ky., 200 ... B6 94
Moorefield, Frontier, Nebr., 55 ... D7 103
Moorefield, Hardy, W. Va., 1,434 ... B6 123
Moorefield, riv., W. Va ... C5 123
Moore Haven, Glades, Fla., 790 ... F5 86
Mooreland, Henry, Ind., 477 ... E7 91
Mooreland, Woodward, Okla., 871 ... A2 112
Mooreland Heights, Knox, Tenn., 900 ... *D10 117
Moorepark, Man., Can ... D2 71
Mooresburg, Hawkins, Tenn., 200 ... C10 117
Moores Corner, Franklin, Mass., 85 ... A2 97
Moores Hill, Dearborn, Ind., 476 ... F7 91
Moore's Mills, N.B., Can., 116 ... D2 74
Moorestown, Missaukee, Mich., 65 ... D5 98
Moorestown, Burlington, N.J., 12,497 ... D3 106
Mooresville, Morgan, Ind., 3,856 ... E5 91
Mooresville, Livingston, Mo., 117 ... B4 101
Mooresville, Iredell, N.C., 6,918 ... B3 109
Mooresville, Marshall, Tenn., 50 ... B5 117
Mooreton, Richland, N. Dak., 164 ... C9 110
Mooreville, Lee, Miss., 200 ... A5 100
Moorewood, Custer, Okla., 35 ... B2 112
Moorhead, Monona, Iowa, 313 ... C2 92
Moorhead, Clay, Minn., 22,934 ... D2 99
Moorhead, Sunflower, Miss., 1,754 ... B3 100
Moorhead, Powder River, Mont ... E11 102
Mooring, Lake, Tenn., 100 ... A2 117
Mooringsport, Caddo, La., 864 ... B2 95
Moor Lake Station, Ont., Can ... A7 72
Moorland, Webster, Iowa, 281 ... B3 92
Moorman, Muhlenberg, Ky., 250 ... C2 94
Moorpark, Ventura, Calif., 2,902 ... E4 82
Moors, The, moors, Scot ... F4 13
Moosburg, Ger., 10,200 ... E6 17
Moose, Teton, Wyo., 15 ... B2 125
Moose, creek, Wyo ... D2 125
Moose, hill, Mass ... h11 97
Moose, isl., Man., Can ... D3 71
Moose, lake, B.C., Can ... C11 69
Moose, lake, Man., Can ... A4 71
Moose, lake, Man., Can ... B1 71
Moose, mtn., Sask., Can ... H4 70
Moose, mtn., N.H ... C2 105
Moose, pond, Maine ... D3 96
Moose, riv., Ont., Can ... F16 67
Moose, riv., Maine ... C2 96
Moose, riv., N.H ... B4 105
Moose, riv., N.Y ... B5 108
Moose, riv., Vt ... B5 120
Moose Creek, Ont., Can., 429 ... B10 72
Moose Creek, buttes, Idaho ... C3 89
Moose Factory, Ont., Can., 689 ... F16 67
Moosehead, Piscataquis, Maine, 15 ... C3 96
Moosehead, lake, Maine ... C3 96
Mooseheart, Kane, Ill., 1,100 ... B5, F1 90
Moose Heights, B.C., Can., 164 ... C6 68
Moosehorn, Man., Can., 208 ... D2 71
Moosehorn, Franklin, Maine ... C2 96
Moose Jaw, Sask., Can., 33,206 ... G3, n7 70
Moose Jaw, creek, Sask., Can ... G3 70
Moose Lake, Man., Can., 283 ... C1 71
Moose Lake, Carlton, Minn., 1,514 ... D6 99
Moose Lake, res., Wis ... B3 124
Mooseleuk, stream, Maine ... B4 96
Mooselookmeguntic, lake, Maine ... D2 96
Moose Mountain, creek, Sask., Can ... H4 70
Moose Mountain, prov. park, Sask., Can ... H4 70
Moose Pass, Alsk., 136 ... C10, g17 79
Moose River, Somerset, Maine, 180 (205▲) ... C2 96
Moosic, Lackawanna, Pa., 4,243 ... B9 114
Moosic, mts., Pa ... A9 114
Moosilauke, mtn., N.H ... B3 105
Moosomin, Sask., Can., 1,781 ... G5 70
Moosonee, Ont., Can., 975 ... o19 72
Moosup, Windham, Conn., 3,000 ... C9 84
Moosup Valley, Providence, R.I., 100 ... C9 84
Mopang, lakes, Maine ... D5 96
Mopeia, Moz ... A6 49
Mopti, Mali, 12,700 ... D4 45
Moquegua, Peru, 4,582 ... E3 58
Moquegua, dept., Peru, 41,072 ... E3 58
Mor, Hung., 11,482 ... B4 24
Mor, isl., Truk ... 52
Mora, Cam ... C2 46
Mora, Atkinson, Ga., 150 ... E4 87
Mora, Kanabec, Minn., 2,329 ... E5 99
Mora, Mora, N. Mex., 400 ... B4 107
Mora, P.R ... B2 65
Mora, Sp., 10,657 ... C4 20
Mora, Swe., 6,032 (12,893▲) ... G6 52
Mora, co., N. Mex., 6,028 ... A5 107
Mora, riv., N. Mex ... B5 107
Morača, riv., Yugo ... D4 22
Morada, San Joaquin, Calif., 2,156 ... *D3 82
Moradabad, India, 180,100 (★191,828) ... C6 39, C7 40
Morada Nova, Braz., 2,475 ... C3 57
Mora de Ebro, Sp., 3,340 ... B6 20
Morafenobé, Malag ... g8 49
Morag, Pol., 2,746 ... B5 26
Moraine, Montgomery, Ohio, 2,262 ... *C3 111
Morales, Guat., 3,587 ... C3 62
Morales, Mex., 3,338 ... k13 63
Morales, Jackson, Tex., 40 ... E4 118
Moramanga, Malag., 3,750 ... g9 49
Moran, Clinton, Ind., 60 ... D4 91
Moran, Allen, Kans., 549 ... E8 93
Moran, Mackinac, Mich., 180 ... B6 98
Moran, Shackelford, Tex., 392 ... C3 118
Moran, Teton, Wyo., 10 ... B2 125
Morann, Clearfield, Pa., 450 ... E5 114
Morant Bay, Jam., 5,053 ... G5 64
Morar, lake, Scot ... D3 13
Morat, lake, Switz ... C3 18
Morata de Tajuña, Sp., 3,801 ... p18 20
Moratalla, Sp., 5,879 ... C5 20
Morattico, Lancaster, Va., 250 ... D6 121
Moratuwa, Cey., 60,215 ... *G6 39
Morava, riv., Czech ... D4 26
Morava, riv., Yugo ... C5 22
Moravia (Morava), reg., Czech., 3,549,700 ... D4 26
Moravia, Appanoose, Iowa, 621 ... D5 92
Moravia, Cayuga, N.Y., 1,575 ... C4 108
Morawhanna, Br. Gu., 305 ... A3 59
Moray, co., Scot., 49,156 ... C5 13
Moraya, Bol ... D2 55
Moray, firth, Scot ... C5 13
Morbach, Ger., 2,400 ... D2 17
Morbihan, dept., Fr., 530,833 ... *D2 14
Morcenx, Fr., 2,370 ... E3 14
Morco, Anderson, Tenn., 150 ... C9 117
Morden, Man., Can., 2,793 ... E2 71
Morden, N.S., Can., 126 ... D5 74
More, mtn., Scot ... C1 13
More, mtn., Scot ... D2 13
More, mtn., Scot ... D4 13
More Assynt, mtn., Scot ... B4 13
Moreau, riv., S. Dak ... B3 116
Moreauville, Avoyelles, La., 815 ... C4 95
Morecambe, Eng., 40,000 ... F6 13
Morecambe, bay, Eng ... C5 10
Moree, Austl., 6,795 ... D7 51
Morehead, Rowan, Ky., 4,170 ... B6 94
Morehead City, Carteret, N.C., 5,583 ... C7 109
Morehouse, New Madrid, Mo., 1,417 ... E8 101
Morehouse, par., La., 33,709 ... B4 95
Mörel, Switz., 456 ... D5 19
Moreland, Pope, Ark., 55 ... B3 81
Moreland, Coweta, Ga., 329 ... C2 87
Moreland, Bingham, Idaho, 250 ... F6 89
Moreland, Lincoln, Ky., 300 ... C5 94
Moreland, Lycoming, Pa ... D8 114
Moreland Hills, Cuyahoga, Ohio, 2,188 ... *A6 111
Morelia, Mex., 100,828 ... D4, n13 63
Morell, P.E.I., Can., 387 ... C7 74
Morella, Sp., 5,037 ... B5 20
Morelos, state, Mex., 381,346 ... D5, n14 63
Morelos, dam, Ariz ... E1 80
Morena, mts., Sp ... C3 20
Morenci, Greenlee, Ariz., 2,431 ... D6 80
Morenci, Lenawee, Mich., 2,053 ... G6 98
Moreno, pt., Fla ... G2 86
Möre og Romsdal, co., Nor., 213,400 ... *F2 25
Moresby, isl., B.C., Can ... C1 68
Moreton, bay, Austl ... C9 51
Moreton, isl., Austl ... C9 51
Moreton-in-Marsh, Eng., 1,798 ... C6 12
Moretown, Washington, Vt., 200 (788▲) ... C3 120
Moreuil, Fr., 3,609 ... E2 15
Morewood, Ont., Can., 189 ... B9 72
Morey, lake, Vt ... D4 120
Morez, Fr., 5,777 ... D7 14
Morgan, Austl., 434 ... G2 51
Morgan, Calhoun, Ga., 293 ... E2 87
Morgan, Pendleton, Ky., 50 ... B5 94
Morgan, Redwood, Minn., 975 ... F4 99
Morgan, Phillips, Mont., 10 ... B9 102
Morgan, Morrow, Oreg ... B7 113
Morgan, Bosque, Texas, 381 ... C4 118
Morgan, Morgan, Utah, 1,299 ... B4 119
Morgan, Orleans, Vt., 40 (260▲) ... B4 120
Morgan, co., Ala., 60,454 ... A3 78
Morgan, co., Colo., 21,192 ... A7 83
Morgan, co., Ga., 10,280 ... C3 87
Morgan, co., Ill., 36,571 ... D3 90
Morgan, co., Ind., 33,875 ... F5 91
Morgan, co., Ky., 11,056 ... C6 94
Morgan, co., Mo., 9,476 ... C5 101
Morgan, co., Ohio, 12,747 ... C6 111
Morgan, co., Tenn., 14,304 ... C9 117
Morgan, co., Utah, 2,837 ... B4 119
Morgan, co., W. Va., 8,376 ... B6 123
Morgan, isl., S.C ... G6 115
Morgan, pt., Conn ... E5 84
Morgana, Edgefield, S.C., 122 ... D3 115
Morgan Center, Orleans, Vt., 75 ... B5 120
Morgan City, St. Mary, La., 13,540 ... C5, E4 95
Morgan City, Leflore, Miss., 250 ... B3 100
Morganfield, Union, Ky., 3,741 ... C2 94
Morgan Hill, Santa Clara, Calif., 3,151 ... C6, D3 82
Morganton, Van Buren, Ark., 75 ... B3 81
Morganton, Fannin, Ga., 211 ... B2 87
Morganton, Burke, N.C., 9,186 ... B2 109
Morgantown, Morgan, Ind., 971 ... F5 91
Morgantown, Butler, Ky., 1,318 ... C3 94
Morgantown, Marion, Miss., 310 ... D4 100
Morgantown, Berks, Pa., 550 ... F10 114
Morgantown, Monongalia, W. Va., 22,487 ... A7, B5 123
Morganville, Dade, Ga., 150 ... B1 87
Morganville, Clay, Kans., 226 ... C6 93
Morganville, Monmouth, N.J., 500 ... C4 106
Morganza, Pointe Coupee, La., 937 ... D4 95
Morges, Switz., 8,420 ... C1 19
Morgex, It., 837 ... D3 18
Morghāb, Iran ... F6 41
Morhange, Fr., 4,786 ... F6 15
Mori, Jap., 12,500 ... E10 37
Moriah, Essex, N.Y., 350 ... A7 108
Moriah, mtn., Nev ... D7 104
Moriah, mtn., N.H ... B4 105
Moriarty, Torrance, N. Mex., 720 ... C3, m8 107
Morice, lake, B.C., Can ... B4 68
Morice, riv., B.C., Can ... B4 68
Moriches, bay, N.Y ... G5 84
Moriguchi, Jap., 102,295 ... *o14 37
Morin Heights, Que., Can., 133 ... D3 73
Morinville, Alta., Can., 935 ... C4 69
Morioka, Jap., 157,441 ... G10 37
Morisset Station, Que., Can., 139 ... C7 73
Moriyama, Jap., 58,798 ... *I9 37
Morjärv, Swe., 655 ... D10 25
Morkill, riv., B.C., Can ... C7 68
Mörkö, Swe ... t35 25
Morlaix, Fr., 18,866 ... C2 14
Morland, Graham, Kans., 317 ... C3 93
Morley, Alta., Can ... D3 69
Morley, Eng., 42,200 ... *A6 12
Morley, Mecosta, Mich., 445 ... E5 98
Morley, Scott, Mo., 472 ... D8 101
Morley, St. Lawrence, N.Y., 300 ... f9 108
Morman, range, Nev ... G7 104
Mormon Lake, Coconino, Ariz ... C4 80
Morningdale, Worcester, Mass., 900 ... B4 97
Morningside, Prince Georges, Md., 1,708 ... *C4 85
Morningside, Hennepin, Minn., 1,981 ... *F5 99
Morningside, Beadle, S. Dak., 150 ... C7 116
Morning Sun, Louisa, Iowa, 875 ... C6 92
Mornington, isl., Chile ... D1 54
Morning View, Kenton, Ky., 150 ... A7 94
Moro, Lee, Ark., 340 ... C5 81
Moro, Madison, Ill., 250 ... A8 101
Moro, Sherman, Oreg., 327 ... B6 113
Moro, creek, Ark ... D3 81
Moro, gulf, Phil ... D6 35
Morobay, Bradley, Ark., 40 ... D3 81
Morobe, N. Gui ... k12 50
Morocco, Newton, Ind., 1,341 ... C3 91
Morocco, country, Afr., 13,150,000 ... C5 42, C3 44
Morococha, Peru, 1,522 ... D2 58
Morogoro, Tan., 14,507 ... C6 48
Moroleón, Mex., 17,955 ... m13 63
Morombé, Malag ... h8 49
Morón, Cuba, 18,629 ... D4 64
Morona, riv., Peru ... B2 58
Morondava, Malag., 5,300 ... h8 49
Morón de la Frontera, Sp., 25,800 (35,248▲) ... D3 20
Moroni, Comoro Is., 6,545 ... *H10 49
Moroni, Sanpete, Utah, 879 ... D4 119
Morong, Phil., 2,115 ... o13 35
Morotai, isl., Indon ... E7 35
Moroto, Ug ... A5 48
Morovis, P.R., 2,428 ... B5 65
Morovis, mun., P.R., 18,094 ... B5 65
Morozovsk, Sov. Un., 28,000 ... D2 29
Morpeth, Ont., Can., 211 ... E3 73
Morpeth, Eng., 12,430 ... E7 13
Morphou, Cyp., 6,097 ... E9 31
Morral, Marion, Ohio, 493 ... B4 111
Morrill, Brown, Kans., 299 ... C8 93
Morrill, Scotts Bluff, Nebr., 884 ... C2 103
Morrill, co., Nebr., 7,057 ... C2 103
Morrilton, Conway, Ark., 5,997 ... B3 81
Morrin, Alta., Can., 316 ... D4 69
Morrinhos, Braz., 9,879 ... E1 57
Morrinsville, N.Z., 4,111 ... L15 51
Morris, Jefferson, Ala., 638 ... B3 78
Morris, Man., Can., 1,370 ... E3 71
Morris, Litchfield, Conn., 200 (1,190▲) ... C4 84
Morris, Quitman, Ga., 150 ... E2 87
Morris, Grundy, Ill., 7,935 ... B5 90
Morris, Ripley, Ind., 400 ... F7 91
Morris, Stevens, Minn., 4,199 ... E3 99
Morris, Otsego, N.Y., 677 ... C5 108
Morris, Okmulgee, Okla., 982 ... B6 112
Morris, co., Kans., 7,392 ... D7 93
Morris, co., N.J., 261,620 ... B3 106
Morris, co., Tex., 12,576 ... C5 118
Morris, isl., S.C ... F8 115
Morris, mtn., N.Y ... A6 108
Morrisburg, Ont., Can., 1,820 ... C9 72
Morris Chapel, Hardin, Tenn., 100 ... B3 117
Morrisdale, Clearfield, Pa., 800 ... E5 114
Morris Jesup, cape, Grnld ... A18 4
Morrison, Jefferson, Colo., 426 ... B5 83
Morrison, Whiteside, Ill., 4,159 ... B4 90
Morrison, Gasconade, Mo., 232 ... C6 101
Morrison, Noble, Okla., 256 ... A6 112
Morrison, Warren, Tenn., 294 ... D8 117
Morrison, Brown, Wis., 125 ... A6 124
Morrison, co., Minn., 26,641 ... D4 99
Morrison City, Sullivan, Tenn., 2,426 ... C11 117
Morrisonville, Christian, Ill., 1,129 ... D4 90
Morris Plains, Morris, N.J., 4,703 ... B4 106
Morris Run, Tioga, Pa., 400 ... C7 114
Morriston, Levy, Fla., 100 ... C4 86
Morristown, Maricopa, Ariz., 200 ... D3, F1 80
Morristown, Shelby, Ind., 709 ... E6 91
Morristown, Rice, Minn., 616 ... F5 99
Morristown, Morris, N.J., 17,712 ... B4 106
Morristown, St. Lawrence, N.Y., 541 ... f9 108
Morristown, Corson, S. Dak., 219 ... B4 116
Morristown, Hamblen, Tenn., 21,267 ... C10 117
Morristown, Lamoille, Vt., 65 (3,347▲) ... B3 120
Morristown, nat. historical park, N.J ... B3 106
Morrisville, Polk, Mo., 228 ... D4 101
Morrisville, Madison, N.Y., 1,304 ... C5 108
Morrisville, Bucks, Pa., 7,790 ... F12 114
Morrisville, Lamoille, Vt., 2,047 ... B3 120
Morrisville, Fauquier, Va., 100 ... C5 121
Morrito, Nic., 387 ... E5 62
Morro, Ec ... B1 58
Morro Bay, San Luis Obispo, Calif., 3,692 ... E3 82
Morro do Chapéu, Braz., 2,039 ... E2 57
Morropón, Peru, 3,909 ... C2 58
Morrosquillo, gulf, Col ... B2 59
Morrow, Clayton, Ga., 580 ... B5, C2 87
Morrow, St. Landry, La., 400 ... D3 95
Morrow, Warren, Ohio, 1,477 ... C3 111
Morrow, co., Ohio, 19,405 ... B5 111
Morrow, co., Oreg., 4,871 ... B7 113
Morrowville, Washington, Kans., 195 ... C6 93
Morse, Sask., Can., 458 ... G2 70
Morse, Acadia, La., 682 ... D3 95
Morse, Hansford, Tex., 150 ... A2 118
Morse, Ashland, Wis., 45 ... B3 124
Morse, res., Ind ... D5 91
Morse Bluff, Saunders, Nebr., 119 ... C9 103

Morse Mill, Jefferson, Mo., 62 ... B7 101
Morses, creek, N.J. ... k8 106
Morshansk, Sov. Un., 48,000 ... C2 29
Mortagne [-au-Perche], Fr., 3,909 ... C4 14
Mortara, It., 10,500 ... B2 21
Morteau, Fr., 5,395 ... D7 14
Morteros, Arg., 5,593 ... A4 54
Mortlach, Sask., Can., 329 .. G2 70
Morton, Tazewell, Ill., 5,325 ... C4 90
Morton, Renville, Minn., 624 ... F4 99
Morton, Scott, Miss., 2,260 .. C4 100
Morton, Delaware, Pa., 2,207 ... *G11 114
Morton, Cochran, Tex., 2,731 ... C1 118
Morton, Lewis, Wash., 1,183 ... C3 122
Morton, Freemont, Wyo., 15 ... B4 125
Morton, co., Kans., 3,354 ... E2 93
Morton, co., N. Dak., 20,992 ... C4 110
Morton Grove, Cook, Ill., 20,533 ... E3 90
Mortons Gap, Hopkins, Ky., 1,308 ... C2 94
Morup, Swe ... B6 24
Moruya, Austl., 1,181 ... G8 51
Morvan, mts., Fr ... D6 14
Morven, Brooks, Ga., 476 ... F3 87
Morven, Anson, N.C., 518 .. C3 109
Morven, mtn., Scot ... B5 13
Morvern, Scot., 457 ... D3 13
Morvi, India, 50,192 ... F3 40
Moryakovskiy Zaton, Sov. Un ... B10 29
Morye, Sov. Un ... r32 25
Mosalsk, Sov. Un., 5,700 .. D10 27
Mosbach, Ger., 11,300 ... D4 17
Mosby, Clay, Mo., 293 ... D2 101
Mosby, Garfield, Mont., 5 ... D9 102
Mosca, Alamosa, Colo., 150 .. D5 83
Moscarello, riv., It ... k9 21
Moscos, is., Bur ... E2 38
Moscow, Jefferson, Ark., 100 .C4 81
Moscow, Latah, Idaho, 11,183 ... C2 89
Moscow, Rush, Ind., 180 ... F6 91
Moscow, Muscatine, Iowa, 208 ... C6 92
Moscow, Stevens, Kans., 211 ... E2 93
Moscow, Clermont, Ohio, 438 ... D3 111
Moscow, Lackawanna, Pa., 1,212 ... B9 114
Moscow (Moskva), Sov. Un., 6,317,000 (*8,350,000) ... D11, n17 27
Moscow, Fayette, Tenn., 368 ... B2 117
Moscow, Lamoille, Vt., 150 ... C3 120
Moscow Mills, Lincoln, Mo., 360 ... C7 101
Mosel, riv., Ger ... C2 17
Moseley, Powhatan, Va., 100 ... D2 121
Moselle, Jones, Miss., 500 .. D4 100
Moselle, dept., Fr., 919,412 ... E6 15
Moselle, riv., Fr ... C7 14
Mosers River, N.S., Can., 382 ... E7 74
Moses, lake, Wash ... B6 122
Moses Coulee, canyon, Wash ... B6 122
Moses Lake, Grant, Wash., 11,299 ... B6 122
Mosgiel, N.Z., 6,456 ... P13 51
Mosheim, Greene, Tenn., 300 ... C11 117
Mosher, Mellette, S. Dak., 25 ... D5 116
Mosherville, N.S., Can., 87 .. D6 74
Moshi, Tan., 13,726 ... B6 48
Moshupa, Bech ... B4 49
Mosier, Wasco, Oreg., 252 ... B5 113
Mosinee, Marathon, Wis., 2,067 ... D4 124
Mosjöen, Nor., 4,600 ... E5 25
Moskee, Crook, Wyo., 15 ... A8 125
Moskva, see Moscow, Sov. Un.
Moskva, riv., Sov. Un ... n17 27
Mosley, creek, B.C., Can ... D5 68
Mosonmagyarovar, Hung., 21,199 ... B3 22
Mosquera, Col., 318 ... C2 60
Mosquero, Harding and San Miguel, N. Mex., 310 ... B6 107
Mosquito, Newf., Can., 40 ... E5 75
Mosquito, creek, Iowa ... D5 92
Mosquito, lagoon, Fla ... D6 86
Mosquito Coast, reg., Hond., Nic ... D6 62
Mosquito Creek, res., Ohio ... A7 111
Mosquitos, gulf, Pan ... F7 62
Moss, Jasper, Miss., 125 ... D4 100
Moss, Nor., 20,600 ... H4, p28 25
Moss, Clay, Tenn., 200 ... C8 117
Moss, mtn., Ark ... C3 81
Mossaka, Con. B ... F3 46
Mossbank, Sask., Can., 568 ... H3 70
Moss Bluff, Liberty, Tex ... F5 118
Mossel Bay, S. Afr., 12,178 .. D3 49
Mossendjo, Con. B ... F2 46
Moss Landing, Monterey, Calif., 400 ... C6 82
Mossleigh, Alta., Can., 40 ... D4 69
Mossoro, Braz., 38,833 ... C3 56
Moss Point, Jackson, Miss., 6,631 ... E3, E5 100
Moss Vale, Austl., 3,040 ... G8 51
Mossville, Newton, Ark., 40 ... B2 81
Mossville, Calcasieu, La., 1,500 ... *D2 95
Mossy, pt., Man., Can ... C2 71
Mossy, riv., Man., Can ... D2 71
Mossy, riv., Sask., Can ... C4 70
Mossy Head, Walton, Fla., 150 ... G2 86
Mossyrock, Lewis, Wash., 344 ... C3 122
Most, Czech., 51,400 ... C2 24
Mostaganem, Alg., 68,921 ... B5 44
Mostar, Yugo., 35,242 ... D3 22
Móstoles, Sp., 2,886 ... p17 20
Mosul, Iraq, 179,646 ... H17 9, D14 31
Motagua, riv., Guat ... C3 62
Motala, Swe., 27,100 ... H6 25
Motatán, Ven., 4,358 ... B3 60
Mothe, isl., Fiji Is ... 52
Motherwell [& Wishaw], Scot., 73,800 ... E5 13
Motihari, India, 32,620 ... D10 40
Motilla del Palancar, Sp., 4,398 ... C5 20
Motley, Morrison, Minn., 430 ... D4 99
Motley, co., Tex., 2,870 ... B2 118
Moto, see Ōshima, Jap.
Moto, mtn., Iwo ... 52
Motril, Sp., 19,185 ... D4 20
Motrul, riv., Rom ... C6 22
Motsa, Isr ... h11 32
Mott, Hettinger, N. Dak., 1,463 ... C3 110
Motta di Livenza, It., 9,255 ... D8 19
Motueka, N.Z., 3,310 ... N14 51
Motuhora, N.Z., 91 ... M16 51
Motul [de Felipe Carrillo Puerto], Mex., 9,965 ... C7 63
Motupe, Peru, 4,396 ... C2 58
Moturiki, isl., Fiji Is ... 52
Mouat Mine, Stillwater, Mont., 50 ... *E7 102
Mouchoir, passage, Ba. Is ... E8 64
Moudhros (Mudros), Grc., 1,720 ... C5 23
Moudjéria, Maur ... C2 45
Moudon, Switz., 2,806 ... C2 19
Moulde Bay, N.W., Ter., Can ... m28 67
Moule, see Le Moule, Guad.
Moulins, Fr., 23,909 (*35,000) ... D5 14
Moulki, Grc., 1,447 ... g10 23
Moulmein, Bur., 108,000 ... D2 38, E10 39
Moulouya, riv., Mor ... C4 44
Moulton, Lawrence, Ala., 1,716 ... A2 78
Moulton, Appanoose, Iowa, 773 ... D5 92
Moulton, valley, Ala ... A2 78
Moultonboro, Carroll, N.H., 150 (840▲) ... C4 105
Moultonville, Carroll, N.H., 215 ... C4 105
Moultrie, Colquitt, Ga., 15,764 ... E3 87
Moultrie, co., Ill., 13,635 ... D5 90
Moultrie, lake, S.C ... E7 115
Mound, Hennepin, Minn., 5,440 ... F5 99
Mound Bayou, Bolivar, Miss., 1,354 ... B3 100
Mound City, Pulaski, Ill., 1,669 ... F4 90
Mound City, Linn, Kans., 661 ... D9 93
Mound City, Holt, Mo., 1,249 ... A2 101
Mound City, Campbell, S. Dak., 144 ... B5 116
Mound City Group, nat. mon., Ohio ... C4 111
Moundou, Chad, 21,866 ... D3 46
Moundridge, McPherson, Kans., 1,214 ... D6 93
Mounds, Crittenden, Ark ... E8 81
Mounds, Pulaski, Ill., 1,835 ... F4 90
Mounds, Creek, Okla., 674 .. B5 112
Mounds View, Ramsey, Minn., 6,416 ... *F5 99
Moundsville, Marshall, W. Va., 15,163 ... B2, B3 123
Mound Valley, Labette, Kans., 481 ... E8 93
Moundville, Hale, Ala., 922 ... C2 78
Moundville, Vernon, Mo., 136 ... D3 101
Mounier, mtn., Fr ... E7 14
Mountain, Pembina, N. Dak., 218 ... A8 110
Mountain, Ritchie, W. Va., 200 ... B4 123
Mountain, Oconto, Wis., 400 ... C5 124
Mountain, prov., Phil., 436,200 ... *B6 35
Mountain, lake, Sask., Can ... B3 70
Mountainair, Torrance, N. Mex., 1,605 ... C3 107
Mountain Ash, Whitley, Ky., 275 ... D5 94
Mountain Brook, Jefferson, Ala., 12,680 ... E5 78
Mountainburg, Crawford, Ark., 402 ... B1 81
Mountain City, Rabun, Ga., 550 ... B3 87
Mountain City, Elko, Nev., 75 ... B6 104
Mountain City, Johnson, Tenn., 1,379 ... C12 117
Mountain Creek, Chilton, Ala., 300 ... C3 78
Mountain Dale, Sullivan, N.Y., 900 ... D6 108
Mountain Dale, Unicoi, Tenn ... C11 117
Mountain Fork, riv., Okla ... C7 112
Mountain Grove, Ont., Can., 135 ... C8 72
Mountain Grove, Wright, Mo., 3,176 ... D5 101
Mountain Grove, Bath, Va., 25 ... C3 121
Mountain Home, Baxter, Ark., 2,105 ... A3 81
Mountain Home, Elmore, Idaho, 10,075 ... F3 89
Mountainhome, Monroe, Pa., 500 ... D11 114
Mountain Home, Kerr, Tex., 25 ... D3 118
Mountain Home, Duchesne, Utah, 50 ... C5 119
Mountain Iron, St. Louis, Minn., 1,808 ... C6 99
Mountain Lake, Cottonwood, Minn., 1,943 ... G4 99
Mountain Lake Park, Garrett, Md., 975 ... D1 85
Mountain Lakes, Morris, N.J., 4,037 ... B4 106
Mountain Nile, see Bahr el Jebel, riv., Sud.
Mountain Park, Alta., Can .. C2 69
Mountain Park, Kiowa, Okla., 403 ... C3 112
Mountain Pine, Garland, Ark., 1,279 ... C2, C5 81
Mountain Province, see Mountain, prov., Phil.
Mountainside, Union, N.J., 6,325 ... B4 106
Mountain Valley, Garland, Ark., 150 ... C2 81
Mountain View, Stone, Ark., 983 ... B3 81
Mountain View, Santa Clara, Calif., 30,889 ... B5 82
Mountain View, Alta., Can., 84 ... E4 69
Mountain View, Clayton, Ga., 1,500 ... *C2 87
Mountainview, Hawaii, Haw., 747 ... D6 88
Mountain View, Ada, Idaho, 4,898 ... *F2 89
Mountain View, Howell, Mo., 936 ... D6 101
Mountain View, Bernalillo, N. Mex., 700 ... C3 107
Mountain View, Chaves, N. Mex., 50 ... D5 107
Mountain View, Kiowa, Okla., 864 ... B3 112
Mountain View, Asotin, Wash ... C8 122
Mountain View, Natrona, Wyo., 1,721 ... *C6 125
Mountain View, Uinta, Wyo., 400 ... D2 125
Mountain Village, Alsk., 300 ... C7 79
Mount Airy, Habersham, Ga., 417 ... B3 87
Mount Airy, Carroll and Frederick, Md., 1,352 ... B3 85
Mount Airy, Hunterdon, N.J., 100 ... C3 106
Mount Airy, Surry, N.C., 7,055 ... A3 109
Mount Airy, Sequatchie, Tenn., 25 ... D8 117
Mount Airy, Pittsylvania, Va., 45 ... E3 121
Mount Albert, Ont., Can., 561 ... C5 72
Mount Andrew, Barbour, Ala., 50 ... D4 78
Mount Angel, Marion, Oreg., 1,428 ... B2, B4 113
Mount Arlington, Morris, N.J., 1,246 ... B3 106
Mount Assiniboine, prov. park, B.C., Can ... D10 68
Mount Athos (Ayion Oros), prov., Grc., 2,687 ... *B5 23
Mount Auburn, Christian, Ill., 502 ... D4 90
Mount Auburn, Benton, Iowa, 186 ... B5 92
Mount Ayr, Newton, Ind., 186 ... C3 91
Mount Ayr, Ringgold, Iowa, 1,738 ... D3 92
Mount Baldy, San Bernardino, Calif., 225 ... F3 82
Mount Barker, Austl., 1,872 ... G2 51
Mount Bellew, Ire., 306 ... D3 11
Mount Berry, Floyd, Ga., 1,000 ... B1 87
Mount Bethel, Somerset, N.J., 600 ... B3 106
Mount Blanchard, Hancock, Ohio, 432 ... B4 111
Mount Blanc, tunnel, Fr., It ... D2 18
Mount Brydges, Ont., Can., 1,016 ... E3 72
Mount Calvary, Fond du Lac, Wis., 650 ... B5, E5 124
Mount Carmel, Montgomery, Ala., 140 ... C3 78
Mount Carmel, Newf., Can., 673 ... E5 75
Mount Carmel, New Haven, Conn. (part of Hamden) .. D4 84
Mount Carmel, Santa Rosa, Fla., 150 ... G2 86
Mount Carmel, Wabash, Ill., 8,594 ... E6 90
Mount Carmel, Franklin, Ind., 142 ... F8 91
Mount Carmel, Cavalier, N. Dak., 50 ... A7 110
Mount Carmel, Clermont, Ohio, 400 ... D2 111
Mount Carmel, Northumberland, Pa., 10,760 ... E9 114
Mount Carmel, McCormick, S.C., 109 ... C3 115
Mount Carmel, Kane, Utah, 85 ... F3 119
Mount Carmel Junction, Kane, Utah, 10 ... F3 119
Mount Carroll, Carroll, Ill., 2,056 ... A4 90
Mount Clare, Harrison, W. Va., 900 ... B4 123
Mount Clemens, Macomb, Mich., 21,016 ... A8, F8 98
Mount Clinton, Rockingham, Va., 170 ... C4 121
Mount Cory, Hancock, Ohio, 301 ... B4 111
Mount Croghan, Chesterfield, S.C., 145 ... B7 115
Mount Darwin, Rh., 485 ... A5 49
Mount Desert, isl., Maine ... D4 96
Mount Dora, Lake, Fla., 3,756 ... D5 86
Mount Dora, Union, N. Mex., 20 ... A6 107
Mount Eaton, Wayne, Ohio, 265 ... B6 111
Mount Eden, Spencer, Ky., 350 ... B4 94
Mount Edgecumbe, Alsk., 1,884 ... *m22 79
Mount Elgin, Ont., Can., 225 ... E4 72
Mount Enterprise, Rusk, Tex., 400 ... D5 118
Mount Ephraim, Camden, N.J., 5,447 ... *D2 106
Mount Erie, Wayne, Ill., 134 .E5 90
Mount Etna, Huntington, Ind., 192 ... C6 91
Mount Etna, Adams, Iowa, 100 ... C3 92
Mount Forest, Ont., Can., 2,623 ... D4 72
Mount Forest, Bay, Mich., 35 ... E6 98
Mount Gambier, Austl., 15,388 ... H3 51
Mount Gay, Logan, W. Va., 3,386 ... *D3 123
Mount Gilead, Montgomery, N.C., 1,229 ... B4 109
Mount Gilead, Morrow, Ohio, 2,788 ... B5 111
Mount Healthy, Hamilton, Ohio, 6,553 ... D2 111
Mount Hebron, Greene, Ala., 40 ... C1 78
Mount Hebron, Siskiyou, Calif., 150 ... B3 82
Mount Hermon, Washington, La., 90 ... D5 95
Mount Hermon, Franklin, Mass., 600 ... A3 97
Mount Heron, Buchanan, Va., 100 ... B3 121
Mount Holly, Union, Ark., 300 ... D3 81
Mount Holly, Burlington, N.J., 13,271 ... C3 106
Mount Holly, Gaston, N.C., 4,037 ... B2 109
Mount Holly, Berkeley, S.C., 150 ... E2, E7 115
Mount Holly, Rutland, Vt., 70 (517▲) ... E3 120
Mount Holly Springs, Cumberland, Pa., 1,840 .. F7 114
Mount Hood, Hood River, Oreg., 50 ... B5 113
Mount Hope, Lawrence, Ala., 100 ... A2 78
Mount Hope, Austl., 129 ... F5 51
Mount Hope, Ont., Can., 807 ... D5 72
Mount Hope, Tolland, Conn ... B8 84
Mount Hope, Sedgwick, Kans., 539 ... B4, E6 93
Mount Hope, Morris, N.J., 600 ... B3 106
Mount Hope, Spokane, Wash .D8 122
Mount Hope, Fayette, W. Va., 2,000 ... D3, D7 123
Mount Hope, Grant, Wis., 218 ... F3 124
Mount Hope, riv., Conn ... B8 84
Mount Horeb, Dane, Wis., 1,991 ... F4 124
Mount Houston, Harris, Tex., 2,500 ... *F5 118
Mount Ida, Montgomery, Ark., 805 ... C2 81
Mount Idaho, Idaho, Idaho, 90 ... D2 89
Mount Isa, Austl., 13,358 ... D6 50
Mount Jackson, Shenandoah, Va., 722 ... B4 121
Mount Jewett, McKean, Pa., 1,226 ... C4 114
Mount Joy, Scott, Iowa, 35 ... D7 92
Mount Joy, Lancaster, Pa., 3,292 ... F9 114
Mount Judea, Newton, Ark., 60 ... B2 81
Mount Juliet, Wilson, Tenn., 750 ... A5 117
Mount Kisco, Westchester, N.Y., 6,805 ... D7, m15 108
Mountlake Terrace, Snohomish, Wash., 9,122 ... B3 122
Mount Laurel, Burlington, N.J., 150 ... D3 106
Mount-Laurier, Que., Can .p20 72
Mount Lebanon, Allegheny, Pa., 35,361 ... F1 114
Mount Lookout, Nicholas, W. Va., 250 ... D7 123
Mount McKinley, nat. park, Alsk ... C9 79
Mount Magnet, Austl., 631 .. E2 50
Mount Meigs, Montgomery, Ala., 85 ... C3 78
Mountmellick, Ire., 2,436 .. D4 11
Mount Misery, pt., N.Y ... F4 84
Mount Montgomery, Mineral, Nev., 10 ... F3 104
Mount Morgan, Austl., 4,000 .A8 51
Mount Moriah, Newf., Can., 716 ... *D2 75
Mount Moriah, Harrison, Mo., 225 ... A4 101
Mount Morris, Ogle, Ill., 3,075 ... A4 90
Mount Morris, Genesee, Mich., 3,484 ... E7 98
Mount Morris, Livingston, N.Y., 3,250 ... C3 108
Mount Morris, Greene, Pa., 700 ... G1 114
Mount Olive, Jefferson, Ala., 1,800 ... B3, E4 78
Mount Olive, Izard, Ark., 50 ... B3 81
Mount Olive, Macoupin, Ill., 2,295 ... D4 90
Mount Olive, Covington, Miss., 841 ... D4 100
Mount Olive, Morris, N.J., 30 ... B3 106
Mount Olive, Wayne, N.C., 4,673 ... B5 109
Mount Olive, Knox, Tenn., 500 ... E11 117
Mount Oliver, Allegheny, Pa., 5,980 ... B6 114
Mount Olivet, Robertson, Ky., 386 ... B5 94
Mount Orab, Brown, Ohio, 1,058 ... C4 111
Mount Pearl Park, Newf., Can., 2,785 ... *f9 75
Mount Penn, Berks, Pa., 3,574 ... *F10 114
Mount Perry, Marion, Ind .. I8 91
Mount Pisgah, Augusta, Va., 100 ... C4 121
Mount Pleasant, Izard, Ark., 250 ... B4 81
Mount Pleasant, New Castle, Del., 65 ... A6 85
Mount Pleasant, Gadsden, Fla., 100 ... B2 86
Mount Pleasant, Henry, Iowa, 7,339 ... D6 92
Mount Pleasant, Frederick, Md., 100 ... B3 85
Mount Pleasant, Isabella, Mich., 14,875 ... E6 98
Mount Pleasant, Marshall, Miss., 150 ... A4 100
Mount Pleasant, Hunterdon, N.J., 100 ... B2 106
Mount Pleasant, Cabarrus, N.C., 1,041 ... B3 109
Mount Pleasant, Jefferson, Ohio, 656 ... B1 123
Mount Pleasant, Westmoreland, Pa., 6,107 ... F2 114
Mount Pleasant, Charleston, S.C., 5,116 ... E3, F8 115
Mount Pleasant, Maury, Tenn., 2,921 ... B4 117
Mount Pleasant, Titus, Tex., 8,027 ... C5 118
Mount Pleasant, Sanpete, Utah, 1,572 ... D4 119
Mount Pocono, Monroe, Pa., 935 ... D11 114
Mount Prospect, Cook, Ill., 22,945 ... A6, E2 90
Mount Pulaski, Logan, Ill., 1,689 ... C4 90
Mountrail, co., N. Dak., 10,077 ... A3 110
Mount Rainier, nat. park, Wash .C4 122
Mount Rainier, Prince Georges, Md., 9,855 ... C1 85
Mount Revelstoke, nat. park, B.C., Can ... D8 68
Mount Robson, prov. park, B.C., Can ... C8 68
Mount Royal, Que., Can., 21,182 ... *D4 73
Mount Royal, Gloucester, N.J., 700 ... D2 106
Mount Rushmore, nat. memorial, S. Dak ... D2 106
Mounts, bay, Eng ... D2 12
Mount Savage, Allegany, Md., 1,639 ... D2 85
Mount Shasta, Siskiyou, Calif., 2,272 ... B2 82
Mount Sherman, Newton, Ark ... A2 81
Mount Sidney, Augusta, Va., 500 ... C4 121
Mount Solon, Augusta, Va., 140 ... C3 121
Mount Sterling, Choctaw, Ala., 125 ... C1 78
Mount Sterling, Brown, Ill., 2,262 ... D3 90
Mount Sterling, Montgomery, Ky., 5,310 ... B6 94
Mount Sterling, Haywood, N.C ... D3 109
Mount Sterling, Madison, Ohio, 1,338 ... C4 111
Mount Stewart, P.E.I., Can., 433 ... C7 74
Mount Storm, Grant, W. Va., 160 ... B5 123
Mount Summit, Henry, Ind., 424 ... D7 91
Mount Tabor, Rutland, Vt., 75 (165▲) ... E3 120
Mount Trumbull, Mohave, Ariz ... E5 80
Mount Uniacke, N.S., Can., 531 ... E6 74
Mount Union, Henry, Iowa, 176 ... C6 92
Mount Union, Huntingdon, Pa., 4,091 ... E6 114
Mount Upton, Chenango, N.Y., 400 ... C5 108
Mount Vernon, Mobile, Ala., 553 ... D1 78
Mount Vernon, Faulkner, Ark., 200 ... B3 81
Mount Vernon, Montgomery, Ga., 1,166 ... D4 87
Mount Vernon, Jefferson, Ill., 15,566 ... E5 90
Mount Vernon, Posey, Ind., 5,970 ... I2 91
Mount Vernon, Linn, Iowa, 2,593 ... C6 92
Mount Vernon, Rockcastle, Ky., 1,177 ... C5 94
Mount Vernon, Kennebec, Maine, 225 (596▲) ... D3 96
Mount Vernon, Somerset, Md., 250 ... D6 85
Mount Vernon, Lawrence, Mo., 2,381 ... D4 101
Mount Vernon, Erie, N.Y., 3,200 ... *C2 108
Mount Vernon, Westchester, N.Y., 76,010 ... h13 108
Mount Vernon, Knox, Ohio, 13,284 ... B5 111
Mount Vernon, Lucas, Ohio, 1,000 ... *A2 111
Mount Vernon, Grant, Oreg., 502 ... C7 113
Mount Vernon, Davison, S. Dak., 379 ... D7 116
Mount Vernon, Monroe, Tenn., 600 ... D9 117
Mount Vernon, Franklin, Tex., 1,338 ... C5 118
Mount Vernon, Fairfax, Va ... B5, C5 121
Mount Vernon, Skagit, Wash., 7,921 ... A3 122
Mount Victory, Hardin, Ohio, 598 ... B4 111
Mount View, Washington, R.I., 500 ... *C11 84
Mountville, Troup, Ga., 139 ... C2 87
Mountville, Lancaster, Pa., 1,411 ... *F9 114
Mountville, Laurens, S.C., 139 ... C4 115
Mount Viso, mtn., It ... E3 18
Mount Washington, Bullitt, Ky., 1,173 ... A4, B4 94
Mount Washington, Berkshire, Mass., 25 (34▲) ... B1 97
Mount Washington, Coos, N.H., 7 ... B4 105
Mount Wolf, York, Pa., 1,514 ... F8 114
Mount Zion, Carroll, Ga., 211 ... C1 87
Mount Zion, Macon, Ill., 925 ... *D5 90
Moura, Braz., 185 ... D5 60
Moura, Port., 9,509 ... C2 20
Mourdi, depression, Chad ... B4 46
Mourmelon-le-Grand, Fr., 3,518 ... E4 15
Mourne, mts., N. Ire ... C5 13
Mouscron, Bel., 36,554 ... D3 15
Mouse Island, Newf., Can., 507 ... E2 75
Mousie, Knott, Ky., 500 ... C7 94
Moutiers [-Tarentaise], Fr., 3,788 ... E7 14
Moutier, Switz., 7,472 ... B3 19
Mouton, isl., N.S., Can ... F5 74
Mouy, Fr., 3,781 ... E2 15
Movico, Mobile, Ala. (part of Mount Vernon) ... D1 78
Moville, Woodbury, Iowa, 1,156 ... B1 92
Moville, Ire., 1,097 ... B4 11
Mowbullan, mtn., Austl ... C8 51
Moweaqua, Shelby, Ill., 1,614 ... D4 90
Mower, co., Minn., 48,498 ... G6 99
Mowich, Klamath, Oreg ... C5 113
Mowrystown, Highland, Ohio, 416 ... C4 111
Moxahala, Perry, Ohio, 300 .. C5 111
Moxee City, Yakima, Wash., 499 ... C5 122
Moxico, dist., Ang., 267,069 ... D3 48
Moxie, mtn., Maine ... C3 96
Moxie, pond, Maine ... C3 96
Moxley, Jefferson, Ga., 50 .. D4 87
Moy, Scot., 528 ... C6 13
Moy, riv., Ire ... C2 11
Moyālē, Eth ... E4 47
Moyale, Ken ... A6 48
Moyamba, S.L ... E2 45
Moycullen, Ire., 127 ... D2 11
Moyers, Pushmataha, Okla., 150 ... C6 112
Moyeuvre-Grande, Fr., 15,146 ... E6 15
Moyie, B.C., Can., 137 ... E10 68
Moyie, range, B.C., Can ... E2 69
Moyie Springs, Boundary, Idaho, 196 ... A2 89
Moylan, Delaware, Pa., 1,000 ... *G10 114
Moynalty, Ire., 128 ... D5 11
Moyobamba, Peru, 8,850 ... C2 58
Moyock, Currituck, N.C., 350 ... A7 109
Moyuta, Guat., 1,478 ... C2 62
Mozambique, Port. dep., Afr., 6,900,000 ... I9 42, B5 49
Mozambique, chan., Afr ... g9 49
Mozart, Sask., Can., 64 ... F3 70
Mozdok, Sov. Un., 32,000 ... E2 29
Mozhaysk, Sov. Un., 10,000 ... D11 27
Mozhga, Sov. Un., 10,000 .. D19 9
Mozyr, Sov. Un., 25,000 ... E7 27
Mpanda, Tan ... C5 48
Mpika, Zambia, 117 ... D5 48
Mporokoso, Zambia ... C5 48
Mpouia, Con. B ... F3 46
Mpulungu, Zambia ... C5 48
Mpwapwa, Tan., 1,612 ... C6 48
Mragowo, Pol., 3,254 ... B6 26
M'Raier, Alg., 6,935 ... C6 44
Mrewa, Rh., 790 ... A5 49
Msec, Czech., 1,007 ... n16 26
Msene, Czech., 886 ... n17 26
M'sila, Alg., 8,645 (71,627▲) ... B5 44
Msta, riv., Sov. Un ... B9 27
Mstislavl, Sov. Un., 10,000 .. D8 27
Mtakuja, Tan ... C5 48
Mtoko, Rh., 975 ... A5 49
Mtorashanga, Rh., 2,270 ... A5 49
Mtsensk, Sov. Un., 10,000 .. E11 27
Mtubatuba, S. Afr ... C5 49
Mtwara, Tan., 10,459 ... D7 48
Muang Fang, Thai., 4,563 ... C3 38
Muang Hot, Thai ... C3 38
Muang Nan, Thai., 13,624 . C4 38
Muari, cape, Pak ... I13 41
Mubi, Nig ... D7 45
Mucajaí, riv., Braz ... C5 60
Mücheln, Ger., 13,200 ... B6 17
Muchkap, Sov. Un., 10,000 .. F14 27
Much Wenlock, Eng., 14,929 ... B5 12
Muck, isl., Scot ... D2 13
Muckalee, creek, Ga ... D2 87
Muckleshoot, Indian res., Wash D2 122
Mucuburi, Moz ... D6 48
Mucuri, Braz., 603 ... E3 57
Mucuri, riv., Braz ... E2 57
Mucusso, Ang ... E3 48
Mud, creek, Ala ... E4 78
Mud, creek, Ga ... B5 87
Mud, creek, Iowa ... D3 92
Mud, creek, Okla ... C4 112
Mud, lake, Maine ... A5 96
Mud, lake, Minn ... C5 99
Mud, lake, Nev ... B2 104
Mud, lake, Nev ... C2 104
Mud, riv., Minn ... B3 99
Mud, riv., W. Va ... C2 123
Mudanya, Tur., 5,900 ... B7 23
Mudawwarah, Jordan, 1,000 ... H10 31
Mud Butte, Meade, S. Dak., 7 ... C3 116
Muddo Gashi, Ken ... A6 48
Muddy, Saline, Ill., 95 ... F5 90
Muddy, creek, Colo ... A4 83
Muddy, creek, Kans ... B7 93
Muddy, creek, Ky ... D2 94
Muddy, creek, Utah ... E4 119
Muddy, creek, Wyo ... B4 125
Muddy, creek, Wyo ... C6 125
Muddy, creek, Wyo ... D2 125
Muddy, creek, Wyo ... D5 125
Muddy, fork, Ind ... A3 94
Muddy, lake, Sask., Can ... E1 70
Muddy, mts., Nev ... G7 104
Muddy, peak, Nev ... G7 104
Muddy Boggy, creek, Okla ... C6 112
Muddy Creek, mtn., Ark ... C2 81
Müden, Ger., 1,600 ... F4 24
Mudgee, Austl., 5,313 ... F7 51
Mudjatik, riv., Sask., Can ... A2 70
Mud Lake, Jefferson, Idaho, 187 ... F6 89
Mud Lick, creek, Ky ... A6 94
Mudon, Bur., 20,123 ... E10 39
Mudros, see Moudhros, Grc.
Mudugh, dist., Som ... D6 47
Mueda, Moz ... D6 48
Muenster, Sask., Can., 182 .. E3 70
Muenster, Cooke, Tex., 1,190 ... C4 118
Muertos, isl., P.R ... D4 65
Muff, Ire., 154 ... B4 11
Mufulira, Zambia 75,900 ... D4 48
Mugía, Sp., 7,061 ... A1 20
Mugla, Tur., 14,000 ... D7 23
Muglad, Sud., 3,735 ... C2 47
Mugodzhary, mts., Sov. Un ... D5 29
Mugulo, Pap ... k11 51
Mugwump, lake, Oreg ... E7 113
Muhammadābād, Iran ... C9 41
Muhammad Qol, Sud ... A4 47
Muheza, Tan ... C6 48
Muhinga, Burundi ... B5 48
Mühlacker, Ger., 12,100 ... E3 17
Mühldorf, Ger., 10,800 ... D6 16
Muhlenberg, co., Ky., 27,791 ... C2 94
Muhlenburg Park, Berks, Pa., 1,000 ... *F10 114
Mühlhausen, Ger., 45,300 .. B5 17

N

Nantucket, sound, Mass ... C7 97
Nantung, China, 260,400 ... H9 36
Nantuxent, pt., N.J. ... E2 106
Nantwich, Eng., 10,454 ... A5 12
Nanty Glo, Cambria, Pa., 4,608 ... F4 114
Nanuet, Rockland, N.Y., 8,700 ... g12 108
Nanuku, passage, Fiji Is ... 52
Nanuku, reef, Fiji Is ... 52
Nanyang, China, 50,000 ... H5 36
Nanyuki, Ken., 4,090 ... A6 48
Nao, cape, Sp ... C6 20
Naoli, riv., China ... C6 37
Naoma, Raleigh, W. Va., 600 ... D6 123
Naomi, lake, Pa ... A2 106
Naomi, peak, Utah ... B4 119
Naoua, Syr ... B8 32
Naousa, Grc., 15,492 ... B4 23
Napa, Napa, Calif., 22,170 ... B5, C2 82
Napa, co., Calif., 65,890 ... C2 82
Napa, riv., Calif ... A5 82
Napadogan, N.B., Can., 167 ... C3 74
Napakiak, Alsk., 190 ... C7 79
Napaktok, bay, Newf., Can ... f9 75
Napamute, Alsk., 20 ... C8 79
Napanee, Ont., Can., 4,500 ... C8 72
Napanoch, Ulster, N.Y., 950 ... D6 108
Napatree, pt., R.I ... D9 84
Napavine, Lewis, Wash., 314 ... C3 122
Nape, Laos ... C6 38
Napeague, bay, N.Y ... E8 84
Napeague, beach, N.Y ... F8 84
Naper, Boyd, Nebr., 198 ... B6 103
Naperville, Du Page, Ill., 12,933 ... B5, F2 90
Napetipi, riv., Que., Can ... C2 75
Napf, mtn., Switz ... C4 19
Napier, N.Z., 27,200 (*36,200) ... M16 51
Napier, mts., Ant ... C18 5
Napierville, Que., Can., 1,812 ... D4 73
Napierville, co., Que., Can., 11,216 ... D4 73
Napinka, Man., Can., 178 ... E1 71
Naples, Collier, Fla., 4,655 ... F5 86
Naples, Boundary, Idaho, 100 ... A2 89
Naples, Scott, Ill., 92 ... D3 90
Naples, see Napoli, It.
Naples, Cumberland, Maine, 350 (735▲) ... E2 96
Naples, Ontario, N.Y., 1,237 ... C3 108
Naples, Clark, S. Dak., 36 ... C8 116
Naples, Morris, Tex., 1,692 ... C5 118
Naples, bay, It ... D5 21
Napo, prov., Ec ... B2 58
Napo, riv., Ec ... B3 58
Napoleon, Ripley, Ind., 290 ... F7 91
Napoleon, Lafayette, Mo., 215 ... B3 101
Napoleon, Logan, N. Dak., 1,078 ... C6 110
Napoleon, Henry, Ohio, 6,739 ... A3 111
Napoleonville, Assumption, La., 1,148 ... C5, E4 95
Napoli (Naples), It., 1,204,900 (*1,750,000) ... D5 21
Naponee, Franklin, Nebr., 206 ... D6 103
Napoopoo, Hawaii, Haw., 90 ... D6 88
Nappanee, Elkhart, Ind., 3,895 ... B5 91
Napton, Saline, Mo., 89 ... B4 101
Na Puukula, peak, Haw ... D6 88
Naqura, Leb ... A7 32
Nara, Jap., 134,577 ... o14 37
Nara, Mali, 2,200 ... C3 45
Nara, pref., Jap., 781,058 ... *I7 37
Nara, canal, Pak ... E2 42
Naracoorte, Austl., 4,410 ... H3 51
Narai, Jap., 3,100 (5,247▲) ... n16 37
Naramata, B.C., Can., 346 ... E8 68
Naranja, Dade, Fla., 2,509 ... F3, G6 86
Naranjito, P.R., 2,719 ... B6 65
Naranjito, mun., P.R., 17,319 ... B5 65
Nararu, mtn., Fiji Is ... 52
Narata, Fiji Is., 110 ... 52
Nara Visa, Quay, N. Mex., 350 ... B6 107
Narayanganj, Pak., 125,792 ... F13 40
Narayanpet, India, 20,504 ... I6 40
Narbada, riv., India ... F6 40
Narberth, Montgomery, Pa., 5,109 ... B11, F11 114
Narberth, Wales, 960 ... C3 12
Narbonne, Fr., 33,891 ... F5 14
Narcisse, Man., Can ... D3 71
Narcoossee, Osceola, Fla., 100 ... D5 86
Nardin, Kay, Okla., 142 ... A4 112
Nardò, It., 24,000 ... D7 21
Nares, strait, Can., Grnld ... B22 4
Narew, riv., Pol ... B6 26
Nariño, dept., Col., 571,940 ... C2 60
Narita, Jap., 17,900 ... n19 37
Narka, Republic, Kans., 166 ... C6 93
Narodnaya, mtn., Sov. Un ... B21 9
Naro-Fominsk, Sov. Un., 10,000 ... D11 27
Narok, Ken ... B6 48
Narol, Man., Can., 592 ... D3 71
Narrabri, Austl., 5,424 ... E7 51
Narragansett, Washington, R.I., 2,000 (3,444▲) ... D11 84
Narragansett, bay, R.I ... C11 84
Narraguagus, riv., Maine ... D5 96
Narran, riv., Austl ... D6 51
Narrandera, Austl., 4,718 ... G6 51
Narraway, riv., Alta., B.C., Can ... B7 68
Narrogin, Austl., 4,620 ... F2 50
Narromine, Austl., 2,282 ... F7 51
Narrows, Giles, Va., 2,508 ... D2 121
Narrows, The, strait, N.Y ... E5 106
Narrows, strait, Vir. Is ... f16 65
Narrows, strait, Wash ... D1 122
Narrowsburg, Sullivan, N.Y., 550 ... D5 108
Narsinghpur, India, 10,000 ... F7 40
Naruna, Burnet, Tex ... D3 118
Naruna, Campbell, Va., 250 ... D3 121
Narva, Sov. Un., 27,600 ... B7 27
Narvik, Nor., 13,300 ... C7 25
Naryan-Mar, Sov. Un., 11,400 ... B19 9
Naryilco, Austl., 150 ... D3 51
Narym, Sov. Un ... D25 9
Naryn, Sov. Un., 16,000 ... E9 29
Naryn, riv., Sov. Un ... E9 29
Nasala, Fiji Is., 71 ... 52
Nasa Manned, spacecraft center, Tex ... F5 118
Nasarawa, Nig ... E6 45
Nasca, Peru, 2,175 ... D3 58
Naschitti, San Juan, N. Mex., 100 ... A1 107
Nase, Jap ... F10 34
Naseby, N.Z., 154 ... P13 51
Nash, Walsh, N. Dak., 33 ... A8 110
Nash, Grant, Okla., 230 ... A3 112
Nash, Bowie, Tex., 1,124 ... C5 118
Nash, co., N.C., 61,002 ... A6 109
Nash, pt., Wales ... C4 12
Nash, stream, N.H ... A4 105
Nashawena, isl., Mass ... D6 97
Nash Creek, N.B., Can., 250 ... B3 74
Nashmead, Mendocino, Calif., 40 ... C2 82
Nashoba, Pushmataha, Okla., 100 ... C6 112
Nashoba, hill, Mass ... f10 97
Nashua, Chickasaw, Iowa, 1,737 ... B5 92
Nashua, Wilkin, Minn., 146 ... D2 99
Nashua, Valley, Mont., 796 ... B10 102
Nashua, Hillsboro, N.H., 39,096 ... E4 105
Nashua, riv., Mass., N.H ... A4 97
Nashville, Howard, Ark., 3,579 ... D2 81
Nashville, Berrien, Ga., 4,070 ... E3 87
Nashville, Washington, Ill., 2,606 ... E4 90
Nashville, Brown, Ind., 489 ... F5 91
Nashville, Kingman, Kans., 137 ... E5 93
Nashville, Barry, Mich., 1,525 ... F5 98
Nashville, Nash., N.C., 1,423 ... B6 109
Nashville, Holmes, Ohio, 234 ... B5 111
Nashville, Davidson, Tenn., 170,874 (*411,500) ... A5, E9 117
Nashwaak, riv., N.B., Can ... C3 74
Nashwaaksis, N.B., Can., 3,702 ... D3 74
Nashwauk, Itasca, Minn., 1,712 ... C5 99
Našice, Yugo., 4,157 ... C4 24
Nasielsk, Pol., 4,028 ... B6 26
Nasijarvi, lake, Fin ... G10 25
Nasik, India, 131,103 (*215,576) ... E5 39, G4 40
Nasir, Sud ... D3 47
Naskaupi, riv., Newf., Can ... g9 75
Naslini, Apache, Ariz ... B6 80
Nason, Jefferson, Ill., 188 ... E4 90
Nasonville, Providence, R.I., 250 ... B10 84
Nass, riv., B.C., Can ... B3 68
Nassau, Ba. Is., 6,000 (*46,125) ... B5 64
Nassau, Lac qui Parle, Minn ... E2 99
Nassau, Rensselaer, N.Y., 1,248 ... C7 108
Nassau, co., Fla., 17,189 ... B5 86
Nassau, co., N.Y., 1,300,171 ... E7 108
Nassau, gulf, Chile ... k12 54
Nassau, pt., N.Y ... F7 84
Nassau, range, W. Irian ... F9 35
Nassau, riv., Fla ... B5 86
Nassau, sound, Fla ... B5 86
Nassauville, Nassau, Fla., 50 ... B5, B6 86
Nassawadox, Northampton, Va., 650 ... D7 121
Nässjö, Swe., 18,400 ... I6 25
Nasugbu, Phil., 5,251 ... o13 35
Nasukoin, mtn., Mont ... B2 102
Natá, Pan., 2,319 ... F7 62
Natagaima, Col., 4,107 ... C2 60
Natal, Braz., 154,276 ... C3, g6 57
Natal, B.C., Can., 829 ... E10 68
Natal, prov., S. Afr., 3,270,000 ... C5 49
Natalbany, Tangipahoa, La., 350 ... D5 95
Natalia, Medina, Tex., 1,154 ... E3 118
Natanes, plat., Ariz ... D5 80
Natanya, Isr., 46,200 ... B6, f10 32
Natashquan, Que., Can ... h9 75
Natashquan, riv., Que., Can ... h9 75
Natawahunan, lake, Man., Can ... B3 71
Natchaug, riv., Conn ... B8 84
Natchez, Adams, Miss., 23,791 ... D2 100
Natchitoches, Natchitoches, La., 13,924 ... C2 95
Natchitoches, par., La., 35,653 ... C2 95
Natewa, bay, Fiji Is ... 52
Nathalie, Halifax, Va., 125 ... E4 121
Nathilau, pt., Fiji Is ... 52
Nathoula, isl., Fiji Is ... 52
Nathrop, Chaffee, Colo., 25 ... C4 83
Natick, Middlesex, Mass., 28,831 ... B5, g10 97
Natimuk, Austl., 595 ... H3 51
Nation, lakes, B.C., Can ... B5 68
Nation, riv., B.C., Can ... B6 68
National, Pierce, Wash., 60 ... C3 122
National, Monongalia, W. Va., 60 ... A7, B4 123
National City, San Diego, Calif., 32,771 ... E2 82
National City, Iosco, Mich., 90 ... D7 98
National Garden, Volusia, Fla., 100 ... C5 86
National Park, Gloucester, N.J., 3,380 ... *D2 106
Natitingou, Dah., 1,900 ... D5 45
Natividade, Braz., 1,243 ... D1 57
Natívitas, Mex., 1,872 ... h9 63
Natoena, isl., Indon ... E3 35
Natoma, Osborne, Kans., 775 ... C4 93
Natron, lake, Tan ... B6 48
Natrona, co., Wyo., 49,623 ... C6 125
Natrona Heights, see Harrison [Township], Pa.
Nattarö, isl., Swe ... u36 25
Nattaung, mtn., Bur ... C2 38
Natuna, isl., Indon ... E3 35
Natural, bridge, Va ... D3 121
Natural Bridge, Winston, Ala., 100 ... A2 78
Natural Bridge, Jefferson, N.Y., 750 ... A5 108
Natural Bridge, Rockbridge, Va., 150 ... D3 121
Natural, bridge, Utah ... F3 119
Natural Bridges, nat. mon., Utah ... F6 119
Naturaliste, cape, Austl ... F2 50
Natural Steps, Pulaski, Ark., 60 ... D5 81
Naturita, Montrose, Colo., 979 ... C2 83
Naubinway, Mackinac, Mich., 100 ... B5 98
Naucalpan de Juárez, Mex., 10,372 ... h9 63
Nauders, Aus., 1,150 ... E5 16
Nauen, Ger., 12,300 ... B6 16
Naugatuck, New Haven, Conn., 19,511 ... D4 84
Naugatuck, riv., Conn ... B4 84
Naughton, Ont., Can., 954 ... A3 72
Naumburg [an der Saale], Ger., 37,700 ... B6 17
Naumburg [in Hessen], Ger., 2,300 ... B4 17
Naunhof, Ger., 5,868 ... B7 17
Naupe, Peru ... C2 58
Nauru, Austl., N.Z. and Br. trust, Oceania, 5,000 ... G10 7
Naushon, isl., Mass ... D6 97
Nautla, Mex., 1,437 ... C5, m15 63
Nauvoo, Walker, Ala., 318 ... B2 78
Nauvoo, Hancock, Ill., 1,039 ... C2 90
Nauwigewauk, N.B., Can., 83 ... D4 74
Nava, lake, Sp ... A3 20
Nava del Rey, Sp., 3,860 ... B3 20
Navahermosa, Sp., 4,761 ... C3 20
Navajo, Apache, Ariz., 15 ... B6 80
Navajo, co., Ariz., 37,994 ... B5 80
Navajo, creek, Utah ... G4 119
Navajo, Indian, res., Ariz., N. Mex ... A6 80
Navajo, mtn., Utah ... F5 119
Navajo, nat. mon., Ariz ... A5 80
Navajo, res., Colo., N. Mex ... A2 107
Navajo, riv., Colo ... D4 83
Navajo Mountain Trading Post, San Juan, Utah, 15 ... F5 119
Naval Base, Charleston, S.C ... F3 115
Navalcarnero, Sp., 4,681 ... B3 20
Navalmoral de la Mata, Sp., 9,073 ... C3 20
Navan, Ont., Can., 190 ... B9, h13 72
Navarin, cape, Sov. Un ... C20 28
Navarino, Shawano, Wis., 110 ... D5 124
Navarino, isl., Chile ... k12 54
Navarra (Navarre), prov., Sp., 402,042 ... *A5 20
Navarre, Stark, Ohio, 1,698 ... B6 111
Navarre, (Navarra), prov., Sp., 402,042 ... *A5 20
Navarre, reg., Sp., 402,042 ... A5 20
Navarro, Arg., 2,547 ... A5, g7 54
Navarro, co., Tex., 34,423 ... C4 118
Navas, de Tolosa, Sp., 1,134 ... C4 20
Navasota, Grimes, Tex., 4,937 ... D4 118
Navassa, Brunswick, N.C., 500 ... C5 109
Navassa, isl., W.I ... F6 64
Nave, isl., Scot ... E2 13
Nävekvarn, Swe., 837 ... u34 25
Naver, lake, Scot ... B4 13
Naver, riv., Scot ... B4 13
Navesink, Monmouth, N.J., 1,500 ... C4 106
Navia, Arg ... A3 54
Navia, riv., Sp ... A2 20
Navidad, Chile ... A2 54
Navina, Logan, Okla., 11 ... B4 112
Naviti, isl., Fiji Is ... 52
Navojoa, Mex., 30,762 ... B3 63
Navola, Fiji Is., 215 ... 52
Navolato, Mex., 7,119 ... C3 63
Navpaktos, Grc., 6,550 ... C3 23
Navplion, Grc., 8,456 ... D4 23
Navrongo, Ghana, 1,170 ... D4 45
Navsari, India, 51,300 (*53,600) ... G4 40
Navy Yard City, Kitsap, Wash., 3,341 ... *B3 122
Nawabshah, Pak., 45,651 ... D2 40
Nawada, India, 17,468 ... E10 40
Naxos, Grc., 2,546 ... D5 23
Naxos, isl., Grc ... D5 23
Nay, Fr., 3,444 ... F3 14
Nayarit, state, Mex., 391,970 ... C4, m11 63
Nāy Band, Iran ... E8 41
Nāy Band, cape, Iran ... E8 41
Naylor, Lowndes, Ga., 272 ... F3 87
Naylor, Ripley, Mo., 499 ... E7 101
Nayoro, Jap., 23,400 ... D11 37
Naytahwaush, Mahnomen, Minn., 300 ... C3 99
Nazaka, Okinawa ... 52
Nazaré, Braz., 14,644 ... D3 57
Nazaré, Port., 9,241 ... C1 20
Nazaré da Mata, Braz., 9,246 ... h6 57
Nazareth, Isr., 26,400 ... B7 32
Nazareth, Nelson, Ky., 500 ... C4 94
Nazareth, Northampton, Pa., 6,209 ... E11 114
Nazareth, Castro, Tex., 100 ... B1 118
Nazas, Mex., 2,294 ... B4 63
Nazas, riv., Mex ... B4 63
Naze, cape, Nor ... H2 25
Naze, headland, Eng ... C9 12
Nāzerābād, Iran ... H11 41
Nāzīk, Iran ... B2 41
Nazilli, Tur., 36,000 ... D7 23, D7 31
Nazimovo, Sov. Un ... D27 9
Naziya, Sov. Un., 10,000 ... s32 25
Nazko, riv., B.C., Can ... C6 68
Nazreth (Adāmā), Eth ... D4 47
Nazyvayevsk, Sov. Un ... B8 29
Ncheu, Malawi ... D6 48
Ndala, Tan ... B5 48
Ndéle, Cen. Afr. Rep ... D4 46
N'Dende, Gabon ... F2 46
Ndjolé, Gabon ... F2 46
Ndola, Zambia, 88,900 ... C5 48
Ndravuni, isl., Fiji Is ... 52
Neagh, lake, N. Ire ... C5 11
Neah Bay, Clallam, Wash., 900 ... A1 122
Neal, Greenwood, Kans., 122 ... E7 93
Nea Palatia, Grc., 999 ... g11 23
Neapolis, Grc., 17,586 ... D4 23
Neapolis, Grc., 3,908 ... E5 23
Nea Psara (Eretria), Grc., 1,731 ... g11 23
Near, is., Alsk ... E2 79
Neath, Wales, 30,600 ... C4 12
Neavitt, Talbot, Md., 312 ... C5 85
Neba, Jap., 900 ... n16 37
Nebel, riv., Ger ... E6 24
Nebine, creek, Austl ... D6 51
Nebish, Beltrami, Minn., 30 ... C4 99
Nebit-Dag, Sov. Un., 40,000 ... B7 41
Nebo, Pike, Ill., 441 ... D3 90
Nebo, Hopkins, Ky., 338 ... C2 94
Nebo, LaSalle, La., 150 ... C3 95
Nebo, McDowell, N.C., 235 ... B2, D4 109
Nebo, mtn., Utah ... D4 119
Nebraska, Jennings, Ind., 120 ... F7 96
Nebraska, state, U.S., 1,411,330 ... B8 76, 103
Nebraska City, Otoe, Nebr., 7,252 ... D10, F3 103
Nebuzely, Czech., 465 ... n18 26
Necedah, Juneau, Wis., 691 ... D3 124
Nechako, mts., B.C., Can ... C5 68
Nechako, riv., B.C., Can ... C5 68
Neche, Pembina, N. Dak., 545 ... A8 110
Neches, riv., Tex ... D5 118
Nechí, Col ... B3 60
Nechi, riv., Col ... B3 60
Neckar, riv., Ger ... D3 17
Neck City, Jasper, Mo., 110 ... D3 101
Necker, isl., Haw ... m15 88
Necochea, Arg., 17,808 ... B5 54
Nederburgh, cape, Indon ... F6 35
Nederland, Boulder, Colo., 272 ... B5 83
Nederland, Jefferson, Tex., 12,036 ... E6 118
Neder Rijn, riv., Neth ... C5 15
Nedrow, Onondaga, N.Y., 2,500 ... *C4 108
Nee, res., Colo ... C8 83
Needham, Norfolk, Mass., 25,793 ... g11 97
Needham Heights, Norfolk, Mass. (part of Needham) ... g11 97
Needle, mtn., Wyo ... A3 125
Needle, mtn., Colo ... D3 83
Needle, range, Utah ... E2 119
Needles, San Bernardino, Calif., 4,590 ... E6 82
Needmore, Echols, Ga., 80 ... F4 87
Needmore, Lawrence, Ind., 150 ... G4 91
Needmore, Fulton, Pa., 145 ... G5 114
Needville, Fort Bend, Tex., 861 ... E5, F4 118
Neel, gap, Ga ... B3 87
Neeley, Power, Idaho, 40 ... G6 89
Neelin, Man., Can., 40 ... E2 71
Neely, Greene, Miss., 100 ... D5 100
Neelyville, Butler, Mo., 385 ... E7 101
Ñeembucu, dept., Par., 50,861 ... E4 55
Neenah, Winnebago, Wis., 18,057 ... A5, D5 124
Neepawa, Man., Can., 3,197 ... D2 71
Neerpelt, Bel., 7,600 ... C5 15
Neeses, Orangeburg, S.C., 347 ... D5 115
Neffs, Belmont, Ohio, 950 ... B7 111
Neffsville, Lancaster, Pa., 900 ... F9 114
Neftegorsk, Sov. Un., 10,000 ... G16 9
Negapattinam, India, 59,063 (*61,305) ... F6 39
Negaunee, Marquette, Mich., 6,126 ... B3 98
Negev, reg., Isr ... D6 32
Negley, Columbiana, Ohio, 500 ... B7 111
Negley, Red River, Tex., 75 ... C5 118
Negoi, peak, Rom ... C7 22
Negotin, Yugo., 8,639 ... C6 22
Negra, range, Peru ... C2 58
Negrais, cape, Bur ... E9 39
Negreira, Sp., 7,725 ... A1 20
Negrine, Alg ... G10 30
Negri, Sembilan, state, Mala., 364,524 ... K4 38
Negrita, C.R ... E6 62
Negro, mtn., Md ... D1 85
Negro, riv., Arg ... B3 54
Negro, riv., Bol ... B3 55
Negro, riv., Braz ... B1 56
Negro, riv., Braz ... D2 56
Negro, riv., S.A ... E1 56
Negro, riv., Ur ... E1 56
Negros, isl., Phil ... D6 35
Negros Occidental, prov., Phil., 1,332,000 ... *C6 35
Negros Oriental, prov., Phil., 598,800 ... *D6 35
Negru Voda, Rom., 3,154 ... D9 22
Neguac, N.B., Can., 559 ... B4 74
Nehalem, Tillamook, Oreg., 233 ... B3 113
Nehalem, riv., Oreg ... B4 113
Nehawka, Cass, Nebr., 262 ... D10, E3 103
Nehbandān, Iran ... F10 41
Neheim-Hüsten, Ger., 33,900 ... B2 17
Neichiang, China, 190,200 ... F5 34
Neiden, Nor ... C13 25
Neidpath, Sask., Can., 80 ... G2 70
Neihart, Cascade, Mont., 150 ... D6 102
Neihsiang, China, 18,000 ... H5 36
Neihuang, China ... G6 36
Neilburg, Sask., Can., 327 ... E1 70
Neill, pt., Wash ... D1 122
Neillsville, Clark, Wis., 2,728 ... D3 124
Neisse, riv., Ger., Pol ... B9 17
Neiva, Col., 54,000 (74,000▲) ... C2 60
Nejd, pol. div., Sau. Ar., 5,000,000 ... *D10 42
Nejdek, Czech., 5,748 ... C7 17
Nekoma, Rush, Kans., 100 ... D4 93
Nekoma, Cavalier, N. Dak., 143 ... A7 110
Nekoosa, Wood, Wis., 2,515 ... D4 124
Neksø, Den., 3,220 ... A3 26
Nelagoney, Osage, Okla., 80 ... A5 112
Nelbi, Sen ... C2 45
Nelidovo, Sov. Un., 25,000 ... C9 27
Neligh, Antelope, Nebr., 1,776 ... B7 103
Nell, isl., Kwajalein ... 52
Nellore, India, 106,776 ... F6 39
Nellysford, Nelson, Va., 140 ... D4 121
Nelma, Sov. Un ... C9 37
Nelson, Yavapai, Ariz., 20 ... B2 80
Nelson, B.C., Can., 7,074 ... E9 68
Nelson, Eng., 32,000 ... *G6 13
Nelson, Pickens and Cherokee, Ga., 658 ... B2 87
Nelson, Lee, Ill., 283 ... B4 90
Nelson, Muhlenberg, Ky ... C2 94
Nelson, Saline, Mo., 126 ... B4 101
Nelson, Nuckolls, Nebr., 695 ... D7 103
Nelson, Clark, Nev., 50 ... H7 104
Nelson, Cheshire, N.H., 75 (222▲) ... E2 105
Nelson, N.Z., 23,971 (*25,321) ... N14 51
Nelson, Tioga, Pa., 400 ... C7 114
Nelson, Buffalo, Wis., 250 ... D1 124
Nelson, co., Ky., 22,168 ... C4 94
Nelson, co., N. Dak., 7,034 ... B7 110
Nelson, co., Va., 12,752 ... C4 121
Nelson, lake, Man., Can ... B1 71
Nelson, riv., Mon., Can ... A4 71
Nelson Forks, B.C., Can ... m18 68
Nelson House, Man., Can ... B2 71
Nelsonville, Athens, Ohio, 4,834 ... C5 111
Nelspruit, S. Afr., 15,344 ... C5 49
Néma, Maur, 3,000 ... C3 45
Nemacolin, Greene, Pa., 1,404 ... G2 114
Nemadji, riv., Minn., Wis ... D6 99, B1 124
Nemaha, Sac, Iowa, 151 ... B2 92
Nemaha, Nemaha, Nebr., 232 ... D10 103
Nemaha, co., Kans., 12,897 ... C7 93
Nemaha, co., Nebr., 9,099 ... D10 103
Nemaha, riv., Nebr ... D10 103
Nemaksciai, Sov. Un ... A7 26
Neman, Sov. Un., 20,000 ... A7 26
Neman, riv., Sov. Un ... E5 27
Nemeiben, lake, Sask., Can ... B3 70
Nemi, lake, It ... h9 21
Nemiscau, Que., Can., 149 ... h11 73
Nemo, Lawrence, S. Dak., 100 ... C2 116
Nemours, Alg., 6,148 (13,245▲) ... B4 44
Nemours, Fr., 6,345 ... C5 14
Nemunas, riv., Sov. Un ... A6 26
Nemuro, Jap., 42,740 ... E12 37
Nemuro, strait, Jap ... E12 37
Nenagh, Ire., 4,317 ... E3 11
Nenana, Alsk., 286 ... C10 79
Nene, riv., Eng ... B8 12
Nenzel, Cherry, Nebr., 43 ... B4 103
Neodesha, Wilson, Kans., 3,594 ... E8 93
Neoga, Cumberland, Ill., 1,145 ... D5 90
Neola, Pottawattamie, Iowa, 870 ... C2 92
Neola, Duchesne, Utah, 300 ... C5 119
Neon, Letcher, Ky., 766 ... C7 94
Neopit, Shawano, Wis., 1,359 ... D5 124
Neosho, Newton, Mo., 7,452 ... E3 101
Neosho, Dodge, Wis., 345 ... E5 124
Neosho, co., Kans., 19,455 ... E8 93
Neosho, riv., Kans., Okla ... E8 93, B6 112
Neosho Falls, Woodson, Kans., 222 ... D8 93
Neosho Rapids, Lyons, Kans., 178 ... D8 93
Nepal, country, Asia, 9,900,000 ... G11 33, D10 40
Nepaug, res., Conn ... B5 84
Nepewassi, lake, Ont., Can ... A4 72
Nephi, Juab, Utah, 2,566 ... D4 119
Nephton, Ont., Can., 86 ... C7 72
Nepisiguit, bay, N.B., Can ... B4 74
Nepisiguit, riv., N.B., Can ... B3 74
Nepomuk, Czech., 1,046 ... D8 17
Neponset, Bureau, Ill., 495 ... B4 90
Neponset, riv., Mass ... h11 97
Nepton, Fleming, Ky., 125 ... B6 94
Neptune, Sask., Can ... H3 70
Neptune, Monmouth, N.J., 13,000 ... C4 106
Neptune, Cheatham, Tenn ... A4 117
Neptune Beach, Duval, Fla., 2,868 ... B5, B6 86
Neptune City, Monmouth, N.J., 4,013 ... *C4 106
Nera, riv., It ... C4 21
Nérac, Fr., 3,917 ... E4 14
Nerane, Syr ... A7 32
Nerchinsk, Sov. Un., 28,700 ... D14 28
Nerekhta, Sov. Un., 19,900 ... C13 27
Neretva, riv., Yugo ... D3 22
Neris, riv., Sov. Un ... A8 26
Nerja, Sp., 7,224 ... D4 20
Nero, Plaquemines, La., 210 ... C8, E6 95
Nerpichye, Sov. Un., 10,000 ... B12 37
Nerstrand, Rice, Minn., 217 ... F5 99
Nerva, Sp., 12,686 ... D2 20
Nesbit, DeSoto, Miss., 130 ... A3 100
Nesbitt, Man., Can., 86 ... E2 71
Nesco, Atlantic, N.J., 400 ... D3 106
Nesconset, Suffolk, N.Y., 2,500 ... F4 84
Nescopeck, Luzerne, Pa., 1,934 ... D9 114
Nesebur, Bul., 2,289 ... D8 22
Neshaminy, creek, Pa ... C2 106
Neshanic, riv., N.J ... C3 106
Neshanic Station, Somerset, N.J., 400 ... B3 106
Nesher, Isr., 1,700 ... B7 32
Neshkoro, Marquette, Wis., 368 ... E4 124
Neshoba, Neshoba, Miss., 250 ... C4 100
Neshoba, co., Miss., 20,927 ... C4 100
Neskaupstadur, Ice., 1,482 ... n26 25
Neskowin, Tillamook, Oreg., 50 ... B3 113
Nesle, Fr., 2,417 ... E2 15
Nesmith, Williamsburg, S.C., 85 ... D8 115
Nesodden, Nor ... p28 25
Nes op Ameland, Neth., 782 ... A5 15
Nespelem, Okanogan, Wash., 358 ... A7 122
Nesquehoning, Carbon, Pa., 2,714 ... E10 114
Ness, co., Kans., 5,470 ... D4 93
Ness, lake, Scot ... C4 13
Ness City, Ness, Kans., 1,653 ... D4 93
Nesselrode, mtn., Alsk., B.C., Can ... E6 66
Nesselwang, Ger., 2,900 ... B6 18
Nesslau, Switz., 2,002 ... B7 19
Nessmersiel, Ger., 530 ... A7 15
Nesterov, Sov. Un ... A7 26
Nesterov, Sov. Un., 10,000 ... C7 26
Nestoria, Baraga, Mich., 20 ... B2 98
Nestorion, Grc., 3,197 ... B3 23
Nestorville, Barbour, W. Va., 100 ... B5 123
Nestos, riv., Grc ... B5 23
Nesvizh, Sov. Un., 10,000 ... E6 27
Nes Ziona, Isr., 10,917 ... h10 32
Netarts, Tillamook, Oreg., 600 ... B3 113
Netawaka, Jackson, Kans., 225 ... C8 93
Netcong, Morris, N.J., 2,765 ... B3 106
Netherhill, Sask., Can., 111 ... F1 70
Netherlands, country, Eur., 12,200,000 ... E10 8, B5 15
Netherlands Antilles (Netherlands West Indies), dep., N.A., 187,000 ... *B4 53, *n15 64
Netherlands Guiana, see Surinam, Neth. dep., S.A.
Netherlands Indies, see Indonesia, country, Asia
Netherlands New Guinea, see West Irian, Indon. dep., Asia
Netherlands West Indies (Netherlands Antilles), dep., N.A., 208,000 ... *B4 53, *n15 64
Nethy Bridge, Scot ... C5 13
Netolice, Czech., 2,066 ... D9 17
Netrakona, Pak., 12,924 ... E13 40
Nett, lake, Minn ... B5 99
Nettie, Nicholas, W. Va., 600 ... C4 123
Nettilling, lake, N.W. Ter., Can ... C18 67
Nett Lake, St. Louis, Minn., 250 ... B5 99
Nettleton, Craighead, Ark. (part of Jonesboro) ... B5 81
Nettleton, Lee and Monroe, Miss., 1,389 ... A5 100
Nettleton, Caldwell, Mo., 63 ... B4 101
Nettuno, It., 14,100 ... k9 21
Netvorice, Czech., 619 ... o18 26
Neubeckum, Ger., 8,900 ... B3 17
Neubert, Knox, Tenn., 600 ... D10, E11 117
Neubrandenburg, Ger., 33,400 ... B6 16
Neuburg, Ger., 16,500 ... E6 17
Neuchâtel, Switz., 33,430 (*45,930) ... B2 19
Neuchâtel, canton, Switz., 147,633 ... C2 19
Neuchâtel, lake, Switz ... C2 19
Neudorf, Sask., Can., 404 ... G4 70
Neue Elde, riv., Ger ... E5 24
Neuenegg, Switz., 2,921 ... C3 19
Neuenkirchen, Ger., 1,500 ... E3 24
Neuenrade, Ger., 5,600 ... B2 17
Neuerburg, Ger., 1,550 ... D6 15
Neufchâteau, Bel., 2,696 ... E5 15
Neufchâteau, Fr., 4,527 ... C6 14
Neufchâtel-en-Bray, Fr., 5,590 ... C4 14
Neufchâtel-sur-Aisne, Fr., 434 ... E4 15
Neufelden, Aus., 1,034 ... D6 16
Neugersdorf, Ger., 12,300 ... C9 17
Neuhaldensleben, Ger., 22,000 ... B6 16
Neuhardt, Crittenden, Ark ... E8 81
Neuharlingersiel, Ger., 180 ... A7 15
Neuhaus, Ger., 10,500 ... B3 17
Neuhaus, Ger., 4,608 ... C6 17
Neuhaus, Ger., 2,774 ... E4 24
Neuilly [-sur-Marne], Fr., 15,082 ... g11 14
Neuilly-sur-Seine, Fr., 72,773 ... g10 14
Neu-Isenburg, Ger., 25,400 ... C3 17
Neukirchen am Grossvenediger, Aus., 1,932 ... B8 18
Neumarkt, Ger., 3,811 ... A8 15
Neumarkt [in der Oberpfalz], Ger., 15,800 ... D6 17
Neumarkt-Sankt Viet, Ger., 3,500 ... A8 18
Neumarkt, see Sroda Slaska, Pol
Neumünster, Ger., 74,800 ... A4 16, D3 24
Neunburg vorm Wald, Ger., 3,500 ... D7 17
Neunkirch, Switz., 1,208 ... A6 19
Neunkirchen, Aus., 10,027 ... E8 16
Neunkirchen, Ger., 46,100 ... D2 17
Neuquén, Arg., 7,498 ... B3 54
Neuquén, prov., Arg., 111,008 ... B3 54
Neuquén, riv., Arg ... B3 54
Neurara, Chile ... D2 55
Neuruppin, Ger., 22,000 ... B6 16
Neuse, riv., N.C ... B5 109
Neusiedler, lake, Aus ... E8 16
Neuss, Ger., 103,600 ... B1 17
Neustadt, Ont., Can., 493 ... C4 72
Neustadt am Rübenberge, Ger., 9,100 ... F3 24
Neustadt [an der Aisch], Ger., 8,900 ... D5 17
Neustadt [an der Dosse], Ger., 2,152 ... B6 16
Neustadt [an der Orla], Ger., 10,600 ... C6 17
Neustadt an der Waldnaab, Ger., 5,400 ... D7 17
Neustadt [an der Weinstrasse], Ger., 31,600 ... D3 17
Neustadt [bei Coburg], Ger., 12,600 ... C6 17
Neustadt-Glewe, Ger., 6,069 ... E5 24
Neustadt [im Schwarzwald], Ger., 6,900 ... B4 18
Neustadt [in Holstein], Ger., 14,500 ... D4 24
Neustadt [in Sachsen], Ger., 6,094 ... B9 17
Neustadt [Kreis Marburg], Ger., 5,000 ... C4 17
Neustrelitz, Ger., 28,000 ... B6 16
Neu-Ulm, Ger., 24,300 ... D5 16

New Riegel, Seneca, Ohio, 349...A4 111
New River, Maricopa, Ariz., 75...D3 80
New River, Bradford, Fla., 20...C4 86
New River, gorge, W. Va...D7 123
New River, inlet, Fla...E3 86
New River, inlet, N.C...C6 109
New River, Scott, Tenn., 300...C9 117
New Road, N.S., Can., 1,109...E6 74
New Roads, Pointe Coupee, La., 3,965...D4 95
New Rochelle, Westchester, N.Y., 76,812...h13, n15 108
New Rockford, Eddy, N. Dak., 2,177...B6 110
New Ross, N.S., Can., 242...E5 74
New Ross, Montgomery, Ind., 332...E4 91
New Ross, Ire., 4,494...E5 11
Newry, Oxford, Maine, 125 (260▲)...D2 96
Newry, N. Ire., 12,450...C5 11
Newry, Oconee, S.C., 762...B2 115
New Salem, Pike, Ill., 172...D3 90
New Salem, Rush, Ind., 250...E7 91
New Salem, Cowley, Kans., 60...E7 93
New Salem, Franklin, Mass., 100 (397▲)...B3 97
New Salem, Morton, N. Dak., 986...C4 110
New Salem, Fayette, Pa., 860...*G2 114
New Salisbury, Harrison, Ind., 200...H5 91
New Sarepta, Alta., Can., 184...C4 69
New Sarpy, St. Charles, La., 1,259...C7 95
New Sharon, Mahaska, Iowa, 1,063...C5 92
New Sharon, Franklin, Maine, 250 (712▲)...D2 96
New Sharon, Mercer & Monmouth, N.J., 50...C3 106
New Shrewsbury, Monmouth, N.J., 7,313...C4 106
New Siberian, see Novosibirskiye, is., Sov. Un.
Newsite, Tallapoosa, Ala., 100...B4 78
New Site, Prentiss, Miss., 7...A5 100
New Smyrna Beach, Volusia, Fla., 8,781...C6 86
Newsom, Davidson, Tenn...E9 117
Newsoms, Southampton, Va., 423...E5 121
New South Wales, state, Austl., 4,160,000...F8 50
New Straitsville, Perry, Ohio, 1,019...C5 111
New Summerfield, Castro, Tex., 525...B1 118
New Sweden, Aroostook, Maine, 250 (713▲)...B4 96
New Tazewell, Claiborne, Tenn., 768...C10 117
Newton, Dale, Ala., 958...D4 78
Newton, Baker, Ga., 529...E2 87
Newton, Jasper, Ill., 2,901...E5 90
Newton, Jasper, Iowa, 15,381...C4 92
Newton, Harvey, Kans., 14,877...A5, D6 93
Newton, Middlesex, Mass., 92,384...B5, g11 97
Newton, Newton, Miss., 3,178...C4 100
Newton, Rockingham, N.H., 175 (1,419▲)...E4 105
Newton, Sussex, N.J., 6,563...A3 106
Newton, Catawba, N.C., 6,658...B2 109
Newton, Newton, Tex., 1,233...D6 118
Newton, Cache, Utah, 480...B3 119
Newton, Roane, W. Va., 100...C3 123
Newton, Manitowoc, Wis., 60...B6 124
Newton, co., Ark., 5,963...B2 81
Newton, co., Ga., 20,999...C3 87
Newton, co., Ind., 11,502...B3 91
Newton, co., Miss., 19,517...C4 100
Newton, co., Mo., 30,093...E3 101
Newton, co., Tex., 10,372...D6 118
Newton, Abbot, Eng., 18,066...D4 12
Newton Brook, Ont., Can...k15 72
Newton Falls, St. Lawrence, N.Y., 750...A6, f9 108
Newton Falls, Trumbull, Ohio, 5,038...A7 111
Newton Grove, Sampson, N.C., 477...B5 109
Newton Hamilton, Mifflin, Pa., 338...F6 114
Newton Junction, Rockingham, N.H., 225...E4 105
Newton Station, B.C., Can...f13 68
Newton Stewart, Scot., 1,980...F4 13
Newtonville, Ont., Can., 331...D6 72
Newtonville, Spencer, Ind., 125...H4 91
Newtonville, Atlantic, N.J., 200...D3 106
Newtonville, Albany, N.Y., 1,500...*C7 108
New Toronto, Ont., Can., 13,384...D5, m14 72
Newtown, Newf., Can., 585...D5 75
Newtown, Fairfield, Conn., 1,261 (11,373▲)...D3 84
Newtown, Fountain, Ind., 321...D3 91
Newtown, Sullivan, Mo., 265...A4 101
New Town, Mountrail, N. Dak., 1,586...B3 110
Newtown, Hamilton, Ohio, 1,750...C3 111
Newtown, Bucks, Pa., 2,323...F12 114
Newtown, Luzerne, Pa., 2,400...*B8 114
Newtown, King and Queen, Va., 65...D5 121
Newtownabbey, N. Ire., 42,200...*C6 11
Newtown [& Llanllwchaiarn], Wales, 5,512...B4 12
Newtownards, N. Ire., 13,090...C6 11
Newtown Crommelin, N. Ire...C5 11
Newtownhamilton, N. Ire., 589...C5 11
Newtownmountkennedy, Ire., 935...D5 11
Newtown Square, Delaware, Pa., 9,270...D2 106
Newtownstewart, N. Ire., 1,265...C4 11
New Trenton, Franklin, Ind., 150...F8 91
New Ulm, Brown, Minn., 11,114...F4 99
New Ulm, Austin, Tex., 500...E4 116
New Underwood, Pennington, S. Dak., 462...C3 116
New Vienna, Dubuque, Iowa, 265...B6 92
New Vienna, Clinton, Ohio, 858...C4 111
New Village, Warren, N.J., 400...B2 106
Newville, Henry, Ala., 546...D4 78
Newville, Cumberland, Pa., 1,656...F7 114
Newville, Braxton, W. Va., 75...C4 123
New Vineyard, Franklin, Maine, 250 (357▲)...D2 96
New Virginia, Warren, Iowa, 381...C4 92
New Washington, Clark, Ind., 700...G6 91
New Washington, Crawford, Ohio, 1,162...B5 111
New Waterford, N.S., Can., 10,592...C9 74
New Waterford, Columbiana, Ohio, 711...B7 111
New Waverly, Cass, Ind., 200...C5 91
New Waverly, Walker, Tex., 426...D5 118
New Westminster, B.C., Can., 33,654...E6, f13 68
New Whiteland, Johnson, Ind., 3,488...*E5 91
New Wilmington, Lawrence, Pa., 2,203...D1 113
New Windsor, Mercer, Ill., 658...B3 90
New Windsor, Carroll, Md., 738...A3 85
New Windsor, Orange, N.Y., 4,500...*D6 108
New Woodstock, Madison, N.Y., 400...C5 108
New World, isl., Newf., Can...D4 75
New Year, lake, Nev...B2 104
New York, Bronx, Kings, New York, Queens, Richmond, N.Y., 7,781,984 (★15,408,100)...E7, h13 108
New York, co. (Manhattan borough), N.Y., 1,698,281 (part of New York City)...k13 108
New York, state, U.S., 16,782,304...B12 76, 108
New York, peak, Calif...E6 82
New York Mills, Otter Tail, Minn., 828...D3 99
New York Mills, Oneida, N.Y., 3,788...*B5 108
New Zealand, country, Oceania, 2,625,000...I10 7, 51
New Zealand Dependencies, see Cook Islands, Niue, and Tokelau
New Zion, Clarendon, S.C., 200...D7 115
Ney, Defiance, Ohio, 338...A3 111
Ney, lake, Ont., Can...B5 71
Neya, Sov. Un...B2 29
Neye, isl., Guam... 52
Neyrīz, Iran, 19,439...G7 41
Neyshābūr, Iran, 25,820...C9 41
Nezhin, Sov. Un., 59,000...F8 27
Nezperce, Lewis, Idaho, 667...C2 89
Nez Perce, co., Idaho, 27,066...C2 89
Nez Perce, pass, Idaho, Mont...D4 89
Nezpique, bayou, La...D3 95
Ngabang, Indon...E3 35
Ngabe, Con. B...F3 46
Ngala, Nig...D7 45
Ngaloa, bay, Fiji Is... 52
Ngaloa, hbr., Fiji Is... 52
Ngamea, isl., Fiji Is... 52
N'Gaoundéré, Cam...D2 46
Ngara, Tan...B5 48
Ngardmau, Palau... 52
Ngaruangl, reef, Palau Is... 52
Ngaruawahia, N.Z., 3,273...L15 51
Ngatapa, N.Z., 284...M16 51
Ngau, isl., Fiji Is... 52
Ngele Levu, isl., Fiji Is... 52
Ngemelis, is., Palau Is... 52
Ngesebus, isl., Palau Is... 52
Ngidinga, Con. L...C2 48
Ngong, Ken...B6 48
Ngoring Nor, lake, China...E4 34
Ngounié, riv., Gabon...F2 46
Nguigmi, Niger, 2,400...D7 45
Nguru, Nig., 23,084...D7 45
Nha Trang, Viet., 49,150...F8 38
Nhill, Austl., 2,233...H3 51
Niafounké, Mali, 4,300...C4 45
Niagara, Grand Forks, N. Dak., 157...B8 110
Niagara, Marinette, Wis., 2,098...C5 124
Niagara, co., N.Y., 242,269...B2 108
Niagara, cave, Minn...G6 99
Niagara, riv., Ont., Can., N.Y...B1 108
Niagara Falls, Ont., Can., 53,365 (★56,621)...D5 72
Niagara Falls, Niagara, N.Y., 102,394...B1 108
Niagara-on-the-Lake, Ont., Can., 2,712...D5 72
Niagara University, Niagara, N.Y., 2,100...*B1 108
Niamey, Niger, 30,030...D5 45
Niangara, Con. L., 3,301...A4 48
Niangua, Webster, Mo., 287...D5 101
Niangua, riv., Mo...D5 101
Niantic, New London, Conn., 3,400...D8 84
Niantic, Macon, Ill., 629...D4 90
Niarada, Sanders, Mont., 5...C2 102
Niassa, prov., Moz...D6 48
Nibe, Den., 2,494...B3 24
Nibley, Cache, Utah, 333...B4 119
Nicaragua, country, N.A., 1,620,000...H12 61, D5 62
Nicaragua, lake, Nic...E5 62
Nicastro, It., 21,500...E6 21
Nicatous, lake, Maine...C4 96
Nice, Fr., 292,958...F7 14
Nice, former prov., Fr., 339,000...*F7 14
Niceville, Okaloosa, Fla., 4,517...G2 86
Nichicun, lake, Que., Can...h12 73
Nichinan, Jap., 34,200 (61,974▲)...*K5 37
Nicholas, co., Ky., 6,677...B6 94
Nicholas, co., W. Va., 25,414...C4 123
Nicholas, chan., Cuba...D3 64
Nicholasville, Jessamine, Ky., 4,275...C5 94
Nicholls, Coffee, Ga., 930...E4 87
Nichols, Fairfield, Conn. (part of Trumbull)...E4 84
Nichols, Muscatine, Iowa, 329...C6 92
Nichols, Greene, Mo., 100...D4 101
Nichols, Tioga, N.Y., 663...C4 108
Nichols, Marion, S.C., 617...C9 115
Nichols Hills, Oklahoma, Okla., 4,897...B4 112
Nicholson, Pearl River, Miss., 500...E4 100
Nicholson, Wyoming, Pa., 942...C10 114
Nicholson, riv., Austl...C6 50
Nicholville, St. Lawrence, N.Y., 400...f10 108
Nickelsville, Scott, Va., 291...B2 121
Nickerie, riv., Sur...A3 59
Nickerson, Reno, Kans., 1,091...A3, D5 93
Nickerson, Dodge, Nebr., 168...C9 103
Nickerson, hill, Conn...D7 84
Nickleville, Venango, Pa., 50...D2 114
Nicobar, is., India...G9 39
Nicodemus, Graham, Kans., 300...C4 93
Nicola, B.C., Can., 159...D7 68
Nicola, riv., B.C., Can...D7 68
Nicolet, Que., Can., 4,441...C5 73
Nicolet, co., Que., Can., 30,827...C5 73
Nicolet, lake, Mich...B6 98
Nicolet, riv., Que., Can...C5 73
Nicoll, pt., N.Y...G4 84
Nicollet, Nicollet, Minn., 493...F4 99
Nicollet, co., Minn., 23,196...F4 99
Nicolls' Town, Ba. Is., 441...C4 63
Nicoma Park, Oklahoma, Okla., 1,263...B4 112
Nicosia, Cyp., 47,000 (★100,000)...E9 31
Nicosia, It., 17,600...F5 21
Nicotera, It., 9,143...E5 21
Nicoya, C.R., 10,461...E5 62
Nicoya, gulf, C.R...F5 62
Nicoya, pen., C.R...F5 62
Nictaux Falls, N.S., Can., 373...E4 74
Nicuadala, Moz...A6 49
Nida, riv., Pol...C6 26
Nidan, rock, Iwo... 52
Nidd, riv., Eng...F7 13
Nidda, Ger., 4,400...C4 17
Nidda, riv., Ger...C4 17
Nidwalden, sub canton, Switz., 22,188...C5 19
Nidzica, Pol., 2,852...B6 26
Niebüll, Ger., 6,300...D2 24
Niederbronn-les-Bains, Fr., 4,074...F7 15
Niedermarsberg, Ger., 9,000...B3 17
Niederösterreich (Lower Austria), state, Aus., 1,374,012...*D7 16
Niedersachsen (Lower Saxony), state, Ger., 6,641,400...A4 17
Nielsville, Polk, Minn., 183...C2 99
Niemen, see Nemunas, riv., Sov. Un.
Niemodlin, Pol., 2,580...C4 26
Nienburg, Ger., 22,100...B4 16
Niers, riv., Ger...C6 15
Nierstein, Ger., 5,500...D3 17
Niesky, Ger., 7,436...B9 17
Nieszawa, Pol., 2,403...B5 26
Niete, mtn., Lib...E3 45
Nietleben, Ger., 5,208...B6 17
Nieuw Amsterdam, Sur...A3 59
Nieuweroord, Neth., 753...B6 15
Nieuw Nickerie, Sur., 3,472...A3 59
Nieuwpoort, Bel., 6,899...C2 15
Nieuw Singkel, see Singkil Baru, Indon.
Nièvre, dept., Fr., 245,921...*D5 14
Nigadoo, N.B., Can., 361...B4 74
Nigde, Tur., 18,000...D10 29
Nigei, isl., B.C., Can...D4 68
Nigel, S. Afr., 34,008...*C4 49
Niger, country, Afr., 3,275,000...E6 42, C6 45
Niger, riv., Afr...E6 42
Niger, riv. mouths, Nig...F6 45
Nigeria, country, Afr., 43,200,000...E6 45, F6 42
Nigg, Scot., 573...C5 13
Nighthawk, Okanogan, Wash., 15...A6 122
Nightingale, isl., Viet...B7 38
Nigrita, Grc., 8,399...B4 23
Nihing, riv., Pak...H11 41
Nihoa, isl., Haw...m15 88
Nii, isl., Japan...I9 37
Niigata, Jap., 314,528...H9 37
Niigata, pref., Jap., 2,442,037...*H9 37
Niihama, Jap., 125,688...J6 37
Niihau, isl., Haw...B1 88
Niijimahon, Jap., 4,827...o18 37
Niimi, Jap., 15,100...I6 37
Niitsu, Jap., 31,500 (56,110▲)...*H9 37
Níjar, Sp., 2,052...D4 20
Nijkerk, Neth., 8,200...B5 15
Nijmegen, Neth., 137,800 (★162,000)...C5 15
Níkaia, Grc., 83,266...*D4 23
Nikep, Allegany, Md., 215...D2 85
Nikitinka, Sov., Un...D9 27
Nikitovka, Sov. Un., 10,000...q21 27
Nikki, Dah...E5 45
Nikko, Jap., 33,348...H9 37
Nikolayev, Sov. Un., 263,000...H9 27
Nikolayevsk, Sov. Un., 40,000...D17 26
Nikolayevskiy, Sov. Un., 30,000...F15 27
Nikolsk, Sov. Un...B3 29
Nikolski, Alsk., 92...E6 79
Nikonovskoye, Sov. Un...n18 27
Nikopol, Bul., 5,409...D7 22
Nikopol, Sov. Un., 95,000...H10 27
Niksar, Tur., 10,600...B11 31
Nīkshahr, Iran...H10 41
Niksic, Yugo., 20,165...D4 22
Niland, Imperial, Calif., 800...F6 82
Nile, Allegany, N.Y., 120...C2 108
Nile, riv., Sud...A3 47
Niles, Cook, Ill., 25,073...E2 90
Niles, Ottawa, Kans., 105...D6 93
Niles, Berrien, Mich., 13,842...G4 98
Niles, Trumbull, Ohio, 19,545...A7 111
Nilópolis, Braz., 65,368...*C4 56
Nilvange, Fr., 9,337...E6 15
Nilwood, Macoupin, Ill., 274...D4 90
Nimaj, India, 10,000...E5 40
Nimba, mts., Guinea, Lib...E3 45
Nimes, Fr., 99,802...F6 14
Nimmons, Clay, Ark., 154...A5 81
Nimmonsburg, Broome, N.Y., 1,500...*C5 108
Nimpkish, riv., B.C., Can...D4 68
Nimrod, Perry, Ark...C2 81
Nimrod, glacier, Ant...B29 5
Nimrod, res., Ark...C2 81
Nimule, Sud...E3 47
Ninaview, Bent, Colo., 5...D7 83
Nine Mile, creek, Kans...B8 93
Nine Mile, creek, Utah...D5 119
Nine Mile, hill, Tenn...E9 117
Nine Mile, pt., Mich...C6 98
Nine Mile Falls, Spokane, Wash., 80...D7 122
Ninette, Man., Can., 673...E2 71
Ninety Mile, beach, Austl...H7 51
Ninety Six, Greenwood, S.C., 1,435...C3 115
Nineveh, Johnson, Ind., 300...F5 91
Nineveh, Greene, Pa., 100...G1 114
Nineveh, ruins, Iraq...D14 31
Ninga, Man., Can., 129...E2 71
Ningan, China, 40,000...C10 34, D4 37
Ningchiang, China...H2 36
Ningchin, China, 15,000...F6 36
Ningching, China...F4 34
Ningerh, China...D11 39
Ninghai, China, 13,000...J9 36
Ninghsien, China, 5,000...D6 34
Ninghua, China, 21,000...K7 36
Ningming, China...A7 38
Ningpo (Ninghsien), China, 237,500...F9 34
Ningsia, see Yinchwan, China
Ningsia Hui, auton. reg., China, 1,822,000...D6 34
Ningte, China, 30,000...K8 36
Ningtu, China, 32,000...K6 36
Ningwu, China...E5 36
Ninh Binh, Viet., 25,000...B6 38
Ninilchik, Alsk., 169...C9, g16 79
Ninnekah, Grady, Okla., 300...C4 112
Ninnescah, riv., Kans...E5 93
Ninnis, glacier, Ant...C27 5
Ninole, Hawaii, Haw., 112...D6 88
Ninove, Bel., 11,831...D4 15
Nioaque, Braz., 2,578...C1 56
Niobe, Ward, N. Dak., 67...A3 110
Niobrara, Knox, Nebr., 736...B7 103
Niobrara, co., Wyo., 3,750...B8 125
Niobrara, creek, Wyo...C8 125
Niobrara, riv., Nebr...B7 103
Nioki, Con. L...B2 48
Nioro, Mali, 6,100...C3 45
Nioro, Sen...D1 45
Niort, Fr., 37,512...D3 14
Niota, Hancock, Ill., 250...C2 90
Niota, McMinn, Tenn., 679...D9 117
Niotaze, Chautauqua, Kans., 124...E8 93
Nipawin, Sask., Can., 3,836...D4 70
Nipawin, prov. park, Sask., Can...C3 70
Nipekamew, lake, Sask., Can...C3 70
Nipigon, Ont., Can., 2,105...o17 72
Nipigon, lake, Ont., Can...o17 72
Nipishish, lake, Newf., Can...g9 75
Nipissing, dist., Ont., Can., 70,568...A5 72
Nipissing, lake, Ont., Can...A5 72
Nipissing Junction, Ont., Can., 323...A5 72
Nipomo, San Luis Obispo, Calif., 550...E3 82
Nippers Harbour, Newf., Can., 236...D4 75
Nipton, San Bernardino, Calif., 40...E6 82
Niquelândia, Braz., 1,262...A3 56
Niquero, Cuba, 5,437...E5 64
Nirasaki, Jap., 11,500...n17 37
Nirmal, India, 19,896...H7 40
Niš (Nish), Yugo., 81,073...D5 22
Nisa, Port., 5,617...C2 20
Nisava, riv., Yugo...D6 22
Nish (Niš), Yugo., 81,073...D5 22
Nishi, Iwo... 52
Nishino, isl., Pac. O...E8 7
Nishinomiya, Jap., 262,608...*o14 37
Nishinotoro, see Dalnyaya, Sov. Un.
Nishio, Jap., 38,200 (67,592▲)...*I9 37
Nishnabotna, riv., Iowa...D2 92
Nisiros, isl., Grc...D6 23
Nisko, Pol., 6,590...C7 26
Nisland, Butte, S. Dak., 211...C2 116
Nisqually, riv., Wash...C3 122
Nissan, riv., Swe...B7 24
Nissum, fjord, Den...B2 24
Nisswa, Crow Wing, Minn., 742...D4 99
Nistowiak, lake, Sask., Can...B3 70
Nisula, Houghton, Mich., 45...B2 98
Niterói, Braz., 228,826...C4, h6 56
Nith, riv., Scot...E5 13
Nitra, Czech., 34,200...D5 26
Nitra, riv., Czech...D5 26
Nitro, Kanawha and Putnam, W. Va., 6,894...C3 123
Nitta Yuma, Sharkey, Miss., 150...B3 100
Nittenau, Ger., 3,300...D7 17
Niue, N.Z. dep., Oceania, 5,000...*H11 7
Nivelles, Bel., 14,345...D4 15
Nivernais, former prov., Fr., 236,000...D5 14
Nivernais, hills, Fr...D5 14
Niverville, Man., Can., 474...E3 71
Nivskiy, Sov. Un...D15 25
Niwka, Pol., 2,500...g10 26
Niwot, Boulder, Colo., 150...A5 83
Nixa, Christian, Mo., 944...D4 101
Nixburg, Coosa, Ala., 30...C3 78
Nixon, Washoe, Nev., 200...D2 104
Nixon, Middlesex, N.J., 10,000...B4 106
Nixon, Gonzales, Tex., 1,751...E4, B4 118
Nizamabad, India, 79,093...H7 40
Nizamsagar, lake, India...H6 40
Nizhmozero, Sov. Un...E17 25
Nizhne-Chirskaya, Sov. Un., 2,000...G14 27
Nizhne-Kolymsk, Sov. Un...C19 28
Nizhneudinsk, Sov. Un., 35,900...D12 28
Nizhneye, Sov. Un., 10,000...q21 27
Nizhniye Narykary, Sov. Un...C21 9
Nizhniy-Lomov, Sov. Un., 5,000...E14 27
Nizhniy-Tagil, Sov. Un., 359,000...B5 29
Nizhnyaya Tunguska, riv., Sov. Un...C12 28
Nizhnyaya Tura, Sov. Un., 20,400...D21 9
Nizmennyy, cape, Sov. Un...E7 37
Nizza Monferrato, It., 9,372...E4 18
Njombe, Tan., 7,560...C5 48
Njurunda, Swe., 1,540...F7 25
Nkai, Rh...A4 49
Nkangsamba, Cam...E1 46
Nkata Bay, Malawi...D5 48
Noah, Coffee, Tenn...B5 117
Noakhali, Pak., 16,677...F13 40
Noank, New London, Conn., 1,200...D9 84
Noasca, It., 963...D3 17
Noatak, Alsk., 275...B7 79
Noatak, riv., Alsk...B7 79
Nobel, Ont., Can., 693...B4 72
Nobeoka, Jap., 100,000 (122,527▲)...J5 37
Noble, Walker, Ga., 200...B1 87
Noble, Richland, Ill., 761...E5 90
Noble, Sabine, La., 206...C2 95
Noble, Cleveland, Okla., 995...B4 112
Noble, co., Ind., 28,162...B7 91
Noble, co., Ohio, 10,982...C6 111
Noble, co., Okla., 10,376...A4 112
Nobleboro, Lincoln, Maine, 75 (679▲)...D3 96
Nobleford, Alta., Can., 309...E4 69
Noble Lake, Jefferson, Ark., 100...C4 81
Nobles, co., Minn., 23,365...G3 99
Noblesville, Hamilton, Ind., 7,664...D5 91
Nobleton, Hernando, Fla., 150...D4 86
Noboribetsu, Jap...E10 37
Nobscot, hill, Mass...B5 97
Nocatee, De Soto, Fla., 750...E5 86
Nocera Inferiore, It., 45,200...*D5 21
Nochixtlán, Mex., 2,571...o15 63
Nocona, Montague, Tex., 3,127...C4 118
Noda, Jap., 30,900 (54,150▲)...*I9 37
Noda, see Chekhov, Sov. Un.
Nodaway, Adams, Iowa, 204...D3 92
Nodaway, co., Mo., 22,215...A3 101
Nodaway, riv., Iowa, Mo...D2 92, A2 101
Node, Niobrara, Wyo., 15...C8 125
Nodoa, China...C8 38
Noel, McDonald, Mo., 736...E3 101
Noel Paul's, brook, Newf., Can...D3 75
Noelville, Ont., Can., 393...A4 72
Noemfoor, isl., W. Irian...F8 35
Nogal, Lincoln, N. Mex., 40...D4 107
Nogal, riv., Som...D6 47
Nogales, Santa Cruz, Ariz., 7,286...F5 80
Nogales, Mex., 37,655...A2 63
Nogales, Mex., 11,179...n15 63
Nogara, It., 7,239...D7 18
Nogata, Jap., 62,179...J5 37
Nogent-en-Bassigny, Fr., 4,208...C6 14
Nogent-le-Rotrou, Fr., 9,428...C4 14
Nogent [-sur-Marne], Fr., 24,501...g10 14
Nogent-sur-Seine, Fr., 3,777...C5 14
Noginsk, Sov. Un., 98,000...B1 29
Nogoa, riv., Austl...B6 51
Nogoyá, Arg., 12,051...A5 54
Nograd, co., Hung., 236,393...*A4 22
Nogueira, Sp., 7,791...A2 20
Nohar, India, 13,728...C5 40
Noheji, Jap., 9,900...F10 37
Nohly, Richland, Mont., 5...C12 102
Noho, China, 5,000...B2 37
Noire, riv., Que., Can...A7 72
Noire, riv., Upper Volta...D4 45
Noirmoutier, isl., Fr...D2 14
Noisy-le-Sec, Fr., 31,187...g10 14
Nojima, cape, Jap...I9 37
Nokkeushi, see Kitami, Jap.
Nok Kundi, Pak...G11 41
Nokomis, Sask., Can., 560...F3 70
Nokomis, Sarasota, Fla., 2,253...E4 86
Nokomis, Montgomery, Ill., 2,476...D4 90
Nokomis, lake, Wis...C4 124
Nokrek, peak, India...E13 40
Nola, Scott, Ark., 25...C2 81
Nola, Cen. Afr. Rep...E3 46
Nola, It., 16,400...D5 21
Nola, Lawrence, Miss., 125...D3 100
Nolan, Nolan, Tex., 100...C2 118
Nolan, Mingo, W. Va., 787...D2 123
Nolan, co., Tex., 18,963...C2 118
Nolensville, Williamson, Tenn., 400...B5 117
Nolin, flood control res., Ky...C3 94
Nolin, riv., Ky...C3 94
Nolinsk, Sov. Un., 9,600...B3 29
Noma, Holmes, Fla., 344...G3 86
Noma, cape, Jap...K5 37
Nomans Land, isl., Mass...D6 97
Nome, Alsk., 2,316...C6 79
Nome, Barnes, N. Dak., 145...C8 110
Nomeny, Fr., 964...F6 15
Nominingue, Que., Can., 744...C2 73
Nomme, Sov. Un., 18,026...*B5 27
Nonacho, lake, N.W. Ter., Can...D11 66
Nonconnah, Shelby, Tenn...E8 117
Nonconnah, creek, Tenn...E8 117
Nondalton, Alsk., 205...C8 79
Nonesuch, riv., Maine...E4 96
Nong Khai, Thai., 16,925...D5 38
Nongoma, S. Afr., 1,650...C5 49
Nonni, riv., China...B9 34, B2 37
Nonoava, Mex., 1,582...B3 63
Noodle, Jones, Tex., 60...C3 118
Nooksack, Whatcom, Wash., 318...A3 122
Nooksack, riv., Wash...A3 122
Noonan, Divide, N. Dak., 625...A2 110
Noord Pagai, isl., Indon...F2 35
Noordoostelijke Polder (North-eastern Polder), reg., Neth., 15,938...B5 15
Noordwijk-Binnen, Neth., 8,300...B4 15
Noorvik, Alsk., 384...B7 79
Nooseneck, Kent, R.I., 40...C10 84
Nootka, isl., B.C., Can...E4 68
Nootka, sound, B.C., Can...E4 68
Nopal, De Witt, Tex., 15...E4 118
No Point, pt., Md...D5 85
Noquebay, lake, Wis...C6 124
Nóqui, Ang., 406...C1 48
Nora, Sask., Can., 72...E4 70
Nora, Jo Daviess, Ill., 229...A4 90
Nora, Marion, Ind., 200...H8 91
Nora, Nuckolls, Nebr., 60...D8 103
Nora, Swe., 4,100...H6 25
Noranda, Que., Can., 11,477...k11 73
Nora Springs, Floyd, Iowa, 1,275...A5 92
Nor-Bayazet, Sov. Un., 8,986...B15 29
Norbeck, Faulk, S. Dak., 10...B6 116
Norborne, Carroll, Mo., 965...B4 101
Norcatur, Decatur, Kans., 302...C3 93
Norco, Riverside, Calif., 4,964...*F3 82
Norco, St. Charles, La., 4,682...B6, D5 95
Norcross, Gwinnett, Ga., 1,605...A5, C2 87
Norcross, Grant, Minn., 153...E2 99
Nord, canal, Fr...D3 15
Nord, dept., Fr., 2,293,112...D3 15
Nord, mts., Hai...F7 64
Nördborg, Den., 2,563...C3 24
Nordby, Den., 1,975...C2 24
Nordby, Den., 313...C4 24
Nordegg, Alta., Can...C2, g7 69
Nordegg, riv., Alta., Can...C3 69
Norden, Ger., 16,200...B3 16
Norden, Keya Paha, Nebr., 15...B5 103
Nordenham, Ger., 26,900...B4 16
Nordenskjöld, arch., Sov. Un...B4 4
Nordenskjold, ice tongue, Ant...e39 5
Norderney, Ger., 7,300...A7 15
Norderney, isl., Ger...A7 15
Nordfjord, fjord, Nor...G1 25
Nordhausen, Ger., 40,800...B5 17
Nordheim, Winnebago, Wis., 900...*D5 124
Nordhorn, Ger., 40,400...B3 16
Nordland, Jefferson, Wash., 100...A3 122
Nordland, co., Nor., 225,394...*D6 25
Nördlingen, Ger., 14,400...E5 17
Nordmaling, Swe., 1,150...F8 25
Nordman, Bonner, Idaho, 25...A2 89
Nordreisa, Nor...C9 25
Nordrhein-Westfalen (North Rhine-Westphalia), state, Ger., 15,901,700...B2 17
Nordstrand, isl., Ger...A4 16
Nord-Tröndelag, co., Nor., 112,185...*E4 25
Nordvik, Sov. Un., 2,500...B14 28
Nore, riv., Ire...E4 11
Norene, Wilson, Tenn., 70...A5 117
Norfield, Lincoln, Miss., 50...D3 100
Norfolk, Litchfield, Conn., 900 (1,827▲)...B4 84
Norfolk, Norfolk, Mass., 350 (3,471▲)...h10 97
Norfolk, Madison, Nebr., 13,640...B8 103
Norfolk, St. Lawrence, N.Y., 1,353...f9 108
Norfolk (Independent City), Va., 305,872 (★578,500)...B7, E6 121
Norfolk, co., Ont., Can., 50,475...E4 72
Norfolk, co., Eng., 561,980...B9 12
Norfolk, co., Mass., 510,256...B5 97
Norfolk, is., Pac. O...H10 7
Norfolk Highlands, Norfolk, Va., 1,000...*E6 121
Norfolk Island, Austl. dep., Oceania, 1,000...H10 7
Norfork, Baxter, Ark., 283...A3 81
Norfork, dam, Ark...A3 81
Norfork, lake, Ark...A3 81
Norge, Grady, Okla., 60...C4 112
Norias, Kenedy, Tex., 25...F4 118
Norilsk, Sov. Un., 117,000...C11 28
Norland, Ont., Can., 257...C6 72
Norland, Dickenson, Va...B2 121
Norlina, Warren, N.C., 927...A5 109
Norma, Salem, N.J., 700...E2 106
Norma, Renville, N. Dak., 84...A4 110
Norma, Scott, Tenn., 250...C9 117
Normal, Madison, Ala., 1,500...A3 78
Normal, McLean, Ill., 13,357...C5 90
Norman, Montgomery, Ark., 482...C2 81
Norman, Jackson, Ind., 130...G5 91
Norman, Kearney, Nebr., 57...D7 103
Norman, Richmond, N.C., 220...B4 109
Norman, Cleveland, Okla., 33,412...B4 112
Norman, co., Minn., 11,253...C2 99
Norman, isl., Vir. Is...F16 65
Norman, riv., Austl...C7 50

Normanby, riv., Austl...B7 50
Normandin, Que., Can., 1,838...*D4 73
Normandy, Duval, Fla., 1,900...*B5 86
Normandy, former prov., Fr., 2,407,000...C4 14
Normandy, St. Louis, Mo., 4,452...A8 101
Normandy, Bedford, Tenn., 119...B5 117
Normandy, hills, Fr...C3 14
Normandy Beach, Ocean, N.J., 100...C4 106
Normandy Park, King, Wash., 3,224...*D2 122
Normangee, Madison and Leon, Tex., 718...D4 118
Normanna, Bee, Tex., 130...E4 118
Norman Park, Colquitt, Ga., 891...E3 87
Norman's Cove, Newf., Can., 571...*D5 75
Normanton, Austl., 234...C7 50
Normantown, Toombs, Ga., 49...D4 87
Norman Wells, N.W. Ter., Can., 297...C7 66
Nornalup, Austl...F2 50
Norphlet, Union, Ark., 457...D3 81
Norquay, Sask., Can., 498...F4 70
Ñorquincó, Arg...C2 54
Norrahammar, Swe., 5,600...A8 24
Norra Värmdö, Swe...t36 25
Norrbotten, co., Swe., 262,600...*E10 25
Nørre Åby, Den., 1,844...C3 24
Nørre Alslev, Den., 1,062...D5 24
Nørresundby, Den., 10,456...A3 24
Norridge, Cook, Ill., 14,087...*E3 90
Norridgewock, Somerset, Maine, 850 (1,634▲)...D3 96
Norrie, Marathon, Wis., 65...D4 124
Norris, Fulton, Ill., 307...C3 90
Norris, Madison, Mont., 25...E5 102
Norris, Pickens, S.C., 594...B2 115
Norris, Mellette, S. Dak., 100...D4 116
Norris, Anderson, Tenn., 1,389...C9 117
Norris, dam, Tenn...C9 117
Norris, lake, Tenn...C10 117
Norris Arm, Newf., Can., 1,226...D4 75
Norris City, White, Ill., 1,243...F5 90
Norris Point, Newf., Can., 711...D3 75
Norristown, Montgomery, Pa., 38,925...A10, F11 114
Norrisville, Harford, Md., 75...A4 85
Norrköping, Swe., 92,300...H7, u34 25
Norrtälje, Swe., 8,900...H8, t36 25
Norseman, Austl., 2,104...F3 50
Norte, chan., Braz...B4 59
Norte, range, Braz...E3 59
Norte de Santander, dept., Col., 403,420...B3 60
North, Orangeburg, S.C., 1,047...D5 115
North, Mathews, Va., 150...D6 121
North, div., Ice., 28,388...*n23 25
North, bay, Utah...B3 119
North (Metedeconk, riv.) branch, N.J...C4 106
North (Lamoille, riv.) branch, Vt...B3 120
North (Winooski, riv.) branch, Vt...C3 120
North, cape, N.S., Can...B9 74
North, cape, N.Z...K14 51
North, cape, Nor...B11 25
North, cape, P.R...e10 65
North, cape, Svalbard...A12 4
North, chan., Ont., Can...A2 72
North, chan., N. Ire...C4 10
North, creek, Ga...B5 87
North (Flathead, riv.) fork, Mont...B2 102
North, fork, Wyo...A3 125
North, inlet, S.C...E9 115
North, isl., N.Z...M14 51
North, isl., S.C...E9 115
North, is., La...E7 95
North, mtn., Okla...C3 112
North, mtn., Pa...D9 114
North, mtn., Va...C4 121
North, park, Pa...A5 114
North, pass, La...E6 95
North, plains, N. Mex...C1 107
North, pt., P.E.I., Can...B6 74
North, pt., Md...B5 85
North, pt., Md...C5 85
North, pt., Mich...C7 98
North, pond, Maine...D3 96
North, pond, Mass...h9 97
North, riv., Ala...B2 78
North, riv., Newf., Can...B3 75
North, riv., Fla...C6 86
North, riv., Mass...h12 97
North, riv., Vt...F3 120
North, riv., Va...D3 121
North, sea, Eur...D9 8
North, sound, Ire...D2 11
North, sound, Scot...A6 13
North Abington, Plymouth, Mass., 3,600...B6, h12 97
North Adams, Berkshire, Mass., 19,905...A1 97
North Adams, Hillsdale, Mich., 494...G6 98
North Albany, Benton, Oreg. C1 113
Northallerton, Eng., 6,720...F7 13
Northam, Austl., 7,200...F2 50
Northam, Eng., 6,572...C3 12
North America, cont., 289,700,000...C14 3, 61
North Amherst, Hampshire, Mass., 1,100...B2 97
North Amity, Aroostook, Maine, (206▲)...C5 96
North Amityville, Suffolk, N.Y., 11,000...*G3 84
Northampton, Austl., 626...E1 50
Northampton, Eng., 105,400...D6 10, B7 12
Northampton, Hampshire, Mass., 30,058...B2 97
Northampton, Northampton, Pa., 8,866...E11 114
Northampton, co., Eng., 398,132...B7 12
Northampton, co., N.C., 26,811...A6 109
Northampton, co., Pa., 201,412...E11 114
Northampton, co., Va., 16,966...D7 121
North Andaman, isl., India...F9 39
North Andover, Essex, Mass., 10,908...A5 97
North Anna, riv., Va...C5 121
North Anson, Somerset, Maine, 700...D3 96
North Apollo, Armstrong, Pa., 1,741...E2 114
North Arlington, Bergen, N.J., 17,477...h8 106
North Asheboro (Balfours), Randolph, N.C., 3,805...*B4 109
North Atlanta, DeKalb, Ga., 12,661...C2 87
North Atlantic, ocean...D18 3
North Attleboro, Bristol, Mass., 14,777...C5 97
North Augusta, Ont., Can., 247...C9 72
North Augusta, Aiken, S.C., 10,348...D4 114
North Aulatsivik, isl., Newf., Can...f9 75
North Aurora, Kane, Ill., 2,088...F1 90
North Babylon, Suffolk, N.Y., 25,000...*G3 84
North Baltimore, Wood, Ohio, 3,011...A4 111
North Bancroft, Aroostook, Maine...C5 96
North Bangor, Franklin, N.Y., 500...f10 108
North Barrackpore, India, 56,683...*F12 40
North Battleford, Sask., Can., 11,230...E1, n7 70
North Battle Mountain, Lander, Nev., 10...C5 104
North Bay, Ont., Can., 23,781...A5, p20 72
North Bay, Dade, Fla., 2,006...*G6 86
North Bay, riv., Newf., Can...E4 75
North Beach, Calvert, Md., 606...C4 85
North Belle Vernon, Westmoreland, Pa., 3,148...*F2 114
North Bellingham, Norfolk, Mass., 400...h10 97
North Bellmore, Nassau, N.Y., 23,000...*G2 84
North Bellport, Suffolk, N.Y., 4,200...*G5 84
North Belmont, Gaston, N.C., 3,000...B2 109
North Bend, B.C., Can., 340...E7 68
North Bend, Dodge, Nebr., 1,174...C9 103
North Bend, Hamilton, Ohio, 622...D1 111
North Bend, Coos, Oreg., 7,512...D2 113
North Bend, Clinton, Pa., 800...D6 114
North Bend, King, Wash., 945...B4 122
North Bend, Jackson, Wis., 100...D2 124
North Bennington, Bennington, Vt., 1,437...F2 120
North Bergen, Hudson, N.J., 42,387...h8 106
North Berwick, York, Maine, 1,295 (1,844▲)...E2 96
North Berwick, Scot., 4,161...D6 13
North Billerica, Middlesex, Mass., 4,000...A5, f10 97
North Bloomfield, Trumbull, Ohio, 350...A7 111
North Bonneville, Skamania, Wash., 494...D4 122
North Borneo, see Sabah, reg., Mala.
Northboro, Page, Iowa, 135...D2 92
Northboro, Worcester, Mass., 2,900 (6,687▲)...B4 97
North Brabant, prov., Neth., 1,512,800...C5 15
North Braddock, Allegheny, Pa., 13,204...F2 114
North Bradford, Penobscot, Maine, 100...C4 96
North Bradley, Midland, Mich., 220...E6 98
North Branch, Allegany, Md., 250...D2 85
North Branch, Lapeer, Mich., 901...E7 98
North Branch, Chisago, Minn., 949...E6 99
North Branch, Somerset, N.J., 700...B3 106
North Branford, New Haven, Conn., 600 (6,771▲)...D5 84
North Brewer, Penobscot, Maine (part of Brewer)...D4 96
Northbridge, Worcester, Mass., 2,180 (10,800▲)...B4 97
North Bridgton, Cumberland, Maine, 300...D2 96
North Brook, Ont., Can., 369...C7 72
Northbrook, Cook, Ill., 11,635...E2 90
North Brookfield, Worcester, Mass., 2,615 (3,616▲)...B3 97
North Brooksville, Hancock, Maine, 100...D4 96
North Brother, mtn., Maine...C4 96
North Brunswick, Middlesex, N.J., 10,099...*C4 106
North Buena Vista, Clayton, Iowa, 50...B7 92
North Calais, Washington, Vt., 35...C4 120
North Caldwell, Essex, N.J., 4,163...B4 106
North Canaan (Town of), Litchfield, Conn. (2,836▲)...*A3 84
North Canadian, riv., Okla...A1 112
North Canton, Hartford, Conn., 250...B5 84
North Canton, Cherokee, Ga., 1,996...B2 87
North Canton, Stark, Ohio, 7,727...B6 111
North Cape, Racine, Wis., 200...F1 124
North Cape May, Cape May, N.J., 3,200...F3 106
North Carolina, state, U.S., 4,556,155...C12 77, 109
North Carrollton, Carroll, Miss., 521...B4 100
North Carver, Plymouth, Mass., 400...C6 97
North Catasauqua, Northampton, Pa., 2,805...*E11 114
North Cedar, Black Hawk, Iowa, 1,500...*B5 92
North Charleroi, Washington, Pa., 2,259...*F2 114
North Charleston, Charleston, S.C., 22,339...F2, F8 115
North Charlestown, Sullivan, N.H., 75...D2 105
North Chelmsford, Middlesex, Mass., 4,500...A5 97
North Chicago, Lake, Ill., 22,938...A6, E2 90
North Chili, Monroe, N.Y., 1,350...*B3 108
North Chillicothe, Peoria, Ill., 2,259...C4 90
North City, King, Wash., 2,000...*B3 122
North Clarendon, Rutland, Vt., 250...D3 120
North Cohasset, Norfolk, Mass., 500...h12 97
North Cohocton, Steuben, N.Y., 300...C3 108
North College Hill, Hamilton, Ohio, 12,035...D2 111
North Collins, Erie, N.Y., 1,574...C2 108
North Concord, Essex, Vt., 60...C5 120
North Conway, Carroll, N.H., 1,104...B4 105
North Corbin, Laurel, Ky., 950...*D5 94
North Cornville, Somerset, Maine...D3 96
North Coroin, Laurel, Ky., 950...D5 94
Northcote, Austl., 56,100...*H5 51
North Coventry, Tolland, Conn...B7 84
Northcraft, Fulton, Pa...G5 114
North Creek, Warren, N.Y., 900...B7 108
Northcrest, Del Norte, Calif., 1,945...*B1 82
North Dakota, state, U.S., 632,446...A7 76, 110
North Danville, Caledonia, Vt., 100...C4 120
North Dartmouth, Bristol, Mass., 4,000...C6 97
North Decatur, De Kalb, Ga., 10,000...*C2 87
North Derby, Orleans, Vt., 40...B4 120
North Dighton, Bristol, Mass., 1,200...C5 97
North Dixmont, Penobscot, Maine, 100...D3 96
North Dorset, Bennington, Vt., 25...E3 120
North Downs, hills, Eng...C8 12
North Druid Hills, De Kalb, Ga., 4,000...*C2 87
North East, Cecil, Md., 1,628...A6 85
North East, Erie, Pa., 4,217...B2 114
Northeast, cape, Alsk...C6 79
North East, isl., Nor...A12 4
North East, is., Truk...52
Northeast, pass, La...E6 95
Northeast, pt., Newf., Can...B4 75
Northeast, pond, N.H...D5 105
Northeast, riv., Md...A6 85
North East Carry, Piscataquis, Maine, 9...C3 96
Northeastern Polder (Noordoostelijke Polder), prov., Neth., 28,800...B5 15
North East Frontier Agency, ter., India, 336,558...*C10 39
Northeast Harbor, Hancock, Maine, 750...D4 96
Northeast New Guinea, reg., N. Gui., 1,320,000...k12 50
North Eastham, Barnstable, Mass., 250...C8 97
North Easton, Bristol, Mass., 3,300...B5 97
Northeast Providence, chan., Ba. Is...C5 64
North Egremont, Berkshire, Mass., 250...B1 97
Northeim, Ger., 19,300...B5 17
North Emporia, Greensville, Va. (part of Emporia)...E5 121
North End, Grafton, N.H...C3 105
North English, Iowa, Iowa, 1,004...C5 92
North Enid, Garfield, Okla., 286...A4 112
Northern, prov., Malawi...D5 48
Northern, prov., Zambia...D5 48
Northern, reg., Ghana...E4 45
Northern, reg., Ken...A6 48
Northern, reg., Nig., 16,840...D6 45
Northern, reg., Sud., 873,059...B2 47
Northern, reg., Tan., 771,426...B6 48
Northern, reg., Ug...A5 48
Northern, head, N.B., Can...E3 74
Northern Arm, Newf., Can., 606...D4 75
Northern Cheyenne, Indian res., Mont...E10 102
North Dvina, riv., Sov. Un...C17 9
Northern Indian, lake, Man., Can...A3 71
Northern Ireland, reg., U.K., 1,460,000...C3 10
Northern Light, lake, Ont., Can. A7 99
Northern Rhodesia, see Zambia, country, Afr.
Northern Sporades, is., Grc...C5 23
Northern Territory, ter., Austl., 51,000...B5 50
North Esk, riv., Scot...D6 13
North Fabius, riv., Mo...A6 101
North Fairfield, Huron, Ohio, 547...A5 111
North Falmouth, Barnstable, Mass., 600...C6 97
North Fayette, Kennebec, Maine, 220...D2 96
North Ferrisburg, Addison, Vt., 100...C2 120
Northfield, B.C., Can., 610...f12 68
Northfield, Litchfield, Conn., 350...C4 84
Northfield, Cook, Ill., 4,005...*E3 90
Northfield, Washington, Maine, 50 (79▲)...D5 96
Northfield, Franklin, Mass., 1,179 (2,320▲)...A3 97
Northfield, Rice, Minn., 8,707...F5 99
Northfield, Merrimack, N.H., 1,243 (1,784▲)...D3 105
Northfield, Atlantic, N.J., 5,849...E3 106
Northfield, Summit, Ohio, 1,055...B2 111
Northfield (P.O.), Summit, Ohio, 2,427...*B2 111
Northfield, Motley, Tex., 60...B2 118
Northfield, Washington, Vt., 2,159 (4,511▲)...C3 120
Northfield, Jackson, Wis., 50...D2 124
Northfield, mts., Vt...C3 120
Northfield Center, Washington, Vt., 170...C3 120
Northfield Falls, Washington, Vt., 325...C3 120
North Fond du Lac, Fond du Lac, Wis., 2,549...B5, E5 124
Northford, New Haven, Conn., 300...D5 84
North Fork, Madera, Calif., 200...D4 82
North Fork, Lemhi, Idaho, 30...D5 89
North Fork Republican, riv., Colo A8 82
North Foster, Providence, R.I., 80...B10 84
North Fox, isl., Mich...C5 98
North Franklin, New London, Conn., 60...C8 84
North Freedom, Sauk, Wis., 579...E4 124
North Frisian, is., Ger...A4 16
North Fryeburg, Oxford, Maine, 150...D2 96
North Galiano, B.C., Can., 40...f12 68
North Gamboa (Gamboa), C.Z., 3,489...k11 62
Northgate, Sask., Can., 70...H4 70
Northgate, Burke, N. Dak., 65...A3 110
North Glen Ellyn, Du Page, Ill., 1,500...*F2 90
North Gower, Ont., Can., 398...B9 72
North Grafton, Worcester, Mass., 3,000...B4 97
North Granby, Hartford, Conn., 200...B5 84
North Gray, Cumberland, Maine...E5 96
North Great River, Suffolk, N.Y., 8,000...*G4 84
North Greenville, Washington, Miss., 2,516...*B2 100
North Grosvenor Dale, Windham, Conn., 2,000...B9 84
North Groton, Grafton, N.H C3 105
North Guilford, New Haven, Conn...D6 84
North Guilford, Piscataquis, Maine, 30...C3 96
North Gulfport, Harrison, Miss., 3,323...*E4 100
North Haledon, Passaic, N.J., 6,026...*B4 106
North Hampton, Rockingham, N.H., 678 (1,910▲)...E5 105
North Hampton, Clark, Ohio, 495...C4 111
North Hanover, Plymouth, Mass., 400...h12 97
North Harlowe, Craven, N.C...C7 109
North Hartland, Windsor, Vt., 250...D4 120
North Hartland, res., Vt...D4 120
North Hartsville, Darlington, S.C., 1,899...*C7 115
North Hatfield, Hampshire, Mass., 200...B2 97
North Hatley, Que., Can., 719...D6 73
North Haven, New Haven, Conn., 15,935...D5 84
North Haven, Knox, Maine, 330 (384▲)...D4 102
North Haven, pen., N.Y...E7 84
North Haverhill, Grafton, N.H., 300...B2 105
North Havre, Hill, Mont., 1,168...B7 102
North Head, N.B., Can., 609...E3 74
North Henderson, Mercer, Ill., 210...B3 90
North Henderson, Vance, N.C., 1,995...*A5 109
North Hero, Grand Isle, Vt., 25 (328▲)...B2 120
North Hero, isl., Vt...B2 120
North Highlands, Sacramento, Calif., 21,271...*A6 82
North Holland (Noordholland), prov., Neth., 2,073,100...B4 15
North Holston, Smyth, Va., 200...B3 121
North Horn, lake, Tenn...E8 117
North Hornell, Steuben, N.Y., 917...*C3 108
North Horr, Ken...A6 48
North Hudson, Essex, N.Y., 65...B7 108
North Hudson, St. Croix, Wis., 1,019...*D1 124
North Hyde Park, Lamoille, Vt., 225...B3 120
North Industry, Stark, Ohio, 1,800...B6 111
North Irwin, Westmoreland, Pa., 1,143...*F2 114
North Isleboro, Waldo, Maine, 50...D4 96
North Jackson, Mahoning, Ohio, 700...A7 111
North Java, Wyoming, N.Y., 250...C2 108
North Jay, Franklin, Maine, 500...D2 96
North Judson, Starke, Ind., 1,942...B4 91
North Kamloops, B.C., Can., 6,456...D7 68
North Kansas City, Clay, Mo., 5,657...E2 101
North Kennebunkport (Arundel), York, Maine (907▲)...E2 96
North Kingstown (Wickford), Washington, R.I., 3,500 (18,977▲)...C11 84
North Kingsville, Ashtabula, Ohio, 1,854...A7 111
North La Junta, Otero, Colo., 950...C7 83
Northlake, Cook, Ill., 12,318...*F2 90
North Lake, Marquette, Mich., 400...B3 98
North Lake, Waukesha, Wis., 300...E1 124
Northland, Marquette, Mich., 45...B3 98
North Laramie, riv., Wyo...C7 125
North Las Vegas, Clark, Nev., 18,422...G6 104
North Lawrence, St. Lawrence, N.Y., 300...f10 108
North Lewisburg, Champaign, Ohio, 879...B4 111
North Liberty, St. Joseph, Ind., 1,241...A5 91
North Liberty, Johnson, Iowa, 334...C6 92
North Lima, Allen, Ohio, 600...B3 111
North Lima, Mahoning, Ohio, 600...B7 111
North Lindenhurst, Suffolk, N.Y., 11,200...*G3 84
North Little Rock, Pulaski, Ark., 58,032...C3, D6 81
North Logan, Cache, Utah, 741...B4 119
North Loup, Valley, Nebr., 453...C7 103
North Loup, riv., Nebr...B5 103
North Lubec, Washington, Maine, 250...D5 96
North Madison, New Haven, Conn....D6 84
North Madison, Jefferson, Ind. (part of Madison)...G7 91
North Magnetic Pole, N.W. Ter., Can...B12 66
North Mam, peak, Colo...B3 83
North Manchester, Wabash, Ind., 4,377...C6 91
North Manitou, isl., Mich...C5 98
North Mankato, Nicollet, Minn., 5,927...F4 99
North Marshfield, Plymouth, Mass., 300...h12 97
North Massapequa, Nassau, N.Y., 24,500...*G3 84
North Merrick, Nassau, N.Y., 15,000...*G2 84
North Miami, Dade, Fla., 28,708...F3, G6 86
North Miami, Ottawa, Okla., 472...A7 112
North Miami Beach, Dade, Fla., 21,405...E3 86
North Middleboro, Plymouth, Mass., 400...C6 97
North Middletown, Bourbon, Ky., 291...B5 94
North Monmouth, Kennebec, Maine, 300...D2 96
North Montpelier, Washington, Vt., 140...C4 120
Northmoor, Platte, Mo., 696...E2 101
North Muskegon, Muskegon, Mich., 3,855...E4 98
North Newcastle, Lincoln, Maine...D3 96
North New Hyde Park, Nassau, N.Y., 15,500...*E7 108
North Newport, Sullivan, N.H...D2 105
North New Portland, Somerset, Maine, 300...D2 96
North New River, canal, Fla...F6 86
North Newry, Oxford, Maine...D2 96
North Newton (Bethel College), Harvey, Kans., 890...A5 93
North Norway, Oxford, Maine, 100...D2 96
North Norwich, Chenango, N.Y., 500...C5 108
North Ogden, Weber, Utah, 2,621...B4 119
North Olmsted, Cuyahoga, Ohio, 16,290...B1 111
Northome, Koochiching, Minn., 291...C4 99
North Orange, Franklin, Mass., 100...A3 97
North Oxford, Worcester, Mass., 1,500...B4 97
North Pacific, ocean...E9 2
North Palm Beach, Palm Beach, Fla., 2,684...*F6 86
North Park, Winnebago, Ill., 1,500...*A4 90
North Park, basin, Colo...A4 83
North Parsonfield, York, Maine, 100...E2 96
North Patchogue, Suffolk, N.Y., 6,000...*G4 84
North Pekin, Tazewell, Ill., 2,025...*C4 90
North Pelham, Westchester, N.Y., 5,326...*h13 108
North Pembroke, Plymouth, Mass., 500...B6 97
North Penobscot, Hancock, Maine, 125...D4 96
North Pitcher, Chenango, N.Y., 120...C5 108
North Plain, Middlesex, Conn....D7 84
North Plainfield, Somerset, N.J., 16,993...B4 106
North Plains, Washington, Oreg., 500...A1, B3 113
North Platte, Lincoln, Nebr., 17,184...C5 103
North Platte, riv., U.S...B7 76
North Pleasanton, Atascosa, Tex., 1,018...*E3 118
North Point, Hong Kong, 269,178...*G7 34
North Pole, Arc. O...4
North Pole, mtn., Idaho...D3 89
North Pomfret, Windsor, Vt., 100...D4 120
Northport, Tuscaloosa, Ala., 5,245...B2 78
Northport, Waldo, Maine, 100 (648▲)...D4 96
Northport, Leelanau, Mich., 530...C5 98
Northport, Morrill, Nebr., 110...C2 103
Northport, Suffolk, N.Y., 6,424...n15 108
Northport, Stevens, Wash., 482...A8 122
North Portal, Sask., Can., 281...H4 70
North Powder, Union, Oreg., 399...B9 113
North Pownal, Cumberland, Maine, 55...E5 96
North Pownal, Bennington, Vt. 300...F2 120
North Prairie, Waukesha, Wis., 489...F5 124
North Providence, Providence, R.I., 18,220...B11 84
North Pyramid, peak, N. Mex...E1 107
North Quidnessett, Washington, R.I., 500...*C11 84
North Range Corner, N.S., Can., 40...E4 74
North Reading, Middlesex, mass., 8,331...f11 97
North Rhine-Westphalia (Nordrhein-Westfalen), state, Ger., 16,540,000...B2 17
North Richland Hills, Tarrant, Tex., 8,662...*B5 118
Northridge, Montgomery, Ohio, 1,500...*C3 111
North Ridgeville, Lorain, Ohio, 8,057...A5, B1 111
North Riding, Yorkshire, see York, co., Eng.
North Rim, Mohave, Ariz...A3 80
North River Bridge, N.S., Can...C9 74
North Riverside, Cook, Ill., 8,401...*F3 90
North Robinson, Crawford, Ohio, 289...B5 111
North Rochester, Strafford, N.H. (part of Rochester)...D5 105
North Rockville Centre, Nassau, N.Y., 800...*G2 84
North Ronaldsay, isl., Scot...A5 10
North Rose, Wayne, N.Y., 850...B4 108
North Royalton, Cuyahoga, Ohio, 9,290...B2 111
North Rustico, P.E.I., Can., 780...C6 74
Norths, highland, Ant...C25 5
North Sacramento, Sacramento, Calif., 12,922...A6 82
North St. Paul, Ramsey, Minn., 8,520...E7 99
North Salem, Hendricks, Ind., 626...E4 91
North Salem, Rockingham, N.H., 400...E4 105
North Salt Lake, Davis, Utah, 1,655...C4 119
North Sandwich, Carroll, N.H., 75...C4 105
North Santee, riv., S.C...E9 115
North Saskatchewan, riv., Alta., Sask., Can...C5 69
North Scarboro, Cumberland, Maine, 75...E5 96
North Scituate, Plymouth, Mass., 2,700...h12 97
North Scituate, Providence, R.I., 500...B10 84
North Searsmont, Waldo, Maine, 50...D3 90
North Shore, St. Tammany, La...B8 95
North Shreveport, Caddo, La., 7,701...*B2 95
North Shrewsbury, Rutland, Vt., 25...D3 120
Northside, Granville, N.C., 100...A5 109
North Sioux City, Union, S. Dak., 736...E9 116
North Slidell, St. Tammany, La. (part of Slidell)...B8 95
North Smithfield (Town of), Providence, R.I., (7,632▲)...*B10 84
North Springfield, Erie, Pa., 250...C1 114
North Springfield, Windsor, Vt., 700...E3 120
North Springfield, Fairfax, Va., 5,000...*B5 121
North Springfield, flood control res., Vt...E4 120
Northstar, Gratiot, Mich., 200...E6 98
North Star, Drake, Ohio, 169...B3 111
North Stonington, New London, Conn., 110 (1,982▲)...D9 84
North Stradbroke, isl., Austl...C9 51
North Stratford, Coos, N.H., 600...A3, B1 105
North Street, St. Clair, Mich., 50...E8 98
North Sudbury, Middlesex, Mass., 700...g10 97
North Sumatra, see Sumatra, isl., Indon.
North Sunderland, Eng., 1,580...E7 13
North Sutton, Merrimack, N.H., 160...D3 105
North Swansea, Bristol, Mass., 700...C5 97
North Sydney, Austl., 52,000...*F8 51
North Sydney, N.S., Can., 8,657...C9 74
North Syracuse, Onondaga, N.Y., 8,076...B4 108
North Tarrytown, Westchester, N.Y., 8,818...g13, m15 108
North Terre Haute, Vigo, Ind., 1,100...E3 91
North Tewksbury, Middlesex, Mass., 900...A5 97
North Thetford, Orange, Vt., 115...D4 120
North Thompson, riv., B.C., Can...D8 68
North Tolsta, Scot...B2 13
North Tonawanda, Niagara, N.Y., 34,757...B2 108
North Troy, Orleans, Vt., 961...B4 120
North Truro, Barnstable, Mass., 400...*B7 97
North Tunbridge, Orange, Vt., 70...D4 120

NORT-OAKS 81X

North Tunica, Tunica, Miss., 1,025 .... *A3 100
North Turner, mtn., Maine C4 96
North Twin, lake, Newf., Can D3 75
North Twin, lake, Wis B4 124
North Tyne, riv., Eng E6 13
North Uist, isl., Scot C1 13
Northumberland, Coos, N.H., 100 (2,586▲) A3 105
Northumberland, Northumberland, Pa., 4,156 .... E8 114
Northumberland, co., N.B., Can., 50,035 .... B3 74
Northumberland, co., Ont., Can., 41,892 .... C6 72
Northumberland, co., Eng., 818,988 .... *C6 10
Northumberland, co., Pa., 104,138 .... D8 114
Northumberland, co., Va., 10,185 .... C6 121
Northumberland, is., Austl D9 50
Northumberland, strait, Can C5 74
North Umpqua, riv., Oreg D4 113
North Uvalde, Uvalde, Tex. (part of Uvalde) E3 118
North Uxbridge, Worcester, Mass., 1,860 .... B4 97
Northvale, Bergen, N.J., 2,892 .... g9 106
North Valley Stream, Nassau, N.Y., 11,700 .... *G2 84
North Vancouver, B.C., Can., 23,656 .... E6, f12 68
North Vandergrift, Armstrong, Pa., 1,827 .... *E2 114
North Vassalboro, Kennebec, Maine, 778 .... D3 96
North Vernon, Jennings, Ind., 4,307 .... F6 91
Northview, Webster, Mo., 200 .... D4 101
Northville, Litchfield, Conn., 200 .... C3 84
Northville, Wayne and Oakville, Mich., 3,967 .... A7 98
Northville, Fulton, N.Y., 1,156 .... B6 108
Northville, Spink, S. Dak., 153 .... B7 116
North Virginia Beach, Princess Anne, Va., 2,587 .... *E7 121
North Wabasca, lake, Alta., Can A3 69
North Waldoboro, Lincoln, Maine, 262 .... D3 96
North Wales, Montgomery, Pa., 3,673 .... F11 114
North Walpole, Cheshire, N.H., 950 .... D2 105
North Walsham, Eng., 5,010 .... B9 12
North Warren, Knox, Maine, 75 .... D3 96
North Warren, Warren, Pa., 1,458 .... C3 114
North Washington, Chickasaw, Iowa, 156 .... A5 92
North Waterford, Oxford, Maine, 300 .... D2 96
North Weare, Hillsboro, N.H., 250 .... D3 105
North Webster, Kosciusko, Ind., 494 .... B6 91
North West, cape, Austl D1 50
North West, hbr., N.Y E7 84
Northwest, highlands, Scot D3 13
North Westchester, New London, Conn., 100 .... C7 84
North Western, prov., Zambia D4 48
North-West Frontier, reg., Pak A3 40
North Westminster, Windham, Vt., 368 .... E4 120
North West Miramichi, riv., N.B., Can B3 74
Northwest Park Apartments, Montgomery, Md., 3,000 .... *B3 85
Northwest Polder, reg., Neth B5 15
North Westport, Bristol, Mass., 1,500 .... C5 97
Northwest Providence, chan., W.I B4 64
North West River, Newf., Can., 753 .... B1, h9 75
Northwest St. Augustin, riv., Que., Can C2 75
Northwest Territories, ter., Can., 22,998 .... C9 66
North West Upsalquitch, riv., N.B., Can B2 74
North Weymouth, Norfolk, Mass. (part of Weymouth) h12 97
North Whittier Heights, Los Angeles, Calif., 12,200 .... *E4 82
Northwich, Eng., 19,374 .... A5 12
North Wilbraham, Hampden, Mass., 700 .... B3 97
North Wildwood, Cape May, N.J., 3,598 .... E3 106
North Wilkesboro, Wilkes, N.C., 4,197 .... A2 109
North Wilmington, Middlesex, Mass., 1,000 .... f11 97
North Windham, Windham, Conn., 500 .... C8 84
North Windham, Cumberland, Maine, 900 .... E2, E4 96
North Winterport, Waldo, Maine D4 96
Northwood, Worth, Iowa, 1,768 .... A4 92
Northwood, Kalamazoo, Mich., 4,000 .... *E5 98
Northwood, Rockingham, N.H., 350 (1,034▲) D4 105
Northwood, Grand Forks, N. Dak., 1,195 .... B8 110
Northwood Center, Rockingham, N.H., 120 .... D4 105
Northwood Narrows, Rockingham, N.H., 200 .... D4 105
Northwood Ridge, Rockingham, N.H., 125 .... D4 105
Northwoods, DeKalb, Ga., 1,000 .... *A5 87
Northwoods, St. Louis, Mo., 4,701 .... *C7 101
North Woodstock, Windham, Conn., 150 .... B8 84
North Woodstock, Grafton, N.H., 600 .... B3 105
North Yarmouth, Cumberland, Maine, 150 (1,140▲) E5 96
North York, York, Pa., 2,290 .... G8 114
North York, moors, Eng C6 10
North Zurich, Madison, Tex., 400 .... D4 118
Norton, N.B., Can., 846 .... D4 74
Norton, Eng., 4,773 .... F8 13
Norton, Norton, Kans., 3,345 .... C4 93
Norton, Bristol, Mass., 1,550 (6,818▲) C5 97
Norton, Jackson, N.C. D3 109
Norton, Rh., 1,800 .... A5 49
Norton, Runnels, Tex., 90 .... D2 118
Norton, Essex, Vt., 150 (241▲) A5 120
Norton (Independent City), Va., 5,013 .... B2 121
Norton, Randolph, W. Va., 400 .... C5 123
Norton, co., Kans., 8,035 .... C4 93
Norton, bay, Alsk C8 79
Norton, pond, Vt B5 120
Norton, pond, Vt D2 120
Norton, res., Mass B12 84
Norton, sound, Alsk C6 79
Norton Center, Summit, Ohio, 2,000 .... *A6 111
Nortons Corner, Maricopa, Ariz., 100 .... G2, D4 80
Nortonville, Jefferson, Kans., 595 .... A7, C8 93
Nortonville, Hopkins, Ky., 775 .... C2 94
Nortonville, La Moure, N. Dak., 105 .... C7 110
Nortorf, Ger., 5,900 .... D3 24
Norvegia, cape, Ant B11 5
Norvell, Crittenden, Ark., 362 .... B5 81
Norvello, Mecklenburg, Va., 75 .... E4 121
Norvelt, Westmoreland, Pa., 1,211 .... *F3 114
Norwalk, Los Angeles, Calif., 88,739 .... *F2 82
Norwalk, Fairfield, Conn., 67,775 .... E3 84
Norwalk, Warren, Iowa, 1,328 .... A7, C4 92
Norwalk, Huron, Ohio, 12,900 .... A5 111
Norwalk, Monroe, Wis., 484 .... E3 124
Norwalk, is., Conn E3 84
Norwalk, riv., Conn E3 84
Norway, Benton, Iowa, 516 .... C6 92
Norway, Republic, Kans., 100 .... C6 93
Norway, Oxford, Maine, 2,654 (3,733▲) D2 96
Norway, Dickinson, Mich., 3,171 .... C3 98
Norway, Coos, Oreg., 175 .... D2 113
Norway, Orangeburg, S.C., 525 .... E5 115
Norway, country, Eur., 3,710,000 .... C11 8, E5 25
Norway, isl., Viet B7 38
Norway, lake, Minn E3 99
Norway House, Man., Can., 543 .... C3 71
Norwayne, Wayne, Mich., 6,000 .... *A7 98
Norwegian, bay, N.W. Ter., Can m33 67
Norwegian, sea, Eur C14 4
Norwell, Plymouth, Mass., 600 (5,207▲) h12 97
Norwich, Ont., Can., 1,703 .... E4 72
Norwich, New London, Conn., 38,506 .... C8 84
Norwich, Eng., 119,500 (*170,000) B9 12
Norwich, Kingman, Kans., 430 .... E6 93
Norwich, Chenango, N.Y., 9,175 .... C5 108
Norwich, McHenry, N. Dak., 75 .... A5 110
Norwich, Windsor, Vt., 800 (1,790▲) D4 120
Norwichtown, New London, Conn. (part of Norwich) .. C8 84
Norwood, Ont., Can., 1,060 .... C7 72
Norwood, San Miguel, Colo., 443 .... C2 83
Norwood, Warren, Ga., 294 .. C4 87
Norwood, Polk, Iowa, 1,500 .. A7 92
Norwood, East Feliciana, La., 427 .... D4 95
Norwood, Norfolk, Mass., 24,898 .... B5, h11 97
Norwood, Carver, Minn., 945 .... F5 99
Norwood, Wright, Mo., 263 .. D5 101
Norwood, Bergen, N.J., 2,852 .... h9 106
Norwood, St. Lawrence, N.Y., 2,200 .... f10 108
Norwood, Stanly, N.C., 1,844 .... B3 109
Norwood, Hamilton, Ohio, 34,580 .... D2 111
Norwood Delaware, Pa., 6,729 .... G11 114
Norwood, Knox, Tenn., 5,000 .... *D10 117
Norwood, lake, N.C B3 108
Norwottock, mtn., Mass B2 97
Nosbonsing, lake, Ont., Can A5 72
Noshiro, Jap., 36,500 (63,002▲) F10 37
Nösjön, lake, Swe A6 24
Noss, head, Scot B6 13
Nossa Senhora das Dores, Braz., 4,740 .... D3 57
Nossen, Ger., 8,505 .... B8 17
Nosy-bé, isl., Malag f9 49
Notasulga, Macon, Ala., 884 .... C4 78
Notch, mtn., Mass A3 97
Notch, peak, Utah D2 119
Notch Hill, B.C., Can., 104 .... D8 68
Notchland, Carroll, N.H B4 105
Notec, riv., Pol B3 26
Notikewin, Alta., Can., 88 .. A2 69
Notikewin, riv., Alta., Can A1 69
Notio, It., 21,000 .... F5 21
Noto, gulf, It F5 21
Noto, isl., Jap H8 37
Notodden, Nor., 7,600 .... H3 25
Notre Dame, N.B., Can., 317 .... C5 74
Notre Dame, St. Joseph, Ind., 6,500 .... *A5 91
Notre Dame, bay, Newf., Can D4 75
Notre Dame, mts., Que., Can D6 73
Notre-Dame [-de-la-Salette], Que., Can., 444 .... D2 73
Notre-Dame-de-Lourdes, Man., Can., 511 .... E2 71
Notre-Dame-de-Rimouski, Que., Can A9 73
Notre-Dame [-des-Bois], Que., Can., 243 .... D6 73
Notre-Dame-du-Lac, Que., Can., 1,695 .... B9 73
Notre-Dame-du-Laus, Que., Can., 565 .... C2 73
Nott, St. Tammany, La B7 95
Nottawa, Ont., Can., 272 .... C4 72
Nottawasaga, bay, Ont., Can .. C4 72
Nottaway, riv., Que., Can F17 67
Nottely, res., Ga B2 87
Nottingham, Eng., 315,100 (*630,000) B6 12
Nottingham, Rockingham, N.H., 100 (623▲) D4 105
Nottingham, Bucks, Pa., 2,500 .... *A12 114
Nottingham, co., Eng., 902,966 .... A7 12
Nottingham, isl., N.W. Ter., Can D17 67
Nottoway, Nottoway, Va., 100 .... D4 121
Nottoway, co., Va., 15,141 .. D4 121
Nottoway, riv., Va E5 121
Notukeu, creek, Sask., Can H2 70
Notus, Canyon, Idaho, 324 .. F2 83
Nouakchott, Maur., 5,807 .... C1 45
Nouméa, N. Cal., 33,500 .. H10 7
Nouna, Upper Volta D4 45
Nounan, Bear Lake, Idaho, 10 .... G7 89
Noupoort, S. Afr., 6,322 .... D3 49
Noutonice, Czech., 172 .... n17 26
Nouvelle-Anvers, Con. L A2 48
Nouzonville, Fr., 6,954 .... C6 14
Nova, Ashland, Ohio, 271 .. A5 111
Nova Chaves, Ang., 293 .... D3 48
Nova Cruz, Braz., 6,780 .. C3, h6 57
Nova Freixo, Moz D6 48
Nova Friburgo, Braz., 49,901 .... C4, h6 56
Nova Gaia, Ang., 1,427 .... D2 48
Nova Granada, Braz., 5,134 .. C3 56
Nova Iguaçu, Braz., 134,708 .. h6 56
Nova Lima, Braz., 21,135 .... E2 57
Nova Lisboa, Ang., 37,381 .. D2 48
Nova Lusitania, Moz A5 49
Nova Mambone, Moz B6 49
Novar, Ont., Can., 344 .... B5 72
Novara, It., 92,000 .. D4 18, B2 21
Nova Russas, Braz., 4,666 .. B2 57
Nova Scotia, prov., Can., 737,007 .... H19 67, 74
Nova Sofala, Moz B5 49
Nova Soure, Braz., 1,760 .... D3 57
Novato, Marin, Calif., 17,881 .... C2 82
Nova Varos, Yugo., 3,186 .. D4 22
Nova Venécia, Braz., 4,567 .. E2 57
Novaya Astrakhan, Sov. Un., 5,000 .... p21 27
Novaya Kazanka, Sov. Un., 10,000 .... F18 9
Novaya Ladoga, Sov. Un., 25,000 .... A9 27
Novaya Lyalya, Sov. Un., 17,700 .... B6 29
Novaya Odessa, Sov. Un H8 27
Novaya Sibir, isl., Sov. Un B17 28
Novaya Zemlya, is., Sov. Un ... B8 28
Nova Zagora, Bul., 11,031 .. D8 22
Novelda, Sp., 8,887 .... C5 20
Novelty, Knox, Mo., 176 .. A5 101
Nové Mesto [nad Vahom], Czech., 12,400 .... D5 26
Nove Straseci, Czech., 2,764 .. n17 26
Nové Zámky, Czech., 22,000 .... E5 26
Novgorod, Sov. Un., 76,000 .. B8 27
Novgorod-Severskiy, Sov. Un., 10,000 .... E9 27
Novi, Oakland, Mich., 6,390 .... A7 98
Novice, Coleman, Tex., 227 .. D3 118
Novigrad, Yugo., 531 .... C2 22
Novi Ligure, It., 26,972 .... B2 21
Novinger, Adair, Mo., 621 .. A5 101
Novi Pazar, Bul., 5,461 .... D8 22
Novi Pazar, Yugo., 20,712 .... D5 22
Novi Sad, Yugo., 102,469 .... C4 22
Noviye Senzhary, Sov. Un., 5,000 .... G10 27
Novo-Annenskiy, Sov. Un., 18,900 .... C2 29
Novoaydar, Sov. Un., 10,000 .... G12, q21 27
Novocherkassk, Sov. Un., 69,000 .... H13 27
Novoekonomicheskoye, Sov. Un., 10,000 .... q20 27
Novograd-Volynskiy, Sov. Un., 38,000 .... F6 27
Novogrudok, Sov. Un., 25,000 .... E5 27
Novo-Kazalinsk, Sov. Un D6 29
Novokurovka, Sov. Un B7 37
Novokuybyshevsk, Sov. Un., 78,000 .... *C3 29
Novokuznetsk, Sov. Un., 410,000 .... E26 9, D11 28
Novo Mesto, Yugo., 6,844 .. C2 22
Novomirgorod, Sov. Un., 10,000 .... G8 27
Novomoskovsk, Sov. Un., 114,000 .... C1 29
Novomoskovsk, Sov. Un., 37,500 .... G10 27
Novonazyvayevka, Sov. Un., 10,000 .... D23 9
Novopokrovskaya, Sov. Un., 10,000 .... F17 9
Novo Redondo, Ang., 1,016 .. D1 48
Novorossiysk, Sov. Un., 104,000 .... I11 27
Novo-Selo, Bul., 4,307 .... C6 22
Novoshakhtinsk, Sov. Un., 108,000 .... H12 27
Novosibirsk, Sov. Un., 990,000 (*1,050,000) B10 29
Novosibirskiye (New Siberian), is., Sov. Un B17 28
Novosil, Sov. Un., 10,000 .. E11 27
Novo-Troitsk, Sov. Un., 69,000 .... *C5 29
Novoukrainka, Sov. Un., 10,000 .... G8 27
Novouzensk, Sov. Un., 32,600 .... C3 29
Novoyeniseyskaya, Sov. Un .. B11 37
Novozybkov, Sov. Un., 35,000 .... E8 27
Nový Bohumín, Czech., 11,000 .... D5 26
Novy Bydzov, Czech., 6,120 .... C3 26
Novy Jicin, Czech., 16,600 .. D5 26
Novyy Oskol, Sov. Un., 10,000 .... F11 27
Novyy Port, Sov. Un C10 28
Novyy Vasyugan, Sov. Un .. B9 29
Nowagrod, Pol B10 17
Nowa Sol., 25,000 .... C3 26
Nowata, Nowata, Okla., 4,163 .... A6 112
Nowata, co., Okla., 10,848 .. A6 112
Nowe Warpno, Pol., 2,154 .. B3 26
Nowlin, Haakon, S. Dak., 40 .... C4 116
Nowogard, Pol., 2,446 .... B3 26
No Wood, Washakie, Wyo .. B5 125
Norwood, creek, Wyo A5, B5 125
Nowra, Austl., 6,221 .... G8 51
Nowshera, Pak., 21,516 (*43,757) B5 39
Nowy Dwor, Pol., 5,046 .... k13 26
Nowy Sacz, Pol., 34,000 .... D6 26
Nowy Targ, Pol., 12,600 .... D6 26
Nowy Tomysl, Pol., 2,700 .. B4 26
Noxapater, Winston, Miss., 549 .... C4 100
Noxen, Wyoming, Pa., 800 .... A7, D9 114
Noxon, Sanders, Mont., 150 .... C1 102
Noxon, res., Mont C1 102
Noxontown, pond, Del B6 85
Noxubee, co., Miss., 16,826 .. B5 100
Noxubee, riv., Miss B5 100
Noxville, Kimble, Tex D3 118
Noya, Sp., 4,236 .... A1 20
Noyack, bay, N.Y E7 84
Noyes, Kittson, Minn., 127 .. B1 99
Noyon, Fr., 9,317 .... C5 14
Nsawam, Ghana, 8,731 (*11,273) E4 45
Nsukka, Nig E6 45
Nuanetsi, Rh B5 49
Nubansit, lake, N.H E2 105
Nuberg, Hart, Ga., 100 .... B4 87
Nubian, des., Sud A3 47
Ñuble, prov., Chile, 284,516 .. B2 54
Nuckolls, co., Nebr., 8,217 .. D7 103
Nucla, Montrose, Colo., 906 .. C2 83
Nudos Ojos del Salado, mtn., Arg E2 55
Nueces, co., Tex., 221,573 .. F4 118
Nueces, riv., Tex E3 118
Nueltin, lake, Man., N.W. Ter., Can D13 66
Nueva Casas Grandes, Mex., 11,735 .... A3 63
Nueva Ecija, prov., Phil., 608,700 .... *B6 35
Nueva Esparta, state, Ven., 89,492 .... A5 60
Nueva Esparta, is., Ven A5 60
Nueva Gerona, Cuba, 2,935 .. E2 64
Nueva Imperial, Chile, 6,450 .... B2 54
Nueva Lubecka, Arg C2 54
Nueva Palmira, Ur., 5,100 .. E1 56
Nueva Rosita, Mex., 32,294 .... B4 63
Nueva San Salvador, Sal., 26,911 .... D3 62
Nueva Vizcaya, prov., Phil., 138,000 .... *B6 35
Nueve de Julio, Arg., 13,678 .... B4 54
Nuevitas, Cuba, 12,390 .... E5 64
Nuevo, gulf, Arg C4 54
Nuevo Laredo, Mex., 92,627 .. B5 63
Nuevo León, state, Mex., 1,063,399 .... B4 63
Nuevo Mundo, mtn., Bol D2 55
Nugget, Lincoln, Wyo D2 125
Nuits [-St Georges], Fr., 3,970 .... D6 14
Nukheila (Merga) (Well), Sud B2 47
Nukualofa, Tonga, 9,202 .. H11 7
Nukus, Sov. Un., 46,000 .... E5 29
Nulato, Alsk., 283 .... C8 79
Nules, Sp., 8,460 .... C5 20
Nulhegan, riv., Vt B5 120
Nullarbor, Austl F5 50
Nullarbor, plain, Austl F4 50
Numa, Appanoose, Iowa, 202 .... D5 92
Numan, Nig., 1,209 .... E7 45
Numazu, Jap., 142,609 (*230,000) I9, n7 37
Nu Mine, Armstrong, Pa., 500 .... E3 114
Nunawading, Austl., 61,100 .... *H5 51
Nunda, Livingston, N.Y., 1,224 .... C3 108
Nunda, Lake, S. Dak., 106 .. C8 116
Nuneaton, Eng., 59,300 .... B6 12
Nunez, Emanuel, Ga., 79 .. D4 87
Nungan, China, 35,000 .... C10 34
Nunica, Ottawa, Mich., 275 .. E4 98
Nunivak, isl., Alsk C6 79
Nunkiang, China, 5,000 .... B10 34
Nunn, Weld, Colo., 228 .... A6 83
Nunnelly, Hickman, Tenn., 200 .... B4 117
Nunukan Timur, isl., Indon E5 35
Nuoro, It., 24,500 .... D2 21
Nuquí, Col., 576 .... B2 60
Nuremberg, see Nürnberg, Ger.
Nuremberg, Luzerne and Schuylkill, Pa., 900 .... E9 114
Nuri, Mex., 808 .... B3 60
Nurmes, Fin., 2,200 .... F13 25
Nürnberg, Ger., 466,200 (*675,000) D6 17
Nurrari, lakes, Austl E5 50
Nursery, Victoria, Tex., 350 .... E4 118
Nürtingen, Ger., 20,500 .... E4 17
Nusaybin, Tur., 5,000 .... D13 31
Nushagak, Alsk., 7 .... D8 79
Nushki, Pak., 2,142 .... C4 39
Nusle, Czech., (part of Prague) n17 26
Nut, lake, Sask., Can E4 70
Nuthe, riv., Ger A8 17
Nutley, Essex, N.J., 29,513 .... B4, h8 106
Nut Mountain, Sask., Can., 164 .... E4 70
Nutrioso, Apache, Ariz., 200 .... D6 80
Nutter Fort, Harrison, W. Va., 2,440 .... B4 123
Nutting Lake, Middlesex, Mass., 2,500 .... f10 97
Nuuanu Pali, pass, Haw g10 88
Nuutele, isl., W. Sam 52
Nuutoi, cape, W. Sam 52
Nuwara Eliya, Cey., 11,983 .. G7 39
Nuwaybi'al Muzayyinah, Eg., U.A.R H10 31
Nuweiba, Eg., U.A.R H10 31
Nuzvid, India, 18,974 .... I8 40
Nvalat, Isr C6, h10 32
Nyac, Alsk., 54 .... C8 79
Nyack, Rockland, N.Y., 5,968 .... D7, m15 108
Nyala, Sud., 12,278 .... C1 47
Nyamandhlovu, Rh., 10,000 .... A4 49
Nyamtumbo, Tan D6 48
Nyandoma, Sov. Un., 17,800 .... A12 27
Nyanza, Rwanda, 1,300 .... B4 48
Nyanza, reg., Ken A5 48
Nyasa, lake, Afr H9 42
Nyasaland, see Malawi, country, Afr.
Nyborg, Den., 11,667 .... C4 24
Nybro, Swe., 8,700 .... I6 25
Nyda, Sov. Un B23 9
Nye, Stillwater, Mont., 75 .. E7 102
Nye, co., Nev., 4,374 .... E5 104
Nyeri, Ken B6 48
Nygami, lake, Bech B3 49
Nyimba, Zambia D5 48
Nyiregyhaza, Hung., 41,800 (59,800▲) B5 22
Nykøbing [på] Falster, Den., 17,850 .... D5 24
Nykøbing [på Mors], Den., 9,326 .... B2 24
Nykøbing [på Sjaelland], Den., 4,803 .... C5 24
Nykoping Swe., 24,300 .... H7, u34 25
Nyland Acres, Ventura, Calif., 1,619 .... *E4 82
Nylstroom, S. Afr., 6,662 .... B4 49
Nymagee, Austl., 197 .... F6 51
Nymburk, Czech., 12,600 .... C3, n19 26
Nymindegab, Den C2 24
Nynäshamn, Swe., 9,400 .... H7, u35 25
Nyngan, Austl., 2,414 .... E6 51
Nyon, Switz., 7,643 .... D1 19
Nyong, riv., Cam E2 46
Nyonga, Tan C5 48
Nyota, Blount, Ala B3 78
Nyrany, Czech., 4,073 .... D2 26
Nyrsko, Czech., 2,559 .... D8 17
Nysa, Pol., 23,000 .... C4 26
Nysa, riv., Pol C4 26
Nyssa, Malheur, Oreg., 2,611 .... D10 113
Nysted, Den., 1,328 .... D5 24
Nyunzu, Con. L C4 48
Nzega, Tan B5 48
Nzérékoré, Guinea, 10,800 .. E3 45

O

Oacoma, Lyman, S. Dak., 312 .... D6 116
Oahe, res., S. Dak C5 116
Oahu, isl., Haw B4 88
Oak, Nuckolls, Nebr., 125 .. D8 103
Oak, hill, Mass f9 97
Oak, isl., Wis B3 124
Oak, lake, Man., Can E1 71
Oak, mtn., Ala B3, F5 78
Oak, mtn., Ga D2 87
Oakalla, Burnet, Tex., 85 .. D4 118
Oak Bay, B.C., Can., 16,935 .... h12 68
Oak Bay, N.B., Can., 287 .. D2 74
Oak Bluffs, Dukes, Mass., 1,419 .... D6 97
Oakboro, Stanly, N.C., 581 .. B3 109
Oakbrook Terrace, DuPage, Ill., 1,121 .... *F2 90
Oakburn, Man., Can., 357 .. D1 71
Oak City, Martin, N.C., 574 .... B6 109
Oak City, Millard, Utah, 312 .... D3 119
Oak Creek, Routt, Colo., 666 .... A4 83
Oak Creek, Milwaukee, Wis., 9,372 .... *F6 124
Oak Creek, canyon, Ariz C4 80
Oakdale, Stanislaus, Calif., 4,980 .... D3 82
Oakdale, New London, Conn., 600 .... D8 84
Oakdale, Washington, Ill., 175 .... E4 90
Oakdale, Allen, La., 6,618 .. D3 95
Oakdale, Worcester, Mass., 500 .... B4 97
Oakdale, Antelope, Nebr., 397 .... B8 103
Oakdale, Suffolk, N.Y., 4,300 .... G4 84
Oakdale, Allegheny, Pa., 1,695 .... B5 114
Oakdale, Morgan, Tenn., 470 .... D9 117
Oakengates, Eng., 12,158 .... B5 12
Oakes, Dickey, N. Dak., 1,650 .... C7 110
Oakesdale, Whitman, Wash., 474 .... B8 122
Oakey, Austl., 1,871 .... C8 51
Oakfield, Worth, Ga., 141 .. E3 87
Oakfield, Aroostook, Maine, 560 (848▲) B4 96
Oakfield, Genesee, N.Y., 2,070 .... B2 108
Oakfield, Madison, Tenn., 175 .... B3 117
Oakfield, Fond du Lac, Wis., 772 .... E5 124
Oakford, Menard, Ill., 301 .. C4 90
Oakford, Howard, Ind., 250 .... D5 91
Oakford, Bucks, Pa., 2,000 .... A12, F12 114
Oak Forest, Cook, Ill., 5,850 .... F3 90
Oakgrove, Carroll, Ark., 151 .... A2 81
Oak Grove, De Kalb, Ga., 3,500 .... *C2 87
Oak Grove, Christian, Ky., 100 .... D2 94
Oak Grove, West Carroll, La., 1,797 .... B4 95
Oak Grove, Livingston, Mich., 125 .... F7 98
Oak Grove, Jackson, Mo., 1,100 .... *B3 101
Oak Grove, Clackamas, Oreg., 4,000 .... B2, B4 113
Oak Grove, Dillon, S.C. C8 115
Oak Grove, Westmoreland, Va., 70 .... C6 121
Oakham, Eng., 4,571 .... B7 12
Oakham, Worcester, Mass., 150 (524▲) B3 97
Oakharbor, Ottawa, Ohio, 2,903 .... A4 111
Oak Harbor, Island, Wash., 3,942 .... A3 122
Oak Hill, Volusia, Fla., 758 .. D6 86
Oak Hill, Clay, Kans., 69 .. C6 93
Oak Hill, Manistee, Mich., 750 .... D4 98
Oak Hill, Crawford, Mo., 20 .... C6 101
Oak Hill, Jackson, Ohio, 1,748 .... D5 111
Oak Hill, Davidson, Tenn., 4,490 .... *A5 117
Oak Hill, Fayette, W. Va., 4,711 .... D3, D7 123
Oakhurst, Monmouth, N.J., 4,500 .... C4 106
Oakhurst, Tulsa and Creek, Okla., 3,000 .... *A5 112
Oak Lake, Man., Can., 430 .. E1 71
Oakland, Lauderdale, Ala., 75 .... A2 78
Oakland, Marion, Ark., 15 .. A3 81
Oakland, Alameda, Calif., 367,548 .... B5, D2 82
Oakland, Ont., Can., 264 .. D4 72
Oakland, Coles, Ill., 939 .... D5 90
Oakland, Pottawattamie, Iowa, 1,340 .... C2 92
Oakland, Warren, Ky., 148 .... C3 94
Oakland, Kennebec, Maine, 1,880 (3,075▲) D3 96
Oakland, Garrett, Md., 1,977 .... D1 85
Oakland, Yalobusha, Miss., 488 .... A4 100
Oakland, St. Louis, Mo., 1,552 .... *C7 101
Oakland, Burt, Nebr., 1,429 .... C9 103
Oakland, Bergen, N.J., 9,446 .... A4 106
Oakland, Transylvania, N.C., 60 .... D3 109
Oakland, Marshall, Okla., 288 .... C5 112
Oakland, Douglas, Oreg., 856 .... D3 113
Oakland, Lawrence, Pa., 2,303 .... *D1 114
Oakland, Susquehanna, Pa., 889 .... C10 114
Oakland, Providence, R.I., 450 .... B10 84
Oakland, Fayette, Tenn., 306 .... B2 117
Oakland, co., Mich., 690,259 .... F7 98
Oakland City, Gibson, Ind., 3,016 .... H3 91
Oakland Gardens, Hartford, Conn., 400 .... *C5 84
Oaklandon, Marion, Ind., 500 .... H8 91
Oakland Park, Broward, Fla., 5,331 .... E3, F6 86
Oakland Park, Franklin, Ohio, 10,000 .... *C5 111
Oaklawn, Cook, Ill., 31,476 .... F3 90
Oaklawn, Sedgwick, Kans., 5,000 .... B5 93
Oaklawn, St. Tammany, La., 150 .... B8 95
Oakleigh, Austl., 50,000 .... *H5 51
Oakley, Contra Costa, Calif., 950 .... *B6 82
Oakley, Cassia, Idaho, 613 .. G5 89
Oakley, Logan, Kans., 2,190 .... C3 93
Oakley, Saginaw, Mich., 417 .... E6 98
Oakley, Hinds, Miss., 300 .... C3 100
Oakley, Buncombe, N.C. (part of Asheville) D3 109
Oakley, Berkeley, S.C., 200 .. E7 115
Oakley, Overton, Tenn C8 117
Oakley, Summit, Utah, 247 .. C4 119
Oakley, Lincoln, Wyo D2 125
Oakley Park, Oakland, Mich., 1,100 .... *A7 98
Oaklyn, Camden, N.J., 4,778 .... *D2 106
Oakman, Walker, Ala., 849 .. B2 78
Oakman, Gordon, Ga., 156 .... B2 87
Oak Mills, Atchison, Kans., 38 .... A8 93
Oakmont, Allegheny, Pa., 7,504 .... A6, E2 114
Oakner, Man., Can D1 71
Oak Orchard, Sussex, Del., 300 .... C7 85
Oak Park, Emanuel, Ga., 302 .... D4 87
Oak Park, Cook, Ill., 61,093 .... F2 90
Oak Park, Oakland, Mich., 36,632 .... F7 98
Oak Point, Man., Can., 238 .... D2 71
Oak Ridge, Morehouse, La., 287 .... B4 95
Oak Ridge, Cape Girardeau, Mo., 175 .... D8 101
Oak Ridge, Guilford, N.C., 500 .... A4 109
Oakridge, Lane, Oreg., 1,973 .... D4 113
Oak Ridge, Armstrong, Pa., 400 .... E3 114
Oak Ridge, Anderson and Roane, Tenn., 27,169 .... C9 117
Oak Ridge, res., N.J A3 106
Oak Ridges, Ont., Can., 1,864 .... k15 72
Oak River, Man., Can., 243 .... D1 71
Oaks, Delaware, Okla., 75 .. A7 112
Oaks, Montgomery, Pa., 950 .... A10 114

82X **OAKT-OLMS**

Oakton, Hickman, Ky., 225 ... B2 94
Oakton, Fairfax, Va., 350 ... B4 121
Oaktown, Knox, Ind., 798 ... G3 91
Oak Vale, Lawrence and Jefferson Davis, Miss., 99 ... D4 100
Oakvale, Mercer, W. Va., 267 ... D4 123
Oak Valley, Elk, Kans., 50 ... E8 93
Oak View, Ventura, Calif., 2,448 ... *E4 82
Oak View, Montgomery, Md., 1,000 ... *C3 85
Oakville, Man., Can., 377 ... E2 71
Oakville, Ont., Can., 42,109 ... D5 72
Oakville, Litchfield, Conn., 7,000 ... C4 84
Oakville, Louisa, Iowa, 346 ... C6 92
Oakville, Delaware, Ind., 250 ... D7 91
Oakville, St. Louis, Mo., 1,300 ... B8 101
Oakville, Shelby, Tenn., 6,000 ... B2, E8 117
Oakville, Appomattox, Va ... D4 121
Oakville, Grays Harbor, Wash., 377 ... C2 123
Oakway, Oconee, S.C., 300 ... B1 115
Oakwood, Hall, Ga., 218 ... B3 87
Oakwood, Vermilion, Ill., 861 ... C6 90
Oakwood, Walsh, N. Dak., 60 ... A8 110
Oakwood, Marion, Mo. (part of Hannibal) ... B6 101
Oakwood (Oakwood Village), Cuyahoga, Ohio, 3,283 ... *B2 111
Oakwood (Far Hills), Montgomery, Ohio, 10,493 ... C3 111
Oakwood, Paulding, Ohio, 686 ... A3 111
Oakwood, Dewey, Okla., 122 ... B3 112
Oakwood, Lawrence, Pa., 2,267 ... *D1 114
Oakwood, Leon, Tex., 716 ... D5 118
Oakwood, Buchanan, Va., 250 ... B3 121
Oakwood, Milwaukee, Wis. (part of Oak Creek) ... F2 124
Oakwood Beach, Salem, N.J., 600 ... D1 106
Oakwood Villa, Duval, Fla., 4,500 ... *B5 86
Oamaru, N.Z., 12,429 ... P13 51
Oami, Jap., 9,600 ... n19 37
Oa Mull, head, Scot ... E2 13
Oasis, Elko, Nev., 15 ... B7 104
Oasis, Millard, Utah, 100 ... D3 119
Oatman, Mohave, Ariz., 75 ... C1 80
Oats, Darlington, S.C., 125 ... C7 115
Oaxaca, Mex., 72,370 ... D5 63
Oaxaca, state, Mex., 1,675,926 ... D5 63
Ob, bay, Sov. Un ... C7 4
Ob, riv., Sov. Un ... D25 9
Oba, Ont., Can., 129 ... G16 67
Obama, Jap., 20,400 ... n14 37
Oban, see Half-moon Bay, N.Z.
Oban, Scot., 6,859 ... D3 13
Oban Station, Sask., Can ... E1 70
O'Bannon, Jefferson, Ky., 300 ... A4 94
Obbia, Som., 1,700 ... D6 47
Obed, Alta., Can., 40 ... C2 69
Obed, riv., Tenn ... C9 117
Obeh, Afg ... D11 41
Oberá, Arg., 4,823 ... E4 55
Oberammergau, Ger., 4,603 ... B7 18
Oberdrauburg, Aus., 770 ... C8 18
Oberhausen, Ger., 260,000 ... B1 17
Oberkirch, Ger., 7,700 ... E3 17
Oberlin, Decatur, Kans., 2,337 ... C3 93
Oberlin, Allen, La., 1,794 ... D3 95
Oberlin, Gladwin, Mich ... D6 98
Oberlin, Lorain, Ohio, 8,198 ... A5 111
Oberlin, Bryan, Okla ... D6 112
Oberlin, Dauphin, Pa., 2,500 ... *F8 114
Obernai, Fr., 4,534 ... C7 14
Obernburg, Ger., 3,500 ... D4 17
Oberon, Benson, N. Dak., 248 ... B6 110
Oberösterreich (Upper Austria), state, Aus., 1,131,623 ... E9 17
Oberstaufen, Ger., 3,300 ... B6 18
Oberstdorf, Ger., 8,300 ... E5 16
Obert, Cedar, Nebr., 42 ... B8 103
Oberursel, Ger., 22,200 ... C3 17
Oberwald, Switz., 309 ... C5 19
Obetz, Franklin, Ohio, 1,984 ... C2, C5 111
Obiam, cape, Saipan ... 52
Obiam, inlet, Saipan ... 52
Óbidos, Braz., 5,901 ... C3 59
Obihiro, Jap., 83,000 (100,915▲) ... E11 37
Obion, Obion, Tenn., 1,097 ... A2 117
Obion, co., Tenn., 26,957 ... A2 117
Obion, creek, Ky ... B2 94
Obion, riv., Tenn ... A2 117
Oblong, Crawford, Ill., 1,817 ... D6 90
Obluchye, Sov. Un., 15,000 ... E16 28
Obo, Cen. Afr. Rep ... D5 46
Obock, Fr. Som., 250 ... C5 47
Oborniki, Pol., 5,266 ... B4 26
Obor Sumun, Mong ... B5 34
Oboyan, Sov. Un., 10,000 ... F11 27
O'Brien, Suwannee, Fla., 100 ... B4 86
O'Brien, Josephine, Oreg., 325 ... E3 113
O'Brien, co., Iowa, 18,840 ... A2 92
Observation, isl., Fla ... F6 86
Observation, peak, Calif ... B3 82
Observation, peak, Oreg ... E4 113
Obsidian, Custer, Idaho, 5 ... F4 89
Obskaya, bay, Sov. Un ... C10 28
Obuasi, Ghana, 15,876 ... E4 45
Obubra, Nig ... E6 45
Obwalden, sub canton, Switz., 23,135 ... C5 19
Ocala, Marion, Fla., 13,598 ... C4 86
Ocampo, Arg ... E4 55
Ocampo, Mex., 373 ... B3 63
Ocaña, Col., 15,214 ... B3 60
Ocaña, Sp., 6,686 ... C4 20
Ocate, Mora, N. Mex., 10 ... A5 107
Occidental, Sonoma, Calif., 200 ... B4 82
Occidental Mindoro, prov., Phil., 84,300 ... *C6 35
Occoquan, Prince William, Va., 301 ... C5 121
Occum, New London, Conn. (part of Norwich) ... C8 84
Ocean, co., N.J., 108,241 ... D4 106
Oceana, Princess Anne, Va., 2,448 ... B7 121
Oceana, Wyoming, W. Va., 1,303 ... D3 123
Oceana, co., Mich., 16,547 ... E4 98
Ocean Beach, Suffolk, N.Y., 104 ... G4 84
Ocean Bluff, Plymouth, Mass., 900 ... B6, h13 97
Ocean City, Worcester, Md., 983 ... D7 85
Ocean City, Cape May, N.J., 7,618 ... E3 106
Ocean Drive Beach, Horry, S.C., 313 ... D10 115
Ocean Falls, B.C., Can., 3,056 ... C4 68
Ocean Gate, Ocean, N.J., 706 ... D4 106
Ocean Grove, Bristol, Mass., 2,000 ... C5 97
Ocean Grove, Monmouth, N.J., 6,000 ... C4 106
Oceanlake, Lincoln, Oreg., 1,342 ... C3 113
Oceano, San Luis Obispo, Calif., 1,317 ... *E3 82
Ocean Park, Pacific, Wash., 750 ... C1 122
Oceanport, Monmouth, N.J., 4,937 ... C4 106
Ocean Ridge, Palm Beach, Fla., 209 ... *F6 86
Oceanside, San Diego, Calif., 24,971 ... F5 82
Oceanside, Nassau, N.Y., 34,000 ... *G2 84
Ocean Springs, Jackson, Miss., 5,025 ... E3, E5 100
Ocean View, Sussex, Del., 422 ... C7 85
Ocean View, Cape May, N.J., 375 ... E3 106
Oceanville, Atlantic, N.J., 600 ... E4 106
Oceanway, Duval, Fla., 1,271 ... B6 86
Ochakov, Sov. Un., 5,000 ... H8 27
Ochamchire, Sov. Un., 6,789 ... A13 31
Ocheda, lake, Minn ... G3 99
Ochelata, Washington, Okla., 312 ... A6 112
Ocheyedan, Osceola, Iowa, 662 ... A2 92
Ocheyedan, mound, Iowa ... A2 92
Ocheyedan, riv., Iowa ... A2 92
Ochiai, see Dolinsk, Sov. Un.
Ochil, hills, Scot ... D5 13
Ochiltree, co., Tex., 9,380 ... A2 118
Ochir, Mong ... B6 36
Ochlochnee, Thomas, Ga., 502 ... F2 87
Ochlockonee, riv., Fla., Ga ... F2 87
Ochoas Ranch, Presidio, Tex ... G2 118
Ochoco, res., Oreg ... C6 113
Ocholt, Ger., 541 ... A7 15
Ochopee, Collier, Fla., 150 ... G5 86
Ochre River, Man., Can., 321 ... D2 71
Ochsenfert, Ger., 7,400 ... D5 17
Ochtrup, Ger., 13,200 ... A2 17
Ocilla, Irwin, Ga., 3,217 ... E3 87
Ockelbo, Swe., 2,490 ... G7 25
Öckerö, isl., Swe ... A5 24
Ocmulgee, nat. mon., Ga ... D3 87
Ocmulgee, riv., Ga ... D3 87
Ocna Sibiului, Rom., 3,752 ... C7 22
Ocnele Mari, Rom., 4,420 ... C7 22
Ocoee, Orange, Fla., 2,628 ... D5 86
Ocoee, Polk, Tenn., 300 ... D9 117
Ocoee, lake, Tenn ... D9 117
Ocoña, Peru, 932 ... E3 58
Oconee, Washington, Ga., 500 ... D4 87
Oconee, Shelby, Ill., 257 ... D4 90
Oconee, co., Ga., 6,304 ... C3 87
Oconee, co., S.C., 40,204 ... B1 115
Oconee, riv., Ga ... D4 87
Oconomowoc, Waukesha, Wis., 6,682 ... E5 124
Oconto, Custer, Nebr., 219 ... C6 103
Oconto, Oconto, Wis., 4,805 ... D6 124
Oconto, co., Wis., 25,110 ... D5 124
Oconto, riv., Wis ... D5 124
Oconto Falls, Oconto, Wis., 2,331 ... D5 124
Ocós, Guat., 340 ... C1 62
Ocosta, Grays Harbor, Wash ... C1 122
Ocotal, Nic., 2,807 ... D4 62
Ocotepeque, Hond., 2,622 ... C3 62
Ocotilla, Maricopa, Ariz., 200 ... G2 80
Ocotlán, Mex., 25,435 ... C4, m12 63
Ocracoke, Hyde, N.C., 600 ... B8 109
Ocracoke, inlet, N.C ... B7 109
Ocracoke, isl., N.C ... B8 109
Ocros, Peru, 1,321 ... D2 58
Octararo, creek, Md., Pa ... G9 114
Octavia, Butler, Nebr., 94 ... C8 103
Octeville, Fr., 6,247 ... C3 14
October Revolution, isl., Sov. Un ... B4 4
Ocumare del Tuy, Ven., 14,019 ... A4 60
Ocussi, reg., Port. Timor ... G6 35
Oda, Ghana, 8,374 ... E4 45
Odanah, Ashland, Wis., 300 ... B3 124
Ōdate, Jap., 28,900 (57,775▲) ... *F10 37
Odawara, Jap., 124,813 ... n18 37
Odd, York, Va. (part of Poquoson) ... B6 121
Odd, Raleigh, W. Va., 400 ... *D3 123
Odda, Nor., 5,197 ... G2 25
Odder, Den., 5,562 ... C4 24
Oddur, Som., 2,600 ... E5 47
Odebolt, Sac, Iowa, 1,331 ... B2 92
Odei, riv., Man., Can ... A3 71
Odell, Livingston, Ill., 936 ... B5 90
Odell, Gage, Nebr., 358 ... D9 103
Odell, Wilbarger, Tex., 131 ... B3 118
Odell, lake, Oreg ... D5 113
Odem, San Patricio, Tex., 2,088 ... F4 118
Odemira, Port., 2,266 ... D1 20
Ödemis, Tur., 28,500 ... C6 23
Oden, Montgomery, Ark., 90 ... C2 81
Odendaalsrus, S. Afr., 15,126 (*21,268) ... C4 49
Odensala, Swe ... t33 25
Odensbacken, Swe., 378 ... t33 25
Odense, Den., 111,145 (*129,833) ... C4 24
Odense, co., Den., 196,213 ... C4 24
Odense Å, riv., Den ... C4 24
Odenton, Anne Arundel, Md., 1,914 ... B4 85
Odenville, St. Clair, Ala., 300 ... B3 78
Odenwald, mts., Ger ... D3 17
Oder (Odra), riv., Ger., Pol ... B7 16, B3 26
Oder-Spree, canal, Ger ... A9 17
Odessa, Ont., Can., 285 ... C8 72
Odessa, Sask., Can., 266 ... G4 70
Odessa, New Castle, Del., 526 ... B6 85
Odessa, Pasco, Fla., 150 ... D4 86
Odessa, Big Stone, Minn., 234 ... E2 99
Odessa, Lafayette, Mo., 2,034 ... C4 101
Odessa, Buffalo, Nebr., 150 ... D6 103
Odessa, Schuyler, N.Y., 573 ... C4 108
Odessa, Sov. Un., 709,000 ... H8 27
Odessa, Ector, Tex., 80,338 ... D1 118
Odessa, Lincoln, Wash., 1,231 ... B7 122
Odienné, I.C., 3,300 ... E3 45
Odin, Marion, Ill., 1,242 ... E4 90
Odin, Barton, Kans., 150 ... D5 93
Odin, Watonwan, Minn., 184 ... G4 99
Odin, mtn., B.C., Can ... D8 68
Odioñgan, Phil., 1,936 ... *C6 35
Odivelas, Port., 6,772 ... f9 20
Odobesti, Rom., 4,977 ... C8 22
Odon, Daviess, Ind., 1,192 ... G4 91
O'Donnell, Dawson and Lynn, Tex., 1,356 ... C2 118
Odorhei, Rom., 14,162 ... B7 22
Odum, Wayne, Ga., 404 ... E4 87
Odweina, Som ... D5 47
Odzi, Rh ... A5 49
Oebisfelde, Ger., 6,968 ... A5 17
Oehringen, Ger., 7,475 ... D4 17
Oeiras, Braz., 6,098 ... C2 57
Oeiras, Port., 4,578 ... f9 20
Oelde, Ger., 13,400 ... B3 17
Oella, Baltimore, Md., 860 ... B4 85
Oelrichs, Fall River, S. Dak., 132 ... D2 116
Oelsnitz, Ger., 18,500 ... C7 17
Oelsnitz [im Vogtland], Ger., 16,400 ... C7 17
Oelwein, Fayette, Iowa, 8,282 ... B6 92
Oensingen, Switz., 2,907 ... B4 19
Oesede, Ger., 6,564 ... A3 17
Ofahoma, Leake, Miss., 300 ... C4 100
O'Fallon, St. Clair, Ill., 4,705 ... E4 90
O'Fallon, St. Charles, Mo., 3,770 ... A7 101
O'Fallon, creek, Mont ... D12 102
Offa, Nig., 20,668 ... *E5 45
Offaly, co., Ire., 51,533 ... D4 11
Offenbach, Ger., 117,500 ... C3 17
Offenburg, Ger., 27,600 ... E2 17
Offerle, Edwards, Kans., 208 ... E4 93
Offerman, Pierce, Ga., 483 ... E4 87
Oficina Avanzada, Chile ... D2 55
Oficina Pepita, Chile ... D2 55
Oficina Rosario, Chile ... D2 55
Oficina San Gregorio, Chile ... D2 55
Ofringen, Switz., 7,731 ... B4 19
Ofunato, Jap., 24,200 ... G10 37
Oga (Funakawa), Jap., 21,500 ... G9 37
Ogaki, Jap., 102,478 ... I8, n15 37
Ogallah, Trego, Kans., 251 ... D4 93
Ogallala, Keith, Nebr., 4,250 ... C4 103
Ogasawara, see Bonin Islands, U.S. occ., Asia
Ogbomosho, Nig., 139,535 ... E5 45
Ogburntown, Forsyth, N.C. (part of Winston-Salem) ... A3 109
Ogden, Little River, Ark., 282 ... D1 81
Ogden, Champaign, Ill., 515 ... C6 90
Ogden, Boone, Iowa, 1,525 ... B3 92
Ogden, Riley, Kans., 1,780 ... C7 93
Ogden, Delaware, Pa., 1,600 ... *G11 114
Ogden, Weber, Utah, 70,197 (*141,400) ... B4 119
Ogden Dunes, Porter, Ind., 947 ... *A3 91
Ogdensburg, Sussex, N.J., 1,212 ... A3 106
Ogdensburg, St. Lawrence, N.Y., 16,122 ... f9 108
Ogdensburg, Tioga, Pa., 275 ... C8 114
Ogeechee, riv., Ga ... C4 87
Ogema, Sask., Can., 458 ... H3 70
Ogema, Becker, Minn., 224 ... C3 99
Ogema, Price, Wis., 250 ... C3 124
Ogemaw, Ouachita, Ark., 125 ... D2 81
Ogemaw, co., Mich., 9,680 ... D6 98
Ogilvie, Kanabec, Minn., 376 ... E5 99
Ogilvie, mts., Yukon, Can ... D5 66
Oglala, Shannon, S. Dak., 45 ... D3 116
Ogle, co., Ill., 38,106 ... A4 90
Ogles, St. Clair, Ill., 1,000 ... *E4 90
Oglesby, La Salle, Ill., 4,215 ... B4 90
Oglesby, Davidson, Tenn., 50 ... E9 117
Oglethorpe, Macon, Ga., 1,169 ... D2 87
Oglethorpe, co., Ga., 7,926 ... C3 87
Ogletown, New Castle, Del., 3,500 ... *A6 85
Oglio, riv., It ... D5 18
Ogoja, Nig ... E6 45
Ogoki, riv., Ont., Can ... o18 72
Ogontz, Somerset, Maine ... C3 96
Ogooué, riv., Gabon ... F2 46
Ogrodzieniec, Pol., 2,700 ... g11 26
Ogulin, Yugo., 3,519 ... C2 22
Ogunquit, York, Maine, 800 ... E2 96
Ogurchinskiy, isl., Sov. Un ... B6 41
Ohakune, N.Z., 1,542 ... M15 51
O'Hanly, riv., Man., Can ... D4 71
Ohara, Jap., 10,500 (23,926▲) ... n19 37
Ohatchee, Calhoun, Ala., 437 ... B3 78
Ohaton, Alta., Can., 88 ... C4 69
O'Higgins, prov., Chile, 259,135 ... A2 54
Ohio, Gunnison, Colo., 35 ... C4 83
Ohio, Bureau, Ill., 489 ... B4 90
Ohio, Herkimer, N.Y., 20 ... B6 108
Ohio, co., Ind., 4,165 ... G7 91
Ohio, co., Ky., 17,725 ... C3 94
Ohio, co., W. Va., 68,437 ... A4 123
Ohio, state, U.S., 9,706,397 ... B11 77, 111
Ohio, caverns, Ohio ... B4 111
Ohio, peak, Colo ... C3 83
Ohio, riv., U.S ... C11 77
Ohio Brush, creek, Ohio ... D4 111
Ohio City, Van Wert, Ohio, 851 ... B3 111
Ohiopyle, Fayette, Pa., 287 ... G3 114
Ohioville, Beaver, Pa., 3,050 ... *E1 114
Ohiowa, Fillmore, Nebr., 195 ... D8 103
Ohlau, see Olawa, Pol.
Ohoopee, Toombs, Ga., 51 ... D4 87
Ohoopee, riv., Ga ... D4 87
Ohopoho, S.W. Afr ... A1 49
Ohrdruf, Ger., 7,474 ... C5 17
Ohre, riv., Czech ... n17 26
Ohrid, Yugo., 16,626 ... E5 22
Ohrigstad, S. Afr ... B5 49
Ohringen, Ger., 10,100 ... D4 17
Oiapoque, riv., Braz ... B4 59
Oich, riv., Scot ... C4 13
Oignon, riv., Fr ... B1 18
Oil, creek, Pa ... D2 114
Oil Center, Lea, N. Mex., 800 ... E6 107
Oil City, Caddo, La., 1,430 ... B2 95
Oil City, Yazoo, Miss ... C3 100
Oil City, Venango, Pa., 17,692 ... D2 114
Oildale, Kern, Calif., 19,000 ... E4 82
Oilmont, Toole, Mont., 100 ... B5 102
Oil Spring, Indian res., N.Y ... C2 108
Oil Springs, Ont., Can., 484 ... E2 72
Oilton, Creek, Okla., 1,100 ... A5 112
Oilton, Webb, Tex., 400 ... F3 118
Oil Trough, Independence, Ark., 237 ... B4 81
Oise, dept., Fr., 481,289 ... E2 15
Oise, canal, Fr ... E3 15
Oise, riv., Fr ... C5 14
Oiseau, riv., Man., Can ... D4 71
Oisemont, Fr., 997 ... E9 12
Oita, Jap., 124,807 (*232,541) ... J5 37
Oita, pref., Jap., 1,239,655 ... *J5 37
Oiticica, Braz ... C2 57
Oizulo, Moz ... D6 48
Ojai, Ventura, Calif., 4,495 ... E4 82
Ojinaga, Mex., 8,384 ... B4 63
Ojito, Rio Arriba, N. Mex., 5 ... A2 107
Ojocaliente, Mex., 6,642 ... C4 63
Ojo Caliente, Taos, N. Mex., 200 ... A4 107
Ojo de Agua, Arg ... E3 55
Ojo Feliz, Mora, N. Mex., 145 ... A4 107
Ojo Sarco, Rio Arriba, N. Mex., 100 ... A4 107
Ojos del Salado, mtn., Arg ... F4 53
Ojus, Dade, Fla., 5,000 ... E3, G6 86
Oka, Que., Can., 1,375 ... D3, q18 73
Oka, riv., Sov. Un ... B2 29
Okaba, W. Irian ... G9 35
Okabena, Jackson, Minn., 244 ... G3 99
Okahandja, S.W. Afr., 1,634 ... B2 49
Okak, is., Newf., Can ... g9 75
Okaloosa, co., Fla., 61,175 ... G2 86
Okanagan, lake, B.C., Can ... D8 68
Okanagan, range, B.C., Can ... E7 68
Okanagan Centre, B.C., Can., 265 ... D8 68
Okanagan Falls, B.C., Can., 353 ... E8 68
Okanagan Landing, B.C., Can., 535 ... D8 68
Okanogan, Okanogan, Wash., 2,001 ... A6 122
Okanogan, co., Wash., 25,520 ... A6 122
Okanogan, riv., Wash ... A6 122
Okapilco, creek, Ga ... E3 87
Okara, Pak., 68,299 ... *B4 40
Okarche, Canadian and Kingfisher, Okla., 584 ... B4 112
Okatibbee, creek, Miss ... C5 100
Okatoma, creek, Miss ... D4 100
Okaton, Jones, S. Dak ... D5 116
Okauchee, Waukesha, Wis., 1,879 ... *E5 124
Okaukuejo, S.W. Afr ... A2 49
Ōkawa, Jap., 34,300 (50,351▲) ... *J5 37
Okawville, Washington, Ill., 931 ... E4 90
Okay, Howard, Ark., 150 ... D2 81
Okay, Wagoner, Okla., 419 ... B6 112
Okaya, Jap., 52,256 ... H9, m17 37
Okayama, Jap., 260,773 ... I6 37
Okayama, pref., Jap., 1,670,454 ... *I6 37
Okazaki, Jap., 137,000 (166,095▲) ... o16 37
O'Kean, Randolph, Ark., 137 ... A5 81
Okeana, Butler, Ohio, 230 ... C1 111
Okecie, Pol ... B6, m13 26
Okeechobee, Okeechobee, Fla., 2,947 ... E6 86
Okeechobee, co., Fla., 6,424 ... E6 86
Okeechobee, lake, Fla ... F6 86
Okeelanta, Palm Beach, Fla., 100 ... F6 86
Okeene, Blaine, Okla., 1,164 ... A3 112
Okefenokee, swamp, Ga ... F4 87
Okehampton, Eng., 3,833 ... D3 12
Okemah, Okfuskee, Okla., 2,836 ... B5 112
Okemos, Ingham, Mich., 1,000 ... *F6 98
Okene, Nig., 32,602 ... *E6 45
Oker, riv., Ger ... A5 17
Okesa, Osage, Okla., 75 ... A5 112
Oketo, Marshall, Kans., 128 ... C7 93
Okfuskee, co., Okla., 11,706 ... B5 112
Okha, India, 9,630 ... F2 40
Okha, Sov. Un., 35,000 ... D17 28
Okhotsk, Sov. Un., 2,000 ... D17 28
Okhotsk, sea, Sov. Un ... D17 28
Okinawa, isl., Ryukyu Is ... 52
Oklahoma, co., Okla., 439,506 ... B4 112
Oklahoma, state, U.S., 2,328,284 ... C8 76, 112
Oklahoma City, Oklahoma, Okla., 324,253 (*493,000) ... B4 112
Oklawaha, Marion, Fla., 600 ... C5 86
Oklawaha, riv., Fla ... C5 86
Oklee, Red Lake, Minn., 529 ... C3 99
Okmulgee, Okmulgee, Okla., 15,951 ... B6 112
Okmulgee, co., Okla., 36,945 ... B6 112
Okoboji, Dickinson, Iowa, 330 ... A2 92
Okobojo, creek, S. Dak ... C5 116
Okolona, Clark, Ark., 344 ... C2 81
Okolona, Jefferson, Ky., 7,000 ... A5 94
Okolona, Chickasaw, Miss., 2,622 ... B5 100
Okome, Swe ... A6 24
Okondja, Gabon ... F2 46
Okotoks, Alta., Can., 1,043 ... D4 69
Okovanggo, swamps, Bech ... A3 49
Okovanggo, riv., Ang., S.W. Afr ... A2 49
Okreek, Todd, S. Dak., 120 ... D5 116
Oktaha, Muskogee, Okla., 199 ... B6 112
Oktibbeha, co., Miss., 26,175 ... B5 100
Oktyabrskiy, Sov. Un., 70,000 ... C4 29
Okuniew, Pol., 1,400 ... k14 26
Okushiri, isl., Jap ... E9 37
Okuma, bay, Ant ... B33 5
Ola, Yell, Ark., 805 ... B2 81
Ola, Gem, Idaho, 20 ... E2 89
Olaa (Keaau), Hawaii, Haw., 1,334 ... D6 88
Ólafsfjördur, Ice., 940 ... m23 25
Ólafsvík, Ice., 826 ... n21 25
Olalla, Kitsap, Wash., 125 ... D1 122
Olamon, Penobscot, Maine, 150 ... C4 96
Olancha, Inyo, Calif., 75 ... D5 82
Olancha, peak, Calif ... D4 82
Olanchito, Hond., 2,785 ... C4 62
Öland, isl., Swe ... I7 25
Olanta, Clearfield, Pa., 80 ... E4 114
Olanta, Florence, S.C., 568 ... D8 115
Olar, Bamberg, S.C., 467 ... E5 115
Olascoaga, Arg., 2,358 ... B4 54
Olathe, Montrose, Colo., 773 ... C3 83
Olathe, Johnson, Kans., 10,987 ... D9 93
Olavarría, Arg., 24,204 ... B4 54
Olawa, Pol., 6,410 ... C4 26
Olazagutia, Sp., 2,097 ... A4 20
Olberg, Pinal, Ariz., 20 ... D4, H3 80
Olbernhau, Ger., 14,300 ... C8 17
Olbia, It., 11,000 ... D2 21
Olcott, Niagara, N.Y., 1,300 ... B2 108
Olcott, Kanawha, W. Va., 300 ... C3, C6 123
Old, chan., Sask., Can ... D4 70
Old Bahama, chan., Cuba ... D4 64
Old Baldy, mtn., Ariz ... F5 80
Old Bennington, Bennington, Vt., 205 ... F2 120
Old Bethpage, Nassau, N.Y., 5,000 ... *G3 84
Old Bight, Ba. Is., 574 ... C6 64
Old Bridge, Middlesex, N.J., 8,000 ... C4 106
Old Brookville, Nassau, N.Y., 1,126 ... *F2 84
Oldbury, Eng., 54,300 ... *B5 12
Old Castile, reg., Sp., 2,218,884 ... B4 20
Oldcastle, Ire., 739 ... D4 11
Old Crow, Yukon, Can., 217 ... C6 66
Old Dock, Columbus, N.C ... C5 109
Oldeani, Tan ... B6 48
Olden, Eastland, Tex., 500 ... C3 118
Oldenburg, Franklin, Ind., 694 ... F7 91
Oldenburg [in Holstein], Ger., 9,350 ... A5 16
Oldenburg [in Oldenburg], Ger., 126,500 ... B4 16, E2 24
Oldenzaal, Neth., 20,300 ... B6 15
Old Faithful, Yellowstone National Park, Wyo ... A2 125
Old Faithful, geyser, Wyo ... A2 125
Old Field, Suffolk, N.Y., 530 ... F4 84
Old Field, pt., N.Y ... F4 84
Old Forge, Herkimer, N.Y., 850 ... B6 108
Old Forge, Lackawanna, Pa., 8,928 ... A9, D10 114
Old Fort, McDowell, N.C., 787 ... D4 109
Old Fort Bay, Que., Can., 102 ... C3 75
Old Greenwich, Fairfield, Conn. (part of Greenwich) ... E2 84
Oldham, Eng., 114,200 ... A5 12
Oldham, Kingsbury, S. Dak., 291 ... C8 116
Oldham, co., Ky., 13,388 ... B4 94
Oldham, co., Tex., 1,928 ... B1 118
Oldham Pines, Plymouth, Mass., 300 ... *B6 97
Oldham Village, Plymouth, Mass., 800 ... *B6 97
Old Harbor, Alsk., 193 ... D9 79
Old Harbor, pt., R.I ... E10 84
Old Head of Kinsale, head, Ire ... F3 11
Old Hickory, Davidson, Tenn., 5,000 ... A5, E9 117
Old Hickory, res., Tenn ... A5, E9 117
Old Hometown, Shelby, Tenn., 2,500 ... *B1 117
Old Lyme, New London, Conn., 400 (3,068▲) ... D7 84
Old Man, mtn., Newf., Can ... D3 75
Oldman, riv., Alta., Can ... E4 69
Old Man of the Mountain (Great Stone Face), mtn., N.H ... B3 105
Oldmans, creek, N.J ... D2 106
Old Marissa, St. Clair, Ill., 217 ... B9 101
Old Meldrum, Scot., 1,083 ... C6 13
Old Mines, Washington, Mo., 400 ... C7 101
Old Monroe, Lincoln, Mo., 290 ... A7, C7 101
Old Mystic, New London, Conn., 500 ... D9 84
Old Ocean, Brazoria, Tex., 950 ... *E5 118
Old Orchard Beach, York, Maine, 4,580 ... E2, E5 96
Old Perlican, Newf., Can., 599 ... D5 75
Old Point Comfort, pt., Va ... B7 121
Old Rhodes, key, Fla ... G6 86
Old River, lake, Ark ... D6 81
Olds, Alta., Can., 2,433 ... D3 69
Olds, Henry, Iowa, 189 ... C6 92
Olds, Chelan, Wash ... B5 122
Old Saybrook, Middlesex, Conn., 2,300 (5,274▲) ... D7 84
Oldsmar, Pinellas, Fla., 878 ... E2 86
Old Spec, mtn., Maine ... D2 96
Old Tampa, bay, Fla ... E2 86
Old Tappam, Bergen, N.J., 2,330 ... *B4 106
Old Tati, Bech ... B4 49
Old Topsail, inlet, N.C ... C6 109
Old Town, Lafayette, Ark., 100 ... D2 81
Old Town, Dixie, Fla., 200 ... C4 86
Oldtown, Bonner, Idaho, 211 ... A1 89
Old Town, Penobscot, Maine, 8,626 ... D4 96
Oldtown, Allegany, Md., 200 ... D2 85
Oldtown, Forsyth, N.C., 1,000 ... *A3 109
Old Trap, Camden, N.C., 300 ... A7 109
Old Washington, Guernsey, Ohio, 369 ... B6 111
Old Westbury, Nassau, N.Y., 2,064 ... *k13 108
Oldwick, Hunterdon, N.J., 400 ... B3 106
Old Wives, Sask., Can ... G3 70
Old Wives, lake, Sask., Can ... G2 70
Olean, Miller, Mo., 135 ... C5 101
Olean, Cattaraugus, N.Y., 21,868 ... C2 108
O'Leary Station, P.E.I., Can., 755 ... C5 74
Olecko, Pol., 1,413 ... A7 26
Oleiros, Sp., 76 ... A1 20
Olekma, riv., Sov. Un ... D15 28
Olekminsk, Sov. Un., 5,000 ... C15 28
Olenek, riv., Sov. Un ... C14 28
Olentangy, riv., Ohio ... B4 111
Oléron, isl., Fr ... E3 14
Olesnica, Pol., 14,300 ... C4 26
Olesno, Pol., 6,058 ... C5 26
Olex, Gilliam, Oreg ... B6 113
Oley, Berks, Pa., 400 ... F10 114
Olga, Cavalier, N. Dak., 96 ... A7 110
Olga, Sov. Un., 1,000 ... E7 37
Olga, mtn., Vt ... F3 120
Olgod, Den., 1,990 ... C2 24
Olgopol, Sov. Un., 10,000 ... G7 27
Olhão, Port., 16,592 ... D2 20
Olifants, riv., S. Afr ... B5 49
Olimpia, Braz., 14,629 ... F1 57
Olimpo, dept., Par., 2,705 ... D4 55
Olin, Jones, Iowa, 703 ... B6 92
Olinda, Braz., 100,545 ... C4, h6 57
Olite, Sp., 2,981 ... A5 20
Oliva, Sp., 14,579 ... C5 20
Oliva de la Frontera, Sp., 12,899 ... C2 20
Olivais, Port., 23,409 ... f9 20
Olive, Powder River, Mont., 5 ... E11 102
Olive (Alexander Park), Norfolk, Va., 7,000 ... *E6 121
Olive Branch, De Soto, Miss., 642 ... A4 100
Olive Hill, Carter, Ky., 1,398 ... B6 94
Olivehill, Hardin, Tenn., 75 ... B3 117
Olivehurst, Yuba, Calif., 4,835 ... C3 82
Oliveira, Braz., 12,919 ... F2 57
Olivenza, Sp., 11,469 ... C2 20
Oliver, Lauderdale, Ala., 50 ... A2 78
Oliver, B.C., Can., 1,774 ... E8 68
Oliver, Gunnison, Colo., 30 ... C3 83
Oliver, Screven, Ga., 192 ... D5 87
Oliver, Fayette, Pa., 1,250 ... G2 114
Oliver, Douglas, Wis., 222 ... B1 124
Oliver, co., N. Dak., 2,610 ... B4 110
Oliverian, Grafton, N.H ... B3 105
Oliver Springs, Anderson and Roane, Tenn., 1,163 ... C9 117
Olives, mtn., Jordan ... h12, m14 32
Olivet, Vermilion, Ill., 350 ... D6 90
Olivet, Osage, Kans., 116 ... D8 93
Olivet, Calvert, Md., 125 ... D5 85
Olivet, Eaton, Mich., 1,185 ... F6 98
Olivet, Hutchinson, S. Dak., 135 ... D8 116
Olivette, St. Louis, Mo., 8,257 ... *C7 101
Olivia, Renville, Minn., 2,355 ... F4 99
Olivia, Hartnett, N.C., 200 ... B4 109
Olivier, Iberia, La., 400 ... E4 95
Olivone, Switz., 930 ... C6 19
Öljaren, lake, Swe ... t34 25
Olkusz, Pol., 10,500 ... g11 26
Olla, LaSalle, La., 1,246 ... C3 95
Ollague, Chile ... D2 55
Ollague, vol., Bol ... D2 55
Ollan, is., Truk ... 52
Ollie, Keokuk, Iowa, 291 ... C5 92
Ollie, Fallon, Mont ... D12 102
Ollita, range, Arg ... A2 54, F2 55
Olmito, Cameron, Tex., 600 ... F4 118
Olmitz, Barton, Kans., 141 ... D5 93
Olmos, Peru, 2,163 ... C2 58
Olmos Park, Bexar, Tex., 2,457 ... B3 118
Olmstead, Pulaski, Ark., 50 ... C3 81
Olmstead, Logan, Ky., 120 ... D2 94
Olmsted, Pulaski, Ill., 475 ... F4 90
Olmsted, Cuyahoga, Ohio, 4,773 ... *B1 111
Olmsted, co., Minn., 65,532 ... G6 99
Olmsted Falls, Cuyahoga, Ohio, 2,144 ... B1 111

Osmanabad, India, 18,868 .. H6 40
Osmancik, Tur., 6,800 .. B10 31
Osmaneli, Tur., 2,700 .. B7 23
Osmaniye, Tur., 29,300 .. D11 31
Osmond, Pierce, Nebr., 719 .. B8 103
Osnabrock, Cavalier, N. Dak., 289 .. A7 110
Osnabrück, Ger., 141,500 .. A3 17
Osório, Braz., 5,739 .. D2 56
Osorno, Chile, 55,100 .. C2 54
Osorno, prov., Chile, 143,955 .. C2 54
Osov, Czech., 398 .. o17 26
Osoyoos, B.C., Can., 1,022 .. E8 68
Osoyoos, lake, B.C., Can., Wash .. A6 122
Ospika, riv., B.C., Can .. A6 68
Osprey, Sarasota, Fla., 800 .. E4 86
Oss, Neth., 30,700 .. C5 15
Ossa, mtn., Austl .. o15 50
Ossabaw, isl., Ga .. E5 87
Ossabaw, sound, Ga .. E5 87
Osseo, Hennepin, Minn., 2,104 .. E6 99
Osseo, Trempealeau, Wis., 1,144 .. D2 124
Ossian, Wells, Ind., 1,108 .. C7 91
Ossian, Winneshiek, Iowa, 827 .. A6 92
Ossineke, Alpena, Mich., 100 .. D7 98
Ossining, Westchester, N.Y., 18,662 .. D7, m15 108
Ossipee, Carroll, N.H., 125 (1,409▲) .. C4 105
Ossipee, lake, N.H .. C4 105
Ossippee, mts., N.H .. C4 105
Ossokmanuan, lake, Newf., Can .. h8 75
Ossora, Sov. Un., 2,300 .. D34 4
Ost, Reno, Kans .. B4 93
Östanå, Swe .. t36 25
Ostashkov, Sov. Un., 10,000 .. C9 27
Oste, riv., Ger .. E3 24
Osteen, Volusia, Fla., 550 .. D5 86
Ostend, see Oostende, Bel.
Osterburg, Ger., 6,893 .. F5 24
Osterburg, Bedford, Pa., 200 .. F4 114
Östergötland, co., Swe., 358,000 .. *H6 25
Osterode, Ger., 16,200 .. B5 17
Osterode, see Ostrod, Pol.
Östersund, Swe., 24,900 .. F6 25
Osterville, Barnstable, Mass., 1,200 .. C7 97
Osterwieck, Ger., 6,283 .. B5 17
Östfold, co., Nor., 202,700 .. *H4 25
Ostia Antica, It .. h8 21
Ostiglia, It., 5,759 .. D7 18
Ostrach, Ger., 1,500 .. B5 18
Ostrander, Fillmore, Minn., 216 .. G6 99
Ostrander, Delaware, Ohio, 438 .. B4 111
Östratorp, Swe .. C7 24
Ostrava, Czech., 244,900 (*380,000) .. D5 26
Ostróda, Pol., 15,200 .. B5 26
Ostrog, Sov. Un., 10,000 .. F6 27
Ostrogozhsk, Sov. Un., 10,000 .. F12 27
Ostroleka, Pol., 11,700 .. B6 26
Ostrov, Czech., 16,600 .. C2 26
Ostrov, Rom., 4,015 .. C8 22
Ostrov, Sov. Un., 10,000 .. C7 27
Ostrow, Pol., 12,900 .. B6 26
Ostrowiec, Pol., 38,000 .. C6 26
Ostrow Lubelski, Pol., 2,604 .. C7 26
Ostrow Wielkopolski, Pol., 42,000 .. C4 26
Ostrzeszow, Pol., 5,403 .. C4 26
Ostuni, It., 23,500 .. D6 21
Osumi, is., Jap .. K5 37
Osumi (Van Diemen), strait, Jap .. K5 37
Osuna, Sp., 19,569 .. D3 20
Oswayo, Potter, Pa., 162 .. C5 114
Oswegatchie, St. Lawrence, N.Y., 300 .. A5 108
Oswegatchie, riv., N.Y .. f9 108
Oswego, Kendall, Ill., 1,510 .. B5, F1 90
Oswego, Labette, Kans., 2,027 .. E8 93
Oswego, Valley, Mont., 50 .. B11 102
Oswego, Oswego, N.Y., 22,155 .. B4 108
Oswego, Sumter, S.C., 100 .. C7 115
Oswego, co., N.Y., 86,118 .. B4 108
Oswego, riv., N.J .. D4 106
Oswego, riv., N.Y .. B4 108
Oswestry, Eng., 11,193 .. B4 12
Oswiecim, Pol., 31,000 .. C5, g10 26
Osyka, Pike, Miss., 712 .. D3 100
Ota, see Minokamo, Jap.
Otago, harbor, N.Z .. P13 51
Otago, pen., N.Z .. P13 51
Otaki, Jap., 4,600 .. n19 37
Otaki, N.Z., 2,973 .. N15 51
Otar, Sov. Un .. E9 29
Otaru, Jap., 198,511 .. E10 37
Otaru, bay, Jap .. E10 37
Otava, riv., Czech .. D8 17
Otavalo, Ec., 8,379 .. A2 58
Otavi, S.W. Afr., 1,303 .. A2 49
Otay, San Diego, Calif., 1,500 .. *F5 82
Otchinjau, Ang .. E1 48
Oteen, Buncombe, N.C., 1,000 .. D3 109
Otego, Jewell, Kans., 9 .. C5 93
Otego, Otsego, N.Y., 875 .. C5 108
Otero, co., Colo., 24,128 .. D7 83
Otero, co., N. Mex., 36,976 .. E3 107
Othello, Adams, Wash., 2,669 .. C6 122
Otho, Webster, Iowa, 593 .. B3 92
Othris, mts., Grc .. C4 23
Oti, riv., Ghana .. E5 45
Otis, Washington, Colo., 568 .. A8 83
Otis, La Porte, Ind., 200 .. A4 91
Otis, Rush, Kans., 362 .. D4 93
Otis, Berkshire, Mass., 150 (473▲) .. B1 97
Otis, Eddy, N. Mex., 100 .. E5 107
Otis, res., Mass .. B1 97
Otisco, Clark, Ind., 250 .. G6 91
Otisco, Waseca, Minn., 100 .. G5 99
Otisco, Onondaga, N.Y., 150 .. C4 108
Otis Orchards, Spokane, Wash., 750 .. D8 122
Otisville, Genesee, Mich., 701 .. E7 98
Otjiwarongo, S.W. Afr., 2,383 .. B2 49
Otley, Marion, Iowa, 177 .. C4 93
Oto, Woodbury, Iowa, 221 .. B2 93
Otočac, Yugo., 3,517 .. C2 22
Otoe, Otoe, Nebr., 225 .. D9, E3 103
Otoe, co., Nebr., 16,503 .. D9 103
Otradnoye, Sov. Un .. s31 25
Otranto, It., 4,309 .. D7 21
Otsego, Allegan, Mich., 4,142 .. F5 98
Otsego, co., Mich., 7,545 .. C6 98
Otsego, co., N.Y., 51,942 .. C5 108
Otsego, lake, N.Y .. C6 108
Otsego Lake, Otsego, Mich .. D6 98
Otsu, Jap., 38,402 .. *o14 37
Otsu, Jap., 113,547 .. o14 37
Otta, isl., Truk .. 52
Ottarp, Swe .. C6 24
Ottauquechee, riv., Vt .. D3 120
Ottawa, Ont., Can., 268,206 (*429,750) .. B9, h12 72
Ottawa, La Salle, Ill., 19,408 .. B5 90
Ottawa, Franklin, Kans., 10,673 .. D8 93
Ottawa, Putnam, Ohio, 3,245 .. A3 111
Ottawa, Boone, W. Va., 200 .. D5 123
Ottawa, co., Kans., 6,779 .. C6 93
Ottawa, co., Mich., 98,719 .. F4 98
Ottawa, co., Ohio, 35,323 .. A4 111
Ottawa, co., Okla., 28,301 .. A7 112
Ottawa, is., N.W. Ter., Can .. E16 67
Ottawa, riv., Ont., Que., Can .. A6 72
Ottawa, riv., Ohio .. A2 111
Ottawa Hills, Lucas, Ohio, 3,870 .. A2, A4 111
Ottawa Lake, Monroe, Mich., 250 .. G7 98
Otter, Powder River, Mont., 5 .. E10 102
Otter, brook, N.H .. E2 105
Otter, creek, Utah .. E4 119
Otter, creek, Vt .. C2 120
Otter, lake, Sask., Can .. B3 70
Otter, riv., Alta., Can .. A2 69
Otter, riv., Eng .. D4 12
Otter, riv., Va .. D3 121
Otterøan, riv., Nor .. H2 25
Otterbein, Benton, Ind., 788 .. D3 91
Otterberg, Ger., 4,000 .. D2 17
Otter Brook, flood control res., N.H .. E2 105
Otterburn, Eng., 624 .. E6 13
Otterburne, Man., Can., 258 .. E3 71
Otter Creek, Levy, Fla., 400 .. C4 86
Otter Creek, Hancock, Maine, 300 .. D4 96
Otter Creek, res., Utah .. E4 119
Otter Lake, Ont., Can .. B4 72
Otter Lake, Lapeer, and Genesee, Mich., 562 .. E7 98
Otter Lake, Oneida, N.Y., 50 .. B5 108
Otterndorf, Ger., 6,600 .. E2 24
Otter River, Worcester, Mass., 600 .. A3 97
Ottersburg, Ger., 3,200 .. E3 24
Ottertail, Otter Tail, Minn., 164 .. D3 99
Otter Tail, co., Minn., 48,960 .. D3 99
Otter Tail, lake, Minn .. D3 99
Otter Tail, riv., Minn .. D2 99
Otterup, Den., 1,687 .. C4 24
Otterville, Ont., Can., 725 .. E4 72
Otterville, Buchanan, Iowa, 25 .. B6 92
Otterville, Cooper, Mo., 416 .. C4 101
Otthon, Sask., Can .. F4 70
Ottignies, Bel., 5,103 .. D4 15
Öttingen, Ger., 3,800 .. E5 17
Otto, Big Horn, Wyo., 50 .. A4 125
Ottokee, Fulton, Ohio, 65 .. A3 111
Ottone, It., 3,183 .. E5 18
Ottosen, Humboldt, Iowa, 92 .. B3 92
Ottoville, Putnam, Ohio, 793 .. B3 111
Ottsville, Bucks, Pa., 60 .. F11 114
Ottumwa, Wapello, Iowa, 33,871 .. C5 92
Ottumwa, Coffey, Kans., 49 .. D8 93
Ottumwa, Haakon, S. Dak., 5 .. C4 116
Ottway, Greene, Tenn .. C11 117
Otukamamoan, lake, Ont., Can .. A6 99
Oturkpo, Nig., 1,367 .. E6 45
Otuzco, Peru, 3,534 .. C2 58
Otway, Carteret, N.C., 350 .. C7 109
Otway, cape, Austl .. I4 51
Otway, sound, Chile .. h11 54
Otwell, Craighead, Ark., 90 .. B5 81
Otwell, Pike, Ind., 550 .. H3 91
Otwock, Pol., 36,000 .. m14 26
Ötztal Alps, mts., Aus., It .. A3 21
Ouachita, co., Ark., 31,641 .. D3 81
Ouachita, par., La., 101,663 .. B3 95
Ouachita, mts., Okla .. C6 112
Ouachita, riv., Ark .. D3 81
Ouachita, riv., La .. B3 95
Ouaddaï, reg., Chad .. C4 46
Ouadi Rimé, riv., Chad .. C3 46
Ouagadougou, Upper Volta, 59,126 .. D4 45
Ouahigouya, Upper Volta, 10,000 .. D4 45
Ouaka, riv., Cen. Afr. Rep .. D4 46
Ouakoro, Mali .. D3 45
Oualata, Maur .. C3 45
Oallam, Niger .. D5 45
Ouanda Djalé, Cen. Afr. Rep .. D4 46
Ouarane, sand dunes, Maur .. B3 45
Ouargla, Alg., 6,456 (27,360▲) .. C6 44
Ouchina (Well), Mali .. C5 45
Ouddorp, Neth., 2,680 .. C3 15
Oudenaarde, Bel., 6,923 .. D3 15
Oude-Pekela, Neth., 5,900 .. A7 15
Oudtshoorn, S. Afr., 22,229 .. D3 49
Oued Zem, Mor., 18,640 .. H3 30
Oueïba (Well), Chad .. B4 46
Ouelle, I.C .. E4 45
Ouelle, riv., Que., Can .. B8 73
Ouellette, Aroostook, Maine .. A4 96
Ouesso, Con. B .. E3 46
Ouezzane, Mor., 26,203 .. C3 44
Ougarta, Alg .. D4 44
Oughter, lake, Ire .. C4 11
Oughterard, Ire., 618 .. D2 11
Ouidah, Dah., 14,000 .. E5 45
Oujda, Mor., 128,645 .. G6 28, C4 44
Oullins, Fr., 24,356 .. E6 14
Oulu, Fin., 63,800 .. E11 25
Oulu, Bayfield, Wis .. B2 124
Oulu, dept., Fin., 338,243 .. *E11 25
Oulujärvi, lake, Fin .. E12 25
Oum Chalouba, Chad .. B4 46
Oum el Asel (Oasis), Mali .. B4 45
Oum Hadjer, Chad, 1,208 .. C3 46
Ounasjoki, riv., Fin .. D11 25
Ounianga Kébir, Chad .. B4 46
Ouray, Ouray, Colo., 785 .. C3 83
Ouray, Uintah, Utah, 100 .. C6 119
Ouray, co., Colo., 1,601 .. C3 83
Ouray, peak, Colo .. C4 83
Ouri, Chad .. A3 46
Ouricurí, Braz., 3,159 .. C2 57
Ourinhos, Braz., 25,717 .. C3 56
Ourique, Port., 2,180 .. D1 20
Ouro Fino, Braz., 8,044 .. C3, m8 56
Ouro Prêto, Braz., 14,722 .. F2 15
Ourthe, riv., Bel .. D5 57
Ourukaen, isl., Bikini .. 52
Ouse, riv., Eng .. D6 10
Outagamie, co., Wis., 101,794 .. D5 124
Outat el Hadj, Mor .. H5 30
Outer, isl., Que., Can .. C2 75
Outer, isl., Wis .. A3 124
Outer Hebrides, is., Scot .. C1 13
Outer Santa Barbara, chan., Calif .. F4 82
Outes, Sp., 869 .. A1 20
Outing, Cass, Minn., 70 .. D5 99
Outjo, S.W. Afr., 1,398 .. B2 49
Outlook, Sask., Can., 1,340 .. F2 70
Outlook, Sheridan, Mont., 226 .. B12 102
Outlook, Yakima, Wash., 325 .. C5 122
Outlying Islands (U.S.), see Baker, Canton, Enderbury, Howland, Jarvis, Johnston and Sand, Midway, Palmyra, Wake Islands and Kingman Reef.
Outreau, Fr., 13,548 .. B4 14
Outremont, Que., Can., 30,753 .. p19 73
Ouville-la-Rivière, Fr., 440 .. E8 12
Ouyen, Austl., 1,695 .. G4 51
Ouzinkie, Alsk., 214 .. D9 79
Ovada, It., 9,594 .. E4 18, B2 21
Oval, Lycoming, Pa., 100 .. D7 114
Oval peak, Wash .. A5 122
Ovalau, isl., Fiji Is .. 52
Ovalle, Chile, 26,000 .. A2 54
Ovando, Powell, Mont., 75 .. C3 102
Ovar, Port., 7,298 .. B1 20
Overath, Ger., 11,500 .. C2 17
Overbrook, Osage, Kans., 509 .. D8 93
Overbrook, Love, Okla., 50 .. C4 112
Overflowing, riv., Man., Sask., Can .. D5 70
Overgaard, Navajo, Ariz., 150 .. C5 80
Overijsche, Bel., 11,290 .. D4 15
Overijssel, prov., Neth., 783,400 .. B6 15
Overisel, Allegan, Mich., 150 .. F4 98
Overland, St. Louis, Mo., 22,763 .. *C7 101
Overland Park, Johnson, Kans., 21,110 .. B9 93
Overlea, Baltimore, Md., 10,795 .. B4, C3 85
Overly, Bottineau, N. Dak., 65 .. A5 110
Overstreet, Gulf, Fla., 100 .. B1, H3 86
Overton, Dawson, Nebr., 523 .. D6 103
Overton, Clark, Nev., 700 .. G7 104
Overton, Rusk, Tex., 1,950 .. C5 118
Overton, co., Tenn., 14,661 .. C8 117
Övertorneå, Swe., 1,536 .. D10 25
Ovett, Jones, Miss., 290 .. D4 100
Ovid, Sedgwick, Colo., 571 .. A8 83
Ovid, Bear Lake, Idaho, 200 .. G7 89
Ovid, Madison, Ind., 95 .. D6 91
Ovid, Clinton, Mich., 1,505 .. E6 98
Ovid, Seneca, N.Y., 789 .. C4 108
Oviedo, Seminole, Fla., 1,926 .. D5 86
Oviedo, Sp., 127,058 .. A3 20
Oviedo, prov., Sp., 989,344 .. *A3 20
Ovitt, Loup, Nebr .. B6 103
Ovruch, Sov. Un., 10,000 .. F7 27
Owaneco, Christian, Ill., 290 .. D4 90
Owanka, Pennington, S. Dak., 60 .. C3 116
Owasco, lake, N.Y .. C4 108
Owasso, Tulsa, Okla., 2,032 .. A6 112
Owatonna, Steele, Minn., 13,409 .. F5 99
Owego, Tioga, N.Y., 5,466 .. C4 108
Owen, Clark, Wis., 1,098 .. D3 124
Owen, co., Ind., 11,400 .. F4 91
Owen, co., Ky., 8,237 .. B5 94
Owen, lake, Wis .. B2 124
Owen, mtn., N.Z .. N14 52
Owen, sound, Ont., Can .. C4 72
Owendale, Huron, Mich., 298 .. E7 98
Owens, Cumberland, N.C., 5,207 .. *B5 109
Owens, creek, Md .. A3 85
Owens, lake, Calif .. D4 82
Owens, riv., Calif .. D4 82
Owensboro, Daviess, Ky., 42,471 .. C3 94
Owensboro East, Daviess, Ky., 2,244 .. *C3 94
Owensboro West, Daviess, Ky., 1,366 .. *C3 94
Owensburg, Greene, Ind., 400 .. G4 91
Owens Cross Roads, Madison, Ala., 600 .. A3 78
Owen Sound, Ont., Can., 17,421 .. C4 72
Owen Stanley, range, Pap .. k12 50
Owensville, Saline, Ark., 100 .. C3, C6 81
Owensville, Gibson, Ind., 1,121 .. H2 91
Owensville, Gasconade, Mo., 2,379 .. C6 101
Owensville, Clermont, Ohio, 609 .. C3 111
Owenton, Owen, Ky., 1,376 .. B5 94
Owerri, Nig., 2,069 .. E6 45
Owey, isl., Ire .. B3 11
Owikeno, lake, B.C., Can .. D4 68
Owings, Calvert, Md., 200 .. C4 85
Owings Mills, Baltimore, Md., 3,810 .. *B4 85
Owingsville, Bath, Ky., 1,040 .. B6 94
O-Wi-Yu-Kuts, mtn., Colo .. A2 83
Owl, creek, Wyo .. B4 125
Owl Creek, mts., Wyo .. B4 125
Owls Head, Knox, Maine, 450 (994▲) .. D3 96
Owosso, Shiawassee, Mich., 17,006 .. E6 98
Owsley, co., Ky., 5,369 .. C6 94
Owyhee, Elko, Nev., 500 .. B5 104
Owyhee, co., Idaho, 6,375 .. G2 89
Owyhee, dam Oreg .. D9 113
Owyhee, res., Oreg .. D9 113
Owyhee, riv., Idaho, Nev., Oreg .. E9 113
Öxabäck, Swe .. A6 24
Oxbow, Sask., Can., 1,359 .. H4 70
Oxbow, Aroostook, Maine, 35 (139▲) .. B4 96
Oxbow, Oakland, Mich., 1,700 .. *F7 98
Oxbow, dam, Idaho .. E2 89
Oxelösund, Swe., 10,000 .. u35 25
Oxford, Calhoun, Ala., 3,603 .. B4 78
Oxford, Izard, Ark., 191 .. A3 81
Oxford, N.S., Can., 1,471 .. D6 74
Oxford, New Haven, Conn., 400 (3,292▲) .. D4 84
Oxford, Eng., 107,100 (*185,000) .. C6 12
Oxford, Sumter, Fla., 287 .. D4 86
Oxford, Newton, Ga., 1,047 .. C3 87
Oxford, Franklin, Idaho, 83 .. G7 89
Oxford, Benton, Ind., 1,108 .. C3 91
Oxford, Johnson, Iowa, 633 .. C6 92
Oxford, Sumner, Kans., 989 .. E6 93
Oxford, De Soto, La., 350 .. C2 95
Oxford, Oxford, Maine, 550 (1,658▲) .. D2 96
Oxford, Talbot, Md., 852 .. C5 85
Oxford, Worcester, Mass., 7,100 (9,282▲) .. B4 97
Oxford, Oakland, Mich., 2,357 .. F7 98
Oxford, Lafayette, Miss., 5,283 .. A4 100
Oxford, Furnas and Harlan, Nebr., 1,090 .. D6 103
Oxford, Warren, N.J., 1,000 .. B3 106
Oxford, Chenango, N.Y., 1,871 .. C5 108
Oxford, Granville, N.C., 6,978 .. A5 109
Oxford, Butler, Ohio, 7,828 .. C3 111
Oxford, Chester, Pa., 3,376 .. G10 114
Oxford, Marquette, Wis., 548 .. E4 124
Oxford, co., Ont., Can., 70,499 .. D4 72
Oxford, co., Eng., 309,458 .. C6 12
Oxford, co., Maine, 44,345 .. D2 96
Oxford, lake, Man., Can .. B4 71
Oxford House, Man., Can .. B4 71
Oxford Junction, N.S., Can., 170 .. D6 74
Oxford Junction, Jones, Iowa, 725 .. C7 92
Oxley, Searcy, Ark., 75 .. B3 81
Oxly, Ripley, Mo., 100 .. E7 101
Oxnard, Ventura, Calif., 40,265 .. E4 82
Oxnard Beach, Ventura, Calif., 2,000 .. *E4 82
Oxon Hill, Prince Georges, Md., 900 .. C1 85
Oxus (Amu Darya), riv., Afg., Sov. Un .. C14 41
Oyama, B.C., Can., 197 .. D8 68
Oyat, riv., Sov. Un .. A10 27
Oyem, Gabon .. E2 46
Oyen, Alta., Can., 780 .. D5 69
Oyens, Plymouth, Iowa, 114 .. B1 92
Öyeren, lake, Nor .. p29 25
Oykell, riv., Scot .. C4 13
Oykell Bridge, Scot .. C4 13
Oymyakon, Sov. Un .. C17 28
Oyo, Nig., 72,133 .. E5 45
Oyonnax, Fr., 14,830 .. D6 14
Oyrot-Tura, see Gorno-Altaysk, Sov. Un.
Oyster, keys, Fla .. G6 86
Oyster Bay, Nassau, N.Y., 6,500 .. E7, n15 108
Oyster Bay Cove, Nassau, N.Y., 988 .. *F2 84
Ozamiz, Phil., 17,940 (44,091▲) .. D6 35
Ozan, Hempstead, Ark., 95 .. D2 81
Ozark, Dale, Ala., 9,534 .. D4 78
Ozark, Franklin, Ark., 1,965 .. B2 81
Ozark, Mackinac, Mich., 10 .. B6 98
Ozark, Christian, Mo., 1,536 .. D4 101
Ozark, co., Mo., 6,744 .. E5 101
Ozark, escarpment, Ark., Mo .. E7 101
Ozark, plat., Okla .. A7 106, A2 81
Ozarks, lake, Mo .. C5 101
Ozarowice, Pol .. g10 26
Ozaukee, co., Wis., 38,441 .. E6 124
Ozawkie, Jefferson, Kans., 265 .. B7 93
Ozd, Hung., 34,155 .. A5 22
Ozero Imandra, lake, Sov. Un .. D15 25
Ozette, lake, Wash .. A1 122
Ozieri, It., 11,884 .. D2 21
Ozona, Pinellas, Fla., 700 .. E1 86
Ozona, Pearl River, Miss., 300 .. E4 100
Ozona, Crockett, Tex., 3,361 .. D2 118
Ozorkow, Pol., 14,800 .. C5 26
Ozu, Jap., 17,100 .. J6 37
Ozuluama, Mex., 1,836 .. C5, m15 63

P

Pa, China .. E7 36
Paan, China .. E4 34
Paar, riv., Ger .. E6 17
Paarl, S. Afr., 41,540 .. D2 49
Paauhau, Hawaii, Haw., 500 .. C6 88
Paauilo, Hawaii, Haw., 1,059 .. C6 88
Pabbay, isl., Scot .. C1 13
Pabianice, Pol., 57,800 .. C5 26
Pablo, Lake, Mont., 300 .. C2 102
Pabna, Pak., 32,240 .. E12 40
Pacaás Novos, mts., Braz .. E2 59
Pacajá, riv., Braz .. C4 59
Pacajá Grande, riv., Braz .. C4 59
Pacaraima, mts., Braz .. C5 60
Pacasmayo, Peru, 6,615 .. C2 58
Pace, Santa Rosa, Fla., 900 .. G2 86
Pachai, China, 3,000 .. K2 36
Pachaug, pond, Conn .. C9 84
Pacheco, Contra Costa, Calif., 1,518 .. *C2 82
Pachmarhi, India .. F7 40
Pachuca [de Soto], Mex., 64,571 .. C5, m14 63
Pachung, China, 16,000 .. I2 36
Pachuta, Clarke, Miss., 271 .. C5 100
Pacific, B.C., Can., 40 .. B3 68
Pacific, Franklin and St. Louis, Mo., 2,795 .. B7, C7 101
Pacific, King, Wash., 1,577 .. D2 122
Pacific, co., Wash., 14,674 .. C2 122
Pacific, creek, Wyo .. C3 125
Pacific, mtn., Calif .. F2 82
Pacific, ocean .. F6, H7 2, 7
Pacific, ranges, B.C., Can .. D4 68
Pacifica, San Mateo, Calif., 20,995 .. *B5 82
Pacific City, Tillamook, Oreg., 350 .. B3 113
Pacific Grove, Monterey, Calif., 12,121 .. C6, D3 82
Pacific Islands Trust Territory, U.S. trust., Oceania, 90,000 .. *F10 7
Pacific Junction, Mills, Iowa, 560 .. C2 92
Packard, Piscataquis, Maine .. C4 96
Packard, mtn., Mass .. B3 97
Pack Monadnock, mtn., N.H .. E3 105
Packwaukee, Marquette, Wis., 300 .. E4 124
Packwood, Jefferson, Iowa, 215 .. C5 92
Pacolet, Spartanburg, S.C., 1,252 .. B4 115
Pacolet, riv., S.C .. A4 115
Pacolet Mills, Spartanburg, S.C., 1,476 .. B4 115
Pacora, Pan., 1,334 .. k12 62
Pacov, Czech., 2,816 .. D9 17
Pacquet, Newf., Can., 328 .. C4 75
Pactola, res., S. Dak .. C2 116
Pactolus, Pitt, N.C., 211 .. B6 109
Paczkow, Pol., 6,955 .. C4 26
Padagi, Iran .. F10 41
Padang, Indon., 143,615 .. F2 35
Padangpandjang, Indon., 25,509 .. F1 35
Padangsidempuan, Indon., 5,709 .. m11, E1 35
Padauiri, riv., Braz .. C5 60
Paddle Prairie, Alta., Can., 339 .. f7 69
Paddling, lake, Sask., Can .. E2 70
Paddockwood, Sask., Can., 219 .. D3 70
Paddy Knob, mtn., W. Va .. C5 123
Paden, Tishomingo, Miss., 134 .. A5 100
Paden, Okfuskee, Okla., 417 .. B5 112
Paden City, Tyler and Wetzel, W. Va., 3,137 .. B4 123
Paderborn, Ger., 57,000 .. B3 17
Pad Idan, Pak .. B2 40
Padilla, Bol., 2,462 .. C3 55
Padova (Padua), It., 207,600 .. D7 18, B3 21
Padre, isl., Tex .. F4 118
Padroni, Logan, Colo., 110 .. A7 83
Padstow, Eng., 2,676 .. D3 12
Padua (Padova), It., 207,600 .. D7 18, B3 21
Paducah, McCracken, Ky., 34,479 .. A2 94
Paducah, Cottle, Tex., 2,392 .. B2 118
Padwa, India, 5,000 .. H9 40
Paepaealeia, cape, W. Sam .. 52
Paeroa, N.Z., 2,894 .. L15 51
Paestum, ruins, It .. D5 21
Pafúri, Moz .. B5 49
Pag, isl., Yugo .. C2 22
Pagadian, Phil., 9,839 .. *D6 35
Pagai Selatan, isl., Indon .. F2 35
Pagai Utara, isl., Indon .. F2 35
Pagan, isl., Mariana Is .. E8 7, F10 34
Pagat, pt., Guam .. 52
Pagatan, Indon .. F4 35
Pagato, riv., Sask., Can .. A4 70
Page, Coconino, Ariz., 2,960 .. A4 80
Page, Holt, Nebr., 230 .. B7 103
Page, Cass, N. Dak., 432 .. B8 110
Page, Le Flore, Okla., 35 .. C7 112
Page, Fayette, W. Va., 800 .. C3, D6 123
Page, co., Iowa, 21,023 .. D2 92
Page, co., Va., 15,572 .. C4 121
Page City, Logan, Kans., 100 .. C2 93
Pagedale, St. Louis, Mo., 5,106 .. *A8 101
Pageland, Chesterfield, S.C., 2,020 .. B7 115
Page Manor, Montgomery, Ohio, 5,000 .. C3 111
Pageton, McDowell, W. Va., 400 .. *D3 123
Paglia, mtn., Switz .. D7 19
Pagny [-sur-Moselle], Fr., 3,301 .. F6 15
Pago, bay, Guam .. 52
Pago, pt., Guam .. 52
Pagoda, peak, Colo .. A3 83
Pago Pago, Am. Sam., 1,251 .. 52
Pago Pago, hbr., Am. Sam .. 52
Pagosa Junction, Archuleta, Colo., 50 .. D3 83
Pagosa Springs, Archuleta, Colo., 1,374 .. D3 83
Paguate, Valencia, N. Mex., 550 .. B2 107
Pahala, Hawaii, Haw., 1,602 .. D6 88
Pahang, state, Mala., 313,058 .. J5 38
Pahang, riv., Mala .. K5 38
Paharpur, Pak .. A3 40
Pahlavi, Iran, 31,349 .. C4 41
Pahoa, Hawaii, Haw., 1,046 .. D7 88
Pahokee, Palm Beach, Fla., 4,709 .. F6 86
Pahra, Afg., 5,000 .. D10 41
Pahranagat, range, Nev .. F6 104
Pahrump, Nye, Nev., 35 .. G5 104
Pahute, mesa, Nev .. F5 104
Pahute, peak, Nev .. B2 104
Paia, Maui, Haw., 3,195 .. C5 88
Paichuan, China, 5,000 .. C3 37
Paignton, Eng., 30,289 .. D4 12
Paiho, China .. H4 36
Päijänne, lake, Fin .. G11 25
Pailingmiao, China .. D4 36
Pailo, Bledsoe, Tenn., 15 .. D8 117
Paincourt, Ont., Can., 289 .. E2 72
Paincourtville, Assumption, La., 500 .. B5 95
Paine Oeste, mtn., Chile .. E2 54
Painesville, Lake, Ohio, 16,116 .. A6 111
Paint, Somerset, Pa., 1,275 .. *F4 114
Paint, creek, Ohio .. C4 111
Paint, creek, W. Va .. D6 123
Paint, lake, Man., Can .. B3 71
Paint, mtn., W. Va .. D6 123
Paint, riv., Mich .. B2 98
Paint Bank, Craig, Va., 100 .. D2 121
Painted Desert, Ariz .. A4 80
Painted Post, Steuben, N.Y., 2,570 .. C3 108
Painter, Accomack, Va., 349 .. D7 121
Painter, Park, Wyo .. A3 125
Paint Lick, Garrard, Ky., 200 .. C5 94
Paint Rock, Jackson, Ala., 264 .. A3 78
Paint Rock, Concho, Tex., 400 .. D3 118
Paintsville, Johnson, Ky., 4,025 .. C7 94
Paisley, Ont., Can., 759 .. C3 72
Paisley, Lake, Fla., 350 .. D5 86
Paisley, Lake, Oreg., 219 .. E6 113
Paisley, Scot., 96,700 .. E4 13
Paita, Peru, 7,177 .. C1 58
Paja, Pan., 570 .. m11 62
Pajala, Swe., 1,407 .. D10 25
Pajarito, Bernalillo, N. Mex., 1,500 .. *B3 107
Pajaro, Monterey, Calif., 1,273 .. *C6 82
Pajaros, isl, Mariana Is .. E8 7
Pajaro, riv., Calif .. C6 82
Pajon, pt., Guam .. 52
Pakanbaru, Indon, 69,147 .. E2 35
Pakaraima, mts., Br. Gu .. A2 59
Pakenham, Ont., Can., 350 .. B8 72
Pakhoi, China, 50,000 .. G6 34
Pakistan, country, Asia, 102,700,000 .. G9, G11 33, C4, D9 39, D2, D12 40
Pakli, China .. C8 38
Pakokku, Bur., 30,943 .. D10 39
Pakowki, lake, Alta., Can .. E5 69
Pakra, riv., Yugo .. C3 22
Paks, Hung., 10,452 .. B4 22
Pakse, Laos, 25,000 .. E6 38
Pakwa, lake, Man., Can .. B2 71
Pala, Chad, 7,451 .. D3 46
Palacois, Matagorda, Tex., 3,676 .. E4 118
Palafrugell, Sp., 7,905 .. B7 20
Palagruza, is., Yugo .. D3 22
Palaiokhora, Grc., 2,130 .. E4 23
Palaion Faliron, Grc., 22,157 .. h11 23
Palaiseau, Fr., 16,326 .. h9 14
Palamas, Grc., 5,370 .. C4 23
Palamós, Sp., 7,639 .. B7 20
Palana, Sov. Un., 1,000 .. D18 28
Palanga, Sov. Un., 4,600 .. D3 27
Palanpur, India, 29,139 .. E4 40
Palapag, Phil., 7,862 .. C7 35
Palapye, Bech., 1,042 .. B4 49
Palas de Rey, Sp., 769 .. A2 20
Palatine, Cook, Ill., 15,189 .. A5, E2 90
Palatka, Putnam, Fla., 11,028 .. C5 86
Palau (Pelew), is., Pac. O .. 52
Palauig, Phil., 1,986 .. o12 35
Palauli, W. Sam., 603 .. 52
Palauli, bay, W. Sam .. 52
Palawan, prov., Phil., 162,900 .. *C5 35
Palawan, isl., Phil .. C5 35
Palayamcottai, India, 51,002 .. *G6 39
Palazzolo Acreide, It., 11,024 .. F5 21
Palco, Rooks, Kans., 575 .. C4 93
Palembang, Indon., 458,661 .. F2 35
Palena, riv., Chile .. C2 54
Palencia, Sp., 48,216 .. A3 20
Palencia, prov., Sp., 231,977 .. *A3 20
Palenque, ruins, Mex .. B1 62
Palenville, Greene, N.Y., 550 .. C6 108
Palermo, It., 614,000 .. E4 21
Palermo, Cape May, N.J., 100 .. E3 106
Palermo, Mountrail, N. Dak., 188 .. A3 110
Palestine, St. Francis, Ark., 532 .. C5 81
Palestine, Crawford, Ill., 1,564 .. D6 90
Palestine, Darke, Ohio, 257 .. B3 111
Palestine, Anderson, Tex., 13,974 .. D5 118
Palestine, Wirt, W. Va., 100 .. B3 123
Palestine (Gaza Strip), see Gaza Area, Eg. occ., Asia
Palestine, reg., Asia .. C7 32
Palestine Potash Company, Jordan .. h13 32
Palestrina, It., 9,154 .. h9 21
Paletwa, Bur., 5,000 .. D9 39
Palezgir Chauki, Pak .. B2 40
Palghat, India, 77,620 .. F6 39
Palgrave, Ont., Can., 234 .. D5 72
Palhoça, Braz., 1,456 .. D3 56
Pali, India, 33,303 .. E4 40
Palidoro (Baebiana), It., 2,169 .. h8 21
Palikea, mtn., Haw .. g9 88
Palikir, pass, Ponape .. 52
Palikir, pt., Ponape .. 52
Palimé, Togo .. E5 45
Palisade, Mesa, Colo., 860 .. B2 83
Palisade, Aitkin, Minn., 180 .. D5 99
Palisade, Hitchcock, Nebr., 544 .. D4 103
Palisade, Eureka, Nev., 25 .. C5 104

Palisades, Bonneville, Idaho, 75 F7 89
Palisades, Douglas, Wash., 15 B6 122
Palisades, The, cliffs, N.J. h9 106
Palisades Park, Bergen, N.J., 11,943 h8 106
Paliseul, Bel., 1,667 E5 15
Palitana, India, 24,581 C5 40
Palk, strait, Cey., India G6 39
Pallaskenry, Ire., 315 E3 11
Pallasovka, Sov. Un. C3 29
Palling, B.C., Can., 139 B5 68
Palliser, cape, N.Z. N15 51
Pall Mall, Fentriss, Tenn., 125 C9 117
Palls, King William, Va. D5 121
Palma, Moz. D7 48
Palma, isl., Sp. (Can. Is.) m13 20
Palma, riv., Braz. D1 57
Palma del Río, Sp., 11,324 D3 20
Palma [de Mallorca], Sp., 159,084 C7 20
Palmares, Braz., 17,327 C3, k6 57
Palmas, Braz., 5,540 D2 56
Palmas, cape, I.C. F3 45
Palmas, Atlas, P.R. B4 65
Palmas de Monte Alto, Braz., 1,279 D2 57
Palma Soriano, Cuba, 33,000 E6 64
Palm Bay, Brevard, Fla., 2,808 D6 86
Palm Beach, Palm Beach, Fla., 6,055 F6 86
Palm Beach, co., Fla., 228,106 F6 86
Palm Beach Shores, Palm Beach, Fla., 885 *F6 86
Palm City, San Diego, Calif. (part of San Diego) E2 82
Palmdale, Los Angeles, Calif., 11,522 E4 82
Palmdale, Glades, Fla., 150 F5 86
Palm Desert, Riverside, Calif., 1,295 *F5 82
Palmeira, Braz., 5,916 D3 56
Palmeira dos Indios, Braz., 15,642 C3, k5 57
Palmeir in Has, pt., Ang. C1 48
Palmer, Alsk., 1,181 C10, g17 79
Palmer, Sask., Can., 104 H2 70
Palmer, Christian, Ill., 265 D4 90
Palmer, Pocahontas, Iowa, 271 B3 92
Palmer, Washington, Kans., 169 C6 93
Palmer, Hampden, Mass., 4,000 (10,358▲) B3 97
Palmer, Marquette, Mich., 850 B3 98
Palmer, Merrick, Nebr., 418 C7 103
Palmer, Grundy, Tenn., 1,069 D8 117
Palmer, Ellis, Tex., 613 B6 118
Palmer, King, Wash., 25 D2 122
Palmer Heights, Northampton, Pa., 2,597 *E11 114
Palmer Lake, El Paso, Colo., 542 B6 83
Palmer Land, reg., Ant. B6 5
Palmer Park, Prince Georges, Md., 4,000 *C4 85
Palmerston, Ont., Can., 1,554 D4 72
Palmerston, N.Z., 868 P13 51
Palmerston North, N.Z., 44,900 (*47,400) N15 51
Palmersville, Weakley, Tenn., 150 A3 117
Palmerton, Carbon, Pa., 5,942 E10 114
Palmerville, Austl. C7 50
Palmetto, Manatee, Fla., 5,556 E4, F2 86
Palmetto, Fulton and Coweta, Ga., 1,466 C2 87
Palmetto, St. Landry, La., 430 D4 95
Palm Harbor, Pinellas, Fla., 1,000 E2 86
Palmi, It., 15,400 E5 21
Palmira, Col., 83,000 C2 60
Palmira, Cuba, 5,865 D3 64
Palmira, Ec. B2 58
Palms, Sanilac, Mich., 50 E8 98
Palms, is., S.C. F8 115
Palm Springs, Riverside, Calif., 13,468 F5 82
Palm Springs, Palm Beach, Fla., 2,503 F6 86
Palm Valley, St. Johns, Fla., 300 C6 86
Palmyra, Macoupin, Ill., 811 D4 90
Palmyra, Harrison, Ind., 470 H5 91
Palmyra, Warren, Iowa, 50 B7 92
Palmyra, Marion, Mo., 2,933 B6 101
Palmyra, Otoe, Nebr., 377 D9, E2 103
Palmyra, Burlington, N.J., 7,036 C2 106
Palmyra, Wayne, N.Y., 3,476 B3 108
Palmyra, Halifax, N.C., 50 A6 109
Palmyra, Lebanon, Pa., 6,999 F8 114
Palmyra, Syr., 8,500 E12 31
Palmyra, Montgomery, Tenn., 100 A4 117
Palmyra, Fluvanna, Va., 350 D4 121
Palmyra, Jefferson, Wis., 1,000 F5 124
Palmyra, isl., Pac. O. F12 7
Palmyras, pt., India G11 40
Palni, India, 39,832 (*56,909) *F6 39
Palo, Linn, Iowa, 387 B6 92
Palo, Ionia, Mich., 250 E4 98
Palo (Alsium), It., 363 h8 21
Palo Alto, Santa Clara, Calif., 52,287 B5, D2 82
Palo Alto, Schuylkill, Pa., 1,445 *E9 114
Palo Alto., co., Iowa, 14,736 A3 92
Palo Blanco, P.R. B4 65
Paloduro, Armstrong, Tex., 30 B2 118
Palo Duro, canyon, Tex. B2 118
Paloich, Sud. C3 47
Palomar, mtn., Calif. F5 82
Palomas, mtn., Ariz. D2 80
Palombara Sabina, It., 6,215 g9 21
Palominos, isl., P.R. f12 65
Palo Pinto, Palo Pinto, Tex., 525 C3 118
Palo Pinto, co., Tex., 20,516 C3 118
Palopo, Indon., 4,208 F6 35
Palos, cape, Sp. D5 20
Palo Seco, P.R., 709 B6 65
Palos Heights, Cook, Ill., 3,775 *F3 90
Palos Hills, Cook, Ill., 3,766 *F2 90
Palos Park, Cook, Ill., 2,169 F2 90
Palos Verdes Estates, Los Angeles, Calif., 9,564 *F2 83
Palourde, lake, La. E4 95
Palouse, Whitman, Wash., 926 C8 122
Palouse, riv., Wash. C7 122
Palo Verde, Maricopa, Ariz., 200 D3, G1 80
Palo Verde, Imperial, Calif., 150 F6 82
Palpa, Peru, 2,171 D3 58
Pålsboda, Swe., 1,140 t33 25
Palua, Ven. B5 60
Paluan, Phil., 1,835 *C6 35
Palung, China D4 34
Pama, Upper Volta D5 45
Pambrun, Sask., Can., 117 H2 70
Pamekasan, Indon., 24,912 G4 35
Pamiers, Fr., 13,297 F4 14
Pamir, mts., China, Sov. Un. H23 9
Pamlico, co., N.C., 9,850 B7 109
Pamlico, riv., N.C. B7 109
Pamlico, sound, N.C. B7 109
Pampa, Gray, Tex., 24,664 B2 118
Pampa Grande, Bol., 727 C3 55
Pampanga, prov., Phil., 615,800 *B6 35
Pampanga, riv., Phil. o13 35
Pampa Peñon, Chile D2 55
Pampas, Peru, 1,622 D3 58
Pampas, reg., Arg. G4 55
Pampilhosa do Botão, Port., 2,779 B1 20
Pamplico, Florence, S.C., 988 D8 115
Pamplin, Appomattox and Prince Edward, Va., 312 D4 121
Pamplona, Col., 16,396 B3 60
Pamplona, Sp., 97,880 A5 20
Pamunkey, riv., Va. D5 121
Pana, Ont., Can. h13 72
Pana, Christian, Ill., 6,432 D4 90
Panaca, Lincoln, Nev., 500 F7 104
Panacea, Wakulla, Fla., 600 B2 86
Panache, lake, Ont., Can. A3 72
Panagyurishte, Bul., 12,015 D7 22
Panaitan, isl., Indon. G3 35
Panama, Montgomery, Ill., 487 D4 90
Panama, Shelby, Iowa, 257 C2 92
Panama, Lancaster, Nebr., 155 D9 103
Panama, Chautauqua, N.Y., 450 C1 108
Panama, LeFlore, Okla., 937 B7 112
Panamá, Pan., 306,000 (*330,000) F8, m11 62
Panama, country, N.A., 1,225,000 I12 61, F7 62
Panama, bay, Pan. F8 62
Panama, canal, C.Z. F8, k11 62
Panama, gulf, Pan. F8 62
Panama Canal Zone, see Canal Zone, U.S. dep., N.A.
Panama City, Bay, Fla., 33,275 G3 86
Panama City Beach, Bay, Fla., 36 G3 86
Panamint, range, Calif. D5 82
Panao, Peru, 954 C2 58
Panarea, isl., It. E5 21
Panaro, riv., It. B3 21
Panay, isl., Phil. C6 35
Pancake, range, Nev. E5 104
Pancevo, Yugo., 40,740 C5 22
Panco, Clay, Ky., 200 C6 94
Pancoastburg, Fayette, Ohio, 75 C4 111
Panda, Moz. E6 49
Pandale, Val Verde, Tex., 10 D2 123
Pandan, Phil., 3,379 *C6 35
Pandharpur, India, 45,421 E5 40
Pandhurna, India G7 40
Pando, Ur., 6,248 E1 56
Pando, dept., Bol., 19,804 B2 55
Pandora, Putnam, Ohio, 782 B4 111
Pandora, Wilson, Tex., 250 B4, E4 123
Pandu, Con. L. A2 48
Panelas, Braz., 1,717 k6 57
Panet, Que., Can., 571 C7 73
Panevezys, Sov. Un., 41,100 D5 27
Panfilov, Sov. Un., 27,300 E9 28
Pangala, Con. B. F2 46
Pangasinan, prov., Phil., 1,124,800 *B6 35
Pangburn, White, Ark., 489 B4 81
Pangfou, see Pengpu, China
Pangi, Con. L. B4 48
Pangim, Goa, 14,213 E5 39
Pañginay, Phil. o13 35
Pangkalanbuun, Indon. F4 35
Pangkalangresik, Indon. F2 35
Pangkalpinang, Indon., 58,540 F3 35
Pangkong, lake, China B6 39
Pangman, Sask., Can., 260 H3 70
Pangnirtung, N.W. Ter., Can., 114 C19 67
Pangong, lake, India B6 39
Pangsau, pass, Bur. C10 39
Panguitch, Garfield, Utah, 1,435 F3 119
Panhandle, Carson, Tex., 1,958 B2 123
Panihati, India, 93,749 *F12 40
Panipat, India, 67,026 C6 40
Paniqui, Phil., 4,789 o13 35
Panjang, isl., Viet. H5 38
Panjao, Afg., 10,000 D13 41
Panjgur, Pak., 754 D3 39
Panjim, India, 31,950 E5 39
Panjpai, Pak. G13 41
Pankshin, Nig., 5,654 E6 45
Panmunjom, Kor. H3 37
Panna, India, 16,737 E8 40
Panola, Sumter, Ala., 250 C1 78
Panola, co., Miss., 28,791 A3 100
Panola, co., Tex., 16,870 C5 123
Panora, Guthrie, Iowa, 1,019 C3 92
Panshan, China C9 36
Panshih, China, 5,000 E2 37
Pantar, isl., Indon. G6 35
Pantego, Beaufort, N.C., 262 B7 109
Pantelleria, It., 2,294 F3 21
Pantelleria, isl., It. F3 21
Pantin, Fr., 46,292 g10 14
Panton, Addison, Vt., 35 (352▲) C2 120
Pantsyan, China C5 36
Pánuco, Mex., 8,688 C5, k14 63
Pánuco, riv., Mex. k14 63
Panulcillo, Chile F1 55
Panzi, Con. L. C2 48
Panzós, Guat., 573 C3 62
Paochang, China D6 36
Paocheng, China, 10,000 H2 36
Paochi, China, 130,100 G2 36
Paoching, China, 5,000 C6 37
Pão de Açúcar, Braz., 4,729 C3 57
Paokang, China, 10,000 I4 36
Paokuotu, China C9 36
Paola, It., 9,197 E6 21
Paola, Miami, Kans., 4,784 D9 93
Paoli, Phillips, Colo., 81 A8 83
Paoli, Orange, Ind., 2,754 G5 91
Paoli, Garvin, Okla., 358 C4 112
Paoli, Chester, Pa., 5,000 A10 114
Paonia, Delta, Colo., 1,083 C3 83
Paoshan, China, 12,000 F4 34
Paote, China E4 36
Paoti, China E7 36
Paoting (Tsingyuan), China, 265,000 E6 36
Paotow, China, 400,000 D4 36
Paoua, Cen. Afr. Rep. D3 46
Paoying, China, 85,000 H8 36
Pap, mtn., Scot. D3 13
Papa, Hawaii, Haw., 50 D6 88
Papa, Hung., 25,629 B3 22
Papaaloa, Hawaii, Haw., 500 D6 88
Papagayo, gulf, C.R. E5 62
Papago, Indian res., Ariz. E3 80
Papaikou, Hawaii, Haw., 1,427 D6 88
Papalaulelei, cape, W. Sam. 52
Papantla, Mex., 18,579 C5, m15 63
Papatele, mtn., Am. Sam. 52
Papaya, Phil., 7,301 o13 35
Papeete, Fr. Polynesia, Oceania, 18,089 H13 7
Papenburg, Ger., 15,000 B3 16
Paper Mill Village, Bennington, Vt., 100 F2 120
Paphos, Cyp., 7,283 E9 31
Papigi, see Parigi, Indon.
Papillion, Sarpy, Nebr., 2,235 C9, E3 103
Papillion, creek, Nebr. E3 103
Papineau, co., Que., Can., 32,697 D2 73
Papineau, lake, Ont., Can. B7 72
Papineauville, Que., Can., 1,300 D2 73
Paposo, Chile E1 55
Papua, Austl. dep., Oceania, 560,000 k12 50
Papua, gulf, N. Gui. k11 50
Papudo, Chile A2 54
Papun, Bur., 1,881 E10 39
Papy, pt., Fla. E2 86
Paquette, Que., Can., 93 D6 73
Paquetville, N.B., Can., 380 B4 74
Pará, state, Braz., 1,550,935 B1 57
Pará, riv., Braz. B1 57
Parabel, Sov. Un. B10 29
Paracale, Phil., 3,204 o14 35
Paracatu, Braz., 5,909 E1 57
Paracatu, riv., Braz. E1 57
Paracel, is., China B4 35
Parachinar, Pak. E15 46
Paraćin, Yugo., 15,627 D5 22
Paracurú, Braz., 2,484 B3 57
Parade, Dewey, S. Dak., 10 B4 116
Paradis, St. Charles, La., 800 C6 95
Paradise, Butte, Calif., 8,268 C3 82
Paradise, Stanislaus, Calif., 5,616 *D3 82
Paradise, Russell, Kans., 134 C5 93
Paradise, Sanders, Mont., 300 C2 102
Paradise, Wallowa, Oreg. B9 113
Paradise, Lancaster, Pa., 750 F9 114
Paradise, Cache, Utah, 368 B4 119
Paradise, riv., Newf., Can. B3 75
Paradise Hill, Sask., Can., 282 D1 70
Paradise Hills, Bernalillo, N. Mex., 2,000 B3, k7 107
Paradise River, Newf., Can., 161 B3 75
Paradise Valley, Maricopa, Ariz., 1,000 G2 80
Paradise Valley, Alta., Can., 182 C5 69
Paradise Valley, Humboldt, Nev., 65 B4 104
Paradox, Montrose, Colo., 50 C2 83
Paradox, valley, Colo. C2 83
Paragon, Morgan, Ind., 560 F4 91
Paragonah, Iron, Utah, 300 F3 119
Paragould, Greene, Ark., 9,947 A5 81
Paragua, riv., Ven. B5 60
Paraguaçu, riv., Braz. D3 57
Paraguaçu Paulista, Braz., 11,391 C2 56
Paraguai, riv., Braz. B1 56
Paraguaná, pen., Ven. A4 60
Paraguarí, Par., 12,405 E4 55
Paraguarí, dept., Par., 159,161 E4 55
Paraguay, country, S.A., 1,920,000 F5 53, D4 55
Paraguay, riv., Par. D4 55
Paraíba, state, Braz., 2,018,023 C3, h6 57
Paraíba, riv., Braz. C4 56
Paraíba do Sul, Braz., 7,675 h6 56
Paraíso, Mex., 2,804 D6 63
Paraisópolis, Braz., 6,582 C3 56
Parakhino-Poddubye, Sov. Un., 20,000 B9 27
Parakou, Dah., 5,700 E5 45
Paraloma, Sevier, Ark., 94 D1 81
Param, isl., Ponape 52
Paramaribo, Sur., 122,600 A3 59
Paramé, Fr., 8,811 C2 14
Paramirim, Braz., 1,776 D2 57
Paramithia, Grc., 2,956 C3 23
Paramonga, Peru D2 58
Paramount, Los Angeles, Calif., 27,249 *F2 82
Paramount, Washington, Md., 200 A2 85
Paramus, Bergen, N.J., 23,238 h8 106
Paraná, Arg., 111,000 A4 54
Paraná, Braz., 970 D1 57
Paraná, state, Braz., 4,227,763 C2 56
Paraná, riv., Arg., Braz. E4 55, C2 56
Paranã, riv., Braz. D1 57
Paranaguá, Braz., 27,728 D3 56
Paranaíba, Braz., 3,853 B2 56
Paranaíba, riv., Braz. B2 56
Paranam, Sur. A3 59
Paranapanema, riv., Braz. C2 56
Parañaque, Phil., 61,898 *C6 35
Paranatinga, riv., Braz. E3 59
Parangaba, Braz., 92,534 *B3 57
Paraopeba, Braz., 3,678 E1 57
Parapetí, riv., Bol. C3 55
Paratinga, Braz., 2,403 D2 57
Paray-le-Monial, Fr., 9,557 D6 14
Parbati, riv., India E6 40
Parbhani, India, 36,795 H6 40
Parchim, Ger., 18,900 B5 16
Parchment, Kalamazoo, Mich., 1,565 F5 98
Parcperdue, Iberia, La. D4 95
Parczew, Pol., 6,173 C7 26
Pardeeville, Columbia, Wis., 1,331 E4 124
Pardess Hanna, Isr., 7,073 B6 32
Pardo, riv., Braz. C2 56
Pardo, riv., Braz. C3 56
Pardo, riv., Braz. E2 57
Pardoe, Mercer, Pa., 120 D1 114
Pardoo, Austl. D2 50
Pardubice, Czech., 55,300 C3 26
Pardum, Blaine, Nebr. B5 103
Parecis, mts., Braz. E2 59
Paredes, de Nava, Sp., 4,733 A3 20
Parent, Que., Can., 1,298 k12 73
Parepare, Indon., 62,683 F5 35
Parga, Grc., 1,722 C3 23
Pargolovo, Sov. Un., 5,000 r31 25
Parguera, P.R. D2 65
Parhams, Catahoula, La., 35 C4 95
Paria, gulf, Ven. A5 60
Paria, pen., Ven. A5 60
Paria, riv., Utah F4 119
Pariaguán, Ven., 6,094 B5 60
Paricutin, vol., Mex. n12 63
Parigi, Indon. F6 35
Parika, Br. Gu., 577 A3 59
Parima, mts., Braz. C5 60
Pariñas, pt., Peru B1 58
Parintins, Braz., 9,068 C3 59
Pario, riv., Ariz. A4 80
Paris, Logan, Ark., 3,007 B2 81
Paris, Ont., Can., 5,820 D4 72
Paris, Fr., 2,790,091 (*7,750,000) C5, g10 14, F2 15
Paris, Bear Lake, Idaho, 746 G7 89
Paris, Edgar, Ill., 9,823 D6 90
Paris, Bourbon, Ky., 7,791 B5 94
Paris, Oxford, Maine, 200 (3,601▲) D2 96
Paris, Calvert, Md., 100 C4 85
Paris, Mecosta, Mich., 180 E5 98
Paris, Lafayette, Miss., 102 A4 100
Paris, Monroe, Mo., 1,393 B5 101
Paris, Greenville, S.C., 1,000 *B3 115
Paris, Henry, Tenn., 9,325 A3 117
Paris, Lamar, Tex., 20,977 C5 118
Paris, Fauquier, Va., 100 B5 121
Paris, Kenosha, Wis. F1 124
Paris Crossing, Jennings, Ind., 135 G6 91
Parish, Oswego, N.Y., 567 B4 108
Parishville, St. Lawrence, N.Y., 400 f10 108
Parisville, Que., Can. C5 63
Park, Grove, Kans., 218 C3 93
Park, co., Colo., 1,822 B5 83
Park, co., Mont., 13,168 E6 102
Park, co., Wyo., 16,874 A3 125
Park, plat., Colo. B3 83
Park, range, Colo., Wyo. B4 83
Parkbeg, Sask., Can., 80 G2 70
Park City, Lake, Ill., 1,408 *A6 90
Park City, Sedgwick, Kans., 2,687 B5 93
Park City, Barren, Ky., 497 C4 94
Park City, Stillwater, Mont., 300 E8 102
Park City, Summit, Utah, 1,366 C4 119
Parkdale, Ashley, Ark., 448 D4 81
Parkdale, P.E.I., Can., 1,735 C6 74
Parkdale, Fremont, Colo., 35 C5 83
Parkdale, Hood River, Oreg., 400 B5 113
Parkdale, Douglas, Wis. B2 124
Parke, co., Ind., 14,804 E3 91
Parker, Yuma, Ariz., 1,642 C1 80
Parker, Douglas, Colo., 100 B6 83
Parker, Bay, Fla., 2,669 G3 86
Parker, Fremont, Idaho, 284 F7 89
Parker, Linn, Kans., 181 D8 93
Parker, Polk, Oreg. C1 113
Parker, Armstrong, Pa., 945 D2 114
Parker, Turner, S. Dak., 1,142 D8 116
Parker, Spotsylvania, Va., 100 C5 121
Parker, Yakima, Wash., 300 C5 122
Parker, co., Tex., 22,880 C4 118
Parker, dam, Ariz. C1 80
Parker, peak, S. Dak. D2 116
Parker City, Randolph, Ind., 1,181 D7 91
Parker Dam, Yuma, Ariz. C1 80
Parker Dam, San Bernardino, Calif., 250 E6 82
Parker Head, Sagadahoc, Maine, 100 E6 96
Parkersburg, Richland, Ill., 253 E5 90
Parkersburg, Butler, Iowa, 1,468 B5 92
Parkersburg, Sampson, N.C., 65 C5 109
Parkersburg, Wood, W. Va., 44,797 B3 123
Parkers Prairie, Otter Tail, Minn., 884 D3 99
Parkerton, Converse, Wyo., 50 C7 125
Parkertown, Ocean, N.J., 400 D4 106
Parkerview, Sask., Can., 59 F4 70
Parkerville, Morris, Kans., 59 D7 93
Parkes, Austl., 8,223 F7 51
Parkesburg, Chester, Pa., 2,759 G10 114
Park Falls, Price, Wis., 2,919 C3 124
Parkfield, Monterey, Calif., 40 E3 82
Park Forest, Cook and Will, Ill., 29,993 F3 90
Park Grove, Valley, Mont., 30 B10 102
Park Hall, St. Marys, Md., 300 D5 85
Park Head, Ont., Can., 58 C3 72
Parkhill, Ont., Can., 1,169 D3 72
Park Hill, Cherokee, Okla., 150 B7 112
Park Hills, Kenton, Ky., 4,076 A7 94
Parkhurst, Aroostook, Maine (part of Presque Isle) B5 96
Parkin, Cross, Ark., 1,489 B5 81
Parkland, Alta., Can., 96 D4 69
Parkland, Bucks, Pa., 1,200 *F12 114
Parkland, Pierce, Wash., 15,000 E1 122
Park Lane, Litchfield, Conn., 350 *C3 84
Parklawn, Fairfax, Va., 1,000 *C5 121
Parkman, Sask., Can. H5 70
Parkman, Piscataquis, Maine, 65 (530▲) C3 96
Parkman, Geauga, Ohio, 300 A6 111
Parkman, Sheridan, Wyo., 25 A5 125
Park Place, Clackamas, Oreg., 100 B2 113
Park Place, Greenville, S.C., 1,600 *B3 115
Park Rapids, Hubbard, Minn., 3,047 D3 99
Park Ridge, Cook, Ill., 35,430 E2 90
Park Ridge, Bergen, N.J., 6,389 g8 106
Park Ridge Manor, Cook, Ill., 1,000 *E2 90
Park River, Walsh, N. Dak., 1,813 A8 110
Parkrose, Multnomah, Oreg., 24,000 *B4 113
Parks, St. Martin, La., 413 D4 95
Parks, Dundy, Nebr., 120 D4 103
Parks, Stephens, Tex. C3 118
Parkside, Sask., Can., 149 D2 70
Parkside, Delaware, Pa., 2,426 *G11 114
Parksley, Accomack, Va., 850 D7 121
Parkston, Hutchinson, S. Dak., 1,514 D8 116
Parksville, B.C., Can., 1,183 E5 68
Parksville, Sullivan, N.Y., 900 D6 108
Parksville, McCormick, S.C., 164 D3 115
Parkton, Baltimore, Md., 180 A4 85
Parkton, Robeson, N.C., 906 C4 109
Park Valley, Box Elder, Utah, 10 B2 119
Park View, Rio Arriba, N. Mex., 300 A3 107
Parkview, Cuyahoga, Ohio, 2,018 *A6 111
Parkview, Allegheny, Pa., 1,000 *E2 114
Parkville, Baltimore, Md., 27,236 C3 85
Parkville, Platte, Mo., 1,229 B3, E2 101
Parkville, York, Pa., 1,300 *G8 114
Parkway Village, Jefferson, Ky., 949 *B4 94
Parkwood, Montgomery, Md., 1,400 *B3 85
Parla, Sp., 1,781 p17 20
Parlakimedi, India, 22,708 H10 40
Parlier, Fresno, Calif., 1,366 *D4 82
Parlin, Gunnison, Colo., 5 *C4 83
Parma, Canyon, Idaho, 1,295 F2 89
Parma, It., 157,300 E6 18, B3 21
Parma, Jackson, Mich., 770 F6 98
Parma, New Madrid, Mo., 1,060 E8 101
Parma, Cuyahoga, Ohio, 82,845 A6, B2 111
Parma, riv., It. E6 18
Parmachenee, lake, Maine C2 96
Parma Heights, Cuyahoga, Ohio, 18,100 B2 111
Parmele, Martin, N.C., 323 B6 109
Parmelee, Todd, S. Dak., 140 D4 116
Parmer, co., Tex., 9,583 B1 118
Parnaguá, Braz., 508 D2 57
Parnaíba, Braz., 39,951 B2 57
Parnaíba, riv., Braz. B2 57
Parnassos, mtn., Grc. C4 23
Parnell, Iowa, Iowa, 200 C6 92
Parnell, Nodaway, Mo., 260 A3 101
Parnis, mtn., Grc. g11 23
Pärnu, Sov. Un., 36,100 B5 27
Paro, Bhu. C8 39
Parole, Anne Arundel, Md. (part of Annapolis) C4 85
Paron, Saline, Ark., 100 C3 81
Paropamisus, range, Afg. D12 41
Paros, Grc., 3,174 D5 23
Paros, isl., Grc. D5 23
Parow, S. Afr., 39,185 *D2 49
Parowan, Iron, Utah, 1,486 F3 119
Parr, Jasper, Ind., 90 B3 91
Parral, Chile, 10,717 B2 54
Parramatta, Austl., 107,100 *F8 51
Parramore, isl., Va. P7 121
Parran, Calvert, Md., 200 C4 85
Parran, Churchill, Nev., 15 D3 104
Parras de la Fuente, Mex., 19,499 B4 63
Parrett, riv., Eng. C5 12
Parrish, Walker, Ala., 1,608 B2 78
Parrish, Manatee, Fla., 800 E4, F2 86
Parrish, Langlade, Wis., 50 C4 124
Parrott, Terrell, Ga., 280 E2 87
Parrott, Pulaski, Va., 650 D2 121
Parrottsville, Cocke, Tenn., 91 C10 117
Parrs, ridge, Md. A3 85
Parrsboro, N.S., Can., 1,834 D5 74
Parry, Sask., Can., 76 H3 70
Parry, cape, N.W. Ter., Can. B8 66
Parry, isl., Ont., Can. B4 72
Parry, isl., Eniwetok 52
Parry, is., N.W. Ter., Can. m29 67
Parry, mtn., B.C., Can. C3 68
Parry Sound, Ont., Can., 6,004 B4, p20 72
Parry Sound, dist., Ont., Can., 29,632 B4 72
Parsberg, Ger., 2,800 D6 17
Parshall, Grand, Colo., 100 B4 83
Parshall, Mountrail, N. Dak., 1,216 B3 110
Parsippany, Morris, N.J., 5,000 *B4 106
Parsippany-Troy Hills, Morris, N.J. (25,557▲) *B4 106
Parsnip, peak, Nev. E7 104
Parsnip, riv., B.C., Can. B6 68
Parsons, Labette, Kans., 13,929 E8 93
Parsons, Decatur, Tenn., 1,859 B3 117
Parsons, Tucker, W. Va., 1,798 B5 123
Parsonsburg, Wicomico, Md., 500 D7 85
Parson's Pond, Newf., Can., 337 C3, h10 75
Partabgarh, India, 14,573 E5 40
Partabpur, India H8 40
Parthenay, Fr., 8,350 D3 14
Parthenen, Aus., 624 C6 18
Parthenon, Newton, Ark., 125 B2 81
Partinico, It., 26,119 E4 21
Partlow, Spotsylvania, Va., 30 C5 121
Partoun, Jaub, Utah, 20 D2 119
Partridge, Reno, Kans., 221 B4, E5 93
Partridge, pt., Newf., Can. C3 75
Partry, Ire. D2 11
Parvan, Afg., 5,000 D11 41
Pasadena, Los Angeles, Calif., 116,407 E4, F2 82
Pasadena, Newf., Can., 288 D3 75
Pasadena, Anne Arundel, Md., 2,000 B2 85
Pasadena, Harris, Tex., 58,737 F5 118
Pasadena Hills, St. Louis, Mo., 1,315 *C7 101
Pasadena Park, Spokane, Wash., 2,000 *B8 122
Pasaje, Ec., 4,864 B2 58
Pasay (Rizal), Phil., 132,673 C6, o13 35
Pasayton, riv., B.C., Can., Wash. A5 122
Pascagoula, Jackson, Miss., 17,155 E3, E5 100
Pascagoula, bay, Miss. E5 100
Pascagoula, riv., Miss. E5 100
Pascani [-Gară], Rom., 15,008 B8 22
Paschall, Warren, N.C. A5 109
Pasco, Franklin, Wash., 14,522 C6 122
Pasco, co., Fla., 36,785 D4 86
Pasco, dept., Peru, 130,507 D2 58
Pascoag, Providence, R.I., 3,400 B10 84
Pascoag, res., R.I. B10 84
Pascola, Pemiscot, Mo., 228 E8 101
Pascualitos, Mex., 237 F6 82
Pas-de-Calais, dept., Fr., 1,366,282 D2 15
Paseley, cape, Austl. F3 50
Pasewalk, Ger., 12,400 B7 16
Pashkovo, Sov. Un., 1,000 B5 37
Pasig, Phil., 62,130 o13 35
Paslek, Pol., 3,278 A5 26
Pasni, Pak., 6,168 C3 39
Paso del Limay, Arg. C2 54
Paso de los Indios, Arg. C3 54
Paso de los Libres, Arg., 11,665 E4 55
Paso de los Toros, Ur., 8,989 E1 56
Paso Río Mayo, Arg. D2 54
Paso Robles, (El Paso de Robles) San Luis Obispo, Calif., 6,677 E3 82
Pasqua, Sask., Can., 40 G3 70
Pasque, isl., Mass. D6 97
Pasquia, hills, Sask., Can. D4 70
Pasquia, riv., Sask., Man., Can. D5 70
Pasquo, Davidson, Tenn., 50 E9 117
Pasquotank, co., N.C., 25,630 A7 109
Pasrur, Pak., 9,403 A5 40
Passaconaway, mtn., N.H. C4 105
Passadumkeag, Penobscot, Maine, 300 (355▲) C4 96
Passadumkeag, mtn., Maine C4 96
Passage East, Ire., 494 E5 11
Passage West, Ire., 2,561 F3 11
Passaic, Passaic, N.J., 53,963 B4, h8 106
Passaic, co., N.J., 406,618 A4 106
Passaic, riv., N.J. h8 106
Passau, Ger., 31,400 E8 17
Pass Christian, Harrison, Miss., 3,881 E2, E4 100
Passekeag, N.B., Can., 180 D4 74
Passero, cape, It. F5 21
Passo Fundo, Braz., 47,299 D2 56
Passos, Braz., 28,555 F1 57
Passugg-Araschgen, Switz. C8 19
Passumpsic, Caledonia, Vt., 200 C4 120
Passumpsic, riv., Vt. C4 120
Passwang, mts., Switz. B4 19
Passy, Fr., 8,458 E2 19

Pastaza, prov., Ec. ... B2 58
Pastaza, riv., Ec., Peru ... B2 58
Pastillo, P.R. ... D5 65
Pasto, Col., 69,000 (115,000▲) ... C2 60
Pastora, peak, Ariz ... A6 80
Pastoria, Jefferson, Ark ... C3 81
Pasto Viejo Central, P.R. ... C7 65
Pastura, Guadalupe, N. Mex., 40 ... C5 107
Pasuruan, Indon., 62,872 ... G4 35
Paswegin, Sask., Can ... F4 70
Patagonia, Santa Cruz, Ariz., 540 ... F5 80
Patan, India, 50,264 (★51,953) ... F4 40
Patan, Nep., 48,600 ... D10 40
Patapedia, riv., N.B., Que., Can ... B2 74
Patapsco, Carroll, Md., 120 ... A4 85
Patapsco, res., Md ... B4 85
Patapsco, riv., Md ... B4 85
Pataskala, Licking, Ohio, 1,046 ... C5 111
Pataz, Peru, 214 ... C2 58
Patchewollock, Austl., 256 ... G4 51
Patchogue, Suffolk, N.Y., 9,039 ... n15 108
Patea, N.Z., 1,989 ... M15 51
Pateley Bridge, Eng., 1,671 ... F7 13
Pateras, mtn., Grc ... g10 23
Paternò, It., 44,400 ... F5 21
Pateros, Okanogan, Wash., 673 ... A6 122
Paterson, Passaic, N.J., 143,663 ... B4, h8 106
Paterson, Benton, Wash., 45 ... D6 122
Patesville, Hancock, Ky., 75 ... C3 94
Pathankot, India, 46,330 (★54,810) ... A5 40
Pathfinder, res., Wyo ... C6 125
Pathfork, Harlan, Ky., 500 ... D6 94
Pathlow, Sask., Can., 108 ... E3 70
Pati, pt., Guam ... 52
Patiala, India, 125,234 ... B6 39, B6 40
Patiala and East Punjab States Union, state, India, 3,493,685 ... *B6 40
Patiali, India, 4,616 ... D7 40
Patillas, P.R., 1,888 ... C6 65
Patillas, mun., P.R., 17,106 ... C6 65
Patmos, Hempstead, Ark., 120 ... D2 81
Patmos, isl., Grc ... D6 23
Patna, India, 363,700 (★450,000) ... C8 39, E10 40
Patnanongan, isl., Phil ... o14 35
Patoka, Marion, Ill., 601 ... E4 90
Patoka, Gibson, Ind., 579 ... H2 91
Patoka, riv., Ind ... H2 91
Paton, Greene, Iowa, 370 ... B3 92
Patos, Braz., 27,275 ... C3 57
Patos de Minas, Braz., 31,471 ... E1 57
Patrai, Grc., 95,364 ... C3 23
Patrai, gulf, Grc ... C3 23
Patricia, Alta., Can., 40 ... D5 69
Patricia, Dawson, Tex., 60 ... C1 118
Patrick, Cherokee, N.C., 200 ... D2 109
Patrick, Chesterfield, S.C., 393 ... B7 115
Patrick, co., Va., 15,282 ... E2 121
Patrick, mtn., Maine ... D3 96
Patricksburg, Owen, Ind., 350 ... F4 91
Patrick Springs, Patrick, Va., 500 ... E2 121
Patriot, Switzerland, Ind., 277 ... G8 91
Patrocínio, Braz., 13,933 ... E1 57
Patroon, Shelby, Tex., 500 ... D6 118
Patsaliga, creek, Ala ... D3 78
Patsville, Elko, Nev., 5 ... B6 104
Pattagumpus, Penobscot, Maine ... C4 96
Pattani, Thai., 16,534 ... I4 38
Pattaquatic, hill, Mass ... B3 97
Patten, Penobscot, Maine, 1,099 ... C4 96
Pattenburg, Hunterdon, N.J., 270 ... B2 106
Pattenville, Middlesex, Mass., 400 ... *A5 97
Patterson, Woodruff, Ark., 324 ... B4 81
Patterson, Stanislaus, Calif., 2,429 ... B6 82
Patterson, Pierce, Ga., 719 ... E4 87
Patterson, Lemhi, Idaho, 24 ... E5 89
Patterson, Greene, Ill., 130 ... D3 90
Patterson, Madison, Iowa, 157 ... C4 92
Patterson, Harvey, Kans ... B4 93
Patterson, St. Mary, La., 2,923 ... E4 95
Patterson, Wayne, Mo., 125 ... D7 101
Patterson, Putnam, N.Y., 900 ... D7 108
Patterson, Buchanan, Va., 400 ... B3 121
Patterson, creek, W. Va ... B5 123
Patterson, mtn., Calif ... C4 82
Patterson Creek, mtn., W. Va ... B6 123
Patterson Knob, mtn., Tenn ... E9 117
Patterson Gardens, Monroe, Mich., 1,747 ... *G7 98
Pattison, Claiborne, Miss., 150 ... D3 100
Patton, Bollinger, Mo., 108 ... D7 101
Patton, Cambria, Pa., 2,880 ... E4 114
Pattonsburg, Daviess, Mo., 753 ... A3 101
Pattullo, mtn., B.C., Can ... A3 68
Patu, Braz., 2,367 ... C3 57
Patuakhali, Pak., 10,289 ... F13 40
Patuca, riv., Hond ... C5 62
Patung, China, 16,000 ... I4 36
Patuxent, Anne Arundel, Md., 60 ... B4 85
Patuxent, riv., Md ... B3 85
Patzau, Douglas, Wis., 50 ... B1 124
Pátzcuaro, Mex., 14,281 ... D4, n13 63
Pátzcuaro, lake, Mex ... n13 63
Patzicía, Guat., 5,021 ... C2 62
Patzún, Guat., 5,103 ... C2 62
Pau, Fr., 59,937 (★82,000) ... F3 24
Paucarbamba, Peru, 1,738 ... D3 58
Paucartambo, riv., Peru ... D3 58
Paudalho, Braz., 6,889 ... C3, h6 57
Pau dos Ferros, Braz., 4,298 ... C3 57
Paugh Lake, Ont., Can ... B7 72
Pauillac, Fr., 2,353 ... E3 14
Pauk, Bur., 5,000 ... D9 39
Paul, Minidoka, Idaho, 701 ... G5 89
Paul, Midland, Tex ... C2 118
Paul, isl., Newf., Can ... g9 75
Paul, stream, Vt ... B5 120
Paulden, Yavapai, Ariz., 15 ... C3 80
Paulding, Ontonagon, Mich., 75 ... A6 98
Paulding, Jasper, Miss., 180 ... C4 100
Paulding, Paulding, Ohio, 2,936 ... A3 111
Paulding, co., Ga., 13,101 ... C2 87
Paulding, co., Ohio, 16,792 ... A3 111
Paulding, bay, Ant ... C25 5
Paulette, Noxubee, Miss., 50 ... B5 100
Paulina (Remy), St. James, La., 1,014 ... *D5 95
Paulina, Warren, N.J., 50 ... B3 106
Paulina, Crook, Oreg., 30 ... C7 113
Paulina, mts., Oreg ... D5 113
Paulina, peak, Oreg ... D5 113
Pauline, Adams, Nebr., 85 ... D7 103
Pauline, Spartanburg, S.C., 200 ... B4 115
Pauline, mtn., B.C., Alta., Can ... C1 69
Paulins, kill, N.J ... A3 106
Paulis, Con. L., 9,700 ... A4 48
Paulistana, Braz., 1,105 ... C2 57
Paull, lake, Sask., Can ... A3 70
Paull, riv., Sask., Can ... B3 70
Paullina, O'Brien, Iowa, 1,329 ... B9 22
Paulo Afonso, falls, Braz ... C3 57
Pauloff Harbor, Alsk., 77 ... E7 79
Paulsboro, Gloucester, N.J., 8,121 ... D2 106
Paul Smiths, Franklin, N.Y., 300 ... f10 108
Paul Spur, Cochise, Ariz., 30 ... F6 80
Pauls Valley, Garvin, Okla., 6,856 ... C4 112
Paungde, Bur., 17,286 ... E10 39
Paupack, Pike, Pa., 250 ... D11 114
Pauwela, Maui, Haw., 300 ... C5 88
Pavant, range, Utah ... E3 119
Pavia, It., 79,400 ... D5 18, B2 21
Pavilion, Genesee, N.Y., 500 ... C2 108
Pavilion, key, Fla ... G5 86
Pavillion, Fremont, Wyo., 190 ... B4 125
Pavlodar, Sov. Un., 120,000 ... C9 29
Pavlof, vol., Alsk ... D7 79
Pavlograd, Sov. Un., 43,000 ... G10 27
Pavlovo, Sov. Un., 55,000 ... D14 27
Pavlovsk, Sov. Un., 30,000 ... s31 25
Pavlovsk, Sov. Un., 30,000 ... F13 27
Pavlovskaya, Sov. Un., 10,000 ... H13 27
Pavlovskiy Posad, Sov. Un., 58,000 ... n18 27
Pavo, Thomas and Brooks, Ga., 817 ... F3 87
Pavonia, Richland, Ohio, 190 ... B5 111
Pawcatuck, New London, Conn., 6,500 ... D9 84
Paw Creek, Mecklenburg, N.C., 2,000 ... B3 109
Pawhuska, Osage, Okla., 5,414 ... A5 112
Pawlet, Rutland, Vt., 150 (1,112▲) ... E2 120
Pawleys Island, Georgetown, S.C., 500 ... E9 115
Pawling, Dutchess, N.Y., 1,734 ... D7 108
Pawnee, Sangamon, Ill., 1,517 ... D4 90
Pawnee, Pawnee, Okla., 2,303 ... A5 112
Pawnee, Bee, Tex., 175 ... E4 118
Pawnee, co., Kans., 10,254 ... D4 93
Pawnee, co., Nebr., 5,356 ... D9 103
Pawnee, co., Okla., 10,884 ... A5 112
Pawnee, creek, Colo ... A7 83
Pawnee, riv., Kans ... D4 93
Pawnee City, Pawnee, Nebr., 1,343 ... D9 103
Pawnee Rock, Barton, Kans., 380 ... D5 93
Pawpaw, Lee, Ill., 725 ... B5 90
Paw Paw, Van Buren, Mich., 2,970 ... F5 98
Paw Paw, Morgan, W. Va., 789 ... B6 123
Pawpaw, creek, W. Va ... A7 123
Paw Paw, riv., Mich ... F4 98
Paw Paw Lake, Berrien, Mich., 3,518 ... *F4 98
Pawtuckaway, pond, N.H ... D4 105
Pawtowicze, Pol ... h9 26
Pawtucket, Providence, R.I., 81,001 ... B11 84
Pawtucket, res., R.I ... A11 84
Pax, Fayette, W. Va., 408 ... D6 123
Paxico, Wabaunsee, Kans., 276 ... C7 93
Paxoi, isl., Grc ... C3 23
Paxtang, Dauphin, Pa., 1,916 ... *F8 114
Paxton, Walton, Fla., 215 ... G3 86
Paxton, Ford, Ill., 4,370 ... C5 90
Paxton, Sullivan, Ind., 275 ... F3 91
Paxton, Worcester, Mass., 600 (2,399▲) ... B4 97
Paxton, Keith, Nebr., 566 ... C4 103
Paxtonville, Snyder, Pa., 350 ... E7 114
Paxville, Clarendon, S.C., 216 ... D7 115
Payen, China, 5,000 ... C3 37
Payenhala, China ... A10 36
Payerne, Switz., 6,024 ... C2 19
Payette, Payette, Idaho, 4,451 ... E2 89
Payette, co., Idaho, 12,363 ... E2 89
Payette, lake, Idaho ... E2 89
Payette, riv., Idaho ... F2 89
Payintala, see Tungliao, China
Payne, Bibb, Ga., 346 ... D3 81
Payne, Paulding, Ohio 1,287 ... A3 111
Payne, co., Okla., 44,231 ... A5 112
Payne, lake, Que., Can ... g12 73
Payne, riv., Que., Can ... E18 67
Payne Bay, Que., Can., 83 ... f12 73
Paynes, Tallahatchie, Miss., 25 ... B3 100
Paynes Creek, Tehama, Calif., 50 ... B3 82
Paynesville, Ontonagon, Mich., 55 ... A6 98
Paynesville, Stearns, Minn., 1,754 ... E4 99
Paynesville, Pike, Mo., 150 ... B7 101
Payneville, Meade, Ky., 113 ... C3 94
Paynton, Sask., Can., 216 ... D1 70
Paysandú, Ur., 51,645 ... E1 56
Paysandú, dept., Ur., 78,400 ... *E1 56
Payson, Gila, Ariz., 800 ... C4 80
Payson, Adams, Ill., 502 ... D2 90
Payson, Lincoln, Okla., 30 ... B5 112
Payson, Utah, Utah, 4,237 ... C4 119
Paz, bay, Mex ... C2 63
Pazardzhik, Bul., 30,430 ... D7 22
Pazin, Yugo., 3,004 ... C1 22
Pea, riv., Ala ... D3 78
Peabody, Marion, Kans., 1,309 ... A6, D6 93
Peabody, Essex, Mass., 32,202 ... A6, f12 97
Peabody, riv., N.H ... B4 105
Peace, riv., Alta., B.C., Can ... E9 66
Peace, riv., Fla ... E5 86
Peace Dale, Washington, R.I., 2,000 ... D11 84
Peace River, Alta., Can., 2,543 ... A2, f7 69
Peach, co., Ga., 13,846 ... D3 87
Peach, pt., Mass ... f12 97
Peacham, Caledonia, Vt., 130 (433▲) ... C4 120
Peach Creek, Logan, W. Va., 700 ... D5 123
Peachland, B.C., Can., 500 ... E8 68
Peachland, Anson, N.C., 563 ... C3 109
Peach Orchard, Clay, Ark., 348 ... A5 81
Peach Orchard Knob, peak, Ky ... C2 94
Peach Springs, Mohave, Ariz., 600 ... B2 80
Peacock, Lake, Mich., 20 ... D5 98
Peacock, hills, N.W. Ter., Can ... C10 66
Peacock, peak, Ariz ... B2 80
Peacock, pt., Wake Isl ... 52
Peacock, sound, Ant ... B2 5
Peak, Newberry, S.C., 86 ... C5 115
Peaked, mtn., Maine ... B4 96
Peak Hill, Austl , 46 ... E2 50
Peale, isl., Wake Isl ... 52
Peale, mtn., Utah ... E6 119
Pea Patch, isl., Del ... D1 106
Pearce, Cochise, Ariz., 25 ... F6 81
Pearce, Alta., Can ... E4 69
Pearcy, Garland, Ark., 100 ... C2, D5 81
Pea Ridge, Benton, Ark., 380 ... A1 81
Pearisburg, Giles, Va., 2,268 ... D2 121
Pearl, Pike, Ill., 348 ... D3 90
Pearl, Rankin, Miss., 5,081 ... *C3 100
Pearl, hbr., Haw ... B4 88
Pearl, riv., Miss ... C3 100
Pearland, Brazoria, Tex., 1,497 ... F5 118
Pearl and Hermes, reef, Haw ... k12 88
Pearl Beach, St. Clair, Mich., 1,224 ... *F8 98
Pearl City, Honolulu, Haw., 8,200 ... B4, g10 88
Pearl City, Stephenson, Ill., 488 ... A4 90
Pearlington, Hancock, Miss., 500 ... E4 100
Pearl River, St. Tammany, La., 964 ... D6 95
Pearl River, Rockland, N.Y., 14,500 ... g12 108
Pearl River, co., Miss., 22,411 ... E4 100
Pear Ridge, Jefferson, Tex., 3,470 ... E2 95
Pearsall, Frio, Tex., 4,957 ... E3 118
Pearsoll, peak, Oreg ... E3 113
Pearson, Cleburne, Ark., 40 ... B3 81
Pearson, Atkinson, Ga., 1,615 ... E4 87
Pearson, Langlade, Wis., 80 ... C4 124
Pearsonia, Osage, Okla ... A5 112
Peary, chan., N.W. Ter., Can ... m30 67
Peary Land, reg., Grnld ... A18 4
Pease, Mille Lacs, Minn., 191 ... E5 99
Peasleeville, Clinton, N.Y., 25 ... f11 108
Peavine, Cumberland, Tenn ... C9 117
Pebane, Moz., 5,000 ... A6 49
Pebble Beach, Monterey, Calif., 900 ... *D3 82
Pebworth, Owsley, Ky., 200 ... C6 94
Peć, Yugo., 28,297 ... D5 22
Peçanha, Braz., 3,602 ... E2 57
Pecan Island, Vermilion, La ... E3 95
Pecatonica, Winnebago, Ill., 1,659 ... A4 90
Pecatonica, riv., Wis ... F3 124
Pechenga, Sov. Un., 13,200 ... C14 25
Pechora, Sov. Un., 30,600 ... C9 4
Pechora, riv., Sov. Un ... C20 9
Pechorskaya, bay, Sov. Un ... B19 9
Peck, Nez Perce, Idaho, 186 ... C2 89
Peck, Sedgwick & Sumner, Kans., 120 ... E6 93
Peck, Sanilac, Mich., 548 ... E8 98
Peckerwood Lake, res., Ark ... C4 81
Peckham, Kay, Okla., 100 ... A4 112
Peckville (Blakely), Lackawanna, Pa., 6,374 ... A9 114
Peconic, Suffolk, N.Y., 400 ... E7 84
Peconic, riv., N.Y ... F6 84
Pecos, San Miguel, N. Mex., 584 ... B4 107
Pecos, Reeves, Tex., 12,728 ... D1, F2 118
Pecos, co., Tex., 11,957 ... D1 118
Pecos, riv., N. Mex., Tex ... D7 76
Pecs, Hung., 127,000 ... B4 22
Peculiar, Cass, Mo., 458 ... C3 101
Pedasí, Pan., 988 ... G7 62
Peddocks, isl., Mass ... g12 97
Pedlar Mills, Amherst, Va., 35 ... D3 121
Pedley, Riverside, Calif., 1,600 ... *F3 82
Pedra Azul, Braz., 8,238 ... F2 57
Pedraza, see Ciudad Bolivia, Ven.
Pedregal, Pan., 631 ... F6 62
Pedregal, Pan ... k12 62
Pedregal, Ven., 1,166 ... A3 60
Pedreiras, Braz., 10,189 ... B2 57
Pedricktown, Salem, N.J., 750 ... D2 106
Pedro, Pennington, S. Dak., 5 ... C3 116
Pedro Afonso, Braz., 3,175 ... C1 57
Pedro Avelino, Braz., 1,399 ... C3 57
Pedro de Valdivia, Chile, 10,989 ... D2 55
Pedro Juan Caballero, Par., 12,521 ... D4 55
Pedro Luro, Arg ... B4 54
Pedro Miguel, C.Z., 603 ... k11 62
Pedro Velho, Braz., 2,041 ... h6 57
Peebinga, Austl., 67 ... G3 51
Peebles, Sask., Can., 40 ... G4 70
Peebles, Adams, Ohio, 1,601 ... D4 111
Peebles, Scot., 5,545 ... E5 13
Peebles, co., Scot., 14,117 ... E5 13
Pee Dee, riv., N.C., S.C ... D9 115
Peekaboo, mtn., Maine ... C5 96
Peekskill, Westchester, N.Y., 18,737 ... D7, m15 108
Peel, N.B., Can., 139 ... C2 74
Peel, I. of Man, 2,487 ... F4 13
Peel, co., Ont., Can., 111,575 ... D5 72
Peel, riv., Yukon, Can ... C5 66
Peel, sound, N.W. Ter., Can ... B13 66
Peeled Chestnut, White, Tenn ... D8 117
Peel Fell, mtn., Scot ... E6 13
Pe Ell, Lewis, Wash., 593 ... C2 122
Peely (Warrior Run), Luzerne, Pa., 833 ... *D10 108
Peene, riv., Ger ... B6 16
Peer, Bel., 5,838 ... C5 15
Peerless, Daniels, Mont., 145 ... B11 102
Peerless, lake, Alta., Can ... A3 69
Peers, Alta., Can., 128 ... C3 69
Peesane, Sask., Can., 65 ... E4 70
Peetz, Logan, Colo., 218 ... A7 83
Peever, Roberts, S. Dak., 208 ... B9 116
Pefferlaw, Ont., Can., 411 ... C5 72
Pegan, hill, Mass ... g10 97
Pegasus, bay, N.Z ... O14 51
Pegau, Ger., 6,754 ... B7 17
Peggs, Cherokee, Okla., 28 ... A6 112
Peggy, Atascosa, Tex., 10 ... E3 118
Pegnitz, Ger., 8,100 ... D6 17
Pegnitz, riv., Ger ... D6 17
Pego, Sp., 8,291 ... C5 20
Pegram, Cheatham, Tenn., 400 ... A4 117
Pegu, Bur., 47,378 ... E10 39
Pegu Yoma, mts., Bur ... C1 38
Pehan, China, 18,000 ... B10 34
Pehčevo, Yugo., 1,750 ... E6 22
Pehuajo, Arg., 13,537 ... B4 54
Pei, China ... G7 36
Pei, China, 69,000 ... G7 36
Peian, China, 70,000 ... *B10 34
Peine, Ger., 29,800 ... A5 17
Peiping, see Peking, China
Peipus, lake, Sov. Un ... B6 27
Peixe, Braz., 822 ... D1 57
Pejepscot, Sagadahoc, Maine, 200 ... E2, E5 96
Pekalongan, Indon., 100,261 ... G3 35
Pekan, Mala., 2,070 ... K5 38
Pekia, China, 1,000 ... A8 40
Pekin, Tazewell, Ill., 28,146 ... C4 90
Pekin (New Pekin), Washington Ind., 661 ... G5 91
Pekin, Nelson, N. Dak., 180 ... B7 110
Peking (Peiping), China, 3,500,000 (6,230,000▲) ... D8 34, E7 36
Pelagie, is., It ... G13 30
Pelagos, isl., Grc ... C5 23
Pelahatchie, Rankin, Miss., 1,066 ... C4 100
Pelaihari, Indon ... F4 35
Pelat, mtn., Fr ... E7 14
Pelee, isl., Ont., Can ... F2 72
Peleliu, isl., Palau Is ... 52
Pelham, Shelby, Ala., 500 ... B3 78
Pelham, Mitchell, Ga., 4,609 ... E2 87
Pelham, Hampshire, Mass., 200 (805▲) ... B3 97
Pelham, Hillsboro, N.H., 150 (2,605▲) ... E4 105
Pelham, Westchester, N.Y., 1,964 ... *D7 108
Pelham, Caswell, N.C., 200 ... A4 109
Pelham, Greenville, S.C., 500 ... B3 115
Pelham, Grundy, Tenn., 300 ... D8 117
Pelham Manor, Westchester, N.Y., 6,114 ... h13 108
Pelhřimov, Czech., 7,200 ... D3 26
Pelican, Alsk., 135 ... k21 79
Pelican, De Soto, La., 250 ... C2 95
Pelican, bay, Man., Can ... C1 71
Pelican, butte, Oreg ... E4 113
Pelican, lake, Alta., Can ... B4 69
Pelican, lake, Man., Can ... C1 71
Pelican, lake, Sask., Can ... B4 70
Pelican, lake, Minn ... B6 99
Pelican, lake, Minn ... D3 99
Pelican, lake, Minn ... D3 99
Pelican, lake, Minn ... D4 99
Pelican, lake, Minn ... E5 99
Pelican, lake, Wis ... C4 124
Pelican, mtn., Alta., Can ... B4 69
Pelican Lake, Palm Beach, Fla., 500 ... F6 86
Pelican Lake, Oneida, Wis., 300 ... C4 124
Pelican Narrows, Sask., Can., 108 ... B4 70
Pelican Rapids, Man., Can., 213 ... C1 71
Pelican Rapids, Otter Tail, Minn., 1,693 ... D2 99
Pelion, Lexington, S.C., 233 ... D5 115
Pella, Marion, Iowa, 5,198 ... C5 92
Pella, prov., Grc., 133,224 ... *B4 23
Pell City, Saint Clair, Ala., 4,165 ... B3 78
Pellejas Central, P.R ... C4 65
Pellice, riv., It ... E3 18
Pell Lake, Walworth, Wis., 900 ... *F5 124
Pellston, Emmet, Mich., 429 ... C6 98
Pellville, Hancock, Ky., 119 ... C3 94
Pellworm, isl., Ger ... A4 16
Pelly, Sask., Can., 476 ... F5 70
Pelly, lake, N.W. Ter., Can ... C12 66
Pelly, mts., Yukon, Can ... D6 66
Pelly, riv., Yukon, Can ... D6 66
Pelly Crossing, Yukon, Can., 151 ... D5 66
Peloncillo, mts., Ariz., N. Mex ... E6 80
Peloponnesos (Peloponnesus), reg., Grc ... D4 23
Pelotas, Braz., 121,280 ... E2 56
Pelotas, riv., Braz ... D2 56
Pelto, lake, La ... E5 95
Pelzer, Anderson, S.C., 106 ... B3 115
Pelzer North, Anderson, S.C., 1,400 ... *B3 115
Pemadumcook, lake, Maine ... C3 96
Pemanggil, isl., Mala ... K6 38
Pemaquid, Lincoln, Maine, 200 ... E3 96
Pematangsiantar, Indon., 112,687 ... K3 38
Pemba, Zambia, 189 ... E4 48
Pemba, isl., Tan ... B6 48
Pemberton, B.C., Can., 181 ... D6 68
Pemberton, Burlington, N.J., 1,250 ... D3 106
Pemberton, Shelby, Ohio, 240 ... B3 111
Pemberville, Wood, Ohio, 1,237 ... A2, A4 111
Pembina, Pembina, N. Dak., 625 ... A8 110
Pembina, co., N. Dak., 12,946 ... A8 110
Pembina, mts., N. Dak ... A7 110
Pembina, riv., Alta., Can ... C3 69
Pembina, riv., Man., Can ... E2 71
Pembine, Marinette, Wis., 550 ... C6 124
Pembroke, Ont., Can., 16,791 ... B7, p20 72
Pembroke, Bryan, Ga., 1,450 ... D5 87
Pembroke, Christian, Ky., 517 ... D2 94
Pembroke, Washington, Maine, 500 (871▲) ... D5 96
Pembroke, Plymouth, Mass., 700 (4,919▲) ... B6 97
Pembroke, Merrimack, N.H., (3,514▲) ... D4 105
Pembroke, Genesee, N.Y., 300 ... C2 108
Pembroke, Robeson, N C., 1,372 ... C4 109
Pembroke, Giles, Va., 1,038 ... D2 121
Pembroke, Wales, 12,737 ... C3 12
Pembroke, co., Wales, 93,980 ... C3 12
Pembroke Pines, Brownard, Fla., 1,429 ... *F6 86
Pembuang, Indon ... F4 35
Pemigewasset, riv., N.H ... C3 105
Pemiscot, co., Mo., 38,095 ... E8 101
Pemmican Portage, Sask., Can., 271 ... D4 70
Pemuco, Chile, 1,703 ... B2 54
Penablanca, Sandoval, N. Mex., 350 ... B3, h8 107
Penafiel, Port., 4,361 ... B1 20
Peñafiel, Sp ... B3 20
Peñalara, mtn., Sp ... B4 20
Penalosa, Kingman, Kans., 84 ... E5 93
Penamacor, Port., 2,740 ... B2 20
Peña Negra, mts., Sp ... A2 20
Penang, Mala., 234,903 (★325,000) ... J4 38
Penang (Penang and Province Wellesley), state, Mala., 572,100 ... J4 38
Penang, isl., Mala ... J4 38
Penápolis, Braz., 14,400 ... C2 56
Peñaranda de Bracamonte, Sp., 5,943 ... B3 20
Pen Argyl, Northampton, Pa., 3,693 ... E11 114
Peña Roya, mtn., Sp ... B5 20
Peñarroya-Pueblonuevo, Sp., 24,152 ... C3 20
Peñas, cape, Sp ... A3 20
Penas, gulf, Chile ... D2 54
Penasco, Taos, N. Mex., 500 ... A4 107
Penasse, Lake of the Woods, Minn., 3 ... A4 99
Penawawa, Whitman, Wash., 30 ... C8 122
Penbrook, Dauphin, Pa., 3,671 ... F8 114
Pence, Warren, Ind., 100 ... D2 91
Pench, trough, Ant ... B12 5
Pendelikon (Pentelicus), mtn., Grc ... g11 23
Pendleton, Anderson, S.C., 2,358 ... B2 115
Pendembu, S.L ... E2 45
Pender, Thurston, Nebr., 1,165 ... B9 103
Pender, co., N.C., 18,508 ... C6 109
Pender, isl., B.C., Can ... g12 68
Pendergrass, Jackson, Ga., 215 ... B3 87
Pender Island, B.C., Can ... g12 68
Pendle Hill, mtn., Eng ... G6 13
Pendleton, Madison, Ind., 2,472 ... E6 91
Pendleton, Umatilla, Oreg., 14,434 ... B8 113
Pendleton, co., Ky., 9,968 ... B5 94
Pendleton, co., W. Va., 8,093 ... C5 123
Pend Oreille, co., Wash., 6,914 ... A8 122
Pend Oreille, lake, Idaho ... A2 89
Pend Oreille, riv., Wash ... A8 122
Pendroy, Teton, Mont., 30 ... B4 102
Penedo, Braz., 17,084 ... D3 57
Penetanguishene, Ont., Can., 5,340 ... C5 72
Penfield, Greene, Ga., 105 ... C3 87
Penfield, Champaign, Ill., 275 ... C6 90
Penfield, Monroe, N.Y., 4,000 ... *B3 108
Penfield, Clearfield, Pa., 700 ... D4 114
Penfield Junction, Lorain, Ohio, 2,300 ... *A5 111
Pengan, China, 13,000 ... I2 36
Penganga, riv., India ... H7 40
Penge, Con. L ... C3 48
Pengibu, isl., Indon ... L7 38
Penglai, China ... F9 36
Pengpu, China, 253,000 ... H7 36
Pengshui, China, 11,000 ... J3 36
Penguin, is., Newf., Can ... E3 75
Penhold, Alta., Can., 319 ... C4 69
Penhook, Franklin, Va., 45 ... E3 121
Peniche, Port., 10,057 ... C1 20
Penicuik, Scot., 5,824 ... E5 13
Peninsula, Washington, Minn., 80 ... E7 99
Peninsula, Summit, Ohio, 644 ... A6 111
Penitas, Hidalgo, Tex., 700 ... F3 118
Penitente, mts., Braz ... C1 57
Penitentiary, mtn., Ala ... A2 78
Penki, China, 449,000 ... C9 34
Penn, Sask., Can ... D2 70
Penn, Ramsey, N. Dak., 70 ... A6 110
Pennant, pt., N.S., Can ... E6 74
Pennant Station, Sask., Can., 289 ... G1 70
Pennask, mtn., B.C., Can ... E7 68
Penndel, Bucks, Pa., 2,158 ... *F12 114
Penne, It., 5,054 ... C4 21
Pennell, mtn., Utah ... F5 119
Pennellville, Oswego, N.Y., 150 ... B4 108
Penneshaw, Austl., 149 ... G1 51
Penney Farms, Clay, Fla., 545 ... C5 86
Pennfield, N.B., Can., 334 ... D3 74
Penn Grove, Sonoma, Calif., 530 ... B5 82
Penn Hills, Allegheny, Pa., 51,512 ... *B6 114
Penniac, N.B., Can., 58 ... C3 74
Pennine Alps, mts., It., Switz ... D4 19
Pennine Chain, mts., Eng ... C5 10
Pennington, Choctaw, Ala., 400 ... C1 78
Pennington, Mercer, N.J., 2,063 ... C3 106
Pennington, co., Minn., 12,468 ... B2 99
Pennington, co., S. Dak., 58,195 ... D2 116
Pennington, mtn., Maine ... B4 96
Pennington Gap, Lee, Va., 1,799 ... B2 121
Pennock, Kandiyohi, Minn., 257 ... E3 99
Pennsauken, Camden, N.J., 33,771 ... D2 106
Pennsboro, Ritchie, W. Va., 1,660 ... B4 123
Pennsburg, Montgomery, Pa., 1,698 ... F11 114
Penns Grove, Salem, N.J., 6,176 ... D2 106
Pennside, Berks, Pa., 3,000 ... *F10 114
Pennsuco, Dade, Fla., 117 ... F3 86
Pennsville, Salem, N.J., 5,000 ... D1 106
Pennsville, Morgan, Ohio, 160 ... C6 111
Pennsylvania, state, U.S., 11,319,366 ... B12 77, 114
Pennsylvania Furnace, Huntingdon, Pa., 50 ... E5 114
Penn Valley, Montgomery, Pa., 3,500 ... *F11 114
Pennville, Jay, Ind., 730 ... D7 91
Pennville, York, Pa., 900 ... *G8 114
Penn Wynne, Montgomery, Pa., 4,500 ... *G11 114
Penny, B.C., Can., 151 ... C7 68
Penn Yan, Yates, N.Y., 5,770 ... C3 108
Pennycutaway, riv., Man., Can ... A5 71
Penny Highland, mts., N.W. Ter., Can ... C19 67
Penny Hill, New Castle, Del., 1,000 ... *A6 85
Penobscot, Hancock, Maine, 150 (706▲) ... D4 96
Penobscot, co., Maine, 126,346 ... C4 96
Penobscot, bay, Maine ... D4 96
Penobscot, lake, Maine ... C2 96
Penobscot, riv., Maine ... C4 96
Penobsquis, N.B., Can., 259 ... D4 74
Penokee, Graham, Kans., 92 ... C4 93
Penola, Caroline, Va., 25 ... D5 121
Penong, Austl., 118 ... F5 50
Penonomé, Pan., 4,266 ... F7 62
Penrith, Eng., 10,931 ... F6 13
Penrose, Fremont, Colo., 200 ... C5 83
Pensacola, Escambia, Fla., 56,752 (★165,400) ... G2 86
Pensacola, Mayes, Okla., 55 ... A6 112
Pensacola, mts., Ant ... A7 5
Pensacola, dam, Okla ... A6 112
Pensaukee, Oconto, Wis., 250 ... D6 124
Pense, Sask., Can., 374 ... G3 70
Pentagon, mtn., Mont ... C3 102
Pentecost, Sunflower, Miss., 100 ... B3 100
Pentecoste, Braz., 5,620 ... B3 57
Penticton, B.C., Can., 13,859 ... E8 68
Pentland, firth, Scot ... B5 13
Pentland, hills, Scot ... E5 13
Penton, DeSota, Miss., 100 ... A3 100
Penton, Salem, N.J., 175 ... D2 106
Pentwater, Oceana, Mich., 1,030 ... E4 98
Peñuelas, P.R., 2,261 ... C4 65
Peñuelas, mun., P.R., 14,887 ... C4 65
Penwell, Ector, Tex., 350 ... D1 118
Pen-y-Ghent, mtn., Eng ... F6 13
Penza, Sov. Un., 296,000 ... C2 29
Penzance, Navajo, Ariz., 10 ... C5 80
Penzance, Sask., Can., 99 ... F3 70
Penzance, Eng., 18,800 ... D2 12
Penzberg, Ger., 10,300 ... E5 16
Penzhina, riv., Sov. Un ... C19 28
Penzhino, Sov. Un., 600 ... C19 28
Penzlin, Ger., 3,811 ... E7 24
Peoa, Summit, Utah, 130 ... C4 119
Peonan, pt., Man., Can ... D2 71
Peone, Spokane, Wash ... D8 122
Peoples, Jackson, Ky., 200 ... C5 94
Peoria, Maricopa, Ariz., 2,593 ... D3, G1 80
Peoria, Peoria, Ill., 103,162 (★265,000) ... C4 90
Peoria, Amite, Miss., 100 ... D3 100
Peoria, Union, Ohio, 200 ... B4 111
Peoria, co., Ill., 189,044 ... C4 90
Peoria Heights, Peoria, Ill., 7,064 ... C4 90
Peotone, Will, Ill., 1,788 ... B6 90
Pep, Roosevelt, N. Mex., 15 ... D6 107
Pepacton, res., N.Y ... C6 108
Pepeekeo, Hawaii, Haw., 750 ... D6 88
Pepin, Pepin, Wis., 825 ... D1 124
Pepin, co., Wis., 7,332 ... D2 124
Pepin, lake, Wis ... D1 124
Pepperell, Middlesex, Mass., 1,200 (4,336▲) ... A4 97
Pepper Pike, Cuyahoga, Ohio, 3,217 ... *B2 111
Pepperton, Butts, Ga., 523 ... C3 87

P.E.P.S.U., see Patiala and East Punjab States Union, state, India
Peqin, Alb., 3,069 .... B2 23
Pequabuck, Litchfield, Conn., 500 .... C5 84
Pequaming, Baraga, Mich. B2 98
Pequannock, Morris, N.J., 3,500 .... B4 106
Pequení, riv., Pan k12 62
Pequest, riv., N.J. B3 106
Pequirí, riv., Braz B1 56
Pequirí, riv., Braz C2 56
Pequop, Elko, Nev., 10 .... B7 104
Pequot Lakes, Crow Wing, Minn., 461 .... D4 99
Perak, isl., Indon J2 38
Perak, riv., Mala J4 38
Perak, state, Mala., 1,221,446 .... J4 38
Perakhóra (Loutrákion-Perakhóra), Grc., 6,168 .... g9 23
Perales, riv., Sp p16 20
Perales de Tajuña, Sp., 1,924 .... p18 20
Peralta, Valencia, N. Mex., 300 .... C3 107
Perchas, P.R B3 65
Percival, Fremont, Iowa, 300 .... D2 92
Percy, Fr., 661 .... C3 14
Percy, Randolph, Ill., 810 .... E4 90
Percy, Marion, Iowa, 30 .... C4 92
Percy, Washington, Miss., 100 .... B3 100
Percy, Coos, N.H., 40 .... A4 105
Perdido, Baldwin, Ala., 900 .... D2 78
Perdido, bay, Fla G1 86
Perdido, mtn., Sp A6 20
Perdido, riv., Fla G1 86
Perdue, Sask., Can., 436 .... E2 70
Perea, McKinley, N. Mex., 50 .... B1 107
Pereira, Col., 121,000 .... C2 60
Pereira Barreto, Braz., 7,173 .... C2 56
Perekop, Sov. Un., 10,000 .... H9 27
Pere Marquette, riv., Mich E4 98
Peremennyy, cape, Ant C23 5
Perené, riv., Peru D3 58
Pereslavl-Zalesskiy, Sov. Un., 22,200 .... C12 27
Pereyaslav-Khmelnitskiy, Sov. Un., 10,000 .... F8 27
Perez, Phil., 1,262 .... o13 35
Pergamino, Arg., 32,382 .... A4 54
Pergine, Valsugana, It., 3,879 .... A3 21
Perham, Aroostook, Maine, 125 (512▲) B4 96
Perham, Otter Tail, Minn., 2,019 .... D3 99
Péribonca, Que., Can., 496 .... A5 73
Perico, Dallam, Tex., 30 .... A1 118
Périgueux, Fr., 38,529 (*51,000) E4 14
Perijá, mts., Ven B3 60
Perim, isl., Aden C5 47
Peristérion, Grc., 79,335 .... *C4 23
Perkasie, Bucks, Pa., 4,650 .... F11 114
Perkins, Sacramento, Calif., 300 .... *A6 82
Perkins, Que., Can., 318 .... D2 73
Perkins, Jenkins, Ga., 250 .... D5 87
Perkins, Delta, Mich., 250 .... C3 98
Perkins, Payne, Okla., 769 .... B4 112
Perkins, co., Nebr., 4,189 .... D4 103
Perkins, co., S. Dak., 5,977 .... B3 116
Perkinston, Stone, Miss., 350 .... E4 100
Perkinstown, Taylor, Wis C3 124
Perkinsville, Windsor, Vt., 167 .... E3 120
Perkiomen, creek, Pa C2 106
Perla, Hot Spring, Ark., 279 .... C3, D6 81
Perlas, arch., Pan F8 62
Perlas, lagoon, Nic D6 62
Perleberg, Ger., 13,500 .... B5 16
Perley, Norman, Minn., 165 .... C2 99
Perlis, state, Mala., 90,885 .... I4 38
Perl-Mack, Adams, Colo., 3,000 .... *B6 83
Perm, Sov. Un., 722,000 .... D20 9
Perma, Sanders, Mont., 25 .... C2 102
Përmet, Alb., 2,302 .... B3 23
Pernambuco, state, Braz., 4,136,900 .... C3, k6 57
Pernell, Garvin, Okla., 150 .... C4 112
Pernik, Bul., 59,930 .... D6 22
Péronne, Fr., 5,081 .... C5 14
Perot, bayou, La C7 95
Perote, Bullock, Ala., 45 .... D4 78
Perpignan, Fr., 83,025 .... F5 14
Perquimans, co., N.C., 9,178 .... A7 109
Perrégaux, Alg., 27,367 .... *B5 44
Perrin, Jack, Tex., 300 .... C3 118
Perrin, Gloucester, Va., 300 .... D6 121
Perrine, Dade, Fla., 6,424 .... F3, G6 86
Perrineville, Monmouth, N.J., 300 .... C4 106
Perris, Riverside, Calif., 2,950 .... F3, F5 82
Perros-Guirec, Fr., 3,495 .... C2 14
Perrot, isl., Que., Can q19 73
Perry, Perry, Ark., 224 .... B3 81
Perry, Taylor, Fla., 7,979 .... B3 86
Perry, Houston, Ga., 6,032 .... D3 87
Perry, Pike, Ill., 442 .... D3 90
Perry, Dallas, Iowa, 6,442 .... C3 92
Perry, Jefferson, Kans., 495 .... B7, C8 93
Perry, Vermilion, La., 150 .... E3 95
Perry, Washington, Maine, 125 (564▲) D5 96
Perry, Shiawassee, Mich., 1,370 .... F6 98
Perry, Ralls, Mo., 802 .... B6 101
Perry, Wyoming, N.Y., 4,629 .... C2 108
Perry, Lake, Ohio, 885 .... A6 111
Perry, Noble, Okla., 5,210 .... A4 112
Perry, Aiken, S.C., 196 .... D5 115
Perry, Box Elder, Utah, 587 .... B3 119
Perry, co., Ala., 17,358 .... C2 78
Perry, co., Ark., 4,927 .... C3 81
Perry, co., Ill., 19,184 .... E4 90
Perry, co., Ind., 17,232 .... H4 91
Perry, co., Ky., 34,961 .... C6 94
Perry, co., Miss., 8,745 .... D4 100
Perry, co., Mo., 14,642 .... D8 101
Perry, co., Ohio, 27,864 .... C3 111
Perry, co., Pa., 26,582 .... F7 114
Perry, co., Tenn., 5,273 .... B4 117
Perry, peak, Mass B1 97
Perry, stream, N.H A1 105
Perrydale, Polk, Oreg., 125 .... B3, C1 113
Perryman, Harford, Md., 700 .... B5 85
Perryopolis, Fayette, Pa., 1,799 .... *F2 114
Perrysburg, Cattaraugus, N.Y., 434 .... C1 108
Perrysburg, Wood, Ohio, 5,519 .... A2, A4 111
Perry's Victory and International Peace Memorial, nat. mon., Ohio A5 111
Perrysville, Vermillion, Ind., 497 .... D3 91
Perrysville, Ashland, Ohio, 769 .... B5 111
Perryton, Ochiltree, Tex., 7,903 .... A2 118
Perryvale, Alta., Can B4 69
Perryville, Alsk., 93 .... D8 79
Perryville, Perry, Ark., 719 .... B3 81
Perryville, Boyle, Ky., 715 .... C5 94
Perryville, Ouachita, La., 100 .... B4 95
Perryville, Cecil, Md., 674 .... A5 85
Perryville, Perry, Mo., 5,117 .... D8 101
Perryville, Washington, R.I., 100 .... D10 84
Perryville, Decatur, Tenn., 250 .... B3 117
Persan, Fr., 5,196 .... E2 15
Persepolis, ruins, Iran G6 41
Pershing (East Germantown), Wayne, Ind., 367 .... E7 91
Pershing, Marion, Iowa, 275 .... C5 92
Pershing, Gasconade, Mo., 40 .... C6 101
Pershing, co., Nev., 3,999 .... C3 104
Persia, Harrison, Iowa, 322 .... C2 92
Persia, see Iran, country, Asia
Persia, Hawkins, Tenn., 150 .... C10 117
Persian, gulf, Asia J19 9
Persimmon Grove, Campbell, Ky., 100 .... A7 94
Persinger, Nicholas, W. Va., 25 .... C4 123
Person, co., N.C., 24,361 .... A4 109
Perstorps, Swe., 4,151 .... B7 24
Pertek, Tur., 3,100 .... C12 31
Perth, Austl., 95,000 (*485,000) F2 50
Perth, N.B., Can., 909 .... C2 74
Perth, Ont., Can., 5,360 .... C8 72
Perth, Sumner, Kans., 100 .... E6 93
Perth, Towner, N. Dak., 73 .... A6 110
Perth, Scot., 41,100 .... D5 13
Perth, co., Ont., Can., 57,452 .... D3 72
Perth, co., Scot., 127,018 .... D4 13
Perth Amboy, Middlesex, N.J., 38,007 .... B4, k7 106
Perthshire, Bolivar, Miss., 500 .... B3 100
Pertuis, Fr., 6,774 .... F6 14
Pertuis Breton, bay, Fr D3 14
Peru, La Salle, Ill., 10,460 .... B4 90
Peru, Miami, Ind., 14,453 .... C5 91
Peru, Madison, Iowa, 265 .... C4 92
Peru, Chautauqua, Kans., 340 .... E7 93
Peru, Berkshire, Mass., 25 (197▲) B1 97
Peru, Nemaha, Nebr., 1,151 .... D10 103
Peru, Clinton, N.Y., 1,000 .... f11 108
Peru, Bennington, Vt., 75 (194▲) E3 120
Peru, country, S.A., 11,500,000 .... E3 53, D3 58
Perugia, It., 75,000 (116,900▲) C4 21
Peruque, St. Charles, Mo., 80 .... A7 101
Peruvian Park, Salt Lake, Utah, 1,000 .... *C4 119
Péruwelz, Bel., 7,668 .... D3 15
Pervomaysk, Sov. Un., 30,000 .... G8 27
Pervomaysk, Sov. Un., 10,000 .... q21 27
Pervouralsk, Sov. Un., 104,000 .... B5 29
Pesaro, It., 49,000 (70,800▲) C4 21
Pescadero, San Mateo, Calif., 400 .... C5, D2 82
Pescara, It., 95,800 .... C5 21
Pescara, riv., It C4 21
Peschani, cape, Sov. Un G19 9
Peschanyy, cape, Sov. Un B10 37
Peshastin, Chelan, Wash., 600 .... B5 122
Peshawar, Pak., 166,273 (*218,691) B5 39
Peshkopi, Alb., 2,524 .... B3 23
Peshtera, Bul., 8,946 .... D7 22
Peshtigo, Marinette, Wis., 2,504 .... C6 124
Peshtigo, riv., Wis C5 124
Peski, Sov. Un., 5,000 .... C7 29
Peski, Sov. Un., 25,500 .... F14 27
Peski, Sov. Un n18 27
Peski Muyun-Kum, des., Sov. Un C23 9
Peso da Régua, Port., 5,623 .... B2 20
Pesotum, Champaign, Ill., 468 .... D5 90
Pesqueira, Braz., 19,778 .... C3, k5 57
Pest, co., Hung., 783,108 .... *B4 22
Petaca, Rio Arriba, N. Mex., 15 .... A3 107
Petah Tiqva, Isr., 58,700 .... B6, g10 32
Petal, Forrest, Miss., 4,007 .... D4 100
Petaluma, Sonoma, Calif., 14,035 .... B5, C2 82
Pétange, Lux., 11,623 .... E5 15
Petare, Ven., 75,441 .... *A4 60
Petatlán, Mex., 3,630 .... D4 63
Petauke, Zambia, 1,410 .... D5 48
Petawawa, Ont., Can., 4,509 .... B7 72
Petawawa, riv., Ont., Can B6 72
Petenwell, res., Wis D4 124
Peter, isl., Vir. Is F16 65
Peterborough, Austl., 3,430 .... F2 51
Peterborough, Ont., Can., 47,185 (*49,902) C6 72
Peterborough, Eng., 63,800 .... B7 12
Peterborough (Peterboro), Hillsboro, N.H., 1,931 .... E3 105
Peterborough, co., Ont., Can., 76,375 .... C6 72
Peter I, isl., Ant C3 5
Petergof, see Petrodvorets, Sov. Un.
Peterhead, Scot., 12,497 .... C7 13
Peterman, Monroe, Ala., 600 .... D2 78
Peter Pond, lake, Sask., Can m7 70
Peters, creek, W. Va C7 123
Peters, mtn., Va., W. Va D4 123
Peter's Arm, Newf., Can., 726 .... *D3 75
Petersburg, Alsk., 1,502 .... D13, m23 79
Petersburg, Menard, Ill., 2,359 .... C4 90
Petersburg, Pike, Ind., 2,939 .... H3 91
Petersburg, Boone, Ky., 390 .... A6 94
Petersburg, Monroe, Mich., 1,018 .... G7 98
Petersburg, Boone, Nebr., 400 .... C7 103
Petersburg, Cape May, N.J., 400 .... E3 106
Petersburg, Rensselaer, N.Y., 400 .... C7 108
Petersburg, Nelson, N. Dak., 272 .... A8 110
Petersburg, Mahoning, Ohio, 600 .... B7 111
Petersburg, Huntingdon, Pa., 552 .... E5 114
Petersburg, Lincoln and Marshall, Tenn., 423 .... B5 117
Petersburg, Hale, Tex., 1,400 .... C2 118
Petersburg (Independent City), Va., 36,750 (*100,370) C7, D5 121
Petersburg, Grant, W. Va., 2,079 .... B5 123
Petersdorf, Ger., 1,800 .... D5 24
Petersfield, Man., Can., 157 .... D3 71
Petersfield, Eng., 7,379 .... D7 12
Petersham, Worcester, Mass., 300 (890▲) B3 97
Peters Landing, Perry, Tenn., 25 .... B4 117
Peterson, Clay, Iowa, 565 .... B2 92
Peterson, Fillmore, Minn., 283 .... G7 99
Peterson, Morgan, Utah, 100 .... B4 119
Peterstown, Monroe, W. Va., 616 .... D4 123
Petersville, Lewis, Ky., 50 .... B6 94
Peter The Great, bay, Sov. Un E5 37
Petilia Policastro, It., 8,662 .... E6 21
Pétionville, Hai., 9,570 .... F7 64
Petit, lake, La C8 95
Petit Bois, isl., Miss E5 100
Petitcodiac, N.B., Can., 902 .... D4 74
Petitcodiac, riv., N.B., Can C5 74
Petite Amite, riv., La B6 95
Petite-de-Grat Bridge, N.S., Can., 865 .... D9 74
Petite Lieure, riv., Que., Can A5 73
Petite-Rivière Bridge, N.S., Can., 310 .... E5 74
Petite-Rivière-de-L'Ile, N.B., Can., 607 .... B5 74
Petit-Étang, N.S., Can., 489 .... C9 74
Petite-Vallée, Que., Can., 237 .... *k14 73
Petit-Goâve, Hai., 5,536 .... F7 64
Petit Jean, creek, Ark B2 81
Petit Jean, mtn., Ark C2 81
Petit Jean, mtn., Ark B3 81
Petit-Rocher, N.B., Can B4 74
Petitsikapau, lake, Newf., Can g8 75
Peto, Mex., 6,995 .... C7 63
Petorca, Chile, 1,098 .... A2 54
Petoskey, Emmet, Mich., 6,138 .... C6 98
Petras, mtn., Ant B36 5
Petrey, Crenshaw, Ala., 165 .... D3 78
Petrich, Bul., 13,456 .... E6 22
Petrified, forest, Miss C3 100
Petrified, forest, N. Dak B2 110
Petrified, forest, S. Dak D2 116
Petrified Forest, nat. park, Ariz B6 80
Petrified Wood, park, S. Dak B3 116
Petrikov, Sov. Un., 10,000 .... E7 27
Petrinja, Yugo., 7,345 .... C3 22
Petrodvorets, Sov. Un., 30,000 .... s30 25
Petrohué, Chile C2 54
Petrokrepost, Sov. Un., 30,000 .... B8 27, s32 25
Petrolândia, Braz., 2,669 .... C3 57
Petroleum, Wells, Ind., 300 .... C7 91
Petroleum, co., Mont., 894 .... C8 102
Petrolia, Ont., Can., 3,708 .... E2 72
Petrolia, Allen, Kans., 125 .... E8 93
Petrolia, Butler, Pa., 527 .... D2 114
Petrolia, Clay, Tex., 631 .... B3 118
Petrolina, Braz., 14,652 .... C2 57
Petropavlovsk, Sov. Un., 153,000 .... C7 29
Petropavlovskiy, Sov. Un D3 29
Petropavlovsk [-Kamchatskiy], Sov. Un., 106,000 .... D18 28
Petrópolis, Braz., 93,849 .... C4, h6 56
Petros, Morgan, Tenn., 850 .... C9 117
Petroseni, Rom., 28,400 (*60,000) C6 22
Petrovgrad, see Zrenjanin, Yugo.
Petrovsk, Sov. Un., 10,000 .... E15 27
Petrovskoye, Sov. Un., 29,000 .... D2 29
Petrovsk-Zabaykalskiy, Sov. Un., 59,000 .... D13 28
Petrozavodsk, Sov. Un., 145,000 .... A10 27
Petterill, riv., Eng F6 13
Pettibone, Kidder, N. Dak., 205 .... B6 110
Pettigoe, Ire., 313 .... C4 11
Pettigrew, Madison, Ark., 150 .... B2 81
Pettis, co., Mo., 35,120 .... C4 101
Pettisville, Fulton, Ohio, 320 .... A3 111
Pettit, Washington, Miss D2 100
Pettus, Lonoke, Ark C4, D6 81
Pettus, Bee, Tex., 450 .... E4 118
Petty Harbour, Newf., Can., 908 .... E5 75
Petukhovo, Sov. Un., 12,300 .... B7 29
Petway, Cheatham, Tenn A4 117
Pevek, Sov. Un., 5,800 .... C33 4
Pevely, Jefferson, Mo., 416 .... B8 101
Pewamo, Ionia, Mich., 416 .... E6 98
Pewaukee, Waukesha, Wis., 2,484 .... E1, E5 124
Pewaukee, lake, Wis E1 124
Pewee Valley, Oldham, Ky., 881 .... A4, B4 94
Peyton, El Paso, Colo., 110 .... B6 83
Pézenas, Fr., 7,198 .... F5 14
Pfaffenhofen, Ger., 8,600 .... E6 17
Pfäffikon, Switz., 5,735 .... B6 19
Pfarrkirchen, Ger., 6,000 .... E7 17
Pfeifer, Ellis, Kans., 200 .... D4 93
Pforzheim, Ger., 85,800 (*125,000) E3 17
Pfunds, Aus., 1,794 .... C6 18
Pfungstadt, Ger., 13,100 .... D3 17
Phair, Aroostook, Maine (part of Presque Isle) B5 96
Phalodi, India, 15,722 .... D4 40
Phaltan, India, 19,003 .... I5 40
Phangan, isl., Thai H4 38
Phan Rang, Viet., 5,000 .... G8 38
Phan Thiet, Viet., 55,180 .... G8 38
Pharoah, Okfuskee, Okla., 250 .... B5 112
Pharr, Hidalgo, Tex., 14,106 .... F3 118
Phatthalung, Thai., 10,147 .... I4 38
Pheba, Clay, Miss., 351 .... B5 100
Phelps, Pike, Ky., 725 .... C7 94
Phelps, Ontario, N.Y., 1,887 .... C3 108
Phelps, Vilas, Wis., 500 .... B4 124
Phelps, co., Mo., 25,396 .... D6 101
Phelps, co., Nebr., 9,800 .... D6 103
Phelps, lake, N.C B7 109
Phelps City, Atchison, Mo., 81 .... A2 101
Phenix City, Russell, Ala., 27,630 .... C4 78
Phet Buri, Thai., 14,288 .... F3 38
Phetchabun, Thai., 5,733 .... D4 38
Phichit, Thai., 9,477 .... D4 38
Philadelphia, Neshoba, Miss., 5,017 .... C4 100
Philadelphia, Marion, Mo., 166 .... B6 101
Philadelphia, Jefferson, N.Y., 868 .... A5 108
Philadelphia, Philadelphia, Pa., 2,002,512 (*3,969,500) B11, G11 114
Philadelphia, Loudon, Tenn., 500 .... D9 117
Philadelphia, co., Pa., 2,002,512 .... G11 114
Philbrook, Todd, Minn., 100 .... D4 99
Phil Campbell, Franklin, Ala., 898 .... A2 78
Philip, Haakon, S. Dak., 1,114 .... C4 116
Philipp, Tallahatchie, Miss., 250 .... B3 100
Philippeville, Alg., 87,922 .... B6 44, F10 30
Philippeville, Bel., 1,559 .... D4 15
Philippi, Barbour, W. Va., 2,228 .... B4 123
Philippi, glacier, Ant C21 5
Philippine, is., Phil B6 35
Philippine, sea, Phil A6 35
Philippines, country, Asia, 31,800,000 .... H15 33, B6 35
Philippolis, S. Afr., 2,078 .... D4 49
Philipsburg, Granite, Mont., 1,107 .... D3 102
Philipsburg, Centre, Pa., 3,872 .... E5 114
Philipsville, Ont., Can., 97 .... C8 72
Philleo, lake, Wash D7 122
Phillip, isl., Austl I5 51
Phillippy, Lake, Tenn., 100 .... A2 111
Phillips, Franklin, Maine, 600 (1,021▲) D2 96
Phillips, Hamilton, Nebr., 192 .... D7 103
Phillips, Coal, Okla., 91 .... C5 112
Phillips, Hutchinson, Tex., 3,605 .... B2 118
Phillips, Price, Wis., 1,524 .... C3 124
Phillips, co., Ark., 43,997 .... C5 81
Phillips, co., Colo., 4,440 .... A8 83
Phillips, co., Kans., 8,709 .... C4 93
Phillips, co., Mont., 6,027 .... B8 102
Phillips, brook, N.H A4, B1 105
Phillips, isl., S.C G6 115
Phillipsburg, Que., Can., 379 .... D4 73
Phillipsburg, Tift, Ga., 2,037 .... *E3 87
Phillipsburg, Phillips, Kans., 3,233 .... C4 93
Phillipsburg, Laclede, Mo., 142 .... D5 101
Phillipsburg, Warren, N.J., 18,502 .... B2 106
Phillipsdale, Providence, R.I. (part of East Providence) B11 84
Phillipston, Worcester, Mass., 100 (695▲) A3 97
Phillipsville, Haywood, N.C., 1,311 .... *D3 109
Philmont, Columbia, N.Y., 1,750 .... C7 108
Philo, Champaign, Ill., 740 .... D5 90
Philo (Taylorsville), Muskingum, Ohio, 913 .... C6 111
Philomath, Benton, Oreg., 1,359 .... C3 113
Philpott, res., Va E2 121
Philrich, Hutchinson, Tex., 2,067 .... *B2 118
Phippen, Sask., Can E1 70
Phippsburg, Routt, Colo., 150 .... A4 83
Phippsburg, Sagadahoc, Maine, 100 (1,121▲) E6 96
Phitsanulok, Thai., 32,659 .... D4 38
Phlox, Langlade, Wis., 150 .... C4 124
Phnom Penh, Camb., 403,500 .... G6 38
Phocis (Fokis), prov., Grc., 47,842 .... *C4 23
Phoebus, Va. (part of Hampton) B6 121
Phoenicia, Ulster, N.Y., 700 .... C6 108
Phoenix, Maricopa, Ariz., 439,170 (*619,600) D3, G2 80
Phoenix, Cook, Ill., 4,203 .... F3 90
Phoenix, Baltimore, Md., 200 .... A4 85
Phoenix, Keweenaw, Mich., 45 .... A2 98
Phoenix, Oswego, N.Y., 2,408 .... B4 108
Phoenix, Jackson, Oreg., 769 .... E4 113
Phoenix, Charlotte, Va., 259 .... D4 121
Phoenix, is., Pac. O G11 7
Phoenixville, Windham, Conn., 150 .... B8 84
Phoenixville, Chester, Pa., 13,797 .... A10, F10 114
Phong Saly, Laos, 10,000 .... B5 38
Phrae, Thai., 15,616 .... C4 38
Phthiotis (Fthiotis), prov., Grc., 160,035 .... *C4 23
Phuket, Thai., 27,021 .... I3 38
Phuket, isl., Thai I3 40
Phu Lai Leng, mtn., Laos C6 38
Phu Quoc, isl., Viet G6 38
Phutthaisong, Thai E5 38
Piaanu, pass, Truk 52
Piacenza, It., 94,900 .... B2 21, D5 18
Pialba, Austl., 3,544 .... B9 51
Pianosa, isl., It C3 21
Pianosa, isl., It C5 21
Piapot, Sask., Can., 246 .... H1 70
Piaseczno, Pol., 13,800 .... m14 26
Piatra-Neamt, Rom., 32,648 .... B8 22
Piatt, co., Ill., 14,960 .... D5 90
Piauí, state, Braz., 1,263,368 .... C2 57
Piauí, mts., Braz C2 57
Piauí, riv., Braz C2 57
Piave, riv., It D8 18
Piazza Armerina, It., 24,887 .... F5 21
Pibor, riv., Sud D3 47
Pibor Post, Sud D3 47
Pibroch, Alta., Can., 118 .... B4 69
Picabo, Blaine, Idaho, 75 .... F4 89
Picacho, Pinal, Ariz., 400 .... E4 80
Picacho, Lincoln, N. Mex., 100 .... D4 107
Picacho, peak, Calif F6 83
Picadome, Fayette, Ky., 900 .... B5 94
Picard, Que., Can B8 73
Picardy (Picardie), former prov., Fr., 1,051,000 .... C5 14
Picayune, Pearl River, Miss., 7,834 .... E4 100
Piccadilly, Newf., Can., 427 .... D2 75
Pic de Tio, mtn., Guinea E3 45
Pic du Midi d'Ossau, mtn., Fr F3 14
Piceance, creek, Colo B2 83
Pichanal, Arg D3 55
Picher, Ottawa, Okla., 2,553 .... A7 112
Pichilemu, Chile A2 54
Pichincha, prov., Ec., 424,655 .... B2 58
Pickardville, Alta., Can., 140 .... B4 69
Pickardville, Sheridan, N. Dak., 23 .... B5 110
Pickaway, co., Ohio, 35,855 .... C4 111
Pick City, Mercer, N. Dak., 101 .... B4 110
Pickens, Desha, Ark., 100 .... D4 81
Pickens, Holmes, Miss., 727 .... C4 100
Pickens, Pickens, S.C., 2,198 .... B2 115
Pickens, Randolph, W. Va., 300 .... C4 123
Pickens, co., Ala., 21,882 .... B1 78
Pickens, co., Ga., 8,903 .... B2 87
Pickens, co., S.C., 46,030 .... B2 115
Pickensville, Pickens, Ala., 150 .... B1 78
Pickerel, Ont., Can., 116 .... B4 72
Pickerel, Langlade, Wis., 60 .... C5 124
Pickerel, lake, Wis C4 124
Pickerel, riv., Ont., Can B4 72
Pickering, Ont., Can., 1,755 .... D5 72
Pickering, Eng., 4,193 .... F8 13
Pickering, Nodaway, Mo., 234 .... A3 101
Pickerington, Fairfield, Ohio, 634 .... C2, C5 111
Pickett, co., Tenn., 4,431 .... C8 118
Pickford, Chippewa and Mackinac, Mich., 650 .... B6 98
Pickle Crow, Ont., Can., 281 .... *E8 72
Pickleville, Rich, Utah, 94 .... B4 119
Pickrell, Gage, Nebr., 130 .... D9 103
Pickstown, Charles Mix, S. Dak., 600 .... E7 116
Pickwick, Winona, Minn., 150 .... G7 99
Pickwick Dam, Hardin, Tenn., 25 .... B3 117
Pickwick, lake, Ala., Miss., Tenn A1 78
Pickworth, pt., Mass f12 97
Pico, isl., Az. Is g8 44
Pico Rivera, Los Angeles, Calif., 49,150 .... *F2 82
Picos, Braz., 8,176 .... C2 57
Pictograph Rocks, Ariz D1 80
Picton, Ont., Can., 4,862 .... D7 72
Picton, N.Z., 2,315 .... N15 51
Pictou, N.S., Can., 4,534 .... D7 74
Pictou, co., N.S., Can., 43,908 .... D7 74
Pictou, isl., N.S., Can D7 74
Pictou Landing, N.S., Can., 405 .... D7 74
Pic Tousidé, mtn., Chad A3 46
Picture, gorge, Oreg C7 113
Picture Butte, Alta., Can., 978 .... E4 69
Pictured, cave, Wis E3 124
Pictured Rocks, Ariz E4 80
Picture Rocks, Lycoming, Pa., 594 .... D8 114
Picuí, Braz., 2,140 .... h5 57
Picún-Leufú, Arg B3 54
Pidcock, Brooks, Ga., 250 .... F3 87
Pidurutalagala, peak, Cey G7 39
Piedade, Braz., 4,812 .... m8 56
Piedmont, Calhoun, Ala., 4,794 .... B4 78
Piedmont, Alameda, Calif., 11,117 .... B5 82
Piedmont, Que., Can., 272 .... D3 73
Piedmont, Greenwood, Kans., 250 .... E7 93
Piedmont, Wayne, Mo., 1,555 .... D7 101
Piedmont, Canadian, Okla., 146 .... B4 112
Piedmont, Anderson and Greenville, S.C., 2,108 .... B3 115
Piedmont, Meade, S. Dak., 200 .... C2 116
Piedmont, Mineral, W. Va., 2,307 .... B5 123
Piedmont, Uinta, Wyo., 10 .... D2 125
Piedmont, reg., It B1 21
Piedmont, res., Ohio B6 111
Piedmont, upland, U.S C2 109
Piedrabuena, Sp., 6,210 .... C3 20
Piedras, pt., Mex D5 63
Piedras, riv., Pan k12 62
Piedras, riv., Peru D3 58
Piedras Blancas, pt., Calif E3 82
Piedras Negras, Guat B2 62
Piedras Negras, Mex., 42,992 .... B4 63
Piedra Sola, Ur E1 56
Piekietko, Pol., 1,000 .... k13 26
Pieksämäki, Fin., 10,600 .... F12 25
Piélagos, Sp., 8,040 .... A4 20
Pielisjarvi, lake, Fin F13 25
Piemonte, pol., dist., It., 3,914,250 .... *B1 21
Piendamó, Col., 1,615 .... C2 60
Pienkaun, China E4 36
Pierce, Weld, Colo., 424 .... A6 83
Pierce, Polk, Fla., 800 .... E5 86
Pierce, Clearwater, Idaho, 522 .... C3 89
Pierce, Pierce, Nebr., 1,216 .... B8 103
Pierce, Tucker, W. Va., 50 .... B5 123
Pierce, co., Ga., 9,678 .... E4 87
Pierce, co., Nebr., 8,722 .... B8 103
Pierce, co., N. Dak., 7,394 .... A5 110
Pierce, co., Wash., 321,590 .... C3 122
Pierce, co., Wis., 22,503 .... D1 124
Pierce, lake, Man., Can B5 71
Pierce, lake, Fla E5 86
Pierce, pond, Maine C2 96
Pierce Bridge, Grafton, N.H B3 105
Pierce City, Lawrence, Mo., 1,006 .... E3 101
Piercefield, St. Lawrence, N.Y., 300 .... A6, f10 108
Pierceland, Sask., Can., 367 .... *n7 70
Pierces Point, Cape May, N.J., 25 .... E3 106
Pierce Station, Obion, Tenn., 25 .... A3 117
Pierceton, Kosciusko, Ind., 1,186 .... B6 91
Pierceville, Finney, Kans., 175 .... E3 93
Piercy, Mendocino, Calif., 50 .... C2 82
Pieria, prov., Grc., 97,697 .... *B4 23
Piermont, Grafton, N.H., 125 (477▲) C2 105
Piermont, Rockland, N.Y., 1,878 .... D7 108
Piermont, mtn., N.H C2 105
Pierowall, Scot A5 13
Pierpont, Ashtabula, Ohio, 250 .... A7 111
Pierpont, Day, S. Dak., 258 .... B8 116
Pierre, Hughes, S. Dak., 10,088 .... C5 116
Pierre, bayou, Miss D3 100
Pierrefitte-sur-Aire, Fr., 256 .... F5 15
Pierrefitte [-sur-Seine], Fr., 14,770 .... g10 14
Pierrefonds, Que., Can., 12,171 .... q19 73
Pierreville, Que., Can., 1,559 .... C5 73
Pierron, Bond and Madison, Ill., 371 .... E4 100
Pierson, Man., Can., 229 .... E1 71
Pierson, Volusia, Fla., 716 .... C5 86
Pierson, Woodbury, Iowa, 425 .... B2 92
Pierz, Morrison, Minn., 816 .... E4 99
Piestany, Czech., 18,700 .... D4 26
Pietermaritzburg, S. Afr., 91,178 (*96,236) C5 49
Pietersaari (Jakobstad), Fin., 7,378 .... F10 25
Pietersburg, S. Afr., 28,071 .... B4 49
Pie Town, Catron, N. Mex., 125 .... C1 107
Pietrasanta, It., 6,600 .... C3 21
Piet Retief, S. Afr., 8,604 .... C5 49
Pieve di Cadore, It., 3,893 .... A4 21
Pigeon, Huron, Mich., 1,191 .... E7 98
Pigeon, bay, Man., Can C3 71
Pigeon, creek, Ala D3 78
Pigeon, creek, Ind H3 91
Pigeon, lake, Alta., Can C3 69
Pigeon, mtn., Ga B1 87
Pigeon, mtn., N.Y B6 108
Pigeon, pt., Calif D2 82
Pigeon, pt., U.S., Can A8 99
Pigeon, riv., Man., Can C3 71
Pigeon, riv., Ind A6 91
Pigeon, riv., Minn A8 99
Pigeon, riv., Wis B6 124
Pigeon Cove, Essex, Mass., 1,600 .... A6 97
Pigeon Falls, Trempealeau, Wis., 207 .... D2 124
Pigeon Forge, Sevier, Tenn., 950 .... D10 117
Pigeon River, Cook, Minn., 35 .... A8 99
Pigg, riv., Va E3 121
Piggott, Clay, Ark., 2,776 .... A5 81
Pigüé, Arg., 5,869 .... B4 54
Piirai, isl., Eniwetok 52
Pijijiapan, Mex., 3,307 .... D6 63
Pike, Pike, Ark., 50 .... C2 81
Pike, Grafton, N.H., 200 .... B2 105
Pike, Wyoming, N.Y., 345 .... C2 108
Pike, Yamhill, Oreg B1 113
Pike, co., Ala., 25,987 .... D4 78
Pike, co., Ark., 7,864 .... C2 81
Pike, co., Ga., 7,138 .... C2 87
Pike, co., Ill., 20,552 .... D3 90
Pike, co., Ind., 12,797 .... H3 91
Pike, co., Ky., 68,264 .... C7 94
Pike, co., Miss., 35,063 .... D3 100
Pike, co., Mo., 16,706 .... B6 101
Pike, co., Ohio, 19,380 .... C4 111
Pike, co., Pa., 9,158 .... D11 114
Pike, riv., Wis C5 124
Pike Rigg, mtn., Eng F6 13
Pike Road, Beaufort, N.C., 400 .... B7 109
Pikes, beach, N.Y G6 84
Pikes, peak, Colo C5 83
Pikes Rocks, mts., Pa C3 114
Pikesville, Baltimore, Md., 18,737 .... C2 85
Piketberg, S. Afr., 3,312 .... D2 49
Piketon, Pike, Ohio, 1,244 .... C4 111
Pikeview, El Paso, Colo., 200 .... C6 83
Pikeville, Pike, Ky., 4,754 .... C7 94
Pikeville, Wayne, N.C., 525 .... B6 109
Pikeville, Bledsoe, Tenn., 951 .... D8 117
Pikwitonei, Man., Can., 175 .... B3 71
Piła, Pol., 27,000 .... B4 26
Pilar, Braz., 7,201 .... C3, k6 57
Pilar, Taos, N. Mex., 100 .... A4 107
Pilar, Par., 10,062 .... E4 55
Pilar de Goiás, Braz., 232 .... A3 56
Pilar [do Sul], Braz., 1,789 .... m8 56
Pilatus, peak, Switz C5 19
Pilcomayo, riv., Par D3 55
Pilger, Sask., Can., 133 .... E3 70
Pilger, Stanton, Nebr., 491 .... B8 103
Pilgram Knob, Buchanan, Va., 100 .... B3 121
Pilgrim Gardens, Delaware, Pa., 5,000 .... *B11 114
Pilibhit, India, 57,527 .... C7 40
Pilica, riv., Pol C5 26
Pillager, Cass, Minn., 338 .... D4 99
Pillar, pt., Calif B5 82
Píllaro, Ec., 2,814 .... B2 58

Pillau, see Baltiysk, Sov. Un.
Pilley's Island, Newf., Can., 478 .... D4 75
Pillow (Uniontown), Dauphin, Pa., 348 .... E8 114
Pillowville, Weakley, Tenn ... A3 117
Pillsbury, Barnes, N. Dak., 76 .... B8 110
Pilos, Grc., 3,130 .... D3 23
Pilot, peak, Nev B7 104
Pilot, range, N.H A4 105
Pilot Butte, Sask., Can., 381 .. G3 70
Pilot Grove, Cooper, Mo., 680 .... C5 101
Pilot Knob, Iron, Mo., 524 ... D7 101
Pilot Knob, mtn., Ark B2 81
Pilot Knob, mtn., Ark C1 81
Pilot Knob, mtn., Idaho D3 89
Pilot Knob, mtn., Mo E4 101
Pilot Knob, mtn., Tenn C8 117
Pilot Knob, ridge, Kans B8 93
Pilot Mound, Man., Can., 802 .... E2 71
Pilot Mound, Boone, Iowa, 196 .... B3 92
Pilot Mountain, Surry, N.C., 1,310 .... A3 109
Pilot Point, Alsk., 61 .... D8 79
Pilot Point, Denton, Tex., 1,254 .... C4 118
Pilot Rock, Umatilla, Oreg., 1,695 .... B8 113
Pilot Station, Alsk., 219 .... C7 79
Pilottown, Plaquemines, La., 150 .... E6 95
Pilsen, Kewaunee, Wis., 30 .. A6 124
Pilvo, Sov. Un A11 37
Pima, Graham, Ariz., 806 ... E6 80
Pima, co., Ariz., 265,660 .... E3 80
Pimba, Austl., 56 .... F6 50
Pimmit Hills, Fairfax, Va., 1,000 .... *B5 121
Pimple, hill, Pa A2 106
Piña, Pan., 229 .... k10 62
Pinal, co., Ariz., 62,673 .... E4 80
Pinal, mts., Ariz D5 80
Pinarbasi, Tur., 5,800 .... C11 31
Pinar del Rio, Cuba, 52,000 .... D2 64
Pinar del Río, prov., Cuba, 448,442 .... D2 64
Pinardville, Hillsboro, N.H., 1,500 .... *E4 105
Pinas, Arg A3 54
Pincher Creek, Alta., Can., 2,961 .... E4 69
Pincher Station, Alta., Can., 79 .... E4 69
Pinckard, Dale, Ala., 578 .... D4 78
Pinckney, Crittenden, Ark ... E8 81
Pinckney, Livingston, Mich., 732 .... F7 98
Pinckney, isl., S.C G6 115
Pinckneyville, Perry, Ill., 3,085 .... E4 90
Pinckneyville, Wilkinson, Miss., 50 .... D2 100
Pinconning, Bay, Mich., 1,329 .... E7 98
Pinczow, Pol., 3,701 .... C6 26
Pindall, Searcy, Ark., 100 .... A3 81
Pindamonhangaba, Braz., 19,144 .... C3 56
Pindare, riv., Braz B1 57
Pindus, mts., Grc C3 23
Pine, Gila, Ariz., 150 .... C4 80
Pine, Jefferson, Colo., 35 .... B5 83
Pine, Ripley, Mo., 150 .... E6 101
Pine, San Miguel, N. Mex., 10 .... B4 107
Pine, co., Minn., 17,004 .... D6 99
Pine, cape, Newf., Can E5 75
Pine, creek, Alta., Can B4 69
Pine, creek, Nev C5 104
Pine, creek, Pa D7 114
Pine, creek, Wash B8 122
Pine, hill, Conn C4 84
Pine, key, Fla F1 86
Pine, lake, Ind A4 91
Pine, lake, Minn D3 99
Pine, lake, Wis C4 124
Pine, mtn., Conn B5 84
Pine, mtn., Ga D2 87
Pine, mtn., Ky., Tenn. D6 94, C9 117
Pine, mtn., Okla C6 112
Pine, mtn., Oreg D6 113
Pine, mtn., Tenn C9 117
Pine, pt., Fla C3 86
Pine, ridge, Nebr B2 103
Pine, ridge, Wyo C8 125
Pine, riv., B.C., Can B6 68
Pine, riv., Man., Can D1 71
Pine, riv., Mich D7 98
Pine, riv., N.H C4 105
Pine, riv., Wis C4 124
Pine Apple, Wilcox, Ala., 355 .... D3 78
Pine Bank, Greene, Pa., 20 .. G1 114
Pine Beach, Ocean, N.J., 985 .... *D4 106
Pine Bluff, Jefferson, Ark., 44,037 .... C3 81
Pinebluff, Moore, N.C., 509 . B4 109
Pinebluff, lake, Sask., Can C4 70
Pine Bluffs, Laramie, Wyo., 1,121 .... D8 125
Pine Bluff Southeast, Jefferson, Ark., 2,679 .... *C4 81
Pinebur, Marion, Miss., 40 . D4 100
Pine Bush, Orange, N.Y., 1,100 .... D6 108
Pine Castle, Orange, Fla., 5,000 .... D5 86
Pine City, Monroe, Ark., 125 .... C4 81
Pine City, Pine, Minn., 1,972 .... E6 99
Pine City, Whitman, Wash., 50 .... B8 122
Pine Creek, Austl., 91 .... B5 50
Pinecreek, Roseau, Minn., 34 .... B3 99
Pine Creek, gorge, Pa C7 114
Pinecrest, Tuolume, Calif., 2,000 .... C4 82
Pinecroft, Spokane, Wash ... D8 122
Pineda, Brevard, Fla., 150 .. D6 86
Pinedale, Navajo, Ariz., 80 ... C5 80
Pinedale, Fresno, Calif., 3,202 .... *D4 82
Pinedale, Sublette, Wyo., 965 .... C3 125
Pine Falls, Man., Can., 1,244 .... D3 71
Pine Forest, mts., Nev B3 104
Pinega, Sov. Un., 3,600 .... C17 9
Pine Grove, Appling, Ga., 100 .... E4 87
Pine Grove, St. Helena, La., 50 .... D5 95
Pine Grove, Burlington, N.J., 180 .... D3 106
Pine Grove, Schuylkill, Pa., 2,267 .... E9 114
Pine Grove, Wetzel, W. Va., 760 .... A6, B4 123
Pine Grove, Brown, Wis., 25 .... A6 124
Pine Grove Mills, Centre, Pa., 900 .... E6 114
Pine Hall, Stokes, N.C., 400 .. A3 109
Pine Hill, Wilcox, Ala., 367 .. D2 78
Pine Hill, Austl A6 51
Pine Hill, Rockcastle, Ky., 600 .... C5 94
Pine Hill, Camden, N.J., 3,939 .... D3 106
Pine Hills, Orange, Fla., 7,000 .... *D5 86
Pinehouse Lake, Sask., Can., 206 .... B2 70
Pinehurst, Dooly, Ga., 457 ... D3 87
Pinehurst, Shoshone, Idaho, 1,432 .... B2 89
Pinehurst, Middlesex, Mass., 3,500 .... f11 97
Pinehurst, Moore, N.C., 1,124 .... B4 109
Pinehurst, Orange, Tex., 1,703 .... *D6 118
Pinehurst, Snohomish, Wash., 3,000 .... B3 122
Pinehurst, lake, Alta., Can B5 69
Pine Island, Goodhue, Minn., 1,308 .... F6 99
Pine Island, Orange, N.Y., 800 .... D6 108
Pine Island, bay, Ant B2 5
Pine Island, sound, Fla F4 86
Pine Knot, McCreary, Ky., 750 .... D5 94
Pine Lake, De Kalb, Ga., 738 .... A5 88
Pinelake, La Porte, Ind., 1,400 .... *A4 91
Pine Lake, Middlesex, Mass., 800 .... g10 97
Pineland, Jasper, S.C., 82 ... F5 115
Pineland, Sabine, Tex., 1,236 .... D6 118
Pine Lawn, St. Louis, Mo., 5,943 .... C7 101
Pine Level, Montgomery, Ala., 150 .... C3 78
Pine Level, Johnston, N.C., 833 .... B5 109
Pinellas, co., Fla., 374,665 .... E4 86
Pinellas, pt., Fla F2 86
Pinellas Park, Pinellas, Fla., 10,848 .... E1, E4 86
Pine Lodge, Lincoln, N. Mex D4 107
Pine Meadow, Litchfield, Conn., 300 .... B5 84
Pine Mountain, Harris, Ga., 790 .... D2 87
Pineora, Effingham, Ga., 210 .... D5 87
Pine Orchard, New Haven, Conn., 500 .... D5 84
Pine Park, Grady, Ga., 82 ... F2 87
Pine Plains, Dutchess, N.Y., 750 .... D7 108
Pine Point, N.W. Ter., Can. D10 66
Pine Point, Cumberland, Maine, 800 .... E2, E5 96
Pine Prairie, Evangeline, La., 387 .... D3 95
Piner, bay, Ant C27 5
Pine Rest, Middlesex, Mass., 750 .... g10 97
Pine Ridge, Montgomery, Ark., 100 .... C2 81
Pine Ridge, Adams, Miss., 50 .... D2 100
Pine Ridge, Shannon, S. Dak., 1,256 .... D3 116
Pine Ridge, Indian res., S. Dak .. D3 116
Pine River, Man., Can., 429 .... D1 71
Pine River, Arenac, Mich ... D5 98
Pine River, Cass, Minn., 775 .... D4 99
Pinerolo, It., 24,500 .... B1 21
Piñeros, isl., P.R B8 65
Pinetop, Navajo, Ariz., 400 ... C5 80
Pinetops, Edgecombe, N.C., 1,372 .... B6 109
Pinetown, Beaufort, N.C., 215 .... B7 109
Pinetta, Madison, Fla., 200 .. B3 86
Pine Valley, San Diego, Calif., 150 .... F5 82
Pine Valley, Hillsboro, N.H., 100 .... E3 105
Pine Valley, LeFlore, Okla .. C7 112
Pine Valley, Washington, Utah, 75 .... F2 119
Pine Valley, mts., Utah F2 119
Pineview, Wilcox, Ga., 369 ... D3 87
Pine View, Harnett, N.C B4 109
Pine Village, Warren, Ind., 309 .... D3 91
Pineville, Bell, Ky., 3,181 ... D6 94
Pineville, Rapides, La., 8,636 .... C3 95
Pineville, Smith, Miss., 100 .. C4 100
Pineville, McDonald, Mo., 454 .... E3 101
Pineville, Mecklenburg, N.C., 1,514 .... B3 109
Pineville, Berkeley, S.C., 100 .... E7 115
Pineville, Wyoming, W. Va., 1,137 .... D3 123
Pinewald, Ocean, N.J., 280 .. D4 106
Pinewater, range, Nev G6 104
Pinewood, Beltrami, Minn., 75 .... C3 99
Pinewood, Sumter, S. C., 570 .... D7 115
Piney, Man., Can., 197 .... E4 71
Piney, creek, Mo D5 101
Piney, creek, W. Va D7 123
Piney, fork, W. Va A6 123
Piney, pt., Fla C3 86
Piney Flats, Sullivan, Tenn., 300 .... C11 117
Piney Fork, Jefferson, Ohio, 800 .... B7 111
Piney Point, Manatee, Fla., 30 .... F2 86
Piney Point, Harris, Tex., 1,790 .... *E5 118
Piney Swamp Knob, mtn., W. Va B5 123
Piney View, Raleigh, W. Va., 800 .... D7 123
Piney Woods, Rankin, Miss .. C3 100
Pingchiang, China J5 36
Pingchuan, China D8 36
Pinghsiang, China, 22,000 .... K5 36
Pingliang, China, 55,000 .... G2 36
Pinglo, China, 10,000 .... G7 38
Pinglo, China, 5,000 .... E2 36
Pingnan, China, 5,000 .... G7 34
Pingree, Bingham, Idaho, 100 .... F6 89
Pingree, Stutsman, N. Dak., 151 .... B7 110
Pingting, China F5 36
Pingtingshan, China, 50,000 . H5 36
Pingtu, China, 10,000 .... F8 36
Pingtung, Taiwan, 93,500 (130,600▲) *G9 35
Pingwu, China, 3,000 .... E5 34
Pinhal, Braz., 14,260 .... C3, m8 56
Pinhal Novo, Port., 6,429 .... f10 20
Pinhead, buttes, Oreg C5 113
Pinheiro, Braz., 6,537 .... B1 57
Pinhel, Port., 3,312 .... B2 20
Pinhsien, China, 6,000 .... D3 37
Pini, isl., Indon E1 35
Pinios, riv., Grc C4 23
Pink, cliffs, Utah F3 119
Pinkham, Sask., Can F1 70
Pink Hill, Lenoir, N.C., 457 . B6 109
Pinkney (South Gastonia), Gaston, N.C., 3,762 .... *B2 109
Pinkstaff, Lawrence, Ill., 300 .... E6 90
Pinnacle, Pulaski, Ark., 25 .... C3, D5 81
Pinnacle, Stokes, N.C., 400 .. A3 109
Pinnacle, butte, Wyo B3 125
Pinnacle, The, mtn., Conn B5 84
Pinnacle, mtn., Mo B7 101
Pinnacle, mtn., N.Y B6 108
Pinnacle, peak, Wyo B2 125
Pinnacle, peaks, B.C., Can D1 69
Pinnacles, nat. mon., Calif D3 82
Pinnaroo, Austl., 621 .... G3 51
Pinneberg, Ger., 28,400 .... E3 24
Pinnebog, Huron, Mich., 110 .... E7 98
Pinó Hachado, pass, Arg B2 54
Pinola, Simpson, Miss., 116 . D4 100
Pinole, Contra Costa, Calif., 6,064 .... B5 82
Pinon, Navajo, Ariz., 100 ... A5 80
Pinon, Fr., 1,636 .... E3 15
Pinon, Otero, N. Mex., 25 ... E4 107
Pinopolis, Berkeley, S.C., 311 .... E7 115
Pinopolis, dam, S.C E8 115
Pinos, Cuba h12 64
Pinos, Mex., 3,327 .... C4 63
Pinos, isl., Cuba E2 64
Pinos, mtn., Calif E4 82
Pinos, pt., Calif D3 82
Pinos Altos, Grant, N. Mex., 150 .... E1 107
Pinos Altos, range, N. Mex D1 107
Pinoso, Sp., 5,114 .... C5 20
Pinos-Puente, Sp., 8,653 .... D4 20
Pinotpandian, Phil o13 35
Pinsk, Sov. Un., 41,548 .... E6 27
Pinsk, marshes, Sov. Un E6 27
Pinson, Jefferson, Ala., 1,121 . E5 78
Pinson, Madison, Tenn., 240 .... B3 117
Pinsonfork, Pike, Ky., 800 . *C7 94
Pinta, isl., Ec f5 58
Pintados, Chile D2 55
Pintendre, Que., Can., 159 .. n17 73
Pinto, Allegany, Md., 150 .... D2 85
Pinto, Sp., 5,360 .... p17 20
Pinto, butte, Sask., Can H2 70
Pinto, creek, Sask., Can H2 70
Pintura, Washington, Utah, 10 .... F2 119
Pinware, riv., Newf., Can C3 75
Pinyon, peak, Idaho E4 89
Pinzolo, It., 3,469 .... C6 18
Pinzón, isl., Ec g5 58
Pioche, Lincoln, Nev., 900 ... F7 104
Piombino, It., 38,200 .... C3 21
Pioneer, Humboldt, Iowa, 448 .... B3 92
Pioneer, West Carroll, La., 154 .... B4 95
Pioneer, Williams, Ohio, 855 A3 111
Pioneer, mts., Idaho F5 89
Pioneer, mts., Mont E3 102
Pioneer Mine, B.C., Can., 226 .... D6 68
Pioner, isl., Sov. Un B5 4
Piopolis, Que., Can., 139 ... D7 73
Piotrkow [Trybunalski], Pol., 54,800 .... C5 26
Piove di Sacco, It., 5,349 .... D8 18
Pipe, Fond du Lac, Wis., 90 .... B5 124
Pipe, creek, Ind D6 91
Pipe, creek, Ohio B3 111
Piper, Bibb, Ala., 15 .... B2 78
Piper, Wyandotte, Kans., 240 .... B8 93
Piper City, Ford, Ill., 807 ... C5 90
Piperi, isl., Grc C5 23
Pipers Gap, Carroll, Va., 25 . E2 121
Pipestone, Ont., Can h12 72
Pipe Spring, nat. mon., Ariz A3 80
Pipestem, Summers, W. Va., 25 .... D4 123
Pipe Stem, creek, N. Dak B6 110
Pipestone, Man., Can., 226 .. E1 71
Pipestone, Pipestone, Minn., 5,324 .... G2 99
Pipestone, co., Minn., 13,605 .... F2 99
Pipestone, creek, Man., Can E1 71
Pipestone, creek, Sask., Can G5 70
Pipestone, nat. mon., Minn G2 99
Pipestone, pass, Mont E4 102
Pipmuacan, res., Que., Can k12 73
Piqua, Woodson, Kans., 258 . E8 93
Piqua, Miami, Ohio, 19,219 . B3 111
Piracanjuba, Braz., 3,869 .... E1 57
Piracicaba, Braz., 80,670 . C3, m8 56
Piracicaba, riv., Braz m8 56
Piraçununga, Braz., 12,546 .... C3, k8 56
Piracuruca, Braz., 4,320 .... B2 57
Piraeus, see Piraievs, Grc.,
Piraievs (Piraeus), Grc., 183,877 .... D4, h11 23
Pirajú, Braz., 10,658 .... C3 56
Pirajuí, Braz., 6,465 .... C3 56
Piramida, mtn., Sov. Un D12 28
Piran, Yugo., 5,464 .... B4 21
Pirané, Arg., 3,561 .... E4 55
Piranga, Braz., 2,169 .... F2 57
Piranhas, Braz., 1,021 .... C3 57
Pirapóra, Braz., 13,772 .... E2 57
Pireway, Columbus, N.C., 100 .... C5 109
Pirgos, Grc., 20,558 .... D3 23
Piriápolis, Ur., 4,400 .... E1 56
Pirin, mts., Bul E6 22
Piripiri, Braz., 9,635 .... B2 57
Pirmasens, Ger., 52,900 .... D2 17
Pirna, Ger., 41,000 .... C8 17
Pirot, Yugo., 18,585 .... D6 22
Pirovskoye, Sov. Un D27 9
Pirtleville, Cochise, Ariz., 850 .... F6 80
Piru, Indon F7 35
Piryatin, Sov. Un., 10,000 .... F9 27
Pis, isl., Truk 52
Pisa, It., 96,400 .... C3 21
Pisagua, Chile, 419 .... C1 55
Piscataqua, riv., N.H., Maine .. D5 105
Piscataquis, co., Maine, 17,379 .... C3 96
Piscataquis, riv., Maine C4 96
Piscataquog, riv., N.H D5 105
Piscataway, creek, Md C4 85
Pisciotta, It., 4,025 .... D5 21
Pisco, Peru, 17,222 .... D2 58
Piseco, lake, N.Y B6 108
Pisek, Czech., 19,500 .... D3 24
Pisek, Walsh, N. Dak., 176 ... A8 110
Pisgah, Jackson, Ala., 214 .... A4 78
Pisgah, Harrison, Iowa, 343 .... C2 92
Pisgah, Charles, Md., 500 ... C3 85
Pisgah, mtn., Vt F3 120
Pisgah, mtn., Wyo B8 125
Pisgah Forest, Transylvania, N.C., 700 .... D3 109
Pishin, Pak., 3,106 .... B1 40
Pishin Lora, riv., Pak C3 39
Pishukan, cape, Pak I11 41
Pisia, riv., Pol m12 26
Pisinimo, Pima, Ariz., 200 ... E3 80
Pismo Beach, San Luis Obispo, Calif., 1,762 .... E3 82
Pisogne, It., 6,848 .... D6 18
Pissis, mtn., Arg E2 55
Pistal River, Curry, Oreg., 50 .... E2 113
Pisticci, It., 13,300 .... D6 21
Pistoia, It., 60,500 (87,300▲) C3 21
Pistolet, bay, Newf., Can C4 75
Pisuerga, riv., Sp A3 20
Pisz, Pol., 1,028 .... B6 26
Pita, Guinea, 6,800 .... D2 45
Pitalito, Col., 3,616 .... C2 60
Pitangui, Braz., 7,421 .... E2 57
Pitcairn, Allegheny, Pa., 5,383 .... F2 114
Pitcairn, Br. dep., Oceania, 100 .... H14 7
Pitchfork, Park, Wyo A3 125
Piteå, Swe., 7,400 .... E9 25
Piteälven, riv., Swe E9 25
Piteşti, Rom., 45,600 .... C7 22
Pithiviers, Fr., 7,318 .... C5 14
Piti, Guam, 777 52
Pitkas Point, Alsk., 28 .... C7 79
Pitkin, Gunnison, Colo., 94 .. C4 83
Pitkin, Vernon, La., 400 .... D3 95
Pitkin, co., Colo., 2,381 .... B4 83
Pitlochry, Scot., 2,501 .... D5 13
Pitman, Gloucester, N.J., 8,644 .... D2 106
Pito, Pan F9 62
Pitreville, St. Landry, La., 30 .... D3 95
Pitrufquén, Chile, 5,193 .... B2 54
Pitsburg, Darke, Ohio, 394 ... C3 111
Pitt, Lake of the Woods, Minn., 25 .... B4 99
Pitt, co., N.C., 69,942 .... B6 109
Pitt, isl., B.C., Can C3 68
Pittman Center, Sevier, Tenn., 45 .... D10 117
Pitts, Wilcox, Ga., 388 .... E3 87
Pittsboro, Hendricks, Ind., 826 .... E5 91
Pittsboro, Calhoun, Miss., 205 .... B4 100
Pittsboro, Chatham, N.C., 1,215 .... B4 109
Pittsburg, Contra Costa, Calif., 19,062 .... B5 82
Pittsburg, Williamson, Ill., 485 .... F5 90
Pittsburg, Carroll, Ind., 250 .. C4 91
Pittsburg, Crawford, Kans., 18,678 .... E9 93
Pittsburg, Laurel, Ky., 810 ... C5 94
Pittsburg, Coos, N.H., 200 (639▲) A1 105
Pittsburg, Pittsburg, Okla., 195 .... C6 112
Pittsburg, Columbia, Oreg., 50 .... B3 113
Pittsburg, Camp, Tex., 3,769 .... C5 118
Pittsburg, co., Okla., 34,360 .... C6 112
Pittsburgh, Allegheny, Pa., 604,332 (*1,957,700) . B6, F1 114
Pittsburg Landing, Hardin, Tenn., 100 .... B3 117
Pittsfield, Pike, Ill., 4,089 ... D3 90
Pittsfield, Somerset, Maine, 3,232 .... D3 96
Pittsfield, Berkshire, Mass., 57,879 (*97,400) B1 97
Pittsfield, Washtenaw, Mich., 1,500 .... *F7 98
Pittsfield, Merrimack, N.H., 1,407 .... D4 105
Pittsfield, Warren, Pa., 500 . C3 114
Pittsfield, Rutland, Vt., 75 (254▲) D3 120
Pittsford, Hillsdale, Mich., 450 .... G6 98
Pittsford, Monroe, N.Y., 1,898 .... B3 108
Pittsford, Rutland, Vt., 671 (2,225▲) D2 120
Pittsford Mills, Rutland, Vt., 100 .... D2 120
Pittston, Luzerne, Pa., 12,407 .... B8, D10 114
Pittstown, Hunterdon, N.J., 150 .... B3 106
Pittsview, Russell, Ala., 300 . C4 78
Pittsville, Wicomico, Md., 488 .... D7 85
Pittsville, Johnson, Mo., 85 ... C4 101
Pittsville, Wood, Wis., 661 ... D3 124
Pittsylvania, co., Va., 58,296 .... E3 121
Pitzuwo, China E10 36
Piuka, Jap., 5,200 .... D11 37
Piura, Peru, 39,800 .... C1 58
Piura, dept., Peru, 431,487 ... C1 58
Piute, co., Utah, 1,436 .... E3 119
Piute, res., Utah E3 119
Piuthan, Nep., 1,350 .... C9 40
Piva, riv., Yugo D4 22
Pixley, Tulare, Calif., 1,327 .... E4 82
Piyang, China H5 36
Pizzo, It., 9,560 .... E6 21
Placentia, Orange, Calif., 5,861 .... *F3 82
Placentia, Newf., Can., 1,610 .... E5 75
Placentia, bay, Newf., Can E4 75
Placer, Josephine, Oreg., 125 .... E3 113
Placer, co., Calif., 56,998 .... C3 82
Placer, mtn., N. Mex k8 107
Placerville, El Dorado, Calif., 4,439 .... C3 82
Placerville, San Miguel, Colo., 50 .... C2 83
Placerville, Boise, Idaho, 12 .. F3 89
Placetas, Cuba, 31,000 .... D4 64
Placid, lake, N.Y f11 108
Placida, Charlotte, Fla., 150 . F4 86
Placita, Taos, N. Mex., 35 . *A4 107
Placitas, Dona Ana, N. Mex., 150 .... E2 107
Placitas, Sandoval, N. Mex., 80 .... B3, k8 107
Plaffeien, Switz., 1,352 .... C3 19
Plain, Sauk, Wis., 677 .... E3 124
Plain City, Union and Madison, Ohio, 2,146 .... B4 111
Plain City, Weber, Utah, 1,152 .... B3 119
Plain Dealing, Bossier, La., 1,357 .... B2 95
Plainfield, Windham, Conn., 2,100 (8,884▲) C9 84
Plainfield, Dodge, Ga., 84 .... D3 87
Plainfield, Will, Ill., 2,183 .... B5, F2 90
Plainfield, Hendricks, Ind., 5,460 .... E5 91
Plainfield, Bremer, Iowa, 445 .... B5 92
Plainfield, Hampshire, Mass., 100 (237▲) A2 97
Plainfield, Sullivan, N.H., 125 (1,071▲) C2 105
Plainfield, Union, N.J., 45,330 .... B4 106
Plainfield, Blount, Tenn., 2,127 .... *D10 117
Plainfield, Washington, Vt., 507 .... C4 120
Plainfield (Town of), Washington, Vt. (966▲) .. *C4 120
Plainfield, Waushara, Wis., 660 .... D4 124
Plainfield Heights, Kent, Mich., 1,000 .... *F5 98
Plains, Sumter, Ga., 572 .... D2 87
Plains (West Plains), Meade, Kans., 780 .... E3 93
Plains, Sanders, Mont., 769 .. C2 102
Plains, Luzerne, Pa., 8,500 .... B8 114
Plains, Yoakum, Tex., 1,195 .. C1 118
Plainsboro, Middlesex, N.J., 600 .... C3 106
Plainsville, Luzerne, Pa., 500 .... *B8 114
Plainview, Yell, Ark., 548 .... C2 81
Plainview, Wabasha, Minn., 1,833 .... F6 99
Plainview, Pierce, Nebr., 1,467 .... B8 103
Plainview, Nassau, N.Y., 30,500 .... *G2 84
Plainview, Hale, Tex., 18,735 .... B2 118
Plainville, Hartford, Conn., 13,149 .... C5 84
Plainville, Adams, Ill., 227 ... D2 90
Plainville, Daviess, Ind., 545 . G3 91
Plainville, Rooks, Kans., 3,104 .... C4 93
Plainville, Norfolk, Mass., 3,810 .... B5 97
Plainwell, Allegan, Mich., 3,125 .... F5 98
Plaisance, Que., Can., 451 ... D2 73
Plaisance, Hai, 2,800 .... F7 64
Plaisance-du-Gers, Fr., 1,490 .... F4 14
Plaisted, Aroostook, Maine, 200 .... A4 96
Plaistow, Rockingham, N.H., 1,500 (2,915▲) E4 105
Plamondon, Alta., Can., 133 . B4 69
Plana, Czech., 2,485 .... D7 17
Planada, Merced, Calif., 1,704 .... *D3 82
Planaltina, Braz., 1,385 .... E1 57
Plandome, Nassau, N.Y., 1,379 .... *F2 84
Plandome Heights, Nassau, N.Y., 1,025 .... *F2 84
Plankinton, Aurora, S. Dak., 644 .... D7 116
Plano (Doyle Colony), Tulare, Calif., 1,500 .... *D4 82
Plano, Kendall, Ill., 3,343 ... B5 90
Plano, Appanoose, Iowa, 87 . D4 92
Plano, Collin, Tex., 3,695 .... A6, C4 118
Plantagenet, Ont., Can., 854 .... B9 72
Plantation, Broward, Fla., 4,772 .... *F6 86
Plant City, Hillsborough, Fla., 15,711 .... D4 86
Plantersville, Dallas, Ala., 650 .... C3 78
Plantersville, Lee, Miss., 572 .... A5 100
Plantersville, Gerogetown, S.C., 150 .... D9 115
Plantsite, Greenlee, Ariz., 1,552 .... D6 80
Plantsville, Hartford, Conn., 2,500 .... C5 84
Plaquemine, Iberville, La., 7,689 .... B5, D4 95
Plaquemines, par., La., 22,545 .... E6 95
Plaquemine Southwest, Iberville, La., 1,272 .... *D4 95
Plasencia, Sp., 21,297 .... B2 20
Plast, Sov. Un., 28,100 .... E21 9
Plaster Rock, N.B., Can., 1,267 .... C2 74
Plastun, Sov. Un D8 37
Plasy, Czech., 1,472 .... D8 17
Plata, mtn., Switz D8 19
Plata, riv., Arg B5 55
Plata Central, P.R B2 65
Platea, Erie, Pa., 357 .... C1 114
Plateau, N.S., Can., 582 .... C8 74
Plateau City, Mesa, Colo., 60 .... B3 83
Plate Cove West, Newf., Can., 228 .... D5 75
Platina, Shasta, Calif., 40 ... B2 82
Platinum, Alsk., 43 .... D7 79
Platner, Washington, Colo., 40 .... A7 83
Plato, Sask., Can., 178 .... F1 70
Plato, Col., 8,039 .... B3 60
Plato, Texas, Mo., 140 .... D5 101
Platt, nat. park, Okla C5 112
Platte, Charles Mix, S. Dak., 1,167 .... D7 116
Platte, co., Mo., 23,350 .... B3 101
Platte, co., Nebr., 23,992 .... C8 103
Platte, co., Wyo., 7,195 .... C7 125
Platte, riv., Iowa, Mo .D3 92, B3 101
Platte, riv., Minn E4 99
Platte, riv., Nebr D6 103
Platte Arkansas, divide, Colo B7 83
Platte Center, Platte, Nebr., 402 .... C8 103
Platte City, Platte, Mo., 1,188 .... B3, D1 101
Plattenville, Assumption, La., 300 .... B5 95
Platter, Bryan, Okla., 200 ... D5 112
Platteville, Weld, Colo., 582 .. A6 83
Platteville, Grant, Wis., 6,957 .... F3 124
Plattling, Ger., 8,400 .... E7 17
Plattsburg, Clinton, Mo., 1,663 .... B3 101
Plattsburgh, Clinton, N.Y., 21,090 .... f11 108
Plattsmouth, Cass, Nebr., 6,244 .... C10, E3 103
Plattsville, Ont., Can., 456 .. D4 72
Plattville, Kendall, Ill., 125 ... B5 90
Plaucheville, Avoyelles, La., 288 .... D3 95
Plauen, Ger., 79,000 .... C7 17
Plauer, lake, Ger E6 24
Plave, riv., Ger A7 65
Playa de Fajardo (Puerto Real), P.R., (part of Fajardo), 2,143 .... B8, f12 17
Playa de Guayanés, P.R C7 65
Playa de Guayanilla, P.R., 1,635 .... C3 65
Playa de Humacao (Punta Santiago), P.R C8, g12 65
Playa de Marianao, Cuba ... h11 64
Playa de Naguabo, P.R C8, g12 65
Playa de Ponce, P.R., (part of Ponce), 15,040 .... D4 65
Playa Grande, P.R B2 65
Playa Salinas, P.R D5 65
Playa Sardinera, P.R ... B8, f12 65
Playgreen, lake, Man., Can B2 71
Plaza, Mountrail, N. Dak., 385 .... A4 110
Plazuela Central, P.R B4 65
Pleasant, bay, Que., Can B8 74
Pleasant, bay, Maine D5 96
Pleasant, lake, Ariz D3 80
Pleasant, lake, Maine C5 96
Pleasant, mtn., Maine D4 96
Pleasant, pond, Maine B4 96
Pleasant, pond, Maine C3 96
Pleasant, pond, N.H D4 105
Pleasant, riv., Maine C3 96
Pleasant Bay, N.S., Can., 109 .... C9 74
Pleasant Beach, Kitsap, Wash. (part of Port Blakely) D1 122
Pleasant City, Guernsey, Ohio, 491 .... C6 111
Pleasantdale, Sask., Can., 151 .... E3 70
Pleasant Dale, Seward, Nebr., 190 .... D8 103
Pleasant Gap, Centre, Pa., 1,389 .... E6 114
Pleasant Garden, Guilford, N.C., 1,000 .... B4 108
Pleasant Grove, Jefferson, Ala., 3,097 .... E4 78
Pleasant Grove, Panola, Miss., 60 .... A3 100
Pleasant Grove, Utah, Utah, 4,772 .... C4 119
Pleasant Hill, Dallas, Ala., 150 .... C3 78
Pleasant Hill, Contra Costa, Calif., 23,844 .... *B5 82
Pleasant Hill, Pike, Ill., 950 .... D3 90
Pleasant Hill, Sabine, La., 907 .... C2 95
Pleasant Hill, De Soto, Miss., 150 .... A4 100
Pleasant Hill, Cass, Mo., 2,689 .... C3 101
Pleasant Hill, Curry, N. Mex., 25 .... C6 107
Pleasant Hill, Miami, Ohio, 1,060 .... B3 111
Pleasant Hill, Lebanon, Pa., 1,200 .... *F9 114
Pleasant Hill, Lancaster, S.C., 150 .... B6 115
Pleasant Hill, Nansemond, Va., 2,636 .... *E6 121
Pleasant Hills, Allegheny, Pa., 8,573 .... *B5, F1 114
Pleasant Hope, Polk, Mo., 216 .... D4 101
Pleasant Lake, Steuben, Ind., 600 .... A7 91
Pleasant Lake, Barnstable, Mass., 125 .... C7 97
Pleasant Lake, Benson, N. Dak., 15 .... A6 110
Pleasant Mills, Adams, Ind., 160 .... C8 91
Pleasant Mount, Wayne, Pa., 160 .... C11 114
Pleasanton, Alameda, Calif., 4,203 .... B6 82
Pleasanton, Decatur, Iowa, 103 .... D4 92
Pleasanton, Linn, Kans., 1,098 .... D9 93
Pleasanton, Buffalo, Nebr., 199 .... D6 103
Pleasanton, Catron, N. Mex., 50 .... D1 107
Pleasanton, Atascosa, Tex., 3,467 .... E3 118
Pleasant Plain, Jefferson, Iowa, 147 .... C6 92
Pleasant Plains, Independence, Ark., 112 .... B4 81
Pleasant Plains, Sangamon, Ill., 518 .... D4 90

Port-au-Port, Newf., Can., 482 ... D2 75
Port au Port, bay, Newf., Can. .. D2 75
Port au Port, pen., Newf., Can. .. D2 75
Port-au-Prince, Haiti, 240,000 ... F7 64
Port Austin, Huron, Mich., 706 ... D8 98
Port Barre, St. Landry, La., 1,876 ... D4 95
Port Bergé, Malag., 1,538 ... g9 49
Port Blair, Andaman Is., 14,075 ... F9 39
Port Blakely, Kitsap, Wash., 500 ... D1 122
Port Blandford, Newf., Can., 716 ... D4 75
Port Bolivar, Galveston, Tex., 600 ... E5, G5 118
Port Borden, P.E.I., Can., 696 ... C6 74
Port Burwell, N.W. Ter., Can ... D20 67
Port Burwell, Ont., Can., 777 ... E4 72
Port Byron, Rock Island, Ill., 1,153 ... B3 90
Port Byron, Cayuga, N.Y., 1,201 ... B4 108
Port Carbon, Schuylkill, Pa., 2,775 ... *E9 114
Port Carling, Ont., Can., 529 ... B5 72
Port-Cartier, Que., Can., 3,458 ... k13 73
Port Chalmers, N.Z., 3,120 ... P13 51
Port Charlotte, Charlotte, Fla., 3,197 ... *F4 86
Port Chester, Westchester, N.Y., 24,960 ... E7, n15 108
Port Chicago, Contra Costa, Calif., 1,746 ... B5 82
Port Clements, B.C., Can., 40 ... C1 68
Port Clinton, Ottawa, Ohio, 6,870 ... A5 111
Port Clyde, N.S., Can., 102 .. F4 74
Port Clyde, Knox, Maine, 350 ... E3 96
Port Colborne, Ont., Can., 14,886 ... E5 72
Port Colden, Warren, N.J., 300 ... B3 106
Port Coquitlam, B.C., Can., 8,111 ... E6, f13 68
Port Crane, Broome, N.Y., 1,200 ... C5 108
Port Credit, Ont., Can., 7,203 ... D5, m14 72
Port-Daniel-Station, Que., Can., 276 ... A5 74
Port-de-Bouc, Fr., 12,510 ... F6 14
Port-de-Paix, Hai., 6,309 ... F7 64
Port Deposit, Cecil, Md., 953 ... A5 85
Port Dickinson, Broome, N.Y., 2,295 ... C5 108
Port Dickson, Mala., 4,415 .. K4 38
Port Discovery, Jefferson, Wash ... A3 122
Port Douglas, Austl., 122 ... C8 50
Port Dover, Ont., Can., 3,064 ... E4 72
Port Eads, Plaquemines, La., 12 ... E6 95
Port Edward, B.C., Can., 887 ... B2 68
Port Edwards, Wood, Wis., 1,849 ... D4 124
Portel, Braz., 1,821 ... C4 59
Port Elgin, N.B., Can., 661 .. C5 74
Port Elgin, Ont., Can., 1,632 ... C3 72
Port Elizabeth, Cumberland, N.J., 500 ... E3 106
Port Elizabeth, S. Afr., 249,211 (*274,180) ... D4 49
Port Ellne, Scot ... E2 13
Porteña, Arg ... A4 54
Porter, Jefferson, Ala., 130 ... B3, E4 78
Porter, Porter, Ind., 2,189 ... A3 91
Porter, Yellow Medicine, Minn., 261 ... F2 98
Porter, Wagoner, Okla., 492 .. B6 112
Porter, Montgomery, Tex., 900 ... D5 118
Porter, Grays Harbor, Wash., 200 ... C2 122
Porter, co., Ind., 60,279 ... B3 91
Porter, lake, Sask., Can ... A2 70
Porter Corners, Saratoga, N.Y., 250 ... B7 108
Porterdale, Newton, Ga., 2,365 ... C3 87
Port Erin, I. of Man, 1,265 .. F4 13
Portersville, Butler, Pa., 344 . E1 114
Portersville, Morgan, Utah, 100 ... *C4 119
Porterville, Tulare, Calif., 7,991 ... D4 82
Porterville, Kemper, Miss., 120 ... C5 100
Porterville West (Burton), Tulare, Calif., 4,635 ... *D4 82
Port Essington, B.C., Can., 40 ... B3 68
Port Étienne, Maur., 1,200 ... B1 45
Port Ewen, Ulster, N.Y., 2,300 ... D7 108
Port Fairy, Austl., 2,434 ... I4 51
Port Fouad (Port Fuad) (Būr Fu'ād), Eg., U.A.R., 1,000 ... C4 32
Port-Francqui, Con. L., 3,553 ... B3 48
Port Fuad (Port Fouad) (Būr Fu'ād), Eg., U.A.R., 1,000 ... C4 32
Port Gamble, Kitsap, Wash., 400 ... B3 122
Port Gamble, Indian res., Wash . B3 122
Port-Gentil, Gabon, 16,600 .. F1 46
Port George, N.S., Can., 74 ... D4 74
Port Gibson, Claiborne, Miss., 2,861 ... D3 100
Port Glasgow, Scot., 22,551 .. E9 13
Portglenone, N. Ire., 609 ... C5 11
Port Graham, Alsk., 139 . D9, h16 79
Port Greville, N.S., Can., 128 ... D5 74
Port Hammond, B.C., Can., 1,267 ... f13 68
Port Harcourt, Nig., 71,634 ... F6 45
Port Hardy, B.C., Can., 606 .. D4 68
Port Harrison, Que., Can., 115 ... g11 73
Port Hastings, N.S., Can., 326 ... D8 74
Port Hawkesbury, N.S., Can., 1,346 ... D8 74
Porthcawl, Wales, 11,082 ... C4 12
Port Hedland, Austl., 328 ... D2 50
Port Heiden, Alsk., 74 ... D8 79
Port Henry, Essex, N.Y., 1,767 ... A7 108
Port Herald, Malawi ... E6 48
Port Hill, P.E.I., Can., 150 ... C6 74
Port Homer, Jefferson, Ohio, 80 ... A2 123
Port Hood, N.S., Can., 511 .. C8 74
Port Hope, Ont., Can., 8,091 ... D6 72
Port Hope, Huron, Mich., 349 ... E8 98
Port Hope Simpson, Newf., Can., 402 ... B3 75
Port Hueneme, Ventura, Calif., 11,067 ... E4 82
Port Huron, St. Clair, Mich., 36,084 (*62,700) ... F8 98
Portia, Lawrence, Ark., 333 . A4 81
Portici, It., 55,900 ... *D5 21
Portillo, Cuba ... F5 64
Portimão, Port., 12,066 ... D1 20
Portis, Osborne, Kans., 232 . C5 93
Port Isabel, Cameron, Tex., 3,575 ... F4 118
Port Jackson, bay, Austl ... F8 51
Port Jefferson, Suffolk, N.Y., 4,000 ... n15 108
Port Jefferson, Shelby, Ohio, 438 ... B3 111
Port Jefferson Station, Suffolk, N.Y., 1,370 ... *n15 108
Port Jervis, Orange, N.Y., 9,268 ... D6 108
Port Kent, Essex, N.Y., 200 ... f11 108
Portland, Ashley, Ark., 566 . D4 81
Portland, Austl., 6,014 ... I3 51
Portland, Ont., Can., 254 ... C8 72
Portland, Fremont, Colo., 73 ... C5 83
Portland, Middlesex, Conn., 7,496 ... C6 84
Portland, Eng., 11,542 ... D5 12
Portland, Walton, Fla., 200 . G3 86
Portland, Jay, Ind., 6,999 ... D8 91
Portland, Cumberland, Maine, 72,566 (*156,000) ... E2, E5 96
Portland, Ionia, Mich., 3,330 ... F6 98
Portland, Callaway, Mo., 125 ... C6 101
Portland, Chautauqua, N.Y., 500 ... C1 108
Portland, Traill, N. Dak., 606 ... B8 110
Portland, Meigs, Ohio, 200 . C6 111
Portland, Multnomah, Oreg., 372,676 (*731,200) ... B2, B4 113
Portland, Northampton, Pa., 589 ... E11 114
Portland, Sumner, Tenn., 2,424 ... A5 117
Portland, San Patricio, Tex., 2,538 ... F4 118
Portland, canal, Alsk ... n24 79
Portland, canal, B.C., Can ... B2 68
Portland, inlet, B.C., Can ... B2 68
Portland, promontory, Que., Can ... g11 73
Portland Bill, pt., Eng ... D5 12
Portland Creek, pond, Newf., Can ... C3 75
Portland Mills, Elk, Pa., 135 ... D4 114
Portlandville, Otsego, N.Y., 128 ... C6 108
Portlaoighise, Ire., 3,133 ... D4 11
Port Lavaca, Calhoun, Tex., 8,864 ... E4 118
Portlaw, Ire., 1,113 ... E4 11
Port Leyden, Lewis, N.Y., 898 ... B5 108
Port Lincoln, Austl., 7,508 .. F6 50
Port Loko, S.L. ... E2 45
Port Loring, Ont., Can., 261 . B4 72
Port-Louis, Fr., 4,140 ... D2 14
Port Louis, Mauritius, 89,096 (*115,000) ... H24 3
Port Ludlow, Jefferson, Wash., 300 ... B3 122
Port McNicoll, Ont., Can., 1,053 ... C5 72
Port Macquarie, Austl., 5,951 ... E9 51
Portmadoc, Wales, 3,419 ... B3 12
Portmagee, Ire., 137 ... F1 11
Portmahomack, Scot ... C5 13
Port Mahon, Kent, Del., 20 . B7 85
Port Maitland, N.S., Can., 469 ... F3 74
Port Maitland, Ont., Can., 103 ... E5 72
Port Maria, Jam., 3,997 ... F5 64
Port Matilda, Centre, Pa., 697 ... E5 114
Port Mayaca, Martin, Fla., 75 ... F6 86
Port Medway, N.S., Can., 310 ... E5 74
Port Mellon, B.C., Can., 284 ... E6 68
Port-Menier, Que., Can., 475 ... k8 75
Port Moller, Alsk., 10 ... D7 79
Port Monmouth, Monmouth, N.J., 5,500 ... C4 106
Port Moody, B.C., Can., 4,789 ... E6, f13 68
Port Moresby, Pap., 29,000 . k12 50
Port-Morien, N.S., Can., 517 ... C10 74
Port Morris, Morris, N.J., 500 ... B3 106
Port-Mouton, N.S., Can., 262 ... F5 74
Port Murray, Warren, N.J., 350 ... B3 106
Port Musgrave, bay, Austl ... B7 50
Portnahaven, Scot ... E2 13
Port Neches, Jefferson, Tex., 8,696 ... E6 118
Port Nelson, Man., Can .. A5, f9 71
Portneuf, Que., Can., 1,380 .. C6 73
Portneuf, co., Que., Can., 50,711 ... C5 73
Portneuf-sur-Mer, Que., Can . A8 73
Port Nolloth, S. Afr., 2,592 ... C2 49
Portnoo, Ire., 173 ... C3 11
Port Norris, Cumberland, N.J., 1,800 ... E2 106
Porto (Oporto), Port., 303,424 (*750,000) ... B1 20
Pôrto Alegre, Braz., 617,629 (*850,000) ... E2 56
Porto Alexandre, Ang., 2,874 ... E1 48
Pôrto Amboim, Ang., 1,537 ... D1 48
Pôrto Amélia, Moz., 10,000 . D7 48
Portobelo, Pan., 591 ... F8, h11 62
Pôrto Calvo, Braz., 3,876 ... C3, k6 57
Port O'Connor, Calhoun, Tex., 500 ... E4 118
Pôrto de Mós, Port., 4,402 .. C1 20
Port de Moz, Braz., 879 ... C4 59
Pôrto Esperanca, Braz., 486 ... B1 56
Pôrto Feliz, Braz. 11,786 ... C3, m8 56
Portoferraio, It., 6,000 ... C3 21
Portofino, It., 1,011 ... B2 21
Port of Ness, Scot ... B2 13
Port-of-Spain, Trin., 93,954 (*170,000) ... A5 60
Porto Garibaldi, It ... E8 18
Portogruaro, It., 7,100 ... B4 21
Pôrto Guaíra, Braz ... C2 56
Portola, Plumas, Calif., 1,874 ... C3 82
Portomaggiore, It., 4,300 ... B3 21
Pôrto Mendes, Braz ... C2 56
Pôrto Murtinho, Braz., 4,476 ... D4 55
Pôrto Nacional, Braz., 4,926 . D1 57
Porto-Novo, Dah., 65,000 ... E5 45
Port Orange, Volusia, Fla., 1,801 ... C6 86
Port Orchard, Kitsap, Wash., 2,778 ... B3, D1 122
Port Orford, Curry, Oreg., 1,171 ... E2 113
Porto Santo, isl., Port. (Madeira Is.) ... C1 44
Portoscuso, It., 2,262 ... E2 21
Pôrto Seguro, Braz., 2,697 .. E3 57
Porto Torres, It., 9,166 ... D2 21
Pôrto União, Braz., 9,954 .. D2 56
Porto-Vecchio, Fr., 2,711 ... D2 21
Pôrto Velho, Braz., 19,387 .. D2 59
Portoviejo, Ec., 18,082 ... B1 58
Portpatrick, Scot., 1,063 ... F3 13
Port Penn, New Castle, Del., 271 ... A6 85
Port Perry, Ont., Can., 2,262 ... C6 72
Port Phillip, bay, Austl ... G7 50
Port Pirie, Austl., 14,003 ... F1 51
Port Radium, N.W., Ter., Can ... C9 66
Port Reading, Middlesex, N.J., 4,000 ... k8 106
Portree, Scot., 1,767 ... C2 13
Portreeve, Sask., Can., 103 .. G1 70
Port Renfrew, B.C., Can., 279 ... E5 68
Port Republic, Atlantic, N.J., 561 ... D4 106
Port Republic, Rockingham, Va., 500 ... C4 121
Port Rexton, Newf., Can., 438 ... D5 75
Port Richey, Pasco, Fla., 1,931 ... D4 86
Port Rowan, Ont., Can., 787 ... E4 72
Port Royal, Henry, Ky., 90 .. B4 94
Port Royal, Juniata, Pa., 805 ... E7 114
Port Royal, Beaufort, S.C., 686 ... G6 115
Port Royal, Montgomery, Tenn., 30 ... A4 117
Port Royal, Caroline, Va., 128 ... C5 121
Port Royal, bay, Bermuda ... E13 77
Port Royal, isl., S.C. ... G6 115
Port Royal, sound, S.C. ... G7 115
Portrush, N. Ire., 4,263 ... B5 12
Port Said (Būr Sa'īd), Eg., U.A.R., 245,318 . C9 31, C4 32, C6 43
Port St. Joe, Gulf, Fla., 4,217 ... C1, H3 86
Port St. Johns, S. Afr., 1,024 ... D4 49
Port-St. Louis [-du-Rhône], Fr., 4,262 ... F6 14
Portsalon, Ire ... B4 12
Port Sanilac, Sanilac, Mich., 361 ... E8 98
Port Saunders, Newf., Can., 504 ... C3, h10 75
Port Sewall, Martin, Fla., 200 ... E6 86
Port Shepstone, S. Afr., 4,238 ... D5 49
Port Simpson, B.C., Can ... B2 68
Portsmouth, Dominica, 1,725 ... o16 64
Portsmouth, Eng., 224,900 (*445,000) ... D6 12
Portsmouth, Shelby, Iowa, 232 ... C2 92
Portsmouth, Rockingham, N.H., 26,900 ... D5 105
Portsmouth, Scioto, Ohio, 33,637 ... D5 111
Portsmouth, Newport, R.I., 3,000 (8,251*) ... C12 84
Portsmouth, (Independent City), Va., 80,039 ... B6, E6 121
Portsoy, Scot., 1,690 ... C6 13
Port Stanley, Ont., Can., 1,460 ... E3 72
Port Stanley (Stanley), Falk. Is., 1,074 ... I5 53
Port Stephens, bay, Austl ... F9 52
Port Sudan, Sud., 56,000 ... B4 47
Port Sulphur, Plaquemines, La., 2,868 ... E6 95
Port-sur-Saône, Fr., 1,725 ... B2 18
Port Sydney, Ont., Can., 192 ... B2 72
Port Talbot, Wales, 51,500 (*125,000) ... C4 12
Port Tampa, Hillsborough, Fla., 1,764 ... E2, E4 86
Port Tobacco, Charles, Md., 75 ... C3 85
Port Townsend, Jefferson, Wash., 5,074 ... A3 122
Portugal, country, Eur., 9,140,000 ... H7 8, C1 20
Portugal Cove, Newf., Can., 1,141 ... *E5 75
Portugal Cove South, Newf., Can., 304 ... E5 75
Portugalete, Sp., 22,584 ... A4 20
Portugalia, Ang ... C3 48
Portuguesa, riv., Ven ... B4 60
Portuguesa, state, Ven., 203,707 ... B4 60
Portuguese Guinea, dep., Afr., 525,000 ... E4 42, D1 45
Portuguese India, see Goa, Damão and Diu, ter., India
Portuguese Timor, dep., Asia, 548,000 ... G7 35
Portumna, Ire., 836 ... D3 11
Port Union, Newf., Can., 645 ... D5 75
Port Union, Butler, Ohio, 75 ... C2 111
Port-Vendres, Fr., 4,504 ... F5 14
Portville, Cattaraugus, N.Y., 1,336 ... C2 108
Port Vincent, Livingston, La., 340 ... B6, D5 95
Port Vue, Allegheny, Pa., 6,635 ... *F2 114
Port Wakefield, Austl., 429 .. G2 52
Port Washington, Nassau, N.Y., 15,800 ... h13 108
Port Washington, Tuscarawas, Ohio, 526 ... B6 111
Port Washington, Ozaukee, Wis., 5,984 ... E6 124
Port Wentworth, Chatham, Ga., 3,705 ... D5 87
Port William, Clinton, Ohio, 360 ... C4 111
Port William, Scot ... F4 13
Port Wing, Bayfield, Wis., 250 ... B2 124
Porum, Muskogee, Okla., 573 ... B6 112
Porvenir, Chile ... h11 54
Porvenir, Presidio, Tex ... F2 118
Porz, Ger., 58,600 ... C2 17
Posadas, Arg., 37,588 ... E4 55
Posadas, Sp., 8,999 ... D3 20
Poschiavo, Switz., 3,743 ... D9 19
Posen, Cook., Ill., 4,517 ... F3 90
Posen, Presque Isle, Mich., 341 ... C7 98
Posen, see Poznan, Pol.
Posey, co., Ind., 19,214 ... H2 91
Poseyville, Posey, Ind., 997 . H2 91
Poshan, China, 250,000 (806,000*) ... F8 36
Poshekhonye-Volodarsk, Sov. Un ... B12 27
Poso, Indon., 2,875 ... F6 35
Poso, lake, Indon ... F6 35
Posse, Braz., 1,953 ... D1 57
Pössneck, Ger., 19,600 ... C6 17
Post, Crook, Oreg., 5 ... C6 113
Post, Garza, Tex., 4,663 ... C2 118
Postell, Cherokee, N.C ... D2 109
Post Falls, Kootenai, Idaho, 1,983 ... B2 89
Postmasburg, S. Afr., 4,701 ... C3 49
Post Mills, Orange, Vt., 200 ... D4 120
Postojna, Yugo., 4,848 ... C2 22
Postville, Allamakee, Iowa, 1,554 ... A6 92
Poston, Florence, S.C., 250 .. D9 115
Potaro Landing, Br. Gu., 353 ... A3 60
Potato Creek, Washabaugh, S. Dak., 40 ... D4 116
Potchefstroom, S. Afr., 41,927 ... C4 49
Poteau, LeFlore, Okla., 4,428 ... B7 112
Poteau, mtn., Ark., Okla ... C1 81
Poteau, riv., Okla ... B7 112
Poteet, Atascosa, Tex., 2,811 ... E3 118
Potenza, It., 30,800 (45,500*) ... D5 21
Potenza, riv., It ... C4 21
Potgietersrus, S. Afr., 11,438 ... B4 49
Poth, Wilson, Tex., 1,119 ... E3 118
Potholes, res., Wash ... B6 122
Poti, Sov. Un., 42,068 ... G17 9
Poti, riv., Braz ... C2 57
Potiskum, Nig., 14,692 ... D7 45
Potlatch, Latah, Idaho, 880 ... C2 89
Poto, Peru, 247 ... D4 58
Potocho, China ... A11 40
Potomac, Vermilion, Ill., 661 ... C6 90
Potomac, Montgomery, Md., 150 ... B3 85
Potomac, Missoula, Mont., 30 ... D3 102
Potomac, riv., Md., Va., W. Va ... C12 77, A1, D4 85
Potomac Park, Allegany, Md., 1,016 ... *D2 85
Potosí, Bol., 54,000 ... C2 55
Potosi, Washington, Mo., 2,805 ... D7 101
Potosi, Grant, Wis., 589 ... F3 124
Potosí, dept., Bol., 534,399 .. C2 55
Pototan, Phil., 4,812 ... *C6 35
Potrerillos, Chile ... E2 55
Potrerillos, Hond., 831 ... C4 62
Potro, mtn., Arg ... E2 55
Potsdam, Ger., 115,300 ... A8 17
Potsdam, St. Lawrence, N.Y., 7,765 ... f10 108
Potsdam, Miami, Ohio, 282 . C3 111
Pottawatomie, co., Kans., 11,957 ... C7 93
Pottawatomie, co., Okla., 41,486 ... B5 112
Pottawatomie, creek, Kans ... D8 93
Pottawatomie Indian res., Kans . C8 93
Pottawattamie, co., Iowa, 83,102 ... C2 92
Pottawattamie Park, La Porte, Ind., 292 ... *A4 91
Potter, Polk, Ark., 120 ... C1 81
Potter, Atchison, Kans., 109 ... A8, C8 93
Potter, Cheyenne, Nebr., 554 ... C2 103
Potter, Calumet, Wis., 225 .. B6 124
Potter, co., Pa., 16,483 ... C6 114
Potter, co., S. Dak., 4,926 ... B6 116
Potter, co., Tex., 115,580 ... B2 118
Potter Hill, Washington, R.I., 285 ... D9 84
Potter Place, Merrimack, N.H., 50 ... D3 105
Pottersdale, Clearfield, Pa., 50 ... D5 114
Potters Mills, Centre, Pa., 130 ... E6 114
Pottersville, Howell, Mo., 45 ... E5 101
Pottersville, Hunterdon and Somerset, N.J., 300 ... B3 106
Pottersville, Warren, N.Y., 500 ... B7 108
Potter Valley, Mendocino, Calif., 220 ... C2 82
Potterville, Taylor, Ga., 400 .. D2 87
Potterville, Eaton, Mich., 1,028 ... *F6 98
Potterville, Bradford, Pa., 65 ... C9 114
Potts, creek, Va., W. Va ... D2 121
Potts, mtn., Va ... D2 121
Potts Camp, Marshall, Miss., 429 ... A4 100
Pottstown, Montgomery, Pa., 26,144 ... F10 114
Pottsville, Pope, Ark., 250 .. B2 81
Pottsville, Schuylkill, Pa., 21,659 ... E9 114
Potwin, Butler, Kans., 635 ... B6, E7 93
Pouce Coupe, B.C., Can., 669 ... B7 68
Pouch Cove, Newf., Can., 1,324 ... E5 75
Poughkeepsie, Sharp, Ark., 250 ... A4 81
Poughkeepsie, Dutchess, N.Y., 38,330 (*112,400) ... D7 108
Poulan, Worth, Ga., 736 ... E3 87
Poulo Condore, is., Viet ... H7 38
Poulsbo, Kitsap, Wash., 1,505 ... B3 122
Poultney, Rutland, Vt., 1,810 (3,009*) ... D2 120
Poultney, riv., Vt ... D2 120
Pound, Wise, Va., 1,135 ... B2 121
Pound, Marinette, Wis., 273 .. C5 124
Pound, gap, Va ... A2 121
Pouso Alegre, Braz., 18,852 ... C3, m9 56
Pouxeux, Fr., 1,783 ... A2 18
Povenets, Sov. Un., 5,000 ... F16 25
Poverty, bay, N.Z. ... M17 51
Póvoa de Varzim, Port., 16,913 ... B1 20
Povorino, Sov. Un., 24,000 .. C2 29
Povorotnyy, cape, Sov. Un ... E6 37
Povungnituk, Que., Can., 434 ... g11 73
Powassan, Ont., Can., 1,064 ... A5 72
Poway, San Diego, Calif., 1,921 ... F5 82
Powder, riv., Mont., Wyo ... D11 102
Powder, riv., Oreg ... C9 113
Powderhorn, Gunnison, Colo., 5 ... C3 83
Powder River, Natrona, Wyo., 50 ... B6 125
Powder River, co., Mont., 2,485 ... E11 102
Powder River, pass, Wyo ... A5 125
Powder Springs, Cobb, Ga., 746 ... A4 87
Powder Springs, Grainger, Tenn., 200 ... C10 117
Powderville, Powder River, Mont., 5 ... E11 102
Powe, Stoddard, Mo., 72 ... E7 101
Powell, McDonald, Mo., 100 ... E3 101
Powell, Delaware, Ohio, 390 ... B4 111
Powell, Bradford, Pa., 250 ... C8 114
Powell, Knox, Tenn., 500 ... E11 117
Powell, Navarro, Tex., 250 ... C4 118
Powell, Park, Wyo., 4,740 ... A4 125
Powell, co., Ky., 6,674 ... C6 94
Powell, co., Mont., 7,002 .. D4 102
Powell, lake, Utah ... F5 119
Powell, mtn., Colo ... B4 83
Powell, mtn., N. Mex ... B1 107
Powell, mtn., Tenn ... C10 117
Powell, peak, Ariz ... C1 80
Powell, riv., Tenn., Va ... C10 117
Powell Butte, Crook, Oreg., 40 ... C5 113
Powell Creek, Austl ... C5 50
Powell Park, basin, Colo ... A2 83
Powell River, B.C., Can., 10,748 ... E5 68
Powellsville, Bertie, N.C., 259 ... A7 109
Powellton, Fayette, W. Va., 1,256 ... C3, D6 123
Powellville, Wicomico, Md., 500 ... D7 85
Powelton, Hancock, Ga., 25 .. C4 87
Powelton, Centre, Pa. (part of Sandy Ridge) ... E5 114
Power, Teton, Mont., 175 ... C5 102
Power, Brooke, W. Va., 175 ... A4, B2 123
Power, co., Idaho, 4,111 ... G6 89
Power, head, Ire ... F3 11
Powers, Jay, Ind., 40 ... D7 91
Powers, Menominee, Mich., 324 ... C3 98
Powers, Coos, Oreg., 1,366 ... E2 113
Powers Lake, Burke, N. Dak., 633 ... A3 110
Powersville, Putnam, Mo., 189 ... A4 101
Powerview, Man., Can., 902 ... *D3 71
Poweshiek, co., Iowa, 19,300 ... C5 92
Powhatan, Jefferson, Ala., 350 ... B2, E4 78
Powhatan, Lawrence, Ark., 136 ... A4 81
Powhatan, Natchitoches, La., 300 ... C2 95
Powhatan, Powhatan, Va., 300 ... D5 121
Powhatan, co., Va., 6,747 ... D5 121
Powhatan Point, Belmont, Ohio, 2,147 ... C7 111
Powhattan, Brown, Kans., 128 ... C8 93
Pownal, Cumberland, Maine, 50 (778*) ... E5 96
Pownal, Bennington, Vt., 325 (1,509*) ... F2 120
Pownal Center, Bennington, Vt., 75 ... F2 120
Poyang, China, 42,000 ... J7 36
Poyang, lake, China ... J7 36
Poyarkovo, Sov. Un ... B4 37
Poyen, Grant, Ark., 312 ... C3 81
Poygan, lake, Wis ... D5 124
Poynette, Columbia, Wis., 1,090 ... E8 124
Poyntzpass, N. Ire., 282 ... C5 11
Poy Sippi, Waushara, Wis., 450 ... D4 124
Požarevac, Yugo., 24,293 ... C5 22
Poznan, Pol., 422,700 ... B4 26
Poznan, prov., Pol., 1,994,000 ... A9 17
Pozo Almonte, Chile ... D2 55
Pozoblanco, Sp., 16,020 ... C3 20
Pozo Redondo, mts., Ariz ... E3 80
Pozuelo de Alarcón, Sp., 9,412 ... p17 20
Pozuzo, Peru, 132 ... D2 58
Pozzallo, It., 12,253 ... F5 21
Pozzuoli, It., 55,000 ... D5 21
Prachatice, Czech., 5,100 ... E9 17
Prachin Buri, Thai., 13,308 .. E4 38
Prachuap Khiri Khan, Thai., 6,799 ... G3 38
Praco, Jefferson, Ala., 900 .. E4 78
Practicos, pt., Cuba ... E5 64
Prada, Switz ... C8 19
Prade Ranch, Real, Tex., 15 ... E3 118
Prades, Fr., 5,676 ... F5 14
Prado, basin, Calif ... F3 82
Praestø, Den., 1,528 ... C6 24
Praestø, co., Den., 123,382 .. C6 24
Praga, Pol. (part of Warsaw) ... k14 26
Prague, Czech., 1,008,900 (*1,105,000) ... C3, n17 26
Prague, Saunders, Nebr., 372 ... C9 103
Prague, Lincoln, Okla., 1,545 ... B5 112
Praha, see Prague, Czech.
Prahran, Austl., 54,700 ... *H5 51
Praia, C.V. Is., 13,100 ... *E3 42
Prainha, Braz., 778 ... C4 59
Prairie, Wilcox, Ala., 50 ... C2 78
Prairie, Monroe, Miss., 112 .. B5 100
Prairie, co., Ark., 10,515 ... C4 81
Prairie, co., Mont., 2,318 ... D11 102
Prairie, bayou, Ark ... D6 81
Prairie, riv., Minn ... C5 99
Prairie, riv., Wis ... C4 124
Prairie City, McDonough, Ill., 613 ... C3 90
Prairie City, Jasper, Iowa, 943 ... C4 92
Prairie City, Grant, Oreg., 801 ... C8 113
Prairie City, Perkins, S. Dak., 50 ... B3 116
Prairie Creek, Vigo, Ind., 240 ... F2 91
Prairie Dog, creek, Kans., Nebr ... C3 93, D6 103
Prairie Dog Town, fork, Okla .. C2 112
Prairie du Chien, Crawford, Wis., 5,649 ... E2 124
Prairie du Rocher, Randolph, Ill., 679 ... E3 90
Prairie du Sac, Sauk, Wis., 1,676 ... E4 124
Prairie Farm, Barron, Wis., 350 ... C2 124
Prairie Grove, Washington, Ark., 1,056 ... B1 81
Prairie Hill, Chariton, Mo., 84 ... B5 101
Prairie Home, Cooper, Mo., 213 ... C5 101
Prairie Home, Lancaster, Nebr., 29 ... E2 103
Prairie Point, Noxubee, Miss., 75 ... B5 100
Prairie River, Sask., Can., 84 ... E4 70
Prairieton, Vigo, Ind., 250 ... F3 91
Prairie View, Logan, Ark., 165 ... B2 81
Prairie View, Phillips, Kans., 188 ... C4 93
Prairie View, Waller, Tex., 2,326 ... *D5 118
Prairie Village, Johnson, Kans., 25,356 ... *B9 93
Prairieville, Ascension, La., 150 ... B5 95
Pralognan-la-Vanoise, Fr., 249 ... D2 18
Pran Buri, Thai ... F3 38
Praszka, Pol., 3,013 ... C5 26
Prata, Braz., 4,725 ... E1 57
Prather, Clark, Ind ... A4 94
Prato, It., 120,400 (*155,000) ... C3 21
Prats-de-Mollo, Fr., 682 ... F5 14
Pratt, Pratt, Kans., 8,156 ... E5 93
Pratt, Kanawha, W. Va., 602 ... *C6 123
Pratt, co., Kans., 12,122 ... E5 93
Pratteln, Switz., 9,492 ... A4 19
Prattsburg, Steuben, N.Y., 690 ... C3 108
Prattsville, Grant, Ark., 150 . C3 81
Prattsville, Greene, N.Y., 500 ... C6 108
Prattville, Autauga, Ala., 6,616 ... C3 78
Prattville, Hillsdale, Mich., 175 ... G6 98
Prattville, Tulsa, Okla., 2,530 ... *A5 112
Pratum, Marion, Oreg., 100 ... C2 113
Pravdinsk (Friedland), Sov. Un., 10,000 ... A6 26
Pravia, Sp., 1,804 ... A2 20
Prawle, pt., Eng ... D4 12
Pray, Park, Mont., 5 ... E6 102
Preble, Adams, Ind., 170 ... C7 91
Preble, Brown, Wis., 12,245 ... A6 124
Preble, co., Ohio, 32,498 ... C3 111
Predazzo, It., 3,783 ... C7 18
Predivinsk, Sov. Un ... D27 9
Preeceville, Sask., Can., 924 . F4 70
Preetz, Ger., 12,800 ... D4 24
Pregel, riv., Sov. Un ... A6 26
Pregnall, Dorchester, S.C., 100 ... E7 115
Prelate, Sask., Can., 618 ... G1 70
Premont, Jim Wells, Tex., 3,049 ... F3 118
Prémontré, Fr., 1,872 ... E3 15
Prenter, Boone, W. Va., 350 ... C3, D6 123
Prentice, Price, Wis., 427 ... C3 124
Prentiss, Penobscot, Maine, 200 (227*) ... C4 96
Prentiss, Jefferson Davis, Miss., 1,321 ... D4 100
Prentiss, Macon, N.C. ... D3 109
Prentiss, co., Miss., 17,949 .. A5 100

Prenzlau, Ger., 19,700 ... B6 16
Prerov, Czech., 30,500 ... D4 26
Prescott, Yavapai, Ariz., 12,861 ... C3 80
Prescott, Nevada, Ark., 3,533 ... D2 81
Prescott, Ont., Can., 5,366 ... C9 72
Prescott, Adams, Iowa, 331 ... C3 92
Prescott, Linn, Kans., 278 ... D9 93
Prescott, Ogemaw, Mich., 308 ... D7 98
Prescott, Columbia, Oreg., 129 ... A4 113
Prescott, Walla Walla, Wash., 269 ... C7 122
Prescott, Pierce, Wis., 1,536 ... D1 124
Prescott, co., Ont., Can., 27,226 ... B10 72
Presho, Lyman, S. Dak., 881 ... D5 116
Presidencia Roque Sáenz Peña, Arg., 23,100 ... E3 55
Presidente Epitácio, Braz., 10,425 ... C2 56
Presidente Hayes, dept., Par., 23,490 ... D4 55
Presidente Prudente, Braz., 54,055 ... C2 56
Presidential, range, N.H ... B4 105
Presidents, isl., Tenn ... E8 117
Presidio, Presidio, Tex., 1,062 ... G2 118
Presidio, co., Tex., 5,460 ... F2 118
Preslav, Bul., 4,114 ... D8 22
Presov, Czech., 35,100 ... D6 26
Presque Isle, Aroostook, Maine, 12,886 ... B4 96
Presque Isle, Presque Isle, Mich., 60 ... C7 98
Presque Isle, Vilas, Wis., 200 ... B4 124
Presque Isle, co., Mich., 13,117 ... C6 98
Pressath, Ger., 3,700 ... D6 17
Pressmens Home, Hawkins, Tenn., 400 ... C10 117
Prestatyn, Wales, 10,771 ... A4 12
Presteigne, Wales, 1,190 ... B4 12
Prestice, Czech., 4,199 ... D8 17
Preston, Austl., 86,600 ... *H5 51
Preston, Ont., Can., 11,577 ... D4 72
Preston, New London, Conn., 200 (4,992*) ... C9 84
Preston, Eng., 111,700 (*230,000) ... A5 12
Preston, Webster, Ga., 232 ... D2 87
Preston, Franklin, Idaho, 3,640 ... G7 89
Preston, Jackson, Iowa, 819 ... B7 92
Preston, Pratt, Kans., 278 ... E5 93
Preston, Bath, Ky., 200 ... B6 94
Preston, Caroline, Md., 469 ... C6 85
Preston, Fillmore, Minn., 1,491 ... G6 99
Preston, Kemper, Miss., 300 ... C5 100
Preston, Hickory, Mo., 117 ... D4 101
Preston, Okmulgee, Okla., 200 ... B6 112
Preston, King, Wash., 250 ... D2 122
Preston, co., W. Va., 27,233 ... B5 123
Preston, peak, Calif ... B2 82
Preston Park, Wayne, Pa., 50 ... C11 114
Prestonburg, Floyd, Ky., 3,133 ... C7 94
Prestonville, Carroll, Ky., 211 ... B4 94
Prestrud, inlet, Ant ... B32 5
Prestwick, Washington, Ala., 60 ... D2 78
Prestwick, Scot., 12,564 ... E4 13
Presumpscot, riv., Maine ... E4 96
Preti, mtn., It ... C8 18
Preto, riv., Braz ... h6 56
Prêto, riv., Braz ... D2 57
Prêto, riv., Braz ... C2 59
Pretoria, S. Afr., 303,684 (*422,590) ... C4 49
Pretty Boy, res., Md ... A4 85
Pretty Prairie, Reno, Kans., 525 ... B4, E5 93
Preveza, Grc., 11,172 ... C3 23
Preveza, prov., Grc., 62,523 ... *C3 23
Prewitt, McKinley, N. Mex., 50 ... B1 107
Prewitt, res., Colo ... A7 82
Prey Veng, Camb., 5,000 ... G6 38
Pribilof, is., Alsk ... D5 79
Priboj, Yugo., 5,501 ... D4 22
Pribram, Czech, 25,700 ... D3 26
Price, Que., Can., 3,094 ... *k13 73
Price, Queen Annes, Md., 126 ... B6 85
Price, Rusk, Tex., 800 ... C5 118
Price, Carbon, Utah, 6,802 ... D5 119
Price, co., Wis., 14,370 ... C3 124
Price, isl., B.C., Can ... C3 68
Price, riv., Utah ... D5 119
Pricedale, Pike, Miss., 80 ... D3 100
Pricedale, Westmoreland, Pa., 1,300 ... *F2 114
Price Hill, Raleigh, W. Va., 200 ... D3, D7 123
Priceville, Ont., Can., 141 ... C4 72
Prichard, Mobile, Ala., 47,371 ... E1 78
Prichard, Wayne, W. Va., 350 ... C2 123
Prides Crossing, Essex, Mass. (part of Beverly) ... f12 97
Priddy, Mills, Tex., 300 ... D3 118
Priego, Sp., 13,801 ... D3 20
Prienai, Sov. Un ... A7 26
Prieska, S. Afr., 6,464 ... C3 49
Priest, lake, Idaho ... A2 89
Priestly, mtn., B.C., Can ... B3 68
Priestly, mtn., Maine ... B3 96
Priest Rapids, dam, Wash ... C6 122
Priest Rapids, res., Wash ... C6 122
Priest River, Bonner, Idaho, 1,749 ... A2 89
Prijedor, Yugo., 11,632 ... C3 22
Prijepolje, Yugo., 4,627 ... D4 22
Prikumsk, Sov. Un ... E7 29
Prilep, Yugo., 37,486 ... E5 22
Priluki, Sov. Un., 40,000 ... F9 27
Prim, pt., P.E.I., Can ... C6 74
Primate, Sask., Can., 129 ... E1 70
Primera, Cameron, Tex., 1,066 ... *F4 118
Primero, riv., Arg ... A4 54
Primghar, O'Brien, Iowa, 1,131 ... A2 92
Primolano, It ... D7 18
Primorsk, Sov. Un., 8,000 ... G13 25
Primorsk (Fischhausen), Sov. Un., 5,000 ... A6 26
Primorsko-Akhtarsk, Sov. Un., 10,000 ... H12 27
Primos, Delaware, Pa., 1,000 ... *B4 114
Primrose, Boone, Nebr., 117 ... C7 103
Primrose, Schuylkill, Pa., 950 ... *E9 114
Primrose, Providence, R.I., 75 ... B10 84
Primrose, lake, Sask., Can ... n7 70
Prince, Sask., Can., 66 ... E1 70
Prince, Lincoln, Nev., 10 ... F7 104
Prince, co., P.E.I., Can., 40,894 ... C5 74
Prince, inlet, S.C ... F4 115
Prince, lake, Va ... B6 121
Prince Albert, Sask., Can., 24,168 ... D3, n7 70
Prince Albert, mts., Ant ... B29 5
Prince Albert, nat. park, Sask., Can ... C2 70
Prince Albert, sound, N.W. Ter., Can ... B9 66
Prince Alfred, cape, N.W. Ter., Can ... B8 66
Prince Charles, isl., N.W. Ter., Can ... C17 67
Prince Charles, mts., Ant ... B19 5
Prince Charles Foreland, isl., Nor ... B14 4
Prince Edward, co., Ont., Can., 21,108 ... C7 72
Prince Edward, co., Va., 14,121 ... D4 121
Prince Edward, isl., P.E.I., Can ... C6 74
Prince Edward, is., Indian O ... J23 3
Prince Edward Island, prov., Can., 104,629 ... G20 67, C6 74
Prince Edward Island, nat. park, P.E.I., Can ... C6 74
Prince Frederick, Calvert, Md., 500 ... C4 85
Prince George, B.C., Can., 13,877 ... C6, n18 68
Prince George, Prince George, Va., 80 ... C7, D5 121
Prince George, co., Va., 20,270 ... D5 121
Prince Georges, co., Md., 357,395 ... C4 85
Prince of Wales, cape, Alsk ... B6 79
Prince of Wales, isl., Alsk ... n23 79
Prince of Wales, isl., Austl ... B7 50
Prince of Wales, isl., N.W. Ter., Can ... B13 66
Prince of Wales, strait, N.W. Ter., Can ... B9 66
Prince Olav, coast, Ant ... C17 5
Prince Patrick, isl., N.W. Ter., Can ... m27 67
Prince Regent, inlet, N.W. Ter., Can ... B14 66
Prince Rupert, B.C., Can., 11,987 ... B2, n16 68
Princesa Isabel, Braz., 3,184 ... C3 57
Princes Risborough, Eng., 3,829 ... C7 12
Princess Anne, Somerset, Md., 1,351 ... D6 85
Princess Anne, Princess Anne, Va., 250 ... B7, E6 121
Princess Astrid, coast, Ant ... B14 5
Princess Charlotte, bay, Austl ... B7 50
Princess Martha, coast, Ant ... B11 5
Princess Ragnhild, coast, Ant ... B16 5
Princess Royal, isl., B.C., Can ... C3 68
Princeton, Jackson, Ala., 150 ... A3 78
Princeton, Dallas, Ark., 57 ... D3 81
Princeton, B.C., Can., 2,163 ... E7 68
Princeton, Newf., Can., 174 ... D5 75
Princeton, Ont., Can., 480 ... D4 72
Princeton, Colusa, Calif., 250 ... C2 82
Princeton, Dade, Fla., 1,719 ... F3, G6 86
Princeton, Latah, Idaho, 90 ... C2 89
Princeton, Gibson, Ind., 7,906 ... H2 91
Princeton, Scott, Iowa, 580 ... C7 92
Princeton, Franklin, Kans., 174 ... D8 93
Princeton, Caldwell, Ky., 5,618 ... C2 94
Princeton, Washington, Maine, 600 (829*) ... C5 96
Princeton, Worcester, Mass., 500 (1,360*) ... B4 97
Princeton, Marquette, Mich., 180 ... B3 98
Princeton, Mille Lacs, Minn., 2,353 ... E5 99
Princeton, Mercer, Mo., 1,443 ... A4 101
Princeton, Mercer, N.J., 11,890 ... C3 106
Princeton, Johnston, N.C., 948 ... B4 109
Princeton, Butler, Ohio, 70 ... C2 111
Princeton, Harney, Oreg., 10 ... D8 113
Princeton, Greenville and Laurens, S.C., 167 ... B3 115
Princeton, Mercer, W. Va., 8,393 ... D3 123
Princeton, Green Lake, Wis., 1,509 ... E4 124
Princeton, mtn., Colo ... C4 83
Princeton Junction, Mercer, N.J., 700 ... C3 106
Princeville, Que., Can., 3,174 ... C6 73
Princeville, Peoria, Ill., 1,281 ... C4 90
Princeville, Edgecombe, N.C., 797 ... B6 109
Prince William, N.B., Can ... D2 74
Prince William, co., Va., 50,164 ... C5 121
Prince William, sound, Alsk ... g18 79
Principe, chan., B.C., Can ... C2 68
Principe, isl., Sao Tome & Principe ... E1 46
Prineville, Crook, Oreg., 3,263 ... C6 113
Prineville, res., Oreg ... C6 113
Prineville Southeast, Crook, Oreg., 1,299 ... *C6 113
Pringle, Luzerne, Pa., 1,418 ... *D10 114
Pringle, Custer, S. Dak., 145 ... D2 116
Prinsburg, Kandiyohi, Minn., 462 ... F3 99
Prinzapolca, Nic., 7,200 ... D6 62
Prinzapolca, riv., Nic ... D6 62
Prior Lake, Scott, Minn., 848 ... F3 99
Priozersk, Sov. Un., 32,800 ... G14 25
Pripyat (Pripet), riv., Sov. Un ... E7 27
Prishib, Sov. Un ... B4 41
Pristina, Yugo., 38,891 ... D5 22
Pritchard, isl., S.C ... G7 115
Pritchardville, Beaufort, S.C., 50 ... G6 115
Pritchett, Baca, Colo., 247 ... D8 83
Pritchett, Upshur, Tex., 100 ... C2 118
Pritzerbe, Ger., 1,943 ... F6 24
Pritzwalk, Ger., 9,416 ... B6 16
Privas, Fr., 8,663 ... E6 14
Privert, lake, Que., Can ... g8 75
Privolnoye, Sov. Un., 9,000 ... H9 27
Prizren, Yugo., 28,050 ... D5 22
Prizzi, It., 9,752 ... F4 21
Probolinggo, Indon., 68,378 ... G4 35
Procious, Clay, W. Va., 75 ... C7 119
Procter, B.C., Can., 213 ... E9 68
Proctor, Logan, Colo., 35 ... A8 83
Proctor, Lee, Ky., 150 ... C6 94
Proctor, St. Louis, Minn., 2,963 ... D6 99
Proctor, Lake, Mont., 10 ... C2 102
Proctor, Elko, Nev., 10 ... C7 104
Proctor, Swain, N.C ... D2 109
Proctor, Adair, Okla., 65 ... B7 112
Proctor, Comanche, Tex., 130 ... D3 118
Proctor, Rutland, Vt., 1,978 (2,102*) ... D2 120
Proctor, Wetzel, W. Va., 130 ... C1 123
Proctorsville, Windsor, Vt., 476 ... E3 120
Proctorville, Robeson, N.C., 188 ... C4 109
Proctorville, Lawrence, Ohio, 831 ... D5 111
Proddatur, India, 50,616 ... *F6 39
Proença-a-Nova, Port., 6,340 ... C2 20
Progreso, Hond., 6,921 ... C4 62
Progreso, Mex., 13,659 ... C7 63
Progreso, Hidalgo, Tex., 900 ... *F4 118
Progress, Pike, Miss., 120 ... D3 100
Progress, Dauphin, Pa., 1,700 ... *F8 114
Prohner, bay, Ger ... D7 24
Project City, Shasta, Calif., 950 ... B2 82
Prokhladnyy, Sov. Un., 28,000 ... E2 29
Prokopyevsk, Sov. Un., 292,000 ... C11 29
Prokuplje, Yugo., 13,690 ... D5 22
Prole, Warren, Iowa, 580 ... B7 92
Proletarsk, Sov. Un., 10,000 ... q21 27
Proletarskaya, Sov. Un., 10,000 ... H13 27
Prome, Bur., 36,997 ... E10 39
Promise, Wallowa, Oreg ... B9 113
Promise City, Wayne, Iowa, 161 ... D4 92
Promontory, mts., Utah ... B3 119
Pronsfeld, Ger., 740 ... D6 15
Prophetstown, Whiteside, Ill., 1,802 ... B4 90
Propriá, Braz., 15,947 ... D3 57
Prorer, bay, Ger ... D7 24
Prorva, Sov. Un ... D4 29
Proskurov, see Khmelnitsky, Sov. Un.
Prosna, riv., Pol ... C5 26
Prosnica, riv., Pol ... A3 26
Prosotsani, Grc., 6,276 ... B4 23
Prospect, N.S., Can., 171 ... E6 74
Prospect, New Haven, Conn., 4,367 ... C5 84
Prospect, Jefferson, Ky., 100 ... A4 94
Prospect, Marion, Ohio, 1,607 ... B4 111
Prospect, Jackson, Oreg., 350 ... E4 113
Prospect, Butler, Pa., 903 ... E1 114
Prospect, Giles, Tenn., 200 ... B5 117
Prospect, Prince Edward, Va., 125 ... D4 121
Prospect, Waukesha, Wis. (part of New Berlin) ... E1 124
Prospect, hill, Mass ... D6 97
Prospect, hill, Mass ... g10 97
Prospect, hill, Oreg ... C1 113
Prospect, mtn., Oreg ... C2 113
Prospect Harbor, Hancock, Maine, 350 ... D4 96
Prospect Heights, Cook, Ill., 2,500 ... *E2 90
Prospect Hill, Caswell, N.C., 65 ... A4 109
Prospect Park, Passaic, N.J., 5,201 ... B4 106
Prospect Park, Delaware, Pa., 6,596 ... B11 114
Prospect Plains, Middlesex, N.J., 35 ... C4 106
Prosper, Cass, N. Dak., 35 ... C9 110
Prosperity, Newberry, S.C., 757 ... C4 115
Prosser, Adams, Nebr., 70 ... D7 103
Prosser, Benton, Wash., 2,763 ... C6 122
Prostejov, Czech., 33,500 ... D4 26
Prostki, Pol ... B7 26
Protection, Comanche, Kans., 780 ... E4 93
Protem, Taney, Mo., 33 ... E5 101
Protivin, Howard, Iowa, 302 ... A5 92
Proton Station, Ont., Can., 53 ... C4 72
Prouts Neck, Cumberland, Maine ... E5 96
Provadiya, Bul., 8,730 ... D8 22
Provadiya, riv., Bul ... D8 22
Provencal, Natchitoches, La., 570 ... C2 95
Provence, former prov., Fr., 1,750,000 ... F7 14
Providence, Polk, Fla., 100 ... C4 86
Providence, Webster, Ky., 3,771 ... C2 94
Providence, Cecil, Md., 85 ... A6 85
Providence, Providence, R.I., 207,498 (*816,200) ... B11 84
Providence, Davidson, Tenn., 3,830 ... *A5 117
Providence, Cache, Utah, 1,189 ... B4 119
Providence, Adams, Wash ... C7 122
Providence, co., R.I., 568,778 ... B10 84
Providence, canyons, Ga ... D2 87
Providence Bay, Ont., Can., 156 ... B2 72
Providence Forge, New Kent, Va., 130 ... D5 121
Providencia, isl., Col ... D7 62
Provincetown, Barnstable, Mass., 3,389 ... B7 97
Proving Ground, Carroll, Ill., 185 ... A3 90
Provins, Fr., 10,310 ... C5 14
Provo, Sevier, Ark., 160 ... C1 81
Provo, Fall River, S. Dak., 160 ... D2 116
Provo, Utah, Utah, 36,047 (*101,000) ... C4 119
Provo, riv., Utah ... C4 119
Provolt, Jackson, Oreg ... E3 113
Provost, Alta., Can., 1,022 ... C5 69
Prowers, co., Colo., 13,296 ... D8 83
Proyecto St. Just., P.R ... B7 65
Prozor, Yugo., 5,506 ... D3 22
Pruden, Claiborne, Tenn., 60 ... C10 117
Prudence, isl., R.I ... C11 84
Prudence Island, Newport, R.I., 60 ... C11 84
Prudentópolis, Braz., 4,524 ... D2 56
Prudenville, Roscommon, Mich., 100 ... D6 98
Prud'homme, Sask., Can., 264 ... E3 70
Prudnik, Pol., 15,200 ... C4 26
Prüm, Ger., 4,000 ... C3 16
Pruszkow, Pol., 37,000 ... B6, m13 26
Prut, riv., Sov. Un ... H7 27
Pruzhany, Sov. Un., 10,000 ... E5 27
Prydz, bay, Ant ... C20 5
Pryor, Huerfano, Colo., 26 ... D6 83
Pryor, Big Horn, Mont., 50 ... E8 102
Pryor (Pryor Creek), Mayes, Okla., 6,476 ... A6 112
Pryor, mts., Mont ... E8 102
Pryorsburg, Graves, Ky., 250 ... B2 94
Przasnysz, Pol., 7,015 ... B6 26
Przedborz, Pol., 3,503 ... C5 26
Przemsza, riv., Pol ... g10 26
Przemysl, Pol., 48,800 ... D7 26
Przeworsk, Pol., 8,569 ... C7 26
Przewoz, Pol ... B9 17
Przhevalsk, Sov. Un., 30,000 ... G24 9
Psakhna, Grc., 4,309 ... C4 23
Psara, isl., Grc ... C5 23
Psary, Pol ... g10 26
Psel, riv., Sov. Un ... G9 27
Pskov, Sov. Un., 101,000 ... C7 27
Pskov, lake, Sov. Un ... B6 27
Pszczyna, Pol., 12,800 ... D5, h9 26
Pszczynka, riv., Pol ... h9 26
Ptarmigan, mtn., Wyo ... A3 125
Ptich, riv., Sov. Un ... E7 27
Ptolemais, Grc., 12,747 ... B3 23
Ptuj, Yugo., 7,365 ... B2 22
Pu, China ... G6 36
Puako, Hawaii, Haw ... D6 88
Puán, Arg., 3,191 ... B4 54
Puapua, W. Sam., 236 ... 52
Pucallpa, Peru, 2,368 ... C3 58
Pucheng, China, 20,000 ... K8 36
Puck, Pol., 3,946 ... A5 26
Puckaway, lake, Wis ... E4 124
Puckett, Rankin, Miss., 302 ... C4 100
Pudasjärvi, Fin ... E12 25
Pudozh, Sov., Un., 2,000 ... A11 27
Pudukkottai, India, 50,488 ... *F6 39
Puebla, Mex., 289,049 ... D5, n14 63
Puebla, state, Mex., 1,957,380 ... D5, n14 63
Puebla de Don Fadrique, Sp., 7,142 ... D4 20
Puebla del Caramiñal, Sp., 8,337 ... A1 20
Pueblito de Ponce, P.R ... B3 65
Pueblo, Pueblo, Colo., 91,181 (*111,000) ... C6 83
Pueblo, co., Colo., 118,707 ... C6 83
Pueblo, mts., Oreg ... E8 113
Pueblo Colorado, wash, Ariz ... B6 80
Pueblo Hundido, Chile ... E2 55
Pueblo Nuevo, Pan., 1,447 ... m11 62
Pueblo Nuevo, P.R ... B3 65
Pueblo Nuevo, Ven., 2,837 ... A4 60
Puebloviejo, Ec., 1,206 ... B2 58
Puenteareas, Sp., 14,634 ... A1 20
Puente Ceso, Sp., 9,780 ... A1 20
Puentedeume, Sp., 7,755 ... A2 20
Puente-Genil, Sp., 25,000 ... D3 20
Puerco, riv., Ariz., N. Mex ... B1 107
Puerto Acosta, Bol., 1,302 ... C2 55
Puerto Asién, Chile, 3,767 ... D2 54
Puerto Alegre, Bol ... B3 55
Puerto Alvaro Obregón, Mex., 8,320 ... D6 63
Puerto Armuelles, Pan., 10,712 ... F6 62
Puerto Arroyo Verde, Arg ... C3 54
Puerto Asís, Col ... C2 60
Puerto Ayacucho, Ven., 5,418 ... B4 60
Puerto Baquerizo, Ec ... g6 58
Puerto Barrios, Guat., 15,155 ... C3 62
Puerto Belgrano, Arg ... B4 54
Puerto Bermúdez, Peru ... D3 58
Puerto Berrío, Col., 8,947 ... B3 60
Puerto Bolívar, Ec., 2,000 ... B2 58
Puerto Cabello, Ven., 50,973 ... A4 60
Puerto Cabezas, Nic., 6,000 ... C6 62
Puerto Carreño, Col., 540 ... B4 60
Puerto Casado, Par., 6,708 ... D4 55
Puerto Chicama, Peru, 2,274 ... C2 58
Puerto Colombia, Col., 5,689 ... A3 60
Puerto Constanza, Arg ... f7 54
Puerto Cortés, Hond., 17,412 ... C4 62
Puerto Cumarebo, Ven., 7,951 ... A4 60
Puerto de Cabras, Sp. (Can. Is.) ... m15 20
Puerto de la Cruz, Sp. (Can. Is.), 5,855 ... m13 20
Puerto de la Paloma, Ur ... E2 56
Puerto del Rosario, Can. Is., 1,459 (4,029*) ... D2 44
Puerto del Son, Sp., 2,221 ... A1 20
Puerto de Luna, Guadalupe, N. Mex., 300 ... C5 107
Puerto Deseado, Arg., 3,392 ... D3 54
Puerto Eten, Peru, 2,576 ... C2 58
Puerto Guaraní, Par., 2,758 ... D4 55
Puerto Heath, Bol ... B2 55
Puerto Iguazú, Arg ... E5 55
Puerto Jobos, P.R., 699 ... D6 65
Puerto la Cruz, Ven., 54,694 ... A5 60
Puerto Leguízamo, Col., 1,433 ... D3 60
Puertollano, Sp., 53,136 ... C3 20
Puerto Madryn, Arg., 3,441 ... C3 54
Puerto Maldonado, Peru, 1,285 ... D4 58
Puerto Manatí, Cuba ... E5 64
Puerto Mineral, Arg ... E4 55
Puerto Montt, Chile, 41,700 ... C2 54
Puerto Morazán, Nic ... D4 62
Puerto Natales, Chile, 8,140 ... E2, h11 54
Puerto Ordoz, Ven ... B5 60
Puerto Padre, Cuba, 6,949 ... E5 64
Puerto Páez, Ven., 677 ... B4 60
Puerto Peñasco, Mex., 2,517 ... A2 63
Puerto Pinasco, Par., 7,576 ... D4 55
Puerto Piramides, Arg ... C4 54
Puerto Plata, Dom. Rep., 19,073 ... F8 64
Puerto Princesa, Phil., 3,326 ... D5 35
Puerto Real, P.R ... C2 65
Puerto Real, Sp., 10,033 ... D2 20
Puerto Rico, U.S. dep., N.A., 2,600,000 ... H14 61, 65
Puerto Sastre, Par., 5,058 ... D4 55
Puerto Siles, Bol., 357 ... B2 55
Puerto Suarez, Bol., 1,159 ... C5 55
Puerto Sucre, Bol., 1,470 ... B2 55
Puerto Supe, Peru, 2,180 ... D2 58
Puerto Tejada, Col., 8,535 ... C2 60
Puerto Vallarta, Mex., 7,397 ... C3, m11 63
Puerto Varas, Chile, 5,797 ... C2 54
Puerto Victoria, Peru ... C3 58
Puerto Viejo, C.R ... F6 62
Puerto Villamizar, Col ... B3 60
Puerto Visser, Arg ... D3 54
Puerto Wilches, Col., 3,451 ... B3 60
Pugachev, Sov. Un., 33,600 ... C3 29
Pugal, India, 5,000 ... C4 40
Puget, sound, Wash ... B3 122
Puget Island, Wahkiakum, Wash ... C2 122
Puget-Théniers, Fr., 919 ... F7 14
Pughtown, Hancock, W. Va., 400 ... A2 123
Puglia, pol. dist., It., 3,421,217 ... *D6 21
Pugwash, N.S., Can., 815 ... D6 74
Puhi, Kauai, Haw., 650 ... B2 88
Puhsi, China, 5,000 ... B2 37
Puigcerdá, Sp., 4,276 ... A6 20
Pujehun, S.L ... E2 45
Pujilí, Ec., 2,149 ... B2 58
Pukalani, Maui, Haw., 600 ... C5 88
Pukchong, Kor., 30,709 ... F4 37
Pukë, Alb., 976 ... A2 23
Pukeamaru, mtn., N.Z ... L17 51
Pukeashun, mtn., B.C., Can ... D8 68
Pukekohe, N.Z., 5,798 ... L15 51
Pukou, China ... H8 36
Pukwana, Brule, S. Dak., 247 ... D6 116
Pula, It., 3,642 ... E2 21
Pula, Yugo., 36,838 ... C1 22
Pulacayo, Bol., 7,984 ... D2 55
Pulantien, China, 12,000 ... D9 34
Pulaski, Candler, Ga., 155 ... D5 87
Pulaski, Pulaski, Ill., 415 ... F4 90
Pulaski, Davis, Iowa, 299 ... D5 92
Pulaski, Scott, Miss., 200 ... C4 100
Pulaski, Oswego, N.Y., 2,256 ... B4 108
Pulaski, Giles, Tenn., 6,616 ... B4 117
Pulaski, Pulaski, Va., 10,469 ... D2 121
Pulaski, Brown, Wis., 1,540 ... D5 124
Pulaski, co., Ark., 242,980 ... C3 81
Pulaski, co., Ga., 8,204 ... D3 87
Pulaski, co., Ill., 10,490 ... F4 90
Pulaski, co., Ind., 12,837 ... B4 91
Pulaski, co., Ky., 34,403 ... C5 94
Pulaski, co., Mo., 46,567 ... D5 101
Pulaski, co., Va., 27,258 ... D2 121
Pulawy, Pol., 11,900 ... C6 26
Pul-i-Khumri, Afg., 12,000 ... D14 41
Pull, pt., Vir. Is ... h17 65
Pullman, Allegan, Mich., 200 ... F4 98
Pullman, Whitman, Wash., 12,957 ... C8 122
Pullman, Ritchie, W. Va., 162 ... B4 123
Pulog, mtn., Phil ... n13 35
Pulozero, Sov. Un ... C15 25
Pulpit Rocks, cavern, N.H ... E3 105
Puluntai, China ... A9 39, D3 34
Puluntohai, see Bulun Tukhoi, China
Pultusk, Pol., 8,787 ... B6 26
Pumphrey, Anne Arundel, Md., 700 ... C2 85
Pumpkin, buttes, Wyo ... B7 125
Pumpkin, creek, Mont ... E11 102
Pumpkin, creek, Nebr ... C2 103
Pumpville, Val Verde, Tex., 40 ... E2 118
Puna, Bol., 852 ... C2 55
Puná, isl., Ec ... B1 58
Punakha (Punaka), Bhu ... D12 40
Punat, Yugo., 1,900 ... C2 22
Punata, Bol., 5,014 ... C2 55
Punchaw, B.C., Can ... C6 68
Pungo, Beaufort, N.C., 160 ... B7 109
Pungo, Princess Anne, Va., 300 ... B7 121
Pungsan, Kor., 17,453 ... F4 37
Pungsan, Kor., 4,300 ... H4 37
Punjab, reg., India, Pak ... B5 39
Punjab, state, India, 20,306,812 ... B6 39
Punnichy, Sask., Can., 408 ... F3 70
Puno, Peru, 18,852 ... E3 58
Puno, dept., Peru, 646,385 ... E3 58
Punta, Torrance, N. Mex., 70 ... C3 107
Punta, mtn., P.R ... C4 65
Punta Alta, Arg., 19,852 ... B4 54
Punta Arenas, Chile, 49,500 ... h11 54
Punta de Díaz, Chile ... E1 55
Punta de Piedras, Ven., 2,257 ... A5 60
Punta de Vacas, Arg ... A3 54
Punta Gorda, Br. Hond., 1,758 ... B3 62
Punta Gorda, Charlotte, Fla., 3,157 ... F4 86
Punta Moreno, Peru ... C2 60
Punta Rassa, Lee, Fla., 20 ... F5 86
Puntarenas, C.R., 19,500 ... F5 62
Puntarenas, prov., C.R., 148,100 ... *F5 62
Punta Fijo, Ven., 15,441 ... A3 60
Puntzi, lake, B.C., Can ... C5 68
Punxsutawney, Jefferson, Pa., 8,805 ... E4 114
Puposky, Beltrami, Minn., 40 ... C4 99
Puquio, Peru, 6,183 ... D3 58
Púquios, Chile ... E2 55
Pur, riv., Sov. Un ... B24 9
Puranpur, India, 11,280 ... C8 40
Purcell, Jasper, Mo., 265 ... D3 101
Purcell, McClain, Okla., 3,729 ... B4 112
Purcell, mts., B.C., Can., Mont ... A1 102
Purcellville, Loudoun, Va., 1,419 ... B5 121
Purdham, hill, Ark ... D6 81
Purdin, Linn., Mo., 207 ... B4 101
Purdum, Blaine, Nebr., 25 ... B5 103
Purdy, Barry, Mo., 467 ... E4 101
Purdy, Greensville, Va., 120 ... E5 121
Purépero, Mex., 10,092 ... n12 63
Purgatoire, riv., Colo ... D7 83
Purgatory, peak, Colo ... D5 83
Puri, India, 60,815 ... H10 40
Puritan, Gogebic, Mich., 150 ... A5 98
Purmerend, Neth., 10,800 ... B4 15
Purna, riv., India ... H6 40
Purnea, India, 40,602 ... E11 40
Purple Springs, Alta., Can ... E5 69
Purpula, mtn., Sov. Un ... D14 28
Pursat, Camb., 25,000 ... F5 38
Pursglove, Monongalia, W. Va., 600 ... B4 123
Purulia, India, 48,134 ... F11 40
Purús, riv., Braz., Peru ... D3 56, D2 59
Purvis, Lamar, Miss., 1,614 ... D4 100
Purvis, Nansemond, Va., 60 ... B6 121
Puryear, Henry, Tenn., 408 ... A3 117
Puryong, Kor ... E4 37
Pusan, Kor., 1,270,600 ... I4 37
Pushaw, lake, Maine ... D4 96
Pushkin, Sov. Un., 55,000 ... B8 27
Pushkino, Sov. Un., 10,000 ... C11, m17 27
Pushmataha, Choctaw, Ala., 200 ... C1 78
Pushmataha, co., Okla., 9,088 ... C6 112
Pushthrough, Newf., Can., 247 ... E3 75
Puspokladany, Hung., 15,735 ... B5 22
Pustelnik, Pol., 5,000 ... k14 26
Pustunich, Mex., 343 ... D6 63
Pustynnove, Sov. Un ... B8 29
Putah, creek, Calif ... A5 82
Putao, Bur., 10,000 ... C10 39
Puteaux, Fr., 39,640 ... g9 14
Putien, China, 14,000 ... F8 34
Putilovo, Sov. Un ... s32 25
Puting, cape, Indon ... F4 35
Putivl, Sov. Un., 10,000 ... F9 27
Putlitz, Ger., 2,763 ... E6 24
Putnam, Marengo, Ala., 175 ... C1 78
Putnam, Windham, Conn., 6,952 (8,412*) ... B9 84
Putnam, Dewey, Okla., 88 ... B3 112
Putnam, Callahan, Tex., 203 ... C3 118
Putnam, co., Fla., 32,212 ... C5 86
Putnam, co., Ga., 7,798 ... C3 87
Putnam, co., Ill., 4,570 ... B4 90
Putnam, co., Ind., 24,927 ... E4 91
Putnam, co., Mo., 6,999 ... A4 101
Putnam, co., N.Y., 31,722 ... D7 108
Putnam, co., Ohio, 28,331 ... B3 111
Putnam, co., Tenn., 29,236 ... C8 117
Putnam, co., W. Va., 23,561 ... C3 123
Putnam Station, Washington, N.Y., 50 ... B7 108
Putnamville, Putnam, Ind., 140 ... E4 91
Putnamville, Washington, Vt., 75 ... C3 120
Putney, Dougherty, Ga., 300 ... E2 87
Putney, Brown, S. Dak., 15 ... B7 116
Putney, Windham, Vt., 500 (1,177*) ... F3 120
Putney, Kanawha, W. Va., 40 ... C3, C6 123
Putre, Chile ... C2 55
Puttalam, Cey., 10,162 ... G6 39
Putte, Neth., 2,000 ... C4 15
Püttlingen, Ger., 14,200 ... D1 17
Putumayo, comisaría, Col., 35,000 ... C2 60
Putumayo, riv., Col ... D3 60
Puturge, Tur., 2,383 ... C12 31
Puukolii, Maui, Haw., 500 ... C5 88
Puu Konahuanui, mtn., Haw ... g10 88
Puulavesi, lake, Fin ... G12 25
Puunene, Maui, Haw., 3,054 ... C5 88
Puurs, Bel., 6,042 ... C4 15
Puu Waawaa, peak, Haw ... D6 88
Puxico, Stoddard, Mo., 743 ... E7 101
Puyallup, Pierce, Wash., 12,063 ... B3, E2 122
Puyallup, riv., Wash ... C3 122
Puyang, China ... G6 36
Puy-de-Dôme, dept., Fr., 508,928 ... *E5 14
Puy de Dome, mtn., Fr ... E5 14
Puy de Sancy, mtn., Fr ... E5 14
Puyehue, Chile ... C2 54
Puyo, Ec., 1,092 ... B2 58
Puzim, cape, Iran ... I10 41
Pweto, Con. L ... C4 48
Pwllheli, Wales, 3,642 ... B3 12
Pyapon, Bur., 19,174 ... E10 39
Pyasina, riv., Sov. Un ... B12 28
Pyatigorsk, Sov. Un., 74,000 ... E2 29
Pyatt, Marion, Ark., 144 ... A3 81
Pyatte, Avery, N.C ... A2, C4 109
Pyavzero, lake, Sov. Un ... D14 25
Pyhäjärvi, lake, Fin ... G10 25
Pyinbugyi, Bur ... F3 38
Pyinmana, Bur., 22,066 ... E10 39
Pyland, Chickashaw, Miss ... B4 100
Pyles, fork, W. Va ... A6 123
Pymatuning, creek, Ohio ... A7 111
Pymatuning, res., Pa ... C1 114
Pyongchang, Kor., 4,300 ... H4 37
Pyongtaek, Kor., 15,200 ... H3 37
Pyŏngyang, Kor., 653,100 ... G2 37
Pyote, Ward, Tex., 420 ... D1 118
Pyramid, lake, Nev ... C2 104
Pyramid, mts., N. Mex ... E1 107
Pyramid, peak, Calif ... C3 82
Pyramid, peak, Wyo ... B2 125
Pyramid Lake, Indian res., Nev ... C2 104
Pyramids, ruins, Eg., U.A.R ... D6 43
Pyrenees, mts., France, Sp ... A5 20, G8 8
Pyrénées-Orientales, dept., Fr., 251,231 ... *F5 14
Pyrites, St. Lawrence, N.Y., 300 ... f9 108
Pyrmont, Carroll, Ind., 70 ... D4 91
Pyrzyce, Pol., 4,179 ... B3 26
Pysht, Clallam, Wash., 50 ... A1 122
Pyskowice, Pol., 21,000 ... g9 26

Pytalovo, Sov. Un., 3,000...C6 27
Pyu, Bur., 10,443...E10 39

Q

Qabātiyah, Jordan, 3,000...B7 32
Qaḍīmah, Sau. Ar...A4 47
Qais, isl., Iran...H6 41
Qala Bist., Afg., 5,000...F12 41
Qala-i-Ghor (Taiwara), Afg., 5,000...E12 41
Qalamshāh, Eg., U.A.R...H8 31
Qala Nau, Afg., 5,000...D11 41
Qala Salih, Iraq, 4,022...F3 41
Qala Shaharak, Afg., 5,000...D12 41
Qala Sharqat, Iraq...E14 31
Qala Sikar, Iraq, 4,913...F3 41
Qal'at al Mu'aẓẓam, Sau. Ar...I11 31
Qaliya, cape, Kuw...G4 41
Qalqīlah, Jordan, 8,000.B6, g10 32
Qalyūb, Eg., U.A.R., 35,800...D3 32
Qamīnis, Libya, 1,100...C4 43
Qana, Leb., 5,000...A7 32
Qārah, Eg., U.A.R...H6 31
Qareh Dāgh, mtn., Iran...B2 41
Qaru, isl., Arabia...G4 41
Qārūm, lake, Eg., U.A.R....D5 43
Qaryat al 'Ulyā, Sau. Ar...H3 41
Qaryat el Inab, Isr., 662...h11 32
Qaṣr al Kharānah, Jordan..G11 31
Qaṣr Banī Walīd, Libya, 2,520...C2 43, C7 44
Qatar, country, Asia, 65,000..I5 41
Qatia, Eg., U.A.R., 1,000...D4 32
Qattah, Eg., U.A.R...D2 32
Qattara (Qaṭṭārah), depression, Eg., U.A.R....D5 43
Qaṭṭarah, see Qattara, depression, Eg., U.A.R.
Qāyen, Iran, 10,000...E9 41
Qazvīn, Iran, 66,420...C4 41
Qeshm, Iran, 15,000...H8 41
Qeshm, isl., Iran...H7 41
Qila Saifullah, Pak...B2 40
Qina, Eg., U.A.R., 47,700...D6 43
Qiryat Anavim, Isr., 286...C7, h11 32
Qiryat Hayim, Isr., (part of Haifa)...B7 32
Qiryat Ono, Isr., 8,137...g10 32
Qiumbele, Ang...C2 48
Qizil Unzun, riv., Iran...C4 41
Qom, Iran, 96,499...D5 41
Quabbin, res., Mass...B3 97
Quaco, head, N.B., Can...D4 74
Quaddick, res., Conn...B9 84
Quakenbrück, Ger., 7,800...B3 16
Quaker City, Guernsey, Ohio, 583...C6 111
Quaker Hill, New London, Conn., 2,000...D8 84
Quakertown, Hunterdon, N.J., 200...B3 106
Quakertown, Bucks, Pa., 6,305...F11 114
Qualicum Beach, B.C., Can., 759...E5 68
Quality, Butler, Ky., 75...C3 94
Qualls, Cherokee, Okla...B6 112
Quamba, Kanabec, Minn., 95...E5 99
Quanah, Hardeman, Tex., 4,564...B3 118
Quang Ngai, Viet., 5,000...E8 38
Quang Tri, Viet., 13,425...D7 38
Quannapowitt, lake, Mass...f11 97
Quantico, Wicomico, Md., 300...D6 85
Quantico, Prince William, Va., 1,015...C5 121
Quapaw, Ottawa, Okla., 850...A7 112
Qu'Appelle, Sask., Can., 565...G4 70
Qu'Appelle, riv., Man., Sask., Can...G4 70
Quaraí, Braz., 10,575...E1 56
Quarai, riv., Braz...E1 56
Quari, riv., Braz...C2 59
Quarry, Manitowoc, Wis., 35.B6 124
Quarryville, N.B., Can., 256.C4 74
Quarryville, Tolland, Conn., 600...*B7 84
Quarryville, Lancaster, Pa., 1,427...G9 114
Quartu Sant'Elena, It., 22,916...E2 21
Quartz, mtn., Oreg...D4 113
Quartz, peak, Nev...G6 104
Quartz Hill, Los Angeles, Calif., 3,325...*E4 82
Quartz Mountain, Lake, Oreg., 5...E6 113
Quartzsite, Yuma, Ariz., 350...D1 80
Quasqueton, Buchanan, Iowa, 373...B6 92
Quassapaug, pond, Conn...C4 84
Quatsino, sound, B.C., Can...D3 68
Quay, Quay, N. Mex., 5...C6 107
Quay, Pawnee and Payne, Okla., 51...A5 112
Quay, co., N. Mex., 12,279..C6 107
Qūchān, Iran, 21,250...C9 41
Quealy, Sweetwater, Wyo., 42... D3 125
Québec, Que., Can., 171,979 (★357,568)...C6, n17 73
Québec, co., Que., Can., 331,307...B5 73
Quebec, prov., Can., 5,259,211...F18 67, 73
Québec-Ouest, Que., Can., 8,733...*C6 73
Quebeck, White, Tenn., 250...D8 117
Quebradillas, P.R., 2,131...B3 65
Quebradillas, mun., P.R., 13,075...B3 65
Quechee, Windsor, Vt., 350..D4 120
Quecreek, Somerset, Pa., 800.F3 113
Quedlinburg, Ger., 31,100...B6 17
Queen, cape, N.W. Ter., Can..D17 67
Queen Alexandra, range, Ant..A28 5
Queen Anne, Talbot, Md., 283...C6 85
Queen Annes, co., Md., 16,569...B5 85
Queen Bess, mtn., B.C., Can...D5 68
Queen Charlotte, B.C., Can..C1 68
Queen Charlotte, is., B.C., Can..C1 68
Queen Charlotte, mts., B.C., Can.C1 68
Queen Charlotte, sound, B.C., Can...n17 68
Queen Charlotte, strait, B.C., Can...D4 68
Queen City, Schuyler, Mo., 599...A5 101
Queen City, Cass, Tex., 1,081...*C6 118
Queen Creek, Maricopa, Ariz., 550...G3 80
Queen Elizabeth, is., N.W. Ter., Can...k32 67
Queen Fabiola, mts., Ant...B16 5
Queen Mary, coast, Ant...C22 5
Queen Maud, gulf, N.W. Ter., Can...C12 66
Queen Maud, range, Ant...A31 5
Queen Maud Land, reg., Ant..B13 5
Queens, borough and co., N.Y., 1,809,578 (part of New York City)...D2 108
Queens, co., N.B., Can., 11,640...D4 74
Queens, co., N.S., Can., 13,155...E4 74
Queens, co., P.E.I., Can., 45,842...C6 74
Queens, chan., Austl...B4 50
Queens, sound, B.C., Can...D3 68
Queensborough, Ont., Can., 117...C7 72
Queen Shoals, Kanawha, W. Va., 65...C6 123
Queensland, Ben Hill, Ga., 60...E3 87
Queensland, state, Austl., 1,606,000...D7 50
Queensport, N.S., Can., 199.D8 74
Queenstown, Austl., 4,601...o15 50
Queenstown, Br., Gu., 1,067...A3 59
Queenstown, Alta., Can., 67...D4 69
Queenstown, N.B., Can., 138.D3 74
Queenstown, Queen Annes, Md., 355...C5 85
Queenstown, N.Z., 1,321...P12 51
Queenstown, S. Afr., 33,182.D4 49
Queguay, Ur...E1 56
Queguay Grande, riv., Ur...E1 56
Queimadas, Braz., 3,553...D3 57
Queixadas, Braz., 745...E2 57
Quela, Ang...C2 48
Quelimane, Moz., 8,000...A6 49
Quemado, Catron, N. Mex., 150...C1 107
Quemado, Maverick, Tex., 300...E2 118
Quemado de Güines, Cuba, 3,276...D3 64
Quemoy (Chinmen), China, 6,000...*G8 34
Quemú Quemú, Arg...B4 54
Quenemo, Osage, Kans., 434...D8 93
Quentin, Franklin, Miss., 300...D3 100
Que Que, Rh., 17,700...A4 49
Quequén, Arg., 4,760...B5 54
Querétaro, Mex., 67,674...C4, m13 63
Querétaro, state, Mex., 353,154...C4, m13 63
Querfurt, Ger., 7,976...B6 17
Quesada, Sp., 7,609...D4 20
Quesnel, B.C., Can., 4,673...C6 68
Quesnel, lake, B.C., Can...C7 68
Quesnel, riv., B.C., Can...C6 68
Questa, Taos, N. Mex., 650..A4 107
Quetena, Bol., 183...D2 55
Quetico, prov. park, Ont., Can..o16 72
Quetta, Pak., 79,493 (★106,633)...B4 39, B1 40
Quezaltenango, Guat., 27,672...C2 62
Quezaltepeque, Sal., 8,471...D3 62
Quezon, prov., Phil., 656,900...*C6 35
Quezon City, Phil., 397,990...C6, o13 35
Quiani, riv., Braz...D5 60
Quibala, Ang., 263...D1 48
Quibell, Ont., Can., 40...E5 71
Quibdó, Col., 11,000 (42,000▲)...B2 60
Quiberon, Fr., 4,103...D2 14
Quiberon, pen., Fr...D2 14
Quicksburg, Shenandoah, Va., 150...C4 121
Quidnessett, Washington, R.I., 1,000...C11 84
Quidnick, Kent, R.I., 2,000...C10 84
Quidnick, res., R.I...C10 84
Quietus, Big Horn, Mont...E10 102
Quiindy, Par., 2,150...E4 55
Quijotoa, Pima, Ariz., 50...E3 80
Quilá, Mex., 1,290...C3 63
Quilan, cape, Chile...C2 54
Quilcene, Jefferson, Wash., 600...B3 122
Quilengues, Ang., 472...D1 48
Quill, lakes, Sask., Can...F3 70
Quillaga, Chile...D2 55
Quillan, Fr., 4,424...F5 14
Quill Lake, Sask., Can., 529...E3 70
Quillota, Chile, 27,000...A2 54
Quilmes, Arg., 310,000...g7 54
Quilon, India, 91,018...G6 39
Quilpie, Austl., 640...C5 51
Quilpué, Chile, 26,000...A2 64
Quilty, Ire., 200...E2 11
Quimby, Cherokee, Iowa, 369...B2 92
Quimby, Arrostook, Maine, 200...B4 96
Quimilí, Arg., 3,686...E3 51
Quimper, Fr., 45,989...C2 14
Quimperlé, Fr., 10,272...D2 14
Quinaby, Marion, Oreg., 50...B4, C1 113
Quinault, Grays Harbor, Wash., 300...B2 122
Quinault, Indian res., Wash...B1 122
Quinault, lake, Wash...B2 122
Quinault, riv., Wash...B1 122
Quincy, Plumas, Calif., 1,700...C3 82
Quincy, Gadsden, Fla., 8,874...B2 86
Quincy, Adams, Ill., 43,793..D2 90
Quincy, Owen, Ind., 150...F4 91
Quincy, Greenwood, Kans., 90...E7 93
Quincy, Lewis, Ky., 300...B6 94
Quincy, Norfolk, Mass., 87,409...B5, h11 97
Quincy, Branch, Mich., 1,602...G6 98
Quincy, Monroe, Miss., 125..B5 100
Quincy, Hickory, Mo., 90...C4 101
Quincy, Grafton, N.H., 85...C3 105
Quincy, Logan, Ohio, 668...B4 111
Quincy, Columbia, Oreg., 200...A3 113
Quincy, Franklin, Pa., 400...G6 114
Quincy, Grant, Wash., 3,269...B6 122
Quincy, bay, Mass...g12 97
Quinebaug, Windham, Conn., 350...A9 84
Quinebaug, riv., Conn...C9 84
Quines, Arg., 3,038...A3 54
Quinhagak, Alsk, 228...D7 79
Qui Nhon, Viet., 10,000...F8 38
Quinlan, Woodward, Okla., 75...A2 112
Quinlan, Hunt, Tex., 621...C4 118
Quinn, Pennington, S. Dak., 162...D3 116
Quinn, riv., Nev...B4 104
Quinn Canon, mts., Nev...F6 104
Quinnesec, Dickinson, Mich., 400...C3 98
Quinnipiac, riv., Conn...D5 84
Quinnville, Providence, R.I., 400...B11 84
Quintana de la Serena, Sp., 7,861...C3 20
Quintanar, Sp., 9,483...C4 20
Quintana Roo, ter., Mex., 52,312...D7 63
Quinter, Gove, Kans., 776...C3 93
Quintero, Chile, 5,563...A2 54
Quinton, Sask., Can., 195...F3 70
Quinton, Pulaski, Ky., 200..D5 94
Quinton, Salem, N.J., 450...D2 106
Quinton, Pittsburg, Okla., 898...B6 112
Quinwood, Greenbrier, W. Va., 506...C4 123
Quipapá, Braz., 3,421...C3, k6 57
Quipungo, Ang...D1 48
Quirauk, mtn., Md...A2 85
Quirindi, Austl., 2,790...E8 51
Quiriquire, Ven., 7,520...B5 60
Quirke, lake, Ont., Can...B8 98
Quiroga, Sp., 8,380...A2 20
Quirpon, isl., Newf., Can...C4 75
Quissanga, Moz...D4 48
Quitaque, Briscoe, Tex., 586...B2 118
Quita Sueño Bank, shoals, Caribbean Sea...C7 62
Quitman, Cleburne, Ark., 305...B3 81
Quitman, Brooks, Ga., 5,071...F3 87
Quitman, Jackson, La., 185..B3 95
Quitman, Clarke, Miss., 2,030...C5 100
Quitman, Nodaway, Mo., 113...A2 101
Quitman, Wood, Tex., 1,237.C5 118
Quitman, co., Ga., 2,432...E1 87
Quitman, co., Miss., 21,019..A3 100
Quitman, mts., Tex...F1 118
Quito, Ec., 355,200...B2 58
Quitsna, Bertie, N.C...B6 109
Quixadá, Braz., 8,747...B3 57
Quixeramobim, Braz., 6,384...C3 57
Qulin, Butler, Mo., 587...E7 101
Qum, riv., Iran...E5 41
Quoi, isl., Truk... 52
Quonochontaug, Washington, R.I., 50...D10 84
Quorn, Austl., 566...F2 51
Quoyness, Scot...B5 13
Qūs, Eg., U.A.R., 23,600...D6 43
Qusrah, Jordan, 2,000...g12 32

R

Raab, riv., Aus...E7 16
Raabs, Aus., 1,132...D7 16
Raahe, Fin., 4,900...E11 25
Raalte, Neth., 3,301...B6 15
Raanana, Isr., 10,656...g10 32
Raasay, isl., Scot...C3 13
Rab, isl., Yugo...C2 22
Raba, Indon, 6,781...G5 35
Rába (Raab), riv., Hung...B3 22
Rabastens, Fr., 2,491...F4 14
Rabat, Mor., 227,445 (★310,000)...G3 30, C3 44
Rabaul, N. Gui., 4,500...G9 7
Rabbit, creek, S. Dak...B3 116
Rabbit Ear, pass, Colo...A4 83
Rabbit Hash, Boone, Ky., 50...A6 94
Rabbit Lake, Sask., Can., 196...D2 70
Rabch, riv., Iran...D9 41
Rabun, Baldwin, Ala., 300..D2 78
Rabun, co., Ga., 7,456...B3 87
Rabun, gap, Ga...B3 87
Rabun Bald, mtn., Ga...B3 87
Råby, Swe...u34 25
Rača Kragujevačka, Yugo., 1,000...C5 22
Raccoon, creek, Ind...E4 91
Raccoon, creek, Ohio...D5 111
Raccoon, mtn., Ala...B3 78
Raccoon, pt., La...E5 95
Raccoon, riv., Iowa...C3 92
Raccourci, isl., La...D4 95
Race, cape, Newf., Can...E5 75
Race, pt., Mass...B7 97
Race, pt., N.Y...D8 84
Race, strait, N.Y...E8 84
Raceland, Greenup, Ky., 1,115...B7 94
Raceland, Lafourche, La., 3,666...C6, E5 95
Racepond, Charlton, Ga., 250...F4 87
Rachaya, Leb...F10 31
Rach, Gia, Viet., 24,000...G6 38
Raciborz, Pol., 32,000...C5 26
Racine, Mower, Minn., 180..G6 99
Racine, Newton, Mo., 150...E3 101
Racine, Meigs, Ohio, 499...D6 111
Racine, Boone, W. Va., 600...C3, D6 123
Racine, Racine, Wis., 89,144 (★115,600)...F2, F6 124
Racine, co., Wis., 141,781...F5 124
Racineves, Czech., 626...n17 26
Rackwick, Scot...B5 13
Raco, Chippewa, Mich., 100...B6 98
Rădăuti, Rom., 15,949...B7 22
Radcliff, Hardin, Ky., 3,384.C4 94
Radcliff, Vinton, Ohio, 200..C5 111
Radcliffe, Hardin, Iowa, 615...B4 92
Råde, Nor...p28 25
Radeberg, Ger., 16,300...B8 17
Radebeul, Ger., 40,200...B8 17
Radersburg, Broadwater, Mont., 80...D5 102
Radford (Independent City), Va., 9,371...D2 121
Radiant Valley, Prince Georges, Md., 1,500...*C4 85
Radisson, Sask., Can., 515...E2 70
Radisson, Sawyer, Wis., 179...C2 124
Radium, Stafford, Kans., 64.D5 93
Radium, Marshall, Minn., 40...B2 99
Radium Hot Springs, B.C., Can., 306...D9 68
Radium Springs, Dona Ana, N. Mex., 75...E3 107
Radley, Crawford, Kans., 235...E9 93
Radnice, Czech., 2,067...D8 17
Radnor, Delaware, Pa., 1,000...*A10 114
Radnor, co., Wales, 18,431...B4 12
Radnor, forest, Wales...D5 12
Radom, Pol., 137,500...C6 26
Radomir, Bul., 5,778...D6 22
Radomsko, Pol., 27,000...C5 26
Radomyshl, Sov. Un., 25,000...F7 27
Radoviš, Yugo., 6,195...E6 22
Radstadt, Aus., 3,311...E6 16
Radville, Sask., Can., 1,067..H3 70
Radway, Alta., Can., 183...B4 69
Radzionkow, Pol., 24,000...g9 26
Radzymin, Pol., 4,356...B6, k14 26
Radzyn., Pol., 4,694...C7 26
Rae, N.W. Ter., Can., 522...D9 66
Rae, strait, N.W. Ter., Can...C14 66
Rae Bareli, India, 29,940...D8 40
Raeford, Hoke, N.C., 3,058..C4 109
Raesfeld, Ger., 3,600...B1 17
Raeville, Boone, Nebr., 80...C7 103
Rafaela, Arg., 23,665...A4 54
Rafah, Gaza Area, 2,000...C6 32
Rafai, Cen. Afr. Rep...D4 46
Raft, riv., Idaho...G5 89
Raft River, mts., Utah...B2 119
Rag, mtn., Tenn...D10 117
Raga, Sud...D2 47
Ragan, Harlan, Nebr., 90...D6 103
Raga Tsangpo, riv., China...C11 40
Ragay, Phil., 1,956...p14 35
Ragay, gulf, Phil...p14 35
Ragged, isl., Maine...E4 96
Ragged, lake, Maine...C3 96
Ragged, pt., Md...C5 85
Ragged Top, mtn., Wyo...D7 125
Raggon, isl., S.C...G1 115
Ragland, St. Clair, Ala., 1,166...B3 78
Raglesville, Daviess, Ind., 45...G4 91
Ragley, Beauregard, La., 25.D2 95
Rago, Kingman, Kans., 60...E5 93
Ragsdale, Knox, Ind., 210...G3 91
Ragunda, Swe., 202...F7 25
Ragusa, It., 48,000 (58,500▲)...F5 21
Rahab el Berdi, Sud...C1 47
Rahden, Ger., 3,500...F2 24
Rahimyar, Khan, Pak., 14,919...C3 40
Rahway, Union, N.J., 27,699...B4, k7 106
Rahway, riv., N.J...k7 106
Raichur, India, 63,329...E6 39
Raiford, Union, Fla., 300...B4 86
Raigarh, India, 36,933...G9 40
Railroad, val., Nev...E6 104
Rainbow, Alsk., 20...g17 79
Rainbow, Hartford, Conn., 300...B6 84
Rainbow, Cascade, Mont., 50...C5 102
Rainbow, falls, Tenn...D10 117
Rainbow, lake, Maine...C3 96
Rainbow, pt., Fla...D4 86
Rainbow, res., Wis...C4 124
Rainbow Bridge, nat. mon., Utah...F5 119
Rainbow City, Etowah, Ala., 1,625...*A3 78
Rainbow Springs, Macon, N.C...D2 109
Rainelle, Greenbrier, W. Va., 649...D4 123
Raines, Crisp, Ga., 35...E3 87
Raines, Shelby, Tenn., (part of Whitehaven)...B1, E8 117
Rainier, Columbia, Oreg., 1,152...A4 113
Rainier, Thurston, Wash., 245...C3 122
Rainier, mtn., Wash...C4 122
Rains, co., Tex., 2,993...C5 118
Rainsboro, Highland, Ohio, 190...C4 111
Rainsville, DeKalb, Ala., 398...A4 78
Rainy, lake, Ont., Can., Minn..B5 99
Rainy, mtn., Okla...C3 112
Rainy, riv., Ont., Can., Minn..B4 99
Rainy River, Ont., Can., 1,168...G14 66
Rainy River, dist., Ont., Can., 26,531...o16 72
Raipur, India, 139,792...D7 39, G8 40
Ra'īs, Sau. Ar...E7 43
Raisin, Victoria, Tex., 50...E4 118
Raismes, Fr., 18,737...D3 15
Raivavae, isl., Fr. Polynesia..*H13 7
Raja, cape, Indon...K2 38
Rajahmundry, India, 130,002...E7 39, I8 40
Rajapalaiyam, India, 71,203...*G6 40
Rajasthan, state, India, 20,155,602...C5 39
Rajkot, India, 193,498 (★194,145)...D5 39, F3 40
Rajmahal, India, 6,801...E11 40
Rajnandgaon, India, 44,678...G8 40
Rajpipla, India, 21,426...G4 40
Rakaia, riv., N.Z...O13 51
Rake, Winnebago, Iowa, 328.A4 92
Rakhov, Sov. Un...A7 22
Rakkestad, Nor., 1,613...p29 25
Rakovnik, Czech., 12,000...C2 26
Rakvere, Sov. Un., 25,000...B6 27
Raleigh, Newf., Can., 307...C4 75
Raleigh, Levy, Fla., 150...C4 86
Raleigh, Saline, Ill., 225...F5 90
Raleigh, Rush, Ind., 120...E7 91
Raleigh, Smith, Miss., 614...C4 100
Raleigh, Wake, N.C., 93,931 (★130,200)...B5 109
Raleigh, Grant, N. Dak., 125.C4 110
Raleigh, Shelby, Tenn., 6,000...B2, E8 117
Raleigh, Raleigh, W. Va., 750...D7 123
Raleigh, co., W. Va., 77,826...D3 123
Raleigh, bay, N.C...C7 109
Rallaovia (Wells), Maur...B2 45
Ralls, Crosby, Tex., 2,229...C2 117
Ralls, co., Mo., 8,078...B6 101
Rally Hill, Maury, Tenn...B5 117
Ralph, Tuscaloosa, Ala., 150.B2 78
Ralph, Dickinson, Mich., 40.B3 98
Ralph, Harding, S. Dak., 20.B2 116
Ralphton, Somerset, Pa., 150.F3 114
Ralston, Carroll and Greene, Iowa, 143...B3 92
Ralston, Douglas, Nebr., 2,977...D3 103
Ralston, Pawnee, Okla., 411.A5 112
Ralston, Lycoming, Pa., 400.D8 114
Ralston, Weakley, Tenn., 50.A3 117
Ralston, Park, Wyo., 20...A4 125
Ralston, val., Nev...E4 104
Ram, riv., Alta., Can...C3 69
Ram, head, Vir. Is...f16 65
Rama, Sask., Can., 288...F4 70
Rama, Nic., 600...D5 62
Ramadan, see Turabah, Sau. Ar.
Ramah, El Paso, Colo., 109..B6 83
Ramah, McKinley, N. Mex., 230...B1 107
Rām Allāh, Jordan, 17,145...C7, h11 32
Ramapo, mts., N.J...A4 106
Ramapo, riv., N.J...A4 106
Ramat Gan, Isr., 95,800.B6, g10 32
Ramat Hakovesh, Isr...g10 32
Ramat Hasharon, Isr., 2,650...g10 32
Ramban, India, 1,490...B6 39
Rambervillers, Fr., 7,042...C7 14
Rambi, isl., Fiji Is... 52
Rambouillet, Fr., 11,382...C4 14
Ramea, Newf., Can., 970...E3 75
Ramea, is., Newf., Can...E3 75
Ramenskoye, Sov. Un., 10,000...D12, n18 27
Ramer, Montgomery, Ala., 500...C3 78
Ramer, McNairy, Tenn., 358...B3 117
Rameshk, Iran, 10,000...H9 41
Ramganga, riv., India...D7 40
Rāmhormoz, Iran, 17,267...F4 41
Ramhurst, Murray, Ga., 100...B2 87
Ramirez, Duval, Tex., 50...F3 118
Ramiriquí, Col., 881...B3 60
Ramirito, Jim Hogg, Tex., 5.F3 118
Ramle, Isr., 23,900...C6, h10 32
Ramnäs, Swe., 1,614...t34 25
Râmnicu-Sărat, Rom., 19,095...C8 22
Râmnicu-Vâlcea, Rom., 18,984...C7 22
Ramona, San Diego, Calif., 2,449...F5 82
Ramona, Marion, Kans., 132...D6 93
Ramona, Washington, Okla., 546...A6 112
Ramona, Lake, S. Dak., 247..C8 116
Ramor, lake, Ire...D4 11
Rampart, Alsk., 49...B9 79
Rampart, range, Colo...B5 83
Rampur, India, 135,407...C6 39, C7 40
Rampur, India, 5,000...G9 40
Rampur-Baolia, Pak., 56,885...E12 40
Ramsay, Gogebic, Mich., 1,158...A5 98
Ramsay, Silver Bow, Mont., 125...D4 102
Ramsayville, Ont., Can., 40.h12 72
Ramseur, Randolph, N.C., 1,258...B4 109
Ramsey, Eng., 5,697...B7 12
Ramsey, Fayette, Ill., 815...D4 90
Ramsey, I. of Man, 3,764...F4 13
Ramsey, Bergen, N.J., 9,527..A4 106
Ramsey, co., Minn., 422,525.E5 99
Ramsey, co., N. Dak., 13,443...A7 110
Ramsgate, Eng., 37,700...C9 12
Ramshorn, mtn., Wyo...B3 125
Ramshorn, peak, Mont...E5 102
Ramu, riv., N. Gui...k11 50
Ranaghat, India, 35,266 (★55,100▲)...F12 40
Ranburne, Cleburne, Ala., 317...B4 78
Rancagua, Chile, 53,300...A2 50
Ranchcreek, Powder River, Mont...E11 102
Rancherie, rock, Oreg...C6 113
Ranches of Taos, Taos, N. Mex., 1,600...A4 107
Ranchester, Sheridan, Wyo., 235...A5 125
Ranchi, India, 122,416 (★140,253)...D8 39, F10 40
Ranchito, Taos, N. Mex., 500...A4 107
Rancho Cordova, Sacramento, Calif., 7,429...*C3 82
Ranco, Chile...C2 54
Ranco, lake, Chile...C2 54
Rancocas, Burlington, N.J., 500...C3 106
Rancocas, creek, N.J...C3 106
Rancocas Woods, Burlington, N.J., 1,200...D3 106
Rand, Jackson, Colo., 12...A4 83
Rand, Kanawha, W. Va., 3,500...C6, C3 123
Randado, Jim Hogg, Tex., 300...F3 118
Randalia, Fayette, Iowa, 114.B6 92
Randall, Hamilton, Iowa, 201...B4 92
Randall, Jewell, Kans., 201..C5 93
Randall, Morrison, Minn., 516...D4 99
Randall, Burnett, Wis...C1 124
Randall, co., Tex., 33,913...B2 118
Randallstown, Baltimore, Md., 2,000...B4 85
Randers, Den., 42,238 (★54,780)...B4 24
Randers, co., Den., 170,802..B4 24
Randfontein, S. Afr., 41,499...*C4 49
Randle, Lewis, Wash., 100...C4 122
Randleman, Randolph, N.C., 2,232...B4 109
Randlett, Cotton, Okla., 356...C3 112
Randlett, Uintah, Utah, 10..C6 119
Randolph, Pinal, Ariz., 400..E4 80
Randolph, Fremont, Iowa, 257...D2 92
Randolph, Kennebec, Maine, 1,724...D3 96
Randolph, Norfolk, Mass., 18,900...B5, h11 97
Randolph, Pontotoc, Miss., 131...A4 100
Randolph, Cedar, Nebr., 1,063...B8 103
Randolph, Coos, N.H., 25 (140▲)...B4 105
Randolph, Cattaraugus, N.Y., 1,414...C2 108
Randolph, Portage, Ohio, 450...A6 111
Randolph, Tipton, Tenn...B2 117
Randolph, Rich, Utah, 537..B4 119
Randolph, Orange, Vt., 2,122 (3,414▲)...D3 120
Randolph, Columbia and Dodge, Wis., 1,507...E4 124
Randolph, co., Ala., 19,477..B4 78
Randolph, co., Ark., 12,520..A4 81
Randolph, co., Ga., 11,078...E2 87
Randolph, co., Ill., 29,988...E4 90
Randolph, co., Ind., 28,434..D7 91
Randolph, co., Mo., 22,014...B5 101
Randolph, co., N.C., 61,497..B4 109
Randolph, co., W. Va., 26,349...C5 123
Randolph Center, Orange, Vt., 140...D3 120
Randolph Field, Bexar, Tex...B4, E3 118
Randolph Hills, Montgomery, Md., 2,000...*B3 85
Random, isl., Newf., Can...D5 75
Random Lake, Sheboygan, Wis., 858...E6 124
Randow, riv., Ger...B7 16
Randsburg, Kern, Calif., 300...E5 82
Randwick, Austl., 110,700..*F8 51
Ranfurly, Alta., Can., 147...C5 69
Rangaunu, bay, N.Z...K14 51
Range, Grant, Oreg...C8 113
Rangely, Rio Blanco, Colo., 1,464...A2 83
Rangeley, Franklin, Maine, 749 (1,087▲)...D2 96
Rangeley, lake, Maine...D2 96
Ranger, Gordon, Ga., 161...B2 87
Ranger, Cherokee, N.C...D2 109
Ranger, Eastland, Tex., 3,313...C3 118
Ranger, Lincoln, W.Va., 300.C2 123
Ranger, lake, N. Mex...D6 107
Rangiora, N.Z., 3,540...O14 51
Rangitata, riv., N.Z...O13 51
Rangoon, Bur., 821,800...D2 38, E10 39
Rangpur, Pak., 31,759...E12 40
Rang-St. Sauveur, N.B., Can., 593...B4 74
Rangsum (Tungpu), China..E4 34
Ranier, Koochiching, Minn., 262...B5 99
Raniganj, India, 30,113...D8 39
Rankin, Vermilion, Ill., 761..C6 90
Rankin, Allegheny, Pa., 5,164...F2 114
Rankin, Cocke, Tenn...C10 117
Rankin, Upton, Tex., 1,214..D2 118
Rankin, co., Miss., 34,322...C4 100
Ranlo, Gaston, N.C., 2,000..*B2 109
Rannes, Austl., 63...B8 51
Rannoch, lake, Scot...D4 13
Rann of Kutch, swamp, India...D4 39
Ranshaw, Northumberland, Pa., 1,078...*E9 114
Ransom, La Salle, Ill., 415...B5 90
Ransom, Ness, Kans., 387...D4 103
Ransom, Lackawanna, Pa., 150...A8 114
Ransom, co., N. Dak., 8,078..C8 110
Ransomville, Niagara, N.Y., 950...B2 108
Ranson, Jefferson, W. Va., 1,974...B7 123
Rantauparapat, Indon...K3 38
Rantoul, Champaign, Ill., 22,116...C5 90
Rantoul, Franklin, Kans., 157...D8 93
Rantowles, Charleston, S.C...F2 115
Ranum, Den., 1,153...B3 24
Raon [-l'Etape], Fr., 7,606...A2 18
Raoui, sand dunes, Alg...D4 44
Rapallo, It., 22,700...B2 21
Rapa, isl., Fr. Polynesia...*H13 7
Rapa Nui (Easter), isl., Pac. O...H15 7
Rapelje, Stillwater, Mont., 100...E7 102
Raphine, Rockbridge, Va., 300...D3 121
Raphoe, Ire., 818...C4 11
Rapid, riv., Minn...B4 99
Rapidan, Culpeper, Va., 220...C4 121
Rapid City, Man., Can., 467.D1 71
Rapid City, Kalkaska, Mich., 300...D5 98
Rapid City, Pennington, S. Dak., 42,399...C2 116
Rapides, Rapides, La...C3 95
Rapides, par., La., 111,351..C3 95
Rapid River, Delta, Mich., 550...C3 98
Rappahannock, co., Va., 5,368...C4 121
Rappahannock, riv., Va...C5 121
Rappahannock Academy, Caroline, Va., 5...C5 121
Rapperswil, Switz., 7,585...B6 19
Raquette, lake, N.Y...B6 108
Raquette, riv., N.Y...f10 108
Raquette Lake, Hamilton, N.Y., 200...B6 108
Rarden, Scioto, Ohio, 250...D4 111
Rardin, Coles, Ill., 130...D5 90

Raritan, Henderson, Ill., 182....C3 90
Raritan, Somerset, N.J., 6,137....B3 106
Raritan, bay, N.J.....C4 106
Raritan, riv., N.J.....C4 106
Rarous (Well), Niger....C6 45
Rasa, pt., Arg....C4 54
Ras al Bidiya, cape, Sau. Ar.....H4 41
Ra's al Khaymah, Tr. Coast, 5,000....C2 39
Ra's al 'Ushsh, Eg., U.A.R....C4 32
Ra's an Naqb, Jordan, 1,000....E7 32
Rasar, Blount, Tenn....D10 117
Ras at Tannura, cape, Sau. Ar.....H5 41
Ra's at Tīn, cape, Libya....F4 31
Rasbokil, Swe....t35 25
Ras Dashan, mtn., Eth....C4 47
Raseiniai, Sov. Un., 6,181....A7 26
Ras el Ain, Syr....D13 31
Ras el Hadd, cape, Om....D2 39
Ras el Milh, cape, Libya....F5 31
Ras en Naqura, cape, Leb....A6 32
Rashad, Sud., 1,683....C3 47
Rashid, see Rosetta, Eg., U.A.R.
Rashkov, Sov. Un....B9 22
Rasht, Iran, 109,491....C4 41
Raška, Yugo., 2,290....D5 22
Raska, riv., Yugo....D5 22
Ras Madraka, cape, Mus. & Om....E2 39
Raso, cape, Arg....C3 54
Raso, cape, Braz....B5 59
Raspberry, peak, Ark....C1 81
Rasskazovo, Sov. Un., 43,500....E13 27
Rastatt, Ger., 24,100....E3 17
Rastede, Ger., 14,200....A8 15
Raszyn, Pol....m13 26
Rat, is., Alsk....E3 79
Rat, lake, Man., Can....A2 71
Rat, lake, Man., Can....B4 71
Rat, riv., Man., Can....A2 71
Rat, riv., Man., Can....E3 71
Ratangarh, India, 26,631....E5 40
Rat Buri, Thai., 19,092....F3 38
Ratcliff, Logan, Ark., 147....B2 81
Ratekau, Ger., 8,900....E4 24
Rathbun, Appanoose, Iowa, 203....D5 92
Rathdrum, Kootenai, Idaho, 710....B2 89
Rathdrum, Ire., 1,128....E5 11
Rathdrum, prairie, Idaho....D8 122
Rathenow, Ger., 28,600....B6 16
Rathfriland, N. Ire., 1,558....C5 11
Rathkeale, Ire., 1,459....E3 11
Rathlin, isl., N. Ire....B5 11
Rathlin, sound, N. Ire....B5 11
Rath Luire, Ire., 1,956....E3 11
Rathmelton, Ire., 808....B4 11
Rathmore, Ire., 417....E2 11
Rathmullen, Ire., 491....B4 11
Rathnew, Ire., 861....D5 11
Rathowen, Ire., 119....D4 11
Rathwell, Man., Can., 197....E2 71
Ratibor, see Raciborz, Pol.
Ratingen, Ger., 36,000....B1 17
Ratlam, India, 87,472....F5 40
Ratnagiri, India, 31,091....I4 40
Ratner, Sask., Can....D3 70
Raton, Colfax, N. Mex., 8,146....A5 107
Raton, mesa, Colo....D6 83
Raton, pass, Colo....D6 83
Ratónes, is., P.R....D5 61
Rattan, Pushmataha, Okla., 300....C6 112
Rattenberg, Aus., 745....E5 16
Rattlesnake, creek, Kans....E4 93
Rattlesnake, creek, Ohio....C4 111
Rattlesnake, creek, Wash....C6 122
Rattlesnake, flat, Wash....C7 122
Rattlesnake, hills, Wash....C6 122
Rattlesnake, mtn., Conn....C5 84
Rattlesnake, range, Wyo....C5 125
Rattling Brook, Newf., Can., 162....D3 75
Rattray, head, Scot....C7 13
Rättvik, Swe., 1,950....G6 25
Ratz, mtn., Alsk., B.C., Can....E6 66
Ratzeburg, Ger., 11,400....E4 24
Ratzeburger, lake, Ger....E4 24
Raub, Benton, Ind., 100....C3 91
Raub, McLean, N. Dak., 15....B3 110
Rauch, Arg., 5,274....B5 54
Rauch, Koochiching, Minn....C5 99
Raue, isl., Nor....p28 25
Raufarhofn, Ice., 483....m24 25
Rauland, Nor....H3 25
Rauma, Fin., 21,700....G9 25
Raus, Bedford, Tenn., 50....B5 117
Rausu, Dake, peak, Jap....D12 37
Rautalampi, Fin., 1,300....F12 25
Rauville, Codington, S. Dak....B8 116
Ravalli, Lake, Mont., 100....C2 102
Ravalli, co., Mont., 12,341....D2 102
Ravanna, Mercer, Mo., 127....A4 101
Rāvar, Iran, 5,074....F8 41
Rava-Russkaya, Sov. Un., 10,000....F4 27
Raven, Tazewell, Va., 900....B3 121
Raven, headland, Ire....B1 12
Ravena, Albany, N.Y., 2,410....C7 108
Ravendale, Lassen, Calif., 40....B3 82
Ravenden, Lawrence, Ark., 231....A4 81
Ravenden Springs, Randolph, Ark., 126....A4 81
Ravenel, Charleston, S.C., 527....F1 115
Ravenglass, Eng., 417....F5 13
Ravenna, It., 57,300 (122,300▲)....E8 19, B4 21
Ravenna, Estill, Ky., 921....C6 94
Ravenna, Muskegon, Mich., 801....E5 98
Ravenna, Buffalo, Nebr., 1,417....C7 103
Ravenna, Portage, Ohio, 10,918....A6 111
Raven Park, basin, Colo....A2 83
Raven Rock, Hunterdon, N.J., 50....C2 106
Ravensburg, Ger., 31,300....E4 16
Ravenscrag, Sask., Can., 40....H1 70
Ravenscroft, White, Tenn., 140....D8 117
Ravensdale, King, Wash., 250....D2 122
Ravensthorpe, Austl., 116....F3 51
Ravenswood, Marion, Ind., 618....H8 91
Ravenswood, Jackson, W. Va., 3,410....C3 123
Ravensworth, Ont., Can....B5 72
Ravenwood, Nodaway, Mo., 282....A3 101
Ravi, riv., Pak....B4 40
Ravia, Johnston, Okla., 307....C5 112
Ravinia, Charles Mix., S. Dak., 164....D7 116
Rawalpindi, Pak., 197,370 (*340,175)....B5 39
Rawalpindi Cantonment, Pak., 142,805....*B5 39
Rawa Mazowiecka, Pol., 6,908....C6 26
Rawdon, Que., Can., 2,388....C4 73
Rawhide, creek, Who....C8 125
Rawhide, lake, Ont., Can....B8 98
Rawicz, Pol., 11,600....C4 26
Rawlings, Allegany, Md., 180....D2 85
Rawlings, Brunswick, Va., 50....E5 121
Rawlinna, Austl., 124....F4 51
Rawlins, Carbon, Wyo., 8,968....E5 125
Rawlins, co., Kans., 5,279....C2 93
Rawlins, hills, Wyo....C5 125
Rawson, Arg....C3 54
Rawson, Arg., 2,425....g6 54
Rawson, McKenzie, N. Dak., 28....B2 110
Rawson, Hancock, Ohio, 407....B4 111
Rawsonville, Windham, Vt., 30....E3 120
Ray, Pinal, Ariz., 1,468....D5 80
Ray, Steuben, Ind., 200....A8 91
Ray, Koochiching, Minn., 55....B5 99
Ray, Williams, N. Dak., 1,049....A2 110
Ray, co., Mo., 16,075....B3 101
Ray, cape, Newf., Can....E2 75
Raya, isl., Indon....J1 38
Rayagada, India, 14,537....H9 40
Ray-Aleksandrovka, Sov. Un....q20 27
Raybon, Brantley, Ga., 400....E5 87
Raychikhinsk, Sov. Un., 30,000....B4 34
Ray City, Berrien, Ga., 713....E3 87
Raygorodka, Sov. Un....q22 27
Rayland, Jefferson, Ohio, 694....B2 123
Rayle, Wilkes, Ga., 200....C4 87
Raymilton, Venango, Pa., 50....D2 114
Raymond, Madera, Calif., 300....D4 82
Raymond, Alta., Can., 2,362....E4 69
Raymond, Coweta, Ga., 300....C2 87
Raymond, Bear Lake, Idaho, 35....G7 89
Raymond, Montgomery, Ill., 871....D4 90
Raymond, Rice, Kans., 143....D5 93
Raymond, Cumberland, Maine 300 (732▲)....E4 96
Raymond, Kandiyohi, Minn., 608....E3 99
Raymond, Hinds, Miss., 1,381....C3 100
Raymond, Sheridan, Mont., 30....B12 102
Raymond, Lancaster, Nebr., 223....D9 103
Raymond, Rockingham, N.H., 800 (1,867▲)....D4 105
Raymond, Clark, S. Dak., 168....C8 116
Raymond, Pacific, Wash., 3,301....C2 122
Raymondville, Texas, Mo., 202....D6 101
Raymondville, St. Lawrence, N.Y., 600....f10 108
Raymondville, Willacy, Tex., 9,385....F4 118
Raymore, Sask., Can., 503....F3 70
Raymore, Cass, Mo., 268....C3 101
Rayne, Acadia, La., 8,634....D3 95
Rayner, glacier, Ant....C17 5
Raynesford, Judith Basin, Mont., 50....C6 102
Raynham, Bristol, Mass., 400 (4,150▲)....C5 97
Raynham Center, Bristol, Mass., 200....C5 97
Rayón, Mex., 1,351....B2 63
Rayong, Thai., 10,776....F4 38
Raystown, branch, Pa....F5 114
Raytown, Taliaferro, Ga., 100....C4 87
Raytown, Jackson, Mo., 17,083....E2 101
Rayville, Richland, La., 4,052....B4 95
Rayville, Ray, Mo., 200....B3 101
Razan, Iran, 3,195....D4 41
Razgrad, Bul., 15,023....D8 22
Razlog, Bul., 6,857....E6 22
Razmak, Pak....B4 39
Razorback, mtn., B.C., Can....D5 68
Ré, isl., Fr....D3 14
Rea, Andrew, Mo., 90....A3 101
Rea, lake, Ire....D3 11
Reader, Ouachita, Ark., 86....D2 81
Reader, Wetzel, W. Va., 500....A6, B4 123
Reader, lake, Man., Can....C1 71
Readfield, Kennebec, Maine, 200 (1,029▲)....D3 96
Reading, Eng., 121,500 (*165,000)....C7 12
Reading, Lyon, Kans., 249....D8 93
Reading, Middlesex, Mass., 19,259....A5, f11 97
Reading, Hillsdale, Mich., 1,128....G6 98
Reading, Nobles, Minn., 160....G3 99
Reading, Hamilton, Ohio, 12,832....C3, D2 111
Reading, Berks, Pa., 98,177 (*192,500)....F10 114
Reading, Windsor, Vt., 165 (472▲)....E3 120
Reading Center, Schuyler, N.Y., 175....C4 108
Readington, Hunterdon, N.J., 200....B3 106
Readland, Chicot, Ark., 100....D4 81
Readlyn, Sask., Can., 85....H3 70
Readlyn, Bremer, Iowa, 547....B5 92
Readsboro, Bennington, Vt., 577 (783▲)....F3 120
Readstown, Vernon, Wis., 469....E3 124
Readyville, Cannon, Tenn., 100....B5 117
Reagan, Henderson, Tenn., 150....B3 117
Reagan, co., Tex., 3,782....D2 118
Reagan Wells, Uvalde, Tex., 35....E3 118
Real, co., Tex., 2,079....E3 118
Real, range, Bol....C2 55
Realicó, Arg....B4 54
Realitos, Duval, Tex., 400....F3 118
Ream, Camb., 5,000....G5 38
Ream, McDowell, W. Va., 800....*D3 123
Reamstown, Lancaster, Pa., 950....F9 114
Reardan, Lincoln, Wash., 474....B8 122
Reasnor, Jasper, Iowa, 224....C4 92
Reata, Mex., 208....B4 63
Reaville, Hunterdon, N.J., 100....C3 106
Rebecca, Turner, Ga., 278....E3 87
Rebersburg, Centre, Pa., 500....E7 114
Rebiana (Oasis), Libya....E4 43
Rebiano, sand sea, Libya....E3 43
Reboly, Sov. Un....F14 25
Rebun, isl., Jap....D10 37
Recalde, Arg....B4 54
Recanati, It., 6,288....C4 21
Recherche, arch., Austl....F3 50
Rechitsa, Sov. Un., 33,800....E8 27
Recife, Braz., 788,569 (*1,100,000)....C4, k6 57
Recinto, Chile....B2 54
Recklinghausen, Ger., 129,700....B2 17
Recluse, Campbell, Wyo., 15....A7 125
Recogne, Bel., 746....E5 15
Reconnaissance, mtn., Guam.... 52
Reconquista, Arg., 12,729....E4 55
Recovery, Decatur, Ga....F2 87
Recreo, Arg., 5,463....E2 55
Rector, Clay, Ark., 1,757....A5 81
Red, bay, N. Ire....B5 11
Red, creek, Miss....E4 100
Red, isl., Newf., Can....E4 75
Red, mtn., Ala....B2 78
Red, mtn., Calif....B2 82
Red, mtn., Mont....C4 102
Red, peak, Colo....B4 83
Red, peak, Idaho....E3 89
Red, riv., Man., Can....E3 71
Red, riv., Ky....C6 94
Red, riv., Tenn....A4 117
Red, riv., U.S....D9 77
Red, riv., Viet....B6 38
Red, riv., Wis....D2 124
Red, sea, Afr., Asia....D9 42
Redang, isl., Mala....J5 38
Redange, Lux., 1,693....E5 15
Red Bank, Monmouth, N.J., 12,482....C4 106
Red Bank, Lexington, S.C., 350....D5 115
Red Banks, Marshall, Miss., 250....A4 100
Red Bank-White Oak, Hamilton, Tenn., 10,777....*D8 117
Red Bay, Franklin, Ala., 1,954....A1 78
Red Bay, Newf., Can., 261....C3, h10 75
Redbay, Walton, Fla., 450....G3 86
Redberry, lake, Sask., Can....E2 70
Redbird, Holt, Nebr....B7 103
Redbird, Wagoner, Okla., 310....B6 112
Red Bird, creek, Ky....C6 94
Red Bluff, Tehama, Calif., 7,202....B2 82
Red Bluff, lake, N. Mex., Tex....E6 107
Red Bluff, res., Tex....E2 118
Red Boiling Springs, Macon, Tenn., 597....C8 117
Red Bud, Randolph, Ill., 1,942....E4 90
Redby, Beltrami, Minn., 300....C4 99
Redcar, Eng., 31,460....F7 13
Red Cedar, lake, Wis....C2 124
Red Cedar, riv., Wis....C2 124
Redcliff, Alta., Can., 2,221....D5 69
Redcliff, Eagle, Colo., 586....B4 83
Red Cliff, Bayfield, Wis., 100....B3 124
Red Cliff, Indian res., Wis....B3 124
Red Cloud, Webster, Nebr., 1,525....D7 103
Red Cloud, peak, Colo....D3 83
Red Creek, Wayne, N.Y., 689....B4 108
Red Cross, lake, Man., Can....B5 71
Red Deer, Alta., Can., 19,612....C4, g8 69
Red Deer, lake, Man., Can....C1 71
Red Deer, riv., Alta., Sask., Can....F10 66
Red Deer, riv., Man., Sask., Can....E4 70
Reddell, Evangeline, La., 500....D3 95
Reddick, Marion, Fla., 594....C4 86
Reddick, Kankakee and Livingston, Ill., 205....B5 90
Reddies River, Wilkes, N.C....A2 109
Redding, Jefferson, Ala....E4 78
Redding, Shasta, Calif., 12,773....B2 82
Redding, Fairfield, Conn., 200 (3,359▲)....D3 84
Redding, Ringgold, Iowa, 129....D3 92
Redding Ridge, Fairfield, Conn., 325....D3 84
Redditch, Eng., 34,077....B6 12
Redditt, Ont., Can....E4 71
Rede, riv., Eng....E6 13
Redearth, lake, Sask., Can....D4 70
Redelm, Ziebach, S. Dak., 10....B4 116
Redenção, Braz., 2,631....B3 57
Redeye, riv., Minn....D3 99
Redeyef, Tun....G11 30
Red Feather Lakes, Larimer, Colo., 150....A5 83
Redfield, Jefferson, Ark., 242....C3 81
Redfield, Dallas, Iowa, 966....C3 92
Redfield, Bourbon, Kans., 133....E9 93
Redfield, Oswego, N.Y., 185....B5 108
Redfield, Spink, S. Dak., 2,952....C7 116
Redford, Clinton, N.Y., 300....f11 108
Redford, Presidio, Tex., 300....G2 118
Redford Heights, Wayne, Mich., 71,276....*F7 98
Redgranite, Waushara, Wis., 588....D4 124
Red Gull, bay, Ont., Can....B6 99
Red Hill, Montgomery, Pa., 1,086....*F11 114
Red Hook, Dutchess, N.Y., 1,719....C7 108
Redhouse, Madison, Ky., 250....C5 94
Red House, Charlotte, Va., 50....D4 121
Red House, Putnam, W. Va., 350....C3 123
Redig, Harding, S. Dak., 5....B2 116
Red Indian, lake, Newf., Can....D3 75
Redington, Morrill, Nebr., 15....C2 103
Redington Beach, Pinellas, Fla., 1,368....*E4 86
Redington Shores, Pinellas, Fla., 917....*E4 86
Red Jacket, Mingo, W. Va., 950....D2 123
Red Key, Jay, Ind., 1,746....D7 91
Red Lake, Ont., Can., 2,051....o16 72
Redlake, Beltrami, Minn., 400....C3 99
Red Lake, co., Minn., 5,830....C2 99
Red Lake, Indian res., Minn....B3 99
Red Lake, riv., Minn....C2 99
Red Lake Falls, Red Lake, Minn., 1,520....C2 99
Redlands, San Bernardino, Calif., 26,829....E5, F3 82
Redlawn, Mecklenburg, Va., 40....E4 121
Red Level, Covington, Ala., 327....D3 78
Red Lick, Jefferson, Miss., 250....D3 100
Red Lion, Logan, Colo....A8 83
Red Lion, York, Pa., 5,594....G8 114
Red Lodge, Carbon, Mont., 2,278....E7 102
Redmesa, La Plata, Colo., 100....D2 83
Redmon, Edgar, Ill., 175....D6 90
Redmond, Deschutes, Oreg., 3,340....C5 113
Redmond, Sevier, Utah, 413....E4 119
Redmond, King, Wash., 1,426....C2 122
Red Mountain, San Bernardino, Calif., 350....E5 82
Red Mountain, pass, Colo....D3 83
Rednitz, riv., Ger....D6 17
Red Oak, Fulton, Ga., 800....B5 87
Red Oak, Montgomery, Iowa, 6,421....D2 92
Red Oak, Nash., N.C., 250....A6 109
Red Oak, Latimer, Okla., 453....C6 112
Red Oak, Ellis, Tex., 415....B5 118
Redoak, Charlotte, Va., 50....E4 121
Redon, Fr., 6,444....D3 14
Redonda, isl., B.C., Can....D5 68
Redondela, Sp., 3,261....A1 20
Redondo, Port., 4,103....C2 20
Redondo, King, Wash., 600....D1 122
Redondo Beach, Los Angeles, Calif., 46,986....F4 82
Redore, St Louis, Minn., 170....C6 99
Redoubt, mtn., Alsk....g15 79
Redowl, Meade, S. Dak., 10....C3 116
Red Pass, B.C., Can., 70....C8 68
Red Pheasant, Sask., Can....E1 70
Red Rapids, N.B., Can., 40....C2 74
Red River, co., Tex., 15,682....C5 118
Red River, par., La., 9,978....B2 95
Red River, Hot Springs, Idaho....D3 89
Red River, Taos, N. Mex., 50....A4 107
Red River of the North, riv., Man., Can., Minn., N. Dak....G13 66
Red Rock, Pinal, Ariz., 30....E4 80
Redrock, Newton, Ark....B2 81
Red Rock, B.C., Can., 182....C6 68
Red Rock, Beaverhead, Mont., 25....F4 102
Redrock, Grant, N. Mex., 25....E1 107
Redrock, Noble, Okla., 262....A4 112
Red Rock, Bastrop, Tex., 50....E4 118
Red Rock, pass, Idaho, Mont....E7 89
Red Rock, riv., Mont....F4 102
Redruth, Eng., 9,600 (part of Camborne-Redruth)....D2 12
Red Slate, mtn., Calif....D4 82
Red Springs, Robeson, N.C., 2,767....C4 109
Redstone, B.C., Can....C6 68
Redstone, Pitkin, Colo., 160....B3 171
Redstone, Sheridan, Mont., 70....B12 102
Redstone, Carroll, N.H., 150....B4 105
Redstone Park, Madison, Ala., 1,000....*A2 78
Red Sucker, lake, Man., Can....B5 71
Red Sucker, riv., Man., Can....B5 71
Red Table, mtn., Colo....B4 83
Red Tank, C.Z....k11 62
Redtop, Dallas, Mo., 128....D4 101
Redvale, Montrose, Colo., 10....C2 83
Redvers, Sask., Can., 642....H5 70
Redwater, Alta., Can., 1,135....C4 69
Redwater, riv., Mont....C11 102
Red Wharf, bay, Wales....A3 12
Red Wing, Huerfano, Colo., 15....D5 83
Red Willow, Alta., Can., 95....C4 69
Red Willow, co., Nebr., 12,940....D5 103
Red Willow, creek, Colo....A8 83
Red Willow, creek, Nebr....D5 103
Redwillow, riv., Alta., B.C., Can....B7 68
Redwine, Morgan, Ky., 88....C6 94
Red Wing, Goodhue, Minn., 10,528....F6 99
Redwood, Warren, Miss., 25....C3 100
Redwood, Jefferson, N.Y., 500....A5, f9 108
Redwood, Salt Lake, Utah, 2,600....*C4 119
Redwood, co., Minn., 21,718....F3 99
Redwood, riv., Minn....F3 99
Redwood City, San Mateo, Calif., 46,290....B5, D2 82
Redwood Estates, Santa Clara, Calif., 930....*C6 82
Redwood Falls, Redwood, Minn., 4,285....F3 99
Redwood Valley, Mendocino, Calif., 200....C2 82
Ree, lake, Ire....D4 11
Reed, Greer, Okla., 100....C2 112
Reed, Lane, Oreg....C3 113
Reed, lake, Man., Can....B1 71
Reed, lake, Sask., Can....G2 70
Reed City, Osceola, Mich., 2,184....E5 98
Reeder, Adams, N. Dak., 321....C3 110
Reedley, Fresno, Calif., 5,850....D4 82
Reedpoint, Stillwater, Mont., 100....E7 102
Reeds, peak, N. Mex....D2 107
Reeds Beach, Cape May, N.J., 25....E3 106
Reedsburg, Sauk, Wis., 4,371....E3 124
Reeds Ferry, Hillsboro, N.H., 300....E4 105
Reeds Lake, Kent, Mich., 10,924....F5 98
Reedsport, Douglas, Oreg., 2,998....D3 113
Reeds Spring, Stone, Mo., 327....E4 101
Reedsville, Meigs, Ohio, 300....C6 111
Reedsville, Mifflin, Pa., 950....E6 114
Reedsville, Preston, W. Va., 398....B5 123
Reedsville, Manitowoc, Wis., 830....A6, D6 124
Reedville, Northumberland, Va., 400....D6 121
Reedy, Roane W. Va., 352....C3 123
Reedy, creek, W. Va....C3 123
Reedy, lake, Fla....E5 86
Reedy, riv., S.C....C3 115
Reef, pt., N.Z....K14 51
Reefton, N.Z., 1,787....O13 51
Ree Heights, Hand, S. Dak., 188....C6 116
Reelfoot, lake, Tenn....A2 117
Reelsville, Putnam, Ind., 100....E4 91
Reeman, Newaygo, Mich., 120....E4 98
Reengus, India, 5,549....D5 40
Reere, isl., Bikini.... 52
Rees, Franklin, Ohio, 650....C2 111
Reese, Greenwood, Kans., 400....E7 93
Reese, Tuscola, Mich., 711....E7 98
Reese, riv., Nev....D4 104
Reese Village, Lubbock, Tex., 1,433....*C2 118
Reeseville, Dodge, Wis., 491....E5 124
Reesville, Clinton, Ohio, 250....C4 111
Reeth, Eng., 588....F7 13
Reeves, co., Tex., 17,644....D1 118
Reeves, mtn., Austl....F7 51
Reevesville, Johnson, Ill., 150....F5 90
Reevesville, Dorchester, S.C., 268....E6 115
Reform, Pickens, Ala., 1,241....B1 78
Reform, Choctaw, Miss., 300....B4 100
Refresco, Chile....E2 55
Reftele, Swe., 1,027....A7 24
Refuge Cove, B.C., Can....D5 68
Refugio, Refugio, Tex., 4,944....E4 118
Refugio, co., Tex., 10,975....E4 118
Rega, riv., Pol....B3 26
Regan, Burleigh, N. Dak., 104....B5 110
Regat, riv., Ger....D5 17
Regen, Ger., 5,400....E8 17
Regen, riv., Ger....D6 16
Regensburg, Ger., 125,300....D7 17
Regent, Man., Can....E1 71
Regent, Hettinger, N. Dak., 388....C3 110
Reger, Sullivan, Mo., 77....A4 101
Reggane, Alg....D5 44
Reggio [di] Calabria, It., 126,000 (155,700▲)....E5 21
Reggio nell'Emilia, It., 90,000 (121,200▲)....B3 21, E6 18
Reghin, Rom., 18,091....B7 22
Regina, Sask., Can., 112,141....G3, n8 70
Regina, Phillips, Mont., 5....C9 102
Regina, Sandoval, N. Mex., 50....A2 107
Regina Beach, Sask., Can., 319....G3 70
Region Occidental (Chaco), dept., Par., 54,277....*D3 55
Registan, des., Afg....I22 9
Register, Bulloch, Ga., 300....D5 87
Regla, Cuba, 26,755....h12 64
Rega, Swe....u33 25
Rego, Orange, Ind., 20....H5 91
Reguengos de Monsaraz, Port., 4,873....C2 20
Rehau, Ger., 10,200....C7 17
Rehna, Ger., 3,519....E5 24
Rehoboth, Bristol, Mass., 300 (4,953▲)....C5 97
Rehoboth, McKinley, N. Mex., 100....B1 107
Rehoboth, S.W Afr., 2,954....B3 49
Rehoboth, bay, Del....C7 85
Rehoboth Beach, Sussex, Del., 1,507....C7 85
Rehovot, Isr., 30,400....C6, h10 32
Reï Bouba, Cam....D2 46
Reichenbach, Ger., 29,600....C7 17
Reichenbach, Ger., 370....A4 18
Reid, lake, Sask., Can....G1 70
Reids Grove, Dorchester, Md., 25....C6 85
Reidsville, Tattnall, Ga., 1,229....D4 87
Reidsville, Rockingham, N.C., 14,267....A4 109
Reidville, Spartanburg, S. C., 242....B3 115
Reigate, Eng., 54,900....C7 12
Reiley, East Feliciana, La....D5 95
Reims, Fr., 133,914....C6 14, E4 15
Reina Adelaida, arch., Chile....E2 54
Reinach, Switz., 5,174....B5 19
Reinbeck, Grundy, Iowa, 1,621....B5 92
Reindeer, isl., Man., Can....C3 71
Reindeer, lake, Man., Sask., Can....E12 66
Reindeer, riv., Sask., Can....B4 70
Reinfeld, Ger., 5,700....E4 24
Reinosa, Sp., 10,044....A3 20
Reipetown, White Pine, Nev., 100....D6 104
Reisterstown, Baltimore, Md., 3,300....B4 85
Reit im Winkl, Ger., 2,300....B8 18
Reitz, S. Afr., 4,990....C4 49
Rekarne, Swe., 214....t34 25
Reliance, N.W. Ter., Can....D11 66
Reliance, Lyman, S. Dak., 201....D6 116
Reliance, Polk, Tenn., 400....D9 117
Reliance, Sweetwater, Wyo., 300....D3 125
Relizane, Alg., 27,120....B5 45
Rêmada, Tun., 1,866....C7 44
Remagen, Ger., 7,200....C2 17
Remanso, Braz., 5,125....C2 57
Rembert, Sumter, S.C., 400....C6 115
Rembertow, Pol., 22,000....B6, k14 26
Rembrandt, Buena Vista, Iowa, 265....B2 92
Remecó, Arg....B4 54
Remedios, Cuba, 10,602....D4 64
Remedios, Pan., 1,125....F7 62
Remer, Cass, Minn., 492....C5 99
Remerton, Lowndes, Ga., 571....F3 87
Remington, Jasper, Ind., 1,207....C3 91
Remington, Fauquier, Va., 288....C5 121
Remiremont, Fr., 9,350....C7 14
Remlap, Blount, Ala., 115....B3 78
Remmel, dam, Ark....D6 81
Remmel, mtn., Wash....A5 121
Rems, riv., Ger....E4 17
Remscheid, Ger., 128,700....B2 17
Remsen, Plymouth, Iowa, 1,338....B2 92
Remsen, Oneida, N.Y., 567....B5 108
Remus, Mecosta, Mich., 600....E5 98
Renaix, see Ronse, Bel.
Renault, Alg., 2,113....F7 30
Renault, Monroe, Ill., 200....E4 90
Rencona, San Miguel, N. Mex., 5....B4 107
Rencontre East, Newf., Can., 293....E4 75
Rendsburg, Ger., 35,700....A4 16
Rendville, Perry, Ohio, 197....C5 111
Renens, Switz., 10,698....C2 19
Renews, Newf., Can., 567....E5 75
Renforth, N.B., Can., 527....D4 74
Renfrew, Ont., Can., 8,935....B8 72
Renfrew, Greenville, S.C., 200....B2 115
Renfrew, co., Ont., Can., 89,635....B7 72
Renfrew, co., Scot., 338,815....E4 13
Renfrow, Grant, Okla., 38....A4 112
Rengo, Chile, 9,115....A2 54
Reni, Sov. Un....C9 22
Renick, Randolph, Mo., 190....B5 101
Renick (Falling Springs), Greenbrier, W. Va., 265....D4 123
Renk, Sud....C3 47
Renmark, Austl....G3 51
Renner, Minnehaha, S. Dak., 100....D9 116
Renner, Collin, Tex., 212....A5 118
Rennerod, Ger., 1,900....C3 17
Rennert, Robeson, N.C., 194....C4 109
Rennes, Fr., 151,948....C3 14
Rennick, bay, Ant....C29 5
Rennie, Man., Can., 135....E4 71
Reno, Bond, Ill., 100....E4 90
Reno, Leavenworth, Kans., 30....B8 93
Reno, Washoe, Nev., 51,470 (*81,500)....D2 104
Reno, Venango, Pa., 600....D2 114
Reno, co., Kans., 59,055....E5 93
Reno, lake, Minn....E3 99
Reno, riv., It....B3 21
Renohill, Johnson, Wyo....B6 125
Renous, N.B., Can., 350....C4 74
Renous, riv., N.B., Can....C3 74
Renovo, Clinton, Pa., 3,316....D6 114
Renown, Sask., Can....F3 70
Rensselaer, Jasper, Ind., 4,740....C3 91
Rensselaer, Rensselaer, N.Y., 10,506....C7 108
Rensselaer, co., N.Y., 142,585....C7 108
Rensselaer Falls, St. Lawrence, N.Y., 375....f9 108
Rensselaerville, Albany, N.Y., 300....C6 108
Rentiesville, McIntosh, Okla., 122....B6 112
Renton, King, Wash., 18,453....B3, D2 122
Rentz, Laurens, Ga., 307....D4 87
Renuss, riv., Switz....C6 19
Renville, Renville, Minn., 1,373....F3 99
Renville, co., Minn., 23,249....F3 99
Renville, co., N. Dak., 4,698....A4 110
Renwick, Humboldt, Iowa, 477....B4 92
Repentigny, Que., Can., 9,139....*D4 73
Repton, Conecuh, Ala., 314....D2 78
Republic, Republic, Kans., 333....C6 93
Republic, Marquette, Mich., 950....B3 98
Republic, Greene, Mo., 1,519....D4 101
Republic, Seneca, Ohio, 729....A4 111
Republic, Fayette, Pa., 1,921....G2 114
Republic, Ferry, Wash., 1,064....A7 122
Republic, co., Kans., 9,768....C6 93
Republican, riv., U.S....C7 76
Republican City, Harlan, Nebr., 189....D6 103
Repulse Bay, N.W. Ter., Can., 116....C15 66
Requa, Del Norte, Calif., 150....B1 82
Requena, Sp., 8,228....C5 20
Rerik, Ger., 4,132....D5 24
Reşadiye, Tur., 2,400....D6 23
Rescue, Isle of Wight, Va., 325....B6, D6 121
Reserve, Sask., Can., 202....E4 70
Reserve, Brown, Kans., 138....C8 93
Reserve, St. John the Baptist, La., 5,297....B6 95
Reserve, Sheridan, Mont., 175....B12 102
Reserve, Catron, N. Mex., 550....D1 107
Reserve, Sawyer, Wis., 140....C2 124
Reservoir, pond, Mass....h11 97
Reservoir 2 (Sudbury res.), Mass....g10 97
Reservoir 1 (Sudbury res.), Mass....g10 97
Reservoir 3 (Sudbury res.), Mass....g10 97
Reshef, Isr....g10 32

Resina, It., 46,600........*D5 21
Resistencia, Arg., 80,000.....E4 55
Reşita, Rom., 46,100 (108,500▲)..........C5 22
Resko, Pol., 1,314..........B3 26
Resolute, N.W. Ter., Can., 153..........B13 66, n32 67
Resolution, isl., N.W. Ter., Can..........D20 67
Resthaven, mtn., Alta., Can.....C1 69
Restigouche, co., N.B., Can., 40,973..........B2 74
Restigouche, riv., N.B., Can.....B2 74
Reston, Man., Can., 529.....E1 71
Reszel, Pol., 5,693.........A6 26
Retalhuleu, Guat., 9,304....C2 62
Retamito, Arg..........A3 54
Rethel, Fr., 7,359..........C6 14
Rethimni (Rhethymnon), prov., Grc., 69,943.......*E5 23
Rethimnon, Grc., 14,999.....E5 23
Reti, Pak..........C2 40
Retie, Bel., 5,820..........C5 15
Retlaw, Alta., Can..........D4 69
Retsil, Kitsap, Wash..........D1 122
Retsof, Livingston, N.Y., 275.C3 108
Reubens, Lewis, Idaho, 113..C2 89
Reunion, Fr. dep., Afr., 385,000..........H24 3
Reus, Sp., 41,014..........B6 20
Reutlingen, Ger., 70,800 (*115,000)..........E4 17
Reutte, Aus., 4,285..........E5 16
Reva, Harding, S. Dak., 5...B2 116
Revda, Sov. Un., 57,000.....B5 29
Revel, Fr., 4,288..........F5 14
Revelo, McCreary, Ky., 500.D5 94
Revelstoke, B.C., Can., 3,624..........D8 68
Reventazón, Peru..........C1 58
Revenue, Sask., Can., 101...E1 70
Revere, Suffolk, Mass., 40,080..........g11 97
Revere, Redwood, Minn., 201..........F3 99
Revere, Clark, Mo., 190.....A6 101
Reverie, Tipton, Tenn., 150..B2 117
Revigny, Fr., 3,287..........F5 15
Revillagigedo, isl., Alsk.......n24 79
Revillagigedo, is., Mex.........D2 63
Revillo, Grant, S. Dak., 202..B9 116
Revin, Fr., 11,244..........E4 15
Revivim, Isr..........C6 32
Revloc, Cambria, Pa., 900...F4 114
Revnice, Czech., 3,033......o17 26
Rew, McKean, Pa., 400.....C4 114
Rewa, Fiji Is..........52
Rewa, India, 43,065.........E8 40
Reward, Sask., Can., 94.....E1 70
Rewari, India, 36,994........C6 40
Rewey, Iowa, Wis., 219.....F3 124
Rex., Clayton, Ga., 120.....B5 87
Rex, mtn., Ant..........B5 5
Rexburg, Madison, Idaho, 4,767..........F7 89
Rexford, Thomas, Kans., 245..........C3 93
Rexford, Lincoln, Mont., 450.B1 102
Rexford, Saratoga, N.Y., 125.C7 108
Rexford, Carter, Tenn......C11 117
Rexhame, Plymouth, Mass., 225..........h13 97
Rexroat, Carter, Okla., 60...C4 112
Rexton, N.B., Can., 668.....C5 74
Rexton, Mackinac, Mich., 90..........B5 98
Reyburn, Hot Spring, Ark...D6 81
Reydell, Jefferson, Ark., 50...C4 81
Reydon, Roger Mills, Okla., 183..........B2 112
Reyes, pt., Calif..........C2 82
Reykjavík, Ice., 75,000 (*92,000)..........n22 25
Reynaud, Sask., Can.........E3 70
Reyno, Randolph, Ark., 348..........A5 81
Reynolds, Taylor, Ga., 1,087..........D2 87
Reynolds, Mercer and Rock Island, Ill., 494..........B3 90
Reynolds, White, Ind., 547..C4 91
Reynolds, Reynolds, Mo., 50.D6 101
Reynolds, Jefferson, Nebr., 131..........D8 103
Reynolds, Grand Forks and Trail, N. Dak., 269........B8 110
Reynolds, co., Mo., 5,161...D6 101
Reynoldsburg, Franklin, Ohio, 7,793..........C2, C5 111
Reynolds Corners, Lucas, Ohio,7,000..........A2 111
Reynolds Knob, mtn., W. Va...C5 123
Reynoldsville, Jefferson, Pa., 3,158..........D4 114
Reynosa, Mex., 74,140.......B5 63
Rezāīyeh (Rizaiyeh, Urmia), Iran, 67,605..........C2 41
Rezé, Fr., 28,276..........D3 14
Rezekne, Sov. Un., 13,139...C2 27
Rezeni, Sov. Un..........B9 22
Rhaetian Alps, mts., It., Switz..D7 19
Rhame, Bowman, N. Dak., 254..........C2 110
Rhazale, Syr..........B8 32
Rhea, co., Tenn., 15,863....D9 117
Rheda, Ger., 13,500..........B3 17
Rheden, Neth., 9,200.........B6 15
Rhein, Sask., Can., 367......F4 70
Rhein (Rhine), riv., Ger.......C6 15
Rheine, Ger., 47,000.........A2 17
Rheinfelden, Switz., 5,197....A4 19
Rheinhausen, Ger., 70,900...B1 17
Rheinkamp, Ger., 40,000...*C6 15
Rheinland-Pfalz (Rhineland-Palatinate), state, Ger., 3,417,100..........D2 17
Rheinsberg, Ger., 4,215.....E6 24
Rheinwaldhorn, mtn., Switz....C7 19
Rhenen, Neth., 6,900.........C5 15
Rhethymnon (Rethimni), prov., Grc., 69,943..........*E5 23
Rheydt, Ger., 96,500........C6 15
Rhin, canal, Ger..........F6 24
Rhinau, Fr., 1,681..........A3 18
Rhine, Dodge, Ga., 485......E3 87
Rhine, riv., Eur..........C2 17
Rhinebeck, Dutchess, N.Y., 2,093..........D7 108
Rhineland, Montgomery, Mo., 190..........C6 101
Rhineland, reg., Ger.........C3 16
Rhinelander, Oneida, Wis., 8,790..........C4 124
Rhineland-Palatinate (Rheinland-Pfalz), state, Ger., 3,545,000..........D2 17
Rhinow, Ger., 2,451.........F6 24
Rhode Island, state, U.S., 859,488..........B13 77, 84
Rhode Island, sound, R.I......D11 84
Rhodell, Raleigh, W. Va., 626..........D3 123
Rhodes, Marshall, Iowa, 358..........C4 92
Rhodes, Gladwin, Mich., 75.E6 98
Rhodes, see Rodhos, isl., Grc.
Rhodes, peak, Idaho..........C4 89
Rhodesia, Br. dep., Afr., 4,200,000..........A4 49
Rhodesia and Nyasaland, Fed. of, see Malawi and Zambia, countries, and Rhodesia, Br. dep., Afr.
Rhodes Point, Somerset, Md., 97..........E5 85
Rhodhiss, Caldwell and Burke, N.C., 837..........B2 109
Rhodope (Rodhopi), prov., Grc., 109,201..........*B5 23
Rhodope, mts., Bul..........E7 22
Rhome, Wise, Tex., 412.....A5 118
Rhondda, Wales, 100,100....C4 12
Rhône, dept., Fr., 1,116,664..........*E6 14
Rhône, riv., Fr., Switz........D3 19
Rhyl, Wales, 21,825.........A4 12
Riacho de Santana, Braz., 1,832..........D2 57
Rialto, San Bernardino, Calif., 18,567..........*F3 82
Rialto, Tipton, Tenn........B2 117
Rianjo, Sp., 9,971..........A1 20
Rib, mtn., Wis..........D4 124
Rib, riv., Wis..........C3 124
Ribadavia, Sp., 7,031.......A1 20
Ribadeo, Sp., 9,567.........A2 20
Ribadesella, Sp., 8,228......A3 20
Ribas, do Rio Pardo, Braz., 1,175..........C2 56
Ribatejo, prov., Port., 464,874..........*C1 20
Ribáuè, Moz..........D6 48
Ribble, riv., Eng..........G6 13
Ribe, Den., 7,809..........C2 24
Ribe, co., Den., 178,501.....C2 24
Ribeauvillé, Fr., 4,314......C7 14
Ribeira do Pombal, Braz., 4,254..........D3 57
Ribeirão Bonito, Braz., 1,921..........m7 56
Ribeirão Branco, Braz., 618..n7 56
Ribeirão Prêto, Braz., 116,153..........C3, k8 56
Ribera, It., 18,547..........F4 21
Ribera, San Miguel, N. Mex., 200..........B4 107
Ribérac, Fr., 2,242..........E4 14
Riberalta, Bol., 6,549.......B2 55
Rib Falls, Marathon, Wis., 80..........D4 124
Rib Lake, Taylor, Wis., 794..C3 124
Ribnitz, Ger., 14,800........D6 24
Ribstone, Alta., Can., 68.....C5 69
Ribstone, creek, Alta., Can.....C5 69
Ricany, Czech., 6,376.......o18 26
Riccione, It., 17,400.........B4 21
Rice, San Bernardino, Calif., 50..........E6 82
Rice, Benton, Minn., 387.....E4 99
Rice, Prince Edward, Va., 300..........D4 121
Rice, co., Kans., 13,909.....D5 93
Rice, co., Minn., 38,988.....F5 99
Rice, creek, Minn..........E7 99
Rice, lake, Ont., Can..........C6 72
Rice, lake, Minn..........C3 99
Rice, lake, Minn..........D5 99
Rice, mtn., N.H..........B2 105
Riceboro, Liberty, Ga., 259..E5 87
Rice Lake, Barron, Wis., 7,303..........C2 124
Rices Landing, Greene, Pa., 693..........G1 114
Riceton, Sask., Can., 130....G3 70
Riceville, Mitchell and Howard, Iowa, 898.......A5 92
Riceville, McMinn, Tenn., 500..........D9 117
Riceville, Pittsylvania, Va...E3 121
Rich, Coahoma, Miss., 100..A3 100
Rich, Mor., 2,455..........H4 30
Rich, co., Utah, 1,685.......B4 119
Rich, cape, Ont., Can..........C4 72
Rich, mtn., Ark., Okla..........C1 81
Rich, mtn., Va..........B3 121
Rich, mtn., W. Va..........C5 123
Richard, Sask., Can., 91.....E2 70
Richard City, Marion, Tenn., 224..........D8 117
Richards, Vernon, Mo., 133..D3 101
Richards, Grimes, Tex., 500..D5 118
Richards, lake, Ariz..........C5 80
Richard's Harbour, Newf., Can., 114..........E3 75
Richardson, Sask., Can......G3 70
Richardson, Lawrence, Ky., 125..........C7 94
Richardson, Dallas, Tex., 16,810..........B6 118
Richardson, co., Nebr., 13,903..........D10 103
Richardson, lakes, Maine......D2 96
Richardson, mts., N.W. Ter., Yukon, Can..........C5 66
Richardsons, Tipton, Tenn..B2 117
Richards Spur, Comanche, Okla., 100..........C3 112
Richardsville, N.B., Can., 897..........*A3 74
Richardton, Stark, N. Dak., 792..........C3 110
Richburg, Allegany, N.Y., 493..........C2 108
Richburg, Chester, S.C., 235..........B5 115
Rich Creek, Giles, Va., 748..D2 121
Richdale, Alta., Can.........D5 69
Riche, pt., Newf., Can.........C3 75
Richelieu, co., Que., Can., 38,565..........C4 73
Richer, Man., Can., 339.....E3 71
Richey, Dawson, Mont., 480..........C11 102
Richfield, Tehama, Calif., 250..........C2 82
Richfield, Lincoln, Idaho, 329..........F4 89
Richfield, Morton, Kans., 122..........E2 93
Richfield, Hennepin, Minn., 42,523..........E7 99
Richfield, Sarpy, Nebr., 48..E3 103
Richfield, Stanly, N.C., 293..B3 109
Richfield, Juniata, Pa., 400..E7 114
Richfield, Sevier, Utah, 4,412..........E3 119
Richfield, Washington, Wis., 250..........E1 124
Richfield Springs, Otsego, N.Y., 1,630..........C5 108
Richford, Tioga, N.Y., 250...C4 108
Richford, Franklin, Vt., 1,663 (2,316▲)..........B3 120
Rich Fountain, Osage, Mo., 150..........C6 101
Rich Hill, Bates, Mo.; 1,699..........C3 101
Richibucto, N.B., Can., 1,375.C5 74
Rich Lake, Alta., Can........B5 69
Richland, Pasco, Fla........D4 86
Richland, Stewart, Ga., 1,472..........D2 87
Richland, Spencer, Ind., 100.I3 91
Richland, Keokuk, Iowa, 546.C6 92
Richland, Pulaski, Mo., 1,662.D5 101
Richland, Valley, Mont., 65..........B10 102
Richland, Colfax, Nebr., 139.C8 103
Richland, Atlantic, N.J., 700.D3 106
Richland, Oswego, N.Y., 450.B4 108
Richland, Baker, Oreg., 228.C9 113
Richland, Lebanon, Pa., 1,276..........*F9 114
Richland, Union, S. Dak., 55..........E9 116
Richland, Benton, Wash., 23,548..........C6 122
Richland, co., Ill., 16,299....E5 90
Richland, co., Mont., 10,504.C12 102
Richland, co., N. Dak., 18,824..........C9 110
Richland, co., Ohio, 117,761..........B5 111
Richland, co., S.C., 200,102.D6 115
Richland, co., Wis., 17,684...E3 124
Richland, par., La., 23,824...B4 95
Richland, creek, Ill..........B9 101
Richland, creek, Tenn..........B5 117
Richland Center, Richland, Wis., 4,746..........E3 124
Richland Hills, Tarrant, Tex., 7,804..........*B5 118
Richlands, Onslow, N.C., 1,079..........C6 109
Richlands, Tazewell, Va., 4,963..........B3 121
Richland Springs, San Saba, Tex., 331..........D3 118
Richlandtown, Bucks, Pa., 741..........F11 114
Richlea, Sask., Can., 84.....F1 70
Richmond, Austl., 775.......D7 50
Richmond, Contra Costa, Calif., 71,854..........B5, D2 82
Richmond, Ont., Can., 1,215..........B9 72
Richmond, P.E.I., Can., 167.C6 74
Richmond, Que., Can., 4,072..........D5 73
Richmond, Eng., 5,764.......F7 13
Richmond, Eng., 41,002.....m11 10
Richmond, McHenry, Ill., 855..........A5, D1 90
Richmond, Wayne, Ind., 44,149..........E8 91
Richmond, Washington, Iowa, 150..........C6 92
Richmond, Franklin, Kans., 352..........D8 93
Richmond, Madison, Ky., 12,168..........C5 94
Richmond, Sagadahoc, Maine, 1,412..........D3, D6 96
Richmond, Berkshire, Mass., 150 (890▲)..........B1 97
Richmond, Macomb, Mich., 2,667..........F8 98
Richmond, Stearns, Minn., 751..........E4 99
Richmond, Ray, Mo., 4,604..B4 101
Richmond, Cheshire, N.H., 70 (295▲)..........E2 105
Richmond, N.Z., 3,482......N14 51
Richmond, Jefferson, Ohio, 728..........A1 123
Richmond, Wheeler, Oreg...C7 113
Richmond (Town of), Washington, R.I. (1,986▲)..........*C10 84
Richmond, S. Afr., 2,410....C5 49
Richmond, S. Afr..........D3 49
Richmond, Bedford, Tenn., 25..........B5 117
Richmond, Fort Bend, Tex., 3,668..........E5, F4 118
Richmond, Cache, Utah, 977..........B4 119
Richmond, Chittenden, Vt., 765 (1,303▲)..........C3 120
Richmond (Independent City), Va., 219,958 (*409,100)..........C7, D5 121
Richmond, co., N.S., Can., 11,374..........D9 74
Richmond, co., Que., Can., 42,232..........D5 73
Richmond, co., Ga., 135,601..........C4 87
Richmond (Staten Island), borough and co., N.Y., 221,991 (part of New York City)..........E6 108
Richmond, co., N.C., 39,202..........B4 109
Richmond, co., Va., 6,375...D6 121
Richmond, gulf, Que., Can....E17 67
Richmond Beach, King, Wash., 2,000..........B3 122
Richmond Dale, Ross, Ohio, 800..........C5 111
Richmond Heights, Dade, Fla., 4,311..........F3 86
Richmond Heights, St. Louis, Mo., 15,622..........B8 101
Richmond Heights, Cuyahoga, Ohio, 5,068..........*B2 111
Richmond Heights, Henrico, Va., 100..........C7 121
Richmond Highlands, King, Wash., 6,000..........*B3 122
Richmond Hill, Alamance, N.C., 2,943..........*A4 109
Richmond Hill, Ont., Can., 16,446..........D5, k15 72
Richmondville, Schoharie, N.Y., 743..........C6 108
Richmound, Sask., Can., 215..........G1 70
Rich Mountain, Polk, Ark...C1 81
Rich Square, Northampton, N.C., 1,134..........A6 109
Richthofen, mtn., Colo.........A5 83
Richton, Perry, Miss., 1,089..........D5 100
Richton Park, Cook, Ill., 933..........*B6 90
Richvale, Ont., Can., 3,392..........*D5 72
Richvalley, Wabash, Ind., 150..........C6 91
Richview, Washington, Ill., 255..........E4 90
Richville, Tuscola, Mich., 400..........E7 98
Richville, Otter Tail, Minn., 91..........D3 99
Richville, St. Lawrence, N.Y., 292..........f9 108
Richville, Bennington, Vt., 90..........E2 120
Richwood, Dooly, Ga., 35...D3 87
Richwood, Boone, Ky., 100..A7 94
Richwood, Union, Ohio, 2,137..........B4 111
Richwood, Nicholas, W. Va., 4,110..........C4 123
Richwoods, Washington, Mo., 250..........C7 101
Ricketts, Crawford, Iowa, 133..........B2 92
Rickman, Overton, Tenn., 400..........C8 117
Rickreall, Polk, Oreg., 150..........C1, C3 113
Rico, Dolores, Colo., 353....D2 83
Rico, mts., Colo..........D2 83
Ridder, see Leninogorsk, Sov. Un.
Riddle, Owyhee, Idaho, 20..G2 89
Riddle, Camden, N.C., 150..A7 109
Riddle, Douglas, Oreg., 992..........E3 113
Riddlesburg, Bedford, Pa., 420..........F5 114
Riderwood, Choctaw, Ala., 150..........C1 78
Ridge, Henrico, Va., 20,000.*D5 121
Ridge, mtn., Va..........B2 121
Ridgebury, Fairfield, Conn., 150..........D2 84
Ridgecrest, Kern, Calif., 5,099..........*E5 82
Ridgecrest, Buncombe, N.C., 300..........D4 109
Ridgecrest, King, Wash., 3,000..........*B3 122
Ridgedale, Sask., Can., 191..D3 70
Ridgedale, Taney, Mo., 135..E4 101
Ridgedale, Knox, Tenn., 1,000..........*D10
Ridge Farm, Vermilion, Ill., 894..........D6 90
Ridgefield, Fairfield, Conn., 3,000 (8,165▲)..........D3 84
Ridgefield, Bergen, N.J., 10,788..........h8 106
Ridgefield Park, Bergen, N.J., 12,701..........B4, h8 106
Ridgeland, Madison, Miss., 875..........C3 100
Ridgeland, Jasper, S.C., 1,192..........G6 115
Ridgeland, Dunn., Wis., 288..........C2 124
Ridgeley, Mineral, W. Va., 1,229..........B6 123
Ridgely, Caroline, Md., 886..C6 85
Ridgely, Lake, Tenn., 1,464..A2 117
Ridgeside, Hamilton, Tenn., 448..........E10 117
Ridge Spring, Saluda, S.C., 649..........D4 115
Ridgetop, Davidson and Robertson, Tenn., 372....A5 117
Ridgetown, Ont., Can., 2,603..........E3 72
Ridgeview, Miami, Ind., 439.C5 91
Ridgeview, Dewey, S. Dak., 40..........B5 116
Ridgeview, Boone, W. Va., 425..........C3, D5 123
Ridgeville, Man., Can., 86...E3 71
Ridgeville, McIntosh, Ga., 200..........E5 87
Ridgeville, Randolph, Ind., 950..........D7 91
Ridgeville, Frederick, Md., 200..........B3 85
Ridgeville, Caswell, N.C.....A4 109
Ridgeville, Dorchester, S.C., 611..........E2, E7 115
Ridgeville Corners, Henry, Ohio, 400..........A3 111
Ridgeway, Ont., Can., 1,871..........E5 72
Ridgeway, Winneshiek, Iowa, 267..........A6 92
Ridgeway, Lenawee, Mich., 180..........F7 98
Ridgeway, Harrison, Mo., 470..........A4 101
Ridgeway, Ocean, N.J., 600..C4 106
Ridgeway, Warren, N.C., 250..........A5 109
Ridgeway, Logan and Hardin, Ohio, 448..........B4 111
Ridgeway, Fairfield, S.C., 417..........C6 115
Ridgeway, Henry, Va., 524...E3 121
Ridgeway, Iowa, Wis., 455...F3 124
Ridgeway, branch, N.J.......C4 106
Ridgewood, Will, Ill., 5,586..........*B5 90
Ridgewood, Bergen, N.J., 25,391..........B4 106
Ridgewood Heights, Montgomery, Ohio, 1,500..........*C3 111
Ridgway, Ouray, Colo., 254.C3 83
Ridgway, Gallatin, Ill., 1,055..........F5 90
Ridgway, Carter, Mont....E12 102
Ridgway, Elk, Pa., 6,387....D4 114
Riding, mtn., Man., Can.....D1 71
Riding Mountain, nat. park, Man., Can..........D1 71
Ridley Farms, Delaware, Pa., 1,500..........*G11 114
Ridley Park, Delaware, Pa., 7,387..........B11 114
Ridlonville, Oxford, Maine (part of Mexico)..........D2 96
Ridott, Stephenson, Ill., 221.A4 90
Ridotta Capuzzo, Libya, 1,983..........C4 43
Ried, Aus., 9,471..........D6 16
Riedlingen, Ger., 5,500.....E4 18
Riedland, McCracken, Ky...A2 94
Riegelsville, Hunterdon and Warren, N.J., 200..........B2 106
Riegelsville, Bucks, Pa., 953..B2 106
Riehen, Switz., 18,077.......A4 19
Rienza, riv., It..........C7 18
Rienzi, Alcorn, Miss., 375...A5 100
Riesa, Ger., 36,800..........B8 17
Riesel, McLennan, Tex., 503..........D4 118
Rieth, Umatilla, Oreg., 300..B8 113
Rieti, It., 24,200..........C4 21
Riffe, Lewis, Wash., 250....C3 122
Riffle, Braxton, W. Va., 10..C4 123
Rifle, Garfield, Colo., 2,135..B3 83
Rifle, riv., Mich..........D6 98
Rift Valley, reg., Ken.......A6 48
Riga, Sov. Un., 632,000.....C5 27
Riga, gulf, Sov. Un..........C4 27
Rigaud, Que., Can., 1,990...D3 73
Rigby, Jefferson, Idaho, 2,281..........F7 89
Riggins, Idaho, Idaho, 588..D2 89
Riggisberg, Switz., 1,949....C3 19
Rigi, peak, Switz..........B6 19
Rigili, isl., Eniwetok..........52
Rigo, Pap..........k12 50
Rigolet, Newf., Can., 108..........A2, g10 75
Riihimäki, Fin., 20,200.....G11 25
Riiser-Larsen, pen., Ant......C16 5
Rijeka, Yugo., 100,989......C2 22
Rijssen, Neth., 14,300.......B6 15
Rijswijk, Neth., 43,200.....*B4 15
Rikers, isl., N.Y..........D6 106
Riley, Vigo, Ind., 248........F3 91
Riley, Riley, Kans., 575.....C7 93
Riley, Marion, Ky., 150......C4 94
Riley, co., Kans., 41,914.....C7 93
Riley, mtn., N. Mex..........F2 107
Rillito, Pima, Ariz., 250.....E4 80
Rilly-la-Montagne, Fr., 1,106..........E4 15
Rimatara, isl., Fr. Polynesia..*H12 7
Rimbey, Alta., Can., 1,266...C3 69
Rimbo, Swe., 1,682..........t36 25
Rimersburg, Clarion, Pa., 1,323..........D2 114
Rimini, It., 69,000 (101,800▲)..........B4 21
Rimouski, Que, Can., 17,739..........A9 73
Rimouski, co., Que., Can., 65,295..........A9 73
Rimouski, riv., Que., Can.......A9 73
Rimouski-Est, Que., Can., 1,581..........A9 73
Rimrock, Yavapai, Ariz., 20..........C4 80
Rimrock, lake, Wash..........C4 122
Rinard, Calhoun, Iowa, 99..B3 92
Rinchhen Ling, China......F3 34
Rincon, Effingham, Ga., 1,057..........D5 87
Rincon, Dona Ana, N. Mex., 200..........E2 107
Rincón, P.R., 1,094..........B1 65
Rincón, mun., P.R., 8,706...B2 65
Rinconada, Arg..........D2 65
Rincón de Romos, Mex., 5,856..........k12 63
Rindge, Cheshire, N.H., 100 (941▲)..........E2 105
Rindjani, peak, Indon.........G5 35
Riner, Montgomery, Va., 125..........D2 121
Rineyville, Hardin, Ky., 350..........C3 94
Rīnge, Den., 2,936..........C4 24
Ringelheim, Ger., 2,640.....A5 17
Ringgold, Catoosa, Ga., 1,311..........B1 87
Ringgold, Bienville, La., 953..........B2 95
Ringgold, Washington, Md., 75..........A2 86
Ringgold, McPherson, Nebr., 23..........C5 103
Ringgold, Montague, Tex., 350..........C4 118
Ringgold, Pittsylvania, Va., 150..........E3 121
Ringgold, co., Iowa, 7,910...D3 92
Ringgold, is., Fiji Is..........52
Ringim, Nig..........D6 45
Ringkøbing, Den., 4,869.....B2 24
Ringkøbing, co., Den., 198,389..........B2 24
Ringkøbing, fjord, Den.........C2 24
Ringling, Meagher, Mont., 85..........D6 102
Ringling, Jefferson, Okla., 1,170..........C4 112
Ringoes, Hunterdon, N.J., 600..........C3 106
Ringold, McCurtain, Okla., 50..........C6 112
Ringos Mills, Fleming, Ky., 45..........B6 94
Ringsaker, Nor..........G4 25
Ringsjön, lake, Swe..........C7 24
Ringso, isl., Swe..........u35 25
Ringsted, Den., 9,694.......C5 24
Ringsted, Emmet, Iowa, 559..........A3 92
Ringvassöy, isl., Nor.........C8 25
Ringville, Ire., 313..........E4 11
Ringwood, Passaic, N.J., 4,182..........A4 106
Ringwood, Major, Okla., 232..........A3 112
Riñihue, Chile..........B2 54
Rinteln, Ger., 9,700.........A4 17
Rio, Martin, Fla., 600.......E6 86
Rio, Knox, Ill., 177..........B3 90
Rio, Hampshire, W. Va., 100..........B6 123
Rio, Columbia, Wis., 788.....E4 124
Rio Arriba, co., N. Mex., 24,193..........A2 107
Río Balsas, Mex., 814..D5, o14 63
Riobamba, Ec., 41,700.......B2 58
Rio Blanco, Rio Blanco, Colo., 5..........B3 83
Río Blanco, P.R......C7, g11 65
Rio Blanco, co., Colo., 5,150..........B2 83
Rio Branco, Braz., 17,245....C4 58
Rio Branco, Ur., 2,697......E2 56
Rio Branco, ter., Braz., 17,245..........C5 60
Rio Branco do Sul, Braz., 715..........D3 56
Rio Bravo del Norte, see Rio Grande, riv., U.S., Mex.
Río Bueno, Chile, 6,259.....C2 54
Río Caribe, Ven., 7,188.....A5 60
Rio Chama, riv., N. Mex.....A3 107
Río Chico, Ven., 2,584......A4 60
Rio Claro, Braz., 48,548..........C3, m8 56
Río Colorado, Arg., 3,304...B4 54
Río Cuarto, Arg., 70,000....A4 54
Rio de Janeiro, Braz., 3,307,163 (*4,700,000).C4, h6 56
Rio de Janeiro, state, Braz., 3,402,728..........C4, h6 56
Río de Jesús, Pan., 1,086....G7 62
Rio Dell, Humboldt, Calif., 3,222..........B1 82
Río de Oro, Col., 1,679.....B3 60
Río Gallegos, Arg., 5,880..........E3, h12 54
Rio Grande, Arg..........h12 54
Rio Grande, Braz., 83,189...E2 56
Rio Grande, Mex., 8,208.....C4 63
Rio Grande, Cape May, N.J., 950..........E3 106
Río Grande, Nic., 173.......D6 62
Rio Grande, Gallia, Ohio, 333..........D3 111
Río Grande, P.R., 2,763.....B7 65
Rio Grande, co., Colo., 11,160..........D4 83
Río Grande, mun., P.R., 17,233..........B7, f11 65
Rio Grande, res., Colo..........D3 83
Rio Grande (Rio Bravo del Norte), riv., U.S., Mex....B4 63, E7 76
Rio Grande City, Starr, Tex., 5,835..........F3 118
Rio Grande do Norte, state, Braz., 1,157,258..........C3, g6 56
Rio Grande do Sul, state, Braz., 5,448,823..........E2 56
Rio Grande Estates, Valencia, N. Mex., 220..........*C3 107
Ríohacha, Col., 5,953.......A3 60
Río Hato, Pan., 2,725........F7 62
Río Hondo, Mex., 1,718......h9 63
Rio Hondo, Cameron, Tex., 1,344..........F4 118
Rio Hondo, riv., N. Mex......D4 107
Rioja, Peru, 3,694..........C2 58
Río Jueyes, P.R..........C5 75
Rio Linda, Sacramento, Calif., 6,000..........*A6 82
Rio Lucio, Taos, N. Mex., 300..........*A4 107
Riom, Fr., 14,418..........E5 14
Rio Maior, Port., 3,055......C1 20
Río Martin, Mor., 3,725.....G4 30
Río Mulato, Bol., 381........C2 55
Rio Muni, reg., Equat. Gui., 195,000..........E1 46
Rion, Fairfield, S.C., 500....C5 115
Riondel, B.C., Can., 681.....E9 68
Rio Negro, Braz., 10,225....D3 56
Río Negro, dept., Ur., 192,595..........*E1 56
Río Negro, prov., Arg., 41,400..........C3 54
Rionero in Vulture, It., 14,378..........D5 21
Rio Pardo, Braz., 14,412....D2 56
Rio Pardo de Minas, Braz., 1,169..........E2 57
Río Penasco, riv., N. Mex.....E5 107
Río Piedras, P.R. (part of San Juan), 65,406..........B6 65
Rio Pomba, Braz., 6,083.....g6 56
Río Primero, Arg..........A4 54
Rio Puerco, riv., N. Mex......B3 107
Rio Salado, riv., N. Mex......C2 107
Río Seco, Chile..........D1 55
Ríosucio (Caldas dept.), Col., 7,363..........B2 60
Ríosucio (Choco dept.), Col., 847..........B2 60
Río Tercero, Arg., 10,683....A4 54
Río Verde, Braz., 11,268.....B2 56
Río Verde (Ríoverde), Mex., 14,294..........m13 63
Rio Vista, Solano, Calif., 2,616..........B3, C3 82
Ripley, Riverside, Calif., 5...F6 82
Ripley, Ont., Can., 464.....C3 72
Ripley, Eng., 17,601.........A6 12
Ripley, Brown, Ill., 167.....C3 90
Ripley, Somerset, Maine, 125 (317▲)..........D3 96
Ripley, Tippah, Miss., 2,668..........A5 100
Ripley, Chautauqua, N.Y., 1,247..........C1 108
Ripley, Brown, Ohio, 2,174..D4 111
Ripley, Payne, Okla., 263...A5 112
Ripley, Lauderdale, Tenn., 3,782..........B2 117
Ripley, Jackson, W. Va., 2,756..........C3 123
Ripley, co., Ind., 20,641.....F7 91
Ripley, co., Mo., 9,096......E7 101
Riplinger, Clark, Wis., 100..D3 124
Ripogenus, lake, Maine.......C3 96
Ripoll, Sp., 9,034..........A7 20
Ripon, San Joaquin, Calif., 1,894..........B6 82
Ripon, Que., Can., 576......D2 73
Ripon, Eng., 10,490.........C6 10
Ripon, Fond du Lac, Wis., 6,163..........E5 124
Rippey, Greene, Iowa, 331..C3 92
Ripple, mtn., B.C., Can......A8 122
Ripples, N.B., Can., 233.....D3 74
Rippowam, riv., Conn., N.Y....A5 106
Ripton, Addison, Vt., 70 (131▲)..........D2 120
Ririe, Bonneville and Jefferson, Idaho, 560..........F7 89
Risco, New Madrid, Mo., 502..........E8 101
Rishiri, isl., Jap..........D10 37
Rishon le-Zion, Isr., 27,998..........C6, h10 32
Rising City, Butler, Nebr., 308..........C8 103
Rising Star, Eastland, Tex., 997..........C3 118
Rising Sun, Ohio, Ind., 2,230..........G8 91
Risingsun, Polk, Iowa, 50...A7 92
Rising Sun., Cecil, Md., 824.A5 86
Risingsun, Wood, Ohio, 815.A4 111
Risle, riv., Fr..........C4 14
Rison, Cleveland, Ark., 889..D3 81
Risör, Nor., 3,100..........H3 25
Ritcher, upland, Ant..........B12 5
Ritchey, Newton, Mo., 128..E3 101
Ritchie, co., W. Va., 10,877..B3 123
Ritidian, pt., Guam..........52
Ritter, Grant, Oreg., 15.....C7 113
Ritter, mtn., Calif..........D4 82
Rittman, Wayne, Ohio, 5,410..........B6 111
Ritzville, Adams, Wash., 2,173..........B7 122
Riva, It., 6,839..........B3 21
Rivadavia, Arg., 5,643.......A3 54
Rivadavia, Arg., 4,925......E4 54
Rivadavia, Arg..........D3 55
Rivadavia, Chile..........E1 55
Rivanna, riv., Va..........D4 121
Rivas, Nic., 8,700..........E5 62
Rive-de-Gier, Fr., 16,565....E6 14
River, Huntington, Ind., 75..C6 91
Rivera, Arg., 2,569.........B4 54
Rivera, Ur., 36,700.........E1 56
Rivera, dept., Ur., 68,700...*E1 56

RIVE-ROIG 95X

Riverbank, Stanislaus, Calif., 2,786 D3 82
River Bourgeois, N.S., Can., 432 D9 74
River Cess, Lib E3 45
Riverdale, Fresno, Calif., 1,012 D4 82
Riverdale, Clayton, Ga., 1,045 *C2 87
Riverdale, Cook, Ill., 12,008 F3 90
Riverdale, Sumner, Kans., 60 E6 93
Riverdale, Prince Georges, Md., 4,389 C2, C4 85
Riverdale, Gratiot, Mich., 380 E6 98
Riverdale, Buffalo, Nebr., 144 D6 103
Riverdale, Morris, N.J., 2,596 B4 106
Riverdale, McLean, N. Dak., 1,055 B4 110
Riverdale, Multnomah, Oreg., 1,500 *B4 113
Riverdale, Weber, Utah, 1,848 B3 119
Riverdale Heights, Prince Georges, Md., 1,800 *C4 85
River Edge, Bergen, N.J., 13,264 h8 106
River Falls, Covington, Ala., 401 D3 78
River Falls, Pierce and St. Croix, Wis., 4,857 D1 124
River Falls, dam, Ala D3 78
River Forest, Cook, Ill., 12,695 F2 90
Rivergaro, It., 4,810 E5 18
River Grove, Cook, Ill., 8,464 E2 90
Riverhead, Suffolk, N.Y., 6,700 n16 108
River Hebert, N.S., Can., 1,382 D5 74
River Heights, Cache, Utah, 880 B4 119
River Hills, Milwaukee, Wis., 1,257 E2 124
Riverhurst, Sask., Can., 281 G2 70
Riverina, reg., Austl G5 51
River John, N.S., Can., 397 D6 74
River Jordan, B.C., Can., 217 h11 68
Riverland Terrace, Charleston, S.C., 2,400 *F2 115
River Oaks, Tarrant, Tex., 8,444 *C4 118
River of Ponds, Newf., Can., 228 C3 75
River Pines, Middlesex, Mass., 1,500 *A5 97
River Plaza, Monmouth, Pa., 4,500 *C4 114
Riverport, N.S., Can., 369 E5 74
River Rouge, Wayne, Mich., 18,147 A7, F7 98
Rivers, Man., Can., 1,574 D1 71
Rivers, inlet, B.C., Can D4 68
Riversdale, N.S., Can., 58 D6 74
Riverside, St. Clair, Ala., 159 B3 78
Riverside, Riverside, Calif., 84,332 F3, F5 82
Riverside, Ont., Can., 18,089 E2 72
Riverside, Douglas, Colo., 180 B5 83
Riverside, Fairfield, Conn. (part of Greenwich) E2 84
Riverside, Colquitt, Ga., 329 E3 87
Riverside, Cook, Ill., 9,750 F2 90
Riverside, Washington, Iowa, 656 C6 92
Riverside, Charles, Md., 100 D3 85
Riverside, Franklin, Mass., 350 *A2 97
Riverside, Platte, Mo., 1,315 B3 101
Riverside, Burlington, N.J., 8,474 C3 106
Riverside, Steuben, N.Y., 1,030 *C3 108
Riverside, Malheur, Oreg., 5 D8 113
Riverside, Northumberland, Pa., 1,580 E8 114
Riverside, Providence, R.I. (part of East Providence) B11 84
Riverside, Greenville, S.C., 1,200 *B3 100
Riverside, Box Elder, Utah, 150 B3 119
Riverside, Okanogan, Wash., 201 A6 122
Riverside, Carbon, Wyo., 87 D6 125
Riverside, Co., Calif., 306,191 F5 82
Riverside, res., Colo A6 83
Riverside Park, Burlington, N.J., 1,200 *C3 106
River Sioux, Harrison, Iowa, 150 C2 92
Riverton, Colbert, Ala., 50 A1 78
Riverton, Man., Can., 808 D3 71
Riverton, Litchfield, Conn., 250 B4 84
Riverton, Sangamon, Ill., 1,591 D4 90
Riverton, Fremont, Iowa, 399 D2 92
Riverton, Cherokee, Kans., 250 E9 93
Riverton, Wicomico, Md., 100 C6 85
Riverton, Crow Wing, Minn., 121 D4 99
Riverton, Franklin, Nebr., 303 D7 103
Riverton, Coos, N.H., 200 B3 105
Riverton, Burlington, N.J., 3,324 C3 106
Riverton, N.Z., 1,225 Q12 51
Riverton, Coos, Oreg., 250 D2 113
Riverton, Salt Lake, Utah, 1,993 C4 119
Riverton, Washington, Vt., 175 C3 120
Riverton, Warren, Va., 250 C4 121
Riverton, Pendleton, W. Va., 150 C5 123
Riverton, Fremont, Wyo., 6,845 B4 125
Riverton Heights, King, Wash., 19,000 *B3 122
River Vale, Bergen, N.J., 5,616 *A5 106
River View, Chambers, Ala., 1,171 C4 78
Riverview, Kern, Calif., 7,000 *E4 82
Riverview, Duval, Fla., 4,000 B6 86
Riverview, Hillsborough, Fla., 1,000 E2 86
Riverview, Wayne, Mich., 7,237 A7 98
Riverview, St. Louis, Mo., 3,706 *C7 101
Riverview (Pasco West), Franklin, Wash., 2,894 *C6 122
Riverview, dam, Ala., Ga C4 88
Riverview Heights, N.B., Can., 2,666 *C5 74
Riverville, Amherst, Va., 50 D4 121
Rives, Dunklin, Mo., 134 E7 101
Rives, Obion, Tenn., 291 A2 117
Rivesaltes, Fr., 5,910 F5 14
Rives Junction, Jackson, Mich., 300 F6 98
Rivesville, Marion, W. Va., 1,191 A7, B4 123
Riviera, Kleberg, Tex., 600 F4 118
Riviera Beach, Palm Beach, Fla., 13,046 F6 86
Riviera Beach, Ocean, N.J., 2,000 C4 106
Rivière-à-Claude, Que., Can., 253 *k13 73
Rivière-à-Pierre, Que., Can., 812 C5 73
Rivière-Bleue, Que., Can., 1,540 B8 73
Rivière du Lievre, riv., Que., Can D2 73
Rivière-du-Loup, Que., Can., 10,835 B8 73
Rivière-du-Loup, co., Que., Can., 40,239 B8 73
Rivière du Loup, riv., Que., Can B8 73
Rivière-du-Milieu, Que., Can B5 73
Rivière-du-Moulin, Que., Can., 4,386 A6 73
Riviere la Madeleine, Que., Can., 289 *k13 73
Rivière-Ouelle, Que., Can., 89 B7 73
Rivière-Raquette, Que., Can., 119 C7 73
Rivière-Trois-Pistoles, Que., Can., 357 A8 73
Rivière Verte, N.B., Can., 918 B1 74
Rivière Verte, Que., Can B8 73
Rivulet, Mineral, Mont., 25 D2 102
Rixford, McKean, Pa., 650 C4 114
Riyadh (Ar Riyāḍ) Sau. Ar., 169,185 I3 41
Rizaiyeh (Rezāīyeh, Urmia), Iran, 67,605 C2 41
Rizal, prov., Phil., 1,463,500 *C6 35
Rize, Tur., 22,300 B13 31
Rizokarpaso, Cyp., 3,667 E10 31
Rjukan, Nor., 5,677 H3 25
Roachdale, Putnam, Ind., 927 E4 91
Roads, Jackson, Ohio, 130 C5 111
Roadstown, Cumberland, N.J., 150 E2 106
Road Town, Vir. Is. (Br.), 891 m14 64, f16 65
Roan, cliffs, Colo., Utah B1 83
Roan, mtn., Tenn C11 117
Roan, plat., Colo., Utah D5 119
Roane, co., Tenn., 39,133 D9 117
Roane, co., W. Va., 15,720 C3 123
Roan High Knob, peak, Tenn C11 117
Roan Mountain, Carter, Tenn., 800 C11 117
Roann, Wabash, Ind., 478 C6 91
Roanne, Fr., 51,723 (★71,000) D5 14
Roanoke, Randolph, Ala., 5,288 B4 78
Roanoke, Woodford, Ill., 1,821 C4 90
Roanoke, Huntington, Ind., 935 C7 91
Roanoke, Jefferson Davis, La., 600 D3 95
Roanoke, Denton, Tex., 585 A5 118
Roanoke (Independent City), Va., 97,110 (★160,400) D3 121
Roanoke, Lewis, W. Va., 100 C4 123
Roanoke, co., Va., 61,693 D2 121
Roanoke, isl., N.C B8 109
Roanoke, pt., N.Y F6 84
Roanoke, riv., N.C., Va E4 121
Roanoke Rapids, Halifax, N.C., 13,320 A6 109
Roanoke Rapids Lake, res., N.C A6 109
Roaring, fork, Colo B4 83
Roaring Branch, Lycoming, Pa., 250 C8 114
Roaring Creek, Columbia, Pa E9 114
Roaring Spring, Blair, Pa., 2,937 F5 114
Roaring Springs, Motley, Tex., 398 C2 118
Roaringwater, bay, Ire F2 11
Roark, Leslie, Ky., 500 C6 94
Roatán, Hond., 1,094 B4 62
Roba, Macon, Ala., 50 C4 78
Robards, Henderson, Ky., 375 C2 94
Robāṭ-e Khān, Iran, 10,000 E8 41
Robb, Alta., Can., 271 C2 69
Robbin, Kittson, Minn., 70 B1 99
Robbins, Cook, Ill., 7,511 F3 90
Robbins, Moore, N.C., 1,294 B4 109
Robbins, Scott, Tenn., 550 C9 117
Robbins, pt., Md B5 85
Robbinsdale, Hennepin, Minn., 16,381 E5, E6 99
Robbinston, Washington, Maine, 250 (476▲) C5 96
Robbinsville, Mercer, N.J., 300 C3 106
Robbinsville, Graham, N.C., 587 D2 109
Robbs, Pope, Ill., 100 F5 90
Robe, riv., Ire D2 11
Robeline, Natchitoches, La., 308 C2 95
Roberdel, Richmond, N.C., 379 C4 109
Robersonville, Martin, N.C., 1,684 B6 109
Robert, Tangipahoa, La., 150 A7, D5 95
Robert, cape, Ont., Can A2 72
Roberta, Crawford, Ga., 714 D2 87
Robert Brown, cape, N.W. Ter., Can C16 67
Robert English, coast, Ant B5 5
Robert Lee, Coke, Tex., 990 D2 118
Roberts, Jefferson, Idaho, 422 F6 89
Roberts, Ford, Ill., 504 C5 90
Roberts, Newton, Miss., 25 C4 100
Roberts, Carbon, Mont., 300 E7 102
Roberts, St. Croix, Wis., 308 D1 124
Roberts, co., S. Dak., 13,190 B8 116
Roberts, co., Tex., 1,075 B2 118
Roberts, peak, B.C., Can C7 68
Roberts, pt., Wash A2 122
Robert's Arm, Newf., Can., 750 D4 75
Robert Scott, glacier, Ant A32 5
Roberts Creek, mtn., Nev D5 104
Robertsdale, Baldwin, Ala., 1,474 E2 78
Robertsdale, Huntingdon, Pa., 800 F3 114
Robertson, S. Afr., 8,166 D3 49
Robertson, Uinta, Wyo., 15 D2 125
Robertson, co., Ky., 2,443 B5 94
Robertson, co., Tenn., 27,335 A5 117
Robertson, co., Tex., 16,157 D4 118
Robertson, bay, Ant B29 5
Robertson, lake, Que., Can C2 75
Robertsonville, Que., Can., 1,156 C6 73
Robertsport, Lib E2 45
Robertstown, White, Ga., 400 B3 87
Robertsville, Litchfield, Conn., 150 B4 84
Robertville, N.B., Can., 680 B4 74
Roberval, Que., Can., 7,739 A5 73
Robeson, co., N.C., 89,102 C4 109
Robesonia, Berks, Pa., 1,579 *F9 114
Robinette, Baker, Oreg C9 113
Robin Hood's Bay, Eng F8 13
Robins, Linn, Iowa, 426 B6 92
Robins, Guernsey, Ohio, 250 C6 111
Robins, isl., N.Y F7 84
Robinson, Crawford, Ill., 7,226 D6 90
Robinson, Brown, Kans., 317 C8 93
Robinson, Kidder, N. Dak., 155 B6 110
Robinson, Indiana, Pa., 900 F3 114
Robinson, McLennan, Tex., 2,111 *D4 118
Robinson, fork, W. Va A6 123
Robinson, fork, W. Va C7 123
Robinson, mtn., Wash A5 122
Robinsons, Aroostook, Maine, 125 B5 96
Robinsons, Newf., Can., 322 D2 75
Robinsonville, Tunica, Miss., 115 A3 100
Robinvale, Austl., 194 G4 51
Robinwood, Jefferson, Ala., 1,000 *B3 78
Roblin, Man., Can., 1,368 D1 71
Roblin, riv., Man., Can A5 71
Robsart, Sask., Can., 110 H1 70
Robson, B.C., Can., 909 E9 68
Robson, mtn., Alta., B.C., Can F9 66
Robstown, Nueces, Tex., 10,266 F4 118
Roby, Tex., Mo., 100 D5 101
Roby, Fisher, Tex., 913 C2 118
Roca, Lancaster, Nebr., 123 F2 103
Roca, cape, Port f9 20
Rocafuerte, Ec., 2,788 B1 58
Rocafuerte, Peru B2 58
Rocanville, Sask., Can., 496 G5 70
Rocas, is., Braz B4 57
Rocca Massima, It., 1,961 h9 21
Roccastrada, It., 3,109 C3 21
Rocha, Ur., 18,200 E2 56
Rocha, dept., Ur., 53,400 *E2 56
Rochdale, Eng., 86,300 A5 12
Rochdale, Worcester, Mass., 1,300 B4 97
Rochechouart, Fr., 1,936 E4 14
Rochefort, Bel., 4,003 D5 15
Rochefort, Fr., 28,648 E3 14
Roche Harbor, San Juan, Wash., 20 A2 122
Rochelaise Central, P.R C2 65
Rochelle, Wilcox, Ga., 1,235 E3 87
Rochelle, Ogle, Ill., 7,008 B4 90
Rochelle, Grant, La., 175 C3 95
Rochelle, McCulloch, Tex., 300 D3 118
Rochelle Park., Bergen, N.J., 6,119 h8 106
Roche-Percée, Sask., Can., 177 H4 70
Rocheport, Boone, Mo., 375 C5 101
Rochester, Alta., Can., 83 B4 69
Rochester, Eng., 51,600 C8 12
Rochester, Sangamon, Ill., 742 D4 90
Rochester, Fulton, Ind., 4,883 B5 91
Rochester, Cedar, Iowa, 40 C6 92
Rochester, Butler, Ky., 314 C3 94
Rochester, Plymouth, Mass., 300 (1,559▲) C6 97
Rochester, Oakland, Mich., 5,431 F7 98
Rochester, Olmsted, Minn., 40,663 F6 99
Rochester, Strafford, N.H., 15,927 D5 105
Rochester, Monroe, N.Y., 305,739 (★594,500) B3 108
Rochester, Lorain, Ohio, 226 A5 111
Rochester, Beaver, Pa., 5,952 E1 114
Rochester, Haskell, Tex., 625 C3 118
Rochester, Windsor, Vt., 350 (879▲) D3 120
Rochester, Thurston, Wash., 350 C2 122
Rochester, Racine, Wis., 413 F1 124
Rochester, mtn., Vt D3 120
Rochfort Bridge, Alta, Can., 85 C3 69
Rochfort Bridge, Ire., 365 D4 11
Rochikarai, isl., Bikini 52
Rochlitz, Ger., 7,872 B7 17
Rociada, San Miguel, N. Mex., 40 B4 107
Rock, Cowley, Kans., 139 E7 93
Rock, Plymouth, Mass., 350 *C6 97
Rock, Delta, Mich., 475 B3 98
Rock, co., Minn., 11,864 G2 99
Rock, co., Nebr., 2,554 B6 103
Rock, co., Wis., 113,913 F4 124
Rock, creek, Sask., Can H2 70
Rock, creek, Ill B4 90
Rock, creek, Kans B4 93
Rock, creek, Md B3 85
Rock, creek, Nebr E1 103
Rock, creek, Nev C5 104
Rock, creek, Wash D5 122
Rock, creek, Wash E8 122
Rock, creek, Wyo D6 125
Rock, isl., Fla C3 86
Rock, isl., Wis C7 124
Rock, lake, Man., Can E2 71
Rock, lake, Wash B8 122
Rock, mtn., Ala B2 78
Rock, mtn., Va E2 121
Rock, riv., Ill., Wis B4 90, E5 124
Rock riv., Iowa, Minn. A1 92, G2 99
Rock, riv., Wash B8 122
Rockall, isl., Scot D16 4
Rockawalkin, Wicomico, Md D6 85
Rockaway, Morris, N.J., 5,413 B3 106
Rockaway, Tillamook, Oreg., 771 B3 113
Rockaway, beach, N.Y k9 106
Rockaway, inlet, N.Y k9 106
Rockaway Beach, Taney, Mo., 117 E4 101
Rock Bay, B.C., Can., 40 D5 68
Rock Bluff, Liberty, Fla., 200 B2 86
Rockbridge, Greene, Ill., 253 D3 90
Rockbridge, Hocking, Ohio, 400 C5 111
Rockbridge, co., Va., 24,039 D3 121
Rockcastle, co., Ky., 12,334 C5 94
Rockcastle, riv., Ky C5 94
Rockcliffe Park, Ont., Can., 2,084 *B9 72
Rock Creek, B.C., Can., 222 E8 68
Rock Creek, Jefferson, Kans., 100 B7 93
Rock Creek, Ashtabula, Ohio, 673 A7 111
Rock Creek, Gilliam, Oreg B6 113
Rock Creek, Pickett, Tenn C9 117
Rock Creek, butte, Oreg C8 113
Rock Creek Hills, Montgomery, Md., 1,500 *B3 85
Rockdale, Austl., 80,000 *G8 51
Rockdale, Will, Ill., 1,272 B5, F2 90
Rockdale, Dubuque, Iowa, 60 B7 92
Rockdale, Baltimore, Md., 1,500 *B4 85
Rockdale, Maury, Tenn., 40 B4 117
Rockdale, Milam, Tex., 4,481 D4 118
Rockdale, co., Ga., 10,572 C3 87
Rockeagle, Goshen, Wyo D8 125
Rock Eagle, mound, Ga C3 87
Rockefeller, plat., Ant A35 5
Rock Elm, Pierce, Wis., 75 D1 124
Rocker, Silver Bow, Mont., 50 D4 102
Rockerville, Pennington, S. Dak., 20 D2 116
Rockfall, Middlesex, Conn., 500 C6 84
Rock Falls, Whiteside, Ill., 10,261 B4 90
Rock Falls, Cerro Gordo, Iowa, 156 A4 92
Rockfield, Carroll, Ind., 350 C4 91
Rockfield, Warren, Ky., 150 D3 94
Rockfield, Washington, Wis., 200 E1 124
Rockford, Coosa, Ala., 328 C3 78
Rockford, Winnebago, Ill., 126,706 (★191,100) A4 90
Rockford, Floyd, Iowa, 941 A5 92
Rockford, Kent, Mich., 2,074 E5 98
Rockford, Wright and Hennepin, Minn., 533 E5 99
Rockford, Mercer, Ohio, 1,155 B3 111
Rockford, Blount, Tenn., 900 D10, E11 117
Rockford, Spokane, Wash., 369 B8 122
Rockford Bay, Kootenai, Idaho, 25 D8 122
Rockglen, Sask., Can., 492 H3 70
Rock Hall, Kent, Md., 1,073 B5 85
Rockham, Faulk, S. Dak., 197 C10 116
Rockhampton, Austl., 44,800 A8 51
Rockhaven, Sask., Can., 83 E1 70
Rock Hill, St. Louis, Mo., 6,523 *C7 101
Rock Hill, York, S.C., 29,404 B6 115
Rockhill Furnace, Huntingdon, Pa., 566 F6 114
Rockholds, Whitley, Ky., 500 D5 94
Rockingham, Bacon, Ga., 40 E4 87
Rockingham, Ray, Mo., 28 B4 101
Rockingham, Richmond, N.C., 5,512 C4 109
Rockingham, Windham, Vt., 65 (5,704▲) E4 120
Rockingham, co., N.H., 99,029 D4 105
Rockingham, co., N.C., 69,629 A4 109
Rockingham, co., Va., 40,485 C4 121
Rock Island, Que., Can., 1,608 D5 73
Rock Island, Rock Island, Ill., 51,863 B3 90
Rock Island, Douglas, Wash., 260 B5 122
Rock Island, co., Ill., 150,991 B3 90
Rocklake, Towner, N. Dak., 350 A6 110
Rockland, Ont., Can., 3,037 B9 72
Rockland, Power, Idaho, 258 G6 89
Rockland, Knox, Maine, 8,769 D3 96
Rockland, Plymouth, Mass., 13,119 B6, h12 97
Rockland, Ontonagon, Mich., 500 A6 98
Rockland, Sullivan, N.Y., 300 D6 108
Rockland, co., N.Y., 162,029 D6 108
Rockledge, Brevard, Fla., 3,481 D6 86
Rockledge, Laurens, Ga., 100 D4 87
Rockledge, Montgomery, Pa., 2,587 A11 114
Rockleigh, Bergen, N.J., 430 g9 106
Rocklin, Placer, Calif., 1,495 *C3 82
Rockmart, Polk, Ga., 3,938 C1 87
Rock Point, Apache, Ariz., 50 A6 80
Rock Point, Charles, Md., 400 D4 85
Rockport, Hot Spring, Ark., 162 D6 81
Rockport, Mendocino, Calif., 90 C2 82
Rockport, Pike, Ill., 300 D2 90
Rockport, Spencer, Ind., 2,474 I3 91
Rockport, Ohio, Ky., 396 C3 94
Rockport, Knox, Maine, 900 (1,893▲) D3 96
Rockport, Essex, Mass., 3,100 (4,616▲) A6 97
Rockport, Copiah, Miss D3 100
Rock Port, Atchison, Mo., 1,310 A2 101
Rockport, Warren, N.J., 60 B3 106
Rockport, Aransas, Tex., 2,989 E4 118
Rockport, Skagit, Wash., 185 A4 122
Rock Rapids, Lyon, Iowa, 2,780 A1 92
Rock River, Albany, Wyo., 497 D7 125
Rock Run, Cherokee, Ala., 150 A4 78
Rocks, Harford, Md., 150 A5 85
Rock Springs, Rosebud, Mont., 5 D10 102
Rocksprings, Edwards, Tex., 1,182 D2 118
Rock Springs, Sauk., Wis., 463 E4 124
Rock Springs, Sweetwater, Wyo., 10,371 D3 125
Rockstone, Br. Gu A3 59
Rockton, Winnebago, Ill., 1,833 A4 90
Rockton, Clearfield, Pa., 200 D4 114
Rockvale, Fremont, Colo., 413 C5 83
Rockvale, Rutherford, Tenn., 150 B5 117
Rock Valley, Sioux, Iowa, 1,693 A1 92
Rockville, Clarke, Ala D2 78
Rockville, Tolland, Conn., 9,478 B7 84
Rockville, Parke, Ind., 2,756 E3 91
Rockville, Montgomery, Md., 26,090 B3 85
Rockville, Norfolk, Mass., 200 h10 97
Rockville, Stearns, Minn., 357 E4 99
Rockville, Bates, Mo., 355 C3 101
Rockville, Sherman, Nebr., 153 C7 103
Rockville, Malheur, Oreg D9 113
Rockville, Washingto ı, R.I., 250 D9 84
Rockville, Washington, Utah, 125 F2 119
Rockville Centre, Nassau, N.Y., 26,355 n15 108
Rockwall, Rockwall, Tex., 2,166 B6, C4 118
Rockwall, co., Tex., 5,878 C4 118
Rockwell, Cerro Gordo, Iowa, 772 B4 92
Rockwell, Rowan, N.C., 948 B3 109
Rockwell City, Calhoun, Iowa, 2,313 B3 92
Rockwood, Franklin, Ala., 200 A2 78
Rockwood, Ont., Can., 863 D4 72
Rockwood, Randolph, Ill., 98 F4 90
Rockwood, Somerset, Maine, 200 C3 96
Rockwood, Wayne, Mich., 2,026 F7 98
Rockwood, Somerset, Pa., 1,101 G3 114
Rockwood, Roane, Tenn., 5,345 D9 117
Rockwood, Coleman, Tex., 80 D3 118
Rocky, Washita, Okla., 343 B2 112
Rocky, bay, Newf., Can B4 75
Rocky, lake, Man., Can B1 71
Rocky, lake, Maine D5 96
Rocky, mtn., Mont C4 102
Rocky, mts., N.A D8 61
Rocky, pt., N.Y E7 84
Rocky, pt., N.Y F2 84
Rocky, riv., Alta., Can C2 69
Rocky, riv., N.C B3 109
Rocky, riv., Ohio B2 111
Rocky, riv., S.C C2 115
Rocky Bar, Elmore, Idaho, 5 F3 89
Rocky Boy, Hill, Mont., 75 B7 102
Rocky Boys, Indian res., Mont B7 102
Rocky Comfort, McDonald, Mo., 151 E3 101
Rocky Coulee, creek, Wash B6 122
Rockyford, Alta., Can., 288 D4 69
Rocky Ford, Otera, Colo., 4,929 C7 83
Rocky Ford, Screven, Ga., 241 D8 87
Rocky Fork Lake, res., Ohio C4 111
Rocky Gap, Bland, Va., 250 D1 121
Rockygrove, Venango, Pa., 3,168 D2 114
Rocky Harbour, Newf., Can., 620 D3 75
Rocky Hill, Hartford, Conn., 7,404 C6 84
Rocky Hill, Edmonson, Ky., 178 C3 94
Rocky Hill, Somerset, N.J., 528 C3 106
Rockyhock, Chowan, N.C., 100 A7 109
Rocky Knob, hill, Ohio C5 111
Rocky Mount, Edgecombe and Nash, N.C., 32,147 B6 109
Rocky Mount, Franklin, Va., 1,412 D3 121
Rocky Mountain, nat. park, Colo A5 83
Rocky Mountain House, Alta., Can., 2,360 C3 69
Rocky Nook, Plymouth, Mass., 300 *C6 97
Rocky Point, Benewah, Idaho, 30 B2 89
Rocky Point, Suffolk, N.Y., 2,300 F5 84
Rocky Point, Pender, N.C., 416 C6 109
Rocky Point, Kitsap, Wash., 1,000 *B3 122
Rockypoint, Campbell, Wyo., 25 A7 125
Rocky Ripple, Marion, Ind., 967 H8 91
Rocky River, Cuyahoga, Ohio, 18,097 A6, B2 111
Rocky River, Van Buren, Tenn D8 117
Rocky Top, mtn., Oreg C4 113
Rocroi, Fr., 1,542 E4 15
Roda, Wise, Va., 300 B2 121
Rodach, Ger., 4,500 C5 17
Rodanthe, Dare, N.C., 95 B8 109
Rodarte, Taos, N. Mex., 105 *A4 107
Rødby, Den., 3,551 D5 24
Rødby Havn, Den D5 24
Roddickton, Newf., Can., 1,185 C3, h10 75
Rødding, Den., 628 C3 24
Rødding, see Spøttrup, Den.
Roddy, Rhea, Tenn., 60 D9 117
Rødekro, Den., 1,621 C3 24
Rodeo, Contra Costa, Calif., 5,400 *B5 82
Rodeo, Hidalgo, N. Mex., 150 F1 107
Roder, riv., Ger B8 17
Roderfield, McDowell, W. Va., 1,020 *D3 123
Roderick, isl., B.C., Can C3 68
Rodessa, Caddo, La., 700 B1 95
Rodewisch, Ger., 12,800 C7 17
Rodey, Dona Ana, N. Mex., 200 E2 107
Rodez, Fr., 20,924 E5 14
Rodgers Forge, Baltimore, Md., 7,645 *B4 85
Rodhopi (Rhodope), prov., Grc., 109,201 *B5 23
Ródhos, Grc., 27,393 D7 23
Ródhos (Rhodes), isl., Grc D6 23
Roding, Ger., 4,000 D7 17
Roding, riv., Eng k13 10
Rodinga, Austl D5 50
Rodman, Palo Alto, Iowa, 144 A3 92
Rodman, Chester, S.C., 225 B5 115
Rodnei, mts., Rom B7 22
Rodney, Ont., Can., 1,041 E3 72
Rodney, Jefferson, Miss., 110 D2 100
Rodney, pond, Newf., Can D4 75
Rodney Village, Kent, Del., 1,200 B6 85
Rödovre, Den., 39,345 *C6 24
Roduco, Gates, N.C., 200 A7 109
Roe, Monroe, Ark., 100 C4 81
Roebling, Burlington, N.J., 3,600 C3 106
Roebourne, Austl., 136 D2 50
Roebuck, Spartanburg, S.C., 300 B4 115
Roebuck, bay, Austl C3 50
Roebuck Plaza, Jefferson, Ala., 1,000 *B3 78
Roeland Park, Johnson, Kans., 8,949 B9 93
Roer, riv., Ger D6 15
Roermond, Neth., 34,500 C5 15
Roeselare, Bel., 35,645 D3 15
Roessleville, Albany, N.Y., 14,000 *C7 108
Roes Welcome, sound, N.W. Ter., Can D15 66
Roetgen, Ger., 2,900 D6 15
Roff, Pontotoc, Okla., 638 C5 112
Rogachev, Sov. Un., 25,000 E8 27
Rogaland, co., Nor., 239,000 *H1 25
Roganville, Jasper, Tex., 240 D6 118
Rogatica, Yugo., 3,044 D4 22
Roger Mills, co., Okla., 5,090 B2 112
Rogers, Benton, Ark., 7,600 A1 81
Rogers, Windham, Conn., 700 B9 84
Rogers, Hennepin, Minn., 378 E5 99
Rogers, Colfax, Nebr., 162 C9 103
Rogers, Roosevelt, N. Mex., 50 D6 107
Rogers, Barnes, N. Dak., 119 B7 110
Rogers, Columbiana, Ohio, 295 B7 111
Rogers, Bell, Tex., 936 D4 118
Rogers, co., Okla., 20,614 A6 112
Rogers, lake, Conn D7 84
Rogers, mtn., Va B3 121
Rogers, pass, Mont C4 102
Rogers City, Presque Isle, Mich., 4,722 C7 98
Rogers Heights, Prince Georges, Md., 2,000 *C4 85
Rogerson, Twin Falls, Idaho, 100 G4 89
Rogersville, Lauderdale, Ala., 766 A2 78
Rogersville, N.B., Can., 1,040 C4 74
Rogersville, Webster, Mo., 447 D4 101
Rogersville, Greene, Pa., 300 G1 114
Rogersville, Hawkins, Tenn., 3,121 C10 117
Roggen, Weld, Colo., 75 A6 83
Rogozno, Pol., 5,536 B4 26
Rogue, riv., Oreg E2 113
Rogue River, Jackson, Oreg., 520 E3 113
Rogue River, range, Oreg E3 113
Rohnerville, Humboldt, Calif., 1,000 *B1 82
Rohrersville, Washington, Md., 170 B2 85
Rohri, canal, Pak D2 40
Rohtak, India, 88,193 *C6 40
Rohwer, Desha, Ark., 86 D4 81
Roi Et, Thai, 12,119 D5 38
Roi, isl., Kwajalein 52
Roig Central, P.R C7 65

Roissy-en-France, Fr., 1,243 .... g11 14
Roj, isl., Ponape 52
Rojas, Arg., 6,608 .... A4 54
Rojo, cape, P.R. D2 67, n13 64
Rokan, riv., Indon L4 38
Rokeby, Sask., Can F4 70
Rokel, riv., S.L. E2 45
Rokitno, Sov. Un., 9,000 .... F6 27
Rokycany, Czech., 12,000 .... D2 26
Roland, Pulaski, Ark., 550 .... C3, D5 81
Roland, Man., Can., 374 .... E3 71
Roland, Story, Iowa, 748 .... B4 92
Roland, Sequoyah, Okla., 100 .... B7 112
Roland, lake, Md C2 85
Roland Terrace, Anne Arundel, Md., 2,000 .... *B4 85
Rolesville, Wake, N.C., 358 .... B5 109
Rolette, Rolette, N. Dak., 524 .... A6 110
Rolette, co., N. Dak., 10,641 .... A6 110
Rolfe, Pocahontas, Iowa, 819 .... B3 92
Rolfsö, isl., Nor B10 25
Roll, Yuma, Ariz., 100 .... E2 80
Roll, Blackford, Ind., 115 .... C7 91
Roll, Roger Mills, Okla., 25 .... B2 112
Rolla, B.C., Can., 69 .... B7 68
Rolla, Morton, Kans., 464 .... E2 93
Rolla, Phelps, Mo., 11,132 .... D6 101
Rolla, Rolette, N. Dak., 1,398 .... A6 110
Rolleville, Ba. Is., 604 .... D5 64
Rolling, fork, Ark C1 81
Rollingbay, Kitsap, Wash., 600 .... D1 122
Rolling Fork, Sharkey, Miss., 1,619 .... C3 100
Rolling Fork, riv., Ky C4 94
Rolling Hills, Los Angeles, Calif., 1,664 .... *F2 82
Rolling Hills, Sedgwick, Kans., 2,000 .... B5 93
Rolling Hills Estates, Los Angeles, Calif., 3,941 .... *F2 82
Rolling Meadows, Cook., Ill., 10,879 .... *E2 90
Rolling Prairie, LaPorte, Ind., 700 .... A4 91
Rollingstone, Winona, Minn., 392 .... F7 99
Rollingwood, Contra Costa, Calif., 2,200 .... *B5 82
Rollins, Lake, Mont., 165 .... C2 102
Rollinsford, Strafford, N.H., 150 (1,935▲) D5 105
Rollo, Switz., 2,677 .... D1 19
Roma, Austl., 5,571 .... C7 51
Roma, Alta., Can A2 69
Roma, see Rome, It.
Roma, Starr, Tex., 1,496 .... F3 118
Romain, cape, S.C F9 115
Romaine, riv., Que., Can h9 75
Roman, Rom., 27,948 .... B8 22
Romania, country, Eur., 19,025,000 .... F13 8, B7 22
Roman Nose, mtn., Md D1 85
Roman Nose, mtn., Oreg D3 113
Romano, cape, Fla G5 86
Romano, isl., Cuba D5 64
Romanshorn, Switz., 7,755 .... A7 19
Romans [sur-Isère], Fr., 26,377 .... E6 14
Romanzof, cape, Alsk C6 79
Romanzof, mts., Alsk B11 79
Romayor, Liberty, Tex., 200 .... D5 118
Rombauer, Butler, Mo., 150 .... E7 101
Romblon, Phil., 5,000 (16,700▲) *C6 35
Romblon, prov., Phil., 132,000 .... *C6 35
Rome, Floyd, Ga., 32,226 .... B1 87
Rome, Jefferson, Ill., 181 .... E5 90
Rome, Peoria, Ill., 1,347 .... C4 90
Rome, Perry, Ind., 60 .... I4 91
Rome, Henry, Iowa, 117 .... D6 92
Rome (Roma), It., 2,379,000 (*2,540,000) D4, h8 21
Rome, Sunflower, Miss., 279 .... B3 100
Rome, Douglas, Mo., 20 .... E5 101
Rome, Oneida, N.Y., 51,646 .... B5 108
Rome, Franklin, Ohio, 1,500 .... *C5 111
Rome, Bradford, Pa., 274 .... C9 114
Rome City, Noble, Ind., 900 .... B7 91
Romema, Isr. (pop. Incl. in Jerusalem) m14 32
Romeo, Conejos, Colo., 339 .... D4 83
Romeo, Will, Ill., 3,574 .... *B5 90
Romeo, Macomb, Mich., 3,327 .... F7 98
Romero, Hartley, Tex., 20 .... B1 118
Romeville, St. James, La., 150 .... B6 95
Romford, Litchfield, Conn., 150 .... C3 84
Romilly [-sur-Seine], Fr., 15,753 .... C5 14
Rominger, Watauga, N.C., 100 .... A2 109
Romita, Mex., 10,377 .... m13 63
Romney, Tippecanoe, Ind., 350 .... D4 91
Romney, Hampshire, W. Va., 2,203 .... B6 123
Romny, Sov. Un., 35,792 .... F9 27
Rømø, isl., Den C2 24
Romona, Owen, Ind F4 91
Romont, Switz., 2,892 .... C2 19
Romorantin, Fr., 11,777 .... D4 14
Rompin, riv., Mala K5 38
Romsdalsfjord, fjord, Nor F2 25
Romsey, Eng., 6,229 .... D6 12
Romulus, Wayne, Mich., 3,500 .... A7 98
Romulus, Seneca, N.Y., 250 .... C4 108
Romurikku, isl., Bikini 52
Ron, Viet D7 38
Rona, isl., Scot C2 13
Ronald, Kittitas, Wash., 250 .... B4 122
Ronan, Lake, Mont., 1,334 .... C2 102
Roncador, mts., Braz E4 59
Roncador Bank, shoals, Caribbean Sea D7 62
Ronceverte, Greenbrier, W. Va., 1,882 .... D4 123
Ronciglione, It., 7,079 .... C4 21
Ronda, Wilkes, N.C., 510 .... A3 109
Ronda, Sp., 17,703 .... D3 20
Rønde, Den., 1,384 .... B4 24
Rondeau, prov. park, Ont., Can E3 72
Rondo, Lee, Ark., 219 .... C5 81
Rondônia, prov., Braz., 70,783 .... E2 59
Rondout, Lake, Ill., 200 .... E2 90
Roneys Point, Ohio, W. Va., 175 .... B2 123
Rong, isl., Camb G5 38
Rongerik, atoll, Marshall Is F10 7
Ronkiti, Ponape 52
Ronkiti, hbr., Ponape 52
Ronkonkoma, Suffolk, N.Y., 7,700 .... F4 84
Ronkonkoma, lake, N.Y F4 84
Rønne, Den., 13,195 .... C8 24
Ronne, entrance, Ant B5 5
Rönne, riv., Swe B6 24
Rönneburg, Ger., 12,000 .... C3 17
Ronse, Bel., 25,106 .... D3 15
Ronuro, riv., Braz E7 59
Roodepoort-Maraisburg, S. Afr., 95,211 .... *C4 49
Roodeschool, Neth., 748 .... A6 15
Roodhouse, Greene, Ill., 2,352 .... D3 90
Roof, butte, Ariz A6 80
Rooks, co., Kans., 9,734 .... C4 93
Roopville, Carroll, Ga., 203 .... C1 87
Roorkee, India, 33,651 (*45,801) *C6 40
Roosendaal, Neth., 41,400 .... C4 15
Roosevelt, Gila, Ariz., 80 .... C3, D4 80
Roosevelt, White, Ark B4 81
Roosevelt, Roseau, Minn., 145 .... B3 99
Roosevelt, Monmouth, N.J., 764 .... C4 106
Roosevelt, Nassau, N.Y., 13,700 .... G2 84
Roosevelt, Kiowa, Okla., 495 .... C2 112
Roosevelt, Kimble, Tex., 80 .... D3 118
Roosevelt, Duchesne, Utah, 1,812 .... C5 119
Roosevelt, Klickitat, Wash., 60 .... D5 122
Roosevelt, co., Mont., 11,731 .... B11 102
Roosevelt, co., N. Mex., 16,198 .... C6 107
Roosevelt, isl., Ant B32 5
Roosevelt, riv., Braz D2 59
Roosevelt Campobello, international park, N.B., Can E3 74
Roosevelt Park, Muskegon, Mich., 2,578 .... E4 98
Root, riv., Minn G7 99
Root, riv., Wis F2 124
Ropczyce, Pol., 2,822 .... C6 26
Roper, Washington, N.C., 771 .... B7 109
Roper, riv., Austl B5 50
Ropesville, Hockley, Tex., 423 .... C1 118
Roque Bluffs, Washington, Maine, 60 (152▲) D5 96
Roquefort, Fr., 1,465 .... E3 14
Roques, is., Ven A4 60
Roques, pt., Cuba h11 64
Roquetas, Sp., 5,514 .... B6 20
Rora, head, Scot B5 13
Roraima, mtn., Ven B5 60
Rorke, lake, Man., Ont., Can B5 71
Rorketon, Man., Can., 273 .... D2 71
Röros, Nor., 2,643 .... F4 25
Rorschach, Switz., 12,759 (*22,358) B7 19
Rosa, St. Landry, La., 80 .... D3 95
Rosa, mtn., It., Switz D3 18
Rosa, pt., Mex B3 63
Rosaire, Que., Can., 544 .... C7 73
Rosales, Phil., 4,411 .... o13 35
Rosalia, Butler, Kans., 200 .... E7 93
Rosalia, Whitman, Wash., 585 .... B8 122
Rosalie, Thurston, Nebr., 182 .... B9 103
Rosalind, Alta., Can., 197 .... C4 69
Rosamond, Kern, Calif., 700 .... E4 82
Rosamond, Christian, Ill., 250 .... D4 90
Rosa Morada, Mex., 1,664 .... k11 63
Rosario, Arg., 595,000 .... A4 54
Rosário, Braz., 6,999 .... B2 57
Rosario, Mex., 11,608 .... C3 63
Rosario, Par., 6,058 .... D4 55
Rosario, Phil., 3,150 .... p13 35
Rosario, P.R C2 65
Rosario, Ur., 7,600 .... E1 56
Rosario, de la Frontera, Arg., 4,927 .... E3 55
Rosário do Sul, Braz., 15,786 .... E2 56
Rosário Oeste, Braz., 2,607 .... A1 56
Rosario Tala, Arg., 10,584 .... A5 54
Rosati, Phelps, Mo., 200 .... C6 101
Rosboro, Pike, Ark., 75 .... C2 81
Rosburg, Wahkiakum, Wash., 50 .... C2 122
Roscoe, Winnebago, Ill., 556 .... A4 90
Roscoe, Stearns, Minn., 168 .... E4 99
Roscoe, St. Clair, Mo., 125 .... D4 101
Roscoe, Carbon, Mont., 50 .... E7 102
Roscoe, Keith, Nebr., 90 .... C4 103
Roscoe, Sullivan, N.Y., 800 .... D6 108
Roscoe, Washington, Pa., 1,315 .... F2 114
Roscoe, Edmunds, S. Dak., 532 .... B6 116
Roscoe, Nolan, Tex., 1,490 .... C2 118
Roscoe, glacier, Ant C22 5
Roscommon, Ire., 1,600 .... D3 11
Roscommon, Roscommon, Mich., 867 .... D6 98
Roscommon, co., Ire., 59,217 .... D3 11
Roscommon, co., Mich., 7,200 .... D6 98
Roscrea, Ire., 3,372 .... E4 11
Rose, Rock, Nebr., 200 .... B6 103
Rose, Wayne, N.C B5 109
Rose, Mayes, Okla., 45 .... A6 112
Rose, peak, Ariz D6 80
Rose, pt., B.C., Can B2 68
Roseau, Dominica, 10,417 .... o16 64
Roseau, Roseau, Minn., 2,146 .... B3 99
Roseau, co., Minn., 12,154 .... B3 99
Roseau, riv., Man., Can E3 71
Roseau, riv., Minn B2 99
Rosebery, B.C., Can., 52 .... D9 68
Rose-Blanche, Newf., Can., 626 .... E2 75
Roseboro, Sampson, N.C., 1,354 .... C5 109
Rose Bud, White, Ark., 120 .... B3 81
Rosebud, Alta., Can., 99 .... D4 69
Rosebud, Gasconade, Mo., 288 .... C6 101
Rosebud, Rosebud, Mont., 140 .... D10 102
Rosebud, Todd, S. Dak., 600 .... D5 116
Rosebud, Falls, Tex., 1,644 .... D4 118
Rosebud, co., Mont., 6,187 .... D10 102
Rosebud, creek, Mont E10 102
Rosebud, Indian res., S. Dak D5 116
Rosebud, riv., Alta., Can D4 69
Roseburg, Douglas, Oreg., 11,467 .... D3 113
Rosebush, Isabella, Mich., 400 .... E6 98
Rose City, Ogemaw, Mich., 435 .... D6 98
Rose Creek, Mower, Minn., 351 .... G6 99
Rosedale, B.C., Can., 654 .... f14 68
Rosedale, Manatee, Fla., 4,085 .... *E4 86
Rosedale, Parke, Ind., 726 .... E3 91
Rosedale, Bolivar, Miss., 2,339 .... B2 100
Rosedale, Anderson, Tenn., 150 .... C9 117
Rosedale, Pierce, Wash., 30 .... D1 122
Rosedale, Braxton, W. Va., 100 .... C4 123
Rosedale Abbey, Eng F8 13
Rosedale Station, Alta., Can D4 69
Roseglen, McLean, N. Dak., 40 .... B4 110
Rosehearty, Scot., 1,140 .... C6 11
Rose Hill, Jasper, Ill., 117 .... D5 90
Rose Hill, Mahaska, Iowa, 223 .... C5 92
Rose Hill, Butler, Kans., 273 .... E6 93
Rose Hill, Jasper, Miss., 100 .... C4 100
Rose Hill, Duplin, N.C., 1,292 .... C5 109
Rose Hill, Lee, Va., 600 .... B1 121
Roseisle, Man., Can., 66 .... E2 71
Roseland, Sonoma, Calif., 4,510 .... *C2 82
Roseland, Indian River, Fla., 145 .... E6 86
Roseland, St. Joseph, Ind., 971 .... A5 91
Roseland, Tangipahoa, La., 1,254 .... D5 95
Roseland, Adams, Nebr., 163 .... D7 103
Roseland, Essex, N.J., 2,804 .... *B4 106
Roseland, Richland, Ohio, 8,204 .... *B5 111
Roselawn, Newton, Ind., 150 .... B3 91
Roselle, DuPage, Ill., 3,581 .... E2 90
Roselle, Union, N.J., 21,032 .... k7 106
Roselle Park, Union, N.J., 12,546 .... k7 106
Rose Lynn, Alta., Can D5 69
Rosemark, Shelby, Tenn., 250 .... B2 117
Rosemary, Alta., Can., 210 .... D4 69
Rosemead, Los Angeles, Calif., 15,476 .... *F2 82
Rosemère, Que., Can., 6,158 .... p19 73
Rose Mills, Nelson, Va D4 121
Rosemont, Cook, Ill., 978 .... *A6 90
Rosemont, St. Clair, Ill., 4,000 .... *E3 90
Rosemont, Hunterdon, N.J., 100 .... C3 106
Rosemont, Delaware and Montgomery, Pa., 4,000 .... *A10 114
Rosemont, Taylor, W. Va., 500 .... B7 123
Rosemount, Dakota, Minn., 1,068 .... F5 99
Rosenberg, Fort Bend, Tex., 9,698 .... F5 118
Rosendael, Fr., 19,960 .... B5 14
Rosendale, Andrew, Mo., 234 .... A3 101
Rosendale, Ulster, N.Y., 1,033 .... *D6 108
Rosendale, Fond du Lac, Wis., 415 .... E5 124
Rosenfeld, Ont., Can., 78 .... C6 72
Rosenfeld, Man., Can., 316 .... E3 71
Rosenhayn, Cumberland, N.J., 700 .... E2 106
Rosenheim, Ger., 31,600 .... E6 16
Rosepine, Vernon, La., 414 .... D2 95
Rose Prairie, B.C., Can A7 68
Roseray, Sask., Can G1 70
Roseto, Northampton, Pa., 1,630 .... E11 114
Roseton, Orange, N.Y., 156 .... D6 108
Rosetown, Sask., Can., 2,450 .... F2, n7 70
Rosetta, Johnson, Ark B2 81
Rosetta (Rashîd), Eg., U.A.R., 32,800 .... C6 43
Rosetta, Wilkinson, Miss., 129 .... D2 100
Rosetta, riv. mouth, Eg., U.A.R. C2 32
Rose Valley, Sask., Can., 627 .... E4 70
Rosevear, Alta., Can C2 69
Roseville, Placer, Calif., 13,421 .... C3 82
Roseville, Warren, Ill., 1,065 .... C3 90
Roseville, Macomb, Mich., 50,195 .... A8 98
Roseville, Ramsey, Minn., 23,997 .... E7 99
Roseville, Muskingum and Perry, Ohio, 1,749 .... C5 111
Roseville, Stafford, Va., 30 .... C5 121
Rosewood, Humboldt, Calif., 1,100 .... *B1 82
Rosewood, Champaign, Ohio, 275 .... B4 111
Rosewood Heights, Madison, Ill., 4,572 .... *E3 90
Rosharon, Brazoria, Tex., 280 .... G5 118
Rosheim, Fr., 3,004 .... F7 15
Rosh Ha'ayin, Isr., 7,500 .... g10 32
Rosholt, Roberts, S. Dak., 423 .... B9 116
Rosholt, Portage, Wis., 497 .... D4 124
Rosh Pina, Isr., 1,200 .... B7 32
Rosiclare, Hardin, Ill., 1,700 .... F5 90
Rosie, Independence, Ark., 150 .... B4 81
Rosier, Burke, Ga., 30 .... D4 87
Rosières-en-Santerre, Fr., 2,381 .... E2 15
Rosignol, Br. Gu., 1,204 .... A3 59
Rosillo, peak, Tex E1 118
Rosine, Ohio, Ky., 350 .... C3 94
Roșiorii-de-Vede, Rom., 17,320 .... C7 22
Rosita, Custer, Colo., 10 .... C5 83
Roskilde, Den., 31,928 .... C6 24
Roskilde, co., Den., 82,223 .... C6 24
Roslavl, Sov. Un., 36,000 .... E9 27
Roslin, Fentress, Tenn., 50 .... C9 117
Roslyn, Nassau, N.Y., 2,681 .... *F2 84
Roslyn, Montgomery, Pa., 8,500 .... *A11 114
Roslyn, Day, S. Dak., 256 .... B8 116
Roslyn, Kittitas, Wash., 1,283 .... B4 122
Roslyn Estates, Nassau, N.Y., 1,289 .... *F2 84
Roslyn Harbor, Nassau, N.Y., 925 .... *F2 84
Roslyn Heights, Nassau, N.Y., 7,600 .... F2 84
Rosman, Transylvania, N.C., 419 .... D3 109
Rosny-sous-Bois, Fr., 21,001 .... g10 14
Ross, Marin, Calif., 2,551 .... *B5 82
Ross, Winston, Miss., 50 .... B4 100
Ross, N.Z., 503 .... O13 51
Ross, Mountrail, N. Dak., 167 .... A3 110
Ross, Butler, Ohio, 800 .... C2, C3 111
Ross, co., Ohio, 61,215 .... C4 111
Ross, dam, Wash A4 122
Ross, ice shelf, Ant B32 5
Ross, isl., Ant B29 5
Ross, isl., Bur F3 38
Ross, isl., Man., Can B3 71
Ross, lake, Wash A4 122
Ross, mtn., N.Z. N15 51
Ross, sea, Ant B31 5
Rossa, Switz., 155 .... D7 19
Ross and Cromarty, co., Scot., 57,607 .... C4 13
Rossano, It., 12,400 .... E6 21
Rossburg, Darke, Ohio, 295 .... B3 111
Rossburn, Man., Can., 591 .... D1 71
Rosscarbery, Ire., 380 .... F2 11
Rosseau, Ont., Can., 233 .... B5 72
Rosseau, Ontonagon, Mich A6 98
Rossendale, Man., Can E2 71
Rosser, Kaufman, Tex., 300 .... B6 118
Rosses, bay, Ire B3 11
Rosses Point, Ire., 319 .... C3 11
Rossford, Wood, Ohio, 4,406 .... A2, A4 111
Ross Fork, Fergus, Mont., 5 .... C7 102
Rossie, St. Lawrence, N.Y., 125 .... f9 108
Rossignol, lake, N.S., Can E4 74
Rossinière, Switz., 504 .... D3 19
Rossiter, Indiana, Pa., 950 .... E4 114
Rossland, B.C., Can., 4,354 .... E9 68
Rosslare, Ire., 529 .... E5 11
Rosslau, Ger., 16,000 .... B7 17
Rosslea, N. Ire., 203 .... C4 11
Rossmoor, Orange, Calif., 9,000 .... *F2 82
Rossmoyne, Hamilton, Ohio, 2,000 .... *D2 111
Rosso, Maur., 2,300 .... C1 45
Ross-on-Wye, Eng., 5,643 .... C5 12
Rossosh, Sov. Un., 10,000 .... F12 27
Ross River, Yukon, Can., 132 .... D6 66
Rosston, Nevada, Ark., 250 .... D2 81
Rosston, Harper, Okla., 58 .... A2 112
Rossville, Walker, Ga., 4,665 .... B1 87
Rossville, Vermilion, Ill., 1,470 .... C6 90
Rossville, Clinton, Ind., 831 .... D4 85
Rossville, Allamakee, Iowa, 100 .... A6 92
Rossville, Shawnee, Kans., 797 .... C8 93
Rossville, Fayette, Tenn., 183 .... B2 117
Rossville, Atascosa, Tex E3 118
Rossway, N.S., Can., 192 .... E4 74
Rosthern, Sask., Can., 1,264 .... E2 70
Rostock, Ger., 166,500 .... A6 14, D6 24
Rostov, Sov. Un., 29,230 .... C12 27
Rostov [-na-Donu], Sov. Un., 689,000 (*780,000) H12 27
Rosul, pass, Rom C6 22
Roswell, El Paso, Colo. (part of Colorado Springs) C6 83
Roswell, Fulton, Ga., 2,983 .... A5, B2 87
Roswell, Canyon, Idaho, 100 .... F2 89
Roswell, Chaves, N. Mex., 39,593 .... D5 107
Roswell, Miner, S. Dak., 39 .... C8 116
Rota, Sp., 16,856 .... D2 20
Rotan, Fisher, Tex., 2,788 .... C2 118
Rotenburg, Ger., 14,500 .... B4 16
Rotenburg [an der Fulda], Ger., 7,700 .... B4 17
Roth, Bottineau, N. Dak., 25 .... A5 110
Roth, Ger., 10,300 .... D6 17
Rothaar, mts., Ger B3 17
Rothbury, Eng., 1,648 .... E6 13
Rothbury, Oceana, Mich., 200 .... E4 98
Röthenbach, Ger., 9,600 .... D6 17
Röthenbach im Emmental, Switz., 1,368 .... C4 19
Rothenburg [in der Lausitz], Ger., 2,587 .... B9 17
Rothenburg ob der Tauber, Ger., 11,100 .... D5 17
Rothenthurm, Switz., 1,159 .... B6 19
Rother, riv., Eng D8 12
Rotherham, Eng., 86,700 .... A6 12
Rothes, Scot., 1,105 .... B5 13
Rothesay, N.B., Can., 782 .... D4 74
Rothesay, Scot., 7,656 .... E3 13
Rothsay, Wilkin, Minn., 457 .... D2 99
Rothschild, Marathon, Wis., 2,550 .... D4 124
Rothsville, Lancaster, Pa., 900 .... F9 114
Rothville, Chariton, Mo., 138 .... B4 101
Rothwell, N.B., Can., 1,357 .... C3 74
Roto, Austl., 127 .... F5 51
Rotondella, It., 5,643 .... D6 21
Rotorua, N.Z., 22,600 (*29,300) M16 51
Rott, riv., Ger E8 17
Rottenburg, Ger., 10,800 .... E3 17
Rottenmann, Aus., 4,139 .... E7 16
Rotterdam, Neth., 731,500 (*1,010,000) C4 15
Rotterdam, Schenectady, N.Y., 22,000 .... *C6 108
Rotterdam Junction, Schenectady, N.Y., 750 .... C6 108
Rottumeroog, isl., Neth A6 15
Rottweil, Ger., 17,900 .... D4 16
Rotuma, isl., Pac. O G10 7
Roubaix, Fr., 112,856 .... B5 14, D3 15
Roudnice nad Labem, Czech., 8,683 .... n17 26
Rouen, Fr., 120,857 (*325,000) C4 14
Rouge, riv., Que., Can D3 73
Rougemont, Fr., 878 .... B2 18
Rougemont, Durham, N.C., 400 .... A5 109
Rough, riv., Ky C3 94
Roughneck, peak, Idaho E3 89
Rougon, Pointe Coupee, La., 375 .... D4 95
Rouleau, Sask., Can., 436 .... G3 70
Roulette, Potter, Pa., 700 .... C5 108
Round, hill, Va B4 121
Round, isl., Miss E3 100
Round, lake, Ont., Can B7 72
Round, lake, Sask., Can G4 70
Round, lake, Wis B2 124
Round, mtn., Austl E9 51
Round, mtn., Kans D4 73
Round, pond, Newf., Can D4 75
Round Bay, Anne Arundel, Md., 600 .... B4 85
Round Harbour, Newf., Can., 63 .... D4 75
Roundhead, Hardin, Ohio, 150 .... B4 111
Round Hill, Alta., Can., 160 .... C4 69
Round Hill, N.S., Can., 300 .... E4 74
Round House, mtn., Kans D4 93
Round Island, passage, Fiji Is 52
Round Knob, mtn., Tenn C3 117
Round Lake, Lake, Ill., 997 .... E2 90
Round Lake, Nobles, Minn., 449 .... G3 99
Roundlake, Bolivar, Miss., 175 .... A3 100
Round Lake, Saratoga, N.Y., 900 .... C7 108
Round Lake Beach, Lake, Ill., 5,011 .... *E2 90
Round Lake Heights, Lake, Ill., 900 .... *E2 90
Round Lake Park, Lake, Ill., 2,565 .... *E2 90
Round Mountain, Franklin, Maine C2 96
Round Mountain, Nye, Nev., 300 .... E4 104
Round Mountain, Blanco, Tex., 75 .... D3 118
Round Oak, Jones, Ga., 200 .... C3 87
Round Pond, St. Francis, Ark., 50 .... B5 81
Round Pond, Lincoln, Maine, 300 .... E3 96
Round Rock, Apache, Ariz., 20 .... A6 80
Round Rock, Williamson, Tex., 1,878 .... D4 118
Round Spring, caverns, Mo D6 101
Roundstone, Ire., 250 .... D2 11
Round Top, hill, Mass B2 97
Roundup, Musselshell, Mont., 2,842 .... D8 102
Round Valley, Indian res., Calif C2 82
Round Valley, res., N.J B3 106
Roura, Fr. Gu., 437 .... B5 59
Rourkela, India, 90,287 .... *F10 40
Rousay, isl., Scot A5 13
Rouses Point, Clinton, N.Y., 2,160 .... f11 108
Rouseville, Venango, Pa., 923 .... D2 114
Rousseau, Ontonagon, Mich A6 98
Roussillon, former prov., Fr., 217,000 .... *F5 14
Routhierville, Que., Can., 219 .... *k13 73
Routon, Henry, Tenn., 40 .... A3 117
Routt, co., Colo., 5,900 .... A3 83
Rouville, co., Que., Can., 25,979 .... D4 73
Rouyn, Que., Can., 18,716 .... k11 73
Rouzerville, Franklin, Pa., 900 .... G6 114
Rovaniemi, Fin., 21,500 .... D11 25
Rovato, It., 6,288 .... B2 21
Rovenki, Sov. Un., 55,000 .... G12, q22 27
Rover, Yell, Ark., 200 .... C2 81
Rover, Bedford, Tenn., 120 .... B5 117
Roveredo, Switz., 1,878 .... D7 19
Rovereto, It., 25,638 .... B3 21
Rovigno, see Rovinj, Yugo.
Rovigo, It., 34,400 (47,500▲) B3 21
Rovinj, Yugo., 7,156 .... C1 22
Rovno, Sov. Un., 77,000 .... F6 27
Rovnoye, Sov. Un., 10,000 .... F16 27
Rowan, Wright, Iowa, 273 .... B4 92
Rowan, co., Ky., 12,808 .... B6 94
Rowan, co., N.C., 82,817 .... B3 109
Rowan, lake, Ont., Can E5 71
Rowan Mill, Rowan, N.C., 1,089 .... *B3 109
Rowan's Ravine, prov. park, Sask., Can G3 70
Rowayton, Fairfield, Conn. (part of Norwalk) E3 84
Rowe, Franklin, Mass., 130 (231▲) A2 97
Rowe, San Miguel, N. Mex., 150 .... B4 107
Rowena, Runnels, Tex., 300 .... D2 118
Rowes Run, Fayette, Pa., 950 .... *F2 114
Rowesville, Orangeburg, S.C., 398 .... E6 109
Rowland, Lincoln, Ky., 200 .... C5 94
Rowland, Robeson, N.C., 1,408 .... C4 109
Rowland, Pike, Pa., 100 .... D11 114
Rowlesburg, Preston, W. Va., 970 .... B5 123
Rowlett, Dallas, Tex., 1,015 .... *C4 118
Rowletts, Hart, Ky., 275 .... C4 94
Rowley, Alta., Can., 65 .... D4 69
Rowley, Buchanan, Iowa, 234 .... B6 92
Rowley, Essex, Mass., 1,500 (2,783▲) A6 97
Rowley Regis, Eng., 49,300 .... *B5 12
Rox, Lincoln, Nev., 15 .... F7 104
Roxabell, Ross, Ohio, 175 .... C4 111
Roxana, Sussex, Del., 100 .... D7 85
Roxana, Madison, Ill., 2,090 .... A8 101
Roxas (Capiz), Phil., 30,033 (49,326▲) C6 35
Roxboro, Person, N.C. 5,147 .... A5 109
Roxburg, Warren, N.J., 140 .... B2 106
Roxburgh, N.Z., 771 .... P12 51
Roxburgh, co., Scot., 43,171 .... E6 13
Roxbury, Litchfield, Conn., 250 (912▲) C3 84
Roxbury, McPherson, Kans., 135 .... D6 93
Roxbury, Oxford, Maine, 250 (344▲) D2 96
Roxbury, Cheshire, N.H., 50 (137▲) E2 105
Roxbury, Delaware, N.Y., 500 .... C6 108
Roxbury, Washington, Vt., 225 (364▲) C3 120
Roxie, Franklin, Miss., 585 .... D2 100
Roxobel, Bertie, N.C., 452 .... A6 109
Roxton, Lamar, Tex., 950 .... C5 118
Roxton Falls, Que., Can., 972 .... D5 73
Roxton Pond, Que., Can., 770 .... D5 73
Roy, Flagler, Fla., 350 .... C5 86
Roy, Bienville, La., 250 .... B2 95
Roy, Fergus, Mont., 175 .... C8 102
Roy, Harding, N. Mex., 633 .... B5 107
Roy, Weber, Utah, 9,239 .... B3 119
Royal, Galland, Ark., 25 .... C2, C5 81
Royal, Sumter, Fla., 200 .... D4 86
Royal, Cary, Iowa, 475 .... A2 92
Royal, Antelope, Nebr., 93 .... B7 103
Royal, Beaufort, N.C., 200 .... B7 109
Royal, canal, Ire D4 11
Royal, gorge, Colo C5 83
Royal, riv., Maine E5 96
Royal Center, Cass, Ind., 966 .... C4 91
Royal Mills, Wake, N.C., 600 .... A5 109
Royal Oak, B.C., Can h12 68
Royal Oak, Talbot, Md., 500 .... C5 85
Royal Oak, Oakland, Mich., 80,612 .... A7, E7 98
Royal Oak Township, Oakland, Mich., 8,147 .... *A7 98
Royalston, Worcester, Mass., 350 (800▲) A3 97
Royalties, Alta., Can., 156 .... D3 69
Royalton, Franklin, Ill., 1,225 .... F4 90
Royalton, Boone, Ind., 60 .... H7 91
Royalton, Magoffin, Ky., 300 .... C6 94
Royalton, Morrison, Minn., 580 .... E4 99
Royalton, Dauphin, Pa., 1,128 .... *F8 114
Royalton, Windsor, Vt., 150 (1,388▲) D3 120
Royalton, Waupaca, Wis., 300 .... D5 124
Royalty, Ward, Tex., 200 .... D1 118
Royan, Fr., 16,521 .... E3 14
Roy Brown, Lander, Nev., 10 .... D4 104
Roye, Fr., 4,912 .... C5 14
Royersford, Montgomery, Pa., 3,969 .... F10 114
Roy Hill, Austl D2 50
Roy Knob, mtn., Tenn D9 117
Royse City, Collin and Rockwall, Tex., 1,274 .... C4 118
Royston, B.C., Can., 700 .... E5 68
Royston, Franklin, Hart and Madison, Ga., 2,333 .... B3 87
Roysville, Lib E2 45
Rozay-en-Brie, Fr., 1,483 .... F2 15
Rozel, Pawnee, Kans., 207 .... D4 93
Rozet, Campbell, Wyo., 15 .... A7 125
Roznava, Czech., 10,200 .... D6 26
Rtishchevo, Sov. Un., 32,000 .... C2 29
Ruac, isl., Truk 52
Ruaha, Tan C6 48
Ruaha, riv., Tan C6 48
Ruapehu, mtn., N.Z. M15 51
Rub al Khali, des., Sau. Ar B6 47
Rubezhnoye, Sov. Un., 50,000 .... p21 27
Rubidoux (West Riverside), Riverside, Calif., 8,000 .... *F3 82
Rubinéia, Braz C2 56
Rubonia, Manatee, Fla., 400 .... F2 86
Rubtsovsk, Sov. Un., 127,000 .... C10 29
Ruby, Alsk., 157 .... C8 79
Ruby, Rapides, La., 25 .... C3 95
Ruby, Chesterfield, S.C., 284 .... B7 115
Ruby, lake, Nev C6 104
Ruby, mts., Nev C6 104
Ruby, range, Colo C3 83
Ruby, range, Mont E4 102
Rubys Inn, Garfield, Utah, 50 .... F3 119
Ruby Valley, Elko, Nev., 20 .... C6 104
Ruby Valley, Indian res., Nev C6 104
Ruchi, isl., Eniwetok 52
Rucker, Rutherford, Tenn., 50 .... B5 117
Ruda, riv., Pol g9 26
Ruda Sląska, Pol., 136,900 .... *C5 26
Rudbar, Afg., 5,000 .... F11 41
Rudd, Floyd, Iowa, 436 .... A5 92
Ruddell, Sask., Can., 100 .... E2 70
Ruddles Mills, Bourbon, Ky., 75 .... B5 94
Ruddock, St. John the Baptist, La B6 95
Rüdesheim, Ger., 7,200 .... D3 16
Rudha Hunish, isl., Scot C2 13
Rudkøbing, Den., 4,336 .... D4 24
Rudolf, lake, Ken A6 48
Rudnichnyy, Sov. Un B4 29
Rudnyy, Sov. Un., 65,000 .... *C6 29
Rudolph, Wood, Ohio, 350 .... A4 111
Rudolph, Kenedy, Tex., 5 .... F4 118
Rudolph, isl., Sov. Un A8 4
Rudolstadt, Ger., 27,700 .... C6 17
Rūd Sar, Iran, 10,000 .... C5 41
Rudyard, Chippewa, Mich., 600 .... B6 98
Rudyard, Hill, Mont., 600 .... B6 102
Rue, Fr., 1,787 .... D9 12
Rueil-Malmaison, Fr., 54,786 .... g9 14
Ruelle [-sur-Touvre], Fr., 5,855 .... E4 14
Rueun, Switz., 506 .... C7 19
Rufa'a, Sud., 9,137 .... C3 47
Rufe, McCurtain, Okla., 80 .... C6 112
Ruffec, Fr., 4,009 .... D4 14

Ruffin, Rockingham, N.C., 500 A4 109
Ruffin, Colleton, S.C., 250 E6 115
Rufiji, riv., Tan C6 48
Rufina Central, P.R. C3 65
Rufino, Arg., 10,987 A4 54
Rufisque, Sen., 49,700 D1 45
Rufus, Sherman, Oreg., 150 B6 113
Rufus Wood Lake, res., Wash A6 122
Rugby, Eng., 54,300 B6 12
Rugby, Pierce, N. Dak., 2,972 A6 110
Rugeley, Eng., 13,012 B6 12
Rügen isl., Ger A6 16
Rugged, mtn., B.C., Can D4 68
Rugozero, Sov. Un. E15 25
Ruhla, Ger., 9,226 C5 17
Ruhland, Ger., 4,533 B8 17
Ruhr, riv., Ger B3 17
Rui, Afg., 5,000 D13 41
Ruidosa, Presidio, Tex., 150 F2 118
Ruidoso, Lincoln, N. Mex., 1,557 D4 107
Ruidoso Downs, Lincoln, N. Mex., 407 D4 107
Ruiz, Mex., 6,490 m11 63
Rujiyoru, isl., Eniwetok 52
Rukoji, isl., Bikini 52
Rukoji, pass, Bikini 52
Rukuruku, bay, Fiji Is 52
Rukwa, lake, Tan C5 48
Rule, Haskell, Tex., 1,347 C3 118
Ruleton, Sherman, Kans., 50 C2 93
Ruleville, Sunflower, Miss., 1,902 B3 100
Rulo, Richardson, Nebr., 412 D10 103
Rum, creek, W. Va D5 123
Rum, isl., Ba. Is D6 64
Rum, isl., Scot C2 13
Rum, riv., Minn E5 99
Rum, sound, Scot D2 13
Ruma, Yugo, 19,570 C4 22
Rumaitha, Iraq, 4,468 F2 41
Rumbek, Sud., 2,944 D2 47
Rumbley, Somerset, Md., 105 D6 85
Rumburk, Czech., 6,759 C9 17
Rumely, Alger, Mich., 25 B3 98
Rumford, Oxford, Maine, 7,233 D2 96
Rumford, Providence, R.I. (part of East Providence) B11 84
Rumford, Fall River, S. Dak., 35 D2 116
Rumford Corner, Oxford, Maine, 60 D2 96
Rumilly, Fr., 3,940 D1 18
Rum Jungle, Austl B5 50
Rummerfield, Bradford, Pa., 50 C9 114
Rumney, Grafton, N.H., 200 (820▲) C3 105
Rumney Depot, Grafton, N.H., 110 C3 105
Rumoe, Jap., 29,100 (35,818▲) E10 37
Rump, mtn., Maine C1 96
Rumpi, Malawi D5 48
Rumsey, Alta., Can., 123 D4 69
Rumsey, McLean, Ky., 252 C2 94
Rumson, Monmouth, N.J., 6,405 C4 106
Runcorn, Eng., 26,035 A5 12
Runge, Karnes, Tex., 1,036 E4 118
Rungwa, Tan C5 48
Runnells, Polk, Iowa, 322 A8, C4 92
Runnels, co., Tex., 15,016 D3 118
Runnelstown, Perry, Miss., 125 D4 100
Runnemede, Camden, N.J., 8,396 D2 106
Running, creek, Colo B6 83
Runnymede, Sask., Can., 120 F5 70
Runtu, S.W. Afr A2 49
Rupanco, Chile C2 54
Rupat, isl., Indon L4 38
Rupert, Minidoka, Idaho, 4,153 G3 89
Rupert, Bennington, Vt., 100 (603▲) E2 120
Rupert, Greenbrier, W. Va., 921 D4 123
Rupert, riv., Que., Can h11 73
Rupert House, Que., Can., 528 h11 73
Rupununi, riv., Br. Gu B3 59
Rural Hall, Forsyth, N.C., 1,503 A3 109
Rural Retreat, Wythe, Va., 413 B3, E1 121
Rurrenabaque, Bol., 1,225 B2 55
Rurui, cape, Jap D13 37
Rurutu, isl., Fr. Polynesia *H12 7
Rusagonis, N.B., Can D3 74
Rusape, Rh., 4,400 A5 49
Ruschuk (Ruse), Bul., 109,900 D7 22
Ruschuk (Ruse), co., Bul., 527,708 *D8 22
Ruse (Ruschuk), Bul., 109,900 D7 22
Ruse (Ruschuk), co., Bul., 527,708 *D8 22
Rusera, India, 13,142 E11 40
Rush, Marion, Ark A3 81
Rush, El Paso, Colo., 25 C6 83
Rush, Ire., 2,118 D5 11
Rush, Boyd, Ky., 300 B7 94
Rush, co., Ind., 20,393 E6 91
Rush, co., Kans, 6,160 D4 93
Rush, creek, Colo C7 83
Rush, creek, Nebr C3 103
Rush, creek, Ohio B4 111
Rush, creek, Okla C4 112
Rush, lake, Minn D3 99
Rush, lake, Wis E5 124
Rush, riv., Wis D1 124
Rush Center, Rush, Kans., 278 D4 93
Rush City, Chisago, Minn., 1,108 E6 99
Rushden, Eng., 17,370 B7 12
Rushford, Fillmore, Minn., 1,335 G7 99
Rushford, Allegany, N.Y., 350 C2 108
Rush Hill, Audrain, Mo., 132 B6 101
Rush Lake, Sask., Can., 213 G2 70
Rushmere, Isle of Wight, Va., 125 B6 121
Rushmore, Nobles, Minn., 382 G3 99
Rush Springs, Grady, Okla., 1,303 C4 112
Rushsylvania, Logan, Ohio, 601 B4 111
Rushville, Schuyler, Ill., 2,819 C3 90
Rushville, Rush, Ind., 7,264 E7 91
Rushville, Buchanan, Mo., 253 B2 101
Rushville, Sheridan, Nebr., 1,228 B3 103
Rushville, Ontario and Yates, N.Y., 465 C3 108
Rushville, Susquehanna, Pa., 40 C9 114
Rusk Cherokee, Tex., 4,900 D5 118
Rusk, co., Tex., 36,421 C5 118
Rusk, co., Wis., 14,794 C2 124
Ruskin, Hillsborough, Fla., 1,894 E4, F2 86
Ruskin, Nuckolls, Nebr., 203 D8 103
Ruskin, Dickson, Tenn., 50 A4 117
Ruso, McLean, N. Dak., 31 B5 110
Russas, Braz., 7,102 B3 57
Russell, White, Ark., 203 B4 81
Russell (Russell City), Alameda, Calif., 1,100 *B5 82
Russell, Man., Can., 1,263 D1 71
Russell, Ont., Can., 587 B9, h13 72
Russell, Clay, Fla., 300 C6 86
Russell, Lucas, Iowa, 577 D4 92
Russell, Russell, Kans., 6,113 D5 93
Russell, Greenup, Ky., 1,458 B7 94
Russell, Hampden, Mass., 600 (1,366▲) B2 97
Russell, Lyon, Minn., 449 F3 99
Russell, St. Lawrence, N.Y., 200 f9 108
Russell, N.Z., 441 K15 51
Russell, Bottineau, N. Dak., 25 A5 110
Russell, Greer, Okla., 100 C2 112
Russell, Warren, Pa., 800 C3 114
Russell, co., Ala., 46,351 C4 78
Russell, co., Ont., Can., 20,892 B9 72
Russell, co., Kans., 11,348 D5 93
Russell, co., Ky., 11,076 D4 94
Russell, co., Va., 26,290 B3 121
Russell, fork, Ky C7 94
Russell, lake, Alta., Can A3 69
Russell, lake, Man., Can A1 71
Russell, mtn., Alsk f15 80
Russell Gardens, Nassau, N.Y., 1,156 *F2 84
Russell Konda, India H10 40
Russell Springs, Logan, Kans., 93 D2 93
Russell Springs, Russell, Ky., 1,125 C4 94
Russellton, Allegheny, Pa., 1,613 *A6 114
Russellville, Franklin, Ala., 6,628 A2 78
Russellville, Pope, Ark., 8,921 B2 81
Russellville, Lawrence, Ill., 197 E6 90
Russellville, Putnam, Ind., 372 E4 91
Russellville, Logan, Ky., 5,861 D3 94
Russellville, Cole, Mo., 442 C5 101
Russellville, Brown, Ohio, 412 D4 111
Russellville, Berkeley, S.C., 100 E8 115
Russellville, Hamblen, Tenn., 750 C10 117
Rüsselsheim, Ger., 45,900 D3 17
Russia, Shelby, Ohio, 300 B3 111
Russia, see Soviet Union, country, Eur., Asia
Russian, riv., Calif C2 82
Russian Soviet Federated Socialist Republic, rep., Sov. Un., 126,300,000 D17 9
Russiaville, Howard, Ind., 1,064 D5 91
Russum, Claiborne, Miss., 30 D2 100
Rustad, Clay, Minn., 25 D2 99
Rustavi, Sov. Un., 72,000 *E7 28
Rustburg, Campbell, Va., 350 D3 121
Rustenburg, S. Afr., 21,016 *C4 49
Rustico, P.E.I., Can., 74 C6 74
Ruston, Lincoln, La., 13,991 B3 95
Ruston, Pierce, Wash., 694 B3, D1 122
Ruswil, Switz., 4,657 B5 19
Ruszow, Pol B10 17
Rutana, Burandi B5 48
Rutba, Iraq F13 31
Rutchenkovo, Sov. Un., 25,000 r20 27
Rute, Sp., 10,077 D3 20
Ruteng, Indon G6 35
Ruth, Huron, Mich., 210 E8 98
Ruth, Lincoln, Miss., 150 D3 100
Ruth, White Pine, Nev., 800 D7 104
Ruth, Rutherford, N.C., 529 D4 109
Ruth, lake, Minn E6 99
Ruthenia, reg., Sov. Un D7 27
Rutherford, Napa, Calif., 150 A5 82
Rutherford, Bergen, N.J., 20,473 B4, h8 106
Rutherford, Gibson, Tenn., 983 A3 117
Rutherford, co., N.C., 45,091 B2 109
Rutherford, co., Tenn., 52,368 B5 117
Rutherford, fork, Tenn A3 117
Rutherford Heights, Dauphin, Pa., 1,700 *F8 114
Rutherfordton, Rutherford, N.C., 3,392 B2, D4 109
Rutherglen, Ont., Can., 50 A5 72
Rutherglen, Scot., 25,067 E4 13
Rutheron, Rio Arriba, N. Mex., 25 A3 107
Ruthilda, Sask., Can., 86 F1 70
Ruthin, Wales, 3,502 A4 12
Ruthton, Pipestone, Minn., 476 F2 99
Ruthven, Wilcox, Ala., 25 D2 78
Ruthven, Palo Alto, Iowa, 712 A3 92
Rüti, Switz, 8,282 B6 19
Rutland, B.C., Can., 1,495 E8 68
Rutland, La Salle, Ill., 509 C4 90
Rutland, Humboldt, Iowa, 221 B3 92
Rutland, Worcester, Mass., 1,800 (3,253▲) B4 97
Rutland, Sargent, N. Dak., 308 C8 110
Rutland, Meigs, Ohio, 687 C5 111
Rutland (Roseville), Tioga, Pa., 162 C8 114
Rutland, Lake, S. Dak., 100 C9 116
Rutland, Rutland, Vt., 18,325 D3 120
Rutland (Town of), Rutland, Vt. (1,542▲) *D3 120
Rutland, co., Eng., 23,956 B7 12
Rutland, co., Vt., 46,719 D2 120
Rutland Station, Sask., Can E1 70
Rutledge, Crenshaw, Ala., 276 D3 78
Rutledge, Morgan, Ga., 478 C3 87
Rutledge, Pine, Minn., 146 D6 99
Rutledge, Scotland, Mo., 158 A5 101
Rutledge, Grainger, Tenn., 793 C10 117
Rutshuru, Con. L B4 48
Rutter, Ont., Can A4 72
Ruunitto, isl., Eniwetok 52
Ruvo [di Pulgia], It., 23,746 D6 21
Ruvuma, riv., Moz., Tan D6 48
Ruwandiz, Iraq, 3,320 C2 41
Ruweiha, ruins, Jordan D7 32
Ruwenzori, mts., Con. L., Ug A4 48
Ruxton, Baltimore, Md., 2,100 C2 85
Ruza, Sov. Un., 7,000 D11 27
Ruzayevka, Sov. Un., 34,500 C3 29
Ruzomberok, Czech., 18,600 D5 26
Rwanda, country, Afr., 2,800,000 B4 48
Ry, Den., 2,004 B3 24
Ryan, Delaware, Iowa, 347 B6 92
Ryan, Jefferson, Okla., 978 C4 112
Ryan, peak, Idaho F4 89
Ryan, riv., Ala A2 78
Ryan Park, Carbon, Wyo., 100 D6 125
Ryazan, Sov. Un., 262,000 C1 29
Ryazhsk, Sov. Un., 10,000 E13 27
Rybatskoye, Sov. Un., 10,000 s31 25
Rybinsk (Shcherbakov), Sov. Un., 195,000 B1 29
Rybinsk, res., Sov. Un B1 29
Rybnik, Pol., 34,000 C5, g9 26
Rybnitsa, Sov. Un B9 22
Rycroft, Alta., Can., 500 B1 69
Rydal, Montgomery, Pa., 1,500 *F11 114
Ryde, Austl., 79,000 *F8 51
Ryde, Eng., 19,800 D6 12
Ryder, Ward, N. Dak., 264 B4 110
Ryderwood, Cowlitz, Wash., 380 C2 122
Rye, Cleveland, Ark., 50 D4 81
Rye, Pueblo, Colo., 179 D6 83
Rye, Eng., 4,429 D8 12
Rye, Rockingham, N.H., 450 (3,244▲) D5 105
Rye, Westchester, N.Y., 14,891 h13, n15 108
Rye, lake, N.Y E2 84
Ryeå, riv., Den A3 24
Rye Beach, Rockingham, N.H., 165 E5 105
Ryegate, Golden Valley, Mont., 314 D7 102
Ryegate, Caledonia, Vt., 35 (894▲) C4 120
Rye Patch, res., Nev C3 104
Ryerson, Sask., Can H5 70
Rygge, Nor p28 25
Ryley, Alta., Can., 469 C4 69
Rylsk, Sov. Un., 10,000 F10 27
Rynda, Sov. Un C17 25
Ryomgaard, Den., 861 B4 24
Ryozu, Jap., 12,100 G9 37
Rypin, Pol., 7,350 B5 26
Ryuku, is., Asia F10 34
Ryukyu Is. (Southern), U.S. occ., Asia, 940,000 F10 34
Rzadza, riv., Pol k14 26
Rzeszow, Pol., 65,700 C6 26
Rzepin, Pol., 2,000 B3 26
Rzhev, Sov. Un., 55,000 C10 27

S

Saale, riv., Ger B6 17
Saaler, bay, Ger D6 24
Saalfield, Ger., 26,900 C6 17
Saalfelden, Aus., 8,901 B8 18
Saanen, Switz., 5,649 D3 19
Saar, state, Ger., 1,116,000 E6 15, D3 16
Saar, riv., Ger E6 15
Saarbrücken, Ger., 132,600 (*360,000) D1 17
Saarburg, Ger., 5,600 E6 15
Saaremaa, isl., Sov. Un B4 27
Saarlouis, Ger., 36,400 D1 17
Saas-Almagell, Switz., 359 D4 19
Saas-Fee, Switz., 739 D4 19
Saavedra, Arg., 2,130 B4 54
Saavedra, Chile B2 54
Sabá, Hond C4 62
Saba, isl., Neth. Antilles n15 64
Sabac, Yugo., 30,231 C4 22
Sabadell, Sp., 105,152 B7 20
Sabael, Hamilton, N.Y., 100 B6 108
Sabah (North Borneo), reg., Mala., 515,000 I14 33, D5 35
Sab'ah, mtn., Libya D3 43
Sabalana, is., Indon G5 35
Sabana, P.R B8, f12 65
Sabana de la Mar, Dom. Rep., 4,032 F9 64
Sabanagrande, Hond., 1,678 D4 62
Sabana Grande, P.R., 3,318 C3 65
Sabana Grande, mun., P.R., 15,910 C3 65
Sabanalarga, Col., 13,982 A3 70
Sabana Llana, P.R C5 65
Sabana Seca, P.R B6 65
Sabang, Indon, 6,855 k11 35
Sabará, Braz., 10,004 E2 57
Sabarmati, riv., India F4 40
Sabaskong, bay, Ont., Can E4 71
Sabastīyah, Jordan, 1,000 f11 32
Sabattus, Androscoggin, Maine, 850 D2 96
Sabattus, pond, Maine D2 96
Sabaudia, It., 6,262 D4 21
Sabbathday, pond, Maine D5 96
Sabderat, Eth B4 47
Sabetha, Nemaha, Kans., 2,318 C8 93
Sabhah, Libya, 3,640 D2 43
Sabillasville, Frederick, Md., 300 A3 85
Sabin, Clay, Minn., 251 D2 99
Sabina, Clinton, Ohio, 2,313 C4 111
Sabinal, Uvalde, Tex., 1,747 E3 118
Sabinas, Mex., 15,953 B4 63
Sabinas Hidalgo, Mex., 11,558 B4 63
Sabine, Jefferson, Tex., 100 E6 118
Sabine, Wyoming, W. Va., 300 D3 123
Sabine, co., Tex., 7,302 D6 118
Sabine, par., La., 18,564 C2 95
Sabine, lake, La E2 95
Sabine, lake, Tex E2 95
Sabine, pass, La E2 95
Sabine, mtn., Ant B29 5
Sabine, riv., La., Tex. C2 95, D6 118
Sabine Pass., Jefferson, Tex., 850 E6 118
Sabinópolis, Braz., 2,957 E2 57
Sabinoso, San Miguel, N. Mex., 25 B5 107
Sabinsville, Tioga, Pa., 300 C6 114
Sable, cape, N.S., Can H19 67
Sable, cape, Fla G5 86
Sable, isl., N.S., Can F10 74
Sable Island, cape, N.S., Can F4 74
Sable River, N.S., Can., 144 F4 74
Sablé [-sur-Sarthe], Fr., 6,885 D3 14
Sabon Birni, Nig D6 45
Sabor, riv., Port B2 20
Sabrina, coast, Ant C25 5
Sabula, Jackson, Iowa, 894 B7 92
Sabula, Iron, Mo., 30 D7 101
Sabula, Clearfield, Pa., 80 D4 114
Sabzawar, Afg., 10,000 E11 41
Sabzevār, Iran, 28,151 C8 41
Sac, co., Iowa, 17,007 B2 92
Sac, riv., Mo D4 101
Sacaba, Bol., 2,752 C2 55
Sacajawea, peak, Oreg B9 113
Sacandaga, lake, N.Y B6 108
Sacandaga, res., N.Y B6 108
Sacaton, Pinal, Ariz., 700 D4 80
Sacavém, Port., 5,569 f9 20
Sacavém, riv., Port f9 20
Sac City, Sac, Iowa, 3,354 B2 92
Sachem Head, New Haven, Conn., 200 E6 84
Sachigo, lake, Ont., Can C5 71
Sachigo, riv., Ont., Can B6 71
Sachse, Dallas, Tex., 359 B6 118
Sachsen, former state, Ger., 5,558,566 B8 17
Sachsen-Anhalt (Saxony-Anhalt), former state, Ger., 4,160,539 B6 17
Sachs Harbour, N.W. Ter., Can., 76 B8 66
Sacile, It., 5,340 D8 18
Sackets Harbor, Jefferson, N.Y., 1,279 B4 108
Sackville, N.B., Can., 3,038 D5 74
Saclay, Fr., 312 h9 14
Saco, Pike, Ala., 150 D4 78
Saco, York, Maine, 10,515 E2, E4 96
Saco, Phillips, Mont., 490 B9 102
Saco, riv., Maine, N.H B4 105
Sacramento, Sacramento, Calif., 191,667 (*536,000) A6, C3 82
Sacramento, McLean, Ky., 429 C2 94
Sacramento, Otero, N. Mex., 75 E4 107
Sacramento, co., Calif., 502,778 C3 82
Sacramento, mts., N. Mex D4 107
Sacramento, riv., Calif C3 84
Sacramento, riv., N. Mex E4 107
Sacramento, val., Calif C2 84
Sacré-Coeur Saguenay, Que., Can., 1,108 A8 73
Sacred Heart, Renville, Minn., 696 F3 99
Sacrofano, It., 1,756 g8 21
Sacul, Nacogdoches, Tex., 200 D5 118
Sá da Bandeira, Ang., 13,867 D1 48
Şa'dah, Yemen, 25,000 B5 47
Saddle, mtn., Colo C5 83
Saddle, mtn., Oreg B3 113
Saddle, mts., Wash C6 122
Saddle (Burnt), riv., Alta., Can B1 69
Saddle, riv., N.J h8 106
Saddleback, mtn., Maine B4 96
Saddleback, mtn., Maine D2 96
Saddle Ball, mtn., Mass A1 97
Saddle Brook, Bergen N.J., 13,834 *A4 106
Saddle Bunch, keys, Fla H5 86
Saddle River, Bergen, N.J., 1,776 *A4 106
Saddle Rock, Nassau, N.Y., 1,109 *G2 84
Saddlerock, mtn., Maine C3 96
Saddlestring, Johnson, Wyo., 5 A6 125
Sadieville, Scott, Ky., 276 B5 94
Sadiya, India, 5,044 C10 39
Sado, isl., Jap G9 37
Sado, riv., Port C1 20
Sadorus, Champaign, Ill., 384 D5 90
Sadska, Czech., 3,047 n18 26
Saeby, Den., 3,669 A4 24
Saegertown, Crawford, Pa., 1,131 C1 114
Saeki, Jap., 32,000 (*51,369) J5 37
Saengchon, Kor G3 37
Safad, Isr., 10,586 B7 32
Safata, bay, W. Sam 52
Safatulafei, W. Sam., 1,108 52
Safety Harbor, Pinellas, Fla., 1,787 D4, E2 86
Safety Valve, entrance, Fla G6 86
Saffell, Lawrence, Ark., 150 B4 81
Safford, Dallas, Ala., 200 C2 78
Safford, Graham, Ariz., 4,648 E6 80
Saffordville, Chase, Kans., 40 D7 93
Saffron Walden, Eng., 7,810 B8 12
Safi, Mor., 81,072 C3 44
Safīdābeh, Iran F10 41
Safonovo, Sov. Un., 24,700 D9 27
Safranbolu, Tur., 7,400 B9 31
Safune, W. Sam., 476 52
Safune, bay, W. Sam 52
Saga, Jap., 129,888 J5 37
Saga, pref., Jap., 942,874 *J5 37
Sagadahoc, co., Maine, 22,793 E3 96
Sagaing, Bur., 15,439 D10 39
Sagami, sea, Jap n18 37
Sagamihara, Jap, 101,655 *n18 37
Sagamore, Barnstable, Mass., 900 C6 97
Sagamore, Armstrong, Pa., 800 E3 114
Sagamore Beach, Barnstable, Mass., 400 *C6 97
Sagamore Hills, Summit, Ohio, 3,848 B2 111
Sagån, riv., Swe t34 25
Saganaga, lake, Ont., Can., Minn B8 99
Sagaponack, Suffolk, N.Y., 100 F7 84
Sagara, Fiji Is 52
Sagara, Jap., 12,000 o17 37
Sage, Lincoln, Wyo., 35 D2 125
Saggart, Ire., 426 D5 11
Sag Harbor, Suffolk, N.Y., 2,346 m16 108
Saginaw, Shelby, Ala., 200 B3 78
Saginaw, Saginaw, Mich., 98,265 (*160,900) E7 98
Saginaw, Lane, Oreg., 100 D3 113
Saginaw, Tarrant, Tex., 1,001 B5 118
Saginaw, co., Mich., 190,752 E6 98
Saginaw, bay, Mich E7 98
Sagiz, Sov. Un D4 29
Sagiz, riv., Sov. Un D5 29
Saglek, bay, Newf., Can f9 75
Sagola, Dickinson, Mich., 150 B2 98
Sagra, mtn., Sp D4 20
Sag Sag, Bis. Arch k12 50
Saguache, Saguache, Colo., 722 C4 83
Saguache, co., Colo., 4,473 C4 83
Saguache, creek, Colo C4 83
Sagua de Tánamo, Cuba, 2,864 D6 64
Sagua la Grande, Cuba, 31,000 C3 64
Saguaro, nat. mon., Ariz E5 80
Saguenay, co., Que., Can., 81,900 A8 73
Saguenay, riv., Que., Can A7 73
Sagunto, Sp., 40,293 C5 20
Saḥāb, Jordan, 1,000 C8 32
Sahagún, Col., 5,910 B2 60
Sahara, des., Afr D5 42
Saharan Atlas, mts., Alg C5 44
Saharanpur, India, 185,213 C6 39, C6 40
Şahrajat al Kubrá, Eg., U.A.R., 1,000 D3 32
Sahuaripa, Mex., 3,836 B3 63
Sahuarita, Pima, Ariz., 250 F5 80
Sahuaro, res., Ariz G3 80
Sahuayo, Mex., 25,673 m12 63
Saïda, Alg., 20,289 G7 30
Saida (Sidon), Leb., 19,853 F10 31
Sa'īdābād, Iran, 8,074 G7 41
Saidaiji, Jap., 21,500 (45,984▲) *I7 37
Saidpur, Pak., 60,628 C9 39
Saigo, Jap., 8,000 H6 37
Saigon, Viet., 1,250,800 (*1,550,000) G7 38
Saijo, Jap., 34,200 (53,187▲) *I6 37
Saikhoa Ghat, India F4 34
Sail, rock, Vir. Is f14 63
Sailor Springs, Clay, Ill., 187 E5 90
Saimaa, lake, Fin G13 25
St. Abb's, head, Scot E6 13
St. Adelphe, Que., Can., 787 C5 73
St. Adolphe, Que., Can D6 73
St. Affrique, Fr., 5,670 F5 14
St. Agapit, Que., Can., 1,117 C6 73
St. Agatha, Aroostook, Maine, 50 (1,137▲) A4 96
Ste. Agathe, Man., Can., 298 E3 71
Ste. Agathe [-de-Lotbinière], Que., Can., 600 C6 73
Ste. Agathe-des-Monts, Que., Can., 5,725 C3 73
Ste. Agnès-de-Dundee, Que., Can D3 73
St. Aimé, Que., Can., 580 D5 73
St. Alban, Que, Can., 786 C5 73
St. Albans, Eng., 50,500 C7 12
St. Albans, Somerset, Maine, 350 (927▲) D3 96
St. Alban's, Newf., Can., 1,547 E4 75
St. Albans, Franklin, Vt., 8,806 B2 120
St. Albans (Town of), Franklin, Vt. (2,303▲) *B2 120
St. Albans, Kanawha, W. Va., 15,103 C3 123
St. Albans, bay, Vt B2 120
St. Albans, head, Eng D5 12
St. Albans Bay, Franklin, Vt., 200 B2 120
St. Albert, Alta., Can., 4,059 C4 69
St. Alexandre [-de-Kamouraska], Que., Can., 872 B8 73
St. Alexandre [-d'Iberville], Que., Can., 425 D4 73
St. Alexis-des-Monts, Que., Can., 1,964 C4 73
St. Alphonse, Que., Can., 103 D5 73
St. Amand-les-Eaux, Fr., 16,674 D3 15
St. Amand-Mont-Rond, Fr., 10,890 D5 14
St. Amant, Ascension, La., 100 B6 95
St. Amarin, Fr., 2,044 B3 18
St. Ambroise, Que., Can., 1,576 A6 73
St. Anaclet, Que., Can., 722 A9 73
St. Andre, cape, Malag g8 49
St. André-Avellin, Que., Can., 1,066 D2 73
St. André [-de-Kamouraska], Que., Can., 550 B8 73
St. André-du-Lac [-St.-Jean], Que., Can., 469 A5 73
St. Andrews, bay, Fla G3 86
St. Andrews, sound, Ga F5 87
St. Andrews, N.B., Can., 1,531 D2 74
St. Andrew's, Newf., Can., 294 E2 75
St. Andrews, Scot., 10,100 D6 13
St. Andrews, Charleston, S.C., 1,500 *F2 115
St. Andrews, Franklin, Tenn., 250 B6 117
St. Andrews, bay, Scot D6 13
St. Andrews East, Que., Can., 1,183 D3 73
Ste. Angele [-de-Monnoir], Que., Can., 314 D4 73
St. Anicet, Que., Can., 132 D3 73
St. Ann., St. Louis, Mo., 12,155 *A8 101
St. Anna, Sheboygan, Wis., 100 B6 124
Ste. Anne, Guad., 2,384 n16 64
St. Anne, Kankakee, Ill., 1,378 B6 90
Ste. Anne, lake, Alta., Can C3 69
Ste. Anne, riv., Que., Can B7 73
Ste. Anne, riv., Que., Can C6 73
Ste. Anne-de-Beaupré, Que., Can., 1,878 B7 73
Ste. Anne [-de-Bellevue], Que., Can., 4,044 q19 73
Ste. Anne-de-la-Pérade, Que., Can., 1,184 C5 73
Ste. Anne-de-Madawaska, N.B., Can., 1,122 B1 74
Ste. Anne-des-Chênes, Man., Can., 653 E3 71
Ste. Anne [-des-Plaines], Que., Can., 1,256 D4 73
Ste. Anne-du-Lac, Que., Can., 423 k11 73
St. Anns, N.S., Can C9 74
St. Ann's Bay, Jam., 5,086 F5 64
St. Anselme, N.B., Can., 715 *C5 74
St. Anselme, Que., Can., 1,131 C7 73
St. Ansgar, Mitchell, Iowa, 1,014 C7 94
St. Anthony, Newf., Can., 1,820 C4 75
St. Anthony, Fremont, Idaho, 2,700 F7 89
St. Anthony, Dubois, Ind., 165 H4 91
St. Anthony, Marshall, Iowa, 130 B4 92
St. Anthony, Hennepin, Minn., 5,084 *F5 99
St. Anthony, Morton, N. Dak., 88 C5 110
St. Antoine-de-Kent, N.B., Can., 718 C5 74
St. Antoine des Laurentides, Que., Can, 3,005 *D3 73
Ste. Antoine [-Lotbinière], Que., Can., 270 C6, o16 73
St. Antoine [-sur-Richelieu], Que., Can., 463 D4 73
St. Antonin, Que., Can., 247 B8 73
St. Apollinaire, Que., Can., 968 C6, o16 73
Ste. Apolline-de-Patton, Que., Can., 353 C7 73
St. Arnaud, Austl., 3,150 H4 51
St. Arsène, Que., Can., 523 B8 73
St. Arthur, N.B., Can., 605 B3 74
St. Athanase, Que., Can., 168 B8 73
St. Aubert, Que., Can., 735 B7 73
St. Augustin, riv., Newf., Que., Can C2 75
St. Augustin-de-Québec, Que., Can., 488 o17 73
St. Augustin [-Deux-Montagnes], Que., Can., 444 p19 73
St. Augustine, St. Johns, Fla., 14,734 C5, C7 86
St. Augustin-Saguenay, Que., Can., 477 C2 75
St. Austell, Eng., 25,027 D3 12
St. Avold, Fr., 15,247 C7 14
Ste. Barbe, Que., Can., 181 D3 73
St. Barnabé-Nord, Que., Can., 541 C5 73
St. Barnabé-Sud, Que., Can., 204 D5 73
St. Barthélémy, Que., Can., 620 C4 73
St. Barthélemy (St. Bartholomew), isl., Guad n15 64
St. Basile, N.B., Can., 1,733 B1 74
St. Basile [-de-Portneuf], Que., Can., 1,709 C6 73
St. Basile-le-Grand, Que., Can., 1,210 *D4 73
Ste. Béatrix, Que., Can C4 73
St. Bees, head, Eng C5 10
St. Benedict, Sask., Can., 205 E3 70
St. Benedict, Kossuth, Iowa, 100 A3 92
St. Benedict, Nemaha, Kans., 75 C7 93
St. Benedict, Marion, Oreg., 450 B2 113
St. Benoît, Que., Can., 571 p18 73
St. Benoît-Labre, Que., Can., 514 C7 73
St. Bernard, Cullman, Ala., 700 A3 78
St. Bernard, Que., Can., 95 D4 73
St. Bernard, St. Bernard, La., 350 C8, E6 95
St. Bernard, Platte, Nebr., 25 C8 103
St. Bernard, Hamilton, Ohio, 6,778 D2 111
St. Bernard, par., La., 32,186 E6 95
St. Bernard, see Grand St. Bernard, pass, Switz., It.
St. Bernard [-de-Dorchester], Que., Can., 496 C6 73
St. Bernice, Perry, Ind., 800 E2 91
St. Bethlehem, Montgomery, Tenn., 200 A4 117
Ste. Blandine, Que., Can A9 73
St. Bonaventure, Que., Can., 384 D5 73
St. Bonaventure, Cattaraugus, N.Y., 1,500 *C2 108
St. Boniface, Man., Can., 37,600 E3 71
St. Boswells, Sask., Can., 40 G2 70

St. Brendan's, Newf., Can., 387 ... D5 75
St. Bride, mtn., Alta., Can ... D3 69
St. Bride's, Newf., Can., 397 ... E4 75
St. Brides, Norfolk, Va., 130 ... E6 121
St. Brides, bay, Wales ... C2 12
St. Brieuc, Fr., 43,142 ... C2 14
St. Brieux, Sask., Can., 364 ... E3 70
Ste. Brigide, Que., Can., 233 ... D4 73
Ste. Brigitte, Que., Can., 124 ... C5 73
St. Bruno-de-Montarville, Que., Can., 6,760 ... *D4 73
St. Bruno-Lac-St. Jean, Que., Can., 1,158 ... A6 73
St. Calais, Fr., 3,045 ... D4 14
St. Calixte, Que., Can., 512 ... D4 73
St. Camille, Que., Can., 204 ... D6 73
St. Camille [-de-Bellechasse], Que., Can., 689 ... C7 73
St. Casimir, Que., Can., 1,386 ... C5 73
St. Catharine, Washington, Ky., 200 ... C4 94
St. Catharines, Ont., Can., 84,472 (*95,577) ... D5 72
Ste. Catherine, Que., Can., 893 ... C6, n16 73
St. Catherine, lake, Vt ... E2 120
St. Catherines, isl., Ga ... E5 87
St. Catherine's, pt., Bermuda ... E14 77
St. Catherines, pt., Eng ... D6 12
St. Catherines, sound, Ga ... E5 87
Ste. Cécile, Que., Can., 141 ... D7 73
St. Célestin, Que., Can., 368 ... C5 73
St. Césaire, Que., Can., 2,097 ... D4 73
St. Chamond, Fr., 17,107 ... E6 14
St. Charles, Arkansas, Ark., 255 ... C4 81
St. Charles, Bear Lake, Idaho, 300 ... G4 89
St. Charles, Kane, Ill., 9,269 ... B5, F1 90
St. Charles, Madison, Iowa, 355 ... C4 92
St. Charles, Hopkins, Ky., 421 ... C2 94
St. Charles, Saginaw, Mich., 1,959 ... E6 98
St. Charles, Winona, Minn., 1,882 ... G6 99
St. Charles, St. Charles, Mo., 21,189 ... A7, C7 101
St. Charles, Gregory, S. Dak., 58 ... D6 116
St. Charles, Lee, Va., 368 ... B2 121
St. Charles, co., Mo., 52,970 ... C7 101
St. Charles, par., La., 21,219 ... E5 95
St. Charles, cape, Newf., Can ... B4 75
St. Charles [-de-Bellechasse], Que., Can., 981 ... C7 73
St. Chély-d'Apcher, Fr., 3,900 ... E5 14
Ste. Christine, Que., Can., 214 ... C6 73
St. Chrysostome, Que., Can., 972 ... D4 73
St. Clair, Burke, Ga., 50 ... C4 87
St. Clair, St. Clair, Mich., 4,538 ... F8 98
St. Clair, Blue Earth, Minn., 373 ... F5 99
St. Clair, Franklin, Mo., 2,711 ... C6 101
St. Clair, Schuylkill, Pa., 5,159 ... E9 114
St. Clair, co., Ala., 25,388 ... B3 78
St. Clair, co., Ill., 262,509 ... E4 90
St. Clair, co., Mich., 107,201 ... F8 98
St. Clair, co., Mo., 8,421 ... C4 101
St. Clair, lake, Ont., Can., Mich ... E2 72
St. Clair, riv., Ont., Can., Mich ... E2 72
St. Claire, Que., Can., 1,338 ... C7 73
St. Clair Hills, St. Clair, Ill., 250 ... B8 101
St. Clair Shores, Macomb, Mich., 76,657 ... A8 98
St. Clairsville, Belmont, Ohio, 3,865 ... B7 111
St. Claude, Man., Can., 609 ... E2 71
St. Claude, Que., Can., 71 ... D6 73
St. Claude [-sur-Bienne], Fr., 12,114 ... D6 14
St. Clément, Que., Can., 400 ... B8 73
St. Cléophas, Que., Can., 227 ... *k13 73
Ste. Clothilde, Que., Can., 359 ... D5 73
St. Cloud, Osceola, Fla., 4,353 ... D5 86
St. Cloud, Fr., 26,476 ... g9 14
St. Cloud, Stearns, Benton and Sherburne, Minn., 33,815 ... E4 99
St. Cloud, Fond du Lac, Wis., 530 ... B5, E5 124
St. Côme, Que., Can., 598 ... C4 73
St. Constant, Que., Can., 2,739 ... q19 73
St. Croix, N.B., Can., 173 ... D2 74
Ste. Croix, Que., Can., 1,363 ... C6, o16 73
Ste. Croix, Perry, Ind., 100 ... H4 91
Ste. Croix, Switz., 6,925 ... C2 19
St. Croix, co., Wis., 29,164 ... C1 124
St. Croix, isl., Vir. Is. (U.S.) ... k17 65
St. Croix, lake, Wis ... D1 124
St. Croix, riv., N.B., Can ... D2 74
St. Croix, riv., Maine ... C5 96
St. Croix, riv., Minn., Wis ... E6 99
St. Croix, stream, Maine ... B4 96
St. Croix Falls, Polk, Wis., 1,249 ... C1 124
St. Cuthbert, Que., Can., 392 ... C4 73
St. Cyprien, Que., Can., 370 ... B8 73
St. Cyrille [-de-L'Islet], Que., Can., 655 ... B7 73
St. Cyrille [-de-Wendover], Que., Can., 1,138 ... D5 73
St. Damase, Que., Can., 879 ... D4 73
St. Damase-de-Matane, Que., Can., 277 ... *k13 73
St. Damase-des-Aulnaies, Que., Can., 256 ... B7 73
St. Damien [-de-Brandon], Que., Can., 431 ... C4 73
St. Damien [-de-Buckland], Que., Can., 1,396 ... C7 73
St. David, Cochise, Ariz., 650 ... F5 80
St. David, Fulton, Ill., 862 ... C3 90
St. David, Aroostook, Maine, 80 ... A4 96
St. David [-de-l'Auberivière], Que., Can., 1,968 ... n17 73
St. David [-d'Yamaska], Que., Can., 277 ... D5 73
St. David's, Newf., Can., 317 ... D2 75
St. Davids, Delaware, Pa., 1,200 ... *A10 114
St. David's, Wales, 1,505 ... C2 12
St. David's, head, Wales ... C2 12
St. David's, isl., Bermuda ... E14 77
St. Denis [-de-la-Bouteillerie], Que., Can., 269 ... B8 73
St. Denis [River Richelieu], Que., Can., 1,063 ... D4 73
St. Denis, Fr., 94,264 ... C5, g10 14
St. Denis, Reunion, 37,688 (65,275*) ... H24 3
St. Didace, Que., Can., 92 ... C4 73
St. Dié, Fr., 23,108 ... C7 14
St. Dizier, Fr., 34,407 ... C6 14
St. Dominique [-de-Bagot], Que., Can., 532 ... D5 73
St. Dominique, Que., Can., 70 ... q18 73
St. Donat-de-Montcalm, Que., Can., 1,414 ... C3 73
St. Donatus, Jackson, Iowa, 100 ... B7 92
Ste. Dorothée, Que., Can., 5,297 ... *D4 73
St. Édouard, Que., Can., 186 ... D4, q19 73
St. Edward, Boone, Nebr., 777 ... C8 103
Ste. Edwige, Que., Can., 205 ... D6 73
St. Eleanors, P.E.I., Can., 1,002 ... C6 74
St. Éleuthère, Que., Can., 1,014 ... B8 73
St. Elias, cape, Alsk ... D11 79
St. Elias, mtn., Alsk., Yukon, Can ... C11 79
St. Elias, mts., Alsk., B.C., Yukon, Can ... C11 79
St. Elie, Fr. Gu ... B4 59
Ste. Élizabeth, Que., Can., 557 ... C4 73
St. Elizabeth, Miller, Mo., 57 ... C5 101
St. Elmo, Mobile, Ala., 600 ... E1 78
St. Elmo, Fayette, Ill., 1,503 ... D5 90
St. Éloi, Que., Can., 252 ... A8 73
Ste. Émélie [-de-l'Énergie], Que., Can., 721 ... C4 73
St. Émile [-de-Suffolk], Que., Can., 244 ... D3 73
St. Ephrem, Que., Can., 898 ... C7 73
Saintes, Fr., 25,717 ... E3 14
St. Esprit, Que., Can., 778 ... D4 73
St. Étienne, Fr., 201,242 (*285,000) ... E6 14
St. Étienne [-de-Beuharnois], Que., Can ... q19 73
St. Étienne [-de-Lauzon], Que., Can ... o17 73
St.-Eugène, Alg., 25,491 ... *B5 44
Ste. Eulalie, Que., Can., 193 ... C5 73
Ste. Euphémie, Que., Can., 158 ... C7 73
St. Eusèbe, Que., Can., 244 ... B9 73
St. Eustache, Que., Can., 5,463 ... D4, p19 73
St. Eustatius, isl., Neth. Antilles ... n15 64
St. Fabien, Que., Can., 1,466 ... A9 73
Ste. Famille, Que., Can ... C7 73
St. Famille d'Aumond, Que., Can, 223 ... C2 73
St. Faustin, Que., Can., 331 ... C3 73
St. Felicien, Que., Can., 5,133 ... A5 73
Ste. Félicité, Que., Can., 1,057 ... *k13 73
St. Félix-de-Valois, Que., Can., 1,399 ... C4 73
St. Ferdinand, Que., Can., 2,706 ... C6 73
St. Féréol, Que., Can., 268 ... B7 73
St. Fidèle, Que., Can., 317 ... B7 73
Saintfield, N. Ire., 604 ... C6 11
St. Fintan's, Newf., Can., 107 ... D2 75
St. Flavien, Que., Can., 610 ... C6 73
Ste. Flore, Que., Can., 622 ... C5 73
St. Florent [-sur-Cher], Fr., 5,453 ... D5 14
St. Florian, Lauderdale, Ala., 100 ... A2 78
St. Flour, Fr., 5,846 ... E5 14
St. Fortunat, Que., Can., 216 ... D6 73
Ste. Foy, Que., Can., 29,716 ... n17 73
Ste. Foy-la-Grande, Fr., 3,152 ... E4 14
St. Francis, Clay, Ark., 224 ... A5 81
St. Francis, Cheyenne, Kans., 1,594 ... C2 93
St. Francis, Aroostook, Maine, 450 (1,058*) ... A4 96
St. Francis, Anoka, Minn., 175 ... E5 99
St. Francis, Todd, S. Dak., 421 ... D4 116
St. Francis, Milwaukee, Wis., 10,065 ... E2 124
St. Francis, co., Ark., 33,303 ... B5 81
St. Francis, cape, Newf., Can ... E5 75
St. Francis, lake, Que., Can ... D6 73
St. Francis, riv., Ark ... C5 81
St. Francis, riv., N.B., Que., Can., Maine ... B8 73
St. Francis, riv., Que., Can ... D5 73
St. Francis, riv., Mo ... E7 101
St. Francisville, Lawrence, Ill., 1,040 ... E6 90
St. Francisville, West Feliciana, La., 1,661 ... D4 95
St. François, Que., Can., 5,122 ... *p19 73
St. Francois, co., Mo., 36,516 ... D7 101
St. François [-du-Lac], Que., Can., 977 ... C5 73
Ste. Françoise, Que., Can., 476 ... A8 73
St. François-Xavier, Que., Can., 433 ... D5 73
St. Frédéric, Que., Can., 307 ... C7 73
St. Froid, lake, Maine ... B4 96
St. Fulgence, Que., Can., 1,094 ... A7 73
St. Gabriel, Iberville, La., 75 ... B5 95
St. Gabriel [-de-Brandon], Que., Can., 3,425 ... C4 73
St. Gallen, see Sankt Gallen, Switz.
St. Gallen, see Sankt Gallen, canton, Switz.
St. Gaudens, Fr., 7,949 ... F4 14
St. Gédéon-de-Beauce, Que., Can., 930 ... D7 73
Ste. Genevieve, Ste., Genevieve, Mo., 4,443 ... D7 101
Ste. Geneviève [-de-Batiscan], Que., Can., 532 ... C5 73
Ste. Genevieve, co., Mo., 12,116 ... D7 101
Ste. Geneviève-de-Pierrefonds, Que., Can., 2,397 ... *D8 73
St. George, Austl., 2,209 ... D7 51
St. George, Bermuda, 1,869 ... E14 77
St. George, N.B., Can., 1,133 ... D3 74
St. George, Ont., Can., 791 ... D4 72
St. George, Charlton, Ga., 582 ... F4 87
St. George, Pottawatomie, Kans., 259 ... C7 93
St. George, St. Louis, Mo., 1,323 ... *C7 101
St. George, Dorchester, S.C., 1,833 ... E6 115
St. George, Greene, Va., 5 ... C4 121
St. George, Washington, Utah, 5,130 ... F2 119
St. George (Town of), Chittenden, Vt. (108*) ... *C2 120
St. George, cape, Newf., Can ... D2 75
St. George, cape, Fla ... C1 86
St. George, cape, N. Gui ... h13 50
St. George, isl., Alsk ... D6 79
St. George, isl., Fla ... C2 86
St. George Island, St. Marys, Md., 200 ... D4 85
St. Georges, Bel., 5,854 ... D5 15
St. George's, Newf., Can., 1,181 ... D2 75
St. Georges, Que., Can., 1,775 ... C5 73
St. Georges, New Castle, Del., 339 ... A6 85
St. Georges, Fr. Gu., 1,502 ... B4 59
St. George's, Grenada, 7,303 (*19,582) ... p16 64
St. George's, bay, Newf., Can ... D2 75
St. George's, chan., Wales ... E3 10
St. George's, isl., Bermuda ... E14 77
St. Georges-de-Malbaie, Que., Can., 252 ... *k14 73
St. Georges [-de-Windsor], Que., Can., 345 ... D6 73
St. Georges-Ouest, Que., Can., 4,755 ... C7 73
St. Gérard, Que., Can., 662 ... D6 73
St. Germain, forest, Fr ... g9 14
St. Germain [-de-Grantham], Que., Can., 1,015 ... D5 73
St. Germain [-de-Kamouraska], Que., Can ... B8 73
St. Germain-en-Laye, Fr., 34,621 ... g9 14
Ste. Germaine-Station, Que., Can., 332 ... C7 73
Ste. Gertrude, Que., Can., 362 ... C5 73
St. Gertrude, St. Tammany, La., 75 ... D5 95
St. Gervais, Que., Can., 576 ... C7 73
St. Gervais-les-Bains, Fr., 1,551 ... D2 18
St. Gilles, Bel., 55,101 ... *D4 15
St. Gilles, Que., Can., 822 ... C6 73
St. Gilles-du-Gard, Fr., 4,791 ... F6 14
St. Gilles-sur-Vie, Fr., 2,511 ... D3 14
St.-Gingolph, Switz., 751 ... D2 19
St. Girons, Fr., 7,368 ... F4 14
St. Goarshausen, see Sankt Goarshausen, Ger.
St. Gobain, Fr., 2,012 ... C5 14
St. Gotthard, tunnel, Switz ... C6 19
St. Goven's, head, Wales ... C2 12
St. Grégoire, Que., Can., 673 ... C5 73
St. Gregor, Sask., Can., 170 ... E3 70
St. Gregory, mtn., Newf., Can ... D2 75
St. Guillaume, Que., Can., 792 ... D5 73
St. Helen, lake, Mich ... D6 98
St. Helena, Napa, Calif., 2,722 ... A5, C2 82
St. Helena, Cedar, Nebr., 63 ... B8 103
St. Helena, Br. dep., Afr., 4,600 ... H5 42
St. Helena, par., La., 9,162 ... D5 95
St. Helena, bay, S. Afr ... D2 49
St. Helena, isl., Atl. O ... H9 6
St. Helena, isl., S.C ... G6 115
St. Helena, mtn., Calif ... A5 82
St. Helena, sound, S.C ... G7 115
Ste. Hélène [-de-Kamouraska], Que., Can., 529 ... B8 73
St. Helens, Eng., 107,500 (*145,000) ... A5 12
St. Helens, Columbia, Oreg., 5,022 ... B4 113
St. Helens, mtn., Wash ... C3 122
St. Hélier, Jersey, 26,500 (*40,000) ... F5 10
Ste. Hénédine, Que., Can., 518 ... C7 73
St. Henri, Que., Can., 782 ... C6, o17 73
St. Henry, Mercer, Ohio, 978 ... B3 111
St. Hermas, Que., Can., 285 ... p18 73
St. Herménégilde, Que., Can., 204 ... D6 73
St. Hilaire, Pennington, Minn., 270 ... B2 99
St. Hilaire [-de-Dorset], Que., Can ... D7 73
St. Hilaire Est, Que., Can., 2,911 ... *D4 73
St. Hilarion, Que., Can., 493 ... B7 73
St. Honoré, Que., Can., 943 ... D7 73
St. Honoré-de-Témiscouata, Que., Can., 528 ... B8 73
St. Hubert, Que., Can., 14,380 ... *D4 73
St. Hubert, Bel., 3,108 ... D5 15
St. Hubert-de-Témiscouata, Que., Can., 724 ... B8 73
St. Hugues, Que., Can., 435 ... D5 73
St. Hyacinthe, Que., Can., 22,354 ... D5 73
St. Hyacinthe, co., Que., Can., 44,993 ... D4 73
St. Ignace, Mackinac, Mich., 3,334 ... C6 98
St. Ignace, N.S., Can., 515 ... C4 74
St. Ignatius, Lake, Mont., 940 ... C2 102
St. Ignatius Mission, Br. Gu ... B3 59
St. Imier, Switz., 6,704 ... B3 19
St. Inigoes, St. Marys, Md., 125 ... D5 85
St. Irénée, Que., Can., 701 ... B7 73
St. Isidore, N.B., Can., 614 ... B4 74
St. Isidore-d'Auckland, Que., Can., 373 ... D6 73
St. Isidore [-de-Laprairie], Que., Can., 241 ... q19 73
St. Isidore-de-Prescott, Ont., Can., 458 ... B10 72
St. Ives, Eng., 4,076 ... B7 12
St. Ives, Eng., 9,337 ... D2 12
St. Jacob, Madison, Ill., 529 ... E4 90
St. Jacobs, Ont., Can., 669 ... D4 72
St. Jacques, N.B., Can., 892 ... B1 74
St. Jacques, Que., Can., 2,038 ... D4 73
St. Jacques, cape, Viet ... H7 38
St. Jacques-le-Mineur, Que., Can., 273 ... q20 73
St. James, Stone, Ark., 30 ... B4 81
St. James, Man., Can., 33,977 ... E3 71
St. James, St. James, La., 280 ... C6 95
St. James, Charlevoix, Mich., 180 ... C5 98
St. James, Watonwan, Minn., 4,174 ... G4 99
St. James, Phelps, Mo., 2,384 ... D6 101
St. James, Suffolk, N.Y., 5,500 ... F4 84
St. James, par., La., 18,369 ... D5 95
St. James, Cedar, Nebr., 50 ... B8 103
St. James, cape, B.C., Can ... D2 68
St. James, is., Vir. Is ... f15 65
St. James City, Lee, Fla., 130 ... F4 86
St. Janvier, Que., Can., 1,811 ... D4, p19 73
St. Jean, Que., Can., 26,988 (*34,576) ... D4 73
St. Jean, co., Que., Can., 38,470 ... D4 73
St. Jean, riv., Que., Can ... A7 73
St. Jean-Baptiste, Man., Can., 521 ... E3 71
St. Jean [-Chrysostome-de-Lévis], Que., Can., 563 ... o17 73
St. Jean-d'Angély, Fr., 8,660 ... E3 14
St. Jean-de-Dieu, Que., Can., 1,177 ... A8 73
St. Jean-de-Luz, Fr., 10,241 ... F3 14
St. Jean-de-Matha, Que., Can., 846 ... C4 73
St. Jean [-de-Maurienne], Fr., 4,252 ... D2 18
St. Jean-Eudes, Que., Can., 2,873 ... *A7 73
St. Jean-Port-Joli, Que., Can., 1,615 ... B7 73
St. Jérôme, Que., Can., 24,546 ... D3 73
St. Jo, Montague, Tex., 977 ... C4 118
St. Joachim [-de-Courval], Que., Can ... D5 73
St. Joachim [-de-Montmorency], Que., Can., 988 ... B7 73
St. Joe, Searcy, Ark., 150 ... A3 81
St. Joe, Benewah, Idaho, 50 ... B2 89
St. Joe, DeKalb, Ind., 499 ... B8 91
St. Joe, riv., Idaho ... B3 89
Saint John, N.B., Can., 55,153 (*95,563) ... D3 74
St. John, Lake, Ind., 1,128 ... B3 91
St. John, Stafford, Kans., 1,753 ... E5 93
St. John, Aroostook, Maine, 400 (407*) ... A4 96
St. John, St. Louis, Mo., 7,342 ... *A8 95
St. John, Rolette, N. Dak., 420 ... A6 110
St. John, Tooele, Utah (part of Vernon) ... C3 119
St. John, Whitman, Wash., 545 ... B8 122
St. John, co., N.B., Can., 89,251 ... D3 74
St. John, bay, Newf., Can ... C3 75
St. John, cape, Newf., Can ... D4 75
St. John, isl., Newf., Can ... C3 75
St. John, isl., Vir. Is. (U.S.) ... f16 65
St. John, lake, Newf., Can ... D4 75
St. John, lake, Que., Can ... A5 73
St. John, riv., Can., Maine ... B5 96
St. John's, Antigua, 21,396 ... n16 64
St. Johns, Apache, Ariz., 1,310 ... C6 80
St. John's, Newf., Can., 63,633 (*90,838) ... E5 75
St. Johns, Perry, Ill., 206 ... E4 90
St. Johns, Clinton, Mich., 5,629 ... E6 98
St. Johns, Auglaize, Ohio, 220 ... B3 111
St. Johns, co., Fla., 30,034 ... C5 86
St. John's, pt., Ire ... C3 11
St. John's, pt., Ire ... C6 11
St. Johns, riv., Fla ... B5 86
St. Johnsbury, Caledonia, Vt., 6,809 (8,869*) ... C4 120
St. Johnsbury Center, Caledonia, Vt., 400 ... C4 120
St. Johns River, entrance, Fla ... B6 86
St. Johnsville, Montgomery, N.Y., 2,196 ... B6 108
St. John the Baptist, par., La., 18,439 ... D5 95
St. Jones, riv., Del ... B6 85
St. Joseph, N.B., Can., 748 ... D5 74
St. Joseph, Dominica, 3,050 ... o16 64
St. Joseph, Champaign, Ill., 1,210 ... C5 90
St. Joseph, Tensas, La., 1,653 ... C4 95
St. Joseph, Berrien, Mich., 11,755 ... F4 98
St. Joseph, Stearns, Minn., 1,487 ... E4 99
St. Joseph, Buchanan, Mo., 79,673 ... B3 101
St. Joseph, Lawrence, Tenn., 547 ... B4 117
St. Joseph, co., Ind., 238,614 ... A5 91
St. Joseph, co., Mich., 42,332 ... G5 98
St. Joseph, bay, Fla ... C1 86
St. Joseph, isl., Ont., Can ... B7 98
St. Joseph, isl., Mich ... B6 98
St. Joseph, isl., Tex ... E4 118
St. Joseph, lake, Ont., Can ... o17 72
St. Joseph, lake, Que., Can ... n16 73
St. Joseph, pt., Fla ... H3 86
St. Joseph, riv., Ind., Mich., Ohio ... B8 91, F5 98, A3 111
St. Joseph-de-Beauce, Que., Can., 2,484 ... C7 73
St. Joseph-de-la-Rive, Que., Can., 335 ... B7 73
St. Joseph-de-St. Hyacinthe, Que., Can., 3,799 ... *D4 73
St. Joseph-de-Sorel, Que., Can., 3,588 ... *C4 73
St. Joseph-du-Lac, Que., Can., 358 ... p18 73
St. Joseph's, Newf., Can., 301 ... E5 75
St. Josephs Hill, Clark and Floyd, Ind., 100 ... A4 94
St. Josephs, sound, Fla ... E1 86
St. Jovite, Que., Can., 2,692 ... C3 73
St. Jovite-Station, Que., Can ... C3 73
St. Jude, Que., Can., 515 ... D5 73
St. Julien, Fr., 2,725 ... D1 19
Ste. Julienne, Que., Can., 753 ... D4 73
Ste. Julie-Station, Que., Can., 242 ... C6 73
St. Junien, Fr., 8,449 ... E4 14
St. Just, Eng., 3,636 ... D2 12
St. Just-en-Chaussée, Fr., 3,575 ... E2 15
Ste. Justine, Que., Can., 513 ... D7 73
St. Keverne, Eng., 1,709 ... D2 12
St. Kilda, Austl., 55,000 ... *H5 51
St. Kitts, isl., St. Kitts-Nevis-Anguilla ... n15 64
St. Kitts-Nevis-Anguilla, Br. dep., N.A., 64,000 ... n15 64
St. Lambert, Que., Can., 14,531 ... p19 73
St. Lambert [-de-Lévis], Que., Can., 502 ... C6 73
St. Landry, Evangeline, La., 425 ... D3 95
St. Landry, par., La., 81,493 ... D3 95
St. Laurent, Man., Can., 869 ... D3 71
St. Laurent, Que., Can., 49,805 ... p19 73
St. Laurent, Fr. Gu., 2,095 ... A4 59
St. Laurent-Blangy, Fr., 3,681 ... D2 15
St. Laurent-de-la-Salanque, Fr., 3,300 ... F5 14
St. Laurent-du-Jura, Fr., 694 ... C1 18
St. Lawrence, Austl., 264 ... D8 50
St. Lawrence, Newf., Can., 2,095 ... E4 75
St. Lawrence, Berks, Pa., 929 ... *F10 114
St. Lawrence, Hand, S. Dak., 290 ... C7 116
St. Lawrence, co., N.Y., 111,239 ... A5 108
St. Lawrence, cape, N.S., Can ... B9 74
St. Lawrence, gulf, Can ... G20 67
St. Lawrence, isl., Alsk ... C5 79
St. Lawrence, riv., Can., N.Y ... G19 67
St. Lazare, Man., Can., 449 ... D1 71
St. Lazare, Que., Can., 513 ... q18 73
St. Leo, Pasco, Fla., 278 ... D4 86
St. Leo, Yellow Medicine, Minn., 129 ... F2 99
St. Léon, Que., Can., 222 ... C5 73
St. Leon, Dearborn, Ind., 319 ... F8 91
St. Léonard, N.B., Can., 1,666 ... B2 74
St. Leonard, Calvert, Md., 140 ... D4 85
St. Léonard [-d'Aston], Que., Can., 852 ... C5 73
St. Léonard [-de-Noblat], Fr., 3,671 ... E4 14
St. Léonard [-de-Portneuf], Que., Can., 454 ... C6 73
St. Léon [-de-Chicoutimi], Que., Can., 432 ... A6 73
St. Léon-de-Standon, Que., Can., 475 ... *C7 73
St. Lewis, riv., Newf., Can ... B3 75
St. Lewis, sound, Newf., Can ... B4 75
St. Liboire, Que., Can., 577 ... D5 73
St. Libory, St. Clair, Ill., 346 ... E4 90
St. Libory, Howard, Nebr., 150 ... C7 103
St. Lô, Fr., 15,388 ... C3 14
St. Louis, P.E.I., Can., 325 ... C5 74
St. Louis, Sask., Can., 344 ... E3 70
St. Louis, Sen., 48,800 ... C1 45
St. Louis, Gratiot, Mich., 3,808 ... E6 98
St. Louis (Independent City), Mo., 750,026 (*2,050,800) ... B8, C7 101
St. Louis, Pottawatomie, Okla., 76 ... B5 102
St. Louis, co., Minn., 231,588 ... C6 99
St. Louis, co., Mo., 703,532 ... C7 101
St. Louis, bay, Miss ... E2 100
St. Louis, lake, Que., Can ... q19 73
St. Louis, riv., Minn ... D6 99
St. Louis-de-Gonzague, Que., Can., 541 ... D3, q19 73
St. Louis-de-Kent, N.B., Can., 861 ... C5 74
St. Louis [-de-Richelieu], Que., Can ... D5 73
St. Louis-du-Ha-Ha, Que., Can., 843 ... B8 73
Ste. Louise, Que., Can., 493 ... B7 73
St. Louis Park, Hennepin, Minn., 43,310 ... E6 99
St. Louisville, Licking, Ohio, 349 ... B5 111
St. Loup-sur-Semouse, Fr., 2,864 ... B2 18
St.-Luc, Switz., 193 ... D4 19
St. Lucas, Fayette, Iowa, 211 ... A6 92
St. Lucia, Br. dep., N.A., 94,000 ... p16 64
St. Lucia, cape, S. Afr ... C5 49
St. Lucia, chan., N.A ... o16 64
Ste. Lucie, Que., Can., 297 ... C7 73
St. Lucie, St. Lucie, Fla., 500 ... E6 86
St. Lucie, co., Fla., 39,294 ... E6 86
St. Lucie, canal, Fla ... E6 86
St. Lucie, inlet, Fla ... E6 86
St. Ludger, Que., Can., 326 ... D7 73
Ste. Madeleine, Que., Can., 964 ... D4 73
St. Magloire, Que., Can., 672 ... C7 73
St. Magnus, bay, Scot ... g10 10
St. Maixent-l'École, Fr., 7,068 ... D3 14
St. Malachie, Que., Can., 338 ... C7 73
St. Malo, Man., Can., 574 ... E3 71
St. Malo, Fr., 17,137 ... C2 14
St. Malo, gulf, Fr ... C3 14
St. Mandé, Fr., 24,325 ... g10 14
St. Marc, Que., Can., 236 ... D4 73
St. Marc, Hai, 10,485 ... F7 64
St. Marc [-des-Carrières], Que., Can., 2,622 ... C5 73
St. Marcel, Que., Can., 258 ... C7 73
St. Marcellin, Fr., 5,298 ... E6 14
St. Margaret, bay, Newf., Can ... C3 75
St. Margarets, Anne Arundel, Md., 75 ... B5 85
St. Margaret's Hope, Scot ... B6 13
Ste. Marguerite, riv., Que., Can ... A7 73
Ste. Marguerite [-de-Dorchester], Que., Can., 324 ... C7 73
Ste. Marguerite Nord-Est, riv., Que., Can ... A7 73
Ste. Marguerite [-Station], Que., Can., 248 ... D3 73
Ste. Marie, Que., Can., 181 ... C5 73
Ste. Marie, Jasper, Ill., 347 ... E5 90
Ste. Marie, cape, Malag ... K8 49
Ste. Marie, isl., Malag ... g9 49
Ste. Marie-aux-Mines, Fr., 7,897 ... A3 18
Ste. Marie-de-Beauce, Que., Can., 3,662 ... C6 73
St. Maries, Benewah, Idaho, 2,435 ... B2 89
Ste. Marie-Sur-Mer., 435 ... B5 74
St. Mark, Sedgwick, Kans ... B5 93
St. Marks, Wakulla, Fla., 350 ... B2 86
Ste. Marthe, Que., Can., 261 ... D3 73
St. Martin, par., La., 29,063 ... D4 95
St. Martin, isl., Fr., Neth. Antilles ... m15 64
St. Martin, isl., Mich ... C4 98
St. Martin, lake, Man., Can ... D2 71
St. Martin, riv., Md ... D7 85
St. Martin-Boulogne, Fr., 10,888 ... D9 12
St. Martin [-de-Ré], Fr., 2,262 ... D3 14
St. Martin-de-Tours, Que., Can., 1,290 ... D7 73
Ste. Martine, Que., Can., 1,695 ... D4, q19 73
St. Martins, N.B., Can., 509 ... D4 74
St. Martin Station, Man., Can., 40 ... D2, g8 71
St. Martinville, St. Martin, La., 6,468 ... D4 95
St. Martory, Fr., 1,066 ... F4 14
St. Mary, Marion, Ky., 250 ... C4 94
St. Mary, par., La., 48,833 ... E4 95
St. Mary, cape, N.S., Can ... E3 74
St. Mary, is., Que., Can ... C2 75
St. Mary, res., Alta., Can ... E4 69
St. Mary, riv., Alta., Can ... E4 69
St. Mary, riv., B.C., Can ... E2 69
St. Mary-of-the-Woods, Vigo, Ind., 700 ... E3 91
St. Mary's, Newf., Can., 434 ... E5 75
St. Marys, Ont., Can., 4,482 ... D3 72
St. Marys, Camden, Ga., 3,272 ... F5 87
St. Marys, St. Joseph, Ind., 900 ... A5 91
St. Marys, Pottawatomie, Kans., 1,509 ... C7 93
St. Marys, Ste. Genevieve, Mo., 620 ... D8 101
St. Marys, Auglaize, Ohio, 7,737 ... B3 111
St. Marys, Elk, Pa., 8,065 ... D4 114
St. Marys, Pleasants, W. Va., 2,443 ... B3 123
St. Marys, co., Md., 38,915 ... D4 85
St. Mary's, bay, Newf., Can ... E5 75
St. Mary's, bay, N.S., Can ... E3 74
St. Mary's, cape, Newf., Can ... E4 75
St. Marys, entrance, Fla ... B5 86
St. Mary's, riv., N.S., Can ... D8 74
St. Marys, riv., Fla., Ga ... B5 80, F5 87
St. Marys, riv., Ind., Ohio ... C8 85, B3 111
St. Marys, riv., Md ... D5 85
St. Marys, riv., Mich ... B6 98
St. Mathieu, Que., Can ... A9 73
St. Mathieu [-de-Laprairie], Que., Can ... q19 73
St. Matthew, isl., Alsk ... C5 79
St. Matthew, isl., Bur ... H3 38
St. Matthews, Jefferson, Ky., 8,738 ... A4, B4 94
St. Matthews, Calhoun, S.C., 2,433 ... D6 115
St. Maur-des-Fossés, Fr., 70,397 ... g10 14, F2 15
St. Maurice, Que., Can., 333 ... C5 73
St. Maurice, Switz., 3,196 ... D3 19
St. Maurice, co., Que., Can., 109,873 ... C4 73
St. Maurice, riv., Que., Can ... C5 73
St. Maxime, Que., Can ... C6 73
St. Meinrad, Spencer, Ind., 850 ... H4 91
Ste. Mélanie, Que., Can., 279 ... C4 73
St. Memmie, Fr., 2,032 ... F4 15
St. Menehould, Fr., 3,406 ... C6 14
St. Méthode, Que., Can., 690 ... C6 73
St. Michael, Alsk., 205 ... C7 79
St. Michael, Alta., Can., 129 ... C4 69

St. Michael, Cambria, Pa., 1,292 .... *F4 114
St. Michaels, Apache, Ariz., 50 .... B6 80
St. Michaels, Talbot, Md., 1,484 .... C5 85
St. Michael, Wright, Minn., 707 .... E5 187
St. Michael, Benson, N. Dak., 40 .... B7 110
St. Michaels, bay, Newf., Can ... B4 75
St. Michel, Que., Can., 55,978 .... p19 73
St. Michel, Fr., 4,502 .... E4 15
St. Michel [-de-Bellechasse], Que., Can., 843 .... C7 73
St. Michel-de-l'Atalaye, Hai., 2,328 .... F7 64
St. Michel [-de-Maurienne], Fr., 2,313 .... D2 18
St. Michel [-de-Napierville], Que., Can., 250 .... q19 73
St. Michel-des-Saints, Que., Can., 1,763 .... C4 73
St. Mihiel, Fr., 5,253 .... C6 14
St. Modeste, Que., Can., 40 .. B8 73
Ste. Monique [-de-Nicolet], Que., Can., 229 .... C5 73
St. Moritz, see Sankt Moritz, Switz.
St. Nazaire, Que., Can., 158 .... D5 73
St. Nazaire, Fr., 58,286 .... D2 14
St. Nazaire [-de-Buckland], Que., Can., 229 .... C7 73
St. Nazaire [-de-Chicoutimi], Que., Can., 816 .... A6 73
St. Nazianz, Manitowoc, Wis., 669 .... B6, D6 124
St. Neots, Eng., 5,570 .... B7 12
St. Nérée, Que., Can., 411 .. C7 73
St. Nicholas, Que., Can., 1,295 .... o17 73
St. Nicolas, see Sint Niklaas, Bel.
St. Nicolas-de-Port, Fr., 5,761 .... F6 15
St. Noël, Que., Can., 1,124 .. *B3 73
St. Norbert, Man., Can., 695 . E3 71
St. Norbert [-d'Arthabaska], Que., Can., 291 .... C6 73
Ste. Odile, Que., Can., 1,293 .... A9 73
St. Odilon, Que., Can., 686 . C7 73
St. Olaf, Clayton, Iowa, 169 . B6 94
St. Olof, Swe., 468 .... C8 24
St. Omer, Que., Can., 470 . k13 73
St. Omer, Fr., 19,283 .... B5 14
St. Onge, Lawrence, S. Dak., 100 .... C2 116
Saintonge, former prov., Fr., 286,000 .... E3 14
St. Ouen, Fr., 51,956 .... g10 14
St. Ours, Que., Can., 711 .. D4 73
St. Pacôme, Que., Can., 1,242 .... B8 73
St. Pamphile, Que., Can., 1,839 .... C8 73
St. Paris, Champaign, Ohio, 1,460 .... B4 111
St. Pascal, Que., Can., 2,144 .... B8 73
St. Patrick, lake, Que., Can A7 72
St. Paul, Madison, Ark., 118 .... B2 81
St. Paul, Alta., Can., 2,823 .. B5 69
St. Paul, Que., Can., 619 .... D5 73
St. Paul, Decatur and Shelby, Ind., 702 .... F6 91
St. Paul, Neosho, Kans., 675 .... E8 93
St. Paul, Ramsey, Minn., 313,411 .... E7, F6 99
St. Paul, St. Charles, Mo., 125 .... A7 101
St. Paul, Howard, Nebr., 1,714 .... C7 103
St. Paul, Marion, Oreg., 254 .... B1 113
St. Paul, Clarendon, S.C., 75 .... D7 115
St. Paul, Wise, Va., 1,156 .. B2 121
St. Paul, isl., Alsk D5 79
St. Paul, isl., N.S., Can B9 74
St. Paul, isl., Indian O I2 2
St. Paul, riv., Newf., Que., Can C3 75
St. Paul, riv., Lib E3 45
St. Paul, rocks, Atl. O E8 6
St. Paul-de-Chester, Que., Can., 317 .... D6 73
St. Paul-de-la-Croix, Que., Can., 318 .... B8 73
St. Paul [-de-Montminy], Que., Can C7 73
St. Paul-du-Nord, Que., Can A8 73
St. Paulin, Que., Can., 920 . C4 73
St. Paul Park, Washington, Minn., 3,267 .... F6, F7 99
St. Pauls, Robeson, N.C., 2,249 .... C5 109
Ste. Perpétue, Que., Can., 203 .... C7 73
Ste. Perpétue-de-L'Islet, Que., Can., 674 .... B8 73
St. Peter, Fayette, Ill., 397 .. E5 90
St. Peter, Graham, Kans., 60 .... C3 93
St. Peter, Nicollett, Minn., 8,484 .... F5 99
St. Peter, Cascade, Mont C5 102
St. Peter, lake, Que., Can C5 73
St. Peter Port, Guernsey, 15,700 (*22,000) F5 10
St. Peters, N.S., Can., 762 .. D9 74
St. Peters, Franklin, Ind., 100 .... F7 91
St. Peters, St. Charles, Mo., 404 .... A7, C7 101
St. Peters Bay, P.E.I., Can., 321 .... C7 74
St. Petersburg, Pinellas, Fla., 181,298 (*355,200) E2, E4 86
St. Petersburg, Clarion, Pa., 417 .... D2 114
St. Petersburg Beach, Pinellas, Fla., 6,268 .... F1 86
Ste. Pétronille, Que., Can., 510 .... n17 73
St. Philémon, Que., Can., 539 .... C7 73
St. Philip, Posey, Ind., 100 .. I2 91
St. Philippe [-de-Laprairie], Que., Can., 424 .... D4, q20 73
St. Philippe-de-Neri, Que., Can., 746 .... B8 73
Ste. Philomène, Que., Can., 386 .... D4, q19 73
St. Pie, Que., Can., 1,434 .. D5 73
St. Pierre, Que., Can., 364 .. *C3 73
St. Pierre, Que., Can., 6,795 .... *D4 73
St. Pierre, Mart., 6,218 .... o16 64
St. Pierre, St. Pierre & Miquelon, 4,362 .... E3 75
St. Pierre, isl., St. Pierre & Miquelon E3 75
St. Pierre & Miquelon, Fr. dep., N.A., 5,000 .... E3 75
St. Pierre d'Albigny, Fr., 838 .... D2 18
St. Pierre-en-Port, Fr., 995 .. E8 12
St. Pierre-Jolys, Man., Can., 856 .... E3 71
St. Pierre [-les-Becquets], Que., Can., 453 .... C5 73
St. Pierre [-Montmagny], Que., Can., 281 .... C7 73
St. Pius, Stark, N. Dak., 75 .. C3 110
St. Placide, Que., Can., 336 .... p18 73
St. Pol-de-Léon, Fr., 6,037 .. C2 14
St. Pol-sur-Mer, Fr., 18,686 . C2 15
St. Pol [-sur-Ternoise], Fr., 5,193 .... B5 14
St. Pourçain [-sur-Sioule], Fr., 3,182 .... D5 14
St. Prime, Que., Can., 659 .. A5 73
St. Prosper, Que., Can., 158 .... C5 73
St. Prosper-de-Dorchester, Que., Can., 1,357 .... C7 73
St. Quentin, N.B., Can., 2,089 .... B2 74
St. Quentin, Fr., 61,071 .... C5 14, E3 15
St. Raphaël, Que., Can., 1,134 .... C7 73
St. Raphaël, Fr., 9,470 .... F7 14
St. Raphaël-sur-Mer, N.B., Can., 643 .... B5 74
St. Raymond, Que., Can., 3,931 .... C6 73
St. Rédempteur, Que., Can. D3 73
St. Rédempteur, Que., Can., 1,035 .... o17 73
St. Regis, Mineral, Mont., 500 .... C1 102
St. Regis, Indian res., N.Y f10 108
St. Regis, riv., N.Y f10 108
St. Regis Falls, Franklin, N.Y., 800 .... f10 108
St. Regis Park, Jefferson, Ky., 1,179 .... *H6 94
St. Rémi, Que., Can., 2,276 .... D4, q19 73
St. Remi-d'Amherst, Que., Can., 396 .... C3 73
St. Rémi [-de-Tingwick], Que., Can., 219 .... D6 73
St. Roch [-de-Richelieu], Que., Can., 468 .... D4 73
St. Roch-des-Aulnaies, Que., Can B7 73
St. Romuald, Que., Can., 5,681 .... C6, n17 73
Ste. Rosalie, Que., Can., 1,255 .... *D5 73
Ste. Rose, Que., Can., 7,571 .... D4, p19 73
Ste. Rose, Guad., 1,288 .... n16 64
St. Rose, St. Charles, La., 1,099 .... C7 95
Ste. Rose-de-Lima, Que., Can., 2,965 .... D2 73
Ste. Rose-du-Dégelé, Que., Can., 1,943 .... B9 73
Ste. Rose-du-Lac, Man., Can., 790 .... D2 71
Ste. Sabine, Que., Can., 444 . C7 73
St. Samuel, Que., Can., 511 .... D7 73
St. Sauveur-des-Monts, Que., Can., 1,702 .... D3 73
Ste. Savine, Fr., 11,864 .... C5 14
Ste. Scholastique, Que., Can., 838 .... D3, p18 73
St. Sébastien-de-Beauce, Que., Can., 516 .... D7 73
St. Sebastien, cape, Malag f9 49
St. Servan [-sur-Mer], Fr., 14,963 .... C3 14
St. Sever, Fr., 2,028 .... F3 14
St. Sévérin, Que., Can., 230 . C6 73
St. Shotts, Newf., Can., 189 .... E5 75
St. Siméon, Que., Can., 1,197 .... B8 73
St. Siméon, Fr., 191 .... E3 73
St. Siméon-de-Bonaventure, Que., Can., 420 .... A4 74
St. Simon-de-Rimouski, Que., Can A8 73
St. Simons, isl., Ga E5 87
St. Simons, sound, Ga E5 87
St. Simons Island, Glynn, Ga., 3,199 .... E5 87
St. Sixte, Que., Can., 86 .... D2 73
Ste. Sophie [-de-Lévrard], Que., Can., 398 .... C5 73
Ste. Sophie [-de-Mégantic], Que., Can., 267 .... C6 73
St. Stephen, N.B., Can., 3,380 .... D2 74
Ste. Stephen, Berkeley, S.C., 1,462 .... E8 115
St. Stephen, Fremont, Wyo., 5 .... C4 125
St. Stephens, Washington, Ala., 150 .... D1 78
St. Sylvère, Que., Can., 223 . C5 73
St. Sylvestre, Que., Can., 652 .... C6 73
St. Tammany, St. Tammany, La., 50 .... B8, D6 95
St. Tammany, par., La., 38,643 .... D5 95
St. Thècle, Que., Can., 2,009 .... C5 73
St. Théodore, Que., Can C5 73
St. Théophile, Que., Can., 510 .... D7 73
Ste. Thérèse-de-Blainville, Que., Can., 11,771 .. D4, p19 73
St. Thomas, Ont., Can., 22,469 .... E3 72
St. Thomas, Que., Can., 508 .... C4 73
St. Thomas, Cole, Mo., 180 .. C5 101
St. Thomas, Pembina, N. Dak., 660 .... A8 110
St. Thomas, Franklin, Pa., 600 .... G6 114
St. Thomas, isl., Vir. Is. (U.S.) .. f15 65
St. Thuribe, Que., Can., 208 .... *C5 73
St. Timothée, Que., Can., 1,003 .... q18 73
St. Tite, Que., Can., 3,250 .. C5 73
St. Tite-des-Caps, Que., Can., 1,227 .... B7 73
St. Tropez, Fr., 3,988 .... F7 14
St. Ubald, Que., Can., 764 .. C5 73
St. Ulric, Que., Can., 1,021 .... *k13 73
St. Urbain-de-Charlevoix, Que., Can., 878 .... B7 73
St. Urbain [-de-Châteauguay], Que., Can., 255 .... q19 73
St. Valère, Que., Can., 197 .. C5 73
St. Valérien, Que., Can., 226 .... D5 73
St. Valéry-en-Caux, Fr., 2,905 .... E8 12
St. Valéry-sur-Somme, Fr., 3,169 .... B4 14
St. Vallier, Que., Can., 540 . C7 73
St. Vallier, Fr., 4,124 .... E6 14
Ste. Véronique, Que., Can., 250 .... C3 73
St. Victor, Que., Can., 931 . C7 73
St. Vincent, Kittson, Minn., 217 .... B1 99
St. Vincent, Br. dep., N.A., 85,000 .... p16 64
St. Vincent, cape, Malag h8 49
St. Vincent, cape, Port D1 20
St. Vincent, gulf, Austl G2 51
St. Vincent, isl., Fla C1 86
St. Vincent, passage, N.A p16 64
St. Vincent-de-Paul, Que., Can., 11,214 .... p19 73
St. Vincent's, Newf., Can., 599 .... E5 75
St. Vith, Bel., 2,708 .... D6 15
St. Vrain, Curry, N. Mex., 10 .... C6 107
St. Walburg, Sask., Can., 689 .... D1 70
St. Wendells, Posey, Ind., 160 .... H2 91
St. Williams, Ont., Can., 399 .... E4 72
St. Xavier, Big Horn., Mont., 100 .... E9 102
St. Yrieix-la-Perche, Fr., 4,368 .... E4 14
St. Yvon, Que., Can., 428 . *k13 73
St. Zacharie, Que., Can., 1,361 .... C7 73
St. Zéphirin, Que., Can., 247 .... C5 73
Saipan, chan., Saipan 52
Saipan, isl., Mariana Is 52
Sa'ir, Jordan, 3,000 .... C7 32
Saitama, pref., Jap., 2,403,871 .... *I9 37
Saiyidabad, Afg., 10,000 .. D14 41
Sajama, mtn., Bol C2 55
Saka, China, 5,000 .... C10 40
Saka, Ken B6 48
Sakai, Jap., 339,863 .... o14 37
Sakaide, Jap., 40,200 (62,142▲) *I6 37
Sakākā, Sau. Ar., 10,000 .. H13 31
Sakami, lake, Que., Can n20 72
Sakania, Con. L., 12,100 .... D4 48
Sakaraha, Malag h8 49
Sakarya (Sangarius), riv., Tur .. B8 31
Sakashita, Jap., 3,400 .... n16 37
Sakata, Jap., 55,600 (97,671▲) G9 37
Sakchu, Kor., 13,568 .... F2 37
Sakhalin, isl., Sov. Un D17 28
Sakiai, Sov. Un A7 26
Sakimotobu, Okinawa, 20,409 .. 52
Sakishima, is., Ryukyu Is G9 34
Sakmara, riv., Sov. Un C5 29
Sakon Nakhon, Thai, 14,940 .... D6 38
Sakonnet, Newport, R.I., 50 .... D12 84
Sakonnet, riv., R.I D12 84
Sak'ot'a, Eth C4 47
Sakripe, Lib E3 45
Sakskøbing, Den., 2,526 (▲4,035) D5 24
Sakti, China A9 40
Sakti, India, 8,125 .... F9 40
Sakwaso, lake, Ont., Can C6 71
Sal, isl., C.V. Is *E3 42
Sal, pt., Calif E3 82
Sal, riv., Sov. Un D2 29
Sala, Swe., 11,000 .... H7, t34 25
Sala Consilina, It., 6,897 .... D5 21
Saladas, Arg., 3,900 .... E4 55
Saladillo, Arg., 7,586 .... B5 54
Salado, riv., Arg A3 54
Salado, riv., Arg B5 54
Salado, riv., Arg E3 55
Salado, riv., Arg E4 55
Salado, riv., Mex B4 63
Salaga, Ghana, 3,156 .... E4 45
Salajar, isl., Indon G6 35
Salamá, Guat., 2,760 .... C4 62
Salamá, Hond., 947 .... C4 62
Salamanca, Chile, 2,819 .... A2 54
Salamanca, Mex., 32,192 .. m13 63
Salamanca, Cattaraugus, N.Y., 8,480 .... C2 108
Salamanca, Sp., 90,498 .... B3 20
Salamanca, prov., Sp., 405,729 .... *B3 20
Salamat, riv., Chad C3 46
Salamaua, N. Gui., 270 .... k12 50
Salamina, Col., 7,940 .... B2 60
Salamis, Grc., 11,161 .. D4, h11 23
Salamis, isl., Grc h10 23
Salamonia, Jay, Ind., 142 .. D8 91
Salamonie, riv., Ind C7 91
Salas, Sp., 2,522 .... A2 20
Salatiga, Idon., 53,706 .... *G4 35
Salavat, Sov. Un., 73,000 .. *C5 29
Salaverry, Peru, 3,403 .... C2 58
Salavina, Arg E3 55
Salawati, is., W. Irian F8 35
Sala-y-Gomez, isl., Pac. O H16 7
Salcedo, Ec B2 58
Saldanha, S. Afr., 2,195 .... D2 49
Saldus, Sov. Un., 10,000 .... C4 27
Sale, Austl., 7,899 .... I6 51
Sale, Eng., 52,600 .... *A5 12
Salé, Mor., 75,799 .... C3 44
Salealua, bay, W. Sam 52
Sale City, Mitchell, Ga., 275 .... E2 87
Sale Creek, Hamilton, Tenn., 800 .... D8 117
Salekhard, Sov. Un., 16,000 .... B22 9
Salem, Lee, Ala., 200 .... C4 78
Salem, Fulton, Ark., 713 .... A4 75
Salem, New London, Conn., 25 (925▲) D7 84
Salem, Taylor, Fla., 200 .... C3 86
Salem, Marion, Ill., 6,165 .... E5 90
Salem, India, 249,145 .... F6 39
Salem, Washington, Ind., 4,546 .... G5 91
Salem, Henry, Iowa, 442 .... D6 92
Salem, Livingston, Ky., 480 . A3 94
Salem, Essex, Mass., 39,211 .... A6, f12 97
Salem, Washtenaw, Mich., 250 .... A7 98
Salem, Dent, Mo., 3,870 .... D6 101
Salem, Richardson, Nebr., 261 .... D10 103
Salem, Rockingham, N.H., 950 (9,210▲) E4 105
Salem, Salem, N.J., 8,941 ... D2 106
Salem, Dona Ana, N. Mex., 150 .... E2 107
Salem, Washington, N.Y., 1,076 .... B7 108
Salem, Columbiana, Ohio, 13,854 .... B7 111
Salem, Marion and Polk, Oreg., 49,142 (*89,900) C1, C4 112
Salem, Oconee, S.C., 206 .... B2 115
Salem, McCook, S. Dak., 1,188 .... D8 116
Salem, Utah, Utah, 920 .... C4 119
Salem, Roanoke, Va., 16,058 .... D2 121
Salem, Harrison, W. Va., 2,366 .... B4, B6 123
Salem, Kenosha, Wis., 500 ... F1 121
Salem, co., N.J., 58,711 .... D2 106
Salem, creek, Ohio A1 123
Salem, fork, W. Va B6 123
Salem, plat., Mo D6 101
Salem, pond, Vt B4 120
Salem, riv., N.J D2 106
Salemburg, Sampson, N.C., 569 .... B5 109
Salem Depot, Rockingham, N.H., 2,523 .... E4 105
Salem Heights, Marion, Oreg., 10,770 .... *C4 113
Salemi, It., 13,300 .... F4 21
Salem Maritime, nat. historic site, Mass f12 97
Salen, Scot D3 13
Salerno, Martin, Fla., 900 .. E6 86
Salerno, It., 125,700 (*195,000) D5 21
Salerno, gulf, It D5 21
Sales, pt., Eng C8 12
Salfīt, Jordan, 2,000 .... B7, g11 32
Salford, Eng., 152,600 .... A5 12
Salge, Bonner, Idaho, 100 .. A2 89
Salgotarjan, Hung., 26,682 . A4 22
Salgueiro, Braz., 8,936 .... C3 57
Salida, Stanislaus, Calif., 1,109 .... *D3 82
Salida, Chaffee, Colo., 4,560 .... C5 83
Salies-de-Béarn, Fr., 2,859 .. F3 14
Salihli, Tur., 24,100 .... C7 31
Salima, Malawi, 1,450 .... D5 48
Salin, Bur., 5,000 .... D1 38
Salina, Saline, Kans., 43,202 .... D6 93
Salina, Mayes, Okla., 972 .... A6 112
Salina, Sevier, Utah, 1,618 .. E4 119
Salina, isl., It E5 21
Salina Cruz, Mex., 14,881 .. D5 63
Salinas, Braz., 5,186 .... E2 57
Salinas, Monterey, Calif., 28,957 .... C6, D3 82
Salinas, Ec., 2,868 .... B1 58
Salinas, P.R., 3,666 .... D5 65
Salinas, mun., P.R., 23,133 .. C5 65
Salinas, bay, P.R D2 65
Salinas, cape, Sp C7 20
Salinas, pampa, Arg A3 54
Salinas, peak, N. Mex D3 107
Salinas, pt., Ang D1 48
Salinas, pt., Peru D2 58
Salinas, pt., P.R B6 65
Salinas, riv., Calif D3 82
Salinas de Garci Mendoza, Bol., 635 .... C2 55
Salinas, Grandes, salt flat, Arg . E3 55
Salina Springs, Apache, Ariz., 200 .... A6 80
Saline, Bienville, La., 329 .... B3 95
Saline, Washtenaw, Mich., 2,334 .... F7 98
Saline, co., Ark., 28,956 .... C3 81
Saline, co., Ill., 26,227 .... F5 90
Saline, co., Kans., 54,715 .... D6 93
Saline, co., Mo., 25,148 .... B4 101
Saline, co., Nebr., 12,542 .... D8 103
Saline, bayou, La B3 95
Saline, riv., Ark C1 81
Saline, riv., Ark D3 81
Saline, riv., Ill F5 90
Saline, riv., Kans C4 93
Salineno, Starr, Tex., 175 .. F3 118
Salineville, Columbiana, Ohio, 1,898 .... B7 111
Salinópolis, Braz., 4,101 .... B1 57
Salins-les-Bains, Fr., 4,476 .. D6 14
Salisbury, N.B., Can., 589 .. C4 74
Salisbury, Litchfield, Conn., 900 (3,309▲) B3 84
Salisbury, Eng., 35,600 .... C6 12
Salisbury, Wicomico, Md., 16,302 .... D6 85
Salisbury, Essex, Mass., 1,000 (3,154▲) A6 97
Salisbury, Chariton, Mo., 1,787 .... B5 101
Salisbury, Merrimack, N.H., 100 (415▲) D3 105
Salisbury, Rowan, N.C., 21,297 .... B3 109
Salisbury, Somerset, Pa., 862 .... G3 114
Salisbury, Rh., 220,000 (*315,300) A5 49
Salisbury, Addison, Vt., 130 (575▲) D2 120
Salisbury, isl., N.W. Ter., Can D17 67
Salisbury, plain, Eng C6 12
Salisbury Beach, Essex, Mass., 400 .... A6 97
Salisbury Center, Herkimer, N.Y., 200 .... B6 108
Salisbury West, Rowan, N.C., 1,323 .... *B3 109
Salitpa, Clarke, Ala., 425 .... D1 78
Salix, Woodbury, Iowa, 394 .... B1 92
Salkehatchie, riv., S.C E5 115
Salkum, Lewis, Wash., 200 . C3 122
Salladasburg, Lycoming, Pa., 255 .... D7 114
Sallanches, Fr., 3,552 .... D2 18
Salley, Aiken, S.C., 403 .... D5 115
Salliquelό, Arg., 3,938 .... B4 54
Sallis, Attala, Miss., 223 .... B4 100
Sallisaw, Sequoyah, Okla., 3,351 .... B7 112
Salm, isl., Sov. Un B9 4
Salmo, B.C., Can., 889 .... E9 68
Salmon, Lemhi, Idaho, 2,944 .... D5 89
Salmon, mtn., N.H A4 105
Salmon, mts., Calif B2 82
Salmon, peak, Tex E2 118
Salmon, riv., B.C., Can B6 68
Salmon, riv., N.B., Can B2 74
Salmon, riv., N.B., Can C4 74
Salmon, riv., Idaho D3 89
Salmon, riv., N.Y f10 108
Salmon Arm, B.C., Can., 1,506 .... D8 68
Salmon Bay, Que., Can., 86 .... C3, h10 75
Salmon Creek, Clark, Wash., 175 .... D3 122
Salmon Creek, res., Idaho G4 89
Salmon Cove, Newf., Can., 655 .... *E5 75
Salmon Falls, Strafford, N.H., 1,210 .... D5 105
Salmon Falls, creek, Nev B7 104
Salmon Falls, riv., Idaho G4 89
Salmon Falls, riv., N.H., Maine D5 105
Salmon Gums, Austl., 61 .... F3 50
Salmon River, mts., Idaho D3 89
Salmon River, res., N.Y B5 108
Salmon Valley, B.C., Can., 309 .... B6 68
Salo, Fin., 11,000 .... G10 25
Saló, It., 5,568 .... B3 18
Salol, Roseau, Minn., 68 .... B3 99
Salome, Yuma, Ariz., 200 .. D2 80
Salon, riv., Fr B1 18
Salon-de-Provence, Fr., 17,267 (21,393▲) F6 14
Salonika (Thessaloniki), Grc., 216,838 .... B4 23
Salonika (Thessaloniki), prov., Grc., 544,394 .... *B4 23
Salonika, gulf, Grc B4 23
Salonta, Rom., 16,276 .... B5 22
Salpi, lake, It D6 21
Salsacate, Arg A3 54
Salsette, isl., India H4 40
Salsk, Sov. Un., 18,500 .... D2 29
Salsomaggiore, It., 8,600 .. B2 21
Salt (As Salt), Jordan, 15,478 .... F10 31
Salt, basin, Tex E2 118
Salt, creek, Ind G5 91
Salt, creek, Kans A3 93
Salt, creek, Nebr E2 103
Salt, creek, N. Mex D5 107
Salt, creek, Ohio C3 111
Salt, creek, Wyo B6 125
Salt, fork, Okla A3 112
Salt, fork, Okla C2 112
Salt, isl., Vir. Is f16 65
Salt, lake, Austl D1 50
Salt, lake, Haw g10 88
Salt, lake, N. Mex E6 107
Salt, marsh, Kans D5 93
Salt, pt., Calif C2 82
Salt, riv., Ariz D4 80
Salt, riv., Ky C4 94
Salt, riv., Mo B5 101
Salta, Arg., 108,000 .... D2 55
Salta, prov., Arg., 412,652 .. D2 55
Saltash, Eng., 7,420 .... D3 12
Saltburn-by-the-Sea, Eng., 3,911 (Saltburn and Marske-by-the-Sea, 12,482) F8 13
Salt Cay, isl., W.I.F f14 65
Saltcoats, Sask., Can., 490 .. F4 70
Saltcoats, Scot., 14,187 .... E4 13
Salt Creek, pass, Oreg D4 113
Saltee, is., Ire E5 11
Salter Path, Carteret, N.C., 135 .... C7 109
Salters, Williamsburg, S.C., 100 .... D8 115
Saltese, Mineral, Mont., 85 . C1 102
Saltfjord, fjord, Nor D6 25
Saltfork, Grant, Okla., 35 .. A4 112
Saltfork, creek, Kans E4 93
Salt Fork of Arkansas, riv., Okla A4 112
Saltholm, isl., Den C6 24
Saltillo, Washington, Ind., 121 .... G5 91
Saltillo, Mex., 98,839 .... B4 63
Saltillo, Lee, Miss., 536 .... A5 100
Saltillo, Huntingdon, Pa., 395 .... F5 114
Saltillo, Hardin, Tenn., 397 . B3 117
Salt Lake, co., Utah, 383,035 .... C3 119
Salt Lake City, Salt Lake, Utah, 189,454 (*410,200) C4 119
Salt Lick, Bath, Ky., 370 .... B6 94
Salto, Braz., 12,643 .... m8 56
Salto, Ur., 57,714 .... E1 56
Salto, dept., Ur., 78,600 .... *E1 56
Salto Grande, Braz., 3,016 .. C2 56
Salton, sea, Calif F6 82
Saltonstall, lake, Conn D5 84
Salt Peter, cave, Ga B2 87
Saltpond, Ghana, 6,968 .... E4 45
Salt River, Bullitt, Ky., 400 .... C4 94
Salt River, Indian res., Ariz G2 80
Salt River, mts., Ariz G2 80
Salt River, range, Wyo C2 125
Saltrou, Hai F7 64
Saltsburg, Indiana, Pa., 1,054 .... F3 114
Saltsjöbaden, Swe., 5,300 .... t36 25
Saltspring, isl., B.C., Can E6 68
Salt Springs, Marion, Fla., 755 .... C5 86
Saltville, Smyth and Washington, Va., 2,844 .. B3 121
Salt Wells, Churchill, Nev., 3 .... D3 104
Saluafata, hbr., W. Sam 52
Salud, Pan., 211 .... k10 62
Saluda, Polk, N.C., 570 .... D4 109
Saluda, Saluda, S.C., 2,089 .... D4 115
Saluda, Middlesex, Va., 300 .... D6 121
Saluda, co., S.C., 14,554 .... C4 115
Saluda, mtn., N.C D3 109
Saluda, riv., S.C C3 115
Saluda Gardens, Lexington, S.C., 2,000 .... *D5 115
Salur, India, 26,111 .... H9 40
Saluvia, Fulton, Pa., 25 .... F5 114
Saluzzo, It., 11,100 .... B1 21
Salvador, Braz., 630,878 .... D3 57
Salvador, Sask., Can., 137 .. E1 70
Salvador, El, see El Salvador, country, N.A.
Salvador, lake, La E5 95
Salvage, Newf., Can., 270 .. D5 75
Salvage, is., Port m14 20
Salvatierra, Mex., 14,417 .. m13 63
Salvisa, Mercer, Ky., 350 .... C5 94
Salween, riv., Bur D10 39
Salyany, Sov. Un., 23,000 .. F3 29
Salyersville, Magoffin, Ky., 1,173 .... C6 94
Salym, marsh, Sov. Un B8 29
Salzach, riv., Aus., Ger A8 18
Salzburg, Aus., 110,500 .... E6 16, B9 18
Salzburg, state, Aus., 347,292 .... B9 18
Salzgitter, Ger., 113,300 .... A5 17
Salzwedel, Ger., 20,700 .... B5 16
Sama, China C8 38
Samadan, Switz., 2,106 .... C5 18
Samaipata, Bol., 1,656 .... C3 55
Samalá, riv., Guat C2 62
Samālūt, Eg., U.A.R., 29,300 .... D6 43
Samaná, Dom. Rep., 3,309 .. F9 64
Samaná, bay, Dom. Rep F9 64
Samana, isl., Ba. Is D7 64
Samaniego, Col., 2,303 .... C2 60
Samannūd, Eg., U.A.R., 23,300 .... D3 32
Samar, prov., Phil., 871,900 .... *C7 35
Samar, isl., Phil C7 35
Samara, riv., Sov. Un E19 9
Samarai, Pap m13 50
Samarga, Sov. Un C9 37
Samaria, Oneida, Idaho, 150 .... G6 89
Samarinda, Indon., 68,095 ... F5 35
Samarkand, Sov. Un., 220,000 .... H22 9
Samarra, Iraq, 8,867 .... D2 41
Samata, W. Sam., 469 52
Sambalpur, India, 38,915 ... G9 40
Sambar, cape, Indon F4 35
Sambas, Indon., 12,000 .... E3 35
Sambava, Malag f10 49
Sambhal, India, 68,940 .... C7 40
Sambhar, India, 14,139 .... D5 40
Sambonifacio, It., 5,470 .... D7 18
Sambor, Sov. Un., 41,200 ... G4 27
Samborombón, bay, Arg B5 54
Sambre, riv., Bel D4 15
Samburg, Obion, Tenn., 451 .... A2 117
Samchŏnpo, Kor., 30,500 (50,800▲) *I4 37
Same, Tan., 4,428 .... B6 48
Samedan, Switz., 1,685 .... C8 19
Samit, Camb G5 38
Sammanish, lake, Wash D2 122
Sammylane, Stone, Mo E4 101
Sam Neua, Laos B6 38
Samnorwood, Collingsworth, Tex., 65 .... B2 118
Samnū, Libya D2 43
Samoa, Humboldt, Calif., 600 .... B1 82
Samoa, American, see American Samoa, U.S. dep., Oceania
Samoa, Western, see Western Samoa, country, Pac. O.
Samokov, Bul., 12,784 .... D6 22
Samos, prov., Grc., 52,022 .... *D6 23
Samos, isl., Grc D6 23
Samoset, Manatee, Fla., 4,824 .... F2 86
Samosir, isl., Indon m11 35
Samosir, mtn., Indon K3 38
Samothraki, isl., Grc B5 23
Sampacho, Arg., 3,554 .... A4 54
Sampit, Indon F4 35
Sampit, riv., S.C E9 115
Sampson, co., N.C., 48,013 .. C5 109
Sampwe, Con. L C4 48
Samrong, Camb E5 38
Samsø, isl., Den C4 24
Samsø Belt, strait, Den C4 24
Samson, Geneva, Ala., 1,932 .... D3 78
Samsun, Tur., 87,688 .... B11 31
Sams Valley, Jackson, Oreg E4 113
Samtown, Rapides, La., 4,008 .... *C3 95
Samtredia, Sov. Un., 10,000 .... A14 31
Samu, Jordan, 3,000 .... C7 32
Samuel, hill, Ky A4 94
Samuels, Bonner, Idaho, 10 .... A2 89
Samui, isl., Thai H4 38
Samus, Sov. Un., 10,000 ... D25 9
Samutprakan, Thai., 21,607 .... *F4 38
Samut Sakhón, Thai., 27,163 .... F4 38
Samwari, Pak C1 40
San, Mali, 7,800 .... D4 45
San, riv., Camb F7 51
San, riv., Pol C7 26
Şan'ā', Yemen, 89,000 .... B5 47
San Acacia, Socorro, N. Mex., 80 .... C3 107
San Acacio, Costilla, Colo., 160 .... D5 83
Sanaga, riv., Cam E2 46
Sanagha, riv., Con. B E3 46
San Agustín, Arg A3 54
San Agustín, Col., 2,493 .... C2 60
San Agustin, cape, Phil D7 35
Sanak, isl., Alsk E7 79
San Ambrosio, isl., Pac. O H17 7
Sanana, isl., Indon F7 35
Sanandaj, Iran, 40,641 .... D3 41
San Andreas, Calaveras, Calif., 1,416 .... C3 82
San Andrés, Col., 2,139 .... D7 62
San Andrés, isl., Col D7 62
San Andres, mts., N. Mex E3 107
San Andres, peak, N. Mex E3 107
San Andrés de Giles, Arg., 5,392 .... g7 54
San Andrés Tetepilco, Mex., 11,266 .... h9 63
San Andrés Tototlepec, Mex., 1,999 .... h9 63
San Andrés Tuxtla, Mex., 19,830 .... D5 63
San Andrés y Providencia, intendencia, Col., 5,330 .. *D7 62
San Angelo, Tom Green, Tex., 58,815 .... D2 118
San Anselmo, Marin, Calif., 11,584 .... *C2 82
San Antioco, isl., It E2 21
San Antonio, Arg D2 55
San Antonio, Chile, 27,000 .... A2 54

Sanshui, China, 25,000......G7 34
San Simeon, San Luis Obispo, Calif., 35..........E3 82
San Simon, Cochise, Ariz., 200..........E6 80
San Simon, creek, Ariz........E6 80
Sansom Park Village, Tarrant, Tex., 4,175..........*B5 118
Sans Souci, Greenville, S.C., 7,000..........*B3 115
Santa, Benewah, Idaho, 100..B2 89
Santa, Peru, 1,089..........C2 58
Santa, riv., Peru..........C2 58
Santa Amaro, isl., Braz.......m8 58
Santa Ana, Bol., 2,225.......B2 55
Santa Ana, Bol., 171........C2 55
Santa Ana, Orange, Calif., 100,350..........F5, F3 82
Santa Ana, Ec., 3,976.......B1 58
Santa Ana, Mex., 3,976.....A2 63
Santa Ana, Peru, 201.......D3 58
Santa Ana, Sal., 72,839.....D3 62
Santa Ana, Ven., 3,584......B3 60
Santa Ana, Indian res., N. Mex.........k7 107
Santa Ana, mts., Calif........F3 82
Santa Ana, riv., Calif........F3 82
Santa Ana Pueblo, Sandoval, N. Mex., 225.........B3, k7 107
Santa Anita, Mex., 4,441.....h9 63
Santa Anna, Coleman, Tex., 1,320..........D3 118
Santa Barbara, Braz., 13,571..........m8 56
Santa Bárbara, Braz., 4,200..E2 57
Santa Barbara, Santa Barbara, Calif., 58,768 (*92,000)....E4 82
Santa Bárbara, Chile, 2,292..........B2 54
Santa Bárbara, Hond., 2,684..........C3 52
Santa Bárbara, Mex., 15,892..........B3 63
Santa Barbara, co., Calif., 168,962..........E3 82
Santa Barbara, chan., Calif....E4 82
Santa Barbara, is., Calif......F4 82
Santa Bárbara Central, P.R..C4 65
Santa Catalina, Arg.........D2 55
Santa Catalina, Chile........E2 55
Santa Catalina, gulf, Calif......F5 82
Santa Catalina, isl., Calif......F4 82
Santa Catalina, mts., Ariz.......E5 80
Santa Catarina, state, Braz., 2,146,909..........D2 56
Santa Catarina, isl., Braz.......D3 56
Santa Clara, Santa Clara, Calif., 58,880.........D3, C6 82
Santa Clara, Cuba, 110,000..D4 64
Santa Clara, Franklin, N.Y., 100..........f10 108
Santa Clara, Ur., 2,499......E2 56
Santa Clara, Washington, Utah, 291..........F2 119
Santa Clara, co., Calif., 642,315..........D3 82
Santa Clara, riv., Calif.....E4, F2 82
Santa Clara, val., Calif........C6 82
Santa Clara Pueblo, Rio Arriba, N. Mex., 300....*B3 107
Santa Claus, Spencer, Ind., 50..........H4 91
Santa Coloma de Farnés, Sp., 4,583..........B7 20
Santa Croce, cape, It...........F5 21
Santa Cruz., Arg..........E3 54
Santa Cruz, Pinal, Ariz...D3, G2 80
Santa Cruz, Bol., 67,000.....C3 55
Santa Cruz, Braz., 5,286..........C3, h6 57
Santa Cruz, Santa Cruz, Calif., 25,596.........D2, C5 82
Santa Cruz, Chile, 2,132....A2 54
Santa Cruz, C.R., 7,430.....E5 62
Santa Cruz, Santa Fe, N. Mex., 450..........B3 107
Santa Cruz, Phil., 3,851....p13 35
Santa Cruz, Phil., 2,189.....o12 35
Santa Cruz, Phil., 1,093.....o13 35
Santa Cruz, co., Ariz., 10,808..........F5 80
Santa Cruz, co., Calif., 84,219..........D2 82
Santa Cruz, dept., Bol., 286,145..........C3 55
Santa Cruz, prov., Arg., 52,853..........D3 54
Santa Cruz, isl., Calif.........F4 82
Santa Cruz, is., Pac. O.........G10 7
Santa Cruz, mts., Calif.........C5 82
Santa Cruz, riv., Ariz..........E4 80
Santa Cruz, Barillas, Guat., 1,296..........C2 62
Santa Cruz de la Palma, Sp. (Can. Is.) 8,835 (11,609▲).......D1 44, m13 20
Santa Cruz de la Zarza, Sp., 5,588..........C4 20
Santa Cruz del Quiché, Guat., 4,211..........C2 62
Santa Cruz del Sur, Cuba, 2,571..........E5 64
Santa Cruz de Tenerife, Sp. (Can. Is.) 133,100.......D1 44, m13 20
Santa Cruz de Tenerife, prov., Sp., 490,655..........*m13 20
Santa Cruz do Rio Pardo, Braz., 13,789..........C3 56
Santa Cruz do Sul, Braz., 18,898..........D2 56
Santa Cruz (Indefatigable), isl., Ec..........g5 58
Santa Elena, Ec., 2,764.......B1 58
Santa Elena, Starr, Tex., 250..........F3 118
Santa Elena, Ven., 620......C5 60
Santa Eugenia [de Ribeira], Sp., 4,543..........A1 20
Santa Eulalia del Río, Sp., 7,564..........C6 20
Santa Fe, Arg., 208,000.....A4 54
Santa Fé, Cuba, 1,098.......E2 64
Santa Fe, Mex., 3,706.......h9 63
Santa Fe, Santa Fe, N. Mex., 33,394..........B4, h9 107
Santa Fe, Auglaize and Logan, Ohio, 170..........B3 111
Santa Fe, Phil., 4,061.......*C6 35
Santafé, Sp., 8,387..........D4 20
Santa Fe, Maury, Tenn., 125..........B4 117
Santa Fe, co., N. Mex., 44,970..........B3 107
Santa Fe, prov., Arg., 1,865,537..........A4 54
Santa Fé, isl., Ec..........g5 58
Santa Fe, lake, Fla..........C4 86
Santa Fe, riv., N. Mex..........h8 107
Santa Fe Baldy, mtn., N. Mex..B4 107
Santa Fe Springs, Los Angeles, Calif., 16,342..........*F2 82
Santa Filomena, Braz., 652..........C1 57
Santai, China, 24,000.......E6 34
Santa Inés, isl., Chile........h11 54
Santa Inés Ahuatempan, Mex., 2,465..........n14 63
Santa Isabel, Arg...........B3 54
Santa Isabel, Chile..........D2 55
Santa Isabel, Equat. Gui., 11,098..........E1 46
Santa Isabel, P.R., 4,712....D5 65
Santa Isabel, see Paso de los Toros, Ur.
Santa Isabel, mun., P.R., 14,542..........D5 65
Santa Isabel de Siguas, Peru, 80..........E3 58
Santa Juana Central, P.R...C6 65
Santa Lucía, Cuba, 1,969....E6 64
Santa Lucía, Ur., 8,258......E1 56
Santa Lucia, range, Calif.......E3 82
Santa Margarita, San Luis Obispo, Calif., 600.......E3 82
Santa Margarita, isl., Mex.....C2 63
Santa María, Arg., 2,052.....E2 55
Santa María, Braz., 78,682..........D2 57
Santa Maria, Santa Barbara, Calif., 20,027..........E3 82
Santa Maria, Phil., 2,510...o13 35
Santa María, P.R...........g13 65
Santa Maria, isl., Az. Is.......h9 44
Santa María, isl., Ec..........g5 58
Santa Maria, mts., Ariz........C3 80
Santa Maria, riv., Ariz........C2 80
Santa María, riv., Mex.......m14 63
Santa María, riv., Mex.......G2 107
Santa María, riv., Pan........F7 62
Santa Maria [Capua Vetere], It., 30,024..........D5 21
Santa María del Oro, Mex., 3,246..........B3 63
Santa Maria di Leuca, cape, It..E7 21
Santa Maria Madalena, Braz., 1,530..........C4 56
Santa Marta, Col., 48,000 (61,000▲)..........A3 60
Santa Marta, Sp., 5,142.....C2 20
Santa Marta, mts., Col.........A3 60
Santa Monica, Los Angeles, Calif., 83,249..........F2 82
Santan, Pinal, Ariz.....D4, G2 80
Santan, mtn., Ariz...........G3 80
Santana, Braz., 4,357........D2 57
Santana, Port. (Madeira Is.) 4,953..........h12 20
Santana do Ipanema, Braz., 8,139..........C3 57
Santander, Col., 5,669.......C2 60
Santander, Sp., 118,435.....A4 20
Santander, prov., Sp., 432,132..........*A4 20
Santander, dept., Col., 804,490..........B3 60
Santander, mts., Col..........B3 60
Santander Jiménez, Mex., 1,358..........C5 63
Sant'Angelo Romano, It., 1,878..........g9 21
Santanoni, peak, N.Y..........A6 108
Santanópole, Braz., 2,218....C3 57
Santañy, Sp., 6,295.........C7 20
Santa Paula, Ventura, Calif., 13,279..........E4 82
Santaquin, Utah, Utah, 1,183..........D4 119
Santa Quitéria, Braz., 2,351..........B2 57
Santarém, Braz., 24,924.....C4 59
Santarém, Port., 13,114.....C1 20
Santaren, chan., W.I..........C4 64
Santa Rita, Braz., 4,427......k8 56
Santa Rita, Braz., 20,623..........C4, h6 57
Santa Rita, Guam, 1,630.......52
Santa Rita, Glacier, Mont., 150..........B4 102
Santa Rita, Grant, N. Mex., 1,700..........E1 107
Santa Rita, Ven., 11,623....A3 60
Santa Rita, mts., Pan..........k11 62
Santa Rita Park, Merced, Calif., 100..........D3 82
Santa Rosa, Arg., 3,564......A3 54
Santa Rosa, Arg., 2,999......A4 54
Santa Rosa, Arg., 14,623....B4 54
Santa Rosa, Bol..........B2 55
Santa Rosa, Braz., 2,761......k8 56
Santa Rosa, Braz., 12,283...D2 56
Santa Rosa, Sonoma, Calif., 31,027..........A5, C2 82
Santa Rosa, Col., 4,668.....B2 60
Santa Rosa, Ec., 4,672.......B2 58
Santa Rosa, Walton, Fla., 300..........G3 86
Santa Rosa, DeKalb, Mo., 75..........B3 101
Santa Rosa, Guadalupe, N. Mex., 2,220..........C5 107
Santa Rosa, Phil., 3,889....o13 35
Santa Rosa, Cameron, Tex., 1,572..........*F4 118
Santa Rosa, co., Fla., 29,547..........G2 86
Santa Rosa, isl., Calif..........F3 82
Santa Rosa, mtn., Guam..........52
Santa Rosa, range, Nev..........B4 104
Santa Rosa Beach, Wlaton, Fla., 300..........G2 86
Santa Rosa de Aguán, Hond., 1,257..........C5 62
Santa Rosa de Copán, Hond., 7,972..........C3 62
Santa Rosa Island. nat. mon., Fla..........G2 86
Santa Rosalía, Mex., 5,361...B2 63
Santa Rosalia, pt., Mex........B2 63
Santa Susana, Ventura, Calif., 2,310..........*E4 82
Santa Teresa, Gallura, It., 2,570..........D2 21
Santa Ursula, Mex., 3,570....h9 63
Santa Venetia, Marin, Calif., 3,000..........*D2 82
Santa Vitória do Palmar, Braz., 8,224..........E2 56
Santa Ynez., Santa Barbara, Calif., 400..........E3 82
Santee, San Diego, Calif., 2,000..........*E2 82
Santee, Knox, Nebr., 65.....B8 103
Santee, dam, S.C..........E7 115
Santee, Indian res., Nebr.......B8 103
Santee, riv., S.C..........E8 115
Sant'Eufemia, gulf, It..........C5 21
Santiago, Bol., 218..........C2 55
Santiago, Braz., 15,140......D2 56
Santiago, Chile, 646,500 (*2,125,000)..........A2 54
Santiago, Dom. Rep., 83,523..........F8 64
Santiago, Mex., 635..........C3 63
Santiago, Pan., 8,746........F7 62
Santiago, Par., 7,834........E4 55
Santiago, Phil., 5,807.......n13 35
Santiago, Sp., 37,916 (57,165▲)..........A1 20
Santiago, prov., Chile, 2,429,539..........A2 54
Santiago, cape, Phil..........p13 35
Santiago, see San Salvador, isl., Ec.
Santiago, isl., Phil..........n12 35
Santiago, isl., P.R..........C8 65
Santiago, mts., Tex..........E1 118
Santiago, peak, Calif..........F3 82
Santiago, riv., Peru..........B2 58
Santiago de Cao, Peru, 957..C2 58
Santiago de Cuba, Cuba, 212,000..........E6 64
Santiago del Estero, Arg., 80,000 (*100,000)..........E3 55
Santiago del Estero, prov., Arg., 477,156..........E3 55
Santiago Ixcuintla, Mex., 10,985..........C3, m11 63
Santiago Morona, prov., Ec., 22,329..........B2 58
Santiago Papasquiaro, Mex., 5,317..........B3 63
Santiago Tepalcatlálpan, Mex., 2,766..........h9 63
Santian, riv., Oreg..........C2 113
Santipur, India, 51,190.....F12 40
Santis, mtn., Switz..........B7 19
Santisteban del Puerto, Sp., 8,678..........C4 20
Santo, Palo Pinto, Tex., 500..........C3 118
Santo Amaro, Braz., 17,226..........D3 57
Santo André, Braz., 230,196..........*C3 56
Santo Ângelo, Braz., 25,415..D2 56
Santo Antão, isl., C.V. Is......*E2 42
Santo Antônio, Braz., 2,978..........C3, h6 57
Santo Antônio de Jesus, Braz., 14,902..........D3 57
Santo Antônio do Zaire, Ang., 528..........C1 48
Santo Domingo, Dom. Rep., 367,053..........F9 64
Santo Domingo, Nic., 3,110..D5 62
Santo Domingo de la Calzada, Sp., 5,436..........A4 20
Santo Domingo de los Colorados, Ec..........B2 58
Santo Domingo, Indian res., N. Mex..........h8 107
Santo Domingo Pueblo, Sandoval, N. Mex., 900..........B3, k8 107
San Tomas, Santa Clara, Calif., 1,500..........*D3 82
Santoña, Sp., 9,082..........A4 20
Santos, Braz., 262,048 (*400,000)..........C3, m8 56
Santos Dumont, Braz., 20,414..........C4, g6 56
Santo Tomás, Peru, 877.....D3 58
Santo Tomas, Ven..........B5 60
Santo Tomé, Arg., 8,348.....E4 55
Santuao, China..........K8 36
Santuc, Union, S.C., 40.....B4 115
Santuit, Barnstable, Mass., 350..........*C7 97
San Valentín, mtn., Chile.......D2 54
San Vicente, Col., 1,002.....C3 60
San Vicente, Sal., 15,189....D3 62
San Vicente Central, P.R....B5 65
San Vicente de Alcántara, Sp., 8,212..........C2 20
San Vicente de la Barquera, Sp., 3,002..........A3 20
San Vito al Tagliamento, It., 5,065..........B4 21
San Xavier, Indian res., Ariz....E4 80
Sanyati, riv., Rh..........A4 49
San Ygnacio, Zapata, Tex., 900..........F3 118
San Ysidro, San Diego, Calif. (part of San Diego)....E2, F5 82
San Ysidro, Sandoval, N. Mex., 50..........B3, h7 107
Sanza Pomba, Ang., 269....C2 48
São Bento do Sul, Braz., 6,470..........D3 56
São Bento do Una, Braz., 5,096..........k5 57
São Bernardo [do Campo], Braz., 61,645..........C3, m8 56
São Borja, Braz., 20,339.....D1 56
São Caetano do Sul, Braz., 114,039..........*C3 56
São Carlos, Braz., 50,010..........C3, m8 56
São Cristóvão, Braz., 7,624..D3 57
São Domingos, Braz., 907....D1 57
São Fidélis, Braz., 6,145.....C4 56
São Francisco, Braz., 4,074...E2 57
São Francisco, Braz., 869.....C5 60
São Francisco, riv., Braz.......C3 57
São Francisco do Sul, Braz., 11,593..........D3 56
São Gabriel, Braz., 22,967....E2 56
São Gonçalo, Braz., 63,776..........*C4 56
São Gotardo, Braz., 6,227....E1 57
São Jerônimo, Braz., 5,568...D2 56
São Jeronimo, mts., Braz.......E1 57
São João, isl., Braz..........B2 57
São João da Barra, Braz., 3,441..........C4 56
São João da Boa Vista, Braz., 25,226..........C3, k8 56
São João das Lampas, Port., 4,637..........f9 20
São João del Rei, Braz., 34,654..........C4, g5 56
São João de Meriti, Braz., 103,495..........*C4 56
São João do Carirí, Braz., 622..........C3, h5 57
São João do Piauí, Braz., 2,688..........C2 57
São João Nepomuceno, Braz., 9,436..........C4, g6 56
São Joaquim, Braz., 3,811....D3 56
São Jorge, isl., Port. (Azores)...g8 44
São José de Mipibú, Braz., 5,179..........h6 57
São José do Rio Pardo, Braz., 14,186..........k8 56
São José do Rio Prêto, Braz., 66,476..........C3 56
São José dos Campos, Braz., 55,349..........C3, m9 56
São José dos Pinhais, Braz., 7,574..........D3 56
São Leopoldo, Braz., 41,023..........D2 56
São Lourenço, Braz., 14,680..C3 56
São Lourenço, riv., Braz.......B1 56
São Lourenço do Sul, Braz., 6,877..........E2 56
São Luís, Braz., 124,606.....B2 57
São Luís do Quitunde, Braz., 2,618..........k6 57
São Luís Gonzaga, Braz., 12,926..........D2 56
São Manuel, Braz., 10,009..........C3, m7 56
São Mateus, Braz., 6,075.....E3 57
São Miguel, isl., Port. (Azores)..h9 44
São Miguel Arcanjo, Braz., 3,633..........m8 56
São Miguel dos Campos, Braz., 6,511..........k5 57
Saône, riv., Fr..........D6 14
Saône-et-Loire, dept., Fr., 535,772..........*D6 14
São Nicolau, isl., C.V. Is.......*E3 42
São Paulo, Braz., 3,825,351 (*4,650,000)..........C3, m8 56
São Paulo, state, Braz., 12,974,699..........C3, m8 56
São Paulo de Olivença, Braz., 1,157..........D4 60
São Pedro, Braz., 4,474......m8 56
São Pedro do Piauí, Braz., 2,139..........C2 57
São Raimundo Nonato, Braz., 3,751..........C2 57
São Roque, Braz., 12,409....m8 56
São Roque, cape, Braz..........C3 57
Saorre, mtn., N.W. Ter., Can..D6 67
São Salvador, Ang., 2,965...C1 48
São Sebastião, cape, Moz.......B6 49
São Sebastião, isl., Braz........C3 56
São Sebastião do Paraíso, Braz., 14,451..........C3 56
São Simão, Braz., 5,742..C3, k8 56
São Tiago, isl., C.V. Is........*E3 42
São Tomé, São Tomé & Principe, 7,817..........E1 46
São Tomé, isl., São Tomé & Principe..........E1 46
São Tomé & Principe, Port. dep., Afr., 65,000..........E1 46
Saoura, riv., Alg..........D4 44
São Vicente, Braz., 73,578....C3 56
São Vicente, Port. (Madeira Is.), 6,663..........h11 20
São Vicente, isl., C.V. Is.......*E3 42
Sapai, Grc., 5,698..........B5 23
Sapatu, isl., Viet..........H8 38
Sapele, Nig., 33,638.........E6 45
Sapello, San Miguel, N. Mex., 15..........B4 107
Sapelo, isl., Ga..........E5 87
Sapelo, sound, Ga..........E5 87
Sapinero, Gunnison, Colo., 10..........C3 83
Saponac, Penobscot, Maine, 20..........C4 96
Saposoa, Peru, 3,243........C2 58
Sapozhok, Sov. Un., 10,000..........E13 27
Sappa, creek, Nebr., Kans.......C3 93
Sappemeer, Neth., 4,565.....A6 15
Sapphire, mts., Mont..........D3 102
Sappho, Clallam, Wash., 100..........A1 122
Sappington, St. Louis, Mo., 10,000..........B8 101
Sappington, Gallatin, Mont., 15..........E5 102
Sapporo, Jap., 523,839 (*615,000)..........E10 37
Sapri, It., 6,188..........D5 21
Sapulpa, Creek, Okla., 14,282..........B5 112
Saqqare, Eg., U.A.R., 8,230..........E3 32
Saqqez, Iran, 10,479........C3 41
Saquarema, Braz., 1,467..........C4, h6 56
Sara, dune, Libya..........E4 43
Sara, riv., Chad, Cen. Afr. Rep..........D3 46
Sara Buri, Thai., 20,245......E4 38
Sarabyum, Eg., U.A.R.......D4 32
Sarafand, Isr., 153.........h10 32
Saragosa, Reeves, Tex., 150..........D1, F2 118
Saragossa, Walker, Ala., 250..........B2 78
Saragossa, Pan..........k11 62
Saragossa, see Zaragoza, prov. and city, Sp.
Saraguro, Ec., 1,334........B2 58
Sarah, Tate, Miss., 125.......A3 100
Sarajevo, Yugo., 143,117....D4 22
Sara Kaeo, Thai..........F5 38
Saraktash, Sov. Un., 10,000..........E20 9
Sarala, Sov. Un., 10,000....E26 9
Saraland, Mobile, Ala., 4,595..........E1 78
Saran, Sov. Un., 52,000.....*D8 29
Saranac, Ionia, Mich., 1,081..F5 98
Saranac, Clinton, N.Y., 600..f11 108
Saranac, lakes, N.Y..........A6 108
Saranac, riv., N.Y..........f11 108
Saranac Inn, Franklin, N.Y., 30..........f10 108
Saranac Lakes, Essex and Franklin, N.Y., 6,421.....f10 108
Saranap, Contra Costa, Calif., 6,450..........*B5 82
Sarandë, Alb., 3,444........C2 23
Sarandí del Yí, Ur., 4,437...E1 56
Sarandí Grande, Ur., 4,539...E1 56
Sarangani, is., Phil..........D6 35
Sarangpur, India, 11,263.....F6 40
Saransk, Sov. Un., 124,000...C3 29
Sarapul, Sov. Un., 78,000....B4 29
Sarasota, Sarasota, Fla., 34,083..........E4, F2 86
Sarasota, co., Fla., 76,895....E4 86
Sarasota, bay, Fla..........E4 86
Sarata, Sov. Un..........B9 22
Saratoga, Howard, Ark., 62..D2 81
Saratoga, Santa Clara, Calif., 14,861..........C5 82
Saratoga, Randolph, Ind., 363..........D8 91
Saratoga, Howard, Iowa, 90..A5 92
Saratoga, Wilson, N.C., 409..B6 109
Saratoga, Hardin, Tex., 800..D5 118
Saratoga, Carbon, Wyo., 1,133..........D6 125
Saratoga, co., N.Y., 89,096...B7 108
Saratoga, lake, N.Y..........C7 108
Saratoga Place, Nansemond, Va., 1,478..........*E6 121
Saratoga Springs, Saratoga, N.Y., 16,630..........B7 108
Saratov, Sov. Un., 644,000 (*770,000)......E18 9, C3 29
Saravane, Laos, 25,000......E7 38
Sarawak, reg., Mala., 845,000..........I14 33, E4 35
Saray, Tur., 5,300..........B6 23
Saray, see Kazim Pasa, Tur.
Saraykoy, Tur., 6,900.......D7 23
Sarbāz, Iran..........H10 41
Sarben, Keith, Nebr., 105....C4 103
Sárbogárd, Hung., 6,859.....B4 22
Sarca, riv., It..........D6 18
Sarcelles, Fr., 35,885.......g10 14
Sarcoxie, Jasper, Mo., 1,056..........D3 101
Sarda, riv., India..........C8 40
Sardalas, Libya..........D2 43
Sardegna, pol. dist., It., 1,419,362..........*E2 21
Sardinia, Decatur, Ind., 170..F6 91
Sardinia, Brown, Ohio, 799..C4 111
Sardinia, isl., It..........D2 21
Sardis, Dallas, Ala., 300.....C3 78
Sardis, B.C., Can., 898......f14 68
Sardis, Burke, Ga., 829......D5 87
Sardis, Mason, Ky., 190......B6 94
Sardis, Panola, Miss., 2,098..A4 100
Sardis, Monroe, Ohio, 500...C7 111
Sardis, Henderson, Tenn., 274..........B3 117
Sardis, dam, Miss..........A4 100
Sardis, res., Miss..........A4 100
Sardo, Eth..........C5 47
Sarektjakko, mtn., Swe.......D7 25
Sarepta, Webster, La., 737...B2 95
Sarepta, Calhoun, Miss., 75..A4 100
Sar-e Yazd, Iran..........F7 41
Sargans, Switz., 2,571.......B7 19
Sargeant, Mower, Minn., 113..........G6 99
Sargent, Coweta, Ga., 900...C2 87
Sargent, Custer, Nebr., 876..C6 103
Sargent, co., N. Dak., 6,856..C8 110
Sargents, Saguache, Colo., 60..........C4 83
Sargodha, Pak., 83,141 (*129,291)..........A4 40
Sarhad, Afg., 5,000..........k17 41
Sāri, Iran, 23,990..........C6 41
Saria, isl., Grc..........E6 23
Sarikamis, Tur., 17,600.....B14 31
Sarine, riv., Switz..........C3 19
Sariñena, Sp., 3,389........B5 20
Sari-Pul, Afg., 5,000.......C12 41
Sarita, Kenedy, Tex., 250....F4 118
Sariwon, Kor., 42,957.......G2 37
Sark, isl., Guernsey..........F5 10
Sarkand, Sov. Un..........F24 9
Sarkisla, Tur., 3,731........C11 31
Sarkoy, Tur., 4,000..........B6 23
Sarlat, Fr., 5,251..........E4 14
Sarles, Cavalier and Towner, N. Dak., 225..........A7 110
Särna, Swe., 1,276..........G5 25
Sarnen, Switz., 6,554.......C5 19
Sarnen, lake, Switz..........C5 19
Sarnia, Ont., Can., 50,976 (*61,293)..........E2 72
Sarny, Sov. Un., 10,000.....F6 27
Särö, Swe., 259..........A5 24
Sarona, Washburn, Wis., 90..C2 124
Saronic, gulf, Grc..........D4 23
Saronno, It., 25,190.........B2 21
Saronville, Clay, Nebr., 71..D8 103
Saros, gulf, Tur..........B6 23
Sarospatak, Hung., 9,610....A5 22
Sarova, Sov. Un., 5,000....D14 27
Sar Planina, mts., Yugo.......D5 22
Sarpsborg, Nor., 13,300.....p29 25
Sarpy, co., Nebr., 31,281....C9 103
Sarrebourg, Fr., 11,080......F7 15
Sarreguemines, Fr., 17,866...C7 14
Sarre-Union, Fr., 2,645......F7 15
Sarria, Sp., 3,935..........A2 20
Sarsfield, Ont., Can., 259...h13 72
Sarstedt, Ger., 10,200.......A4 17
Sarstun, riv., Guat..........C3 62
Sartell, Stearns, Minn., 791..E4 99
Sartène, Fr., 4,067..........D2 21
Sarthe, dept., Fr., 443,019..*D4 14
Sarthe, riv., Fr..........D3 14
Sartrouville, Fr., 31,267......g9 14
Sarufutsu, Jap., 2,900.......D11 37
Sarus, see Seyhan, riv., Tur.
Sarvar, Hung., 11,021........B3 22
Sarvestān, Iran..........G6 41
Sarybyevo, Sov. Un..........O18 27
Sary-Ishikotrau, des., Sov. Un....D9 29
Sary-Ozek, Sov. Un..........E9 29
Sarysu, riv., Sov. Un..........D7 29
Sarzana, It., 8,600..........B2 21
Sasabe, Pima, Ariz., 50......F4 80
Sasaginnigak, lake, Man., Can..........D4 71
Sasakwa, Seminole, Okla., 253..........C5 112
Sasalaguan, mtn., Guam..........52
Sasaram, India, 37,782.......E10 40
Sasebo, Jap., 262,484.........J4 37
Saskatchewan, prov., Can., 925,181..........F11 66, 70
Saskatchewan, riv., Man., Sask., Can..........F12 66
Saskatoon, Sask., Can., 95,526..........E2, n7 70
Sasovo, Sov. Un., 26,000.....C2 29
Saspamco, Wilson, Tex., 300..........B4 118
Sassafras, mtn., S.C..........A2 115
Sassafras, riv., Md..........B5 85
Sassandra, I.C., 2,600.......E3 45
Sassandra, riv., I.C..........E3 45
Sassari, It., 94,200..........D2 21
Sassenberg, Ger., 3,700......B3 17
Sasser, Terrell, Ga., 382.....E2 87
Sassnitz, Ger., 13,400.......A6 16
Sasso Marconi, It., 1,308....E7 18
Sassuolo, It., 10,300........E6 18
Sastre, Arg., 2,308..........A4 54
Sasuri, Kor..........F3 37
Sasykkol, lake, Sov. Un.......D10 29
Satah, mtn., B.C., Can..........C5 68
Satalo, W. Sam., 181..........52
Satanta, Haskell, Kans., 686..........E3 93
Satapuala, W. Sam., 637.......52
Satara, India, 44,353........I4 40
Satartia, Yazoo, Miss., 126..C3 100
Sataua, bay, W. Sam..........52
Säter, Swe., 4,500..........G6 25
Saticoy, Ventura, Calif., 2,283..........E4 82
Satilla, riv., Ga..........E4 87
Satipo, Peru..........D3 58
Satka, Sov. Un., 38,900.....B5 29
Satmala, range, India..........H7 40
Satna, India, 38,046........E8 40
Satoraljaujhely, Hung., 16,197..........A5 22
Satpura, range, India..........G5 40
Sätrabrunn, Swe., 169......t34 25
Satrup, Ger., 1,750..........D3 24
Satsop, Grays Harbor, Wash., 150..........B2 122
Satsuma, Mobile, Ala., 1,491..........E1 78
Satsuma, Putnam, Fla., 300..C5 86
Sattahip, Thai., 4,478.......F4 38
Sattler, Comal, Tex., 30......A4 118
Satu-Mare, Rom., 60,800....B6 22
Satun, Thai., 5,615..........I4 38
Satupaitea, Samoa, 1,047......52
Saturna, isl., B.C., Can.......E6 68
Satus, creek, Wash..........C5 122
Sauage, Scott, Minn., 1,094..........F5, F6 99
Sauce, Arg., 3,017..........A5 54
Sauceda, mts., Ariz..........E3 80
Saucier, Harrison, Miss., 300..........E4 100
Saucillo, Mex., 6,820........B3 63
Sauda, Nor., 3,055..........H2 25
Saudi Arabia, country, Asia, 7,000,000..........G7 33
Saugatuck, Fairfield, Conn. (part of Westport)........E3 84
Saugatuck, Allegan, Mich., 927..........F4 98
Saugatuck, riv., Conn..........D3 84
Saugerties, Ulster, N.Y., 4,286..........C7 108
Saugor, India, 85,491 (*104,676)..........F7 40
Saugus, Los Angeles, Calif., 200..........F2 82
Saugus, Essex, Mass., 20,666..........B5, g11 98
Saugus, riv., Mass..........g11 97
Sauk, co., Wis., 36,179......E4 124
Sauk, riv., Minn..........E4 99
Sauk, riv., Wash..........A4 122
Sauk Centre, Stearns, Minn., 3,573..........E4 99
Sauk City, Sauk, Wis., 2,095..........E4 124
Sauk Rapids, Benton, Minn., 4,038..........E4 99
Sauk Village, Cook, Ill., 5,774..........*B6 90
Saukville, Ozaukee, Wis., 1,038..........E6 124
Saulgrub, Ger., 1,100.......B7 18
Saulnierville, N.S., Can., 450..........E3 74
Saulsbury, Hardeman, Tenn., 141..........B2 117
Saulston, Wayne, N.C., 100..........B6 109
Sault-au-Mouton, Que., Can., 876..........A8 73
Sault Ste. Marie, Ont., Can., 43,088 (*58,460)........p18 72
Sault Ste. Marie, Chippewa, Mich., 18,722..........B6 98
Saumlakki, Indon..........G8 35
Saumur, Fr., 20,773.........D4 14
Saunders, Alta., Can.......C10 68
Saunders, co., Nebr., 17,270..........C9 84
Saunderstown, Washington, R.I., 400..........C11 84
Saundersville, Sumner, Tenn., 100..........E9 117
Saunemin, Livingston, Ill., 392..........C5 90
Saurashtra, state, India, 4,137,359..........*G3 40
Saurashtra, pen., India........D4 39
Sausalito, Marin, Calif., 5,331..........B5, D2 82
Sauveterre, Fr., 334.........E5 14
Sava, riv., Yugo..........C4 22
Savage, Howard, Md., 1,341..........B4 85
Savage, Scott, Minn., 1,094..........F5, F6 99
Savage, Tate, Miss., 75......A3 100
Savage, Richland, Mont., 300..........C12 102
Savage, riv., Md..........D1 85
Savageton, Campbell, Wyo..B7 125
Savaii, isl., W. Sam..........52
Savalan, mtn., Iran..........B3 41
Savalou, Dah., 4,100.........E5 45
Savanna, Carroll, Ill., 4,950..A3 90
Savanna, Pittsburg, Okla., 620..........C6 112
Savannah, Chatham, Ga., 149,245 (*189,200)........D5 87
Savannah, Andrew, Mo., 2,455..........B3 101
Savannah, Wayne, N.Y., 602..........B4 108
Savannah, Ashland, Ohio, 409..........B5 111
Savannah, Hardin, Tenn., 4,315..........B3 117
Savannah, lake, Md..........D6 85
Savannah, riv., Ga., S.C.......F5 115
Savannah Beach, Chatham, Ga., 1,385..........D6 87
Savannakhet, Laos..........D6 38
Savanna-la-Mar, Jam., 9,783..........F4 64
Savé, Dah., 5,100..........E5 45
Save, riv., Moz..........B5 49
Sāveh, Iran, 15,365..........D5 41
Saveni, Rom., 6,470..........B8 22
Saverne, Fr., 9,056..........C7 14
Saverton, Ralls, Mo., 135....B6 101
Savery, Carbon, Wyo., 25...D5 125
Savigliano, It., 14,800.......B1 21
Savigny [-sur-Orgel] Fr., 24,316..........F2 15
Savo, riv., It..........h9 21
Savoie, dept., Fr., 266,678...D2 18
Savona, B.C., Can., 532.....D7 68
Savona, It., 75,100 (*108,000)..........B2 21
Savona, Steuben, N.Y., 904..C3 108
Savonburg Allen, Kans., 131..........E8 93
Savonlinna, Fin., 14,700....G13 25
Savoonga, Alsk., 200........C5 79
Savoy, Berkshire, Mass., 25 (277▲)..........A1 97
Savoy, Blaine, Mont..........B8 102
Savoy (Savoie), former prov., Fr., 546,000..........E7 14
Savran, Sov. Un., 10,000....G8 27
Sävsjö, Swe., 5,100........A8 24
Savu, is., Indon..........B3 50

Selma, Drew, Ark., 300 D4 81
Selma, Fresno, Calif., 6,934 D4 82
Selma, Delaware, Ind., 562 D7 91
Selma, Grant, La. C3 95
Selma, Johnston, N.C., 3,102 B5 109
Selma, Josephine, Oreg., 30 E3 113
Selmah, N.S., Can., 135 D6 74
Selman, Harper, Okla., 60 A2 112
Selmer, McNairy, Tenn., 1,897 B3 117
Selsey, Eng., 3,889 D7 12
Selsey Bill, pt., Eng D7 12
Selukwe, Rh., 1,200 A5 49
Selva, Arg E3 55
Selvas, forests, Braz D4 53
Selvin, Warrick, Ind., 150 H3 91
Selway, riv., Idaho C3 89
Selwyn, Austl D7 50
Selwyn, lake, N.W. Ter., Sask. Can k8 70
Selwyn, mtn., B.C., Can A6 68
Selwyn, mts., N.W. Ter., Yukon, Can D6 66
Selz, Pierce, N. Dak., 150 B6 110
Seman, Elmore, Ala., 70 C3 78
Seman, riv., Alb B2 23
Semans, Sask., Can., 386 F3 70
Semarang, Indon., 487,006 G4 35
Semenov, Sov. Un., 98,000 D17 9
Semenovka, Sov. Un., 9,000 E9 27
Seminary, Covington, Miss., 288 D4 100
Seminoe, mts., Wyo C6 125
Seminoe, res., Wyo D6 125
Seminoe Dam, Carbon, Wyo., 55 C6 125
Seminole, Baldwin, Ala., 200 E2 78
Seminole, Pinellas, Fla., 1,500 *E4 86
Seminole, Seminole, Okla., 11,464 B5 112
Seminole, Gaines, Tex., 5,737 C1 118
Seminole, co., Fla., 54,947 D5 86
Seminole, co., Ga., 6,802 F2 87
Seminole, co., Okla., 28,066 B5 112
Seminole, Indian res., Fla F6 86
Seminole (Big Cypress), Indian res., Fla F5 86
Seminole (Brighton), Indian res., Fla E5 86
Semipalatinsk, Sov. Un., 188,000 C10 29
Semitau, Indon E4 35
Semiyarskoye, Sov. Un C9 29
Semliki, riv., Con. L A4 48
Semmens, lake, Man., Can B4 71
Semmering, pass, Aus E7 16
Semnān, Iran, 23,078 D6 41
Semora, Caswell, N.C., 350 A4 109
Semoy, riv., Bel E5 15
Sempach, Switz., 1,345 B5 19
Sempacher, lake, Switz B5 19
Semur-en-Auxois, Fr., 3,399 D6 14
Sen, riv., Camb F6 38
Sena, San Miguel, N. Mex., 45 B4 107
Senaca, La Salle, Ill., 1,719 B5 90
Senachwine, lake, Ill B4 90
Senador Pompeu, Braz., 8,210 C3 57
Sena Madureira, Braz., 1,962 C4 58
Senanga, Zambia, 2,785 E3 48
Senate, Sask., Can H1 70
Senath, Dunklin, Mo., 1,369 E7 101
Senatobia, Tate, Miss., 3,259 A4 100
Sendai, Jap., 425,272 (*515,000) G10 37
Sendai (Kagoshima pref.), Jap., 25,600 (61,322▲) K5 37
Sendai, bay, Jap G10 37
Seneca, Gila, Ariz., 50 D5 80
Seneca, La Salle, Ill., 1,719 B5 90
Seneca, Nemaha, Kans., 2,072 C7 93
Seneca, Newton, Mo., 1,478 E3 101
Seneca, Thomas, Nebr., 160 B5 103
Seneca, Union, N. Mex., 5 A6 107
Seneca, Grant, Oreg., 400 C8 113
Seneca, Venango, Pa., 950 D2 114
Seneca, Oconee, S.C., 5,227 B2 115
Seneca, Faulk, S. Dak., 161 B6 116
Seneca, Crawford, Wis., 180 E3 124
Seneca, co., N.Y., 31,984 C4 108
Seneca, co., Ohio, 59,326 A4 111
Seneca, caverns, W. Va C5 123
Seneca, lake, N.Y C4 108
Seneca, mtn., N.Y C2 108
Seneca, rocks, W. Va C5 123
Seneca Falls, Seneca, N.Y., 7,439 C4 108
Seneca Gardens, Jefferson, Ky., 928 *H6 94
Senecaville, Guernsey, Ohio, 575 C6 111
Senecaville, res., Ohio C6 111
Seneffe, Bel., 2,971 D4 15
Senegal, country, Afr., 3,480,000 D2 45, E4 42
Sénégal, riv., Maur., Sen C2 45
Senekal, S. Afr., 7,409 C4 49
Seney, Schoolcraft, Mich., 80 B5 98
Senftenberg, Ger., 21,000 B9 17
Senga Hill, Zambia C5 48
Senguerr, riv., Arg D3 54
Senhor do Bonfim, Braz., 13,958 D2 57
Senhoshi, Jap D10 37
Senigallia, It., 16,700 C4 21
Senj, Yugo., 3,909 C2 22
Senja, isl., Nor C7 25
Senlac, Sask., Can., 127 E1 70
Senlis, Fr., 9,371 C5 14
Sennār, Sud., 8,093 C3 47
Senneterre, Que., Can., 3,246 k11 73
Senneville, Que., Can., 1,262 *p19 73
Senoia, Coweta, Ga., 782 C2 87
Sens, Fr., 20,015 C5 14
Sense, riv., Switz C3 19
Senta, Yugo., 24,987 C5 22
Sentery, Con. L C4 48
Sentinel, Maricopa, Ariz., 20 E2 80
Sentinel, Washita, Okla., 1,154 B2 112
Sentinel, peak, B.C., Can B6 68
Sentinel, butte, N. Dak C2 110
Sentinel, range, Ant B4 5
Sentinel Butte, Golden Valley, N. Dak., 160 C2 110
Senzu, Jap n17 37
Seo de Urgel, Sp., 7,195 A6 20
Seoni, India, 30,274 F7 40
Seoul (Sŏul), Kor., 2,983,300 (*3,060,000) H3 37
Separ, Grant, N. Mex., 10 E1 107
Sepik, riv., N. Gui h11 50
Sepolno, Pol., 4,214 B4 26
Sept Îles (Seven Islands), Que., Can., 14,196 h13 73
Sepulga, riv., Ala D3 78
Sequatchie, Marion, Tenn., 400 D8 117
Sequatchie, co., Tenn., 5,915 D8 117
Sequatchie, riv., Tenn D7 117
Sequim, Clallam, Wash., 1,164 A2 122
Sequoia, nat. park, Calif D4 82
Sequoia National Park, Tulare, Calif D4 82
Sequoyah, co., Okla., 18,001 B7 112
Serafimovich, Sov. Un., 8,800 D2 29
Serafina, San Miguel, N. Mex., 50 B4 107
Seraing, Bel., 41,239 D5 15
Serakhs, Sov. Un C10 41
Serampore, India, 91,521 *F12 40
Serang, Indon., 11,163 G3 35
Serasan, is., Indon K8 38
Serbia, reg., Yugo D5 22
Serbia, rep., Yugo., 7,629,113 *D5 22
Serdobsk, Sov. Un., 10,000 E15 27
Sered, Czech., 6,208 D4 26
Sereflikochisar, Tur., 8,700 C9 31
Seremban, Mala., 52,091 K4 38
Serengeti, plain, Tan B5 48
Serenje, Zambia, 510 D5 48
Sereni, Som E5 47
Sergeant, McKean, Pa., 120 C4 114
Sergeant Bluff, Woodbury, Iowa, 813 B1 92
Sergeantsville, Hunterdon, N.J., 200 C3 106
Sergipe, state, Braz., 760,273 D3 57
Seria, Brunei, 17,595 E4 35
Serifos, Grc., 2,372 D5 23
Serifos, isl., Grc D5 23
Seringapatam, India, 11,423 F6 39
Serles, Hardeman, Tenn., 25 B2 117
Sermaize, Fr., 2,964 F4 15
Sernyy Zavod, Sov. Un B9 41
Seroei, W. Irian, 2,200 F9 35
Serón, Sp., 7,091 D4 20
Serov, Sov. Un., 102,000 B6 29
Serowe, Bech., 15,935 B4 49
Serpa, Port., 7,273 D2 20
Serpentine, lakes, Austl E4 50
Serpentine, prov. park, Newf., Can D2 75
Serpukhov, Sov. Un., 113,000 C1 29
Serra dos Aimorés, disputed reg., Braz., 384,297 *E2 57
Serrai, Grc., 40,063 B4 23
Serrai, prov., Grc., 248,041 *B4 23
Serrana Bank, shoals, Caribbean Sea C7 62
Serra Negra, Braz., 5,221 m8 56
Serranilla Bank, shoals, Caribbean Sea C8 62
Serra Talhada, Braz., 5,353 C3 57
Serres, Fr., 770 E1 18
Serrezuela, Arg A3 54
Serrinha, Braz., 10,284 C3 57
Sêrro, Braz., 4,594 E2 57
Sertã, Port., 7,281 C1 20
Sertânia, Braz., 7,556 C3 57
Serua, isl., Indon G8 35
Seruli, Bech B4 49
Servia, Grc., 3,236 B4 23
Servia, Wabash, Ind., 150 C6 91
Service, Choctaw, Ala., 100 D1 78
Service, buttes, Oreg B7 113
Service Creek, Wheeler, Oreg C7 113
Sese, isl., Ug B5 48
Sesheke, Zambia, 124 E3 48
Sèsia, riv., It D4 18
Sesoko, isl., Okinawa 52
Sesoko, Okinawa 52
Sesser, Franklin, Ill., 1,764 E4 90
Sessums, Oktibbeha, Miss., 100 B5 100
Sesto [Fiorentino], It., 22,453 C3 21
Sestokai, Sov. Un A7 26
Sesto San Giovanni, It., 79,500 D5 18
Sestriere, It., 73 E2 18
Sestri Levante, It., 9,100 B2 21
Sestroretsk, Sov. Un., 34,000 (part of Leningrad) A8 27
Setana, Jap., 4,100 E9 37
Setauket, Suffolk, N.Y., 1,500 F4 84
Sète (Cette), Fr., 36,301 F5 14
Sete Lagoas, Braz., 36,302 E2 57
Sete Quedas, falls, Braz C2 55
Seth, Boone, W. Va., 800 C3, D6 123
Seth Ward, Hale, Tex., 1,328 *B2 118
Sétif, Alg., 93,561 B6 44
Seto, Jap., 82,101 I8, n16 37
Seton Portage, B.C., Can., 107 D6 68
Settat, Mor., 29,617 C3 44
Setté-Cama, Gabon F1 46
Settee, lake, Sask., Can B3 70
Setting, lake, Man., Can B2 71
Settle, Eng., 2,297 F6 13
Setúbal, Port., 44,435 C1 20
Setubal, bay, Port C1 20
Seul, lake, Ont., Can o16 72
Seul Choix, pt., Mich C5 98
Sevan, lake, Sov. Un G18 9
Sevastopol, Sov. Un., 169,000 I9 27
Seven, heads, Ire F3 11
Seven Devils, mts., Idaho D2 89
Seven Harbors, Oakland, Mich., 2,748 F7 98
Seven Hills, Cuyahoga, Ohio, 5,708 *A6 111
Seven Islands, see Sept Îles, Que., Can.
Seven Islands, bay, Newf., Can f9 75
Seven Mile, Butler, Ohio, 690 C3 111
Seven Mile, beach, N.J E3 106
Sevenoaks, Eng., 17,604 C8 12
Seven Persons, Alta., Can., 40 E5 69
Seven Rivers, Eddy, N. Mex., 50 E5 107
Seven Sisters, Duval, Tex., 75 E3 118
Seven Sisters, peaks, B.C., Can B3 68
Seven Springs, Wayne, N.C., 207 B6 109
70 Mile House, B.C., Can D7 68
Severance, Weld, Colo., 70 A6 83
Severance, Doniphan, Kans., 146 C8 93
Severka, riv., Sov. Un n18 27
Severn, Anne Arundel, Md., 280 B4 85
Severn, Northampton, N.C., 310 A6 109
Severn, Gloucester, Va., 300 D6 121
Severn, mouth, Eng C5 12
Severn, riv., Ont., Can n17 72
Severn, riv., Eng B5 12
Severn, riv., Md B4 85
Severna Park, Anne Arundel, Md., 3,100 B4 85
Severnaya Zemlya, is., Sov. Un B13 28
Severomorsk, Sov. Un., 30,000 C15 25
Severouralsk, Sov. Un., 23,200 C20 9
Severy, Greenwood, Kans., 492 E7 93
Sevier, Sevier, Utah, 10 E3 119
Sevier, co., Ark., 10,156 D1 81
Sevier, co., Tenn., 24,251 D10 117
Sevier, co., Utah, 10,565 E4 119
Sevier, des., Utah D3 119
Sevier, lake, Utah E2 119
Sevier, riv., Utah D3 119
Sevier Bridge, res., Utah D4 119
Sevierville, Sevier, Tenn., 2,890 D10 117
Sevilla, Col., 17,210 C2 60
Sevilla (Seville), Sp., 442,300 D3 20
Sevilla (Seville), prov., Sp., 1,234,435 *D3 20
Seville, Volusia, Fla., 623 C5 86
Seville, Wilcox, Ga., 179 E3 87
Seville, Medina, Ohio, 1,190 A6 111
Sevlievo, Bul., 9,856 D7 22
Sevogle, riv., N.B., Can B3 74
Sevran, Fr., 17,969 g11 14
Sèvre, riv., Fr D3 14
Sèvre Niortaise, riv., Fr D3 14
Sèvres, Fr., 20,129 g9 14
Sewal, Wayne, Iowa, 100 D4 92
Sewanee, Franklin, Tenn., 1,464 B6 117
Seward, Alsk., 1,891 C10, g17 79
Seward, Winnebago, Ill., 150 A4 90
Seward, Stafford, Kans., 92 D5 93
Seward, Seward, Nebr., 4,208 D8 103
Seward, Logan, Okla., 49 B4 112
Seward, Westmoreland, Pa., 754 F3 114
Seward, co., Kans., 15,930 E3 93
Seward, co., Nebr., 13,581 D8 103
Seward, pen., Alsk B7 79
Seward Roads, chan., Midway Is 52
Sewaren, Middlesex, N.J., 1,500 k7 106
Sewell, Chile, 9,009 A2 54
Sewell, Breathitt, Ky., 265 C6 94
Sewell, Glouchester, N.J., 1,700 D2 106
Sewickley, Allegheny, Pa., 6,157 A5, E1 114
Sewickley Heights, Allegheny, Pa., 931 *E1 114
Sexsmith, Alta., Can., 531 B1 69
Sextonville, Richland, Wis., 250 E3 124
Seychelles, Br. dep., Afr., 47,000 G24 3
Seychelles, is., Indian O G24 3
Seydisehir, Tur., 6,300 D8 31
Seydisfjördur, Ice., 742 n25 25
Seyhan (Sarus), riv., Tur C10 31
Seym, riv., Sov. Un F9 27
Seymchan, Sov. Un C18 28
Seymour, Austl., 5,103 H5 51
Seymour, New Haven, Conn., 10,100 D4 84
Seymour, Jackson, Ind., 11,629 G6 91
Seymour, Wayne, Iowa, 1,117 D4 92
Seymour, Webster, Mo., 1,046 D5 101
Seymour, Sevier, Tenn., 40 D10, E12 117
Seymour, Baylor, Tex., 3,789 C3 118
Seymour, Outagamie, Wis., 2,045 A5, D5 124
Seymour, inlet, B.C., Can D4 68
Seymour, lake, Vt B4 120
Seymourville, Iberville, La., 1,788 B5 95
Sézanne, Fr., 5,300 C5 14
Sezimbra, Port., 6,957 C1 20
Sezze, It., 7,544 D4 21
Sfantul-Gheorghe, Rom., 17,638 C7 22
Sfax, Tun., 65,645 C7 44, G12 30
Sfax, prov., Tun., 338,268 *C7 44
Sgarbhbreae, mtn., Scot F2 13
's Gravenhage, see The Hague, Neth.
Sgurr Mor, mtn., Scot C3 13
Sha, China K7 36
Shabalē, riv., Eth D5 47
Shabani, Rh., 10,800 B5 49
Shabbona, DeKalb, Ill., 690 B5 90
Shabogamo, lake, Newf., Can h8 75
Shabrakhit, Eg., U.A.R., 1,000 C2 41
Shabunda, Con. L B4 48
Shabwah, S. Arabia B4 47
Shackelford, co., Tex., 3,990 C3 118
Shackleton, Sask., Can., 96 G1 70
Shackleton, glacier, Ant A31 5
Shackleton, ice shelf, Ant C22 5
Shackleton, range, Ant A10 5
Shade, riv., Ohio C5 111
Shadehill, Perkins, S. Dak., 20 B3 116
Shadehill, dam, S. Dak B3 116
Shadehill, res., S. Dak B3 116
Shades, creek, Ala E4 78
Shades, mtn., Ala E4 78
Shadeville, Franklin, Ohio, 250 C2 111
Shadrinsk, Sov. Un., 62,000 B6 29
Shady Cove, Jackson, Oreg., 875 E4 113
Shady Dale, Jasper, Ga., 201 C3 87
Shady Grove, Pike, Ala., 100 D3 78
Shady Grove, Taylor, Fla., 300 B3 86
Shady Grove, Crittenden, Ky., 50 A3, C2 94
Shadygrove, Franklin, Pa., 500 G6 114
Shadypoint, LeFlore, Okla., 300 B7 112
Shady Rill, Washington, Vt., 60 C3 120
Shady Side, Anne Arundel, Md., 749 C4 85
Shadyside, Belmont, Ohio, 5,028 C7 111
Shady Spring, Raleigh, W. Va., 850 D3 123
Shady Valley, Johnson, Tenn., 50 C12 117
Shafer, lake, Ind C4 91
Shaft (William Penn), Schuylkill, Pa., 850 *E9 114
Shafter, Kern, Calif., 4,576 E4 82
Shafter, Elko, Nev., 10 C7 104
Shafter, Presidio, Tex., 975 F2 118
Shaftesbury, Eng., 3,366 D5 12
Shaftsbury, Bennington, Vt., 700 (1,939▲) E2 120
Shaftsbury Center, Bennington, Vt., 100 F2 120
Shag, rocks, Atl. O J7 6
Shagamu, Nig., 30,099 *E5 45
Shageluk, Alsk., 155 C8 79
Shag Harbour, N.S., Can., 249 F4 74
Shagwong, pt., N.Y E9 84
Shah, riv., Iran C5 41
Shahdād (Khabis), Iran, 15,000 F8 41
Shahdadkot, Pak., 8,994 D1 40
Shah Fuladi, mtn., Afg D13 41
Shahgarh, India D4 40
Shaḩḩāt, Libya, 4,149 C4 43
Shahi, isl., Iran C2 41
Shahjahanpur, India, 110,432 (*117,702) C6 38, D7 40
Shahjui, Afg., 5,000 E13 41
Shahpur, India, 11,776 I6 40
Shāhpūr (Dilmān), Iran, 13,161 B2 41
Shahpur, Pak C4 39
Shahpura, India, 12,165 E5 40
Shahr-e Bābak, Iran, 10,000 F7 41
Shahreẕā, Iran, 23,980 E5 41
Shāhrūd, Iran, 23,132 C7 41
Shahsavār, Iran, 5,046 C5 41
Shaib al Qur, wadi, Sau. Ar G13 31
Shaib Hub, riv., Iraq G14 31
Shaikh Shuaib, isl., Iran H6 41
Shaker Heights, Cuyahoga, Ohio, 36,460 A6, B2 111
Shakhrisyabz, Sov. Un., 15,000 B13 41
Shakhtersk, Sov. Un., 65,000 *G12 27
Shakhty, Sov. Un., 201,000 H13 27
Shakhunya, Sov. Un B3 29
Shaki, Nig., 22,983 E5 45
Shakopee, Scott, Minn., 5,201 F5 99
Shakotan, cape, Jap E10 37
Shaktoolik, Alsk., 187 C7 79
Shalalth, B.C., Can., 182 D6 68
Shaler, mts., N.W. Ter., Can B10 66
Shalimar, Okaloosa, Fla., 754 G2 86
Shallmar, Garrett, Md., 100 D1 85
Shallotte, Brunswick, N.C., 480 D3 109
Shallotte, inlet, N.C D5 109
Shallow Lake, Ont., Can., 340 C3 72
Shallow Water, Scott, Kans., 85 D3 93
Shallowater, Lubbock, Tex., 1,001 C2 118
Shamattawa, Man., Can., 256 B5 71
Shambat, Sud., 6,611 B3 47
Shambaugh, Page, Iowa, 206 D2 92
Shambe, Sud D3 47
Shamīl, Iran, 5,000 H8 41
Shamokin, Northumberland, Pa., 13,674 E8 114
Shamokin Dam, Snyder, Pa., 1,093 E8 114
Shamrock, Sask., Can., 126 G2 70
Shamrock, Dixie, Fla., 600 C3 86
Shamrock, Natchitoches, La., 70 C2 95
Shamrock, Creek, Okla., 211 B5 112
Shamrock, Wheeler, Tex., 3,113 B2 118
Shamva, Rh A5 49
Shandaken, Ulster, N.Y., 500 C6 108
Shandon, San Luis Obispo, Calif., 500 E3 82
Shandon, Butler, Ohio, 300 C2 111
Shanee, Park, Colo., 100 B5 83
Shang, China, 6,000 H3 36
Shangchiu, China, 134,400 G6 36
Shanghai, China, 6,900,000 (9,500,000▲) E9 34, I9 36
Shangjao, China, 50,000 J8 36
Shangnan, China I4 36
Shangssu, China A7 38
Shangtu, China D5 36
Shaniko, Wasco, Oreg., 39 B6 113
Shannock, Washington, R.I., 500 D10 84
Shannon, Floyd, Ga., 1,629 B1 87
Shannon, Carroll, Ill., 766 A4 90
Shannon, Lee, Miss., 554 A5 100
Shannon, Clay, Tex., 75 C3 118
Shannon, co., Mo., 7,087 D6 101
Shannon, co., S. Dak., 6,000 D3 116
Shannon, airport, Ire E3 11
Shannon, isl., Grnld B16 4
Shannon, lake, Wash A4 122
Shannon, riv., Ire E2 11
Shannon, riv. mouth, Ire E2 11
Shannon City, Union and Ringgold, Iowa, 127 D3 92
Shannontown, Sumter, S.C., 7,064 *D7 115
Shanshan (Pichan), China C3 34
Shansi, prov., China, 15,960,000 D7 34
Shantar, is., Sov. Un D16 28
Shantung, prov., China, 54,030,000 D8 34
Shantung, pen., China D9 34, F9 36
Shanwa, Tan B5 48
Shaohsing, China, 130,600 E9 34, I9 36
Shaopo, China H8 36
Shaowu, China, 12,000 K7 36
Shaoyang, China, 117,700 F7 34, K4 36
Shap, Eng., 1,152 F6 13
Shapinsay, isl., Scot A6 13
Shapio, lake, Newf., Can g9 75
Shapki, Sov. Un s32 25
Sharafkhāneh, Iran, 1,260 B2 41
Sharangad, Mong B2 36
Sharasume (Chenghwa), China, 25,000 B2 34
Sharbot Lake, Ont., Can., 481 C8 72
Shari, Jap., 8,100 E12 37
Sharita, cape, Mus. & Om H8 41
Shark, bay, Austl E1 50
Shark, pt., Fla G5 86
Sharkey, co., Miss., 10,738 C3 100
Sharkh, Mus. & Om D2 39
Sharktooth, mtn., B.C., Can E7 66
Sharon, Litchfield, Conn., 700 (2,141▲) B3 84
Sharon, Taliaferro, Ga., 264 C4 87
Sharon, Barber, Kans., 272 E5 93
Sharon, Norfolk, Mass., 10,070 B5, h11 97
Sharon, Madison, Miss., 50 C4 100
Sharon, Hillsboro, N.H., 50 (78▲) E3 105
Sharon, Schoharie, N.Y., 90 C6 108
Sharon, Steele, N. Dak., 251 B8 110
Sharon, Woodward, Okla., 97 A2 112
Sharon, Mercer, Pa., 25,267 D1 114
Sharon, York, S.C., 280 B5 115
Sharon, Weakley, Tenn., 966 A3 117
Sharon, Windsor, Vt., 150 (485▲) D4 120
Sharon, Spokane, Wash C7 122
Sharon, Kanawha, W. Va., 100 D6 123
Sharon, Walworth, Wis., 1,167 F5 124
Sharon Grove, Todd, Ky., 100 D2 94
Sharon Hill, Delaware, Pa., 7,123 G11 114
Sharon Springs, Wallace, Kans., 966 D2 93
Sharon Springs, Schoharie, N.Y., 351 C6 108
Sharon Valley, Litchfield, Conn., 200 B3 84
Sharonville, Hamilton, Ohio, 6,457 D2 111
Sharp, co., Ark., 6,319 A4 81
Sharpe, lake, Man., Can B5 71
Sharpes, Brevard, Fla., 700 D6 86
Sharples, Logan, W. Va., 40 D3, D5 123
Sharpsburg, Taylor, Iowa, 130 D3 92
Sharpsburg, Bath, Ky., 311 B6 94
Sharpsburg, Washington, Md., 861 B2 85
Sharpsburg, Nash, Edgecombe and Wilson, N.C., 490 B5 109
Sharpsburg, Allegheny, Pa., 6,096 A5 114
Sharps Chapel, Union, Tenn., 25 C10 117
Sharpsville, Tipton, Ind., 663 D5 91
Sharpsville, Mercer, Pa., 6,067 D1 114
Sharp Top, mtn., Ark C2 81
Sharptown, Wicomico, Md., 620 C6 85
Sharptown, Salem, N.J., 200 D2 106
Sharya, Sov. Un., 21,700 B3 29
Shāshamani, Eth D4 47
Shashi, riv., Bech., Rh B4 49
Shashke, Sov. Un C7 29
Shasi, China, 85,800 E7 34
Shasta, co., Calif., 59,468 B3 82
Shasta, lake, Calif B2 82
Shasta, mtn., Calif B2 82
Shastsk, Sov. Un., 10,000 D13 27
Shatney, mtn., N.H A1 105
Shatra, Iraq, 9,543 F3 41
Shattuck, Ellis, Okla., 1,625 A2 112
Shattuckville, Franklin, Mass., 150 A2 97
Shatura, Sov. Un., 50,000 D12 27
Shauck, Morrow, Ohio, 200 B5 111
Shaunavon, Sask., Can., 2,154 H1 70
Shavano, mtn., Colo C4 83
Shaver, mtn., W. Va C5 123
Shavers, fork, W. Va C5 123
Shavertown, Luzerne, Pa., 2,000 *B8 114
Shaw, Lincoln, Colo B7 83
Shaw, St. Louis, Minn., 50 C6 99
Shaw, Bolivar, Miss., 2,062 B3 100
Shaw, Marion, Oreg., 75 C2 113
Shaw, Mineral, W. Va., 200 B5 123
Shawā, prov., Eth D4 47
Shawanaga, Ont., Can B4 72
Shawangunk, mts., N.Y D6 108
Shawano, Shawano, Wis., 6,103 D5 124
Shawano, co., Wis., 34,351 D5 124
Shawano, lake, Wis D5 124
Shawatun, China D9 36
Shawboro, Currituck, N.C., 60 A7 109
Shawbridge, Que., Can., 1,034 D3 73
Shawhan, Bourbon, Ky., 250 B5 94
Shawinigan, Que., Can., 32,169 (*63,518) C5 73
Shawinigan Lake, B.C., Can., 436 g12 68
Shawinigan-Sud, Que., Can., 12,683 C5 73
Shawmut, Chambers, Ala., 1,898 C4 78
Shawmut, Pike, Ark C2 81
Shawmut, Somerset, Maine, 225 D3 96
Shawmut, Wheatland, Mont., 70 D7 102
Shawnee, Johnson, Kans., 9,072 B8 93
Shawnee, Perry, Ohio, 1,000 C5 111
Shawnee, Pottawatomie, Okla., 24,326 B5 112
Shawnee, Converse, Wyo., 18 C7 125
Shawnee, co., Kans., 141,286 D8 93
Shawneetown, Gallatin, Ill., 1,399 F5 90
Shawsheen, riv., Mass f11 97
Shawsville, Hartford, Md., 250 A4 85
Shawsville, Montgomery, Va., 300 D2 121
Shawver Mill, Tazewell, Va B3 121
Shawville, Que., Can., 1,534 B8 72
Shayang, China I5 36
Shchekino, Sov. Un., 30,000 D11 27
Shchelkovo, Sov. Un., 66,000 n18 27
Shcherbakov, see Rybinsk, Sov. Un.
Shchetovo, Sov. Un., 10,000 q22 27
Shchigry, Sov. Un., 10,000 F11 27
Shchors, Sov. Un., 10,000 F8 27
Shchuchinsk, Sov. Un C8 29
Shchurovo, Sov. Un., 15,000 n18 27
Shearstown, Newf., Can., 680 *E5 75
Sheaville, Malheur, Oreg D9 113
Sheboygan, Sheboygan, Wis., 45,747 B6, E6 124
Sheboygan, co., Wis., 86,484 E6 124
Sheboygan, riv., Wis B5 124
Sheboygan Falls, Sheboygan, Wis., 4,061 B6, E6 124
Shebshi, mts., Nig E7 45
Shechichen, China H5 36
Shedd, Linn, Oreg., 150 C3 113
Shedden, Ont., Can., 295 E3 72
Shediac, N.B., Can., 2,159 C5 74
Sheelin, lake, Ire D4 11
Sheenjek, riv., Alsk B11 79
Sheep, creek, Alta., Can C1 69
Sheep, mtn., Ariz E1 80
Sheep, mtn., Wyo B2 125
Sheep, mtn., Wyo B3 125
Sheep, peak, Nev G6 104
Sheep, range, Nev G6 104
Sheep Haven, bay, Ire B4 11
Sheep Heaven, mtn., Mass A1 97
Sheerness, Alta., Can., 93 D5 69
Sheerness, Eng., 14,123 C8 12
Sheet Harbour, N.S., Can., 883 E7 74
Sheffield, Colbert, Ala., 13,491 A2 78
Sheffield, Eng., 495,300 (*735,000) A6 12
Sheffield, Bureau, Ill., 1,078 B4 90
Sheffield, Franklin, Iowa, 1,156 B4 92
Sheffield, Berkshire, Mass., 500 (2,138▲) B1 97
Sheffield, N.Z., 151 O14 51
Sheffield, Lorain, Ohio, 1,664 A5 111
Sheffield, Warren, Pa., 1,971 C3 114
Sheffield, Pecos, Tex., 350 D2 118
Sheffield, Caledonia, Vt., 150 (342▲) B4 120
Sheffield, lake, Newf., Can D3 75
Sheffield Lake, Lorain, Ohio, 6,884 *A5 111
Shefford, co., Que., Can., 54,963 D5 73
Sheguiandah, Ont., Can., 116 B3 72
Sheho, Sask., Can., 391 F4 70
Shehsien, China J8 36
Shehy, mts., Ire F2 11
Sheikh, Som D6 47
Sheikhupura, Pak., 41,635 *B4 40
Sheila, N.B., Can., 553 B5 74
Shekar Dzong, China, 5,000 C11 40
Shelagski, cape, Sov. Un B33 4
Shelagyote, peak, B.C., Can B4 68
Shelbiana, Pike, Ky., 500 C7 94
Shelbina, Shelby, Mo., 2,067 B5 101
Shelburn, Sullivan, Ind., 1,299 F3 91
Shelburn, Linn, Oreg., 40 C2, C4 113
Shelburne, N.S., Can., 2,408 F4 74
Shelburne, Ont., Can., 1,239 C4 72
Shelburne, Franklin, Mass., 100 (1,739▲) A2 97
Shelburne, Coos, N.H., 50 (226▲) B4 105
Shelburne, Chittenden, Vt., 200 (1,805▲) C2 120
Shelburne, co., N.S., Can., 15,208 F4 74
Shelburne, pond, Vt C2 120
Shelburne Falls, Franklin, Mass., 2,097 A2 97
Shelburne Falls, Chittenden, Vt., 100 C2 120
Shelby, Shelby, Ala., 600 B3 78
Shelby, Lake, Ind., 500 B3 91
Shelby, Shelby, Iowa, 533 C2 92
Shelby, Oceana, Mich., 1,603 E4 98
Shelby, Bolivar, Miss., 2,384 B3 100
Shelby, Toole, Mont., 4,017 B5 102
Shelby, Polk, Nebr., 613 C8 103
Shelby, Cleveland, N.C., 17,698 B2 109
Shelby, Richland, Ohio, 9,106 B5 111
Shelby, co., Ala., 32,132 B3 78
Shelby, co., Ill., 23,404 D5 90
Shelby, co., Ind., 34,093 E6 91
Shelby, co., Iowa, 15,825 C2 92
Shelby, co., Ky., 18,493 B4 94
Shelby, co., Mo., 9,063 B5 101
Shelby, co., Ohio, 33,586 B3 111
Shelby, co., Tenn., 627,019 B2 117
Shelby, co., Tex., 20,479 B5 118

Shelby City, Boyle, Ky., 500 C5 94
Shelby Village, Macomb, Mich., 1,900 *F7 98
Shelbyville, Shelby, Ill., 4,821 D5 90
Shelbyville, Shelby, Ind., 14,317 E6 91
Shelbyville, Shelby, Ky., 4,525 B4 94
Shelbyville, Shelby, Mo., 657 B5 101
Shelbyville, Bedford, Tenn., 10,466 B5 117
Sheldahl, Boone, Polk, and Story, Iowa, 279 A7 92
Sheldon, Iroquois, Ill., 1,137 C6 90
Sheldon, O'Brien, Iowa, 4,251 A2 92
Sheldon, Vernon, Mo., 434 D3 101
Sheldon, Ransom, N. Dak., 221 C8 110
Sheldon, Beaufort, S.C., 200 F6 115
Sheldon, Harris, Tex., 100 F5 118
Sheldon, Franklin, Vt., 300 (1,281▲) B3 120
Sheldon, Rusk, Wis., 240 C3 124
Sheldon Springs, Franklin, Vt., 250 B3 120
Sheldonville, Norfolk, Mass., 300 B5 97
Shelekhov, gulf, Sov. Un C18 28
Shelikof, strait, Alsk D9 79
Shell, creek, Wyo A5 125
Shell, lake, Minn D3 99
Shell, lake, Wis C1 124
Shell, riv., Man., Can D1 71
Shell Beach, San Luis Obispo, Calif., 1,820 *E3 82
Shell Beach, St. Bernard, La., 125 E6 95
Shellbrook, Sask., Can., 1,042 D2 70
Shell Camp, Gregg, Tex., 500 *C5 118
Shell Creek, Carter, Tenn., 400 C11 117
Shell Creek, range, Nev D7 104
Shelley, B.C., Can., 148 C6 68
Shelley, Bingham, Idaho, 2,612 F6 89
Shell Lake, Sask., Can., 241 D2 70
Shell Lake, Washburn, Wis., 1,016 C2 124
Shellman, Randolph, Ga., 1,050 E2 87
Shellman Bluff, McIntosh, Ga., 150 E5 87
Shellmouth, Man., Can., 98 D1 71
Shell Rock, Butler, Iowa, 1,112 B5 92
Shellrock, riv., Iowa B4, B5 92
Shellsburg, Benton, Iowa, 625 B6 92
Shelly, Norman, Minn., 310 C2 99
Shelter, isl., N.Y E7 84
Shelter Island, Suffolk, N.Y., 550 E7 84
Shelter Island Heights, Suffolk, N.Y., 500 E7 84
Shelton, Fairfield, Conn., 18,190 D4 84
Shelton, Buffalo, Nebr., 904 D7 103
Shelton, Fairfield, S.C., 150 C5 115
Shelton, Mason, Wash., 5,651 B2 122
Shemogue, N.B., Can., 93 C5 74
Shenandoah, Page, Iowa, 6,567 D2 92
Shenandoah, Schuylkill, Pa., 11,073 E9 114
Shenandoah, Page, Va., 1,839 C4 121
Shenandoah, co., Va., 21,825 C4 121
Shenandoah, mtn., Va C3 121
Shenandoah, nat. park, Va C4 121
Shenandoah, riv., Va B5 121
Shenandoah, val., Va C4 121
Shenandoah Heights, Schuylkill, Pa., 1,721 *E9 114
Shenandoah Tower, mtn., Va., W. Va C3 121, C5 123
Shenchiu, China H6 36
Shendi, Sud., 11,031 B3 47
Shenipsit, lake, Conn B7 84
Shenmu, China, 10,000 D7 34
Shenorock, Westchester, N.Y., 1,600 *D7 108
Shensi, prov., China, 18,130,000 E6 34
Shentsa Dzong, China, 5,000 B12 40
Shenyang, see Mukden, China
Sheopur, India, 14,591 E6 40
Shepard, Alta., Can., 66 D4 69
Shepard, isl., Ant B35 5
Shepardsville, Vigo, Ind., 350 E3 91
Shepaug, riv., Conn C3 84
Shepetovka, Sov. Un., 10,000 F6 27
Shepherd, Isabella, Mich., 1,293 E6 98
Shepherd, Yellowstone, Mont., 100 E8 102
Shepherd, San Jacinto, Tex., 800 D5 118
Shepherd Brook, mtn., Maine B3 96
Shepherdstown, Jefferson, W. Va., 1,328 B7 123
Shepherdsville, Bullitt, Ky., 1,525 A4, C4 94
Shepp, Haywood, Tenn., 40 B2 117
Sheppards, Buckingham, Va D4 121
Shepparton, Austl., 13,579 H5 51
Sheppey, isl., Eng C8 12
Sheppton, Schuylkill, Pa., 800 E9 114
Shepton Mallet, Eng., 5,518 C5 12
Sherard, Coahoma, Miss., 60 A3 100
Sherborn, Middlesex, Mass., 500 (1,806▲) h10 97
Sherborne, Eng., 6,062 D5 12
Sherbro, isl., S.L. E2 45
Sherbrooke, N.S., Can., 384 D8 74
Sherbrooke, Que., Can., 66,554 (★70,253) C2, k12 73
Sherbrooke, co., Que., Can., 80,490 D5 73
Sherbrooke, lake, N.S., Can E5 74
Sherburn, Martin, Minn., 1,227 G4 99
Sherburne, Chenango, N.Y., 1,647 C5 108
Sherburne (Town of), Rutland, Vt. (266▲) *D3 120
Sherburne, co., Minn., 12,861 E5 99
Shercock, Ire., 254 D5 11
Shereik, Sud B3 47
Shereshevo, Sov. Un., 10,000 B8 26
Shergarh, India D4 40
Sheridan, Grant, Ark., 1,938 C3 81
Sheridan, Arapahoe, Colo., 3,559 B6 83
Sheridan, La Salle, Ill., 704 B5 90
Sheridan, Hamilton, Ind., 2,165 D5 91
Sheridan, Crittenden, Ky., 60 A3 94
Sheridan, Aroostook, Maine, 350 B4 96
Sheridan, Montcalm, Mich., 606 E5 98
Sheridan, Worth, Mo., 277 A3 101
Sheridan, Madison, Mont., 539 E4 102
Sheridan, Yamhill, Oreg., 1,763 B3 113
Sheridan, Sheridan, Wyo., 11,651 A6 125
Sheridan, co., Kans., 4,267 C3 93
Sheridan, co., Mont., 6,458 B12 102
Sheridan, co., Nebr., 9,049 B3 103
Sheridan, co., N. Dak., 4,350 B5 104
Sheridan, co., Wyo., 18,989 A5 125
Sheridan, mtn., Wyo A2 125
Sheridan Beach, King, Wash., 1,500 *B3 122
Sheridan Lake, Kiowa, Colo., 90 C8 83
Sheringham, Eng., 4,836 B9 12
Sherkaly, Sov. Un C22 9
Sherman, Fairfield, Conn., 250 (825▲) C3 84
Sherman, Aroostook, Maine, 100 (1,034▲) C4 96
Sherman, Pontotoc and Union, Miss., 403 A5 100
Sherman, St. Louis, Mo., 300 A7 101
Sherman, Grant, N. Mex., 25 E2 107
Sherman, Chautauqua, N.Y., 873 C1 108
Sherman, Summit, Ohio, 1,000 *B6 111
Sherman, Major, Okla A3 112
Sherman, Minnehaha, S. Dak., 116 D9 116
Sherman, Grayson, Tex., 24,988 C4 118
Sherman, co., Kans., 6,682 C2 93
Sherman, co., Nebr., 5,382 C6 103
Sherman, co., Oreg., 2,446 B6 113
Sherman, co., Tex., 2,605 A2 118
Sherman, mtn., Ark A2 81
Sherman, res., Nebr C7 103
Sherman Mills, Aroostook, Maine, 450 C4 96
Sherman Station, Penobscot, Maine, 375 C4 96
Sherpur, Pak., 19,312 E12 40
Sherrard, Mercer, Ill., 574 B3 90
Sherridon, Man., Can., 40 B1 71
Sherrill, Jefferson, Ark., 241 C4 81
Sherrill, Oneida, N.Y., 2,922 B5 108
Sherrodsville, Carroll, Ohio, 480 B6 111
's Hertogenbosch, Neth., 75,700 (★120,000) C5 15
Sherwood, Pulaski, Ark., 1,222 D5 81
Sherwood, P.E.I., Can., 1,580 C6 74
Sherwood, Choctaw, Miss., 65 B5 100
Sherwood, Renville, N. Dak., 360 A4 110
Sherwood, Defiance, Ohio, 578 A3 111
Sherwood, McCurtain, Okla., 100 C7 112
Sherwood, Washington, Oreg., 680 B2 113
Sherwood, Franklin, Tenn., 650 B6 117
Sherwood, Irion, Tex., 200 D2 118
Sherwood, Calumet, Wis., 300 A5 124
Sherwood Manor, Hartford, Conn., 900 *B6 84
Sherwood Park, Alta., Can., 2,923 C4 69
Sheshebee, Aitkin, Minn., 100 D5 99
Shetek, lake, Minn F3 99
Shetland, co., Scot., 17,500 *g10 10
Shetland, is., Scot g10 10
Shetucket, riv., Conn C8 84
Shevchenko, Sov. Un E4 29
Shevlin, Clearwater, Minn., 203 C3 99
Shevlin, Klamath, Oreg D5 113
Sheyenne, Eddy, N. Dak., 423 B6 110
Sheyenne, riv., N. Dak C8 110
Shfaram, Isr., 5,029 B7 32
Shfayim, Isr., 713 g10 32
Shiant, isl., Scot C2 13
Shiawassee, co., Mich., 53,446 F6 98
Shibarghan (Shibargan), Afg., 22,464 C12 41
Shibata, Jap., 36,400 (73,886▲) *H9 37
Shibetsu, Jap., 12,750 D11 37
Shibīn al Kawm, Eg., U.A.R., 47,100 D3 32
Shībin al Qanāṭir, Eg., U.A.R., 11,610 D3 32
Shichito, isl., Pac. O D8 7
Shickley, Fillmore, Nebr., 371 D8 103
Shickshinny, Luzerne, Pa., 1,843 D9 114
Shideler, Delaware, Ind., 240 D7 91
Shiderty, riv., Sov. Un C8 29
Shidler, Osage, Okla., 870 A5 112
Shieldaig, Scot C3 13
Shields, Lane, Kans., 50 D3 93
Shields, Harlan, Ky., 900 *D6 94
Shields, Grant, N. Dak., 100 C4 110
Shiga, pref., Jap., 842,695 *I8 37
Shigawake, Que., Can., 125 *B4 73
Shihchiachuang, China, 126,000 E6 36
Shihchuan, China, 5,000 H3 36
Shihkiachwang, China, 598,000 D7 34
Shihmen, China, 5,000 J4 36
Shihshou, China, 19,000 J5 36
Shihtaokuo, China F10 36
Shikarpur, Pak., 53,910 C4 38, D2 40
Shikoku, isl., Jap J6 37
Shikuka, see Poronaysk, Sov. Un.
Shilka, Sov. Un., 23,000 D14 28
Shilla, peak, India A7 40
Shillington, Berks, Pa., 5,639 F10 114
Shillong, India, 72,438 (★102,389) C9 39
Shiloh, Marengo, Ala., 100 C2 78
Shiloh, Cleburne, Ark., 6 B3 81
Shiloh, Harris, Ga., 250 D2 87
Shiloh, St. Clair, Ill., 701 B9 101
Shiloh, Cumberland, N.J., 554 E2 106
Shiloh, Camden, N.C. (part of Asheville) A7 109
Shiloh, Montgomery, Ohio, 9,500 C3 111
Shiloh, Richland, Ohio, 724 B5 111
Shiloh, York, Pa., 1,500 *G8 114
Shiloh, Montgomery, Tenn., 40 A4 117
Shiloh, nat. military park and cemetery, Tenn B3 117
Shimabara, Jap., 28,200 (45,205▲) J5 37
Shimada, Jap., 36,500 (53,900▲) o17 37
Shimane, pref., Jap., 888,886 *I6 37
Shimanovsk, Sov. Un., 17,000 D15 28
Shimizu, Jap., 142,983 I9, n17 37
Shimo, isl., Jap J5 37
Shimoda, Jap., 16,200 o17 37
Shimodate, Jap., 23,000 (51,257▲) m18 37
Shimoga, India, 63,764 F6 39
Shimonoseki, Jap., 246,941 I5 37
Shimotsuma, Jap., 9,700 m18 37
Shin, lake, Scot B4 13
Shinall, mtn., Ark D5 81
Shiner, Lavaca, Tex., 1,945 E4 118
Shinewell, McCurtain, Okla., 50 D7 112
Shingbwiyang, Bur., 5,000 C10 39
Shinglehouse, Potter, Pa., 1,298 C5 114
Shingleton, Alger, Mich., 450 B4 98
Shingu, Jap., 39,114 J7 37
Shinjo, Jap., 22,100 G10 37
Shinkolobwe, Con. L., 10,900 D4 48
Shinnecock, bay, N.Y F6 84
Shinnston, Harrison, W. Va., 2,724 A7, B4 123
Shin Pond, Penobscot, Maine, 40 B4 96
Shinshiro, Jap., 14,100 o16 37
Shinyanga, Tan., 2,907 B5 48
Shio, cape, Jap J7 37
Shiocton, Outagamie, Wis., 685 A5, D5 124
Shiogama, Jap., 55,325 G10 37
Shiojiri, Jap., 13,500 m16 37
Shioya, cape, Jap H10 37
Ship, isl., Miss E5 100
Ship Bottom, Ocean, N.J., 717 D4 106
Ship Cove, Newf., Can., 66 E4 75
Ship Harbour, N.S., Can., 212 E7 74
Shipiskan, lake, Newf., Can g9 75
Ship Island, pass., Miss E2 100
Shipka, pass, Bul D7 22
Shipki, pass, India B7 40
Shipman, Sask., Can., 40 D3 70
Shipman, Macoupin, Ill., 417 D3 90
Shipman, Nelson, Va., 500 D4 121
Shippegan, N.B., Can., 1,631 B5 74
Shippegan, isl., N.B., Can B5 74
Shippegan Gully, N.B., Can., 761 *B5 74
Shippensburg, Cumberland and Franklin, Pa., 6,138 F6 114
Shippenville, Clarion, Pa., 599 D3 114
Shiprock, San Juan, N. Mex., 1,000 A1 107
Ship Rock, mtn., N. Mex. A1 107
Shipshewana, Lagrange, Ind., 312 A6 91
Shirabad, Sov. Un C13 41
Shirase, glacier, Ant. B17 5
Shiratori, Jap., 5,819 n15 37
Shīrāz, Iran, 170,659 G6 41
Shirbīn, Eg., U.A.R., 13,293 C8 31
Shire, riv., Malawi, Moz E5 48
Shiremanstown, Cumberland, Pa., 1,212 *F8 114
Shire Nor, China E3 34
Shiretoko, cape, Jap D12 37
Shireza, Pak C4 39
Shiriya, cape, Jap C4 39
Shir Kuh, mtn., Iran F7 41
Shirley, Van Buren, Ark., 197 B3 81
Shirley, McLean, Ill., 130 C4 90
Shirley, Hancock and Henry, Ind., 1,038 E6 91
Shirley, Middlesex, Mass., 1,850 (5,202▲) A4 97
Shirley, Custer, Mont. D11 102
Shirley, Suffolk, N.Y., 4,500 *F5 84
Shirley, Tyler, W. Va., 150 A6 123
Shirley, Carbon, Wyo C6 125
Shirley, basin, Wyo C6 125
Shirley Center, Middlesex, Mass., 150 A4 97
Shirley Mills, Piscataquis, Maine, 200 (214▲) C3 96
Shirleysburg, Huntingdon, Pa., 170 F6 114
Şhirntoru, see Makarov, Sov. Un.
Shishaldin, vol., Alsk E7 79
Shishido, Jap., 11,018 m19 37
Shishmaref, Alsk., 217 B6 79
Shively, Humboldt, Calif., 100 B2 82
Shively, Jefferson, Ky., 15,155 A4, B4 94
Shivers, Simpson, Miss., 10 D4 100
Shivpuri, India, 28,681 E6 40
Shivwits, Washington, Utah, 50 F2 119
Shivwits, Indian res., Utah F2 119
Shizuoka, Jap., 323,819 (★485,000) I9, o17 37
Shizuoka, pref., Jap., 2,756,271 *I9 37
Shkodër (Scutari), Alb., 43,234 A2 23
Shkodër (Scutari), pref., Alb., 150,000 *A2 23
Shkotovo, Sov. Un E6 37
Shoal, creek, Tenn B4 117
Shoal, lake, Ont., Can B6 99
Shoal, lake, Ont., Man., Can. E4 71
Shoal, lakes, Man., Can D3 71
Shoal, riv., Man., Can C1 71
Shoal Harbour, Newf., Can., 544 D4 75
Shoal Lake, Man., Can., 774 D1 71
Shoals, Martin, Ind., 1,022 G4 91
Shoalwater, cape, Wash C1 122
Shobankazgan, Sov. Un E6 29
Shobonier, Fayette, Ill., 200 E4 90
Shoe Cove, Newf., Can., 152 D4 75
Shoeheel, creek, S.C. B9 115
Shoemakersville, Berks, Pa., 1,464 E10 114
Shōfō, see Changsong, Kor.
Shola, lake, Eth D4 47
Sholapur, India, 337,583 E6 39, I5 40
Sholes, Wayne, Nebr., 26 B8 103
Shona, isl., Scot D2 13
Shongopovi, Navajo, Ariz., 120 B5 80
Shonkin, Chouteau, Mont., 5 C6 102
Shonto, Navajo, Ariz., 15 A5 80
Shooks, Beltrami, Minn., 25 C4 99
Shooting Creek, Clay, N.C., 50 D2 109
Shop Spring, Wilson, Tenn., 175 A5 117
Shore Acres, Contra Costa, Calif., 3,093 *B5 82
Shoreacres, B.C., Can., 80 E9 68
Shore Acres, Plymouth, Mass., 900 h13 97
Shoreham, Berrien, Mich., 443 F4 98
Shoreham, Suffolk, N.Y., 224 F5 84
Shoreham, Addison, Vt., 150 (786▲) D2 120
Shoreham Center, Addison, Vt., 60 D2 120
Shoreview, Ramsey, Minn., 7,157 *F5 99
Shorewood, Hennepin, Minn., 3,197 *F5 99
Shorewood, Milwaukee, Wis., 15,990 E2, E6 124
Shorewood Hills, Dane, Wis., 2,320 *E4 124
Short, Sequoyah, Okla B7 112
Short, creek, Ohio B1 123
Short, mtn., Tenn B6 117
Short, mtn., Tenn C10 117
Short Beach, New Haven, Conn., 1,500 D5 84
Short Creek, Mohave, Ariz., 200 A3 80
Short Creek, Brooke, W. Va., 400 B2 123
Shorter, Macon, Ala., 200 C4 78
Shorterville, Henry, Ala., 300 D4 78
Short Falls, Merrimack, N.H., 100 D4 105
Shorts Creek, Carroll, Va., 50 E2 121
Shortsville, Ontario, N.Y., 1,382 C3 108
Shoshone, Garfield, Colo., 15 B3 83
Shoshone, Lincoln, Idaho, 1,416 G4 89
Shoshone, co., Idaho, 20,876 B3 89
Shoshone, basin, Wyo B4 125
Shoshone, falls, Idaho G4 89
Shoshone, lake, Wyo A2 125
Shoshone, mtn., Nev G5 104
Shoshone, mts., Nev E4 104
Shoshone, peak, Nev D4 104
Shoshone, riv., Wyo A4 125
Shoshone Cavern, nat. mon., Wyo A3 125
Shoshoni, Fremont, Wyo., 766 B4 125
Shostka, Sov. Un., 30,000 F9 27
Shou, China H7 36
Shouldice, Alta., Can D4 69
Shouns, Johnson, Tenn., 250 C12 117
Shoup, Lemhi, Idaho, 10 D4 89
Showak, Sud., 2,171 C4 47
Showell, Worcester, Md., 200 D7 85
Show Low, Navajo, Ariz., 1,625 C5 80
Shpola, Sov. Un., 10,000 G8 27
Shreve, Wayne, Ohio, 1,617 B5 111
Shreveport, Caddo, La., 164,372 (★245,200) B2 95
Shrewsbury, Eng., 50,700 B5 12
Shrewsbury, Worcester, Mass., 16,622 B4 97
Shrewsbury, St. Louis, Mo., 4,730 *C7 101
Shrewsbury, Monmouth, N.J., 3,222 C4 106
Shrewsbury, York, Pa., 943 G8 114
Shrewsbury, riv., N.J C5 106
Shropshire, co., Eng., 297,313 B5 12
Shrub Oak, Westchester, N.Y., 2,200 *D7 108
Shrule, Ire., 250 D2 11
Shuangcheng, China, 81,000 B10 34, D3 37
Shuangchiang, China G4 34
Shuangshan, China, 5,000 E1 37
Shuangyang, China, 5,000 E2 37
Shuangyashan, China, 50,000 B11 34
Shubenacadie, N.S., Can., 579 D6 74
Shubenacadie, lake, N.S., Can. E6 74
Shubert, Richardson, Nebr., 231 D10 103
Shubrā Khit, Eg., U.A.R., 1,000 C2 32
Shubuta, Clarke, Miss., 718 D5 100
Shucheng, China I7 36
Shufat, Jordan, 2,000 h11 32
Shuford, Panola, Miss., 60 A4 100
Shujabad, Pak., 14,602 C3 40
Shuksan, mtn., Wash A4 122
Shulan, China, 5,000 D3 37
Shulaps, peak, B.C., Can D6 68
Shulerville, Berkeley, S.C., 250 E8 115
Shullsburg, Lafayette, Wis., 1,324 F3 124
Shumagin, isl., Alsk D7 79
Shuman House, Alsk., 20 B11 79
Shumaykh, Libya I13 30
Shumen, co., Bul., 1,408,188 *D8 22
Shumerlya, Sov. Un., 26,800 B3 29
Shumikha, Sov. Un B6 29
Shunan, China, 6,000 J8 36
Shunat Nimrin, Jordan, 1,000 h13 32
Shunchang, China, 4,000 K7 36
Shungnak, Alsk., 135 B8 79
Shunk, Sullivan, Pa., 65 C8 114
Shunner Fell, mtn., Eng F6 13
Shunning, China G4 34
Shuo, China E5 36
Shuqrā', S. Arabia C6 47
Shuqualak, Noxubee, Miss., 550 C5 100
Shur, riv., Iran D5 41
Shur, riv., Iran F7 41
Shur, riv., Iran F10 41
Shur, riv., Iran H7 41
Shūrāb, Iran G10 41
Shūrāb, Iran G10 41
Shuri, Okinawa, 17,537 52
Sūsh, Iran E4 41
Shushan, Washington, N.Y., 350 B7 108
Shushong, Bech B4 49
Shūshtar, Iran, 23,654 E4 41
Shusht el Maghara, mtn., Eg D5 32
Shuswap, lake, B.C., Can D8 68
Shuswap, riv., B.C., Can D8 68
Shutesbury, Franklin, Mass., 150 (265▲) B3 97
Shuwaykah, Jordan, 3,000 f11 32
Shuya, Sov. Un., 67,000 B2 29
Shuzenji, Jap., 7,800 o17 37
Shwangliao (Chengchiatun), China, 120,100 C9 34
Shwebo, Bur., 17,842 D10 39
Shwegyin, Bur., 10,000 D2 38
Si, riv., China G7 34
Siah Band, mtn., Afg E11 41
Siahan, range, Iran, Pak H11 41
Sialkot, Pak., 143,889 (★164,346) B5 39, A5 40
Sialum, N. Gui k12 50
Siam, see Thailand, country, Asia
Siam, gulf, Asia G4 38
Sian (Hsian), China, 1,310,000 E6 34
Siangtan, China, 183,600 F7 34, K5 36
Siantan, isl., Indon K7 38
Siasconset, Nantucket, Mass., 200 D8 97
Siatista, Grc., 4,969 B3 23
Siaton, Phil., 2,364 *D6 35
Siau, isl., Indon E7 35
Siauliai, Sov. Un., 68,000 D4 27
Sibay, Sov. Un C5 29
Sibbald, Alta., Can., 75 D5 69
Sibenik, Yugo., 26,253 D2 22
Sibert, Clay, Ky., 700 C6 94
Siberut, isl., Indon F1 35
Sibi, Pak., 11,842 C4 39
Sibiryakov, isl., Sov. Un. B7 4
Sibiti, Con. B F2 46
Sibiu, Rom., 98,400 C7 22
Sibley, Ford, Ill., 386 C5 90
Sibley, Osceola, Iowa, 2,852 A2 92
Sibley, Webster, La., 595 B2 95
Sibley, Adams, Miss., 50 D2 100
Sibley, Jackson, Mo., 177 E3 101
Sibley, co., Minn., 16,228 F4 99
Sibolga, Indon., 37,171 L3 38
Sibsagar, India, 15,106 C9 39
Sibu, Mala., 29,630 E4 35
Sibuatan, mtn., Indon K3 38
Sibuko, Phil., 2,136 *D6 35
Sibutu, isl., Phil E5 35
Sibuyan, sea, Phil C6 35
Sicamous, B.C., Can. D8 68
Sicapoo, mtn., Phil B6 35
Sicard, Ouachita, La., 2,000 *B3 95
Sichomovi, Navajo, Ariz., 100 B5 80
Sicilia, pol. dist., It., 4,810,000 *F4 21
Sicily, isl., It F4 21
Sicily Island, Catahoula, La., 761 C4 95
Sicklerville, Camden, N.J., 750 D3 106
Sico, riv., Hond C5 62
Sicuaní, Peru, 7,036 D3 58
Sidādah, Libya C2 43
Sidāmo, prov., Eth. E4 47
Sideling, hill, Md., W. Va A1 85
Sideling Hill, creek, Md A1 85
Sidell, Vermilion, Ill., 614 D6 90
Siderno Marina, It., 6,915 E6 21
Sidheros, cape, Grc E6 23
Sidhirokastron, Grc., 9,022 B4 23
Sidi Abdalkah Ben Ali, Alg D5 44
Sidi Abd el Hakem, Alg D5 44
Sīdī Barrānī, Eg., U.A.R., 1,000 G6 31
Sidi-bel-Abbès, Alg., 105,357 B4 44
Sidi Bennour, Mor., 5,479 C3 44, H2 30
Sidi bou Haous, Alg H8 30
Sidi Hadjed Dine, Alg C5 44
Sidi Ifni, Ifni, 12,751 D2 44
Sidi Kacem, Mor., 19,478 G4 30
Sidikalang, Indon m11 35
Sīdī Sālim, Eg., U.A.R., 1,000 C2 32
Sidlaw, hills, Scot D5 13
Sidley, mtn., Ant B36 5
Sidmouth, Eng., 11,139 D4 12
Sidnaw, Houghton, Mich., 200 B2 98
Sidney, Sharp, Ark., 97 A4 81
Sidney, B.C., Can., 1,558 E6, g12 68
Sidney, Man., Can., 154 E2 71
Sidney, Champaign, Ill., 686 C5 90
Sidney, Kosciusko, Ind., 208 B6 91
Sidney, Fremont, Iowa, 1,057 D2 92
Sidney, Kennebec, Maine, 50 (988▲) D3 96
Sidney, Richland, Mont., 4,564 C12 102
Sidney, Cheyenne, Nebr., 8,004 C3 103
Sidney, Hunterdon, N.J., 75 B3 106
Sidney, Delaware, N.Y., 5,157 C5 108
Sidney, Shelby, Ohio, 14,663 B3 111
Sidney Center, Delaware, N.Y., 500 C5 108
Sidney Lanier, lake, Ga B3 87
Sidon, White, Ark., 90 B4 81
Sidon, see Saida, Leb.
Sidon, Leflore, Miss., 410 B3 100
Sidonia, Weakley, Tenn., 120 A3 117
Sidorovka, Sov. Un., 10,000 D25 9
Sidra (Khalij Surt), gulf, Libya C3 43
Siedlce, Pol., 32,000 B7 26
Sieg, riv., Ger C3 16
Siegburg, Ger., 34,000 C2 17
Siegen, Ger., 49,500 (★125,000) C3 17
Sieglar, Ger., 19,500 C2 17
Siemianowice Slaskie, Pol., 64,600 g10 26
Siemiatycze, Pol., 4,106 B7 26
Siem Reap, Camb., 10,000 F5 38
Siena, It., 48,200 (62,900▲) C3 21
Sieper, Rapides, La., 150 C3 95
Sieradz, Pol., 11,700 C5 26
Siero, Sp., 30,931 A3 20
Sierpc, Pol., 10,200 B5 26
Sierra, co., Calif., 2,247 C3 82
Sierra, co., N. Mex., 6,409 D2 107
Sierra Ancha, mts., Ariz D4 80
Sierra Blanca, Hudspeth, Tex., 800 F1 118
Sierra Blanca, peak, N. Mex. D4 107
Sierra City, Sierra, Calif., 150 C3 82
Sierra Colorada, Arg C3 54
Sierra Del Carmen, mts., Tex E1 118
Sierra Del Pinacate, mtn., Ariz F2 80
Sierra Diablo, mts., Tex F2 118
Sierra Estrella, mts., Ariz G1 80
Sierra Gordo, Chile D2 55
Sierra Leone, country, Afr., 2,250,000 E2 45, F4 42
Sierra Madre, Los Angeles, Calif., 9,732 F2 82
Sierra Madre, mts., Wyo D6 125
Sierra Mojada, Mex., 954 B4 63
Sierra Nacimiento, mts., N. Mex. B3 107
Sierra Nevada, mts., Calif D4 82
Sierra Oscura, mts., N. Mex D3 107
Sierraville, Sierra, Calif., 150 C3 82
Sierra Vista, Cochise, Ariz., 3,121 F5 80
Sierre, Switz., 8,690 D4 19
Siesta, key, Fla E4 86
Siewierz, Pol., 2,385 g10 26
Sifnos, isl., Grc D5 23
Sifton, Man., Can., 245 D1 71
Sigean, Fr., 2,346 F5 14
Sigel, Shelby, Ill., 387 D5 90
Sigel, Jefferson, Pa., 190 D3 114
Sighet, Rom., 22,361 B6 22
Sighişoara, Rom., 20,363 B7 22
Sighty Crag, mtn, Eng E6 13
Sigli, Indon., 3,327 J1 38
Siglufjördur, Ice., 2,756 m23 25
Sigma, Phil., 1,218 *C6 35
Sigmaringen, Ger., 6,578 A5 18
Signakhi, Sov. Un., 4,338 B15 31
Signal, mtn., Vt. C4 120
Signal, mtn., Va B4 121
Signal, peak, Utah F2 119
Signal Hill, Los Angeles, Calif., 4,627 *F2 82
Signal Hill, St. Clair, Ill., 1,200 *E3 90
Signal Mountain, Hamilton, Tenn., 3,413 D8, E10 117
Signau, Switz., 2,555 C4 19
Signy-l' Abbaye, Fr., 1,486 E4 15
Sigourney, Keokuk, Iowa, 2,387 C5 92
Sigsig, Ec., 1,632 B2 58
Sigtuna, Swe., 3,200 t35 25
Siguatepeque, Hond., 2,618 C4 62
Sigüenza, Sp., 4,620 B4 20
Siguiri, Guinea, 11,400 D3 45
Sigurd, Sevier, Utah, 339 E3 119
Siirt, Tur., 22,900 D13 31
Sikar, India, 50,636 D5 40
Sikasso, Mali, 13,600 D3 45
Sikes, Winn, La., 233 B3 95
Sikeston, Scott, Mo., 13,765 E8 101
Sikhote-Alin, mts., Sov. Un D7 37
Sikia, Grc., 2,457 B4 23
Sikinos, isl., Grc D5 23
Sikionia, Grc., 5,113 C4 23
Sikkim, country, Asia, 170,000 C8 39, D12 40
Siklos, Hung., 5,905 C4 22
Sil, riv., Sp A2 20
Silandro, It., 3,958 A3 21
Silang, Phil., 4,920 o13 35
Silao, Mex., 24,138 m13 63
Silas, Choctaw, Ala., 353 D1 78
Sīlat adh Dhahr, Jordan, 3,000 f11 32
Silay, Phil., 19,569 (60,324▲) *C6 35
Silchar, India, 41,062 D9 39
Sile, Tur., 2,700 B7 23
Siler City, Chatham, N.C., 4,455 B4 109
Silerton, Hardeman, Tenn., 84 B3 117
Silesia, Prince Georges, Md., 60 C3 85
Silesia, Carbon, Mont., 100 E8 102
Silesia, reg., Pol C4 26

Siletz, Lincoln, Oreg., 583...C3 113
Silex, Lincoln, Mo., 176...B6 101
Silgarhi, Doti, Nep., 1,461...C8 40
Silhuas, Peru, 1,432...C2 58
Silica, Lucas, Ohio, 100...A1 111
Silifke, Tur., 9,200...D9 31
Silīguri, India, 65,471...D12 40
Silistra, Bul., 16,180...C8 22
Silivri, Tur., 4,129...B7 23
Siljan, Nor...p27 25
Siljan, lake, Swe...G6 25
Silkeborg, Den., 24,465...B3 24
Sillery, Que., Can., 14,109...n17 73
Silloth, Eng., 3,081...F5 13
Sil Nakya, Pima, Ariz., 60...E4 80
Siloam, Greene, Ga., 321...C3 87
Siloam Springs, Benton, Ark., 3,953...A1 81
Siloam Springs, Howell, Mo., 35...E5 101
Silsbee, Hardin, Tex., 6,277...D5 118
Silsby, lake, Man., Can...B4 71
Sils im Domleschg, Switz., 737...D8 19
Silt, Garfield, Colo., 384...B3 83
Silton, Sask., Can., 97...G3 70
Siltou, well, Chad...B3 46
Siluria, Shelby, Ala., 736...B3 78
Silute, Sov. Un., 5,000...A6 26
Silva, Wayne, Mo., 100...D7 101
Silva, Pierce, N. Dak., 56...A6 110
Silva Jardim, Braz., 1,774...h6 57
Silva Porto, Ang., 12,146...D2 48
Silver, Clarendon, S.C., 50...D7 96
Silver, creek, Ill...B9 101
Silver, creek, Ind...H6 91
Silver, creek, Nebr...D2 103
Silver, creek, Oreg...D7 113
Silver, lake, Ont., Can...E4 71
Silver, lake, Iowa...A3 92
Silver, lake, Maine...C3 96
Silver, lake, Nev...B5 104
Silver, lake, N.H...C4 105
Silver, lake, N.H...E2 105
Silver, lake, Oreg...D6 113
Silver, lake, Oreg...D7 113
Silver, lake, Wash...D7 122
Silver, riv., N.S., Can...E4 74
Silver Bank, passage, Ba. Is...E8 64
Silver Bay, Lake, Minn., 3,723...C7 99
Silver Bay, Warren, N.Y., 80...B7 108
Silver Bell, Pima, Ariz., 700...E4 80
Silverbow, Silver Bow, Mont., 40...E4 102
Silver Bow, co., Mont., 46,454...E4 102
Silver Bow Park, Silver Bow, Mont., 4,798...D4 102
Silver City (Rainbow City), C.Z., 3,688...k11 62
Silver City, Owyhee, Idaho...F2 89
Silver City, Mills, Iowa, 281...C2 93
Silver City, Humphreys, Miss., 431...B3 100
Silver City, Lyon, Nev., 120...D2 104
Silver City, Grant, N. Mex., 6,972...E1 107
Silver City, Pennington, S. Dak., 150...C2 116
Silver City, Juab, Utah...D3 119
Silver Cliff, Custer, Colo., 153...C5 83
Silver Creek, Floyd, Ga., 200...B1 87
Silver Creek, Lawrence, Miss., 229...D3 100
Silver Creek, Merrick, Nebr., 431...C8 103
Silver Creek, Chautauqua, N.Y., 3,310...C1 108
Silverdale, Cowley, Kans., 50...E7 93
Silverdale, Onslow, N.C...C6 109
Silverdale, Kitsap, Wash., 950...B3, D1 122
Silver Gate, Park, Mont., 20...E6 102
Silver Grove, Campbell, Ky., 1,207...A7 94
Silverhill, Baldwin, Ala., 417...E2 78
Silver Hill, Prince Georges, Md. (part of Suitland)...C1 85
Silver Island, range, Utah...C2 119
Silver Lake, Kosciusko, Ind., 514...B6 91
Silver Lake, Shawnee, Kans., 392...C8 93
Silver Lake, Middlesex, Mass., 4,700...f11 97
Silver Lake, McLeod, Minn., 646...F4 99
Silver Lake, Carroll, N.H., 150...C4 105
Silver Lake, Summit, Ohio, 2,655...*A6 111
Silver Lake, Lake, Oreg., 97...D5 113
Silverlake, Cowlitz, Wash., 300...C3 122
Silver Lake, Kenosha, Wis., 1,077...F1, F5 124
Silvermines, Ire., 222...E3 11
Silverpeak, Esmeralda, Nev., 45...F4 104
Silver Point, Putnam, Tenn., 150...C8 117
Silver Run, Carroll, Md., 125...A3 85
Silver Spring, Montgomery, Md., 66,348...C1, C3 85
Silver Springs, Marion, Fla., 300...C4 86
Silver Springs, Lyon, Nev., 60...D2 104
Silver Springs, Wyoming, N.Y., 726...C2 108
Silver Star, Madison, Mont., 75...E4 102
Silver Star, mtn., Wash...A4 122
Silverstreet, Newberry, S.C., 181...C4 115
Silverthrone, mtn., B.C., Can...D4 68
Silvertip, mtn., Mont...C3 102
Silverton, B.C., Can., 285...E9 68
Silverton, San Juan, Colo., 822...D3 83
Silverton, Shoshone, Idaho, 700...B3 89
Silverton, Ocean, N.J., 1,500...C4 106
Silverton, Hamilton, Ohio, 6,682...D2 111
Silverton, Marion, Oreg., 3,081...B4, C2 113
Silverton, Briscoe, Tex., 1,098...B2 118
Silves, Port., 4,361...D1 20
Silvia, Col., 2,499...C2 60
Silvies, Grant, Oreg...C8 113
Silvies, riv., Oreg...D7 113
Silvis, Rock Island, Ill., 3,973...B3 90
Silvis Heights, Rock Island, Ill., 1,500...*B3 90
Silwān, Jordan, 5,000...h11, m14 32
Simanggang, Mala., 5,648...E4 35
Simav, Tur., 6,300...C7 23
Simav, riv., Tur...C7 23
Simcoe, Ont., Can., 8,754...E4 72
Simcoe, McHenry, N. Dak., 100...A5 110
Simcoe, co., Ont., Can., 141,271...C4 72
Simcoe, creek, Wash...C5 122
Simcoe, lake, Ont., Can...C5 72
Simcoe, mtn., Wash...C5 122
Simcoe, mts., Wash...C5 122
Simdega, India, 10,438...F10 40
Simeulue, isl., Indon...K1 38
Simferopol, Sov. Un., 203,000...I10 27
Simi, Ventura, Calif., 2,107...*E4 82
Simi, isl., Grc...D6 23
Similkameen, riv., B.C., Can...E7 68
Simití, Col., 1,742...B3 60
Simla, Elbert, Colo., 450...B6 83
Simla, India, 42,597...B6 39
Simleul-Silvaniei, Rom., 8,560...B6 22
Simme, riv., Switz...C3 19
Simmern, Ger., 5,200...D2 17
Simmesport, Avoyelles, La., 2,125...D4 95
Simmie, Sask., Can., 136...H1 70
Simmons, Texas, Mo., 85...D5 101
Simmons, cave, Mo...D5 101
Simms, Cascade, Mont., 200...C5 102
Simnasho, Wasco, Oreg...C5 113
Simonette, riv., Alta., Can...B1 69
Simonhouse, lake, Man., Can...B1 71
Simonstorp, Swe., 238...u34 25
Simonsville, Windsor, Vt., 40...E3 120
Simoom Sound, B.C., Can...D4 68
Simpang Kiri, riv., Indon...K2 38
Simplício Mendes, Braz., 1,682...C2 57
Simplon, pass, Switz...D5 19
Simplon, tunnel, Switz., It...D5 19
Simpson, Sask., Can., 340...F3 70
Simpson, Johnson, Ill., 89...F5 90
Simpson, Mitchell, Kans., 154...C6 93
Simpson, Vernon, La., 400...C2 95
Simpson, Olmsted, Minn., 100...G6 99
Simpson, Hill, Mont., 10...B6 102
Simpson, Pitt., N.C., 302...B6 109
Simpson, Lackawanna, Pa., 1,800...C11 114
Simpson, Taylor, W. Va., 250...B7 123
Simpson, co., Ky., 11,548...D3 94
Simpson, co., Miss., 20,454...D4 100
Simpson, creek, W. Va...B7 123
Simpson, des., Austl...E6 50
Simpson, pen., N.W. Ter., Can...C15 66
Simpsonville, Shelby, Ky., 220...B4 94
Simpsonville, Greenville, S.C., 2,282...B3 115
Simrishamn, Swe., 7,300...J6 25
Sims, Wayne, Ill., 376...E5 90
Sims, Grant, Ind., 225...D6 91
Sims, Wilson, N.C., 205...B5 109
Sims, stream, N.H...A4, B1 105
Simsboro, Lincoln, La., 363...B3 95
Simsbury, Hartford, Conn., 3,200 (10,138▲)...B5 84
Sims Chapel, Washington, Ala., 50...D1 78
Simunjan, Mala., 1,679...E4 35
Sinabang, Indon...K2 38
Sinai, Brookings, S. Dak., 166...C8 116
Sinai, pen., Eg., U.A.R...C4 41
Sinaia, Rom., 9,006...C7 22
Sinajana, Guam, 2,861...52
Sinaloa, Mex., 1,284...B3 63
Sinaloa, state, Mex., 790,679...C3 63
Sinanju, Kor., 16,493...G2 37
Sinarū, Eg., U.A.R., 1,000...E2 32
Sināwan, Libya, 609...C2 43
Sinawi, Afg., 10,000...D15 41
Sincé, Col., 7,112...B2 60
Sincelejo, Col., 21,625...B2 60
Sinclair, Carbon, Wyo., 621...D5 125
Sinclair's, bay, Scot...B5 13
Sinclair, Man., Can., 85...E1 71
Sinclairville, Chautauqua, N.Y., 726...C1 108
Sind, reg., Pak...C4 39
Sind, riv., India...D7 40
Sindal, Den., 1,400...A4 24
Sindara, Gabon...F2 46
Sindelfingen, Ger., 26,100...E3 17
Sindirgi, Tur., 3,209...C7 23
Sinelnikovo, Sov. Un., 10,000...G10 27
Sines, Port., 4,893...D1 20
Singa, Sud., 9,436...C3 47
Singapore, Mala., 925,241 (*1,476,694)...L5 38
Singapore, reg., Mala., 1,840,000...I13 33, L5 38
Singapore, strait, Asia...L5 38
Singaradja, Indon., 12,345...G5 35
Singen, Ger., 33,300...E4 18
Singer, Beauregard, La., 150...D2 95
Singers Glen, Rockingham, Va., 102...C4 121
Singhampton, Ont., Can., 138...C4 72
Singida, Tan., 3,938...B5 48
Singitic, gulf, Grc...B4 23
Singkawang, Indon., 7,127...L8 38
Singkep, isl., Indon...F2 35
Singkil, Indon...E1, m11 35
Singleton, Austl., 4,523...F8 51
Singu, Bur...B1 38
Sinhai, China, 207,600...G8 36
Sinhsien, China...D7 34
Sinhung, Kor., 7,583...F3 37
Sining (Hsining), China, 300,000...D5 34
Siniscola, It., 6,559...D2 21
Sinj, Yugo., 4,133...D3 22
Sinjil, Jordan, 2,000...g12 32
Sinkat, Sud., 5,175...B4 47
Sinkiang Uighur, prov., China, 5,640,000...C2 34
Sinking, creek, Ky...D3 94
Sinking Springs, Highland, Ohio, 202...C4 111
Sinking Spring, Berks, Pa., 2,244...*F9 114
Sinks Grove, Monroe, W. Va., 100...D4 123
Sinnamahoning, Cameron, Pa., 400...D5 114
Sinnamahoning, creek, Pa...D5 114
Sinnamary, Fr. Gu., 1,373...A4 59
Sinnuris, Eg., U.A.R., 23,537...E2 32
Sinoia, Rh., 4,200...A5 49
Sinop, Tur., 9,900...A10 31
Sinsiang, China, 170,500...G5 36
Sintaluta, Sask., Can., 376...G4 70
Sint-Amandsberg Bel., 24,359...C3 15
Sintang, Indon., 4,474...E4 35
Sint Jacobiparochie, Neth., 1,199...A5 15
Sint-Lenaarts, Bel., 4,301...C4 15
Sint-Niklaas, Bel., 47,819...C4 15
Sinton, San Patricio, Tex., 6,008...E4 118
Sintra, Port., 7,150...f9 20
Sint-Truiden, Bel., 20,341...D5 15
Sinú, riv., Col...B2 60
Sinuiju, Kor., 118,414...F2 37
Sinyavino, Sov. Un...s32 25
Sinzig, Ger., 6,100...C2 17
Sion, Switz., 16,051...D3 19
Sioux, co., Iowa, 26,375...A1 92
Sioux, co., Nebr., 2,575...B2 103
Sioux, co., N. Dak., 3,662...C4 110
Sioux Center, Sioux, Iowa, 2,275...A1 92
Sioux City, Woodbury, Iowa, 89,159 (*101,500)...B1 92
Sioux Falls, Minnehaha, S. Dak., 65,466...D9 116
Sioux Lookout, Ont., Can., 2,453...o17 72
Sioux Rapids, Buena Vista, Iowa, 962...B2 92
Sipanok, chan., Sask., Can...D4 70
Sipes (Midway), Seminole, Fla., 1,500...*D5 86
Sipiwesk, Man., Can...E13 66
Sipiwesk, lake, Man., Can...B3 71
Siple, mtn., Ant...B36 5
Sipolilo, Rh...A5 49
Sipsey, Walker, Ala., 900...B2 78
Sipsey, riv., Ala...B2 78
Sipura, isl., Indon...F1 35
Siquirres, C.R., 4,053...E6 62
Siquisique, Ven., 2,354...A4 60
Sir Abu Nuair, isl., Sau. Ar...I7 41
Siracusa, It., 93,368...F5 21
Sirājganj, Pak., 47,152...E12 40
Sir Alexander, mtn., B.C., Can...C7 68
Sirdar, B.C., Can...E9 68
Sir Douglas, mtn., Alta., B.C., Can...D3 69
Sir Edward Pellew Group, is., Austl...C6 50
Siren, Burnett, Wis., 679...C1 124
Siret, Rom., 5,664...B8 22
Siretul, riv., Rom...B8 22
Sir Francis Drake's, chan., Vir. Is...f16 65
Sirḥān, wadi, Libya...G3 31
Sīrīk, Iran, 5,000...H8 41
Sirinhaém, Braz., 1,772...k6 57
Sir James MacBrien, mtn., N.W. Ter., Can...D7 66
Sirmione, It., 712...D6 18
Sirnai, isl., Grc...D6 23
Sironj, India, 17,288...E6 40
Siros, Grc., 16,953...D5 23
Siros, isl., Grc...D5 23
Sirpur, India, 4,466...H7 40
Sirretta, peak, Calif...E4 82
Sirri, isl., Iran...I7 41
Sirsa, India, 33,363...C5 40
Sir Sanford, mtn., B.C., Can...D9 68
Sirte (Surt), Libya, 890...C3 43
Sirvintos, Sov. Un...A8 26
Sir Wilfrid, mtn., Que...C2 73
Sir Wilfrid Laurier, mtn., B.C., Can...C8 68
Sisak, Yugo., 19,238...C3 22
Sisaket, Thai., 9,778...E6 38
Sisib, lake, Man., Can...C2 71
Sisipuk, lake, Man., Sask., Can...B1 71
Siskiyou, co., Calif., 32,885...B2 82
Siskiyou, gap, Oreg...E4 113
Siskiyou, mts., Calif., Oreg...F3 113
Sisophon, Camb...F5 38
Sisquoc, Santa Barbara, Calif., 40...E3 82
Sissach, Switz., 4,574...B4 19
Sisseton, Roberts, S. Dak., 3,218...B8 116
Sissiboo, riv., N.S., Can...E4 74
Sisson Branch, res., N.B., Can...B2 74
Sissonville, Kanawha, W. Va., 900...C3 123
Sister Bay, Door, Wis., 520...C6 124
Sisterdale, Kendall, Tex., 50...E3 118
Sisteron, Fr., 3,286...E6 14
Sisters, Deschutes, Oreg., 602...C5 113
Sisterville, Tyler, W. Va., 2,331...B4 123
Sitapur, India, 53,884...D8 40
Site Six, Mohave, Ariz...C1 80
Sitia, Grc., 4,393...E6 23
Sítio da Abadia, Braz., 482...A3 56
Sitionuevo, Col., 4,694...A3 60
Sitka, Alsk., 3,237...D12, m22 79
Sitka, Sharp, Ark., 50...A4 81
Sitka, Clark, Kans., 115...E4 93
Sitka, nat. mon., Alsk...D12 79
Sitka, sound, Alsk...m22 79
Sitkum, Coos, Oreg., 50...D3 113
Sittang, riv., Bur...E10 39
Sittard, Neth., 30,700...D5 15
Sitter, riv., Switz...A7 19
Siushui, China...G25 9
Situ, W. Sam., 1,284...52
Situmet, vol., Indon...G3 35
Sivas, Tur., 93,368...C11 31
Siverek, Tur., 26,100...D12 31
Sivrihisar, Tur., 7,200...C8 31
Siwah (Siwa) (Oasis), Eg., U.A.R., 878...D5 43
Siwalik, range, India Nep...C7 40
Siwana, India...E4 40
Siwani, cape, Pak...I10 41
Six Mile, Pickens, S.C., 218...B2 115
Sixmile, creek, Fla...C6 86
Sixmile, lake, La...E4 95
Sixmilecross, N. Ire., 245...C4 11
Sixteen Island Lake, Que., Can., 271...D3 73
6th. Cataract (Nile River), Sud...B3 47
Sizerville, Cameron, Pa., 30...C5 114
Sjaelland, isl., Den...C5 24
Sjenica, Yugo., 5,499...D5 22
Sjöbo, Swe., 2,419...C7 24
Skaelskør, Den., 2,889...C5 24
Skaerbaek, Den., 1,989...C2 24
Skagen, Den., 10,390...A4 24
Skagen, cape, Den...A4 24
Skagerrak, chan., Eur...I3 25
Skagit, co., Wash., 51,350...A4 122
Skagit, riv., Wash...A4 122
Skagway, Alsk., 659...D12, k22 79
Skälderviken, bay, Swe...B6 24
Skamania, Skamania, Wash., 325...D3 122
Skamania, co., Wash., 5,207...D4 122
Skamokawa, Wahkiakum, Wash., 200...C2 122
Skanderborg, Den., 5,482...B3 24
Skanderborg, co., Den., 136,495...C3 24
Skaneateles, Onondaga, N.Y., 2,921...C4 108
Skaneateles, lake, N.Y...C4 108
Skanee, Baraga, Mich., 55...B2 98
Skanör, Swe., 900...C6 24
Skantzoura, isl., Grc...C5 23
Skara, Swe., 9,100...H5 25
Skaraborg, co., Swe., 249,900...*H6 25
Skarkar, Afg., 5,000...C15 41
Skarven, lake, Swe...t35 25
Skawa, riv., Pol...h11 26
Skawina, Pol., 3,638...D5 26
Skedee, Pawnee, Okla., 128...A5 112
Skeena, mts., B.C., Can...A3 68
Skeena, riv., B.C., Can...B3 68
Skegness, Eng., 12,843...A8 12
Skeldon, Br. Gu., 2,654...A3 59
Skeleton, lake, Ont., Can...B5 72
Skellefteå, Swe., 22,700...E9 25
Skellefteälven, riv., Swe...E8 25
Skellytown, Carson, Tex., 967...B2 118
Skelton, Raleigh, W. Va., 500...D7 123
Skelton, glacier, Ant...f40 5
Skene, Bolivar, Miss., 200...B3 100
Skerries, Ire., 2,721...D5 11
Skhimatarion, Grc., 1,369...g11 23
Skiathos, isl., Grc...C4 23
Skiatook, Tulsa and Osage, Okla., 2,503...A5 112
Skibbereen, Ire., 2,028...F2 11
Skibby, Den., 1,040...C5 24
Skiddaw, mtn., Eng...F5 13
Skidegate, B.C., Can., 40...C2 68
Skidegate, inlet, B.C., Can...C2 68
Skidmore, Nodaway, Mo., 425...A2 101
Skidmore, Bee, Tex., 550...E4 118
Skien, Nor., 15,500 (*56,000)...H3, p27 25
Skierniewice, Pol., 22,000...C6 26
Skiff, Alta., Can...E5 69
Skihist, mtn., B.C., Can...D7 68
Skiles, Bertie, N.C...B7 109
Skillet, fork, Ill...E5 90
Skillman, Somerset, N.J., 50...C3 106
Skime, Roseau, Minn., 5...B3 99
Skipperville, Dale, Ala., 60...D4 78
Skipton, Eng., 12,988...G7 13
Skiros, Grc., 3,395...C5 23
Skiros, isl., Grc...C5 23
Skive, riv., Den...B3 24
Skjern, Den., 5,349...C2 24
Skjern Å, riv., Den...C2 24
Skoczow, Pol., 4,480...h9 26
Skofja Loka, Yugo., 3,367...B2 22
Skokie, Cook, Ill., 65,281...E3 90
Skokomish, Indian res., Wash...B2 122
Skokomish, mtn., Wash...B2 122
Skole, Sov. Un., 5,000...D7 26
Skönnarbo, Swe...u33 25
Skopelos, isl., Grc...C4 23
Skopin, Sov. Un., 10,000...E13 27
Skopje (Skoplje), Yugo., 165,529...D5 22
Skørping, Den., 1,461...B3 24
Skotovataya, Sov. Un., 6,400...q20 27
Skotselv, Nor., 183...p27 25
Skövde, Swe., 23,900...H5 25
Skovorodino, Sov. Un., 26,000...D15 28
Skowhegan, Somerset, Maine, 6,667...D3 96
Skownan, Man., Can., 40...D2 71
Skradin, Yugo., 928...D2 22
Skreen, Ire...C3 11
Skull Valley, Yavapai, Ariz., 100...C3 80
Skull Valley, Indian res., Utah...C3 119
Skuna, riv., Miss...B4 100
Skunk, riv., Iowa...C4 92
Skurup, Swe., 4,700...C7 24
Skvira, Sov. Un., 10,000...G7 27
Skwentna, riv., Alsk...g16 79
Skwierzyna, Pol., 2,822...B3 26
Skye, isl., Scot...C3 13
Skykomish, King, Wash., 366...B4 122
Skykomish, riv., Wash...B4 122
Skyland, De Kalb, Ga., 2,000...*C2 87
Skyland, Buncombe, N.C., 1,500...D3 109
Skylight, Oldham, Ky., 100...A4 94
Skylight, mtn., Ark...B1 81
Skyline, Jackson, Ala., 100...A3 78
Sky Manor, Ocean, N.J., 900...C4 106
Skyring, lake, Chile...E2 54
Slade, Powell, Ky., 200...C6 94
Sladesville, Hyde, N.C., 50...B7 109
Slagelse, Den., 20,562...C5 24
Slagle, Vernon, La., 100...C2 95
Slamet, vol., Indon...G3 35
Slane, Ire., 421...D5 11
Slaney, riv., Ire...E5 11
Slangerup, Den., 1,638...C6 24
Slănic-Prahova, Rom., 6,842...C7 22
Slany, Czech., 12,000...n17 26
Slapy, Czech., 704...o17 26
Slate, Wood, W. Va., 125...B3 123
Slater, Moffat, Colo., 3...A3 83
Slater, Story, Iowa, 717...A7, C4 92
Slater, Saline, Mo., 2,767...B4 101
Slater, Greenville, S.C., 900...A3 105
Slater, Platte, Wyo., 15...D8 121
Slatersville, Providence, R.I., 1,200...B10 84
Slate Run, Lycoming, Pa., 75...D6 114
Slate Spring, Calhoun, Miss., 123...B4 100
Slatina, Rom., 13,381...C7 22
Slatington, Lehigh, Pa., 4,316...E10 114
Slaton, Lubbock, Tex., 6,568...C2 118
Slätthög, Swe...A8 24
Slaughter, East Feliciana, La., 403...D4 95
Slaughter Beach, Sussex, Del., 107...C7 85
Slaughters, Webster, Ky., 284...C2 94
Slave, riv., Alta., N.W. Ter., Can...f8 69
Slave Lake, Alta., Can., 468...B3 69
Slavgorod, Sov. Un., 38,413...C9 29
Slavonia, reg., Yugo...C3 22
Slavonska Požega, Yugo., 13,112...C3 22
Slavsk, Sov. Un...A6 26
Slavyanoserbsk, Sov. Un., 5,000...q21 27
Slavyansk, Sov. Un., 86,000...G11, q20 27
Slavyanskaya, Sov. Un., 83,000...I12 27
Slawkow, Pol...g10 26
Slawno, Pol., 4,845...A4 26
Slayden, Marshall, Miss., 100...A4 100
Slayton, Murray, Minn., 2,487...G3 99
Slea, head, Ire...E1 11
Sleaford, Eng., 7,834...A7 12
Sleat, pt., Scot...C2 13
Sleat, sound, Scot...C3 13
Sled, lake, Sask., Can...C2 70
Sledge, Quitman, Miss., 440...F3 100
Sleeper, Laclede, Mo., 111...D5 101
Sleeping Bear, pt., Mich...D4 98
Sleeping Deer, mtn., Idaho...E4 89
Sleepy Creek, Morgan, W. Va., 200...B6 123
Sleepy Eye, Brown, Minn., 3,492...F4 99
Sleepy Hollow, Marin, Calif., 1,200...*B5 82
Sleepy Hollow, Fairfax, Va., 1,200...*C5 121
Sleepy, pt., Fiji Is...52
Sleetmute, Alsk., 122...C8 79
Sliabh Gaoil, mtn., Scot...E3 13
Slick, Creek, Okla., 151...B5 112
Slick Rock, San Miguel, Colo...C2 83
Slickville, Westmoreland, Pa., 950...F2 114
Slide, mtn., N.Y...C6 108
Slidell, St. Tammany, La., 6,356...B8, D6 95
Sliderock, mtn., Mont...D3 102
Slieve Aughty, mts., Ire...D3 11
Slieve Beagh, mtn., N. Ire...C4 11
Slieve Bloom, mts., Ire...D4 11
Slieve Callan, mtn., Ire...E2 11
Slieve Car, mtn., Ire...C2 11
Slieve Croob, mtn., N. Ire...C5 11
Slieve Donard, mtn., N. Ire...C6 11
Slieve Gamph, mts., Ire...C3 11
Slieve Mish, mts., Ire...E2 11
Slieve Miskish, mts., Ire...F2 11
Slievenaman, mtn., Ire...E4 11
Sligo, Weld, Colo...A6 83
Sligo, Ire., 13,145...C3 11
Sligo, Clarion, Pa., 814...D3 114
Sligo, co., Ire., 53,561...C3 11
Slinger, Washington, Wis., 1,141...E1, E5 124
Slingerlands, Albany, N.Y., 1,500...*C7 108
Slippery Rock, Butler, Pa., 2,563...D1 114
Sliven, Bul., 46,175...D8 22
Slivenec, Czech., 1,726...n17 26
Sloan, Woodbury, Iowa, 704...B1 92
Sloan, Clark, Nev., 40...H6 104
Sloan, Erie, N.Y., 5,824...C2 108
Sloans Valley, Pulaski, Ky., 250...D5 94
Sloat, Plumas, Calif., 200...C3 82
Sloatsburg, Rockland, N.Y., 2,812...A4 106
Slobodskoy, Sov. Un., 28,700...B4 29
Slobozia, Rom., 9,632...C8 22
Slocan, B.C., Can., 293...E9 68
Slocan, lake, B.C., Can...E9 68
Slocomb, Geneva, Ala., 1,368...D4 78
Slocum, Washington, R.I., 150...C10 84
Slonim, Sov. Un., 10,000...E5 27
Slope, co., N. Dak., 1,893...C2 110
Slough, Eng., 84,200...C7 12
Slovac, Prairie, Ark., 30...C4 81
Slovakia (Slovensko), reg., Czech., 4,175,000...D5 26
Slovaktown, Prairie, Ark...C4 81
Slovan, Washington, Pa., 1,018...F1 114
Slovenia, reg., Yugo...C2 22
Slovenia, rep., Yugo., 1,584,368...*C2 22
Slubice, Pol., 1,689...A9 17
Sluch, riv., Sov. Un...F6 27
Slunj, Yugo., 1,260...C2 22
Slupa, riv., Pol...A4 26
Slupca, Pol., 5,133...B4 26
Slupsk, Pol., 55,800...A4 26
Slutsk, Sov. Un., 5,000...s31 25
Slutsk, Sov. Un., 20,000...E6 27
Slyne, head, Ire...D1 11
Slyudyanka, Sov. Un., 17,500...D13 28
Smackover, Union, Ark., 2,434...D3 81
Smackover, creek, Ark...D2 81
Smaalandsfarvandet, bay, Den...C5 24
Smali Anadolu, mts., Tur...B11 31
Small, pt., Maine...E6 96
Small Point Beach, Sagadahoc, Maine, 25...E6 96
Smara, Sp. Sahara, 395...D2 44
Smarr, Monroe, Ga., 70...D3 87
Smarts, mtn., N.H...C2 105
Smartt, Warren, Tenn., 125...D8 117
Smeaton, Sask., Can., 322...D3 70
Smecno, Czech., 2,446...n17 26
Smederevo, Yugo., 27,104...C5 22
Smela, Sov. Un., 44,534...G8 27
Smeltertown, El Paso, Tex. (part of El Paso)...E1 118
Smelterville, Shoshone, Idaho, 1,127...B2 89
Smethport, McKean, Pa., 1,725...C5 114
Smethwick, Eng., 68,500...B6 12
Smicksburg, Indiana, Pa., 80...E3 114
Smidovich, Sov. Un., 5,000...B6 37
Smiley, Sask., Can., 232...F1 70
Smiley, Gonzales, Tex., 455...B4, E4 118
Smith, Alta., Can., 86...B3, f8 69
Smith, Lyon, Nev., 35...E2 104
Smith, co., Kans., 7,776...C5 93
Smith, co., Miss., 14,303...C4 100
Smith, co., Tenn., 12,059...C8 117
Smith, co., Tex., 86,350...C5 118
Smith, bay, Alsk...A9 79
Smith, cape, Ont., Can...B3 72
Smith, isl., Ant...C6 5
Smith, isl., Md., Va...D5 85, D6 121
Smith, isl., Va...D7 121
Smith, peak, Idaho...A2 89
Smith, pen., Ant...B6 5
Smith, pt., N.S., Can...D6 74
Smith, pt., Mass...D7 97
Smith, pt., Va...D6 121
Smith, res., Ala...A2 78
Smith, riv., Mont...D5 102
Smith, riv., Va...E3 121
Smith, sound, B.C., Can...D4 68
Smithboro, Bond, Ill., 213...E4 90
Smithburg, Doddridge, W. Va., 200...B4, B6 123
Smith Center, Smith, Kans., 2,379...C5 93
Smith Creek, Wakulla, Fla., 40...B2 86
Smithdale, Amite, Miss., 75...D3 100
Smithers, B.C., Can., 2,487...B4 68
Smithers, Fayette, W. Va., 1,696...C3, C6 123
Smithfield (Town of), Providence, R.I. (9,442▲)...*B10 84
Smithfield, Fulton, Ill., 329...C3 90
Smithfield, Somerset, Maine, 200 (382▲)...D3 96
Smithfield, Jasper, Mo...D3 101
Smithfield, Gosper, Nebr., 85...D6 103
Smithfield, Johnston, N.C., 6,117...B5 109
Smithfield, Jefferson, Ohio, 1,312...B7 111
Smithfield, Fayette, Pa., 939...G2 114
Smithfield, Tarrant, Tex...B5 118
Smithfield, Cache, Utah, 2,512...B4 119
Smithfield, Isle of Wight, Va., 917...B6, E6 121
Smithfield, Wetzel, W. Va., 361...A6 123
Smithland, Woodbury, Iowa, 349...B2 92
Smithland, Livingston, Ky., 541...A3 94
Smithland, Marion, Tex., 100...C5 118
Smithmill, Clearfield, Pa., 600...E5 114
Smith Mills, Henderson, Ky., 300...C2 94
Smithonia, Oglethorpe, Ga., 30...B3 87
Smith River, Del Norte, Calif., 600...B1 82
Smiths, Lee, Ala., 950...C4 78
Smithsburg, Washington, Md., 586...A2 85
Smith's Cove, N.S., Can., 408...E4 74
Smiths Falls, Ont., Can., 9,603...C8 72
Smiths Ferry, Valley, Idaho, 15...E2 89
Smiths Grove, Warren, Ky., 613...C3 94
Smithshire, Warren, Ill., 140...C3 90
Smiths Lake, McKinley, N. Mex., 30...B1 107
Smithsons Valley, Comal, Tex...A4 118
Smithton, Clark, Ark., 75...D2 81
Smithton, Austl., 2,671...o15 50
Smithton, St. Clair, Ill., 629...E4 90
Smithton, Pettis, Mo., 395...C4 101
Smith Town, McCreary, Ky., 300...D5 94
Smithtown, Rockingham, N.H., 150...E5 105
Smithtown, Suffolk, N.Y., 9,600...F4 84
Smithtown, bay, N.Y...F4 84
Smithville, Lawrence, Ark., 75...A4 81
Smithville, Ont., Can., 947...D5 72
Smithville, Lee, Ga., 865...E2 87
Smithville, Monroe, Ind., 400...F4 91
Smithville, Monroe, Miss., 489...A5 100
Smithville, Clay, Mo., 1,254...B3, D2 101
Smithville, Atlantic, N.J., 100...E4 106
Smithville, Burlington, N.J., 100...D3 106
Smithville, Wayne, Ohio, 1,024...B6 111

Smithville, McCurtain, Okla., 110....C7 112
Smithville, DeKalb, Tenn., 2,348....D8 117
Smithville, Bastrop, Tex., 2,933....D4 118
Smithville, Ritchie, W. Va., 350....B3 123
Smithville Flats, Chenango, N.Y., 200....C5 108
Smithwick, Fall River, S. Dak., 60....D2 116
Smittle, cave, Mo....D5 101
Smoaks, Colleton, S.C., 145..E6 115
Smock, Fayette, Pa., 1,012..*G2 114
Smoke Bend, Ascension, La., 450....B5 95
Smoke Creek, Washoe, Nev., 16,618....C2 104
Smoke Creek, des., Nev....C2 104
Smokerun, Clearfield, Pa., 250....E5 114
Smoky, cape, Austl....E9 51
Smoky, cape, N.S., Can....C9 74
Smoky, mts., Idaho....F4 89
Smoky, riv., Alta., Can....B1 69
Smoky Hill, riv., Kans....D5 93
Smoky Junction, Scott, Tenn., 200....C9 117
Smoky Lake, Alta., Can., 626....B4 69
Smöla, isl., Nor....F2 25
Smolan, Saline, Kans., 210..D6 93
Smolensk, Sov. Un., 170,000....D8 27
Smolyan, Bul., 3,395....E7 22
Smoot, Lincoln, Wyo., 100..C2 121
Smooth Rock Falls, Ont., Can., 1,131....o19 72
Smoothstone, lake, Sask., Can....C2 70
Smoothstone, riv., Sask., Can....B2 70
Smoots, creek, Kans....B4 93
Smyadovo, Bul., 5,939....D8 22
Smyley, cape, Ant....B4 5
Smyre, Gaston, N.C., 1,197....*B2 109
Smyrna, Kent, Del., 3,241..B6 85
Smyrna, Cobb, Ga., 10,157....A5, C2 87
Smyrna, Chenango, N.Y., 286....C5 108
Smyrna, York, S.C., 52....A5 115
Smyrna, Rutherford, Tenn., 3,612....B5 117
Smyrna, see Izmir, Tur.
Smyrna, riv., Del....B6 85
Smyrna Mills, Aroostook, Maine, 200 (331▲)....B4 96
Smyth, co., Va., 31,066....B3 121
Smythe, mtn., B.C., Can....E8 66
Snaefell, mtn., I of Man....F4 13
Snag, Yukon, Can....C29 4
Snake, creek, Nebr....B2 103
Snake, falls, Nebr....B5 103
Snake, lake, Sask., Can....B2 70
Snake, mtn., N.C....A2 109
Snake, mtn., Vt....C2 120
Snake, range, Nev....E7 104
Snake, riv., Minn....B1 99
Snake, riv., Minn....D5 99
Snake, riv., Oreg....B10 113
Snake, riv., U.S....B4 76
Snake, riv., Wash....C7 122
Snake Indian, riv., Alta., Can..C1 69
Snake River, canyon, Idaho, Oreg....D2 89, C10 113
Snake River, plain, Idaho....F2 89
Snake River, range, Idaho, Wyo....F7 89
Snares, is., N.Z....R11 51
Sneads, Jackson, Fla., 1,399....B1 86
Sneads Ferry, Onslow, N.C., 500....C6 109
Snedsted, Den., 1,030....B2 24
Sneedville, Hancock, Tenn., 799....C10 117
Sneek, Neth., 21,100....A5 15
Sneem, Ire., 282....F2 11
Snelling, Barnwell, S.C., 100....E5 115
Snellville, Gwinnett, Ga., 468....A6 87
Snezhnoye, Sov. Un., 55,000....q21 27
Snezhnvy, peak, Sov. Un....D14 28
Sniardwy, lake, Pol....B7 26
Snipe, keys, Fla....H5 86
Snipe, lake, Alta., Can....B2 69
Snizort, bay, Scot....C2 13
Snöhetta, mtn., Nor....F3 25
Snohomish, Snohomish, Wash., 3,894....B3 122
Snohomish, co., Wash., 172,199....A4 122
Snomac, Seminole, Okla., 100....B5 112
Snoqualmie, King, Wash., 1,216....B4 122
Snov, riv., Sov. Un....F8 27
Snover, Sanilac, Mich., 250....E8 98
Snow, Pushmataha, Okla., 20....C6 112
Snow, mtn., Maine....C2 96
Snow, peak, Wash....A7 122
Snowball, Searcy, Ark., 125....B3 81
Snowbank, lake, Minn....B7 99
Snow Camp, Alamance, N.C., 130....B4 109
Snowden, Sask., Can., 79....D3 70
Snowdon, mtn., Wales....A3 12
Snowdon, mts., Wales....A4 12
Snowdoun, Montgomery, Ala., 250....C3 78
Snowfield, peak, Wash....A4 122
Snowflake, Navajo, Ariz., 982....C5 80
Snowflake, Man., Can., 73..E2 71
Snow Hill, Wilcox, Ala., 120....D2 78
Snow Hill, Ouachita, Ark., 50....D3 81
Snow Hill, Worcester, Md., 2,311....D7 85
Snow Hill, Greene, N.C., 1,043....B6 109
Snowking, mtn., Wash....A4 122
Snow Lake, Desha, Ark., 119....C4 81
Snow Lake, Man., Can., 881....B1 71
Snowmass, Petkin, Colo., 8..B4 83
Snowmass, mtn., Colo....B3 83
Snow Road Station, Ont., Can., 60....C8 72
Snow Shoe, Centre, Pa., 714....D6 114
Snowshoe, lake, Maine....B4 96
Snowshoe, peak, Mont....B1 102
Snowville, Box Elder, Utah, 159....B3 119
Snowville, Pulaski, Va., 100....D2 121
Snow Water, lake, Nev....C7 104
Snowy, mtn., N.Y....B6 108
Snowyside, mtn., Idaho....F4 89
Snyatyn, Sov. Un., 10,000..A7 22
Snyder, Ashley, Ark., 75....D4 81
Snyder, Morgan, Colo., 200....A7 83
Snyder, Dodge, Nebr., 325..C9 103
Snyder, Kiowa, Okla., 1,663....C3 112
Snyder, Scurry, Tex., 13,850....C2 118
Snyder, co., Pa., 25,922....E7 114
Snyder Knob, mtn., W. Va....C4 123
Soai Rieng, Camb., 5,000....G6 38
Soalala, Malag., 759....g9 49
Soap Lake, Grant, Wash., 1,591....B6 122
Soar, riv., Eng....B6 12
Soatá, Col., 3,116....B3 60
Soay, isl., Scot....C2 13
Sobat, riv., Sud....D3 47
Sobeslav, Czech., 4,299....D9 17
Sobieski, Oconto, Wis., 80..D5 124
Sobinka, Sov. Un., 10,000....D13 27
Sobota Rimavska, Czech., 10,700....D6 26
Sobral, Braz., 32,281....B2 57
Sobti (Well), Mali....B4 45
Søby, Den., 728....D4 24
Sochaczew, Pol., 13,300....B6 26
Sochaux, Fr., 7,557....A2 19
Soche, see Yarkand, China
Sochi, Sov. Un., 174,000..G16 9
Social Circle, Walton, Ga., 1,780....C3 87
Social Hill, Hot Spring, Ark., 100....D6 81
Society, is., Fr. Polynesia....H12 7
Society Hill, Darlington, S.C., 677....B8 115
Socmbawa, isl., Indon....G5 35
Socorro, Braz., 6,402....m8 56
Socorro, Col., 11,842....B3 60
Socorro, Socorro, N. Mex., 5,271....C3 107
Socorro, El Paso, Tex., 400....*F1 118
Socorro, co., N. Mex., 10,168....D2 107
Socotra, isl., S. Arabia....H8 33
Socrum, Polk, Fla., 175....D4 86
Soc Trang, Viet., 16,890....H6 38
Socuéllamos, Sp., 14,828....C4 20
Soda Creek, B.C., Can., 113....C6 68
Sodankylä, Fin., 2,500....D12 25
Soda Springs, Caribou, Idaho, 2,424....G7 89
Sodaville, Linn, Oreg., 145..C4 113
Soddy, Hamilton, Tenn., 2,206....D8, E10 117
Söderala, Swe., 499....G7 25
Söderhamn, Swe., 13,000....G7 25
Söderköping, Swe., 3,648....H7 25
Södermanland, co., Swe., 230,400....H7 25
Södertälje, Swe., 35,300....t35 25
Sodiri, Sud., 1,804....C2 47
Sodo, Eth....D4 47
Sodus, Berrien, Mich., 50....F4 98
Sodus, Wayne, N.Y., 1,645....B3 108
Sodus Point, Wayne, N.Y., 909....B4 108
Soela, isl., Indon....F6 35
Soenda (Sunda), strait, Indon....G3 35
Soest, Ger., 33,300....B3 17
Sofadhes, Grc., 4,046....C4 23
Sofia (Sofiya), Bul., 695,400 (*769,700)....D6 22
Sofia, riv., Malag....g9 49
Sofiya, see Sofia, Bul.
Sofiya, co., Bul., 1,457,742....*D6 22
Sofiyevka, Sov. Un., 10,000....G9 27
Sofre, Pan., 193....F7 62
Sofu-Gan, isl., Pac. O....E8 7
Sogamoso, Col., 13,574....B3 60
Sögel, Ger., 2,900....B7 15
Sognefjord, fjord, Nor....G1 25
Sogn og Fjordane, co., Nor., 99,900....*G1 25
Sogod, Phil., 3,344....*C7 35
Sogut, Tur., 2,900....C8 23
Sohagpur, India, 9,382....F8 40
Soham, San Miguel, N. Mex., 200....B4 107
Soignies, Bel., 10,874....D4 15
Sointula, B.C., Can., 682....D4 68
Soissons, Fr., 23,150....C5 14
Sokal, Sov. Un., 10,000....F5 27
Sokcho, Kor., 50,700....*G4 37
Soke, Tur., 23,400....D6 23
Soke of Peterborough, co., Eng., 74,442....*D6 10
Sokhondo, mtn., Sov. Un....E14 28
Sokhta Chinar, Afg., 5,000....D13 41
Sokodé, Togo....E5 45
Sokol, Sov. Un., 36,000....B13 27
Sokolka, Pol., 4,879....B7 26
Sokolo, Mali....D3 45
Sokolov, Czech., 17,600....C7 17
Sokolow, Pol., 7,515....B7 26
Sokoto, Nig., 47,643....D6 45
Solana, Charlotte, Fla., 1,309....*F4 86
Solana Beach, San Diego, Calif., 3,000....*F5 76
Solander, isl., N.Z....Q11 51
Solano, Harding, N. Mex., 30....B5 107
Solano, Phil., 9,497....n13 35
Solano, co., Calif., 134,597....C2 82
Solbad Hall [in Tirol], Aus., 10,750....E5 16
Soldatovo, Sov. Un....F26 9
Soldier, Monona, Iowa, 284....C2 92
Soldier, Jackson, Kans., 171....C8 93
Soldier, Carter, Ky., 150....B6 94
Soldier, key, Fla....F3 86
Soldier, riv., Iowa....C2 92
Soldier Pond, Aroostook, Maine, 500....A4 96
Soldiers Grove, Crawford, Wis., 663....E3 124
Soldier Summit, Wasatch, Utah, 33....D4 119
Soledad, Monterey, Calif., 2,837....D3 82
Soledad, Col., 20,158....A3 60
Soledad, Ven., 5,259....B5 60
Soleduck, riv., Wash....B1 122
Solen, Sioux, N. Dak., 250....C5 110
Solent, chan., Eng....D6 12
Solesmes, Fr., 5,722....D3 15
Solihull, Eng., 100,700....B6 12
Solikamsk, Sov. Un., 82,000....B5 29
Sol-Iletsk, Sov. Un., 19,100....C5 29
Soliman, Tun., 6,980....F12 30
Solimões (Amazon), riv., Braz., Peru....B4 58
Solingen, Ger., 172,300....B2 17
Solitar, mtn., Tex....B3 118
Sollas, Scot....C1 13
Sollefteå, Swe., 9,900....F7 25
Sóller, Sp., 6,817....C7 20
Soller Central, P.R....B3 65
Sölleröd, Den., 25,877....*C6 24
Sollihögda, Nor....p28 25
Sollum, gulf, Eg., U.A.R....G5 31
Sollyu-Bong, mts., Kor....G2 37
Solna, Swe., 53,700....H7 25
Solok, Indon., 6,214....F2 35
Solomea, Samoa....52
Solomon, Graham, Ariz., 500....E6 80
Solomon, Dickinson, Kans., 1,008....D6 93
Solomon Is. (Austl.), reg., N. Gui., 62,000....*G9 7
Solomon Is., British, dep., Oceania, 133,000....*G9 7
Solomon, riv., Kans....C6 93
Solomons, Calvert, Md., 183....D5 85
Solon, Johnson, Iowa, 604..C6 92
Solon, Somerset, Maine, 500 (669▲)....D3 96
Solon, Cuyahoga, Ohio, 6,333....A6 111
Solonika, see Thessaloniki, Grc.
Solon Mills, McHenry, Ill., 130....D2 90
Solon Springs, Douglas, Wis., 530....B2 124
Solothurn, Switz., 17,800....B4 19
Solothurn, Switz., 18,394 (*30,405)....B4 19
Solothurn, canton, Switz., 200,816....B4 19
Solovyevsk, Sov. Un., 10,000....D15 28
Solsberry, Greene, Ind., 150....F4 91
Solsgirth, Man., Can., 78....D1 71
Solta, isl., Yugo....D3 22
Soltau, Ger., 14,400....B4 16
Solvang, Santa Barbara, Calif., 1,325....*E3 82
Solvay, Onondaga, N.Y., 8,732....B4 108
Sölvesborg, Swe., 6,000....B8 24
Solway, Beltrami, Minn., 100....C3 99
Solway, firth, Eng., Scot....F5 13
Solwezi, Zambia....D4 48
Soma, Tur., 13,100....C6 23
Somaliland, French, see French Somaliland, dep., Afr.
Somali Republic, country, Afr., 2,350,000....E10 42, E5 47
Sombor, Yugo., 37,802....C4 22
Sombra, Ont., Can., 520....E2 72
Sombrerete, Mex., 9,260....C4 63
Sombrero, chan., India....G9 39
Somerdale, Camden, N.J., 4,839....D2 106
Somers, Tolland, Conn., 850 (3,702▲)....B7 84
Somers, Calhoun, Iowa, 203....B3 92
Somers, Flathead, Mont., 800....B2 102
Somers, Kenosha, Wis., 200....F2, F6 124
Somerset, Man., Can., 587....E2 71
Somerset, Gunnison, Colo., 250....C3 83
Somerset, Wabash, Ind., 250....C6 91
Somerset, Miami, Kans., 100....D9 93
Somerset, Pulaski, Ky., 7,112....C5 94
Somerset, Montgomery, Md., 1,444....*C3 85
Somerset, Bristol, Mass., 12,196....C5 97
Somerset, Somerset, N.J., 11,500....B3 106
Somerset, Perry, Ohio, 1,361....C5 111
Somerset, Somerset, Pa., 6,347....F3 114
Somerset, Bexar, Tex., 700..B3 118
Somerset, St. Croix, Wis., 729....C1 124
Somerset, co., Eng., 598,556....C5 12
Somerset, co., Maine, 39,749....C2 96
Somerset, co., Md., 19,623..D6 85
Somerset, co., N.J., 143,913....C3 106
Somerset, co., Pa., 77,450....G3 114
Somerset, isl., Bermuda....E13 77
Somerset, isl., N.W. Ter., Can....B14 66
Somerset, res., Vt....E3 120
Somerset Bridge, Bermuda..E13 77
Somerset East, S. Afr., 9,779....D4 49
Somers Point, Atlantic, N.J., 4,504....E3 106
Somersville, Tolland, Conn., 700....B7 84
Somersworth, Strafford, N.H., 8,529....D5 105
Somerton, Yuma, Ariz., 1,613....E1 80
Somervell, co., Tex., 2,577..C4 118
Somerville, Morgan, Ala., 166....A3 78
Somerville, Gibson, Ind., 317....H3 91
Somerville, Middlesex, Mass., 94,697....B5, g11 97
Somerville, Somerset, N.J., 12,458....B3 106
Somerville, Butler, Ohio, 478....C3 111
Somerville, Fayette, Tenn., 1,820....B2 117
Somerville, Burleson, Tex., 1,177....D4 118
Somesul, riv., Rom....B6 22
Somme, dept., Fr., 488,225..E2 15
Somme, riv., Fr....B4 14
Sommepy, Fr., 588....E4 15
Sömmerda, Ger., 13,800....B6 17
Sommesous, Fr., 540....F4 15
Somogy, co., Hung., 371,783....*B3 22
Somonauk, DeKalb, Ill., 899....B5 90
Somosomo, strait, Fiji Is....52
Somoto, Nic., 2,322....D4 62
Sompeta, India, 10,588....H10 40
Somuncura, plat., Arg....C3 54
Somvix, Switz., 2,004....C6 19
Son, riv., India....E9 40
Soná, Pan., 3,176....F7 62
Sonchon, Kor., 22,725....G2 40
Soncino, It., 9,809....D5 15
Sønder, riv., Den....D3 24
Sønderborg, Den., 20,653..D3 24
Sønderborg, co., Den., 49,604....D3 24
Sønderho, Den., 410....C2 24
Sonderhausen, Ger., 19,000..B5 17
Sønder Omme, Den., 1,308..C2 24
Søndervig, Den....B2 24
Sondheimer, East Carroll, La., 350....B4 95
Sondrio, It., 20,200....A2 21
Sonestown, Sullivan, Pa., 250....D8 114
Song, Nig....E7 45
Songarh, India, 2,858....G4 40
Song Cau, Viet., 5,000....F8 38
Songchon, Kor., 9,148....G3 37
Songea, Tan., 1,401....D6 48
Songjin, see Kimchaek, Kor.
Songkhla, Thai., 31,014....I4 38
Songololo, Con. L....C1 48
Sonhat, India....F9 40
Son La, Viet., 10,000....B5 38
Sonmiani, Pak....C4 39
Sonmiani, bay, Pak....I12 41
Sonneberg, Ger., 28,900....C6 17
Sonnette, Powder River, Mont., 5....E11 102
Sonningdale, Sask., Can., 129....E2 70
Sono, riv., Braz....C1 57
Sonobe, Jap., 7,300....n14 37
Sonoita, Santa Cruz, Ariz., 5....F5 80
Sonoita, Mex., 1,275....A2 63
Sonoma, Sonoma, Calif., 3,023....B5, C2 82
Sonoma, co., Calif., 147,375..C2 82
Sonoma, peak, Nev....C4 104
Sonoma, range, Nev....C4 104
Sonora, Pinal, Ariz., 1,244....D4 80
Sonora, Tuolumne, Calif., 2,725....D3 82
Sonora, Hardin, Ky., 268....C4 94
Sonora, Muskingum, Ohio, 200....C6 111
Sonora, Sutton, Tex., 2,619..D2 118
Sonora, state, Mex., 771,663..B2 63
Sonora, riv., Mex....G5 80
Sonoraville, Gordon, Ga., 78....B2 87
Sonpur, India, 7,108....G9 40
Sonqor, Iran, 12,126....D3 41
Sonsón, Col., 10,913....B2 60
Sonsonate, Sal., 23,137....D3 62
Sontag, Lawrence, Miss., 200....D3 100
Son Tay, Viet., 16,640....B6 38
Sonyea, Livingston, N.Y., 500....C3 108
Soo, locks, Mich....B6 98
Soochow (Suchou), China, 633,000....E9 34
Soo Junction, Luce, Mich..B5 98
Sooke, B.C., Can., 1,121....E6, h12 68
Sopchoppy, Wakulla, Fla., 450....B2 86
Soper, Choctaw, Okla., 309..C6 112
Soperton, Treutlen, Ga., 2,317....D4 87
Soperton, Forest, Wis. (part of Wabeno)....C5 124
Sophia, Randolph, N.C., 250....B4 109
Sophia, Raleigh, W. Va., 1,284....D3 123
Sopot, Pol., 44,000....A5 26
Sopris, Las Animas, Colo., 950....D6 83
Sopron, Hung., 43,400....B3 22
Soquel, Santa Cruz, Calif., 950....C6 82
Sôr, riv., Port....C1 20
Sora, It., 9,000....D4 21
Sorak-San, peak, Kor....G4 37
Sorata, Bol., 2,087....C2 55
Sorau, see Zary, Pol.
Sorbas, Sp., 5,961....D4 20
Sorel, Que., Can., 17,147....C4 73
Sorell, cape, Austl....o15 50
Sorento, Bond, Ill., 681....E4 90
Soresina, It., 9,100....B2 21
Soria, Sp., 19,301....B4 20
Soria, prov., Sp., 147,052..*B4 20
Soriano, Ur., 1,003....f7 54
Soriano, dept., Ur., 70,500..*E1 56
Sorø, Den., 5,494....C5 24
Sorø, co., Den., 128,176....C5 24
Sorocaba, Braz., 109,258....C3, m8 56
Sorochinsk, Sov. Un., 18,400....C4 29
Soroco, P.R....B8, f12 65
Soroki, Sov. Un., 15,000....G7 27
Sorong, W. Irian, 8,000....F8 35
Soroti, Ug., 6,645....A5 48
Söröy, isl., Nor....B10 25
Sorraia, riv., Port....C1 20
Sorrento, Lake, Fla., 500....D5 86
Sorrento, It., 8,900....D5 21
Sorrento, Ascension, La., 1,151....B6, D5 95
Sorris Sorris, S. W. Afr....B1 49
Sør-Rondane, mts., Ant....B15 5
Sorsogon, Phil., 14,000 (35,500▲)....C6 35
Sorsogon, prov., Phil., 348,700....*C6 35
Sortavala, Sov. Un., 16,400....G14 25
Sör-Tröndelag, co., Nor., 211,700....*F4 25
Sorum, Perkins, S. Dak., 10..B3 116
Sörumsand, Nor., 726....p29 25
Sosan, Kor., 13,500....H3 37
Sosnogorsk, Sov. Un....C19 9
Sosnovka, Sov. Un., 10,000....E13 27
Sosnowiec, Pol., 135,500....C5, g10 26
Soso, Jones, Miss., 150....D4 100
Sosvinskaya, Sov. Un....C21 9
Sota, riv., Pol....h10 26
Sottern, lake, Swe....t33 25
Sotteville-lès-Rouen, Fr., 25,625....C4 14
Souanké, Con. B....E2 46
Soubré, I.C., 1,300....E3 45
Soucook, riv., N.H....D4 105
Soudan, St. Louis, Minn., 810....C6 99
Souderton, Montgomery, Pa., 5,381....F11 114
Souflion, Grc., 7,435....B6 23
Soufriere, St. Lucia, 3,550..p16 64
Souhegan, riv., Mass., N.H....E3 105
Souk Ahras, Alg., 17,444....F10 28
Souk el Arba, Tun., 6,469....F11 28
Souk el Arba, prov., Tun., 196,113....*C6 44
Sŏul, see Seoul, Kor.
Soulac [-sur-Mer], Fr., 1,192....E3 14
Soulanges, co., Que., Can., 10,075....D3 73
Sound Beach, Suffolk, N.Y., 1,800....*F5 84
Sounding, creek, Alta., Can....D5 69
Sounding, lake, Alta., Can....C5 69
Sound View, New London, Conn., 40....D7 84
Sources, mtn., Bas., S. Afr....C4 49
Sourdnahunk, lake, Maine....B3 96
Soure, Braz., 6,666....C5 59
Soure, Port., 9,117....B1 20
Souris, Man., Can., 1,841....E1 71
Souris, Bottineau, N. Dak., 213....A5 111
Souris, riv., Man., Sask., Can., N. Dak....G12 66
Souris East, P.E.I., Can., 1,537....C7 74
Sourlake, Hardin, Tex., 1,602....D5 118
Sourland, mtn., N.J....C3 106
Sous, riv., Mor....C3 44
Sousa, Braz., 12,350....C3 57
Sousse, Tun., 48,185....B7 44
Sousse, prov., Tun., 447,093....*B7 44
Soustons, Fr., 1,901....F3 14
South, div., Ice., 13,416....*n21 25
South, bay, Ont., Can....B3 72
South, bay, Utah....B3 119
South (Rancocas, creek) branch, N.J....D3 106
South (Raritan, riv.) branch, N.J....B3 106
South, cape, N.Z....Q11 51
South, cape, Nor....B13 4
South (Flathead, riv.) fork, Mont....C3 102
South, isl., N.Z....O12 51
South, isl., S.C....E9 115
South, isl., Truk....52
South, mtn., Idaho....G2 89
South, mtn., Md....A2 85
South, mtn., N. Mex....k8 107
South, mtn., Pa....C1 106
South, mts., N.C....B2 109
South, pass, Kwajalein....52
South, pass, La....F6 95
South, pass, Wyo....C4 125
South, pt., Newf., Can....C4 75
South, pt., Md....D7 85
South, pt., Mich....D7 98
South, riv., Ont., Can....A5 72
South, riv., Ga....B5 87
South, riv., Iowa....C4 92
South, riv., Md....C4 85
South, riv., N.C....C5 109
South Acton, Middlesex, Mass., 1,100....g10 97
South Acworth, Sullivan, N.H., 100....D2 105
South Addison, Washington, Maine, 150....D5 96
South Africa, country, Afr., 17,700,000....C3 49
South Amboy, Middlesex, N.J., 8,422....C4, m7 106
South America, cont., 160,800,000....H17 3, 53
South Amherst, Hampshire, Mass., 600....B2 97
South Amherst, Lorain, Ohio, 1,657....*A5 111
Southampton, N.S., Can., 188....D5 74
Southampton, Ont., Can., 1,818....C3 72
Southampton, Eng., 207,200 (*355,000)....D6 12
Southampton, Hampshire, Mass., 400 (2,192▲)....B2 97
Southampton, Suffolk, N.Y., 4,582....n16 108
Southampton, Bucks, Pa., 4,500....*F11 114
Southampton (Hampshire), Co., Eng., 1,336,084....C6 12
Southampton, co., Va., 27,195....E5 121
Southampton, beach, N.Y....F7 84
Southampton, cape, N.W. Ter., Can....D16 67
Southampton, isl., N.W. Ter., Can....D15 67
South Andaman, isl., India....F9 39
South Anna, riv., Va....D5 121
South Apopka, Orange, Fla., 2,484....*D5 86
South Arabia, Br. prot., Asia, 1,050,000....C6 47
Southard, Monmouth, N.J., 300....C4 106
Southard, Blaine, Okla., 385....A3 112
South Ashburnham, Worcester, Mass., 800....A4 97
South Ashfield, Franklin, Mass., 100....A2 97
South Atlantic, ocean....H20 3
South Aulatsivik, isl., Newf., Can....g9 75
South Australia, state, Austl., 1,042,000....F6 50
South Baker, Baker, Oreg. (part of Baker)....C9 113
South Baldy, mtn., N. Mex....D2 107
South Bancroft, Aroostook, Maine....C5 96
Southbank, B.C., Can., 149..C5 68
South Barnstead, Belknap, N.H., 45....D4 105
South Barre, Worcester, Mass., 800....B3 97
South Barre, Washington, Vt., 650....C3 120
South Bathurst, N.B., Can., 1,390....*B4 74
South Bay, Palm Beach, Fla., 1,631....F6 86
South Bellingham, Norfolk, Mass., 3,000....B5 97
South Belmar, Monmouth, N.J., 1,537....C4 106
South Belmont, Gaston, N.C., 2,286....*B2 109
South Beloit, Winnebago, Ill., 3,781....A4 90
South Bend, Lincoln, Ark..*C4 81
South Bend, St. Joseph, Ind., 132,445 (*265,100)....A5 91
South Bend, Cass, Nebr., 86....E2 103
South Bend, Young, Tex., 130....C3 118
South Bend, Pacific, Wash., 1,671....C2 122
South Benfleet, Eng., 32,372....C8 12
South Bennettsville, Marlboro, S.C., 1,025....*B8 115
South Bentinck Arm, chan., B.C., Can....C4 68
South Berwick, York, Maine, 1,773....E2 96
South Bethlehem, Albany, N.Y., 400....C7 108
South Bitter, creek, Wyo....D4 125
South Bloomfield, Pickaway, Ohio, 424....C5 111
South Boardman, Kalkaska, Mich., 175....D5 98
South Bocagrande, Lee, Fla..F4 86
South Boise, Ada, Idaho, 1,452....*F2 89
South Bolton, Que., Can....D5 73
Southboro, Worcester, Mass., 1,114 (3,996▲)....B4, g9 97
South Boston (Independent City), Va., 5,974....E4 121
South Bound, Brook, Somerset, N.J., 3,626....B3 106
South Branch, Newf., Can., 311....E2 75
Southbranch, Ogemaw, Mich., 80....D7 98
South Branch, lake, Maine....C4 96
South Branch, mtn., W. Va....B6 123
Southbridge, Worcester, Mass., 16,523....B3 97
South Bridgeview, Cook, Ill., 1,000....*B6 90
South Bristol, Lincoln, Maine, 550 (610▲)....E3 96
South Britain, New Haven, Conn., 550....D3 84
South Broadway, Yakima, Wash., 3,661....*C5 122
South Brook, Newf., Can., 621....*D3 75
South Brookfield, N.S., Can., 240....E5 74
South Brooksville, Hancock, Maine, 90....D4 96
South Burlington, Chittenden, Vt., 6,903....C2 120
Southbury, New Haven, Conn., 600 (5,186▲)....D4 84
South Byfield, Essex, Mass., 100....A6 97
South Byron, Genesee, N.Y., 250....B2 108
South Canaan, Wayne, Pa., 150....C11 114
South Carolina, state, U.S., 2,382,594....D11 77, 115
South Carver, Plymouth, Mass., 400....C6 97
South Chaplin, Windham, Conn., 500....*C8 84
South Charleston, Clark, Ohio, 1,505....C4 111
South Charleston, Kanawha, W. Va., 19,180....C6 123
South Charlestown, Sullivan, N.H., 100....D2 105
South Chatham, Barnstable, Mass., 400....C7 97
South Chatham, Carroll, N.H., 50....B4 105
South Chelmsford, Middlesex, Mass., 500....f10 97
South Cheney, Spokane, Wash....D7 122
South Chicago Heights, Cook, Ill., 4,043....F3 90
South China, Kennebec, Maine, 115....D3 96
South China, sea, Asia....H14 33
South Cle Elum, Kittitas, Wash., 383....B5 122
South Clement, creek, Md....D4 85
South Cleveland, Bradley, Tenn, 1,512....*D9 117
South Clinton, Anderson, Tenn., 1,356....*C9 117
South Coatesville, Chester, Pa., 2,032....*G10 114
South Coffeyville, Nowata, Okla., 622....A6 112
South Colby, Kitsap, Wash., 350....D1 122
South Colton, St. Lawrence, N.Y., 500....f10 108
South Connellsville, Fayette, Pa., 2,434....G2 114
South Corning, Steuben, N.Y., 1,448....*C3 108
South Covington, Va. (part of Covington)....D2 121
South Dakota, state, U.S., 680,514....B7 76, 116
South Danbury, Merrimack, N.H., 35....D3 105
South Danville, Rockingham, N.H., 100....E4 105
South Dartmouth, Bristol, Mass., 5,500....C6 97
South Dayton, Cattaraugus, N.Y., 696....C1 108
South Daytona, Volusia, Fla., 1,954....C5 86
South Decatur, De Kalb, Ga., 15,000....*C2 87

South Deerfield, Franklin, Mass., 1,253 ..... B2 97
South Deerfield, Rockingham, N.H., 50 ..... D4 105
South Deer Isle, Hancock, Maine, 115 ..... D4 96
South Dennis, Barnstable, Mass., 600 ..... C7 97
South Dennis, Cape May, N.J., 350 ..... E3 106
South Dorset, Bennington, Vt., 160 ..... E2 120
South Downs, hills, Eng D7 12
South Dum-Dum, India, 111,284 ..... *F12 40
South Durham, Que., Can., 438 ..... D5 73
South Duxbury, Plymouth, Mass., 1,000 ..... B6 97
Southeast, pass, La E6 95
South Easton, Bristol, Mass., 900 ..... B5 97
South Effingham, Carroll, N.H., 80 ..... C5 105
South Egremont, Berkshire, Mass., 400 ..... B1 97
South Elgin, Kane, Ill., 2,624 ..... E2 90
South El Monte, Los Angeles, Calif., 4,850 ..... *E5 82
South Elwood, Madison, Ind., 400 ..... D6 91
Southend-on-Sea, Eng., 165,900 ..... C8 12
South English, Keokuk, Iowa, 217 ..... C5 92
Southern, prov., Malawi E5 48
Southern, prov., Zambia E4 48
Southern, reg., Ken B6 48
Southern, reg., Tan., 1,014,265 ..... D6 48
Southern, uplands, Scot E4 13
Southern Alps, mts., N.Z. O13 51
Southern Bug, riv., Sov. Un H8 27
Southern Cross, Austl., 760 ..... F2 50
Southern Cross, Deer Lodge, Mont D3 102
Southern Highlands, reg., Tan., 1,030,041 ..... C5 48
Southern Indian, lake, Man., Can A2 71
Southern Pines, Moore, N.C., 5,198 ..... B4 109
Southern Rhodesia, see Rhodesia, Br. dep., Afr.
Southern Slopes (Lone Oak), Spartanburg, S.C., 1,435 ..... *B4 115
Southern Ute, Indian res., Colo D3 83
Southern View, Sangamon, Ill., 1,485 ..... *D4 90
South Erradale, Scot C3 13
South Esk., riv., Scot D6 13
South Essex, Essex, Mass., 600 ..... A6 97
South Euclid, Cuyahoga, Ohio, 27,569 ..... B2 111
Southey, Sask., Can., 483 ..... G3 70
South Fabius, riv., Mo A6 101
South Fallsburg, Sullivan, N.Y., 1,290 ..... D6 108
South Farmingdale, Nassau, N.Y., 18,000 ..... *G1 84
South Fayetteville, Cumberland, N.C., 3,411 ..... *B5 109
Southfield, Berkshire, Mass., 150 ..... B1 97
Southfield, Oakland, Mich., 31,501 ..... *F7 98
South Flevoland Polder, reg., Neth B5 15
South Floral Park, Nassau, N.Y., 1,090 ..... *G2 84
South Fork, Humboldt, Calif., 75 ..... B2 82
South Fork, Sask., Can H1 70
South Fork, Rio Grande, Colo., 175 ..... D4 83
South Fork, Cambria, Pa., 2,053 ..... F4 114
South Fork, res., Wash B4 122
South Fork Republican, riv., Colo B8 83
South Fort George, B.C., Can., 1,964 ..... C6 68
South Fort Mitchell, Kenton, Ky., 4,086 ..... A7 94
South Fort Smith, Sebastian, Ark. (part of Fort Smith) B1 81
South Foster, Providence, R.I., 150 ..... B10 84
South Fox, isl., Mich C5 98
South Freeport, Cumberland, Maine, 350 ..... E5 96
South Fulton, Obion, Tenn., 2,512 ..... A3 117
South Gamboa, C.Z. k11 62
South Gardiner, Kennebec, Maine (part of Gardiner) D3 96
South Gate, Los Angeles, Calif., 53,831 ..... F2 82
Southgate, Campbell, Ky., 2,070 ..... A7 94
Southgate, Wayne, Mich., 29,404 ..... *F7 98
South Georgia, isl., Atl. O. J18 3
South Gifford, Macon, Mo., 93 ..... A5 101
South Glastonbury, Hartford, Conn., 1,000 ..... C6 84
South Glens Falls, Saratoga, N.Y., 4,129 ..... *B7 108
South Grafton, Worcester, Mass., 3,000 ..... B4 97
South Grand, riv., Mo C3 101
South Gray, Cumberland, Maine, 70 ..... E5 96
South Greenfield, Dade, Mo., 179 ..... D4 101
South Greensburg, Westmoreland, Pa., 3,058 ..... *F2 114
South Greenwood, Greenwood, S.C., 2,520 ..... C3 115
South Groveland, Essex, Mass., 400 ..... A5 97
South Guam, McKinley, N. Mex B1 107
South Hackensack, Bergen, N.J., 1,841 ..... *B4 106
South Hadley, Hampshire, Mass., 4,000 (14,956▲) B2 97
South Hadley Falls, Hampshire, Mass., 8,000 ..... B2 97
South Hamilton, Essex, Mass., 3,000 ..... A6, f12 97
South Hampton, Rockingham, N.H., 100 (443▲) E5 105
South Hanover, Plymouth, Mass., 600 ..... h12 97
South Harpswell, Cumberland, Maine, 500 ..... E5 96
South Harriman, Roane, Tenn., 2,884 ..... *D9 117
South Harris, pen., Scot C2 13
South Harwich, Barnstable, Mass., 650 ..... C7 97
South Haven, Sumner, Kans., 408 ..... E6 93
South Haven, Van Buren, Mich., 6,149 ..... F4 98
South Heart, Stark, N. Dak., 97 ..... C2 110
South Heart, riv., Alta., Can B2 69
South Hempstead, Nassau, N.Y., 3,000 ..... *G2 84
South Henderson, Vance, N.C., 2,017 ..... *A5 115
South Hero, Grand Isle, Vt., 300 (614▲) B2 120
South Hero, isl., Vt B2 120
South Hill, Mecklenburg, Va., 2,569 ..... E4 121
South Holland, Cook, Ill., 12,603 ..... *F3 90
South Holland (Zuidholland), prov., Neth., 2,726,200 ..... B4 15
South Holston, lake, Tenn., Va C11 117, B2 121
South Holston Lake, res., Tenn., Va C11 117, B3 121
South Hooksett, Merrimack, N.H., 1,700 ..... D4 105
South Hopkinton, Washington, R.I., 500 ..... *D9 84
South Houston, Harris, Tex., 7,523 ..... F5 118
South Humboldt, riv., Nev C6 104
South Huntingdon (Smithfield), Huntingdon, Pa., 2,547 ..... *E5 114
South Hutchinson, Reno, Kans., 1,672 ..... A4 93
South Indian Lake, Man., Can., 103 ..... A2 71
Southington, Hartford, Conn., 14,000 (22,797▲) C5 84
South International Falls, Koochiching, Minn., 2,479 ..... B5 99
South Jacksonville, Morgan, Ill., 2,340 ..... D3 90
South Jordan, Salt Lake, Utah, 1,354 ..... C3 119
South Junction, Man., Can., 233 ..... E4 71
South Junction, Wasco, Oreg., 35 ..... B5 113
South Kent, Litchfield, Conn., 250 ..... C3 84
Southkent, Kent, Mich., 15,000 ..... *F5 98
South Killingly, Windham, Conn., 200 ..... B9 84
South Kingston, Rockingham, N.H., 100 ..... E4 105
South Kingstown (Town of), Washington, R.I. (11,942▲) *D10 84
South Klamath, Klamath, Oreg E5 113
South Laguna, Orange, Calif., 2,000 ..... *F5 82
Southlake, Tarrant, Tex., 1,023 ..... *C4 118
South Lancaster, Worcester, Mass., 2,100 ..... B4 97
Southland, Jackson, Mich., 2,000 ..... *F6 98
Southland, Garza, Tex., 153 ..... C2 118
South Lansing, Tompkins, N.Y., 100 ..... C4 108
Southlawn, Sangamon, Ill., 2,300 ..... *D4 90
South Lebanon, Warren, Ohio, 2,720 ..... C3 111
South Lee, Berkshire, Mass., 360 ..... B1 97
South Lee, Strafford, N.H. D4 105
South Liberty, Waldo, Maine, 100 ..... D3 96
South Lincoln, Addison, Vt., 35 ..... C3 120
South Londonderry, Windham, Vt., 300 ..... E3 120
South Loup, riv., Nebr C6 103
South Lubec, Washington, Maine, 230 ..... D5 96
South Lunenburg, Essex, Vt., 60 ..... C5 120
South Lyme, New London, Conn., 350 ..... D7 84
South Lyndeboro, Hillsboro, N.H., 150 ..... E3 105
South Lyon, Oakland, Mich., 1,753 ..... A6, F7 98
South Macon, Bibb, Ga., 9,000 ..... *D3 87
Southmag, Ont., Can B4 72
South Magnetic Pole, Ant C27 5
South Manitou, isl., Mich C4 98
South Mansfield, De Soto, La., 616 ..... B2 95
South Marsh, isl., Md D5 85
South Medford, Jackson, Oreg., 2,306 ..... *E4 113
South Meriden, New Haven, Conn. (part of Meriden) C5 84
South Merrimack, Hillsboro, N.H., 125 ..... E3 105
South Miami, Dade, Fla., 9,846 ..... F3, G6 86
South Middleboro, Plymouth, Mass., 400 ..... C6 97
South Milford, Lagrange, Ind., 350 ..... A7 91
South Milford, Hillsboro, N.H E3 105
South Mills, Camden, N.C., 479 ..... A7 109
South Milwaukee, Milwaukee, Wis., 20,307 ..... F2, F6 124
Southminster, Eng., 1,444 ..... C8 12
South Modesto, Stanislaus, Calif., 9,000 ..... *D3 82
South Molton, Eng., 2,994 ..... C4 12
South Monroe, Monroe, Mich., 2,919 ..... *G7 98
Southmont, Davidson, N.C., 700 ..... B3 109
Southmont, Cambria, Pa., 2,857 ..... *F4 114
South Montrose, Susquehanna, Pa., 250 ..... C10 114
South Mountain, Franklin, Pa., 600 ..... G7 114
South Naknek, Alsk., 33 ..... D8 79
South Natuna, is., Indon E3 35
South Nelson, N.B., Can., 792 ..... *C4 74
South Nelson Village, B.C., Can., 939 ..... *E9 68
South New Berlin, Chenango, N.Y., 400 ..... C5 108
South Newburg, Penobscot, Maine D4 96
South Newbury, Merrimack, N.H., 70 ..... D2 105
South Newbury, Orange, Vt., 60 ..... C4 120
South Newfane, Windham, Vt., 120 ..... F3 120
South New River, canal, Fla E3 86
South Northfield, Washington, Vt., 110 ..... C3 120
South Nyack, Rockland, N.Y., 3,113 ..... g9 106
South Ogden, Weber, Utah, 7,405 ..... B4 119
Southold, Suffolk, N.Y., 1,000 ..... m16 108
South Orange, Essex, N.J., 16,175 ..... B4 106
South Orkney, is., Ant C8 5
South Oroville, Butte, Calif., 3,704 ..... *C3 82
South Orrington, Penobscot, Maine, 600 ..... D4 96
South Otselic, Chenango, N.Y., 400 ..... C5 108
South Oyster, bay, N.Y G3 84
South Pacific, ocean H12 2
South Paris, Oxford, Maine, 2,063 ..... D2 96
South Park, Sonoma, Calif., 3,261 ..... *C2 82
South Park, Kane, Ill., 2,063 ..... *B5 90
South Pasadena, Los Angeles, Calif., 19,706 ..... F2 82
South Pass City, Fremont, Wyo., 15 ..... C4 125
South Peacham, Caledonia, Vt., 25 ..... C4 120
South Pekin, Tazewell, Ill., 1,007 ..... C4 90
South Penobscot, Hancock, Maine, 100 ..... D4 96
South Pittsburg, Marion, Tenn., 4,130 ..... D8 117
South Plainfield, Middlesex. N.J., 17,879 ..... B4 106
South Platte, riv., Colo., Nebr B5 84, C4 103
South Point, Lawrence, Ohio, 1,663 ..... *D5 111
South Polar, plateau, Ant A9 5
South Pole, Ant ..... A 5
South Pomfret, Windsor, Vt., 25 ..... D3 120
South Porcupine, Ont., Can., 5,144 ..... o19 72
Southport (South Coast), Austl., 33,716 ..... C9 51
Southport, Fairfield, Conn. (part of Fairfield) E3 84
Southport, Eng., 80,200 ..... A4 12
Southport, Bay, Fla., 900 ..... G3 86
Southport, Marion, Ind., 892 ..... E5, I8 91
Southport (Elmira Southeast), Chemung, N.Y., 6,900 ..... *C4 108
Southport, Brunswick, N.C., 2,034 ..... D5 109
South Portland, Cumberland, Maine, 22,788 ..... E2, E5 96
South Portsmouth, Greenup, Ky., 600 ..... B7 94
South Pottstown, Chester, Pa., 1,850 ..... *F10 114
South Poultney, Rutland, Vt., 200 ..... E2 120
South Prairie, Pierce, Wash., 214 ..... B3 118
South Queensferry, Scot., 2,700 ..... E5 13
South Range, Houghton, Mich., 760 ..... A2 98
South Range, Douglas, Wis., 100 ..... B2 124
South Reading, Windsor, Vt., 75 ..... E3 120
South Renovo, Clinton, Pa., 777 ..... D6 114
South Revelstoke, B.C., Can., 737 ..... D8 68
South River, Ont., Can., 1,044 ..... B5 72
South River, Middlesex, N.J., 13,397 ..... C4 106
South Robbinston, Washington, Maine C5 96
South Rockwood, Monroe, Mich., 1,337 ..... *F7 98
South Ronaldsay, isl., Scot B6 13
South Roxana, Madison, Ill., 2,010 ..... *E3 90
South Roxton, Que., Can., 86 ..... *D5 73
South Royalston, Worcester, Mass., 400 ..... A3 97
South Royalton, Windsor, Vt., 400 ..... D3 120
South Russell, Geauga, Ohio, 1,276 ..... *A6 111
South Ryegate, Caledonia, Vt., 360 ..... C4 120
South Sacramento, Sacramento, Calif., 10,960 ..... *C3 82
South St. Paul, Dakota, Minn., 22,032 ..... E7, F5 99
South Salem, Ross, Ohio, 180 ..... C4 111
South Salisbury, Rowan, N.C., 3,065 ..... *B3 109
South Salt Lake, Salt Lake, Utah, 9,520 ..... C4 119
South Sandwich, is., Atl. O. J19 3
South Sanford, York, Maine E2 96
South San Francisco, San Mateo, Calif., 39,418 ..... B5 82
South San Gabriel, Los Angeles, Calif., 26,213 ..... *F2 82
South San Leandro, Alameda, Calif., 17,150 ..... *B5 82
South Saskatchewan, riv., Alta., Sask., Can G1 70
South Seaville, Cape May, N.J., 300 ..... E3 106
South Shetland, is., Ant C7 5
South Shields, Eng., 109,100 ..... C6 10
South Shore, St. Charles, Mo., 200 ..... A7 101
South Shore, Codington, S. Dak., 259 ..... B9 116
Southside, Lincoln, N.C., 645 ..... B2 109
Southside, Montgomery, Tenn., 100 ..... A4 117
Southside Estates, Duval, Fla., 4,000 ..... *B5 86
South Side Place, Harris, Tex., 1,282 ..... F5 118
South Sioux City, Dakota, Nebr., 7,200 ..... B9 103
South Slocan, B.C., Can., 168 ..... E9 68
South Solon, Madison, Ohio, 414 ..... C4 111
South Spencer, Worcester, Mass., 75 ..... B3 97
South Sterling, Wayne, Pa., 150 ..... D11 114
South Stickney, Cook, Ill., 23,000 ..... *B6 90
South Strafford, Orange, Vt., 85 ..... D4 120
South Streator, Livingston, Ill., 1,923 ..... *B5 90
South Suburbs, India, 185,811 ..... *F12 40
South Sumatra, see Sumatra, isl., Indon.
South Superior, Sweetwater, Wyo., 401 ..... D4 125
South Sutton, Merrimack, N.H., 100 ..... D3 105
South Swansea, Bristol, Mass., 1,000 ..... C5 97
South Taft, Kern, Calif., 1,910 ..... *E4 82
South Tamworth, Carroll, N.H., 160 ..... C4 105
South Temple, Berks, Pa., 1,500 ..... *F10 114
South Toms River, Ocean, N.J., 1,603 ..... D4 106
South Torrington, Goshen, Wyo., 950 ..... C8 125
South Trail (Hayden), Sarasota, Fla., 5,471 ..... *E4 86
South Tucson, Pima, Ariz., 7,004 ..... E5 80
South Tunnel, Sumner, Tenn., 200 ..... A5 117
South Turlock, Stanislaus, Calif., 1,577 ..... *D3 82
South Twin, lake, Newf., Can D4 75
South Twin, mtn., N.H B3 105
South Tyne, riv., Eng F6 13
South Uist, isl., Scot C1 13
South Uniontown, Fayette, Pa., 3,603 ..... *G2 114
South Vienna, Clark, Ohio, 440 ..... C4 111
Southville, Worcester, Mass., 450 ..... g9 97
South Wabasca, lake, Alta., Can B4 69
South Wadesboro, Anson, N.C., 189 ..... C3 109
South Wallingford, Rutland, Vt., 60 ..... E3 120
South Walpole, Norfolk, Mass., 600 ..... h10 97
South Wareham, Plymouth, Mass., 180 ..... C6 97
South Waterford, Oxford, Maine, 230 ..... D2 96
South Waverly, Bradford, Pa., 1,382 ..... C8 114
South Wayne, Lafayette, Wis., 354 ..... F4 124
South Weare, Hillsboro, N.H., 30 ..... D3 105
South Weber, Davis, Utah, 382 ..... *B4 119
South Webster, Scioto, Ohio, 803 ..... D5 111
South Wellfleet, Barnstable, Mass., 500 ..... C8 97
South Wellington, B.C., Can., 409 ..... f12 68
South Wenatchee, Chelan, Wash B5 122
Southwest, Westmoreland, Pa., 800 ..... F2 114
South West, div., Ice., 77,976 ..... *n22 25
Southwest, cape, Que., Can B7 74
Southwest, cape, Vir. Is k17 65
Southwest, chan., Fla E4 86
Southwest, head, N.B., Can E3 74
Southwest, pass, La E3 95
Southwest, pass, La F6 95
Southwest, pt., R.I E10 84
South West Africa, S. Afr. mandate, Afr., 555,000 ..... B2 49, I7 42
South Westbury, Nassau, N.Y., 12,300 ..... *G2 84
South West City, McDonald, Mo., 504 ..... E3 101
Southwest Dillon, Dillon, S.C., 1,048 ..... *C9 115
Southwestern, mts., Va C4 121
South West Fargo, Cass., N. Dak., 3,328 ..... C9 110
Southwest Greensburg, Westmoreland, Pa., 3,264 ..... *F2 114
Southwest Harbor, Hancock, Maine, 900 (1,480▲) D4 96
South Westminster, B.C., Can., 500 ..... *E6 68
South Weymouth, Norfolk, Mass. (part of Weymouth) h12 97
South Whitley, Whitley, Ind., 1,325 ..... B6 91
Southwick, Nez Perce, Idaho, 50 ..... C2 89
Southwick, Hampden, Mass., 1,400 (5,139▲) B2 97
South Williamson, Pike, Ky., 1,097 ..... C7 94
South Williamsport, Lycoming, Pa., 6,972 ..... D7 114
South Willington, Tolland, Conn., 250 ..... B7 84
South Wilmington, Grundy, Ill., 730 ..... B5 90
South Windermere, Charleston, S.C., 1,500 ..... *F8 115
South Windham, Windham, Conn., 380 ..... C8 84
South Windham, Cumberland, Maine, 1,142 ..... E2, E4 96
South Windsor, Hartford, Conn., 800 (9,460▲) B6 84
Southwold, Eng., 2,228 ..... B9 12
South Wolf, isl., Newf., Can B4 75
South Wolfeboro, Carroll, N.H., 150 ..... C4 105
Southwood Acres, Hartford, Conn., 5,000 ..... *B6 84
South Woodbury, Washington, Vt., 75 ..... C4 120
South Woodstock, Windham, Conn., 400 ..... B9 84
South Woodstock, Windsor, Vt., 100 ..... D3 120
South Worthington, Hampshire, Mass., 25 ..... B2 97
South Yarmouth, Barnstable, Mass., 2,100 ..... C7 97
South Zanesville, Muskingum, Ohio, 1,557 ..... C5 111
Soverato, It., 4,750 ..... E6 21
Sovereign, Sask., Can., 125 ..... F2 70
Sovetsk (Tilsit), Sov. Un., 85,900 ..... A6 26, D3 27
Sovetskaya Gavan, Sov. Un., 49,000 ..... E16 28, B10 37
Soviet Union (U.S.S.R.), country, Eur., Asia, 229,500,000 ..... 28, D11 33
Soya, cape, Jap D10 37
Sozopol, Bul., 3,178 ..... D8 22
Spa, Bel., 9,055 ..... D5 15
Spadra, Johnson, Ark., 300 ..... B2 81
Spain, country, Eur., 31,500,000 ..... G8 8, 20
Spalding, Austl., 240 ..... F2 51
Spalding, Sask., Can., 416 ..... E3 70
Spalding, Eng., 14,821 ..... B7 12
Spalding, Nez Perce, Idaho, 200 ..... C2 89
Spalding, Greeley, Nebr., 683 ..... C7 103
Spalding co., Ga., 35,404 ..... C2 87
Spanaway, Pierce, Wash., 2,500 ..... B3 122
Spangle, Spokane, Wash., 208 ..... B8, D7 122
Spangler, Cambria, Pa., 2,658 ..... E4 114
Spangler, hill, Ohio C2 111
Spaniard's Bay, Newf., Can., 1,289 ..... E5 75
Spanish, Ont., Can., 1,536 ..... A2 72
Spanish, peak, Oreg C7 113
Spanish, riv., Ont., Can A2 72
Spanishburg, Mercer, W. Va., 200 ..... D3 123
Spanish Fork, Utah, Utah, 6,472 ..... C4 119
Spanish Fort, Montague, Tex., 100 ..... C4 118
Spanish Possessions in North Africa, see Ceuta, Melilla, dep., Afr.
Spanish Ranch, Plumas, Calif., 150 ..... C3 82
Spanish Sahara, dep., Afr., 45,000 ..... E2 44
Spanish Town, Jam., 14,439 ..... G5 64
Sparenberg, Dawson, Tex., 25 ..... C2 118
Sparkill, Rockland, N.Y., 1,200 ..... C5 106
Sparkman, Dallas, Ark., 787 ..... D3 81
Sparks, Cook, Ga., 1,158 ..... E3 87
Sparks, Cherry, Nebr., 5 ..... B5 103
Sparks, Washoe, Nev., 16,618 ..... D2 104
Sparks, Lincoln, Okla., 186 ..... B5 112
Sparksville, Jackson, Ind., 100 ..... G5 91
Sparksville, Adair, Ky., 150 ..... C4 94
Sparland, Marshall, Ill., 534 ..... B4 90
Sparr, Marion, Fla., 400 ..... C4 86
Sparreholm, Swe., 974 ..... t34 25
Sparrow Lake, Ont., Can., 40 ..... C5 72
Sparrows Point, Baltimore, Md., 3,300 ..... B5 85
Sparta, Hancock, Ga., 1,921 ..... C4 87
Sparta, see Spárti, Grc.
Sparta, Randolph, Ill., 3,452 ..... E4 90
Sparta, Gallatin, Ky., 235 ..... B5 94
Sparta, Kent, Mich., 2,749 ..... E5 98
Sparta, Christian, Mo., 272 ..... E4 101
Sparta, Sussex, N.J., 700 ..... A3 106
Sparta, Alleghany, N.C., 1,047 ..... A2 109
Sparta, Morrow, Ohio, 228 ..... B5 111
Sparta, Baker, Oreg C9 113
Sparta, White, Tenn., 4,510 ..... D8 117
Sparta, Monroe, Wis., 6,080 ..... E3 124
Sparta, mts., N.J B3 106
Spartanburg, Randolph, Ind., 200 ..... D8 91
Spartanburg, Spartanburg, S.C., 44,352 ..... B4 115
Spartanburg, co., S.C., 156,830 ..... B4 115
Spartansburg, Crawford, Pa., 500 ..... C2 114
Spárti (Sparta), Grc., 10,412 ..... D4 23
Spas-Demensk, Sov. Un., 4,000 ..... D10 27
Spassk-Dalniy, Sov. Un., 29,400 ..... E16 28
Spassk-Ryazanskiy, Sov. Un., 14,500 ..... D13 27
Spaulding, Jefferson, Ala., 300 ..... E4 78
Spaulding, Hughes, Okla., 150 ..... B5 112
Spavinaw, Mayes, Okla., 319 ..... A6 112
Spavinaw, creek, Okla A7 112
Spean Bridge, Scot D4 13
Spear, Avery, N.C., 170 ..... C4 109
Spear, cape, Newf., Can E5 75
Spearfish, Lawrence, S. Dak., 3,682 ..... C2 116
Spearhill, Man., Can., 75 ..... D2 71
Spearman, Hansford, Tex., 3,555 ..... A2 118
Spearsville, Union, La., 90 ..... B3 95
Spearville, Ford, Kans., 602 ..... E4 93
Spectacle, pond, Maine D4 96
Speculator, Hamilton, N.Y., 372 ..... B6 108
Spedden, Alta., Can., 123 ..... B5 69
Spednik, lake, N.B., Can D2 74
Speed, Clark, Ind., 950 ..... H6 91
Speed, Phillips, Kans., 75 ..... C4 93
Speed, Edgecombe, N.C., 142 ..... B6 109
Speedway, Marion, Ind., 9,624 ..... E5, H7 91
Speedwell, Claiborne, Tenn., 75 ..... C10 117
Speedwell, Wythe, Va., 200 ..... E1 121
Speer, Laramie, Wyo D8 125
Speers, Sask., Can., 175 ..... E2 70
Speers, Washington, Pa., 1,479 ..... *F2 108
Speigener, Elmore, Ala., 125 ..... C3 78
Speight, Pike, Ky., 500 ..... C7 94
Spelter, Harrison, W. Va., 500 ..... B7 123
Spenard, Alsk., 9,074 ..... *g17 79
Spencer, Clark, Idaho, 100 ..... E6 89
Spencer, Owen, Ind., 2,557 ..... F4 91
Spencer, Clay, Iowa, 8,864 ..... A2 92
Spencer, Somerset, Maine C2 96
Spencer, Worcester, Mass., 5,593 (7,838▲) B4 97
Spencer, Boyd, Nebr., 671 ..... B7 103
Spencer, Tioga, N.Y., 767 ..... C4 108
Spencer, Rowan, N.C., 2,904 ..... B3 109
Spencer, Medina, Ohio, 742 ..... A5 111
Spencer, Oklahoma, Okla., 1,189 ..... *B4 112
Spencer, McCook, S. Dak., 460 ..... D8 116
Spencer, Van Buren, Tenn., 870 ..... D8 117
Spencer, Henry, Va., 200 ..... E2 121
Spencer, Roane, W. Va., 2,660 ..... C3 123
Spencer, Marathon, Wis., 897 ..... D3 124
Spencer, co., Ind., 16,074 ..... H4 91
Spencer, co., Ky., 5,680 ..... B4 94
Spencer, butte, Oreg D3 113
Spencer, cape, Alsk k21 79
Spencer, gulf, Austl F6 50
Spencer, lake, Maine C2 96
Spencer, mts., Maine C3 96
Spencer, pond, Maine C3 96
Spencerport, Monroe, N.Y., 2,676 ..... B3 108
Spencer's Island, N.S., Can., 109 ..... D5 74
Spencerville, DeKalb, Ind., 340 ..... B8 91
Spencerville, Montgomery, Md., 900 ..... B4 85
Spencerville, Allen, Ohio, 2,061 ..... B3 111
Spences Bridge, B.C., Can., 239 ..... D7 68
Spennymoor, Eng., 19,104 ..... F7 13
Sperkhios, riv., Grc C4 23
Sperling, Man., Can., 172 ..... E3 71
Sperrin, mts., N. Ire C4 11
Sperry, Des Moines, Iowa, 70 ..... D6 92
Sperry, Tulsa, Okla., 883 ..... A6 112
Sperryville, Rappahannock, Va., 300 ..... C4 121
Spesutie, isl., Md B5 85
Spey, riv., Scot C5 13
Speyer, Ger., 40,100 ..... D3 17
Spiceland, Henry, Ind., 863 ..... E7 91
Spicer, Kandiyohi, Minn., 589 ..... E4 99
Spicer, is., N.W. Ter., Can. C17 67
Spickard, Grundy, Mo., 450 ..... A4 101
Spider, lake, Wis B2 124
Spiekeroog, Ger., 770 ..... A7 15
Spiekeroog, isl., Ger B3 16
Spielman, Washington, Md., 75 ..... A2 85
Spiez, Switz., 8,168 ..... C4 19
Spigno Monferrato, It., 3,014 ..... E4 18
Spillville, Winneshiek, Iowa, 389 ..... A6 92
Spilsby, Eng., 1,486 ..... A8 12
Spinazzola, It., 10,850 ..... D6 21
Spindale, Rutherford, N.C., 4,082 ..... B2, D4 109
Spink, Union, S. Dak., 25 ..... E9 116
Spink, co., S. Dak., 11,706 ..... C7 116
Spink Colony, Spink, S. Dak., 100 ..... C7 116
Spirit, Price, Wis C3 124
Spirit, lake, Iowa A2 92
Spirit, lake, Wash C3 122
Spirit, res., Wis C4 124
Spirit Lake, Kootenai, Idaho, 693 ..... B2 89
Spirit Lake, Dickinson, Iowa, 2,685 ..... A2 92
Spirit River, Alta., Can., 890 ..... B1 69
Spiritwood, Sask., Can., 548 ..... D2 70
Spiritwood, Stutsman, N. Dak., 90 ..... C7 110
Spiro, LeFlore, Okla., 1,450 ..... B7 112
Spisská Nová Ves., Czech., 16,900 ..... D6 26
Spithead, roadstead, Eng D6 12
Spitsbergen, see Svalbard, is., Nor.
Spittal, Aus., 10,045 ..... E6 16
Spivey, Kingman, Kans., 98 ..... E5 93
Split, Yugo., 99,462 ..... D3 22
Split, cape, N.S., Can D5 74
Split, lake, Man., Can A3 71
Splügen, Switz., 346 ..... C7 19
Splügen, pass, Switz C7 19
Spofford, Cheshire, N.H., 300 ..... E2 105
Spofford, Kinney, Tex., 138 ..... E2 118
Spofford, lake, N.H E2 105
Spokane, Spokane, Wash., 181,608 (★252,000) B8, D7 122
Spokane, co., Wash., 278,333 ..... B8 122
Spokane, mtn., Wash B8 122

Stella, mtn., It. C5 18
Stellarton, N.S., Can., 5,327 D7 74
Stellenbosch, S. Afr., 22,333 *D2 49
Stelvio, pass., Switz. C9 19
Stem, Granville, NC., 221 A5 109
Stemmers Run, Baltimore, Md. (part of Essex) B7 85
Stenay, Fr., 3,829 E5 15
Stendal, Ger., 37,000 B5 16
Stendal, Pike, Ind., 180 H3 91
Stenen, Sask., Can., 275 F4 70
Stengårdshult, Swe A7 24
Stennes, lake, Scot A5 13
Stensele, Swe., 870 E7 25
Stepanakert, Sov. Un., 22,000 F3 29
Stepenitz, riv., Ger E5 24
Stephan, Hyde, S. Dak., 300 C6 116
Stephen, Marshall, Minn., 858 B2 99
Stephens, Ouachita, Ark., 1,275 D2 81
Stephens, Oglethorpe, Ga., 150 C3 87
Stephens, co., Ga., 18,391 B3 87
Stephens, co., Okla., 37,990 C4 112
Stephens, co., Tex., 8,885 C3 118
Stephens, passage, Alsk m23 79
Stephensburg, Morris, N.J., 100 B3 106
Stephens City, Frederick, Va., 876 B4 121
Stephenson, Menominee, Mich., 820 C3 98
Stephenson, co., Ill., 46,207 A4 90
Stephensport, Breckinridge, Ky., 150 D3 94
Stephenson, mtn., Ant. C6 5
Stephenston, Warrick, Ind., 60 H3 91
Stephenville, Newf., Can., 6,043 D2 75
Stephenville, Erath, Tex., 7,359 C3 118
Stephenville Crossing, Newf., Can., 2,209 D2 75
Stepnoy, Sov. Un D3 29
Stepnyak, Sov. Un., 20,000 C8 29
Steps, pt., Am. Sam 52
Steptoe, White Pine, Nev., 5 D7 104
Steptoe, Whitman, Wash., 100 B8 122
Steptoe, creek, Nev E7 104
Sterkstroom, S. Afr., 3,744 D4 49
Sterley, Floyd, Tex., 100 B2 111
Sterling, Logan, Colo., 10,751 A7 83
Sterling, Windham, Conn., 400 (1,397▲) C9 84
Sterling, Bingham, Idaho, 70 F6 89
Sterling, Whiteside, Ill., 15,688 B4 90
Sterling, Fountain, Ind., 430 D3 91
Sterling, Rice, Kans., 2,303 D5 93
Sterling, Worcester, Mass., 950 (3,193▲) B4 97
Sterling, Arenac, Mich., 470 D6 98
Sterling, Johnson, Nebr., 471 D9 103
Sterling, Burleigh, N. Dak., 100 C5 110
Sterling, Comanche, Okla., 562 C3 112
Sterling, Sanpete, Utah, 137 D4 119
Sterling, Loudoun, Va., 300 A4, B5 121
Sterling, co., Scot., 190,500 D4 13
Sterling, co., Tex., 1,177 D2 118
Sterling, res., Colo A7 83
Sterling City, Sterling, Tex., 854 D2 118
Sterling Junction, Worcester, Mass., 400 *B4 97
Sterling Run, Cameron, Pa., 150 D5 114
Sterlington, Ouachita, La., 1,200 B3 95
Sterlitamak, Sov. Un., 131,000 C5 29
Sternberg, Ger., 4,479 E5 24
Sternberk, Czech., 11,200 D4 26
Sterrett, Shelby, Ala., 450 B3 78
Steti, Czech., 1,716 C9 17
Stetson, Penobscot, Maine 150 (420▲) D3 96
Stetson, mtn., Maine C5 96
Stetsonville, Taylor, Wis., 319 C3 124
Stettin, see Szczecin, Pol.
Stettin, lagoon, Ger., Pol E8 24
Stettler, Alta., Can., 3,638 C4 69
Steuben, Washington, Maine, 350 (673▲) D5 96
Steuben, Schoolcraft, Mich., 15 B4 98
Steuben, Crawford, Wis., 193 E3 124
Steuben, co., Ind., 17,184 A7 91
Steuben, co., N.Y., 97,691 C3 108
Steubenville, Jefferson, Ohio, 32,495 (*121,300) B7 111
Steve, Yell, Ark., 10 C2 81
Stevenage, Eng., 50,300 E6 12
Stevens, Burlington, N.J., 300 C3 106
Stevens, co., Kans., 4,400 E2 93
Stevens, co., Minn., 11,262 E3 99
Stevens, co., Wash., 17,884 A8 122
Stevens, peak, Idaho, Mont C1 102
Stevenson, Jackson, Ala., 1,456 A4 78
Stevenson, Fairfield, Conn., 400 D4 84
Stevenson, Skamania, Wash., 927 D4 122
Stevenson, lake, Man., Can C4 71
Stevenson, mtn., Ark B1 81
Stevenson, mtn., Oreg C6 113
Stevenson, riv., Man., Can B4 71
Stevens Point, Portage, Wis., 17,837 D4 124
Stevens Pottery, Baldwin, Ga., 300 D3 87
Stevens Village, Alsk., 102 B10 79
Stevensville, Queen Annes, Md., 400 C5 85
Stevensville, Berrien, Mich., 697 F4 98
Stevensville, Ravalli, Mont., 784 D2 102
Steveston, B.C., Can., 4,000 f12 68
Steward, Lee, Ill., 264 B4 90
Stewardson, Shelby, Ill., 656 D5 90
Stewart, Hale, Ala., 50 C2 78
Stewart, B.C., Can., 327 B3, m17 68
Stewart, McLeod, Minn., 676 F4 99
Stewart, Montgomery, Miss., 162 B4 100
Stewart, Ormsby, Nev., 900 D2 104
Stewart, Athens, Ohio, 300 C6 111
Stewart, Houston, Tenn., 150 A4 117
Stewart, co., Ga., 7,371 D2 87
Stewart, co., Tenn., 7,851 A4 117
Stewart, isl., N.Z. Q11 51
Stewart, riv., Yukon, Can D5 66
Stewart Manor, Nassau, N.Y., 2,422 *G2 84
Stewarton, Scot., 3,387 E4 13
Stewartstown, Coos, N.H., 125 (918▲) B1 105
Stewartstown, N. Ire., 620 C5 11
Stewartstown, York, Pa., 1,164 G8 114
Stewartsville, Coosa, Ala., 60 B3 78
Stewartsville, Posey, Ind., 235 H2 91
Stewartsville, DeKalb, Mo., 466 B3 101
Stewartsville, Warren, N.J., 950 B2 106
Stewartsville, Bedford, Va., 150 D3 121
Stewart Valley, Sask., Can., 181 G2 70
Stewartville, Olmsted, Minn., 1,670 G6 99
Stewiacke, N.S., Can., 1,042 D6 74
Steynsburg, S. Afr., 3,365 D4 49
Steyr, Aus., 38,306 D7 16
Stibnite, Valley, Idaho, 25 E3 89
Stickney, Cook, Ill., 6,239 *F3 90
Stickney, Aurora, S. Dak., 456 D7 116
Stigler, Haskell, Okla., 1,923 B6 112
Stikine, riv., Alsk., B.C., Can E6 66
Stiles, Macon, N.C. D2 109
Stiles, Reagan, Tex., 15 D2 118
Stilesville, Hendricks, Ind., 361 E4 91
Stilis, Grc., 3,606 C4 23
Stillaguamish, riv., Wash A4 122
Stillman Valley, Ogle, Ill., 598 A4 90
Stillmore, Emanuel, Ga., 354 D4 87
Still Pond, Kent, Md., 350 B5 85
Still River, Worcester, Mass., 150 B4 97
Stillwater, B.C., Can., 165 E5 68
Stillwater, Penobscot, Maine (part of Old Town) D4 96
Stillwater, Washington, Minn., 8,310 E6, E8 99
Stillwater, Churchill, Nev., 20 D3 104
Stillwater, Sussex, N.J., 300 A3 106
Stillwater, Saratoga, N.Y., 1,398 C7 108
Stillwater, Payne, Okla., 23,965 A4 112
Stillwater, Columbia, Pa., 193 D9 114
Stillwater, Providence, R.I., 150 B10 84
Stillwater, co., Mont., 5,526 E7 102
Stillwater, range, Nev D3 104
Stillwater, res., N.Y. B5 108
Stillwell, Effingham, Ga., 50 D5 87
Stillwell, LaPorte, Ind., 225 A4 91
Stilson, Bullock, Ga., 160 D5 87
Stilwell, Johnson, Kans., 162 D9 93
Stilwell, Adair, Okla., 1,916 B7 112
Stimson, mtn., Mont B3 102
Stinchar, riv., Scot F4 13
Stine, mtn., Mont E3 102
Stinear Nunataks, peaks, Ant C19 5
Stinesville, Monroe, Ind., 288 F4 91
Stinnett, Hutchinson, Tex., 2,695 B2 118
Stinson Lake, Grafton, N.H., 40 C3 105
Stip, Yugo., 18,650 E6 22
Stirling, Alta., Can., 468 E4 69
Stirling, Ont., Can., 1,315 C7 72
Stirling, Que., Can B5 73
Stirling, Morris, N.J., 1,500 B4 106
Stirling, Scot., 27,553 D5 13
Stirling, co., Scot., 194,858 D4 13
Stirling City, Butte, Calif., 350 C3 82
Stirrat, Logan, W. Va., 900 D3 123
Stirum, Sargent, N. Dak., 80 C8 110
Stissing, mtn., N.Y. B2 84
Stites, Idaho, Idaho, 299 C2 89
Stittsville, Ont., Can., 1,508 B9 72
Stjördal, Nor., 6,133 F4 25
Stoa Pikt, Pima, Ariz., 25 E3 80
Stobnica, Pol., 2,000 E8 24
Stockbridge, Henry, Ga., 1,201 C2 87
Stockbridge, Berkshire, Mass., 900 (2,161▲) B1 97
Stockbridge, Ingham, Mich., 1,097 F6 98
Stockbridge, Windsor, Vt., 40 (392▲) D3 120
Stockbridge, Calumet, Wis., 476 B5, D5 124
Stockbridge, Indian res., Wis D4 124
Stockdale, Pike, Ohio, 175 D5 111
Stockdale, Wilson, Tex., 1,111 B4, E4 118
Stockerau, Aus., 11,853 D8 16
Stockertown, Northampton, Pa., 777 E11 114
Stockett, Cascade, Mont., 400 C5 102
Stockham, Hamilton, Nebr., 69 D8 103
Stockholm, Sask., Can., 238 G4 70
Stockholm, Aroostook, Maine, 500 (649▲) A4 96
Stockholm, Sussex, N.J., 200 A3 106
Stockholm, Grant, S. Dak., 155 B9 116
Stockholm, Swe., 802,100 (*1,160,000) H8, t36 25
Stockholm, Pepin, Wis., 106 D1 124
Stockholm, co., Swe., 487,100 *H8 25
Stockhorn, mtn., Switz C4 19
Stockland, Iroquois, Ill., 150 C6 90
Stockport, Eng., 142,700 A5 12
Stockport, Van Buren, Iowa, 342 D6 92
Stockport, Morgan, Ohio, 458 C6 111
Stockton, Baldwin, Ala., 900 E2 78
Stockton, San Joaquin, Calif., 86,321 (*160,000) B6, D3 82
Stockton, Man., Can., 61 E2 71
Stockton, Lanier, Ga., 500 F4 87
Stockton, Jo Daviess, Ill., 1,800 A3 90
Stockton, Rooks, Kans., 2,073 C4 93
Stockton, Worcester, Md., 300 D7 85
Stockton, Cedar, Mo., 838 D4 101
Stockton, Hunterdon, N.J., 520 C3 106
Stockton, Chautauqua, N.Y., 300 C1 108
Stockton, Tooele, Utah, 362 C3 119
Stockton, isl., Wis B3 124
Stockton-on-Tees, Eng., 83,700 C6 10
Stockton Springs, Waldo, Maine, 400 (980▲) D4 96
Stockville, Frontier, Nebr., 91 D5 103
Stockwell, Tippecanoe, Ind., 400 D4 91
Stod, Czech., 2,502 D8 17
Stoddard, Cheshire, N.H., 100 (146▲) D2 105
Stoddard, Vernon, Wis., 552 E2 124
Stoddard, co., Mo., 29,490 E8 101
Stoeckl, mtn., B.C., Can A2 68
Stoke Centre, Que., Can D6 73
Stoke-on-Trent, Eng., 266,100 (*440,000) A5 12
Stokes, Pitt, N.C., 195 B6 109
Stokes, co., N.C., 22,314 A3 109
Stokesdale, Guilford, N.C., 900 A4 109
Stokesley, Eng., 1,980 F7 13
Stokke, Nor p28 25
Stolac, Yugo., 2,950 D3 22
Stolberg, Ger., 37,500 C3 16
Stolbovaya, Sov. Un n17 27
Stollberg, Ger., 13,000 C7 17
Stolbovoy, isl., Sov. Un B1 4
Stolzenau, Ger., 2,800 F3 24
Stone, Eng., 8,791 B5 12
Stone, Oneida, Idaho, 20 G6 89
Stone, Pike, Ky., 728 C7 94
Stone, co., Ark., 6,294 B3 81
Stone, co., Miss., 7,013 E4 100
Stone, co., Mo., 8,176 E4 101
Stone, lake, Wis C5 124
Stone, mtn., Ga C2 89
Stone, mtn., Tenn D10 117
Stone, mtn., Vt B5 120
Stone, mts., Tenn C12 117
Stonebluff, Fountain, Ind., 170 D3 91
Stoneboro, Mercer, Pa., 1,267 D1 114
Stoneboro, Kershaw, S.C., 100 B6 115
Stone City, Pueblo, Colo., 35 C6 83
Stone City, Jones, Iowa, 200 B6 92
Stone Corral, lake, Oreg E7 113
Stonefort, Saline and Williamson, Ill., 349 F5 90
Stonega, Wise, Va., 800 B2 121
Stoneham, Weld, Colo., 80 A7 83
Stoneham, Middlesex, Mass., 17,821 g11 97
Stone Harbor, Cape May, N.J., 834 E3 106
Stonehaven, N.B., Can., 95 B4 74
Stonehaven, Scot., 4,500 D6 13
Stonehenge, Austl., 38 B4 51
Stone Lake, Sawyer, Wis., 175 C2 124
Stoneleigh, Baltimore, Md., 8,000 *B4 85
Stone Mountain, De Kalb, Ga., 1,976 B5, C2 87
Stone Park, Cook, Ill., 3,038 *F2 90
Stoner, B.C., Can., 163 C6 68
Stoner, Montezuma, Colo., 30 D2 83
Stones, riv., Tenn A5 117
Stones River, nat. battlefield and cemetery, Tenn B5 117
Stones River Homes, Rutherford, Tenn., 1,800 *B5 117
Stoneville, Washington, Miss., 300 B3 100
Stoneville, Rockingham, N.C., 951 A4 109
Stoneville, Meade, S. Dak., 9 C3 116
Stonewall, Man., Can., 1,420 D3 71
Stonewall, Fulton, Ga., 800 B4 87
Stonewall, De Soto, La., 100 B2 95
Stonewall, Clarke, Miss., 1,126 C5 100
Stonewall, Pontotoc, Okla., 584 C5 112
Stonewall, Gillespie, Tex., 170 D3 118
Stonewall, co., Tex., 3,017 C2 118
Stonewood, Harrison, W. Va., 2,202 *B4 123
Stoney, creek, Va D5 121
Stoney Creek, Ont., Can., 6,043 D5 72
Stonington, Baca, Colo., 36 D8 83
Stonington, New London, Conn., 1,622 (13,969▲) D8 84
Stonington, Christian, Ill., 1,076 D4 90
Stonington, Hancock, Maine, 800 (1,408▲) D4 96
Stonington, Delta, Mich., 25 C4 98
Stono, inlet, S.C. F8 115
Stono, riv., S.C. F2 115
Stony, brook, N.J. C3 106
Stony, isl., Newf., Can B4 75
Stony, isl., N.Y. B4 108
Stony, lake, Ont., Can C6 72
Stony, riv., W. Va B5 123
Stony Beach, Sask., Can., 40 G3 70
Stony Brook, Suffolk, N.Y., 4,000 F4 84
Stony Brook, hbr., N.Y. F4 84
Stony Creek, New Haven, Conn., 600 D5 84
Stony Creek, Warren, N.Y., 450 B7 108
Stony Creek, Sussex, Va., 437 E5 121
Stony Creek Mills, Berks, Pa., 1,500 *F10 114
Stonyford, Colusa, Calif., 125 C2 82
Stony Mountain, Man., Can., 1,130 D3 71
Stony Plain, Alta., Can., 1,311 C3 69
Stony Point, Rockland, N.Y., 3,000 A5 106
Stony Point, Alexander, N.C., 1,015 B2 109
Stony Rapids, Sask., Can., 107 m7 70
Stony Ridge, Wood, Ohio, 335 A2 111
Stor, riv., Ger B4 16
Storaa, riv., Den B2 24
Stora Luleträsk, lake, Swe D8 25
Stora Sundby, Swe t34 25
Storavan, lake, Swe E8 25
Storden, Cottonwood, Minn., 390 F3 99
Store Belt, strait, Den C4 24
Store-Heddinge, Den., 2,082 C6 24
Storey, co., Nev., 568 D2 104
Storfjord, fjord, Nor F2 25
Storkow, Ger., 4,738 A8 17
Storla, Aurora, S. Dak., 50 D7 116
Storm, lake, Iowa B2 92
Storm Lake, Buena Vista, Iowa, 7,728 B2 92
Stormont, co., Ont., Can., 57,867 B9 72
Stornoway, Sask., Can., 89 F4 70
Stornoway, Scot., 5,221 B2 13
Storozhinets, Sov. Un., 10,000 G5 27
Storr, mtn., Scot C2 13
Storrs, Tolland, Conn., 8,000 B7 84
Storsjön, lake, Swe F6 25
Storsjö, Swe F5 25
Storthoaks, Sask., Can., 227 H5 70
Storuman, lake, Swe E7 25
Story, Sheridan, Wyo., 200 A6 125
Story, co., Iowa, 49,327 B4 92
Story City, Story, Iowa, 1,773 B4 92
Story Prairie, Sandusky, Ohio, 1,720 *A4 111
Stotesbury, Vernon, Mo., 64 D3 101
Stotts City, Lawrence, Mo., 221 D4 101
Stottville, Columbia, N.Y., 1,040 C7 108
Stouffville, Ont., Can., 3,188 D5, k15 72
Stoughton, Sask., Can., 606 H4 70
Stoughton, Norfolk, Mass., 16,328 B5, h11 97
Stoughton, Dane, Wis., 5,555 F4 124
Stour, riv., Eng C8 12
Stour, riv., Eng C9 12
Stour, riv., Eng D5 12
Stourbridge, Eng., 44,900 B5 12
Stourport-on-Severn, Eng., 11,751 B5 12
Stout, Grundy, Iowa, 145 B5 92
Stout (Rome), Adams, Ohio, 149 D4 111
Stoutland, Camden, Mo., 172 D5 101
Stoutsville, Monroe, Mo., 109 B6 101
Stoutsville, Fairfield, Ohio, 500 C5 111
Stovall, Meriwether, Ga., 250 D2 87
Stovall, Coahoma, Miss., 125 A3 100
Stovall, Granville, N.C., 570 A5 109
Stove Creek, Sask., Can E4 70
Stover, Tallahatchie, Miss., 150 A3 100
Stover, Morgan, Mo., 757 C4 101
Støvring, Den., 1,373 B3 24
Stow, Oxford, Maine., 25 (108▲) D2 96
Stow, Middlesex, Mass., 950 (2,573▲) B4, g9 97
Stow, Summit, Ohio, 12,194 A6 111
Stow, creek, N.J. E2 106
Stowe [Township], Allegheny, Pa., 11,730 *B5 114
Stowe, Montgomery, Pa., 3,501 F10 114
Stowe, Lamoille, Vt., 534 (1,901▲) C3 120
Stowmarket, Eng., 7,790 B8 12
Stoy, Crawford, Ill., 185 D6 90
Stoyoma, mtn., B.C., Can E7 68
Stoystown, Somerset, Pa., 468 F4 114
Strabane, N. Ire., 7,786 C4 11
Strabane, Washington, Pa., 1,940 F1 114
Strachur, Scot., 578 D3 13
Stradbally, Ire., 792 D4 11
Strader, Tangipahoa, La B7 95
Stradone, Ire., 113 D4 11
Strafford, Greene, Mo., 300 D4 101
Strafford, Strafford, N.H., 135 (722▲) D4 105
Strafford, Chester, Pa., 2,500 *A10 114
Strafford, Orange, Vt., 75 (548▲) D4 120
Strafford, co., N.H., 59,799 D4 105
Straffordville, Ont., Can., 487 E4 72
Strakonice, Czech., 14,100 D2 26
Straldzha, Bul., 5,348 D8 22
Stralsund, Ger., 67,000 A6 16
Strandburg, Grant, S. Dak., 105 B9 116
Strandby, Den., 1,303 A4 24
Strandhill, Ire., 301 C3 11
Strandquist, Marshall, Minn., 160 B2 99
Strang, Fillmore, Nebr., 68 D8 103
Strang, Mayes, Okla., 176 A6 112
Stranger, creek, Kans B8 93
Strangford, N. Ire., 413 C6 11
Strangford, lake, N. Ire C6 11
Strängnäs, Swe., 8,300 t35 25
Strångsjö, Swe., 241 u34 25
Stranraer, Sask., Can., 78 F1 70
Stranraer, Scot., 9,249 F3 13
Strasbourg, Sask., Can., 636 F3 70
Strasbourg, Fr., 228,971 (*320,000) C7 14, F7 15
Strasburg, Adams and Arapahoe, Colo., 439 B6 83
Strasburg, Ger., 6,994 E7 24
Strasburg, Shelby, Ill., 467 D5 90
Strasburg, Cass, Mo., 213 C3 101
Strasburg, Emmons, N. Dak., 612 C5 110
Strasburg, Tuscarawas, Ohio, 1,687 B6 111
Strasburg, Lancaster, Pa., 1,416 G9 114
Strasburg, Shenandoah, Va., 2,428 C4 121
Strass, Aus., 495 B7 18
Strasswalchen, Aus., 4,163 B9 18
Stratford, Kings, Calif., 500 D4 82
Stratford, Ont., Can., 20,467 D3 72
Stratford, Fairfield, Conn., 45,012 E4 84
Stratford, Hamilton and Webster, Iowa, 703 B4 92
Stratford, Coos, N.H., 130 (1,029▲) A3 105
Stratford, Camden, N.J., 4,308 D2 106
Stratford, Fulton, N.Y., 250 B6 108
Stratford, N.Z., 5,273 M15 51
Stratford, Garvin, Okla., 1,058 C5 112
Stratford, Brown, S. Dak., 109 B7 116
Stratford, Sherman, Tex., 1,380 A1 118
Stratford, Marathon, Wis., 1,106 D3 124
Stratford, pt., Conn E4 84
Stratford Centre, Que., Can., 461 D6 73
Stratford Hills, Chesterfield, Va., 2,500 *D5 121
Stratford-on-Avon, Eng., 17,000 B6 12
Stratham, Rockingham, N.H., 160 (1,033▲) D5 105
Strathaven, Scot., 5,867 E4 13
Strathclair, Man., Can., 465 D1 71
Strathcona, Ont., Can., 106 C8 72
Strathcona, Roseau, Minn., 64 B2 99
Strathcona, prov. park, B.C., Can E5 68
Strathlorne, N.S., Can., 176 C8 74
Strathmere, Cape May, N.J., 100 E3 106
Strathmore, Tulare, Calif., 1,095 D4 82
Strathmore, Alta., Can., 924 D4 69
Strathroy, Ont., Can., 5,150 E3 72
Strattanville, Clarion, Pa., 547 D3 114
Stratton, Ont., Can., 112 *D5 72
Stratton, Kit Carson, Colo., 680 B8 83
Stratton, Franklin, Maine, 500 C2 96
Stratton, Hitchcock, Nebr., 492 D4 103
Stratton, Jefferson, Ohio, 311 B7 111
Stratton (Town of), Windham, Vt. (38▲) *E3 120
Stratton, mtn., Vt E3 120
Straubing, Ger., 36,300 E7 17
Straubville, Sargent, N. Dak., 40 C8 110
Straughn, Henry, Ind., 349 E7 91
Strausberg, Ger., 13,800 F7 24
Strausstown, Berks, Pa., 380 F9 114
Straw, Fergus, Mont D7 102
Strawberry, Lawrence, Ark., 200 B4 81
Strawberry, mtn., Oreg C8 113
Strawberry, mts., Oreg C8 113
Strawberry, pt., Mass B6 97
Strawberry, res., Utah C4 119
Strawberry, riv., Ark A4 81
Strawberry, riv., Utah C5 119
Strawberry Plains, Jefferson, Tenn., 400 C10 117
Strawberry Point, Marin, Calif., 1,500 *B5 82
Strawberry Point, Clayton, Iowa, 1,303 B6 92
Strawberry Daniels, pass, Utah C4 119
Strawn, Livingston, Ill., 152 B5 90
Strawn, Coffey, Kans., 100 D8 93
Strawn, Palo Pinto, Tex., 817 C3 118
Straznice, Czech., 4,989 D4 26
Streamstown, Alta., Can., 55 C5 69
Streamwood, Cook, Ill., 6,751 *A5 90
Streator, La Salle and Livingston, Ill., 16,868 B5 90
Streator East, La Salle, Ill., 1,517 *B5 90
Streeter, Stutsman, N. Dak., 491 C6 110
Streeter, Mason, Tex., 30 D3 118
Streetman, Freestone and Navarro, Tex., 300 D4 118
Streetsboro, Portage, Ohio, 1,000 *A6 111
Streetsville, Ont., Can., 5,056 m14 72
Strehaia, Rom., 8,545 C6 22
Strehlen, see Strzelin, Pol.
Strelka, Sov. Un C13 28
Strelka, Sov. Un D27 9
Stresa, It., 2,953 B2 18
Stretford, Eng., 60,600 *A5 12
Stribling, Stewart, Tenn A4 117
Stribro, Czech., 3,950 D8 17
Strichen, Scot., 1,949 C6 13
Strimon, gulf, Grc B4 23
Strimon, riv., Grc B4 23
Stringer, Jasper, Miss., 150 D4 100
Stringtown, Lake, Colo., 500 B4 83
Stringtown, Anderson, Ky., 300 B5 94
Stringtown, Bolivar, Miss., 150 B3 100
Stringtown, Atoka, Okla., 414 C5 112
Strofadhes, isl., Grc D3 23
Stroh, Lagrange, Ind., 475 A7 91
Strokestown, Ire., 707 D3 11
Stroma, isl., Scot B5 13
Stromboli, isl., It E5 21
Strome, Alta., Can., 311 C4 69
Strome Ferry, Scot C3 13
Stromness, Scot., 1,477 B5 13
Stromsburg, Polk, Nebr., 1,244 C8 103
Stronach, Manistee, Mich., 350 D4 98
Stroner, Crook, Wyo., 5 A8 125
Strong, Union, Ark., 741 D3 81
Strong, Franklin, Maine, 300 (976▲) D2 96
Strong, Monroe, Miss., 300 B5 100
Strong, riv., Miss C4 100
Strong City, Chase, Kans., 659 D7 93
Strong City, Roger Mills, Okla., 51 B2 112
Strongfield, Sask., Can., 218 F2 70
Stronghurst, Henderson, Ill., 815 C3 90
Strongs, Chippewa, Mich., 225 B6 98
Strongsville, Cuyahoga, Ohio, 8,504 A6, B2 111
Stronsay, firth, Scot A6 13
Stronsay, isl., Scot A6 13
Strontian, Scot D3 13
Stroud, Eng., 17,461 C5 12
Stroud, Lincoln, Okla., 2,456 B5 112
Stroudsburg, Monroe, Pa., 6,070 E11 114
Stroudsburg West, Monroe, Pa., 1,569 *E11 114
Struble, Plymouth, Iowa, 74 B1 92
Struer, Den., 8,335 B2 24
Struga, Yugo., 6,871 E5 22
Strule, riv., Ire C4 11
Strum, Trempealeau, Wis., 663 D2 124
Struma, riv., Bul E6 22
Strumble, head, Wales B2 12
Strumica, Yugo., 15,978 E6 22
Strunk, McCreary, Ky., 450 D5 94
Struthers, Mahoning, Ohio, 15,631 A7 111
Stryama, riv., Bul D7 22
Stryker, Lincoln, Mont., 65 B2 102
Stryker, Williams, Ohio, 1,205 A3 111
Strykersville, Wyoming, N.Y., 400 C2 108
Stryy, Sov. Un., 36,180 G4 27
Stryy, riv., Sov. Un D7 26
Strzegom, Pol., 7,137 C4 26
Strzelce, Pol., 10,300 C5 26
Strzelce. Krajenskie, Pol., 1,552 B3 26
Strzelecki, creek, Austl D3 51
Strzelin, Pol., 7,334 C4 26
Strzelno, Pol., 5,264 B5 26
Strzemieszyce, Pol g10 26
Stuart, Martin, Fla., 4,791 E6 86
Stuart, Guthrie and Adair, Iowa, 1,486 C3 92
Stuart, Holt, Nebr., 794 B6 103
Stuart, Hughes, Okla., 271 C5 112
Stuart, Patrick, Va., 974 E2 121
Stuart, lake, B.C., Can B5 68
Stuart, mtn., Wash B4 122
Stuart, riv., B.C., Can B5 68
Stuart, range, Austl E5 50
Stuarts Draft, Augusta, Va., 600 C3 121
Stub, hill, N.H A2 105
Stubbekøbing, Den., 2,097 D6 24
Studley, Sheridan, Kans., 60 C3 93
Stull, Douglas, Kans., 35 B7 93
Stull, lake, Ont., Can B5 71
Stull, riv., Man., Can B5 71
Stump, lake, N. Dak B7 110
Stump Creek, Jefferson, Pa. D4 114
Stumptown, Gilmer, W. Va., 100 C4 123
Stumpy Point, Dare, N.C., 250 B8 109
Stung Treng, Camb., 10,000 F6 38
Stupart, riv., Man., Can B4 71
Stupino, Sov. Un., 36,000 D12 27
Stura, riv., It D3 18
Sturbridge, Worcester, Mass., 800 (3,604▲) B3 97
Sturgeon, Boone, Mo., 619 B5 101
Sturgeon, Allegheny, Pa., 1,000 *F1 114
Sturgeon, bay, Man., Can C3 71
Sturgeon, lake, Alta., Can B2 69
Sturgeon, lake, Ont., Can C6 72
Sturgeon, riv., Sask., Can D2 70
Sturgeon Bay, Door, Wis., 7,353 D6 124
Sturgeon Falls, Ont., Can., 6,288 A5 72
Sturgeon Lake, Pine, Minn., 151 D6 99
Sturgeon Landing, Sask., Can., 104 C5 70
Sturgeon-weir, riv., Sask., Can C4 70
Sturgis, Sask., Can., 611 F4 70
Sturgis, Union, Ky., 2,209 C2 94
Sturgis, St. Joseph, Mich., 8,915 G5 98
Sturgis, Oktibbeha, Miss., 358 B4 100
Sturgis, Meade, S. Dak., 4,639 C2 116
Sturmill, Dallas, Ark D3 80
Sturt, creek, Austr C4 50
Sturtevant, Racine, Wis., 1,488 F2, F6 124
Stutsman, co., N. Dak., 25,137 B6 110
Stutterheim, S. Afr., 9,015 D4 49
Stuttgart, Arkansas, Ark., 9,661 C4 81
Stuttgart, Ger., 634,700 (*1,415,000) E4 17
Stuttgart, Phillips, Kans., 100 C4 93
Styr, riv., Sov. Un F5 27

Styria, reg., Aus. E7 16
Su, China H7 36
Suakin, Sud., 4,228 B4 47
Suao, Taiwan, 5,000 *G9 34
Subiaco, Logan, Ark., 290 B2 81
Subi-Besar, isl., Indon K8 38
Subic, Phil., 2,000 (13,000▲) C6, o13 35
Subic, bay, Phil o13 35
Sublette, Lee, Ill., 306 B4 90
Sublette, Haskell, Kans., 1,077 E3 93
Sublette, co., Wyo., 3,778 C2 125
Sublimity, Marion, Oreg., 490 C2, C4 113
Subotica, Yugo., 74,832 B4 22
Sucarnoochee, Kemper, Miss., 100 C5 100
Sucarnoochee, creek, Ala., Miss C5 100
Succasunna, Morris, N.J., 3,300 B3 106
Success, Clay, Ark., 226 A5 81
Success, Sask., Can., 117 G1 70
Suceava, Rom., 23,200 (58,800▲) B8 22
Suceava, riv., Rom B7 22
Sucha, Pol., 5,866 D5 26
Suchan, Sov. Un., 48,505 E6 37
Suchdol, Czech., 3,730 n17 26
Suches, Union, Ga., 600 B2 87
Suchitoto, Sal., 4,380 D3 62
Suchocin, Pol., 500 k13 26
Suchou, see Soochow, China
Suchow, China, 676,000 E8 34
Suck, riv., Ire D3 11
Sucre, Bol., 55,000 C2 55
Sucre, state, Ven., 401,992 A5 60
Suçuapara, Braz., 1,860 B3 59
Sucuriú, riv., Braz B2 56
Sucy-en-Brie, Fr., 13,258 g11 14
Sudan, Lamb, Tex., 1,235 B1 118
Sudan, country, Afr., 13,350,000 E8 42, C2 47
Sudan, reg., Afr E7 42
Sudbury, Ont., Can., 80,120 (*110,694) A4, p19 72
Sudbury, Eng., 6,643 B8 12
Sudbury, Middlesex, Mass., 1,200 (7,447▲) B5, g10 97
Sudbury, Rutland, Vt., 30 (249▲) D2 120
Sudbury, dist., Ont., Can., 165,862 A3 72
Sudbury, res., Mass g9 97
Sudbury, riv., Mass B5 97
Sudbury Center, Middlesex, Mass., 800 *B5 97
Sudd, swamp, Sud D2 47
Süderbrarup, Ger., 3,200 D4 15
Sudetes, mts., Pol C4 26
Sudlersville, Queen Annes, Md., 394 B6 85
Sudley, Anne Arundel, Md., 80 C4 85
Sud-Nord, canal, Ger B7 15
Sudogda, Sov. Un., 10,500 D13 27
Sudzha, Sov. Un., 10,000 F10 27
Sue, cape, Sov. Un G19 9
Sueca, Sp., 20,612 C5 20
Suez, Eg., U.A.R., 203,610 C6 43
Suez, canal, Eg., U.A.R C6 43
Suez, gulf, Afr D6 43
Suffern, Rockland, N.Y., 5,504 D6, m14 108
Suffield, Alta., Can., 130 D5 69
Suffield, Hartford, Conn., 1,110 (6,779▲) B6 84
Suffolk, Fergus, Mont., 10 C7 102
Suffolk (Independent City), Va., 12,609 B6, E6 121
Suffolk (East Suffolk, West Suffolk), co., Eng., 472,665 B8 12
Suffolk, co., Mass., 791,329 B5 97
Suffolk, co., N.Y., 666,784 n15 108
Sufu, see Kashgar, China
Sugar, creek, Ind F6 91
Sugar, creek, Ind E3 91
Sugar, creek, Pa C8 114
Sugar, isl., Mich B6 98
Sugar, riv., N.H D2 105
Sugar, riv., Wis F4 124
Sugar City, Crowley, Colo., 409 C7 83
Sugar City, Madison, Idaho, 584 F7 89
Sugar Creek, Jackson, Mo., 2,663 E2 101
Sugarcreek, Tuscarawas, Ohio, 982 *B6 111
Sugar Grove, Logan, Ark., 100 B2 81
Sugar Grove, Watauga, N.C., 500 A2 109
Sugar Grove, Fairfield, Ohio, 479 C5 111
Sugargrove, Warren, Pa., 636 C3 114
Sugar Grove, Smyth, Va., 800 B3, E1 121
Sugar Grove, Pendleton, W. Va., 50 C5 123
Sugar Hill, Gwinnett, Ga., 1,175 B2 87
Sugar Hill, Grafton, N.H., 100 B3 105
Sugar Land, Fort Bend, Tex., 2,802 E5 F4 118
Sugarloaf, hill, Ohio A6 111
Sugarloaf, mtn., Maine C2 96
Sugar Loaf, mtn., Md B3 85
Sugarloaf, mtn., Mont C4 102
Sugarloaf, mtn., N.H A4, B1 105
Sugarloaf, mts., Okla B7 112
Sugar Notch, Luzerne, Pa., 1,524 B8 114
Sugarpine, mtn., Oreg D5 113
Sugar Run, Bradford, Pa., 65 C9 114
Sugar Tree, Decatur, Tenn., 40 B3 117
Sugar Valley, Gordon, Ga., 165 B1 87
Sugden, Jefferson, Okla., 68 C4 112
Suget, pass, China, India B6 39
Suggi, lake, Sask., Can C4 70
Suggsville, Clarke, Ala., 100 D2 78
Sugluk, Que., Can., 255 f11 73
Suhār, Mus. & Om., 5,000 D2 39
Suhl, Ger., 25,500 C5 17
Sui, China G6 36
Suiattle, riv., Wash A4 122
Suichi, China, 1,000 B9 38
Suichiang, China, 5,000 F5 34
Suichuan, China, 13,000 F7 34
Suichung, China D9 36
Suifenho, China C11 34
Suihsien, China, 31,000 E7 34
Suihua (Peilintzu), China, 40,000 B10 34
Suilai, see Manas, China
Suileng, China, 5,000 C3 37
Suilu, China A7 38
Suipacha, Arg., 3,006 g7 54
Suipacha, Bol D2 55
Suipin, China, 5,000 C5 37
Suippes, Fr., 2,738 E4 15
Suir, riv., Ire E4 11
Suisun City, Solano, Calif., 2,470 B5 82
Suita, Jap., 116,765 *o14 37
Suite, China, 15,000 D7 34
Suiter, Bland, Va D1 121
Suitland, Prince Georges, Md., 10,300 C2 85
Suitung, China C9 36
Sukabumi, Indon, 78,806 G3 35
Sukadana, Indon F3 35
Sukarnapura, W. Irian, 16,300 F10 35
Sukhaya Tunguska, Sov. Un B26 9
Sukhobuzimskoye, Sov. Un., 10,000 D27 9
Sukhona, riv., Sov. Un C17 9
Sukhumi, Sov. Un., 81,000 G17 9
Sukkur, Pak., 103,216 C4 38, D2 40
Sukunka, riv., B.C., Can B7 68
Sul, chan., Braz C5 59
Sula, Ravalli, Mont., 5 E3 102
Sula, isl., Indon F6 35
Sula, riv., Sov. Un F9 27
Sulaiman, range, Pak C4 40
Sulecin, Pol., 2,566 B3 26
Sulgen, Switz., 1,252 *A7 19
Sulina, Rom., 3,622 C9 22
Sulingen, Ger., 7,300 F2 24
Sulitjelma, mtn., Swe D7 25
Suliwula, mtn., China D4 34
Sullana, Peru, 26,330 B1 58
Sulligent, Lamar, Ala., 1,346 B1 78
Sullivan, Moultrie, Ill., 3,946 D5 90
Sullivan, Sullivan, Ind., 4,979 F3 91
Sullivan, Union, Ky., 250 C2 94
Sullivan, Franklin and Crawford, Mo., 4,098 C6 101
Sullivan, Cheshire, N.H., 35 (261▲) D2 105
Sullivan, Ashland, Ohio, 340 A5 111
Sullivan, Jefferson, Wis., 418 E5 124
Sullivan, co., Ind., 21,721 F3 91
Sullivan, co., Mo., 8,783 A4 101
Sullivan, co., N.H., 28,067 D2 105
Sullivan, co., N.Y., 45,272 D6 108
Sullivan, co., Pa., 6,251 D8 114
Sullivan, co., Tenn., 114,139 C11 117
Sullivan, isl., Bur G3 38
Sullivan, lake, Alta., Can D5 69
Sullivans Island, Charleston, S.C., 1,358 F3 115
Sully, Jasper, Iowa, 508 C5 92
Sully, co., S. Dak., 2,607 C5 111
Sulmona, It., 18,400 C4 26
Sulphide, Ont., Can., 217 C7 72
Sulphur, Henry, Ky., 275 B4 94
Sulphur, Calcasieu, La., 11,429 D2 95
Sulphur, Murray, Okla., 4,737 C5 112
Sulphur, fork, Tenn A4 117
Sulphur, riv., Ark., Tex D1 75, C5 118
Sulphur, riv., Alta., Can C1 69
Sulphurdale, Beaver, Utah, 20 E3 119
Sulphur Rock, Independence, Ark., 225 B4 81
Sulphur South, Calcasieu, La., 1,351 *D2 95
Sulphur Spring, val., Ariz E6 80
Sulphur Springs, Benton, Ark., 460 A1 81
Sulphur Springs, Henry, Ind., 400 D7 91
Sulphur Springs, Jefferson, Mo., 110 B8 101
Sulphur Springs, Crawford, Ohio, 350 B5 111
Sulphur Springs, Douglas, Oreg D3 113
Sulphur Springs, Hopkins, Tex., 9,160 C5 118
Sultan, Snohomish, Wash., 821 B4 122
Sultanabad, India H7 40
Sultanabad, see Arāk, Iran
Sultanpur, India, 26,081 D9 40
Sulu, prov., Phil., 327,100 *D6 35
Sulu, arch., Phil D6 35
Sulu, riv., China C4 34
Sulu, sea, Phil D6 35
Sulūq, Libya, 1,000 C4 43
Sulyukta, Sov. Un., 15,000 H22 9
Sulzbach, Ger., 23,800 D2 17
Sulzbach-Rosenberg, Ger., 19,600 D6 17
Sulzberger bay, Ant B33 5
Sumach, Yakima, Wash., 1,345 *C5 122
Sumas, Whatcom, Wash., 629 A3 122
Sumatra, Liberty, Fla., 250 B2 86
Sumatra, Rosebud, Mont., 25 D9 102
Sumatra, isl., Indon E2 35
Sumava Resorts, Newton, Ind., 200 B2 91
Sumay, Guam 52
Sumba, isl., Indon G6 35
Sumbar, riv., Sov. Un B7 41
Sumbawa, Indon G5 35
Sumbawanga, Tan, 4,590 C5 48
Sumbay, Peru E3 58
Sumburgh, pt., Scot h10 10
Sumeg, Hung., 5,941 B3 24
Sumenep, Indon., 17,824 G4 35
Sumgait, Sov. Un., 68,000 A4 41
Sumiswald, Switz., 5,525 B4 19
Sumiton, Walker, Ala., 1,287 B2 78
Summan, des., Sau. Ar H3 41
Summer, isl., Mich C4 98
Summer, lake, Oreg E6 113
Summerberry, Sask., Can., 84 G4 70
Summerberry, riv., Man., Can C1 71
Summerdale, Baldwin, Ala., 533 E2 78
Summerdale, Cumberland, Pa., 1,200 *F8 114
Summerfield, Marion, Fla., 450 C4 86
Summerfield, Marshall, Kans., 237 C7 93
Summerfield, Claiborne, La., 200 B3 95
Summerfield, Maries, Mo., 100 C6 101
Summerfield, Guilford, N.C., 700 A4 109
Summerfield, Noble, Ohio, 352 C6 111
Summerfield, Castro, Tex., 45 B1 118
Summerford, Newf., Can., 570 D4 75
Summer Hill, Pike, Ill., 150 D3 90
Summerhill, Ire., 97 D5 11
Summer Lake, Lake, Oreg., 5 E6 113
Summerland, B.C., Can., 4,307 E8 68
Summerland Key, Monroe, Fla., 350 H5 87
Summers, co., W. Va., 15,640 D4 123
Summerset, Warren, Iowa B7 92
Summer Shade, Metcalfe, Ky., 250 D4 94
Summerside, P.E.I., Can., 8,611 C6 74
Summersville, Green, Ky., 350 D4 94
Summersville, Texas, Mo., 356 D6 101
Summersville, Nicholas, W. Va., 2,008 C4, C7 123
Summerton, Clarendon, S.C., 1,504 D7 115
Summertown, Emanuel, Ga., 100 D4 87
Summertown, Lawrence, Tenn., 900 B4 117
Summerville, Chattooga, Ga., 4,706 B1 87
Summerville, Union, Oreg., 76 B8 113
Summerville, Jefferson, Pa., 895 D3 114
Summerville, Dorchester, S.C., 3,633 E2, E7 115
Summit, Marion, Ark., 239 A3 81
Summit, San Bernardino, Calif., 150 F3 82
Summit, C.Z., 48 k11 62
Summit, Cook, Ill., 10,374 F2 90
Summit, Pike, Miss., 1,663 D3 100
Summit, Union, N.J., 23,677 B4 106
Summit, Benton, Oreg., 50 C3 114
Summit, Kent, R.I., 130 C10 84
Summit, Roberts, S. Dak., 283 B8 116
Summit, Hamilton, Tenn., 200 E10 117
Summit, Iron, Utah, 140 F3 119
Summit, co., Colo., 2,073 B4 83
Summit, co., Ohio, 513,569 A6 111
Summit, co., Utah, 5,673 C5 119
Summit, lake, Iowa C3 92
Summit, mtn., Nev D5 104
Summit, mtn., N.Z N16 51
Summit, peak, Colo D4 83
Summit Hill, Carbon, Pa., 4,386 E10 114
Summit Lake, B.C., Can., 117 B6 68
Summit Lake, Indian res., Nev B3 104
Summit Point, Jefferson, W. Va., 150 B7 123
Summit Station, Licking, Ohio, 400 C2 111
Summitville, Rio Grande, Colo., 20 D4 83
Summitville, Madison, Ind., 1,048 D6 91
Summitville, Coffee, Tenn., 400 B6 117
Summum, Fulton, Ill., 225 C3 90
Sumner, Worth, Ga., 193 E3 87
Sumner, Lawrence, Ill., 1,035 E6 90
Sumner, Bremer, Iowa, 2,170 B5 92
Sumner, Gratiot, Mich., 85 E6 98
Sumner, Tallahatchie, Miss., 551 B3 100
Sumner, Chariton, Mo., 234 B4 101
Sumner, Dawson, Nebr., 254 D6 103
Sumner, Noble, Okla., 27 A4 112
Sumner, Pierce, Wash., 3,156 B3 122
Sumner, co., Kans., 25,316 E6 93
Sumner, co., Tenn., 36,217 A5 117
Sumner, strait, Alsk m23 79
Sumoto, Jap., 34,000 (48,497▲) I7 37
Sumperk, Czech., 19,400 D4 26
Sumpter, Baker, Oreg., 96 C8 113
Sumrall, Lamar, Miss., 797 D4 100
Sumter, Sumter, Ga., 100 E2 87
Sumter, Sumter, S.C., 23,062 D7 115
Sumter, co., Ala., 20,041 C1 78
Sumter, co., Fla., 11,869 D4 86
Sumter, co., Ga., 24,652 D2 87
Sumter, co., S.C., 74,941 D7 115
Sumterville, Sumter, Ala., 50 C1 78
Sumurr, Maricopa, Ariz E3 80
Sumy, Sov. Un., 117,000 F10 27
Sun, St. Tammany, La., 224 D6 95
Sun, riv., Mont C4 102
Suna, Tan C5 48
Sunagawa, Jap., 24,200 E10 37
Sunapee, Sullivan, N.H., (1,164▲) D2 105
Sunapee, lake, N.H D2 105
Sunapee, mtn., N.H D2 105
Sunart, inlet, Scot D3 13
Sunbeam, Custer, Idaho, 5 E4 89
Sunbright, Morgan, Tenn., 550 C9 117
Sunbright, Scott, Va B2 121
Sunburg, Kandiyohi, Minn., 161 E3 99
Sunburst, Toole, Mont., 882 B5 102
Sunbury, Livingston, Ill. B5 90
Sunbury, Gates, N.C., 450 A7 109
Sunbury, Delaware, Ohio, 1,360 B5 111
Sunbury, Northumberland, Pa., 13,687 E8 114
Sunbury, co., N.B., Can., 22,796 D3 74
Sunchales, Arg., 5,048 A4 54
Suncho Corral, Arg., 3,020 E2 55
Sunchon, Kor., 20,682 G2 37
Sunchon, Kor., 46,000 (72,000▲) I3 37
Sun City, Maricopa, Ariz., 2,000 *D3 80
Sun City, Hillsborough, Fla., 300 F2 86
Sun City, Barber, Kans., 188 E5 93
Suncook, Merrimack, N.H., 3,807 D4 105
Suncook, ponds, N.H D4 105
Suncook, riv., N.H D4 105
Sun Crest, San Diego, Calif., 1,166 *F5 82
Sunda, is., Asia G3 2
Sunda (Soenda), strait, Indon G3 35
Sundance, Crook, Wyo., 908 A8 125
Sundance, mtn., Wyo A8 125
Sunday, strait, Austl C3 50
Sundbyberg, Swe., 27,100 t35 25
Sundarbans, swamp, India G12 40
Sunderland, Ont., Can., 634 C5 72
Sunderland, Eng., 190,500 (*250,000) C6 10
Sunderland, Calvert, Md., 25 C4 85
Sunderland, Franklin, Mass., 500 (1,279▲) B2 97
Sunderland, Bennington, Vt., 240 (566▲) E2 120
Sundown, Man., Can., 196 E3 71
Sundown, Hockley, Tex., 1,186 C1 118
Sundre, Alta., Can., 853 D3 69
Sundridge, Ont., Can., 756 B5 72
Sunds, Den., 1,039 B3 24
Sundsvall, Swe., 30,300 (*44,000) F7 25
Sunfield, Eaton, Mich., 626 F5 98
Sunflower, Maricopa, Ariz., 5 D4 80
Sunflower, Sunflower, Miss., 662 B3 100
Sunflower, co., Miss., 45,750 B3 100
Sunflower, mtn., Kans C2 93
Sunflower, riv., Miss B3 100
Sungaiguntung, Indon E2 35
Sungari, res., China E3 37
Sungari, riv., China C5 37
Sungchiang, China, 70,000 I9 36
Sungei Patani, Mala., 22,916 J4 38
Sunghsien, China E7 34
Sungkan, China J2 36
Sungtao, China, 5,000 J3 36
Sungurlu, Tur., 10,500 B10 31
Sunland Park, Dona Ana, N. Mex., 900 F3 107
Sunlight, creek, Wyo A3 125
Sunman, Ripley, Ind., 446 F7 91
Sunne, Swe., 3,300 H5 25
Suniland, Dade, Fla., 1,500 *G6 86
Sunny Acres, Kenton, Ky., 844 *A7 94
Sunnybrae, N.S., Can., 180 D7 74
Sunnybrook, Alta., Can., 40 C3 69
Sunnydale, Sedgwick, Kans B5 93
Sunnyland, Sarasota, Fla., 4,761 *E4 86
Sunnyland, Tazewell, Ill., 1,000 *C4 90
Sunnymead, Riverside, Calif., 3,404 *F5 82
Sunnynook, Alta., Can., 76 D5 69
Sunnyside, Newf., Can., 533 E5 75
Sunnyside, Bay, Fla., 125 G3 86
Sunnyside, Leflore, Miss B3 100
Sunnyside, Carbon, Utah, 1,740 D5 119
Sunnyside, Yakima, Wash., 6,208 C5 122
Sunnyslope, Alta., Can., 61 D4 69
Sunny South, Wilcox, Ala., 200 D2 78
Sunnyvale, Santa Clara, Calif., 52,898 B5 82
Sunnyvale, Dallas, Tex., 969 *A6 118
Sunnyview, Brookings, S. Dak., 75 C9 116
Sunol, Alameda, Calif., 750 B6 82
Sunol, Cheyenne, Nebr., 100 C3 103
Sun Prairie, Dane, Wis., 4,008 E4 124
Sunray, Moore, Tex., 1,967 B2 118
Sunrise, Falls, Tex., 1,708 *D4 118
Sunrise, Platte, Wyo., 300 C8 125
Sunrise, mtn., N.J A3 106
Sunrise Heights, Calhoun, Mich., 1,569 *F5 98
Sun River, Cascade, Mont., 100 C5 102
Sunset, St. Landry, La., 1,307 D3 95
Sunset, Hancock, Maine, 150 D4 96
Sunset, Montague, Tex., 500 C4 118
Sunset, Davis, Utah, 4,235 B3 119
Sunset, hill, Conn B8 84
Sunset, lake, Vt E3 120
Sunset Beach, Orange, Calif., 1,300 *F2 82
Sunset Crater, nat. mon., Ariz B4 80
Sunset Hills, St. Louis, Mo., 3,525 *B8 101
Sunset Park, Sedgwick, Kans., 1,000 *B5 93
Sunshine, Austl., 64,800 *H5 51
Sunshine, Los Angeles, Calif., 9,000 *F4 82
Sunshine, Hancock, Maine, 120 D4 96
Sunshine, Park, Wyo A4 125
Sunspot, Otero, N. Mex., 100 E4 107
Suntar, Sov. Un C14 28
Suntaug, lake, Mass f11 97
Suntex, Harney, Oreg D7 113
Suntrana, Alsk., 81 C10 79
Sun Valley, Blaine, Idaho, 317 F4 89
Sunwui, China, 85,000 G7 34
Sunyani, Ghana, 4,570 E4 45
Suo, sea, Jap J5 37
Suoyarvi, Sov. Un F15 25
Supai, Coconino, Ariz., 140 A3 80
Superb, Sask., Can., 40 F1 70
Superior, Pinal, Ariz., 4,875 D4 80
Superior, Boulder, Colo., 173 B5 83
Superior, Dickinson, Iowa, 190 A3 92
Superior, Mineral, Mont., 1,242 C2 102
Superior, Nuckolls, Nebr., 2,935 D7 103
Superior, Lawrence, Ohio, 5 D5 111
Superior, Douglas, Wis., 33,563 B1 124
Superior, Sweetwater, Wyo., 241 D4 125
Superior, lake, U.S., Can A10 77
Superior, McDowell, W. Va., 900 *D3 123
Suphan Buri, Thai., 14,258 E4 38
Supi Oidak, Pima, Ariz., 75 F4 80
Suplee, Crook, Oreg C7 113
Supply, Randolph, Ark A5 81
Supply, Brunswick, N.C., 95 C5 109
Suprise, Maricopa, Ariz., 1,574 G1 80
Suqash Shuyukh, Iraq, 7,735 F3 41
Suquamish, Kitsap, Wash., 950 B3 122
Sur, see Tyre, Leb.
Şur, Mus. & Om D2 39
Sura, riv., Sov. Un C3 29
Surabaja (Soerabaja), Indon., 989,734 (*1,050,000) G4 35
Surakarta (Soerakarta), Indon., 363,167 G4 35
Surakhany, Sov. Un E4 29
Surany, Czech., 5,381 D5 26
Surat, Austl., 406 C7 51
Surat, India, 288,026 D5 39, G4 40
Suratgarh, India, 8,330 C4 40
Surat Thani, Thai., 18,460 H3 38
Surazh, Sov. Un., 10,000 E9 27
Şūr Bāhir, Jordan k11 32
Surbiton, Eng., 62,940 m11 10, C7 12
Suresnes, Fr., 39,100 g9 14
Suretka, C.R F6 62
Surette Island, N.S., Can., 212 F4 74
Surf City, Ocean, N.J., 419 D4 106
Surfside, Dade, Fla., 3,157 F3 86
Surgères, Fr., 4,839 D3 14
Surgoinsville, Hawkins, Tenn., 1,132 C11 117
Surgut, Sov. Un., 3,500 C23 9
Suri, India, 22,841 F11 40
Suriapet, India, 12,443 I7 40
Suribachi, mtn., Iwo 52
Surigao, Phil., 12,870 D7 35
Surigao, prov., Phil., 360,100 *D7 35
Surinam (Netherlands Guiana), Neth dep., S.A., 385,000 C5 53, B3 59
Suriname, riv., Sur B3 59
Suring, Oconto, Wis., 513 D5 124
Surkhan Darya, riv., Sov. Un C13 41
Surprise, Butler, Nebr., 79 C8 103
Surrency, Appling, Ga., 312 E4 87
Surrey, Ward, N. Dak., 309 A4 110
Surrey, co., Eng., 1,733,036 C7 12
Surrey, Hancock, Maine, 180 (547▲) D4 96
Surry, Cheshire, N.H., 200 (362▲) D2 105
Surry, Surry, Va., 288 B5, D6 121
Surry, co., N.C., 48,205 A3 109
Surry, co., Va., 6,220 D6 121
Sursee, Switz., 5,324 B5 19
Surt, see Sirte, Libya
Suruc, Tur., 3,632 D12 31
Surud Ad, mtn., Som C6 47
Suruga, bay, Jap o17 37
Surveyor, Raleigh, W. Va., 125 D6 123
Susa, It., 5,891 B1 21
Susac, isl., Yugo D3 22
Susak, isl., Yugo C2 22
Susana Knolls, Ventrua, Calif., 900 *E4 82
Susanino, Sov. Un s31 25
Susank, Barton, Kans., 87 D5 93
Susanville, Lassen, Calif., 5,598 B3 82
Susanville, Grant, Oreg C8 113
Susice, Czech., 6,793 D2 26
Susitna, Alsk., 42 g16 79
Susitna, riv., Alsk C10 79
Susquehanna, Susquehanna, Pa., 2,591 C10 114
Susquehanna, co., Pa., 33,137 C10 114
Susquehanna, riv., Md., N.Y., Pa C9, G9 114
Susques, Arg D2 55
Sussex, N.B., Can., 3,457 D4 74
Sussex, Sussex, N.J., 1,656 A3 106
Sussex, Sussex, Va., 75 E5 121
Sussex, Waukesha, Wis., 1,087 E1 124
Sussex, Johnson, Wyo., 5 B6 125
Sussex, co., Del., 73,195 C6 85
Sussex, co., Eng., 1,075,893 D8 12
Sussex, co., N.J., 49,255 A3 106
Sussex, co., Va., 12,411 E5 121
Sustut, riv., B.C., Can A4 68
Susua, P.R C3 65
Susung, China I7 36
Susurluk, Tur., 6,147 C7 23
Sutcliffe, Washoe, Nev., 80 D2 104
Sutersville, Westmoreland, Pa., 964 *F2 114
Sutherland, O'Brien, Iowa, 883 B2 92
Sutherland, Lincoln, Nebr., 867 C4 103
Sutherland, S. Afr., 1,809 D3 49
Sutherland, Dinwiddie, Va., 65 C7, D5 121
Sutherland, co., Scot., 13,442 B4 13
Sutherland, res. and canal system, Nebr D5 103
Sutherland Springs, Wilson, Tex., 300 B4 118
Sutherlin, Douglas, Oreg., 2,452 D3 113
Sutlej, riv., India, Pak B4 40
Sutter, Sutter, Calif., 1,219 *C3 82
Sutter, co., Calif., 33,380 C3 82
Sutter Creek, Amador, Calif., 1,161 C3 82
Suttle, Perry, Ala., 250 C2 78
Sutton, Nevada, Ark., 70 D2 81
Sutton, Que., Can., 1,755 D5 73
Sutton, Eng., 78,969 m12 10
Sutton, Worcester, Mass., 500 (3,638▲) *B4 97
Sutton, Clay, Nebr., 1,252 D8 103
Sutton, Merrimack, N.H., 200 (487▲) D3 105
Sutton, Griggs, N. Dak., 150 B7 110
Sutton, Caledonia, Vt., 100 (476▲) B4 120
Sutton, Braxton, W. Va., 967 C4 123
Sutton, co., Tex., 3,738 D2 118
Sutton, res., W. Va C4 123
Sutton Coldfield, Eng., 76,600 B6 12
Sutton-in-Ashfield, Eng., 40,700 A6 12
Suttons Bay, Leelanau, Mich., 421 D5 98
Sutton West, Ont., Can., 1,470 C5 72
Suttsu, Jap., 6,200 E10 37
Suujiin Hudag, Mong A2 36
Suva, Fiji Is., 47,850 52
Suva, hbr., Fiji Is 52
Suver, Polk, Oreg C1 113
Suveydiye, Tur D10 31
Suwa, Jap., 31,400 (44,035▲) m17 37
Suwalki, Pol., 20,000 A7 26
Suwanee, Gwinnett, Ga., 541 B2 87
Suwannee, lake, Man., Can A1 71
Suwanee, mtn., Ga B2 87
Suwannee, Dixie, Fla., 200 C3 86
Suwannee, co., Fla., 14,961 B3 86
Suwannee, riv., Fla C4 86
Suwannee, riv., Ga F4 87
Suwannee, sound, Fla C3 86
Suwanoochee, creek, Ga F4 87
Suwanose, isl., Jap L4 37
Şuwaylih, Jordan, 2,000 B7 32
Suwŏn, Kor., 113,300 *H3 37
Suyo, Peru, 744 B1 58
Suzu, cape, Jap H8 37
Suzuka, Jap., 44,800 (90,499▲) o15 37
Suzuka-Sammyaku, mts., Jap o15 37
Suzzara, It., 6,631 E6 18
Svalbard, Nor. dep., Eur B13 4
Svaneke, Den., 1,167 A3 26
Svärtagård, Swe., 2,392 u35 25
Svartån, riv., Swe t34 25
Svartisen, mtn., Nor D5 25
Svatovo, Sov. Un., 10,000 G12 27
Svedala, Swe., 3,114 C7 24
Sveg, Swe., 2,300 F6 25
Svendborg, Den., 23,892 C4 24
Svendborg, co., Den., 150,365 C4 24
Svene, Nor p27 25
Svenljunga, Swe., 2,600 A7 24
Svensen, Clatsop, Oreg., 50 A3 113
Svenstrup, Den., 1,254 B3 24
Sverdlovsk, Sov. Un., 66,000 q22 27
Sverdlovsk, Sov. Un., 869,000 (*1,015,000) D21 9, B6 29
Sverdrup, isl., Sov. Un B7 4
Sverdrup, is., N.W. Ter., Can m31 67
Svetlaya, Sov. Un., 10,000 C9 37
Svicha, riv., Sov. Un D8 26
Svilajnac, Yugo., 5,905 C5 22
Svilengrad, Bul., 9,918 E8 22
Svindal, Nor p29 25
Svinninge, Den., 1,437 C5 24
Svir, riv., Sov. Un A10 27
Svirstroy, Sov. Un., 10,000 A9 27
Svishtov, Bul., 12,949 D7 22
Svitavy, Czech., 13,900 D4 26
Svobodnyy, Sov. Un., 58,000 D15 28
Svobodnyy, cape, Sov. Un B11 37
Svyatoy, cape, Sov. Un B16 28
Swadlincote, Eng., 19,222 B6 12
Swaffham, Eng., 3,210 B8 12
Swain, co., N.C., 8,387 D2 109
Swain, mtn., Ark A5 81
Swain, reefs, Austl D9 50
Swains, isl., Pac. O G11 7
Swainsboro, Emanuel, Ga., 5,943 D4 87
Swakopmund, S.W. Afr., 2,842 B1 49
Swale, riv., Eng C6 10
Swaledale, Cerro Gordo, Iowa, 217 B4 92
Swalwell, Alta., Can., 85 D4 69
Swamp, riv., N.Y C2 84
Swampers, Franklin, La., 20 B4 95
Swampscott, Essex, Mass., 13,294 B6, g12 97
Swan, Marion, Iowa, 168 C4 92
Swan, creek, Ohio A2 111
Swan, falls, Idaho F2 89
Swan, hills, Alta., Can B3 69
Swan, is., Caribbean Sea B6 72
Swan, lake, Man., Can C1 71
Swan, lake, Maine D4 96
Swan, lake, Nebr C3 103
Swan, lake, Wash D2 122
Swan, peak, Mont C3 102
Swan, pt., Md B5 85
Swan, range, Mont C3 102
Swan, riv., Austl F2 50
Swan, riv., Alta., Can B3 69
Swan, riv., Man., Sask., Can C1 71
Swanage, Eng., 8,112 D6 12
Swan Creek, Warren, Ill., 125 C3 90
Swandale, Clay, W. Va., 200 C7, C4 123
Swan Hill, Austl., 6,185 G4 51
Swan Hills, Alta., Can., 643 B3 69
Swanington, Benton, Ind., 150 C3 91
Swan Lake, Man., Can., 307 E2 71
Swan Lake, Bannock, Idaho, 150 G6 89
Swan Lake, Tallahatchie, Miss., 300 B3 100
Swan Lake, Lake, Mont., 200 C3 102
Swanlinbar, Ire., 306 C4 11
Swannanoa, Buncombe, N.C., 2,189 D4 109
Swanquarter, Hyde, N.C., 200 B7 109
Swan River, Man., Can., 3,163 C1 71

Swan River, Itasca, Minn., 150 ... C5 99
Swans, isl., Maine ... D4 96
Swansboro, Onslow, N.C., 1,104 ... C6 109
Swansea, Ont., Can., 9,628 ... m15 72
Swansea, St. Clair, Ill., 3,018 ... B9 101
Swansea, Bristol, Mass., 300 (9,916*) ... C5 97
Swansea, Lexington, S.C., 776 ... D5 115
Swansea, Wales, 170,400 (*270,000) ... C4 12
Swansea, bay, Wales ... C4 12
Swansea Center, Bristol, Mass., 700 ... *C5 97
Swans Island, Hancock, Maine, 300 (402*) ... D4 96
Swanson, Sask., Can. ... F2 70
Swanson Lake, res., Kans. ... B2 93
Swanton, Garrett, Md., 100 ... E1 85
Swanton, Saline, Nebr., 190 ... D8 103
Swanton, Fulton, Ohio, 2,306 ... A4 111
Swanton, Franklin, Vt., 2,390 (3,946*) ... B2 120
Swan Valley, Bonneville, Idaho, 217 ... F7 89
Swanville, Morrison, Minn., 342 ... E4 99
Swanzey, Cheshire, N.H., 150 (3,626*) ... E2 105
Swarthmore, Delaware, Pa., 5,753 ... B10 114
Swarthwood, Sussex, N.J., 150 ... A3 106
Swartswood, lake, N.J. ... A3 106
Swartz, Ouachita, La., 300 ... B4 95
Swartz Creek, Genesee, Mich., 3,006 ... F7 98
Swatara, Aitkin, Minn., 90 ... D5 99
Swatow (Shantou), China, 280,400 ... G8 34
Swayzee, Grant, Ind., 863 ... C6 91
Swaziland, Br. dep., Afr., 295,000 ... C5 49
Swea City, Kossuth, Iowa, 805 ... A3 92
Sweatman, Montgomery, Miss., 25 ... B4 100
Swedeborg, Pulaski, Mo., 175 ... D5 101
Swedeburg, Saunders, Nebr., 65 ... E2 103
Swedeland, Montgomery, Pa., 950 ... A11 114
Sweden, country, Eur., 7,675,000 ... C12 8, F7 25
Swedesboro, Gloucester, N.J., 2,449 ... D2 106
Swedesburg, Montgomery, Pa., 950 ... *A11 114
Sweeny, Brazoria, Tex., 3,087 ... G4 118
Sweet, Gem, Idaho, 100 ... F2 89
Sweet Briar, Amherst, Va., 850 ... D3 121
Sweetgrass, Toole, Mont., 205 ... B5 102
Sweet Grass, co., Mont., 3,290 ... E7 102
Sweet Hall, King William, Va., 50 ... D6 121
Sweet Home, Pulaski, Ark., 900 ... C3, D6 81
Sweet Home, Linn, Oreg., 3,353 ... C4 113
Sweet Home, Lavaca, Tex., 300 ... E4 118
Sweetsburg, Que., Can., 958 ... D5 73
Sweetsers, Grant, Ind., 896 ... C6 91
Sweet Springs, Saline, Mo., 1,452 ... C4 101
Sweetsprings, Monroe, W. Va., 500 ... D4 123
Sweet Valley, Luzerne, Pa., 250 ... D9 114
Sweet Water, Marengo, Ala., 300 ... C2 78
Sweetwater, Dade, Fla., 645 ... *G6 86
Sweetwater, Nez Perce, Idaho, 80 ... C2 89
Sweetwater, Beckham and Roger Mills, Okla., 50 ... B2 112
Sweetwater, Monroe, Tenn., 4,145 ... D8 117
Sweetwater, Nolan, Tex., 13,914 ... C2 118
Sweetwater, co., Wyo., 17,920 ... D3 125
Sweetwater, riv., Wyo. ... C4 125
Sweime, Jordan, 1,000 ... h13 32
Swenson, Stonewall, Tex., 150 ... C2 118
Swepsonville, Alamance, N.C., 800 ... A4 109
Swider, riv., Pol. ... m14 26
Swidnica, Pol., 39,000 ... C4 26
Świdwin, Pol., 6,098 ... B3 26
Swiebodzice, Pol., 6,078 ... C4 26
Swiebodzin, Pol., 11,200 ... B3 26
Swiecie, Pol., 8,358 ... B5 26
Swietochlowice, Pol., 58,200 ... g9 26
Swift, Roseau, Minn., 30 ... B3 99
Swift, Hardin, Tenn. ... B3 117
Swift, co., Minn., 14,936 ... E3 99
Swift, creek, N.C. ... B6 109
Swift, creek, Va. ... C7 121
Swift, res., Wash. ... C3 122
Swift, riv., N.H. ... C4 105
Swift, riv., N.H. ... B4 105
Swift Current, Sask., Can., 12,186 ... G2, n7 70
Swiftcurrent, creek, Sask., Can. ... H1 70
Swift Diamond, riv., N.H. ... B2 105
Swifton, Jackson, Ark., 601 ... B4 81
Swiftown, Leflore, Miss., 125 ... B3 100
Swiftwater, Grafton, N.H., 60 ... B3 105
Swilly, inlet, Ire. ... B4 11
Swinburne, cape, N.W. Ter., Can. ... B13 66
Swindle, isl., B.C., Can. ... C3 68
Swindon, Eng., 96,200 ... C6 12
Swinemünde, see Swinoujscie, Pol.
Swinford, Ire., 1,115 ... D3 11
Swink, Otero, Colo., 348 ... C7 83
Swinomish, Indian res., Wash. ... A3 122
Swinoujscie, Pol., 10,600 ... A3 26
Swinton & Pendlebury, Eng., 41,200 ... *A5 12
Swisher, Johnson, Iowa, 271 ... C6 92
Swisher, co., Tex., 10,607 ... B2 118
Swiss, Yancey, N.C. ... C3 109
Swiss, Nicholas, W. Va., 500 ... C3, C7 123
Swissvale, Allegheny, Pa., 15,089 ... B6 114
Switz City, Greene, Ind., 339 ... F3 91
Switzer, Logan, W. Va., 1,131 ... D3 123
Switzerland, St. Johns, Fla., 150 ... C6 86
Switzerland, Jasper, S.C., 50 ... G5 115
Switzerland, co., Ind., 7,092 ... G7 91
Switzerland, country, Eur., 6,075,000 ... F10 8, 19
Swords, Morgan, Ga., 200 ... C3 87
Swords, Ire., 1,816 ... D5 11
Swoyersville, Luzerne, Pa., 6,751 ... B8, D10 114
Sycamore, Talladega, Ala., 900 ... B3 78
Sycamore, Turner, Ga., 501 ... E3 87
Sycamore, De Kalb, Ill., 6,961 ... B5 90
Sycamore, Montgomery, Kans., 187 ... E8 93
Sycamore, Ozark, Mo., 42 ... E5 101
Sycamore, Wyandot, Ohio, 998 ... B4 111
Sycamore, Allendale, S.C., 401 ... E5 115
Sycamore, Pittsylvania, Va. ... D3 121
Sycamore, creek, Tenn. ... A4 117
Sycamore, creek, W. Va. ... C7 123
Sychevka, Sov. Un. ... D10 27
Sycow, Pol., 2,108 ... C4 26
Sydenham, Ont., Can., 803 ... C8 72
Sydney, Austl., 168,800 (*2,315,000) ... F8 51
Sydney, N.S., Can., 33,617 (*40,300) ... C9 74
Sydney Mines, N.S., Can., 9,122 ... C9 74
Sykeston, Wells, N. Dak., 236 ... B6 110
Sykesville, Carroll, Md., 1,196 ... B4 85
Sykesville, Burlington, N.J., 150 ... C3 106
Sykesville, Jefferson, Pa., 1,479 ... D4 114
Syktyvkar, Sov. Un., 84,000 ... C19 9
Sylacauga, Talladega, Ala., 12,857 ... B3 78
Sylamore, Izard, Ark., 45 ... B3 81
Sylhet, Pak., 37,740 ... D9 39
Sylling, Nor., 268 ... p28 25
Sylt, isl., Ger. ... D2 24
Sylva, Jackson, N.C., 1,564 ... D3 109
Sylvan, Multnomah, Oreg., 600 ... B2 113
Sylvan, Franklin, Pa., 20 ... G5 114
Sylvan, lake, Alta., Can. ... C10 68
Sylvan, lake, Ind. ... B7 91
Sylvan Beach, Oneida, N.Y., 600 ... B5 108
Sylvan Grove, Lincoln, Kans., 400 ... C5 93
Sylvan Hills, Pulaski, Ark., 2,000 ... *C3 81
Sylvania, DeKalb, Ala., 400 ... A4 78
Sylvania, Sask., Can., 116 ... E3 70
Sylvania, Screven, Ga., 3,469 ... D5 87
Sylvania, Jefferson, Ky., 1,200 ... A3 94
Sylvania, Lucas, Ohio, 5,187 ... A1, A4 111
Sylvania, Bradford, Pa., 243 ... C8 114
Sylvan Lake, Alta., Can., 1,381 ... C3 69
Sylvan Lake, Oakland, Mich., 2,004 ... F7 98
Sylvan Shores, Lake, Fla., 1,214 ... *D5 86
Sylvarena, Smith, Miss., 69 ... C4 100
Sylvester, Worth, Ga., 3,610 ... E3 87
Sylvester, Fisher, Tex., 405 ... C2 118
Sylvester, mtn., Newf., Can. ... D4 75
Sylvia, Reno, Kans., 402 ... E5 93
Sylvia, Dickson, Tenn., 100 ... A4 117
Sym, riv., Sov. Un. ... C26 9
Symmes, creek, Ohio ... D5 111
Symsonia, Graves, Ky., 400 ... A2 94
Syosset, Nassau, N.Y., 21,500 ... F3 84
Syracuse, Kosciusko, Ind., 1,595 ... B6 91
Syracuse, Hamilton, Kans., 1,888 ... E2 93
Syracuse, Morgan, Mo., 180 ... C5 101
Syracuse, Otoe, Nebr., 1,261 ... D9, F3 103
Syracuse, Onondaga, N.Y., 216,038 (*442,300) ... B4 108
Syracuse, Meigs, Ohio, 731 ... D6 111
Syracuse, Davis, Utah, 1,061 ... B3 119
Syr Darya, riv., Sov. Un. ... G22 9
Syria, country, Asia, 5,100,000 ... E12 31, F6 33
Syriam, Bur., 15,070 ... D2 38
Sysladobsis, lake, Maine ... C4 96
Sysola, riv., Sov. Un. ... C19 9
Syzran, Sov. Un., 159,000 ... C3 29
Szabadszallas, Hung., 4,878 ... B4 22
Szabolcs-Szatmar, co., Hung., 587,257 ... *B5 22
Szamos, riv., Hung. ... A6 22
Szamotuly, Pol., 10,800 ... B4 26
Szarvas, Hung., 12,277 ... B5 22
Szczakowa, Pol., 4,285 ... g10 26
Szczebrzeszyn, Pol., 5,122 ... C7 26
Szczecin (Stettin), Pol., 286,300 ... E8 24, B3 26
Szczecinek, Pol., 23,000 ... B4 26
Szczuczyn, Pol., 2,479 ... B7 26
Szczytno, Pol., 3,645 ... B6 26
Szechwan, prov., China, 72,160,000 ... E5 34
Szeged, Hung., 107,300 ... B5 22
Szekesfehervar, Hung., 61,400 ... B4 22
Szekszard, Hung., 16,409 (19,347*) ... B4 22
Szengen, China ... G6 34
Szentendre, Hung., 10,307 ... B4 22
Szentes, Hung., 24,807 (31,175*) ... B5 22
Szeping, China, 125,900 ... C9 32
Szigetvar, Hung., 7,395 ... B3 22
Szolnok, Hung., 51,300 ... B5 22
Szolnok, co., Hung., 462,516 ... *B5 22
Szombathely, Hung., 57,600 ... B3 22
Szprotawa, Pol., 2,672 ... C3 26
Sztum, Pol., 3,111 ... B5 26
Szubin, Pol., 3,742 ... B4 26
Szydlowiec, Pol., 4,010 ... C6 26
Szymanow, Pol., 2,000 ... m12 26

T

Taal, Phil., 4,752 ... p13 35
Taal, lake, Phil. ... p13 35
Taasinge, isl., Den. ... C4 24
Tab, Warren, Ind., 100 ... D3 91
Tabaco, Phil., 8,308 ... *C6 35
Ţabah, Sau. Ar. ... I14 31
Tabas, Iran ... E8 41
Ţabas, Iran ... E8 41
Ţabas, Iran, 17,743 ... E10 41
Tabasco, state, Mex., 471,808 ... D6 63
Tabatinga, mts., Braz. ... D2 57
Tabayoc, mtn., Phil. ... n13 35
Tabbys, peak, Utah ... C3 119
Tabelbala, Alg. ... D4 44
Taber, Alta., Can., 3,951 ... E4 69
Taberg, Oneida, N.Y., 400 ... B5 108
Tabernacle, Burlington, N.J., 40 ... D3 106
Tabernas, Sp., 4,121 ... D4 20
Tabernash, Grand, Colo., 275 ... B5 83
Taberville, St. Clair, Mo., 100 ... C4 101
Tabik, isl., Kwajalein ... 52
Tabiona, Duchesne, Utah, 167 ... C5 119
Tablas, cape, Chile ... A2 54
Tablas, isl., Phil. ... C6 35
Table, bay, Newf., Can. ... B3 75
Table, bay, S. Afr. ... D2 49
Table, head, Newf., Can. ... B4 75
Table, mtn., Ariz. ... E5 80
Table, mtn., Newf., Can. ... E2 75
Table, rock, Oreg. ... C4 113
Table Grove, Fulton, Ill., 500 ... C3 90
Table Rock, Pawnee, Nebr., 422 ... D9 103
Table Rock, Jackson, Oreg. ... E4 113
Tables, isl., Scot. ... C2 13
Table Top, mtn., Ariz. ... E3 80
Tablónes, P.R. ... C8, g12 65
Taboada, Sp., 8,162 ... A2 20
Tabor, Czech., 19,600 ... D3 26
Tabor, Fremont and Mills, Iowa, 909 ... D2 92
Tabor, Polk, Minn., 100 ... B2 99
Tabor (Mount Tabor), Morris, N.J., 1,500 ... *B4 106
Tabor, Bon Homme, S. Dak., 378 ... E8 116
Tabor, mtn., Isr. ... B3 32
Tabora, Tan., 15,361 ... C5 48
Tabor City, Columbus, N.C., 2,338 ... C5 109
Tabou, I.C., 2,100 ... F3 45
Tabrīz, Iran, 289,996 ... B3 41
Tabūk, Sau. Ar., 10,000 ... D7 43
Tabusintac, riv., N.B., Can. ... B4 74
Tacámbaro de Codallos, Mex., 7,286 ... n13 63
Tacheng, China ... E7 36
Tachie, riv., B.C., Can. ... B5 68
Tachiiwa, pt., Iwo ... 52
Tachikawa, Jap., 67,949 ... n18 37
Táchira, state, Ven., 399,163 ... B3 60
Tachov, Czech., 5,200 ... D7 17
Tacloban, Phil., 35,974 (53,551*) ... C6 35
Tacna, Yuma, Ariz., 150 ... E1 80
Tacna, Peru, 13,514 ... E3 58
Tacna, dept., Peru, 42,874 ... E3 58
Tacoma, La Plata, Colo., 15 ... D3 83
Tacoma, Pierce, Wash., 147,979 (*298,000) ... B3, D1 122
Tacoma Park, Brown, S. Dak., 25 ... B7 116
Taconic, Litchfield, Conn., 200 ... A3 84
Taconic, range, Mass. ... A1 97
Tacoronte, Sp. (Can. Is.), 10,282 ... m13 20
Tacuarembó, Ur., 21,200 ... E1 56
Tacuarembó, dept., Ur., 71,100 ... *E1 56
Tacuatí, Par., 1,538 ... D4 55
Tacubaya, Mex. (part of Mexico City) ... h9 63
Tad, Kanawha, W. Va., 500 ... C6 123
Tadanac, B.C., Can., 347 ... *E9 68
Tademait, plat., Alg. ... D5 44
Tadent, riv., Alg. ... E6 44
Tadjoura, Fr. Som., 1,150 ... C5 47
Tadoule, lake, Man., Can. ... f8 71
Tadoussac, Que., Can., 1,083 ... A8 73
Tadzhik, S.S.R., rep., Sov. Un., 2,410,000 ... F9 28
Taegu, Kor., 716,600 ... I4 37
Taejon, Kor., 268,800 ... H3 37
Taeyudong, Kor., 5,000 ... F2 37
Tafalla, Sp., 7,320 ... A5 20
Tafí Viejo, Arg., 15,374 ... E2 55
Taft, Kern, Calif., 3,822 ... E4 82
Taft, Orange, Fla., 1,214 ... D5 86
Taft, St. Charles, La., 260 ... B6 75
Taft, Muskogee, Okla., 386 ... B6 112
Taft, Lincoln, Oreg., 577 ... C3 113
Taft, Lincoln, Tenn., 200 ... B5 117
Taft, San Patricio, Tex., 3,463 ... F4 118
Taft Heights, Kern, Calif., 2,661 ... *E4 82
Taft Southwest, San Patricio, Texas, 1,927 ... *F4 118
Taftsville, Windsor, Vt., 150 ... D4 120
Taftville, New London, Conn. (part of Norwich) ... C8 84
Tagachan, pt., Guam ... 52
Taganrog, Sov. Un., 220,000 ... H12 27
Taganrog, gulf, Sov. Un. ... H12 27
Tagawa, Jap., 100,071 ... *J5 37
Tagbileran, Phil., 5,879 ... D6 35
Taghrifat, Libya ... D3 43
Taghmaconnell, Ire. ... D5 11
Taghmon, Ire., 347 ... E5 11
Tagliamento, riv., It. ... C8 18
Tagolo, pt., Phil. ... D6 35
Tagouranet (Well), Maur. ... C3 45
Taguan, pt., Guam ... 52
Taguatinga, Braz., 1,496 ... D1 57
Taguchi, Jap., 4,400 ... n16 37
Tagus, Mountrail, N. Dak., 72 ... A4 110
Tagus see Tejo, riv., Port.
Tagus, see Tajo, riv., Sp.
Tahan, mtn., Mala. ... J5 38
Tahat, mtn., Alg. ... D6 44
Tahiti, isl., Society Is. ... H13 7
Tahlequah, Cherokee, Okla., 5,840 ... B7 112
Tahoe, lake, Calif., Nev. ... C3 82
Tahoe City, Placer, Calif., 350 ... C3 82
Tahoka, Lynn, Tex., 3,012 ... C2 118
Taholah, Grays Harbor, Wash., 400 ... B1 122
Tahoma, Placer, Calif., 50 ... C3 82
Tahona, LeFlore, Okla., 35 ... B7 112
Tahoua, Niger, 12,400 ... D6 45
Tahquamenon, falls, Mich. ... B5 98
Tahsien, China, 26,000 ... I2 36
Tahsis, B.C., Can., 686 ... E4 68
Ţahţā, Eg., U.A.R., 41,400 ... D6 43
Tahtsa, lake, B.C., Can. ... C4 68
Tahtsa, peak, B.C., Can. ... C4 68
Tahtsa, riv., B.C., Can. ... C4 68
Tahuya, Mason, Wash., 150 ... B2 122
Tai, China ... E5 36
Tai, China, 159,800 ... H8 36
Taï, I.C. ... E3 45
Tai, lake, China ... I9 36
Taian, China ... D10 36
Taian, China, 80,000 ... F7 36
Taiban, De Baca, N. Mex., 20 ... C5 107
Taiban, creek, N. Mex. ... C5 107
Taichao, see Giamda, China
Taichinatala, China ... B9 36
T'aichung, Taiwan, 221,000 (320,200*) ... G9 34
Taihape, N.Z., 2,682 ... M15 51
Taikang, China, 5,000 ... C2 37
Taiku, China ... F5 36
Tailagoin, mts., Mong. ... C6 34
Tailai, China, 5,000 ... C1 37
Tailem Bend, Austl., 2,049 ... G2 51
Tailevu, pt., Fiji Is. ... 52
Tain, Scot., 1,699 ... C4 13
T'ainan, Taiwan, 278,000 (362,700*) ... G9 34
Taining, China ... K7 36
Taipei (Taihoku), Taiwan, 979,100 (*1,375,000) ... G9 34
Taiping, Mala., 48,206 ... J4 38
Taipu, Braz., 1,162 ... g6 57
Taira, Jap., 71,115 (*103,000) ... H10 37
Taishun, China, 11,000 ... K8 36
Taitao, pen., Chile ... D1 54
Taitiarato, Pap. ... k11 50
T'aitung, Taiwan, 29,010 ... G9 34
Taivalkoski, Fin., 850 ... E13 25
Taiwan (Formosa), country (Nationalist China), Asia, 12,250,000 ... G9 34
Taiwan, isl., Asia ... G9 34
Taiwara, see Qala-i-Ghor, Afg.
Taiyüan (Yangkü), China, 1,020,000 ... D7 34, F5 36
Tajarhi, Libya ... E2 43
Tajimi, Jap., 53,793 ... I8, n16 37
Tajique, Torrance, N. Mex., 170 ... C3 107
Tajo (Tagus), riv., Sp. ... C3 20
Tajumulco, peak, Guat. ... C2 62
Tajuna, riv., Sp. ... B4 20
Tājūrā', Libya, 2,670 ... C2 43
Tak, Thai., 12,918 ... D3 38
Taka Banare, isl., Okinawa ... 52
Takabba, Ken. ... A7 48
Takada, Jap., 46,200 (73,238*) ... H9 37
Takahe, mtn., Ant. ... B1 5
Takaka, N.Z., 769 ... N14 51
Takamatsu, Jap., 228,172 ... I7 37
Takaoka, Jap., 135,190 ... H8 37
Takarazuka, Jap., 66,491 ... *I7 37
Takasago, Jap., 53,565 ... *I7 37
Takasaki, Jap., 125,000 (142,152*) ... H9, m18 37
Takata, Jap., 23,025 ... H9 37
Takato, Jap., 4,100 ... n17 37
Takatsuki, Jap., 79,043 ... o14 37
Takaw, Bur. ... B3 38
Takawa, Jap., 95,911 ... *J5 37
Takayama, Jap., 34,800 (50,588*) ... H8, m16 37
Takazze, riv., Eth. ... C4 47
Take, isl., Jap. ... H5 37
Takefu, Jap., 37,100 (62,610*) ... n15 37
Takeo, Camb., 5,000 ... G6 38
Tākestān, Iran, 10,543 ... C4 41
Takhta-Bazar, Sov. Un. ... D11 41
Takhta-Kupyr, Sov. Un. ... E6 29
Takht-i-Sulaiman, mtn., Iran ... C5 41
Takihara, Jap., 4,457 ... o15 37
Takilma, Josephine, Oreg., 50 ... E3 113
Takingeun, Indon., 1,411 ... J2 38
Takiyuak, lake, N.W. Ter., Can. ... C10 66
Takla, lake, B.C., Can. ... B5 68
Taklakhar, China ... B8 40
Takla Makan, des., China ... F11 33
Takoma Park, Montgomery and Prince Georges, Md., 16,799 ... C1 85
Takotna, Alsk., 40 ... C8 79
Takouchen, China ... D7 36
Taku, China ... E7 36
Taku Pa, Thai., 5,646 ... H3 38
Takut, Bur., 5,000 ... B3 38
Ţalā, Eg., U.A.R., 18,570 ... D2 32
Tala, Mex., 12,541 ... m12 63
Tala, Ur., 1,957 ... E1 56
Talaga, Phil., 1,746 ... p13 35
Talagante, Chile, 7,966 ... A2 54
Talai, China, 24,921 ... D2 37
Talakan, Sov. Un. ... B6 37
Talakmau, mtn., Indon. ... E2 35
Talala, Rogers, Okla., 147 ... A6 112
Talamanca, mts., C.R. ... F6 62
Talanga, Hond., 2,312 ... C4 62
Talanquera, pt., Cuba ... h12 64
Talara, Peru, 12,985 ... B1 58
Talas, Sov. Un., 10,000 ... E8 29
Talaud, is., Indon. ... E7 35
Talavera de la Reina, Sp., 31,900 ... B2 20
Talayan, Phil., 9,240 ... *D6 35
Talbert, Breathitt, Ky., 150 ... C6 94
Talbiya, Isr. (part of Jerusalem) ... m14 32
Talbot, Benton, Ind., 100 ... D3 89
Talbot, Marion, Oreg., 65 ... C1 113
Talbot, co., Ga., 7,127 ... D2 87
Talbot, co., Md., 21,578 ... C5 85
Talbot, isl., Fla. ... B5 86
Talbot, lake, Alta., Can. ... C1 69
Talbot, lake, Man., Can. ... B2 71
Talbotton, Talbot, Ga., 1,163 ... D2 87
Talca, Chile, 68,100 ... B2 54
Talca, prov., Chile, 205,448 ... B2 54
Talcahuano, Chile, 83,000 ... B2 54
Talcher, India, 8,147 ... G10 40
Talco, Titus, Tex., 1,024 ... C5 118
Talcott, Summers, W. Va., 600 ... D4 123
Talcottville, Tolland, Conn., 520 ... B7 84
Talcottville, Lewis, N.Y., 100 ... B5 108
Taldy-Kurgan, Sov. Un., 41,000 ... D9 29, F24 9
Talent, Jackson, Oreg., 868 ... E4 113
Talha, Chad ... A4 46
Tali, China, 9,000 ... F5 34
Tali, China, 15,000 ... G4 36
Taliabu, isl., Indon. ... F6 35
Taliaferro, co., Ga., 3,370 ... C4 87
Talien, see Dairen, China
Talihina, LeFlore, Okla., 1,048 ... C6 112
Talim, isl., Phil. ... o13 35
Tali Post, Sud. ... D3 47
Talisay, Phil., 1,512 ... o14 35
Talisayan, Phil., 10,646 ... *D6 35
Talish, mts., Iran, Sov. Un. ... B4 41
Talitsa, Sov. Un., 17,300 ... B6 29
Täljeån, riv., Swe. ... t33 25
Talkeetna, Alsk., 76 ... C9, f16 79
Talkeetna, mts., Alsk. ... f17 79
Talkhā, Eg., U.A.R., 13,216 ... C3 32
Talking Rock, Pickens, Ga., 84 ... B2 87
Tallaboa, P.R. ... C4 65
Talladega, Talladega, Ala., 17,742 ... B3 78
Talladega, co., Ala., 65,495 ... B3 78
Talladega, mts., Ala. ... B4 78
Talladega Springs, Talladega, Ala., 177 ... B3 78
Tallahala, creek, Miss. ... D4 100
Tallahassee, Leon, Fla., 48,174 ... B2 86
Tallahatchie, co., Miss., 24,081 ... B3 100
Tallahatchie, riv., Miss. ... B3 100
Tallangatta, Austl., 853 ... H6 51
Tallant, Osage, Okla., 25 ... A5 112
Tallapoosa, Haralson, Ga., 2,744 ... C1 87
Tallapoosa, New Madrid, Mo., 225 ... E8 101
Tallapoosa, co., Ala., 35,007 ... C4 78
Tallapoosa, riv., Ala. ... C3 78
Tallard, Fr., 550 ... E7 18
Tallassee, Elmore and Tallapoosa, Ala., 4,934 ... C4 78
Tallevast, Manatee, Fla., 500 ... F2 86
Talleyville, New Castle, Del., 1,000 ... *A6 85
Tallieu, Assumption, La. ... C5 95
Tallinn, Sov. Un., 311,000 ... B5 27
Tallmadge, Summit, Ohio, 10,246 ... A6 111
Tallow, Ire., 819 ... E3 11
Tallula, Menard, Ill., 547 ... D4 90
Tallula, Issaquena, Miss., 100 ... C2 100
Tallulah, Madison, La., 9,413 ... B4 95
Tallulah, mts., Ga. ... B3 87
Tallūza, Jordan, 2,000 ... f12 32
Talmage, Sask., Can., 63 ... H4 70
Talmage, Dickinson, Kans., 200 ... C6 93
Talmage, Otoe, Nebr., 361 ... D9 103
Talmage, Duchesne, Utah, 10 ... C5 119
Talnoye, Sov. Un., 10,000 ... G8 27
Talo, mtn., Eth. ... C4 47
Talodi, Sud., 2,736 ... C3 47
Talofofo, Guam, 947 ... 52
Talofofo, bay, Guam ... 52
Taloga, Dewey, Okla., 322 ... A3 112
Talon, lake, Ont., Can. ... A5 72
Talowah, Lamar, Miss., 50 ... D4 100
Talpa, Coleman, Tex., 195 ... D3 118
Talpa de Allende, Mex., 3,157 ... m11 63
Talquin, lake, Fla. ... B2 86
Talsi, Sov. Un., 10,000 ... C4 27
Taltal, Chile, 4,901 ... E1 55
Tama, Tama, Iowa, 2,925 ... C5 92
Tama, co., Iowa, 21,413 ... B5 92
Tamaha, Haskell, Okla., 80 ... B7 112
Tamalameque, Col., 1,843 ... B3 60
Tamale, Ghana, 40,400 ... E4 45
Tamalpais, mtn., Calif. ... B5 82
Tamalpais Valley, Marin, Calif., 1,500 ... *B5 82
Taman, Sov. Un., 10,000 ... I11 27
Tamanar, Mor., 783 ... C3 44
Tamano, Jap., 65,292 ... I6 37
Tamanrasset, see Fort Laperrine, Alg.
Tamanrasset, riv., Alg. ... E5 44
Tamaqua, Shuylkill, Pa., 10,173 ... E10 114
Tamar, riv., Eng. ... D3 12
Tamarack, Adams, Idaho, 50 ... E2 89
Tamarack, Aitkin, Minn., 112 ... D5 99
Tamarite, Sp., 4,272 ... B6 20
Tamaroa, Perry, Ill., 696 ... E4 90
Tamashima, Jap., 30,400 (51,928*) ... *I6 37
Tamassee, Oconee, S.C., 350 ... B1 115
Tamatave, Malag., 39,627 ... g9 49
Tamatave, prov., Malag. ... g9 49
Tamaulipas, state, Mex., 1,009,800 ... C5 63
Tamazula de Gordiano, Mex., 10,784 ... n12 63
Tamazunchale, Mex., 8,393 ... C5, m14 63
Tambach, Ken. ... A6 48
Tambacounda, Sen., 4,600 ... D2 45
També, Braz., 4,149 ... C3, h6 57
Tambelan, is., Indon. ... E3 35
Tambellaga (Well), Niger ... C6 45
Tambo, Austl., 404 ... B6 51
Tambo, riv., Peru ... D3 58
Tambo, riv., Peru ... E3 58
Tambo Grande, Peru, 4,078 ... B1 58
Tambov, Sov. Un., 194,000 ... C2 29
Tambre, riv., Sp. ... A1 20
Tamdy-Bulak, Sov. Un. ... E6 29
Tambura, Sud. ... D2 47
Tamchakett, Maur. ... C2 45
Tame, Col., 1,383 ... B3 60
Tamega, riv., Port. ... B2 20
Tamel Aike, Arg. ... D2 54
Tamgue, mtn., Guinea ... D2 45
Tamiahua, Mex., 4,055 ... C5, m15 63
Tamiahua, lagoon, Mex. ... C5 63
Tamiami, canal, Fla. ... G6 86
Tamiao, China ... C4 36
Tamina, Montgomery, Tex., 130 ... D5 118
Tamina, riv., Switz. ... C7 19
Taming, China ... F6 36
Tamins, Switz., 881 ... C7 19
Tamis, riv., Yugo. ... C5 22
Tam Ky, Viet. ... E8 38
Tamms, Alexander, Ill., 548 ... F4 90
Ţammūn, Jordan, 2,000 ... B7, f12 32
Tamney, Ire. ... B4 11
Tamo, Jefferson, Ark., 100 ... C4 81
Tamola, Kemper, Miss., 50 ... C5 100
Tamora, Seward, Nebr., 88 ... D8 103
Tamora, Ponape ... 52
Tamoroi, Ponape ... 52
Tampa, Hillsborough, Fla., 274,970 (*356,200) ... E2, E4 86
Tampa, Marion, Kans., 145 ... D6 93
Tampa, bay, Fla. ... E4 86
Tampasak, Mala. ... D5 35
Tampere, Fin., 133,300 (*172,000) ... G10 25
Tampico, Whiteside, Ill., 790 ... B4 90
Tampico, Jackson, Ind., 100 ... G6 91
Tampico, Mex., 122,535 (*180,000) ... C5, k15 63
Tampico, Valley, Mont., 50 ... B10 102
Tampico, Grainger, Tenn. ... C10 117
Tams, Raleigh, W. Va., 500 ... D3 123
Tamworth, Austl., 18,984 ... E8 51
Tamworth, Ont., Can., 375 ... C8 72
Tamworth, Eng., 13,555 ... B6 12
Tamworth, Carroll, N.H., 250 (1,016*) ... C4 105
Tana, Chile ... C2 55
Tana, lake, Eth. ... C4 47
Tana, riv., Ken. ... B7 48
Tanabe, Jap., 48,673 ... J7 37
Tanacross, Alsk., 102 ... C11 79
Tanaelv, riv., Fin. ... C11 25
Tanafjord, fjord, Nor. ... B13 25
Tanaga, isl., Alsk. ... E4 79
Tanahbala, isl., Indon. ... F1 35
Tanahgrogot, Indon. ... F5 35
Tanahmasa, isl., Indon. ... F1 35
Tanakpur, India ... C8 40
Tanami, Austl. ... D4 50
Tanana, Alsk., 349 ... B9 79
Tanana, riv., Alsk. ... C11 79
Tananarive, Malag., 254,271 ... g9 49
Tananarive, prov., Malag. ... g9 49
Tanapag, Saipan ... 52
Tanapag, hbr., Saipan ... 52
Tanaro, riv., It. ... B2 21
Tanauan, Phil., 4,265 ... o13 35
Tanaunella, It., 208 ... D2 21
Tanavuso, pt., Fiji Is. ... 52
Tancheng, China ... G8 36
Tanchon, Kor., 32,761 ... F4 37
Tancook Island, N.S., Can., 323 ... E5 74
Tanda, India, 32,687 ... D9 40
Tandag, Phil., 6,735 ... *D7 35
Tandarei, Rom., 2,353 ... C8 24
Tandil, Arg., 32,309 ... B5 54
Tandjung, Indon. ... F5 35
Tandjungbalai, Indon., 27,315 ... E1, m11 35
Tandjungpandan, Indon., 15,708 ... F3 35
Tandjungselor, Indon., 1,991 ... E5 35
Tando-Adam, Pak., 21,275 ... E2 40
Tandou, lake, Austl. ... F4 51
Tanega, isl., Jap. ... K5 37
Tanega, strait, Jap. ... K5 37
Taney, co., Mo., 10,238 ... E9 101
Taneycomo, lake, Mo. ... E5 101
Taneytown, Carroll, Md., 1,519 ... A3 85
Taneyville, Taney, Mo., 134 ... E4 101
Tanezrouft, des., Alg., Mali ... E4 44
Tanga, Tan., 38,053 ... C6 48
Tanga, reg., Tan., 687,846 ... C6 48
Tangancícuaro [de Arista], Mex., 9,428 ... n12 63
Tanganyika, see Tanzania, country, Afr.
Tanganyika, lake, Afr. ... C4 48
Tangent, Linn, Oreg., 150 ... C3, D1 113
Tanger (Tangier), Mor., 141,714 ... B3 44
Tangerhütte, Ger., 6,679 ... A6 17
Tangermünde, Ger., 13,800 ... B5 16
Tangho, China ... H5 36
Tangier, N.S., Can., 230 ... E7 74
Tangier, Parke, Ind., 95 ... E3 91
Tangier, see Tanger, Mor.
Tangier, Woodward, Okla. ... A2 112

Townsend, Northampton, Va., 120 ..... D7 121
Townshend, Windham, Vt., 170 (643▲) E3 120
Townshend, res., Vt E3 120
Townsville, Austl., 54,000 ..... C8 50
Townsville, Vance, N.C., 195 ..... A5 109
Townville, Crawford, Pa., 361 ..... C2 114
Townville, Anderson, S.C., 200 ..... B2 115
Towson, Baltimore, Md., 17,000 ..... B4, C2 85
Towuti, lake, Indon F6 35
Towyn, Wales, 4,466 ..... B3 12
Toxey, Choctaw, Ala., 157 ..... D1 78
Toy, Pershing, Nev., 15 ..... C3 104
Toyah, Reeves, Tex., 294 ..... F2 118
Toyahvale, Reeves, Tex., 20 ..... F2 118
Toyama, Jap., 207,266 ..... H8 37
Toyama, pref., Jap., 1,032,614 ..... *H8 37
Toyama, bay, Jap H8 37
Toyohashi, Jap., 215,515 ..... I8, o16 37
Toyohira, Jap., 58,900 (77,312▲) *E10 37
Toyokawa, Jap., 44,900 (65,313▲) *o16 37
Toyonaka, Jap., 199,065 ..... I7, o14 37
Tozeur, Tun., 11,820 ..... C6 44
Tozghi Koh, min., Pak G11 41
Trabancos, riv., Sp B3 20
Traben-Trarbach, Ger., 5,700 ..... D2 17
Trabzon (Trebizond), Tur., 53,039 ..... B12 31
Tracadie, N.B., Can., 1,651 ..... B5 74
Tracadie, N.S., Can., 321 ..... D8 74
Tracadie, riv., N.B., Can B4 74
Tracadie Cross, P.E.I., Can., 158 ..... *C7 74
Tracy, San Joaquin, Calif., 11,289 ..... B6, D3 82
Tracy, N.B., Can., 655 ..... D3 74
Tracy, New Haven, Conn. (part of Wallingford) C5 84
Tracy, Marion, Iowa, 300 ..... C5 92
Tracy, Barren, Ky., 50 ..... D4 94
Tracy, Lyon, Minn., 2,862 ..... F3 99
Tracy, Platte, Mo., 208 ..... B3, D1 101
Tracy, brook, Md C4 85
Tracy City, Grundy, Tenn., 1,577 ..... D8 117
Tracyton, Kitsap, Wash., 300 ..... D1 122
Trade, Johnson, Tenn., 40 ..... C12 117
Trade, lake, Sask., Can B4 70
Tradesville, Lancaster, S.C., 75 ..... B6 115
Tradewater, riv., Ky C2 94
Trading Post, Linn., Kans., 50 ..... D9 93
Traer, Tama, Iowa 1,623 ..... B5 92
Traer, Decatur, Kans., 52 ..... C3 93
Trafalgar, Johnson, Ind., 459 ..... F5 91
Trafford, Westmoreland and Allegheny, Pa., 4,330 ..... B7 114
Trafford, lake, Fla F5 86
Traiguén, Chile, 8,806 ..... B2 54
Trail, B.C., Can., 11,580 ..... E9, o19 68
Trail, Polk, Minn., 100 ..... C3 99
Trail, Jackson, Oreg., 40 ..... E4 113
Trail, ridge, Ga F4 87
Trail City, Dewey, S. Dak., 100 ..... B5 116
Trail Creek, LaPorte, Ind., 1,552 ..... A5 91
Trailer Estates, Manatee, Fla., 1,562 ..... *E4 86
Traill, co., N. Dak., 10,583 ..... B8 110
Traill, isl., Grnld B17 4
Trainer, Delaware, Pa., 2,358 ..... *G11 114
Traipu, Braz., 2,393 ..... C3 57
Trairí, riv., Braz h6 57
Tralee, Ire., 10,723 ..... E2 11
Tramelan Dessus, Switz., 5,567 ..... B3 19
Tramore, Ire., 2,882 ..... E4 11
Trampas, Taos, N. Mex., 100 ..... A4 107
Tramping, lake, Sask., Can E1 70
Tramping Lake, Sask., Can., 288 ..... E1 70
Tranås, Swe., 15,400 ..... H6 25
Trancas, Arg E2 55
Trancoso, Port., 3,537 ..... B2 20
Tranebjerg, Den., 729 ..... C4 24
Tranemo, Swe., 1,983 ..... A7 24
Trang, Thai., 16,393 ..... I3 38
Trangan, isl., Indon G8 35
Trani, It., 38,129 ..... D6 21
Tranquility, Sussex, N.J., 50 ..... B3 106
Tranquillity, Fresno, Calif., 750 ..... D3 82
Transcona, Man., Can., 14,248 ..... E3 71
Transfer, Mercer, Pa., 300 ..... D1 114
Trans-Ili Alatau, mts., Sov. Un E9 29
Transilvania, prov., Rom., 3,420,859 ..... *B6 22
Transjordan, see Jordan, country, Asia
Transvaal, prov., S. Afr., 7,020,000 ..... B4 49
Transylvania, East Carroll, La., 50 ..... B4 95
Transylvania, co., N.C., 16,372 ..... D3 109
Transylvania, reg., Rom B6 22
Transylvanian Alps, mts., Rom C6 22
Trap, mtn., Ark D5 81
Trapani, It., 78,800 ..... E4 21
Trapiche, Guat B2 62
Trappe, Talbot, Md., 358 ..... C5 85
Trappe, Montgomery, Pa., 1,264 ..... *F11 114
Trappe, creek, Md D7 85
Trapper, peak, Mont E2 102
Traralgon, Austl., 12,300 ..... I6 51
Traryd, Swe., 687 ..... B7 24
Trasimeno, lake, It C4 21
Traskwood, Saline, Ark., 205 ..... C3 81
Trás-os-Montes, reg., Port., 558,700 ..... B2 20
Trás-os-Montes e Alto Douro, prov., Port., 639,846 ..... *B2 20
Trat, Thai., 3,633 ..... F5 38
Traun, lake, Aus E6 16
Traun, riv., Aus D7 16
Traunik, Alger, Mich., 50 ..... B4 98
Traunstein, Ger., 14,400 ..... E6 16
Trave, riv., Ger E4 24
Travelers Rest, Greenville, S.C., 1,973 ..... B3 115
Travers, Alta., Can., 50 ..... D4 69
Travers, Switz., 1,550 ..... C2 19
Travers, res., Alta., Can D4 69
Traverse, co., Minn., 7,503 ..... E2 99
Traverse, isl., Mich A2 98
Traverse, lake, Minn E2 99
Traverse City, Grand Traverse, Mich., 18,432 ..... D5 98
Traverspine, riv., Newf., Can B1 75
Tra Vinh, Viet., 39,700 ..... H7 38
Travis, co., Tex., 212,136 ..... D4 118
Travnik, Yugo., 9,984 ..... C3 22
Trawbreaga, bay, Ire B4 11
Tray, mtn., Ga B3 87
Treadway, Hancock, Tenn., 75 ..... C10 117
Treadway, lake, Ill C3 90
Treasure, co., Mont., 1,345 ..... D9 102
Treasure Island, Pinellas, Fla., 3,506 ..... *E4 86
Trebbia, riv., It E5 18
Trebel, riv., Ger E6 24
Trebic, Czech, 19,200 ..... D3 26
Trebinje, Yugo., 4,072 ..... D4 22
Trebisov, Czech, 9,300 ..... D6 26
Trebizond (Trabzon), Tur., 53,039 ..... B12 31
Treble, mtn., B.C., Can B3 68
Trebnitz, see Trzebnica, Pol.
Trebon, Czech., 4,172 ..... D3 26
Treece, Cherokee, Kans., 280 ..... E9 93
Tregaron, Wales, 1,243 ..... B4 12
Tregarva, Sask., Can G3 70
Trego, Lincoln, Mont., 15 ..... B2 102
Trego, Washburn, Wis., 175 ..... C2 124
Trego, co., Kans., 5,473 ..... D4 93
Tréguier, Fr., 2,885 ..... C2 14
Treherne, Man., Can., 569 ..... E2 71
Treig, lake, Scot D4 13
Treinta y Tres, Ur., 18,600 ..... E2 56
Treinta y Tres, dept., Ur., 41,400 ..... *E2 56
Treis, Ger., 2,000 ..... C2 12
Trélazé, Fr., 9,400 ..... D3 14
Trelew, Arg., 5,880 ..... C3 54
Trelleborg, Swe., 19,200 ..... J5 25
Tremadoc, bay, Wales B3 12
Tremblant, mtn., Que., Can C3 73
Tremblay [-lès-Gonesse], Fr., 7,854 ..... g11 14
Trembleur, lake, B.C., Can B5 68
Trementina, San Miguel, N. Mex., 10 ..... B5 107
Tremiti, is., It C5 21
Tremont, Tazewell, Ill., 1,558 ..... C4 90
Tremont, Itawamba, Miss., 300 ..... A5 100
Tremont, Schuylkill, Pa., 1,893 ..... E9 114
Tremont City, Clark, Ohio, 414 ..... B4 111
Tremonton, Box Elder, Utah, 2,115 ..... B3 119
Tremosna, Czech., 3,176 ..... D8 17
Tremp, Sp., 4,466 ..... A6 20
Trempealeau, Trempealeau, Wis., 704 ..... D2 124
Trempealeau, co., Wis., 23,377 ..... D2 124
Trempealeau, riv., Wis D2 124
Trenary, Alger, Mich., 180 ..... B4 98
Trenche, riv., Que., Can B5 73
Trencin, Czech., 22,300 ..... D5 26
Trengganu, state, Mala., 278,269 ..... J7 38
Trenque, Lauquén, Arg., 10,887 (631) B4 54
Trent, Ger., 1,872 ..... D7 24
Trent, Lane, Oreg., 40 ..... D4 113
Trent, Moody, S. Dak., 232 ..... D9 116
Trent, Taylor, Tex., 298 ..... C2 118
Trent, riv., Eng A7 12
Trent, riv., N.C B6 109
Trentino-Alto Adige, pol. dist., It., 785,967 ..... C7 18
Trento, It., 80,300 ..... A3 21, C7 18
Trenton, Jackson, Ala., 80 ..... A3 78
Trenton, N.S., Can., 3,140 ..... D7 74
Trenton, Ont., Can., 13,183 ..... C7 72
Trenton, Gilchrist, Fla., 941 ..... C4 86
Trenton, Dade, Ga., 1,301 ..... B1 87
Trenton, Clinton, Ill., 1,866 ..... E4 90
Trenton, Todd, Ky., 542 ..... D2 94
Trenton, Wayne, Mich., 18,439 ..... B7, F7 98
Trenton, Grundy, Mo., 6,262 ..... A4 101
Trenton, Hitchcock, Nebr., 914 ..... D4 103
Trenton, Mercer, N.J., 114,167 (*279,800) C3 106
Trenton, Jones, N.C., 404 ..... B6 109
Trenton, Williams, N. Dak., 125 ..... A2 110
Trenton, Butler, Ohio, 3,064 ..... C3 111
Trenton, Edgefield, S.C., 314 ..... D4 115
Trenton, Gibson, Tenn., 4,225 ..... B3 117
Trenton, Fannin, Tex., 712 ..... C4 118
Trenton, Cache, Utah, 448 ..... B4 119
Trentwood, Spokane, Wash., 1,387 ..... *B8 122
Trepassey, Newf., Can., 495 ..... E5 75
Trepassey, bay, Newf., Can E5 75
Tres Algarrobos, Arg B4 54
Tres Arboles, Ur E1 56
Tres Arroyos, Arg., 29,996 ..... B4 54
Tres Cerros, Arg D3 54
Tresckow, Carbon, Pa., 1,145 ..... E10 114
Três Corações, Braz., 17,498 ..... C3 56
Tres Esquinas, Col C2 60
Tres Forcas, cape, Mor G5 36
Três Lagoas, Braz., 14,520 ..... C2 50
Tresle Creek, Bonner, Idaho, 50 ..... A2 89
Tres Lomas, Arg., 3,425 ..... B4 54
Tres Marías, is., Mex C3 63
Três Marias, res., Braz B3 56
Tres Piedras, Taos, N. Mex., 100 ..... A4 107
Tres Pinos, San Benito, Calif., 150 ..... C6 82
Tres Puntas, cape, Arg D3 54
Tres Ritos, Taos, N. Mex., 25 ..... A4 107
Tre Teste, riv., It h9 21
Treuchtlingen, Ger., 6,700 ..... E5 17
Treuenbrietzen, Ger., 8,569 ..... A7 17
Treuter, mts., N.W. Ter., Can A16 66
Treutlen, co., Ga., 5,874 ..... D4 87
Treviglio, It., 23,413 ..... B2 21
Treviño, Sp A4 20
Treviso, It., 79,200 ..... B4 21, D8 18
Trevor, Kenosha, Wis., 250 ..... F1 124
Trevorton, Northumberland, Pa., 2,597 ..... E8 114
Trevose, Bucks, Pa., 6,000 ..... *A12 114
Trevose, head, Eng D2 12
Trevose Heights, Bucks, Pa., 1,500 ..... *F12 114
Treynor, Pottawattamie, Iowa, 368 ..... C2 92
Treysa, Ger., 7,800 ..... C4 17
Trezevant, Carroll, Tenn., 944 ..... A3 117
Trhove Sviny, Czech., 2,485 ..... E9 17
Triadelphia, Ohio, W. Va., 600 ..... A4, B2 123
Triadelphia, res., Md B3 85
Triangle, Prince William, Va., 2,948 ..... C5 121
Triangle Lake, Lane, Oreg. 100 ..... C3 113
Triaucourt, Fr., 588 ..... F5 15
Tribbet, Washington, Miss., 200 ..... B3 100
Tribbey, Pottawatomie, Okla., 150 ..... B4 112
Tribune, Sask., Can., 153 ..... H4 70
Tribune, Greeley, Kans., 1,036 ..... D2 93
Trichinopoly, see Tiruchirappalli, India
Trichur, India, 73,038 ..... F6 39
Tridell, Uintah, Utah, 10 ..... C6 119
Trident, Gallatin, Mont., 100 ..... E5 102
Trident, peak, Nev B3 104
Trier, Ger., 86,800 ..... D1 17
Trieste, It., 277,600 ..... B4 21
Trieste, gulf, Italy B4 21
Trigg, co., Ky., 8,870 ..... D2 94
Triglav, mtn., Yugo B1 22
Trigo, mts., Ariz D1 80
Trigueros, Sp., 6,454 ..... D2 20
Trikkala, Grc., 27,876 ..... C3 23
Trikkala, prov., Grc., 142,781 ..... *C3 23
Tri Lakes, Whitley, Ind., 1,089 ..... *B7 91
Trilby, Pasco, Fla., 700 ..... D4 86
Trilby, Lucas, Ohio, 5,000 ..... A2 111
Trilla, Coles and Cumberland, Ill., 225 ..... D5 90
Trillick, N. Ire., 220 ..... C4 11
Trim, Ire., 1,371 ..... D5 11
Trimble, La Plata, Colo., 20 ..... D3 83
Trimble, Clinton, Mo., 185 ..... B3 101
Trimble, Dyer, Tenn., 581 ..... A2 117
Trimble, co., Ky., 5,102 ..... B4 94
Trimble, isl., Wash D1 122
Trimont, Martin, Minn., 942 ..... G4 99
Trimountain, Houghton, Mich., 400 ..... A2 98
Trinchera, Las Animas, Colo. 150 ..... D6 83
Trinchera, creek, Colo D5 83
Trinchera, peak, Colo D5 83
Trincomalee, Cey., 26,356 ..... G7 39
Tring-Jonction, Que., Can., 1,214 ..... C6 73
Trinidad, Bol., 8,695 ..... B3 65
Trinidad, Humboldt, Calif., 289 ..... *B1 82
Trinidad, Las Animas, Colo., 10,691 ..... D6 83
Trinidad, Cuba, 16,756 ..... E4 64
Trinidad, Henderson, Tex., 786 ..... C4 118
Trinidad, Ur., 13,600 ..... E1 56
Trinidad & Tobago, country, N.A., 960,000 ..... A5 60
Trinidad, bay, Pan k11 62
Trinidad, isl., Arg B4 54
Trinidad, isl., Trin A5 60
Trinidade, isl., Braz H8 6
Trinité, Mart., 7,732 ..... o16 74
Trinity, Morgan, Ala., 454 ..... A2 78
Trinity, Newf., Can., 362 ..... D5 75
Trinity, Newf., Can., 692 ..... D5 75
Trinity, Randolph, N.C., 881 ..... B4 109
Trinity, Trinity, Tex., 1,787 ..... D5 118
Trinity, co., Calif., 9,706 ..... B2 82
Trinity, co., Tex., 7,539 ..... D5 118
Trinity, bay, Newf., Can D5 75
Trinity, isl., Alsk D9 79
Trinity, mtn., Idaho F3 89
Trinity, mts., Nev C3 104
Trinity, mts., Calif B2 82
Trinity, range, Nev C3 104
Trinity, res., Calif B2 82
Trinity, riv., Calif B2 82
Trinity, riv., Tex D5 118
Trinity Center, Trinity, Calif., 100 ..... B2 82
Trinity Springs, Martin, Ind., 125 ..... G4 91
Trino, It., 8,100 ..... B2 21
Trinway, Muskingum, Ohio, 500 ..... B5 111
Trio, Williamsburg, S.C., 174 ..... E8 115
Trion, Chattooga, Ga., 2,227 ..... B1 87
Triplett, Chariton, Mo., 231 ..... B4 101
Tripoli, Bremer, Iowa, 1,179 ..... B5 92
Tripoli, see Tarabulus, Leb.
Tripoli (Tarābulus), Libya, 212,600 ..... C2 43
Tripoli, Oneida, Wis., 45 ..... C4 124
Tripolis, Grc., 18,500 ..... D4 23
Tripolitania (Tarābulus), prov., Libya, 746,064 ..... C2 43
Tripp, Hutchinson, S. Dak., 837 ..... D8 116
Tripp, co., S. Dak., 8,761 ..... D6 116
Tripura, ter., India, 1,142,005 ..... *D9 39
Trischen, isl., Ger A4 16
Tristan da Cunha, is., Atl. O I9 6
Tristate Village, Du Page, Ill., 1,000 ..... *B6 90
Triste, gulf, Ven A4 60
Tritle, mtn., Ariz C3 80
Triumph, Plaquemines, La., 900 ..... E6 95
Triune, Williamson, Tenn., 100 ..... B5 117
Triunfo, Braz., 3,123 ..... C3 57
Trivandrum, India, 239,815 (*302,214) G6 39
Trnava, Czech., 31,700 ..... D4 26
Trobriand, is., Pap k13 50
Trochu, Alta., Can., 671 ..... D4 69
Trogir, Yugo., 4,995 ..... D3 22
Trögstad, Nor p29 25
Troisdorf, Ger., 16,700 ..... C2 17
Trois-Pistoles, Que., Can., 4,349 ..... A8 73
Trois-Rivières, Que., Can., 56,413 (*87,432) C5 73
Trois-Saumons, Que., Can., 60 ..... B7 73
Troisvierges, Lux., 2,006 ..... D6 13
Troitsk, Sov. Un., 80,000 ..... C6 29
Troitskoye, Sov. Un., 1,000 ..... B8 37
Trojan, Lawrence, S. Dak., 5 ..... C2 116
Trolldalen, Nor., 141 ..... p28 25
Trollhättan, Swe., 33,100 ..... H5 25
Trombetas, riv., Braz C3 59
Trombudo [Central], Braz., 732 ..... D3 56
Tromper, bay, Ger D7 24
Troms, co., Nor., 127,500 ..... *C8 25
Tromsö, Nor., 12,400 (*19,500) C8 25
Trona, San Bernardino, Calif., 1,138 ..... E5 82
Tronador, mtn., Arg C2 54
Trondheim, Nor., 58,600 (*109,000) F3 25
Trondheimsfjord, fjord, Nor F3 25
Troodos, mtn., Cyp E9 31
Troon, Scot., 9,932 ..... E4 13
Tropea, It., 6,702 ..... E5 21
Trophy, mtn., B.C., Can D8 68
Tropic, Garfield, Utah, 382 ..... F3 119
Trosa, Swe., 1,300 ..... u35 25
Trosky, Pipestone, Minn., 122 ..... G2 99
Trossachs, Sask., Can., 89 ..... H3 70
Trostan, mtn., N. Ire B5 11
Trotters, Golden Valley, N. Dak., 2 ..... B2 110
Trotwood, Montgomery, Ohio, 4,992 ..... C3 111
Trough Creek, Huntingdon, Pa., 50 ..... E5 114
Troup, Cherokee and Smith, Tex., 1,667 ..... C5 118
Troup, co., Ga., 47,189 ..... C1 87
Trousdale, Edwards, Kans., 83 ..... E4 93
Trousdale, co., Ten., 4,914 ..... A5 117
Trousers, lake, N.B., Can B3 74
Trout, La Salle, La., 500 ..... C3 95
Trout, creek, Fla B6 86
Trout, lake, B.C., Can D9 68
Trout, lake, N.W. Ter., Can D8 66
Trout, lake, Ont., Can A5 72
Trout, lake, Ont., Can o16 72
Trout, lake, Minn B6 99
Trout, lake, Wis B4 124
Trout, peak, Wyo A3 125
Trout, riv., Alta., Can A3 69
Trout, riv., Vt B3 120
Trout Creek, Ont., Can., 510 ..... B5 72
Trout Creek, Ontonagon, Mich., 350 ..... A6 98
Trout Creek, Sanders, Mont., 100 ..... C1 102
Trout Creek, Juab, Utah, 15 ..... D2 119
Trout Creek, pass, Colo C5 83
Troutdale, Somerset, Maine C3 96
Trout Dale, Grayson, Va., 273 ..... B3, E1 121
Trout Lake, Chippewa, Mich., 200 ..... B5 98
Trout Lake, Klickitat, Wash., 450 ..... D4 122
Troutman, Stewart, Ga., 100 ..... E2 87
Troutman, Iredell, N.C., 648 ..... B3 109
Trout River, Newf., Can., 696 ..... D2 75
Trout Run, Lycoming, Pa., 370 ..... D7 114
Troutville, Botetourt, Va., 524 ..... D3 121
Trouville, Fr., 6,622 ..... C3 14
Trowbridge, Eng., 15,833 ..... C5 12
Troy, Pike, Ala., 10,234 ..... D4 78
Troy, Latah, Idaho, 555 ..... C2 89
Troy, Madison, Ill., 1,778 ..... E4 90
Troy, Perry, Ind., 528 ..... H4 91
Troy, Davis, Iowa, 95 ..... D5 92
Troy, Doniphan, Kans., 1,051 ..... C8 93
Troy, Oakland, Mich., 19,382 ..... *F7 98
Troy, Pontotoc, Miss., 250 ..... A5 100
Troy, Lincoln, Mo., 1,779 ..... C7 101
Troy, Lincoln, Mont., 855 ..... B1 102
Troy, Cheshire, N.H., 950 ..... E2 105
Troy, Rensselaer, N.Y., 67,492 ..... C7 108
Troy, Montgomery, N.C., 2,346 ..... B4 109
Troy, Miami, Ohio, 13,685 ..... B3 111
Troy, Johnston, Okla., 100 ..... C5 112
Troy, Wallowa, Oreg., 100 ..... B9 113
Troy, Bradford, Pa., 1,478 ..... C8 114
Troy, Greenwood, S.C., 260 ..... C3 115
Troy, Grant, S. Dak., 15 ..... B9 116
Troy, Obion, Tenn., 587 ..... A2 117
Troy, Bell, Tex., 500 ..... D4 118
Troy, Orleans, Vt., 150 (1,613▲) B4 120
Troy, Gilmer, W. Va., 110 ..... B4 123
Troy, peak, Nev E6 104
Troy, ruins, Tur C6 23
Troyes, Fr., 67,406 (*101,000) C6 14
Troy Grove, La Salle, Ill., 271 ..... B4 90
Troy Mills, Linn, Iowa, 150 ..... B6 92
Trstenik, Yugo., 5,577 ..... D5 22
Truax, Sask., Can., 76 ..... H3 70
Trubchevsk, Sov. Un., 10,000 ..... E9 27
Trubschachen, Switz., 1,665 ..... C4 19
Truchas, Rio Arriba, N. Mex., 400 ..... A4 107
Truchas, peak, N. Mex B4 107
Trucial Coast, country, Asia, 120,000 ..... I7 41
Truckee, Nevada, Calif., 950 ..... C3 82
Truckee, riv., Nev D2 104
Trucksville, Luzerne, Pa., 2,300 ..... *B8 114
Truesdell, Kenosha, Wis., 10 ..... F2 124
Truhart, King and Queen, Va., 55 ..... D6 121
Trujillo, Hond., 2,957 ..... C4 62
Trujillo, San Miguel, N. Mex., 10 ..... B5 107
Trujillo, Peru, 99,800 ..... C2 58
Trujillo, Sp., 13,326 ..... C3 20
Trujillo, Ven., 19,358 ..... B3 60
Trujillo, state, Ven., 326,634 ..... B3 60
Trujillo Alto, P.R., 1,297 ..... B6 65
Trujillo Alto, mun., P.R., 18,251 ..... B6 65
Truk, is., Caroline Is 52
Truman, Martin, Minn., 1,256 ..... G4 99
Trumann, Poinsett, Ark., 4,511 ..... B5 81
Trumansburg, Tompkins, N.Y., 1,768 ..... C4 108
Trumbull, Fairfield, Conn., 20,379 ..... D4 84
Trumbull, Clay and Adams, Nebr., 173 ..... D7 103
Trumbull, co., Ohio, 208,526 ..... A7 111
Trun, Bul., 2,169 ..... D6 22
Truro, N.S., Can., 12,421 ..... D6 74
Truro, Eng., 13,328 ..... D2 12
Truro, Madison, Iowa 338 ..... C4 92
Truro, Barnstable, Mass., 400 (1,002▲) C7 97
Truscott, Knox, Tex., 150 ..... C3 118
Trussville, Jefferson, Ala., 2,510 ..... B3, E5 78
Truth or Consequences, Sierra, N. Mex., 4,269 ..... D2 107
Trutnov, Czech., 23,000 ..... C3 26
Truxton, Mohave, Ariz., 15 ..... B2 80
Truxton, Lincoln, Mo., 85 ..... B6 101
Truxton, Cortland, N.Y., 250 ..... C4 108
Tryon, McPherson, Nebr., 150 ..... C5 103
Tryon, Polk, N.C., 2,223 ..... D4 109
Tryon, Lincoln, Okla., 254 ..... B5 112
Trysil, Nor G5 25
Trzcianka, Pol., 4,482 ..... B4 26
Trzebiatowo, Pol., 5,995 ..... A3 26
Trzebinia, Pol., 4,140 ..... C5, g10 26
Trzebnica, Pol., 3,170 ..... C4 26
Tsabong, Bech C3 49
Tsagaan Hamar, Mong C2 36
Tsala Apopka, lake, Fla D4 86
Tsane, Bech B3 49
Tsang, China E7 36
Tsanghsien, China, 60,000 ..... *D8 34
Tsangpo (Brahmaputra), riv., China C8 39
Tsangwu, see Wuchow, China
Tsaratanana, Malag., 1,145 ..... g9 49
Tsau, Bech B3 49
Tsavo, Ken B6 48
Tschetter Colony, Hutchinson, S. Dak., 75 ..... D8 116
Tschida, lake, N. Dak C4 110
Tselinograd (Akmolinsk), Sov. Un., 139,000 ..... C8 29
Tsentralnyy, Sov. Un D26 9
Tsetsey Suma, Mong C1 36
Tshela, Con. L B1 48
Tshikapa, Con. L., 6,400 ..... C3 48
Tshilongo, Con. L C4 48
Tshimbo, Con. L C4 48
Tshofa C4 48
Tshuapa, riv., Con. L B3 48
Tsiafajavona, mtn., Malag g9 49
Tsihombe, Malag., 600 ..... k9 49
Tsimlyansk, res., Sov. Un D2 29
Tsinan (Chinan), China, 862,000 ..... D8 34
Tsinghai (Chinghai), prov., China, 2,050,000 ..... D4 34
Tsinghai, seekoko-Nor, lake, China
Tsingma, China C8 38
Tsingtao (Chingtao), China, 1,121,000 ..... D9 34, F9 36
Tsingyuan, see Paoting, China
Tsinling Shan, mts., China E6 34
Tsintsabis, S.W. Afr A2 49
Tsiroanomandidy, Malag g9 49
Tsis, isl., Truk 52
Tsitsihar (Ch'i-ch'i-ha-erh), China, 668,000 ..... B9 34
Tsitsutl, peak, B.C., Can C5 68
Tsivory, Malag., 800 ..... h9 49
Tskhakaya, Sov. Un., 10,000 ..... A13 31
Tskhinvali, Sov. Un., 24,000 ..... E2 29
Tsna, riv., Sov. Un C2 29
Tsodilo, mtn., Bech A3 49
Tsoshui, China, 2,000 ..... H3 36
Tsu, Jap., 110,900 ..... I8, o15 37
Tsuchiura, Jap., 47,500 (71,474▲) H10, m19 37
Tsugaru, strait, Jap F10 37
Tsukan, isl., Okinawa 52
Tsulukidze, Sov. Un., 9,700 ..... A14 31
Tsumeb, S.W. Afr A2 49
Tsumis, S.W. Afr B2 49
Tsunami, Okinawa 52
Tsunghua, China, 1,000 ..... G7 36
Tsunhua, China, 15,000 ..... D7 36
Tsuni, China, 97,500 ..... K2 36
Tsun Wan, Hong Kong, 150,000 ..... *G7 34
Tsurikake, Jap 6,800 ..... E9 37
Tsuruga, Jap., 36,000 (53,493▲) I8, n15 37
Tsuruoka, Jap., 56,300 (83,149▲) G9 37
Tsushima, Jap., 43,198 ..... n15 37
Tsu-Shima, isl., Jap I4 37
Tsushima, strait, Jap I4 37
Tsuyama, Jap., 44,800 (78,549▲) I7 37
Tsuyung, China F5 34
Túa, riv., Port B2 20
Tual, Indon G8 35
Tualatin, riv., Oreg B1 113
Tuam, Ire., 3,500 ..... D3 11
Tuamotu (Low), arch., Fr. Polynesia H13 7
Tuangku, isl., Indon, 634 ..... K2 38
Tuapse, Sov. Un., 36,650 ..... G16 9
Tuasivi, Cape, W. Sam 52
Tuatapere, N.Z., 872 ..... Q11 51
Tuath, bay, Scot D2 13
Tubac, Santa Cruz, Ariz., 100 ..... F4 80
Tuba City, Coconino, Ariz., 500 ..... A4 80
Tubarão, Braz., 29,615 ..... D3 56
Tubas, Jordan, 5,000 ..... B7, f12 32
Tuberose, Sask., Can G1 70
Tübingen, Ger., 52,000 ..... E4 17
Tu Bong, Viet F8 38
Tubre, It., 941 ..... C6 18
Tubrug (Tobruk), Libya, 4,995 ..... C4 43
Tubuai, is., Fr. Polynesia *H13 7
Tucacas, Ven., 3,783 ..... A4 60
Tucannon, canyon, Wash C8 122
Tucannon, riv., Wash C8 122
Tucano, Braz., 4,007 ..... D3 57
Tuchola, Pol., 5,750 ..... B4 26
Tuchuan, China B9 36
Tuckahoe, Cape May, N.J., 750 ..... E3 106
Tuckahoe, Westchester, N.Y., 6,423 ..... h13 108
Tuckahoe, creek, Md C6 85
Tuckahoe, riv., N.J E3 106
Tucker, Jefferson, Ark., 350 ..... C4 81
Tucker, De Kalb, Ga., 5,000 ..... A5 87
Tucker, Jones, Miss., 25 ..... D4 100
Tucker, Anderson, Tex., 75 ..... D5 118
Tucker, co., W. Va., 7,750 ..... B5 123
Tucker, isl., N.J D4 106
Tuckerman, Jackson, Ark., 1,539 ..... B4 81
Tuckernuck, isl., Mass D7 97
Tuckerton, Ocean, N.J., 1,536 ..... D4 106
Tucson, Pima, Ariz., 212,892 (*243,000) E5 80
Tucumán, Arg., 280,000 ..... E2 55
Tucumán, prov., Arg., 780,348 ..... E2 55
Tucumcari, Quay, N. Mex., 8,143 ..... B6 107
Tucumcari, mtn., N. Mex B6 107
Tucupita, Ven., 9,575 ..... B5 60
Tucuruí, Braz., 3,403 ..... C5 59
Tuczna, riv., Pol m13 26
Tucznobaby, Pol g10 26
Tudela, Sp., 16,456 ..... A5 20
Tufi, Pap k12 50
Tug, fork, W. Va., Ky C2 123
Tugaloo, riv., S.C B1 115
Tugaske, Sask., Can., 267 ..... G2 70
Tuguegarao, Phil., 23,584 ..... B6 35
Tuira, riv., Pan F9 62
Tukangbesi, is., Indon G6 35
Tükrah (Tocra), Libya, 4,643 ..... C4 43
Tuktoyaktuk, N.W. Ter., Can., 409 ..... C6 66
Tukums, Sov. Un., 10,000 ..... C4 27
Tukuyu, Tan, 3,563 ..... C5 48
Tukwila, King, Wash., 1,804 ..... D1 122
Tukzar, Afg., 5,000 ..... D13 41
Tula, Mex., 7,559 ..... C5 63
Tula, Lafayette, Miss., 175 ..... A4 100
Tula, Sov. Un., 351,000 ..... C1 29
Tulalip, Indian res., Wash A3 122
Tulancingo, Mex., 26,663 ..... C5, m14 63
Tulare Tulare, Calif., 13,824 ..... D4 82
Tulare, Spink, S. Dak., 225 ..... C7 116
Tulare, co., Calif., 168,403 ..... D4 82
Tularosa, Otero, N. Mex., 3,200 ..... D3 107
Tularosa, mts., N. Mex D1 107
Tularosa, val., N. Mex E3 107
Tulcán, Ec., 10,658 ..... A2 58
Tulcea, Rom., 24,639 ..... C9 22
Tulchin, Sov. Un., 10,000 ..... G7 27
Tulear, Malag., 18,648 ..... h8 49
Tule River, Indian res., Calif E4 82
Tuli, Rh B4 49
Tulia, Swisher, Tex., 4,410 ..... B2 118
Tül Karm, Jordan, 21,872 ..... B7, f11 32
Tulla, Ire., 389 ..... E3 11
Tullahassee, Wagoner, Okla., 199 ..... B6 112
Tullahoma, Coffee, Tenn., 12,242 ..... B5 117
Tullamore, Ire., 6,243 ..... D4 11
Tulle, Fr., 19,084 ..... E4 14
Tullins, Fr., 3,680 ..... E6 14
Tulln, Aus., 6,306 ..... D8 16
Tullos, La Salle, La., 594 ..... C3 95
Tullow, Ire., 1,725 ..... E5 11
Tully, Austl., 2,678 ..... C8 50
Tully, Onondaga, N.Y., 803 ..... C4 108
Tully, res., Mass A3 97
Tullytown, Bucks, Pa., 2,452 ..... *F2 114
Tulmaythah, Libya, 350 ..... F3 31
Tuloma, riv., Sov. Un C15 25
Tulot, Poinsett, Ark., 80 ..... B5 81
Tulsa, Tulsa, Okla., 261,685 (*387,100) A6 112
Tulsa, co., Okla., 346,038 ..... B6 112
Tulsequah, B.C., Can E6 66
Tulsk, Ire D3 11
Tuluá, Col., 28,715 ..... C2 60
Tulufan, see Turfan, China
Tulun, Sov. Un., 34,000 ..... D13 28
Tulu Wallel, mtn., Eth D3 47
Tulyehualco, Mex., 4,089 ..... h9 63
Tuma, riv., Nic D5 63
Tumaco, Col., 12,692 ..... C2 60
Tumaco, bay, Col C2 60
Tumacacori, Santa Cruz, Ariz., 80 ..... F4 80
Tumacacori, nat. mon., Ariz F4 80
Tumatumari, Br. Gu A3 59
Tumba, Swe., 6,618 ..... t35 25
Tumba, lake, Con. L B2 48

Union, Union, Oreg., 1,490..B9 113
Union, Union, S.C., 10,191..B4 115
Union, Salt Lake, Utah, 1,500..........*C4 119
Union, Mason, Wash., 500..B2 122
Union, Monroe, W. Va., 411..........D4 123
Union, co., Ark., 49,518.....D3 81
Union, co., Fla., 6,043......B4 86
Union, co., Ga., 6,510.......B2 87
Union, co., Ill., 17,645......F4 90
Union, co., Ind., 6,457......E8 91
Union, co., Iowa, 13,712....C8 92
Union, co., Ky., 14,537.....C2 94
Union, co., Miss., 18,904....A4 100
Union, co., N.J., 504,255....B4 106
Union, co., N. Mex., 6,068..A6 107
Union, co., N.C., 44,670.....B3 109
Union, co., Ohio, 22,853.....B4 111
Union, co., Oreg., 18,180....B8 113
Union, co., Pa., 25,646......E7 114
Union, co., S.C., 30,015......B4 115
Union, co., S. Dak., 10,197..E9 116
Union, co., Tenn., 8,498...C10 117
Union, par., La., 17,624.....B3 95
Union, lake, N.J...........E2 106
Union, riv., Maine..........D4 96
Union Bay, B.C., Can., 600..E5 68
Union Beach, Monmouth, N.J., 5,862..........C4 106
Union Bridge, Carroll, Md., 833..........A3 85
Union Center, Meade, S. Dak., 35..........C3 116
Union Center, Juneau, Wis., 252..........E3 124
Union City, Alameda, Calif., 6,618..........B5 82
Union City, Fulton, Ga., 2,118..........B4, C2 87
Union City, Randolph, Ind., 4,047..........D8 91
Union City, Branch and Calhoun, Mich., 1,669....F5 98
Union City, Hudson, N.J., 52,180..........h8 106
Union City, Darke, Ohio, 1,657..........*B3 111
Union City, Erie, Pa., 3,819..........C2 114
Union City, Obion, Tenn., 8,837..........A2 117
Union Creek, Jackson, Oreg., 25..........E4 113
Uniondale, Wells, Ind., 311..C7 91
Uniondale, Nassau, N.Y., 20,500..........*G2 84
Union Dale, Susquehanna, Pa., 287..........C11 114
Unión de Reyes, Cuba, 5,503..........D3 64
Unión de Tula, Mex., 5,584..........m11 63
Union Flat, creek, Wash.......C8 122
Union Furnace, Hocking, Ohio, 300..........C5 111
Union Gap, Yakima, Wash., 2,100..........C5 122
Union Grove, Racine, Wis., 1,970..........F1, F5 124
Union Hall, Franklin, Va., 50..........D3 121
Unionhill, Independence, Ark., 25..........B4 81
Union Lake, Oakland, Mich., 2,000..........*F7 98
Union Mills, LaPorte, Ind., 450..........B4 91
Union Mills, Carroll, Md., 60..........A3 85
Union of South Africa, see South Africa, country, Afr.
Union of Soviet Socialist Republics, country, Eur., Asia, 216,151,000......26, D11 33
Union Park, Orange, Fla., 1,000..........*D5 86
Union Pier, Berrien, Mich., 900..........G4 98
Union Point, Greene, Ga., 1,615..........C3 87
Union Springs, Bullock, Ala., 3,704..........C4 78
Union Springs, Cayuga, N.Y., 1,066..........C4 108
Union Star, DeKalb, Mo., 392..........B3 101
Uniontown, Perry, Ala., 1,993..........C2 78
Uniontown, Perry, Ind., 20..H5 91
Uniontown, Bourbon, Kans., 211..........E9 93
Uniontown, Union, Ky., 1,255..........C2 94
Uniontown, Carroll, Md., 260..........A3 96
Uniontown, Perry, Mo., 125..........D8 101
Uniontown, Stark, Ohio, 1,668..........B6 111
Uniontown, Fayette, Pa., 17,942..........G2 114
Uniontown, Whitman, Wash., 242..........C8 122
Union Village, Providence, R.I., 1,500..........B10 84
Union Village, Orange and Windsor, Vt., 70....D4 120
Union Village, flood control res., Vt...........D4 120
Unionville, Ont., Can., 945..........D5, k15 72
Unionville, Hartford, Conn., 2,300..........B5 84
Unionville, Bibb, Ga., 1,000..........*D3 87
Unionville, Tift, Ga., 1,607..........*E3 87
Unionville, Whiteside, Ill., 100..........B3 90
Unionville, Appanoose, Iowa, 185..........D5 92
Unionville, Washington, Maine..........D5 96
Unionville, Tuscola, Mich., 629..........E7 98
Unionville, Putnam, Mo., 1,896..........A4 101
Unionville, Union, N.C., 119..........B3 109
Unionville, Ashtabula and Lake, Ohio, 500..........A7 111
Unionville, Bedford, Tenn., 100..........B5 117
Unionville, Orange, Va., 250..........C5 121
Unionville Center, Union, Ohio, 305..........B4 111
Unisan, Phil., 1,890.........p13 35
United, Westmoreland, Pa., 2,044..........F3 114
United Arab Republic (Egypt), country, Afr., 29,000,000..........H6 31, D5 43
United Kingdom of Great Britain and Northern Ireland, country, Eur., 54,500,000..........E9 8,10
United Nations Headquarters, N.Y...........h13 108
United Provinces, see Uttar Pradesh, state, India
United Pueblos, Indian res., N. Mex...........A3 107
United States, country, N.A., 193,850,000..........F11 61, 77
U.S. Air Force Academy, El Paso, Colo., 5,000......C6 83
U.S. Naval Ammunition Depot, Mineral, Nev..........E3 104
Unity, Sask., Can., 1,902....E1 70
Unity, Alexander, Ill., 110...F4 90
Unity, Waldo, Maine, 400 (983▲)..........D3 96
Unity, Sullivan, N.H., 50 (708▲)..........D2 105
Unity, Baker, Oreg., 150....C8 113
Unity, Marathon and Clark, Wis., 386..........D3 124
Unity, dam, Oreg...........C8 113
Unity, pond, Maine..........D4 96
Unityville, McCook, S. Dak., 70..........D8 116
Universal, Vermillion, Ind., 424..........E3 91
Universales, mts., Sp.........B5 20
University, Tuscaloosa, Ala. (part of Tuscaloosa).......B2 78
University, Lafayette, Miss., 3,597..........A4 100
University City, St. Louis, Mo., 51,249..........A8, C7 101
University Gardens, Prince Georges, Md., 1,000.....*C4 85
University Heights, Cuyahoga, Ohio, 16,641........B2 111
University Hills, Prince Georges, Md., 1,700.......*C4 85
University Park, Mahaska, Iowa, 569..........C5 92
University Park, Prince Georges, Md., 3,098........*C4 85
University Park, Dona Ana, N. Mex., 3,800.........E3 107
University Park, Dallas, Tex., 23,202..........B5 118
University View, Franklin, Ohio, 1,000..........*C2 111
Unlingen, Ger., 900.........A5 18
Unna, Ger., 31,500.........B2 17
Unnen, lake, Swe...........B7 24
Unsan, Kor..........G2 37
Unsernherrn, Ger., 5,900....E6 17
Unst, isl., Scot...........g10 10
Unstrut, riv., Ger...........B5 17
Unterwalden, canton, Switz., 45,323..........C5 19
Unterwasser, Switz.........B7 19
Unuk, riv., B.C., Can........A2 68
Unuwhao, mtn., N.Z.........K14 51
Unwin, Sask., Can..........E1 70
Unye, Tur., 11,400.........B11 31
Unzha, riv., Sov. Un........D17 9
Uondo, Eth..........D4 47
Uorra Ilu, Eth..........C4 47
Upalco, Duchesne, Utah, 50..........C5 119
Upemba, lake, Con. L........C4 48
Upernavik, Grnld., 555.....B20 4
Upham, McHenry, N. Dak., 333..........A5 110
Upia, riv., Col...........C3 60
Upington, S. Afr., 20,366....C3 49
Upland, San Bernardino, Calif., 15,918..........E5, F3 82
Upland, Grant, Ind., 1,999..........D7 91
Upland, Franklin, Nebr., 237..........D7 103
Upland, Delaware, Pa., 4,343..........*G10 114
Upolu, isl., W. Sam........... 52
Upolu, pt., Haw...........C6 88
Upper, reg., Ghana..........D4 45
Upper Ammonoosuc, riv., N.H...A4 105
Upper Arlington, Franklin, Ohio, 28,486..........C2, C4 111
Upper Arrow, lake, B.C., Can...D9 68
Upper Black Eddy, Bucks, Pa., 400..........E11 114
Upper Blackville, N.B., Can., 438..........C4 74
Upper Brookville, Nassau, N.Y., 1,045..........*n15 108
Upperco, Baltimore, Md., 150..........A4 85
Upper Darby, Delaware, Pa., 44,000..........B11, G11 114
Upper Dilia, Guadalupe, N. Mex., 60..........*B4 107
Upper Erne, lake, N. Ire.......C4 11
Upper Fairmount, Somerset, Md., 550..........D6 85
Upper Falls, Baltimore, Md., 100..........B5 85
Upper Fraser, B.C., Can., 172..........B7 68
Upper Frenchville, Aroostook, Maine, 200..........A4 96
Upper Gagetown, N.B., Can., 244..........D3 74
Upper Ganges, canal, India....C6 40
Upper Giuba, dist., Som......E5 47
Upper Gloucester, Cumberland, Maine, 150..........D5, E2 96
Upper Graniteville, Washington, Vt., 500..........C4 120
Upper Gullies, Newf., Can., 547..........*E5 75
Upper Humber, riv., Newf., Can...........D3 75
Upper Indian, pond, Newf., Can...........D3 75
Upper Iowa, riv., Iowa........A6 92
Upper Island Cove, Newf., Can., 1,668..........E5 75
Upper Jay, Essex, N.Y., 200..........f11 108
Upper Kapuas, mts., Indon., Mala..........E4 35
Upper Kent, N.B., Can., 174..........C2 74
Upper Klamath, lake, Oreg.....E5 113
Upper Lake, Lake, Calif., 400..........C2 82
Upper Marlboro, Prince Georges, Md., 673.......C4 85
Upper Musquodoboit, N.S., Can., 328..........D7 74
Upper New York, bay, N.J......k8 106
Upper Nile, reg., Sud., 888,611..........D3 47
Upper Nyack, Rockland, N.Y., 1,833..........*D7 108
Upper Red, lake, Minn........B4 99
Upper Sackville, N.B., Can., 254..........D5 74
Upper Saddle River, Bergen, N.J., 3,570..........A4 106
Upper Sandusky, Wyandot, Ohio, 4,941..........B4 111
Upper Seal, lake, Que., Can...g12 73
Upper Sheila, N.B., Can., 752..........B5 74
Upper Silesia, reg., Pol......g9 26
Upper Strasburg, Franklin, Pa., 75..........F6 114
Upper Tract, Pendleton, W. Va., 85..........C5 123
Upperville, Fauquier, Va., 400..........C5 121
Upper Volta, country, Afr., 4,775,000........E5 42, D4 45
Upper Wilson, pond, Maine....C3 96
Upper Wood Harbour, N.S., Can, 130..........F4 74
Uppsala, Swe., 80,500...H7, t35 25
Uppsala, co., Swe., 170,000..........*H7 25
Upsala, Morrison, Minn., 356..........E4 104
Upsalquitch, N.B., Can., 165..........B3 74
Upsalquitch, riv., N.B., Can...B3 74
Upshur, co., Tex., 19,793....C5 118
Upshur, co., W. Va., 18,292..........C4 123
Upson, co., Ga., 23,800......D2 87
Upson, Iron, Wis., 150.......B3 124
Uptanum, ridge, Wash..........C5 122
Upton, Que., Can., 830......D5 73
Upton, Hardin and Larue, Ky., 547..........C4 94
Upton, Oxford, Maine, 30 (35▲)..........D2 96
Upton, Worcester, Mass., 1,150 (3,127▲)..........B4, h9 97
Upton, Texas, Mo., 56.......D5 101
Upton, Weston, Wyo., 1,224..........A8 125
Upton, co., Tex., 6,239......D1 118
Urabá, gulf, Col...........B2 60
Uracas, isl., Mariana Is.......E8 7
Uracoa, Ven., 849..........B5 50
Urakawa, Jap., 12,300......E11 37
Ural, Lincoln, Mont.........B1 102
Ural, mts., Sov. Un..........D20 9
Ural, riv., Sov. Un...........E20 9
Uralsk, Sov. Un., 111,000...C4 29
Urandi, Braz., 1,497.........D2 57
Urania, La Salle, La., 1,063..C3 95
Uranium City, Sask., Can., 1,665..........m7 70
Uraicoera, riv., Braz..........C5 60
Ura-Tyube, Sov. Un., 20,000..........H22 9
Uravan, Montrose, Colo., 1,005..........C2 83
Urawa, Jap., 168,757....I9, n18 37
Urbana, Union, Ark., 400...D3 81
Urbana, Champaign, Ill., 27,294..........C5 90
Urbana, Wabash, Ind., 350..C6 91
Urbana, Benton, Iowa, 544..B6 92
Urbana, Frederick, Md., 100..........B3 85
Urbana, Dallas, Mo., 348...D4 101
Urbana, Champaign, Ohio, 10,461..........B4 111
Urbancrest, Franklin, Ohio, 1,029..........C2 111
Urbandale, Polk, Iowa, 5,821..........A7, C4 92
Urbank, Otter Tail, Minn., 177..........D3 99
Urbanna, Middlesex, Va., 512..........D6 121
Urbino, It., 6,500..........C4 21
Urcos, Peru, 2,096..........D3 58
Urdaneta, Phil., 4,474.......o13 35
Urdzhar, Sov. Un., 3,500...D10 29
Ure, riv., Eng...........F7 13
Ures, Mex., 3,456..........B2 63
Urfa, Tur., 59,863..........D12 31
Urga, Sov. Un..........E5 29
Urgench, Sov. Un., 55,000...E6 29
Urgun, Afg., 5,000..........E14 41
Urgut, Sov. Un..........B13 41
Uri, canton, Switz., 32,021..C6 19
Uriah, Monroe, Ala., 800....D2 78
Uribia, Col., 1,101..........A3 69
Urich, Henry, Mo., 408......C4 101
Urique, Mex., 256..........B3 63
Uritsk, Sov. Un..........s31 25
Urk, Neth., 5,800..........B5 15
Urla, Tur., 10,800..........C6 23
Urlingford, Ire., 562........E4 11
Urmi, riv., Sov. Un..........B6 37
Urmia, see Rezāīyeh, Iran
Urmia, salt lake, Iran........C2 41
Urmston, Eng., 43,100......*A5 12
Uroyan, mts., P.R...........C3 65
Urr, riv., Scot...........F5 13
Urrao, Col., 5,958..........B2 60
Ursa, Adams, Ill., 325.......C2 90
Ursatyevskaya, Sov. Un., 12,300..........E7 29
Ursina, Somerset, Pa., 313...G3 114
Ursine, Lincoln, Nev., 60....F7 104
Uruapan, Mex., 45,727..........D4, n13 63
Urubamba, Peru, 3,481......D3 58
Urubamba, riv., Peru.........D3 58
Urubú, riv., Braz...........C3 59
Urucará, Braz., 1,203........C3 59
Uruçuí, Braz., 2,253.........C2 57
Urucuia, riv., Braz...........E1 57
Uruguai, riv., Braz...........D2 56
Uruguaiana, Braz., 48,358...D1 56
Uruguay, country, S.A., 2,600,000..........G5 53, E1 56
Uruguay, riv., Arg., Ur.......A5 54
Urukthapel, isl., Palau Is.......... 52
Urumchi (Tihwa), China, 275,000..........C2 34
Urungu, riv., China..........B2 34
Uruno, pt., Guam.......... 52
Urusha, Sov. Un., 10,000...D15 28
Uryupinsk, Sov. Un., 29,900..........C2 29
Urzhum, Sov. Un., 11,200...B3 29
Urziceni, Rom., 6,061.......C8 22
Usa, riv., Sov. Un...........B20 9
Usak, Tur., 22,000..........C7 23
Usakos, S.W. Afr., 2,355....B2 49
Usedom, Ger., 2,562.........E7 24
Usedom, isl., Ger...........E8 24
Ushaki, Sov. Un..........s32 25
Usher, Levy, Fla., 70........C4 86
Ushi, pt., Tinian.......... 52
Ushiro, see Orlovo, Sov. Un.
Ush-Tobe, Sov. Un., 16,300..........D9 29
Ushturinan Kuh, mtn., Iran.....E4 41
Ushuaia, Arg., 1,950........h12 54
Usingen, Ger., 3,800........C3 17
Usk, B.C., Can., 73.........B3 68
Usk, Pend Oreille, Wash., 300..........A8 122
Uskudar, Tur., 60,722..........B7 23, B7 31
Uslar, Ger., 6,400..........B4 17
Uslava, riv., Czech...........D8 17
Usman, Sov. Un., 50,000...E12 27
Usolye-Sibirskoye, Sov. Un., 60,000..........D13 28
Uspallata, pass, Arg., Chile....A3 54
Uspenskiy, Sov. Un., 2,600..........D8 29
Usquepaugh, Washington, R.I., 300..........C10 84
Ussel, Fr., 6,797..........E5 14
Ussuri, riv., China, Sov. Un....C7 37
Ussuriysk, Sov. Un., 113,000..........E6 37, E16 28
Ust-Aldan, Sov. Un.........C15 28
Ust-Bolsheretsh, Sov. Un...D18 28
Uster, Switz., 17,252.........B6 19
Ustica, isl., It...........E4 21
Ustick, Ada, Idaho, 125......F2 89
Ústí nad Labem, Czech., 66,700..........C3 26
Usti nad Labem (Ustecky), prov., Czech., 622,747.....C8 17
Ust-Ishim, Sov. Un..........B8 29
Ustka, Pol., 2,807..........A4 26
Ust-Kamchatsk, Sov. Un...D19 28
Ust-Kamenogorsk, Sov. Un., 195,000..........C10 29
Ust-Kut, Sov. Un., 21,900..........D13 28
Ust-Maya, Sov. Un., 2,300..........C16 28
Ust-Olenek, Sov. Un.......B14 28
Ust-Shchugor, Sov. Un......C9 4
Ust-Srednikan, Sov. Un., 800..........C18 28
Ust-Tsilma, Sov. Un., 7,900..........B19 9
Ust-Tym, Sov. Un..........B9 29
Ust-Tyrma, Sov. Un.........A5 37
Ust-Urt, plat., Sov. Un.......G20 9
Ust-Usa, Sov. Un., 2,500...B20 9
Ustyuzhna, Sov. Un., 10,000..........B11 27
Usulután, Sal., 12,094......D3 62
Utah, co., Utah, 106,991....C4 119
Utah, state, U.S., 890,627..........C5 76, 119
Utah, lake, Utah..........C4 119
Utajärvi, Fin., 700..........E12 25
Ute, Monona, Iowa, 511....B2 92
Ute, creek, N. Mex..........A6 107
Ute Mountain, Indian res., Colo., N. Mex..........A1 107
Ute Park, Colfax, N. Mex., 60..........A4 107
Utete, Tan., 970..........C6 48
Utica (North Utica), La Salle, Ill., 1,014........B4 90
Utica, Clark, Ind., 800.....H6 91
Utica, Ness, Kans., 322.....D3 93
Utica, Daviess, Ky., 300.....C2 94
Utica, Macomb, Mich., 1,454..........A8, F7 98
Utica, Hinds, Miss., 764.....C3 100
Utica, Livingston, Mo., 450..B4 101
Utica, Judith Basin, Mont., 50..........D6 102
Utica, Seward, Nebr., 564...D8 103
Utica, Oneida, N.Y., 100,410 (*284,000)..........B5 108
Utica, Licking, Ohio, 1,854...B5 111
Utica, Bryan, Okla., 100.....D5 112
Utica, Venango, Pa., 274....D2 114
Utica, Oconee, S.C., 1,294..*B1 115
Utica, Yankton, S. Dak., 70..E8 116
Utica Heights, Macomb, Mich., 2,700..........*F8 98
Utiel, Sp., 10,076..........C5 20
Utik, lake, Man. Can...........B4 71
Utikuma, lake, Alta., Can......B3 69
Utleyville, Baca, Colo., 5....D7 83
Utö, isl., Swe...........u36 25
Utopia, Uvalde, Tex., 500...E3 118
Utopia, lake, N.B., Can........D3 74
Utrata, riv., Pol...........m13 26
Utrecht, Neth., 264,200 (*410,000)..........B5 15
Utrecht, prov., Neth., 686,600..........B5 15
Utrera, Sp., 35,200 (41,126▲)..........D3 20
Utsjoki, Fin., 1,200........C12 25
Utsunomiya, Jap., 193,000 (239,007▲)..........H9 37
Utsuryō-Tō, see Ullŭng, isl., Kor.
Uttaradit, Thai., 9,372......D4 38
Uttar Pradesh, state, India, 73,746,401..........C6 39
Utterson, Ont., Can., 184....B5 72
Uttoxeter, Eng., 8,168.......B6 12
Utuado, P.R., 9,870..........B4 65
Utuado, mun., P.R., 40,449..B4 65
Utulei, Am. Sam., 719.......... 52
Uusikaupunki, Fin., 4,500....G9 25
Uusimaa, dept. Fin., 668,211..........*G11 25
Uva, Platte, Wyo..........C8 121
Uvada, Iron, Utah, 10.......F1 119
Uvalda, Montgomery, Ga., 589..........D4 87
Uvalde, Uvalde, Tex., 10,293..........E3 118
Uvalde, co., Tex., 16,814....E3 118
Uvaly, Czech., 4,706........n18 26
Uvarovo, Sov. Un., 10,000..........F14 27
Uvat, Sov. Un..........B7 29
Uverite, pt., Fiji Is........... 52
Uvinza, Tan., 1,880..........C5 48
Uvira, Con. L., 970..........B4 48
Uwajima, Jap., 49,500 (68,106▲)..........J6 37
Uxbridge, Ont., Can., 2,316..........C5 72
Uxbridge, Eng., 63,762.......C7 12
Uxbridge, Worcester, Mass., 3,400 (7,789▲)..........B4 97
Uyak, Alsk., 11..........D9 79
Uyar, Sov. Un., 10,000....D27 9
Uyuni, Bol., 6,968..........D2 55
Uyuni, salt flat, Bol..........D2 55
Uzbek S.S.R., rep., Sov. Un., 10,050,000..........G21 9
Uzès, Fr., 4,390..........E6 14
Uzh, riv., Sov. Un...........F7 27
Uzhgorod, Sov. Un., 55,000..........G4 27
Uzlovaya, Sov. Un., 53,000..........E16 9
Uzunkopru, Tur., 18,300....B6 23

V

Vaal, riv., S. Afr..........C4 49
Vaals, Neth., 6,700..........D5 15
Vaasa, Fin., 44,400..........F9 25
Vaasa, dept., Fin., 603,964..........*F9 25
Vac, Hung., 24,748..........B4 22
Vaca, key, Fla..........H5 86
Vaca, mtn., Calif..........A5 82
Vaca, pt., P.R...........f13, g12 65
Vacaria, Braz., 15,489.......D2 56
Vacaville, Solano, Calif., 10,898..........B5, C3 82
Vaccina, riv., It...........h8 21
Vacha, Ger., 4,383..........C5 17
Vacherie, St. James, La., 950..........B6 95
Vacia Talega, pt., P.R........B7 65
Vader, Lewis, Wash., 380....C3 122
Vadis, Lewis, W. Va., 125...B4 123
Vadito, Taos, N. Mex., 100..........A4 107
Vadnais Heights, Ramsey, Minn., 2,459..........*F5 99
Vado, Dona Ana, N. Mex., 200..........E3 107
Vadsö, Nor., 3,000.........B13 25
Vaduz, Liech., 3,398........B5 18
Vagay, Sov. Un..........B7 29
Vagnhärad, Swe., 857.......u35 25
Vagos, Port., 2,180..........B1 20
Vah, riv., Czech..........D4 26
Vaiden, Carroll, Miss., 475..B4 100
Vaigai, riv., India..........G6 39
Vaigalu, Sam., 802.......... 52
Vaihingen [an der Enz], Ger., 6,300..........E3 17
Vail, Pima, Ariz., 150.......E5 80
Vail, Crawford, Iowa, 473...B2 92
Vail, lake, Scot..........D4 13
Vailele, bay, W. Sam.......... 52
Vail Homes, Monmouth, N.J., 1,204..........*C4 106
Vails, Warren, N.J., 50......B2 106
Vaitele, bay, W. Sam.......... 52
Vakfikebir (Buyukliman), Tur., 1,341..........B12 31
Vakh, riv., Sov. Un...........C25 9
Vakhrushev, Sov. Un.......B11 37
Valais, canton, Switz., 177,783..........D3 19
Valatie, Columbia, N.Y., 1,237..........C7 108
Val-Barrette, Que., Can., 557..........C2 73
Valcartier Station, Que., Can., 121..........n16 73
Valcartier Village, Que., Can., 163..........C6, n17 73
Valcheta, Arg..........C3 54
Valcourt, Que., Can., 843...D5 73
Valdagno, It., 23,000........D7 18
Val-David, Que., Can., 1,118..........C3 73
Valday, Sov. Un., 14,400....C9 27
Valday, hills, Sov. Un........C9 27
Valdemarsvik, Swe., 3,200...H7 25
Valdemorillo, Sp., 1,470..........D6, p17 20
Valdepeñas, Sp., 25,706.....C4 20
Valders, Manitowoc, Wis., 622..........B6, D6 124
Valdes, isl., B.C., Can..........f12 68
Valdés, pen., Arg..........C4 54
Valdese, Burke, N.C., 2,941..........B2 109
Valdez, Alsk., 555.....C10, g18 79
Valdez, Las Animas, Colo., 400..........D6 83
Valdez, Taos, N. Mex., 135..........A4 107
Valdilecha, Sp., 1,539.......p18 20
Valdivia, Chile, 61,300......B2 54
Valdivia, Col., 1,169........B2 60
Valdivia, prov., Chile, 255,109..........B2 54
Valdobbiadene, It., 11,430...D7 18
Val-d'Or, Que., Can., 10,983..........k11 73
Valdosta, Lowndes, Ga., 30,652..........F3 87
Våle, Nor..........p28 25
Vale, Malheur, Oreg., 1,491..........D9 113
Vale, Butte, S. Dak., 108....C2 116
Vale, Carroll, Tenn., 125....A3 117
Vale, Jefferson, Ind., 70....H5 91
Valemount, B.C., Can., 631..C8 68
Valença, Braz., 17,137.......D3 57
Valença, Port., 2,825.........A1 20
Valença do Piauí, Braz., 3,046..........C2 57
Valence, Fr., 52,532 (*68,000)..........E6 14
Valencia, Maricopa, Ariz., 750..........G1 80
Valencia, Butler, Pa., 310...E2 114
Valencia, Sp., 13,159........C2 20
Valencia, Sp., 505,066 (*660,000)..........C5 20
Valencia, Ven., 161,413......A4 60
Valencia, co., N. Mex., 39,085..........C1 107
Valencia, prov., Sp., 1,429,708..........*C5 20
Valencia, reg., Sp., 2,480,879..........C5 20
Valencia, isl., Ire..........F1 11
Valenciennes, Fr., 45,379 (*172,000)..........B5 14
Valendas, Switz., 417.......C7 19
Valentigney, Fr., 11,241.....D7 14
Valentine, Mohave, Ariz., 50..........B2 80
Valentine, Pulaski, Ark..C3, D6 81
Valentine, Fergus, Mont....C8 102
Valentine, Cherry, Nebr., 2,875..........B5 103
Valentine, Jeff Davis, Tex., 420..........F2 118
Valera, Ven., 44,566.........B3 60
Valga, Sov. Un., 13,400....*C6 27
Valhalla, Westchester, N.Y., 4,500..........D7, m15 108
Valhermosa Springs, Morgan, Ala., 500..........A3 78
Valier, Franklin, Ill., 649....E4 90
Valier, Pondera, Mont., 724..B4 102
Valier, Jefferson, Pa., 800....E3 114
Val-Jalbert, Que., Can., 39..A5 73
Valjevo, Yugo., 22,070.......C4 22
Valka, Sov. Un., 25,000......C6 27
Valkeakoski, Fin., 14,200...G11 25
Valkenswaard, Neth., 19,300..........C3 15
Valki, Sov. Un., 10,000....G10 27
Valladolid, Ec..........B2 58
Valladolid, Mex., 9,306......C7 63
Valladolid, Sp., 151,807.....B3 20
Valladolid, prov., Sp., 363,106..........*B3 20
Vallauris, Fr., 4,337.........F7 14
Vall de Uxó. Sp., 18,596.....C5 20
Valle, La Plata, Colo.......D3 83
Vallecito, res., Colo..........D3 83
Vallecitos, Rio Arriba, N. Mex., 300..........A3 107
Valle d'Aosta, It., pol. dist., 100,959..........*B1 21
Valle de Bravo, Mex., 4,459..........n13 63
Valle de Cauca, dept., Col., 1,396,630..........C2 60
Valle de la Pascua, Ven., 24,051..........B4 60
Valle de Santiago, Mex., 20,879..........m13 63
Valledupar, Col., 9,011......A3 60
Vallée-Jonction, Que., Can., 1,405..........C7 73
Valle Grande, Bol., 5,094....C3 55
Vallejo, Solano, Calif., 60,877..........B5, C2 82
Vallenar, Chile, 9,677.......E1 55
Valles Mines, Jefferson, Mo., 225..........C7 101
Valletta, Malta, 18,300 (*208,000)..........G14 30
Valley, Douglas, Nebr., 1,452..........C9, D2 103
Valley, Avery, N.C..........C4 109
Valley, Stevens, Wash., 250..........A8 122
Valley, Park, Wyo., 15.......A3 125
Valley, co., Idaho, 3,663.....E3 89
Valley, co., Mont., 17,080..B10 102
Valley, co., Nebr., 6,590....C6 103
Valley, creek, Ala..........E4 81
Valley, riv., Man., Can.......D1 71
Valley Bend, Randolph, W. Va., 500..........C4 123
Valley Brook, Oklahoma, Okla., 1,378..........*B4 112
Valley Center, Sedgwick, Kans., 2,570..........B5, E6 93
Valley Centre, Sask., Can., 40..........F2 70
Valley City, Pike, Ill., 109...D3 90
Valley City, Barnes, N. Dak., 7,809..........C7 110
Valley City, Medina, Ohio, 400..........A6 111
Valley Cottage, Rockland, N.Y., 3,000..........g13 108
Valleydale, Los Angeles, Calif., 1,000..........*F3 82
Valley Falls, Jefferson, Kans., 1,193..........B7, C8 93
Valley Falls, Lake, Oreg.....E6 113
Valley Farms, Pinal, Ariz., 200..........E4 80
Valleyfield, Newf., Can., 509..........D5 75
Valleyfield, Que., Can., 27,297 (*29,849).......D3, q18 73
Valleyford, Spokane, Wash., 100..........B8, D8 122
Valley Forge, Chester, Pa., 450..........A10 114
Valley Grove, Ohio, W. Va., 548..........A4, B2 123
Valley Head, De Kalb, Ala., 424..........A4 78
Valley Head, Randolph, W. Va., 600..........C4 123
Valley Lee, St. Marys, Md., 300..........D4 85
Valley Mills, Marion, Ind., 150..........H7 91
Valley Mills, Bosque, Tex., 1,061..........D4 118
Valley Park, Issaquena, Miss., 100..........C3 100
Valley Park, St. Louis, Mo., 3,452..........B7 101
Valley Spring, Llano, Tex., 60..........D3 118
Valley Springs, Boone, Ark., 150..........A3 81
Valley Springs, Minnehaha, S. Dak., 472..........D9 116
Valley Station, Jefferson, Ky., 10,553..........A4 94
Valley Stream, Nassau, N.Y., 38,629..........k13 180
Valleyview, Alta., Can., 1,077..........B2 69
Valley View, Kane, Ill., 1,741..........*A5 91
Valley View, Madison, Ky., 200..........C5 94
Valley View, Cuyahoga, Ohio, 1,221..........*A6 111
Valley View, Schuylkill, Pa., 1,540..........E8 114
Valley View, Cooke, Tex., 500..........C4 118
Valliant, McCurtain, Okla., 477..........D6 112
Valli di Comacchio, lake, It....E8 18
Vallimanca, riv., Arg.........B4 54
Vallo della Lucania, It., 6,863..........D5 21
Vallonia, Jackson, Ind., 150..........G5 91
Vallorbe, Switz., 3,990......C1 19
Valls, Sp., 11,886..........B6 20
Vallscreek, McDowell, W. Va., 500..........D3 123
Val Marie, Sask., Can., 443..........H2 70
Valmeyer, Monroe, Ill., 709..E3 90
Valmiera, Sov. Un., 10,000..........C5 27
Valmont, Que., Can., 230...C5 73
Valmontone, It., 7,314......h9 21

Vic [-sur-Seille], Fr., 1,213...F6 15
Victor, Teller, Colo., 434....C5 83
Victor, Teton, Idaho, 240....F7 89
Victor, Iowa and Poweshiek, Iowa, 870..........C5 92
Victor, Ravalli, Mont., 400..D2 102
Victor, Ontario, N.Y., 1,180..........C3 108
Victor, Roberts, S. Dak., 30..B9 116
Victor Harbor, Austl., 2,036..........G2 52
Victoria, Coffee, Ala........D4 78
Victoria, Arg., 17,711.......A4 54
Victoria, Cam., 8,025........F6 45
Victoria, B.C., Can., 54,941 (*154,152)....E6, h12 68
Victoria, Newf., Can., 1,506..........E5 75
Victoria, P.E.I., Can., 148..C6 74
Victoria, Chile, 10,671.......B2 54
Victoria, Hong Kong, 674,962 (*2,800,000).......G7 34
Victoria, Knox, Ill., 453....B3 90
Victoria, Ellis, Kans., 1,170..D4 93
Victoria, Marshall, Miss., 500..........A4 100
Victoria, Jefferson, Mo., 150..........C7 101
Victoria, Phil, 5,672........o13 35
Victoria, P.R..........B2 65
Victoria, Seychelles, 11,380..........*G24 3
Victoria, Marion, Tenn., 600..........D8 117
Victoria, Victoria, Tex., 33,047..........E4 118
Victoria, Lunenburg, Va., 1,737..........E4 121
Victoria, co., N.B., Can., 19,712..........B2 74
Victoria, co., N.S., Can., 8,226..........C9 74
Victoria, co., Ont., Can., 29,750..........C6 72
Victoria, co., Tex., 46,475...E2 118
Victoria, state, Austl. 3,155,000..........G7 51
Victoria, falls, Rh., Zambia...A4 49
Victoria, isl., N.W. Ter., Can..........B10 66
Victoria, lake, Austl..........F3 51
Victoria, lake, Newf., Can......D3 75
Victoria, lake, Tan., Ug........B5 48
Victoria, mtn., Pap..........k12 50
Victoria, riv., Austl..........C5 50
Victoria, riv., Newf., Can.......D3 75
Victoria, strait, N.W. Ter., Can..........C12 66
Victoria Beach, Man., Can., 74..........D3 71
Victoria Central, P.R.........B7 65
Victoria di las Tunas, Cuba, 12,754..........E5 64
Victoria Falls, Rh., 1,455....A4 49
Victoria Harbour, Ont., Can., 1,066..........C5 72
Victoria Land, reg., Ant......B29 5
Victoria Mine, Ont., Can ...E3 74
Victoria Park, Los Angeles, Calif., 2,400..........*F2 82
Victoria Point, Bur., 1,519..........F10 39
Victoria River Downs, Austl..........C5 50
Victoria Road, Ont., Can., 125..........C6 72
Victoriaville, Que., Can., 18,720..........C6 73
Victoria West, S. Afr., 3,745..........D3 49
Victorica, Arg..........B3 54
Victorino de la Plaza, Arg....B4 54
Victor Mills, Spartanburg, S.C., 2,018..........*B3 115
Victorville, San Bernardino, Calif., 5,000..........E5 82
Victory, Cumberland, N.C...B5 109
Victory (Town of), Essex, Vt. (46*)..........*C5 120
Victory, Vernon, Wis., 143...E2 124
Victory Gardens, Morris, N.J., 1,085..........*B3 106
Victory Heights, Chemung, N.Y., 600..........*C4 108
Vicuña, Chile, 3,415.........F1 55
Vida, McCone, Mont., 85..C11 102
Vidal, San Bernardino, Calif., 100..........E6 82
Vidalia, Toombs, Ga., 7,569..........D4 87
Vidalia, Concordia, La., 4,313..........C4 95
Vidette, Burke, Ga., 103....C4 87
Vidin, Bul., 18,580.........D6 22
Vidor, Orange, Tex., 4,938..D5 118
Vidora, Sask., Can........H1 70
Viechtach, Ger., 3,600......D7 17
Viedma, Arg., 4,683.........C4 54
Vieja, peak, Tex..........F2 118
Vielsalm, Bel., 3,698........D5 15
Vienenburg, Ger., 6,700.....B5 17
Vienna (Wien), Aus., 1,631,400 (*1,995,000)....D8 16
Vienna, Ont., Can., 373......E4 72
Vienna, Dooly, Ga., 2,099...D3 87
Vienna, Johnson, Ill., 1,094..F5 90
Vienna, Dorchester, Md., 420..........D6 85
Vienna, Maries, Mo., 536...C6 101
Vienna, Warren, N.J., 300...B3 106
Vienna, Clark, S. Dak., 191..........C8 116
Vienna, Fairfax, Va., 11,440..........B4, C5 121
Vienna, Wood, W. Va., 9,381..........B3 123
Vienne, Fr., 26,977..........E6 14
Vienne, dept., Fr., 331,619..........*D4 14
Vienne, riv., Fr..........D4 14
Vientiane, Laos, 162,000....D5 38
Vieques, P.R., 2,487.......g13 65
Vieques, mun., P.R., 7,210..g13 65
Vieques, isl., P.R..........g13 65
Vieques, sound, P.R..........g13 5
Viernheim, Ger., 19,900.....D3 17
Viersen, Ger., 42,100.......C6 15
Vierzon, Fr., 31,549........D5 14
Viesca, Mex., 3,043.........B4 63
Vieste, It., 12,679..........D6 21
Vietnam, reg., Asia..........E8 38, H13 33
Vietnam, North, country, Asia, 17,500,000..........C6 38
Vietnam, South, country, Asia, 15,900,000..........F8 38
Viewfield, Meade, S. Dak., 5..........C3 116
View Park, Los Angeles, Calif., 2,500..........*E4 82
Vigan, Phil., 7,424..........B6 35
Viger, Que., Can..........B8 73
Vigevano, It., 61,500.......B2 21
Vignola, It., 5,868..........E7 18
Vigo, Sp., 144,914..........A1 20
Vigo, co., Ind., 108,458.....F3 91
Vigso, bay, Den..........A2 24
Vihowa, Pak., 2,827..........B5 39, B3 40
Vijayapuri, India, 30,500...*E6 39
Vijayavada, India, 230,397..E7 39
Vik, Ice., 339..........o23 25
Viken, Swe., 750..........B6 24
Vikesund, Nor., 1,267......p27 25
Viking, Alta., Can., 1,043...C5 69
Viking, Marshall, Minn., 128..........B2 99
Vikramasingapuram, India, 32,978 (*75,657)..........*G6 39
Vila, New Hebr., 800.......*H10 7
Vila Cabral, Moz..........D6 48
Vila da Feira, Port.........B1 20
Vila da Ponte, Ang., 329....D2 48
Vila de Aljustrel, Ang.......D2 48
Vila de João Belo, Moz., 1,936..........C5 49
Vila de Manica, Moz.........A5 49
Vila de Rei, Port., 5,982....C1 20
Vila do Conde, Port., 7,772..........B1 20
Vila Fontes, Moz..........A6 49
Vila Franca de Xira, Port., 8,296..........C1 20
Vila Gago Coutinho, Ang., 1,411..........D3 48
Vila General Machado, Ang., 2,387..........D2 48
Vila João de Almeida, Ang...E1 48
Vila Junqueiro, Moz.........A6 49
Vilaine, riv., Fr..........D2 14
Vila Luso, Ang., 2,821.......D2 48
Vila Macedo de Cavaleiros, Ang..........D2 48
Vila Marechal Carmona, Ang., 8,300..........C2 48
Vila Mariano Machado, Ang., 349..........D1 48
Vilanculos, Moz..........B6 49
Vila Nova de Foz Coa, Port., 3,481..........B2 20
Vila Nova de Gaia, Port., 45,739..........B1 20
Vila Nova de Milfontes, Port., 2,460..........D1 20
Vila Nova de Seles, Ang., 1,115..........D1 48
Vila Pereira d' Eça, Ang., 416..........E2 48
Vila Pery, Moz..........A5 49
Vila Real, Port., 9,285......B2 20
Vila Real de Santo António, Port, 6,086..........D2 20
Vila Robert Williams, Ang., 3,679..........D2 48
Vila Salazar, Ang., 2,105....C1 48
Vilas, Baca, Colo., 107......D8 83
Vilas, Liberty, Fla., 15......B2 86
Vilas, Miner, S. Dak., 49....C8 116
Vilas, co., Wis., 9,332.......B4 124
Vila Serpa Pinto, Ang., 387..D2 48
Vila Teixeira da Silva, Ang., 4,897..........D2 48
Vila Vasco de Gama, Moz ..D5 48
Vila Viçosa, Port., 3,802....C2 20
Vila Vila, Bol., 658.........C2 55
Vildbjerg, Den., 1,108.......B2 24
Vildo, Hardeman, Tenn., 40..........B2 117
Vileyka, Sov., Un., 10,000...D6 27
Vilhelmina, Swe., 3,000......E7 25
Viljandi, Sov. Un., 12,941...B5 27
Vilkaviskis, Sov. Un., 8,699..A7 26
Vilkitsky, isl., Sov. Un........B7 4
Vilkovo, Sov. Un., 20,000....I7 27
Villa Acuña, Mex., 20,204...B4 63
Villa Ahumada, Mex., 2,489..........A3 63
Villa Alhucemas, Mor., 11,262..........G5 30
Villa Angela, Arg., 7,345.....E3 55
Villa Aroma, Bol., 1,486.....C2 55
Villa Bella, Bol., 88..........B2 55
Villablino, Sp., 7,647........A2 20
Villacañas, Sp., 10,113......C4 20
Villacarrillo, Sp., 13,090....C4 20
Villach, Aus., 32,971.........E6 16
Villacidro, It., 11,266.......E2 21
Villa Cisneros, Sp Sahara, 1,011..........E1 44
Villa Colón, C.R., 4,309.....F5 62
Villa Constitución, Arg., 9,183..........A4 54
Villa Crespo, Arg., 4,289....A4 54
Villa Cuauhtémoc, Mex., 2,436..........k15 63
Villa de Cura, Ven., 19,644..........A4 60
Villa del Rosario, Arg., 4,461..........A4 54
Villa Dolores, Arg., 13,835..A3 54
Villafamés, Sp., 3,652.......C5 20
Villa Federal, Arg., 9,158....A5 54
Villafranca, It., 15,712.......B3 21
Villafranca del Bierzo, Sp., 4,512..........A2 20
Villafranca de los Barros, Sp., 16,671..........C2 20
Villafranca del Panadés, Sp., 11,985..........B6 20
Villafranca di Verona, It., 6,015..........D6 18
Villa García, Mex., 1,877...k13 63
Villagarcía de Arosa, Sp., 4,986..........A1 20
Village, Columbia, Ark., 85..D2 81
Village, Richmond, Va., 140..........D6 121
Village, creek, Ala..........E4 78
Village-Richelieu, Que., Can., 1,612..........*D4 73
Village Springs, Blount, Ala., 125..........B3 78
Villaggio Duca degli Abruzzi, Som., 9,000 (15,900*).......E6 47
Villa Grove, Saguache, Colo., 100..........C5 83
Villa Grove, Douglas, Ill., 2,308..........D5 90
Villaguay, Arg., 17,607......A5 54
Villa Hayes, Par., 12,590....E4 55
Villa Heights, Prince Georges, Md., 1,000..........*C4 85
Villahermosa, Mex., 52,262..D6 63
Villa Huidobro, Arg.........A4 54
Villa Iris, Arg., 2,422.......B4 54
Villajoyosa, Sp., 9,412......C5 20
Villalba, P.R., 1,892........C5 65
Villalba, Sp., 3,180.........A2 20
Villalba, mun., P.R., 16,239..........C5 65
Villaldama, Mex., 2,529.....B4 63
Villalon, Cuba..........k11 64
Villalonga, Arg..........B4 54
Villalpando, Sp., 2,590......B3 20
Villa María, Arg., 30,362....A4 54
Villamartín, Sp., 9,849......D3 20
Villamil, Ec..........g5 58
Villa Montes, Bol., 3,105....D3 55
Villanova, Delaware, Pa., 4,000..........*A10 114
Villanueva, Col., 5,830......A3 60
Villanueva, San Miguel, N. Mex., 300..........B4 107
Villanueva de Córdoba, Sp., 15,719..........C3 20
Villanueva del Arzobispo, Sp., 9,712..........C4 20
Villanueva de la Serena, Sp., 20,812..........C3 20
Villanueva [del Río y Minas], Sp., 10,982..........D3 20
Villanueva y Geltrú, Sp., 25,669..........B6 20
Villa Obregón, Mex., 25,908..........h9 63
Villa Oliva, Par., 4,042......E4 55
Villa Park, DuPage, Ill., 23,294..........F2 90
Villa Pedro Montoya, Mex., 4,443..........m14 63
Villa Pérez, P.R..........C3 65
Villaputzu, It., 3,731.......E2 21
Villa Ranchaero, Pennington, S. Dak., 3,000..........C3 116
Villard, Pope, Minn., 235....E3 99
Villard-Bonnot, Fr., 6,499...E6 14
Villa Rica, Carroll and Douglas, Ga., 3,450.......C1 87
Villa Ridge, Pulaski, Ill., 550..........F4 90
Villa Ridge, Franklin, Mo., 150..........C7 101
Villarreal, Sp., 19,700.......C5 20
Villarrica, Chile, 7,036.....B2 54
Villarrica, Par., 15,600.....E4 55
Villarrobledo, Sp., 21,356...C4 20
Villarrubia, Sp., 9,043......C4 20
Villars-le-Terroir, Switz., 511..........D3 19
Villas, Cape May, N.J., 2,500..........E3 106
Villa Unión, Arg..........E2 55
Villa Unión, Mex., 4,199....C3 63
Villa Valeria, Arg..........A4 54
Villavicencio, Col., 20,000 (39,000*)..........C3 60
Villaviciosa, Sp., 2,322......A3 20
Villazon, Bol., 6,261........D2 55
Villazón, Bol..........D3 55
Villé, Fr., 1,326..........A3 18
Ville-de-Tracy, Que., Can., 8,171..........C4 73
Villefranche [-de-Rouergue], Fr., 7,969..........E5 14
Villefranche-sur-Saône, Fr., 24,516..........E6 14
Villegreen, Las Animas, Colo., 10..........D7 83
Villejuif, Fr., 46,116........g10 14
Ville Marie, Que., Can., 1,710..........p20 72
Villemomble, Fr., 24,540....g10 14
Villena, Sp., 15,687.........C5 20
Villenauxe-la-Grande, Fr., 1,925..........F3 15
Villeneuve, Que., Can., 1,934..........*C6 73
Villeneuve-le-Roi, Fr., 22,300..........h10 14
Villeneuve-St. Georges, Fr., 28,231..........h10 14
Villeneuve-sur-Lot, Fr., 15,296 (17,295*).........E4 14
Villeneuve-sur-Yonne, Fr., 3,655..........C5 14
Villepinte, Fr., 483..........g11 14
Ville Platte, Evangeline, La., 7,512..........D3 95
Villeroy, Que., Can., 198....C6 72
Villers-Bretonneux, Fr., 3,342..........E2 15
Villers-Cotterêts, Fr., 5,489..C5 14
Villers-Outréaux, Fr., 2,420..D3 15
Villers-Semeuse, Fr., 3,389...E4 15
Villerupt, Fr., 14,377.......C6 14
Ville St. Georges, Que., Can., 4,082..........C7 73
Villeta, Par., 14,729........E4 55
Villeurbanne, Fr., 105,416...E6 14
Villia, Grc., 3,151..........g10 23
Villingen, Ger., 31,900......D4 16
Villisca, Montgomery, Iowa, 1,690..........D3 92
Vilna, Alta., Can., 400......B5 69
Vilnius, Sov. Un., 271,000...D5 27
Vilonia, Faulkner, Ark., 234..........B3 81
Vilppula, Fin., 1,800........F11 25
Vils, riv., Ger..........E7 17
Vils, riv., Ger..........D6 17
Vilsbiburg, Ger., 5,900......E7 17
Vilseck, Ger., 2,200.........D6 17
Vilshofen, Ger., 5,800.......E8 17
Vilvoorde, Bel., 31,441.....D4 15
Vilyuy, riv., Sov. Un.........C15 28
Vilyuysk, Sov. Un., 3,600...C15 28
Vim, Slope, N. Dak..........C2 110
Vimianzo, Sp., 654..........A1 20
Vimmerby, Swe., 6,400.......I6 25
Vimperk, Czech., 2,940.....D2 26
Vina, Franklin, Ala., 184....A1 78
Vina, Tehama, Calif., 200...C2 82
Viña del Mar, Chile, 115,500..........A2 54
Vinalhaven, Knox, Maine, 950 (1,273*).......D4 96
Vinalhaven, isl., Maine......D4 96
Vinaroz, Sp., 10,968.........B6 20
Vincennes, Fr., 50,436.......g10 14
Vincennes, Knox, Ind., 18,046..........G2 91
Vincennes, bay, Ant..........C24 5
Vincent, Shelby, Ala., 1,402..B3 78
Vincent, Crittenden, Ark., 100..........E8 81
Vincent, Webster, Iowa, 173..........B3 92
Vincent, Calcasieu, La., 75..D2 95
Vincent, Lorain, Ohio, 2,100..........*A5 111
Vincent, Washington, Ohio, 340..........C6 111
Vincent, Howard, Tex., 50..C2 118
Vincentown, Burlington, N.J., 600..........D3 106
Vinces, Ec., 4,129..........B2 58
Vinchina, Arg..........E2 55
Vinco, Payne, Okla., 50.....B4 112
Vindelälven, riv., Swe.........E8 25
Vinderup, Den., 1,910.......B2 24
Vindex, Garrett, Md., 80....D1 85
Vindhya, mts., India..........F6 37
Vine, brook, Mass..........g11 97
Vine Grove, Hardin, Ky., 2,435..........C4 94
Vine Hill (Martinez East) Contra Costa, Calif., 3,958.......*C2 82
Vineland, Orange, Fla., 100..........D5 86
Vineland, Cumberland, N.J., 37,685..........E2 106
Vinemont, Cullman, Ala., 500..........A3 78
Vineyard, Lee, Ark..........C5 81
Vineyard, sound, Mass.........D6 97
Vineyard Haven (Tisbury), Dukes, Mass., 2,169..........D6 97
Vingåker, Swe., 4,300........t33 25
Vinh, Viet., 43,954.........C6 38
Vinhais, Port., 2,911.........B2 20
Vinh Long, Viet., 30,000....G6 38
Vinh Yen, Viet., 3,820......B6 38
Vining, Clay, Kans., 128....C6 93
Vining, Otter Tail, Minn., 136..........D3 99
Vinings, Cobb, Ga..........A5 87
Vinita, Craig, Okla., 6,027..A6 112
Vinita Park, St. Louis, Mo., 2,204..........*C7 101
Vinkovci, Yugo., 23,113.....C4 22
Vinnitsa, Sov. Un., 139,000..G7 27
Vinson, Harmon, Okla., 75..C2 112
Vinson Massif, mtn., Ant......B4 5
Vinton, Benton, Iowa, 4,781..........B5 92
Vinton, Calcasieu, La., 2,987..........D2 95
Vinton, Gallia, Ohio, 374...D5 111
Vinton, Roanoke, Va., 3,432..........D3 121
Vinton, co., Ohio, 10,274....C5 111
Vintondale, Cambria, Pa., 938..........F4 114
Viola, Fulton, Ark., 196....A4 81
Viola, Kent, Del., 159.......B6 85
Viola, Latah, Idaho, 60......C1 89
Viola, Mercer, Ill., 812......B3 90
Viola, Sedgwick, Kans., 203..E6 93
Viola, Warren, Tenn., 206...D8 117
Viola, Richland and Vernon, Wis., 721..........E3 124
Viola, Lincoln, Wyo.........C2 125
Violet, St. Bernard, La., 900..........C8 95
Vipiteno, It., 3,151..........C7 18
Virac, Phil., 8,539..........*C6 35
Virden, Man., Can., 2,708...E1 71
Virden, Macoupin, Ill., 3,309..........D4 90
Virden, Hidalgo, N. Mex., 135..........E1 107
Vire, Fr., 9,518..........C3 14
Vire, riv., Fr..........C3 14
Virgelle, Chouteau, Mont., 25..........B6 102
Virgenes, cape, Arg..........E3 54
Virgil, Greenwood, Kans., 229..........E7 93
Virgil, Beadle, S. Dak., 81...C7 116
Virgil, Cortland, N.Y., 200..........C4 108
Virgilina, Halifax, Va., 286..E4 121
Virgin, Washington, Utah, 124..........F2 119
Virgin, mts., Nev..........G7 104
Virgin, riv., Utah..........G2 119
Virgin Gorda, isl., Vir. Is. (Br.)..........m14 64
Virgin Islands, nat. park, Vir. Is..........f15 65
Virgin Islands, Br. dep., N.A., 8,000..........f15 65
Virgin Islands of the U.S., dep., N.A., 38,000....m14 64, f15 65
Virginia, Bannock, Idaho, 50..........G6 89
Virginia, Cass, Ill., 1,669....D3 90
Virginia, Ire., 515..........D4 11
Virginia, St. Louis, Minn., 14,034..........C6 99
Virginia, Gage, Nebr., 88...D9 103
Virginia, S. Afr., 18,273 (*40,359)..........*C4 49
Virginia, state, U.S., 3,966,949..........C12 77, 121
Virginia, peak, Nev..........D2 104
Virginia, peak, Wyo..........C2 125
Virginia Beach (Independent City), Va., 8,091.....B7, E7 121
Virginia City, Madison, Mont., 194..........E5 102
Virginia City, Storey, Nev., 500..........D2 104
Virginia Gardens, Dade, Fla., 2,159..........*G6 87
Viroflay, Fr., 16,004.........g9 14
Viroqua, Vernon, Wis., 3,926..........E3 124
Virovitica, Yugo., 14,027....C3 22
Vir-Pazar, Yugo, 323.......D4 22
Virrat, Fin., 1,600.........F10 25
Virserum, Swe., 2,414........I6 25
Virton, Bel., 3,421..........E5 15
Virú, Peru, 2,573..........C2 58
Virudhunagar, India, 54,827..........*G6 39
Vis, Yugo., 2,844..........D3 22
Vis, isl., Yugo..........D3 22
Visakhapatnam, India, 182,004..........E7 39, I9 40
Visalia, Tulare, Calif., 15,791..........D4 82
Visalia, Kenton, Ky., 253....A7 94
Visalia North (Crowley), Tulare, Calif., 3,950..........*D4 82
Visayan, sea, Phil..........C6 35
Visby, Swe., 16,000..........I8 25
Visconde do Rio Branco, Braz., 12,363..........C4 56
Viscount, Sask., Can., 303...F3 70
Viscount Melville, sound, N.W. Ter., Can..........B10 66
Visé, Bel., 6,018..........D5 15
Višegrad, Yugo., 3,316......D4 22
Viseu, Braz., 1,606..........B1 57
Viseu, Port., 13,190.........B2 20
Vishera, riv., Sov. Un.........A5 29
Vislanda, Swe., 1,400........B8 24
Viso, mtn., It..........B1 21, E3 18
Visoko, Yugo., 7,461.........D4 22
Visonau, Fiji Is..........52
Visp, Switz., 3,658..........D4 19
Vista, San Diego, Calif., 14,795..........F5 82
Vista, Man., Can., 79.......D1 71
Vista, St. Clair, Mo., 50....D4 101
Vista, Washoe, Nev., 25....D2 104
Vista Park, Kern, Calif., 3,500..........*E4 82
Vistillas, Lake, Ore.........E6 113
Vistula (Frisches Haff), lagoon, Sov. Un..........A5 26
Vita, Man., Can., 316.......E3 71
Vitanovak, Yugo., 1,127.....D5 22
Vitebsk, Sov. Un., 174,000...D8 27
Viterbo, It., 29,000 (50,100*)..........C4 21
Viti Levu, bay, Fiji Is..........52
Viti Levu, isl., Fiji Is..........52
Vitim, Sov. Un., 2,300.....D14 28
Vitim, riv., Sov. Un........D14 28
Vitor, Peru, 2,343..........E3 58
Vitória, Braz., 82,748 (*165,000)..........F2 57
Vitória, Braz..........k5 57
Vitória, Braz..........C4 61
Vitoria, Sp., 73,701.........A4 20
Vitória da Conquista, Braz., 46,778..........D2 57
Vitória [de Santo Antão], Braz., 27,053..........C3, k6 57
Vitória do Mearim, Braz., 1,494..........B2 57
Vitré, Fr., 10,380..........C3 14
Vitry-le-François, Fr., 14,795..........C6 14
Vitry [-sur-Seine], Fr., 65,734..........g10 14
Vittel, Fr., 5,012..........C6 14
Vittoria, Ont., Can., 407....E4 72
Vittoria, It., 45,000.........F5 21
Vittorio Veneto, It., 21,500..B4 21
Vivero, Sp., 3,628..........A2 20
Vivian, Caddo, La., 2,624...B2 95
Vivian, Lyman, S. Dak., 300..........D5 116
Vivian, McDowell, W. Va., 900..........D3 123
Vivian Park, Utah, Utah, 45..........C4 119
Vivoratá, Arg..........B5 54
Viwa, isl., Fiji Is..........52
Vizcaíno, des., Mex..........B2 63
Vizcaíno, mts., Mex..........B2 63
Vizcaya, prov., Sp., 754,383..........*A4 20
Vize, Tur., 6,200..........B6 23
Vizianagram, India, 76,808..........E7 39, H9 40
Vizille, Fr., 6,493..........E6 14
Viziru, Rom., 5,414..........C8 22
Vizzini, It., 10,806..........F5 21
Vlaardingen, Neth., 71,900..C4 15
Vladimir, Sov. Un., 181,000..........B2 29
Vladimiro-Aleksandrovskoye, Sov. Un., 10,000..........E6 37
Vladimirovo, Sov. Un........D3 29
Vladimir-Volynskiy, Sov. Un., 10,000..........F5 27
Vladivostok, Sov. Un., 338,000..........E5 37, E16 28
Vlasenica, Yugo., 3,047.....C4 22
Vlasim, Czech., 5,066.......D9 17
Vlasotince, Yugo., 5,924....D6 22
Vlčany, Czech., 4,555........D4 26
Vlieland, Neth., 700..........A5 15
Vlieland, isl., Neth..........A4 15
Vlissingen, Neth., 28,900....C3 15
Vlkava, Czech., 526.........n18 26
Vlkava, riv., Czech..........n18 26
Vlonë (Valona), Alb., 41,285..........B2 23
Vlonë, pref., Alb., 58,000...*B2 23
Vlotho, Ger., 8,100..........A3 17
Vltava, riv., Czech..........n17 26
Voca, McCulloch, Tex., 100..........D3 118
Vodlozero, lake, Sov. Un......F17 25
Vodnany, Czech., 4,576.....D9 17
Voeune Sai, Camb., 10,000..........F7 38
Vogelkop, pen., W. Irian.......F8 35
Voghera, It., 35,747.........B2 21
Vohenstrauss, Ger., 3,700....D7 17
Vohipeno, Malag..........h9 49
Voi, Ken..........B6 48
Void, Fr., 1,118..........F5 15
Voiotia (Boeotia), prov., Grc., 114,256..........*C4 23
Voiron, Fr., 11,150..........E6 14
Voisin, lake, Sask., Can.......C2 70
Voitsberg, Aus., 6,353.......E7 16
Voivis, lake, Grc..........C4 23
Vojens, Den., 3,563..........C3 24
Vokhma, Sov. Un..........C15 27
Volary, Czech., 2,278.......E8 17
Volborg, Custer, Mont., 5...E11 102
Volcano, isl., Phil..........o13 35
Volchansk, Sov. Un., 10,000..........F11 27
Volga, Clayton, Iowa, 361...B6 92
Volga, Brookings, S. Dak., 780..........C9 116
Volga, Barbour, W. Va., 125..........B4 123
Volga, plat., Sov. Un..........C15 27
Volga, riv., Sov. Un..........F18 9
Volga, riv. mouths, Sov. Un....F18 9
Volgograd, Sov. Un., 663,000 (*775,000)..........F17 9, D2 29
Volgograd, res., Sov. Un.......D3 29
Volin, Yankton, S. Dak., 171..........E8 116
Volkach, Ger., 3,600........D5 17
Volkhov, Sov. Un., 16,500...B9 27
Volkhov, riv., Sov. Un........B8 27
Völklingen, Ger., 42,400.....D1 17
Volkovysk, Sov. Un., 10,000..........E5 27
Vollenhove, Neth., 1,918....B5 15
Volney, Grayson, Va., 40....E1 121
Volnovakha, Sov. Un., 10,000..........H11 27
Volo, Lake, Ill., 150.........E2 90
Volochayevka Vtoraya, Sov. Un..........B7 37
Volochisk, Sov. Un., 10,000..........G6 27
Volodarskiy, Sov. Un., 10,000..........s31 25
Volodarskoye, Sov. Un.......C7 29
Vologda, Sov. Un., 152,000..........B1 29
Volokolamsk, Sov. Un., 10,000..........C10 27
Volos, Grc., 49,221 (*67,424)..........C4 23
Volos, gulf, Grc..........C4 23
Volsk, Sov. Un., 67,000....C3 29
Volta, reg., Ghana..........E5 45
Volta, riv., Ghana..........E4 45
Voltaire, McHenry, N. Dak., 70..........A5 110
Volta Redonda, Braz., 83,973 (*135,000)..........C4, h5 56
Volterra, It., 9,300..........C3 21
Volturno, riv., It..........D5 21
Voluntown, New London, Conn., 700 (1,028*)........C9 84
Volusia, co., Fla., 125,319...C5 86
Volzhskiy, Sov. Un., 76,000..........F17 9
Vona, Kit Carson, Colo., 130..........B8 83
Vonda, Sask., Can., 238.....E2 70
Von Frank, mtn., Alsk..........C8 79
Vonitsa, Grc., 2,800.........C3 23
Vonore, Monroe, Tenn., 525..........D9 117
Von Ormy, Bexar, Tex., 350..........B3 118
Voorburg, Neth., 45,600....*B4 15
Voorheesville, Albany, N.Y., 1,228..........*C7 108
Vopnafjordur, Ice., 388.....n25 25
Vorarlberg, state, Aus., 226,323..........B5 18
Vorderthal, Switz., 918......B6 19
Vordingborg, Den., 11,780..C5 24
Vorkuta, Sov. Un., 60,000..B21 9
Vorona, riv., Sov. Un..........E14 27
Voronezh, Sov. Un., 535,000..........C1 29
Voronezh, riv., Sov. Un.......E12 27
Voronya, riv., Sov. Un........C16 25
Voroshilov, see Ussuriysk, Sov. Un.
Voroshilovgrad, see Lugansk, Sov. Un.
Vorskla, riv., Sov. Un........G10 27
Vørterkaka, mtn., Ant.........B15 5
Vosburg, S. Afr., 718........D3 49
Vosges, dept., Fr., 380,676...A2 18
Vosges, mts., Fr..........C7 14
Voskresensk, Sov. Un., 39,000..........n18 27
Voss, Nor..........G2 56
Voss, Walsh, N. Dak., 40....A8 110
Vossburg, Jasper, Miss., 250..........D5 100
Vostochnyy, Sov. Un........B11 37
Vostok, U.S.S.R. scientific station, Ant..........B23 5
Vostok, isl., Pac. O..........G12 7
Votaw, Hardin, Tex., 350...D5 118
Votice, Czech, 1,933........D9 17
Votkinsk, Sov. Un., 68,000..B4 29
Vouga, riv., Port..........B1 20
Vouliagmeni, Grc., 694.....h11 23
Vouvray, Fr., 1,616..........D4 14
Vouziers, Fr., 3,973..........C6 14
Voyeykov, ice shelf, Ant.......C25 5
Vozhega, Sov. Un., 2,000...A13 27
Voznesensk, Sov. Un., 10,000..........H8 27
Voznesenskoye, Sov. Un., 1,000..........A8 37
Voznesenye, Sov. Un., 2,000..........A10 27
Vrå, Den., 1,994..........A3 24
Vrå, Swe..........B7 24
Vranany, Czech., 659........n17 26
Vranje, Yugo., 16,457.......D5 22
Vratsa, Bul., 19,448.........D6 22
Vratsa, co., Bul., 771,486....D6 22
Vrbas, Yugo., 19,272.........C4 22
Vrbas, riv., Yugo..........C3 22
Vrchlabi, Czech., 9,900......C3 26
Vrede, S. Afr., 6,770.........C4 49
Vreden, Ger., 7,200..........A1 17
Vredenburgh, Monroe, Ala., 632..........D2 78
Vrena, Swe., 590..........u34 25
Vriezenveen, Neth., 7,200...B6 15
Vrigstad, Swe., 820..........A8 24
Vrin, Switz., 393..........C7 19
Vršac, Yugo., 31,551.........C5 22
Vrsovice, Czech., 43,663 (part of Prague)..........n17 26
Vryburg, S. Afr., 14,597....C3 49
Vryheid, S. Afr., 10,753.....C5 49
Vsetaty, Czech., 1,636.......n18 26
Vsetin, Czech., 18,200.......D4 26
Vsevidof, mtn., Alsk..........E6 79
Vsevolozhskiy, Sov. Un., 5,000..........r31 25
Vucha, riv., Bul..........E7 22
Vukovar, Yugo., 25,826......C4 22
Vulcan, Alta., Can., 1,310...D4 69
Vulcan, Dickinson, Mich., 450..........C3 98
Vulcan, Iron, Mo., 100.......D7 101
Vulcano, isl., It..........E5 21
Vulchedrum, Bul., 8,068.....D6 22
Vuoloyarvi, Sov. Un.........r31 25
Vuya, pt., Fiji Is..........52
Vyartsilya, Sov. Un.........F14 25
Vyatka, riv., Sov. Un........D18 9
Vyatskiye Polyany, Sov. Un., 23,200..........B4 29
Vyazemskiy, Sov. Un., 10,000..........C7 37
Vyazma, Sov. Un., 26,700..D10 27
Vyazma, riv., Sov. Un.......n18 27
Vyazniki, Sov. Un., 39,392..........C14 27
Vyborg, Sov. Un., 57,000..........G13 25, A7 27
Vychegda, riv., Sov. Un.......C18 9
Vygozero, lake, Sov. Un.......F16 25
Vyksa, Sov. Un., 28,600....D14 27
Vym, riv., Sov. Un..........C19 9
Vyritsa, Sov. Un., 5,000.....s31 25
Vyrovka, riv., Czech..........n19 26
Vyshniy Volochek, Sov. Un., 71,000..........C10 27
Vyskov, Czech., 12,400......D4 26
Vysoka u Melnika, Czech., 392..........n18 26
Vysoke Myto, Czech., 7,983..........D4 26
Vysoké Tatry, Czech., 9,000..........D6 26
Vyssi Brod., Czech., 1,066...E9 17
Vytegra, Sov. Un., 11,800..A11 27

W

Wa, Ghana, 5,165..........D4 45
Waal, riv., Neth..........C5 15
Waalwijk, Neth., 18,200.....C5 15
Wabamun, Alta., Can., 444..C3 69
Wabamun, lake, Alta., Can.....C3 69

Wabana (Bell Island) Newf., Can., 8,026 .... E5 75
Wabasca, Alta., Can., 381 .... B4 69
Wabasca, riv., Alta., Can A3 69
Wabash, Phillips, Ark., 115 .. C5 81
Wabash, Wabash, Ind., 12,621 .... C6 91
Wabash, Cass, Nebr., 30 .... E2 103
Wabash, co., Ill., 14,047 .... E6 90
Wabash, co., Ind., 32,605 .. C6 91
Wabash, riv., U.S. C10 77
Wabasha, Wabasha, Minn., 2,500 .... F6 99
Wabasha, co., Minn., 17,007 .... F6 99
Wabasso, Indian River, Fla., 500 .... E6 86
Wabasso, Redwood, Minn., 789 .... F3 99
Wabaunsee, Wabaunsee, Kans., 100 .... C7 93
Wabaunsee, co., Kans., 6,648 .... D7 93
Wabbaseka, Jefferson, Ark., 432 .... C4 81
Wabek, Mountrail, N. Dak., 14 .... B4 110
Wabeno, Forest, Wis., 800 .. C5 124
Wabigoon, Ont., Can., 433 .. E5 71
Wabigoon, lake, Ont., Can E5 71
Wabigoon, riv., Ont., Can E5 71
Wabiskaw, riv., Alta., Can E9 66
Wabowden, Man., Can., 327 .... B2, g8 71
Wabrzezno, Pol., 9,320 .... B5 26
Wabush, Newf., Can., 151 ... h8 75
Wabuska, Lyon, Nev., 60 ... D2 104
Waccamaw, riv., N.C., S.C. .. D5 109
Waccasassa, bay, Fla. C4 86
Wachapreague, Accomack, Va., 507 .... D7 121
Wachusett, mtn., Mass. B4 97
Wachusett, res., Mass. B4 97
Wacissa, Jefferson, Fla., 300 .. B3 86
Waco, Haralson, Ga., 381 ... C1 87
Waco, York, Nebr., 166 .... D8 103
Waco, Cleveland, N.C., 256 .... B2 109
Waco, McLennan, Tex., 97,808 (*129,000) D4 118
Waconia, Carver, Minn., 2,048 .... F5 99
Waddān, Libya D3 43
Waddān, mtn., Libya D3 43
Waddell, Maricopa, Ariz., 5 .... D3, G1 80
Wadden, sea, Neth A5 15
Wädenswil, Switz., 11,677 .. B6 19
Waddington, St. Lawrence, N.Y., 921 .... f9 108
Waddington, mtn., B.C., Can .. D5 68
Waddy, Shelby, Ky., 300 ... B4 94
Waddy, lake, Sask., Can A7 40
Wade, Cumberland, N.C. B5 109
Wade, Bryan, Okla., 150 ... D5 112
Wade, mtn., Ant A31 5
Wadena, Sask., Can., 1,311 .. F4 70
Wadena, Fayette, Iowa, 275 .... B6 92
Wadena, Wadena, Minn., 4,381 .... D3 99
Wadena, co., Minn., 12,199 .... D4 99
Wadesboro, Tangipahoa, La., 150 .... B6 95
Wadesboro, Anson, N.C., 3,744 .... C3 109
Wadesville, Posey, Ind., 300 .... H2 91
Wadham, is., Newf., Can D5 75
Wadhams, Essex, N.Y., 150 .... A7, f11 108
Wadhwan, India, 27,104 .... F3 40
Wādī ar Ratam, Jordan m14 32
Wadi el Joz, Jordan m14 32
Wadi Halfa, Sud., 11,006 ... A3 47
Wading, riv., N.J. D3 106
Wading River, Burlington, N.J., 100 .... D4 106
Wading River, Suffolk, N.Y., 900 .... n16 108
Wadi Sirhān, val., Sau. Ar .. D8 43
Wadley, Randolph, Ala., 605 .... B4 78
Wadley, Jefferson, Ga., 1,898 .... D4 87
Wadmalaw, isl., S.C. G2 115
Wad Medani, Sud., 56,000 .. C3 47
Wadowice, Pol., 7,123 .. D5, h10 26
Wadsworth, Autauga, Ala., 40 .... C3 78
Wadsworth, Lake, Ill., 150 ... E2 90
Wadsworth, Leavenworth, Kans. B8, C9 93
Wadsworth, Washoe, Nev., 200 .... D2 104
Wadsworth, Medina, Ohio, 10,635 .... A6 111
Waelder, Gonzales, Tex., 1,270 .... E4 118
Wagener, Aiken, S.C., 614 .. D5 115
Wager, bay, N.W. Ter., Can C15 66
Wagga, Sud., 4,676 .... B4 47
Wagga Wagga, Austl., 22,087 .... G6 51
Waggoner, Montgomery, Ill., 219 .... D4 90
Waging [am See], Ger., 1,900 .... B8 18
Waginger See, lake, Ger E6 18
Wagner, Phillips, Mont., 40 .... B8 102
Wagner, Charles Mix, S. Dak., 1,586 .... D7 116
Wagoner, Yavapai, Ariz., 5 .. C3 80
Wagoner, Wagoner, Okla., 4,469 .... B6 112
Wagoner, co., Okla., 15,673 .. B6 112
Wagon Mound, Mora, N. Mex., 760 .... A5 107
Wagontire, mtn., Oreg D6 113
Wagon Wheel Gap, Mineral, Colo D4 83
Wagon Wheel Gap, res., Colo .. D4 83
Wagram, Scotland, N.C., 562 .... C4 109
Wagrowiec, Pol., 10,800 .... B4 26
Wahai, Indon F7 35
Wahak Hotrontk, Pima, Ariz E3 80
Wahiawa, Honolulu, Haw., 15,512 .... B3, f9 88
Wahkiakum, co., Wash., 3,426 .... C2 122
Wahkon, Mille Lacs, Minn., 172 .... D5 99
Wahlern, Switz., 4,723 .... C3 19
Wahneta, Polk, Fla., 1,796 .. *E5 86
Wahoo, Saunders, Nebr., 3,610 .... C9, D2 103
Wahoo, creek, Nebr E1 103
Wahpeton, Richland, N. Dak., 5,876 .... C9 110
Wahsatch, Summit, Utah, 10 .... B4 119
Wah Wah, mts., Utah E2 119
Waia, isl., Fiji Is 52
Waiakoa, Maui, Haw., 450 .... C5 88
Waialee, Honolulu, Haw., 75 .... B3, f9 88
Waialua (Waialua Mill), Honolulu, Haw., 2,689 .... B3, f9 88
Waianae, Honolulu, Haw., 4,120 .... B3, g9 88
Waianae, mts., Haw g9 88
Waiawa, riv., Haw g10 88
Waiblingen, Ger., 22,600 .... E4 17
Waidhofen, Aus., 3,748 .... D7 16
Waidhofen [an der Ybbs], Aus., 5,586 .... E7 16
Waigeo, isl., W. Irian E8 35
Waihee, Maui, Haw., 500 .. C5 88
Waikabubak, Indon G5 35
Waikalo, Indon G5 35
Waikane, Honolulu, Haw., 40 .... g10 88
Waikapu, Maui, Haw., 549 .. C5 88
Waikari, N.Z., 378 .... O14 51
Waikato, riv., N.Z. L15 51
Waikawa, N.Z., 82 .... Q12 51
Waikerie, Austl, 950 .... G2 51
Waikii, Hawaii, Haw., 45 ... D6 88
Wailangilala, isl., Fiji Is 52
Wailea, Hawaii, Haw., 250 .. D6 88
Wailua (Wailua Houselots), Kauai, Haw., 1,129 .... A2 28
Wailuku, Maui, Haw., 6,969 .... C5 88
Wailuku, riv., Haw D6 88
Waimanalo, Honolulu, Haw., 3,011 .... B4, g11 88
Waimanalo, bay, Haw g11 88
Waimate, N.Z., 3,310 .... P13 51
Waimea, Honolulu, Haw., 400 .... f9 88
Waimea, Kauai, Haw., 1,312 .... B2 88
Wainganga, riv., India G7 40
Waingapu, Indon., 2,217 .... G6 35
Waini, pt., Br. Gu A3 59
Wainola, Ontonagon, Mich. A6 98
Wainunu, bay, Fiji Is 52
Wainwright, Alsk., 253 .... A7 79
Wainwright, Alta., Can., 3,351 .... C5 69
Wainwright, East Carroll, La B4 95
Wainwright, Tuscarawas, Ohio, 400 .... B6 111
Wainwright, Muskogee, Okla., 114 .... B6 112
Waiohinu, Hawaii, Haw., 163 .... D6 88
Waipahu, Honolulu, Haw., 7,650 .... B3, g9 88
Waipara, N.Z., 349 .. O14 51
Waipawa, N.Z., 1,714 .... M16 51
Waipio, Hawaii, Haw C6 88
Waipio Acres, Honolulu, Haw., 1,158 .... g9 88
Waipukurau, N.Z., 3,250 .. N16 51
Wairoa, N.Z., 4,303 .... M16 51
Waitaki, riv., N.Z. P13 51
Waitara, N.Z., 4,372 .... M15 51
Waite, Washington, Maine, 65 (73▲) C5 96
Waite Park, Stearns, Minn., 2,016 .... E4 99
Waiteville, Monroe, W. Va., 200 .... D4 123
Waits, riv., Vt C4 120
Waitsburg, Walla Walla, Wash., 1,010 .... C7 122
Waitsfield, Washington, Vt., 250 (658▲) C3 120
Waits River, Orange, Vt., 50 .... C4 120
Waitville, Sask., Can E3 70
Waiwo, W. Irian F8 35
Wajima, Jap., 18,000 .... H8 37
Wajir, Ken A7 48
Waka, Con. L A3 48
Waka, Ochiltree, Tex., 100 .... A2 118
Wakamatsu, Jap., 70,200 (99,546▲) H9 37
Wakarusa, Elkhart, Ind., 1,145 .... A5 91
Wakarusa, Shawnee, Kans., 90 .... D8 93
Wakarusa, riv., Kans D8 93
Wakasa, bay, Jap I7 37
Wakatipu, lake, N.Z. P12 41
Wakatomika, creek, Ohio B5 111
Wakaw, Sask., Can., 974 .... E3 70
Wakaya, isl., Fiji Is 52
Wakayama, Jap., 285,155 .... I7, o14 37
Wakayama, pref., Jap., 1,002,191 .... *I7 37
Wake, co., N.C., 169,082 .... B5 109
Wake, isl., Oceania 52
WaKeeney, Trego, Kans., 2,808 .... C4 93
Wakefield, Que., Can., 381 .. D2 73
Wakefield, Eng., 60,400 .... A6 12
Wakefield, Clay, Kans., 603 .... C6 93
Wakefield, Middlesex, Mass., 24,295 .... B5, f11 97
Wakefield, Gogebic, Mich., 3,231 .... A5 98
Wakefield, Dixon and Wayne, Nebr., 1,068 .... B9 103
Wakefield, Carroll, N.H., 100 (1,223▲) C4 105
Wakefield, Pike, Ohio, 135 .. D4 111
Wakefield, Washington, R.I., 4,000 .... D11 84
Wakefield, Sussex, Va., 1,015 .. E6 121
Wake Forest, Wake, N.C., 2,664 .... B5 109
Wakeham Bay, Que., Can., 112 .... f12 73
Wake Island, U.S. dep., Oceania, 1,200 52
Wakeman, Huron, Ohio, 728 .... A5 111
Wakenda, Carroll, Mo., 146 .... B4 101
Wake Village, Bowie, Texas, 1,140 .... *C5 118
Wakita, Grant, Okla., 452 .. A4 112
Wakkanai, Jap., 42,100 (51,113▲) D10 37
Wakkerstroom, S. Afr., 2,495 .... C5 49
Wakomata, lake, Ont., Can B7 98
Wakonda, Clay, S. Dak., 382 .... E8 116
Wakopa, Man., Can E2 71
Wakpala, Corson, S. Dak., 200 .... B5 116
Wakuach, lake, Que., Can g8 75
Wakulla, Wakulla, Fla., 200 .... B2 87
Wakulla, co., Fla., 5,257 .... B2 86
Wakwekobi, lake, Ont., Can B7 98
Walachia, reg., Rom C7 22
Walagā, Eth. prov D4 47
Walang, India C10 39
Walbourg, Fr., 463 .... F7 15
Walbridge, Wood, Ohio, 2,142 .... A2 111
Walbrzych, Pol., 120,800 (*155,000) C4 26
Walchen, lake, Ger B7 18
Walcott, Greene, Ark., 75 .. A5 81
Walcott, Scott, Iowa, 664 ... C7 92
Walcott, Richland, N. Dak., 30 .... C9 110
Walcott, Carbon, Wyo., 30 .. D6 125
Walcz, Pol., 13,600 .... B4 26
Wald, Switz., 7,778 .... B6 19
Waldbröl, Ger., 13,000 .... C2 17
Waldeck, Sask., Can., 237 .. G2 70
Walden, Jackson, Colo., 809 .... A4 83
Walden, Orange, N.Y., 4,851 .... D6 108
Walden, Caledonia, Vt., 35 (427▲) C4 120
Walden, pond, Mass g10 97
Walden, ridge, Tenn D7 117
Waldenburg, Poinsett, Ark., 113 .... B4 81
Walden Heights, Caledonia, Vt., 30 .... C4 120
Waldheim, Sask., Can., 515 .... E2 70
Waldheim, Ger., 11,400 .... B8 17
Waldheim, St. Tammany, La D5 95
Waldkappel, Ger., 1,900 .... B4 17
Waldkirchen, Ger., 2,400 .... E8 17
Waldmünchen, Ger., 4,100 .. D7 17
Waldo, Columbia, Ark., 1,722 .... D2 81
Waldo, B.C., Can E10 68
Waldo, Alachua, Fla., 735 .. C4 86
Waldo, Russell, Kans., 178 .. C5 93
Waldo, Santa Fe, N. Mex k8 107
Waldo, Marion, Ohio, 374 .. B4 111
Waldo, co., Maine, 22,632 .. D3 96
Waldo, hills, Oreg C2 113
Waldo, lake, Mass h11 97
Waldo, lake, Oreg D4 113
Waldoboro, Lincoln, Maine, 705 (2,882▲) D3 96
Waldorf, Charles, Md., 1,048 .... C4 85
Waldorf, Waseca, Minn., 270 .... G5 99
Waldport, Lincoln, Oreg., 667 .... C2 113
Waldron, Scott, Ark., 1,758 .... C1 81
Waldron, Sask., Can., 99 .... G4 70
Waldron, Shelby, Ind., 700 .. F6 91
Waldron, Harper, Kans., 38 .... E5 93
Waldron, Hillsdale, Mich., 454 .... G6 98
Waldron, Platte, Mo., 200 ... E1 101
Waldsassen, Ger., 7,600 .... C7 17
Waldshut, Ger., 10,900 .... E4 16
Waldwick, Bergen, N.J., 10,495 .... A4 106
Wales, Alsk., 128 .... B6 99
Wales, Hampden, Mass., 300 (659▲) B3 97
Wales, Lake, Minn., 40 .... C7 99
Wales, Cavalier, N. Dak., 151 .... A7 110
Wales, Giles, Tenn., 100 .... B4 117
Wales, Sanpete, Utah, 130 .. D4 119
Wales, reg., U.K., 2,675,000 .... D5 10, B4 12
Waleska, Cherokee, Ga., 479 .... B2 87
Walford Station, Ont., Can., 153 .... A2 72
Walgett, Austl., 1,726 .... E7 51
Walgreen, coast, Ant B2 5
Walhachin, B.C., Can., 40 .. D7 68
Walhalla, Mason, Mich., 300 .... E4 98
Walhalla, Pembina, N. Dak., 1,432 .... A8 110
Walhalla, Oconee, S.C., 3,431 .... B1 115
Walhonding, riv., Ohio B5 111
Walikale, Con. L B4 48
Walker, Yavapai, Ariz., 30 .. C3 80
Walker, Linn, Iowa, 584 .... B6 92
Walker, Ellis, Kans., 100 .... D4 93
Walker, Livingston, La., 912 .... A6 95
Walker, Cass, Minn., 1,180 .. C4 99
Walker, Vernon, Mo., 235 ... D3 101
Walker, Corson, S. Dak., 20 .... B4 116
Walker, co., Ala., 54,211 .... B2 76
Walker, co., Ga., 45,264 .... B1 87
Walker, co., Tex., 21,475 .... D5 118
Walker, creek, Wyo C7 125
Walker, lake, Man., Can B3 71
Walker, lake, Nev E3 104
Walker, mtn., Ga B3 87
Walker, mtn., Oreg D5 113
Walker, mtn., Va D1 121
Walker, rim, Oreg D5 113
Walker Knob, mtn., Tenn D8 117
Walker River, Indian res., Nev .. E3 104
Walker Springs, Clarke, Ala., 500 .... D2 78
Walkersville, Frederick, Md., 1,020 .... B3 85
Walkersville, Lewis, W. Va., 200 .... C4 123
Walkerton, Ont., Can., 3,851 .... C3 72
Walkerton, St. Joseph, Ind., 2,044 .... B5 91
Walkertown, Forsyth, N.C., 1,240 .... A3 109
Walkerville, Oceana, Mich., 261 .... E4 98
Walkerville, Silver Bow, Mont., 1,453 .... D4 102
Wall, Allegheny, Pa., 1,493 .... *F2 114
Wall, Pennington, S. Dak., 629 .... D3 116
Wall, lake, Iowa B4 92
Wallace, Escambia, Ala., 150 .... D2 78
Wallace, N.S., Can., 276 .... D6 74
Wallace, Ont., Can B6 72
Wallace, Shoshone, Idaho, 2,412 .... B3 89
Wallace, Wallace, Kans., 110 .... D2 93
Wallace, Menominee, Mich., 120 .... C3 98
Wallace, Lincoln, Nebr., 293 .... D4 103
Wallace, Steuben, N.Y., 250 .... C3 108
Wallace, Duplin, N.C., 2,285 .... C5 109
Wallace, Codington, S. Dak., 132 .... B8 116
Wallace, Washington, Va., 200 .... B3 121
Wallace, Harrison, W. Va., 200 .... A6, B4 123
Wallace, co., Kans., 2,069 .. D2 93
Wallace, creek, Wyo E5 125
Wallaceburg, Ont., Can., 7,881 .... E2 72
Wallacetown, Ont., Can., 200 .... E3 72
Wallagrass, Aroostook, Maine, (818▲) A4 96
Wallal Downs, Austl C3 50
Walland, Blount, Tenn., 250 .... D10 117
Wallaroo, Austl., 2,237 .... F6 50
Wallasey, Eng., 103,400 .... A4 12
Walla Walla, Walla Walla, Wash., 24,536 .... C7 122
Walla Walla, co., Wash., 42,195 .... C7 122
Walla Walla, riv., Wash C7 122
Walla Walla West (Garrett), Walla Walla, Wash., 1,641 .... *C7 122
Walldürn, Ger., 7,400 .... D4 17
Walled Lake, Oakland, Mich., 3,550 .... A7 98
Wallen, Allen, Ind B7 91
Wallen, lake, Switz B7 19
Wallenpaupack, lake, Pa D11 114
Wallenstadt, Switz., 3,296 .. B7 19
Waller, Waller, Tex., 900 .... E5 118
Waller, co., Tex., 12,071 .... E4 118
Wallerville, Union, Miss. A5 100
Walling, mtn., Mass B1 97
Wallingford, New Haven, Conn., 29,920 .... D5 84
Wallingford, Eng., 4,829 .... C6 12
Wallingford, Emmet, Iowa, 228 .... A3 92
Wallingford, Delaware, Pa., 3,000 .... *B10 114
Wallingford, Rutland, Vt., 800 (1,439▲) E3 120
Wallington, Eng., 32,500 ... m12 10
Wallington, Bergen, N.J., 9,261 .... h8 106
Wallis, Austin, Tex., 950 .... E4 118
Wallis & Futuna Is., Fr. dep., Oceania, 9,000 .... *G11 7
Wallkill, Ulster, N.Y., 1,215 .... D6 108
Wallkill, riv., N.Y. D6 108
Wall Lake, Sac, Iowa, 812 .. B2 92
Wallo, prov., Eth C4 47
Walloomsac, riv., Vt F2 120
Walloon, lake, Mich C6 98
Wallowa, Wallowa, Oreg., 989 .... B9 113
Wallowa, co., Oreg., 7,102 .. B9 113
Wallowa, mts., Oreg B9 113
Wallpack Center, Sussex, N.J., 25 .... A3 106
Walls, West Baton Rouge, La D4 95
Walls, De Soto, Miss., 300 ... A3 100
Wallsburg, Wasatch, Utah, 180 .... C4 119
Wallsend, Eng., 49,600 .... C6 10
Wallula, Walla Walla, Wash., 150 .... C7 122
Wallum, lake, R.I. A9 84
Wallville, Calvert, Md D4 85
Walney, isl., Eng C5 10
Walnut, Los Angeles, Calif., 934 .... *F3 82
Walnut, Bureau, Ill., 1,192 .. B4 90
Walnut, Pottawattamie, Iowa, 777 .... C2 92
Walnut, Crawford, Kans., 381 .... E8 93
Walnut, Tippah, Miss., 390 .. A5 100
Walnut, Madison, N.C., 450 .... C3 109
Walnut, creek, Kans D4 93
Walnut, hill, Mass B2 97
Walnut, mtn., Conn B4 84
Walnut, riv., Kans E7 93
Walnut Bottom, Cumberland, Pa., 325 .... F7 114
Walnut Canyon, nat. mon., Ariz B4 80
Walnut Cove, Stokes, N.C., 1,288 .... A3 109
Walnut Creek, Contra Costa, Calif., 9,903 .... B5 82
Walnut Grove, Etowah, Ala., 237 .... A3 78
Walnut Grove, Sacramento, Calif., 725 .... B6 82
Walnut Grove, Redwood, Minn., 886 .... F3 99
Walnut Grove, Leake, Miss., 433 .... C4 100
Walnut Grove, Greene, Mo., 373 .... D4 101
Walnut Heights, Contra Costa, Calif., 5,080 .... *B5 82
Walnut Hill, Lafayette, Ark., 25 .... D2 81
Walnut Hill, Escambia, Fla., 150 .... C1 86
Walnut Hill, Cumberland, Maine E5 96
Walnut Park, Los Angeles, Calif., 7,500 .... *F2 82
Walnutport, Northampton, Pa., 1,609 .... E10 114
Walnut Ridge, Lawrence, Ark., 3,547 .... A5 81
Walpole, Sask., Can H5 70
Walpole, Norfolk, Mass., 7,700 (14,068▲) B5, h10 97
Walpole, Cheshire, N.H., 800 (2,825▲) D2 105
Walsall, Eng., 120,600 .... B5 12
Walsenburg, Huerfano, Colo., 5,071 .... D6 83
Walsh, Alta., Can., 97 .... E5 69
Walsh, Baca, Colo., 856 .... D8 83
Walsh, co., N. Dak., 17,997 .... A8 110
Walsingham, cape, N.W. Ter., Can C20 67
Walsrode, Ger., 13,000 .... F3 24
Walston, Jefferson, Pa., 350 .. E4 114
Walsum, Ger., 46,800 .... *C6 15
Walter Bathurst, cape, N.W. Ter., Can B17 67
Walterboro, Colleton, S.C., 5,417 .... F6 115
Walterhill, Rutherford, Tenn., 100 .... B5 117
Walters, Mississippi, Ark B5 81
Walters, Faribault, Minn., 133 .... G5 99
Walters, Cotton, Okla., 2,825 .... C3 112
Walters, Isle of Wight, Va., 135 .... E6 121
Walters Falls, Ont., Can., 140 .... C4 72
Waltershausen, Ger., 13,400 .... C5 17
Waltersville, Warren, Miss., 400 .... C3 100
Walterville, Lane, Oreg., 170 .... C4 113
Walthall, Webster, Miss., 153 .... B4 100
Walthall, Chesterfield, Va., 230 .... C7 121
Walthall, co., Miss., 13,512 .. D3 100
Waltham, Hancock, Maine, 30 (153▲) D4 96
Waltham, Middlesex, Mass., 55,413 .... B5, g11 97
Waltham, Mower, Minn., 207 .... G6 99
Waltham, Chouteau, Mont., 5 .... C6 102
Waltham (Town of), Addison, Vt. (186▲) *C2 120
Waltham Station, Que., Can., 413 .... B8 102
Walthamstow, Eng., 108,788 .... k12 10
Walthill, Thurston, Nebr., 844 .... B9 103
Walthourville, Long, Ga., 600 .... E5 87
Waltman, Natrona, Wyo., 5 .. B5 125
Walton, N.S., Can., 393 .... D6 74
Walton, Ont., Can., 62 .... D3 72
Walton, St. Lucie, Fla., 300 .... E6 86
Walton, Cass, Ind., 1,079 .... C5 91
Walton, Harvey, Kans., 225 .... A5, D6 93
Walton, Boone, Ky., 1,530 .... A7, B5 94
Walton, Lancaster, Nebr., 80 .... E2 103
Walton, Delaware, N.Y., 3,855 .... C5 108
Walton, Roane, W. Va., 300 .... C3 123
Walton, co., Fla., 15,576 .... G3 86
Walton, co., Ga., 20,481 .... C3 87
Walton Hills, Cuyahoga, Ohio, 1,776 .... *A6 111
Waltonville, Jefferson, Ill., 394 .... E4 90
Waltreak, Yell, Ark., 50 .... C2 81
Walum, Griggs, N. Dak., 65 .. B7 110
Walville, peak, Wash C2 122
Walvis Bay, S. Afr., 12,235 .... B1 49
Walworth, Wayne, N.Y., 400 .... B3 108
Walworth, Walworth, Wis., 1,494 .... F5 124
Walworth, co., S. Dak., 8,097 .... B5 116
Walworth, co., Wis., 52,368 .... F5 124
Wama, Afg., 5,000 .... D15 41
Wamac, Marion, Clinton and Washington, Ill., 1,394 .... E4 90
Wamba, Con. L A4 48
Wamba, Nig E6 45
Wamba, riv., Con. L C2 48
Wamego, Pottawatomie, Kans., 2,363 .... C7 93
Wamesit, Middlesex, Mass., 450 .... A5, f10 97
Wamgumbaug, lake, Conn B7 84
Wami, riv., Tan C6 48
Wamic, Wasco, Oreg., 125 .. B5 113
Wampoo, Pulaski, Ark E6 81
Wampsville, Madison, N.Y., 564 .... B5 108
Wampum, Lawrence, Pa., 1,085 .... E1 114
Wamsutter, Sweetwater, Wyo., 110 .... E4 125
Wana, Pak A2 40
Wanaaring, Austl., 76 .... D5 51
Wanakah, Erie, N.Y., 1,500 .... *C2 108
Wanakena, St. Lawrence, N.Y., 250 .... A6 108
Wanamaker, Marion, Ind., 600 .... H8 91
Wanamassa, Monmouth, N.J., 2,100 .... C4 106
Wanamie, Luzerne, Pa., 950 .... D9 114
Wanamingo, Goodhue, Minn., 540 .... F6 99
Wanan, China, 3,000 .... K6 36
Wananish, Columbus, N.C. (part of Lake Waccamon) C5 109
Wanapitei, riv., Ont., Can A4 72
Wanaque, Passaic, N.J., 7,126 .... A4 106
Wanaque, res., N.J. A4 106
Wanatah, La Porte, Ind., 800 .... B4 91
Wanblee, Washabaugh, S. Dak., 200 .... D4 116
Wanchese, Dare, N.C., 600 .... B8 109
Wandering River, Alta., Can. B4 69
Wando, Kor., 7,800 .... I3 37
Wando, Berkeley, S.C., 100 .... E8, F3 115
Wando, riv., S.C. F8 115
Wandoan, Austl., 370 .... C7 51
Wandsworth, Eng., 347,209 (part of London) C7 12
Wanette, Pottawatomie, Okla., 381 .... C4 112
Wanganui, N.Z., 35,400 (*37,900) M15 51
Wangaratta, Austl., 13,783 .. H6 51
Wangava, isl., Fiji Is 52
Wangching (Paitsaokou), China C10 34
Wangen, Ger., 13,300 .... B5 18
Wangerooge, isl., Ger B3 16
Wangkuei, China, 5,000 .... C3 37
Wangyehmiao, China., 51,400 .... A10 36
Wanham, Alta., Can., 251 .. B1 69
Wanhsien, China D6 34
Wanhsien, China, 90,000 .... I3 36
Wanilla, Lawrence, Miss., 100 .... D3 100
Wanipigow, riv., Man., Can .. D4 71
Wankie, Rh., 20,200 .... A4 49
Wankie, nat. park, Rh A4 49
Wann, Saunders, Nebr., 35 .. E2 103
Wann, Nowata, Okla., 157 .. A6 112
Wannaska, Roseau, Minn., 50 .... B3 99
Wanne-Eickel, Ger., 108,300 .... *C7 15
Wanship, Summit, Utah, 150 .... C4 119
Wansreck, riv., Eng E6 13
Wantagh, Nassau, N.Y., 34,000 .... G3 84
Watnsai, China, 15,000 .... J6 36
Wanup, Ont., Can A4 72
Wapakoneta, Auglaize, Ohio, 6,756 .... B3 111
Wapanucka, Johnson, Okla., 459 .... C5 112
Wapato, Yakima, Wash., 3,137 .... C5 122
Wapawekka, hills, Sask., Can .. C3 70
Wapawekka, lake, Sask., Can .. C3 70
Wapella, Sask., Can., 584 .. G5 70
Wapella, DeWitt, Ill., 526 .. C5 90
Wapello, Louisa, Iowa, 1,745 .... C6 92
Wapello, co., Iowa, 46,126 .. C5 92
Wapisu, lake, Man., Can B2 71
Wapiti, pass., B.C., Can B7 68
Wapiti, range, Wyo A3 125
Wapiti, riv., B.C., Alta., Can .. B7 68
Wappapello, Wayne, Mo., 150 .... E7 101
Wappapello, res., Mo D7 101
Wapping, Hartford, Conn., 600 .... B6 84
Wappinger, creek, N.Y. B1 84
Wappingers Falls, Dutchess, N.Y., 4,447 .... D7 108
Wapsipinicon, riv., Iowa B5 92
Wapske, N.B., Can., 182 .. C2 74
Wapus, lake, Sask., Can A4 70
Wapwallopen, Luzerne, Pa., 200 .... D9 114
Wāqid, Eg., U.A.R D2 32
Waqqāş, Jordan, 1,000 .... B7 32
Waquoit, Barnstable, Mass., 336 .... C6 97
War, McDowell, W. Va., 3,006 .... D3 123
War, ridge, W. Va D7 123
Warabi, Jap., 50,952 .... *I9 37
Waramaug, lake, Conn C3 84
Warangal, India, 156,106 .... E6 38, H7 40
Warba, Itasca, Minn., 162 .. C5 99
Warburg, Alta., Can., 285 .. C3 69
Warburg, Ger., 9,200 .... B4 17
Warburton, Austl., 1,630 .... H5 51
Warburton, riv., Austl C2 51
Ward, Sumter, Ala., 100 .... C1 78
Ward, Lonoke, Ark., 470 .... B4 81
Ward, Saluda, S.C., 162 .... D4 115
Ward, Moody, S. Dak., 74 .. C9 116
Ward, Kanawha, W. Va., 1,109 .... C6 123
Ward, co., N. Dak., 47,072 .. A4 110
Ward, co., Tex., 14,917 .... D1 118
Ward, mtn., Ant B6 5
Ward, mtn., Mont D2 102
Wardān, Eg., U.A.R., 3,000 .... D2 32
Wardell, Pemiscot, Mo., 331 .... E8 101
Warden, Que., Can., 355 .... D5 73
Warden, Grant, Wash., 949 .. C6 122
Warden Junction, Alta., Can C4 69
Wardensville, Hardy, W. Va., 289 .... B6 123
Warder, lake, Ger E4 24
Wardha, India, 49,113 .... G7 40
Wardlow, Alta., Can D5 69
Wardner, B.C., Can., 171 .. E10 68
Wardner, Shoshone, Idaho, 577 .... B2 89
Ward Ridge, Gulf, Fla., 45 .... *C1 86
Wardsboro, Windham, Vt., 125 (322▲) E3 120
Wardsville, Ont., Can., 345 .. E3 72
Wardville, Rapides, La., 1,086 .... *C3 95
Wardville, Atoka, Okla., 150 .... C5 112
Ware, Pocahontas, Iowa, 25 .... B3 92
Ware, Hampshire, Mass., 6,700 (7,517▲) B3 97
Ware, co., Ga., 34,219 .... E4 87
Ware, riv., Mass B3 97
Wareagle, Benton, Ark., 40 .. A2 81
War Eagle, Mingo, W. Va., 180 .... D3 123
War Eagle, creek, Ark A2 81
Wareham, Eng, 3,094 .... E5 10
Wareham, Plymouth, Mass., 2,100 (9,451▲) C6 97
Warehouse Point, Hartford, Conn., 1,400 .... B6 84
Waren, Ger., 19,700 .... B6 16
Waren, W. Irian F9 35
Warendorf, Ger., 15,800 .... B2 17
Waresboro, Ware, Ga., 350 .. E4 87
Ware Shoals, Greenwood, S.C., 2,671 .... C3 115
Waretown, Ocean, N.J., 700 .... D4 106
Warfield, B.C., Can., 2,212 .. E9 68
Warfield, Martin, Ky., 295 .. C7 94
Warfield, Brunswick, Va., 80 .... E5 121
Warfordsburg, Fulton, Pa., 100 .... G5 114
Warin, Ger., 3,652 .... E5 24
Waring, Kendall, Tex., 75 ... E3 118
Wark, Eng., 690 .... E6 13
Warkworth, Ont., Can., 514 .. C7 72
Warkworth, N.Z., 991 .... L15 51
Warland, Lincoln, Mont., 40 .... B1 102
Warman, Sask., Can., 659 .. E2 70
Warmbad, S. Afr., 6,351 .... B4 49
Warmbad, S.W. Afr., 177 .. C2 49

Warm Beach, Snohomish, Wash., 300 ..... A3 122
Warminster, Bucks, Pa., 3,000 ..... *F11 114
Warminster, Eng., 9,855 ..... C5 12
Warm River, Fremont, Idaho, 20 ..... E7 89
Warm Springs, Randolph, Ark., 40 ..... A4 81
Warm Springs, Meriwether, Ga., 538 ..... D2 87
Warm Springs, Deer Lodge, Mont., 500 ..... D4 102
Warm Springs, Nye, Nev., 5 ..... E5 104
Warm Springs, Jefferson, Oreg., 250 ..... C5 113
Warm Springs, Bath, Va., 300 ..... C3 121
Warm Springs, Indian res., Oreg C5 113
Warm Springs, res., Oreg D8 113
Warner, Alta., Can., 472 ..... E4 69
Warner, Henry, Ill., 20 ..... D7 92
Warner, Merrimack, N.H., 750 (1,004▲) D3 105
Warner, Washington, Ohio, 200 ..... C6 111
Warner, Muskogee, Okla., 881 ..... B6 112
Warner, Brown, S. Dak., 135 ..... B7 116
Warner, mtn., Mass B1 97
Warner, mts., Calif., Oreg F6 113
Warner Robins, Houston, Ga., 18,633 ..... D3 87
Warner Springs, San Diego, Calif., 150 ..... F5 82
Warnerton, Washington, La., 35 ..... D5 95
Warnes, Bolivia, 1,581 ..... C3 55
Warnow, riv., Ger B6 16
Warpath, riv., Man., Can C2 71
Warracknabeal, Austl., 3,061 ..... H4 51
Warr Acres, Oklahoma, Okla., 7,135 ..... B4 112
Warragul, Austl., 6,404 ..... I5 51
Warren, Bradley, Ark., 6,752 ..... D3 81
Warren, Austl., 1,505 ..... E6 51
Warren, Ont., Can., 557 ..... A4 72
Warren, Litchfield, Conn., 75 (600▲) C3 84
Warren, Idaho, Idaho, 30 ..... D3 89
Warren, Jo Daviess, Ill., 1,470 ..... A4 90
Warren, Huntington, Ind., 1,241 ..... C7 91
Warren, Knox, Maine, 850 750 (1,678▲) D3 96
Warren, Worcester, Mass., 1,616 (3,383▲) B3 97
Warren, Macomb, Mich., 89,246 ..... F7 98
Warren, Marshall, Minn., 2,007 ..... B2 99
Warren, Carbon, Mont., 10 ..... E8 102
Warren, Grafton, N.H., 400 (548▲) C3 105
Warren, Herkimer, N.Y., 80 ..... C6 108
Warren, Trumbull, Ohio, 59,648 ..... A7 111
Warren, Warren, Pa., 14,505 ..... C3 114
Warren, Bristol, R.I., 8,750 ..... C12 84
Warren, Tyler, Tex., 360 ..... D5 117
Warren, Washington, Vt., 200 (469▲) C3 120
Warren, co., Ga., 7,360 ..... C4 87
Warren, co., Ill., 21,587 ..... C3 90
Warren, co., Ind., 8,545 ..... D3 91
Warren, co., Iowa, 20,829 ..... C4 92
Warren, co., Ky., 45,491 ..... D3 94
Warren, co., Miss., 42,206 ..... C3 100
Warren, co., Mo., 8,750 ..... C6 101
Warren, co., N.J., 63,220 ..... B3 106
Warren, co., N.Y., 44,002 ..... B7 108
Warren, co., N.C., 19,652 ..... A5 109
Warren, co., Ohio, 65,711 ..... C3 111
Warren, co., Pa., 45,582 ..... C3 114
Warren, co., Tenn., 23,102 ..... D8 117
Warren, co., Va., 14,655 ..... C4 121
Warren Center, Bradford, Pa., 75 ..... C9 114
Warrendale, Allegheny, Pa., 800 ..... A5 114
Warren Park, Marion, Ind., 852 ..... H8 91
Warrenpoint, N. Ire., 3,238 ..... C5 11
Warrens, Monroe, Wis., 280 ..... D3 124
Warrensburg, Macon, Ill., 681 ..... D4 90
Warrensburg, Johnson, Mo., 9,689 ..... C4 101
Warrensburg, Warren, N.Y., 2,240 ..... B7 108
Warrensburg, Greene, Tenn., 100 ..... C10 117
Warrensville, Cuyahoga, Ohio, 10,609 ..... B2 111
Warrensville, Lycoming, Pa., 200 ..... D8 114
Warrenton, Warren, Ga., 1,770 ..... C4 87
Warrenton, Warren, Mo., 1,869 ..... C6 101
Warrenton, Warren, N.C., 1,124 ..... A5 109
Warrenton, Clatsop, Oreg., 1,717 ..... A3 113
Warrenton, S. Afr., 5,980 ..... C3 49
Warrenton, Fauquier, Va., 3,522 ..... C5 121
Warrentown, Fayette, Ky B5 94
Warrenville, Windham, Conn., 50 ..... B8 84
Warrenville, Du Page, Ill., 3,134 ..... F2 90
Warrenville, Aiken, S.C., 1,128 ..... D4 115
Warri, Nig., 10,726 ..... E6 45
Warrick, co., Ind., 23,577 ..... H3 91
Warrington, Eng., 76,000 (*130,000) A5 12
Warrington, Escambia, Fla., 16,752 ..... G2 86
Warrior, Jefferson, Ala., 2,448 ..... B3 78
Warrior, mtn., Md D2 85
Warriors, Mark, Huntingdon, Pa., 220 ..... E5 114
Warrnambool, Austl., 15,702 ..... I4 51
Warroad, Roseau, Minn., 1,309 ..... B3 99
Warsaw, Ont., Can., 258 ..... C6 72
Warsaw, Hancock, Ill., 1,938 ..... C2 90
Warsaw, Kosciusko, Ind., 7,234 ..... B6 91
Warsaw, Gallatin, Ky., 981 ..... B5, B6 94
Warsaw, Benton, Mo., 1,054 ..... C4 101
Warsaw, Wyoming, N.Y., 3,653 ..... C2 108
Warsaw, Duplin, N.C., 2,221 ..... B5 109
Warsaw, Coshocton, Ohio, 594 ..... B5 111
Warsaw (Warszawa), Pol., 1,189,000 (*1,550,000) B6, m14 26
Warsaw, Richmond, Va., 549 ..... D6 121
Warson Woods, St. Louis, Mo., 1,746 ..... *C7 101
Warspite, Alta Can., 153 ..... B4 69
Warstein, Ger., 9,000 ..... B3 17
Warszawa, see Warsaw, Pol.
Warta, Pol., 2,896 ..... C5 26
Warta, riv., Pol B5 26
Wartburg, Morgan, Tenn., 800 ..... C9 117
Warth, Aus., 120 ..... B6 18
Warthen, Washington, Ga., 275 ..... C4 87
Wartime, Sask., Can., 96 ..... F1 70
Wartrace, Bedford, Tenn., 545 ..... B5 117
Warwick, Austl., 9,843 ..... D9 51
Warwick, Ont., Can., 110 ..... D3 72
Warwick, Que., Can., 2,487 ..... D6 73
Warwick, Eng., 16,600 ..... B6 12
Warwick, Worth, Ga., 434 ..... E3 87
Warwick, Cecil, Md., 350 ..... B6 85
Warwick, Franklin, Mass., 150 (426▲) A3 97
Warwick, Orange, N.Y., 3,218 ..... D2, m14 108
Warwick, Benson, N. Dak., 204 ..... B7 110
Warwick, Lincoln, Okla., 250 ..... B5 112
Warwick, Chester, Pa., 120 ..... F10 114
Warwick, Kent, R.I., 68,504 ..... C11 84
Warwick, co., Eng., 2,023,289 ..... B6 11
Wasaga Beach, Ont., Can., 431 ..... C4 72
Wasatch, co., Utah, 5,308 ..... C4 119
Wasatch, mts., Utah C4 119
Wasatch, plat., Utah D4 119
Wasco, Kern, Calif., 6,841 ..... E4 82
Wasco, Sherman, Oreg., 348 ..... B6 113
Wasco, co., Oreg., 20,205 ..... B5 113
Waseca, Sask., Can., 103 ..... D1 70
Waseca, Waseca, Minn., 5,898 ..... F5 99
Waseca, co., Minn., 16,041 ..... F5 99
Wash, The, bay, Eng B8 12
Washabaugh, co., S. Dak., 1,042 ..... D4 116
Washademoak, lake, N.B., Can D4 74
Washago, Ont., Can., 355 ..... C5 72
Washakie, Box Elder, Utah, 54 ..... B3 119
Washakie, co., Wyo., 8,883 ..... B5 125
Washakie Needles, mtn., Wyo B3 125
Washburn, Woodford and Marshall, Ill., 1,064 ..... C4 90
Washburn, Black Hawk, Iowa, 900 ..... B5 92
Washburn, Aroostook, Maine, 1,055 (2,083▲) B4 96
Washburn, Barry, Mo., 325 ..... E4 101
Washburn, McLean, N. Dak., 993 ..... B4 110
Washburn, Bayfield, Wis., 1,896 ..... B3 124
Washburn, co., Wis., 10,301 ..... C2 124
Washington, Hempstead, Ark., 321 ..... D2 81
Washington, Litchfield, Conn., 500 (2,603▲) C3 84
Washington, D.C., 763,956 (*2,053,600) C1, C3 85
Washington, Wilkes, Ga., 4,440 ..... C4 87
Washington, Tazewell, Ill., 5,919 ..... C4 90
Washington, Daviess, Ind., 10,846 ..... G3 91
Washington, Washington, Iowa, 6,037 ..... C6 92
Washington, Washington, Kans., 1,506 ..... C6 93
Washington, Mason, Ky., 600 ..... B6 94
Washington, St. Landry, La., 1,291 ..... D3 95
Washington, Berkshire, Mass., 50 (290▲) B1 97
Washington, Adams, Miss., 200 ..... D2 100
Washington, Franklin, Mo., 7,961 ..... C6 101
Washington, Washington, Nebr., 44 ..... D2 103
Washington, Sullivan, N.H., 100 (162▲) D2 105
Washington, Warren, N.J., 5,723 ..... B3 106
Washington, Beaufort, N.C., 9,939 ..... B7 109
Washington, McClain, Okla., 278 ..... B4 112
Washington, Washington, Pa., 23,545 ..... F1 114
Washington, Rhea, Tenn., 90 ..... D9 117
Washington, Washington, Utah, 445 ..... F2 119
Washington, Orange, Vt., 225 (565▲) C4 120
Washington, Rappahannock, Va., 255 ..... C4 121
Washington, Wood, W. Va., 50 ..... B3 123
Washington, co., Ala., 15,372 ..... D1 78
Washington, co., Ark., 55,797 ..... A1 81
Washington, co., Colo., 6,625 ..... B7 83
Washington, co., Fla., 11,249 ..... G3 86
Washington, co., Ga., 18,903 ..... C4 87
Washington, co., Idaho, 8,378 ..... E2 89
Washington, co., Ill., 13,569 ..... E4 90
Washington, co., Ind., 17,819 ..... G5 91
Washington, co., Iowa, 19,406 ..... C6 92
Washington, co., Kans., 10,739 ..... C7 93
Washington, co., Ky., 11,168 ..... C4 94
Washington, co., Maine, 32,908 ..... D5 96
Washington, co., Md., 91,219 ..... A2 85
Washington, co., Minn., 52,432 ..... E6 99
Washington, co., Miss., 78,638 ..... B3 100
Washington, co., Mo., 14,346 ..... D2 101
Washington, co., Nebr., 12,103 ..... C9 103
Washington, co., N.Y., 48,476 ..... B7 108
Washington, co., N.C., 13,488 ..... B7 109
Washington, co., Ohio, 51,489 ..... C6 111
Washington, co., Okla., 42,347 ..... A6 112
Washington, co., Oreg., 92,237 ..... B3 113
Washington, co., Pa., 217,271 ..... F1 114
Washington, co., R.I., 59,054 ..... D10 84
Washington, co., Tenn., 64,832 ..... C11 117
Washington, co., Tex., 19,145 ..... D4 118
Washington, co., Utah, 10,271 ..... F2 119
Washington, co., Vt., 42,860 ..... C3 120
Washington, co., Va., 38,076 ..... B3 121
Washington, co., Wis., 46,119 ..... E5 124
Washington, par., La., 44,015 ..... D5 95
Washington, state, U.S., 2,853,214 ..... A3 76, 122
Washington, cape, Fiji Is 52
Washington, isl., Pac. O F12 7
Washington, isl., Wis C7 124
Washington, lake, Fla D6 86
Washington, lake, Minn E4 99
Washington, lake, Miss B2 100
Washington, lake, Wash D2 122
Washington, mtn., N.H B4 105
Washington Bald, mtn., Maine D2 74
Washington Court House, Fayette, Ohio, 12,388 ..... C4 111
Washington Crossing, Mercer, N.J., 1,000 ..... C3 106
Washington Depot, Litchfield, Conn., 600 ..... C3 84
Washington Heights, Orange, N.Y., 1,231 ..... *D6 108
Washington North, Washington, Pa., 2,077 ..... *F1 122
Washington Park, St. Clair, Ill., 6,601 ..... E3 90
Washington Place, Marion, Ind., 2,000 ..... *E5 91
Washington Terrace, Weber, Utah, 6,441 ..... B4 119
Washingtonville, Montour, Pa., 198 ..... D8 114
Washington West, Washington, Pa., 3,951 ..... *F1 114
Washir, Afg., 10,000 ..... E11 41
Washita, co., Okla., 18,121 ..... B2 112
Washita, riv., Okla B3 112
Washoe, Washoe, Nev., 175 ..... D2 104
Washoe, co., Nev., 84,743 ..... C2 104
Washougal, Clark, Wash., 2,672 ..... D3 122
Washow, bay, Man., Can D3 71
Washta, Cherokee, Iowa, 310 ..... B2 92
Washtenaw, co., Mich., 172,440 ..... F7 98
Washtucna, Adams, Wash., 331 ..... C7 122
Washunga, Kay, Okla., 60 ..... A5 112
Wasilkow, Pol., 3,948 ..... B7 26
Wasilla, Alsk., 112 ..... C10, g17 79
Waskada, Man., Can., 297 ..... E1 71
Washaiowaka, lake, Man., Can A3 71
Waskana, creek, Sask., Can G3 70
Waskatenau, Alta., Can., 305 ..... B4 69
Waskesiu, lake, Sask., Can C2 70
Waskigomog, lake, Ont., Can B5 72
Waskish, Beltrami, Minn., 35 ..... B4 99
Waskom, Harrison, Tex., 1,336 ..... C5 118
Wasque, pt., Mass D7 97
Wass, lake, Man., Can C4 71
Wassaw, sound, Ga E6 87
Wassenaar, Neth., 25,400 ..... B4 15
Wasseralfingen, Ger., 10,900 ..... E5 17
Wasserburg am Inn, Ger., 6,500 ..... A8 18
Wasserkuppe, mtn., Ger C4 17
Wassokeag, lake, Maine C3 96
Wasson, Saline, Ill., 100 ..... F5 90
Wassuk, range, Nev E3 104
Wassy-sur-Blaise, Fr., 2,818 ..... F4 15
Wasta, Pennington, S. Dak., 196 ..... C3 116
Waswanipi, Que., Can o20 72
Wataga, Knox, Ill., 570 ..... B3 90
Watalula, Franklin, Ark B2 81
Watampone, Indon., 2,515 ..... F6 35
Watapi, lake, Sask., Can B6 69
Wataroa, N.Z., 159 ..... O13 51
Watatic, mtn., Mass A4 97
Watauga, Corson, S. Dak., 74 ..... B4 116
Watauga, Carter, Tenn., 500 ..... C11 117
Watauga, co., N.C., 17,529 ..... A2 109
Watauga, res., Tenn C11 117
Watauga, riv., Tenn C12 117
Watchang, pond, R.I D10 84
Watchet, Eng., 2,596 ..... C4 12
Watch Hill, Washington, R.I., 350 ..... D9 84
Watchung, Somerset, N.J., 3,312 ..... *B4 106
Water, isl., Vir. Is I15 65
Waterboro, York, Maine, 300 (1,059▲) E2 96
Waterbury, New Haven, Conn., 107,130 (*181,100) C4 84
Waterbury, Dixon, Nebr., 81 ..... B9 103
Waterbury, Washington, Vt., 2,984 (4,303▲) C3 120
Waterbury, res., Vt C3 120
Waterbury, riv., Vt C3 120
Waterbury Center, Washington, Vt., 400 ..... C3 120
Waterdown, Ont., Can., 1,844 ..... D5 72
Wateree, Richland, S.C., 75 ..... D6 115
Wateree, res., S.C C6 115
Wateree, riv., S.C D6 115
Waterflow, San Juan, N. Mex., 50 ..... A1 107
Waterford, Stanislaus, Calif., 1,780 ..... *D3 82
Waterford, Ont., Can., 2,221 ..... E4 72
Waterford, P.E.I., Can., 109 ..... C5 74
Waterford, New London, Conn., 6,000 (15,391▲) D8 84
Waterford, LaPorte, Ind., 200 ..... A4 91
Waterford, Ire., 28,216 ..... E4 11
Waterford, Spencer, Ky., 60 ..... A4 94
Waterford, Oakland, Mich., 1,000 ..... *F7 98
Waterford, Marshall, Miss., 175 ..... A4 100
Waterford, Saratoga, N.Y., 2,915 ..... C7 108
Waterford, Washington, Ohio, 450 ..... C6 111
Waterford, Erie, Pa., 1,390 ..... C1 114
Waterford, Providence, R.I., 300 ..... *A10 84
Waterford, Loudoun, Va., 247 ..... B5 121
Waterford (Town of), Caledonia, Vt., (460▲) *B4 120
Waterford, Racine, Wis., 1,500 ..... F1, F5 124
Waterford, co., Ire., 71,439 ..... E4 11
Waterford, hbr., Ire E5 11
Waterford Mills, Elkhart, Ind., 150 ..... A6 91
Waterford Works, Camden, N.J., 700 ..... D3 106
Watergrasshill, Ire., 143 ..... E3 11
Waterhen, lake, Man., Can C2 71
Waterhen, lake, Sask., Can C1 70
Waterloo, Lauderdale Ala., 215 ..... A1 78
Waterloo, Nevada, Ark., 200 ..... D2 81
Waterloo, Bel., 11,846 ..... D4 15
Waterloo, Ont., Can., 21,366 ..... D4 72
Waterloo, Que., Can., 4,543 ..... D5 73
Waterloo, Monroe, Ill., 3,739 ..... E3 90
Waterloo, DeKalb, Ind., 1,432 ..... B7 91
Waterloo, Black Hawk, Iowa, 71,755 (*114,300) B5 92
Waterloo, Kingham, Kans., 35 ..... B4 93
Waterloo, Madison, Mont., 100 ..... E4 102
Waterloo, Douglas, Nebr., 516 ..... D2 103
Waterloo, Seneca, N.Y., 5,098 ..... C4 108
Waterloo, Linn, Oreg., 151 ..... C4 113
Waterloo, S.L., 2,312 ..... E2 45
Waterloo, Laurens, S.C., 148 ..... C3 115
Waterloo, Jefferson, Wis., 1,947 ..... E5 124
Waterloo, co., Ont., Can., 176,754 ..... D4 72
Waterman, DeKalb, Ill., 916 ..... B5 90
Waterman, Wheeler, Oreg C7 113
Water Mill, Suffolk, N.Y., 850 ..... F7 84
Waterport, Orleans, N.Y., 200 ..... B2 108
Water Proof, Tensas, La., 1,412 ..... C4 95
Waters, Otsego, Mich., 35 ..... D6 98
Watersmeet, Gogebic, Mich., 500 ..... A6 98
Waterton, riv., Alta., Can E4 69
Waterton-Glacier International Peace Park, Can., U.S A5 76
Waterton Lakes, nat. park, Alta., Can E3 69
Waterton Park, Alta., Can E4 69
Watertown, Litchfield, Conn., 6,000 (14,837▲) C4 84
Watertown, Columbia, Fla., 2,109 ..... B4 86
Watertown, Middlesex, Mass., 39,092 ..... g11 97
Watertown, Carver, Minn., 1,046 ..... *F5 99
Watertown, Jefferson, N.Y., 33,306 ..... B5 108
Watertown, Washington, Ohio, 160 ..... C6 111
Watertown, Codington, S. Dak., 14,077 ..... C8 116
Watertown, Wilson, Tenn., 919 ..... A5 117
Watertown, Dodge and Jefferson, Wis., 13,943 ..... E5 124
Water Valley, Graves, Ky., 267 ..... B2 94
Water Valley, Yalobusha, Miss., 3,206 ..... A4 100
Water Valley, Tom Green, Tex., 150 ..... D2 118
Water View, Middlesex, Va., 150 ..... D6 121
Water Village, Carroll, N.H., 50 ..... C4 105
Waterville, N.S., Can., 886 ..... D5 74
Waterville, Que., Can., 1,330 ..... D6 73
Waterville, Allamakee, Iowa, 184 ..... A6 92
Waterville, Ire., 702 ..... F1 11
Waterville, Marshall, Kans., 700 ..... C7 93
Waterville, Kennebec, Maine, 18,695 ..... D3 96
Waterville, Worcester, Mass., 500 ..... A3 97
Waterville, LeSueur, Minn., 1,623 ..... F5 99
Waterville, Grafton, N.H., 11 (14▲) C3 105
Waterville, Oneida, N.Y., 1,901 ..... C5 108
Waterville, Lucas, Ohio, 1,856 ..... A1, A4 111
Waterville, Lycoming, Pa., 125 ..... D7 114
Waterville, Lamoille, Vt., 100 (332▲) B3 120
Waterville, Douglas, Wash., 1,013 ..... B5 122
Watervliet, Bel., 1,922 ..... C3 15
Watervliet, Berrien, Mich., 1,818 ..... F4 98
Watervliet, Albany, N.Y., 13,917 ..... C7 108
Waterways, Alta., Can A5 69
Watford, Ont., Can., 1,293 ..... E3 72
Watford, Eng., 75,800 ..... C7 12
Watford City, McKenzie, N. Dak., 1,865 ..... B2 110
Watha, Pender, N.C., 174 ..... C5 109
Wathena, Doniphan, Kans., 837 ..... C9 93
Watino, Alta., Can., 93 ..... B2 69
Watkins, Benton, Iowa, 120 ..... C6 92
Watkins, Meeker, Minn., 744 ..... E4 99
Watkins Glen, Schuyler, N.Y., 2,813 ..... C4 108
Watkinsville, Oconee, Ga., 758 ..... C3 87
Watlam, China A9 38
Watling, see San Salvador, isl., Ba. Is.
Watonga, Blaine, Okla., 3,252 ..... B3 112
Watonwan, co., Minn., 14,460 ..... F4 99
Watonwan, riv., Minn F4 99
Watou, Bel., 2,671 ..... D2 15
Watova, Nowata, Okla., 80 ..... A6 112
Watrous, Sask., Can., 1,461 ..... F3 70
Watrous, Mora, N. Mex., 150 ..... B5 107
Watsa, Con. L., 6,000 ..... A4 48
Watseka, Iroquois, Ill., 5,219 ..... C6 90
Watson, Desha, Ark., 312 ..... D4 81
Watson, Sask., Can., 910 ..... E3 70
Watson, Effingham, Ill., 247 ..... D5 90
Watson, Clark, Ind., 500 ..... A4 94
Watson, Chippewa, Minn., 267 ..... E3 99
Watson, Atchison, Mo., 181 ..... A2 101
Watson Lake, Yukon, Can., 597 ..... D7 66
Watsontown, Northumberland, Pa., 2,431 ..... D8 114
Watsonville, Santa Cruz., Calif., 13,293 ..... C6, D3 82
Watten, Fr., 3,100 ..... D10 12
Watten, lake, Scot B5 13
Wattenberg, Weld, Colo., 150 ..... A6 83
Wattensaw, bayou, Ark C4 81
Wattenscheid, Ger., 79,800 ..... *C7 15
Wattis, Carbon, Utah, 60 ..... D4 119
Watton, Eng., 3,104 ..... B8 12
Watton, Baraga, Mich., 70 ..... B2 98
Wattrelos, Fr., 41,319 ..... B5 14
Watts, Adair, Okla., 268 ..... A7 112
Watts Bar, lake, Tenn D9 117
Watts Bar Dam, Rhea, Tenn., 25 ..... D9 117
Wattsburg, Erie, Pa., 401 ..... C2 114
Wattsville, St. Clair, Ala., 700 ..... B3 78
Wattsville, Laurens, S.C., 1,438 ..... B4 115
Wattwil, Switz., 7,480 ..... B7 19
Watu, Con. L B3 48
Watuppa, pond, Mass C5 97
Wau, Sud., 8,009 ..... D2 47
Waubamick, Ont., Can., 170 ..... B4 72
Waubaushene, Ont., Can., 597 ..... C5 72
Waubay, Day, S. Dak., 851 ..... B8 116
Waubay, lake, S. Dak B8 116
Waubun, Mahnomen, Minn., 350 ..... C3 99
Wauchope, Sask., Can., 83 ..... H5 70
Wauchula, Hardee, Fla., 3,411 ..... E5 86
Waucoma, Fayette, Iowa, 364 ..... A5 92
Wauconda, Lake, Ill., 3,227 ..... E2 90
Waukau, Winnebago, Wis., 150 ..... E5 124
Waukee, Dallas, Iowa, 687 ..... C4 92
Waukeenah, Jefferson, Fla., 300 ..... B3 86
Waukegan, Lake, Ill., 55,719 ..... A6, E2 90
Waukesha, Waukesha, Wis., 30,004 ..... E1, F5 124
Waukesha, co., Wis., 158,249 ..... E5 124
Waukomis, Garfield, Okla., 516 ..... A4 112
Waukon, Allamakee, Iowa, 3,639 ..... A6 92
Wauna, Clatsop, Oreg., 175 ..... A3 113
Wauna, Pierce, Wash., 130 ..... D1 122
Waunakee, Dane, Wis., 1,611 ..... E4 124
Wauneta, Chase, Nebr., 794 ..... D4 103
Waupaca, Waupaca, Wis., 3,984 ..... D4 124
Waupaca, co., Wis., 35,340 ..... D5 124
Waupun, Dodge and Fond du Lac, Wis., 7,935 ..... E5 124
Wauregan, Windham, Conn., 950 ..... B9 84
Waurika, Jefferson, Okla., 1,933 ..... C4 112
Wausa, Knox, Nebr., 724 ..... B8 103
Wausau, Washington, Fla., 300 ..... G3 86
Wausau, Marathon, Wis., 31,943 ..... D4 124
Wausaukee, Marinette, Wis., 608 ..... C6 124
Wauseon, Fulton, Ohio, 4,311 ..... A3 111
Waushara, co., Wis., 13,497 ..... D4 124
Wautoma, Waushara, Wis., 1,466 ..... D4 124
Wauwatosa, Milwaukee, Wis., 56,923 ..... E1 124
Wauzeka, Crawford, Wis., 494 ..... E3 124
Wave, Dallas, Ark C3 81
Wave Hill, Austl., 75 ..... C5 50
Waveland, Montgomery, Ind., 549 ..... E3 91
Waveland, Hancock, Miss., 1,106 ..... E1, E4 100
Waveney, riv., Eng B9 12
Waverly, Chambers and Lee, Ala., 250 ..... C4 78
Waverly, Crittendon, Ark E8 117
Waverley, Austl., 65,100 ..... *F8 51
Waverley, Austl., 53,200 ..... *H5 51
Waverly, N.S., Can., 1,142 ..... E6 74
Waverly, Polk, Fla., 1,160 ..... *E5 86
Waverly, Camden, Ga., 165 ..... E5 87
Waverly, Morgan, Ill., 1,375 ..... D4 90
Waverly, Morgan, Ind., 150 ..... E5 91
Waverly, Bremer, Iowa, 6,357 ..... B5 92
Waverly, Coffey, Kans., 381 ..... D8 93
Waverly, Union, Ky., 331 ..... C2 94
Waverly, Madison, La., 75 ..... B4 95
Waverly, Middlesex, Mass. (part of Belmont) g11 97
Waverly, Wright, Minn., 574 ..... E5 99
Waverly, Lafayette, Mo., 837 ..... B4 101
Waverly, Lancaster, Nebr., 511 ..... D9, E2 103
Waverly, Tioga, N.Y., 5,950 ..... C4 108
Waverly, Pike, Ohio, 3,830 ..... C5 111
Waverly, Humphreys, Tenn., 2,891 ..... A4 117
Waverly, Sussex, Va., 1,601 ..... D5 121
Waverly, Wood, W. Va., 300 ..... B3 123
Waverly Hall, Harris, Ga., 712 ..... D2 87
Wavre, Bel., 9,706 ..... D4 15
Wawa, Ont., Can., 4,040 ..... o18 72
Wawaka, Noble, Ind., 300 ..... B7 91
Waw al Kabir, Libya D3 43
Wawanesa, Man., Can., 456 ..... E2 71
Waw an Nāmūs (Well), Libya E3 43
Wawasee, lake, Ind B6 91
Wawayanda, lake, N.J A4 106
Wawayanda, mtn., N.J A4 106
Waweig, N.B., Can., 179 ..... D2 74
Wawota, Sask., Can., 453 ..... H4 70
Waxahachie, Ellis, Tex., 12,749 ..... B5, C4 118
Waxhaw, Union, N.C., 729 ..... C3 109
Waxia, St. Landry, La D4 95
Waxweiler, Ger., 950 ..... D6 15
Way, Madison, Miss., 50 ..... C3 100
Way, is., Viet H5 38
Wayagamack, lake, Que., Can B5 73
Wayan, Caribou, Idaho, 10 ..... G7 89
Waycross, Ware, Ga., 20,944 ..... E4 87
Wayland, Henry, Iowa, 597 ..... C6 92
Wayland, Floyd, Ky., 1,340 ..... C7 94
Wayland, Middlesex, Mass., 950 (10,444▲) g10 97
Wayland, Allegan, Mich., 2,019 ..... F5 98
Wayland, Clark, Mo., 384 ..... A6 101
Wayland, Steuben, N.Y., 2,003 ..... C3 108
Wayland Springs, Lawrence, Tenn., 200 ..... B4 117
Waymart, Wayne, Pa., 1,106 ..... C11 114
Wayne, Alta., Can., 116 ..... D4 69
Wayne, Du Page, Ill., 373 ..... E2 90
Wayne, Republic, Kans., 50 ..... C6 93
Wayne, Wayne, Mich., 16,034 ..... A7 98
Wayne, Wayne, Nebr., 4,217 ..... B8 103
Wayne, Passaic, N.J., 29,353 ..... B4 106
Wayne, Schuyler, N.Y., 400 ..... C3 108
Wayne, Wood, Ohio, 949 ..... A4 111
Wayne, McClain, Okla., 517 ..... C4 112
Wayne, Delaware, Pa., 10,000 ..... A10, F11 114
Wayne, Wayne, W. Va., 1,274 ..... C2 123
Wayne, co., Ga., 17,921 ..... E5 87
Wayne, co., Ill., 19,008 ..... E5 90
Wayne, co., Ind., 74,039 ..... E7 91
Wayne, co., Iowa, 9,800 ..... D4 92
Wayne, co., Ky., 14,700 ..... D5 94
Wayne, co., Mich., 2,666,297 ..... F7 98
Wayne, co., Miss., 16,258 ..... D5 100
Wayne, co., Mo., 8,638 ..... D7 101
Wayne, co., Nebr., 9,959 ..... B8 103
Wayne, co., N.Y., 67,989 ..... B3 108
Wayne, co., N.C., 82,059 ..... B5 109
Wayne, co., Ohio, 75,497 ..... B6 111
Wayne, co., Pa., 28,237 ..... C11 114
Wayne, co., Tenn., 11,908 ..... B4 117
Wayne, co., Utah, 1,728 ..... E4 119
Wayne, co., W. Va., 38,977 ..... C2 123
Wayne City, Wayne, Ill., 903 ..... E5 90
Waynesboro, Burke, Ga., 5,359 ..... C4 87
Waynesboro, Wayne, Miss., 3,892 ..... D5 100
Waynesboro, Franklin, Pa., 10,427 ..... G6 114
Waynesboro, Wayne, Tenn., 1,343 ..... B4 117
Waynesboro (Independent City), Va., 15,694 ..... C4 121
Waynesburg, Lincoln, Ky., 450 ..... C5 94
Waynesburg, Stark, Ohio, 1,442 ..... B6 111
Waynesburg, Greene, Pa., 5,188 ..... G1 114
Waynesville, Brantley, Ga., 250 ..... E5 87

West Enosburg, Franklin, Vt., 75 ..... B3 120
West Epping, Rockingham, N.H., 350 ..... D4 105
Westerkappeln, Ger., 8,500 .. A2 17
Westerland, Ger., 8,700 ..... A4 16
Westerly, Washington, R.I., 10,300 (14,267▲) D9 84
Western, Saline, Nebr., 351 .. D8 103
Western, prov., Zambia D4 48
Western, reg., Ghana E4 45
Western, reg., Nig., 6,087,000 ..... E5 45
Western, reg., Tan., 955,852 ..... C5 48
Western, reg., Ug A5 48
Western, downs, Eng D5 13
Western, head, Newf., Can D2 75
Western, head, N.S., Can F5 74
Western, isl., Newf., Can C4 75
Western Australia, state, Austl., 814,000 ..... D3 50
Western Azerbaijan, see Azerbaijan, reg., Iran
Western Ghats, range, India E5 39
Western Grove, Newton, Ark., 148 ..... A3 81
Western Hills, Adams, Colo., 1,500 ..... *B6 83
Western Peninsula, div., Ice., 11,394 ..... *m21 25
Westernport, Allegany, Md., 3,559 ..... D2 85
Western Samoa, country, Oceania, 124,000 52
Western Shore, N.S., Can., 653 ..... E5 74
Western Shoshone, Indian res., Idaho, Nev B5 104
Western Springs, Cook, Ill., 10,838 ..... F2 90
Wester Schelde, chan., Neth C3 15
Westerstede, Ger., 15,400 .... A7 15
Westervelt, Shelby, Ill., 180 ..... D5 90
Westerville, Custer, Nebr., 40 ..... C6 103
Westerville, Franklin, Ohio, 7,011 ..... B5 111
Westerwald, mts., Ger C2 17
West Fairlee, Orange, Vt., 150 (333▲) D4 120
West Fairview, Cumberland, Pa., 1,718 ..... F8 114
Westfall, Lincoln, Kans., 75 .. D5 93
Westfall, Malheur, Oreg., 8 ..... D9 113
West Falmouth, Cumberland, Maine (part of Falmouth) . E5 96
West Falmouth, Barnstable, Mass., 725 ..... C6 97
West Fargo, Cass, N. Dak., 93 ..... C9 110
West Farmington, Franklin, Maine, 500 ..... D2 96
West Farmington, Trumbull, Ohio, 614 ..... A7 111
West Farms, Monmouth, N.J., 200 ..... C4 106
West Feliciana, par., La., 12,395 ..... D4 95
Westfield, Jefferson, Ala., 2,000 ..... E4 78
Westfield, N.B., Can D3 74
Westfield, Clark, Ill., 636 .... D6 90
Westfield, Hamilton, Ind., 1,217 ..... D5 91
Westfield, Plymouth, Iowa, 187 ..... B1 92
Westfield, Aroostook, Maine, 350 (569▲) B5 96
Westfield, Hampden, Mass., 26,302 ..... B2 97
Westfield, Union, N.J., 31,447 ..... B4 106
Westfield, Chautauqua, N.Y., 3,878 ..... C1 108
Westfield, Surry, N.C., 200 ..... A3 109
Westfield, Emmons, N. Dak., 40 ..... C5 110
Westfield, Tioga, Pa., 1,333 .. C6 114
Westfield, Orleans, Vt., 100 (347▲) B4 120
Westfield, Marquette, Wis., 919 ..... E4 124
Westfield, riv., Mass B2 97
Westfir, Lane, Oreg., 500 .... D4 113
West Flanders, prov., Bel., 1,068,976 ..... C3 15
Westford, Windham, Conn., 200 ..... B8 84
Westford, Middlesex, Mass., 800 (6,261▲) f10 97
Westford, Chittenden, Vt., 60 (680▲) B2 120
West Fork, Washington, Ark., 350 ..... B1 81
West Fork, riv., W. Va B4 123
West Forks, Somerset, Maine, (930▲) C3 96
West Frankfort, Franklin, Ill., 9,027 ..... F5 90
West Freehold, Monmouth, N.J., 150 ..... C4 106
West Friendship, Howard, Md., 50 ..... B4 85
West Frisian, is., Neth A5 15
West Gardiner, Kennebec, Maine, 35 (1,144▲) D3 96
Westgate, Palm Beach, Fla., 2,500 ..... F6 86
Westgate, Fayette, Iowa, 214 ..... B6 92
West Glacier, Flathead, Mont., 350 ..... B3 102
West Glens Falls, Warren, N.Y., 2,725 ..... *B7 108
West Glocester, Providence, R.I., 150 ..... B9 84
West Glover, Orleans, Vt., 64 ..... B4 120
West Gorham, Cumberland, Maine, 40 ..... E4 96
West Goshen, Litchfield, Conn., 400 ..... B3 84
West Gouldsboro, Hancock, Maine, 90 ..... D4 96
West Granby, Hartford, Conn., 300 ..... B5 84
West Granville, Hampden, Mass., 125 ..... B2 97
West Gravenhurst, Ont., Can C5 72
West Gray, Cumberland, Maine, 75 ..... E2, E5 96
West Green, Coffee, Ga., 300 ..... E4 87
West Greene, Greene, Ala., 60 ..... C1 96
West Greenwich (Town of), Kent, R.I. (1,169▲) *C10 84
West Groton, Middlesex, Mass., 650 ..... A4 97
West Grove, Davis, Iowa, 100 ..... D5 92
West Grove, Chester, Pa., 1,607 ..... G10 114
West Halifax, Windham, Vt., 150 ..... F3 120
WestHam, Eng., 157,186 ..... k13 10, C8 12
West Hamlin, Lincoln, W. Va., 788 ..... C2 123
West Hampstead, Rockingham, N.H., 150 ..... E4 105
Westhampton, Hampshire, Mass., 200 (583▲) B2 97
Westhampton, Suffolk, N.Y., 900 ..... F6 84
Westhampton, beach, N.Y G6 84
Westhampton Beach, Suffolk, N.Y., 1,460 ..... n16 108
West Hanover, Plymouth, Mass., 700 ..... h12 97
West Harrison, Dearborn, Ind., 341 ..... F8 91
West Hartford, Hartford, Conn., 62,382 ..... B5 84
West Hartford, Windsor, Vt., 125 ..... D4 120
West Hartland, Hartford, Conn., 150 ..... A5 84
West Hartlepool, Eng., 78,600 ..... C6 10
West Harwich, Barnstable, Mass., 350 ..... *C7 97
West Hatfield, Hampshire, Mass., 100 ..... B2 97
West Haven, New Haven, Conn., 43,002 ..... D5 84
West Haven, Va. (part of Portsmouth) B6 121
West Haverstraw, Rockland, N.Y., 5,020 ..... *D7 108
West Hazleton, Luzerne, Pa., 6,278 ..... E9 114
West Helena, Phillips, Ark., 8,385 ..... C5 81
West Hempstead, Nassau, N.Y., 26,500 ..... *G2 84
West Hickory, Forest, Pa., 450 ..... C3 114
West Hill, Ont., Can D5, k15 72
West Hill, res., Mass B4, h9 97
Westhoff, De Witt, Tex., 400 ..... E4 118
West Hollywood, Los Angeles, Calif., 28,870 ..... *F2 82
West Hollywood, Broward, Fla., 52,000 ..... E3 86
West Homestead, Allegheny, Pa., 4,155 ..... *F2 114
Westhope, Bottineau, N. Dak., 824 ..... A4 110
West Hopkinton, Merrimack, N.H., 45 ..... D3 105
West Hyannisport, Barnstable, Mass., 500 ..... C7 97
West Indies, is., N.A G13 61, 64
West Irian, Indon. dep., Asia, 775,000 ..... F9 35
West Islip, Suffolk, N.Y., 23,000 ..... *G3 84
West Java, see Java, isl., Indon.
West Jefferson, Ashe, N.C., 1,000 ..... A2 109
West Jefferson, Madison, Ohio, 2,774 ..... C1, C4 111
West Jonesport, Washington, Maine, 540 ..... D5 96
West Jordan, Salt Lake, Utah, 3,009 ..... C4 119
West Junction, Shelby, Tenn., 4,000 ..... B1, E8 117
West Kankakee, Kankakee, Ill., 3,197 ..... B6 90
Westkapelle, Bel., 2,355 .... C3 15
Westkapelle, Neth., 2,400 ..... C3 15
West Keansburg, Monmouth, N.J., 3,200 ..... *C4 106
West Kennebunk, York, Maine, 350 ..... E2 96
West Kildonan, Man., Can., 20,077 ..... E3 71
West Kingston, Washington, R.I., 900 ..... D10 84
West La Crosse, La Crosse, Wis., 1,440 ..... *E2 124
West Lafayette, Tippecanoe, Ind., 12,680 ..... D4 91
West Lafayette, Coshocton, Ohio, 1,476 ..... B6 111
Westlake, Calcasieu, La., 3,311 ..... D2 95
Westlake, Cuyahoga, Ohio, 12,906 ..... B1 111
Westlake, Lane, Oreg., 150 ..... D2 113
Westland, Tarrant, Tex., 1,000 ..... *B5 118
Westlands, Middlesex, Mass., 2,000 ..... f10 97
West Lanham Hills, Prince Georges, Md., 1,000 ..... *C4 85
West Las Vegas, see Las Vegas, N. Mex.
West Lawn, Berks, Pa., 2,059 ..... F10 114
West Lawn, Fairfax, Va., 1,400 ..... *C5 121
West Layton, Davis, Utah, 150 ..... *B3 119
West Lebanon, Warren, Ind., 720 ..... D3 91
West Lebanon, York, Maine, 160 ..... E2 96
West Lebanon, Grafton, N.H. (part of Lebanon) C2 105
West Lebanon, Lebanon, Pa., 1,054 ..... *F9 114
West Leechburg, Westmoreland, Pa., 1,323 ..... *E2 114
West Leisenring, Fayette, Pa., 800 ..... G2 114
Westley, Stanislaus, Calif., 250 ..... B6 82
West Leyden, Lewis, N.Y., 200 ..... B5 108
West Liberty, Jasper, Ill., 160 ..... E5 90
West Liberty, Muscatine, Iowa, 2,042 ..... C6 92
West Liberty, Morgan, Ky., 1,165 ..... C6 94
West Liberty, Logan, Ohio, 1,522 ..... B4 111
West Liberty, Ohio, W. Va., 1,500 ..... B2 123
West Lima, Richland, Wis., 140 ..... E3 124
West Lincoln, Lancaster, Nebr., 507 ..... E1 103
West Lincoln, Addison, Vt., 50 ..... C2 120
Westline, McKean, Pa., 160 ..... C4 114
West Linn, Clackamas, Oreg., 3,933 ..... B2, B4 113
Westlock, Alta., Can., 1,838 ..... B4 69
West Long Branch, Monmouth, N.J., 5,337 ..... C4 106
West Lorne, Ont., Can., 1,070 ..... E3 72
West Lothian, co., Scot., 92,764 ..... E5 13
West Louisville, Daviess, Ky., 250 ..... C2 94
West Lubec, Washington, Maine, 150 ..... D5 96
West Manayunk, Montgomery, Pa., 1,900 ..... *F11 114
West Manchester, Preble, Ohio, 460 ..... C3 111
West Mansfield, Bristol, Mass., 800 ..... B5 97
West Mansfield, Logan, Ohio, 791 ..... B4 111
West Marion, Marion, S.C., 45 ..... C9 115
West Mayfield, Beaver, Pa., 2,201 ..... *E1 114
Westmeath, Ont., Can., 260 ..... B8 72
Westmeath, co., Ire., 52,861 ..... D4 11
West Medway, Norfolk, Mass., 2,000 ..... B5, h10 97
West Melbourne, Brevard, Fla., 2,266 ..... *D6 86
West Memphis, Crittenden, Ark., 19,374 ..... B5 81
Westmere, Albany, N.Y., 4,000 ..... *C7 108
West Methow, riv., Wash A5 122
West Miami, Dade, Fla., 5,296 ..... F3 86
West Middlesex, Mercer, Pa., 1,301 ..... D1 114
West Middleton, Howard, Ind., 280 ..... D5 91
West Mifflin, Allegheny, Pa., 27,289 ..... F2 114
West Milan, Coos, N.H., 100 ..... A4 105
West Milford, Passaic, N.J., 1,000 ..... A4 106
West Milford, Harrison, W. Va., 367 ..... B4 123
West Milton, Miami, Ohio, 2,972 ..... C3 111
West Milton, Union, Pa., 750 ..... D8 114
West Milwaukee, Milwaukee, Wis., 5,043 ..... E2 124
West Mineral, Cherokee, Kans., 262 ..... E9 93
Westminster, Orange, Calif., 25,750 ..... *F3 82
Westminster, Adams, Colo., 13,850 ..... B5 83
Westminster, Carroll, Md., 6,123 ..... A4 85
Westminster, Worcester, Mass., 1,400 (4,022▲) A4 97
Westminster, Oconee, S.C., 2,413 ..... B1 115
Westminster, Windham, Vt., 333 (1,602▲) E4 120
Westminster Station, Windham, Vt., 150 ..... E4 120
Westminster West, Windham, Vt., 60 ..... E3 120
West Monroe, Ouachita, La., 15,215 ..... B3 95
Westmont, Du Page, Ill., 5,997 ..... F2 90
Westmont, Camden, N.J., 8,000 ..... D2 106
Westmont, Cambria, Pa., 6,573 ..... F4 114
West Monterey, Clarion, Pa., 300 ..... D2 114
Westmoreland, Pottawatomie, Kans., 460 ..... C7 93
Westmoreland, Cheshire, N.H., 100 (921▲) E2 105
Westmoreland, Sumner, Tenn., 865 ..... A5 117
Westmoreland, co., Pa., 352,629 ..... F2 114
Westmoreland, co., Va., 11,042 ..... C6 121
Westmoreland City, Westmoreland, Pa., 1,300 ..... *F2 114
Westmorland, Imperial, Calif., 1,404 ..... F6 82
Westmorland, co., N.B., Can., 93,679 ..... C4 74
Westmorland, co., Eng., 67,222 ..... *C5 10
Westmount, Que., Can., 25,012 ..... *D4 73
West Muncie, Delaware, Ind., 300 ..... D7 91
West Musquash, lake, Maine .. C5 96
West Mystic, New London, Conn., 650 ..... *D9 84
West Nanticoke, Luzerne, Pa., 800 ..... *B7 114
West Newbury, Essex, Mass., 600 (1,844▲) A6 97
West Newbury, Orange, Vt., 50 ..... C4 120
West Newfield, York, Maine, 100 ..... E2 96
West New Guinea, see West Irian, Indon. dep., Asia
West Newton, Marion, Ind., 400 ..... I7 91
West Newton, Westmoreland, Pa., 3,982 ..... F2 114
West New York, Hudson, N.J., 35,547 ..... h8 106
West Nicholson, Rh B4 49
West Nishnabotna, riv., Iowa .. C2 92
West Norfolk, Norfolk, Va., 500 ..... B6 121
West Nottingham, Rockingham, N.H., 50 ..... D4 105
West Nyack, Rockland, N.Y., 4,000 ..... *D7 108
West Olive, Ottawa, Mich., 60 ..... F4 98
Weston, Ont., Can., 9,715 .. m14 72
Weston, Las Animas, Colo., 350 ..... D6 83
Weston, Fairfield, Conn., 700 (4,039▲) E3 84
Weston, Webster, Ga., 120 .. E2 87
Weston, Franklin, Idaho, 284 ..... G7 89
Weston, McLean, Ill., 150 .. C5 90
Weston, Aroostook, Maine, 50 (202▲) C5 96
Weston, Middlesex, Mass., 8,261 ..... g10 97
Weston, Platte, Mo., 1,057 ..... B3, D1 101
Weston, Saunders, Nebr., 340 ..... C9 103
Weston, Wood, Ohio, 1,075 ..... A4 111
Weston, Umatilla, Oreg., 783 ..... B8 113
Weston, Windsor, Vt., 200 (442▲) E3 120
Weston, Lewis, W. Va., 8,754 ..... B4 123
Weston, Dunn, Wis., 40 .... D1 124
Weston, co., Wyo., 7,929 .... B8 125
Weston-super-Mare, Eng., 43,200 ..... C5 12
West Orange, Franklin, Mass., 50 ..... A3 97
West Orange, Essex, N.J., 39,895 ..... B4 106
West Orange, Orange, Tex., 4,848 ..... *D6 118
West Ossipee, Carroll, N.H., 100 ..... C4 105
Westover, Shelby, Ala., 350 ..... B3 78
Westover, Somerset, Md., 250 ..... D6 85
Westover, Broome, N.Y., 600 ..... *C5 108
Westover, Clearfield, Pa., 492 ..... E4 114
Westover, Monongalia, W. Va., 4,749 ..... A7, B5 123
West Pakistan, prov., Pak., 42,976,261 ..... *C5 39
West Palm Beach, Palm Beach, Fla., 56,208 (*157,200) F6 86
West Paris, Oxford, Maine, 600 (1,050▲) D2 96
West Park, Ulster, N.Y., 500 ..... D7 108
West Paterson, Passaic N.J., 7,602 ..... *B4 106
West Pawlet, Rutland, Vt., 300 ..... E2 120
West Pearl, riv., La D6 95
West Pelham, Hampshire, Mass., 400 ..... *B2 9
West Pelzer, Anderson, S.C., 687 ..... B2 115
West Pembroke, Washington, Maine, 400 ..... D5 96
West Pensacola, Escambia, Fla., 25,000 ..... G2 86
West Peru, Oxford, Maine, 350 ..... D2 96
West Peterborough, Hillsboro, N.H., 325 ..... E3 105
West Petersburg, Alsk., 20 .. m23 79
Westphalia, Knox, Ind., 300 ..... G3 91
Westphalia, Anderson, Kans., 249 ..... D8 93
Westphalia, Clinton, Mich., 560 ..... F6 98
Westphalia, Osage, Mo., 316 ..... C5 101
Westphalia, reg., Ger C3 16
West Pittsburg (Shell Point), Contra Costa, Calif., 5,188 . *B6 82
West Pittsburg, Lawrence, Pa., 850 ..... E1 114
West Pittston, Luzerne, Pa., 6,998 ..... B8 114
West Plains, Howell, Mo., 5,836 ..... E6 101
West Point, Cullman, Ala., 200 ..... A3 78
West Point, White, Ark., 97 ..... B4 81
West Point, Calaveras, Calif., 900 ..... C3 82
West Point, Troup, Ga., 4,610 ..... D1 87
West Point, Hancock, Ill., 234 ..... C2 90
Westpoint, Tippecanoe, Ind., 350 ..... D3 91
West Point, Lee Iowa, 758 ..... D6 92
West Point, Hardin, Ky., 2,005 ..... C4 94
Westpoint, Sagadahoc, Maine, 170 ..... E6 96
West Point, Clay, Miss., 8,550 ..... B5 100
West Point, Cuming, Nebr., 2,921 ..... C9 103
West Point, Orange, N.Y., 4,500 ..... D2, m15 108
Westpoint, Lawrence, Tenn., 300 ..... B4 117
West Point, Davis, Utah, 599 ..... *B3 119
West Point, King William, Va., 1,678 ..... D6 121
West Point, mtn., Alsk C11 79
Westport, Newf., Can., 222 ..... D3, k10 75
Westport, N.S., Can., 413 .... E3 74
Westport, Ont., Can., 711 .... C8 72
Westport, Fairfield, Conn., 20,955 ..... E3 84
Westport, Decatur, Ind., 833 ..... F6 91
Westport, Ire., 2,882 ..... D2 11
Westport, Oldham, Ky., 125 ..... A4, B4 94
Westport, Bristol, Mass., 600 (6,641▲) C5 97
Westport, Pope, Minn., 87 .... E3 99
Westport, Cheshire, N.H., 170 ..... E2 105
Westport, Essex, N.Y., 723 ..... A7, f11 108
Westport, N.Z., 5,460 ..... N13 51
Westport, Clatsop, Oreg., 300 ..... A3 113
Westport, Brown, S. Dak., 35 ..... B7 116
Westport, Carroll, Tenn., 125 ..... B3 117
Westport, Grays Harbor, Wash., 976 ..... C1 122
West Portland, Multnomah, Oreg., 2,000 ..... *B4 113
Westport Point, Bristol, Mass., 350 ..... C5 97
West Portsmouth, Scioto, Ohio, 3,100 ..... D4 111
West Prairie, riv., Alta., Can B2 69
West Pubnico, N.S., Can., 247 ..... F4 74
West Pueblo, Pueblo, Colo., 1,700 ..... *C6 83
West Punjab, reg., Pak B3 40
West Quoddy Head, cape, Maine D6 96
Westray, firth, Scot A5 13
Westray, isl., Scot A5 13
West Reading, Berks, Pa., 4,938 ..... F10 114
West Redding, Fairfield, Conn., 250 ..... D3 84
Westrhauderfehn, Ger., 4,500 ..... A7 15
West Richland, Benton, Wash., 1,347 ..... *C6 122
West Riding, Yorkshire, see York, co., Eng.
West Rindge, Cheshire, N.H., 130 ..... E2 105
West River, Anne Arundel, Md., 100 ..... C4 85
West Road, riv., B.C., Can C5 68
West Roag, bay, Scot B1 13
West Roanoke Rapids, Halifax, N.C., 2,000 ..... *A6 109
West Rockingham, Richmond, N.C., 1,128 ..... *C4 109
West Rumney, Grafton, N.H., 40 ..... C3 105
West Rupert, Bennington, Vt., 250 ..... E2 120
West Rutland, Rutland, Vt., 2,302 ..... D2 120
West Rye, Rockingham, N.H., 150 ..... E5 105
West Sacramento, Yolo, Calif., 10,000 ..... *A6 82
West St. Modeste, Newf., Can., 141 ..... C3 75
West St. Paul, Dakota, Minn., 13,101 ..... E7 99
West Salem, Edwards, Ill., 956 ..... E5 90
West Salem, Wayne, Ohio, 1,017 ..... B5 111
West Salem, Polk, Oreg. (part of Salem) C1, C3 113
West Salem, La Crosse, Wis., 1,707 ..... E2 124
West Sayville, Suffolk, N.Y., 3,500 ..... G4 84
West Scarboro, Cumberland, Maine, 900 ..... E2, E4 96
West Sebois, Penobscot, Maine, 50 ..... C4 96
West Seneca, Erie, N.Y., 39,653 ..... *C2 108
West Shefford, Que., Can., 406 ..... D5 73
West Siberian, plain, Sov. Un .. A6 29
Westside, Crawford, Iowa, 367 ..... B2 92
West Side, Lake, Oreg E6 113
West Simsbury, Hartford, Conn., 400 ..... B5 84
West Slope, Washington, Oreg., 9,000 ..... B2 113
West Somerset, Pulaski, Ky., 400 ..... C5 94
West Spanish, peak, Colo D6 83
West Spitsbergen, isl., Nor A13 4
West Springfield, Hampden, Mass., 24,924 ..... B2 97
West Springfield, Sullivan, N.H., 35 ..... D2 105
West Stafford, Tolland, Conn., 210 ..... B7 84
West Sterling, Whiteside, Ill., 1,430 ..... *B4 90
West Stewartstown, Coos, N.H., 225 ..... A1 105
West Stockbridge, Berkshire, Mass., 900 (1,244▲) B1 97
West Suffield, Hartford, Conn., 400 ..... B6 84
West Sullivan, Hancock, Maine, 125 ..... D4 96
West Sumner, Oxford, Maine, 125 ..... D2 96
West Sunbury, Butler, Pa., 252 ..... E2 114
West Swanzey, Cheshire, N.H., 900 ..... E2 105
Westsyde, B.C., Can., 942 .. D7 68
West Tarbert, bay, Scot C1 13
West Terre Haute, Vigo, Ind., 3,006 ..... F3 91
Westterschelling, Neth., 1,995 ..... A5 15
West Thornton, Grafton, N.H., 130 ..... C3 105
West Tisbury, Dukes, Mass., 240 (360▲) D6 97
West Tocoi, Clay, Fla., 30 .. C5 86
West Topsham, Orange, Vt., 150 ..... C4 120
West Townsend, Middlesex, Mass., 600 ..... A4 97
West Townshend, Windham, Vt., 150 ..... E3 120
West Union, Clark, Ill., 400 . D6 90
West Union, Fayette, Iowa, 2,551 ..... B6 92
West Union, Adams, Ohio, 1,762 ..... D4 111
West Union, Oconee, S.C., 443 ..... B2 115
West Union, Doddridge, W. Va., 1,186 ..... B4, B6 123
West Unity, Williams, Ohio, 1,192 ..... A3 111
West University Place, Harris, Tex., 14,628 ..... F4 118
West Upton, Worcester, Mass., 1,100 ..... B4, h9 97
Westvale, Onondaga, N.Y., 9,500 ..... *B4 108
West Valley, Cattaraugus, N.Y., 400 ..... C2 108
West Van Lear, Johnson, Ky., 900 ..... C7 94
West Vernon, Wilbarger, Tex. (part of Vernon) B3 118
Westview, Cuyahoga, Ohio, 1,303 ..... B1 111
West View, Allegheny, Pa., 8,079 ..... A5 114
Westview Heights, New Haven, Conn., 900 ..... *C4 84
West View Park, Sullivan, Tenn., 1,000 ..... C11 117
Westville, N.S., Can., 4,159 . D7 74
Westville, Holmes, Fla., 250 ..... G3 86
Westville, Vermilion, Ill., 3,497 ..... C6 90
Westville, LaPorte, Ind., 789 ..... A4 91
Westville, Rockingham, N.H., 400 ..... E4 105
Westville, Gloucester, N.J., 4,951 ..... D2 106
Westville, Champaign, Ohio, 180 ..... B4 111
Westville, Adair, Okla., 727 .. B7 112
Westville, Jefferson, Pa., 160 ..... D4 114
Westville, Kershaw, S.C., 200 ..... C4 115
Westville, res., Mass B3 97
Westville Grove, Gloucester, N.J., 3,000 ..... *D2 106
West Virginia, state, U.S., 1,860,421 ..... C11 77, 123
West Walker, riv., Nev E2 104
West Wardsboro, Windham, Vt., 100 ..... E3 120
West Wareham, Plymouth, Mass., 500 ..... C6 97
West Warren, Worcester, Mass, 1,124 ..... B3 97
West Warwick, Kent, R.I., 21,414 ..... C10 84
Westwego, Jefferson, La., 9,815 ..... C7, E5 95
West Wenatchee, Chelan, Washington, 2,518 ..... *B5 122
West Wickham, Eng. (part of Beckenham) m12 10
West Willington, Tolland, Conn., 200 ..... B7 84
West Wilton, Hillsboro, N.H., 100 ..... E3 105
West Windsor (Town of), Windsor, Vt. (539▲) *E4 120
West Winfield, Herkimer, N.Y., 960 ..... C5 108
West Winfield, Butler, Pa., 300 ..... E2 114
West Winter Haven, Polk, Fla., 5,050 ..... *D5 86
Westwold, B.C., Can., 327 .. D8 68
Westwood, Lassen, Calif., 1,209 ..... B3 82
Westwood, Johnson, Kans., 2,040 ..... *D9 93
Westwood, Boyd, Ky., 6,000 ..... B7 94
Westwood, Norfolk, Mass., 7,200 (10,354▲) B5, h11 97
Westwood, Kalamazoo, Mich., 6,500 ..... *F5 98
Westwood, Bergen, N.J., 9,046 ..... B4, h8 106
Westwood Lakes, Dade, Fla., 22,517 ..... F3 86
West Woodstock, Windham, Conn., 75 ..... *B8 84
West Woodstock, Windsor, Vt., 100 ..... D3 120
Westworth Village, Tarrant, Tex., 3,321 ..... *C4 118
West Wyalong, Austl., 2,399 ..... F6 51
West Wyoming, Luzerne, Pa., 3,166 ..... B8 114
West Wyomissing, Berks, Pa., 2,500 ..... *F9 114
West Yarmouth, Barnstable, Mass., 2,100 ..... C7 97
West Yellowstone, Gallatin, Mont., 150 ..... F5 102
West York, Crawford, Ill., 250 ..... D6 90
West York, York, Pa., 5,526 . G8 114
Wet, mts., Colo C5 83
Wetar, isl., Indon G7 35
Wetaskiwin, Alta., Can., 5,300 ..... C4 69
Wethersfield, Hartford, Conn., 20,561 ..... C6 84
Wetmore, Custer, Colo., 100 . C5 83
Wetmore, Nemaha, Kans., 390 ..... C8 93
Wetmore, Alger, Mich., 200 . B4 98
Wetonka, McPherson, S. Dak., 46 ..... B7 116
Wettingen, Switz., 17,613 ... *B5 19
Wetumka, Hughes, Okla., 1,798 ..... B5 112
Wetumpka, Elmore, Ala., 3,672 ..... C3 78
Wetzel, co., W. Va., 19,347 .. B4 123
Wetzikon, Switz., 10,421 .... B6 19
Wetzlar, Ger., 37,900 (*70,000) C3 17
Wevelgem, Bel., 12,805 ..... D3 15
Wever, Lee, Iowa, 100 ..... D6 92
Wewahitchka, Gulf, Fla., 1,436 ..... B1 86
Wewahotee, Orange, Fla. ... D5 86
Wewak, N. Gui., 59 ..... h11 50
Wewela, Tripp, S. Dak., 22 ..... D6 116
Wewoka, Seminole, Okla., 5,954 ..... B5 112
Wexford, Ire., 11,328 ..... E5 12
Wexford, co., Ire., 83,308 .... E5 12
Wexford, co., Mich., 18,466 ..... D5 98
Wexford, bay, Ire E5 12
Weyakwin, lake, Sask., Can .. C3 70
Weyanoke, West Feliciana, La., 50 ..... D4 95
Weyauwega, Waupaca, Wis., 1,239 ..... D5 124
Weybridge [& Walton], Eng., 46,700 ..... *C7 12
Weyburn, Sask., Can., 9,101 ..... H4, o8 70
Weyerhauser, Rusk, Wis., 339 ..... C2 124
Weyers Cave, Augusta, Va., 300 ..... C4 121
Weymouth, N.S., Can., 671 .. E4 74
Weymouth, Eng., 40,962 .... E5 12
Weymouth, Norfolk, Mass., 48,177 ..... B6, h12 97
Weymouth, Atlantic, N.J., 300 ..... D3 106
Weymouth, bay, Eng D5 12
Weymouth [& Melcombe Regis], Eng., 41,800 ..... D5 12
Whakatane, N.Z., 7,167 .... L16 51
Whalan, Fillmore, Minn., 146 ..... G7 99
Whale, riv., Que., Can g8 75
Whales, bay, Ant B32 5
Whaley, pond, N.Y C2 84

Willcox, Cochise, Ariz., 2,441....E6 80
Willemstad, Neth. Antilles, 43,500 (*94,000)....A4 60
Willemstad, Neth., 905....C4 15
Willernie, Washington, Minn., 664....E7 99
Willesden, Eng., 170,835....k11 10
Willet, Cortland, N.Y., 200..C5 108
Willette, Macon, Tenn., 100....C8 117
Willetts, Concordia, La.....C4 95
Willey House, Carroll, N.H., 8....B4 105
William, lake, Man., Can.....C2 71
William Creek, Austl.....E6 50
Williams, Coconino, Ariz., 3,559....B3 80
Williams, Colusa, Calif., 1,370....C2 82
Williams, Lawrence, Ind., 400....C4 91
Williams, Hamilton, Iowa, 490....B4 92
Williams, Lake of the Woods, Minn., 317....B4 99
Williams, Le Flore, Okla., 100....B7 112
Williams, Colleton, S.C., 194....E6 115
Williams, co., N. Dak., 22,051....A2 110
Williams, co., Ohio, 29,968..A3 111
Williams, cape, Ant.....C29 5
Williams, mtn., Okla.....C7 112
Williams, riv., Ariz.....C1 80
Williams, riv., Vt.....E3 120
Williams, riv., W. Va.....C4 123
Williams Bay, Walworth, Wis., 1,347....F5 124
Williamsburg, Ont., Can., 442....C9 72
Williamsburg, Wayne, Ind., 400....E8 91
Williamsburg, Iowa, Iowa, 1,342....C5 92
Williamsburg, Franklin, Kans., 255....D8 93
Williamsburg, Whitley, Ky., 3,478....D5 94
Williamsburg, Dorchester, Md., 400....C6 85
Williamsburg, Hampshire, Mass., 800 (2,186▲)....B2 97
Williamsburg, Grand Traverse, Mich., 140....D5 98
Williamsburg, Sierra, N. Mex., 350....D2 107
Williamsburg, Clermont, Ohio, 1,956....C3 111
Williamsburg, Blair, Pa., 1,792....F5 114
Williamsburg (Independent City), Va., 6,832....D6 121
Williamsburg, Greenbrier, W. Va., 250....D4 123
Williamsburg, co., S.C., 40,932....D8 115
Williamsfield, Knox, Ill., 548....C3 90
Williams Lake, B.C., Can., 2,120....C6, n18 68
Williamson, Pike, Ga., 215..C2 87
Williamson, Madison, Ill., 324....A9 101
Williamson, Lucas, Iowa, 262....C4 92
Williamson, Wayne, N.Y., 1,690....B3 108
Williamson, Mingo, W. Va., 6,746....D2 123
Williamson, co., Ill., 46,117..F5 90
Williamson, co., Tenn., 25,267....A5 117
Williamson, co., Tex., 35,044....D4 118
Williamson, head, Ant.....C28 5
Williams Park, Lake, Ill., 900....*E2 90
Williamsport, Newf., Can., 151....C3 75
Williamsport, Warren, Ind., 1,353....D3 91
Williamsport, Washington, Md., 1,853....A2 85
Williamsport, Pickaway, Ohio, 840....C4 111
Williamsport, Lycoming, Pa., 41,967....D7 114
Williamsport, Maury, Tenn., 100....B4 117
Williamston, Ingham, Mich., 2,214....F6 98
Williamston, Martin, N.C., 6,924....B6 109
Williamston, Anderson, S.C., 3,721....B3 115
Williamstown, Ont., Can., 325....B10 72
Williamstown, Jefferson, Kans., 70....B7 93
Williamstown, Grant, Ky., 1,611....B5 94
Williamstown, Berkshire, Mass., 5,500 (7,322▲)....A1 97
Williamstown, Lewis, Mo., 125....A6 101
Williamstown, Gloucester, N.J., 2,800....D3 106
Williamstown, Oswego, N.Y., 350....B5 108
Williamstown, Hancock, Ohio, 100....B4 111
Williamstown, Dauphin, Pa., 2,097....E8 114
Williamstown, Orange, Vt., 650 (1,553▲)....C3 120
Williamstown, Wood, W. Va., 2,632....B3 123
Williamsville, Sangamon, Ill., 735....D4 90
Williamsville, Attala, Miss., 100....B4 100
Williamsville, Wayne, Mo., 412....E7 101
Williamsville, Erie, N.Y., 6,316....C2 108
Williamsville, Windham, Vt., 160....F3 120
Williaumez, pen., Bis. Arch........ 51
Williford, Sharp, Ark., 195...A4 81
Williford, Gilchrist, Fla., 75..C4 86
Willimantic, Windham, Conn., 13,881....C8 84
Willimantic, riv., Conn.....B7 84
Willingboro, Burlington, N.J., 11,861....C3 106
Willingdon, Alta., Can., 429....C4 69
Willington (Town of), Tolland, Conn. (2,005▲)..*B7 84
Willis, Brown, Kans., 109....C8 93
Willis, Washtenaw, Mich., 175....A7 98
Willis, Marshall, Okla., 10..D5 112
Willis, Montgomery, Tex., 975....D5 118
Willis, Floyd, Va., 70....E2 121
Willis, isl., Newf., Can.....D5 75
Willis Beach, Dakota, Nebr., 100....B9 103
Willisburg, Washington, Ky., 300....C4 94
Williston, Levy, Fla., 1,582..C4 86
Williston, Carteret, N.C., 300....C7 109
Williston, Williams, N. Dak., 11,866....A2 110
Williston, Ottawa, Ohio, 500....A2 111
Williston, Barnwell, S.C., 2,722....E5 115
Williston, Fayette, Tenn., 150....B2 117
Williston, S. Afr., 2,873....D3 49
Williston, Chittenden, Vt., 150 (1,484▲)....C2 120
Williston, basin, Mont.....B11 102
Williston Park, Nassau, N.Y., 8,255....G2 84
Willisville, Nevada, Ark., 100....D2 81
Willisville, Perry, Ill., 532..F4 90
Willis Wharf, Northampton, Va., 528....D7 121
Willits, Mendocino, Calif., 3,410....C2 82
Willmar, Sask., Can., 51....H4 70
Willmar, Kandiyohi, Minn., 10,417....E3 99
Willoughby, Austl., 54,100..*F8 51
Willoughby, Lake, Ohio, 15,058....A6 111
Willoughby, lake, Vt.....B4 120
Willoughby Hills, Lake, Ohio, 4,241....*A6 111
Willow, Alsk., 78....g16 79
Willow, Dallas, Ark., 60....C3 81
Willow, Greer, Okla., 187...B2 112
Willow, creek, Alta., Can....D4 69
Willow, creek, Utah....D6 119
Willow, creek, Wyo.....B6 125
Willow, res., Wis.....C3 124
Willow, riv., B.C., Can.....C6 68
Willow Branch, Hancock, Ind., 200....E6 91
Willow Brook, Los Angeles, Calif., 22,000....*F2 82
Willowbrook, Sask., Can., 86....F4 70
Willow Bunch, Sask., Can., 698....H3 70
Willow Bunch, lake, Sask., Can....H3 70
Willow City, Bottineau, N. Dak., 494....A5 110
Willow City, Gillespie, Tex., 75....D3 118
Willow Creek, Gallatin, Mont., 150....E5 102
Willowcreek, Malheur, Oreg., 50....C9 113
Willowdale, Ont., Can. .D5, k15 72
Willowgrove, Kent, Del., 100....B6 85
Willow Grove, Montgomery, Pa., 10,000....A11, F11 114
Willow Hill, Jasper, Ill., 335....E5 90
Willow Hill, Franklin, Pa., 30....F6 114
Willowick, Lake, Ohio, 18,749....B2 111
Willow Island, Dawson, Nebr., 85....D5 93
Willow Lake, Clark, S. Dak., 467....C8 116
Willow Lawn, Henrice, Va., 2,500....*D5 121
Willowmore, S. Afr., 3,454....D3 49
Willow Ranch, Modoc, Calif., 300....B3 82
Willow River, B.C., Can., 331....B6 68
Willow River, Pine, Minn., 343....D6 99
Willow Run, Washtenaw, Mich., 4,100....*F7 98
Willows, Glenn, Calif., 4,139....C2 82
Willows, Sask., Can....H3 70
Willows, Gilliam, Oreg.....B6 113
Willow Springs, Cook, Ill., 2,348....F2 90
Willow Springs, Howell, Mo., 1,913....E6 101
Wills, creek, W. Va.....C6 123
Wills, hill, Mass.....f11 97
Wills, mtn., Md.....D2 85
Wills, riv., Ala.....A3 78
Wills, val., Ala.....A4 78
Willsboro, Essex, N.Y.,....f11 108
Willshire, Van Wert, Ohio, 601....B3 111
Wills Point, Van Zandt, Tex., 2,281....*C5 118
Wilmar, Drew, Ark., 718....D4 81
Wilmer, Mobile, Ala., 200...E1 78
Wilmer, Dallas, Tex., 1,785..B6 118
Wilmerding, Allegheny, Pa., 4,349....B6 114
Wilmersdorf, Ger., 398....E7 24
Wilmette, Cook, Ill., 28,268....A6, E3 90
Wilmington, New Castle, Del., 95,827 (*318,700)....A6 85
Wilmington, Will, Ill., 4,210....B5 90
Wilmington, Middlesex, Mass., 3,000 (12,475▲)....A5, f11 97
Wilmington, Essex, N.Y., 500....f11 108
Wilmington, New Hanover, N.C., 44,013....C6 109
Wilmington, Clinton, Ohio, 8,915....C4 111
Wilmington, Windham, Vt., 591 (1,245▲)....F3 120
Wilmington, lake, Fla.....E6 86
Wilmont, Nobles, Minn., 473....G3 99
Wilmore, Comanche, Kans., 99....E4 93
Wilmore, Jessamine, Ky., 2,773....C5 94
Wilmot, Ashley, Ark., 732..D4 81
Wilmot, Cowley, Kans., 60..E7 93
Wilmot, Merrimack, N.H., 75 (391▲)....D3 105
Wilmot, Stark, Ohio, 402....B6 111
Wilmot, Roberts, S. Dak., 545....B9 116
Wilmot Flat, Merrimack, N.H., 75....D3 105
Wilmot Station, N.S., Can., 363....E4 74
Wilmslow, Eng., 21,393....A5 12
Wilmurt, Herkimer, N.Y., 100....B6 108
Wilno, Ont., Can., 161....B7 72
Wilno, see Vilnius, Sov. Un.
Wilsall, Park, Mont., 200....E6 102
Wilsey, Morris, Kans., 224..D7 93
Wilson, Mississippi, Ark., 1,191....B5 81
Wilson, Hartford, Conn., 3,000....B5 84
Wilson, Brevard, Fla., 100...D6 86
Wilson, Ellsworth, Kans., 905....D5 93
Wilson, East Feliciana, La., 300....D4 95
Wilson, Menominee, Mich., 70....C3 98
Wilson, Niagara, N.Y., 1,320....B2 108
Wilson, Wilson, N.C., 28,753....B6 109
Wilson, Carter, Okla., 1,647....C4 112
Wilson, Northampton, Pa., 8,465....E11 114
Wilson, Lynn, Tex., 403....C2 118
Wilson, Weber, Utah, 300...B3 119
Wilson, Teton, Wyo., 35....B2 125
Wilson, co., Kans., 13,077...E8 93
Wilson, co., N.C., 57,716....B6 109
Wilson, co., Tenn., 27,668...A5 117
Wilson, co., Tex., 13,267....E3 118
Wilson, creek, Wash.....B5 122
Wilson, creek, Wash.....B6 122
Wilson, dam, Ala.....A2 78
Wilson, mtn., Calif.....F2 82
Wilson, mtn., Nev.....E7 104
Wilson, mtn., Oreg.....B5 113
Wilson, peak, Colo.....D3 83
Wilson, pond, Maine....C3 96
Wilson, riv., Austl.....C4 51
Wilson Creek, Grant, Wash., 252....B6 122
Wilson Mills (Lincoln Plantation), Oxford, Maine, 65 (99▲)....D1 96
Wilson Mills, Johnston, N.C., 280....B5 109
Wilson Piedmont, glacier, Ant. .e39 5
Wilsons, Dinwiddie, Va., 150....D5 121
Wilson's promontory, Austl.....I6 51
Wilsons Beach, N.B., Can., 768....E3 74
Wilsonville, Shelby, Ala., 683....B3 78
Wilsonville, Windham, Conn., 150....A9 84
Wilsonville, Macoupin, Ill., 688....D4 90
Wilsonville, Spencer, Ky., 30....A4 94
Wilsonville, Furnas, Nebr., 289....D5 103
Wilsonville, Clackamas, Oreg., 185....B2 113
Wilstedt, Ger., 1,150....E3 18
Wilster, Ger., 4,900....E3 18
Wilton, Shelby, Ala., 428...B3 78
Wilton, Little River, Ark., 329....D1 81
Wilton, Fairfield, Conn., 5,500 (8,026▲)....E3 84
Wilton, Franklin, Maine, 1,761 (3,274▲)....D2 96
Wilton, Beltrami, Minn., 112....C3 99
Wilton, Hillsboro, N.H., 1,425 (2,025▲)....E3 105
Wilton, Saratoga, N.Y., 200....B7 108
Wilton, Burleigh and McLean, N. Dak., 739....B5 110
Wilton, Monroe, Wis., 578...E3 124
Wilton Junction (Wilton), Muscatine, Iowa, 1,750....C6 92
Wilton Manors, Broward, Fla., 8,257....*F6 86
Wiltshire, co., Eng., 422,753....C6 12
Wiltz, Lux, 3,904....E5 15
Wiluna, Austl., 576....E3 51
Wimapedi, riv., Man., Can.....B2 71
Wimauma, Hillsborough, Fla., 583....E4 86
Wimbledon, Eng., 56,994....m12 10, C7 12
Wimbledon, Barnes, N. Dak., 402....B7 110
Wimborne, Alta., Can., 80...D4 69
Wimborne, Eng., 4,156....D6 12
Wimer, Jackson, Oreg.....E3 113
Wimico, lake, Fla.....C1 86
Winagami, lake, Alta., Can.....B2 69
Winamac, Pulaski, Ind., 2,375....B4 90
Winburg, S. Afr., 4,968....C4 49
Winburne, Clearfield, Pa., 800....E5 114
Wincheck, pond, R.I.....C9 84
Winchell, mtn., Mass.....B2 97
Winchendon, Worcester, Mass., 3,800 (6,237▲)....A3 97
Winchendon Springs, Worcester, Mass., 300....A3 97
Winchester, Drew, Ark., 185....D4 81
Winchester, Riverside, Calif., 200....F3 82
Winchester, Ont., Can., 1,429....B9 72
Winchester, Eng., 29,500....C6 12
Winchester, Lewis, Idaho, 427....C2 89
Winchester, Scott, Ill., 1,657....D3 90
Winchester, Randolph, Ind., 5,742....D8 91
Winchester, Jefferson, Kans., 428....B7 93
Winchester, Clark, Ky., 10,187....C5 94
Winchester, Middlesex, Mass., 19,376....g11 97
Winchester, Wayne, Miss., 50....D5 100
Winchester, Clark, Mo.....A6 101
Winchester, St. Louis, Mo., 1,299....*B7 101
Winchester, Clark, Nev., 600....G6 104
Winchester, Cheshire, N.H., 950 (2,411▲)....E2 105
Winchester, Adams, Ohio, 788....D4 111
Winchester, Franklin, Tenn., 4,760....B5 117
Winchester (Independent City), Va., 15,110....B4 121
Winchester, Washakie, Wyo., 20....B4 125
Winchester Bay, Douglas, Oreg., 500....D2 113
Winchester Center, Litchfield, Conn., 170 (10,496▲)....B4 84
Wind, lake, Wis.....F1 124
Wind, riv., Wash.....D4 122
Wind, riv., Wyo.....B7 125
Wind, riv., Wyo.....B3 125
Windber, Somerset, Pa., 6,994....F4 114
Wind Cave, nat. park, S. Dak. .D2 116
Windemere, Ingham, Mich., 2,000....*F6 98
Winder, Barrow, Ga., 5,555..C3 87
Windermere, B.C., Can., 391....D10 68
Windermere, Ont., Can., 137....B5 72
Windermere, Tolland, Conn., 75....B7 84
Windermere, Eng., 6,556....C5 10
Windermere, lake, Eng.....F6 13
Windfall, Alta., Can., 101...B2 69
Windfall, Tipton, Ind., 1,135....D6 91
Windgap, Northampton, Pa., 1,930....E11 114
Windham, Windham, Conn., 500 (16,973▲)....C8 84
Windham, Judith Basin, Mont., 125....C6 102
Windham, Rockingham, N.H., 30 (1,317▲)....E4 105
Windham, Greene, N.Y., 300....C6 108
Windham, Portage, Ohio, 3,777....A6 111
Windham, co., Conn., 68,572....B8 84
Windham, co., Vt., 29,776..F3 120
Windhoek, S.W. Afr., 36,051....B2 49
Windigo Lake, Ont., Can....n17 72
Windigo, riv., Que., Can.....A4 73
Winding Stair, mtn., Okla.....C7 112
Wind Lake, Racine, Wis., 1,305....F5 124
Windmill, pt., Va.....D6 121
Windom, McPherson, Kans., 168....D6 93
Windom, Cottonwood, Minn., 3,691....G3 99
Wind, peak, Colo.....D3 83
Windorah, Austl., 48....B4 51
Window Rock, Apache, Ariz., 500....B6 80
Wind Ridge, Greene, Pa., 250....G1 114
Wind River, Fremont, Wyo. (part of Fort Washakie)....C4 125
Wind River, basin, Wyo.....B4 125
Wind River, Indian res., Wyo.....B3 125
Wind River, range, Wyo.....B3 125
Windsbach, Ger., 2,900....D5 17
Windsheim, Ger., 8,200....D5 17
Windsor, Sonoma, Calif., 600....A5 82
Windsor, Newf., Can., 5,505....D4 75
Windsor, N.S., Can., 3,823..E5 74
Windsor, Ont., Can., 114,367 (*193,365)....E1 72
Windsor, Que., Can., 6,589..D5 73
Windsor, Weld, Colo., 1,509....A6 83
Windsor, Hartford, Conn., 13,500 (19,467▲)....B6 84
Windsor, Eng., 28,300....C7 12
Windsor, Shelby, Ill., 1,021..D5 90
Windsor, Berkshire, Mass., 55 (384▲)....A1 97
Windsor, Henry, Mo., 2,714....C4 101
Windsor, Mercer, N.J., 300..C3 106
Windsor, Broome, N.Y., 1,026....*C5 108
Windsor, Bertie, N.C., 1,813....B7 109
Windsor, Stutsman, N. Dak., 55....C6 110
Windsor, York, Pa., 1,029....G8 114
Windsor, Aiken, S.C., 200...E4 115
Windsor, Windsor, Vt., 3,256 (4,468▲)....E4 120
Windsor, Isle of Wight, Va., 579....B6, E6 121
Windsor, co., Vt., 42,483....D3 120
Windsor Heights, Polk, Iowa, 4,715....C4 92
Windsor Hills, Los Angeles, Calif., 3,500....*F2 82
Windsor Locks, Hartford, Conn., 11,411....B6 84
Windsorville, Hartford, Conn., 300....B6 84
Windthorst, Sask., Can., 202.G4 70
Windthorst, Archer, Tex., 170....C3 118
Windward, passage, N.A.....F6 64
Windward Islands, see Dominica, Grenada, St. Lucia, and St. Vincent, Br. dep., N.A....o16 64
Windy, Wirt, W. Va., 15....B3 123
Windy, lake, Sask., Can.....C4 70
Windy, peak, Wash.....A6 122
Windy, pt., Newf., Can.....C4 75
Windygates, Man., Can....E2 71
Windy Hill, Florence, S.C., 2,201....*C8 115
Windy Hills, Jefferson, Ky., 1,371....*H6 94
Wine, isl., La.....E5 95
Winefred, lake, Alta., Can.....B5 69
Winefred, riv., Alta., Can.....B5 69
Winesap, Cumberland, Tenn.D8 117
Winesap, Chelan, Wash....B5 122
Winfall, Perquimans, N.C., 269....A7 109
Winfield, Marion, Ala., 2,907....B2 78
Winfield, Alta., Can., 238...C3 69
Winfield, Du Page, Ill., 1,575....*F2 90
Winfield, Henry, Iowa, 862..C6 92
Winfield, Cowley, Kans., 11,117....E7 93
Winfield, Carroll, Md., 100..B3 85
Winfield, Lincoln, Mo., 564....A7, C7 101
Winfield, Union, N.J., 2,458 ..k7 106
Winfield, Union, Pa., 270....E8 114
Winfield, Scott, Tenn., 200..C9 117
Winfield, Putnam, W. Va., 318....C3 123
Winfred, Lake, S. Dak., 137....C8 116
Wing, Covington, Ala., 82...D3 78
Wing, Yell, Ark., 15....C2 81
Wing, Burleigh, N. Dak., 303....B5 110
Wing, riv., Minn.....D3 99
Wingate, Eng., 12,688....F7 13
Wingate, Montgomery, Ind., 431....D3 91
Wingate, Dorchester, Md., 400....D5 85
Wingate, Union, N.C., 1,304....C3 109
Wingate, Centre, Pa., 100...E6 114
Wingdale, Dutchess, N.Y., 100....D7 108
Winger, Polk, Minn., 292...C3 99
Wingham, Ont., Can., 2,922....D3 72
Wing Lake, Oakland, Mich., 1,500....*F7 98
Wingo, Graves, Ky., 340....B2 94
Winhall (Town of), Bennington, Vt. (245▲)...*E3 120
Winifred, Fergus, Mont., 220....C7 102
Winifreda, Arg.....B4 54
Winifrede, Kanawha, W. Va., 300....D6 123
Winigan, Sullivan, Mo., 100.A5 101
Winisk, Ont., Can....n18 72
Winisk, lake, Ont., Can....n18 72
Winisk, riv., Ont., Can....n18 72
Wink, Winkler, Tex., 1,863..D1 118
Winkelman, Gila, Ariz., 1,123....E5 80
Winkle, Highland, Ohio, 150....C4 111
Winkler, Man., Can., 2,529..E3 71
Winkler, co., Tex., 13,652...D1 118
Winlaw, B.C., Can., 392....E9 68
Winlock, Wheeler, Oreg.....C7 113
Winlock, Lewis, Wash., 808..C3 122
Winn, Penobscot, Maine, 200 (526▲)....C4 96
Winn, Isabella, Mich., 300...E6 98
Winn, par., La., 16,034....C3 95
Winnabow, Brunswick, N.C., 150....C5 109
Winneba, Ghana, 15,171....E4 45
Winnebago, Winnebago, Ill., 1,059....A4 90
Winnebago, Faribault, Minn., 2,088....G4 99
Winnebago, Thurston, Nebr., 682....B9 103
Winnebago, Winnebago, Wis., 150....B5 124
Winnebago, co., Ill., 209,765....A4 90
Winnebago, co., Iowa, 13,099....A4 92
Winnebago, co., Wis., 107,928....D5 124
Winnebago, Indian res., Nebr.....B9 103
Winnebago, lake, Wis.....D5 124
Winneconne, Winnebago, Wis., 1,273....D5 124
Winnegance, Sagadahoc, Maine, 125....E3, E6 96
Winnemucca, Humboldt, Nev., 3,453....C4 104
Winnemucca, lake, Nev.....C2 104
Winner, Tripp, S. Dak., 3,705....D6 116
Winneshiek, co., Iowa, 21,651....A6 92
Winnetka, Cook, Ill., 13,368....A6, E3 90
Winnetoon, Knox, Nebr., 85....B8 103
Winnett, Petroleum, Mont., 360....D8 102
Winnfield, Winn, La., 7,022....C3 95
Winnibigoshish, lake, Minn.....C4 99
Winnie, Chambers, Texas, 1,114....*E5 118
Winnifred, Alta., Can....E5 69
Winning Pool, Austl.....D1 50
Winnipeg, Man., Can., 265,429 (*475,989)....E3, h8 71
Winnipeg, lake, Man., Can.....C3 71
Winnipeg, riv., Man., Can.....D4 71
Winnipeg Beach, Man., Can., 807....D3 71
Winnipegosis, Man., Can., 980....D2 71
Winnipegosis, lake, Man., Can. .C2 71
Winnepesaukee, lake, N.H.....C4 105
Winnisquam, Belknap, N.H., 80....C3 105
Winnisquam, lake, N.H.....C3 105
Winnsboro, Franklin, La., 4,437....B4 95
Winnsboro, Fairfield, S.C., 3,479....C5 115
Winnsboro, Franklin and Wood, Tex., 2,675....C5 118
Winokur, Charlton, Ga., 75..E4 87
Winona, Ont., Can., 294...*D5 72
Winona, Starke, Ind., 100...B4 91
Winona, Logan, Kans., 393....C2 93
Winona, Houghton, Mich., 120....B2 98
Winona, Winona, Minn., 24,895....F7 99
Winona, Montgomery, Miss., 4,282....B4 100
Winona, Shannon, Mo., 562....D6 101
Winona, Whitman, Wash., 100....C8 122
Winona, Fayette, W. Va., 650....C4, D7 123
Winona, co., Minn., 40,937..F7 99
Winona Lake, Kosciusko, Ind., 1,928....B6 91
Winona Lakes, Orange, N.Y., 1,655....*D6 108
Winooski, Chittenden, Vt., 7,420....C2 120
Winooski, riv., Vt.....C3 120
Winschoten, Neth., 16,600...A7 15
Winsen, Ger., 9,700....E4 24
Winsford, Eng., 12,738....A5 12
Winside, Wayne, Nebr., 416....B8 103
Winslow, Navajo, Ariz., 8,862....C5 80
Winslow, Washington, Ark., 183....B1 81
Winslow, Stephenson, Ill., 366....A4 90
Winslow, Pike, Ind., 1,089...H3 91
Winslow, Kennebec, Maine, 3,640 (5,891▲)....D3 96
Winslow, Dodge, Nebr., 136.C9 97
Winslow, Camden, N.J., 300.D3 106
Winslow, Kitsap, Wash., 919....D1 122
Winsted, Litchfield, Conn., 8,136....B4 84
Winsted, McLeod, Minn., 1,163....F4 99
Winston, Polk, Fla., 3,323...D4 86
Winston, Daviess, Mo., 236.B3 101
Winston, Broadwater, Mont., 35....D5 102
Winston, Sierra, N. Mex., 60....D2 107
Winston, Douglas, Oreg., 2,395....*D3 113
Winston, co., Ala., 14,858....A2 78
Winston, co., Miss., 19,246..B4 100
Winston-Salem, Forsyth, N.C., 111,135 (*185,700)..A3 109
Winstonville, Bolivar, Miss., 413....B3 100
Winsum, Neth., 996....A6 15
Winter, Sask., Can., 65....E1 70
Winter, Sawyer, Wis., 500...C2 124
Winter Beach, Indian River, Fla., 700....E6 86
Winterberg, Ger., 3,400....B3 17
Winter Garden, Orange, Fla., 5,513....D5 86
Winter Gardens, San Diego, Calif., 1,000....*E2 82
Winter Harbor, Hancock, Maine, 500 (756▲)....D4 96
Winter Harbour, B.C., Can., 103....D3 68
Winterhaven, Imperial, Calif., 800....F6 82
Winter Haven, Polk, Fla., 16,277....D5 86
Wintering, lake, Man., Can.....B3 71
Winter Park, Grand, Colo., 50....B5 83
Winter Park, Orange, Fla., 17,162....D5 86
Winterpock, Chesterfield, Va., 130....D5 121
Winterport, Waldo, Maine, 900 (2,088▲)....D4 96
Winter Rim, mts., Oreg.....E6 113
Winters, Yolo, Calif., 1,700....A5, C3 82
Winters, Runnels, Tex., 3,266....D3 118
Winterset, Madison, Iowa, 3,639....C3 92
Wintersville, Jefferson, Ohio, 3,597....B7 111
Winterswijk, Neth., 15,000...C6 15
Winterthur, Switz., 86,700 (*105,000)....A6 19
Winterton, Newf., Can., 808.E5 75
Winterville, Clarke, Ga., 497....C3 87
Winterville, Aroostook, Maine, 100 (215▲)....B4 96
Winterville, Washington, Miss., 300....B2 100
Winterville, Pitt, N.C., 1,418....B6 109
Winthrop, Little River, Ark., 225....D1 81
Winthrop, Middlesex, Conn., 400....*D7 84
Winthrop, Buchanan, Iowa, 649....B6 92
Winthrop, Kennebec, Maine, 2,260 (3,537▲)....D3 96
Winthrop, Suffolk, Mass., 20,303....B6, g12 97
Winthrop, Sibley, Minn., 1,381....F4 99
Winthrop, Buchanan, Mo., 80....B2 101
Winthrop, St. Lawrence, N.Y., 500....f10 108
Winthrop, Okanogan, Wash.,....A5 122
Winthrop, lake, Mass.....h10 97
Winthrop Harbor, Lake, Ill., 3,848....A6, D2 90
Winton, Austl., 1,784....D7 50
Winton, St. Louis, Minn., 182....C7 99
Winton, Hertford, N.C., 835....A6 109
Winton, see Jessup, Pa.
Winton, Sweetwater, Wyo. ..D3 125
Wintzenheim, Fr., 2,762....A3 18
Winyah, bay, S.C.....E9 115
Wiota, Cass, Iowa, 195....C3 92
Wirral, N.B., Can., 123....D3 74
Wirt, Itasca, Minn., 60....C5 99
Wirt, Carter, Okla., 500....C4 112
Wirt, co., W. Va., 4,391....B3 123
Wirtz, Franklin, Va., 75....D3 121
Wisbech, Eng., 17,512....B8 12
Wiscasset, Lincoln, Maine, 950 (1,800▲)....D3 96
Wisconsin, state, U.S., 3,951,777....B10 77, 124
Wisconsin, riv., Wis.....E3 124
Wisconsin Dells, Columbia, Wis., 2,105....E4 124
Wisconsin Rapids, Wood, Wis., 15,042....D4 124
Wisdom, Beaverhead, Mont., 180....E3 102
Wise, Warren, N.C., 350....A5 109
Wise, Wise, Va., 2,614....B2 121
Wise, co., Tex., 17,012....C4 118
Wise, co., Va., 43,579....B2 121
Wiseman, Alsk., 12....B9 79
Wise River, Beaverhead, Mont., 70....E4 102
Wiseton, Sask., Can., 246...F2 70
Wishart, Sask., Can., 273....F3 70
Wishaw, Scot. (part of Motherwell & Wishaw)...E5 13
Wishek, McIntosh, N. Dak., 1,290....C6 110
Wishram, Klickitat, Wash., 750....D4 122
Wisla, riv., Pol.....B5 26
Wislok, riv., Pol.....C7 26
Wisloka, riv., Pol.....D6 26
Wismar, Br. Gu.....A3 59
Wismar, Ger., 56,600....B5 16

X

Y

Yaak, Lincoln, Mont., 50....B1 102
Yaan, China, 55,200........F5 34
Yabbenohr, isl., Kwajalein........ 52
Yablis, Nic..............C6 62
Yablonovy, mts., Sov. Un.......D14 28
Yabucoa, P.R., 3,734........C7 65
Yabucoa, mun., P.R., 29,782..............C7 65
Ya'bud, Jordan, 3,000.......B7 32
Yachats, Lincoln, Oreg., 250..............C2 113
Yaco, riv., Braz............C4 60
Yacolt, Clark, Wash., 375...D3 122
Yacuiba, Bol., 5,027........D3 55
Yadkin, co., N.C., 22,804....A3 109
Yadkin, riv., N.C............B3 109
Yadkin Valley, Caldwell, N.C., 125..............A2 109
Yadkinville, Yadkin, N.C., 1,644................A3 109
Yagi, Jap., 8,372..........o14 37
Yaguachi, Ec., 2,879........B2 58
Yaguajay, Cuba, 4,867.......D4 64
Yaguas, riv., Peru...........B3 58
Yahk, B.C., Can., 243........E9 68
Yahuma, Con. L..............A3 48
Yainax, butte, Oreg..........E5 113
Yaizu, Jap., 50,600 (72,118▲)..............o17 37
Yakima, Yakima, Wash., 43,284................C5 122
Yakima, co., Wash., 145,112..................C5 122
Yakima, ridge, Wash..........C5 122
Yakima, riv., Wash...........C5 122
Yakima, val., Wash...........C5 122
Yakoma, Con. L..............A3 48
Yaku, isl., Jap...............K5 37
Yakutat, Alsk., 230.........D12 79
Yakutat, bay, Alsk...........D12 79
Yakutsk, Sov. Un., 82,000..C15 28
Yalaha, Lake, Fla., 650.....D5 86
Yale, B.C., Can., 297........E7 68
Yale, Jasper, Ill., 123.......D5 90
Yale, Guthrie, Iowa, 260....C3 92
Yale, St. Clair, Mich., 1,621................E8 98
Yale, Payne, Okla., 1,369...A5 112
Yale, Beadle, S. Dak., 171...C8 116
Yale, Sussex, Va., 150........E5 121
Yale, mtn., Colo.............C4 83
Yale, res., Wash.............C3 122
Yalesville, New Haven, Conn. (part of Wallingford).....D5 84
Yalinga, Cen. Afr. Rep.......D4 46
Yalobusha, co., Miss., 12,502..................A4 100
Yalobusha, riv., Miss........B4 100
Yalova, Tur., 11,500.........B7 23
Yalta, Sov., Un., 43,994....I10 27
Yalu, China, 10,000..........B9 34
Yalu, riv., China, Kor.......D11 36
Yalung, riv., China..........E5 34
Yalutrovsk, Sov. Un., 18,700..................B7 29
Yalvac, Tur., 10,400.........C8 31
Yama, Sov. Un., 5,000......q21 27
Yamachiche, Que., Can., 1,186..................C5 73
Yamagata, Jap., 125,000 (188,597▲)..........G10 37
Yamagata, pref., Jap., 1,320,664............*G10 37
Yamaguchi, Jap., 54,400 (87,695▲)..............I5 37
Yamaguchi, pref., Jap., 1,602,207..............*I5 37
Yamanashi, pref., Jap., 782,062................*I9 37
Yamantau, mtn., Sov. Un........C5 29
Yamaska, Que., Can., 454...C5 73
Yamaska, co., Que., Can., 16,058.................C5 73
Yambio, Sud., 3,890..........E2 47
Yambol, Bul., 30,311........D8 22
Yamdrok, lake, China.........C9 39
Yamethin, Bur., 12,030.....D10 39
Yamhill, Yamhill, Oreg., 407....................B1 113
Yamhill, co., Oreg., 32,478..................B3 113
Yamkino, Sov. Un., 1,000...n18 27
Yamma Yamma, lake, Austl....C3 51
Yampa, Routt, Colo., 312....A4 83
Yampa, mtn., Colo............A3 83
Yampa, plat., Colo., Utah.....C6 119
Yampa, riv., Colo.............A2 83
Yamparaez, Bol., 725........C2 55
Yamsey, mtn., Oreg..........E5 113
Yamsk, Sov. Un., 800.......D18 28
Yamunanagar, India, 51,700.................*B6 40
Yana, riv., Sov. Un..........C16 28
Yanam, India, 7,032..........E7 39, I9 40
Yanao, Austl., 252...........H3 51
Yanaoca, Peru, 1,384........D3 58
Yanaul, Sov. Un., 10,000..D20 9
Yanbu', Sau. Ar., 10,000.....E7 43
Yancey, co., N.C., 14,008...C4 109
Yanceyville, Caswell, N.C., 1,113.................A4 109
Yanfolila, Mali..............D3 45
Yang, China.................H2 36
Yangambi, Con. L., 12,800...A3 48
Yangasa Cluster, is., Fiji Is........ 52
Yangchiang, China, 31,000..G7 34
Yangchow, China, 180,200...E8 34
Yangchüan, China, 177,400................*F5 36
Yangchun, China, 11,000....G7 34
Yangeshiri, isl., Jap........D10 37
Yangi-Yul, Sov. Un., 30,000...............G22 9
Yangku, see Taiyuan, China
Yangtze, riv., China..........H9 36
Yangyang, Kor., 4,900.......G4 37
Yankeetown, Citrus and Levy, Fla., 425.................C4 86
Yankeetown, Warrick, Ind., 250....................I3 91
Yankton, Yankton, S. Dak., 9,279..................E8 116
Yankton, co., S. Dak., 17,551...................D8 116
Yanonge, Con. L............A3 48
Yantic, New London, Conn. (part of Norwich).........C8 84
Yantley, Chactaw, Ala., 200.....................C1 78
Yantra, riv., Bul.............D7 22
Yanush, Latimer, Okla., 60..C6 112
Yao, Chad, 3,679...........C3 46
Yao, Jap., 122,832........*o14 37
Yaosca, Nic.................D5 62
Yaoundé, Cam., 92,600....................E2 46
Yap, isl., Pac. O..............F8 7
Yaphank, Suffolk, N.Y., 1,500.....................F5 84
Yaque del Norte, riv., Dom. Rep...................F8 64
Yaqui, riv., Mex.............B3 63
Yar, Sov. Un................B4 29
Yaracuy, state, Ven., 175,291...................A4 60
Yaraka, Austl., 27...........B5 52
Yarbo, Washington, Ala., 125.....................D1 78
Yarda, well, Chad............B3 46
Yardley, Bucks, Pa., 2,271...................F12 114
Yardville, Mercer, N.J., 7,500....................C3 106
Yarensk, Sov. Un., 2,600...C18 9
Yarí, riv., Col...............C3 60
Yariga-Take, peak, Jap........H8 37
Yaritagua, Ven., 6,036.......A4 60
Yarkand (Soche), China, 80,000...................H24 9
Yarker, Ont., Can., 314......C8 72
Yarkon, riv., Isr.........B6, g10 32
Yarkovo, Sov. Un............B7 29
Yarmouth, N.S., Can., 8,636....................F3 74
Yarmouth, Des Moines, Iowa, 175.....................C6 92
Yarmouth, Cumberland, Maine, 2,913 (3,517▲).E2, E5 96
Yarmouth, Barnstable, Mass., 300 (5,504▲).............C7 97
Yarmouth, co., N.S., Can., 23,386...................F4 74
Yarmouth Port, Barnstable, Mass., 450...............*C7 97
Yarmuk, riv., Jordan and Syr....B7 32
Yarnell, Yavapai, Ariz., 500.....................C3 80
Yarnema, Sov. Un..........F18 25
Yaroslavl, Sov. Un., 454,000..................B1 29
Yaroslavl, pref., Sov. Un.......B8 29
Yarovskoye, marsh, Sov. Un......B8 29
Yarraden, Austl.............B7 50
Yarram, Austl., 2,053........I6 51
Yarrow, B.C., Can., 985.....f13 68
Yarrowsburg, Washington, Md., 175.....................B2 85
Yartsevo, Sov. Un., 25,800..D9 27
Yarumal, Col., 10,349.......B2 60
Yasana, Con. L..............A4 48
Yasawa, isl., Fiji Is........... 52
Yasawa Group, is., Fiji Is....... 52
Yashi, Nig..................D6 45
Yasinovataya, Sov. Un., 10,000..................q20 27
Yasinya, Sov. Un............A7 22
Yasothon, Thai., 10,851......E6 38
Yata, Bol....................B2 55
Yates, co., N.Y., 18,614.....C3 108
Yatesboro, Armstrong, Pa., 900.....................E3 114
Yates Center, Woodson, Kans., 2,080...............E8 93
Yates City, Knox, Ill., 802...C3 90
Yatesville, Upson, Ga., 354..D2 87
Yathata, isl., Fiji Is........... 52
Yathkyed, lake, N.W. Ter., Can......................D13 66
Yatsuga Take, peak, Jap.......I9 37
Yatsushiro, Jap., 68,000 (100,566▲)...............J5 37
Yatsushiro, sea, Jap..........J5 37
Yaṭṭah, Jordan, 5,000........C7 32
Yatung, China...............D12 40
Yauca, Peru, 596............E3 58
Yauco, P.R., 8,996..........C5 65
Yauco, mun., P.R., 34,780...................C5 65
Yauco, riv., P.R.............C5 65
Yauli, Peru, 821.............D2 58
Yaupi, Ec...................B2 58
Yauri, Peru, 1,487...........D3 58
Yautepec, Mex., 8,649.......n14 63
Yauyos, Peru, 1,058.........D2 58
Yavapai, co., Ariz., 28,912...D3 80
Yavarí, riv., Braz., Peru........B3 58
Yavne, Isr., 5,397.......C6, h9 32
Yavneel, Isr., 1,884.........B7 32
Yavorov, Sov. Un., 10,000...G4 27
Yawata, isl., Truk............ 52
Yawatahama, Jap., 35,200 (52,527▲)...............J6 37
Yawhee, plat., Oreg..........E5 113
Yawngseng, Bur.............A3 38
Yazd (Yezd), Iran, 63,502...F7 41
Yazdan, Iran................E10 41
Yazd-e Khvāst, Iran, 5,000..F6 41
Yazoo, co., Miss., 31,653....C3 100
Yazoo, riv., Miss............C3 100
Yazoo City, Yazoo, Miss., 11,236..................C3 100
Ybbs, riv., Aus...............D7 16
Yding Skovhøj, hill, Den.......C3 14
Ye, Bur., 12,743............E10 39
Yeadon, Delaware, Pa., 11,610..................B11 114
Yeager, Hughes, Okla., 129..B5 112
Yeagertown, Mifflin, Pa., 1,349.....................E6 114
Yebbi Bou, Chad, 146........A3 46
Yecla, Sp., 18,400...........C5 20
Yeddo, Fountain, Ind., 150.......................D3 91
Yefremov, Sov. Un., 42,900.E12 27
Yegendybulak, Sov. Un.......D9 29
Yegoryevsk, Sov. Un., 61,000..................B1 29
Yeguas, pt., P.R.............C7 65
Yehpaishou, China...........D8 36
Yei, Sud., 739...............E3 47
Yekaterinoslavka, Sov. Un., 5,000....................A4 39
Yelabuga, Sov. Un., 16,900..................D19 9
Yelan, Sov. Un., 10,000....F14 27
Yelanskoye, Sov. Un........C15 28
Yelets, Sov. Un., 85,000.....C1 29
Yélimané, Mali..............C2 45
Yelizarovo, Sov. Un........C22 9
Yell, co., Ark., 11,940........B2 81
Yell, isl., Scot..............g10 10
Yellandalpad, India, 10,955..I8 40
Yelleq, mtn., Eg., U.A.R.......D5 32
Yellow, cliff, Ky.............D5 94
Yellow, creek, Ohio...........A4 111
Yellow, creek, Tenn...........A4 117
Yellow, lake, Wis.............C1 124
Yellow, riv., see Hwang Ho, China
Yellow, riv., Fla.............G2 86
Yellow, riv., Ga..............A6 87
Yellow, riv., Ind.............B4 91
Yellow, riv., Wis.............D3 124
Yellow, sea, China...........D9 34
Yellow Bluff, Wilcox, Ala., 25......................D2 78
Yellow Creek, Sask., Can., 182.....................E3 70
Yellow Grass, Sask., Can., 527.....................H3 70
Yellowhead, pass, Alta., B.C., Can........................C1 69
Yellow Jacket, Montezuma, Colo., 3...................D2 83
Yellow Jacket, mts., Idaho......D4 89
Yellowknife, N.W. Ter., Can., 3,141...............D10 66
Yellow Medicine, co., Minn., 15,523...................F2 99
Yellow Pine, Washington, Ala., 150..................D1 78
Yellow Pine, Valley, Idaho, 45......................E3 89
Yellow Springs, Frederick, Md., 130...................B3 85
Yellow Springs, Greene, Ohio, 4,167.................C4 111
Yellowstone, co., Mont., 79,016..................D8 102
Yellowstone, lake, Wyo........A2 125
Yellowstone, nat. park, Idaho, Mont., Wyo...............A1 125
Yellowstone, riv., Mont., Wyo.......................D10 102
Yellowstone National Park (part), co., Wyo., 420.....A2 125
Yellowstone Park, Yellowstone National Park, Wyo., 300..A2 125
Yellowtail, res., Mont........E8 102
Yellville, Marion, Ark., 636.....................A3 81
Yelm, Thurston, Wash., 479.....................C3 122
Yelnya, Sov. Un., 10,500....D9 27
Yeltes, riv., Sp..............B2 20
Yelverton, bay, N.W. Ter., Can.......................k35 67
Yelvington, Daviess, Ky., 100.....................C3 94
Yelwa, Nig., 2,142..........D5 45
Yemanzhelinsk, Sov. Un., 33,500..................C6 29
Yemassee, Beaufort and Hampton, S. C., 473......F6 115
Yemen, country, Asia, 5,000,000..................H7 33
Yen, riv., China.............G8 36
Yena, Sov. Un...............D14 25
Yenakiyevo, Sov. Un., 92,000...............G12, q21 27
Yenan, (Fushih), China.......D6 34
Yenangyat, Bur...............B1 38
Yenangyaung, Bur., 11,098..B1 38
Yen Bay, Viet., 10,000......B6 38
Yencheng, China............H5 36
Yencheng, China, 105,000...H9 36
Yenchi (Chutzuchieh), China, 70,000..............C10 34
Yendi, Ghana, 7,694.........E4 45
Yendua, isl., Fiji Is............ 52
Yenice, riv., Tur.............B9 31
Yenisey, riv., Sov. Un........C11 28
Yeniseysk, Sov. Un., 18,300..................D12 28
Yeniseyskiy Kryazh, mts., Sov. Un......................D27 9
Yenki, see Kara Shahr, China
Yenshan, China..............E7 36
Yenshih, China..............G5 36
Yenshou, China, 5,000.......D4 37
Yentna, riv., Alsk............f16 79
Yeo, lake, Austl..............E3 50
Yeoman, Carroll, Ind., 172..C4 91
Yeotmal, India, 45,587.......G7 40
Yeovil, Eng., 24,552........D5 12
Yerania, mtn., Grc...........g10 23
Yerba Buena, Chile..........E1 55
Yerevan, Sov. Un., 578,000.............G17 9, E2 29
Yerington, Lyon, Nev., 1,764...................E2 104
Yerkéhida (Well), Niger......B7 45
Yermakovskoye, Sov. Un...E27 9
Yermo, San Bernardino, Calif., 800.................E5 82
Yermolayevo, Sov. Un........C5 29
Yerres, Fr., 10,747..........h10 14
Yerres, riv., Fr..............F2 15
Yerseke, Neth., 5,000........C4 15
Yershov, Sov. Un., 16,500...C3 29
Yerupaja, mtn., Peru.........D2 58
Yesilova, Tur., 1,165........D7 23
Yeso, De Baca, N. Mex., 200....................C5 107
Yessentuki, Sov. Un., 32,600..................G17 9
Yessey, Sov. Un., 10,000...C13 28
Yeste, Sp., 9,997............C4 20
Yetter, Calhoun, Iowa, 85...B3 92
Yeu, isl., Fr................D2 14
Yevlakh, Sov. Un., 15,000...E3 29
Yevpatoriya, Sov. Un., 61,000...................I9 27
Yew, mtn., W. Va...........C4 123
Yeysk, Sov. Un., 61,000....H12 27
Yezd, see Yazd, Iran
Yezd, reg., Iran.............F6 41
Yí, riv., Ur..................E1 56
Yiannitsa, Grc., 19,693......B4 23
Yiaros, isl., Grc.............D5 23
Yinchwan (Ningsia), China, 84,000...................E2 36
Ying, China.................E5 36
Yingkow, China, 131,400...D10 36
Yingshang, China............H7 36
Yingtak, China..............G7 34
Yin Shan, mtn., China........D4 36
Yioura, isl., Grc.............C5 23
Yirol, Sud., 1,895...........D3 47
Yithion, Grc., 7,110.........D4 23
Ylig, bay, Guam............... 52
Ylikitka, lake, Fin...........D13 25
Ymer, isl., Grnld...........B17 4
Ymir, B.C., Can., 323........E9 68
Ymir, mtn., B.C., Can........E2 69
Yoakum, DeWitt and Lavaca, Tex., 5,761..............E4 118
Yoakum, co., Tex., 8,032....C1 118
Yockanookany, riv., Miss......C4 100
Yocona, riv., Miss...........A4 100
Yoder, Arkansas, Ark........C4 81
Yoder, El Paso, Colo., 30....C6 83
Yoder, Allen, Ind., 200.......C7 91
Yoder, Reno, Kans., 75......B4 93
Yoder, Goshen, Wyo., 83....D8 125
Yoho, nat. park, B.C., Can.....D9 68
Yoichi, Jap., 18,600.........E10 37
Yojoa, lake, Hond...........C3 62
Yokadouma, Cam.............E2 46
Yokkaichi, Jap., 195,974...............I8, o15 37
Yoko, Cam..................D2 46
Yokoate, isl., Jap............L4 37
Yokohama, Jap., 1,375,710...........I9, n18 37
Yokoshiba, Jap., 3,900.....n19 37
Yokosuka, Jap., 287,309...............I9, n18 37
Yokosuka, Jap., 6,000.......o16 37
Yokote, Jap., 24,700.........G10 37
Yokun Seat, mtn., Mass........B1 97
Yola, Nig., 8,573............E7 45
Yolaina, mts., Nic...........E5 62
Yolo, co., Calif., 65,727.....C2 82
Yolyn, Logan, W. Va., 800..D5 123
Yom, riv., Thai..............C4 38
Yomakyo, mtn., Bur...........C2 38
Yona, Guam, 1,105............ 52
Yonago, Jap., 62,900 (94,808▲)..................I6 37
Yoncalla, Douglas, Oreg., 698.....................D3 113
Yonezawa, Jap., 60,300 (96,991▲)...............H10 37
Yongan, Kor.................F4 37
Yonges Island, Charleston, S.C., 250...........G1, G7 115
Yonghung, Kor., 18,445......G3 37
Yongil, bay, Kor.............H4 37
Yonkers, Westchester, N.Y., 190,634...............E7, n15 108
Yonkers, Wagoner, Okla.....A6 112
Yonne, dept., Fr., 269,826..................*D5 14
Yonne, riv., Fr..............C5 14
Yorba Linda, Orange, Calif., 1,198...................*F5 82
York, Sumter, Ala., 2,932...C1 78
York, Austl., 1,524...........F2 50
York, Eng., 104,300.........D6 10
York, York, Maine, 950 (4,663▲)..................E1 96
York, York, Nebr., 6,173....D8 103
York, Benson, N. Dak., 148......................A6 110
York, York, Pa., 54,504 (*146,600)...............G8 114
York, York, S.C., 4,758......B5 115
York, co., N.B., Can., 52,672....................C3 74
York, co., Ont., Can., 1,733,108.................D5 72
York, co., Eng., 4,722,661...A7 12
York, co., Maine, 99,402.....E2 96
York, co., Nebr., 13,724.....D8 103
York, co., Pa., 238,336......G8 114
York, co., S.C., 78,760......A5 115
York, co., Va., 21,583.......D6 121
York, pt., Newf., Can.........C4 75
York, riv., Ont., Can.........B7 72
York, riv., Va...............D6 121
York Beach, York, Maine, 400.....................E2 96
York Center, Du Page, Ill., 1,100...................*B6 90
York Corners, York, Maine (part of York)...........E2 96
Yorke, pen., Austl...........F6 50
York Factory, Man., Can.A5, f9 71
Yorkfield, Du Page, Ill., 1,200...................*B6 90
York Harbor, York, Maine, 850.....................E2 96
York Haven, York, Pa., 736..F8 114
Yorklyn, New Castle, Del., 400.....................A6 85
Yorkshire, Cattaraugus, N.Y., 450.....................C2 108
Yorkshire, York, Pa., 1,000.*G8 114
Yorkshire, Prince William, Va., 1,500.................*C5 121
York Springs, Adams, Pa., 384.....................F7 114
Yorkton, Sask., Can., 9,995.................F4, n8 70
Yorktown, Lincoln, Ark., 200.....................C4 81
Yorktown, Delaware, Ind., 1,137...................D6 91
Yorktown, Page, Iowa, 150..D2 92
Yorktown, Salem, N.J., 150..D2 106
Yorktown, DeWitt, Tex., 2,527...................E4 118
Yorktown, York, Va., 311..................A6, D6 121
Yorktown Heights, Westchester, N.Y., 7,500................A5 106
Yorktown Manor, Washington, R.I., 1,300.............C11 84
Yorkville, Kendall, Ill., 1,568.....................B5 90
Yorkville, Oneida, N.Y., 3,749.....................B5 108
Yorkville, Belmont and Jefferson, Ohio, 1,801......B7 111
Yorkville, Gibson, Tenn., 250......................A2 117
Yorkville, Racine, Wis., 35...F1 124
York Wolds, hills, Eng.......C6 10
Yoro, Hond., 1,471..........C4 62
Yoseki, Con. L...............A3 48
Yosemite, nat. park, Calif......D4 82
Yosemite National Park, Mariposa, Calif., 900.....D4 82
Yosemite, Casey, Ky., 200...C5 94
Yoshiwara, Jap., 80,944 (*174,000)...............n17 37
Yoshkar-Ola, Sov. Un., 116,000..................B3 29
Yost, Box Elder, Utah, 87...B2 119
Yosu, Kor., 78,000 (89,400▲)..................I3 37
Yotala, Bol., 1,554..........C2 55
Youbou, B.C., Can., 1,153..................g11 68
Youghal, Ire., 5,043..........F4 11
Youghal, bay, Ire............F4 11
Youghiogheny, riv., Md., Pa.............D1 85, F1 114
Youghiogheny River, res., Pa...G3 114
Youkounkoun, Guinea, 700..D2 45
Young, Gila, Ariz., 30........C5 80
Young, Austl., 5,448.........G7 51
Young, Sask., Can., 341......F3 70
Young, Ur., 4,923...........E1 56
Young, co., Tex., 17,254.....C3 118
Young America, Cass, Ind., 250.....................C5 91
Young Harris, Towns, Ga., 743.....................B3 87
Youngs Creek, Orange, Ind., 45......................H4 91
Youngs Point, Ont., Can., 206.....................C6 72
Youngstown, Alta., Can., 321.....................D5 69
Youngstown, Bay, Fla., 600................B1, G3 86
Youngstown, Vigo, Ind., 200.....................F3 91
Youngstown, Polk, Iowa.....A7 92
Youngstown, Niagara, N.Y., 1,848...................B1 108
Youngstown, Trumbull and Mahoning, Ohio, 166,689 (*467,600)..............A7 111
Youngsville, Lafayette, La., 946......................D3 95
Youngsville, Rio Arriba, N. Mex., 130..............A3 107
Youngsville, Franklin, N.C., 596.....................A5 109
Youngsville, Warren, Pa., 2,211.....................C3 114
Youngtown, Maricopa, Ariz., 1,559...................G1 80
Youngwood, Westmoreland, Pa., 2,813...................F2 114
Yountville, Napa, Calif., 600.....................A5 82
Youssoufia, Mor., 4,835.....C3 44
Yozgat, Tur., 18,300.........C10 31
Ypacaraí, Par., 8,118........E4 55
Ypané, riv., Par.............D4 55
Ypres, see Ieper, Bel.
Ypsilanti, Washtenaw, Mich., 20,957...............A6, F7 98
Ypsilanti, Stutsman, N. Dak., 110.....................C7 110
Yreka, Siskiyou, Calif., 4,759.B2 82
Ysleta, El Paso, Tex. (part of El Paso)...........F1 118
Yssingeaux, Fr., 2,702.......E6 14
Ystad, Swe., 13,700.........J5 25
Ythan, riv., Scot............C6 13
Yü, China...................E6 36
Yü, riv., China..............G6 34
Yuan, riv., China...........J4 36
Yuanan, China, 13,000........I4 36
Yuanchiang, China...........G5 34
Yuanling, China, 28,000.....J4 36
Yuanshih, China.............F6 36
Yuba, co., Calif., 33,859.....C3 82
Yuba, riv., Calif.............C3 82
Yuba City, Sutter, Calif., 11,507....................C3 82
Yuba City South, Sutter, Calif., 3,200...................*C3 82
Yubari, Jap., 107,972........E10 37
Yubi, cape, Sp. Sahara........D2 44
Yucaipa, San Bernardino, Calif., 6,000...................*F3 82
Yucatán, state, Mex., 612,047.C7 63
Yucatán, chan., Mex..........C7 63
Yucca, Mohave, Ariz., 100..C1 80
Yucca, mtn., Nev............G5 104
Yucheng, China..............F7 36
Yuchi, China, 4,000.........K8 36
Yudoma, riv., Sov. Un.......D1 4
Yuehyang, China............J5 36
Yug, riv., Sov. Un...........A3 29
Yugoslavia, country, Eur., 19,400,000.......G12 8, C3 22
Yuhuan, China, 9,000........J9 36
Yukhnov, Sov. Un., 5,100..D10 27
Yukon, Duval, Fla., 2,000.B5, B6 86
Yukon, Canadian, Okla., 3,076....................B4 112
Yukon, McDowell, W. Va., 400.....................D3 123
Yukon, ter., Can., 14,628....D5 66
Yukon, riv., Alsk., Yukon, Can..C9 79
Yuksekkum, Tur.............D7 23
Yule, bay, Ant..............B29 5
Yulee, Nassau, Fla., 500..B5, B6 86
Yuli, Nig...................E7 45
Yulin, China................C8 38
Yulin, China................E3 36
Yulin, Phil..................C8 35
Yuma, Yuma, Ariz., 23,974...E1 80
Yuma, Yuma, Colo., 1,919...A8 83
Yuma, Wexford, Mich., 50...D5 98
Yuma, Carroll, Tenn., 80.....B3 117
Yuma, co., Ariz., 46,235.....D1 80
Yuma, co., Colo., 8,912......A8 83
Yuma, des., Ariz.............E1 80
Yuma, Indian res., Calif.......F6 82
Yumari, peak, Ven...........C4 60
Yumbi, Con L................B4 48
Yumen, China, 50,000........C4 34
Yunabaru, Okinawa............ 52
Yuncheng, China.............G4 36
Yunes, riv., P.R.............B4 65
Yungan, China, 12,000..........F8 34, L7 36
Yungas, mts., Bol............C2 55
Yungay, Chile, 3,671.........B2 54
Yungay, Peru, 2,517..........C2 58
Yungchi, China, 10,000......G4 36
Yungching, China............E5 34
Yungchow, see Lingling, China
Yungera, Austl...............G4 51
Yunghsiu, China, 7,000......J6 36
Yungkia, see Wenchow, China
Yungnien, China.............F6 36
Yungning (Nanning), China, 264,000...............G6 34
Yungshou, China, 6,000......G2 36
Yungshun, China.............J3 36
Yungsui, China..............J3 36
Yunho, China, 3,000.........J8 36
Yunhsiao, China, 18,000.....G8 34
Yunhsien, China, 20,000.....G5 34
Yunhsien, China.............H4 36
Yunnan, plat., China..........F5 34
Yunnan, prov., China 19,100,000..................G5 34
Yunnanfu, see Kunming, China
Yunta, Austl., 111............F2 51
Yurécuaro, Mex., 12,088....m12 63
Yurga, Sov. Un., 52,000....D25 9
Yurimaguas, Peru, 5,918.....C2 58
Yurino, Sov. Un., 5,000.....C16 27
Yuriria, Mex., 10,221........m13 63
Yurochi, isl., Bikini........... 52
Yuryevets, Sov. Un., 10,000..................C14 27
Yuryev-Polskiy, Sov. Un., 10,000..................C12 27
Yuscarán, Hond., 1,189....D4 62
Yüshan, China, 16,000.......J8 36
Yushih, China...............G6 36
Yushkozero, Sov. Un........E15 25
Yuta, China.................F8 34
Yutan, Saunders, Nebr., 335................C9, D2 103
Yutien, China...............E7 36
Yutu, China, 16,000.........F8 34
Yuty, Par., 16,262...........E4 55
Yutzu, China, 60,000........E2 34
Yuwang, China...............F2 36
Yuyang, China, 18,000.......J3 36
Yuyao, China, 26,000........J9 36
Yuyü, China.................D5 36
Yuzha, Sov. Un., 25,000...C13 27
Yuzhno-Sakhalinsk (Toyohara), Sov. Un., 87,000..................C11 37
Yuzhnoye, Sov. Un., 10,000..................C11 37
Yverdon, Switz., 16,338.....C2 19
Yvetot, Fr., 7,932...........C4 14
Yvonand, Switz., 1,290......C2 19
Ywathit, Bur.................C2 38

Z

Zaandam, Neth., 52,600......B4 15
Zabkowice, Pol., 10,127.....C4 26
Zabkowice, Pol., 2,544......g10 26
Zābol, Iran..................F10 41
Zābolī, Iran.................H10 41
Zabrze, Pol., 196,900....C5, g9 26
Zacapa, Guat., 8,260.........C3 62
Zacapu, Mex., 22,241........n13 63
Zacatecas, Mex., 31,701.....C4 63
Zacatecas, state, Mex., 798,232.................C4, m12 63
Zacatecoluca, Sal., 11,173...D3 62
Zachary, East Baton Rouge, La., 3,268.....................D4 95
Zachun, Ger., 273............E5 24
Zack, Searcy, Ark...........B3 81
Zacoalco [de Torres], Mex., 8,675.....................C4, m12 63
Zacualpan, Mex., 1,657.....m14 63
Zacualtipán, Mex., 3,661....m14 63
Zadar, Yugo., 25,132.........C2 22
Zadonsk, Sov. Un., 10,000..................E12 27
Zadzbork, see Mragowo, Pol.
Za'farānah, Eg., U.A.R.....H9 31
Zafra, Sp., 10,723............C2 20
Zagan, Pol., 15,300..........C3 26
Zaghouan, Tun...............B7 44
Zagora, Grc., 3,223..........C4 23
Zagora, Mor., 2,200..........C3 44
Zagorsk, Sov. Un., 78,000...B1 29
Zagreb, Yugo., 430,802......C2 22
Zagros, mts., Iran............E3 41
Zagyva, riv., Hung...........B5 22
Zāhedān, Iran, 5,000........G10 41
Zahl, Williams, N. Dak., 100......................A2 110
Zahle, Leb., 30,387..........F10 31
Zahna, Ger., 5,992...........B7 17
Zaindeh, riv., Iran...........E5 41
Zaire, dist., Ang., 89,755....C1 48
Zaječar, Yugo., 18,545......D6 22
Zaka, Rh....................B5 49
Zakataly, Sov. Un., 5,603..B16 31
Zákinthos, Grc., 9,506.......D3 23
Zákinthos (Zante), prov., Grc., 35,509.....................*D3 23
Zákinthos (Zante), isl., Grc.....D3 23
Zakopane, Pol., 25,000.......D6 26
Zakroczym, Pol., 3,358......k13 26
Zala, co., Hung., 274,161...*B3 22
Zala, riv., Hung.............B3 22
Zalaegerszeg, Hung., 23,738..B3 22
Zalamea de la Serena, Sp., 8,543.....................C3 20
Zalamea la Real, Sp., 6,065.....................D2 20
Zalău, Rom., 13,378.........B6 22
Zaleski, Vinton, Ohio, 336...C5 111
Zalewo, Pol., 2,634..........B5 26
Zalingei, Sud., 3,314.........C1 47
Zalma, Bollinger, Mo., 141..D7 101
Zaltan, mts., Libya...........D3 43
Zaltbommel, Neth., 6,000....C5 15
Zama, Attala, Miss., 150.....C4 96
Zambales, prov., Phil., 213,600..................B6 35
Zambezi, riv., Afr...........H8 42
Zambézia, prov., Moz........A6 49
Zambia (Northern Rhodesia), country, Afr., 3,650,000...D4 48
Zamboanga, Phil., 25,000 (131,489▲)..................D6 35
Zamboanga del Norte, prov., Phil., 280,400..............*D6 35
Zamboanga del Sur, prov., Phil., 744,500..............*D6 35
Zambrano, Col., 5,863.......B3 60
Zambrow, Pol., 4,150........B7 26
Zamora, Ec., 485.............B2 58
Zamora, Mex., 31,991..C4, m12 63
Zamora, Bernalillo, N. Mex., 70......................k8 107
Zamora, Sp., 42,060.........B3 20
Zamora, prov., Sp., 301,129.*B3 20
Zamora, riv., Ec.............B2 58
Zamość, Pol., 28,000........C7 26
Zampa, pt., Okinawa........... 52
Zamsar, China..............B13 40
Zamzam, Wadi, Libya........C2 43
Zanaga, Con. B..............F2 46
Zandvoort, Neth., 14,400.....B4 15
Zane, Iron, Utah, 10.........F2 119
Zanesville, Wells, Ind., 400..C7 91
Zanesville, Miskingum, Ohio, 39,077..............C6 111
Zanja Blanca, P.R...........C5 65
Zanjān, Iran, 47,159..........C4 41
Zante (Zakinthos), prov., Grc., 35,509.....................*D3 23
Zante, see Zákinthos, isl., Grc.
Zanzibar, Tan., 57,923.......C6 48
Zanzibar, see Tanzania, country, Afr.
Zanzibar, isl., Tan...........C6 48
Zaoviet Tahtania, Alg........C4 44
Zap, Mercer, N. Dak., 339...B4 110
Zapadna Morava, riv., Yugo....D5 22
Zapala, Arg., 3,387..........B2 54
Zapallar, Arg.................E4 55
Zapata, Zapata, Tex., 2,031.....................F3 118
Zapata, co., Tex., 4,393......F3 118
Zapata, pen., Cuba..........D3 64
Zapatoca, Col., 5,629.........B3 60
Zaporozhye, Sov. Un., 507,000...................H10 27
Zapotillo, Ec.................B1 58
Zapotitlán, Mex., 3,248.......h9 63
Zaqaziq, see Zagazig, Eg., U.A.R.
Zara, Tur., 7,400.............C11 31
Zaragoza, Col., 1,732.........B3 60
Zaragoza, Mex., 5,334........B4 63
Zaragoza, Mex., 2,464........k13 63
Zaragoza, Sp., 326,316......B5 20
Zaragoza, prov., Sp., 656,772.....................*B5 20
Zarand, Iran, 4,493..........F8 41
Zárate, Arg., 35,197......A5, g7 54
Zaraysk, Sov. Un., 10,000..D12 27